BASEBALL PROSPECTUS

2015

The Essential Guide to the 2015 Season

Edited by Sam Miller and Jason Wojciechowski

R.J. Anderson, J.P. Breen, Ben Carsley, Patrick Dubuque, Ken Funck, Ryan Ghan, Craig Goldstein, Bryan Grosnick, Andrew Koo, Dustin Nosler, Tommy Rancel, Daniel Rathman, Mauricio Rubio Jr., Bret Sayre, Sahadev Sharma, Adam Sobsey, Paul Sporer, Matt Sussman, Doug Thorburn, Will Woods, Geoff Young

Dave Pease, Publisher

WILEY

Wiley General Trade, an imprint of Turner Publishing Company
424 Church Street • Suite 2240 • Nashville, Tennessee 37219
445 Park Avenue • 9th Floor • New York, New York 10022
www.turnerpublishing.com

For general information about our other products and services, please contact Ingram Publisher Services at (866) 400-5351.

Library of Congress Cataloging-in-Publication Data:
ISBN 978-1-1184-7145-6 (pbk); 978-1-1184-7148-7 (ebk)

Printed in the United States of America
10 9 8 7 6 5 4 3 2 1

Cuban League statistics courtesy Clay Davenport

Header image by W. Conway, 1951. From *http://eephusleague. com/2011/05/field-schematic/*

Design and layout by Bryan Davidson and Jon Franke

TABLE OF CONTENTS

Foreword

by Brian Bannister, Boston Red Sox Pro Scouting Department

There were two things I wanted to be when I grew up: A major-league baseball player or a filmmaker. These might not seem to have a lot in common—beyond extremely long odds—but Baseball Prospectus helped me see what they shared.

Take *Shawshank Redemption*, one of my favorite movies of all time. It's a story of wrongful imprisonment and, ultimately, the titular redemption. The protagonist, Andy Dufresne, is a common man who uses extraordinary ingenuity to escape a life sentence. He overcomes a system heavily weighted against him, refusing to accept circumstances that others might have accepted as reality.

Of course, the story is just one part of what makes the movie great. So too do the technical aspects that the casual viewer might enjoy without ever appreciating: the Oscar-nominated camerawork of cinematographer Roger Deakins; the "moss-dark, saturated images" that, one critic wrote, make "you feel as if you could reach out and touch the prison walls;" the shadows and lighting teasing out themes of imprisonment and freedom; the recurrent motifs, slow reveals and perfectly detailed mise-en-scene. The inspiration of the story is important, but there is also a technical side to creating the final product. A cinematographer has to know the equipment and process better than anybody. From the construction of the lenses, to the physics of the lights, to the development of the film stock, there is very little margin for error. It's the science within the art.

I always found similarities between the movie's story and themes and my own baseball career. As a high school senior, I was 5-feet-9 and weighed 175 pounds. I distinctly remember running a 7.6-second 60-yard dash at a baseball showcase (despite going to speed camps and training on high-speed treadmills for several years). My best fastball topped out at 84 mph. I was the epitome of a nonprospect, seemingly doomed to a life sentence in the low minors because of my paltry physical tools. Like Andy Dufresne, I had to think outside the box and approach my circumstance in a different way to succeed.

This meant that I needed to know the science within my craft—just as a great cinematographer would. I had to understand the math, not just the traditional approaches. As a pitcher in the minor leagues, I didn't have good velocity or much rise on my fastball, and I recognized that I gave up too many fly balls that would eventually become home runs if I made it to the big leagues. In the Arizona Fall League in 2004, I developed a cutter and made it my main pitch because it had a much better batted-ball profile. While I never had the stuff of a Cy Young winner, methodically making adjustments like this at each progressively more difficult professional level allowed me to keep playing the game I loved. Even if I wouldn't ever outperform players with twice the natural ability, at least I was getting the most out of my physical ability.

Baseball will always have an element of probability and chance that we can't control, but putting the odds in your favor on a consistent basis is the responsibility of every professional player and team. Baseball Prospectus has been at the forefront of explaining the math, science and inner workings of the game for two decades now. Whether its authors are writing illuminatingly about scouting, player development or analytics (or all of the above), Baseball Prospectus has consistently furnished the baseball community with much-needed original critical thinking. It has been a major resource for my career and the careers of those around me.

Now that I have the privilege of working with the incredibly talented individuals at the Boston Red Sox, the skills and critical thinking that I developed as a player are put into use every day. No two players are the same, and no two baseball teams or farm systems or free-agent markets are ever the same. Understanding the incredibly complex interconnectedness of the baseball universe, and applying proper evaluation, development, projection and valuation techniques can be overwhelming. Being able to separate the information from the noise makes all the difference in the world, and Baseball Prospectus continues to provide that incredible value in its Annual and on its site daily.

If I'd grown up to be a cinematographer, I'd use science, math and years of experience to produce something that requires none of those to enjoy—a movie. Likewise, a good baseball team uses science, math and years of experience to produce something that requires none of those skills to enjoy—a championship. Whether you tend to enjoy baseball on an intellectual level or an emotional level—or, more likely, both—I promise you will find incredible value in the talented and passionate writers of Baseball Prospectus. They will further your understanding of this great game. Enjoy the show. ■

Preface

by Peter Gammons

I was somewhere on either side of a line of age 40, and in the words of Jackson Browne thought I knew where I was going after close to 15 years on the baseball beat. Now, my vantage point had already begun to evolve, thanks to Bill James and Steve Hirdt and his Elias books, brilliant writing and analysis that I labeled the tributaries from the main streams of the Mississippi and Hudson.

I traveled with a team. On the road, I worked out every day when the Red Sox took early batting practice, and while the landscape was invaluable in appreciating the skills and athleticism and the work that separated the extraordinary from the ordinary, that landscape was often conventional.

Darned right I loved the way Alfredo Griffin played shortstop. Most everyone did. He was flashy, he was energetic, he was flossy in the field, and when the 1985 Bill James book arrived, James shot down Alfredo Griffin. Four walks in 140 games. Second base partner Damaso Garcia had 16 walks. And that was why the Blue Jays left their tools in a shed too often. I was covering Wade Boggs—who in that '85 season began an OBP run of .450, .453, .461, .471—and Dwight Evans.

And I never viewed the game the same again. I had Rickey Henderson and Wade Boggs within 200 miles of one another, and Tim Raines less than an hour flight away, and the tools…

From the James and Elias schools Baseball Prospectus was born, and for all of us who always sought different angles and views and opinions, it became each day's must-read, be it by Will Carroll or Kevin Goldstein, Keith Law or any of what seem like hundreds of minds producing analytical perspectives. This is the 20th edition of the Baseball Prospectus annual, hence the 20th year the book has been part of my spring training traveling circus. I yanked the 2003 book off the shelf. Nate Silver "Introducing PECOTA." Carroll. Clay Davenport. And on and on.

What has made this annual compilation so fascinating is that its inception came just as the analytics revolution was rising from the Sloane School to Paul DePodesta to Silicon Valley. It was novel, but it has morphed into several intellectual shapes over 20 years. I honestly do not remember what statistics were held as closest to absolutes 20 years ago. Probably not WAR. Probably not OPS+.

The Billy Beane-Paul DePodesta Athletics, the Theo Epstein Red Sox, the Mark Shapiro-Chris Antonetti Indians and some other teams were already heavily into the use of analytics after the turn of the century. Epstein and Shapiro were strong believers in the blend between the seen and the analytical, and Prospectus has been a tugboat bringing an entire industry forward across the bay of tradition.

For instance, most of us could see defense with our eyes, but it was Prospectus that first brought team defensive metrics to a site where we in the media could use them. In time, teams like the Rays and Pirates became revolutionaries in their own fashions, before the much-applauded approach of the Houston Astros. And, in time, the rational debates about what great scouting eyes can deduce and what can be proven or unproven—such as whether or not Jack Morris really was a big game pitcher and pitched to the score—became a huge part of the joy that is arguing Alan Trammell vs. Ozzie Smith, or Mike Mussina vs. John Smoltz. Because most of us know that every day someone can make an argument that changes our opinions and theories, and that, as James has often said, the more he's worked for a team the more he appreciates there are elements that simply cannot be explained.

I have been covering baseball on a full-time basis since 1972, and just as 30 years ago the Alfredo Griffin-Damaso Garcia light went off, it seems that my eyes have been opened one way or another every year since. Baseball Prospectus the site and Baseball Prospectus the annual have been major contributors to what I see as the never-ending educational thought progression. They will be an important guide as we watch the counteraction of defensive shifts, and as we test the theories that an inordinate amount of shifting might hurt the defensive ratings of players like Andrew McCutchen or Jose Altuve.

And somewhere this spring, maybe in Yeehaw Junction, Florida or in Surprise, Arizona, I will read something in this book, use some notation, then enter it into my laptop when I get to my hotel and pull it out in April or June when discussing a particular team and its issues. As someone who loves the game and has been talking and writing about it for all of Mike Trout's lifetime, the best thing to do is to thank Baseball Prospectus for all it has done to expand our baseball horizons.

Statistical Introduction

Why don't you get your nose out of those numbers and watch a game?

It's a false dilemma, of course. We would wager that Baseball Prospectus readers watch more games than the typical fan. They also probably pay better attention when they do. The numbers do not replace observation; they supplement it. Having the numbers allows you to learn things not readily seen by mere watching and to keep up on many more players than any one person could.

So this book doesn't ask you to choose between the two. Instead, we combine numerical analysis with the observations of a lot of very bright people. They won't always agree. Just as the eyes don't always see what the numbers do, the reverse can be true. In order to get the most out of this book, however, it helps to understand the numbers we're presenting and why.

Offense

The core of our offense measurements is True Average, which attempts to quantify everything a player does at the plate—hitting for power, taking walks, striking out and even "productive" outs—and scale it to batting average. A player with a TAv of .260 is average, .300 exceptional, .200 rather awful.

True Average also accounts for the context a player performs in. That means we adjust it based on the mix of parks a player plays in. Also, rather than use a blanket park-adjustment for every player on a team, a player who plays a disproportionate number of his games at home will see that reflected in his numbers. We also adjust based upon league quality: The average player in the AL is better than the average player in the NL, and True Average accounts for this.

Because hitting runs isn't the entirety of scoring runs, we also look at a player's Baserunning Runs. BRR accounts for the value of a player's ability to steal bases, of course, but also accounts for his ability to go first to third on a single, or advance on a fly ball.

Defense

Defense is a much thornier issue. The general move in the sabermetric community has been toward stats based on zone data, where human stringers record the type of batted ball (grounder, liner, fly ball) and its presumed landing location. That data is used to compile expected outs for comparing a fielder's actual performance.

The trouble with zone data is twofold. First, unlike the data we use in the calculation of the statistics you see in this book, zone data wasn't made publicly available; it was recorded by commercial data providers who kept the raw data private, only disclosing it to a select few who paid for it. Second, as we've seen the field of zone-based defensive analysis open up—more data and more metrics based upon that data coming to light—we see that the conclusions of zone-based defensive metrics don't hold up to outside scrutiny. Different data providers can come to very different conclusions about the same events. And even two metrics based on the same data set can come to radically different conclusions based upon their starting assumptions, assumptions that haven't been tested, using methods that can't be duplicated or verified by outside analysts.

The quality of the fielder can bias the data: Zone-based fielding metrics will tend to attribute more expected outs to good fielders than bad fielders, irrespective of the distribution of batted balls. Scorers who work in parks with high press boxes will tend to score more line drives than scorers who work in parks with low press boxes.

Our FRAA incorporates play-by-play data, allowing us to study the issue of defense at a granular level, without resorting to the sorts of subjective data used in some other fielding metrics. We count how many plays a player made, as well as expected plays for the average player at that position based on a pitcher's estimated groundball tendencies and the handedness of the batter. There are also adjustments for park and the base-out situations.

Pitching

Of course, how we measure fielding influences how we measure pitching.

Most sabermetric analysis of pitching has been inspired by Voros McCracken, who stated, "There is little if any difference among major-league pitchers in their ability to prevent hits on balls hit in the field of play." When first published, this statement was extremely controversial, but later research has, by and large, validated it. McCracken (and others) went forth from that finding to create a variety of defense-independent pitching measures. One that you'll see in the book is FIP, Fielding Independent Pitching, which accounts for walks, strikeouts, hit-by-pitches and homers accumulated by a pitcher and puts them into one number on an ERA scale.

The trouble is that many efforts to separate pitching from fielding have ended up separating pitching from *pitching*—looking at only a handful of variables in isolation from the situation in which they occurred. What we've done instead is take a pitcher's actual results—not just what happened, but when it happened—and adjust it for the quality of a pitcher's defensive support, as measured by FRAA.

Applying FRAA to pitchers in this sense is easier than applying it to fielders. We don't have to worry about figuring out which fielder is responsible for making an out, only identifying the likelihood of an out being made. So there is far less uncertainty here than there is in fielding analysis.

Note that Fair RA intentionally omits the "E": Looking only at earned runs tends over time to overrate three kinds of pitchers:

1. Pitchers who play in parks where scorers hand out more errors. Looking at error rates between parks tells us scorers differ significantly in how likely they are to score any given play as an error (as opposed to an infield hit);
2. Groundball pitchers, because a substantial proportion of errors occurs on groundballs; and
3. Pitchers who aren't very good. Good pitchers tend to allow fewer unearned runs than bad pitchers, because good pitchers have more ways to get out of jams than bad pitchers. They're more likely to get a strikeout to end the inning, and less likely to give up a home run.

Projections

Of course, many of you aren't turning to this book just for a look at what a player has done, but a look at what a player is going to do: The PECOTA projections.

PECOTA, initially developed by Nate Silver (who has moved on to greater fame as a political analyst), consists of three parts:

1. Major league equivalencies, to allow us to use minor-league stats to project how a player will perform in the majors;
2. Baseline forecasts, which use weighted averages and regression to the mean to produce an estimate of a player's true talent level; and
3. A career-path adjustment, which incorporates information on how comparable players' stats changed over time.

Now that we've gone over the stats, let's go over what's in the book.

The Team Prospectus

The bulk of this book comprises team chapters, with one for each of the 30 major-league franchises. On the first page of each chapter, you will be greeted by a box laying out some key statistics for each team. The one for the Rangers is shown here at the upper right.

2014 W-L is exactly as it sounds, the unadjusted tally of wins and losses. "Pythag" tallies wins and losses on an adjusted basis by taking the runs scored per game (RS/G) and allowed (RA/G) by a team in a season and running them through a version of Bill James' Pythagorean formula refined and developed by David Smyth and Brandon Heipp called "Pythagenpat."

A team's runs scored is accompanied by True Average and Baserunning Runs to give a picture of how a team scores its runs. In terms of run-prevention ability, we present a team's TAv against ("TAv-P"), FIP and Defensive Efficiency Rating ("DER"), which is its rate of balls in play turned into outs.

Then we have several measures not directly related to on-field performance. B-Age and P-Age tell us the average age of a team's batters and pitchers, respectively. Salary tells us how much the team cost to put on the field, and Doug Pappas' Marginal Dollars

RANGERS PROSPECTUS
2014 W-L: 67-95, 5TH IN AL WEST

Pythag	.411	30th		DER	.690	26th
RS/G	3.93	17th		B-Age	28.4	14th
RA/G	4.77	28th		P-Age	27.8	8th
TAv	.256	21st		Salary	$132.7M	10th
BRR	4.3	7th		M$/MW	$6.5M	29th
TAv-P	.281	30th		DL Days	2218	30th
FIP	4.25	29th		$ on DL	38%	29th

Three-Year Park Factors

Runs	Runs/RH	Runs/LH	HR/RH	HR/LH
101	101	101	81	85

Top Hitter WARP	4.9	Adrian Beltre
Top Pitcher WARP	3.8	Yu Darvish
Top Prospect		Joey Gallo

per Marginal Win (M$/MW) tells us how much a team paid above the bare minimum it had to pay and how much production above replacement it received for that money.

Finally, we count up the number of disabled-list days a team has, as well as the amount of salary paid to players while they were on the DL, expressed as a percentage of the total payroll.

Position Players

After a bylined opening essay about each team, the chapters move to the player comments, which are bylined this year for the first time, though the vagaries of player movement and the group-project nature of the book means that the names you see at the head of each chapter are more a rough guide than a precise accounting of the division of labor. Each player is listed with the major-league team by whom he was employed as of mid-December 2014, meaning that players who changed teams via free agency, trade or otherwise later in the offseason will be listed under their previous employer. As an example, take a look at the winter's record-breaking player, Giancarlo Stanton, shown at the bottom of the page.

The player-specific sections begin with biographical information before moving onto the column headers and actual data. The column headers begin with more standard information like year, team, level (majors or level of the minors), and the raw, untranslated tallies found on the back of a baseball card: PA (Plate Appearances), R (Runs), 2B (doubles), 3B (triples), HR (home runs), RBI (runs batted in), BB (walks), K (strikeouts), SB (stolen

Giancarlo Stanton   RF

Born: 11/8/89   Age: 25   Bats: R   Throws: R   Height: 6' 6"   Weight: 240

YEAR	TEAM	LVL	AGE	PA	R	2B	3B	HR	RBI	BB	K	SB	CS	AVG/OBP/SLG	TAv	BABIP	BRR	FRAA	WARP
2012	MIA	MLB	22	501	75	30	1	37	86	46	143	6	2	.290/.361/.608	.342	.344	0.1	RF(117): 6.0	6.1
2013	MIA	MLB	23	504	62	26	0	24	62	74	140	1	0	.249/.365/.480	.316	.313	0.2	RF(116): 0.4	3.8
2014	MIA	MLB	24	638	89	31	1	37	105	94	170	13	1	.288/.395/.555	.342	.353	2.3	RF(143): 11.3	8.2
2015	MIA	MLB	25	575	84	28	2	33	96	67	157	7	1	.269/.359/.531	.326	.322	0.6	RF 8	5.8

Breakout: 5%   Improve: 68%   Collapse: 1%   Attrition: 4%   MLB: 99%   Comparables: Mickey Mantle, Ryan Braun, Darryl Strawberry

bases) and CS (caught stealing). (While these stats and the similar ones for pitchers are easy to find in American organized baseball, stats from games played farther afield are harder. Thanks, then, to Clay Davenport for his site claydavenport.com, where we sourced the Cuban stats reported for certain players here.)

Following those are untranslated "slash" statistics: batting average (AVG), on-base percentage (OBP) and slugging percentage (SLG). The slash line is followed by True Average (TAv), which rolls all those things and more into one easy-to-digest number.

BABIP stands for Batting Average on Balls in Play, and is what it sounds like: How often did a ball put in play by the hitter fall for a hit? An especially low or high BABIP may mean a hitter was especially lucky or unlucky. However, hitters who hit the ball hard tend to have especially high BABIPs from season to season; so do speedy hitters who are able to beat out more grounders for base hits.

Next is Baserunning Runs (BRR) which, as mentioned earlier, covers all sorts of baserunning accomplishments, not just stolen bases. Then comes Fielding Runs Above Average; for historical stats, we have the number of games played at each position in parenthesis.

The last column is Wins Above Replacement Player. WARP is our total-value stat that combines a player's batting runs above average (derived from True Average), BRR, FRAA, an adjustment based upon position played and a credit for plate appearances based upon the difference between the "replacement level" (derived from looking at the quality of players added to a team's roster after the start of the season) and the league average.

The final line below the comment is PECOTA data, which is discussed further below.

Pitchers

Now let's look at how pitchers are presented, using the American League's reigning Cy Young: Corey Kluber, below

The first line and the YEAR, TM, LVL, and AGE columns are the same as in the hitter's example above. The next set of columns—W (Wins), L (Losses), SV (Saves), G (Games pitched), GS (Games started), IP (Innings Pitched), H (Hits), HR, BB, K, BB/9 (walks per nine innings), K/9 (strikeouts per nine innings)—are the actual, unadjusted cumulative stats compiled by the pitcher during each season.

Next is GB%, which is the percentage of all batted balls that were hit on the ground, including both outs and hits. The average GB% for a major-league pitcher in 2007 was about 45%; a pitcher with a GB% anywhere north of 50% can be considered a good groundball pitcher. As mentioned above, this is based upon the observation of human stringers and can be skewed based upon a number of factors. We've included the number as a guide, but please approach it skeptically.

BABIP is the same statistic as for batters, but often tells you more in the case of pitchers, because most pitchers have very little control over their batting average on balls in play. A high BABIP is most likely due to a poor defense or bad luck rather than a pitcher's own abilities, and may be a good indicator of a potential rebound. A typical league-average BABIP is around .290–.300.

WHIP and ERA are common to most fans, with the former measuring the number of walks and hits allowed on a per-inning basis while the latter prorates earned runs allowed on a nine innings basis. Neither is translated or adjusted in any way.

FIP was discussed above: It puts onto an ERA scale a measurement of how the pitcher performed on the events that do not involve the fielders behind him.

Fair RA (FRA), as also described above, is the basis of WARP for pitchers. Incorporating play-by-play data allows us to set different replacement levels for starting pitchers and relievers. Relief pitchers have several advantages over starters: They can give their best effort on every pitch and hitters have fewer chances to pick up on what they're doing. That means that it's significantly easier to find decent replacements for relief pitchers than it is for starting pitchers, and that's reflected in the replacement level for each.

We also credit starters for pitching deeper into games and "saving the pen"—a starting pitcher who's able to go deep in to a game (while pitching effectively) allows a manager to keep his worst relievers in the pen and bring his best relievers out to preserve a lead.

All of this means that WARP values for relief pitchers (especially closers) will seem lower than what we've seen in the past and may conflict with how we feel about relief aces coming in and "saving" the game. Saves give extra credit to the closer for what his teammates did to put him in a save spot to begin with; WARP is incapable of feeling excitement over a successful save, and judges them dispassionately.

PECOTA

Both pitchers and hitters have PECOTA projections for next season, as well as a set of biographical details that describe the performance of that player's comparable players according to PECOTA.

The 2015 line is the PECOTA projection for the player at the date we went to press. Note that the player is projected into the league and park context as indicated by his team abbreviation. All PECOTAs represent a player's projected major-league performance. The numbers beneath the player's name—Breakout, Improve, Collapse and Attrition—are also a part of PECOTA. These estimate the likelihood of changes in performance relative to a player's previously established level of production, based upon the performance of the comparable players:

- *Breakout Rate* is the percent chance that a player's production will improve by at least 20 percent relative to

Corey Kluber   RHP

Born: 4/10/86   Age: 29   Bats: R   Throws: R   Height: 6'4"   Weight: 215

YEAR	TEAM	LVL	AGE	W	L	SV	G	GS	IP	H	HR	BB	K	BB/9	K/9	GB%	BABIP	WHIP	ERA	FIP	FRA	WARP
2012	COH	AAA	26	11	7	0	21	21	125^1	121	9	49	128	3.5	9.2	48%	.316	1.36	3.59	3.34	4.56	1.6
2012	CLE	MLB	26	2	5	0	12	12	63	76	9	18	54	2.6	7.7	46%	.342	1.49	5.14	4.24	4.81	0.3
2013	COH	AAA	27	1	1	0	2	2	12^1	14	2	3	12	2.2	8.8	51%	.343	1.38	6.57	4.10	4.99	0.0
2013	CLE	MLB	27	11	5	0	26	24	147^1	153	15	33	136	2.0	8.3	48%	.329	1.26	3.85	3.33	3.97	2.0
2014	CLE	MLB	28	18	9	0	34	34	236^2	207	14	51	269	1.9	10.3	50%	.316	1.09	2.44	2.37	2.84	6.0
2015	CLE	MLB	29	11	10	0	30	30	181^1	182	16	55	181	2.7	9.0	44%	.321	1.30	3.99	3.72	4.33	1.4

Breakout: 19%   Improve: 41%   Collapse: 12%   Attrition: 18%   MLB: 68%   Comparables: *Wade LeBlanc, Marco Estrada, Rich Hill* the weighted average of his performance over his most recent seasons.

- *Improve Rate* is the percent chance that a player's production will improve at all relative to his baseline performance. A player who is expected to perform just the same as he has in the recent past will have an Improve Rate of 50 percent.
- *Collapse Rate* is the percent chance that a position player's runs produced per plate appearance will decline by at least 25 percent relative to his baseline performance over his past three seasons.
- *Attrition Rate* operates on playing time rather than performance. Specifically, it measures the likelihood that a player's playing time will decrease by at least 50 percent relative to his established level.

Breakout Rate and Collapse Rate can sometimes be counterintuitive for players who have already experienced a radical change in their performance levels. It's also worth noting that the projected decline in a given player's rate performances might not be indicative of an expected decline in underlying ability or skill, but rather something of an anticipated correction following a breakout season.

MLB% is the percentage of similar players who played in the major leagues in their relevant season.

The final pieces of information are the player's three highest-scoring comparable players as determined by PECOTA. Occasionally, a player's top comparables will not be representative of the larger sample that PECOTA uses. All comparables represent a snapshot of how the listed player was performing at the same age as the current player, so if a 23-year-old hitter is compared to Sammy Sosa, he's actually being compared to a 23-year-old Sammy Sosa, not the decrepit Orioles version of Sosa, nor to Sosa's career as a whole.

Lineouts

The stats box in the Lineouts section contains all the same information, but only has the 2014 stats for each player.

Managers

Each team chapter ends with a manager's comment and data breaking down his tactical tendencies. Though it's often difficult to isolate a manager's contribution to a team, comparing specific data modeled after well-documented plays and styles to the league average helps determine what a manager likes to do, even if we are still unable to translate that information into actual wins and losses.

Following the year, team and the actual record, Pythag +/- lets us know by how many games the team under- or overperformed its Pythagenpat record. That isn't necessarily a reflection on the manager, but it does tell us how well a team performed compared to a somewhat less noisy assessment of the underlying talent.

Pitching staff usage follows, first with AVG PC reporting the average pitch count of his starting pitchers; 100+P and 120+P track the number of games in which the starters exceeded those pitch thresholds. QS is the number of quality starts—a start of at least six innings and with no more than three runs allowed—that a manager received from his starting pitchers. BQS is Blown Quality Starts, a Baseball Prospectus stat that measures games

in which the starter delivered a quality start through six innings before losing it in the seventh inning or later. That said, a Blown Quality Start is not necessarily an indictment of a manager's abilities or tactics—a number of factors, ranging from excellent offensive support to extremely poor bullpen support, can lead a manager to leave his starter in a game after he's thrown six quality innings. Conversely, the decision by a manager to "bank" quality starts by restricting his starters to only six innings can have downsides as well, as it increases the bullpen's workload and gives it more opportunities to blow games in which the starter was cruising.

The next stats in the manager table tally how many pitching changes a manager made over the course of the season (REL) and how many times the reliever called upon didn't allow any runners, his own or inherited, to score (REL w Zero R). Bequeathed runners also count against "REL w Zero R," meaning that relievers who exit with runners on that subsequently score prevent a manager from "padding" his tally here. Concluding the pitching section, IBB is simply the number of intentional walks the manager ordered during the given season, which can be a mark of managerial strategy so long as outlying intentional-walk recipients like Miguel Cabrera are accounted for.

Managers do more than manage pitchers, however; their usage of the bench can lead to added or lost performance. PH is the number of pinch-hitters used, and PH Avg and PH HR report the offensive statistics of pinch-hitters called upon.

We then turn to the so-called small-ball tactics, starting with the running game. The manger's aggressiveness on the bases is broken down by successful steals of second and third base (SB2, SB3) and times caught (CS2, CS3). We also provide the number of sacrifices a team attempted (SAC Att) and their success rate (SAC %). Be sure to keep in mind the differences between leagues as National League sacrifice attempts are greatly inflated by the fact that pitchers bat. To correct for this, we list the number of times a manager got a successful sacrifice from a position player (POS SAC), which allows for comparisons between the two leagues. We finish up with Squeeze, which counts the number of successful squeeze plays the team executed over the season. Finally, we have a couple of statistics that attempt to measure the manager's hit-and-run tactics. Swing is the number of times a hitter swung at a pitch while the runners were in motion, while In Play reflects how many times hitters swung and made contact while those runners were off to the races. Granted, swings on steal attempts do not always translate to hit-and-run attempts, but managers who greatly deviate from the average can be assumed to be staunch proponents or opponents of the strategy.

PECOTA Leaderboards

As a result of the way it weights previous seasons, PECOTA can tend to appear bullish on players coming off a bad year and bearish on players coming off a great year. And because we list the 50th percentile projections—the middle of the range the system thinks this player is capable of producing—it rarely predicts any player will hit 40 home runs or strike out 200 batters. At the end of this book, though, we've ranked the top players according to their projections. It's often as helpful to know who the system thinks will be the top second baseman as what his actual stats are likely to be. ∎

ARIZONA DIAMONDBACKS

by David Raposa

Chief Baseball Operator Tony La Russa talking up the franchise's sterling reputation, new manager Chip Hale talking up Tony La Russa's sterling reputation as a baseball leader and the need for players to learn the fundamentals, new general manager Dave Stewart talking up the team's potential starting pitching depth—after a season when the personnel off the field outshone the personnel on the field in the worst possible way, it must be nice for Diamondbacks fans to hear some good old-fashioned baseball boilerplate from the new bosses. These sorts of bland nothings might not be the whispers knowledgeable ticket buyers necessarily want to hear, but given what polluted the airwaves previously, it's the sweetest music imaginable. Granted, continuous loogie-hawking or tone-deaf *American Idol* hopefuls would've been preferable listening alternatives to the awkward and overblown chest-puffed hyper-masculine nonsense the Kevin Towers–Kirk Gibson brain trust had to offer during their error-riddled reign.

A compilation of the duo's greatest hits reads like the unhinged rantings of an end-of-the-bar loon three beers past his cutoff point trying to tell people who aren't listening how much he's packing in his pants. There's Towers in October 2013 saying to KTAR 620 AM that "come spring training, it will be duly noted that it's going to be an eye for an eye and we're going to protect one another." There's Towers, in the same radio interview, saying he would've "fired [a carton of baseballs] into the dugout from where I was sitting behind home plate" because of how the Diamondbacks were taking an embarrassing loss to the Dodgers. There's Gibson, in August 2013, publicly sassing noted Diamondback / National League nemesis Ryan Braun for dragging his feet on his public apology for PED usage ("He's probably practicing at the theater school somewhere.") and promising to ask him a question "right to his face." There's Gibson, on camera, giving Diamondbacks reliever Evan Marshall an emphatic round of applause after Marshall plugged Braun in the back to load the bases in a June 2014 game. (Of course, Jonathan Lucroy hit a grand slam off Marshall's replacement to give the Brewers the win.) And while the notable August 2014 incident involving Andrew McCutchen and a fastball aimed squarely at his back (presumably in retaliation for Paul Goldschmidt getting his hand broken by an errant fastball in

a game where the Pirates were up five runs) didn't necessarily involve anything stupid being said by either Towers or Gibson, it's the sort of incident that speaks volumes about these men and their hilariously regressive ideas about baseball.

It'd be one thing if that kind of head-hunting buffoonery was accompanied by positive on-the-field results. Instead, the Diamondbacks followed up their surprising 2011 first-place campaign with two lackluster break-even seasons, and followed that up this past year with an honest to goodness disasterpiece. While it'd be hard for any team to overcome the unfortunate combination of downtime and down years that afflicted Arizona in 2014, it's not a stretch to suggest the team would've eaten asphalt even at full strength. The manic tinkering Towers indulged in following 2011 bore the bitterest fruit in 2014, especially when it came to the move that best exemplifies his folly. When he traded Justin Upton to the Braves, it was supposed to send a message, both to Diamondbacks fans and to the baseball world at large: It didn't matter if you were a good player—even Justin Upton good—if you weren't the right kind of player for the Diamondbacks. Given the player this statement was centered around, it didn't seem like the most sensible or defensible philosophy. The problem, however, wasn't so much the notion that Upton wasn't a "real Diamondback," but that it never seemed like Towers knew who that "real Diamondback" actually was.

Sometimes, that player was a fitfully effective reliever credited with an impressive number of saves but whose better days were well in the past (or, at the very least, nowhere near Chase Field). Sometimes, that player was a back-of-the-rotation starting pitcher mistakenly viewed (and paid) as a reliable rotational workhorse. Sometimes, that player was a stocky, defensively challenged power hitting outfielder whose power may or may not be a reliable asset. And there was that one time it was Martin Prado, a perfectly fine and versatile player for whom Towers traded a much better player. Worse than Towers' catch-as-catch-can acquisitional wanderlust, though, was his impatience with those acquisitions. Most of the notable players he signed or traded for didn't make it to their second anniversary in the Arizona clubhouse, and the brevity of their Diamondback tenure often came at a steep price. Post-

DIAMONDBACKS PROSPECTUS
2014 W-L: 64-98, 5TH IN NL WEST

Pythag	.414	29th	DER	.688	28th
RS/G	3.8	25th	B-Age	27.5	7th
RA/G	4.58	26th	P-Age	27.9	10th
TAv	.248	29th	Salary	$112M	11th
BRR	1.81	13th	M$/MW	$6.4M	28th
TAv-P	.267	22nd	DL Days	1,260	28th
FIP	3.8	20th	$ on DL	18%	20th

Three-Year Park Factors

Runs	Runs/RH	Runs/LH	HR/RH	HR/LH
104	103	101	101	101

Top Hitter WARP	4.8	Paul Goldschmidt
Top Pitcher WARP	1.0	Josh Collmenter
Top Prospect		Archie Bradley

purchase moves like flipping Brandon McCarthy to the Yankees for the useful Vidal Nuno in advance of the former's free agency were the rare exception. (And, of course, when McCarthy credited his Yankees success to returning to a pitch—the cut fastball—Arizona wouldn't let him throw, Towers responded by taking the low road: "[I]t's always good to place blame on others once you leave the organization.") Getting a 24-year-old Double-A corner infield prospect for the player who cost you Justin Upton is more in line with what Towers ultimately "accomplished." In the end, he mistook making moves for making progress, and left the Diamondbacks holding a sizable bill.

The good news is that, after this season, that bill shrinks a bit. Once 2015 is in the books, Arizona won't have to pay Trevor Cahill $12 million to hide in the bullpen or the minors anymore. (This assumes he doesn't put together a campaign that makes the new front office actually consider picking up his $13 million team option.) Bronson Arroyo's slightly more reasonable $8.5 million salary also comes off the books. Unfortunately, the same can't be said for Aaron Hill ($12 million each of the next two seasons) or that still-inexplicable contract given to Cody Ross, which has him earning $17 million over the next two years.

In addition, here are the farmhands Arizona gave up over the past three seasons: Ryan Cook, Jarrod Parker, Trevor Bauer, Bryan Shaw, Adam Eaton, Tyler Skaggs and Matt Davidson. That's a decent set of cost-controlled starting pitchers (injuries notwithstanding), a quality reliever, a solid outfielder (who is a lot cheaper and younger than Cody Ross) and a 22-year-old corner infield prospect. It's probably just a coincidence that there's a significant overlap between the kinds of rookies Towers shipped out and the kinds of veterans he brought in. Also, those players—young, cost-controlled, full of promise—would be a lot to lose for a team that could correct its mistakes by offering triple-digit contracts to the best free agents available; for a medium-market team like Arizona, it's a loss of disastrous proportions. What makes these trades even worse is how little the Diamondbacks got back. After moving all that talent, the 2015 Arizona Diamondbacks can call upon the diminishing Trevor Cahill, a less-than-inspiring Mark Trumbo, the inconsistent established-closer stylings of Addison Reed, a handful of less-established minor leaguers and whatever unsold Justin Upton jerseys they have in storage.

Despite the best efforts of the Towers regime, though, the Diamondbacks aren't necessarily in the worst position imaginable. They have one of the best sluggers in the game—Paul Goldschmidt—inked to a very favorable contract. Despite all of Towers' wheeling and dealing, they still have a young, homegrown starting staff that's shown the potential to be good, if not great, and that's not even taking into account remaining Upton trade chit Randall Delgado or any of the pitchers they still have on the farm. (Flipping Wade Miley to the Red Sox for more young arms and minor-league depth is exactly the sort of move that should be made with this surplus.) Assuming he stays healthy

and builds on his promising rookie campaign, A.J. Pollock will help Arizona fans forget about the loss of Adam Eaton. In moving Didi Gregorius (the key piece acquired in the Trevor Bauer trade), the Diamondbacks are showing faith that Chris Owings can build on his work last year. In addition to the dead weight coming off their books in 2015, the Diamondbacks found a buyer for the $40 million remaining on Miguel Montero's contract; there's a chance someone will take Aaron Hill and Cody Ross, and the tens of millions of dollars owed both players, off Arizona's hands as well. Seriously contending with either the deep-pocketed Dodgers, the transactionally scrappy Giants or the suddenly maniacal Padres is still a few years away, but there's a solid foundation to build on. It's just a matter of capitalizing on the strong base by making the right moves, or at the very least not making the wrong moves (i.e. doing a lot of what the previous regime did).

So far, the La Russa-Stewart cabal seems to be in the business of taking some shrewd, if still potentially questionable, gambles. Signing Cuban émigré Yasmany Tomas to a six-year deal for $68 million might not seem the move a hole-riddled 64-win team should make, but the potential of getting a player entering his athletic prime who produces at a level well above his $11 million price tag outweighs the risk of being saddled with another double-digit millstone. Slightly less justifiable is trading two farmhands for the services of onetime FIP-flouter Jeremy Hellickson. Stewart's on record saying that the Diamondbacks are in the market for pitching, but (a) the number of major league-ready pitchers they already have (or, in the case of the injured Patrick Corbin, will soon have) belies that need, and (b) Hellickson's lackluster performance the past two seasons makes him the sort of guy who creates a need for pitching help rather than fills one. Still, Hellickson's cheaper than some of the other space-filling veterans currently on the roster, he has some track record of success and the players Stewart gave to Tampa Bay are young enough that it'll take a few years for this trade to look lopsided, if it ever does. Even cutting bait on Gregorius—instead of installing him as half of a long-term double-play combo with Owings—can be spun in the Diamondbacks' favor, if you see the acquisition of Robbie Ray and Domingo Leyba as the Diamondbacks adding back organizational depth they needlessly lost over the past few years.

These handful of moves seem to be getting the franchise pointed in the right direction. They won't all work, but at least they're understandable pieces of a plan to build a talented baseball team rather than a squad of knuckleheaded beanbrawlers. There's nothing explosive or inflammatory or inexplicable about these transactions; in a sense, they're just boring, run-of-the-mill baseball moves. Given the volatility and silliness that typified the last Diamondbacks regime, some boredom—blissful, yawn-inducing, ulcer-quieting boredom—is just what the doctor ordered. ∎

—David Raposa has written for, among others, The Classical, the Village Voice, Pitchfork *and The Awl.*

Player comments by Tommy Rancel, Craig Goldstein and Baseball Prospectus Authors

Hitters

Nick Ahmed   SS

Born: 3/15/90   Age: 25   Bats: R   Throws: R   Height: 6' 3"   Weight: 205

YEAR	TEAM	LVL	AGE	PA	R	2B	3B	HR	RBI	BB	K	SB	CS	AVG/OBP/SLG	TAv	BABIP	BRR	FRAA	WARP
2012	LYN	A+	22	571	84	36	4	6	49	49	102	40	10	.269/.337/.391	.270	.325	5.6	SS(128): 17.5	5.6
2013	MOB	AA	23	538	58	21	5	4	46	33	72	26	7	.236/.288/.324	.231	.266	1.3	SS(133): 21.5, 2B(2): -0.2	3.0
2014	RNO	AAA	24	452	57	26	4	4	47	37	55	14	6	.312/.373/.425	.270	.352	0.3	SS(91): 12.9, 2B(14): 0.1	3.8
2014	ARI	MLB	24	75	9	2	0	1	4	3	10	0	1	.200/.233/.271	.200	.220	1.0	SS(18): -2.3, 2B(2): -0.0	-0.3
2015	ARI	MLB	25	250	27	11	2	2	18	13	47	7	2	.239/.280/.333	.228	.284	0.5	SS 6, 2B -0	1.0

Breakout: 5%   Improve: 14%   Collapse: 6%   Attrition: 19%   MLB: 32%   Comparables: *Darwin Barney, Ozzie Martinez, Anderson Hernandez*

Score another one for the Pacific Coast League's offensive environment. Ahmed, a light-hitting infielder, put up a gaudy slash line as a member of the Reno Aces but failed while facing the aces (and also-rans) at the highest level. The former second-round pick from UConn is neither a defensive dynamo nor a burner on the bases. By all accounts he is hard working and has a full-throttle approach, but Sheriff Towers doesn't patrol these parts anymore, son. The skill set appears unambiguous: a potential utility infielder adept at breaking up potential game-ending double plays.

Sergio Alcantara   SS

Born: 7/10/96   Age: 18   Bats: B   Throws: R   Height: 5'10   Weight: 150

YEAR	TEAM	LVL	AGE	PA	R	2B	3B	HR	RBI	BB	K	SB	CS	AVG/OBP/SLG	TAv	BABIP	BRR	FRAA	WARP
2015	ARI	MLB	18	250	21	8	1	1	15	23	71	0	0	.190/.268/.249	.199	.266	-0.3	SS 4	-0.2

Breakout: 0%   Improve: 0%   Collapse: 0%   Attrition: 0%   MLB: 0%   Comparables: *Ruben Tejada, Tyler Pastornicky, L.J. Hoes*

Alcantara is Anderson Hernandez's nephew—only here, in these pages, in this safe space where you and I share this time, would that sentence mean a thing—and signed for $700,000 in July 2012. He doesn't lack for tools, displaying a quick first step, soft hands and a fantastic arm. Alcantara's precocious strike-zone knowledge sets him apart, and allowed him to walk 15 percent of the time despite his spotting the average pitcher three years of life experience. There's risk here, as there is with any player this age, and his most likely outcome involves a utility future. Still, there's a chance Alcantara hits his 90th percentile outcome and becomes a first-division starter.

Zach Borenstein   LF

Born: 7/23/90   Age: 24   Bats: L   Throws: R   Height: 6' 0"   Weight: 225

YEAR	TEAM	LVL	AGE	PA	R	2B	3B	HR	RBI	BB	K	SB	CS	AVG/OBP/SLG	TAv	BABIP	BRR	FRAA	WARP
2012	CDR	A	21	327	42	25	3	11	50	27	60	13	5	.266/.339/.485	.286	.300	0.3	LF(66): -4.0, RF(6): -0.7	1.4
2013	INL	A+	22	465	76	22	7	28	95	43	88	5	5	.337/.403/.631	.368	.366	-4.5		5.7
2014	ARK	AA	23	207	23	13	2	5	28	21	53	6	4	.266/.338/.440	.280	.344	2.6	LF(42): -3.0	0.9
2014	MOB	AA	23	102	13	4	2	3	14	12	17	3	0	.241/.333/.437	.290	.261	0.4	LF(21): -0.2	0.2
2014	RNO	AAA	23	81	12	4	1	5	15	7	22	0	1	.260/.321/.548	.282	.298	-0.7	RF(19): 0.7, LF(1): 0.0	0.2
2014	SLC	AAA	23	123	11	4	0	2	22	3	33	0	2	.256/.279/.342	.223	.337	-1.8	LF(29): -1.8, RF(1): -0.1	-0.8
2015	ARI	MLB	24	250	27	11	2	9	31	15	67	3	2	.242/.291/.417	.257	.298	-0.2	LF -2, RF -0	0.1

Breakout: 0%   Improve: 18%   Collapse: 11%   Attrition: 16%   MLB: 41%   Comparables: *Corey Dickerson, Eric Thames, Kyle Parker*

Acquired for Joe Thatcher, Borenstein is a bat-first player who has made a name for himself with an advanced approach and California League Power. Of the many ways of pooh-poohing a player's pop, that one is probably less damning than Warning Track Power but maybe a bit less promising than Five O'Clock Power. He employs a toe-tap timing mechanism, uses only a slight load, and can get to balls down and in (classic left-hander). But without a big-league power tool, nobody will want to live with his defense. He's weak enough against same-side arms that he profiles as a left-handed platoon bat.

Socrates Brito   RF

Born: 9/6/92   Age: 22   Bats: L   Throws: L   Height: 6' 2"   Weight: 200

YEAR	TEAM	LVL	AGE	PA	R	2B	3B	HR	RBI	BB	K	SB	CS	AVG/OBP/SLG	TAv	BABIP	BRR	FRAA	WARP
2013	SBN	A	20	566	61	24	9	2	49	37	124	27	9	.264/.313/.356	.248	.340	0.0	RF(105): 3.8, CF(25): -0.3	0.0
2014	VIS	A+	21	561	82	30	5	10	62	36	109	38	10	.293/.339/.429	.275	.351	6.9	RF(72): 6.8, CF(43): -0.1	3.2
2015	ARI	MLB	22	250	22	10	2	2	19	9	69	8	3	.224/.250/.302	.206	.303	0.8	RF 2, CF 0	-0.6

Breakout: 0%   Improve: 0%   Collapse: 0%   Attrition: 0%   MLB: 0%   Comparables: *Denis Phipps, Brennan Boesch, Abraham Almonte*

Neck-and-neck with Jose Jose as top name in the the system, Brito has benefitted from the slow-and-low development beat. He's still raw in many facets of the game, and while his High-A stat line looks good, put it in context and he was actually below league average offensively. His power and hit tools are often questioned, and neither projects to be even mediocre. He can still be an everyday player, thanks to his arm, glove and speed all rating above average.

Brandon Drury   3B

Born: 8/21/92   Age: 22   Bats: R   Throws: R   Height: 6' 2"   Weight: 190

YEAR	TEAM	LVL	AGE	PA	R	2B	3B	HR	RBI	BB	K	SB	CS	AVG/OBP/SLG	TAv	BABIP	BRR	FRAA	WARP
2012	ROM	A	19	480	47	22	3	6	51	20	73	3	4	.229/.270/.333	.215	.259	-3.6	1B(55): -1.9, 3B(44): -0.9	-2.2
2013	SBN	A	20	583	78	51	4	15	85	47	92	1	1	.302/.362/.500	.308	.340	-3.8	3B(108): 4.1	4.9
2014	VIS	A+	21	478	73	35	1	19	81	41	76	4	3	.300/.366/.519	.306	.326	-2.7	3B(94): 2.1	3.8
2014	MOB	AA	21	116	12	7	0	4	14	7	19	0	0	.295/.345/.476	.306	.321	0.8	3B(28): -1.8, 2B(2): -0.0	0.9
2015	ARI	MLB	22	250	22	13	1	6	27	10	58	0	0	.233/.266/.371	.233	.280	-0.4	3B -0, 1B -0	-0.3

Breakout: 0%   Improve: 0%   Collapse: 0%   Attrition: 0%   MLB: 0%   Comparables: *Neil Walker, Josh Vitters, Mat Gamel*

Acquired as part of the Justin Upton trade, Drury lacks the over-the-fence power associated with the hot corner archetype. That might feel like a funny thing to read, given that he set a new career high in home runs, but 19 of the 23 came with Visalia, which inflates numbers like a sleazy accountant. It's not a mechanical defect—he shifts his weight well—he would just rather make contact than sell out for extra thump. Drury's emphasis on the gaps requires secondary skills for his bat to play the position, so consider it a positive that he sustained his improved walk rate. He should return to Double-A, after closing out the year there.

Paul Goldschmidt 1B

Born: 9/10/87   Age: 27   Bats: R   Throws: R   Height: 6' 3"   Weight: 245

YEAR	TEAM	LVL	AGE	PA	R	2B	3B	HR	RBI	BB	K	SB	CS	AVG/OBP/SLG	TAv	BABIP	BRR	FRAA	WARP
2012	ARI	MLB	24	587	82	43	1	20	82	60	130	18	3	.286/.359/.490	.307	.340	2.2	1B(139): -2.8	3.4
2013	ARI	MLB	25	710	103	36	3	36	125	99	145	15	7	.302/.401/.551	.325	.343	-0.3	1B(159): 15.9	7.5
2014	ARI	MLB	26	479	75	39	1	19	69	64	110	9	3	.300/.396/.542	.332	.368	3.9	1B(109): 3.3	4.8
2015	ARI	MLB	27	493	70	27	2	22	74	61	114	10	3	.283/.372/.512	.320	.333	1.2	1B 2	3.9

Breakout: 2%   Improve: 58%   Collapse: 6%   Attrition: 6%   MLB: 99%   *Comparables: Joey Votto, Miguel Cabrera, Prince Fielder*

The Kevin Towers Era will not be looked upon favorably in Arizona's history, but his early 2013 extension of Goldschmidt is a deal that will be lauded for years to come. A broken hand limited the slugger to just 109 games but the production up until that point was an almost hit-for-hit, walk-for-walk, HBP-for-HBP match for his near-MVP 2013 season. Not only is he a stud with the bat, but is non-zero with the glove and can cut a rug on the bases about as well as any man of his size. His only downfall is the nickname "Goldy." See how easily "Gold Man Jacks" rolls off the tongue?

Aaron Hill 2B

Born: 3/21/82   Age: 33   Bats: R   Throws: R   Height: 5' 11"   Weight: 205

YEAR	TEAM	LVL	AGE	PA	R	2B	3B	HR	RBI	BB	K	SB	CS	AVG/OBP/SLG	TAv	BABIP	BRR	FRAA	WARP
2012	ARI	MLB	30	668	93	44	6	26	85	52	86	14	5	.302/.360/.522	.296	.317	-0.3	2B(153): 23.2	6.8
2013	RNO	AAA	31	26	8	1	1	0	6	1	3	0	0	.375/.385/.500	.281	.409	0.1	2B(6): 0.7	0.2
2013	ARI	MLB	31	362	45	21	1	11	41	29	48	1	4	.291/.356/.462	.288	.312	-0.1	2B(84): -0.8	1.8
2014	ARI	MLB	32	541	52	26	3	10	60	28	92	4	3	.244/.287/.367	.234	.276	-2.6	2B(116): 5.3, 3B(7): 0.1	0.2
2015	ARI	MLB	33	476	57	23	2	12	48	30	74	6	3	.252/.304/.398	.257	.275	-0.8	2B 5, 3B 0	1.9

Breakout: 1%   Improve: 37%   Collapse: 5%   Attrition: 7%   MLB: 94%   *Comparables: Brandon Phillips, Mark Ellis, Orlando Hudson*

Hill was healthy for most of the 2014 season, which is good, but that is about the only positive to take away from what was otherwise a dismal season. He struck out at the highest rate of his career while walking at the lowest. He is a non-factor in the running game, and FRAA is the only kid at advanced defensive metrics camp who still considers him a plus defender at the keystone. Hill still hits pitches with velocity, which is a good sign for his bat speed, but pitches with wiggle give him fits. He has rebounded from poor performances in the past, but he is owed $24 million through 2016 and will be 33 when the first pitch of 2015 is thrown. With several talented youngsters available up the middle, the Arizona infield is no country for old men.

Ender Inciarte CF

Born: 10/29/90   Age: 24   Bats: L   Throws: L   Height: 5' 10"   Weight: 165

YEAR	TEAM	LVL	AGE	PA	R	2B	3B	HR	RBI	BB	K	SB	CS	AVG/OBP/SLG	TAv	BABIP	BRR	FRAA	WARP
2012	SBN	A	21	264	36	16	5	1	30	31	31	18	4	.293/.375/.422	.310	.332	0.4	CF(64): 7.6	3.0
2012	VIS	A+	21	279	46	12	5	1	17	22	32	28	8	.319/.377/.419	.292	.361	2.9	CF(29): 2.9, LF(21): 1.2	2.1
2013	MOB	AA	22	516	68	17	3	5	25	27	47	43	8	.281/.327/.362	.269	.303	8.4	CF(94): 8.0, RF(22): -0.6	4.2
2014	RNO	AAA	23	120	22	4	2	2	12	10	21	7	2	.312/.367/.440	.273	.368	2.2	CF(25): -3.1	0.5
2014	ARI	MLB	23	447	54	18	2	4	27	25	53	19	3	.278/.318/.359	.251	.310	2.3	CF(76): 7.8, LF(37): 3.2	2.8
2015	ARI	MLB	24	410	48	17	3	4	31	20	60	20	4	.268/.305/.362	.247	.301	1.4	CF 6, LF 2	1.6

Breakout: 6%   Improve: 25%   Collapse: 7%   Attrition: 21%   MLB: 60%   *Comparables: Ben Revere, Julio Borbon, Michael Brantley*

Inciarte is in the running for Best Season By A Player Not Included In Last Year's BP Annual. A.J. Pollock's broken hand forced Inciarte into regular duty for most of the summer, and though the former Rule 5 pick lacks the incumbent's offensive acumen, he's a burner who provided plenty of value on the basepaths and on defense. He started slowly at the plate, but was able to bring his numbers to a respectable level by season's end. He has an aggressive approach, reaching out of the zone regularly, but also has good bat-to-ball skills. This leads to a decent average—buoyed by the ability to leg out infield hits—and a mediocre on-base percentage. In an ideal world he is nifty fourth outfielder without a platoon hole. In the Diamondbacks' less-than-ideal 2014 season, though, Inciarte held his own.

Jacob Lamb 3B

Born: 10/9/90   Age: 24   Bats: L   Throws: R   Height: 6' 3"   Weight: 220

YEAR	TEAM	LVL	AGE	PA	R	2B	3B	HR	RBI	BB	K	SB	CS	AVG/OBP/SLG	TAv	BABIP	BRR	FRAA	WARP
2013	VIS	A+	22	283	44	20	0	13	47	48	70	0	0	.303/.424/.558	.331	.380	-0.1	3B(55): -2.3	2.8
2014	MOB	AA	23	439	60	35	5	14	79	50	99	0	0	.318/.399/.551	.340	.389	-1.1	3B(97): 2.4	4.8
2014	RNO	AAA	23	21	3	4	0	1	5	3	4	2	0	.500/.571/.889	.464	.615	0.1	3B(5): -0.2, 1B(1): -0.1	0.5
2014	ARI	MLB	23	133	15	4	1	4	11	6	37	1	1	.230/.263/.373	.226	.291	0.4	3B(34): 0.4	0.0
2015	ARI	MLB	24	250	27	13	1	7	31	20	70	1	0	.251/.315/.418	.269	.326	-0.2	3B 0, 1B -0	0.8

Breakout: 0%   Improve: 22%   Collapse: 26%   Attrition: 32%   MLB: 68%   *Comparables: Mat Gamel, Alex Liddi, Chase Headley*

After fewer than 400 at-bats in the upper minors, Lamb was led to the slaughter. Impressive as his Double-A work had been, the promotion was based more on the Diamondbacks' needs than any true conviction he could handle the jump. He's got plenty of swing-and-miss within the zone, particularly above the belt, where his whiff rate was roughly double the major-league average. NL pitchers had no trouble exploiting that flaw, repeatedly. At just 23, there's no reason to write him off, but he's a cautionary tale for scouting the stat line, as everything he did in the minors implied an ability to hit better than he probably will.

Peter O'Brien   C

Born: 7/15/90   Age: 24   Bats: R   Throws: R   Height: 6' 3"   Weight: 215

YEAR	TEAM	LVL	AGE	PA	R	2B	3B	HR	RBI	BB	K	SB	CS	AVG/OBP/SLG	TAv	BABIP	BRR	FRAA	WARP
2012	STA	A-	21	213	27	8	0	10	32	10	61	0	1	.202/.249/.394	.248	.233	-1.3	C(33): 1.2	0.3
2013	CSC	A	22	226	47	22	1	11	41	22	58	0	0	.325/.394/.619	.396	.397	0.9	C(53): -0.2	4.6
2013	TAM	A+	22	280	31	17	3	11	55	19	76	0	1	.265/.314/.486	.280	.326	0.1	3B(38): -3.9, C(12): -0.1	1.0
2014	TAM	A+	23	119	19	9	1	10	19	4	29	0	0	.321/.353/.688	.349	.351	-0.1	C(24): -0.3, RF(6): 0.1	1.6
2014	TRN	AA	23	294	47	14	1	23	51	16	77	0	0	.245/.296/.555	.291	.253	-0.9	1B(27): -0.2, C(19): 0.1	1.0
2015	ARI	MLB	24	250	29	11	1	13	38	10	81	0	0	.234/.270/.462	.264	.289	-0.4	C -0, 1B -0	0.7

Breakout: 2%   Improve: 16%   Collapse: 18%   Attrition: 23%   MLB: 43%   *Comparables: Xavier Scruggs, Travis d'Arnaud, Matt Clark*

Acquired from the Yankees for Martin Prado at the trade deadline, O'Brien enjoyed a breakout 2014. His strong performance earned him a spot in both the Futures Game and on the Eastern League All-Star team, as well as a trip to the Arizona Fall League. O'Brien employs a swing longer than *The English Patient*, and packs nearly as much power—helping him finish the season with 34 home runs, good for fifth in the minor leagues. It remains to be seen where Arizona will play O'Brien, as the Yankees had been using him at catcher, first, third and designated hitter. The Diamondbacks hope that O'Brien can mature into a Mark Trumbo-type hitter, as he already resembles the slugger in the field.

Chris Owings   SS

Born: 8/12/91   Age: 23   Bats: R   Throws: R   Height: 5' 10"   Weight: 190

YEAR	TEAM	LVL	AGE	PA	R	2B	3B	HR	RBI	BB	K	SB	CS	AVG/OBP/SLG	TAv	BABIP	BRR	FRAA	WARP
2012	VIS	A+	20	257	51	16	2	11	24	13	63	8	3	.324/.362/.544	.317	.399	1.4	SS(55): 1.0	3.0
2012	MOB	AA	20	310	35	10	3	6	28	11	69	4	3	.263/.291/.377	.230	.324	-0.2	SS(67): 6.5	1.1
2013	RNO	AAA	21	575	104	31	8	12	81	22	99	20	7	.330/.359/.482	.272	.386	6.3	SS(111): 8.7, 2B(11): -0.8	4.2
2013	ARI	MLB	21	61	5	5	0	0	5	6	10	2	0	.291/.361/.382	.254	.356	-0.9	SS(13): -0.6, 2B(3): 0.2	0.0
2014	RNO	AAA	22	40	6	1	0	0	1	0	9	3	0	.250/.250/.275	.177	.323	0.8	2B(8): 1.0, SS(1): -0.0	-0.2
2014	ARI	MLB	22	332	34	15	6	6	26	16	67	8	1	.261/.300/.406	.249	.314	-0.8	SS(61): -1.6, 2B(18): -0.5	0.3
2015	ARI	MLB	23	333	38	15	3	7	31	10	75	8	2	.262/.286/.390	.247	.320	-1.1	SS 3, 2B 0	1.1

Breakout: 11%   Improve: 42%   Collapse: 6%   Attrition: 23%   MLB: 63%   *Comparables: Tony Abreu, Grant Green, Howie Kendrick*

After his promising debut, Owings' sequel got chipped away by all sorts of second-year taxes: Right-handers with a plan bullied him with breaking stuff; his previous strike-zone issues resurfaced; and a shoulder injury wiped out two months of his summer (and ultimately required offseason surgery). Results aside, C.O. has star qualities. He is rangy with a good throwing arm, has simple hitting mechanics, and makes loud contact for a player his size. He absolutely tears down the first base line, and as a rule would rather run (rather well) than walk anywhere. He doesn't just have good instincts, he has great ones, as in an April 4th highlight: He dove into the hole to field a ball, hopped up, considered a play at third, but did the algebra just in time to spin and get a force out at second. Provided his shoulder holds up, Owings still stands a chance to be the best of a young group of infielders.

Cliff Pennington   SS

Born: 6/15/84   Age: 31   Bats: B   Throws: R   Height: 5' 10"   Weight: 195

YEAR	TEAM	LVL	AGE	PA	R	2B	3B	HR	RBI	BB	K	SB	CS	AVG/OBP/SLG	TAv	BABIP	BRR	FRAA	WARP
2012	OAK	MLB	28	462	50	18	2	6	28	35	90	15	6	.215/.278/.311	.234	.259	2.9	SS(93): 6.4, 2B(32): 3.2	1.8
2013	ARI	MLB	29	299	25	13	1	1	18	26	54	2	0	.242/.310/.309	.233	.298	3.0	SS(51): 2.0, 2B(29): 0.5	0.9
2014	ARI	MLB	30	201	21	5	3	2	10	20	36	6	1	.254/.340/.350	.271	.309	0.2	SS(23): -0.8, 2B(18): 0.7	1.1
2015	ARI	MLB	31	250	26	11	2	3	22	20	48	6	2	.250/.313/.356	.250	.298	1.1	SS 1, 2B 1	1.1

Breakout: 0%   Improve: 37%   Collapse: 5%   Attrition: 4%   MLB: 95%   *Comparables: Barry Larkin, Nick Punto, Julio Lugo*

Pennington succeeded as a suitable substitute substance, except when disabling thumb supination required the Diamondbacks to summon a superutility subcontractor for the summer. He appeared at three different positions defensively, with most of his work coming up the middle. The 30-year-old does not have standout tools but is more than capable of defending at shortstop and second base. A drop in swings on pitches out of the zone resulted in a higher walk rate and more on-base opportunities. Meanwhile, his bat overall remains relatively harmless. There are younger and cheaper players who could do a similar job, but seven figures is a fair price to pay for reliable infield depth.

David Peralta   OF

Born: 8/14/87   Age: 27   Bats: L   Throws: L   Height: 6' 2"   Weight: 215

YEAR	TEAM	LVL	AGE	PA	R	2B	3B	HR	RBI	BB	K	SB	CS	AVG/OBP/SLG	TAv	BABIP	BRR	FRAA	WARP
2013	VIS	A+	25	219	29	15	0	8	42	9	28	1	0	.346/.370/.534	.300	.368	0.5	LF(36): 1.2, RF(8): -0.6	1.5
2014	MOB	AA	26	223	33	17	1	6	46	18	21	2	0	.297/.359/.480	.317	.307	1.8	LF(43): 2.0, CF(4): -0.4	2.3
2014	ARI	MLB	26	348	40	12	9	8	36	16	60	6	3	.286/.320/.450	.272	.328	0.1	RF(40): 0.2, LF(36): -3.7	0.8
2015	ARI	MLB	27	317	32	15	4	7	37	14	54	4	1	.274/.307/.422	.266	.310	0.2	LF -1, RF -0	0.5

Breakout: 5%   Improve: 42%   Collapse: 10%   Attrition: 21%   MLB: 84%   *Comparables: Juan Rivera, Andy Dirks, Ben Francisco*

Peralta isn't old enough to be a journeyman, but check out this journey, man: A native of Venezuela, he came stateside as a pitcher in the Cardinals' organization. Multiple shoulder surgeries later, he was out of the affiliated world, having never passed rookie ball. Four *years* later, he showed up as an outfielder for the independent Rio Grande WhiteWings in 2011. The next year, a Diamondbacks scout filed a positive report on Peralta—who was by then a Wichita Wingnut—and a year after that, while he was playing for the Amarillo Sox, Arizona signed him and sent him to A-Ball. His athleticism and hard style of play caught the attention of top executives the following spring training, so much so that he was called up on June 1st and took over as the team's primary right fielder. In just 88 games, Peralta produced 29 extra-base hits, showing a blend of pop and speed. Defensively there are still kinks to work out, but he has a strong arm (duh!) and will likely be okay in a corner. He's unlikely to grow into a star, but he'll never have to suck on a hot sauce packet for lunch again.

A.J. Pollock   CF

Born: 12/5/87   Age: 27   Bats: R   Throws: R   Height: 6' 1"   Weight: 195

YEAR	TEAM	LVL	AGE	PA	R	2B	3B	HR	RBI	BB	K	SB	CS	AVG/OBP/SLG	TAv	BABIP	BRR	FRAA	WARP
2012	RNO	AAA	24	471	65	25	3	3	52	32	52	21	8	.318/.369/.411	.261	.353	3.4	CF(63): 2.6, RF(29): -0.5	1.6
2012	ARI	MLB	24	93	8	4	1	2	8	9	11	1	2	.247/.315/.395	.253	.257	-1.5	CF(14): 0.7, LF(7): 0.4	0.2
2013	ARI	MLB	25	482	64	28	5	8	38	33	82	12	3	.269/.322/.409	.259	.314	2.8	CF(110): -3.0, RF(7): -0.4	1.4
2014	RNO	AAA	26	52	4	1	1	0	9	2	4	0	0	.163/.192/.224	.146	.174	1.1	CF(13): -0.1	-0.4
2014	ARI	MLB	26	287	41	19	6	7	24	19	46	14	3	.302/.353/.498	.306	.344	1.9	CF(68): -3.2, LF(2): -0.1	1.8
2015	ARI	MLB	27	317	38	16	3	5	28	20	54	10	3	.266/.314/.392	.260	.307	0.8	CF -2, LF -0	0.7

Breakout: 11%   Improve: 39%   Collapse: 5%   Attrition: 18%   MLB: 92%   *Comparables: Jon Jay, Desmond Jennings, Franklin Gutierrez*

Pollock was headed for a breakout season until an inside pitch from Johnny Cueto broke his right hand in late May. The three missed months kept him from chasing a 20/20 season or flagging down the Gold Glove consideration he deserves. He has good contact skills and his power extends beyond the wall thanks to a strong upper-body swing. Pollock can get passive and take strikes that should be offered at. His lower body is relatively quiet through his swing process but once the ball is in play his legs are a tremendous asset. Those last dozen words are true on defense, too: His long limbs allow him to close quickly and provide extended reach. Though he is a heady ballplayer with proficient awareness, he has the occasional misread; however, the physical tools typically bail him out. There will be a lot of turnover in Arizona in 2015, but Pollock should pick up where he left off.

Cody Ross   OF

Born: 12/23/80   Age: 34   Bats: R   Throws: L   Height: 5' 10"   Weight: 195

YEAR	TEAM	LVL	AGE	PA	R	2B	3B	HR	RBI	BB	K	SB	CS	AVG/OBP/SLG	TAv	BABIP	BRR	FRAA	WARP
2012	BOS	MLB	31	528	70	34	1	22	81	42	129	2	3	.267/.326/.481	.289	.317	0.2	RF(96): 0.0, LF(22): -2.4	2.4
2013	ARI	MLB	32	351	33	17	1	8	38	25	50	3	2	.278/.331/.413	.267	.303	-0.7	LF(46): -0.7, RF(44): 4.1	1.4
2014	RNO	AAA	33	32	2	1	0	0	7	1	5	0	0	.290/.313/.323	.221	.346	-0.2	LF(6): -0.2, RF(3): -0.1	-0.2
2014	ARI	MLB	33	219	15	8	0	2	15	15	44	0	0	.252/.306/.322	.233	.312	-0.2	LF(37): -4.3, RF(20): -0.4	-0.9
2015	ARI	MLB	34	250	26	12	1	6	29	18	54	1	1	.254/.311/.398	.262	.302	0.0	RF 1, LF -2	0.4

Breakout: 0%   Improve: 31%   Collapse: 13%   Attrition: 20%   MLB: 90%   *Comparables: Billy Williams, Rondell White, Jacque Jones*

Remember that awful moment in 2013, when Ross was running calmly to first and his hip suddenly fractured? The slow recovery from such a painful break was as predictable as the injury itself was unpredictable. Ross was limited to just 83 games (a calf strain also got in the way), and it might have been 83 too many. His bat speed decayed, he had trouble turning on fastballs, and his resulting slugging percentage wouldn't win a batting title. Worse, the sneaky-great defense he had shown the previous year was gone; depending on your metric of choice, he was around 10 or 20 runs worse in 2014. Entering his age 34 season, the $9.5 million question: Is he a rebound candidate or a sunk cost? Unfortunately, probably the latter.

Yasmany Tomas   OF

Born: 11/14/90   Age: 24   Bats: R   Throws: R   Height: 6' 2"   Weight: 230

What we know about Tomas—who signed for six years and $68.5 million—is that we don't know enough. He's a thick 6-feet-1, 230 pounds, and while he's a good athlete for his size, his build does affect his range, likely limiting him to left field. His power is his carrying tool, but its plus-plus potential could be shorn by an inability to make consistent, hard contact. While his swing isn't overly long, approach issues are going to lead to elevated strikeout totals. The final package is a work in progress; Tomas is raw in many areas but older than most premier prospects. This leaves him in a sort of purgatory, as his large contract is going to lead to large expectations. There is significant boom-or-bust potential here, so while the average annual value of the deal justifies modest expectations, a deterioration in physique or a stalled hit tool could have the Arizona faithful begging "no mas" by year six. Something in the vein of Khris Davis' 2014 seems like a reasonable middle ground.

Stryker Trahan   C

Born: 4/25/94   Age: 21   Bats: L   Throws: R   Height: 5' 11"   Weight: 215

YEAR	TEAM	LVL	AGE	PA	R	2B	3B	HR	RBI	BB	K	SB	CS	AVG/OBP/SLG	TAv	BABIP	BRR	FRAA	WARP
2014	SBN	A	20	407	47	21	1	13	52	30	146	3	0	.198/.264/.367	.232	.282	5.9	RF(66): -4.3, LF(19): -1.2	0.2
2014	YAK	A-	20	131	15	7	1	6	22	15	23	2	2	.257/.344/.496	.317	.267	0.8	C(15): -0.2, RF(6): -0.3	1.1
2015	ARI	MLB	21	250	21	8	1	7	26	14	94	0	0	.182/.231/.310	.201	.264	-0.3	RF -2, C -0	-1.2

Breakout: 0%   Improve: 0%   Collapse: 0%   Attrition: 0%   MLB: 0%   *Comparables: Jamie Romak, Yorman Rodriguez, Steven Moya*

With a name and frame like this, you might expect Trahan to be a linebacker, American Gladiator or fitness consigliere. Truth is, his role with South Bend last season was so ill-defined that he actually *might* have snuck in some time as one of those, at least when a lefty was on the mound. Although most catchers' bats would welcome a move from the position, Trahan's did not. Things got so bad the D'backs demoted him to short-season ball and relocated him to his old spot behind the dish. Trahan soon started hitting again, leaving management in a tough spot. Wherever he plays, he remains a project the scale of the Big Dig. Luckily for him, the high ceiling will buy him time.

Mark Trumbo   LF

Born: 1/16/86   Age: 29   Bats: R   Throws: R   Height: 6' 4"   Weight: 235

YEAR	TEAM	LVL	AGE	PA	R	2B	3B	HR	RBI	BB	K	SB	CS	AVG/OBP/SLG	TAv	BABIP	BRR	FRAA	WARP
2012	ANA	MLB	26	586	66	19	3	32	95	36	153	4	5	.268/.317/.491	.287	.316	-3.3	LF(66): -1.0, RF(35): -2.6	1.7
2013	ANA	MLB	27	678	85	30	2	34	100	54	184	5	2	.234/.294/.453	.274	.273	-3.5	1B(123): 6.3, RF(19): -0.4	2.0
2014	ARI	MLB	28	362	37	15	1	14	61	28	89	2	3	.235/.293/.415	.254	.274	-2.2	1B(43): -3.4, LF(41): -2.2	-0.6
2015	ARI	MLB	29	407	51	18	2	20	61	27	103	3	2	.253/.304/.471	.282	.293	-1.8	1B 0, LF -0	1.3

Breakout: 3%   Improve: 53%   Collapse: 1%   Attrition: 1%   MLB: 94%   *Comparables: Jonny Gomes, George Foster, Albert Belle*

There were many different takes on the trade that brought Trumbo to Arizona, but the consensus was that his right-handed power bat and Chase Field would become fast friends. That might still ring true, but 2014 was an altogether disappointment. He broke his left hoof in early April and took about 80 days to heal, and even upon returning didn't provide the oomph expected. His Isolated Power was actually slightly higher on the road than it was at home and his paltry on-base percentages will never off-set a power slide. For the second straight season an injury to his team's primary first baseman allowed him to hide at the cold corner. Losing your best player in order to hide Trumbo's defensive shortcomings should not be any team's game plan. On the other hand, getting Trumbo back to mashing home runs, and shading the center fielder 15 feet to his right, might work.

Pitchers

Chase Anderson   RHP

Born: 11/30/87   Age: 27   Bats: R   Throws: R   Height: 6'0"   Weight: 190

YEAR	TEAM	LVL	AGE	W	L	SV	G	GS	IP	H	HR	BB	K	BB/9	K/9	GB%	BABIP	WHIP	ERA	FIP	FRA	WARP
2012	MOB	AA	24	5	4	0	21	21	104	91	9	25	97	2.2	8.4	46%	.290	1.12	2.86	3.36	4.41	1.0
2013	RNO	AAA	25	4	7	0	26	13	88	107	11	33	80	3.4	8.2	38%	.350	1.59	5.73	4.54	4.83	1.4
2014	MOB	AA	26	4	2	0	6	6	39	22	1	6	38	1.4	8.8	48%	.212	0.72	0.69	2.19	2.81	0.9
2014	ARI	MLB	26	9	7	0	21	21	114¹	117	16	40	105	3.1	8.3	42%	.313	1.37	4.01	4.19	4.63	0.6
2015	ARI	MLB	27	5	10	0	23	23	119	116	14	34	105	2.5	8.0	41%	.316	1.25	4.13	4.07	4.48	0.6

Breakout: 39%   Improve: 56%   Collapse: 14%   Attrition: 33%   MLB: 79%   Comparables: Cory Luebke, Charlie Furbush, Rick VandenHurk

The only Chase in MLB whose last name doesn't end in -ley (Headley, Utley, Whitley), Anderson made his major-league debut without much fanfare. It was Anderson—not crown jewel Archie Bradley—who picked up the slack for the ailing Diamondbacks rotation, starting more than 20 games. Lacking a big fastball, he survives thanks to his ability to locate, and a changeup that features more tumble than your dryer. He can manipulate the pitch as well, telling Eno Sarris of FanGraphs, "I almost throw two changeups—a strike changeup and a strikeout changeup." In essence, Anderson has added a pitch to his repertoire, giving him something else to lean on when his fastball isn't fooling anyone.

Bronson Arroyo   RHP

Born: 2/24/77   Age: 38   Bats: R   Throws: R   Height: 6'3"   Weight: 195

YEAR	TEAM	LVL	AGE	W	L	SV	G	GS	IP	H	HR	BB	K	BB/9	K/9	GB%	BABIP	WHIP	ERA	FIP	FRA	WARP
2012	CIN	MLB	35	12	10	0	32	32	202	209	26	35	129	1.6	5.7	43%	.286	1.21	3.74	4.13	4.39	2.1
2013	CIN	MLB	36	14	12	0	32	32	202	199	32	34	124	1.5	5.5	47%	.267	1.15	3.79	4.46	5.10	-0.1
2014	ARI	MLB	37	7	4	0	14	14	86	92	10	19	47	2.0	4.9	55%	.295	1.29	4.08	4.29	5.14	0.0
2015	ARI	MLB	38	4	7	0	14	14	89¹	92	13	19	53	1.9	5.3	44%	.296	1.24	4.31	4.83	4.68	0.1

Breakout: 8%   Improve: 26%   Collapse: 11%   Attrition: 13%   MLB: 62%   Comparables: Livan Hernandez, Paul Byrd, Brian Moehler

The teflon blonde waited until February to sign what appeared to be a modest two-year deal with the Diamondbacks. After nearly a decade of impressive endurance, it stood to reason that Arroyo would provide Arizona's rotation with stability if nothing else. Whoops! Not only did the 37-year-old land on the disabled list for the first time in his career, but his injured elbow required Tommy John surgery. This means that he will spend the majority of his guaranteed contract rehabbing and most likely collect a $4.5 million buyout for his age-39 season. So much for modesty.

Jake Barrett   RHP

Born: 7/22/91   Age: 23   Bats: R   Throws: R   Height: 6'3"   Weight: 230

YEAR	TEAM	LVL	AGE	W	L	SV	G	GS	IP	H	HR	BB	K	BB/9	K/9	GB%	BABIP	WHIP	ERA	FIP	FRA	WARP
2012	SBN	A	20	0	3	6	25	0	24²	28	2	13	25	4.7	9.1	57%	.347	1.66	5.84	4.20	5.75	-0.1
2013	VIS	A+	21	2	1	15	28	0	27¹	21	2	9	37	3.0	12.2	49%	.284	1.10	1.98	3.33	3.66	0.7
2013	MOB	AA	21	1	1	14	24	0	24²	18	2	3	22	1.1	8.0	46%	.232	0.85	0.36	2.55	3.64	0.3
2014	MOB	AA	22	1	2	12	25	0	26¹	25	0	12	24	4.1	8.2	46%	.338	1.41	2.39	2.73	2.91	0.5
2014	RNO	AAA	22	1	0	16	30	0	29	22	3	15	23	4.7	7.1	45%	.268	1.28	3.72	5.11	5.31	0.2
2015	ARI	MLB	23	2	1	2	46	0	46²	44	5	17	41	3.3	8.0	46%	.315	1.31	4.07	4.20	4.43	0.2

Breakout: 0%   Improve: 0%   Collapse: 0%   Attrition: 0%   MLB: 0%   Comparables: Fernando Hernandez, Chase Whitley, Carson Smith

Two years after being drafted in the third round, Barrett finds himself on the brink of the majors. He was absolutely dominant in his express trip through the lower minors in 2013, and while his 2014 stats didn't shine quite so brightly, he still boasts high-quality offerings. Both his fastball and slider rate as plus pitches and he generally pitches around the zone, though his command within it can get loose. This could explain the spike in home runs upon his arrival in the PCL; "his arrival in the PCL" could also explain the spike in home runs upon his arrival in the PCL. The Diamondbacks ran through relief options without calling on him last summer, but that won't happen again in 2015. If he boosts his command and control by a grade, he'll be in high leverage.

Blake Beavan   RHP

Born: 1/17/89   Age: 26   Bats: R   Throws: R   Height: 6'7"   Weight: 245

YEAR	TEAM	LVL	AGE	W	L	SV	G	GS	IP	H	HR	BB	K	BB/9	K/9	GB%	BABIP	WHIP	ERA	FIP	FRA	WARP
2012	TAC	AAA	23	0	0	0	6	6	38	39	3	9	15	2.1	3.6	42%	.277	1.26	2.61	4.77	4.55	0.3
2012	SEA	MLB	23	11	11	0	26	26	152¹	168	23	24	67	1.4	4.0	39%	.280	1.26	4.43	4.80	4.96	0.1
2013	TAC	AAA	24	6	6	0	16	16	94	120	15	23	47	2.2	4.5	45%	.327	1.52	5.55	5.54	5.79	0.0
2013	SEA	MLB	24	0	2	0	12	2	39²	46	8	8	27	1.8	6.1	40%	.292	1.36	6.13	5.02	5.59	-0.4
2014	TAC	AAA	25	4	1	0	19	2	39	38	7	14	31	3.2	7.2	31%	.272	1.33	3.69	5.60	5.38	0.0
2014	SEA	MLB	25	0	1	0	1	1	4	6	2	0	1	0.0	2.2	33%	.308	1.50	4.50	9.16	8.21	-0.1
2015	ARI	MLB	26	2	4	0	11	9	56¹	63	8	10	32	1.5	5.0	41%	.312	1.29	4.77	4.72	5.19	-0.2

Breakout: 33%   Improve: 58%   Collapse: 9%   Attrition: 21%   MLB: 80%   Comparables: David Huff, Edgar Gonzalez, Taylor Buchholz

You remember college. You remember what it was like to open the empty cupboard, to start boiling the last box of macaroni & "cheese" only to find that your roommate already drank the last of the milk. You remember trying to eat it with double the butter instead. You will always remember. That's why you keep the box of old plain oatmeal in the pantry, even though you're a responsible adult who can buy four meals a day if you want. You keep that oatmeal because you never know when you might go hungry, and you pray that you never feel that despair again. Because you remember how that oatmeal tastes, and you know that somehow it tastes even worse now, based on its spot on the aging curve.

Blake Beavan is a box of old plain oatmeal.

Aaron Blair   RHP

Born: 5/26/92   Age: 23   Bats: R   Throws: R   Height: 6'5"   Weight: 230

YEAR	TEAM	LVL	AGE	W	L	SV	G	GS	IP	H	HR	BB	K	BB/9	K/9	GB%	BABIP	WHIP	ERA	FIP	FRA	WARP
2013	SBN	A	21	0	2	0	3	3	18²	19	0	4	13	2.0	6.6	45%	.328	1.30	3.57	2.72	3.25	0.4
2013	YAK	A-	21	1	1	0	8	8	31	25	2	13	28	3.8	8.1	42%	.280	1.23	2.90	3.80	4.68	0.2
2014	SBN	A	22	1	2	0	6	6	35²	25	2	14	44	3.5	11.1	42%	.258	1.09	4.04	3.01	3.81	0.7
2014	VIS	A+	22	4	2	0	13	13	72¹	70	6	21	81	2.6	10.1	38%	.328	1.26	4.35	3.86	3.86	1.7
2014	MOB	AA	22	4	1	0	8	8	46¹	30	4	16	46	3.1	8.9	44%	.228	0.99	1.94	3.49	4.19	0.6
2015	ARI	MLB	23	5	10	0	22	22	115²	113	13	44	101	3.4	7.9	40%	.317	1.35	4.44	4.37	4.82	0.1

Breakout: 0%   Improve: 0%   Collapse: 0%   Attrition: 0%   MLB: 0%   Comparables: *Sean Nolin, Chad Bettis, Scott Barnes*

The second of Arizona's two first-rounders in 2013, Blair has lived up to his polished reputation by moving fast through the system. Though he continues to miss bats, his four-pitch arsenal is heavier on quantity than quality. His fastball and changeup could become plus pitches, but he lacks overall projection. Credit his command and pitchability, which should allow him to exceed the sum of his parts. Look for Blair to reach the majors soon, where he should settle in as an innings eater and—if his .214/.267/.429 batting line in Double-A is a hint—a pitcher who can turn on a fastball.

Archie Bradley   RHP

Born: 8/10/92   Age: 22   Bats: R   Throws: R   Height: 6'4"   Weight: 235

YEAR	TEAM	LVL	AGE	W	L	SV	G	GS	IP	H	HR	BB	K	BB/9	K/9	GB%	BABIP	WHIP	ERA	FIP	FRA	WARP
2012	SBN	A	19	12	6	0	27	27	136	87	6	84	152	5.6	10.1	57%	.248	1.26	3.84	3.87	4.50	1.5
2013	VIS	A+	20	2	0	0	5	5	28²	22	1	10	43	3.1	13.5	44%	.362	1.12	1.26	2.48	2.41	1.2
2013	MOB	AA	20	12	5	0	21	21	123¹	93	5	59	119	4.3	8.7	47%	.276	1.23	1.97	3.04	3.70	1.4
2014	MOB	AA	21	2	3	0	12	12	54²	45	2	36	46	5.9	7.6	44%	.285	1.48	4.12	4.23	6.15	-0.5
2014	RNO	AAA	21	1	4	0	5	5	24¹	26	0	12	23	4.4	8.5	46%	.373	1.56	5.18	3.78	4.40	0.9
2015	ARI	MLB	22	3	7	0	16	16	80¹	73	7	42	75	4.7	8.4	47%	.316	1.43	4.43	4.34	4.81	0.1

Breakout: 0%   Improve: 0%   Collapse: 0%   Attrition: 0%   MLB: 0%   Comparables: *Zack Wheeler, Jeurys Familia, Chris Archer*

Bradley came to big-league camp poised to compete for a rotation spot. Instead, he struggled in camp, suffered an elbow injury, and then was roughed up in Double-A. Physically, he threw in the mid-90s instead of the uppers. Further, he continued to have command issues linked to his delivery, as he starts with an extremely high leg kick before hesitating and reaching back. For all the perceived negative, Bradley is still a top talent. His fastball, even at a slightly slower speed, is still a plus pitch, and so is his knuckle curve. A high school star and then top draft pick and top prospect, he was at times visibly frustrated going through his first struggles since ... forever? But his ceiling remains a top-of-the-rotation pitcher with the floor of an impact reliever. For all we know, getting knocked on his ass might help him land on his feet.

Trevor Cahill   RHP

Born: 3/1/88   Age: 27   Bats: R   Throws: R   Height: 6'4"   Weight: 220

YEAR	TEAM	LVL	AGE	W	L	SV	G	GS	IP	H	HR	BB	K	BB/9	K/9	GB%	BABIP	WHIP	ERA	FIP	FRA	WARP
2012	ARI	MLB	24	13	12	0	32	32	200	184	16	74	156	3.3	7.0	63%	.289	1.29	3.78	3.89	4.95	0.4
2013	RNO	AAA	25	0	2	0	3	3	16²	16	3	9	13	4.9	7.0	60%	.289	1.50	5.94	5.97	7.14	-0.3
2013	ARI	MLB	25	8	10	0	26	25	146²	143	13	65	102	4.0	6.3	58%	.289	1.42	3.99	4.23	5.24	0.1
2014	RNO	AAA	26	2	2	0	6	6	28¹	21	4	20	27	6.4	8.6	63%	.254	1.45	3.49	5.75	6.58	0.1
2014	ARI	MLB	26	3	12	1	32	17	110²	123	9	55	105	4.5	8.5	50%	.350	1.61	5.61	3.86	4.27	0.9
2015	ARI	MLB	27	5	10	0	22	22	129¹	121	13	47	104	3.3	7.2	56%	.308	1.30	4.08	4.26	4.43	0.6

Breakout: 29%   Improve: 54%   Collapse: 22%   Attrition: 25%   MLB: 96%   Comparables: *Dontrelle Willis, Anibal Sanchez, Edwin Jackson*

Not often do you find a former 18-game winner accepting a trip to the minor leagues at age 26, but Cahill had to if he wanted to collect the nearly $20 million still owed him. It was a bit of an unusual situation: Cahill had been dropped to the bullpen in April, then pitched pretty well for two months (3.04 ERA as a reliever), so Kirk Gibson wanted him back in the rotation. But to stretch him back out, he first had to be ... designated for assignment, and so he was. The bulk of the right-hander's issues stem from poor command of his sinker. He relies heavily upon the low-90s offering to generate groundballs and play up his secondary options. The sinker didn't sink, the groundballs weren't generated and his secondary option became Reno. Eventually Gibson got his starter back, and while Cahill's peripherals in the second half improved, the results didn't. He is owed $12 million for 2015, with a 2016 club option that he can void if he finishes in the top two in Cy Young voting.

Andrew Chafin   LHP

Born: 6/17/90   Age: 25   Bats: R   Throws: L   Height: 6'2"   Weight: 220

YEAR	TEAM	LVL	AGE	W	L	SV	G	GS	IP	H	HR	BB	K	BB/9	K/9	GB%	BABIP	WHIP	ERA	FIP	FRA	WARP
2012	VIS	A+	22	6	6	0	30	22	122¹	112	12	69	150	5.1	11.0	53%	.324	1.48	4.93	4.38	5.41	1.9
2013	VIS	A+	23	3	1	0	6	6	31	32	1	14	32	4.1	9.3	47%	.341	1.48	4.65	3.48	4.18	0.8
2013	MOB	AA	23	10	7	0	21	21	126¹	118	5	41	87	2.9	6.2	53%	.292	1.26	2.85	3.09	4.24	0.8
2014	MOB	AA	24	4	1	0	9	9	55	49	4	19	41	3.1	6.7	46%	.280	1.24	1.96	3.73	4.28	0.4
2014	RNO	AAA	24	5	6	0	17	16	93²	111	11	39	73	3.8	7.1	52%	.339	1.62	5.34	4.99	5.97	0.8
2014	ARI	MLB	24	0	1	0	3	3	14	13	0	8	10	5.1	6.4	56%	.317	1.50	3.86	3.60	3.75	0.3
2015	ARI	MLB	25	5	12	0	26	26	140	139	14	55	108	3.5	7.0	49%	.316	1.38	4.41	4.38	4.79	0.2

Breakout: 27%   Improve: 38%   Collapse: 6%   Attrition: 31%   MLB: 52%   Comparables: *John Gast, Alex Colome, Jimmy Barthmaier*

The 43rd pick in the 2011 draft, Chafin was one of 11 baby 'backs who made big-league debuts. The first thing you will notice about the left-hander is his sizeable leg kick: He brings his knee to his chest as he turns his back to the plate. There is a lot going on pre-release, which makes his delivery tough to repeat. As sure as a hangover follows a frat party, his fastball command suffers, as he tends to fly open. His low-80s slider can be an out pitch, his changeup has improved to serviceable, and when he keeps the ball down he can rack up easy outs on the ground. He overcame concerns about workload this season, but ultimately mechanics and command will determine his long-term fate.

Josh Collmenter   RHP

Born: 2/7/86   Age: 29   Bats: R   Throws: R   Height: 6'4"   Weight: 235

YEAR	TEAM	LVL	AGE	W	L	SV	G	GS	IP	H	HR	BB	K	BB/9	K/9	GB%	BABIP	WHIP	ERA	FIP	FRA	WARP
2012	ARI	MLB	26	5	3	0	28	11	90¹	92	13	22	80	2.2	8.0	40%	.304	1.26	3.69	3.97	4.50	1.0
2013	ARI	MLB	27	5	5	0	49	0	92	79	8	33	85	3.2	8.3	36%	.277	1.22	3.13	3.44	3.00	1.8
2014	ARI	MLB	28	11	9	1	33	28	179¹	163	18	39	115	2.0	5.8	41%	.267	1.13	3.46	3.84	4.47	1.0
2015	ARI	MLB	29	5	7	0	37	17	133²	126	14	32	105	2.2	7.1	39%	.301	1.18	3.54	3.91	3.85	1.6

Breakout: 30%   Improve: 43%   Collapse: 19%   Attrition: 14%   MLB: 85%   Comparables: Brandon McCarthy, Brian Bannister, Sergio Mitre

What a weird dude. On looks alone, one would think the burly Collmenter is the type to light up radar guns. In reality, his cut-fastball is thrown in the mid-80s; on special occasions it might struggle toward 90. He employs a strange wrist-hook motion and over-the-top snap release, which might lead you to believe he would have issues controlling the ball. In fact, "Tomahawk"—a nickname earned because of the motion—walked fewer than two batters per nine innings. He works primarily off of two pitches, but not, as you'd expect, a fastball and breaking ball. Instead, it's the cutter and an upper-70s changeup. He does throw a knuckle curveball, but less than every 10th pitch. Despite the irregularities, Collmenter was successful because he manipulated location and changed speeds enough to unsettle batters who couldn't square up what is basically mediocre stuff. The parts don't seem to add up to a starting pitcher, but with Collmenter nothing is as it seems.

Patrick Corbin   LHP

Born: 7/19/89   Age: 25   Bats: L   Throws: L   Height: 6'2"   Weight: 185

YEAR	TEAM	LVL	AGE	W	L	SV	G	GS	IP	H	HR	BB	K	BB/9	K/9	GB%	BABIP	WHIP	ERA	FIP	FRA	WARP
2012	MOB	AA	22	2	0	0	4	4	27	22	0	8	25	2.7	8.3	50%	.306	1.11	1.67	2.29	2.50	0.9
2012	RNO	AAA	22	3	2	0	9	9	52¹	57	4	15	55	2.6	9.5	51%	.349	1.38	3.44	3.47	4.28	1.3
2012	ARI	MLB	22	6	8	1	22	17	107	117	14	25	86	2.1	7.2	46%	.317	1.33	4.54	4.04	4.54	1.2
2013	ARI	MLB	23	14	8	0	32	32	208¹	189	19	54	178	2.3	7.7	48%	.283	1.17	3.41	3.40	4.13	2.9
2015	ARI	MLB	25	2	3	0	6	6	37²	36	4	9	33	2.2	7.8	47%	.315	1.21	3.81	3.75	4.14	0.3

Breakout: 33%   Improve: 55%   Collapse: 19%   Attrition: 18%   MLB: 92%   Comparables: Jon Niese, Luke Hochevar, Vance Worley

An up-and-coming All-Star in 2013, Corbin was a camp casualty, undergoing Tommy John surgery in March. The profile of a no. 2 or 3 starter remains if his control and command return to the mound with him in 2015. Until we know whether that'll happen, we recommend going back and reading whatever dross we wrote about him last year.

Eury De La Rosa   LHP

Born: 2/24/90   Age: 25   Bats: L   Throws: L   Height: 5'9"   Weight: 165

YEAR	TEAM	LVL	AGE	W	L	SV	G	GS	IP	H	HR	BB	K	BB/9	K/9	GB%	BABIP	WHIP	ERA	FIP	FRA	WARP
2012	MOB	AA	22	4	4	8	53	0	63¹	47	3	17	68	2.4	9.7	36%	.277	1.01	2.84	2.51	3.69	1.1
2013	RNO	AAA	23	3	5	0	44	0	49²	52	6	27	49	4.9	8.9	44%	.326	1.59	5.26	4.92	5.46	0.6
2013	ARI	MLB	23	0	1	0	19	0	14²	13	5	5	16	3.1	9.8	39%	.222	1.23	7.36	6.29	7.54	-0.4
2014	RNO	AAA	24	2	4	2	36	0	39¹	33	3	20	36	4.6	8.2	44%	.269	1.35	2.52	4.77	5.00	0.6
2014	ARI	MLB	24	2	0	0	25	0	36²	37	2	14	32	3.4	7.9	45%	.327	1.39	2.95	3.46	3.37	0.5
2015	ARI	MLB	25	3	1	0	56	0	66²	60	7	24	63	3.3	8.5	43%	.307	1.26	3.87	4.02	4.21	0.4

Breakout: 21%   Improve: 31%   Collapse: 21%   Attrition: 47%   MLB: 61%   Comparables: Sam Demel, Robbie Weinhardt, David Carpenter

The former international free agent who was acquired in a minor December trade continues to defy the odds as he overcomes a lack of size and stuff. De La Rosa is an atypical reliever, topping out around 90 mph with a starter's assortment of pitches. He has some of the characteristics of a finesse lefty, but fastball control is not one of them. His best offering is a mid-80s slider that he uses against batters on both sides of the dish. The ability to bust the pitch in on the hands of right-handed batters produced uncommon splits for his ilk, especially since his changeup is just average. People love an underdog, though his bullpenmates might not love this one: He allowed 77 percent of their bequeathed baserunners to score. At some point lack of production trumps a good story.

Rubby De La Rosa   RHP

Born: 3/4/89   Age: 26   Bats: R   Throws: R   Height: 6'1"   Weight: 205

YEAR	TEAM	LVL	AGE	W	L	SV	G	GS	IP	H	HR	BB	K	BB/9	K/9	GB%	BABIP	WHIP	ERA	FIP	FRA	WARP
2012	LAN	MLB	23	0	0	0	1	0	0²	0	0	2	0	27.0	0.0	0%	.000	3.00	27.00	12.14	13.83	-0.1
2013	PAW	AAA	24	3	3	0	24	20	80¹	65	9	48	76	5.4	8.5	44%	.265	1.41	4.26	4.82	5.24	0.3
2013	BOS	MLB	24	0	2	0	11	0	11¹	15	2	2	6	1.6	4.8	48%	.325	1.50	5.56	5.63	6.02	-0.1
2014	PAW	AAA	25	2	4	0	12	12	60	50	1	25	57	3.8	8.6	55%	.299	1.25	3.45	2.97	3.47	1.1
2014	BOS	MLB	25	4	8	0	19	18	101²	116	12	35	74	3.1	6.6	47%	.327	1.49	4.43	4.33	4.89	0.1
2015	ARI	MLB	26	5	12	0	28	28	134¹	128	14	53	116	3.5	7.8	49%	.315	1.34	4.28	4.28	4.66	0.5

Breakout: 35%   Improve: 65%   Collapse: 15%   Attrition: 21%   MLB: 94%   Comparables: Jason Hammel, Felipe Paulino, Rick VandenHurk

Does De La Rosa best profile as a starter or reliever? After an up-and-down 2014 campaign, we still don't know. He entered 2014 having never thrown more than 110 innings in a season, and he clearly wore down toward the end of the year as he pushed past 160, his cumulative ERA for the season jumping from 3.32 to 4.29 in just the final 34 innings. When it's all clicking, De La Rosa looks the part of a no. 3 starter: heavy mid-90s fastball, changeup that occasionally dazzles. But when he tires he leaves pitches up in the zone, a problem that could be mitigated by a move to the bullpen. He probably deserves one more crack at a starting spot, but much like the second b in his first name, De La Rosa's ultimate purpose remains unclear.

Randall Delgado   RHP

Born: 2/9/90   Age: 25   Bats: R   Throws: R   Height: 6'3"   Weight: 200

YEAR	TEAM	LVL	AGE	W	L	SV	G	GS	IP	H	HR	BB	K	BB/9	K/9	GB%	BABIP	WHIP	ERA	FIP	FRA	WARP
2012	GWN	AAA	22	4	3	0	8	8	44¹	47	6	21	51	4.3	10.4	44%	.353	1.53	4.06	4.11	5.23	0.1
2012	ATL	MLB	22	4	9	0	18	17	92²	89	8	42	76	4.1	7.4	52%	.299	1.41	4.37	4.11	4.59	1.0
2013	RNO	AAA	23	2	5	0	13	13	64	69	9	35	57	4.9	8.0	54%	.327	1.62	5.91	5.44	6.91	0.1
2013	ARI	MLB	23	5	7	0	20	19	116¹	116	24	23	79	1.8	6.1	43%	.266	1.19	4.26	4.96	5.42	-0.2
2014	ARI	MLB	24	4	4	0	47	4	77²	71	6	35	86	4.1	10.0	37%	.311	1.36	4.87	3.36	4.03	0.9
2015	ARI	MLB	25	3	6	0	20	14	82²	79	11	30	73	3.3	8.0	45%	.309	1.32	4.40	4.53	4.78	0.1

Breakout: 35%   Improve: 54%   Collapse: 24%   Attrition: 25%   MLB: 90%   Comparables: *Rick VandenHurk, Garrett Olson, J.P. Howell*

Hi, my name is Randall. I'm 25, I'm an Aquarius and I spend most of my summer in Arizona. Previously I tried to force long-term relationships, but this year I figured out that going out once with somebody is just better for my particular personality. I am great on first dates, as long as they don't drag on all night. With my new lease on life I found that I work harder and a bit faster. I am no stranger to change. It might actually be my best attribute. I can do a mean cha-cha slide but am better going to the right ... to the right. I am young enough that I might give the long-term stuff another chance; however, now I am single and ready to mingle.

Jeremy Hellickson   RHP

Born: 4/8/87   Age: 28   Bats: R   Throws: R   Height: 6'1"   Weight: 190

YEAR	TEAM	LVL	AGE	W	L	SV	G	GS	IP	H	HR	BB	K	BB/9	K/9	GB%	BABIP	WHIP	ERA	FIP	FRA	WARP
2012	TBA	MLB	25	10	11	0	31	31	177	163	25	59	124	3.0	6.3	43%	.262	1.25	3.10	4.55	4.59	1.0
2013	TBA	MLB	26	12	10	0	32	31	174	185	24	50	135	2.6	7.0	41%	.307	1.35	5.17	4.25	4.60	0.7
2014	DUR	AAA	27	1	4	0	5	5	18²	38	1	5	16	2.4	7.7	41%	.493	2.30	7.23	3.46	4.20	0.4
2014	TBA	MLB	27	1	5	0	13	13	63²	71	8	21	54	3.0	7.6	38%	.321	1.45	4.52	4.18	4.20	0.7
2015	ARI	MLB	28	5	8	0	19	19	107	102	12	29	87	2.5	7.3	39%	.306	1.22	3.91	4.07	4.25	0.8

Breakout: 23%   Improve: 49%   Collapse: 16%   Attrition: 12%   MLB: 79%   Comparables: *Jeff Francis, Wade Davis, Homer Bailey*

Bone spurs discovered in his right elbow wiped out the first half of the season for Hellickson. When he returned, he was inconsistent at best and struggled with pitch efficiency. When he is on, the former Rookie of the Year blends a low-90s fastball with a low-80s changeup and a curveball in the mid-70s. The change of speeds keeps hitters off-balance, resulting in weak aerial contact. At his worst, he loses command, leaving pitches up in the zone and over the fence. (The shift from Tampa Bay to Arizona isn't going to help on this front.) The secondary offerings—particularly the changeup—are very effective, but are often negated by a poor performance from the fastball. The crux of those issues seems to be poor command to his glove side. Still, Hellickson is on the right side of 30 with two years of team control remaining, which is why the Diamondbacks gave up a couple of prospects of moderate value to acquire him.

Daniel Hudson   RHP

Born: 3/9/87   Age: 28   Bats: R   Throws: R   Height: 6'3"   Weight: 225

YEAR	TEAM	LVL	AGE	W	L	SV	G	GS	IP	H	HR	BB	K	BB/9	K/9	GB%	BABIP	WHIP	ERA	FIP	FRA	WARP
2012	ARI	MLB	25	3	2	0	9	9	45¹	62	9	12	37	2.4	7.3	39%	.368	1.63	7.35	4.88	6.07	-0.2
2014	ARI	MLB	27	0	1	0	3	0	2²	4	0	0	2	0.0	6.8	46%	.364	1.50	13.50	1.60	1.07	0.1
2015	ARI	MLB	28	2	3	0	7	7	38¹	35	4	9	33	2.2	7.8	42%	.309	1.16	3.61	3.74	3.92	0.4

Breakout: 20%   Improve: 53%   Collapse: 12%   Attrition: 9%   MLB: 84%   Comparables: *Gavin Floyd, Brandon McCarthy, Jason Hammel*

Hudson went 799 days between appearances as a two-time survivor of Tommy John surgery. The right-hander returned to a major-league mound on September 3rd and threw the 13 most important pitches of his life. The first, a 94-mph fastball, fell low for ball one. On the next, another fastball, he registered his first strike since June 26, 2012, three days before Yasiel Puig *was signed*. After falling behind 2-1, he coaxed a groundout with a fourth heater. Hudson started the next batter with a called strike. This one was a mid-80s changeup; formerly his signature offering. He then threw a slider that was fouled off before another fastball was lined to left field for out number two. Hudson jumped 1-2 on the third batter with three fastballs. Perhaps feeling his oats a bit, he tossed a 96-mph fastball too far inside, which evened the count. The 13th pitch of the inning—another changeup—was grounded to second for a 4-3 put out. Three up. Three down. Welcome back.

Evan Marshall   RHP

Born: 4/18/90   Age: 25   Bats: R   Throws: R   Height: 6'2"   Weight: 220

YEAR	TEAM	LVL	AGE	W	L	SV	G	GS	IP	H	HR	BB	K	BB/9	K/9	GB%	BABIP	WHIP	ERA	FIP	FRA	WARP
2012	MOB	AA	22	6	3	16	42	0	48²	55	2	16	27	3.0	5.0	60%	.315	1.46	3.51	3.68	5.17	-0.2
2013	RNO	AAA	23	3	6	3	54	0	58	75	2	30	59	4.7	9.2	60%	.412	1.81	4.34	3.79	4.85	0.9
2014	RNO	AAA	24	0	1	1	14	0	16²	10	0	5	19	2.7	10.3	61%	.303	0.90	0.54	2.32	3.03	0.5
2014	ARI	MLB	24	4	4	0	57	0	49¹	50	3	17	54	3.1	9.9	61%	.351	1.36	2.74	2.86	2.94	0.8
2015	ARI	MLB	25	3	1	0	54	0	56²	55	5	19	52	2.9	8.3	55%	.331	1.30	3.97	3.75	4.31	0.3

Breakout: 23%   Improve: 33%   Collapse: 21%   Attrition: 41%   MLB: 66%   Comparables: *Chris Resop, Robbie Weinhardt, Josh Spence*

Marshall made his major-league debut in 2014 and stuck around after a strong showing. The right-hander drops down low before slinging the ball toward the plate with a short arm action that has some violence to it. He's a three-pitch reliever with a mid-90s fastball and a pair of secondary offerings that each register eight to 10 miles slower, including a top-shelf slider. Though his changeup is effective against lefties, he has a pronounced split. This is likely because he cuts himself off from the inner half against southpaws and works almost everything away. The ability to work glove-side *is* within his repertoire, as Marshall routinely goes away from righties with the heater. The ingredients for a late-inning reliever are all there. He just needs some more work in the kitchen.

Vidal Nuno   LHP

Born: 7/26/87   Age: 27   Bats: L   Throws: L   Height: 5'11"   Weight: 195

YEAR	TEAM	LVL	AGE	W	L	SV	G	GS	IP	H	HR	BB	K	BB/9	K/9	GB%	BABIP	WHIP	ERA	FIP	FRA	WARP
2012	TAM	A+	24	1	1	0	11	1	24¹	22	2	6	26	2.2	9.6	44%	.299	1.15	2.96	3.19	4.06	0.4
2012	TRN	AA	24	9	5	0	20	20	114	109	10	27	100	2.1	7.9	38%	.304	1.19	2.45	3.35	4.06	1.7
2013	SWB	AAA	25	2	0	0	5	5	25	14	2	2	30	0.7	10.8	44%	.211	0.64	1.44	2.08	2.85	0.6
2013	NYA	MLB	25	1	2	0	5	3	20	16	2	6	9	2.7	4.1	36%	.219	1.10	2.25	4.53	4.75	0.1
2014	ARI	MLB	26	0	7	0	14	14	83²	71	10	20	69	2.2	7.4	39%	.257	1.09	3.76	3.87	4.95	0.2
2014	NYA	MLB	26	2	5	0	17	14	78	86	15	26	60	3.0	6.9	39%	.301	1.44	5.42	5.20	6.12	-0.6
2015	ARI	MLB	27	5	9	0	26	19	123¹	121	16	32	102	2.3	7.4	38%	.310	1.24	4.18	4.26	4.54	0.5

Breakout: 40%   Improve: 63%   Collapse: 12%   Attrition: 31%   MLB: 86%   Comparables: Wade LeBlanc, Josh Tomlin, Hector Noesi

Nuno has pitched in 10 different leagues as a professional, but it looks like the National League might be home. Shipped from the Yankees to the Diamondbacks mid-season, the left-hander turned in a solid performance as a member of the senior circuit. Trading the designated hitter for opposing pitchers, he increased his strikeouts and dropped his walks, dominating lefties with a two-punch combination of glove-side fastballs and sliders. None of his five pitches—pair of fastballs, slider, curveball and changeup—tops 90, and the inability (or lack of confidence) to place fastballs on the corners against right-handers leaves too many pitches over the plate. The move west brought forth an emphasis on fastballs, especially elevated, especially with two strikes. The next homer will always be looming, given his fly-ball approach, but you could do worse in the back of a rotation.

Oliver Perez   LHP

Born: 8/15/81   Age: 33   Bats: L   Throws: L   Height: 6'3"   Weight: 220

YEAR	TEAM	LVL	AGE	W	L	SV	G	GS	IP	H	HR	BB	K	BB/9	K/9	GB%	BABIP	WHIP	ERA	FIP	FRA	WARP
2012	TAC	AAA	30	2	2	1	22	0	31	33	4	19	42	5.5	12.2	41%	.382	1.68	4.65	4.47	4.25	0.7
2012	SEA	MLB	30	1	3	0	33	0	29²	27	1	10	24	3.0	7.3	35%	.295	1.25	2.12	2.88	2.92	0.5
2013	SEA	MLB	31	3	3	2	61	0	53	50	6	26	74	4.4	12.6	31%	.361	1.43	3.74	3.28	3.44	0.7
2014	ARI	MLB	32	3	4	0	68	0	58²	50	5	24	76	3.7	11.7	47%	.312	1.26	2.91	3.20	3.07	0.8
2015	ARI	MLB	33	2	2	1	41	3	51²	48	6	23	52	4.0	9.2	38%	.325	1.39	4.54	4.36	4.93	-0.1

Breakout: 17%   Improve: 27%   Collapse: 15%   Attrition: 24%   MLB: 48%   Comparables: John Wasdin, Casey Fossum, Ryota Igarashi

For whatever reason, Perez stayed on the open market until March, when Arizona scooped him up to a two-year deal worth less than $5 million. The converted starter posted another stellar season in relief, but not in the conventional sense. We could easily write it off as just one of those things, though his knee-high slider command was significantly better against righties, who whiffed on half their swings at this pitch. If he can mix some of his past results against lefties with his newfound success over right-handers, he could turn out to be quite the bargain. That would be in stark contrast to the names people were calling him a few years ago.

Robbie Ray   LHP

Born: 10/1/91   Age: 23   Bats: L   Throws: L   Height: 6'2"   Weight: 195

YEAR	TEAM	LVL	AGE	W	L	SV	G	GS	IP	H	HR	BB	K	BB/9	K/9	GB%	BABIP	WHIP	ERA	FIP	FRA	WARP
2012	POT	A+	20	4	12	0	22	21	105²	122	14	49	86	4.2	7.3	35%	.332	1.62	6.56	5.18	6.02	-0.2
2013	POT	A+	21	6	3	0	16	16	84	60	9	41	100	4.4	10.7	45%	.273	1.20	3.11	3.97	4.77	1.2
2013	HAR	AA	21	5	2	0	11	11	58	56	4	21	60	3.3	9.3	45%	.317	1.33	3.72	3.55	3.59	1.1
2014	TOL	AAA	22	7	6	0	20	19	100¹	106	6	44	75	3.9	6.7	36%	.326	1.50	4.22	4.05	4.48	1.1
2014	DET	MLB	22	1	4	0	9	6	28²	43	5	11	19	3.5	6.0	40%	.376	1.88	8.16	5.25	6.18	0.1
2015	ARI	MLB	23	4	11	0	24	24	117	122	14	50	95	3.8	7.3	39%	.325	1.46	5.07	4.74	5.51	-0.7

Breakout: 20%   Improve: 27%   Collapse: 3%   Attrition: 22%   MLB: 35%   Comparables: Carlos Carrasco, Eric Hurley, Travis Blackley

Ray is a Columbia House Baseball Trades member and he keeps forgetting to send back the stupid card that says "Don't trade me this winter." Arizona's probably a better place for Ray than Detroit: He won't have the pressure of answering "This is all we got for Fister?" questions from fans. ("This is all we got for Gregorius" doesn't yet have the same sting.) As for his actual abilities, Ray's curveball will determine his capacity as a starter; it's still not major-league ready. He'd be more helpful (and effective) out of the bullpen, with a gradual transition into the rotation in 2016, depending on that curve or any decent third pitch.

Addison Reed   RHP

Born: 12/27/88   Age: 26   Bats: L   Throws: R   Height: 6'4"   Weight: 220

YEAR	TEAM	LVL	AGE	W	L	SV	G	GS	IP	H	HR	BB	K	BB/9	K/9	GB%	BABIP	WHIP	ERA	FIP	FRA	WARP
2012	CHA	MLB	23	3	2	29	62	0	55	57	6	18	54	2.9	8.8	33%	.323	1.36	4.75	3.59	4.07	0.8
2013	CHA	MLB	24	5	4	40	68	0	71¹	56	6	23	72	2.9	9.1	35%	.260	1.11	3.79	3.20	3.38	1.1
2014	ARI	MLB	25	1	7	32	62	0	59¹	57	11	15	69	2.3	10.5	28%	.295	1.21	4.25	4.00	4.36	0.4
2015	ARI	MLB	26	3	1	31	52	0	58	48	5	14	66	2.2	10.1	35%	.310	1.08	3.00	2.95	3.26	1.0

Breakout: 31%   Improve: 49%   Collapse: 18%   Attrition: 11%   MLB: 83%   Comparables: Bill Bray, Sean Doolittle, Drew Storen

In his first season with the Snakes, the former White Sox closer posted a career best in strikeouts and walks. Reed's only problem was being a fly-ball pitcher in a hitters paradise. That turned out to be a doozy, with six of the homers he allowed putting the Diamondbacks behind, and two others tying the ballgame. In his brief career, he has officially iced 101 games as a closer and is arbitration eligible for the first time, which means mid-seven figures is in his future.

Braden Shipley   RHP

Born: 2/22/92   Age: 23   Bats: R   Throws: R   Height: 6'3"   Weight: 190

YEAR	TEAM	LVL	AGE	W	L	SV	G	GS	IP	H	HR	BB	K	BB/9	K/9	GB%	BABIP	WHIP	ERA	FIP	FRA	WARP
2013	SBN	A	21	0	1	0	4	4	20²	14	2	8	16	3.5	7.0	46%	.218	1.06	2.61	4.35	4.92	0.1
2013	YAK	A-	21	0	2	0	8	8	19	30	1	6	24	2.8	11.4	44%	.475	1.89	7.58	2.58	3.65	0.5
2014	SBN	A	22	4	2	0	8	8	45²	46	1	11	41	2.2	8.1	47%	.336	1.25	3.74	2.83	3.92	0.6
2014	VIS	A+	22	2	4	0	10	10	60¹	57	7	21	68	3.1	10.1	46%	.336	1.29	4.03	4.39	5.47	0.7
2014	MOB	AA	22	1	2	0	4	4	20	14	3	10	18	4.5	8.1	56%	.216	1.20	3.60	4.84	5.40	0.1
2015	ARI	MLB	23	3	9	0	19	19	93²	95	11	39	77	3.7	7.4	44%	.323	1.43	4.83	4.67	5.25	-0.3

Breakout: 0%   Improve: 0%   Collapse: 0%   Attrition: 0%   MLB: 0%   Comparables: *Dan Straily, Alex Colome, Aneury Rodriguez*

Veracity is considered a positive quality in most scenarios, but apply it to a fastball and that connotation starts to wane. Shipley's fastball straightens out at the upper levels of his velocity band, becoming a bit too true. Enter Shipley's changeup, a mendacious little pitch, which grades out as plus at present with room to grow. He disguises it well, pounds the lower quadrants, and manipulates velocity at will. The key to his ascension, though, will be the development of his third pitch. Shipley throws a curveball of the spike persuasion, giving him another swing-and-miss offering that has been notoriously difficult for him to command. Already at Double-A, the former college shortstop is on the fast track to the major leagues. It would be a surprise not to see him in Arizona at some point in 2015, truth be told.

Matt Stites   RHP

Born: 5/28/90   Age: 25   Bats: L   Throws: R   Height: 5'11"   Weight: 195

YEAR	TEAM	LVL	AGE	W	L	SV	G	GS	IP	H	HR	BB	K	BB/9	K/9	GB%	BABIP	WHIP	ERA	FIP	FRA	WARP
2012	FTW	A	22	2	0	13	42	0	48²	25	4	3	60	0.6	11.1	34%	.196	0.58	0.74	2.20	2.98	1.2
2013	SAN	AA	23	2	2	14	46	0	52	37	6	8	51	1.4	8.8	47%	.228	0.87	2.08	3.11	4.14	0.4
2014	MOB	AA	24	0	1	3	12	0	12	10	0	3	8	2.2	6.0	54%	.286	1.08	3.75	2.60	4.11	0.1
2014	RNO	AAA	24	0	0	12	17	0	16	13	1	6	15	3.4	8.4	49%	.286	1.19	2.25	3.76	3.95	0.3
2014	ARI	MLB	24	0	0	0	37	0	33	33	6	16	26	4.4	7.1	45%	.273	1.48	5.73	5.44	6.65	-0.7
2015	ARI	MLB	25	3	1	0	49	0	53¹	48	6	16	48	2.7	8.1	42%	.300	1.20	3.81	4.01	4.14	0.4

Breakout: 22%   Improve: 29%   Collapse: 27%   Attrition: 49%   MLB: 64%   Comparables: *Robbie Weinhardt, Chris Resop, David Carpenter*

An undersized college starter turned professional reliever, Stites has a big fastball that approaches triple digits. A short arm action only enhances what is already a high-octane offering. Despite the lack of size, he can elevate the fastball above bats—or at least high enough to deaden contact when wood is put to it. Stites backs the heater with a swing-missing slider that lives in the neighborhood of 85-88 mph. His changeup has some semblance of an average offering but can also look like a weak fastball. Even without the off-speed pitch, he was able to produce reverse splits—perhaps the quick action combined with velocity did not allow for the other hand to get a good read. Stites showed good control against weaker competition in the minors but struggled with location against the best hitters. Like many fireballers before him, control and command will determine if he is a have or have not.

Allen Webster   RHP

Born: 2/10/90   Age: 25   Bats: R   Throws: R   Height: 6'2"   Weight: 190

YEAR	TEAM	LVL	AGE	W	L	SV	G	GS	IP	H	HR	BB	K	BB/9	K/9	GB%	BABIP	WHIP	ERA	FIP	FRA	WARP
2012	CHT	AA	22	6	8	0	27	22	121²	120	1	57	117	4.2	8.7	59%	.336	1.45	3.55	3.15	4.28	1.6
2013	PAW	AAA	23	8	4	0	21	21	105	71	9	43	116	3.7	9.9	51%	.246	1.09	3.60	3.80	4.21	1.3
2013	BOS	MLB	23	1	2	0	8	7	30¹	37	7	18	23	5.3	6.8	44%	.316	1.81	8.60	6.54	7.21	-0.5
2014	PAW	AAA	24	4	4	1	21	20	122	107	9	44	100	3.2	7.4	49%	.279	1.24	3.10	3.88	4.94	0.2
2014	BOS	MLB	24	5	3	0	11	11	59	58	3	28	36	4.3	5.5	47%	.297	1.46	5.03	4.38	5.20	0.0
2015	ARI	MLB	25	6	13	0	29	29	152¹	149	15	60	125	3.5	7.4	50%	.316	1.37	4.56	4.42	4.96	-0.1

Breakout: 29%   Improve: 54%   Collapse: 15%   Attrition: 35%   MLB: 79%   Comparables: *Andre Rienzo, Esmil Rogers, Blake Wood*

Webster is what we get when we fall in love with a starting pitcher who offers only two good pitches. For years we've been taunted by his athleticism, his lively fastball and his legitimately great changeup, waiting for him to add a third pitch and to iron out his command issues. Vladimir and Estragon will be done waiting before we are. Webster still loses his fastball command from one batter to the next, and he still lacks a consistent third weapon to rely on when his changeup isn't working. Add in a general unwillingness to attack the strike zone, and you get a pitcher who's often exposed the second turn through a lineup. Webster could try to survive as a back-end option for a few years, but his best chance of achieving sustained success is in relief, where he can use his fastball-changeup combo to deceive smaller batches of hitters at a time. At the very least, such a transition would spare the world from more "Webster's defines a walk as ..." jokes.

Brad Ziegler   RHP

Born: 10/10/79   Age: 35   Bats: R   Throws: R   Height: 6'4"   Weight: 210

YEAR	TEAM	LVL	AGE	W	L	SV	G	GS	IP	H	HR	BB	K	BB/9	K/9	GB%	BABIP	WHIP	ERA	FIP	FRA	WARP
2012	ARI	MLB	32	6	1	0	77	0	68²	54	2	21	42	2.8	5.5	76%	.264	1.09	2.49	3.25	4.89	0.6
2013	ARI	MLB	33	8	1	13	78	0	73	61	3	22	44	2.7	5.4	71%	.258	1.14	2.22	3.38	4.28	0.5
2014	ARI	MLB	34	5	3	1	68	0	67	60	5	24	54	3.2	7.3	65%	.284	1.25	3.49	3.67	5.13	-0.1
2015	ARI	MLB	35	4	1	4	67	0	62¹	56	4	19	47	2.8	6.9	62%	.302	1.21	3.46	3.65	3.76	0.7

Breakout: 23%   Improve: 42%   Collapse: 25%   Attrition: 10%   MLB: 83%   Comparables: *Matt Guerrier, Scott Downs, Steve Kline*

In a world of power bullpens, Ziegler's mid-80s fastball has been one of the league's most effective pitches since he was acquired in 2011. The side-arming sinkerballer continues to post extreme groundball rates, but his location was off at times in 2014, diminishing his outlier status a bit and leading to more hard contact. The sweeping slider is a nightmare for right-handed batters and completed almost 80 percent of his strikeouts. Improved command of his changeup in recent seasons has closed what was a sizeable platoon split and now leaves him useful against both hands. The 35-year-old's arm is in good shape, but late-season microfracture surgery on his left knee could delay the start of his 2015 campaign..

Lineouts

Hitters

NAME	POS	TEAM	LVL	AGE	PA	R	2B	3B	HR	RBI	BB	K	SB	CS	AVG/OBP/SLG	TAv	BABIP	BRR	FRAA	WARP
Tyler Bortnick	2B	RNO	AAA	26	98	13	2	1	0	5	10	21	3	0	.224/.313/.271	.220	.297	0.5	2B(22): 1.7, 3B(6): -0.0	0.0
Tuffy Gosewisch	C	ARI	MLB	30	132	6	8	0	1	7	3	24	0	0	.225/.242/.310	.211	.269	0.5	C(35): 0.4	0.3
Mitch Haniger	RF	MOB	AA	23	30	5	3	0	0	5	3	4	0	0	.333/.433/.458	.369	.381	0.9	RF(7): -0.5	0.6
	RF	HUN	AA	23	271	41	7	1	10	34	19	41	4	0	.255/.316/.416	.286	.267	-0.4	RF(47): -5.7, CF(25): 1.5	0.8
Mike Jacobs	1B	RNO	AAA	33	575	79	37	0	19	97	60	120	0	0	.299/.370/.487	.283	.351	-4.1	1B(102): 0.6	1.8
Domingo Leyba	SS	WMI	A	18	124	20	7	0	1	7	6	13	1	2	.397/.431/.483	.344	.441	1.0	SS(17): 0.4, 2B(13): 0.5	2.0
	2B	ONE	A-	18	154	20	11	1	1	17	8	17	1	2	.264/.303/.375	.252	.294	1.9	2B(35): -5.2, SS(3): 0.1	-0.1
Andy Marte	3B	RNO	AAA	30	531	81	32	3	19	80	48	62	1	0	.329/.388/.531	.288	.343	-5.0	3B(121): 2.8, 1B(2): 0.2	3.5
	3B	ARI	MLB	30	16	1	0	0	1	3	0	3	0	0	.188/.188/.375	.209	.167	0.0	3B(4): 0.1	0.0
Jordan Pacheco	C	COL	MLB	28	80	4	6	1	0	8	6	15	0	0	.236/.300/.347	.218	.293	-2.2	C(19): 0.1, 1B(4): 0.1	-0.4
	1B	ARI	MLB	28	85	6	4	0	0	8	3	12	0	0	.272/.298/.321	.219	.319	-0.4	1B(11): -0.4, 3B(3): -0.4	-0.3
Nolan Reimold	LF	BOW	AA	30	69	10	3	0	2	9	12	13	1	1	.315/.420/.481	.351	.357	-0.9	LF(8): 0.1	0.7
	LF	ARI	MLB	30	18	2	1	0	1	4	0	10	0	0	.294/.278/.529	.277	.571	0.0	LF(4): 0.0	0.1
	RF	TOR	MLB	30	60	3	4	0	2	9	6	22	1	0	.212/.283/.404	.266	.300	0.4	RF(10): 0.6	0.2
Danny Worth	2B	TOL	AAA	28	251	19	15	1	1	18	27	87	9	0	.211/.296/.300	.208	.341	-0.1	2B(43): 0.3, SS(12): 0.5	-1.1
	SS	DET	MLB	28	46	5	1	0	0	5	2	12	0	1	.167/.217/.190	.159	.226	-0.2	SS(13): -0.1, 2B(3): -0.2	-0.3

Tyler Bortnick struggled in a return trip to Reno, then strained a hamstring in June and didn't return. A reserve role may await him at the highest level. "My son's name is also Bortnick," he tossed in lazily, gratuitously, pathetically. ❖ Drafted 70th overall, **Isan Diaz** has the athleticism and actions for short, but the arm for the keystone. ❖ What if I told you that on April 24, 2014 **James Benjamin "Tuffy" Gosewisch** would hit the first home run of his career at age 30? This is *30 for 30: Tuffs the Legend*. ❖ In his last big-league trade, Kevin Towers sent Gerardo Parra to Milwaukee and had to pick his prize from one of the game's worst farm systems. He chose **Mitch Haniger,** who at least has an outside shot to be a big-league center fielder, with a likely role as a fourth outfielder. ❖ **Mike Jacobs,** pronounced J-AAAA-cobs. ❖ The switch-hitting **Domingo Leyba** impressed defensively at second in short-season ball, then hit safely in 24 of 30 games at the next level. He could be a big-league second baseman, but at just 19, he has time to declare another major. ❖ This marks the 10th anniversary of BP2005's "The best prospect in baseball and a future superstar" comment for **Andy Marte**. Which anniversary is the 10th, again? Crystal? Silk? Or, no, wait, it's the Salty Tears Of Lost Potential Anniversary. ❖ A catcher—even a below-average one—who can play multiple positions is worthy of a spot somewhere in an organization, but boy oh boy does **Jordan Pacheco** make you reconsider. ❖ Though he tore his hamstring after just 13 games, **Matt Railey** could be a third-round steal. He has plus speed and raw power from an up-the-middle position. He also had recurring hamstring issues throughout high school. ❖ **Nolan Reimold** bounced around the league, wearing three uniforms in 2014. He was unsigned at press time, but in a league-wide power outage, he is likely to get another chance to get hurt. ❖ A second-round pick in 2014, **Marcus Wilson** is the classic toolsy, athletic, boom-or-bust profile. The hit tool is the big question mark here, as his plus bat speed could be deadly if he makes enough contact. ❖ In a world of good-gloved shortstops with singles power, **Danny Worth** revealed he can throw a league-average knuckleball, thereby creating his own Internet cult.

Pitchers

NAME	TEAM	LVL	AGE	W	L	SV	G	GS	IP	H	HR	BB	K	BB/9	K/9	GB%	BABIP	WHIP	ERA	FIP	FRA	WARP
Silvino Bracho	SBN	A	21	3	2	26	45	0	43¹	25	3	8	70	1.7	14.5	40%	.275	0.76	2.08	1.85	2.44	1.3
Julio DePaula	BOW	AA	31	1	5	3	21	1	38	44	2	13	43	3.1	10.2	52%	.375	1.50	4.97	2.96	2.93	1.3
Derek Eitel	RNO	AAA	26	5	1	0	30	0	46²	44	5	23	60	4.4	11.6	57%	.358	1.44	2.70	4.06	3.23	1.4
Lucas Harrell	RNO	AAA	29	6	4	0	22	20	106²	115	12	77	67	6.5	5.7	63%	.311	1.80	5.15	6.21	7.44	-0.3
	HOU	MLB	29	0	3	0	3	3	12¹	19	2	9	9	6.6	6.6	50%	.370	2.27	9.49	6.00	6.74	-0.2
J.J. Putz	ARI	MLB	37	1	1	0	18	0	13²	17	1	6	14	4.0	9.2	56%	.400	1.68	6.59	3.54	3.51	0.1
Jimmie Sherfy	VIS	A+	22	2	0	6	11	0	11	6	2	5	23	4.1	18.8	53%	.308	1.00	3.27	3.56	3.94	0.2
	MOB	AA	22	3	1	1	37	0	38	34	4	18	45	4.3	10.7	48%	.316	1.37	4.97	3.92	4.47	0.2

A dominant strikeout rate paired with a miniscule walk rate is nothing to ignore, but it's worth noting that while **Silvino Bracho** does boast above-average stuff, he carries all the risks associated with a short, slight frame, and he is already relieving in Low-A. ❖ **Julio DePaula,** who hasn't appeared in an MLB game since 2007, began the year in an independent league, joined Double-A, got called up to the bigs for a day, then was designated for assignment. Aw, so close. ❖ The move to the bullpen has agreed heartily with **Derek Eitel,** who has seen his stuff tick up since the shift, though not quite as much as his strikeout rate implies. He should function in middle relief as soon as 2015. ❖ A tough season for **Lucas Harrell,** dropped twice by big-league organizations and once by a line drive to the head. His groundball tendencies might earn him another look down the road, but for now, he'll continue his career in Korea. ❖ Once a closer candidate, **David Hernandez** is just looking for a role after missing the 2014 season due to Tommy John surgery. ❖ With a frame that hinted at a future in the bullpen but stuff that screamed starter, **Jose Martinez's** Tommy John surgery didn't alter his ceiling so much as it made his chances of reaching it less likely. ❖ **Jefferson Mejia** caught eyes with a velocity jump, and he's got major-league size at 6-feet-7, but he's got a *lot* of other stuff to work on: mechanics, secondaries, command. Pitching, basically. ❖ One hopes **J.J. Putz** has set up a good 401(k) plan. ❖ With a frame built for eating innings and the potential for four average or better pitches, all signs point to 2014 second-round pick **Cody Reed** being an option toward the back end of the rotation if things go smoothly. ❖ **Matt Reynolds** redshirted the 2014 season recovering from Tommy John surgery. Prior to injury he was on the verge of becoming a serviceable middle reliever. ❖ There's no truth to the rumor that ABC named *Wipeout* after **Jimmie Sherfy's** slider; literally cannot even imagine how such an illogical rumor might have been started. Armed with a 96-98 mph fastball and a max-effort delivery, Sherfy has a chance to be a special reliever. ❖ With a name straight out of the bayou and stuff nastier than bog water, **Touki Toussaint's** potential to be a frontline starter is undercut by his reliever-ready command.

Manager

Chip Hale

Though Hale is a California native, his hiring represents a homecoming of sorts. He attended the University of Arizona, managed for six seasons in the Diamondbacks' minor-league system, coached third base under Bob Melvin for the Diamondbacks and continued to live in Tucson even after he'd moved on to jobs with the Mets (third-base coach) and Athletics (bench coach, again under Melvin).

All those cutesy ties aside, Hale wasn't appointed to generate feel-good PR for the franchise—besides, who pines for the old third-base coach? He was hired for the same reasons he almost won over the Mets and Mariners in the past: He's a quality, competent managerial prospect. Various sources have described Hale as energetic, competitive and a stickler. Factor in how he's spent years around Melvin, seemingly a good manager in his own right, and there's reason for optimism in the desert.

ATLANTA BRAVES

by Alex Remington

From 2012 to 2013, no team won more regular-season games than the Atlanta Braves. They won a division title in 2013 while boasting the youngest offense and third-youngest pitching staff in the National League. Not only did they have the third-best 25-and-Under core in the game (per the BP prospect staff's rankings), but by early 2014 the front office had locked up four of the 25U core—Andrelton Simmons, Craig Kimbrel, Freddie Freeman and Julio Teheran—to long, club-friendly extensions. True, their first-round exit in the 2013 NLDS marked the seventh straight time that the Braves had failed to advance in the playoffs, but that's a First World Problem. It was easy to assume that the team was on its way to greater glory, and on July 31st, with the club's playoff odds at a healthy 51 percent, GM Frank Wren added a superutility player and an excellent left-handed reliever for the pennant run.

And the next time you heard Frank Wren's name, just seven weeks later, he'd been fired.

Okay, maybe you heard his name once in the interim, when Braves CEO Terry McGuirk implicitly put Wren on a wobby chair by telling the *Atlanta Journal-Constitution* in late August, "Everybody is accountable … . I'm holding myself accountable." The Braves were reeling when he'd made the comment, having gone 9-11 and lost 4 1/2 games in the division race in the first three weeks of The Emilio Bonifacio Era; they would go 12-22 in the month-plus after McGuirk's quote appeared. It was just their third losing season since Chipper Jones was drafted, and the 17-win drop from 2013 was Atlanta's biggest decline in a non-strike year since 1975.

Understandably, this all upset upper management—especially the two executives most frequently quoted, team president John Schuerholz and former manager Bobby Cox. Wren was hardly out the door before they slammed it on him. Brass started spreading rumors that Wren had rubbed a ton of people the wrong way. "The decision has been building for nearly three years," wrote MLB.com's Tracy Ringolsby after getting an interview with Schuerholz.

Somewhere between McGuirk's quote and Schuerholz's, the question of accountability gets very murky. The former implied that *somebody* had to suffer for the Braves' sins in 2014, and Wren and AGM Bruce Manno—and, other than a couple coaches, nobody else—were those somebodies. But the latter quote

suggested that there might have been no number of games that Atlanta could have won to save Wren's job—or, at least, to do any more than postpone the inevitable severance.

Either way, the question has to be asked: Did Wren get screwed?

First Hypothesis: Bad Luck Screwed Frank Wren.

Evidence: Two-fifths of the projected starting rotation—Kris Medlen and Brandon Beachy—went down in spring training with Tommy John surgery. Further, it was the second such surgery for each, a phenomenon that is becoming more common but is still the exception. This forced the team to scramble to replace the pair on the free agent market, ultimately spending nearly $20 million and a draft pick on Gavin Floyd and Ervin Santana. After a month of pitching effectively, Floyd went down with one of the rarest baseball injuries ever, breaking the olecranon bone in his right arm while throwing a pitch, the same bone break that ended Joel Zumaya's career.

It's hard for any team to survive the loss of three starters—not to mention relief star Jonny Venters, who had his *third* Tommy John surgery. Could the Braves be somehow to blame for the injuries? Perhaps, but an epidemic is bound to affect some households more than others, and it's hard to say Wren should have somehow avoided a problem that has afflicted all 29 other teams.

Counterargument: In the end, the pitching was up to Atlanta's usual standard. The Braves were third best in the National League in FIP and runs allowed per game. Their three non-injured young pitchers—Mike Minor, Alex Wood and Julio Teheran—produced two and a half good seasons, Minor's first half the exception. Aaron Harang had his best year since he was a Red, and his healthiest, too. You can't blame pitching injuries when the problem isn't pitching.

Further, the offense was exceptionally healthy, with only Evan Gattis missing any substantial time. Now, whether that's lucky or unlucky...

Second Hypothesis: Bad Coaching Screwed Frank Wren.

Evidence: ESPN's David Schoenfield noticed that, by Baseball-Reference's model of WAR, the Braves had the worst production in baseball at three positions—respectively, they received -3.1 wins

BRAVES PROSPECTUS
2013 W-L: 81-81, 2ND IN NL WEST

Pythag	.482	18th	DER	.700	20th
RS/G	3.54	29th	B-Age	26.7	2nd
RA/G	3.69	6th	P-Age	27.6	6th
TAv	.253	27th	Salary	$110.5M	13th
BRR	3.54	9th	M$/MW	$3.2M	17th
TAv-P	0.26	13th	DL Days	1,011	22nd
FIP	3.44	3rd	$ on DL	14%	13th

Three-Year Park Factors

Runs	Runs/RH	Runs/LH	HR/RH	HR/LH
95	95	93	97	82

Top Hitter WARP	6.0	Jason Heyward
Top Pitcher WARP	2.4	Alex Wood
Top Prospect		Lucas Sims

above average at 3B, -2.8 at 2B, and -2.6 in CF. Not coincidentally, each of those positions was occupied by an immovable player signed to a long-term deal:

- 3B Chris Johnson was signed to a three-year, $23.5 million extension following his 2.9-WARP 2013
- 2B Dan Uggla was traded for and signed to a five-year, $62 million extension following his 6.2-WARP 2010
- CF B.J. Upton was signed to a five-year, $75.25 million contract following his 2.2-WARP 2012.

How, you might ask, is signing lousy players listed here as exculpatory evidence? There's a serious case to be made that the players were failed by their coaches, and we don't just mean tactical in-game failings.

After almost any bad season, the coaches are the first people blamed, and there's a strong element of theater: It's a lot easier to fire the lowest-paid people on the team than it is to fire the players. So there was little surprise when hitting coach Greg Walker resigned in late September, or when assistant hitting coach Scott Fletcher and third base coach Doug Dascenzo were booted as well.

But if we believe coaching means anything, it's easy to conclude that the Braves' coaching staff failed to put its hitters in a position to succeed. Nearly every Braves hitter with at least 100 plate appearances performed worse in 2014 than in 2013, and on average the cohort produced a True Average 13 points lower than PECOTA had projected before the season.

While it's possible that they all got unlucky together, whatever stung them afflicted nearly every aspect of the Braves' hitting. The pinch-hitters were the second worst in the National League. The Braves *pitchers* were among the worst hitting pitchers, for goodness sakes.

Moreover, it wasn't just an everyday failure to hit that sank their season. It was the truly epic September collapse (they went 7-18) that took the team from a half-game lead for the second wild card to nine games out of contention. Manager Fredi Gonzalez presided over exactly such a collapse three years prior, when the 2011 Braves went 9-18 in September, blowing an 8 1/2 game wild card lead over the Cardinals. Once is a dot, but twice starts to look like a line.

Counterargument: The worst players on the team were B.J. Upton and Uggla, who were terrible in 2013, and there was no contingency plan for their continued failure—that's on the man who builds the roster. Johnson was asked to repeat a career year, and once that hope proved illusory, there was no plan B there, either. The managers and coaching staff weren't able to make chicken salad out of the ingredients they were given—hint: not chicken—but that suggests that the team's true failing was its roster.

Wren could blame the players themselves, and B.J. Upton, Uggla and Johnson clearly deserve some scorn: They were abominably bad. But as explanations go, to quote the Yiddishist Michael Wex, it "can't be accused of trying too hard." It doesn't answer the why. The players were in the lineup because Frank Wren signed them. They stayed in the lineup because he filled the bench with stiffs, and because the upper ranks of his farm were thin.

Third Hypothesis: Thrifty Ownership Screwed Frank Wren.

Evidence: Atlanta is the 11th-largest metropolitan area in the country, and more than that have an almost incomparably large regional advantage—no team but perhaps the Red Sox can claim such a large swath of American real estate as its own. Yet the Braves opened the 2014 season with just the 17th-largest payroll in baseball, $97.9 million. That's barely up from the $91.1 million they spent in 2001, when they had the sixth-highest payroll in baseball.

That year, incidentally, was the last time the Braves won a playoff series.

Payrolls across the league, meanwhile, have been going up, largely because of lucrative cable deals, a revenue stream that the Braves have been unable to tap due to a sweetheart below-market deal that Time Warner signed with itself, back when it owned both the Braves and the channels that broadcast the team. But current ownership can't claim poverty based on that. The deal was well known when Liberty Media bought the team, and should have been factored into the price. The owner of the Braves is Liberty Media CEO John Malone, a man who made billions of dollars on cable television in the 1980s and is one of the largest private landowners in the United States. In each of these respects, he is extremely similar to the Braves' previous owner, Ted Turner, except that Turner was an eccentric cable TV billionaire landowner who *liked* lavishing money on his team. The current owner has decided to impose very strict limits on the team, and the roster has suffered along with the payroll.

Counterargument: Payroll is not determinant. The Braves, as noted, had the 17th-highest payroll in 2014; the team with the 18th-highest was the Royals, who beat the A's (22nd-highest payroll) and the Orioles (14th) to win the American League pennant. What's more, when the team lost two starting pitchers in spring training, Liberty Media specifically authorized spending $14 million to bring in Santana on a one-year contract, so Wren could hardly cry poverty—particularly when more than $30 million was spent fielding the three worst positions in the league.

Fourth hypothesis: Wren was scapegoated, but not unfairly.

Evidence: When you have eliminated the impossible, whatever remains, however improbable, must be the truth.

Or, put another way: The answer is a little bit of all of the above. And Wren is the thread that links all of the above.

Does that make him a bad GM? Certainly not. The team won 96 games in 2013 with almost the same lineup. The majority of the team was drafted and developed internally, then locked up for years to come. If the front office is to be blamed for the 79-win season in 2014, it deserves credit for the 190 wins the previous two seasons.

But the Braves got unlucky with pitching injuries, which stretched their budget, which meant that the front office didn't have the financial wherewithal to improve the team on the fly. The farm system had become mediocre after some disappointing drafts, which meant they didn't have a surplus to trade from, and they didn't have help on the farm once the offense began to struggle. Wren's inability to prepare for that extremely likely eventuality is what damned him.

So is that what McGuirk meant when he said everybody would be held accountable? For some reason, the team did not see any reason to hold the team's two recent September collapses against manager Gonzalez. It's possible that his lame duck status is meant to allow the team to rebuild in 2015, then hire a new manager for 2016 with an immediate mandate to succeed.

Or perhaps not. The team is loyal to its people and opaque in its dealings. Wren was promoted to replace Schuerholz without a search; Gonzalez, one of Cox's former coaches, was hired to replace Cox without a search. The current GM tandem, President of Baseball Operations John Hart and Assistant GM John Coppolella, were promoted from within, without a search. The Braves' rhetoric after firing Wren suggested that the real problem was a personality conflict, not success or failure on the field. It's very possible that the same calculus applies to Gonzalez: that his job security depends not on whether he is good at his job, but on whether his bosses like him.

The Braves are a large organization with an aging brain trust. President Schuerholz has been with the team since 1990; former manager Cox isn't listed on the team's front office page, but he's been with the team for the better part of four decades, as manager from 1978-1981 and from 1990-2010, as GM in between, and as an éminence grise in his post-retirement years. Together, they won 14 straight division titles from 1991 to 2005 (not counting the 1994 strike year).

But they're old men. The 2014 team exposed failures in both amateur and professional scouting, leading to the poor drafts and the terrible Upton, Uggla and Johnson contracts; in player development, as seen by the graduated rookies who failed to help the team; in coaching, as symbolized by the departed hitting coaches; in the health and training staff, who failed to keep pitchers healthy or to diagnose player maladies in a timely fashion. (Gattis was out for nearly two weeks with strep throat; more than a week after the initial diagnosis, the team realized that he actually had a kidney stone.)

As GM, Wren surely deserves responsibility for overseeing a team with all of these failures, and for hiring many of the personnel who played a direct role. But Cox and Schuerholz oversaw *him*. There is some cognitive dissonance between the notions that "Everyone is accountable" and that Wren's eventual firing was "building for nearly three years," and the ultimate reality that among the team's top staff, only Wren and Manno were canned.

Yes, Cox and Schuerholz are Hall of Famers, among the greatest baseball men ever to grace the game. But now may be the time for them to gracefully bow out. ■

—Alex Remington writes for the Hardball Times and manages Braves Journal. He is a product manager at The Washington Post *and a fellow at the Reynolds Journalism Institute.*

Player comments by R.J. Anderson and Baseball Prospectus Authors

Hitters

Christian Bethancourt C
Born: 9/2/91   Age: 23   Bats: R   Throws: R   Height: 6' 2"   Weight: 205

YEAR	TEAM	LVL	AGE	PA	R	2B	3B	HR	RBI	BB	K	SB	CS	AVG/OBP/SLG	TAv	BABIP	BRR	FRAA	WARP
2012	MIS	AA	20	288	30	5	1	2	26	11	45	8	6	.243/.275/.291	.228	.281	-2.0	C(69): 2.5	0.2
2013	MIS	AA	21	388	42	21	0	12	45	16	57	11	7	.277/.305/.436	.273	.294	-0.4	C(85): 0.8	2.4
2013	ATL	MLB	21	1	0	0	0	0	0	0	1	0	0	.000/.000/.000	.053	—	0.0		0.0
2014	GWN	AAA	22	365	33	17	1	8	48	13	61	7	1	.283/.308/.408	.244	.318	0.3	C(80): 0.7	1.0
2014	ATL	MLB	22	117	7	3	0	0	9	3	26	1	1	.248/.274/.274	.210	.322	0.2	C(31): 0.3	0.0
2015	ATL	MLB	23	250	26	10	0	5	22	5	55	4	2	.245/.261/.352	.235	.291	-0.2	C 1	0.4

Breakout: 5%   Improve: 16%   Collapse: 2%   Attrition: 15%   MLB: 23%   Comparables: Wilson Ramos, Audry Perez, Tony Cruz

Nearly everyone who has watched Bethancourt catch over the past few years has a story about his arm. Take the time against the Phillies last season, when he retrieved a ball from the back of the cutout, turned, dodged the umpire and made a throw to second as electric and straight as an eel, nailing the baserunner by feet. That play had it all: athleticism, instincts and yes, an elite arm. The other parts of Bethancourt's game remain less polished. He's not a quiet receiver, which affects his overall defensive value, and his approach at the plate is so bad that we're not going to waste words on it. Nonetheless, Bethancourt is the catcher of the future in Atlanta, meaning basestealers are about to become a thing of the past.

Emilio Bonifacio CF
Born: 4/23/85   Age: 30   Bats: B   Throws: R   Height: 5' 11"   Weight: 205

YEAR	TEAM	LVL	AGE	PA	R	2B	3B	HR	RBI	BB	K	SB	CS	AVG/OBP/SLG	TAv	BABIP	BRR	FRAA	WARP
2012	JUP	A+	27	36	6	1	0	0	4	6	9	3	1	.167/.306/.200	.206	.238	0.9	CF(9): -0.2	0.0
2012	MIA	MLB	27	274	30	3	4	1	11	25	52	30	3	.258/.330/.316	.246	.325	1.3	CF(51): -3.7, 2B(15): 0.7	0.0
2013	KCA	MLB	28	179	21	6	2	0	11	17	37	16	2	.285/.352/.348	.258	.369	3.7	2B(31): -1.3, 3B(6): -0.1	0.7
2013	TOR	MLB	28	282	33	16	1	3	20	13	66	12	6	.218/.258/.321	.217	.277	2.6	2B(59): 0.8, LF(20): 0.9	0.0
2014	ATL	MLB	29	128	12	3	1	1	6	10	36	12	2	.212/.273/.280	.220	.296	-1.5	CF(17): -0.4, RF(6): 0.0	-0.4
2014	CHN	MLB	29	298	35	14	3	2	18	16	49	14	6	.279/.318/.373	.261	.333	3.6	CF(48): -2.2, 2B(26): -2.5	1.0
2015	ATL	MLB	30	411	50	15	3	2	26	30	91	27	7	.253/.308/.328	.245	.319	1.9	2B -2, CF -4	0.2

Breakout: 1%   Improve: 47%   Collapse: 2%   Attrition: 6%   MLB: 96%   Comparables: Kenny Lofton, Michael Bourn, Manny Mota

Sometimes one month is all it takes. Bonifacio hit .337 for the Cubs in April before entering a slump that swallowed nearly the entire season. Along the way, he spent time on the disabled list with a strained oblique, and changed teams (with the Braves plucking him and James Russell at the deadline). Bonifacio can run and defend adequately at enough positions to hold down a super-sub job; sort of a faster Jerry Hairston Jr. Problem is, everyone keeps waiting for a repeat of his 2011, which means anytime he gets hot for a few weeks people assume he has everything figured out, be it the dimensions of the strike zone or a channel to Patience Worth. He never does, and likely never will.

Alberto Callaspo   2B

Born: 4/19/83   Age: 32   Bats: B   Throws: R   Height: 5' 9"   Weight: 225

YEAR	TEAM	LVL	AGE	PA	R	2B	3B	HR	RBI	BB	K	SB	CS	AVG/OBP/SLG	TAv	BABIP	BRR	FRAA	WARP
2012	ANA	MLB	29	520	55	20	0	10	53	56	59	4	3	.252/.331/.361	.266	.268	1.8	3B(131): 3.2	2.8
2013	ANA	MLB	30	336	32	13	0	5	36	34	22	0	2	.252/.324/.347	.253	.254	-1.9	3B(84): 0.3	0.5
2013	OAK	MLB	30	180	20	7	0	5	22	19	25	0	0	.270/.350/.409	.286	.292	1.2	2B(32): -3.7, 3B(9): 0.1	0.6
2014	OAK	MLB	31	451	37	15	0	4	39	40	50	0	1	.223/.290/.290	.231	.242	-4.4	2B(46): 0.2, 1B(23): 1.9	-0.7
2015	ATL	MLB	32	439	42	17	0	6	39	39	53	2	1	.253/.317/.343	.259	.275	-0.6	3B 2, 2B -2	1.0

Breakout: 2%   Improve: 38%   Collapse: 3%   Attrition: 10%   MLB: 97%   *Comparables: Placido Polanco, Jeff Keppinger, Jose Vidro*

Callaspo's value lies in his versatility as a switch-hitter who can play three infield positions. The problem is that he's not especially good at any of those things. His .616 OPS as a left-handed batter was barely playable for a non-shortstop, and the 100 points of OPS he lost from the right side sent him below replacement level. He can handle second or third base in a utility role, but Callaspo is miscast as an everyday solution. The A's compounded the issue by starting him at designated hitter 34 times in 2014, and though his high-contact approach can pay some dividends at the plate, that deployment simultaneously weakened the lineup and robbed the team of the very versatility that makes him worth a roster spot in the first place. This didn't fit anywhere else, but: At this point, Callaspo is in the discussion for slowest sub-six-foot player ever.

Todd Cunningham   CF

Born: 3/20/89   Age: 26   Bats: B   Throws: R   Height: 6' 0"   Weight: 205

YEAR	TEAM	LVL	AGE	PA	R	2B	3B	HR	RBI	BB	K	SB	CS	AVG/OBP/SLG	TAv	BABIP	BRR	FRAA	WARP
2012	MIS	AA	23	519	77	23	6	3	51	38	51	24	8	.309/.364/.403	.289	.340	5.3	CF(97): -11.7, RF(17): -1.0	2.7
2013	GWN	AAA	24	487	60	13	5	2	38	41	62	20	7	.265/.342/.333	.244	.305	3.6	CF(110): -1.1, RF(3): 0.4	1.4
2013	ATL	MLB	24	8	2	0	0	0	0	0	3	0	0	.250/.250/.250	.150	.400	-0.1	LF(5): -0.1, RF(2): -0.0	-0.1
2014	GWN	AAA	25	531	59	28	2	8	58	35	79	19	8	.287/.347/.406	.262	.329	0.8	CF(119): 12.7	3.4
2015	ATL	MLB	26	250	28	10	1	3	19	13	45	8	3	.256/.304/.346	.250	.299	0.4	CF -1, RF -0	0.4

Breakout: 3%   Improve: 22%   Collapse: 14%   Attrition: 27%   MLB: 46%   *Comparables: Logan Schafer, Jamie Hoffmann, Darin Mastroianni*

The Pynchoniest Braves prospect, in that it's not clear where this is headed or if any of it makes sense. Cunningham repeated Triple-A, improved upon his first go-round, and hit .316 with a .409 on-base percentage in the second half. Think he received a September call-up? Nope. Bewildering as that might be, the Braves' handling of him earlier in the season confused us even more, as they had him take grounders at second base but abandoned the experiment without using him there in-game. Do the Braves think he isn't ready for the limelight, or are they worried his singles-heavy approach won't work in the majors? As T.P. once wrote, If they can get you asking the wrong questions, they don't have to worry about answers. (Huh?)

Braxton Davidson   OF

Born: 6/18/96   Age: 19   Bats: L   Throws: L   Height: 6'2   Weight: 210

YEAR	TEAM	LVL	AGE	PA	R	2B	3B	HR	RBI	BB	K	SB	CS	AVG/OBP/SLG	TAv	BABIP	BRR	FRAA	WARP
2015	ATL	MLB	19	250	17	7	0	2	18	17	81	0	0	.181/.242/.238	.192	.268	-0.4	LF 2	-1.1

Breakout: 0%   Improve: 0%   Collapse: 0%   Attrition: 0%   MLB: 0%   *Comparables: Dalton Pompey, Caleb Gindl, Aaron Hicks*

Anytime a teenager whose best defensive position is first base gets drafted on the first day, you can bet his bat is the selling point. Scouts believe Davidson, selected with the compensatory pick gained from Brian McCann's departure, could develop into a middle-of-the-order hitter who contributes plenty of average and power. Unfortunately those same scouts are unconvinced that Davidson has the athleticism or instincts to play a passable outfield, making him an awkward fit for the franchise that owes Freddie Freeman roughly twice the GDP of Nauru through the 2021 season. Just 19, Davidson is far enough from the majors that the Braves have time to figure out where to play him—or, at minimum, where *not* to play him.

Ryan Doumit   C

Born: 4/3/81   Age: 34   Bats: B   Throws: R   Height: 6' 1"   Weight: 220

YEAR	TEAM	LVL	AGE	PA	R	2B	3B	HR	RBI	BB	K	SB	CS	AVG/OBP/SLG	TAv	BABIP	BRR	FRAA	WARP
2012	MIN	MLB	31	528	56	34	1	18	75	29	98	0	0	.275/.320/.461	.269	.306	1.7	C(59): 0.2, LF(16): 1.2	2.1
2013	MIN	MLB	32	538	49	28	1	14	55	48	99	1	0	.247/.314/.396	.264	.282	-0.8	C(43): 0.2, RF(32): -1.3	1.5
2014	ATL	MLB	33	166	11	4	0	5	17	7	49	1	0	.197/.235/.318	.217	.250	-0.2	LF(9): 0.3, RF(9): 0.6	-0.5
2015	ATL	MLB	34	250	24	11	0	6	28	17	56	0	0	.241/.298/.374	.257	.289	0.1	C 0, RF -0	0.6

Breakout: 0%   Improve: 31%   Collapse: 13%   Attrition: 21%   MLB: 91%   *Comparables: Dusty Baker, Leon Wagner, Billy Williams*

"Glove, Doumit! That's the biggest trap of all," said a bald inventor named Wallace. Ain't that the truth? Were it not for Doumit's widely panned defense behind the plate and history of concussions, he probably spends last season starting at catcher for an offensively needy team. Instead he was miscast by the Braves as a designated pinch-hitter. Doumit took to the role about as well as Hutch the Rabbit would, leaving him with some of the worst offensive production of any player who appeared in more than half his team's games. On the bright side: He was behind the plate only long enough (18 innings) to cost his pitchers five strikes with his receiving technique.

Freddie Freeman   1B

Born: 9/12/89   Age: 25   Bats: L   Throws: R   Height: 6' 5"   Weight: 225

YEAR	TEAM	LVL	AGE	PA	R	2B	3B	HR	RBI	BB	K	SB	CS	AVG/OBP/SLG	TAv	BABIP	BRR	FRAA	WARP
2012	ATL	MLB	22	620	91	33	2	23	94	64	129	2	0	.259/.340/.456	.284	.295	1.9	1B(146): -7.2	1.5
2013	ATL	MLB	23	629	89	27	2	23	109	66	121	1	0	.319/.396/.501	.324	.371	-2.6	1B(147): 2.1	5.0
2014	ATL	MLB	24	708	93	43	4	18	78	90	145	3	4	.288/.386/.461	.315	.351	-1.4	1B(162): 0.1	4.1
2015	ATL	MLB	25	651	76	33	1	20	84	63	139	2	2	.279/.354/.448	.304	.332	-0.7	1B -3	3.2

Breakout: 3%   Improve: 63%   Collapse: 1%   Attrition: 3%   MLB: 100%   *Comparables: Prince Fielder, Albert Pujols, Billy Butler*

Freeman? Not anytime soon. Those reading this who ignore contractual matters in baseball are in for a real treat, because the Braves went on an extension frenzy last year. Freeman was part of the bunch, signing an eight-year deal worth $135 million. He's a good player; he hits for average, walks, hits for power and, while there's disagreement about his defensive value, is at worst a tolerable gloveman. The one drawback is his position. The league is covering the injuries and/or poor play of other big-monied first basemen (Joey Votto, Prince Fielder, Mark Teixeira, etc.), which raises the question: Were the Braves smart to lock in their own? Given Freeman's age and upside (he could go all prime Adrian Gonzalez on the league some year), there's a good chance he earns this deal. Now, about his next one …

Evan Gattis   C

Born: 8/18/86   Age: 28   Bats: R   Throws: R   Height: 6' 4"   Weight: 260

YEAR	TEAM	LVL	AGE	PA	R	2B	3B	HR	RBI	BB	K	SB	CS	AVG/OBP/SLG	TAv	BABIP	BRR	FRAA	WARP
2012	LYN	A+	25	94	14	7	0	9	29	10	12	1	1	.385/.468/.821	.414	.356	-0.5	C(10): 0.0, LF(3): -0.1	1.9
2012	MIS	AA	25	207	24	13	4	9	37	20	29	1	1	.258/.343/.522	.273	.262	0.2	LF(30): -1.3, C(17): -0.4	0.7
2013	GWN	AAA	26	22	1	4	0	1	1	0	4	0	0	.333/.364/.667	.344	.375	-0.6	C(1): -0.0, LF(1): -0.1	0.2
2013	ATL	MLB	26	382	44	21	0	21	65	21	81	0	0	.243/.291/.480	.271	.255	0.6	LF(48): -0.9, C(42): 0.7	2.0
2014	ATL	MLB	27	401	41	17	1	22	52	22	97	0	0	.263/.317/.493	.297	.298	-5.1	C(93): -0.3	2.6
2015	*ATL*	*MLB*	*28*	*378*	*45*	*18*	*1*	*19*	*57*	*21*	*87*	*0*	*0*	*.252/.303/.470*	*.289*	*.280*	*-1.5*	*C -0, LF -1*	*2.2*

Breakout: 1%   Improve: 46%   Collapse: 5%   Attrition: 9%   MLB: 95%   *Comparables:*   *Geovany Soto, Allen Craig, Mark Trumbo*

"He's a polar bear," Fredi Gonzalez explained to David O'Brien, of the *Atlanta Journal-Constitution*, after Gattis started the season smoking hot in cold temperatures. Ol' Breezly managed to top his rookie-year production due to a fattened batting average, but none of his other performance indicators improved (and his strikeout rate got worse, as pitchers spun more and more breaking stuff his way), so take those gains for what you will. Murmurs about a move back to left field persisted because of his shortcomings behind the plate. He's a quality framer, yet his size (6-feet-4, 260-plus) hinders him from blocking balls that his catching colleagues do. Additionally, that body is already dealing with back problems. Gattis would make sense as someone's DH. The Braves lack that option, so he could be moved in a trade—ideally to someplace cooler than Atlanta.

Phil Gosselin   IF

Born: 10/3/88   Age: 26   Bats: R   Throws: R   Height: 6' 1"   Weight: 200

YEAR	TEAM	LVL	AGE	PA	R	2B	3B	HR	RBI	BB	K	SB	CS	AVG/OBP/SLG	TAv	BABIP	BRR	FRAA	WARP
2012	MIS	AA	23	547	55	23	3	3	46	46	90	12	4	.242/.317/.320	.249	.289	3.1	2B(120): -2.1, LF(5): 0.2	1.2
2013	MIS	AA	24	241	27	10	1	1	23	12	31	5	1	.243/.291/.312	.244	.275	0.4	2B(35): 6.4, LF(16): -1.1	0.5
2013	GWN	AAA	24	228	17	4	1	2	15	12	38	1	0	.266/.308/.324	.234	.315	1.3	2B(46): 5.1, LF(4): 0.2	0.6
2013	ATL	MLB	24	7	2	0	0	0	0	1	2	0	0	.333/.429/.333	.258	.500	0.2	2B(3): -0.0	0.0
2014	GWN	AAA	25	407	58	29	5	5	31	19	62	6	1	.344/.379/.487	.296	.401	2.1	3B(41): 0.3, 2B(25): -0.7	2.8
2014	ATL	MLB	25	136	17	4	0	1	3	5	27	2	2	.266/.304/.320	.268	.330	1.5	2B(26): -0.8, 3B(9): -0.1	0.7
2015	*ATL*	*MLB*	*26*	*250*	*25*	*11*	*1*	*2*	*19*	*10*	*53*	*3*	*1*	*.251/.286/.338*	*.243*	*.306*	*-0.1*	*2B 1, 3B -0*	*0.3*

Breakout: 3%   Improve: 13%   Collapse: 8%   Attrition: 16%   MLB: 27%   *Comparables:*   *Danny Worth, Russell Mitchell, Luis Jimenez*

Regarded by many (us included) as an org player entering the season, Gosselin made the most of his opportunity late in the year. Was it enough to change minds? Eh, not really. He didn't walk or bop, and his hit tool isn't good enough to expect this kind of average moving forward. The glove is nice and so are the instincts, but he's a utility infielder at best.

Chris Johnson   3B

Born: 10/1/84   Age: 30   Bats: R   Throws: R   Height: 6' 3"   Weight: 225

YEAR	TEAM	LVL	AGE	PA	R	2B	3B	HR	RBI	BB	K	SB	CS	AVG/OBP/SLG	TAv	BABIP	BRR	FRAA	WARP
2012	ARI	MLB	27	160	12	7	2	7	35	8	40	1	0	.286/.321/.503	.282	.340	-2.6	3B(39): -2.4	0.2
2012	HOU	MLB	27	368	36	21	3	8	41	23	92	4	1	.279/.329/.428	.262	.360	-1.0	3B(88): -9.1, 1B(6): 0.6	0.1
2013	ATL	MLB	28	547	54	34	0	12	68	29	116	0	0	.321/.358/.457	.283	.394	2.3	3B(125): -3.8, 1B(12): 0.6	2.9
2014	ATL	MLB	29	611	43	27	0	10	58	23	159	6	0	.263/.292/.361	.238	.345	-0.3	3B(150): -17.6, 1B(1): -0.0	-1.9
2015	*ATL*	*MLB*	*30*	*561*	*54*	*28*	*2*	*12*	*62*	*25*	*143*	*3*	*1*	*.268/.303/.394*	*.264*	*.342*	*-0.6*	*3B -14, 1B 0*	*0.0*

Breakout: 6%   Improve: 46%   Collapse: 2%   Attrition: 8%   MLB: 87%   *Comparables:*   *Kevin Kouzmanoff, Ty Wigginton, Hank Blalock*

What was Wren thinking when he extended Johnson for three years and $23 million? Here's a guess: He wanted to save money by avoiding the arbitration process. Why would that be an issue, you ask? Johnson is the exact kind of player a smart agent can sell to arbitrators. He hits for a solid-to-good average based on singles and doubles, and does nothing else well. He doesn't defend or walk enough, and he even strikes out more than he should. Basically, he's the kind of player who is always one bad year away from being non-tendered. Unless, of course, he had agreed to a three-year extension months earlier.

Kyle Kubitza   3B

Born: 7/15/90   Age: 24   Bats: L   Throws: R   Height: 6' 3"   Weight: 215

YEAR	TEAM	LVL	AGE	PA	R	2B	3B	HR	RBI	BB	K	SB	CS	AVG/OBP/SLG	TAv	BABIP	BRR	FRAA	WARP
2012	ROM	A	21	531	68	24	9	9	59	73	127	18	11	.239/.349/.393	.267	.310	0.7	3B(90): -1.4	1.9
2013	LYN	A+	22	527	75	28	6	12	57	80	132	8	16	.260/.380/.434	.283	.344	-2.9	3B(125): -1.2	1.9
2014	MIS	AA	23	529	76	31	11	8	55	77	133	21	6	.295/.405/.470	.335	.401	3.7	3B(120): -5.2, LF(1): -0.0	5.8
2015	*ATL*	*MLB*	*24*	*250*	*25*	*9*	*2*	*4*	*23*	*27*	*81*	*5*	*2*	*.215/.305/.333*	*.249*	*.316*	*0.1*	*3B -2*	*0.1*

Breakout: 0%   Improve: 7%   Collapse: 10%   Attrition: 12%   MLB: 24%   *Comparables:*   *Matt Tuiasosopo, Josh Fields, Adam Duvall*

Many wondered what Chris Johnson's extension meant for Kubitza's future in Atlanta. Maybe nothing, given their respective seasons. Kubitza's knowledge of the strike zone is second only to that of Twitter users, as evidenced by his Southern League-leading on-base percentage. His average power manifests itself through doubles rather than home runs, but could be limited in the majors by a hitch in his swing. A strong arm and fluid movements lend credence to the idea that Kubitza should be a competent defender at the hot corner. Altogether, that leaves him somewhere between second-division starter and bench player, which should be enough to land him the starting gig if Johnson continues to struggle.

Gerald Laird C

Born: 11/13/79   Age: 35   Bats: R   Throws: R   Height: 6' 1"   Weight: 230

YEAR	TEAM	LVL	AGE	PA	R	2B	3B	HR	RBI	BB	K	SB	CS	AVG/OBP/SLG	TAv	BABIP	BRR	FRAA	WARP
2012	DET	MLB	32	191	24	8	1	2	11	14	21	0	0	.282/.337/.374	.249	.309	0.5	C(56): 0.1	0.7
2013	ATL	MLB	33	141	12	8	0	1	13	14	23	1	1	.281/.367/.372	.280	.337	-1.1	C(40): 0.2	0.9
2014	ATL	MLB	34	167	12	8	0	0	10	14	33	0	0	.204/.275/.257	.194	.261	-1.0	C(48): 0.0	-0.4
2015	ATL	MLB	35	250	21	11	1	2	19	18	49	1	0	.228/.291/.305	.232	.277	-0.5	C 1	0.3

Breakout: 0%   Improve: 32%   Collapse: 11%   Attrition: 25%   MLB: 84%   Comparables: Matt Treanor, Yorvit Torrealba, Ron Hassey

Jazayerli's Law of Backup Catchers states that every reserve backstop will, given enough trials, have a season where he hits .300. In other words: Unless there's good reason to buy in, slow your roll. Laird hasn't hit .300, but he posted a .280-plus average in consecutive seasons, which caused us to wonder whether his swing tinkering might have resulted in an upped talent level. His 2014 said phooey to all that. So which small sample do we trust? Or do we just chalk it up to the decline you'd expect from a career catcher reaching his mid-30s? The Braves didn't stick around to find out.

Nick Markakis RF

Born: 11/17/83   Age: 31   Bats: L   Throws: L   Height: 6' 1"   Weight: 190

YEAR	TEAM	LVL	AGE	PA	R	2B	3B	HR	RBI	BB	K	SB	CS	AVG/OBP/SLG	TAv	BABIP	BRR	FRAA	WARP
2012	BAL	MLB	28	471	59	28	3	13	54	42	51	1	1	.298/.363/.471	.285	.310	0.4	RF(102): -2.7	1.8
2013	BAL	MLB	29	700	89	24	0	10	59	55	76	1	2	.271/.329/.356	.255	.291	1.9	RF(155): 0.8	1.2
2014	BAL	MLB	30	710	81	27	1	14	50	62	84	4	2	.276/.342/.386	.271	.299	-1.8	RF(147): 1.9, 1B(2): -0.1	2.3
2015	ATL	MLB	31	665	74	29	2	9	58	56	93	3	2	.272/.335/.372	.272	.305	0.3	RF -2, 1B -0	1.8

Breakout: 0%   Improve: 33%   Collapse: 3%   Attrition: 7%   MLB: 92%   Comparables: Tony Gwynn, David DeJesus, Floyd Robinson

Markakis isn't your prototypical leadoff hitter, but then again the prototypical leadoff hitter is Rickey Henderson, so nobody ever will be again. He's no longer even your prototypical Markakis—that guy sprayed extra-base hits all over the field. But a decent OBP and one of the game's best strike-out rates make him an effective tablesetter, and his right field arm still has some zing. Yes, he's arguably overpaid—when someone earns $44 million on singles and isn't the co-founder of eHarmony, he'll get that reputation—but he should still be an above-average player for at least the first half of his four-year stay in Atlanta.

Ramiro Pena SS

Born: 7/18/85   Age: 29   Bats: B   Throws: R   Height: 5' 11"   Weight: 200

YEAR	TEAM	LVL	AGE	PA	R	2B	3B	HR	RBI	BB	K	SB	CS	AVG/OBP/SLG	TAv	BABIP	BRR	FRAA	WARP
2012	SWB	AAA	26	404	40	13	3	2	29	34	74	1	3	.258/.325/.328	.248	.317	-1.1	SS(69): 7.4, 2B(18): -1.9	1.4
2012	NYA	MLB	26	4	0	0	0	0	0	0	0	0	0	.250/.250/.250	.180	.250	0.2	SS(1): 0.1	0.0
2013	ATL	MLB	27	107	14	5	1	3	12	8	18	0	2	.278/.330/.443	.292	.312	-0.4	3B(32): 0.4, 2B(10): -0.4	0.8
2014	ATL	MLB	28	165	9	6	0	3	9	13	38	1	0	.245/.304/.347	.265	.308	-1.1	2B(38): -1.3, 3B(17): -0.5	0.3
2015	ATL	MLB	29	250	22	9	1	3	21	16	53	1	1	.238/.289/.323	.240	.289	-0.5	SS 1, 2B -2	0.3

Breakout: 2%   Improve: 18%   Collapse: 20%   Attrition: 20%   MLB: 56%   Comparables: Matt Tolbert, Russ Adams, Jason Donald

The stars aligned for Pena to build upon his solid 2013 in a larger role, yet he failed to capitalize on the opportunity. Fredi Gonzalez's Plan B at second base after Dan Uggla disappointed (and before Tommy La Stella arrived), Pena started 12 games at the keystone in May and lived up to his Yankees nickname ("Derek Jeter's Glove") at the plate. La Stella soon took the starting job, pushing Pena to the bench, then Phil Gosselin emerged late in the year and made Pena the tertiary option across the infield. His fielding should keep him on a bench somewhere, but he'll need to keep some change-of-address forms handy; he was outrighted in November.

Jose Peraza 2B

Born: 4/30/94   Age: 21   Bats: R   Throws: R   Height: 6' 0"   Weight: 165

YEAR	TEAM	LVL	AGE	PA	R	2B	3B	HR	RBI	BB	K	SB	CS	AVG/OBP/SLG	TAv	BABIP	BRR	FRAA	WARP
2013	ROM	A	19	504	72	18	8	1	47	34	64	64	15	.288/.341/.371	.275	.328	7.0	SS(104): 20.4	5.6
2014	LYN	A+	20	304	44	13	8	1	27	10	32	35	7	.342/.365/.454	.302	.376	4.9	2B(58): -6.2, SS(7): 0.6	2.2
2014	MIS	AA	20	195	35	7	3	1	17	7	15	25	8	.335/.363/.422	.295	.361	5.2	2B(41): -2.9	1.4
2015	ATL	MLB	21	250	31	8	2	1	15	6	47	21	5	.257/.278/.330	.234	.307	2.5	2B -3, SS 4	0.6

Breakout: 0%   Improve: 0%   Collapse: 0%   Attrition: 0%   MLB: 0%   Comparables: Jose Altuve, Jean Segura, Luis Sardinas

In most organizations, Peraza would serve as the Shortstop of the Future; not in Atlanta, not with Andrelton Simmons around. So the Braves made preparations last season, sliding Peraza to the other side of the bag. He took to the position just fine, thanks for asking, and did so while making a newsworthy adjustment at the plate: slotting his hands deeper so his bat enters the hitting zone quicker. That adjustment helped Peraza storm through Lynchburg and keep pace at Mississippi, despite being one of the youngest players in the league. Atlanta continues to groom Peraza and his near-elite speed for the leadoff spot, even though his walk rate resides in Alfredo Griffin's neighborhood. Given how the Braves have challenged Peraza and other top prospects before, they could bring him to the majors earlier than expected—with or without an improved approach.

Victor Reyes RF

Born: 10/5/94   Age: 20   Bats: B   Throws: R   Height: 6' 3"   Weight: 170

YEAR	TEAM	LVL	AGE	PA	R	2B	3B	HR	RBI	BB	K	SB	CS	AVG/OBP/SLG	TAv	BABIP	BRR	FRAA	WARP
2014	ROM	A	19	361	32	13	0	0	34	24	58	12	7	.259/.309/.298	.231	.312	-3.3	RF(79): 3.2	-0.7
2015	ATL	MLB	20	250	18	8	0	1	17	11	69	3	2	.207/.244/.257	.199	.283	-0.4	RF 1, LF 0	-1.1

Breakout: 0%   Improve: 0%   Collapse: 0%   Attrition: 0%   MLB: 0%   Comparables: Lorenzo Cain, Aaron Cunningham, Ender Inciarte

The gangly Reyes had a gangly season. He was phenomenal early, hitting .342 over his first 44 games, yet struggled to a .181 mark over his final 45, at which point he suffered a campaign-ending leg contusion. There are legitimate drawbacks to Reyes' game—he's not going to hit many home runs or play a premium defensive position—but his supporters believe he has the best barrel control this side of Donkey Kong, which should lead to a high average and doubles power.

Andrelton Simmons   SS

Born: 9/4/89   Age: 25   Bats: R   Throws: R   Height: 6' 2"   Weight: 195

YEAR	TEAM	LVL	AGE	PA	R	2B	3B	HR	RBI	BB	K	SB	CS	AVG/OBP/SLG	TAv	BABIP	BRR	FRAA	WARP
2012	MIS	AA	22	203	29	9	2	3	21	20	20	10	2	.293/.372/.420	.288	.314	-0.7	SS(44): 6.8	2.2
2012	ATL	MLB	22	182	17	8	2	3	19	12	21	1	0	.289/.335/.416	.265	.310	1.9	SS(49): 7.5	1.8
2013	ATL	MLB	23	658	76	27	6	17	59	40	55	6	5	.248/.296/.396	.257	.247	-1.0	SS(156): 26.5	5.4
2014	ATL	MLB	24	576	44	18	4	7	46	32	60	4	5	.244/.286/.331	.230	.263	3.6	SS(146): 10.0	2.1
2015	ATL	MLB	25	557	56	22	4	10	55	32	61	6	4	.256/.301/.375	.262	.269	1.5	SS 19	4.7

Breakout: 0%   Improve: 63%   Collapse: 2%   Attrition: 4%   MLB: 100%   Comparables: *Elvis Andrus, Jose Reyes, J.J. Hardy*

The things this guy can do with cowhide would make Leatherface jealous; unfortunately, Simmons hits like he's swinging a chainsaw. It's hard to reconcile how someone so smooth and skillful in the field can look so unbalanced and lost at the dish. There's little positive to be found in his offensive year, unless you're really generous and credit him for hitting fewer popups. His strikeout rate increased, his power production skydived and his walk rate dipped for a second consecutive season. He's not even a good smallballer, since he can't steal bases or bunt well. The Braves signed him to a seven-year extension worth $58 million—the largest average annual value for a player with his service time—because they love his glove that much, but jeez did he fit in a bit too comfortably with the other automatic outs in the lineup.

B.J. Upton   CF

Born: 8/21/84   Age: 30   Bats: R   Throws: R   Height: 6' 3"   Weight: 185

YEAR	TEAM	LVL	AGE	PA	R	2B	3B	HR	RBI	BB	K	SB	CS	AVG/OBP/SLG	TAv	BABIP	BRR	FRAA	WARP
2012	TBA	MLB	27	633	79	29	3	28	78	45	169	31	6	.246/.298/.454	.274	.294	2.9	CF(142): -9.6	2.2
2013	ATL	MLB	28	446	30	14	0	9	26	44	151	12	5	.184/.268/.289	.212	.266	-1.8	CF(118): -10.8	-2.1
2014	ATL	MLB	29	582	67	19	5	12	35	57	173	20	7	.208/.287/.333	.242	.286	6.1	CF(139): -6.0	0.7
2015	ATL	MLB	30	521	68	21	2	14	49	48	154	20	6	.221/.294/.368	.255	.293	1.4	CF -5	0.8

Breakout: 6%   Improve: 55%   Collapse: 5%   Attrition: 3%   MLB: 100%   Comparables: *Rick Monday, Mack Jones, Larry Walker*

Two disappointing seasons down, three to go? Technically, Upton improved in his second year in Atlanta, but it merely reinforced that this is his new level. Fans considered him an overpaid bum anyway, so their boos are of no concern here. More worrisome is how the coaching staff and front office's faith started cracking. Gonzalez, who—despite constant criticism—had batted Upton near the top of the order all year in the name of comfort, relented in August, dropping him to the eighth spot, where he belonged, or at least belonged more. (If only the Braves' lineup went to 11 ...) Gonzalez's concession occurred around the same time that reports surfaced linking Wren to an NBA-style swap involving Upton, the Cubs and Upton's former teammate Edwin Jackson.

Through it all, Upton worked and tinkered—or leastways gave the appearance of working. Always known for his tweaking, Upton's continued struggles pushed him to compulsive territory. He tried darn near everything to get back on the right path. He worked with his father over the winter; he started wearing glasses; he asked Chipper Jones for advice; he opened this; closed that; broadened this; narrowed that; and nothing worked. Upton had seemingly found a good spot late in the year, when he improved his bat path by fixing his back shoulder, yet the resulting month wasn't even the best of his otherwise dreadful season.

So what's next? To find out, we consulted history. The extent of Upton's collapse makes it tough enough to find comparisons, so we focused only on the offensive part of the game. All we wanted were players who posted True Averages of .270 or better in back-to-back years, then slid to .250 or lower in consecutive seasons. Here are the five players we found:

- Paul Blair, 1973-1976
- Enos Cabell, 1977-1980
- Terry Kennedy, 1982-1985
- Mookie Wilson, 1987-1990
- Tim Wallach, 1989-1992

Those players don't have a ton in common—their positions and ages vary, though most were in their late 20s or early 30s; so too do their reasons for decline—but here's one thing they all shared: None posted an average-or-better TAv in the next season. (Kennedy and Blair, both at .249, came closest.) A few of the players did enjoy success later in their careers—Cabell and Wallach had two above-average seasons, Kennedy had one—but it didn't come right away and it didn't last for long.

So things aren't looking good for Upton. But why? Where did it all go wrong? Did the pressure to live up to a king-sized free-agent deal sink him? Was it his brother's presence that doomed him? Or Joe Maddon's absence? Did he leave more than an empty dome in St. Petersburg? Did he lose bat speed and eye talent quicker than expected? Or did he quit caring? We'll never know. What we do know is, if Upton is working as hard as he looks to be from the outside, he deserves to find success.

Justin Upton   LF

Born: 8/25/87   Age: 27   Bats: R   Throws: R   Height: 6' 2"   Weight: 205

YEAR	TEAM	LVL	AGE	PA	R	2B	3B	HR	RBI	BB	K	SB	CS	AVG/OBP/SLG	TAv	BABIP	BRR	FRAA	WARP
2012	ARI	MLB	24	628	107	24	4	17	67	63	121	18	8	.280/.355/.430	.279	.327	0.5	RF(149): 10.6	3.6
2013	ATL	MLB	25	643	94	27	2	27	70	75	161	8	1	.263/.354/.464	.293	.321	2.9	LF(108): 4.5, RF(54): -0.9	3.9
2014	ATL	MLB	26	641	77	34	2	29	102	60	171	8	4	.270/.342/.491	.313	.332	0.4	LF(150): -1.2	4.5
2015	ATL	MLB	27	602	76	26	2	22	79	59	145	11	4	.265/.342/.445	.298	.321	0.8	LF 2, RF 1	3.9

Breakout: 3%   Improve: 57%   Collapse: 4%   Attrition: 4%   MLB: 100%   Comparables: *Kal Daniels, Barry Bonds, Grady Sizemore*

While the older Upton languished, the younger Upton flourished. The Braves hadn't received that kind of production from left field since Chipper's third base sabbatical. Before then? Try the early days of Ryan Klesko, or Lonnie Smith. The notoriously streaky Upton put together four fantastic months, leading to his finest offensive campaign since his banner 2011. Worth noting: He introduced a new, more aggressive approach that saw him swing more inside and outside the zone. That's generally a frowned-upon development, especially the second part, and he walked less and struck out more—but he did hit for more average and power. If Upton proves his new level of production is sustainable—and it would be even more impressive coming in Petco—then plenty of teams will expand their zones to land him as a free agent at season's end.

Pitchers

Luis Avilan   LHP

Born: 7/19/89   Age: 25   Bats: L   Throws: L   Height: 6'2"   Weight: 220

YEAR	TEAM	LVL	AGE	W	L	SV	G	GS	IP	H	HR	BB	K	BB/9	K/9	GB%	BABIP	WHIP	ERA	FIP	FRA	WARP
2012	MIS	AA	22	3	6	1	16	12	61¹	50	7	31	55	4.5	8.1	53%	.259	1.32	3.23	4.40	5.82	-0.1
2012	ATL	MLB	22	1	0	0	31	0	36	27	1	10	33	2.5	8.2	48%	.268	1.03	2.00	2.58	2.82	0.6
2013	ATL	MLB	23	5	0	0	75	0	65	40	1	22	38	3.0	5.3	58%	.204	0.95	1.52	3.25	3.66	0.9
2014	GWN	AAA	24	0	1	0	9	0	11²	13	0	11	6	8.5	4.6	50%	.342	2.06	5.40	5.16	7.34	-0.2
2014	ATL	MLB	24	4	1	0	62	0	43¹	47	2	21	25	4.4	5.2	58%	.317	1.57	4.57	4.21	4.79	-0.3
2015	ATL	MLB	25	3	2	0	37	4	52	48	5	19	39	3.4	6.8	48%	.296	1.29	3.89	4.32	4.23	0.1

Breakout: 29%   Improve: 49%   Collapse: 18%   Attrition: 27%   MLB: 82%   Comparables: *Alex Burnett, Brad Thompson, Jensen Lewis*

Something you'll notice reading through this part of the chapter is how many left-handed relievers in the Braves system are near the majors. That makes Avilan's misstep of a season even less opportune for the Avilan estate. A strikeout artist in his rookie campaign, Avilan has since morphed into a pitch-to-contact double-play sculptor. The results he found with the new look in 2013 deteriorated as he allowed more hits, home runs, and walks (albeit some intentionally) and tallied fewer strikeouts. Lefties of Avilan's age and career ERA tend to have job security to spare. Not this guy, not anymore.

Ryan Buchter   LHP

Born: 2/13/87   Age: 28   Bats: L   Throws: L   Height: 6'3"   Weight: 240

YEAR	TEAM	LVL	AGE	W	L	SV	G	GS	IP	H	HR	BB	K	BB/9	K/9	GB%	BABIP	WHIP	ERA	FIP	FRA	WARP
2012	MIS	AA	25	3	1	4	35	0	41¹	24	1	19	50	4.1	10.9	39%	.247	1.04	1.31	2.56	3.29	0.7
2013	GWN	AAA	26	4	0	5	51	0	62	36	5	51	103	7.4	15.0	46%	.287	1.40	2.76	3.59	3.64	1.2
2014	GWN	AAA	27	3	3	1	49	0	63	51	5	40	63	5.7	9.0	35%	.286	1.44	3.29	4.39	4.83	0.6
2014	ATL	MLB	27	1	0	0	1	0	1	0	0	1	1	9.0	9.0	100%	.000	1.00	1.00	4.10	4.42	0.0
2015	ATL	MLB	28	2	1	2	46	0	55²	44	5	35	67	5.7	10.8	41%	.313	1.41	4.00	4.15	4.35	0.0

Breakout: 7%   Improve: 7%   Collapse: 6%   Attrition: 6%   MLB: 15%   Comparables: *John Gaub, Kevin Whelan, Leyson Septimo*

Wanna see how knowledgeable the Braves fan in your life is about the team? Ask 'em if they remember Buchter on the Opening Day roster. The prize from 2011's Rodrigo Lopez trade didn't appear in a big-league game—not until later, anyway—and was soon optioned to make room for Pedro Beato, but sneaked into a June game for a lone appearance. Expect Buchter to once again be barely a rumor in Atlanta this year, because this wild thing will do his walking in Gwinnett until his control improves.

Mauricio Cabrera   RHP

Born: 9/22/93   Age: 21   Bats: R   Throws: R   Height: 6'2"   Weight: 180

YEAR	TEAM	LVL	AGE	W	L	SV	G	GS	IP	H	HR	BB	K	BB/9	K/9	GB%	BABIP	WHIP	ERA	FIP	FRA	WARP
2013	ROM	A	19	3	8	0	24	24	131¹	118	3	71	107	4.9	7.3	51%	.298	1.44	4.18	3.91	5.01	0.2
2014	LYN	A+	20	1	1	0	19	3	29	24	1	19	28	5.9	8.7	65%	.295	1.48	5.59	4.41	5.65	0.0
2015	ATL	MLB	21	2	3	0	13	8	44²	47	5	26	30	5.2	6.0	47%	.317	1.62	5.43	5.41	5.90	-0.7

Breakout: 0%   Improve: 0%   Collapse: 0%   Attrition: 0%   MLB: 0%   Comparables: *Chaz Roe, Vin Mazzaro, Allen Webster*

Nearly every interesting pitching prospect in the Braves system missed time due to injury in 2014, and since Cabrera is an interesting arm . . . well, you can connect the dots. The malady, a strained forearm, sidelined Cabrera for three months. He took things slow upon his return, easing off his fastball to keep from re-aggravating his moneymaker. Add those injury concerns to his lagging command and unpolished secondaries as reasons to think he'll soon move to the bullpen. No shame in that—Cabrera has the potential be a late-inning monster—but it'd be a letdown against what was expected not so long ago.

David Carpenter   RHP

Born: 7/15/85   Age: 29   Bats: R   Throws: R   Height: 6'2"   Weight: 230

YEAR	TEAM	LVL	AGE	W	L	SV	G	GS	IP	H	HR	BB	K	BB/9	K/9	GB%	BABIP	WHIP	ERA	FIP	FRA	WARP
2012	LVG	AAA	26	0	1	1	16	0	17²	15	1	7	19	3.6	9.7	43%	.292	1.25	3.57	3.61	4.19	0.3
2012	HOU	MLB	26	0	2	0	30	0	29²	43	4	14	27	4.2	8.2	43%	.402	1.92	6.07	4.59	4.59	0.2
2012	TOR	MLB	26	0	0	0	3	0	2²	8	1	2	4	6.8	13.5	54%	.583	3.75	30.38	8.30	6.92	-0.1
2013	GWN	AAA	27	1	2	0	6	0	15¹	17	1	4	11	2.3	6.5	56%	.340	1.37	3.52	3.60	5.43	0.0
2013	ATL	MLB	27	4	1	0	56	0	65²	45	5	20	74	2.7	10.1	39%	.260	0.99	1.78	2.81	3.38	0.8
2014	ATL	MLB	28	6	4	3	65	0	61	61	5	16	67	2.4	9.9	39%	.333	1.26	3.54	2.91	3.17	0.8
2015	ATL	MLB	29	3	1	1	57	0	60	53	5	18	63	2.7	9.5	41%	.322	1.18	3.37	3.34	3.66	0.5

Breakout: 29%   Improve: 51%   Collapse: 12%   Attrition: 12%   MLB: 78%   Comparables: *Jerry Blevins, Shawn Kelley, Matt Reynolds*

One of the few players whose story can inspire weak-hitting catchers and wild relievers alike. Carpenter's winding career dates back to his days as a backstop in the Cardinals system. He traded his mitt for the mound in 2008, and soon began a journey across the league. First the Cardinals traded him to the Astros for Pedro Feliz, then the Astros included him as part of their 10-player swap with Toronto. Months later, the Blue Jays sent him to the Red Sox for Mike Aviles. Carpenter never appeared in a game for the Red Sox before being awarded to the Braves off waivers. He's since learned how to control his upper-90s fastball, which has in turn increased his slider's effectiveness. The Braves make it look so easy that you forget these results aren't common.

David Hale   RHP

Born: 9/27/87   Age: 27   Bats: R   Throws: R   Height: 6'2"   Weight: 210

YEAR	TEAM	LVL	AGE	W	L	SV	G	GS	IP	H	HR	BB	K	BB/9	K/9	GB%	BABIP	WHIP	ERA	FIP	FRA	WARP
2012	MIS	AA	24	8	4	0	27	27	145²	121	11	67	124	4.1	7.7	48%	.271	1.29	3.77	4.01	5.47	-0.7
2013	GWN	AAA	25	6	9	0	22	20	114²	123	8	36	77	2.8	6.0	54%	.313	1.39	3.22	3.89	4.91	0.3
2013	ATL	MLB	25	1	0	0	2	2	11	11	0	1	14	0.8	11.5	61%	.355	1.09	0.82	0.75	0.97	0.5
2014	ATL	MLB	26	4	5	0	45	6	87¹	89	5	39	44	4.0	4.5	57%	.288	1.47	3.30	4.28	4.91	-0.7
2015	ATL	MLB	27	4	5	0	22	12	81²	84	8	32	57	3.5	6.3	50%	.316	1.42	4.64	4.56	5.05	-0.6

Breakout: 27%   Improve: 37%   Collapse: 10%   Attrition: 34%   MLB: 55%   Comparables: Zach Jackson, Sean Henn, Jared Hughes

We're obligated to mention Hale attended Princeton. With that out of the way, let's address his weird season. He began the year as part of Atlanta's makeshift rotation, then slid to the bullpen in late April when Mike Minor returned. From there Gonzalez used him as one would a starter-turned-reliever: by having him record four-plus outs in about half his appearances. All the while Hale did his best Cla Meredith impression: lotta walks, few strikeouts and just enough double-play balls to maintain a respectable ERA. It's not a bad career if you can have it; if Hale can't, at least he'll put his education to good use. He went to Princeton.

Aaron Harang   RHP

Born: 5/9/78   Age: 37   Bats: R   Throws: R   Height: 6'7"   Weight: 260

YEAR	TEAM	LVL	AGE	W	L	SV	G	GS	IP	H	HR	BB	K	BB/9	K/9	GB%	BABIP	WHIP	ERA	FIP	FRA	WARP
2012	LAN	MLB	34	10	10	0	31	31	179²	167	14	85	131	4.3	6.6	41%	.277	1.40	3.61	4.18	4.56	0.6
2013	NYN	MLB	35	0	1	0	4	4	23	20	5	12	26	4.7	10.2	31%	.268	1.39	3.52	5.28	5.42	-0.1
2013	SEA	MLB	35	5	11	0	22	22	120¹	133	21	28	87	2.1	6.5	38%	.291	1.34	5.76	4.72	5.24	-0.2
2014	ATL	MLB	36	12	12	0	33	33	204¹	215	15	71	161	3.1	7.1	42%	.318	1.40	3.57	3.54	3.82	1.4
2015	ATL	MLB	37	9	11	0	27	27	161¹	168	18	55	127	3.0	7.1	40%	.323	1.38	4.52	4.33	4.92	-0.9

Breakout: 6%   Improve: 31%   Collapse: 19%   Attrition: 17%   MLB: 72%   Comparables: Kevin Millwood, Ryan Dempster, A.J. Burnett

"We thought he would get better, and, frankly, with the injuries we were desperate and he was the best and easiest guy to get. We got lucky," Braves assistant GM John Coppolella told us in April, after Harang had raced out to a majors-best 0.85 ERA through five starts. You know what comes next: Yes, he pitched worse from that point forward. But not *that* much worse. Harang recorded a career-best quality-start rate and his raw numbers, though respectable enough, would've been better were it not for a few bloody encounters with those pesky Marlins. (Insert your *Old Man and the Sea* jokes here.) Harang didn't necessarily reinvent himself with a better pitch or tightened mechanics, but he did reestablish that he's a tolerable back-of-the-rotation option, albeit one nobody had cared to throw a bunch of money at as this book went out the door.

Jason Hursh   RHP

Born: 10/2/91   Age: 23   Bats: R   Throws: R   Height: 6'3"   Weight: 200

YEAR	TEAM	LVL	AGE	W	L	SV	G	GS	IP	H	HR	BB	K	BB/9	K/9	GB%	BABIP	WHIP	ERA	FIP	FRA	WARP
2013	ROM	A	21	1	1	0	9	9	27	20	1	10	15	3.3	5.0	63%	.235	1.11	0.67	4.07	5.04	0.3
2014	MIS	AA	22	11	7	0	27	26	148¹	151	5	43	83	2.6	5.0	59%	.306	1.31	3.58	3.52	4.56	-0.3
2015	ATL	MLB	23	6	8	0	22	22	104²	112	10	34	59	2.9	5.1	54%	.315	1.40	4.58	4.58	4.98	-0.5

Breakout: 0%   Improve: 0%   Collapse: 0%   Attrition: 0%   MLB: 0%   Comparables: Drew VerHagen, Zeke Spruill, Jake Buchanan

Hursh continued to whirr through the system as expected, putting himself in position to debut this season, likely as a middle reliever. Problem is there's no guarantee he outgrows the role. His fastball is a quality offering, and he has the size to start, but his strikeout rate is scary low due to uninspiring secondaries. Others have found the key to pitching starts in the bullpen, so it's possible Hursh does the same. Just don't consider enlightenment a given based on his current vibrations.

Juan Jaime   RHP

Born: 8/2/87   Age: 27   Bats: R   Throws: R   Height: 6'2"   Weight: 250

YEAR	TEAM	LVL	AGE	W	L	SV	G	GS	IP	H	HR	BB	K	BB/9	K/9	GB%	BABIP	WHIP	ERA	FIP	FRA	WARP
2012	LYN	A+	24	1	3	18	42	0	51¹	31	4	33	73	5.8	12.8	36%	.257	1.25	3.16	3.72	4.15	0.7
2013	MIS	AA	25	2	5	0	35	0	42	30	1	28	70	6.0	15.0	31%	.345	1.38	4.07	2.25	2.28	1.2
2014	GWN	AAA	26	1	0	18	43	0	41	27	1	36	63	7.9	13.8	41%	.306	1.54	3.51	3.24	3.82	0.8
2014	ATL	MLB	26	0	0	0	16	0	12¹	14	1	9	18	6.6	13.1	41%	.394	1.86	5.84	3.67	3.83	0.0
2015	ATL	MLB	27	2	1	0	46	0	49¹	35	3	29	69	5.3	12.6	38%	.324	1.30	3.31	3.17	3.60	0.5

Breakout: 15%   Improve: 22%   Collapse: 15%   Attrition: 19%   MLB: 45%   Comparables: John Gaub, Jason Motte, Ryan Buchter

The new Carlos Marmol? Nah—Marmol had a knockout secondary offering. Jaime is a better thought than machine. He throws the ball as hard as anyone on the continent, but would walk Wang Zhizhi on five pitches. Know how Atlanta's instructors are renowned for helping pitchers find their control? Jaime is about to enter his fourth season with the organization and his walk rate has *increased* in each. It's possible for wild relievers to succeed—e.g. A.J. Ramos or Alex Torres—but Jaime takes the formula to such an extreme that he's the *Yeezus* of pitchers: You'll either love him or hate him, but there's nothing else like him.

Tyrell Jenkins   RHP

Born: 7/20/92   Age: 22   Bats: R   Throws: R   Height: 6'4"   Weight: 204

YEAR	TEAM	LVL	AGE	W	L	SV	G	GS	IP	H	HR	BB	K	BB/9	K/9	GB%	BABIP	WHIP	ERA	FIP	FRA	WARP
2012	QUD	A	19	4	4	0	19	19	82¹	84	5	36	80	3.9	8.7	56%	.336	1.46	5.14	3.62	4.70	0.8
2013	PEO	A	20	4	4	0	10	10	49¹	51	4	24	34	4.4	6.2	58%	.303	1.52	4.74	4.53	5.12	0.2
2013	PMB	A+	20	0	0	0	3	3	10	13	0	1	6	0.9	5.4	58%	.361	1.40	4.50	2.34	3.71	0.2
2014	PMB	A+	21	6	5	0	13	13	74	74	6	23	41	2.8	5.0	50%	.286	1.31	3.28	4.31	5.32	-0.3
2015	ATL	MLB	22	3	5	0	12	12	60¹	67	7	28	38	4.2	5.7	51%	.324	1.57	5.42	5.14	5.89	-0.9

Breakout: 0%   Improve: 0%   Collapse: 0%   Attrition: 0%   MLB: 0%   Comparables: T.J. House, Michael Belfiore, J.C. Ramirez

A former top prep pick with an ideal frame and easy mid-90s heat, Jenkins has seen his developmental timetable delayed by shoulder woes and his command, control and off-speed offerings remain works in progress. Last fall's trade to the Braves may be just the ticket to jump-start his career, as Jenkins goes from being yet another lightning arm in a loaded Cardinals system to a prized centerpiece in Atlanta. Healthy and effective in the Arizona Fall League, Jenkins flashed improving command of his power curve, but his changeup is still missing in action. If he can find something to make lefties uncomfortable he could grow into a mid-rotation starter; if not, the late innings beckon.

Jim Johnson   RHP

Born: 6/27/83   Age: 32   Bats: R   Throws: R   Height: 6'6"   Weight: 240

YEAR	TEAM	LVL	AGE	W	L	SV	G	GS	IP	H	HR	BB	K	BB/9	K/9	GB%	BABIP	WHIP	ERA	FIP	FRA	WARP
2012	BAL	MLB	29	2	1	51	71	0	68²	55	3	15	41	2.0	5.4	64%	.251	1.02	2.49	3.21	4.16	0.7
2013	BAL	MLB	30	3	8	50	74	0	70¹	72	5	18	56	2.3	7.2	59%	.327	1.28	2.94	3.47	4.01	0.6
2014	DET	MLB	31	1	0	0	16	0	13	9	0	12	14	8.3	9.7	68%	.265	1.62	6.92	4.47	4.12	0.1
2014	OAK	MLB	31	4	2	2	38	0	40¹	60	5	23	28	5.1	6.2	60%	.390	2.06	7.14	5.32	5.80	-0.7
2015	*ATL*	*MLB*	*32*	*3*	*1*	*20*	*58*	*0*	*61²*	*58*	*4*	*17*	*50*	*2.5*	*7.2*	*57%*	*.314*	*1.21*	*3.38*	*3.51*	*3.68*	*0.5*

Breakout: 24%   Improve: 46%   Collapse: 27%   Attrition: 14%   MLB: 92%   *Comparables: Matt Lindstrom, Danys Baez, Chad Bradford*

Proof that even Billy Beane makes bad trades, Johnson was demoted from the A's closer role a week into the season and released by August. The desperate Tigers signed him hoping that three awful months was nothing more than a small sample size. It wasn't. Johnson's command disappeared from the face of the earth and is circling the planet in perpetual orbit. The only other reliever to post back-to-back 50-save seasons was Eric Gagne, and even his flameout took a few years. Johnson's velocity is a tick slower, but the main issue is throwing strikes. If he can do that in spring training, he just might win a job in a tiebreak against some rookie reliever, but lets just say Kimbrel's job is safe.

Craig Kimbrel   RHP

Born: 5/28/88   Age: 27   Bats: R   Throws: R   Height: 5'11"   Weight: 220

YEAR	TEAM	LVL	AGE	W	L	SV	G	GS	IP	H	HR	BB	K	BB/9	K/9	GB%	BABIP	WHIP	ERA	FIP	FRA	WARP
2012	ATL	MLB	24	3	1	42	63	0	62²	27	3	14	116	2.0	16.7	50%	.250	0.65	1.01	0.82	1.41	2.2
2013	ATL	MLB	25	4	3	50	68	0	67	39	4	20	98	2.7	13.2	47%	.263	0.88	1.21	1.90	2.06	1.9
2014	ATL	MLB	26	0	3	47	63	0	61²	30	2	26	95	3.8	13.9	43%	.237	0.91	1.61	1.81	2.14	1.5
2015	*ATL*	*MLB*	*27*	*3*	*2*	*46*	*59*	*0*	*58*	*31*	*3*	*20*	*94*	*3.1*	*14.6*	*46%*	*.298*	*0.87*	*1.29*	*1.78*	*1.41*	*2.2*

Breakout: 29%   Improve: 49%   Collapse: 33%   Attrition: 14%   MLB: 94%   *Comparables: Francisco Rodriguez, Jonathan Broxton, Carlos Marmol*

It's time to get statty. Three closers have recorded a sub-2.00 ERA in three consecutive seasons while also throwing at least 50 innings and saving at least 30 games: Joe Nathan, Mariano Rivera and Kimbrel. No wonder the Braves last winter felt comfortable giving the best closer in baseball a four-year deal worth $42 million (not including a club option that would cost an additional $13 million). The upshot for the Braves is they probably saved money by avoiding arbitration—at minimum, they won't poison the relationship through the process. The attrition rate with relievers is scary—there's a reason why Rivera is so special, after all—but if there is one in all the game worth marrying, it's Kimbrel.

By the way, Rivera did it four years in a row. Yeah. Your turn, Mr. Kimbrel.

Michael Kohn   RHP

Born: 6/26/86   Age: 29   Bats: R   Throws: R   Height: 6'2"   Weight: 200

YEAR	TEAM	LVL	AGE	W	L	SV	G	GS	IP	H	HR	BB	K	BB/9	K/9	GB%	BABIP	WHIP	ERA	FIP	FRA	WARP
2013	ANA	MLB	27	1	4	0	63	0	53	42	7	28	52	4.8	8.8	24%	.248	1.32	3.74	4.58	3.20	0.5
2014	SLC	AAA	28	1	1	8	33	0	34	28	6	27	33	7.1	8.7	33%	.253	1.62	4.76	6.52	8.75	-0.6
2014	ANA	MLB	28	2	1	0	25	0	23²	11	1	20	26	7.6	9.9	26%	.192	1.31	3.04	4.30	4.94	-0.2
2015	*ATL*	*MLB*	*29*	*3*	*1*	*0*	*57*	*0*	*53²*	*42*	*5*	*28*	*60*	*4.6*	*10.1*	*35%*	*.296*	*1.29*	*3.67*	*3.99*	*3.99*	*0.2*

Breakout: 17%   Improve: 38%   Collapse: 14%   Attrition: 15%   MLB: 66%   *Comparables: Derrick Turnbow, Steve Delabar, Denny Bautista*

Kohn is a relic of the old Angels system, a feel-good story that involves the *daughter* of scouting legend Tom Kotchman coming across the exploratory bullpen session of a failed collegiate position player. A quick phone call to dad ultimately landed Kohn a 13th-round selection in that year's draft. His super-short arm action and "sneaky" fastball up in the zone gave minor-league hitters fits as he ascended the system, but major-league hitters were never quite as willing to chase upstairs. He failed to manage his walk rate, lacked a consistent secondary pitch, coughed up too many dingers and shoulder issues cost him a season while forcing fundamental changes to his mechanics. Through it all, he still fanned nearly a batter an inning, prompting the Braves to roll the dice on him this offseason. He'd once predicted something like this, MLB.com's Mark Bowman revealed, posting a note Kohn had written and signed when he was 10 years old: "I Michael Thomas Kohn. Will make Pro baseball for the Atlanta Braves and make all My Goal."

Cody Martin   RHP

Born: 9/4/89   Age: 25   Bats: R   Throws: R   Height: 6'3"   Weight: 230

YEAR	TEAM	LVL	AGE	W	L	SV	G	GS	IP	H	HR	BB	K	BB/9	K/9	GB%	BABIP	WHIP	ERA	FIP	FRA	WARP
2012	LYN	A+	22	12	7	0	22	19	107¹	93	7	34	123	2.9	10.3	40%	.314	1.18	2.93	3.09	3.62	2.1
2013	MIS	AA	23	3	3	0	16	11	67	63	3	27	71	3.6	9.5	42%	.333	1.34	2.82	2.58	2.84	1.7
2013	GWN	AAA	23	3	4	1	13	11	69²	59	6	31	66	4.0	8.5	42%	.283	1.29	3.49	3.85	4.69	0.5
2014	GWN	AAA	24	7	8	1	27	26	156	151	17	56	142	3.2	8.2	40%	.302	1.33	3.52	4.17	4.73	1.7
2015	*ATL*	*MLB*	*25*	*8*	*7*	*0*	*32*	*21*	*137¹*	*123*	*14*	*49*	*137*	*3.2*	*9.0*	*40%*	*.316*	*1.25*	*3.77*	*3.83*	*4.10*	*0.6*

Breakout: 19%   Improve: 34%   Collapse: 10%   Attrition: 35%   MLB: 50%   *Comparables: Matt Maloney, George Kontos, Brad Peacock*

Martin, whose father pitched in the minors for the Braves back in the day, is another fast-moving collegiate arm slated to debut in 2015. He is, as the bloodlines suggest, well acquainted with the ins and outs of pitching. A good thing, because while he could boast four average or better pitches, the only standout offering is a plus cutter. Throw Martin's instincts, repertoire and control in a pot, add water and heat and you'll be looking at ... a whole lot of boiling water. Martin's a back-end starter at best.

Shelby Miller   RHP

Born: 10/10/90   Age: 24   Bats: R   Throws: R   Height: 6'3"   Weight: 215

YEAR	TEAM	LVL	AGE	W	L	SV	G	GS	IP	H	HR	BB	K	BB/9	K/9	GB%	BABIP	WHIP	ERA	FIP	FRA	WARP
2012	MEM	AAA	21	11	10	0	27	27	136²	138	24	50	160	3.3	10.5	35%	.322	1.38	4.74	4.95	4.72	1.5
2012	SLN	MLB	21	1	0	0	6	1	14²	9	0	4	16	2.6	10.5	42%	.273	0.95	1.32	1.89	2.41	0.5
2013	SLN	MLB	22	15	9	0	31	31	173¹	152	20	57	169	3.0	8.8	40%	.280	1.21	3.06	3.64	3.88	2.0
2014	SLN	MLB	23	10	9	0	32	31	183	160	22	73	127	3.6	6.2	42%	.256	1.27	3.74	4.51	4.92	0.4
2015	ATL	MLB	24	9	9	0	27	27	151²	132	16	50	154	3.0	9.1	40%	.307	1.20	3.53	3.75	3.83	1.2

Breakout: 31%   Improve: 65%   Collapse: 12%   Attrition: 15%   MLB: 92%   Comparables: David Price, Tommy Hanson, Drew Smyly

Miller was unable to build on his impressive rookie campaign and struggled to find consistency, earning a brief demotion to the bullpen before putting together a nice run of starts down the stretch. The big Texan held opposing hitters to a .189/.224/.279 line in September, earning a spot on the St. Louis playoff roster and fueling optimism for his future in Atlanta. Like Lance Lynn, Miller's approach is all about his fastball, which he is now delivering in three flavors (two-seam, four-seam, cut) and is good enough to earn outs on its own. He's essentially ditched his changeup—it was a two-faced friend anyway—and is relying more on a slower, bigger-breaking curveball against lefties, with some success. It's easy to forget that Miller is still only 24, and while few believe he'll ever turn into the ace his stuff and pedigree foretold, the tools are still there to become a solid second starter.

Mike Minor   LHP

Born: 12/26/87   Age: 27   Bats: R   Throws: L   Height: 6'4"   Weight: 220

YEAR	TEAM	LVL	AGE	W	L	SV	G	GS	IP	H	HR	BB	K	BB/9	K/9	GB%	BABIP	WHIP	ERA	FIP	FRA	WARP
2012	ATL	MLB	24	11	10	0	30	30	179¹	151	26	56	145	2.8	7.3	37%	.252	1.15	4.12	4.42	5.07	0.5
2013	ATL	MLB	25	13	9	0	32	32	204²	177	22	46	181	2.0	8.0	37%	.272	1.09	3.21	3.34	4.07	2.3
2014	ATL	MLB	26	6	12	0	25	25	145¹	165	21	44	120	2.7	7.4	43%	.323	1.44	4.77	4.36	4.67	0.1
2015	ATL	MLB	27	9	9	0	26	26	153²	140	18	40	144	2.3	8.4	40%	.307	1.17	3.61	3.83	3.93	0.9

Breakout: 23%   Improve: 57%   Collapse: 15%   Attrition: 15%   MLB: 86%   Comparables: Ian Snell, Kevin Slowey, Dan Haren

Shelved for the first month with shoulder inflammation, Minor returned in May with a quality start against the Giants. Then the worst season of his big-league career began. The next two months were so bad that Minor exited July with an ERA north of 5.20. Chief among the causes for his implosion were, as noted by the attentive folks at Talking Chop, an elevated arm slot and worse posture—leading to flat pitches and worse command. Minor also tinkered with his pitch selection, all but benching his changeup over the final few weeks. He did find success late, reeling off six quality starts in a row, and his peripherals remained solid. Even so, it's understandable if Braves fans are guarded in their expectations for Minor heading forward.

Aaron Northcraft   RHP

Born: 5/28/90   Age: 25   Bats: R   Throws: R   Height: 6'4"   Weight: 230

YEAR	TEAM	LVL	AGE	W	L	SV	G	GS	IP	H	HR	BB	K	BB/9	K/9	GB%	BABIP	WHIP	ERA	FIP	FRA	WARP
2012	LYN	A+	22	10	11	0	27	27	151²	143	4	53	160	3.1	9.5	62%	.328	1.29	3.98	2.82	4.54	1.0
2013	MIS	AA	23	8	8	0	26	26	137	124	7	51	121	3.4	7.9	58%	.296	1.28	3.42	3.23	4.81	-0.6
2014	MIS	AA	24	7	3	0	13	12	65²	57	2	24	62	3.3	8.5	52%	.293	1.23	2.88	2.93	3.14	1.4
2014	GWN	AAA	24	0	7	0	13	12	64²	86	6	31	51	4.3	7.1	48%	.370	1.81	6.54	4.80	5.39	0.2
2015	ATL	MLB	25	6	8	0	22	22	117	119	11	48	96	3.7	7.4	52%	.327	1.43	4.63	4.35	5.03	-0.7

Breakout: 0%   Improve: 0%   Collapse: 0%   Attrition: 0%   MLB: 0%   Comparables: Erik Goeddel, Chris Carpenter, Josh Collmenter

All the injuries in the Braves rotation must have tempted Northcraft to slide into Frank Wren's (or Faux Frank Wren's) DMs with updates on his Mississippi starts. Those messages would have stopped after his promotion to Gwinnett; not only did his peripherals get worse, but he had only two starts where he allowed fewer than three runs—one of those being his debut, which came on short rest and lasted five batters. Because Northcraft's arsenal was thin to begin with, there was always a chance he'd move to the bullpen. If his second try at Triple-A mimics the first, we'll be able to write his next comment in fewer than 140 characters.

Carlos Perez   LHP

Born: 11/20/91   Age: 23   Bats: L   Throws: L   Height: 6'3"   Weight: 220

YEAR	TEAM	LVL	AGE	W	L	SV	G	GS	IP	H	HR	BB	K	BB/9	K/9	GB%	BABIP	WHIP	ERA	FIP	FRA	WARP
2012	ROM	A	20	0	3	0	7	4	19	33	3	19	12	9.0	5.7	43%	.417	2.74	12.79	7.53	6.84	-0.2
2013	ROM	A	21	3	0	2	20	0	32	20	1	8	37	2.2	10.4	57%	.253	0.88	2.25	2.42	3.25	0.6
2013	LYN	A+	21	0	0	1	9	0	13²	6	1	11	15	7.2	9.9	41%	.161	1.24	3.95	4.74	6.38	-0.1
2015	ATL	MLB	23	1	2	0	14	4	34	35	4	22	26	5.7	6.9	46%	.322	1.66	5.56	5.44	6.04	-0.6

Breakout: 0%   Improve: 0%   Collapse: 0%   Attrition: 0%   MLB: 0%   Comparables: Javy Guerra, Kevin Jepsen, Gregory Infante

Not to be confused with the current Astros prospect or the former Tigers prospect. Oh no, this Perez had a curious enough year without any identity mixups. He opened the season with Mississippi and appeared in four games before disappearing for two months due to a viral infection. A slow and steady rehab stint in the Gulf Coast League followed, but he escaped the complex just in time to finish the regular season with Rome. Though Perez's starting days are just a memory, his velocity and funkiness should make him an effective lefty-on-lefty reliever. Shy of that, he can always claim he used to pitch for the Dodgers.

James Russell   LHP

Born: 1/8/86   Age: 29   Bats: L   Throws: L   Height: 6'4"   Weight: 200

YEAR	TEAM	LVL	AGE	W	L	SV	G	GS	IP	H	HR	BB	K	BB/9	K/9	GB%	BABIP	WHIP	ERA	FIP	FRA	WARP
2012	CHN	MLB	26	7	1	2	77	0	69¹	67	5	23	55	3.0	7.1	40%	.293	1.30	3.25	3.53	3.08	1.1
2013	CHN	MLB	27	1	6	0	74	0	52²	46	7	18	37	3.1	6.3	34%	.258	1.22	3.59	4.43	5.79	-0.6
2014	ATL	MLB	28	0	0	0	22	1	24¹	21	0	4	16	1.5	5.9	42%	.276	1.03	2.22	2.28	2.47	0.4
2014	CHN	MLB	28	0	2	1	44	0	33¹	24	3	16	26	4.3	7.0	44%	.219	1.20	3.51	4.24	4.69	-0.1
2015	ATL	MLB	29	3	1	2	61	0	50¹	46	6	13	43	2.3	7.6	39%	.297	1.17	3.66	4.08	3.98	0.2

Breakout: 31%   Improve: 44%   Collapse: 25%   Attrition: 19%   MLB: 82%   Comparables: Matt Capps, Brandon Lyon, Ryan Madson

"... he needs to be spotted carefully or northpaws will eat him alive," we concluded about Russell last year. Oops. Included in the same three-player trade that netted Bonifacio, Russell left Chicago for Atlanta yet continued to confound with an odd season. Historically a lefty killer and righty thriller, the results were flipped in 2014. There's no reason to think the slider-heavy Russell is vulnerable to same-handed batters—ditto for his improved performance against righties—but it goes to show that funky things can happen to specialists in small samples. Even to those who look like Jesus.

Gus Schlosser   RHP
Born: 10/20/88 Age: 26 Bats: R Throws: R Height: 6'4" Weight: 225

YEAR	TEAM	LVL	AGE	W	L	SV	G	GS	IP	H	HR	BB	K	BB/9	K/9	GB%	BABIP	WHIP	ERA	FIP	FRA	WARP
2012	LYN	A+	23	13	7	0	27	27	165¹	156	9	33	139	1.8	7.6	55%	.305	1.14	3.38	3.12	4.56	1.0
2013	MIS	AA	24	7	6	0	25	25	135¹	118	5	44	101	2.9	6.7	58%	.282	1.20	2.39	2.99	3.71	1.5
2014	GWN	AAA	25	7	6	0	25	15	99¹	93	7	48	70	4.3	6.3	54%	.288	1.42	4.17	4.53	5.88	0.1
2014	ATL	MLB	25	0	1	0	15	0	17²	23	2	6	8	3.1	4.1	35%	.328	1.64	7.64	4.86	5.34	-0.2
2015	ATL	MLB	26	6	6	0	27	16	107¹	106	10	36	80	3.0	6.7	52%	.313	1.32	4.11	4.18	4.47	-0.1

Breakout: 25%   Improve: 36%   Collapse: 8%   Attrition: 38%   MLB: 51%   Comparables: Stephen Fife, Kevin Mulvey, Bryan Bullington

There are only so many roles in life for a man named August Schlosser. Big-league pitcher is one of them, Jane Austen character is another and rule-of-threes muse is a third. Schlosser is a sinker-slider side-armer who, despite success in the minors as a starter, could be looking at a smaller platform in The Show as a specialist. Expect him to make more appearances (and tie more tongues) for the Braves in 2015.

Chasen Shreve   LHP
Born: 7/12/90 Age: 24 Bats: L Throws: L Height: 6'3" Weight: 190

YEAR	TEAM	LVL	AGE	W	L	SV	G	GS	IP	H	HR	BB	K	BB/9	K/9	GB%	BABIP	WHIP	ERA	FIP	FRA	WARP
2012	LYN	A+	21	4	4	1	32	0	46	44	2	17	41	3.3	8.0	56%	.323	1.33	2.15	3.28	3.89	0.6
2012	MIS	AA	21	2	1	0	11	0	18¹	17	1	16	16	7.9	7.9	41%	.302	1.80	3.93	4.73	5.14	-0.1
2013	LYN	A+	22	0	1	2	14	0	19²	15	1	8	15	3.7	6.9	46%	.233	1.17	2.75	3.71	3.56	0.4
2013	MIS	AA	22	3	1	0	36	0	42²	43	1	22	28	4.6	5.9	47%	.298	1.52	4.43	3.45	4.82	-0.3
2014	MIS	AA	23	3	2	7	36	0	54¹	42	2	9	76	1.5	12.6	46%	.336	0.94	2.48	1.42	1.98	1.9
2014	ATL	MLB	23	0	0	0	15	0	12¹	10	0	3	15	2.2	10.9	50%	.312	1.05	0.73	1.40	1.55	0.4
2015	ATL	MLB	24	2	1	0	42	0	61²	58	5	24	58	3.5	8.5	46%	.324	1.33	4.01	3.71	4.35	0.0

Breakout: 8%   Improve: 14%   Collapse: 4%   Attrition: 10%   MLB: 21%   Comparables: Edgmer Escalona, Rich Thompson, Daniel Herrera

At one point late in the season, the Braves telecast highlighted how Shreve—who wears no. 61—resembles actor Barry Pepper—or as he's known in the flick 61*, Roger Maris. We don't see it. We do see Shreve, a product of the same Nevada JuCo as Bryce Harper, looking a lot like a quality left-handed reliever for the foreseeable future. He throws strikes, misses bats and does it all with a capable three-pitch mix that should keep his platoon split in check. You might say it's like he's reading from a script.

Shae Simmons   RHP
Born: 9/3/90 Age: 24 Bats: R Throws: R Height: 5'11" Weight: 175

YEAR	TEAM	LVL	AGE	W	L	SV	G	GS	IP	H	HR	BB	K	BB/9	K/9	GB%	BABIP	WHIP	ERA	FIP	FRA	WARP
2013	ROM	A	22	1	1	24	39	0	42¹	26	0	15	66	3.2	14.0	61%	.289	0.97	1.49	1.71	2.09	1.4
2013	MIS	AA	22	0	0	0	11	0	11	5	0	7	16	5.7	13.1	52%	.238	1.09	2.45	1.91	3.00	0.2
2014	MIS	AA	23	0	0	14	20	0	23	15	0	6	30	2.3	11.7	65%	.288	0.91	0.78	1.49	2.17	0.7
2014	ATL	MLB	23	1	2	1	26	0	21²	15	1	11	23	4.6	9.6	56%	.259	1.20	2.91	3.10	4.11	0.0
2015	ATL	MLB	24	2	1	1	38	0	41¹	32	3	17	49	3.8	10.7	51%	.314	1.20	3.12	3.17	3.39	0.5

Breakout: 14%   Improve: 29%   Collapse: 10%   Attrition: 25%   MLB: 53%   Comparables: David Robertson, Stephen Pryor, Eduardo Sanchez

During his time in the majors, Simmons looked like the latest in a long line of quality homegrown relievers. The Braves, perhaps eager to avoid the health woes that plagued . . . well, almost all of those before him, wisely shut Simmons down after he landed on the disabled list with a strained shoulder. Expect to hear more Kimbrel comparisons heading forward, and not because we're all just lazy. Simmons *does* have similarities to the best closer in baseball—like a high-grade fastball-slider combination—though in a lesser overall package. Health provided, Simmons should be another Braves reliever worth watching.

Lucas Sims   RHP
Born: 5/10/94 Age: 21 Bats: R Throws: R Height: 6'2" Weight: 195

YEAR	TEAM	LVL	AGE	W	L	SV	G	GS	IP	H	HR	BB	K	BB/9	K/9	GB%	BABIP	WHIP	ERA	FIP	FRA	WARP
2013	ROM	A	19	12	4	0	28	18	116²	83	3	46	134	3.5	10.3	44%	.284	1.11	2.62	3.09	3.47	2.0
2014	LYN	A+	20	8	11	0	28	28	156²	146	12	57	107	3.3	6.1	42%	.277	1.30	4.19	4.56	5.76	-0.5
2015	ATL	MLB	21	7	10	0	26	26	132	128	14	58	100	4.0	6.8	41%	.307	1.41	4.61	4.77	5.01	-0.7

Breakout: 0%   Improve: 0%   Collapse: 0%   Attrition: 0%   MLB: 0%   Comparables: Tyler Chatwood, Robbie Ray, Michael Pineda

Arguably the best arm in the system, Sims opened the season as the youngest pitcher in the Carolina League. That youth excuses the mediocre numbers, and the lack of fastball command, for the most part. Sims has two potential plus offerings in his fastball and curveball, along with a developing change, and should develop into a middle-of-the-rotation starter. He's a good athlete with a smart approach to pitching, and he's even got a—get back! get back! dag gummit, too late—quality pickoff move.

Julio Teheran   RHP
Born: 1/27/91 Age: 24 Bats: R Throws: R Height: 6'2" Weight: 200

YEAR	TEAM	LVL	AGE	W	L	SV	G	GS	IP	H	HR	BB	K	BB/9	K/9	GB%	BABIP	WHIP	ERA	FIP	FRA	WARP
2012	GWN	AAA	21	7	9	0	26	26	131	146	18	43	97	3.0	6.7	38%	.318	1.44	5.08	4.79	5.51	0.1
2012	ATL	MLB	21	0	0	0	2	1	6¹	5	0	1	5	1.4	7.1	22%	.278	0.95	5.68	2.03	2.45	0.1
2013	ATL	MLB	22	14	8	0	30	30	185²	173	22	45	170	2.2	8.2	39%	.288	1.17	3.20	3.67	4.04	2.2
2014	ATL	MLB	23	14	13	0	33	33	221	188	22	51	186	2.1	7.6	37%	.267	1.08	2.89	3.46	4.15	1.3
2015	ATL	MLB	24	11	10	0	30	30	175²	157	19	46	158	2.4	8.1	38%	.300	1.16	3.48	3.86	3.79	1.4

Breakout: 29%   Improve: 63%   Collapse: 13%   Attrition: 17%   MLB: 93%   Comparables: David Price, John Danks, Ervin Santana

Inked to a six-year, $32 million extension as part of Atlanta's efforts to lock in its core, Teheran is the right kind of pitcher to embrace for the long haul. He's smart and athletic with good stuff, a balky pickoff move that umpires have apparently grandfathered in, and quality results. To find negatives about Teheran—besides the at-first tricky pronunciation (TEY-ron) of his name—you have to nitpick. To wit: He remains a little susceptible to left-handed hitters. Oh, and there's this: The three most recent 23-year-olds to throw 200-plus innings in a season for the Braves were Tommy Hanson, Jair Jurrjens and Steve Avery—or, three fellas who saw their careers derailed by injuries. Hold Teheran tight, Braves fans. Just not *too* tight.

Ian Thomas   LHP

Born: 4/20/87   Age: 28   Bats: R   Throws: L   Height: 6'4"   Weight: 215

YEAR	TEAM	LVL	AGE	W	L	SV	G	GS	IP	H	HR	BB	K	BB/9	K/9	GB%	BABIP	WHIP	ERA	FIP	FRA	WARP
2012	ROM	A	25	5	0	6	26	0	45²	45	4	15	58	3.0	11.4	45%	.353	1.31	3.15	3.16	3.22	1.4
2013	MIS	AA	26	7	8	1	39	13	104¹	72	7	37	123	3.2	10.6	43%	.259	1.04	2.76	2.52	4.33	0.7
2014	GWN	AAA	27	0	1	1	6	1	13²	12	1	5	16	3.3	10.5	46%	.324	1.24	3.95	3.06	3.90	0.1
2014	ATL	MLB	27	1	2	0	16	0	10²	10	0	6	13	5.1	11.0	41%	.345	1.50	4.22	2.35	2.63	0.1
2015	*ATL*	*MLB*	*28*	*2*	*1*	*0*	*21*	*4*	*40²*	*34*	*4*	*15*	*46*	*3.3*	*10.0*	*42%*	*.317*	*1.21*	*3.36*	*3.51*	*3.65*	*0.4*

Breakout: 9%   Improve: 18%   Collapse: 8%   Attrition: 17%   MLB: 28%   Comparables: *Robert Coello, Scott Mathieson, Christian Garcia*

Every year the Braves seem to get a quality performance from an unknown reliever they found God knows where. Thomas, who made the Opening Day roster despite having appeared in more games for various indy teams than for Braves affiliates, looked like a good candidate for the honors. Nope. When he wasn't on the minor-league disabled list, battling shoulder tendinitis, he made 16 forgettable big-league appearances. Our two strongest memories of Thomas: 1) When he walked two batters, uncorked two wild pitches and failed to cover first base in a six-batter meltdown against the Red Sox; and 2) when he hugged impassive bullpen coach Eddie Perez on Turner Field's "Hug Cam."

Arodys Vizcaino   RHP

Born: 11/13/90   Age: 24   Bats: R   Throws: R   Height: 6'0"   Weight: 190

YEAR	TEAM	LVL	AGE	W	L	SV	G	GS	IP	H	HR	BB	K	BB/9	K/9	GB%	BABIP	WHIP	ERA	FIP	FRA	WARP
2014	TEN	AA	23	1	1	1	14	0	13²	7	1	3	16	2.0	10.5	52%	.200	0.73	2.63	2.67	3.64	0.2
2014	IOW	AAA	23	0	0	0	17	0	18¹	25	1	11	16	5.4	7.9	47%	.393	1.96	5.40	4.79	4.56	0.2
2014	CHN	MLB	23	0	0	0	5	0	5	5	1	3	4	5.4	7.2	40%	.286	1.60	5.40	5.90	6.45	-0.1
2015	*ATL*	*MLB*	*24*	*2*	*2*	*0*	*20*	*4*	*37*	*34*	*3*	*13*	*34*	*3.1*	*8.3*	*43%*	*.314*	*1.27*	*3.77*	*3.67*	*4.10*	*0.2*

Breakout: 28%   Improve: 52%   Collapse: 19%   Attrition: 28%   MLB: 77%   Comparables: *Jason Windsor, Jess Todd, Nick Maronde*

What do Javier Vazquez, Boone Logan, Reed Johnson, Paul Maholm and Tommy La Stella have in common, other than their abiding love of Basque folk art and Ariana Grande? They've all been traded for Vizcaino. Reacquired by the team that traded him two-and-a-half years ago, he produced just five big-league innings (and 46 total innings) under the Cubs' care. There hasn't ever been much doubt about his talent, but health is destiny. He was inconsistent in the upper levels last year, showing varying velocity and often struggling with his command, both problems stemming from mechanical issues. If Vizcaino can stay off the disabled list and develop consistency with his delivery, he has the upper-90s fastball and nasty breaking ball to make him a dominant late-inning arm.

Alex Wood   LHP

Born: 1/12/91   Age: 24   Bats: R   Throws: L   Height: 6'4"   Weight: 215

YEAR	TEAM	LVL	AGE	W	L	SV	G	GS	IP	H	HR	BB	K	BB/9	K/9	GB%	BABIP	WHIP	ERA	FIP	FRA	WARP
2012	ROM	A	21	4	3	0	13	13	52²	39	1	14	52	2.4	8.9	62%	.277	1.01	2.22	2.76	3.89	1.2
2013	MIS	AA	22	4	2	0	10	10	57	41	1	15	57	2.4	9.0	56%	.261	0.98	1.26	1.98	2.79	1.2
2013	ATL	MLB	22	3	3	0	31	11	77²	76	3	27	77	3.1	8.9	50%	.333	1.33	3.13	2.62	3.06	1.3
2014	ATL	MLB	23	11	11	0	35	24	171²	151	16	45	170	2.4	8.9	48%	.295	1.14	2.78	3.22	3.41	2.4
2015	*ATL*	*MLB*	*24*	*9*	*8*	*0*	*27*	*27*	*145¹*	*126*	*11*	*39*	*145*	*2.4*	*9.0*	*49%*	*.314*	*1.14*	*3.12*	*3.19*	*3.40*	*2.0*

Breakout: 24%   Improve: 59%   Collapse: 18%   Attrition: 22%   MLB: 98%   Comparables: *Brian Matusz, Mat Latos, Matt Cain*

When people sentence a pitcher to life in the bullpen, it's almost always for at least one of three crimes: bad command, lack of a third pitch and/or physical issues. The last tends to be the toughest conviction to shake. Take Wood. He's more than a season's worth of starts into his big-league career, during which he's posted fantastic numbers without requiring a trip to the disabled list, yet poll 50 people on his future role and you'd still get a split response. Blame jumpy mechanics and an elbow scar from a previous Tommy John surgery for the skepticism. Blame stubbornness if another good, healthy season from Wood doesn't convince some he should be in the rotation rather than wasting away in the 'pen.

Lineouts

Hitters

NAME	POS	TEAM	LVL	AGE	PA	R	2B	3B	HR	RBI	BB	K	SB	CS	AVG/OBP/SLG	TAv	BABIP	BRR	FRAA	WARP
Johan Camargo	SS	ROM	A	20	478	53	16	4	0	40	34	50	7	6	.267/.320/.324	.254	.297	-3.4	SS(114): 1.6	1.8
	SS	LYN	A+	20	62	7	2	0	1	6	1	13	0	0	.259/.262/.345	.239	.304	0.7	SS(17): 0.1	0.3
Josh Elander	LF	LYN	A+	23	163	19	9	0	2	21	20	32	6	0	.219/.319/.328	.244	.262	0.4	LF(32): 1.0	-0.1
Sean Godfrey	CF	ROM	A	22	153	23	4	3	3	24	7	27	11	0	.275/.313/.408	.252	.321	2.0	CF(11): -0.8, LF(7): -0.3	0.7
	CF	LYN	A+	22	47	3	4	1	0	6	1	9	4	2	.333/.391/.476	.335	.424	0.2	CF(11): -0.2	0.5
Steven Lerud	C	GWN	AAA	29	200	23	9	1	4	19	28	43	1	0	.250/.376/.390	.265	.316	1.0	C(54): 0.1	1.1
Tyler Pastornicky	2B	GWN	AAA	24	189	13	5	1	1	17	11	23	7	2	.290/.330/.347	.230	.327	-1.5	2B(41): -3.8, CF(1): 0.0	-0.6
	2B	ATL	MLB	24	47	4	0	1	0	2	6	11	0	1	.200/.304/.250	.222	.276	-0.3	2B(10): -0.1	-0.2
Elmer Reyes	SS	MIS	AA	23	228	25	16	1	2	28	7	48	3	2	.303/.339/.417	.284	.378	-4.2	SS(44): 0.9, 2B(9): 0.3	0.9
	SS	GWN	AAA	23	221	27	16	2	3	24	5	45	2	0	.286/.318/.427	.254	.348	-4.7	SS(54): -4.7	0.3
Edward Salcedo	RF	GWN	AAA	22	413	50	21	5	10	44	40	97	13	5	.212/.294/.357	.229	.257	1.9	RF(48): -5.6, 3B(47): -0.5	-0.9
Joey Terdoslavich	1B	GWN	AAA	25	569	62	18	1	15	61	61	106	1	3	.256/.337/.385	.244	.298	-2.8	1B(65): -0.1, RF(29): 0.5	-0.6
	1B	ATL	MLB	25	11	1	2	0	0	2	0	3	0	0	.300/.364/.500	.308	.429	-0.6	1B(2): -0.0, RF(2): 0.0	0.0

Remember teenage shortstop **Ozhaino Albies**' name. (As if you had a choice.) ❖ Just as **Johan Camargo's** top-heavy swing will prevent him from hitting for power, his clodhoppers will force a move off shortstop. It's a fringe life for him. ❖ Converted catcher **Josh Elander** missed most of the year with shoulder woes. He's a bat-only prospect, and if he doesn't start hitting soon, he never will. ❖ **Sean Godfrey,** a senior selected in the 22nd round, doesn't have loud tools. He does, however, have the distinction of being the first Ball State player drafted by the Braves since Gregory Dikos. ❖ In our younger, more naive days, we would have spent this space raging about how on-base machine **Steven Lerud** lost all his playing time to some walk-allergic kid whose value is derived from his defense. ❖ In addition to serving as the answer to a trivia question—who was the last short-stop to start for the Braves on Opening Day before Andrelton Simmons?—**Tyler Pastornicky** should reprise his role as organizational depth. ❖ Nic-araguan infielder **Elmer Reyes** is a better fielder than hitter, but not so good as to avoid being glued to the bench for most of the game. ❖ **Edward Salcedo** can't hit advanced pitching, field third base, or offer value to a big-league club. He's basically the average 23-year-old—except he has a spot in the lineup (and in this book) because he once signed for $1.6 million. ❖ For years folks have wondered what position **Joey Terdoslavich** would play in the majors. Another season like last from him and we won't have to wonder anymore.

Pitchers

NAME	TEAM	LVL	AGE	W	L	SV	G	GS	IP	H	HR	BB	K	BB/9	K/9	GB%	BABIP	WHIP	ERA	FIP	FRA	WARP
Pedro Beato	GWN	AAA	27	2	0	6	42	2	48¹	43	7	17	45	3.2	8.4	36%	.279	1.24	4.10	4.43	5.82	0.3
	ATL	MLB	27	0	0	0	3	0	4¹	3	0	3	3	6.2	6.2	23%	.231	1.38	0.00	3.79	3.43	0.0
James Hoyt	MIS	AA	27	2	2	6	28	0	31²	19	1	10	43	2.8	12.2	47%	.250	0.92	1.14	1.83	1.99	1.0
	GWN	AAA	27	1	1	1	24	0	28	38	4	14	34	4.5	10.9	44%	.395	1.86	5.46	4.50	3.66	0.7
Aaron Kurcz	PME	AA	23	3	2	3	34	0	42	32	0	22	54	4.7	11.6	42%	.308	1.29	2.14	2.50	2.52	1.3
Wes Parsons	LYN	A+	21	4	7	0	23	23	113¹	119	10	34	96	2.7	7.6	53%	.321	1.35	5.00	4.19	5.43	0.3
Williams Perez	MIS	AA	23	7	6	0	26	25	133	119	4	39	94	2.6	6.4	59%	.283	1.19	2.91	3.29	4.26	0.1
Carlos Salazar	ROM	A	19	1	6	0	10	10	35²	47	4	38	27	9.6	6.8	33%	.372	2.38	10.60	6.34	6.92	-0.3
Donnie Veal	CHR	AAA	29	4	5	4	37	0	50	57	4	27	49	4.9	8.8	46%	.353	1.68	5.94	4.48	5.31	0.2
	CHA	MLB	29	0	0	0	7	0	6	6	0	7	6	10.5	9.0	39%	.333	2.17	7.50	5.16	3.46	0.1
Daniel Winkler	TUL	AA	24	5	2	0	12	12	70	33	5	17	71	2.2	9.1	38%	.172	0.71	1.41	3.01	3.54	1.1

Brandon Beachy's comp trajectory tells it all: PECOTA likened him to Pedro and Wainwright before 2013; then Rich Hill and J.P. Howell before last year. Now he can only be comped to the small (but growing) number of two-time Tommy Johnners. ❖ **Pedro Beato** is only 28, but has been pursuing a usable secondary longer than Ethan Edwards searched for Debbie. His fastball would need to be an 80 for him to have any future with his current mix. ❖ Souring on second-rounder **Garrett Fulenchek** because he struggled in rookie ball is like watching "The Shining" and concluding mazes are terrifying—it misses the point. Fulencheck is a projectable righty with the chance for two plus pitches. Give him time. ❖ **Alec Grosser's** middle name is Del, meaning his name kinda sorta translates to Alec The Grosser. He's not there yet, but he has the fastball and physical ingredients to become just that. ❖ Before signing with the Braves, **James Hoyt** worked on boats and pitched under Jose Canseco in an independent league. His mid-90s fastball and biting slider will earn him a spot in the big-league bullpen someday, where he should entertain teammates with tales from depths unknown. Plus boat stories. ❖ Part of Boston's return in the Theo Epstein trade, **Aaron Kurcz** recovered from Tommy John surgery to post encouraging numbers in 2014 and got himself traded to Atlanta for Anthony Varvaro, which is more of a compliment than it sounds at first blush. ❖ **Kris Medlen** underwent his second Tommy John surgery in March but his mid-rotation upside makes him a nice gamble for the Royals. ❖ For the skimmers in the crowd, there are two certainties when it comes to the Braves and pitching: 1) They know how to find it and 2) they don't know how to keep it healthy. Both statements apply to **Wes Parsons,** a non-drafted free agent with middle-of-the-rotation potential, who allowed 19 runs in 21 innings following a bout with arm discomfort. Ruh roh. ❖ **Williams Perez** throws strikes and coerces groundballs with an average arsenal. His name works better when flipped. ❖ **Carlos Salazar** flashes three usable pitches, but throws as many strikes as a skunk ape in a bowling alley. ❖ **Donnie Veal** should finally be arbitration eligible next winter, and his last name will be the only thing keeping him from being labeled a non-tender candidate. ❖ **Jonny Venters** is proof that these kids with scarred elbows can still enjoy big-league glory. Alas, he's also proof that those same kids could have their careers derailed by forces beyond their control. Venters underwent his *third* Tommy John surgery and isn't expected back this sea-son. Unless he lost his punch card, his next one is free. ❖ You'll rarely see upper-80s velocity and a 27 percent strikeout rate flirting with each other, but **Daniel Winkler's** deception has played a wonderful matchmaker. Can their potential major-league marriage survive their first tiff, Tommy John surgery?

Manager

Fredi Gonzalez

YEAR	TEAM	W	L	Py-thag +/-	Avg PC	100+ P	120+ P	QS	BQS	REL	REL w Zero R	IBB	PH	PH Avg	PH HR	SB2	CS2	SB3	CS3	SAC Att	SAC%	POS SAC	Squeeze	Swing	In Play
2012	ATL	94	68	1	93.3	53	1	79	3	460	404	40	249	.158	4	83	25	17	5	85	62.4%	18	3	288	93
2013	ATL	96	66	-3	95.3	48	1	102	5	466	422	35	213	.247	6	60	28	4	2	99	58.6%	21	3	241	76
2014	ATL	79	83	1	98.2	78	3	110	6	472	393	36	205	.180	2	90	29	5	3	89	59.6%	19	3	273	78

You can ask many questions of Gonzalez—for instance: Why did he bat B.J. Upton first or second 91 times, or why didn't he move the other Upton up to the second slot?—but the one that Braves fans asked the most during the offseason was: Why are you still here?

That the Braves retained their unpopular manager despite dismissing Wren created the need for an explanation. Did management overvalue his clubhouse skills and his previous record? Did they acknowledge he was dealt a shoddy roster (10 of the 15 hitters with triple-digit plate appearances posted below-average OBPs)? Or did they retain him because he used to be on Bobby Cox's staffs? The truth is probably contained in the first few attempts—especially since Wren's dismissal seems tied to his interpersonal skills rather than a disappointing 2014.

If there is a positive for Braves fans to embrace, it's that Gonzalez's impact on the record is overstated. He wasn't the catalyst behind last year's lackluster record, just as he wasn't the driving force behind the Braves' recent winning teams. For better or worse, talent tends to overcome.

BALTIMORE ORIOLES

by Jeff Long

The Orioles of recent years have given us in the outside-analyst game a lot of fodder for discussion about Pythagorean records and what makes a team an outlier. The conversation began when the 2012 team shocked everyone with a run to the playoffs, outperforming their Pythagorean record by 11 wins in the process. Their 2013 season reinforced the "overrated" narrative, as the team came back to earth with 85 wins and no postseason games. On the other hand, that win total exactly matched their Pythagorean wins, suggesting the team might actually be improving despite a drop in the standings. Last year, the O's once again posted an actual win total that closely matched their Pythagorean win total, 96 to 94, finishing tied for second in baseball and 12 games ahead of the Yankees in their division.

In last year's annual, Ben Lindbergh's essay included a chart showing the Orioles' Pythagorean win total versus their actual win total; I've replicated and updated it below. All in all, the club has improved its Pythagorean record each of the last four seasons, despite up-and-down results in the actual standings. At this point, the argument that the Orioles are a fluke doesn't hold water.

Still, there are obstacles in the road ahead, as there are for every organization. During the next two offseasons, for instance, the O's will need to work through several core players hitting free agency, including Matt Wieters, Steve Pearce, Chris Davis and Darren O'Day. But Dan Duquette and Buck Showalter have deftly handled everything thrown their way, leading to the best three-year run of success Baltimore has had since 1982-84. The fascinating part isn't what the Orioles did in 2014; the fascinating part was how they did it.

✦ ✦ ✦

Many years ago, the Orioles instituted an organization-wide philosophy: "The Oriole Way." It emphasized fundamentals and resulted in a run of strong O's teams: The club won at least 53 percent of its games 21 times in those 24 years, won 100-plus five times and reached six World Series, winning three. Earl Weaver managed the team for 15 of those years, and summed up his approach succinctly: "The key to winning baseball games is pitching, fundamentals, and three-run homers."

The Orioles of the '60s, '70s and early '80s were a genuine dynasty, even if World Championships came less often than for the Ruth-Gehrig-DiMaggio-Mantle Yankees. "Only three," scoffs New York, but the club was competitive nearly every season over in that period, particularly considering the American League's expansion in 1969 and 1977. Baltimore's rosters were stocked with players who learned The Oriole Way as they advanced through the minor-league system. The concepts of solid fundamentals, a tenacious attitude and an emphasis on the long ball were old hat to young Orioles. It's no surprise that Ron Hansen, Curt Blefary, Al Bumbry, Eddie Murray and Cal Ripken Jr. won Rookie of the Year awards. The team's leadership, including the aforementioned Weaver, farm director Don Pries and then-minor-league manager Cal Ripken Sr. all played roles in guiding the baby birds to become key contributors in the bigs.

✦ ✦ ✦

The Orioles' current run of success has been guided by a different philosophy: none at all. Duquette and Showalter have built a winner through emphasis on the periphery of the roster. Though there are a handful of homegrown contributors, this isn't a team that looks like the Cubs soon will, with a lineup full of players promoted from the minors. Instead, it was built through outside acquisition and centered around a manager who can quickly and effectively integrate new Orioles into their roles.

One could argue that the 2014 Orioles are emphatically anti-

ORIOLES PROSPECTUS
2014 W-L: 96-66, 1ST IN AL EAST

Pythag	.578	4th	DER	.720	4th
RS/G	4.35	8th	B-Age	28.4	14th
RA/G	3.66	5th	P-Age	27.7	7th
TAv	.273	4th	Salary	$105.7M	15th
BRR	-11.47	28th	M$/MW	$1.9M	7th
TAv-P	.257	11th	DL Days	928	17th
FIP	3.99	25th	$ on DL	13%	11th

Three-Year Park Factors

Runs	Runs/RH	Runs/LH	HR/RH	HR/LH
100	99	99	86	89

Top Hitter WARP	4.8	Steve Pearce
Top Pitcher WARP	1.8	Wei-Yin Chen
Top Prospect	Dylan Bundy	

Orioles Way, at least in its traditional form. Sure, the club hit a lot of home runs, but not because of any particular philosophy that Duquette and Showalter hold dear. They're simply the byproduct of obtaining undervalued, flawed-but-talented players. The Astros and Cubs are spending millions of dollars and years of draft picks acquiring players with elite pedigrees who they can develop and grow into contributors. That's much closer to The Oriole Way than what the O's are currently doing: assembling a winning team that's greater than the sum of its parts.

In building his 2014 roster, Duquette focused on relatively cheap improvements to augment his successful core. This included bringing in an immobile power hitter who had missed a third of 2013 to a PED suspension, signing a veteran hurler whose capricious mechanics made him extremely volatile and creating a gladitorial tournament for the bench spots. The goal was simple: to minimize the drop off when the inevitable happened. Nelson Cruz and Ubaldo Jimenez were the headliners of Duquette's offseason, but adding guys like David Lough and Ryan Webb was equally important.

The Orioles knew going into 2014 that Manny Machado would be a late addition to the squad, as he was still recovering from offseason knee surgery. They likely didn't foresee the other calamities that would hit: Machado recovered well and finally started to put together a solid season before going down with another knee injury in August; Chris Davis imploded after missing 12 games early in the season with an oblique strain, and his catastrophic fall from grace was punctuated by a September suspension for amphetamine use that held him out of the lineup down the stretch; and Matt Wieters started hot but went down with Tommy John surgery after just 26 games.

All that lost production was quickly and cheaply replaced by Duquette's fringe-of-the-roster additions. The table shows how much WARP every team received from its bench in 2014, where bench players are defined as those who appeared in at least 40 games while averaging fewer than 3.3 plate appearances per game. The Orioles' high ranking shows how important the periphery of the roster was to the team's success. David Lough (1.4 WARP), Delmon Young (1.0) and Ryan Flaherty (0.6) were particularly key contributors despite WARP totals that fall in the eyes-glaze-over portion of the leaderboards.

The table understates the value Duquette added on the edge of the roster, though. Caleb Joseph, who was expected to be the starting catcher at Triple-A Norfolk, ended up producing 0.8

Team	Bench WARP
Dodgers	7.5
Mets	5.3
Padres	4.6
Orioles	3.5
Pirates	3.1
Reds	1.9
Athletics	1.9
Brewers	1.9
Rays	1.8
Angels	1.7
Giants	1.6
Royals	1.5
Twins	1.2
Tigers	0.8
Yankees	0.5
Mariners	0.4
Marlins	0.3
Blue Jays	0.1
Rangers	0.1
Phillies	-0.1
Red Sox	-0.1
Rockies	-0.2
Braves	-0.5
Nationals	-0.6
Diamondbacks	-0.7
Cardinals	-1.0
Astros	-1.2
Indians	-1.6
Cubs	-1.8
White Sox	-2.1

WARP as one of the two primary backstops following Wieters' injury. Joseph didn't qualify for the bench player list because his plate appearances per game left him just over the threshold for a true reserve. Steve Pearce also does not qualify on account of receiving too many plate appearances, but he too is more realistically lumped in with the reserves than the genuine starters. Pearce was actually cut in late April, but re-signed two days later; he went on to produce 4.8 WARP on the year, more than 28 teams got from their entire bench combined.

Those two, both bench players pressed into full-time duty, became huge contributors to the success of the 2014 Orioles. Joseph became a favorite of the pitching staff as a result of his elite pitch framing skills, adding, by our numbers, more than 10 runs above average on top of his WARP through pitch-framing. Pearce came into the season as a reserve corner bat—one who averaged just 121 plate appearances per season over his first seven years in the majors—and ended it as one of the top offensive players in the American League.

The production the O's were able to get out of these specific players was surprising, but the underlying method of relying on the back end of the roster was not. Duquette has shown a propensity to build a portfolio of assets for Showalter, who is then tasked with deploying them in a way that maximizes their talents. It's this dynamic that has helped the Orioles excel despite a myriad of obstacles in their path. There will inevitably be hurdles in 2015, but Duquette and Showalter's willingness to adapt to changed circumstances bodes better for their ability to avoid catastrophe than any overarching system or philosophy, any Way, could. ∎

—Jeff Long writes the weekly Pitching Backward column for Baseball Prospectus and covers the Orioles for Baltimore Sports and Life.

Player comments by Matt Sussman, Craig Goldstein and Baseball Prospectus Authors

Hitters

Dariel Alvarez   OF

Born: 11/7/88   Age: 26   Bats: R   Throws: R   Height: 6' 2"   Weight: 180

YEAR	TEAM	LVL	AGE	PA	R	2B	3B	HR	RBI	BB	K	SB	CS	AVG/OBP/SLG	TAv	BABIP	BRR	FRAA	WARP
2013	FRD	A+	24	41	5	2	0	2	7	2	1	1	2	.436/.463/.641	.362	.417	-0.3	RF(10): -0.6, CF(1): 0.1	0.5
2013	BOW	AA	24	32	2	0	0	1	1	1	9	0	0	.194/.219/.290	.165	.238	0.0	RF(9): 1.2	-0.1
2014	BOW	AA	25	381	52	20	1	14	68	13	35	7	4	.309/.332/.487	.287	.307	-0.7	CF(90): 0.6	2.5
2014	NOR	AAA	25	183	23	17	2	1	19	8	27	1	1	.301/.328/.439	.262	.347	-0.6	RF(37): -1.2, CF(6): -0.0	0.4
2015	BAL	MLB	26	250	24	12	1	6	27	7	43	2	1	.260/.282/.389	.253	.292	-0.3	CF 0, RF -0	0.4

Breakout: 5%   Improve: 14%   Collapse: 10%   Attrition: 24%   MLB: 33%   Comparables: Jason Pridie, Lou Montanez, Eugenio Velez

A three true outcomes player Alvarez is not. He doesn't walk, he doesn't strike out and over-the-fence power isn't his specialty. What he does do is make contact at an excellent clip, and while the home runs might not be there, he's not an empty average either. While the power will never be elite, Alvarez did cut down on his noisy pre-swing set up, allowing his already plus bat speed to play up. The question on Alvarez isn't if he'll play in the majors, but where, as he's stretched in center and might not have the power profile for right.

Chris Davis   1B

Born: 3/17/86   Age: 29   Bats: L   Throws: R   Height: 6' 3"   Weight: 230

YEAR	TEAM	LVL	AGE	PA	R	2B	3B	HR	RBI	BB	K	SB	CS	AVG/OBP/SLG	TAv	BABIP	BRR	FRAA	WARP
2012	BAL	MLB	26	562	75	20	0	33	85	37	169	2	3	.270/.326/.501	.282	.335	0.7	1B(38): 1.7, RF(30): 1.5	2.4
2013	BAL	MLB	27	673	103	42	1	53	138	72	199	4	1	.286/.370/.634	.358	.336	1.9	1B(155): -9.8	7.0
2014	BAL	MLB	28	525	65	16	0	26	72	60	173	2	1	.196/.300/.404	.271	.242	-3.1	1B(115): -3.3, 3B(21): -1.1	0.7
2015	BAL	MLB	29	523	67	24	0	26	79	44	160	2	1	.251/.322/.473	.293	.318	0.0	1B -3, 3B -1	2.0

Breakout: 6%   Improve: 57%   Collapse: 2%   Attrition: 3%   MLB: 96%   Comparables: *Ryan Howard, Mark Reynolds, Dick Allen*

Since the dawn of history, Man has never been able to hit 50 home runs forever. For Chris Davis, the power didn't disappear altogether, but 26 home runs looks bad compared to 53. A scout told BP last August that his hands and timing at the plate are "a mess." All that really improved was his walk rate—a moderately promising indicator that opposing pitchers still respect the threat of his thump—but the 300 points in decreased OPS indicates most other pitchers figured him out. To compound his frustration, a 25-game suspension for unpermitted Adderall use abruptly ended his season mid-September. The good news is 2015 is another year and a home run every 17 at-bats is still really nice and good.

Glynn Davis   OF

Born: 12/7/91   Age: 23   Bats: R   Throws: R   Height: 6' 3"   Weight: 170

YEAR	TEAM	LVL	AGE	PA	R	2B	3B	HR	RBI	BB	K	SB	CS	AVG/OBP/SLG	TAv	BABIP	BRR	FRAA	WARP
2012	DEL	A	20	465	53	16	2	0	25	51	91	29	9	.252/.342/.302	.260	.322	1.7	CF(98): -4.9, LF(2): -0.1	1.4
2012	FRD	A+	20	97	11	1	1	0	4	12	25	8	1	.256/.358/.293	.249	.368	1.3	CF(19): -0.7, LF(3): -0.3	0.2
2013	FRD	A+	21	410	42	17	3	2	32	43	74	19	7	.234/.316/.313	.232	.288	-0.1	CF(91): -4.0, LF(4): -0.1	-0.7
2014	FRD	A+	22	395	65	21	4	1	31	36	69	20	8	.295/.363/.386	.274	.364	-0.6	CF(88): -6.8	1.3
2014	BOW	AA	22	104	9	6	0	1	12	2	20	3	1	.313/.330/.406	.274	.372	0.9	LF(20): -0.1, CF(6): -0.8	0.4
2015	BAL	MLB	23	250	25	9	1	1	14	16	62	7	3	.220/.272/.276	.215	.291	0.3	CF -3, LF -0	-0.8

Breakout: 0%   Improve: 0%   Collapse: 0%   Attrition: 0%   MLB: 0%   Comparables: *Quintin Berry, Kevin Kiermaier, Antoan Richardson*

Davis made an appearance in High-A for the fourth consecutive (and second full) season. The 22-year-old finally got the hang of it, earning a promotion to Double-A by season's end, where he was undoubtedly disappointed at how similar the post-game spreads were. A career-high batting average was buoyed by an aberrant BABIP, but Davis also recorded the highest ISO of his career, showing true progress. His glove and speed both grade out as plus, making him a real threat to reach the major leagues even if the bat is developing to the beat of John Cage's Organ[2]/ASLSP. <— cool joke

Alejandro De Aza   OF

Born: 4/11/84   Age: 31   Bats: L   Throws: L   Height: 6' 0"   Weight: 195

YEAR	TEAM	LVL	AGE	PA	R	2B	3B	HR	RBI	BB	K	SB	CS	AVG/OBP/SLG	TAv	BABIP	BRR	FRAA	WARP
2012	CHR	AAA	28	21	3	1	0	1	2	1	3	0	0	.250/.286/.450	.248	.250	0.9	CF(3): 0.0	0.1
2012	CHA	MLB	28	585	81	29	6	9	50	47	109	26	12	.281/.349/.410	.271	.339	2.9	CF(125): 4.7, LF(11): 0.1	3.0
2013	CHA	MLB	29	675	84	27	4	17	62	50	147	20	8	.264/.323/.405	.266	.318	1.8	CF(107): 5.6, LF(79): 1.3	3.2
2014	BAL	MLB	30	89	11	5	3	3	10	6	19	2	3	.293/.341/.537	.311	.350	-1.3	LF(20): 1.1, CF(2): -0.1	0.7
2014	CHA	MLB	30	439	45	19	5	5	31	33	100	15	7	.243/.309/.354	.244	.311	-2.0	LF(112): 1.1, CF(14): 2.2	0.5
2015	BAL	MLB	31	525	65	25	4	7	44	38	109	19	9	.263/.322/.381	.266	.320	-0.1	LF 1, CF 3	2.0

Breakout: 0%   Improve: 38%   Collapse: 8%   Attrition: 14%   MLB: 82%   Comparables: *Scott Hairston, Fred Lewis, Esteban German*

While there is no literal English equivalent, most etymologists agree "Alejandro De Aza" has roots in ancient Iberian dialects and roughly translates to "Alexander of League Average." As a center fielder who can steal bases, he doesn't reach base nearly enough to attempt it. To his credit, he has cut down on his fielding follies and baserunning boners. Routine center fielders aren't cheap, and neither is he, which is why if he can't add any pop or patience to his game, Mark Kotsay might sue him for career arc infringement.

J.J. Hardy   SS

Born: 8/19/82   Age: 32   Bats: R   Throws: R   Height: 6' 1"   Weight: 190

YEAR	TEAM	LVL	AGE	PA	R	2B	3B	HR	RBI	BB	K	SB	CS	AVG/OBP/SLG	TAv	BABIP	BRR	FRAA	WARP
2012	BAL	MLB	29	713	85	30	2	22	68	38	106	0	0	.238/.282/.389	.229	.253	0.9	SS(158): 21.0	3.1
2013	BAL	MLB	30	644	66	27	0	25	76	38	73	2	1	.263/.306/.433	.268	.263	-3.8	SS(159): -12.6	1.5
2014	BAL	MLB	31	569	56	28	0	9	52	29	104	0	0	.268/.309/.372	.255	.317	-0.9	SS(141): -0.0	2.2
2015	BAL	MLB	32	550	53	24	1	14	63	31	89	1	0	.250/.294/.384	.257	.273	-0.9	SS 3	2.4

Breakout: 0%   Improve: 46%   Collapse: 5%   Attrition: 9%   MLB: 94%   Comparables: *Michael Young, Edgar Renteria, Alan Trammell*

Never go to the grocery store hungry, and never announce a contract extension during the postseason. The three-year, $38 million extension was made public after the Orioles rolled through the ALDS and before they were swept out of the ALCS. If Hardy quickly becomes an old middle infielder, everyone will blame the timing. But three years is a conservative bet on his expiration date, and even if the range starts to give toward the end of the contract, second base is just right over there (although he has never defended anywhere else as a pro). He still owns one of the snazziest gloves around and ranks as a top-three power-hitting shortstop, even if his overall game is atypical. No other shortstop in history has more than 5,000 plate appearances and fewer than 10 stolen bases.

Nick Hundley   C

Born: 9/8/83   Age: 31   Bats: R   Throws: R   Height: 6' 1"   Weight: 200

YEAR	TEAM	LVL	AGE	PA	R	2B	3B	HR	RBI	BB	K	SB	CS	AVG/OBP/SLG	TAv	BABIP	BRR	FRAA	WARP
2012	TUC	AAA	28	47	4	1	1	0	7	4	9	0	1	.190/.255/.262	.178	.235	-0.3	C(13): -0.1	-0.2
2012	SDN	MLB	28	225	14	7	1	3	22	15	56	0	3	.157/.219/.245	.173	.196	0.4	C(56): 1.8	-0.5
2013	SDN	MLB	29	408	35	19	0	13	44	26	98	1	4	.233/.290/.389	.251	.279	-1.9	C(112): 0.5	0.9
2014	BAL	MLB	30	174	17	4	0	5	19	10	50	1	0	.233/.273/.452	.244	.299	-0.4	C(49): 0.7	0.4
2014	SDN	MLB	30	59	1	3	0	1	3	0	13	0	0	.271/.271/.373	.240	.333	-0.6	C(14): 0.2	0.1
2015	BAL	MLB	31	254	25	11	1	6	26	16	62	1	1	.231/.285/.366	.247	.283	-0.5	C 1	0.7

Breakout: 0%   Improve: 34%   Collapse: 15%   Attrition: 14%   MLB: 99%   Comparables: *Don Pavletich, Gene Oliver, Javy Lopez*

Early extensions rarely backfire on a club, but Hundley's was one of the few that did, as San Diego had to eat money to unload the final few months of his three-year, $9 million contract. Hundley was a late bloomer who signed the deal after a breakout age-27 season, which in retrospect is more accurately described as a breakout two months: He was hitting .202/.222/.307 on 8/1/2011, before slashing .367/.404/.656 in his final two months and setting up all sorts of unrealistic expectations. Hundley is better cast as a backup, with the ability to hit for power, mentor a pitching staff and provide leadership in a clubhouse, but not much else. Actually, he's got one other hidden talent: quickly and tactfully responding, "No, I'm not related to former major-league catchers Todd and Randy Hundley."

Kelly Johnson 3B

Born: 2/22/82   Age: 33   Bats: L   Throws: R   Height: 6' 1"   Weight: 200

YEAR	TEAM	LVL	AGE	PA	R	2B	3B	HR	RBI	BB	K	SB	CS	AVG/OBP/SLG	TAv	BABIP	BRR	FRAA	WARP
2012	TOR	MLB	30	581	61	19	2	16	55	62	159	14	2	.225/.313/.365	.246	.292	1.1	2B(136): -6.1	0.3
2013	TBA	MLB	31	407	41	12	2	16	52	35	99	7	4	.235/.305/.410	.268	.276	1.5	LF(53): -2.3, 2B(22): 0.6	1.6
2014	BAL	MLB	32	45	7	4	0	1	4	6	11	0	1	.231/.333/.410	.302	.296	-0.9	3B(17): -0.7, 2B(3): -0.2	0.1
2014	BOS	MLB	32	25	1	1	0	0	1	0	10	0	0	.160/.160/.200	.119	.267	0.2	1B(5): -0.1, 3B(2): 0.1	-0.3
2014	NYA	MLB	32	227	21	9	2	6	22	23	50	2	1	.219/.304/.373	.253	.260	-4.8	3B(41): 0.4, 1B(27): 3.4	0.1
2015	BAL	MLB	33	302	35	12	1	8	32	29	77	5	2	.228/.307/.375	.259	.284	-0.7	2B -1, 3B 0	0.5

Breakout: 1%   Improve: 31%   Collapse: 3%   Attrition: 4%   MLB: 93%   Comparables: Corey Koskie, Howard Johnson, Ron Cey

Johnson lapped the competition in Trivial Pursuit: AL East Edition, collecting wedges for all five teams in a span of just three years. If there was a long, drawn-out nine-inning game, you can bet that Johnson has been a part of it. He was flipped at the trade deadline from New York to Boston for Stephen Drew, then again at "the other" deadline to Baltimore for Jemile Weeks, among others. Further pursuits of Johnson are likely to be equally trivial, as he's increasingly a groundball hitter with no speed, and decreasingly qualified to defend either the keystone or a patch of outfield. One hopes than when he announces his retirement tour, rather than receive a gift from every visiting stadium, he is traded to all 30 teams in a single season, and plays five different positions with his veteran moxie and can-do attitude.

Adam Jones CF

Born: 8/1/85   Age: 29   Bats: R   Throws: R   Height: 6' 3"   Weight: 225

YEAR	TEAM	LVL	AGE	PA	R	2B	3B	HR	RBI	BB	K	SB	CS	AVG/OBP/SLG	TAv	BABIP	BRR	FRAA	WARP
2012	BAL	MLB	26	697	103	39	3	32	82	34	126	16	7	.287/.334/.505	.289	.313	2.0	CF(162): 15.5	6.4
2013	BAL	MLB	27	689	100	35	1	33	108	25	136	14	3	.285/.318/.493	.294	.314	2.2	CF(156): -18.4	3.0
2014	BAL	MLB	28	682	88	30	2	29	96	19	133	7	1	.281/.311/.469	.290	.311	2.1	CF(155): -8.1	4.0
2015	BAL	MLB	29	642	76	29	2	24	85	26	126	11	3	.274/.313/.448	.287	.308	1.6	CF -3	3.4

Breakout: 3%   Improve: 49%   Collapse: 2%   Attrition: 5%   MLB: 97%   Comparables: Andre Dawson, Hunter Pence, Carlos Beltran

But he hasn't done well in the playoffs yet! When the conversation invariably reaches that point, we are agreeing that the player is a downright behemoth in the regular season, and Jones has little left to prove April though October. Sure, he barely walks. If Jones magically converted 50 outs a year into walks, presto: now he's Ken Griffey, Jr. If he adds 40 points of average, he's Mike Trout. If he had wild hair he'd be Andrew McCutchen. Nobody mentioned in this paragraph has won a World Series yet. Despite the worst walk rate in the last two years, an average contact rate and a commonplace haircut, Jones is a consistent All-Star. Perhaps it's time to look inward for why Jones isn't considered a superstar of the game; the numbers are mostly there, as is the defense and the personality. The best theory on the table is he has the same name as an embattled NFL player. If his name was Adam Coolcenterfielder, maybe more people would consider him to be the face of baseball.

Caleb Joseph C

Born: 6/18/86   Age: 29   Bats: R   Throws: R   Height: 6' 3"   Weight: 180

YEAR	TEAM	LVL	AGE	PA	R	2B	3B	HR	RBI	BB	K	SB	CS	AVG/OBP/SLG	TAv	BABIP	BRR	FRAA	WARP
2012	BOW	AA	26	317	38	17	1	12	48	29	60	2	0	.272/.343/.470	.289	.303	-3.8	C(61): 0.0	1.9
2012	NOR	AAA	26	76	6	4	1	0	7	8	10	0	0	.206/.289/.294	.210	.241	0.0	C(20): -0.0	0.0
2013	BOW	AA	27	570	74	31	2	22	97	39	92	4	2	.299/.346/.494	.302	.321	0.8	C(64): 0.7, LF(16): -1.5	4.0
2014	NOR	AAA	28	95	8	7	0	2	11	3	22	0	0	.261/.284/.402	.257	.324	0.6	C(21): 0.2	0.5
2014	BAL	MLB	28	275	22	9	0	9	28	17	69	0	1	.207/.264/.354	.231	.246	-1.4	C(78): 1.1, 1B(4): -0.0	0.8
2015	BAL	MLB	29	286	28	12	0	9	34	15	64	0	0	.238/.281/.387	.251	.275	-0.5	C 0, LF -0	0.7

Breakout: 6%   Improve: 20%   Collapse: 12%   Attrition: 29%   MLB: 43%   Comparables: Shawn Riggans, John Hester, Rene Rivera

Domestic players who finally reach the big leagues at 28 typically don't stay there much longer, so it's paramount that they make the most of their opportunity. Joseph was drafted in 2008, the same year as All-Stars Buster Posey, Alex Avila and Jason Castro. His big milestone in 2014 was finally starting a season in Triple-A. If Matt Wieters stayed healthy, Joseph wouldn't be in this book at all, just another organizational catcher climbing a ladder that is unknowingly sinking in quicksand. But an impending DL trip for the All-Star prompted Joseph's May call-up; in a 30-AB stretch of August he hit five homers and slugged .900; in a 30-AB stretch of September he went hitless. The final slash stats are caricatural of a career backup catcher, but his 40 percent basestealer-vanquishment rate led the AL. (Even Wieters never threw out 40 percent in a season.) With okay power against lefties he can be the 27th- or 28th-best backup in the league, but his throwing arm and strong framing abilities will keep the late bloomer on the 40-man roster for a few more years.

Steve Lombardozzi 2B

Born: 9/20/88   Age: 26   Bats: B   Throws: R   Height: 6' 0"   Weight: 200

YEAR	TEAM	LVL	AGE	PA	R	2B	3B	HR	RBI	BB	K	SB	CS	AVG/OBP/SLG	TAv	BABIP	BRR	FRAA	WARP
2012	WAS	MLB	23	416	40	16	3	3	27	19	46	5	3	.273/.317/.354	.248	.304	-2.5	2B(51): 5.7, LF(41): -0.5	0.8
2013	WAS	MLB	24	307	25	15	1	2	22	8	34	4	3	.259/.278/.338	.226	.284	1.7	2B(48): 3.2, LF(23): 0.2	0.3
2014	NOR	AAA	25	295	26	9	1	0	30	17	32	6	4	.270/.307/.311	.228	.299	-1.6	2B(38): 1.6, LF(22): 0.4	-0.2
2014	BAL	MLB	25	74	6	1	1	0	2	0	14	1	0	.288/.297/.329	.223	.356	0.4	2B(20): -0.6	-0.3
2015	BAL	MLB	26	250	23	10	1	2	20	11	34	4	2	.261/.297/.342	.243	.290	-0.1	2B 0, LF 0	0.3

Breakout: 7%   Improve: 42%   Collapse: 11%   Attrition: 28%   MLB: 77%   Comparables: Darwin Barney, Donovan Solano, Kevin Frandsen

Being traded twice last year—once as a throw-in for a good pitcher, once for the aging husk of a shortstop—means Lombardozzi has different value to everyone. Each team can probably agree he can play multiple positions, and versatility is next to godliness. Of course, when somebody can play four positions (second, short, third, left) it *typically* means he's not a viable solution at any, either because of light offensive production, inconsistent defense, or both. On the right team he can last an entire season. On a contending team he's the Triple-A affiliate's favorite player and number one jersey seller.

David Lough   LF

Born: 1/20/86   Age: 29   Bats: L   Throws: L   Height: 5' 11"   Weight: 180

YEAR	TEAM	LVL	AGE	PA	R	2B	3B	HR	RBI	BB	K	SB	CS	AVG/OBP/SLG	TAv	BABIP	BRR	FRAA	WARP
2012	OMA	AAA	26	544	69	19	11	10	69	25	65	26	4	.275/.317/.420	.262	.296	5.2	RF(70): 13.2, CF(38): 3.5	3.4
2012	KCA	MLB	26	65	9	2	1	0	2	4	9	1	0	.237/.292/.305	.210	.275	-0.1	CF(12): -0.2, RF(5): -0.6	-0.2
2013	OMA	AAA	27	172	29	6	3	3	17	11	21	5	5	.338/.391/.474	.326	.374	-0.6	LF(30): 1.7, CF(9): -0.6	1.9
2013	KCA	MLB	27	335	35	17	4	5	33	10	52	5	2	.286/.311/.413	.274	.326	-0.1	RF(74): -3.9, LF(15): 1.1	1.0
2014	BAL	MLB	28	197	31	6	3	4	16	15	33	8	5	.247/.309/.385	.264	.283	1.9	LF(85): 5.1, CF(16): 0.8	1.4
2015	BAL	MLB	29	250	25	10	3	4	24	11	42	7	3	.253/.293/.368	.252	.285	0.4	LF 2, RF 1	0.6

Breakout: 0%   Improve: 18%   Collapse: 17%   Attrition: 26%   MLB: 61%   Comparables: *Nyjer Morgan, Jeremy Reed, Lou Montanez*

This ideal fourth outfielder should start very few games, and here's why. Imagine the seventh-inning stretch and Lough strolling onto the field with a microphone, belting this classic baseball tune: "Put me into the ballgame, put me in for my glove, replace the slugger who can't throw well, I don't care if I ever will bat, for it's U-Z-R that's important, in one-run late-inning games, for it's one, two, three outfield spots at the Lough ballgame!"

Manny Machado   3B

Born: 7/6/92   Age: 22   Bats: R   Throws: R   Height: 6' 2"   Weight: 180

YEAR	TEAM	LVL	AGE	PA	R	2B	3B	HR	RBI	BB	K	SB	CS	AVG/OBP/SLG	TAv	BABIP	BRR	FRAA	WARP
2012	BOW	AA	19	459	60	26	5	11	59	48	70	13	4	.266/.352/.438	.280	.297	1.0	SS(104): -7.7, 3B(2): -0.0	2.4
2012	BAL	MLB	19	202	24	8	3	7	26	9	38	2	0	.262/.294/.445	.256	.293	-0.1	3B(51): 0.9	0.6
2013	BAL	MLB	20	710	88	51	3	14	71	29	113	6	7	.283/.314/.432	.268	.322	0.7	3B(156): 28.4	6.0
2014	BAL	MLB	21	354	38	14	0	12	32	20	68	2	0	.278/.324/.431	.273	.317	-1.2	3B(82): 6.9	2.4
2015	BAL	MLB	22	405	47	22	2	9	41	21	71	4	0	.270/.312/.414	.274	.306	0.0	3B 11, SS -0	2.7

Breakout: 1%   Improve: 60%   Collapse: 3%   Attrition: 7%   MLB: 93%   Comparables: *Ryan Zimmerman, Starlin Castro, David Wright*

Here's the good news: Machado is still a mere 22 years old and he still should be a high-end third-baseman-or-maybe-shortstop for years. The bad: He has already had both knees repaired, and a third injury-plagued season would be a Grady-Size'd red flag, particularly if he manages to injure a third knee. Fortunately, you #cantpredictinjuries, so for the sake of simplicity let's assume he continues without any more severe season-shortening maladies. He'll make outstanding plays as well as the routine ones; he'll hit for enough power to justify batting him fifth. He'll mature and develop a marketable personality. If he remains in the lineup, he'll wedge himself back onto the short list of the league's best infielders. Basically, we're talking about a guy whose first three years draw comparisons to Nomar Garciaparra's—and he's still younger than Garciaparra was in his major-league debut. We're just also talking about a guy with the same head start on Garciaparra's injury log.

Steve Pearce   LF

Born: 4/13/83   Age: 32   Bats: R   Throws: R   Height: 5' 11"   Weight: 210

YEAR	TEAM	LVL	AGE	PA	R	2B	3B	HR	RBI	BB	K	SB	CS	AVG/OBP/SLG	TAv	BABIP	BRR	FRAA	WARP
2012	SWB	AAA	29	227	37	15	0	11	30	29	33	3	1	.318/.419/.568	.335	.336	-0.6	1B(48): -0.1, 3B(3): 0.1	2.2
2012	BAL	MLB	29	83	8	4	0	3	14	8	17	0	1	.254/.341/.437	.282	.283	0.1	LF(20): 0.0, RF(9): -0.5	0.4
2012	HOU	MLB	29	75	2	4	1	0	8	7	16	1	1	.254/.347/.349	.246	.327	0.1	1B(10): -0.6, RF(10): -1.0	-0.3
2012	NYA	MLB	29	30	6	0	0	1	4	5	8	0	0	.160/.300/.280	.221	.188	0.2	1B(9): 0.2	-0.1
2013	BAL	MLB	30	138	14	7	0	4	13	15	25	1	0	.261/.362/.420	.301	.300	-0.7	LF(15): -0.4, RF(3): -0.0	0.7
2014	BAL	MLB	31	383	51	26	0	21	49	40	76	5	0	.293/.373/.556	.344	.322	-2.1	1B(51): 5.2, LF(35): 2.1	4.8
2015	BAL	MLB	32	313	37	15	1	10	39	32	65	3	1	.258/.342/.429	.292	.299	-0.7	1B 1, LF 1	1.6

Breakout: 2%   Improve: 27%   Collapse: 4%   Attrition: 6%   MLB: 90%   Comparables: *Luke Scott, Kevin Youkilis, Justin Morneau*

Scholars don't typically keep track of such records, but Pearce might have had the best season ever by someone whose own team released him in the same season. He was re-signed two days after Chris Davis got injured in April, and by a technicality—the Orioles fielded a 24-man roster for a day—they were able to circumvent the 30-day waiting period to re-add Pearce to the active roster. Few experience breakout years at age 31, but Pearce outhit even Davis' PECOTA projection, and was also a valuable defender, being credited with nine Defensive Runs Saved (best in the AL) in just 400 innings at the position. The margins are small for lefty-mashing corner guys, even after such a charmed season, but Pearce's .279/.360/.496 line against righties buys him at least three or four months of not having to check the lineup card each day.

Jonathan Schoop   2B

Born: 10/16/91   Age: 23   Bats: R   Throws: R   Height: 6' 2"   Weight: 210

YEAR	TEAM	LVL	AGE	PA	R	2B	3B	HR	RBI	BB	K	SB	CS	AVG/OBP/SLG	TAv	BABIP	BRR	FRAA	WARP
2012	BOW	AA	20	555	68	24	1	14	56	50	103	5	3	.245/.324/.386	.254	.282	-2.7	2B(88): -2.0, SS(39): -5.0	0.3
2013	NOR	AAA	21	289	30	11	0	9	34	13	55	1	2	.256/.301/.396	.247	.290	0.1	2B(48): -0.1, SS(20): 2.8	0.7
2013	BAL	MLB	21	15	5	0	0	1	1	1	2	0	0	.286/.333/.500	.257	.273	0.0	2B(4): -0.4	0.0
2014	BAL	MLB	22	481	48	18	0	16	45	13	122	2	0	.209/.244/.354	.220	.249	0.3	2B(123): 1.2, 3B(17): -0.4	-0.6
2015	BAL	MLB	23	398	40	15	0	12	43	18	93	2	1	.227/.271/.367	.243	.265	0.0	2B -1, 3B -0	0.6

Breakout: 4%   Improve: 37%   Collapse: 4%   Attrition: 11%   MLB: 52%   Comparables: *Robinson Cano, Asdrubal Cabrera, Nick Franklin*

Hold your thumb over his defensive position and Schoop has the rookie numbers of Jonathan Singleton; big fly or bust. With a career-best mark in home runs (including minors), the pleasant surprise is he plays second base and is good at it. And he's only 22, so give the kid a break. His probably-too-aggressive approach netted him one of the league's worst BABIPs and line drive rates, but it did pay off in some dramatic late-inning moments. "Swing and hope" isn't a major-league approach (although it does sound like a decent wedding band), but real power and above-average defense at the major-league minimum is the stuff that 90-win seasons are made of.

Chance Sisco   C

Born: 2/24/95   Age: 20   Bats: L   Throws: R   Height: 6' 2"   Weight: 193

YEAR	TEAM	LVL	AGE	PA	R	2B	3B	HR	RBI	BB	K	SB	CS	AVG/OBP/SLG	TAv	BABIP	BRR	FRAA	WARP
2014	DEL	A	19	478	56	27	2	5	63	42	79	1	2	.340/.406/.448	.311	.406	-1.2	C(74): -0.9	3.8
2015	BAL	MLB	20	250	20	10	0	3	22	15	62	0	0	.236/.288/.317	.233	.307	-0.5	C -0	0.0

Breakout: 0%   Improve: 0%   Collapse: 0%   Attrition: 0%   MLB: 0%   Comparables: *J.R. Murphy, Hank Conger, Travis d'Arnaud*

It's possible that Sisco's 40 games at designated hitter were a reflection of the loud concerns about his ability to stay behind the plate—he frames poorly, doesn't move his feet to block balls and takes way too long to unload a throw to second—but it's more likely the Orioles just wanted to get him more reps at the plate without wearing him out. A deviation from the low-average/big-power bats we're used to seeing from a backstop, Sisco's balanced swing brought home the South Atlantic League batting title. Wherever Sisco lands, his athleticism (he played shortstop in high school) should help him adjust, but the real draw here is that ba-ba-ba-ba-bat.

Christian Walker   1B

Born: 3/28/91   Age: 24   Bats: R   Throws: R   Height: 6' 0"   Weight: 220

YEAR	TEAM	LVL	AGE	PA	R	2B	3B	HR	RBI	BB	K	SB	CS	AVG/OBP/SLG	TAv	BABIP	BRR	FRAA	WARP
2012	ABE	A-	21	93	12	5	0	2	9	10	14	2	1	.284/.376/.420	.313	.323	1.0	1B(17): 0.8	0.8
2013	DEL	A	22	131	19	5	0	3	20	11	16	0	3	.353/.420/.474	.345	.388	-1.9	1B(29): 4.3	1.6
2013	FRD	A+	22	239	25	17	0	8	35	17	41	2	0	.288/.343/.479	.283	.318	-1.0	1B(52): -2.1	0.5
2013	BOW	AA	22	69	7	5	0	0	1	6	10	0	0	.242/.319/.323	.266	.288	-1.6	1B(14): -0.5	-0.1
2014	BOW	AA	23	411	58	15	2	20	77	38	83	2	1	.301/.367/.516	.315	.337	0.9	1B(91): 1.8	3.2
2014	NOR	AAA	23	188	15	10	0	6	19	18	49	0	0	.259/.335/.428	.274	.327	-2.8	1B(44): -1.4, 3B(1): -0.0	0.0
2014	BAL	MLB	23	19	1	1	0	1	1	1	9	0	0	.167/.211/.389	.227	.250	0.0	1B(6): 0.1	0.0
2015	BAL	MLB	24	250	26	10	0	8	30	16	63	0	0	.245/.299/.395	.264	.300	-0.5	1B 0	0.3

Breakout: 1%   Improve: 12%   Collapse: 12%   Attrition: 21%   MLB: 34%   Comparables: *Jesus Aguilar, Neftali Soto, Brock Peterson*

It took fewer than three seasons for Walker to go from fourth-round pick to major leaguer. Normally a contact hitter, Walker muscled up for 26 home runs in 2014, a full 200 percent of his previous career *total*. The added power is likely a benefit of repeating Double-A and being more familiar with the pitching he was facing, as well as cleaning up his physique. Whether Walker can sustain that type of power output is the true question, as he's not athletic enough to slot in anywhere but first base. Unless or until Walker starts incorporating his lower half into his swing, the odds of this power production sticking around are slimmish, bordering on noneish. More likely, he's a guy with a nice hit tool who could fit on a team that isn't hung up on the typical first base profile.

Matt Wieters   C

Born: 5/21/86   Age: 29   Bats: B   Throws: R   Height: 6' 5"   Weight: 240

YEAR	TEAM	LVL	AGE	PA	R	2B	3B	HR	RBI	BB	K	SB	CS	AVG/OBP/SLG	TAv	BABIP	BRR	FRAA	WARP
2012	BAL	MLB	26	593	67	27	1	23	83	60	112	3	0	.249/.329/.435	.265	.274	-5.6	C(134): -2.3	2.4
2013	BAL	MLB	27	579	59	29	0	22	79	43	104	2	0	.235/.287/.417	.262	.247	0.7	C(140): 0.7	3.1
2014	BAL	MLB	28	112	13	5	0	5	18	6	19	0	1	.308/.339/.500	.312	.329	-0.2	C(22): -0.3	0.9
2015	BAL	MLB	29	250	27	11	0	8	30	21	46	1	0	.246/.311/.401	.269	.273	-0.9	C 0	1.1

Breakout: 4%   Improve: 47%   Collapse: 2%   Attrition: 9%   MLB: 99%   Comparables: *Ted Simmons, Yogi Berra, Gary Carter*

Here's the positive thing about Tommy John surgery on a non-pitcher, if you can call it positive: The timetable for a return is a lot shorter when the patient doesn't aspire to hurl 95 mph heat. Wieters, named an All-Star by the fans after 25 really good games, should be ready to start the season on time, and even get plenty of spring training at-bats to bring back his timing. That leaves only the question of his throwing arm, which had thrown out one-third of attempted base thieves. There's very little to go on, historically. According to Jon Roegele's exhaustive list of Tommy John survivors, just five major-league catchers have ever had the surgery, none since John Baker in 2010, and none nearly as distinguished defensively as Wieters. All other parts of his body remain durable and he should have no problem enduring another 130 games behind the plate.

Michael Yastrzemski   OF

Born: 8/23/90   Age: 24   Bats: L   Throws: L   Height: 5' 11"   Weight: 180

YEAR	TEAM	LVL	AGE	PA	R	2B	3B	HR	RBI	BB	K	SB	CS	AVG/OBP/SLG	TAv	BABIP	BRR	FRAA	WARP
2013	ABE	A-	22	235	28	13	4	3	25	24	44	8	8	.273/.362/.420	.309	.333	-2.2	CF(34): 2.8, RF(14): 0.1	2.4
2014	DEL	A	23	288	52	14	10	10	44	19	64	12	4	.306/.365/.554	.319	.371	4.3	RF(54): 1.9, CF(6): 0.1	3.3
2014	FRD	A+	23	107	21	7	2	1	19	8	16	5	0	.312/.364/.462	.298	.350	0.5	LF(14): 0.1, RF(9): -0.6	0.7
2014	BOW	AA	23	201	23	13	4	3	12	14	34	1	2	.250/.310/.413	.257	.293	-0.5	CF(38): 3.3, LF(4): -0.1	0.8
2015	BAL	MLB	24	250	26	10	2	5	21	13	64	3	1	.225/.273/.349	.236	.286	0.1	RF 0, CF 2	0.2

Breakout: 0%   Improve: 0%   Collapse: 0%   Attrition: 0%   MLB: 0%   Comparables: *Scott Van Slyke, Alfredo Marte, Chris Pettit*

Yes, of *the* Yastrzemskis. The grandson of Carl, Mike spent four years at Vanderbilt before being selected in the 14th round by Baltimore. What he lacks in talent, Yastrzemski makes up for in work ethic, though there's a fair amount of talent in the .288/.346/.490 line slashed across three levels. One of two players in the minor leagues who had double-digit homers, triples, doubles and steals, Yastrzemski is a polished hitter with gap power, and profiles best as a fourth outfielder. He should continue to move aggressively because of his age, and he should continue to succeed because of his makeup.

Delmon Young   DH

Born: 9/14/85   Age: 29   Bats: R   Throws: R   Height: 6' 3"   Weight: 240

YEAR	TEAM	LVL	AGE	PA	R	2B	3B	HR	RBI	BB	K	SB	CS	AVG/OBP/SLG	TAv	BABIP	BRR	FRAA	WARP
2012	DET	MLB	26	608	54	27	1	18	74	20	112	0	2	.267/.296/.411	.249	.299	-3.4	LF(31): -1.1	-0.5
2013	MNT	AA	27	31	4	0	0	1	3	1	7	0	0	.233/.258/.333	.211	.273	-0.1		-0.1
2013	PHI	MLB	27	291	22	13	0	8	31	14	69	0	0	.261/.302/.397	.253	.320	-2.8	RF(64): -1.3	-0.1
2013	TBA	MLB	27	70	8	3	0	3	7	6	9	0	0	.258/.329/.452	.301	.255	-0.9	RF(1): -0.0	0.3
2014	BAL	MLB	28	255	27	11	1	7	30	10	51	2	0	.302/.337/.442	.287	.359	0.4	LF(27): -0.9, RF(2): 0.0	1.0
2015	BAL	MLB	29	268	27	13	0	7	32	12	50	1	0	.265/.303/.406	.269	.302	-1.1	RF -0, LF -1	0.5

| Breakout: 6% | Improve: 52% | Collapse: 7% | Attrition: 9% | MLB: 97% | Comparables: | Ted Kluszewski, Hank Blalock, Chad Tracy |

So your team has paid for the services of Delmon Young. Congratulations: Your team must be expected to reach the playoffs. Postseason DH isn't officially a position but Young has constantly battled character flaws, image issues, legal quagmires and how to wear a baseball mitt to appear in four straight postseasons for three separate franchises, making an impact each time. His postseason OPS is 98 points higher than his regular-season mark, and while the odds of him making an All-Star game or MVP ballot are hilariously five miles behind the bandwagon, he's still in his 20s and is one of the preferred choices to be a platoon DH, pinch-hitter and postseason force. This is still way better than several no. 1 overall picks, but also way more disappointing than all the famous ones.

Pitchers

Tim Berry   LHP

Born: 3/18/91   Age: 24   Bats: L   Throws: L   Height: 6'3"   Weight: 180

YEAR	TEAM	LVL	AGE	W	L	SV	G	GS	IP	H	HR	BB	K	BB/9	K/9	GB%	BABIP	WHIP	ERA	FIP	FRA	WARP
2012	DEL	A	21	2	7	0	10	10	52	60	3	17	44	2.9	7.6	43%	.335	1.48	5.02	3.79	4.19	0.8
2012	FRD	A+	21	5	5	0	15	13	75	83	6	20	61	2.4	7.3	50%	.336	1.37	4.32	3.84	4.97	0.6
2013	FRD	A+	22	11	7	0	27	27	152	156	13	40	119	2.4	7.0	47%	.310	1.29	3.85	3.84	4.61	2.1
2014	BOW	AA	23	6	7	0	23	23	133¹	122	12	45	108	3.0	7.3	45%	.288	1.25	3.51	4.10	4.47	1.4
2015	BAL	MLB	24	5	9	0	21	21	109	123	14	46	70	3.8	5.8	44%	.306	1.55	5.29	5.44	5.75	-0.9

| Breakout: 0% | Improve: 0% | Collapse: 0% | Attrition: 0% | MLB: 0% | Comparables: | Alex Wilson, Yohan Flande, Rob Rasmussen |

After an initial burst, Berry settles in as more of a mild option that leaves you wanting more, flavor-wise. Slight of build, he can lose velocity as he gets deeper into games. With a deceptive delivery and three pitches to choose from, he could be a sweet option out of the bullpen, and a tart at-bat for left-handed batters. As a reliever, he could see the majors next season, but as a starter, he'll need additional time to ripen, but that might be grasping at straws. Wait wait. But that might leave seeds in your teeth. No, wait, got it, his stuff might play best in a pancake. Uhhh, he's tarter as a starter? He'll need to show he can get out of a jam? /ding ding ding, music plays, confetti falls, family runs out of the audience. Promotional considerations by Pepsodent; if you want your teeth their whitest, you need Pepsodent.

Brad Brach   RHP

Born: 4/12/86   Age: 29   Bats: R   Throws: R   Height: 6'6"   Weight: 215

YEAR	TEAM	LVL	AGE	W	L	SV	G	GS	IP	H	HR	BB	K	BB/9	K/9	GB%	BABIP	WHIP	ERA	FIP	FRA	WARP
2012	SDN	MLB	26	2	4	0	67	0	66²	50	11	33	75	4.5	10.1	36%	.245	1.25	3.78	4.61	4.60	-0.3
2013	TUC	AAA	27	4	3	3	33	0	44¹	43	5	14	44	2.8	8.9	40%	.306	1.29	2.84	4.13	3.88	0.9
2013	SDN	MLB	27	1	0	0	33	0	31	36	3	19	31	5.5	9.0	40%	.375	1.77	3.19	4.12	4.44	0.0
2014	NOR	AAA	28	3	1	1	17	0	23¹	26	1	6	43	2.3	16.6	31%	.490	1.37	3.47	1.00	1.05	1.3
2014	BAL	MLB	28	7	1	0	46	0	62¹	48	6	25	54	3.6	7.8	41%	.250	1.17	3.18	3.93	4.37	0.2
2015	BAL	MLB	29	3	1	0	64	0	71¹	65	8	26	76	3.3	9.6	39%	.300	1.27	3.53	4.05	3.84	0.8

| Breakout: 21% | Improve: 40% | Collapse: 16% | Attrition: 18% | MLB: 73% | Comparables: | Jason Motte, Will Harris, Michael Wuertz |

Brach delivers as if he's about to throw underhand (or possibly faceplant toward the third base dugout), then straightens out and chucks it from a deceptive 3/4 angle, or 3/5 angle, or whatever you want to call it. The former 42nd-rounder's money pitches are a slider and a splitter that are the same velocity and stay on the same plane but veer in radically different directions. The slider is one of the league's sweepiest, and he has added a tick and a half to his fastball velocity. Brach is a solid middle-innings pawn, if a bit of a gimmick who always seems on the cusp of being figured out.

Zach Britton   LHP

Born: 12/22/87   Age: 27   Bats: L   Throws: L   Height: 6'3"   Weight: 195

YEAR	TEAM	LVL	AGE	W	L	SV	G	GS	IP	H	HR	BB	K	BB/9	K/9	GB%	BABIP	WHIP	ERA	FIP	FRA	WARP
2012	BOW	AA	24	1	0	0	2	2	12	8	0	3	11	2.2	8.2	73%	.242	0.92	0.75	2.37	3.74	0.2
2012	NOR	AAA	24	4	2	0	9	9	51¹	49	5	20	37	3.5	6.5	56%	.278	1.34	4.91	4.15	5.65	-0.3
2012	BAL	MLB	24	5	3	0	12	11	60¹	61	6	32	53	4.8	7.9	61%	.311	1.54	5.07	4.27	5.26	0.4
2013	NOR	AAA	25	6	5	0	19	19	103¹	112	5	46	75	4.0	6.5	63%	.324	1.53	4.27	3.86	5.51	-0.4
2013	BAL	MLB	25	2	3	0	8	7	40	52	4	17	18	3.8	4.1	59%	.338	1.73	4.95	4.83	5.13	0.0
2014	BAL	MLB	26	3	2	37	71	0	76¹	46	4	23	62	2.7	7.3	76%	.215	0.90	1.65	3.16	4.90	-0.1
2015	BAL	MLB	27	4	4	4	21	11	70¹	71	6	27	50	3.4	6.5	59%	.297	1.39	4.11	4.49	4.47	0.4

| Breakout: 29% | Improve: 60% | Collapse: 14% | Attrition: 12% | MLB: 85% | Comparables: | Ross Detwiler, Dana Eveland, Tyson Ross |

By October 2013, Britton looked like a pitcher destined for a series of tumultuous waiver deals and minor-league assignments. Instead, the former starter made the Opening Day roster as a reliever and mowed down the competition in middle innings until opportunity gave him a closing role, which he took and ran into the ground. (As a groundballer, the metaphor is positive for him.) Now he's one of about four left-handed closers in the majors, and the only one of those to average less than one strikeout per inning. His control issues occasionally fester (as in the postseason) and only great closers last forever, so while he will begin the season holding down the ninth he should know there's always another Zach Britton lurking behind him.

Dylan Bundy   RHP

Born: 11/15/92   Age: 22   Bats: B   Throws: R   Height: 6'1"   Weight: 195

YEAR	TEAM	LVL	AGE	W	L	SV	G	GS	IP	H	HR	BB	K	BB/9	K/9	GB%	BABIP	WHIP	ERA	FIP	FRA	WARP
2012	DEL	A	19	1	0	0	8	8	30	5	0	2	40	0.6	12.0	51%	.091	0.23	0.00	1.31	2.52	1.1
2012	FRD	A+	19	6	3	0	12	12	57	48	5	18	66	2.8	10.4	36%	.312	1.16	2.84	3.21	3.46	1.3
2012	BOW	AA	19	2	0	0	3	3	16²	14	1	8	13	4.3	7.0	46%	.265	1.32	3.24	3.86	4.55	0.1
2012	BAL	MLB	19	0	0	0	2	0	1²	1	0	1	0	5.4	0.0	20%	.200	1.20	0.00	4.85	6.60	0.0
2014	ABE	A-	21	0	1	0	3	3	15	10	0	3	22	1.8	13.2	55%	.323	0.87	0.60	1.11	1.32	0.7
2014	FRD	A+	21	1	2	0	6	6	26¹	28	0	13	15	4.4	5.1	47%	.318	1.56	4.78	3.97	4.80	0.3
2015	BAL	MLB	22	2	3	0	7	7	34¹	34	3	15	29	3.9	7.6	43%	.297	1.41	4.23	4.41	4.60	0.2

Breakout: 15%   Improve: 23%   Collapse: 5%   Attrition: 17%   MLB: 34%   *Comparables:*   *Alex Wood, Nick Tropeano, Jarrod Parker*

Pitching in games that mattered for the first time since 2012, Bundy rebounded solidly from Tommy John surgery. He was able to touch his old velocity, but generally sat a tick below, at 91-94 mph. The Orioles continued to play the role of helicopter parent, limiting him to five innings in all but one start and refusing to let him get involved with the cutter even if everybody else's parents let *them* throw it. That's because 2014 was all about health for Bundy; his tepid performance at Frederick is likely to be swept under the rug. Even without his previous velocity, Bundy stands a good chance of reaching the major leagues in the coming season, as he continues to refine the consistency of his plus breaking ball and usable changeup and eventually is allowed to pitch without limits.

Wei-Yin Chen   LHP

Born: 7/21/85   Age: 29   Bats: L   Throws: L   Height: 6'0"   Weight: 195

YEAR	TEAM	LVL	AGE	W	L	SV	G	GS	IP	H	HR	BB	K	BB/9	K/9	GB%	BABIP	WHIP	ERA	FIP	FRA	WARP
2012	BAL	MLB	26	12	11	0	32	32	192²	186	29	57	154	2.7	7.2	39%	.274	1.26	4.02	4.37	5.02	1.4
2013	BOW	AA	27	1	0	0	2	2	12	9	0	2	8	1.5	6.0	50%	.265	0.92	3.00	2.49	3.35	0.3
2013	BAL	MLB	27	7	7	0	23	23	137	142	17	39	104	2.6	6.8	36%	.305	1.32	4.07	4.07	4.10	1.6
2014	BAL	MLB	28	16	6	0	31	31	185²	193	23	35	136	1.7	6.6	42%	.296	1.23	3.54	3.92	4.12	1.8
2015	BAL	MLB	29	8	10	0	25	25	153	154	17	37	119	2.2	7.0	39%	.294	1.25	3.83	4.25	4.17	1.3

Breakout: 21%   Improve: 39%   Collapse: 21%   Attrition: 6%   MLB: 95%   *Comparables:*   *Jeff Francis, Odalis Perez, Brad Penny*

The Taiwanese mid-rotation starter struck again with his third consecutive underappreciated season, this time improving his walk rate to fifth-best in the AL. For the second year he was even better with RISP, resembling a clean-cut orange-jerseyed Clayton Kershaw with a .555 OPS against in those situations. His main weakness is charity to righthanders, particularly allowing them home runs, but 70 percent came with bases empty and his struggles aren't egregious anyway. As long as he continues to command his fastball and plethora of breaking pitches, the fly balls should stay within the boundaries of hyperventilation and eventually his accomplishments will become properly appreciated. At the very least people will stop wondering if he's Bruce Chen's brother or something.

Zachary Davies   RHP

Born: 2/7/93   Age: 22   Bats: R   Throws: R   Height: 6'0"   Weight: 150

YEAR	TEAM	LVL	AGE	W	L	SV	G	GS	IP	H	HR	BB	K	BB/9	K/9	GB%	BABIP	WHIP	ERA	FIP	FRA	WARP
2012	DEL	A	19	5	7	1	25	17	114¹	109	11	46	91	3.6	7.2	55%	.294	1.36	3.86	4.52	5.28	0.7
2013	FRD	A+	20	7	9	0	26	26	148²	145	10	38	132	2.3	8.0	52%	.310	1.23	3.69	3.28	4.12	2.9
2014	BOW	AA	21	10	7	0	21	20	110	106	8	32	109	2.6	8.9	54%	.314	1.25	3.35	3.30	4.13	1.7
2015	BAL	MLB	22	5	7	0	18	18	97¹	104	11	36	72	3.3	6.6	50%	.304	1.44	4.61	4.78	5.01	0.0

Breakout: 0%   Improve: 0%   Collapse: 0%   Attrition: 0%   MLB: 0%   *Comparables:*   *Patrick Corbin, Hector Rondon, Cesar Carrillo*

Listed weights are often out of date, but even so, there aren't many starting pitchers at any level of pro ball who tip the scales at a mere 150 pounds. Davies might be a bit heavier than that by now, but not enough to stop scouts from questioning his future in the rotation. Everything he throws has movement, which is good because he lacks good downhill plane. He's never going to get by on stuff alone, so his ability to locate is paramount. As is, his command, plus change up and willingness to pitch backward have bought him time in the rotation. Now somebody buy him a burger.

Kevin Gausman   RHP

Born: 1/6/91   Age: 24   Bats: L   Throws: R   Height: 6'3"   Weight: 190

YEAR	TEAM	LVL	AGE	W	L	SV	G	GS	IP	H	HR	BB	K	BB/9	K/9	GB%	BABIP	WHIP	ERA	FIP	FRA	WARP
2013	BOW	AA	22	2	4	0	8	8	46¹	44	3	5	49	1.0	9.5	54%	.313	1.06	3.11	2.57	2.73	1.5
2013	NOR	AAA	22	1	2	0	8	7	35²	36	1	9	33	2.3	8.3	48%	.354	1.26	4.04	2.56	3.81	0.7
2013	BAL	MLB	22	3	5	0	20	5	47²	51	8	13	49	2.5	9.3	45%	.328	1.34	5.66	4.02	4.68	0.4
2014	NOR	AAA	23	1	3	0	11	11	43¹	41	5	18	44	3.7	9.1	47%	.298	1.36	3.32	4.07	4.47	0.7
2014	BAL	MLB	23	7	7	0	20	20	113¹	111	7	38	88	3.0	7.0	44%	.304	1.31	3.57	3.44	3.45	1.8
2015	BAL	MLB	24	7	9	0	27	27	132¹	130	13	37	117	2.5	7.9	45%	.304	1.26	3.74	3.98	4.06	1.6

Breakout: 29%   Improve: 66%   Collapse: 10%   Attrition: 16%   MLB: 95%   *Comparables:*   *Brett Cecil, Jered Weaver, Brett Anderson*

The Orioles found the solution to The Strasburg Conundrum, the one where an ace on an innings limit runs out of leash in mid-August and has to either be shut down for the stretch run or ridden into the danger zone. Baltimore sent Gausman on periodic visits to Triple-A Norfolk, where he could pitch on regular rest, as a starter, all season long—but in mostly four- or five-inning outings, occasionally padded with a few extra days off. Come September, he was the Orioles' best starter as they put the finishing touches on the AL East, sitting at 96 mph and twirling a 2.87 ERA in September, without topping 170 innings on the year. That total includes the eight dominant innings he threw over three multi-frame postseason appearances, when his 96 mph became 99 coming out of the bullpen. His slider can be a put-away pitch some day, but as Keith Law wrote last year, rushing him to the big leagues could have hurt his chance to develop it. Looking ahead, that pitch is the margin between a very good starter and a Cy Young award.

Miguel Gonzalez   RHP

Born: 5/27/84   Age: 31   Bats: R   Throws: R   Height: 6'1"   Weight: 170

YEAR	TEAM	LVL	AGE	W	L	SV	G	GS	IP	H	HR	BB	K	BB/9	K/9	GB%	BABIP	WHIP	ERA	FIP	FRA	WARP
2012	NOR	AAA	28	3	2	1	14	6	44²	22	1	10	53	2.0	10.7	42%	.208	0.72	1.61	1.75	3.24	1.2
2012	BAL	MLB	28	9	4	0	18	15	105¹	92	13	35	77	3.0	6.6	37%	.260	1.21	3.25	4.33	4.47	1.1
2013	BAL	MLB	29	11	8	0	30	28	171¹	157	24	53	120	2.8	6.3	41%	.260	1.23	3.78	4.48	4.92	0.7
2014	BAL	MLB	30	10	9	0	27	26	159	155	25	51	111	2.9	6.3	39%	.273	1.30	3.23	4.92	4.73	0.2
2015	BAL	MLB	31	8	10	0	26	26	146²	142	18	47	106	2.9	6.5	39%	.279	1.29	4.04	4.84	4.39	0.9

Breakout: 14%   Improve: 39%   Collapse: 9%   Attrition: 15%   MLB: 59%   *Comparables:*   *Jeremy Guthrie, Jeremy Bonderman, Chris Narveson*

Half the Orioles rotation was pretty okay but overrated, and the other half pretty okay but underrated. Gonzalez was part of the latter. He's a late bloomer, was a non-prospect, and his peripherals could belong to almost any Quad-A starter, but the record of success is adding up: He's now at 450 career innings of FIP resistance, and his ERA+ over the past three years is better than Jon Lester's or Madison Bumgarner's. We probably shouldn't have gone there, but you get the point.

So where does that FIP/ERA discrepancy come in? His career BABIP, at .266, is one of the league's lowest, partly because he gets far more fly balls than the typical pitcher, without all the extra line drives that sometimes come along with that. Partly it's because fewer of the line drives he has allowed end up base hits—maybe that's the Orioles' frequent shifting, or maybe luck, or maybe it just has to do with how batted balls in Camden Yards get classified, but it has saved him about 16 hard-stung hits in his career. Finally, while he hasn't generally been clusterlucky, an exceptionally high percentage of his home runs allowed have come with bases empty—76 percent, compared to the 58 percent league average.

Each of those factors has a different expectation of regression, but it's not outlandish to conclude that between his batted ball tendencies, the Orioles' defense, and maybe a little moxie there's reason to at least hope he'll defy FIP a bit more. But it's fairly clear he's in no position to improve beyond pretty okay back-end starter. At 30 years old and under team control for three more seasons, he'll never earn the chance to become an over-paid starting pitcher. Or, probably, an overrated one.

Hunter Harvey   RHP

Born: 12/9/94   Age: 20   Bats: R   Throws: R   Height: 6'3"   Weight: 175

YEAR	TEAM	LVL	AGE	W	L	SV	G	GS	IP	H	HR	BB	K	BB/9	K/9	GB%	BABIP	WHIP	ERA	FIP	FRA	WARP
2013	ABE	A-	18	0	1	0	3	3	12	11	0	4	15	3.0	11.2	68%	.355	1.25	2.25	1.60	2.71	0.3
2014	DEL	A	19	7	5	0	17	17	87²	66	5	33	106	3.4	10.9	46%	.290	1.13	3.18	3.42	4.27	1.5
2015	BAL	MLB	20	3	5	0	13	13	61²	60	7	31	57	4.5	8.3	45%	.302	1.47	4.55	4.92	4.95	0.1

Breakout: 0%   Improve: 0%   Collapse: 0%   Attrition: 0%   MLB: 0%   Comparables: *Carlos Martinez, Shelby Miller, Robbie Ray*

Aggression and confidence are part and parcel to Harvey's success. Both were evident in his decision not to commit to a college program before being drafted, and both are present in his on-field demeanor. With two plus pitches in his pocket, and a no-nonsense approach, it's easy to see why some scouts have Harvey as a high-impact bullpen arm, a la his father Bryan. His best pitch is a curve that's as bent as the Soviet sickle and as hard as the hammer that crosses it. Shut down toward the end of the season with elbow inflammation, Harvey will need to show progress with his changeup and the ability to log a full-season workload to reach his no. 2 starter ceiling.

Matthew Hobgood   RHP

Born: 8/3/90   Age: 24   Bats: R   Throws: R   Height: 6'4"   Weight: 245

YEAR	TEAM	LVL	AGE	W	L	SV	G	GS	IP	H	HR	BB	K	BB/9	K/9	GB%	BABIP	WHIP	ERA	FIP	FRA	WARP
2013	DEL	A	22	7	3	1	24	1	63	61	2	28	47	4.0	6.7	61%	.307	1.41	3.71	3.83	4.59	0.0
2013	FRD	A+	22	2	1	0	9	0	30²	29	2	11	25	3.2	7.3	57%	.307	1.30	5.58	4.13	6.20	-0.1
2014	FRD	A+	23	3	4	4	29	0	64¹	64	3	30	48	4.2	6.7	53%	.295	1.46	4.48	4.22	5.68	-0.3
2015	BAL	MLB	24	1	1	1	21	3	57	68	7	32	25	5.1	4.0	52%	.303	1.76	6.03	6.28	6.55	-1.0

Breakout: 0%   Improve: 0%   Collapse: 0%   Attrition: 0%   MLB: 0%   Comparables: *Jesus Delgado, Scott Rice, Rommie Lewis*

The fifth overall pick in 2009, Hobgood has never thrown 100 innings in a season, hasn't posted a strikeout rate above 20 percent since 2011 and hasn't progressed past High-A after six years. Some of that can be blamed on the shoulder injury that wiped out his 2012 season, but he was trending toward bust before then. Baltimore might salvage something out of him in the bullpen, but he's going to need to limit the free passes, and miss a lot more bats, and he's going to have to do it before hitting minor-league free agency next winter. As is, it's a lot like Matt Not-Good, if you ask me.

Tommy Hunter   RHP

Born: 7/3/86   Age: 28   Bats: R   Throws: R   Height: 6'3"   Weight: 260

YEAR	TEAM	LVL	AGE	W	L	SV	G	GS	IP	H	HR	BB	K	BB/9	K/9	GB%	BABIP	WHIP	ERA	FIP	FRA	WARP
2012	BOW	AA	25	1	0	1	2	1	10	3	0	1	6	0.9	5.4	59%	.111	0.40	0.00	2.30	3.95	0.1
2012	NOR	AAA	25	2	1	0	3	3	19¹	20	2	5	14	2.3	6.5	52%	.305	1.29	4.66	3.83	4.38	0.1
2012	BAL	MLB	25	7	8	0	33	20	133²	161	32	27	77	1.8	5.2	48%	.298	1.41	5.45	5.70	6.46	-0.8
2013	BAL	MLB	26	6	5	4	68	0	86¹	71	11	14	68	1.5	7.1	40%	.249	0.98	2.81	3.71	4.07	0.6
2014	BAL	MLB	27	3	2	11	60	0	60²	55	4	12	45	1.8	6.7	53%	.285	1.10	2.97	3.18	3.85	0.4
2015	BAL	MLB	28	3	2	1	25	5	54¹	56	7	11	35	1.8	5.8	45%	.285	1.23	3.96	4.68	4.31	0.4

Breakout: 22%   Improve: 52%   Collapse: 15%   Attrition: 12%   MLB: 82%   Comparables: *Andy Sonnanstine, Joe Blanton, Sean Marshall*

The 2014 Orioles used a closer-by-whatever-failed-starting-pitcher-we-have-lying-around-committee, and Hunter was, for a time, the starting pitcher who was most lying around. He hung on for about a month before two legendary ninth-inning meltdowns took him out of the role. Following a mid-May demotion, Hunter posted a 1.77 ERA and 0.85 WHIP. Sure, they were in lower leverage, but Hunter also changed his approach, focusing more on a sinking fastball and turning more pitches into grounders than fly balls for the first time in his career. Check out those home run totals since he joined Baltimore and tell us that it wasn't a wise idea. With his simplified and refined pitch list, the rotation is likely not in his future, but closing still might be.

Ubaldo Jimenez   RHP

Born: 1/22/84   Age: 31   Bats: R   Throws: R   Height: 6'5"   Weight: 210

YEAR	TEAM	LVL	AGE	W	L	SV	G	GS	IP	H	HR	BB	K	BB/9	K/9	GB%	BABIP	WHIP	ERA	FIP	FRA	WARP
2012	CLE	MLB	28	9	17	0	31	31	176²	190	25	95	143	4.8	7.3	40%	.309	1.61	5.40	5.02	5.09	0.7
2013	CLE	MLB	29	13	9	0	32	32	182²	163	16	80	194	3.9	9.6	45%	.304	1.33	3.30	3.45	4.01	2.1
2014	BAL	MLB	30	6	9	0	25	22	125¹	113	14	77	116	5.5	8.3	43%	.289	1.52	4.81	4.70	5.37	-0.4
2015	BAL	MLB	31	7	8	0	22	22	126	115	11	58	119	4.1	8.5	44%	.294	1.37	3.99	4.31	4.33	0.9

Breakout: 16%   Improve: 46%   Collapse: 24%   Attrition: 22%   MLB: 91%   Comparables: *Matt Clement, Chris Young, Ted Lilly*

Jimenez has the mechanics of a kid playing pin the tail on the donkey; each throw is more of a hypothesis than a theory. He's *often* facing the right direction, but once he starts going off course he's a threat to the kitty litter. Or, more specifically, he's a threat to his own walk rate, which went uncorrected in 2014 and undid all the optimism of his finally-figured-things-out 2013 season. As runaway division winners, the Orioles survived the summer with Jimenez and were able to locate four starters and a long-man better than him, so he was left off the postseason roster. That's awk-ward, to say the least, for a pitcher in the first year of a long-term contract, but all those zeroes will ensure he gets another shot in the rotation this year, and next, until he either sticks that pin right on the donkey, or right into his cousin's eye.

Brian Matusz LHP

Born: 2/11/87 Age: 28 Bats: L Throws: L Height: 6'4" Weight: 200

YEAR	TEAM	LVL	AGE	W	L	SV	G	GS	IP	H	HR	BB	K	BB/9	K/9	GB%	BABIP	WHIP	ERA	FIP	FRA	WARP
2012	NOR	AAA	25	2	1	1	10	6	47	43	2	15	32	2.9	6.1	43%	.281	1.23	4.21	3.31	4.64	0.2
2012	BAL	MLB	25	6	10	0	34	16	98	112	15	41	81	3.8	7.4	43%	.319	1.56	4.87	4.64	4.75	0.8
2013	BAL	MLB	26	2	1	0	65	0	51	43	3	16	50	2.8	8.8	40%	.292	1.16	3.53	2.94	3.52	0.6
2014	BAL	MLB	27	2	3	0	63	0	51²	51	7	17	53	3.0	9.2	36%	.301	1.32	3.48	4.03	3.96	0.3
2015	BAL	MLB	28	2	2	0	24	6	44²	45	5	16	37	3.1	7.5	39%	.302	1.37	4.32	4.51	4.69	0.1

Breakout: 23% Improve: 43% Collapse: 13% Attrition: 12% MLB: 79% Comparables: *Manny Parra, Jason Hammel, Wade Davis*

Mariano Rivera ruined it for the 90s, as did Eric Gagne in the 2000s and Wade Davis this decade. When floundering starters become relievers, we expect them to be lights-out good or consider them disappointments. As Matusz enters his third full season in the bullpen, he's accepted the fact that right-handers are going to devour his fastballs for brunch, and that he is therefore likely to be pulled before the right-hander steps to the plate. His 2013 season was probably his ceiling, and 2014 better resembled his profile. That is to say, he'll give up the occasional home run since he lives and dies by the fly ball, and sometimes even lefties will beat him. But he's a big-league middle-inning reliever, and two years ago he was on pace to be a Triple-A starter. In the end Matusz remains a converted-reliever success story, just not the one you hoped for.

T.J. McFarland LHP

Born: 6/8/89 Age: 26 Bats: L Throws: L Height: 6'3" Weight: 220

YEAR	TEAM	LVL	AGE	W	L	SV	G	GS	IP	H	HR	BB	K	BB/9	K/9	GB%	BABIP	WHIP	ERA	FIP	FRA	WARP
2012	AKR	AA	23	8	2	0	10	10	60¹	61	1	12	41	1.8	6.1	59%	.328	1.21	2.69	2.80	4.21	0.6
2012	COH	AAA	23	8	6	0	17	17	102²	112	9	33	55	2.9	4.8	56%	.306	1.41	4.82	4.22	5.92	-0.1
2013	BAL	MLB	24	4	1	0	38	1	74²	83	7	28	58	3.4	7.0	60%	.319	1.49	4.22	3.87	4.76	0.2
2014	NOR	AAA	25	0	1	0	5	5	24	21	0	8	25	3.0	9.4	71%	.309	1.21	3.75	2.77	3.39	0.6
2014	BAL	MLB	25	4	2	0	37	1	58²	70	2	13	34	2.0	5.2	65%	.337	1.41	2.76	3.31	4.48	0.1
2015	BAL	MLB	26	3	4	0	20	9	71	78	6	24	44	3.0	5.5	57%	.306	1.44	4.48	4.58	4.87	0.0

Breakout: 40% Improve: 61% Collapse: 16% Attrition: 23% MLB: 81% Comparables: *Luis Mendoza, Juan Gutierrez, Chien-Ming Wang*

Virtually all left-handers fall into three categories: starter, LOOGY, long reliever. Biblically these categories correspond to heaven, hell and purgatory. McFarland, a minor-league starter, has now spent two seasons with the Orioles in purgatory, longer than most left-handers. It must be frustrating having a permanent temporary role, because the long man in the regular season gets bumped from the playoff roster by the fifth starter, and that's what happened to him. He has the pitch array to start and his fastball added two ticks in 2014, so he'll fight for the classier role out of spring training. The only thing working against him is that a good long reliever is hard to find.

Evan Meek RHP

Born: 5/12/83 Age: 32 Bats: R Throws: R Height: 6'0" Weight: 225

YEAR	TEAM	LVL	AGE	W	L	SV	G	GS	IP	H	HR	BB	K	BB/9	K/9	GB%	BABIP	WHIP	ERA	FIP	FRA	WARP
2012	IND	AAA	29	3	2	1	36	0	46	33	3	26	41	5.1	8.0	62%	.242	1.28	2.74	4.18	5.73	-0.3
2012	PIT	MLB	29	0	0	0	12	0	12	14	1	6	8	4.5	6.0	36%	.317	1.67	6.75	4.64	4.31	0.1
2013	ROU	AAA	30	6	9	4	33	15	108	115	9	46	80	3.8	6.7	57%	.315	1.49	4.50	4.75	5.65	-0.4
2014	NOR	AAA	31	2	0	16	39	0	41²	33	2	4	37	0.9	8.0	61%	.265	0.89	1.94	2.49	3.50	0.8
2014	BAL	MLB	31	0	4	0	23	0	23¹	26	3	11	16	4.2	6.2	53%	.307	1.59	5.79	5.13	5.43	-0.2
2015	BAL	MLB	32	3	2	1	42	4	61¹	59	6	24	47	3.5	6.9	54%	.287	1.35	4.02	4.69	4.37	0.3

Breakout: 16% Improve: 28% Collapse: 6% Attrition: 18% MLB: 41% Comparables: *Rick Bauer, Tommy Phelps, Randy Flores*

Few besides the team's traveling secretary remember those interchangeable bullpenners who scuttle between Triple-A and the majors. This is Meek's life, five years removed from starring as the Pirates' obligatory All-Star, but now with a second feather in his cap: He'll forever be the man who was on the mound during Derek Jeter's final hit, swing and game-winning memory in Yankee Stadium. Blessed is the Meek, for he shall inherit runners in the sixth.

Bud Norris RHP

Born: 3/2/85 Age: 30 Bats: R Throws: R Height: 6'0" Weight: 220

YEAR	TEAM	LVL	AGE	W	L	SV	G	GS	IP	H	HR	BB	K	BB/9	K/9	GB%	BABIP	WHIP	ERA	FIP	FRA	WARP
2012	HOU	MLB	27	7	13	0	29	29	168¹	165	23	66	165	3.5	8.8	40%	.301	1.37	4.65	4.27	4.45	1.6
2013	BAL	MLB	28	4	3	0	11	9	50²	61	6	24	57	4.3	10.1	45%	.382	1.68	4.80	3.84	3.31	1.2
2013	HOU	MLB	28	6	9	0	21	21	126	135	11	43	90	3.1	6.4	41%	.316	1.41	3.93	3.90	3.98	2.0
2014	BAL	MLB	29	15	8	0	28	28	165¹	149	20	52	139	2.8	7.6	44%	.279	1.22	3.65	4.25	4.53	1.0
2015	BAL	MLB	30	7	10	0	24	24	143	143	17	54	129	3.4	8.1	42%	.305	1.38	4.37	4.60	4.75	0.3

Breakout: 18% Improve: 41% Collapse: 23% Attrition: 15% MLB: 83% Comparables: *John Patterson, Ted Lilly, Ervin Santana*

Norris isn't improving much but he sure is getting more expensive. The traditional fastball-changeup-slider pitcher continues to be thwarted by his arch-nemesis, Unnamed Lefty Slugger, and doesn't work deep enough into games to put "no. 2 starter" on his resume—even if he has mostly been on teams where he qualified as the no. 2 starter. Years of trade rumors likely inflated expectations, but it's best not to expect much more than 5 2/3 innings and a real shot at coming back against the other team's bullpen.

Darren O'Day RHP

Born: 10/22/82 Age: 32 Bats: R Throws: R Height: 6'4" Weight: 220

YEAR	TEAM	LVL	AGE	W	L	SV	G	GS	IP	H	HR	BB	K	BB/9	K/9	GB%	BABIP	WHIP	ERA	FIP	FRA	WARP
2012	BAL	MLB	29	7	1	0	69	0	67	49	6	14	69	1.9	9.3	36%	.251	0.94	2.28	2.91	3.05	1.3
2013	BAL	MLB	30	5	3	2	68	0	62	47	7	15	59	2.2	8.6	40%	.250	1.00	2.18	3.61	4.12	0.5
2014	BAL	MLB	31	5	2	4	68	0	68²	42	6	19	73	2.5	9.6	47%	.218	0.89	1.70	3.35	3.92	0.6
2015	BAL	MLB	32	3	1	2	58	0	57	46	6	14	57	2.2	8.9	41%	.268	1.05	2.90	3.86	3.16	1.1

Breakout: 21% Improve: 42% Collapse: 28% Attrition: 7% MLB: 88% Comparables: *Jason Frasor, Will Ohman, Frank Francisco*

Sidearmers of a feather stick together. Throw from that weird angle and O'Day becomes Chad Bradford with fewer movie references, or Peter Moylan with a different flush to his toilet. But put your hand over the right hand side of your screen and focus only on results, and O'Day joins the cool-kids club: Since 2009 there have been just five relievers (min. 200 IP) with better WHIPs, and all five—Sergio Romo, Craig Kimbrel, Koji Uehara, Mariano Rivera and Joaquin Benoit—have been closers. O'Day could close but he won't, not with that nerdy arm slot, so the eighth inning will be in good, knuckle-scraped hands.

Stephen Tarpley   LHP

Born: 2/17/93   Age: 22   Bats: R   Throws: L   Height: 6'1"   Weight: 180

YEAR	TEAM	LVL	AGE	W	L	SV	G	GS	IP	H	HR	BB	K	BB/9	K/9	GB%	BABIP	WHIP	ERA	FIP	FRA	WARP
2014	ABE	A-	21	3	5	0	13	12	66¹	69	4	24	60	3.3	8.1	61%	.339	1.40	3.66	3.91	4.48	0.3
2015	BAL	MLB	22	2	4	0	10	10	46¹	54	6	26	28	5.0	5.5	49%	.312	1.73	5.90	6.00	6.42	-0.6

Breakout: 0%   Improve: 0%   Collapse: 0%   Attrition: 0%   MLB: 0%   Comparables: Adam Warren, Nick Maronde, Mario Hollands

Elaine Benes once described George Costanza as a short, stocky, slow-witted bald man, and while we make no claims against Tarpley's wits or hair, he fulfills the former two attributes. A southpaw with the potential for three average or better pitches, Tarpley carries as much risk in his profile as he does promise. He's yet to reach full-season ball, and requires significant growth from both his secondary offerings, as well as his command. The upside is a back-end starting pitcher, while the probability is middle relief. This is what depth looks like.

Chris Tillman   RHP

Born: 4/15/88   Age: 27   Bats: R   Throws: R   Height: 6'5"   Weight: 210

YEAR	TEAM	LVL	AGE	W	L	SV	G	GS	IP	H	HR	BB	K	BB/9	K/9	GB%	BABIP	WHIP	ERA	FIP	FRA	WARP
2012	NOR	AAA	24	8	8	0	16	15	89¹	85	5	30	92	3.0	9.3	51%	.323	1.29	3.63	2.93	3.91	1.1
2012	BAL	MLB	24	9	3	0	15	15	86	66	12	24	66	2.5	6.9	36%	.221	1.05	2.93	4.20	4.45	0.3
2013	BAL	MLB	25	16	7	0	33	33	206¹	184	33	68	179	3.0	7.8	40%	.269	1.22	3.71	4.45	4.58	1.0
2014	BAL	MLB	26	13	6	0	34	34	207¹	189	21	66	150	2.9	6.5	42%	.267	1.23	3.34	4.04	4.51	0.9
2015	BAL	MLB	27	9	11	0	31	31	175²	168	21	59	138	3.0	7.1	41%	.282	1.29	3.92	4.66	4.26	1.4

Breakout: 23%   Improve: 51%   Collapse: 15%   Attrition: 13%   MLB: 85%   Comparables: Homer Bailey, Jeff Francis, Jeremy Hellickson

The last time an Orioles pitcher posted back-to-back 200-inning seasons with an above-average ERA+ was Mike Mussina. Of all the hypothetical future aces Baltimore fans imagined would supplant him, none looked like Tillman. He doesn't throw mid-90s or have a signature pitch, although he can muscle up to 93, throw a really sharp knuckle curve, field his position, and—lately—limit home runs and walks, so maybe he's more like Mussina than originally thought. With apologies to his pretty good pop-up rate, it's his control of the running game that most interests us; in the past two seasons, runners are just 2-for-13 against him. He comes set in the most peculiar way, rocking back and forth in a series of false "set" positions before finally coming to rest; at which point he varies the length of his pause to either freeze or get the jump on a baserunner. It's maybe worth only a few runs a year, but it's nice to know your ace isn't doing anything frivolously.

Ryan Webb   RHP

Born: 2/5/86   Age: 29   Bats: R   Throws: R   Height: 6'6"   Weight: 245

YEAR	TEAM	LVL	AGE	W	L	SV	G	GS	IP	H	HR	BB	K	BB/9	K/9	GB%	BABIP	WHIP	ERA	FIP	FRA	WARP
2012	MIA	MLB	26	4	3	0	65	0	60¹	72	2	20	44	3.0	6.6	52%	.350	1.52	4.03	3.30	3.18	0.6
2013	MIA	MLB	27	2	6	0	66	0	80¹	70	5	27	54	3.0	6.0	59%	.266	1.21	2.91	3.57	3.87	0.6
2014	NOR	AAA	28	0	2	0	11	0	11¹	13	1	2	10	1.6	7.9	50%	.324	1.32	4.76	3.27	4.69	0.1
2014	BAL	MLB	28	3	3	0	51	0	49¹	50	2	12	37	2.2	6.8	52%	.310	1.26	3.83	2.98	3.68	0.5
2015	BAL	MLB	29	3	1	0	53	0	54²	55	4	16	40	2.7	6.5	55%	.301	1.31	3.78	4.02	4.11	0.4

Breakout: 40%   Improve: 54%   Collapse: 27%   Attrition: 24%   MLB: 91%   Comparables: Tony Pena, Brandon League, Bobby Parnell

Webb has a very special place in BP's heart as the pitcher with the most games ever finished without recording a save, currently at 87. The journeyman righthander throws strikes but not strikeouts, explaining both his value to a bullpen and his limitations in leverage. The mid-90s fastball is no longer there, but it still has some strong sink and compels batters of either handedness to pepper it into the grass. Reliable as ever in 2014, he was nonetheless squeezed out of a crowded Baltimore bullpen in the summer and the postseason. But at some point, the save opportunity will be there for Webb, because baseball will always have tired closers, doubleheaders and extra-inning marathons. At this point it's his white whale, though one doubts he's aware of how much we're talking about it.

Tyler Wilson   RHP

Born: 9/25/89   Age: 25   Bats: R   Throws: R   Height: 6'2"   Weight: 185

YEAR	TEAM	LVL	AGE	W	L	SV	G	GS	IP	H	HR	BB	K	BB/9	K/9	GB%	BABIP	WHIP	ERA	FIP	FRA	WARP
2012	DEL	A	22	3	3	0	6	6	32	30	4	11	29	3.1	8.2	53%	.295	1.28	5.06	4.52	5.38	0.2
2012	FRD	A+	22	7	7	0	19	19	111	95	12	19	114	1.5	9.2	43%	.285	1.03	3.49	3.41	4.07	1.8
2013	FRD	A+	23	1	1	0	11	11	62¹	57	4	25	48	3.6	6.9	44%	.285	1.32	4.48	3.89	4.80	0.7
2013	BOW	AA	23	7	5	0	16	16	89¹	85	13	22	70	2.2	7.1	35%	.270	1.20	3.83	4.45	5.25	0.3
2014	BOW	AA	24	10	5	0	16	16	96²	101	10	22	91	2.0	8.5	52%	.320	1.27	3.72	3.53	4.08	1.5
2014	NOR	AAA	24	4	3	0	12	12	70	61	8	21	66	2.7	8.5	44%	.280	1.17	3.60	3.90	4.33	0.9
2015	BAL	MLB	25	7	10	0	25	25	137²	142	19	41	105	2.7	6.9	43%	.292	1.33	4.36	4.84	4.73	0.4

Breakout: 16%   Improve: 26%   Collapse: 9%   Attrition: 24%   MLB: 42%   Comparables: Charles Brewer, Tyler Lyons, Kyle Gibson

True to form, Wilson pitched at two levels in 2014, compiling a 3.67 ERA between them. He gets by with a low-90s fastball, average slider and fringy changeup. Wilson is often around the plate—too often, the latest thinking goes, as his missed locations tend to travel very quickly in the other direction. In order to limit how many of those mistakes land in the bullpen, he's likely to end up there himself.

Lineouts

Hitters

NAME	POS	TEAM	LVL	AGE	PA	R	2B	3B	HR	RBI	BB	K	SB	CS	AVG/OBP/SLG	TAv	BABIP	BRR	FRAA	WARP
Michael Almanzar	3B	PME	AA	23	188	18	9	0	5	25	12	39	2	0	.277/.356/.422	.274	.333	0.2	3B(39): 3.2, 1B(8): -0.4	1.4
Quintin Berry	LF	NOR	AAA	29	432	53	19	1	3	35	57	84	25	6	.285/.382/.367	.267	.359	-1.7	LF(76): 7.7, CF(23): 2.3	2.4
	LF	BAL	MLB	29	2	3	0	0	0	0	0	1	1	0	.000/.000/.000	-.006	.000	0.6	LF(3): 0.0, RF(1): -0.0	0.0
Alexi Casilla	2B	NOR	AAA	29	213	25	8	0	1	19	14	28	9	2	.264/.315/.320	.221	.302	2.0	2B(34): 2.1, SS(21): -1.9	0.1
	3B	BAL	MLB	29	4	0	0	0	0	0	0	1	0	0	.000/.000/.000	.021	.000	0.0	3B(1): -0.1, 2B(1): -0.0	-0.1
Steve Clevenger	C	NOR	AAA	28	254	28	13	0	2	30	23	30	1	0	.305/.366/.389	.259	.338	-2.4	C(48): 0.0, 1B(3): 0.1	0.5
	C	BAL	MLB	28	97	8	8	1	0	8	8	19	0	0	.225/.289/.337	.238	.286	-0.9	C(25): -0.1, 1B(3): -0.0	-0.1
Drew Dosch	3B	DEL	A	22	558	76	22	4	5	50	47	97	5	3	.314/.379/.404	.296	.381	-1.3	3B(120): -3.4	3.4
Jason Esposito	3B	FRD	A+	23	498	50	31	5	9	50	17	103	4	4	.272/.301/.417	.248	.327	-3.6	3B(118): 9.5	1.2
Ryan Flaherty	3B	BAL	MLB	27	312	33	15	1	7	32	22	68	1	0	.221/.288/.356	.241	.266	0.8	3B(43): 1.2, 2B(30): 1.0	0.6
Derrik Gibson	CF	PME	AA	24	340	49	15	3	2	26	38	54	8	7	.302/.390/.395	.293	.363	1.9	CF(40): -5.2, LF(18): 0.1	2.0
	2B	PAW	AAA	24	85	9	2	2	2	9	4	15	2	0	.244/.282/.397	.227	.270	0.0	2B(10): -0.8, CF(7): -0.7	-0.2
Josh Hart	CF	DEL	A	19	353	22	5	1	1	28	21	86	11	5	.255/.301/.285	.225	.339	-0.6	CF(85): -5.8	-0.9
Alex Hassan	RF	PAW	AAA	26	474	66	31	4	8	55	60	105	2	2	.287/.378/.426	.290	.369	-3.1	RF(66): 0.8, LF(24): 1.9	2.4
	RF	BOS	MLB	26	9	1	0	0	0	0	1	5	0	0	.125/.222/.125	.153	.333	0.0	RF(2): -0.2	-0.1
Adrian Marin	SS	FRD	A+	20	460	40	30	1	5	42	21	103	12	4	.232/.271/.341	.224	.292	-0.8	SS(115): -8.5	-0.9
Michael Ohlman	C	BOW	AA	23	454	40	25	1	2	33	43	86	0	0	.236/.310/.318	.242	.292	-2.4	C(91): 0.6	0.4
Jimmy Paredes	3B	OMA	AAA	25	280	37	18	4	5	36	11	78	17	1	.305/.332/.457	.273	.414	1.3	3B(28): 1.5, SS(14): -1.0	1.6
	3B	NOR	AAA	25	140	11	7	1	3	23	6	31	4	0	.258/.286/.394	.229	.310	0.7	3B(27): -2.6, 2B(5): -0.3	-0.3
	3B	BAL	MLB	25	55	9	4	0	2	8	2	13	2	0	.302/.327/.491	.296	.368	0.2	3B(13): 0.3, 2B(1): -0.0	0.4
	3B	KCA	MLB	25	10	3	0	0	0	0	0	3	2	0	.200/.200/.200	.162	.286	0.1	3B(3): -0.1, 2B(2): -0.0	-0.1
Henry Urrutia	RF	NOR	AAA	27	211	14	12	1	0	17	5	50	2	1	.270/.284/.338	.213	.353	0.1	RF(19): -0.1, LF(16): 1.4	-0.8

A Rule 5 pick by the Orioles, **Michael Almanzar** was returned to Boston in July, only to be reacquired by Baltimore as a non-Rule 5er in August. His ability to play all over the infield is a boon, but his bat makes him organizational depth. ❖ Senator **Quintin Berry** (Independent, Norfolk) is the primary sponsor of a bill that requires major-league teams carry at least one pinch-runner. ❖ The Orioles recalled **Alexi Casilla** in September and wish they could forget. ❖ Then there's **Steve Clevenger**, who, upon getting regular starts (as in the case of Matt Wieters' season-ending injury), inspires his club to immediately seek better alternatives (as in the case of Caleb Joseph & The Traveling Hundley). ❖ A sweet-swinging left-hander, **Drew Dosch** shows a good eye at the plate and pairs it with a low strikeout rate. He transfers his weight early at times, robbing himself of power, something he can't afford to do given the lack of loft in his swing. ❖ **Jason Esposito** improved across the board in 2014, but it was a repeat at the level and he lacks the power to compensate for his utter inability to walk. ❖ **Ryan Flaherty** is a six-position utilityman who looks most comfortable at second base but doesn't possess the batting chops to stay there daily. ❖ **Derrik Gibson** finally solved Double-A in his third stint at the level, but he has never lived up to the promise many saw when he was drafted in the second round in 2008. ❖ **Josh Hart**'s sub-70 percent success rate on stolen bases was by far his finest offensive achievement. ❖ If Daniel Nava is Jango Fett, **Alex Hassan** is a Stormtrooper, cut from the same cloth but lacking in originality and, as Boston finally allowed, totally disposable. ❖ It's starting to look like the triple **Adrian Marin** hit off of Joey Gallo at the NHSI tournament is going to be his most famous hitting highlight. A capable if not superlative defender at short, his offense took a step backward from an already tenuous position. ❖ At 6-feet-4, **Michael Ohlman** is a catcher in name only. He doesn't use his size well at the dish, and it hinders him behind it. ❖ Oft-waived utilityman **Jimmy Paredes** was claimed by three different teams last offseason, then repurchased by Baltimore; he strung a good month together and played in the postseason. He hasn't spent the majority of a season in the majors because the good months don't outweigh the lean ones. ❖ One of the more forgettable Cuban signees in recent memory, a sports hernia limited **Henry Urrutia** to 51 games and a sub-700 OPS at Triple-A.

Pitchers

NAME	TEAM	LVL	AGE	W	L	SV	G	GS	IP	H	HR	BB	K	BB/9	K/9	GB%	BABIP	WHIP	ERA	FIP	FRA	WARP
Parker Bridwell	FRD	A+	22	7	10	0	26	26	141²	123	11	70	142	4.4	9.0	41%	.299	1.36	4.45	4.20	5.07	0.7
Patrick Connaughton	ABE	A-	21	0	1	0	6	4	14²	13	0	3	10	1.8	6.1	58%	.271	1.09	2.45	2.90	3.74	0.3
Eddie Gamboa	BOW	AA	29	1	2	0	5	5	31	19	1	18	30	5.2	8.7	31%	.220	1.19	3.19	3.68	4.11	0.4
	NOR	AAA	29	4	5	0	14	12	77²	70	7	28	74	3.2	8.6	44%	.289	1.26	4.06	3.90	5.22	0.4
Mychal Givens	FRD	A+	24	1	2	3	18	0	33¹	21	2	16	27	4.3	7.3	62%	.202	1.11	3.24	4.30	5.76	-0.2
	BOW	AA	24	0	0	0	18	0	25¹	19	0	23	28	8.2	9.9	66%	.292	1.66	3.91	4.58	4.61	0.2
Jason Gurka	BOW	AA	26	3	1	0	30	3	64¹	50	4	18	60	2.5	8.4	63%	.261	1.06	2.38	3.23	4.75	0.7
Steve Johnson	NOR	AAA	26	0	2	0	13	13	38	47	9	30	32	7.1	7.6	32%	.322	2.03	7.11	7.28	7.83	-0.4
Branden Kline	FRD	A+	22	8	6	0	23	23	126²	143	9	32	95	2.3	6.8	47%	.332	1.38	3.84	3.77	4.58	1.1
	BOW	AA	22	0	2	0	3	3	16²	18	1	11	9	5.9	4.9	43%	.321	1.74	5.94	5.03	5.08	0.1
Patrick McCoy	ERI	AA	25	1	0	1	9	0	13²	16	0	3	9	2.0	5.9	54%	.333	1.39	3.95	2.70	3.96	0.2
	TOL	AAA	25	2	0	0	21	0	31¹	25	3	6	25	1.7	7.2	41%	.259	0.99	2.59	3.68	4.11	0.3
	DET	MLB	25	0	0	0	14	0	14	21	0	13	11	8.4	7.1	62%	.420	2.43	3.86	4.37	4.23	0.1
John Means	ABE	A-	21	1	3	0	10	9	37	42	1	2	33	0.5	7.9	43%	.357	1.19	3.41	2.41	2.82	1.0
Clay Rapada	TAC	AAA	33	4	1	0	19	0	19²	17	5	7	16	3.2	7.3	42%	.222	1.22	4.12	6.60	7.53	-0.3
	NOR	AAA	33	2	0	1	18	0	18²	28	2	7	12	3.4	5.8	31%	.382	1.88	7.23	4.59	5.10	0.0
Joe Saunders	OMA	AAA	33	1	2	0	4	4	18²	27	4	5	6	2.4	2.9	57%	.329	1.71	6.75	6.65	7.45	-0.3
	NOR	AAA	33	0	1	0	10	0	12	11	0	6	8	4.5	6.0	51%	.297	1.42	1.50	3.52	3.69	0.2
	ROU	AAA	33	0	1	0	2	2	12	15	1	5	8	3.8	6.0	64%	.368	1.67	2.25	4.70	3.96	0.3
	BAL	MLB	33	0	0	0	6	0	3¹	3	0	4	1	10.8	2.7	46%	.200	2.10	13.50	10.96	15.17	-0.3
	TEX	MLB	33	0	5	0	8	8	39²	62	8	20	22	4.5	5.0	48%	.367	2.07	6.13	6.26	6.46	-0.5
Mike Wright	NOR	AAA	24	5	11	0	26	26	142²	159	10	41	103	2.6	6.5	39%	.322	1.40	4.61	3.79	4.37	1.6
Suk-Min Yoon	NOR	AAA	27	4	8	0	23	18	95²	125	15	26	67	2.4	6.3	40%	.348	1.58	5.74	4.97	5.99	-0.4

Despite a name that sounds like a high-end fashion line, **Parker Bridwell** has pitched more like a knockoff. ❖ The Orioles have allowed fourth-rounder **Patrick Connaughton** to finish out his basketball career at Notre Dame before turning his full attention to the mound. He's got the raw ingredients for a mid-rotation starter, including the ability to touch the mid-90s. ❖ One of two players the Orioles actively turned into knuckle-ballers, **Eddie Gamboa** actually throws two of them. There's the slow one (65-69 MPH) and the fast one (75-80), and he complements them with a low-90s heater. He can start or relieve, and should be a useful piece as soon as 2015. ❖ At 24, **Mychal Givens** made the transition from strong-armed shortstop to minor-league pitcher. In one season on the bump he reached Double-A, a level he never achieved over four seasons as a position player. ❖ A third-rounder, and the Orioles' top pick in the 2014 draft, **Brian Gonzalez** lacks the typical projection associated with prep products. Standing 6-feet-3 and weighing 230 pounds, he boasts the polished repertoire to move quickly. ❖ Slight of build and short on premium stuff, **Jason Gurka** has that left-handed thing going for him. He fits in as bullpen depth, and could be an effective LOOGY thanks to the movement on his fastball, and good bite on his slider. ❖ **Steve Johnson** walked nearly as many as he struck out in Triple-A, failing to crack the major-league roster of a team that made a habit of shuttling relievers between the two levels in 2014. ❖ While he'll be tried as a starter for as long as possible, **Branden Kline**'s history and stuff point to a bullpen future. He profiles as a seventh-inning type when he does make the conversion. ❖ Left-handed reliever **Patrick McCoy** doesn't stand out in any great fashion other than showing control in the minors. Well, that and the cowboy name. ❖ A lanky lefty, **John Means** uses his height well, attacking with a low-90s fastball that features arm-side run, complementing it with a fringy changeup. It is currently unknown how seriously he takes his business. ❖ For the first time since 2006, we missed the side-sweeping left arm of **Clay Rapada,** who reposed among the tumbleweeds of two Triple-A cities. While there, he faced more righties than lefties. Did they even read the Clay Rapada instruction manual? ❖ **Johan Santana**'s comeback bid ended, ironically enough, on a comebacker; it hit off him and he tore his Achilles chasing it in extended spring training. He hasn't thrown a pitch in anger in more than two years; something tells us he has done lots of other things in anger in that absence. ❖ There is a strange man going from team to team pretending to be **Joe Saunders,** only worse. If you see him, call Major League Baseball and report him immediately, then grab a bat, because you're going to want to get in on this. ❖ Another big ERA filling out the Triple-A rotation for Baltimore, **Mike Wright** doesn't quite miss enough bats to remain a starter. That's not a bad thing; he'll get his pension as a reliever, eventually. ❖ Combine 15 homers allowed in 23 games with an inability to miss bats, and you'll receive **Suk-Min Yoon**'s rough debut season. The down year evened the Orioles' records on Asian imports, after they succeeded with Koji Uehara and Wei-Yin Chen and missed on Tsuyoshi Wada.

Manager

Buck Showalter

YEAR	TEAM	W	L	Py-thag +/-	Avg PC	100+ P	120+ P	QS	BQS	REL	REL w Zero R	IBB	PH	PH Avg	PH HR	SB2	CS2	SB3	CS3	SAC Att	SAC%	POS SAC	Squeeze	Swing	In Play
2012	BAL	93	69	11	95.6	66	1	78	6	492	415	36	69	0.161	0	55	21	3	8	51	74.5%	34	1	282	102
2013	BAL	85	77	0	95.9	75	0	78	5	473	380	32	65	0.143	0	70	26	9	2	39	69.2%	23	0	236	68
2014	BAL	96	66	1	97.9	80	1	78	7	479	405	25	74	0.308	2	37	16	6	3	56	62.5%	32	1	205	60

It's hard not to like Showalter. He owns multiple basset hounds, gives great quips (including this one about Michael Pineda's pine-tar usage, via MLB.com's Bryan Hoch: "Our guy's going to have it loaded down too, so I'm going to let them do whatever they want.") and grades as a good manager.

Showalter earned praise during the postseason for his aggressive managing of the bullpen. Much of that likely had to do with his distrust of a mediocre rotation, but the slick moves proved he was willing to approach the game in a bold, creative manner. Ditto for his decision to intentionally walk Nick Castellanos in the decisive game of the ALDS, thereby setting up a series-ending double-play ball.

For the most part, Showalter stayed true to his disdain for small ball during the regular season, as the Orioles ranked 30th in stolen bases and hit-and-runs. The exception was the seventh-most position-player sacrifices in the majors. Don't fear—the main offenders were David Lough, Ryan Flaherty, Caleb Joseph and Jonathan Schoop, four players who weren't offensive factors to begin with, meaning even when Showalter deigned he did so in a cost-effective way.

Although an appearance in the World Series remains overdue, it's nice to see Showalter managing deep into the postseason with a club he built—particularly after he missed the parades in New York and Arizona.

BOSTON RED SOX

by Tim Britton

"What is difficult is not to have been someone but to stay that way."
- Roger Martin du Gard

Why is success so difficult to sustain in Major League Baseball these days? I understand that this is an odd question to pose when the same franchise has won three of the last five World Series, but even the Giants' even-year reign has been hole-punched by odd-year mediocrity. One can, in fact, argue that San Francisco is the greatest inspiration for our query: Why hasn't a team good enough to win the World Series even contended for a playoff spot the year after? The Spurs and Devils had the decency to do that during their own drawn-out so-called dynasties.

The issue of sustenance is an especially pressing question for a Red Sox organization that has endured worst-to-first-to-worst vertigo these past 1,000 days. Boston's pinballing between poles has made it difficult to evaluate this slice of its history: In three years under GM Ben Cherington, the Red Sox have twice lost 90 or more games, which they hadn't done even once in the 45 seasons that preceded his promotion.

Of course, in the one other season, they won the World Series, with Cherington's wily offseason maneuvers among the primary reasons why. And entering 2014, it could be said that the Red Sox had seldom in their history been better positioned for more. They were coming off a third World Series title in a decade, they had two franchise icons locked into team-friendly deals that would likely keep each from ever wearing another uniform, and they possessed a farm system that even rebuilding teams would envy. On top of all that, their much-ballyhooed division was closer to Least than Beast on the spectrum of overused geographical puns.

Ahh, but from that spring whence comfort seemed to come, discomfort swelled, to cop some Shakespeare.

The Red Sox fell from 97 wins to 91 losses and a last-place finish. It was the worst title-defense effort in modern baseball history, so long as we don't count what the 1998 Marlins did as effort. Boston became only the third team in the past decade to lose 90 games the year after *making* the playoffs, let alone winning them.

How did that happen? We can actually try to compress any detailed conversation about the myriad differences between what went right in 2013 and what went wrong in 2014 into a simple comparison of the respective seasons of one Mike Carp.

2013: Designated by a Seattle team that would lose 91 games, Carp is acquired for cash considerations. In a reserve role, he slashes .296/.362/.523, or 120 points better in OPS than his Steamer projection. A year after getting hurt on Opening Day for the Mariners, Carp is healthy all season and thus becomes an incredible luxury on a team that leads the league in runs. He is totally fine with his relatively limited role, memorably slugging a pinch-hit grand slam to break a 10th-inning tie at the Trop. He starts Game Two of the ALCS instead of Mike Napoli, and this is completely justifiable.

2014: The subject of ample trade speculation in the spring because he is too good to be a mere bench player, Carp underperforms with Boston to the tune of .198/.320/.279, or 163 points worse in OPS than his Steamer projection. When Napoli goes on the disabled list on Memorial Day in Atlanta, an intrepid reporter asks Carp how much he is looking forward to seeing regular at-bats at first base. Carp defers comment until those at-bats actually came in an American League park, which they never do because he breaks his foot later that same afternoon—meaning he not only gets hurt this time around, but at the absolute worst moment. He does not hit any home runs, let alone memorable ones, for an offense bereft of pop. He is unhappy enough to request a trade once healthy and is DFA'd in July by the Sox, picked up by the Rangers and DFA'd again.

It's banal to say that everything went right in 2013 and everything went wrong in 2014—Clay Buchholz got hurt when he was 8-0 with a 1.62 ERA in June 2013, after all—but Carp can serve as shorthand for the preponderance of things that leaned in the right direction for a championship team one season and those that listed toward disaster a year later.

Worse yet, many of these negative developments aren't three-sigma data points to be written off as outliers. Dustin Pedroia hasn't hit for power in two years, and that universally lauded team-friendly extension doesn't seem like the same kind of bargain a year after we last checked in on it. Red Sox fans went from wanting Buchholz to pitch through whatever injury he had in 2013 to wanting Buchholz to concoct any injury possible to avoid

RED SOX PROSPECTUS
2014 W-L: 71-91, 5TH IN AL EAST

Pythag	0.445	25th	DER	.699	21st
RS/G	3.91	18th	B-Age	29.2	22nd
RA/G	4.41	24th	P-Age	29.5	26th
TAv	.254	25th	Salary	$151.9M	6th
BRR	-2.47	22nd	M$/MW	$6.2M	27th
TAv-P	.267	22nd	DL Days	606	6th
FIP	3.95	22nd	$ on DL	13%	11th

Three-Year Park Factors

Runs	Runs/RH	Runs/LH	HR/RH	HR/LH
103	101	105	78	75

Top Hitter WARP	3.6	Dustin Pedroia
Top Pitcher WARP	3.2	Jon Lester
Top Prospect		Blake Swihart

pitching in 2014. Jackie Bradley Jr., a highly rated prospect with a seemingly reliable floor, proceeded to occupy a Strangelovian mineshaft while posting the worst slugging percentage of anyone with 400 plate appearances since the strike.

These are developments that not only derail one season but alter expectations for the next. The Red Sox don't really know—can't really know?—what to reasonably project for players like Pedroia, like Buchholz, like Bradley and Xander Bogaerts and Mookie Betts and Allen Craig and the honest-to-goodness dozen starting pitchers whose talent level resides somewhere between (inclusively) Triple-A and the majors. It's no wonder that, when he appeared at the annual Saber Seminar in Boston in August, Cherington focused on the topic of projections, of finding a way to operate more consistently on their higher end than the organization did throughout 2014.

If we've summarized the how, the why remains opaque: What caused the Red Sox to go so wrong? Our most interesting failures are the unexpected, seemingly inexplicable ones, which is what makes this Boston downfall more intriguing than, say, that of the Philadelphia 76ers. (We know why the Sixers are bad.)

The Red Sox probably should have compiled better backup plans behind Bogaerts, Bradley and Will Middlebrooks. But then again, it's not particularly easy to convince a reliable veteran to sign and sit, and often those guys don't work out well either (see Mark Ellis' season in St. Louis or Craig Gentry's in Oakland). A full season of Stephen Drew—the simplest and most expensive insurance policy—wouldn't have saved anything.

Certainly Boston should have more aggressively pursued an extension with Jon Lester. On the one hand, writing on this side of the 2014 season surely makes it easier to forget that, two-thirds of the way through 2013, Lester's ERA was just about a run higher than Felix Doubront's. On the other, even Gobias Industries thought four years and $70 million was a bad negotiating tactic. This poor personnel decision, though, affected 2015 and beyond more than it did the on-field performance in 2014: The Sox were in last place even before they traded Lester and John Lackey.

How, then, to explain a descent in the standings worthy of Hieronymous Bosch? Why did a Red Sox team that brought back so much from its championship-winning core and which wasn't the victim of obvious mismanagement suffer such collective regression?

Is the best answer to this a shrug and the old managerial standby of *That's baseball?*

Maybe it is, in fact, what baseball has become. To steal more Shakespeare, Major League Baseball has suffered a sea change into something rich and strange. In essence, it's becoming the NFL, with parity upsetting what had been a rather rigid hierarchy a little more than a decade ago.

For two decades, the safest way of predicting an NFL season has been to take half of the previous year's dozen playoff teams and throw them out of the picture: The league averaged roughly a 50 percent turnover in postseason participants. In the first decade of baseball's wild card era, such turnover happened only periodically; you could pretty much write the Yankees, Red Sox, Indians and Braves into your playoff bracket before Opening Day.

Over the past nine years, though, playoff turnover has soared in MLB. In each season during that time period, at least half of the previous year's playoff teams have missed the tournament. From 1995-2005, a team that made the playoffs one season made it the next about 60 percent of the time. Since then, it's 42 percent. This has happened while the other three major North American sports

have shown only minor and probably negligible movement in that same direction, as you can see in the table below.

Percentage of Returning Playoff Teams				
	MLB	**NFL**	**NBA**	**NHL**
1995-2005	59.8	52.5	76.2	72.5
2006-2014	42.3	50.9	74.3	69.5

There are reasons for this, although we'd probably all divide the pie graph differently. The rising tide of revenue across baseball since the 2006 Collective Bargaining Agreement has left fewer have-nots, and closed the gap between them and the haves. To wit: In 2004, the median payroll across MLB was barely $60 million. Last season, it crossed into nine figures for the first time. There are now only a half-dozen franchises yet to sport a $100 million payroll in any one season. The top has risen, too, though more slowly: The three highest spenders in 2014 dished out 52 percent more cash than they did in 2004. The median, meanwhile, is 71 percent higher than it was back in '04.

One can see the particular impact this might have on the Red Sox and their big-spending brethren in the Bronx; even as Boston and New York's payrolls have grown over the past decade-plus, they've grown at a slower rate than that of their competitors. The Red Sox have seen their payroll go from $125 million in 2004 to $163 million this past season, a growth of 30 percent. The Yankees spent only 12 percent more in 2014 than they did a decade earlier.

Meanwhile, the Brewers, Tigers and Nationals increased their payroll threefold in that time span. An additional eight franchises have more than doubled what they spend on players. The average payroll of AL East rivals Baltimore, Tampa Bay and Toronto has grown 142 percent.

Furthermore, even if Boston elected to increase its payroll at a greater rate and go beyond the competitive balance tax for the first time since 2011, the marginal benefits for doing so have diminished. As more and more teams are able to buy out the free-agent years of their best players, the open market can price-gouge worse than the Kwik-E-Mart.

Imagine, for instance, how much different the dynamic would have been this winter had Clayton Kershaw, Evan Longoria and Carlos Gonzalez—each of them with six years of service time to date—all been free agents, and if Miami's chances of re-signing Giancarlo Stanton were as remote as we had all assumed they were from the start.

Finally, front offices are not only smarter, but smarter in the same way. There is a uniformity of approach across the game, such that locating marginal advantages has become more difficult with each passing year. Take Cherington, from the spring:

"The other thing that's changed, I think, is every front office is full of competent people. There are smart, hard-working people everywhere. Every team in baseball is trying to gain an advantage some way that fits their model or fits their market, whereas 20 years ago, teams were trying to gain an advantage mostly through player analysis—trying to find value in the player market with undervalued players.... So you have to continue to find other ways to gain an advantage. I think teams are just looking through a broader lens in where they're trying to gain an advantage."

We think of this intellectual flattening as a disadvantage to smart small-market clubs, who lose one weapon to overcoming their payroll destiny, but it's a threat to outright dominance by any team, rich or poor. In the past, Boston's payroll and front-office advantage meant that good but flawed Red Sox teams—hello, 2005 iteration and ALDS Game One starter Matt Clement—had enough margin for error to feast on the AL's downtrodden. From 1998 through 2007—The Devil Ray Era—Boston won 60 percent of its games against Baltimore, Tampa Bay and Toronto.

In the seven seasons and 384 contests since, the Sox are but six games over .500 against that triumvirate. The margin for error isn't gone, but it has lost a lot of weight.

The funny thing is that it was this exact environment of flux that allowed the Red Sox to rise from the ashes of 2012 in the first place. They didn't have to climb over the kind of behemoth Yankees team that so often stood in their way in the late 1990s and early aughts, since the Yankees have to deal with the same issues as the Sox. Boston's bottoming out so completely in both

2012 and 2014 allowed it to commence the revamping process mid-season—an example where knowing you're bad is better than pretending you're not.

While we like to think that league-wide parity mainly props up and peddles hope to the Pittsburghs of the world, the last few years have shown it can be just as helpful and just as motivating to those by the Bay and in the Bay State. Which is kind of what makes the past two World Series champs the perfect emblems of this time in baseball, what with teams riding a compressed sine wave of performance. Parity works both ways: What makes it easier to fall back to the pack also lowers the escape velocity for breaking away again. That's baseball. ■

—Tim Britton is the Red Sox beat writer for the Providence Journal.

Player comments by Ben Carsley and Baseball Prospectus Authors

Hitters ────────────────────────────────

Mookie Betts   2B

Born: 10/7/92   Age: 22   Bats: R   Throws: R   Height: 5' 9"   Weight: 155

YEAR	TEAM	LVL	AGE	PA	R	2B	3B	HR	RBI	BB	K	SB	CS	AVG/OBP/SLG	TAv	BABIP	BRR	FRAA	WARP
2012	LOW	A-	19	292	34	8	1	0	31	32	30	20	4	.267/.352/.307	.293	.298	2.2	2B(58): 1.0, SS(13): 1.5	2.6
2013	GRN	A	20	340	63	24	1	8	26	58	40	18	2	.296/.418/.477	.329	.322	4.7	2B(76): -4.0	3.4
2013	SLM	A+	20	211	30	12	3	7	39	23	17	20	2	.341/.414/.551	.331	.346	3.0	2B(50): 7.1	3.5
2014	PME	AA	21	253	56	18	3	6	34	35	20	22	3	.355/.443/.551	.346	.366	6.2	2B(40): 1.4, CF(12): 0.8	3.9
2014	PAW	AAA	21	211	31	12	2	5	31	26	30	11	4	.335/.417/.503	.317	.380	2.4	CF(33): 0.0, 2B(6): 0.1	2.1
2014	BOS	MLB	21	213	34	12	1	5	18	21	31	7	3	.291/.368/.444	.300	.327	3.2	CF(28): -1.6, 2B(14): -0.5	1.7
2015	BOS	MLB	22	293	40	16	1	5	27	31	45	13	3	.281/.358/.415	.291	.318	2.4	2B 1, CF -1	2.1

Breakout: 4%   Improve: 40%   Collapse: 8%   Attrition: 13%   MLB: 69%   Comparables: Daric Barton, Oscar Taveras, Colby Rasmus

There must be something Betts can't do on a baseball diamond—pitch, catch, groundskeeping—but he hasn't revealed his limitations yet. Betts was unfathomably good in Portland and Pawtucket in 2014, forcing his way to the big leagues despite starting the year with no experience above High-A. He hit for more power than he had previously shown, successfully stole bases at a high clip at every level and maintained his patient approach in the majors. Betts even handled a move from second base to center field, spent some time in right field, then without skipping a beat moved back to second base when Dustin Pedroia was injured. He is a potential franchise cornerstone because he has no weaknesses, and he plays with an understated swagger that tells you he knows how good he is. This is going to be a really, really fun career to watch.

Xander Bogaerts   SS

Born: 10/1/92   Age: 22   Bats: R   Throws: R   Height: 6' 1"   Weight: 210

YEAR	TEAM	LVL	AGE	PA	R	2B	3B	HR	RBI	BB	K	SB	CS	AVG/OBP/SLG	TAv	BABIP	BRR	FRAA	WARP
2012	SLM	A+	19	435	59	27	3	15	64	43	85	4	4	.302/.378/.505	.306	.353	-2.0	SS(98): -7.1	3.3
2012	PME	AA	19	97	12	10	0	5	17	1	21	1	1	.326/.351/.598	.325	.373	-1.4	SS(21): 2.8	1.2
2013	PME	AA	20	259	40	12	6	6	35	35	51	5	1	.311/.407/.502	.324	.378	1.9	SS(47): -3.1	2.4
2013	PAW	AAA	20	256	32	11	0	9	32	28	44	2	2	.284/.369/.453	.285	.320	1.5	SS(49): -5.9, 3B(10): -0.7	1.2
2013	BOS	MLB	20	50	7	2	0	1	5	5	13	1	0	.250/.320/.364	.300	.323	1.1	3B(9): -0.4, SS(8): 0.9	0.5
2014	BOS	MLB	21	594	60	28	1	12	46	39	138	2	3	.240/.297/.362	.247	.296	3.0	SS(99): -5.3, 3B(44): -2.6	0.7
2015	BOS	MLB	22	511	52	25	2	12	57	39	118	3	2	.256/.318/.397	.271	.314	2.3	SS -3, 3B -2	2.1

Breakout: 3%   Improve: 50%   Collapse: 2%   Attrition: 15%   MLB: 79%   Comparables: Troy Tulowitzki, B.J. Upton, Eric Hosmer

No Red Sox regular better represented man's hubris in a dark and dismal 2014 season than Bogaerts. He was The Savior, The Chosen One. He was to bring balance and a long-term solution to the shortstop position for the first time since Boston's last wunderkind, Nomar Garciaparra, left town in 2004. After watching Bogaerts excel in the postseason in 2013, it seemed unfathomable he'd do anything but take the league by storm. He did indeed show flashes of that player in 2014, but overall his rookie campaign was a major disappointment. He struck out in nearly a quarter of his plate appearances. He hit just .143 against sliders, per Brooks Baseball. He made several errors that ended up costing the Red Sox games. And he appeared mentally unequipped to handle a temporary move from shortstop to third base, giving sports talk radio admirers in Boston even more ammunition against the Drew family. Of course, it wasn't *all* bad. Bogaerts hit quite well in April, May and September, slammed 12 homers and appeared to make defensive progress as the season went on. But while he's hardly the first young player to be humbled by the game of baseball, Bogaerts left us with more questions than he answered. He's still arguably the most important player in Boston's organization, and his ceiling remains statue-outside-of-Fenway high. But it's time to stop putting the cart before the horse, and let Bogaerts prove he can start every day for a first-division team before anointing him Garciaparra's spiritual successor.

Jackie Bradley   CF

Born: 4/19/90   Age: 25   Bats: L   Throws: R   Height: 5' 10"   Weight: 195

YEAR	TEAM	LVL	AGE	PA	R	2B	3B	HR	RBI	BB	K	SB	CS	AVG/OBP/SLG	TAv	BABIP	BRR	FRAA	WARP
2012	SLM	A+	22	304	53	26	2	3	34	52	40	16	6	.359/.480/.526	.365	.407	0.3	CF(66): 1.5, RF(1): -0.1	4.5
2012	PME	AA	22	271	37	16	2	6	29	35	49	8	3	.271/.373/.437	.291	.316	-2.4	CF(48): -0.0	1.4
2013	PAW	AAA	23	374	57	26	3	10	35	41	75	7	7	.275/.374/.469	.302	.331	0.1	CF(58): 3.0, RF(7): 0.4	3.3
2013	BOS	MLB	23	107	18	5	0	3	10	10	31	2	0	.189/.280/.337	.236	.246	-2.2	CF(19): 0.5, LF(14): -0.1	-0.3
2014	PAW	AAA	24	69	6	1	0	1	5	3	18	0	1	.212/.246/.273	.186	.277	0.3	CF(14): 0.7	-0.1
2014	BOS	MLB	24	423	45	19	2	1	30	31	121	8	0	.198/.265/.266	.198	.284	0.4	CF(113): 10.0, RF(12): -0.2	0.0
2015	BOS	MLB	25	389	44	21	2	5	31	36	96	7	2	.234/.315/.345	.252	.305	-1.5	CF 5, RF -0	1.1

Breakout: 6%   Improve: 45%   Collapse: 12%   Attrition: 32%   MLB: 82%   Comparables: *Ryan Kalish, Brian Anderson, Andre Ethier*

After watching years of baseball, one gains a sense as to when a batted ball *should* be caught, *could* be caught or *won't* be caught. Throw all of that out the window with Bradley; he catches balls your brain tells you will fall in for hits, and he does so with what looks like a profound lack of urgency. Indeed, Bradley's diving plays often aren't his best. Rather, it's the plays in which he perfectly syncs himself with a ball's flight path, and tracks down liners you were *sure* were going to fall for extra-base hits. His jumps are so good it looks like he's reacting to premonitions, and he has enough speed to cover decent ground. When you couple those traits with his plus-plus arm, you get a potentially generational talent in center field.

Yet while Bradley's defense wows like a Michael Bay action sequence, his at-bats are like a Michael Bay plot. An adjustment to his swing in July allowed him to hit .339/.391/.424 over an 18-game span, but that was the lone offensive bright spot in his 2014 season. Shortly after a demotion to Triple-A in August, reports surfaced that the Red Sox viewed Bradley as stubborn and unwilling to change his approach. That flies in the face of his reputation as a high-makeup prospect, but would help explain how Bradley remained so awful at the plate for so long.

It will be a tremendous shame if Bradley's bat robs fans of the chance to watch him roam the outfield on a daily basis, because he is a truly breathtaking defender in center field. But as of now, he's hopeless against left-handed pitchers and anyone with a half-decent breaking ball. His dazzling defensive displays don't absolve him of all offensive responsibility. They do give him a much longer leash than most, thank heavens.

Rusney Castillo   CF

Born: 9/7/87   Age: 27   Bats: R   Throws: R   Height: 5' 8"   Weight: 186

YEAR	TEAM	LVL	AGE	PA	R	2B	3B	HR	RBI	BB	K	SB	CS	AVG/OBP/SLG	TAv	BABIP	BRR	FRAA	WARP
2014	BOS	MLB	26	40	6	1	0	2	6	3	6	3	0	.333/.400/.528	.319	.357	0.7	CF(10): 0.8	0.6
2015	BOS	MLB	27	250	32	12	1	7	28	20	45	9	2	.272/.338/.428	.287	.310	0.6	CF 3	1.8

Breakout: 4%   Improve: 52%   Collapse: 8%   Attrition: 11%   MLB: 100%   Comparables: *Chet Lemon, Adam Jones, Cesar Cedeno*

Castillo's seven-year, $72.5 million contract is sure to lead to some unreasonable expectations, but the truth is the Red Sox didn't sign him to be a superstar. Instead, his acquisition represents an acknowledgement that the Red Sox needed more MLB-ready talent if they are to compete in 2015 and 2016, and Castillo will help on that front. We can't be entirely sure what to expect from the Cuban, but even a brief glimpse at his abilities last season tells us that he's a plus to plus-plus defensive center fielder, and that he has enough pop to keep pitchers honest. He's not terribly fast down the line, but he's an excellent runner underway and a legitimate threat to steal bases. Castillo would likely be miscast in a leadoff role, but he's a luxury to a team if he bats in the lower third of the order, and he has the athleticism and tools to be a first-division starter.

Garin Cecchini   3B

Born: 4/20/91   Age: 24   Bats: L   Throws: R   Height: 6' 3"   Weight: 220

YEAR	TEAM	LVL	AGE	PA	R	2B	3B	HR	RBI	BB	K	SB	CS	AVG/OBP/SLG	TAv	BABIP	BRR	FRAA	WARP
2012	GRN	A	21	526	84	38	4	4	62	61	90	51	6	.305/.394/.433	.278	.371	6.8	3B(99): -2.3	3.1
2013	SLM	A+	22	262	44	19	4	5	33	43	34	15	7	.350/.469/.547	.349	.400	2.2	3B(59): -8.2	2.9
2013	PME	AA	22	295	36	14	3	2	28	51	52	8	2	.296/.420/.404	.312	.367	0.6	3B(44): 3.4	3.2
2014	PAW	AAA	23	458	52	21	1	7	57	44	99	11	1	.263/.341/.371	.257	.331	2.0	3B(84): -3.4, LF(26): -0.0	1.0
2014	BOS	MLB	23	36	6	3	0	1	4	3	11	0	0	.258/.361/.452	.313	.368	-0.5	3B(9): -0.5	0.3
2015	BOS	MLB	24	250	25	13	1	2	22	25	58	6	1	.251/.333/.345	.259	.327	0.4	3B -2, LF 0	0.4

Breakout: 2%   Improve: 10%   Collapse: 9%   Attrition: 16%   MLB: 31%   Comparables: *Zach Lutz, James Darnell, Eric Campbell*

Ask one scout and here's a fringy second-division player without no true plus tool. Ask another, and now Cecchini is a first-division threat, an adequate man at the hot corner and the Italian God of Walks at the plate. Cecchini's poor performance during the middle months of 2014 pushed the prospect community's deviations still further. Some contend there are real holes in Cecchini's swing that were exploited from Mayday on, a three-month stretch in which he hit .220/292/.318 in Pawtucket. Others reference Cecchini's solid bookends, and write off the mid-season struggles as a typical developmental hiccup for a 23-year-old getting his first taste of Triple-A. No matter where you stand, Cecchini has an admittedly odd profile for a third baseman. He's not likely to hit for a lot of power and isn't terribly athletic. But believers in the hit tool see someone who can challenge for a .290 average with a strong walk rate and enough pop to keep pitchers honest. What they all agree on: He's got plus-plus makeup and seems likely to get the most out of his natural abilities.

Michael Chavis   SS

Born: 8/11/95   Age: 19   Bats: R   Throws: R   Height: 5' 10"   Weight: 190

YEAR	TEAM	LVL	AGE	PA	R	2B	3B	HR	RBI	BB	K	SB	CS	AVG/OBP/SLG	TAv	BABIP	BRR	FRAA	WARP
2015	BOS	MLB	19	250	18	10	1	2	19	12	76	3	2	.198/.239/.268	.193	.279	-0.2	3B -0, SS 0	-1.1

Breakout: 0%   Improve: 0%   Collapse: 0%   Attrition: 0%   MLB: 0%   Comparables: *Maikel Franco, Josh Vitters, Matt Davidson*

The 26th overall pick last June, Chavis is another athletic player with a plus hit tool in a farm system that has graduated several such talents in recent years. Currently a shortstop, he profiles best as a third baseman or second baseman down the line. The bat will make such a move acceptable. With quick wrists, athleticism and more power than his stature would suggest, Chavis has the ingredients to hit for a good average and for meaningful power. Like most high school picks, Chavis will take time to advance to the majors, but the potential payoff is a first-division starter, with offensive comps ranging from Martin Prado to Clint Frazier to "dear god, stop making comparisons, he's 19 years old."

Sean Coyle   2B

Born: 1/17/92   Age: 23   Bats: R   Throws: R   Height: 5' 8"   Weight: 175

YEAR	TEAM	LVL	AGE	PA	R	2B	3B	HR	RBI	BB	K	SB	CS	AVG/OBP/SLG	TAv	BABIP	BRR	FRAA	WARP
2012	SLM	A+	20	484	60	31	2	9	63	29	116	16	0	.249/.316/.391	.258	.317	0.9	2B(111): 7.3	2.2
2013	GRN	A	21	28	4	3	0	1	4	3	9	0	1	.320/.393/.560	.282	.467	-0.4	2B(5): -0.3	0.1
2013	SLM	A+	21	224	41	9	1	14	28	24	65	11	0	.241/.321/.513	.286	.275	4.2	2B(36): -0.6	1.7
2014	PME	AA	22	384	60	23	1	16	61	38	95	13	1	.295/.371/.512	.311	.362	0.8	2B(61): -0.8, 3B(18): -2.0	3.1
2015	BOS	MLB	23	250	30	11	0	7	25	17	76	5	0	.227/.288/.374	.250	.302	0.5	2B 1, 3B -1	0.5

Breakout: 2%   Improve: 15%   Collapse: 2%   Attrition: 8%   MLB: 35%   Comparables: Josh Barfield, George Springer, Mark Reynolds

Coyle is such a scrappy, dirt dog-type player that it's a miracle Kevin Towers never found a way to trade for him. His size belies a compact swing with legitimate pop behind it, and while injuries continued to plague him in 2014 he stayed on the field often enough to show off an intriguing power/speed combination. A second baseman by trade, Coyle saw some time at third base in 2014 but doesn't have the arm to profile as an everyday player there. At present he lacks the defensive versatility to project as a utility infielder in the majors, but could hit his way toward a role as a second-division starter at the keystone, where he'll be compared to Dustin Pedroia every day of his career.

Allen Craig   1B

Born: 7/18/84   Age: 30   Bats: R   Throws: R   Height: 6' 2"   Weight: 215

YEAR	TEAM	LVL	AGE	PA	R	2B	3B	HR	RBI	BB	K	SB	CS	AVG/OBP/SLG	TAv	BABIP	BRR	FRAA	WARP
2012	SLN	MLB	27	514	76	35	0	22	92	37	89	2	1	.307/.354/.522	.306	.334	-3.6	1B(91): -7.5, RF(23): -0.3	1.7
2013	SLN	MLB	28	563	71	29	2	13	97	40	100	2	0	.315/.373/.457	.297	.368	-2.5	1B(95): 1.5, LF(25): -0.6	2.3
2014	BOS	MLB	29	107	7	3	0	1	2	9	36	1	0	.128/.234/.191	.177	.193	-0.2	1B(17): 0.9, RF(12): 0.1	-0.8
2014	SLN	MLB	29	398	34	17	1	7	44	26	77	1	1	.237/.291/.346	.234	.281	-3.6	RF(70): -4.4, 1B(24): 1.2	-1.2
2015	BOS	MLB	30	487	52	28	1	12	58	37	99	2	1	.270/.330/.421	.281	.318	-2.5	1B -1, RF -3	1.0

Breakout: 2%   Improve: 42%   Collapse: 2%   Attrition: 16%   MLB: 97%   Comparables: Xavier Nady, Ben Francisco, Ryan Church

Craig was quite good from 2011-2013. That seems to be the entire basis for the theory that he's a solid rebound candidate moving forward; he's done it before. That's all well and good, but where can we reasonably expect Craig to improve? Even before his rough 2014, Craig's power took a nosedive in 2013, masked only by his ridiculous performance with runners in scoring position. He's been hitting the ball on the ground more for three consecutive years, and he'll be 31 for much of the 2015 season. Sandwich Craig's worsening batted ball trends between his Maginot Line out-fielding and his litany of injuries, and it's tough to be terribly optimistic that he'll be anything but optimistically terrible.

Rafael Devers   3B

Born: 10/24/96   Age: 18   Bats: L   Throws: R   Height: 6' 0"   Weight: 195

YEAR	TEAM	LVL	AGE	PA	R	2B	3B	HR	RBI	BB	K	SB	CS	AVG/OBP/SLG	TAv	BABIP	BRR	FRAA	WARP
2015	BOS	MLB	18	250	17	9	1	3	20	10	75	0	0	.197/.234/.275	.193	.272	-0.4	3B 4	-0.8

Breakout: 0%   Improve: 0%   Collapse: 0%   Attrition: 0%   MLB: 0%   Comparables: Josh Vitters, Maikel Franco, Alex Liddi

In his first professional season, Devers wasted no time showing why he was regarded as one of the 2013 international signing period's best prospects. Younger than the Tampa Bay Rays franchise and with a sweet, left-handed swing that promises power, Devers laid waste to the Dominican Summer League before helping lead Boston's GCL affiliate to a championship. He hit for power and average and controlled the strike zone, and while he might eventually outgrow third base he has the instincts and arm for the position. Despite the bevy of young talent they've nurtured, the Red Sox have struggled to develop reliable sources of power in recent years. Devers is still three to five years away from the majors, but he has a chance to buck that trend.

Ryan Hanigan   C

Born: 8/16/80   Age: 34   Bats: R   Throws: R   Height: 6' 0"   Weight: 210

YEAR	TEAM	LVL	AGE	PA	R	2B	3B	HR	RBI	BB	K	SB	CS	AVG/OBP/SLG	TAv	BABIP	BRR	FRAA	WARP
2012	CIN	MLB	31	371	25	14	0	2	24	44	37	0	0	.274/.365/.338	.258	.302	0.8	C(110): -0.2	2.3
2013	CIN	MLB	32	260	17	8	0	2	21	29	27	0	1	.198/.306/.261	.219	.216	-1.1	C(72): 0.9	0.2
2014	PCH	A+	33	24	4	0	0	1	2	2	3	0	0	.250/.375/.400	.294	.250	-0.1	C(3): -0.0	0.1
2014	TBA	MLB	33	263	18	9	0	5	34	31	39	1	0	.218/.318/.324	.248	.240	-1.6	C(79): -0.6	0.7
2015	BOS	MLB	34	251	24	9	0	2	20	28	31	0	0	.241/.336/.311	.259	.268	-0.3	C -0	0.9

Breakout: 2%   Improve: 28%   Collapse: 8%   Attrition: 13%   MLB: 87%   Comparables: Jason Kendall, Paul Lo Duca, Carlos Ruiz

In search of a catcher to take some of the pressure off Jose Molina, the Rays traded for Hanigan—taking on the salary of Heath Bell in the process—and gave him a three-year extension before he put on his chest protector. For the most part, the backstop performed as advertised. He was close to the league average with the bat and handled the pitching staff expertly. He remains an excellent receiver and blocker. His caught-stealing rate dropped but the Rays' staff is not known for its ability to hold runners. Many predicted a drop in walks as he moved from batting eighth in the National League to the bottom of an American League lineup, but as it turns out, Hanigan just has a good feel for balls and strikes and walked at a rate in line with his career norms. The biggest disappointment from his season in Tampa Bay was the 60-plus days spent on the disabled list with hamstring and oblique injuries. He'll be veteran leadership to a young Boston catching corps this year.

Brock Holt   UT

Born: 6/11/88   Age: 27   Bats: L   Throws: R   Height: 5' 10"   Weight: 185

YEAR	TEAM	LVL	AGE	PA	R	2B	3B	HR	RBI	BB	K	SB	CS	AVG/OBP/SLG	TAv	BABIP	BRR	FRAA	WARP
2012	ALT	AA	24	432	52	24	6	2	43	40	51	11	11	.322/.389/.432	.291	.364	-0.6	SS(98): 0.5	3.2
2012	IND	AAA	24	106	13	7	0	1	7	9	9	5	2	.432/.476/.537	.362	.465	1.0	2B(14): 1.0, SS(9): 0.3	1.7
2012	PIT	MLB	24	72	6	2	1	0	3	4	14	0	0	.292/.329/.354	.249	.365	-0.6	2B(14): 0.2	0.0
2013	PAW	AAA	25	329	35	6	0	3	24	30	54	8	3	.258/.327/.309	.244	.303	-0.1	2B(44): -4.0, SS(32): -1.8	-0.2
2013	BOS	MLB	25	72	9	2	0	0	11	7	4	1	0	.203/.275/.237	.230	.207	0.7	3B(20): -0.9, 2B(5): 0.0	0.0
2014	PAW	AAA	26	121	21	8	1	2	7	8	12	7	1	.315/.380/.454	.304	.344	0.5	SS(19): -0.7, 2B(4): 1.5	1.3
2014	BOS	MLB	26	492	68	23	5	4	29	33	98	12	2	.281/.331/.381	.261	.349	3.8	3B(39): 0.9, RF(35): 0.9	1.6
2015	BOS	MLB	27	436	48	21	3	2	33	31	76	10	3	.277/.330/.364	.260	.327	1.4	3B -0, SS -0	1.3

| Breakout: 5% | Improve: 32% | Collapse: 10% | Attrition: 25% | MLB: 77% | | *Comparables:* | *Luis Valbuena, Brent Morel, Jordan Pacheco* |

Don't read the comments—unless you're Brock Holt. With a grind-it-out attitude that makes high school coaches weak in the knees, Holt's the sort of player the casual fan always wants to see more of—a superutility type who is always just the spark the lineup needs, if you ask me. After tearing the cover off the ball for the better part of three months, Holt came crashing down to earth in the second half, hitting just .253/.305/.333 from July 1st onward. He's not a starter for a first-division team, but Holt has transformed himself from a Quad-A guy to one of the more intriguingly versatile players in the league. He also has a glorious, glorious head of hair.

Manuel Margot CF

Born: 9/28/94 Age: 20 Bats: R Throws: R Height: 5' 11" Weight: 170

YEAR	TEAM	LVL	AGE	PA	R	2B	3B	HR	RBI	BB	K	SB	CS	AVG/OBP/SLG	TAv	BABIP	BRR	FRAA	WARP
2013	LOW	A-	18	216	29	8	2	1	21	22	40	18	8	.270/.346/.351	.283	.333	2.9	CF(47): 10.5	2.4
2014	GRN	A	19	413	61	20	5	10	45	37	49	39	13	.286/.355/.449	.283	.309	2.8	CF(96): 11.7	4.0
2014	SLM	A+	19	56	4	5	0	2	14	2	5	3	2	.340/.364/.560	.313	.333	0.0	CF(16): -0.1	0.5
2015	*BOS*	*MLB*	*20*	*250*	*28*	*10*	*1*	*4*	*21*	*14*	*54*	*13*	*6*	*.229/.277/.333*	*.230*	*.277*	*0.8*	*CF 6, RF 0*	*0.7*

| Breakout: 0% | Improve: 0% | Collapse: 0% | Attrition: 0% | MLB: 0% | | *Comparables:* | *Cedric Hunter, Aaron Hicks, Fernando Martinez* |

Once upon a time, "Manny being Manny" in Boston meant a home run, some GIF-worthy defensive butchery or a piss break behind a major landmark. Margot has a chance to add a bit more refinement to the phrase some day. The 20-year-old burst onto the prospect scene in 2014, hitting for average with some power and stealing 42 bases between Greenville and Salem. His best tool, though, is his glove, as he impresses with his instincts and range in center field. Margot is still a few years away from the majors, but he has the tools to profile as a top-of-the-order hitter who brings a plus glove to a premium defensive position if it all clicks.

Deven Marrero SS

Born: 8/25/90 Age: 24 Bats: R Throws: R Height: 6' 1" Weight: 195

YEAR	TEAM	LVL	AGE	PA	R	2B	3B	HR	RBI	BB	K	SB	CS	AVG/OBP/SLG	TAv	BABIP	BRR	FRAA	WARP
2012	LOW	A-	21	284	45	14	3	2	24	34	48	24	6	.268/.358/.374	.291	.325	2.3	SS(29): 1.0	2.0
2013	SLM	A+	22	376	50	20	0	2	21	42	60	21	2	.256/.341/.334	.238	.307	-0.5	SS(85): 5.2	1.3
2013	PME	AA	22	85	7	0	0	0	5	10	16	6	0	.236/.321/.236	.229	.293	1.9	SS(19): 4.4	0.8
2014	PME	AA	23	307	42	19	2	5	39	34	57	12	7	.291/.371/.433	.290	.349	-1.3	SS(66): -3.7	1.9
2014	PAW	AAA	23	202	23	11	0	1	20	12	37	4	1	.210/.260/.285	.190	.255	0.7	SS(50): -1.4	-0.7
2015	*BOS*	*MLB*	*24*	*250*	*26*	*12*	*0*	*1*	*16*	*20*	*57*	*7*	*2*	*.226/.290/.300*	*.228*	*.291*	*0.3*	*SS 1*	*0.4*

| Breakout: 2% | Improve: 7% | Collapse: 4% | Attrition: 19% | MLB: 20% | | *Comparables:* | *Ehire Adrianza, Nick Noonan, Dean Anna* |

The Red Sox are clearly believers in the age-old adage, "You can never have enough defensively gifted middle infielders from Arizona State." Marrero was a known quantity as a standout defender when drafted in the first round in 2012, and he's lived up to that reputation throughout his minor-league career. His bat was less of a sure thing, and so it remains after a season in which Marrero crushed Double-A pitching but found himself at the mercy of Triple-A arms. Marrero will reach the majors in some capacity because of his glove, but he'll need to hit more and improve his baserunning (66 percent stolen base success rate) if he wants to be more than a utility infielder.

Mike Napoli 1B

Born: 10/31/81 Age: 33 Bats: R Throws: R Height: 6' 0" Weight: 220

YEAR	TEAM	LVL	AGE	PA	R	2B	3B	HR	RBI	BB	K	SB	CS	AVG/OBP/SLG	TAv	BABIP	BRR	FRAA	WARP
2012	TEX	MLB	30	417	53	9	2	24	56	56	125	1	0	.227/.343/.469	.287	.273	0.5	C(72): 1.1, 1B(28): -0.5	2.6
2013	BOS	MLB	31	578	79	38	2	23	92	73	187	1	1	.259/.360/.482	.294	.367	-0.3	1B(131): 3.2	2.7
2014	BOS	MLB	32	500	49	20	0	17	55	78	133	3	2	.248/.370/.419	.294	.321	-1.8	1B(110): 0.2	2.0
2015	*BOS*	*MLB*	*33*	*485*	*61*	*22*	*1*	*20*	*67*	*61*	*138*	*2*	*1*	*.246/.348/.450*	*.296*	*.314*	*-0.4*	*1B 1, C 0*	*2.5*

| Breakout: 1% | Improve: 22% | Collapse: 6% | Attrition: 6% | MLB: 93% | | *Comparables:* | *Ryan Howard, Richie Sexson, Carlos Pena* |

Torii Hunter might be Spiderman and Noah Syndergaard Thor, but not branding Napoli as Wolverine is a collective oversight committed by us all. On top of the impressive beard and appropriate build, Napoli seems to possess regenerative abilities. Avascular necrosis—emphasis on the "necrosis" here—couldn't slow him down. He treated a dislocated finger like mortal men would treat a papercut. Add in the damage we've seen Napoli do to his liver, and it becomes increasingly obvious that he can't be harmed. Napoli added a degree of selectivity to his two-strike approach in 2014, cutting down on his strikeouts and boosting his walk rate. Unfortunately, said improvements might have come at the expense of power; he still hit a few balls to Logan, but Napoli posted the lowest slugging percentage of his career. For the heart of the Red Sox order to really get going, Wolverine's primary mission next year will involve looking to his origins and recuperating some of his pop.

Daniel Nava RF

Born: 2/22/83 Age: 32 Bats: B Throws: L Height: 5' 11" Weight: 200

YEAR	TEAM	LVL	AGE	PA	R	2B	3B	HR	RBI	BB	K	SB	CS	AVG/OBP/SLG	TAv	BABIP	BRR	FRAA	WARP
2012	PAW	AAA	29	120	20	7	1	4	18	16	15	1	1	.313/.425/.525	.352	.333	-0.2	LF(16): -0.5, RF(3): 0.1	1.3
2012	BOS	MLB	29	317	38	21	0	6	33	37	63	3	0	.243/.352/.390	.268	.295	2.2	LF(76): -5.6, RF(4): -0.1	0.9
2013	BOS	MLB	30	536	77	29	0	12	66	51	93	0	2	.303/.385/.445	.309	.352	-2.1	RF(69): -4.6, LF(63): -2.0	2.8
2014	PAW	AAA	31	98	12	3	0	3	14	12	21	2	1	.253/.347/.398	.261	.295	-2.2	LF(8): 0.3, RF(6): 0.5	-0.1
2014	BOS	MLB	31	408	41	21	0	4	37	33	81	4	2	.270/.346/.361	.271	.336	1.7	RF(69): 3.3, LF(38): -0.3	1.8
2015	*BOS*	*MLB*	*32*	*423*	*43*	*22*	*1*	*6*	*42*	*41*	*87*	*3*	*2*	*.260/.348/.373*	*.276*	*.321*	*0.4*	*RF -0, LF -1*	*1.4*

| Breakout: 1% | Improve: 32% | Collapse: 4% | Attrition: 11% | MLB: 82% | | *Comparables:* | *Bobby Kielty, Ryan Spilborghs, Rocky Colavito* |

After the 2013 season, we no longer needed to qualify every nice thing said about Nava with a reference to his background, as he finished fifth in the AL in OBP and played almost every day for a World Series-winning team. That means we can't make excuses for his failures either, and Nava was awful to start 2014. Yes, he hit .297/.369/.382 from May 24th onward after resurfacing from a demotion to Pawtucket. But he still hit just .159/.209/.190 against southpaws on the season, and he really has no business facing them with any regularity. Nava is a platoon player through and through, and while there are negative connotations associated with that term he's a pretty good one, especially with his improved outfield defense.

David Ortiz   DH

Born: 11/18/75   Age: 39   Bats: L   Throws: L   Height: 6' 4"   Weight: 230

YEAR	TEAM	LVL	AGE	PA	R	2B	3B	HR	RBI	BB	K	SB	CS	AVG/OBP/SLG	TAv	BABIP	BRR	FRAA	WARP
2012	BOS	MLB	36	383	65	26	0	23	60	56	51	0	1	.318/.415/.611	.343	.316	-3.1	1B(7): 0.1	3.4
2013	BOS	MLB	37	600	84	38	2	30	103	76	88	4	0	.309/.395/.564	.332	.321	-2.2	1B(6): -0.4	4.9
2014	BOS	MLB	38	602	59	27	0	35	104	75	95	0	0	.263/.355/.517	.306	.256	-7.7	1B(5): 0.2	2.6
2015	BOS	MLB	39	567	74	31	1	24	83	70	101	1	0	.271/.362/.485	.309	.294	-3.9	1B -0	3.2

Breakout: 0%   Improve: 17%   Collapse: 10%   Attrition: 14%   MLB: 79%   Comparables: Hank Aaron, Manny Ramirez, Jason Giambi

Throw out anything you think you know about aging curves or the rules of baseball in general; they don't apply to Ortiz. Since the last Annual publication, Ortiz added another 35 homers to his total, surpassed the 1,500 RBI mark, signed a new contract and finished third in the city of Boston in a Mayoral race in which he did not run. Some BABIP fluctuation led to a lower average, but Ortiz posted identical ISO marks in 2013 and 2014, and markedly similar walk and strikeout rates, too. Ortiz will be 39 for the entirety of the 2015 season, but there's no reason to expect anything but more of the same out of him. There's going to be a statue outside Fenway with his likeness some day, and a plaque in Cooperstown with his face on it, too. Enjoy the ride while it lasts, because there's never going to be anyone quite like Ortiz ever again.

Dustin Pedroia   2B

Born: 8/17/83   Age: 31   Bats: R   Throws: R   Height: 5' 8"   Weight: 165

YEAR	TEAM	LVL	AGE	PA	R	2B	3B	HR	RBI	BB	K	SB	CS	AVG/OBP/SLG	TAv	BABIP	BRR	FRAA	WARP
2012	BOS	MLB	28	623	81	39	3	15	65	48	60	20	6	.290/.347/.449	.281	.300	-0.9	2B(139): -10.5	2.0
2013	BOS	MLB	29	724	91	42	2	9	84	73	75	17	5	.301/.372/.415	.289	.326	-1.4	2B(160): 4.4	4.5
2014	BOS	MLB	30	609	72	33	0	7	53	51	75	6	6	.278/.337/.376	.268	.307	2.9	2B(135): 6.5	3.6
2015	BOS	MLB	31	595	65	33	1	9	61	58	71	13	5	.282/.353/.402	.285	.307	-0.2	2B -2	3.3

Breakout: 0%   Improve: 42%   Collapse: 1%   Attrition: 2%   MLB: 96%   Comparables: Ian Kinsler, Jose Vidro, Maicer Izturis

The New England Patriots have convinced Bostonians that following The Patriot Way—a kind moniker for the method by which they unceremoniously dump old, expensive players—is the only way to win. It's why people clamored for Jimmy Garoppolo after two bad games from Tom Brady, and it's why some wondered out loud if the Red Sox would be better off trading Pedroia and going with Mookie Betts at second base. That's a very silly idea. Sure, Pedroia is no longer the 20-steal, 20-homer threat he was in his mid-20s, as his power has unquestionably diminished. Yet he's still an elite defender, he still sees a ton of pitches per plate appearance and he's still potent at the plate when healthy. The "when healthy" caveat is a big one, and the day when we debate whether Pedroia should still be a top-of-the-order hitter might be closer than the Sox would prefer. But he's on an insanely team-friendly contract, can still post several 4-plus WARP seasons and is exactly the type of baseball nut you want around to help groom younger players. Boston doesn't deserve nice things.

Hanley Ramirez   SS

Born: 12/23/83   Age: 31   Bats: R   Throws: R   Height: 6' 2"   Weight: 225

YEAR	TEAM	LVL	AGE	PA	R	2B	3B	HR	RBI	BB	K	SB	CS	AVG/OBP/SLG	TAv	BABIP	BRR	FRAA	WARP
2012	LAN	MLB	28	272	30	11	2	10	44	17	60	7	3	.271/.324/.450	.280	.319	1.8	SS(57): -3.3, 3B(8): 0.1	1.7
2012	MIA	MLB	28	395	49	18	2	14	48	37	72	14	4	.246/.322/.428	.275	.271	3.1	3B(90): -12.6	0.8
2013	LAN	MLB	29	336	62	25	2	20	57	27	52	10	2	.345/.402/.638	.360	.363	-1.6	SS(76): 0.3	4.8
2014	LAN	MLB	30	512	64	35	0	13	71	56	84	14	5	.283/.369/.448	.304	.323	0.9	SS(115): -16.9	2.7
2015	BOS	MLB	31	448	57	25	1	13	55	44	77	14	5	.275/.351/.443	.297	.310	0.7	SS -9, 3B -2	2.4

Breakout: 0%   Improve: 42%   Collapse: 4%   Attrition: 1%   MLB: 98%   Comparables: Chase Utley, Robinson Cano, David Wright

Ramirez's 2014 stat line was only a disappointment if you thought he'd somehow established the historic dominance he showed in half a season in 2013 as his new baseline. In reality, he hit exactly as you'd expect a 30-year-old with a prior-to-2013 career line of .298/.371/.495 to hit. He also defended exactly as you'd expect a 30-year-old "shortstop" with about -60 runs of defensive value in his career to defend, which helps explain Boston's plan to play Ramirez in left field despite not a single professional inning at the position. When healthy, he remains one of baseball's most dangerous hitters, but "healthy" is a relative term for Ramirez, whose injury history reads like a really long list of injuries.

David Ross   C

Born: 3/19/77   Age: 38   Bats: R   Throws: R   Height: 6' 2"   Weight: 230

YEAR	TEAM	LVL	AGE	PA	R	2B	3B	HR	RBI	BB	K	SB	CS	AVG/OBP/SLG	TAv	BABIP	BRR	FRAA	WARP
2012	ATL	MLB	35	196	18	7	0	9	23	18	60	1	0	.256/.321/.449	.274	.330	-1.7	C(54): -0.0	1.1
2013	BOS	MLB	36	116	11	5	0	4	10	11	42	1	0	.216/.298/.382	.240	.321	0.0	C(36): -0.2	0.5
2014	BOS	MLB	37	171	16	7	0	7	15	16	58	0	1	.184/.260/.368	.228	.239	-0.8	C(50): -1.1	-0.2
2015	BOS	MLB	38	250	26	11	0	7	26	24	77	1	1	.221/.298/.366	.248	.299	-0.8	C -0	0.6

Breakout: 0%   Improve: 14%   Collapse: 15%   Attrition: 25%   MLB: 75%   Comparables: Jason Varitek, Darryl Strawberry, Joe Adcock

Ross has so much veteran grizzle that, the idea goes, if he gives his body a good shake the whole room gets covered with it. He's a good defensive catcher with a reputation for strong game-calling skills—he must have loved working with A.J. Pierzynski—and he reportedly served as a mentor to Christian Vazquez last season. Unfortunately, his adherence to the backup-catcher archetype includes a lack of offense, and his value behind the plate won't mitigate his troubles at it for much longer. Ross seemed to possess an acute sense of his baseball mortality toward the end of 2014, requesting the start in Derek Jeter's final game, just in case that was the end of his road, too. It wasn't: He signed on for another year, aiming for the baseball immortality of winning a ring with the Cubs.

Pablo Sandoval   3B

Born: 8/11/86   Age: 28   Bats: B   Throws: R   Height: 5' 11"   Weight: 245

YEAR	TEAM	LVL	AGE	PA	R	2B	3B	HR	RBI	BB	K	SB	CS	AVG/OBP/SLG	TAv	BABIP	BRR	FRAA	WARP
2012	SJO	A+	25	23	1	2	0	1	1	1	5	0	0	.273/.304/.500	.272	.313	0.0	3B(4): -0.7	0.0
2012	SFN	MLB	25	442	59	25	2	12	63	38	59	1	1	.283/.342/.447	.292	.301	-0.2	3B(102): 8.1, 1B(3): 0.1	3.6
2013	SFN	MLB	26	584	52	27	2	14	79	47	79	0	0	.278/.341/.417	.275	.301	-4.8	3B(137): -14.9	0.4
2014	SFN	MLB	27	638	68	26	3	16	73	39	85	0	0	.279/.324/.415	.284	.300	-4.7	3B(151): 4.0	3.1
2015	BOS	MLB	28	589	63	32	2	16	73	44	80	1	1	.281/.336/.439	.289	.301	-2.9	3B -1, 1B -0	2.7

Breakout: 0%   Improve: 44%   Collapse: 1%   Attrition: 5%   MLB: 98%   *Comparables: George Brett, Edwin Encarnacion, Chad Tracy*

The list of homegrown Giants players who've left the organization to sign multi-year pacts elsewhere is short. Before Sandoval bolted for Boston, its most recent entrant was Pedro Feliz, a fellow third baseman who got $8.5 million over two years from the Phillies after 2007, eventually clearing the way for the Panda. Far more nimble than his rotund figure would suggest, and equipped with an excellent arm, Sandoval was one of the league's top defenders at the hot corner in 2014. The offensive numbers above also obscure a .308 average and .799 OPS from May 11th through the end of the regular season, followed by a major-league-record 26 postseason hits. Whether or not Fenway Park breathes life into the Panda's feeble right-handed swing, he should justify the Red Sox' investment for as long as his fielding remains tolerable.

Travis Shaw   1B

Born: 4/16/90   Age: 25   Bats: L   Throws: R   Height: 6' 4"   Weight: 225

YEAR	TEAM	LVL	AGE	PA	R	2B	3B	HR	RBI	BB	K	SB	CS	AVG/OBP/SLG	TAv	BABIP	BRR	FRAA	WARP
2012	SLM	A+	22	423	69	31	3	16	73	59	81	11	2	.305/.411/.545	.326	.354	1.6	1B(79): 4.7, 3B(10): 0.4	4.3
2012	PME	AA	22	133	13	13	0	3	12	21	34	1	1	.227/.353/.427	.275	.297	-0.1	1B(30): -0.1, 3B(1): -0.1	0.4
2013	PME	AA	23	529	57	21	4	16	50	78	117	7	3	.221/.342/.394	.270	.262	-2.4	1B(111): -1.9, 3B(4): -0.2	0.5
2014	PME	AA	24	208	35	8	1	11	37	29	23	5	3	.305/.406/.548	.319	.301	-1.8	1B(35): -3.2, 3B(6): -0.2	1.1
2014	PAW	AAA	24	346	43	21	1	10	41	28	76	2	0	.262/.321/.431	.262	.312	-2.1	1B(75): 2.2, 3B(6): -0.0	0.7
2015	BOS	MLB	25	250	27	12	1	7	28	27	60	2	1	.232/.320/.386	.264	.285	-0.2	1B -0, 3B -0	0.3

Breakout: 10%   Improve: 16%   Collapse: 12%   Attrition: 30%   MLB: 38%   *Comparables: Chris McGuiness, Tommy Medica, Jeff Larish*

Shaw continued his proud history of mastering one level of the minors, then struggling after a promotion. The power-hitting left-hander mashed 21 homers between Portland and Pawtucket, and he now sits on the precipice of the finally attaining a $99 per diem. Unfortunately, he can't hit left-handed pitching, has a penchant for striking out and is confined to first base. Still, Shaw's done well enough against righties in his career to profile as a second-division platoon player, and he has the type of carrying tool that should allow him to stick around in the majors for several years. For a player drafted in the ninth round, that's a big developmental win.

Blake Swihart   C

Born: 4/3/92   Age: 23   Bats: B   Throws: R   Height: 6' 1"   Weight: 175

YEAR	TEAM	LVL	AGE	PA	R	2B	3B	HR	RBI	BB	K	SB	CS	AVG/OBP/SLG	TAv	BABIP	BRR	FRAA	WARP
2012	GRN	A	20	378	44	17	4	7	53	26	68	6	2	.262/.307/.395	.257	.300	0.4	C(66): -1.1	1.0
2013	SLM	A+	21	422	45	29	7	2	42	41	63	7	8	.298/.366/.428	.271	.350	-6.9	C(101): 2.6	2.4
2014	PME	AA	22	380	47	23	3	12	55	29	65	7	1	.300/.353/.487	.303	.337	2.2	C(81): 0.7	4.2
2014	PAW	AAA	22	71	6	3	1	1	9	2	15	1	0	.261/.282/.377	.213	.321	0.1	C(16): 0.2	0.0
2015	BOS	MLB	23	250	22	12	2	3	24	14	57	2	1	.243/.285/.352	.240	.302	-0.1	C 0	0.5

Breakout: 7%   Improve: 19%   Collapse: 2%   Attrition: 18%   MLB: 27%   *Comparables: Jonathan Lucroy, Austin Romine, Miguel Montero*

There's nothing quite so seductive as a blue chip catching prospect, and Swihart blossomed into such a siren in 2014. More well rounded than special in any one area of the game, Swihart's power started to stand out in Portland, as he added nearly 60 points of isolated power from his 2013 campaign in Salem. A switch-hitter who profiles as a slightly above-average defender, Swihart is the ever-rare player who should be able to hit in the first two-thirds of a batting order for a first-division team while catching in excess of 120 games. His development has been exceptionally smooth and markedly linear for a prep catching prospect.

Christian Vazquez   C

Born: 8/21/90   Age: 24   Bats: R   Throws: R   Height: 5' 9"   Weight: 195

YEAR	TEAM	LVL	AGE	PA	R	2B	3B	HR	RBI	BB	K	SB	CS	AVG/OBP/SLG	TAv	BABIP	BRR	FRAA	WARP
2012	SLM	A+	21	342	43	17	0	7	41	40	70	2	2	.266/.360/.396	.275	.326	-0.8	C(76): 1.5	2.9
2012	PME	AA	21	82	11	4	0	0	5	8	9	0	0	.205/.280/.260	.191	.231	0.7	C(20): 0.3	-0.3
2013	PME	AA	22	399	48	19	1	5	48	47	44	7	5	.289/.376/.395	.285	.316	1.2	C(93): 0.7	3.7
2014	PAW	AAA	23	270	35	17	0	3	20	21	52	0	1	.279/.336/.385	.254	.340	0.8	C(52): -1.4	1.1
2014	BOS	MLB	23	201	15	9	0	1	20	19	33	0	0	.240/.308/.309	.239	.283	-1.8	C(54): -0.4	0.7
2015	BOS	MLB	24	250	22	12	0	2	20	22	47	1	1	.245/.313/.328	.245	.295	-0.9	C 0	0.5

Breakout: 4%   Improve: 15%   Collapse: 8%   Attrition: 12%   MLB: 33%   *Comparables: Francisco Cervelli, Jason Castro, Chris Herrmann*

If Fausto Carmona and Leo Nunez fooled you with their *noms de play*, you can be forgiven. But if you've truly been duped into believing Vazquez isn't the fourth Molina brother, you're not paying attention. Just 55 games into his MLB career, Vazquez already has a well earned reputation as one of the majors' best defensive catchers. He's an excellent pitch-framer, blocks the ball well and has an absurd arm, throwing out 15 of 29 would-be basestealers in the majors last season with pop times under 1.8 seconds. While he'll need to hit better than he did in 2014 to start for a contender, the bar is set at merely "passable" given the glove's value. The dream is that he ends up somewhere between Yadier and Bengie on the Molina scale for offense, but even if it's more likely he settles between Bengie and Jose, he's still an exciting young backstop.

Shane Victorino   RF

Born: 11/30/80   Age: 34   Bats: R   Throws: R   Height: 5' 9"   Weight: 190

YEAR	TEAM	LVL	AGE	PA	R	2B	3B	HR	RBI	BB	K	SB	CS	AVG/OBP/SLG	TAv	BABIP	BRR	FRAA	WARP
2012	LAN	MLB	31	235	26	12	2	2	15	18	31	15	2	.245/.316/.351	.260	.278	0.4	LF(48): 6.1, CF(8): 0.0	1.3
2012	PHI	MLB	31	431	46	17	5	9	40	35	49	24	4	.261/.324/.401	.266	.278	1.9	CF(101): -0.8	1.9
2013	BOS	MLB	32	532	82	26	2	15	61	25	75	21	3	.294/.351/.451	.292	.321	-0.6	RF(110): 20.8, CF(15): 0.5	5.2
2014	PAW	AAA	33	29	3	1	0	0	0	0	6	0	0	.138/.138/.172	.112	.174	0.3	RF(9): -1.1	-0.5
2014	BOS	MLB	33	133	14	6	1	2	12	6	21	2	0	.268/.303/.382	.250	.304	-0.7	RF(30): -0.7	-0.1
2015	BOS	MLB	34	250	32	11	3	4	22	19	34	10	2	.261/.326/.397	.271	.284	-0.1	RF 5, CF 0	1.4

Breakout: 1%   Improve: 30%   Collapse: 19%   Attrition: 22%   MLB: 93%   *Comparables: Tommy Holmes, Trot Nixon, Gabe Kapler*

The omen laid right before us, and we missed it. Prior to the 2014 season, Major League Baseball enacted a new rule stating that walk-up music could not run longer than 15 seconds. This mandate cut short Victorino's 20-second sample of Bob Marley's "Three Little Birds," eliminating its reassuring refrain, "every little thing, is gonna be alright." So it went for Victorino and the Red Sox as a whole in 2014. The Flyin' Hawaiian was grounded with leg and back injuries for a majority of the year, eventually undergoing back surgery in early August. His production at the plate and prowess in right field were sorely missed. Victorino was one of the catalysts of Boston's 2013 championship run, but there's no telling what he's capable of producing moving forward. He'd be expensive for a fourth outfielder, but relying on him as an everyday contributor would be more "Waiting in Vain" than "Three Little Birds."

Pitchers ────────────────────────────────

Burke Badenhop   RHP

Born: 2/8/83   Age: 32   Bats: R   Throws: R   Height: 6'5"   Weight: 220

YEAR	TEAM	LVL	AGE	W	L	SV	G	GS	IP	H	HR	BB	K	BB/9	K/9	GB%	BABIP	WHIP	ERA	FIP	FRA	WARP
2012	TBA	MLB	29	3	2	0	66	0	62¹	63	6	12	42	1.7	6.1	55%	.284	1.20	3.03	3.58	4.32	0.3
2013	MIL	MLB	30	2	3	1	63	0	62¹	62	6	12	42	1.7	6.1	56%	.289	1.19	3.47	3.50	4.39	0.3
2014	BOS	MLB	31	0	3	1	70	0	70²	70	1	19	40	2.4	5.1	62%	.304	1.26	2.29	3.10	3.69	0.8
2015	BOS	MLB	32	3	1	1	54	0	56²	59	3	17	37	2.7	5.9	55%	.304	1.34	4.04	3.93	4.39	0.4

Breakout: 21%   Improve: 41%   Collapse: 28%   Attrition: 19%   MLB: 87%   Comparables: Matt Wise, Geoff Geary, Braden Looper

Few of Boston's offseason moves go unheralded—at the very least, they're *Boston Herald*ed—yet no one seemed to notice or care last winter when the Red Sox stole Badenhop from the Brewers, with whom he'd enjoyed an unremarkable season in 2013. The sinkerballer was Boston's third-best reliever in 2014, as he generated groundballs at a 61 percent clip and induced 14 double plays, stranding nearly three-fourths of inherited runners in the process. It's truly amazing that some teams keep overspending to add former closers when pitchers like Badenhop can be acquired for the price of one Luis Ortega.

Trey Ball   LHP

Born: 6/27/94   Age: 21   Bats: L   Throws: L   Height: 6'6"   Weight: 185

YEAR	TEAM	LVL	AGE	W	L	SV	G	GS	IP	H	HR	BB	K	BB/9	K/9	GB%	BABIP	WHIP	ERA	FIP	FRA	WARP
2014	GRN	A	20	5	10	0	22	22	100	111	9	39	68	3.5	6.1	38%	.309	1.50	4.68	4.66	5.57	1.1
2015	BOS	MLB	21	4	6	0	17	17	68¹	85	8	36	32	4.8	4.3	39%	.314	1.77	6.23	5.95	6.77	-1.0

Breakout: 0%   Improve: 0%   Collapse: 0%   Attrition: 0%   MLB: 0%   Comparables: Brett Marshall, Mike Foltynewicz, T.J. House

Some evaluators viewed Ball as a better outfielder than pitcher before he was selected seventh overall in the 2013 draft. The Red Sox, wishing to add another entry to the Bob Walk/Grant Balfour/Homer Bailey pantheon of unfortunate pitcher names, decided to develop Ball on the mound instead. That looked like a mistake during the first half of the 2014 season, when Ball owned a 6.59 ERA through July 11th. The left-hander had trouble commanding his fastball/changeup combo and his curveball remains an unreliable weapon. However, Ball was much better over his final eight starts, sporting a 2.11 ERA thanks to a reduced walk rate and more swinging strikes. Ball might have failed to meet the lofty expectations placed upon a player of his draft status, but his comparative lack of high school pitching experience earns him a long leash.

Matt Barnes   RHP

Born: 6/17/90   Age: 25   Bats: R   Throws: R   Height: 6'4"   Weight: 205

YEAR	TEAM	LVL	AGE	W	L	SV	G	GS	IP	H	HR	BB	K	BB/9	K/9	GB%	BABIP	WHIP	ERA	FIP	FRA	WARP
2012	GRN	A	22	2	0	0	5	5	26²	12	0	4	42	1.4	14.2	60%	.240	0.60	0.34	0.99	1.43	1.3
2012	SLM	A+	22	5	5	0	20	20	93	85	6	25	91	2.4	8.8	48%	.312	1.18	3.58	3.33	4.14	1.4
2013	PME	AA	23	5	10	0	24	24	108	112	11	46	135	3.8	11.2	46%	.356	1.46	4.33	3.54	3.51	2.9
2014	PAW	AAA	24	8	9	0	23	22	127²	119	8	46	103	3.2	7.3	44%	.294	1.29	3.95	3.71	4.45	1.0
2014	BOS	MLB	24	0	0	0	5	0	9	11	1	2	8	2.0	8.0	34%	.357	1.44	4.00	3.49	2.72	0.2
2015	BOS	MLB	25	7	7	0	22	22	111	114	10	44	100	3.5	8.1	45%	.315	1.42	4.31	4.23	4.68	0.6

Breakout: 24%   Improve: 43%   Collapse: 13%   Attrition: 36%   MLB: 65%   Comparables: Brad Peacock, Brad Mills, Scott Barnes

Barnes has all the tools he needs to succeed as a major-league starter. His fastball grades out as plus or plus-plus, his curveball is a strong second weapon and his changeup also flashes above-average potential. Yet he hasn't put together a good season from start-to-finish since he graduated to the mid-minors. He missed some time with a shoulder injury to begin the 2014 season and got off to an abysmal start in Pawtucket. He eventually showed improvement over his final 10 starts, but there's still plenty of Barnes raising* to be done before he can be relied upon as a starter at the highest level. The UConn product got a cup of coffee as a reliever in Boston at the end of the year, and while he'd likely be dominant in that role the Red Sox have to hope he figures it out in the rotation.
*So sorry

Craig Breslow   LHP

Born: 8/8/80   Age: 34   Bats: L   Throws: L   Height: 6'1"   Weight: 190

YEAR	TEAM	LVL	AGE	W	L	SV	G	GS	IP	H	HR	BB	K	BB/9	K/9	GB%	BABIP	WHIP	ERA	FIP	FRA	WARP
2012	ARI	MLB	31	2	0	0	40	0	43¹	38	5	13	42	2.7	8.7	44%	.277	1.18	2.70	3.67	4.14	0.3
2012	BOS	MLB	31	1	0	0	23	0	20	14	0	9	19	4.1	8.6	52%	.269	1.15	2.70	2.65	3.06	0.4
2013	BOS	MLB	32	5	2	0	61	0	59²	49	3	18	33	2.7	5.0	45%	.254	1.12	1.81	3.63	3.97	0.5
2014	BOS	MLB	33	2	4	1	60	0	54¹	73	8	28	37	4.6	6.1	38%	.351	1.86	5.96	5.37	5.53	-0.5
2015	BOS	MLB	34	3	1	1	56	0	53	54	5	21	42	3.6	7.2	40%	.302	1.42	4.34	4.51	4.71	0.1

Breakout: 13%   Improve: 22%   Collapse: 31%   Attrition: 11%   MLB: 73%   Comparables: Aaron Fultz, Brandon Lyon, Matt Guerrier

Breslow has changed his arsenal and batted-ball profiles as his career progressed. He has sporadically shown reverse platoon splits. His walk and strikeout rates have fluctuated wildly. With all that in mind, it was perhaps foolish to expect consistency from Breslow, but it was still surprising to see him struggle so badly in what was his age-33 season. Breslow pitched to a significant workload in 2013, throwing 71 innings including a rehab stint and the postseason. That might have contributed to his recession, but his velocity has been declining for four straight seasons. Breslow's fall from key World Series cog to having his $4 million option declined is an unfortunate reminder of how fungible bullpen arms can be.

Clay Buchholz RHP

Born: 8/14/84   Age: 30   Bats: L   Throws: R   Height: 6'3"   Weight: 190

YEAR	TEAM	LVL	AGE	W	L	SV	G	GS	IP	H	HR	BB	K	BB/9	K/9	GB%	BABIP	WHIP	ERA	FIP	FRA	WARP
2012	BOS	MLB	27	11	8	0	29	29	189¹	187	25	64	129	3.0	6.1	49%	.284	1.33	4.56	4.60	5.53	-0.3
2013	BOS	MLB	28	12	1	0	16	16	108¹	75	4	36	96	3.0	8.0	49%	.254	1.02	1.74	2.81	3.53	1.8
2014	PAW	AAA	29	0	1	0	2	2	10²	6	2	2	10	1.7	8.4	42%	.167	0.75	2.53	4.76	5.35	0.0
2014	BOS	MLB	29	8	11	0	28	28	170¹	182	17	54	132	2.9	7.0	48%	.315	1.39	5.34	4.03	4.65	0.7
2015	BOS	MLB	30	10	7	0	24	24	145¹	137	12	51	111	3.2	6.9	48%	.289	1.30	3.77	4.28	4.10	1.6

Breakout: 13%   Improve: 34%   Collapse: 28%   Attrition: 13%   MLB: 86%   Comparables: *Jason Hammel, Tim Hudson, Josh Johnson*

After eight seasons and 915 total innings pitched in the majors, here's what we can say we know about Buchholz: ¯\(シ)/¯. He continues to be one of the game's most frustrating, talented and inconsistent pitchers, and he doubled down on that reputation in 2014. On August 3rd, he had a 6.20 ERA, having given up .303/.368/.466 line in 102 innings. Yet over his final 10 outings he threw six quality starts, held batters to a .224/.279/.332 line and posted a 4.06 ERA. Buchholz has truly entered the Tyson Zone for pitchers, wherein a two-out, 11-run performance and a perfect game seem equally feasible outcomes every time he toes the rubber. See-saws have fewer ups and downs.

Edwin Escobar LHP

Born: 4/22/92   Age: 23   Bats: L   Throws: L   Height: 6'1"   Weight: 185

YEAR	TEAM	LVL	AGE	W	L	SV	G	GS	IP	H	HR	BB	K	BB/9	K/9	GB%	BABIP	WHIP	ERA	FIP	FRA	WARP
2012	AUG	A	20	7	8	0	22	22	130²	121	7	32	122	2.2	8.4	46%	.301	1.17	2.96	3.30	3.89	1.9
2013	SJO	A+	21	3	4	0	16	14	74²	68	3	17	92	2.0	11.1	41%	.323	1.14	2.89	2.55	2.93	2.3
2013	RIC	AA	21	5	4	0	10	10	54	44	2	13	54	2.2	9.0	44%	.286	1.06	2.67	2.64	3.31	1.2
2014	FRE	AAA	22	3	8	0	20	20	111	128	16	37	96	3.0	7.8	44%	.326	1.49	5.11	5.01	5.31	0.8
2014	PAW	AAA	22	0	2	0	5	5	27¹	33	3	8	20	2.6	6.6	40%	.337	1.50	4.28	4.20	4.68	0.1
2014	BOS	MLB	22	0	0	0	2	0	2	1	0	0	2	0.0	9.0	20%	.200	0.50	4.50	2.66	2.86	0.0
2015	BOS	MLB	23	7	8	0	22	22	115¹	126	12	44	88	3.4	6.9	42%	.314	1.47	4.95	4.68	5.38	-0.3

Breakout: 0%   Improve: 0%   Collapse: 0%   Attrition: 0%   MLB: 0%   Comparables: *Burch Smith, Hector Rondon, Nick Tropeano*

The good news is Escobar's floor is quality LOOGY on a playoff-bound club, and he should be ready to fulfill that role at some point in 2015. The bad news is his value crashed from "borderline top-100 prospect" to "complementary piece in a Jake Peavy trade" in under a calendar year. His terrific Double-A numbers at Richmond belied his lack of a plus breaking pitch or sexy velocity, and while the PCL can be a cruel place to pitch, Escobar's poor 2014 season might ultimately be more representative of his skill set. Six-plus years of control of a back-end starter or reliever would be a fine return for a spare part like Peavy, but don't let his numbers from the mid-minors fool you into thinking he's a future star.

Brian Johnson LHP

Born: 12/7/90   Age: 24   Bats: L   Throws: L   Height: 6'3"   Weight: 225

YEAR	TEAM	LVL	AGE	W	L	SV	G	GS	IP	H	HR	BB	K	BB/9	K/9	GB%	BABIP	WHIP	ERA	FIP	FRA	WARP
2013	GRN	A	22	1	6	0	15	15	69	50	4	28	69	3.7	9.0	47%	.251	1.13	2.87	3.63	4.38	1.0
2013	SLM	A+	22	1	0	0	2	2	11	9	0	5	8	4.1	6.5	59%	.281	1.27	1.64	3.26	4.09	0.2
2014	SLM	A+	23	3	1	0	5	5	25²	23	0	7	33	2.5	11.6	41%	.333	1.17	3.86	1.76	2.52	1.0
2014	PME	AA	23	10	2	0	20	20	118	78	6	32	99	2.4	7.6	48%	.229	0.93	1.75	3.15	3.69	2.1
2015	BOS	MLB	24	7	6	0	21	21	105	100	9	43	84	3.7	7.2	46%	.291	1.36	4.00	4.40	4.34	1.0

Breakout: 15%   Improve: 32%   Collapse: 13%   Attrition: 28%   MLB: 50%   Comparables: *Adam Warren, Lance Lynn, Anthony Ranaudo*

Johnson lends credence to the oft-issued warning not to scout the stat sheet. If you look at his ERA, WHIP and walk rate at Double-A, you might assume he's on his way to pitching near the front of a major-league rotation. The harsh reality is that Johnson lacks an out pitch, relying on good command and a wide variety of solid offerings to keep hitters off balance. That type of approach can befuddle batters in the mid-to-low minors, but does not always fool major-league hitters more used to pitch sequencing. There's a chance that the whole is greater than the parts here, and Johnson may be able to pitch at the back end of a major-league rotation, but the upside is modest.

Joe Kelly RHP

Born: 6/9/88   Age: 27   Bats: R   Throws: R   Height: 6'1"   Weight: 175

YEAR	TEAM	LVL	AGE	W	L	SV	G	GS	IP	H	HR	BB	K	BB/9	K/9	GB%	BABIP	WHIP	ERA	FIP	FRA	WARP
2012	MEM	AAA	24	2	5	0	12	12	72¹	75	2	21	45	2.6	5.6	56%	.322	1.33	2.86	3.82	4.30	1.5
2012	SLN	MLB	24	5	7	0	24	16	107	112	10	36	75	3.0	6.3	53%	.306	1.38	3.53	4.04	4.99	0.2
2013	SLN	MLB	25	10	5	0	37	15	124	124	10	44	79	3.2	5.7	52%	.289	1.35	2.69	3.98	4.25	0.9
2014	MEM	AAA	26	0	0	0	3	3	10¹	8	1	6	4	5.2	3.5	56%	.226	1.35	2.61	5.93	6.97	-0.1
2014	BOS	MLB	26	4	2	0	10	10	61¹	47	5	32	41	4.7	6.0	57%	.237	1.29	4.11	4.64	5.72	-0.3
2014	SLN	MLB	26	2	2	0	7	7	35	41	3	10	25	2.6	6.4	55%	.330	1.46	4.37	3.90	4.19	0.3
2015	BOS	MLB	27	5	5	0	19	14	87¹	94	7	38	59	3.9	6.0	54%	.309	1.51	4.70	4.76	5.10	0.0

Breakout: 27%   Improve: 53%   Collapse: 13%   Attrition: 15%   MLB: 77%   Comparables: *Sergio Mitre, Dana Eveland, Ross Detwiler*

If we're going on pure stuff and not taking into account all of the other things that make a good pitcher good, Kelly should be better than he is. His power sinker features a ton of movement, his changeup, slider and curveball all have life and he generates plenty of groundballs. But Kelly struggles with command, and that has a starkly limiting effect on the overall effectiveness of his repertoire. It's not just the walks that hurt Kelly; it's his inability to place strikes where he wants them, and his inability to entice batters to swing at pitches just outside of the strike zone, and his inability to pitch from ahead in the count. Kelly has the ingredients needed to serve as a mid-rotation pitcher, but he's going to be more of a back-end option unless he gets better at working in and on the periphery of the strike zone, which is the premise of a lot more rejected screenplays than pictures in production.

Michael Kopech   RHP
Born: 4/30/96   Age: 19   Bats: R   Throws: R   Height: 6'3"   Weight: 195

YEAR	TEAM	LVL	AGE	W	L	SV	G	GS	IP	H	HR	BB	K	BB/9	K/9	GB%	BABIP	WHIP	ERA	FIP	FRA	WARP
2015	BOS	MLB	19	2	3	0	7	7	31	38	4	21	16	6.0	4.7	45%	.317	1.89	6.54	6.56	7.11	-0.6

Breakout: 0%   Improve: 0%   Collapse: 0%   Attrition: 0%   MLB: 0%   Comparables: *Mike Foltynewicz, Edwin Escobar, Jenrry Mejia*

Back in 2005, the Red Sox drafted Jacoby Ellsbury with the pick they received when Orlando Cabrera signed with the Angels. Compensation picks are a flat circle, and nine years later, the Sox nabbed Kopech with the pick they received when Ellsbury signed with the Yankees. A prototypical big-bodied right-hander from Texas, Kopech has velocity and a natural feel for his secondaries on his side. He's reached the upper 90s when he really lets it fly, and there's still room for him to fill out. That being said, it will take some work to clean up Kopech's high-effort delivery, and he has the profile of a pitcher who could take four or five years in the minors to round into form.

Tom Layne   LHP
Born: 11/2/84   Age: 30   Bats: L   Throws: L   Height: 6'2"   Weight: 190

YEAR	TEAM	LVL	AGE	W	L	SV	G	GS	IP	H	HR	BB	K	BB/9	K/9	GB%	BABIP	WHIP	ERA	FIP	FRA	WARP
2012	SAN	AA	27	0	5	1	32	2	35²	31	2	16	36	4.0	9.1	64%	.305	1.32	3.28	3.34	7.12	0.2
2012	RNO	AAA	27	0	2	0	5	4	20	30	4	9	14	4.1	6.3	48%	.366	1.95	10.35	6.52	8.37	0.1
2012	TUC	AAA	27	0	3	0	5	5	22	28	4	15	19	6.1	7.8	56%	.348	1.95	7.77	6.76	7.35	-0.1
2012	SDN	MLB	27	2	0	2	26	0	16²	9	0	3	25	1.6	13.5	51%	.243	0.72	3.24	1.22	2.76	0.3
2013	TUC	AAA	28	2	4	0	49	0	46	49	1	27	41	5.3	8.0	52%	.338	1.65	4.50	4.09	4.44	0.7
2013	SDN	MLB	28	0	2	0	14	0	8²	10	1	5	6	5.2	6.2	54%	.360	1.73	2.08	5.56	6.39	-0.2
2014	PAW	AAA	29	5	1	11	37	0	48	29	1	20	53	3.8	9.9	61%	.243	1.02	1.50	2.73	2.74	1.1
2014	BOS	MLB	29	2	1	0	30	0	19	14	0	8	14	3.8	6.6	51%	.264	1.16	0.95	3.11	4.27	0.0
2015	BOS	MLB	30	3	2	1	33	4	51	54	4	23	34	4.1	6.0	54%	.303	1.52	4.82	4.81	5.24	-0.1

Breakout: 6%   Improve: 8%   Collapse: 0%   Attrition: 5%   MLB: 11%   Comparables: *Matt Palmer, Anastacio Martinez, Frankie De La Cruz*

Guys like Layne must drive GMs absolutely nuts. Year after year, teams spend big money on relievers, only to watch their investments crumble before their eyes. Then the Red Sox go dumpster diving and unearth a player like Layne, who couldn't cut it in Petco Park (not enough is made of the fact that Layne was once teammates with a closer named Street) but hasn't had trouble in Fenway. Layne is generally thought of as a LOOGY because of his lack of command and troubles against right-handers, but he managed right-handers well in Pawtucket and Boston. He can miss bats and induce groundballs, so he's a useful depth piece in a bullpen as long as he keeps his walks under control.

Justin Masterson   RHP
Born: 3/22/85   Age: 30   Bats: R   Throws: R   Height: 6'6"   Weight: 250

YEAR	TEAM	LVL	AGE	W	L	SV	G	GS	IP	H	HR	BB	K	BB/9	K/9	GB%	BABIP	WHIP	ERA	FIP	FRA	WARP
2012	CLE	MLB	27	11	15	0	34	34	206¹	212	18	88	159	3.8	6.9	57%	.309	1.45	4.93	4.11	5.31	0.2
2013	CLE	MLB	28	14	10	0	32	29	193	156	13	76	195	3.5	9.1	60%	.285	1.20	3.45	3.38	4.27	1.8
2014	COH	AAA	29	0	1	0	2	2	11²	9	0	8	10	6.2	7.7	47%	.281	1.46	5.40	3.70	5.42	0.0
2014	CLE	MLB	29	4	6	0	19	19	98	106	6	56	93	5.1	8.5	61%	.350	1.65	5.51	4.11	4.48	1.1
2014	SLN	MLB	29	3	3	0	9	6	30²	35	6	13	23	3.8	6.8	59%	.309	1.57	7.04	5.81	6.02	-0.3
2015	BOS	MLB	30	8	7	0	22	22	130¹	131	8	54	111	3.7	7.7	56%	.315	1.42	4.19	4.09	4.56	0.7

Breakout: 15%   Improve: 35%   Collapse: 29%   Attrition: 16%   MLB: 90%   Comparables: *Ubaldo Jimenez, Carlos Zambrano, Jon Lester*

When a struggling Masterson was traded to St. Louis last summer, the Cardinals clearly believed that pitching in front of one of the league's best infield defenses would shake the long-time sinkerball impresario out of the doldrums. Six starts and an ERA best suited for a Boeing jet later, it was clear the problem was with Masterson, not the fielders behind him. He has often struggled to retire lefties, but last year a puzzling drop in velocity combined with shaky command allowed hitters of all stripes to tee off, and his walk and strikeout rates moved in the wrong direction. He still produces more groundball outs than anyone, but if Masterson can't regain some zip on his fastball he may need to move to the 'pen, where he'll be better positioned to torture righties with impunity.

Wade Miley   LHP
Born: 11/13/86   Age: 28   Bats: L   Throws: L   Height: 6'0"   Weight: 220

YEAR	TEAM	LVL	AGE	W	L	SV	G	GS	IP	H	HR	BB	K	BB/9	K/9	GB%	BABIP	WHIP	ERA	FIP	FRA	WARP
2012	ARI	MLB	25	16	11	0	32	29	194²	193	14	37	144	1.7	6.7	45%	.293	1.18	3.33	3.19	3.90	2.9
2013	ARI	MLB	26	10	10	0	33	33	202²	201	21	66	147	2.9	6.5	54%	.296	1.32	3.55	3.95	4.81	0.2
2014	ARI	MLB	27	8	12	0	33	33	201¹	207	20	75	183	3.4	8.2	52%	.317	1.40	4.34	3.95	4.79	0.7
2015	BOS	MLB	28	10	9	0	26	26	159¹	169	14	56	117	3.2	6.6	51%	.309	1.41	4.37	4.34	4.75	0.5

Breakout: 24%   Improve: 51%   Collapse: 13%   Attrition: 18%   MLB: 84%   Comparables: *Dillon Gee, Brian Bannister, Dave Bush*

Miley, a barrel-chested left-hander, comes over the top as though he's pulling down a curtain. The effect generates a good number of groundballs, the saving grace of many a pitcher who allows too frequent baserunners. The Red Sox added him to an all-grounder-machine rotation this winter, and even if there are reasons to expect little—the walk rate has gotten loose, and command lapses with both the heat and the changeup lead to belt-high stingers—the durability will play. He crossed the 200-inning mark for a second consecutive season and hasn't missed a start in three years.

Edward Mujica   RHP
Born: 5/10/84   Age: 31   Bats: R   Throws: R   Height: 6'3"   Weight: 225

YEAR	TEAM	LVL	AGE	W	L	SV	G	GS	IP	H	HR	BB	K	BB/9	K/9	GB%	BABIP	WHIP	ERA	FIP	FRA	WARP
2012	MIA	MLB	28	0	3	2	41	0	39	36	6	9	26	2.1	6.0	53%	.252	1.15	4.38	4.57	5.70	-0.4
2012	SLN	MLB	28	0	0	0	29	0	26¹	20	1	3	21	1.0	7.2	51%	.264	0.87	1.03	2.38	3.70	0.3
2013	SLN	MLB	29	2	1	37	65	0	64²	60	9	5	46	0.7	6.4	46%	.263	1.01	2.78	3.69	3.81	0.7
2014	BOS	MLB	30	2	4	8	64	0	60	69	6	14	43	2.1	6.4	44%	.332	1.38	3.90	3.73	4.26	0.4
2015	BOS	MLB	31	3	3	13	54	0	54	52	6	9	44	1.5	7.3	47%	.291	1.14	3.49	3.91	3.80	0.7

Breakout: 22%   Improve: 45%   Collapse: 26%   Attrition: 9%   MLB: 86%   Comparables: *Jon Rauch, Luis Ayala, Dan Wheeler*

Mujica joins Edgar Renteria and the 2004 and 2013 World Series as proof that Cardinals Voodoo Magic doesn't make it through security at Logan Airport. After saving 37 games for St. Louis in 2013, an abysmal April saw Mujica allow 10 earned runs in nine innings and quickly led to his demotion from primary set-up man to mop-up reliever. He fought his way back to relevancy as the year went on, posting a 1.71 ERA in 24 games in August and September and filling in for Koji Uehara as closer near the season's end. He shouldn't function as a team's primary or even secondary right-handed reliever, but he's a fine depth piece.

Henry Owens   LHP

Born: 7/21/92   Age: 22   Bats: L   Throws: L   Height: 6'6"   Weight: 205

YEAR	TEAM	LVL	AGE	W	L	SV	G	GS	IP	H	HR	BB	K	BB/9	K/9	GB%	BABIP	WHIP	ERA	FIP	FRA	WARP
2012	GRN	A	19	12	5	0	23	22	101²	100	10	47	130	4.2	11.5	38%	.350	1.45	4.87	3.86	3.79	3.0
2013	SLM	A+	20	8	5	0	20	20	104²	66	6	53	123	4.6	10.6	45%	.249	1.14	2.92	3.46	4.28	2.1
2013	PME	AA	20	3	1	0	6	6	30¹	18	3	15	46	4.5	13.6	29%	.254	1.09	1.78	3.26	3.67	0.7
2014	PME	AA	21	14	4	0	20	20	121	89	6	47	126	3.5	9.4	48%	.267	1.12	2.60	3.16	3.84	2.2
2014	PAW	AAA	21	3	1	0	6	6	38	32	4	12	44	2.8	10.4	44%	.301	1.16	4.03	3.59	4.58	0.1
2015	BOS	MLB	22	8	7	0	24	24	125²	113	11	61	132	4.4	9.5	42%	.301	1.39	3.98	4.16	4.32	1.2

Breakout: 0%   Improve: 0%   Collapse: 0%   Attrition: 0%   MLB: 0%   Comparables: *Tommy Hanson, Gerrit Cole, Trevor May*

A lanky left-hander who relies on a unique combination of deception, size and legitimately good stuff, Owens toyed with Double-A hitters in 2014. With a low-90s fastball, a devastating changeup and a curveball that should serve as a useful change-of-pace pitch, Owens has the arsenal to succeed at the next level. However, opinions vary on whether he can be a no. 2 starter or more of a no. 3/4 type; his fastball is likely to get hit harder in the majors, so he'll need to improve his command to reach a loftier ceiling. Owens found Triple-A to be more daunting than Portland, and he should end up in Pawtucket to start the 2015 season. That being said, it's easy to see him breaking into the majors at some point this year.

Rick Porcello   RHP

Born: 12/27/88   Age: 26   Bats: R   Throws: R   Height: 6'5"   Weight: 200

YEAR	TEAM	LVL	AGE	W	L	SV	G	GS	IP	H	HR	BB	K	BB/9	K/9	GB%	BABIP	WHIP	ERA	FIP	FRA	WARP
2012	DET	MLB	23	10	12	0	31	31	176¹	226	16	44	107	2.2	5.5	55%	.344	1.53	4.59	3.86	4.76	1.6
2013	DET	MLB	24	13	8	0	32	29	177	185	18	42	142	2.1	7.2	56%	.315	1.28	4.32	3.56	4.76	1.0
2014	DET	MLB	25	15	13	0	32	31	204²	211	18	41	129	1.8	5.7	51%	.298	1.23	3.43	3.70	4.36	1.5
2015	BOS	MLB	26	11	9	0	28	28	166²	180	12	41	115	2.2	6.2	52%	.315	1.33	4.06	3.94	4.41	1.2

Breakout: 17%   Improve: 49%   Collapse: 20%   Attrition: 14%   MLB: 96%   Comparables: *Dontrelle Willis, Mike Leake, Trevor Cahill*

Porcello believers finally saw the season they had been seeking—or, at least, half of it, as the sinker started elevating down the stretch. The AL leader in shutouts—he had never previously thrown even a complete game—finally had a decent infield defense to support his pitch-to-contact tendencies. As his strikeout rate went down, so did his walk rate, and up went his smile rate. He's still young but it's suddenly his last year of arbitration eligibility, which made him available for Boston's winter rotation rebuild.

Anthony Ranaudo   RHP

Born: 9/9/89   Age: 25   Bats: R   Throws: R   Height: 6'7"   Weight: 230

YEAR	TEAM	LVL	AGE	W	L	SV	G	GS	IP	H	HR	BB	K	BB/9	K/9	GB%	BABIP	WHIP	ERA	FIP	FRA	WARP
2012	PME	AA	22	1	3	0	9	9	37²	41	4	27	27	6.5	6.5	36%	.311	1.81	6.69	5.54	6.61	-0.3
2013	PME	AA	23	8	4	0	19	19	109²	80	9	40	106	3.3	8.7	44%	.250	1.09	2.95	3.63	3.87	2.0
2013	PAW	AAA	23	3	1	0	6	5	30¹	32	1	7	21	2.1	6.2	46%	.320	1.29	2.97	2.94	3.95	0.5
2014	PAW	AAA	24	14	4	0	24	24	138	112	9	54	111	3.5	7.2	37%	.264	1.20	2.61	3.86	3.98	1.6
2014	BOS	MLB	24	4	3	0	7	7	39¹	39	10	16	15	3.7	3.4	35%	.225	1.40	4.81	6.92	7.50	-1.0
2015	BOS	MLB	25	9	9	0	26	26	138¹	140	14	60	98	3.9	6.4	40%	.292	1.45	4.55	4.92	4.95	0.3

Breakout: 33%   Improve: 53%   Collapse: 10%   Attrition: 37%   MLB: 71%   Comparables: *Wade Miley, Kevin Mulvey, Jeff Manship*

It might not seem like it now, but getting Ranaudo to the point where he comfortably profiles as a major leaguer is a developmental win for the Red Sox. It's easy to remember what Ranaudo was at LSU in 2009 and wonder why he can't be that now, but the truth is that version of Ranaudo was never coming back. In fact, that's not even who the Sox drafted in 2010, when they took a gamble on Ranaudo in the supplemental first round. That the Sox have transformed him into major-league currency is an achievement, even if Ranaudo's flat fastball and sporadic command issues give him a probable outcome as a reliever. There's still a chance he survives at the back end of a rotation instead, but his changeup and command would both need to take steps forward.

Eduardo Rodriguez   LHP

Born: 4/7/93   Age: 22   Bats: L   Throws: L   Height: 6'2"   Weight: 200

YEAR	TEAM	LVL	AGE	W	L	SV	G	GS	IP	H	HR	BB	K	BB/9	K/9	GB%	BABIP	WHIP	ERA	FIP	FRA	WARP
2012	DEL	A	19	5	7	0	22	22	107	103	4	30	73	2.5	6.1	53%	.289	1.24	3.70	3.68	5.08	0.8
2013	FRD	A+	20	6	4	0	14	14	85¹	78	4	25	66	2.6	7.0	48%	.292	1.21	2.85	3.36	4.18	1.6
2013	BOW	AA	20	4	3	0	11	11	59²	53	5	24	59	3.6	8.9	42%	.296	1.29	4.22	3.74	3.77	1.3
2014	BOW	AA	21	3	7	0	16	16	82²	90	5	29	69	3.2	7.5	46%	.328	1.44	4.79	3.52	3.61	1.8
2014	PME	AA	21	3	1	0	6	6	37¹	30	1	8	39	1.9	9.4	47%	.299	1.02	0.96	2.42	2.62	1.2
2015	BOS	MLB	22	6	7	0	20	20	103¹	112	9	41	71	3.6	6.2	46%	.310	1.48	4.73	4.62	5.14	0.0

Breakout: 15%   Improve: 26%   Collapse: 5%   Attrition: 23%   MLB: 38%   Comparables: *David Holmberg, Patrick Corbin, Casey Kelly*

Andrew Miller is a phenomenal reliever, but it's incredible to think that the Red Sox talked the Orioles into giving up six years of Rodriguez's services for two-plus months of a set-up man. Rodriguez earned his way onto most top-100 prospect lists before the 2014 season thanks to a solid 2013 performance in High-A and Double-A and a bat-missing plus-fastball/plus-slider combo. There's still debate over whether he's a future no. 3 or just back-of-the-rotation chum, but Rodriguez should be ready to start in the majors fairly soon.

Zeke Spruill   RHP

Born: 9/11/89   Age: 25   Bats: R   Throws: R   Height: 6'5"   Weight: 190

YEAR	TEAM	LVL	AGE	W	L	SV	G	GS	IP	H	HR	BB	K	BB/9	K/9	GB%	BABIP	WHIP	ERA	FIP	FRA	WARP
2012	MIS	AA	22	9	11	0	27	27	161²	158	8	46	106	2.6	5.9	52%	.295	1.26	3.67	3.44	4.71	0.9
2013	MOB	AA	23	0	3	0	5	5	31²	24	0	12	20	3.4	5.7	54%	.267	1.14	1.42	2.79	3.52	0.5
2013	RNO	AAA	23	6	5	0	16	16	92	98	8	33	48	3.2	4.7	54%	.290	1.42	4.21	4.83	5.98	0.6
2013	ARI	MLB	23	0	2	0	6	2	11¹	17	3	5	9	4.0	7.1	42%	.378	1.94	5.56	6.46	5.19	0.0
2014	RNO	AAA	24	3	7	1	28	11	79	89	10	21	71	2.4	8.1	48%	.324	1.39	6.04	4.57	6.10	0.9
2014	ARI	MLB	24	1	1	0	6	1	22²	27	0	4	14	1.6	5.6	54%	.338	1.37	3.57	2.53	3.34	0.4
2015	BOS	MLB	25	6	6	0	16	16	94	105	9	31	51	3.0	4.9	50%	.301	1.44	4.78	4.87	5.20	-0.1

Breakout: 28%   Improve: 41%   Collapse: 7%   Attrition: 34%   MLB: 55%   Comparables: Brandon Cumpton, Kevin Mulvey, Juan Gutierrez

Spruill took a step back after making the leap from Double-A to the big leagues in 2013. He was knocked around the Pacific Coast League, was side-lined with an elbow ailment and finished the season as a major-league mop-up man in a last-place bullpen. Spruill is a long right-hander who uses his size and release point to generate downward action. His changeup is advertised to be the best of his secondary options, but he has preferred throwing a pair of breaking balls in his brief big-league career. He showed an upper-70s curveball and low-80s slider, but both were hit hard at the top level. There is still some hope for Spruill as a starter, but as the ratio of butts to seats in the rotation becomes more complex he might find him-self working in relief, where his strengths can be highlighted.

Junichi Tazawa   RHP

Born: 6/6/86   Age: 29   Bats: R   Throws: R   Height: 5'11"   Weight: 200

YEAR	TEAM	LVL	AGE	W	L	SV	G	GS	IP	H	HR	BB	K	BB/9	K/9	GB%	BABIP	WHIP	ERA	FIP	FRA	WARP
2012	PAW	AAA	26	3	2	4	25	0	42¹	34	2	17	56	3.6	11.9	49%	.308	1.20	2.55	2.33	3.17	0.9
2012	BOS	MLB	26	1	1	1	37	0	44	37	1	5	45	1.0	9.2	49%	.303	0.95	1.43	1.77	2.68	1.1
2013	BOS	MLB	27	5	4	0	71	0	68¹	70	9	12	72	1.6	9.5	35%	.321	1.20	3.16	3.25	3.37	1.1
2014	BOS	MLB	28	4	3	0	71	0	63	58	5	17	64	2.4	9.1	38%	.303	1.19	2.86	2.97	3.89	0.7
2015	BOS	MLB	29	3	1	1	48	0	55¹	52	5	15	57	2.4	9.3	40%	.310	1.20	3.40	3.56	3.70	0.8

Breakout: 34%   Improve: 59%   Collapse: 13%   Attrition: 10%   MLB: 86%   Comparables: Jerry Blevins, Santiago Casilla, Fernando Salas

Though his ERA has fluctuated pretty wildly over the past three years, Tazawa's been a very consistent, above-average reliever since 2012. He's a bit homer prone and his walk rate jumped last year, but Tazawa misses a lot of bats, hasn't lost any velocity on his fastball despite significant work-loads, and doesn't offer much in the way of a platoon split. Just keep him away from the Blue Jays—he craps the bed in Canada enough to be an honorary member of Terrance and Phillip—and you have a good middle reliever who's fine as a second or third right-hander out of the 'pen.

Koji Uehara   RHP

Born: 4/3/75   Age: 40   Bats: R   Throws: R   Height: 6'2"   Weight: 195

YEAR	TEAM	LVL	AGE	W	L	SV	G	GS	IP	H	HR	BB	K	BB/9	K/9	GB%	BABIP	WHIP	ERA	FIP	FRA	WARP
2012	TEX	MLB	37	0	0	1	37	0	36	20	4	3	43	0.8	10.8	33%	.200	0.64	1.75	2.35	3.74	0.6
2013	BOS	MLB	38	4	1	21	73	0	74¹	33	5	9	101	1.1	12.2	42%	.188	0.57	1.09	1.64	2.13	2.1
2014	BOS	MLB	39	6	5	26	64	0	64¹	51	10	8	80	1.1	11.2	35%	.273	0.92	2.52	3.11	3.55	0.9
2015	BOS	MLB	40	3	2	8	35	4	56	42	5	10	71	1.6	11.4	36%	.276	0.92	2.02	2.68	2.19	1.9

Breakout: 12%   Improve: 23%   Collapse: 24%   Attrition: 4%   MLB: 67%   Comparables: Takashi Saito, Tom Gordon, Octavio Dotel

The Red Sox decided to do away with any drama regarding a Uehara reunion, re-signing the free-agent-to-be less than 24 hours after the World Series ended. His two-year deal might seem to be a bit much for a 40-year-old reliever, but Uehara's performance dictates the special treatment. Yes, he tapered off toward the end of the 2014 season, but even with his late collapse he finished with 10 times as many strikeouts as walks and an ERA well below 3.00. The Red Sox will have to be judicious in how they use Uehara, and he'll probably be limited to around 60 innings a year. But if he continues to perform at his 2013-2014 level and is deployed properly, there are plenty more high-fives in Boston's future.

Anthony Varvaro   RHP

Born: 10/31/84   Age: 30   Bats: R   Throws: R   Height: 6'0"   Weight: 190

YEAR	TEAM	LVL	AGE	W	L	SV	G	GS	IP	H	HR	BB	K	BB/9	K/9	GB%	BABIP	WHIP	ERA	FIP	FRA	WARP
2012	GWN	AAA	27	0	2	6	33	1	44¹	39	1	24	47	4.9	9.5	42%	.311	1.42	2.23	3.02	2.73	1.2
2012	ATL	MLB	27	1	1	0	12	0	16²	16	2	9	21	4.9	11.3	43%	.333	1.50	5.40	4.16	3.88	0.2
2013	ATL	MLB	28	3	1	1	62	0	73¹	68	3	25	43	3.1	5.3	48%	.278	1.27	2.82	3.44	3.53	0.8
2014	ATL	MLB	29	3	3	0	61	0	54²	46	5	13	50	2.1	8.2	50%	.273	1.08	2.63	3.18	3.49	0.3
2015	BOS	MLB	30	2	1	0	41	0	49²	41	4	20	47	3.7	8.6	45%	.298	1.24	3.40	3.75	3.70	0.4

Breakout: 13%   Improve: 38%   Collapse: 12%   Attrition: 14%   MLB: 61%   Comparables: Bobby Seay, Josh Roenicke, Leo Rosales

Another waiver claim turned quality reliever, Varvaro continued his odd trend of being better without the platoon advantage. In fact, he was more effective against left-handed hitters than many left-handed relievers were, including Tony Watson, Will Smith and Javier Lopez; those guys were pretty darn effective. A new development saw Varvaro incorporate his changeup more against those lefties, particularly in hitter's counts, giving him a third look to offer in addition to his fastball and curve. That variety was part of the reason why he was Fredi Gonzalez's best non-Kimbrel option when it came to retiring lefties. In a Boston bullpen that could have just Drake Britton from the left side, he could fill the same role.

Brandon Workman   RHP

Born: 8/13/88   Age: 26   Bats: R   Throws: R   Height: 6'5"   Weight: 225

YEAR	TEAM	LVL	AGE	W	L	SV	G	GS	IP	H	HR	BB	K	BB/9	K/9	GB%	BABIP	WHIP	ERA	FIP	FRA	WARP
2012	SLM	A+	23	7	7	0	20	20	113²	104	10	20	107	1.6	8.5	48%	.297	1.09	3.40	3.20	4.54	1.1
2012	PME	AA	23	3	1	0	5	5	25	23	2	5	23	1.8	8.3	38%	.296	1.12	3.96	3.00	4.12	0.4
2013	PME	AA	24	5	1	0	11	10	65²	51	6	17	74	2.3	10.1	36%	.281	1.04	3.43	3.08	3.10	1.7
2013	PAW	AAA	24	3	1	0	6	6	35¹	39	6	13	34	3.3	8.7	42%	.340	1.47	2.80	4.76	4.45	0.4
2013	BOS	MLB	24	6	3	0	20	3	41²	44	5	15	47	3.2	10.2	42%	.345	1.42	4.97	3.46	3.48	0.7
2014	PAW	AAA	25	7	1	0	11	11	61¹	61	10	17	55	2.5	8.1	37%	.298	1.27	4.11	4.52	4.85	0.2
2014	BOS	MLB	25	1	10	0	19	15	87	88	11	36	70	3.7	7.2	42%	.296	1.43	5.17	4.47	4.93	0.0
2015	BOS	MLB	26	8	7	0	23	23	123¹	129	15	43	103	3.1	7.5	41%	.308	1.40	4.46	4.61	4.84	0.4

Breakout: 27%   Improve: 44%   Collapse: 20%   Attrition: 27%   MLB: 79%   *Comparables: Juan Nicasio, Hector Rondon, Esmil Rogers*

If it looks like a reliever, loses velocity when starting like a reliever, and lacks a strong third pitch like a reliever, it's probably a reliever. Workman pitched well enough as a starter in 2013 that you can't blame the Red Sox for trying it again, but the follow-up proved that Workman belongs in the bullpen. His fastball has ticked up to the mid-90s in relief, and his hammer curveball provides him with the second weapon he needs to induce swinging strikes. That's a more appealing package than what he brings to a rotation, where his fastball sits 90-91 and his curveball loses bite. If he can throw 80-plus innings and serve as part of a set-up crew, he's still plenty valuable.

Lineouts

Hitters

NAME	POS	TEAM	LVL	AGE	PA	R	2B	3B	HR	RBI	BB	K	SB	CS	AVG/OBP/SLG	TAv	BABIP	BRR	FRAA	WARP
Carlos Asuaje	3B	GRN	A	22	383	59	24	10	11	73	41	56	7	4	.305/.391/.542	.318	.333	0.0	3B(38): -0.3, 2B(24): 1.5	3.5
	LF	SLM	A+	22	176	27	14	2	4	28	18	34	1	3	.323/.398/.516	.313	.390	1.0	LF(19): 0.5, 2B(16): 0.2	1.7
Bryce Brentz	LF	PAW	AAA	25	267	42	11	2	12	53	32	58	0	1	.243/.341/.465	.277	.272	0.7	LF(28): 1.1, RF(23): -1.1	1.3
	LF	BOS	MLB	25	26	5	2	0	0	2	0	9	0	0	.308/.308/.385	.281	.471	1.0	LF(6): 0.3, RF(2): -0.0	0.2
Dan Butler	C	PAW	AAA	27	325	35	19	0	4	30	29	71	0	0	.241/.317/.350	.254	.301	-2.7	C(54): -0.0	0.6
	C	BOS	MLB	27	20	1	3	0	0	2	1	5	0	0	.211/.250/.368	.198	.286	-0.2	C(7): 0.1	-0.1
Keury De La Cruz	LF	PME	AA	22	275	30	15	0	7	30	14	55	3	2	.295/.327/.434	.268	.347	-2.5	LF(62): 3.0	0.6
Nick Longhi	LF	LOW	A-	18	121	19	10	1	0	10	11	22	0	3	.330/.388/.440	.309	.409	-0.2	LF(13): -1.4, RF(12): -0.2	0.5
Henry Ramos	RF	PME	AA	22	194	26	9	2	2	23	11	38	2	4	.326/.384/.431	.291	.404	-2.5	RF(39): -2.7, CF(7): 0.1	0.4
Wendell Rijo	2B	GRN	A	18	473	56	27	6	9	46	56	103	16	6	.254/.348/.416	.273	.318	-4.2	2B(106): 4.8	1.8
Sam Travis	1B	GRN	A	20	115	12	11	1	3	14	7	14	0	1	.290/.330/.495	.279	.308	-1.3	1B(23): 0.5	0.3
	1B	LOW	A-	20	174	28	5	1	4	30	4	18	5	1	.333/.364/.448	.292	.357	-0.7	1B(33): -1.5	0.5
Jemile Weeks	2B	NOR	AAA	27	257	29	12	4	1	19	37	30	8	4	.280/.392/.391	.281	.318	1.5	2B(30): 0.4, SS(17): 0.0	1.5
	2B	BAL	MLB	27	13	2	0	1	0	0	0	0	1	0	.273/.273/.455	.294	.273	0.1	2B(1): -0.0	0.1
	2B	BOS	MLB	27	32	6	3	0	0	3	4	2	2	0	.308/.406/.423	.318	.320	-0.2	2B(6): 0.0, SS(3): -0.1	0.2

Carlos Asuaje comes from the Dustin Pedroia/Sean Coyle school of short infielders with plus hit tools. He's got second-division upside, which is a big jump from 11th-round downside. ❖ The word "literally" is overused nowadays, but **Bryce Brentz** is a man who *literally* shot himself in the foot before the 2013 season. Things have mostly gone south for him since—on the field, at least; he hasn't shot any other body parts—though he recorded a few big hits in Boston as a September call-up. ❖ **Dan Butler** is salt-of-the-earth backup backstop whose summoning to the major leagues last season was a testament to human resiliency and the value of hard work. And if he sees any significant MLB time in 2015, something went horribly wrong and everybody in Boston will be miserable. ❖ **Keury De La Cruz** doesn't have the physical tools for an impact profile, but he's hit at every stop and continued that trend in Portland. He'll probably settle in as a Quad-A type. ❖ With impressive defensive chops at shortstop, plenty of swagger and a bat that stops short of hopeless, **Javier Guerra** started turning some heads in the GCL last season. He's got a chance to jump up the prospect rankings if he learns to take a walk once or twice a month. ❖ A 30th-round pick from the 2013 draft who signed for well over slot, **Nick Longhi** impressed with his hit tool and approach in Lowell before suffering a season-ending thumb injury. He's full of helium if he can stay on the field in 2015. ❖ A potential future fourth outfielder, **Henry Ramos** was having a great year in Portland before he suffered a stress fracture to his left leg in late May, ending his season. There aren't any standout tools here, but Ramos doesn't have glaring deficiencies, either. ❖ Billed as the "next Mookie Betts" before Betts became the Betts we know today, **Wendell Rijo** had a so-so year in Greenville, demonstrating a patient approach but failing to hit particularly well. Still, he could someday supplant Wendell Kim as the best Wendell in Red Sox history. ❖ A second-rounder out of Indiana, **Sam Travis** has a 1:1 ratio of first names to tools. Fortunately, the two are hit and power, good attributes for somebody confined to first base or left field. ❖ Things generally aren't looking up in your career when you're traded for Kelly Johnson, but **Jemile Weeks** hit in Triple-A and looked surprisingly adequate at shortstop in September. He's useful depth.

Pitchers

NAME	TEAM	LVL	AGE	W	L	SV	G	GS	IP	H	HR	BB	K	BB/9	K/9	GB%	BABIP	WHIP	ERA	FIP	FRA	WARP
Drake Britton	PAW	AAA	25	2	3	5	45	0	58¹	77	8	38	37	5.9	5.7	46%	.354	1.97	5.86	5.83	6.93	-1.4
	BOS	MLB	25	0	0	0	7	0	6²	5	0	2	4	2.7	5.4	33%	.238	1.05	0.00	2.86	3.05	0.1
Ty Buttrey	GRN	A	21	0	5	0	11	11	46	59	5	24	40	4.7	7.8	44%	.358	1.80	6.85	4.89	5.34	0.6
	LOW	A-	21	0	0	0	3	2	11²	11	0	7	12	5.4	9.3	48%	.333	1.54	3.09	3.18	3.08	0.3
Keith Couch	PME	AA	24	8	2	1	18	17	100¹	105	3	22	72	2.0	6.5	54%	.315	1.27	2.96	3.15	3.95	1.6
Luis Diaz	SLM	A+	22	6	3	0	13	13	67²	71	3	18	48	2.4	6.4	46%	.311	1.32	3.33	3.61	4.30	0.9
	PME	AA	22	3	4	0	13	13	77¹	71	7	26	63	3.0	7.3	41%	.286	1.25	3.72	4.03	4.74	0.6
Jeffry Fernandez	LOW	A-	21	0	3	0	4	4	18²	22	2	6	4	2.9	1.9	57%	.278	1.50	5.30	5.69	7.71	-0.5
Justin Haley	SLM	A+	23	7	4	1	19	13	92²	77	4	23	74	2.2	7.2	52%	.275	1.08	2.82	3.42	4.37	1.0
	PME	AA	23	3	2	0	6	6	37²	30	2	16	33	3.8	7.9	52%	.275	1.22	1.19	3.73	4.32	0.4
Heath Hembree	FRE	AAA	25	1	3	18	41	0	39¹	40	5	13	46	3.0	10.5	31%	.337	1.35	3.89	4.16	4.50	0.7
	BOS	MLB	25	0	0	0	10	0	11	11	1	5	6	4.5	5.4	28%	.323	1.60	4.50	4.76	4.99	-0.1
Dalier Hinojosa	PAW	AAA	28	3	5	3	41	0	61²	39	5	33	65	4.8	9.5	34%	.227	1.17	3.79	3.96	4.54	0.4
Cody Kukuk	GRN	A	21	3	0	0	5	5	24	18	1	12	29	4.5	10.9	46%	.315	1.25	1.88	3.21	3.19	0.7
	SLM	A+	21	4	7	0	20	20	78²	71	2	71	87	8.1	10.0	52%	.342	1.81	5.26	4.46	5.17	0.6
Simon Mercedes	LOW	A-	22	0	0	0	3	1	11	13	0	3	5	2.5	4.1	55%	.342	1.45	1.64	3.35	4.45	0.1
	SLM	A+	22	5	10	1	19	14	85	85	6	38	74	4.0	7.8	52%	.316	1.45	4.76	4.14	5.21	0.1
Nestor Molina	BIR	AA	25	7	4	7	44	0	61¹	58	7	22	46	3.2	6.8	59%	.274	1.30	4.55	4.44	5.33	-0.2
Noe Ramirez	PME	AA	24	2	1	18	42	0	67¹	56	0	16	56	2.1	7.5	51%	.290	1.07	2.14	2.54	3.38	1.2
Teddy Stankiewicz	GRN	A	20	11	8	0	25	25	140¹	141	9	29	102	1.9	6.5	44%	.299	1.21	3.72	3.63	4.47	2.3
Steven Wright	PAW	AAA	29	5	5	0	15	15	95	86	9	22	68	2.1	6.4	48%	.269	1.14	3.41	3.88	4.69	0.5
	BOS	MLB	29	0	1	0	6	1	21	21	4	4	22	1.7	9.4	57%	.328	1.19	2.57	2.87	3.30	0.5

Christopher Acosta was part of Boston's impressive haul of international talent last July. A 6-foot-3 Dominican teenager with an impressive feel for a changeup, Acosta is a lottery ticket, but one of those shiny $20 ones reserved for milestone birthdays. ❖ By sucking in Pawtucket, **Drake Britton** missed an opportunity to cement himself as part of Boston's bullpen. He was better in limited major-league duty in September, but at this point is still best known for looking like a Keebler Elf. ❖ **Ty Buttrey** was an above-slot signing in 2012, but gives out too many free passes and missed time with a hand injury last year. When asked to name the best pitcher on Greenville's staff, many scouts reluctantly admit they can't believe it's not Buttrey, given his draft pedigree. All things considered, that joke is probably still better than the one in Matt Barnes' comment. ❖ **Keith Couch** is a groundball artist who limited walks and taters in Double-A. He lacks a true out pitch, but gets glowing reviews for his makeup. ❖ You can't predict baseball, but maybe **Ryan Dempster** can: He elected not to partake in the train wreck that was Boston's 2014 season, spending the entire year on the restricted list in a state of quasi-retirement. ❖ **Luis Diaz** keeps getting better as he climbs through the minors, but it's really tough to imagine his secondaries working well enough for him to start in the majors, good command or not. ❖ Rated in some circles as the best pitcher in last July's international signing class, **Anderson Espinoza** is a 16-year-old right-hander who already hits 94. Pitchers this young always live up to their full potential, so he's a near lock to be an ace by 2019. Anderson Acepinoza, we'll call him, certainly. ❖ If you're looking for a sleeper prospect, **Jeffry Fernandez** is a terrific candidate, albeit a horrible speller. Fully recovered from Tommy John surgery, Fernandez can hit the upper 90s with his fastball, features a promising slider and should reach full-season ball in 2015. ❖ He's unlikely to ever be a big-time prospect, but **Justin Haley** took a long step forward in 2014, improving his command and moving up two levels. He needs better secondaries to avoid the bullpen, but has the fastball and size to start. ❖ **Joel Hanrahan** signed a $1 million deal with the Tigers last May while recovering from Tommy John surgery. He basically earned money to remain injured, which sounds kinkier than it actually was, but in doing so he was the only Tigers closer not to blow a save. ❖ Once billed as San Francisco's "closer of the future," **Heath Hembree** now looks like he'll profile more as a solid. unspectacular seventh-inning arm. He's homer-prone, which is dangerous in Fenway. ❖ Cuban righty **Dalier Hinojosa** had a rough transition to stateside pitching, with a 5.24 ERA at June's end. Six earned runs in his final 29 innings helped the final line, however, and he could see Fenway by late 2015. ❖ **Cody Kukuk** walked nearly as many batters as he struck out in High-A, but because he's a lefty with velocity he'll—whoa, says here he was arrested in November on suspicion of robbing a Kansas apartment at gunpoint. Nevermind. ❖ Unless **Simon Mercedes** bends his curveball with more consistency, he'll find himself in the bullpen as he moves up through the minor leagues. ❖ At this point, the Sox should move **Nestor Molina** behind the plate and see if his last name leads to a plus defensive profile. He's devoid of upside on the mound. ❖ If **Noe Ramirez** can limit homers in the majors as he did in Double-A, he'll have a meaningful career as a middle reliever. He'd be best suited to a big, power-killing home park, which is not exactly a unique trait among pitchers. ❖ Boston's second-round pick in 2013, **Teddy Stankiewicz** had a solid, if unspectacular, first full professional season. He has a nice fastball/slider/changeup combo but trouble repeating his delivery. ❖ Much as there must always be a Stark in Winterfell, there must always be a knuckleballer in Boston ... or at least in Pawtucket. **Steven Wright** held the throne last season, and will keep providing Quad-A depth moving forward.

Manager

John Farrell

YEAR	TEAM	W	L	Py-thag +/-	Avg PC	100+ P	120+ P	QS	BQS	REL	REL w Zero R	IBB	PH	PH Avg	PH HR	SB2	CS2	SB3	CS3	SAC Att	SAC%	POS SAC	Squeeze	Swing	In Play
2012	TOR	73	89	-1	91.9	52	0	74	3	495	396	20	80	.205	1	89	31	33	8	67	49.3%	32	3	406	138
2013	BOS	97	65	-5	100	88	5	95	6	450	355	10	81	.235	6	104	17	17	2	38	63.2%	21	0	336	104
2014	BOS	71	91	0	97.9	74	2	87	6	493	410	19	91	.231	2	43	21	19	3	34	58.8%	19	1	301	79

Bill James once proposed the hypothesis that managers do their best work early in their tenures. Farrell, who shares an organization with James these days, has obeyed the theory at both of his managerial stops. His Boston team, much like his Toronto team, performed better in his first year than his second. Of course, winning the World Series in '13 meant Farrell's second Boston team had to repeat as champions to avoid a letdown. They didn't, but there were other issues at play that caused friction.

Fudging with top prospects is among the few things that can end a championship-inspired honeymoon between a manager and the fanbase. While Farrell inspired complaints that went beyond his handling of the kids—for instance, he stuck with Brock Holt in the leadoff spot for too long—none was more spirited or meaningful to Boston's future. The tricky part is Farrell did not act on his own when he had Bogaerts change positions twice, or mookie Betts play all over; management signed and traded Stephen Drew, forcing Xander Bogaerts to third then back to short, and management had Betts move around while in the minors. That so many Boston rookies struggled last season amid inconsistent roles should raise questions about the Red Sox' introductory processes, or at minimum, their criteria when it comes to promoting players to The Show.

But none of the above is solely on Farrell's hands. And between his reputation and Boston's state as a team in transition, there's no reason to think the Sox should be concerned about moving forward under his watch. In other words, Farrell should prove to be an exception to James' hypothesis.

CHICAGO CUBS

by Sahadev Sharma

When Theo Epstein sat in a hotel room surrounded by Chicago reporters at the winter meetings in 2013, the Cubs were at the outset of an offseason that proved to be uneventful. A few small moves here and there, but nothing to inject a fan base that was starting to get restless with any real excitement. Epstein was, as is common for him, very straightforward about the state of his team.

"To make a big impact in the winter, you need one of two different kinds of currency in the game, or both," Epstein said. "The most important currency in the game right now, from a baseball standpoint, is either massive amounts of payroll flexibility or a real surplus of above-average, young players who are major-league ready or already making impact in the big leagues. If you look at the Cubs right now in December of 2013, we're not yet where we need to be in either of those areas. We don't have lots of currency in either area. But we're going to, we're getting there."

No Cubs fans wanted to hear Epstein essentially admit that they didn't have enough money or assets to be big players during the offseason, but he did it anyway. It was deflating at the time, but some took comfort that Epstein was confident they would be in a position to make a splash soon. This winter Epstein and general manager Jed Hoyer took quite a different tone, making it clear that the Cubs would no longer be building. Rather, as Epstein said, they were finally "transitioning away from a three-year period where we were essentially only accumulating young talent, and now we're competing."

Fans certainly didn't love all the losing that had become familiar during the Epstein era, but many have understood the goal. At Epstein's introductory press conference, he said it was essential to build from the ground up, focusing on scouting and player development; he, Hoyer and Jason McLeod, the Senior Vice President for Player Development and Amateur Scouting, have followed through. Epstein's been open about the fact that many of the team's signings in winters past—Paul Maholm, Scott Feldman, Jason Hammel—were added with the intent to flip them in trades.

It now appears that the Cubs are meeting their goals even sooner than they expected: Epstein has been quoted saying that they've done five years' worth of work in just three. They've revamped the player-development department, built state-of-the-art facilities in both Arizona and the Dominican Republic and transformed their farm system into one of the best in baseball.

Now, finally, it appears all that effort should start to add up to wins at the major-league level. For an organization whose fans certainly deserve a stretch of success, 2015 is the first time in a while that they can actually expect positive results: The team last finished above .500 in 2009. More importantly, 2015 is meant to be just the first in a series of good teams, something the Cubs haven't experienced in generations: The last time they strung together three seasons over .500 was 2007–09. At least four consecutive seasons over .500? You have to look all the way back to 1967–72.

The word 'process' gets thrown around a lot in baseball and the analytics community. It's easy to point to a sound process and say everything will work out in the end. But the bottom line is that no matter how perfectly a team plans and executes, results aren't guaranteed, and in the end, results are what matter. The Cubs appear to have made many smart moves over the past three years; things certainly haven't gone perfectly, but for the most part, they've hit the right notes. They have generally avoided the high-end free-agent market as a method of filling present holes on the roster and parlayed the consequent rough seasons into high draft picks. Those picks, under the current draft regime, translate to more money to spend in the draft, and the Cubs' bad final records have also given them additional room to spend on the international free agent market. Further, by working the periphery of free agency and scouring the waiver wire for value, they've done a remarkable job accumulating talent.

Hector Rondon, who served as the team's closer in 2014 and appears to have a bright future in the role, or at least as a high-leverage reliever, was picked up in the Rule 5 draft. Luis Valbuena was plucked off the waiver wire in April 2012, but he's a tough out at the plate and has a strong glove at third base. He shouldn't be a starter in the long run, but he could be a very valuable piece off the bench, capable of spot starts and injury-replacement duty at multiple positions. Trade acquisitions Anthony Rizzo and Jake Arrieta have emerged as stars, legit pieces around which to build a lineup and rotation.

Those moves were based on a sound strategy, but it also takes

CUBS PROSPECTUS
2014 W-L: 73-89, 5TH IN NL CENTRAL

Pythag	.436	26th	DER	.696	22nd
RS/G	3.79	26th	B-Age	26.7	2nd
RA/G	4.36	23rd	P-Age	28.1	15th
TAv	.257	20th	Salary	$92.6M	18th
BRR	3.39	10th	M$/MW	$3.2M	18th
TAv-P	.261	18th	DL Days	715	11th
FIP	3.48	6th	$ on DL	12%	8th

Three-Year Park Factors

Runs	Runs/RH	Runs/LH	HR/RH	HR/LH
98	93	99	95	88

Top Hitter WARP	7.5	Anthony Rizzo
Top Pitcher WARP	2.5	Jake Arrieta
Top Prospect		Addison Russell

luck. Kris Bryant has emerged as possibly the best prospect in baseball in under two years with the Cubs organization, but had the Astros, picking first overall, passed on Mark Appel, it's likely the Cubs, who were rumored to be interested in him, would have taken him at no. 2. Appel still has a chance at a bright future, but college aces are supposed to dominate A-ball, not get lit up for a 9.74 ERA, as Appel did in 2014. Had the chips fallen slightly differently, figuring him out could be the Cubs' problem rather than the Astros'.

In the most recent draft, the Cubs chose Kyle Schwarber fourth overall, a move many viewed as a reach. But not only did Schwarber hit at such a high level after signing (.344/.428/.634, mostly at High-A) that few question the pick anymore, he also signed for well below his slot value, allowing the Cubs to spend money on hard-to-sign pitchers like Carson Sands, Justin Steele and Dylan Cease in later rounds. Strategy is a major factor, of course: The Cubs obviously planned to spend less than the slot allotment on Schwarber. But there's good fortune in Schwarber producing like a player who could have been drafted no. 4 on his own merits.

A bit of luck showed up again with the Cubs' monster 2013 international class. Two arms acquired that year, Jefferson Mejia and Jen-Ho Tseng, have performed better than many expected prior to their stateside arrival. Tseng's velocity was down when many scouts saw him, but that wasn't the case when the Cubs' eyes were turned his way. Their brass believed the uptick was sustainable, and while the young Taiwanese righty doesn't hold much projection, he is a strong option to hold a spot in the middle of the Cubs' rotation a few years down the line. The Cubs were able to convince Mejia, who was eligible to sign in the previous international class, to wait for more money from them and he has rewarded them. The 6-foot-7 Dominican has seen an uptick in velocity and his secondaries are started to come around.

And of course there is the acquisition of two of the team's top-ten prospects—Addison Russell and Billy McKinney—last summer in a trade with the Oakland A's. Sure, Jeff Samardzija is proving to be one of the better pitchers in the game, and Jason Hammel was wrapping up a very impressive first half of the season, but it's rare for a general manager in this era to give up so much talent and so many years of control for anybody, even players like Samardzija and Hammel. However, Billy Beane was clearly willing to "overpay" for a chance to improve his team immediately and push them from very good to elite. Alas, it didn't work out for Beane and the A's, but the North Siders certainly won't be granting any requests for a mulligan. After struggling in the first half, McKinney found his stroke with the Cubs, hitting well in the normally pitcher-friendly Florida State League. Russell got healthy and has the all-around game at shortstop to be one of the few players who could justify a ranking ahead of Bryant on prospect lists. In a market where David Price and Jon Lester were also available, the Cubs were in the right place at the right time for Russell and McKinney to fall into their laps. But it wasn't pure chance, of course: The Cubs' willingness to make their big sale nearly a month before the trade deadline, while the Red Sox and Rays didn't make their moves until the last minute, surely played a major role.

Cubs prospects have also stayed healthy, avoiding any major injuries over the last few years. Even when they are saddled with issues, it doesn't hold them back on the field, particularly in the case of Jorge Soler. Since coming from Cuba in 2012, Soler has battled various ailments, including numerous lower-body muscular issues. After missing much of the first half in 2014, he returned healthy and rocketed through the system, hitting everything in sight and earning a late-season call-up, whereupon he delivered a .292/.330/.573 line in 24 big-league games. C.J. Edwards also missed much of last season with shoulder problems, but he never required surgery and was a standout in the Arizona Fall League. Pierce Johnson missed time on separate occasions with calf and hamstring problems, but he ended the season in dominating fashion (1.80 ERA with 69 strikeouts and 30 walks in his final 65 innings pitched), developing a feel for his impressive cutter in the process.

None of this is to say there haven't been misses: The Edwin Jackson signing has been an unmitigated disaster; the ill-fated trade for Ian Stewart cost them Gold Glove second baseman D.J. LeMahieu; and Scott Baker, Jose Veras and James McDonald did not pan out, failing to contribute to the big-league club or convince any other general managers to give up any goodies to acquire them. But misses are to be expected; no front office bats 1.000. Organizations just have to hope the good outweighs the bad, minimize disastrous moves and, every once in a while, hit a home run.

There are high hopes for 2015, but this season isn't the final step of the process. It isn't easy to flip a switch and transition from a long stretch of extreme losing to reach contender status. While new manager Joe Maddon did oversee that type of dramatic turnaround in Tampa, nobody should sound the alarms if the Cubs fail to contend for the playoffs this summer. It certainly is the goal, as Epstein has plainly stated on numerous occasions, but a big step forward in the win department while hanging on the periphery of the Wild-Card race late into the season should be seen as legitimate progress.

The organization has pointed to the Cardinals as a literal model of consistency. And while Epstein has gone out of his way to compliment what St. Louis has done to build its team, he's also made clear that he expects the Cubs not to look up at them forever, but to surpass them and become everybody else's model franchise. This team is no longer lying in wait; things are expected to turn in Wrigleyville, and the hope is that 2015 will be the coming-out party. ■

—Sahadev Sharma is an editor and writer for Baseball Prospectus. When not at Wrigley Field or The Cell, he carves out time to spend with his family.

Player comments by Sahadev Sharma and Baseball Prospectus Authors

Hitters

Arismendy Alcantara   CF

Born: 10/29/91   Age: 23   Bats: B   Throws: R   Height: 5' 10"   Weight: 170

YEAR	TEAM	LVL	AGE	PA	R	2B	3B	HR	RBI	BB	K	SB	CS	AVG/OBP/SLG	TAv	BABIP	BRR	FRAA	WARP
2012	DAY	A+	20	359	47	13	7	7	51	19	61	25	4	.302/.339/.447	.278	.347	4.1	SS(71): -4.6, 3B(8): 0.6	2.1
2013	TEN	AA	21	571	69	36	4	15	69	62	125	31	6	.271/.352/.451	.287	.332	5.2	SS(66): 4.1, 2B(64): -0.1	4.2
2014	IOW	AAA	22	366	62	25	11	10	41	25	83	21	3	.307/.353/.537	.300	.380	3.8	2B(70): -2.8, CF(11): -0.2	2.6
2014	CHN	MLB	22	300	31	11	2	10	29	17	93	8	5	.205/.254/.367	.228	.266	0.7	CF(48): -2.7, 2B(25): 0.8	-0.3
2015	*CHN*	*MLB*	*23*	*345*	*44*	*16*	*3*	*8*	*32*	*20*	*93*	*14*	*4*	*.240/.285/.387*	*.251*	*.306*	*1.3*	*2B -1, CF -1*	*0.7*

Breakout: 1%   Improve: 27%   Collapse: 5%   Attrition: 12%   MLB: 49%   Comparables: *Josh Barfield, Howie Kendrick, Nick Franklin*

Alcantara came up through the Cubs' system as a shortstop, but with their embarrassment of riches at the position he developed more versatility by playing second base and center field. As befits an ex-shortstop, he displayed good range at second and showed plus defensive skills there overall. As befits an ex-infielder, his routes and reads in center were rough, though they've improved quickly, and Alcantara has the speed to outrun his mistakes. As befits nothing in particular, he swung and missed a lot in the majors and looked hopeless against breaking stuff. Alcantara's offseason will be spent working on his selectivity; if he can correct that, his speed-power combination, which has drawn (insane) comparisons to Jose Reyes and Jimmy Rollins, may bear fruit.

Albert Almora   CF

Born: 4/16/94   Age: 21   Bats: R   Throws: R   Height: 6' 2"   Weight: 180

YEAR	TEAM	LVL	AGE	PA	R	2B	3B	HR	RBI	BB	K	SB	CS	AVG/OBP/SLG	TAv	BABIP	BRR	FRAA	WARP
2012	BOI	A-	18	65	9	7	0	1	6	0	5	0	1	.292/.292/.446	.232	.305	-3.0	CF(15): 1.9	0.0
2013	KNC	A	19	272	39	17	4	3	23	17	30	4	4	.329/.376/.466	.286	.362	-0.7	CF(59): 9.2	2.7
2014	DAY	A+	20	385	55	20	2	7	50	12	46	6	3	.283/.306/.406	.254	.305	0.9	CF(87): 4.2	1.6
2014	TEN	AA	20	144	20	7	2	2	10	2	23	1	1	.234/.250/.355	.214	.267	-0.1	CF(32): -1.1	-0.4
2015	*CHN*	*MLB*	*21*	*250*	*23*	*12*	*1*	*3*	*20*	*5*	*51*	*1*	*1*	*.237/.255/.336*	*.225*	*.285*	*-0.4*	*CF 3*	*0.1*

Breakout: 0%   Improve: 0%   Collapse: 0%   Attrition: 0%   MLB: 0%   Comparables: *Engel Beltre, Rafael Ortega, Xavier Avery*

Don't make the mistake of scouting Almora's 2014 stat line and assuming he failed. There are two things that can't be questioned: He plays some of the best center-field defense in the minors and his makeup is off the charts. His extreme confidence could rub some the wrong way, but it is admired in a baseball clubhouse. Almora is a very aggressive hitter with innate contact skills who had rarely struggled before posting an ugly .241/.264/.317 line in his first 62 games at Daytona. The Cubs' development staff took the opportunity to work with him on his approach, imploring him not to channel a young Josh Vitters and swing at anything he can reach. Armed with a better plan of attack and a slight mechanical adjustment, Almora mashed to a .988 OPS in his last 27 games at High-A before being promoted. He might never take walks, but many scouts believe in Almora's hit tool and trust that, in addition to his glove and leadership, he'll do enough with the bat to have a successful big-league career.

Javier Baez   2B

Born: 12/1/92   Age: 22   Bats: R   Throws: R   Height: 6' 0"   Weight: 190

YEAR	TEAM	LVL	AGE	PA	R	2B	3B	HR	RBI	BB	K	SB	CS	AVG/OBP/SLG	TAv	BABIP	BRR	FRAA	WARP
2012	PEO	A	19	235	41	10	5	12	33	9	48	20	3	.333/.383/.596	.347	.378	4.4	SS(52): 5.1	3.9
2012	DAY	A+	19	86	9	3	1	4	13	5	21	4	2	.188/.244/.400	.206	.200	-0.9	SS(23): -1.0	-0.4
2013	DAY	A+	20	337	59	19	4	17	57	21	78	12	2	.274/.338/.535	.299	.310	2.2	SS(73): 2.9	3.3
2013	TEN	AA	20	240	39	15	0	20	54	19	69	8	2	.294/.346/.638	.343	.333	1.0	SS(50): 1.5	3.4
2014	IOW	AAA	21	434	64	24	2	23	80	34	130	16	8	.260/.323/.510	.282	.322	2.8	SS(85): -6.2, 2B(16): 0.7	2.8
2014	CHN	MLB	21	229	25	6	0	9	20	15	95	5	1	.169/.227/.324	.197	.248	1.2	SS(30): -0.4, 2B(25): -3.3	-1.0
2015	*CHN*	*MLB*	*22*	*303*	*38*	*12*	*1*	*14*	*41*	*15*	*101*	*8*	*3*	*.225/.270/.427*	*.260*	*.289*	*0.5*	*SS -0, 2B -1*	*1.1*

Breakout: 4%   Improve: 30%   Collapse: 3%   Attrition: 14%   MLB: 54%   Comparables: *Chris Davis, Travis Snider, Chris Carter*

The report on Baez was out before he even arrived in the big leagues: The super-prospect will swing early and often, looking to launch the ball as far as possible every time. Result? The incredible 42 percent strikeout rate you see above. With a history of struggling early at higher levels, Baez has shown the ability to correct flaws. Indeed, part of the reason he was promoted at the end of season was to jump-start the adjustments he'll need to make in 2015 and beyond. With some big-league at-bats now on video, Baez and the coaching/development staff have something to break down and analyze over the winter so they can develop a plan for the spring. Despite a toned-down bat waggle, Baez still has an unconventional swing, though most suggest that improvements to his approach, not cleaner mechanics, are the key to future success. (Noticing a theme?) If Baez can learn a little more patience at the plate, his obscene power from a middle infield position will make him an All Star.

John Baker   C

Born: 1/20/81   Age: 34   Bats: L   Throws: R   Height: 6' 1"   Weight: 215

YEAR	TEAM	LVL	AGE	PA	R	2B	3B	HR	RBI	BB	K	SB	CS	AVG/OBP/SLG	TAv	BABIP	BRR	FRAA	WARP
2012	SDN	MLB	31	214	17	8	0	0	14	20	41	2	1	.238/.310/.280	.229	.303	-1.8	C(56): 0.5	-0.2
2013	ABQ	AAA	32	153	14	1	0	4	17	18	33	0	1	.203/.294/.301	.222	.235	1.2	C(37): -0.2	0.2
2013	SDN	MLB	32	46	0	0	0	0	2	6	12	0	0	.150/.261/.150	.140	.214	0.1	C(14): 0.0	-0.3
2014	CHN	MLB	33	208	9	7	0	0	15	19	58	0	0	.192/.273/.231	.198	.278	-3.9	C(55): -0.8, P(1): -0.0	-1.2
2015	*CHN*	*MLB*	*34*	*250*	*20*	*8*	*1*	*1*	*17*	*24*	*62*	*1*	*0*	*.206/.284/.264*	*.217*	*.275*	*-1.8*	*C -1*	*-0.4*

Breakout: 1%   Improve: 35%   Collapse: 11%   Attrition: 28%   MLB: 85%   Comparables: *Chad Moeller, Wil Nieves, Johnny Roseboro*

Don't expect any visible value out of Baker and you won't be disappointed. He's a veteran backstop who's worthless at the plate and isn't a standout defensively, but he calls a solid game, builds strong relationships with his pitchers and has been known to occasionally deliver an entertaining position-player-on-the-mound performance. He earns his roster spot with leadership by example in the clubhouse: He works hard, studies film and is, in a phrase, a student of the game. The fact that he does it all without the pious over-seriousness that sometimes afflicts his kind is icing on the cake. He cracks jokes and befriends all around him, showing his younger teammates that the job can balance hard work and fun. If you think this all sounds like a managerial candidate waiting to happen, you're not wrong.

Kris Bryant   3B
Born: 1/4/92   Age: 23   Bats: R   Throws: R   Height: 6'5"   Weight: 215

YEAR	TEAM	LVL	AGE	PA	R	2B	3B	HR	RBI	BB	K	SB	CS	AVG/OBP/SLG	TAv	BABIP	BRR	FRAA	WARP
2013	BOI	A-	21	77	13	8	1	4	16	8	17	0	0	.354/.416/.692	.372	.404	-0.2	3B(16): 1.5	1.1
2013	DAY	A+	21	62	9	5	1	5	14	3	17	1	0	.333/.387/.719	.362	.400	-0.6	3B(13): 1.4	1.0
2014	TEN	AA	22	297	61	20	0	22	58	43	77	8	2	.355/.458/.702	.405	.440	0.1	3B(62): 1.5	6.0
2014	IOW	AAA	22	297	57	14	1	21	52	43	85	7	2	.295/.418/.619	.358	.367	-2.2	3B(67): 5.3	4.4
2015	CHN	MLB	23	250	37	10	0	14	41	27	79	4	1	.261/.351/.514	.321	.336	0.0	3B 4	2.5

Breakout: 1%   Improve: 34%   Collapse: 2%   Attrition: 13%   MLB: 73%   *Comparables: Giancarlo Stanton, Chris Carter, Chris Davis*

It's hard to imagine a better season for Bryant that doesn't end with him in the majors. He won every imaginable minor-league award and you'd be pressed to find someone who didn't feel he deserved the accolades. Those slash lines above combine to .325/.438/.661 and the 43 home runs led the minors. All this in his first full professional season. If not for MLB's punitive-to-players service time rules, Bryant could have arrived at Wrigley in September; alas, he likely won't hit the bigs until an extra year of team control is guaranteed. (See Jason Heyward's service time for the results of an Opening Day assignment.)

Bryant has an advanced approach and is constantly honing his craft, with his only apparent flaw being his strikeout rate, which peaked at 29 percent in Triple-A. As with many great hitters, the strikeouts are a byproduct of comfort hitting with two strikes and a willingness to wait for his pitch, resulting in deep counts. His adjustment to major-league pitching should be easier than for most young players, even most top prospects, and his combination of talent and makeup make him one of few prospects scouts feel comfortable labeling "can't-miss." Add the baseball skills to a frankly absurd degree of handsomeness and you've got a potential Face of MLB knocking down the door.

Welington Castillo   C
Born: 4/24/87   Age: 28   Bats: R   Throws: R   Height: 5'10"   Weight: 210

YEAR	TEAM	LVL	AGE	PA	R	2B	3B	HR	RBI	BB	K	SB	CS	AVG/OBP/SLG	TAv	BABIP	BRR	FRAA	WARP
2012	IOW	AAA	25	176	22	6	0	6	22	23	37	0	0	.260/.375/.425	.286	.305	-0.1	C(41): -0.8	1.2
2012	CHN	MLB	25	190	16	11	0	5	22	17	51	0	0	.265/.337/.418	.271	.348	-0.6	C(49): -1.5, 1B(1): -0.0	0.8
2013	CHN	MLB	26	428	41	23	0	8	32	34	97	2	0	.274/.349/.397	.266	.347	-1.0	C(111): -0.1	2.5
2014	CHN	MLB	27	417	28	19	0	13	46	26	102	0	0	.237/.296/.389	.261	.288	-1.9	C(106): 0.6	2.3
2015	CHN	MLB	28	395	41	18	0	11	46	30	99	1	0	.243/.312/.391	.267	.301	-1.0	C -1, 1B 0	1.7

Breakout: 2%   Improve: 43%   Collapse: 10%   Attrition: 22%   MLB: 90%   *Comparables: Michael McKenry, Geovany Soto, Matt LaPorta*

Castillo keeps most everything in front of him, displays a strong arm and has solid mechanics behind the plate. That wasn't always the case, but after spending time working with catching coach Mike Borzello, Castillo has improved by leaps and bounds, or by squats and shuffles, or whatever catchers improve by. Framing is still an issue despite the hard work, which might mean that he's already at his (very low) ceiling in that area. Castillo was once considered a bat-first prospect; he didn't turn into an All-Star hitter and his sub-.300 on-base percentage in 2014 makes right-thinking fans wrinkle their noses, but his bat is league-average overall and well above the average for his position. The arrival of Miguel Montero will affect Castillo's playing time if he stays in Wrigleyville, but given his history of battering southpaws he's well-suited for platoon duty.

Starlin Castro   SS
Born: 3/24/90   Age: 25   Bats: R   Throws: R   Height: 6'0"   Weight: 190

YEAR	TEAM	LVL	AGE	PA	R	2B	3B	HR	RBI	BB	K	SB	CS	AVG/OBP/SLG	TAv	BABIP	BRR	FRAA	WARP
2012	CHN	MLB	22	691	78	29	12	14	78	36	100	25	13	.283/.323/.430	.269	.315	1.1	SS(162): -0.7	3.9
2013	CHN	MLB	23	705	59	34	2	10	44	30	129	9	6	.245/.284/.347	.228	.290	0.1	SS(159): -4.0	0.0
2014	CHN	MLB	24	569	58	33	1	14	65	35	100	4	4	.292/.339/.438	.279	.337	-2.6	SS(133): 4.9	3.6
2015	CHN	MLB	25	562	56	29	4	8	57	29	91	10	6	.278/.318/.396	.271	.320	-0.4	SS -1	2.9

Breakout: 1%   Improve: 70%   Collapse: 2%   Attrition: 3%   MLB: 100%   *Comparables: Jose Reyes, Nomar Garciaparra, J.J. Hardy*

The narrative on Castro has fluctuated quite a bit in a short period of time. The Cubs saw instant impact on his arrival in the majors when he homered in his first at-bat and added a triple later that night. The next season, Castro led the league in hits and made his first All-Star team. Then came the Epstein/Hoyer takeover; it was clear the new group valued Castro, but believed they could get more out of him. After hitting coach Rudy Jaramillo was let go during the 2012 season, manager Dale Sveum and interim hitting coach James Rowson went to work adjusting Castro's aggressive approach. Utter disaster. Not only were the 2013 numbers bad, but Castro seemed to lose all self-confidence. A player who came to the big leagues with one of the highest-rated hit tools in the minors was a liability in the box. Then Sveum and Rowson were let go and new manager Rick Renteria dedicated himself to rebuilding Castro's swagger; this included allowing him to return to the free-swinging style that had carried him to the majors in the first place. Castro rewarded Renteria with a career-best season at the plate, though he lost the final month to a high-ankle sprain.

While some might say that the year-and-a-half experiment adjusting Castro's approach was a failure, the results suggest that 2014 actually represented the synthesis of Castro's natural approach and the Sveum-Rowson teaching. Though he technically *can* cover a few inches off the plate, Castro took more of those pitches, swinging at a career-low 30 percent of the pitches he saw outside the zone. He drove the ball with more frequency when he saw strikes. While he gets dinged for lapses of concentration that lead to sloppy errors or baserunning mistakes, they were infrequent last year.

Castro remains a polarizing player, but his third career All-Star appearance served to scold those in the baseball world who wrote him off too hastily after 2013.

Chris Coghlan   LF
Born: 6/18/85   Age: 30   Bats: L   Throws: R   Height: 6'0"   Weight: 195

YEAR	TEAM	LVL	AGE	PA	R	2B	3B	HR	RBI	BB	K	SB	CS	AVG/OBP/SLG	TAv	BABIP	BRR	FRAA	WARP
2012	NWO	AAA	27	368	42	21	3	7	31	46	44	10	2	.284/.375/.435	.300	.309	0.2	RF(41): 3.5, LF(36): 1.3	2.9
2012	MIA	MLB	27	105	10	1	0	1	10	9	12	0	2	.140/.212/.183	.156	.146	0.7	LF(21): 0.8, CF(13): -0.7	-0.9
2013	JUP	A+	28	28	1	0	1	0	2	1	6	0	0	.185/.214/.259	.165	.238	0.4	3B(6): -0.9	-0.3
2013	MIA	MLB	28	214	10	10	3	1	10	17	43	2	0	.256/.318/.354	.263	.322	-0.1	LF(18): 2.0, CF(17): 0.8	0.7
2014	IOW	AAA	29	88	9	5	0	0	6	13	18	6	1	.243/.379/.314	.264	.321	0.5	RF(16): 0.6, 1B(5): -0.1	0.2
2014	CHN	MLB	29	432	50	28	5	9	41	39	81	7	4	.283/.352/.452	.293	.337	2.4	LF(101): 3.2, RF(4): 0.2	3.0
2015	CHN	MLB	30	381	38	19	2	5	36	34	70	7	3	.244/.316/.359	.257	.289	1.2	LF 2, RF 1	1.1

Breakout: 0%		Improve: 37%		Collapse: 5%		Attrition: 21%		MLB: 89%			*Comparables:*	*Mitch Maier, Eric Byrnes, Willie Harris*								

Mostly an afterthought after suffering numerous injuries over the past four seasons—including knee and back issues—Coghlan was healthy and, in turn, productive, for the first time since his 2009 Rookie of the Year campaign. Though the bat was quite strong, the defense left much to be desired. Yes, he's hidden in left field, but he chases batted balls with all the awkward gusto of your uncle's Thanksgiving-table speech about Kim Kardashian's posterior. It's not a disaster if Coghlan is your Opening Day left fielder, but he fits much better for a contender as a bat-first fourth outfielder.

Eloy Jimenez   OF
Born: 11/27/96 Age: 18 Bats: R Throws: R Height: 6' 4" Weight: 205

YEAR	TEAM	LVL	AGE	PA	R	2B	3B	HR	RBI	BB	K	SB	CS	AVG/OBP/SLG	TAv	BABIP	BRR	FRAA	WARP
2015	CHN	MLB	18	250	16	9	1	2	19	10	77	1	0	.189/.225/.259	.186	.264	-0.3	RF -1, LF -0	-1.6

Breakout: 0%	Improve: 0%	Collapse: 0%	Attrition: 0%	MLB: 0%	*Comparables:*	*Zoilo Almonte, Gregory Polanco, Caleb Gindl*

After receiving the highest bonus ($2.8 million) in the 2013 international free agent class, Jimenez impressed enough to spend the summer stateside despite not even turning 18 until November. You could forgive the Cubs for thinking he's actually 25, because the hulking corner outfielder is built like anything but a teenager. As you'd expect, he projects to have top-tier power, as the ball jumps off his bat. The swing mechanics, on the other hand, are more akin to your Geocities home page, the one with the questionable overuse of <blink> tags and the "Always Under Construction!" animated GIF. But hey, you got smarter, signed up for a WordPress account, and now look. The Cubs' development staff is, to torture a metaphor, logging in now.

Tommy La Stella   2B
Born: 1/31/89 Age: 26 Bats: L Throws: R Height: 5' 11" Weight: 185

YEAR	TEAM	LVL	AGE	PA	R	2B	3B	HR	RBI	BB	K	SB	CS	AVG/OBP/SLG	TAv	BABIP	BRR	FRAA	WARP
2012	LYN	A+	23	358	43	22	5	5	56	36	24	13	2	.302/.386/.460	.315	.305	-0.3	2B(75): -6.6	2.7
2013	LYN	A+	24	29	7	1	0	1	4	8	1	1	1	.550/.690/.750	.488	.556	0.9	2B(3): 0.1	0.9
2013	MIS	AA	24	324	32	21	2	4	41	37	34	7	1	.343/.422/.473	.339	.380	-1.8	2B(73): -3.2	3.1
2014	GWN	AAA	25	199	18	6	1	1	23	25	14	1	1	.293/.384/.359	.274	.308	0.0	2B(40): 1.7	1.1
2014	ATL	MLB	25	360	22	16	1	1	31	36	40	2	1	.251/.328/.317	.239	.283	-0.2	2B(88): -2.3	0.2
2015	CHN	MLB	26	338	32	17	2	3	31	33	43	2	1	.267/.343/.362	.270	.299	0.0	2B -3	1.1

Breakout: 2%	Improve: 42%	Collapse: 10%	Attrition: 20%	MLB: 64%	*Comparables:*	*Alberto Callaspo, Chris Getz, Johnny Giavotella*

Long viewed as the antidote to Dan Uggla's toxin in Atlanta, La Stella played as well as he could early on. He hit for a high average, walked and gave the Braves an archetypal no. 2 hitter, complete with exceptional bat control. After two months of peak La Stella, everything went downhill. Blame it on a few minor bumps, the boogie or the league adjusting with better defensive positioning, but the degree of the drop-off is worrisome. Why? La Stella doesn't do anything else well enough to earn his keep. If he's not hitting singles and getting on base, he's not a big-league player, especially now that he's a Cub and has to compete with their plethora of infield youngsters for a spot.

Junior Lake   LF
Born: 3/27/90 Age: 25 Bats: R Throws: R Height: 6' 3" Weight: 215

YEAR	TEAM	LVL	AGE	PA	R	2B	3B	HR	RBI	BB	K	SB	CS	AVG/OBP/SLG	TAv	BABIP	BRR	FRAA	WARP
2012	TEN	AA	22	448	56	26	3	10	50	35	105	21	12	.279/.341/.432	.281	.353	-0.4	SS(72): 0.8, 3B(29): 0.5	2.6
2013	IOW	AAA	23	170	30	10	2	4	18	10	33	14	5	.295/.341/.462	.287	.347	1.9	3B(36): 2.1, RF(6): -0.2	1.2
2013	CHN	MLB	23	254	26	16	0	6	16	13	68	4	4	.284/.332/.428	.280	.377	0.2	LF(32): 0.2, CF(27): -0.4	1.5
2014	IOW	AAA	24	71	11	3	0	2	7	6	15	2	1	.262/.324/.400	.291	.313	0.4	LF(8): -0.7, CF(5): -0.0	0.4
2014	CHN	MLB	24	326	30	10	3	9	25	14	110	7	3	.211/.246/.351	.223	.293	0.8	LF(53): 4.5, CF(36): -2.8	-0.3
2015	CHN	MLB	25	323	34	15	1	7	33	17	92	9	4	.241/.285/.373	.251	.319	0.2	LF 2, CF -2	0.7

Breakout: 2%	Improve: 38%	Collapse: 8%	Attrition: 25%	MLB: 83%	*Comparables:*	*Starling Marte, Wladimir Balentien, Aaron Cunningham*

Lake looks the part, but the holes in his game aren't closing. The athletic former infielder has a cannon but no accuracy in the outfield. His fielding instincts and routes are poor. He whiffs indiscriminately, even relative to his strikeout-era peers. He looks fastball at all times—when someone's dumb or unlucky enough to give him one out over the plate, he'll scatter pedestrians on Waveland. But if a pitcher has bendy and/or slow stuff or any semblance of command, Lake is overmatched, and the percentage of pitchers in the big leagues with command or good secondaries is overwhelming. There's still a chance Lake could have value as a fourth outfielder, especially if his defense upgrades to center-fieldable, but the likelihood of anything more is unrealistic. We should have been calling him "Pond" all along.

Billy McKinney   CF
Born: 8/23/94 Age: 20 Bats: L Throws: L Height: 6' 1" Weight: 195

YEAR	TEAM	LVL	AGE	PA	R	2B	3B	HR	RBI	BB	K	SB	CS	AVG/OBP/SLG	TAv	BABIP	BRR	FRAA	WARP
2013	VER	A-	18	37	5	2	1	1	6	3	4	1	1	.353/.405/.559	.371	.379	-0.5	CF(9): 0.6	0.6
2014	DAY	A+	19	210	30	12	4	1	36	25	42	1	0	.301/.390/.432	.306	.377	2.4	RF(29): 2.6, CF(4): -0.1	1.8
2014	STO	A+	19	333	42	12	2	10	33	36	58	5	3	.241/.330/.400	.257	.267	-0.7	CF(67): -3.8, RF(7): 0.2	0.3
2015	CHN	MLB	20	250	24	9	1	3	19	19	62	0	0	.214/.280/.304	.226	.277	-0.2	CF -2, RF 1	-0.5

Breakout: 0%	Improve: 0%	Collapse: 0%	Attrition: 0%	MLB: 0%	*Comparables:*	*Aaron Hicks, Cedric Hunter, Che-Hsuan Lin*

McKinney was the less-heralded piece acquired by the Cubs when they sent Jeff Samardzija and Jason Hammel to Oakland in early July. However, he opened eyes with an impressive showing at Daytona, displaying both notable bat-to-ball skills and the mature approach of a stereotypical A's draft pick. McKinney isn't projected to hit for much power and will be limited to a corner in the future, with a weak arm and questionable defense even for left field, but a plus hit tool is a plus hit tool. He makes contact, draws walks and uses his lefty swing to spray liners all over the field. McKinney has the tools and approach to succeed this summer as a 20-year-old in Double-A, making him yet another impressive bat in a fully stocked farm system.

Miguel Montero   C
Born: 7/9/83   Age: 31   Bats: L   Throws: R   Height: 5' 11"   Weight: 210

YEAR	TEAM	LVL	AGE	PA	R	2B	3B	HR	RBI	BB	K	SB	CS	AVG/OBP/SLG	TAv	BABIP	BRR	FRAA	WARP
2012	ARI	MLB	28	573	65	25	2	15	88	73	130	0	0	.286/.391/.438	.296	.362	-5.9	C(139): 2.2	4.6
2013	ARI	MLB	29	475	44	14	0	11	42	51	110	0	0	.230/.318/.344	.240	.282	-2.0	C(112): 0.5	0.9
2014	ARI	MLB	30	560	40	23	0	13	72	56	97	0	4	.243/.329/.370	.260	.275	-4.6	C(131): 0.4	1.8
2015	CHN	MLB	31	512	52	23	0	11	56	52	109	1	1	.248/.332/.377	.271	.300	-3.2	C 1	2.4

Breakout: 1%   Improve: 34%   Collapse: 4%   Attrition: 10%   MLB: 94%   Comparables: *Ted Simmons, Geovany Soto, Russell Martin*

After missing part of the 2013 season with a back injury, Montero returned to play almost 140 games in 2014. But whether absence, age or injury is to blame, he's not quite the star he once was. A natural pull hitter, the 31-year-old is putting the ball on the ground more, playing into the shifting nature of opposing defenses and zapping his average. To his credit, he has tried to use the opposite field (with some success) and managed double-digit infield hits, including a few bunts. Montero continues to walk at a decent rate and makes a solid amount of contact. Defensively, he is adept at stealing strikes, a skill that has not been shown to decay with age, though he lacks mobility on balls in the dirt. Even on the wrong side of 30, he is still a starter at catcher; however, the margins for his health are slim, and he's probably not worth the $40 million the Cubs will pay him over the next three seasons.

Mike Olt   3B
Born: 8/27/88   Age: 26   Bats: R   Throws: R   Height: 6' 2"   Weight: 210

YEAR	TEAM	LVL	AGE	PA	R	2B	3B	HR	RBI	BB	K	SB	CS	AVG/OBP/SLG	TAv	BABIP	BRR	FRAA	WARP
2012	FRI	AA	23	421	65	17	1	28	82	61	101	4	0	.288/.398/.579	.344	.327	1.7	3B(78): 0.9, 1B(13): -0.9	5.4
2012	TEX	MLB	23	40	2	1	0	0	5	5	13	1	1	.152/.250/.182	.205	.227	-1.3	1B(8): 0.8, 3B(5): 0.3	-0.2
2013	IOW	AAA	24	152	11	3	1	3	8	20	37	0	0	.168/.276/.275	.213	.207	-0.9	3B(38): 2.5	0.0
2013	ROU	AAA	24	268	37	15	0	11	32	35	89	0	0	.213/.317/.422	.268	.288	0.6	3B(63): 5.1	1.5
2014	IOW	AAA	25	115	16	9	0	7	24	8	33	1	0	.302/.348/.585	.320	.373	-0.7	1B(26): 0.6, 3B(2): -0.1	-0.9
2014	CHN	MLB	25	258	23	8	0	12	33	25	100	0	1	.160/.248/.356	.235	.203	-0.3	3B(52): -1.3, 1B(12): 0.4	-0.3
2015	CHN	MLB	26	260	29	10	0	11	34	27	85	1	0	.211/.295/.399	.263	.275	-0.4	3B 2, 1B 0	0.8

Breakout: 3%   Improve: 22%   Collapse: 10%   Attrition: 27%   MLB: 64%   Comparables: *Josh Fields, Zach Lutz, Brandon Allen*

The Cubs handed Olt the keys to the hot corner last spring, and the former Ranger promptly backed over Jimmy's tricycle, through the peonies and into the neighbor's lemonade stand, as his complete inability to make contact earned him a demotion to Triple-A in late July. Olt admitted he'd developed bad habits at the plate and worked to correct them in Iowa, revamping his stance and swing, which led to better results. The strikeouts remained high, but one major issue—swinging through pitches in the zone—seemed to be less of a bugaboo. Olt has tremendous raw power and some versatility as a multi-corner player, which will give him a shot at big-league relevance even as he's rudely shoved aside by the arrival of Kris Bryant.

Manny Ramirez   DH
Born: 5/30/72   Age: 43   Bats: R   Throws: R   Height: 6' 0"   Weight: 225

YEAR	TEAM	LVL	AGE	PA	R	2B	3B	HR	RBI	BB	K	SB	CS	AVG/OBP/SLG	TAv	BABIP	BRR	FRAA	WARP
2012	SAC	AAA	40	69	8	3	0	0	14	5	17	0	0	.302/.348/.349	.228	.404	0.5		-0.1
2013	ROU	AAA	41	119	7	3	0	3	13	10	14	0	0	.259/.328/.370	.251	.275	-1.6		-0.2
2014	IOW	AAA	42	77	6	2	0	3	10	5	27	0	0	.222/.273/.375	.234	.310	-0.5	LF(4): -0.2	-0.2
2015	CHN	MLB	43	250	22	10	0	3	23	24	60	0	0	.228/.307/.319	.242	.294	-0.5	LF 0	-0.1

Breakout: 7%   Improve: 9%   Collapse: 25%   Attrition: 27%   MLB: 49%   Comparables: *Darrell Evans, Hank Aaron, Jason Giambi*

When Ramirez joined the Cubs' Triple-A team as a player/coach in July, Theo Epstein made it clear to him that while he'd get sporadic playing time, he was there primarily to pass along his vast hitting knowledge to the team's precocious prospects, and he had zero chance of being called up. By all accounts Ramirez's coaching was a rousing success, enriching three of the Cubs' best prospects—Kris Bryant, Javier Baez and Jorge Soler. While Ramirez proved that he may have a future in coaching (get in your time machine, find yourself 10 years ago, and show them this comment; beware of heart attacks!), he's never wavered from his desire to return to a big-league lineup. The quirky 43-year-old hasn't made an active roster since 2011, but has flatly stated that will change this season. Being realistic is boring, so let's just wish him luck.

Anthony Rizzo   1B
Born: 8/8/89   Age: 25   Bats: L   Throws: L   Height: 6' 3"   Weight: 240

YEAR	TEAM	LVL	AGE	PA	R	2B	3B	HR	RBI	BB	K	SB	CS	AVG/OBP/SLG	TAv	BABIP	BRR	FRAA	WARP
2012	IOW	AAA	22	284	48	18	2	23	62	23	52	2	2	.342/.405/.696	.375	.357	-3.2	1B(66): 10.4	4.8
2012	CHN	MLB	22	368	44	15	0	15	48	27	62	3	2	.285/.342/.463	.288	.310	-0.7	1B(85): -0.8	1.6
2013	CHN	MLB	23	690	71	40	2	23	80	76	127	6	5	.233/.323/.419	.264	.258	-1.8	1B(159): 11.1	2.3
2014	CHN	MLB	24	616	89	28	1	32	78	73	116	5	4	.286/.386/.527	.336	.311	2.1	1B(140): -0.6	5.6
2015	CHN	MLB	25	593	76	30	1	25	84	59	123	5	4	.262/.343/.470	.305	.294	-0.1	1B 5	3.9

Breakout: 2%   Improve: 60%   Collapse: 1%   Attrition: 5%   MLB: 100%   Comparables: *Prince Fielder, Ike Davis, Brandon Belt*

The Cubs' lineup lacked many things entering the season, but two big holes—a consistent bat and a team leader—were filled by the end of the year by Rizzo. The big lefty had a monster season, making solid strides in his plate approach, developing more consistent mechanics and finding a way to hit, nay, crush lefties (.928 OPS). Rizzo's emergence as arguably one of the 10 best bats in the game was huge, but he also seemed to embrace the leadership role that has been thrust upon him. Despite being a particularly mature young man, Rizzo never gravitated to being an outspoken clubhouse voice; in 2014, though, he realized the team needed him to rise to that task, and he excelled.

Addison Russell   SS

Born: 1/23/94   Age: 21   Bats: R   Throws: R   Height: 6' 0"   Weight: 195

YEAR	TEAM	LVL	AGE	PA	R	2B	3B	HR	RBI	BB	K	SB	CS	AVG/OBP/SLG	TAv	BABIP	BRR	FRAA	WARP
2012	BUR	A	18	66	8	4	2	0	9	5	12	5	1	.310/.369/.448	.298	.383	1.5	SS(15): -0.2	0.9
2012	VER	A-	18	57	9	2	2	1	7	4	13	2	0	.340/.386/.509	.348	.436	0.2	SS(12): 0.5	0.8
2013	STO	A+	19	504	85	29	10	17	60	61	116	21	3	.275/.377/.508	.321	.338	1.0	SS(105): -4.6	5.3
2014	MID	AA	20	57	7	3	1	1	8	8	8	3	2	.333/.439/.500	.293	.385	-0.3	SS(11): -1.1	0.3
2014	TEN	AA	20	205	32	11	0	12	36	9	35	2	2	.294/.332/.536	.309	.306	0.2	SS(47): 4.6	2.6
2015	CHN	MLB	21	250	30	11	2	7	25	17	66	5	2	.240/.299/.387	.261	.304	0.2	SS -0	1.1

Breakout: 4%   Improve: 14%   Collapse: 7%   Attrition: 11%   MLB: 35%   Comparables: Xander Bogaerts, B.J. Upton, Reid Brignac

Russell played only 68 games last season, but did nothing to diminish his status as an elite prospect. He projects as a solid enough defender, with a strong arm, good hands and enough skill to allow him to stick at shortstop. His offense is what excites, though: He should have the kind of plus power that gets a player voted into all-star games. If it weren't for Javier Baez's freakish bat speed, Russell would get more love for his. With Starlin Castro currently manning short, Russell does not have a spot carved out for him, but talent has a way of forcing itself into the lineup, so don't be surprised to see him contributing in the majors this year.

Kyle Schwarber   C

Born: 3/5/93   Age: 22   Bats: L   Throws: R   Height: 6' 0"   Weight: 235

YEAR	TEAM	LVL	AGE	PA	R	2B	3B	HR	RBI	BB	K	SB	CS	AVG/OBP/SLG	TAv	BABIP	BRR	FRAA	WARP
2014	KNC	A	21	96	17	8	0	4	15	11	17	1	1	.361/.448/.602	.295	.419	-0.1	LF(2): -0.0, C(1): -0.0	0.2
2014	BOI	A-	21	24	7	1	1	4	10	2	2	0	1	.600/.625/1.350	.612	.533	0.0		0.0
2014	DAY	A+	21	191	31	9	1	10	28	26	38	4	0	.302/.393/.560	.323	.328	-0.7	LF(26): 1.6, C(9): 0.1	2.0
2015	CHN	MLB	22	250	26	10	1	8	30	22	68	1	0	.228/.300/.383	.257	.285	-0.3	LF 2, C 0	0.7

Breakout: 2%   Improve: 20%   Collapse: 0%   Attrition: 13%   MLB: 37%   Comparables: Thomas Neal, Jaff Decker, Jamie Romak

The Cubs picked Schwarber fourth overall in the 2014 draft, raising eyebrows. He was seen as a bat-only prospect without much projection on defense. Even if he can't catch, though, the Cubs think he'll stick in left; they note impressive athleticism despite his being a, uh, big-bodied young man. In his three months in the system, Schwarber exceeded all expectations: He crushed the ball at three levels and displayed the perfect combination of average, power and approach. He also has a dogged work ethic and desire to prove the naysayers wrong about his defense.

The conundrum for the Cubs: Do you move him up the chain as fast as his bat calls for (very fast) or do you slow him down, pair him with your best catching coach and let him try to learn that craft? Two years ago, this would have been no debate: The major-league team's daily goal was merely to not be *too* embarrassed, so there was no reason to rush anyone. As the Cubs transition into contention, though, the gap between Schwarber and a random left fielder could make enough difference to be worth giving up on dreams of the next Mike Piazza.

Jorge Soler   RF

Born: 2/25/92   Age: 23   Bats: R   Throws: R   Height: 6' 4"   Weight: 215

YEAR	TEAM	LVL	AGE	PA	R	2B	3B	HR	RBI	BB	K	SB	CS	AVG/OBP/SLG	TAv	BABIP	BRR	FRAA	WARP
2012	PEO	A	20	88	14	5	0	3	15	6	6	4	1	.338/.398/.513	.331	.338	0.4	RF(19): 0.5	0.8
2013	DAY	A+	21	237	38	13	1	8	35	21	38	5	1	.281/.343/.467	.283	.304	1.8	RF(55): -0.9	1.1
2014	TEN	AA	22	79	13	9	1	6	22	12	15	0	0	.415/.494/.862	.461	.457	-0.3	RF(16): -1.3	1.6
2014	IOW	AAA	22	127	22	11	1	8	29	17	26	0	1	.282/.378/.618	.320	.303	-0.1	RF(27): 1.3	1.1
2014	CHN	MLB	22	97	11	8	1	5	20	6	24	1	0	.292/.330/.573	.325	.339	-0.2	RF(24): -0.8	0.6
2015	CHN	MLB	23	250	29	13	1	10	35	19	57	2	1	.258/.316/.457	.287	.299	-0.2	RF -2	0.9

Breakout: 2%   Improve: 33%   Collapse: 4%   Attrition: 13%   MLB: 69%   Comparables: Wil Myers, Wladimir Balentien, Domonic Brown

After suffering multiple muscle injuries early in the season, Soler finally got healthy and rocketed his way through the system, earning a call-up in late August. The powerful righty never skipped a beat at any level, displaying a strong approach and the ability to make quick adjustments to advanced pitching. These traits were open questions heading into 2014 because he hadn't faced much live action due to injuries and his defection from Cuba. The defense in right also appears to be strong, as he shows the athleticism to cover plenty of ground and an imposing arm. Nitpicking, because we have to say *something* he can improve on, Soler's two-strike approach could use some honing. More reps will be key to doing so, and the Cubs worked hard to make sure he'll get those reps, revamping his training regimen and diet and ensuring he was properly hydrated.

Ryan Sweeney   CF

Born: 2/20/85   Age: 30   Bats: L   Throws: L   Height: 6' 4"   Weight: 225

YEAR	TEAM	LVL	AGE	PA	R	2B	3B	HR	RBI	BB	K	SB	CS	AVG/OBP/SLG	TAv	BABIP	BRR	FRAA	WARP
2012	BOS	MLB	27	219	22	19	2	0	16	12	43	0	0	.260/.303/.373	.234	.327	0.5	RF(49): 2.2, CF(19): -0.3	0.1
2013	IOW	AAA	28	91	12	2	2	6	16	8	15	1	0	.337/.396/.627	.337	.355	-0.6	RF(16): -0.8, LF(4): 0.1	0.6
2013	CHN	MLB	28	212	19	13	2	6	19	17	31	1	0	.266/.324/.448	.282	.288	-2.0	CF(45): 5.4, LF(10): 0.6	1.7
2014	CHN	MLB	29	226	22	9	0	3	20	15	33	0	0	.251/.304/.338	.250	.285	-0.7	CF(24): -1.4, RF(22): 0.1	0.1
2015	CHN	MLB	30	250	22	13	2	3	24	20	42	1	0	.261/.320/.366	.263	.305	-0.6	CF 1, RF -0	0.8

Breakout: 0%   Improve: 48%   Collapse: 5%   Attrition: 9%   MLB: 98%   Comparables: Angel Pagan, Coco Crisp, Franklin Gutierrez

After a solid showing toward the end of 2013, Sweeney signed a two-year deal with the Cubs. Alas, all that new power disappeared like leaves before locusts. Sweeney is unlikely to add value with the bat, even in center field. Still, the ability to play all three positions and man the long side of a platoon makes him a solid fourth outfielder. Sweeney is as good an example as any of the gap between a jeans-selling physical specimen and an above-average baseball player.

Gleyber Torres SS

Born: 12/13/96 Age: 18 Bats: R Throws: R Height: 6' 1" Weight: 175

YEAR	TEAM	LVL	AGE	PA	R	2B	3B	HR	RBI	BB	K	SB	CS	AVG/OBP/SLG	TAv	BABIP	BRR	FRAA	WARP
2014	BOI	A-	17	32	4	2	3	1	4	4	7	2	0	.393/.469/.786	.374	.500	0.6	SS(7): 0.5	0.7
2015	CHN	MLB	18	250	23	9	1	2	16	14	72	4	2	.198/.248/.273	.201	.272	-0.2	SS 3	-0.1

Breakout: 0% Improve: 0% Collapse: 0% Attrition: 0% MLB: 0% Comparables: Jonathan Schoop, Argenis Diaz, Adrian Cardenas

Like Eloy Jimenez, the Cubs brought Torres stateside even though he spent the entire summer being 17. Unlike Jimenez, Torres put up solid numbers in the Arizona League and earned a brief promotion to Boise. Also unlike Jimenez, Torres doesn't project to have much power, but he has a smooth swing that lends itself to lining balls all over the field. His patient approach belies his age and enhances his impressive bat-to-ball skills. Add in that he has a chance to stick at shortstop, where he displays a strong arm and impressive athleticism, and it's no wonder Torres is one of the top prospects to watch heading into this season.

Luis Valbuena 3B

Born: 11/30/85 Age: 29 Bats: L Throws: R Height: 5' 10" Weight: 200

YEAR	TEAM	LVL	AGE	PA	R	2B	3B	HR	RBI	BB	K	SB	CS	AVG/OBP/SLG	TAv	BABIP	BRR	FRAA	WARP
2012	IOW	AAA	26	246	38	17	1	8	31	28	50	1	1	.303/.378/.507	.311	.352	0.8	SS(44): 1.8, 2B(9): 0.2	2.5
2012	CHN	MLB	26	303	26	20	0	4	28	36	55	0	2	.219/.310/.340	.237	.260	-0.5	3B(82): -0.6, 2B(5): -0.2	0.3
2013	CHN	MLB	27	391	34	15	1	12	37	53	63	1	4	.218/.331/.378	.260	.233	-0.2	3B(94): -1.8, 2B(6): -0.1	1.2
2014	CHN	MLB	28	547	68	33	4	16	51	65	113	1	2	.249/.341/.435	.294	.294	-0.2	3B(124): -5.4, 2B(21): -0.9	2.2
2015	CHN	MLB	29	484	49	23	1	11	52	53	101	2	2	.235/.320/.372	.264	.279	0.0	3B -4, 2B -0	1.0

Breakout: 1% Improve: 30% Collapse: 10% Attrition: 19% MLB: 92% Comparables: Andy LaRoche, Casey McGehee, Brian Buscher

The quirky infielder has quickly catapulted himself into the realm of "fan favorite" on the North Side. With interesting habits like appealing his own check-swings (even when the home plate ump seems perfectly content with giving him a ball), bat-flipping harmless pop-outs and reacting not at all to no-doubt home runs, it's no wonder Valbuena developed a cult following. However, he also brings legitimate on-field value, playing multiple infield positions, seeing a lot of pitches and, at least in 2014, delivering some pop. Valbuena can be a solid enough starter going forward, but is probably best deployed as a heavily used utility infielder.

Christian Villanueva 3B

Born: 6/19/91 Age: 24 Bats: R Throws: R Height: 5' 11" Weight: 210

YEAR	TEAM	LVL	AGE	PA	R	2B	3B	HR	RBI	BB	K	SB	CS	AVG/OBP/SLG	TAv	BABIP	BRR	FRAA	WARP
2012	DAY	A+	21	95	14	5	0	4	9	10	24	5	2	.250/.337/.452	.264	.304	-0.1	3B(24): 4.5	1.0
2012	MYR	A+	21	425	45	19	1	10	59	24	83	9	9	.285/.356/.421	.298	.338	-2.4	3B(90): -8.1, 2B(4): 0.5	2.5
2013	TEN	AA	22	542	60	41	2	19	72	34	117	5	7	.261/.317/.469	.275	.303	1.8	3B(124): -1.1	2.3
2014	TEN	AA	23	259	31	20	0	4	32	19	42	0	1	.248/.310/.385	.253	.284	-1.0	3B(61): 2.8, 2B(3): -0.1	0.7
2014	IOW	AAA	23	248	22	18	0	6	26	21	64	2	1	.211/.283/.372	.229	.266	-0.1	3B(63): 8.0	0.7
2015	CHN	MLB	24	250	23	13	0	6	26	12	66	2	1	.224/.271/.360	.237	.282	-0.6	3B 3, 2B 0	0.2

Breakout: 2% Improve: 6% Collapse: 5% Attrition: 10% MLB: 15% Comparables: Danny Valencia, Neil Walker, James D'Antona

Villanueva has always wowed scouts with his glove, earning praise for his work at the hot corner, but after a breakthrough 2013 with the bat, he struggled at Triple-A and was demoted back to Tennessee to make way roster space for Kris Bryant. Like Matt Dominguez, Villanueva could find himself on a major-league roster sometime in 2015 on the strength of his defense alone. (For Villanueva's sake, pretend we're talking about 2013's above-average Dominguez, not 2014's below-replacement Dominguez.) His swing could benefit from some significant rework, but there's still time for him to do so without destroying his chances for a career.

Josh Vitters LF

Born: 8/27/89 Age: 25 Bats: R Throws: R Height: 6' 2" Weight: 200

YEAR	TEAM	LVL	AGE	PA	R	2B	3B	HR	RBI	BB	K	SB	CS	AVG/OBP/SLG	TAv	BABIP	BRR	FRAA	WARP
2012	IOW	AAA	22	452	54	32	2	17	68	30	77	6	3	.304/.356/.513	.303	.337	0.1	3B(95): -2.2, 1B(9): -0.6	2.8
2012	CHN	MLB	22	109	7	2	0	2	5	7	33	2	0	.121/.193/.202	.153	.154	-0.7	3B(29): -1.1	-1.2
2013	IOW	AAA	23	100	14	4	0	5	12	11	19	1	0	.295/.380/.511	.305	.328	0.0	3B(18): -2.0, 1B(4): 0.1	0.6
2014	IOW	AAA	24	404	33	14	0	11	38	23	107	4	1	.213/.268/.339	.212	.268	1.2	LF(73): -7.5, 1B(16): -0.1	-1.9
2015	CHN	MLB	25	250	24	11	0	7	28	14	64	2	1	.223/.273/.360	.242	.276	-0.2	LF -2, 3B -2	-0.4

Breakout: 6% Improve: 14% Collapse: 10% Attrition: 21% MLB: 33% Comparables: Zoilo Almonte, Caleb Gindl, John Mayberry

The third pick in the 2007 draft, Vitters was once the crown jewel of the Cubs' farm system. He has been described as having one of the most beautiful swings scouts have seen from the right side. The problem appears to be that he uses it too much, rarely getting deep into counts or drawing walks. Vitters overcame that issue in the minors by hitting for a high average, at least before his horrendous showing in 2014. Some question whether he has put in the time and effort needed to succeed, but whether it's work ethic, lack of confidence or general disinterest, you'd be hard-pressed to find optimism about his future, even if we're still years shy of being able to write him off entirely. Stranger things than a Vitters turnaround at age 25 have been reported, though they're usually consumed in weekly tabloid form.

Dan Vogelbach 1B

Born: 12/17/92 Age: 22 Bats: L Throws: R Height: 6' 0" Weight: 250

YEAR	TEAM	LVL	AGE	PA	R	2B	3B	HR	RBI	BB	K	SB	CS	AVG/OBP/SLG	TAv	BABIP	BRR	FRAA	WARP
2012	BOI	A-	19	168	23	9	1	10	31	23	34	0	1	.322/.423/.608	.340	.364	-0.3	1B(29): -2.5	1.2
2013	KNC	A	20	502	55	21	0	17	71	57	76	4	4	.284/.364/.450	.288	.305	-5.6	1B(85): -0.7	1.4
2013	DAY	A+	20	66	13	2	0	2	5	16	13	1	0	.280/.455/.440	.322	.343	0.7	1B(7): -0.2	0.6
2014	DAY	A+	21	560	71	28	1	16	76	66	91	4	4	.268/.357/.429	.280	.296	-3.1	1B(103): -9.2	0.5
2015	CHN	MLB	22	250	25	10	0	7	28	23	60	0	0	.226/.298/.367	.252	.272	-0.5	1B -3	-0.3

Breakout: 0% Improve: 0% Collapse: 0% Attrition: 0% MLB: 0% Comparables: Mike Carp, Chris Marrero, Logan Morrison

Vogelbach opened eyes last spring when he came into camp down 30 pounds. The big-bodied (cough) first baseman worked hard in the offseason to shed the weight and the "DH only" label that came with it, though it doesn't mean the total disappearance of questions about his ability to play first: Whether he's 250 pounds or 220, he's not exactly Olerudian around the bag. Still, he remains staunch at the plate with an advanced approach and a plus hit tool. He's also been consistently inconsistent, as one scout pointed out that he inevitably bounces back from slow Aprils, watching balls that died on the warning track in the spring start to carry over the fence or fall for extra-bases as the season progresses and the weather warms up. Anthony Rizzo's re-breakout probably makes Vogelbach trade bait, though at 22 and without a high-minors plate appearance to his name, there's no rush.

Logan Watkins   2B

Born: 8/29/89   Age: 25   Bats: L   Throws: R   Height: 5' 11"   Weight: 195

YEAR	TEAM	LVL	AGE	PA	R	2B	3B	HR	RBI	BB	K	SB	CS	AVG/OBP/SLG	TAv	BABIP	BRR	FRAA	WARP
2012	TEN	AA	22	588	93	20	11	9	52	76	97	28	7	.281/.383/.422	.286	.332	4.0	2B(95): 0.6, SS(29): -1.4	3.4
2013	IOW	AAA	23	472	51	18	7	8	26	52	98	10	9	.243/.333/.379	.263	.300	0.1	2B(90): -4.8, SS(13): -1.4	0.9
2013	CHN	MLB	23	42	2	1	0	0	0	3	14	0	0	.211/.268/.237	.195	.333	0.4	2B(9): -0.5	-0.2
2014	IOW	AAA	24	368	59	21	1	4	38	33	77	23	4	.256/.327/.364	.245	.322	4.0	2B(44): -5.2, SS(16): -0.4	0.4
2014	CHN	MLB	24	68	10	3	0	1	6	1	16	1	0	.246/.269/.338	.225	.313	-0.1	2B(16): -0.4, RF(2): 0.0	-0.1
2015	*CHN*	*MLB*	*25*	*250*	*29*	*10*	*2*	*3*	*18*	*21*	*58*	*8*	*2*	*.229/.300/.331*	*.238*	*.288*	*0.7*	*2B -2, SS -1*	*-0.1*

Breakout: 1%   Improve: 4%   Collapse: 11%   Attrition: 23%   MLB: 34%   *Comparables: Tommy Field, Brendan Harris, Travis Denker*

Watkins provides value with his versatility and solid plate approach. He doesn't project to be a stand-out regular, but he can play all over the infield and even in center. With the bat, he won't provide much in terms of power, but he's shown a patient approach in the minors. Watkins was drafted three picks after Lucas Luetge, who also appears in this book, in the 21st round in 2008. He was drafted seven picks after Mathieu LeBlanc Poirier, who had a nice run in the low minors considering he's 5-feet-10, stocky and best known for a sitcom that ended its run in 2004.

Pitchers

Jake Arrieta   RHP

Born: 3/6/86   Age: 29   Bats: R   Throws: R   Height: 6'4"   Weight: 225

YEAR	TEAM	LVL	AGE	W	L	SV	G	GS	IP	H	HR	BB	K	BB/9	K/9	GB%	BABIP	WHIP	ERA	FIP	FRA	WARP
2012	NOR	AAA	26	5	4	0	10	10	56	46	3	28	54	4.5	8.7	48%	.287	1.32	4.02	3.64	4.76	0.1
2012	BAL	MLB	26	3	9	0	24	18	114²	122	16	35	109	2.7	8.6	46%	.320	1.37	6.20	4.01	4.79	1.1
2013	IOW	AAA	27	2	2	0	7	7	30¹	32	2	16	39	4.7	11.6	51%	.390	1.58	3.56	3.64	4.24	0.7
2013	NOR	AAA	27	5	3	0	9	8	49	45	4	14	38	2.6	7.0	52%	.285	1.20	4.41	3.63	4.80	0.2
2013	BAL	MLB	27	1	2	0	5	5	23²	25	2	17	23	6.5	8.7	33%	.343	1.77	7.23	4.64	4.87	0.1
2013	CHN	MLB	27	4	2	0	9	9	51²	34	7	24	37	4.2	6.4	46%	.190	1.12	3.66	4.92	5.88	-0.2
2014	TEN	AA	28	1	1	0	4	4	14¹	9	0	5	11	3.1	6.9	62%	.200	0.91	1.26	2.70	3.92	0.3
2014	CHN	MLB	28	10	5	0	25	25	156²	114	5	41	167	2.4	9.6	51%	.272	0.99	2.53	2.23	2.87	4.0
2015	*CHN*	*MLB*	*29*	*8*	*9*	*0*	*25*	*25*	*140¹*	*121*	*12*	*52*	*127*	*3.4*	*8.1*	*47%*	*.299*	*1.23*	*3.59*	*3.84*	*3.90*	*1.2*

Breakout: 27%   Improve: 43%   Collapse: 22%   Attrition: 14%   MLB: 81%   *Comparables: John Maine, Chris Young, Jeff Niemann*

Arrieta started the season on the disabled list with shoulder issues, but once he took the mound in early May, he started pitching like one of the best arms in the National League. Under the tutelage of Chris Bosio, the former Orioles top prospect tweaked his mechanics, found consistency in his delivery and revived his career, posting numbers that, if prorated over a full season, would put him near the top of Cy Young ballots. Arrieta also seemed the most confident he's been in his major-league career, expecting success rather than hoping for it, and when he did struggle, he showed the mental fortitude to quickly rectify the problem and bounce back strong. The key to 2015 is health; if he can pitch a full season, Arrieta is primed to continue his ascent and emerge as one of the top arms in all of baseball.

Dallas Beeler   RHP

Born: 6/12/89   Age: 26   Bats: R   Throws: R   Height: 6'5"   Weight: 210

YEAR	TEAM	LVL	AGE	W	L	SV	G	GS	IP	H	HR	BB	K	BB/9	K/9	GB%	BABIP	WHIP	ERA	FIP	FRA	WARP
2012	TEN	AA	23	6	7	0	27	27	136	166	11	48	70	3.2	4.6	56%	.330	1.57	4.24	4.31	5.99	-1.2
2013	TEN	AA	24	2	7	0	9	9	54²	43	3	17	35	2.8	5.8	71%	.241	1.10	3.13	3.61	4.76	0.1
2014	IOW	AAA	25	9	6	0	20	20	124¹	112	8	32	83	2.3	6.0	58%	.280	1.16	3.40	4.07	4.69	1.4
2014	CHN	MLB	25	0	2	0	2	2	11	10	0	7	6	5.7	4.9	61%	.303	1.55	3.27	3.92	3.97	0.1
2015	*CHN*	*MLB*	*26*	*5*	*7*	*0*	*18*	*18*	*98¹*	*104*	*10*	*29*	*56*	*2.7*	*5.2*	*56%*	*.310*	*1.35*	*4.41*	*4.55*	*4.79*	*-0.2*

Breakout: 16%   Improve: 22%   Collapse: 5%   Attrition: 18%   MLB: 31%   *Comparables: Cesar Ramos, Brian Duensing, Thad Weber*

For Beeler to reach his fourth-starter ceiling in the big leagues, he's going to have to avoid ball four and induce groundballs. Lacking a true swing-and-miss offering, Beeler works low in the zone, hoping to induce weak contact with his sinker or splitter and relying on his defense to get the job done. His 2013 was cut short by a finger injury, but he did enough in the Arizona Fall League to make the Cubs' 40-man roster and eventually have a brief trial in the majors. Beeler did half of what he was supposed to do in that limited sample, inducing grounders but not limiting walks, leaving him one trick short of a touring act. One wonders whether Beeler's parents really had his best interests in mind when they named him "Dallas" despite living in Oklahoma.

Paul Blackburn   RHP

Born: 12/4/93   Age: 21   Bats: R   Throws: R   Height: 6'2"   Weight: 185

YEAR	TEAM	LVL	AGE	W	L	SV	G	GS	IP	H	HR	BB	K	BB/9	K/9	GB%	BABIP	WHIP	ERA	FIP	FRA	WARP
2013	BOI	A-	19	2	3	0	13	12	46	41	3	29	38	5.7	7.4	55%	.290	1.52	3.33	4.47	5.76	0.1
2014	KNC	A	20	9	4	0	24	24	117	108	6	31	75	2.4	5.8	58%	.279	1.19	3.23	3.84	5.35	-0.1
2015	*CHN*	*MLB*	*21*	*4*	*8*	*0*	*21*	*21*	*86²*	*98*	*10*	*39*	*42*	*4.1*	*4.4*	*50%*	*.315*	*1.58*	*5.43*	*5.43*	*5.91*	*-1.1*

Breakout: 0%   Improve: 0%   Collapse: 0%   Attrition: 0%   MLB: 0%   *Comparables: Zach Britton, Robert Carson, Xavier Cedeno*

Blackburn surprised many in the Cubs' front office when he posted an eye-opening 14 percent walk rate in short-season ball in 2013. However, team officials were adamant that if he stopped nibbling and trusted his stuff, he'd transform back into the prospect they thought they drafted. Last year Blackburn delivered on that promise, reducing his walk rate and causing numerous scouts to pen overwrought odes to his command. His fringy stuff, featuring a fastball that sits at 90 and a curve best described as a work in progress, leaves you wanting more, though Blackburn could gain velocity as he fills out his lean frame. If everything breaks right, Blackburn could grow into a back-end rotation option, though a swingman future is more likely.

C.J. Edwards RHP

Born: 9/3/91   Age: 23   Bats: R   Throws: R   Height: 6'2"   Weight: 155

YEAR	TEAM	LVL	AGE	W	L	SV	G	GS	IP	H	HR	BB	K	BB/9	K/9	GB%	BABIP	WHIP	ERA	FIP	FRA	WARP
2012	SPO	A-	20	2	3	0	10	10	47	26	0	19	60	3.6	11.5	50%	.250	0.96	2.11	2.11	2.83	1.5
2013	HIC	A	21	8	2	0	18	18	93¹	62	0	34	122	3.3	11.8	54%	.268	1.03	1.83	2.06	2.57	2.9
2013	DAY	A+	21	0	0	0	6	6	23	14	1	7	33	2.7	12.9	43%	.260	0.91	1.96	1.85	2.37	0.7
2014	TEN	AA	22	1	2	0	10	10	48	30	1	21	46	3.9	8.6	47%	.234	1.06	2.44	2.92	3.57	0.9
2015	*CHN*	*MLB*	*23*	*3*	*4*	*0*	*11*	*11*	*53¹*	*44*	*4*	*24*	*53*	*4.0*	*9.0*	*47%*	*.305*	*1.27*	*3.55*	*3.77*	*3.86*	*0.6*

Breakout: 21%   Improve: 31%   Collapse: 5%   Attrition: 25%   MLB: 42%   Comparables: *Zack Wheeler, Tyler Thornburg, Jake Arrieta*

After a breakout 2013, Edwards missed a large chunk of last summer with a minor shoulder problem. The rail-thin righty has a four-seamer that can touch the upper 90s, but leans more on his two-seamer while using a plus curve as his swing-and-miss pitch. Edwards' build leads to questions about his ability to survive the rigors of a big league rotation, although lack of fastball command may be just as big an obstacle. Last year's injury left him ill-placed to prove doubters wrong, but if he can deliver a hush-your-mouth 2015, he profiles as a mid-rotation starter. More likely, he ends up a high-leverage reliever who could be ready in the second half this year.

Justin Grimm RHP

Born: 8/16/88   Age: 26   Bats: R   Throws: R   Height: 6'3"   Weight: 210

YEAR	TEAM	LVL	AGE	W	L	SV	G	GS	IP	H	HR	BB	K	BB/9	K/9	GB%	BABIP	WHIP	ERA	FIP	FRA	WARP
2012	FRI	AA	23	9	3	0	16	14	83²	70	3	14	73	1.5	7.9	50%	.288	1.00	1.72	2.54	3.59	1.5
2012	ROU	AAA	23	2	3	0	9	8	51	53	2	16	30	2.8	5.3	54%	.307	1.35	4.59	4.18	5.19	0.2
2012	TEX	MLB	23	1	1	0	5	2	14	22	1	3	13	1.9	8.4	45%	.438	1.79	9.00	2.76	3.81	0.3
2013	IOW	AAA	24	2	3	0	8	8	42¹	46	1	17	41	3.6	8.7	51%	.354	1.49	4.68	3.14	3.38	0.9
2013	CHN	MLB	24	0	2	0	10	0	9	4	0	3	8	3.0	8.0	38%	.167	0.78	2.00	2.58	2.84	0.1
2013	TEX	MLB	24	7	7	0	17	17	89	116	15	31	68	3.1	6.9	45%	.347	1.65	6.37	4.82	5.35	0.0
2014	CHN	MLB	25	5	2	0	73	0	69	59	4	27	70	3.5	9.1	51%	.294	1.25	3.78	3.18	4.01	0.2
2015	*CHN*	*MLB*	*26*	*4*	*4*	*0*	*25*	*11*	*75²*	*73*	*6*	*24*	*63*	*2.9*	*7.5*	*48%*	*.320*	*1.29*	*3.95*	*3.76*	*4.29*	*0.3*

Breakout: 38%   Improve: 66%   Collapse: 14%   Attrition: 18%   MLB: 93%   Comparables: *Scott Baker, Zach McAllister, Taylor Buchholz*

The story of Grimm's career is still unwritten, and could take multiple paths. Last season was a solid one for him out of the 'pen, but he has the repertoire—and desire—to start again. His slider has improved significantly since he last found regular work as a starter, so the added weapon could help compensate for the inevitable drop in fastball velocity that would accompany a transition back to the rotation. If his new slide-piece doesn't turn into a pumpkin there's a chance he could hold down a fourth starter role; if not, he'll earn his pension as a swingman.

Jason Hammel RHP

Born: 9/2/82   Age: 32   Bats: R   Throws: R   Height: 6'6"   Weight: 225

YEAR	TEAM	LVL	AGE	W	L	SV	G	GS	IP	H	HR	BB	K	BB/9	K/9	GB%	BABIP	WHIP	ERA	FIP	FRA	WARP
2012	BAL	MLB	29	8	6	0	20	20	118	104	9	42	113	3.2	8.6	54%	.291	1.24	3.43	3.24	3.64	2.8
2013	BAL	MLB	30	7	8	1	26	23	139¹	155	22	48	96	3.1	6.2	42%	.304	1.46	4.97	4.96	5.18	-0.5
2014	CHN	MLB	31	8	5	0	17	17	108²	88	10	23	104	1.9	8.6	41%	.272	1.02	2.98	3.16	3.46	1.4
2014	OAK	MLB	31	2	6	0	13	12	67²	66	13	21	54	2.8	7.2	38%	.272	1.29	4.26	5.13	5.61	-0.5
2015	*CHN*	*MLB*	*32*	*8*	*9*	*0*	*25*	*25*	*147*	*137*	*14*	*43*	*121*	*2.6*	*7.4*	*45%*	*.307*	*1.23*	*3.78*	*3.93*	*4.10*	*0.8*

Breakout: 14%   Improve: 39%   Collapse: 23%   Attrition: 7%   MLB: 74%   Comparables: *Gil Meche, John Lackey, Freddy Garcia*

Hammel was in the midst of a career-best season when he was traded to the A's in July, but the breakout broke down upon his arrival in Oakland. His perceived fall from grace was overly dramatized, partially due to the outlandish expectations generated by his first-half flourish; his performance for the green and gold was better than his Baltimore fiasco in 2013, and Hammel finished the season strong, spinning quality starts in five of his final seven turns in the rotation. The real culprit behind Hammel's struggles was a badly escalated rate of homers allowed, as the right-hander gave up more bombs in 67 innings for Oakland than he did in 108 innings for the Cubs. Expect all-around performance at the midpoint of his last few seasons, but at 32 and without an enormous base of physical talent to draw on, watch out for utter collapse.

Kyle Hendricks RHP

Born: 12/7/89   Age: 25   Bats: R   Throws: R   Height: 6'3"   Weight: 190

YEAR	TEAM	LVL	AGE	W	L	SV	G	GS	IP	H	HR	BB	K	BB/9	K/9	GB%	BABIP	WHIP	ERA	FIP	FRA	WARP
2012	DAY	A+	22	1	0	0	5	4	17	17	3	3	11	1.6	5.8	46%	.264	1.18	4.24	5.10	6.53	0.0
2012	MYR	A+	22	5	8	0	20	20	130²	123	8	15	112	1.0	7.7	54%	.304	1.06	2.82	2.95	3.95	1.3
2013	TEN	AA	23	10	3	0	21	21	126¹	107	3	26	101	1.9	7.2	59%	.279	1.05	1.85	2.36	3.81	2.5
2013	IOW	AAA	23	3	1	0	6	6	40	35	2	8	27	1.8	6.1	62%	.273	1.08	2.47	3.54	4.10	0.5
2014	IOW	AAA	24	10	5	0	17	17	102²	98	5	23	97	2.0	8.5	56%	.322	1.18	3.59	3.17	4.06	1.5
2014	CHN	MLB	24	7	2	0	13	13	80¹	72	4	15	47	1.7	5.3	51%	.271	1.08	2.46	3.29	3.65	1.2
2015	*CHN*	*MLB*	*25*	*9*	*9*	*0*	*25*	*25*	*153*	*143*	*11*	*32*	*114*	*1.9*	*6.7*	*52%*	*.306*	*1.14*	*3.30*	*3.47*	*3.59*	*1.8*

Breakout: 21%   Improve: 44%   Collapse: 15%   Attrition: 23%   MLB: 78%   Comparables: *Zach McAllister, Juan Nicasio, A.J. Griffin*

"Know thyself" comes down from Apollo himself, and who are we to argue with the god of the sun? You won't catch Hendricks disagreeing: He doesn't blow anyone away with his mundane offerings, but he knows his limitations, learns from his mistakes and makes the most of what he has. One of them Ivy League types (Dartmouth, economics), Hendricks relies on plus command to induce weak contact. After arriving in the big leagues in the wake of the Cubs' trade of Jeff Samardzija and Jason Hammel, he immediately took advantage of the advanced scouting and video available to him, soaking in as much knowledge about how to attack his opponents as possible. His changeup has swing-and-miss potential, so an uptick in strikeouts is not out of the question. Even a small increase, as long as the walks stay low and the ball stays in the park, could make him a very valuable asset, particularly at the (league-minimum) price. Apollo also gave us, "On reaching the end be without sorrow," and Hendricks seems likely to wring out every ounce of success his fringy stuff will support before the game is done with him.

Edwin Jackson   RHP

Born: 9/9/83   Age: 31   Bats: R   Throws: R   Height: 6'3"   Weight: 210

YEAR	TEAM	LVL	AGE	W	L	SV	G	GS	IP	H	HR	BB	K	BB/9	K/9	GB%	BABIP	WHIP	ERA	FIP	FRA	WARP
2012	WAS	MLB	28	10	11	0	31	31	189²	173	23	58	168	2.8	8.0	48%	.278	1.22	4.03	3.89	4.72	1.3
2013	CHN	MLB	29	8	18	0	31	31	175¹	197	16	59	135	3.0	6.9	53%	.322	1.46	4.98	3.76	4.69	0.4
2014	CHN	MLB	30	6	15	0	28	27	140²	168	18	63	123	4.0	7.9	41%	.352	1.64	6.33	4.42	4.63	0.6
2015	CHN	MLB	31	7	9	0	22	22	128²	130	12	43	111	3.0	7.8	47%	.330	1.34	4.33	3.89	4.71	-0.2

Breakout: 13%   Improve: 51%   Collapse: 14%   Attrition: 23%   MLB: 91%   *Comparables: Ervin Santana, Nate Robertson, Jeff Weaver*

After signing his first long-term deal prior to 2013, Jackson has delivered easily the two worst seasons of his career. The shape of Jackson's ugly performance in 2013 left some room for hope: His FIP *way* outperformed his ERA, his groundball rate was very good and his strand rate was the worst in the league. Indeed, his comment in last year's edition of this book can be summed up as "Positive regression alert!" But then 2014 was all "rofl nope." Jackson's velocity fell for the third straight year and he did the one thing you thought you could count on him not to do: get hurt. His return from his first disabled list trip since 2004 saw a dreadful start followed by a banishment to the bullpen, whence he made just his fourth relief appearance since becoming a starter in 2007. Optimism for 2015 is ill-advised.

Pierce Johnson   RHP

Born: 5/10/91   Age: 24   Bats: R   Throws: R   Height: 6'3"   Weight: 170

YEAR	TEAM	LVL	AGE	W	L	SV	G	GS	IP	H	HR	BB	K	BB/9	K/9	GB%	BABIP	WHIP	ERA	FIP	FRA	WARP
2013	KNC	A	22	5	5	0	13	13	69²	68	4	22	74	2.8	9.6	52%	.335	1.29	3.10	3.12	3.52	1.8
2013	DAY	A+	22	6	1	0	10	8	48²	41	1	21	50	3.9	9.2	43%	.333	1.27	2.22	2.99	4.23	0.6
2014	KNC	A	23	0	1	0	2	2	11	4	1	3	8	2.5	6.5	63%	.115	0.64	2.45	4.30	5.83	0.0
2014	TEN	AA	23	5	4	0	18	17	91²	60	8	54	91	5.3	8.9	44%	.242	1.24	2.55	4.27	4.51	0.5
2015	CHN	MLB	24	5	6	0	18	18	86¹	77	8	42	80	4.4	8.3	45%	.313	1.39	4.23	4.30	4.60	0.1

Breakout: 17%   Improve: 31%   Collapse: 8%   Attrition: 27%   MLB: 42%   *Comparables: Jose Cisnero, Chris Dwyer, Andre Rienzo*

Johnson missed much of spring training with a hamstring issue, battled his control to the tune of a 21 percent walk rate in six starts, lost a month to a calf injury, then finally looked like himself on his return from *that* injury. He still walked too many batters, even throwing out the early part of the season, but the leg problems and the disruption they caused serve as a useful excuse. Johnson is also developing his cutter, which he had stopped using at the Cubs' behest while he worked on his changeup, but unleashed to great effect last year. Adding another weapon to his arsenal, which already includes a low-to-mid-90s fastball and plus slider, helps him make the case for a debut as early as midsummer 2015 if a rotation spot opens up.

Jon Lester   LHP

Born: 1/7/84   Age: 31   Bats: L   Throws: L   Height: 6'4"   Weight: 240

YEAR	TEAM	LVL	AGE	W	L	SV	G	GS	IP	H	HR	BB	K	BB/9	K/9	GB%	BABIP	WHIP	ERA	FIP	FRA	WARP
2012	BOS	MLB	28	9	14	0	33	33	205¹	216	25	68	166	3.0	7.3	51%	.312	1.38	4.82	4.06	5.07	1.2
2013	BOS	MLB	29	15	8	0	33	33	213¹	209	19	67	177	2.8	7.5	46%	.300	1.29	3.75	3.61	4.03	2.7
2014	BOS	MLB	30	10	7	0	21	21	143	128	9	32	149	2.0	9.4	46%	.308	1.12	2.52	2.65	3.03	3.2
2014	OAK	MLB	30	6	4	0	11	11	76²	66	7	16	71	1.9	8.3	43%	.281	1.07	2.35	3.16	3.46	1.0
2015	CHN	MLB	31	12	11	0	31	31	197	167	15	58	191	2.7	8.7	48%	.307	1.15	3.22	3.34	3.50	2.5

Breakout: 13%   Improve: 46%   Collapse: 18%   Attrition: 13%   MLB: 90%   *Comparables: Gavin Floyd, Adam Wainwright, CC Sabathia*

There was a lot of bad juju surrounding the trade that sent Lester to Oakland at the deadline in exchange for Yoenis Cespedes. The A's went into the tank immediately following the deal, yet Lester did his part to steer the ship through the suddenly shallow waters, tossing a quality start in all 11 of his regular-season outings. But when he took the ball in the Wild Card play-in game, he went dizzy from thieving Royals and wound up allowing six earned runs. While that fiasco exposed a possible weakness in controlling the running game (exemplified by the almost inconceivable stat that he did not throw over to first *even one single time* in 2014; on the other hand, his caught-stealing rates have been around the league average), such transgressions are overshadowed by his giant improvement in minimizing the free pass.

James McDonald   RHP

Born: 10/19/84   Age: 30   Bats: L   Throws: R   Height: 6'5"   Weight: 205

YEAR	TEAM	LVL	AGE	W	L	SV	G	GS	IP	H	HR	BB	K	BB/9	K/9	GB%	BABIP	WHIP	ERA	FIP	FRA	WARP
2012	PIT	MLB	27	12	8	0	30	29	171	147	21	69	151	3.6	7.9	42%	.269	1.26	4.21	4.25	4.58	1.5
2013	IND	AAA	28	1	3	0	4	4	20²	26	2	9	12	3.9	5.2	39%	.348	1.69	6.53	4.90	5.77	-0.1
2013	PIT	MLB	28	2	2	0	6	6	29²	29	1	20	25	6.1	7.6	42%	.315	1.65	5.76	4.10	4.42	0.3
2015	CHN	MLB	30	2	3	0	7	7	36²	34	4	15	33	3.7	8.2	40%	.310	1.33	4.17	4.28	4.54	0.0

Breakout: 22%   Improve: 37%   Collapse: 19%   Attrition: 18%   MLB: 69%   *Comparables: Ian Snell, Oliver Perez, Byung-Hyun Kim*

The last time McDonald pitched in a non-rehab, non-spring training game was April 30, 2013; he's been either out with or rehabbing from right shoulder soreness and tendinitis since then. Even if he hadn't been hurt for nearly two full years, and hurt in the most alarming way possible for a pitcher, he's 30 and thus subject to the whole gamut of alarm bells about declining stuff and decreased effectiveness and projectile dysfunction that we trot out for pitchers of a certain age. McDonald was a top prospect once upon a time, then he was an okay pitcher and now he's a wild card with a murky future and a terrifically depressing list of pitchers who've missed two seasons with shoulder injuries bearing down on him.

Neil Ramirez   RHP

Born: 5/25/89   Age: 26   Bats: R   Throws: R   Height: 6'4"   Weight: 190

YEAR	TEAM	LVL	AGE	W	L	SV	G	GS	IP	H	HR	BB	K	BB/9	K/9	GB%	BABIP	WHIP	ERA	FIP	FRA	WARP
2012	FRI	AA	23	2	5	0	13	12	49¹	47	6	16	45	2.9	8.2	34%	.301	1.28	4.20	4.31	4.31	0.7
2012	ROU	AAA	23	6	8	0	15	15	74	78	12	31	63	3.8	7.7	30%	.301	1.47	7.66	5.57	5.93	0.1
2013	FRI	AA	24	9	3	0	21	21	103	77	8	42	127	3.7	11.1	44%	.295	1.16	3.84	2.97	3.56	2.1
2014	CHN	MLB	25	3	3	3	50	0	43²	29	2	17	53	3.5	10.9	30%	.262	1.05	1.44	2.58	2.69	0.8
2015	CHN	MLB	26	3	4	0	19	11	55	48	6	22	57	3.7	9.3	35%	.311	1.27	3.91	4.05	4.25	0.3

Breakout: 21%   Improve: 30%   Collapse: 15%   Attrition: 31%   MLB: 54%   Comparables: *Steve Johnson, J.A. Happ, Joel Carreno*

Ramirez had been dogged by shoulder injuries for much of his time in the Rangers' system; when the Cubs acquired him in the summer of 2013, they stated that keeping him healthy was their top goal. So far, so good, as Ramirez enjoyed an impressive first season in the big leagues, emerging as the Cubs' primary setup man. He has a starter's repertoire (and it's not out of the question that he could return to that role in the future), but the stuff plays up impressively out of the 'pen. With the bulldog attitude managers love to see from their high-leverage bullpen arms and three swing-and-miss pitches (mid-90s fastball, slider and curve), Ramirez has the goods to thrive in the late innings.

Armando Rivero   RHP

Born: 2/1/88   Age: 27   Bats: R   Throws: R   Height: 6'4"   Weight: 190

YEAR	TEAM	LVL	AGE	W	L	SV	G	GS	IP	H	HR	BB	K	BB/9	K/9	GB%	BABIP	WHIP	ERA	FIP	FRA	WARP
2013	KNC	A	25	0	0	1	11	0	18¹	19	4	9	28	4.4	13.7	58%	.366	1.53	5.40	4.76	5.93	0.1
2014	TEN	AA	26	2	1	10	26	0	34²	18	2	16	54	4.2	14.0	39%	.250	0.98	1.56	2.29	2.64	0.8
2014	IOW	AAA	26	3	0	1	23	0	30¹	25	4	12	46	3.6	13.6	44%	.328	1.22	2.97	3.57	3.42	0.8
2015	CHN	MLB	27	2	1	2	38	0	53	40	4	20	69	3.4	11.7	44%	.317	1.13	2.93	2.90	3.18	0.8

Breakout: 8%   Improve: 14%   Collapse: 14%   Attrition: 18%   MLB: 34%   Comparables: *Anthony Slama, Jason Motte, John Gaub*

Rivero is yet another power-armed reliever poised to make the Wrigley scene this summer. Signed to a $3.1 million bonus prior to the 2013 season, the young Cuban comes equipped with a high-effort delivery, a mitt-popping mid-90s heater and the potential to work high-leverage situations, posthaste. His slider and change are still more concept than prototype, but if they continue to develop and Rivero can improve his command, he could grow into an eighth-inning option.

Hector Rondon   RHP

Born: 2/26/88   Age: 27   Bats: R   Throws: R   Height: 6'3"   Weight: 180

YEAR	TEAM	LVL	AGE	W	L	SV	G	GS	IP	H	HR	BB	K	BB/9	K/9	GB%	BABIP	WHIP	ERA	FIP	FRA	WARP
2013	CHN	MLB	25	2	1	0	45	0	54²	52	6	25	44	4.1	7.2	46%	.280	1.41	4.77	4.37	5.11	-0.1
2014	CHN	MLB	26	4	4	29	64	0	63¹	52	2	15	63	2.1	9.0	50%	.286	1.06	2.42	2.23	3.05	1.0
2015	CHN	MLB	27	3	1	8	50	0	54²	49	5	16	53	2.6	8.7	44%	.311	1.19	3.44	3.55	3.73	0.5

Breakout: 28%   Improve: 58%   Collapse: 15%   Attrition: 15%   MLB: 86%   Comparables: *Carlos Villanueva, Boone Logan, Ryan Madson*

It doesn't take long to name every Rule 5 draft success story. (Let's try! Roberto Clementa, Johan Santana, Josh Hamilton, Dan Uggla, Joakim Soria, Everth Cabrera, Darren O'Day, Luis Ayala, Jay Gibbons. Bar trivia!) Rondon may be getting close to the list, as he started hitting the upper 90s with regularity late in 2013 and the trend continued last year, leading to good, if sparse, work in the closer's role. He's not all blazing guns, either: He breaks out a two-plane slider as a put-away pitch, especially to righties. It has the kind of short, tight movement that physicist Alan Nathan has identified as the likely cause of the baseball concept of "late break," a term that also aptly describes Rondon's newfound opportunity to earn the Proven Closer label, and the riches it implies.

Pedro Strop   RHP

Born: 6/13/85   Age: 30   Bats: R   Throws: R   Height: 6'1"   Weight: 220

YEAR	TEAM	LVL	AGE	W	L	SV	G	GS	IP	H	HR	BB	K	BB/9	K/9	GB%	BABIP	WHIP	ERA	FIP	FRA	WARP
2012	BAL	MLB	27	5	2	3	70	0	66¹	52	2	37	58	5.0	7.9	64%	.275	1.34	2.44	3.54	3.95	0.9
2013	BAL	MLB	28	0	3	0	29	0	22¹	23	4	15	24	6.0	9.7	52%	.292	1.70	7.25	5.54	6.71	-0.4
2013	CHN	MLB	28	2	2	1	37	0	35	22	1	11	42	2.8	10.8	54%	.247	0.94	2.83	2.28	2.70	0.7
2014	CHN	MLB	29	2	4	2	65	0	61	40	2	25	71	3.7	10.5	56%	.268	1.07	2.21	2.63	2.92	1.1
2015	CHN	MLB	30	3	1	1	55	0	53¹	41	3	23	59	3.8	9.9	53%	.308	1.20	3.07	3.27	3.34	0.7

Breakout: 23%   Improve: 46%   Collapse: 20%   Attrition: 19%   MLB: 84%   Comparables: *Fernando Rodney, Jared Burton, Michael Wuertz*

The question with Strop has always been whether he could keep opponents off the basepaths via the free pass. As a groundballer with a good strike-out rate, he doesn't need to be Greg Maddux to be a successful reliever; he just needs to avoid being late-career Carlos Marmol. So far with the Cubs, he's done that. He also possesses one of the nastiest pitches in baseball: his slider. The pitch was used to get 58 of his 71 strikeouts in 2014 and his 63 percent whiffs-per-swing rate was bested by only a few pitches (min. 50): Rich Hill's curve (67 percent), Logan Ondrusek's splitter (74) and Aroldis Chapman's changeup (95; yes, that's the percentage, not the velocity).

Daury Torrez   RHP

Born: 6/11/93   Age: 22   Bats: R   Throws: R   Height: 6'3"   Weight: 170

YEAR	TEAM	LVL	AGE	W	L	SV	G	GS	IP	H	HR	BB	K	BB/9	K/9	GB%	BABIP	WHIP	ERA	FIP	FRA	WARP
2014	KNC	A	21	11	7	0	23	23	131¹	110	8	21	81	1.4	5.6	52%	.251	1.00	2.74	3.64	5.19	0.0
2015	CHN	MLB	22	4	6	0	21	13	95²	108	11	33	44	3.1	4.1	46%	.309	1.47	5.17	5.14	5.62	-1.1

Breakout: 0%   Improve: 0%   Collapse: 0%   Attrition: 0%   MLB: 0%   Comparables: *Yorman Bazardo, Brad Bergesen, Ivan Nova*

Torrez popped onto prospect radar screens in 2014 with a strong showing in a talent-laden Kane County rotation. He displays a plus fastball, sitting 90-94 with impressive life and the ability to spot it, a quality slider and feel for a changeup, but scouts differ on which of the two secondaries is stronger. This is as good a place to drop this Fun Fact as any: That talented Kane County rotation could do a lot of things, but they could not field the baseball. Torrez, Tyler Skulina, Jen-Ho Tseng, Paul Blackburn and Duane Underwood combined for 12 errors in just 145 chances, a .917 fielding percentage. You want major-league context? That's worse than Pedro Alvarez.

Jen-Ho Tseng   RHP

Born: 10/3/94   Age: 20   Bats: L   Throws: R   Height: 6'1"   Weight: 210

YEAR	TEAM	LVL	AGE	W	L	SV	G	GS	IP	H	HR	BB	K	BB/9	K/9	GB%	BABIP	WHIP	ERA	FIP	FRA	WARP
2014	KNC	A	19	6	1	0	19	17	105	76	7	15	85	1.3	7.3	48%	.239	0.87	2.40	3.28	4.20	1.0
2015	CHN	MLB	20	3	4	0	13	11	68²	70	7	24	45	3.1	5.9	45%	.308	1.37	4.54	4.56	4.93	-0.2

Breakout: 0%   Improve: 0%   Collapse: 0%   Attrition: 0%   MLB: 0%   Comparables: Casey Kelly, Ian Krol, Jacob Turner

Part of the Cubs' huge international haul in 2013, Tseng was aggressively assigned to Kane County in his first professional season. The Cubs were rewarded for their faith, as the 19-year-old proved to be a steady presence, earning the organization's minor league pitcher of the year award. Tseng earns praise from talent evaluators for his polish, but lacks the projection to be a top-tier prospect. The feeling is "what you see is what you get," which is not an insult so much as a statement of reality. Tseng got the benefit of facing advanced talent at a young age as a member of Taiwan's World Baseball Classic squad. It has proven useful stateside, as his mound presence and confidence frequently impressed observers. Tseng works primarily with a low-90s fastball, a strong changeup and a plus curveball, all of which he commands quite well. He belongs in the argument for the best pitching prospect in the system, but that says as much about the distribution of Baby Cub talent as it does about Tseng: He projects as a mid-rotation contributor.

Duane Underwood   RHP

Born: 7/20/94   Age: 20   Bats: R   Throws: R   Height: 6'2"   Weight: 205

YEAR	TEAM	LVL	AGE	W	L	SV	G	GS	IP	H	HR	BB	K	BB/9	K/9	GB%	BABIP	WHIP	ERA	FIP	FRA	WARP
2013	BOI	A-	18	3	4	0	14	11	54¹	62	4	27	36	4.5	6.0	58%	.310	1.64	4.97	4.77	5.66	-0.1
2014	KNC	A	19	6	4	0	22	21	100²	85	10	36	84	3.2	7.5	50%	.273	1.20	2.50	4.42	5.41	0.0
2015	CHN	MLB	20	4	7	0	19	19	77¹	83	9	38	46	4.4	5.4	47%	.314	1.57	5.48	5.37	5.96	-1.0

Breakout: 0%   Improve: 0%   Collapse: 0%   Attrition: 0%   MLB: 0%   Comparables: T.J. House, Jeurys Familia, Brett Marshall

Underwood has some of the best stuff in the Cubs' system, but he came into his first spring training out of shape and unmotivated. After a rough season, Underwood realized that talent alone wasn't going to get him where he wanted to be, unless where he wanted to be was at Sears selling Lady Kenmores. He showed up focused and in shape in 2014 and carried that positive approach into the season. Reducing his walk rate to respectable levels might have been his biggest accomplishment because scouts have long questioned his command (stemming from difficulties repeating his delivery), not his stuff. Underwood features a mid-90s fastball with solid movement, a strong curveball and a developing changeup that could become a plus pitch. His profile still screams potential over polish: The promise of a mid-rotation starter is clearly there, but he's still a few years of development away from fulfilling it.

Carlos Villanueva   RHP

Born: 11/28/83   Age: 31   Bats: R   Throws: R   Height: 6'2"   Weight: 215

YEAR	TEAM	LVL	AGE	W	L	SV	G	GS	IP	H	HR	BB	K	BB/9	K/9	GB%	BABIP	WHIP	ERA	FIP	FRA	WARP
2012	TOR	MLB	28	7	7	0	38	16	125¹	113	23	46	122	3.3	8.8	38%	.275	1.27	4.16	4.66	4.77	1.2
2013	CHN	MLB	29	7	8	0	47	15	128²	117	14	40	103	2.8	7.2	43%	.283	1.22	4.06	3.84	4.64	0.1
2014	CHN	MLB	30	5	7	2	42	5	77²	89	6	19	72	2.2	8.3	45%	.342	1.39	4.64	3.10	3.52	0.9
2015	CHN	MLB	31	4	3	0	29	9	77²	71	8	23	70	2.7	8.1	39%	.307	1.21	3.68	3.83	4.00	0.5

Breakout: 15%   Improve: 48%   Collapse: 14%   Attrition: 21%   MLB: 84%   Comparables: Kelvim Escobar, Glendon Rusch, Rodrigo Lopez

A useful swingman and a clubhouse character, Villanueva won't wow anyone with his stats, but when used effectively, he'll eat multiple innings out of the 'pen and occasionally be good for a solid spot start. He also at times sports a quality, finely coiffed mustache, perfect for carrying extra soup to the mound during long, cold September evenings spent working multiple relief innings for a non-contender.

Travis Wood   LHP

Born: 2/6/87   Age: 28   Bats: R   Throws: L   Height: 5'11"   Weight: 175

YEAR	TEAM	LVL	AGE	W	L	SV	G	GS	IP	H	HR	BB	K	BB/9	K/9	GB%	BABIP	WHIP	ERA	FIP	FRA	WARP
2012	IOW	AAA	25	3	3	0	7	7	41¹	48	5	11	39	2.4	8.5	39%	.358	1.43	4.57	4.22	4.72	0.9
2012	CHN	MLB	25	6	13	0	26	26	156	133	25	54	119	3.1	6.9	37%	.244	1.20	4.27	4.89	5.32	0.9
2013	CHN	MLB	26	9	12	0	32	32	200	163	18	66	144	3.0	6.5	35%	.248	1.14	3.11	3.86	4.43	1.7
2014	CHN	MLB	27	8	13	0	31	31	173²	190	20	76	146	3.9	7.6	37%	.320	1.53	5.03	4.35	4.54	2.1
2015	CHN	MLB	28	9	10	0	27	27	158¹	145	16	50	130	2.8	7.4	37%	.302	1.23	3.78	4.08	4.11	0.9

Breakout: 26%   Improve: 50%   Collapse: 15%   Attrition: 11%   MLB: 80%   Comparables: Wade Davis, Gavin Floyd, Jesse Litsch

After an All-Star performance in 2013, nothing seemed to go right for Wood last season. His command, which needs to be on point for him to succeed, seemed to disappear at times, leading to a higher walk rate and too many pitches in bad parts of the zone, allowing opponents to tee off for a .782 OPS. His true talent probably lies in between his 2013 and 2014 performances, which, hey, look at 2012. That's a back-end rotation candidate, something the Cubs need even after signing Jon Lester and Jason Hammel to man the top and the middle.

Lineouts

Hitters

NAME	POS	TEAM	LVL	AGE	PA	R	2B	3B	HR	RBI	BB	K	SB	CS	AVG/OBP/SLG	TAv	BABIP	BRR	FRAA	WARP
Jeimer Candelario	3B	KNC	A	20	263	32	19	3	6	37	18	45	0	1	.250/.300/.426	.263	.284	-0.6	3B(62): 2.6	1.5
	3B	DAY	A+	20	244	24	10	2	5	26	23	44	0	3	.193/.275/.326	.224	.218	-2.0	3B(57): 5.5	0.4
Victor Caratini	C	KNC	A	20	58	7	4	1	0	13	4	10	0	0	.264/.310/.377	.252	.318	-0.2	C(9): -0.1	0.1
	C	ROM	A	20	365	42	18	4	5	42	34	59	1	1	.279/.352/.406	.271	.324	-4.0	C(70): 0.2, 3B(10): -0.5	1.5
Jacob Hannemann	CF	KNC	A	23	386	57	14	5	6	39	31	77	32	4	.254/.321/.377	.268	.309	5.2	CF(76): -3.0, RF(9): -0.2	1.8
	CF	DAY	A+	23	159	17	9	0	2	12	11	34	5	3	.241/.299/.345	.232	.303	-1.1	CF(36): 2.2	0.1
Jonathan Herrera	2B	PAW	AAA	29	61	11	2	1	0	4	4	11	1	1	.309/.350/.382	.256	.378	1.4	2B(11): 0.8, SS(2): -0.3	0.3
	SS	BOS	MLB	29	104	10	1	2	0	9	7	24	1	1	.233/.307/.289	.222	.313	-1.1	SS(16): -0.0, 3B(14): -0.2	0.0
Rafael Lopez	C	TEN	AA	26	177	21	13	0	4	24	29	26	1	1	.297/.412/.466	.321	.339	-1.1	C(39): 0.3	2.1
	C	IOW	AAA	26	239	17	4	1	1	27	28	52	0	0	.285/.378/.329	.248	.377	0.6	C(56): 0.0	0.8
	C	CHN	MLB	26	14	0	0	0	0	1	2	4	0	0	.182/.286/.182	.225	.250	-0.1	C(4): 0.1	0.1
Matthew Szczur	CF	IOW	AAA	24	457	52	16	1	1	24	30	78	30	7	.261/.315/.312	.228	.318	2.1	CF(79): 3.4, LF(20): 1.2	0.4
	RF	CHN	MLB	24	66	6	2	0	2	5	4	11	0	0	.226/.273/.355	.217	.245	0.0	RF(13): 1.2, CF(9): 0.2	0.0
Chris Valaika	1B	IOW	AAA	28	397	43	21	0	10	50	31	76	2	1	.278/.344/.423	.274	.325	-1.8	1B(52): 0.8, SS(15): -1.9	1.2
	1B	CHN	MLB	28	131	10	4	0	3	13	7	35	1	0	.231/.282/.339	.227	.298	0.3	1B(15): -0.2, 2B(12): 0.1	-0.1
Mark Zagunis	C	BOI	A-	21	191	32	9	2	2	27	31	31	11	2	.299/.429/.422	.250	.361	1.3	C(4): -0.1, LF(3): 0.1	0.2
	RF	KNC	A	21	62	11	6	1	0	4	10	9	5	0	.280/.419/.440	.319	.341	0.9	RF(4): 0.4, C(3): -0.0	0.7

Jeimer Candelario has a line-drive stroke but struggled in his first taste of High-A. His nickname is Candy, which then evolved into Baby Ruth, which is dangerously close to becoming Butterfingers; Cubs just hope he'll pop rocks. ❖ **Victor Caratini** is a catcher with a *maaaaaybe* plus hit tool, which is plenty. ❖ **Jacob Hannemann** is a speedy former BYU football player who is chronologically old for his minor-league levels but young in terms of experience and skills-development. ❖ What is there to say about **Jonathan Herrera** that wasn't already said about Aaron Miles seven or eight years ago? He's a jack-of-all-trades, master-of-none, run-of-the-mill utility infielder who lost his job in Boston to Brock Holt's hair. ❖ **Rafael Lopez** made a brief debut in 2014 and has always posted good walk rates in the minors; he's no wunderkind, but he could be a nice option as a backup catcher. ❖ **Matt Szczur**'s speed and solid defense make up for a lack of power; if the hit tool plays up, he could develop into a strong fourth outfielder. ❖ **Chris Valaika** is a utility infielder with enough stick not to embarrass himself and strong prospects for an enviable collection of Triple-A hats. ❖ **Mark Zagunis**' bat has always impressed and that didn't change in his pro debut; if his skills behind the plate continue to develop, he's another strong catching prospect in a system that was sorely lacking in the department just a year ago.

Pitchers

NAME	TEAM	LVL	AGE	W	L	SV	G	GS	IP	H	HR	BB	K	BB/9	K/9	GB%	BABIP	WHIP	ERA	FIP	FRA	WARP
Corey Black	TEN	AA	22	6	7	0	26	25	124¹	100	13	71	119	5.1	8.6	45%	.269	1.38	3.47	4.68	5.32	0.1
Felix Doubront	IOW	AAA	26	0	1	0	2	2	10	12	0	3	11	2.7	9.9	48%	.414	1.50	5.40	2.70	3.70	0.3
	BOS	MLB	26	2	4	0	17	10	59¹	69	10	26	43	3.9	6.5	37%	.301	1.60	6.07	5.32	6.20	-0.5
	CHN	MLB	26	2	1	0	4	4	20¹	22	2	7	8	3.1	3.5	47%	.286	1.43	3.98	4.63	5.94	-0.1
Eric Jokisch	IOW	AAA	24	9	10	0	26	26	158¹	155	12	31	143	1.8	8.1	46%	.311	1.17	3.58	3.54	4.12	3.2
	CHN	MLB	24	0	0	0	4	1	14¹	18	3	4	10	2.5	6.3	54%	.306	1.53	1.88	5.27	5.60	-0.1
Juan Paniagua	KNC	A	24	6	4	1	17	14	80¹	71	7	36	75	4.0	8.4	51%	.299	1.33	3.36	4.21	5.26	0.3
	DAY	A+	24	2	4	0	8	7	29¹	36	4	21	23	6.4	7.1	32%	.340	1.94	6.14	5.74	6.06	-0.2
Blake Parker	IOW	AAA	29	0	1	25	35	0	35²	28	3	13	52	3.3	13.1	44%	.325	1.15	1.77	2.97	3.33	0.9
	CHN	MLB	29	1	1	0	18	0	21	24	3	4	24	1.7	10.3	32%	.350	1.33	5.14	3.25	4.27	0.0
Jasvir Rakkar	KNC	A	23	3	1	1	12	0	20²	10	0	6	21	2.6	9.1	38%	.200	0.77	0.87	2.47	2.37	0.6
	BOI	A-	23	0	1	0	7	0	14²	21	2	5	17	3.1	10.4	35%	.413	1.77	7.98	4.29	4.97	0.2
Donn Roach	ELP	AAA	24	4	6	0	19	13	77¹	98	2	40	44	4.7	5.1	59%	.352	1.78	5.24	4.72	5.91	0.6
	SDN	MLB	24	1	0	0	16	1	30¹	36	2	15	17	4.5	5.0	65%	.333	1.68	4.75	4.72	5.10	0.0
Zac Rosscup	IOW	AAA	26	2	0	4	29	0	30	18	0	15	38	4.5	11.4	29%	.265	1.10	2.10	2.67	2.57	1.0
	CHN	MLB	26	1	0	0	18	0	13¹	14	2	12	21	8.1	14.2	30%	.387	1.95	9.45	4.60	5.19	-0.1
Brian Schlitter	CHN	MLB	28	2	3	0	61	0	56¹	58	4	19	31	3.0	5.0	63%	.298	1.37	4.15	3.58	4.74	0.0
Dan Straily	SAC	AAA	25	4	3	0	10	10	63	54	9	26	67	3.7	9.6	33%	.296	1.27	4.71	4.76	5.48	-0.1
	IOW	AAA	25	3	5	0	10	10	55	59	7	20	56	3.3	9.2	34%	.327	1.44	4.09	4.57	4.22	1.2
	OAK	MLB	25	1	2	0	7	7	38¹	33	9	15	34	3.5	8.0	36%	.240	1.25	4.93	5.69	6.16	-0.5
	CHN	MLB	25	0	1	0	7	1	13²	20	1	9	13	5.9	8.6	35%	.396	2.12	11.85	4.35	5.36	-0.1
Tsuyoshi Wada	IOW	AAA	33	10	6	0	19	18	113²	104	13	28	120	2.2	9.5	42%	.302	1.16	2.77	3.87	4.13	2.4
	CHN	MLB	33	4	4	0	13	13	69¹	67	7	19	57	2.5	7.4	39%	.296	1.24	3.25	3.72	3.72	0.9
Ryan Williams	BOI	A-	22	1	1	1	9	0	24²	20	2	3	26	1.1	9.5	54%	.286	0.93	1.46	3.13	3.79	0.3
Wesley Wright	CHN	MLB	29	0	3	0	58	0	48¹	48	2	19	37	3.5	6.9	56%	.309	1.39	3.17	3.41	3.98	0.1

The Cubs are going to let sub-six-foot righty **Corey Black** start as long as they can, and for the sake of his development they're probably wise to do so, but his realistic projection is power reliever. ❖ **Felix Doubront** is only missing two elements from a starter's toolbox: command and consistent stuff. Those are also the elements you are missing. ❖ **Eric Jokisch** is a heady Northwestern product who relies on weak contact, groundballs and wordplay. He amuses the clubhouse with puns and limericks, which are known by his teammates as "Jokisch Things." ❖ **Juan Paniagua** flashes three plus pitches, and if the command comes along, he would end up at worst a late-inning reliever. That's an "if" on par with the cable tech showing up at the beginning of your six-hour service window, though: "I mean, it *could* happen!" ❖ On the one hand, **Blake Parker**'s peripherals were better than his ERA. On the other hand, he's a 30-year-old reliever named "Blake Parker." ❖ Jon Hamm's not knocking down his door yet, but **Jasvir Rakkar** has a chance to make history and become the first player of Indian heritage in the majors; if he does, it'll be as a middle reliever. ❖ **Donn Roach** started the season in San Diego and ended it in El Paso, with his pitches meeting too many bats in both places. The groundball specialist moved to the bullpen in August; if he has a future, that's probably where it lies. ❖ If **Zac Rosscup** can reduce the walks, his low-90s fastball and slider could make him a useful reliever. If your dog can reduce the walks, you might spend less time freezing on the street corner at 2 a.m. ❖ **Carson Sands** is a big-bonus fourth-rounder who impressed many during his short initial stint in pro ball. His clean mechanics and recent jump in velocity and overall stuff make him an intriguing arm to follow. ❖ **Brian Schlitter** won't rack up strikeouts, but his splitter is a legit weapon that gives him value in need-a-groundball situations. ❖ **Justin Steele** is another projectable, over-slot arm snagged by the Cubs in the 2014 draft; the lefty has a mid-90s fastball and a chance for his breaking ball and change to develop into average or better pitches. ❖ **Jake Stinnett** is a former two-way player with a plus fastball, a potentially plus slider and a changeup that holds the key to unlocking his mid-rotation potential. ❖ **Dan Straily** is 26 and has an option remaining, so there's time for him to recover his lost velocity and command. On the other hand, he may have simply reached his peak in 2013; there's no mechanical fix for aging. ❖ Finally healthy, **Tsuyoshi Wada** got his first taste of the bigs and became the no. 3/4 starter the Orioles originally signed him to be three winters ago. ❖ The Cubs saw plenty of **Ryan Williams** while scouting Jeff Hoffman at East Carolina and paid him the new-10th-round-normal $1,000 to sign; the righty has a strong slider and a helluva career line (for now), but his profile makes him strictly a reliever. ❖ **Wesley Wright**'s strikeout and walk rates were down from previous seasons; his phonetic spoonerism, meanwhile, is what Ted DiBiase checks off on his Census forms.

Manager

Joe Maddon

YEAR	TEAM	W	L	Py-thag +/-	Avg PC	100+ P	120+ P	QS	BQS	REL	REL w Zero R	IBB	PH	PH Avg	PH HR	SB2	CS2	SB3	CS3	SAC Att	SAC%	POS SAC	Squeeze	Swing	In Play
2012	TBA	90	72	-6	99.9	91	7	90	2	471	415	35	135	.178	3	122	38	11	5	62	54.8%	32	3	354	105
2013	TBA	92	71	4	94.9	65	2	80	2	485	399	38	169	.235	1	61	34	12	3	39	61.5%	24	0	292	93
2014	TBA	77	85	-2	97.3	78	0	84	1	494	418	27	130	.218	1	52	24	11	2	73	58.9%	42	3	313	106

Well, this is an unexpected development. Back when Epstein was hunting for Grady Little's replacement, he interviewed Maddon, then the Angels' bench coach, for the job. Epstein passed, opting instead for Terry Francona, who would deliver the World Series in his first season. Maddon took over the Devil Rays two years later, and everything worked out well for everyone involved.

More than a decade later, Maddon has joined Epstein in Chicago, the result of an offseason dance that saw the Cubs ditch Rick Renteria after one season once Maddon evoked an opt-out clause in his contract and bolted to the highest bidder. There is shared ground between where the Cubs are now and where the D-Rays were back then, namely both teams nearing their competitive window thanks to a bunch of talented youngsters, but there are myriad differences, too. Maddon wasn't as revered back then—he didn't look so deft with the bullpen when Jon Switzer was his top left-handed reliever—and he hasn't faced the kind of scrutiny he will in Chicago.

Then there's how Maddon is unfamiliar with the NL brand of ball, although that shouldn't be an issue. Maddon has inherited many of Gene Mauch's quirks, ranging from squeeze plays and bunts to defensive positioning and platoons, and has developed a few of his own. You won't see many managers willingly shed the DH as part of a double switch, but that's what Maddon did during his days with the Rays. He's smart and flexible enough that taking to the NL style should be a breeze.

And so the optimism in and around Wrigley Field is just. Maddon is undeniably one of the best managers in the game; a skilled communicator, bold strategist and intelligent leader who knows better than to throw his players under the bus. What he's not is a miracle worker, and Padre Pio himself wouldn't have led these recent Cubs teams to glory. Maddon will deploy the pieces better than Renteria could, but the real fun won't begin until the pieces themselves are improved.

CHICAGO WHITE SOX

by Tim Marchman

The Chicago White Sox might be the most ordinary franchise in baseball, the one that would be closest to the center if you used pretty much any two criteria you can think of and laid out every team in the game on one of those big quadrant charts. It's not a bad thing, but it is a slightly strange thing. The team's defining trait is that they don't have one.

If you just think of the most basic traits a ballclub can have, you'll see there's something to this. The Sox certainly aren't a small-market team, but also aren't really a big-market one in practice, given that they tend to draw their fans from the less densely populated and less affluent parts of Chicagoland. Their park, U.S. Cellular Field, is the last one built before Camden Yards started the fake bandbox craze, which makes it both obsolete and nowhere near old-fashioned enough to have any real retro charm. And while they've been a little too successful over the years to lay claim to a curse or any kind of long-term suffering, they haven't really been successful enough to be defined by a storied history and noble traditions, either. All of this can make it a little exasperating to be a Sox fan—here you are, rooting for a second city's second team, and you don't even get to lay claim to the local inferiority complex.

All of this ordinariness has some real advantages, though, and the main one is that while they may almost never be really great, the Sox are also almost never really lousy. The run they're on, in which they've been losers two years running, is their first since the three-year stretch from 1997 to 1999, and that doesn't *really* count given that two of those teams won 80 games. Properly speaking, this has been the first truly bad Sox team since the four years immediately preceding Frank Thomas' 1990 debut, in which they lost 90 games three out of four years and sank all the way to the bottom of the league in attendance. That's pretty okay. There are a whole lot of fans who would take it.

✦✦✦

One of the strange things about what you could call, a little arbitrarily but not unfairly, the Thomas era—say it began when he debuted in the majors and ended last year with his induction into the Hall of Fame and the retirement of the last Sox to have played with him, Paul Konerko—was the way pretty okayness

worked as an operating principle. For the most part, a team defined by one of the greatest hitters in major-league history didn't seem to have much use for great players. They had some very good ones, like Robin Ventura and Ray Durham and Magglio Ordóñez, but whether it was the draft, the international market, the trade market or the free agent market, the Sox rarely seemed to go after the best available talent.

A lot of this, of course, had to do with owner Jerry Reinsdorf. He's always been happy to spend money, but he's preferred to spread that money around, especially since signing Albert Belle to the biggest contract in baseball in 1996, only to watch Belle do nothing much his first year and then scram after putting up a great one the year after that.

It also, though, had to do with an organizational philosophy that was something more than just an expression of what was convenient to Reinsdorf's interests. All through this era, after all, the Sox *did* have some of the best talent in baseball—it just wasn't necessarily on the field. First there was legendary hitting coach Walt Hriniak; later there was pitching coach Don Cooper; and trainer Herm Schneider was there all along, keeping the Sox one of the healthiest teams in the game.

The Sox' philosophy could, during this period, have been expressed through two axioms: First, that a team is stronger when it isn't overly reliant on one or two players, and, second, that if you have a strong enough coaching and training staff, you can coax exceptional performances out of unexceptional talent. The ultimate expression of all of this was the 2005 World Series championship, won by a truly great team that not only didn't have any great players, but didn't even have any good ones playing over their head. (The team's best players, starters Mark Buehrle and Jon Garland, were maybe fringe All-Stars.) That team wasn't great because it had any transcendent talents, but because pretty much everyone who got any playing time was at least okay. It was the triumph of a philosophy that prized the system above the individual, and, in a way, of risk aversion.

As the big flag with a trophy on it hanging up over the outfield at U.S. Cellular shows, that's a perfectly viable team-building philosophy. As the fact that the Sox haven't had a winning record two years in a row since 2005-06 shows, it's also maybe a little dated, not least because it goes so overwhelmingly against the

WHITE SOX PROSPECTUS
2014 W-L: 73-89, 4TH IN AL CENTRAL

Pythag	.436	26th	DER	.694	23rd
RS/G	4.07	13th	B-Age	27.7	10th
RA/G	4.68	27th	P-Age	27.2	4th
TAv	.258	16th	Salary	$90.1M	21st
BRR	-15.88	30th	M$/MW	$3.1M	16th
TAv-P	.271	28th	DL Days	727	13th
FIP	4.12	28th	$ on DL	9%	1st

Three-Year Park Factors

Runs	Runs/RH	Runs/LH	HR/RH	HR/LH
104	105	103	88	83

Top Hitter WARP	5.5	Jose Abreu
Top Pitcher WARP	4.7	Chris Sale
Top Prospect		Tim Anderson

basic, central findings of whatever we're now calling baseball's quantitative revolution.

No one in baseball ever needed Bill James or a properly calculated replacement level to know that stars were incredibly valuable, but for anyone who grew up before Baseball Prospectus and Baseball-Reference and FanGraphs, the actual numbers can still be a little unnerving. We're now pretty sure that a star is (depending on just how much of a star he is) as valuable as three or four or five perfectly average players put together. And when you think of things in those terms, the idea of picking up as many good players as you can and subsidizing the expense by avoiding great ones seems a bit obstinate. It may do a lot to ensure you're never embarrassingly bad, but it will also ensure that you need everything to go right to be great.

All of this is why this year's Sox team is the most encouraging the Sox have fielded in a very long time.

When the White Sox signed Cuban defector Jose Abreu to a six-year, $68 million contract in 2013, the deal was several things, all of them unexpected. It was the largest contract any Cuban had ever signed, half-again as rich as the next-largest; it was the largest contract the White Sox had ever given out; and it was a serious risk. This unprecedented contract, after all, was going to a player who, even if he looked like the rough equivalent of Miguel Cabrera on paper, not only hadn't ever taken an at-bat against major-league pitching, but who by the nature of what he was—a slow first baseman—would have to be a really serious hitter just to justify his contract, and a great one to be a star.

Abreu, of course, turned out to be a great hitter, as good as any in the American League. He was top-five in all the Triple Crown categories and on-base percentage, led in slugging, and in all he hit as well as any White Sox other than Thomas or Dick Allen ever has. More than that, he hit with some serious style; he would just stand there, sleepy-eyed, letting his bat lope toward sliders and fastballs away, driving these impossibly straight line drives up and out into the right-field seats, and the Sox's bad record and thin pitching didn't seem to matter very much at all. For a while—through, say, the middle of June—it seemed he was more or less a pure power hitter; then pitchers started treating him a little more carefully and he started getting a little pickier and the Sox' sketchy play seemed to matter even less when he was up. In his last 90 games, he hit .352 and walked about once every 10 plate appearances. He was, basically, Miguel Cabrera.

He also wasn't the best player on the team; that was Chris Sale, who wasn't only the best starter in the league (at least on a per-inning basis) and probably the most entertaining, given his propensity for doing things like making hitters swing so hard their batting helmets fell off, but seemed at times to be on the verge of discovering some inner mystery of pitching. At one point he walked four batters in 44 innings. It was, and still is, very easy to believe that he has it in him to put up one of those Maddux or Martinez years in which a pitcher totally masters the strike zone and does whatever he wants with it.

It's pretty obvious that if a team has arguably the best hitter and the best pitcher in the league and it still loses 89 games, a lot went wrong. That's especially so for the Sox, given that 25-year-old center fielder Adam Eaton basically played like peak Tim Raines in between injuries that cost him a quarter of the season and that fellow 25-year-old Jose Quintana established himself as a reliable no. 2 starter. What happened was that they basically fielded a lot of really terrible players. Depending on the variety of WAR you like, playing sub-replacement level talent seems to have cost them something like 15 games. If they'd been able to scare up enough scrubs, this team might well have made the playoffs. It made for a lot of painful baseball, but for anyone with an eye on the long term, it also made for some real hope that the Sox might someday soon be better than okay.

✦✦✦

One way that the Sox' reliance on the system, rather than the individual, has long played out is in their continuity. General Manager Rick Hahn, who's been with the team since 2000, is actually the new guy in comparison to, say, manager Robin Ventura or his boss, former GM Kenny Williams. This stability has, over the years, led to a certain consistency of results; it's also led to a certain amount of doing things the way they've always been done because that's the way they're done. What's important about what's happened over the last year is that this seems to be changing.

There was the Abreu signing, of course, but there was also what the Sox did with the no. 3 overall draft pick: They took college left-hander Carlos Rodon, a former no. 1 overall candidate whose velocity had dropped about five miles per hour in his draft year, and gave him the highest bonus any amateur player got. That he almost immediately, and somewhat mysteriously, added the velocity back on as soon as he hit the minors, putting himself in contention for the 2015 staff, is an outstanding thing in its own right, but the more significant thing, as with Abreu's deal, is that this represents a bet on excellence.

So does what Hahn did in early December, when, in the space of a week, he traded nothing much at all for starter Jeff Samardzjia, signed reliever David Robertston and, finally, signed outfielder Melky Cabrera, filling some of the deeper holes on the roster with reliably outstanding players. On the one hand, all three are more very good than great; on the other hand, each was arguably the very best player available at his position.

As ideals in baseball go, there are worse ones than a team consisting of 25 players clustered right around the center of the bell curve, winning because they make the most of their talents and because no one is letting the side down. There are better ones, too, though, and the highest recognize that great teams comprise great players. Any competent front office—and recent results aside, the Sox have one that's a lot better than that—can figure a way to zero out those 15 wins the Sox lost by fielding players who didn't play at a major-league level. That will leave you with an okay team; to do better than that takes something more, which the Sox have done. It's not a great and glamorous thing, but a whole lot of fans would take it.

The promise of this time for the Sox isn't so much that they have a couple of great players and, having spent some money well, serious complementary talent. It's that they're showing every sign of finally recognizing the value of truly exceptional baseball players. If they can marry that to the kind of commitment to steady, inglorious and decent play that's kept them very rarely anything less than respectable for a very long time—and Hahn's very nice December shows they probably can—they could do something that would finally define them: Reach the top of a league that's there for the taking, and stay there. ∎

—Tim Marchman is an editor at Deadspin.

Player comments by Ben Carsley, Mauricio Rubio and Baseball Prospectus Authors

Hitters

Jose Abreu   1B

Born: 1/29/87   Age: 28   Bats: R   Throws: R   Height: 6' 3"   Weight: 255

YEAR	TEAM	LVL	AGE	PA	R	2B	3B	HR	RBI	BB	K	SB	CS	AVG/OBP/SLG	TAv	BABIP	BRR	FRAA	WARP
2012	CFG	CNS	25	385	74	18	1	37	103	80	43	1	0	.394/.543/.835	.459	.363	--	--	--
2013	CFG	CNS	26	349	61	17	0	19	60	58	43	1	6	.344/.479/.604	.377	.350	--	--	--
2014	CHA	MLB	27	622	80	35	2	36	107	51	131	3	1	.317/.383/.581	.341	.356	-1.0	1B(109): 0.4	5.5
2015	CHA	MLB	28	460	63	23	2	23	74	36	100	2	1	.295/.360/.528	.326	.336	-0.5	1B -0	3.5

Breakout: 1%   Improve: 52%   Collapse: 2%   Attrition: 2%   MLB: 100%   Comparables: *Miguel Cabrera, Mark Teixeira, Prince Fielder*

A year ago at this time, people were questioning whether Abreu had enough bat speed for the majors, or the ability to adjust to advanced pitching, whether he'd be able to survive in the field, whether he'd be worth $68 million. Thirty-six homers and a unanimously awarded Rookie of the Year prize later, the answer to all of the above is emphatic. Abreu showed that his massive power translated to game action early and often in 2014, hitting 25 homers through July 1st. When his power pace slowed in the second half, he compensated by getting on base more in July, August and September. His solid defense at first base was a pleasant surprise, and he impressed many with his ability to make mid-game and even mid-at-bat adjustments. He's a legitimate cornerstone player, and one of the game's premier power hitters—no question about it.

Tim Anderson   SS

Born: 6/23/93   Age: 22   Bats: R   Throws: R   Height: 6' 1"   Weight: 180

YEAR	TEAM	LVL	AGE	PA	R	2B	3B	HR	RBI	BB	K	SB	CS	AVG/OBP/SLG	TAv	BABIP	BRR	FRAA	WARP
2013	KAN	A	20	301	45	10	5	1	21	23	78	24	4	.277/.348/.363	.272	.384	6.3	SS(63): 2.8	2.6
2014	WNS	A+	21	300	48	18	7	6	31	7	68	10	3	.297/.323/.472	.264	.369	3.6	SS(66): 0.2	1.7
2014	BIR	AA	21	45	7	3	0	1	7	0	9	0	1	.364/.364/.500	.327	.441	-0.1	SS(10): 0.5	0.5
2015	CHA	MLB	22	250	26	9	2	3	19	8	75	6	2	.230/.262/.330	.220	.315	0.6	SS 2	0.3

Breakout: 0%   Improve: 0%   Collapse: 0%   Attrition: 0%   MLB: 0%   Comparables: *Zach Walters, Chris Nelson, Daniel Santana*

Anderson didn't start playing baseball until his junior year at Tuscaloosa's Hillcrest High, where he was a basketball star. With a glaring lack of "baseball" on his resume, he garnered little draft attention and went the JuCo route, finally emerging as a first-round pick in the 2013 draft. Which is all to say: This is the textbook example of raw, and he'll need playing time, playing time and more playing time to smooth out his edges. He has natural bat-to-ball skills at the plate and some thunder in the lumber, he's fast as hell and while he's miscast as a shortstop he could be an impact player in center or solid at second. The lack of plate discipline—seriously, that strikeout-to-walk ratio—is the red flag, even if it's partly to be expected at this stage of his development. He has the ability to be special, but he has to connect the athletic to the cerebral.

Keon Barnum   1B

Born: 1/16/93   Age: 22   Bats: L   Throws: L   Height: 6' 5"   Weight: 225

YEAR	TEAM	LVL	AGE	PA	R	2B	3B	HR	RBI	BB	K	SB	CS	AVG/OBP/SLG	TAv	BABIP	BRR	FRAA	WARP
2013	KAN	A	20	223	22	13	1	5	26	19	65	0	0	.254/.315/.403	.267	.346	-1.6	1B(54): -0.8	0.1
2014	WNS	A+	21	533	49	29	1	8	60	37	163	3	0	.253/.306/.365	.231	.360	-3.9	1B(130): 1.3	-1.5
2015	CHA	MLB	22	250	19	9	1	4	23	13	90	0	0	.200/.243/.295	.201	.300	-0.4	1B -0	-1.3

Breakout: 0%   Improve: 0%   Collapse: 0%   Attrition: 0%   MLB: 0%   Comparables: *Paul Goldschmidt, Mauro Gomez, Brandon Allen*

Rick Hahn had an impressive 2014 draft, and the White Sox' system is improving, which means the few holdovers from the previous regime are sliding out of the top spots on team prospect lists. Barnum, a hulking lefty with big raw power and an even bigger hole in his swing is one such player. He has yet to pull together an attack for his at-bats, which has left him exposed at upper levels. Swing-and-miss was always going to be part of his game, but it bordered on vulgar in High-A, especially considering that .102 isolated power. Time is on his side and the raw borders on elite, but he's more likely to be remembered as a symbol of the White Sox' past than be a principal of their future.

Melky Cabrera   LF

Born: 8/11/84   Age: 30   Bats: B   Throws: L   Height: 5' 10"   Weight: 210

YEAR	TEAM	LVL	AGE	PA	R	2B	3B	HR	RBI	BB	K	SB	CS	AVG/OBP/SLG	TAv	BABIP	BRR	FRAA	WARP
2012	SFN	MLB	27	501	84	25	10	11	60	36	63	13	5	.346/.390/.516	.330	.379	0.6	LF(106): 2.0, RF(11): -1.0	5.2
2013	TOR	MLB	28	372	39	15	2	3	30	23	47	2	2	.279/.322/.360	.252	.313	-0.2	LF(77): -3.2	-0.1
2014	TOR	MLB	29	621	81	35	3	16	73	43	67	6	2	.301/.351/.458	.291	.316	-1.8	LF(133): -5.0, RF(4): 0.1	2.9
2015	CHA	MLB	30	537	64	27	4	10	52	35	77	8	3	.291/.336/.420	.281	.322	-0.5	LF -2, RF -0	1.9

Breakout: 1%   Improve: 43%   Collapse: 2%   Attrition: 12%   MLB: 99%   Comparables: *Juan Rivera, Kevin Mench, Carl Crawford*

Cabrera returned to form last year with incredible consistency, finishing with the American League's eighth-best batting average. It never sat below .290 after March 31st, and he hit for moderate power too, leading the Blue Jays in doubles. In short, scrap 2012 and 2013 as anomalies, perhaps the latter as karmic retribution for the former. Cabrera played every game but one until early September, when an untimely pinky injury—fractured getting picked off—put him out for the season, the third straight year he's missed the last month. He'll return from surgery in time for spring training, but his ability to properly grip a bat and generate power in the White Sox lineup isn't guaranteed.

Jordan Danks CF

Born: 8/7/86 Age: 28 Bats: L Throws: R Height: 6' 4" Weight: 215

YEAR	TEAM	LVL	AGE	PA	R	2B	3B	HR	RBI	BB	K	SB	CS	AVG/OBP/SLG	TAv	BABIP	BRR	FRAA	WARP
2012	CHR	AAA	25	264	37	17	1	8	30	44	66	6	3	.317/.428/.514	.334	.418	-0.5	CF(59): -1.1, RF(4): -0.1	2.9
2012	CHA	MLB	25	75	12	1	0	1	4	6	16	3	1	.224/.280/.284	.206	.269	-0.5	LF(21): 0.1, CF(14): -0.3	-0.3
2013	CHR	AAA	26	238	35	9	2	6	28	26	57	3	1	.279/.363/.428	.287	.356	0.8	CF(22): -3.5, LF(20): 1.7	0.8
2013	CHA	MLB	26	179	15	7	0	5	12	18	57	7	2	.231/.313/.369	.250	.327	-0.7	CF(47): -2.2, RF(20): 0.1	-0.3
2014	CHR	AAA	27	406	51	18	0	16	57	47	103	2	0	.270/.355/.460	.268	.329	-0.2	CF(87): 6.0, RF(3): -0.2	2.1
2014	CHA	MLB	27	132	14	2	0	2	10	14	46	5	3	.222/.303/.291	.241	.343	-1.9	CF(28): 2.0, LF(12): 0.2	0.0
2015	CHA	MLB	28	250	28	9	1	6	27	26	74	5	2	.241/.322/.376	.263	.328	-1.1	CF -1, RF -0	0.5

Breakout: 6% Improve: 29% Collapse: 17% Attrition: 31% MLB: 70% *Comparables: Clete Thomas, Brandon Boggs, John Mayberry*

John Danks produced 0.2 WARP for the White Sox in 2014. He still had a better year than Jordan. The good news is that Danks the younger hit pretty well in Charlotte in 2014, showing more power than he has in years past. The bad is that he continued to strike out swinging, and while he's not afraid to take a walk he can't barrel enough balls to keep pitchers honest. Barring a big-league power spike, he'll fall short even of fourth outfielder value. The DVD sequel—Jordan Danks-Dayan Viciedo-Alejandro De Aza—didn't work out any better than the original.

Matt Davidson 3B

Born: 3/26/91 Age: 24 Bats: R Throws: R Height: 6' 2" Weight: 225

YEAR	TEAM	LVL	AGE	PA	R	2B	3B	HR	RBI	BB	K	SB	CS	AVG/OBP/SLG	TAv	BABIP	BRR	FRAA	WARP
2012	MOB	AA	21	576	81	28	2	23	76	69	126	3	4	.261/.367/.469	.296	.304	-5.2	3B(127): -2.6	3.2
2013	RNO	AAA	22	500	55	32	3	17	74	46	134	1	0	.280/.350/.481	.264	.359	-2.6	3B(108): -0.7	1.5
2013	ARI	MLB	22	87	8	6	0	3	12	10	24	0	1	.237/.333/.434	.258	.306	-0.8	3B(20): -2.0	-0.2
2014	CHR	AAA	23	539	59	18	0	20	55	49	164	0	0	.199/.283/.362	.224	.253	-5.2	3B(111): -5.6, SS(2): -0.1	-1.5
2015	CHA	MLB	24	250	25	10	0	8	30	20	77	0	0	.219/.289/.379	.249	.288	-0.5	3B -2, SS -0	0.0

Breakout: 1% Improve: 14% Collapse: 17% Attrition: 23% MLB: 40% *Comparables: Mat Gamel, Alex Liddi, Mike Costanzo*

One of Kevin Towers' many castoffs—a collective that could reconvene and probably challenge for third place—Davidson was supposed to ascend to a throne that still bears Joe Crede's buttgroove. Instead, he endured a brutal April (and, later, May, July and August) in Triple-A while Conor Gillaspie chose "right now" to have a career year. Clearly, he'll need to get back on track if he wants another shot at the job, but he's got plenty of pop for the position, and his minor-league stats are close enough to Crede's to suggest his tush would be comfortable.

Adam Eaton CF

Born: 12/6/88 Age: 26 Bats: L Throws: L Height: 5' 8" Weight: 185

YEAR	TEAM	LVL	AGE	PA	R	2B	3B	HR	RBI	BB	K	SB	CS	AVG/OBP/SLG	TAv	BABIP	BRR	FRAA	WARP
2012	MOB	AA	23	51	11	1	0	0	3	6	8	6	1	.300/.451/.325	.300	.375	1.3	CF(11): -0.3	0.7
2012	RNO	AAA	23	562	119	46	5	7	45	53	68	38	10	.381/.456/.539	.323	.432	4.6	CF(82): 1.9, RF(29): 2.7	6.6
2012	ARI	MLB	23	103	19	3	2	2	5	14	15	2	3	.259/.382/.412	.292	.294	2.0	CF(21): -2.7, LF(1): -0.0	0.6
2013	VIS	A+	24	64	12	3	0	1	6	10	6	8	1	.321/.438/.434	.298	.348	1.8	CF(4): -0.2	0.5
2013	RNO	AAA	24	40	5	2	0	1	5	3	8	0	0	.143/.225/.286	.180	.148	-0.7	CF(2): 0.0	-0.4
2013	ARI	MLB	24	277	40	10	4	3	22	17	44	5	2	.252/.314/.360	.239	.294	2.1	LF(35): -1.3, CF(30): -4.6	-0.3
2014	CHA	MLB	25	538	76	26	10	1	35	43	83	15	9	.300/.362/.401	.281	.359	0.6	CF(121): 1.2	2.8
2015	CHA	MLB	26	469	57	22	5	4	37	37	81	16	7	.283/.351/.386	.276	.337	2.2	CF -3, LF -1	1.9

Breakout: 5% Improve: 54% Collapse: 17% Attrition: 21% MLB: 94% *Comparables: Denard Span, Julio Borbon, Jacoby Ellsbury*

At what point do we label a player injury prone? Eaton probably shouldn't have that reputation yet, but he might be getting dangerously close. After playing in just 66 games in 2013 thanks to an elbow injury, he missed more than 30 games with various hamstring, wrist and abdomen issues in 2014. He still accumulated more than 500 plate appearances, but the myriad boo-boos are concerning at such a rigorous defensive position. Obtaining Eaton for the low, low cost of one Hector Santiago last offseason remains a terrific move for the White Sox, and Eaton is a perfectly functioning leadoff man with a great beard when he's on the field. If he misses another 100-plus plate appearances in 2015, though, expect to see the "when he's on the field" caveat pop up a lot more often.

Tyler Flowers C

Born: 1/24/86 Age: 29 Bats: R Throws: R Height: 6' 4" Weight: 245

YEAR	TEAM	LVL	AGE	PA	R	2B	3B	HR	RBI	BB	K	SB	CS	AVG/OBP/SLG	TAv	BABIP	BRR	FRAA	WARP
2012	CHA	MLB	26	153	19	6	0	7	13	12	56	2	1	.213/.296/.412	.232	.301	-0.4	C(49): -0.8, 1B(2): -0.1	0.1
2013	CHA	MLB	27	275	24	11	0	10	24	14	94	0	1	.195/.247/.355	.212	.261	-1.0	C(84): 0.8	-0.2
2014	CHA	MLB	28	442	42	16	1	15	50	25	159	0	1	.241/.297/.396	.249	.355	-0.5	C(124): -1.8	1.4
2015	CHA	MLB	29	382	42	14	1	13	44	33	132	1	1	.216/.296/.379	.253	.304	-0.5	C -1, 1B 0	1.1

Breakout: 9% Improve: 41% Collapse: 11% Attrition: 18% MLB: 86% *Comparables: Kelly Shoppach, Josh Phelps, Taylor Teagarden*

We've been waiting for Flowers to blossom for quite a while now, but he rose to the occasion in the second half of 2014. Vision proved to be a thorn in his side early in the year (check those irises), leading to a .218/.273/.304 first-half line. But he turned over a new leaf at the halfway point, hitting .280/.337/.553. The 29-year-old has made perennial improvements defensively, and while he's not divine, he doesn't need to be supplanted by a backup late in games. We don't need to joke orchid about his game calling, either. The White Sox haven't kept mum about giving him full-time play in 2015, but pay no mind tulip service; if a better option sprouts up, they'll pounce. Still, there's no doubt that Flowers is easier to root for today than he was a year ago, and while it took him longer than expected to have his day in the sun, Flowers has finally bloomed.

Leury Garcia 2B

Born: 3/18/91   Age: 24   Bats: B   Throws: R   Height: 5' 8"   Weight: 170

YEAR	TEAM	LVL	AGE	PA	R	2B	3B	HR	RBI	BB	K	SB	CS	AVG/OBP/SLG	TAv	BABIP	BRR	FRAA	WARP
2012	FRI	AA	21	416	55	12	11	2	30	22	79	31	7	.292/.337/.398	.281	.361	4.7	2B(57): 9.5, SS(39): -0.7	3.6
2013	CHR	AAA	22	32	3	1	0	0	1	1	8	3	0	.267/.313/.300	.209	.364	0.2	2B(5): 0.0, SS(2): -0.1	-0.1
2013	ROU	AAA	22	208	31	8	4	4	19	14	53	12	4	.264/.314/.409	.257	.346	1.8	SS(42): 3.5, CF(5): -0.4	1.6
2013	CHA	MLB	22	54	2	1	0	0	1	4	18	6	2	.204/.259/.224	.200	.313	0.2	2B(9): 0.2, CF(6): -0.1	-0.1
2013	TEX	MLB	22	57	8	0	1	0	1	3	16	1	0	.192/.236/.231	.187	.278	0.4	2B(12): 0.3, SS(4): 0.2	-0.2
2014	CHA	MLB	23	155	13	3	0	1	6	5	48	11	1	.166/.192/.207	.152	.237	1.4	3B(15): 0.9, CF(14): -1.1	-1.4
2015	CHA	MLB	24	250	29	8	3	2	16	11	68	16	3	.234/.270/.319	.220	.310	1.0	2B 2, SS 1	0.1

Breakout: 2%   Improve: 18%   Collapse: 6%   Attrition: 17%   MLB: 38%   *Comparables: Emilio Bonifacio, Hernan Iribarren, Erick Aybar*

Garcia played every position but first base and catcher for the White Sox in 2014. He even pitched, allowing two runs in an inning. That's an impressive feat; few players have the versatility to adequately fill in defensively across the board, and Garcia gives Robin Ventura lots of late-inning options. The bad news is that batting is a part of baseball, and Garcia is soft as baby thighs at the plate. He's still quite young and his unique defensive skill set will give him a fighting chance to stick for a long time, but ultimately Garcia needs to hit less like a pitcher (or pitch less like a hitter) to secure his future.

Avisail Garcia RF

Born: 6/12/91   Age: 24   Bats: R   Throws: R   Height: 6' 4"   Weight: 240

YEAR	TEAM	LVL	AGE	PA	R	2B	3B	HR	RBI	BB	K	SB	CS	AVG/OBP/SLG	TAv	BABIP	BRR	FRAA	WARP
2012	LAK	A+	21	287	47	8	5	8	36	11	57	14	4	.289/.324/.447	.265	.335	1.8	RF(62): 2.2, CF(3): 0.2	1.3
2012	ERI	AA	21	226	31	9	3	6	22	7	38	9	4	.312/.345/.465	.274	.357	1.5	CF(44): 1.1, RF(9): 0.5	1.3
2012	DET	MLB	21	51	7	0	0	0	3	3	10	0	2	.319/.373/.319	.241	.405	0.1	RF(18): -0.5, LF(2): 0.1	0.0
2013	LAK	A+	22	28	9	0	2	1	4	4	1	2	0	.417/.500/.708	.393	.409	0.7	CF(2): -0.1, RF(2): 0.0	0.5
2013	CHR	AAA	22	32	6	0	1	1	9	4	4	0	0	.370/.469/.556	.387	.409	-0.4	CF(7): -0.6	0.4
2013	TOL	AAA	22	156	23	7	1	5	23	8	32	4	2	.374/.410/.537	.342	.455	0.6	CF(25): 0.2, RF(6): -0.6	1.8
2013	CHA	MLB	22	168	19	4	2	5	21	5	38	3	2	.304/.327/.447	.272	.370	-1.1	RF(36): -2.2, CF(8): -0.6	0.1
2013	DET	MLB	22	88	12	3	1	2	10	4	21	0	1	.241/.273/.373	.246	.295	0.3	CF(23): -0.6, RF(5): 0.1	-0.1
2014	CHR	AAA	23	53	9	3	0	1	3	1	16	0	0	.340/.377/.460	.283	.485	0.8	RF(7): -0.0	0.3
2014	CHA	MLB	23	190	19	8	0	7	29	14	44	4	1	.244/.305/.413	.256	.285	-1.8	RF(46): -3.3	-0.3
2015	CHA	MLB	24	250	27	9	2	7	29	10	60	4	2	.275/.310/.415	.271	.339	-0.6	RF -2, CF -1	0.5

Breakout: 4%   Improve: 39%   Collapse: 6%   Attrition: 15%   MLB: 81%   *Comparables: Victor Diaz, Aaron Cunningham, Carlos Gonzalez*

Way on down the path of "physically gifted player" the road diverges and the player is left looking down the trails of greatness, mediocrity and irrelevance. Avisail Garcia has arrived at those crossroads. A torn labrum (from which he recovered with preternatural speed) delayed the inevitable journey down any of those paths but now there isn't much time for Garcia to enjoy the scenery. Soon he will have to coalesce his natural gifts (he's faster than he looks and he puts on an absolute show from 5 to 7 p.m.) into a career, the shape of which we're still to discern. The promise of youth quickly loses its glimmer as we advance from our young 20s to our middle 20s.

Conor Gillaspie 3B

Born: 7/18/87   Age: 27   Bats: L   Throws: R   Height: 6' 1"   Weight: 195

YEAR	TEAM	LVL	AGE	PA	R	2B	3B	HR	RBI	BB	K	SB	CS	AVG/OBP/SLG	TAv	BABIP	BRR	FRAA	WARP
2012	FRE	AAA	24	465	60	18	3	14	49	41	54	0	0	.281/.345/.441	.272	.291	-0.6	3B(81): -1.5, 1B(20): 0.2	1.6
2012	SFN	MLB	24	20	2	1	0	0	2	0	2	0	0	.150/.150/.200	.122	.167	0.0	3B(5): -0.3	-0.3
2013	CHA	MLB	25	452	46	14	3	13	40	37	79	0	1	.245/.305/.390	.259	.270	-1.4	3B(113): 1.3, 1B(12): 0.6	1.6
2014	CHA	MLB	26	506	50	31	5	7	57	36	78	0	4	.282/.336/.416	.276	.325	-1.9	3B(127): -6.1	1.6
2015	CHA	MLB	27	466	45	20	3	9	50	38	83	1	2	.256/.317/.387	.260	.293	-1.1	3B -1, 1B 0	0.8

Breakout: 6%   Improve: 40%   Collapse: 7%   Attrition: 17%   MLB: 82%   *Comparables: Luis Valbuena, Ruben Gotay, Danny Valencia*

Gillaspie isn't a very good defensive third baseman and he should be spared from left-handers at all costs, but he does some things well. He hit .300/.360/.444 against right-handers last year (.278/.340/.425 for his career), and he's proven capable of hitting double-digit bombs before. Gillaspie is a second-division starter through and through, which is about six divisions higher than you'd have predicted when he was with the Giants.

Courtney Hawkins CF

Born: 11/12/93   Age: 21   Bats: R   Throws: R   Height: 6' 3"   Weight: 220

YEAR	TEAM	LVL	AGE	PA	R	2B	3B	HR	RBI	BB	K	SB	CS	AVG/OBP/SLG	TAv	BABIP	BRR	FRAA	WARP
2012	KAN	A	18	72	11	5	2	4	15	4	17	3	2	.308/.352/.631	.331	.356	0.0	CF(16): -0.6	0.8
2013	WNS	A+	19	425	48	16	3	19	62	29	160	10	5	.178/.249/.384	.216	.236	1.7	CF(100): 2.3	-0.7
2014	WNS	A+	20	515	65	25	4	19	84	53	143	11	3	.249/.331/.450	.272	.316	2.0	LF(108): -3.2, CF(6): -0.0	1.4
2015	CHA	MLB	21	250	25	8	1	9	29	14	94	3	1	.194/.246/.349	.222	.274	0.0	LF -1, CF -0	-0.4

Breakout: 0%   Improve: 0%   Collapse: 0%   Attrition: 0%   MLB: 0%   *Comparables: Chris Davis, Michael Choice, Marcell Ozuna*

If you squint you can still see what the White Sox saw in the former first-rounder. In a repeat of High-A after a disastrous 2013, Hawkins struck out less, walked more and recovered a more respectable BABIP, boosting his production across the row. Still, as it stands, the bat won't get him to the majors, as his "good" weight has turned bad and sentenced him to a 1B/DH role. The swing is long, he doesn't recognize off-speed stuff and even with the improvements he struck out at an alarming rate, especially considering the level. He's not even to Double-A and it's tempting to call him a Quad-A prospect.

Micah Johnson   2B

Born: 12/18/90   Age: 24   Bats: L   Throws: R   Height: 6' 0"   Weight: 190

YEAR	TEAM	LVL	AGE	PA	R	2B	3B	HR	RBI	BB	K	SB	CS	AVG/OBP/SLG	TAv	BABIP	BRR	FRAA	WARP
2013	KAN	A	22	351	76	17	11	6	42	40	67	61	19	.342/.422/.530	.357	.422	5.5	2B(72): 8.2	6.0
2013	WNS	A+	22	228	28	7	4	1	15	10	27	22	7	.275/.309/.360	.234	.310	-1.0	2B(47): 6.6	0.4
2013	BIR	AA	22	22	2	0	0	0	1	0	4	1	0	.238/.227/.238	.175	.278	0.3	2B(5): 0.1	-0.1
2014	BIR	AA	23	170	18	9	1	3	16	21	27	10	7	.329/.414/.466	.318	.385	1.1	2B(30): -1.2	1.5
2014	CHR	AAA	23	302	30	10	5	2	28	16	42	12	6	.275/.314/.370	.242	.315	1.5	2B(58): -4.6	-0.4
2015	CHA	MLB	24	250	31	8	3	3	18	15	56	13	6	.251/.298/.348	.240	.309	0.8	2B 1	0.5

Breakout: 7%   Improve: 15%   Collapse: 8%   Attrition: 29%   MLB: 41%   Comparables: *Eric Young, Cesar Hernandez, Jose Pirela*

Johnson is a true burner—those stolen base numbers don't really capture it—but there've always been doubts about how much of his production would move up the ladder with him. He's got an idea of how to handle the strike zone, with a good overall approach and solid bat-to-ball skills, but he's got flimsy power, poor instincts and a below-average defensive skill set. There's a player here—and one whose line at Birmingham has already proved some skeptics wrong—but super fast won't be enough; he'll need to learn to slow the game down, too.

Paul Konerko   DH

Born: 3/5/76   Age: 39   Bats: R   Throws: R   Height: 6' 2"   Weight: 220

YEAR	TEAM	LVL	AGE	PA	R	2B	3B	HR	RBI	BB	K	SB	CS	AVG/OBP/SLG	TAv	BABIP	BRR	FRAA	WARP
2012	CHA	MLB	36	598	66	22	0	26	75	56	83	0	0	.298/.371/.486	.293	.312	-3.0	1B(105): -6.2	1.7
2013	CHA	MLB	37	520	41	16	0	12	54	45	74	0	0	.244/.313/.355	.246	.265	-6.1	1B(76): -1.1	-1.0
2014	CHA	MLB	38	224	15	8	0	5	22	10	51	0	0	.207/.254/.317	.202	.247	-0.6	1B(23): 0.1	-1.1
2015	CHA	MLB	39	271	31	10	0	9	34	24	49	0	0	.266/.336/.424	.281	.296	-1.6	1B -2	0.5

Breakout: 0%   Improve: 15%   Collapse: 5%   Attrition: 10%   MLB: 73%   Comparables: *Stan Musial, Hideki Matsui, Rafael Palmeiro*

Every hero, from the low-key local variety to the grander protagonist of legend, has a moment when he steps out from a seemingly normal story arc into something other, something bigger. For Paul Konerko the moment came on October 23, 2005, World Series Game Two, the bottom of the seventh inning, the bases loaded and two outs, Sox down 6-4, home-field advantage hanging in the balance. Up until Chad Qualls delivered a fastball that caught too much plate, Konerko was known as a good-not-great player, but one with an uncertain future in the White Sox organization. On that rainy October night, his story—and that of the White Sox—changed when he hit the most important home run in the organization's history.

After Konerko gave the series-winning ball to White Sox owner Jerry Reinsdorf—nice touch—he and the White Sox agreed to a five-year deal that winter. He lasted another nine seasons before retiring with minimal fanfare this year. All is said and done, and baseball at large will regard Konerko as a good-not-great player, but his place in the White Sox organization is undisputed. For those who crowded the front row of U.S. Cellular Field to see the captain take a final farewell lap around the field, and for anyone who watched Konerko's career with the White Sox close to their hearts, he will always be something more.

Adam LaRoche   1B

Born: 11/6/79   Age: 35   Bats: L   Throws: L   Height: 6' 3"   Weight: 205

YEAR	TEAM	LVL	AGE	PA	R	2B	3B	HR	RBI	BB	K	SB	CS	AVG/OBP/SLG	TAv	BABIP	BRR	FRAA	WARP
2012	WAS	MLB	32	647	76	35	1	33	100	67	138	1	1	.271/.343/.510	.301	.298	-2.9	1B(153): 11.1	4.2
2013	WAS	MLB	33	590	70	19	3	20	62	72	131	4	1	.237/.332/.403	.265	.277	-0.6	1B(149): 1.3	0.8
2014	WAS	MLB	34	586	73	19	0	26	92	82	108	3	0	.259/.362/.455	.305	.277	-2.6	1B(136): 4.0	3.8
2015	CHA	MLB	35	552	64	22	1	20	71	60	134	2	1	.239/.323/.415	.274	.284	-1.6	1B 6	1.8

Breakout: 1%   Improve: 21%   Collapse: 12%   Attrition: 17%   MLB: 95%   Comparables: *Roy Sievers, Eric Hinske, Davey Johnson*

Another notch in the belt for Laroche, who reached the 20-homer plateau for the ninth time in the past 10 years (only Miguel Cabrera and David Ortiz have gone 10-for-10). He also maintained a 20-grade beard. The one noticeable difference, however, was the improvement in plate discipline statistics, as LaRoche secured both the second-best walk rate and second-best strikeout rate of his long career. Not surprisingly, this led to his best TAv in five seasons. There's no reason to believe LaRoche will stop being productive over the next couple of seasons for Chicago, even if Father Time (or, God willing, a razor) finally catches up with him.

Jacob May   CF

Born: 1/23/92   Age: 23   Bats: B   Throws: R   Height: 5' 10"   Weight: 180

YEAR	TEAM	LVL	AGE	PA	R	2B	3B	HR	RBI	BB	K	SB	CS	AVG/OBP/SLG	TAv	BABIP	BRR	FRAA	WARP
2013	KAN	A	21	230	36	6	3	8	28	16	43	19	5	.286/.346/.461	.309	.325	1.6	CF(50): -5.1	1.7
2014	WNS	A+	22	472	66	31	10	2	27	42	71	37	8	.258/.326/.395	.252	.305	5.1	CF(92): -8.0, LF(2): -0.0	0.6
2015	CHA	MLB	23	250	30	10	2	3	17	15	58	14	4	.224/.274/.326	.222	.278	1.7	CF -5, LF -0	-0.7

Breakout: 0%   Improve: 0%   Collapse: 0%   Attrition: 0%   MLB: 0%   Comparables: *Blake Tekotte, Jacoby Ellsbury, Shane Robinson*

If you were born around 1975, this is the moment you groan "I'm so ollllld": May is the *grandson* of the Big Bopper, Lee May, who hit 354 home runs and was smiling up from packs of baseball cards that *you* bought. Jacob's a much different player than the old man—he's a burner and a switch-hitter who made a lot of contact and laid down a lot of bunts in his first full season. He has the speed to play center field but needs to learn the position better to avoid a future in left field. He still has a lot to prove and refinements to make, especially from the left side, but the skill set is a flashy one. You, meanwhile, are one minute older than you were when you started reading this comment.

Trey Michalczewski   3B

Born: 2/27/95   Age: 20   Bats: B   Throws: R   Height: 6' 3"   Weight: 210

YEAR	TEAM	LVL	AGE	PA	R	2B	3B	HR	RBI	BB	K	SB	CS	AVG/OBP/SLG	TAv	BABIP	BRR	FRAA	WARP
2014	KAN	A	19	495	57	25	7	10	70	45	140	6	3	.273/.348/.433	.279	.375	0.9	3B(114): -10.0	2.0
2014	WNS	A+	19	84	5	2	0	0	5	9	21	1	0	.194/.293/.222	.220	.275	-0.8	3B(17): -0.3	-0.3
2015	CHA	MLB	20	250	19	8	1	3	22	16	87	1	0	.199/.256/.291	.207	.296	-0.3	3B -4	-1.3

Breakout: 0%   Improve: 0%   Collapse: 0%   Attrition: 0%   MLB: 0%   Comparables: *Steven Souza, Matt Davidson, Alex Liddi*

Michalczewski is a switch-hitting third baseman with a strong arm and power, which can be a very valuable package. More valuable: He's got the "seat" of power, a bubbly protrusion that you can see on a county map. It's built upon the strong foundation of two sturdy legs and a good pair of hips, which are an underrated factor in the butt equation. When it comes to A+ asses, the hips are a proverbial fastball on the black that sets up the power curve that is the rear, and Michalczewski's hips and rear rival Kershaw's fastball/curve combo in their own special way.

Jared Mitchell   LF
Born: 10/13/88   Age: 26   Bats: L   Throws: L   Height: 6' 0"   Weight: 205

YEAR	TEAM	LVL	AGE	PA	R	2B	3B	HR	RBI	BB	K	SB	CS	AVG/OBP/SLG	TAv	BABIP	BRR	FRAA	WARP
2012	BIR	AA	23	408	51	13	12	10	54	62	126	20	5	.240/.368/.440	.293	.350	0.5	CF(80): 1.1, LF(7): -1.2	2.6
2012	CHR	AAA	23	141	18	11	1	1	13	16	53	1	1	.231/.329/.364	.257	.397	1.7	LF(21): -0.3, CF(15): -2.0	0.1
2013	BIR	AA	24	291	23	6	2	5	20	41	96	13	5	.174/.297/.275	.215	.260	-0.4	LF(34): 2.8, CF(32): 0.7	-0.3
2013	CHR	AAA	24	65	7	2	0	0	3	10	27	4	1	.132/.277/.170	.198	.259	0.4	CF(11): -0.5, LF(3): 0.0	-0.4
2014	BIR	AA	25	179	32	5	3	10	20	16	40	4	5	.299/.367/.561	.316	.339	-0.8	CF(21): -1.4, LF(18): 1.1	1.3
2014	CHR	AAA	25	336	41	8	2	9	30	49	111	11	7	.230/.360/.375	.250	.344	0.9	LF(56): -3.9, CF(20): -1.4	-0.2
2015	CHA	MLB	26	250	31	7	2	6	21	27	92	7	3	.200/.297/.333	.237	.307	0.4	LF -0, CF -1	-0.2

Breakout: 0%   Improve: 3%   Collapse: 5%   Attrition: 11%   MLB: 14%   Comparables: *John-Ford Griffin, Brad Snyder, Danny Putnam*

Oft-injured Mitchell survived the season unscathed and logged 515 plate appearances, his highest total since 2012, but otherwise the year was a push. This was once a noticeable athlete and a top-100 prospect, but age and injury have dulled his physical gifts and sent him on that depressing trek from center field to left. He slugged the kids in Double-A but couldn't pick on pitchers his own age. Simply put: He's got limited utility, he's not getting better and he is getting older. Nobody tell him about Lee May's grandkid.

Adrian Nieto   C
Born: 11/12/89   Age: 25   Bats: B   Throws: R   Height: 6' 0"   Weight: 200

YEAR	TEAM	LVL	AGE	PA	R	2B	3B	HR	RBI	BB	K	SB	CS	AVG/OBP/SLG	TAv	BABIP	BRR	FRAA	WARP
2012	HAG	A	22	299	32	17	0	6	39	35	64	4	2	.257/.346/.393	.263	.314	1.4	C(65): -0.4	1.5
2012	ESP	INT	22	20	3	2	0	0	1	3	3	0	0	.313/.421/.438	.311	.385	0.0		0.0
2013	POT	A+	23	452	68	29	1	11	53	53	82	4	2	.285/.373/.449	.280	.332	-0.4	C(86): 0.9	3.0
2014	CHA	MLB	24	118	8	5	0	2	7	8	38	0	1	.236/.296/.340	.238	.348	-0.2	C(46): 0.3	0.1
2015	CHA	MLB	25	250	22	10	0	5	25	19	69	1	0	.225/.288/.337	.234	.295	-0.5	C 0	0.2

Breakout: 5%   Improve: 11%   Collapse: 8%   Attrition: 22%   MLB: 34%   Comparables: *Guillermo Quiroz, Rob Bowen, Jose Lobaton*

The Rule 5 draft is often a useless exercise these days, but the White Sox nabbed Nieto from the Nationals and managed to keep him on the big-league roster all year. This could very well end up a Pyrrhic victory. Nieto is young, but he looked like a player who required more minor-league seasoning in 2014. He had a poor approach at the plate and offered little pop, but even more concerning was his performance behind the dish. Nieto received below-average measures for his pitch framing, doesn't move well behind the plate, got trounced by opposing basestealers and didn't seem to make a difference with his game-calling. He's Chicago's property now, and given how hard it is to find quality catching, you can understand why the Sox took a gamble on his youth and upside. But he's best off finally getting to Triple-A.

Alexei Ramirez   SS
Born: 9/22/81   Age: 33   Bats: R   Throws: R   Height: 6' 2"   Weight: 180

YEAR	TEAM	LVL	AGE	PA	R	2B	3B	HR	RBI	BB	K	SB	CS	AVG/OBP/SLG	TAv	BABIP	BRR	FRAA	WARP
2012	CHA	MLB	30	621	59	24	4	9	73	16	77	20	7	.265/.287/.364	.229	.290	1.4	SS(158): 8.0	1.7
2013	CHA	MLB	31	674	68	39	2	6	48	26	68	30	9	.284/.313/.380	.254	.309	1.6	SS(158): -3.2	2.4
2014	CHA	MLB	32	657	82	35	2	15	74	24	81	21	4	.273/.305/.408	.251	.292	-0.1	SS(158): 8.1	3.2
2015	CHA	MLB	33	621	71	30	3	8	51	25	87	21	6	.267/.299/.369	.249	.297	0.4	SS 7	2.7

Breakout: 0%   Improve: 34%   Collapse: 5%   Attrition: 8%   MLB: 91%   Comparables: *Edgar Renteria, Julio Lugo, Jack Wilson*

Harken back, if you will, to the days before Yoenis Cespedes, Jorge Soler and Yasiel Puig, and way before the days of Jose Abreu, Yasmany Tomas and Rusney Castillo. Before the current run of talented Cubans, there was Ramirez, to whom the White Sox have paid less than $40 million in exchange for 18.5 WARP over the past seven years. The 33-year-old recovered some of his pop in 2014 without sacrificing much OBP; with passable defense at short and meaningful speed, he continues to be a valuable player. He doesn't walk and he makes more than his fair share of errors, but not every valuable player needs to do it pretty. His $16 million club option for 2016 will make for an interesting decision.

Carlos Sanchez   2B
Born: 6/29/92   Age: 23   Bats: B   Throws: R   Height: 5' 11"   Weight: 195

YEAR	TEAM	LVL	AGE	PA	R	2B	3B	HR	RBI	BB	K	SB	CS	AVG/OBP/SLG	TAv	BABIP	BRR	FRAA	WARP
2012	WNS	A+	20	416	58	14	6	1	42	31	64	19	10	.315/.374/.395	.278	.373	-1.0	SS(47): -0.4, 2B(45): -0.2	2.0
2012	BIR	AA	20	133	17	9	1	0	13	10	22	7	5	.370/.424/.462	.338	.449	-1.3	2B(14): -0.6, SS(11): 1.5	1.4
2012	CHR	AAA	20	39	4	2	0	0	1	0	6	0	0	.256/.256/.308	.206	.303	0.1	SS(10): -0.4, 2B(1): -0.1	-0.2
2013	CHR	AAA	21	479	50	20	2	0	28	29	76	16	10	.241/.293/.296	.220	.290	-1.9	2B(61): -2.2, SS(52): 1.6	-1.2
2014	CHR	AAA	22	494	60	19	6	7	57	36	84	16	4	.293/.349/.412	.251	.344	1.8	2B(64): -0.7, SS(44): 1.6	1.4
2014	CHA	MLB	22	104	6	5	0	0	5	3	25	1	1	.250/.269/.300	.220	.329	-1.5	2B(27): -1.9, SS(1): 0.1	-0.7
2015	CHA	MLB	23	250	26	10	2	2	18	12	52	6	3	.258/.298/.337	.238	.315	0.3	2B -2, SS 0	0.2

Breakout: 6%   Improve: 22%   Collapse: 3%   Attrition: 10%   MLB: 31%   Comparables: *Jose Pirela, Luis Valbuena, Alexi Amarista*

Sanchez has a lot of positive attributes. He's a plus defender at second base. He's a switch-hitter. He can run a bit, make some contact. He's not allergic to walks, or grass, or the sun, or any of the other things that would disqualify him from this profession. Most importantly, he's not Gordon Beckham. Unfortunately, we have to talk about what Sanchez can't do, too, and that's a list that includes hitting for power, throwing hard or hitting well enough to bat near the top of a lineup. If everything breaks right for Sanchez, he's an everyday, down-the-order second baseman who saves plenty of runs with his glove and does enough at the plate to warrant at-bats. If he doesn't maximize his talent, he can still serve as a utility infielder, pinch-runner and Not Gordon Beckham.

Trayce Thompson   CF

Born: 3/15/91   Age: 24   Bats: R   Throws: R   Height: 6' 3"   Weight: 210

YEAR	TEAM	LVL	AGE	PA	R	2B	3B	HR	RBI	BB	K	SB	CS	AVG/OBP/SLG	TAv	BABIP	BRR	FRAA	WARP
2012	WNS	A+	21	510	77	28	5	22	90	45	144	18	3	.254/.325/.486	.288	.316	0.9	CF(110): 5.0, RF(6): -0.1	3.9
2012	BIR	AA	21	58	10	1	1	3	6	8	16	2	0	.280/.379/.520	.327	.355	-0.5	CF(13): -1.2, RF(1): -0.1	0.5
2012	CHR	AAA	21	20	1	2	0	0	0	2	6	1	0	.167/.250/.278	.184	.250	0.3	CF(4): 0.3, LF(1): 0.1	-0.1
2013	BIR	AA	22	590	78	23	5	15	73	60	139	25	8	.229/.321/.383	.274	.280	3.8	CF(67): -10.1, RF(62): 2.0	2.0
2014	BIR	AA	23	595	86	34	6	16	59	65	151	20	5	.237/.324/.419	.274	.301	4.0	CF(81): 4.6, LF(48): 3.4	3.6
2015	CHA	MLB	24	250	27	10	1	7	27	19	79	7	2	.213/.279/.364	.240	.287	0.7	CF -0, LF 1	0.2

Breakout: 1%   Improve: 5%   Collapse: 4%   Attrition: 9%   MLB: 16%   Comparables: *Melky Mesa, Matt Den Dekker, Thomas Pham*

Thompson was part of the Kenny Williams' Raw And Toolsy Middle-Of-The-Diamond Boys, a lad group that looked good in magazine spreads but didn't produce many hits. Last year marked his third engagement at Double-A, and at this point he's been slow-cooking long enough to have smoke rings. Problem is, the extended stay in Birmingham hasn't seen much in the way of improvement or refinement. He's a capable defender with a promising pop, but his struggles with breaking balls are sad enough to make Clint Eastwood cry. That limits the hit tool and ultimately caps his in-game power potential. He'll cook some more in 2015.

Dayan Viciedo   RF

Born: 3/10/89   Age: 26   Bats: R   Throws: R   Height: 5' 11"   Weight: 240

YEAR	TEAM	LVL	AGE	PA	R	2B	3B	HR	RBI	BB	K	SB	CS	AVG/OBP/SLG	TAv	BABIP	BRR	FRAA	WARP
2012	CHA	MLB	23	543	64	18	1	25	78	28	120	0	2	.255/.300/.444	.259	.286	-1.6	LF(131): 2.9	1.2
2013	CHA	MLB	24	473	43	23	3	14	56	24	98	0	0	.265/.304/.426	.264	.308	-0.3	LF(109): -11.3	0.0
2014	CHA	MLB	25	563	65	22	3	21	58	32	122	0	1	.231/.281/.405	.247	.261	1.7	RF(84): -5.6, LF(55): -1.5	-0.8
2015	CHA	MLB	26	513	56	22	2	17	63	27	112	0	1	.257/.302/.421	.270	.299	0.1	LF -3, RF -4	0.8

Breakout: 5%   Improve: 57%   Collapse: 8%   Attrition: 7%   MLB: 96%   Comparables: *Travis Snider, Andre Ethier, J.D. Martinez*

Finesse is not a part of Viciedo's game. He has violent raw power that has sent 60 homers and 63 doubles flying over the past three years. He's an atrocious fielder, stumbling around the outfield with the grace of a frightened boar. His approach is unbalanced, as he consistently strikes out in about a fifth of his plate appearances while walking every 20th. Viciedo has been getting older and worse, so as the White Sox continue to get younger and better it'll be tough for him to squeeze into the lineup. He was a popular non-tender candidate this offseason, and if he fails to impress again in 2015, he gone.

Pitchers ─────────────────────────────

Ronald Belisario   RHP

Born: 12/31/82   Age: 32   Bats: R   Throws: R   Height: 6'3"   Weight: 240

YEAR	TEAM	LVL	AGE	W	L	SV	G	GS	IP	H	HR	BB	K	BB/9	K/9	GB%	BABIP	WHIP	ERA	FIP	FRA	WARP
2012	LAN	MLB	29	8	1	1	68	0	71	47	3	29	69	3.7	8.7	65%	.243	1.07	2.54	3.14	4.02	0.3
2013	LAN	MLB	30	5	7	1	77	0	68	72	3	28	49	3.7	6.5	62%	.321	1.47	3.97	3.61	4.28	0.3
2014	CHA	MLB	31	4	8	8	62	0	66¹	78	4	18	47	2.4	6.4	61%	.339	1.45	5.56	3.57	3.65	1.0
2015	CHA	MLB	32	3	1	3	59	0	58²	59	5	21	48	3.2	7.3	58%	.307	1.36	4.01	4.26	4.36	0.4

Breakout: 29%   Improve: 48%   Collapse: 29%   Attrition: 12%   MLB: 93%   Comparables: *Matt Lindstrom, Danys Baez, Ray King*

Middle relievers are difficult properties to manage effectively, but the White Sox mishandled Belisario. First, they made him a closer, even though he's not that good. Then, they designated him for assignment when he's really not that bad, either. Yes, the ERA is ugly and he was woefully miscast in high-leverage situations, but Belisario generates a ton of groundballs and his FIP suggests his ERA should've been two full runs lower, which would be more in line with his career average. Plus, he's a perennial contender for the league lead in FACE (Facial Area Circumference Equivalent), up there with Bartolo Colon, Aaron Harang, Juan Uribe and Delmon Young. If he's used as a groundball generator in the sixth or seventh inning, he can still return some value.

Tyler Danish   RHP

Born: 9/12/94   Age: 20   Bats: R   Throws: R   Height: 6'0"   Weight: 205

YEAR	TEAM	LVL	AGE	W	L	SV	G	GS	IP	H	HR	BB	K	BB/9	K/9	GB%	BABIP	WHIP	ERA	FIP	FRA	WARP
2014	KAN	A	19	3	0	0	7	7	38	28	0	10	25	2.4	5.9	66%	.252	1.00	0.71	3.06	4.09	0.7
2014	WNS	A+	19	5	3	0	18	18	91²	87	7	23	78	2.3	7.7	62%	.301	1.20	2.65	3.69	4.63	1.1
2015	CHA	MLB	20	4	6	0	21	14	86²	96	10	35	59	3.6	6.1	56%	.306	1.51	4.99	5.09	5.42	-0.2

Breakout: 0%   Improve: 0%   Collapse: 0%   Attrition: 0%   MLB: 0%   Comparables: *Jacob Turner, Casey Kelly, Ian Krol*

Danish is of modest build and he doesn't have a big fastball but he gets after it on the mound. He made his professional full-season debut in 2014 and impressed, employing a funky and deceptive low-three-quarters delivery that divides scouts. He attacks hitters with a heavy low-90s fastball and a good slider that's developing into a weapon. He spent some time on the disabled list in 2014 and he'll have to fight hard against the perception that his body can't hold up to a starter's workload but Danish is the type to use that as extra motivation. Scouts love his competitiveness, so if you're going to wager against him, bet against the windup, not the makeup.

John Danks   LHP

Born: 4/15/85   Age: 30   Bats: L   Throws: L   Height: 6'1"   Weight: 210

YEAR	TEAM	LVL	AGE	W	L	SV	G	GS	IP	H	HR	BB	K	BB/9	K/9	GB%	BABIP	WHIP	ERA	FIP	FRA	WARP
2012	CHA	MLB	27	3	4	0	9	9	53²	57	7	23	30	3.9	5.0	46%	.282	1.49	5.70	4.97	5.46	0.1
2013	CHR	AAA	28	1	0	0	3	3	15²	13	1	12	14	6.9	8.0	49%	.286	1.60	3.45	4.93	6.18	-0.2
2013	CHA	MLB	28	4	14	0	22	22	138¹	151	28	27	89	1.8	5.8	42%	.283	1.29	4.75	5.09	5.55	-0.6
2014	CHA	MLB	29	11	11	0	32	32	193²	205	25	74	129	3.4	6.0	44%	.291	1.44	4.74	4.79	5.05	0.2
2015	CHA	MLB	30	9	10	0	27	27	164²	173	19	50	124	2.7	6.8	44%	.300	1.36	4.41	4.59	4.79	0.6

Breakout: 16%   Improve: 41%   Collapse: 20%   Attrition: 12%   MLB: 84%   Comparables: *Jeff Francis, Jason Vargas, Cliff Lee*

Danks found different ways to deliver similar, mediocre results in 2014 and 2013. He cut his staggering-even-for-the-Cell home run rate by a third, but walked twice as many hitters, a push/pull effect common to mediocre pitchers humping up to hit 89 mph. He's a financial liability at this point, and should be relegated to the very back end of a rotation. The best chance he has at success is finding himself in a less homer-friendly park, but with nearly $30 million owed to him through 2016, he'll be tough to move.

Zach Duke   LHP

Born: 4/19/83   Age: 32   Bats: L   Throws: L   Height: 6'2"   Weight: 210

YEAR	TEAM	LVL	AGE	W	L	SV	G	GS	IP	H	HR	BB	K	BB/9	K/9	GB%	BABIP	WHIP	ERA	FIP	FRA	WARP
2012	SYR	AAA	29	15	5	0	26	26	164¹	178	16	39	91	2.1	5.0	53%	.297	1.32	3.51	4.05	5.83	-1.2
2012	WAS	MLB	29	1	0	0	8	0	13²	11	0	4	10	2.6	6.6	40%	.262	1.10	1.32	2.55	2.51	0.4
2013	LOU	AAA	30	2	0	2	26	0	27²	19	2	5	34	1.6	11.1	52%	.274	0.87	1.30	2.34	4.50	0.3
2013	CIN	MLB	30	0	1	0	14	0	10²	8	1	2	7	1.7	5.9	41%	.226	0.94	0.84	3.49	2.46	0.3
2013	WAS	MLB	30	1	1	0	12	1	20²	31	2	8	11	3.5	4.8	54%	.367	1.89	8.71	4.52	5.04	-0.1
2014	MIL	MLB	31	5	1	0	74	0	58²	49	3	17	74	2.6	11.4	60%	.322	1.12	2.45	2.11	2.70	1.3
2015	CHA	MLB	32	2	2	0	22	5	46	54	6	13	32	2.6	6.2	50%	.319	1.45	4.91	4.81	5.34	-0.1

Breakout: 14%   Improve: 36%   Collapse: 11%   Attrition: 11%   MLB: 48%   Comparables: *Jerome Williams, Josh Towers, Jae Weong Seo*

Transitions to the bullpen are for failed back-end starters what a 12-pack of beer is at the end of a lousy work week: resurrection, if something of a dead-end. What makes Duke's breakout campaign so interesting is that it wasn't the role switch so much as a successful arm-slot experiment. The left-hander kept dropping down until he was a nearly sidewinding, and it transformed him from a journeyman who had thrown nearly 200 Triple-A innings over the previous three years into a dominant reliever with the 12th-best FIP (2.14) among qualified relievers in 2014. Seriously, look at this silliness:

9. Greg Holland
10. Kenley Jansen
11. Mark Melancon
12. Zach Duke, renowned failure

His swinging-strike rate jumped from 9.9 percent in 2013 to 12.3 percent in 2014, which is a career high by a mile. He struck out 35.2 percent of the lefties he faced, and held righties to an even lower slugging than lefties managed. Ron Roenicke used him as a high-leverage reliever in the second half, rather than simply as a lefty specialist. It was the right move: He's much more than a specialist going forward. Cheers.

Onelki Garcia   LHP

Born: 8/2/89   Age: 25   Bats: L   Throws: L   Height: 6'3"   Weight: 225

YEAR	TEAM	LVL	AGE	W	L	SV	G	GS	IP	H	HR	BB	K	BB/9	K/9	GB%	BABIP	WHIP	ERA	FIP	FRA	WARP
2013	CHT	AA	23	2	3	1	25	6	52¹	41	3	32	53	5.5	9.1	61%	.277	1.39	2.75	3.58	5.81	0.4
2013	LAN	MLB	23	0	0	0	3	0	1¹	1	1	4	1	27.0	6.8	75%	.000	3.75	13.50	20.27	25.75	-0.3
2015	CHA	MLB	25	1	1	0	19	3	33²	33	3	17	34	4.6	8.9	52%	.309	1.48	4.44	4.30	4.83	0.1

Breakout: 17%   Improve: 24%   Collapse: 11%   Attrition: 27%   MLB: 40%   Comparables: *Jon Meloan, Juan Morillo, Tanner Scheppers*

Garcia had one of the liveliest arms in the Dodgers organization, but he hasn't been able to stay healthy, which is why he was available to the White Sox on waivers this winter. He had elbow surgery (though not of the Tommy John variety) in November 2013 and knee surgery in January 2014. Which, hey, at least he's putting that health insurance plan to good use. It's anyone's guess if he'll ever regain the stuff that made the Cuban a third-round selection in 2012.

Javy Guerra   RHP

Born: 10/31/85   Age: 29   Bats: R   Throws: R   Height: 6'1"   Weight: 190

YEAR	TEAM	LVL	AGE	W	L	SV	G	GS	IP	H	HR	BB	K	BB/9	K/9	GB%	BABIP	WHIP	ERA	FIP	FRA	WARP
2012	LAN	MLB	26	2	3	8	45	0	45	44	1	23	37	4.6	7.4	50%	.321	1.49	2.60	3.38	3.69	0.5
2013	ABQ	AAA	27	0	4	12	27	4	39¹	46	6	14	36	3.2	8.2	49%	.345	1.53	3.66	4.94	5.08	0.4
2013	LAN	MLB	27	0	0	0	9	0	10²	15	1	6	12	5.1	10.1	39%	.400	1.97	6.75	3.96	4.18	0.0
2014	CHR	AAA	28	1	1	3	14	0	19¹	19	1	8	11	3.7	5.1	56%	.310	1.40	2.33	4.44	5.42	0.1
2014	CHA	MLB	28	2	4	1	42	0	46¹	41	3	20	38	3.9	7.4	44%	.288	1.32	2.91	3.98	4.71	0.0
2015	CHA	MLB	29	2	1	2	49	0	53¹	53	5	23	44	3.8	7.5	47%	.307	1.43	4.33	4.61	4.70	0.2

Breakout: 30%   Improve: 48%   Collapse: 23%   Attrition: 16%   MLB: 78%   Comparables: *Matt Lindstrom, Javier Lopez, Vinnie Chulk*

It's like a Buy One, Get One Free offer, except only one of the two you get actually works. The White Sox plucked Guerra and Ronald Belisario from the Dodgers' scrap heap, and while Belisario burned Guerra smoked, toning down command issues and adding a little velocity back to his fastball. The end result: A strikeout rate right in line with his career average, but a lower BB/9 and fewer homers despite moving from a big park to a small. It's reasonable to be skeptical of that homer-suppressing success moving forward, but while Guerra's days as a closer are long over, he can once again survive in an major-league bullpen. Or just fall apart, who knows.

Dan Jennings   LHP

Born: 4/17/87   Age: 28   Bats: L   Throws: L   Height: 6'3"   Weight: 210

YEAR	TEAM	LVL	AGE	W	L	SV	G	GS	IP	H	HR	BB	K	BB/9	K/9	GB%	BABIP	WHIP	ERA	FIP	FRA	WARP
2012	NWO	AAA	25	1	3	2	42	0	51²	48	2	16	48	2.8	8.4	60%	.315	1.24	3.14	3.24	3.54	1.2
2012	MIA	MLB	25	1	0	0	22	0	19	18	2	11	8	5.2	3.8	46%	.254	1.53	1.89	5.72	6.63	-0.5
2013	NWO	AAA	26	4	2	1	18	0	25	19	1	11	25	4.0	9.0	68%	.265	1.20	1.80	3.41	3.98	0.3
2013	MIA	MLB	26	2	4	0	47	0	40²	39	1	16	38	3.5	8.4	49%	.328	1.35	3.76	2.65	2.80	0.7
2014	MIA	MLB	27	0	2	0	47	0	40¹	45	1	17	38	3.8	8.5	50%	.339	1.54	1.34	3.45	3.68	0.3
2015	CHA	MLB	28	2	1	1	45	0	48	49	4	21	43	4.0	8.1	54%	.316	1.46	4.34	4.23	4.72	0.1

Breakout: 22%   Improve: 36%   Collapse: 12%   Attrition: 21%   MLB: 59%   Comparables: *Royce Ring, Derrick Turnbow, Javy Guerra*

Luck is a big part of baseball, but it's relative. Take Jennings. The lefty pitched very well by ERA standards, posting a 1.34 mark over the course of the season. It wasn't a BABIP mirage or great luck on fly balls, but the product of a fortunate strand rate (88.2 percent). From another perspective, Jennings was also the victim of terrible luck, as a Jordy Mercer line drive careened off his skull and knocked him out of commission with a concussion for much of August. But luck is a capricious thing—instead of causing a career- or life-threatening injury, Jennings was able to return in September and finish out the season.

Erik Johnson   RHP
Born: 12/30/89   Age: 25   Bats: R   Throws: R   Height: 6'3"   Weight: 230

YEAR	TEAM	LVL	AGE	W	L	SV	G	GS	IP	H	HR	BB	K	BB/9	K/9	GB%	BABIP	WHIP	ERA	FIP	FRA	WARP
2012	KAN	A	22	2	2	0	9	9	43	39	3	19	39	4.0	8.2	49%	.290	1.35	2.30	4.14	4.47	0.8
2012	WNS	A+	22	4	3	0	8	8	49¹	43	0	10	48	1.8	8.8	49%	.305	1.07	2.74	2.11	2.74	1.5
2013	BIR	AA	23	8	2	0	14	14	84²	57	6	21	74	2.2	7.9	50%	.228	0.92	2.23	2.90	4.40	0.7
2013	CHR	AAA	23	4	1	0	10	10	57¹	43	1	19	57	3.0	8.9	48%	.295	1.08	1.57	2.59	3.38	0.9
2013	CHA	MLB	23	3	2	0	5	5	27²	32	5	11	18	3.6	5.9	48%	.290	1.55	3.25	5.42	4.87	0.1
2014	CHR	AAA	24	5	7	0	20	20	105²	136	11	54	63	4.6	5.4	45%	.346	1.80	6.73	5.19	6.50	-0.6
2014	CHA	MLB	24	1	1	0	5	5	23²	27	1	15	18	5.7	6.0	40%	.356	1.77	6.46	4.34	5.18	0.0
2015	*CHA*	*MLB*	*25*	*6*	*8*	*0*	*22*	*22*	*119*	*127*	*12*	*48*	*92*	*3.6*	*7.0*	*45%*	*.310*	*1.47*	*4.67*	*4.68*	*5.07*	*0.1*

Breakout: 27%   Improve: 53%   Collapse: 15%   Attrition: 32%   MLB: 83%   Comparables: Garrett Richards, Shairon Martis, Aneury Rodriguez

Score one for the TINSTAAPP crowd. A year ago, Johnson looked poised to slot toward the back of the White Sox' rotation and accumulate value as a low-upside, low-risk option. The Cal product suffered a disastrous 2014, however, getting abused both in Triple-A and the majors. Most alarmingly, his velocity dropped after a career-high workload in 2013. That's a scary symptom from a 24-year-old pitcher who didn't have premium gas to begin with, and it led the Sox to shut him down with shoulder fatigue late in the season. There are plenty of scenarios in which it's easy to envision Johnson rebounding, from mechanical changes to simple rest and recovery. They all require some optimistic forecasting, though, and if Johnson's issues prove chronic it will be a blow to an organization without much pitching talent in the upper minors.

Nate Jones   RHP
Born: 1/28/86   Age: 29   Bats: R   Throws: R   Height: 6'5"   Weight: 220

YEAR	TEAM	LVL	AGE	W	L	SV	G	GS	IP	H	HR	BB	K	BB/9	K/9	GB%	BABIP	WHIP	ERA	FIP	FRA	WARP
2012	CHA	MLB	26	8	0	0	65	0	71²	67	4	32	65	4.0	8.2	48%	.317	1.38	2.39	3.34	4.39	0.8
2013	CHA	MLB	27	4	5	0	70	0	78	69	5	26	89	3.0	10.3	52%	.330	1.22	4.15	2.66	3.35	1.4
2014	CHA	MLB	28	0	0	0	2	0	0	2	0	3	0	—	—	0%	1.000	—	—	—	30.82	-0.2
2015	*CHA*	*MLB*	*29*	*1*	*1*	*1*	*28*	*0*	*34*	*35*	*3*	*15*	*31*	*4.0*	*8.2*	*47%*	*.323*	*1.48*	*4.47*	*4.30*	*4.85*	*0.1*

Breakout: 15%   Improve: 39%   Collapse: 11%   Attrition: 15%   MLB: 61%   Comparables: Tom Wilhelmsen, Sean Henn, Dustin Nippert

After the White Sox traded Addison Reed one winter ago, Jones looked poised for a breakout season, with an upper-90s fastball and wipeout slider straight out of the Closer's Cookbook. But after two bad outings, he spent a majority of the season recovering form back surgery and, in the process of recovering, felt a burning sensation in his elbow. This led to Tommy John surgery in late July. (He ended up as one of two pitchers in the majors with an undefined ERA. Read the rest of the book closely and you'll know the other.) We've likely seen the last of Jones until 2016, at which point he'll be 30. He still has a fighting chance to make an impact, but, as in a William Faulkner novel or a Christopher Nolan film, time is the enemy.

Matt Lindstrom   RHP
Born: 2/11/80   Age: 35   Bats: R   Throws: R   Height: 6'3"   Weight: 215

YEAR	TEAM	LVL	AGE	W	L	SV	G	GS	IP	H	HR	BB	K	BB/9	K/9	GB%	BABIP	WHIP	ERA	FIP	FRA	WARP
2012	ARI	MLB	32	0	0	0	12	0	10²	10	0	2	10	1.7	8.4	53%	.312	1.12	2.53	2.10	3.02	0.1
2012	BAL	MLB	32	1	0	0	34	0	36¹	35	2	12	30	3.0	7.4	51%	.308	1.29	2.72	3.43	4.42	0.4
2013	CHA	MLB	33	2	4	0	76	0	60²	64	2	23	46	3.4	6.8	57%	.330	1.43	3.12	3.17	3.39	0.9
2014	CHA	MLB	34	2	2	6	35	0	34	47	3	12	18	3.2	4.8	55%	.355	1.74	5.03	4.40	5.49	-0.3
2015	*CHA*	*MLB*	*35*	*2*	*1*	*2*	*44*	*0*	*39*	*43*	*3*	*13*	*30*	*3.0*	*7.0*	*50%*	*.322*	*1.42*	*4.35*	*4.17*	*4.73*	*0.1*

Breakout: 20%   Improve: 34%   Collapse: 20%   Attrition: 10%   MLB: 69%   Comparables: Joe Beimel, Matt Guerrier, Scott Downs

It was a contract year for Lindstrom, and the well-traveled right-hander could've put himself in contention for a guaranteed deal somewhere. He suffered through injuries and ineffectiveness instead, losing nearly two full mph off his fastball. Maybe that's due in part to the ankle injury he suffered, or maybe it's just because he's going to be 35 soon and pitchers exist in large part to remind us of life's fleeting, impermanent nature. Either way, he posted the lowest strikeout rate of his career, generating fewer groundballs and giving up more homers than in years past. If he looks healthier and is throwing harder this offseason, someone will let Lindstrom work in low-leverage situations in 2015. If not, the end is nigh.

Francellis Montas   RHP
Born: 3/21/93   Age: 22   Bats: R   Throws: R   Height: 6'2"   Weight: 185

YEAR	TEAM	LVL	AGE	W	L	SV	G	GS	IP	H	HR	BB	K	BB/9	K/9	GB%	BABIP	WHIP	ERA	FIP	FRA	WARP
2013	GRN	A	20	2	9	0	19	18	85¹	94	10	32	96	3.4	10.1	39%	.349	1.48	5.70	3.98	4.70	0.7
2013	KAN	A	20	3	2	0	5	5	25²	20	1	18	31	6.3	10.9	47%	.302	1.48	4.56	3.68	4.04	0.3
2014	WNS	A+	21	4	0	0	10	10	62	45	2	14	56	2.0	8.1	54%	.256	0.95	1.60	2.90	3.56	1.5
2015	*CHA*	*MLB*	*22*	*3*	*6*	*0*	*14*	*14*	*65²*	*72*	*8*	*33*	*51*	*4.6*	*7.0*	*44%*	*.312*	*1.60*	*5.32*	*5.28*	*5.79*	*-0.3*

Breakout: 0%   Improve: 0%   Collapse: 0%   Attrition: 0%   MLB: 0%   Comparables: Matt Magill, Dan Straily, Andrew Heaney

The 21-year-old Montas—acquired as part of the haul from Boston in the Jake Peavy deal—was shut down for knee surgery (his second) in June, but when he was healthy he hit 102 mph and showed improving control. He made some strides in correcting the max-effort delivery he worked with prior to 2014, producing some hope he can stick as a starter—indeed, AGM Buddy Bell told MLB.com that "he could compete for a big league starting job" in 2015. Still, it's difficult to get past his mechanics, as there's still a lot of labor there. While his ultimate role is uncertain, his upside is pretty real.

Felipe Paulino RHP
Born: 10/5/83   Age: 31   Bats: R   Throws: R   Height: 6'3"   Weight: 270

YEAR	TEAM	LVL	AGE	W	L	SV	G	GS	IP	H	HR	BB	K	BB/9	K/9	GB%	BABIP	WHIP	ERA	FIP	FRA	WARP
2012	NWA	AA	28	1	0	0	3	3	13¹	12	3	4	14	2.7	9.4	47%	.257	1.20	4.05	5.01	5.20	0.1
2012	KCA	MLB	28	3	1	0	7	7	37²	31	3	15	39	3.6	9.3	44%	.283	1.22	1.67	3.21	3.55	0.9
2013	OMA	AAA	29	0	3	0	5	5	19²	30	2	11	18	5.0	8.2	44%	.418	2.08	8.24	5.04	5.20	0.1
2014	CHR	AAA	30	0	3	0	5	5	19²	29	5	16	16	7.3	7.3	38%	.375	2.29	9.61	7.63	8.46	-0.4
2014	CHA	MLB	30	0	2	0	4	4	18¹	35	6	12	14	5.9	6.9	45%	.414	2.56	11.29	8.01	6.66	-0.3
2015	CHA	MLB	31	2	3	0	7	7	36²	39	4	17	35	4.1	8.7	44%	.327	1.52	4.88	4.64	5.30	0.0

Breakout: 20%   Improve: 48%   Collapse: 15%   Attrition: 26%   MLB: 71%   Comparables: Brandon Duckworth, Jonathan Sanchez, Tom Gorzelanny

Elbow injuries and Tommy John surgery tend to dominate the goddang-all-these-pitchers conversation, but Paulino offers further proof that shoulder injuries are scarier. The 31-year-old missed the vast majority of the 2014 season dealing with shoulder tendinitis, and that's after undergoing surgery last offseason to remove a cyst from his shoulder and clean up his rotator cuff and labrum. It's been two years since Paulino has been healthy or good, and with the White Sox declining his $4 million club option for 2015, it's tough to see him landing another guaranteed contract until he has put at least six healthy weeks together.

Jake Petricka RHP
Born: 6/5/88   Age: 27   Bats: R   Throws: R   Height: 6'5"   Weight: 205

YEAR	TEAM	LVL	AGE	W	L	SV	G	GS	IP	H	HR	BB	K	BB/9	K/9	GB%	BABIP	WHIP	ERA	FIP	FRA	WARP
2012	WNS	A+	24	5	5	0	19	19	82²	93	2	46	84	5.0	9.1	63%	.374	1.68	5.33	3.45	4.91	0.6
2012	BIR	AA	24	3	3	0	10	10	57²	63	7	35	27	5.5	4.2	51%	.298	1.70	5.46	5.61	6.65	-0.9
2013	BIR	AA	25	3	0	0	21	1	39¹	36	1	18	41	4.1	9.4	57%	.350	1.37	2.06	2.61	3.25	0.8
2013	CHR	AAA	25	2	0	1	10	0	15¹	9	0	7	17	4.1	10.0	60%	.237	1.04	1.17	2.36	3.62	0.2
2013	CHA	MLB	25	1	1	0	16	0	19¹	20	0	10	10	4.7	4.7	64%	.312	1.55	3.26	3.75	4.57	0.1
2014	CHA	MLB	26	1	6	14	67	0	73	67	3	33	55	4.1	6.8	65%	.299	1.37	2.96	3.63	4.32	0.4
2015	CHA	MLB	27	3	3	2	24	8	58¹	64	5	31	43	4.7	6.7	55%	.319	1.62	5.17	4.94	5.62	-0.3

Breakout: 27%   Improve: 43%   Collapse: 12%   Attrition: 32%   MLB: 64%   Comparables: Lenny DiNardo, Jon Switzer, Matt Roney

A big right-hander with shoddy control and no idea how to pronounce his own last name, Petricka finished the 2014 season with 14 saves, which should tell you all you need to know about Chicago's bullpen. He's pretty much a one-trick pony, with a heavy sinker that induces a ton of groundballs; he combines to throw his flimsy secondary pitches, a changeup and a slider, less than 30 percent of the time. Petricka's command has taken a step forward from his days as a starting prospect, but it's still subpar and it limits his ceiling to that of a fairly generic middle reliever—which, thankfully, is all the White Sox will ask of him now.

Zach Putnam RHP
Born: 7/3/87   Age: 27   Bats: R   Throws: R   Height: 6'2"   Weight: 225

YEAR	TEAM	LVL	AGE	W	L	SV	G	GS	IP	H	HR	BB	K	BB/9	K/9	GB%	BABIP	WHIP	ERA	FIP	FRA	WARP
2012	CSP	AAA	24	3	4	12	49	0	60²	73	5	27	49	4.0	7.3	46%	.351	1.65	4.15	4.51	4.97	0.7
2012	COL	MLB	24	0	0	0	2	0	2	3	0	1	0	4.5	0.0	50%	.375	2.00	0.00	4.64	7.68	0.0
2013	IOW	AAA	25	1	1	4	17	0	19¹	20	0	6	22	2.8	10.2	73%	.364	1.34	3.26	2.22	3.00	0.6
2013	CHN	MLB	25	0	0	0	5	0	3¹	9	1	0	4	0.0	10.8	53%	.571	2.70	18.90	4.52	5.32	0.0
2014	CHA	MLB	26	5	3	6	49	0	54²	39	2	20	46	3.3	7.6	56%	.257	1.08	1.98	3.10	3.45	0.7
2015	CHA	MLB	27	2	1	2	35	0	43	43	4	14	40	3.0	8.3	49%	.311	1.33	3.84	3.94	4.18	0.4

Breakout: 21%   Improve: 34%   Collapse: 17%   Attrition: 27%   MLB: 61%   Comparables: Cody Eppley, Cesar Jimenez, Sam Demel

In a season that could have been the sweeps-week episode of *When Buildings Collapse*, this minor-league free agent stood out for sturdiness. Putnam used a heavy splitter to generate groundballs, and while lefties hit him hard, he was tougher on righties than Dellin Betances. Even the .260 BABIP can regress a good long way before he stops being useful, assuming health: Putnam has been plagued by arm injuries for much of his career, having missed time in 2012 and 2013 with elbow trouble and in 2014 with shoulder inflammation.

Jose Quintana LHP
Born: 1/24/89   Age: 26   Bats: R   Throws: L   Height: 6'1"   Weight: 220

YEAR	TEAM	LVL	AGE	W	L	SV	G	GS	IP	H	HR	BB	K	BB/9	K/9	GB%	BABIP	WHIP	ERA	FIP	FRA	WARP
2012	BIR	AA	23	1	3	0	9	9	48²	43	1	14	41	2.6	7.6	55%	.300	1.17	2.77	2.59	3.33	0.9
2012	CHA	MLB	23	6	6	0	25	22	136¹	142	14	42	81	2.8	5.3	50%	.299	1.35	3.76	4.18	4.89	1.1
2013	CHA	MLB	24	9	7	0	33	33	200	188	23	56	164	2.5	7.4	44%	.283	1.22	3.51	3.85	3.93	2.7
2014	CHA	MLB	25	9	11	0	32	32	200¹	197	10	52	178	2.3	8.0	47%	.318	1.24	3.32	2.84	3.16	4.5
2015	CHA	MLB	26	10	10	0	29	29	169¹	169	14	47	141	2.5	7.5	46%	.305	1.28	3.69	3.84	4.01	2.2

Breakout: 31%   Improve: 68%   Collapse: 14%   Attrition: 14%   MLB: 95%   Comparables: Jon Lester, Matt Garza, Jaime Garcia

Teams spend millions and millions of dollars on efforts to scout, draft, acquire, develop and protect starting pitchers. Yet aside from the White Sox, it seems the entire baseball industry, fans and insiders alike, missed the boat on Quintana, who has gone from anonymous to one of the game's best left-handed starters in just three seasons. Thanks to the five-year, $21 million extension (with two very affordable option years) that he signed last offseason, he's one of the game's best bargains, too.

Quintana posted career-best marks in strikeout, walk and home run percentage in 2014 with a modest uptick in velocity across the board. He also further improved upon the success he had against right-handed hitters in 2013, holding them to a .243 TAv. Quintana threw his cutter and sinker less often and his changeup and curveball more often, and he's a sequencing savant. We probably can't expect Quintana to limit hitters to just 10 bombs again, but even if regression strikes, the rest of his performance appears sustainable.

Look at Quintana's similarity scores, and you see names like Jon Lester, Matt Garza, David Price, Anibal Sanchez and whoa okay now let's just ignore Tom Gorzelanny. Does he have the raw talent of Lester or Price? No. But Quintana isn't the back-end starter many believed he'd be after his promising 2012 debut. He's a legitimate middle-of-the-rotation guy, and, as we saw in 2014, in his best years he's a strong no. 2. That's not bad for a minor-league free agent, especially if, unlike Ernie Johnson, you actually know what that term means.

David Robertson   RHP

Born: 4/9/85   Age: 30   Bats: R   Throws: R   Height: 5'11"   Weight: 195

YEAR	TEAM	LVL	AGE	W	L	SV	G	GS	IP	H	HR	BB	K	BB/9	K/9	GB%	BABIP	WHIP	ERA	FIP	FRA	WARP
2012	NYA	MLB	27	2	7	2	65	0	60²	52	5	19	81	2.8	12.0	45%	.331	1.17	2.67	2.44	2.89	1.5
2013	NYA	MLB	28	5	1	3	70	0	66¹	51	5	18	77	2.4	10.4	52%	.287	1.04	2.04	2.64	3.32	1.0
2014	NYA	MLB	29	4	5	39	63	0	64¹	45	7	23	96	3.2	13.4	47%	.288	1.06	3.08	2.71	3.05	1.3
2015	CHA	MLB	30	3	1	13	57	0	54²	43	4	21	74	3.4	12.2	46%	.312	1.16	2.65	3.00	2.88	1.4

Breakout: 33%   Improve: 42%   Collapse: 31%   Attrition: 9%   MLB: 92%   Comparables: *Francisco Rodriguez, Jonathan Papelbon, B.J. Ryan*

We didn't get to see how Robertson handles Mariano Rivera's playoff legacy, but he mimed the regular-season version quite capably. He put together his usual excellent sixty-ish innings, only one frame later than he had in the past. His psyche remained intact. Like his predecessor, there's very little mystery in Robertson's game: When he's behind, he throws his (technically, Mariano's) cutter; when he's ahead, he throws his curve. The latter drew a whiff nearly a quarter of the times it was thrown, and even when hitters did manage to make contact with it, nothing special happened. Armchair game theorists might click their tongues at Robertson's predictability, but sometimes all the warning in the world will do no good. We'll soon find out whether Robertson can find similar success staring down the legacy of Jake Petricka.

Carlos Rodon   LHP

Born: 4/7/93   Age: 22   Bats: L   Throws: L   Height: 6'2"   Weight: 200

YEAR	TEAM	LVL	AGE	W	L	SV	G	GS	IP	H	HR	BB	K	BB/9	K/9	GB%	BABIP	WHIP	ERA	FIP	FRA	WARP
2014	CHR	AAA	21	0	0	0	3	3	12	9	0	8	18	6.0	13.5	42%	.346	1.42	3.00	2.61	3.03	0.5
2015	CHA	MLB	22	2	2	0	12	6	34²	31	3	15	40	4.0	10.4	46%	.312	1.34	3.75	3.73	4.07	0.5

Breakout: 19%   Improve: 25%   Collapse: 4%   Attrition: 13%   MLB: 34%   Comparables: *Tommy Hanson, Fautino De Los Santos, Zach Braddock*

Aside from his ability on the mound, Rodon has another plus tool working in his favor: The man knows how to wear stirrups. "Stirrup Swag," he once called his style in an Instagram caption, propelling his calfwear past Bryce Harper's eyeblack, Yasiel Puig's fauxhawk and Mike Trout's "That'$ Really Neat" gold chain to the top of the Young Stars Style Power Rankings. To less important matters: Rodon works with some hot cheese and a nasty slider combination—hmmmmm, hot, nasty cheesesliders—that has made both pro and amateur opponents sick to their stomachs. North Carolina State rode the talented lefty hard during the season, pushing his pitch counts into the extreme, 125-plus territory and scaring some evaluators away. But the White Sox selected him third overall and let him idle as they worked out his draft bonus. When he finally debuted in full-season ball, he struck out the side in his first inning, earned a promotion to Triple-A after two weeks, and punched out 13.5 per nine in three starts there. That nearly earned him a September call-up, but the White Sox worried about rushing him into an undefined role, and want to see better fastball command from him. If that and a more refined changeup come together, we're talking about a bona fide no. 2 starter.

Chris Sale   LHP

Born: 3/30/89   Age: 26   Bats: L   Throws: L   Height: 6'6"   Weight: 180

YEAR	TEAM	LVL	AGE	W	L	SV	G	GS	IP	H	HR	BB	K	BB/9	K/9	GB%	BABIP	WHIP	ERA	FIP	FRA	WARP
2012	CHA	MLB	23	17	8	0	30	29	192	167	19	51	192	2.4	9.0	46%	.294	1.14	3.05	3.22	3.70	3.7
2013	CHA	MLB	24	11	14	0	30	30	214¹	184	23	46	226	1.9	9.5	47%	.289	1.07	3.07	3.20	3.53	4.0
2014	CHA	MLB	25	12	4	0	26	26	174	129	13	39	208	2.0	10.8	43%	.280	0.97	2.17	2.60	2.75	4.7
2015	CHA	MLB	26	10	7	1	35	21	156¹	130	13	37	182	2.1	10.5	45%	.298	1.07	2.65	3.09	2.88	4.1

Breakout: 21%   Improve: 53%   Collapse: 19%   Attrition: 8%   MLB: 97%   Comparables: *Clayton Kershaw, Tim Lincecum, Felix Hernandez*

Jameson Taillon, Drew Pomeranz and Matt Harvey were all taken before Sale in the 2010 draft. This isn't the beginning of a "can you believe Sale's been better" comment; it's not unusual for a mid-first rounder to outproduce some guys ahead of him, and Taillon, Pomeranz and Harvey all have plenty of value. But what's fascinating is that all three of those players were considered relatively safe at the time of the draft, and all have broken at some point. Sale, who has a delivery that makes anyone with eyes and an arm cringe, just keeps pitching.

Yes, Sale has missed time with shoulder and elbow injuries during his career, but he has avoided the knife to this point and logged 85 starts over the past three years. Maybe the baseball gods take him away some day, but at this point, saying "I told you so" if he does break will look petty. No one thought Sale would last this long. His dominance is beyond question, and he's as good a candidate as any to win the AL Cy Young in 2015. Savor his starts and relish the fact that, for once, we can be happy at how little we know about pitchers.

Jeff Samardzija   RHP

Born: 1/23/85   Age: 30   Bats: R   Throws: R   Height: 6'5"   Weight: 225

YEAR	TEAM	LVL	AGE	W	L	SV	G	GS	IP	H	HR	BB	K	BB/9	K/9	GB%	BABIP	WHIP	ERA	FIP	FRA	WARP
2012	CHN	MLB	27	9	13	0	28	28	174²	157	20	56	180	2.9	9.3	46%	.296	1.22	3.81	3.59	4.11	2.3
2013	CHN	MLB	28	8	13	0	33	33	213²	210	25	78	214	3.3	9.0	50%	.314	1.35	4.34	3.75	4.10	2.4
2014	CHN	MLB	29	2	7	0	17	17	108	99	7	31	103	2.6	8.6	54%	.306	1.20	2.83	3.07	3.91	1.1
2014	OAK	MLB	29	5	6	0	16	16	111²	92	13	12	99	1.0	8.0	49%	.262	0.93	3.14	3.33	4.17	0.8
2015	CHA	MLB	30	9	9	1	42	23	171	161	19	62	171	3.3	9.0	46%	.303	1.31	3.95	4.20	4.29	1.5

Breakout: 17%   Improve: 33%   Collapse: 24%   Attrition: 13%   MLB: 75%   Comparables: *John Maine, Felipe Paulino, Jorge De La Rosa*

The Shark was chomping at the opportunity to swim in playoff waters, an opportunity that was granted with the July trade that sent him to Northern California. He handled a potentially awkward moment with aplomb when he sat in the AL dugout in Oakland colors for the All-Star Game a mere 10 days after the already elected NL representative changed leagues. Samardzija has held his plus-plus velocity over the past several years, throwing just as hard as he did in 2011 and coming within a half-tick of his peak. He offsets the fastball with a late-fading splitter and a slider-cutter combination. The similar speed of his pitches helps mask their trajectory and illustrates that there is no ideal way to build an arsenal: Some pitchers want as much separation as they can stand; others want their pitches indistinguishable until the last possible second. The magic for pitching coaches and player development staff is figuring out the best approach for each individual.

Nolan Sanburn   RHP

Born: 7/21/91   Age: 23   Bats: R   Throws: R   Height: 6'0"   Weight: 175

YEAR	TEAM	LVL	AGE	W	L	SV	G	GS	IP	H	HR	BB	K	BB/9	K/9	GB%	BABIP	WHIP	ERA	FIP	FRA	WARP
2012	VER	A-	20	0	1	0	7	7	18²	23	2	6	19	2.9	9.2	53%	.375	1.55	3.86	3.65	3.83	0.3
2013	BLT	A	21	1	3	0	14	1	26	17	1	9	20	3.1	6.9	47%	.225	1.00	1.38	3.34	4.47	0.3
2014	STO	A+	22	3	1	6	42	0	71¹	78	6	25	73	3.2	9.2	58%	.358	1.44	3.28	3.92	3.83	1.8
2015	CHA	MLB	23	2	1	1	27	3	52	58	6	24	40	4.1	6.8	49%	.318	1.57	5.14	5.06	5.58	-0.3

Breakout: 0%   Improve: 0%   Collapse: 0%   Attrition: 0%   MLB: 0%   Comparables: Jake Dunning, Aaron Loup, Blaine Hardy

Converted from the outfield, Sanburn was part of the package the White Sox got for Adam Dunn, who in a sense was also converted from the outfield. Sanburn's got a power arm that can reach 97, and a curveball that shows potential. "Once I get stretched out into a starter, I don't want to ever go back," he once told a reporter, but he never did get stretched out; between his size, durability concerns and some minor shoulder injuries, the A's kept him in the bullpen. That seems to be where his future is, but he does have a deeper repertoire than most relievers, and Rick Hahn praised his pitchability, so who knows.

Eric Surkamp   LHP

Born: 7/16/87   Age: 27   Bats: L   Throws: L   Height: 6'5"   Weight: 220

YEAR	TEAM	LVL	AGE	W	L	SV	G	GS	IP	H	HR	BB	K	BB/9	K/9	GB%	BABIP	WHIP	ERA	FIP	FRA	WARP
2013	SJO	A+	25	0	0	0	5	5	15¹	8	2	3	17	1.8	10.0	40%	.182	0.72	2.93	3.84	4.52	0.3
2013	FRE	AAA	25	7	1	0	11	11	71¹	56	4	20	54	2.5	6.8	41%	.259	1.07	2.78	3.71	4.03	1.1
2013	SFN	MLB	25	0	1	0	1	1	2²	9	2	0	0	0.0	0.0	19%	.500	3.38	23.62	15.02	13.73	-0.3
2014	CHR	AAA	26	4	5	0	18	11	78²	95	8	20	86	2.3	9.8	46%	.383	1.46	4.69	3.52	4.45	1.5
2014	CHA	MLB	26	2	0	0	35	0	24¹	22	3	13	20	4.8	7.4	44%	.271	1.44	4.81	4.84	4.91	0.0
2015	CHA	MLB	27	5	5	0	24	14	87	87	8	31	79	3.2	8.2	42%	.310	1.35	4.08	4.14	4.43	0.7

Breakout: 31%   Improve: 39%   Collapse: 15%   Attrition: 32%   MLB: 65%   Comparables: Brad Mills, Dustin Nippert, Dan Meyer

Left-handers who can throw strikes stick around forever, and Surkamp is the gum on the sole of your shoe. The southpaw worked as a starter to middling effect in Charlotte until June, at which point he was summoned to the majors and used as something of a LOOGY. He did fairly well against left-handers but the sample is too small to be meaningful, and his overall numbers are lackluster. With Zach Duke and Onelki Garcia joining the White Sox bullpen, Surkamp faces a longer road to playing time in 2015, but it'll happen.

Daniel Webb   RHP

Born: 8/18/89   Age: 25   Bats: R   Throws: R   Height: 6'3"   Weight: 215

YEAR	TEAM	LVL	AGE	W	L	SV	G	GS	IP	H	HR	BB	K	BB/9	K/9	GB%	BABIP	WHIP	ERA	FIP	FRA	WARP
2012	KAN	A	22	1	8	3	31	4	62	73	2	27	50	3.9	7.3	51%	.346	1.61	5.81	3.84	4.55	0.8
2013	WNS	A+	23	1	0	2	8	0	15	10	0	5	19	3.0	11.4	56%	.278	1.00	0.00	1.82	2.16	0.6
2013	BIR	AA	23	0	0	4	13	0	20¹	11	0	5	21	2.2	9.3	39%	.216	0.79	1.77	1.73	3.06	0.4
2013	CHR	AAA	23	1	1	4	21	0	27¹	24	1	17	38	5.6	12.5	39%	.333	1.50	2.96	2.77	2.83	0.7
2013	CHA	MLB	23	0	0	0	9	0	11¹	9	0	4	10	3.2	7.9	56%	.281	1.15	3.18	2.37	2.59	0.3
2014	CHA	MLB	24	6	5	0	57	0	67²	59	6	42	58	5.6	7.7	53%	.282	1.49	3.99	4.55	4.15	0.4
2015	CHA	MLB	25	2	2	0	33	3	56²	60	6	30	45	4.7	7.1	48%	.310	1.58	5.18	5.08	5.63	-0.3

Breakout: 39%   Improve: 52%   Collapse: 12%   Attrition: 20%   MLB: 72%   Comparables: Logan Kensing, Macay McBride, Randor Bierd

Charlotte's Webb became Chicago's Webb on a permanent basis in 2014, and his first full season in the majors left plenty to be desired. His premium velocity, promising slider and hard change should lead to good results, but the 25-year-old simply lacks the command to make his arsenal work. He walked every seventh batter he faced last year, and it's tough to have a good week with such a steady occurrence of Mondays. Webb still has youth and arm strength on his side, and he could work his way into a setup role at some point. But ultimately, this Webb is more likely to spell "humble" than "terrific," "radiant" or "some pig."

Michael Ynoa   RHP

Born: 9/24/91   Age: 23   Bats: R   Throws: R   Height: 6'7"   Weight: 210

YEAR	TEAM	LVL	AGE	W	L	SV	G	GS	IP	H	HR	BB	K	BB/9	K/9	GB%	BABIP	WHIP	ERA	FIP	FRA	WARP
2012	VER	A-	20	1	3	0	8	6	20²	20	2	16	19	7.0	8.3	24%	.295	1.74	6.97	5.51	6.16	-0.1
2013	BLT	A	21	2	1	0	15	15	54²	45	3	18	48	3.0	7.9	51%	.275	1.15	2.14	3.67	4.50	1.1
2013	STO	A+	21	1	2	1	7	6	21	23	2	17	20	7.3	8.6	37%	.333	1.90	7.71	5.82	6.80	-0.1
2014	STO	A+	22	4	2	0	31	0	45²	42	5	21	64	4.1	12.6	40%	.349	1.38	5.52	4.07	4.13	1.1
2015	CHA	MLB	23	2	3	0	18	8	42	45	5	23	35	5.0	7.6	41%	.315	1.63	5.37	5.36	5.83	-0.2

Breakout: 0%   Improve: 0%   Collapse: 0%   Attrition: 0%   MLB: 0%   Comparables: Brayan Villarreal, Jhonny Nunez, Henry Sosa

The one-time wunderkind has struggled to stay on the mound, with 2013's total of 75 innings representing the high-water mark in his pro career. Injuries have stunted his development, and Ynoa was shifted to the bullpen in an effort to accelerate his path to the majors. The tall right-hander cost the A's a spot on the 40-man last season despite his pitching in High-A, but ignoring the contract issues reveals a young pitcher who showed promise against players in his age range. He racked up strikeouts for the first time in his career, armed with a mid-90s fastball and a tight slider with late vertical dive. His simple delivery features a strong combination of stability and power, providing the foundation for mechanical consistency, though he is far behind the typical curve in terms of reps. His inclusion in the Samardzija deal was a roster-crunch issue as much as anything, but he's got the potential to add real value to Chicago's side.

Lineouts

Hitters

NAME	POS	TEAM	LVL	AGE	PA	R	2B	3B	HR	RBI	BB	K	SB	CS	AVG/OBP/SLG	TAv	BABIP	BRR	FRAA	WARP
Eddy Alvarez	2B	KAN	A	24	80	12	6	0	3	14	7	10	4	4	.431/.488/.639	.413	.475	0.1	2B(9): -1.2, SS(6): 1.1	1.7
Rob Brantly	C	NWO	AAA	24	392	38	15	2	4	37	20	61	0	0	.255/.291/.341	.235	.291	-2.3	C(92): 0.6	0.6
Tony Campana	CF	SLC	AAA	28	227	31	6	2	0	17	18	39	9	9	.267/.330/.317	.236	.331	0.8	CF(48): 4.3, LF(4): -0.6	0.3
	CF	RNO	AAA	28	181	31	5	4	0	17	12	28	8	2	.288/.343/.368	.256	.346	0.8	CF(34): -2.3, LF(4): 0.1	0.4
	CF	ANA	MLB	28	15	6	0	0	0	2	0	6	0	1	.333/.333/.333	.246	.556	0.2	CF(10): -0.1, LF(3): 0.1	0.1
	CF	ARI	MLB	28	61	4	1	1	0	3	0	10	4	1	.150/.164/.200	.154	.180	-0.2	CF(13): 0.9, LF(3): -0.1	-0.5
Adam Engel	CF	KAN	A	22	341	54	14	7	6	30	29	86	28	11	.261/.344/.410	.273	.344	3.3	CF(74): -1.5	2.0
	CF	WNS	A+	22	100	11	0	0	0	5	6	21	9	1	.239/.296/.239	.207	.304	1.4	CF(18): 0.8	0.3
Cleuluis Rondon	SS	KAN	A	20	336	35	9	0	0	16	26	65	13	8	.233/.295/.262	.216	.293	0.5	SS(77): 7.2	1.1
	SS	WNS	A+	20	222	24	10	4	1	24	19	33	3	4	.247/.315/.354	.246	.291	0.4	SS(53): -0.2	0.6
J.B. Shuck	CF	SLC	AAA	27	465	64	18	9	5	57	43	30	9	6	.320/.382/.446	.274	.329	0.1	CF(35): -1.2, RF(28): 0.6	1.6
	LF	ANA	MLB	27	88	10	1	0	2	9	3	11	2	0	.167/.195/.250	.187	.169	1.2	LF(21): 0.6, RF(2): 0.2	-0.1
	RF	CLE	MLB	27	26	2	0	0	0	0	0	1	0	0	.077/.077/.077	.045	.080	0.4	RF(6): 0.2, LF(4): 0.0	-0.5
Michael Taylor	RF	SAC	AAA	28	258	34	14	1	5	31	33	50	7	2	.243/.357/.385	.278	.293	-1.6	RF(56): 0.1, LF(2): 0.1	0.6
	RF	CHR	AAA	28	254	41	18	2	6	38	29	50	1	0	.306/.386/.489	.290	.365	0.1	RF(49): 0.9, LF(7): -0.3	1.6
	LF	CHA	MLB	28	33	3	1	0	0	0	5	9	0	0	.250/.364/.286	.246	.368	-0.1	LF(8): -0.0	-0.1
Andy Wilkins	1B	CHR	AAA	25	529	79	38	1	30	85	34	91	0	1	.293/.338/.558	.281	.306	-3.3	1B(99): -5.2	1.0
	1B	CHA	MLB	25	45	2	2	0	0	2	2	22	0	0	.140/.178/.186	.134	.286	0.2	1B(13): 0.2	-0.5

He struggled out of the gate but **Micker Adolfo** has a well-rounded tool set, in which plus power is the hammer and a big outfield arm is the extension socket bit. ❖ **Eddy Alvarez** medaled as a speed skater in Sochi and will now try to revive the baseball career he left behind at Salt Lake Community College. The speed translated to dirt, but his instincts need some smoothing over. ❖ In 2012, **Rob Brantly** was the Marlins' catcher of the future. By 2017, he'll be the White Sox' organizational depth of the past. ❖ The Angels acquired **Tony Campana** to serve as speed specialist through their playoff push, but the speed specialist is always the first left off the postseason roster when the bullpen needs a 10th reliever. ❖ **Adam Engel** was a burner out of Louisville but the bat wasn't special and he had less power than Scott Podsednik in his prime. He's still a burner and the bat still isn't special and Scott Podsednik's prime isn't getting any better. ❖ **Cleuluis Rondon**—which is Drunk Uncle for "Carlos Rodon"—can pick it, but he bulked up and now lacks the range to play a true shortstop. ❖ Home Depot was out of power tools when **J.B. Shuck** went shopping. ❖ A top-20 prospect not *that* long ago, **Michael Taylor** has settled into a role as the Andre Ethier of Triple-A. He's older than Billy Butler. ❖ **Andy Wilkins** mashed at Triple-A and got the call to U.S. Cellular, but he can only play the corners and looks like filler.

Pitchers

NAME	TEAM	LVL	AGE	W	L	SV	G	GS	IP	H	HR	BB	K	BB/9	K/9	GB%	BABIP	WHIP	ERA	FIP	FRA	WARP
Chris Beck	BIR	AA	23	5	8	0	20	20	116²	116	7	31	57	2.4	4.4	49%	.278	1.26	3.39	3.92	4.71	0.5
	CHR	AAA	23	1	3	0	7	7	33¹	36	1	13	28	3.5	7.6	49%	.324	1.47	4.05	3.42	4.45	0.7
Scott Carroll	CHR	AAA	29	3	1	0	4	4	23	18	0	9	13	3.5	5.1	64%	.273	1.17	1.57	3.40	4.96	0.2
	CHA	MLB	29	5	10	0	26	19	129¹	147	13	45	64	3.1	4.5	56%	.305	1.48	4.80	4.80	6.01	-1.0
Maikel Cleto	CHR	AAA	25	3	0	3	22	0	35	37	7	15	50	3.9	12.9	30%	.375	1.49	5.91	4.39	5.46	0.2
	CHA	MLB	25	0	1	0	28	0	29¹	24	3	23	32	7.1	9.8	44%	.273	1.60	4.60	4.97	5.63	-0.2
F. De Los Santos	CHR	AAA	26	1	1	0	24	0	36	46	3	17	17	4.2	4.2	50%	.341	1.75	5.75	5.00	7.27	-0.4
Raul Fernandez	WNS	A+	24	2	3	0	14	0	21²	14	1	17	20	7.1	8.3	52%	.245	1.43	2.49	4.90	5.33	0.0
	MOD	A+	24	0	1	7	29	0	27	37	2	15	20	5.0	6.7	45%	.365	1.93	7.00	5.11	5.90	0.1
Tommy Hanson	CHR	AAA	27	3	5	0	10	10	49²	49	9	28	32	5.1	5.8	41%	.261	1.55	6.16	6.24	7.19	-0.3
Andrew Mitchell	KAN	A	22	4	3	0	31	5	65¹	51	3	67	83	9.2	11.4	41%	.322	1.81	5.37	4.95	5.82	0.2
Hector Noesi	CHA	MLB	27	8	11	0	28	27	166	167	27	54	117	2.9	6.3	40%	.281	1.33	4.88	5.11	4.51	-0.1
	TEX	MLB	27	0	0	0	3	0	5¹	11	0	2	4	3.4	6.8	50%	.500	2.44	11.81	2.78	3.59	0.1
	SEA	MLB	27	0	1	0	2	0	1	2	1	0	2	0.0	18.0	0%	.333	2.00	27.00	12.16	9.38	-0.1
Braulio Ortiz	WNS	A+	22	0	8	3	20	9	51²	64	3	33	51	5.7	8.9	38%	.389	1.88	5.05	4.33	4.79	0.5
	BIR	AA	22	0	2	1	15	0	18	16	0	30	25	15.0	12.5	44%	.372	2.56	9.00	5.91	7.27	-0.4
Scott Snodgress	BIR	AA	24	6	7	0	21	21	122²	119	9	52	79	3.8	5.8	49%	.289	1.39	3.89	4.30	4.81	0.6
	CHR	AAA	24	0	1	0	8	0	16¹	17	4	4	16	2.2	8.8	43%	.289	1.29	4.96	5.32	6.98	-0.1
	CHA	MLB	24	0	0	0	4	0	2¹	8	1	3	1	11.6	3.9	47%	.500	4.71	15.43	11.73	8.42	-0.1

Spencer Adams has a good fastball, a developing breaking ball, and one hell of a basketball highlight reel on YouTube. ❖ **Chris Beck** has middling stuff and doesn't miss bats, but he could reach innings-eater status with a few breaks (i.e. his curveball comes around). ❖ **Scott Carroll** might be the most anonymous player to have thrown over 120 innings in 2014. The White Sox non-tendered him in December, making for a sad Christmas Carroll. ❖ **Maikel Cleto** still throws really hard and is somehow just 25, but in the time it takes you to finish reading this sentence he'll have walked six people. ❖ Nine lousy batters. **Frank De Los Santos** walked nine of the 67 lefties he faced, producing a .278/.381/.315 lefty-on-lefty slash line and changing the story of his season from "maybe a specialist" to "sucked against everybody." ❖ For the converted catcher **Raul Fernandez**, life was good, life was predictable, life was Jeopardy! at 7 o'clock and 12-packs of Coke always being on sale. Then his walk rate doubled and suddenly he was playing for Chicago. ❖ These pages are lousy with stories of former ace pitching prospects derailed by injuries, but even in that big pond **Tommy Hanson** is a big fish. ❖ Someday, **Andrew Mitchell** will be the answer to a really hard trivia question, but we have no idea what it'll be. ❖ There's no easy way to explain how major-league baseball teams gave **Hector Noesi** 172 1/3 innings last season. Were life a meritocracy, that number would decrease by 172 1/3 in 2015. ❖ Don't scout the statline, they tell us. "**Braulio Ortiz** walked 30 batters in 18 innings," we tell them. You win this round, they tell us. ❖ **Scott Snodgress** gains some life to his fastball as a reliever but has just enough stuff to survive as a fifth starter, which sounds like a pretty good swingman.

Manager

Robin Ventura

YEAR	TEAM	W	L	Py-thag +/-	Avg PC	100+ P	120+ P	QS	BQS	REL	REL w Zero R	IBB	PH	PH Avg	PH HR	SB2	CS2	SB3	CS3	SAC Att	SAC%	POS SAC	Squeeze	Swing	In Play
2012	CHA	85	77	-4	98.8	91	6	86	4	466	381	29	63	.135	1	107	41	2	1	45	68.9%	29	0	317	88
2013	CHA	63	99	-3	100.5	96	4	90	3	470	389	24	67	.125	1	102	41	2	1	27	70.4%	15	0	315	102
2014	CHA	73	89	3	100.2	92	4	89	5	453	332	42	72	.290	1	81	33	4	2	28	67.9%	18	0	276	80

There are two predicaments that all but invalidate managerial assessments: 1) His team is rebuilding, and 2) His bullpen is poor; both spur the manager to act in different, even irrational ways. Much to Ventura's misfortune, he had to deal with both issues last season.

Ventura managed the youngest White Sox lineup (weighed by plate appearances) since the 2000 crew that included youngsters Paul Konerko (24), Carlos Lee (24) and Magglio Ordonez (26). That team, like its 2014 counterpart, had just three players aged 30 or older tally more than 300 plate appearances; two of last year's vets finished on other squads.

In addition to overseeing a roster in medias res, Ventura stomached the AL's second-worst bullpen, according to ERA. He reacted as you'd expect, leaning on his veteran rotation to pick up the slack; as a result, the White Sox finished second in pitches per start and starts with 120 or more pitches thrown. When Ventura opted for the bullpen, he asked his relievers to cover multiple innings. Daniel Webb and Ronald Belisario combined for 47 appearances in which they notched four or more outs, enough to rank fourth and fifth in the majors. (More than a third of those outings came in situations where the score differential exceeded three runs either way.)

Through it all, we didn't learn much about Ventura. Unless the White Sox have another 2012-like surprise run in them, we won't learn much about him in 2015, either.

CINCINNATI REDS

by R.J. Anderson

There's an old Cherokee parable you might have read or heard before. It involves a grandfather, his grandchild and two metaphorical wolves located inside the soul. The wolves, the grandfather explains, have opposite temperaments—one is peaceful, the other angry—but share in a fight to dominate the soul. The grandchild asks who'll win, to which the grandfather replies, "The one I feed."

General managers pick between wolves each time they make a move. Their wolves don't represent spiritual harmony and disarray—nothing that trivial concerns baseball executives—but rather their lineup and pitching staff, and their wolves devour tangible instead of intangible resources: money, prospects and draft picks. The exercise is, in essence, an extension of the age-old debate over what wins games—hitting or pitching?

Back in 1980 James K. Skipper, of SABR's *Baseball Research Journal*, sought the industry's answer to the question. He sent questionnaires to 50 general managers, field managers and media members (broadcasters and writers), asking them to estimate the roles pitching, hitting, defense and other factors played in victories. The overall responses were interesting enough— the respondents, on average, credited pitching with 60 percent of the responsibility—but what's telling is who voted how.

The 14 media members believed pitchers contributed 65 percent of a W—thus explaining the origin and endurance of the "pitching wins championships" adage—while the managers checked in at 63 percent. Conversely, the 22 general managers gave pitchers just 54 percent of the pie, meaning general managers were the only ones who considered hitting-plus-fielding to be about as important to winning games as pitching alone; the only group who viewed position players— the other wolf—as an equal.

Reds GM Walt Jocketty wasn't around to answer Skipper's survey. If he had been, perhaps we would have anticipated his offseason moves—decisions he made out of necessity rather than desire, as time and financial constraints forced him to make the kind of franchise-defining decisions that most GMs can kick down the road.

Jocketty entered the winter with an obvious dilemma. Once the 2015 season concluded, Homer Bailey—who, it must be noted, had the highest ERA of the bunch in '14—would be the

Reds' only starting pitcher under contract. The other four— Johnny Cueto, Mat Latos, Mike Leake and Alfredo Simon—were scheduled to become free agents after making about 60 percent of Cincinnati's starts over the past three seasons. The possible exodus couldn't have come at a worst time for Jocketty, who had to entertain tweaking a lineup that produced as poorly as any other in franchise history.

Just how bad was Cincinnati's lineup in 2014? It was the first time in more than 30 years the Reds had failed to score at least 600 runs. The offensive woes comprised the lowest isolated slugging since 1992, and the third-worst strikeout rate and worst walk rate of any Cincinnati team since the 1960s. For those who'd rather not compare numbers across eras, take discomfort in knowing the Reds posted their lowest True Average since 2009—that club gave Paul Janish, Adam Rosales, Willy Taveras, Jerry Hairston Jr. and Alex Gonzalez more than 1,600 combined plate appearances.

Ideally Jocketty could have fed both wolves—heaven knows he needed to. He could have re-signed two starters and added punch to a kickless lineup. But idealism gave way to realism last winter, as it is wont to do, and so Jocketty had to shave the payroll for the first time since 2009.

In truth, Jocketty didn't have a fluffy cash beard to begin with. The Reds' $114 million Opening Day payroll, though a new franchise record, was less impressive than it appeared. The league-average mark, for context, checked in at $115 million—a figure admittedly skewed by high rollers. Still, the Reds ranked 11th in payroll—and that was with them overspending, as their local TV deal is regarded as one of the worst in the league; hence the need for extreme cost-cutting measures.

When Jocketty wanted a morale boost, he could compare situations with those of his peers in Oakland and St. Petersburg. Alternatively, he could daydream about 2016, when the Reds' TV deal expires. Yet, even then reality intruded upon his reverie, because the Reds have already spent money with a revenue boost in mind.

Take the contracts the Reds have guaranteed for the 2016 season, including the buyout due to Skip Schumaker, and that leaves you with five players owed $70 million. Fill the roster with 20 players making the minimum, and the Reds have $35 million

REDS PROSPECTUS
2014 W-L: 76-86, 4TH IN NL CENTRAL

Pythag	.487	17th	DER	.723	3rd
RS/G	3.67	28th	B-Age	29	21st
RA/G	3.78	8th	P-Age	27.9	10th
TAv	.251	28th	Salary	$111.7M	12th
BRR	-2.09	21st	M$/MW	$3.6M	21st
TAv-P	.260	13th	DL Days	958	19th
FIP	3.98	24th	$ on DL	24%	26th

Three-Year Park Factors

Runs	Runs/RH	Runs/LH	HR/RH	HR/LH
98	97	96	102	104

Top Hitter WARP	4.9	Devin Mesoraco
Top Pitcher WARP	3.1	Johnny Cueto
Top Prospect		Robert Stephenson

to spend before setting a new franchise record; not as luxurious as it seems, not when a qualifying offer or extension for Cueto would cost at least half that on its own—oh, and that's without any outside additions or internal raises.

And so Jocketty, lacking financial might and flexibility, entered the winter with many choices to make, none of which was whether it was time to retool—that decision had already been made for him. Instead Jocketty had to deliberate about which starters to move and, in turn, which wolf to feed through the trades. It's too early to know if Jocketty chose correctly, but his decisions appear defensible:

- He traded Latos and Simon, his second and third-best starters last year, by ERA+.
- He acquired two young right-handed pitchers as part of the return.
- He shed salary that, one suspects, is earmarked for efforts to extend or re-sign Cueto or Leake.

The offense, meanwhile, went largely unruffled. Jocketty's thought process likely focused foremost on the context surrounding the Reds' offense last season. Long story made short, the lineup was bad because its best players missed time or had down seasons, not because it is inherently bad. Todd Frazier and Billy Hamilton were the only Cincinnati hitters to record more than 550 plate appearances, and the player-to-player comparisons are jarring. The club's best hitter, Joey Votto, finished with one more trip to the plate than Schumaker; backup catcher Brayan Pena played in one more game than young stud Devin Mesoraco; and all-glove shortstop Zack Cozart appeared in 26 more games than the declining-but-tolerable Phillips.

Include some other catalysts—the possibility for positive regression after 27-year-old Bruce's career-worst campaign; the likelihood that Hamilton sprouts from his rookie season, etc.—and Jocketty must have felt the potential for organic growth exists in 2015 and 2016. The Reds sure hope his hunch is correct, because Bruce is their only main position player who isn't under contract or under team control through the 2017 season. As such, the only positions where upgrades seemed feasible were shortstop and left field.* The market is never flooded with real shortstops who can hit, but the opposite is true for left field. Jocketty, having pulled Ryan Ludwick from the scrapheap a few years back, had to feel he could find an improvement who didn't require a long or lucrative contract.

(*Perhaps there's some complacency in that line of thinking, but the Reds aren't going to find better players at catcher or the corner-infield positions, and don't seem likely to move or move on from Hamilton or Phillips.)

What about Jocketty's reasons for favoring Cueto and Leake over Latos and Simon? It's not hard to fashion a decent explanation. Consider that both Cueto and Latos—the two front-end types—had dealt with injuries before; difference being Latos' issues arose in '14 while Cueto remained healthy. Likewise, Leake and Simon might fit the same role—back-end inning eater—yet Simon's ascent came at a later age and without the same track record. When Jocketty selected his keeper from each group, he chose to retain the safer, homegrown option—and who could blame him?

Well, perhaps those not sweet on the return Jocketty received—right-handed pitchers Jonathon Crawford and Anthony DeSclafani, shortstop Eugenio Suarez and catcher Chad Wallach. Or, in terms of realistic roles: two potential middle-of-the-rotation starters or high-leverage relievers, a probable utility infielder and a possible backup catcher. There's no plausible superstar in the group, but there's enough upside, safeness and proximity to the majors for the Reds to benefit soon and later.

That development is welcomed for the obvious, on-the-field reasons and the secondary, off-the-field reasons—i.e. the more cheap talent the Reds employ, the more freedom they have to re-sign their transcendent talents, like Cueto. But say the Reds can't re-sign Cueto: Do the trades still make sense?

Yes, albeit for slightly different reasons. The additions of those players improve an already healthy farm system. While outfielder Jesse Winker ought to soon take left field as his own, the Reds' prospect milk and honey is on the mound. In addition to Crawford and DeSclafani, right-handers Robert Stephenson and Michael Lorenzen—two potential above-average starters—could be ready to join the rotation in a year's time. Add in Tony Cingrani and some other, lesser arms in the system, and it's possible the Reds can rebuild the middle and back of their rotation through internal means, thereby cutting costs without slaying their competitive hopes.

Unrealistic, you say—these aren't the Cardinals, who seem to bake fully formed prospects like boxed-mix brownies. But one of the great ironies of the Reds is how Jocketty has built a monument to the sabermetric ideal—a roster full of homegrown talent and players developmental wins—despite not offering the friendly face to the movement that Theo Epstein or Andrew Friedman does. The Reds were fielding lineups with six or seven homegrown position players and a rotation with three Cincy-developed pitchers—and that's excluding the players who were nurtured to success by the Reds, like Phillips and Simon.

Perhaps that's the thread Reds fans should cling to about these deals. Success is never guaranteed in baseball—not with draftees or prospects—yet by going out and acquiring four prospects instead of banking on a draft pick, Jocketty ensured his staff a head start on molding that talent—call it the time value of player development. Crawford and DeSclafani won't master third pitches or improve their command just by donning the uniform, but the Reds' track record suggests there's a chance it happens. Besides, if the Reds had kept Latos and gained a draft pick, the odds are they would've picked someone like those two—a promising arm who needed guidance to get over the proverbial hump.

Invariably, Jocketty considered a lot over the winter. He weighed the condition of his roster, his budget and his farm system. In the end, Jocketty chose to feed his pitching wolf. Whether these deals help the Reds sustain or not, the outcome could've been worse—Jocketty could've starved both wolves. ∎

—R.J. Anderson lives in Florida and joined Prospectus in 2011. In the past, Anderson's work has appeared on ESPN and Wired.com, as well as in Newsweek.

Player comments by J.P. Breen and Baseball Prospectus Authors

Hitters

Tucker Barnhart   C
Born: 1/7/91   Age: 24   Bats: B   Throws: R   Height: 5' 11"   Weight: 195

YEAR	TEAM	LVL	AGE	PA	R	2B	3B	HR	RBI	BB	K	SB	CS	AVG/OBP/SLG	TAv	BABIP	BRR	FRAA	WARP
2012	BAK	A+	21	231	26	12	1	4	22	29	45	0	2	.278/.371/.409	.281	.340	-5.3	C(59): 0.3	1.6
2012	PEN	AA	21	142	10	4	1	2	12	11	22	1	1	.200/.262/.292	.189	.226	1.3	C(41): 0.2	-0.2
2013	PEN	AA	22	395	31	19	1	3	44	45	57	1	0	.260/.348/.348	.262	.300	-2.3	C(96): 1.9	2.2
2014	LOU	AAA	23	292	18	9	3	1	29	28	34	0	1	.246/.319/.316	.232	.277	-3.0	C(75): -1.3	0.4
2014	CIN	MLB	23	60	3	0	0	1	1	4	10	0	0	.185/.241/.241	.207	.209	-0.4	C(20): -0.0	0.1
2015	CIN	MLB	24	250	21	9	1	3	21	20	48	0	0	.222/.285/.309	.228	.263	-0.4	C 0	0.1

Breakout: 1%   Improve: 3%   Collapse: 5%   Attrition: 9%   MLB: 11%   Comparables: *Steve Clevenger, Jordan Pacheco, Sandy Leon*

Boy, Barnhart can really throw. Golly can he throw. Kid can throw like the dickens. Got an arm on him like you wouldn't believe, like a pirate ship's cannon hopped up on bath salts. Woo buddy, you see baserunners, some of these guys are quick like rabbits but they look like a possum caught in molasses against Barnhart. Heard one time he threw someone out so bad the guy just plum retired right there on second base. Or a couple feet from second base, really. Just gave it up. That's his arm.

   (It's actually not even so much that Barnhart's throwing is *that* good as that we're trying not to say anything uncouth about his bat.)

Alex Blandino   SS
Born: 11/6/92   Age: 22   Bats: R   Throws: R   Height: 6' 0"   Weight: 190

YEAR	TEAM	LVL	AGE	PA	R	2B	3B	HR	RBI	BB	K	SB	CS	AVG/OBP/SLG	TAv	BABIP	BRR	FRAA	WARP
2014	DYT	A	21	152	20	10	1	4	16	13	42	1	2	.261/.329/.440	.289	.341	0.3	SS(34): 3.7	1.7
2015	CIN	MLB	22	250	24	9	1	5	20	16	77	1	1	.198/.255/.305	.214	.268	-0.5	SS 4	0.3

Breakout: 0%   Improve: 0%   Collapse: 0%   Attrition: 0%   MLB: 0%   Comparables: *Todd Frazier, Ryan Flaherty, Zach Walters*

A first-round pick in 2014 out of Stanford, Blandino earned a quick promotion to A-Ball after destroying the Pioneer League in a 29-game cameo. He displayed power, patience and a strong hit tool. Scouts don't believe he'll be able to stick at shortstop long term, but whether he ends up at second or third base, the bat should play. He projects to be a high-average hitter with average power, but he doesn't have strong speed. He's old for the levels at which he played, but he displays a quiet swagger on the diamond and understands what he brings to the table. If everything congeals, Blandino could be an everyday bat for a first-division squad.

Brennan Boesch   RF
Born: 4/12/85   Age: 30   Bats: L   Throws: L   Height: 6' 4"   Weight: 235

YEAR	TEAM	LVL	AGE	PA	R	2B	3B	HR	RBI	BB	K	SB	CS	AVG/OBP/SLG	TAv	BABIP	BRR	FRAA	WARP
2012	DET	MLB	27	503	52	22	2	12	54	26	104	6	3	.240/.286/.372	.235	.284	1.0	RF(121): -5.0	-0.8
2013	SWB	AAA	28	37	6	2	0	0	2	7	8	0	0	.200/.351/.267	.283	.273	0.6	RF(7): -0.3	0.2
2013	NYA	MLB	28	53	6	2	1	3	8	2	9	0	0	.275/.302/.529	.273	.282	-1.2	RF(15): 0.6	0.1
2014	SLC	AAA	29	407	68	25	7	25	85	29	86	10	4	.332/.381/.636	.325	.374	1.8	RF(56): -10.1, CF(20): -1.2	2.6
2014	ANA	MLB	29	79	6	2	0	2	7	2	19	3	0	.187/.203/.293	.203	.214	0.2	RF(9): 0.4, LF(3): -0.2	-0.3
2015	CIN	MLB	30	250	28	11	1	8	30	17	56	4	1	.244/.301/.405	.267	.288	-0.1	RF -2, CF -0	0.4

Breakout: 0%   Improve: 38%   Collapse: 4%   Attrition: 17%   MLB: 95%   Comparables: *Ben Francisco, Will Venable, Larry Bigbie*

The Angels gave journeyman Boesch every opportunity to rekindle some of that old Tigers magic and earn the lefty half of a DH platoon in time for the postseason. Alas, he faltered, leaving right-handed teammate C.J. Cron platoonless and the punchless Efren Navarro as the lefty "power" off the bench in the ALDS. Boesch's big-league plate appearances were disastrous; he hacked at more pitches outside the strike zone than Josh Hamilton while posting an isolated power of zero against hard stuff. To be fair, that wasn't the whole Boesch tale in 2014: Between stints of futility with the big-league club, he won the PCL batting title, joining Willie McCovey, Edgar Martinez and Bobby Bonds in the only conceivable list that includes the four of them. He signed a minor-league deal with the Reds, but he has a pretty clean look at a big-league job unless Skip Schumaker is supposed to stand in his way.

Jay Bruce   RF
Born: 4/3/87   Age: 28   Bats: L   Throws: L   Height: 6' 3"   Weight: 215

YEAR	TEAM	LVL	AGE	PA	R	2B	3B	HR	RBI	BB	K	SB	CS	AVG/OBP/SLG	TAv	BABIP	BRR	FRAA	WARP
2012	CIN	MLB	25	633	89	35	5	34	99	62	155	9	3	.252/.327/.514	.294	.283	-4.2	RF(154): 8.8	3.8
2013	CIN	MLB	26	697	89	43	1	30	109	63	185	7	3	.262/.329/.478	.290	.322	1.9	RF(160): 9.2	5.1
2014	CIN	MLB	27	545	71	21	1	18	66	44	149	12	3	.217/.281/.373	.245	.269	4.2	RF(131): -2.8, 1B(3): -0.1	0.4
2015	CIN	MLB	28	542	67	25	2	22	73	52	139	9	3	.243/.317/.440	.282	.292	0.2	RF 5, 1B -0	2.8

Breakout: 1%   Improve: 66%   Collapse: 1%   Attrition: 5%   MLB: 100%   Comparables: *Roger Maris, David Justice, Manny Ramirez*

Bruce suffered through his worst season as a professional in 2014. His strikeout rate edged up to a career-high 27 percent and his walk rate dropped for the third straight year, but the most problematic feature of his offense was his 45 percent rate of grounders, which played right into the hands of the shifts he frequently faced. Was it the left knee (i.e. his back leg at the plate) meniscus surgery in May from which he returned in 16 days despite reports that he was supposed to be out three to four weeks? He had his best month *after* the surgery and stole a career-high number of bases at a career-high rate, so that doesn't fully track. Is his bat already slowing despite having two more seasons until he turns 30? Is his plate discipline eroding? Is his plate discipline eroding because he has to cheat to make up for a slowed bat? Was it a weird blip? Please send your answers to Baseball Prospectus, One Baseball Prospectus Plaza, Baseballprospectusland, CA. One winner will be chosen at random from the 20 best submissions. Previous winners and family of Baseball Prospectus employees not eligible.

Zack Cozart   SS

Born: 8/12/85   Age: 29   Bats: R   Throws: R   Height: 6' 0"   Weight: 195

YEAR	TEAM	LVL	AGE	PA	R	2B	3B	HR	RBI	BB	K	SB	CS	AVG/OBP/SLG	TAv	BABIP	BRR	FRAA	WARP
2012	CIN	MLB	26	600	72	33	4	15	35	31	113	4	0	.246/.288/.399	.248	.282	2.0	SS(138): 2.7	2.4
2013	CIN	MLB	27	618	74	30	3	12	63	26	102	0	0	.254/.284/.381	.242	.285	6.9	SS(150): -3.7	2.0
2014	CIN	MLB	28	543	48	18	5	4	38	25	79	7	0	.221/.268/.300	.213	.255	2.0	SS(147): 7.3	0.9
2015	*CIN*	*MLB*	*29*	*525*	*55*	*24*	*3*	*9*	*46*	*26*	*91*	*4*	*0*	*.242/.283/.358*	*.244*	*.274*	*2.7*	*SS 3*	*1.9*

Breakout: 3%   Improve: 49%   Collapse: 8%   Attrition: 15%   MLB: 97%   Comparables: *Ronny Cedeno, Angel Berroa, Michael Young*

Cozart has found himself on the Brendan Ryan Plan. He offers plus defense at shortstop, which allows him to keep his job despite a putrid bat. His .213 TAv ranked second-worst in all of baseball among regulars. The 29-year-old won't steal bases (though he's never been caught stealing), hit for average, hit for power or walk. He's a one-asset portfolio, and it's all on the defensive end. Fortunately for the former second-round pick, above-average defenders aren't easy to find at shortstop. It should also be noted that he's not the first Cozart to play in the majors. Charlie pitched eight innings for the Boston Braves, walking 31 percent of the batters he faced and retiring with a 10.13 ERA. So stick or no stick, it seems safe to say that Zack is the greatest Cozart to ever play the game.

Phillip Ervin   OF

Born: 7/15/92   Age: 22   Bats: R   Throws: R   Height: 5' 10"   Weight: 205

YEAR	TEAM	LVL	AGE	PA	R	2B	3B	HR	RBI	BB	K	SB	CS	AVG/OBP/SLG	TAv	BABIP	BRR	FRAA	WARP
2013	DYT	A	20	51	7	2	0	1	6	8	10	2	1	.349/.451/.465	.354	.438	-1.4	CF(8): -0.1, RF(4): -0.3	0.5
2014	DYT	A	21	562	68	34	7	7	68	46	110	30	5	.237/.305/.376	.263	.284	3.1	CF(68): -2.9, LF(38): -1.9	1.1
2015	*CIN*	*MLB*	*22*	*250*	*23*	*10*	*1*	*4*	*21*	*16*	*66*	*7*	*2*	*.205/.260/.304*	*.220*	*.266*	*0.6*	*CF -1, LF -1*	*-0.6*

Breakout: 0%   Improve: 0%   Collapse: 0%   Attrition: 0%   MLB: 0%   Comparables: *Xavier Avery, J.B. Shuck, Trayvon Robinson*

A first-round pick in 2013, Ervin face-planted in Low-A Dayton, the first time he's failed anywhere. Part of the issue seems to have come from his offseason wrist surgery, a notoriously difficult area of the body to rehab, or to trust *after* rehab. Ervin became too pull-conscious and developed bad habits at the plate, affecting his pitch selection and hit tool. Many believe he's destined for right field, where he should be adequate defensively, so the bat must bounce back in 2015. The 22-year-old could still offer double-digit homers with 20 stolen bases in the majors someday; it's just difficult to see past the struggles of last season.

Todd Frazier   3B

Born: 2/12/86   Age: 29   Bats: R   Throws: R   Height: 6' 3"   Weight: 220

YEAR	TEAM	LVL	AGE	PA	R	2B	3B	HR	RBI	BB	K	SB	CS	AVG/OBP/SLG	TAv	BABIP	BRR	FRAA	WARP
2012	LOU	AAA	26	41	4	2	0	1	7	2	11	3	0	.231/.268/.359	.226	.296	0.2	3B(8): -0.0, LF(1): -0.1	-0.1
2012	CIN	MLB	26	465	55	26	6	19	67	36	103	3	2	.273/.331/.498	.291	.316	0.1	3B(73): -1.5, 1B(39): -0.2	2.5
2013	CIN	MLB	27	600	63	29	3	19	73	50	125	6	5	.234/.314/.407	.260	.269	1.7	3B(147): -2.2, LF(2): -0.1	1.9
2014	CIN	MLB	28	660	88	22	1	29	80	52	139	20	8	.273/.336/.459	.299	.309	3.2	3B(124): -4.0, 1B(43): -0.8	4.5
2015	*CIN*	*MLB*	*29*	*608*	*74*	*26*	*2*	*22*	*77*	*48*	*137*	*12*	*5*	*.247/.315/.425*	*.281*	*.287*	*1.5*	*3B -3, 1B -0*	*2.4*

Breakout: 2%   Improve: 36%   Collapse: 4%   Attrition: 11%   MLB: 97%   Comparables: *Chase Headley, David Freese, Garrett Atkins*

The re-breakout at the plate was nice, but who knew Frazier had a major-league 20-20 season in him? You put your hand down, Wayne Krivsky; sure, sure, we've heard it before, you drafted the guy, and yeah, you Rule 5'd Josh Hamilton, and we know, you picked up Brandon Phillips for Jeff Stevens, and yes, yes, you inherited the Eric Milton and Ken Griffey contracts that ate up a quarter of your payroll, but ... well, hold on, where were we? This isn't Wayne Krivsky's comment. Frazier's total stolen-base record came in below the break-even mark because he was caught too many times, but he was a positive baserunner anyway, largely due to very good work advancing on hits. He and Billy Hamilton had nearly the same run value in nearly the same number of hit-advancement opportunities in 2014. To put Frazier's overall +3.2 baserunning runs in context, he finished in the top 50 in baseball in the stat. The leader was Denard Span at +6.8; it's hard to distinguish oneself on the bases, at least in the ways we can reliably measure with objective data.

Billy Hamilton   CF

Born: 9/9/90   Age: 24   Bats: B   Throws: R   Height: 6' 0"   Weight: 160

YEAR	TEAM	LVL	AGE	PA	R	2B	3B	HR	RBI	BB	K	SB	CS	AVG/OBP/SLG	TAv	BABIP	BRR	FRAA	WARP
2012	BAK	A+	21	392	79	18	9	1	30	50	70	104	21	.323/.413/.439	.316	.404	13.1	SS(77): 8.9	6.2
2012	PEN	AA	21	213	33	4	5	1	15	36	43	51	16	.286/.406/.383	.294	.371	3.9	SS(48): 1.2	2.3
2013	LOU	AAA	22	547	75	18	4	6	41	38	102	75	15	.256/.308/.343	.232	.310	10.7	CF(118): 18.7, SS(1): 0.0	3.0
2013	CIN	MLB	22	22	9	2	0	0	1	2	4	13	1	.368/.429/.474	.358	.467	1.1	CF(7): 0.5	0.5
2014	CIN	MLB	23	611	72	25	8	6	48	34	117	56	23	.250/.292/.355	.244	.304	5.4	CF(144): 10.5	3.1
2015	*CIN*	*MLB*	*24*	*522*	*76*	*19*	*5*	*5*	*33*	*37*	*110*	*58*	*17*	*.248/.302/.344*	*.246*	*.304*	*4.1*	*CF 11, SS 1*	*2.5*

Breakout: 6%   Improve: 32%   Collapse: 7%   Attrition: 16%   MLB: 61%   Comparables: *Willy Taveras, Julio Borbon, Jacoby Ellsbury*

Wellllll, that only sorta worked. Hamilton got the regular at-bats speed freaks have been jonesing for, but he didn't do anything with them: His .244 TAv was a smidge better than B.J. Upton's mark, and Upton's futility at the plate has been a running joke for two years now. Unlike Upton, however, the defensive metrics like Hamilton's work in center field, which lowers the bar significantly for his offensive output. He would probably benefit from hitting the ball on the ground more often: Six homers is impressive for a guy listed at 160 pounds, and he posted a higher ISO than in full seasons in both Double- and Triple-A, but with his speed, he should not have a groundball rate below the league average.

Hamilton was also caught stealing more often than was hoped, but he's still right in range of the break-even mark, so with further study of the pitchers around the league (as long as he maintains most of his speed as he ages), he could turn back into the elite basestealer he was in the minors. Of course, Hamilton was never known as one of those clever-type thieves; his M.O. was always *fast*, not *fast and smart*.

Gavin LaValley   3B

Born: 12/28/94   Age: 20   Bats: R   Throws: R   Height: 6' 3"   Weight: 235

YEAR	TEAM	LVL	AGE	PA	R	2B	3B	HR	RBI	BB	K	SB	CS	AVG/OBP/SLG	TAv	BABIP	BRR	FRAA	WARP
2015	CIN	MLB	20	250	18	7	0	4	21	12	82	0	0	.181/.226/.267	.189	.254	-0.4	3B -5	-1.9

Breakout: 0%   Improve: 0%   Collapse: 0%   Attrition: 0%   MLB: 0%   Comparables: Mat Gamel, Josh Bell, Alex Liddi

LaValley was the Reds' 2014 fourth-round pick out of high school in Oklahoma. He's old for a prep pick, will switch from third base to first soon enough, didn't face a lot of high-level competition as an amateur and is more of a masher than a hitter. That's a lot of issues! Which goes to show just how much weight power carries with teams: LaValley's grades out as a potential 60, which is enough to make the problems worth bearing to see if he can reach his ceiling, though it's not enough to make him a first-division player even if everything goes right.

Ryan Ludwick   LF

Born: 7/13/78   Age: 36   Bats: R   Throws: L   Height: 6' 2"   Weight: 215

YEAR	TEAM	LVL	AGE	PA	R	2B	3B	HR	RBI	BB	K	SB	CS	AVG/OBP/SLG	TAv	BABIP	BRR	FRAA	WARP
2012	CIN	MLB	33	472	53	28	1	26	80	42	97	0	1	.275/.346/.531	.299	.299	-0.1	LF(108): -2.8	2.6
2013	LOU	AAA	34	39	2	1	0	1	4	0	9	0	0	.132/.154/.237	.132	.143	-0.1	LF(10): -0.7	-0.6
2013	CIN	MLB	34	140	7	5	0	2	12	10	29	0	0	.240/.293/.326	.211	.293	-0.4	LF(32): -2.1	-0.8
2014	CIN	MLB	35	400	28	20	0	9	45	31	94	0	2	.244/.308/.375	.260	.302	-4.4	LF(92): -2.2	0.1
2015	CIN	MLB	36	327	33	14	0	9	38	26	77	0	1	.235/.302/.383	.260	.282	-1.1	LF -4	0.2

Breakout: 0%   Improve: 27%   Collapse: 8%   Attrition: 19%   MLB: 80%   Comparables: Mark DeRosa, Andres Torres, Raul Ibanez

Ludwick is now 36 years old and his pale blue eyes occasionally reflect an inner sadness. His skills have eroded to the point that he's a mere bench player without a true defensive home. A sub-.700 OPS from a bench bat is acceptable when he's a utility infielder, but not from someone lumbering around left field. Ludwick is, as ever, a free swinger. In his heyday, he made that work with plus power, but that's been gone for two years. It's unclear what skills he brings to the table at this point, aside from the "veteran presence" players supposedly have once they've become a shell of their former selves.

Devin Mesoraco   C

Born: 6/19/88   Age: 27   Bats: R   Throws: R   Height: 6' 1"   Weight: 220

YEAR	TEAM	LVL	AGE	PA	R	2B	3B	HR	RBI	BB	K	SB	CS	AVG/OBP/SLG	TAv	BABIP	BRR	FRAA	WARP
2012	CIN	MLB	24	184	17	8	0	5	14	17	33	1	1	.212/.288/.352	.236	.234	-0.2	C(53): 0.9	0.5
2013	CIN	MLB	25	352	31	13	0	9	42	24	61	0	2	.238/.287/.362	.233	.264	-1.2	C(97): 1.0	0.8
2014	CIN	MLB	26	440	54	25	0	25	80	41	103	1	3	.273/.359/.534	.336	.309	-6.2	C(109): 0.9	4.8
2015	CIN	MLB	27	399	46	19	0	14	49	34	80	1	2	.246/.317/.420	.277	.276	-2.1	C 1	2.2

Breakout: 5%   Improve: 49%   Collapse: 6%   Attrition: 9%   MLB: 96%   Comparables: Victor Martinez, Jason Kubel, Miguel Montero

Boy howdy, *that's* a breakout. Nearly tripling your home run output, adding 100 points to your TAv and sextupling your WARP? That's how you live up to those top-100 prospect rankings that, after two disappointing years, had started to feel distant. Mesoraco's .260 ISO ranked sixth in baseball among hitters with at least 400 plate appearances. He was easily tops among catchers, outripping even Evan Gattis by 30 points, and Gattis is a catcher the way Keanu Reeves is an actor: He puts on the gear and goes through the motions, but you're never entirely convinced. (*John Wick* was friggin' awesome, though.) While Mesoraco did enormous damage to lefties (.418 OBP), he actually hit righties for more power (.272 ISO).

Kristopher Negron   INF

Born: 2/1/86   Age: 29   Bats: R   Throws: R   Height: 6' 0"   Weight: 195

YEAR	TEAM	LVL	AGE	PA	R	2B	3B	HR	RBI	BB	K	SB	CS	AVG/OBP/SLG	TAv	BABIP	BRR	FRAA	WARP
2012	LOU	AAA	26	319	34	13	2	6	20	22	77	17	3	.218/.287/.342	.225	.276	4.2	SS(21): -0.5, CF(18): 1.3	1.0
2012	CIN	MLB	26	5	2	0	0	0	0	1	2	0	0	.250/.400/.250	.373	.500	-0.1	CF(1): -0.0	0.1
2013	LOU	AAA	27	379	31	14	1	5	30	26	93	11	3	.225/.295/.317	.223	.292	1.3	SS(73): -4.9, 3B(12): 0.7	-0.3
2014	LOU	AAA	28	240	33	15	3	3	25	14	54	9	2	.269/.328/.406	.250	.346	2.5	SS(47): 1.1, CF(14): -0.3	1.1
2014	CIN	MLB	28	158	19	10	1	6	17	12	40	5	0	.271/.331/.479	.292	.337	2.6	3B(25): -0.2, 2B(17): 0.6	1.5
2015	CIN	MLB	29	250	26	10	1	5	23	15	70	7	1	.218/.275/.336	.233	.283	0.8	SS -0, 3B 1	0.4

Breakout: 0%   Improve: 2%   Collapse: 8%   Attrition: 12%   MLB: 21%   Comparables: Tommy Manzella, Jose Leon, Brent Dlugach

Negron reached the majors in mid-July and, from August 1st on, started 32 games at second and third base while also making brief appearances in left field and at shortstop. The very best thing a fringe utility player can do for his career is catch lightning in a bottle when he gets his first shot at playing time; Negron's best seasonal OPS in the minors was the .765 mark he posted between Rookie and short-season ball as a 20-year-old in 2006. Which is to say that the .810 figure he put up in Cincinnati is, how do you say, a fluke. The man can steal a base and his versatility is useful on a bench, but don't think Negron's outburst makes Brandon Phillips expendable. Not that you were thinking that. We're just saying.

Brandon Phillips   2B

Born: 6/28/81   Age: 34   Bats: R   Throws: R   Height: 6' 0"   Weight: 200

YEAR	TEAM	LVL	AGE	PA	R	2B	3B	HR	RBI	BB	K	SB	CS	AVG/OBP/SLG	TAv	BABIP	BRR	FRAA	WARP
2012	CIN	MLB	31	623	86	30	1	18	77	28	79	15	2	.281/.321/.429	.263	.298	1.7	2B(146): -5.0	1.3
2013	CIN	MLB	32	666	80	24	2	18	103	39	98	5	3	.261/.310/.396	.257	.281	-1.1	2B(151): 7.7	3.6
2014	CIN	MLB	33	499	44	25	0	8	51	23	74	2	3	.266/.306/.372	.255	.298	-2.2	2B(121): -7.6	0.0
2015	CIN	MLB	34	504	50	22	1	10	53	28	75	6	3	.259/.307/.379	.261	.284	-0.7	2B -2	1.5

Breakout: 0%   Improve: 28%   Collapse: 12%   Attrition: 14%   MLB: 87%   Comparables: Freddy Sanchez, Mark Ellis, Ronnie Belliard

Phillips is trending in the wrong direction across the board. His isolated power has dropped in each of the past four seasons from .157 in 2011 to just .106 in 2014. Phillips hasn't added anything at the plate (more contact, more walks) to make up for the falling power, so his TAv has plummeted from .285 to .255 in that time. Other defensive systems and many eyes think Phillips can still pick it at second base, so he remains useful, especially because the second basemen around the league are a sack of moldy oranges right now. But even measured against that lackluster set of peers, he's simply no longer a top-tier player.

Yorman Rodriguez   RF

Born: 8/15/92   Age: 22   Bats: R   Throws: R   Height: 6' 3"   Weight: 195

YEAR	TEAM	LVL	AGE	PA	R	2B	3B	HR	RBI	BB	K	SB	CS	AVG/OBP/SLG	TAv	BABIP	BRR	FRAA	WARP
2012	DYT	A	19	277	35	17	3	6	44	12	61	7	5	.271/.307/.430	.267	.332	1.4	RF(57): -3.9, CF(1): -0.1	0.2
2012	BAK	A+	19	94	7	4	0	0	7	3	39	4	0	.156/.181/.200	.150	.269	1.0	RF(19): -1.2, CF(4): 0.5	-0.9
2013	BAK	A+	20	278	41	20	4	9	35	22	77	6	3	.251/.319/.470	.265	.327	0.9	CF(55): -10.5, RF(1): -0.0	0.0
2013	PEN	AA	20	289	30	15	2	4	31	25	76	4	0	.267/.329/.385	.261	.359	-0.3	RF(66): -4.1	0.5
2014	PEN	AA	21	502	69	20	5	9	40	47	117	12	5	.262/.331/.389	.269	.333	2.7	CF(88): -3.0, RF(20): 0.2	2.2
2014	CIN	MLB	21	29	3	0	0	0	2	1	12	0	1	.222/.276/.222	.194	.400	0.5	RF(4): 0.1, CF(2): -0.1	0.0
2015	CIN	MLB	22	250	22	10	1	4	23	13	78	3	1	.217/.261/.325	.224	.301	-0.1	CF -3, RF -1	-0.8

Breakout: 0%   Improve: 0%   Collapse: 0%   Attrition: 0%   MLB: 0%   Comparables: Felix Pie, Elijah Dukes, Michael Saunders

A $2.5 million bonus baby out of Venezuela, Rodriguez disappointed in his second shot at Double-A, but scouts still drool over his tools: He has a huge arm in the outfield, a great baseball body, plus power potential and good speed. That's almost everything you want in a big leaguer, and he has the chance to be a first-division starter, but notice what's not mentioned: His hit tool remains in question. It's hard to justify a place in the corner outfield without hitting; it's even harder to tap into power without hitting. All told, Rodriguez's profile is sexy but dangerous, like flammable panties.

Ramon Santiago   3B

Born: 8/31/79   Age: 35   Bats: B   Throws: R   Height: 5' 11"   Weight: 175

YEAR	TEAM	LVL	AGE	PA	R	2B	3B	HR	RBI	BB	K	SB	CS	AVG/OBP/SLG	TAv	BABIP	BRR	FRAA	WARP
2012	DET	MLB	32	259	19	7	1	2	17	20	39	1	0	.206/.283/.272	.198	.239	1.1	2B(71): 2.4, SS(20): -1.1	-0.9
2013	DET	MLB	33	234	27	8	1	1	14	21	32	0	1	.224/.298/.288	.230	.260	-0.7	2B(33): 0.3, 3B(27): 0.6	0.2
2014	CIN	MLB	34	214	20	8	0	2	17	24	38	2	1	.246/.343/.324	.263	.300	-0.4	3B(28): 0.5, SS(20): 0.4	0.9
2015	CIN	MLB	35	250	22	8	1	2	20	21	43	1	1	.228/.302/.304	.234	.263	0.0	2B 0, SS 1	0.4

Breakout: 0%   Improve: 29%   Collapse: 8%   Attrition: 24%   MLB: 91%   Comparables: Carney Lansford, Buddy Bell, Bill Spiers

If you take Philippa Foot's thought experiment, the trolley problem, but say that Santiago has to hit a single to switch the runaway trolley to the side track, well, too bad for those people who are about to get run over because Santiago's not going to hit that single.

Skip Schumaker   LF

Born: 2/3/80   Age: 35   Bats: L   Throws: R   Height: 5' 10"   Weight: 195

YEAR	TEAM	LVL	AGE	PA	R	2B	3B	HR	RBI	BB	K	SB	CS	AVG/OBP/SLG	TAv	BABIP	BRR	FRAA	WARP
2012	MEM	AAA	32	25	5	2	0	0	0	4	3	1	0	.286/.400/.381	.316	.333	0.3	2B(4): -0.6, CF(2): -0.0	0.2
2012	SLN	MLB	32	304	37	14	4	1	28	27	50	1	1	.276/.339/.368	.256	.332	-0.3	2B(61): 0.4, CF(15): 0.0	0.8
2013	LAN	MLB	33	356	31	16	0	2	30	28	54	2	2	.263/.332/.332	.242	.312	-1.6	2B(44): -4.7, LF(35): -0.5	-0.8
2014	CIN	MLB	34	271	22	12	0	2	22	18	50	2	1	.235/.287/.308	.234	.284	0.8	LF(33): -1.4, 2B(19): -0.3	-0.4
2015	CIN	MLB	35	273	24	12	1	2	22	21	46	2	1	.248/.309/.323	.244	.292	-0.2	2B -1, LF -1	0.0

Breakout: 1%   Improve: 28%   Collapse: 11%   Attrition: 20%   MLB: 80%   Comparables: Tim Raines, Shannon Stewart, Chone Figgins

Schumaker has Randy Velarde's physique but not his ability to put up a .275 TAv. His contract is cheap in a sense because what's $2.5 million in today's market? On the other hand, he's 35 and spent the last two years playing more corner outfield than second base and turning in sub-replacement performance. He's not a utility infielder because he doesn't play on the left side and he's not really a fourth outfielder because you don't want to put him in center. So given all that, why pay him major-league money at all? Hope he still carries around some residual Cardinals devil magic?

Marquez Smith   3B

Born: 3/20/85   Age: 30   Bats: R   Throws: R   Height: 5' 10"   Weight: 205

YEAR	TEAM	LVL	AGE	PA	R	2B	3B	HR	RBI	BB	K	SB	CS	AVG/OBP/SLG	TAv	BABIP	BRR	FRAA	WARP
2012	PME	AA	27	314	43	22	1	8	37	23	52	1	0	.293/.350/.464	.287	.330	0.1	3B(55): 8.4, 2B(13): -0.4	3.0
2013	BAK	A+	28	217	33	11	2	8	26	26	34	2	1	.301/.406/.514	.334	.331	0.2	1B(21): -0.5, 3B(11): 1.7	2.1
2013	PEN	AA	28	80	9	5	0	3	11	9	13	0	0	.214/.300/.414	.282	.218	0.0	1B(20): 0.4	0.0
2014	BAK	A+	29	520	89	32	4	29	126	83	93	1	0	.323/.438/.623	.349	.352	-0.4	1B(83): 0.1, 3B(29): 0.8	5.9
2014	PEN	AA	29	34	4	2	0	1	5	2	12	0	0	.156/.206/.313	.163	.211	0.0	1B(7): -0.1	-0.3
2015	CIN	MLB	30	250	27	10	1	8	30	24	59	0	0	.234/.314/.394	.269	.279	-0.4	1B -0, 3B 1	0.6

Breakout: 1%   Improve: 2%   Collapse: 5%   Attrition: 13%   MLB: 17%   Comparables: Bobby Scales, Luis Antonio Jimenez, Kevin Barker

You know your friend who likes to play MLB: The Show and hit .350 with 70 homers and 150 RBI ... while refusing to increase the difficulty level from "Beginner"? That's Smith, who laid waste to the Cal League last year at 29. The league returned the favor on September 1st, when Smith made a pitching appearance against Visalia: He faced two batters, gave up a single and a double and is now the proud owner of an undefined professional ERA (1 ER, 0 IP). Smith reached Triple-A back in 2010 with the Cubs, OPS'd .958, repeated the league in 2011 and lost 130 points of slugging percentage, spent half of 2012 in the Atlantic and Mexican Leagues and has played most of the last two years at Bakersfield. The Reds have precious little going on at first base in their minor-league system, so theoretically Smith can stick around and mash baseballs as long as he's content to do so. This may all feel faintly depressing, Wooderson at the pool hall, but that feeling is rooted in the notion that there's something intrinsically valuable about growing up and leaving childish dreams behind; who are we, holding this book in our hands, to look askance at Smith's choices? Cheer instead for him to find joy and, perhaps, a big-league cup of coffee.

Eugenio Suarez   SS

Born: 7/18/91   Age: 23   Bats: R   Throws: R   Height: 5' 11"   Weight: 180

YEAR	TEAM	LVL	AGE	PA	R	2B	3B	HR	RBI	BB	K	SB	CS	AVG/OBP/SLG	TAv	BABIP	BRR	FRAA	WARP
2012	WMI	A	20	604	82	34	5	6	67	65	116	21	9	.288/.380/.409	.302	.356	-4.4	SS(119): -0.6, 2B(15): 0.5	4.8
2013	LAK	A+	21	122	17	6	2	1	12	14	25	2	3	.311/.410/.437	.305	.397	-0.3	SS(24): 1.1, 2B(1): 0.1	1.4
2013	ERI	AA	21	496	53	24	4	9	45	46	98	9	11	.253/.332/.387	.268	.307	-0.3	SS(111): 4.3	3.2
2014	ERI	AA	22	170	26	14	1	6	29	15	38	7	2	.284/.347/.503	.295	.342	-0.5	SS(42): -0.9	1.3
2014	TOL	AAA	22	52	6	4	0	2	7	6	9	2	0	.302/.404/.535	.304	.333	0.6	SS(12): -1.3	0.5
2014	DET	MLB	22	277	33	9	1	4	23	22	67	3	2	.242/.316/.336	.247	.316	1.1	SS(81): 0.2, 3B(2): -0.1	0.9
2015	CIN	MLB	23	312	35	13	1	6	26	24	80	5	3	.230/.298/.346	.247	.296	0.4	SS -0, 2B 0	0.9

Breakout: 4%   Improve: 27%   Collapse: 2%   Attrition: 16%   MLB: 38%   *Comparables: Josh Rodriguez, Jonathan Villar, Brad Miller*

Year after year Suarez's offensive production has been all over the map, but he picked the right time to rake in Double-A and Triple-A. With Jose Iglesias on the mend and the Tigers employing a lazy Susan's horde of Quad-A shortstops, Suarez earned a promotion, making him the team's fourth starting shortstop of the year. He started great in June, peaked in his eighth career game, cooled off the rest of the year and didn't make a postseason start. He might need to begin the year in Triple-A to polish his defense and reenergize his confidence at the plate, but in the end his makeup could allow him to carve out a nice little Felipe Lopez career. He could push Zack Cozart as soon as this year, which was presumably part of the point of the Reds acquiring him in the Alfredo Simon deal.

Joey Votto   1B
Born: 9/10/83   Age: 31   Bats: L   Throws: R   Height: 6' 2"   Weight: 220

YEAR	TEAM	LVL	AGE	PA	R	2B	3B	HR	RBI	BB	K	SB	CS	AVG/OBP/SLG	TAv	BABIP	BRR	FRAA	WARP
2012	CIN	MLB	28	475	59	44	0	14	56	94	85	5	3	.337/.474/.567	.360	.404	-3.2	1B(109): 4.7	6.1
2013	CIN	MLB	29	726	101	30	3	24	73	135	138	6	3	.305/.435/.491	.329	.360	0.5	1B(161): 7.7	6.7
2014	CIN	MLB	30	272	32	16	0	6	23	47	49	1	1	.255/.390/.409	.306	.299	-0.7	1B(61): 2.3	1.8
2015	*CIN*	*MLB*	*31*	*347*	*47*	*18*	*1*	*12*	*47*	*57*	*68*	*3*	*2*	*.288/.408/.481*	*.331*	*.338*	*-0.7*	*1B 4*	*3.2*

Breakout: 2%   Improve: 40%   Collapse: 6%   Attrition: 6%   MLB: 100%   *Comparables: Lance Berkman, Frank Thomas, Adrian Gonzalez*

The unbreakable machine experienced technical difficulties last year. He strained each thigh once, losing nearly a month early in the year to the left-leg injury and the Reds' final 76 games to the right. In between, his power disappeared and he did absolutely nothing pulling the ball, hitting just .226 with a .113 isolated power to the right side. For a hitter of his caliber, with his physical strength and general batting acumen, those are shockingly poor numbers. If he can get his base healthy, though, and get back to crushing inside stuff (from 2008 to 2013, Votto slugged .600 on pitches on the inner third and off the plate inside; in 2014, .283), he should again be an MVP candidate. Even if he can't, though, note that he posted nearly two WARP last year in well under half a season of playing time; Votto's on-base skills, doubles pop and defense are such that he can be a contributor even in a state diminished from his MVP-candidate prime. The problem is that the Reds didn't commit to $25 million per year through 2023 to get the 2014 version of Votto.

Chad Wallach   C
Born: 11/4/91   Age: 23   Bats: R   Throws: R   Height: 6' 3"   Weight: 210

YEAR	TEAM	LVL	AGE	PA	R	2B	3B	HR	RBI	BB	K	SB	CS	AVG/OBP/SLG	TAv	BABIP	BRR	FRAA	WARP
2013	BAT	A-	21	163	19	6	0	0	13	11	27	0	0	.226/.294/.267	.229	.273	-0.3	C(43): 0.3	0.2
2014	GRB	A	22	330	50	19	1	7	49	50	39	3	0	.321/.430/.476	.312	.351	-1.7	C(73): 0.1	3.4
2014	JUP	A+	22	78	4	3	0	0	8	12	7	0	0	.328/.436/.375	.319	.362	0.2	C(18): -0.4	0.8
2015	*CIN*	*MLB*	*23*	*250*	*22*	*10*	*0*	*3*	*23*	*25*	*53*	*0*	*0*	*.225/.309/.316*	*.242*	*.277*	*-0.4*	*C -0*	*0.5*

Breakout: 3%   Improve: 18%   Collapse: 1%   Attrition: 13%   MLB: 26%   *Comparables: George Kottaras, Christian Vazquez, Curtis Casali*

Son of Tim has a smart pedigree and a tasty 2014 batting record, but there's little chance he'll continue to hit 50 percent better than his league's average. Yes, he's got a fine approach, but that could just be taking advantage of Class-A pitching. A brief stop at the Arizona Fall League—a fairer fight—was not a resounding success, and Wallach doesn't have a set of carrying tools. He's a large target behind the plate, and reportedly has solid makeup, so there's a chance he could still develop. But he's less the next Wallach than the latest Chad, best filed under org depth.

Jesse Winker   LF
Born: 8/17/93   Age: 21   Bats: L   Throws: L   Height: 6' 3"   Weight: 210

YEAR	TEAM	LVL	AGE	PA	R	2B	3B	HR	RBI	BB	K	SB	CS	AVG/OBP/SLG	TAv	BABIP	BRR	FRAA	WARP
2013	DYT	A	19	486	73	18	5	16	76	63	75	6	1	.281/.379/.463	.290	.308	-1.6	LF(100): -6.1, RF(1): -0.0	2.1
2014	BAK	A+	20	249	42	15	0	13	49	40	46	5	1	.317/.426/.580	.324	.349	-2.2	LF(48): -2.7	1.9
2014	PEN	AA	20	92	15	5	0	2	8	14	22	0	0	.208/.326/.351	.260	.259	0.4	LF(20): 0.9	0.4
2015	*CIN*	*MLB*	*21*	*250*	*26*	*9*	*1*	*7*	*28*	*26*	*62*	*0*	*0*	*.221/.305/.362*	*.254*	*.270*	*-0.3*	*LF -1, RF -0*	*0.1*

Breakout: 0%   Improve: 0%   Collapse: 0%   Attrition: 0%   MLB: 0%   *Comparables: Wil Myers, Jaff Decker, Joc Pederson*

Winker doesn't get the hype someone with his bat normally would because of his left field-only defensive profile. He possesses one of the best swings in the minors, controls the strike zone and works baseballs all over the field with his plus hit tool. A July car crash resulted in a partially torn tendon in his right wrist and, though he initially tried to play through it, he was eventually shut down for the remainder of the minor-league season. He did not require surgery, however, and he was healthy enough to play in the Arizona Fall League. Wrist and hand injuries can be death to a hitter, but as long as Winker's doesn't linger, he should remain of the safest prospects around, extremely likely to make the majors and hit once he gets there, even if his overall profile doesn't come with game-breaking potential.   ;-)

Pitchers

Dylan Axelrod   RHP
Born: 7/30/85   Age: 29   Bats: R   Throws: R   Height: 6'0"   Weight: 195

YEAR	TEAM	LVL	AGE	W	L	SV	G	GS	IP	H	HR	BB	K	BB/9	K/9	GB%	BABIP	WHIP	ERA	FIP	FRA	WARP
2012	CHR	AAA	26	7	5	0	16	16	97	81	8	31	92	2.9	8.5	38%	.283	1.15	2.88	3.35	4.43	0.7
2012	CHA	MLB	26	2	2	0	14	7	51	56	8	21	40	3.7	7.1	45%	.304	1.51	5.47	4.99	5.53	0.2
2013	CHA	MLB	27	4	11	0	30	20	128¹	170	24	43	73	3.0	5.1	45%	.330	1.66	5.68	5.47	5.66	-0.7
2014	CHR	AAA	28	6	7	0	18	16	88	96	9	36	76	3.7	7.8	46%	.341	1.50	4.50	4.36	5.28	0.9
2014	LOU	AAA	28	2	2	0	6	6	42¹	31	3	7	32	1.5	6.8	43%	.231	0.90	2.98	3.26	4.93	0.3
2014	CIN	MLB	28	2	1	0	5	4	18¹	14	5	4	20	2.0	9.8	33%	.209	0.98	2.95	5.12	5.08	0.1
2015	*CIN*	*MLB*	*29*	*7*	*9*	*0*	*23*	*23*	*131¹*	*125*	*15*	*38*	*105*	*2.6*	*7.2*	*42%*	*.303*	*1.24*	*4.01*	*4.22*	*4.36*	*0.4*

Breakout: 19%   Improve: 32%   Collapse: 17%   Attrition: 26%   MLB: 60%   *Comparables: Alfredo Figaro, Guillermo Moscoso, Garrett Mock*

Axelrod throws 90 mph with his right hand. He's not tall and his delivery isn't funky. He was a 30th-round pick. And yet here he is, with 34 starts under his belt in the big leagues. Not good starts, mind you! Even when he's good (the 2.95 ERA with the Reds last year) he isn't good (5.12 FIP driven by 2.5 HR/9). Nonetheless: starts! More starts than Daniel Moskos, who was taken 923 spots ahead of Axelrod in the draft. More starts than every other 927th-overall pick in history. More starts than Axelrod himself made in his first four seasons in the minor leagues. What we're saying is that predicting baseball is hard, maybe impossible. That said, we're confident in the following prediction: Axelrod will not catch up to Jesse Orosco's record for most games pitched by a graduate of Santa Barbara High School.

Homer Bailey   RHP

Born: 5/3/86   Age: 29   Bats: R   Throws: R   Height: 6'4"   Weight: 230

YEAR	TEAM	LVL	AGE	W	L	SV	G	GS	IP	H	HR	BB	K	BB/9	K/9	GB%	BABIP	WHIP	ERA	FIP	FRA	WARP
2012	CIN	MLB	26	13	10	0	33	33	208	206	26	52	168	2.2	7.3	46%	.290	1.24	3.68	4.01	4.05	2.3
2013	CIN	MLB	27	11	12	0	32	32	209	181	20	54	199	2.3	8.6	48%	.284	1.12	3.49	3.28	3.77	3.4
2014	CIN	MLB	28	9	5	0	23	23	145²	134	16	45	124	2.8	7.7	52%	.286	1.23	3.71	3.90	4.44	0.6
2015	CIN	MLB	29	7	8	0	21	21	132²	119	14	35	117	2.4	7.9	45%	.302	1.16	3.49	3.87	3.79	1.2

Breakout: 27%   Improve: 45%   Collapse: 17%   Attrition: 8%   MLB: 92%   *Comparables:*   Anibal Sanchez, Aaron Harang, Gil Meche

Everyone panicked when Bailey surrendered six runs in 3 2/3 innings against the Phillies on May 17th. His ERA ballooned to 5.44 and people began wondering how long the Reds could tolerate him in the rotation. However, his underlying performance was still solid: He was missing bats, limiting walks and inducing groundballs. Sure enough, the right-hander turned it around and compiled 10 quality starts in his next 14 outings. Unfortunately, Bailey suffered a forearm injury and didn't pitch after August 7th, so he missed his chance to push his rate stats all the way back to 2013 levels. He avoided major surgery, though, and plans to be back around Opening Day. As long as he keeps owies at bay, the outlook is positive: He has pounded the strike zone for the last four years, but his swinging-strike rate increased to a career-high 11 percent in 2014 and he cracked the 50 percent groundball mark for the first time. His contract turns rather pricey in 2016 (albeit with an interesting structure where money is deferred until November of each year); nobody will begrudge him the cash if he turns in quality-plus-quantity seasons like 2013, but if that was his peak, the $91 million guaranteed left on his deal could turn into a millstone.

Aroldis Chapman   LHP

Born: 2/28/88   Age: 27   Bats: L   Throws: L   Height: 6'4"   Weight: 205

YEAR	TEAM	LVL	AGE	W	L	SV	G	GS	IP	H	HR	BB	K	BB/9	K/9	GB%	BABIP	WHIP	ERA	FIP	FRA	WARP
2012	CIN	MLB	24	5	5	38	68	0	71²	35	4	23	122	2.9	15.3	37%	.252	0.81	1.51	1.59	1.91	2.4
2013	CIN	MLB	25	4	5	38	68	0	63²	37	7	29	112	4.1	15.8	34%	.280	1.04	2.54	2.44	2.78	1.2
2014	CIN	MLB	26	0	3	36	54	0	54	21	1	24	106	4.0	17.7	44%	.290	0.83	2.00	0.86	1.73	1.6
2015	CIN	MLB	27	3	2	11	24	6	51²	29	3	23	82	4.1	14.3	43%	.303	1.02	2.02	2.28	2.20	1.6

Breakout: 33%   Improve: 55%   Collapse: 24%   Attrition: 17%   MLB: 88%   *Comparables:*   David Robertson, Carlos Marmol, Hong-Chih Kuo

It's time to admit that Chapman, who's still only 27, is simply playing a different game than everyone else. Not only did he *average* a ludicrous 101 mph on his fastball in 2014, the southpaw also struck out 53 percent of the batters he faced. That's the highest single-season percentage in history, with a minimum of 10 innings pitched. (Fun fact: if you set the minimum at zero innings, it only falls to 17th.) It now appears unlikely that Chapman will make that long-discussed conversion to the rotation; however, he has introduced a changeup to his already filthy repertoire, giving him an arsenal that could theoretically stand the transition. That noise you heard in the distance was the collective National League screaming in terror.

Tony Cingrani   LHP

Born: 7/5/89   Age: 25   Bats: L   Throws: L   Height: 6'4"   Weight: 215

YEAR	TEAM	LVL	AGE	W	L	SV	G	GS	IP	H	HR	BB	K	BB/9	K/9	GB%	BABIP	WHIP	ERA	FIP	FRA	WARP
2012	BAK	A+	22	5	1	0	10	10	56²	39	2	13	71	2.1	11.3	45%	.276	0.92	1.11	2.46	2.48	2.2
2012	PEN	AA	22	5	3	0	16	15	89¹	59	7	39	101	3.9	10.2	44%	.257	1.10	2.12	3.24	3.81	1.6
2012	CIN	MLB	22	0	0	0	3	0	5	4	1	2	9	3.6	16.2	64%	.300	1.20	1.80	3.34	2.74	0.1
2013	LOU	AAA	23	3	0	0	6	6	31¹	14	1	11	49	3.2	14.1	50%	.236	0.80	1.15	1.64	2.42	1.0
2013	CIN	MLB	23	7	4	0	23	18	104²	72	14	43	120	3.7	10.3	36%	.241	1.10	2.92	3.76	4.32	1.2
2014	CIN	MLB	24	2	8	0	13	11	63¹	62	12	35	61	5.0	8.7	37%	.292	1.53	4.55	5.34	5.47	-0.6
2015	CIN	MLB	25	4	4	0	13	13	66²	51	8	27	73	3.7	9.9	41%	.288	1.18	3.34	4.01	3.63	0.8

Breakout: 44%   Improve: 67%   Collapse: 20%   Attrition: 25%   MLB: 94%   *Comparables:*   Gio Gonzalez, Rick VandenHurk, Matt Moore

After his third-round selection in 2011, Cingrani plowed through pro hitters; his stat box above is missing only his 51-inning stint in Rookie ball in his draft year, so his meteoric rise out of Rice is fully within view. Cingrani made a brief debut in 2012; just two other players from his draft round have pitched in the majors at all (Carter Capps and Nick Maronde), though both also pitched in the bigs just a season after being drafted. The crash came hard last year, though, as the top hitters in the world adjusted to Cingrani's fastball-heavy approach, teeing off on the pitch for a .210 isolated power. He worked his slider and changeup into the mix enough that he threw less than three-quarters of the time, but even that reduced rate fits in the leaderboards around relievers like Trevor Rosenthal, Kelvin Herrera and Craig Kimbrel rather than down around the other starting pitchers. Those guys all throw 98, by the way; Cingrani throws 92. To add injury to insult, Cingrani pitched only a partial year because of shoulder tendinitis, and had his throwing program shut down in August after he felt renewed pain. Forget about getting back to where he was in 2013; for now, he's just got to get back on the mound period.

Carlos Contreras   RHP

Born: 1/8/91   Age: 24   Bats: R   Throws: R   Height: 5'11"   Weight: 205

YEAR	TEAM	LVL	AGE	W	L	SV	G	GS	IP	H	HR	BB	K	BB/9	K/9	GB%	BABIP	WHIP	ERA	FIP	FRA	WARP
2012	DYT	A	21	0	1	16	40	0	50²	29	6	19	51	3.4	9.1	46%	.183	0.95	3.20	4.18	5.35	0.0
2012	BAK	A+	21	1	0	4	9	0	10	9	1	5	12	4.5	10.8	67%	.276	1.40	2.70	4.21	4.26	0.2
2013	BAK	A+	22	5	7	0	18	18	90	70	9	41	96	4.1	9.6	43%	.269	1.23	3.80	4.44	5.20	1.1
2013	PEN	AA	22	3	2	0	8	8	42¹	36	2	21	26	4.5	5.5	48%	.262	1.35	2.76	4.07	4.70	0.0
2014	PEN	AA	23	2	1	0	9	3	20	15	0	11	27	4.9	12.1	40%	.300	1.30	2.70	2.29	3.24	0.6
2014	CIN	MLB	23	0	1	0	17	0	19¹	19	2	17	19	7.9	8.8	36%	.304	1.86	6.52	5.12	6.35	-0.4
2015	CIN	MLB	24	2	2	0	22	5	50²	45	6	26	43	4.7	7.7	42%	.295	1.42	4.42	4.88	4.80	-0.1

Breakout: 19%   Improve: 24%   Collapse: 15%   Attrition: 23%   MLB: 43%   *Comparables:*   Nick Maronde, Felipe Paulino, Josh Outman

Making the jump from Double-A to the big leagues at 23 isn't easy, but you can't just wave away Contreras walking nearly a batter per inning last year. He can sit mid-90s all he wants, but his height makes it hard for him to create downward plane, so his minor-league walk rates should have been seen as a trainwreck waiting to happen: If you're going to give up homers and doubles, better that there not be free baserunners hanging around when you do.

Jonathon Crawford   RHP

Born: 11/1/91   Age: 23   Bats: R   Throws: R   Height: 6'2"   Weight: 205

YEAR	TEAM	LVL	AGE	W	L	SV	G	GS	IP	H	HR	BB	K	BB/9	K/9	GB%	BABIP	WHIP	ERA	FIP	FRA	WARP
2013	ONE	A-	21	0	2	0	8	8	19	15	0	9	21	4.3	9.9	60%	.288	1.26	1.89	2.46	3.22	0.4
2014	WMI	A	22	8	3	0	23	23	123	93	3	50	85	3.7	6.2	55%	.261	1.16	2.85	3.88	5.13	-0.3
2015	*CIN*	*MLB*	*23*	*4*	*7*	*0*	*18*	*18*	*84*	*87*	*10*	*44*	*50*	*4.8*	*5.4*	*49%*	*.305*	*1.56*	*5.24*	*5.53*	*5.70*	*-0.9*

Breakout: 0%   Improve: 0%   Collapse: 0%   Attrition: 0%   MLB: 0%   Comparables: *Charlie Leesman, Rafael Dolis, Bryan Morris*

It was a difficult year to stand out in West Michigan. Case in point: Crawford, the Tigers' 2013 first-rounder, was sixth in the Midwest League in ERA, but third on his own team. He was fifth in WHIP, and fourth among Whitecaps. You'd expect someone with his pedigree to be the ace of the staff, yet here we are. He had long stretches of struggles: In June and July he piled up more walks than strikeouts (25 to 22 in 48 innings). His starter ceiling is slowly trending downward, but now that he's out of Detroit, there may be less rush to convert him into a high-end reliever. (This is the problem with having a tire-fire bullpen on a win-now team. Every 22-year-old starting pitching prospect begins to look like a pretty good reliever, like how a hungry man in a cartoon sees everything as a giant ham.)

Johnny Cueto   RHP

Born: 2/15/86   Age: 29   Bats: R   Throws: R   Height: 5'11"   Weight: 215

YEAR	TEAM	LVL	AGE	W	L	SV	G	GS	IP	H	HR	BB	K	BB/9	K/9	GB%	BABIP	WHIP	ERA	FIP	FRA	WARP
2012	CIN	MLB	26	19	9	0	33	33	217	205	15	49	170	2.0	7.1	50%	.296	1.17	2.78	3.31	4.07	2.8
2013	CIN	MLB	27	5	2	0	11	11	60²	46	7	18	51	2.7	7.6	53%	.236	1.05	2.82	3.78	4.46	0.3
2014	CIN	MLB	28	20	9	0	34	34	243²	169	22	65	242	2.4	8.9	48%	.238	0.96	2.25	3.28	3.63	3.1
2015	*CIN*	*MLB*	*29*	*10*	*9*	*0*	*27*	*27*	*174¹*	*142*	*14*	*45*	*151*	*2.3*	*7.8*	*48%*	*.283*	*1.07*	*2.96*	*3.55*	*3.21*	*2.9*

Breakout: 13%   Improve: 36%   Collapse: 21%   Attrition: 6%   MLB: 92%   Comparables: *Josh Johnson, Brandon Webb, Adam Wainwright*

Cueto may have flown under the radar coming into last year because of the 2013 lat injury that cost him 117 games in three separate stints on the disabled list. This turned out to be loony: He had a 116 ERA+ through 2012 and finished fourth in that year's National League Cy Young voting and re-asserted his acehood last season, leading the league in innings and finishing second in ERA. The lat problem did not raise its head in terms of injury or pitch selection: Cueto's average fastball was a skosh above 94 mph and he did not shy away from throwing the cutter even though it's regarded in some circles as more taxing on the arm. His money pitch remains the changeup, though: Batters swung at it over half the time he threw it, whiffed on 35 percent of those swings and only hit .113 when they did make contact.

Anthony DeSclafani   RHP

Born: 4/18/90   Age: 25   Bats: R   Throws: R   Height: 6'1"   Weight: 190

YEAR	TEAM	LVL	AGE	W	L	SV	G	GS	IP	H	HR	BB	K	BB/9	K/9	GB%	BABIP	WHIP	ERA	FIP	FRA	WARP
2012	LNS	A	22	11	3	0	28	21	123	145	3	25	92	1.8	6.7	58%	.367	1.38	3.37	2.85	4.54	1.8
2013	JUP	A+	23	4	2	0	12	12	54	48	3	9	53	1.5	8.8	54%	.304	1.06	1.67	2.56	3.94	0.6
2013	JAX	AA	23	5	4	0	13	13	75	74	7	14	62	1.7	7.4	49%	.309	1.17	3.36	3.19	4.69	0.4
2014	JAX	AA	24	3	3	0	8	8	43	40	4	10	38	2.1	8.0	46%	.333	1.28	4.19	3.33	4.77	0.3
2014	NWO	AAA	24	3	3	0	12	11	59¹	48	2	21	59	3.2	8.9	44%	.284	1.16	3.49	3.41	3.68	1.2
2014	MIA	MLB	24	2	2	0	13	5	33	40	4	5	26	1.4	7.1	42%	.330	1.36	6.27	3.74	4.65	-0.1
2015	*CIN*	*MLB*	*25*	*6*	*8*	*0*	*23*	*23*	*114²*	*116*	*13*	*32*	*91*	*2.5*	*7.1*	*48%*	*.319*	*1.29*	*4.13*	*4.20*	*4.49*	*0.3*

Breakout: 23%   Improve: 44%   Collapse: 13%   Attrition: 33%   MLB: 73%   Comparables: *Dillon Gee, Jeff Locke, Brandon Workman*

DeSclafani has gone from a low-ceiling afterthought in the Jose Reyes-Mark Buehrle trade to, well, his ceiling still isn't very high, but at least he was the main piece in the Mat Latos deal. He showed enough promise to land on Marlins top prospect lists and performed solidly across three levels and the Arizona Fall League in 2014. His trek across the southern U.S. took him from Jacksonville to New Orleans and culminated in a short, intriguing trip to Miami before a victory lap in the Arizona Fall League. It was there that DeSclafani showed the best-case scenario: leveraging his fastball-slider combo, control and aggressive mentality to hold down a back-of-the-rotation starter slot. If nothing else, he can always fall back on a spot in the bullpen.

Jose Diaz   RHP

Born: 2/27/84   Age: 31   Bats: R   Throws: R   Height: 6'4"   Weight: 315

YEAR	TEAM	LVL	AGE	W	L	SV	G	GS	IP	H	HR	BB	K	BB/9	K/9	GB%	BABIP	WHIP	ERA	FIP	FRA	WARP
2012	IND	AAA	28	1	2	3	41	0	45	43	3	19	37	3.8	7.4	38%	.299	1.38	3.60	3.91	4.29	0.4
2013	LOU	AAA	29	3	4	13	44	0	54¹	35	5	21	60	3.5	9.9	51%	.231	1.03	1.66	3.41	3.79	0.8
2014	LOU	AAA	30	2	2	18	30	0	33¹	25	1	10	31	2.7	8.4	48%	.267	1.05	1.35	2.97	3.45	0.7
2014	CIN	MLB	30	0	1	0	36	0	34²	29	3	14	37	3.6	9.6	41%	.295	1.24	3.38	3.30	3.75	0.3
2015	*CIN*	*MLB*	*31*	*3*	*1*	*0*	*54*	*0*	*57*	*49*	*6*	*22*	*55*	*3.5*	*8.7*	*43%*	*.299*	*1.24*	*3.61*	*4.05*	*3.93*	*0.4*

Breakout: 5%   Improve: 11%   Collapse: 4%   Attrition: 4%   MLB: 14%   Comparables: *Fernando Cabrera, Jose Valdez, Tim Hamulack*

"Jumbo" Diaz would have made headlines in 2014 for finally debuting after 13 long years in the minor leagues in five different organizations even if he hadn't dropped 70 pounds in the offseason, weighing in at 278 in spring training. He's always thrown hard and his graduation to the PITCHf/x league substantiated minor-league reports: He averaged 98 mph with his fastballs in the majors. When Tony Cingrani's struggles piled on top of Sean Marshall's shoulder injury in June, Diaz was promoted and never looked back: He allowed more fly balls than he had in Triple-A, but his walk and strikeout numbers didn't take a hit. He's better against righties because of his fastball-slider combination; lefties knocked him around a little bit because his splitter lags behind in quality. He should have a straightforward shot at a middle relief, or even setup, role in 2015.

Amir Garrett   LHP

Born: 5/3/92   Age: 23   Bats: L   Throws: L   Height: 6'5"   Weight: 210

YEAR	TEAM	LVL	AGE	W	L	SV	G	GS	IP	H	HR	BB	K	BB/9	K/9	GB%	BABIP	WHIP	ERA	FIP	FRA	WARP
2013	DYT	A	21	1	3	0	8	8	34	40	4	16	15	4.2	4.0	40%	.305	1.65	6.88	5.57	6.87	-0.2
2014	DYT	A	22	7	8	0	27	27	133¹	115	11	51	127	3.4	8.6	50%	.282	1.25	3.64	3.87	5.15	0.1
2015	CIN	MLB	23	4	10	0	23	23	101²	107	13	52	63	4.6	5.5	48%	.306	1.57	5.49	5.50	5.97	-1.4

Breakout: 0%   Improve: 0%   Collapse: 0%   Attrition: 0%   MLB: 0%   Comparables: Ryan Cook, Evan Reed, Charlie Leesman

Garrett is perhaps best known for playing collegiate basketball at St. John's, but the young lefty is beginning to make a name for himself on the mound. He flirted with a no-hitter in June and scouts love his fastball-slider combination and quick arm; he could be a no. 3 starter if everything clicks and should at least be a reliever if only a few things click. Due to his extensive basketball background, though, he's still building the arm strength and consistency that most other pitchers develop as amateurs, so extra patience is advised. In particular, while Garrett is chronologically old for his level, and will likely remain so, he should be judged differently in this regard than the other exciting pitching prospects you're keeping an eye on.

Ismael Guillon   LHP

Born: 2/13/92   Age: 23   Bats: L   Throws: L   Height: 6'2"   Weight: 210

YEAR	TEAM	LVL	AGE	W	L	SV	G	GS	IP	H	HR	BB	K	BB/9	K/9	GB%	BABIP	WHIP	ERA	FIP	FRA	WARP
2012	DYT	A	20	2	0	0	4	4	24²	22	2	7	27	2.6	9.9	41%	.323	1.18	2.55	3.07	3.75	0.4
2013	DYT	A	21	7	8	0	27	26	121¹	95	14	95	134	7.0	9.9	29%	.275	1.57	4.75	5.00	5.47	1.0
2014	DYT	A	22	4	1	0	13	12	65¹	41	3	27	69	3.7	9.5	36%	.250	1.04	3.17	3.26	5.06	0.0
2014	BAK	A+	22	1	6	0	12	11	58¹	68	13	28	45	4.3	6.9	38%	.307	1.65	6.79	6.79	7.63	-0.2
2015	CIN	MLB	23	4	10	0	22	22	104	101	15	68	85	5.9	7.3	34%	.304	1.62	5.51	5.75	5.99	-1.5

Breakout: 0%   Improve: 0%   Collapse: 0%   Attrition: 0%   MLB: 0%   Comparables: Bryan Mitchell, Anthony Varvaro, Steve Johnson

Currently being groomed as a starter, Guillon features promising, though inconsistent, stuff. His fastball can touch 95 mph, but scouts are most excited about his changeup, which allows him to be effective against righties and allows us to see a potential starter. He's been on the 40-man roster for two years already, so 2015 should be his third year of optional assignment; he's going to have to move quickly. This obviously raises the possibility of a transition to the bullpen, where he can let his stuff fly in short stints and perhaps have enough success to justify a call to the majors. Changeup or not, that may be for the best anyway given his continuing struggles with control. If he does make it to Cincinnati as a reliever, keep an eye on his splits and his usage: He needs to tighten up his slider to have a good second pitch against lefties, so he'd be ill-served by slotting into a specialist role.

J.J. Hoover   RHP

Born: 8/13/87   Age: 27   Bats: R   Throws: R   Height: 6'3"   Weight: 230

YEAR	TEAM	LVL	AGE	W	L	SV	G	GS	IP	H	HR	BB	K	BB/9	K/9	GB%	BABIP	WHIP	ERA	FIP	FRA	WARP
2012	LOU	AAA	24	4	0	13	30	0	37	15	1	12	55	2.9	13.4	33%	.203	0.73	1.22	1.59	2.66	0.9
2012	CIN	MLB	24	1	0	1	28	0	30²	17	2	13	31	3.8	9.1	27%	.195	0.98	2.05	3.23	3.32	0.5
2013	CIN	MLB	25	5	5	3	69	0	66	47	6	26	67	3.5	9.1	33%	.244	1.11	2.86	3.44	4.48	0.3
2014	CIN	MLB	26	1	10	0	54	0	62²	56	13	31	75	4.5	10.8	29%	.277	1.39	4.88	4.94	5.18	-0.3
2015	CIN	MLB	27	3	2	1	46	3	62	49	6	25	65	3.6	9.5	34%	.287	1.18	3.38	3.79	3.67	0.6

Breakout: 36%   Improve: 61%   Collapse: 12%   Attrition: 19%   MLB: 82%   Comparables: Scott Elbert, Andrew Bailey, Bobby Parnell

Hoover found success in 2012-2013 with a mid-90s fastball, an overpowering curve and a mystifying lack of homers given an exceedingly low groundball rate. Hoover found trouble in 2014 with a mid-90s fastball, an overpowering curve and a homer every five innings. He pitches in a band-box, sure, but five of his homers allowed came in 26 road innings, so he can't just chalk it up to the Great American Tater Park. In any event, he's still, as of this writing, a Red, so he's going to have to deal with that park for 30 more innings this year unless Bryan Price gets creative with his usage. (He pitched 10 more frames at home than on the road in 2014.) Hoover also got pasted by lefties last year after two seasons of reverse splits; he's probably not suddenly a ROOGY, but throw those issues into the pot with the homer troubles, the poor walk rate and the August demotion to the minors, spice liberally with "never trust a reliever" and you've got yourself a nice stew of "watch out, he might be done."

Nick Howard   RHP

Born: 4/6/93   Age: 22   Bats: R   Throws: R   Height: 6'3"   Weight: 215

YEAR	TEAM	LVL	AGE	W	L	SV	G	GS	IP	H	HR	BB	K	BB/9	K/9	GB%	BABIP	WHIP	ERA	FIP	FRA	WARP
2014	DYT	A	21	2	1	0	11	5	33²	28	4	11	23	2.9	6.1	53%	.274	1.16	3.74	4.73	5.67	-0.3
2015	CIN	MLB	22	1	3	0	9	6	34²	38	5	17	19	4.3	4.8	46%	.310	1.59	5.57	5.87	6.06	-0.5

Breakout: 0%   Improve: 0%   Collapse: 0%   Attrition: 0%   MLB: 0%   Comparables: Maikel Cleto, Ivan Nova, T.J. McFarland

A first-round pick in the 2014 draft, Howard excelled as a closer in college but the Reds believe he can start. His ceiling is probably no higher than mid-rotation, but a workhorse no. 3 with a low-90s fastball and a swing-and-miss slider is nothing to sneeze at. Some scouts suggest that serious mechanical changes are in order for Howard to develop the consistency to start. It would be easier to trust that he can make those adjustments and reach his potential if not for his completely untrustworthy two-first-names status. Compounding the problem, he pitched for the Virginia Cavaliers, who are also known as the "Wahoos" ... even though that has absolutely nothing to do with a cavalier. A cavalier is either an English swashbuckler or a reliable Chevy. A wahoo is a tropical fish. All of this is very upsetting.

Mike Leake   RHP

Born: 11/12/87   Age: 27   Bats: R   Throws: R   Height: 5'10"   Weight: 190

YEAR	TEAM	LVL	AGE	W	L	SV	G	GS	IP	H	HR	BB	K	BB/9	K/9	GB%	BABIP	WHIP	ERA	FIP	FRA	WARP
2012	CIN	MLB	24	8	9	0	30	30	179	201	26	41	116	2.1	5.8	50%	.306	1.35	4.58	4.47	5.01	1.6
2013	CIN	MLB	25	14	7	0	31	31	192¹	193	21	48	122	2.2	5.7	50%	.285	1.25	3.37	4.01	4.64	0.9
2014	CIN	MLB	26	11	13	0	33	33	214¹	217	23	50	164	2.1	6.9	55%	.298	1.25	3.70	3.85	4.73	0.9
2015	CIN	MLB	27	9	12	0	29	29	180²	177	21	41	131	2.1	6.5	50%	.305	1.21	4.00	4.20	4.35	0.4

Breakout: 25%   Improve: 58%   Collapse: 21%   Attrition: 17%   MLB: 96%   Comparables: Wei-Yin Chen, Ben Sheets, Scott Olsen

Despite a lack of natural downward plane, Leake pushed himself into the upper reaches of the worm-slaying leaderboards last year: Among pitchers with at least 180 innings, Leake finished ninth in groundball rate, and he now throws his sinker nearly half the time. He also amped up the whiffs on his slider, inducing more whiffs per swing while keeping batters' swing rate the same; this helped result in the jump you see above from a well-be-low-average strikeout rate to one only a little below average. Add all that to durability and you've got a solid no. 3 or 4 starter. Brandon McCarthy with health, you might say, or Jason Vargas with groundballs; both of those guys got four-year deals in free agency.

Sam LeCure   RHP

Born: 5/4/84   Age: 31   Bats: R   Throws: R   Height: 6'0"   Weight: 205

YEAR	TEAM	LVL	AGE	W	L	SV	G	GS	IP	H	HR	BB	K	BB/9	K/9	GB%	BABIP	WHIP	ERA	FIP	FRA	WARP
2012	CIN	MLB	28	3	3	0	48	0	57¹	46	3	23	61	3.6	9.6	48%	.289	1.20	3.14	2.94	3.41	1.1
2013	CIN	MLB	29	2	1	1	63	0	61	50	4	24	66	3.5	9.7	44%	.295	1.21	2.66	2.94	3.07	0.9
2014	CIN	MLB	30	1	4	0	62	0	56²	62	6	24	48	3.8	7.6	45%	.329	1.52	3.81	4.21	4.00	0.2
2015	CIN	MLB	31	3	1	0	49	0	54¹	46	5	19	51	3.2	8.5	47%	.301	1.49	3.49	3.80	3.80	0.4

Breakout: 24%   Improve: 37%   Collapse: 21%   Attrition: 22%   MLB: 71%   Comparables: *Alfredo Aceves, Justin Miller, Matt Belisle*

After LeCure pitched just like heaven in 2013, many thought he could compete for a back-end bullpen role. The walk rate held steady last year, but, as he lost velocity, his strikeout rate declined to a wrong number. He's always handled lefties well thanks to a good curveball, but one good pitch is never enough in the big leagues unless it's Marianoesque. "Why can't I be you," LeCure probably wondered as he watched righties pound his diminished stuff for a sky-high .333/.384/.468 line. Big boys don't cry about turns of fortune in the majors, though, and LeCure will surely just say yes to a middle-relief role in 2015, hoping the curve continues to act as a lullaby to lefty hitters.

Ben Lively   RHP

Born: 3/5/92   Age: 23   Bats: R   Throws: R   Height: 6'4"   Weight: 190

YEAR	TEAM	LVL	AGE	W	L	SV	G	GS	IP	H	HR	BB	K	BB/9	K/9	GB%	BABIP	WHIP	ERA	FIP	FRA	WARP
2014	BAK	A+	22	10	1	0	13	13	79	57	6	16	95	1.8	10.8	37%	.277	0.92	2.28	2.97	3.10	2.7
2014	PEN	AA	22	3	6	0	13	13	72	60	7	36	76	4.5	9.5	37%	.290	1.33	3.88	4.01	4.19	1.2
2015	CIN	MLB	23	6	8	0	22	22	110²	95	12	44	109	3.6	8.9	39%	.301	1.26	3.69	4.08	4.01	0.9

Breakout: 20%   Improve: 29%   Collapse: 4%   Attrition: 23%   MLB: 40%   Comparables: *Matt Barnes, Matt Harvey, Jake McGee*

Lively burst onto the prospect radar in 2014 with his dream statistical performance in the very unforgiving Cal League. That extreme success caused scouts to perk up, wondering what allowed him to dominate. Turns out Lively features a low-90s fastball and a trio of off-speed pitches, with his slider the best of the bunch, though even that is only flashing above-average potential at the moment. His overall profile is based on command and deception rather than stuff. Some believe he can make all this work as a back-end starter, but one scout questioned his ability to consistently perform in the rotation at the highest level, saying he had "reliever mechanics" and doubting that his secondaries would fool left-handers. Don't take one scouting report as a death knell, but do take this as a reminder not to scout by stats alone. Of course, even if you made that mistake, you'd note the Double-A performance and, in particular, the more-than-double walk rate.

Michael Lorenzen   RHP

Born: 1/4/92   Age: 23   Bats: R   Throws: R   Height: 6'3"   Weight: 195

YEAR	TEAM	LVL	AGE	W	L	SV	G	GS	IP	H	HR	BB	K	BB/9	K/9	GB%	BABIP	WHIP	ERA	FIP	FRA	WARP
2014	PEN	AA	22	4	6	0	24	24	120²	112	9	44	84	3.3	6.3	53%	.285	1.29	3.13	4.01	5.05	1.0
2015	CIN	MLB	23	4	6	1	27	15	84²	85	10	35	56	3.7	6.0	49%	.304	1.42	4.80	4.99	5.21	-0.5

Breakout: 0%   Improve: 0%   Collapse: 0%   Attrition: 0%   MLB: 0%   Comparables: *John Gast, Lance Broadway, Chaz Roe*

Lorenzen was a sandwich-round pick in 2013 out of Cal State Fullerton who many had pegged for the bullpen before he showed a nice three-pitch mix early last year. The right-hander could develop into a mid-rotation starter with a mid-90s fastball, a biting slider and a developing changeup that flashed average. His stuff plays up in short bursts, so the downside might still be a dominant reliever. Along with the same things every minor-league pitcher has to work on (command, sharpening his secondaries), Lorenzen must build endurance: Scouts reported that his stuff declined in the late innings and that he was worn out as the summer came to a close. He's skinny, but he's not Chris Sale, and plenty of players with his build wind up perfectly durable big-league starters. The Reds have had a pitching staff of titans in recent years (think Latos, Simon, Broxton, Marshall, Ondrusek, Diaz) but they also employ Johnny Cueto and Mike Leake, so they know as well as anyone that there's more than one way to pitch a baseball.

Carlos Marmol   RHP

Born: 10/14/82   Age: 32   Bats: R   Throws: R   Height: 6'1"   Weight: 235

YEAR	TEAM	LVL	AGE	W	L	SV	G	GS	IP	H	HR	BB	K	BB/9	K/9	GB%	BABIP	WHIP	ERA	FIP	FRA	WARP
2012	CHN	MLB	29	3	3	20	61	0	55¹	40	4	45	72	7.3	11.7	41%	.290	1.54	3.42	4.02	4.12	0.5
2013	CHN	MLB	30	2	4	2	31	0	27²	26	6	21	32	6.8	10.4	42%	.299	1.70	5.86	6.13	6.85	-0.5
2013	LAN	MLB	30	0	0	0	21	0	21¹	14	1	19	27	8.0	11.4	43%	.271	1.55	2.53	3.91	4.08	0.2
2014	MIA	MLB	31	0	3	0	15	0	13¹	16	3	10	14	6.8	9.4	46%	.342	1.95	8.10	6.40	7.91	-0.6
2015	CIN	MLB	32	2	1	1	39	0	36²	24	3	23	51	5.6	12.6	40%	.304	1.29	3.28	3.64	3.56	0.4

Breakout: 22%   Improve: 44%   Collapse: 22%   Attrition: 9%   MLB: 85%   Comparables: *Brad Lidge, Michael Gonzalez, Damaso Marte*

It may finally be the end for Marmol. He broke camp with the Marlins and the league promptly broke him. The Reds tossed a rope into the abyss and offered him a minor-league deal so he could extricate himself from the darkness, but after three appearances, six walks and a 7.36 ERA, Cincinnati declared "enough" and cut bait. If he is done, Marmol concludes his career with the highest walk rate (6.2 BB/9) of any pitcher with at least 500 innings since 1995 and the sixth-highest walk rate in the history of baseball. Someone drop some crackers down there, at least.

Logan Ondrusek   RHP

Born: 2/13/85   Age: 30   Bats: R   Throws: R   Height: 6'8"   Weight: 230

YEAR	TEAM	LVL	AGE	W	L	SV	G	GS	IP	H	HR	BB	K	BB/9	K/9	GB%	BABIP	WHIP	ERA	FIP	FRA	WARP
2012	CIN	MLB	27	5	2	2	63	0	54²	51	8	31	39	5.1	6.4	44%	.265	1.50	3.46	5.48	5.59	-0.4
2013	CIN	MLB	28	3	1	0	52	0	55	53	8	16	53	2.6	8.7	48%	.290	1.25	4.09	3.91	4.46	0.2
2014	CIN	MLB	29	3	3	0	40	0	41	50	5	16	42	3.5	9.2	45%	.360	1.61	5.49	3.88	4.91	-0.3
2015	CIN	MLB	30	2	1	1	45	0	43¹	39	5	16	37	3.3	7.6	47%	.298	1.27	3.76	4.32	4.08	0.2

Breakout: 27%   Improve: 48%   Collapse: 13%   Attrition: 13%   MLB: 69%   *Comparables:*   *Chris Ray, Juan Gutierrez, Brandon League*

The bigger they are, the harder they fall. Ondrusek found himself non-tendered this winter by the Reds after giving up hit upon hit upon hit and missing a month in the second half with a shoulder strain in 2014. He's a five-pitch reliever with a fastball in the mid-90s, which means he should be five times as good as Kenley Jansen or Sean Doolittle, one-pitch relievers who throw in the mid-90s. Math is hard. So is pitching.

Manny Parra   LHP

Born: 10/30/82   Age: 32   Bats: L   Throws: L   Height: 6'3"   Weight: 215

YEAR	TEAM	LVL	AGE	W	L	SV	G	GS	IP	H	HR	BB	K	BB/9	K/9	GB%	BABIP	WHIP	ERA	FIP	FRA	WARP
2012	MIL	MLB	29	2	3	0	62	0	58²	62	3	35	61	5.4	9.4	49%	.345	1.65	5.06	3.66	3.59	1.0
2013	CIN	MLB	30	2	3	0	57	0	46	40	5	15	56	2.9	11.0	46%	.315	1.20	3.33	3.04	3.74	0.5
2014	CIN	MLB	31	0	3	1	53	0	36²	39	4	18	34	4.4	8.3	54%	.327	1.55	4.66	4.22	4.99	-0.2
2015	*CIN*	*MLB*	*32*	*2*	*1*	*0*	*44*	*0*	*36²*	*33*	*4*	*16*	*37*	*3.8*	*9.1*	*48%*	*.320*	*1.33*	*3.94*	*4.13*	*4.28*	*0.1*

Breakout: 27%   Improve: 48%   Collapse: 16%   Attrition: 5%   MLB: 81%   *Comparables:*   *Dennys Reyes, Juan Cruz, Kevin Gregg*

Parra has always possessed legitimate swing-and-miss stuff from the left side. His 94 mph fastball, low-80s slider and devastating splitter have combined to produce lofty strikeout rates, but his inability to limit free passes in Milwaukee ultimately wore out his welcome. His walk rate declined to 8 percent in his inaugural season with the Reds but jumped back to his career 11 percent rate in 2014. Guess what happened to his ERA. Or don't guess: It's in the box up there ↑↑↑. Now, you'd think that Parra's leverage index would have gone ↓↓↓ as a result, but the trend line on the leverage of the situations he entered was actually slightly *positive*. Don't roar your terrible roars and gnash your terrible teeth just yet, Reds fans: Aroldis Chapman, Sean Marshall, Jonathan Broxton, Trevor Bell, Tony Cingrani and Logan Ondrusek, bullpenners one and all, missed time on the disabled list last year. Bryan Price could only work with what he had.

Robert Stephenson   RHP

Born: 2/24/93   Age: 22   Bats: R   Throws: R   Height: 6'3"   Weight: 195

YEAR	TEAM	LVL	AGE	W	L	SV	G	GS	IP	H	HR	BB	K	BB/9	K/9	GB%	BABIP	WHIP	ERA	FIP	FRA	WARP
2012	DYT	A	19	2	4	0	8	8	34¹	32	4	15	35	3.9	9.2	40%	.301	1.37	4.19	4.40	5.55	0.0
2013	DYT	A	20	5	3	0	14	14	77	56	5	20	96	2.3	11.2	51%	.279	0.99	2.57	2.59	4.12	1.4
2013	BAK	A+	20	2	2	0	4	4	20²	19	3	2	22	0.9	9.6	39%	.286	1.02	3.05	3.82	3.97	0.5
2013	PEN	AA	20	0	2	0	4	4	16²	17	2	13	18	7.0	9.7	34%	.357	1.80	4.86	4.65	4.20	0.1
2014	PEN	AA	21	7	10	0	27	26	136²	114	18	74	140	4.9	9.2	38%	.264	1.38	4.74	4.58	5.43	0.3
2015	*CIN*	*MLB*	*22*	*6*	*9*	*0*	*23*	*23*	*114²*	*103*	*15*	*53*	*107*	*4.1*	*8.4*	*41%*	*.299*	*1.36*	*4.48*	*4.70*	*4.87*	*-0.2*

Breakout: 0%   Improve: 0%   Collapse: 0%   Attrition: 0%   MLB: 0%   *Comparables:*   *Yordano Ventura, Robbie Ray, Jake Odorizzi*

Some fans have begun to jump ship on Stephenson. Scouts say he has some of the best stuff in the minors, but then he puts up a 4.74 ERA in Double-A. There was plenty of "future reliever" talk even before that ugly result. Stephenson touches triple digits with the fastball and backs it up with a nasty curve. The changeup flashes above-average potential, but it's a project. Still, he's a future big leaguer: With his stuff and makeup, Stephenson's upside is no. 2 starter with a floor of shutdown late-innings relief. (Assuming health, as always.) The struggles at Double-A are worrisome, but he's only 22, so he won't be behind any eight-balls in terms of developmental expectations even if he has to spend all of 2015 repeating the level.

Nick Travieso   RHP

Born: 1/31/94   Age: 21   Bats: R   Throws: R   Height: 6'2"   Weight: 215

YEAR	TEAM	LVL	AGE	W	L	SV	G	GS	IP	H	HR	BB	K	BB/9	K/9	GB%	BABIP	WHIP	ERA	FIP	FRA	WARP
2013	DYT	A	19	7	4	0	17	17	81²	83	7	27	61	3.0	6.7	40%	.305	1.35	4.63	4.10	5.15	0.9
2014	DYT	A	20	14	5	0	26	26	142²	123	10	44	114	2.8	7.2	50%	.272	1.17	3.03	3.93	5.04	-0.4
2015	*CIN*	*MLB*	*21*	*5*	*10*	*0*	*23*	*23*	*111²*	*119*	*15*	*50*	*62*	*4.0*	*5.0*	*42%*	*.302*	*1.51*	*5.30*	*5.56*	*5.77*	*-1.3*

Breakout: 0%   Improve: 0%   Collapse: 0%   Attrition: 0%   MLB: 0%   *Comparables:*   *Brett Marshall, T.J. House, Mike Foltynewicz*

In his second go at the Midwest League, Travieso did what you're supposed to do on a repeat assignment: He pitched better. In particular, he surrendered only 11 runs in his final nine starts. The right-hander sits at 88 to 92 mph with his fastball and backs it up with an improving slider. His changeup is nothing special but could be average down the road. There's a significant risk that Travieso's secondary pitches never develop, as there is with every young pitcher, but his thick build also leads to worries that he'll wind up carrying bad weight as he ages further from the weird miracle metabolism gifted to teenage boys. He could be a mid-rotation starter, but don't bet your house on it.

Lineouts

Hitters

NAME	POS	TEAM	LVL	AGE	PA	R	2B	3B	HR	RBI	BB	K	SB	CS	AVG/OBP/SLG	TAv	BABIP	BRR	FRAA	WARP
Ramon Cabrera	C	ALT	AA	24	49	5	5	0	1	5	3	6	0	1	.239/.286/.413	.269	.256	-1.8	C(11): -0.2	0.0
	C	ERI	AA	24	431	42	17	0	5	47	33	37	1	0	.277/.329/.358	.250	.292	-1.1	C(73): -0.8	0.6
Ivan De Jesus	SS	NOR	AAA	27	469	54	19	5	5	56	50	84	2	1	.282/.358/.389	.259	.340	-2.9	SS(98): -7.4, 2B(8): -0.3	0.7
Juan Duran	RF	PEN	AA	22	364	40	18	3	17	51	23	130	1	1	.243/.297/.464	.274	.340	0.3	RF(72): -0.8, LF(13): 1.4	1.3
Sebastian Elizalde	LF	DYT	A	22	229	29	12	1	7	34	41	48	9	10	.311/.439/.503	.353	.385	-0.4	LF(20): -1.1, 1B(18): -0.5	2.4
	LF	BAK	A+	22	267	35	17	1	9	37	19	44	10	7	.272/.330/.461	.266	.297	-0.1	LF(41): 0.0, RF(18): 0.9	0.9
Donald Lutz	LF	PEN	AA	25	97	16	7	2	6	16	7	17	1	0	.360/.412/.685	.382	.394	1.0	LF(22): 2.0	1.7
	LF	LOU	AAA	25	218	26	9	2	6	33	17	68	4	0	.236/.307/.395	.238	.325	-0.4	LF(31): -2.1, 1B(15): 1.4	0.0
	1B	CIN	MLB	25	54	2	4	0	0	1	3	19	0	0	.176/.222/.255	.183	.281	-0.1	1B(6): -0.1, LF(4): -0.1	-0.1
Seth Mejias-Brean	3B	BAK	A+	23	313	56	8	3	11	45	44	49	7	1	.300/.396/.476	.296	.330	2.1	3B(64): 4.5, 3B(4): 4.5	2.8
	3B	PEN	AA	23	264	23	7	2	3	22	32	50	1	4	.235/.333/.323	.246	.287	-1.6	3B(63): -0.7	0.3
Brayan Pena	1B	CIN	MLB	32	372	23	18	1	5	26	20	42	2	3	.253/.291/.353	.241	.273	-6.5	1B(53): -0.0, C(46): -0.1	-0.4
Josh Satin	3B	LVG	AAA	29	440	50	27	1	9	49	61	79	1	3	.289/.386/.439	.276	.341	-1.7	3B(59): 5.5, 1B(25): 0.0	2.1
	1B	NYN	MLB	29	43	2	2	0	0	3	6	14	0	0	.086/.256/.143	.151	.143	-0.8	1B(8): -0.2, 3B(1): 0.0	-0.6
Kyle Skipworth	C	NWO	AAA	24	227	24	7	1	10	30	16	75	1	2	.216/.292/.407	.241	.286	1.9	C(60): 0.8	0.6
Neftali Soto	3B	LOU	AAA	25	303	27	23	0	2	34	21	41	0	0	.302/.350/.406	.250	.345	-4.3	3B(37): 0.5, 1B(35): 0.1	-0.1
	1B	CIN	MLB	25	31	1	1	0	0	1	0	8	1	0	.100/.097/.133	.100	.130	0.2	1B(7): -0.1, 3B(2): -0.1	-0.5
Kyle Waldrop	RF	BAK	A+	22	289	54	20	1	6	32	22	56	11	2	.359/.409/.516	.317	.432	0.7	RF(44): -2.7, LF(8): -0.3	2.1
	RF	PEN	AA	22	252	27	17	3	8	35	17	44	3	4	.315/.359/.517	.309	.357	-0.5	RF(30): -0.6, LF(29): 0.5	2.1

Switch-hitting catcher **Ramon Cabrera** returned to his original organization after an August waiver claim. He's little more than ballast, but you can't spell ballast without balla. ❖ The last time the Red Sox acquired **Ivan De Jesus** in a midseason trade, they won the World Series the following year. That'd be a silly motive to explain why they swapped for him again in August, but considering they let him leave for Cincinnati immediately after the season, it's on you to top it. ❖ **Juan Duran** is a 6-foot-7 monster with raw power for days and serious issues making contact: His career minor-league strikeout rate is 10 percentage points higher than Richie Sexson's major-league rate. ❖ **Sebastian Elizalde** had a very good all-around debut and reached High-A after signing out of Mexico; scouts worry that he'll be exploited by left-handed pitching, especially on the outer half. ❖ **Donald Lutz** has a left field or first base defensive profile, but he doesn't hit for average and his power hasn't manifested against high-level pitching. Let's focus on the positive: He hit four triples in 2014. Get it? ❖ Young Cuban prospects often draw lofty parallels, but 21-year-old **Reydel Medina** began his professional career in Rookie ball and hit .244/.265/.449 with a 32 percent strikeout rate; forget Yoenis Cespedes and Yasiel Puig, Medina may not even be the next Leslie Anderson. ❖ Although **Seth Mejias-Brean** is one of the more polished hitters in the Reds' system and has dominated the lower levels, questions about his ability to handle advanced pitching linger after he struggled in his first taste of Double-A. ❖ **Brayan Pena**'s switch-hitting offense is sufficient for backup catching; he got a Rolex from Max Scherzer after the latter won the Cy Young Award in 2013. These statements aren't really related. ❖ "Organizational bat" is a bitter pill to swallow, but **Josh Satin** just doesn't have the power to play first base or the defensive skills to get by elsewhere. ❖ After **Kyle Skipworth** was taken with the sixth overall pick in 2008, his bat—much like the market for Crystal Pepsi—never developed like the suits expected. ❖ **Neftali Soto** is limited to first base and has a .410 career slugging percentage at Triple-A. That's Daric Barton, except Barton has a 60-point on-base percentage edge and a *very* slick glove, which is to say that Soto isn't a big leaguer unless 17 things go wrong. ❖ **Taylor Sparks** has a good power-speed combination at third base, but the 2014 second-rounder is far too aggressive and will need time to develop his approach. ❖ **Mitch Trees** is a high school catcher out of Illinois who the Reds picked in the 11th round and signed away from a Louisville commitment; reports on his pop times and arm are off the charts, but his bat ... well, he went in the 11th round, not the first. ❖ **Chadwick Tromp** is not a lacrosse player from Massachusetts; he's an Aruban catcher who hit .323/.354/.505 with three homers in 25 games in the Arizona League before receiving a five-game promotion to Low-A Dayton. ❖ **Kyle Waldrop** repeated the Cal League to start 2014, had a batting average–driven .925 OPS, got promoted to Double-A, and kept hitting. He has some power, but he's going to have to hit for a high average to keep his OBP acceptable, and his left field–only profile means the bar for "acceptable" is quite high.

Pitchers

NAME	TEAM	LVL	AGE	W	L	SV	G	GS	IP	H	HR	BB	K	BB/9	K/9	GB%	BABIP	WHIP	ERA	FIP	FRA	WARP
Jose Cisnero	OKL	AAA	25	0	0	0	6	0	11	5	1	4	18	3.3	14.7	41%	.190	0.82	2.45	2.70	3.32	0.3
	HOU	MLB	25	0	0	0	5	0	4²	8	0	4	5	7.7	9.6	31%	.500	2.57	9.64	3.59	5.76	-0.1
Daniel Corcino	PEN	AA	23	10	11	0	26	25	143²	123	16	70	113	4.4	7.1	33%	.258	1.34	4.13	4.86	5.35	0.5
	CIN	MLB	23	0	2	0	5	3	18²	13	2	10	15	4.8	7.2	32%	.212	1.23	4.34	4.66	5.36	0.0
Ryan Dennick	LOU	AAA	27	4	0	3	57	0	49²	42	0	18	39	3.3	7.1	55%	.288	1.21	2.36	2.93	4.37	0.6
	CIN	MLB	27	0	0	0	8	0	4²	7	2	4	3	7.7	5.8	28%	.312	2.36	11.57	9.96	12.20	-0.4
Wilmer Font	FRI	AA	24	2	1	3	29	0	31	25	2	17	31	4.9	9.0	39%	.271	1.35	3.48	3.70	3.85	0.4
David Holmberg	LOU	AAA	22	2	6	0	18	18	92²	119	4	33	56	3.2	5.4	41%	.353	1.64	4.66	3.81	4.82	0.8
	CIN	MLB	22	2	2	0	7	5	30	27	8	16	18	4.8	5.4	40%	.213	1.43	4.80	7.57	7.82	-0.7
Matt Magill	ABQ	AAA	24	7	6	0	36	12	84²	98	8	59	70	6.3	7.4	46%	.298	1.64	5.21	5.58	6.07	0.5
Sean Marshall	CIN	MLB	31	0	0	0	15	0	14	23	1	12	14	7.7	9.0	58%	.431	2.50	7.71	5.03	4.45	-0.2
Jon Moscot	PEN	AA	22	7	10	0	25	25	149¹	145	11	43	111	2.6	6.7	38%	.291	1.26	3.13	3.68	4.41	1.1
	LOU	AAA	22	1	1	0	3	3	17¹	15	5	7	9	3.6	4.7	22%	.189	1.27	5.71	7.28	7.26	-0.3
Curtis Partch	LOU	AAA	27	4	1	6	41	2	47¹	46	3	25	54	4.8	10.3	45%	.336	1.50	4.75	3.74	3.84	0.8
	CIN	MLB	27	1	0	0	6	0	7	2	0	7	6	9.0	7.7	47%	.118	1.29	0.00	4.39	3.19	0.1
Chad Rogers	LOU	AAA	24	2	0	1	35	0	53	58	4	37	34	6.3	5.8	36%	.291	1.79	4.08	6.11	6.98	-1.0
Salvatore Romano	DYT	A	20	8	11	0	28	28	148²	169	9	42	128	2.5	7.7	54%	.352	1.42	4.12	3.56	4.72	0.7
Jackson Stephens	DYT	A	20	2	7	0	14	14	67¹	70	8	22	54	2.9	7.2	54%	.307	1.37	4.81	4.72	5.61	-0.2
Pedro Villarreal	LOU	AAA	26	6	2	2	42	2	56¹	57	5	13	50	2.1	8.0	40%	.313	1.24	3.20	3.59	4.42	0.7
	CIN	MLB	26	0	2	0	12	0	14²	11	1	7	12	4.3	7.4	36%	.244	1.23	4.30	3.99	3.60	0.1
Daniel Wright	DYT	A	23	3	2	0	10	7	43²	36	5	7	42	1.4	8.7	52%	.272	0.98	2.06	3.74	4.56	0.0
	BAK	A+	23	11	5	0	18	18	108²	105	15	15	99	1.2	8.2	50%	.289	1.10	4.14	4.35	4.95	1.8

It had been a long road, but fastball specialist **Jose Cisnero** finally appeared to be establishing himself in Houston's bullpen as the 2014 calendar flipped to May, but then his elbow perished, he had Tommy John surgery and he lost his roster spot in November. Now he's back to that damn road. ❖ **Jacob Constante** is a 6-foot-4 Dominican lefty who signed for $730,000 in 2012; he sits in the low 90s with his fastball and has a potentially above-average slider. ❖ **Daniel Corcino** is a sinker/slider pitcher who touches 90 on a good day, walks too many hitters and doesn't miss bats. Other than that, Mrs. Lincoln ... ❖ **Ryan Dennick** is a lefty without overpowering stuff who cruised through Triple-A; if that sounds like a specialist reliever to you, hey, great minds think alike. ❖ **Wilmer Font** is a Venezuelan fireballer who looked like he was heading toward a role in the Rangers' bullpen in 2014 but ended up stalling out in Frisco before needing surgery for bone spurs in his elbow; he signed a minor-league deal with the Reds after being unceremoniously designated for assignment in October to make room for Alfredo Figaro. ❖ **David Holmberg** is a lefty who sits at 87 mph and has the home run rate to prove it. ❖ **Raisel Iglesias**, who signed last June, is a smallish Cuban right-hander with a low-to-mid-90s fastball and a variety of breaking balls, all of which he throws from a multitude of angles. The Reds think he's a starter, but other teams see a reliever; either way, he could see Cincinnati this summer. ❖ **Matt Magill** is a former top-10 prospect who has yet to learn how to control his solid-average stuff. He pitched in the Arizona Fall League and is making the time-honored transition to the bullpen. ❖ **Sean Marshall** suffered yet another injury in 2014, this time resulting in a shoulder debridement in June. Consistency is beautiful in all forms. ❖ **Jon Moscot** lacks a plus pitch and could be a back-end starter as soon as this year if everything goes perfectly; autocorrect really wants to call him "Mascot." ❖ Pitchers who can average over 95 mph on their fastball, like **Curtis Partch**, will receive ample opportunity to put it together on the mound; in two brief cups of coffee with the Reds, though, he had more walks (24) than strikeouts (22). ❖ **Chad Rogers** survived an attack by a bull shark in the Gulf of Mexico and still surfs there, so the big leagues won't scare him; maybe they should, though, because he hasn't missed bats in the minors. ❖ **Sal Romano** features a low-90s fastball, a big curve that flashes plus and the foundations of a changeup, which might congeal into a back-end starter. Or two-day-old pizza. Either one. ❖ **Jackson Stephens** repeated the Midwest League and saw incremental deterioration of all his relevant rates; he's only 21, but this isn't how low-minors do-overs are supposed to go. ❖ A third-rounder out of Southern Cal in the 2014 draft, **Wyatt Strahan** is a hard-throwing fastball-curve guy who should eventually end up in the bullpen. ❖ **Pedro Villareal** is a right-handed specialist who doesn't handle righties all that well. He's had brief cups of coffee the last three years, but they've been more Folgers at 10 p.m. than Doi Chaang Arabica on a lazy late-fall morning. ❖ **Daniel Wright** was a new-model 10th-rounder in 2013, a cheap ($10,000) sign who leaves cap room to throw at other picks, but with 184 strikeouts to 27 walks in 195 pro innings, he's outperforming expectations and should pitch at Double-A this year.

Manager

Bryan Price

YEAR	TEAM	W	L	Py-thag +/-	Avg PC	100+ P	120+ P	QS	BQS	REL	REL w Zero R	IBB	PH	PH Avg	PH HR	SB2	CS2	SB3	CS3	SAC Att	SAC%	POS SAC	Squeeze	Swing	In Play
2014	CIN	76	86	-3	97.5	74	2	103	2	428	337	33	219	.246	6	103	42	19	7	103	73.8%	38	1	309	77

Readers outside of Ohio might be amused to learn that Price—or "Not Dusty Baker," as some know him—oversaw a Reds team that led the NL in position-player sacrifices during his first year as manager. Okay, that's misleading; the Reds ranked first due to their personnel rather than any fascination with giving away outs. Billy Hamilton bunted a lot because the bunt is a weapon against the opposition when you're that fast, while Ramon Santiago, Skip Schumaker and Zack Cozart each bunted a few times because swinging away is a weapon against your own team when you're that bad.

In addition to the bunts, the main arguments against Baker in Cincinnati revolved around poor lineups and uninspired usage of Aroldis Chapman. (For all the criticisms about abusing pitchers and ignoring rookies, Baker didn't have problems with either during his Reds tenure.) Unsurprisingly, Price's approach to both strayed from his predecessor's. Price didn't have a Shin-Soo Choo to throw at the top of the order in 2014, so he placed Hamilton there and prayed the speed would eclipse the shaky on-base skills. The biggest difference was how Price used the second spot in the order. Whereas Baker parked Cozart, a no-hit shortstop, there for the purposes of bunting the runner over, Price gave turns to the likes of Joey Votto, Todd Frazier and Jay Bruce. Ultimately, Votto's injury and Bruce's underachieving season sabotaged an otherwise sensible arrangement.

As for Chapman, he made more multi-inning appearances and entered more games before the ninth inning, or with the Reds trailing, than he had in '13. None of the increases was by a large amount—usually one or two extra appearances, tops—but consider it a positive that Price was more aggressive with his best arm in a lost year than Baker was during a pennant chase.

CLEVELAND INDIANS

by Bryan Joiner

In just a slightly different universe, this essay is about how close the Cleveland Indians came to winning last year's World Series, and what they could do to put themselves over the top in 2015. In this slightly different universe, the Indians play the role of last year's Royals, finishing the year 90 feet from stardom, their fan base still holding its breath, waiting for the absolution that never came.

There's no reason to think the Indians *would* have done the same thing in the playoffs, given a few regular-season bounces here and a smidgen of good fortune there, but there's every reason, on the shores of Lake Erie, to dream it. Maybe Yan Gomes plays the role of Salvador Perez, singling home the winning run in the bottom of the 12th of the Wild Card game; maybe Lorenzo Cain is replaced by Carlos Santana, who terrorizes Orioles pitching in the ALCS; and maybe Michael Brantley brings them to the brink of immortality in Game Seven of the World Series with a near-four-bagger, only to be stranded on third by Gomes. (I am not bold enough to suggest Madison Bumgarner could have been beaten last year.)

The numbers tell us that this dream isn't so far-fetched. Baseball Prospectus' third-order winning percentage, which adjusts standings based on a team's underlying statistics and quality of opponents, rated the Indians at 82 wins last season to Kansas City's paltry 79. They were both lucky to finish where they did, but the Royals just got a bit luckier. Then they got hot and the rest is near-history that still resonates.

Back in reality, the Indians finished four games behind the Royals and didn't make it to the postseason party, forced to watch as their division rivals almost completed their Cinderella season. Their consolation prize was a Cy Young Award for ace Corey Kluber. It's a good one as far as consolation prizes go, but it's not what they want. New trophies are given out every year, but flags fly forever.

For Kansas City, their eventual World Series loss felt awfully close to a win. They wanted a championship, but championship relevance was a close second. Cleveland, the city and the franchise, might not have been so sanguine. The history to which Cleveland clings is of perpetual disappointment marked by high-profile failures illustrated by an anachronistic red-faced logo that is ostensibly, as the blogger Peter "Cleveland Frowns"

Pattakos wrote, "a portrait of great Indian ballplayer Louis Sockalexis, who logged 367 at-bats with the Cleveland team before ruining his career by jumping from a second-story window of a whorehouse." Pattakos has written about the "Curse of Chief Wahoo" affecting all Cleveland sports teams through sheer force of bad karma.

The distance between last year's Indians and the curse-breaking dream isn't great. It is as simple as getting in the tournament and hoping the one-game playoff launches you on a story-book path, be you Bucky Dent, the Indians of *Major League* or the 2014 Royals. In today's MLB, that's the goal: get to October. It is a low enough threshold to clear, in such a transparently chaotic environment, that the only real barrier is getting in the door. It's not about history. It's like life: It's about showing up.

If the "Curse of Chief Wahoo" exists, it is powerless before the randomness of the expanded Major League Baseball playoffs. In a world where you can easily imagine last year's team nearly going all the way, there is every reason to think that small improvements in the present reality could crush the curse once and for all.

✦ ✦ ✦

The Indians will return a very similar team to the one they fielded at the end of 2014. Kluber will anchor a young, exciting pitching staff, while the offense will nominally be led by Michael Brantley, who hit .327/.385/.506 in what likely will end up his career-best season.

The pitchers present the biggest reason for enthusiasm. The Indians were the only team that didn't start anyone age 30 or over last year, and they got younger midyear when they shipped 29-year-old Justin Masterson to St. Louis for minor-league outfielder James Ramsey. Heading into the season, then, the Indians' likely rotation consists of:

- Corey Kluber, 29, and has some stats
- Carlos Carrasco 28, also has some stats
- Danny Salazar, 25, wouldn't you know? Stats!
- Trevor Bauer, 24, not stats. Just kidding! Stats
- Gavin Floyd, 32, has stats, but is mainly notable for signing a free-agent contract in December that ruins the whole "under-30" theme

INDIANS PROSPECTUS
2014 W-L: 85-77, 3RD IN AL CENTRAL

Pythag	.511	13th	DER	.691	25th
RS/G	4.13	11th	B-Age	28.5	17th
RA/G	4.03	16th	P-Age	27.0	2nd
TAv	.261	11th	Salary	$83.1M	25th
BRR	4.05	8th	M$/MW	$1.9M	6th
TAv-P	.258	12th	DL Days	474	2nd
FIP	3.45	4th	$ on DL	18%	20th

Three-Year Park Factors

Runs	Runs/RH	Runs/LH	HR/RH	HR/LH
101	103	101	84	89

Top Hitter WARP	6.0	Michael Brantley
Top Pitcher WARP	6.0	Corey Kluber
Top Prospect		Francisco Lindor

You know about Kluber. Salazar and Bauer, as electric former prospects, have been making their way to full-time starter status for a while. Bauer has been a particularly sneaky post-hype sleeper, posting a 4.18 ERA in a full season at age 23. That's nothing to sneeze at in the American League. Floyd's a good-when-healthy type, and, as we know, those guys are never healthy, so it's good that Zach McAllister and T.J. House are a perfectly nice back-end combination who can step in when Floyd bails.

But Carrasco, the reliever-turned-no. 2 starter, is the most interesting player in the group. For years, he couldn't harness his obvious talent in the majors, but Cleveland stuck with him. Last April, the Indians finally tired of waiting and sent him to the bullpen after four starts. He says he learned how to relax, and when he returned to the rotation in August with the departure of Masterson, he was a revelation. Pitching exclusively out of the stretch, he used a new hybrid slider/splitter out-pitch that combined top decile swing, whiff and groundball rates to form a truly elite pitch to play off his 96 mph fastball. Carrasco pitched 78 innings (some in relief) after the All-Star break with a 1.72 ERA and more than six strikeouts for every walk. His numbers in this stretch matched Kluber's performance almost perfectly: The ace put up a 1.73 ERA after the All-Star break, with a 1.12 ERA in five starts down the stretch.

Carrasco also features a nasty sinker that doesn't fit well with Cleveland's Jason Kipnis/Lonnie Chisenhall infield defense, so his counting stats could tick upward, but he should still perform well within a range that's great for Cleveland. If he and Kluber can stay healthy and at least one of Salazar, Bauer, Floyd, McAllister or House works out, Cleveland should be sitting pretty. More than that and the sky's the limit.

That defense will still suffer Kipnis and Chisenhall, but it could improve this year through the efforts of 21-year-old Francisco Lindor, the crowning jewel of the Indians' minor-league system, who will be up to make Web Gems and sell jerseys this year. Lindor is a defensive wizard who might not see the majors until May, though Jose Ramirez is an able-gloved fill-in keeping the position warm until then. Lindor probably won't hit much, especially at first, but even if he doesn't, and even if Brantley regresses, the Indians can afford it: With two notable and expensive exceptions, their hitters are talented and/or entering their primes at reasonable prices. This is a situation you want.

The most compelling of these players is Gomes, who is signed cheaply through 2019 and won the 2014 Silver Slugger at catcher. He doesn't walk often and strikes out at a generous rate, but when he hits the ball, he hits it hard and hits it far. His career slugging percentage is .463, which is far better than it has to be for an everyday catcher, especially one who can actually catch. He was the team's defensive player of the year in 2013 and Kluber has said he "can't put a value" on Gomes's pitch-calling and framing. (Baseball Prospectus *has* put a number on his framing and agrees that he's above average.)

Kipnis had a disappointing age-27 season last year, but he has youth, talent and injury excuses on his side, so hope remains. Moving up the age ladder, the Tribe got 31-year-old outfielder Brandon Moss for second base prospect Joey Wendle in the Oakland A's juice-cleanse offseason. The left-handed Moss is likely a platoon player, and he's coming off October hip surgery, but he costs almost nothing. The real problems are Nick Swisher, 34, and Michael Bourn, 32, who are scheduled to make $28.5 million between them after posting a combined -0.6 WARP last year. That's bad, but the core of the team is such that any contribution whatsoever from the pair would be found money.

The pieces, in short, are there for Terry Francona, a man who seems to exist in full only at the ballpark, to oversee the overthrow of the "Curse of Chief Wahoo" just as he tossed off the yoke of the "Curse of the Bambino." That we can contemplate this outcome is a credit to the work of General Manager Chris Antonetti, who has built a team full of good-to-very-good players in their mid- to late-20s, signed at reasonable prices. He is betting on the value of the athletic prime.

It's a smart bet. There is no question that most baseball players hit their primes in their late 20s. It is the furthest thing from rocket science. If we have a large enough sample size on anything, it is that. Still, it's one thing to have a team with an average age in the fat middle of that prime; it's another to have most of your *core* players that age. (Far more important to have a prime third baseman than a prime middle reliever, after all.) If there's a way to add wins to a team returning the vast majority of its roster, it's to have a bunch of players in their prime, not likely to lose performance to aging, along with veterans poised for a bounce-back. These are your 2015 Indians. This is good. This is their time.

With Detroit's core largely *past* its prime and shedding players in an attempt to balance the budget while keeping the window open, more is at stake than just a Wild Card spot. Despite everything Kansas City did last year, the Indians should be considered favorites to topple the Tigers, maybe favorites outright. (Or at least co-favorites with the aggressive White Sox.) Of course, the AL Central isn't the ultimate goal for a city humiliated by its sports franchises: It doesn't mean a thing without the ring. For this team in this town at this time, there's only one thing left to do. ∎

—Bryan Joiner was born in Boston and lives in Brooklyn, where he's writing about sports when he's not "producing" the "news."

Player comments by Doug Thorburn, Mauricio Rubio and Baseball Prospectus Authors

Hitters

Jesus Aguilar   1B
Born: 6/30/90 Age: 25 Bats: R Throws: R Height: 6' 3" Weight: 250

YEAR	TEAM	LVL	AGE	PA	R	2B	3B	HR	RBI	BB	K	SB	CS	AVG/OBP/SLG	TAv	BABIP	BRR	FRAA	WARP
2012	CAR	A+	22	427	63	25	2	12	58	45	91	0	1	.277/.365/.454	.294	.333	-2.2	1B(104): 8.5	2.9
2012	AKR	AA	22	87	12	6	0	3	13	13	24	0	0	.292/.402/.500	.331	.391	-1.2	1B(13): 1.0	0.7
2013	AKR	AA	23	567	66	28	0	16	105	56	107	0	1	.275/.349/.427	.284	.316	-5.1	1B(128): -0.6	1.6
2014	COH	AAA	24	499	69	31	0	19	77	64	96	0	0	.304/.395/.511	.298	.350	-3.1	1B(82): 1.5, 3B(1): -0.1	2.5
2014	CLE	MLB	24	38	2	0	0	0	3	4	13	0	0	.121/.211/.121	.159	.190	-0.2	1B(12): 0.2, 3B(1): -0.0	-0.4
2015	CLE	MLB	25	250	26	11	0	7	29	22	62	0	0	.246/.316/.393	.268	.305	-0.5	1B 1, 3B -0	0.6

Breakout: 7%   Improve: 19%   Collapse: 8%   Attrition: 25%   MLB: 38%   Comparables: *Ryan Garko, Lars Anderson, Tommy Medica*

Having big raw power is well and good but being able to utilize it in games is a completely different issue. Aguilar has the pop, but it's all drawn from his natural strength; his bat looks slow and his hit tool is severely lacking. He was a September call-up and was overmatched by major-league pitching. You've heard the Triple-A First Baseman's Lament before: Aguilar's bat will have to carry him, but it doesn't look like he has enough in his skill set to turn his physical strength into baseball power.

Mike Aviles   3B
Born: 3/13/81 Age: 34 Bats: R Throws: R Height: 5' 10" Weight: 205

YEAR	TEAM	LVL	AGE	PA	R	2B	3B	HR	RBI	BB	K	SB	CS	AVG/OBP/SLG	TAv	BABIP	BRR	FRAA	WARP
2012	BOS	MLB	31	546	57	28	0	13	60	23	77	14	6	.250/.282/.381	.243	.269	3.5	SS(128): -1.0, 2B(2): -0.0	1.4
2013	CLE	MLB	32	394	54	15	0	9	46	15	41	8	5	.252/.282/.368	.241	.257	1.4	3B(56): -2.2, SS(46): 1.1	0.5
2014	CLE	MLB	33	374	38	16	1	5	39	13	49	14	5	.247/.273/.343	.231	.271	2.0	3B(36): 0.6, 2B(33): 2.3	0.1
2015	CLE	MLB	34	355	37	15	1	6	32	14	53	11	5	.250/.280/.360	.238	.272	1.4	SS 1, 3B -0	0.6

Breakout: 0%   Improve: 29%   Collapse: 15%   Attrition: 15%   MLB: 87%   Comparables: *Jack Wilson, Kazuo Matsui, Freddy Sanchez*

Say hello to a HACKING MASS All-Star. Over the past four seasons, Aviles has posted an aggregate on-base percentage of .281 across more than 1,600 plate appearances, and the bat doesn't figure to improve much as the 34-year-old slips further into the decline phase of his career. His defensive versatility is handy off the bench or to cover for injury, but having him penciled into the starting lineup 100 times per year dooms his bat to overexposure. Aviles' offensive stylings are like the hard mattresses and inadequate pillows at Motel 6: Predictability only goes so far.

Michael Bourn   CF
Born: 12/27/82 Age: 32 Bats: L Throws: R Height: 5' 10" Weight: 180

YEAR	TEAM	LVL	AGE	PA	R	2B	3B	HR	RBI	BB	K	SB	CS	AVG/OBP/SLG	TAv	BABIP	BRR	FRAA	WARP
2012	ATL	MLB	29	703	96	26	10	9	57	70	155	42	13	.274/.348/.391	.271	.349	11.3	CF(153): 1.2	4.4
2013	CLE	MLB	30	575	75	21	6	6	50	40	132	23	12	.263/.316/.360	.251	.338	5.4	CF(128): -6.5	1.2
2014	AKR	AA	31	25	0	0	0	0	0	2	10	1	0	.087/.160/.087	.120	.154	-1.0	CF(6): 0.5	-0.4
2014	COH	AAA	31	20	1	1	0	0	2	0	3	0	0	.150/.150/.200	.118	.176	-0.6	CF(3): 0.4	-0.3
2014	CLE	MLB	31	487	57	17	10	3	28	35	114	10	6	.257/.314/.360	.248	.337	1.8	CF(105): -5.8	0.4
2015	CLE	MLB	32	483	56	19	5	3	33	38	108	21	8	.258/.319/.344	.250	.329	4.1	CF -3	1.0

Breakout: 2%   Improve: 42%   Collapse: 2%   Attrition: 8%   MLB: 94%   Comparables: *Reed Johnson, Ken Griffey, Tony Gonzalez*

For the second consecutive season, the wheels that define Bourn's value were out of alignment, an ominous characteristic for the man who was Cleveland's second-highest-paid player and still has two years remaining on his deal. His range in center field took another hit and he had by far the worst stolen-base rate of his career, both in terms of frequency and success. Making matters worse was the faulty left hamstring that required surgery, delayed the start to his 2014 season and shelved him for another month over the summer. Hamstring injuries are like cold sores for speed-first players: They keep coming back and will sap a player of his game.

Michael Brantley   LF
Born: 5/15/87 Age: 28 Bats: L Throws: L Height: 6' 2" Weight: 200

YEAR	TEAM	LVL	AGE	PA	R	2B	3B	HR	RBI	BB	K	SB	CS	AVG/OBP/SLG	TAv	BABIP	BRR	FRAA	WARP
2012	CLE	MLB	25	609	63	37	4	6	60	53	56	12	9	.288/.348/.402	.271	.310	2.7	CF(144): -11.5	1.5
2013	CLE	MLB	26	611	66	26	3	10	73	40	67	17	4	.284/.332/.396	.271	.304	2.4	LF(151): 0.5, CF(1): -0.0	2.5
2014	CLE	MLB	27	676	94	45	2	20	97	52	56	23	1	.327/.385/.506	.323	.333	5.1	LF(107): -6.2, CF(46): 1.4	6.0
2015	CLE	MLB	28	622	67	32	4	9	64	47	73	17	4	.286/.341/.404	.278	.309	3.0	LF -3, CF -2	2.4

Breakout: 0%   Improve: 48%   Collapse: 4%   Attrition: 11%   MLB: 94%   Comparables: *Conor Jackson, Mike Greenwell, Martin Prado*

It pays to have a dad in the baseball business. After offseason work with his father, former big-league hitting coach Mickey Brantley, Dr. Smooth laid waste to the American League with an offensive spike in his age-27 season that lines up perfectly with the statistical cliché. He doubled his previous high in homers, set personal marks in the slash stats, compiled more WARP than he had in his entire career entering the season and topped it off with a third-place finish in the AL MVP voting.

Underlying the success was remarkable consistency: He dropped about 90 points of slugging against lefties but held his on-base percentage steady; ripped off-speed pitches for the first time in his career, teeing off on changeups and splitters after years of swinging over those pitches; and started hitting to the opposite field with authority, garnering nine doubles to left. His next left-of-center homer will be his first, but that's no knock: Opposite-field power isn't easy to come by. The magnitude of Brantley's improvement was robust and far-reaching, and there's comfort in knowing that if he falls off track, dad is just a phone call away.

Lonnie Chisenhall 3B

Born: 10/4/88 Age: 26 Bats: L Throws: R Height: 6' 2" Weight: 190

YEAR	TEAM	LVL	AGE	PA	R	2B	3B	HR	RBI	BB	K	SB	CS	AVG/OBP/SLG	TAv	BABIP	BRR	FRAA	WARP
2012	COH	AAA	23	126	16	12	0	4	17	4	22	0	0	.314/.341/.517	.270	.351	0.4	3B(27): 3.2	1.0
2012	CLE	MLB	23	151	16	6	1	5	16	8	27	2	1	.268/.311/.430	.267	.300	-1.0	3B(30): -0.3	0.4
2013	COH	AAA	24	125	21	8	2	6	26	12	24	2	0	.390/.456/.676	.388	.443	-1.3	3B(27): 0.6	2.2
2013	CLE	MLB	24	308	30	17	0	11	36	16	56	1	0	.225/.270/.398	.251	.243	0.6	3B(88): 0.2	0.7
2014	CLE	MLB	25	533	62	29	1	13	59	39	99	3	1	.280/.343/.427	.281	.328	-1.8	3B(114): -6.9, 1B(11): -0.5	1.4
2015	CLE	MLB	26	470	51	25	2	13	53	29	92	2	1	.263/.315/.417	.273	.303	-0.8	3B -0, 1B -0	1.6

Breakout: 2%   Improve: 58%   Collapse: 4%   Attrition: 9%   MLB: 99%   *Comparables: Kyle Seager, Edwin Encarnacion, Kevin Kouzmanoff*

Maybe Dr. Jekyll gave way to Mr. Hyde, or perhaps Chiserella lost her glass slipper, but it takes a metaphor drawn from fantastical fiction to describe the tale of two seasons that was Chisenhall's 2014 campaign. He was on absolute fire for the first three months, carrying a line of .344/.401/.559 into Independence Day, but the demons of arbitrary endpoints (or perhaps it was the alien invasion) sucked the life out of his bat for the rest of the year, with a .223/.289/.307 line in his final 72 games. His offensive skills cratered across the board, infiltrating all splits and manifesting against all pitch types. Chisenhall's performance against fastballs fell off a cliff and he stopped going the other way with any authority, dropping from eight opposite-field doubles in the first half to zero extra-base hits to left in the second. His defensive liabilities at the hot corner exacerbate the pessimism as Chisenhall navigates through his theoretical prime.

Chris Dickerson   LF

Born: 4/10/82 Age: 33 Bats: L Throws: L Height: 6' 4" Weight: 230

YEAR	TEAM	LVL	AGE	PA	R	2B	3B	HR	RBI	BB	K	SB	CS	AVG/OBP/SLG	TAv	BABIP	BRR	FRAA	WARP
2012	SWB	AAA	30	321	57	24	4	7	25	49	73	17	3	.316/.417/.515	.328	.403	4.5	CF(40): 2.4, LF(13): -1.0	3.7
2012	NYA	MLB	30	17	5	0	0	2	5	3	5	3	0	.286/.412/.714	.347	.286	-0.1	LF(18): -0.3, RF(5): -0.1	0.2
2013	NOR	AAA	31	160	24	7	2	2	8	21	35	1	1	.243/.350/.368	.254	.310	1.4	RF(16): 1.1, CF(12): -0.1	0.5
2013	BAL	MLB	31	109	17	5	0	4	13	4	36	5	1	.238/.266/.400	.247	.323	0.7	LF(17): 0.2, RF(6): 0.3	0.2
2014	IND	AAA	32	280	44	15	2	7	30	33	65	12	5	.309/.407/.479	.309	.395	0.8	CF(63): 3.2	2.8
2014	CLE	MLB	32	112	12	4	0	2	6	12	38	3	0	.224/.309/.327	.232	.345	0.6	LF(19): -0.6, RF(11): 0.1	0.0
2015	CLE	MLB	33	250	31	11	1	4	21	24	73	9	2	.242/.320/.362	.260	.332	0.3	CF 1, RF 0	0.7

Breakout: 1%   Improve: 8%   Collapse: 8%   Attrition: 21%   MLB: 44%   *Comparables: Mark Little, Ruben Rivera, Ryan Langerhans*

Terry Francona did everything in his power to maximize Dickerson's value, including a usage pattern that featured 88 percent of his plate appearances with the platoon advantage. Dickerson responded by resurrecting his walk rate, which spiked above 10 percent for the first meaningful stretch since 2009, but his bat was otherwise lifeless. Playing for his fifth organization in as many years, the 33-year-old outfielder was just trying to squeeze a couple more big-league paychecks out of his playing career, and is likely to continue his Triple-A tour in 2015 while waiting for an injury-induced opening for big-league playing time.

Clint Frazier   OF

Born: 9/6/94 Age: 20 Bats: R Throws: R Height: 6' 1" Weight: 190

YEAR	TEAM	LVL	AGE	PA	R	2B	3B	HR	RBI	BB	K	SB	CS	AVG/OBP/SLG	TAv	BABIP	BRR	FRAA	WARP
2014	LKC	A	19	542	70	18	6	13	50	56	161	12	6	.266/.349/.411	.276	.372	0.8	CF(111): -13.7, RF(1): 0.1	1.0
2015	CLE	MLB	20	250	24	8	1	4	20	17	91	2	1	.197/.256/.299	.212	.299	-0.2	CF -6, RF 0	-1.2

Breakout: 0%   Improve: 0%   Collapse: 0%   Attrition: 0%   MLB: 0%   *Comparables: Oswaldo Arcia, Robbie Grossman, Chris Parmelee*

Big expectations have a way of setting up big hiccups for prospects. You hear it over and over: Prospects don't progress at a linear rate but in fits and starts, with great leaps forward and even greater tumbles back; still, it's worth repeating to keep prospect struggles (and "struggles") in context. Frazier entered 2014 with high hopes pinned to his name; the main drawback in his scouting profile was the color of his hair. (Quick, name all the star redheads in baseball history.) Thus, while the above stat line as a 19-year-old in full-season ball looks great in a vacuum, it was in a sense a disappointment through the lens of the expectations he built during his Rookie league campaign. The prodigious power he teased in 2013 was nonexistent through the first third of 2014. Frazier did improve as the season wore on, as he made adjustments and went on a tear in the middle of the year. Frazier's tremendous upside as an up-the-middle player with serious pop hasn't gone anywhere; he'll just have to continue working through the hiccups to get there.

Jason Giambi   DH

Born: 1/8/71 Age: 44 Bats: L Throws: R Height: 6' 3" Weight: 240

YEAR	TEAM	LVL	AGE	PA	R	2B	3B	HR	RBI	BB	K	SB	CS	AVG/OBP/SLG	TAv	BABIP	BRR	FRAA	WARP
2012	COL	MLB	41	113	7	4	0	1	8	20	24	0	0	.225/.372/.303	.237	.288	-0.3	1B(13): -0.2	-0.2
2013	CLE	MLB	42	216	21	8	0	9	31	23	56	0	1	.183/.282/.371	.235	.202	-2.9		-0.6
2014	CLE	MLB	43	70	3	2	0	2	5	9	12	0	0	.133/.257/.267	.187	.130	0.2		-0.4
2015	CLE	MLB	44	250	26	9	0	7	27	30	67	0	0	.200/.307/.341	.248	.250	-1.0	1B -0	0.0

Breakout: 0%   Improve: 11%   Collapse: 0%   Attrition: 25%   MLB: 52%   *Comparables: Carlton Fisk, Dave Winfield, Carl Yastrzemski*

You're excused if you saw Captain Graybeard in the Cleveland dugout and thought he was a coach: The 20-year veteran's mentoring abilities surely brought more value to the ballclub than his way-below-replacement bat in 2014. Terry Francona did everything in his power or anyone else's to maximize Giambi's production: All 70 of Giambi's plate appearances came against righties. As of this writing, he hasn't announced whether he's going to keep making a go of it on the field, but it's hard to think of a team that will want to expend a roster spot on him. On the other hand, it's hard to think of a team that *wouldn't* want him in the player-coach role Manny Ramirez filled for the Iowa Cubs for a few months last summer.

Yan Gomes   C

Born: 7/19/87   Age: 27   Bats: R   Throws: R   Height: 6' 2"   Weight: 215

YEAR	TEAM	LVL	AGE	PA	R	2B	3B	HR	RBI	BB	K	SB	CS	AVG/OBP/SLG	TAv	BABIP	BRR	FRAA	WARP
2012	LVG	AAA	24	335	44	29	1	13	59	25	72	4	0	.328/.380/.557	.310	.392	-3.7	C(35): 0.2, 3B(24): -1.4	2.6
2012	TOR	MLB	24	111	9	4	0	4	13	6	32	0	0	.204/.264/.367	.233	.246	-1.0	1B(20): 0.4, C(9): -0.1	-0.2
2013	COH	AAA	25	24	2	4	0	0	3	4	4	0	0	.300/.417/.500	.309	.375	-0.4	C(6): -0.1	0.1
2013	CLE	MLB	25	322	45	18	2	11	38	18	67	2	0	.294/.345/.481	.296	.342	0.1	C(85): 1.4, 1B(1): -0.0	3.1
2014	CLE	MLB	26	518	61	25	3	21	74	24	120	0	0	.278/.313/.472	.283	.326	-0.1	C(126): -1.0	3.7
2015	CLE	MLB	27	450	51	24	2	15	56	25	108	1	0	.268/.314/.443	.281	.323	-0.4	C -0, 1B 0	2.6

Breakout: 4%   Improve: 53%   Collapse: 7%   Attrition: 8%   MLB: 95%   *Comparables:*   *J.P. Arencibia, Ryan Doumit, Mike Jacobs*

Formerly one of the best-kept secrets in the American League, Gomes is now firmly on the radar following a full season of across-the-board contributions. He doesn't walk much, but his bat-to-ball skills and burgeoning power are valuable traits, especially for a backstop, *especially* one who can hold his own with the glove and control the running game. He went through a defensive lapse at the beginning of the season, but work with Sandy Alomar Jr. corrected the issue; Gomes also receives plus marks for his pitch-framing abilities. He brings balance to a left-leaning lineup that struggled against southpaws in 2014 and the six-year pact he signed prior to the 2014 campaign is already looking like a steal at just $23 million.

Erik Gonzalez   SS

Born: 8/31/91   Age: 23   Bats: R   Throws: R   Height: 6' 0"   Weight: 175

YEAR	TEAM	LVL	AGE	PA	R	2B	3B	HR	RBI	BB	K	SB	CS	AVG/OBP/SLG	TAv	BABIP	BRR	FRAA	WARP
2012	MHV	A-	20	230	30	9	1	2	18	11	50	9	1	.220/.264/.299	.231	.278	2.1	1B(27): 2.1, 3B(24): 5.2	1.1
2013	LKC	A	21	383	59	23	7	9	49	24	71	10	4	.259/.307/.439	.261	.301	2.4	3B(65): 10.6, SS(16): -0.7	2.7
2013	CAR	A+	21	163	16	9	5	0	27	5	38	1	2	.242/.259/.366	.207	.311	-0.5	SS(39): 2.7	0.0
2014	CAR	A+	22	336	44	14	7	3	46	23	65	15	6	.289/.336/.409	.261	.355	1.2	SS(74): -2.4	1.3
2014	AKR	AA	22	136	21	6	3	1	16	7	23	6	1	.357/.390/.473	.294	.429	2.9	SS(30): -1.7	1.0
2015	CLE	MLB	23	250	21	10	2	3	21	9	66	5	2	.227/.254/.323	.216	.298	0.4	SS -1, 3B 2	0.0

Breakout: 6%   Improve: 15%   Collapse: 4%   Attrition: 16%   MLB: 21%   *Comparables:*   *Jeff Bianchi, Hector Gomez, Zack Cozart*

The Indians have moved the lanky Gonzalez from position to position in his career, but it looks like he's finally found a home at shortstop. He has a smooth glove, good range, fine instincts and a strong left-side arm. Gonzalez had a solid year with the bat in 2014, but it's still a work in progress and the glove is definitely ahead developmentally. Still, if you dance like Gene Kelly and act like Grace Kelly while singing like Jim Kelly, well, we'll overlook that as long as you can hum a few bars. Which is to say that even as Gonzalez doesn't profile as an offensive contributor, guys who play short as well as he has tend to find major-league jobs.

Jason Kipnis   2B

Born: 4/3/87   Age: 28   Bats: L   Throws: R   Height: 5' 11"   Weight: 190

YEAR	TEAM	LVL	AGE	PA	R	2B	3B	HR	RBI	BB	K	SB	CS	AVG/OBP/SLG	TAv	BABIP	BRR	FRAA	WARP
2012	CLE	MLB	25	672	86	22	4	14	76	67	109	31	7	.257/.335/.379	.262	.291	3.0	2B(146): -8.9	1.3
2013	CLE	MLB	26	658	86	36	4	17	84	76	143	30	7	.284/.366/.452	.309	.345	-0.8	2B(147): -2.5	4.9
2014	CLE	MLB	27	555	61	25	1	6	41	50	100	22	3	.240/.310/.330	.239	.288	4.6	2B(123): 9.5	2.1
2015	CLE	MLB	28	543	63	24	4	11	56	53	108	22	4	.256/.331/.390	.272	.304	1.4	2B 0	2.7

Breakout: 0%   Improve: 47%   Collapse: 1%   Attrition: 5%   MLB: 95%   *Comparables:*   *Marcus Giles, Neil Walker, Kelly Johnson*

Kipnis has been a streaky hitter in his big-league tenure, equally likely to put the offense on his shoulders as to fall into a pit of despair for a month at a time. He forgot the hot streaks in 2014, though his shelving for the month of May with an oblique injury and performance upon his return suggests that the oblique continued to nag him throughout the season. The lower-leg woes he endured down the stretch further compromised his foundation. Kipnis salvaged his value with defense that FRAA liked (though other metrics disagreed) and baserunning (in particular a Rainesesque 88 percent stolen-base rate). With four very different seasons of performance on his resume, it's anyone's guess which version of Kipnis will show up for 2015.

Francisco Lindor   SS

Born: 11/14/93   Age: 21   Bats: B   Throws: R   Height: 5' 11"   Weight: 175

YEAR	TEAM	LVL	AGE	PA	R	2B	3B	HR	RBI	BB	K	SB	CS	AVG/OBP/SLG	TAv	BABIP	BRR	FRAA	WARP
2012	LKC	A	18	568	83	24	3	6	42	61	78	27	12	.257/.352/.355	.260	.295	3.3	SS(120): 6.1	3.4
2013	CAR	A+	19	373	51	19	6	1	27	35	39	20	5	.306/.373/.410	.274	.341	-2.3	SS(82): 2.6	2.5
2013	AKR	AA	19	91	14	3	1	1	7	14	7	5	2	.289/.407/.395	.305	.309	-0.8	SS(21): -2.0	0.5
2014	AKR	AA	20	387	51	12	4	6	48	40	61	25	9	.278/.352/.389	.274	.320	0.1	SS(88): 5.4	3.1
2014	COH	AAA	20	180	24	4	0	5	14	9	36	3	7	.273/.307/.388	.231	.317	0.7	SS(38): 0.9	0.5
2015	CLE	MLB	21	250	29	9	1	3	18	18	51	9	4	.240/.298/.329	.239	.291	0.2	SS 1	0.7

Breakout: 0%   Improve: 0%   Collapse: 0%   Attrition: 0%   MLB: 0%   *Comparables:*   *Tyler Pastornicky, Jose Pirela, Carlos Sanchez*

If you closed your eyes and set your mind to imagining the prototypical defensive shortstop, Francisco Lindor would appear with a quick first step. He would display superior range and show off arm strength and accuracy with a seed delivered to the first baseman's chest from deep in the hole. Maybe at the end he would wink at you. Lindor's glove has a way of overshadowing his contributions at the plate, which are developing in a positive direction: He has good barrel control, a quick bat and a plan at the plate that foretells a possible future as a good offensive player, but, as you can see above, he's not there yet. He runs well enough to envision a few seasons in the 20s in stolen bases, but he's not going to break any land speed records. Or air speed records, for that matter. Or water. Are there any other speed records?

Francisco Mejia   C

Born: 10/27/95   Age: 19   Bats: B   Throws: R   Height: 5' 10"   Weight: 175

YEAR	TEAM	LVL	AGE	PA	R	2B	3B	HR	RBI	BB	K	SB	CS	AVG/OBP/SLG	TAv	BABIP	BRR	FRAA	WARP
2014	MHV	A-	18	274	32	17	4	2	36	18	47	2	4	.282/.339/.407	.277	.337	0.0	C(52): 0.1	1.9
2015	CLE	MLB	19	250	17	10	1	3	21	8	71	0	0	.207/.238/.291	.199	.277	-0.4	C 0, LF 0	-0.7

Breakout: 0%   Improve: 0%   Collapse: 0%   Attrition: 0%   MLB: 0%   Comparables: Tomas Telis, Miguel Gonzalez, Wilson Ramos

Switch-hitting catchers with 1.87 pop times melt hearts. Add in the barrel-to-ball skills that Mejia showed in 2014 and you've got a full-fledged heart-throb. Mejia's an aggressive hitter: He has good bat speed and isn't afraid to show it off, and there's some power potential mixed in as well, albeit belied by the mediocre ISO he showed at Mahoning Valley. His framing will need some work, as he's still a raw receiver, but he blocks well and the arm is borderline elite. We say it with every top prospect: Take a deep breath, expect bumps. We say it with every catching prospect: Take a really deep breath, expect serious bumps. We say it with every kid who graduates Rookie ball before he turns 20 and thus inflames our prospect loins with dreams of a 25-year major-league career: Take 10 deep breaths, he's probably not a Hall-of-Famer. So, regarding Mejia: breathe.

Brandon Moss   1B

Born: 9/16/83   Age: 31   Bats: L   Throws: R   Height: 6' 0"   Weight: 210

YEAR	TEAM	LVL	AGE	PA	R	2B	3B	HR	RBI	BB	K	SB	CS	AVG/OBP/SLG	TAv	BABIP	BRR	FRAA	WARP
2012	SAC	AAA	28	224	32	11	1	15	33	22	40	4	0	.286/.371/.582	.322	.289	-0.6	LF(14): -0.2, 1B(13): -0.6	1.9
2012	OAK	MLB	28	296	48	18	0	21	52	26	90	1	1	.291/.358/.596	.335	.359	-0.3	1B(55): -3.4, RF(13): 0.1	2.3
2013	OAK	MLB	29	505	73	23	3	30	87	50	140	4	2	.256/.337/.522	.328	.301	-1.9	1B(111): -5.4, RF(27): 0.3	3.5
2014	OAK	MLB	30	580	70	23	2	25	81	67	153	1	0	.234/.334/.438	.288	.283	0.7	1B(67): -2.7, LF(56): 0.4	2.4
2015	CLE	MLB	31	530	66	24	1	25	77	49	146	3	1	.245/.323/.460	.290	.299	-0.4	1B -5, LF 0	1.7

Breakout: 1%   Improve: 33%   Collapse: 9%   Attrition: 10%   MLB: 83%   Comparables: Carlos Pena, Marcus Thames, Josh Phelps

Moss has been mashing home runs for bargain-basement prices for the past three seasons, and though he helped lead the charge as Oakland carved out the majors' best run differential over the first half of 2014, his bat went silent for the final nine weeks of the regular season. The player that knocked 23 balls over the wall in the first four months mustered just two bombs among eight extra-base hits over the final two, but his bat suddenly came alive during the Wild Card game, ripping a pair of homers to carry the team's run-scoring efforts at the most opportune time. It wasn't enough in the end, and one game is just one game, but late October left-hip surgery lent some perspective to his power disappearance while inspiring optimism for 2015. Moss came to Cleveland in December as part of the A's sell-off; there are worse places for someone lacking in hip to land.

David Murphy   RF

Born: 10/18/81   Age: 33   Bats: L   Throws: L   Height: 6' 3"   Weight: 210

YEAR	TEAM	LVL	AGE	PA	R	2B	3B	HR	RBI	BB	K	SB	CS	AVG/OBP/SLG	TAv	BABIP	BRR	FRAA	WARP
2012	TEX	MLB	30	521	65	29	3	15	61	54	74	10	5	.304/.380/.479	.307	.333	3.2	LF(120): -2.0, RF(17): -0.2	3.6
2013	TEX	MLB	31	476	51	26	1	13	45	37	59	1	4	.220/.282/.374	.234	.227	-0.9	LF(128): -4.6, RF(1): 0.1	-0.5
2014	CLE	MLB	32	462	40	25	1	8	58	36	61	2	3	.262/.319/.385	.268	.285	-4.4	RF(120): -1.9, LF(2): -0.1	0.3
2015	CLE	MLB	33	436	46	22	1	8	44	36	68	4	4	.260/.321/.386	.268	.292	-0.6	RF -1, LF -1	0.9

Breakout: 2%   Improve: 24%   Collapse: 2%   Attrition: 8%   MLB: 97%   Comparables: David DeJesus, Shane Victorino, Rocky Colavito

Murphy took a vacation from his quest to check off every number between 10 and 20 on the seasonal home run count, finishing with single-digit jacks for the first time in his seven seasons as a full-time big leaguer. His departure from the cozy confines of the Arlington launching pad likely played a role in the power outage. Vulnerable against southpaws, Murphy is a good fit for the platoon-heavy scheme in Cleveland, where he faced right-handed pitchers in 81 percent of his plate appearances last season. If he can't even crack a .270 TAv with that heavy slate of righties, though, his two-year run of mediocrity and his defensive liabilities call his future utility into question.

Tyler Naquin   CF

Born: 4/24/91   Age: 24   Bats: L   Throws: R   Height: 6' 3"   Weight: 190

YEAR	TEAM	LVL	AGE	PA	R	2B	3B	HR	RBI	BB	K	SB	CS	AVG/OBP/SLG	TAv	BABIP	BRR	FRAA	WARP
2012	MHV	A-	21	161	22	11	2	0	13	17	26	4	3	.270/.379/.380	.272	.333	-0.3	CF(34): 4.0	1.1
2013	CAR	A+	22	498	69	27	6	9	42	41	112	14	7	.277/.345/.424	.264	.351	0.9	CF(102): 1.6	2.8
2013	AKR	AA	22	85	9	3	0	1	6	5	22	1	3	.225/.271/.300	.237	.298	-1.0	CF(18): -1.0	-0.1
2014	AKR	AA	23	341	54	12	5	4	30	29	71	14	3	.313/.371/.424	.292	.389	-0.1	CF(73): 0.7, RF(1): 0.1	2.6
2015	CLE	MLB	24	250	26	10	2	3	19	15	69	5	2	.234/.283/.330	.233	.316	0.2	CF 0, RF 0	0.0

Breakout: 8%   Improve: 12%   Collapse: 17%   Attrition: 24%   MLB: 34%   Comparables: Lane Adams, James Jones, Lorenzo Cain

Naquin silenced critics for a second straight year in 2014 with a strong showing with both the bat and the glove. Naquin makes good contact via solid bat speed and an ability to track pitches well. He doesn't have the natural lift for over-the-fence power but he can attack the gaps and hit his share of doubles. Naquin's loudest tool is his arm, rating plus-plus. It's a weapon and it should be a tremendous asset in center. This might also make you think "right field," but he doesn't have the power to carry a first-division profile in a corner, so his upside takes a big hit if he has to move.

Michael Papi   LF

Born: 9/19/92   Age: 22   Bats: L   Throws: R   Height: 6' 2"   Weight: 190

YEAR	TEAM	LVL	AGE	PA	R	2B	3B	HR	RBI	BB	K	SB	CS	AVG/OBP/SLG	TAv	BABIP	BRR	FRAA	WARP
2014	LKC	A	21	166	21	4	0	3	15	26	32	2	0	.178/.305/.274	.232	.204	0.7	RF(33): -1.8, 1B(2): 0.0	-0.4
2015	CLE	MLB	22	250	20	8	1	3	21	23	67	1	0	.195/.271/.283	.215	.258	-0.3	RF -3, 1B 0	-1.1

Breakout: 0%   Improve: 0%   Collapse: 0%   Attrition: 0%   MLB: 0%   Comparables: Rene Tosoni, Lorenzo Cain, Brandon Jones

Cleveland selected Papi, who sadly is not terribly Big by ballplayer standards, with a competitive balance pick in 2014. He had a big bat as a Virginia Cavalier and has the raw tools to carry the success over to his professional career: good bat speed and a compact swing coupled with some pull-side power. Papi is not a gifted athlete, so the defense leaves something to be desired in the outfield. In particular, he's basically a left fielder only because his arm isn't suited for right. (He's nowhere near fast enough to handle center. And yes, we know Nick Swisher has played center in the major leagues.) Still, a left field home will be kinder to his offensive package than first base.

Dorssys Paulino   SS

Born: 11/21/94   Age: 20   Bats: R   Throws: R   Height: 6' 0"   Weight: 175

YEAR	TEAM	LVL	AGE	PA	R	2B	3B	HR	RBI	BB	K	SB	CS	AVG/OBP/SLG	TAv	BABIP	BRR	FRAA	WARP
2012	MHV	A-	17	62	5	5	0	1	8	3	14	2	1	.271/.306/.407	.251	.341	0.5	SS(15): -1.3	0.0
2013	LKC	A	18	523	56	28	3	5	46	30	91	12	7	.246/.297/.349	.229	.294	0.0	SS(116): -10.3	-0.8
2014	LKC	A	19	472	51	25	5	3	35	33	101	5	6	.251/.311/.354	.242	.319	-2.0	LF(75): 2.6, SS(24): -5.9	-0.4
2015	CLE	MLB	20	250	20	11	1	2	16	9	67	1	1	.206/.237/.279	.196	.274	-0.4	SS -4, LF 1	-1.3

Breakout: 0%   Improve: 0%   Collapse: 0%   Attrition: 0%   MLB: 0%   Comparables: *Alfredo Marte, Luis Durango, Joc Pederson*

Paulino repeated the Midwest League in search of the hit tool that had made him an exciting prospect before 2013; he came away instead with more question marks about his ultimate defensive home, as Cleveland moved him to the outfield. Ross Atkins, the team's Vice President for Player Development, wins the Positive Spin Award for 2014 by writing in an email to *The Cleveland Plain Dealer*'s Tim Warsinskey, "The errors at shortstop were impacting his ability to focus on controllables because of how much he cares about his teammates." Paulino is still winning in the age department, but that's a battle we all lose eventually, so he'll need to show actual baseball skills in the meantime.

Ryan Raburn   DH

Born: 4/17/81   Age: 34   Bats: R   Throws: R   Height: 6' 0"   Weight: 185

YEAR	TEAM	LVL	AGE	PA	R	2B	3B	HR	RBI	BB	K	SB	CS	AVG/OBP/SLG	TAv	BABIP	BRR	FRAA	WARP
2012	TOL	AAA	31	66	8	2	0	4	12	5	15	1	0	.250/.318/.483	.249	.268	0.2	2B(11): -1.2, LF(6): 0.4	0.1
2012	DET	MLB	31	222	14	14	0	1	12	13	53	1	1	.171/.226/.254	.175	.224	-0.2	2B(32): -1.1, LF(30): -0.1	-1.8
2013	CLE	MLB	32	277	40	18	0	16	55	29	67	0	0	.272/.357/.543	.327	.311	0.7	RF(54): -1.1, LF(13): 0.0	2.4
2014	CLE	MLB	33	212	18	7	0	4	22	13	51	0	0	.200/.250/.297	.198	.245	-0.4	RF(25): -1.7, LF(20): -0.6	-1.2
2015	CLE	MLB	34	250	25	12	0	7	27	17	66	0	0	.232/.290/.379	.251	.292	0.1	RF -2, LF 0	0.0

Breakout: 0%   Improve: 26%   Collapse: 6%   Attrition: 14%   MLB: 92%   Comparables: *Fred McGriff, Orlando Cepeda, Phil Nevin*

He can be a very useful player when his power generator is working, but in 2014 the Raburn machine was on the fritz for the second time in three seasons. His days of playing second base appear to be over and his glove has never been much of an asset overall, putting more pressure on his bat. Those 2012 and 2014 lines you see above do not represent adequate responses to that pressure. The 34-year-old's hold on a roster spot appears to be hanging by a thread.

Jose Ramirez   SS

Born: 9/17/92   Age: 22   Bats: B   Throws: R   Height: 5' 9"   Weight: 165

YEAR	TEAM	LVL	AGE	PA	R	2B	3B	HR	RBI	BB	K	SB	CS	AVG/OBP/SLG	TAv	BABIP	BRR	FRAA	WARP
2012	LKC	A	19	313	54	13	4	3	27	24	26	15	6	.354/.403/.462	.327	.378	-2.4	2B(62): 3.4, SS(2): 0.1	3.3
2013	AKR	AA	20	533	78	16	6	3	38	39	41	38	16	.272/.325/.349	.261	.290	3.0	2B(53): -0.6, SS(50): 3.0	3.0
2013	CLE	MLB	20	14	5	0	1	0	0	2	2	0	1	.333/.429/.500	.338	.400	0.5	2B(5): 0.3, SS(2): -0.0	0.3
2014	COH	AAA	21	277	37	15	2	5	29	25	30	19	11	.302/.360/.441	.270	.321	-1.8	2B(35): 4.5, SS(21): 0.9	1.8
2014	CLE	MLB	21	266	27	10	2	2	17	13	35	10	1	.262/.300/.346	.235	.297	2.1	SS(56): 0.5, 2B(11): -0.4	0.7
2015	CLE	MLB	22	304	36	12	2	3	22	16	42	14	6	.264/.303/.353	.244	.290	0.6	SS 1, 2B 1	1.0

Breakout: 4%   Improve: 28%   Collapse: 13%   Attrition: 22%   MLB: 49%   Comparables: *Tyler Pastornicky, Joe Panik, Ruben Tejada*

Twenty-one-year-old shortstops who hold their own at the highest level don't grow on trees, and though the presence of Francisco Lindor in the system somewhat marginalizes Ramirez's potential impact, having too many up-the-middle players under cost control is a good problem for Cleveland. At times he was treated like a player whose bat was not quite ready, with 13 sacrifices (tied atop a major-league leaderboard heavily populated by NL pitchers) despite playing in just 68 games, yet his manager thought enough of his offense to pencil him into the two-hole 42 times as the Indians fought to remain in playoff contention. Ramirez has shown a wide swath of offensive skills in the minors, with dabs of power and speed to complement a hit tool that has produced a .306 average across 1,344 plate appearances.

James Ramsey   CF

Born: 12/19/89   Age: 25   Bats: L   Throws: R   Height: 6' 0"   Weight: 190

YEAR	TEAM	LVL	AGE	PA	R	2B	3B	HR	RBI	BB	K	SB	CS	AVG/OBP/SLG	TAv	BABIP	BRR	FRAA	WARP
2012	PMB	A+	22	247	36	9	3	1	14	33	59	10	2	.229/.333/.314	.248	.309	2.7	CF(53): -7.8	0.3
2013	PMB	A+	23	77	17	5	2	1	7	12	12	1	0	.361/.481/.557	.396	.429	0.4	CF(18): 0.7	1.5
2013	SFD	AA	23	416	61	11	2	15	44	53	108	8	4	.251/.356/.424	.273	.316	3.0	CF(76): -4.3, RF(12): -0.9	1.6
2014	SFD	AA	24	281	47	14	1	13	36	31	66	4	2	.300/.389/.527	.312	.364	-1.1	CF(36): 2.0, RF(25): 0.2	2.3
2014	COH	AAA	24	127	17	9	1	3	16	13	34	1	0	.284/.365/.468	.279	.378	0.2	CF(26): 2.2, LF(2): 0.1	0.9
2015	CLE	MLB	25	250	30	10	1	6	24	24	72	2	1	.234/.316/.374	.260	.309	-0.1	CF -1, RF -0	0.5

Breakout: 8%   Improve: 21%   Collapse: 7%   Attrition: 34%   MLB: 49%   Comparables: *Brian Barton, Joe Benson, Casper Wells*

You can't spend more than 17 seconds in a Google search for Ramsey without bumping into a story about his amazing makeup and his Rhodes Scholar candidacy at Florida State. (He fell short in his attempt to follow in the footsteps of Myron Rolle, but falling short of being a Rhodes Scholar is like ... well, it's sorta like falling short of becoming a major-league ballplayer.) He has experienced a power spike over the past two seasons as he shortened his swing; he's already outperforming the power scouts projected him to have when he was drafted in 2012. He's not athletic enough to stick in center, so in the long run Ramsey is likely a corner outfielder with a bit of pop and a strong enough arm to play right field.

Carlos Santana   1B

Born: 4/8/86   Age: 29   Bats: B   Throws: R   Height: 5' 11"   Weight: 210

YEAR	TEAM	LVL	AGE	PA	R	2B	3B	HR	RBI	BB	K	SB	CS	AVG/OBP/SLG	TAv	BABIP	BRR	FRAA	WARP
2012	CLE	MLB	26	609	72	27	2	18	76	91	101	3	5	.252/.365/.420	.288	.278	-2.2	C(100): -0.7, 1B(21): 0.0	3.7
2013	CLE	MLB	27	642	75	39	1	20	74	93	110	3	1	.268/.377/.455	.312	.301	-2.6	C(84): -1.4, 1B(29): 0.1	4.8
2014	CLE	MLB	28	660	68	25	0	27	85	113	124	5	2	.231/.365/.427	.294	.249	-1.8	1B(94): 3.5, 3B(26): -2.2	3.9
2015	CLE	MLB	29	616	76	30	1	21	79	94	116	4	2	.249/.366/.432	.301	.280	-1.7	1B 2, C -0	3.7

Breakout: 2%   Improve: 48%   Collapse: 3%   Attrition: 4%   MLB: 96%   Comparables: *Justin Morneau, Todd Helton, Carlos Quentin*

The rise of Yan Gomes allowed Santana to take a reprieve from catching duties, splitting time between first, third and designated hitter, though he still got into the crouch for 10 games over the first couple of months to help preserve his catcher eligibility for fantasy-league managers. It was a temporary stay of execution, as he didn't play an inning behind the plate after a foul-tip rattled his cage and required a stint on the 7-day disabled list for a concussion; the switch-hitter's bat is too valuable to risk unnecessarily, and he may never again don the tools of ignorance. The ever-patient Santana led the majors in walks and watched a higher percentage of "ball" calls than any player in baseball, while his rate of 4.3 pitches per plate appearance was the fourth-highest mark in the game. His offensive production is valuable from anywhere on the diamond, but if he can at least nominally play third, the additional flexibility granted Terry Francona is one of those bits of value that doesn't show up in any public flavor of WAR.

Nick Swisher   1B

Born: 11/25/80   Age: 34   Bats: B   Throws: L   Height: 6' 0"   Weight: 200

YEAR	TEAM	LVL	AGE	PA	R	2B	3B	HR	RBI	BB	K	SB	CS	AVG/OBP/SLG	TAv	BABIP	BRR	FRAA	WARP
2012	NYA	MLB	31	624	75	36	0	24	93	77	141	2	3	.272/.364/.473	.292	.324	0.3	RF(109): 8.0, 1B(41): 3.8	4.4
2013	CLE	MLB	32	634	74	27	2	22	63	77	138	1	0	.246/.341/.423	.283	.288	-1.6	1B(112): 5.6, RF(27): -0.1	3.2
2014	CLE	MLB	33	401	33	20	0	8	42	36	111	0	0	.208/.278/.331	.236	.273	-1.7	1B(52): -0.2, RF(4): -0.3	-1.0
2015	CLE	MLB	34	424	53	20	1	12	45	47	101	1	1	.248/.334/.406	.278	.303	-0.6	1B 3, RF 1	1.7

Breakout: 0%   Improve: 34%   Collapse: 5%   Attrition: 8%   MLB: 91%   Comparables: Norm Cash, Paul Konerko, Adam LaRoche

Entering last season, Swisher had gone nine full years since his last visit to the disabled list and had played in 145 or more games for eight consecutive seasons, but the wear and tear finally caught up to him. He underwent surgery in August to repair the meniscus of both knees, limiting him to just 97 games. He hit fewer than 20 bombs for the first time since his 2004 cup of coffee. Prior to going under the knife, Cleveland's highest-paid player had been mired in a season-long slump that resulted in career-worst slash stats and an OPS 200 points below his career average. It remains to be seen whether fixing his knees will cause the return of Swisher's mojo, but sources indicate that he may have violated the Bro Code and been punitively stripped of his Playbook. As penance for this infraction, he was forced to suit up on national television as part of FOX's coverage of the World Series.

Giovanny Urshela   3B

Born: 10/11/91   Age: 23   Bats: R   Throws: R   Height: 6' 0"   Weight: 197

YEAR	TEAM	LVL	AGE	PA	R	2B	3B	HR	RBI	BB	K	SB	CS	AVG/OBP/SLG	TAv	BABIP	BRR	FRAA	WARP
2012	CAR	A+	20	475	50	30	1	14	59	16	60	1	1	.278/.309/.446	.266	.290	-1.8	3B(113): -7.4	1.0
2013	AKR	AA	21	466	42	23	2	8	43	14	48	1	1	.270/.292/.384	.240	.286	-2.7	3B(107): -3.6, SS(3): 0.0	0.4
2014	AKR	AA	22	98	15	9	0	5	19	6	16	1	1	.300/.347/.567	.305	.314	2.2	3B(23): 1.1	1.1
2014	COH	AAA	22	430	63	27	6	13	65	30	51	0	2	.276/.331/.473	.268	.289	-0.6	3B(98): -0.6, SS(1): -0.1	1.7
2015	CLE	MLB	23	250	22	12	1	6	28	7	42	0	0	.246/.271/.384	.245	.271	-0.4	3B -1, SS -0	0.0

Breakout: 4%   Improve: 17%   Collapse: 9%   Attrition: 19%   MLB: 34%   Comparables: Henry Rodriguez, Brent Morel, Cody Asche

Weirdly not yet nicknamed "The Sea Witch," Urshela is a former glove-first, bat-maybe prospect who has come a long way from his free-swinging days and sub-5 percent walk rates. He's been aggressively promoted throughout his career, so he's been more than two years younger than the average hitter at each of his stateside stops. The power spike he's enjoying now is encouraging, but the improved approach is even more important, in part because a great way to hit the ball harder is to wait for good pitches to hit. Urshela's profile doesn't scream "star" by any means, but he'll find his way onto a major-league roster.

Zach Walters   UT

Born: 9/5/89   Age: 25   Bats: B   Throws: R   Height: 6' 2"   Weight: 210

YEAR	TEAM	LVL	AGE	PA	R	2B	3B	HR	RBI	BB	K	SB	CS	AVG/OBP/SLG	TAv	BABIP	BRR	FRAA	WARP
2012	POT	A+	22	207	24	8	1	5	24	10	43	6	3	.269/.304/.399	.252	.318	0.6	SS(33): -0.1, 3B(9): -0.9	0.5
2012	HAR	AA	22	172	23	11	4	6	19	8	38	1	0	.293/.326/.518	.288	.350	0.1	SS(43): 1.3	1.3
2012	SYR	AAA	22	105	9	4	0	1	6	6	28	0	0	.214/.260/.286	.209	.290	-0.3	SS(29): 3.8	0.2
2013	SYR	AAA	23	521	69	32	5	29	77	20	134	4	3	.253/.286/.517	.276	.285	-0.7	SS(102): -0.7, 3B(27): 1.5	2.8
2013	WAS	MLB	23	9	2	0	1	0	1	1	0	0	0	.375/.444/.625	.332	.375	-0.2	3B(2): 0.0, SS(2): 0.1	0.1
2014	COH	AAA	24	31	4	4	0	2	8	0	5	0	0	.387/.387/.710	.379	.417	-0.3	2B(3): 0.3, LF(2): 0.1	0.5
2014	SYR	AAA	24	261	38	18	5	15	48	20	62	0	2	.300/.358/.608	.314	.348	-0.7	2B(27): -0.1, SS(14): -0.4	2.5
2014	CLE	MLB	24	94	9	2	0	7	12	5	32	0	1	.170/.223/.432	.235	.163	-0.6	LF(5): 0.1, 2B(4): -0.0	-0.2
2014	WAS	MLB	24	43	7	1	0	3	5	4	16	0	0	.205/.279/.462	.291	.250	1.0	3B(3): -0.1, SS(3): 0.1	0.3
2015	CLE	MLB	25	250	28	12	2	11	36	10	71	1	1	.240/.274/.449	.266	.290	-0.3	SS 1, 2B 0	1.1

Breakout: 6%   Improve: 23%   Collapse: 13%   Attrition: 24%   MLB: 57%   Comparables: Juan Francisco, Mike Jacobs, Sean Rodriguez

Go big or go home. Walters has legit power, with a combined slugging percentage of .554 over the past two seasons in the minors, but the results of his first extended major-league look were truly all-or-nothing. Of his 23 hits last season, 10 left the yard, an absurd ratio that would make Dave Kingman blush. Acquired from Washington in the Asdrubal Cabrera trade, Walters is already in his third organization, but he might have found a home in Cleveland; the team is expert at maximizing value by minimizing exposure to weakness, and his positional versatility is a big drawing card for a club that relishes lineup flexibility.

Bradley Zimmer   CF

Born: 11/27/92   Age: 22   Bats: L   Throws: R   Height: 6' 4"   Weight: 185

YEAR	TEAM	LVL	AGE	PA	R	2B	3B	HR	RBI	BB	K	SB	CS	AVG/OBP/SLG	TAv	BABIP	BRR	FRAA	WARP
2014	MHV	A-	21	197	32	11	2	4	30	19	30	11	4	.304/.401/.464	.326	.348	2.4	CF(42): 1.9	2.4
2015	CLE	MLB	22	250	25	9	1	5	24	15	70	6	2	.211/.268/.325	.226	.274	0.3	CF 1, RF -0	0.0

Breakout: 0%   Improve: 0%   Collapse: 0%   Attrition: 0%   MLB: 0%   Comparables: Nick Markakis, Felix Pie, Trayvon Robinson

Cleveland took Zimmer 21st overall in 2014 and he quickly went to work in the New York-Penn League, just missing an aesthetically perfect .300/.400/.500 line. (Fun fact: the closest a qualified MLB hitter has come to that line was Gavvy Cravath in 1914 at .299/.402/.499.) He has a broad frame that likely precludes him from center when he fills out. Ultimately, though, Zimmer is a solid prospect despite no carrying tool because his composite skill set meshes well and should help him exceed the sum of his parts. He was a nice pick at this draft spot as a solid complementary piece at a price that allowed the Indians to take a gamble on some prep arms later.

Pitchers

Cody Allen RHP

Born: 11/20/88   Age: 26   Bats: R   Throws: R   Height: 6'1"   Weight: 210

YEAR	TEAM	LVL	AGE	W	L	SV	G	GS	IP	H	HR	BB	K	BB/9	K/9	GB%	BABIP	WHIP	ERA	FIP	FRA	WARP
2012	COH	AAA	23	3	2	2	24	0	31²	22	3	9	35	2.6	9.9	42%	.244	0.98	2.27	3.03	3.61	0.6
2012	CLE	MLB	23	0	1	0	27	0	29	29	2	15	27	4.7	8.4	42%	.329	1.52	3.72	3.63	4.02	0.2
2013	CLE	MLB	24	6	1	2	77	0	70¹	62	7	26	88	3.3	11.3	33%	.307	1.25	2.43	3.02	2.91	1.3
2014	CLE	MLB	25	6	4	24	76	0	69²	48	7	26	91	3.4	11.8	40%	.266	1.06	2.07	3.02	3.49	0.9
2015	CLE	MLB	26	3	1	5	52	0	59¹	49	5	21	72	3.1	10.9	39%	.297	1.17	2.98	3.28	3.24	1.1

Breakout: 30%   Improve: 51%   Collapse: 17%   Attrition: 11%   MLB: 84%   Comparables: Sean Doolittle, Bill Bray, Rex Brothers

Allen has been the best reliever on the Cleveland staff for the past two seasons, and he was the ace in the 'pen from day one of the 2014 campaign, yet he had to wrestle the closer job away from newcomer John Axford. Terry Francona used him liberally, resulting in 76 appearances, tied for second-most in the circuit. Allen's curveball is a true wipeout offering, with 12-to-6 shape despite a low three-quarters arm slot; it falls off the table to invoke whiffs on 52 percent of swings. With upper-90s velocity and that killer curve, he is equipped with the stuff to get away with missed targets, and he has elite-reliever upside if he can further harness his command.

Scott Atchison RHP

Born: 3/29/76   Age: 39   Bats: R   Throws: R   Height: 6'2"   Weight: 200

YEAR	TEAM	LVL	AGE	W	L	SV	G	GS	IP	H	HR	BB	K	BB/9	K/9	GB%	BABIP	WHIP	ERA	FIP	FRA	WARP
2012	BOS	MLB	36	2	1	0	42	0	51¹	42	2	9	36	1.6	6.3	57%	.261	0.99	1.58	2.68	3.64	0.8
2013	NYN	MLB	37	3	3	0	50	0	45¹	45	4	12	28	2.4	5.6	49%	.273	1.26	4.37	3.73	4.51	-0.1
2014	CLE	MLB	38	6	0	2	70	0	72	60	4	14	49	1.8	6.1	61%	.263	1.03	2.75	3.10	3.57	0.8
2015	CLE	MLB	39	2	1	1	43	0	55²	55	5	13	42	2.2	6.7	50%	.292	1.22	3.50	3.95	3.81	0.7

Breakout: 20%   Improve: 36%   Collapse: 10%   Attrition: 9%   MLB: 64%   Comparables: Darren Oliver, LaTroy Hawkins, Elmer Dessens

It is easy to look at his birthdate and assume that Atchison is embarking on his swan song, but the 39-year-old is showing few signs of the typical aging pattern. His fastball averaged 93 mph in 2014, a full tick higher than 2013 and two mph harder than the velocity he established in his mid-30s. He also threw more innings in the majors last season than in any other year of his career, and his 70 games pitched put him among the top 20 in the American League. Atchison will be at it again in 2015, thanks to an extension he signed midseason that includes a club option for his age-40 season.

Dylan Baker RHP

Born: 4/6/92   Age: 23   Bats: R   Throws: R   Height: 6'2"   Weight: 215

YEAR	TEAM	LVL	AGE	W	L	SV	G	GS	IP	H	HR	BB	K	BB/9	K/9	GB%	BABIP	WHIP	ERA	FIP	FRA	WARP
2013	LKC	A	21	7	6	0	27	25	143²	124	3	62	117	3.9	7.3	55%	.285	1.29	3.63	3.36	4.47	1.9
2014	CAR	A+	22	3	3	0	9	9	46²	45	3	18	28	3.5	5.4	58%	.278	1.35	4.05	4.37	5.13	0.2
2015	CLE	MLB	23	3	4	0	12	12	54²	62	6	29	32	4.7	5.3	51%	.305	1.66	5.53	5.59	6.01	-0.5

Breakout: 0%   Improve: 0%   Collapse: 0%   Attrition: 0%   MLB: 0%   Comparables: Rafael Dolis, Kevin Siegrist, Esmil Rogers

Much like his actor namesake, Baker seems destined for a succession of supporting roles. He has a lively fastball, a solid curve and a changeup that doesn't earn any adjective in particular. Baker lost some opportunity for further development of that change by breaking his ankle in 2014. He is thick and slow to the plate, and if he doesn't improve the changeup (and most players in his position never do), that adds up to "middle reliever." Which, when you think about it, analogizes pretty well to "played the Attorney General in one episode of The West Wing."

Trevor Bauer RHP

Born: 1/17/91   Age: 24   Bats: R   Throws: R   Height: 6'1"   Weight: 190

YEAR	TEAM	LVL	AGE	W	L	SV	G	GS	IP	H	HR	BB	K	BB/9	K/9	GB%	BABIP	WHIP	ERA	FIP	FRA	WARP
2012	MOB	AA	21	7	1	0	8	8	48¹	33	1	26	60	4.8	11.2	48%	.286	1.22	1.68	2.67	3.10	1.1
2012	RNO	AAA	21	5	1	0	14	14	82	74	8	35	97	3.8	10.6	46%	.319	1.33	2.85	3.85	4.00	2.1
2012	ARI	MLB	21	1	2	0	4	4	16¹	14	2	13	17	7.2	9.4	48%	.273	1.65	6.06	5.22	6.29	-0.1
2013	COH	AAA	22	6	7	0	22	22	121¹	119	14	73	106	5.4	7.9	43%	.307	1.58	4.15	5.08	5.78	-0.2
2013	CLE	MLB	22	1	2	0	4	4	17	15	3	16	11	8.5	5.8	36%	.240	1.82	5.29	7.08	8.39	-0.4
2014	COH	AAA	23	4	1	0	7	7	46	36	5	14	44	2.7	8.6	40%	.263	1.09	2.15	3.84	4.67	0.6
2014	CLE	MLB	23	5	8	0	26	26	153	151	16	60	143	3.5	8.4	37%	.312	1.38	4.18	4.04	4.26	1.2
2015	CLE	MLB	24	9	10	0	29	29	158¹	150	17	73	156	4.1	8.9	41%	.302	1.41	4.30	4.55	4.68	0.7

Breakout: 33%   Improve: 66%   Collapse: 14%   Attrition: 17%   MLB: 90%   Comparables: Homer Bailey, Mike Minor, Danny Duffy

After years of Bauer embracing the inner complexities of pitching, the right-hander simplified his process in order to harness the one critical aspect that had eluded him for his professional career: consistency. From a perspective of repertoire or mechanics, Bauer was playing chess before he had mastered checkers, but his advanced understanding of pitching will only prove its worth once he has mastered the basics of balance and repetition. He could age well, throwing in wrinkles of complication as his physical peak fades, but for now the key is to trust his stuff and hit his spots; he made great strides in that direction in 2014.

Charles Brewer RHP

Born: 4/7/88   Age: 27   Bats: R   Throws: R   Height: 6'3"   Weight: 205

YEAR	TEAM	LVL	AGE	W	L	SV	G	GS	IP	H	HR	BB	K	BB/9	K/9	GB%	BABIP	WHIP	ERA	FIP	FRA	WARP
2012	MOB	AA	24	0	0	0	3	3	17¹	19	2	2	13	1.0	6.8	48%	.304	1.21	4.15	3.49	4.75	0.1
2012	RNO	AAA	24	11	7	0	24	24	133²	177	26	34	104	2.3	7.0	44%	.345	1.58	5.99	5.47	6.50	0.8
2013	RNO	AAA	25	5	12	0	25	22	139²	158	13	43	107	2.8	6.9	51%	.334	1.44	4.90	4.36	5.17	1.7
2013	ARI	MLB	25	0	0	0	4	0	6	8	0	2	5	3.0	7.5	45%	.400	1.67	3.00	2.35	2.44	0.2
2014	MOB	AA	26	3	2	0	7	7	43¹	36	3	14	42	2.9	8.7	44%	.297	1.15	2.91	3.19	4.12	0.5
2014	RNO	AAA	26	8	10	0	22	22	126¹	146	10	34	96	2.4	6.8	47%	.340	1.42	4.99	4.13	4.67	2.6
2015	CLE	MLB	27	8	8	0	25	25	135¹	146	16	38	104	2.6	6.9	46%	.310	1.36	4.38	4.52	4.76	0.4

Breakout: 12%   Improve: 16%   Collapse: 14%   Attrition: 18%   MLB: 33%   *Comparables: Phil Irwin, Matt Shoemaker, Yohan Pino*

In 2013, Brewer, an Arizona native, fulfilled his lifelong dream of pitching for his boyhood team. In 2014, it was back to reality as the 26-year-old was once again a split resident of Reno and Mobile, the respective hosts of the Diamondbacks' Triple- and Double-A clubs. More of an organizational arm than a prospect, he has a good feel for the strike zone and keeps the ball in the yard. The latter is quite the accomplishment considering his time in the Pacific Coast League. He might have had a crack at the 12th pitching spot in Arizona, but he's more like 15th in Cleveland.

Carlos Carrasco   RHP

Born: 3/21/87   Age: 28   Bats: R   Throws: R   Height: 6'3"   Weight: 210

YEAR	TEAM	LVL	AGE	W	L	SV	G	GS	IP	H	HR	BB	K	BB/9	K/9	GB%	BABIP	WHIP	ERA	FIP	FRA	WARP
2013	COH	AAA	26	3	1	1	16	14	71²	59	6	21	79	2.6	9.9	45%	.285	1.12	3.14	3.22	4.03	1.2
2013	CLE	MLB	26	1	4	0	15	7	46²	64	4	18	30	3.5	5.8	50%	.364	1.76	6.75	4.13	4.76	0.2
2014	CLE	MLB	27	8	7	1	40	14	134	103	7	29	140	1.9	9.4	54%	.274	0.99	2.55	2.47	2.86	3.1
2015	CLE	MLB	28	6	5	0	26	16	107²	105	10	32	95	2.7	7.9	49%	.301	1.27	3.77	3.99	4.10	1.1

Breakout: 19%   Improve: 52%   Collapse: 15%   Attrition: 20%   MLB: 85%   *Comparables: Jeff Niemann, John Maine, Boof Bonser*

Carrasco completely reinvented himself in 2014 and he stands on the precipice of a big season if the improvements from late in the year carry over. His fastball velocity has increased by three ticks since the right-hander underwent Tommy John surgery in 2011, averaging 96 last season. He also features a pair of breaking pitches and a hard changeup, all of which proved to be unhittable. He began the year as a starter but was ineffective through four games, after which he was shuttled to the bullpen. He ditched his windup at that point, which allowed him to simplify his mechanics to a single timing pattern without losing effectiveness. Success in the 'pen brought him back to the starter's role, where he maintained the all-stretch approach, a simple fix that converted Carrasco into a pitcher with excellent command of his explosive stuff.

Kyle Crockett   LHP

Born: 12/15/91   Age: 23   Bats: L   Throws: L   Height: 6'2"   Weight: 170

YEAR	TEAM	LVL	AGE	W	L	SV	G	GS	IP	H	HR	BB	K	BB/9	K/9	GB%	BABIP	WHIP	ERA	FIP	FRA	WARP
2013	AKR	AA	21	1	0	0	9	0	10¹	7	0	2	9	1.7	7.8	67%	.259	0.87	0.00	2.16	2.75	0.2
2014	AKR	AA	22	0	0	6	15	0	15²	8	0	3	17	1.7	9.8	60%	.211	0.70	0.57	1.95	2.32	0.5
2014	CLE	MLB	22	4	1	0	43	0	30	26	2	8	28	2.4	8.4	57%	.296	1.13	1.80	3.26	3.19	0.4
2015	CLE	MLB	23	2	1	1	43	0	39²	37	3	11	38	2.5	8.6	52%	.299	1.20	3.33	3.57	3.62	0.6

Breakout: 20%   Improve: 27%   Collapse: 13%   Attrition: 17%   MLB: 48%   *Comparables: Drew Storen, Kelvin Herrera, Chance Ruffin*

The college left-hander made his MLB debut at Progressive Field less than one year after the Indians selected him in the fourth round of the 2013 draft. He relies on deception to increase his effectiveness, with a modest fastball that averaged 90 mph last season but which features good movement to encourage weak contact. He also has a sweeping breaker with curveball velocity but the two-plane trajectory of a slider. The former college closer may lack the raw stuff typically associated with the stopper role, but he is quickly carving a place for himself as a lefty specialist and mop-up reliever. Crockett's delivery starts with a normal leg lift and a slight lean to the third-base side during his stride, but he suddenly drops down to a near-submarine level after foot strike, finishing with a sidearm slot and a release point that falls into Pat Neshek territory.

Gavin Floyd   RHP

Born: 6/9/88   Age: 27   Bats: R   Throws: R   Height: 6'1"   Weight: 175

YEAR	TEAM	LVL	AGE	W	L	SV	G	GS	IP	H	HR	BB	K	BB/9	K/9	GB%	BABIP	WHIP	ERA	FIP	FRA	WARP
2012	CHA	MLB	29	12	11	0	29	29	168	166	22	63	144	3.4	7.7	48%	.299	1.36	4.29	4.41	5.00	1.6
2013	CHA	MLB	30	0	4	0	5	5	24¹	27	4	12	25	4.4	9.2	52%	.333	1.60	5.18	4.64	4.84	0.1
2014	GWN	AAA	31	1	1	0	5	5	19¹	17	3	9	11	4.2	5.1	52%	.241	1.34	3.26	5.79	6.40	-0.1
2014	ATL	MLB	31	2	2	0	9	9	54¹	55	6	13	45	2.2	7.5	53%	.302	1.25	2.65	3.77	4.38	0.3
2015	CLE	MLB	32	3	3	0	10	10	56	56	6	16	47	2.6	7.6	47%	.305	1.29	3.94	4.29	4.28	0.5

Breakout: 21%   Improve: 43%   Collapse: 24%   Attrition: 9%   MLB: 80%   *Comparables: Wandy Rodriguez, Brett Myers, John Lackey*

Though Floyd missed most of 2013 due to Tommy John surgery, he gambled on himself during the offseason when he turned down a multi-year deal in favor of a one-year agreement with the Braves. His performance through most of nine starts vindicated his decision, as his ERA and strikeout-to-walk rate were in career-best shape. "Most of" because Floyd then felt a pop in his arm during a start at Washington, which he assumed had to do with leftover scar tissue from the operation. Nope. Turned out he fractured his olecranon, ending his season and ruining what should have been a happy homecoming. (He grew up in nearby Annapolis, Maryland.) Floyd showed enough in his nine starts for Chris Antonetti to guarantee him a rotation spot, inasmuch as anything is ever guaranteed in Floyd's life.

Nick Hagadone   LHP

Born: 1/1/86   Age: 29   Bats: L   Throws: L   Height: 6'5"   Weight: 230

YEAR	TEAM	LVL	AGE	W	L	SV	G	GS	IP	H	HR	BB	K	BB/9	K/9	GB%	BABIP	WHIP	ERA	FIP	FRA	WARP
2012	CLE	MLB	26	1	0	1	27	0	25¹	26	4	15	26	5.3	9.2	37%	.310	1.62	6.39	4.82	5.22	0.0
2013	COH	AAA	27	2	3	7	27	0	32¹	24	1	17	46	4.7	12.8	40%	.315	1.27	2.51	2.34	2.30	1.1
2013	CLE	MLB	27	0	1	0	36	0	31¹	24	4	21	30	6.0	8.6	40%	.256	1.44	5.46	4.83	5.57	-0.4
2014	COH	AAA	28	3	4	1	23	0	28²	26	5	12	41	3.8	12.9	43%	.333	1.33	3.77	4.13	5.51	0.1
2014	CLE	MLB	28	1	0	0	35	0	23¹	18	3	6	27	2.3	10.4	36%	.273	1.03	2.70	3.29	3.33	0.3
2015	CLE	MLB	29	2	1	0	40	0	44²	40	5	22	47	4.5	9.5	41%	.298	1.39	3.90	4.47	4.23	0.3

Breakout: 13%   Improve: 22%   Collapse: 20%   Attrition: 26%   MLB: 52%   *Comparables: Dan Runzler, Donnie Veal, Clay Zavada*

Hagadone has prototypical size for a pitcher, but his release height breaks the mold. The theoretical king of downhill plane has the tallest release point in the majors, averaging close to seven and a half feet of vertical height as he invokes all of the mechanical strategies at his disposal to coax extra elevation: He creates massive spine tilt to manipulate an over-the-top arm slot, uses very little flex in his knees to raise his foundation and has long limbs that help to exaggerate these "stay tall" methods. He also serves as a counterexample to the conventional fallacy that downhill plane promotes higher groundball rates, with a fly-heavy profile that leaves him vulnerable to long drives when he catches too much plate with his fastball.

T.J. House   LHP

Born: 9/29/89   Age: 25   Bats: R   Throws: L   Height: 6'1"   Weight: 205

YEAR	TEAM	LVL	AGE	W	L	SV	G	GS	IP	H	HR	BB	K	BB/9	K/9	GB%	BABIP	WHIP	ERA	FIP	FRA	WARP
2012	CAR	A+	22	2	0	0	4	4	25	17	1	6	26	2.2	9.4	56%	.246	0.92	1.44	2.91	3.48	0.5
2012	AKR	AA	22	8	5	0	23	23	124¹	114	7	44	90	3.2	6.5	52%	.285	1.27	3.98	3.72	5.10	0.2
2013	AKR	AA	23	2	1	0	4	4	22¹	20	1	3	27	1.2	10.9	57%	.333	1.03	3.22	1.89	2.47	0.8
2013	COH	AAA	23	7	10	0	24	24	141²	163	11	54	110	3.4	7.0	56%	.338	1.53	4.32	3.89	5.01	0.6
2014	COH	AAA	24	1	4	0	10	10	57	56	3	16	42	2.5	6.6	60%	.312	1.26	3.79	3.52	5.26	0.3
2014	CLE	MLB	24	5	3	0	19	18	102	113	10	22	80	1.9	7.1	62%	.332	1.32	3.35	3.72	3.96	1.3
2015	*CLE*	*MLB*	*25*	*7*	*9*	*0*	*24*	*24*	*133²*	*149*	*14*	*50*	*91*	*3.3*	*6.1*	*50%*	*.312*	*1.48*	*4.89*	*4.85*	*5.32*	*-0.4*

Breakout: 33%   Improve: 55%   Collapse: 13%   Attrition: 39%   MLB: 81%   Comparables: *Wade Miley, Anthony Swarzak, Clayton Mortensen*

T.J. threw a House party in Cleveland after Justin Masterson left town, replacing him in the rotation with a mirrored approach from the south side of the rubber. His delivery is part Felix Hernandez, part Alex Wood and part Chris Sale (it looks as funky as it sounds), not to mention a mustache that hails from the Rod Beck Studio of Facial Fuzz. House's slider was his premier pitch, with a low sweeping break that coaxed 65 percent of his strikeouts in his rookie season, but the sinker and changeup were hit hard. The three-pitch mix comes from a near-sidearm slot and all of his pitches are masked by a common trajectory out of his hand. Most intriguing is the exceedingly low walk rate from a pitcher whose arm slot dictates a ton of lateral variation on his pitches, such that mistimed offerings tend to miss wide of the zone. He rarely elevated pitches above the belt in 2014, and he could get a full season to film House Party 2 if he can continue to keep it down.

Corey Kluber   RHP

Born: 4/10/86   Age: 29   Bats: R   Throws: R   Height: 6'4"   Weight: 215

YEAR	TEAM	LVL	AGE	W	L	SV	G	GS	IP	H	HR	BB	K	BB/9	K/9	GB%	BABIP	WHIP	ERA	FIP	FRA	WARP
2012	COH	AAA	26	11	7	0	21	21	125¹	121	9	49	128	3.5	9.2	48%	.316	1.36	3.59	3.34	4.56	1.6
2012	CLE	MLB	26	2	5	0	12	12	63	76	9	18	54	2.6	7.7	46%	.342	1.49	5.14	4.24	4.81	0.3
2013	COH	AAA	27	1	1	0	2	2	12¹	14	2	3	12	2.2	8.8	51%	.343	1.38	6.57	4.10	4.99	0.0
2013	CLE	MLB	27	11	5	0	26	24	147¹	153	15	33	136	2.0	8.3	48%	.329	1.26	3.85	3.33	3.97	2.0
2014	CLE	MLB	28	18	9	0	34	34	235²	207	14	51	269	1.9	10.3	50%	.316	1.09	2.44	2.37	2.84	6.0
2015	*CLE*	*MLB*	*29*	*11*	*10*	*0*	*30*	*30*	*181¹*	*182*	*16*	*55*	*181*	*2.7*	*9.0*	*44%*	*.321*	*1.30*	*3.99*	*3.72*	*4.33*	*1.4*

Breakout: 19%   Improve: 41%   Collapse: 12%   Attrition: 18%   MLB: 68%   Comparables: *Wade LeBlanc, Marco Estrada, Rich Hill*

If Kluber's 2013 season was the breakout, then last year was the breakthrough. After a slow start, the right-handed locomotive picked up steam as the season progressed and finished with an electric five-start run that included a 1.12 ERA and 54 strikeouts against five walks in 40 innings of work, not to mention five consecutive W's that surely helped win the hearts of the voters for certain hardware. He flew past a Vulture from Chicago, trounced a pack of trophy-winning Tigers and dethroned the King of Seattle to capture the AL Cy Young crown. Kluber receives a rare "A" grade for his mechanics, a critical aspect that underlies his excellent command of mid-90s velocity. He backs that up with an exploding slider that has been known to give Crash Davis nightmares. He throws the breaking ball with two distinct shapes, yet similar velocity, including a 12-to-6 version and another that has two-plane movement, and the pitch was his finishing move for 128 of his 269 strikeouts. And he did all this pitching in front of the team with the worst defensive efficiency in the league, leading to an ERA that, as good as it was, actually underperformed his FIP.

C.C. Lee   RHP

Born: 10/21/86   Age: 28   Bats: R   Throws: R   Height: 5'11"   Weight: 190

YEAR	TEAM	LVL	AGE	W	L	SV	G	GS	IP	H	HR	BB	K	BB/9	K/9	GB%	BABIP	WHIP	ERA	FIP	FRA	WARP
2013	COH	AAA	26	1	0	0	19	0	19	14	1	5	24	2.4	11.4	46%	.310	1.00	2.37	2.31	3.23	0.4
2013	CLE	MLB	26	0	0	0	8	0	4¹	4	0	3	4	6.2	8.3	29%	.286	1.62	4.15	4.00	5.02	0.0
2014	COH	AAA	27	0	1	3	25	0	30	29	1	9	37	2.7	11.1	42%	.359	1.27	3.30	2.42	3.01	0.8
2014	CLE	MLB	27	1	1	0	37	0	28	30	3	12	26	3.9	8.4	43%	.325	1.50	4.50	4.30	4.41	0.1
2015	*CLE*	*MLB*	*28*	*2*	*1*	*0*	*41*	*0*	*47²*	*42*	*4*	*17*	*53*	*3.2*	*10.0*	*48%*	*.306*	*1.24*	*3.47*	*3.65*	*3.77*	*0.6*

Breakout: 11%   Improve: 16%   Collapse: 17%   Attrition: 27%   MLB: 45%   Comparables: *Brandon Gomes, Scott Maine, Michael Schwimer*

Despite superficially representing the perfect amalgamation of former Cleveland superheroes CC Sabathia and Cliff Lee, the current Indians sidewinder is actually more of a bizarro version of those two pitchers, what with his relief work, right-handedness, lack of command and even a Tommy John surgery on his resume. With a combined total of 61 strikeouts against 14 walks across 49 innings in his past two seasons in the minors, Lee earned an extended look at the highest level. In the majors, his walk rate rose while his mid-90s sinker and high-frequency slider proved to be minimally effective in his first extended tour of duty, but the combination of deception and velocity should earn him multiple opportunities to succeed.

Shaun Marcum   RHP

Born: 12/14/81   Age: 33   Bats: R   Throws: R   Height: 6'0"   Weight: 195

YEAR	TEAM	LVL	AGE	W	L	SV	G	GS	IP	H	HR	BB	K	BB/9	K/9	GB%	BABIP	WHIP	ERA	FIP	FRA	WARP
2012	WIS	A	30	1	0	0	3	3	12²	9	1	3	10	2.1	7.1	40%	.222	0.95	2.84	3.51	4.19	0.2
2012	MIL	MLB	30	7	4	0	21	21	124	116	16	41	109	3.0	7.9	37%	.280	1.27	3.70	4.14	4.30	1.3
2013	NYN	MLB	31	1	10	0	14	12	78¹	85	7	21	60	2.4	6.9	38%	.322	1.35	5.29	3.61	3.86	0.7
2014	COH	AAA	32	1	0	0	8	1	15¹	10	1	6	10	3.5	5.9	40%	.214	1.04	2.35	4.27	5.12	-0.1
2015	*CLE*	*MLB*	*33*	*2*	*2*	*0*	*6*	*6*	*35²*	*35*	*4*	*10*	*29*	*2.4*	*7.4*	*38%*	*.292*	*1.25*	*3.74*	*4.32*	*4.07*	*0.4*

Breakout: 6%   Improve: 36%   Collapse: 18%   Attrition: 17%   MLB: 81%   Comparables: *Freddy Garcia, Jake Peavy, John Lackey*

Marcum became yet another victim of thoracic outlet syndrome, a debilitating nerve condition that ravages the pitcher's throwing shoulder. The procedure required to fix it proved to be a death knell for the career of Cardinals ace Chris Carpenter and Marcum might be following in those footsteps. Never known for his velocity, he now faces an uphill battle to recapture even the modest speed of his youth; his big-league future hangs in the balance.

Zach McAllister   RHP

Born: 12/8/87   Age: 27   Bats: R   Throws: R   Height: 6'6"   Weight: 240

YEAR	TEAM	LVL	AGE	W	L	SV	G	GS	IP	H	HR	BB	K	BB/9	K/9	GB%	BABIP	WHIP	ERA	FIP	FRA	WARP
2012	COH	AAA	24	5	2	0	11	11	63¹	59	5	19	52	2.7	7.4	40%	.300	1.23	2.98	3.54	4.47	0.9
2012	CLE	MLB	24	6	8	0	22	22	125¹	133	19	38	110	2.7	7.9	41%	.304	1.36	4.24	4.20	4.67	0.7
2013	CLE	MLB	25	9	9	0	24	24	134¹	134	13	49	101	3.3	6.8	39%	.295	1.36	3.75	4.06	4.31	0.8
2014	COH	AAA	26	7	1	0	11	11	69	57	3	14	59	1.8	7.7	44%	.276	1.03	2.09	2.86	3.78	1.2
2014	CLE	MLB	26	4	7	0	22	15	86	96	7	28	74	2.9	7.7	43%	.332	1.44	5.23	3.47	4.48	0.6
2015	CLE	MLB	27	8	8	0	24	24	133¹	141	14	38	104	2.6	7.0	40%	.309	1.34	4.23	4.31	4.59	0.7

Breakout: 32%   Improve: 63%   Collapse: 12%   Attrition: 17%   MLB: 86%   Comparables: *Dillon Gee, Juan Nicasio, Anthony Reyes*

The Indians used McAllister to start games as well as finish them, but his fastball-heavy repertoire and questionable secondaries should hasten a full-time transition to the bullpen. He brings mid-90s heat with arm-side run and dials it up nearly 75 percent of the time. The breaking stuff is light on movement despite large velocity differentials; it includes two distinct pitches that both follow single-plane flight paths with vertical depth but a lack of lateral movement. The peripherals suggest that McAllister was an innocent victim of the vagaries of balls in play, but the narrative is distorted by an approach that was relatively easy for opposing batters to decipher, resulting in a 28 percent line-drive rate on his fastball that ranked in the top (the bad kind of top) decile of pitchers.

Adam Miller   RHP

Born: 11/26/84   Age: 30   Bats: R   Throws: R   Height: 6'4"   Weight: 215

YEAR	TEAM	LVL	AGE	W	L	SV	G	GS	IP	H	HR	BB	K	BB/9	K/9	GB%	BABIP	WHIP	ERA	FIP	FRA	WARP
2012	TRN	AA	27	0	3	0	8	8	39	57	2	13	14	3.0	3.2	51%	.362	1.79	5.08	4.30	6.04	-0.2
2012	SWB	AAA	27	0	1	0	5	0	10	13	0	4	4	3.6	3.6	58%	.361	1.70	4.50	3.56	4.65	0.0
2014	AKR	AA	29	1	2	0	28	0	41¹	39	6	14	43	3.0	9.4	52%	.289	1.28	5.44	4.32	5.63	-0.2
2015	CLE	MLB	30	1	1	1	18	2	33	39	4	14	21	3.8	5.7	48%	.320	1.60	5.41	5.38	5.88	-0.3

Breakout: 2%   Improve: 2%   Collapse: 0%   Attrition: 2%   MLB: 4%   Comparables: *Amauri Sanit, Zack Segovia, Scott Randall*

Six years ago, we called Miller "the Tribe's answer to Rich Harden." The five-time *Baseball America* top-100 prospect with the one-time triple-digit heat responded by not pitching at all in 2009 and 2010. Since then, he's put up bad ERAs, largely out of the bullpen, in both organized and independent ball, including spending all of 2013 striking out just over one batter per walk for the Sugar Land Skeeters. His return to Double-A last season was not exactly a triumph, but a strikeout per inning is a strikeout per inning. After all the travails, he's only now 30, and weirder things than Miller pitching in the big leagues have happened. How could you not root for a guy who was once quoted saying, about the middle finger on which he's had four surgeries, "I looked down at the finger and stuff was just spewing out of there."

Marc Rzepczynski   LHP

Born: 8/29/85   Age: 29   Bats: L   Throws: L   Height: 6'2"   Weight: 220

YEAR	TEAM	LVL	AGE	W	L	SV	G	GS	IP	H	HR	BB	K	BB/9	K/9	GB%	BABIP	WHIP	ERA	FIP	FRA	WARP
2012	SLN	MLB	26	1	3	0	70	0	46²	46	7	17	33	3.3	6.4	59%	.281	1.35	4.24	4.76	5.65	-0.5
2013	MEM	AAA	27	1	2	0	32	0	44	44	1	18	31	3.7	6.3	57%	.297	1.41	3.07	3.75	4.03	0.8
2013	CLE	MLB	27	0	0	0	27	0	20¹	11	1	6	20	2.7	8.9	58%	.204	0.84	0.89	3.08	3.76	0.1
2013	SLN	MLB	27	0	0	0	11	0	10¹	16	1	4	9	3.5	7.8	56%	.429	1.94	7.84	3.99	4.38	0.0
2014	CLE	MLB	28	0	3	1	73	0	46	42	1	19	46	3.7	9.0	61%	.323	1.33	2.74	2.88	3.22	0.5
2015	CLE	MLB	29	3	1	1	54	0	44	43	4	17	40	3.5	8.1	55%	.306	1.36	4.13	4.22	4.48	0.2

Breakout: 44%   Improve: 62%   Collapse: 16%   Attrition: 13%   MLB: 88%   Comparables: *Nick Masset, J.P. Howell, Rafael Perez*

The token LOOGY in a bullpen full of every-other-day relievers. Rzepczynski nailed the role, with 73 percent of his appearances lasting fewer than three outs, and 55 percent of his opponents standing in the left-handed batter's box. The southpaw is seemingly impervious to the velocity attrition that plagues most pitchers' fastballs, having averaged a consistent 92.5 mph on his heat for the past four seasons. His approach is simple: Sinkers early and sliders late in the count, mix in the changeup when he gets ahead of right-handed bats. Wash. Rinse. Repeat.

Danny Salazar   RHP

Born: 1/11/90   Age: 25   Bats: L   Throws: R   Height: 6'0"   Weight: 190

YEAR	TEAM	LVL	AGE	W	L	SV	G	GS	IP	H	HR	BB	K	BB/9	K/9	GB%	BABIP	WHIP	ERA	FIP	FRA	WARP
2012	CAR	A+	22	1	2	0	16	16	53²	46	3	19	53	3.2	8.9	42%	.307	1.21	2.68	3.20	4.07	1.0
2012	AKR	AA	22	4	0	0	6	6	34	25	1	8	23	2.1	6.1	48%	.240	0.97	1.85	2.94	3.69	0.5
2013	AKR	AA	23	2	3	0	7	7	33²	27	1	10	51	2.7	13.6	33%	.366	1.10	2.67	1.57	2.39	1.2
2013	COH	AAA	23	4	2	1	14	13	59¹	44	4	14	78	2.1	11.8	42%	.303	0.98	2.73	2.26	3.44	1.4
2013	CLE	MLB	23	2	3	0	10	10	52	44	7	15	65	2.6	11.2	37%	.298	1.13	3.12	3.19	3.61	0.8
2014	COH	AAA	24	4	6	0	11	11	60²	58	7	28	76	4.2	11.3	38%	.323	1.42	3.71	3.79	4.40	0.8
2014	CLE	MLB	24	6	8	0	20	20	110	117	13	35	120	2.9	9.8	36%	.343	1.38	4.25	3.55	4.09	1.4
2015	CLE	MLB	25	11	10	0	32	32	166²	156	18	54	181	2.9	9.8	38%	.312	1.26	3.64	3.81	3.96	2.2

Breakout: 39%   Improve: 63%   Collapse: 19%   Attrition: 17%   MLB: 91%   Comparables: *Danny Duffy, Jordan Zimmermann, Francisco Liriano*

Salazar was a shell of himself to start last season, as his mechanics fell out of whack and he struggled to stabilize his high-powered delivery. The right-hander's fastball was shy a couple of ticks in the early going and he was sent down to the minors to iron out the wrinkles. He made some improvements and resurfaced in Cleveland over the summer, pitching well over the second half of the season, though he lacked the overpowering stuff and mechanical efficiency that hallmarked his 2013 performance. Salazar has the talent and athleticism to recapture those skills, combined with a strong coaching staff that has earned a reputation for coaxing the best from its moundsmen.

Bryan Shaw   RHP

Born: 11/8/87   Age: 27   Bats: B   Throws: R   Height: 6'1"   Weight: 210

YEAR	TEAM	LVL	AGE	W	L	SV	G	GS	IP	H	HR	BB	K	BB/9	K/9	GB%	BABIP	WHIP	ERA	FIP	FRA	WARP
2012	ARI	MLB	24	1	6	2	64	0	59¹	60	4	24	41	3.6	6.2	57%	.309	1.42	3.49	3.95	4.82	0.0
2013	CLE	MLB	25	7	3	1	70	0	75	60	4	28	73	3.4	8.8	46%	.271	1.17	3.24	3.10	3.22	1.3
2014	CLE	MLB	26	5	5	2	80	0	76¹	61	6	22	64	2.6	7.5	50%	.251	1.09	2.59	3.45	3.82	0.7
2015	CLE	MLB	27	3	1	2	64	0	63²	60	5	22	53	3.1	7.4	50%	.290	1.28	3.68	4.08	4.00	0.7

Breakout: 34%   Improve: 54%   Collapse: 17%   Attrition: 16%   MLB: 84%   Comparables: Jeremy Accardo, Brandon League, Darren O'Day

The Indians put their bullpen to work in 2014, and Shaw logged the most hours of the crew, leading baseball in and setting a team record for appearances. He's one of those pitchers who gets a lot more local love than national because of his usage as an effective set-up man rather than a closer. Shaw's bread and butter is a cut fastball at 92 to 95 mph that he throws 70 percent of the time; he pairs it with a low-80s put-away slider. The breaking ball has more of a vertical shape when he hits targets on the arm side but noticeable two-plane break when thrown to the left side of the zone, and the subtle explosiveness of his cutter keeps batters too busy tracking incoming projectiles to adjust effectively.

Justus Sheffield   RHP

Born: 5/13/96   Age: 19   Bats: L   Throws: L   Height: 5'10"   Weight: 195

YEAR	TEAM	LVL	AGE	W	L	SV	G	GS	IP	H	HR	BB	K	BB/9	K/9	GB%	BABIP	WHIP	ERA	FIP	FRA	WARP
2015	CLE	MLB	19	1	1	0	8	2	31²	37	4	20	20	5.6	5.7	45%	.315	1.79	6.12	6.12	6.66	-0.4

Breakout: 0%   Improve: 0%   Collapse: 0%   Attrition: 0%   MLB: 0%   Comparables: Matt Moore, Michael Blazek, Joe Wieland

Athleticism and bloodlines are the key words for Sheffield, nephew of The Iron Sheff himself. The Indians were able to lure Sheffield The Younger away from Vanderbilt for a touch under slot money. He has an athletic delivery, four pitches and a feel for the changeup, which is both rare and critical considering his age, handedness and lack of typical pitcher size. These are the raw ingredients of a mid-rotation starter. They are also, however, the raw ingredients of everything else on the baseball map; at just 19, Sheffield's got a lot of time left in the oven before we can pull him out and see what he is.

Josh Tomlin   RHP

Born: 10/19/84   Age: 30   Bats: R   Throws: R   Height: 6'1"   Weight: 190

YEAR	TEAM	LVL	AGE	W	L	SV	G	GS	IP	H	HR	BB	K	BB/9	K/9	GB%	BABIP	WHIP	ERA	FIP	FRA	WARP
2012	CLE	MLB	27	5	8	0	21	16	103¹	126	18	25	56	2.2	4.9	43%	.309	1.46	6.36	5.04	5.96	-0.7
2013	COH	AAA	28	2	0	0	3	3	15	12	0	0	11	0.0	6.6	28%	.279	0.80	2.40	2.14	3.19	0.4
2013	CLE	MLB	28	0	0	0	1	0	2	2	0	0	0	0.0	0.0	38%	.250	1.00	0.00	3.08	3.80	0.0
2014	COH	AAA	29	2	1	0	6	6	40	26	5	10	33	2.2	7.4	37%	.210	0.90	2.25	4.08	5.24	0.3
2014	CLE	MLB	29	6	9	0	25	16	104	120	18	14	94	1.2	8.1	39%	.320	1.29	4.76	4.03	4.93	0.0
2015	CLE	MLB	30	6	6	0	18	18	104²	108	14	21	72	1.8	6.2	39%	.286	1.24	4.11	4.63	4.47	0.7

Breakout: 13%   Improve: 32%   Collapse: 18%   Attrition: 14%   MLB: 70%   Comparables: Andy Sonnanstine, Glen Perkins, Kevin Slowey

A common repercussion of Tommy John surgery, even for those who make a full recovery, is poor control in the short term as the pitcher rediscovers his release point. Tomlin had no such issues, throwing as many strikes as ever while posting a 3 percent walk rate that was the lowest of his career. His velocity was also unharmed, with a 90 mph average on his fastball that was a near lock for his radar-gun readings of 2012. If anything, Tomlin stayed too close to the strike zone with his modest repertoire: His fly-ball tendencies led to copious slow trots from opposing batters, and for the second time in his career the right-hander surrendered more homers than he did free passes. At least he squelched the running game: Opposing baserunners were just 1-for-3 on stolen base attempts in 2014.

Lineouts

Hitters

NAME	POS	TEAM	LVL	AGE	PA	R	2B	3B	HR	RBI	BB	K	SB	CS	AVG/OBP/SLG	TAv	BABIP	BRR	FRAA	WARP
Tyler Holt	LF	AKR	AA	25	156	13	4	1	0	14	27	26	11	2	.298/.416/.347	.307	.366	-1.4	LF(17): -0.6, RF(10): -0.8	0.9
	CF	COH	AAA	25	272	61	15	0	2	16	39	45	20	4	.308/.416/.401	.276	.378	4.0	CF(53): 2.4, LF(5): -0.0	2.2
	RF	CLE	MLB	25	76	4	2	0	0	2	3	25	2	0	.268/.307/.296	.223	.413	-0.1	RF(28): 0.0, CF(9): -0.1	-0.1
Bryan LaHair	1B	AKR	AA	31	417	38	17	2	5	60	50	91	1	1	.234/.324/.332	.244	.295	-6.1	1B(80): 0.5	-0.9
	1B	COH	AAA	31	36	2	2	0	0	4	1	10	0	0	.114/.139/.171	.116	.160	-0.5	1B(3): 0.0, RF(2): -0.1	-0.6
Sicnarf Loopstok	C	LKC	A	21	41	7	2	1	1	2	3	7	2	0	.278/.366/.472	.312	.321	0.3	C(10): 0.2	0.4
Carlos Moncrief	RF	COH	AAA	25	530	64	33	4	12	63	38	130	8	3	.271/.328/.431	.254	.347	0.0	RF(127): 9.5, CF(2): -0.0	2.2
Nyjer Morgan	CF	COH	AAA	33	64	4	4	0	1	7	3	16	1	0	.200/.234/.317	.182	.250	-0.3	CF(13): -0.8	-0.5
	CF	CLE	MLB	33	52	8	1	0	1	6	7	6	3	0	.341/.429/.439	.342	.371	0.5	CF(12): -0.3, LF(2): -0.0	0.7
Roberto Perez	C	COH	AAA	25	209	29	11	1	8	43	29	51	1	0	.305/.405/.517	.299	.388	-1.2	C(53): 0.8	2.0
	C	CLE	MLB	25	95	10	5	0	1	4	5	26	0	0	.271/.311/.365	.245	.379	-1.5	C(29): -0.3	0.1
Luigi Rodriguez	RF	CAR	A+	21	393	50	13	4	6	30	50	88	15	8	.250/.347/.366	.273	.320	-0.6	RF(63): 4.9, LF(17): 1.0	1.4
Ronny Rodriguez	2B	AKR	AA	22	447	52	25	0	5	34	25	92	4	5	.228/.270/.324	.222	.276	4.0	2B(45): 0.9, 3B(40): -1.8	-0.6
Tony Wolters	C	AKR	AA	22	387	36	15	2	1	34	35	74	3	2	.249/.319/.314	.242	.309	2.9	C(66): -0.9, 2B(10): -0.4	1.4

Bobby Bradley, a lefty first baseman with significant power out of a Mississippi high school, was Cleveland's third-round pick, though he required second-round money to sway him from college. ❖ **Tyler Holt** has a patient approach, good speed and baserunning IQ and a ton of frequent-flyer miles from his constant shuttling between Columbus and Cleveland. ❖ **Bryan LaHair** couldn't hack it in Nippon Professional Baseball, signed a minor-league deal with Cleveland and proved that his bat had regressed below even Double-A level; don't look for him in the 2016 edition of this book. ❖ **Sicnarf Loopstok** missed most of 2014 with injury; his name's writing checks that his body can't cash. ❖ **Carlos Moncrief** started on the mound thanks to a fastball that touched the mid-90s, but he switched to the outfield after spate of arm issues; he's obviously got an elite outfield arm, but there's plus power to go along with it. ❖ **Nyjer Morgan** came back from Japan on a minor-league deal with Cleveland, hit well in the majors for a few weeks, had his right knee buckle while chasing a fly ball in mid-May, came off the disabled list in August just in time to be released and signed in December with the Hanwha Eagles in Korea. ❖ **Roberto Perez** was stricken by Bell's Palsy early in the season but that can't stop someone nicknamed "Robocop." He graduated to the majors in July and assumed the role of unheralded backup catcher. ❖ **Luigi Rodriguez** is a switch-hitting center fielder who took a step back in High-A, denting his chances of becoming the first Luigi in major-league history. ❖ **Ronny Rodriguez** had his second straight year of backsliding after a breakout 2012; he's playing the corner infield spots a lot more these days, another hit to his stock. ❖ **Tony Wolters** converted from the middle infield in 2013 and is now donning the tools of ignorance; as you'd expect, he has a long way to go on the nuances of defense behind the plate.

Pitchers

NAME	TEAM	LVL	AGE	W	L	SV	G	GS	IP	H	HR	BB	K	BB/9	K/9	GB%	BABIP	WHIP	ERA	FIP	FRA	WARP
Austin Adams	COH	AAA	27	3	2	5	42	0	54	44	4	16	52	2.7	8.7	49%	.282	1.11	2.50	3.28	4.18	0.7
	CLE	MLB	27	0	0	0	6	0	7	9	1	1	4	1.3	5.1	56%	.333	1.43	9.00	4.30	6.49	-0.1
Cody Anderson	AKR	AA	23	4	11	0	25	25	125²	141	17	45	81	3.2	5.8	46%	.312	1.48	5.44	4.62	5.78	0.0
Tyler Cloyd	COH	AAA	27	10	8	0	27	26	166²	181	26	31	118	1.7	6.4	44%	.301	1.27	3.89	4.62	5.78	0.0
Kyle Davies	AKR	AA	30	2	1	0	5	5	29²	28	7	7	18	2.1	5.5	36%	.239	1.18	3.03	6.12	7.34	-0.5
	COH	AAA	30	9	8	0	21	21	124²	130	10	33	80	2.4	5.8	44%	.303	1.31	4.11	3.98	5.06	0.7
J.P. Feyereisen	MHV	A-	21	3	0	4	15	0	17	9	0	1	24	0.5	12.7	36%	.273	0.59	0.00	0.97	1.84	0.3
Luis Lugo	LKC	A	20	10	9	0	27	22	126¹	124	16	40	146	2.8	10.4	41%	.325	1.30	4.92	3.86	4.76	1.4
Nick Maronde	ANA	MLB	24	0	0	0	11	0	6¹	12	0	7	7	9.9	9.9	39%	.522	3.00	12.79	4.74	5.20	-0.1
Adam Plutko	LKC	A	22	3	1	0	10	10	52²	49	1	12	66	2.1	11.3	44%	.350	1.16	3.93	1.97	2.98	1.6
	CAR	A+	22	4	9	0	18	18	97	99	11	18	78	1.7	7.2	33%	.306	1.21	4.08	4.00	4.70	1.0
Bryan Price	AKR	AA	27	1	0	1	8	0	10	7	2	2	16	1.8	14.4	38%	.263	0.90	1.80	3.35	2.92	0.3
	COH	AAA	27	0	1	4	20	0	26¹	19	3	10	28	3.4	9.6	39%	.242	1.10	2.73	3.85	6.10	-0.2
	CLE	MLB	27	0	0	0	3	0	2²	8	3	1	1	3.4	3.4	33%	.417	3.38	20.25	20.41	14.98	-0.3
Giovanni Soto	AKR	AA	23	0	2	1	37	0	53	45	2	12	49	2.0	8.3	59%	.291	1.08	3.23	2.73	3.60	1.0

Austin Adams throws smoke, sitting in the upper 90s with his fastball and scraping triple digits, and he flashed a potential plus changeup that fooled Miguel Cabrera. ❖ Repeating Double-A did broad righty **Cody Anderson** no favors as he got hit around again in 2014. He has a four-pitch mix but none of them miss bats. ❖ **Tyler Cloyd** spent a full season on the farm, feeding batters a blend of fastball variations that failed to crack 90 mph. He keeps the ball around the zone, which minimizes walks but leaves a lot of slop in the trough for hitters to feast on. ❖ **Kyle Davies** has spent the last three years trying to come back from right shoulder surgery, re-climbing the minor-league ladder through two organizations after missing the entire 2012 season; he's now just one rung away. ❖ **J.P. Feyereisen** has a strong, thick, maxed-out frame. He also had *literally* the best pitching line in professional baseball last year, and his surname sounds like what a pitching coach would say with a mouth full of chewing tobacco. ❖ **Luis Lugo** has the prototypical starter's body but he's lacking prototypical major-league arm speed; a back-end future is still possible. ❖ The velocity of 2012 failed to return for **Nick Maronde**, and a midseason strain of his throwing shoulder revealed the time bomb that had been loudly ticking; he was designated for assignment in mid-December. ❖ **Adam Plutko** threw in the mid-90s in high school but the velocity has been sliding backward ever since, so now he's a 90 mph strike-thrower, which is unlikely to work at higher levels. ❖ After seven seasons in the minors, The Other **Bryan Price** finally got his first crack at the big time when rosters expanded in September, but he was greeted rudely to the tune of three homers in just 19 batters faced; he was outrighted in December. ❖ Once thought of as a budding starter, **Giovanni Soto** is transitioning into a LOOGY role that will take advantage of his command/control profile.

Manager

Terry Francona

YEAR	TEAM	W	L	Py-thag +/-	Avg PC	100+ P	120+ P	QS	BQS	REL	REL w Zero R	IBB	PH	PH Avg	PH HR	SB2	CS2	SB3	CS3	SAC Att	SAC%	POS SAC	Squeeze	Swing	In Play
2013	CLE	92	70	1	94.9	68	0	73	5	540	454	26	58	.255	3	96	33	21	3	41	75.6%	30	0	332	85
2014	CLE	85	77	2	94.7	61	0	78	5	573	507	51	103	.233	0	96	23	8	4	63	81.0%	49	0	290	92

Francona has not guided a team to fewer than 85 wins since 2000. During that span, he has won two World Series and reached the postseason four additional times. Point is, Francona has been around a while, and has done enough in that while to earn a pass if he's uninterested in babying young pitchers.

Yet Francona did not take advantage of his legacy last season. Instead he refused to compromise his inexperienced rotation, which ended the season with two pitchers who had more than 50 career big-league starts. Among the group, Kluber—ùone of the relative graybeards—and Bauer were the only Cleveland starters to average 100 pitches per start, and together they accounted for 39 of the club's 66 triple-digit starts. Salazar and House meanwhile, each 24 years old, were afforded 100 pitches or more in just six of their 38 combined starts.

Rather than push his young starters, Francona placed the innings burden on his bullpen. That practice saw three Indians—Bryan Shaw, Chad Allen and Scott Atchison—finish in the top 10 in the majors in appearances made on zero days' rest. Another, Marc Rzepczynski, ranked second in the majors in appearances in which he entered with at least one runner on base (he did so in 40 of his 73 outings). Unsurprisingly, Cleveland as a whole paced the majors in both categories.

In an ideal world, Francona could have split the workload between the units. Since Francona didn't work in an ideal world, and since he had an unusual set of circumstances—a green rotation, competitive aspirations and a number of quality relievers—he seemingly made the correct call to put the pressure on his 'pen.

COLORADO ROCKIES

by David Roth

The best-case scenario is, naturally, the rarest. In this case, the team you care about is owned by a wealthy person who cares roughly equally about the community in which the team plays and the team's success, and understands the cultivation of the latter as a service to the former. In this model, the team is understood as a sort of public good—more popular and better-followed than the water company, although the effectiveness of the bullpen can move the needle there—and the owner's role is seen as a sort of trusteeship.

This type of owner would not jam fellow citizens with a nine-figure tab for a dubiously necessary new stadium; this type of owner would endeavor to hire the best people and treat those people well, deferring to the experts whenever possible and holding them to account as needed. This type of owner would understand which matters are the owner's concern and gladly stay the hell out of those that are not, so as better to focus on some responsible rich person hobby, like building hospitals in the developing world or dressage. This type of owner is nearly extinct in the wild.

In this world, we do not get to choose our team-owning rich guys, and the team-owning rich guys get to do a great deal of choosing. If we are lucky, we get to cheer for a team owned by the rare specimen rich enough to own a team and decent enough to understand that responsibility and role in an adult way. If we are not lucky, we get Dick and Charlie Monfort. The Colorado Rockies have their problems, both prosaic baseball-team problems and longstanding organizational failures big and small. But also they are unlucky. They got the Monforts. Oh brother do they ever have the Monforts.

❖ ❖ ❖

"I live in fear all the time," Dick Monfort told the *Denver Post*'s Mark Kiszla on July 8th. "Fear of losing." The Rockies had lost 32 of their previous 43 games at the time of the conversation. This was not the bottom.

The headlines scrolling up the side of the *Post*'s website tell the story of Monfort's next few days. July 10th: *Rockies owner Dick Monfort reaches out to fan after controversial email*, which email included the words "maybe Denver doesn't deserve a franchise, maybe time for it to find a new home." ("I do remember I was rapid-firing it," Monfort said later. "I don't even have an idea what I meant to say.") July 11th: *Rockies owner Dick Monfort issues formal apology to fans he's offended*. The team lost the next two games, to the Twins, by a combined 14 runs. The All-Star break began on July 14th. On July 17th, the headline was: *Rockies losing support from fed-up fans*. While they continued to draw well—this 66-win team ranked fifth in the National League in attendance—the season was, in most every other way, a disaster. Even the ways in which the season was less than disastrous had a faint whiff of the Hindenburg about them: The Rockies were a solid 45–36 at home, which—to spare you some very depressing arithmetic—meant they were an astonishing 21–60 away from Coors Field.

It is the subject of some debate in the Ownerologist community whether a team is worse off with an owner who does not care about the team's fortunes at all or whether it and its fans will suffer more under an owner who desperately wants a winning team but believes such a goal can only be realized through a maximum of micromanagerial oversight and ham-headed assertiveness from the owner's box. There are compelling and easily made cases for both sides, but the Monfort Administration Rockies offer strong evidence for the second argument.

During the last decade and a half, the Rockies have been both extremely bad and extremely stable, with General Manager Dan O'Dowd atop the org chart for a retrospectively inexplicable 15 years. As strange as O'Dowd's tenure was for those years of almost uninterrupted un-success—only the recently rejuvenated Orioles (five GMs during Colorado's Dan O'Dowd Era), Pirates (three GMs plus one interim) and Royals (three GMs) lost more games during those 15 years than did the Rockies—the fallout from O'Dowd's resignation at the end of the 2014 season revealed a degree of organizational weirdness that was stranger still. O'Dowd, it seemed, had been usurped to a great degree by associate GM Bill Geivett, and resigned only after turning down Monfort's offer of a reassignment and an opportunity to work alongside new GM and former farm director Jeff Bridich. (Geivett, whom Monfort blamed for the team's poor performance at the tail end of that July oversharing spree—because Geivett was "responsible for

ROCKIES PROSPECTUS
2014 W-L: 66-96, 4TH IN NL WEST

Pythag	.462	22nd	DER	.693	24th
RS/G	4.66	3rd	B-Age	27.2	4th
RA/G	5.05	30th	P-Age	27.9	10th
TAv	.258	16th	Salary	$92.6M	17th
BRR	-0.36	18th	M$/MW	$4.5M	24th
TAv-P	.269	26th	DL Days	1,052	26th
FIP	4.4	30th	$ on DL	35%	28th

Three-Year Park Factors

Runs	Runs/RH	Runs/LH	HR/RH	HR/LH
118	120	113	115	114

Top Hitter WARP	4.3	Nolan Arenado
Top Pitcher WARP	1.8	Tyler Matzek
Top Prospect		Jonathan Gray

the major league team"—also resigned at season's end.)

This is about as close to a fresh start as the Rockies are likely to have under the Monforts, who prize the team's distinctive culture—which includes a semi-public evangelical Christian component, courtesy of both born-again co-owner Charlie Monfort and O'Dowd—to a degree that would be laudable if it did not also preclude both executive accountability and an organizational strategy beyond Don't Stop Believing. It is not the Monforts' fault that the team's success is largely dependent on a pair of brittle but brilliant stars in Carlos Gonzalez and Troy Tulowitzki. Neither is it really the Monforts' fault that the team used 15 starting pitchers in 2014, among them Jair Jurrjens (24 baserunners and 11 earned runs over two starts/nine innings) and the un-magic Christians Friedrich and Bergman, who combined for a 5.93 ERA over 79 innings, 26 appearances and 13 starts.

But it is, finally, on the Monforts that this roster—and the farm system that offered no greater answers than We Actually Have This Other Guy Named Christian Who Also Pitches when injuries hit—was constructed by the same people, Good Baseball Men all, who had been entrusted with that task for 15 years, during which time the Rockies managed four seasons over .500. Whatever residual poignancy there is in Dick Monfort's evident and apparently authentic upset at his team's failure is canceled out, in the end, by his unwillingness or inability to notice that the same people had been giving him roughly the same team since Larry Summers was Treasury Secretary. Bridich, the ostensible new blood in the front office, has been with the organization since 2004.

✦✦✦

"We understand how difficult it is to build a culture in a world that's valued only on performance," O'Dowd said in 2012, "but we're going to continue to build a culture of value." In this sense, and more or less only in this sense, O'Dowd and his bosses succeeded. The Rockies are for better and mostly for worse one of the most distinctive organizations in Major League Baseball, one that adheres to its own cockeyed consistency even as it zigs and zags indefatigably in its effort to avoid the game's generally accepted best practices.

On-field results aside, baseball fans—humans in general, really—do not need another organization run with ruthless, umpteenth-decimal-point efficiency by an army of Robocop quants, and need it least of all in their leisure time. But there's nothing especially pleasant or likable about an organization that runs, always and everywhere, as the opposite, in which gut and culture are all and decision-makers are not so much held accountable as prayed-for and worried-about in private, and given fulsome votes of confidence in public. And there is nothing about that way of doing things that suggests it would, could or should produce a winning team with any more frequency than the Monfort/O'Dowd Rockies ever did. During that period, the Rockies had one team get dazzlingly hot and streak all the way to the World Series—which they lost in a tidy four-game sweep—in 2007, and 11 seasons of fewer than 76 wins. In each of the last four years, the team has finished at least 18 games out of first place.

It is fitting, then, that the Rockies appear certain to more or less stay the course in 2015. Monfort has been very clear about his unwillingness to trade either Gonzalez or Tulowitzki, despite their sizable contracts and sizable value. This is less unreasonable than it sounds—Gonzalez's value is at a low ebb

after a characteristically injury-marred and uncharacteristically poor season in 2014; Tulowitzki is unfailingly among the most valuable players in the game when healthy, but has averaged 88 games over the past three seasons, and has managed 150 games just twice in his eight big-league campaigns, and as such is unlikely to return satisfying value in a trade.

There is no reason for the Rockies to trade either of their cornerstone stars for financial relief or an appetizer-sampler of scatter-armed short-season prospects named Kale and Codee. Monfort has vetoed such trades in the past—late last season, he shut down a deal that would've sent ace-by-default Jorge De La Rosa to the Orioles—and is not necessarily wrong to do it. Some such deals have worked out well, and a great many haven't, but the Rockies have no real need to trade their best and most popular players simply for the sake of shaking things up. There is, also and anyway, no reason to think the Monfort-run Rockies are inclined to shake anything up. Could lead to dancing.

✦✦✦

As a result, the 2015 roster may look a lot like the 2014 one. Michael Cuddyer, who hit very well and fielded very poorly over three injury-limited seasons, left as a free agent; the team gets a first-round draft pick back. There have been rumblings that the team is willing to deal catcher Wilin Rosario, who is still just 26 and one disappointing 2014 campaign away from a two-year stretch in which he hit 49 homers. Rosario's plate approach can best be described as avant-garde and his defensive value as mulch-like, but he is one of the few Rockies whose future production is not dishearteningly easy to guess. It is difficult to imagine the Rockies trading Rosario, but only because of how difficult it has become to imagine any sort of change in this organization.

The thing is, it's easy to see why—beyond the hope-springs-eternal thing—Monfort and his inner circle of long-tenured, defiantly minimalist Baseball Men could believe that making some minor tweaks to the previous year's 74-win team could be enough to get the Rockies back into contention. If Tulowitzki manages one of his quadrennial semi-full seasons, he will almost certainly contend for the National League MVP. If Gonzalez is healthy enough, he will be one of the more productive all-around players in the league.

And if Justin Morneau can continue the late-career, Coors-aided renaissance he hinted at in 2014; if Charlie Blackmon and Corey Dickerson are as reliable going forward as they were in their low-key 2014 breakouts; if Rosario figures things out and if Nolan Arenado continues to develop and if the pitching is a little healthier and a little luckier and if Walt Weiss, the team's inexperienced and intermittently overmatched second-year manager, gets it together a bit and mixes in a defensive shift every now and then. Ifs on ifs on ifs, yes, but none of this is entirely unreasonable. It is just so very tired, the same brand of hope that the organization has been asking fans to buy—and, more worryingly, buying itself, in bulk—for 15 mostly moribund years.

The likely 2015 arrival of pitching prospects Eddie Butler—who was roughed up in his brief 2014 audition and suffered a mysterious near-halving of his strikeout rate at Double-A Tulsa—and Jonathan Gray will improve the rotation and provide the depth necessary to prevent an encore performance by Jair And The Interchangeable Dudes Named Christian. Gray, who is still among the better pitching prospects in the minors after a mostly uninspiring Double-A campaign in 2014, could eventually head the rotation, and is the team's most recent attempt at a homegrown answer to the decades-old and possibly unanswerable question "what kind of pitcher can get major leaguers out at altitude?" Some promising bats are scattered lower in the farm system, which is not going to mean much to the team in 2015 but seems like a nice thing to mention.

There are some valuable things to find amid the wreckage of the Rockies' 2014 season, if the new-ish people entrusted to run things can bear to pull on their purple hazmat suits and look. A more proactive recognition of the fact that a team with so many achy, breaky stars cannot afford to be so stubbornly and thoroughly depth-less, for example, should ensure that the team won't flirt with 100 losses again. (Daniel Descalso's addition in December addresses the lack of infield depth in that his official label is "infielder" and he owns a bunch of gloves, if perhaps in no other way.) But there is, everywhere but the places in which it would matter most, an understanding that the Rockies cannot afford to keep doing the same things and waiting to be proved right. "It's supposed to be about winning," an exasperated player told Patrick Saunders of the *Post* near

the end of the season. "We change a few players, but we never have enough talent. Things never change upstairs. Other teams make changes, but we never will."

Never is a long time, and certainly long enough to see what Raimel Tapia can do in the upper minors. And the end of O'Dowd and Geivett is, at least and at last, the first suggestion that the Rockies realize the need to change. It's just that, after a decade and a half of principled inaction and culture-first mediocrity, it has become nearly impossible to imagine the Rockies doing anything but what they've done. One place to start might be hiring a new team president, an astute and experienced front-office type who can look at the organization and assess what the team has, what it needs and how it can best develop the former and acquire the latter. There are people who do this for a living and who might be willing to do it for the Rockies. The problem, as ever, is that the owners already believe they have the right man for the job: the team's chairman and chief executive officer, Dick Monfort. ∎

—David Roth is a co-founder and editor of The Classical, and a contributing editor at Vice Sports.

Player comments by Andrew Koo and Baseball Prospectus Authors

Hitters

Nolan Arenado 3B

Born: 4/16/91   Age: 24   Bats: R   Throws: R   Height: 6' 2"   Weight: 205

YEAR	TEAM	LVL	AGE	PA	R	2B	3B	HR	RBI	BB	K	SB	CS	AVG/OBP/SLG	TAv	BABIP	BRR	FRAA	WARP
2012	TUL	AA	21	573	55	36	1	12	56	39	58	0	2	.285/.337/.428	.281	.296	-4.1	3B(133): 27.4	6.5
2013	CSP	AAA	22	75	14	11	0	3	21	5	9	0	2	.364/.392/.667	.337	.368	-1.6	3B(17): 2.6	1.2
2013	COL	MLB	22	514	49	29	4	10	52	23	72	2	0	.267/.301/.405	.236	.296	1.1	3B(130): 14.8	2.4
2014	CSP	AAA	23	20	2	2	0	0	3	0	3	0	0	.350/.350/.450	.245	.412	0.1	3B(4): -0.2	0.0
2014	COL	MLB	23	467	58	34	2	18	61	25	58	2	1	.287/.328/.500	.273	.294	1.3	3B(111): 14.3	4.3
2015	COL	MLB	24	460	48	29	2	13	57	22	62	2	1	.282/.319/.448	.263	.300	0.7	3B 11	2.5

Breakout: 2%   Improve: 51%   Collapse: 3%   Attrition: 8%   MLB: 93%   Comparables: Mike Moustakas, Matt Dominguez, Robinson Cano

In 2013, Arenado was two TAv points away from Mike Moustakas as the worst-hitting third baseman. In 2014, Arenado added nearly 40 points while Moose retained a firm hold on the cellar spot. In fact, Arenado led third basemen in isolated power (min. 350 PA) in his sophomore year, the youngest to do that since Troy Glaus in 2000. This doesn't surprise anyone who followed his minor-league upbringing, during which Arenado mashed 50 extra-base hits annually. Though 16 of his 18 home runs came in cozy Coors, he hit better than league average on the road, too. Arenado never excited anyone on defense in the minors, yet he has two well-deserved Gold Gloves to his name now. Did we mention he's only 23 and arbitration eligible when the 2016 annual prints?

Brandon Barnes RF

Born: 5/15/86   Age: 29   Bats: R   Throws: R   Height: 6' 2"   Weight: 210

YEAR	TEAM	LVL	AGE	PA	R	2B	3B	HR	RBI	BB	K	SB	CS	AVG/OBP/SLG	TAv	BABIP	BRR	FRAA	WARP
2012	CCH	AA	26	183	30	20	0	7	31	14	42	7	2	.317/.377/.567	.331	.385	0.7	CF(37): 0.3, RF(4): 0.2	2.2
2012	OKL	AAA	26	263	51	19	1	5	38	23	49	14	4	.323/.383/.477	.296	.388	3.5	CF(57): 8.2, RF(3): 0.0	3.1
2012	HOU	MLB	26	105	8	3	0	1	7	5	29	1	1	.204/.250/.265	.194	.279	0.2	CF(32): 2.0, RF(5): -0.2	-0.1
2013	HOU	MLB	27	445	46	17	1	8	41	21	127	11	11	.240/.289/.346	.242	.327	0.5	CF(116): 11.7, RF(13): 0.1	1.7
2014	COL	MLB	28	313	37	17	4	8	27	15	100	5	4	.257/.293/.425	.235	.364	0.2	RF(55): -0.3, LF(18): -0.6	-0.4
2015	COL	MLB	29	320	36	17	2	7	33	17	86	8	5	.261/.306/.401	.247	.336	0.3	CF 3, RF -0	0.7

Breakout: 3%   Improve: 43%   Collapse: 11%   Attrition: 13%   MLB: 85%   Comparables: Craig Monroe, Will Venable, Jeremy Hermida

In the span of nine games in June, Barnes hit two inside-the-park home runs, a feat not seen in nearly 27 years, when Ruben Sierra did it in the same game. As the Rockies' fourth outfielder, Barnes occasionally lit up SportsCenter like this, especially with defensive highlights, yet there was nothing he did more than swing—and miss. No batter with 200 plate appearances swung at a higher rate than Barnes, who offered at nearly 60 percent of pitches. This extreme deviation from his career norm was caused by the Rockies frequently deploying him as a pinch-hitter, where he clearly adopted the "be aggressive" mindset to an extreme. Barnes' 38 percent swinging strike rate off the bench didn't earn him many walks, but he did lead the league in pinch-hits, with nine of the 17 going for extra bases. It's a creative way to use Barnes, a below-replacement hitter whose defense and Brett Lawrie-like energy should otherwise maintain rosterability.

Charlie Blackmon   RF

Born: 7/1/86   Age: 28   Bats: L   Throws: L   Height: 6' 3"   Weight: 210

YEAR	TEAM	LVL	AGE	PA	R	2B	3B	HR	RBI	BB	K	SB	CS	AVG/OBP/SLG	TAv	BABIP	BRR	FRAA	WARP
2012	TRI	A-	25	69	8	5	0	1	3	7	10	3	0	.237/.348/.373	.300	.271	-0.9	CF(9): -0.5, LF(1): 0.0	0.3
2012	CSP	AAA	25	264	55	18	4	5	34	29	42	10	0	.303/.385/.482	.291	.350	1.5	CF(55): -3.5, LF(3): -0.1	1.7
2012	COL	MLB	25	121	15	8	0	2	9	4	17	1	2	.283/.325/.407	.236	.319	0.9	RF(17): -0.1, LF(15): 1.5	0.4
2013	CSP	AAA	26	299	56	15	6	3	40	35	41	7	5	.288/.376/.428	.266	.329	2.0	CF(65): -4.9	0.9
2013	COL	MLB	26	258	35	17	2	6	22	7	49	7	0	.309/.336/.467	.273	.366	3.0	RF(34): -0.4, CF(25): -2.5	1.3
2014	COL	MLB	27	648	82	27	3	19	72	31	96	28	10	.288/.335/.440	.260	.315	0.0	RF(73): -1.1, CF(69): 1.7	1.5
2015	COL	MLB	28	567	74	27	4	13	56	32	92	19	6	.278/.327/.422	.259	.311	1.4	CF -4, RF -1	1.0

Breakout: 3%   Improve: 41%   Collapse: 15%   Attrition: 25%   MLB: 84%   Comparables: *Felix Pie, Nate Schierholtz, Matt Murton*

With Blackmon's swing aggression well documented, pitchers adjusted by throwing more pitches out of the zone to him. Chuck Nazty responded by swinging even more—on pitches *in* the zone. The big change from 2013 was Blackmon laying off balls down and inside, leading to a doubled BB:K ratio. He still doesn't take nearly as many pitches as one would prefer from a leadoff man, and his park-adjusted production overall is just average. Fortunately, his ability to play three outfield positions will keep him in the lineup, and his ability to sculpt that beard will keep him a facial hair icon.

Charlie Culberson   INF

Born: 4/10/89   Age: 26   Bats: R   Throws: R   Height: 6' 0"   Weight: 200

YEAR	TEAM	LVL	AGE	PA	R	2B	3B	HR	RBI	BB	K	SB	CS	AVG/OBP/SLG	TAv	BABIP	BRR	FRAA	WARP
2012	CSP	AAA	23	128	17	11	1	2	12	1	18	6	2	.336/.344/.488	.281	.377	1.1	2B(28): 1.3	0.9
2012	FRE	AAA	23	380	53	14	6	10	53	20	76	8	2	.236/.283/.396	.240	.272	1.4	2B(88): -3.0	-0.1
2012	SFN	MLB	23	20	0	0	0	0	1	0	7	0	0	.136/.136/.136	.100	.200	0.5	2B(6): -0.4	-0.3
2013	CSP	AAA	24	419	63	27	8	14	64	17	74	13	9	.310/.338/.524	.275	.350	2.9	SS(46): 2.9, 2B(46): 2.9	3.3
2013	COL	MLB	24	104	12	5	0	2	12	4	23	5	1	.293/.317/.404	.236	.360	0.0	LF(27): 0.6, 2B(4): -0.1	0.2
2014	COL	MLB	25	233	17	7	2	3	24	12	62	2	2	.195/.253/.290	.194	.259	0.8	3B(32): 2.4, SS(23): 0.3	-0.7
2015	COL	MLB	26	250	26	11	2	6	27	9	56	5	3	.250/.282/.393	.235	.299	0.2	2B -0, SS 1	0.4

Breakout: 2%   Improve: 15%   Collapse: 7%   Attrition: 22%   MLB: 36%   Comparables: *Travis Metcalf, Donnie Murphy, Michael Morse*

Culberson, acquired from the Giants in the Marco Scutaro trade of 2012, claimed the distinction of being the Rockies' worst player by WARP in 2014, and earned the NL's lowest TAv among batters who collected 200 plate appearances. At least his walk rate climbed above 5 percent this year? What he gave away with the bat, he attempted to recoup in positional flexibility as an able body at second, third and short. Once a former supplemental first-rounder, Culberson joins Colorado's list of failed experiments to find a permanent second baseman—a long scroll of DJ LeMahieu, Josh Rutledge, Jonathan Herrera, Eric Young Jr., Chris Nelson, Alfredo Amezaga ... the days of Clint Barmes have never looked more appealing.

David Dahl   CF

Born: 4/1/94   Age: 21   Bats: L   Throws: R   Height: 6' 2"   Weight: 195

YEAR	TEAM	LVL	AGE	PA	R	2B	3B	HR	RBI	BB	K	SB	CS	AVG/OBP/SLG	TAv	BABIP	BRR	FRAA	WARP
2013	ASH	A	19	42	9	4	1	0	7	2	8	2	0	.275/.310/.425	.259	.344	-0.1	CF(8): -1.1	0.0
2014	ASH	A	20	422	69	33	6	10	41	23	65	18	5	.309/.347/.500	.280	.348	3.3	CF(70): 8.0, LF(7): 0.3	3.5
2014	MOD	A+	20	125	14	8	2	4	14	5	27	3	0	.267/.296/.467	.274	.315	1.7	CF(29): 3.2	1.1
2015	COL	MLB	21	250	27	12	2	5	22	7	58	5	1	.247/.269/.376	.220	.301	0.5	CF 3, LF 0	0.0

Breakout: 0%   Improve: 0%   Collapse: 0%   Attrition: 0%   MLB: 0%   Comparables: *Jordan Schafer, Felix Pie, Austin Jackson*

After losing the previous year to injury, Dahl came back roaring in his age-20 season. The 10th overall pick in 2012 showed no developmental loss as he completed his first full stint in Low-A, featuring all five tools and outstanding makeup. He even flew to High-A Modesto for a month and slugged enough to rank third on the team in OPS, before returning to Asheville for a championship run. Dahl is an elite center fielder with great speed and impeccable reads. The glove fights the bat for the title of Dahl's best tool; with his bat speed and natural ability to go opposite field, you could make a case for either one. With further growth, the line-drive swing will turn the 49 doubles and triples into more home runs, giving the Rockies an All-Star profile in center field for years to come.

Daniel Descalso   INF

Born: 10/19/86   Age: 28   Bats: L   Throws: R   Height: 5' 10"   Weight: 190

YEAR	TEAM	LVL	AGE	PA	R	2B	3B	HR	RBI	BB	K	SB	CS	AVG/OBP/SLG	TAv	BABIP	BRR	FRAA	WARP
2012	SLN	MLB	25	426	41	10	7	4	26	37	83	6	3	.227/.303/.324	.240	.279	5.0	2B(96): 4.8, SS(26): 1.8	1.2
2013	SLN	MLB	26	358	43	25	1	5	43	22	56	6	3	.238/.290/.366	.243	.271	3.9	SS(55): 0.8, 2B(39): 1.5	1.5
2014	SLN	MLB	27	184	20	11	0	0	10	20	33	1	3	.242/.333/.311	.245	.305	-0.6	2B(21): 1.6, SS(19): -1.0	0.1
2015	COL	MLB	28	250	25	13	2	3	23	20	40	3	2	.261/.326/.378	.248	.299	1.5	2B 1, SS 0	0.8

Breakout: 4%   Improve: 45%   Collapse: 1%   Attrition: 9%   MLB: 91%   Comparables: *Paul Janish, Cliff Pennington, Jason Bartlett*

A utility tool the Cardinals plugged in all over the diamond, Descalso is starting to resemble a Swiss Army knife with a dull blade and a missing toothpick. Never much of a hitter, he saw frequent use in prior years when the St. Louis middle infield was in flux and his lefty bat was the best of several bad options, but the signing of Jhonny Peralta and the emergence of Matt Carpenter and Kolten Wong led to a significantly reduced role. Non-tendered, he got a two-year deal from the Rockies. Descalso posted a random .364/.475/.424 line against lefty pitchers last year, a fact that is far more likely to excite Strat-o-Matic players than it is to scare any southpaws that have to face him in the future. His defensive versatility has value in the double-switch league, but might not be enough to trump his declining range and hollow bat for much longer.

Corey Dickerson LF

Born: 5/22/89   Age: 26   Bats: L   Throws: R   Height: 6' 1"   Weight: 205

YEAR	TEAM	LVL	AGE	PA	R	2B	3B	HR	RBI	BB	K	SB	CS	AVG/OBP/SLG	TAv	BABIP	BRR	FRAA	WARP
2012	MOD	A+	23	270	43	24	4	9	43	25	42	9	5	.338/.396/.583	.352	.373	1.1	RF(30): -0.9, LF(18): 2.1	3.4
2012	TUL	AA	23	290	40	16	3	13	38	18	51	7	3	.274/.322/.504	.295	.293	2.4	LF(67): -7.6	1.0
2013	CSP	AAA	24	345	61	21	14	11	50	26	49	6	10	.371/.414/.632	.332	.409	-1.1	LF(63): -1.4, RF(5): -0.6	3.2
2013	COL	MLB	24	213	32	13	5	5	17	16	41	2	2	.263/.316/.459	.269	.307	0.3	LF(36): -0.2, CF(15): 0.8	0.9
2014	COL	MLB	25	478	74	27	6	24	76	37	101	8	7	.312/.364/.567	.304	.356	-2.4	LF(99): -1.5, CF(9): -0.5	2.3
2015	COL	MLB	26	440	55	24	6	17	62	29	87	7	6	.293/.338/.507	.289	.332	-1.3	LF -3, CF 0	1.9

Breakout: 6%   Improve: 48%   Collapse: 6%   Attrition: 9%   MLB: 88%   Comparables: *Eric Thames, Mike Carp, Chase Headley*

Has there been a player so heavily platooned as Dickerson who also led a team in home runs? Dickerson started just 13 games against lefties, resulting in 478 total plate appearances—not enough even to qualify for the batting title. It was second-fewest PA among teams' home run leaders, next to Yasmani Grandal, who didn't lead a team so much as he led a group of underfed street urchins. Dickerson's quick bat allows him to make contact to all fields, particularly those that comprise Coors Field's wide gaps. He also hit the *highest* home run of the season—actually, of the past five years, according to Hit Tracker—a towering, angled blast off Dan Haren that reached an apex of 171 feet before falling on Coors' right field porch. In the square of his prime, Dickerson's hitting compensates for the lack of other tools, but any decline in the bat will hurt him, especially if he keeps chasing those breaking balls.

Carlos Gonzalez LF

Born: 10/17/85   Age: 29   Bats: L   Throws: L   Height: 6' 1"   Weight: 220

YEAR	TEAM	LVL	AGE	PA	R	2B	3B	HR	RBI	BB	K	SB	CS	AVG/OBP/SLG	TAv	BABIP	BRR	FRAA	WARP
2012	COL	MLB	26	579	89	31	5	22	85	56	115	20	5	.303/.371/.510	.279	.352	0.5	LF(131): -3.9	1.7
2013	COL	MLB	27	436	72	23	6	26	70	41	118	21	3	.302/.367/.591	.313	.368	1.9	LF(106): 0.4	3.6
2014	COL	MLB	28	281	35	15	1	11	38	19	70	3	0	.238/.292/.431	.234	.283	1.2	LF(48): -3.4, RF(17): -0.7	-0.7
2015	COL	MLB	29	298	42	15	2	14	45	23	66	10	2	.293/.351/.518	.298	.339	0.6	LF -2, RF -0	1.6

Breakout: 2%   Improve: 61%   Collapse: 1%   Attrition: 3%   MLB: 98%   Comparables: *Albert Belle, Matt Holliday, Kevin Mitchell*

Lacerations, sprains, fractures, contusions, tendonitis, inflammation—Gonzalez has suffered it all, and everywhere: fingers, feet, knees, wrists, groin, back, thighs, ankles. Never before 2014 though, did he require surgery; then he underwent three such operations in the span of eight months. First, an emergency appendectomy in January; he missed June after having a tumor removed from his left index finger; finally, an August bursectomy put him on crutches, knocking him out for good. The latter was a result of left-knee tendonitis that plagued him since spring training, explaining why he hit like Mark Trumbo all year. Yet through it all, his True Average at Coors Field was .286, giving you an idea of how good he is even when battered by injury. He's at risk of missing the start of 2015, but you knew that.

DJ LeMahieu 2B

Born: 7/13/88   Age: 26   Bats: R   Throws: R   Height: 6' 4"   Weight: 205

YEAR	TEAM	LVL	AGE	PA	R	2B	3B	HR	RBI	BB	K	SB	CS	AVG/OBP/SLG	TAv	BABIP	BRR	FRAA	WARP
2012	CSP	AAA	23	280	33	14	2	1	31	23	29	13	6	.314/.368/.396	.266	.348	-1.0	2B(52): -1.4, 3B(7): 0.0	0.8
2012	COL	MLB	23	247	26	12	4	2	22	13	42	1	2	.297/.332/.410	.249	.353	2.6	2B(67): 7.4, 3B(9): -0.2	1.5
2013	CSP	AAA	24	158	34	8	5	1	22	10	19	8	2	.364/.405/.510	.292	.405	3.4	SS(30): 3.7, 2B(2): 0.0	2.2
2013	COL	MLB	24	434	39	21	3	2	28	19	67	18	7	.280/.311/.361	.228	.328	0.7	2B(90): 3.1, 3B(14): 0.5	0.2
2014	COL	MLB	25	538	59	15	5	5	42	33	97	10	10	.267/.315/.348	.226	.322	3.7	2B(144): 4.0, 3B(7): -0.4	0.2
2015	COL	MLB	26	504	52	22	4	5	43	25	81	13	8	.282/.317/.376	.241	.324	2.2	2B 4, 3B 0	1.4

Breakout: 7%   Improve: 42%   Collapse: 8%   Attrition: 22%   MLB: 84%   Comparables: *Ronny Cedeno, Donovan Solano, Russ Adams*

Convinced Coors can aggrandize any hitter? See the powerless LeMahieu. His True Average at home was .250, 10 points below league average, or what 37-year-old Lyle Overbay hit all year. Like we articulated last year, LeMahieu's competitors for the second base job were Infield Humidor and Denver Wind Current, and while LeMahieu might hit like air, he has hands to hold a glove and can wield it competently too, winning him the job for at least another year. He lifted his walk rate as a sign of improvement, but still hits too many weak grounders to produce any batting value. Championed with his first Gold Glove, there might not have been another second baseman who had a hand in more groundballs—fielded *and* hit.

Michael McKenry C

Born: 3/4/85   Age: 30   Bats: R   Throws: R   Height: 5' 10"   Weight: 205

YEAR	TEAM	LVL	AGE	PA	R	2B	3B	HR	RBI	BB	K	SB	CS	AVG/OBP/SLG	TAv	BABIP	BRR	FRAA	WARP
2012	PIT	MLB	27	275	25	14	0	12	39	29	73	0	0	.233/.320/.442	.283	.278	-0.4	C(80): 1.4	2.1
2013	PIT	MLB	28	122	9	6	0	3	14	5	24	0	0	.217/.262/.348	.223	.250	-0.8	C(31): 0.7	-0.2
2014	CSP	AAA	29	93	15	6	0	3	12	7	13	3	0	.313/.370/.494	.266	.338	1.3	C(22): -0.4	0.3
2014	COL	MLB	29	192	23	9	0	8	22	22	42	0	3	.315/.398/.512	.291	.381	-0.6	C(50): -0.9	1.0
2015	COL	MLB	30	250	28	12	1	7	29	21	58	1	1	.254/.320/.412	.255	.305	-0.4	C 0	0.9

Breakout: 5%   Improve: 27%   Collapse: 8%   Attrition: 22%   MLB: 74%   Comparables: *Travis Ishikawa, George Kottaras, Javier Valentin*

McKenry dubs himself @theFortMcKenry on Twitter, but his negative blocking runs don't agree with that defensive representation. Maybe he's metaphorically referring to the cannons that defend the national monument's walls? His career 19 percent rate of throwing runners out doesn't support that, either. Hmm. Well, that aside, McKenry flourished offensively behind Wilin Rosario, posting the league's best True Average among second-string backstops. The walks and power aren't new, but unsustainably hitting 35 percent of his batted balls for line drives is. That's also Joey Votto's line drive rate in 2014; McKenry might be a fort but he's not Joey Votto. Expect the batting average to fall.

Ryan McMahon 3B

Born: 12/14/94   Age: 20   Bats: L   Throws: R   Height: 6' 2"   Weight: 185

YEAR	TEAM	LVL	AGE	PA	R	2B	3B	HR	RBI	BB	K	SB	CS	AVG/OBP/SLG	TAv	BABIP	BRR	FRAA	WARP
2014	ASH	A	19	552	93	46	3	18	102	54	143	8	5	.282/.358/.502	.284	.360	-0.3	3B(118): 8.1	4.0
2015	COL	MLB	20	250	23	11	1	7	28	16	80	1	1	.221/.277/.364	.222	.303	-0.4	3B 3	-0.1

Breakout: 0%   Improve: 0%   Collapse: 0%   Attrition: 0%   MLB: 0%   Comparables: Matt Davidson, Matt Dominguez, Mike Moustakas

McMahon led the championship-winning Asheville Tourists in plate appearances last year; he was also just 48 hours older than the team's youngest position player. Left-handed, power-hitting third basemen are uncommon types, especially realized so young: Joey Gallo and Rio Ruiz would be McMahon's few contemporaries. In fact, McMahon would fit nicely in the middle on the Gallo-Ruiz spectrum: While he doesn't possess the gunpowder that Gallo does, his power is more game-ready than Ruiz's; McMahon would also benefit from Ruiz's professional hitting approach, as he swings and misses a fair amount, albeit, again, not at Gallo levels. McMahon struggles against lefties and his aggression can be exposed by breaking balls, but at age 19, call 2014 an excellent full-season debut.

Justin Morneau 1B

Born: 5/15/81   Age: 34   Bats: L   Throws: R   Height: 6' 4"   Weight: 220

YEAR	TEAM	LVL	AGE	PA	R	2B	3B	HR	RBI	BB	K	SB	CS	AVG/OBP/SLG	TAv	BABIP	BRR	FRAA	WARP
2012	MIN	MLB	31	570	63	26	2	19	77	49	102	1	0	.267/.333/.440	.269	.294	-4.2	1B(99): -4.6	0.4
2013	MIN	MLB	32	543	56	32	0	17	74	37	98	0	0	.259/.315/.426	.274	.288	-0.6	1B(112): -5.3	0.6
2013	PIT	MLB	32	92	6	4	0	0	3	13	12	0	0	.260/.370/.312	.246	.303	-0.4	1B(25): -0.9	-0.2
2014	COL	MLB	33	550	62	32	3	17	82	34	60	0	3	.319/.364/.496	.298	.330	-0.7	1B(131): 2.7	3.0
2015	COL	MLB	34	534	59	29	2	16	68	42	86	1	1	.283/.343/.449	.273	.311	-1.4	1B -4	0.6

Breakout: 0%   Improve: 30%   Collapse: 2%   Attrition: 11%   MLB: 92%   Comparables: Aubrey Huff, Mike Sweeney, Ted Kluszewski

Already an MVP, Morneau added batting champion to his name, next to his best title, Canadian. Call it home cooking, but Morneau showed good manners on the road too: Park-adjust his numbers, and his True Average was better away (.321) than at home (.277), a split rarely seen in a Rockies uniform. How rarely? No other Rockie regular had a road TAv within 18 points of his home TAv. The craziest thing: Even with that sizable reverse split, his unadjusted raw numbers at home were still better than on the road, a reminder not to sleep on post-humidor Coors Field absurdity.

Morneau's swing rates jumped with Colorado, producing the lowest walk and strikeout rates of his career, but the extra contact allowed him to enjoy the BABIP benefits of Coors Field. His consistency earned him more opportunities against left-handed pitching, a growing weakness as he's aged, although his performance (.236 TAv in 139 plate appearances) suggests a relegation to platoon duty soon.

Kyle Parker RF

Born: 9/30/89   Age: 25   Bats: R   Throws: R   Height: 6' 0"   Weight: 205

YEAR	TEAM	LVL	AGE	PA	R	2B	3B	HR	RBI	BB	K	SB	CS	AVG/OBP/SLG	TAv	BABIP	BRR	FRAA	WARP
2012	MOD	A+	22	463	86	18	6	23	73	66	88	1	2	.308/.415/.562	.338	.346	-0.3	RF(77): -3.7	4.1
2013	TUL	AA	23	528	70	23	3	23	74	40	99	6	6	.288/.345/.492	.300	.318	-2.0	LF(77): -7.0, RF(20): -0.8	2.0
2014	CSP	AAA	24	542	73	30	3	15	72	33	102	4	3	.289/.336/.450	.260	.335	-3.3	RF(74): -10.4, 1B(40): 1.4	-0.2
2014	COL	MLB	24	26	1	1	0	0	1	0	14	0	0	.192/.192/.231	.154	.417	-0.1	RF(4): -0.1, 1B(2): -0.1	-0.3
2015	COL	MLB	25	250	27	11	1	8	32	16	56	1	1	.265/.314/.433	.261	.313	-0.3	RF -2, LF -1	0.1

Breakout: 4%   Improve: 17%   Collapse: 9%   Attrition: 29%   MLB: 41%   Comparables: Bronson Sardinha, Josh Kroeger, Joey Terdoslavich

Parker, short but strong, was made to hit home runs; at least, that's what the Rockies will tell you after they lured him away from football with $1.4 million in 2010. While his Triple-A numbers look consistent with the rest of his minor-league career, one might've expected more power from Parker in the Pacific Coast League. He doesn't hit anything but fastballs and he catches only what's placed directly into his glove, and you probably know how narrow the margins are for such a player. Parker might become a useful bench player one day, feasting on reliever fastballs, but that would be a low return on the first-round pick Colorado spent on him five years ago.

Ben Paulsen 1B

Born: 10/27/87   Age: 27   Bats: L   Throws: R   Height: 6' 4"   Weight: 205

YEAR	TEAM	LVL	AGE	PA	R	2B	3B	HR	RBI	BB	K	SB	CS	AVG/OBP/SLG	TAv	BABIP	BRR	FRAA	WARP
2012	TUL	AA	24	478	58	18	3	13	53	37	113	1	4	.255/.314/.399	.260	.313	0.6	1B(99): -4.0	0.2
2013	CSP	AAA	25	502	64	32	10	18	79	37	128	2	2	.292/.345/.523	.291	.366	0.8	1B(116): 6.5	2.9
2014	CSP	AAA	26	497	76	32	6	20	76	58	119	4	5	.294/.378/.533	.296	.362	-1.5	1B(93): 11.3, RF(4): 0.1	3.4
2014	COL	MLB	26	66	8	4	0	4	10	2	19	0	0	.317/.348/.571	.294	.400	-1.5	1B(15): 1.2, RF(3): 0.0	0.2
2015	COL	MLB	27	250	27	12	2	8	32	17	68	1	1	.256/.309/.438	.258	.324	-0.3	1B 1, RF 0	0.4

Breakout: 1%   Improve: 3%   Collapse: 5%   Attrition: 11%   MLB: 16%   Comparables: Steven Hill, Mauro Gomez, Eric Crozier

After a Triple-A breakout in 2013, Paulsen followed up with another solid season in Colorado Springs, earning four call-ups throughout the year. The former third-rounder has a decent hit tool and developed power, but his career .238 True Average versus lefties in the minors limits his usage (of course, he hit three home runs in 12 major-league plate appearances against southpaws). Worse, he played first base his entire minor-league career until a few experimental outfield starts last year; Justin Morneau's not exactly Todd Helton in Rockies franchise history, but he'll block the cold corner for at least another year. Just look at Paulsen's age to see how damning that is.

Wilin Rosario C

Born: 2/23/89   Age: 26   Bats: R   Throws: R   Height: 5' 11"   Weight: 220

YEAR	TEAM	LVL	AGE	PA	R	2B	3B	HR	RBI	BB	K	SB	CS	AVG/OBP/SLG	TAv	BABIP	BRR	FRAA	WARP
2012	COL	MLB	23	426	67	19	0	28	71	25	99	4	5	.270/.312/.530	.268	.289	-1.2	C(105): 0.6, 3B(3): -0.0	2.2
2013	COL	MLB	24	466	63	22	1	21	79	15	109	4	3	.292/.315/.486	.268	.344	3.1	C(106): -0.8, 1B(4): -0.1	2.5
2014	COL	MLB	25	410	46	25	0	13	54	23	70	1	0	.267/.305/.435	.238	.293	-1.8	C(96): 0.1, 1B(4): -0.1	0.4
2015	COL	MLB	26	397	47	19	1	18	57	17	88	2	1	.267/.299/.467	.263	.301	0.2	C -0, 1B -0	1.6

Breakout: 3%   Improve: 61%   Collapse: 8%   Attrition: 8%   MLB: 98%   Comparables: Dan Graham, Carlton Fisk, Jorge Cantu

Rosario's pitches per plate appearance fell from 3.5 to 3.2 last year, a curious development that saw him increase his contact and walk rates. Despite that and the decreased strikeout rate, 2014 was the worst offensive season of Rosario's career, and it came just as he headed into his first arbitration payday. After he hit .344 on balls in play in 2013, the BABIP gods sentenced him back to career levels, and he didn't find any luck with the health gods, either, missing time with wrist troubles and, in May, a viral infection. For that matter, he also found no favor with the passed ball gods, leading the NL in that embarrassing category for a third straight year. When you've lost even the passed ball gods, it's usually time to switch religions.

Trevor Story SS

Born: 11/15/92 Age: 22 Bats: R Throws: R Height: 6' 1" Weight: 175

YEAR	TEAM	LVL	AGE	PA	R	2B	3B	HR	RBI	BB	K	SB	CS	AVG/OBP/SLG	TAv	BABIP	BRR	FRAA	WARP
2012	ASH	A	19	548	96	43	6	18	63	60	121	15	3	.277/.367/.505	.290	.335	3.3	SS(85): 7.9, 3B(21): 1.8	5.0
2013	MOD	A+	20	554	71	34	5	12	65	45	183	23	1	.233/.305/.394	.270	.343	1.8	SS(125): -4.7, 3B(4): -0.1	3.0
2014	MOD	A+	21	218	38	17	7	5	28	31	59	20	4	.332/.436/.582	.348	.467	2.7	SS(39): 0.2, 3B(8): -0.3	3.2
2014	TUL	AA	21	237	29	8	1	9	20	28	82	3	1	.200/.302/.380	.250	.281	0.8	SS(43): -7.6, 3B(6): 0.7	-0.2
2015	COL	MLB	22	250	26	11	2	6	27	19	82	6	1	.225/.289/.375	.232	.316	0.7	SS -2, 3B 0	0.2

Breakout: 0% Improve: 0% Collapse: 0% Attrition: 0% MLB: 0% Comparables: *Brandon Wood, Derek Dietrich, Mark Reynolds*

However you slice Story's career trajectory thus far, he's a power-hitting shortstop with speed. His poor 2013 at High-A Modesto sunk him on every prospect list, but the power-hitting shortstop with speed rebounded last year, repeating and acing the level before swinging and missing all over again in Double-A. If Story didn't play shortstop while hitting with power and speed, he'd be beyond discarded. Consider this: Only three full-season shortstops produced a higher ISO in the minors than Story in 2014. Yet none of them—not even *Javier Baez*—struck out at a higher rate. His position, where he displays a solid arm and range, gives him a long leash to learn pitch recognition; so too do the power and speed. He also finished his fourth season before turning 22, and at that age, he's a power-hitting shortstop with speed who is still worth investing in.

Drew Stubbs CF

Born: 10/4/84 Age: 30 Bats: R Throws: R Height: 6' 4" Weight: 205

YEAR	TEAM	LVL	AGE	PA	R	2B	3B	HR	RBI	BB	K	SB	CS	AVG/OBP/SLG	TAv	BABIP	BRR	FRAA	WARP
2012	CIN	MLB	27	544	75	13	2	14	40	42	166	30	7	.213/.277/.333	.226	.290	3.7	CF(135): -10.3	-0.8
2013	CLE	MLB	28	481	59	21	2	10	45	44	141	17	2	.233/.305/.360	.254	.319	2.4	RF(105): 2.5, CF(43): 2.2	2.0
2014	COL	MLB	29	424	67	22	4	15	43	30	136	20	3	.289/.339/.482	.270	.404	2.1	CF(113): -8.6	1.1
2015	COL	MLB	30	410	56	16	3	11	40	35	119	19	4	.251/.318/.396	.251	.334	1.7	CF -2, RF 1	0.7

Breakout: 2% Improve: 50% Collapse: 6% Attrition: 4% MLB: 99% Comparables: *Shane Mack, Rick Monday, Reggie Sanders*

Is Stubbs baseball's splitsiest regular? His True Average gap between lefties and righties (.297 and .256) and home and away (.307 and .229) might say so. Stubbs used to be a spicy power/speed threat when he rose through the ranks, but the upside has been leveled by a barrage of swing-and-miss. When Stubbs wasn't striking air every four swings, Coors Field blessed him with a .440 home BABIP, a high figure that tends to emerge for serial whiffers with power. His defense is trustworthy in center, and should stay that way into his early 30s.

Raimel Tapia RF

Born: 2/4/94 Age: 21 Bats: L Throws: L Height: 6' 2" Weight: 160

YEAR	TEAM	LVL	AGE	PA	R	2B	3B	HR	RBI	BB	K	SB	CS	AVG/OBP/SLG	TAv	BABIP	BRR	FRAA	WARP
2014	ASH	A	20	539	93	32	1	9	72	35	90	33	16	.326/.382/.453	.289	.383	3.1	LF(43): -1.4, CF(42): 2.0	2.7
2015	COL	MLB	21	250	25	11	1	3	22	9	59	8	4	.252/.285/.347	.219	.315	-0.2	CF 1, RF -1	-0.6

Breakout: 0% Improve: 0% Collapse: 0% Attrition: 0% MLB: 0% Comparables: *Xavier Avery, Peter Bourjos, Dexter Fowler*

An international free agent signed at age 16, Tapia progressively crushed three short rookie league seasons before his national coming-out party in Asheville last year. He led the Sally League champs in steals and hits, the latter his primary calling card among multiple skills. Within his twig-skinny frame, Tapia possesses sublime bat speed and balance, demonstrating natural bat-to-ball ability despite unorthodox movements in his stance. His aggressive approach—almost an overeagerness to hit baseballs—will be tested as he rises up the chain, but he'll develop further power too, giving him a chance to feature all five tools.

Troy Tulowitzki SS

Born: 10/10/84 Age: 30 Bats: R Throws: R Height: 6' 3" Weight: 215

YEAR	TEAM	LVL	AGE	PA	R	2B	3B	HR	RBI	BB	K	SB	CS	AVG/OBP/SLG	TAv	BABIP	BRR	FRAA	WARP
2012	COL	MLB	27	203	33	8	2	8	27	19	19	2	2	.287/.360/.486	.270	.284	1.0	SS(47): 0.6	1.3
2013	COL	MLB	28	512	72	27	0	25	82	57	85	1	0	.312/.391/.540	.306	.334	0.7	SS(121): 4.6	4.9
2014	COL	MLB	29	375	71	18	1	21	52	50	57	1	1	.340/.432/.603	.331	.355	-2.1	SS(89): 1.7	4.0
2015	COL	MLB	30	380	53	20	1	18	60	38	56	2	1	.306/.378/.534	.313	.319	0.0	SS 1	3.8

Breakout: 1% Improve: 53% Collapse: 2% Attrition: 6% MLB: 100% Comparables: *Hanley Ramirez, David Wright, Chase Utley*

Adjust for Coors all you want, but Tulowitzki is still among the league's top hitters. A torn labrum prevented yet another full season, but Tulo was largely responsible for the offense that led to Colorado's 23-16 start, a fleeting high when Rockies fans felt excitement and hope and the munchies. Their franchise player hit for a .392 True Average during this run and punctuated it with Andrelton-is-stealing-my-Gold-Glove defense, featuring his laser-accurate arm that completed an elite double-play combination with DJ LeMahieu. Tulo has strung memorable hitting streaks together before—recall his 14 home runs in 15 games during September 2011—but none lasted three months. If the left-hip surgery indeed remedies recurring leg issues, Tulowitzki could play healthier than ever, with few precious prime years left to chase his first MVP award.

Forrest Wall 2B

Born: 11/20/95 Age: 28 Bats: L Throws: R Height: 6' 0" Weight: 175

YEAR	TEAM	LVL	AGE	PA	R	2B	3B	HR	RBI	BB	K	SB	CS	AVG/OBP/SLG	TAv	BABIP	BRR	FRAA	WARP
2015	COL	MLB	19	250	27	9	2	3	17	14	71	9	3	.209/.255/.296	.192	.282	0.8	2B -2	-1.1

Breakout: 0% Improve: 0% Collapse: 0% Attrition: 0% MLB: 0% Comparables: *Ozzie Martinez, Starlin Castro, L.J. Hoes*

Wall is the rare second baseman taken as high as the sandwich round. Shoulder surgery limits his arm's playability to the right side of the infield, and while most first-round picks are shortstops who might eventually move to second, Wall demonstrated his hitting and speed was worth the 35th overall selection and a $2 million bonus. He carried his natural contact skill into the Pioneer League and should grow into average to above-average power; even if he's eventually a little less than that, he'll fill a position in Colorado that hasn't seen an above-average hitter since Kazuo Matsui in 2006.

Pitchers

Brett Anderson   LHP

Born: 2/1/88   Age: 27   Bats: L   Throws: L   Height: 6'4"   Weight: 225

YEAR	TEAM	LVL	AGE	W	L	SV	G	GS	IP	H	HR	BB	K	BB/9	K/9	GB%	BABIP	WHIP	ERA	FIP	FRA	WARP
2012	SAC	AAA	24	1	1	0	5	5	23¹	27	4	5	18	1.9	6.9	51%	.324	1.37	4.24	5.12	4.61	0.3
2012	OAK	MLB	24	4	2	0	6	6	35	29	1	7	25	1.8	6.4	61%	.272	1.03	2.57	2.68	3.31	0.6
2013	OAK	MLB	25	1	4	3	16	5	44²	51	5	21	46	4.2	9.3	62%	.359	1.61	6.04	3.88	4.27	0.4
2014	COL	MLB	26	1	3	0	8	8	43¹	44	4	13	29	2.7	6.0	63%	.314	1.32	2.91	2.96	3.44	1.1
2015	COL	MLB	27	3	3	0	8	8	45	48	4	12	35	2.4	6.9	55%	.334	1.32	4.36	3.87	4.74	0.4

Breakout: 31%   Improve: 60%   Collapse: 18%   Attrition: 20%   MLB: 95%   *Comparables: Jaime Garcia, Paul Maholm, Jon Niese*

It took three starts for Anderson to return home to the 60-day disabled list. With two stints last year, his career total of games missed on the DL surpassed his career total of innings pitched (he's averaged 82 over his six seasons). He hasn't reinjured his surgically repaired left elbow, but Anderson's myriad other injuries have prevented a full season for five years now. In 2014, it was his lower back and his left index finger that screwed everything all to hell. Somehow, all this added up to a $10 million contract from the Dodgers. Maybe they're counting on him taking over the team's Twitter account.

Tyler Anderson   LHP

Born: 12/30/89   Age: 25   Bats: L   Throws: L   Height: 6'4"   Weight: 215

YEAR	TEAM	LVL	AGE	W	L	SV	G	GS	IP	H	HR	BB	K	BB/9	K/9	GB%	BABIP	WHIP	ERA	FIP	FRA	WARP
2012	ASH	A	22	12	3	0	20	20	120¹	102	5	28	81	2.1	6.1	54%	.270	1.08	2.47	3.55	4.62	1.9
2013	TRI	A-	23	1	1	0	3	3	15	9	0	3	13	1.8	7.8	66%	.205	0.80	0.60	2.18	3.30	0.3
2013	MOD	A+	23	3	2	0	13	13	74²	62	10	24	63	2.9	7.6	47%	.250	1.15	3.25	4.87	5.07	0.5
2014	TUL	AA	24	7	4	0	23	23	118¹	91	3	40	106	3.0	8.1	52%	.274	1.11	1.98	2.77	3.47	2.7
2015	COL	MLB	25	5	7	0	17	17	93	100	11	34	59	3.3	5.7	49%	.316	1.44	4.96	4.85	5.39	0.1

Breakout: 20%   Improve: 24%   Collapse: 6%   Attrition: 26%   MLB: 34%   *Comparables: Rob Scahill, Chris Heston, Gus Schlosser*

Anderson was named Texas League pitcher of the year with a 1.98 ERA and .218 TAv against, both tops among hurlers with at least 15 starts. Drafted 20th overall in 2011, the lanky lefty might've been expected to pitch for the big-league club at this point. Injuries wiped out most of 2013 and Anderson couldn't avoid them last year either, dropping out of the playoffs with elbow soreness. Still, his Double-A performance should assuage developmental concerns. Anderson throws with an awkward hitch, but commands his upper-80s fastball well and shows the same arm speed on his changeup, the leading trick in his box of deception. It runs in the low 80s with sinking action, coercing copious groundballs. It's a polished package of the sort that traditionally plays well in the minors; he should reach the majors in 2015, where he'll chase his mid-rotation upside.

Christian Bergman   RHP

Born: 5/4/88   Age: 27   Bats: R   Throws: R   Height: 6'1"   Weight: 180

YEAR	TEAM	LVL	AGE	W	L	SV	G	GS	IP	H	HR	BB	K	BB/9	K/9	GB%	BABIP	WHIP	ERA	FIP	FRA	WARP
2012	MOD	A+	24	16	5	0	27	27	162²	161	16	37	121	2.0	6.7	41%	.295	1.22	3.65	4.34	5.08	1.6
2013	TUL	AA	25	8	7	0	27	27	171	162	25	23	111	1.2	5.8	50%	.265	1.08	3.37	4.15	4.91	0.4
2014	CSP	AAA	26	5	5	0	15	15	92¹	96	11	18	60	1.8	5.8	43%	.287	1.23	4.19	4.60	5.58	0.2
2014	COL	MLB	26	3	5	0	10	10	54²	75	9	10	31	1.6	5.1	33%	.333	1.55	5.93	4.71	5.68	-0.1
2015	COL	MLB	27	7	9	0	22	22	132²	156	20	32	70	2.2	4.7	43%	.320	1.41	5.27	5.12	5.73	-0.4

Breakout: 11%   Improve: 22%   Collapse: 10%   Attrition: 17%   MLB: 36%   *Comparables: Bobby Livingston, Ryan Feierabend, Daniel Barone*

Bergman throws four workable pitches, walks very few batters and the list of baseball positives ends there. His control is so good that he throws the ball right into the strike zone where batters can hit it, especially when it floats toward them in the upper 80s. He surrendered one of the league's highest contact rates and, with it, many, many fly balls and line drives. Pitching to contact carried him through the minor leagues as an innings-eater, and he might manage that in the majors at the back of a rotation. As a 24th-rounder five years ago, the Rockies would consider it a win.

Chad Bettis   RHP

Born: 4/26/89   Age: 26   Bats: R   Throws: R   Height: 6'1"   Weight: 200

YEAR	TEAM	LVL	AGE	W	L	SV	G	GS	IP	H	HR	BB	K	BB/9	K/9	GB%	BABIP	WHIP	ERA	FIP	FRA	WARP
2013	TUL	AA	24	3	4	0	12	12	63	60	9	13	68	1.9	9.7	50%	.307	1.16	3.71	3.52	4.26	0.7
2013	COL	MLB	24	1	3	0	16	8	44²	55	6	20	30	4.0	6.0	49%	.327	1.68	5.64	4.90	5.04	0.4
2014	CSP	AAA	25	3	4	3	20	5	55¹	45	1	21	55	3.4	8.9	60%	.303	1.19	3.09	3.25	4.65	0.9
2014	COL	MLB	25	0	2	0	21	0	24²	42	4	10	13	3.6	4.7	53%	.384	2.11	9.12	5.49	7.87	-0.4
2015	COL	MLB	26	4	4	0	20	11	75¹	79	9	25	61	3.0	7.2	48%	.328	1.38	4.76	4.41	5.17	0.3

Breakout: 28%   Improve: 45%   Collapse: 21%   Attrition: 29%   MLB: 79%   *Comparables: John Maine, Christian Friedrich, David Phelps*

Can you name the two other pitchers in the past seven seasons to finish with an ERA over nine pitching in at least 20 games? *Hint:* they own the same surname. Bettis' sophomore year was one to forget, but his prospect status afforded him a moderate leash. The Rockies shuffled him between Denver (altitude: 5,280 feet) and Colorado Springs (altitude: 6,035 feet), and opponents torched him in each home park. With his sinker and changeup, Bettis relies on groundball outs, but he's failed to produce weak contact: Major-league batters hit .340 on them, well above the .250 league average. He retired starting in August with the Sky Sox until his right shoulder, the same joint that caused him to miss 2012, acted up. That might be a sign; with rushed mechanics and deteriorating, post-surgery breaking ball, Bettis is better suited for multi-inning relief. *(Trivia answer: Victor Marte 2010, Damaso Marte 2009.)*

Rex Brothers   LHP

Born: 12/18/87   Age: 27   Bats: L   Throws: L   Height: 6'0"   Weight: 210

YEAR	TEAM	LVL	AGE	W	L	SV	G	GS	IP	H	HR	BB	K	BB/9	K/9	GB%	BABIP	WHIP	ERA	FIP	FRA	WARP
2012	COL	MLB	24	8	2	0	75	0	67²	63	5	37	83	4.9	11.0	48%	.343	1.48	3.86	3.33	3.66	1.2
2013	COL	MLB	25	2	1	19	72	0	67¹	51	5	36	76	4.8	10.2	50%	.280	1.29	1.74	3.33	3.61	1.0
2014	COL	MLB	26	4	6	0	74	0	56¹	65	7	39	55	6.2	8.8	41%	.343	1.85	5.59	4.95	5.78	-0.3
2015	COL	MLB	27	3	1	5	64	0	57¹	48	5	28	68	4.5	10.8	47%	.331	1.33	3.77	3.59	4.10	0.8

| Breakout: 35% | Improve: 52% | Collapse: 25% | Attrition: 16% | MLB: 87% | | *Comparables:* | *Brian Bruney, Jon Coutlangus, Manny Delcarmen* |

Last year, Brothers became the first reliever ever to pitch 70 games in consecutive seasons and triple his ERA. Triple! The control problems that kept Brothers on the cliff's edge finally tipped him over: His walk rate rose to 14 percent, and with the strikeout rate falling below reliever average, he failed to strand those free passes. Nevertheless, Walt Weiss stuck with Brothers all season in the set-up role, next in line for the closer role that LaTroy Hawkins never relinquished. To keep his value down heading into his first arbitration year, Brothers might've been barred from getting that chance anyway, but nothing about his 2014 suggests he's ready. Throw some strikes, bro.

Brooks Brown RHP
Born: 6/20/85 Age: 30 Bats: L Throws: R Height: 6'3" Weight: 205

YEAR	TEAM	LVL	AGE	W	L	SV	G	GS	IP	H	HR	BB	K	BB/9	K/9	GB%	BABIP	WHIP	ERA	FIP	FRA	WARP
2012	TOL	AAA	27	4	4	0	29	19	112	125	11	58	81	4.7	6.5	47%	.329	1.63	4.90	4.68	5.51	-0.8
2013	IND	AAA	28	6	5	0	37	8	91	95	11	24	69	2.4	6.8	52%	.316	1.31	4.75	4.12	6.24	0.2
2014	CSP	AAA	29	1	1	7	37	0	47¹	50	4	17	46	3.2	8.7	52%	.336	1.42	4.18	4.25	5.26	0.7
2014	COL	MLB	29	0	1	0	28	0	26	20	3	5	21	1.7	7.3	60%	.230	0.96	2.77	3.68	5.60	0.1
2015	*COL*	*MLB*	*30*	*3*	*3*	*0*	*26*	*8*	*65²*	*75*	*9*	*23*	*42*	*3.1*	*5.8*	*49%*	*.331*	*1.49*	*5.36*	*5.08*	*5.83*	*-0.2*

| Breakout: 4% | Improve: 4% | Collapse: 0% | Attrition: 4% | MLB: 7% | | *Comparables:* | *Brad Thomas, Jack Egbert, Mario Ramos* |

Looking for a fashionable coat? Visit Brooks Brothers. Looking for Colorado's hottest reliever? That's Brooks Brown, at least by earned run average. On a snowy April night some weeks from now, both will be welcome in the Rockies' frigid bullpen. The 2006 supplemental-round pick lost his prospect status in 2010, his BP Annual comment in 2011 and his starter hopes in 2013. So Brown shifted to relief, where he climbed back up by going down. His sinking fastball and slider played well in Denver, generating groundballs on 60 percent of his batted balls. A nifty changeup combated lefties, too. A full two runs of ERA better than his relief counterparts in Colorado, Brown should get higher leverage next year.

Eddie Butler RHP
Born: 3/13/91 Age: 24 Bats: R Throws: R Height: 6'2" Weight: 180

YEAR	TEAM	LVL	AGE	W	L	SV	G	GS	IP	H	HR	BB	K	BB/9	K/9	GB%	BABIP	WHIP	ERA	FIP	FRA	WARP
2013	ASH	A	22	5	1	0	9	9	54¹	25	2	25	51	4.1	8.4	76%	.172	0.92	1.66	3.63	5.30	0.3
2013	MOD	A+	22	3	4	0	13	13	67²	58	7	21	67	2.8	8.9	49%	.280	1.17	2.39	4.16	4.67	0.9
2013	TUL	AA	22	1	0	0	6	6	27²	13	0	6	25	2.0	8.1	58%	.188	0.69	0.65	2.01	2.44	0.9
2014	TUL	AA	23	6	9	0	18	18	108	104	10	32	63	2.7	5.2	47%	.274	1.26	3.58	4.10	4.76	0.2
2014	COL	MLB	23	1	1	0	3	3	16	23	2	7	3	3.9	1.7	56%	.328	1.88	6.75	5.67	6.50	-0.2
2015	*COL*	*MLB*	*24*	*6*	*8*	*0*	*21*	*21*	*114¹*	*125*	*14*	*44*	*63*	*3.4*	*5.0*	*51%*	*.312*	*1.48*	*5.20*	*5.15*	*5.65*	*-0.1*

| Breakout: 11% | Improve: 15% | Collapse: 7% | Attrition: 18% | MLB: 27% | | *Comparables:* | *Ivan Nova, Daryl Thompson, Troy Patton* |

Those enchanted by Butler's brilliant 2013 were probably destined for a small letdown. With his enduring, mid-90s fastball well established, Butler worked on sharpening his diverse repertoire in Tulsa and submitted to the Rockies' organizational groundball philosophy. He got the call-up in June, made one start, and then joined half the staff on the disabled list with rotator cuff inflammation in his right shoulder. He returned in late September for two starts and flashed his fancy changeup, a pitch that touches the upper 80s and induces both whiffs and grounders. Butler will have plenty of time to break in his other toys—two breaking balls and an excellent cutter—and with time, should emerge as a mid-rotation force.

Jhoulys Chacin RHP
Born: 1/7/88 Age: 27 Bats: R Throws: R Height: 6'3" Weight: 215

YEAR	TEAM	LVL	AGE	W	L	SV	G	GS	IP	H	HR	BB	K	BB/9	K/9	GB%	BABIP	WHIP	ERA	FIP	FRA	WARP
2012	CSP	AAA	24	1	1	0	2	2	13²	10	1	5	5	3.3	3.3	62%	.205	1.10	2.63	4.98	6.90	-0.1
2012	COL	MLB	24	3	5	0	14	14	69	80	10	32	45	4.2	5.9	40%	.311	1.62	4.43	5.19	5.47	1.0
2013	COL	MLB	25	14	10	0	31	31	197¹	188	11	61	126	2.8	5.7	48%	.288	1.26	3.47	3.44	3.95	3.5
2014	CSP	AAA	26	1	1	0	2	2	10²	9	0	5	8	4.2	6.8	52%	.273	1.31	2.53	3.89	4.09	0.1
2014	COL	MLB	26	1	7	0	11	11	63¹	63	8	28	42	4.0	6.0	44%	.285	1.44	5.40	4.79	5.88	0.2
2015	*COL*	*MLB*	*27*	*5*	*5*	*0*	*15*	*15*	*86²*	*82*	*8*	*32*	*68*	*3.3*	*7.0*	*49%*	*.307*	*1.31*	*4.19*	*4.19*	*4.56*	*0.9*

| Breakout: 30% | Improve: 57% | Collapse: 21% | Attrition: 21% | MLB: 95% | | *Comparables:* | *Anibal Sanchez, Jair Jurrjens, Josh Johnson* |

Chacin missed spring training and April with right shoulder stiffness, and judging by his sub-90s velocity upon return, never healed completely. An MRI in early July, prompted by a dead arm, revealed multiple issues in the shoulder. The Rockies opted for rehabilitation rather than surgery; Chacin's season ended regardless, becoming one of over a dozen injuries to the big club's pitching staff. He lost most of 2012 with inflammation in the same shoulder, and as long as Chacin throws with poor posture, leaning toward first base at release, he'll continue carrying that injury liability.

Tyler Chatwood RHP
Born: 12/16/89 Age: 25 Bats: R Throws: R Height: 6'0" Weight: 185

YEAR	TEAM	LVL	AGE	W	L	SV	G	GS	IP	H	HR	BB	K	BB/9	K/9	GB%	BABIP	WHIP	ERA	FIP	FRA	WARP
2012	TUL	AA	22	1	1	0	4	4	24	17	2	7	22	2.6	8.2	67%	.242	1.00	3.00	3.41	4.33	0.3
2012	CSP	AAA	22	0	2	0	9	9	37¹	52	2	19	31	4.6	7.5	59%	.394	1.90	5.79	4.39	4.66	1.0
2012	COL	MLB	22	5	6	1	19	12	64²	74	9	33	41	4.6	5.7	58%	.308	1.65	5.43	5.21	5.78	0.2
2013	CSP	AAA	23	2	1	0	6	6	34	37	0	7	33	1.9	8.7	65%	.366	1.29	2.91	2.33	3.29	1.4
2013	COL	MLB	23	8	5	0	20	20	111¹	118	5	41	66	3.3	5.3	60%	.314	1.43	3.15	3.63	4.11	2.4
2014	COL	MLB	24	1	0	0	4	4	24	21	4	8	20	3.0	7.5	46%	.254	1.21	4.50	4.85	6.49	-0.2
2015	*COL*	*MLB*	*25*	*2*	*3*	*0*	*8*	*8*	*40²*	*45*	*4*	*17*	*27*	*3.7*	*5.9*	*53%*	*.331*	*1.52*	*5.20*	*4.73*	*5.66*	*0.0*

| Breakout: 32% | Improve: 56% | Collapse: 17% | Attrition: 15% | MLB: 90% | | *Comparables:* | *Jon Lester, Tom Gorzelanny, Anibal Sanchez* |

Chatwood didn't get a chance to prove his 2013 doubters right or wrong, and he might not this year, either. After missing the beginning of 2014 with a strained hamstring, Chatwood made four starts before elbow inflammation shelved him. He encountered more issues during rehab, and a July diagnosis led to Tommy John surgery. With one operation (at age 16) already under his belt, he joins 50-odd players on the repeat list.

Jorge De La Rosa   LHP

Born: 4/5/81   Age: 34   Bats: L   Throws: L   Height: 6'1"   Weight: 215

YEAR	TEAM	LVL	AGE	W	L	SV	G	GS	IP	H	HR	BB	K	BB/9	K/9	GB%	BABIP	WHIP	ERA	FIP	FRA	WARP
2012	COL	MLB	31	0	2	0	3	3	10²	17	5	2	6	1.7	5.1	36%	.300	1.78	9.28	8.67	8.14	-0.3
2013	COL	MLB	32	16	6	0	30	30	167²	170	11	62	112	3.3	6.0	50%	.303	1.38	3.49	3.74	4.36	1.7
2014	COL	MLB	33	14	11	0	32	32	184¹	161	21	67	139	3.3	6.8	53%	.264	1.24	4.10	4.31	5.40	0.5
2015	COL	MLB	34	8	10	0	28	28	149¹	146	17	54	117	3.3	7.1	49%	.313	1.34	4.51	4.48	4.90	1.1

Breakout: 17%   Improve: 41%   Collapse: 15%   Attrition: 11%   MLB: 76%   Comparables: *Matt Clement, Vicente Padilla, Barry Zito*

Injury bugs were flying in Colorado all year, but De La Rosa proved immune as the only starter to pitch a full season. Perhaps he already paid his debts to the disabled list when he missed nearly two years from 2011 to 2012. De La Rosa's velocity hasn't returned to pre-Tommy John levels—and he's 34, so it might never—but he threw a tick harder last year and relied more on his cutter, another pitch he used to combat righties. With his clean health sheet and the Rockies' desperate need of stable pitching, De La Rosa got a two-year extension in September.

Jairo Diaz   RHP

Born: 5/27/91   Age: 24   Bats: R   Throws: R   Height: 6'0"   Weight: 195

YEAR	TEAM	LVL	AGE	W	L	SV	G	GS	IP	H	HR	BB	K	BB/9	K/9	GB%	BABIP	WHIP	ERA	FIP	FRA	WARP
2012	CDR	A	21	2	7	0	13	13	69	99	8	29	45	3.8	5.9	52%	.373	1.86	7.70	5.08	6.58	-0.5
2013	BUR	A	22	0	3	8	32	0	34	27	3	11	28	2.9	7.4	54%	.253	1.12	3.97	4.16	6.64	-0.3
2013	INL	A+	22	2	0	0	13	0	22¹	38	3	14	21	5.6	8.5	53%	.438	2.33	8.87	5.52	6.40	0.0
2014	INL	A+	23	2	3	4	29	0	32	31	2	10	37	2.8	10.4	53%	.322	1.28	4.78	3.27	3.77	0.6
2014	ARK	AA	23	2	1	11	27	0	32²	30	2	10	48	2.8	13.2	53%	.384	1.22	2.20	1.99	2.24	1.0
2014	ANA	MLB	23	0	0	0	5	0	5²	4	0	3	8	4.8	12.7	46%	.308	1.24	3.18	1.92	1.45	0.2
2015	COL	MLB	24	2	3	0	24	7	56²	70	8	27	38	4.3	6.0	49%	.350	1.70	6.30	5.51	6.85	-0.8

Breakout: 0%   Improve: 0%   Collapse: 0%   Attrition: 0%   MLB: 0%   Comparables: *Jeremy Horst, Buddy Boshers, Randy Wells*

Diaz has travelled a path familiar to many of those who wind up successful relievers: total obscurity. His career minor-league ERA over five seasons sits at 5.36, but prior to 2014 he would occasionally hit triple digits on the gun, which is of course the one thing that always guarantees more chances. He didn't notch enough strikes with the fastball in his MLB arrival to claim a postseason roster spot—he overthrew more often than not and his release point varies from pitch to pitch—but he did make heat-geared hitters look silly chasing his slider. The peripherals were better in the high minors, which is where the Rockies will likely send him in 2015 to prove worthiness for a high-leverage role.

Yohan Flande   LHP

Born: 1/27/86   Age: 29   Bats: L   Throws: L   Height: 6'2"   Weight: 180

YEAR	TEAM	LVL	AGE	W	L	SV	G	GS	IP	H	HR	BB	K	BB/9	K/9	GB%	BABIP	WHIP	ERA	FIP	FRA	WARP
2012	GWN	AAA	26	6	11	0	29	27	147²	153	11	55	106	3.4	6.5	52%	.308	1.41	4.21	3.91	5.42	0.1
2013	GWN	AAA	27	9	7	1	31	19	131¹	142	9	46	92	3.2	6.3	53%	.314	1.43	4.18	3.84	5.11	0.4
2014	CSP	AAA	28	3	11	0	18	16	88¹	112	9	33	67	3.4	6.8	55%	.361	1.64	5.60	4.70	5.85	0.1
2014	COL	MLB	28	0	6	0	16	10	59	55	5	16	34	2.4	5.2	60%	.272	1.20	5.19	3.97	5.86	0.0
2015	COL	MLB	29	6	8	0	27	20	121	142	14	39	72	2.9	5.4	51%	.335	1.49	5.32	4.76	5.78	-0.3

Breakout: 9%   Improve: 14%   Collapse: 5%   Attrition: 12%   MLB: 22%   Comparables: *Graham Godfrey, Robert Ray, Chris Seddon*

Our last comment on the extra-hittable Flande came in 2011 when he signed a minor-league contract with the Braves. Since then, he became the Gwinnett franchise record holder in (tracked) groundballs, prompting the Rockies to sign him and test his darting changeup's abilities in Colorado. His low-90s fastball remained extra hittable in Triple-A Colorado Springs, but with the Rockies short on starting pitching, Flande earned several call-ups and affirmed that he could at least rack up loads of grounders. Despite failing to last seven innings in any start, Flande limited lefties to a .167 TAv in a small sample, leaving our 2010 prognosis of him—limited stuff might only work in situational relief—in its original mint condition.

Kyle Freeland   LHP

Born: 5/14/93   Age: 22   Bats: L   Throws: L   Height: 6'3"   Weight: 170

YEAR	TEAM	LVL	AGE	W	L	SV	G	GS	IP	H	HR	BB	K	BB/9	K/9	GB%	BABIP	WHIP	ERA	FIP	FRA	WARP
2014	ASH	A	21	2	0	0	5	5	21²	14	1	4	18	1.7	7.5	52%	.220	0.83	0.83	3.08	3.74	0.6
2015	COL	MLB	22	2	3	0	8	8	34¹	40	4	16	21	4.1	5.4	48%	.332	1.63	5.87	5.27	6.39	-0.2

Breakout: 0%   Improve: 0%   Collapse: 0%   Attrition: 0%   MLB: 0%   Comparables: *Alex Cobb, Robbie Ross, Zach Phillips*

Freeland, the eighth overall pick out of Evansville in the 2014 draft, breezed through short-season ball after signing for $900,000 less than his $3.2 million slot value. Originally drafted in the 35th round three years ago by the Phillies, Freeland turned down ninth-round bonus money to attend college. There, he produced a 10:1 K:BB ratio in his junior year and ascended draft boards. He has a low-90s fastball and an 80s slider—er, to clarify, the latter isn't *from* the 1980s, but Freeland throws it in two varieties and two speeds, covering a wide velocity band. One is a more traditional, low-80s, sweeping slider; the other, in the mid-to-upper 80s, grooves more to the tune of a cutter. As his out pitch, it's bad medicine for hitters. For Freeland, with his stellar command, it's mid-rotation upside.

Christian Friedrich   LHP

Born: 7/8/87   Age: 27   Bats: R   Throws: L   Height: 6'4"   Weight: 215

YEAR	TEAM	LVL	AGE	W	L	SV	G	GS	IP	H	HR	BB	K	BB/9	K/9	GB%	BABIP	WHIP	ERA	FIP	FRA	WARP
2012	CSP	AAA	24	2	1	0	5	5	30	23	1	4	27	1.2	8.1	52%	.259	0.90	3.00	2.80	3.59	0.8
2012	COL	MLB	24	5	8	0	16	16	84²	102	14	30	74	3.2	7.9	45%	.342	1.56	6.17	4.67	5.44	0.6
2013	CSP	AAA	25	0	1	0	4	4	14²	13	1	8	8	4.9	4.9	58%	.245	1.43	4.30	5.00	6.33	0.1
2014	CSP	AAA	26	2	9	1	27	13	91¹	114	16	39	83	3.8	8.2	57%	.354	1.68	7.00	5.54	6.50	0.1
2014	COL	MLB	26	0	4	0	16	3	24¹	25	3	10	27	3.7	10.0	38%	.324	1.44	5.92	3.97	4.42	0.3
2015	COL	MLB	27	4	7	0	16	16	85²	98	13	30	66	3.1	6.9	46%	.337	1.49	5.44	4.98	5.91	-0.3

Breakout: 32%   Improve: 46%   Collapse: 17%   Attrition: 32%   MLB: 67%   Comparables: *Billy Buckner, Jon Rauch, Brad Lincoln*

After back problems cut off his 2013 season, the Rockies gave Friedrich several chances to return to starting form. Even with a 7.89 ERA at Triple-A Colorado Springs, he was sent up to the big-league club for three starts. When those didn't go any better (9.45 ERA), the club finally relegated its former first-rounder to the bullpen. Back to Colorado Springs. Friedrich researched his bullpen role for a month and taxied to Denver in late August, armed with a fastball/hard slider combo that tore hitters apart. His WHIP in that role was 0.55 over 11 innings, during which he struck out 36 percent of the batters he faced. The hope is he can be a solid LOOGY; the dream is he can start again.

Jonathan Gray RHP

Born: 11/5/91   Age: 23   Bats: R   Throws: R   Height: 6'4"   Weight: 235

YEAR	TEAM	LVL	AGE	W	L	SV	G	GS	IP	H	HR	BB	K	BB/9	K/9	GB%	BABIP	WHIP	ERA	FIP	FRA	WARP
2013	MOD	A+	21	4	0	0	5	5	24	10	0	6	36	2.2	13.5	50%	.227	0.67	0.75	1.52	2.42	0.9
2014	TUL	AA	22	10	5	0	24	24	124¹	107	10	41	113	3.0	8.2	40%	.285	1.19	3.91	3.43	4.42	0.7
2015	COL	MLB	23	5	7	0	19	19	91¹	94	10	32	76	3.1	7.5	41%	.327	1.37	4.51	4.26	4.91	0.7

Breakout: 19%   Improve: 30%   Collapse: 8%   Attrition: 26%   MLB: 44%   Comparables: Matt Barnes, Chad Bettis, Drew Smyly

Gray joined the Texas League as its third-youngest starter and spent his high-minors debut improving his changeup and command. They're the rougher elements of Gray's power game, and learning to harness consistency caused an erratic year in Tulsa. His upper-90s heater and wicked slider are mastered commodities, born and ready to punish big-league hitters; the former retains dominant velocity deep into games, and the latter ties up hitters with sadistic vertical movement. Tall and strong, it's ace potential if he refines his command. Restrain yourself; when he pitches in the majors, it won't be safe for work.

LaTroy Hawkins RHP

Born: 12/21/72   Age: 42   Bats: R   Throws: R   Height: 6'5"   Weight: 220

YEAR	TEAM	LVL	AGE	W	L	SV	G	GS	IP	H	HR	BB	K	BB/9	K/9	GB%	BABIP	WHIP	ERA	FIP	FRA	WARP
2012	ANA	MLB	39	2	3	1	48	0	42	45	5	13	23	2.8	4.9	58%	.292	1.38	3.64	4.43	5.33	-0.2
2013	NYN	MLB	40	3	2	13	72	0	70²	71	6	10	55	1.3	7.0	51%	.301	1.15	2.93	3.03	3.24	0.9
2014	COL	MLB	41	4	3	23	57	0	54¹	52	3	13	32	2.2	5.3	48%	.275	1.20	3.31	3.36	4.16	0.7
2015	COL	MLB	42	3	1	9	54	0	50²	55	5	12	33	2.1	5.9	50%	.322	1.32	4.32	4.09	4.69	0.4

Breakout: 8%   Improve: 17%   Collapse: 28%   Attrition: 16%   MLB: 62%   Comparables: Mike Timlin, Doug Brocail, Trevor Hoffman

Hawkins is the only pitcher in every Baseball Prospectus Annual ever. He might not have outwitted or outplayed, but he's certainly outlasted over a thousand other pitchers who began major-league journeys after 1995 and didn't make it to 2014. In 20 years of taking the mound and Annual comments, Hawkins has never made more than $5 million a season, and our highest compliment of him probably came in 2006: "We are often forced to remind ourselves that this guy is still a decent reliever."

Hawkins first pitched for Minnesota on April 29, 1995, facing 13 batters and allowing seven runs. It was the start of a five-year experiment gone very wrong, and he made his 98th and final start in September of 1999, switching to relief next April—soon becoming the Twins' closer. Fourteen years and five months later, he trotted out of the bullpen for his 1,000th big-league appearance, the closer tag still hanging loosely on him as he retired Darwin Barney on a deep fly ball. Teammate Brett Anderson on Twitter: "Hopefully one day @LaTroyHawkins32 can teach me how to stay healthy…" Hawkins will be staying a few more days, alright. Still pumping 94 mph, throwing strikes and pitching to contact, Hawkins registered the second-best ERA among Rockies relievers, and Colorado exercised its 2015 option. See you here next year.

Tommy Kahnle RHP

Born: 8/7/89   Age: 25   Bats: R   Throws: R   Height: 6'1"   Weight: 230

YEAR	TEAM	LVL	AGE	W	L	SV	G	GS	IP	H	HR	BB	K	BB/9	K/9	GB%	BABIP	WHIP	ERA	FIP	FRA	WARP
2012	TAM	A+	22	2	1	6	30	0	55	30	3	24	72	3.9	11.8	35%	.223	0.98	2.45	2.90	3.19	1.3
2013	TRN	AA	23	1	3	15	46	0	60	38	4	45	74	6.8	11.1	45%	.254	1.38	2.85	3.97	3.69	0.9
2014	COL	MLB	24	2	1	0	54	0	68²	51	7	31	63	4.1	8.3	48%	.240	1.19	4.19	3.99	4.60	0.2
2015	COL	MLB	25	2	1	1	36	0	56²	49	6	30	58	4.7	9.3	43%	.314	1.40	4.19	4.38	4.55	0.5

Breakout: 15%   Improve: 26%   Collapse: 5%   Attrition: 23%   MLB: 38%   Comparables: David Holmberg, Patrick Corbin, Casey Kelly

The Rockies selected Kahnle in the Rule 5 draft from the Yankees' system, where he closed for Double-A Trenton. For his first major-league game, they thrust him into a two-out, one-out jam created by Franklin Morales. That was the first of many multi-inning appearances for Kahnle, who averaged 1.7 innings per game in the minor leagues. By the All-Star break, he trailed only Dellin Betances in bullpen appearances of more than three outs, and had pitched the fourth-most relief innings in the league, all with a .208 TAv against. Kahnle relies on a mid-90s fastball, mid-80s slider and hard changeup, the latter especially good against lefties. He struggles with command and had a poor second half, but Kahnle, at least for 2014, can be declared a Rule 5 success.

Boone Logan LHP

Born: 8/13/84   Age: 30   Bats: R   Throws: L   Height: 6'5"   Weight: 215

YEAR	TEAM	LVL	AGE	W	L	SV	G	GS	IP	H	HR	BB	K	BB/9	K/9	GB%	BABIP	WHIP	ERA	FIP	FRA	WARP
2012	NYA	MLB	27	7	2	1	80	0	55¹	48	6	28	68	4.6	11.1	40%	.311	1.37	3.74	3.62	3.52	0.8
2013	NYA	MLB	28	5	2	0	61	0	39	33	7	13	50	3.0	11.5	51%	.292	1.18	3.23	3.84	5.12	-0.3
2014	COL	MLB	29	2	3	0	35	0	25	31	6	11	32	4.0	11.5	54%	.379	1.68	6.84	5.10	5.63	-0.2
2015	COL	MLB	30	3	1	2	55	0	37	34	4	13	41	3.2	10.0	45%	.334	1.28	3.92	3.64	4.26	0.5

Breakout: 33%   Improve: 48%   Collapse: 25%   Attrition: 12%   MLB: 87%   Comparables: Frank Francisco, Shawn Kelley, Tony Sipp

For a guy whose name literally means "beneficial," Logan's year was nothing but bad luck exacerbated by his own mistakes. He spent four different stints with the Colorado Travelin' Disableds, and when the groundballer was on the mound he saw roughly a quarter of his fly balls go over the wall. Thirty percent of his batted balls went for line drives, leading to an astronomical .379 BABIP. Each of those failings has an element of "aw dagnabit" intertwined with an element of "get 'im outta there," so Logan is both a solid bounceback candidate—based on his 27 percent strikeout rate and an increased groundball frequency—and a good bet to underperform the $5.5 million the Rockies will pay him in the second third of his three-year deal. The September elbow surgery to remove a bone spur is the most troubling indicator, considering he had the same operation in October 2013.

Jordan Lyles   RHP

Born: 10/19/90   Age: 24   Bats: R   Throws: R   Height: 6'4"   Weight: 215

YEAR	TEAM	LVL	AGE	W	L	SV	G	GS	IP	H	HR	BB	K	BB/9	K/9	GB%	BABIP	WHIP	ERA	FIP	FRA	WARP
2012	OKL	AAA	21	5	0	0	7	7	40²	41	2	8	33	1.8	7.3	59%	.331	1.20	3.54	3.71	5.00	0.6
2012	HOU	MLB	21	5	12	0	25	25	141¹	159	20	42	99	2.7	6.3	55%	.302	1.42	5.09	4.57	5.05	0.6
2013	OKL	AAA	22	2	2	0	6	5	23²	30	1	6	11	2.3	4.2	62%	.345	1.52	5.32	3.95	5.43	0.1
2013	HOU	MLB	22	7	9	1	27	25	141²	165	17	49	93	3.1	5.9	50%	.314	1.51	5.59	4.59	5.28	0.0
2014	COL	MLB	23	7	4	0	22	22	126²	127	12	46	90	3.3	6.4	53%	.295	1.37	4.33	4.19	4.70	1.4
2015	COL	MLB	24	6	9	0	21	21	118²	135	14	34	80	2.6	6.1	48%	.334	1.43	5.20	4.60	5.65	-0.2

Breakout: 26%   Improve: 63%   Collapse: 15%   Attrition: 20%   MLB: 93%   Comparables: *Chris Volstad, Jesse Litsch, Brett Cecil*

When we think of durable young starters, Lyles probably doesn't come to mind, but he's got more than 500 innings through age 23 and ranked second on the Rockies last year. Eventually he couldn't avoid the DL either, suffering a left-hand fracture on a home plate collision and becoming one of 15 disabled-list transactions on the staff—one every 13 days of the season! Lyles' height and sinker are instrumental tools for maintaining his high groundball rate, the candy that lured Dan O'Dowd into trading Dexter Fowler for the former first-rounder. Yet inside the shiny wrapper, Lyles doesn't throw very hard and lacks a strikeout pitch—the third time through the order, he's probably stale. At least you can get him in bulk.

Nick Masset   RHP

Born: 5/17/82   Age: 33   Bats: R   Throws: R   Height: 6'5"   Weight: 235

YEAR	TEAM	LVL	AGE	W	L	SV	G	GS	IP	H	HR	BB	K	BB/9	K/9	GB%	BABIP	WHIP	ERA	FIP	FRA	WARP
2014	COL	MLB	32	2	0	0	51	0	45	56	3	24	36	4.8	7.2	55%	.371	1.78	5.80	4.30	5.39	0.0
2015	COL	MLB	33	2	1	1	44	0	40²	40	3	16	38	3.5	8.4	49%	.335	1.37	4.17	3.74	4.53	0.4

Breakout: 23%   Improve: 44%   Collapse: 29%   Attrition: 12%   MLB: 87%   Comparables: *Jason Frasor, Santiago Casilla, Will Ohman*

Another groundball specialist targeted by the Rockies, Masset signed a minor-league deal last winter after spending two dire years recovering from *three* surgeries on his right shoulder. Though he lost two mph off his fastball, Masset's curve remained lethal: Not only did batters whiff on 41 percent of swings, but in 101 throws righties *never* hit it the air, neither line drives nor fly balls. The curve has severe tilt and tails away from righties, or in on lefties (watch out, you might get nicked). Resist the pitch, and it'll likely go for a ball, though with the strike zone's recent shift downward, can a hitter ever be sure? Masset's reduced velocity will keep him from showing the consistency and reliability of his Cincinnati years, but middle relief is a fine outcome after a two-year absence.

Tyler Matzek   LHP

Born: 10/19/90   Age: 24   Bats: L   Throws: L   Height: 6'3"   Weight: 210

YEAR	TEAM	LVL	AGE	W	L	SV	G	GS	IP	H	HR	BB	K	BB/9	K/9	GB%	BABIP	WHIP	ERA	FIP	FRA	WARP
2012	MOD	A+	21	6	8	0	28	28	142¹	134	7	95	153	6.0	9.7	44%	.326	1.61	4.62	4.41	4.80	1.9
2013	TUL	AA	22	8	9	0	26	26	142¹	147	13	76	95	4.8	6.0	42%	.306	1.57	3.79	4.62	5.38	0.1
2014	CSP	AAA	23	5	4	0	12	12	66²	70	8	31	61	4.2	8.2	51%	.302	1.51	4.05	4.82	5.76	0.8
2014	COL	MLB	23	6	11	0	20	19	117²	120	9	44	91	3.4	7.0	52%	.312	1.39	4.05	3.75	4.30	1.8
2015	COL	MLB	24	7	11	0	27	27	143²	152	16	84	108	5.2	6.8	43%	.328	1.64	5.46	5.19	5.94	-0.5

Breakout: 36%   Improve: 55%   Collapse: 16%   Attrition: 30%   MLB: 77%   Comparables: *Ubaldo Jimenez, Brad Hand, Kyle Drabek*

The 11th overall pick in 2009, Matzek finally took big steps with his command in Colorado Springs. He built on his improvement in Tulsa and got the call-up with the Rockies in June, immediately joining the rotation. His walk rate finished at 9 percent with Colorado, satisfying progress since his days of walking 21 percent of batters in 2011. When Matzek's mechanics are under, uh, control, his deep arsenal can dominate lineups, starting with a fastball that touches the mid-90s. He complements it with two breaking balls, plus a working changeup against righties that would benefit from more velocity separation. That stuff, alone, has mid-rotation upside, but the spotty command will likely result in intermittent frustration and brilliance, lest he becomes a reliever with too much of the former.

Franklin Morales   LHP

Born: 1/24/86   Age: 29   Bats: L   Throws: L   Height: 6'1"   Weight: 210

YEAR	TEAM	LVL	AGE	W	L	SV	G	GS	IP	H	HR	BB	K	BB/9	K/9	GB%	BABIP	WHIP	ERA	FIP	FRA	WARP
2012	BOS	MLB	26	3	4	1	37	9	76¹	64	11	30	76	3.5	9.0	40%	.262	1.23	3.77	4.34	4.82	0.7
2013	PAW	AAA	27	0	1	0	5	2	11¹	5	3	3	12	2.4	9.5	35%	.087	0.71	4.76	5.32	9.44	-0.1
2013	BOS	MLB	27	2	2	0	20	1	25¹	24	2	15	21	5.3	7.5	40%	.310	1.54	4.62	4.58	5.31	-0.1
2014	COL	MLB	28	6	9	0	38	22	142¹	166	24	65	100	4.1	6.3	45%	.315	1.62	5.37	5.39	6.05	0.1
2015	COL	MLB	29	5	5	0	55	13	108²	108	15	47	94	3.9	7.8	40%	.316	1.43	4.86	4.91	5.28	0.3

Breakout: 33%   Improve: 49%   Collapse: 12%   Attrition: 11%   MLB: 73%   Comparables: *Todd Wellemeyer, David Hernandez, Byung-Hyun Kim*

Fresh off winning a World Series ring with the Red Sox, Morales returned to the Rockies determined to make it as a starter again. Colorado welcomed him with its usual homer-happy air, while Walt Weiss alternated between roles for Morales throughout the season. Despite being pulled from the rotation twice, he made 22 starts—tied for second most on the team—while his ERA rarely wandered below five. Franklin was bashed especially by righties, as his .310 TAv against was worse than only Travis Wood's (min. 350 PA). Once a top prospect, Morales has been injured, ineffective and incapable of throwing strikes, and has totaled just 1.1 WARP in his major-league career, yet you look up and he's entering his ninth season.

Adam Ottavino   RHP

Born: 11/22/85   Age: 29   Bats: B   Throws: R   Height: 6'5"   Weight: 230

YEAR	TEAM	LVL	AGE	W	L	SV	G	GS	IP	H	HR	BB	K	BB/9	K/9	GB%	BABIP	WHIP	ERA	FIP	FRA	WARP
2012	CSP	AAA	26	0	0	0	13	0	19²	22	2	7	25	3.2	11.4	44%	.364	1.47	3.20	3.51	3.37	0.7
2012	COL	MLB	26	5	1	0	53	0	79	76	9	34	81	3.9	9.2	49%	.313	1.39	4.56	3.90	4.55	0.9
2013	COL	MLB	27	1	3	0	51	0	78¹	73	5	31	70	3.6	9.0	48%	.311	1.33	2.64	3.12	3.84	1.1
2014	COL	MLB	28	1	4	0	75	0	65	67	6	16	70	2.2	9.7	47%	.347	1.28	3.60	3.07	3.93	0.9
2015	COL	MLB	29	3	2	0	34	4	59	59	6	20	55	3.1	8.4	47%	.334	1.35	4.39	3.91	4.77	0.4

Breakout: 24%   Improve: 54%   Collapse: 14%   Attrition: 14%   MLB: 81%   Comparables: *Jon Rauch, Juan Gutierrez, Dan Wheeler*

Last year, Ottavino recorded his third straight season in Colorado with an ERA+ over 100. With his role shifting to set-up man, he no longer pitched multiple innings: After 24 games getting six outs or more in 2013, only one such game occured in 2014. As a result, Ottavino faced his kryptonite, lefties, less frequently. Just 30 percent of his batters hit left-handed, softening the effect of their .297 True Average against. Against righties, the story with Ottavino hasn't changed: slider, slider, slider. He threw his two-plane weapon 60 percent of the time; whether he was starting off or finishing off a batter, it didn't matter. With fellow comrades Matt Belisle and Rex Brothers tailing off, Ottavino became the Rockies' most reliable reliever under the age of 40.

Lineouts

Hitters

NAME	POS	TEAM	LVL	AGE	PA	R	2B	3B	HR	RBI	BB	K	SB	CS	AVG/OBP/SLG	TAv	BABIP	BRR	FRAA	WARP
Cristhian Adames	SS	TUL	AA	22	380	42	9	4	2	38	29	58	7	9	.267/.324/.336	.261	.312	-0.4	SS(50): 2.5, 2B(14): -1.3	1.3
	SS	CSP	AAA	22	163	19	12	0	1	14	13	25	5	1	.338/.392/.441	.282	.403	0.7	SS(18): 0.1, 3B(16): 2.0	1.2
	SS	COL	MLB	22	15	1	0	0	0	0	0	5	0	0	.067/.067/.067	.030	.100	0.0	SS(5): 0.1, 2B(2): 0.1	-0.4
Ryan Casteel	1B	TUL	AA	23	481	63	22	1	16	56	39	94	3	3	.280/.341/.445	.287	.322	-3.2	1B(59): -0.7, C(39): -0.6	2.1
Rosell Herrera	SS	MOD	A+	21	302	31	11	1	4	23	24	52	9	7	.244/.302/.335	.234	.285	0.1	SS(35): 1.0, 3B(29): -0.4	0.7
Matt McBride	RF	CSP	AAA	29	206	27	11	1	7	35	12	19	0	1	.305/.345/.487	.286	.301	-0.8	RF(26): 0.1, 1B(7): 0.3	0.7
	1B	COL	MLB	29	34	6	2	0	2	6	2	12	0	0	.226/.294/.484	.255	.294	0.0	1B(5): 0.1, RF(3): -0.1	0.1
Tom Murphy	C	TUL	AA	23	109	16	4	0	5	15	14	27	0	0	.213/.321/.415	.257	.242	-0.6	C(23): -0.1	0.1
Jordan Patterson	RF	ASH	A	22	532	69	27	0	14	66	46	118	25	8	.278/.359/.430	.270	.338	-1.5	RF(102): -7.4, 1B(11): 2.8	1.0
Wilfredo Rodriguez	C	ASH	A	20	315	36	16	0	3	37	21	33	2	3	.310/.359/.399	.268	.335	-4.9	C(44): -0.8	0.6
Will Swanner	C	MOD	A+	22	348	36	16	3	9	41	32	106	7	5	.261/.331/.419	.267	.364	-0.2	C(40): 0.9, 1B(28): -0.5	1.0
	1B	TUL	AA	22	108	12	5	0	4	14	4	35	1	4	.279/.306/.442	.271	.385	-1.5	1B(11): -0.4, C(8): 0.1	0.3
Patrick Valaika	SS	ASH	A	21	144	25	12	1	4	23	9	26	6	2	.370/.407/.575	.289	.430	-1.1	SS(31): -1.1	1.5
	SS	MOD	A+	21	362	46	14	5	8	47	24	101	7	6	.272/.321/.417	.265	.366	3.1	SS(49): 7.9, 2B(22): -0.5	2.3
Tim Wheeler	LF	CSP	AAA	26	472	51	25	3	11	45	36	109	9	10	.233/.313/.387	.247	.289	-1.7	LF(62): -0.9, RF(27): 0.1	-0.1
Rafael Ynoa	SS	CSP	AAA	26	473	66	31	3	5	32	38	78	7	7	.297/.356/.419	.263	.353	-1.6	SS(46): 2.8, 3B(44): 2.6	2.4
	3B	COL	MLB	26	71	5	6	1	0	13	4	9	0	0	.343/.380/.463	.295	.397	-0.9	3B(13): 1.5, SS(2): 0.4	0.7

Cristhian Adames grew from teenager to adult in the Rockies organization since signing as an amateur at 16; unfortunately, his hitting hasn't matured as much, making him a defense-only solution. ❖ After just two home runs in high-scoring Low-A Asheville, **Ryan Casteel** broke out in low-scoring High-A Modesto, hitting 22. He proved it was no fluke in neutral-scoring Double-A Tulsa, but it won't matter if he can't stick at catcher. ❖ *Well, you've made a long journey from Asheville to Modesto, Rosell, Rosell. You've never stopped hoping; soon you'll be in Colorado, Rosell, Rosell.* But first you'll have to hit, **Rosell Herrera**. ❖ Does anything spell AAAA more than a strikeout rate nearly four times higher in the big leagues than in Triple-A? Many thanks for the major-league memories, **Matt McBride**. ❖ In 23 games, runners stole 18 of 22 bases off **Tom Murphy** in Tulsa. The nightmares it gave his shoulder eventually gave way to a season-ending injury in May. ❖ **Dom Nunez**'s hands and athleticism merited a season at middle infield, but they're rarer tools at the backstop, his natural position. He repeated the Pioneer League there and threw out 36 percent of runners. ❖ **Jordan Patterson**'s power and arm project prototypical right fielder, and his Low-A splits (.295 home TAv, .244 away) project prototypical Rockies hitter. ❖ **Wilfredo Rodriguez** hit slightly better than his Asheville catching counterpart, Jose Briceno, but W-Rod's good receiving couldn't save him from the fact that Briceno threw out four times as many runners. ❖ Walt Weiss awaits the day he can send the slugging **Will Swanner** to pinch-hit, as there won't be many other times he'll say "Will in for Wilin." ❖ Though the Valaika brothers are many accomplishments away from supplanting the infamous Molinas, **Patrick Valaika** could emerge as a defense-first utility infielder while brother Chris continues swinging with futility. ❖ In his third season at Colorado Springs, **Tim Wheeler** doubled his home run count for the second time; his batting average also fell another 30 points, foreboding his descent into Triple-A purgatory. ❖ **Rafael Ynoa** never broke past Double-A in his eight seasons in the Dodgers' system, but he found BABIP magic in Colorado Springs and sparkled as a September utility infielder.

Pitchers

NAME	TEAM	LVL	AGE	W	L	SV	G	GS	IP	H	HR	BB	K	BB/9	K/9	GB%	BABIP	WHIP	ERA	FIP	FRA	WARP
Jayson Aquino	MOD	A+	21	5	10	0	16	16	95	113	7	30	74	2.8	7.0	59%	.353	1.51	5.40	4.47	5.73	0.6
	TUL	AA	21	0	0	0	2	2	12	9	0	8	9	6.0	6.8	69%	.257	1.42	3.00	3.62	5.43	-0.1
Shane Broyles	MOD	A+	22	2	2	1	41	0	63	55	7	21	68	3.0	9.7	49%	.296	1.21	3.43	4.07	4.70	0.9
Ryan Castellani	TRI	A-	18	1	2	0	10	10	37	35	2	9	25	2.2	6.1	56%	.282	1.19	3.65	4.22	5.49	0.2
Pedro Hernandez	CSP	AAA	25	6	7	0	19	17	88¹	125	10	30	53	3.1	5.4	50%	.365	1.75	6.42	5.09	5.65	0.5
	COL	MLB	25	0	1	0	1	1	5²	6	0	2	2	3.2	3.2	63%	.316	1.41	4.76	3.98	6.95	-0.2
Austin House	STO	A+	23	3	4	19	46	0	54²	47	4	19	79	3.1	13.0	55%	.347	1.21	3.46	3.01	3.48	1.6
Aaron Laffey	SYR	AAA	29	12	6	0	25	21	147	159	8	37	91	2.3	5.6	53%	.307	1.33	3.67	3.64	4.78	0.7
Chris Martin	CSP	AAA	28	1	3	5	25	0	26²	33	2	9	36	3.0	12.1	51%	.431	1.58	4.39	3.21	3.59	0.7
	COL	MLB	28	0	0	0	16	0	15²	22	2	4	14	2.3	8.0	61%	.408	1.66	6.89	3.74	4.35	0.2
Justin Miller	TOL	AAA	27	2	1	5	38	0	44²	30	2	12	39	2.4	7.9	42%	.241	0.94	1.81	3.27	3.40	0.8
	DET	MLB	27	1	0	0	8	0	12¹	14	2	2	5	1.5	3.6	41%	.273	1.30	5.11	4.94	6.36	-0.2
Scott Oberg	TUL	AA	24	0	1	15	27	0	27¹	22	1	6	21	2.0	6.9	52%	.262	1.02	2.63	2.83	3.70	0.3
Jose Ortega	TOL	AAA	25	2	2	1	43	1	58	50	4	36	48	5.6	7.4	52%	.275	1.48	3.57	4.62	5.56	0.1
	DET	MLB	25	0	1	0	1	0	1¹	0	0	4	1	27.0	6.8	67%	.000	3.00	27.00	12.91	20.36	-0.2
Jorge Rondon	MEM	AAA	26	5	4	10	51	0	62¹	59	3	20	51	2.9	7.4	56%	.297	1.27	3.03	3.80	3.86	0.9
	SLN	MLB	26	0	0	0	1	0	1	0	0	1	0	9.0	0.0	67%	.000	1.00	0.00	6.10	4.71	0.0
Kraig Sitton	TUL	AA	25	4	8	4	48	0	66	63	8	24	43	3.3	5.9	55%	.268	1.32	3.68	4.53	5.62	-0.5

Jayson Aquino's command-dependent fastball/changeup combination loves groundballs and hates home runs, but he has not developed a trustworthy breaking ball in his five years in the Rockies' system. ❖ One of the oldest players to ever undergo Tommy John surgery, **Rafael Betancourt** pitched in rookie league just nine months after the operation. Finished with striking out hitters half his age, he'll look to come back with the Rockies in 2015. ❖ Without a third pitch complementing his low-90s fastball and slider, 14th-round pick **Shane Broyles** flipped to full-time relief last year and posted a 1.20 ERA after April, expediting his path to the major leagues. ❖ High schooler **Ryan Castellani** throws a hard sinker fit for groundballs at Coors Field. It's a good start for the second-rounder; his secondary pitches need significant work. ❖ **Pedro Hernandez** induced groundballs on half his batted balls in Triple-A—oh forget it, it's impossible to positively spin Pedro Hernandez. ❖ High-A batters could not solve **Austin House**, whose sinker-changeup combination led to a ton of empty swings; he struck out 10 more hitters in 2014 than the year prior despite 38 fewer innings, the result of full-time work in the bullpen, where this House felt more at home. ❖ If unused Nationals reliever **Aaron Laffey** had to do it over again, he'd probably have signed with an organization less stocked in pitching depth and/or a Triple-A city with better Vietnamese food. The Rockies meet the first qualification. ❖ A torn labrum ended **Chris Martin**'s baseball dreams in 2006. He turned to warehouse work, lifting boxes for four years, where he magically rehabbed his shoulder, dated Jennifer Lawrence and now throws 97 out of the bullpen. ❖ **Justin Miller** overcame Tommy John surgery in 2012 to make the 40-man in Detroit and debuted in May, but couldn't miss a bat to save his life and was outrighted midseason. He'll mop up what you spill. ❖ **Scott Oberg** throws in the low-to-mid-90s with a big 12-to-6 curve, and with that one-two he has seized the closer job at every level he's tried. ❖ The Tigers had always tolerated **Jose Ortega**'s walk rate, because that's what you do with an upper-90s pitcher, but upper-90s became low-to-mid-90s and it still missed the plate, so the team evicted him from the 40-man. ❖ Flamethrowing **Jorge Rondon** finally learned some control last summer in a Triple-A bullpen, and if he continues to avoid ball four his mid-90s heat could be handy in the seventh inning. ❖ Twenty-six and stuffed on the 40-man away from Rule 5 leachers, **Kraig Sitton** held lefties to a .186 TAv in Double-A, showing distant LOOGY potential. Don't look at the other side of that split though (.312 TAv). I said don't look!

Manager

Walt Weiss

YEAR	TEAM	W	L	Py-thag +/-	Avg PC	100+ P	120+ P	QS	BQS	REL	REL w Zero R	IBB	PH	PH Avg	PH HR	SB2	CS2	SB3	CS3	SAC Att	SAC%	POS SAC	Squeeze	Swing	In Play
2013	COL	74	88	-1	90.2	22	0	65	0	502	366	52	257	.282	6	97	28	15	4	100	65.0%	34	2	301	91
2014	COL	66	96	-9	92	33	0	70	4	547	404	32	265	.259	5	70	40	15	6	92	64.1%	33	2	313	79

With a bald head and gray-speckled beard, Weiss looks like the stereotypical manager. He behaves like one, too.

Sabermetric convention holds that any manager who embraces small-ball tactics inside Coors Field deserves to lose—ùsomething Weiss has done plenty of times over the past two years. That he remained faithful to his ultra-conservative ways last season, despite questionable results, raises concerns about his ability and willingness to adjust. The Rockies, though 29th in stolen-base percentage, ran often enough to finish in the top half of the majors in attempts. When the ineffective basestealers weren't giving up outs, Weiss was by calling for the second-most position-player sacrifices in the NL. If there is a silver lining—or a blue mountain, so to speak—it's that the most common bunters were offensive non-entities (Barnes, Culberson and LeMahieu). Otherwise, oof.

Unsurprisingly, Weiss played as loose with his hook as he did with his outs. He afforded Colorado's starters the third-lowest average pitch count in the NL, and his relievers led the league in appearances lasting fewer than three outs. (His impatient approach didn't help: no team blew more saves or allowed a higher rate of inherited runners to score than the Rockies did.) Weiss also deployed closer LaTroy Hawkins in a predictably rigid manner. Hawkins notched more than three outs or entered before the ninth just once each—ùthose feats came, respectively, during the late stages of a 16-inning affair and in the season's penultimate game, in which he faced one batter before departing.

Were it not for his indistinct nature, odds are people wouldn't think highly of Weiss as a manager. As such, being indistinguishable might be Weiss' best attribute.

DETROIT TIGERS

by Ken Funck

The Detroit Tigers enter the 2015 season having won four consecutive American League Central titles and are favored to win their fifth. The franchise has won 366 games during that span, the most in baseball. Their roster is littered with stars, including a generational batting talent and several ace starters, one of whom is dating a supermodel. Their owner is committed to winning a championship and allows his well-regarded general manager to pay his big-league players more than the City of Detroit budgets for its fire department. The three most recent AL Cy Young winners were toiling in the Tigers' rotation last September. Everything, as our friend Russell Carleton is wont to say, should be peace, love, happiness and banana pudding.

So why aren't the Tigers *great*?

Here at Baseball Prospectus, we like to quantify as much as we possibly can to learn what does and doesn't help a baseball team win. But that's not what this is about. This is about perception, and few would disagree that the recent Dombrowski-Cabrera-Verlander Tigers are not viewed as a memorably, historically great team, not in the way the Big Red Machine or the Core Four Yankees or Earl Weaver's Orioles teams were considered great.

Yet Detroit's accomplishment of winning four straight division titles is notably rare. For comparison's sake, the Boston Red Sox—often considered a great team—have won four division titles *in total* since Sha Na Na preceded Jimi Hendrix at Woodstock. Only five other clubs have managed to win four in a row since the first divisional structure was implemented in 1969:

Oakland Athletics, 1971–1975. Charlie Finley's Swingin' A's won three straight World Series titles during the Watergate years, gifting the people of Oakland with smiles wider than their ties. If you doubt whether The Mustache Gang are considered an all-time great, consider that they are one of only seven teams listed in the "MLB Dynasty" entry at Wikipedia, which must be the online version of winning a People's Choice Award.

Atlanta Braves, 1991–2005. The lone franchise ever to break the laws of time and space by winning fourteen straight division titles in fifteen years (since 1994 never actually happened), the Braves also broke the laws of probability by only winning a single World Series title in all that time. Yet they dominated the

National League for a decade with one of the most memorable rotations in baseball history, and most would agree they were an all-time great team.

Cleveland Indians, 1995–1999. Perhaps the closest approximation to today's Tigers, the Indians slugged their way to two World Series appearances but lost them both before fading into the shadow cast by the …

New York Yankees, 1998–2006. Of course.

Philadelphia Phillies, 2007–2011. The Phightin' Phils won a World Series, lost another one and featured a star-studded lineup and a rotation some thought might turn into one of the best ever. That transformation never happened, and after the Phillies sank under the weight of their bloated contracts it became doubtful that they would become a pantheon team.

No other "dynasty" has managed to win four straight division titles. Not the Big Red Machine. Not the great Orioles teams, or Cito's Blue Jays, or Brett's Royals, or any team associated with Tony La Russa and Dave Duncan. Yet each of those teams is more likely to be considered an all-timer than the Tigers of recent vintage. Detroit's lack of dynastic credibility among casual fans suffers in four areas:

1. No World Championship: Obviously. Until Miguel Cabrera or some other Tigers star gets to share a charmingly awkward moment with the Chevy Guy, the Tigers will never shed their also-ran label. Winning it all doesn't guarantee a place on the dynasty list—cough Phillies cough—but without it you won't even be in the discussion.

Again, this is optics. When you win a World Series, the public's final image of you is a champagne-soaked clubhouse reverie. The Giants are clearly considered today's dynasty because they won three championships in five years, despite not making the playoffs at all those other two years. The Cardinals have played the most postseason games over the last four seasons, launching their gloves in triumph at the end of seven different series, including the 2011 World Series and a Wild Card play-in game. Those franchises have become synonymous with winning.

TIGERS PROSPECTUS
2014 W-L: 90-72, 1ST IN AL CENTRAL

Pythag	.533	9th	DER	.688	28th
RS/G	4.67	2nd	B-Age	29.9	28th
RA/G	4.35	22nd	P-Age	28.1	15th
TAv	.271	5th	Salary	$163.1M	4th
BRR	3.15	11th	M$/MW	$3.6M	23rd
TAv-P	.260	13th	DL Days	1,055	27th
FIP	3.62	11th	$ on DL	9%	1st

Three-Year Park Factors

Runs	Runs/RH	Runs/LH	HR/RH	HR/LH
107	114	100	89	82

Top Hitter WARP	5.5	Miguel Cabrera
Top Pitcher WARP	5.0	Max Scherzer
Top Prospect		Derek Hill

The Tigers have split their eight postseason series since 2011, which sounds reasonably good, but dig a little deeper. Twice they've sent Oakland home, but that doesn't earn any style points in the popular imagination. Everyone knows Billy Beane's shiz doesn't work in the playoffs. Detroit's other two victories were against New York, which ended not with headlines screaming "Tigers Win!" so much as "Yankees Lose And A-Rod Sucks." Detroit wasn't viewed as the 2012 AL Champion; they were an instrument of karmic vengeance, with Delmon Young of all people delivering the overdue *coup de grace* to the evil empire.

Detroit's four playoff exits were more memorable. Texas bullied them 15-5 in the clinching game of the 2011 ALCS. The Giants swept them in the 2012 World Series. The 2013 ALCS was defined by Big Papi's game-tying eighth-inning grand slam in Game Two that pivoted the momentum to Boston. Last year Detroit exited with the softest of whimpers, swept by the Orioles. When last we saw the Tigers, they had been unable to solve the workaday offerings of Bud Norris, and were forced to stare icily from the dugout as Baltimore celebrated on the Comerica grass. That's America's image of this Tigers team, fair or not.

Winning the big one may put all those bad memories to rest, but that's easier said than done. The heavy lifting is out of the way: The Tigers have a team good enough to make the postseason dance year after year. After that, it's a crapshoot. Playing a short series against another very good team is pretty much a fifty-fifty proposition, and numerous analysts (including ours) have made processors smoke looking for the "secret sauce" that leads to playoff success, to no avail. Some may claim Detroit is "due" after four straight playoff exits, but those are the same folks who allow casinos to thrive off their sketchy understanding of probability. Hope isn't a plan, but having built a leviathan that rampages through the regular season, hope is all a team can buy itself once October comes around.

2. Weak Competition: Not every division is created equal, and Detroit's reputation has suffered from the relative lightweights that have populated the AL Central during their recent dominance. Their divisional opponents have averaged 75.5 wins annually since 2011, the worst set of opponents in baseball, lending credence to the argument that the Tigers feast on the Little Sisters of the Poor during the regular season but can't compete with the big boys come October. That's not a charge you generally hear leveled against St. Louis, even though their division-mates have averaged just 77.3 wins during the same time span, higher only than the Tigers. But they're the Cardinals, and life isn't fair.

Detroit has also missed out on the benefit of a consistent divisional rival to overcome, one that sparks breathtaking pennant races and the perception that the Tigers are battle-tested. Cleveland, the second-best team in the division over the last four years, is just 18th in wins overall. The Tigers have edged out the White Sox, Indians and Royals for their last three division crowns, but the common refrain among observers hasn't been respect for Detroit's fortitude in holding off their divisional rivals, but disappointment that the Tigers didn't dominate from the get-go.

3. That Whole Don Kelly Thing: He's probably a cool guy and has his uses, but a truly great franchise wouldn't keep Don Kelly on the roster for a half-decade, let alone start him in center field

in a playoff elimination game. Full stop.

4. Lack of Home-Grown Talent: This may be the unkindest cut of all, but given today's prospect-aware baseball fandom, Detroit's consistently low farm-system rankings marks them down a grade in the court of public opinion. Never mind Justin Verlander, Alex Avila, Nick Castellanos and the long-serving Rick Porcello, home-grown talents all. Never mind the use of young players (such as Cameron Maybin, Andrew Miller and Drew Smyly) as trade bait to acquire talent (such as Miguel Cabrera and David Price) to help win a championship right now. There's a perception among some that winning with players you've brought in from the outside rather than run through your own employee training program is a kind of cheating. Of course, even St. Louis traded for Adam Wainwright and Matt Holliday and signed Jhonny Peralta as a free agent, but they're the Cardinals, and life isn't fair.

✦✦✦

Can the Tigers overcome these obstacles and finally be considered a dynasty? Certainly they can. The acquisitions of outfielders Anthony Gose and Yoenis Cespedes may finally bring an end to the Don Kelly Era. Kansas City's miracle playoff run last season, along with offseason improvements in Chicago and Cleveland and the potential arrival of some jaw-dropping talent in Minnesota, will make the AL Central crown a more impressive prize. Most importantly, Detroit's top-shelf talent will once again make them divisional favorites and thus potential champions, though for how much longer is an open question.

We've written in these pages several times about the moves Dave Dombrowski engineered starting in late 2009—primarily the trade of Curtis Granderson to bring in ace starter Max Scherzer and center fielder Austin Jackson—that set the Tigers up for a long run of dominance. Dombrowski restructured the team's payroll so that they could afford to pay for the prime years of Verlander, Cabrera and Victor Martinez by relying on the production they received from inexpensive players like Scherzer, Jackson, Porcello, Avila and Doug Fister. As each year has passed without a championship, however, Dombrowski has been twisting knobs ever more frantically to keep the entire edifice from tumbling down around him.

The exemplar of this is Scherzer, who in five years has gone from a bargain to a player on the verge of a $200 million contract. At press time he was unsigned, and while Dombrowski has been known to pull more than one rabbit out of his hat during an offseason, few expected him to return to Detroit. To prepare for his departure from the top of the rotation, the Tigers traded for Price, but the cost in big-league talent was high: Jackson, Smyly and prospect Willy Adames. The addition of Price gives Detroit an enviable Big Three with Anibal Sanchez and Justin Verlander, but the lefty will be a free agent at the end of the season.

The loss of Jackson caused Dombrowski to trade top prospect Devon Travis for Gose, an offense-challenged fly-catcher, to play center, and send Porcello, fresh off a breakout year, to Boston for Cespedes to shore up Detroit's always-potent lineup. That in turn left a void in the rotation, which engendered the trades of yet more prospects for Redlegs rotation refugee Alfredo Simon and unproven groundball stylist Shane Greene from the Yankees.

Few general managers can match Dombrowski's reputation as a savvy trader, so Tigers fans are right to expect that Gose's bat will improve and he'll make a solid platoon partner with Rajai Davis in center, that Cespedes will provide the lineup thump that Torii Hunter didn't last season and that Simon will build on his one productive season in a big-league rotation, and Greene on his one productive month, to successfully fill out the bottom of the rotation. There's also hope for improvement from young third baseman Castellanos, a full season of Jose Iglesias flashing the leather at shortstop, a bounceback from Verlander and fewer disasters from one of baseball's worst bullpens. If most of that happens, and it well might, the Tigers will again win the Central.

But next fall, Detroit will still have a hollowed-out farm system and be facing the possible loss of Price with a roster that is one year older, one year more expensive and one year closer to the day when Dombrowski runs out of patches and has to face a rebuild. When we were heaping praise on Detroit's salary structure several years ago, Verlander, Cabrera and Martinez were signed through their mid-thirties, when they would just be entering their decline phases. After signing Verlander and

Cabrera to monstrous extensions prior to the 2013 season, and Martinez to a new four-year deal after his tremendous comeback last year, the Tigers now owe them huge stacks of cash well past their peaks. Baseball's money spigot continues to gush, and it may be that those contracts will look quaint before they expire, but the Tigers are now in danger of spending their way into the same payroll morass Dombrowski had to dig himself out of back in 2009.

If that happens, he has shown in the past that he has the guts and intelligence to make the hard choices needed to right the organization's ship, but it won't be easy. Detroit has been blessed with a very good baseball team, if not a "great" one, for years. They'll take yet another stab at immortality this summer, but with their division improving around them and their roster aging underneath them, the wolves are at the door. ■

—Ken Funck is an author at Baseball Prospectus and has contributed to the Annual since 2010.

Player comments by Matt Sussman and Baseball Prospectus Authors

Hitters

Xavier Avery   LF

Born: 1/1/90   Age: 25   Bats: L   Throws: L   Height: 6' 0"   Weight: 190

YEAR	TEAM	LVL	AGE	PA	R	2B	3B	HR	RBI	BB	K	SB	CS	AVG/OBP/SLG	TAv	BABIP	BRR	FRAA	WARP
2012	NOR	AAA	22	458	57	13	5	8	34	51	106	22	7	.236/.330/.356	.245	.301	3.5	CF(78): -10.3, LF(23): 0.1	-0.2
2012	BAL	MLB	22	107	14	6	1	1	6	11	23	6	3	.223/.305/.340	.232	.286	0.6	LF(27): 0.5, CF(1): -0.0	0.0
2013	BOW	AA	23	186	34	10	2	1	12	23	44	12	3	.300/.391/.406	.302	.409	2.3	CF(30): -0.4, LF(7): 0.2	1.6
2013	NOR	AAA	23	333	36	12	2	2	23	31	73	17	5	.237/.312/.312	.230	.306	0.1	LF(42): -2.5, CF(37): -1.7	-0.7
2014	TAC	AAA	24	447	70	21	2	10	38	42	91	31	8	.275/.344/.413	.274	.332	2.5	LF(70): 1.8, CF(31): -1.5	2.0
2015	DET	MLB	25	250	31	10	2	3	19	21	59	13	4	.241/.308/.348	.241	.303	1.3	LF -0, CF -2	0.0

Breakout: 8%   Improve: 16%   Collapse: 4%   Attrition: 14%   MLB: 25%   Comparables: *Bryan Petersen, Trevor Crowe, Chris Pettit*

Avery is a collection of archetypes, often with hyphens: the toolsy-but-rough second-round draft choice, the lean, long-legged fourth-outfield-er-in-waiting, the prospect-named-Xavier who disappoints you. He was also a symbol of wasted development, so after a failed cup of coffee and a lost 2013 in the minors, the Orioles shipped him to Seattle for the privilege of suiting up Mike Morse. For all his failures, Avery quietly improved his hitting in his age-23 season from egregious to unpleasant, and only the presence of Tool Twin James Jones prevented a late-season call-up. Avery should be ready to start for the Tigers at a moment's notice: Disgust with Anthony Gose's bat has been known to set in suddenly. He may have a shot at a bench job out of spring training, depending on how much more of Rajai Davis the team can take in center.

Alex Avila   C

Born: 1/29/87   Age: 28   Bats: L   Throws: R   Height: 5' 11"   Weight: 210

YEAR	TEAM	LVL	AGE	PA	R	2B	3B	HR	RBI	BB	K	SB	CS	AVG/OBP/SLG	TAv	BABIP	BRR	FRAA	WARP
2012	DET	MLB	25	434	42	21	2	9	48	61	104	2	0	.243/.352/.384	.257	.313	-1.0	C(113): -2.8	1.8
2013	TOL	AAA	26	51	5	3	0	1	5	7	12	0	0	.250/.353/.386	.260	.323	0.4	C(6): 0.1	0.1
2013	DET	MLB	26	379	39	14	1	11	47	44	112	0	0	.227/.317/.376	.253	.305	-2.8	C(98): -0.1	0.9
2014	DET	MLB	27	457	44	22	0	11	47	61	151	0	3	.218/.327/.359	.251	.322	-5.5	C(122): -1.3, 1B(1): -0.0	0.9
2015	DET	MLB	28	420	47	19	2	10	45	53	113	1	1	.241/.339/.387	.268	.316	-2.5	C -1	1.6

Breakout: 4%   Improve: 46%   Collapse: 0%   Attrition: 5%   MLB: 99%   Comparables: *Joe Ferguson, Tom Haller, Wes Westrum*

The ball has always found Avila well. Unfortunately it's usually a 90 mph pitch tipped by a bat finding his body. The veteran catcher suffered three concussions last year, including one in the final game of the season, leading many to wonder how much he can contribute to a team and, more importantly, whether he should. Catchers have moved to first base to extend their careers before. However, Avila does not have first base hitting skills; he has defense-first-catcher hitting skills: okay power, terrible contact and a nice walk rate. He's played corner infield sparingly but poorly. Still, better to roll the dice on a new position than a central nervous system.

Miguel Cabrera   1B

Born: 4/18/83   Age: 32   Bats: R   Throws: R   Height: 6' 4"   Weight: 240

YEAR	TEAM	LVL	AGE	PA	R	2B	3B	HR	RBI	BB	K	SB	CS	AVG/OBP/SLG	TAv	BABIP	BRR	FRAA	WARP
2012	DET	MLB	29	697	109	40	0	44	139	66	98	4	1	.330/.393/.606	.326	.331	-5.6	3B(154): -2.4, 1B(2): -0.0	6.3
2013	DET	MLB	30	652	103	26	1	44	137	90	94	3	0	.348/.442/.636	.372	.356	-3.0	3B(145): -11.8	7.9
2014	DET	MLB	31	685	101	52	1	25	109	60	117	1	1	.313/.371/.524	.309	.346	3.0	1B(126): 5.4, 3B(10): -0.2	5.5
2015	DET	MLB	32	637	92	37	2	31	103	75	99	2	1	.318/.399/.557	.340	.338	-1.6	3B -4, 1B -2	5.5

Breakout: 0%   Improve: 27%   Collapse: 2%   Attrition: 5%   MLB: 98%   Comparables: *David Ortiz, Albert Pujols, Lance Berkman*

Hobbled over the past two years by injuries that would put a lesser man in the infirmary, Cabrera began the season fresh, and was playing like typical Miguel Cabrera by May; as the regular season congealed to a conclusion, his overall offense was terrific even as his slugging reached a 10-year low. Bone spurs in his ankle limited Cabrera's general movement in the second half, but he pushed forward to hit eight home runs in September, earning Player of the Month honors. Maybe bone spurs are a good thing? Who knows; we're writers, not doctors, and the bone spurs were surgically removed this offseason. An undiagnosed stress fracture was also corrected while they were rooting around in there, so maybe the Tigers' doctors are writers, too.

Assuming no setbacks during the printing and speedy delivery of this book, Cabrera should be ready for camp as his fearsome, wholesome, happy-go-lucky self, but a slow start might be expected given how little he was able to dedicate to conditioning this winter. Now 32, Cabrera is creeping into the bad-body-old-slugger archetype and the next couple of seasons will determine whether he's a Hank Aaron diamond mine, a Ryan Howard iron pyrite statue or a Dick Allen vintage muscle car. Now for the good news: His move to first base was a welcome sight and FRAA commended him for the first time ever. Little known fact: The FRAA formula adjusts for number of bone spurs.

Nick Castellanos 3B

Born: 3/4/92   Age: 23   Bats: R   Throws: R   Height: 6' 4"   Weight: 210

YEAR	TEAM	LVL	AGE	PA	R	2B	3B	HR	RBI	BB	K	SB	CS	AVG/OBP/SLG	TAv	BABIP	BRR	FRAA	WARP
2012	LAK	A+	20	243	37	17	3	3	32	22	42	3	2	.405/.461/.553	.339	.486	0.6	3B(51): -0.9	2.7
2012	ERI	AA	20	341	35	15	1	7	25	14	76	5	4	.264/.296/.382	.226	.322	-3.8	RF(51): -2.9, 3B(27): -0.8	-1.4
2013	TOL	AAA	21	595	81	37	1	18	76	54	100	4	1	.276/.343/.450	.282	.307	-0.6	LF(130): 2.6	3.1
2013	DET	MLB	21	18	1	0	0	0	0	0	1	0	0	.278/.278/.278	.206	.294	-0.1	LF(9): -0.3	-0.1
2014	DET	MLB	22	579	50	31	4	11	66	36	140	2	2	.259/.306/.394	.254	.326	-3.0	3B(145): -6.3	1.0
2015	DET	MLB	23	503	49	25	2	11	56	29	111	2	1	.264/.307/.401	.259	.320	-1.6	3B -5, LF 0	0.4

Breakout: 3%   Improve: 39%   Collapse: 5%   Attrition: 19%   MLB: 68%   Comparables: Brett Lawrie, Edwin Encarnacion, Blake DeWitt

Tossed about like a Little League home run ball, the former-third-baseman-cum-left-fielder was moved back to third upon Miguel Cabrera's evacuation for first base. The rookie struggled and slumped but adjusted better than some mature batters, displaying a good inside-out swing and a slight bit of power that could ultimately mature into homers in the mid-20s in his mid-20s. His third base defense leaves much room for improvement, particularly to his lateral range, but he ought to stay there for now. If he realizes his offensive potential he could get away with first base.

Yoenis Cespedes LF

Born: 10/18/85   Age: 29   Bats: R   Throws: R   Height: 5' 10"   Weight: 210

YEAR	TEAM	LVL	AGE	PA	R	2B	3B	HR	RBI	BB	K	SB	CS	AVG/OBP/SLG	TAv	BABIP	BRR	FRAA	WARP
2012	OAK	MLB	26	540	70	25	5	23	82	43	102	16	4	.292/.356/.505	.320	.326	0.0	LF(56): -1.4, CF(48): -0.8	4.7
2013	OAK	MLB	27	574	74	21	4	26	80	37	137	7	7	.240/.294/.442	.279	.274	-0.1	LF(94): -0.1, CF(18): -0.7	2.2
2014	BOS	MLB	28	213	27	10	3	5	33	7	48	4	0	.269/.296/.423	.269	.325	-0.1	LF(43): -0.9	1.1
2014	OAK	MLB	28	432	62	26	3	17	67	28	80	3	2	.256/.303/.464	.287	.278	1.7	LF(82): 0.4, CF(9): 0.0	2.7
2015	DET	MLB	29	593	72	27	6	23	81	38	123	10	4	.270/.320/.467	.287	.306	0.3	LF -1, CF -1	2.8

Breakout: 2%   Improve: 45%   Collapse: 1%   Attrition: 4%   MLB: 95%   Comparables: Matt Holliday, Kevin Mitchell, Rocky Colavito

Cespedes has launched more narratives than Helen of Troy, what with cursing the A's offense and supposedly earning of the enmity of the Red Sox coaching staff. Yet if we focus on what Cespedes actually brings to the table, a mundane truth emerges: He's more of a strong complementary piece than a franchise cornerstone worthy of all this attention. The 29-year-old sacrificed some power for more contact in 2014, lowering his strikeout rate and slightly improving his OBP. However, his walk rate has dipped twice since his rookie year, and he's not the threat on the bases many once hoped he'd be. Cespedes might put up flashier counting stats at Comerica, a better hitter's park than the A's have, but his approach remains something of an Achilles' heel.

Tyler Collins RF

Born: 6/6/90   Age: 25   Bats: L   Throws: L   Height: 5' 11"   Weight: 215

YEAR	TEAM	LVL	AGE	PA	R	2B	3B	HR	RBI	BB	K	SB	CS	AVG/OBP/SLG	TAv	BABIP	BRR	FRAA	WARP
2012	LAK	A+	22	542	68	35	5	7	66	58	64	20	3	.290/.371/.429	.272	.319	0.8	LF(82): 1.0, RF(34): 1.2	2.2
2013	ERI	AA	23	530	67	29	0	21	79	51	122	4	5	.240/.323/.438	.282	.277	0.9	LF(88): 1.3, RF(18): 1.0	2.0
2014	TOL	AAA	24	526	63	17	2	18	62	49	116	12	4	.263/.335/.423	.261	.310	-1.8	LF(92): -2.4, RF(22): -0.4	1.1
2014	DET	MLB	24	25	3	0	0	1	4	1	4	0	0	.250/.280/.375	.231	.263	-0.4	LF(5): 0.5, RF(5): -0.1	-0.1
2015	DET	MLB	25	250	27	10	1	7	29	18	57	3	1	.239/.297/.391	.253	.284	-0.1	LF 0, RF 0	0.4

Breakout: 8%   Improve: 19%   Collapse: 14%   Attrition: 32%   MLB: 43%   Comparables: Todd Frazier, Paul McAnulty, Chris Pettit

Conventional wisdom is that younger players should be able to play every day, and their level assignment should be one that lets them do that. Collins, a surprise Opening Day roster selection, languished on the Tigers' bench before he was sent to a full Triple-A season in which he essentially replicated his Double-A numbers. A bit more polish wouldn't hurt him, but he's likely playing his way into a role as some team's Ross Gload. Nobody grows up with intent to be Ross Gload, except perhaps Ross Gload's kids, and even they're probably aiming for Andrew McCutchen. Collins flashed an ability last September to pinch-hit, play some outfield and watch a ton of games from the dugout.

Rajai Davis LF

Born: 10/19/80   Age: 34   Bats: R   Throws: R   Height: 5' 9"   Weight: 195

YEAR	TEAM	LVL	AGE	PA	R	2B	3B	HR	RBI	BB	K	SB	CS	AVG/OBP/SLG	TAv	BABIP	BRR	FRAA	WARP
2012	TOR	MLB	31	487	64	24	3	8	43	29	102	46	13	.257/.309/.378	.240	.314	0.1	LF(114): 0.6, RF(24): 0.9	0.3
2013	TOR	MLB	32	360	49	16	2	6	24	21	67	45	6	.260/.312/.375	.251	.308	6.7	LF(57): 2.9, RF(35): -0.5	1.5
2014	DET	MLB	33	494	64	27	2	8	51	22	75	36	11	.282/.320/.401	.263	.320	4.8	LF(99): 0.6, CF(48): 1.8	1.9
2015	DET	MLB	34	439	59	21	3	4	29	21	78	40	10	.261/.301/.357	.244	.310	2.4	LF 1, CF -0	0.6

Breakout: 0%   Improve: 30%   Collapse: 14%   Attrition: 12%   MLB: 94%   Comparables: Reed Johnson, Cesar Cedeno, Jay Payton

As a fast person for hire, Davis was exactly what the 2014 Tigers needed: ludicrous speed out of a league-average hitter. In April he stole eight bases, tying the 2013 Tigers' team leader. For the season he had more steals than the entire 2013 team, and the most by an individual Tiger in nine years. Speed is what keeps him in the everyday lineup, even if he is batting ninth against righties. Poor reads, poor breaks and a hero complex that causes him to dive for balls out of reach are what keep him mostly in left field. But what a pleasant platoon fourth outfielder and pinch-runner he makes for slow teams.

Anthony Gose   CF

Born: 8/10/90   Age: 24   Bats: L   Throws: L   Height: 6' 1"   Weight: 190

YEAR	TEAM	LVL	AGE	PA	R	2B	3B	HR	RBI	BB	K	SB	CS	AVG/OBP/SLG	TAv	BABIP	BRR	FRAA	WARP
2012	LVG	AAA	21	482	87	21	10	5	43	49	101	34	12	.286/.366/.419	.273	.365	7.4	CF(98): -6.9, LF(3): -0.4	2.3
2012	TOR	MLB	21	189	25	7	3	1	11	17	59	15	3	.223/.303/.319	.225	.340	1.8	RF(24): -0.3, CF(22): 1.5	0.1
2013	BUF	AAA	22	448	64	17	6	3	27	38	121	22	13	.239/.316/.336	.233	.336	4.0	CF(85): -6.9, RF(14): 1.1	-0.3
2013	TOR	MLB	22	153	15	6	5	2	12	5	37	4	3	.259/.283/.408	.233	.333	0.0	CF(34): -2.3, LF(15): -0.3	-0.2
2014	BUF	AAA	23	224	29	5	2	4	25	17	65	21	8	.244/.305/.348	.223	.338	1.4	CF(31): 2.6, RF(18): -1.6	-0.1
2014	TOR	MLB	23	274	31	8	1	2	13	25	74	15	5	.226/.311/.293	.225	.317	4.3	CF(65): 0.5, RF(14): 0.7	0.4
2015	*DET*	*MLB*	*24*	*320*	*39*	*11*	*4*	*3*	*21*	*23*	*87*	*18*	*7*	*.236/.299/.331*	*.234*	*.321*	*1.4*	*CF -1, RF -0*	*0.0*

Breakout: 10%   Improve: 30%   Collapse: 3%   Attrition: 11%   MLB: 46%   Comparables: *Austin Jackson, Dexter Fowler, Jordan Schafer*

In his third season, Gose finally played more games with Toronto than Buffalo. He still flew south on five separate occasions—once each month until September—but didn't hit better in Triple-A than the majors. His walk rate climbed back to his career minor-league rate, but the frequent swing-and-miss caused trouble, especially because Gose didn't slug for extra bases even when he did make contact. His very low fly-ball rate is probably good given his high-speed, low-power profile; his very low line-drive rate is just bad. That speed (and his arm) aids him as a rangy center fielder, but defense is beginning to look like his only playable major-league skill.

Derek Hill   CF

Born: 12/30/95   Age: 19   Bats: R   Throws: R   Height: 6' 2"   Weight: 195

YEAR	TEAM	LVL	AGE	PA	R	2B	3B	HR	RBI	BB	K	SB	CS	AVG/OBP/SLG	TAv	BABIP	BRR	FRAA	WARP
2014	ONE	A-	18	78	8	1	1	0	3	2	26	2	1	.203/.244/.243	.178	.313	0.0	—	0.0

Detroit fell into good fortune with the opportunity to draft a pure center fielder with the 23rd overall pick. The Austin Jackson comparisons began almost immediately, and with Jackson being traded at the deadline, the picture of Hill roving Comerica Park's spacious outfield became clearer, though that image will take more than a few years to develop. In the meantime, expect grainy YouTube clips of terrific catches in various minor-league ballparks. The hitting numbers will also come later: Hill was visibly overmatched in his first pro season. In the end, a five-tool player is possible, but three-and-a-half will turn you into a millionaire too.

Jose Iglesias   SS

Born: 1/5/90   Age: 25   Bats: R   Throws: R   Height: 5' 11"   Weight: 185

YEAR	TEAM	LVL	AGE	PA	R	2B	3B	HR	RBI	BB	K	SB	CS	AVG/OBP/SLG	TAv	BABIP	BRR	FRAA	WARP
2012	PAW	AAA	22	396	46	9	1	1	23	27	46	12	3	.266/.318/.306	.232	.299	0.3	SS(88): 11.4	1.6
2012	BOS	MLB	22	77	5	2	0	1	2	4	16	1	0	.118/.200/.191	.151	.137	0.9	SS(24): 0.8	-0.3
2013	PAW	AAA	23	133	17	2	0	4	15	9	18	5	3	.202/.262/.319	.203	.204	1.2	SS(32): 2.5, 3B(1): -0.1	0.0
2013	BOS	MLB	23	234	27	10	2	1	19	11	30	3	1	.330/.376/.409	.285	.376	0.1	3B(34): -0.9, SS(29): -0.1	1.5
2013	DET	MLB	23	148	12	6	0	2	10	4	30	2	1	.259/.306/.348	.236	.320	-0.4	SS(42): 1.0, 3B(3): 0.2	0.5
2015	*DET*	*MLB*	*25*	*250*	*24*	*9*	*1*	*2*	*20*	*12*	*38*	*5*	*1*	*.257/.300/.331*	*.237*	*.291*	*0.1*	*SS 3, 3B -0*	*0.6*

Breakout: 4%   Improve: 46%   Collapse: 6%   Attrition: 32%   MLB: 69%   Comparables: *Dee Gordon, Marwin Gonzalez, Alcides Escobar*

Shins were always in issue for Iglesias, and the Tigers knew this when they acquired him in 2013. But the pain wouldn't go away last March, and further medical tests revealed longstanding fractures, forcing the team to shut him down. He's a highlight factory of a shortstop under team control through 2018, so using one year of rest to get value out of the next four was a necessary trade-off. Should Iglesias' bionic shins hold up (and all reports point to "yes"), his Vizquelian glove should keep him in the everyday lineup batting eighth.

Don Kelly   3B

Born: 2/15/80   Age: 35   Bats: L   Throws: R   Height: 6' 4"   Weight: 190

YEAR	TEAM	LVL	AGE	PA	R	2B	3B	HR	RBI	BB	K	SB	CS	AVG/OBP/SLG	TAv	BABIP	BRR	FRAA	WARP
2012	TOL	AAA	32	85	8	2	0	1	12	12	17	4	1	.233/.341/.301	.239	.291	-0.9	3B(14): 0.6, LF(4): 0.6	0.2
2012	DET	MLB	32	127	14	2	1	1	7	14	22	2	0	.186/.276/.248	.199	.222	1.7	RF(35): 0.2, LF(18): -0.5	-0.4
2013	DET	MLB	33	251	33	6	1	6	23	27	28	2	0	.222/.309/.343	.252	.226	0.9	LF(38): -1.5, CF(25): -1.5	0.2
2014	DET	MLB	34	185	24	5	1	0	7	20	29	6	1	.245/.332/.288	.225	.299	-0.9	3B(41): 0.3, 1B(30): 0.0	-0.3
2015	*DET*	*MLB*	*35*	*250*	*24*	*7*	*2*	*4*	*23*	*20*	*39*	*4*	*1*	*.233/.297/.332*	*.237*	*.261*	*0.4*	*3B 1, RF -0*	*0.1*

Breakout: 1%   Improve: 31%   Collapse: 3%   Attrition: 22%   MLB: 82%   Comparables: *Buddy Bell, Carney Lansford, Denny Walling*

Jim Leyland's good-luck charm played his first season under a new manager since 2008. He started fewer games but was used mostly how Leyland used him, which is all over the darn field. He's the 15th player in MLB history to start at least 50 games at first base, third base and each outfield position in his career. If he's on your roster, the starting Triple-A lineup secretly detests him since he is basically six Quad-A players squished into one scrawny frame, none of whom can really swing the bat. Kelly did show more patience at the plate, earning a career high in OBP, but that's about it. If John McDonald can play in the league at 40, Kelly can at 35.

Ian Kinsler   2B

Born: 6/22/82   Age: 33   Bats: R   Throws: R   Height: 6' 0"   Weight: 200

YEAR	TEAM	LVL	AGE	PA	R	2B	3B	HR	RBI	BB	K	SB	CS	AVG/OBP/SLG	TAv	BABIP	BRR	FRAA	WARP
2012	TEX	MLB	30	731	105	42	5	19	72	60	90	21	9	.256/.326/.423	.260	.270	7.0	2B(144): -3.8, 3B(1): -0.0	2.0
2013	TEX	MLB	31	614	85	31	2	13	72	51	59	15	11	.277/.344/.413	.291	.288	3.5	2B(124): 13.3	5.4
2014	DET	MLB	32	726	100	40	4	17	92	29	79	15	4	.275/.307/.420	.257	.288	3.0	2B(160): 5.3	2.5
2015	*DET*	*MLB*	*33*	*661*	*84*	*33*	*4*	*14*	*63*	*55*	*79*	*18*	*7*	*.262/.329/.403*	*.272*	*.278*	*3.9*	*2B 6*	*4.1*

Breakout: 2%   Improve: 27%   Collapse: 6%   Attrition: 10%   MLB: 93%   Comparables: *Placido Polanco, Brian Roberts, Skip Schumaker*

The longtime Ranger couldn't, realistically, have asked for a better first year away from Texas. He was an All-Star selection, a Wilson Defensive Player of the Year, had no threat of losing his position to a young stud and made a new best friend in noted BABIP victim Rick Porcello. Highlight plays from a middle infielder had been as rare in Detroit as a budget surplus, and being the guy received straight up for the disappointing Prince Fielder only endeared him to fans more. Now for the bad news: His freewheeling approach at the plate resulted in a career-low OBP and TAv, he'll make eight figures in each of the next three years and he has a hefty buyout in 2018. Second basemen in their early 30s can fall off the cliff at a moment's notice. Kinsler is durable, gritty and covers ground, but the same can be said of a good leafblower.

Victor Martinez   DH

Born: 12/23/78   Age: 36   Bats: B   Throws: R   Height: 6' 2"   Weight: 210

YEAR	TEAM	LVL	AGE	PA	R	2B	3B	HR	RBI	BB	K	SB	CS	AVG/OBP/SLG	TAv	BABIP	BRR	FRAA	WARP
2013	DET	MLB	34	668	68	36	0	14	83	54	62	0	2	.301/.355/.430	.280	.313	-6.2	1B(11): 0.8, C(3): 0.1	1.6
2014	DET	MLB	35	641	87	33	0	32	103	70	42	3	2	.335/.409/.565	.335	.316	-5.9	1B(35): -3.5, C(2): -0.0	4.8
2015	DET	MLB	36	608	68	32	2	15	75	49	59	2	1	.302/.358/.450	.295	.312	-4.3	1B 0, C -0	2.6

Breakout: 0%   Improve: 24%   Collapse: 3%   Attrition: 6%   MLB: 85%   Comparables: Hideki Matsui, Todd Helton, Aubrey Huff

After missing all of 2012 with a torn ACL and struggling a bit to start 2013, Martinez hit his stride later that season and in 2014 carried on that success. As great as Martinez is, he's not who you'd show your Little League team as far as approach: He swings a *lot*; it works for him because he also hits a *lot*. He took just eight called third strikes on the year, hit a career high in home runs and garnered the most intentional walks ever by a switch-hitter. All at age 35. That ACL injury has continued to limit his speed and mobility, as well as his capacity to play any defense short of first base maybe once a week, and the power is due for hard regression, but he should still crank out a few more .300 years and drive strikeout pitchers to the loony bin.

J.D. Martinez   LF

Born: 8/21/87   Age: 27   Bats: R   Throws: R   Height: 6' 3"   Weight: 220

YEAR	TEAM	LVL	AGE	PA	R	2B	3B	HR	RBI	BB	K	SB	CS	AVG/OBP/SLG	TAv	BABIP	BRR	FRAA	WARP
2012	OKL	AAA	24	95	6	6	0	0	4	4	17	0	1	.233/.263/.300	.191	.284	-1.7	LF(19): -2.7	-0.8
2012	HOU	MLB	24	439	34	14	3	11	55	40	96	0	2	.241/.311/.375	.238	.290	-4.0	LF(100): -10.4	-1.7
2013	CCH	AA	25	20	1	2	0	1	5	0	1	0	0	.300/.300/.550	.287	.278	0.0	LF(2): -0.3, RF(2): -0.3	0.0
2013	HOU	MLB	25	310	24	17	0	7	36	10	82	2	0	.250/.272/.378	.244	.319	-2.3	LF(50): -5.5, RF(25): -2.0	-1.1
2014	TOL	AAA	26	71	16	3	1	10	22	3	17	0	2	.308/.366/.846	.353	.263	-0.5	LF(12): -0.3	0.9
2014	DET	MLB	26	480	57	30	3	23	76	30	126	6	3	.315/.358/.553	.320	.389	0.6	LF(83): -0.4, RF(34): -1.8	4.0
2015	DET	MLB	27	430	48	22	2	14	55	27	97	3	2	.271/.319/.442	.278	.323	-1.5	LF -5, RF -2	0.7

Breakout: 5%   Improve: 56%   Collapse: 5%   Attrition: 8%   MLB: 95%   Comparables: Brennan Boesch, Mark Trumbo, Carlos Gonzalez

Last year, we wrote that "mediocrity ... will be what sends Martinez to pasture for good." Sure, Detroit's population is dwindling but "pastoral" is not entirely descriptive. His perceived mediocrity led him there, though, as he was released by the Astros during spring training. Thereafter, he became anything but mediocre. A piping hot April in Triple-A forced him into Detroit's patchwork outfield and he eventually secured the left field job for the season. Martinez took the initiative to retool his swing and became a feared no. 5 hitter, leading the AL in late-inning home runs: closers love fastballs and so does he. He'll deserve to start in a corner, but expecting another batting line straight from the George Brett archives would be a bit much.

James McCann   C

Born: 6/13/90   Age: 25   Bats: R   Throws: R   Height: 6' 2"   Weight: 210

YEAR	TEAM	LVL	AGE	PA	R	2B	3B	HR	RBI	BB	K	SB	CS	AVG/OBP/SLG	TAv	BABIP	BRR	FRAA	WARP
2012	LAK	A+	22	177	24	10	0	0	20	10	29	3	0	.288/.345/.350	.259	.346	-0.3	C(45): 0.1	1.0
2012	ERI	AA	22	230	15	12	0	2	19	8	44	2	2	.200/.227/.282	.177	.240	-2.2	C(64): -0.3	-1.3
2013	ERI	AA	23	486	50	30	1	8	54	30	85	3	3	.277/.328/.404	.266	.321	-0.5	C(100): -0.3	2.0
2014	TOL	AAA	24	460	49	34	0	7	54	25	90	9	2	.295/.343/.427	.265	.355	0.7	C(98): -1.0, 3B(1): 0.0	2.3
2014	DET	MLB	24	12	2	1	0	0	0	0	2	1	0	.250/.250/.333	.211	.300	0.1	C(6): -0.0	0.0
2015	DET	MLB	25	250	21	13	1	3	24	9	54	2	1	.246/.278/.350	.231	.300	-0.2	C -0, 3B 0	0.1

Breakout: 4%   Improve: 6%   Collapse: 14%   Attrition: 19%   MLB: 25%   Comparables: Caleb Joseph, Miguel Perez, Josh Phegley

Throughout McCann's minor-league career, the profile has been echoed ad nauseum: backup catcher, backup catcher, backup catcher. Then again, if you're not Mike Zunino or Buster Posey, all catchers coming up the system look like backups until disproved. In McCann's first taste of Triple-A, the former Arkansas Razorback posted career highs in average, OBP and slugging thanks to a bevy of doubles, finally earning that elusive September call-up. Since he matches up against righties just fine and lefties extremely fine, he's ready right now to be a backup, especially having thrown out at least 40 percent of baserunners three years in a row. The potential to be a regular is real, but he needs to develop a bit more power to reach it.

Steven Moya   RF

Born: 8/9/91   Age: 23   Bats: L   Throws: R   Height: 6' 6"   Weight: 230

YEAR	TEAM	LVL	AGE	PA	R	2B	3B	HR	RBI	BB	K	SB	CS	AVG/OBP/SLG	TAv	BABIP	BRR	FRAA	WARP
2012	WMI	A	20	258	28	14	3	9	47	11	59	5	3	.288/.319/.481	.296	.345	-2.5	RF(57): -1.0	1.0
2013	LAK	A+	21	388	52	19	5	12	55	18	106	6	0	.255/.296/.433	.254	.327	1.3	RF(78): -4.0	-0.1
2014	ERI	AA	22	549	81	33	3	35	105	23	161	16	4	.276/.306/.555	.298	.327	1.4	RF(131): 2.8	3.5
2014	DET	MLB	22	8	2	0	0	0	0	0	2	0	0	.375/.375/.375	.289	.500	0.0	RF(5): -0.0	0.0
2015	DET	MLB	23	250	28	11	1	11	33	7	81	4	1	.235/.257/.424	.246	.303	0.4	RF -0	0.1

Breakout: 1%   Improve: 15%   Collapse: 1%   Attrition: 7%   MLB: 24%   Comparables: Bryce Brentz, Carlos Peguero, Matt LaPorta

Most scouts agree that Moya is a tall drink who packs a punch, which means he's basically a large Mountain Dew. That's where the agreement ceases. The Eastern League MVP had a downright Darin Rufian season, but without the downsides: Moya trumps the comparison in age, athleticism and defensive value. Still, his 7:1 strikeout-to-walk ratio in the Eastern League has been reached by only three major leaguers, and Moya isn't Adam Jones, nor is he a catcher like Miguel Olivo and Benito Santiago. Whether Moya has a career is going to come down to whether he improves his plate approach. If the issue is pitch identification, he'll face an uphill climb. If the problem is lack of focus, just cut back on the Mountain Dew.

Andrew Romine   SS

Born: 12/24/85   Age: 29   Bats: B   Throws: R   Height: 6' 1"   Weight: 200

YEAR	TEAM	LVL	AGE	PA	R	2B	3B	HR	RBI	BB	K	SB	CS	AVG/OBP/SLG	TAv	BABIP	BRR	FRAA	WARP
2012	SLC	AAA	26	388	57	11	7	4	39	24	46	23	10	.285/.336/.390	.263	.317	4.8	SS(64): -0.5, 3B(13): 0.0	2.5
2012	ANA	MLB	26	21	2	0	0	0	1	3	3	1	0	.412/.500/.412	.356	.500	0.2	SS(8): 0.3, 3B(1): -0.0	0.3
2013	SLC	AAA	27	416	61	16	5	4	39	43	68	15	6	.287/.367/.391	.259	.341	1.8	SS(59): 1.7, 2B(20): -1.1	2.0
2013	ANA	MLB	27	123	9	3	0	0	10	7	24	1	0	.259/.308/.287	.226	.329	2.2	3B(24): -0.3, SS(17): -0.3	0.1
2014	DET	MLB	28	273	30	6	0	2	12	18	60	12	2	.227/.279/.275	.214	.291	3.3	SS(83): 0.5, 2B(12): -0.3	0.1
2015	DET	MLB	29	276	30	8	2	1	17	20	55	10	3	.241/.300/.304	.230	.295	1.9	SS 2, 3B 0	0.6

Breakout: 2%   Improve: 11%   Collapse: 6%   Attrition: 16%   MLB: 27%   *Comparables: Ivan Ochoa, Ramon Santiago, Mike Rouse*

You can't predict baseball, except when you can. Romine was billed as an all-glove, no-bat shortstop, and that's exactly what the Tigers got. In a world where the Royals can be one inning away from winning the World Series, it's refreshing to observe a player like Romine, make an educated conclusion about what he'll do and be right every single time.

Pitchers

Al Alburquerque   RHP

Born: 6/10/86   Age: 29   Bats: R   Throws: R   Height: 6'0"   Weight: 195

YEAR	TEAM	LVL	AGE	W	L	SV	G	GS	IP	H	HR	BB	K	BB/9	K/9	GB%	BABIP	WHIP	ERA	FIP	FRA	WARP
2012	TOL	AAA	26	1	0	0	9	0	10²	9	1	4	18	3.4	15.2	44%	.364	1.22	1.69	2.41	3.02	0.3
2012	DET	MLB	26	0	0	0	8	0	13¹	6	0	8	18	5.4	12.1	67%	.222	1.05	0.68	2.15	2.54	0.4
2013	TOL	AAA	27	0	1	1	10	0	14¹	9	2	13	27	8.2	17.0	17%	.318	1.53	3.14	3.97	4.44	0.1
2013	DET	MLB	27	4	3	0	53	0	49	39	5	34	70	6.2	12.9	40%	.312	1.49	4.59	3.75	4.18	0.4
2014	DET	MLB	28	3	1	1	72	0	57¹	46	7	21	63	3.3	9.9	46%	.275	1.17	2.51	3.81	4.31	0.4
2015	DET	MLB	29	3	1	0	51	0	49²	39	4	26	65	4.8	11.8	45%	.303	1.31	3.31	3.64	3.60	0.9

Breakout: 30%   Improve: 50%   Collapse: 23%   Attrition: 13%   MLB: 87%   *Comparables: Sergio Santos, Will Ohman, Jose Valverde*

White Castle's menu has other options besides sliders, although they're not very good. The same can be said of Alburquerque's pitch selection. He has a fastball, but he doesn't throw it for strikes. So how on earth did his walk rate go down? In three-ball counts, rather than stick to conventional logic and try to throw a fastball over the plate, he just stuck with the slider, which kind of worked.

Joba Chamberlain   RHP

Born: 9/23/85   Age: 29   Bats: R   Throws: R   Height: 6'2"   Weight: 250

YEAR	TEAM	LVL	AGE	W	L	SV	G	GS	IP	H	HR	BB	K	BB/9	K/9	GB%	BABIP	WHIP	ERA	FIP	FRA	WARP
2012	NYA	MLB	26	1	0	0	22	0	20²	26	3	6	22	2.6	9.6	46%	.371	1.55	4.35	3.97	3.80	0.4
2013	NYA	MLB	27	2	1	1	45	0	42	47	8	26	38	5.6	8.1	43%	.315	1.74	4.93	5.67	5.97	-0.5
2014	DET	MLB	28	2	5	2	69	0	63	57	3	24	59	3.4	8.4	55%	.310	1.29	3.57	3.19	4.17	0.5
2015	DET	MLB	29	3	1	1	54	0	51	50	5	18	49	3.2	8.6	48%	.314	1.34	3.91	4.08	4.25	0.5

Breakout: 31%   Improve: 49%   Collapse: 26%   Attrition: 18%   MLB: 85%   *Comparables: Jose Mijares, Jesse Crain, Scott Linebrink*

He survived bugs, unmet expectations, a trampoline accident and Tommy John surgery in New York, but never did nail down that second respectable season until he went to Detroit. The Tigers took a flier on him because their bullpen was basically a stack of fliers. Chamberlain was blindly thrust into the eighth-inning role and for a large part of the year was Detroit's only dependable bullpen arm. His command started wavering as the season progressed, and when the dust settled on his body of work, he had a postseason ERA of 1.08 and a beard down to his stomach. The offseason gave him the chance to trim just one of the two.

Phil Coke   LHP

Born: 7/19/82   Age: 32   Bats: L   Throws: L   Height: 6'1"   Weight: 210

YEAR	TEAM	LVL	AGE	W	L	SV	G	GS	IP	H	HR	BB	K	BB/9	K/9	GB%	BABIP	WHIP	ERA	FIP	FRA	WARP
2012	DET	MLB	29	2	3	1	66	0	54	71	5	18	51	3.0	8.5	50%	.388	1.65	4.00	3.42	3.52	1.0
2013	DET	MLB	30	0	5	1	49	0	38¹	43	3	21	30	4.9	7.0	48%	.325	1.67	5.40	4.17	5.21	-0.1
2014	DET	MLB	31	5	2	1	62	0	58	69	5	20	41	3.1	6.4	56%	.340	1.53	3.88	4.00	5.23	-0.2
2015	DET	MLB	32	3	2	0	41	3	48¹	53	4	18	37	3.4	6.9	45%	.325	1.48	4.61	4.35	5.01	0.1

Breakout: 26%   Improve: 49%   Collapse: 26%   Attrition: 12%   MLB: 91%   *Comparables: Dennys Reyes, Jeremy Affeldt, John Grabow*

Velocity wonks adore the veteran Coke: He's one of the few lefty relievers with both experience and a 95 mph fastball, and they all can't be Aroldis Chapman. But control wonks will ask what good a speedy fastball is if you can't locate it. Strikeout fanatics will clamor that a 95 mph fastball should miss some bats, and Coke rarely does, but pitch-to-contact gurus will counter by saying Coke is evolving into a groundball pitcher. Imagine all these groups locked in a room arguing about Phil Coke, and try to figure out their end game. But they all agree his strength is against lefties, and his weaknesses include righties and endless committee-based debate.

Buck Farmer   RHP

Born: 2/20/91   Age: 24   Bats: L   Throws: R   Height: 6'4"   Weight: 225

YEAR	TEAM	LVL	AGE	W	L	SV	G	GS	IP	H	HR	BB	K	BB/9	K/9	GB%	BABIP	WHIP	ERA	FIP	FRA	WARP
2013	ONE	A-	22	0	3	0	12	11	32	32	1	7	33	2.0	9.3	44%	.333	1.22	3.09	2.10	3.08	0.8
2014	WMI	A	23	10	5	0	18	18	103²	91	6	24	116	2.1	10.1	48%	.314	1.11	2.60	2.78	3.62	1.4
2014	ERI	AA	23	1	0	0	2	2	12	10	1	4	11	3.0	8.2	50%	.273	1.17	3.00	3.60	3.59	0.3
2014	DET	MLB	23	0	1	0	4	2	9¹	12	2	5	11	4.8	10.6	32%	.385	1.82	11.57	5.84	6.14	-0.1
2015	DET	MLB	24	5	7	0	20	20	92	101	11	38	72	3.8	7.1	44%	.315	1.52	5.07	4.96	5.51	0.0

Breakout: 20%   Improve: 41%   Collapse: 8%   Attrition: 23%   MLB: 55%   Comparables: *Felix Doubront, Matt Magill, Travis Blackley*

Risking a severe case of minor-league bends, Farmer went from West Michigan to the majors in a three-week span. The 2013 fifth-rounder didn't necessarily torch the Midwest League, but the Tigers needed someone for a day. His spot start was appreciated, if not effective. He followed it by not escaping the first inning in his next Triple-A start, only to be yanked back into a Tigers doubleheader, which went about as you'd predict. He has a solid fastball and decent breaking pitches, but don't count on another major-league appearance this year.

Shane Greene   RHP

Born: 11/17/88   Age: 26   Bats: R   Throws: R   Height: 6'4"   Weight: 210

YEAR	TEAM	LVL	AGE	W	L	SV	G	GS	IP	H	HR	BB	K	BB/9	K/9	GB%	BABIP	WHIP	ERA	FIP	FRA	WARP
2012	TAM	A+	23	4	7	0	24	23	112	113	5	63	101	5.1	8.1	54%	.331	1.57	5.22	4.13	5.84	0.0
2013	TAM	A+	24	4	6	0	13	13	75	83	4	10	69	1.2	8.3	49%	.348	1.24	3.60	2.61	3.94	0.9
2013	TRN	AA	24	8	4	0	14	13	79¹	92	6	20	68	2.3	7.7	51%	.347	1.41	3.18	3.61	4.00	1.0
2014	SWB	AAA	25	5	0	0	15	13	66¹	79	3	26	57	3.5	7.7	52%	.360	1.58	4.61	3.40	4.45	0.8
2014	NYA	MLB	25	5	4	0	15	14	78²	81	8	29	81	3.3	9.3	51%	.330	1.40	3.78	3.76	4.02	1.0
2015	DET	MLB	26	6	9	0	23	23	121²	143	13	53	91	4.0	6.7	49%	.328	1.61	5.51	4.97	5.99	-0.8

Breakout: 19%   Improve: 35%   Collapse: 15%   Attrition: 33%   MLB: 60%   Comparables: *Brad Peacock, J.D. Durbin, Hayden Penn*

Perhaps one of the reasons people hate the Yankees is because of guys like Greene: 15th-round fringe relieving prospects with bad Triple-A stats forced into starting duty by injuries who don't even have the decency to implode entertainingly. It just isn't fair. Greene throws six different pitches, four of them unrecognizable; PITCHf/x catches on fire trying to describe him. His sinker has a higher average velocity than the four-seam. His deadliest pitch is either a curve that doesn't drop like a curve or a slider that breaks differently than the slider we already know he throws. It also might stop working tomorrow. As a pitcher, he's either a madman or a genius or both. The track record and the comps both cry reliever, and not even a very good reliever, but the Tigers may well stick him at the back of their rotation and pray.

Blaine Hardy   LHP

Born: 3/14/87   Age: 28   Bats: L   Throws: L   Height: 6'2"   Weight: 230

YEAR	TEAM	LVL	AGE	W	L	SV	G	GS	IP	H	HR	BB	K	BB/9	K/9	GB%	BABIP	WHIP	ERA	FIP	FRA	WARP
2012	NWA	AA	25	1	1	3	10	0	20²	17	3	9	13	3.9	5.7	45%	.237	1.26	2.61	5.51	6.20	-0.2
2012	OMA	AAA	25	3	2	1	30	0	54²	68	6	22	45	3.6	7.4	41%	.363	1.65	3.79	4.65	4.41	0.9
2013	ERI	AA	26	2	2	1	16	0	27²	16	1	12	26	3.9	8.5	34%	.217	1.01	1.63	3.21	3.28	0.6
2013	TOL	AAA	26	6	1	0	14	9	64	46	7	19	53	2.7	7.5	29%	.227	1.02	1.69	3.95	4.42	0.4
2014	TOL	AAA	27	3	2	0	20	6	47	35	2	13	53	2.5	10.1	50%	.284	1.02	2.68	2.55	3.84	0.8
2014	DET	MLB	27	2	1	0	38	0	39	34	1	20	31	4.6	7.2	54%	.289	1.38	2.54	3.52	3.50	0.6
2015	DET	MLB	28	3	2	0	37	3	70²	70	8	27	54	3.5	6.9	40%	.290	1.38	4.27	4.76	4.64	0.4

Breakout: 9%   Improve: 15%   Collapse: 7%   Attrition: 17%   MLB: 30%   Comparables: *Romulo Sanchez, John Ennis, Jon Huber*

By WARP, Hardy was the most valuable Tigers relief pitcher, and even after the end of this sentence you're not entirely sure who Hardy is. A 22nd-round pick by the Royals in 2008 out of Lewis-Clark State College (Keith Foulke, stand up!), Hardy narrowly missed making the Tigers' Opening Day roster but eventually forced his way into the bullpen as Detroit searched for anyone who would bring his own fire extinguisher. For a few months he was better in pressure situations than mop-up duty, although he was never assigned "his own inning." Come September the command of his out-pitch curve began to ebb and by October he was left off the postseason roster. Spring training will determine his fate again.

Ian Krol   LHP

Born: 5/9/91   Age: 24   Bats: L   Throws: L   Height: 6'1"   Weight: 210

YEAR	TEAM	LVL	AGE	W	L	SV	G	GS	IP	H	HR	BB	K	BB/9	K/9	GB%	BABIP	WHIP	ERA	FIP	FRA	WARP
2012	STO	A+	21	1	7	0	21	15	86¹	95	13	24	79	2.5	8.2	46%	.315	1.38	5.21	4.88	5.16	1.1
2012	MID	AA	21	1	2	0	8	0	10²	11	0	2	10	1.7	8.4	62%	.379	1.22	5.06	1.97	3.22	0.2
2013	HAR	AA	22	0	0	1	21	0	26	14	1	7	29	2.4	10.0	48%	.210	0.81	0.69	2.63	2.55	0.7
2013	WAS	MLB	22	2	1	0	32	0	27¹	28	5	8	22	2.6	7.2	40%	.280	1.32	3.95	4.67	4.83	-0.1
2014	DET	MLB	23	0	0	1	45	0	32²	42	6	13	28	3.6	7.7	42%	.343	1.68	4.96	5.21	5.99	-0.3
2015	DET	MLB	24	2	2	0	28	3	38²	42	5	13	28	3.1	6.6	44%	.304	1.43	4.81	5.00	5.23	0.0

Breakout: 36%   Improve: 59%   Collapse: 11%   Attrition: 29%   MLB: 83%   Comparables: *Alex Burnett, Trevor Bell, Jordan Walden*

A throw-in bullpen piece in the Doug Fister-Robbie Ray deal, Krol went from late-inning possibility to big-league pitching machine to Triple-A project in a ridiculously short time. His command was so out of whack, the team neglected to call him back up in September. His results indicate he should become a situational lefty; an anonymous poll of right-handed sluggers disagrees. Of the six home runs he allowed, five were to righties, four were with runners on base, three were to Cleveland, two were to turtle doves and one was to Xavier Nady, who, yes, did play in the majors in 2014.

Austin Kubitza RHP

Born: 11/16/91 Age: 23 Bats: R Throws: R Height: 6'5" Weight: 225

YEAR	TEAM	LVL	AGE	W	L	SV	G	GS	IP	H	HR	BB	K	BB/9	K/9	GB%	BABIP	WHIP	ERA	FIP	FRA	WARP
2013	LAK	A+	21	0	1	0	8	1	17	16	0	10	14	5.3	7.4	55%	.327	1.53	5.82	4.24	6.21	-0.2
2014	WMI	A	22	10	2	0	23	23	131	98	5	43	140	3.0	9.6	72%	.271	1.08	2.34	2.99	4.38	1.1
2015	DET	MLB	23	4	6	0	21	14	88	94	9	44	67	4.5	6.8	59%	.308	1.56	5.07	5.08	5.51	-0.2

Breakout: 0%   Improve: 0%   Collapse: 0%   Attrition: 0%   MLB: 0%   Comparables: Glen Perkins, Wade Davis, D.J. Mitchell

We didn't mention the 2013 fourth-rounder out of Rice in last year's Annual; apologies to his future fan base. So many power arms, so few pages. He forced his way in this year by being named the Tigers' Minor League Pitcher Of The Year. Kubitza overmatched the Midwest League with his sinker-slider combo, holding the competition to an arousing .202/.275/.272 line and showing no real platoon extreme. If his changeup doesn't fool Double-A, he'd be a fool not to accept a fast-track path to a big-league bullpen, but he passed his first test with straight A's. By the way, a good name for that future fan base would be the Kibitzas.

Kyle Lobstein LHP

Born: 8/12/89 Age: 25 Bats: L Throws: L Height: 6'3" Weight: 200

YEAR	TEAM	LVL	AGE	W	L	SV	G	GS	IP	H	HR	BB	K	BB/9	K/9	GB%	BABIP	WHIP	ERA	FIP	FRA	WARP
2012	MNT	AA	22	8	7	0	27	27	144	140	12	69	129	4.3	8.1	42%	.311	1.45	4.06	3.91	4.49	1.6
2013	ERI	AA	23	7	4	0	15	15	95¹	92	6	27	83	2.5	7.8	50%	.322	1.25	3.12	3.25	3.67	1.7
2013	TOL	AAA	23	6	3	0	13	13	72¹	73	2	25	65	3.1	8.1	47%	.330	1.35	3.48	2.97	4.14	0.7
2014	TOL	AAA	24	9	11	0	26	25	146	174	10	42	127	2.6	7.8	49%	.360	1.48	4.07	3.45	4.34	1.7
2014	DET	MLB	24	1	2	0	7	6	39¹	35	3	14	27	3.2	6.2	46%	.267	1.25	4.35	3.85	4.83	0.2
2015	DET	MLB	25	8	11	0	27	27	153	175	18	55	107	3.2	6.3	42%	.317	1.50	5.04	4.88	5.48	-0.3

Breakout: 18%   Improve: 33%   Collapse: 12%   Attrition: 35%   MLB: 55%   Comparables: Chris Schwinden, Philip Humber, Daryl Thompson

A Triple-A ERA north of 4.00 doesn't normally compel a team to rush a prospect into the rotation. But after the Tigers blew through the Yellow Pages looking for a fresh body for a doubleheader, Lobstein threw 5 2/3 innings of fifth-starter stuff and earned a spot for the remainder of the season. With four pitches, none too overpowering (his fastball goes to about 90 on a warm day), Lobber's prime directive is "pitch to contact." His velocity faded to a max of 89 in his final start, possibly due to a career high in innings, but his presence as a left-hander who can throw strikes will always put him in the running to be a fifth starter, sixth starter, long reliever or just another guy whose name sounds like a crustacean rabbi.

Melvin Mercedes RHP

Born: 11/2/90 Age: 24 Bats: R Throws: R Height: 6'3" Weight: 250

YEAR	TEAM	LVL	AGE	W	L	SV	G	GS	IP	H	HR	BB	K	BB/9	K/9	GB%	BABIP	WHIP	ERA	FIP	FRA	WARP
2012	WMI	A	21	0	3	9	37	0	64¹	54	3	23	43	3.2	6.0	57%	.268	1.20	2.80	3.79	4.83	0.2
2013	LAK	A+	22	3	1	11	24	0	28	23	1	5	17	1.6	5.5	54%	.256	1.00	0.96	3.13	3.77	0.3
2013	ERI	AA	22	2	1	12	26	0	25	23	3	9	19	3.2	6.8	40%	.256	1.28	1.44	4.68	5.01	0.1
2014	TOL	AAA	23	0	3	3	46	0	60¹	69	8	16	31	2.4	4.6	49%	.295	1.41	4.92	4.85	6.10	-0.6
2014	DET	MLB	23	0	0	0	1	0	2	0	0	0	2	0.0	9.0	75%	.000	0.00	0.00	1.16	2.59	0.0
2015	DET	MLB	24	2	1	1	36	0	49¹	58	6	21	23	3.8	4.2	49%	.299	1.60	5.57	5.69	6.05	-0.5

Breakout: 0%   Improve: 0%   Collapse: 0%   Attrition: 0%   MLB: 0%   Comparables: Frank Mata, Bobby Cassevah, Dan Otero

Mercedes—who is not, as you're assuming, an anthropomorphized automobile in a police pamphlet warning about the dangers of drunk driving on prom night—made his major-league debut because the Tigers were desperate for anybody who could get three outs out of the bullpen, all the other desperation bids we've named in this chapter having already failed. It's not like he blew away Triple-A, but being on the 40-man roster is the sort of skill you can't teach. (Mercedes received an object lesson in this fact when he was DFA'd in December.) With a wide build, his weight can be an issue, but he commands a nice power sinker with intent to generate bad contact and ultimately could become a seventh-inning fireman.

Joe Nathan RHP

Born: 11/22/74 Age: 40 Bats: R Throws: R Height: 6'4" Weight: 230

YEAR	TEAM	LVL	AGE	W	L	SV	G	GS	IP	H	HR	BB	K	BB/9	K/9	GB%	BABIP	WHIP	ERA	FIP	FRA	WARP
2012	TEX	MLB	37	3	5	37	66	0	64¹	55	7	13	78	1.8	10.9	46%	.306	1.06	2.80	2.74	3.32	1.4
2013	TEX	MLB	38	6	2	43	67	0	64²	36	2	22	73	3.1	10.2	34%	.224	0.90	1.39	2.29	2.43	1.7
2014	DET	MLB	39	5	4	35	62	0	58	60	5	29	54	4.5	8.4	44%	.324	1.53	4.81	3.97	4.56	0.3
2015	DET	MLB	40	3	1	35	56	0	53	47	5	18	55	3.1	9.3	40%	.296	1.23	3.37	3.81	3.66	0.9

Breakout: 20%   Improve: 29%   Collapse: 25%   Attrition: 3%   MLB: 70%   Comparables: Tom Gordon, Arthur Rhodes, Mike Remlinger

Following a most glorious bullpen flameout in 2013, nobody could accuse the Tigers of apathy when they inked Nathan, coming off two straight All-Star seasons, to a two-year deal. Nathan fit right in almost immediately, blowing saves and losing bite on his fastball and slider, becoming the latest epicenter of ire for Tigers fans. The organization remained patient as he tried mechanical adjustments, but he sucked all the way. To his very small credit, he and Anibal Sanchez were the only Tigers relievers to appear in a postseason game and not allow a run. The 40-year-old is due $10 million this year, so the expectation is he'll be the Opening Day closer with a short leash.

David Price LHP

Born: 8/26/85 Age: 29 Bats: L Throws: L Height: 6'6" Weight: 210

YEAR	TEAM	LVL	AGE	W	L	SV	G	GS	IP	H	HR	BB	K	BB/9	K/9	GB%	BABIP	WHIP	ERA	FIP	FRA	WARP
2012	TBA	MLB	26	20	5	0	31	31	211¹	173	16	59	205	2.5	8.7	53%	.285	1.10	2.56	3.00	3.75	3.3
2013	TBA	MLB	27	10	8	0	27	27	186²	178	16	27	151	1.3	7.3	47%	.298	1.10	3.33	3.05	3.53	3.1
2014	DET	MLB	28	4	4	0	11	11	77²	74	5	15	82	1.7	9.5	45%	.317	1.15	3.59	2.46	2.91	2.1
2014	TBA	MLB	28	11	8	0	23	23	170²	156	20	23	189	1.2	10.0	42%	.301	1.05	3.11	2.96	3.75	1.7
2015	DET	MLB	29	13	10	0	30	30	203¹	191	17	46	193	2.0	8.5	45%	.303	1.17	3.23	3.45	3.51	3.9

Breakout: 20%   Improve: 44%   Collapse: 14%   Attrition: 4%   MLB: 95%   Comparables: Zack Greinke, Cole Hamels, CC Sabathia

Forty years ago, 40 pitchers faced at least 1,000 batters in a season. In the last four seasons, one did: this guy, last year. It's no wonder Price, the ace of a waffling contender, endured a typhoon of trade rumors. Finally he was freighted to Detroit to supplement the Best Starting Rotation Ever, which was still not enough to win a postseason game. The Tigers might have anticipated a Randy Johnson/CC Sabathia-type performance down the stretch, but received the same old stoic eight-inning vignettes. Now in his final year of team control, he could face another 1,000 batters, spell the bullpen even on his mediocre nights and run away with the gross tonnage of Scrooge McDuck's swimming pool next winter.

Evan Reed   RHP

Born: 12/31/85   Age: 29   Bats: R   Throws: R   Height: 6'4"   Weight: 255

YEAR	TEAM	LVL	AGE	W	L	SV	G	GS	IP	H	HR	BB	K	BB/9	K/9	GB%	BABIP	WHIP	ERA	FIP	FRA	WARP
2012	JAX	AA	26	3	1	12	27	0	34²	24	1	11	43	2.9	11.2	43%	.280	1.01	2.34	1.99	2.71	0.9
2012	NWO	AAA	26	2	3	1	23	0	32²	43	2	16	27	4.4	7.4	50%	.369	1.81	7.16	4.28	5.01	0.1
2013	TOL	AAA	27	1	4	1	32	0	49²	38	1	20	49	3.6	8.9	47%	.296	1.17	2.54	2.70	3.51	0.7
2013	DET	MLB	27	0	1	0	16	0	23¹	28	2	8	17	3.1	6.6	53%	.338	1.54	4.24	3.89	4.83	0.0
2014	TOL	AAA	28	0	1	0	17	1	23¹	26	0	5	26	1.9	10.0	37%	.400	1.33	4.24	1.77	2.57	0.8
2014	DET	MLB	28	0	1	0	32	0	32¹	39	2	12	26	3.3	7.2	56%	.363	1.58	4.18	3.75	3.97	0.4
2015	DET	MLB	29	2	1	0	38	0	49²	53	4	19	41	3.4	7.4	46%	.320	1.44	4.39	4.15	4.77	0.2

Breakout: 16%   Improve: 25%   Collapse: 19%   Attrition: 26%   MLB: 47%   *Comparables: Josh Roenicke, Chris Leroux, Ehren Wassermann*

If youth is wasted on the young, then an upper-90s fastball is wasted on Reed, who can throw it but isn't quite sure how to maximize its potential. He had a tumultuous season that included a journey off the 40-man roster, and he pitched under the very dark cloud of rape allegations for much of the year. This may be confusing correlation with causation, but after the charges were dismissed, Reed pitched better and earned a late-August call-up, throwing some decent innings. However, the charges were reinstated on appeal in November. Some teams have a reputation for balancing character issues against talent differently than others; Reed may soon find himself seeking those teams out for employment.

Bruce Rondon   RHP

Born: 12/9/90   Age: 24   Bats: R   Throws: R   Height: 6'3"   Weight: 275

YEAR	TEAM	LVL	AGE	W	L	SV	G	GS	IP	H	HR	BB	K	BB/9	K/9	GB%	BABIP	WHIP	ERA	FIP	FRA	WARP
2012	LAK	A+	21	1	0	15	22	0	23¹	12	1	10	34	3.9	13.1	57%	.239	0.94	1.93	2.45	3.79	0.4
2012	ERI	AA	21	0	1	12	21	0	21²	15	1	9	23	3.7	9.6	52%	.264	1.11	0.83	3.48	3.86	0.3
2013	TOL	AAA	22	1	1	14	30	0	29²	14	1	13	40	3.9	12.1	51%	.210	0.91	1.52	2.46	3.67	0.4
2013	DET	MLB	22	1	2	1	30	0	28²	28	2	11	30	3.5	9.4	47%	.329	1.36	3.45	3.04	3.29	0.5
2015	DET	MLB	24	2	1	1	35	0	34²	30	3	18	38	4.6	9.9	48%	.298	1.37	3.82	4.22	4.15	0.4

Breakout: 13%   Improve: 24%   Collapse: 10%   Attrition: 26%   MLB: 50%   *Comparables: Stephen Pryor, Eduardo Sanchez, David Robertson*

We can only speculate what Rondon's 2014 season would have been with a healthy UCL. More than likely he'd have been handed the eighth-inning role out of spring training, wowed us all with 100-plus mph fastballs, earned a few save opportunities when the inexorable spectre of age decided to crank call Joe Nathan. Or he could have struggled to throw strikes, then been banished to the world of dust and Toledo to work on that. All that's known is he missed a whole season (and probably the beginning of this one) yet is the manifestation of The Next Great Tigers Closer, chasing the shadows of Fernando Rodney, Ryan Perry, Franklyn German and Matt Anderson. Of those, at least Rondon casts the biggest shadow.

Anibal Sanchez   RHP

Born: 2/27/84   Age: 31   Bats: R   Throws: R   Height: 6'0"   Weight: 205

YEAR	TEAM	LVL	AGE	W	L	SV	G	GS	IP	H	HR	BB	K	BB/9	K/9	GB%	BABIP	WHIP	ERA	FIP	FRA	WARP
2012	DET	MLB	28	4	6	0	12	12	74²	81	8	15	57	1.8	6.9	47%	.313	1.29	3.74	3.64	4.23	1.1
2012	MIA	MLB	28	5	7	0	19	19	121	119	12	33	110	2.5	8.2	49%	.308	1.26	3.94	3.47	3.83	1.3
2013	DET	MLB	29	14	8	0	29	29	182	156	9	54	202	2.7	10.0	48%	.307	1.15	2.57	2.42	2.98	4.5
2014	DET	MLB	30	8	5	0	22	21	126	108	4	30	102	2.1	7.3	48%	.277	1.10	3.43	2.74	3.54	2.6
2015	DET	MLB	31	7	6	0	18	18	113²	112	9	32	101	2.5	8.0	46%	.307	1.26	3.64	3.71	3.96	1.7

Breakout: 10%   Improve: 47%   Collapse: 19%   Attrition: 11%   MLB: 91%   *Comparables: Adam Wainwright, Gavin Floyd, John Lackey*

If the cast of *Friends* typified the deep Tigers rotation, Sanchez reached Lisa Kudrow levels of overlooked brilliance when he matter-of-factly won the 2013 ERA title. It was when he missed two months in separate DL stints last year that his absence suddenly exposed Detroit's lack of depth. He returned at the denouement of the season, but as a reliever because the stamina wasn't there. He threw two innings in an ALDS game and that's all they'd let him last. When he's at full strength, the smooth corkscrew delivery keeps hitters off balance with a fastball, slider, curve and two different flavors of changeup. His velocity fell a single tick, and his strikeout rate slid back to his career average, but moving forward his innings will remain high in quality, if not in quantity.

Max Scherzer   RHP

Born: 7/27/84   Age: 30   Bats: R   Throws: R   Height: 6'3"   Weight: 220

YEAR	TEAM	LVL	AGE	W	L	SV	G	GS	IP	H	HR	BB	K	BB/9	K/9	GB%	BABIP	WHIP	ERA	FIP	FRA	WARP
2012	DET	MLB	27	16	7	0	32	32	187²	179	23	60	231	2.9	11.1	38%	.333	1.27	3.74	3.22	3.50	4.2
2013	DET	MLB	28	21	3	0	32	32	214¹	152	18	56	240	2.4	10.1	38%	.259	0.97	2.90	2.77	3.23	4.8
2014	DET	MLB	29	18	5	0	33	33	220¹	196	18	63	252	2.6	10.3	38%	.315	1.18	3.15	2.87	3.11	5.0
2015	DET	MLB	30	12	9	0	30	30	185¹	168	18	54	201	2.6	9.7	39%	.305	1.20	3.39	3.57	3.68	3.3

Breakout: 13%   Improve: 39%   Collapse: 27%   Attrition: 8%   MLB: 89%   *Comparables: Jake Peavy, Tim Lincecum, Johan Santana*

It took six years, 179 starts, 81 wins, but Max Scherzer finally earned his first complete game, becoming the first pitcher to throw his first one *after* winning a Cy Young. That sounds like the sort of thing traditionalists would needle him for, but he's actually a workhorse, just a new-age kind of one: He tossed six-plus frames in 28 starts and now ranks sixth in the majors in innings (and fourth in pitches) since 2013. As an extreme fly-baller he might give up solo homers in smaller parks, but little else. His intelligence is off the charts and into the next guy's chart, so even if his mechanics ever revert to 2009-era Scherzer, he still has the brainpower and armpower to gut through six innings on a bad day.

Alfredo Simon   RHP

Born: 5/8/81   Age: 34   Bats: R   Throws: R   Height: 6'6"   Weight: 265

YEAR	TEAM	LVL	AGE	W	L	SV	G	GS	IP	H	HR	BB	K	BB/9	K/9	GB%	BABIP	WHIP	ERA	FIP	FRA	WARP
2012	CIN	MLB	31	3	2	1	36	0	61	65	2	22	52	3.2	7.7	56%	.337	1.43	2.66	3.23	3.45	1.0
2013	CIN	MLB	32	6	4	1	63	0	87²	68	8	26	63	2.7	6.5	47%	.236	1.07	2.87	3.93	4.78	0.0
2014	CIN	MLB	33	15	10	0	32	32	196¹	181	22	56	127	2.6	5.8	50%	.265	1.21	3.44	4.30	5.05	-0.6
2015	DET	MLB	34	6	6	0	45	15	134²	144	15	45	91	3.0	6.1	47%	.297	1.40	4.63	4.87	5.03	0.3

Breakout: 18%   Improve: 31%   Collapse: 16%   Attrition: 14%   MLB: 71%   *Comparables: Dustin Hermanson, Brian Tallet, John Halama*

The big right-hander had spent the previous two seasons in the Reds' bullpen and found ample success, but he seamlessly transitioned to the rotation in 2014. He poured in the strikes, kept the ball on the ground and allowed one of the league's best defenses to clean up after him. As a reliever, the 6-foot-6 sinkerballer didn't need his splitter very often. As a starter, though, he threw it 30 percent of the time against lefties, which helped limit their overall effectiveness. In fact, his 15 percent whiff rate on the pitch came almost exclusively against lefties. Some doubters have pointed to his FIP and argued his .265 BABIP suggests he benefited from a plethora of luck; however, it's not significantly above his career .282 BABIP, and one would expect a groundball pitcher with a good defense to post a good BABIP. The Kinsler-Iglesias pair behind him will help soften the blow of waving goodbye to Zack Cozart.

Joakim Soria   RHP

Born: 5/18/84   Age: 31   Bats: R   Throws: R   Height: 6'3"   Weight: 200

YEAR	TEAM	LVL	AGE	W	L	SV	G	GS	IP	H	HR	BB	K	BB/9	K/9	GB%	BABIP	WHIP	ERA	FIP	FRA	WARP
2013	TEX	MLB	29	1	0	0	26	0	23²	18	2	14	28	5.3	10.6	53%	.286	1.35	3.80	3.71	4.33	0.2
2014	DET	MLB	30	1	1	1	13	0	11	13	2	2	6	1.6	4.9	52%	.289	1.36	4.91	5.25	5.93	-0.1
2014	TEX	MLB	30	1	3	17	35	0	33¹	25	0	4	42	1.1	11.3	42%	.291	0.87	2.70	1.09	1.57	1.3
2015	DET	MLB	31	2	1	5	38	0	36¹	32	3	10	38	2.5	9.4	45%	.299	1.17	3.22	3.40	3.51	0.7

Breakout: 21%   Improve: 35%   Collapse: 29%   Attrition: 13%   MLB: 81%   *Comparables: Ryan Madson, Sergio Romo, Nick Masset*

If nobody ever again trades for a proven closer at the deadline, it's going to be Soria's fault. Detroit paid a steep price for two months of the ex-Rangers closer, which later became one month thanks to an injury. The other month he was used in odd low-leverage spots, then became a postseason punching bag. Detroit did pick up his $7 million option, banking that his two-month tenure was a painful outlier in his otherwise reliable late-inning career. The thing is, most relievers don't age like a fine wine, but rather like an ice cream cone.

It is worth noting, here in Soria's ninth Baseball Prospectus comment, that if you mispronounce the "a" in his surname, he's the most Canadian player ever.

Justin Verlander   RHP

Born: 2/20/83   Age: 32   Bats: R   Throws: R   Height: 6'5"   Weight: 225

YEAR	TEAM	LVL	AGE	W	L	SV	G	GS	IP	H	HR	BB	K	BB/9	K/9	GB%	BABIP	WHIP	ERA	FIP	FRA	WARP
2012	DET	MLB	29	17	8	0	33	33	238¹	192	19	60	239	2.3	9.0	43%	.273	1.06	2.64	2.90	3.12	5.7
2013	DET	MLB	30	13	12	0	34	34	218¹	212	19	75	217	3.1	8.9	40%	.316	1.31	3.46	3.30	3.39	4.4
2014	DET	MLB	31	15	12	0	32	32	206	223	18	65	159	2.8	6.9	41%	.317	1.40	4.54	3.77	4.00	2.9
2015	DET	MLB	32	12	9	0	27	27	187	169	15	54	177	2.6	8.5	41%	.293	1.19	3.24	3.60	3.52	3.6

Breakout: 17%   Improve: 36%   Collapse: 30%   Attrition: 7%   MLB: 83%   *Comparables: Adam Wainwright, Josh Beckett, Johan Santana*

Little else could have gone horribly wrong for Verlander last year—he can't even say "at least nude photos of me weren't leaked on the Internet." Three years after winning an MVP award, two years after a Cy Young runner-up, one year after being an All-Star, he found himself with the eighth-worst ERA among qualified pitchers. The talking point from the Tigers was that an unannounced core muscle surgery last offseason required Verlander to take extra time to rebuild his strength, and he probably should have started the season on the disabled list. What that elides is that he's an aging pitcher who can no longer throw 99. He still has terrific secondary stuff but moving forward must ultimately accept that his fastball is an average pitch, or else every postseason he's going to be the popular choice for the Tim Lincecum Bullpen and Cheerleading role.

Josh Zeid   RHP

Born: 3/24/87   Age: 28   Bats: R   Throws: R   Height: 6'4"   Weight: 235

YEAR	TEAM	LVL	AGE	W	L	SV	G	GS	IP	H	HR	BB	K	BB/9	K/9	GB%	BABIP	WHIP	ERA	FIP	FRA	WARP
2012	CCH	AA	25	2	0	1	47	0	56¹	57	6	20	66	3.2	10.5	40%	.338	1.37	5.59	3.60	5.47	0.0
2013	OKL	AAA	26	4	1	13	43	0	43²	36	3	27	53	5.6	10.9	38%	.311	1.44	3.50	3.89	4.38	0.6
2013	HOU	MLB	26	0	1	1	25	0	27²	26	3	12	24	3.9	7.8	52%	.295	1.37	3.90	4.16	4.87	-0.1
2014	OKL	AAA	27	2	2	7	17	0	18²	14	2	9	21	4.3	10.1	50%	.261	1.23	2.41	4.29	4.00	0.3
2014	HOU	MLB	27	0	0	0	23	0	20²	30	6	7	18	3.0	7.8	43%	.364	1.79	6.97	6.35	6.51	-0.5
2015	DET	MLB	28	2	1	0	29	2	38¹	42	5	17	33	4.0	7.7	42%	.314	1.54	5.08	4.98	5.52	-0.1

Breakout: 12%   Improve: 19%   Collapse: 12%   Attrition: 20%   MLB: 38%   *Comparables: B.J. Rosenberg, Marcos Mateo, Jeremy Horst*

For relief prospects, stuff trumps results most every time. When Houston called to invite Zeid to major-league camp back in 2013, even he was surprised, initially thinking it was a prank. All he had done, after all, was post an ERA north of 5.00 as a reliever in Double-A. Twice. He rewarded the organization for its faith by mastering a split-change that spring; accompanying his power arsenal, that new plus pitch helped hold major-league lefties to a .178 batting average in 2013. He couldn't take another step forward last year—quite literally: He had surgeries to both feet—and the Astros faced a roster crunch with their young power arms, but Detroit eagerly snatched Zeid off of waivers. Remember, stuff trumps results.

Kevin Ziomek   LHP

Born: 3/21/92   Age: 23   Bats: R   Throws: L   Height: 6'3"   Weight: 200

YEAR	TEAM	LVL	AGE	W	L	SV	G	GS	IP	H	HR	BB	K	BB/9	K/9	GB%	BABIP	WHIP	ERA	FIP	FRA	WARP
2014	WMI	A	22	10	6	0	23	23	123	89	5	53	152	3.9	11.1	47%	.286	1.15	2.27	2.98	3.27	2.5
2015	DET	MLB	23	4	6	0	17	17	80²	82	9	44	74	4.9	8.2	44%	.310	1.55	4.88	5.00	5.30	0.1

Breakout: 0%   Improve: 0%   Collapse: 0%   Attrition: 0%   MLB: 0%   *Comparables: Jake Arrieta, Jose Cisnero, Tyler Thornburg*

Detroit's love affair with Vanderbilt pitchers deepened with the acquisition of David Price, but with Ziomek, their 2013 second-rounder, having an immaculate Low-A season, they're ready to propose. His mechanical concerns remain, as does poor command, but he tattered the strike zone the final two months to the tune of 76 strikeouts and 14 walks. He throws no singular overpowering pitch but has three usable ones working in harmony—the Neapolitan ice cream of pitchers—which forces him to mix and, as the old-timers call it, "pitch, not throw." This isn't a bad habit to master as he moves up the ladder.

Lineouts

Hitters

NAME	POS	TEAM	LVL	AGE	PA	R	2B	3B	HR	RBI	BB	K	SB	CS	AVG/OBP/SLG	TAv	BABIP	BRR	FRAA	WARP
Daniel Fields	CF	ERI	AA	23	35	4	3	1	0	9	6	7	2	0	.286/.429/.464	.337	.381	-1.0	CF(8): -0.6	0.2
	CF	TOL	AAA	23	299	29	10	3	6	26	15	76	8	2	.219/.273/.343	.228	.278	0.1	CF(67): -1.1, LF(5): 0.3	-0.3
Alex Gonzalez	SS	DET	MLB	37	32	4	0	1	0	2	2	4	0	0	.167/.219/.233	.192	.192	-0.8	SS(9): 0.4, 3B(1): -0.0	-0.2
Grayson Greiner	C	WMI	A	21	104	11	5	0	2	16	11	18	0	0	.322/.394/.444	.299	.375	0.0		0.0
Mike Hessman	3B	TOL	AAA	36	485	62	18	2	28	64	53	116	5	2	.248/.330/.500	.283	.267	-1.3	3B(86): 7.5, 1B(2): -0.0	3.1
Bryan Holaday	C	DET	MLB	26	171	14	5	1	0	15	8	37	1	1	.231/.266/.276	.206	.293	0.4	C(58): -0.2	-0.1
Jordan Lennerton	1B	TOL	AAA	28	488	54	26	2	10	53	73	114	0	1	.249/.362/.395	.264	.319	-0.2	1B(121): -1.2, P(2): -0.0	0.7
Dixon Machado	SS	LAK	A+	22	187	30	8	1	1	8	23	34	2	1	.252/.348/.333	.253	.312	0.8	SS(41): -1.8	0.4
	SS	ERI	AA	22	342	45	23	1	5	32	40	36	8	5	.305/.391/.442	.297	.331	2.4	SS(90): -1.3	3.1
Jefry Marte	3B	MID	AA	23	460	50	17	0	10	53	45	69	9	3	.259/.333/.375	.261	.286	-1.4	3B(91): 9.9, 1B(3): 0.3	2.0
Joseph Pankake	3B	ONE	A-	21	267	37	16	2	2	36	22	44	2	0	.292/.345/.400	.278	.342	-0.5	3B(34): -4.9, SS(16): 0.5	0.8
Hernan Perez	SS	TOL	AAA	23	596	69	32	7	6	53	36	65	21	6	.287/.331/.404	.249	.315	5.8	SS(118): -3.9, 2B(14): 0.1	2.2
	2B	DET	MLB	23	6	1	0	0	0	0	1	1	0	0	.200/.333/.200	.230	.250	-0.1	2B(5): 0.0, 3B(2): -0.0	0.0

A quality season could have ascended **Daniel Fields**, a defensively sound center fielder, to the big leagues, but he missed several weeks with a broken hand and then there's that whole "hitting the ball" skill. ❖ This was not a fever dream: The 37-year-old **Alex Gonzalez** was acquired in the wake of Jose Iglesias' shin injuries, hit a walk-off single on Opening Day and was released 20 days later during a harshly timed market correction. ❖ Third-round pick **Grayson Greiner** knocked around Single-A pitching before a Single-A pitch knocked around his wrist bone. ❖ The ageless and tenacious **Mike Hessman** last year became the International League record-holder for career homers and is 16 shy of the mark across all minors. He should reach that this year (knees permitting), at which point he'll immediately transform into Kevin Costner. ❖ All young backup catchers try to stand out somehow in an attempt to receive more playing time; **Bryan Holaday**'s superpower is bunt singles, of which he had five. ❖ Outrighted off the Tigers' 40-man roster in May, **Jordan Lennerton** is an aging gap-slashing first baseman with MLB-caliber defense who constantly refreshes Craigslist to see if Daric Barton requires an understudy. ❖ The lanky, rangy **Dixon Machado** lost his spot on the 40-man in 2013 due to poor hitting but finally broke into Double-A last year and reached base in 40 of his last 42 games. He still may be an organizational infielder, but a year later at least the question gives us pause. ❖ **Jefry Marte** keeps trying to carve out a career in a corner despite nonexistent power; some folks are always trying to ice skate uphill. ❖ **Joey Pankake** showed off his hitting prowess in his first pro season, but two primary questions remain for Pankake: (1) what position will he play and (2) is he exclusively a breakfast meal? ❖ Middle-infield depth filler **Hernan Perez** spent the year playing a decent Triple-A shortstop, then was a surprise addition to the Tigers' postseason roster and ended their season on a GIDP. But now he has playoff experience!

Pitchers

NAME	TEAM	LVL	AGE	W	L	SV	G	GS	IP	H	HR	BB	K	BB/9	K/9	GB%	BABIP	WHIP	ERA	FIP	FRA	WARP
Endrys Briceno	LAK	A+	22	0	0	0	3	3	16	16	1	3	7	1.7	3.9	54%	.273	1.19	3.38	3.89	4.86	0.1
Casey Crosby	TOL	AAA	25	0	0	0	11	0	17¹	15	2	13	12	6.8	6.2	40%	.236	1.62	5.71	5.90	7.04	-0.4
Joe Jimenez	ONE	A-	19	3	2	4	23	0	26²	22	1	6	41	2.0	13.8	44%	.350	1.05	2.70	1.75	3.22	0.6
Angel Nesbitt	LAK	A+	23	2	0	14	24	0	34¹	23	0	8	36	2.1	9.4	55%	.264	0.90	0.79	1.99	3.22	0.7
	ERI	AA	23	1	0	6	24	0	32¹	20	3	15	36	4.2	10.0	42%	.227	1.08	2.23	3.82	3.96	0.5
Luke Putkonen	DET	MLB	28	0	0	0	2	0	2²	6	2	2	1	6.8	3.4	43%	.333	3.00	27.00	15.53	15.96	-0.3
Kyle Ryan	ERI	AA	22	7	10	0	21	21	126²	140	15	32	78	2.3	5.5	49%	.309	1.36	4.55	4.44	5.07	0.7
	TOL	AAA	22	3	0	0	5	5	33	21	0	5	20	1.4	5.5	52%	.221	0.79	1.64	2.60	3.45	0.6
	DET	MLB	22	2	0	0	6	1	10¹	10	0	2	4	1.7	3.5	77%	.286	1.16	2.61	2.97	3.78	0.1
Daniel Schlereth	IND	AAA	28	1	2	0	21	0	18²	18	2	18	18	8.7	8.7	52%	.296	1.93	7.23	6.52	8.60	-0.6
	TOL	AAA	28	1	1	0	17	0	18	19	1	11	16	5.5	8.0	56%	.321	1.67	4.50	4.47	5.90	-0.1
Chad Smith	ERI	AA	24	1	0	1	12	0	20	15	0	6	18	2.7	8.1	74%	.278	1.05	1.35	2.45	3.53	0.4
	TOL	AAA	24	4	3	0	22	0	27	38	2	5	22	1.7	7.3	51%	.400	1.59	5.00	3.25	3.87	0.4
	DET	MLB	24	0	0	0	10	0	11²	15	1	3	9	2.3	6.9	37%	.378	1.54	5.40	3.50	3.67	0.2
Will Startup	ERI	AA	29	5	1	0	36	0	49¹	59	7	21	31	3.8	5.7	40%	.313	1.62	5.47	5.40	6.12	-0.3
Josh Turley	LAK	A+	23	7	1	0	18	13	97¹	70	2	23	81	2.1	7.5	50%	.258	0.96	1.85	2.73	3.71	1.2
	ERI	AA	23	3	4	0	9	9	50	53	8	16	28	2.9	5.0	43%	.283	1.38	3.78	5.27	5.48	0.1
Spencer Turnbull	ONE	A-	21	0	2	0	11	11	28¹	31	1	14	19	4.4	6.0	68%	.347	1.59	4.45	4.15	5.34	0.0
Jose Valdez	ERI	AA	24	2	3	18	47	0	57	56	6	26	66	4.1	10.4	43%	.340	1.44	4.11	3.83	3.65	1.1
Drew VerHagen	TOL	AAA	23	6	7	0	19	19	110¹	117	5	25	63	2.0	5.1	56%	.308	1.29	3.67	3.70	4.74	0.7
	DET	MLB	23	0	1	0	1	1	5	5	0	4	4	5.4	7.2	46%	.385	1.60	5.40	3.36	4.68	0.0
Alex Wilson	PAW	AAA	27	6	1	5	35	0	41¹	38	2	23	40	5.0	8.7	38%	.316	1.48	4.35	3.87	4.79	0.2
	BOS	MLB	27	1	0	0	18	0	28¹	20	3	5	19	1.6	6.0	45%	.213	0.88	1.91	3.94	4.32	0.2

One of the Tigers' litany of Venezuelan prospects, **Endrys Briceno**'s chance to shoot up the starting pitching prospect charts was tapered by an unfortunate visit to UCL Replacement Land, the most painful amusement park in the world. ❖ **Casey Crosby** has two potentially plus pitches that he can't control. Injuries during a transition to the bullpen ultimately led to his outright release from the Tigers. ❖ Mature young reliever **Joe Jimenez** may have starter potential, but he has been used exclusively in late innings, striking out anything with a bat, which isn't a bad specialty either. ❖ **Angel Nesbitt** could help a team in the bullpen this year. He could command that upper-90s fastball better. He could do lots of things. ❖ The hard-throwing **Luke Putkonen** had more injury setbacks than innings pitched, qualifying him for the Joel Zumaya Lifetime Achievement Award. ❖ **Kyle Ryan**'s major-league debut lasted six shutout innings, but with mid-80s stuff and pitch-to-contact command, the lanky lefty will toy with aggressive Triple-A hitters between big-league spot starts. ❖ Minor-league hot potato **Daniel Schlereth** found himself back in Toledo in his endless search for the fabled strike zone. He's getting warmer! ❖ Former Red Hot Chili Peppers drummer **Chad Smith** released an eclectic album titled "The Process" in November. This is more interesting than anything about the nondescript relief pitcher who earned an MLB call-up but started and ended the season in Double-A. ❖ **Will Startup** fits the definition of a replacement-level lefty, as well as the definition of a replacement-level office computer. ❖ Don't call him a knuckleball pitcher, but **Josh Turley** did begin incorporating the Internet's Favorite Pitch into his already deep arsenal and silenced High-A bats partly because of it. ❖ Second-rounder **Spencer Turnbull** features a power arm, a mid-90s fastball and experience pitching in the SEC, hitting all three checkboxes required to be a True Tigers Pitching Prospect. ❖ **Jose Valdez**, who signed out of the Dominican Republic at 19, has slowly ascended the charts as a minor-league reliever with a big sinking fastball that can strike out batters or magically give them first base, depending on the phase of the moon. ❖ **Drew VerHagen** made his major-league debut out of need rather than merit, as he still must craft other pitches around his strong sinker. A stress fracture in his back (at 6-feet-6, he has a big back) ended his season in August. ❖ **Alex Wilson** has gone from rotation prospect to bullpen prospect to fringe MLB reliever to trade throw-in, which means he'll save 20 games for the Padres someday.

Manager

Brad Ausmus

YEAR	TEAM	W	L	Py-thag +/-	Avg PC	100+ P	120+ P	QS	BQS	REL	REL w Zero R	IBB	PH	PH Avg	PH HR	SB2	CS2	SB3	CS3	SAC Att	SAC%	POS SAC	Squeeze	Swing	In Play
2014	DET	90	72	3	101.1	105	3	90	9	473	367	34	71	.164	1	90	34	16	7	40	60.0%	20	1	296	83

If there's an area where you'd bet on a rookie manager struggling, it has to be handling the pitching staff. The game moves faster from the bench, where more variables are at play than on the field. Even former catchers, like Ausmus, have to adjust to supervising a great number of players and working through more complex scenarios, such as when to warm a reliever. Expectedly, that's where Ausmus took most of his lumps during his first season in charge. But it wasn't for the reasons you'd think. The Tigers led the majors with nine blown quality starts in '14, a product of his unwillingness to turn things over to a leaky bullpen. Sometimes Ausmus' stubbornness proved correct, though those successes were quickly lost to the past. Instead folks remember the failures.

Chief among them: standing by Joe Nathan's side all season. Giving a veteran with Nathan's track record time to get things right is defensible; sticking with him as a high-leverage option when he's at the tail end of a miserable season is more questionable. Ausmus was in a tough spot either way, since he lacked good alternatives. Even Joakim Soria, added at the deadline to shore things up, missed time with injury and returned in an ineffective state.

None of that excuses Ausmus entirely. He erred plenty throughout the year, including when he cracked an absentminded joke about domestic violence. But Ausmus wasn't a total lost cause or numbskull out there. If anything, his willingness to lose with his starter in the game shows that he comprehended his personnel's limitations too well; a different manager might have deluded himself into thinking the relief options could hold a lead, no matter how many times they'd proved otherwise.

HOUSTON ASTROS

by Ted Walker

There is one franchise in baseball for which a 70-win season could be considered a major victory. The 2014 Houston Astros' 19-win jump from 2013, an improvement that trails only the Angels as far as turnarounds go, reminds how utterly abysmal this team had been over the previous few years. Seventy wins gave this franchise and its fans the chance to look down and see some other teams below them for once, even if the view back up is still dizzying.

The brightest Astro to shine in 2014, and one among several notable causes for the uptick: the young All-Star second baseman, Jose Altuve. The statistical and spiritual center of the 2014 Astros, Altuve begins any conversation about Houston baseball over the past year, even as supporting cast members emerged to share the load. With strokes of doubles down the third-base line and grounders skimming through the left side, he sketched a portrait of an undeniable and unlikely hero. During a season in which the front office's plan threatened to once again draw more attention than any particular on-field accomplishment, Altuve reminded Astros fans that elite play at the major-league level can happen in Houston and that none of us can ever know, really, what success will look like.

Truly. To wit, the starting rotation's twin pillars: Dallas Keuchel and Collin McHugh, undercover aces. Against the odds and amongst a chorus of sort of pleasantly surprised commentators, these pitchers put together years of high value. Keuchel's 3.9 WAR and McHugh's 3.3 represented hundreds of innings of quality work

To wit: The 345 thrilling, electrifying, hard-swinging, rain-making plate appearances of George Springer. The years of expectations finally bearing fruit. He would raise the barn single-handedly, and we'd all live in it until this winter was over. Twenty home runs, including a euphoric stretch in which he hit seven in as many games; outfield catches made slung across the turf; cuts so mighty that even a swing and miss was a thing. This was a sturm und drang of a different order altogether. And when he came up lame in July, his thunderous peals quieted just as quickly as they arose, stirring a great anticipation that, like all things Astro, tomorrow we will be quenched.

The improvement feels, to the optimistic, like the upward swing from the sickening drop that began with a 56-win 2011 season and sunk yet further as the major-league roster was dismantled in quest of infinite minor leaguers. The trust-us nature of such a Process meant General Manager Jeff Luhnow's job has been ambassador for the plan as much as front office dealmaker, but 2014 was perhaps his first opportunity to field a playable team. He was the first to advance such a notion. Indeed, the team's payroll in 2014 leapt to a Hearstian $50 million, up from $26 million the year before. Luhnow went so far as to sign a veteran to a multi-year deal, the ancient 31-year-old Scott Feldman, and trade a young pitcher, Jordan Lyles, for the elderly 28-year-old Dexter Fowler. Luhnow gave this team some rein and dedicated resources to the main event, with positive results, even if some of those results were driven by unpredictable performances.

Seventy wins. Proof that, if nothing else, the Astros could exceed their allotted 56.

✦✦✦

And yet, even as 2014 represented some semblance of a reentry into the baseball conversation, Astros fans have forestalled the much-hoped-for renaissance on Crawford Street. In fact, it would be fair to suggest that 2014 was the worst season, as a whole, in franchise history.

Each step forward on the field was accompanied by a hailstorm of humiliations and misfires, amplified all the more because of the attention brought to the team by Luhnow and Co.'s unabashed dedication to the style of rebuild that few teams outside of Miami have forced their fans to endure.

The parade of gaffes in Houston even resounded on a national scale, with plot turns and subplots that captured the attention of outlets that in years past would have gladly posted a D-minus A-Rod story over anything out of the third coast.

Luhnow and Co. have become known for their maneuvering and manipulation of the mechanisms of player management. They've made the most of the rulebook in the past few years by saving on first-pick bonuses and spending big on later picks in the amateur draft, maximizing the waiver wire to acquire MLB-ready players like McHugh and reliever Tony Sipp, and letting the payroll slide to uncomfortably low levels. Distinctive in style is the sense of transparency that accompanies the tactics. This is what we're about, the moves suggest, with disarming honesty. In 2014, that honesty made them sitting ducks.

Four fiascos define the strange nature of this seemingly

ASTROS PROSPECTUS
2014 W-L: 70-92, 4TH IN AL WEST

Pythag	.436	26th	DER	.701	19th
RS/G	3.88	21st	B-Age	25.4	1st
RA/G	4.46	25th	P-Age	27.4	5th
TAv	.258	16th	Salary	$50.5M	29th
BRR	1.78	15th	M$/MW	$1.7M	4th
TAv-P	.269	26th	DL Days	1,024	24th
FIP	3.95	22nd	$ on DL	21%	25th

Three-Year Park Factors

Runs	Runs/RH	Runs/LH	HR/RH	HR/LH
100	99	101	86	90

Top Hitter WARP	4.8	Jose Altuve
Top Pitcher WARP	2.7	Collin McHugh
Top Prospect		Carlos Correa

successful season, each of which feels out of place in a city that prides itself on warm welcomes and congenial competence over scheming and exploiting.

First: The Astros failed to sign the no. 1 overall draft pick—over, reportedly, the smallest margin in draft negotiation history: The length of a ligament. With the opportunity to designate, draft and sign the player of their choice, they balked on their offer to Brady Aiken and flubbed the resulting re-negotiation. This team failing to sign the nation's top prospect rings so antithetical to Luhnowball as to seem outright incorrect, like a headline writer's mistake. This cancellation of the Astros fan's Super Bowl presented the grand plan in a harsh and near-farcical light, as their unfettered pick (and other contingent picks who bolted for college when, for complicated but related reasons, the Astros could no longer offer them out-of-slot bonuses) slipped away in a fog of fuzzy decision science.

"I do feel genuine empathy for the players involved," Luhnow told Sports Illustrated's Ben Reiter. "It was bad luck all around. I understand that from a fan's perspective, we got nothing." Luck is convenient ballast when the ship is scraping bottom, but more importantly for the fan, the process of process starts to drown out the pleasures of the game. The "nothing" Luhnow refers to seems, in an odd way, to acknowledge that the decision was made despite the fan, as a kind of lamentation that the cost of a decision indeed goes far beyond the dollars and the draft slots.

Second: Less than half of the cable-viewing public had access to Astros baseball games in 2014. Comcast SportsNet Houston, which the Astros and the Houston Rockets owned a majority stake in, suffered from stalled negotiations with cable providers. It ultimately ended up in bankruptcy court and showed a chronic inability to expand its viewership beyond almost unbelievably low levels. Sports Illustrated, Deadspin and Yahoo! Sports were among the outlets to deridingly report the multiple instances in which Astros broadcasts received a 0.0 Nielsen rating.

Luhnow has, for his part, remained remarkably positive in his messaging, even as a significant portion of the fan base decries the team's business side. In combination with the team's largely unwelcome jump to the American League (accompanied by the west-coast schedule that remains counter-convenient for this writer and presumably many more Texans), those who are not hopelessly addicted to MLB have had plenty of opportunities to write off baseball in Houston. On a positive note, AT&T and DirecTV bought the channel out of bankruptcy this offseason and launched a new channel to millions more viewers. In a calculating tone that is the perceived persona of the team—maybe by now it's become the real tone of the team—Astros owner Jim Crane said of the new deal, "Comcast wasn't paying us, and now we have that behind us. We will get paid, and most importantly, we will get the fans to see the product."

Third: Ground Control. In late June, Deadspin reported a leak of the Astros' internal transaction management software, which goes by that admittedly pretty creative name. Reams of internal notes were scattered to the winds for all of us to pore over and poke fun at (with strategic and political implications that we can't even begin to speculate upon). There is a silver lining to this serious security breach: humanity. While the entire episode was no doubt heartbreaking for Luhnow—it's terrifying to consider anyone's private digital communication showing up on Deadspin—it put a human face on the transaction business. The sheer excitement of a world of possibilities comes through. Giancarlo Stanton! Dylan Bundy! Gregory Polanco! These are

the notes of people working every day, poking around the league, dropping inquiries and teasing out possibilities. This sounds like … fun. Still, though, pretty terrible. For a team that is process first and prides itself on strategy, this was a blow to the collective ecosystem, if not the win-loss table.

Fourth: Near the end of the season, Luhnow relieved manager Bo Porter of his duties. A vastly improved record for a team that writes off losses as business expenses is hardly the scenario one envisions for an execution. There were attempts to tie the move to a visit from top prospect Mark Appel, a visit about which the GM failed to forewarn his manager. Luhnow himself referred less to any specific factors and more to general distaste. "It's something that I had been considering for a few weeks, but there's no one event that led to it," he told the Houston Chronicle at the time. The air slowly leaked out of the balloon. The motivational posters that the media pumped up as a sign of a manager committed to winning without excuses became fodder for ridicule. Ken Rosenthal cited a rift-in-the-making due to "the emotional Porter and deeply analytical Luhnow."

Porter's departure added to the general sense that the mega-planners were planning on the fly. Communication, which is in many ways at the core of the team's identity both internally and externally, was breaking down even as victories accumulated. The focus, the order, the direction—the plan—that the franchise has sold to its fans seemed stymied by the human elements of a game played by, managed by and enjoyed by humans.

✦✦✦

The real achievement of the 2014 season in Houston is not measured in wins or losses, but in Altuves.

The Astros defied all predictive sense, because, through all of the above, Jose Altuve hit. The team lost and he hit. They won a little and he hit. Young players burned bright, faltered and froze up. He hit. Porter and Luhnow soured, the plan marched on, and Jose Altuve just kept on hitting. The batting championship is a dusty, outmoded metric, all the way until your man's singles keep the hope alive. Late in the season, when the adrenaline rush of Springer had faded, when the doldrums of late non-contention threatened, Jose Altuve popped and sprayed and sprinted and hit .341.

What a number: a towering monument looming above a Great Plains of plainness.

When there was no pennant race left, no draft blunders or trade news, Astros fans checked in to see if Altuve got his hit, if he chased down Craig Biggio's team-record 210, if he, my god, if he won the batting title!

Every single that dropped over the shortstop's head and every double that rattled the scoreboard in front of the Crawford Boxes had some sense of significance beyond its immediate context, even if the game did not. When Altuve rapped his 211th hit of the year, he stood at first base after the single and tipped his helmet humbly toward Biggio, while a half-capacity crowd raised its voices. The young second baseman sucked wind on first base, not because of the sprint—it was a seeing-eye single with no play—but perhaps because he'd found himself in "a moment," which, in his young career on the worst team in baseball, was as rare as wins were. I felt—and maybe as he stood there huffing, he did too—a through-line from that moment to the great Astros of the mid-2000s and the 1990s and the '80s, that he and his teammates were tethered as they weren't before to the team's history: a new generation arriving.

The hitter who looks so much the kid playing a kid's game played the steely veteran when he rapped two hits on the last day of the 2014 season to lock in his title over the resurgent Victor Martinez (a friend and fellow Venezuelan). Altuve entered the season with a modest 1.3 WAR under his belt from 2013 and a ZiPS projection predicting another 1.8 for the 2014 season. But 225 hits and 56 stolen bases later he's a Silver Slugger, an All-Star, a beloved bit of belt in an otherwise unremarkable lineup.

Two hundred twenty-five hits. Jose de Jesus Ortiz noted early in the year that a retooled swing brought more rhythm to the load and more balance to the approach in 2014. There are plenty of analysts who can do a better job than I of describing what

tendencies and trends define the nature of Altuve's 168 singles, 48 doubles, three triples and seven home runs. For me, it's good enough to consider his hands, so quick he seems to wait until the pitch has arrived to start his swing, and his bat head, a blur at the point of contact; his quick hands the confluence of style and effort and skill that make for great major leaguers.

In a season you could chart by the fiasco or fiat, Altuve's accomplishment lent levity and charm to what could have easily been another tedious march toward only the future, the future never, really, being the point. ∎

—Ted Walker lives and works in his home town, Houston, Texas.

Player comments by Matt Sussman, Ryan Ghan and Baseball Prospectus Authors

Hitters

Jose Altuve   2B

Born: 5/6/90   Age: 25   Bats: R   Throws: R   Height: 5' 6"   Weight: 175

YEAR	TEAM	LVL	AGE	PA	R	2B	3B	HR	RBI	BB	K	SB	CS	AVG/OBP/SLG	TAv	BABIP	BRR	FRAA	WARP
2012	HOU	MLB	22	630	80	34	4	7	37	40	74	33	11	.290/.340/.399	.271	.321	3.6	2B(147): 6.1	3.9
2013	HOU	MLB	23	672	64	31	2	5	52	32	85	35	13	.283/.316/.363	.243	.316	0.9	2B(145): -6.9	-0.1
2014	HOU	MLB	24	707	85	47	3	7	59	36	53	56	9	.341/.377/.453	.302	.360	5.9	2B(156): -5.9	4.8
2015	*HOU*	*MLB*	*25*	*657*	*84*	*35*	*4*	*6*	*52*	*30*	*75*	*39*	*10*	*.300/.334/.399*	*.277*	*.327*	*2.4*	*2B -3*	*3.2*

Breakout: 0%   Improve: 63%   Collapse: 4%   Attrition: 9%   MLB: 100%   Comparables: *Jose Lopez, Martin Prado, Jose Reyes*

There are certain batting seasons we can recognize almost immediately—"I can name that tune in two stats"—and Altuve's 2014 ought to be one of them. It's a dead ringer for Ichiro's 2001, another memorable campaign, though Altuve's has the mnemonic benefit of including both the bold and beautiful (his average, hits and steals all led the AL) and the discordantly plain: How *does* an everyday leadoff man crack 220 hits and steal 50 bases without scoring even 90 runs? Oh, right, Astros. He's young, under team control and plays an important position both in the field—although only averagely; his leaping grabs are routine liners to others—and at the plate, where he's one of the few pure leadoff men that statheads and Dusty Baker could agree on. The complete list of previous 66-inch players to record 200 hits in a season since 1900: Phil Rizzuto, Hack Wilson, Joe Sewell—all Hall of Famers. More impressive: To make height for that list, Altuve had to play the entire season wearing moon boots.

Chris Carter   DH

Born: 12/18/86   Age: 28   Bats: R   Throws: R   Height: 6' 4"   Weight: 250

YEAR	TEAM	LVL	AGE	PA	R	2B	3B	HR	RBI	BB	K	SB	CS	AVG/OBP/SLG	TAv	BABIP	BRR	FRAA	WARP
2012	SAC	AAA	25	324	48	19	1	12	53	38	74	5	1	.279/.367/.486	.293	.332	0.3	1B(47): -4.5	1.0
2012	OAK	MLB	25	260	38	12	0	16	39	39	83	0	0	.239/.350/.514	.315	.295	-1.4	1B(55): 0.3	1.6
2013	HOU	MLB	26	585	64	24	2	29	82	70	212	2	0	.223/.320/.451	.281	.311	-2.0	1B(61): -3.4, LF(49): -4.6	0.8
2014	HOU	MLB	27	572	68	21	1	37	88	56	182	5	2	.227/.308/.491	.293	.267	0.3	1B(14): 0.6, LF(6): 0.0	2.6
2015	*HOU*	*MLB*	*28*	*540*	*68*	*21*	*1*	*27*	*79*	*58*	*172*	*3*	*1*	*.225/.312/.445*	*.282*	*.285*	*-1.0*	*1B -2, LF -2*	*1.5*

Breakout: 3%   Improve: 34%   Collapse: 5%   Attrition: 13%   MLB: 80%   Comparables: *Josh Phelps, Chris Davis, Jonny Gomes*

It finally happened. Carter displayed the full season of power everyone envisioned back when he was still climbing Oakland's organizational ladder. Yes, he'll swing and miss far too much, and no he doesn't walk enough to be heir to the Adam Dunn throne, but this is the clay model of the modern-day designated hitter: home runs and attempted home runs. Let him occasionally play the field to fine-tune his body, then slap some on-base guys ahead of him, serve and enjoy.

Jason Castro   C

Born: 6/18/87   Age: 28   Bats: L   Throws: R   Height: 6' 3"   Weight: 215

YEAR	TEAM	LVL	AGE	PA	R	2B	3B	HR	RBI	BB	K	SB	CS	AVG/OBP/SLG	TAv	BABIP	BRR	FRAA	WARP
2012	HOU	MLB	25	295	29	15	2	6	29	31	61	0	0	.257/.334/.401	.264	.309	-0.1	C(79): -1.7	0.9
2013	HOU	MLB	26	491	63	35	1	18	56	50	130	2	1	.276/.350/.485	.305	.351	2.1	C(98): -0.2	4.3
2014	HOU	MLB	27	512	43	21	2	14	56	34	151	1	0	.222/.286/.366	.245	.294	-2.3	C(114): -1.8	1.0
2015	*HOU*	*MLB*	*28*	*477*	*48*	*22*	*1*	*11*	*52*	*43*	*119*	*1*	*0*	*.240/.312/.377*	*.263*	*.302*	*-0.1*	*C -1*	*1.8*

Breakout: 3%   Improve: 40%   Collapse: 3%   Attrition: 8%   MLB: 97%   Comparables: *Chris Snyder, Ryan Doumit, John Buck*

Hug your starting catcher. Hug him when he's an All-Star, because who knows when that day will come again. Castro is still an effective defender and pitch framer (11th in runs saved) but his lumber did not float: fewer hits, fewer extra-base hits, fewer walks and more strikeouts. (More HBPs, though, so perhaps more enemies?) There's no smoking gun in his contact, plate discipline or batted ball tendencies, which is perhaps the most troubling thing: 2013, not 2014, is likely to be the outlier when we look back at his career. Consider: Castro's *2013* PECOTA projection was .240/.321/.362, which didn't come close to his actual, BABIP-fuelled line, but instead is a pretty solid match for his 2014 performance. At this point, his ability to stay healthy and in a squat is his greatest asset. Maybe it's best, then, not to hug him too hard.

Hank Conger   C

Born: 1/29/88   Age: 27   Bats: B   Throws: R   Height: 6' 2"   Weight: 220

YEAR	TEAM	LVL	AGE	PA	R	2B	3B	HR	RBI	BB	K	SB	CS	AVG/OBP/SLG	TAv	BABIP	BRR	FRAA	WARP
2012	SLC	AAA	24	288	48	17	0	10	42	19	49	2	0	.295/.347/.473	.273	.329	1.4	C(59): 0.1	1.7
2012	ANA	MLB	24	22	0	0	0	0	1	1	0	0	0	.167/.238/.167	.161	.158	-0.2	C(7): 0.1	-0.1
2013	ANA	MLB	25	255	23	13	1	7	21	17	61	0	1	.249/.310/.403	.259	.307	-0.2	C(71): -0.2	0.9
2014	ANA	MLB	26	260	24	12	0	4	25	22	57	0	2	.221/.293/.325	.232	.275	0.8	C(79): 0.7	0.6
2015	HOU	MLB	27	250	25	11	1	6	26	21	52	1	1	.238/.306/.369	.256	.280	0.3	C 0	0.9

Breakout: 7%   Improve: 40%   Collapse: 11%   Attrition: 23%   MLB: 86%   Comparables: JD Closser, Francisco Cervelli, Lou Marson

Hank Conger, defensive specialist? Exactly nobody projected that particular outcome back when the Halos selected Hammerin' Hank 25th overall in 2006; even as he moved up the minors, there was talk that he might have to hit enough to DH. Yet his most notable 2014 contributions—really, his only contributions—came from behind the dish, where pitch framing metrics estimate that he conned 20-plus runs worth of extra strike calls from gullible umpires, implying world-class hands. He nevertheless lost playing time to Chris Iannetta due to significant regression in his offensive game. Back in 2013, Hank rarely missed a mistake, slugging .929 on pitches in the middle third of the plate and .533 on fastballs generally. In 2014, those numbers dropped to .343 and .376 respectively, which seems fluky, and might indicate that he's just a mechanical tweak away from rebounding mightily in 2015. The Astros are certainly hopeful, but you don't sense that the organization that hired Mike Fast missed all the stuff mentioned in the top half of this comment.

Carlos Corporan   C

Born: 1/7/84   Age: 31   Bats: B   Throws: R   Height: 6' 2"   Weight: 245

YEAR	TEAM	LVL	AGE	PA	R	2B	3B	HR	RBI	BB	K	SB	CS	AVG/OBP/SLG	TAv	BABIP	BRR	FRAA	WARP
2012	OKL	AAA	28	229	35	15	0	6	31	15	46	2	0	.286/.349/.447	.285	.340	0.3	C(67): -0.1	2.0
2012	HOU	MLB	28	85	5	2	0	4	13	4	19	0	1	.269/.310/.449	.257	.304	-0.2	C(24): 0.6	0.4
2013	HOU	MLB	29	210	16	5	0	7	20	10	60	0	0	.225/.287/.361	.242	.288	-1.8	C(57): -1.1, 1B(1): -0.0	0.4
2014	HOU	MLB	30	190	22	6	0	6	19	14	37	0	0	.235/.302/.376	.251	.264	-1.6	C(54): -1.0	0.3
2015	HOU	MLB	31	250	24	10	0	6	25	14	63	0	0	.226/.282/.350	.240	.280	-1.0	C -0, 1B -0	0.3

Breakout: 1%   Improve: 25%   Collapse: 23%   Attrition: 29%   MLB: 87%   Comparables: Chad Moeller, Javier Valentin, Miguel Ojeda

Corporan's profile has been backup catcher ever since the minors. Shoot, he was probably a backup catcher in Little League. ("That kid's gonna be something special," his coach might have said, noting how leadershippy Corporan's lugging of the catcher's equipment from truck to dugout was.) Not one skill stands out—okay power, okay contact rate, decent arm, average pitch framer—but without being a liability in any facet, isn't that the type of player you want starting a couple times a week? There will always be a roster spot for Corporan, especially as he ages into his 30s, as he ripens from inexpensive young backup to inexpensive journeyman backup.

Carlos Correa   SS

Born: 9/22/94   Age: 20   Bats: R   Throws: R   Height: 6' 4"   Weight: 205

YEAR	TEAM	LVL	AGE	PA	R	2B	3B	HR	RBI	BB	K	SB	CS	AVG/OBP/SLG	TAv	BABIP	BRR	FRAA	WARP
2013	QUD	A	18	519	73	33	3	9	86	58	83	10	10	.320/.405/.467	.314	.375	-2.3	SS(115): -6.8	4.7
2014	LNC	A+	19	293	50	16	6	6	57	36	45	20	4	.325/.416/.510	.317	.373	1.1	SS(59): 9.4	3.8
2015	HOU	MLB	20	250	24	11	1	3	23	19	58	5	2	.240/.304/.340	.249	.305	0.0	SS 1	0.9

Breakout: 0%   Improve: 0%   Collapse: 0%   Attrition: 0%   MLB: 0%   Comparables: Jurickson Profar, Brad Harman, Jonathan Schoop

If one sets aside Correa's inability to maintain two intact fibulas, then the consensus top-10 prospect's season was a smashing success. Both his strikeout and walk rates trended in the best direction, and he slammed righties to the tune of a four-digit OPS. That last tidbit is interesting, both because it underscores Correa's immunity to A-Ball bendy stuff, and also because it stands in contradiction to a rather bewildering inability to square up southpaws, who fanned him at a 29 percent rate while inducing groundballs 67 percent of the time on contact. The only pitcher he faced all year who was younger than him was the Dodgers' mini-lefty uber-prospect Julio Urias, who whiffed him in three of five confrontations. Apparently, if you want to get Correa out, you have to be left-handed, and it helps to be 17.

Matt Dominguez   3B

Born: 8/28/89   Age: 25   Bats: R   Throws: R   Height: 6' 1"   Weight: 215

YEAR	TEAM	LVL	AGE	PA	R	2B	3B	HR	RBI	BB	K	SB	CS	AVG/OBP/SLG	TAv	BABIP	BRR	FRAA	WARP
2012	NWO	AAA	22	315	27	14	0	7	46	23	31	0	1	.234/.291/.357	.240	.239	-3.2	3B(78): -3.1	-0.3
2012	OKL	AAA	22	177	21	10	0	2	23	11	21	0	0	.298/.347/.398	.275	.329	0.6	3B(45): -0.8	0.8
2012	HOU	MLB	22	113	14	2	2	5	16	4	17	0	0	.284/.310/.477	.268	.299	-2.6	3B(31): 0.1	0.3
2013	HOU	MLB	23	589	56	25	0	21	77	30	96	0	1	.241/.286/.403	.249	.254	-0.3	3B(149): 11.9	2.8
2014	HOU	MLB	24	607	51	17	0	16	57	29	125	0	1	.215/.256/.330	.212	.244	-0.4	3B(153): -4.1	-1.4
2015	HOU	MLB	25	567	51	22	1	15	63	28	99	0	0	.233/.275/.364	.242	.256	-1.0	3B 3	0.4

Breakout: 6%   Improve: 61%   Collapse: 11%   Attrition: 17%   MLB: 98%   Comparables: Jose Castillo, Mike Moustakas, Steve Lombardozzi

The Astros enjoyed a year of promising youth. Unfortunately for Dominguez, he wasn't part of that resurgence. While his name was scribbled into the lineup nearly every day, all that held up from his 2013 breakout were his power numbers; everything else took a nasty turn, especially in the summer, with a .472 second-half OPS that was 100 points worse than any teammate's. His reputation as a reliable defender with a bit of power will be on the line this year. A team can stay a bit more patient with a 25-year-old, but if he starts struggling again early, the Astros might waste little time yanking him for someone who can get on base.

Derek Fisher   OF

Born: 8/21/93   Age: 21   Bats: L   Throws: R   Height: 6' 1"   Weight: 207

YEAR	TEAM	LVL	AGE	PA	R	2B	3B	HR	RBI	BB	K	SB	CS	AVG/OBP/SLG	TAv	BABIP	BRR	FRAA	WARP
2014	TCV	A-	20	172	31	4	3	2	18	16	35	17	4	.303/.378/.408	.299	.379	-0.6	LF(38): 0.0, CF(1): -0.0	1.1
2015	HOU	MLB	21	250	23	8	1	2	18	13	73	9	3	.201/.249/.274	.203	.277	0.8	LF 0	-0.8

Breakout: 0%   Improve: 0%   Collapse: 0%   Attrition: 0%   MLB: 0%   Comparables: Aaron Cunningham, Xavier Paul, Shane Peterson

For Fisher, all roads lead to Texas. The Rangers tried to corral the power-speed threat out of high school in 2011, drafting him in the sixth round and offering over-slot money. Fisher declined, electing to attend the University of Virginia instead. Three years later, with pre-draft scouting reports projecting Fisher's hit and power tools as among the tops of his draft class, Houston tapped him in the supplemental first round and brought him to the Lone Star state with a $1.5 million bonus. His pro debut was more solid than spectacular, much like his college numbers, but Houston is making a long-term bet that the sweet swing and discerning eye will eventually shift the narrative of The Aiken Draft to that of The Fisher Draft.

Dexter Fowler   CF

Born: 3/22/86   Age: 29   Bats: B   Throws: R   Height: 6' 4"   Weight: 190

YEAR	TEAM	LVL	AGE	PA	R	2B	3B	HR	RBI	BB	K	SB	CS	AVG/OBP/SLG	TAv	BABIP	BRR	FRAA	WARP
2012	COL	MLB	26	530	72	18	11	13	53	68	128	12	5	.300/.389/.474	.278	.390	1.6	CF(131): -9.1	1.7
2013	COL	MLB	27	492	71	18	3	12	42	65	105	19	9	.263/.369/.407	.265	.323	3.9	CF(110): -7.4	1.1
2014	HOU	MLB	28	505	61	21	4	8	35	66	108	11	4	.276/.375/.399	.292	.351	-0.9	CF(111): -11.3	1.5
2015	HOU	MLB	29	475	58	19	6	7	40	57	114	12	5	.249/.344/.373	.274	.323	0.9	CF -5	1.6

Breakout: 5%   Improve: 40%   Collapse: 2%   Attrition: 7%   MLB: 98%   *Comparables: Nate McLouth, Chet Lemon, Chris Young*

There's always an inherent danger in acquiring an outfielder from Colorado, not unlike gas station sandwiches. But Fowler was never power-dependent, and his eight-point drop in slugging percentage is hardly stale bread. That he more or less replicated his overall batting results in Minute Maid Park suggest some relative improvement under the Astros' coaching, but his baseline is so darn steady that even silent-era projection systems have a good understanding of what his 2015 will look like: see 2014, 2013, 2012, 2011 and so on, all the way to the beginning of time, when Fowler's Cro-Magnon ancestors all hit .270/.370/.410 in any given dinosaur mating ground.

Marwin Gonzalez   SS

Born: 3/14/89   Age: 26   Bats: B   Throws: R   Height: 6' 1"   Weight: 205

YEAR	TEAM	LVL	AGE	PA	R	2B	3B	HR	RBI	BB	K	SB	CS	AVG/OBP/SLG	TAv	BABIP	BRR	FRAA	WARP
2012	OKL	AAA	23	43	2	4	0	1	10	3	7	0	0	.333/.395/.513	.336	.387	-1.3	SS(10): -2.3	0.2
2012	HOU	MLB	23	219	21	13	0	2	12	13	29	3	3	.234/.280/.327	.215	.264	-3.0	SS(47): -0.2, 3B(14): 0.4	-0.4
2013	OKL	AAA	24	183	16	10	1	1	15	8	23	4	1	.262/.293/.349	.234	.295	-0.5	SS(29): -3.5, 2B(13): 1.6	-0.1
2013	HOU	MLB	24	222	22	8	0	4	14	9	37	6	2	.221/.252/.319	.222	.250	1.1	SS(53): -4.3, 2B(10): 1.7	0.1
2014	HOU	MLB	25	310	33	15	1	6	23	17	58	2	4	.277/.327/.400	.261	.330	-0.6	SS(71): 1.0, 2B(11): 0.1	1.4
2015	HOU	MLB	26	296	29	14	1	4	27	15	50	4	3	.250/.291/.354	.246	.285	-0.6	SS -1, 2B 1	0.8

Breakout: 7%   Improve: 47%   Collapse: 8%   Attrition: 18%   MLB: 95%   *Comparables: Yuniesky Betancourt, Erick Aybar, Omar Infante*

Time was a-ticking, and Gonzalez's numbers weren't getting any better. His career options included: law school, Japan or becoming a superutilityman. Gonzalez chose Door No. 3, as the middle infielder saw his first pro playing time in the corner outfield and even sampled an inning at first base. As an added bonus Gonzalez began squaring the ball up better, and a higher line-drive percentage led to an above-average OPS. As a switch-hitter and owner of several gloves, Gonzalez can fit as a team's 25th man. Law school will always be there if he wants it, and Japan will always need attorneys.

Robbie Grossman   LF

Born: 9/16/89   Age: 25   Bats: B   Throws: L   Height: 6' 0"   Weight: 195

YEAR	TEAM	LVL	AGE	PA	R	2B	3B	HR	RBI	BB	K	SB	CS	AVG/OBP/SLG	TAv	BABIP	BRR	FRAA	WARP
2012	ALT	AA	22	417	59	20	4	7	36	59	78	9	10	.266/.378/.406	.285	.325	0.4	CF(94): -12.1	1.3
2012	CCH	AA	22	160	22	8	2	3	11	18	43	4	1	.267/.371/.422	.286	.367	1.2	CF(27): -1.3, LF(6): 0.6	1.0
2013	OKL	AAA	23	310	42	11	2	2	20	48	66	15	8	.281/.396/.364	.277	.371	-0.2	CF(33): -2.4, LF(32): -2.9	0.9
2013	HOU	MLB	23	288	29	14	0	4	21	23	70	6	7	.268/.332/.370	.259	.353	2.0	LF(45): -1.7, CF(29): -2.6	0.2
2014	OKL	AAA	24	199	30	16	0	4	15	22	38	10	8	.337/.417/.497	.316	.414	0.9	CF(35): -0.8, LF(7): 0.4	1.8
2014	HOU	MLB	24	422	42	14	2	6	37	55	105	9	3	.233/.337/.333	.258	.311	-2.0	LF(67): -0.9, RF(32): -1.4	0.0
2015	HOU	MLB	25	436	53	18	2	6	35	47	108	11	7	.245/.332/.351	.260	.319	-0.4	LF -2, CF -4	0.3

Breakout: 8%   Improve: 46%   Collapse: 8%   Attrition: 23%   MLB: 78%   *Comparables: Andre Ethier, J.D. Martinez, Domonic Brown*

If a genie offers to grant you two true outcomes, it's probably a trick; you *could* become Barry Bonds, but the genie's knowing smirk suggests you'll probably be Robbie Grossman. The slash line was comparable to Ruben Tejada's, or a 43-year-old Rickey Henderson, whichever you prefer. Among players with 400 PAs, he had the seventh-lowest swing percentage and was eighth in the league in called third strikes. You might think of him as the anti-MacGyver: He has *exactly* the tool he needs for each situation, but can't figure out how to use it. Defensively he'll provide average range and performance, which means he does own a baseball mitt, or at least has baseball mitt-sized hands, which would explain why he has difficulty swinging a baseball bat.

Teoscar Hernandez   CF

Born: 10/15/92   Age: 22   Bats: R   Throws: R   Height: 6' 2"   Weight: 180

YEAR	TEAM	LVL	AGE	PA	R	2B	3B	HR	RBI	BB	K	SB	CS	AVG/OBP/SLG	TAv	BABIP	BRR	FRAA	WARP
2012	LEX	A	19	30	2	2	0	1	5	3	12	1	0	.240/.310/.440	.271	.385	-0.8	CF(5): -0.5, RF(3): -0.3	-0.1
2013	QUD	A	20	565	97	25	9	13	55	41	135	24	11	.271/.328/.435	.280	.344	6.4	CF(108): -11.0, RF(15): -0.2	2.8
2014	LNC	A+	21	455	72	33	8	17	75	49	117	31	6	.294/.376/.550	.315	.374	3.3	CF(96): 4.2	4.9
2014	CCH	AA	21	98	12	4	1	4	10	2	36	2	3	.284/.299/.474	.284	.418	-1.0	CF(21): -0.3, RF(2): 0.1	0.4
2015	HOU	MLB	22	250	29	10	2	6	22	13	82	8	3	.219/.263/.350	.231	.302	0.6	CF -2, RF 0	-0.2

Breakout: 3%   Improve: 15%   Collapse: 1%   Attrition: 11%   MLB: 30%   *Comparables: Jordan Schafer, Felix Pie, Michael Saunders*

Without a plus-plus tool, 21-year-old Hernandez is going to have a hell of a time standing out in Houston's current gaggle of young outfielders. He does most everything well, playing an adequate center, running the bases aggressively and effectively, hitting for gap and distance pop and walking enough in Rookie and A-Ball to avoid the hacker tag. The trouble is, he doesn't do any of those things well enough to take at-bats away from higher-ceilinged Domingo Santana, Nick Marisnick and that George Springer fellow. He'll continue to bang away in the minors, but earning even a fifth-outfielder gig behind all of those righty bats will be a challenge.

Anthony Kemp 2B

Born: 10/31/91   Age: 23   Bats: L   Throws: R   Height: 5' 6"   Weight: 165

YEAR	TEAM	LVL	AGE	PA	R	2B	3B	HR	RBI	BB	K	SB	CS	AVG/OBP/SLG	TAv	BABIP	BRR	FRAA	WARP
2013	QUD	A	21	120	21	1	1	1	9	19	18	4	2	.255/.387/.316	.269	.304	0.9	2B(17): 1.1, CF(3): -0.2	0.7
2013	TCV	A-	21	204	25	7	2	1	13	21	29	17	9	.282/.355/.362	.278	.325	-1.1	2B(47): 1.2, LF(3): 0.1	0.9
2014	LNC	A+	22	356	79	19	4	4	37	45	35	28	7	.336/.433/.468	.318	.367	7.2	2B(64): -2.7	3.7
2014	CCH	AA	22	275	42	11	4	4	21	28	32	13	6	.292/.381/.425	.286	.322	5.7	2B(56): -1.9, LF(3): 0.1	1.9
2015	HOU	MLB	23	250	29	9	2	2	17	22	45	9	3	.243/.320/.323	.248	.290	0.5	2B -1, LF 0	0.4

Breakout: 3%   Improve: 20%   Collapse: 1%   Attrition: 8%   MLB: 29%   Comparables: *Eric Sogard, Johnny Giavotella, Dustin Ackley*

In any other system, a five-and-a-half-foot package of explosive baseball athleticism putting up these kinds of numbers would have attracted more attention. At the very least, you would see a devoted following of super-fans harassing the national prospect pundits and distributing their own #freeTonyKemp t-shirts. But he does play for the Astros, who have this Altuve guy playing for them, a second baseman who shares all of Kemp's compelling qualities and then some. Look for the Astros to experiment with Kemp on the left side of the infield in 2015 in the hopes that he can function in superutility. He might just wind up as half of the shortest one-two punch in big-league history.

Jed Lowrie SS

Born: 4/17/84   Age: 31   Bats: B   Throws: R   Height: 6' 0"   Weight: 190

YEAR	TEAM	LVL	AGE	PA	R	2B	3B	HR	RBI	BB	K	SB	CS	AVG/OBP/SLG	TAv	BABIP	BRR	FRAA	WARP
2012	HOU	MLB	28	387	43	18	0	16	42	43	65	2	0	.244/.331/.438	.283	.257	0.6	SS(93): 5.0	3.3
2013	OAK	MLB	29	662	80	45	2	15	75	50	91	1	0	.290/.344/.446	.291	.319	-0.1	SS(119): -6.7, 2B(24): -3.3	3.7
2014	OAK	MLB	30	566	59	29	3	6	50	51	79	0	0	.249/.321/.355	.257	.281	-1.9	SS(130): -7.8	1.0
2015	HOU	MLB	31	552	55	29	2	12	61	46	91	1	0	.259/.323/.397	.273	.291	-0.5	SS -5, 2B -0	2.4

Breakout: 0%   Improve: 37%   Collapse: 7%   Attrition: 4%   MLB: 95%   Comparables: *Stephen Drew, Nomar Garciaparra, Jimmy Rollins*

Today's Tom Sawyer established a modicum of health during his two years in Oakland following an injury-riddled start to his career. Lowrie's 2014 performance told a different story than years past, including the worst full-season OPS of his career and an evaporation of the power that previously allowed teams to forgive his lackluster defense at shortstop. A's writers became fond of an apology for Lowrie's defensive skills that went, "He makes plays on the balls he gets to." True enough, but hardly the point: His lack of range has become a serious liability, particularly now that he's playing on a team with no second base exit chute.

Jake Marisnick CF

Born: 3/30/91   Age: 24   Bats: R   Throws: R   Height: 6' 4"   Weight: 225

YEAR	TEAM	LVL	AGE	PA	R	2B	3B	HR	RBI	BB	K	SB	CS	AVG/OBP/SLG	TAv	BABIP	BRR	FRAA	WARP
2012	DUN	A+	21	306	41	18	7	6	35	26	55	10	5	.263/.349/.451	.271	.309	-1.2	CF(63): 2.1	1.8
2012	NHP	AA	21	247	25	11	3	2	15	11	45	14	4	.233/.286/.336	.238	.278	2.5	CF(55): 3.3	0.9
2013	JAX	AA	22	298	43	13	3	12	46	17	68	11	6	.294/.358/.502	.311	.351	1.9	CF(54): 3.4, LF(11): 0.3	3.3
2013	MIA	MLB	22	118	6	2	1	1	5	6	27	3	1	.183/.231/.248	.193	.232	0.4	CF(32): 0.8	-0.1
2014	NWO	AAA	23	377	50	16	4	10	40	17	64	24	6	.277/.326/.434	.274	.314	1.7	CF(81): -0.9, RF(4): 0.1	2.0
2014	MIA	MLB	23	51	3	0	0	0	0	3	19	5	0	.167/.216/.167	.150	.276	0.1	CF(13): 2.4	-0.2
2014	HOU	MLB	23	186	18	8	3	0	19	5	48	6	3	.272/.299/.370	.247	.352	1.1	RF(31): 2.5, CF(17): 1.4	0.9
2015	HOU	MLB	24	292	35	11	2	6	24	11	71	12	3	.235/.277/.356	.239	.289	0.6	CF 3, RF 1	0.7

Breakout: 13%   Improve: 38%   Collapse: 6%   Attrition: 21%   MLB: 55%   Comparables: *Felix Pie, Franklin Gutierrez, Jordan Schafer*

It was clear that the Marlins had no room for Marisnick in their young outfield when he didn't make the 2014 Opening Day roster. His brief call-up didn't help his case either. Just when the season was going downhill, he was dealt to Houston, where, as a center fielder, he could go uphill in both the metaphorical and topographical sense. He shows little patience at the plate and has trouble picking up breaking pitches, but he can still play a mean center field. The Astros outfield could get crowded; if Marisnick wants to plant his flag on Tal's Hill, he might want to consider an OBP on the good side of .300.

Colin Moran SS

Born: 10/1/92   Age: 22   Bats: L   Throws: R   Height: 6' 4"   Weight: 215

YEAR	TEAM	LVL	AGE	PA	R	2B	3B	HR	RBI	BB	K	SB	CS	AVG/OBP/SLG	TAv	BABIP	BRR	FRAA	WARP
2013	GRB	A	20	175	19	8	1	4	23	15	25	1	0	.299/.354/.442	.300	.323	-1.0	3B(33): -0.5	1.0
2014	JUP	A+	21	392	34	21	0	5	33	28	53	1	2	.294/.342/.393	.271	.330	-2.3	3B(86): -4.1	1.1
2014	CCH	AA	21	123	12	6	0	2	22	9	23	0	1	.304/.350/.411	.269	.360	-0.7	3B(28): 0.4	0.5
2015	HOU	MLB	22	250	20	11	1	4	24	13	56	0	0	.239/.280/.337	.236	.294	-0.5	3B -2	-0.3

Breakout: 0%   Improve: 0%   Collapse: 0%   Attrition: 0%   MLB: 0%   Comparables: *Neil Walker, Ryan Wheeler, Jake Smolinski*

Moran and Matt Dominguez share some obvious traits: They are both high-profile expat (or "castoff") third basemen who got their starts in the Marlins system. Both now collect Astros paychecks. Less obvious commonalities include near-*identical* minor-league career strikeout and walk rates, and a mere 24-point spread in farm OPS. Their age-21 peripherals were especially close. That's not a favorable comparison for offense-first Moran, who's been riding the "polished college bat" rep since Florida took him sixth overall in the 2013 draft. To take Dominguez's job, he'll have to do a better job delivering on that label in 2015.

Gregorio Petit SS

Born: 12/10/84   Age: 30   Bats: R   Throws: R   Height: 5' 10"   Weight: 195

YEAR	TEAM	LVL	AGE	PA	R	2B	3B	HR	RBI	BB	K	SB	CS	AVG/OBP/SLG	TAv	BABIP	BRR	FRAA	WARP
2012	COH	AAA	27	422	51	24	0	10	45	29	75	1	2	.260/.320/.403	.241	.297	-1.1	SS(82): 12.9, 3B(30): 3.4	2.6
2013	TUC	AAA	28	555	55	26	3	4	61	40	75	5	3	.292/.344/.380	.253	.334	1.0	SS(91): -1.2, 3B(48): -1.7	1.5
2014	OKL	AAA	29	347	46	19	1	10	43	20	52	1	3	.297/.340/.457	.281	.324	0.5	SS(65): 10.0, 3B(12): 0.5	3.2
2014	HOU	MLB	29	100	14	8	0	2	9	1	25	0	0	.278/.300/.423	.263	.357	0.5	SS(19): -0.9, 3B(12): 0.1	0.5
2015	HOU	MLB	30	250	22	11	1	3	22	12	51	1	1	.241/.281/.339	.237	.288	-0.6	SS 2, 3B 0	0.6

Breakout: 0%   Improve: 5%   Collapse: 1%   Attrition: 5%   MLB: 11%   Comparables: *Blake Davis, Jason Alfaro, Brian Barden*

In one of the year's quieter feel-good stories, Petit returned to the majors four seasons removed from his last appearance. Credit it to persistence, or stubbornness, or maybe some quality Triple-A numbers for once. The well-traveled minor leaguer was rewarded for his finest power numbers with two months as the Astros' backup infielder. At worst he's a Triple-A mentor who had one lucky season, but he could be a cheap replacement-level utilityman, which isn't much to most but it's the world to him.

Brett Phillips CF

Born: 5/30/94   Age: 21   Bats: L   Throws: R   Height: 6' 0"   Weight: 175

YEAR	TEAM	LVL	AGE	PA	R	2B	3B	HR	RBI	BB	K	SB	CS	AVG/OBP/SLG	TAv	BABIP	BRR	FRAA	WARP
2013	QUD	A	19	44	4	2	0	0	3	3	10	1	1	.231/.286/.282	.233	.310	-0.5	CF(12): 0.7	0.0
2014	QUD	A	20	443	68	21	12	13	58	36	76	18	10	.302/.362/.521	.320	.341	2.3	RF(60): 5.3, CF(44): -2.1	4.5
2014	LNC	A+	20	128	19	8	2	4	10	14	20	5	4	.339/.421/.560	.341	.384	0.4	CF(27): -2.1	1.4
2015	HOU	MLB	21	250	28	9	2	4	21	14	62	5	3	.230/.278/.349	.234	.283	-0.1	CF -1, RF 1	0.0

Breakout: 0%   Improve: 0%   Collapse: 0%   Attrition: 0%   MLB: 0%   Comparables: Austin Jackson, Joc Pederson, Andrew McCutchen

Phillips flashed five-tool numbers in a breakout ascent through the Midwest and California Leagues, earning him legitimate prospect status and hardware as the Astros' farm player of the year. Scouts remain split when projecting the all-important hit and power tools, however, and skeptics will point out that five of thirteen Midwest League homers landed on the hitter-friendly porch in Quad Cities' right field. To convince folks that he's more Joc Pederson than fourth outfielder, Phillips will have to mash when he gets his shot at Double-A, most likely in the second half of 2015. Like other Astros' outfield prospects, he has a good half-dozen bodies to climb over to earn a full-time big-league gig, though hitting left-handed gives him a boost toward irregular playing time.

Andrew Reed 1B

Born: 5/10/93   Age: 22   Bats: L   Throws: L   Height: 6' 4"   Weight: 240

YEAR	TEAM	LVL	AGE	PA	R	2B	3B	HR	RBI	BB	K	SB	CS	AVG/OBP/SLG	TAv	BABIP	BRR	FRAA	WARP
2014	QUD	A	21	135	21	9	1	7	24	8	32	0	0	.272/.326/.528	.297	.314	-2.3	1B(18): -1.3	0.4
2014	TCV	A-	21	150	22	11	0	5	30	22	22	2	0	.306/.420/.516	.349	.337	-1.8	1B(31): -0.5	1.3
2015	HOU	MLB	22	250	23	9	1	7	28	13	70	0	0	.215/.263/.355	.234	.272	-0.3	1B -3	-0.7

Breakout: 0%   Improve: 0%   Collapse: 0%   Attrition: 0%   MLB: 0%   Comparables: Chris Marrero, Jesus Aguilar, Jerry Sands

A monster junior season for the University of Kentucky filled Reed's trophy room with sparkly stuff, including the Golden Spikes Award, ABCA National Player of the Year, SEC Player of the Year, SEC Male Athlete of the Year, the John Olerud Trophy and the Dick Howser Trophy. Others, too. Point is, he was the best collegiate player in the country, hands down, serving as the Wildcats' Friday-night starter while putting up a .336/.476/.735 slash line that has no place in college baseball's new dead-bat era. Obviously a guy like that sits out the first round on draft day. Obviously. Scouting is strange business.

Rio Ruiz 3B

Born: 5/22/94   Age: 21   Bats: L   Throws: R   Height: 6' 2"   Weight: 215

YEAR	TEAM	LVL	AGE	PA	R	2B	3B	HR	RBI	BB	K	SB	CS	AVG/OBP/SLG	TAv	BABIP	BRR	FRAA	WARP
2013	QUD	A	19	472	46	33	1	12	63	50	92	12	3	.260/.335/.430	.275	.303	-3.6	3B(111): -8.0	1.3
2014	LNC	A+	20	602	76	37	2	11	77	82	91	4	4	.293/.387/.436	.286	.335	-4.0	3B(122): -9.4	2.8
2015	HOU	MLB	21	250	21	11	1	3	22	21	59	1	0	.218/.286/.312	.232	.277	-0.4	3B -4	-0.6

Breakout: 0%   Improve: 0%   Collapse: 0%   Attrition: 0%   MLB: 0%   Comparables: Taylor Green, Jake Smolinski, Matt Dominguez

After watching his Lancaster teammates out-slug him throughout the first half, Ruiz finally began to lift the ball into the midsummer desert winds, fueling a long-awaited .333/.424/.590 July power surge. The numbers tanked in August, corresponding with the quad injury that eventually benched him, but he returned to slash .333/.459/.519 in Lancaster's successful California League playoff run. Positive trends in contact and walk rate scream elite hitter in the making, but scouts remain skeptical of his distance power, which (but for July) exists predominantly as a projection based on body type and his knack for good contact. His poor Arizona Fall League showing did nothing to change that perception. Through it all he fielded well enough to not lose third base, which might sound like faint praise, but represents a big victory for a guy whose easiest path to Houston is as a sort of anti-Matt Dominguez.

Domingo Santana LF

Born: 8/5/92   Age: 22   Bats: R   Throws: R   Height: 6' 5"   Weight: 225

YEAR	TEAM	LVL	AGE	PA	R	2B	3B	HR	RBI	BB	K	SB	CS	AVG/OBP/SLG	TAv	BABIP	BRR	FRAA	WARP
2012	LNC	A+	19	525	87	26	6	23	97	55	148	7	1	.302/.385/.536	.311	.397	-1.1	RF(114): -7.8	2.9
2013	CCH	AA	20	476	72	23	2	25	64	46	139	12	5	.252/.345/.498	.296	.316	0.2	RF(100): -3.9, CF(8): 0.0	2.9
2014	OKL	AAA	21	513	63	27	2	16	81	64	149	6	4	.296/.384/.474	.302	.408	0.7	RF(59): 0.6, LF(49): 2.3	3.5
2014	HOU	MLB	21	18	1	0	0	0	1	1	14	0	0	.000/.056/.000	.065	.000	0.1	LF(3): -0.4, RF(2): -0.1	-0.4
2015	HOU	MLB	22	250	28	10	1	8	30	21	85	2	1	.229/.302/.392	.265	.324	-0.2	RF -2, LF 0	0.4

Breakout: 2%   Improve: 29%   Collapse: 1%   Attrition: 14%   MLB: 51%   Comparables: Michael Choice, Oswaldo Arcia, Chris Carter

Santana paced all Triple-A hitters with a .408 BABIP and yet still couldn't quite touch a .300 batting average. It doesn't seem entirely fluky, either: He hits tons of line drives and groundballs, hits them with plenty of authority to the opposite field, and he runs well, which all support the BABIP; but he struck out in a full 29 percent of his PA's, suppressing his batting average. He also won't add much to his average with big flies, despite the obvious big-human power, because less than a quarter of his contact goes for outfield fly balls. That's an equilibrium that seems, well, unique. To stick in the majors, he'll have to trade some of the inevitable regression to his BABIP for either more home runs or fewer strikeouts, with the former seeming most likely.

Joe Sclafani   UT

Born: 4/22/90   Age: 25   Bats: B   Throws: R   Height: 5' 11"   Weight: 190

YEAR	TEAM	LVL	AGE	PA	R	2B	3B	HR	RBI	BB	K	SB	CS	AVG/OBP/SLG	TAv	BABIP	BRR	FRAA	WARP
2012	TCV	A-	22	311	39	9	3	1	36	33	40	16	3	.271/.355/.338	.283	.310	2.0	SS(70): -5.9	1.4
2013	QUD	A	23	81	13	3	0	0	9	17	7	3	2	.241/.430/.293	.320	.269	0.8	2B(10): -0.1, SS(10): 1.0	1.0
2013	LNC	A+	23	406	81	28	5	7	53	52	60	16	3	.302/.396/.474	.296	.345	2.3	3B(28): 0.3, SS(23): -0.6	3.1
2014	CCH	AA	24	157	14	4	2	1	15	10	13	2	2	.285/.333/.361	.259	.305	-0.1	3B(17): 0.1, 2B(12): -0.6	0.3
2014	OKL	AAA	24	226	38	7	3	2	25	26	27	7	2	.339/.420/.438	.299	.387	0.2	2B(42): 2.6, 3B(14): 0.7	2.0
2015	HOU	MLB	25	250	26	10	2	1	17	21	45	4	1	.244/.313/.320	.245	.292	0.1	2B 0, SS -0	0.4

Breakout: 1%   Improve: 2%   Collapse: 9%   Attrition: 19%   MLB: 25%   Comparables: *Callix Crabbe, Cole Figueroa, Jake Elmore*

Ideally, you'd like to see a Dartmouth draftee bring some serious WASP to a system's name pool: Chester Emerson, Art Quirk, Zeke Bella and Rusty Yarnall were all upper-crusty Dartmouth alums who made notable contributions to the big leagues. Sclafini lacks the Boston Brahmin handle, but he has made a rapid three-season ascent through the Astros' system, and most recently impressed in the Arizona Fall League. While he's never shown much home run power, the switch-hitter makes up for it with positional versatility, an elite contact rate and a career .813 OPS against right-handed pitching. Sclafani could see MLB playing time all over the field these next few years, first as bridge to the bigger name-prospects, then potentially as a long-term utility guy and finally as a tenured classics professor with flexible office hours.

Jonathan Singleton   1B

Born: 9/18/91   Age: 23   Bats: L   Throws: L   Height: 6' 2"   Weight: 255

YEAR	TEAM	LVL	AGE	PA	R	2B	3B	HR	RBI	BB	K	SB	CS	AVG/OBP/SLG	TAv	BABIP	BRR	FRAA	WARP
2012	CCH	AA	20	555	94	27	4	21	79	88	131	7	2	.284/.396/.497	.317	.350	1.0	1B(113): 5.5, LF(19): -1.6	4.2
2013	QUD	A	21	25	6	2	0	3	5	4	5	0	0	.286/.400/.810	.420	.231	0.5	1B(5): 0.3	0.6
2013	CCH	AA	21	48	5	2	1	2	8	9	16	0	0	.263/.396/.526	.351	.381	-0.7	1B(10): -0.5	0.4
2013	OKL	AAA	21	294	31	13	0	6	31	46	89	1	0	.220/.340/.347	.247	.314	-1.4	1B(68): -5.0	-1.1
2014	OKL	AAA	22	239	37	10	1	14	43	42	52	1	1	.267/.397/.544	.307	.292	-0.9	1B(51): -1.6	1.3
2014	HOU	MLB	22	362	42	13	0	13	44	50	134	2	3	.168/.285/.335	.241	.238	-0.5	1B(91): 1.9	-0.2
2015	HOU	MLB	23	347	39	13	1	12	42	47	109	2	1	.213/.321/.381	.268	.288	0.1	1B 0, LF -0	0.7

Breakout: 3%   Improve: 24%   Collapse: 6%   Attrition: 17%   MLB: 55%   Comparables: *Kyle Blanks, Anthony Rizzo, Ryan Lavarnway*

Singleton's June call-up was a shockwaver for the players union, since it coincided with the signing of a five-year, $10 million extension that included club option years through arbitration. One interpretation of the timing suggests a tacit form of coercion; if he's an All-Star in five years, he probably got bilked out of millions. It's early, but so far Singleton is winning the contract; his rookie season numbers didn't quite pass muster. It's not a completely clear picture: The extreme struggles against righties aren't backed up by any sort of minor-league history, and the core of his problems is a low batting average, an overrated measure for a slugger. On the other hand, slugger or not, an average should at minimum begin with a dot followed by a two. There's still plenty of time for him to grow into, at least, an above-average lefty platoon bat alongside Carter, whose own initiation into the league shows a fine resemblance to Singleton's.

George Springer   RF

Born: 9/19/89   Age: 25   Bats: R   Throws: R   Height: 6' 3"   Weight: 205

YEAR	TEAM	LVL	AGE	PA	R	2B	3B	HR	RBI	BB	K	SB	CS	AVG/OBP/SLG	TAv	BABIP	BRR	FRAA	WARP
2012	LNC	A+	22	500	101	18	10	22	82	56	131	28	6	.316/.398/.557	.327	.404	8.9	CF(103): -1.7	5.9
2012	CCH	AA	22	81	8	3	0	2	5	6	25	4	2	.219/.288/.342	.233	.304	1.4	CF(13): 0.3, RF(7): -0.3	0.1
2013	CCH	AA	23	323	56	20	0	19	55	42	96	23	5	.297/.399/.579	.350	.390	4.9	CF(70): -2.8, LF(3): -0.0	4.4
2013	OKL	AAA	23	267	50	7	4	18	53	41	65	22	3	.311/.425/.626	.373	.362	1.6	CF(47): -0.7, RF(11): -0.4	4.1
2014	OKL	AAA	24	61	17	4	1	3	9	9	15	4	0	.353/.459/.647	.367	.455	1.4	RF(7): -0.3	1.0
2014	HOU	MLB	24	345	45	8	1	20	51	39	114	5	2	.231/.336/.468	.304	.294	0.5	RF(71): 0.5, CF(8): 0.9	2.3
2015	HOU	MLB	25	336	47	11	2	16	48	35	108	12	3	.246/.334/.459	.300	.325	0.9	RF -1, CF -1	2.1

Breakout: 4%   Improve: 42%   Collapse: 3%   Attrition: 16%   MLB: 83%   Comparables: *Dallas McPherson, Jonny Gomes, Paul Goldschmidt*

If we're going to fault Springer for striking out too much, then we need to fault every teenager who stares at his phone during a family dinner. They're going to do it because it's their generation's modus operandi, so let's commend them on what else they bring to the table. Springer had the worst contact rate of any player in 2013 (minimum 300 PAs) at 61 percent. That's bad. However, his walk rate was 11 percent, which is above average. There have been about 50 rookies in history to knock 20 homers and walk 10 percent of the time, but none struck out as much. Fred McGriff and Kevin Maas came close, but neither grew up with unlimited texting and data, either. Live with the strikeouts, enjoy the OPS.

Max Stassi   DH

Born: 3/15/91   Age: 24   Bats: R   Throws: R   Height: 5' 10"   Weight: 200

YEAR	TEAM	LVL	AGE	PA	R	2B	3B	HR	RBI	BB	K	SB	CS	AVG/OBP/SLG	TAv	BABIP	BRR	FRAA	WARP
2012	STO	A+	21	360	48	18	0	15	45	27	83	3	1	.268/.331/.468	.289	.304	-1.5	C(66): -0.3	2.1
2013	CCH	AA	22	323	40	20	1	17	60	19	68	1	1	.277/.333/.529	.299	.301	-3.4	C(50): 0.3	2.2
2013	HOU	MLB	22	8	0	0	0	0	1	0	2	0	0	.286/.375/.286	.210	.400	-0.4	C(1): -0.0	-0.1
2014	OKL	AAA	23	425	49	20	2	9	45	22	103	1	0	.247/.296/.378	.243	.312	-4.5	C(72): -1.2	0.2
2014	HOU	MLB	23	20	2	2	0	0	4	0	6	0	0	.350/.350/.450	.299	.500	0.9	C(6): -0.0	0.3
2015	HOU	MLB	24	250	23	10	1	7	28	10	69	0	0	.227/.268/.364	.240	.285	-0.4	C -0	0.2

Breakout: 5%   Improve: 16%   Collapse: 14%   Attrition: 30%   MLB: 35%   Comparables: *Welington Castillo, Yan Gomes, Lucas May*

There is a theory about action films arguing that audiences must see the male hero suffer, be physically brutalized, in order to value his kick-assing that follows. If baseball were that movie, than Stassi is that hero—he must be the only guy in the game ever to earn his first major-league RBI by taking a fastball to the face, and seemingly every year some crucial joint in his body spontaneously implodes—but he finally stayed healthy enough to reach 400 plate appearances for the first time since 2010. He has sufficient catch-and-throw skills and enough occasional pop to play a reserve role now, so look for him to serve as Jason Castro's caddy or platoon partner for a couple of years. Because injuries have so disrupted his development and perceived ceiling, it might take that long for the Astros to determine whether or not he's their catcher and hero of the future.

Ronald Torreyes 2B

Born: 9/2/92 Age: 22 Bats: R Throws: R Height: 5' 10" Weight: 150

YEAR	TEAM	LVL	AGE	PA	R	2B	3B	HR	RBI	BB	K	SB	CS	AVG/OBP/SLG	TAv	BABIP	BRR	FRAA	WARP
2012	DAY	A+	19	474	62	23	5	6	47	32	29	13	4	.264/.326/.385	.253	.268	3.9	2B(91): -5.4, SS(20): -1.8	0.7
2013	CCH	AA	20	162	19	6	2	0	12	6	14	1	1	.278/.310/.344	.240	.307	0.2	SS(23): 0.6, 2B(15): -0.4	0.3
2013	TEN	AA	20	265	32	13	4	2	25	22	15	4	0	.263/.340/.384	.256	.270	-2.7	2B(54): -2.0	0.0
2014	OKL	AAA	21	519	65	20	5	2	46	25	26	12	9	.298/.345/.376	.270	.310	3.9	2B(73): -1.2, 3B(24): -0.0	2.9
2015	HOU	MLB	22	250	24	10	2	1	17	9	28	3	2	.249/.287/.327	.236	.267	-0.1	2B -1, SS -0	0.1

Breakout: 0% Improve: 0% Collapse: 0% Attrition: 0% MLB: 0% Comparables: Johnny Giavotella, Chris Getz, Alexi Amarista

At just 22, Torreyes is the youngest of a growing pool of potential utility types Houston has accumulated in its upper levels. It's a tough big-league profile: Right-handed hitters who lack secondary skills and are pushed off shortstop at 20 tend not to have the best outcomes, but Torreyes fanned just 25 times in 519 plate appearances last season against competition averaging almost six years his senior. That kind of precocious performance earns more looks, if not devotion, from parent clubs. Twice-traded already, it's easy to envision the Astros packaging him again should he lose the utility scramble.

Danry Vasquez LF

Born: 1/8/94 Age: 21 Bats: L Throws: R Height: 6' 3" Weight: 177

YEAR	TEAM	LVL	AGE	PA	R	2B	3B	HR	RBI	BB	K	SB	CS	AVG/OBP/SLG	TAv	BABIP	BRR	FRAA	WARP
2012	WMI	A	18	112	5	3	0	1	7	7	20	0	0	.162/.218/.222	.173	.185	1.3	LF(28): -0.7	-0.8
2012	ONE	A-	18	311	36	16	2	2	35	13	45	6	4	.311/.341/.401	.303	.361	-2.1	LF(62): -0.1, RF(9): 1.1	2.1
2013	QUD	A	19	128	12	2	1	3	20	6	15	2	0	.288/.323/.398	.285	.304	-1.1	LF(32): 1.3	0.5
2013	WMI	A	19	423	47	16	5	6	40	31	56	9	8	.283/.334/.400	.279	.313	-0.7	LF(96): 0.2	1.3
2014	LNC	A+	20	475	67	30	2	5	47	40	68	1	2	.291/.353/.407	.266	.335	-1.6	RF(62): -6.2, LF(31): 0.6	0.0
2015	HOU	MLB	21	250	18	10	1	2	21	10	54	1	1	.226/.258/.306	.215	.274	-0.4	LF 0, RF -1	-0.8

Breakout: 0% Improve: 0% Collapse: 0% Attrition: 0% MLB: 0% Comparables: Yangervis Solarte, Matt Joyce, Ryan Sweeney

The key get in the Jose Veras trade, Danry Vasquez has been a trendy sleeper pick for three years running now, which says something about how much of a sleeper he really is. Look past the decent 2014 rate stats, because they're entirely the product of Lancaster's windy brand of barely baseball: On the road, Vasquez's OPS plummeted by more than 300 points. He redeemed himself somewhat with a good winter campaign in his native Venezuela, but still didn't show the over-the-fence inclinations necessary to overcome his defensive limitations. He was the 12th-youngest player in the California League last year, so it stands to reason that the Astros will send him back to Lancaster, hoping, as with many a young man his age, he finally quits hitting snooze.

Jonathan Villar SS

Born: 5/2/91 Age: 24 Bats: B Throws: R Height: 6' 1" Weight: 205

YEAR	TEAM	LVL	AGE	PA	R	2B	3B	HR	RBI	BB	K	SB	CS	AVG/OBP/SLG	TAv	BABIP	BRR	FRAA	WARP
2012	CCH	AA	21	377	54	7	2	11	50	35	87	39	8	.261/.336/.396	.269	.319	3.9	SS(85): 7.2	3.1
2013	OKL	AAA	22	386	47	16	8	8	41	32	93	31	7	.277/.341/.442	.272	.358	1.2	SS(88): 9.3	3.5
2013	HOU	MLB	22	241	26	9	2	1	8	24	71	18	6	.243/.321/.319	.237	.362	3.4	SS(58): -6.2	0.0
2014	OKL	AAA	23	225	34	2	3	3	27	31	61	24	6	.258/.363/.347	.267	.362	4.4	SS(48): 2.2	1.6
2014	HOU	MLB	23	289	31	13	2	7	27	19	80	17	4	.209/.267/.354	.227	.271	4.0	SS(82): 6.6	1.2
2015	HOU	MLB	24	342	46	11	3	6	26	27	97	24	6	.230/.294/.343	.240	.303	3.4	SS 1	1.3

Breakout: 6% Improve: 32% Collapse: 5% Attrition: 15% MLB: 67% Comparables: Stephen Drew, Jhonny Peralta, Mark Teahen

Villar "won" the Astros' starting shortstop job, but by the end of June his OBP was .255 and he was OTW to OKC. He returned to Houston in September but had merely added "error prone" to his problems. The main advancement in his game has been becoming a smarter baserunner, as he slowed the overzealousness that cost him outs in his rookie season. And he's still young enough to figure out how to reach first base and to refine his shortstop defense; or more bluntly, the two things that separate a starting shortstop from a full-time pinch runner.

Pitchers

Matt Albers RHP

Born: 1/20/83 Age: 32 Bats: L Throws: R Height: 6'1" Weight: 225

YEAR	TEAM	LVL	AGE	W	L	SV	G	GS	IP	H	HR	BB	K	BB/9	K/9	GB%	BABIP	WHIP	ERA	FIP	FRA	WARP
2012	ARI	MLB	29	1	1	0	23	0	21	16	3	7	19	3.0	8.1	60%	.241	1.10	2.57	4.33	5.19	-0.1
2012	BOS	MLB	29	2	0	0	40	0	39¹	30	6	15	25	3.4	5.7	56%	.218	1.14	2.29	4.98	5.95	-0.3
2013	CLE	MLB	30	3	1	0	56	0	63	57	2	23	35	3.3	5.0	66%	.274	1.27	3.14	3.52	4.52	0.1
2014	HOU	MLB	31	0	0	0	8	0	10	10	0	3	8	2.7	7.2	53%	.333	1.30	0.90	2.76	2.03	0.3
2015	HOU	MLB	32	2	1	0	32	0	34²	33	3	14	27	3.6	7.1	53%	.288	1.36	4.01	4.44	4.36	0.2

Breakout: 21% Improve: 46% Collapse: 31% Attrition: 15% MLB: 95% Comparables: Danys Baez, Peter Moylan, Jeremy Affeldt

In an alternative Xbox reality where injuries were turned off, Albers enjoyed a surprising breakout year, turning into the league's best closer and aligning himself to be one of the most coveted midseason trade acquisitions. Instead he missed the last five months of the season due to right shoulder tendinitis and a motorcade of setbacks. As wonderful as the April sample looks (in one inning batters swung and missed eight times on 14 pitches), he'll likely polymorph back into a mortal late-inning sinker-slider soldier spy.

Mark Appel   RHP

Born: 7/15/91   Age: 23   Bats: R   Throws: R   Height: 6'5"   Weight: 225

YEAR	TEAM	LVL	AGE	W	L	SV	G	GS	IP	H	HR	BB	K	BB/9	K/9	GB%	BABIP	WHIP	ERA	FIP	FRA	WARP
2013	QUD	A	21	3	1	0	8	8	33	30	2	9	27	2.5	7.4	54%	.277	1.18	3.82	3.40	4.58	0.4
2014	LNC	A+	22	2	5	0	12	12	44¹	74	9	11	40	2.2	8.1	49%	.414	1.92	9.74	5.32	6.10	0.5
2014	CCH	AA	22	1	2	0	7	6	39	35	2	13	38	3.0	8.8	46%	.300	1.23	3.69	2.99	3.36	0.6
2015	HOU	MLB	23	4	5	0	15	15	66	76	8	24	45	3.3	6.2	47%	.314	1.51	5.08	5.04	5.52	-0.3

Breakout: 0%   Improve: 0%   Collapse: 0%   Attrition: 0%   MLB: 0%   Comparables: *Kyle Lobstein, Brandon Workman, Anthony Swarzak*

You could almost hear the baseball prospecting world sigh in relief when Appel met *relative* success in Double-A upon leaving his Lancaster nightmare. Yet even at Corpus Christi, he still K'd righties at a meager 16 percent rate, and those same-handed hitters' line-drive rate spiked at the higher level. The substantial change came against Texas League lefties, whom he fanned at a 33 percent rate while inducing grounders on nearly half of balls put in play, and pop-ups on one in 10. The touted slider may have too often turned to slush, but his changeup took a big step forward. In the Arizona Fall League, the slider again drew rave reviews, but righties continued to fan only at a mediocre 19 percent rate, so evaluators may have to rewrite the book on Appel yet. He's going to be a major-league starter, and possibly a quite good one, but probably not in quite the same mold that scouts had envisioned prior to both of his first-round selections.

Jake Buchanan   RHP

Born: 9/24/89   Age: 25   Bats: R   Throws: R   Height: 6'0"   Weight: 235

YEAR	TEAM	LVL	AGE	W	L	SV	G	GS	IP	H	HR	BB	K	BB/9	K/9	GB%	BABIP	WHIP	ERA	FIP	FRA	WARP
2012	CCH	AA	22	5	9	0	27	19	134¹	171	11	33	83	2.2	5.6	57%	.346	1.52	4.96	3.98	5.48	-0.5
2013	CCH	AA	23	7	2	1	18	13	82	67	4	9	44	1.0	4.8	57%	.250	0.93	2.09	3.02	4.52	0.8
2013	OKL	AAA	23	5	5	0	12	12	76¹	85	6	13	55	1.5	6.5	58%	.326	1.28	3.89	3.66	4.40	0.8
2014	OKL	AAA	24	7	5	0	16	15	88¹	95	7	16	46	1.6	4.7	65%	.296	1.26	3.87	4.33	6.07	0.0
2014	HOU	MLB	24	1	3	0	17	2	35¹	41	4	12	20	3.1	5.1	62%	.316	1.50	4.58	4.60	4.96	-0.1
2015	HOU	MLB	25	6	6	0	22	16	109	123	11	27	55	2.2	4.5	56%	.301	1.37	4.41	4.74	4.80	0.1

Breakout: 28%   Improve: 37%   Collapse: 6%   Attrition: 31%   MLB: 51%   Comparables: *Brandon Cumpton, Chad Jenkins, Anthony Vasquez*

Jake Buchanan is a one-trick guy. He induced a 60 percent groundball rate in the majors last year—a hair under what he managed in Triple-A—which easily would have placed him in the top ten on that particular leaderboard had he pitched more innings. Since 2011, there have been 41 MLB pitching seasons of 70 innings or more that feature 50 percent-plus groundball rates and sub-15 percent strikeout rates. Together, those pitchers have averaged ERAs and FIPs that are 0.4 runs above the MLB average. Buchanan will no doubt earn more opportunities as a spot starter and swingman, but his one-trick predecessors offer little precedent for him becoming more than replacement-level filler.

Kevin Chapman   LHP

Born: 2/19/88   Age: 27   Bats: L   Throws: L   Height: 6'3"   Weight: 225

YEAR	TEAM	LVL	AGE	W	L	SV	G	GS	IP	H	HR	BB	K	BB/9	K/9	GB%	BABIP	WHIP	ERA	FIP	FRA	WARP
2012	CCH	AA	24	6	3	2	49	0	58	49	2	32	59	5.0	9.2	48%	.290	1.40	2.64	3.40	4.01	0.7
2013	OKL	AAA	25	1	2	2	45	0	50²	42	2	36	61	6.4	10.8	55%	.310	1.54	3.20	3.87	3.67	1.0
2013	HOU	MLB	25	1	1	1	25	0	20¹	13	1	13	15	5.8	6.6	45%	.211	1.28	1.77	4.30	3.88	0.1
2014	OKL	AAA	26	2	1	9	43	0	44	38	0	25	64	5.1	13.1	55%	.373	1.43	1.23	2.56	2.09	1.8
2014	HOU	MLB	26	2	0	0	21	0	21¹	22	3	11	19	4.6	8.0	52%	.297	1.55	4.64	4.75	4.77	0.0
2015	HOU	MLB	27	3	1	3	50	0	57²	52	5	31	62	4.8	9.7	49%	.305	1.43	3.98	4.25	4.33	0.3

Breakout: 21%   Improve: 31%   Collapse: 23%   Attrition: 29%   MLB: 60%   Comparables: *Pedro Strop, Cory Gearrin, Royce Ring*

Take out Chapman's horrendous April trial with the Astros, during which he yielded seven walks and two home runs in only 3 2/3 innings, and suddenly the hard-throwing southpaw looks the part of future bullpen mainstay. After returning to the big leagues for good in mid-August, he put up a 2.30 ERA in 16 surprisingly high-leverage innings, with just two walks surrendered. He was a different pitcher down the stretch, throwing a) more sinkers to double his groundball rate, b) way more strikes, going from 5th percentile among MLB pitchers to 85th percentile, and c) more change ups to righties, which correlated with increasingly lethal results against opposite-handers. Which is the real Chapman? Well, between big-league stints, he struck out 33 percent of PCL opponents while inducing a 51 percent groundball rate, so the tonnage is on his side. Chapman is a big reason why Houston's league-worst relief unit is going to be ... well, probably no worse than 29th best this year.

Samuel Deduno   RHP

Born: 7/2/83   Age: 31   Bats: R   Throws: R   Height: 6'3"   Weight: 190

YEAR	TEAM	LVL	AGE	W	L	SV	G	GS	IP	H	HR	BB	K	BB/9	K/9	GB%	BABIP	WHIP	ERA	FIP	FRA	WARP
2012	ROC	AAA	28	1	2	0	9	9	42	27	2	22	46	4.7	9.9	65%	.250	1.17	2.14	3.44	4.90	0.1
2012	MIN	MLB	28	6	5	0	15	15	79	69	10	53	57	6.0	6.5	60%	.266	1.54	4.44	5.45	6.55	-0.6
2013	ROC	AAA	29	0	0	0	3	3	16²	14	1	10	17	5.4	9.2	50%	.317	1.44	2.70	3.74	4.10	0.2
2013	MIN	MLB	29	8	8	0	18	18	108	105	7	41	67	3.4	5.6	62%	.291	1.35	3.83	4.07	5.01	0.2
2014	MIN	MLB	30	2	5	0	30	8	92	92	9	41	74	4.0	7.2	55%	.303	1.45	4.60	4.49	5.29	0.0
2014	HOU	MLB	30	0	1	0	5	1	8²	5	0	5	9	5.2	9.3	62%	.238	1.15	3.12	2.81	3.43	0.2
2015	HOU	MLB	31	5	5	0	24	13	89¹	83	8	44	74	4.4	7.4	55%	.290	1.43	4.23	4.81	4.60	0.3

Breakout: 17%   Improve: 27%   Collapse: 9%   Attrition: 15%   MLB: 47%   Comparables: *Clay Hensley, Rich Hill, Luke Hudson*

After two years as a mediocre starter, Deduno moved into the next phase of Dedunoness: Mediocre swingman. He still got his customary 100 innings of work, the final nine coming after the Astros claimed him in late August. He didn't get a velocity bump as a reliever, but something about the role suited him: He struck out nearly a batter per inning (with a Twins-friendly 5.7 Ks per nine as a starter) and produced an ERA 2.50 runs lower in relief. Still, he's bottom of the depth chart in either role.

Scott Feldman   RHP

Born: 2/7/83   Age: 32   Bats: L   Throws: R   Height: 6'7"   Weight: 230

YEAR	TEAM	LVL	AGE	W	L	SV	G	GS	IP	H	HR	BB	K	BB/9	K/9	GB%	BABIP	WHIP	ERA	FIP	FRA	WARP
2012	TEX	MLB	29	6	11	0	29	21	123²	139	14	32	96	2.3	7.0	42%	.318	1.38	5.09	3.77	4.55	1.7
2013	BAL	MLB	30	5	6	0	15	15	90²	80	9	31	65	3.1	6.5	51%	.262	1.22	4.27	4.16	4.62	0.4
2013	CHN	MLB	30	7	6	0	15	15	91	79	10	25	67	2.5	6.6	53%	.255	1.14	3.46	3.90	4.53	0.9
2014	HOU	MLB	31	8	12	0	29	29	180¹	185	16	50	107	2.5	5.3	49%	.291	1.30	3.74	4.14	4.68	0.3
2015	HOU	MLB	32	9	9	0	26	26	152²	160	15	43	104	2.5	6.2	47%	.296	1.32	4.20	4.47	4.56	0.6

Breakout: 17%   Improve: 42%   Collapse: 23%   Attrition: 8%   MLB: 76%   *Comparables: Kyle Lohse, Jake Westbrook, Chien-Ming Wang*

Ten years into a pitcher's career, you hope you know what you're getting, and Feldman's approach (and results) have rarely wavered. This is why Houston forked over multi-year money: He'll stay in the rotation, pitch to contact and not embarrass the team. Only twice in 2014 did he not pitch at least five innings, but only Mark Buehrle had a worse strikeout rate among qualified pitchers. He was also Houston's Opening Day starter, an experience Feldman shouldn't have again unless the entire rest of the pitching staff contracts food poisoning (in which case we should really be asking why Feldman wasn't dining with his teammates). But as rotation slots go, he's a solid no. 4; let him go three times through the order then encouragingly slap his back and thank him for keeping it close.

Michael Feliz   RHP

Born: 6/28/93   Age: 22   Bats: R   Throws: R   Height: 6'4"   Weight: 210

YEAR	TEAM	LVL	AGE	W	L	SV	G	GS	IP	H	HR	BB	K	BB/9	K/9	GB%	BABIP	WHIP	ERA	FIP	FRA	WARP
2013	TCV	A-	19	4	2	1	14	10	69	53	2	13	78	1.7	10.2	53%	.288	0.96	1.96	1.91	2.96	1.7
2014	QUD	A	21	8	6	0	25	19	102²	104	6	37	111	3.2	9.7	41%	.348	1.37	4.03	3.31	3.88	1.7
2015	HOU	MLB	22	3	5	0	17	13	77	88	9	39	54	4.5	6.3	44%	.316	1.64	5.54	5.41	6.02	-0.8

Breakout: 0%   Improve: 0%   Collapse: 0%   Attrition: 0%   MLB: 0%   *Comparables: Charlie Furbush, Jo-Jo Reyes, Shane Greene*

As Feliz's Futures Game went, so went his season. He faced five hitters on the big Minnesota stage, two righties and three lefties, one of whom happened to be Joey Gallo. He looked fantastic burying the two righties, neither of whom could touch his mid-90s heat, though Cubs prospect Kris Bryant just missed a poorly conceived changeup that drifted up and middle. It was the three lefties who hurt him, punctuated by a Gallo homer on a middle fastball. Any pitcher could suffer Gallo's lash, but all six of Feliz's other home runs allowed in 2014 went to lefties, and they OPS'd 267 points better off him than the same-handed guys. That's all a way of saying that he'd better work on his changeup and feel for spotting pitches to opposite-hand hitters.

Josh Fields   RHP

Born: 8/19/85   Age: 29   Bats: R   Throws: R   Height: 6'0"   Weight: 190

YEAR	TEAM	LVL	AGE	W	L	SV	G	GS	IP	H	HR	BB	K	BB/9	K/9	GB%	BABIP	WHIP	ERA	FIP	FRA	WARP
2012	PME	AA	26	3	3	8	32	0	44²	30	4	16	59	3.2	11.9	46%	.255	1.03	2.62	2.87	3.32	1.1
2012	PAW	AAA	26	1	0	4	10	0	13²	8	0	2	19	1.3	12.5	36%	.286	0.73	0.00	0.82	0.74	0.7
2013	HOU	MLB	27	1	3	5	41	0	38	31	8	18	40	4.3	9.5	38%	.245	1.29	4.97	5.13	4.79	-0.1
2014	HOU	MLB	28	4	6	4	54	0	54²	50	2	17	70	2.8	11.5	33%	.343	1.23	4.45	2.12	2.70	1.2
2015	HOU	MLB	29	2	1	2	40	0	47²	40	4	21	53	4.0	10.1	42%	.294	1.28	3.46	3.84	3.76	0.6

Breakout: 16%   Improve: 30%   Collapse: 21%   Attrition: 23%   MLB: 68%   *Comparables: Mitch Stetter, Will Harris, Denny Bautista*

If they made blockbuster movies about Astros relievers, we'd be living in a strange society, but Fields' 2014 season had all the twists and turns for one. The plot begins with Fields as Opening Day closer, picking up where he left off in 2013. But a rocky April costs him the ninth-inning job, and after a 2/3-inning, five-run laugher in early May, he gets back to basics and begins posting zeroes. Brief Stan Lee cameo; did you catch it? Then, after a DL trip in June, Fields picks up where he left off, throwing good innings—including working his new changeup more often—and in September returns to the closer's role for two saves before an oblique injury ends his season. High five. Roll credits. Post-credits stinger. Where are my keys? I heard them fall in between the seats. Can't wait for the sequel.

Mike Foltynewicz   RHP

Born: 10/7/91   Age: 23   Bats: R   Throws: R   Height: 6'4"   Weight: 220

YEAR	TEAM	LVL	AGE	W	L	SV	G	GS	IP	H	HR	BB	K	BB/9	K/9	GB%	BABIP	WHIP	ERA	FIP	FRA	WARP
2012	LEX	A	20	14	4	0	27	27	152	145	11	62	125	3.7	7.4	50%	.298	1.36	3.14	4.20	4.62	2.3
2013	LNC	A+	21	1	0	0	7	5	26	31	4	14	29	4.8	10.0	46%	.360	1.73	3.81	5.16	4.63	0.9
2013	CCH	AA	21	5	3	3	23	16	103¹	75	8	52	95	4.5	8.3	55%	.254	1.23	2.87	3.88	4.71	1.0
2014	OKL	AAA	22	7	7	0	21	18	102²	98	10	52	102	4.6	8.9	49%	.322	1.46	5.08	4.79	5.61	0.6
2014	HOU	MLB	22	0	1	0	16	0	18²	23	3	7	14	3.4	6.8	29%	.333	1.61	5.30	4.87	4.43	0.1
2015	HOU	MLB	23	5	7	0	23	18	102¹	108	12	52	75	4.6	6.6	46%	.302	1.56	5.10	5.35	5.54	-0.6

Breakout: 17%   Improve: 24%   Collapse: 3%   Attrition: 23%   MLB: 32%   *Comparables: Felix Doubront, Anthony Ranaudo, Carlos Carrasco*

Foltynewicz notched his first MLB strikeout by firing four consecutive 99 mph bullets at a flailing Jose Bautista. Who could fault the Astros and their fans for imagining, at that moment, that they might have the next coming of Nolan Ryan? Alas, Folty's next 11 innings went less smoothly, due to the same cocktail of walks, home runs and untimely contact that had tormented him in the PCL. Still, the fastball gives him a very good chance of handling high-leverage innings with competence soon, should the Astros elect to keep him in the bullpen. Barring a mind-blowing spring training, he will head back to the minors and keep developing as a starter. And lastly, the WTF: His straight, low-to-mid-80s change became a weapon against righties as the season wound down, generating a 38 percent whiff rate. Who saw that coming?

Luke Gregerson   RHP

Born: 5/14/84   Age: 31   Bats: L   Throws: R   Height: 6'3"   Weight: 200

YEAR	TEAM	LVL	AGE	W	L	SV	G	GS	IP	H	HR	BB	K	BB/9	K/9	GB%	BABIP	WHIP	ERA	FIP	FRA	WARP
2012	SDN	MLB	28	2	0	9	77	0	71²	57	7	21	72	2.6	9.0	52%	.262	1.09	2.39	3.40	3.36	1.1
2013	SDN	MLB	29	6	8	4	73	0	66¹	49	3	18	64	2.4	8.7	47%	.257	1.01	2.71	2.67	2.99	1.1
2014	OAK	MLB	30	5	5	3	72	0	72¹	58	6	15	59	1.9	7.3	54%	.256	1.01	2.12	3.27	4.17	0.2
2015	HOU	MLB	31	3	2	3	64	0	59²	51	5	15	56	2.2	8.5	49%	.281	1.11	2.95	3.59	3.21	1.1

Breakout: 22%   Improve: 41%   Collapse: 29%   Attrition: 13%   MLB: 84%   Comparables: *Aaron Heilman, Jon Rauch, Scott Linebrink*

Gregerson posted his lowest ERA and stingiest walk rate (despite the move into the American League) in six big-league seasons, though his other peripheral stats took a step backward. His modest fastball plays up due to strong command and subtle movement, but he lives and dies by the slider, a pitch with steep vertical break that accounted for 83 percent of his strikeouts in 2014 and which he threw three-quarters of the time when the count reached two strikes. Gregerson offers excellent consistency with a long track record of pitching in high-leverage situations, attributes that will allow him to slide into the closer role if the need arises in Houston. The piratical facial hair he added with the A's will serve him well in any role.

Josh Hader   LHP

Born: 4/7/94   Age: 21   Bats: L   Throws: L   Height: 6'3"   Weight: 160

YEAR	TEAM	LVL	AGE	W	L	SV	G	GS	IP	H	HR	BB	K	BB/9	K/9	GB%	BABIP	WHIP	ERA	FIP	FRA	WARP
2013	DEL	A	19	3	6	0	17	17	85	67	4	42	79	4.4	8.4	46%	.266	1.28	2.65	3.93	4.79	0.3
2013	QUD	A	19	2	0	0	5	5	22¹	14	0	12	16	4.8	6.4	56%	.230	1.16	3.22	4.05	6.40	-0.1
2014	LNC	A+	20	9	2	2	22	15	103¹	76	9	38	112	3.3	9.8	42%	.266	1.10	2.70	4.10	4.45	1.9
2014	CCH	AA	20	1	1	0	5	4	20	16	2	16	24	7.2	10.8	35%	.286	1.60	6.30	4.87	5.14	0.1
2015	HOU	MLB	21	5	6	0	25	15	97¹	94	10	52	80	4.8	7.4	43%	.292	1.50	4.68	5.12	5.09	-0.1

Breakout: 0%   Improve: 0%   Collapse: 0%   Attrition: 0%   MLB: 0%   Comparables: *Aaron Sanchez, Mauricio Robles, Zack Wheeler*

It's very likely that at some point in 2015, a debuting Josh Hader will begin his windup, do his funky little stutter step as he rocks back and have every one of the 3,000 or so fans tuned in to Root Sports Southwest wondering if the network is sending out a glitchy feed. The tick in his delivery is just the beginning of his funk: He generally plays it tight to the first-base side of the rubber, and remains closed for a long time before slinging the ball from a low arm slot. In a system loaded with high-90s arms, it was the "string bean southpaw" who paced Houston's farm with 136 strikeouts, so the funk is working. A former 19th-round prep pick who came to the Astros via the Bud Norris trade, Hader can touch 95 and get swinging strikes when he elevates up in the zone, and he generally made California League hitters look bad, even in wind-tunnel Lancaster. He found the going tougher in Corpus Cristi, where Double-A hitters refused to chase his mediocre off-speed stuff, leading to too many walks. He will need to adjust. Houston viewers worrying about their satellite dishes won't.

Will Harris   RHP

Born: 8/28/84   Age: 30   Bats: R   Throws: R   Height: 6'4"   Weight: 225

YEAR	TEAM	LVL	AGE	W	L	SV	G	GS	IP	H	HR	BB	K	BB/9	K/9	GB%	BABIP	WHIP	ERA	FIP	FRA	WARP
2012	TUL	AA	27	2	1	1	31	0	34¹	26	2	12	46	3.1	12.1	54%	.304	1.11	2.62	2.49	3.24	0.7
2012	CSP	AAA	27	2	0	0	13	0	17²	9	0	1	20	0.5	10.2	64%	.214	0.57	1.02	1.57	2.70	0.6
2012	COL	MLB	27	1	1	0	20	0	17²	27	3	6	19	3.1	9.7	36%	.400	1.87	8.15	4.38	6.21	-0.1
2013	RNO	AAA	28	0	0	2	12	0	11²	12	1	6	23	4.6	17.7	31%	.440	1.54	4.63	2.28	2.46	0.5
2013	ARI	MLB	28	4	1	0	61	0	52²	50	3	15	53	2.6	9.1	49%	.326	1.23	2.91	2.72	3.21	0.7
2014	RNO	AAA	29	3	2	1	43	0	45²	34	3	20	44	3.9	8.7	45%	.259	1.18	0.99	4.27	4.48	0.8
2014	ARI	MLB	29	0	3	0	29	0	29	27	3	9	35	2.8	10.9	36%	.338	1.24	4.34	3.17	3.31	0.4
2015	HOU	MLB	30	3	1	1	57	0	60²	54	5	21	67	3.1	9.9	45%	.305	1.24	3.38	3.57	3.68	0.8

Breakout: 12%   Improve: 30%   Collapse: 12%   Attrition: 22%   MLB: 55%   Comparables: *Mitch Stetter, Juan Salas, Doug Slaten*

A classic two-pitch reliever, Harris continues to toil in middle relief with decent success. He combines a fastball in the range of 91-94 mph with a curveball that comes in about 12 mph slower. In addition to the speed differential, he uses the tandem to manipulate eye levels. The curve typically works the lower half of the zone while the fastball tends to live above the belt. He has a decent idea of where both pitches are going once they leave his hand, but the curve can hang, which leads to some hard-hit balls.

Dallas Keuchel   LHP

Born: 1/1/88   Age: 27   Bats: L   Throws: L   Height: 6'3"   Weight: 210

YEAR	TEAM	LVL	AGE	W	L	SV	G	GS	IP	H	HR	BB	K	BB/9	K/9	GB%	BABIP	WHIP	ERA	FIP	FRA	WARP
2012	OKL	AAA	24	6	4	0	16	16	92¹	92	5	20	50	1.9	4.9	59%	.290	1.21	3.90	3.94	5.13	1.0
2012	HOU	MLB	24	3	8	0	16	16	85¹	93	14	39	38	4.1	4.0	54%	.277	1.55	5.27	5.78	6.91	-0.9
2013	HOU	MLB	25	6	10	0	31	22	153²	184	20	52	123	3.0	7.2	58%	.340	1.54	5.15	4.28	4.47	1.2
2014	HOU	MLB	26	12	9	0	29	29	200	187	11	48	146	2.2	6.6	65%	.296	1.17	2.92	3.24	4.31	1.9
2015	HOU	MLB	27	9	9	0	26	26	159²	169	15	44	102	2.5	5.8	57%	.300	1.34	4.14	4.43	4.50	0.7

Breakout: 26%   Improve: 60%   Collapse: 9%   Attrition: 12%   MLB: 79%   Comparables: *Wade Miley, Ross Detwiler, Clayton Richard*

They weren't ace numbers, but Houston isn't an ace town, which explains how he was the first Astro in 17 years to throw at least five complete games. Keuchel's primary adjustment from the previous year was ditching his curveball and focusing more on his slider, which was thrown at the same velocity and release point as his changeup. This kept righties who had mashed his fastball in previous years guessing, and he induced more popups, groundballs and broken hearts while at the same time limiting homers, line drives and early showers. His two-seamer's groundball rate (77 percent of balls in play) was the highest for any pitcher since Justin Masterson in 2009; if the Astros really want to make the Internet explode, they'll throw us a bone and try a five-man infield behind him. Alternately, they could simply invest in a shortstop with above-average range.

Lance McCullers   RHP

Born: 10/2/93   Age: 21   Bats: L   Throws: R   Height: 6'2"   Weight: 205

YEAR	TEAM	LVL	AGE	W	L	SV	G	GS	IP	H	HR	BB	K	BB/9	K/9	GB%	BABIP	WHIP	ERA	FIP	FRA	WARP
2013	QUD	A	19	6	5	0	25	19	104²	92	3	49	117	4.2	10.1	57%	.327	1.35	3.18	3.05	3.99	1.9
2014	LNC	A+	20	3	6	4	25	18	97	95	18	56	115	5.2	10.7	48%	.321	1.56	5.47	5.73	6.68	0.7
2015	HOU	MLB	21	4	6	0	21	16	82²	85	10	47	74	5.2	8.0	48%	.310	1.61	5.18	5.24	5.63	-0.5

Breakout: 0%   Improve: 0%   Collapse: 0%   Attrition: 0%   MLB: 0%   Comparables: Enny Romero, Gio Gonzalez, Casey Crosby

Lancaster is home to a musical road. Seriously. It plays the *Lone Ranger* theme song to drivers in the middle of the desert. (Originally it was downtown, but folks complained about the noise.) Imagine McCullers barreling down that road before home starts, music pulsating from the ribbed asphalt, the endless desert horizon whirling, his blood pounding. Then, fully amped up, McCullers ascends the mound, screams "Hi-Yo Silver" into the high winds sweeping the ballpark and fires silver bullet mid-90's fastballs and hammer curveballs at the opposition. With single-minded determination, he boosts his home strikeout rate all the way up to 31 percent (an 8 percent gain over games played in cities lacking musical roads) in a desperate bid to minimize contact. The desert elements nevertheless win, and McCullers is undone by a catastrophic 2.8 homers per nine rate that balloons his home ERA to 5.95. "Who was that masked man?" asks no one as dejected fans trickle away. Lancaster is a crazy place.

Collin McHugh   RHP

Born: 6/19/87   Age: 28   Bats: R   Throws: R   Height: 6'2"   Weight: 195

YEAR	TEAM	LVL	AGE	W	L	SV	G	GS	IP	H	HR	BB	K	BB/9	K/9	GB%	BABIP	WHIP	ERA	FIP	FRA	WARP
2012	BIN	AA	25	5	5	0	12	12	74²	63	4	17	65	2.0	7.8	47%	.278	1.07	2.41	3.04	3.79	1.3
2012	BUF	AAA	25	2	4	0	13	13	73²	60	8	29	70	3.5	8.6	50%	.256	1.21	3.42	3.93	4.84	0.4
2012	NYN	MLB	25	0	4	0	8	4	21¹	27	5	8	17	3.4	7.2	39%	.328	1.64	7.59	6.00	6.23	-0.1
2013	TUL	AA	26	1	1	0	2	2	13	9	1	0	12	0.0	8.3	48%	.250	0.69	1.38	2.21	3.02	0.2
2013	CSP	AAA	26	2	2	0	9	9	46²	52	2	14	47	2.7	9.1	46%	.355	1.41	4.63	3.21	4.02	1.1
2013	LVG	AAA	26	3	2	0	9	9	53¹	57	3	13	41	2.2	6.9	47%	.329	1.31	2.87	3.72	4.01	1.4
2013	COL	MLB	26	0	3	0	4	4	19	33	4	2	8	0.9	3.8	40%	.377	1.84	9.95	5.23	6.83	-0.2
2013	NYN	MLB	26	0	1	0	3	1	7	12	2	3	3	3.9	3.9	50%	.385	2.14	10.29	7.16	6.61	-0.2
2014	OKL	AAA	27	0	0	0	5	3	19	15	0	6	13	2.8	6.2	33%	.263	1.11	3.79	3.28	3.60	0.4
2014	HOU	MLB	27	11	9	0	25	25	154²	117	13	41	157	2.4	9.1	45%	.259	1.02	2.73	3.13	3.55	2.7
2015	HOU	MLB	28	8	8	0	24	24	136¹	133	14	43	118	2.8	7.8	46%	.299	1.29	3.96	4.26	4.30	1.0

Breakout: 31%   Improve: 44%   Collapse: 16%   Attrition: 32%   MLB: 66%   Comparables: Guillermo Moscoso, Mike Fiers, Marco Estrada

For the past two years, we wondered in this space whether McHugh, a failing, flailing starting pitcher, could even make it as a reliever, given a career ERA that was just under nine. After being plucked off waivers by Houston, he made the standard mechanical tweaks one does with a career ERA just under nine and was thrust into the Astros rotation. With a higher and more consistent arm slot, he seemed to trade movement for command and a bit more zip, and batters suddenly couldn't square him up. Lo and behold, he was in the Rookie of the Year conversation. (That conversation: "Who do you think should be Rookie of the Year?" "Jose Abreu." "Yeah. Who do you think should finish fourth?") The fact that he owned the league's sixth-lowest BABIP means batters will have better luck this year, since through his struggles and shining moments, he's always thrown oodles of strikes. But it's finally time to say it: He's no reliever.

Pat Neshek   RHP

Born: 9/4/80   Age: 34   Bats: B   Throws: R   Height: 6'3"   Weight: 210

YEAR	TEAM	LVL	AGE	W	L	SV	G	GS	IP	H	HR	BB	K	BB/9	K/9	GB%	BABIP	WHIP	ERA	FIP	FRA	WARP
2012	NOR	AAA	31	3	2	11	35	0	44	42	1	7	49	1.4	10.0	42%	.345	1.11	2.66	1.77	2.85	1.0
2012	OAK	MLB	31	2	1	0	24	0	19²	10	3	6	16	2.7	7.3	35%	.137	0.81	1.37	4.47	4.71	0.1
2013	OAK	MLB	32	2	1	0	45	0	40¹	40	6	15	29	3.3	6.5	35%	.268	1.36	3.35	4.69	4.36	0.1
2014	SLN	MLB	33	7	2	6	71	0	67¹	44	4	9	68	1.2	9.1	37%	.233	0.79	1.87	2.35	2.81	1.4
2015	HOU	MLB	34	3	1	2	50	0	49¹	46	6	16	43	2.9	7.8	39%	.283	1.25	3.67	4.50	3.99	0.5

Breakout: 15%   Improve: 26%   Collapse: 21%   Attrition: 8%   MLB: 52%   Comparables: Brian Sanches, John Bale, Geoff Geary

Fun math fact: The number of National League pitchers who worked more innings than Neshek last year and bettered his .186 TAv allowed is equal to the total number of monkeys that have flown out of Garth Algar's butt. The veteran submariner came out of nowhere to dominate in a set-up role, relying heavily on an improved power sinker that was impossible to square up, along with his normally impressive slider and a glacial changeup that takes five heartbeats to reach the plate. Other highlights included his first All-Star Game appearance and the autographed Babe Ruth baseball John Lackey traded him for the right to wear number 41. Neshek can't possibly keep this up, but he's a good bet to continue his career-long success against same-side hitters, and if he can continue to hold his own against lefties he can work high-leverage innings in Houston.

Brett Oberholtzer   LHP

Born: 7/1/89   Age: 25   Bats: L   Throws: L   Height: 6'1"   Weight: 225

YEAR	TEAM	LVL	AGE	W	L	SV	G	GS	IP	H	HR	BB	K	BB/9	K/9	GB%	BABIP	WHIP	ERA	FIP	FRA	WARP
2012	CCH	AA	22	5	3	0	13	13	77	81	11	21	68	2.5	7.9	54%	.304	1.32	4.21	4.23	4.71	1.0
2012	OKL	AAA	22	5	7	0	15	15	89²	105	13	19	69	1.9	6.9	41%	.324	1.38	4.52	4.71	4.99	1.0
2013	OKL	AAA	23	6	6	0	16	16	80¹	77	9	25	72	2.8	8.1	51%	.296	1.27	4.37	4.24	5.50	0.5
2013	HOU	MLB	23	4	5	0	13	10	71²	66	7	13	45	1.6	5.7	36%	.260	1.10	2.76	3.68	3.92	0.9
2014	OKL	AAA	24	1	2	0	5	5	31	35	9	3	31	0.9	9.0	44%	.306	1.23	4.65	5.86	6.06	-0.1
2014	HOU	MLB	24	5	13	0	24	24	143²	170	12	28	94	1.8	5.9	39%	.325	1.38	4.39	3.58	3.92	1.7
2015	HOU	MLB	25	8	9	0	25	25	147¹	160	17	37	106	2.2	6.5	43%	.305	1.34	4.45	4.47	4.83	0.2

Breakout: 26%   Improve: 46%   Collapse: 16%   Attrition: 28%   MLB: 82%   Comparables: Liam Hendriks, Justin Grimm, Edgar Gonzalez

One argument against putting snakes in a teammate's locker is that they might get revenge by not scoring runs or catching line drives in the games you're pitching. Granted, there's no proof Oberholtzer did this to teammates, but how else *but* snakes in lockers do you explain his ERA coming in 0.83 points higher than his FIP, or the fact that he had the lowest run support (min. 140 IP) in the American League? Luck, perhaps? Maybe left-handed hitters just got the ball in play more often? Pft. Pitchers create their own luck, by not orchestrating snake-in-the-locker pranks on fellow humans. He's a young pitcher with exceptional command who can still lean on a nice 2013 debut. But he'll have to learn.

Brad Peacock   RHP

Born: 2/2/88   Age: 27   Bats: R   Throws: R   Height: 6'1"   Weight: 210

YEAR	TEAM	LVL	AGE	W	L	SV	G	GS	IP	H	HR	BB	K	BB/9	K/9	GB%	BABIP	WHIP	ERA	FIP	FRA	WARP
2012	SAC	AAA	24	12	9	0	28	25	134²	147	16	66	139	4.4	9.3	35%	.340	1.58	6.01	4.73	4.54	1.9
2013	OKL	AAA	25	6	2	0	14	13	79	65	9	22	76	2.5	8.7	39%	.273	1.10	2.73	4.00	4.14	1.0
2013	HOU	MLB	25	5	6	0	18	14	83¹	78	15	37	77	4.0	8.3	39%	.270	1.38	5.18	5.01	4.95	0.3
2014	HOU	MLB	26	4	9	0	28	24	131²	136	20	70	119	4.8	8.1	40%	.309	1.56	4.72	5.01	5.22	0.0
2015	*HOU*	*MLB*	*27*	*7*	*8*	*0*	*23*	*23*	*124*	*119*	*16*	*51*	*118*	*3.7*	*8.6*	*39%*	*.296*	*1.37*	*4.34*	*4.68*	*4.72*	*0.4*

Breakout: 40%   Improve: 62%   Collapse: 13%   Attrition: 28%   MLB: 83%   *Comparables: Rick VandenHurk, Charlie Furbush, Wade LeBlanc*

It's the classic pitcher's comeback story. PItcher gets kicked out of the rotation, pitcher has something to prove out of the bullpen, pitcher earns his way back and proves everyone wrong. Peacock's story is that exact narrative, except the opposite. He did get demoted to the bullpen out of camp, but was lit up as a reliever, then was given a starting job out of necessity and still struggled. He was sent to Triple-A for a start, was recalled and continued to fall behind batters. His main issue is locating his fastball, locating his knuckle curve, locating his changeup and locating his slider. Other than that, his control is worthy of being in the rotation again.

Chad Qualls   RHP

Born: 8/17/78   Age: 36   Bats: R   Throws: R   Height: 6'4"   Weight: 240

YEAR	TEAM	LVL	AGE	W	L	SV	G	GS	IP	H	HR	BB	K	BB/9	K/9	GB%	BABIP	WHIP	ERA	FIP	FRA	WARP
2012	NYA	MLB	33	1	0	0	8	0	7¹	10	0	3	2	3.7	2.5	54%	.357	1.77	6.14	3.73	4.74	0.0
2012	PHI	MLB	33	1	1	0	35	0	31¹	39	7	9	19	2.6	5.5	56%	.308	1.53	4.60	5.69	6.52	-0.5
2012	PIT	MLB	33	0	0	0	17	0	13²	14	0	2	6	1.3	4.0	60%	.280	1.17	6.59	2.70	3.30	0.2
2013	MIA	MLB	34	5	2	0	66	0	62	57	4	19	49	2.8	7.1	65%	.298	1.23	2.61	3.29	3.82	0.4
2014	HOU	MLB	35	1	5	19	58	0	51¹	54	5	5	43	0.9	7.5	58%	.310	1.15	3.33	3.16	3.69	0.6
2015	*HOU*	*MLB*	*36*	*2*	*1*	*4*	*48*	*0*	*44¹*	*48*	*5*	*11*	*33*	*2.3*	*6.6*	*55%*	*.310*	*1.34*	*4.20*	*4.35*	*4.56*	*0.1*

Breakout: 18%   Improve: 38%   Collapse: 33%   Attrition: 6%   MLB: 75%   *Comparables: Jamie Walker, LaTroy Hawkins, Bob Howry*

The peripherals never looked gaudy for a reliever, but Qualls parlayed a productive 2013 into a multi-year contract in Houston. Now here's the dilemma: Qualls lives in Texas during the offseason and became an Astro, his original team, with intent to retire there. But if he continues to pitch this well—he issued only three unintentional walks all year—he'll continue to be trade bait. Detroit claimed him and engaged in trade talks in August, though no deal was completed. Such reports might give Chad qualms.

Thomas Shirley   LHP

Born: 11/11/88   Age: 26   Bats: L   Throws: L   Height: 6'5"   Weight: 220

YEAR	TEAM	LVL	AGE	W	L	SV	G	GS	IP	H	HR	BB	K	BB/9	K/9	GB%	BABIP	WHIP	ERA	FIP	FRA	WARP
2012	LEX	A	23	2	4	1	16	1	35¹	32	2	16	45	4.1	11.5	57%	.341	1.36	3.06	3.38	3.38	0.9
2013	LNC	A+	24	1	4	1	27	9	75¹	66	6	24	64	2.9	7.6	45%	.279	1.19	3.35	4.06	4.47	1.4
2014	CCH	AA	25	7	3	1	17	13	86¹	63	7	17	78	1.8	8.1	55%	.242	0.93	1.88	3.20	3.79	1.4
2014	OKL	AAA	25	0	2	0	13	3	31	34	1	15	22	4.4	6.4	60%	.347	1.58	4.35	4.15	5.95	0.3
2015	*HOU*	*MLB*	*26*	*4*	*4*	*1*	*29*	*10*	*88²*	*88*	*9*	*33*	*70*	*3.4*	*7.1*	*50%*	*.297*	*1.36*	*4.11*	*4.56*	*4.46*	*0.5*

Breakout: 18%   Improve: 27%   Collapse: 6%   Attrition: 17%   MLB: 35%   *Comparables: Carlos Fisher, Jack Egbert, Bryan Morris*

Thirty-four. Fifty-four. The first number is what's going to get the southpaw to the big leagues: The rate at which he fanned left-handed hitters across three levels in 2014. The second number is what's going to get him consideration for a role more significant than staff LOOGY in the majors: The rate at which he coaxed groundballs on contact from righties. Other numbers matter, too: He's 26, he's a former ninth-rounder, he spent four years in the minors and he was born on a date that suggests he's "elusive," "self-destructive" and "misunderstood." "Oh now you're giving Zodiac readings?" you ask. "Surely you can't be serious." We are serious.

Tony Sipp   LHP

Born: 7/12/83   Age: 31   Bats: L   Throws: L   Height: 6'0"   Weight: 190

YEAR	TEAM	LVL	AGE	W	L	SV	G	GS	IP	H	HR	BB	K	BB/9	K/9	GB%	BABIP	WHIP	ERA	FIP	FRA	WARP
2012	CLE	MLB	28	1	2	1	63	0	55	47	9	23	51	3.8	8.3	37%	.255	1.27	4.42	4.63	5.22	-0.2
2013	RNO	AAA	29	1	0	1	9	0	10	3	0	5	12	4.5	10.8	44%	.130	0.80	0.00	2.67	1.80	0.4
2013	ARI	MLB	29	3	2	0	56	0	37²	35	6	22	42	5.3	10.0	28%	.284	1.51	4.78	4.85	4.23	0.2
2014	ELP	AAA	30	1	1	0	11	0	14²	14	1	2	21	1.2	12.9	38%	.361	1.09	4.30	2.34	3.24	0.4
2014	HOU	MLB	30	4	3	4	56	0	50²	28	5	17	63	3.0	11.2	35%	.205	0.89	3.38	2.96	4.33	0.3
2015	*HOU*	*MLB*	*31*	*3*	*1*	*1*	*58*	*0*	*50²*	*42*	*6*	*22*	*56*	*3.9*	*9.9*	*35%*	*.275*	*1.26*	*3.62*	*4.31*	*3.94*	*0.5*

Breakout: 27%   Improve: 42%   Collapse: 25%   Attrition: 16%   MLB: 89%   *Comparables: Jorge Julio, Frank Francisco, Jose Valverde*

And this is why left-handers earn endless chances. After a dismal 2013, San Diego signed Sipp but had no room for him in their bullpen, so he was granted his release from Triple-A to sign with Houston in early May. All he did was post a career-best walk rate, hit rate, strikeout rate and FIP—basically the fantastic four of reliever stats. He also had his fastest fastball (93 mph), a jump of nearly two full ticks, perhaps the most noticeable difference from a scouting standpoint. The other change was his split-finger; he's always had one, but he used it much more (nearly one in four pitches) to stymie right-handers. He's a lefty and gets lefties out, but he's by no means a specialist. Sipp is a dependable back-end reliever who just happens to throw with the weird arm.

Vincent Velasquez   RHP

Born: 6/7/92   Age: 23   Bats: B   Throws: R   Height: 6'3"   Weight: 203

YEAR	TEAM	LVL	AGE	W	L	SV	G	GS	IP	H	HR	BB	K	BB/9	K/9	GB%	BABIP	WHIP	ERA	FIP	FRA	WARP
2012	TCV	A-	20	4	1	0	9	9	45²	37	2	17	51	3.4	10.1	44%	.299	1.18	3.35	2.98	3.87	0.6
2013	QUD	A	21	9	4	3	25	16	110	90	7	33	123	2.7	10.1	52%	.292	1.12	3.19	2.99	4.24	1.8
2013	LNC	A+	21	0	2	0	3	3	14²	14	2	8	19	4.9	11.7	33%	.353	1.50	6.14	5.00	5.75	0.1
2014	LNC	A+	22	7	4	0	15	10	55¹	45	6	23	72	3.7	11.7	40%	.312	1.23	3.74	3.96	3.75	1.6
2015	HOU	MLB	23	3	4	0	14	11	60²	60	7	28	56	4.2	8.3	44%	.305	1.46	4.61	4.78	5.01	0.0

Breakout: 0%   Improve: 0%   Collapse: 0%   Attrition: 0%   MLB: 0%   Comparables: Thomas Diamond, Bud Norris, Henry Sosa

Valasquez posted the highest strikeout rate among starters in the Astros system, which distinguishes him among some pretty good company. He sits in the low-to-mid-90s and shows that tantalizing ability to ramp up the velocity as he works deeper into games. The heat also sets up a plus changeup that gets swings and misses from both lefties and righties and makes his 95 look all the tougher. His curve might be average, but that's okay because he'll use it mostly as a show-me pitch. A groin injury limited his 2014 innings more effectively than the Astros' plan to piggy-back his starts, and he's been inconsistent since returning, especially in a bruising Arizona Fall League stint. He'll have to be stretched out carefully in 2015.

Jose Veras   RHP

Born: 10/20/80   Age: 34   Bats: R   Throws: R   Height: 6'6"   Weight: 240

YEAR	TEAM	LVL	AGE	W	L	SV	G	GS	IP	H	HR	BB	K	BB/9	K/9	GB%	BABIP	WHIP	ERA	FIP	FRA	WARP
2012	MIL	MLB	31	5	4	1	72	0	67	61	5	40	79	5.4	10.6	46%	.322	1.51	3.63	3.63	3.74	1.0
2013	DET	MLB	32	0	1	2	25	0	19²	16	2	8	16	3.7	7.3	38%	.241	1.22	3.20	4.14	4.35	0.1
2013	HOU	MLB	32	0	4	19	42	0	43	29	4	14	44	2.9	9.2	46%	.240	1.00	2.93	3.42	4.17	0.4
2014	CHN	MLB	33	0	1	0	12	0	13¹	12	2	11	13	7.4	8.8	57%	.286	1.73	8.10	6.25	7.05	-0.4
2014	HOU	MLB	33	4	0	1	34	0	32²	25	4	16	37	4.4	10.2	43%	.256	1.26	3.03	3.96	4.03	0.3
2015	HOU	MLB	34	3	1	6	50	0	46²	39	4	22	51	4.3	9.8	43%	.287	1.31	3.59	4.01	3.90	0.5

Breakout: 14%   Improve: 31%   Collapse: 37%   Attrition: 10%   MLB: 84%   Comparables: Kerry Wood, Jay Witasick, Michael Gonzalez

In the summer of 2013, the Astros dealt Veras to the Tigers for outfield prospect Danry Vasquez. After he signed with, then flamed out with, the Cubs, the Astros signed him again in the summer of 2014, perhaps in a quest to strike gold twice, or because their roster of relievers looked a little despondent. He regained a bit of his command, but not enough for Houston to hoodwink another team at the deadline. His velocity and effectiveness are on a steady decline but baseball teams adore veteran relievers who have pitched late innings, and Veras certainly has done that. He probably won't be bolstering a contender's bullpen again, unless a GM sees that his name is an anagram for "Jose Saver" and thinks "Ooh that just might work."

Asher Wojciechowski   RHP

Born: 12/21/88   Age: 26   Bats: R   Throws: R   Height: 6'4"   Weight: 240

YEAR	TEAM	LVL	AGE	W	L	SV	G	GS	IP	H	HR	BB	K	BB/9	K/9	GB%	BABIP	WHIP	ERA	FIP	FRA	WARP
2012	DUN	A+	23	7	3	0	18	18	93¹	91	3	22	76	2.1	7.3	46%	.320	1.21	3.57	3.05	3.89	1.8
2012	CCH	AA	23	2	2	0	8	8	43²	30	0	14	34	2.9	7.0	44%	.240	1.01	2.06	3.03	3.92	0.4
2013	CCH	AA	24	2	1	1	6	3	26	17	1	7	27	2.4	9.3	52%	.254	0.92	2.08	2.29	2.90	0.6
2013	OKL	AAA	24	9	7	0	22	21	134	116	10	44	104	3.0	7.0	35%	.268	1.19	3.56	4.00	4.52	1.5
2014	OKL	AAA	25	4	4	0	15	14	76	89	10	21	59	2.5	7.0	33%	.335	1.45	4.74	4.84	5.45	0.4
2015	HOU	MLB	26	5	5	0	15	15	78¹	81	9	25	55	2.8	6.3	40%	.295	1.35	4.24	4.74	4.61	0.3

Breakout: 15%   Improve: 25%   Collapse: 7%   Attrition: 27%   MLB: 35%   Comparables: Phil Irwin, Hector Ambriz, Matt Shoemaker

Arriving in the Astros' system in the J.A. Happ/Brandon Lyon trade (if that's what we're reduced to calling it), Wojciechowski has long projected to be a potential innings-eater in the back of a rotation. The problem—well, one of the problems, in addition to the slew of injuries that chopped up his 2014 season—is that he's evolved into something of a fly-ball pitcher who lacks elite stuff or command. He pitched terribly between aches and pains in June and July, but looked more competent in August. Lefties ate him for lunch, hitting .338/.377/.542 overall. Unless his slider or change take a significant step forward, Wojciechowski currently projects as an occasional spot starter and swingman through his option years, then perhaps a middle reliever if he gets lucky.

Lineouts

Hitters

NAME	POS	TEAM	LVL	AGE	PA	R	2B	3B	HR	RBI	BB	K	SB	CS	AVG/OBP/SLG	TAv	BABIP	BRR	FRAA	WARP
Andrew Aplin	RF	CCH	AA	23	434	49	11	1	6	50	65	56	21	8	.267/.379/.354	.273	.298	0.4	RF(55): 2.0, CF(42): -1.8	1.9
	CF	OKL	AAA	23	116	14	3	1	0	15	15	15	5	3	.260/.348/.313	.248	.294	-0.3	CF(23): 2.1, RF(6): 0.2	0.5
Bobby Borchering	1B	LNC	A+	23	71	3	4	1	0	7	8	24	0	0	.238/.324/.333	.231	.385	-2.4	1B(13): -0.7, 1B(1): -0.7	-0.4
Jonathan Davis	3B	QUD	A	21	171	20	9	0	8	32	13	41	4	0	.303/.363/.516	.312	.364	0.5	3B(41): -1.8	1.4
	3B	TCV	A-	21	131	18	7	1	5	20	15	25	1	0	.279/.382/.495	.320	.317	-0.3	3B(27): 4.2, RF(1): 0.1	1.6
Nolan Fontana	2B	CCH	AA	23	305	33	21	1	1	26	61	76	5	8	.262/.418/.376	.296	.383	-2.7	2B(41): -0.0, SS(25): 2.1	2.1
Jesus Guzman	1B	HOU	MLB	30	184	10	4	0	2	9	19	52	3	0	.188/.272/.248	.203	.261	-1.0	1B(52): -1.2, LF(8): -0.5	-1.1
L.J. Hoes	CF	OKL	AAA	24	148	21	6	2	2	15	16	30	5	4	.297/.381/.391	.278	.371	-1.5	CF(23): 0.7, LF(9): -0.2	0.6
	LF	HOU	MLB	24	136	12	5	0	3	11	10	31	0	0	.172/.230/.287	.197	.198	-1.4	LF(36): -0.8, RF(12): 0.4	-0.7
Telvin Nash	1B	CCH	AA	23	321	46	4	0	22	49	34	112	1	1	.227/.330/.484	.280	.284	-0.2	1B(68): 3.2	1.2
Roberto Pena	C	LNC	A+	22	387	48	19	0	13	54	25	63	1	2	.249/.306/.414	.246	.265	-0.8	C(79): -0.2, C(9): -0.2	1.7
Alex Presley	LF	HOU	MLB	28	271	22	6	1	6	19	13	44	5	1	.244/.281/.346	.238	.272	0.8	LF(43): -0.8, CF(21): -0.9	-0.5
Preston Tucker	RF	CCH	AA	23	290	41	17	1	17	43	26	46	3	3	.276/.348/.536	.305	.278	-1.5	RF(34): 2.8, LF(15): -0.5	1.9
	LF	OKL	AAA	23	309	38	18	0	7	51	31	74	2	0	.287/.356/.429	.269	.365	-0.8	LF(44): -0.2, RF(12): -0.3	0.8

In a different system, former fifth-rounder **Andrew Aplin**'s quick and competent rise would have earned him a place on the depth chart; with Houston, he'll likely remain ninth outfielder, if that's even a thing. ❖ One by one, the 24 players taken ahead of Mike Trout in 2009 will fall out of the league, like victims in a *Scream* sequel. After his release in November, this just might be **Bobby Borchering**'s moment to run shrieking into the darkness. ❖ **J.D. Davis** could not have had a better pro debut, playing an almost credible third base while showing serious right-handed thump across two levels. Astros fans cheered but scouts yawned, saying to wake them when he's in the Texas League. ❖ **Nolan Fontana** broke his wee little pinky finger in June, costing himself half a season of opportunities to show he belongs on the depth chart in an organization featuring Carlos Correa. ❖ It says here that **Jesus Guzman** is a first baseman. And it's true: You could definitely put Guzman at first base and see how that goes for you. ❖ Trivia question: Which left fielder was kept on the roster so that the Astros could release J.D. Martinez? That would be **L.J. Hoes**. You get 100 points and can pick another question from the category "Regrettable Rosterings." ❖ Seventeen-year-old Dominican shortstop **Joan Mauricio** earned the ink here by playing his way stateside, but we could have just as easily mentioned fellow teens Jonathan Matute, Frankeny Fernandez and Wander Franco, who put up equally impressive numbers in the Dominican Summer League. That's a significant number of teenage lottery tickets, and some are bound to pay out. ❖ The 2013 Astros struck out more than any other team in big-league history; if they want to chase those glory days, they can always call up **Telvin Nash**. ❖ Having put down a staggering 57 percent of would-be basestealers, **Roberto Pena** has the catch-and-throw skills to which other backstops aspire. He just aspires to hit .250. ❖ If you're looking for a dependable fourth outfielder who can hit and play defense, consider signing him. Then sign **Alex Presley** just in case that guy gets hurt. ❖ Presumably panicked at their lack of toolsy, right-handed hitting outfield prospects, the Astros shelled out $1.5 million for Dominican teenager **Ronny Rafael** in July. ❖ Jonathon Singleton's struggles could translate into MLB playing time for **Preston Tucker** next year, but to turn that window into a career, he'll have to really pick up his production against righties.

Pitchers

NAME	TEAM	LVL	AGE	W	L	SV	G	GS	IP	H	HR	BB	K	BB/9	K/9	GB%	BABIP	WHIP	ERA	FIP	FRA	WARP
Luis Cruz	CCH	AA	23	7	6	1	21	17	100¹	86	12	25	92	2.2	8.3	40%	.269	1.11	3.14	3.74	4.53	1.2
	OKL	AAA	23	1	2	0	5	5	24¹	31	4	13	26	4.8	9.6	29%	.397	1.81	5.92	5.43	5.62	0.0
Darin Downs	OKL	AAA	29	1	2	0	9	0	13	17	0	4	15	2.8	10.4	32%	.425	1.62	5.54	2.31	3.06	0.4
	HOU	MLB	29	2	1	0	45	0	34²	28	2	19	27	4.9	7.0	46%	.268	1.36	5.45	4.26	5.01	-0.1
Kent Emanuel	QUD	A	22	0	2	0	6	4	22	20	3	4	17	1.6	7.0	46%	.270	1.09	2.45	4.26	5.64	0.0
	LNC	A+	22	9	5	2	21	14	102	111	12	19	76	1.7	6.7	45%	.312	1.27	4.59	4.46	5.25	1.4
Kyle Farnsworth	NYN	MLB	38	0	3	3	19	0	17	18	2	6	10	3.2	5.3	36%	.302	1.41	3.18	4.51	4.49	0.0
	HOU	MLB	38	0	0	0	16	0	11²	14	0	9	8	6.9	6.2	42%	.350	1.97	6.17	4.10	4.65	0.0
Jordan Jankowski	CCH	AA	25	5	6	3	30	14	108	90	12	26	120	2.2	10.0	38%	.287	1.07	3.58	3.15	4.03	1.7
Richard Rodriguez	LNC	A+	24	0	0	0	7	0	10²	10	2	2	16	1.7	13.5	36%	.348	1.12	5.06	3.74	6.16	0.1
	CCH	AA	24	0	2	0	11	0	20²	21	1	2	28	0.9	12.2	44%	.377	1.11	3.05	1.47	2.03	0.8
	OKL	AAA	24	2	0	0	16	0	28¹	19	3	6	23	1.9	7.3	49%	.216	0.88	3.49	4.30	4.96	0.1
Kyle Smith	LNC	A+	21	4	0	0	7	3	27²	18	3	12	31	3.9	10.1	45%	.221	1.08	2.60	4.21	6.19	0.5
	CCH	AA	21	5	5	0	21	13	95¹	92	14	25	96	2.4	9.1	43%	.300	1.23	4.34	3.86	3.95	1.1
Alex White	OKL	AAA	25	3	6	0	25	10	63²	78	7	31	53	4.4	7.5	44%	.351	1.71	6.50	5.11	5.60	0.3

The last time **Jesse Crain** threw a pitch was in June 2013, for the White Sox. Since then he has been traded to the Rays and signed by the Astros, neither of which got to see him pitch. If injury setbacks are his specialty, maybe Crain can make it three in a row. ❖ The 5-foot-9 lefty **Luis Cruz** owns property on the 40-man roster, despite getting roughed up in a Triple-A debut that took seven years to come. He's LOOGY depth and a potential spot starter. ❖ **Darin Downs**' ERA rose like a beautiful sunrise. Since he's left-handed, teams will give him every chance to see if it sets. ❖ At 6-feet-8 and 225 pounds, **Brock Dykxhoorn** is a massive hulk of a human, with a massive hulk of a name. His stuff is presently neither massive nor hulking, but big guys like this often make unpredictable development leaps, so the 2014 sixth-rounder will get plenty of time to go from Rookie ball curiosity to bullpen strongman. ❖ **Kent Emanuel** put up a road ERA of 2.62 in the California League. At home in Lancaster, it was 7.21. Lancaster is hard on pitchers, but, as a particular philosopher said, "It is not God's will merely that we should be happy, but that we should make ourselves happy." ❖ **Kyle Farnsworth** still pitches in glasses and should strongly consider franchising a LensCrafters. ❖ **Jordan Jankwoski** is a Texas-Leaguer-made-good story who fails to get much recognition in a crowded system, but he spins one of the organization's better sliders and consistently posts strong peripherals. ❖ **Richard Rodriguez** throws hard, throws strikes and completed two innings in more than half of his 34 relief appearances across three levels. ❖ Short righties get no love; short righties with mediocre Texas League stats get forgotten, so **Kyle Smith** has to get it done in 2015. ❖ Still trying to build arm strength after Tommy John surgery in 2012, **Alex White** was forced to pitch against Triple-A bats with reduced velocity and a can-do attitude. The former is a threat to the latter.

Manager

A.J. Hinch

A logical match. Hinch is among the most well-schooled managers in the game. He earned a psychology degree from Stanford, caught in the majors for parts of seven seasons [Ed note: redundant], managed the Diamondbacks for more than 200 games and in the intervening periods filled a variety of front office roles—including last year as the Padres interim GM—that left him with a greater understanding of analytics. Take someone with that range and wed him to a front-office whose approach was summed up by *BusinessWeek* as "Extreme Moneyball" and what do you get? Who knows.

While Hinch seems like Mr. Perfect for the Astros, it's hard to ignore his similarities to Bo Porter—the erstwhile Houston manager who, coincidentally enough, served on Hinch's Arizona staff. Both were identified as quality managerial prospects equipped with the necessary skills to work alongside a progressive GM like Luhnow. For whatever reason—likely bad communication, given what's been reported by the *Houston Chronicle*'s Evan Drellich, among others—Porter and Luhnow never meshed. Yet Houston's communication failures persisted even after Porter was dismissed late in the year. On the season's final day, some 24 hours before Hinch's introductory press conference, the Astros became entangled in another PR mess, benching Altuve against his will to preserve his batting title. Management later relented, allowing Altuve to play and win the crown, but it was the latest preventable blunder.

The hope is Hinch can settle what seems to be an unsettled organization, that he can serve as a better conduit for the front office—to the press, public and players alike—and that he can be a better in-game tactician than Porter ever was. However there is a chance this relationship, like the one before it, goes south for reasons beyond results. That would be too bad; on paper, this pairing feels too rational to fail.

KANSAS CITY ROYALS

by Andy McCullough

On July 14, 2014, a day before three Royals represented their franchise in the All-Star Game, a phone rang in Arkansas. David Glass picked up on the third ring. He had been the owner of the Royals for 14 seasons; the team posted a winning record in two of those. He is not renowned for his dealings with the press—in part because he prefers the shadows to the spotlight and in part because there has been little positive to discuss during his stewardship of the franchise—so his kindly affect can be disarming.

The upward momentum of Glass' team had stalled. They spent a few days in first place only to cede control back to Detroit. The Tigers had just thumped the club in a series to end the first half. The renaissance of the Royals appeared, as ever, delayed.

Glass did not sound particularly thrilled about these events. But he maintained a confident tone.

"I think we'll have a better team next year than we'll have this year," Glass said.

At the time, the statement sounded improbable. The season likely marked the last one involving James Shields, who was expected to depart in free agency. Yet Glass' viewpoint aligned with that of general manager Dayton Moore. The public—and plenty of those within the game—demarcated 2014 as a make-or-break season for the Royals. The team itself opted to perceive the situation in a more fluid manner.

The Royals did not view The Trade, the deal to acquire James Shields and Wade Davis from Tampa Bay for a package of players including Wil Myers and Jake Odorizzi, in the same way you or I did. The team did not view this as The Trade. They saw it as a trade. There would be life after Shields left, the team felt, and the Royals would benefit even in his absence.

"A lot of the attention last year was 'well, if it doesn't work out, and the Royals don't make it to the playoffs ...'" Moore said in February 2014. "No. It's the first of many trades we're going to have to do if we're going to win," adding, "That's what we'll always have to do."

To the general baseball public, the team's window of competitiveness would close with the departure of Shields after 2014. To the Royals, before Shields arrived, a window did not even exist. They would live with the consequences. If Shields fulfilled his role, his presence would not even be required in the future.

Moore cast Shields not just as a baseball player, a lone addition to the 25-man roster; he saw him as a catalytic agent, one capable of influencing and improving the other 24 men assembled around him. The Royals have never been known as a forward-thinking organization, but Moore placed his faith in human nature and saw this rewarded in 2014.

James Shields was a transformative figure in the history of the Kansas City Royals. The coming years will decide just how large his legacy looms.

+ + +

Rany Jazayerli has written three Russian novels' worth of material on this trade, but he summed up his position early in a lengthy take-down at Grantland. His column ran on December 10, 2012, a day after the Royals and Rays consummated their swap.

"This is a terrible trade for the Royals," he wrote, "deeply flawed in both its theory and execution, and while it might make the Royals marginally more likely to make the playoffs in 2013, it does irreparable damage to their chances of building a perennial winner."

This was the general consensus of The Baseball Internet. So stipulated, we can continue.

+ + +

When his team acquired Shields, Moore gambled in three ways. The First Gamble: The team would win enough to justify mortgaging those assets. He proved right here: A World Series berth is plenty for a club that hadn't made the playoffs in nearly three decades.

+ + +

Dave Cameron made a good point about this trade, even though he did not like it.

"Two winning seasons in 20 years can make a franchise desperate for respectability," Cameron wrote at FanGraphs. "And desperate teams often do desperate things. But I don't think anyone saw the Royals doing something *this desperate*."

Yes. I do believe this trade was made in the context of desperation, even if most Royals officials would not directly voice that thought. During spring training, I was discussing the deal with pitching coach Dave Eiland.

ROYALS PROSPECTUS
2014 W-L: 89-73, 2ND IN AL CENTRAL

Pythag	.519	11th	DER	.708	12th
RS/G	4.02	14th	B-Age	28.2	12th
RA/G	3.85	12th	P-Age	29.2	23rd
TAv	.254	25th	Salary	$89.4M	22nd
BRR	18.52	1st	M$/MW	$1.9M	5th
TAv-P	.256	9th	DL Days	575	5th
FIP	3.72	16th	$ on DL	11%	6th

Three-Year Park Factors

Runs	Runs/RH	Runs/LH	HR/RH	HR/LH
103	103	99	78	78

Top Hitter WARP	5.5	Alex Gordon
Top Pitcher WARP	2.9	James Shields
Top Prospect		Raul Mondesi

– 158 –

"If we don't trade Wil Myers for James Shields, we don't win 86 games last year," Eiland said. "And none of us may be standing here right now."

He was right. You heard this refrain, almost always on background and not for attribution, from various Kansas City officials throughout the season. After the 2012 season—when Eric Hosmer regressed and Danny Duffy blew out and the team lost 90 games *again*—the club had reached something of a crossroads. Moore had been the general manager since 2007. That's six full seasons of futility. Six full seasons, and their best record was a 75–87 mark in 2008. Their farm system was the class of the industry, but their big-league club was still a doormat.

They needed to do *something*.

So one night that December, in a suite at Nashville's Gaylord Opryland Resort during the Winter Meetings, Moore grabbed a marker and approached a whiteboard. He started writing all the names of the team's top prospects.

✦ ✦ ✦

This next point is important. I will keep it simple. Here goes: Prospects are bullshit.

You may not agree with it, but I am pretty sure it's true. There is no better con in sports than rebuilding and there is no greater fallacy than the one built around prospects. Prospects do not always get better. Sometimes they stagnate. Sometimes they get worse. Sometimes they get hurt. Sometimes they just fade away.

If you talk to enough people involve in player development, you'll hear a variation on this phrase often: "Prospects always surprise you." They almost never turn out as good—or as bad—as you think they will. Few lines are straight.

Remember Neftali Feliz? Remember all the debate about whether he should start or relieve? He required Tommy John surgery in 2012 and was last seen striking out six batters per nine with a 4.93 FIP in 2014.

The Royals traded Wil Myers because he was a prospect and because James Shields was James Shields. For a moment, let's ignore the off-field stuff. We will discuss The Shields Effect soon enough, but for now, let's limit this to in-game contributions. Kansas City traded for James Shields because they knew, more or less, exactly what Shields would give them every fifth day. With Myers, as with any prospect, the range of his possible contributions was far broader.

Remember Ike Davis? Remember all the talk about him replacing David Wright as the face of the Mets' franchise? He boomed 32 homers in 2012, but his approach at the plate had mutated into something grotesque. The team traded him to Pittsburgh in 2014, and the A's acquired him for international slot money this winter.

In the past decade, as media coverage of minor-league baseball proliferated, fans became enamored with prospect rankings. Baseball had lagged behind football and basketball in the mock-draft craze, mostly because baseball writers understand trying to predict how a draft will aid a team is utter folly. But prospect rankings allowed for a more educated equivalent. Fans gobble up this sort of content. It's why the Royals were considered a failure in the first place in 2012. If their farm system hadn't been so highly praised in the years prior, fewer folks would have cared about their 90-loss campaign that season. (To be clear, prospect *writers* aren't the problem. They can only work with the materials they have, i.e. prospects. As noted, those materials are bullshit.)

Baseball America rated Wil Myers the no. 4 prospect in the game before the 2013 season. Here is a review of some other no. 4 prospects:

2004: Edwin Jackson (One of the more bizarre careers in recent memories: He's been traded six times and continually underperforms his peripherals. He's been in the majors for 12 seasons and has 11.6 WARP. He signed a four-year deal with the Cubs before 2013 and promptly became atrocious.)

2005: Ian Stewart (He hit 25 homers in 2009, which appears to have been a creation of Coors Field. His last notable moment was being suspended by the Cubs for ranting about them keeping him in Triple-A.)

2006: Jeremy Hermida (My only discernible memories of Hermida (worth 4.7 WARP for his career and tilting at windmills in Milwaukee's farm system in 2014) involve striking him out in MLB: The Show 2007.)

2007: Phil Hughes (The book isn't finished on Hughes, but, by God, it's going to be a long book. He was a potential savior in New York, then a bust, then a good reliever on a World Series team, then a good starter, then a decent starter, then a bad starter. He looked revived in Minnesota in 2014. Who knows?)

2008: Clay Buchholz (He's a two-time All-Star and he's put together some good years. He's also never made 30 starts in a season. He was terrible in 2014. James Shields is better.)

2009: Tommy Hanson (Put together a few tantalizing years in Atlanta before breaking down. When he was traded to Los Angeles, another baseball writer joked to me that Frank Wren wanted to cut costs and couldn't afford the flowers for the funeral for Hanson's right arm.)

2010: Jesus Montero (In 2014, he showed up to camp 40 pounds overweight. He was so blubbery a scout sent him an ice cream sandwich in the middle of a minor-league game. The scout worked for the Mariners.)

2011: Domonic Brown (His sterling first half in 2013 looked like a breakout campaign. Turns out, it was a mirage. Brown slumped in the second half, then bumbled through another discouraging season in 2014. He turned 27 in September and it's still unclear if he's a big-league regular.)

2012: Yu Darvish (Okay, he's good.)

Prospects are bullshit.

✦ ✦ ✦

The Second Gamble: Shields would imbue his younger teammates with an understanding of meaningful baseball. Moore proved right here: A glance at Lorenzo Cain or Yordano Ventura or Eric Hosmer in October feels like a representative example.

✦ ✦ ✦

On that December night, when all the names were on the whiteboard, Dayton Moore began slashing ink through some.

- He crossed off Wil Myers.
- He crossed off Jake Odorizzi.
- He crossed off Mike Montgomery.
- He crossed off Patrick Leonard.

This was the package necessary to acquire James Shields (and Wade Davis). Moore turned to his lieutenants assembled around him. He asked him if their farm system would still be strong without these players.

The answer was affirmative.

Leonard, now 22, had a decent year in the Florida State League in 2014. Whoop-de-damn-do, as Derrick Coleman once said. Montgomery, 24, posted a 4.29 ERA in his second consecutive year with Triple-A Durham. Odorizzi, 25, underperformed his peripherals a tad, but he still struck out 9.3 batters per nine with a 3.78 FIP in 168 big-league innings. That's a nice year.

But the trade hinges on Myers. He played 88 good games for Tampa Bay in 2013. He struck out a bunch, but he still hit 13 homers and punched up an .831 OPS. He won the American League Rookie of the Year over such luminaries as Jose Iglesias, Chris Archer (actually a really good pitcher), Dan Straily and J.B. Shuck.

Wil Myers played 87 bad games for Tampa Bay in 2014. His plate approach did not improve. He still struck out a bunch, but this time his batted-ball luck cratered and his power evaporated. He broke his wrist in May and missed nearly three months.

Tampa Bay won 92 games and then the Wild Card game in 2013 before crashing out in the American League Division Series. As with Myers, little went right for them last year. They started losing early and never really stopped. They traded David Price. In the fall, Friedman bolted for the Dodgers. A week later, manager Joe Maddon unhitched his RV and took a road trip to Wrigley Field. The franchise scrambled to rearrange itself. This was not the fault of Wil Myers, but it was hard to imagine him being relevant in October for Tampa Bay, which may be why new Rays GM Matt Silverman flipped him to San Diego in December. (For prospects.)

✦✦✦

James Shields pitched well in 2014, but he was not exactly dominant. His ERA was 3.21, but he gave up 14 unearned runs. His FIP was a credible but merely decent 3.62. He pitched only one complete game. In the playoffs he was pretty much terrible, and far too many people made unfunny cracks about his nickname.

But here are the things he did do, which the Royals had come to count on: He made all 34 of his starts. He logged 227 innings. He mentored Danny Duffy. He aided Jeremy Guthrie with his changeup. He dimmed the spotlight on Yordano Ventura. The 86 wins in 2013 convinced Jason Vargas, in part, to sign with Kansas City.

I say in part because Vargas also needed a four-year, $32 million contract offer to convince him. It is worth wondering whether Glass would have approved that expenditure if the club had not won 86 games in 2013. Never will Glass be confused with George Steinbrenner. His temperament is far too reasonable, and his spending is far too thrifty.

But the Royals added salary before the waiver-wire trading deadline last August (financial considerations had scotched a series of possible upgrades before the July 31st deadline, like potential deals for Marlon Byrd, A.J. Burnett and Alex Rios). They hosted the American League Wild Card game at the end of September and did not lose again until the first game of the

World Series. Their payroll is expected to jump past $100 million for the first time in franchise history. This is not all because of James Shields. But it is hard to imagine the Royals reaching this stage in 2014 without him.

✦✦✦

The Third Gamble was both the most nebulous and the most critical to the franchise's future. A rising tide lifts all boats, but Moore gambled on his players staying afloat after Shields receded with the tide for the riches of free agency.

✦✦✦

Moore learned his trade in the Atlanta organization. The Braves vied for October every season he worked there, from 1994 to 2006. He believed contention operated as a forge. Players developed better. They learned winning habits. Otherwise, he suspected, they only cared about themselves. His first few seasons in Kansas City confirmed this. On a losing team, players became obsessed with their contracts, with their statistics, with their future. On a winning team, players became obsessed with winning.

It is probably too simplistic to say the Royals lived this axiom in 2014. They were a mediocre team for much of the season. On July 21st, they resided two games below .500 and eight behind Detroit in the American League Central. That afternoon, veteran Raul Ibanez decided a players-only meeting was in order. The first person he sought out to organize the meeting was Shields.

Then, for whatever reason, they started to win. They survived a rocky September to clinch a playoff berth. And in the playoffs, a strange thing happened: The younger players began to play better. Cain stopped giving away at-bats. Moustakas crushed pitches over the middle and even slapped a few opposite-field hits. Hosmer resembled the star he could become.

Does Shields deserve credit for this? No. But, yes.

✦✦✦

Glass earned his fortune as an executive at Walmart. His voice still retains the honeyed twang of the Ozarks. He grew up in Mountain View, Missouri, about four hours south of Kauffman Stadium, the namesake of his close friend, Ewing Kauffman, the man who brought the Royals to Kansas City.

For nearly two decades, Glass was seen as the man who allowed Kauffman's baseball franchise to rot. All that changed last October. The Royals made the playoffs. They played seven games in the World Series. They wormed their way into the heart of the sporting public.

When asked during the playoffs, Glass repeated his notion the team would be better in 2015. Only now the statement did not sound so improbable. Even without James Shields, the Royals may not recede with the tide. ∎

—Andy McCullough covers the Royals for The Kansas City Star. *You can follow him on Twitter @McCulloughStar.*

Player comments by Ken Funck and Baseball Prospectus Authors

Hitters

Lane Adams   OF

Born: 11/13/89 Age: 25 Bats: R Throws: R Height: 6' 4" Weight: 190

YEAR	TEAM	LVL	AGE	PA	R	2B	3B	HR	RBI	BB	K	SB	CS	AVG/OBP/SLG	TAv	BABIP	BRR	FRAA	WARP
2012	KNC	A	22	291	40	13	4	5	44	21	48	11	1	.298/.349/.435	.296	.343	1.5	CF(55): 1.5, LF(10): -0.9	2.3
2012	WIL	A+	22	285	37	10	1	6	25	21	64	8	4	.240/.302/.355	.244	.297	1.6	RF(48): 8.0, CF(13): 0.4	1.1
2013	WIL	A+	23	370	56	23	2	7	39	43	66	23	6	.276/.362/.424	.294	.325	2.6	CF(85): -2.6	2.7
2013	NWA	AA	23	177	30	7	1	5	26	18	45	15	0	.244/.333/.397	.272	.311	2.9	RF(18): -0.6, LF(15): 0.8	0.7
2014	NWA	AA	24	465	65	25	3	11	36	45	86	38	9	.269/.352/.427	.279	.314	3.2	CF(104): 5.1	3.5
2014	KCA	MLB	24	3	1	0	0	0	0	0	2	0	0	.000/.000/.000	.011	.000	0.1	LF(2): 0.1, CF(2): -0.0	0.0
2015	*KCA*	*MLB*	*25*	*250*	*28*	*11*	*1*	*4*	*23*	*16*	*59*	*13*	*2*	*.238/.293/.355*	*.245*	*.297*	*1.5*	*CF 1, RF 0*	*0.6*

Breakout: 9%   Improve: 30%   Collapse: 5%   Attrition: 32%   MLB: 49%   Comparables: Ben Francisco, Xavier Paul, Brian Bogusevic

Tall and athletic, Adams has game-changing speed of the sort Kansas City rode to the World Series last year. He's a solid center fielder with an accurate arm, and has shown he can steal bases at a high success rate. Adams has never quite grown into the power that his size and swing portend, although he can out-slug Jarrod Dyson, and between the walks and the doubles and the plus defense he'll make a nice fourth outfielder.

Norichika Aoki   RF

Born: 1/5/82 Age: 33 Bats: L Throws: R Height: 5'9" Weight: 180

YEAR	TEAM	LVL	AGE	PA	R	2B	3B	HR	RBI	BB	K	SB	CS	AVG/OBP/SLG	TAv	BABIP	BRR	FRAA	WARP
2012	MIL	MLB	30	588	81	37	4	10	50	43	55	30	8	.288/.355/.433	.281	.304	1.5	RF(107): 2.8, CF(19): -2.4	2.9
2013	MIL	MLB	31	674	80	20	3	8	37	55	40	20	12	.286/.356/.370	.269	.295	-4.2	RF(149): -0.9, CF(2): -0.1	1.6
2014	KCA	MLB	32	549	63	22	6	1	43	43	49	17	8	.285/.349/.360	.267	.314	3.6	RF(119): -7.7, LF(5): -0.0	1.0
2015	*KCA*	*MLB*	*33*	*542*	*63*	*24*	*3*	*2*	*38*	*39*	*48*	*18*	*8*	*.278/.340/.357*	*.266*	*.296*	*-0.2*	*RF -3, CF -0*	*0.9*

Breakout: 1%   Improve: 30%   Collapse: 6%   Attrition: 11%   MLB: 94%   Comparables: Juan Pierre, Ichiro Suzuki, Luis Castillo

Aoki was a big part of Kansas City's stretch run last year, setting the table with his .317/.377/.408 second-half line and playing a very good right field. On the whole, though, he's a player in decline. An outstanding contact hitter who slaps more groundballs than any player in baseball, Aoki works his way on base and hangs in well against lefties, but he no longer has the range for center field or the power for a corner. His on-base percentage is useful but not elite, he isn't stealing bases at a high enough rate and last year his heretofore oddly persistent ability to reach base on error was nowhere to be seen. Aoki is a solid two-hole hitter and would be a definite asset if he were a middle infielder, but in an outfield corner his on-base chops and declining speed will have trouble trumping his lack of power.

Jorge Bonifacio   RF

Born: 6/4/93 Age: 22 Bats: R Throws: R Height: 6' 1" Weight: 195

YEAR	TEAM	LVL	AGE	PA	R	2B	3B	HR	RBI	BB	K	SB	CS	AVG/OBP/SLG	TAv	BABIP	BRR	FRAA	WARP
2012	KNC	A	19	448	54	20	6	10	61	30	84	6	3	.282/.336/.432	.272	.333	-2.1	RF(96): -6.3, 3B(1): 0.0	0.7
2013	WIL	A+	20	234	32	11	3	2	29	23	40	0	2	.296/.368/.408	.289	.353	-1.7	RF(50): 0.9	1.1
2013	NWA	AA	20	105	15	7	0	2	19	11	23	2	1	.301/.371/.441	.302	.377	0.8	RF(23): -1.8	0.8
2014	NWA	AA	21	566	49	20	4	4	51	50	127	2	3	.230/.302/.309	.227	.295	3.3	RF(125): -9.4, LF(2): -0.1	-1.8
2015	*KCA*	*MLB*	*22*	*250*	*20*	*10*	*2*	*2*	*21*	*14*	*62*	*1*	*1*	*.230/.276/.318*	*.225*	*.300*	*-0.1*	*RF -3, LF -0*	*-0.9*

Breakout: 0%   Improve: 0%   Collapse: 0%   Attrition: 0%   MLB: 0%   Comparables: Moises Sierra, Brandon Jones, Rene Tosoni

If minor league baseball has a weeder class it's Double-A, and Bonifacio showed last year he wasn't ready to make the grade. He has the raw power and cannon arm of a prototypical right fielder, but has yet to translate them into production on the field, and was certifiably awful at the plate last year. Off-speed pitches continue to give him fits, and his approach leads neither to walks nor to counts where he can lay into get-me-over fastballs with impunity. Bonifacio is still young, of course, but there's a lot of work to do.

Lorenzo Cain   CF

Born: 4/13/86 Age: 29 Bats: R Throws: R Height: 6' 2" Weight: 205

YEAR	TEAM	LVL	AGE	PA	R	2B	3B	HR	RBI	BB	K	SB	CS	AVG/OBP/SLG	TAv	BABIP	BRR	FRAA	WARP
2012	NWA	AA	26	24	4	1	0	1	1	0	6	0	0	.208/.208/.375	.230	.235	0.2	CF(5): 0.3	0.0
2012	OMA	AAA	26	31	4	3	0	1	6	2	4	0	0	.321/.355/.536	.307	.333	-0.5	CF(5): -0.2	0.1
2012	KCA	MLB	26	244	27	9	2	7	31	15	56	10	0	.266/.316/.419	.265	.319	0.6	CF(50): 2.0, RF(9): 0.6	1.3
2013	KCA	MLB	27	442	54	21	3	4	46	33	90	14	6	.251/.310/.348	.245	.309	-1.3	CF(92): 6.6, RF(32): 1.3	1.4
2014	KCA	MLB	28	502	55	29	4	5	53	24	108	28	5	.301/.339/.412	.269	.380	3.2	CF(93): 3.4, RF(77): 3.9	2.9
2015	*KCA*	*MLB*	*29*	*461*	*49*	*22*	*4*	*5*	*43*	*28*	*98*	*19*	*5*	*.271/.320/.379*	*.261*	*.335*	*0.4*	*CF 3, RF 1*	*1.7*

Breakout: 0%   Improve: 27%   Collapse: 21%   Attrition: 24%   MLB: 85%   Comparables: Roger Bernadina, Rajai Davis, Chris Duffy

It wasn't quite Brooks Robinson circa 1970, but Cain put on a show in the playoffs that was the talk of baseball. The ALCS MVP was a human highlight reel in center field, making spectacular diving catches and running down gappers with ease. At the plate, Cain hit line drives all over the yard and posted a .333/.388/.417 playoff line, building on a successful season that saw him hit for a high average and become an elite threat on the bases. He doesn't draw walks or hit for power, and he's not likely to duplicate last season's high batting average on balls in play, but his speed and defense should more than make up for any regression from his bat.

Christian Colon   2B

Born: 5/14/89   Age: 26   Bats: R   Throws: R   Height: 5' 10"   Weight: 190

YEAR	TEAM	LVL	AGE	PA	R	2B	3B	HR	RBI	BB	K	SB	CS	AVG/OBP/SLG	TAv	BABIP	BRR	FRAA	WARP
2012	NWA	AA	23	315	33	9	2	5	27	31	27	12	6	.289/.364/.392	.272	.305	-2.6	SS(54): 2.3, 2B(17): 0.1	1.5
2012	OMA	AAA	23	21	4	1	0	1	5	2	1	0	0	.412/.429/.647	.380	.353	-0.3	SS(4): -0.8, 2B(1): -0.0	0.2
2013	OMA	AAA	24	577	72	12	3	12	58	41	57	15	4	.273/.335/.379	.256	.288	2.1	2B(75): 2.4, SS(54): -5.4	1.9
2014	OMA	AAA	25	388	55	18	0	8	47	30	29	15	4	.311/.366/.433	.276	.317	0.6	2B(35): 2.0, SS(35): 2.4	2.4
2014	KCA	MLB	25	49	8	5	1	0	6	3	4	2	0	.333/.375/.489	.317	.366	0.8	2B(11): 0.4, 3B(5): -0.0	0.6
2015	KCA	MLB	26	250	29	10	1	3	20	15	29	7	2	.265/.313/.360	.250	.283	0.4	2B 1, SS 1	0.9

Breakout: 3%   Improve: 23%   Collapse: 4%   Attrition: 23%   MLB: 36%   Comparables: *Jarrett Hoffpauir, Jeff Keppinger, Matt Tolbert*

Colon added plenty of drama to Kansas City's miracle comeback win in last year's Wild Card playoff, chopping a high-hop single that plated Eric Hosmer with the tying run in the bottom of the 12th, nearly getting picked off to end the inning before stealing second on the next pitch, then coming around to score the winner on a Salvador Perez single. It won't be the last contribution Colon makes to the Royals, as the former top pick has finally arrived as a solid utility option. Stretched at shortstop, he's a plus defensive second baseman and provides a right-handed option at third base to pair with Mike Moustakas. At the plate, he brings a professional approach, solid contact and doubles power. Add all that to excellent makeup and gamer instincts and Colon is ready to be a primary infield backup with enough vestigial upside to eventually support a full-time gig at second base.

Cheslor Cuthbert   3B

Born: 11/16/92   Age: 22   Bats: R   Throws: R   Height: 6' 1"   Weight: 190

YEAR	TEAM	LVL	AGE	PA	R	2B	3B	HR	RBI	BB	K	SB	CS	AVG/OBP/SLG	TAv	BABIP	BRR	FRAA	WARP
2012	WIL	A+	19	517	47	18	0	7	59	37	80	6	3	.240/.296/.322	.252	.274	-5.0	3B(120): -8.8	-0.1
2013	WIL	A+	20	254	32	21	2	2	31	27	37	1	2	.280/.354/.418	.283	.324	-2.2	3B(57): -2.0	1.0
2013	NWA	AA	20	264	25	16	0	6	28	20	51	5	2	.215/.279/.359	.218	.246	-2.9	3B(59): 4.4	-0.3
2014	NWA	AA	21	395	35	19	1	10	48	36	67	9	3	.276/.342/.420	.268	.313	-2.1	3B(60): 2.3, 1B(28): 1.3	1.0
2014	OMA	AAA	21	100	12	5	0	2	16	9	12	1	1	.264/.330/.385	.231	.286	0.3	3B(15): -0.7, 1B(9): -1.1	-0.2
2015	KCA	MLB	22	250	22	12	0	4	23	14	49	2	1	.235/.279/.338	.235	.279	-0.3	3B -1, 1B -0	-0.2

Breakout: 0%   Improve: 0%   Collapse: 0%   Attrition: 0%   MLB: 0%   Comparables: *Jake Smolinski, Neil Walker, Ryan Wheeler*

After five minor-league seasons, the most frequent thing we've written about Cuthbert is "young for his level," which remained true when he reached Triple-A as a 21-year-old last summer. What also remained true is that Cuthbert has a strong arm but little mobility, making him below-average at the hot corner, and his move to first base last summer was discouraging because his bat isn't loud enough to carry him there. The Royals have had him taking grounders at the keystone, where his bat-to-ball skills are a better fit, but you could read the list of subpar corner men who thrived in the middle infield in the time it takes to watch one Vine.

Hunter Dozier   3B

Born: 8/22/91   Age: 23   Bats: R   Throws: R   Height: 6' 4"   Weight: 220

YEAR	TEAM	LVL	AGE	PA	R	2B	3B	HR	RBI	BB	K	SB	CS	AVG/OBP/SLG	TAv	BABIP	BRR	FRAA	WARP
2013	LEX	A	21	59	6	6	0	0	9	3	5	0	0	.327/.373/.436	.322	.360	-0.5	3B(13): 0.1	0.6
2014	WIL	A+	22	267	36	18	0	4	39	35	56	7	3	.295/.397/.429	.318	.371	2.2	3B(62): -5.8	2.0
2014	NWA	AA	22	267	33	12	0	4	21	31	70	3	2	.209/.303/.312	.218	.280	0.9	3B(61): -4.0	-0.9
2015	KCA	MLB	23	250	22	11	0	3	22	21	65	2	1	.222/.292/.315	.231	.294	-0.4	3B -4, SS -0	-0.7

Breakout: 0%   Improve: 0%   Collapse: 0%   Attrition: 0%   MLB: 0%   Comparables: *Chris Gimenez, Zelous Wheeler, Jesus Guzman*

Dozier showed off his advanced approach and line-drive stroke in his full-season debut, posting a high on-base percentage and moderate, gap-to-gap power in Wilmington before hitting the wall in Double-A. He's a converted shortstop with a plus arm, but he's still a work in progress at third base; most scouts agree he will eventually be average there. He's a gamer with a simple swing that serves him well, and he uses the whole field, draws walks and flashes plus bat speed that hints at untapped wells of future home run power. Look for Dozier to solve more advanced pitching this summer, and if he starts launching a few more over the fence, watch out.

Jarrod Dyson   CF

Born: 8/15/84   Age: 30   Bats: L   Throws: R   Height: 5' 10"   Weight: 160

YEAR	TEAM	LVL	AGE	PA	R	2B	3B	HR	RBI	BB	K	SB	CS	AVG/OBP/SLG	TAv	BABIP	BRR	FRAA	WARP
2012	OMA	AAA	27	71	12	3	3	0	5	4	5	7	1	.333/.373/.476	.262	.362	2.6	CF(14): 0.8	0.7
2012	KCA	MLB	27	330	52	8	5	0	9	30	56	30	5	.260/.328/.322	.240	.318	6.0	CF(88): 8.8	2.0
2013	OMA	AAA	28	58	8	2	0	0	1	3	12	5	0	.154/.228/.192	.185	.200	0.6	CF(14): 0.1	-0.2
2013	KCA	MLB	28	239	30	9	4	2	17	21	45	34	6	.258/.326/.366	.246	.317	3.2	CF(73): 0.6	0.9
2014	KCA	MLB	29	290	33	4	4	1	24	22	52	36	7	.269/.324/.327	.242	.330	4.7	CF(106): 5.4, LF(3): 0.2	1.5
2015	KCA	MLB	30	269	33	9	3	0	16	20	50	29	5	.248/.308/.316	.236	.301	3.1	CF 5, LF 0	1.0

Breakout: 5%   Improve: 40%   Collapse: 8%   Attrition: 21%   MLB: 79%   Comparables: *Joey Gathright, Alfredo Amezaga, Gregor Blanco*

There's a lot more to baseball than hitting and pitching, as Dyson showed last year with his leather and spikes. Faster than a Robin Williams character-shift, he ranked among the league leaders in producing runs with his legs (despite starting only 66 games) by stealing bases at a high success rate, taking every extra base that wasn't tied down and generally driving opposing defenses and pitchers to distraction. With virtually no power and limited on-base skills, he never has and never will hit enough to start, but Mr. Zoombiya is a true weapon off the bench.

Alcides Escobar   SS

Born: 12/16/86   Age: 28   Bats: R   Throws: R   Height: 6' 1"   Weight: 185

YEAR	TEAM	LVL	AGE	PA	R	2B	3B	HR	RBI	BB	K	SB	CS	AVG/OBP/SLG	TAv	BABIP	BRR	FRAA	WARP
2012	KCA	MLB	25	648	68	30	7	5	52	27	100	35	5	.293/.331/.390	.252	.344	1.6	SS(155): -11.5	1.4
2013	KCA	MLB	26	642	57	20	4	4	52	19	84	22	0	.234/.259/.300	.205	.264	2.2	SS(158): -0.3	-0.7
2014	KCA	MLB	27	620	74	34	5	3	50	23	83	31	6	.285/.317/.377	.255	.326	5.3	SS(162): -0.1	2.5
2015	KCA	MLB	28	587	58	25	6	3	44	24	81	26	4	.261/.296/.343	.239	.294	1.7	SS -3	1.1

Breakout: 0%   Improve: 40%   Collapse: 6%   Attrition: 5%   MLB: 93%   Comparables: *Cristian Guzman, Jack Wilson, Tony Fernandez*

You can't spell Alcides without ALCS, and Escobar starred against the Orioles last fall, posting a .278/.316/.500 line to go with his typically Royals blend of speed and defense. An unapologetic free swinger, Escobar is more prone than most to the vagaries of BABIP, and with more safeties falling in last summer he bounced back from a woeful 2013 at the plate. His speed and marginal power and manager have often miscast him as a table-setter, but with Nori Aoki on hand last year to actually serve up tasty morsels for the heart of the order, Escobar hacked away at the bottom. Of course, Escobar was the leadoff man throughout Kansas City's immortal playoff run, and if the organization doesn't remember the old saw about correlation and causation they may wind up giving away a few runs by keeping him in that role this year. Regardless, Escobar remains a nifty, strong-armed shortstop who can hit a little, is tremendous on the basepaths, has never seen the disabled list and should be well worth his reasonable club options through 2017.

Johnny Giavotella 2B

Born: 7/10/87 Age: 27 Bats: R Throws: R Height: 5' 8" Weight: 185

YEAR	TEAM	LVL	AGE	PA	R	2B	3B	HR	RBI	BB	K	SB	CS	AVG/OBP/SLG	TAv	BABIP	BRR	FRAA	WARP
2012	OMA	AAA	24	418	67	20	2	10	71	46	40	7	1	.323/.404/.472	.308	.339	0.1	2B(79): -1.7, 3B(4): 0.2	3.3
2012	KCA	MLB	24	189	21	7	1	1	15	8	35	3	0	.238/.270/.304	.210	.290	0.3	2B(45): -5.1	-1.0
2013	OMA	AAA	25	426	48	24	0	7	46	51	59	8	0	.286/.369/.408	.286	.320	0.2	2B(46): -0.8, 3B(29): 0.7	2.4
2013	KCA	MLB	25	48	4	3	0	0	4	5	4	0	0	.220/.333/.293	.253	.243	-0.6	2B(13): -0.0	0.0
2014	OMA	AAA	26	493	66	33	2	7	61	47	36	20	4	.308/.373/.440	.292	.321	0.5	2B(65): -7.2, 3B(29): -1.0	2.7
2014	KCA	MLB	26	41	8	1	0	1	5	1	5	0	1	.216/.268/.324	.258	.219	0.8	2B(12): 0.8	0.2
2015	KCA	MLB	27	250	24	13	1	2	23	18	35	5	1	.267/.320/.365	.259	.302	0.3	2B -2, 3B -0	0.5

Breakout: 5%   Improve: 22%   Collapse: 14%   Attrition: 26%   MLB: 56%   Comparables: Eric Sogard, Jake Elmore, Jeff Keppinger

A scrappy second-round pick who has never quite arrived, Giavotella has lately dedicated his summers to demonstrating the yawning fissure between Charlie Leesman and Chris Sale. The Big Easy native has feasted on the has-beens and won't-becomes in Triple-A, posting a career .315/.384/.451 line, but big-league pitchers knock the bat clean out of his hands. With a fringy arm and subpar range, Giavotella can stand in at second or third base but doesn't provide the speed or defense teams look for in a utilityman. Dream about the day his patient approach, gap power and plus surname translate to the big stage if you want, but Giavotella, who the Royals designated for assignment in December, is in Southern California now; dreams are especially cheap there.

Alex Gordon LF

Born: 2/10/84 Age: 31 Bats: L Throws: R Height: 6' 1" Weight: 220

YEAR	TEAM	LVL	AGE	PA	R	2B	3B	HR	RBI	BB	K	SB	CS	AVG/OBP/SLG	TAv	BABIP	BRR	FRAA	WARP
2012	KCA	MLB	28	721	93	51	5	14	72	73	140	10	5	.294/.368/.455	.285	.356	0.5	LF(160): 8.4	4.8
2013	KCA	MLB	29	700	90	27	6	20	81	52	141	11	3	.265/.327/.422	.277	.310	4.2	LF(155): 3.4	4.1
2014	KCA	MLB	30	643	87	34	1	19	74	65	126	12	3	.266/.351/.432	.286	.310	4.2	LF(156): 12.2	5.5
2015	KCA	MLB	31	615	70	33	3	15	71	59	132	11	4	.267/.344/.421	.284	.322	2.2	LF 8	4.0

Breakout: 0%   Improve: 40%   Collapse: 6%   Attrition: 8%   MLB: 96%   Comparables: Andy Pafko, Josh Willingham, Rico Carty

Only five position players have demonstrated the health, production and consistency to post at least four WARP in each of the last four seasons: Miguel Cabrera, Robinson Cano, Andrew McCutchen, Adrian Beltre and Gordon. The Royals' outfielder continues to excel in every facet of the game, winning his fourth Gold Glove last fall, adding runs on the basepaths at a rate that makes even Dee jealous and tattooing pitchers of every stripe, including lefties like Madison Bumgarner. Gordon has never had the immense power of a steroid-era corner outfielder, but his line-drive stroke and discriminating eye are fine for today's game. Rarely mentioned among baseball's current greats, perhaps last season's World Series appearance and an offseason spent endlessly debating whether he could have out-run Brandon Crawford's arm will finally provide Gordon the attention he deserves.

Terrance Gore OF

Born: 6/8/91 Age: 24 Bats: R Throws: R Height: 5' 7" Weight: 165

YEAR	TEAM	LVL	AGE	PA	R	2B	3B	HR	RBI	BB	K	SB	CS	AVG/OBP/SLG	TAv	BABIP	BRR	FRAA	WARP
2013	LEX	A	22	541	76	6	3	0	24	62	120	68	8	.215/.334/.242	.244	.293	12.3	LF(119): 14.4, CF(10): 0.1	3.0
2014	WIL	A+	23	287	34	8	1	0	15	20	66	36	4	.218/.284/.258	.239	.293	4.2	LF(81): 19.0, CF(8): -0.7	2.2
2014	OMA	AAA	23	26	8	0	0	0	0	2	4	11	3	.250/.348/.250	.230	.313	1.9	LF(7): -0.0	0.1
2014	KCA	MLB	23	2	5	0	0	0	0	0	0	0	5	0	.000/.500/.000	.292	.000	1.0	LF(2): 0.0	0.1
2015	KCA	MLB	24	250	30	7	1	0	11	17	65	22	3	.203/.272/.243	.201	.275	3.2	LF 10, CF 0	0.5

Breakout: 0%   Improve: 0%   Collapse: 0%   Attrition: 0%   MLB: 0%   Comparables: Jarrod Dyson, Tyler Graham, Kyle Hudson

A human-cheetah hybrid, Gore has speed that makes even the Royals' collection of rocket cars look like they're in second gear. He can run down outfield flies with the best of them, but unfortunately he slots in midway between Jarrod Dyson and Herb Washington at the plate. "Punchless" doesn't go nearly far enough to describe a player with a career .271 slugging percentage and .034 isolated power, earned mostly in the low minors: Juan Pierre's career MLB isolated power was .066. Gore will likely never develop enough on-base panache to be a viable fourth outfielder, but it's still a gas to watch him run, something a smart contender should let us do every September.

Eric Hosmer 1B

Born: 10/24/89 Age: 25 Bats: L Throws: L Height: 6' 4" Weight: 225

YEAR	TEAM	LVL	AGE	PA	R	2B	3B	HR	RBI	BB	K	SB	CS	AVG/OBP/SLG	TAv	BABIP	BRR	FRAA	WARP
2012	KCA	MLB	22	598	65	22	2	14	60	56	95	16	1	.232/.304/.359	.241	.255	1.7	1B(148): 5.8, RF(3): -0.2	0.3
2013	KCA	MLB	23	680	86	34	3	17	79	51	100	11	4	.302/.353/.448	.291	.335	-0.4	1B(158): 8.1, RF(1): -0.1	3.7
2014	KCA	MLB	24	547	54	35	1	9	58	35	93	4	2	.270/.318/.398	.262	.312	-1.9	1B(130): 6.7	1.4
2015	KCA	MLB	25	542	59	27	2	12	62	40	86	8	2	.279/.331/.417	.278	.312	-0.5	1B 3, RF -0	1.7

Breakout: 2%   Improve: 66%   Collapse: 0%   Attrition: 2%   MLB: 99%   Comparables: Ron Blomberg, Billy Butler, Sean Casey

You know you've arrived when TMZ starts reporting on your celebratory series-clinching bar tabs. While Alex Gordon is the star of the Kansas City lineup, Hosmer was its beating heart last fall. After struggling through another disappointing summer at the plate and losing a month to a broken hand, Hosmer returned to slug .290/.347/.495 down the stretch and become the vocal leading man in the Royals' hit playoff show. He worked with hitting coach Dale Sveum to retool his swing during his forced August absence, loading up earlier and taking a shorter path to the ball, with season-saving results. Of course, that narrative ignores the scorching hot July he logged *before* his trip to the swing clinic, but never mind. Hosmer is still only 25, has already earned two Gold Gloves and seems to have finally made the adjustments to turn his prodigious natural gifts into consistent production.

Raul Ibanez   DH

Born: 6/2/72   Age: 43   Bats: L   Throws: R   Height: 6' 2"   Weight: 225

YEAR	TEAM	LVL	AGE	PA	R	2B	3B	HR	RBI	BB	K	SB	CS	AVG/OBP/SLG	TAv	BABIP	BRR	FRAA	WARP
2012	NYA	MLB	40	425	50	19	3	19	62	35	67	3	0	.240/.308/.453	.264	.243	0.7	LF(80): 0.2, RF(13): -1.1	0.9
2013	SEA	MLB	41	496	54	20	2	29	65	42	128	0	0	.242/.306/.487	.288	.273	-1.9	LF(99): -4.1, RF(1): -0.1	1.3
2014	ANA	MLB	42	190	16	5	2	3	21	23	43	3	2	.157/.258/.265	.218	.190	-1.5	LF(16): 0.8, 1B(1): -0.1	-0.8
2014	KCA	MLB	42	90	7	3	1	2	5	10	16	0	0	.188/.278/.325	.225	.210	-1.6	LF(6): 0.7, RF(5): 0.0	-0.1
2015	KCA	MLB	43	306	30	13	2	8	34	24	61	2	1	.230/.291/.373	.250	.265	-0.9	LF -2, RF -0	-0.1

Breakout: 4%   Improve: 6%   Collapse: 25%   Attrition: 27%   MLB: 41%   Comparables: Hank Aaron, Darrell Evans, Jason Giambi

We tend to reserve full comments for players who may actually contribute to a team's future, but we'll make an exception for Ibanez, whose career has been one lengthy exception. It's rare to find a player who doesn't earn a full-time big-league job before turning 30 but still goes on to have the productivity and longevity Ibanez has had. His relative anonymity is underscored by his one All-Star appearance despite earning MVP votes in three separate seasons, and the lefty slugger's .279 career TAv is nearly identical to those of Alan Trammell, Paul Konerko, Ryne Sandberg and Cal Ripken. A 36th-round pick long known as a hard worker and a "good clubhouse guy," it seems only a matter of time before Ibanez joins baseball's coaching fraternity. Indeed, he was a finalist for the Rays' managerial position over the winter before pulling out of the race; Marc Topkin reported that the reason was "family considerations."

Omar Infante   2B

Born: 12/26/81   Age: 33   Bats: R   Throws: R   Height: 5' 11"   Weight: 195

YEAR	TEAM	LVL	AGE	PA	R	2B	3B	HR	RBI	BB	K	SB	CS	AVG/OBP/SLG	TAv	BABIP	BRR	FRAA	WARP
2012	DET	MLB	30	241	27	7	5	4	20	9	23	7	2	.257/.283/.385	.238	.269	0.3	2B(61): 0.7, 3B(6): -0.3	0.0
2012	MIA	MLB	30	347	42	23	2	8	33	12	42	10	1	.287/.312/.442	.268	.307	5.0	2B(83): 4.6	2.5
2013	TOL	AAA	31	21	1	0	0	0	1	2	2	0	0	.211/.286/.211	.160	.235	0.3	2B(4): -0.4	-0.2
2013	DET	MLB	31	476	54	24	3	10	51	20	44	5	2	.318/.345/.450	.285	.333	-0.2	2B(118): 4.8	3.1
2014	KCA	MLB	32	575	50	21	3	6	66	33	68	9	3	.252/.295/.337	.234	.275	2.9	2B(134): -14.6	-1.2
2015	KCA	MLB	33	525	57	22	4	6	44	24	61	8	3	.278/.310/.377	.256	.300	1.9	2B 3, 3B -0	2.1

Breakout: 1%   Improve: 34%   Collapse: 3%   Attrition: 7%   MLB: 90%   Comparables: Cristian Guzman, Freddy Sanchez, Skip Schumaker

Infante struggled through shoulder and back woes that cut into his playing time and his production. When healthy, he's usually agile and rangy at the keystone and his contact skills and occasional power can help out the bottom of the lineup, but his bat and glove were both MIA last year. There's a well-documented pattern of second basemen breaking down around Infante's age, and since the Royals will be paying him for at least three more seasons, they're hoping a winter's rest helps him buck the trend.

Erik Kratz   C

Born: 6/15/80   Age: 35   Bats: R   Throws: R   Height: 6' 4"   Weight: 240

YEAR	TEAM	LVL	AGE	PA	R	2B	3B	HR	RBI	BB	K	SB	CS	AVG/OBP/SLG	TAv	BABIP	BRR	FRAA	WARP
2012	LEH	AAA	32	141	17	10	0	8	30	10	20	0	0	.266/.326/.540	.278	.250	-1.1	C(31): -0.6	0.8
2012	PHI	MLB	32	157	14	9	0	9	26	11	34	0	0	.248/.306/.504	.285	.257	-1.4	C(41): 0.8	1.4
2013	PHI	MLB	33	218	21	7	0	9	26	18	45	0	0	.213/.280/.386	.223	.228	1.1	C(60): -0.5	0.1
2014	BUF	AAA	34	100	13	10	0	3	17	9	18	0	1	.299/.354/.517	.295	.333	-0.2	C(20): -0.1	0.7
2014	KCA	MLB	34	31	4	1	0	2	3	1	10	0	0	.276/.290/.517	.270	.333	0.1	C(11): -0.1	0.1
2014	TOR	MLB	34	84	8	3	0	3	10	3	12	0	0	.198/.226/.346	.201	.197	-0.5	C(25): -0.2	-0.2
2015	KCA	MLB	35	250	27	12	0	8	29	17	51	0	0	.236/.297/.397	.256	.267	-0.2	C 0	0.8

Breakout: 1%   Improve: 21%   Collapse: 15%   Attrition: 27%   MLB: 60%   Comparables: Raul Casanova, Corky Miller, Tom Wilson

Kratz is your typical backup backstop, with solid catch-and-throw skills, a good reputation as a game-caller, the ability to occasionally turn on a fastball and plus cheerleading skills. "Turkey Bacon" is fine running the staff for a few games at a time, but if he has to catch every day for a month his bat will be exposed for the cheap substitute it is. Now that the Royals are bona fide contenders, they may need to be a little more aspirational in their bench choices.

Raul Mondesi   SS

Born: 7/27/95   Age: 19   Bats: B   Throws: R   Height: 6' 1"   Weight: 165

YEAR	TEAM	LVL	AGE	PA	R	2B	3B	HR	RBI	BB	K	SB	CS	AVG/OBP/SLG	TAv	BABIP	BRR	FRAA	WARP
2013	LEX	A	17	536	61	13	7	7	47	34	118	24	10	.261/.311/.361	.257	.331	1.1	SS(108): 2.3	2.0
2014	WIL	A+	18	472	54	14	12	8	33	24	122	17	4	.211/.256/.354	.229	.274	1.3	SS(106): -0.3	0.8
2015	KCA	MLB	19	250	24	7	3	3	17	7	71	6	2	.216/.239/.305	.201	.284	0.8	SS 1	-0.4

Breakout: 0%   Improve: 0%   Collapse: 0%   Attrition: 0%   MLB: 0%   Comparables: Eduardo Nunez, Arismendy Alcantara, Chris Owings

Mondesi may be the top position prospect in the Royals' system, but you wouldn't know it from his minor-league numbers. He spent last summer as an 18-year-old in High-A, where more experienced pitchers hazed him like a fraternity pledge. Mondesi is a true shortstop with blazing speed and a cannon arm, but if they had thrown a kitchen sink at him last year he would have swung at it. He has yet to develop any pitch recognition or a sense of the strike zone, but he has the quick bat and power potential to become a lineup force if the skills come around. Few prospects have as full a tool chest as Mondesi, and a more reasonable assignment (like a repeat engagement with High-A) this year will give him a better chance to start using them to build a career.

Kendrys Morales DH

Born: 6/20/83   Age: 32   Bats: B   Throws: R   Height: 6' 1"   Weight: 225

YEAR	TEAM	LVL	AGE	PA	R	2B	3B	HR	RBI	BB	K	SB	CS	AVG/OBP/SLG	TAv	BABIP	BRR	FRAA	WARP
2012	ANA	MLB	29	522	61	26	1	22	73	31	116	0	1	.273/.320/.467	.294	.315	-2.5	1B(28): 0.5	2.1
2013	SEA	MLB	30	657	64	34	0	23	80	49	114	0	0	.277/.336/.449	.290	.309	-4.5	1B(31): -1.3	2.0
2014	MIN	MLB	31	162	12	11	0	1	18	6	27	0	0	.234/.259/.325	.222	.273	-0.3	1B(13): -0.9	-0.6
2014	SEA	MLB	31	239	16	9	0	7	24	21	41	0	0	.207/.285/.347	.250	.222	-1.2	1B(14): -0.9	-0.3
2015	KCA	MLB	32	428	45	21	1	13	53	28	78	0	0	.266/.318/.422	.278	.299	-1.8	1B -1	1.1

Breakout: 1%   Improve: 34%   Collapse: 2%   Attrition: 10%   MLB: 95%   Comparables: Bob Watson, Michael Cuddyer, Rafael Palmeiro

It's the familiar old story: boy finds team, boy loses team, boy sits around his house for a few months playing Halo and losing millions of dollars, boy finds team again, they live unhappily ever after. In this version of the tale, none of the characters' motivations make any sense. Morales rejected several islands' worth of money from the Mariners last offseason and wound up with them anyway, and everyone paid dearly, fans most of all. Sitting out for months clearly impaired his hitting, and hitting was the only skill he still had at age 31. Somehow, this led to a two-year deal with the Royals. Maybe we're all supposed to treat 2014 like season two of *Friday Night Lights*: It never happened.

Mike Moustakas 3B

Born: 9/11/88   Age: 26   Bats: L   Throws: R   Height: 6' 0"   Weight: 195

YEAR	TEAM	LVL	AGE	PA	R	2B	3B	HR	RBI	BB	K	SB	CS	AVG/OBP/SLG	TAv	BABIP	BRR	FRAA	WARP
2012	KCA	MLB	23	614	69	34	1	20	73	39	124	5	2	.242/.296/.412	.252	.274	-2.4	3B(149): 17.9	3.4
2013	KCA	MLB	24	514	42	26	0	12	42	32	83	2	4	.233/.287/.364	.234	.257	-3.0	3B(134): 3.8	0.5
2014	OMA	AAA	25	34	3	3	0	1	5	3	6	0	0	.355/.412/.548	.325	.417	0.1	3B(7): 0.4	0.5
2014	KCA	MLB	25	500	45	21	1	15	54	35	74	1	0	.212/.271/.361	.233	.220	1.7	3B(138): 6.0	1.2
2015	KCA	MLB	26	478	46	24	1	12	53	30	83	2	1	.242/.293/.382	.252	.270	-0.8	3B 7	1.4

Breakout: 1%   Improve: 54%   Collapse: 0%   Attrition: 6%   MLB: 98%   Comparables: Hank Blalock, Puddin Head Jones, Jeff Cirillo

Postseason heroics aside, few players pose more of a conundrum than Moustakas. As a prospect he was considered a can't-miss slugger with a strong arm but iffy defensive skills; in the big leagues he's become a sterling defensive third baseman who can't hit a lick. The bat speed and contact skills that had scouts predicting he'd become a middle-of-the-order force are still evident, but his approach completely undermines his tools. Moose tries to pull everything he sees into the right-field bleachers but he only has average power, leading to middling home run totals along with copious fly-ball outs, pop ups and groundballs into the shift. Moustakas needs to focus on hitting rather than slugging because his glove won't be able to make excuses for his bat forever.

Carlos Peguero RF

Born: 2/22/87   Age: 28   Bats: L   Throws: L   Height: 6' 5"   Weight: 250

YEAR	TEAM	LVL	AGE	PA	R	2B	3B	HR	RBI	BB	K	SB	CS	AVG/OBP/SLG	TAv	BABIP	BRR	FRAA	WARP
2012	TAC	AAA	25	322	47	13	1	21	54	29	103	2	2	.285/.366/.562	.334	.369	-1.4	RF(51): 3.3, LF(23): -3.5	3.0
2012	SEA	MLB	25	57	2	2	1	2	7	1	28	0	0	.179/.193/.357	.210	.308	-0.1	RF(11): 0.8, LF(2): 0.1	0.0
2013	TAC	AAA	26	505	60	28	3	19	83	42	156	11	8	.260/.321/.460	.275	.346	1.6	RF(80): -4.4, LF(11): -0.5	1.7
2013	SEA	MLB	26	7	1	0	0	1	1	1	2	1	0	.333/.429/.833	.441	.333	0.0	RF(2): -0.0	0.1
2014	OMA	AAA	27	418	64	17	1	30	76	45	138	11	4	.266/.349/.563	.299	.337	-0.6	LF(40): -4.5, RF(23): 1.9	2.3
2014	KCA	MLB	27	10	1	1	0	0	1	1	5	0	0	.222/.300/.333	.221	.500	0.2	RF(4): -0.2	0.0
2015	KCA	MLB	28	250	31	10	1	11	34	16	87	4	2	.237/.292/.437	.266	.323	0.0	RF 1, LF -1	0.6

Breakout: 2%   Improve: 12%   Collapse: 9%   Attrition: 18%   MLB: 36%   Comparables: Brad Eldred, Jason Dubois, Shelley Duncan

With Wily Mo Pena probably gone from these shores for good, Peguero inherits his mantle as the player most likely to literally launch a pitch into orbit. Assuming, that is, the hulking Quad-A slugger happened to randomly make contact with it. And yet, with power hitters in high demand, Peguero is stuck in the PCL smashing 30 bombs while watching the big club succeed with their slap-and-dash offense. The reason is Peguero's insanely hacktastic approach, which major-league hurlers continually exploit. If he were to spend a full season in the bigs, Peguero's 33 percent Triple-A strikeout rate would look like Rod Carew compared to what AL pitchers would inflict on him. It's easy for us to say he should take a few more pitches or shorten up with two strikes, but let's be honest: If you could put that kind of a hurt on a baseball, wouldn't you swing for the fences every time too?

Salvador Perez C

Born: 5/10/90   Age: 25   Bats: R   Throws: R   Height: 6' 3"   Weight: 240

YEAR	TEAM	LVL	AGE	PA	R	2B	3B	HR	RBI	BB	K	SB	CS	AVG/OBP/SLG	TAv	BABIP	BRR	FRAA	WARP
2012	OMA	AAA	22	53	11	2	0	0	7	2	5	0	0	.340/.365/.380	.252	.378	-0.7	C(8): 0.0	0.0
2012	KCA	MLB	22	305	38	16	0	11	39	12	27	0	0	.301/.328/.471	.270	.299	-1.8	C(74): -1.7	1.9
2013	KCA	MLB	23	526	48	25	3	13	79	21	63	0	0	.292/.323/.433	.277	.311	-2.3	C(137): -1.6, 1B(1): -0.0	3.4
2014	KCA	MLB	24	606	57	28	2	17	70	22	85	1	0	.260/.289/.403	.251	.278	-3.6	C(146): -2.7	1.5
2015	KCA	MLB	25	553	54	28	2	13	65	20	70	0	0	.283/.312/.421	.274	.302	-2.4	C -2, 1B -0	2.5

Breakout: 1%   Improve: 62%   Collapse: 3%   Attrition: 4%   MLB: 96%   Comparables: Wilson Ramos, Kurt Suzuki, James Loney

Perez has two Gold Gloves on his mantle and was an iron man last season, catching a major-league record 158 games, counting the postseason, but he'll need to improve his Will Rogers plate approach if he wants to reach his gaudy potential. He doesn't rank among baseball's best pitch-framers, but he calls a good game, is surprisingly agile for a big man and controls baserunners. Perez also avoids strikeouts and has above-average power, but last year he didn't meet a pitch he didn't like. He continually offered at stuff out of the zone, leading to weak contact and pitchers learning they needn't throw strikes to retire him. Even his game-winning hit in the Wild Card game came when he pulled a pitch that was low and away. If Perez can't become a little more selective, he'll turn into A.J. Pierzynski with better defense and a lower batting average; that's not a bad player, but it also isn't the Junior Circuit's version of Yadier Molina.

Bubba Starling   CF

Born: 8/3/92   Age: 22   Bats: R   Throws: R   Height: 6' 4"   Weight: 180

YEAR	TEAM	LVL	AGE	PA	R	2B	3B	HR	RBI	BB	K	SB	CS	AVG/OBP/SLG	TAv	BABIP	BRR	FRAA	WARP
2013	LEX	A	20	498	51	21	4	13	63	53	128	22	3	.241/.329/.398	.287	.309	1.0	CF(117): 2.2	3.3
2014	WIL	A+	21	549	67	23	4	9	54	49	150	17	2	.218/.304/.338	.256	.293	4.9	CF(130): -9.3	1.7
2015	KCA	MLB	22	250	23	9	1	5	24	16	77	4	1	.207/.265/.318	.221	.284	0.4	CF -1	-0.4

Breakout: 0%   Improve: 0%   Collapse: 0%   Attrition: 0%   MLB: 0%   Comparables: Corey Brown, Elijah Dukes, Michael Saunders

A multi-sport home-town hero who received the highest draft bonus in club history, Starling's career has stalled due to his continuing inability to solidly strike a spherical projectile with a cylindrical cudgel. Tall and athletic, he's excellent with the glove and has the speed and power potential of a future All-Star center fielder, but hitting remains a mystery to him. He's not an inveterate hacker, as Starling has improved his pitch recognition and knows the strike zone, but he simply struggles to make contact when he gets his pitch. The Royals will be patient with him given his youth and relative inexperience, but unless he develops the skills to leverage his talent he'll have to rely on every five-tool washout's backup career plan: groundbreaking general manager.

Pitchers

Miguel Almonte   RHP

Born: 4/4/93   Age: 22   Bats: R   Throws: R   Height: 6'2"   Weight: 180

YEAR	TEAM	LVL	AGE	W	L	SV	G	GS	IP	H	HR	BB	K	BB/9	K/9	GB%	BABIP	WHIP	ERA	FIP	FRA	WARP
2013	LEX	A	20	6	9	0	25	25	130²	115	6	36	132	2.5	9.1	47%	.297	1.16	3.10	3.04	3.98	1.1
2014	WIL	A+	21	6	8	0	23	22	110¹	107	9	32	101	2.6	8.2	48%	.316	1.26	4.49	3.92	4.41	0.7
2015	KCA	MLB	22	5	7	0	18	18	91	104	11	36	58	3.6	5.7	45%	.313	1.54	5.20	5.26	5.65	-0.5

Breakout: 0%   Improve: 0%   Collapse: 0%   Attrition: 0%   MLB: 0%   Comparables: Kyle Drabek, Andrew Heaney, Adam Wilk

At an age when most people are concerned with mixtapes, keggers and mastering the art of ironic detachment, Almonte is charged with honing the skills that may or may not earn him millions. Blessed with a mid-90s fastball and a changeup that could one day rank among baseball's best, the young Dominican has the goods to be a mid-rotation starter but didn't dominate last year in High-A. He struggled with fastball command, although his control was fine, and his slurvy breaking ball made some progress but still has miles to go. He works fast and there's some deception in his delivery, but his comparatively slight frame and struggles to develop a third pitch have some thinking his future lies in relief. The Royals will give him every opportunity to stick in the rotation, but if that falls through his stuff will play well in the late innings.

Christian Binford   RHP

Born: 12/20/92   Age: 22   Bats: R   Throws: R   Height: 6'6"   Weight: 217

YEAR	TEAM	LVL	AGE	W	L	SV	G	GS	IP	H	HR	BB	K	BB/9	K/9	GB%	BABIP	WHIP	ERA	FIP	FRA	WARP
2013	LEX	A	20	8	7	0	23	23	135	129	7	25	130	1.7	8.7	56%	.319	1.14	2.67	2.94	3.68	1.9
2014	WIL	A+	21	5	4	0	14	14	82²	72	2	11	92	1.2	10.0	45%	.315	1.00	2.40	2.08	2.83	1.9
2014	NWA	AA	21.	3	2	0	8	8	48	45	7	6	38	1.1	7.1	51%	.270	1.06	3.19	3.93	4.85	0.3
2014	OMA	AAA	21	0	1	0	4	0	10	16	1	5	9	4.5	8.1	46%	.417	2.10	5.40	5.00	4.75	0.1
2015	KCA	MLB	22	6	7	0	20	20	112	131	12	31	73	2.5	5.8	48%	.318	1.45	4.76	4.63	5.17	-0.1

Breakout: 0%   Improve: 0%   Collapse: 0%   Attrition: 0%   MLB: 0%   Comparables: Patrick Corbin, David Holmberg, Joe Wieland

Binford stood out in the Wilmington rotation last year, both for his towering build and for a level of production that dwarfed more heralded prospects Miguel Almonte and Sean Manaea. He stood out at the Futures Game, too, as the former 30th-round pick is a low-velocity strike-thrower whose upper-80s fastball seemed out of place among the gaudy tools on display in Minneapolis. Binford knows how to pitch, commands his fastball well and has a serviceable slide piece, though his changeup still lags. He held his own in Double-A but struggled in a brief bullpen audition in Omaha; still, that the Royals were considering him to bolster their relief corps down the stretch highlights the progress he's made. If he continues to avoid walks and miss a few bats he could eventually slot in at the end of a big-league rotation, though a career in middle relief seems more likely.

Francisley Bueno   LHP

Born: 3/5/81   Age: 34   Bats: L   Throws: L   Height: 5'11"   Weight: 205

YEAR	TEAM	LVL	AGE	W	L	SV	G	GS	IP	H	HR	BB	K	BB/9	K/9	GB%	BABIP	WHIP	ERA	FIP	FRA	WARP
2012	OMA	AAA	31	1	4	6	35	0	55²	43	5	15	54	2.4	8.7	50%	.253	1.04	2.75	3.86	5.14	0.4
2012	KCA	MLB	31	1	1	0	18	0	17¹	16	0	2	7	1.0	3.6	59%	.271	1.04	1.56	2.76	3.85	0.2
2013	OMA	AAA	32	3	3	1	36	1	67²	64	6	24	56	3.2	7.4	47%	.296	1.30	2.66	3.98	4.54	0.6
2013	KCA	MLB	32	1	0	0	7	0	8¹	4	0	2	5	2.2	5.4	58%	.167	0.72	0.00	2.60	3.98	0.1
2014	OMA	AAA	33	0	2	0	9	3	14²	14	1	4	17	2.5	10.4	56%	.325	1.23	5.52	3.49	6.27	0.2
2014	KCA	MLB	33	0	0	0	30	0	32¹	36	3	7	20	1.9	5.6	46%	.297	1.33	4.18	3.87	4.66	0.1
2015	KCA	MLB	34	2	1	0	33	0	46	46	4	13	33	2.5	6.5	47%	.295	1.28	3.93	4.23	4.27	0.3

Breakout: 7%   Improve: 17%   Collapse: 13%   Attrition: 14%   MLB: 35%   Comparables: Roman Colon, Randy Choate, Vinnie Chulk

You know that restaurant on the other side of town with a menu the size of *Infinite Jest*? The one where everything is okay, but nothing ever stands out? That's Bueno, who changes speeds and uses a wide assortment of off-speed junk to distract hitters from his upper-80s four-seamer. The Royals never really tried to protect him from right-handed batters, and Bueno has never perfected a recipe to retire them, but his career .217/.252/.278 line against same-side hitters paints him as a possible LOOGY. The Royals released him last fall, making him available to add a little Cuban spice to another team's bullpen stew.

Bruce Chen LHP

Born: 6/19/77   Age: 38   Bats: L   Throws: L   Height: 6'2"   Weight: 215

YEAR	TEAM	LVL	AGE	W	L	SV	G	GS	IP	H	HR	BB	K	BB/9	K/9	GB%	BABIP	WHIP	ERA	FIP	FRA	WARP
2012	KCA	MLB	35	11	14	0	34	34	191²	215	33	47	140	2.2	6.6	34%	.304	1.37	5.07	4.68	4.65	2.3
2013	KCA	MLB	36	9	4	0	34	15	121	107	13	36	78	2.7	5.8	29%	.255	1.18	3.27	4.15	4.20	1.3
2014	OMA	AAA	37	0	1	0	3	3	12¹	21	1	3	13	2.2	9.5	32%	.500	1.95	8.76	3.38	4.56	0.3
2014	KCA	MLB	37	2	4	0	13	7	48¹	69	7	16	36	3.0	6.7	34%	.380	1.76	7.45	4.61	4.91	0.1
2015	KCA	MLB	38	4	4	0	12	12	66	71	8	21	47	2.8	6.3	35%	.301	1.39	4.57	4.79	4.97	0.1

Breakout: 8%   Improve: 26%   Collapse: 14%   Attrition: 10%   MLB: 62%   Comparables: *Ted Lilly, Kevin Millwood, Mike Hampton*

The most important role the soft-tossing Chen filled on the Royals' staff last year was as Yordano Ventura's translator, which meant that whatever the young Dominican said in Spanish likely came out much slower in English. Also funnier and wiser, as Chen's limited value as a pitcher has been superseded by his clubhouse role as class clown and mentor. One of the most studious pitchers around, Chen has relaunched his career a half-dozen times but has seemingly run out of ways to hide his mid-80s heater from professional bats; he earned his release last August. If this truly is the end, he leaves having matched Mariano Rivera with 82 wins, a record for Panamanian pitchers. Proof, Chen will no doubt explain, that they were equally successful.

Casey Coleman RHP

Born: 7/3/87   Age: 27   Bats: L   Throws: R   Height: 6'0"   Weight: 185

YEAR	TEAM	LVL	AGE	W	L	SV	G	GS	IP	H	HR	BB	K	BB/9	K/9	GB%	BABIP	WHIP	ERA	FIP	FRA	WARP
2012	IOW	AAA	24	2	4	0	13	11	58	53	4	25	52	3.9	8.1	48%	.299	1.34	4.34	4.17	5.00	1.1
2012	CHN	MLB	24	0	2	0	17	1	24¹	37	5	12	16	4.4	5.9	43%	.372	2.01	7.40	5.97	6.64	-0.4
2013	IOW	AAA	25	5	3	3	41	4	88¹	77	7	36	66	3.7	6.7	44%	.267	1.28	3.16	4.36	4.53	0.7
2014	OMA	AAA	26	5	1	3	34	0	67	51	4	26	53	3.5	7.1	57%	.254	1.15	2.15	4.10	4.76	0.7
2014	KCA	MLB	26	1	0	0	10	0	12	16	0	6	5	4.5	3.8	64%	.364	1.83	5.25	3.83	4.31	0.1
2015	KCA	MLB	27	3	3	0	24	7	66²	71	6	26	42	3.5	5.7	49%	.298	1.46	4.56	4.76	4.95	0.1

Breakout: 29%   Improve: 53%   Collapse: 13%   Attrition: 26%   MLB: 81%   Comparables: *Mitchell Boggs, Jim Johnson, Josh Outman*

This Coleman throws harder than the other Coleman who spat seeds in the Royals' bullpen last year and is a beat writer's dream to boot. A "Notes" column made flesh, Casey is the son and grandson of All-Star starters (Joe, in both cases), making these particular Colemen the first three-generation pitching family in major-league history. Other bullet points: Coleman pitched with Chris Sale at Florida Gulf Coast and beat him to the majors, and a mechanical change helped his fastball jump three full ticks since coming to Kansas City last spring. He has a decent slider to abet his mid-90s heater and found success in the Omaha 'pen last year, but walked more men than he whiffed in his Royals cameo. He should get another shot at low-leverage work.

Louis Coleman RHP

Born: 4/4/86   Age: 29   Bats: R   Throws: R   Height: 6'4"   Weight: 205

YEAR	TEAM	LVL	AGE	W	L	SV	G	GS	IP	H	HR	BB	K	BB/9	K/9	GB%	BABIP	WHIP	ERA	FIP	FRA	WARP
2012	OMA	AAA	26	0	2	3	11	1	19²	13	1	8	26	3.7	11.9	28%	.267	1.07	3.20	2.90	3.48	0.6
2012	KCA	MLB	26	0	0	0	42	0	51	41	10	26	65	4.6	11.5	22%	.270	1.31	3.71	4.63	5.07	-0.1
2013	OMA	AAA	27	3	2	6	24	0	44²	36	1	17	52	3.4	10.5	37%	.304	1.19	1.61	2.67	2.74	1.4
2013	KCA	MLB	27	3	0	0	27	0	29²	19	1	6	32	1.8	9.7	42%	.257	0.84	0.61	2.06	2.29	0.7
2014	OMA	AAA	28	2	1	7	28	1	39²	32	6	15	53	3.4	12.0	37%	.283	1.18	3.86	4.28	3.27	1.1
2014	KCA	MLB	28	1	0	1	31	0	34	39	6	18	24	4.8	6.4	44%	.314	1.68	5.56	5.72	6.16	-0.5
2015	KCA	MLB	29	3	1	0	50	0	65²	56	7	25	74	3.4	10.1	35%	.290	1.22	3.36	3.95	3.65	1.0

Breakout: 11%   Improve: 19%   Collapse: 21%   Attrition: 19%   MLB: 49%   Comparables: *Philip Humber, Cha Seung Baek, Dave Williams*

The side-winding Coleman continues to ride the stage between Kansas City and Omaha, but struggled mightily with the big club last year. Normally poison to same-side batters, righties tuned him up, posting a .274/.352/.489 line between the majors and Triple-A and launching eleven bombs. Coleman struggled all year to command his upper-80s fastball and his slider came in flat, which led to consistent hard contact and too many episodes of handing the ball to a scowling Ned Yost. Relievers live in a reality defined by small sample sizes, so Coleman may well bounce back this year and provide solid work in the 'pen. Then again, maybe he won't. If we knew for sure, we'd probably sell that information to Dayton Moore.

Tim Collins LHP

Born: 8/21/89   Age: 25   Bats: L   Throws: L   Height: 5'7"   Weight: 170

YEAR	TEAM	LVL	AGE	W	L	SV	G	GS	IP	H	HR	BB	K	BB/9	K/9	GB%	BABIP	WHIP	ERA	FIP	FRA	WARP
2012	KCA	MLB	22	5	4	0	72	0	69²	55	8	34	93	4.4	12.0	43%	.297	1.28	3.36	3.42	3.71	1.1
2013	KCA	MLB	23	3	6	0	66	0	53¹	49	3	28	52	4.7	8.8	40%	.307	1.44	3.54	3.43	4.18	0.4
2014	OMA	AAA	24	2	1	3	23	1	42¹	26	6	16	56	3.4	11.9	41%	.233	0.99	2.76	4.17	4.08	0.6
2014	KCA	MLB	24	0	3	0	22	0	21	18	2	11	15	4.7	6.4	42%	.267	1.38	3.86	4.83	5.12	-0.1
2015	KCA	MLB	25	3	1	1	51	0	51	42	4	24	59	4.3	10.4	40%	.293	1.30	3.37	3.77	3.66	0.8

Breakout: 27%   Improve: 61%   Collapse: 18%   Attrition: 14%   MLB: 91%   Comparables: *Chris Perez, Joel Zumaya, Taylor Tankersley*

Collins struggled at the outset last season, losing April to an elbow strain (which beats losing her to a goof like Andy Dwyer), then struggling with his command before a June demotion. Tiny Tim righted the ship in Omaha, racking up strikeouts at the rate to which we have grown accustomed and pitching his way onto the postseason roster. Collins supplements his plus lefty velocity with a solid curve and changeup that allow him to be effective against opposite-side hitters. He issues too many free passes to be trusted in the late innings, but is a solid option in the sixth.

Wade Davis   RHP

Born: 9/7/85   Age: 29   Bats: R   Throws: R   Height: 6'5"   Weight: 220

YEAR	TEAM	LVL	AGE	W	L	SV	G	GS	IP	H	HR	BB	K	BB/9	K/9	GB%	BABIP	WHIP	ERA	FIP	FRA	WARP
2012	TBA	MLB	26	3	0	0	54	0	70¹	48	5	29	87	3.7	11.1	40%	.264	1.09	2.43	2.73	2.82	1.6
2013	KCA	MLB	27	8	11	0	31	24	135¹	169	15	58	114	3.9	7.6	42%	.361	1.68	5.32	4.21	4.92	0.6
2014	KCA	MLB	28	9	2	3	71	0	72	38	0	23	109	2.9	13.6	49%	.264	0.85	1.00	1.22	1.63	2.4
2015	KCA	MLB	29	4	3	0	28	8	68²	69	6	24	58	3.2	7.6	41%	.306	1.36	4.14	4.13	4.50	0.4

Breakout: 15%   Improve: 39%   Collapse: 22%   Attrition: 8%   MLB: 92%   Comparables: John Lackey, Freddy Garcia, Edwin Jackson

Can we all just agree now that Davis should stay in the bullpen? It's a baseball adage that a starter's stuff will play up when he moves to relief, but what Davis did last season nearly defies explanation. When the Rays first tried him in the 'pen in 2012, he gained two miles per hour on his fastball and found success. This time, he added three ticks to every offering, unleashed a devastating knuckle-curve and swapped his dodgy slider for a cutter that causes blindness if viewed directly. Per the PITCHf/x savants at Brooks Baseball, his cutter "generates an extremely high number of swings and misses[,] generates an extreme number of groundballs[,] is blazing fast and has strong cutting action." You could sum that up as "totally freakin' unhittable." Batters posted a .172 TAv against Davis, the lowest in the Junior Circuit. With three dominant pitches, the middle cog of HDH was the best reliever in baseball last year, and while his salary takes a jump this year, his ability to shorten games will make him more than worth it.

Scott Downs   LHP

Born: 3/17/76   Age: 39   Bats: L   Throws: L   Height: 6'2"   Weight: 220

YEAR	TEAM	LVL	AGE	W	L	SV	G	GS	IP	H	HR	BB	K	BB/9	K/9	GB%	BABIP	WHIP	ERA	FIP	FRA	WARP
2012	ANA	MLB	36	1	1	9	57	0	45²	43	3	17	32	3.4	6.3	61%	.282	1.31	3.15	3.62	4.51	0.1
2013	ANA	MLB	37	2	3	0	43	0	29¹	26	1	11	22	3.4	6.8	63%	.291	1.26	1.84	3.35	3.47	0.3
2013	ATL	MLB	37	2	1	0	25	0	14	19	0	8	15	5.1	9.6	68%	.432	1.93	3.86	2.59	2.17	0.4
2014	CHA	MLB	38	0	2	1	38	0	23²	24	1	15	22	5.7	8.4	59%	.329	1.65	6.08	3.75	3.55	0.3
2014	KCA	MLB	38	0	2	0	17	0	14¹	12	1	5	3	3.1	1.9	65%	.229	1.19	3.14	4.69	6.14	-0.2
2015	KCA	MLB	39	2	1	2	46	0	34²	35	2	13	24	3.3	6.3	57%	.298	1.37	3.84	4.13	4.17	0.3

Breakout: 17%   Improve: 45%   Collapse: 11%   Attrition: 8%   MLB: 69%   Comparables: Jamey Wright, Rheal Cormier, Mike Stanton

Downs and his vaunted sinker kill more worms before breakfast than most hurlers do all day, but there's more to pitching than groundball outs. His walk and strikeout rates set off klaxons last season and he posted a shudder-inducing ERA, so his days as a solid seventh-inning guy are long gone. But Downs can still put a chill into same-side batters and induce his share of double-play grounders, so there's no reason he can't fill a situational role as long as he's spotted correctly and his arm remains fully attached.

Danny Duffy   LHP

Born: 12/21/88   Age: 26   Bats: L   Throws: L   Height: 6'3"   Weight: 205

YEAR	TEAM	LVL	AGE	W	L	SV	G	GS	IP²	H	HR	BB	K	BB/9	K/9	GB%	BABIP	WHIP	ERA	FIP	FRA	WARP
2012	KCA	MLB	23	2	2	0	6	6	27²	26	2	18	28	5.9	9.1	33%	.329	1.59	3.90	3.91	4.22	0.4
2013	NWA	AA	24	0	2	0	4	4	16	16	3	5	28	2.8	15.8	38%	.448	1.31	3.94	3.49	4.01	0.3
2013	OMA	AAA	24	3	0	0	12	10	53	50	4	25	59	4.2	10.0	38%	.329	1.42	4.08	3.85	4.04	0.8
2013	KCA	MLB	24	2	0	0	5	5	24¹	19	0	14	22	5.2	8.1	31%	.284	1.36	1.85	3.12	3.41	0.5
2014	KCA	MLB	25	9	12	0	31	25	149¹	113	12	53	113	3.2	6.8	38%	.239	1.11	2.53	3.86	4.52	0.9
2015	KCA	MLB	26	7	7	0	23	23	117¹	111	11	45	108	3.5	8.3	39%	.299	1.33	3.88	4.22	4.22	1.3

Breakout: 37%   Improve: 67%   Collapse: 12%   Attrition: 13%   MLB: 95%   Comparables: Gio Gonzalez, Francisco Liriano, Felix Doubront

Oh yeah! After watching him lose almost two seasons to elbow woes, Royals Nation was totally ready to Get Duffed last summer, and the young lefty delivered. Duffy entered the rotation in May and pitched well, posting a triumphant sub-three ERA. His peripherals paint a different picture, however, as his pedestrian walk and strikeout rates could drive a stat-head to drink. An extreme fly-ball pitcher who benefits greatly from Kansas City's collection of outfield speedsters, Duffy works his rising low-90s fastball up in the zone and generates plenty of pop-ups and managed to keep most batters in the yard last year. That won't last: Duffy is as sure a bet as there is in baseball for gopher-ball regression this season. He also missed time last September with an inflamed rotator cuff and worked out of the 'pen in the playoffs due to a stress reaction in his ribcage. If he can stay healthy, Duffy can be a solid fourth starter, but he isn't an ace-in-waiting.

Brandon Finnegan   LHP

Born: 4/14/93   Age: 22   Bats: L   Throws: L   Height: 5'11"   Weight: 185

YEAR	TEAM	LVL	AGE	W	L	SV	G	GS	IP	H	HR	BB	K	BB/9	K/9	GB%	BABIP	WHIP	ERA	FIP	FRA	WARP
2014	WIL	A+	21	0	1	0	5	5	15	5	1	2	13	1.2	7.8	50%	.121	0.47	0.60	3.05	3.65	0.2
2014	NWA	AA	21	0	3	0	8	0	12	15	2	2	13	1.5	9.8	52%	.342	1.42	2.25	3.87	4.63	0.1
2014	KCA	MLB	21	0	1	0	7	0	7	6	0	1	10	1.3	12.9	59%	.353	1.00	1.29	0.73	1.95	0.2
2015	KCA	MLB	22	2	1	1	19	4	35¹	35	3	10	31	2.6	7.9	47%	.308	1.30	3.90	3.81	4.24	0.3

Breakout: 24%   Improve: 38%   Collapse: 8%   Attrition: 12%   MLB: 53%   Comparables: Carter Capps, Zach Putnam, Mat Latos

They call James Shields "Big Game," but it was Finnegan who made history last year by being the first pitcher ever to work both the College World Series and the Fall Classic in the same year. Drafted in the first round out of Texas Christian, he was tabbed as a fast mover and made good by working only 27 minor-league innings before getting big outs for the Royals 'pen down the stretch and in the playoffs. He shows impressive command of a mature arsenal, with a fastball that can reach the mid-90s in bursts, a solid changeup and a potentially devastating slider. His high-effort delivery and short stature have many expecting a full-time bullpen role. Finnegan made only five professional starts, all of them in High-A, but he has three quality pitches and a plan of attack, so the Royals would be best served by stretching him out as a Triple-A starter to see if he can reach his mid-rotation potential.

Brian Flynn   LHP

Born: 4/19/90   Age: 25   Bats: L   Throws: L   Height: 6'7"   Weight: 250

YEAR	TEAM	LVL	AGE	W	L	SV	G	GS	IP	H	HR	BB	K	BB/9	K/9	GB%	BABIP	WHIP	ERA	FIP	FRA	WARP
2012	LAK	A+	22	8	4	0	18	18	102	113	5	32	84	2.8	7.4	46%	.341	1.42	3.71	3.41	4.62	1.2
2012	JAX	AA	22	3	0	0	8	8	45	48	3	13	32	2.6	6.4	47%	.315	1.36	3.80	3.72	5.06	0.2
2013	JAX	AA	23	1	1	0	4	4	23	18	2	3	25	1.2	9.8	47%	.298	0.91	1.57	2.39	2.41	0.7
2013	NWO	AAA	23	6	11	0	23	23	138	127	7	40	122	2.6	8.0	55%	.302	1.21	2.80	3.42	3.79	2.1
2013	MIA	MLB	23	0	2	0	4	4	18	27	4	13	15	6.5	7.5	40%	.411	2.22	8.50	6.41	7.12	-0.3
2014	NWO	AAA	24	8	10	0	25	25	139²	169	13	50	104	3.2	6.7	47%	.342	1.57	4.06	4.62	4.77	1.3
2014	MIA	MLB	24	0	1	0	2	1	7	12	0	3	6	3.9	7.7	50%	.462	2.14	9.00	2.67	2.64	0.2
2015	KCA	MLB	25	7	9	0	22	22	124¹	148	12	43	80	3.1	5.8	46%	.325	1.53	5.00	4.71	5.44	-0.5

Breakout: 27%   Improve: 43%   Collapse: 10%   Attrition: 35%   MLB: 59%   Comparables: *Scott Diamond, Kevin Mulvey, Jeff Locke*

How about that Anibal Sanchez trade for the Marlins? With Jacob Turner released to the Cubs and Rob Brantly turning into a pumpkin, Flynn was Miami's last best hope to salvage something out of that debacle of a deal. Something, it turns out, was Aaron Crow, an arb-eligible reliever with a strikeout rate around five per nine last year. How about that freakin' Anibal Sanchez trade?

For Flynn's acquiring team, there's still upside here, despite the pitcher taking a step back in his repeat performance at New Orleans last season. A tall lefty with questionable mechanics, he struggles with release points and, as a result, his control. His once-impressive fastball looks like it is stalling out or, worse, losing a few ticks from his high-water mark a few seasons back in the minors. But he comes to the table with four solid offerings, which makes him a candidate to stay in the rotation, rather than land in the no-man's-land of middle relief.

Jason Frasor   RHP

Born: 8/9/77   Age: 37   Bats: R   Throws: R   Height: 5'9"   Weight: 180

YEAR	TEAM	LVL	AGE	W	L	SV	G	GS	IP	H	HR	BB	K	BB/9	K/9	GB%	BABIP	WHIP	ERA	FIP	FRA	WARP
2012	TOR	MLB	34	1	1	0	50	0	43²	42	6	22	53	4.5	10.9	42%	.333	1.47	4.12	4.05	5.23	0.2
2013	TEX	MLB	35	4	3	0	61	0	49	36	4	20	48	3.7	8.8	47%	.250	1.14	2.57	3.40	3.70	0.5
2014	TEX	MLB	36	1	1	0	38	0	29²	27	2	14	30	4.2	9.1	48%	.305	1.38	3.34	3.53	3.81	0.3
2014	KCA	MLB	36	3	0	0	23	0	17²	13	1	4	16	2.0	8.2	46%	.267	0.96	1.53	2.93	3.45	0.2
2015	KCA	MLB	37	2	1	0	46	0	39¹	37	3	16	39	3.6	9.0	44%	.307	1.34	3.85	3.92	4.18	0.3

Breakout: 15%   Improve: 33%   Collapse: 17%   Attrition: 9%   MLB: 72%   Comparables: *Arthur Rhodes, Trever Miller, Brian Fuentes*

If it feels like Frasor has been around forever, it's because he has. The diminutive righty continues to provide just enough to be an asset in a big-league bullpen. He commands his low-90s fastball well, can get righties to pound his slider into the ground and his splitter keeps lefties honest. The Royals traded for him last summer and re-upped him this fall to do what he always does: work 40 reliable innings in middle relief. They'll get what they paid for and probably a little more.

Jeremy Guthrie   RHP

Born: 4/8/79   Age: 36   Bats: R   Throws: R   Height: 6'1"   Weight: 205

YEAR	TEAM	LVL	AGE	W	L	SV	G	GS	IP	H	HR	BB	K	BB/9	K/9	GB%	BABIP	WHIP	ERA	FIP	FRA	WARP
2012	COL	MLB	33	3	9	0	19	15	90²	122	21	31	45	3.1	4.5	43%	.318	1.69	6.35	6.41	6.89	-0.7
2012	KCA	MLB	33	5	3	0	14	14	91	84	9	19	56	1.9	5.5	40%	.268	1.13	3.16	3.79	4.50	0.9
2013	KCA	MLB	34	15	12	0	33	33	211²	236	30	59	111	2.5	4.7	45%	.296	1.39	4.04	4.82	5.18	0.3
2014	KCA	MLB	35	13	11	0	32	32	202²	215	23	49	124	2.2	5.5	45%	.294	1.30	4.13	4.34	4.70	0.7
2015	KCA	MLB	36	10	11	0	28	28	173²	189	21	47	101	2.4	5.2	42%	.294	1.36	4.57	4.99	4.97	0.1

Breakout: 19%   Improve: 41%   Collapse: 11%   Attrition: 12%   MLB: 69%   Comparables: *Bronson Arroyo, Jarrod Washburn, Kevin Millwood*

To dismiss Guthrie as an innings-eater is to misunderstand his value, as the veteran righty's continuing ability to start 30 games, work 200 innings and give his team a chance in most of his starts is the definition of a big-league fourth starter. Read through this book and see how many prospects we project with similar or higher ceilings, then reflect on how few of them will ever match Guthrie by turning in eight average seasons in a rotation. Guthrie's time in Kansas City has been the perfect marriage of skill and environment: His strike-throwing, pitch-to-contact style benefits greatly from the vacuum gloves and burners playing behind him. Vanilla may not be the most exotic flavor around, but it's hard to bake anything delicious without it.

Kelvin Herrera   RHP

Born: 12/31/89   Age: 25   Bats: R   Throws: R   Height: 5'10"   Weight: 200

YEAR	TEAM	LVL	AGE	W	L	SV	G	GS	IP	H	HR	BB	K	BB/9	K/9	GB%	BABIP	WHIP	ERA	FIP	FRA	WARP
2012	KCA	MLB	22	4	3	3	76	0	84¹	79	4	21	77	2.2	8.2	57%	.312	1.19	2.35	2.66	3.24	1.6
2013	OMA	AAA	23	0	1	2	10	3	16	6	1	6	22	3.4	12.4	47%	.161	0.75	1.12	3.13	4.12	0.4
2013	KCA	MLB	23	5	7	2	59	0	58¹	48	9	21	74	3.2	11.4	49%	.281	1.18	3.86	3.73	3.37	1.0
2014	KCA	MLB	24	4	3	0	70	0	70	54	0	26	59	3.3	7.6	52%	.274	1.14	1.41	2.72	2.85	1.4
2015	KCA	MLB	25	3	1	1	54	0	60¹	53	5	18	60	2.8	9.0	51%	.293	1.18	3.14	3.65	3.41	1.1

Breakout: 27%   Improve: 54%   Collapse: 26%   Attrition: 19%   MLB: 91%   Comparables: *Addison Reed, Adam Wainwright, Drew Storen*

Herrera ended the season as the lead consonant in Kansas City's now-legendary HDH bullpen, but entered it as just another bullpen arm. Well, okay, just another bullpen arm with a triple-digit fastball and devastating changeup. The difference for him last year was the gopher ball, or lack thereof. His strikeout rate surprisingly clocked in right at league average, but most of the missing third strikes were replaced by lazy two-hoppers, so never fear. Ned Yost's admirable decision to use Herrera in multi-inning playoff appearances speaks to his value, and as long as he keeps his fastball down, he'll remain an elite late-inning beast.

Greg Holland   RHP

Born: 11/20/85   Age: 29   Bats: R   Throws: R   Height: 5'10"   Weight: 205

YEAR	TEAM	LVL	AGE	W	L	SV	G	GS	IP	H	HR	BB	K	BB/9	K/9	GB%	BABIP	WHIP	ERA	FIP	FRA	WARP
2012	KCA	MLB	26	7	4	16	67	0	67	58	2	34	91	4.6	12.2	47%	.346	1.37	2.96	2.24	2.03	2.3
2013	KCA	MLB	27	2	1	47	68	0	67	40	3	18	103	2.4	13.8	40%	.282	0.87	1.21	1.39	1.49	2.2
2014	KCA	MLB	28	1	3	46	65	0	62¹	37	3	20	90	2.9	13.0	49%	.268	0.91	1.44	1.86	2.43	1.6
2015	KCA	MLB	29	3	1	35	48	0	51²	38	3	19	69	3.3	12.1	45%	.299	1.10	2.30	2.71	2.50	1.5

Breakout: 28%   Improve: 51%   Collapse: 26%   Attrition: 13%   MLB: 91%   Comparables: Sergio Santos, Bill Bray, Brian Wilson

How fantastic is Holland's slider? Hitters don't miss it; their bats are merely too star-struck to approach it. Salvador Perez could flash his signs above his head and batters still wouldn't touch it. Joe Morgan refuses to call it a "slide piece" because it's too noble a beast for such dismissive informality. The most common name for baby girls in Kansas City last year was "Emma," but "Hollandslider" came in second. Batters whiff on it nearly 60 percent of the time, and when they do put it in play they pound it into the ground 60 percent of *that* time. (One of these sentences is true.) As long as Holland can pair it with his plus fastball and remain healthy, he'll be a top-shelf closer.

Sean Manaea   LHP

Born: 2/1/92   Age: 23   Bats: L   Throws: L   Height: 6'5"   Weight: 235

YEAR	TEAM	LVL	AGE	W	L	SV	G	GS	IP	H	HR	BB	K	BB/9	K/9	GB%	BABIP	WHIP	ERA	FIP	FRA	WARP
2014	WIL	A+	22	7	8	0	25	25	121²	102	5	54	146	4.0	10.8	45%	.319	1.28	3.11	3.11	4.00	1.3
2015	KCA	MLB	23	5	6	0	17	17	81²	84	8	38	74	4.2	8.2	43%	.317	1.49	4.57	4.54	4.97	0.2

Breakout: 17%   Improve: 23%   Collapse: 5%   Attrition: 24%   MLB: 34%   Comparables: Jake McGee, Christian Friedrich, Chris Dwyer

A supplemental first-rounder in 2013 whose raw stuff far exceeded his draft position, Manaea fell into Kansas City's lap due to hip surgery that put his future in question. He made great strides in his first professional season, improving as the year went on and showing glimpses of a future rotation stalwart. Blessed with an ideal starter's frame, Manaea's fastball has plenty of wiggle and can reach 95 while his sharp-breaking slider and developing changeup play up due to his deceptive delivery. Mechanical changes saw him flashing much-improved command, and if the Manaea scouts saw in August shows up again this spring, he could easily grow into a second starter.

Michael Mariot   RHP

Born: 10/20/88   Age: 26   Bats: R   Throws: R   Height: 6'0"   Weight: 190

YEAR	TEAM	LVL	AGE	W	L	SV	G	GS	IP	H	HR	BB	K	BB/9	K/9	GB%	BABIP	WHIP	ERA	FIP	FRA	WARP
2012	NWA	AA	23	6	3	1	31	14	113²	111	12	30	81	2.4	6.4	45%	.289	1.24	3.40	4.12	4.95	0.4
2013	OMA	AAA	24	4	5	11	47	1	60²	59	4	25	66	3.7	9.8	45%	.335	1.38	3.56	3.59	3.78	0.9
2014	OMA	AAA	25	2	1	2	14	0	20	19	2	7	25	3.2	11.2	38%	.321	1.30	4.95	3.55	3.36	0.5
2014	KCA	MLB	25	1	0	0	17	0	25	31	2	12	21	4.3	7.6	38%	.349	1.72	6.48	3.96	4.40	0.2
2015	KCA	MLB	26	2	1	0	18	3	42	46	4	15	30	3.2	6.3	43%	.309	1.45	4.71	4.52	5.12	-0.1

Breakout: 18%   Improve: 28%   Collapse: 2%   Attrition: 19%   MLB: 35%   Comparables: Luis Marte, Davis Romero, Steven Shell

There's little to differentiate Mariot from the legion of arms striving to work low-leverage innings in the Royals 'pen. Last year he grew familiar with the majestic vistas of I-29, ping-ponging between solid work in Omaha and struggles in Kansas City before a late-August hamstring pull ended his season. His workaday assortment baffles the farm kids but is fringy at best for the big leagues, so he'll likely continue on as Triple-A insurance policy. Whispers that he's been matched with Paris Hilton in an arranged marriage to settle a long-running resort war could not be confirmed before we went to press.

James Shields   RHP

Born: 12/20/81   Age: 33   Bats: R   Throws: R   Height: 6'3"   Weight: 215

YEAR	TEAM	LVL	AGE	W	L	SV	G	GS	IP	H	HR	BB	K	BB/9	K/9	GB%	BABIP	WHIP	ERA	FIP	FRA	WARP
2012	TBA	MLB	30	15	10	0	33	33	227²	208	25	58	223	2.3	8.8	53%	.292	1.17	3.52	3.42	4.19	1.7
2013	KCA	MLB	31	13	9	0	34	34	228²	215	20	68	196	2.7	7.7	43%	.298	1.24	3.15	3.50	4.02	2.6
2014	KCA	MLB	32	14	8	0	34	34	227	224	23	44	180	1.7	7.1	47%	.295	1.18	3.21	3.62	4.13	2.9
2015	KCA	MLB	33	12	10	0	28	28	193¹	194	20	46	168	2.1	7.8	45%	.306	1.24	3.80	3.97	4.13	1.8

Breakout: 7%   Improve: 37%   Collapse: 28%   Attrition: 19%   MLB: 86%   Comparables: Johan Santana, Hisashi Iwakuma, Josh Beckett

Many believe last year's World Series appearance validates Dayton Moore's decision to trade for Shields two years ago, while others retort that winning at Keno does not prove that playing Keno is a smart move. Either way, Shields provided the Royals with exactly what they should have expected: The health, consistency and production of an excellent second starter. Shields struggled with his famous changeup at times last year but got more mileage from his cutter and wound up trading a few strikeouts for groundballs. He's not an ace, but he's solid, durable and likely to take the ball and provide above-average outings for years to come.

Jason Vargas   LHP

Born: 2/2/83   Age: 32   Bats: L   Throws: L   Height: 6'0"   Weight: 215

YEAR	TEAM	LVL	AGE	W	L	SV	G	GS	IP	H	HR	BB	K	BB/9	K/9	GB%	BABIP	WHIP	ERA	FIP	FRA	WARP
2012	SEA	MLB	29	14	11	0	33	33	217¹	201	35	55	141	2.3	5.8	42%	.254	1.18	3.85	4.64	5.27	-0.3
2013	ANA	MLB	30	9	8	0	24	24	150	162	17	46	109	2.8	6.5	42%	.310	1.39	4.02	4.12	4.38	0.9
2014	KCA	MLB	31	11	10	0	30	30	187	197	19	41	128	2.0	6.2	41%	.299	1.27	3.71	3.87	4.23	2.0
2015	KCA	MLB	32	9	9	0	24	24	154¹	167	18	41	98	2.4	5.7	39%	.296	1.35	4.37	4.70	4.75	0.4

Breakout: 15%   Improve: 40%   Collapse: 22%   Attrition: 9%   MLB: 78%   Comparables: Paul Maholm, Brad Penny, Kevin Correia

Vargas is a slightly younger, slightly better, somewhat less durable lefty version of Jeremy Guthrie, and has thus far made good on his reasonable four-year deal. Like Guthrie, Vargas pitches to contact and avoids walks, throwing his standout changeup over a third of the time to keep hitters from gearing up for his delectable upper-80s fastball. He missed time last year with appendicitis and the year before with a blood clot in his shoulder, but his elbow, rotator cuff and labrum have yet to unravel. Vargas may not have the most eye-popping arsenal in the game, but there are far worse options cluttering up big-league rotations.

Yordano Ventura   RHP

Born: 6/3/91   Age: 24   Bats: R   Throws: R   Height: 6'0"   Weight: 180

YEAR	TEAM	LVL	AGE	W	L	SV	G	GS	IP	H	HR	BB	K	BB/9	K/9	GB%	BABIP	WHIP	ERA	FIP	FRA	WARP
2012	WIL	A+	21	3	5	0	16	16	76¹	66	7	28	98	3.3	11.6	43%	.314	1.23	3.30	3.31	3.56	1.4
2012	NWA	AA	21	1	2	0	6	6	29¹	23	1	13	25	4.0	7.7	52%	.275	1.23	4.60	3.76	4.39	0.3
2013	NWA	AA	22	3	2	0	11	11	57²	39	3	20	74	3.1	11.5	43%	.279	1.02	2.34	2.41	2.91	1.6
2013	OMA	AAA	22	5	4	0	15	14	77	80	4	33	81	3.9	9.5	42%	.357	1.47	3.74	3.54	3.53	1.7
2013	KCA	MLB	22	0	1	0	3	3	15¹	13	3	6	11	3.5	6.5	51%	.227	1.24	3.52	5.36	5.17	0.0
2014	KCA	MLB	23	14	10	0	31	30	183	168	14	69	159	3.4	7.8	48%	.288	1.30	3.20	3.63	4.22	1.9
2015	KCA	MLB	24	9	9	0	29	29	150¹	147	13	58	136	3.5	8.1	44%	.306	1.37	4.08	4.16	4.44	1.2

Breakout: 27%   Improve: 65%   Collapse: 15%   Attrition: 17%   MLB: 90%   Comparables: Homer Bailey, Michael Pineda, Jarrod Parker

Ah, to be young, gifted and have a howitzer for an arm. Ventura was the hardest-throwing starter in baseball last year, with a fastball that can reach triple-digits, a hammer curve, a changeup that out-sprints Jason Vargas' fastball and a mid-90s cutter that could develop into a true worm killer. His stuff has never been in question, but his slight frame has long made scouts wonder if Ventura can bear up under a starter's workload. Last year he missed a few days with a valgus extension overload—kids, don't try that at home—and a sore back, but he's maintained his velocity deep into starts and early returns have been positive. If the Royals treat his young arm with care and build up his strength, Ventura could develop into a true ace as soon as this summer.

Kyle Zimmer   RHP

Born: 9/13/91   Age: 23   Bats: R   Throws: R   Height: 6'3"   Weight: 215

YEAR	TEAM	LVL	AGE	W	L	SV	G	GS	IP	H	HR	BB	K	BB/9	K/9	GB%	BABIP	WHIP	ERA	FIP	FRA	WARP
2012	KNC	A	20	2	3	0	6	6	29²	34	1	8	29	2.4	8.8	57%	.367	1.42	2.43	3.05	4.25	0.5
2013	WIL	A+	21	4	8	0	18	18	89²	80	9	31	113	3.1	11.3	55%	.318	1.24	4.82	3.27	4.37	1.3
2013	NWA	AA	21	2	1	0	4	4	18²	11	2	5	27	2.4	13.0	56%	.231	0.86	1.93	2.68	3.21	0.5
2015	KCA	MLB	23	2	3	0	8	8	34¹	35	4	13	32	3.5	8.5	51%	.315	1.41	4.41	4.53	4.79	0.2

Breakout: 0%   Improve: 0%   Collapse: 0%   Attrition: 0%   MLB: 0%   Comparables: Christian Friedrich, Eric Surkamp, Matt Barnes

Babelfish tells us that "Zimmer" is German for "room," and given his frequent doctor visits the last few years we can only assume that "Kyle" means "waiting." When healthy, the former no. 5 overall pick can unleash front-line stuff, with a fastball that reaches the upper 90s and a plus power curve. He's yet to remain healthy through a professional season, however, enduring both elbow surgery and chronic shoulder woes that culminated in a clean-up procedure last fall. "Minor shoulder surgery" and "pitcher" mix like vodka and gasoline, but the Royals expect Zimmer back on the mound in time for spring training. If he can put his health woes in the rear-view mirror, build up his strength and find success in the high minors, Zimmer still has the goods to front a big-league rotation.

Lineouts

Hitters

NAME	POS	TEAM	LVL	AGE	PA	R	2B	3B	HR	RBI	BB	K	SB	CS	AVG/OBP/SLG	TAv	BABIP	BRR	FRAA	WARP
Orlando Calixte	SS	NWA	AA	22	412	43	15	1	11	37	27	92	9	5	.241/.288/.374	.243	.286	-0.9	SS(92): -3.1, 3B(1): 0.0	0.5
Reymond Fuentes	CF	SAN	AA	23	194	25	6	2	4	17	16	37	12	1	.324/.386/.453	.306	.392	0.9	CF(39): -0.2, LF(2): 0.2	1.7
	LF	ELP	AAA	23	178	29	9	3	1	16	17	27	13	2	.261/.337/.376	.285	.310	1.4	LF(27): 1.1, CF(17): 1.0	0.3
Cameron Gallagher	C	WIL	A+	21	361	24	18	0	5	34	37	38	1	0	.228/.306/.333	.247	.240	-3.4	C(89): -1.4	0.9
Elier Hernandez	RF	LEX	A	19	446	54	19	4	9	34	16	99	5	5	.264/.296/.393	.246	.324	-2.6	RF(77): 1.1, CF(23): -0.9	-0.3
Jack Lopez	2B	WIL	A+	21	443	34	19	2	1	29	27	66	23	9	.215/.274/.279	.213	.254	1.2	2B(76): 2.6, SS(29): 0.2	-0.6
Justin Maxwell	RF	OMA	AAA	30	233	32	11	1	8	29	20	75	3	2	.285/.352/.464	.275	.402	-1.9	RF(34): 1.2, CF(18): 0.8	1.0
	RF	KCA	MLB	30	45	4	1	0	0	3	2	20	0	1	.150/.222/.175	.170	.286	1.1	RF(7): -1.2, CF(6): -0.5	-0.4
Paulo Orlando	CF	OMA	AAA	28	554	61	21	9	6	63	39	86	34	9	.301/.355/.415	.275	.351	3.6	CF(80): 8.7, RF(42): 7.1	4.5
Francisco Pena	C	OMA	AAA	24	370	53	13	0	27	61	16	65	0	3	.240/.280/.515	.268	.216	0.7	C(90): 1.0	2.6
Moises Sierra	RF	CHA	MLB	25	135	20	8	2	2	7	7	34	3	1	.276/.311/.417	.270	.359	-0.4	RF(64): -2.0, LF(7): 0.2	0.3
	RF	TOR	MLB	25	35	2	0	0	0	2	1	9	0	0	.059/.086/.059	.061	.080	-0.1	RF(6): 0.2, LF(2): -0.0	-0.7
Josh Willingham	LF	ROC	AAA	35	29	3	2	0	1	3	1	8	0	0	.185/.241/.370	.182	.222	-0.1	LF(4): 0.0	-0.2
	LF	MIN	MLB	35	278	34	5	1	12	34	42	78	1	0	.210/.345/.402	.283	.252	0.0	LF(53): 0.0	1.1
	RF	KCA	MLB	35	86	14	5	0	2	6	11	24	1	0	.233/.349/.384	.250	.319	0.9	RF(1): 0.0	0.1

Orlando Calixte avoids the standard cliché by being a good field, *some*-hit shortstop: He's slick and rangy and can muscle up some home run thump, but unless he suddenly improves his pitch recognition and makes more contact, he's a future utility guy. ❖ Toronto washout **Balbino Fuenmayor** revived his career and put on a laser show in the Can-Am League; signed by the Royals, there's some chance he could be the next Chris Colabello, and a better chance he won't be. ❖ Future spare outfielder **Reymond Fuentes** floundered at Triple-A, re-established his game in a third stab at Double-A and finished strong on returning to the higher level before a right hip flexor strain ended his season on July 26th. ❖ Lancastrian (we're assuming that's what natives of Lancaster, PA call themselves) backstop **Cam Gallagher** is a rock behind the dish and treats potential basestealers like Yorkist usurpers, but his projected power has yet to develop; he's only 22, so the Royals can afford to let him bake a little longer. ❖ Dominican bonus baby **Elier Hernandez** has the prototypical right-field tool kit, but struggled to make contact and recognize spin during his full-season debut; eyes are more telling than numbers at this point, so let's wait until the kid is old enough to order a Zima before we start to worry. ❖ Slick infielder **Jack Lopez** can't hit a lick but his vacuum glove, good range and shortstop's arm make him one of the best defensive second basemen around; when he looks up at his ceiling he sees Darwin Barney. Which is kind of creepy when you start thinking about it. Get down from there, Darwin Barney. ❖ Quad-A outfielder **Justin Maxwell** has always looked the part, but injuries, bad timing and inconsistent performance have kept him from the career his tools have long foretold; now on the wrong side of 30, he's just about out of chances. ❖ Lefty thumper **Ryan O'Hearn** took Pioneer League pitchers to the woodshed on his way to MVP honors; he's no whiz with the leather at first base or in the outfield, so he'll have to keep raking to keep moving. ❖ Brazilian outfielder **Paulo Orlando** parlayed a solid season in the Omaha outfield into his third Lineout in these pages since 2009 and, less importantly, a spot on the 40-man roster; with blazing speed and a plus glove, he's *so* Royals, which no longer sounds like a pejorative. ❖ Strong-armed receiver **Francisco Pena** earned a September call-up after smacking 27 Triple-A home runs, tripling his career high; never known for his bat, if Pena can continue to lay into a few misplaced fastballs he could carve out a career as a backup. ❖ **Moises Sierra**'s modest power and fairly high strikeout rates have reduced him to a Quad-A player, causing a whole new generation to associate "Sierra missed" with disappointing pop.

❖ Supplemental first-rounder **Chase Vallot** is raw behind the dish and struck out in more than a third of his Rookie-level plate appearances last season, but since he wasn't even old enough to vote there's plenty of time to leverage his impressive power potential into a career. ❖ Late-blooming slugger **Josh Willingham** finally made it to the playoffs, then decided to hang 'em up after 11 big-league seasons; his offensive value was often obscured by the large ballparks he played in, but he'll retire with the same .295 TAv as Don Mattingly, Carl Yastrzemski, Kirk Gibson and Fred Lynn.

Pitchers

NAME	TEAM	LVL	AGE	W	L	SV	G	GS	IP	H	HR	BB	K	BB/9	K/9	GB%	BABIP	WHIP	ERA	FIP	FRA	WARP
Angel Baez	NWA	AA	23	1	5	0	35	0	62	58	9	29	71	4.2	10.3	39%	.312	1.40	4.65	4.41	4.37	0.6
Aaron Brooks	OMA	AAA	24	12	3	1	25	23	139	151	14	25	97	1.6	6.3	48%	.311	1.27	3.88	4.17	4.73	1.6
	KCA	MLB	24	0	1	0	2	1	2²	12	1	3	2	10.1	6.8	47%	.688	5.62	43.88	12.16	13.39	-0.3
Chris Dwyer	OMA	AAA	26	4	4	2	28	5	66	64	8	39	65	5.3	8.9	39%	.308	1.56	5.59	5.21	6.08	0.4
Jandel Gustave	QUD	A	21	5	5	2	23	14	79	94	3	29	82	3.3	9.3	48%	.374	1.56	5.01	3.50	4.08	1.5
John Lamb	OMA	AAA	23	8	10	0	27	26	138¹	137	19	68	131	4.4	8.5	41%	.303	1.48	3.97	5.26	5.21	1.5
Joe Paterson	RNO	AAA	28	0	2	0	56	0	42²	45	1	19	33	4.0	7.0	54%	.333	1.50	2.95	3.93	4.29	1.0
	ARI	MLB	28	0	0	0	3	0	1¹	4	0	1	0	6.8	0.0	12%	.500	3.75	33.75	7.60	11.47	-0.1
Yohan Pino	ROC	AAA	30	10	2	0	16	9	73	47	9	24	72	3.0	8.9	36%	.209	0.97	2.47	4.10	5.28	0.4
	MIN	MLB	30	2	5	0	11	11	60¹	66	8	14	50	2.1	7.5	30%	.314	1.33	5.07	3.97	4.16	0.8
Reid Redman	JUP	A+	25	4	1	6	35	0	48²	42	1	9	58	1.7	10.7	45%	.328	1.05	2.22	1.95	2.99	1.1
	JAX	AA	25	1	0	1	9	0	13	8	0	3	10	2.1	6.9	30%	.216	0.85	1.38	2.34	2.51	0.3
Sam Selman	NWA	AA	23	4	6	0	28	16	93	81	7	49	87	4.7	8.4	48%	.287	1.40	3.87	4.03	4.86	0.6
Glenn Sparkman	WIL	A+	22	8	3	1	29	18	121	94	2	25	117	1.9	8.7	44%	.281	0.98	1.56	2.42	2.89	2.8

Fireballer **Angel Baez** can generate significant swing-and-miss with his moving mid-90s fastball, slider and change, but lack of command results in sky-high walk and home run rates; like countless relievers before him, he'll have a bullpen career if he can graduate from thrower to pitcher. ❖ New York prep righty **Scott Blewett** has an ideal frame, a mid-90s fastball, a power curve and easily the worst pitcher name this side of Grant Balfour; just pray he's never a closer. ❖ **Aaron Brooks** doesn't wow you with electric stuff, but he commands his low-90s fastball, slider and changeup, gets groundballs, and would rather watch 18 straight hours of *Full House* than issue a free pass. ❖ Observers once expected lefty **Chris Dwyer** to work big-league innings for the next great Royals team, but few expected them to be three innings during a September call-up that Dwyer "earned" after posting a 5.59 ERA out of the Omaha bullpen. If there's such a thing as a post-post-post-hype sleeper, Dwyer isn't even that. ❖ Long-limbed prep lefty **Foster Griffin** is miles away from The K, but with good velocity and two off-speed offerings that can flash plus, he's a potential mid-rotation workhorse; the only things that can stop him now are injury, or inconsistency, or lack of command, or gopheritis, or walks, or … ❖ Triple-digit heat, not the numbers, keep **Jandel Gustave** on the prospect radar. ❖ No sooner did **Luke Hochevar** resurrect his career in the bullpen than the fickle gods of baseball saw fit to release gremlins in his elbow; he'll be back from Tommy John surgery later this summer, and anyone with a soul should hope he makes it all the way back. ❖ Former top prospect **John Lamb** worked a full season in Triple-A and is again missing bats, but has yet to regain the velocity and command he showed before his 2011 elbow surgery. ❖ After allowing 11 earned runs in 34 innings as a Rule 5 pick in 2011, **Joe Paterson** has allowed 17 in just six over the past three years. Garsh, though, he's left-handed so I guess we'll try again. ❖ After throwing 1,000 innings over 10 minor-league seasons, including solid work last year in Triple-A, soft-tossing **Yohan Pino** made his major-league debut and took 11 forgettable turns in the Minnesota rotation before earning his release at season's end; we're sure there's a lesson about fortitude in there somewhere. ❖ **Reid Redman**'s name is an anagram for "Damn, I erred." Since admitting it, the converted infielder has seen nothing but success on the mound: Sparkling at two levels and the AFL in 2014, he's moving fast toward major-league relevance, and the Royals plucked him in the Aaron Crow trade. ❖ Poor control has long plagued lefty **Sam Selman**, but a midseason move to the bullpen has him back on the prospect trail; he still issues too many walks, but with his fastball/slider combo playing up in short bursts, he now whiffs enough batters to make up for it. ❖ Towering **Eric Skoglund** struck out more than a batter per inning in his Pioneer League debut, which is what a third-round college lefty needs to do to avoid setting off alarm bells; time will tell whether he'll grow into the fourth starter his frame and average stuff can support. ❖ Note to 20th-round picks: If you want to get your organization's attention, follow **Glenn Sparkman**'s lead and post a buck-fifty ERA in your full-season debut; it's an open question whether tremendous command of his fringy arsenal can baffle more advanced hitters, but at least he has scouts asking.

Manager

Ned Yost

YEAR	TEAM	W	L	Py-thag +/-	Avg PC	100+ P	120+ P	QS	BQS	REL	REL w Zero R	IBB	PH	PH Avg	PH HR	SB2	CS2	SB3	CS3	SAC Att	SAC%	POS SAC	Squeeze	Swing	In Play
2012	KCA	72	90	-1	90.5	55	0	69	4	500	411	44	55	.208	3	109	34	22	4	42	61.9%	25	1	334	97
2013	KCA	86	76	-1	98.6	79	2	95	5	427	374	21	74	.210	1	133	30	19	2	56	66.1%	36	1	369	99
2014	KCA	89	73	5	98.8	90	2	95	4	451	399	14	43	.250	2	124	29	29	7	55	60.0%	30	1	344	112

The book on Yost entering the playoffs went something like this: He bunts his team out of big innings, refuses to use his bench well and is far too rigid with his bullpen and lineup. There was truth to it all, of course. The Royals finished 10th in the majors in position-player sacrifices, and anyone who watched them late in the season or during the postseason knows they cost themselves some rich run-scoring opportunities. Yost used 28 fewer pinch-hitters than any team during the regular season. He slotted kevin Herrera, Wade Davis and Greg Holland into the final three frames and often figured out the first six later. And yes, he went a month without changing his starting lineup, much to Perez's detriment.

But you know what? Yost deserves some credit for the postseason run. As the *Kansas City Star*'s Andy McCullough noted during a chat on Baseball Prospectus, Yost altered his relief usage at the urging of pitching coach Dave Eiland. It would've been hard to imagine Yost tapping Herrera for the sixth inning during the regular season, let alone the third, as he did in Game Seven. In fact, Yost leaned so heavily on those relievers during the final game that you can almost forgive him sticking by Jeremy Guthrie as long as he did.

None of this makes Yost Earl Weaver. He has his faults, and is probably one of the worst tactical managers in the game, no matter how you reach that opinion. But faced with his first playoff run, one that carried a lot of pressure from the city and for the organization, Yost was willing to adjust his worldview for the better; just not enough, as it turned out, to bring a trophy to Kansas City.

LOS ANGELES ANGELS

by Daniel Volmar

1. Doom Metal

In 2013, Angels Baseball LP—the corporation through which Arte Moreno took ownership of the franchise in 2003—commemorated its decennial with a dirge to its worst season ever. The grim procession seemed as though it might stretch as far as 2022, when the team's last swollen mega-contract finally lays to rest. Even the famous front office omerta cracked enough to reveal Arte Moreno pacing the boathouse like Michael Corleone, weighing the price of a brother's betrayal. No one knew whether the manager or the general manager would be out on the lake, but Mike Scioscia's own indulgent pact, sealed until 2020, seemed more likely to save him than Fredo. Such must have felt the chill on Jerry Dipoto's neck as he sent invitations to last year's spring training.

Of course, no truly fallen franchise suddenly recovers 20 wins and conquers the league. At the same time, hardly "everything," or even "nearly everything," favored a team hauling so much stubborn baggage, clattering and careening and kicking up sparks behind it. Rather, the same tired rattletrap regained its former spectacle just by shaking itself to pieces. Each night we watched the old millstone roll farther and faster down the hill; we thrilled as the wreck dissolved into a white-hot sluice; and we cheered for momentum itself to carry the molten slag-heap past the finish. Congealing in another postseason quench-bath, the Angels pushed their vertiginous run to a remarkable 98 wins, flouting immutable laws of inertia, entropy, and hydrodynamics, but strangely, no softer rules of statistical inference. Mike Scioscia's own lucky car-keys, which once unlocked so much unsustainable Pythagorean over-performance, must have got lost in the wash, because not even his reckless driving could push the needle beyond the empirical red-line. If 2014 fades like a green flash into the twilight of decadent mediocrity, then at least we will have seen an exceptionally rare and beautiful sight, with nothing so abnormal as the appearance of normality itself.

2. Some Strange Comfort

How do we reconcile ourselves with events that seem to go right only by going wrong? I am not convinced we should. This is not to say, as the traditionalists do, that an explanation would somehow diminish the wonder. Even the shrillest cries against the "human drama" retreating into "mom's basement" shout their own narratives from the newsprint numbers of sports-page psychoanalysis. Indeed, the "sabermetric revolution" could not have taken the path it did without baseball's century-long traditionalist obsession with counting, scoring, and compiling everything around the diamond. What began as an industrial-age efficiency for managing wages became, rather curiously, a media-cultural hobby for customers as well. To the pure enthusiast, the tension is not between events on a field and rows on a spreadsheet; it is between the satisfaction of spectatorship and the agony of powerlessness. Unfortunately, Angels Baseball LP is about to remind fans like me that we are not the crowd as much as we are the ball. Our interests are not theirs and need not be reconciled with theirs, though strangely enough, we always find some relief in breaking down their balance sheet.

And did any successful team have a ledger so provocative as the Angels? Their 25 player-season commitment to Albert Pujols, Josh Hamilton, Jered Weaver and C.J. Wilson vested another $12 million on top of the $61.1 million paid out in 2013, when the four athletes, all on the wrong side of 30, combined for only 8.4 WARP. Although the "Albertross" raised his sunk cost slightly, the others more than offset any gain from that account. Hamilton played nearly as disappointingly, but half as often, while Weaver aged further into an "ace emeritus" and Wilson contributed more in three interleague plate-appearances than in 175⅔ innings pitched. Including final payments to Joe Blanton and Vernon Wells, who enjoyed them from their living rooms, the Angels shed $100 million for 5.6 WARP from four roster spots. In other words, their Opening Day payroll, despite ranking sixth in the league, allotted just $55 million—barely Houston money—to buy the additional 30+ WARP typical of a competitive performance.

Here I can salvage the obvious punchline only by teasing it out. The trick is in the troublesome L-word, a nettlesome term with its sting not in sabermetrics, but in the philosophy of economics itself. Luck—or "chance" or "fortune," as you prefer: even the most contemplative among us will never disentangle what we have achieved from that which we may have unwittingly

---

ANGELS PROSPECTUS
2014 W-L: 98-64, 1ST IN AL WEST

Pythag	.594	2nd		DER	.715	6th
RS/G	4.77	1st		B-Age	29.3	23rd
RA/G	3.89	14th		P-Age	28.2	17th
TAv	.277	1st		Salary	$158.8M	5th
BRR	8.26	2nd		M$/MW	$2.9M	15th
TAv-P	.252	4th		DL Days	993	21st
FIP	3.60	10th		$ on DL	11%	6th

Three-Year Park Factors

Runs	Runs/RH	Runs/LH	HR/RH	HR/LH
96	95	93	83	76

Top Hitter WARP	9.4	Mike Trout
Top Pitcher WARP	2.4	Garrett Richards
Top Prospect		Andrew Heaney

---

accrued, because the alternatives remain forever unknowable. Fan-based analyses will confront the problem sooner or later, if they have not already begun to do so, because sabermetrics is itself a theory of economic value. By defining, assessing, and forecasting the performance of certain commodities, better than most commodity-managers themselves, it is being incorporated into enterprises far graver than forum threads or fantasy leagues. For Angels fans too, a time of reckoning is at hand, one that will trivialize the last great disputation.

2.1. More heat than light

By the end of the last decade, Angels Baseball LP had divided its critics into a predictable contest; "Moneyball" against "Morenoball," some called it, and the latter was running up the score. From 2007 to 2011, the stricken Athletics finished an average 19 games out, even as Brad Pitt's charm and Aaron Sorkin's wit exalted Billy Beane into a Hollywood prestige-film, which was way better than Angels in the Outfield, but with fewer shots of the Oakland Coliseum. While the trade paperback killed time for frequent fliers caught between a late takeoff and a Hudson News, the Angels won 58 percent of their games and five of six division titles between 2004 and 2009. All they got, besides a few flags, was the awkward "of Anaheim" they wore like a polyester suit. By cheating Pythagoras for 30 games in the regular season, then dropping 19 of 29 of them in the playoffs, the Angels never earned the baseball legitimacy their executives felt they deserved. Each winter exposed the front office to the same bruising one-two: a cross of postseason humiliation, followed by a jab of analytical disrespect.

Fans shrugged it off the way that fans do, with parry and counterpunch. Michael Lewis was, after all, just another A's fan, and when saber heavyweights Dave Cameron and Jeff Sullivan emerged as Seattle's seconds, it seemed that Texas would be the only rival willing to fight on the field instead of the Internet. The brawl acquired that peculiarly web-centric sort of rowdiness, with statistical outliers, thrown like bludgeons, crashing against Hippasus, whom Pythagoras supposedly had drowned for discovering the irrational numbers. It also had a spontaneous authenticity absent on the nostalgic sports beat, where Arte Moreno's brand of "nice-guy capitalism" was a shirt-sleeve small-business fantasy worth defending from the wolves who wrecked Wall Street, and Mike Scioscia's own cult-of-personality offered the perfect foil to Billy's bean counters. Springtime press junkets always brought another round of admiring old-media backslapping for the bashful billionaire and his beloved blue-collar Clausewitz, to whom pitching was merely catching by other means. If Abner Doubleday could have seen a swollen-faced station-to-station offense, or a single-batter switch in the bullpen, he might have etched Angels Baseball® into the dirt at Cooperstown, or so we were told.

But within a community that had produced such saber-sized luminaries as Sean Smith and Rich Lederer, pundits who confused Paul DePodesta's biography with Jonah Hill's filmography found less traction than ridicule. "Morenoball," like Ross Perot, was never so much a thing as not-that-other thing, with all the grotesque self-flattery of a funhouse mirror. The distortions must have amused someone, however, because with no opponent in sight, Angels Baseball LP mimicked its own twisting reflections instead of settling into a robust equilibrium. A ceaseless slurry of gritty veterans, light-hitting track stars, pitch-whispering backstops, and role-playing relievers congested the organizational pipeline and poisoned its shallowing well. So long as House Moreno could sweep the breakage under its divisional doormats, no one dared to expose its store-brand loafers as blundering Hessian parade-boots. Nevertheless, by 2011 the confrontation had clearly spilled over from Pythagoras to, dare I say, privilege.

2.2. Perestroika

The irony is that no Scioscia campaign had won its division without the top run-differential before 2014, though one did lose to a team that had not (the resulting World Series title was consolation enough). The tragedy was that a tremendous payroll advantage tempted whoever was holding the checkbook—and reports have varied on that essential detail—into mistakes competitors could not even consider. Dodging a bullet in Carl Crawford, just to dive on a grenade named Vernon Wells, belied panic instead of planning, while unforced errors, like Pujols and Hamilton, dismissed pragmatism for pageantry. Each glimpse into the organization, once praised for its straight-shooting stability, has shown us an insecure, contested, or perhaps merely incoherent picture, cloaked in the conspiratorial loyalty of a hedge fund. Dipoto, the outside reformer, may yet find himself as Mikhail Gorbachev did, hastening the collapse of the regime the more he tries to modernize it. Although his baseball bonafides seem to have restrained Scioscia, albeit unhappily, sources suggest that the meddlesome mismanagement has only shifted to the ownership group.

Table 1: The win deviation for each of Mike Scioscia's teams (*sdev*), derived from run differential, compared with that of their season rival (*rdev*), i.e. the team that finished first when they did not, or second when they did. The relative wins between them (*relw*) and the relative wins predicted (*relp*) follow the relationship *relp - relw = rdev - sdev*.

	sdev	rdev	relw	relp
2000	+1.5	−1.5	−9.5	−12.5
2001	−2.0	+6.0	−41.0	−33.0
2002	−3.0	+7.0	−4.0	+6.0
2003	−3.5	+2.0	−19.0	−13.5
2004	+1.0	+5.0	+1.0	+5.0
2005	+1.5	−5.0	+7.0	+0.5
2006	+4.5	+7.5	−4.0	−1.0
2007	+4.0	+9.0	+6.0	+11.0
2008	+12.0	+3.5	+21.0	+12.5
2009	+4.5	+1.5	+10.0	+7.0
2010	+1.5	−1.5	−10.0	−13.0
2011	+1.0	−2.5	−10.0	−13.5
2012	+1.0	+2.0	−5.0	−4.0
2013	−2.5	+0.0	−18.0	−15.5
2014	+2.0	−10.5	+10.0	−2.5
Mean	+1.5	+1.5	−4.5	−4.5

Sleepless nights must also remind him that the two heads that came together to acquire his most valuable assets soon rolled to make way for his. So if Pythagoras is the red herring of modern Angels history, then the 2009 Amateur Draft, Tony Reagins and Eddie Bane presiding, is The Fluke. Finally, the groan-worthy punchline, and another proof of "Salmon's Law": any sufficiently long discussion about the Angels will inevitably degenerate into fish puns. Ultimately, the team that needed to find 30 WARP in about $55 million recouped a third of it from one player entitled to a league-minimum salary. Before hoisting the world on Mike Trout's mighty shoulders, however, consider that finding 20 WARP in $55 million is a difficult problem too. On that same account, the 2013 Angels traded $65 million for 10.7 WARP, and they lost 84 games. Jerry DiPoto must have truly done something right this time, because even his otherwise infallible center fielder slipped up a little.

3. Roll The Bones

Without a doubt, Mike Trout earned every last vote toward his unanimous MVP award, and 29 other teams would have loved to see one of their own ski the slopes of Mount Olympus. He stumbled all the same into his first sustained "slump," batting an uncharacteristically mortal .257/.347/.502 in the second half. Although his plate discipline remained fairly consistent, Trout seemed especially pressed against the league's expanding strike zone. He fell behind 18 percent more often than in 2013, due at least partly to disproportionately unfavorable calls on borderline pitches. Despite a plunging BB/K rate, his ISO jumped 40 points on a league-beating 84 extra-base hits. He even battled with notorious baseball-killer Giancarlo Stanton for both the longest average and the longest individual home run hit last year. (Trout's best: a 483-foot splashdown that nearly cleared the left-center field fountain in Kansas City.) Recall the prospect who hit 10 HR per 600 minor-league PA and imagine power like it.

So the predictable "kids aren't all right" stories that followed Trout into his disappointing October never seemed fair to me. What I observed was a young man diverging—not declining—from the five-tool phenom scouts saw as a teenager, as well as a few cheeky umpires especially eager to "put him in his place." This Mike Trout might be a straight-up outfield slugger in the right-handed image of Gary Sheffield or Manny Ramirez, neither of whom was entirely unathletic in his youth. At the same age, Trout actually has 40 pounds and two inches on the both of them, so notwithstanding all those Very Bad Things they did, who knows how he might develop? He is still impressively nimble, of course, but he only turned 23 in August. Ten years from now we may not remember we ever cared about his speed down the line or his reach at the fence.

Table 2: The relative change in outcomes for Mike Trout on borderline pitches with two strikes: how often he saw one (Δpitch), swung at it (Δswing), missed when he did (Δmiss), or lost the call when he did not (Δlook). He is compared to the average right-handed batter last year. The compass points follow the catcher's perspective, so "northeast" is "up and away."

	Δpitch	Δswing	Δmiss	Δlook
NW	0.33	-0.09	0.89	0.19
N	0.79	-0.24	0.72	0.17
NE	0.09	-0.18	0.34	0.30
W	0.34	-0.09	0.66	-0.14
E	-0.17	-0.10	0.01	0.34
SW	-0.17	0.12	-0.84	-0.28
S	-0.05	-0.02	-0.23	-1.00
SE	-0.19	-0.14	-0.20	0.10

All this leads to a supremely important question. Why did an organization that has withheld no extravagance from older, lesser stars extend a potentially generational player so conservatively? A six-year, $145 million deal, announced just in time for Opening Day, will eventually open bidding on a 29 year-old who, in his first three seasons, had already surpassed several Hall of Famers (albeit not very good ones) on the all-time bWAR list. While the Angels might have secured the best of Trout's career, suppose that in 2004, the St. Louis Cardinals had signed Albert Pujols, who was actually 18 months older and arguably less remarkable at the time, for only three seasons beyond his arbitration years, instead of the eventual five. Even the stunning terms recently offered to Giancarlo Stanton would have barely included Trout's 36th birthday. If Angels Baseball LP indeed refused to negotiate

a longer tenure, as Trout's representatives have claimed, then either they project him like Andruw Jones (a poor bet for going all-in), or else their strategic thinking is, shall we say, less than obvious. Before sharing my own suspicions, however, I still need to explain how the Angels surged into 2014 even with their highest of high tides ebbing slightly from the previous season.

3.1. A rogue wave?

Dipoto's approach to his limited "effective payrolls" has been to swap his pricier 12-sided dice for twice their number in six-sided ones—going for security, not ceiling. His signature moves have shaken out mostly through immediate trade-ins for workaday pitching—perhaps his only play, given the immediate pressure, but an often disappointing one. The 2014 roster put 54 different players, 31 of them pitchers, onto the field, churning more like a flailing team than one leading its league in wins, runs, WARP, and TAv. Surprisingly, their offensive success actually makes some sense. Instead of surrounding Trout, their shooting star, with black holes, the starting nine remained healthy and productive enough to offset a thin bench and some fat salaries. The same cannot be said for the pitching, which entered the season threadbare, yet strangely held strongest right at the point of snapping completely. For the second time in as many years, Dipoto thoroughly reshuffled the entire staff, and though he did draw a winning hand eventually, he nearly emptied the deck in the process.

While Hector Santiago pitched well enough, and Tyler Skaggs impressed intermittently before meeting with Tommy John, the greatest lift, and the most ominous letdown, both came from Garrett Richards, who ranked among the league's finest until a catastrophic injury laid him low as well. While Richards had been a top prospect as recently as 2012, few knew the 27 year-old Matt Shoemaker until the two right-handers nearly matched performances over the summer. In fact, between July 31st, the day Skaggs went down, and September 15th, when Shoemaker started ailing himself, the team played an astonishing 30–13 record, despite losing Richards in between. A refurbished bullpen, which improved as the season progressed, deserves significant credit for this fantastic run, especially Cory Rasmus, last year's return on Scott Downs, who did excellent work as a "permanent emergency" starter. Dipoto also scored flawless victories with Mike Morin, a 2012 draft pick, and Jason Grilli, as Ernesto Frieri continued his three-true-outcome death-spiral in Pittsburgh. Among many others, even Rich Hill jogged from the Angels bullpen last year, retiring none of the four batters he faced, so that was fun. They can actually keep 11 of the 12 pitchers they took to the playoffs, so as much as they might prefer to never see C.J. Wilson again, at least Richards should return before mid-season, and Skaggs could pitch in September as well.

4. Welcome to Anaheim

The wave that clears the breakwater is a complicated thing. Although the underlying processes are deterministic, its height cannot be predicted, only compared with its likelihood after the event. Perhaps now, with five years between playoff appearances, we can finally say something sensible about "Morenoball," which has changed pitch and tempo under Jerry Dipoto, but definitely not its tune. What the Angels experience is, in essence, merely an exaggerated symptom of the league's overall liquidity problem: all the thirtysomething pensioners collecting the wages they earned in their primes. High-revenue franchises, with stakes in regional sports-networks, hold a disproportionate number of non-fungible "albatrosses" who by draining prospects, soaking up playing time, getting injured, and blocking potential replacements, also inflate the price for players under team control. The old-fashioned arbitrage that Michael Lewis called "Moneyball" does not much help when the market is bursting with assets that are either too toxic to "buy low" or too valuable to "sell high." While payroll is still a significant predictor of team success, the correlation has weakened over the last decade.

Table 3: Significant *p*-values for team payroll, adjusted for salary inflation, as a predictor of wins above replacement (*warp*), win-loss percentage (*wpct*), expected win-loss percentage (*wpat*) and whether or not the team played in the postseason (*post*) observed in two-year running samples (*n* = 60) and expressed as –*log p*. (Note that the significance levels *p* < 0.10 and *p* < 0.01 become *1.00* and *2.00* when written as –*log p*.) The *p*-values for each column as a function of the sampling interval are *0.903, 0.108, 0.099,* and *0.036,* respectively.

	warp	wpct	wpat	post
2000-2001	1.91	1.87	1.61	1.18
2001-2002	4.13	2.65	2.95	1.47
2002-2003	4.33	3.08	3.62	1.32
2003-2004	3.68	3.84	3.39	2.44
2004-2005	3.24	4.51	3.52	2.93
2005-2006	2.56	4.29	3.01	2.03
2006-2007	3.42	4.44	4.38	1.56
2007-2008	2.79	2.87	4.02	1.31
2008-2009	3.41	2.94	3.30	1.62
2009-2010	3.74	3.09	2.52	1.49
2010-2011	3.95	2.40	2.31	0.80
2011-2012	4.25	1.73	2.13	0.90
2012-2013	2.90	1.41	1.35	0.56
2013-2014	2.30	1.67	1.06	0.63

As an organization, the Angels badly need to refuel; Dipoto had never drafted in the first round before 2014, and he missed the second round in 2012 as well. Nevertheless, his luxury players are just good enough to keep the big-league club nominally competitive year to year, and so the throttle remains wide open. Under the circumstances, an executive in Dipoto's position might have little alternative to playing an aggressive dice game with middle performers. Hank Conger has already been sent to Houston for the young arm on Nick Tropeano, as well as Carlos Perez, who has never caught above Triple-A. Still, the Angels this year are more likely to discover another J.B. Shuck instead of a Kole Calhoun, or Jerome Williams instead of Matt Shoemaker (early bets are on Daniel Robertson and Yoslan Herrera). So far as I can tell, the next few seasons project the same as the previous three, when the team that left spring training could have won 95 games or 75 games and not surprised me either way. On average, they finished right in the middle, which leaves us waiting on the

next rogue wave, and whether it comes in one year or five, no one can say.

I can accept that; certainly other teams have it worse. In our bedroom analyses, awe is admiring the unlikely and joy is explaining the unpredictable, while an innocuous blog can safely excoriate our favorite team for reaching different conclusions than we do. But who else or what else can represent our stake? Although spectatorship does feed back into the sport, rarely do we see what the shareholders do: a firm, to which the 25-man roster is so much exposed pipe-fitting in the great unseen plumbing that sloshes capital between real and media properties. Whether or not the superstars perform on the field, the accounts payable get amortized into fixed-term annuities and through the black art of financial valuation spout dividends all the same. A going concern like Angels Baseball LP can still appreciate by 50 percent, despite missing four postseasons in a row, because the partners are playing a different game. Arte Moreno, who owes half his dynastic wealth to a single investment, is now in business with Fox, who are less interested in projecting PECOTAs than speculating on your cable bill. SportsNet LA has already shown Dodgers fans just how deep the pipes are buried, and sewage, as they say, always runs downhill.

In Anaheim, the latest excitement might have been the last of the calm, before all those other things become impossible to ignore. If Wells, Pujols, and Hamilton all followed the immediate pursuit of television lucre, then what comes for the franchise seeking public subsidies for a redevelopment mega-project? The three seasons after the next will all trigger the opt-out clause on the Angel Stadium lease, and the relevant interests are expecting to cash out with billions. After failing to keep Rob Manfred from the commissioner's chair, Moreno looks to be the latest draw in a 20-year shootout over some decommissioned military bases in south Orange County, and while otherwise auditioning well for the role, I suspect he hedged on his commitment to Mike Trout. Orange County, a Cold War car-topia built around Disney and defense spending, was the birthplace of Richard Nixon, the redoubt of Ronald Reagan, and the flashpoint of the California Tax Rebellion. Strong as his municipal-industrial complex might be, the competition is probably stronger, and whoever wins, the homeowners will sue over the traffic impact. Should his frustration consequently become ours, bringing higher prices for less interesting products, then sabermetrics, like the classic Chinatown, speaks only the cathartic lesson to "forget it, Jake. It's Anaheim." ∎

—Daniel Volmar is a PhD candidate in the Department of the History of Science at Harvard University and a frequent contributor to Halos Heaven.

Player comments by Ryan Ghan and Baseball Prospectus Authors

Hitters

Erick Aybar   SS

Born: 1/14/84   Age: 31   Bats: B   Throws: R   Height: 5' 10"   Weight: 180

YEAR	TEAM	LVL	AGE	PA	R	2B	3B	HR	RBI	BB	K	SB	CS	AVG/OBP/SLG	TAv	BABIP	BRR	FRAA	WARP
2012	ANA	MLB	28	554	67	31	5	8	45	22	61	20	4	.290/.324/.416	.277	.316	1.4	SS(139): -5.4	2.8
2013	ANA	MLB	29	589	68	33	5	6	54	23	59	12	7	.271/.301/.382	.250	.292	4.0	SS(138): -10.5	1.1
2014	ANA	MLB	30	641	77	30	4	7	68	36	62	16	9	.278/.321/.379	.269	.297	5.5	SS(155): -11.8	2.3
2015	ANA	MLB	31	593	60	28	4	6	50	29	73	16	7	.266/.306/.365	.259	.291	2.8	SS -7	2.1

Breakout: 0%   Improve: 34%   Collapse: 2%   Attrition: 2%   MLB: 98%   *Comparables:*   Alexei Ramirez, Rafael Furcal, Cristian Guzman

Aybar's glove confounds the defensive metrics, but his bat is a known quantity, best summed up by his distinction for being the only player to appear on the top 10 list for fewest pitches seen per plate appearance in each of the past four seasons. Yeah, those lists exists, though one doubts

Aybar is aware of them. He's actually in some pretty good company there—Jose Altuve, Yadier Molina and Alexei Ramirez each hacked their way on three times, and even Robinson Cano made an appearance—and some of those guys turned their free-swinging aggression and up-the-middle defensive reps into big paydays. Aybar never quite had that BABIP-driven monster season or power spike to bump himself up the salary scale, which has worked out great for the Angels, who continue to pay him pennies on the dollar for his contributions while he consistently turns in some of the better shortstop seasons in the league.

Roberto Baldoquin   INF

Born: 5/15/94   Age: 21   Bats: R   Throws: R   Height: 5' 11"   Weight: 175

YEAR	TEAM	LVL	AGE	PA	R	2B	3B	HR	RBI	BB	K	SB	CS	AVG/OBP/SLG	TAv	BABIP	BRR	FRAA	WARP
2012	Tunas	CBA	18	12	3	0	0	0	1	1	4	0	1	.167/.231/.167	—	—	—	—	—
2013	Tunas	CBA	19	51	10	0	1	0	4	3	7	1	1	.235/.278/.275	—	—	—	—	—
2014	Tunas	CBA	20	68	11	0	0	1	8	4	10	2	2	.279/.377/.324	—	—	—	—	—

The Angels committed $8 million to this 20 year-old Cuban expat to address imminent turnover to the roster. By the end of 2016, the Angels will likely have bid farewell to all the non-Pujols members of their infield; meanwhile, they've traded pretty much every potential replacement from their minor-league system. Baldoquin could hypothetically fill any one of the three holes. Hypothetically. Reports peg his glove as adequate at shortstop, even if he lacks standout defensive tools, but questions remain about whether he'll show enough bat to match the production of the Angels' current middle infield duo. The profile sniffs of utility, but you don't shell out that much dough on a future bench piece, so the Halos are betting big that Baldoquin—who will play the upcoming season as the equivalent of a college junior—has more ceiling to his offensive game.

Jett Bandy   C

Born: 3/26/90   Age: 25   Bats: R   Throws: R   Height: 6' 4"   Weight: 235

YEAR	TEAM	LVL	AGE	PA	R	2B	3B	HR	RBI	BB	K	SB	CS	AVG/OBP/SLG	TAv	BABIP	BRR	FRAA	WARP
2012	INL	A+	22	365	42	22	1	7	46	20	51	1	1	.247/.318/.386	.274	.271	-2.3		1.9
2013	ARK	AA	23	272	26	17	2	4	28	14	39	0	1	.241/.303/.376	.250	.268	-3.0	C(76): 1.3	0.6
2014	ARK	AA	24	363	38	12	0	13	40	33	63	2	4	.250/.348/.413	.296	.273	-3.4	C(91): -0.2	3.1
2015	ANA	MLB	25	250	23	11	0	5	24	12	50	0	0	.225/.281/.341	.245	.262	-0.5	C 0, 1B 0	0.6

Breakout: 3%   Improve: 9%   Collapse: 9%   Attrition: 20%   MLB: 28%   Comparables: Jason Jaramillo, Bobby Wilson, Tony Sanchez

The Conger trade opens up the backup catcher gig, so a strong spring might push Jett Bandy into another tax bracket faster than anticipated. He once appeared a lock to join the One Percent when a strong sophomore campaign at the University of Arizona lifted him into upper-round consideration, but he tanked as a junior and fell all the way to the 31st round, where the Halos signed him for peanuts. He's proven to be a deft glove behind the plate, with surprisingly smooth agility for a big guy. Last year, his strength finally translated at the plate, and he showed more consistent pull power than ever before. Whether or not he makes the Angels out of spring training, he'll see plenty of MLB playing time through his option years.

Gordon Beckham   2B

Born: 9/16/86   Age: 28   Bats: R   Throws: R   Height: 6' 0"   Weight: 185

YEAR	TEAM	LVL	AGE	PA	R	2B	3B	HR	RBI	BB	K	SB	CS	AVG/OBP/SLG	TAv	BABIP	BRR	FRAA	WARP
2012	CHA	MLB	25	582	62	24	0	16	60	40	89	5	4	.234/.296/.371	.242	.254	-0.8	2B(149): -0.4	0.5
2013	CHR	AAA	26	38	7	2	0	0	5	2	6	0	0	.333/.368/.389	.264	.400	0.7	2B(5): 0.2, SS(2): 0.3	0.3
2013	CHA	MLB	26	408	46	22	1	5	24	28	56	5	1	.267/.322/.372	.260	.299	1.3	2B(103): -4.0, SS(2): -0.1	0.8
2014	BIR	AA	27	47	5	2	0	1	6	4	6	1	0	.163/.234/.279	.196	.167	0.5	2B(6): 0.6	-0.1
2014	ANA	MLB	27	61	10	3	0	2	8	3	11	0	0	.268/.328/.429	.254	.302	0.4	3B(13): 0.1, SS(6): 0.2	0.3
2014	CHA	MLB	27	422	43	24	0	7	36	19	70	3	0	.221/.263/.336	.222	.248	2.6	2B(100): 5.8	0.3
2015	ANA	MLB	28	450	46	21	1	6	36	26	80	4	1	.236/.289/.336	.248	.272	0.9	2B 1, 3B 0	1.1

Breakout: 2%   Improve: 63%   Collapse: 1%   Attrition: 4%   MLB: 98%   Comparables: Jose Vidro, Omar Infante, Bill Doran

Beckham accomplished *something* just by forcing the Angels to consider offering him arbitration; it seemed a foregone conclusion he'd be non-tendered while he was with Chicago, but a .306/.342/.472 September—his best single month since 2010—made him a useful utility infielder on a postseason roster. The Angels non-tendered him anyway, but still.

Kole Calhoun   RF

Born: 10/14/87   Age: 27   Bats: L   Throws: L   Height: 5' 10"   Weight: 200

YEAR	TEAM	LVL	AGE	PA	R	2B	3B	HR	RBI	BB	K	SB	CS	AVG/OBP/SLG	TAv	BABIP	BRR	FRAA	WARP
2012	SLC	AAA	24	463	79	30	7	14	73	44	88	12	3	.298/.369/.507	.290	.346	5.3	CF(52): 2.5, RF(41): -2.7	3.4
2012	ANA	MLB	24	25	2	1	0	0	1	2	6	1	0	.174/.240/.217	.183	.235	0.6	RF(14): 0.2, LF(4): -0.0	-0.1
2013	SLC	AAA	25	274	48	15	6	12	49	32	32	10	2	.354/.431/.617	.332	.371	-0.4	CF(31): -1.1, RF(17): -1.5	2.4
2013	ANA	MLB	25	222	29	7	2	8	32	21	41	2	2	.282/.347/.462	.294	.311	1.5	RF(54): 4.3, 1B(6): 0.5	1.8
2014	SLC	AAA	26	22	7	2	1	1	5	0	3	0	1	.500/.500/.818	.388	.556	-0.3	RF(4): -0.0	0.3
2014	ANA	MLB	26	537	90	31	3	17	58	38	104	5	3	.272/.325/.450	.293	.313	3.9	RF(123): -0.8, 1B(2): -0.0	3.0
2015	ANA	MLB	27	478	61	23	3	14	52	38	97	7	3	.265/.325/.430	.288	.308	2.8	RF -1, CF 0	2.5

Breakout: 5%   Improve: 56%   Collapse: 7%   Attrition: 15%   MLB: 94%   Comparables: Shin-Soo Choo, Lucas Duda, Matt Joyce

Despite declining social mobility since 1980, belief in the American Dream remains alive and well in 2014 because of the Kole Calhouns of the world. Starting with nothing but a hit tool and a dream, he went undrafted and unrecruited following high school, slogged his way through a local JuCo's coursework, finally played onto a Pac 10 roster and wound up a cash-saving, ninth-round senior sign. He was seen by some as immobile, limited perhaps to DH and PH duties, but as a minor leaguer willed himself into a plus right fielder and baserunner. For now, he's starring in countless fluff pieces; if he keeps it up, his legend might ultimately end up in coaches' pep talks around the country. It's stories like these that keep thousands of kids playing nationwide, long after it's rational to move on, clinging to the faith that they can earn their place within a grit-fueled meritocracy.

Kaleb Cowart   3B

Born: 6/2/92   Age: 23   Bats: L   Throws: R   Height: 6' 3"   Weight: 225

YEAR	TEAM	LVL	AGE	PA	R	2B	3B	HR	RBI	BB	K	SB	CS	AVG/OBP/SLG	TAv	BABIP	BRR	FRAA	WARP
2012	CDR	A	20	290	42	16	3	9	54	22	44	9	4	.293/.348/.479	.283	.319	2.2	3B(63): 7.6	2.6
2012	INL	A+	20	316	48	15	4	7	49	45	67	5	3	.259/.366/.426	.307	.316	-1.3		2.9
2013	ARK	AA	21	546	48	20	1	6	42	38	124	14	5	.221/.279/.301	.216	.280	3.1	3B(131): -10.8	-1.5
2014	ARK	AA	22	487	48	18	4	6	54	43	99	26	7	.223/.295/.324	.229	.272	1.7	3B(120): -2.4	-0.2
2015	ANA	MLB	23	250	22	9	1	3	20	16	63	7	2	.211/.262/.298	.221	.272	0.5	3B -1	-0.5

Breakout: 0%   Improve: 0%   Collapse: 0%   Attrition: 0%   MLB: 0%   Comparables: Matt Hague, Jesus Guzman, Ryan Rua

In a recent survey of middle management, 63 percent of bosses reported putting off difficult conversations with employees due to apprehension about how that person would react. Kaleb Cowart works for one of those bosses. He even wrangled another Arizona Fall League stint, a last-ditch effort to prove that there's juice in his bat yet, but the results were no different than they had been in 1,100-plus previous plate appearances. If Jerry Dipoto finally does get around to having that difficult conversation with Cowart this offseason—the one where they both agree that the whole position player thing just didn't work out—it's only going to net the Angels a single season window in which to develop the former first-rounder as a pitcher before having to add him to the 40-man roster. That's likely too little time to extract any value, though Doolittler things have happened. Let this be a lesson to bosses everywhere.

Collin Cowgill   OF

Born: 5/22/86   Age: 29   Bats: R   Throws: L   Height: 5' 9"   Weight: 185

YEAR	TEAM	LVL	AGE	PA	R	2B	3B	HR	RBI	BB	K	SB	CS	AVG/OBP/SLG	TAv	BABIP	BRR	FRAA	WARP
2012	SAC	AAA	26	285	33	17	1	4	37	20	50	8	2	.254/.312/.373	.261	.298	-0.4	CF(30): 0.9, LF(18): 0.1	1.0
2012	OAK	MLB	26	116	10	2	0	1	9	11	27	3	4	.269/.336/.317	.238	.351	-1.0	LF(16): 0.9, CF(15): -0.5	0.2
2013	LVG	AAA	27	145	22	6	0	5	12	17	25	4	0	.268/.366/.439	.267	.301	2.8	LF(18): 2.9, CF(14): -0.4	1.1
2013	ANA	MLB	27	99	11	3	2	2	8	5	27	1	0	.231/.271/.374	.256	.306	0.4	LF(26): -1.0, RF(17): 1.0	0.1
2013	NYN	MLB	27	63	7	2	0	2	8	2	15	0	0	.180/.206/.311	.209	.205	-0.4	CF(17): -1.5, LF(6): -0.2	-0.4
2014	ANA	MLB	28	293	37	10	1	5	21	26	74	4	0	.250/.330/.354	.267	.331	3.5	RF(49): 3.6, LF(44): 2.2	1.8
2015	ANA	MLB	29	271	31	10	1	4	23	20	63	5	1	.244/.305/.349	.258	.305	1.1	RF 2, LF 2	1.1

Breakout: 0%   Improve: 16%   Collapse: 17%   Attrition: 27%   MLB: 60%   Comparables: Brian Bogusevic, Travis Buck, Delwyn Young

When Jerry Dipoto acquired Cowgill from the Mets back in June 2013, it appeared to be the latest move in a full-blown trend of collecting former Diamondbacks' organizational "good guys," the just plain likable types he knew from his time in Arizona. Cowgill was reunited with Barry Enright and Billy Buckner, replacement-level talents who displaced or blocked homegrown assets for more than a year. Cowgill's miserable debut with the Angels that summer, followed by the trade of higher-ceilinged-but-suddenly-redundant Peter Bourjos, seemed to affirm the folly of that policy. Then, in April, Josh Hamilton tackled first base, snapped a ligament in his thumb, and Cowgill stepped up to hit .277/.354/.407 through the first half while playing stellar defense. Loyalty rewarded. Cowgill eventually met overexposure against same-handed pitching in 2014, dragging down his overall numbers, but the ability to mash lefties will continue to make him a valuable depth piece on a club committed to Hamilton for three more years.

C.J. Cron   DH

Born: 1/5/90   Age: 25   Bats: R   Throws: R   Height: 6' 4"   Weight: 235

YEAR	TEAM	LVL	AGE	PA	R	2B	3B	HR	RBI	BB	K	SB	CS	AVG/OBP/SLG	TAv	BABIP	BRR	FRAA	WARP
2012	INL	A+	22	557	73	32	2	27	123	17	72	3	4	.293/.327/.516	.302	.295	-5.2		2.8
2013	ARK	AA	23	565	56	36	1	14	83	23	83	8	4	.274/.319/.428	.278	.298	-1.5	1B(124): 2.2	1.6
2014	SLC	AAA	24	213	30	14	1	7	33	18	40	2	1	.316/.385/.511	.297	.368	1.7	1B(42): -0.5	1.3
2014	ANA	MLB	24	253	28	12	1	11	37	10	61	0	0	.256/.289/.450	.265	.300	-1.6	1B(36): -0.7	0.1
2015	ANA	MLB	25	286	28	14	1	8	34	9	59	1	1	.248/.279/.397	.259	.284	-0.8	1B -0	0.2

Breakout: 3%   Improve: 14%   Collapse: 8%   Attrition: 18%   MLB: 38%   Comparables: Scott Thorman, Nick Evans, Wes Bankston

The Angels masterfully wrung every last drop of juice from Cron's bat to support the playoff push while minimizing the young slugger's inevitable overexposure. Injuries to outfield cornermen opened the door to a rushed promotion at the beginning of May, and for a while Cron helped carry the offense; he hit his high-water mark on June 27th, when he went to bed with a .301/.328/.577 batting line and eight homers. And 26 strikeouts to just four walks. Predictably, he wilted, hitting just .211/.241/.276 over the next 22 games before finding himself on a flight back to Salt Lake; he was back for the stretch run and a 1-for-9 postseason as the Angels' full-time DH in October. Good plate coverage across the breadth of the plate (and beyond), and some ability to hit whatever breaking stuff chugged through the zone, delayed pitchers from picking him apart, but his propensity for chasing and missing above and below the zone will likely land him back in the minors for further seasoning in 2015.

Natanael Delgado   RF

Born: 10/23/95   Age: 19   Bats: L   Throws: L   Height: 6' 1"   Weight: 170

YEAR	TEAM	LVL	AGE	PA	R	2B	3B	HR	RBI	BB	K	SB	CS	AVG/OBP/SLG	TAv	BABIP	BRR	FRAA	WARP
2015	ANA	MLB	19	250	15	8	1	2	19	5	79	0	0	.189/.208/.256	.181	.264	-0.3	LF -2, CF -0	-1.8

Breakout: 0%   Improve: 0%   Collapse: 0%   Attrition: 0%   MLB: 0%   Comparables: Ender Inciarte, Zoilo Almonte, Jordan Schafer

Delgado would likely not warrant a comment in any other team's section. Maybe a lineout. Maybe. There, it had to be said. He's a perfectly good guy to have in your system, a 19-year-old who just held his own in Rookie ball as the equivalent of a graduating high school senior, but he didn't really hit anything with squiggle, bend or fade last summer. He saw fastballs—lots of Rookie ball fastballs—and turned those around with little trouble. There's bat speed, some power projection and a talent for barreling heat, but evaluators worry that he's going to reach his ceiling of competence quickly in any league where pitchers can and do turn to the proverbial "book" for help in exploiting the opposition.

Kody Eaves   2B

Born: 7/8/93   Age: 21   Bats: L   Throws: R   Height: 6' 0"   Weight: 175

YEAR	TEAM	LVL	AGE	PA	R	2B	3B	HR	RBI	BB	K	SB	CS	AVG/OBP/SLG	TAv	BABIP	BRR	FRAA	WARP
2014	BUR	A	20	587	74	37	7	10	45	29	142	25	10	.268/.308/.415	.262	.342	3.4	2B(126): -1.6	1.7
2015	ANA	MLB	21	250	23	10	1	2	16	6	75	6	3	.202/.223/.282	.196	.277	0.3	2B -1, SS 0	-1.0

Breakout: 0%   Improve: 0%   Collapse: 0%   Attrition: 0%   MLB: 0%   Comparables: *Hernan Perez, Sean Kazmar, Jimmy Paredes*

In a system as bereft of impact hitters as this one, Eaves' tools stand out. The 2012 prep-draftee ranked third in total bases in the Midwest League, smashing a league leading 37 doubles as the 15th-youngest hitter in the league. His strength is his ability to square up heat, especially to the opposite field, though he has a much tougher time with breaking and off-speed stuff. He won't get much national attention due to the unsightly K/BB ratio and OBP, but modest growth in his approach would mean helium.

David Freese   3B

Born: 4/28/83   Age: 32   Bats: R   Throws: R   Height: 6' 2"   Weight: 225

YEAR	TEAM	LVL	AGE	PA	R	2B	3B	HR	RBI	BB	K	SB	CS	AVG/OBP/SLG	TAv	BABIP	BRR	FRAA	WARP
2012	SLN	MLB	29	567	70	25	1	20	79	57	122	3	3	.293/.372/.467	.290	.352	-3.5	3B(134): 2.3	3.2
2013	SLN	MLB	30	521	53	26	1	9	60	47	106	1	2	.262/.340/.381	.252	.320	-1.6	3B(132): -14.6	-0.4
2014	ANA	MLB	31	511	53	25	1	10	55	38	124	1	3	.260/.321/.383	.269	.330	-0.4	3B(122): -7.2	1.1
2015	ANA	MLB	32	486	49	21	1	10	52	39	113	2	2	.259/.327/.381	.275	.324	-1.2	3B -5	1.2

Breakout: 1%   Improve: 37%   Collapse: 6%   Attrition: 7%   MLB: 97%   Comparables: *Joe Torre, Bobby Bonilla, Al Rosen*

On one count, Freese delivered: In Game One of the ALDS, he hit what seemed at the time to be a crucial home run, and wound up posting the second-best OPS of the club's brief postseason run. That provided the Angels with a little "Big Game" pyrrhic victory in a season where Freese generally disappointed. He produced the 24th-best WARP of all MLB third basemen, and merely matched Peter Bourjos (who received just 60 percent of Freese's playing time) in that category. Meanwhile, Randal Grichuk—the other guy the Angels gave up to get Freese—took the reins in the Cardinals' right field, made their postseason roster and slammed a Clayton Kershaw curveball into the seats. Entering the 2015 offseason, the Halos are reportedly looking to go either better or cheaper at third base, so yeah, Angels fans have every reason to hold a grudge.

Grant Green   LF

Born: 9/27/87   Age: 27   Bats: R   Throws: R   Height: 6' 3"   Weight: 180

YEAR	TEAM	LVL	AGE	PA	R	2B	3B	HR	RBI	BB	K	SB	CS	AVG/OBP/SLG	TAv	BABIP	BRR	FRAA	WARP
2012	SAC	AAA	24	562	73	28	6	15	75	33	75	13	9	.296/.338/.458	.276	.320	1.7	LF(49): -2.1, CF(30): -0.8	2.6
2013	SAC	AAA	25	415	66	27	3	11	50	27	70	4	1	.325/.379/.500	.313	.376	-0.6	2B(73): -11.4, 1B(1): -0.1	2.3
2013	SLC	AAA	25	28	2	1	0	0	3	3	7	0	1	.333/.393/.375	.285	.444	0.0	3B(4): 0.3, 2B(2): 0.0	0.2
2013	ANA	MLB	25	137	16	8	1	1	16	10	38	0	0	.280/.336/.384	.260	.391	-0.9	2B(40): -3.1	-0.2
2013	OAK	MLB	25	16	0	0	0	0	1	0	6	0	0	.000/.000/.000	.027	.000	0.0	2B(5): -0.4	-0.5
2014	SLC	AAA	26	214	38	17	3	5	42	13	31	4	2	.333/.379/.525	.295	.374	1.0	SS(18): -0.8, 3B(15): -1.6	1.3
2014	ANA	MLB	26	103	7	5	0	1	11	2	20	1	4	.273/.282/.354	.250	.325	-2.0	LF(17): -1.5, 2B(10): 0.5	-0.3
2015	ANA	MLB	27	250	27	12	1	4	23	11	51	3	2	.263/.298/.382	.265	.314	-1.1	2B -2, LF -0	0.4

Breakout: 3%   Improve: 22%   Collapse: 13%   Attrition: 24%   MLB: 54%   Comparables: *Lou Montanez, Alejandro De Aza, Jorge Piedra*

The Angels ended last April short three regulars, one game over .500, and 3 1/2 games back of the A's. Then Green took over left field for a month (while filling in occasionally at second and third) and put up a gaudy .361/.375/.475 slash line. May ended and Green's opportunities and efficacy both disappeared, but, hey, he'll always have that 16-12 month to claim credit for. The Angels had emptied their system of middle-infield depth in recent years but began reversing that trend in late summer, so Green's future role is now murkier. Could be that the club thinks that we've already seen the best of him.

Josh Hamilton   LF

Born: 5/21/81   Age: 34   Bats: L   Throws: L   Height: 6' 4"   Weight: 240

YEAR	TEAM	LVL	AGE	PA	R	2B	3B	HR	RBI	BB	K	SB	CS	AVG/OBP/SLG	TAv	BABIP	BRR	FRAA	WARP
2012	TEX	MLB	31	636	103	31	2	43	128	60	162	7	4	.285/.354/.577	.310	.320	1.7	CF(95): -3.6, LF(84): -0.2	4.5
2013	ANA	MLB	32	636	73	32	5	21	79	47	158	4	0	.250/.307/.432	.269	.303	3.3	RF(83): 2.5, LF(19): 3.1	2.6
2014	ANA	MLB	33	381	43	21	0	10	44	32	108	3	3	.263/.331/.414	.287	.350	-3.3	LF(68): 6.4, CF(7): 0.2	2.2
2015	ANA	MLB	34	411	49	20	2	16	56	30	100	4	2	.268/.325/.460	.295	.320	0.4	LF 3, RF 0	2.6

Breakout: 1%   Improve: 31%   Collapse: 10%   Attrition: 14%   MLB: 95%   Comparables: *Ryan Ludwick, Josh Willingham, Alfonso Soriano*

Sequencing is everything. Had Josh Hamilton's season ended on an eight-game, .444/.545/.741 tear, he'd have single-handedly extended the Angels' playoff run, redeemed an otherwise dismal season, and be looking forward to an April filled with loud cheers instead of the boos that will rain down at the first hint of struggle. Alas, those eight magic games came out of the gate last season, and the tear ended abruptly with a headlong dive into first. It was almost two full months before he returned, and then slashed .248/.310/.386 through the end of the season. He made it back from an eyebrow-raising rib injury and went 0 for frigg'n 13 to an increasing cacophony of boos during the Division Series. He saw 47 pitches in October, and swung and missed 13 times.

Interestingly, away from the scrutiny of the home crowd, he hit .278/.347/.572 over the season. Who says they make up make-up?

Chad Hinshaw   CF

Born: 9/10/90   Age: 24   Bats: R   Throws: R   Height: 6' 1"   Weight: 205

YEAR	TEAM	LVL	AGE	PA	R	2B	3B	HR	RBI	BB	K	SB	CS	AVG/OBP/SLG	TAv	BABIP	BRR	FRAA	WARP
2014	BUR	A	23	249	51	13	3	6	24	28	63	25	8	.282/.403/.461	.316	.380	0.5	CF(49): -0.4, LF(9): 0.3	2.3
2014	INL	A+	23	298	49	14	8	10	46	15	65	16	7	.261/.333/.489	.298	.307	0.7		2.8
2015	ANA	MLB	24	250	31	8	2	5	19	13	73	11	5	.210/.276/.322	.236	.284	0.8	CF 1, LF 0	0.3

Breakout: 7%   Improve: 11%   Collapse: 3%   Attrition: 12%   MLB: 21%   Comparables: *Matt Den Dekker, Jordan Danks, Thomas Pham*

As a 15th-round senior pick, Hinshaw entered his first full professional season with a very low profile, even in a thin system. By several measures of aggregate performance, he turned in the top performance on the Angels' farm last year, and followed it up with a strong showing in the Arizona Fall League, so his profile is a little higher heading into 2015. That is to say, some of the Angels' most informed fans will recognize the name when he takes his token spring training at-bats. His legs and glove give him fourth-outfielder potential; the strikeouts give him night sweats.

Chris Iannetta   C

Born: 4/8/83   Age: 32   Bats: R   Throws: R   Height: 6' 0"   Weight: 230

YEAR	TEAM	LVL	AGE	PA	R	2B	3B	HR	RBI	BB	K	SB	CS	AVG/OBP/SLG	TAv	BABIP	BRR	FRAA	WARP
2012	SLC	AAA	29	25	3	2	0	0	2	3	7	0	0	.273/.360/.364	.261	.400	-0.2	C(4): -0.0	0.1
2012	ANA	MLB	29	253	27	6	1	9	26	29	60	1	3	.240/.332/.398	.268	.288	0.1	C(78): -0.5	1.5
2013	ANA	MLB	30	399	40	15	0	11	39	68	100	0	1	.225/.358/.372	.275	.284	-3.1	C(113): -0.9	1.4
2014	ANA	MLB	31	373	41	22	0	7	43	54	91	3	0	.252/.373/.392	.298	.329	-0.3	C(104): -1.5	2.9
2015	ANA	MLB	32	356	41	13	0	9	37	50	87	2	1	.222/.338/.360	.273	.279	-0.7	C -0	1.8

Breakout: 1%   Improve: 23%   Collapse: 12%   Attrition: 14%   MLB: 92%   Comparables: Chris Snyder, Ted Simmons, Erubiel Durazo

For the rest of his life, Iannetta will be the guy who allowed Billy Butler to swipe a bag in Game Three of the ALDS. He'll wake up in cold sweats, consumed by visions of the big man breaking toward second base and lumbering his way to glory. He'll writhe in his blankets, desperately trying to find a better grip on a ball that is no longer there, shrieking in humiliation as he sees his own throw bounce pathetically in front of the bag while Butler slides in safely. Postseason trauma aside, Iannetta's season was a smashing success as he reclaimed the full-time catching job through a combination of successful smashing and tolerable defense. Still. Billy Butler. Forever and ever, amen.

Matt Joyce   LF

Born: 8/3/84   Age: 30   Bats: L   Throws: R   Height: 6' 2"   Weight: 200

YEAR	TEAM	LVL	AGE	PA	R	2B	3B	HR	RBI	BB	K	SB	CS	AVG/OBP/SLG	TAv	BABIP	BRR	FRAA	WARP
2012	TBA	MLB	27	462	55	18	3	17	59	55	102	4	3	.241/.341/.429	.277	.281	2.3	RF(89): -2.2, LF(33): -0.8	1.4
2013	TBA	MLB	28	481	61	22	0	18	47	59	87	7	3	.235/.328/.419	.285	.251	-1.2	RF(58): -2.7, LF(58): 2.8	1.8
2014	TBA	MLB	29	493	51	23	2	9	52	62	111	2	5	.254/.349/.383	.276	.316	-0.3	LF(81): 0.3, RF(15): -0.4	1.7
2015	ANA	MLB	30	461	52	22	2	13	54	53	99	5	3	.247/.337/.407	.284	.293	0.2	LF 1, RF -1	2.1

Breakout: 3%   Improve: 59%   Collapse: 0%   Attrition: 5%   MLB: 99%   Comparables: Milton Bradley, Seth Smith, Carl Yastrzemski

Picture a carefree teenager wanting to live her life every day to its fullest. Meanwhile, her dad, while cooler and more free-spirited than most other pops on the block, wants what is best for his daughter. This means a strict curfew and, most importantly, keeping her away from "that boy." She knows he means well but does not understand why she can't make her own choices. Dad tries to explain his side as best as he can but even his friends tell him, "Come on, let her live a little" and, "You were young once; let her make some mistakes." He remains steadfast in his decision to shelter her, keeping everyone's best interest in mind. All the while, the ne'er-do-well down the street is just waiting for his chance to disrupt the household's order. You've figured this out by now, but: Joyce is the daughter, Joe Maddon is the father and that dastardly boy is all of the left-handed pitchers in the league. Now that the family is broken up, will step-dad Mike Scioscia try to win the kid over by relaxing the rules?

John McDonald   3B

Born: 9/24/74   Age: 40   Bats: R   Throws: R   Height: 5' 9"   Weight: 185

YEAR	TEAM	LVL	AGE	PA	R	2B	3B	HR	RBI	BB	K	SB	CS	AVG/OBP/SLG	TAv	BABIP	BRR	FRAA	WARP
2012	ARI	MLB	37	213	16	9	0	6	22	12	33	0	1	.249/.295/.386	.233	.272	1.2	SS(54): -0.6, 3B(5): -0.0	0.3
2013	IND	AAA	38	37	5	1	0	0	1	2	3	1	0	.265/.324/.294	.214	.290	0.3	SS(6): 0.3, 2B(4): -0.0	0.0
2013	BOS	MLB	38	9	1	0	0	0	0	1	3	0	0	.250/.333/.250	.248	.400	0.0	2B(6): -0.3	0.0
2013	CLE	MLB	38	8	2	0	0	0	0	1	1	0	0	.000/.125/.000	.091	.000	0.2	3B(8): -0.0	0.0
2013	PHI	MLB	38	25	5	0	0	1	3	1	4	0	0	.174/.208/.304	.178	.167	-0.5	3B(8): 0.2, SS(6): 0.1	-0.1
2013	PIT	MLB	38	35	0	1	0	0	1	3	8	0	0	.065/.171/.097	.129	.087	0.0	SS(13): -0.6, 2B(4): 0.1	-0.5
2014	ANA	MLB	39	91	4	2	0	0	5	7	18	1	1	.171/.256/.197	.203	.220	0.1	3B(73): 1.9, SS(16): 0.0	-0.1
2015	ANA	MLB	40	250	20	9	1	2	19	12	43	2	1	.214/.256/.291	.219	.245	0.3	SS 1, 3B 2	0.2

Breakout: 1%   Improve: 18%   Collapse: 10%   Attrition: 25%   MLB: 64%   Comparables: Cal Ripken Jr., Tony Taylor, Jamey Carroll

Over the past two seasons, John McDonald has hit an empty buck forty-five. Over the past two seasons, John McDonald has taken the field with *four* clubs that ultimately made the playoffs. If this were the 1970s, Ronald Reagan would be calling him the Welfare Queen and pledging to cleanse the system of fraud and waste. It's 2015, though, so McDonald will likely spend the first four months of the season angling for a trade to a contender.

Efren Navarro   UT

Born: 5/14/86   Age: 29   Bats: L   Throws: L   Height: 6' 0"   Weight: 210

YEAR	TEAM	LVL	AGE	PA	R	2B	3B	HR	RBI	BB	K	SB	CS	AVG/OBP/SLG	TAv	BABIP	BRR	FRAA	WARP
2012	SLC	AAA	26	577	79	35	1	7	74	36	70	3	2	.294/.336/.403	.259	.321	1.1	1B(140): 1.7	1.4
2013	SLC	AAA	27	586	83	39	3	7	81	68	99	8	5	.326/.404/.454	.288	.390	1.7	1B(130): 2.8	3.2
2013	ANA	MLB	27	6	0	0	0	0	1	2	1	1	0	.250/.500/.250	.326	.333	0.1	1B(2): 0.1	0.1
2014	SLC	AAA	28	318	45	19	3	4	50	43	47	2	1	.326/.418/.462	.302	.381	-0.8	1B(31): 2.9, RF(17): -1.1	1.9
2014	ANA	MLB	28	174	17	10	1	1	14	13	27	1	3	.245/.302/.340	.245	.290	1.3	1B(28): -1.5, LF(23): 1.3	0.2
2015	ANA	MLB	29	250	21	12	1	2	21	19	47	2	1	.250/.306/.332	.249	.302	-0.5	1B 0, LF 1	0.1

Breakout: 0%   Improve: 1%   Collapse: 7%   Attrition: 14%   MLB: 14%   Comparables: Blake Lalli, Brian Dinkelman, Michael Aubrey

The ever-so-minor downside of Pujols remaining relatively healthy in 2014 was that it denied Halos fans the pleasure of watching Navarro, long-standing organizational soldier, field his natural position. At his defensive peak, Navarro surfaced repeatedly as an outlier in multiple defensive metrics—one industry member even referred to him as breaking the system—and won the Rawlings Minor League gold glove in 2011. His Angels' slash line was underwhelming, but solid minor-league peripherals, including a 26 percent line-drive rate, translated well to the majors, so he might hit enough in 2015 to maintain his spot on a big-league roster.

Shawn O'Malley   UT

Born: 12/28/87   Age: 27   Bats: B   Throws: R   Height: 5' 11"   Weight: 165

YEAR	TEAM	LVL	AGE	PA	R	2B	3B	HR	RBI	BB	K	SB	CS	AVG/OBP/SLG	TAv	BABIP	BRR	FRAA	WARP
2012	MNT	AA	24	144	22	3	3	0	5	17	24	7	3	.231/.333/.306	.240	.286	1.6	SS(22): -0.5, LF(8): 0.7	0.4
2012	DUR	AAA	24	247	32	4	2	2	18	17	49	11	1	.245/.304/.310	.229	.302	2.9	2B(34): 2.6, SS(22): 0.4	0.3
2013	MNT	AA	25	373	53	12	6	3	32	32	60	24	3	.262/.337/.364	.268	.310	4.5	SS(89): -5.8, 2B(1): 0.1	1.6
2014	ARK	AA	26	41	3	0	1	0	5	6	8	1	0	.188/.308/.250	.268	.240	0.2	CF(3): -0.3, 2B(1): 0.1	0.1
2014	SLC	AAA	26	376	60	19	9	3	38	39	44	13	4	.330/.411/.475	.300	.372	3.9	SS(56): -3.9, 2B(13): 1.8	3.5
2014	ANA	MLB	26	16	3	0	0	0	1	0	8	2	0	.188/.188/.188	.167	.375	0.3	LF(5): -0.3, 2B(1): 0.0	-0.2
2015	ANA	MLB	27	250	26	8	3	1	16	17	51	9	2	.237/.298/.308	.236	.290	1.3	SS -2, 2B 0	0.2

Breakout: 5%   Improve: 18%   Collapse: 2%   Attrition: 16%   MLB: 24%   Comparables: Andrew Romine, Eider Torres, Kris Negron

Despite having only just turned 27, O'Malley is already the veteran of nine minor-league campaigns. The Halos invited him to spring training last year, and general system thinness opened the door for him to take his slap-hitting, I-have-a-glove-for-every-position schtick to Salt Lake, earn his roster spot, notch a few September big-league hits and claim his playoff share. Alas, even after such a feel-good year with the organization, he couldn't keep his 40-man spot through the winter.

Carlos Perez   C

Born: 10/27/90   Age: 24   Bats: R   Throws: R   Height: 6' 0"   Weight: 210

YEAR	TEAM	LVL	AGE	PA	R	2B	3B	HR	RBI	BB	K	SB	CS	AVG/OBP/SLG	TAv	BABIP	BRR	FRAA	WARP
2012	LNS	A	21	319	48	22	5	5	40	35	38	3	2	.275/.358/.447	.293	.298	1.3	C(71): 1.8	2.9
2012	LNC	A+	21	97	11	6	1	0	10	6	17	0	1	.318/.368/.409	.257	.394	0.2	C(26): 0.7	0.9
2013	CCH	AA	22	60	6	4	0	1	5	4	11	0	0	.283/.356/.415	.259	.341	0.0	C(12): -0.2	0.3
2013	OKL	AAA	22	296	29	14	0	2	32	25	39	1	1	.269/.328/.345	.254	.304	-1.0	C(71): 0.7	1.5
2014	OKL	AAA	23	340	33	16	2	6	34	29	54	3	0	.259/.323/.385	.252	.295	-0.5	C(74): -0.1, 1B(5): -0.2	1.0
2015	ANA	MLB	24	250	21	11	1	2	20	16	49	1	0	.231/.282/.316	.235	.276	-0.3	C 0, 1B -0	0.3

Breakout: 3%   Improve: 5%   Collapse: 3%   Attrition: 10%   MLB: 11%   Comparables: Jordan Pacheco, Steve Clevenger, Tony Sanchez

Not to be confused with the current Astros prospect or the former Tigers prospect. Oh no, *this* Perez had a curious enough year without any identity mixups. He opened the season with Mississippi and appeared in four games before disappearing for two months due to a viral infection. A slow and steady rehab stint in the Gulf Coast League followed, but he escaped the complex just in time to finish the regular season with Rome. Though Perez's starting days are just a memory, his velocity and funkiness should make him an effective lefty-on-lefty reliever. Shy of that, he can always claim he used to pitch for the Dodgers.

Albert Pujols   1B

Born: 1/16/80   Age: 35   Bats: R   Throws: R   Height: 6' 3"   Weight: 230

YEAR	TEAM	LVL	AGE	PA	R	2B	3B	HR	RBI	BB	K	SB	CS	AVG/OBP/SLG	TAv	BABIP	BRR	FRAA	WARP
2012	ANA	MLB	32	670	85	50	0	30	105	52	76	8	1	.285/.343/.516	.302	.282	-2.8	1B(120): 7.1, 3B(3): -0.0	4.0
2013	ANA	MLB	33	443	49	19	0	17	64	40	55	1	1	.258/.330/.437	.285	.258	1.7	1B(34): 2.1	2.2
2014	ANA	MLB	34	695	89	37	1	28	105	48	71	5	1	.272/.324/.466	.296	.265	-2.1	1B(116): -4.0, 3B(1): 0.0	2.9
2015	ANA	MLB	35	603	76	30	1	25	86	53	74	5	1	.273/.339/.472	.306	.272	-1.0	1B 5, 3B 0	4.0

Breakout: 1%   Improve: 28%   Collapse: 4%   Attrition: 8%   MLB: 96%   Comparables: Vladimir Guerrero, Todd Helton, Hideki Matsui

Back on July 20th, Pujols responded to a preemptive Fernando Rodney arrow celebration by lacing a game-tying double down the first-base line, then unleashing an imaginary arrow of his own at the guy Angels fans remember as "Fraudney." That moment of swagger defined the Angels' second-half surge, and earned Albert the loving acceptance that had mostly eluded him during his first two-and-a-half seasons in Anaheim. This sort of symbolism is important when earning $23 million for 2.9 WARP worth of work. He entered this offseason vowing to strengthen his injury-be-leaguered lower half in order to reassert his opposite-field pop. That would do more to restore his former self than anything else: In 2010, his last MVP-caliber season, he slugged .909 on pitches in the outer third of the strike zone; in 2014 it was just .512, up from .473 the previous year, but still far short of his glory days, when he didn't need to be snarky to get fans on his side.

Daniel Robertson   OF

Born: 9/30/85   Age: 29   Bats: R   Throws: R   Height: 5' 8"   Weight: 170

YEAR	TEAM	LVL	AGE	PA	R	2B	3B	HR	RBI	BB	K	SB	CS	AVG/OBP/SLG	TAv	BABIP	BRR	FRAA	WARP
2012	TUC	AAA	26	553	70	28	4	2	38	48	58	18	8	.302/.371/.388	.263	.339	1.5	CF(80): 1.7, LF(33): -0.4	2.0
2013	TUC	AAA	27	565	91	24	9	2	53	60	63	23	6	.285/.371/.384	.268	.320	6.0	RF(72): -0.6, CF(64): 5.7	2.9
2014	ELP	AAA	28	23	6	2	0	2	5	1	3	0	0	.364/.391/.727	.358	.353	0.6	2B(5): 0.4, RF(1): -0.0	0.0
2014	ROU	AAA	28	33	6	1	1	1	3	5	4	2	0	.250/.364/.464	.277	.261	0.5	LF(5): -0.0, CF(2): -0.0	0.1
2014	TEX	MLB	28	197	23	9	1	0	21	17	28	6	4	.271/.333/.333	.248	.320	1.1	LF(30): -0.8, CF(21): -1.2	0.4
2015	ANA	MLB	29	250	27	10	1	1	16	20	40	7	3	.245/.311/.310	.247	.287	0.2	CF 0, RF -0	0.3

Breakout: 1%   Improve: 13%   Collapse: 12%   Attrition: 18%   MLB: 35%   Comparables: Jose Constanza, Tommy Watkins, Mike Edwards

The diminutive outfielder was called upon to do one thing when the Rangers picked him up from the Padres' organization in April: hit left-handed pitching. Robertson did just that, which is good for him because he isn't qualified to do much else. The .330/.398/.423 line he posted against south-paws was fueled by lots of contact, a solid walk rate and his customary doubles-only power. Robertson only homered 27 times as a minor leaguer in seven seasons, despite spending three seasons combined in Lake Elsinore and Tuscon. He'll compete for a reserve outfielder role with the Angels after being acquired in a minor early-winter trade.

Josh Rutledge   SS

Born: 4/21/89   Age: 26   Bats: R   Throws: R   Height: 6' 1"   Weight: 190

YEAR	TEAM	LVL	AGE	PA	R	2B	3B	HR	RBI	BB	K	SB	CS	AVG/OBP/SLG	TAv	BABIP	BRR	FRAA	WARP
2012	TUL	AA	23	379	57	27	3	13	35	14	69	14	4	.306/.338/.508	.316	.345	1.7	SS(67): -6.3, 2B(22): -0.0	3.0
2012	COL	MLB	23	291	37	20	5	8	37	9	54	7	0	.274/.306/.469	.252	.315	-0.3	SS(57): -3.5, 2B(7): -0.3	0.2
2013	CSP	AAA	24	162	24	17	1	4	24	12	21	1	2	.371/.444/.587	.336	.415	-0.4	SS(22): -0.4, 2B(16): 0.7	1.8
2013	COL	MLB	24	314	45	6	1	7	19	22	62	12	0	.235/.294/.337	.229	.276	4.2	2B(58): 1.4, SS(14): -0.4	0.7
2014	CSP	AAA	25	64	7	3	0	1	5	7	12	3	3	.333/.413/.444	.303	.405	1.2	SS(13): -0.3, 2B(2): -0.1	0.6
2014	COL	MLB	25	342	44	16	7	4	33	20	83	2	3	.269/.323/.405	.242	.353	2.2	SS(69): -6.3, 2B(17): -1.2	0.2
2015	ANA	MLB	26	345	39	16	2	6	31	16	78	7	2	.249/.293/.374	.257	.303	1.1	SS -5, 2B -0	0.7

Breakout: 7%   Improve: 60%   Collapse: 11%   Attrition: 17%   MLB: 96%   Comparables: Felipe Lopez, Khalil Greene, Ian Desmond

For the third straight year, Rutledge sat patiently on the bench awaiting Troy Tulowitzki's next injury. If this comment was a lineout, it would simply end with, "He got his chance on July 19th and, in an entire second half, failed to produce even one-third of Tulo's season output." With the extra space though, we'll note this: Tulowitzki's injuries gave Rutledge more than 200 games to prove himself, and that he did not, unless he proved he'll swing at anything off-speed. He's expected to replace Howie Kendrick at second base, which is to say, he not expected to *replace* Howie Kendrick at second base.

Mike Trout   CF

Born: 8/7/91   Age: 23   Bats: R   Throws: R   Height: 6' 2"   Weight: 230

YEAR	TEAM	LVL	AGE	PA	R	2B	3B	HR	RBI	BB	K	SB	CS	AVG/OBP/SLG	TAv	BABIP	BRR	FRAA	WARP
2012	SLC	AAA	20	93	21	4	5	1	13	11	16	6	1	.403/.467/.623	.360	.476	-0.4	CF(8): -0.9, LF(5): 0.2	1.1
2012	ANA	MLB	20	639	129	27	8	30	83	67	139	49	5	.326/.399/.564	.351	.383	7.9	CF(110): 3.9, LF(67): 2.2	9.0
2013	ANA	MLB	21	716	109	39	9	27	97	110	136	33	7	.323/.432/.557	.367	.376	1.7	CF(111): 0.1, LF(47): 2.2	10.4
2014	ANA	MLB	22	705	115	39	9	36	111	83	184	16	2	.287/.377/.561	.353	.349	4.7	CF(149): 1.5	9.4
2015	ANA	MLB	23	665	106	31	8	26	86	76	149	28	5	.298/.383/.518	.337	.354	3.2	CF -1, LF 2	7.4

Breakout: 4%   Improve: 55%   Collapse: 2%   Attrition: 6%   MLB: 98%   Comparables: Giancarlo Stanton, Miguel Cabrera, Jason Heyward

Back on June 7th, Chris Sale threw a perfectly good changeup below the outer edge of the strike zone, and Trout turned it around some 410 feet to dead center. With that home run, Trout put the pitchers of the world on notice: *Your* pitch, that buried secondary, is not *your* pitch. It is *my* pitch. Throw it, and I will hurt you. Trout slugged .686 below the strike zone, .833 in the bottom third of the strike zone and .915 on changeups generally. Perhaps the real marvel was that pitchers reacted so minimally to that message: In the second half of 2014, they stayed out of Trout's low (and really low) kill zones just 3 percent less often than they did in the first half. They went upstairs only 5 percent more often, long after Trout's heat maps detailed in brilliant color that his whiff rate tripled and his slugging dropped 600 points from the bottom third of the zone. Pitchers had the opportunity to make baseball's superhero a mere mortal, and it only changed their habits with one in 20 pitches. Egad.

Oh, and Trout is spectacular. The BBWAA finally took notice. Happy MVP, Mike.

Alex Yarbrough   2B

Born: 8/3/91   Age: 23   Bats: B   Throws: R   Height: 6' 0"   Weight: 195

YEAR	TEAM	LVL	AGE	PA	R	2B	3B	HR	RBI	BB	K	SB	CS	AVG/OBP/SLG	TAv	BABIP	BRR	FRAA	WARP
2012	CDR	A	20	257	35	12	9	0	27	10	20	9	2	.287/.320/.410	.253	.313	0.6	2B(58): -1.1	0.4
2013	INL	A+	21	615	77	32	10	11	80	27	106	14	4	.313/.341/.459	.302	.364	0.5		2.4
2014	ARK	AA	22	592	66	38	4	5	77	33	124	6	6	.285/.321/.397	.266	.352	-0.2	2B(132): -15.2	0.5
2015	ANA	MLB	23	250	19	12	2	2	21	6	56	2	1	.246/.264/.333	.231	.309	-0.2	2B -6	-0.6

Breakout: 2%   Improve: 7%   Collapse: 4%   Attrition: 8%   MLB: 15%   Comparables: German Duran, Jordany Valdespin, Scooter Gennett

Counting stats are kind of Yarbrough's thing: He is generally a league leader in categories like games played, hits and doubles, and trails those leagues in errors committed. These types of numbers win him no small share of good will, landing him hardware like this year's Texas League Player of the Year Award, labels like Best Defensive Cal League Second Baseman in 2013, and a smattering of feature articles that no doubt make his loved ones proud. Yet, for the second year running, Fielding Runs Above Average has given him the shank. The system, usually so polite, so willing to generate modest, significantly regressed numbers that convey just the barest hint of growing pains in the field, maintains that Yarbrough has cost Angels' affiliates 35 runs in the field these past two years. He walks little, strikes out a bit too often, and doesn't hit for significant power, which further deflates sub-replacement level PECOTA projections. In the past two years, it's been possible to assume a gradual merging of baseball man wisdom and advanced metrics, but here they are, taking polar opposite positions with Yarbrough. With his pedigree, he'll no doubt get major-league time, but the Halos would be making a mighty old-school bet if they hand the position over to him.

Pitchers

Alfonso Alcantara   RHP

Born: 4/3/93   Age: 22   Bats: R   Throws: R   Height: 6'2"   Weight: 190

YEAR	TEAM	LVL	AGE	W	L	SV	G	GS	IP	H	HR	BB	K	BB/9	K/9	GB%	BABIP	WHIP	ERA	FIP	FRA	WARP
2014	BUR	A	21	7	6	1	27	20	125¹	98	6	60	117	4.3	8.4	58%	.277	1.26	3.81	3.77	5.15	0.1
2015	ANA	MLB	22	5	6	0	20	16	88²	96	10	54	60	5.5	6.1	51%	.305	1.70	5.37	5.71	5.83	-0.9

Breakout: 0%   Improve: 0%   Collapse: 0%   Attrition: 0%   MLB: 0%   Comparables: Jon Lester, Jose Cisnero, Jimmy Barthmaier

Back in the fall of 2012, a Dominican prospect by the name of Alfonso Alcantara entered the United States to the very faint appreciation of die-hard prospect followers, who were amped at rumors that the lanky 19-year-old had touched triple digits in complex games. That guy spent a forgettable summer with the Orem Owlz; hitting 94 mph a couple of times in August was enough to evoke celebratory words from the press box. We here at Baseball Prospectus are, like, 90 percent sure that this Victor Alcantara, who reportedly touched 100 mph again in the Midwest League, is the same fellow. Maybe he's risen from the ashes of the combusted Alfonso, to emerge once again as the only right-handed power arm in the system with a chance at remaining a starter. Trouble is, most analysts project him as a reliever in the end due to a rigid, exhausting delivery, come-and-go command, and a high-80s changeup/slider combo that's drawn poor scouting grades but induced a lot of whiffs in A-Ball. In a system bereft of potential impact talent, all eyes will be on Alfonso. I mean, Victor.

Sean Burnett   LHP

Born: 9/17/82   Age: 32   Bats: L   Throws: L   Height: 6'1"   Weight: 180

YEAR	TEAM	LVL	AGE	W	L	SV	G	GS	IP	H	HR	BB	K	BB/9	K/9	GB%	BABIP	WHIP	ERA	FIP	FRA	WARP
2012	WAS	MLB	29	1	2	2	70	0	56²	58	4	12	57	1.9	9.1	60%	.331	1.24	2.38	2.84	3.15	1.0
2013	ANA	MLB	30	0	0	0	13	0	9²	9	1	4	7	3.7	6.5	66%	.286	1.34	0.93	4.21	4.58	0.0
2014	ANA	MLB	31	0	0	0	3	0	0²	1	0	0	0	0.0	0.0	67%	.333	1.50	13.50	3.16	3.93	0.0
2015	ANA	MLB	32	2	1	1	44	0	35²	33	3	11	32	2.7	8.0	53%	.296	1.23	3.30	3.84	3.59	0.5

Breakout: 25%   Improve: 49%   Collapse: 25%   Attrition: 11%   MLB: 92%   Comparables: *Matt Lindstrom, Pedro Feliciano, John Grabow*

History will remember the Josh Hamilton signing on 12/15/12, but the two weeks preceding it weren't exactly Jerry Dipoto's finest fortnight. In an attempt to rebuild a less costly pitching staff around Dan Haren and Ervin Santana's departures, he traded Jordan Walden for Tommy Hanson, signed Joe Blanton, and, to replace Walden, signed Burnett; all three players were under club control for at least two years. Hanson was non-tendered after a year. Blanton was released after a year. And Burnett was the last one standing.

Perhaps that's the wrong word to describe Burnett's state of recline. You're more likely to find him lying down (as in an MRI machine) or perhaps lounging around (as on a beach) than standing up (as on a mound). Back-to-back Tommy John surgeries have limited him to three batters faced since May 2013. The Angels bought out the 2015 option, and the book was closed on the December 2012 trio: 216 innings, 145 runs. At least the moves freed up some money to sign Josh Hamilton ...

Tyler DeLoach   LHP

Born: 4/12/91   Age: 24   Bats: R   Throws: L   Height: 6'6"   Weight: 240

YEAR	TEAM	LVL	AGE	W	L	SV	G	GS	IP	H	HR	BB	K	BB/9	K/9	GB%	BABIP	WHIP	ERA	FIP	FRA	WARP
2013	BUR	A	22	5	5	0	13	13	70	50	5	22	79	2.8	10.2	40%	.263	1.03	3.34	3.21	4.20	1.0
2014	INL	A+	23	10	4	0	21	19	112	87	6	49	122	3.9	9.8	44%	.283	1.21	3.21	4.00	3.70	2.4
2014	ARK	AA	23	4	0	0	6	6	35¹	17	3	17	39	4.3	9.9	34%	.182	0.96	2.29	3.97	4.29	0.2
2015	ANA	MLB	24	7	6	0	20	20	109²	103	10	53	96	4.3	7.9	40%	.292	1.42	4.27	4.71	4.64	0.2

Breakout: 20%   Improve: 32%   Collapse: 8%   Attrition: 29%   MLB: 42%   Comparables: *Jose Cisnero, Andre Rienzo, Kyle Weiland*

DeLoach is a fraud. On paper, the dude oozes power: He led the California League in punchouts and hit batsmen upon graduating from the circuit in July; he's a hulk, towering over everything at a full six-and-a-half feet; and he pounds hitters inside, frequently closing each sting by elevating for the whiff or pop-up. Yet the gun reads that fastball as 86-89 mph. Will advanced hitters catch on to his act, and nail DeLoach and his bag of tricks to the wall? Probably. He walks too many, and makes mistakes up that should cost him more than they have so far. But maybe, just maybe he'll pull off that fabled long con.

Joe Gatto   RHP

Born: 6/14/95   Age: 19   Bats: R   Throws: R   Height: 6'3"   Weight: 204

YEAR	TEAM	LVL	AGE	W	L	SV	G	GS	IP	H	HR	BB	K	BB/9	K/9	GB%	BABIP	WHIP	ERA	FIP	FRA	WARP
2015	ANA	MLB	20	1	2	0	9	4	31	39	4	19	13	5.7	3.7	46%	.310	1.88	6.59	6.56	7.16	-0.6

Breakout: 0%   Improve: 0%   Collapse: 0%   Attrition: 0%   MLB: 0%   Comparables: *Hunter Strickland, Jake Odorizzi, Allen Webster*

For the second year running, the Angels used a top pick on a high school arm. And, for the second year running, they received uninspiring early returns. Like Hunter Green before him, Gatto—who sits in the low 90s with ease, and occasionally delivers a nice deuce—showed only the massive gulf between potential ceiling and present skills. Under the old administration, the Angels invested heavily in prep arms: Tyler Skaggs, Kevin Jepsen and Cam Bedrosian came out of that strategy, as did Tyler Chatwood, Jordan Walden and Nick Adenhart. Dipoto's preps have a long way to go to match that group.

Hunter Green   LHP

Born: 7/12/95   Age: 19   Bats: L   Throws: L   Height: 6'4"   Weight: 175

YEAR	TEAM	LVL	AGE	W	L	SV	G	GS	IP	H	HR	BB	K	BB/9	K/9	GB%	BABIP	WHIP	ERA	FIP	FRA	WARP
2015	ANA	MLB	19	2	3	0	8	8	30²	38	4	20	13	5.9	3.7	43%	.309	1.90	6.61	6.69	7.18	-0.7

Breakout: 0%   Improve: 0%   Collapse: 0%   Attrition: 0%   MLB: 0%   Comparables: *Kyle Ryan, Brandon Maurer, Mike Foltynewicz*

The Angels had simple goals for Green: Get healthy and build up innings. He met neither, instead spending the summer rehabbing a back issue. The year of lost development time isn't a massive blow—Green is a long-term play—but it certainly didn't help. He enters 2015 with the same goals.

Jason Grilli   RHP

Born: 11/11/76   Age: 38   Bats: R   Throws: R   Height: 6'4"   Weight: 235

YEAR	TEAM	LVL	AGE	W	L	SV	G	GS	IP	H	HR	BB	K	BB/9	K/9	GB%	BABIP	WHIP	ERA	FIP	FRA	WARP
2012	PIT	MLB	35	1	6	2	64	0	58²	45	7	22	90	3.4	13.8	32%	.309	1.14	2.91	2.85	2.46	1.4
2013	PIT	MLB	36	0	2	33	54	0	50	40	4	13	74	2.3	13.3	36%	.327	1.06	2.70	1.94	2.38	1.3
2014	ANA	MLB	37	1	3	1	40	0	33²	29	0	10	36	2.7	9.6	42%	.312	1.16	3.48	2.18	2.01	0.9
2014	PIT	MLB	37	0	2	11	22	0	20¹	22	4	11	21	4.9	9.3	28%	.321	1.62	4.87	5.36	4.81	-0.2
2015	ANA	MLB	38	3	1	16	50	0	48	39	4	17	61	3.2	11.5	39%	.305	1.16	2.88	3.23	3.13	0.9

Breakout: 18%   Improve: 38%   Collapse: 18%   Attrition: 7%   MLB: 76%   Comparables: *Al Reyes, Rudy Seanez, Tim Byrdak*

If Jerry Dipoto winds up a legendary general manager of folklore and biopics, his acquisition of Grilli might go down as his first chart-topping hit; girls screaming, rich businessmen with dollar signs in their eyes, montages of the standings going up up up in the Angels' direction. In late June, Dipoto sent failed closer Ernesto Frieri, then sporting a 29 percent strikeout rate and 7 percent walk rate, to the Pirates for failed closer Grilli, whose rates were 23 percent and 12 percent respectively. Both had longball issues, but Frieri was nine years younger, threw harder and still had two additional years of club control remaining. Grilli's peripherals immediately reversed in 35-plus innings of dingerless moundwork in Anaheim, while Frieri's "change of scenery" devolved into epic collapse; he was out of the big leagues by August while Grilli was in the postseason by October. Finding a signal in the noise of bullpen performances is one of a GM's most difficult jobs, so Dipoto's swap was really two masterpieces of player evaluation in one transaction. If instead of a legend Dipoto winds up a general managerial bust, then this trade will just be a confusing footnote.

Andrew Heaney   LHP

Born: 12/7/90   Age: 24   Bats: L   Throws: L   Height: 6'3"   Weight: 225

YEAR	TEAM	LVL	AGE	W	L	SV	G	GS	IP	H	HR	BB	K	BB/9	K/9	GB%	BABIP	WHIP	ERA	FIP	FRA	WARP
2012	GRB	A	21	1	2	0	4	4	20	25	0	4	21	1.8	9.4	54%	.373	1.45	4.95	2.23	3.15	0.7
2013	JUP	A+	22	5	2	0	13	12	61²	45	2	17	66	2.5	9.6	49%	.257	1.01	0.88	2.64	3.00	1.4
2013	JAX	AA	22	4	1	0	6	6	33²	31	2	9	23	2.4	6.1	41%	.279	1.19	2.94	3.12	3.13	0.6
2014	JAX	AA	23	4	2	0	9	8	53²	45	2	13	52	2.2	8.7	47%	.285	1.08	2.35	2.46	3.13	1.4
2014	NWO	AAA	23	5	4	0	15	15	83²	75	9	23	91	2.5	9.8	49%	.296	1.17	3.87	3.89	4.25	1.6
2014	MIA	MLB	23	0	3	0	7	5	29¹	32	6	7	20	2.1	6.1	48%	.289	1.33	5.83	5.42	5.94	-0.4
2015	ANA	MLB	24	8	7	0	24	24	124²	122	13	34	105	2.5	7.6	45%	.295	1.25	3.75	4.18	4.08	1.1

Breakout: 23%   Improve: 54%   Collapse: 15%   Attrition: 25%   MLB: 75%   Comparables: *Jake Odorizzi, Alex Cobb, Brett Oberholtzer*

Can Heaney stand to improve both his command and his changeup? Sure. But he's also one of the premier pitching prospects in pro ball, blessed with hot, hot heat and an already-menacing slider. The fact that he's struck out nearly a batter per inning—or better—at each minor-league stop adds the performance factor to what scouts have been talking up since before he was the Marlins' first-round pick back in 2012. He's instantly the Angels' best prospect, even if there is a hrmmmmm aspect of two teams trading him away in the span of a couple hours. His floor is high, especially as a southpaw who already features two plus pitches and a changeup on the way.

Wade LeBlanc   LHP

Born: 8/7/84   Age: 30   Bats: L   Throws: L   Height: 6'3"   Weight: 215

YEAR	TEAM	LVL	AGE	W	L	SV	G	GS	IP	H	HR	BB	K	BB/9	K/9	GB%	BABIP	WHIP	ERA	FIP	FRA	WARP
2012	NWO	AAA	27	5	5	0	16	16	98²	91	10	20	91	1.8	8.3	46%	.288	1.12	3.74	3.78	4.48	1.2
2012	MIA	MLB	27	2	5	0	25	9	68²	71	7	19	43	2.5	5.6	38%	.299	1.31	3.67	4.08	4.30	0.6
2013	OKL	AAA	28	3	1	1	19	7	49²	55	5	16	47	2.9	8.5	49%	.340	1.43	4.71	3.95	4.57	0.7
2013	HOU	MLB	28	0	0	0	4	0	6¹	9	1	5	2	7.1	2.8	38%	.286	2.21	7.11	7.34	7.88	-0.2
2013	MIA	MLB	28	1	5	0	13	7	48²	63	6	15	31	2.8	5.7	43%	.339	1.60	5.18	4.40	4.65	-0.1
2014	SLC	AAA	29	10	4	0	22	22	128	143	11	42	119	3.0	8.4	41%	.352	1.45	4.43	4.04	4.49	2.6
2014	ANA	MLB	29	1	1	0	10	3	28²	25	2	6	21	1.9	6.6	42%	.274	1.08	3.45	3.33	3.79	0.3
2014	NYA	MLB	29	0	0	0	1	0	1	2	0	1	0	9.0	0.0	60%	.400	3.00	18.00	9.16	12.10	-0.1
2015	ANA	MLB	30	8	6	0	29	20	127	136	14	36	96	2.5	6.8	41%	.307	1.35	4.29	4.41	4.66	0.1

Breakout: 11%   Improve: 19%   Collapse: 21%   Attrition: 19%   MLB: 49%   Comparables: *Philip Humber, Cha Seung Baek, Dave Williams*

LeBlanc's skill set earned him with a ton of MLBTR coverage in 2014—he was DFA'd three times and called five different clubhouses home—but it doesn't merit more than minor-league contracts at this point. It's a cold, hard fact for a guy who did exactly what he was supposed to do, serving as Triple-A depth and major-league spotter; it's just that he's used up his options and therefore must face the whims of the waiver wire whenever the big-league club has a more pressing roster need. He actually throws harder now than when he entered the bigs back in 2008. That'll earn him plenty of NPBTR coverage—he signed with the Seibu Lions for 2015.

Michael Morin   RHP

Born: 5/3/91   Age: 24   Bats: R   Throws: R   Height: 6'4"   Weight: 220

YEAR	TEAM	LVL	AGE	W	L	SV	G	GS	IP	H	HR	BB	K	BB/9	K/9	GB%	BABIP	WHIP	ERA	FIP	FRA	WARP
2013	INL	A+	22	3	1	13	30	0	39	30	2	5	43	1.2	9.9	42%	.297	0.90	1.85	2.69	3.33	0.9
2013	ARK	AA	22	0	2	10	26	0	31	26	2	5	33	1.5	9.6	51%	.296	1.00	2.03	2.44	2.76	0.7
2014	ANA	MLB	23	4	4	0	60	0	59	51	3	19	54	2.9	8.2	48%	.287	1.19	2.90	3.11	3.11	0.7
2015	ANA	MLB	24	3	1	1	51	0	58¹	54	5	17	54	2.6	8.3	45%	.300	1.21	3.31	3.77	3.60	0.7

Breakout: 22%   Improve: 43%   Collapse: 12%   Attrition: 25%   MLB: 73%   Comparables: *Josh Spence, Cla Meredith, Addison Reed*

Everyone knows that Morin has a dynamite changeup and a ho-hum four-seam fastball. Everyone. Morin nonetheless surprised with a better-than-expected slider and a developing sinker that generates crazy groundball rates. He's got more weapons than everyone expected, so look for him to continue to evolve as bullpen mainstay, potentially climbing as high as set-up man or a Huston Street-style closer down the road.

Sean Newcomb   LHP

Born: 6/12/93   Age: 22   Bats: L   Throws: L   Height: 6'5"   Weight: 240

YEAR	TEAM	LVL	AGE	W	L	SV	G	GS	IP	H	HR	BB	K	BB/9	K/9	GB%	BABIP	WHIP	ERA	FIP	FRA	WARP
2014	BUR	A	21	0	1	0	4	4	11²	13	1	5	15	3.9	11.6	28%	.387	1.54	6.94	3.31	4.75	0.2
2015	ANA	MLB	22	2	3	0	8	8	33	36	4	16	23	4.3	6.4	42%	.310	1.58	5.12	5.44	5.56	-0.2

Breakout: 0%   Improve: 0%   Collapse: 0%   Attrition: 0%   MLB: 0%   Comparables: *Andrew Heaney, Justin Wilson, Jose A. Ramirez*

Over his first three starts with the Angels' Midwest League affiliate, instant-organizational-top-prospect Newcomb coughed up 11 hits, six walks and nine runs in 7 2/3. He struck out just six, despite 97 mph gas. That's raw with a capital 'R' and a few extra a's for emphasis, which might offer some insight into why Hartford's ace unexpectedly dropped to the Angels at the 15th overall pick. Then, in his final two outings, including a playoff start, he allowed just six hits and one run over nine innings while fanning 16 to just one walk. Newcomb threw enough strikes with his secondaries to keep A-Ball hitters guessing, and they couldn't touch the low- to mid-90s heat up in the zone, which gives you some insight into why his slippage to no. 15 was unexpected. The Angels brass will now try to help Newcomb sort through and prioritize work on his slider, changeup and curve, all of which have a shot at becoming plus pitches.

Vinnie Pestano   RHP

Born: 2/20/85   Age: 30   Bats: R   Throws: R   Height: 6'0"   Weight: 200

YEAR	TEAM	LVL	AGE	W	L	SV	G	GS	IP	H	HR	BB	K	BB/9	K/9	GB%	BABIP	WHIP	ERA	FIP	FRA	WARP
2012	CLE	MLB	27	3	3	2	70	0	70	53	7	24	76	3.1	9.8	41%	.263	1.10	2.57	3.38	3.41	1.0
2013	COH	AAA	28	0	0	0	14	0	13²	13	0	4	13	2.6	8.6	38%	.351	1.24	3.29	2.40	3.33	0.2
2013	CLE	MLB	28	1	2	6	37	0	35¹	37	6	21	37	5.3	9.4	36%	.330	1.64	4.08	5.06	4.79	0.0
2014	COH	AAA	29	2	4	6	32	0	30¹	23	0	12	37	3.6	11.0	37%	.303	1.15	1.78	2.20	2.39	1.0
2014	ANA	MLB	29	0	0	0	12	0	9²	5	1	4	13	3.7	12.1	33%	.200	0.93	0.93	3.06	2.78	0.2
2014	CLE	MLB	29	0	1	0	13	0	9	13	2	1	13	1.0	13.0	38%	.458	1.56	5.00	3.49	2.21	0.1
2015	ANA	MLB	30	3	1	3	52	0	49¹	40	4	18	59	3.3	10.7	42%	.298	1.18	2.96	3.39	3.22	0.8

Breakout: 21%   Improve: 46%   Collapse: 19%   Attrition: 18%   MLB: 83%   *Comparables: Steve Delabar, Jason Motte, Pat Neshek*

The Angels carried *nine* relievers on their postseason roster, and six of them had been acquired after the 2013 season ended. Pestano was the last add by the ever-restless Dipoto, who acquired the can-you-believe-he's-only-29-years-old 29-year-old in August for a C-minus pitching prospect. Pestano's velocity is down nearly three ticks since his 2010-2011 run as a dominant set-up man in Cleveland, and he's bumped along a command rollercoaster in the intervening years, but he spotted his 90 mph fastball sufficiently to fan 13 batters in 9 2/3 innings during his trial run with the Angels. He even made their postseason bullpen though, admittedly, who didn't?

Cesar Ramos   LHP

Born: 6/22/84   Age: 31   Bats: L   Throws: L   Height: 6'2"   Weight: 200

YEAR	TEAM	LVL	AGE	W	L	SV	G	GS	IP	H	HR	BB	K	BB/9	K/9	GB%	BABIP	WHIP	ERA	FIP	FRA	WARP
2012	DUR	AAA	28	5	5	1	25	7	62	58	10	16	46	2.3	6.7	43%	.262	1.19	3.77	4.54	5.55	0.2
2012	TBA	MLB	28	1	0	0	17	1	30	19	2	10	29	3.0	8.7	53%	.221	0.97	2.10	3.18	3.14	0.6
2013	TBA	MLB	29	2	2	1	48	0	67¹	66	6	22	53	2.9	7.1	42%	.293	1.31	4.14	3.73	4.20	0.4
2014	TBA	MLB	30	2	6	0	43	7	82²	73	8	39	66	4.2	7.2	46%	.265	1.35	3.70	4.27	4.63	0.0
2015	ANA	MLB	31	3	2	0	47	4	69¹	68	7	26	52	3.4	6.8	45%	.289	1.36	3.97	4.60	4.31	0.3

Breakout: 15%   Improve: 20%   Collapse: 17%   Attrition: 16%   MLB: 49%   *Comparables: Matt Wise, Adam Bernero, Chris Resop*

The wealth of pitching cultivated by the Rays' organization has been a selling point of the franchise since they dropped the "Devil" in 2008. So naturally, Ramos, with 143 career relief appearances and three starts, broke camp as the club's fifth starter. What?!? In lieu of rushing a prospect to cover injuries in the rotation, Ramos was pressed into starting duty until a healthy alternative arrived. The transition was relatively painless as Ramos, even as a reliever, works with a four-pitch selection—fastball, curveball, slider, changeup—and served as the de facto long man in the bullpen. Meanwhile, endurance proved to be his biggest hurdle as he struggled working late into games. After a handful of starts, his work in the rotation was complete and he was relegated back to his low-leverage perch in the 'pen. The Angels gave up a prospect to get him, and will appreciate the depth he provides in each role.

Cory Rasmus   RHP

Born: 11/6/87   Age: 27   Bats: R   Throws: R   Height: 6'0"   Weight: 200

YEAR	TEAM	LVL	AGE	W	L	SV	G	GS	IP	H	HR	BB	K	BB/9	K/9	GB%	BABIP	WHIP	ERA	FIP	FRA	WARP
2012	MIS	AA	24	3	5	7	50	0	58²	45	3	32	62	4.9	9.5	37%	.284	1.31	3.68	3.43	3.74	0.8
2013	GWN	AAA	25	3	1	14	37	0	36²	20	2	22	48	5.4	11.8	42%	.240	1.15	1.72	3.18	3.50	0.7
2013	ANA	MLB	25	1	1	0	16	0	15	16	2	10	14	6.0	8.4	33%	.304	1.73	4.20	4.94	5.15	0.0
2013	ATL	MLB	25	0	0	0	3	0	6²	8	4	3	6	4.1	8.1	27%	.222	1.65	8.10	10.37	9.88	-0.3
2014	SLC	AAA	26	2	1	2	22	0	28	23	2	16	24	5.1	7.7	43%	.259	1.39	4.18	4.63	5.05	0.3
2014	ANA	MLB	26	3	2	0	30	6	56	42	5	17	57	2.7	9.2	39%	.253	1.05	2.57	3.20	3.43	0.9
2015	ANA	MLB	27	3	2	0	49	3	67	61	7	32	62	4.2	8.3	39%	.287	1.39	4.11	4.61	4.47	0.2

Breakout: 24%   Improve: 43%   Collapse: 7%   Attrition: 23%   MLB: 59%   *Comparables: Francisco Rosario, Brayan Villarreal, Michael Stutes*

As the Angels' bullpen went, so went Rasmus, though one might argue that the reverse was more important. Through late June he was erratic and sometimes terrible, then righted the ship before the All-Star break and was dominant through August. When Garrett Richards went down, it was Rasmus who got the call to lead off the Johnny All-Staff starts that made for some of the team's most memorable stretch-run victories. They were just mini-starts—usually three innings per, even when he was twirling a shutout—but he pitched well enough to make a case for a rotation spot in 2015, and it's not bonkers to see him excelling in that role: His secondary pitches, especially his changeup, have evolved into real weapons since his days as Braves' fringe prospect, and major leaguers managed just a .130/.259/.148 slash line when facing him for the second time in a day. If you're looking for a longshot, Collin McHugh-type breakout candidate for your fantasy team, Rasmus might be your man.

Garrett Richards   RHP

Born: 5/27/88   Age: 27   Bats: R   Throws: R   Height: 6'3"   Weight: 210

YEAR	TEAM	LVL	AGE	W	L	SV	G	GS	IP	H	HR	BB	K	BB/9	K/9	GB%	BABIP	WHIP	ERA	FIP	FRA	WARP
2012	SLC	AAA	24	7	3	0	14	14	77	87	5	35	65	4.1	7.6	52%	.346	1.58	4.21	4.42	4.38	1.6
2012	ANA	MLB	24	4	3	1	30	9	71	77	7	34	47	4.3	6.0	47%	.308	1.56	4.69	4.57	5.06	-0.2
2013	ANA	MLB	25	7	8	1	47	17	145	151	12	44	101	2.7	6.3	60%	.302	1.34	4.16	3.69	4.62	0.3
2014	ANA	MLB	26	13	4	0	26	26	168²	124	5	51	164	2.7	8.8	52%	.264	1.04	2.61	2.63	3.41	2.4
2015	ANA	MLB	27	9	6	0	32	20	134²	129	10	46	107	3.1	7.2	51%	.293	1.30	3.66	4.06	3.98	1.2

Breakout: 29%   Improve: 57%   Collapse: 15%   Attrition: 12%   MLB: 83%   *Comparables: Dana Eveland, Tyson Ross, Sergio Mitre*

When asked what was the difference between his two-and-a-half years as underperforming swingman and his breakout 2014 season, the Angels' new ace replied, "The game slowed down for me." The new state of mound nirvana sped things up for hitters, manifesting in a tick-and-a-half velocity bump in all of Richard's pitches. He accrued strikes at the same rate as 2013, even while pitching out of the zone more often and throwing more breaking balls. He sequenced the strikes better too, allowing him to pitch from ahead in the count more often in 2014 than he had previously. When hitters did put the bat on the ball, they failed to pull for any power. The only thing that Richards didn't do better last year was to maintain the integrity of his left patellar tendon. We can only hope that the damage to his landing leg doesn't permanently disrupt the perfection of his less-than-textbook delivery and send him back into his pre-nirvana, early-career funk.

Michael Roth   LHP

Born: 2/15/90   Age: 25   Bats: L   Throws: L   Height: 6'1"   Weight: 210

YEAR	TEAM	LVL	AGE	W	L	SV	G	GS	IP	H	HR	BB	K	BB/9	K/9	GB%	BABIP	WHIP	ERA	FIP	FRA	WARP
2013	ARK	AA	23	6	3	0	17	15	79¹	77	8	36	51	4.1	5.8	50%	.290	1.42	4.20	4.78	5.60	-0.5
2013	ANA	MLB	23	1	1	0	15	1	20	24	0	6	17	2.7	7.7	42%	.375	1.50	7.20	2.43	3.24	0.4
2014	ARK	AA	24	11	7	0	22	22	140²	121	9	53	79	3.4	5.1	51%	.258	1.24	2.62	4.02	4.64	-0.1
2014	ANA	MLB	24	1	0	0	7	0	12¹	16	2	9	9	6.6	6.6	59%	.378	2.03	8.76	6.73	6.27	-0.3
2015	ANA	MLB	25	7	7	0	30	20	115²	129	12	49	62	3.9	4.9	48%	.299	1.54	5.03	5.32	5.47	-0.8

Breakout: 33%   Improve: 47%   Collapse: 11%   Attrition: 38%   MLB: 68%   *Comparables: Mitchell Boggs, Zach Jackson, Yorman Bazardo*

How far will character take you? Will your attitude, not your aptitude, determine your altitude in life? These are questions that Roth, former College World Series hero, ninth-round draftee and present marginal pro, ponders, both on those endless Texas League bus rides and on flights to and from Santa Ana's John Wayne Airport. When on the mound, he slings mid-80s sinkers and 75 mph junk, not at the zone, but rather toward those spots just off the black where a hitter might accidentally stick his bat. Roth's limitations got him booted from the 40-man roster early in the season, but the Angels' gut-shot rotation and thin system briefly opened the door to a long relief role in the summer, same as in 2013. If there were any justice in the world, his double addition to the 40-man roster would entitle him to a double share of the playoff money, in compensation for the indignity of it all. Instead, it entitled him to free agency when he passed through waivers a second time.

Drew Rucinski   RHP

Born: 12/30/88   Age: 26   Bats: R   Throws: R   Height: 6'2"   Weight: 190

YEAR	TEAM	LVL	AGE	W	L	SV	G	GS	IP	H	HR	BB	K	BB/9	K/9	GB%	BABIP	WHIP	ERA	FIP	FRA	WARP
2013	INL	A+	24	2	2	0	5	5	29	29	0	4	21	1.2	6.5	44%	.326	1.14	1.86	2.84	3.94	0.5
2014	ARK	AA	25	10	6	0	26	26	148²	142	7	41	140	2.5	8.5	52%	.325	1.23	3.15	2.80	3.05	3.1
2014	ANA	MLB	25	0	0	0	3	0	7¹	7	0	2	8	2.5	9.8	44%	.391	1.50	4.91	2.21	2.89	0.2
2015	ANA	MLB	26	6	5	0	28	16	110¹	116	9	34	86	2.8	7.0	48%	.315	1.36	4.17	4.11	4.53	0.2

Breakout: 16%   Improve: 30%   Collapse: 16%   Attrition: 39%   MLB: 56%   *Comparables: Dan Meyer, Marco Estrada, Vidal Nuno*

Rucinski caught the attention of Angels' scouts back in the summer of 2013 while pitching for the independent-ball Rockford Aviators. He signed, and within four weeks had pitched the Inland Empire 66ers to the Cal League title. Late last July, Arkansas manager Phillip Wellman slapped Rucinski on the back, said "As long as you have a heartbeat and a jersey on your back, you have a chance," and showed him the door. To Anaheim. He notched his first major-league strikeout five days later. Rucinski features average fastball velocity, a deceptive delivery, and a five-pitch arsenal, which together put him on the Halos' depth chart and make him a candidate to join Matt Shoemaker as the only duo of American-born, undrafted rotation mates in the modern era. Look for the full story in next year's edition of *Chicken Soup for the Baseball Soul*.

Fernando Salas   RHP

Born: 5/30/85   Age: 30   Bats: R   Throws: R   Height: 6'2"   Weight: 210

YEAR	TEAM	LVL	AGE	W	L	SV	G	GS	IP	H	HR	BB	K	BB/9	K/9	GB%	BABIP	WHIP	ERA	FIP	FRA	WARP
2012	SLN	MLB	27	1	4	0	65	0	58²	56	5	27	60	4.1	9.2	40%	.313	1.41	4.30	3.63	3.48	0.6
2013	MEM	AAA	28	1	2	12	22	0	23²	15	1	5	21	1.9	8.0	36%	.222	0.85	1.90	3.10	3.55	0.4
2013	SLN	MLB	28	0	3	0	27	0	28	27	3	6	22	1.9	7.1	34%	.279	1.18	4.50	3.59	4.08	0.2
2014	ANA	MLB	29	5	0	0	57	0	58²	50	5	14	61	2.1	9.4	32%	.285	1.09	3.38	2.96	2.97	1.0
2015	ANA	MLB	30	3	1	1	50	0	51¹	43	4	15	52	2.6	9.1	37%	.284	1.13	2.96	3.49	3.22	0.9

Breakout: 27%   Improve: 49%   Collapse: 14%   Attrition: 11%   MLB: 82%   *Comparables: Darren O'Day, Santiago Casilla, Bill Bray*

Rumor has it that the Cards intended to non-tender Salas last offseason, so they jumped at the opportunity to package him with David Freese and send him to Anaheim. The former closing candidate certainly looked past his prime in April, when he inherited six runners and let them all score. He didn't get a crack at a situation with men on base again until June 5th, when he inherited three more runners, and again, let them all score. Overall, he allowed 75 percent of inherited runners to cross the plate last year. Command problems in the first half further blemish his year, and his velocity declined all season. Then, something clicked. He basically stopped walking people in the second half, and achieved more whiffs on his fastball than at any time since 2010—despite dropping into the high 80s by September. Two home runs undid the ERA in September, and one of those high-80s fastballs cost the Angels Game One of the ALDS. But them's the breaks.

Hector Santiago   LHP

Born: 12/16/87   Age: 27   Bats: R   Throws: L   Height: 6'0"   Weight: 210

YEAR	TEAM	LVL	AGE	W	L	SV	G	GS	IP	H	HR	BB	K	BB/9	K/9	GB%	BABIP	WHIP	ERA	FIP	FRA	WARP
2012	CHR	AAA	24	1	0	0	3	3	14²	9	0	6	13	3.7	8.0	51%	.257	1.02	0.00	2.61	3.37	0.3
2012	CHA	MLB	24	4	1	4	42	4	70¹	54	10	40	79	5.1	10.1	39%	.259	1.34	3.33	4.65	4.97	0.4
2013	CHA	MLB	25	4	9	0	34	23	149	137	17	72	137	4.3	8.3	39%	.289	1.40	3.56	4.47	4.24	1.4
2014	SLC	AAA	26	1	1	0	3	3	14	23	0	7	9	4.5	5.8	48%	.426	2.14	6.43	4.13	4.94	0.2
2014	ANA	MLB	26	6	9	0	30	24	127¹	120	15	53	108	3.7	7.6	32%	.288	1.36	3.75	4.31	4.64	0.4
2015	ANA	MLB	27	8	6	0	33	20	123²	115	12	53	111	3.9	8.1	39%	.292	1.36	3.93	4.49	4.27	0.7

Breakout: 20%   Improve: 56%   Collapse: 17%   Attrition: 13%   MLB: 86%   *Comparables: Erik Bedard, Juan Cruz, Gavin Floyd*

According to spring training hype, Santiago was supposed to come out of the gate firing a screwball, the only such pitch known to be in a major leaguer's repertoire today. Didn't happen. Instead, he threw breaking balls, to piss-poor results: No one whiffed, righties slugged .652, and even lefties managed to hit a cool .300 on the pitch. It'll surprise Angels fans to learn that his 2014 season represented career bests in K/BB ratio and FIP, but the contours of the season—terrible start, terrible finish—ruined his stat line early and got him kicked out of the postseason rotation. The really frustrating thing about him is that it takes about 25 pitches for him to settle in—he struck out just 16 percent of guys while walking 10 percent to begin games. But from pitch 26 to pitch 75, he's nails, dropping his walk rate to 8 percent and pumping his K rate up to 23 percent. After pitch 75, things get ugly again. Now that you mention it, yes: Santiago's season was a perfect replica of a Santiago start.

Matt Shoemaker   RHP

Born: 9/27/86   Age: 28   Bats: R   Throws: R   Height: 6'2"   Weight: 225

YEAR	TEAM	LVL	AGE	W	L	SV	G	GS	IP	H	HR	BB	K	BB/9	K/9	GB%	BABIP	WHIP	ERA	FIP	FRA	WARP
2012	SLC	AAA	25	11	10	0	29	29	176²	229	25	45	124	2.3	6.3	42%	.350	1.55	5.65	4.95	5.48	1.8
2013	SLC	AAA	26	11	13	0	29	29	184¹	212	27	29	160	1.4	7.8	44%	.332	1.31	4.64	4.34	5.04	2.5
2013	ANA	MLB	26	0	0	0	1	1	5	2	0	2	5	3.6	9.0	42%	.167	0.80	0.00	2.28	3.22	0.1
2014	SLC	AAA	27	1	0	0	5	5	25²	34	2	9	26	3.2	9.1	47%	.421	1.68	6.31	3.97	4.69	0.5
2014	ANA	MLB	27	16	4	0	27	20	136	122	14	24	124	1.6	8.2	43%	.286	1.07	3.04	3.29	3.88	1.3
2015	ANA	MLB	28	9	7	0	22	22	138²	146	17	34	110	2.2	7.1	42%	.303	1.29	4.14	4.42	4.50	0.3

Breakout: 20%   Improve: 28%   Collapse: 10%   Attrition: 23%   MLB: 40%   Comparables: John Ely, Daniel McCutchen, Felix Diaz

Among non-Jose Abreus, Matt Shoemaker placed first in American League Rookie of the Year voting, capping an improbable season in which the former undrafted free agent "saved" the Angels' season (in the words of Mike Scioscia, who's known far more for his understatement than hyperbole). At one critical juncture after another in the season, he made the difference: He upended a four-game losing streak on August 9th by pitching three scoreless innings out of the bullpen on two days rest, picking up the W in the 19th inning. Two weeks later, on the day after Garrett Richards went down with a season-ending injury, Shoemaker took a no-hitter into the eighth before allowing a double to Will "Butt Hole" Middlebrooks (in the words of Shoemaker's wife, who *is* known for her hyperbole). Finally, he returned from an oblique strain in the ALDS to hurl six innings of one-run playoff baseball before the Royals won in extra innings. That's how far one trick pitch, outstanding command, and an otherwise below-average arsenal can take a guy.

Tyler Skaggs   LHP

Born: 7/13/91   Age: 23   Bats: L   Throws: L   Height: 6'4"   Weight: 215

YEAR	TEAM	LVL	AGE	W	L	SV	G	GS	IP	H	HR	BB	K	BB/9	K/9	GB%	BABIP	WHIP	ERA	FIP	FRA	WARP
2012	MOB	AA	20	5	4	0	13	13	69²	63	8	21	71	2.7	9.2	45%	.291	1.21	2.84	3.55	4.35	1.1
2012	RNO	AAA	20	4	2	0	9	9	52²	49	4	16	45	2.7	7.7	47%	.306	1.23	2.91	3.91	4.74	1.1
2012	ARI	MLB	20	1	3	0	6	6	29¹	30	6	13	21	4.0	6.4	36%	.264	1.47	5.83	5.90	7.01	-0.6
2013	RNO	AAA	21	6	10	0	19	17	104	114	5	39	107	3.4	9.3	45%	.353	1.47	4.59	3.44	4.10	2.1
2013	ARI	MLB	21	2	3	0	7	7	38²	38	7	15	36	3.5	8.4	45%	.282	1.37	5.12	4.83	4.95	0.3
2014	ANA	MLB	22	5	5	0	18	18	113	107	9	30	86	2.4	6.8	51%	.293	1.21	4.30	3.58	4.47	0.2
2015	ANA	MLB	23	7	5	0	18	18	103²	100	10	34	91	2.9	7.9	46%	.298	1.29	3.74	4.15	4.06	0.9

Breakout: 22%   Improve: 67%   Collapse: 10%   Attrition: 20%   MLB: 89%   Comparables: Brett Cecil, Brian Matusz, Danny Duffy

Skaggs' return to the Angels organization corresponded with the return of his fastball, which jumped a full three notches over his 2013 mark and put a serious feather into the caps of beleaguered organizational pitching coaches. The velocity bump transformed his two-seamer from fringy offering to true weapon, especially against right-handers, and made Skaggs a legit groundball pitcher for the first time in his career. All of those fastballs meant more strikes, his lowest walk rate since A-Ball, and the luxury of frequently pitching when ahead in the count. However, the curveball failed to live up to longstanding billing as an out pitch, leading to a decline in his overall strikeout rate and a doubtlessly frustrating reverse split against lefties. Now he faces two big challenges: The first is to simply recover velocity and command following his August Tommy John surgery, and the second is to hone a more devastating strikeout weapon for his arsenal. If he manages just the recovery, he'll be a solid no. 4 in the Angels' rotation for years to come. If he manages both, he has no. 2 potential.

Joe Smith   RHP

Born: 3/22/84   Age: 31   Bats: R   Throws: R   Height: 6'2"   Weight: 205

YEAR	TEAM	LVL	AGE	W	L	SV	G	GS	IP	H	HR	BB	K	BB/9	K/9	GB%	BABIP	WHIP	ERA	FIP	FRA	WARP
2012	CLE	MLB	28	7	4	0	72	0	67	53	4	25	53	3.4	7.1	60%	.253	1.16	2.96	3.45	4.38	0.4
2013	CLE	MLB	29	6	2	3	70	0	63	54	5	23	54	3.3	7.7	52%	.282	1.22	2.29	3.63	3.63	0.7
2014	ANA	MLB	30	7	2	15	76	0	74²	45	4	15	68	1.8	8.2	61%	.214	0.80	1.81	2.88	3.91	0.5
2015	ANA	MLB	31	3	2	5	63	0	59	49	4	20	50	3.0	7.6	55%	.273	1.17	2.91	3.83	3.16	1.1

Breakout: 28%   Improve: 46%   Collapse: 27%   Attrition: 19%   MLB: 87%   Comparables: Chad Bradford, Ronald Belisario, Jim Johnson

In 2013 the Angels bullpen ranked 26th in ERA, 25th in FIP. Over the offseason, they made Joe Smith their biggest free agent acquisition, betting that the veteran sidearmer and some positive regression among the holdovers would smother the garbage fire. Nope! But the failure wasn't Smith's fault: He put up his finest season yet, posting career bests in strikeout and walk rates and batting average allowed. The Angels leaned on him heavily, first as set-up man, then emergency closer, and again as set-up man, leading to a career high in innings. The club made enough actual improvements to the bullpen as the year went on that Smith won't be asked to set a new one this year.

Nate Smith   LHP

Born: 8/28/91   Age: 23   Bats: L   Throws: L   Height: 6'3"   Weight: 200

YEAR	TEAM	LVL	AGE	W	L	SV	G	GS	IP	H	HR	BB	K	BB/9	K/9	GB%	BABIP	WHIP	ERA	FIP	FRA	WARP
2014	INL	A+	22	6	3	0	10	10	55²	41	3	14	51	2.3	8.2	41%	.250	0.99	3.07	3.36	3.22	1.3
2014	ARK	AA	22	5	3	0	11	11	62¹	48	3	30	67	4.3	9.7	34%	.290	1.25	2.89	3.04	3.28	1.1
2015	ANA	MLB	23	5	5	0	17	17	82²	82	8	34	67	3.8	7.3	40%	.298	1.41	4.28	4.55	4.65	0.2

Breakout: 0%   Improve: 0%   Collapse: 0%   Attrition: 0%   MLB: 0%   Comparables: Sean Nolin, Scott Barnes, Tyson Ross

Plus changeups are hot. The best ones miss bats, but they also yield the least damage on contact, and tend to make their owners' fastballs play above their scouting grades. Nate Smith is hot. His plus changeup misses lots of bats, he consistently yields a below-average BABIP and ISO, and finds himself accruing whiffs on 88 mph heat when frustrated hitters begin to sit on the off-speed. Righties at two levels staggered to a pathetic .196/.275/.348 line against him. Lefties were better—Smith's curveball kind of sucks—but his whole was most definitely better than the sum of his parts. Had he not gone down with a pinky injury at the end of July, he might very well have secured his pension when the Angels' rotation disintegrated in August. Instead, the injury earned him a spot in the Arizona Fall League, where he fanned a higher percentage of hitters than Mark Appel.

Huston Street   RHP

Born: 8/2/83   Age: 31   Bats: R   Throws: R   Height: 6'0"   Weight: 195

YEAR	TEAM	LVL	AGE	W	L	SV	G	GS	IP	H	HR	BB	K	BB/9	K/9	GB%	BABIP	WHIP	ERA	FIP	FRA	WARP
2012	SDN	MLB	28	2	1	23	40	0	39	17	2	11	47	2.5	10.8	43%	.179	0.72	1.85	2.24	2.80	0.7
2013	SDN	MLB	29	2	5	33	58	0	56²	44	12	14	46	2.2	7.3	32%	.213	1.02	2.70	4.89	5.14	-0.4
2014	ANA	MLB	30	1	2	17	28	0	26¹	24	1	7	23	2.4	7.9	33%	.299	1.18	1.71	2.70	2.74	0.5
2014	SDN	MLB	30	1	0	24	33	0	33	18	3	7	34	1.9	9.3	42%	.195	0.76	1.09	2.86	3.47	0.2
2015	ANA	MLB	31	3	1	31	52	0	49²	42	5	11	49	1.9	8.9	39%	.277	1.05	2.72	3.58	2.95	1.0

Breakout: 22%   Improve: 40%   Collapse: 26%   Attrition: 12%   MLB: 85%   Comparables: Dan Wheeler, Darren O'Day, Sergio Romo

The all-important second hit song in the Jerry Dipoto biopic movie we're apparently writing: Bucking the consensus that the Angels needed another "proven big-league starter," and instead going all in for the best pitcher available ... at the price he could afford. That was Street. The return on investment outstripped the most optimistic projections, as Street kept his ERA under 2 with his usual blend of Ks and soggy contact. Had the Angels gone on to win it all—a realistic sequence—the addition of Street would be considered a masterstroke, putting the Angels built-on-the-fly bullpen over the top and making it one of the deepest in baseball, a unit so good it successfully took over a rotation slot in the season's final six weeks. The Angels didn't win it all, but if Street is pitching high-leverage innings again this October, the trade will still be a clear victory, and we might get our script's Act Three.

Joe Thatcher   LHP

Born: 10/4/81   Age: 33   Bats: L   Throws: L   Height: 6'2"   Weight: 230

YEAR	TEAM	LVL	AGE	W	L	SV	G	GS	IP	H	HR	BB	K	BB/9	K/9	GB%	BABIP	WHIP	ERA	FIP	FRA	WARP
2012	SDN	MLB	30	1	4	1	55	0	31²	30	2	14	39	4.0	11.1	45%	.337	1.39	3.41	3.10	2.25	0.5
2013	ARI	MLB	31	0	1	0	22	0	9¹	12	1	6	7	5.8	6.8	23%	.379	1.93	6.75	4.84	3.64	0.0
2013	SDN	MLB	31	3	1	0	50	0	30	28	3	4	29	1.2	8.7	44%	.298	1.07	2.10	2.89	3.63	0.2
2014	ANA	MLB	32	1	1	0	16	0	6¹	13	0	1	2	1.4	2.8	62%	.448	2.21	8.53	3.95	4.21	0.0
2014	ARI	MLB	32	1	0	0	37	0	24	23	3	3	25	1.1	9.4	27%	.299	1.08	2.62	3.27	2.90	0.3
2015	ANA	MLB	33	3	1	1	62	0	35²	33	3	10	37	2.5	9.4	42%	.305	1.19	3.18	3.55	3.46	0.6

Breakout: 18%   Improve: 44%   Collapse: 30%   Attrition: 12%   MLB: 89%   Comparables: Heath Bell, Will Ohman, Jason Frasor

Thatcher was yet another reliever picked up for scraps by Dipoto, and he was supposed to fill a longstanding organizational LOOGY void. He had performed well in San Diego before journeying up the I-5, but he pitched himself out of a near-certain playoff roster spot by coughing up 13 hits on a 93 percent contact rate while striking out just two of 35 hitters faced. Small was the sample, but bitter the taste.

Nick Tropeano   RHP

Born: 8/27/90   Age: 24   Bats: R   Throws: R   Height: 6'4"   Weight: 200

YEAR	TEAM	LVL	AGE	W	L	SV	G	GS	IP	H	HR	BB	K	BB/9	K/9	GB%	BABIP	WHIP	ERA	FIP	FRA	WARP
2012	LEX	A	21	6	4	0	15	14	87¹	77	3	26	97	2.7	10.0	49%	.323	1.18	2.78	2.77	3.40	2.4
2012	LNC	A+	21	6	3	0	12	12	70²	72	8	21	69	2.7	8.8	43%	.323	1.32	3.31	4.35	4.85	1.4
2013	CCH	AA	22	7	10	5	28	20	133²	140	15	39	130	2.6	8.8	45%	.333	1.34	4.11	3.51	4.22	2.3
2014	OKL	AAA	23	9	5	0	23	20	124²	90	11	33	120	2.4	8.7	40%	.248	0.99	3.03	3.81	4.27	1.8
2014	HOU	MLB	23	1	3	0	4	4	21²	19	0	9	13	3.7	5.4	43%	.279	1.29	4.57	3.34	3.92	0.2
2015	ANA	MLB	24	8	6	0	22	22	118	112	11	39	101	2.9	7.7	43%	.296	1.28	3.67	4.14	3.98	1.1

Breakout: 19%   Improve: 44%   Collapse: 13%   Attrition: 26%   MLB: 64%   Comparables: Jake Odorizzi, Eric Surkamp, Garrett Richards

The emergence of Tropeano's changeup was one of the single most important developments on the Astros' farm last year, transforming the big righty from decent depth-chart piece into a significant trade chip. The improved off-speed arsenal decimated minor-league lefties. Tropeano missed more bats, but the real secret sauce was in limiting those opposite-handed hitters to a .196 BABIP and a .156 batting average overall by inducing more weak contact in the air. He handled his debut in September with enough poise to convince the Angels that the improvements would translate, so they sent Hank Conger to Houston and will give Tropeano a crack at their 2015 rotation. His mechanics are worth keeping an eye on: Coaches will seek to protect his shoulder from the unconventional arm action; fans will want to catch the butt wiggle that occasionally initiates his delivery, a tick that flashes more salsa than twerk, and which is frankly mesmerizing.

Jered Weaver   RHP

Born: 10/4/82   Age: 32   Bats: R   Throws: R   Height: 6'7"   Weight: 210

YEAR	TEAM	LVL	AGE	W	L	SV	G	GS	IP	H	HR	BB	K	BB/9	K/9	GB%	BABIP	WHIP	ERA	FIP	FRA	WARP
2012	ANA	MLB	29	20	5	0	30	30	188²	147	20	45	142	2.1	6.8	37%	.241	1.02	2.81	3.70	4.37	1.4
2013	ANA	MLB	30	11	8	0	24	24	154¹	139	17	37	117	2.2	6.8	32%	.268	1.14	3.27	3.85	4.52	0.6
2014	ANA	MLB	31	18	9	0	34	34	213¹	193	27	65	169	2.7	7.1	35%	.267	1.21	3.59	4.22	4.59	0.5
2015	ANA	MLB	32	13	7	0	27	27	178¹	155	18	45	153	2.3	7.7	35%	.271	1.12	3.00	3.96	3.27	3.1

Breakout: 17%   Improve: 37%   Collapse: 31%   Attrition: 8%   MLB: 81%   Comparables: Johan Santana, John Lackey, Chris Carpenter

Back on September 13th, the fabric of space-time tore just a smidge, permitting the Jered Weaver of yesteryear—the guy who could rear back for 92 mph heat at will—to smite the hitters of 2014. Armed with a one-night-only, three-tick velocity bump over *this* dimension's Jered Weaver, the time-traveling Jered Weaver induced a 15 percent whiff rate with the fastball alone. His whole arsenal ratcheted up with additional heat, and the whiff rates on his curveball and changeup doubled. Alas: It was just for that night, that one magic night. *Our* Jered Weaver, the one who averaged 86 mph with the fastball over his other 34 starts, continues to say things like, "If I can put the ball where I want to, it doesn't really matter how hard I throw," but he can't really believe that. It's a safe bet that even now he's seeking to summon back vintage Jered Weaver across the mysteries of the fourth dimension.

C.J. Wilson   LHP

Born: 11/18/80   Age: 34   Bats: L   Throws: L   Height: 6'1"   Weight: 210

YEAR	TEAM	LVL	AGE	W	L	SV	G	GS	IP	H	HR	BB	K	BB/9	K/9	GB%	BABIP	WHIP	ERA	FIP	FRA	WARP
2012	ANA	MLB	31	13	10	0	34	34	202¹	181	19	91	173	4.0	7.7	50%	.281	1.34	3.83	4.00	4.27	2.0
2013	ANA	MLB	32	17	7	0	33	33	212¹	200	15	85	188	3.6	8.0	46%	.300	1.34	3.39	3.54	3.77	3.0
2014	ANA	MLB	33	13	10	0	31	31	175²	169	17	85	151	4.4	7.7	49%	.306	1.45	4.51	4.34	4.97	-0.1
2015	ANA	MLB	34	11	8	0	27	27	164¹	147	12	66	146	3.6	8.0	48%	.292	1.30	3.59	4.05	3.91	1.6

Breakout: 16%   Improve: 41%   Collapse: 20%   Attrition: 14%   MLB: 86%   Comparables: Doug Davis, Erik Bedard, Ryan Dempster

The last time Wilson faltered down the stretch, doctors vacuumed bone chips from his elbow and returned him stronger than ever the following season. Wilson imploded again in the second half of 2014, but this time there's no clear fix, because mostly he just wilted when the going got tough. In high-leverage situations, his strikeout rate dropped by half, while hitters increased their walk rate by five percentage points and their slugging by 150 points. He was just about the last arm in the organization that you'd want starting an elimination game, but that's exactly what happened on the Angels' final gasp in October. The symbolism there feels important, because the team's future playoff hopes will likely continue to depend on Wilson getting fixed. Maybe those doctors can take the old chips from his elbow and build him a new backbone.

Austin Wood   RHP

Born: 7/11/90   Age: 24   Bats: R   Throws: R   Height: 6'4"   Weight: 225

YEAR	TEAM	LVL	AGE	W	L	SV	G	GS	IP	H	HR	BB	K	BB/9	K/9	GB%	BABIP	WHIP	ERA	FIP	FRA	WARP
2012	CDR	A	21	5	12	0	26	26	127²	125	4	72	109	5.1	7.7	56%	.330	1.54	4.30	3.88	5.54	0.5
2013	INL	A+	22	0	3	0	5	5	21²	25	1	12	18	5.0	7.5	51%	.348	1.71	4.15	4.37	4.86	0.3
2014	INL	A+	23	0	0	0	4	4	10¹	6	0	3	9	2.6	7.8	66%	.207	0.87	1.74	3.16	3.83	0.3
2015	ANA	MLB	24	2	3	0	7	7	32¹	36	3	19	21	5.4	5.8	50%	.311	1.71	5.53	5.38	6.01	-0.4

Breakout: 0%   Improve: 0%   Collapse: 0%   Attrition: 0%   MLB: 0%   Comparables: Bryan Morris, Ryan Cook, Jimmy Nelson

Wood enters 2015 as the dark horse of the Angels' farm. He wasn't much of a prospect before going down with the ol' Tommy John in July of 2013, but those who saw him on the occasional good day dreamed big—really big—on his boring 98 mph heat and flashes of brilliance in the secondaries. He came back firing bullets in 2014, with a career-low walk rate to boot. Wood's post-recovery performance might explain why Dipoto has felt comfortable trading away so much of the farm's right-handed heat since June.

Lineouts

Hitters

NAME	POS	TEAM	LVL	AGE	PA	R	2B	3B	HR	RBI	BB	K	SB	CS	AVG/OBP/SLG	TAv	BABIP	BRR	FRAA	WARP
John Buck	C	SLC	AAA	33	135	13	8	0	2	15	13	22	0	0	.294/.370/.412	.262	.344	-0.6	C(22): -0.4, 1B(2): 0.0	0.3
	C	ANA	MLB	33	5	0	0	0	0	0	0	2	0	0	.200/.200/.200	.165	.333	-0.1	C(5): -0.0	0.0
	C	SEA	MLB	33	92	9	2	0	1	6	8	24	0	0	.226/.293/.286	.245	.305	0.8	C(19): -0.0, 1B(1): 0.0	0.2
Drew Butera	C	LAN	MLB	30	192	16	6	1	3	14	17	41	0	0	.188/.267/.288	.213	.227	-0.2	C(57): 0.5, P(2): -0.0	0.0
Taylor Featherston	2B	TUL	AA	24	550	69	33	4	16	57	38	114	14	6	.260/.322/.439	.273	.305	-2.1	2B(72): 8.1, SS(39): 0.1	3.2
Zachary Houchins	3B	BUR	A	21	120	8	6	0	0	10	7	26	3	0	.200/.258/.255	.206	.259	-0.5	3B(21): -0.4, SS(5): -0.2	-0.4
Sherman Johnson	2B	INL	A+	21	629	107	23	13	17	78	88	104	26	12	.276/.382/.465	.316	.314	5.4		5.0
Roger Kieschnick	RF	RNO	AAA	27	401	57	25	2	15	49	28	88	5	1	.260/.317/.461	.250	.303	1.2	RF(55): 6.4, CF(30): -1.6	0.9
	LF	ARI	MLB	27	41	2	1	0	1	2	0	16	0	0	.195/.195/.293	.180	.292	0.2	LF(5): -0.2, RF(3): -0.0	-0.3
Marc Krauss	1B	OKL	AAA	26	184	22	12	0	5	38	22	43	1	0	.289/.375/.459	.289	.363	-1.9	1B(25): -0.4, RF(5): 0.2	0.5
	1B	HOU	MLB	26	208	16	6	0	6	21	21	54	0	0	.194/.279/.323	.219	.238	-1.8	1B(33): 0.3, LF(19): -0.4	-0.8
Alfredo Marte	LF	RNO	AAA	25	317	46	15	3	11	45	39	60	6	0	.319/.407/.519	.300	.369	-2.4	LF(48): -2.1, RF(24): -0.4	1.6
	LF	ARI	MLB	25	114	8	5	1	2	9	6	34	1	0	.170/.221/.292	.180	.229	-0.9	LF(20): 0.4, RF(7): -0.5	-0.9
Dennis Raben	1B	INL	A+	26	448	63	15	3	31	94	38	96	4	3	.292/.362/.579	.348	.309	-2.8		5.1
Angel Rosa	3B	BUR	A	21	429	43	23	3	7	46	25	103	15	5	.246/.300/.372	.243	.315	1.5	3B(73): 7.4, SS(22): 0.3	1.9
	SS	INL	A+	21	124	14	7	3	0	18	6	21	4	3	.348/.390/.464	.333	.419	0.6		1.4
Eric Stamets	SS	ARK	AA	22	382	46	13	1	4	23	24	62	11	1	.235/.293/.314	.243	.275	3.5	SS(106): 21.7	4.2
Ian Stewart	1B	SLC	AAA	29	142	21	3	0	5	13	18	42	1	0	.198/.310/.347	.232	.253	0.4	1B(14): 0.2, 3B(9): -0.9	-0.1
	3B	ANA	MLB	29	72	8	2	3	2	7	3	31	1	0	.176/.222/.382	.209	.286	-0.5	3B(16): -1.5, 1B(6): 0.2	-0.3
Cal Towey	3B	INL	A+	24	547	72	24	6	10	63	51	137	21	15	.279/.364/.417	.288	.369	5.0		3.3
Bo Way	CF	BUR	A	22	133	21	4	2	2	10	13	16	6	4	.339/.424/.461	.320	.381	-1.3	CF(25): 1.2, RF(1): 0.0	1.3
Ryan Wheeler	3B	SLC	AAA	25	102	13	1	0	2	15	8	19	0	0	.326/.373/.402	.259	.384	-0.5	3B(10): 0.3, 1B(8): 0.0	0.1
	3B	CSP	AAA	25	230	18	9	0	4	20	15	43	0	2	.243/.293/.343	.224	.283	-1.6	3B(46): -1.3, LF(5): -0.2	-0.9
	3B	COL	MLB	25	64	6	2	0	2	13	5	12	0	0	.232/.281/.375	.244	.244	-0.7	3B(12): -0.1, 1B(5): -0.0	0.1

John Buck has quietly had himself a nice 11-year career. Highlights: When he was an All-Star! Non-highlights: When he was an Angel. ❖ As far as backup catchers go, **Drew Butera** isn't one of the best. As far as mop-up relief pitchers go, he also isn't one of the best, though he did touch 91 mph in his first relief appearance of 2014. ❖ Eleventh-rounder **Andrew Daniel** mashed in his pro debut while playing a tolerable second base, so he now has a legitimate—if long—shot to carve out a role in the next Angels infield. ❖ The Angels have recently traded away some of their fringe-bat middle infielders. **Taylor Featherston**, a 2011 fifth-round pick of the Rockies who led the Texas League in total bases, was acquired to refill the pool. ❖ Social media magnifies the scope and consequences of youthful indiscretion; just ask **Zachary Houchins**, who lost thousands in the draft after some objectionable tweets and a defense that never works: "I'm not racist. My closest friends literally are all black." The Halos capitalized. ❖ **Sherman Johnson** has outhit and outfielded most every other player in the Angels' system over the past two years, but remains strangely sidelined. A good 2015 will make him the Angels' utility player of the future. ❖ Once a power prospect, **Roger Kieschnick** will join his third organization in three years following an early-October waiver claim. ❖ Weirdly, **Marc Krauss** owns a career OPS 330 points higher on the road than at home. Given his home has always been Minute Maid Park, he could have a chronic fear of hills, trains, or citrus. ❖ Until the Angels claimed him off waivers in October, **Alfredo Marte** was somehow the second-longest-tenured player on the Diamondbacks' 40-man roster. He has the tools to contribute at the major-league level, but the flaws to limit him to a fourth-outfielder role. ❖ The Angels signed **Dennis Raben** to provide a little sock in their otherwise lightweight A-Ball lineups. Thirty-one long balls later, he's due to get his first crack at the high minors come spring. ❖ Midwest League pitchers had swell gloveman **Angel Rosa** figured out: He can't hit the slider. California League pitchers never got the memo. ❖ Major-league glove, A-Ball bat: **Eric Stamets** has a skill set that will keep him employed for a long time, but not as a regular. ❖ **Ian Stewart** ended 2014 with a higher OPS for the Angels than Raul Ibanez and Brennan Boesch, an achievement that appears in the most depressing free agent binder ever. ❖ Posting a .492 OBP anywhere, even in the Pioneer League, will put you on the map; **Cal Towey** has performed reasonably well since that magical summer, earning himself an Arizona Fall League look, but he likely lacks the punch to contribute. ❖ If Kody Eaves was typical of the Angels' system half a decade ago, **Bo Way** is the typical guy now. He's a senior sign with a polished approach and modest tools who outperforms at every level, and if he can show enough pop, he just might make it as fourth outfielder. ❖ After not producing enough to stick with the hapless Rockies, **Ryan Wheeler** failed to stick with the hapful Angels and lost his roster spot again. He remains on Salt Lake's roster at press time, so will come to camp looking to claim the left-handed bat job that's been up for grabs for two years.

Pitchers

NAME	TEAM	LVL	AGE	W	L	SV	G	GS	IP	H	HR	BB	K	BB/9	K/9	GB%	BABIP	WHIP	ERA	FIP	FRA	WARP
Cam Bedrosian	ARK	AA	22	1	0	15	30	0	32¹	10	1	10	57	2.8	15.9	57%	.196	0.62	1.11	0.92	1.96	1.0
	ANA	MLB	22	0	1	0	17	0	19¹	23	2	12	20	5.6	9.3	43%	.356	1.81	6.52	4.30	3.67	0.1
Harrison Cooney	BUR	A	22	9	8	1	25	22	129	108	5	51	91	3.6	6.3	50%	.268	1.23	2.65	4.02	4.73	0.6
Dane De La Rosa	SLC	AAA	31	3	2	3	27	0	25¹	21	2	18	21	6.4	7.5	50%	.264	1.54	5.33	5.20	5.56	0.1
	ANA	MLB	31	0	0	0	3	0	2¹	3	0	3	0	11.6	0.0	40%	.300	2.57	11.57	7.02	7.50	-0.1
Trevor Gott	LEL	A+	21	2	4	16	29	0	31¹	28	3	9	31	2.6	8.9	59%	.281	1.18	3.16	3.96	4.49	0.4
	SAN	AA	21	0	0	0	10	0	11²	11	0	9	11	6.9	8.5	60%	.314	1.71	4.63	3.55	4.79	0.0
	ARK	AA	21	2	1	2	13	0	17²	11	0	7	18	3.6	9.2	58%	.256	1.02	1.53	2.27	3.55	0.2
Yoslan Herrera	SLC	AAA	33	4	4	5	41	0	50	51	3	16	47	2.9	8.5	53%	.322	1.34	2.52	3.74	4.72	0.8
	ANA	MLB	33	1	1	0	20	0	16²	22	0	9	13	4.9	7.0	51%	.400	1.86	2.70	3.22	3.11	0.3
Daniel Hurtado	BUR	A	21	2	4	0	16	12	64	63	7	20	64	2.8	9.0	37%	.329	1.30	2.95	4.22	4.48	0.8
Edgar Ibarra	NBR	AA	25	2	1	1	9	0	14¹	17	1	5	16	3.1	10.0	60%	.390	1.53	6.91	3.28	3.81	0.2
	ROC	AAA	25	5	0	0	31	0	49²	50	3	23	42	4.2	7.6	43%	.313	1.47	3.44	3.84	3.87	0.8
Anthony Lerew	SLC	AAA	31	4	6	0	22	14	82²	116	12	34	56	3.7	6.1	45%	.365	1.81	6.75	5.54	5.70	0.6
Joel Pineiro	TEN	AA	35	0	1	0	4	4	22¹	29	5	4	10	1.6	4.0	55%	.293	1.48	4.43	5.87	6.59	-0.3
	SLC	AAA	35	1	2	0	4	4	21²	36	3	7	11	2.9	4.6	52%	.402	1.98	7.48	5.45	5.99	0.1
Daniel Reynolds	INL	A+	23	0	0	0	11	0	20	11	0	7	19	3.2	8.6	63%	.216	0.90	1.80	3.04	4.18	0.2
	ARK	AA	23	3	2	2	30	0	40	42	1	15	41	3.4	9.2	47%	.360	1.42	3.60	2.75	2.82	0.8
Chris Volstad	SLC	AAA	27	2	1	0	7	7	39¹	48	7	12	24	2.7	5.5	48%	.306	1.53	6.18	5.78	7.54	-0.4
Randy Wolf	SLC	AAA	37	1	1	0	7	7	37²	45	5	12	31	2.9	7.4	46%	.342	1.51	4.78	4.81	5.51	0.4
	RNO	AAA	37	5	1	0	6	6	34	40	1	18	35	4.8	9.3	46%	.398	1.71	4.50	3.61	3.71	1.1
	NOR	AAA	37	0	0	0	6	1	15	18	1	5	12	3.0	7.2	36%	.347	1.53	4.20	3.62	3.19	0.3
	MIA	MLB	37	1	3	1	6	4	25²	33	4	6	19	2.1	6.7	41%	.345	1.52	5.26	4.35	5.09	-0.1

Before catching a case of the yips in his major-league call-up, **Cam Bedrosian** was dominating hitters at two levels with good command and a fastball-down/fastball-up approach. He's got the stuff to be a first-division closer. ❖ Tommy John surgery robbed hard-throwing relief prospect and long-time Angels' farmhand **Ryan Brasier** of one last shot to make the Angels bullpen. ❖ A lively fastball will likely get **Harrison Cooney** to the majors, but unless his command improves tremendously, it'll be as a middle reliever. ❖ **Dane De La Rosa**'s fastball steadily gained speed in 2013, peaking at 96 mph in September, mirroring his ascent in the Angels' bullpen. The pitch was on the wrong side of 90 last spring, and quickly made him a non-factor. Sometimes, pitchers just break. ❖ A guy like third-rounder **Chris Ellis** keeps pitching coaches up at nights. The Ole Miss alum flashes three average or better pitches, and zero pitchability. ❖ The Angels received power reliever **Trevor Gott** in the Huston Street deal; if he reaches his set-up man ceiling he could turn out to be the most valuable of the five prospects involved in the transaction, which would just be the mic drop to end all mic drops. ❖ Back in 2008, **Yoslan Herrera** got a cup of coffee with the Pirates, but faded quickly; in 2014, Herrera—this time with four additional ticks on his fastball and a decent split-change—got another chance with the Angels, but big-league lefties chased him back to the minors in short order. ❖ Scouting reports don't paint a particularly rosy picture for **Daniel Hurtado**, sketching out fringy stuff and extreme fly-ball tendencies, but the outs keep coming. ❖ Lefty reliever **Edgar Ibarra** can tell his grandkids about that mid-90s heater and those 10 glorious months on a 40-man roster, but he might be less forthcoming about how his complete lack of fastball command always kept him out of the big leagues. ❖ **Jake Jewell**'s worm-killing sinker was awfully good in the Arizona League, but Pioneer League offenses ran that Jewell fast. ❖ After spending three seasons abroad in Japan and Korea, former major leaguer **Anthony Lerew** returned home, playing first in independent ball before getting a break with the pitching-starved Angels; now it's back to his nomadic existence. ❖ At 17, **Crusito Mieses** put up the best pitching performance by far on the Angels' Dominican Summer League team, making him one of the more interesting names to track (or just to say) in the coming year. ❖ Former Angels' rotation anchor **Joel Pineiro** joined the organization in June, no doubt hoping to play hero in a thinning system. His sinker failed him in Salt Lake, robbing him of the opportunity. ❖ The Angels protected **Daniel Reynolds** and his mid-90s fastball by adding him to the roster in November. He throws hard but without deception, so if he doesn't put that heat exactly where he wants it come March, the roster spot won't last long. ❖ In a boring system, bonus baby lefty **Ricardo Sanchez** remains one of the least boring prospects, despite boring results. ❖ After a brief stint in Korea to start 2014, **Chris Volstad** returned to sign a minor-league deal, only to sprain his elbow one month later. Back to forks for him. ❖ **Randy Wolf** is the first pitcher ever to spend time with the Orioles, Mariners, Marlins, Diamondbacks and Angels in one season. Probably, right? Has to be.

Manager

Mike Scioscia

YEAR	TEAM	W	L	Py-thag +/-	Avg PC	100+ P	120+ P	QS	BQS	REL	REL w Zero R	IBB	PH	PH Avg	PH HR	SB2	CS2	SB3	CS3	SAC Att	SAC%	POS SAC	Squeeze	Swing	In Play
2012	ANA	89	73	1	97.4	87	4	91	3	444	365	20	68	.203	2	121	27	12	4	72	65.3%	43	3	419	132
2013	ANA	78	84	-3	97.5	77	6	87	5	496	400	36	83	.214	3	71	32	10	1	54	68.5%	35	0	349	110
2014	ANA	98	64	1	94.2	72	3	80	5	543	467	41	103	.233	1	72	37	9	2	42	61.9%	24	1	315	88

The longest-tenured manager in baseball, Scioscia was hired in November 1999; no other active skipper was hired at his current position before 2006. In fact, Scioscia has been around so long that he's managed nearly 30 percent of the games in franchise history.

For an old dog—or, rather, celestial attendant—Scioscia remains interested in new tricks. It's generally a bad thing when a team sets new franchise records for batters and pitchers used in a single season. Not so with the 2014 Angels. Faced with a system void of prospects, the Angels loaded their 40-man roster with useful situational talents and carried a 39-man roster throughout September; Scioscia, in turn, put those players in situations to succeed. Conventional? Hardly, but it showed creativity and adaptability.

Those same attributes were present in Scioscia's aggressive usage of his bullpen. Everyone will remember him yanking Wilson during the first inning of a playoff game, but the Angels finished the regular season with 28 starts of 80 pitches or fewer—tied for the most in the majors. Unsurprisingly, Scioscia was the only manager within hollering distance of Terry Francona when it came to relief appearances with zero days' rest, as he worked his bullpen hard to fill the gaps.

Scioscia should no longer be on the hot seat, as he was as recently as a year ago. Instead, the Angels will chase their eighth postseason berth under him in '15.

LOS ANGELES DODGERS

by Molly Knight

At the end of the movie version of *Moneyball*, Brad Pitt's Billy Beane is handed an envelope with a pledge inside to make him the best-paid general manager in the history of American sports. He carries that envelope back from Boston to Oakland, terrified to open it. He knows that when he sees that offer with his own eyes—when all those zeros zap his subconscious and the faces of brilliant players he could never afford become real possibilities dancing in his imagination—he might not be able to say no. But saying yes would mean leaving the darling, poor A's franchise he turned into a perennial contender for the big, bad Red Sox. And that would make him a sellout.

But there was perhaps a more practical reason that compelled movie-Beane to turn down the Boston job. As the GM in Oakland, he had mastered the arts of waiver trawling and back-page trading, of getting the most out of his players and getting the most in return for them. Since he never had the cash for a trade-and-sign of, say, a Curt Schilling or a Josh Beckett (and then to ink some other ace if either one blew up), Beane focused on dozens of smaller moves. His A's would be too small to punch the rest of the league in the mouth, so he set about paper cutting the competition to death. It worked, and the more it worked the better he got at it. Succeeding on a small budget required a different skill set; and, in turn, it returned different rewards. There was more joy in being the underdog, so Beane said no. If we want to know how Beane would have done in Boston, we'll have to wait for Bennett Miller's speculative sequel.

But we might have just as much fun watching the next decade of the Dodgers. They succeeded where the Red Sox once failed, persuading Tampa Bay Rays GM Andrew Friedman to say yes to an opportunity much like the one Beane turned down. The question facing Friedman is the same one that challenged Beane, and it's the same one, ironically, that challenged Ned Colletti: Is it harder to be a great general manager when money is no object?

Friedman takes over the Dodgers' baseball ops from Colletti, a general manager whose decision-making process turned out to be poorly served by having more money than he knew what to do with. Before the Guggenheim Group bought the franchise for an American record $2.15 billion, and before the Dodgers began throwing solid gold bricks at as many All-Stars as the league could

produce, Colletti and his crew excelled when they went small. Consider how for years they loaded the Dodgers bullpen with cheap, low-risk, high-reward castoffs and afterthoughts: Ronald Belisario, Joe Beimel, Takashi Saito, Hong-Chih Kuo. When the Dodgers' crook former owner, Frank McCourt, was replaced by men willing to spend money, Colletti seemed to drown in his freedom, even as unlimited payroll all but guaranteed him an NL frontrunner.

Emboldened with millions of dollars he was apparently allowed to light on fire, he filled the club's bullpen with expensive former closers. He was hell-bent on overpaying the over-the-hill. Watching the Dodgers bullpen in 2014 was like walking into the biggest, most beautiful mansion on a hill only to find it decorated with three-legged futons and spaghetti stuck to the walls.

Table 1 lists every pitcher who threw 25 or more innings in relief for the Dodgers in 2012—with the exception of deadline acquisition League, it was the last bullpen Colletti constructed before the Dodgers were sold—alongside the relievers who pitched 25-plus innings for the Dodgers 'pen in 2014.

Even worse than the money, which was already sunk: When the men on the right struggled, they couldn't be sent to the minors, because they didn't have options. In that sense, the Dodgers lost twice.

Los Angeles won 94 games in 2014 by drubbing bad and average teams. But against teams over .500, their 26-33 record was the worst of any of the 10 clubs that made the playoffs. The Dodgers spent more than $110 million dollars on pitching last season—and more

DODGERS PROSPECTUS
2014 W-L: 94-68, 1ST IN NL WEST

Pythag	.569	5th	DER	.707	13th
RS/G	4.43	6th	B-Age	29.3	23rd
RA/G	3.81	10th	P-Age	30.1	28th
TAv	.276	2nd	Salary	$236.2M	1st
BRR	1.15	16th	M$/MW	$4.9M	25th
TAv-P	.255	8th	DL Days	1,015	23rd
FIP	3.45	4th	$ on DL	16%	18th

Three-Year Park Factors

Runs	Runs/RH	Runs/LH	HR/RH	HR/LH
97	95	98	99	109

Top Hitter WARP	5.8	Yasiel Puig
Top Pitcher WARP	6.1	Clayton Kershaw
Top Prospect		Corey Seager

Table 1: Dodgers 25+ Inning Pitchers

2012 Reliever	Salary	ERA+	2014 Reliever	Salary	ERA+
K. Jansen	$0.5M	162	K. Jansen	$4.3M	127
R. Belisario	$0.5M	150	B. Wilson	$10.0M	75
J. Wright	$0.9M	102	B. League	$8.5M	136
J. Lindblom	$0.5M	127	J. Howell	$5.5M	147
J. Guerra	$0.5M	147	J. Wright	$1.8M	80
S. Tolleson	$0.5M	89	P. Maholm	$1.5M	72
S. Elbert	$0.5M	174	C. Perez	$2.3M	82
B. League	$1.7M	167	C. Frias	$0.5M	58
Total	**$5.6M**			**$34.4M**	

than $30 million on the bullpen—but when they faced off against the Cardinals in the first round of the playoffs, their lack of reliable arms was laid shockingly bare. In Game One of the NLDS, an exhausted Clayton Kershaw was forced to go seven on a 100-degree day because Don Mattingly didn't trust any of his relievers other than closer Kenley Jansen, who he was considering bringing in for the eighth. Even the relative strengths in the "2014 Reliever" column—League and Howell—were dead to Mattingly, League having folded in the second half, Howell having produced an 11.81 ERA in September. Kershaw had been brilliant through six. But when the Cardinals finally solved him in the seventh, he had to wear it until eight earned runs were in.

Then Zack Greinke threw seven scoreless innings in Game Two, only to watch Howell cough up a game-tying two-run home run in the eighth. And because Mattingly didn't trust any of the aforementioned veteran relievers, he handed the ball to little-used Scott Elbert with Game Three tied 1-1 in the seventh. Elbert gave up a two-run homer. The Dodgers lost the series. Colletti lost his job.

Colletti won't ever be confused for his successor. The cowboy-booted GM preferred to rule with gut instinct instead of by spreadsheet. When the Guggenheim Group bought the Dodgers in 2012, the organization had an analytics "department" of one person. Though the Dodgers' amateur scouting director, Logan White, did well enough in the draft, the club's brain trust lagged behind the field in developing those players, and in then figuring out what to do with them. A depleted farm system gave Colletti license to spend, but that license came with expectations. That's the rub: Only Colletti, among baseball's 30 GMs, could win back-to-back division titles, could win 186 games in two seasons, and be seen as a failure.

The skills required are different when you have money. The expectations are different when you have money. Colletti lacked the former and was doomed by the latter.

✦✦✦

Those who knew Andrew Friedman well said he would never leave the Rays. Like Beane, Friedman had excelled as a member of the sport's mathematical underclass by inventing new ways to evaluate talent that his small-market club could afford. He thrived with salary restrictions—for instance, his relievers had the second-best ERA in the American League over the past five years, despite his only once giving out a multi-year contract to one—and the expectations of a bottom-10 payroll were kind to him: His Rays never won a World Series and cleared the first round of the playoffs just once, yet his regime was never for an instant seen as anything less than a miraculous turnaround for Tampa Bay baseball. He worked for and with men who were loyal to him and to each other. So deep was the organizational trust that Friedman didn't even have a multi-year contract, a standard industry perk even for GMs with little true job security. And, with a reputation as one of the brightest minds in the game—maybe *the* brightest mind in the game—he turned down opportunities to perform on a bigger stage. He said no to the Cubs, the Angels, even his hometown Astros to stay with the Rays.

But in Los Angeles, the Guggenheim executives watched the $2 billion team fail to make the World Series yet again—twice in two years; unacceptable!—and set their sights on Friedman. Red Sox owner John Henry had let Billy Beane say no. But as Friedman, and Rays fans, came to find out, Dodgers chief Mark

Walter is a man who gets what he wants, whatever the cost.

What he wants, of course, isn't Friedman as an end unto itself, but a championship—the first for Los Angeles since the year Clayton Kershaw was born. Rivals fear the combination of the game's sharpest mind with the game's largest payroll: Is it possible to win 170 games in a 162-game season? (At press time, the other 29 clubs had not yet forfeited the 2015 season.)

The last time the Dodgers hired a small-market genius, Paul DePodesta lasted just 20 months before getting fired. But if Friedman is worried about a Moneyball With Money curse—see Queens, NY for another still-developing example—he didn't show it, doubling down by hiring Farhan Zaidi from the A's front office to be his general manager. Zaidi, like Friedman, had worked in only one organization, and operated in only one financial state: Broke. Friedman arguably tripled down by installing Josh Byrnes—late of the Padres—to be senior vice president of baseball ops, though at least Byrnes has seen the inside of a rich team's board room, having served as an assistant GM in Boston.

Friedman and Zaidi have a tall task ahead of them, not because the Dodgers need much help to be great—they're already a lock to be PECOTA's NL favorite this season—but because money changes the definition of success. For the Dodgers, for the Guggenheim group, success will mean perfection, and the Dodgers need a lot of help to be perfect. To help shore up a rotation that was forced to start Roberto Hernandez and Kevin Correia last year, Zaidi signed his old buddy from Oakland, Brandon McCarthy, who should make for a fantastic no. 4 starter if he stays healthy. For bullpen depth, Friedman struck a deal with his old team to add Tampa workhorse Joel Peralta.

Friedman and company also demonstrated right away that they were willing to make unpopular moves to try to get better. They let fan favorite Hanley Ramirez walk because he gets injured, he pouts and he can no longer field the shortstop position. They traded second baseman Dee Gordon, another favorite, to the Marlins for prospects, then flipped one of those prospects—Andrew Heaney—to the Angels for Howie Kendrick. Though, coaches, teammates and fans loved Gordon for the effort he gave and the joy he exuded, Friedman was right to sell high—Gordon's OBP was too low for the top of a rich team's lineup and his gaudy stolen base totals inflated perception of how good he really is.

But the trade this new front office will be remembered for—for better or worse—is the one that sent Matt Kemp to the Padres for catcher Yasmani Grandal and prospects. The Dodgers' outfield logjam in 2014 became a daily headache, and that was before the club called up superprospect Joc Pederson. Heading into the winter meetings, the Dodgers had SEVEN major-league outfielders and no shortstop. So, Friedman, Zaidi and Byrnes traded the club's longest-tenured player, Kemp, for a return that landed them catching help and a prospect they were able to flip to the Phillies for Jimmy Rollins. While some fans hated the trade, there wasn't much way around it. The Dodgers got younger, acquired a shortstop, eased the outfield gridlock and freed up the cash to sign a fourth starter. Five teams were involved, 18 players, hundreds of millions in salaries. It all happened in about 10 hours.

Though dealing away popular veterans will be tough for the fan base to swallow, Friedman knows he must incorporate young talent into an aging roster, a challenge that has vexed the big-market Yankees, Red Sox and Phillies. The Dodgers must also build a rotation deep enough that Kershaw won't have to pitch yet another October on short rest, and they must shore up their bullpen with the sort of live arms that can be demoted if they implode. They must learn from Colletti's mistakes: In the bullpen, and elsewhere, money can be the root of all evil if you use it wrong.

Money can do amazing things. Had the Yankees been broke, they wouldn't have been able to spend $45 million on Alex Rodriguez and Derek Jeter in each player's prime. But money also has a long history of making people do stupid things. Had the Yankees been broke, they wouldn't be stuck with Rodriguez today, and they wouldn't have fielded a 40-year-old, sub-replacement shortstop last season. Friedman has never spent more than $100 million on a player before—Evan Longoria's extension was his max—and neither has Zaidi, but the pair inherited five such contracts. They will have to get used to handing over that kind of promissory note, while also resisting

the urge to nuke the competition with an overbid for a guy they want just because they can afford him.

The Dodgers spent an MLB record $279 million on player payroll in 2014. They won exactly one playoff game. Friedman knows money can't ensure that the Dodgers win a World Series championship. Intelligence, perhaps, can: The Red Sox won it the year after Beane said no to them, under the direction of a man who employed many of the same tactics. No one knows if Friedman will have the same success in Los Angeles. It will sure be fun to find out. ∎

—Molly Knight lives in Los Angeles and has written for ESPN The Magazine *and* The New York Times Magazine, *among others. Her book on the Dodgers' attempt to build a dynasty,* The Best Team Money Can Buy, *will be published by Simon & Schuster in July.*

Player comments by Dustin Nosler and Baseball Prospectus Authors

Hitters

Erisbel Arruebarrena   SS

Born: 3/25/90   Age: 25   Bats: R   Throws: R   Height: 6'0"   Weight: 200

YEAR	TEAM	LVL	AGE	PA	R	2B	3B	HR	RBI	BB	K	SB	CS	AVG/OBP/SLG	TAv	BABIP	BRR	FRAA	WARP
2014	RCU	A+	24	54	8	4	1	2	11	2	24	1	0	.245/.259/.490	.316	.385	0.1	3B(8): 0.0, SS(4): -0.2	0.5
2014	CHT	AA	24	105	10	4	1	1	6	4	31	0	0	.208/.252/.302	.206	.292	0.3	SS(25): -0.4	-0.2
2014	ABQ	AAA	24	95	7	3	2	1	11	10	26	1	1	.333/.400/.452	.282	.466	-0.4	SS(18): 1.7, 3B(4): 0.7	0.8
2014	LAN	MLB	24	45	4	1	0	0	4	3	17	0	0	.195/.244/.220	.184	.320	-0.9	SS(21): -1.3	-0.4
2015	LAN	MLB	25	250	20	9	1	3	20	13	87	1	0	.204/.247/.295	.210	.302	-0.2	SS -1, 3B 1	-0.4

Breakout: 1%   Improve: 10%   Collapse: 7%   Attrition: 15%   MLB: 23%   Comparables: *Enrique Cruz, Tyler Greene, Brandon Hicks*

The Dodgers signed the third of their three major Cuban imports when they inked Arruebarrena to a $25 million deal in February 2014. He's a defensive wizard—literally; he makes baserunners disappear—but he spent most of his first professional season in the minor leagues. The pre-signing scouting reports on him were accurate: He didn't hit a lick. Unfortunately, Arruebarrena made news for things other than his ability to play the game. At the end of July, he was in the middle of a full-scale brawl in Triple-A that included him pimping a home run and throwing a helmet. He also, reportedly, didn't like playing in day games. If he's going to be a big leaguer, he'll have to shape up.

Austin Barnes   C

Born: 12/28/89   Age: 25   Bats: R   Throws: R   Height: 5'9"   Weight: 185

YEAR	TEAM	LVL	AGE	PA	R	2B	3B	HR	RBI	BB	K	SB	CS	AVG/OBP/SLG	TAv	BABIP	BRR	FRAA	WARP
2012	GRB	A	22	566	76	36	3	12	65	59	61	9	2	.318/.401/.481	.304	.343	-0.2	2B(104): 5.5, C(16): 0.0	4.9
2013	JUP	A+	23	417	42	15	1	4	38	52	59	5	2	.260/.367/.343	.272	.298	-0.1	C(64): 0.9	2.0
2013	JAX	AA	23	74	10	2	2	1	7	12	10	0	0	.339/.446/.484	.346	.392	0.0	C(11): -0.1, 2B(4): 0.0	0.9
2014	JUP	A+	24	200	24	11	2	1	14	19	25	3	3	.317/.385/.417	.285	.364	-3.3	C(44): -0.8	1.2
2014	JAX	AA	24	348	56	20	2	12	43	50	36	8	0	.296/.406/.507	.339	.299	0.7	2B(30): -0.1, C(29): -0.5	4.2
2015	LAN	MLB	25	250	28	11	1	5	23	23	47	1	0	.245/.319/.366	.263	.284	-0.2	C -0, 2B 0	0.9

Breakout: 2%   Improve: 9%   Collapse: 12%   Attrition: 24%   MLB: 35%   Comparables: *John Jaso, Curtis Casali, Dan Butler*

He may not have been the *best* prospect in Miami's system, but Barnes was making a strong case as the most interesting before he was included in the Dee Gordon deal. His ascent through the minors has been slowed by the Marlins' deep cast of catching prospects, but he showed last year why he has a major-league future. Barnes pairs solid, but not great, defensive ability at two critical positions: catcher and second base. That's plus-plus utility. Without any loud tools, his carrying skill should still be his bat. He has a solid approach and a short swing that lends itself to line-drive power. He really stroked at Jacksonville last year, and if he was a little old for the league, well, shoot, isn't Foreigner a little old to be touring? That doesn't stop us from rocking out to *Head Games* more than once in a while.

Carl Crawford   LF

Born: 8/5/81   Age: 33   Bats: L   Throws: L   Height: 6'2"   Weight: 225

YEAR	TEAM	LVL	AGE	PA	R	2B	3B	HR	RBI	BB	K	SB	CS	AVG/OBP/SLG	TAv	BABIP	BRR	FRAA	WARP
2012	BOS	MLB	30	125	23	10	2	3	19	3	22	5	0	.282/.306/.479	.266	.319	0.8	LF(30): -1.9	0.1
2013	LAN	MLB	31	469	62	30	3	6	31	28	66	15	4	.283/.329/.407	.273	.321	1.9	LF(107): 6.9	2.6
2014	LAN	MLB	32	370	56	14	3	8	46	16	55	23	6	.300/.339/.429	.296	.335	3.9	LF(94): 0.8	2.7
2015	LAN	MLB	33	370	46	18	4	7	33	18	66	15	4	.270/.308/.402	.271	.311	1.6	LF 3	1.8

Breakout: 0%   Improve: 28%   Collapse: 5%   Attrition: 4%   MLB: 98%   Comparables: *Matt Diaz, Vernon Wells, Eric Byrnes*

Carl Crawford WARP, 2010: 5.8. Carl Crawford WARP, 2011-14: 6.3. Maybe the devil magic actually resides in St. Petersburg? Crawford's last two seasons with the Dodgers are about as good as he's going to be now that he's easing toward his mid-30s, and it's not so much that he's *bad* as that he's due $67 million over the next three years to be solid, decent, above average. He's also missed a month each of the past two years with leg injuries, which is alarming for a player reliant on speed for both defensive and offensive value, and which also highlights the need for the Dodgers to have a good extra outfielder at the ready. If there's anything the Dodgers have in spades, though, it's good extra outfielders.

A.J. Ellis C
Born: 4/9/81   Age: 34   Bats: R   Throws: R   Height: 6' 3"   Weight: 220

YEAR	TEAM	LVL	AGE	PA	R	2B	3B	HR	RBI	BB	K	SB	CS	AVG/OBP/SLG	TAv	BABIP	BRR	FRAA	WARP
2012	LAN	MLB	31	505	44	20	1	13	52	65	107	0	0	.270/.373/.414	.288	.329	-2.9	C(131): -0.0	3.7
2013	LAN	MLB	32	448	43	17	1	10	52	45	78	0	2	.238/.318/.364	.265	.269	-0.6	C(113): -1.3	2.3
2014	LAN	MLB	33	347	21	9	0	3	25	53	57	0	0	.191/.323/.254	.227	.225	-4.1	C(92): -1.2	-0.2
2015	LAN	MLB	34	348	35	13	1	5	32	42	66	0	1	.232/.333/.335	.263	.274	-1.6	C -1	1.2

Breakout: 0%   Improve: 31%   Collapse: 14%   Attrition: 17%   MLB: 86%   Comparables: Nick Johnson, Doug Mientkiewicz, Ron Hassey

It took a long time for Ellis to get his chance in the majors. He was entrenched as the Dodgers' starting catcher the past three years, but his 2014 campaign was, on the whole, miserable. He posted the lowest batting average and TAv of any regular catcher (non-Jose Molina division). Ellis' only saving grace in the regular season was his career-best walk rate of 15 percent. It may have been a lengthy con, as he turned into Babe Ruth in the NLDS against the Cardinals, hitting .538/.647/.846 in the four games. Ellis is bad at framing (by our metrics, he cost his team the second-most runs in baseball last year, behind only Jarrod Saltalamacchia), but Clayton Kershaw adores him and he works well with the rest of the pitching staff. Those are decent notches to have in one's belt.

Andre Ethier OF
Born: 4/10/82   Age: 33   Bats: L   Throws: L   Height: 6' 2"   Weight: 200

YEAR	TEAM	LVL	AGE	PA	R	2B	3B	HR	RBI	BB	K	SB	CS	AVG/OBP/SLG	TAv	BABIP	BRR	FRAA	WARP
2012	LAN	MLB	30	618	79	36	1	20	89	50	124	2	2	.284/.351/.460	.307	.333	-0.6	RF(146): -8.2, CF(1): 0.1	3.1
2013	LAN	MLB	31	553	54	33	2	12	52	61	95	4	3	.272/.360/.423	.284	.315	-2.0	CF(74): -8.3, RF(54): 1.9	1.8
2014	LAN	MLB	32	380	29	17	6	4	42	31	74	2	2	.249/.322/.370	.262	.307	-4.3	CF(68): -1.6, LF(16): -1.2	0.4
2015	LAN	MLB	33	391	42	20	1	9	45	34	77	2	1	.265/.335/.412	.285	.312	-1.4	CF -4, RF -1	1.1

Breakout: 0%   Improve: 28%   Collapse: 3%   Attrition: 6%   MLB: 98%   Comparables: Bernie Williams, Carlos Beltran, Torii Hunter

Few players have fallen as hard and fast as Ethier in recent years; Tim Lincecum comes to mind, but at least he has World Series rings to show for it. Ethier's days of being a full-time player might have come to an end with his dismal 2014 season that saw him post career lows in every offensive category that matters, plus a bunch you've never heard of. And this isn't a case where the superficial numbers belie underlying indicators that show a run of bad luck amid retained skills: Any in-depth investigation will reinforce rather than undermine the conclusion that Ethier is through. He might be the most expensive pinch-hitter in the history of baseball for the next four years.

Chone Figgins UT
Born: 1/22/78   Age: 37   Bats: B   Throws: R   Height: 5' 8"   Weight: 180

YEAR	TEAM	LVL	AGE	PA	R	2B	3B	HR	RBI	BB	K	SB	CS	AVG/OBP/SLG	TAv	BABIP	BRR	FRAA	WARP
2012	SEA	MLB	34	194	18	5	2	2	11	19	48	4	1	.181/.262/.271	.208	.237	-0.8	LF(38): -2.5, 3B(10): 0.6	-0.8
2014	ABQ	AAA	36	74	12	3	0	0	3	11	14	2	1	.286/.392/.333	.255	.367	-0.2	3B(5): 0.6, 2B(4): 0.3	0.2
2014	LAN	MLB	36	76	8	3	0	0	1	14	15	4	1	.217/.373/.267	.260	.289	2.6	3B(10): 0.9, 2B(5): 0.1	0.7
2015	LAN	MLB	37	250	27	9	1	1	15	23	47	8	3	.224/.297/.287	.231	.270	0.5	LF -1, 3B 1	-0.2

Breakout: 1%   Improve: 33%   Collapse: 9%   Attrition: 16%   MLB: 81%   Comparables: Jeff Cirillo, Craig Counsell, Buddy Bell

One of the best spoonerisms on the team, Fone Chiggins (or, if you're a phonetic absolutist, Fawn Shiggins) actually provided value for the Dodgers in 2014. After he basically did not try in Seattle, the Dodgers took a flyer on the former six-win player, and Figgins rewarded them with more than half a win in 38 games before being designated for assignment on August 6th. It was a low-risk, low-reward move for the Dodgers, and they definitely got their money's worth out of what was probably Figgins' final go-'round in the majors.

Adrian Gonzalez 1B
Born: 5/8/82   Age: 33   Bats: L   Throws: L   Height: 6' 2"   Weight: 225

YEAR	TEAM	LVL	AGE	PA	R	2B	3B	HR	RBI	BB	K	SB	CS	AVG/OBP/SLG	TAv	BABIP	BRR	FRAA	WARP
2012	BOS	MLB	30	527	63	37	0	15	86	31	81	0	0	.300/.343/.469	.286	.329	-0.4	1B(115): 12.4, RF(18): -1.2	3.1
2012	LAN	MLB	30	157	12	10	1	3	22	11	29	2	0	.297/.344/.441	.288	.351	-2.7	1B(36): 1.6	0.6
2013	LAN	MLB	31	641	69	32	0	22	100	47	98	1	0	.293/.342/.461	.293	.315	-3.8	1B(151): -2.4	2.1
2014	LAN	MLB	32	660	83	41	0	27	116	56	112	1	1	.276/.335/.482	.300	.294	-5.3	1B(157): 11.4	4.0
2015	LAN	MLB	33	616	71	33	1	21	82	51	108	1	0	.284/.342/.458	.298	.315	-3.3	1B 8, RF -0	3.4

Breakout: 1%   Improve: 26%   Collapse: 6%   Attrition: 8%   MLB: 95%   Comparables: Ted Kluszewski, Paul Konerko, Mark Teixeira

Gonzalez will never again be the wonder he was in San Diego, but last year was his best campaign since 2011: He led the Dodgers in home runs, led the majors in RBIs (big deal) and played stellar defense at first base (ask Hanley Ramirez), which added up to a seventh-place finish in the MVP voting. Granted, he was only the third-most-valuable player on his own team, behind Yasiel Puig and Clayton Kershaw, but the descent into his mid-30s (and the final $88 million remaining on his contract) should go a lot more smoothly than the pre-2014 vantage point suggested it might. His daddish facial hair belies a fire in the belly that fueled a notable confrontation with Yadier Molina in last year's playoffs. Either that or the madness of the Dodgers' clubhouse caused temporary insanity.

Alexander Guerrero UT
Born: 11/20/86   Age: 28   Bats: R   Throws: R   Height: 5' 10"   Weight: 205

YEAR	TEAM	LVL	AGE	PA	R	2B	3B	HR	RBI	BB	K	SB	CS	AVG/OBP/SLG	TAv	BABIP	BRR	FRAA	WARP
2012	LTU	CNS	26	338	54	15	1	22	56	40	33	2	5	.286/.394/.568	.325	.256	--	--	--
2014	RCU	A+	27	21	3	4	1	0	2	2	2	0	0	.368/.429/.684	.358	.412	-0.1	3B(2): -0.1, 2B(2): -0.2	0.3
2014	ABQ	AAA	27	258	38	14	5	15	49	10	44	4	0	.329/.364/.613	.310	.351	1.5	2B(51): -3.3, LF(9): -0.5	1.8
2014	LAN	MLB	27	13	0	0	0	0	0	0	6	0	0	.077/.077/.077	.061	.143	0.2	LF(3): -0.0	-0.2
2015	LAN	MLB	28	250	27	11	2	9	32	9	58	2	0	.248/.281/.425	.266	.288	0.1	2B -2, LF -0	0.6

Breakout: 4%   Improve: 17%   Collapse: 10%   Attrition: 17%   MLB: 29%   Comparables: Brooks Conrad, Matt Carson, Craig Brazell

Guerrero was the Dodgers' second foray into the market of Cuban escapees since Guggenheim Partners took over ownership of the organization in

2012. They hit *really* big on Yasiel Puig the first time and were hoping Guerrero would be better (offensively) than anyone they've had at second base since Jeff Kent. A shortstop in Cuba, a move to second shouldn't have been difficult. It was. Guerrero spent most of his debut season in Triple-A, and even that was interrupted by attempted cannibalism by Miguel Olivo, who took a chomp out of Guerrero's ear in a dugout altercation. He came up in September and was a pinch-hitter, playing all of 14 innings in the majors, and those came in left field. Perhaps the Dodgers spent $28 million on a utility player, but it isn't a good sign when a shortstop-turned-second-baseman-turned-utility player doesn't make much of an impact in his debut year at age 27.

Enrique Hernandez   INF

Born: 8/24/91   Age: 23   Bats: R   Throws: R   Height: 5' 11"   Weight: 170

YEAR	TEAM	LVL	AGE	PA	R	2B	3B	HR	RBI	BB	K	SB	CS	AVG/OBP/SLG	TAv	BABIP	BRR	FRAA	WARP
2012	LNC	A+	20	411	52	25	7	5	49	22	43	4	2	.275/.318/.418	.257	.297	0.8	2B(99): -3.3, LF(4): 0.2	1.1
2012	CCH	AA	20	88	7	2	0	1	3	4	9	2	2	.247/.299/.309	.225	.268	-0.6	2B(23): -2.8	-0.5
2013	CCH	AA	21	483	53	18	2	13	46	34	70	5	3	.236/.297/.375	.240	.253	-0.5	2B(104): -6.8, SS(5): 0.1	-0.2
2014	CCH	AA	22	43	9	3	0	1	5	3	3	0	0	.325/.372/.475	.292	.333	0.1	2B(10): 0.5	0.4
2014	NWO	AAA	22	84	8	5	0	2	6	10	13	0	1	.250/.345/.403	.282	.276	-0.5	2B(11): -0.4, SS(8): -0.6	0.4
2014	OKL	AAA	22	289	41	17	2	8	31	18	25	6	5	.337/.380/.508	.292	.346	1.7	2B(26): -1.6, 3B(14): 1.6	2.3
2014	HOU	MLB	22	89	10	4	2	1	8	8	11	0	0	.284/.348/.420	.283	.319	0.3	CF(11): 0.9, LF(8): -0.7	0.5
2014	MIA	MLB	22	45	3	2	1	2	6	4	10	0	0	.175/.267/.425	.267	.179	0.0	CF(7): 0.1, RF(3): -0.1	0.3
2015	LAN	MLB	23	250	23	11	1	5	24	12	41	2	1	.235/.274/.353	.238	.262	-0.3	2B -2, SS 0	0.1

Breakout: 5%   Improve: 26%   Collapse: 0%   Attrition: 7%   MLB: 32%   Comparables: *Luis Valbuena, Alexi Amarista, Daniel Descalso*

If you could say one thing about Hernandez's 2014 season, it would be that he got around. Few players don five different uniforms in the course of a regular season, and even fewer play so many positions on the diamond for each of those squads. He suited up in eighteen different team-and-position combinations in 2014 alone. Of course, the reason most utility players *are* utility players is because they don't do any one thing particularly well. Hernandez has no carrying tool and, aside from his semi-breakout in 2014, he hasn't shown a propensity to hit much better than league-average at any level. To run it down: no speed on the basepaths, no power, average-ish defense and mediocre contact ability. He's the $3 stocking stuffer at eye-level near the hardware store checkout, the imperfect tool for any job. He'll be in some team's toolkit for a decade, but without punching much higher than replacement level.

Matt Kemp   RF

Born: 9/23/84   Age: 30   Bats: R   Throws: R   Height: 6' 4"   Weight: 215

YEAR	TEAM	LVL	AGE	PA	R	2B	3B	HR	RBI	BB	K	SB	CS	AVG/OBP/SLG	TAv	BABIP	BRR	FRAA	WARP
2012	LAN	MLB	27	449	74	22	2	23	69	40	103	9	4	.303/.367/.538	.325	.354	0.9	CF(105): -7.0	4.0
2013	LAN	MLB	28	290	35	15	0	6	33	22	76	9	0	.270/.328/.395	.252	.353	3.6	CF(70): -5.2	0.8
2014	LAN	MLB	29	599	77	38	3	25	89	52	145	8	5	.287/.346/.506	.306	.345	-0.8	RF(59): -1.8, LF(44): -1.2	3.8
2015	LAN	MLB	30	505	67	25	2	22	72	42	126	12	4	.274/.335/.482	.303	.329	1.0	CF -5, RF -1	2.8

Breakout: 1%   Improve: 41%   Collapse: 0%   Attrition: 9%   MLB: 100%   Comparables: *Hank Aaron, Darryl Strawberry, Albert Belle*

Maybe, like the narrative went, injuries have caused Kemp's loudquietloud performances since the start of 2012. After all, we learned in December, via a leaker of doubtful ethics and morals, that Kemp has two arthritic hips. Still, maybe the dude is just streaky. He might have been the best hitter in baseball in the second half last year, batting .309/.365/.606 after the break, the third year in a row that he hit like an MVP in one half and a league-average (or worse) corner outfielder in the other.

Smooth out the swings and it starts to look like Kemp hasn't really changed as a hitter since signing his eight-year extension after the 2011 season: He had a 134 OPS+ in the three seasons before inking, and 135 in the years since. What has changed, possibly as a result of those hips, is that he's no longer a center fielder, starting a career-low 34 games there in 2014. Nor is he any longer even a passable corner outfielder. FRAA was by far the rosiest of the defensive metrics; by UZR, he was 26 runs below average last year (and 50 below over the past three), while DRS had him at negative 23 (40 since 2012). Defense isn't supposed to slump like offense does, but it rarely goes through hot streaks, either, which means Kemp will have to put two big halves together if he's ever going to get another MVP vote.

Year	First-half OPS	Second-half OPS
2012	1.163	.792
2013	.666	1.042
2014	.760	.971

His trade to San Diego started out merely surprising for its destination but turned into a clusterfluff of the highest order when the aforementioned hip condition held up the deal. Undoing the trade would have unwound the Dodgers' acquisition of Jimmy Rollins (because Zach Eflin was in both deals), the Padres-Rays-Nats Wil Myers deal (because of Yasmani Grandal) and maybe even the Derek Norris trade as well (for the same reason). For us outside analysts, though, it was a nice illustration of the folly of evaluating transactions in a vacuum; everything is interdependent.

Howie Kendrick   2B

Born: 7/12/83   Age: 31   Bats: R   Throws: R   Height: 5' 10"   Weight: 210

YEAR	TEAM	LVL	AGE	PA	R	2B	3B	HR	RBI	BB	K	SB	CS	AVG/OBP/SLG	TAv	BABIP	BRR	FRAA	WARP
2012	ANA	MLB	28	594	57	32	3	8	67	29	115	14	6	.287/.325/.400	.263	.347	3.8	2B(143): 9.6, 1B(2): 0.0	3.4
2013	ANA	MLB	29	513	55	21	4	13	54	23	89	6	3	.297/.335/.439	.290	.340	-6.6	2B(118): -1.2, LF(1): 0.0	2.0
2014	ANA	MLB	30	674	85	33	5	7	75	48	110	14	5	.293/.347/.397	.278	.347	-2.2	2B(154): 4.1	2.9
2015	LAN	MLB	31	601	62	32	4	11	64	31	113	11	4	.278/.319/.407	.276	.325	-1.6	2B 0, LF -0	2.8

Breakout: 0%   Improve: 46%   Collapse: 3%   Attrition: 1%   MLB: 94%   Comparables: *Brandon Phillips, Aaron Hill, Ryne Sandberg*

Upon completion of the American League Division Series, daily Howie Kendrick trade rumors replaced the daily box score in Angels fans' routines; same as the year before, but louder. This time, the smoke really did indicate fire. On the surface, a trade made sense for the Angels: With a weak free-agent group, Kendrick was the best second baseman available, plus he's entering his walk year and is both eminently affordable to most teams ($9.5 million) and a financial burden to a club with an obstinate—and nonsensical—focus on staying under the luxury tax threshold.

Kendrick is coming off a season in which he failed to slug .400 and posted a career-worst 60 percent groundball rate, but his consistency—if not his explosiveness—made him an invaluable cleanup guy (a role in which he hit .320/.366/.513) when Josh Hamilton went MIA. The Dodgers are counting on one more vintage Howie Kendrick season to anchor, along with Jimmy Rollins, their remade middle infield: a .290/.340/.420 line with 14 steals (he's stolen exactly 14 in four of the last five seasons), 10 dingers, 30 doubles and above-average defense would suit them fine. It would suit anyone fine. PECOTA sees less, but that's the danger of being 31: PECOTA's a real killjoy for players that age.

Julian Leon C

Born: 1/24/96   Age: 19   Bats: R   Throws: R   Height: 5' 11"   Weight: 215

YEAR	TEAM	LVL	AGE	PA	R	2B	3B	HR	RBI	BB	K	SB	CS	AVG/OBP/SLG	TAv	BABIP	BRR	FRAA	WARP
2015	LAN	MLB	19	250	20	8	0	6	25	12	78	0	0	.200/.245/.313	.215	.268	-0.4	C -0	-0.4

Breakout: 0%   Improve: 0%   Collapse: 0%   Attrition: 0%   MLB: 0%   Comparables: *Brandon Snyder, Miguel Gonzalez, Travis Snider*

The Dodgers struck gold in Mexico in 2012, but it wasn't just because of Julio Urias. Leon was signed in April 2012 in a package deal with three other prospects (Victor Gonzalez, Lenix Osuna, William Soto) for about a million bucks. Leon's first season of pro ball could not have gone better, as he displayed everything the organization wanted to see out of him: good hitter, hit for power, walked and was solid behind the plate. The 19-year-old will have to prove his impressive offense output wasn't a product of the hitter-friendly Pioneer League environment. With the Dodgers having almost literally no catching depth in the minors, Leon might be the heir apparent to Yasmani Grandal.

Joc Pederson CF

Born: 4/21/92   Age: 23   Bats: L   Throws: L   Height: 6' 1"   Weight: 185

YEAR	TEAM	LVL	AGE	PA	R	2B	3B	HR	RBI	BB	K	SB	CS	AVG/OBP/SLG	TAv	BABIP	BRR	FRAA	WARP
2012	RCU	A+	20	499	96	26	4	18	70	51	81	26	14	.313/.396/.516	.329	.350	5.7	CF(76): -6.1, LF(33): 1.4	5.4
2013	CHT	AA	21	519	81	24	3	22	58	70	114	31	8	.278/.381/.497	.313	.327	3.9	CF(106): -0.3, LF(6): 0.5	5.3
2014	ABQ	AAA	22	553	106	17	4	33	78	100	149	30	13	.303/.435/.582	.325	.385	3.7	CF(99): -0.4, LF(12): -0.5	5.9
2014	LAN	MLB	22	38	1	0	0	0	0	9	11	0	0	.143/.351/.143	.210	.235	-0.4	CF(7): 0.0, RF(5): -0.0	0.0
2015	LAN	MLB	23	250	38	9	1	10	29	29	68	10	3	.244/.336/.433	.289	.302	0.4	CF -1, LF 0	1.4

Breakout: 2%   Improve: 24%   Collapse: 6%   Attrition: 17%   MLB: 64%   Comparables: *Brett Jackson, Michael Choice, Brandon Belt*

Pederson opened eyes in spring training when he hit three home runs in 38 at-bats, but his Triple-A destiny was written by the realities of the Dodgers' outfield depth chart. In Albuquerque, he posted historic numbers and was named Pacific Coast League MVP: He was the first 30/30 player in *80 years*. His strikeout rate was too high, but his overall skill set does not point to a likely flameout through excessive whiffage in the majors. That's especially true because he can play center field, where the offensive standards aren't anywhere near as high as in left, home to every lumbering dinosaur unlucky enough to be blocked at first base by some even more lumbering dinosaur.

Yasiel Puig RF

Born: 12/7/90   Age: 24   Bats: R   Throws: R   Height: 6' 3"   Weight: 235

YEAR	TEAM	LVL	AGE	PA	R	2B	3B	HR	RBI	BB	K	SB	CS	AVG/OBP/SLG	TAv	BABIP	BRR	FRAA	WARP
2012	RCU	A+	21	59	10	2	0	1	4	6	8	7	4	.327/.407/.423	.335	.372	-0.1	RF(8): -0.4	0.5
2013	CHT	AA	22	167	26	12	3	8	37	15	29	13	5	.313/.383/.599	.348	.339	1.0	RF(31): 0.9, CF(4): -0.2	2.1
2013	LAN	MLB	22	432	66	21	2	19	42	36	97	11	8	.319/.391/.534	.329	.383	0.6	RF(93): -4.2, CF(10): -0.5	4.0
2014	LAN	MLB	23	640	92	37	9	16	69	67	124	11	7	.296/.382/.480	.320	.356	3.5	RF(91): -2.7, CF(53): -1.5	5.8
2015	LAN	MLB	24	580	84	29	5	19	69	51	122	14	8	.289/.362/.476	.316	.342	1.6	RF -4, CF -2	4.0

Breakout: 3%   Improve: 61%   Collapse: 1%   Attrition: 3%   MLB: 97%   Comparables: *Justin Upton, Jason Heyward, Travis Buck*

Just two players with listed weights higher than Yasiel Puig's 235 pounds have ever appeared in more than 50 games in center field in a season: Marlon Byrd (245 pounds, eight different seasons) and Josh Hamilton (240, four seasons). (Baseball players and humans in general are getting bigger, so this is the place to note Baby Doll Jacobson, who managed the feat nine times from 1917 to 1926 while weighing in at 215; it would have been ten times but for his year of service in the Great War.) Puig doesn't *really* belong at the position, but he can handle it better than Andre Ethier and Matt Kemp, which, hey, that's why he was out there in the first place.

Puig followed up his star-making rookie season by essentially holding steady, trading some homers for doubles and triples and some singles for walks. Most importantly, he stayed healthy despite a playing style best described as "Animaniacs on crank." As he ages and his back starts barking at him for slamming into a fence one too many times, he might start to preserve himself a little better. But he might not, in which case you just have to hope the aforementioned 235 pounds, of which approximately 275 pounds is muscle, shields his tender innards. He also needs to stop showing up late because nothing pisses off Baseball Men like showing up late.

Jimmy Rollins SS

Born: 11/27/78   Age: 36   Bats: B   Throws: R   Height: 5' 8"   Weight: 180

YEAR	TEAM	LVL	AGE	PA	R	2B	3B	HR	RBI	BB	K	SB	CS	AVG/OBP/SLG	TAv	BABIP	BRR	FRAA	WARP
2012	PHI	MLB	33	699	102	33	5	23	68	62	96	30	5	.250/.316/.427	.269	.262	5.4	SS(156): -9.2	3.3
2013	PHI	MLB	34	666	65	36	2	6	39	59	93	22	6	.252/.318/.348	.241	.288	1.9	SS(153): -4.0	1.2
2014	PHI	MLB	35	609	78	22	4	17	55	64	100	28	6	.243/.323/.394	.275	.269	-0.8	SS(131): 9.2	4.3
2015	LAN	MLB	36	584	73	23	2	11	49	51	82	23	5	.240/.306/.355	.257	.262	1.2	SS -2	2.3

Breakout: 0%   Improve: 22%   Collapse: 4%   Attrition: 9%   MLB: 84%   Comparables: *Marco Scutaro, Mark Loretta, Barry Larkin*

There were parts of Jimmy Rollins' resurgence that were easy to see coming—most notably his mysteriously low HR/FB rate in 2013, which would have made sense in a world where the Phillies were playing 161 games in Petco Park, but not in this one. He jacked that back up to 9.6 percent (from 3.1 percent in 2013, against a career rate of 7.8 percent), and the found power gave him the fourth-best ISO among all shortstops. There were parts of his resurgence that weren't easy to see coming—and, even in retrospect, aren't that easy to see now, like the 13-run improvement in his defense. Hey, don't look at us: Baseball-Reference's metrics had him improving by *19* runs, and Fielding Bible voters moved him from [No Votes Received] to ninth among shortstops last year. He was a local icon, but he's expensive and this is his walk year, so consider his consenting to go to Los Angeles one final gift to the City of Brotherly Love.

Scott Schebler LF

Born: 10/6/90   Age: 24   Bats: L   Throws: R   Height: 6' 1"   Weight: 208

YEAR	TEAM	LVL	AGE	PA	R	2B	3B	HR	RBI	BB	K	SB	CS	AVG/OBP/SLG	TAv	BABIP	BRR	FRAA	WARP
2012	GRL	A	21	560	67	32	8	6	67	30	99	17	11	.260/.312/.388	.261	.310	1.1	LF(108): -8.2, RF(24): 0.8	1.0
2013	RCU	A+	22	534	95	29	13	27	91	35	140	16	5	.296/.360/.581	.321	.364	2.3	RF(76): -5.7, LF(50): -3.2	3.5
2014	CHT	AA	23	560	82	23	14	28	73	45	110	10	4	.280/.365/.556	.312	.308	0.8	LF(87): 1.2, RF(45): -2.5	4.5
2015	LAN	MLB	24	250	26	10	2	8	30	10	69	3	1	.228/.273/.399	.252	.283	0.2	LF -1, RF -1	0.1

Breakout: 0%   Improve: 14%   Collapse: 9%   Attrition: 15%   MLB: 35%   *Comparables: Eric Thames, Corey Dickerson, Kyle Parker*

The 2013 winner of the Dodgers' Branch Rickey Award (given for community service) proved his production in the California League wasn't a fluke. He went to the neutral Southern League and filled up the proverbial stat sheet. Schebler led that league in home runs (though only because Cubs prospect Kris Bryant got promoted), triples, total bases and, the most painful, hit-by-pitches. He's a corner outfielder, and if there's anything the Dodgers need, it's another outfielder. His future likely lies with another organization, but Schebler has done a lot to put his name on the prospect map. He'll either be a fourth outfielder on a first-division team or a starter on a second-division team.

Corey Seager   SS

Born: 4/27/94   Age: 21   Bats: L   Throws: R   Height: 6' 4"   Weight: 215

YEAR	TEAM	LVL	AGE	PA	R	2B	3B	HR	RBI	BB	K	SB	CS	AVG/OBP/SLG	TAv	BABIP	BRR	FRAA	WARP
2013	GRL	A	19	312	45	18	3	12	57	34	58	9	4	.309/.389/.529	.330	.353	-0.5	SS(74): -5.5	3.2
2013	RCU	A+	19	114	10	2	1	4	15	12	31	1	0	.160/.246/.320	.221	.179	0.2	SS(25): -4.1, 3B(1): -0.0	-0.6
2014	RCU	A+	20	365	61	34	2	18	70	30	76	5	1	.352/.411/.633	.365	.411	1.8	SS(77): 8.8	6.9
2014	CHT	AA	20	161	28	16	3	2	27	10	39	1	1	.345/.381/.534	.310	.450	1.4	SS(35): -2.2	1.6
2015	*LAN*	*MLB*	*21*	*250*	*25*	*12*	*1*	*7*	*30*	*13*	*69*	*1*	*0*	*.246/.287/.401*	*.259*	*.311*	*-0.3*	*SS -2, 3B -0*	*0.7*

Breakout: 4%   Improve: 14%   Collapse: 8%   Attrition: 11%   MLB: 31%   *Comparables: Xander Bogaerts, Reid Brignac, Joel Guzman*

In the Logan White era (2002 to not quite the present), the Dodgers have gone pitcher-heavy in the first round of the draft. A rare exception was Seager in 2012, which is looking like a brilliant move. The Dodgers' co-Minor League Player of the Year had success at both High-A and Double-A: He was named California League MVP despite a 38-game promotion to the Southern League. Barring anything unforeseen, he could be the first legitimate hitting prospect the Dodgers have developed in a long time. (Puig didn't need much in the way of development.) Despite the organization's insistence that he's a shortstop, he will need to move to third base at some point, though if he manages even 500 innings at short, he'll tie Cal Ripken and Andy Fox as the tallest such shortstops in MLB history.

Darnell Sweeney   2B

Born: 2/1/91   Age: 24   Bats: B   Throws: R   Height: 6' 1"   Weight: 180

YEAR	TEAM	LVL	AGE	PA	R	2B	3B	HR	RBI	BB	K	SB	CS	AVG/OBP/SLG	TAv	BABIP	BRR	FRAA	WARP
2012	GRL	A	21	229	34	8	4	5	23	24	41	17	4	.291/.372/.447	.290	.344	4.9	SS(49): -5.5	1.7
2013	RCU	A+	22	613	79	34	16	11	77	43	151	48	20	.275/.329/.455	.276	.355	4.7	SS(107): -10.9, 2B(29): 2.7	3.2
2014	CHT	AA	23	586	88	34	5	14	57	77	117	15	16	.288/.387/.463	.297	.350	3.2	2B(81): -1.1, SS(28): -4.1	3.6
2015	*LAN*	*MLB*	*24*	*250*	*29*	*10*	*2*	*4*	*20*	*18*	*68*	*7*	*4*	*.228/.286/.346*	*.238*	*.296*	*-0.1*	*SS -4, 2B 0*	*0.0*

Breakout: 2%   Improve: 6%   Collapse: 3%   Attrition: 13%   MLB: 18%   *Comparables: Ryan Flaherty, Kevin Melillo, Ryan Adams*

There's a negative connotation to "utility player," but there are valuable utility players on every team in baseball. Sweeney is on his way to becoming one. Drafted as a shortstop in 2012, he wasn't able to handle the position defensively. He started playing some second base last season, and that was his position for most of 2014. He dabbled in center field and could become the rare second baseman-center fielder; in other words, the next Skip Schumaker. But no matter how hard Sweeney works, he's unlikely to ever come close to being as good as Schumaker. Sweeney led the Southern League in walks, which would normally be good news for a speedster, but he was just 15-for-31 in stolen base attempts. He's always been a better runner once he's underway.

Justin Turner   INF

Born: 11/23/84   Age: 30   Bats: R   Throws: R   Height: 6' 0"   Weight: 210

YEAR	TEAM	LVL	AGE	PA	R	2B	3B	HR	RBI	BB	K	SB	CS	AVG/OBP/SLG	TAv	BABIP	BRR	FRAA	WARP
2012	NYN	MLB	27	185	20	13	1	2	19	9	24	1	1	.269/.319/.392	.274	.301	0.7	2B(14): -0.4, 1B(11): -1.2	0.6
2013	NYN	MLB	28	214	12	13	1	2	16	11	34	0	1	.280/.319/.385	.262	.327	0.3	3B(23): -1.1, SS(18): -0.8	0.4
2014	LAN	MLB	29	322	46	21	1	7	43	28	58	6	1	.340/.404/.493	.339	.404	1.0	3B(59): 2.1, SS(15): 0.7	4.0
2015	*LAN*	*MLB*	*30*	*286*	*28*	*17*	*1*	*4*	*29*	*19*	*44*	*3*	*1*	*.272/.329/.390*	*.277*	*.310*	*0.6*	*3B -1, SS -1*	*1.1*

Breakout: 0%   Improve: 33%   Collapse: 4%   Attrition: 7%   MLB: 85%   *Comparables: Brendan Harris, Martin Prado, Morgan Ensberg*

The Mets have done a lot of questionable things over the last few years (decades), but non-tendering Turner after 2013 takes the red velvet cake. The Dodgers signed him for a million bucks and it paid off by ... well, you can read the stats above. Really, take a minute. Turner filled in for Juan Uribe when the third baseman was injured, then, over the next three months (52 games, 31 starts), teamed with Scott Van Slyke to form the majors' best bench. He won't hit like 2014 again, wrote The Obvious Prognosticator, but that doesn't mean he's not a useful, valuable utilityman who hits more than many teams get from their middle-infield starters. And even if he decides to completely fall off the map with his bat, he'll still be the life of the clubhouse clinch party: Turner brought a mason jar of Blackberry Ole Smoky Tennessee Moonshine to the Dodgers' celebration after claiming the NL West crown in late September. If it sounds horrifying, that's because it is.

Juan Uribe   3B

Born: 3/22/79   Age: 36   Bats: R   Throws: R   Height: 6' 0"   Weight: 235

YEAR	TEAM	LVL	AGE	PA	R	2B	3B	HR	RBI	BB	K	SB	CS	AVG/OBP/SLG	TAv	BABIP	BRR	FRAA	WARP
2012	LAN	MLB	33	179	15	9	0	2	17	13	37	0	1	.191/.258/.284	.200	.234	1.8	3B(46): 2.5, SS(1): -0.1	-0.1
2013	LAN	MLB	34	426	47	22	2	12	50	30	81	5	0	.278/.331/.438	.279	.322	1.9	3B(123): 9.3, 1B(4): 0.1	3.9
2014	LAN	MLB	35	404	36	23	0	9	54	15	77	0	1	.311/.337/.440	.280	.368	0.4	3B(102): 7.4	3.7
2015	*LAN*	*MLB*	*36*	*387*	*39*	*18*	*1*	*9*	*41*	*21*	*78*	*2*	*1*	*.244/.289/.375*	*.253*	*.283*	*1.3*	*3B 8, 1B 0*	*1.7*

Breakout: 0%   Improve: 27%   Collapse: 10%   Attrition: 21%   MLB: 76%   *Comparables: Doug Decinces, Eric Chavez, Johnny Bench*

You'll notice a mini-theme running through this book, which is that we can be really dumb sometimes. So here's what we said in the 2013 version about Juan Uribe: "The bet here is that the Dodgers cut bait by Opening Day." Nearly 8 WARP over two seasons later, here's what we have to say about that: ooooooops. His swing isn't picturesque and neither is his body, but after the rough (horrible, terrible, awful) first two years with the Dodgers that prompted the comment above, Uribe is now one of the most valuable members of the team. He hits plenty for third base, particularly given his consistently above-average defense, and in return for the wins he puts on the board, the Dodgers will pay him a whopping $6.5 million this season.

Scott Van Slyke   OF

Born: 7/24/86   Age: 28   Bats: R   Throws: R   Height: 6' 5"   Weight: 220

YEAR	TEAM	LVL	AGE	PA	R	2B	3B	HR	RBI	BB	K	SB	CS	AVG/OBP/SLG	TAv	BABIP	BRR	FRAA	WARP
2012	ABQ	AAA	25	411	68	34	1	18	67	46	64	5	3	.327/.404/.578	.312	.354	-1.2	RF(43): -1.7, 1B(39): -1.4	2.3
2012	LAN	MLB	25	57	4	2	0	2	7	2	14	1	0	.167/.196/.315	.188	.184	0.9	RF(12): 0.5, LF(11): 0.1	-0.2
2013	ABQ	AAA	26	263	55	17	2	12	48	50	61	8	2	.348/.479/.627	.338	.437	1.0	1B(51): 2.2, LF(8): 0.1	3.1
2013	LAN	MLB	26	152	13	8	0	7	19	20	37	1	1	.240/.342/.465	.285	.276	-1.0	LF(30): 0.4, RF(13): 0.3	0.6
2014	LAN	MLB	27	246	32	13	1	11	29	28	71	4	2	.297/.386/.524	.330	.394	-0.1	LF(32): 0.9, CF(21): 0.1	2.7
2015	LAN	MLB	28	250	32	12	0	10	34	28	63	3	1	.256/.342/.449	.298	.311	0.0	LF 1, 1B 0	1.6

Breakout: 3%   Improve: 38%   Collapse: 13%   Attrition: 17%   MLB: 80%   Comparables: Mike Carp, Josh Willingham, Casper Wells

Van Slyke is probably most famous for his 2013 NLCS Game Six post-anthem standoff with Joe Kelly, but his play on the field in 2014 opened some eyes. Not only did his playing time increase, so did his production. While he made his living mashing lefties (.317/.415/.630), he hit righties well enough to draw some starts against them (.279/.353/.413). With Carl Crawford and Andre Ethier on the roster, there were plenty of at-bats against left-handed pitchers to go around. The most comical part about Van Slyke's season was Don Mattingly starting him in center field for 17 games when the Dodgers didn't have anyone else. Some see a Jayson Werth-like player if given the opportunity, and that might be true, but for now, he'll have to settle for being Scott Van Slyke, Destroyer of Lefties.

Alex Verdugo   CF

Born: 5/15/96   Age: 19   Bats: L   Throws: L   Height: 6' 0"   Weight: 200

YEAR	TEAM	LVL	AGE	PA	R	2B	3B	HR	RBI	BB	K	SB	CS	AVG/OBP/SLG	TAv	BABIP	BRR	FRAA	WARP
2015	LAN	MLB	19	250	18	9	1	2	20	8	68	2	0	.203/.234/.278	.198	.270	0.0	CF -1, LF 0	-1.0

Breakout: 0%   Improve: 0%   Collapse: 0%   Attrition: 0%   MLB: 0%   Comparables: Oscar Taveras, Joe Benson, Che-Hsuan Lin

Most teams liked Verdugo as a pitcher out of high school, but the Dodgers liked him as a hitter, partly because Verdugo himself wanted to be a hitter. Based on his debut season, that just may have been the right move: Verdugo hit .353/.421/.511 across two levels. What was most impressive is the fact he walked more than he struck out. The last prominent Dodgers draftee to do that was James Loney. Verdugo also played a competent center field. Logan White put a Joc Pederson comparison on him shortly after the draft and so far, that looks quite apt. A better determination will be made once he starts facing advanced competition, possibly as soon as this year.

Pitchers

Chris Anderson   RHP

Born: 7/29/92   Age: 22   Bats: R   Throws: R   Height: 6'4"   Weight: 215

YEAR	TEAM	LVL	AGE	W	L	SV	G	GS	IP	H	HR	BB	K	BB/9	K/9	GB%	BABIP	WHIP	ERA	FIP	FRA	WARP
2013	GRL	A	20	3	0	0	12	12	46	32	0	24	50	4.7	9.8	40%	.288	1.22	1.96	2.79	3.15	1.2
2014	RCU	A+	21	7	7	0	27	25	134¹	147	11	63	146	4.2	9.8	42%	.366	1.56	4.62	4.26	5.02	1.7
2015	LAN	MLB	22	6	8	0	23	23	109	107	11	51	90	4.2	7.5	41%	.323	1.45	4.60	4.58	5.00	-0.4

Breakout: 0%   Improve: 0%   Collapse: 0%   Attrition: 0%   MLB: 0%   Comparables: Jeurys Familia, Anthony Ranaudo, Dan Cortes

The big right-hander definitely struggled with command in his first full season of professional ball, but he also showed flashes of the potential that made him a first-round draft pick in 2013. With a fastball that sits in the low to mid-90s and touches the high 90s, a slider that flashes plus at times and a potentially average changeup, Anderson has all the makings of a no. 3 starter. The Dodgers' player development department tinkered with his delivery and mechanics midway through the season, and it seemed to help: He finished his season with three consecutive games of 10 or more strikeouts; he also walked only seven batters in his final six starts. Correlation/causation and all that, so **DON'T** anoint him but **DO** keep an eye out.

Pedro Baez   RHP

Born: 3/11/88   Age: 27   Bats: R   Throws: R   Height: 6'2"   Weight: 230

YEAR	TEAM	LVL	AGE	W	L	SV	G	GS	IP	H	HR	BB	K	BB/9	K/9	GB%	BABIP	WHIP	ERA	FIP	FRA	WARP
2013	RCU	A+	25	2	2	2	32	0	34²	41	3	15	32	3.9	8.3	39%	.349	1.62	3.63	4.69	4.58	0.5
2013	CHT	AA	25	1	1	0	16	0	23¹	26	3	8	23	3.1	8.9	44%	.338	1.46	4.24	3.64	4.25	0.4
2014	CHT	AA	26	2	1	6	17	0	19¹	15	0	9	18	4.2	8.4	35%	.278	1.24	2.79	2.88	2.39	0.6
2014	ABQ	AAA	26	0	0	6	23	0	22²	27	4	4	20	1.6	7.9	46%	.343	1.37	4.76	5.02	5.66	0.1
2014	LAN	MLB	26	0	0	0	20	0	24	16	3	5	18	1.9	6.8	38%	.197	0.88	2.62	3.85	3.92	0.1
2015	LAN	MLB	27	3	1	0	50	0	57²	55	6	18	47	2.8	7.3	41%	.306	1.26	4.05	4.11	4.40	0.0

Breakout: 19%   Improve: 27%   Collapse: 12%   Attrition: 24%   MLB: 45%   Comparables: Caleb Thielbar, Warner Madrigal, Luis Perdomo

It took a bit more than a year for Baez to convert from minor-league third baseman to major-league pitcher, which is impressive even if the end result is not. Mattingly fell in love with Baez's mid-90s fastball, but it's too straight to avoid hard contact, and he has no effective secondary pitch to cover it. Case in point: After Clayton Kershaw's Game One meltdown in the NLDS, Baez was brought in. He threw six fastballs in a row to Randal Grichuk and issued a walk; then a first-pitch fastball to Matt Holliday, who homered. Amusingly for a former infielder, he has an .885 fielding percentage as a pitcher.

Josh Beckett   RHP

Born: 5/15/80   Age: 35   Bats: R   Throws: R   Height: 6'5"   Weight: 230

YEAR	TEAM	LVL	AGE	W	L	SV	G	GS	IP	H	HR	BB	K	BB/9	K/9	GB%	BABIP	WHIP	ERA	FIP	FRA	WARP
2012	BOS	MLB	32	5	11	0	21	21	127¹	131	16	38	94	2.7	6.6	42%	.292	1.33	5.23	4.22	5.38	0.5
2012	LAN	MLB	32	2	3	0	7	7	43	43	5	14	38	2.9	8.0	51%	.302	1.33	2.93	3.86	3.72	0.3
2013	LAN	MLB	33	0	5	0	8	8	43¹	50	8	15	41	3.1	8.5	42%	.323	1.50	5.19	4.64	4.82	0.1
2014	LAN	MLB	34	6	6	0	20	20	115²	96	17	39	107	3.0	8.3	44%	.258	1.17	2.88	4.30	4.38	0.3
2015	LAN	MLB	35	5	5	0	15	15	89	80	11	24	80	2.5	8.1	43%	.296	1.17	3.66	4.06	3.98	0.6

Breakout: 13%   Improve: 35%   Collapse: 16%   Attrition: 11%   MLB: 83%   Comparables: Erik Bedard, Johan Santana, John Lackey

Beckett really threw a wrench into the whole "every other year he's good" theory by struggling in 2013 with his performance and health, then getting off to a fast start in 2014, so fast that at one time he was the Dodgers' second- or third-best active starting pitcher. His season reached its pinnacle on May 25th, when he threw a no-hitter in Philadelphia. Beckett was a legitimate contender for the All-Star team, but he was ultimately passed over.

After 11 more starts, a hip injury that he tried to pitch through (what could possibly go wrong?) ended his season and, ultimately, his career. "I just don't see me going through that rehab and coming back to pitch at this point in my life," Beckett said, and who can blame him? He's younger than you might have guessed, a product of an age-21 debut, but he's got 345 big-league starts (counting the playoffs) under his belt and nearly that many stints on the disabled list. With nine figures in career earnings, an aeronautics engineer wife, a couple of rugrats and a 7,000-acre ranch in Texas, what's the point of doing the whole post-rehab audition thing just to get some second-tier contender to consider signing you? You work until you can't work anymore, and then you kick your feet up until you die. Here's to a long, happy retirement.

Or a really fun comeback attempt four years from now.

Chad Billingsley RHP

Born: 7/29/84   Age: 30   Bats: R   Throws: R   Height: 6'1"   Weight: 240

YEAR	TEAM	LVL	AGE	W	L	SV	G	GS	IP	H	HR	BB	K	BB/9	K/9	GB%	BABIP	WHIP	ERA	FIP	FRA	WARP
2012	LAN	MLB	27	10	9	0	25	25	149²	148	11	45	128	2.7	7.7	47%	.308	1.29	3.55	3.38	3.80	2.4
2013	LAN	MLB	28	1	0	0	2	2	12	12	1	5	6	3.8	4.5	45%	.297	1.42	3.00	4.35	5.94	-0.2
2015	LAN	MLB	30	2	2	0	7	7	37¹	35	3	12	31	2.9	7.5	47%	.315	1.27	3.93	3.75	4.27	0.1

Breakout: 14%   Improve: 38%   Collapse: 28%   Attrition: 14%   MLB: 88%   *Comparables: Jason Jennings, Kip Wells, Ervin Santana*

Another case of a pitcher trying to play through an injury, Billingsley had his 2013 season cut short after two starts because he needed Tommy John surgery. He tried to rehab the injury prior to the season, and did so unsuccessfully. He was ahead of schedule—according to some—during spring training in 2014, but he suffered a setback and never appeared in a game. Then he made two rehab appearances before another setback, this time a partially torn flexor tendon in his right elbow. Two years, two surgeries, 12 innings pitched. Not exactly what he or the Dodgers had in mind. Billingsley's inability to pitch led to the Dodgers *needing* to acquire Roberto Hernandez in August, a need that opens a super-secret hidden dimension on Maslow's hierarchy.

Zachary Bird RHP

Born: 7/14/94   Age: 20   Bats: R   Throws: R   Height: 6'4"   Weight: 205

YEAR	TEAM	LVL	AGE	W	L	SV	G	GS	IP	H	HR	BB	K	BB/9	K/9	GB%	BABIP	WHIP	ERA	FIP	FRA	WARP
2013	GRL	A	18	2	5	0	19	11	60	56	5	45	50	6.8	7.5	48%	.290	1.68	5.10	5.11	5.94	0.1
2014	GRL	A	19	6	17	0	26	24	118²	118	9	55	110	4.2	8.3	43%	.316	1.46	4.25	4.13	4.57	0.6
2015	LAN	MLB	20	5	9	0	23	23	101²	108	13	59	66	5.3	5.8	45%	.314	1.65	5.65	5.66	6.14	-1.6

Breakout: 0%   Improve: 0%   Collapse: 0%   Attrition: 0%   MLB: 0%   *Comparables: Jeurys Familia, T.J. House, Edwin Escobar*

An unheralded ninth-round pick in 2012, Bird has drawn easy (some would say lazy) (some would say worse) comparisons to former Dodgers pitching prospects Edwin Jackson and James McDonald. If Bird ever gets to that level, it'd be a win. Because of his over-the-top delivery, he struggles to find the strike zone at times. Still, his peripherals weren't 17-loss bad, so take Bird as another example of why pitcher wins (and, conversely and equally, losses) don't mean a whole lot. He has a starter's repertoire and frame, but he hasn't shown the ability that turned him from forgettable ninth-rounder to sleeper prospect. Advancing to the California League might not do him any favors.

Michael Bolsinger RHP

Born: 1/29/88   Age: 27   Bats: R   Throws: R   Height: 6'2"   Weight: 210

YEAR	TEAM	LVL	AGE	W	L	SV	G	GS	IP	H	HR	BB	K	BB/9	K/9	GB%	BABIP	WHIP	ERA	FIP	FRA	WARP
2012	VIS	A+	24	3	2	0	7	7	38	31	1	13	49	3.1	11.6	50%	.312	1.16	2.37	2.68	3.03	1.4
2012	MOB	AA	24	4	3	0	15	15	77²	82	5	38	64	4.4	7.4	45%	.341	1.55	3.82	3.88	4.86	0.5
2013	MOB	AA	25	4	0	0	9	6	43	35	0	15	31	3.1	6.5	57%	.271	1.16	2.51	2.59	3.69	0.5
2013	RNO	AAA	25	7	7	0	17	17	101	116	12	39	97	3.5	8.6	53%	.348	1.53	4.72	4.47	5.15	1.0
2014	RNO	AAA	26	8	3	0	17	16	91²	92	6	32	88	3.1	8.6	56%	.331	1.35	3.93	3.78	4.83	1.6
2014	ARI	MLB	26	1	6	0	10	9	52¹	66	7	17	48	2.9	8.3	54%	.355	1.59	5.50	3.98	4.62	0.0
2015	LAN	MLB	27	7	8	0	23	23	127²	124	13	41	107	2.9	7.5	51%	.317	1.29	4.11	4.02	4.46	0.1

Breakout: 36%   Improve: 43%   Collapse: 10%   Attrition: 28%   MLB: 59%   *Comparables: Dan Meyer, Brad Mills, Collin McHugh*

A three-time draftee, Bolsinger made his big-league debut in 2014. The right-hander looks the part of a starting pitcher with a sturdy frame, a three-pitch medley and control. However, looks can be deceiving, and the Texas native has some hurdles to overcome, most notably that not every strike he throws is quality. The upper-80s fastball and cutter often take the path of most resistance to the catcher's glove, passing through what a PITCHf/x aficionado might know as "Zone 12" and what a Hollywood Squares devotee might call "The Paul Lynde." A loopy, upper-70s bender is by far his best pitch, a major-league-quality offering that he throws for strikes or chases. If he picks up command over one or both of the hard pitches, the Dodgers have the makings of a back-end starter. That's worth the risk of sending a little cash to Arizona to grab him.

Jharel Cotton RHP

Born: 1/19/92   Age: 23   Bats: R   Throws: R   Height: 5'11"   Weight: 195

YEAR	TEAM	LVL	AGE	W	L	SV	G	GS	IP	H	HR	BB	K	BB/9	K/9	GB%	BABIP	WHIP	ERA	FIP	FRA	WARP
2013	GRL	A	21	2	5	0	11	9	58¹	42	4	17	58	2.6	8.9	42%	.253	1.01	3.55	3.17	4.05	0.9
2013	CHT	AA	21	0	2	0	8	0	10	15	0	3	11	2.7	9.9	41%	.441	1.80	8.10	1.61	2.91	0.2
2014	RCU	A+	22	6	10	0	25	20	126²	113	18	34	138	2.4	9.8	45%	.290	1.16	4.05	4.24	5.20	1.2
2015	LAN	MLB	23	5	6	0	24	15	102²	98	12	35	86	3.0	7.5	42%	.306	1.29	4.13	4.31	4.49	0.0

Breakout: 0%   Improve: 0%   Collapse: 0%   Attrition: 0%   MLB: 0%   *Comparables: Sean Nolin, Nick Tropeano, Dan Straily*

Coming into 2014, Cotton was an afterthought for most prospectors. He struggled with performance and health in 2013, so it was easy to overlook him. Then he got off to a horrific start in 2014 (7.07 ERA in his first 42 innings), and it looked like a lost season for the Virgin Islands native. But former Rancho Cucamonga pitching coach Matt Herges and his staff noticed Cotton might have been tipping his pitches. After they corrected that, he went on a hot streak, posting a Bob Gibson-esque 1.11 ERA in his final 48 2/3 innings and establishing himself as a legitimate prospect. He has four pitches, but lives off his fastball-changeup combination, so he'll need to improve his bendy stuff if he wishes to remain a starter.

Jose De Leon   RHP

Born: 8/7/92   Age: 22   Bats: R   Throws: R   Height: 6'2"   Weight: 185

YEAR	TEAM	LVL	AGE	W	L	SV	G	GS	IP	H	HR	BB	K	BB/9	K/9	GB%	BABIP	WHIP	ERA	FIP	FRA	WARP
2014	GRL	A	21	2	0	0	4	4	22²	14	1	2	42	0.8	16.7	31%	.317	0.71	1.19	0.62	1.12	1.2
2015	LAN	MLB	22	3	4	0	13	13	62²	59	7	29	60	4.2	8.6	44%	.321	1.41	4.41	4.43	4.80	-0.1

Breakout: 0%   Improve: 0%   Collapse: 0%   Attrition: 0%   MLB: 0%   Comparables: *Michael Stutes, Tony Cingrani, Clay Buchholz*

No relation to Ponce, probably, though keep an eye on his aging curve, De Leon opened eyes in the Pioneer League by striking out 12 in his second start, and then pitched better after a promotion to Great Lakes. He uses a low-90s fastball that tops out at 96, a slider and a changeup, the latter being the pitch he likes to throw most. De Leon is too young to be called the next great Dodgers pitcher, but the bat-missing looks legit and, in any event, as a 24th-round pick, he'll be considered a wild success the day he makes his big-league debut.

Scott Elbert   LHP

Born: 8/13/85   Age: 29   Bats: L   Throws: L   Height: 6'2"   Weight: 225

YEAR	TEAM	LVL	AGE	W	L	SV	G	GS	IP	H	HR	BB	K	BB/9	K/9	GB%	BABIP	WHIP	ERA	FIP	FRA	WARP
2012	LAN	MLB	26	1	1	0	43	0	32²	27	3	13	29	3.6	8.0	37%	.276	1.22	2.20	3.84	4.42	0.0
2014	ABQ	AAA	28	0	2	0	18	0	14²	17	2	15	14	4.3	9.2	42%	.366	1.64	4.91	5.06	6.25	0.1
2014	LAN	MLB	28	1	0	0	7	0	4¹	4	0	1	2	2.1	4.2	47%	.267	1.15	2.08	2.87	2.83	0.0
2015	LAN	MLB	29	2	1	1	48	0	37¹	32	3	16	36	3.8	8.8	43%	.304	1.27	3.57	3.81	3.88	0.3

Breakout: 16%   Improve: 38%   Collapse: 18%   Attrition: 19%   MLB: 68%   Comparables: *Esmerling Vasquez, Tom Wilhelmsen, Chris Resop*

The Dodgers' first pick of the 2004 draft (six picks ahead of Phil Hughes; 16 picks behind Matt Bush) has had scar tissue surgeries in his elbow and shoulder, surgery on a damaged area of cartilage in his elbow and the Tommy John procedure. Also an appendectomy because, what the hell, gotta fill up that punch card if you're ever going to get that free cup of coffee, right? He somehow made the Dodgers' postseason roster last year and boy did that ever pay off. For the Cardinals, that is, since he gave up Kolten Wong's Game Three–winning homer. After all this, he's still just 29, so there's still time for him to luck into a run of health and make a little money before the game spits him out completely.

Carlos Frias   RHP

Born: 11/13/89   Age: 25   Bats: R   Throws: R   Height: 6'4"   Weight: 170

YEAR	TEAM	LVL	AGE	W	L	SV	G	GS	IP	H	HR	BB	K	BB/9	K/9	GB%	BABIP	WHIP	ERA	FIP	FRA	WARP
2013	GRL	A	23	5	3	0	12	12	68¹	66	3	23	49	3.0	6.5	48%	.304	1.30	2.63	3.66	4.65	0.5
2013	RCU	A+	23	2	3	0	8	8	46	52	4	11	48	2.2	9.4	47%	.353	1.37	4.11	3.60	3.75	1.2
2013	CHT	AA	23	1	1	0	8	2	16	15	2	7	8	3.9	4.5	55%	.265	1.38	3.94	5.23	7.45	-0.4
2014	CHT	AA	24	2	1	0	5	5	32	34	2	9	14	2.5	3.9	55%	.294	1.34	3.38	4.16	5.78	0.0
2014	ABQ	AAA	24	8	4	0	16	15	91²	114	4	21	65	2.1	6.4	50%	.358	1.47	5.01	3.60	4.48	1.8
2014	LAN	MLB	24	1	1	0	15	2	32¹	33	4	7	29	1.9	8.1	52%	.299	1.24	6.12	3.57	4.47	0.1
2015	LAN	MLB	25	7	8	0	32	21	132²	138	13	43	85	2.9	5.8	47%	.315	1.37	4.47	4.42	4.86	-0.5

Breakout: 23%   Improve: 37%   Collapse: 10%   Attrition: 34%   MLB: 54%   Comparables: *Josh Hall, Alfredo Figaro, Jeff Manship*

When the Dodgers added Frias to the 25-man roster in August, a great "who?" arose in Los Angeles. He signed out of the Dominican Republic in 2007 and made his debut after seven years in the minors. Armed with a low-to-mid-90s fastball, a slider and a changeup, Frias was involved in a couple of memorable games for the Dodgers. He made his first career start against Washington on September 3rd, tossing six scoreless frames, only to see the Dodgers lose in 14 as the bullpen imploded on multiple occasions. Later, Frias drew a start in Colorado and recorded just two outs while allowing 10 hits and eight runs. The Dodgers lost 16-2. Despite that, he has the talent to contribute out of the bullpen.

Zack Greinke   RHP

Born: 10/21/83   Age: 31   Bats: R   Throws: R   Height: 6'2"   Weight: 195

YEAR	TEAM	LVL	AGE	W	L	SV	G	GS	IP	H	HR	BB	K	BB/9	K/9	GB%	BABIP	WHIP	ERA	FIP	FRA	WARP
2012	ANA	MLB	28	6	2	0	13	13	89¹	80	11	26	78	2.6	7.9	45%	.279	1.19	3.53	3.84	4.42	0.7
2012	MIL	MLB	28	9	3	0	21	21	123	120	7	28	122	2.0	8.9	55%	.326	1.20	3.44	2.58	3.17	3.7
2013	LAN	MLB	29	15	4	0	28	28	177²	152	13	46	148	2.3	7.5	48%	.276	1.11	2.63	3.20	3.81	3.6
2014	LAN	MLB	30	17	8	0	32	32	202¹	190	19	43	207	1.9	9.2	50%	.311	1.15	2.71	2.94	3.27	4.7
2015	LAN	MLB	31	11	9	0	27	27	169¹	148	15	37	162	2.0	8.6	48%	.309	1.09	3.14	3.26	3.41	2.3

Breakout: 14%   Improve: 49%   Collapse: 16%   Attrition: 11%   MLB: 94%   Comparables: *John Lackey, Scott Baker, Jered Weaver*

Zack Greinke is good at pitching. Zack Greinke has been healthy, having only been placed on the DL for a mood disorder, a rib fractured playing basketball and a clavicle broken by a charging Carlos Quentin. Zack Greinke is still only 31. Yada yada yada. He's great. He's super. Let's get to the quotes:

On pitching at home: "Sometimes, in the hotels they have bad coffee." On the playoffs (while with Milwaukee): "It'll be tough just to get there, so if you're not first place, you've got to win the Wild Card. That's probably tough, too. I don't have much playoff experience, so I don't know how it all works." On Chipotle: "They changed their guacamole from $1.50 to $1.80. I mean, $1.50 is already pretty darn high. So they changed it to $1.80, and I'll never again get guacamole." On Brad Pitt playing him in a movie: "No, I'm too boring for him." On baseball: "I don't want to name names, but there were guys I played with that were so stupid that they're really good, because their mind never gets in the way." On the name of his barber: "I wish I knew." On telling his wife how happy he was to get traded to Milwaukee: "I was happy when we got married, too."

Chris Hatcher   RHP

Born: 1/12/85   Age: 30   Bats: B   Throws: R   Height: 6'1"   Weight: 205

YEAR	TEAM	LVL	AGE	W	L	SV	G	GS	IP	H	HR	BB	K	BB/9	K/9	GB%	BABIP	WHIP	ERA	FIP	FRA	WARP
2012	NWO	AAA	27	1	0	11	37	0	47	33	1	15	45	2.9	8.6	33%	.256	1.02	0.77	3.11	2.35	1.6
2012	MIA	MLB	27	0	0	0	11	0	14²	17	3	6	10	3.7	6.1	37%	.304	1.57	4.30	5.86	6.54	-0.2
2013	NWO	AAA	28	4	3	33	60	0	67¹	69	8	28	65	3.7	8.7	46%	.314	1.44	3.61	4.48	3.93	1.0
2013	MIA	MLB	28	0	1	0	7	0	8²	13	1	4	7	4.2	7.3	39%	.375	1.96	12.46	4.29	4.71	0.0
2014	NWO	AAA	29	1	2	5	15	0	22¹	16	2	6	25	2.4	10.1	48%	.259	0.99	2.01	3.43	3.16	0.6
2014	MIA	MLB	29	0	3	0	52	0	56	55	4	12	60	1.9	9.6	49%	.327	1.20	3.38	2.53	3.30	0.7
2015	LAN	MLB	30	3	1	1	60	0	69¹	61	7	21	67	2.7	8.7	43%	.306	1.18	3.39	3.65	3.68	0.6

Breakout: 8%	Improve: 20%	Collapse: 10%	Attrition: 17%	MLB: 40%	Comparables: Shawn Camp, Jonathan Albaladejo, Matt Daley

If you were wondering how many years it takes to complete a conversion from minor-league catcher to major-league pitcher, it appears to be about four. That's how long it has taken Hatcher to harness the juice in his arm, limit his walks and develop a slider that won't embarrass him. Control is a key word here, not only because his breakout 2014 was dependent on a drastic slash in his walk rate (down from around 9 percent in the minors to about 5 percent in Miami), but also because in April he broke bullpen-mate Sam Dyson's jaw in a Nashville bar and was suspended by the organization for five games.

Roberto Hernandez   RHP

Born: 8/30/80   Age: 34   Bats: R   Throws: R   Height: 6'4"   Weight: 230

YEAR	TEAM	LVL	AGE	W	L	SV	G	GS	IP	H	HR	BB	K	BB/9	K/9	GB%	BABIP	WHIP	ERA	FIP	FRA	WARP
2012	LKC	A	31	1	1	0	2	2	12¹	12	5	1	13	0.7	9.5	54%	.233	1.05	3.65	6.76	7.75	-0.3
2012	COH	AAA	31	1	0	0	2	2	12	13	0	3	7	2.2	5.2	56%	.317	1.33	4.50	2.74	4.12	0.3
2012	CLE	MLB	31	0	3	0	3	3	14¹	17	4	3	2	1.9	1.3	50%	.250	1.40	7.53	7.23	7.04	-0.4
2013	TBA	MLB	32	6	13	1	32	24	151	164	24	38	113	2.3	6.7	56%	.308	1.34	4.89	4.66	5.34	-1.4
2014	LAN	MLB	33	2	3	0	9	9	43²	48	8	18	30	3.7	6.2	45%	.292	1.51	4.74	5.48	6.25	-0.6
2014	PHI	MLB	33	6	8	0	23	20	121	108	11	55	75	4.1	5.6	53%	.256	1.35	3.87	4.58	4.55	0.0
2015	LAN	MLB	34	8	9	0	24	24	140	140	17	42	95	2.7	6.1	53%	.301	1.29	4.34	4.65	4.71	-0.3

Breakout: 14%	Improve: 41%	Collapse: 14%	Attrition: 10%	MLB: 77%	Comparables: Jason Marquis, Jason Johnson, Jake Westbrook

A lot is made of who this guy used to be, but we can't help but mention it: He used to be really good! Back when he was a Cy Young candidate for the Indians, he threw his sinker 95, but 2014 marked a new low, at 91. His changeup, somehow, has held most of its velocity, with the result being a substandard 7 mph difference between the heat and the off-speed. In late July he managed to put together two excellent starts—15 innings and two earned runs, though only four batters K'd—and the Dodgers jumped, giving up two C+ prospects to add him in early August. The surface improvements he showed with Philadelphia disappeared, and for the postseason the Dodgers made sure he did, too.

Grant Holmes   RHP

Born: 3/22/96   Age: 19   Bats: L   Throws: R   Height: 6'1"   Weight: 215

YEAR	TEAM	LVL	AGE	W	L	SV	G	GS	IP	H	HR	BB	K	BB/9	K/9	GB%	BABIP	WHIP	ERA	FIP	FRA	WARP
2015	LAN	MLB	19	2	3	0	7	7	34²	37	4	19	23	4.9	5.9	51%	.316	1.61	5.50	5.32	5.97	-0.5

Breakout: 0%	Improve: 0%	Collapse: 0%	Attrition: 0%	MLB: 0%	Comparables: Edwin Escobar, Jonathan Pettibone, Jenrry Mejia

When Holmes inexplicably fell to no. 22 in the 2014 draft, popping him was a no-brainer for the Dodgers. He was a projected top-12 pick and didn't disappoint in the Arizona League before a late-season promotion. His ERA at Ogden doesn't tell the full story, as it was marred by one bad start. In any case, the components are what have the Dodgers excited, not the minor-league runs allowed, as he showed great feel for pitching and the stuff to make him a no. 2 or 3 starter. Holmes featured a low-to-mid-90s fastball, a power curve, a slider and a changeup. As a stocky kid, he reminds a lot of evaluators of Chad Billingsley.

J.P. Howell   LHP

Born: 4/25/83   Age: 32   Bats: L   Throws: L   Height: 6'0"   Weight: 185

YEAR	TEAM	LVL	AGE	W	L	SV	G	GS	IP	H	HR	BB	K	BB/9	K/9	GB%	BABIP	WHIP	ERA	FIP	FRA	WARP
2012	TBA	MLB	29	1	0	0	55	0	50¹	39	7	22	42	3.9	7.5	53%	.250	1.21	3.04	4.74	5.13	-0.1
2013	LAN	MLB	30	4	1	0	67	0	62	42	2	23	54	3.3	7.8	59%	.241	1.05	2.03	2.86	2.76	1.1
2014	LAN	MLB	31	3	3	0	68	0	49	31	2	25	48	4.6	8.8	59%	.236	1.14	2.39	3.27	3.36	0.4
2015	LAN	MLB	32	3	1	0	55	0	45¹	36	4	18	43	3.6	8.5	52%	.288	1.20	3.35	3.91	3.64	0.4

Breakout: 26%	Improve: 48%	Collapse: 22%	Attrition: 10%	MLB: 89%	Comparables: Pedro Feliciano, Santiago Casilla, Jason Frasor

Howell was such a nice surprise for the Dodgers in 2013 that they took the normally ill-advised step of signing a 30-plus sub-elite reliever to a two-year contract before 2014. So far, though, it's worked out. Howell was masterful through the season's first five months, posting a 1.24 ERA through the end of August and striking out nearly a batter per inning. Things fell apart in September, perhaps due to overwork as the team's primary lefty through the first five months. In Dodgerland, that's known as a case of Paco Rodriguezitis. It's a predictable affliction, but still sad every time it happens.

Kenley Jansen   RHP

Born: 9/30/87   Age: 27   Bats: B   Throws: R   Height: 6'5"   Weight: 265

YEAR	TEAM	LVL	AGE	W	L	SV	G	GS	IP	H	HR	BB	K	BB/9	K/9	GB%	BABIP	WHIP	ERA	FIP	FRA	WARP
2012	LAN	MLB	24	5	3	25	65	0	65	33	6	22	99	3.0	13.7	33%	.221	0.85	2.35	2.44	2.78	1.3
2013	LAN	MLB	25	4	3	28	75	0	76²	48	6	18	111	2.1	13.0	39%	.273	0.86	1.88	1.96	2.46	1.8
2014	LAN	MLB	26	2	3	44	68	0	65¹	55	5	19	101	2.6	13.9	36%	.350	1.13	2.76	1.88	2.14	1.5
2015	LAN	MLB	27	4	2	31	63	0	64	39	4	20	98	2.7	13.7	36%	.305	0.91	1.68	2.00	1.82	2.1

Breakout: 27%	Improve: 48%	Collapse: 34%	Attrition: 14%	MLB: 95%	Comparables: Francisco Rodriguez, Jonathan Broxton, Carlos Marmol

This is the stupidest thing to say, but Jansen's dominance as a closer practically invites stupid comparisons, in particular his dominance as a closer with one incredible pitch, in particular in particular because that pitch is a cutter, so we're just going to go ahead and say it: Through his age-26 season, Kenley Jansen has 106 saves; through *his* age-26 season, Mariano Rivera had five. (Warned you that it was stupid.) Anyway, it's weird that Jansen has never received even a single Cy Young vote, right? Henderson Alvarez, Francisco Liriano and Kyle Lohse have received votes in the last three years, though so have Aroldis Chapman and Craig Kimbrel, which illustrates the problem: However good Jansen is, he's "only" the third-best closer in the National League. Baseball nerd ideology says the Dodgers should let him walk to someone dumb enough to pay him after 2016 and home-grow some new closer in the meantime, but baseball nerds don't have a 10-figure local media deal.

Clayton Kershaw   LHP

Born: 3/19/88   Age: 27   Bats: L   Throws: L   Height: 6'3"   Weight: 225

YEAR	TEAM	LVL	AGE	W	L	SV	G	GS	IP	H	HR	BB	K	BB/9	K/9	GB%	BABIP	WHIP	ERA	FIP	FRA	WARP
2012	LAN	MLB	24	14	9	0	33	33	227²	170	16	63	229	2.5	9.1	49%	.262	1.02	2.53	2.93	3.41	3.7
2013	LAN	MLB	25	16	9	0	33	33	236	164	11	52	232	2.0	8.8	49%	.252	0.92	1.83	2.36	2.90	5.7
2014	LAN	MLB	26	21	3	0	27	27	198¹	139	9	31	239	1.4	10.8	53%	.278	0.86	1.77	1.78	2.40	6.1
2015	LAN	MLB	27	12	7	0	25	25	178	130	12	37	191	1.9	9.6	46%	.284	0.94	2.17	2.67	2.36	5.0

Breakout: 23%   Improve: 60%   Collapse: 20%   Attrition: 13%   MLB: 99%   *Comparables: Felix Hernandez, Tim Lincecum, Rich Harden*

What can be said about Kershaw that hasn't already been said about bacon, sex and baseball? He's the best, and he proved it with an historic 2014 campaign. He threw a no-hitter and won his third Cy Young in four years along with his first MVP (and the Dodgers' first since 1988). It was the first time a pitcher had won an MVP Award in the NL since 1968. His no-hitter, according to Game Score, was the second-best nine-inning start ever, just behind Kerry Wood's 20-strikeout, should-have-been-a-perfect-game performance in 1998. Kershaw was always a good prospect (he was drafted seventh overall) and had All-Star upside, but when he added a slider to his repertoire, he made the leap from merely very good to historically great. The comparisons to Sandy Koufax look less absurd by the day, and it's worth noting that Kershaw turned the corner and became *Clayton Kershaw* two years younger than Koufax did. Here's hoping modern medicine means we get 15 more years.

Brandon League   RHP
Born: 3/16/83   Age: 32   Bats: R   Throws: R   Height: 6'2"   Weight: 215

YEAR	TEAM	LVL	AGE	W	L	SV	G	GS	IP	H	HR	BB	K	BB/9	K/9	GB%	BABIP	WHIP	ERA	FIP	FRA	WARP
2012	SEA	MLB	29	0	5	9	46	0	44²	48	1	19	27	3.8	5.4	48%	.322	1.50	3.63	3.40	3.63	0.4
2012	LAN	MLB	29	2	1	6	28	0	27¹	17	0	14	27	4.6	8.9	58%	.258	1.13	2.30	2.81	2.86	0.4
2013	LAN	MLB	30	6	4	14	58	0	54¹	69	8	15	28	2.5	4.6	60%	.313	1.55	5.30	4.90	5.23	-0.4
2014	LAN	MLB	31	2	3	0	63	0	63	65	0	27	38	3.9	5.4	69%	.320	1.46	2.57	3.37	4.95	-0.4
2015	LAN	MLB	32	3	1	4	59	0	57¹	54	4	17	41	2.7	6.5	56%	.303	1.24	3.74	3.79	4.07	0.2

Breakout: 20%   Improve: 44%   Collapse: 27%   Attrition: 12%   MLB: 95%   *Comparables: Braden Looper, Danys Baez, Matt Guerrier*

Despite a shiny ERA in 2014, it was difficult to trust League, especially in high-leverage situations. But his season was much better than, say, his 2013. Pitching a home run shutout for the season was even more impressive considering left-handed hitters posted a .313 batting average against him. If there's such a thing as a right-handed specialist, League is it. He was, inexplicably, given a three-year deal by the Dodgers after 2012, so they're on the hook for one more season, but a repeat of 2014 would go a long way to turning the contract from an utter failure to merely a regular failure.

Zach Lee   RHP
Born: 9/13/91   Age: 23   Bats: R   Throws: R   Height: 6'3"   Weight: 195

YEAR	TEAM	LVL	AGE	W	L	SV	G	GS	IP	H	HR	BB	K	BB/9	K/9	GB%	BABIP	WHIP	ERA	FIP	FRA	WARP
2012	RCU	A+	20	2	3	0	12	12	55¹	60	9	10	52	1.6	8.5	48%	.315	1.27	4.55	4.65	4.64	1.2
2012	CHT	AA	20	4	3	0	13	13	65²	69	6	22	51	3.0	7.0	48%	.313	1.39	4.25	3.83	4.85	0.1
2013	CHT	AA	21	10	10	0	28	25	142²	132	13	35	131	2.2	8.3	49%	.298	1.17	3.22	3.08	4.02	1.2
2014	ABQ	AAA	22	7	13	0	28	27	150²	177	18	54	97	3.2	5.8	52%	.323	1.53	5.38	5.16	5.91	1.9
2015	LAN	MLB	23	7	9	0	26	26	133¹	136	17	38	92	2.5	6.2	47%	.308	1.30	4.51	4.60	4.90	-0.4

Breakout: 0%   Improve: 0%   Collapse: 0%   Attrition: 0%   MLB: 0%   *Comparables: Brett Oberholtzer, Kyle Lobstein, Anthony Swarzak*

You can buy a lot of things for $5.25 million—a 21 percent share in the Dodgers' new Triple-A team, the Oklahoma City Redhawks; front-row field box MVP level Dodgers season tickets for a family of four for 135 years; 10,500,000 Jack in the Box tacos—but the Dodgers bought a former high school quarterback to be their next ace. Instead, Lee has been more of a middle-of-the-rotation pitcher since the Dodgers drafted him in 2010. Talent evaluators expected his stuff to take a step forward, but it never has. It doesn't mean he's a bust, it just means he was a little overrated. The lack of a true out pitch is what limits Lee's ceiling, as he doesn't have elite velocity and relies on control and command to get hitters out.

Adam Liberatore   LHP
Born: 5/12/87   Age: 28   Bats: L   Throws: L   Height: 6'3"   Weight: 225

YEAR	TEAM	LVL	AGE	W	L	SV	G	GS	IP	H	HR	BB	K	BB/9	K/9	GB%	BABIP	WHIP	ERA	FIP	FRA	WARP
2012	MNT	AA	25	3	4	8	33	0	52	53	4	20	27	3.5	4.7	64%	.295	1.40	2.94	4.61	6.23	-0.5
2012	DUR	AAA	25	1	1	1	16	0	21	18	0	8	21	3.4	9.0	52%	.300	1.24	1.29	2.30	3.27	0.4
2013	DUR	AAA	26	5	3	0	43	0	60¹	50	1	25	69	3.7	10.3	49%	.308	1.24	3.58	2.43	3.46	1.3
2014	DUR	AAA	27	6	1	4	54	0	65	43	1	15	86	2.1	11.9	46%	.292	0.89	1.66	1.65	2.50	1.9
2015	LAN	MLB	28	2	1	2	35	0	54²	49	4	18	48	2.9	8.0	51%	.309	1.22	3.49	3.61	3.79	0.4

Breakout: 4%   Improve: 4%   Collapse: 5%   Attrition: 9%   MLB: 13%   *Comparables: Dale Thayer, Dane De La Rosa, Matt Langwell*

A classic three-year Triple-A project, Liberatore has gone from just a big body to a big-league-ready fireman. He beat out Durham's entire starting rotation for the team's Most Valuable Pitcher Award, was named the Rays' minor-league Reliever of the Year and was by most statistical measures the best reliever in the International League. Liberatore's increasingly heavy, 93 mph fastball was responsible for most of his success, along with a workable slider, a show-me changeup and (more importantly) maturity that allowed him to assume Durham's closer role late in the season. The 2010 21st-rounder should make his big-league debut this year; his sub-.500 OPS allowed to lefties over three Triple-A seasons recommends him for situational use, but he handles righties, too.

Paul Maholm   LHP
Born: 6/25/82   Age: 33   Bats: L   Throws: L   Height: 6'2"   Weight: 245

YEAR	TEAM	LVL	AGE	W	L	SV	G	GS	IP	H	HR	BB	K	BB/9	K/9	GB%	BABIP	WHIP	ERA	FIP	FRA	WARP
2012	CHN	MLB	30	9	6	0	21	20	120¹	115	12	34	81	2.5	6.1	51%	.281	1.24	3.74	4.18	4.79	0.1
2012	ATL	MLB	30	4	5	0	11	11	68²	63	8	19	59	2.5	7.7	54%	.281	1.19	3.54	3.81	4.44	0.3
2013	ATL	MLB	31	10	11	0	26	26	153	169	17	47	105	2.8	6.2	53%	.310	1.41	4.41	4.21	4.71	0.0
2014	LAN	MLB	32	1	5	0	30	8	70²	82	8	28	34	3.6	4.3	57%	.311	1.56	4.84	4.93	5.25	-0.4
2015	LAN	MLB	33	4	5	0	13	13	76²	78	8	21	51	2.5	6.0	51%	.311	1.29	4.34	4.36	4.71	-0.2

Breakout: 6%   Improve: 32%   Collapse: 21%   Attrition: 24%   MLB: 80%   *Comparables: Jeff Suppan, Kris Benson, Joe Saunders*

Now that he's past his 2011 to 2012 peak, Maholm's main value is as evidence that you definitely pronounce the "l" in "calm" and "palm." The Dodgers seemed to think he had pitching value, though, and signed him early in spring training to add starter depth and a true long reliever. He played that role, but not as well as the Dodgers hoped. Hitters just don't miss his pitches: Maholm had the 10th-lowest whiff rate among pitchers with at least 50 innings. His season ended with an ugly left-knee injury.

Brandon McCarthy   RHP

Born: 7/7/83   Age: 31   Bats: R   Throws: R   Height: 6'7"   Weight: 200

YEAR	TEAM	LVL	AGE	W	L	SV	G	GS	IP	H	HR	BB	K	BB/9	K/9	GB%	BABIP	WHIP	ERA	FIP	FRA	WARP
2012	OAK	MLB	28	8	6	0	18	18	111	115	10	24	73	1.9	5.9	43%	.295	1.25	3.24	3.71	3.98	1.3
2013	RNO	AAA	29	0	0	0	2	2	10¹	15	2	3	4	2.6	3.5	55%	.325	1.74	6.97	6.47	7.58	-0.1
2013	ARI	MLB	29	5	11	0	22	22	135	161	13	21	76	1.4	5.1	50%	.320	1.35	4.53	3.72	4.35	0.4
2014	ARI	MLB	30	3	10	0	18	18	109²	131	15	20	93	1.6	7.6	56%	.345	1.38	5.01	3.79	4.50	0.6
2014	NYA	MLB	30	7	5	0	14	14	90¹	91	10	13	82	1.3	8.2	51%	.307	1.15	2.89	3.25	3.97	1.1
2015	LAN	MLB	31	10	9	0	27	27	170	169	17	24	131	1.3	6.9	48%	.314	1.14	3.55	3.57	3.86	1.3

Breakout: 12%   Improve: 46%   Collapse: 14%   Attrition: 12%   MLB: 84%   *Comparables: Bronson Arroyo, Jeff Karstens, Jeff Francis*

It's never been easy for our young hero, forced to reinvent himself multiple times throughout his career. Injuries and stamina always being a concern, McCarthy set out to improve his durability through a liberal shake weight regimen; the result was his first 200-inning season. But fate had new obstacles in store, including a grisly Diamondbacks offense and a curse that sent 20 percent of his fly balls out of the yard.

Everyone knows that the best way to solve your problems is to move to a new city and change absolutely nothing else about yourself. So McCarthy did, in a deadline deal with the Yankees, where his fortunes magically reversed. With Brian McCann's help, McCarthy did actually make some adjustments, working up in the zone sometimes to pull a hitter's attention away from his excellent sinker, resulting in a career-best strikeout rate. This particular chapter has a happy ending, with a well-deserved and generous contract to play in Los Angeles.

Juan Nicasio   RHP

Born: 8/31/86   Age: 28   Bats: R   Throws: R   Height: 6'3"   Weight: 210

YEAR	TEAM	LVL	AGE	W	L	SV	G	GS	IP	H	HR	BB	K	BB/9	K/9	GB%	BABIP	WHIP	ERA	FIP	FRA	WARP
2012	COL	MLB	25	2	3	0	11	11	58	72	7	22	54	3.4	8.4	41%	.376	1.62	5.28	4.03	4.94	0.7
2013	CSP	AAA	26	1	0	0	2	2	11	8	0	1	8	0.8	6.5	62%	.250	0.82	0.82	2.39	3.16	0.4
2013	COL	MLB	26	9	9	0	31	31	157²	168	17	64	119	3.7	6.8	46%	.303	1.47	5.14	4.23	4.81	1.2
2014	CSP	AAA	27	3	2	1	10	4	35²	41	4	15	36	3.8	9.1	43%	.378	1.57	4.54	4.48	5.27	0.3
2014	COL	MLB	27	6	6	0	33	14	93²	107	19	31	63	3.0	6.1	49%	.298	1.47	5.38	5.42	6.11	-0.5
2015	LAN	MLB	28	7	8	0	23	23	122	118	14	34	104	2.5	7.7	44%	.314	1.24	3.97	4.01	4.31	0.4

Breakout: 21%   Improve: 46%   Collapse: 21%   Attrition: 32%   MLB: 80%   *Comparables: Chad Durbin, Armando Galarraga, Ross Ohlendorf*

Nicasio avoided injury once again in 2014 but couldn't avoid the inevitable demotion to the bullpen. Allowing six runs per nine innings and striking out just 14 percent of batters as a starter, Nicasio went back to Colorado Springs for relief pitcher summer school in June. He returned in August, working mostly in low-leverage situations (are there any others, with the Rockies?) but throwing two mph harder. The results: a .246 TAv against, 51 points better than his starter figure. With his mid-90s fastball and go-to slider, Nicasio never really forged a reliable changeup. As a reliever, he likely won't need it.

Joel Peralta   RHP

Born: 3/23/76   Age: 39   Bats: R   Throws: R   Height: 5'11"   Weight: 210

YEAR	TEAM	LVL	AGE	W	L	SV	G	GS	IP	H	HR	BB	K	BB/9	K/9	GB%	BABIP	WHIP	ERA	FIP	FRA	WARP
2012	TBA	MLB	36	2	6	2	76	0	67	49	9	17	84	2.3	11.3	32%	.261	0.99	3.63	3.09	3.52	0.9
2013	TBA	MLB	37	3	8	1	80	0	71¹	47	7	34	74	4.3	9.3	27%	.227	1.14	3.41	3.71	3.38	0.8
2014	TBA	MLB	38	3	4	1	69	0	63¹	60	9	15	74	2.1	10.5	35%	.307	1.18	4.41	3.43	3.21	1.0
2015	LAN	MLB	39	4	2	1	68	0	62¹	48	6	16	67	2.3	9.7	33%	.284	1.02	2.74	3.21	2.98	1.1

Breakout: 18%   Improve: 32%   Collapse: 21%   Attrition: 12%   MLB: 70%   *Comparables: Russ Springer, Tom Gordon, Trevor Hoffman*

Con el corazón del león, Peralta desafía las probabilidades de ser relevista eficaz de las entradas tardes a pesar de su edad y falta de pitcheo. Aunque a veces los enemigos producen contacto sólido en varias apariencias, su producción en general sube el promedio. Uso de pitcheos secundarios ha sido parte clave de su éxito, ya que Peralta tira una curva de 79 millas por hora con la misma frecuencia que su recta de 89 millas por hora mientras mezcla un splitter como tercer pitcheo. Aparte de su trabajo en el montículo, se ve a Peralta como líder del clubhouse, embajador de la organización y uno que promueve una energía positiva.

Chris Reed   LHP

Born: 5/20/90   Age: 25   Bats: L   Throws: L   Height: 6'4"   Weight: 195

YEAR	TEAM	LVL	AGE	W	L	SV	G	GS	IP	H	HR	BB	K	BB/9	K/9	GB%	BABIP	WHIP	ERA	FIP	FRA	WARP
2012	RCU	A+	22	1	4	0	7	6	35	25	1	14	38	3.6	9.8	60%	.279	1.11	3.09	3.30	4.51	0.7
2012	CHT	AA	22	0	4	0	12	11	35¹	31	2	20	29	5.1	7.4	61%	.290	1.44	4.84	4.28	5.03	0.3
2013	CHT	AA	23	4	11	0	29	25	137²	128	9	63	106	4.1	6.9	62%	.295	1.39	3.86	3.73	5.60	0.0
2014	CHT	AA	24	4	8	0	23	23	137	114	10	55	116	3.6	7.6	54%	.267	1.23	3.22	3.80	4.77	1.7
2014	ABQ	AAA	24	0	3	0	5	5	21¹	37	5	11	18	4.6	7.6	49%	.416	2.25	10.97	6.89	6.81	0.1
2015	LAN	MLB	25	7	10	0	28	28	134²	129	15	53	103	3.5	6.9	54%	.307	1.35	4.43	4.58	4.81	-0.3

Breakout: 21%   Improve: 27%   Collapse: 1%   Attrition: 22%   MLB: 31%   *Comparables: Alex Wilson, Chris Dwyer, Erik Goeddel*

Recently departed scouting director Logan White made countless prescient draft choices, but it's tough to convert a college reliever into a professional starter, and Reed hasn't proven able to defy the trend. His 2014 started off well enough, as he posted a 1.71 ERA in April, but he wasn't able to sustain it, as he finished the last four months with a 4.90 ERA. A late-season promotion to Albuquerque didn't do any favors for those who bemoan his draft selection. A move back to the bullpen is likely sooner rather than later, which would be best for all parties involved.

Paco Rodriguez LHP

Born: 4/16/91 Age: 24 Bats: L Throws: L Height: 6'3" Weight: 220

YEAR	TEAM	LVL	AGE	W	L	SV	G	GS	IP	H	HR	BB	K	BB/9	K/9	GB%	BABIP	WHIP	ERA	FIP	FRA	WARP
2012	CHT	AA	21	1	0	3	15	0	13²	7	0	6	22	4.0	14.5	46%	.269	0.95	1.32	1.46	1.93	0.5
2012	LAN	MLB	21	0	1	0	11	0	6²	3	0	4	6	5.4	8.1	44%	.188	1.05	1.35	3.14	2.19	0.1
2013	LAN	MLB	22	3	4	2	76	0	54¹	30	5	19	63	3.1	10.4	50%	.210	0.90	2.32	3.06	3.26	0.5
2014	ABQ	AAA	23	2	3	1	32	0	28²	25	4	17	35	5.3	11.0	51%	.300	1.47	4.40	4.85	4.72	0.5
2014	LAN	MLB	23	1	0	0	19	0	14	12	1	4	14	2.6	9.0	51%	.324	1.14	3.86	2.89	3.08	0.1
2015	LAN	MLB	24	3	1	2	54	0	41²	30	3	14	50	3.0	10.8	48%	.294	1.05	2.57	2.89	2.79	0.9

Breakout: 28% Improve: 60% Collapse: 13% Attrition: 29% MLB: 93% Comparables: *Tim Collins, Chris Perez, Kelvin Herrera*

Eighty-one players were picked before Rodriguez in the 2012 draft, and just six have debuted in the majors; Rodriguez, meanwhile, is already a grizzled three-year veteran who might be in his decline phase. After scuffling in the final month-plus of 2013, a couple bad April outings got him sent to the minors, where left-handed batters knocked an extra-base hit every 10 plate appearances. He finally returned to Los Angeles late in the season, throwing not as hard, and he was left off the postseason roster. It was a disappointing year in a lot of ways: Mark Mulder's comeback attempt, which was inspired by Rodriguez's funky delivery, flopped in spring training. Better days might be ahead, as PECOTA still thinks he's the Dodgers' second-best reliever. Rodriguez, that is, not Mulder, though Mulder might be third.

Hyun-jin Ryu LHP

Born: 3/25/87 Age: 28 Bats: R Throws: L Height: 6'2" Weight: 255

YEAR	TEAM	LVL	AGE	W	L	SV	G	GS	IP	H	HR	BB	K	BB/9	K/9	GB%	BABIP	WHIP	ERA	FIP	FRA	WARP
2013	LAN	MLB	26	14	8	0	30	30	192	182	15	49	154	2.3	7.2	52%	.296	1.20	3.00	3.21	3.84	2.4
2014	LAN	MLB	27	14	7	0	26	26	152	152	8	29	139	1.7	8.2	50%	.319	1.19	3.38	2.59	3.13	3.2
2015	LAN	MLB	28	9	7	0	23	23	137¹	126	11	28	117	1.8	7.7	49%	.310	1.12	3.14	3.31	3.41	1.9

Breakout: 23% Improve: 60% Collapse: 16% Attrition: 6% MLB: 96% Comparables: *John Danks, Cole Hamels, CC Sabathia*

When the Dodgers signed Ryu in late 2012, some thought he wouldn't be more than a back-of-the-rotation starter or even a reliever. Ryu has since hushed the doubters and he may not be done improving. He dealt with injuries to his shoulder and hip in 2014, preventing him from adding to his innings total, but the quality of those innings was excellent: He slotted in between Felix Hernandez and Chris Sale on the major-league FIP leaderboard. Ryu was mostly a fastball-changeup pitcher in 2013, but he refined his curve and slider to the point where they were actually better weapons than the change. Add 2013 (or better) quantity to 2014 quality and you've got a Cy Young Award candidate.

Oh, and the entertainment he provides with Juan Uribe is good enough to land them their own sitcom on the Dodgers' regional sports network. Seriously, how has SportsNet LA not made this a thing yet? Time Warner Cable is paying the Dodgers $8 billion over 25 years for TV rights; it might as well try to make some of that money back with *"The Ryuribe Show."*

Ross Stripling RHP

Born: 11/23/89 Age: 25 Bats: R Throws: R Height: 6'3" Weight: 190

YEAR	TEAM	LVL	AGE	W	L	SV	G	GS	IP	H	HR	BB	K	BB/9	K/9	GB%	BABIP	WHIP	ERA	FIP	FRA	WARP
2013	RCU	A+	23	2	0	0	6	6	33²	24	1	11	34	2.9	9.1	57%	.261	1.04	2.94	3.12	3.13	1.0
2013	CHT	AA	23	6	4	1	21	16	94	91	4	19	83	1.8	7.9	54%	.310	1.17	2.78	2.31	3.87	1.4
2015	LAN	MLB	25	2	3	0	8	8	37¹	37	4	10	28	2.5	6.8	52%	.311	1.26	3.92	4.12	4.26	0.2

Breakout: 0% Improve: 0% Collapse: 0% Attrition: 0% MLB: 0% Comparables: *David Phelps, Gus Schlosser, Chris Heston*

The Dodgers' 2014 search for starting-pitcher depth wouldn't have been so arduous if Stripling hadn't suffered a torn UCL in spring training. The 2012 fifth-rounder underwent Tommy John surgery and could be back by the middle of 2015, but the Dodgers could have really used him last year, given their loss of confidence in Zach Lee. Before the injury, Stripling featured a low-90s fastball, a curveball that flashed plus potential, a solid changeup and a developing slider, giving him the ceiling of a middle-of-the-rotation starter. The mix of pitches and lack of overwhelming top-line stuff means that he may actually project better as a starter than a reliever. Of course, he has to come back healthy to reach that ceiling, and we say it every year: Tommy John surgery feels like a sure thing these days, but it's not.

Julio Urias LHP

Born: 8/12/96 Age: 18 Bats: L Throws: L Height: 5'11" Weight: 160

YEAR	TEAM	LVL	AGE	W	L	SV	G	GS	IP	H	HR	BB	K	BB/9	K/9	GB%	BABIP	WHIP	ERA	FIP	FRA	WARP
2013	GRL	A	16	2	0	0	18	18	54¹	44	5	16	67	2.7	11.1	54%	.320	1.10	2.48	3.01	3.59	1.4
2014	RCU	A+	17	2	2	0	25	20	87²	60	4	37	109	3.8	11.2	45%	.281	1.11	2.36	3.35	3.88	1.8
2015	LAN	MLB	18	4	5	0	20	20	71	62	8	28	69	3.6	8.7	45%	.305	1.27	3.82	4.13	4.15	0.6

Breakout: 0% Improve: 0% Collapse: 0% Attrition: 0% MLB: 0% Comparables: *Taijuan Walker, Madison Bumgarner, Jordan Lyles*

Urias is left-handed, Mexican, a Dodger and might debut while he's still a teenager. Therefore, we are legally, ethically, morally and magically bound to say the name "Fernando." There, we said it.

Urias has the pure stuff to be more than a brief, bright flash, with a fastball into the mid-90s and two off-speed pitches that are at least average. He is also, perhaps more importantly, praised for his poise, a quality that will be tested soon, whether in the high minors or the majors, when Urias starts dealing with the best hitters in the world. Nobody is good enough not to have bad stretches, not even the youngest pitcher ever to pitch in the Futures Game.

Brian Wilson RHP

Born: 3/16/82 Age: 33 Bats: R Throws: R Height: 6'1" Weight: 205

YEAR	TEAM	LVL	AGE	W	L	SV	G	GS	IP	H	HR	BB	K	BB/9	K/9	GB%	BABIP	WHIP	ERA	FIP	FRA	WARP
2012	SFN	MLB	30	0	0	1	2	0	2	4	0	2	2	9.0	9.0	25%	.500	3.00	9.00	4.14	6.53	0.0
2013	LAN	MLB	31	2	1	0	18	0	13²	8	0	4	13	2.6	8.6	56%	.250	0.88	0.66	2.74	2.10	0.3
2014	LAN	MLB	32	2	4	1	61	0	48¹	49	5	29	54	5.4	10.1	39%	.336	1.61	4.66	4.26	4.09	0.1
2015	LAN	MLB	33	3	1	1	50	0	43¹	35	3	17	47	3.5	9.8	47%	.311	1.20	3.22	3.27	3.50	0.5

Breakout: 20% Improve: 49% Collapse: 30% Attrition: 12% MLB: 92% Comparables: *Fernando Rodney, Pedro Feliciano, Scot Shields*

Wilson would be an amazing used car salesman. He'd show you all the good stuff (sweet stereo, beautiful purr of the engine, super cool ground effects lighting), then you'd drive it off the lot and three months later you'd be left with a heap of metal that makes a nasty *chu-chunk* noise when you turn the key. Wilson was signed in late 2013, put on a good show for the Dodgers and earned himself a two-year contract. In 2014, the wheels came off, to torture a metaphor. Wilson started it off by hurting himself in San Diego in the team's third game. He spent time on the disabled list, came back and couldn't get hitters out. He didn't have the zip on his fastball he once had, his cutter was flat and he couldn't command his pitches. All of this is great news! For the opponents. For some reason, Don Mattingly continued to use Wilson in high-leverage situations; the subpar results, shockingly, also continued. The new Dodgers regime decided not to toss good innings after bad and designated him for assignment in December.

Tom Windle   LHP

Born: 3/10/92   Age: 23   Bats: L   Throws: L   Height: 6'4"   Weight: 215

YEAR	TEAM	LVL	AGE	W	L	SV	G	GS	IP	H	HR	BB	K	BB/9	K/9	GB%	BABIP	WHIP	ERA	FIP	FRA	WARP
2013	GRL	A	21	5	1	0	13	12	53²	50	2	20	51	3.4	8.6	44%	.308	1.30	2.68	3.15	3.71	1.2
2014	RCU	A+	22	12	8	0	26	25	139¹	147	14	44	111	2.8	7.2	56%	.309	1.37	4.26	4.53	5.89	0.7
2015	LAN	MLB	23	6	8	0	22	22	112	117	12	41	69	3.3	5.6	48%	.308	1.41	4.69	4.74	5.10	-0.6

Breakout: 0%   Improve: 0%   Collapse: 0%   Attrition: 0%   MLB: 0%   Comparables: T.J. House, Anthony Ortega, John Gast

The 2013 second-round pick came with question marks. In particular: Is his arm action going to work as a starting pitcher? The Dodgers have worked with Windle to help make it more palatable, leaving some hope that he's not "just" a reliever. Windle started decently in 2014 (3.94 ERA in his first six games) before seemingly running out of gas down the stretch (5.10 in his last 10). He has a solid fastball and a potentially plus slider, so Philadelphia got a good relief prospect in the Jimmy Rollins deal even if Windle doesn't develop his changeup and increase his stamina. There's more hope for him than for Chris Reed, an easy comparison because of handedness and background.

Chris Withrow   RHP

Born: 4/1/89   Age: 26   Bats: R   Throws: R   Height: 6'4"   Weight: 215

YEAR	TEAM	LVL	AGE	W	L	SV	G	GS	IP	H	HR	BB	K	BB/9	K/9	GB%	BABIP	WHIP	ERA	FIP	FRA	WARP
2012	CHT	AA	23	3	3	2	22	7	60	52	3	36	64	5.4	9.6	53%	.306	1.47	4.65	3.56	5.42	0.4
2013	ABQ	AAA	24	4	0	0	25	0	26¹	25	0	13	33	4.4	11.3	56%	.362	1.44	1.71	2.54	2.50	1.1
2013	LAN	MLB	24	3	0	1	26	0	34²	20	5	13	43	3.4	11.2	37%	.205	0.95	2.60	3.54	4.06	0.2
2014	LAN	MLB	25	0	0	0	20	0	21¹	10	1	18	28	7.6	11.8	46%	.214	1.31	2.95	3.76	4.37	0.0
2015	LAN	MLB	26	2	2	0	16	4	36²	32	4	18	35	4.4	8.6	44%	.305	1.37	4.26	4.43	4.64	0.0

Breakout: 22%   Improve: 34%   Collapse: 17%   Attrition: 25%   MLB: 60%   Comparables: Michael Kirkman, Justin Wilson, Brayan Villarreal

Withrow and his mustache (though it's possible the order there is wrong) emerged in 2013 after a midyear promotion from Triple-A. The former first-round pick used his starter's arsenal to become one of the most effective Dodgers relievers. He continued his good work to a degree in 2014, though his walk rate was obviously unacceptable, before—you guessed it—Tommy John surgery ended his season. It was a big blow to an already shaky bullpen, and Withrow's absence glared ever brighter as the season progressed. Most of his 2015 season will be lost, too, but the future still shines for Withrow because of his pure stuff, most particularly his 96 mph fastball. Best-case scenario puts him back around midseason.

Lineouts

Hitters

NAME	POS	TEAM	LVL	AGE	PA	R	2B	3B	HR	RBI	BB	K	SB	CS	AVG/OBP/SLG	TAv	BABIP	BRR	FRAA	WARP
Devan Ahart	CF	GRL	A	21	72	5	6	0	0	4	1	8	3	0	.304/.310/.391	.265	.339	0.9	CF(12): 0.3, LF(5): -0.3	0.3
Darwin Barney	SS	ABQ	AAA	28	38	5	1	0	0	1	3	5	0	0	.257/.316/.286	.218	.300	0.9	SS(6): 0.2, 3B(3): -0.3	0.0
	2B	CHN	MLB	28	217	18	10	2	2	16	9	31	1	0	.230/.265/.328	.229	.262	2.4	2B(67): -0.8	0.0
	2B	LAN	MLB	28	45	6	1	0	1	7	8	3	0	0	.303/.467/.424	.362	.300	0.0	2B(12): -0.4, SS(2): 0.1	0.5
Mike Baxter	RF	ABQ	AAA	29	468	72	25	8	7	36	45	87	12	5	.289/.365/.439	.264	.349	3.6	RF(88): -2.6, LF(22): -2.3	0.3
	LF	LAN	MLB	29	8	0	0	0	0	0	1	2	0	0	.000/.125/.000	.038	.000	0.0	LF(1): 0.1	0.0
Roger Bernadina	LF	ABQ	AAA	30	71	8	2	2	0	2	12	23	2	0	.246/.380/.351	.272	.400	0.3	LF(12): -0.2, RF(3): -0.2	0.2
	LF	CIN	MLB	30	71	3	3	0	0	5	10	16	2	1	.153/.286/.203	.193	.209	-0.9	LF(15): -0.0, RF(8): -0.2	-0.5
	RF	LAN	MLB	30	9	2	0	0	1	4	0	3	0	0	.286/.444/.714	.431	.333	0.2	RF(2): -0.1, LF(2): -0.0	0.2
Justin Chigbogu	1B	GRL	A	19	96	13	4	1	3	12	5	39	1	0	.156/.200/.322	.193	.229	0.5	1B(22): -1.2	-0.8
Tim Federowicz	C	ABQ	AAA	26	329	51	26	0	14	48	26	66	1	0	.328/.383/.555	.305	.380	-1.7	C(69): 0.2	3.2
	C	LAN	MLB	26	78	2	3	0	1	5	3	18	0	0	.113/.158/.197	.132	.132	0.2	C(22): 0.3	-0.5
Chris Heisey	LF	CIN	MLB	29	299	34	15	2	8	22	15	64	9	2	.222/.265/.378	.247	.259	1.0	LF(53): 3.4, CF(16): 1.3	0.8
Kyle Jensen	RF	NWO	AAA	26	556	70	29	6	27	92	48	147	1	0	.260/.331/.481	.286	.312	0.7	RF(68): -5.5, LF(33): 2.7	2.4
Ryan Lavarnway	1B	PAW	AAA	26	257	22	10	0	3	20	33	45	0	0	.283/.389/.370	.283	.345	-2.2	1B(31): -1.9, C(15): -0.0	0.7
	1B	BOS	MLB	26	10	0	0	0	0	0	0	3	0	0	.000/.000/.000	-.024	.000	0.2	1B(6): 0.2	-0.2
Miguel Olivo	C	ABQ	AAA	35	81	10	6	0	4	20	3	25	0	0	.368/.407/.605	.310	.511	0.3	C(18): 0.5	0.9
	C	LAN	MLB	35	25	4	0	1	0	2	1	12	0	0	.217/.240/.304	.197	.417	0.0	C(8): 0.1	0.0
Clint Robinson	1B	ABQ	AAA	29	499	77	31	5	18	80	64	84	0	0	.312/.401/.534	.306	.350	-1.1	1B(99): -5.4, RF(2): 0.2	2.6
	1B	LAN	MLB	29	10	3	0	0	0	1	1	1	0	0	.333/.400/.333	.252	.375	0.3	1B(3): -0.1	0.0

Sixteenth-round college outfielder **Devan Ahart** was expected to do well in Rookie ball, and he did, well enough to get a brief taste of a full-season league. ❖ When the Dodgers acquired **Darwin Barney** before the July 31st trade deadline, not much was made of the move, and rightly so, but Barney got on base in nearly half of his 45 plate appearances, which really just goes to show you. ❖ **Mike Baxter** was the only Dodgers position player to go hitless in 2014 (0-for-7). He made the Australia trip and was quickly sent to Triple-A, but he is in *R.B.I. Baseball 14*. ❖ **Roger Bernadina** led the Dodgers in OPS. It sounds impressive, but he only had nine plate appearances. ❖ With one of the best names in the system, **Justin Chigbogu** is a Ryan Howard clone with a lot of power, but low-minors first basemen with his contact rates don't typically turn into success stories. ❖ Rafa Nadal's got an argument but needs a few more years of longevity, Pete Sampras was terrible at Roland Garros, Bjorn Borg quit too soon and it's just too difficult to compare Rod Laver to modern players. They're all great, but **Tim Federowicz** remains the best of all time. ❖ Based on the draft slot (23rd round), **Andrew Godbold** will be playing indy ball in two years. Based on the name, Andrew G*d**bold** is a future All-Star. Split the difference and call him a future regular. That's how scouting works, right? ❖ It's great to have a fourth outfielder who offers above-average defense at all three spots and can occasionally run into one at the plate; now that he's a Dodger, that's all **Chris Heisey** should have to be. ❖ Sure, he's got right-handed power, but **Kyle Jensen** still strikes out too much at Triple-A to hold any sort of big-league corner outfield job. ❖ **Ryan Lavarnway**, once touted as a power-hitting catching prospect, has stopped hitting for power and stopped catching. His value has declined to "guy claimed on waivers" accordingly. ❖ Best known for trying to eat Alex Guerrero in a Triple-A game, **Miguel Olivo** was promptly released after the incident. He signed on with the Tijuana Toros of the Mexican League. ❖ A career minor leaguer, **Clint Robinson**'s biggest contribution to the Dodgers was a pinch-hit RBI single in a 1-0 victory over Corey Kluber on June 30th. ❖ **Lucas Tirado** received the largest Dodgers international signing bonus in 2013 ($1 million), then struggled in an aggressive assignment to the Arizona League. He didn't turn 18 until after the World Series, though, so don't get worked up.

Pitchers

NAME	TEAM	LVL	AGE	W	L	SV	G	GS	IP	H	HR	BB	K	BB/9	K/9	GB%	BABIP	WHIP	ERA	FIP	FRA	WARP
Kevin Correia	LAN	MLB	33	2	4	0	9	3	24²	34	7	8	18	2.9	6.6	55%	.329	1.70	8.03	6.31	7.84	-0.6
	MIN	MLB	33	5	13	0	23	23	129¹	157	13	32	61	2.2	4.2	43%	.312	1.46	4.94	4.38	4.86	1.0
Daniel Coulombe	RCU	A+	24	3	0	5	31	0	44¹	33	3	17	61	3.5	12.4	50%	.303	1.13	3.05	3.09	2.91	1.4
	CHT	AA	24	0	0	1	18	0	21	18	1	10	31	4.3	13.3	59%	.354	1.33	2.57	2.57	2.56	0.7
	LAN	MLB	24	0	0	0	5	0	4¹	5	1	2	4	4.2	8.3	44%	.267	1.62	4.15	5.64	5.19	0.0
Stephen Fife	ABQ	AAA	27	2	2	0	11	9	43²	65	2	15	27	3.1	5.6	55%	.394	1.83	7.01	4.23	4.56	0.9
	LAN	MLB	27	0	0	0	1	1	6	7	3	1	5	1.5	7.5	55%	.235	1.33	6.00	8.94	10.32	-0.3
Yimi Garcia	ABQ	AAA	23	4	2	5	47	0	61	58	5	18	69	2.7	10.2	30%	.327	1.25	3.10	3.63	3.21	1.9
	LAN	MLB	23	0	0	0	8	0	10	6	2	1	9	0.9	8.1	42%	.167	0.70	1.80	4.20	4.77	0.0
Jarret Martin	CHT	AA	24	1	1	7	46	0	54²	34	1	48	64	7.9	10.5	52%	.256	1.50	3.29	4.05	5.37	-0.1
Chris Perez	LAN	MLB	28	1	3	1	49	0	46¹	38	6	25	39	4.9	7.6	39%	.256	1.36	4.27	5.05	5.57	-0.6
Jamey Wright	LAN	MLB	39	5	4	1	61	1	70¹	72	3	27	54	3.5	6.9	60%	.314	1.41	4.35	3.44	4.02	0.6

Kevin Correia has pitched in 12 major-league seasons, made an All-Star team and thrown over 1,400 career innings, all as a replacement-level pitcher. Life, man. ❖ A short lefty, **Daniel Coulombe** earned a surprise late-season call-up and was decent with a low-90s fastball and a potentially plus curve. ❖ **Stephen Fife** began 2014 in the minors because the Dodgers had too many starting pitchers, posted an ugly but sadly not atypical stat line in Albuquerque, then had Tommy John surgery, ill-timed given his minor-league free agency. He might not pitch again until 2016. ❖ Still no flying cars or robot maids, but at least we know **Yimi Garcia** has a high spin rate on his fastball, and that it helps the pitch play up. The future is pretty cool. ❖ A somewhat curious addition to the Dodgers' 40-man roster prior to 2014, **Jarret Martin** has good stuff but zero idea where said stuff is going. If he can cut his walks by, say, 80 percent, he could contribute to this year's bullpen. ❖ **Chris Perez** still throws in the mid-90s and added a changeup in 2014, but that didn't stop him from being a bad pitcher; PECOTA sees a useful pitcher worth a flier because his 2012 remains in sight. ❖ **Kam Uter**, a 12th-round pick who got $200,000 to skip Wake Forest's football scholarship, is so far notable for being the subject of an intraoffice war over whether Uter Zorker jokes or "commuter" jokes are funnier. Check *Baseball Prospectus 2016* to find out who won. ❖ **Jamey Wright** had a string of eight consecutive years of getting a non-roster invite before earning a major-league contract, but bucked that trend in 2014 by signing a guaranteed deal with the Dodgers. The results were essentially the same.

Manager

Don Mattingly

YEAR	TEAM	W	L	Py-thag +/-	Avg PC	100+ P	120+ P	QS	BQS	REL	REL w Zero R	IBB	PH	PH Avg	PH HR	SB2	CS2	SB3	CS3	SAC Att	SAC%	POS SAC	Squeeze	Swing	In Play
2012	LAN	86	76	0	96.2	66	0	93	5	506	426	62	241	.281	2	93	39	10	2	122	67.2%	33	2	329	97
2013	LAN	92	70	2	95.1	69	2	93	2	504	424	44	208	.209	4	74	22	4	5	113	62.8%	32	0	283	93
2014	LAN	94	68	1	95.2	73	1	100	1	496	395	35	235	.231	1	123	46	14	3	82	57.3%	15	1	340	104

Comparing Mattingly to Joe Torre is lazy, predictable and valid. Just as Torre was never known for his tactical chops, Mattingly is considered a substandard strategist—look no further than his work in the postseason, which included benching Yasiel then using him as a pinch-runner rather than as a pinch-hitter. Both managers earned their keep behind closed doors, calming clubhouses flooding in big egos, personalities and contracts. Last season alone, Mattingly had to juggle an outfield situation that left someone with an eight-figure salary on the bench most days. Somehow he did it without a riot developing.

The Torre comparison works on another level, too: job security. Torre had to endure endless rumors about his employment during his time with the Yankees. Mattingly first experienced those whispers in 2013, but signed a three-year extension after the Dodgers finished strong. No matter, folks began to wonder if he'd be fired during the postseason, then once again following Andrew's hiring. Poor guy.

There's no reason to think Mattingly will win as many championships as Torre did—or, to be more accurate, that Mattingly's teams will win as many championships as Torre's teams did—but both deserve more credit than those focused only on their in-game work permit them. Friedman, at least for now, seems to agree; Mattingly will return for the '15 season.

MIAMI MARLINS

by Bryan Grosnick

The Marlins aren't like other major-league franchises, because the Marlins cannot be trusted. It's a cliché at this point, but after a dozen years of Jeffrey Loria twirling his mustache like Snidely Whiplash, here we all are. Admittedly, multibillionaires don't typically enjoy sterling reputations with the average Joe, but Miami has been cursed with two of the most hated owners in professional sports, two owners who meddled in all the worst ways and who never saw the business sense in showing loyalty, be it to their city, to their fans, or even (with the bizarre exception of Greg Dobbs) to their players.

Think, for a moment, about what your all-time Marlins lineup would look like. Probably something like this?

C. Charles Johnson
1B. Jeff Conine
2B. Luis Castillo
SS. Hanley Ramirez
3B. Miguel Cabrera
LF. Cliff Floyd
CF. Juan Pierre
RF. Giancarlo Stanton
SP. Dontrelle Willis
RP. Robb Nen

Every single one of them, save Stanton, was traded. So too were Dan Uggla and Mike Lowell, Kevin Brown and Livan Hernandez, Gary Sheffield and Josh Johnson. The top 20 Marlins in history, by Baseball-Reference's Wins Above Replacement, include just three players who weren't traded away: Cody Ross, A.J. Burnett and Stanton.

The song has always been the same in South Beach: Grow a superstar, trade him, lay the lyrics over a raised dance beat and there's your lead single. Instead of paying premiums to keep franchise figureheads, just sell to the highest bidder. Can you fault rival GMs, gossip writers, and even Miami's die-hardiest fans for assuming the pattern would continue?

Coming into the 2014 season, the Marlins had the best right fielder in the world and, arguably, the best right-handed starter in the world. Each was under 25. Plenty of GMs would kill to start building with those two in place, but it seemed inevitable that this, too, would pass. Stanton would be traded.

Here's what we didn't expect. The Marlins changed. They signed their best player, he of the nigh-limitless potential and massive biceps, he who will someday wear the first Marlins cap on a plaque in Cooperstown, to a 13-year contract. Most shockingly of all: It came with a no-trade clause, a prize that

for once seemed to pledge allegiance to a player, a perk that the Marlins had refused to bestow before now—a privilege they wouldn't even grant to Albert Pujols. For Stanton, they made an exception. Which means Stanton might be an exception: He could be, should be… a Marlin for life.

A leaf had been turned. The Marlins entered negotiation talks with Jose Fernandez, and with outfield wunderkinds Christian Yelich and Marcell Ozuna, and with defensive wizard-slash-enigma Adeiny Hechavarria. The new Marlins, under the leadership of President Michael Hill and General Manager Dan Jennings, have finally embraced loyalty to their players.

Of course, the Marlins cannot be trusted.

✦✦✦

It was a good season for an 85-loss team. A year earlier, the Marlins had been a dumpster fire, or a fail whale, or whatever turn of phrase is appropriate to describe something that's well and truly horrible. They were the baseball equivalent of a Guy Fieri selfie. After a 100-loss effort, they entered the 2014 season with the most discordant collection of commons in the game: Casey McGehee, who had last been seen wandering roads to sad piano music like Bill Bixby in the old Hulk TV show, would bat cleanup. Rafael Furcal, held together by paper spray-painted to look like duct tape, would start at second. Reed Johnson, Ed Lucas and Tom Koehler were to get substantive playing time.

Bad scene, everyone's fault.

And yet, even in a season bracketed by season-ending injuries—to Jose Fernandez early, to Stanton late—you don't have to squint to see a successful campaign. Henderson Alvarez went to the All-Star game, Yelich and Ozuna emerged and suddenly the Marlins had half a good lineup and half a good rotation. Attendance improved a little bit, as they carried a .500 record (and wild card dreams) into late August.

But perhaps the most fascinating development came at the trade deadline, when the Marlins actually traded away prospects *for* a semi-established major leaguer, Jarred Cosart. They sent Colin Moran, Jake Marisnick and a compensation draft pick to Houston, and the contrast between the trade partners was notable: The Astros have been rebuilding forever, and show no urgency to enter the next phase. The Marlins, just 18 months after a total teardown, had declared they would be credible.

MARLINS PROSPECTUS
2014 W-L: 77-85, 4TH IN NL EAST

Pythag	.480	19th	DER	.690	26th
RS/G	3.98	16th	B-Age	27.2	4th
RA/G	4.16	19th	P-Age	26.1	1st
TAv	.261	11th	Salary	$42.4M	30th
BRR	.170	17th	M$/MW	$1.0M	1st
TAv-P	.268	24th	DL Days	754	15th
FIP	3.53	7th	$ on DL	15%	15th

Three-Year Park Factors

Runs	Runs/RH	Runs/LH	HR/RH	HR/LH
97	98	91	88	76

Top Hitter WARP	8.2	Giancarlo Stanton
Top Pitcher WARP	1.6	Nathan Eovaldi
Top Prospect		Tyler Kolek

The goal of most bad teams, from a player personnel perspective, should be to identify which players on the roster are worth keeping around, and develop and retain those players. In an 85-loss season, the Marlins identified Alvarez, Cosart, Ozuna, Yelich and Hechavarria as long-term pieces to complement Stanton and Fernandez. They improved by 15 wins, and they weren't done. By mid-December, they had traded for Dee Gordon and Mat Latos, the latter under contract for just one more season. The Marlins were going for it.

+ + +

I'm not certain anyone expected Stanton to be a Marlin for life, perhaps not even Stanton himself. After the infamous offloading of veterans after 2012, Stanton took to Twitter: "Alright, I'm Pissed off! Plain & Simple." In August 2014, he told Yahoo's Tim Brown, "Five months doesn't change five years."

So what's going on with the contract he signed three months later, a deal that includes some of the most intriguing opt-outs, backloading and trade limitations we've ever seen, but one that seems to undercut Stanton's declared suspicion of his employers?

Start with the backloading: Stanton will pull down $107 million over the first three years. Had he simply gone through the arbitration process he likely would have made more than $30 million in the next two years, according to MLB Trade Rumors contributor Matt Swartz. And he likely would have made around $30 million in year three alone, his first free-agency year. Those first six years represent a huge pay cut.

The last seven will pay him $218 million, which brings us to the opt-out: Stanton can walk away from the deal and test free agency after the sixth season. He'll be 30, the same age Miguel Cabrera was when he signed his recent $292 million extension, the same age Robinson Cano was when he signed his $240 million contract. On the other hand, nothing's guaranteed about any baseball player six years from now.

(According to the Pirates president Frank Coonelly, Loria admitted he's counting on this. "I just couldn't get my head around the $325 million," Coonelly said in December. "They said to me, 'You don't understand. Those first six years are only going to cost $107 million. After that, he'll leave and play for somebody else. So, it's not really $325 million.'")

All of this, put together, crafts a pretty compelling narrative: Stanton is so cheap in the first several years of his contract that the Marlins should have the flexibility to spend big and build a contender with alacrity … or at least tender extensions to their other talented youngsters. If the Marlins don't build that contender, well, Stanton can opt out after six more years in the orange grove, but then he'll be passing up most of his glorious, record-breaking deal. And he will have sacrificed about $50 million in earnings to spend his peak years playing for the Marlins.

In essence, Stanton is putting his faith in a team that hasn't done much to earn that trust. He's banking on Loria, Jennings and Hill to build a strong team with the money he's saving them. If the Marlins are really committing to competing over the next six years, Stanton gets what he wants: a championship run in the near short term, and financial security in the long run. If they don't build rapidly to contention, well, that's when things will get very ugly. Stanton will be left under team contract, and his only way out will be to wave goodbye to all that cash—or waive his no-trade clause. Given the qualities of the contract and the qualities of the team's owner, one has to assume this would please Loria to no end.

+ + +

The Marlins still have weaknesses, including what most would consider a soft analytics department. While the public doesn't have exact details of the front office's relationship with modern analytics, an educated guess might be "little." The brass talks less than most about how they use modern analytics, creating a vacuum of information that is quickly filled by memories of Heath Bell signing a three-year deal.

The best Marlins fact from the 2014 season: They were the only team, by Baseball Info Solutions' defensive shift metric, to actually cost themselves runs by shifting on defense. A couple of other squads didn't add value, per BIS, but over the course of the year, the Marlins actually made their team worse by moving players into more "advantageous" positions.

But there are things they do well: Their first-round haul from 2010 to 2012 (Yelich, Fernandez and Andrew Heaney) rivals any team's, for instance. But maybe their best quality, from a crass competitive standpoint, is the one thing that makes them so despised: Their total lack of loyalty. They are almost never stuck with a player's decline phase. They are quick to admit a mistake and cash out before the mistake becomes an albatross. Mark Buehrle's pit bull sure doesn't appreciate it, but the Marlins' flash rebuild two winters ago netted them Alvarez, bat-first utility infielder Derek Dietrich and the pieces to later acquire Cosart and Latos. It spared them the terrifying specter of Jose Reyes' hamstrings in middle age. When a team isn't beholden to a player for loyalty's sake, which the Marlins are often not, then they also don't wind up paying for the player's worst years.

So what does that mean for Stanton? In his case, loyalty is less about the Marlins keeping him around—one way or another, it seems he and the club will each have plenty of opportunities to dissolve the marriage—as it is justifying his decision to take a big pay cut. Loyalty will mean a good-faith effort to deliver Stanton a World Series contender in the next six years, as often as possible over the next six years. That depends in part on the Marlins' front office's integrity, in part of its skill and in part on balancing the smart-move aspects of player dumping with the present-day demands of Stanton's competitive window.

They are not, despite the recent moves, likely to be a great team in 2015. Fernandez will miss most of the first half, acquisitions Gordon and Latos have question marks (regression and health, respectively), and much of the lineup is young enough to project exposure as easily as growth.

But at the same time, they're no further off than most teams in the National League, and they've done what was absolutely necessary: removed Donovan Solano and Tom Koehler from the relying-on-you levels of the depth chart. You can make a compelling argument that 10 of the 15 NL squads are in roughly the same position as the Marlins, at least in terms of their win curves. Only one team in the NL East is significantly better on paper, which, in the 10-playoff-team era, puts the Marlins in the thick of things.

The question, though, is what happens beyond. If you can squint and see a contender, you can squint and see a 65-win season, too. What happens in that scenario? What happens if it's 70 wins, or 75? The Marlins are trapped between a history of ambivalence and an uncertain future. The front office has the capability and, unquestionably, the verve to make the moves to propel the team into the thrilling realm of real contention. Enough of the breaks have gone their way: They have young hitters, young pitchers, upside and reliable stars to lean on.

But the Marlins aren't like other major-league franchises, because the Marlins cannot be trusted. Ultimately, Stanton must know, they'll be content to pull back instead of push forward if the momentum slows—particularly if the return on investment remains solid.

✦ ✦ ✦

The future is unwritten for everybody, but for the Marlins there's not even a definite outline. There's a sense this is a team ready to ride its young roster and see where it takes them. A core of Stanton, Fernandez, Alvarez and Yelich could be competitive—it

could!—if supplemented with talented veterans and role players. Call those four Posey, Bumgarner, Cain and Sandoval and you've got the Giants' dynasty. Why not the Marlins?

But the Marlins have to show not just the willingness to push forward, but the ability to execute, to pull off the tiered acquisitions (Tier 1: Gregor Blanco; Tier 2: Tim Hudson; Tier 3: Hunter Pence) that turn a core into a roster. They have to do it with the baggage of being known as the team without loyalty, with the payroll of a 1.7-million attendance club and with the front office that might be really smart—or might be incapable of figuring out shifts.

They don't have to earn our trust. What's important for them is that they earned Stanton's. It just remains to be seen whether it was justified. ■

—Bryan Grosnick is the Managing Editor and lead writer at Beyond the Box Score.

Player comments by Bryan Grosnick and Baseball Prospectus Authors

Hitters

Jeff Baker   PH

Born: 6/21/81   Age: 34   Bats: R   Throws: R   Height: 6' 2"   Weight: 220

YEAR	TEAM	LVL	AGE	PA	R	2B	3B	HR	RBI	BB	K	SB	CS	AVG/OBP/SLG	TAv	BABIP	BRR	FRAA	WARP
2012	ATL	MLB	31	20	1	0	0	0	1	1	10	0	0	.105/.150/.105	.102	.222	0.0	LF(3): -0.1, 2B(1): 0.0	-0.3
2012	CHN	MLB	31	144	16	10	1	4	20	8	28	4	1	.269/.306/.448	.263	.308	-0.3	1B(20): -2.4, RF(14): 0.1	0.0
2012	DET	MLB	31	37	1	2	0	0	4	2	10	0	0	.200/.243/.257	.202	.280	-0.1	RF(11): -0.2, 3B(4): 0.0	-0.2
2013	TEX	MLB	32	175	21	8	0	11	21	18	48	1	0	.279/.360/.545	.318	.333	-1.8	LF(21): -0.3, 1B(21): -1.2	0.9
2014	MIA	MLB	33	225	27	10	4	3	28	13	51	1	0	.264/.307/.394	.267	.331	-2.0	1B(43): -2.8, 2B(21): 0.6	0.1
2015	MIA	MLB	34	250	23	12	2	4	25	15	60	2	0	.248/.295/.367	.257	.314	-1.2	1B -4, 2B 0	-0.2

Breakout: 0%   Improve: 22%   Collapse: 5%   Attrition: 14%   MLB: 94%   Comparables: *George Hendrick, Orlando Cepeda, Willie Horton*

Ideally, Baker would never have to bat against a righty, as he sports a .231/.283/.353 split against righties over his 10-year career. But there are limits to what a manager can get away with, and for an NL bat like Baker, 89 plate appearances—42 percent of his workload—is about as good as it gets, and still enough to torpedo a slash line. Baker can still hit lefties (.313 TAv over his career, .311 in 2014) and should find the soft side of a platoon for a few more years, but he's better suited for the AL, where he's not asked to pinch-hit against righties. Though he has a reputation as a multi-position player, advanced metrics say you want him on the field as little as possible.

Derek Dietrich   2B

Born: 7/18/89   Age: 25   Bats: L   Throws: R   Height: 6' 0"   Weight: 205

YEAR	TEAM	LVL	AGE	PA	R	2B	3B	HR	RBI	BB	K	SB	CS	AVG/OBP/SLG	TAv	BABIP	BRR	FRAA	WARP
2012	PCH	A+	22	417	49	21	9	10	58	25	78	4	2	.282/.343/.468	.280	.329	3.2	SS(75): -6.9, 2B(17): -2.8	1.9
2012	MNT	AA	22	146	22	7	1	4	17	7	36	0	1	.271/.324/.429	.255	.340	0.2	2B(34): 1.1	0.6
2013	JAX	AA	23	257	35	13	3	11	38	29	60	3	0	.271/.381/.509	.316	.327	0.2	2B(50): -3.7, 3B(8): -0.5	1.9
2013	MIA	MLB	23	233	32	10	2	9	23	11	56	1	0	.214/.275/.405	.260	.247	0.7	2B(57): -2.6	0.3
2014	NWO	AAA	24	92	15	3	0	7	16	4	18	1	0	.317/.391/.610	.355	.333	0.0	2B(21): -0.6	1.2
2014	MIA	MLB	24	183	31	6	2	5	17	13	38	1	0	.228/.326/.386	.277	.270	2.9	2B(44): 2.2, 3B(1): -0.0	1.3
2015	MIA	MLB	25	250	26	10	2	8	30	13	61	1	0	.240/.300/.406	.267	.290	1.2	2B -1, SS -0	1.0

Breakout: 4%   Improve: 33%   Collapse: 11%   Attrition: 20%   MLB: 84%   Comparables: *Jedd Gyorko, Danny Espinosa, Neil Walker*

The facts here are starting to crystallize. Dietrich comes with a promising left-handed bat, offering 20-homer potential and enough contact ability to make pitchers sweat their defense-independent stats. (You know, if pitchers cared about such things.) A wrist injury made a dog's dinner out of his 2014 season, but he's an offensive bright spot in an otherwise-dismal mix on the dirt in Miami.

Unfortunately, he's also a bit offensive near the second sack. For a guy who's a talented juggler off the field, Dietrich has a lot of trouble with small round objects. He was always kinda questionable with the leather, but was actually worse than advertised in his limited action last season. Rumors have him sliding over to first or third base, but his bat doesn't have the kind of upside that teams look for at the corner cushions. Dietrich's best bet might be to devote himself to becoming average at second, lest he become the second coming of Dan Uggla, but, y'know, worse.

Rafael Furcal   2B

Born: 10/24/77   Age: 37   Bats: B   Throws: R   Height: 5' 8"   Weight: 195

YEAR	TEAM	LVL	AGE	PA	R	2B	3B	HR	RBI	BB	K	SB	CS	AVG/OBP/SLG	TAv	BABIP	BRR	FRAA	WARP
2012	SLN	MLB	34	531	69	18	3	5	49	44	57	12	4	.264/.325/.346	.246	.289	4.3	SS(120): 0.5	2.3
2014	JUP	A+	36	44	6	0	0	0	1	5	5	1	0	.316/.409/.316	.285	.364	-0.9	2B(11): 1.2	0.0
2014	JAX	AA	36	40	5	2	0	0	0	3	2	4	0	.297/.350/.351	.249	.314	0.2	2B(10): 0.4	0.1
2014	MIA	MLB	36	37	4	0	1	0	2	2	7	0	0	.171/.216/.229	.186	.214	0.6	2B(8): -0.8	-0.2
2015	MIA	MLB	37	250	27	10	2	2	18	20	33	6	2	.253/.314/.340	.257	.283	1.4	SS 2, 2B -1	1.1

Breakout: 0%   Improve: 23%   Collapse: 25%   Attrition: 13%   MLB: 79%   Comparables: *Jerry Hairston, Marco Scutaro, Mark Ellis*

Two weeks in June. For some, it's a summer vacation, but for the Marlins, it was the punctuation to a disastrous $3.5 million dollar investment in Furcal. The Fish probably expected Furcal to miss some time with his ever-present injury issues, but a balky left hamstring and right groin kept him off the field for all but nine big-league games. In his brief, shining moment, from June 13th to June 21st, Furcal was *awful*, as depressing as the last wahwaaahwaaaaaaaa moment when the batteries go dead. A 2013 Tommy John surgery robbed Furcal of his signature skill, that railgun of an arm, and forced a move to second base. And at the dish? He never got his legs under him (injury joke) and posted the kind of numbers that make Jeff Mathis look like Buster Posey. Can Furcal stay upright and on the diamond enough to provide value in 2015? Middle infield is an open question for so many clubs come summer, but recent history suggests clubs would need another vacation after traveling with Furcal.

Dee Gordon 2B

Born: 4/22/88   Age: 27   Bats: L   Throws: R   Height: 5' 11"   Weight: 170

YEAR	TEAM	LVL	AGE	PA	R	2B	3B	HR	RBI	BB	K	SB	CS	AVG/OBP/SLG	TAv	BABIP	BRR	FRAA	WARP
2012	ABQ	AAA	24	32	3	0	1	0	1	2	3	2	1	.267/.313/.333	.200	.296	0.6	SS(8): -0.4	-0.1
2012	LAN	MLB	24	330	38	9	2	1	17	20	62	32	10	.228/.280/.281	.222	.281	1.6	SS(79): -4.1	-0.3
2013	ABQ	AAA	25	433	65	17	9	0	33	51	70	49	11	.297/.385/.390	.277	.364	7.2	SS(73): 9.8, 2B(20): -0.5	4.3
2013	LAN	MLB	25	106	9	1	1	1	6	10	21	10	2	.234/.314/.298	.234	.292	1.4	SS(27): 1.3, 2B(3): 0.1	0.5
2014	LAN	MLB	26	650	92	24	12	2	34	31	107	64	19	.289/.326/.378	.267	.346	4.0	2B(144): -2.8	2.4
2015	MIA	MLB	27	554	71	19	7	0	31	32	90	52	14	.269/.315/.336	.249	.321	2.5	2B -2, SS -0	1.4

Breakout: 7%   Improve: 45%   Collapse: 3%   Attrition: 14%   MLB: 90%   Comparables: *Alexi Casilla, Luis Gonzalez, Chris Getz*

Gordon was just about done as a Dodger in almost every respect. He had been handed the starting shortstop job in 2012, which went poorly. Like sub-replacement poorly. After a 2013 spent mostly in the PCL, with trade rumors swirling, the Dodgers gave him a chance to win the second base job in spring training in 2014. Lo and behold, he seized it. Despite offensive limitations (mostly little things like never walking or hitting for power), he wound up with an above-average hitting line and led the league in steals and triples. He's too old to expect great leaps forward, but he's too young to start thinking about cratering; it isn't unreasonable to think he could match his 2014 offensive production this year. Smart money, on the other hand, takes into account Gordon's entire body of work and calls for some regression, as PECOTA does. Still, with solid work at second base, value added on the bases and a reasonable salary, you see what the Marlins were attracted to.

Adeiny Hechavarria SS

Born: 4/15/89   Age: 26   Bats: R   Throws: R   Height: 5' 11"   Weight: 185

YEAR	TEAM	LVL	AGE	PA	R	2B	3B	HR	RBI	BB	K	SB	CS	AVG/OBP/SLG	TAv	BABIP	BRR	FRAA	WARP
2012	LVG	AAA	23	490	78	20	6	6	63	38	86	8	2	.312/.363/.424	.259	.371	1.6	SS(95): 4.5, 2B(8): 1.9	2.7
2012	TOR	MLB	23	137	10	8	0	2	15	4	32	0	0	.254/.280/.365	.227	.323	0.2	3B(18): 0.8, SS(17): -0.8	0.0
2013	MIA	MLB	24	578	30	14	8	3	42	30	96	11	10	.227/.267/.298	.204	.270	-5.5	SS(148): -5.2	-2.3
2014	MIA	MLB	25	574	53	20	10	1	34	26	86	7	5	.276/.308/.356	.243	.323	3.6	SS(146): 7.6	2.8
2015	MIA	MLB	26	542	47	19	6	2	41	27	97	8	5	.253/.290/.329	.239	.302	-0.4	SS 0, 3B 0	1.1

Breakout: 8%   Improve: 47%   Collapse: 10%   Attrition: 15%   MLB: 96%   Comparables: *Angel Berroa, Erick Aybar, Alcides Escobar*

Hechavarria's glove is the baseball equivalent of Schrödinger's Cat; his reputation as a great defender is both alive and dead simultaneously. On the side of the angels, Hecha was a finalist for the Gold Glove at shortstop, comes with a sterling defensive rep from scouts and improved his FRAA to eighth among shortstops last season. On the other hand, he was the most critical part of a Marlins defense that had the fifth-worst park-adjusted defensive efficiency as a team, and the common defensive metrics UZR and DRS shook their statistically generated heads at him for the second straight season. The data collection company Inside Edge might get closest to his true nature, revealing that he excels on difficult plays but is merely average or worse on the easy ones. Fair to say, though, that the actual value of his leather remains a mystery on par with the JFK assassination or how magnets work.

   Hechavarria's bat and baserunning skills improved considerably from 2013, moving him from the "garbage fire at the plate" tier of hitters to the "just not very good" level. Given the complete lack of middle-infield options in Miami, his job is probably safe, no matter what advanced metrics say about his glove, or how poorly he hits.

Garrett Jones 1B

Born: 6/21/81   Age: 34   Bats: L   Throws: L   Height: 6' 5"   Weight: 235

YEAR	TEAM	LVL	AGE	PA	R	2B	3B	HR	RBI	BB	K	SB	CS	AVG/OBP/SLG	TAv	BABIP	BRR	FRAA	WARP
2012	PIT	MLB	31	515	68	28	3	27	86	33	103	2	0	.274/.317/.516	.306	.293	-3.2	1B(72): -1.2, RF(66): -1.3	2.4
2013	PIT	MLB	32	440	41	26	2	15	51	31	101	2	0	.233/.289/.419	.260	.271	-3.7	1B(83): 0.4, RF(32): -1.4	0.0
2014	MIA	MLB	33	547	59	33	2	15	53	46	116	0	1	.246/.309/.411	.267	.290	-2.1	1B(129): -3.7, RF(9): -0.7	0.1
2015	MIA	MLB	34	493	50	25	2	14	58	38	108	2	1	.240/.298/.399	.264	.282	-2.6	1B -2, RF -1	0.3

Breakout: 0%   Improve: 30%   Collapse: 4%   Attrition: 13%   MLB: 91%   Comparables: *Bob Watson, Roy Sievers, Fred McGriff*

Here's what you probably know about Jones: Mashes righties, sucks at anything requiring full-body motion and digs Metallica. Now, one by one: Against righties, he's been one of the least effective starting first basemen in the National League (.246/.305/.435) over the past two seasons. Against lefties? It's a really vulgar scene. Further, the Marlins couldn't protect him from them crooked vultures the way the Pirates did, with 87 percent of his plate appearances coming against righties, down from 95 percent in Pittsburgh a year earlier. He produced his fourth consecutive year with a below-average FRAA (and his reputation with the glove is arguably worse still), and a seventh consecutive year costing his team runs on the basepaths. Jones' value is tied inexorably to his bat. And the bat hasn't been good enough to play regularly at first since 2012. If he continues to decline, his output could be *Lulu*-level bad.

Jeff Mathis C

Born: 3/31/83   Age: 32   Bats: R   Throws: R   Height: 6' 0"   Weight: 205

YEAR	TEAM	LVL	AGE	PA	R	2B	3B	HR	RBI	BB	K	SB	CS	AVG/OBP/SLG	TAv	BABIP	BRR	FRAA	WARP
2012	TOR	MLB	29	227	25	13	0	8	27	9	68	1	0	.218/.249/.393	.218	.279	-1.7	C(66): -1.2, P(2): -0.0	0.0
2013	MIA	MLB	30	256	14	7	1	5	29	21	76	0	0	.181/.251/.284	.204	.243	1.0	C(73): -0.9	0.0
2014	MIA	MLB	31	195	12	7	0	2	12	15	64	0	0	.200/.263/.274	.204	.303	0.8	C(62): 1.1	0.0
2015	MIA	MLB	32	250	20	9	1	4	21	14	75	0	0	.199/.248/.294	.208	.267	0.0	C 0	-0.3

Breakout: 5%   Improve: 34%   Collapse: 13%   Attrition: 28%   MLB: 92%   Comparables: *Damian Miller, Hank Foiles, Benito Santiago*

He can't hit. He just *can't*. Last year could be considered a good offensive season for one of sabermetrics' long-standing punchlines, because Mathis was only about 50 percent worse than league average with the stick. And, hey, he was 70 percent better than the league-average pitcher with the stick. However, with the advent of BP's regressed pitch-framing metrics, the world is better able to measure those things that Mathis does well.

Despite logging only 473 innings, Mathis added more framing value than all but 20 big-league catchers, adding about eight runs to the proper side of his ledger. That drags him up from the depths of replacement level to a place Mathis hasn't often found himself over the past decade.

(But he still can't hit.)

Casey McGehee 3B

Born: 10/12/82   Age: 32   Bats: R   Throws: R   Height: 6' 1"   Weight: 220

YEAR	TEAM	LVL	AGE	PA	R	2B	3B	HR	RBI	BB	K	SB	CS	AVG/OBP/SLG	TAv	BABIP	BRR	FRAA	WARP
2012	CSC	A	29	27	4	3	0	0	8	2	4	0	0	.360/.407/.480	.350	.429	0.0	3B(3): 0.0, 1B(1): 0.0	0.4
2012	NYA	MLB	29	59	9	3	0	1	6	5	10	0	0	.151/.220/.264	.192	.163	-0.3	3B(12): -1.3, 1B(8): -0.2	-0.5
2012	PIT	MLB	29	293	27	13	1	8	35	24	60	1	1	.230/.297/.377	.252	.266	-1.5	1B(77): 2.6, 3B(9): 0.1	0.3
2014	MIA	MLB	31	691	56	29	1	4	76	67	102	4	2	.287/.355/.357	.265	.335	-6.0	3B(158): -19.4	0.0
2015	MIA	MLB	32	511	45	23	1	6	48	39	86	2	1	.250/.307/.347	.255	.290	-3.0	3B -8, 1B 0	-0.3

Breakout: 2%   Improve: 48%   Collapse: 4%   Attrition: 6%   MLB: 92%   *Comparables: Buddy Bell, Brooks Robinson, Bill Madlock*

Gold stars for everyone who predicted McGehee would be a fine stopgap for the Marlins at third base in 2014. Come collect your gold stars. Anyone? Anybody? Good, because we forgot to buy any gold stars. Coming off a year playing in Japan, and two dismal years in MLB before that, McGehee was an actual, honest-to-goodness stalwart in the Marlins' lineup. He played 160 games, all but two at the hot corner, and provided the third-best OBP of any qualified third baseman in the big leagues.

Expecting him to replicate his 2014 performance this year for the Giants would be a bit unwise, though. During his good seasons, McGehee has hit the ball hard and seen a nice BABIP bump, but without the power he showed in his previous seasons, he's more prone to bad luck dragging down his production than the typical third sacker. But going from token *gaijin* for the Tohoku Rakuten Golden Eagles to a real-live everyday third baseman is no small feat. Give that man a gold star!

Michael Morse   LF

Born: 3/22/82   Age: 33   Bats: R   Throws: R   Height: 6' 5"   Weight: 245

YEAR	TEAM	LVL	AGE	PA	R	2B	3B	HR	RBI	BB	K	SB	CS	AVG/OBP/SLG	TAv	BABIP	BRR	FRAA	WARP
2012	WAS	MLB	30	430	53	17	1	18	62	16	97	0	1	.291/.321/.470	.273	.339	-4.3	LF(67): -3.6, RF(36): 1.6	0.5
2013	TAC	AAA	31	26	3	1	0	1	2	2	6	0	0	.250/.308/.417	.240	.294	0.2	RF(3): 0.1	0.0
2013	SEA	MLB	31	307	31	13	0	13	27	20	80	0	0	.226/.283/.410	.259	.267	-1.5	RF(53): -2.9, LF(11): 0.1	-0.1
2013	BAL	MLB	31	30	3	0	0	0	0	1	7	0	0	.103/.133/.103	.092	.136	-0.2	LF(8): 0.4, RF(2): 0.1	-0.5
2014	SFN	MLB	32	482	48	32	3	16	61	31	121	0	0	.279/.336/.475	.296	.348	-3.2	LF(84): -3.3, RF(43): 1.1	1.9
2015	MIA	MLB	33	427	47	20	2	15	57	25	105	0	0	.262/.313/.440	.284	.316	-2.5	LF -2, RF -0	1.3

Breakout: 1%   Improve: 27%   Collapse: 6%   Attrition: 6%   MLB: 92%   *Comparables: Ryan Ludwick, Alfonso Soriano, Geoff Jenkins*

Cherry-picking data is a perilous venture fraught with distortion risk, but sometimes, when you can explain away the rejected items, it has its merits. Cast aside Morse's 2013 campaign, when he played his way through the entire Operation card set, then sum up his remaining body of work since 2010, and you'll get a .291/.343/.505 slash line, respectable by any standards, but particularly considering most of it was assembled in neutral or pitcher-friendly parks. An enormous human with Stantonian raw strength, Morse can clear any fence, and the force with which he clobbers baseballs explains his seemingly inflated BABIPs.

There's no denying that the Floridian's medical chart is thick, but he has always been a productive power hitter in a league where beasts of his breed are increasingly rare. Morse has traveled farther than perhaps anybody in history on the defensive spectrum, from rookie shortstop to veteran whose glove is best locked away, but the Marlins looked past that to gain the benefit of a bat that plays above average at any position.

Marcell Ozuna   CF

Born: 11/12/90   Age: 24   Bats: R   Throws: R   Height: 6' 1"   Weight: 230

YEAR	TEAM	LVL	AGE	PA	R	2B	3B	HR	RBI	BB	K	SB	CS	AVG/OBP/SLG	TAv	BABIP	BRR	FRAA	WARP
2012	JUP	A+	21	539	89	27	2	24	95	44	116	8	3	.266/.328/.476	.281	.301	1.1	RF(107): 17.7, CF(14): -0.5	4.3
2013	JAX	AA	22	47	6	3	1	5	15	3	9	1	0	.333/.383/.810	.414	.310	0.4	RF(10): -0.6	0.9
2013	MIA	MLB	22	291	31	17	4	3	32	13	57	5	1	.265/.303/.389	.258	.326	1.4	RF(36): 1.9, CF(33): -2.3	1.0
2014	MIA	MLB	23	612	72	26	5	23	85	41	164	3	1	.269/.317/.455	.286	.337	-1.0	CF(140): -11.3, LF(11): 1.1	2.9
2015	MIA	MLB	24	518	55	24	3	16	65	30	129	4	1	.257/.301/.424	.275	.314	0.1	CF -7, RF 2	1.6

Breakout: 3%   Improve: 49%   Collapse: 5%   Attrition: 7%   MLB: 98%   *Comparables: Adam Jones, Matt Kemp, Chris Young*

It's probably due to the presence of wunderstars Christian Yelich and Giancarlo Stanton in the Miami outfield, but Ozuna doesn't get the respect he deserves. In a different organization, he'd be almost a Jay Bruce-lite. Sure, there are question marks in the approach, but he's got weapons, namely a cannon arm, plus power and an ability to hit both right- and left-handed pitching. The defense in center is a bit of an open question, as the major defensive metrics disagree on his range and value. But in the current flanking, Marlins fans will be happy with Ozuna playing the Porthos to Yelich's Athos and Stanton's Aramis.

J.T. Realmuto   C

Born: 3/18/91   Age: 24   Bats: R   Throws: R   Height: 6' 1"   Weight: 215

YEAR	TEAM	LVL	AGE	PA	R	2B	3B	HR	RBI	BB	K	SB	CS	AVG/OBP/SLG	TAv	BABIP	BRR	FRAA	WARP
2012	JUP	A+	21	499	63	16	0	8	46	37	64	13	5	.256/.319/.345	.241	.279	-0.9	C(95): 1.1, 1B(1): -0.0	0.9
2013	JAX	AA	22	416	41	21	3	5	39	36	68	9	1	.239/.310/.353	.253	.275	-1.6	C(99): -1.2	1.5
2014	JAX	AA	23	423	66	25	6	8	62	41	59	18	5	.299/.369/.461	.308	.333	5.6	C(88): -1.3	4.8
2014	MIA	MLB	23	30	4	1	1	0	9	1	8	0	0	.241/.267/.345	.227	.333	0.0	C(9): -0.2	0.0
2015	MIA	MLB	24	250	22	11	2	3	22	15	49	5	1	.238/.287/.336	.241	.286	0.4	C -0, 1B -0	0.5

Breakout: 7%   Improve: 11%   Collapse: 6%   Attrition: 16%   MLB: 30%   *Comparables: Austin Romine, Curtis Casali, Tim Federowicz*

Late to the catching game after coming up as a middle infielder, Realmuto has taken to the tools of ignorance like a duck to water, learning quickly how to leverage his athleticism into solid receiving skills. He can run especially well for a catcher (at least for now), makes contact and flashes batting-practice power that could translate to a dozen dingers at the highest level. Best of all (for a catcher at least), he earns high marks for his intangibles and ability to learn. While the Marlins' Minor League Player of the Year might not have the tools to carry your fantasy team, his ability to do just about everything at a role-5 level, and still improve, makes for a pretty useful catcher.

Miguel Rojas   INF

Born: 2/24/89   Age: 26   Bats: R   Throws: R   Height: 6' 0"   Weight: 150

YEAR	TEAM	LVL	AGE	PA	R	2B	3B	HR	RBI	BB	K	SB	CS	AVG/OBP/SLG	TAv	BABIP	BRR	FRAA	WARP
2012	PEN	AA	23	160	14	1	0	0	10	16	17	2	3	.210/.294/.217	.189	.238	-0.6	2B(25): 2.0, 3B(14): -1.2	-0.4
2012	LOU	AAA	23	144	9	3	0	1	7	7	16	0	0	.186/.226/.233	.186	.204	0.4	SS(37): -0.7, 2B(3): 0.4	-0.5
2013	CHT	AA	24	478	45	12	2	5	32	40	49	10	4	.233/.303/.307	.227	.253	3.1	SS(129): 19.3, 2B(3): -0.0	2.9
2014	ABQ	AAA	25	173	27	9	0	4	13	10	21	7	3	.302/.353/.434	.270	.326	1.2	SS(23): -0.3, 3B(16): 1.0	1.1
2014	LAN	MLB	25	162	16	3	0	1	9	10	28	0	0	.181/.242/.221	.175	.217	0.5	SS(66): 2.3, 3B(19): 0.8	-0.3
2015	MIA	MLB	26	250	20	8	1	1	17	14	37	3	1	.219/.267/.276	.213	.249	-0.1	SS 5, 3B 0	0.4

Breakout: 3%   Improve: 15%   Collapse: 4%   Attrition: 11%   MLB: 26%   Comparables: Andres Blanco, Melvin Dorta, Alberto Gonzalez

When then-GM Ned Colletti mentioned Rojas as a possibility for the second base job last winter, it felt more like an empty Dad threat than anything: "I'll turn this car around if you don't shut yer yappers," that sort of thing. Rojas is a suitable September addition, where he can serve as a defensive replacement without stretching the roster thin. The Dodgers used him that way, replacing Hanley Ramirez after the seventh inning of nearly every game that month, and his defensive ratings were off the charts. He's basically Rafael Belliard. Belliard played 17 years and produced -5.4 career WARP.

Avery Romero   2B

Born: 5/11/93   Age: 22   Bats: R   Throws: R   Height: 5' 8"   Weight: 190

YEAR	TEAM	LVL	AGE	PA	R	2B	3B	HR	RBI	BB	K	SB	CS	AVG/OBP/SLG	TAv	BABIP	BRR	FRAA	WARP
2012	JAM	A-	19	25	3	0	0	0	4	3	0	1	0	.381/.458/.381	.299	.381	-0.6	3B(5): -0.1, 2B(3): -0.2	0.1
2013	GRB	A	20	40	5	1	0	1	5	4	5	0	0	.147/.237/.265	.204	.143	-0.1	2B(9): -0.8	-0.2
2013	BAT	A-	20	235	27	18	0	2	30	15	34	3	4	.297/.357/.411	.289	.339	-1.2	2B(53): 6.6	2.0
2014	GRB	A	21	399	51	23	1	5	46	25	47	6	4	.320/.366/.429	.287	.354	-0.2	2B(77): -3.0	1.8
2014	JUP	A+	21	108	12	8	0	0	10	7	13	4	1	.320/.370/.400	.285	.368	0.9	2B(16): 0.4, 3B(6): -0.5	0.7
2015	MIA	MLB	22	250	18	11	1	1	20	11	51	1	1	.235/.272/.301	.223	.290	-0.4	2B -0, 3B -0	-0.3

Breakout: 0%   Improve: 0%   Collapse: 0%   Attrition: 0%   MLB: 0%   Comparables: Luis Valbuena, Daniel Descalso, Enrique Hernandez

So far, so good. Still young, and still more projection than performance, Romero has batting practice power that hasn't flashed in game action yet, and a sneaky hit tool powered by an ability to make contact on pitches inside. As he's not particularly refined in his approach, the likely end result isn't a superstar, but rather someone on the spectrum between a quad-A bench option and a first-division starter. The outcome will toggle on his defense, as he's still adjusting to life in the middle of the infield. He works hard, but doesn't have the athleticism or reaction to show too much fluidity up the middle. He'll live and die on his bat, which could make iffy defense in the center of the diamond an idiosyncrasy, not a death sentence.

Jarrod Saltalamacchia   C

Born: 5/2/85   Age: 30   Bats: B   Throws: R   Height: 6' 3"   Weight: 235

YEAR	TEAM	LVL	AGE	PA	R	2B	3B	HR	RBI	BB	K	SB	CS	AVG/OBP/SLG	TAv	BABIP	BRR	FRAA	WARP
2012	BOS	MLB	27	448	55	17	1	25	59	38	139	0	1	.222/.288/.454	.265	.265	-0.4	C(104): 0.5, 1B(1): -0.0	2.1
2013	BOS	MLB	28	470	68	40	1	14	65	43	139	4	1	.273/.338/.466	.288	.372	0.8	C(119): -0.2	3.4
2014	MIA	MLB	29	435	43	20	0	11	44	55	143	0	1	.220/.320/.362	.259	.317	0.1	C(107): -1.0	1.2
2015	MIA	MLB	30	417	43	20	2	13	50	38	126	1	1	.227/.299/.392	.261	.302	0.2	C -1	1.6

Breakout: 0%   Improve: 47%   Collapse: 6%   Attrition: 14%   MLB: 95%   Comparables: Kelly Shoppach, Stan Lopata, Johnny Bench

At first glance, the man with the longest last name in baseball looks like a pretty solid backstop. Salty's ability to take a free pass (13 percent walk rate) gets him to first base and produces at least some offensive value, even as his power takes a sharp turn south. But recently, Saltalamacchia has revealed an Achilles' heel: he's a stabber. As the catcher's ability to sneak extra strikes becomes more scrutinized—and therefore more valuable—Saltalamacchia has become the poster boy for what not to do. BP's pitch-framing metrics rate him the worst framer in baseball, giving back nearly 20 runs due to receiving inadequacy. If you factor that into his overall contributions, the man with the longest last name in baseball looks like a replacement-level contributor taking home 13 percent of his team's payroll.

Donovan Solano   2B

Born: 12/17/87   Age: 27   Bats: R   Throws: R   Height: 5' 9"   Weight: 205

YEAR	TEAM	LVL	AGE	PA	R	2B	3B	HR	RBI	BB	K	SB	CS	AVG/OBP/SLG	TAv	BABIP	BRR	FRAA	WARP
2012	NWO	AAA	24	160	14	7	1	0	14	10	27	4	0	.262/.327/.326	.237	.322	-0.4	2B(18): 2.3, SS(17): -1.2	0.2
2012	MIA	MLB	24	316	29	11	3	2	28	21	58	7	0	.295/.342/.375	.266	.357	2.1	2B(58): 4.6, LF(10): -0.3	1.8
2013	NWO	AAA	25	73	8	3	1	2	9	4	11	0	0	.379/.411/.545	.366	.418	0.0	2B(9): 0.2, 3B(4): -0.0	1.2
2013	MIA	MLB	25	395	33	13	1	3	34	23	57	3	1	.249/.305/.316	.230	.287	-1.8	2B(93): 8.1, 3B(2): -0.0	0.5
2014	NWO	AAA	26	22	2	1	0	0	3	0	5	0	0	.095/.091/.143	.066	.118	0.1	3B(3): 0.5, 2B(1): -0.1	-0.3
2014	MIA	MLB	26	340	26	11	1	3	28	19	61	1	2	.252/.300/.323	.239	.304	-1.3	2B(73): 3.3, SS(4): 0.1	0.1
2015	MIA	MLB	27	344	35	13	2	2	26	19	60	3	1	.260/.308/.340	.250	.306	-0.4	2B 6, SS 0	1.4

Breakout: 7%   Improve: 54%   Collapse: 2%   Attrition: 12%   MLB: 98%   Comparables: Hector Luna, Luis Rivas, Darwin Barney

In the film *High Fidelity*, the depressed, worn-out, sad-sack Rob Gordon says this about his two even-sadder-sack record store employees: "I can't fire them. I hired these guys for three days a week and they just started showing up every day. That was four years ago." (Cue sad-sack Beta Band song.) That's Donovan Solano in a nutshell. Signed as a minor-league free agent in 2011, Solano was probably meant to be organizational depth. Instead, he's fallen head-first into 300-plus plate appearances each season by sheer virtue of playing for the Marlins. Does Solano have any useful big-league skills? Probably not. He's played a few innings off of his native position, second base, but he doesn't have elite defensive chops and hasn't been trusted with much time off the pivot. He's certainly not a good hitter, with a career TAv of .244. Unless something changes in Solano's bat or his glove, he's more likely to make a long-term impact as a record store employee than as an MLB second baseman, but as long as he keeps showing up ...

Giancarlo Stanton   RF

Born: 11/8/89   Age: 25   Bats: R   Throws: R   Height: 6' 6"   Weight: 240

YEAR	TEAM	LVL	AGE	PA	R	2B	3B	HR	RBI	BB	K	SB	CS	AVG/OBP/SLG	TAv	BABIP	BRR	FRAA	WARP
2012	MIA	MLB	22	501	75	30	1	37	86	46	143	6	2	.290/.361/.608	.342	.344	0.1	RF(117): 6.0	6.1
2013	MIA	MLB	23	504	62	26	0	24	62	74	140	1	0	.249/.365/.480	.316	.313	0.2	RF(116): 0.4	3.8
2014	MIA	MLB	24	638	89	31	1	37	105	94	170	13	1	.288/.395/.555	.342	.353	2.3	RF(143): 11.3	8.2
2015	MIA	MLB	25	575	84	28	2	33	96	67	157	7	1	.269/.359/.531	.326	.322	0.6	RF 8	5.8

Breakout: 5%   Improve: 68%   Collapse: 1%   Attrition: 4%   MLB: 99%   Comparables: Mickey Mantle, Ryan Braun, Darryl Strawberry

Baseball lifers and armchair analysts bemoan the dearth of right-handed power throughout the league, but Stanton remains the prototype of the slugging right fielder. His massive build cuts the image of a superhero in the batter's box: Incredible Hulk with self-control, or Mighty Thor with an even more powerful hammer. He cut his strikeout rate slightly while maintaining his signature power, setting career bests in doubles, walks (both intentional and unintentional) and plate appearances. He played in each of the Marlins' first 145 games, his first injury-free season in three years, until ...

All heroes have weaknesses, some subtle and some as direct as a fastball to the face. Giancarlo was the MVP frontrunner before a Mike Fiers fastball came up and in and caused multiple fractures and lacerations, ending his season in mid-September. Since the horror show that closed his season did not appear to damage his orbital bone or cause a serious concussion, the prognosis is a full recovery. With no real weaknesses on the basepaths or in the field, he begins 2015 the same way he ended 2014: As the MVP frontrunner.

Miguel Tejada   INF

Born: 5/25/74   Age: 41   Bats: R   Throws: R   Height: 5' 9"   Weight: 220

YEAR	TEAM	LVL	AGE	PA	R	2B	3B	HR	RBI	BB	K	SB	CS	AVG/OBP/SLG	TAv	BABIP	BRR	FRAA	WARP
2012	NOR	AAA	38	151	10	5	0	0	18	11	16	1	0	.259/.325/.296	.235	.289	-0.9	3B(30): -0.2, SS(3): -0.4	-0.1
2013	KCA	MLB	39	167	15	5	0	3	20	6	25	1	0	.288/.317/.378	.256	.326	-0.1	2B(26): -1.1, 3B(22): -0.4	0.1
2015	MIA	MLB	41	250	19	10	1	1	20	9	31	2	1	.247/.280/.312	.233	.274	-0.3	3B 2, 2B -1	0.1

Breakout: 0%   Improve: 17%   Collapse: 9%   Attrition: 19%   MLB: 61%   Comparables: Lou Piniella, Wade Boggs, B.J. Surhoff

Between a 105-game PED suspension handed down in August 2013, and a this-time-we-really-mean-it release 12 months later, Tejada played four games for the Marlins' Triple-A affiliate. His exit from baseball was not celebrated in the way of his also-retiring contemporary, Derek Jeter, despite the two players posting career WARPs within eight wins of each other. Tejada had not the consistency nor the charm nor the postseason success—he never did win a postseason series—and we'll remember him more for the abbreviation B-12 than MVP, but he was a force during several of his 17 seasons in the big leagues. He was good enough that for the next 20 years you'll be able to get a rise out of Yankees fans just by noting that Tejada and Jeter posted career WARPs within eight wins of each other.

Justin Twine   SS

Born: 10/7/95   Age: 19   Bats: R   Throws: R   Height: 5' 11"   Weight: 205

YEAR	TEAM	LVL	AGE	PA	R	2B	3B	HR	RBI	BB	K	SB	CS	AVG/OBP/SLG	TAv	BABIP	BRR	FRAA	WARP
2015	MIA	MLB	19	250	16	8	1	1	18	9	79	2	1	.188/.222/.250	.184	.269	-0.1	SS 1	-0.8

Breakout: 0%   Improve: 0%   Collapse: 0%   Attrition: 0%   MLB: 0%   Comparables: Adrian Cardenas, Carlos Rivero, Neftali Soto

Twine's calling-card skill is ridiculous speed and athleticism—as a sophomore he once rushed for more than 500 yards in a high school game. Averaged 25 yards per carry that night, and wasn't even playing running back, but rather QB. Running fast enough to make up for his arm seems to be a persistent theme in his athletic career, as there are concerns about his throws at shortstop, along with questions about most of the rest of his game at this point. It's all about projection, because right now he's raw as ceviche. He has no approach to speak of, and he has never displayed over-the-fence power, even in high school. But he's got a quick-twitch bat and very fast hands, flashing a raw ability to come around on the ball. If all else fails: Run.

Christian Yelich   LF

Born: 12/5/91   Age: 23   Bats: L   Throws: R   Height: 6' 3"   Weight: 200

YEAR	TEAM	LVL	AGE	PA	R	2B	3B	HR	RBI	BB	K	SB	CS	AVG/OBP/SLG	TAv	BABIP	BRR	FRAA	WARP
2012	JUP	A+	20	447	76	29	5	12	48	49	85	20	6	.330/.404/.519	.323	.397	2.4	CF(96): -0.0, LF(7): -0.3	4.6
2013	JUP	A+	21	30	3	0	0	2	4	4	8	0	0	.231/.333/.462	.271	.250	0.2	CF(6): -1.3	0.1
2013	JAX	AA	21	222	33	13	6	7	29	26	52	5	5	.280/.365/.518	.322	.346	-1.0	CF(27): -0.9, LF(22): -1.0	1.9
2013	MIA	MLB	21	273	34	12	1	4	16	31	66	10	0	.288/.370/.396	.295	.380	3.3	LF(59): -0.4, CF(5): 0.1	1.7
2014	MIA	MLB	22	660	94	30	6	9	54	70	137	21	7	.284/.362/.402	.286	.356	2.6	LF(138): -1.7, CF(12): -1.3	3.0
2015	MIA	MLB	23	578	74	27	5	11	54	56	133	17	5	.272/.344/.404	.286	.344	2.1	LF -1, CF -2	2.8

Breakout: 5%   Improve: 56%   Collapse: 2%   Attrition: 4%   MLB: 94%   Comparables: B.J. Upton, Matt Kemp, David Wright

It doesn't take long for a player to hit the "post-hype" label, especially with so many touted outfield prospects popping up like Whac-A-Mole every season. It can be easy to forget that a left field wunderkind like Yelich just completed his age-22 season, or that he's already the second-best everyday player on the Marlins. The value metrics speak for themselves—various WARs and WARP all range between three and four wins in 2014—but they do so in a robotic monotone. If you want a clear, living-color picture of Yelich's value, watch his game on September 14th against the Phillies. He made a tremendous running catch to show off Gold Glove-winning defense, roped two singles to demonstrate his plus contact ability and even took a walk, as if to say "yes, my approach is strong, and I will reach base with great frequency." It's cool that Yelich can do a passable Alex Gordon impersonation for the Fish, and it's even cooler that he can do it at an age in which most young men are gearing up for a fifth year of college. Even Gordon was still in Double-A.

Pitchers

Henderson Alvarez   RHP

Born: 4/18/90   Age: 25   Bats: R   Throws: R   Height: 6'0"   Weight: 205

YEAR	TEAM	LVL	AGE	W	L	SV	G	GS	IP	H	HR	BB	K	BB/9	K/9	GB%	BABIP	WHIP	ERA	FIP	FRA	WARP
2012	TOR	MLB	22	9	14	0	31	31	187¹	216	29	54	79	2.6	3.8	58%	.291	1.44	4.85	5.13	6.35	-1.0
2013	JUP	A+	23	1	0	0	2	2	10	9	1	1	2	0.9	1.8	53%	.242	1.00	2.70	4.44	5.31	-0.1
2013	JAX	AA	23	1	0	0	2	2	14¹	5	0	0	13	0.0	8.2	77%	.143	0.35	0.00	1.10	2.49	0.5
2013	MIA	MLB	23	5	6	0	17	17	103²	90	2	27	57	2.4	5.0	55%	.271	1.14	3.59	3.16	4.23	1.1
2014	MIA	MLB	24	12	7	0	30	30	187	198	14	33	111	1.6	5.3	56%	.304	1.24	2.65	3.55	4.36	1.3
2015	*MIA*	*MLB*	*25*	*9*	*8*	*0*	*24*	*24*	*146¹*	*148*	*12*	*30*	*83*	*1.9*	*5.1*	*53%*	*.306*	*1.22*	*3.85*	*3.98*	*4.18*	*0.5*

Breakout: 25%   Improve: 56%   Collapse: 12%   Attrition: 9%   MLB: 95%   Comparables: *Chris Volstad, Mike Pelfrey, Jesse Litsch*

If you had to pick a hurler who epitomizes the Marlins' pitching philosophy, it wouldn't be superstar ace Jose Fernandez. It would be non-superstar, non-ace Henderson Alvarez. The young Venezuelan has emerged as a solid cog in the Miami rotation since coming over from Toronto, and he's succeeding using the team's primary pitching philosophy: throw hard, pound the strike zone, get groundball outs, pitch efficiently. Alvarez has a heavy, hasty sinker and a changeup, and he lives low in the strike zone. Good news for him: MLB's de facto strike zone is getting lower and lower as the years go on, earning him more swings and costing him fewer bad counts and bases on balls. Of course, Alvarez still doesn't strike anyone out. His K% went up just a bit in 2014, as hitters had more swings and misses at his offerings outside the zone. Despite how rarely he walks anyone, Henderson is unlikely to be a defense-independent superstar, or an elite starter. But every team in baseball would love to have him, if not quite as much as the Marlins do.

Carter Capps   RHP

Born: 8/7/90   Age: 24   Bats: R   Throws: R   Height: 6'4"   Weight: 230

YEAR	TEAM	LVL	AGE	W	L	SV	G	GS	IP	H	HR	BB	K	BB/9	K/9	GB%	BABIP	WHIP	ERA	FIP	FRA	WARP
2012	WTN	AA	21	2	3	19	38	0	50	40	2	12	72	2.2	13.0	44%	.328	1.04	1.26	1.56	1.73	2.1
2012	SEA	MLB	21	0	0	0	18	0	25	25	0	11	28	4.0	10.1	41%	.357	1.44	3.96	2.13	2.35	0.7
2013	TAC	AAA	22	0	0	0	7	0	11	6	0	4	9	3.3	7.4	54%	.214	0.91	1.64	3.84	3.78	0.1
2013	SEA	MLB	22	3	3	0	53	0	59	73	12	23	66	3.5	10.1	41%	.365	1.63	5.49	4.75	4.39	0.1
2014	NWO	AAA	23	0	1	0	7	0	11	8	0	6	17	4.9	13.9	56%	.348	1.27	1.64	2.24	1.78	0.4
2014	MIA	MLB	23	0	0	0	17	0	20¹	19	1	5	25	2.2	11.1	39%	.340	1.18	3.98	2.32	3.61	0.2
2015	*MIA*	*MLB*	*24*	*2*	*1*	*0*	*28*	*1*	*38*	*33*	*3*	*12*	*42*	*2.8*	*10.0*	*41%*	*.330*	*1.19*	*3.26*	*3.13*	*3.54*	*0.4*

Breakout: 30%   Improve: 58%   Collapse: 15%   Attrition: 23%   MLB: 92%   Comparables: *Kelvin Herrera, Tim Collins, Bill Bray*

Was 2014 a lost season for Capps? He missed three mid-year months rehabbing right elbow issues, and he bookended his season with good but not great performance in low-leverage relief work. Possessed of a righteous 97 mph fastball and only cursory command of the strike zone, Capps is the prototype of the hit-or-miss young reliever: all of the potential, none of the run prevention. In 2015, we'll get to keep playing the "if" game. *If* he can stay healthy, and *if* he can keep his walk rate as low as he kept it in 2014, and *if* he eats all his vegetables, he'll find his way to the business end of a bullpen.

Steve Cishek   RHP

Born: 6/18/86   Age: 29   Bats: R   Throws: R   Height: 6'6"   Weight: 215

YEAR	TEAM	LVL	AGE	W	L	SV	G	GS	IP	H	HR	BB	K	BB/9	K/9	GB%	BABIP	WHIP	ERA	FIP	FRA	WARP
2012	MIA	MLB	26	5	2	15	68	0	63²	54	3	29	68	4.1	9.6	54%	.302	1.30	2.69	3.26	3.15	0.7
2013	MIA	MLB	27	4	6	34	69	0	69²	53	3	22	74	2.8	9.6	55%	.278	1.08	2.33	2.49	2.95	1.1
2014	MIA	MLB	28	4	5	39	67	0	65¹	58	3	21	84	2.9	11.6	46%	.331	1.21	3.17	2.14	2.63	1.3
2015	*MIA*	*MLB*	*29*	*3*	*1*	*28*	*58*	*0*	*60²*	*49*	*3*	*20*	*64*	*2.9*	*9.5*	*49%*	*.310*	*1.13*	*2.88*	*2.94*	*3.13*	*1.0*

Breakout: 34%   Improve: 55%   Collapse: 22%   Attrition: 16%   MLB: 88%   Comparables: *Kevin Jepsen, Brian Wilson, Luke Gregerson*

From a birds-eye view, Cishek's 2014 was a lot like his 2013. He was a boring, successful closer on an unsuccessful team, armed with lots of saves and strong overall numbers. A deeper look shows some interesting but not necessarily *good* changes from 2013. His strikeout rate spiked, pushing him up over 30 percent for the season. But that didn't come with an increased number of whiffs, as his swinging strike rate stayed the same. Also, instead of burning worms with a 54 percent groundball rate (his average over his three previous seasons), Cishek induced grounders on just 46 percent of batted balls. What does it all mean? Well, that's kind of a deep, philosophical question that's not usually covered in a player comment. But in regards to Cishek, he seems to be in his prime, but needs either his groundball rate to regress or his strikeout rate to not.

Jarred Cosart   RHP

Born: 5/25/90   Age: 25   Bats: R   Throws: R   Height: 6'3"   Weight: 195

YEAR	TEAM	LVL	AGE	W	L	SV	G	GS	IP	H	HR	BB	K	BB/9	K/9	GB%	BABIP	WHIP	ERA	FIP	FRA	WARP
2012	CCH	AA	22	5	5	0	15	15	87	83	3	38	68	3.9	7.0	63%	.300	1.39	3.52	3.72	4.52	1.1
2012	OKL	AAA	22	1	2	0	6	5	27²	26	0	13	24	4.2	7.8	59%	.325	1.41	2.60	3.45	3.96	0.7
2013	OKL	AAA	23	7	4	0	18	17	93	74	5	50	93	4.8	9.0	60%	.276	1.33	3.29	3.98	4.80	1.0
2013	HOU	MLB	23	1	1	0	10	10	60	46	3	35	33	5.2	4.9	55%	.246	1.35	1.95	4.38	4.91	0.1
2014	HOU	MLB	24	9	7	0	20	20	116¹	119	7	51	75	3.9	5.8	58%	.302	1.46	4.41	4.05	4.44	1.0
2014	MIA	MLB	24	4	4	0	10	10	64	54	2	22	40	3.1	5.6	52%	.267	1.19	2.39	3.29	3.88	0.7
2015	*MIA*	*MLB*	*25*	*9*	*9*	*0*	*28*	*28*	*155²*	*142*	*8*	*65*	*109*	*3.8*	*6.3*	*54%*	*.301*	*1.33*	*3.76*	*3.95*	*4.08*	*0.8*

Breakout: 31%   Improve: 61%   Collapse: 15%   Attrition: 21%   MLB: 91%   Comparables: *Zach Britton, Vin Mazzaro, Ivan Nova*

First impressions are absolutely, positively this guy's bag. The plan for the tall Texan should be to debut for a new franchise in the middle of each season. The reason? Cosart's late-2013 big-league debut with the Astros and his post-deadline starts with the Marlins each made him look like a real run-preventer, but bookended an otherwise uninspiring 2014 season.

Cosart is, in many ways, the ideal Marlins stereotype, with a 94 mph average fastball, a pitch-to-contact sinker, prospect pedigree—and, by both peripheral and traditional measures, pretty lousy results so far. They had enough faith in his ripping fastball and worm-burning ways to part with a pair of highly touted (if somewhat dimmed) prospects to acquire him, despite having organizational depth in the rotation. Given his lack of strikeouts at *all* levels of pro ball, there's little hope for Cosart to develop into a star. Yet the Marlins have shown that their ground-and-pound pitching philosophy can have success, and if he can avoid the control issues that have plagued him in the past, there's a recipe for Henderson Alvarez-like success. Or Jacob Turner-like failure.

Aaron Crow   RHP

Born: 11/10/86   Age: 28   Bats: R   Throws: R   Height: 6'3"   Weight: 195

YEAR	TEAM	LVL	AGE	W	L	SV	G	GS	IP	H	HR	BB	K	BB/9	K/9	GB%	BABIP	WHIP	ERA	FIP	FRA	WARP
2012	KCA	MLB	25	3	1	2	73	0	64²	54	4	22	65	3.1	9.0	53%	.298	1.18	3.48	2.91	3.95	0.7
2013	KCA	MLB	26	7	5	1	57	0	48	49	6	22	44	4.1	8.2	51%	.316	1.48	3.38	4.37	4.44	0.0
2014	KCA	MLB	27	6	1	3	67	0	59	52	10	24	34	3.7	5.2	45%	.239	1.29	4.12	5.43	6.56	-0.9
2015	MIA	MLB	28	3	1	1	57	0	53	49	5	21	47	3.5	7.9	52%	.311	1.31	3.91	4.04	4.25	0.1

Breakout: 28%   Improve: 50%   Collapse: 20%   Attrition: 21%   MLB: 78%   Comparables: Wesley Wright, Marc Rzepczynski, Angel Guzman

Crow's fourth full year in the Royals' bullpen turned out to be his last, as the Topeka native was shipped off to Miami in November. A former top pick, Crow's peripherals have been headed in the wrong direction for years and last year wandered clean off the map. His velocity was down from its mid-90s peak, his sinker didn't have much sink and his woeful walk and strikeout rates helped Crow post baseball's worst FIP among relievers who worked at least 50 innings. The Marlins, always willing to try new ways to fail, are toying with the idea of putting him in the rotation. Curious, to say the least, given how few bats he missed when he was throwing all-out in relief. Think Tanner Scheppers.

Mike Dunn   LHP

Born: 5/23/85   Age: 30   Bats: L   Throws: L   Height: 6'0"   Weight: 210

YEAR	TEAM	LVL	AGE	W	L	SV	G	GS	IP	H	HR	BB	K	BB/9	K/9	GB%	BABIP	WHIP	ERA	FIP	FRA	WARP
2012	NWO	AAA	27	1	1	0	12	0	17²	19	0	7	24	3.6	12.2	49%	.404	1.47	4.58	2.14	2.25	0.7
2012	MIA	MLB	27	0	3	1	60	0	44	49	3	29	47	5.9	9.6	36%	.357	1.77	4.91	3.86	3.64	0.4
2013	MIA	MLB	28	3	4	2	75	0	67²	53	5	28	72	3.7	9.6	42%	.271	1.20	2.66	3.09	3.86	0.5
2014	MIA	MLB	29	10	6	1	75	0	57	47	4	22	67	3.5	10.6	37%	.291	1.21	3.16	3.03	3.42	0.5
2015	MIA	MLB	30	3	1	1	64	0	54	43	4	23	61	3.8	10.1	40%	.313	1.23	3.28	3.40	3.56	0.6

Breakout: 25%   Improve: 44%   Collapse: 22%   Attrition: 12%   MLB: 84%   Comparables: Sergio Santos, Bill Bray, Jose Valverde

If you need proof that pitcher wins are kind of a crapshoot—and since you're reading a BP Annual in 2015, you probably don't—look at the consistently inconsistent Dunn. He pilfered 10 W's, good for second on the Marlins, despite doing his work in the seventh and eighth frames as a southpaw setup man. He melted down as often as he shut it down, but the overall package was a solid, if unspectacular, late-inning lefty. Dunn leaned harder on his slider, a potent whiff-inducing weapon against same-handed hitters. At the same time, his strikeout rate spiked slightly against right-handed hitters (up to 32 percent, hooray!), as did his walk rate (up to 11 percent, boo!). That walk rate is the thing keeping the Nevada product from graduating from solid setup arm on a second-division team to the sort of reliever who'll get a three-year contract when he finally hits free agency.

Sam Dyson   RHP

Born: 5/7/88   Age: 27   Bats: R   Throws: R   Height: 6'1"   Weight: 205

YEAR	TEAM	LVL	AGE	W	L	SV	G	GS	IP	H	HR	BB	K	BB/9	K/9	GB%	BABIP	WHIP	ERA	FIP	FRA	WARP
2012	DUN	A+	24	2	0	0	6	6	28²	35	1	5	16	1.6	5.0	68%	.337	1.40	4.08	3.36	5.09	0.2
2012	NHP	AA	24	2	2	9	33	0	45¹	38	2	15	22	3.0	4.4	67%	.248	1.17	2.38	4.06	6.30	-0.6
2012	TOR	MLB	24	0	0	0	2	0	0²	4	0	2	1	27.0	13.5	80%	.800	9.00	40.50	9.05	6.43	0.0
2013	JAX	AA	25	3	7	0	16	15	75¹	72	0	23	41	2.7	4.9	64%	.287	1.26	2.63	3.14	4.73	0.3
2013	NWO	AAA	25	1	3	0	5	5	31	23	1	12	16	3.5	4.6	62%	.232	1.13	2.61	4.21	4.49	0.5
2013	MIA	MLB	25	0	2	0	5	1	11	16	2	5	5	4.1	4.1	70%	.341	1.91	9.00	6.11	7.75	-0.3
2014	NWO	AAA	26	2	1	1	13	0	25¹	21	0	10	20	3.6	7.1	66%	.296	1.22	2.49	3.54	3.72	0.5
2014	MIA	MLB	26	3	1	0	31	0	42	41	1	15	33	3.2	7.1	67%	.310	1.33	2.14	3.13	4.45	-0.1
2015	MIA	MLB	27	3	3	0	28	7	65²	68	4	22	37	3.0	5.0	59%	.312	1.37	4.20	4.20	4.56	-0.1

Breakout: 31%   Improve: 42%   Collapse: 6%   Attrition: 28%   MLB: 57%   Comparables: Enerio Del Rosario, Jordan Smith, Miguel Asencio

Groundball Specialist probably rates behind closer, set-up man, long man, and LOOGY in the every-team-needs-one bullpen rankings, but it certainly doesn't hurt to have a guy available in the seventh who can induce a double play on demand. Ostensibly, that's Dyson's job—his groundball rate was among the 10 highest among relievers last year. While his ERA was low, low, low and his sinker comes in hot, hot, hot, Dyson gave up about a hit per inning, and his strikeout and walk rates don't allow his groundball stuff to translate into anything special. He's good at getting groundballs, but he's just not that good.

Nathan Eovaldi   RHP

Born: 2/13/90   Age: 25   Bats: R   Throws: R   Height: 6'2"   Weight: 215

YEAR	TEAM	LVL	AGE	W	L	SV	G	GS	IP	H	HR	BB	K	BB/9	K/9	GB%	BABIP	WHIP	ERA	FIP	FRA	WARP
2012	CHT	AA	22	2	2	0	9	8	35	30	2	13	30	3.3	7.7	57%	.298	1.23	3.09	3.46	5.11	0.7
2012	LAN	MLB	22	1	6	0	10	10	56¹	63	5	20	34	3.2	5.4	49%	.319	1.47	4.15	4.15	4.82	-0.1
2012	MIA	MLB	22	3	7	0	12	12	63	70	5	27	44	3.9	6.3	45%	.316	1.54	4.43	4.20	4.97	0.2
2013	JAX	AA	23	1	0	0	3	3	11²	13	0	4	9	3.1	6.9	50%	.342	1.46	5.40	2.40	3.73	0.1
2013	MIA	MLB	23	4	6	0	18	18	106¹	100	7	40	78	3.4	6.6	46%	.287	1.32	3.39	3.57	4.01	1.0
2014	MIA	MLB	24	6	14	0	33	33	199²	223	14	43	142	1.9	6.4	46%	.323	1.33	4.37	3.34	3.97	1.6
2015	MIA	MLB	25	9	10	0	28	28	156	158	11	50	109	2.9	6.3	47%	.320	1.33	4.07	3.91	4.43	0.2

Breakout: 27%   Improve: 56%   Collapse: 12%   Attrition: 11%   MLB: 94%   Comparables: Chris Volstad, Edwin Jackson, Jose Quintana

Things went pretty well for Eovaldi last year, except when they didn't. The fireballing righty still hasn't found a way to translate his prodigious fastball velocity into strikeouts—he had the fourth-fastest heat but the 70th-best K rate among qualified starters—but he has cut down on walks and started leaning more heavily on an improved slider. Throwing just under 200 innings during his age-24 season is a pretty neat trick as well. At the same time, he had a tough time stranding runners due to his lack of swing-and-miss stuff and propensity for pounding the zone. He had the second-lowest left-on-base percentage (66 percent) in baseball and the fourth-most hits allowed (223). He'll battle with Chris Capuano for starts in New York's rotation, which is fitting: They're essentially opposite pitchers who get almost the same results.

Jose Fernandez RHP

Born: 7/31/92 Age: 22 Bats: R Throws: R Height: 6'2" Weight: 225

YEAR	TEAM	LVL	AGE	W	L	SV	G	GS	IP	H	HR	BB	K	BB/9	K/9	GB%	BABIP	WHIP	ERA	FIP	FRA	WARP
2012	GRB	A	19	7	0	0	14	14	79	51	2	18	99	2.1	11.3	47%	.282	0.87	1.59	2.16	2.83	2.5
2012	JUP	A+	19	7	1	0	11	11	55	38	0	17	59	2.8	9.7	47%	.273	1.00	1.96	2.34	3.37	1.3
2013	MIA	MLB	20	12	6	0	28	28	172²	111	10	58	187	3.0	9.7	47%	.240	0.98	2.19	2.70	3.31	3.4
2014	MIA	MLB	21	4	2	0	8	8	51²	36	4	13	70	2.3	12.2	50%	.271	0.95	2.44	2.15	3.49	0.7
2015	MIA	MLB	22	4	3	0	11	11	61²	45	4	18	70	2.6	10.2	46%	.297	1.03	2.39	2.82	2.60	1.6

Breakout: 36%   Improve: 58%   Collapse: 18%   Attrition: 16%   MLB: 93%   Comparables: Stephen Strasburg, Phil Hughes, Clayton Kershaw

After a revelation of a 2013 debut season that won him the NL Rookie of the Year award despite the best efforts of fellow Cuban emigre Yasiel Puig, Fernandez's 2014 was supposed to be a sequel that outstripped the original—*The Empire Strikes Back* to 2013's *Star Wars*, the *Run The Jewels 2* to 2013's *Run The Jewels*. Despite coming in hot during eight glorious starts, eventually legendary sequel-ruiner "torn UCL" showed up. The 21-year-old needed Tommy John surgery on May 16th, ending his season.

Fernandez is expected to return to the big leagues sometime around the 2015 All-Star Game, at which time he'll have to face many of the classic obstacles for pitchers returning from TJS. Will he be able to locate his eponymous curveball with the same alacrity he's had in the past? Will the velocity stay tight after the layoff? "Can baseball be trusted with a pitcher this good?" we asked on the cover of BP 2014. The answer was no, but the hope remains yes.

Dan Haren RHP

Born: 9/17/80 Age: 34 Bats: R Throws: R Height: 6'5" Weight: 215

YEAR	TEAM	LVL	AGE	W	L	SV	G	GS	IP	H	HR	BB	K	BB/9	K/9	GB%	BABIP	WHIP	ERA	FIP	FRA	WARP
2012	ANA	MLB	31	12	13	0	30	30	176²	190	28	38	142	1.9	7.2	41%	.302	1.29	4.33	4.20	4.42	1.3
2013	WAS	MLB	32	10	14	1	31	30	169²	179	28	31	151	1.6	8.0	39%	.302	1.24	4.67	4.06	4.47	1.5
2014	LAN	MLB	33	13	11	0	32	32	186	183	27	36	145	1.7	7.0	43%	.277	1.18	4.02	4.06	4.33	1.0
2015	MIA	MLB	34	9	9	0	26	26	156¹	152	17	29	130	1.7	7.5	41%	.310	1.16	3.71	3.71	4.03	0.8

Breakout: 18%   Improve: 43%   Collapse: 12%   Attrition: 5%   MLB: 83%   Comparables: Aaron Harang, Javier Vazquez, Ben Sheets

It's hard to believe Haren, a Pepperdine alumnus from La Puente, California with a free-flowing head of hair, had never pitched for Los Angeles before 2014. He had a reverse roller coaster season in his Dodgers debut: a 2.03 ERA in his first 31 innings, a 5.64 mark over his next 96, then 2.43 in the final 59. His stuff isn't what it once was (91 mph fastball, fall-off-the-table splitter, sharp cutter): His fastball now tops out at 89 (hence the excellent Twitter handle @ithrow88), his splitter is a little flat, he's relying more and more on his cutter and all the pitches are blending together a little bit. You know that animation that shows five pitches with radically different movement and velocity all issuing from one Yu Darvish release point? Haren's the opposite of that.

Still, teams have done and will do worse for $12.5 million. (Haren hit nearly all the performance incentives in his contract and made an additional $2.5 million on top of his $10 million base.) Haren's 2015 option vested, but we're all stuck here waiting to see if he's going to retire after a mid-winter trade from Los Angeles. You already know, because you live in the future. Lucky dog.

Tom Koehler RHP

Born: 6/29/86 Age: 29 Bats: R Throws: R Height: 6'2" Weight: 235

YEAR	TEAM	LVL	AGE	W	L	SV	G	GS	IP	H	HR	BB	K	BB/9	K/9	GB%	BABIP	WHIP	ERA	FIP	FRA	WARP
2012	NWO	AAA	26	12	11	0	28	27	151	154	15	61	138	3.6	8.2	48%	.317	1.42	4.17	4.46	4.96	1.3
2012	MIA	MLB	26	0	1	0	8	1	13¹	15	4	2	13	1.4	8.8	24%	.297	1.27	5.40	5.54	6.54	-0.2
2013	NWO	AAA	27	0	2	0	4	4	23	16	2	12	18	4.7	7.0	48%	.230	1.22	2.74	4.70	5.19	-0.1
2013	MIA	MLB	27	5	10	0	29	23	143	140	14	54	92	3.4	5.8	49%	.289	1.36	4.41	4.24	4.95	-0.7
2014	MIA	MLB	28	10	10	0	32	32	191¹	177	16	71	153	3.3	7.2	46%	.290	1.30	3.81	3.81	4.39	0.2
2015	MIA	MLB	29	9	10	0	28	28	155²	149	15	56	117	3.3	6.7	44%	.306	1.32	4.15	4.44	4.51	0.0

Breakout: 17%   Improve: 34%   Collapse: 9%   Attrition: 15%   MLB: 51%   Comparables: Dustin Moseley, Chris Narveson, Dave Williams

Compared to the young guns on the rest of the Marlins pitching staff, this 28-year-old hurler has earned his nickname: "The Dino." But along with being older than his rotation compatriots, Koehler also lacks their upside. He doesn't really have swing-and-miss stuff, despite a shockingly effective knuckle-curve, and his command is short of crafty-veteran height requirements. Despite a replacement-level performance over 190-plus innings in 2014, he's likely to get pushed from the rotation. At least we'll know why this dino went extinct.

Tyler Kolek RHP

Born: 12/15/95 Age: 19 Bats: R Throws: R Height: 6'5" Weight: 260

YEAR	TEAM	LVL	AGE	W	L	SV	G	GS	IP	H	HR	BB	K	BB/9	K/9	GB%	BABIP	WHIP	ERA	FIP	FRA	WARP
2015	MIA	MLB	19	1	2	0	8	6	33¹	39	3	20	16	5.3	4.2	46%	.323	1.75	6.05	5.61	6.57	-0.6

Breakout: 0%   Improve: 0%   Collapse: 0%   Attrition: 0%   MLB: 0%   Comparables: David Holmberg, Roman Mendez, Kelvin Herrera

The no. 2 overall pick in June didn't get off to a dominant start in the GCL, but who cares? Nobody takes the GCL seriously. From a pure "holy hell, did you see that pitch?" standpoint, Kolek is a sight. His fastball is a rarity, a potential 80-grade heater that regularly flashes triple-digits from his max-effort delivery. Between his unreal velocity, his massive frame and his youth, scouts don't even have to squint to see a front-of-the-rotation ace. But before that dream of acehood comes to life, Kolek will have to take some serious developmental steps. Though he's flashed some feel for a slider, he's basically a one-pitch wonder at this point, and he'll need to really refine his breaking and off-speed offerings to be more than a velo freakshow. The bad news is that starting pitching prospects this young and this raw have a lot of injuries to dodge before they amount to anything of worth. The good news? Kolek has the physical abilities you can't teach, and his premium velocity grants him more upside than nearly any player in the Miami system.

Mat Latos   RHP

Born: 12/9/87   Age: 27   Bats: R   Throws: R   Height: 6'6"   Weight: 245

YEAR	TEAM	LVL	AGE	W	L	SV	G	GS	IP	H	HR	BB	K	BB/9	K/9	GB%	BABIP	WHIP	ERA	FIP	FRA	WARP
2012	CIN	MLB	24	14	4	0	33	33	209¹	179	25	64	185	2.8	8.0	47%	.266	1.16	3.48	3.90	4.51	2.1
2013	CIN	MLB	25	14	7	0	32	32	210²	197	14	58	187	2.5	8.0	47%	.299	1.21	3.16	3.08	3.50	3.2
2014	LOU	AAA	26	2	0	0	4	4	19¹	17	1	7	13	3.3	6.1	43%	.281	1.24	2.33	3.77	4.78	0.2
2014	CIN	MLB	26	5	5	0	16	16	102¹	92	9	26	74	2.3	6.5	41%	.269	1.15	3.25	3.62	4.05	0.5
2015	MIA	MLB	27	8	6	0	19	19	122	107	8	31	105	2.3	7.8	45%	.303	1.13	3.03	3.26	3.30	1.8

Breakout: 31%   Improve: 64%   Collapse: 20%   Attrition: 22%   MLB: 97%   Comparables: Johnny Cueto, John Danks, Hyun-jin Ryu

Latos missed much of the first half recovering from left-knee meniscus surgery, didn't pitch after September 7th because of a bone bruise in his pitching elbow and had stem cells put into that elbow in November. In between all this, he gave up more fly balls than usual, didn't miss bats at his normal rate, lost two mph off his fastball and halved his slider usage. Add that to Latos being just one year from free agency and you begin to see why the Marlins "only" had to give up Anthony DeSclafani and Chad Wallach to acquire the reliably above-average righty. This could be a tidy buy-low move for the Marlins and, even if it's not, they're only out a decent pitching prospect, a mediocre minor-league catcher and a 2015 salary figure depressed by Latos' injury problems. The major question is whether Cat Latos fits on a team named for a fish.

Bryan Morris   RHP

Born: 3/28/87   Age: 28   Bats: L   Throws: R   Height: 6'3"   Weight: 225

YEAR	TEAM	LVL	AGE	W	L	SV	G	GS	IP	H	HR	BB	K	BB/9	K/9	GB%	BABIP	WHIP	ERA	FIP	FRA	WARP
2012	IND	AAA	25	2	2	5	46	0	81	76	8	17	79	1.9	8.8	59%	.294	1.15	2.67	3.12	4.29	0.7
2012	PIT	MLB	25	0	0	0	5	0	5	2	0	2	6	3.6	10.8	73%	.182	0.80	1.80	2.54	3.02	0.1
2013	PIT	MLB	26	5	7	0	55	0	65	57	8	28	37	3.9	5.1	58%	.251	1.31	3.46	4.87	6.17	-1.0
2014	PIT	MLB	27	4	0	0	21	0	23²	25	4	12	14	4.6	5.3	68%	.296	1.56	3.80	5.89	6.26	-0.5
2014	MIA	MLB	27	4	1	0	39	0	40²	33	2	12	36	2.7	8.0	57%	.265	1.11	0.66	3.00	3.54	0.4
2015	MIA	MLB	28	2	1	1	43	0	58¹	54	5	20	47	3.1	7.2	56%	.306	1.28	3.82	3.97	4.15	0.2

Breakout: 32%   Improve: 46%   Collapse: 11%   Attrition: 17%   MLB: 65%   Comparables: Kevin Gregg, Matt Lindstrom, Jeff Bennett

After watching his career begin to implode in Pittsburgh, a mid-season deal to Miami was exactly what this right-hander needed. The change of scenery didn't totally flip the script, but it put Morris in a ballpark where his arch-enemy, the home run, couldn't hurt him as badly. Sure, that sparkling 0.66 ERA with the Marlins doesn't exactly tell the whole story, as he allowed as many unearned runs as earned in his half-season in South Beach, though that's still sterling. Appropriately for a guy who lives and dies with his slider (his most-used pitch), he punished righties but was ineffective against lefties.

Justin Nicolino   LHP

Born: 11/22/91   Age: 23   Bats: L   Throws: L   Height: 6'3"   Weight: 190

YEAR	TEAM	LVL	AGE	W	L	SV	G	GS	IP	H	HR	BB	K	BB/9	K/9	GB%	BABIP	WHIP	ERA	FIP	FRA	WARP
2012	LNS	A	20	10	4	0	28	22	124¹	112	6	21	119	1.5	8.6	55%	.308	1.07	2.46	2.69	4.17	2.1
2013	JUP	A+	21	5	2	0	18	18	96²	89	4	18	64	1.7	6.0	50%	.286	1.11	2.23	3.08	4.38	0.5
2013	JAX	AA	21	3	2	0	9	9	45¹	63	2	12	31	2.4	6.2	42%	.386	1.65	4.96	3.04	4.02	0.6
2014	JAX	AA	22	14	4	0	28	28	170¹	162	10	20	81	1.1	4.3	49%	.267	1.07	2.85	3.44	4.55	1.2
2015	MIA	MLB	23	8	9	0	26	26	137²	147	11	32	77	2.1	5.0	48%	.315	1.30	4.15	4.05	4.51	0.1

Breakout: 0%   Improve: 0%   Collapse: 0%   Attrition: 0%   MLB: 0%   Comparables: Adam Wilk, Zach McAllister, Dallas Keuchel

The Marlins Minor League Pitcher of the Year doesn't wow scouts with his stuff or ability to miss bats, but his floor is higher than a South Beach penthouse. He's already proved capable of throwing 170-plus innings in a season, and any team can use a guy capable of showing up that often. The lanky lefty doesn't have an overpowering heater, and his best weapon is a confounding changeup that he delivers with the same arm speed as his barely-in-the-90s fastball. With lots of competition for slots in the Miami rotation, Nicolino might be looking at a stint in New Orleans in 2015, where he'll look to leverage his plus command into a Mark Buehrle profile.

Brad Penny   RHP

Born: 5/24/78   Age: 37   Bats: R   Throws: R   Height: 6'4"   Weight: 230

YEAR	TEAM	LVL	AGE	W	L	SV	G	GS	IP	H	HR	BB	K	BB/9	K/9	GB%	BABIP	WHIP	ERA	FIP	FRA	WARP
2012	SFN	MLB	34	0	1	0	22	0	28	42	4	9	10	2.9	3.2	53%	.349	1.82	6.11	5.35	5.24	-0.2
2014	JUP	A+	36	0	2	0	2	2	10²	10	0	0	4	0.0	3.4	46%	.270	0.94	5.06	2.92	4.22	0.1
2014	NWO	AAA	36	2	2	0	5	5	27²	26	0	9	26	2.9	8.5	55%	.338	1.27	2.28	2.90	3.24	0.5
2014	MIA	MLB	36	2	1	0	8	4	26	34	3	13	13	4.5	4.5	54%	.344	1.81	6.58	5.22	5.91	-0.1
2015	MIA	MLB	37	2	3	0	12	7	44¹	50	4	14	23	2.8	4.6	50%	.327	1.44	4.88	4.51	5.30	-0.4

Breakout: 12%   Improve: 35%   Collapse: 18%   Attrition: 23%   MLB: 68%   Comparables: Mike Hampton, Jeff Suppan, Brian Moehler

We assume that in 2013, his year off from baseball, Penny walked the earth like Kwai Chang Caine, solving the problems of strangers by throwing straight-as-arrow 92 mph fastballs that were impossible to miss. In 2014, however, Penny's performance was just a rerun of the old episodes we'd seen before. He posted basically the same sub-replacement numbers he did when he pitched for the Giants in 2012, the only difference being that 2014's performance came mostly as a starting pitcher. Penny can't strike out a hitter to save his life, and even on the low-K Marlins, the numbers probably aren't good enough to get another shot. Nevertheless, he does have a knack for always turning up, like a bad ... rash.

A.J. Ramos   RHP

Born: 9/20/86   Age: 28   Bats: R   Throws: R   Height: 5'10"   Weight: 205

YEAR	TEAM	LVL	AGE	W	L	SV	G	GS	IP	H	HR	BB	K	BB/9	K/9	GB%	BABIP	WHIP	ERA	FIP	FRA	WARP
2012	JAX	AA	25	3	3	21	55	0	69²	36	3	21	89	2.8	11.7	48%	.223	0.83	1.44	2.04	3.21	1.4
2012	MIA	MLB	25	0	0	0	11	0	9¹	8	2	4	13	3.9	12.5	32%	.300	1.29	3.86	4.74	5.24	0.0
2013	MIA	MLB	26	3	4	0	68	0	80	58	4	43	86	4.8	9.7	40%	.266	1.26	3.15	3.21	3.95	0.6
2014	MIA	MLB	27	7	2	0	68	0	64	36	1	43	73	6.0	10.3	45%	.233	1.23	2.11	3.18	3.12	0.7
2015	MIA	MLB	28	3	1	1	57	0	62¹	46	4	29	71	4.2	10.3	43%	.298	1.19	2.86	3.35	3.11	1.0

Breakout: 28%   Improve: 41%   Collapse: 22%   Attrition: 16%   MLB: 75%   Comparables: Vinnie Pestano, Al Alburquerque, Jose Valverde

Sometimes it's just more fun to watch those pitchers with lightning stuff and frightening control. The guys who walk the bases loaded, strike out the side and scratch the sign of The Marmol into the mound dirt. Despite walking 15 percent of the batters he faced, Ramos managed a sterling ERA and a good (if not great) FIP. His secret? Whiffs. Shhhhhhh. Don't tell anybody, but the secret is whiffs. Also a minuscule home run rate and low BABIPs, same as Marmol always had. If Ramos is ever able to control that iffy walk rate, he's a guy who could slot in as a closer.

Jose Urena   RHP

Born: 9/12/91   Age: 23   Bats: R   Throws: R   Height: 6'2"   Weight: 195

YEAR	TEAM	LVL	AGE	W	L	SV	G	GS	IP	H	HR	BB	K	BB/9	K/9	GB%	BABIP	WHIP	ERA	FIP	FRA	WARP
2012	GRB	A	20	9	6	2	27	22	138¹	143	13	29	101	1.9	6.6	48%	.304	1.24	3.38	3.99	4.97	1.6
2013	JUP	A+	21	10	7	0	27	26	149²	148	8	29	107	1.7	6.4	50%	.299	1.18	3.73	3.21	4.45	0.3
2014	JAX	AA	22	13	8	0	26	25	162	155	14	29	121	1.6	6.7	48%	.290	1.14	3.33	3.39	4.73	0.7
2015	MIA	MLB	23	7	9	0	23	23	131¹	139	13	37	79	2.5	5.4	46%	.313	1.34	4.40	4.35	4.79	-0.4

Breakout: 0%   Improve: 0%   Collapse: 0%   Attrition: 0%   MLB: 0%   Comparables: Dallas Keuchel, Adam Wilk, Elih Villanueva

An easy, active fastball is a great first step to success. Adding an improved changeup to pair with it, well, that makes Urena quite the interesting prospect. The performance in full-season ball hasn't exactly caught up to the prospect profile yet, but there's still room for the Dominican fireballer to progress into a mid-rotation starter or late-inning relief option. While the latter is more likely long-term—it is for almost every pitching prospect—there's projection and possibility with the potential to stay relevant in a rotation. He'll need to improve his slurvy breaking ball.

Trevor Williams   RHP

Born: 4/25/92   Age: 23   Bats: R   Throws: R   Height: 6'3"   Weight: 228

YEAR	TEAM	LVL	AGE	W	L	SV	G	GS	IP	H	HR	BB	K	BB/9	K/9	GB%	BABIP	WHIP	ERA	FIP	FRA	WARP
2013	BAT	A-	21	0	2	0	10	10	29	26	0	8	20	2.5	6.2	61%	.274	1.17	2.48	2.65	4.68	0.2
2014	JUP	A+	22	8	6	0	23	23	129	138	5	29	90	2.0	6.3	52%	.322	1.29	2.79	3.17	4.48	0.9
2014	JAX	AA	22	0	1	0	3	3	15	22	0	6	14	3.6	8.4	69%	.431	1.87	6.00	2.52	3.53	0.2
2015	MIA	MLB	23	6	8	0	23	23	107²	119	9	36	64	3.0	5.3	50%	.326	1.44	4.65	4.34	5.05	-0.5

Breakout: 0%   Improve: 0%   Collapse: 0%   Attrition: 0%   MLB: 0%   Comparables: Brandon Workman, Adam Wilk, Robbie Ross

Perhaps no prospect in the Marlins' system is a better fit for the team's pitching philosophy than the big righty out of Arizona State. A year after getting drafted, he carried a 3:1 strikeout-to-walk ratio through a full season at Jupiter. He's recently improved on a heavy two-seam fastball with good sink, which he will live or die on as he works his way through the upper minors. If he can continue to build on the two-seamer and his secondary offerings, he could eat innings in the middle of a rotation. If not, middle relief is probably his last, best hope.

Lineouts

Hitters

NAME	POS	TEAM	LVL	AGE	PA	R	2B	3B	HR	RBI	BB	K	SB	CS	AVG/OBP/SLG	TAv	BABIP	BRR	FRAA	WARP
Brian Anderson	3B	GRB	A	21	172	27	7	0	8	37	13	28	0	0	.314/.378/.516	.324	.336	-1.6	3B(26): 0.6, 2B(9): -0.3	1.8
	2B	BAT	A-	21	85	11	3	1	3	12	6	11	1	1	.273/.333/.455	.270	.286	-0.1	2B(17): -1.5	0.1
Justin Bohn	SS	GRB	A	21	285	39	16	2	6	47	39	49	4	2	.293/.397/.452	.312	.346	0.8	SS(34): 0.2, 2B(23): -0.9	2.6
	SS	JUP	A+	21	217	29	9	3	0	12	16	45	7	3	.296/.347/.372	.268	.381	0.9	SS(40): -1.2, 2B(5): -0.9	1.0
Justin Bour	1B	NWO	AAA	26	430	59	27	0	18	72	39	57	3	1	.306/.372/.517	.316	.319	-1.6	1B(91): 4.5	3.5
	1B	MIA	MLB	26	83	10	3	0	1	11	9	19	0	1	.284/.361/.365	.279	.370	-0.6	1B(15): 0.5	0.3
Reid Brignac	2B	LEH	AAA	28	149	23	8	1	5	21	16	31	3	0	.266/.340/.461	.285	.305	0.5	2B(16): -0.5, 3B(8): -0.9	0.7
	3B	PHI	MLB	28	91	4	5	1	1	10	9	33	1	1	.222/.300/.346	.238	.362	-0.2	3B(20): -1.3, 3B(3): 0.1	-0.1
Zack Cox	3B	NWO	AAA	25	344	40	18	3	8	35	29	65	2	0	.282/.344/.436	.282	.333	1.3	3B(73): -2.9, P(1): -0.0	1.6
Austin Dean	LF	GRB	A	20	449	67	20	4	9	58	38	72	4	4	.308/.371/.444	.293	.354	3.8	LF(81): -7.5, CF(1): -0.1	1.9
Cole Gillespie	RF	BUF	AAA	30	104	15	4	1	2	16	14	14	3	0	.354/.423/.500	.341	.370	-1.0	RF(11): 0.6, LF(9): 0.0	1.2
	LF	TAC	AAA	30	68	14	5	1	5	14	9	9	2	0	.362/.456/.741	.425	.364	1.2	LF(9): -0.2, RF(6): -0.5	1.4
	RF	TOR	MLB	30	3	0	0	0	0	0	0	0	0	0	.000/.000/.000	-.006	.000	0.0	RF(1): -0.0	-0.1
	LF	SEA	MLB	30	78	9	2	0	1	5	6	13	2	2	.254/.312/.324	.227	.298	0.6	LF(16): 1.4, RF(9): 0.2	0.0
Christopher Hoo	C	GRB	A	22	48	5	2	0	0	3	9	8	0	0	.382/.543/.441	.360	.500	-1.0	C(12): 0.1	0.9
	C	BAT	A-	22	34	1	4	0	0	1	1	3	0	0	.321/.424/.464	.294	.360	-0.3	C(5): 0.1	0.2
Reed Johnson	LF	MIA	MLB	37	201	24	15	0	2	25	1	37	0	1	.235/.266/.348	.236	.278	0.8	LF(23): -2.1, RF(11): -0.9	-0.3
Austin Nola	SS	JAX	AA	24	595	68	21	5	1	53	77	94	8	5	.259/.368/.327	.273	.313	-4.0	SS(125): 1.1, 2B(7): -0.0	3.1
Viosergy Rosa	1B	JUP	A+	24	498	52	25	1	13	78	42	98	0	0	.291/.355/.439	.281	.344	-5.1	1B(102): 0.1	1.1
	1B	JAX	AA	24	89	15	4	1	2	17	14	13	0	0	.292/.416/.458	.317	.328	-0.1	1B(20): 0.5	0.7
Jhonatan Solano	C	SYR	AAA	28	374	45	15	1	10	53	23	49	1	0	.251/.305/.388	.234	.265	-6.4	C(81): -0.4	-0.4
Jesus Solorzano	RF	JUP	A+	23	320	27	8	4	3	19	9	78	18	7	.233/.255/.316	.217	.300	1.2	RF(63): 3.2, CF(22): 1.4	-0.4
Jordany Valdespin	2B	NWO	AAA	26	265	39	9	2	8	29	36	29	15	10	.270/.374/.437	.302	.278	-1.1	2B(35): -0.4, RF(14): -0.5	1.8

High-school catcher **Blake Anderson** wasn't a Top 200 draft prospect last year, but that didn't stop the Marlins from betting big on his makeup, arm and rough potential in the supplemental round. ❖ **Brian Anderson** is an average-ish defender at second base, but looks unlikely to hit any better than the synonymous former Diamondbacks starting pitcher. ❖ Not to be confused with Justin Bour, **Justin Bohn** is a low-ceiling shortstop prospect without much power. He is unlikely to make an impact with the big-league Marlins. ❖ Not to be confused with Justin Bohn, **Justin Bour** is a low-ceiling first base prospect without much power. He is unlikely to make an impact with the big-league Marlins. ❖ **Reid Brignac** posted his first .800-plus OPS since 2006, but it came in Triple-A at the age of 28, and in a small sample to boot. ❖ Scouts saw a polished college third baseman with a chance to really hit when **Zack Cox** was drafted in 2010. PECOTA, however, sees an aging prospect unlikely to hit enough to be a regular at the five. ❖ **Austin Dean** was the youngest player on the Single-A Greensboro Grasshoppers last year, and arguably the team's best hitter, but he still needs to bring his big raw power into games. ❖ There's one every year—a traveling fringeman who dons at least six different jerseys in one season. **Cole Gillespie**, who journeyed though the Seattle and Toronto systems, took that crown from Steve Clevenger, whose 2013 comprised play for the Chicago Cubs, Iowa Cubs, GCL Orioles, Aberdeen IronBirds, Norfolk Tides and Baltimore Orioles. ❖ A startling line in his first taste of professional ball doesn't make **Christopher Hoo** a prospect; it makes him a guy too advanced for Single-A but without the bat speed of a big-league hitter. ❖ **Reed Johnson** is basically a zombie, but instead of eating brains, he has subsisted on right-handed pitching. Alas, the zombie aging curve is steep at the end; he has almost fully decomposed, and is no longer a threat. ❖ Brother of Phillies prospect Aaron, **Austin Nola** acquitted himself well in the Arizona Fall League, showcasing his prodigious plate discipline. Drafted after a full term at LSU, he has been old for his levels but has hit like a freshman. ❖ **Viosergy Rosa** is really too old to have only tasted Double-A pitching. As a lumbering first-base-only player, he needs to double his power output and halve his age to stay relevant another year. ❖ What is there to say about **Jhonatan Solano**, except that the missing H stood for Hitting and the extra H stands for—no, we're nicer than that. ❖ **Jesus Solorzano** needed to prove he could overcome a sketchy approach; instead he backslid at High-A and his power slipped away, as well. ❖ **Jordany Valdespin** is still most famous for having a terrible clubhouse reputation and getting hit in the beans with a pitch. He has no calling-card tools, despite flashing a little power and a little speed, and he has no positional home. If you hear his name again, it'll almost certainly be beans-related.

Pitchers

NAME	TEAM	LVL	AGE	W	L	SV	G	GS	IP	H	HR	BB	K	BB/9	K/9	GB%	BABIP	WHIP	ERA	FIP	FRA	WARP
A. Caminero	NWO	AAA	27	4	1	10	42	0	63	70	7	30	79	4.3	11.3	41%	.362	1.59	4.86	4.40	4.39	0.7
	MIA	MLB	27	0	1	0	6	0	6²	8	2	4	8	5.4	10.8	37%	.353	1.80	10.80	6.40	9.73	-0.3
Adam Conley	NWO	AAA	24	3	5	0	12	11	60	65	3	26	48	3.9	7.2	53%	.333	1.52	6.00	4.20	4.75	0.2
Grant Dayton	JAX	AA	26	0	1	3	11	0	16¹	17	0	4	18	2.2	9.9	41%	.347	1.29	1.10	1.72	2.31	0.5
	NWO	AAA	26	2	2	1	39	0	55²	53	10	22	61	3.6	9.9	39%	.299	1.35	3.72	5.08	5.19	0.1
Jarlin Garcia	GRB	A	21	10	5	0	25	25	133²	152	13	21	111	1.4	7.5	49%	.332	1.29	4.38	3.78	4.62	1.7
Domingo German	GRB	A	21	9	3	0	25	25	123¹	116	6	25	113	1.8	8.2	51%	.315	1.14	2.48	3.26	4.21	2.3
Kevin Gregg	MIA	MLB	36	0	0	0	12	0	9	11	2	5	6	5.0	6.0	37%	.321	1.78	10.00	6.32	6.34	-0.2
Brad Hand	JUP	A+	24	0	0	0	2	2	12	4	0	2	14	1.5	10.5	84%	.160	0.50	0.75	1.56	3.40	0.2
	NWO	AAA	24	2	0	0	4	4	22	18	3	9	22	3.7	9.0	54%	.268	1.23	3.27	4.70	4.42	0.5
	MIA	MLB	24	3	8	1	32	16	111	112	10	39	67	3.2	5.4	53%	.287	1.36	4.38	4.17	5.15	-0.2
Michael Mader	BAT	A-	20	1	0	0	12	12	45	31	3	16	28	3.2	5.6	51%	.228	1.04	2.00	4.46	5.83	-0.2
Ryan Newell	GRB	A	23	8	7	0	19	19	109²	110	8	21	94	1.7	7.7	56%	.315	1.19	3.36	3.45	4.60	1.4
Matthew Ramsey	MNT	AA	24	3	0	6	24	0	33²	16	0	23	46	6.1	12.3	64%	.242	1.16	1.07	2.50	2.93	0.7
	JAX	AA	24	0	2	8	20	0	27²	19	2	7	34	2.3	11.1	48%	.258	0.94	1.95	2.43	3.56	0.6
Andre Rienzo	CHR	AAA	25	1	4	0	10	9	46²	44	4	24	43	4.6	8.3	47%	.290	1.46	4.05	4.24	4.41	0.8
	CHA	MLB	25	4	5	0	18	11	64²	82	12	33	51	4.6	7.1	47%	.332	1.78	6.82	5.76	6.11	-0.6
Colby Suggs	JUP	A+	22	1	6	3	46	0	58¹	59	6	25	47	3.9	7.3	48%	.320	1.44	5.09	4.09	5.07	0.0
Sean Townsley	GRB	A	23	6	3	3	20	14	96	88	2	18	87	1.7	8.2	55%	.307	1.10	2.25	2.83	3.64	2.4
Nick Wittgren	JAX	AA	23	5	5	20	52	0	66	73	6	14	56	1.9	7.6	42%	.332	1.32	3.55	3.40	3.86	0.9

Arquimedes Caminero shares a first name with a legendary mathematician who's been dead for 2,200 years. He's got maybe one more chance to prove he can stick in the bigs, or he'll be history too. ❖ At one point after elbow injuries derailed **Adam Conley**'s season, there were rumors he'd be traded to the Athletics for Jim Johnson, which is the sort of wake-up call that has no snooze bar. ❖ **Grant Dayton** saw his stock slip with his strike-out rate in 2014. Unfortunately for him, there's little use for another lefty in this Marlins bullpen. ❖ For the past two seasons, young lefty **Jarlin Garcia** has seen his future earnings potential steadily rise. He's all projection, and needs to add strength, stamina and a better change before cementing himself as a legit starter prospect. ❖ In a first year putting real mileage on his arm, Dominican-born **Domingo German** was excellent, blowing his fastball past Sally League hitters and earning a trip to the Futures Game. Note that his name translates to German Sunday and not German Sundae, which typically comprises potatoes, saurkraut, cheese, sour cream, bacon bits and olives. ❖ **Kevin Gregg**'s career deserves a tombstone, and the epitaph might read: "More career saves than Brian Wilson. He probably never should have been a closer." ❖ Over the past two seasons, **Brad Hand** has added velocity, added to his career innings count, and remained a below-replacement pitcher. ❖ Nearly every young pitcher needs to develop secondary offerings. Third-rounder **Michael Mader** has the big left-handed body and the early success in short-season ball, but he is like nearly every young pitcher. ❖ His sinker and slider could be big-league offerings, but **Ryan Newell**'s trouble with lefties casts him as a middle reliever. ❖ **Matthew Ramsey** has shown a big-time ability to miss bats and strike zones. If he irons out his consistency issues, he's ready for bullpen action this year. ❖ **Andre Rienzo** split time between starting and relieving and Charlotte and Chicago in 2014. The Brazilian doesn't have the command or the out pitch to survive in a rotation in the long run, so assume the Marlins acquired him for their bullpen. ❖ The 2013 second-rounder **Colby Suggs** is a former college closer who saw his strikeout rate crater in his first full season. Might be the first guy you can write off from the top of that draft. ❖ Man cannot live on knuckle-curves alone, so 6-foot-7 lefty **Sean Townsley** might end up in the bullpen begging for scraps. ❖ **Nick Wittgren** powered through an early season "dead-arm" period and held it down as co-closer for the Double-A Jacksonville Suns. Command and deception will take him to The Show, but high-level hitters aren't so easily bullied by command and deception as the kids in A-Ball were.

Manager

Mike Redmond

YEAR	TEAM	W	L	Py-thag +/-	Avg PC	100+ P	120+ P	QS	BQS	REL	REL w Zero R	IBB	PH	PH Avg	PH HR	SB2	CS2	SB3	CS3	SAC Att	SAC%	POS SAC	Squeeze	Swing	In Play
2013	MIA	62	100	-1	91.4	41	0	82	1	471	368	58	237	0.235	1	64	24	14	5	90	63.30%	27	0	291	85
2014	MIA	77	85	0	90.3	37	0	86	1	487	391	35	275	0.183	5	50	19	8	2	102	69.60%	31	2	264	85

Redmond has spent the past two seasons in relative obscurity, his name surfacing only when Jose Fernandez or Giancarlo Stanton's accomplishments required a managerial sound bite. There's reason to think that won't be the case much longer, and that his stock is on the rise, right alongside his team's.

Redmond behaved like a solid tactician last season. He was among the game's most pinch-hit-happy managers, stemming in part from his aggressive platooning of Garrett Jones (who faced righties in almost 90 percent of his plate appearances) and Jeff Baker (nearly 60 percent lefties). Otherwise, Redmond played it cool by doing nothing. He didn't hit-and-run or call for a ton of steals; he didn't issue many intentional walks for a National Leauge manager, or ride his young arms into Tommyjohntown chasing faint playoff hopes; and when he bunted, it was mostly with pitchers and light-hitting infielders (Adeiny Hechavarria, Jordany Valdespin, Donovan Solano and Jeff Mathis). Redmond understood the subtleties of his roster and didn't force it to play like something it wasn't. Smart.

Unfortunately, there is one thing that could prevent Redmond from guiding the Marlins to the postseason someday soon: the club's owner. Since purchasing the franchise in 2002, Jeffrey Loria has disposed of managers the way most do cotton swabs. Redmond will attempt to become the second captain under Loria to last a third consecutive season, joining Fredi Gonzalez. Redmond would become the longest-tenured skipper in franchise history if he's able to manage through the end of his recent contract extension, which runs through the 2017 season. Whether Redmond can avoid Loria's Steinbrenner-like wandering eyes for that long is anyone's guess. If not, you can bet he'll find work elsewhere.

MILWAUKEE BREWERS

by J.P. Breen

$\textbf{G}$oing All In™ has become a ubiquitous baseball trope. Teams supposedly sacrifice their futures for immediate gratification, trading numerous prospects for high-impact rentals or giving five-year contracts to acquire the player they really only want for the next two seasons. Such a model has been deemed unsustainable, especially for small-market organizations. The acquired talent leaves via free agency and the depleted farm system is unable to fill the void; or it just hangs around, getting older and prohibitively more expensive.

However, in an environment in which expanding payrolls and increased competitiveness can entice free agents to small-market clubs, it seems plausible that repeatedly cashing in assets to maximize single-season performance isn't as much of a death sentence as it used to be. That is to say, small-to-mid-market teams can now have the appeal and the money to cope with a depleted farm system and extend their windows of competition longer than we might otherwise have assumed.

The Brewers serve as an interesting case study. Former BP author Nate Silver has illustrated that Milwaukee is one of the two smallest markets in Major League Baseball. Yet playing against small-market type, the Brewers have authored numerous blockbuster trades in the past seven years, resulting in postseason appearances in 2008 and 2011. Those trades hollowed out the Brewers' minor leagues, and BP has consequently ranked the organization's system in the bottom five for the past three years. Cumulatively, one could argue that this is perhaps the bleakest picture one could paint of a club.

Yet the Brewers are still finding ways to compete. Their late-season swoon last year overshadowed five good months, in which they topped the NL Central from April 5th through August 31st, and maxed out at 19 games over .500 near the season's midpoint. A 9-17 record in September cost them a happy winter, but the Brewers were close. Had they really mortgaged the future in 2008 and 2011, if this is that future?

Before exploring how the Brewers have managed to remain relevant, it's imperative to define the transactions in question:

- July 7, 2008: Brewers acquire CC Sabathia from the Indians for 1B Matt LaPorta, OF Michael Brantley, RHP Rob Bryson and LHP Zach Jackson

- December 6, 2010: Brewers acquire Shaun Marcum from the Blue Jays for 3B Brett Lawrie
- December 19, 2010: Brewers acquire Zack Greinke and Yuniesky Betancourt from the Royals for SS Alcides Escobar, RHP Jake Odorizzi, OF Lorenzo Cain and RHP Jeremy Jeffress
- March 25, 2013: Brewers sign free-agent RHP Kyle Lohse, sacrifice first-round draft pick

All four of the moves were made to maximize the immediate product on the field, at the expense of substantial assets in the minor-league system (or, in the case of Escobar, young major-league talent). The list of exports is formidable: An MVP candidate, this year's ALCS MVP and the key piece used by Toronto to acquire Josh Donaldson this winter.

The question, however, is not whether the Brewers were better off in the short term due to these acquisitions. That's indisputable: Milwaukee made the playoffs in 2008 and 2011 following the major trades, and Lohse has pitched 400 valuable, above-average innings. Rather, it becomes a question of how the Brewers replaced the lost production. Furthermore, it is a question of whether waiting for the young talent to mature would have been worthwhile.

It's common knowledge that all prospects don't pan out. Teams are largely afraid to dish out massive packages of prospects because they don't want to look foolish, like the Braves did after dealing for Mark Teixeira, or the Diamondbacks after acquiring Trevor Cahill, but the truth is that most prospects turn out to be irrelevant. That's apparent in the above list of transactions: LaPorta, Jackson and Jeffress were top prospects, and they all accomplished nothing significant with their new clubs. Jeffress is finally a good major leaguer—with Milwaukee, to whom he returned as a scrap-heap pickup last April, posting a 1.88 ERA in their bullpen.

But allowing that some of the prospects did turn into valuable players, it isn't as though GM Doug Melvin could address the deficiencies created by the "all in" trades.

Michael Brantley: 10.0 WARP

Brantley presumably would have played in center field if he had stayed in Milwaukee, as Ryan Braun and Corey Hart had the corner outfield spots locked down. However, Brantley wouldn't

---

BREWERS PROSPECTUS
2014 W-L: 82-80, 3RD IN NL CENTRAL

Pythag	.495	15th	DER	.711	9th
RS/G	4.01	15th	B-Age	28.8	20th
RA/G	4.06	17th	P-Age	28.9	21st
TAv	.261	11th	Salary	$103.4M	16th
BRR	2.11	12th	MS/MW	$2.7M	13th
TAv-P	.260	13th	DL Days	559	4th
FIP	3.86	21st	$ on DL	10%	5th

Three-Year Park Factors

Runs	Runs/RH	Runs/LH	HR/RH	HR/LH
100	98	97	98	104

Top Hitter WARP	6.0	Jonathan Lucroy
Top Pitcher WARP	1.3	Zach Duke
Top Prospect		Orlando Arcia

have been needed until 2010, at the earliest, as Mike Cameron handled center field in 2008 and 2009, posting a 111 OPS+ and a combined 6.2 WARP. When Cameron left, though, the Brewers felt the absence of Brantley. To plug the hole, Melvin traded shortstop J.J. Hardy for center fielder Carlos Gomez.

Gomez has amassed 14.8 WARP since joining the Brewers in 2010. Thus, the Brewers (briefly) acquired the best pitcher in franchise history, CC Sabathia, and also ended up with the better center fielder. One could argue Brantley would still be useful, as he's better than Milwaukee's current left fielder, but even Khris Davis posted a 2.8 WARP at the league minimum last year. As it played out the Brewers were wholly better off—both in the long and short terms—following the Sabathia deal, highlighting that even when a prospect is traded away and turns into something great, his team might not miss him. Better still, the Brewers didn't invest four years waiting for Brantley to develop into a useful major leaguer.

Brett Lawrie: 9.9 WARP

In the Shaun Marcum trade, the Brewers sacrificed their former first-rounder and no. 1 prospect, Brett Lawrie. He would have played third base for the organization after the departure of Casey McGehee, though he wouldn't have had a clear path until after McGehee's production dropped off dramatically in 2011.

Again, the Brewers' farm system lacked an internal replacement for the chasm at third base when McGehee hit .223/.280/.346 in 2011. Lawrie would've been a welcome addition; however, Doug Melvin worked the free-agent market and acquired Aramis Ramirez on a three-year, $36 million deal that included a mutual option for 2015. Another big-league acquisition to cover the hole made through going "all in" during the 2011 season.

Ramirez has only been worth 5.2 WARP over the past three years, which is lower than Lawrie's 6.9 WARP. Other total-value metrics vary, but there's basic agreement that both players have been around average third basemen. Doug Melvin once again found a way to recoup the overall value that could have been offered by the prospect traded away, at an obvious cost (the money) but for obvious benefit (Marcum's 200 high-quality innings on a postseason club). Milwaukee once again showed it could stay competitive by augmenting the big-league squad when the minor-league option was no longer available.

Alcides Escobar, Jake Odorizzi and Lorenzo Cain: 12.4 WARP

One could immediately argue that the loss of Cain was offset by the acquisition of Gomez, as he would have had little use on the 2014 Brewers. And one wonders how relevant Odorizzi would be as a Brewer, as his big-league success has been tied to a new changeup learned since joining Tampa Bay. Thus, the one true vacancy that needs to be addressed is at shortstop.

Escobar's departure left a significant hole in the Brewers' roster. The organization managed to skate by with Yuniesky Betancourt in 2011, as he provided 1.5 WARP and a warm body that could handle the position. He even hit .310/.326/.500 in the postseason for the Brewers, which you'd chalk up to a big scoop of luck for Milwaukee, but value is value.

Things got ugly in 2012. The Brewers suffered through a weird combination of Cody Ransom, Cesar Izturis, Alex Gonzalez, Jeff Bianchi and Edwin Maysonet before the organization ultimately traded Zack Greinke for a package

that included Jean Segura. Segura was a replacement-level performer through the remainder of 2012, and the bar was so low that even that was an improvement over the smorgasbord of sadness that preceded him.

But over the past two years, Segura has added tremendous value as a excellent defensive shortstop. While Escobar produced about four WARP from 2011 through 2014, Segura has 9.4 WARP over the past two alone. As always, other metrics vary, and low estimates of his defense put him around four wins over the past two seasons, but that's still equivalent to, or a bit better than, what Escobar has provided in Kansas City. And Segura is under team control for another four seasons.

Conclusion

The Brewers have consistently shown both creativity and the willingness to spend on free agents to cover the holes created by Going All In™. The pieces that would normally cause teams to regret the trades were all covered by subsequent moves. Carlos Gomez is an elite outfielder and has provided more overall value than either Brantley or Cain. Aramis Ramirez, Kyle Lohse and Matt Garza have all addressed vacancies left by Lawrie and Odorizzi, at higher costs but without overwhelming the overall budget. Finally, a shrewd move to acquire Jean Segura plugged the hole left by Escobar's departure. Milwaukee acquired impact pieces to make the postseason in 2008 and 2011 without, in the end, sacrificing the club's ultimate future, as they were still competing with the replacements in 2014.

Of course, the Brewers *could* be in a position where they'd have Brantley, Cain, Odorizzi, Escobar, etc., and have saved that free agent money to allocate elsewhere. While conceding that's a possibility, those transactions were necessary: The Brewers wouldn't have made the postseason in 2008 and 2011, and if they were in a better position to do so now it would have come at the expense of an entire generation of Brewers—Prince Fielder, J.J. Hardy, Rickie Weeks, etc. You can't wait on prospects forever, banking on a magical moment when they all come together perfectly and a 10-year window of competition opens up. At some point, the day needs to be seized.

This is all to say that the Brewers should have maximized their chance to win last summer, that the lesson of 2008 and 2011 is a team should never waste a chance like Doug Melvin had in 2014. David Price was within reach over the summer. It would've cost Jimmy Nelson and a few prospects, but the club could have once again "mortgaged the future" to win now. The worst-case scenario would have been entering 2015 with David Price as the club's ace and another chance to compete.

Baseball writers have grown accustomed to thinking of every short-term move as a future deficit. The Brewers have shown that's not the case. Such moves make things more difficult, but in baseball's lucrative era the Brewers can afford to acquire mid-tier free agents to replace lost young talent. Those free-agent options are less available to a team without some recent history of winning; the Brewers struggled to attract free agents before reaching the playoffs in 2008. After that success, and after drawing 3 million fans, Milwaukee became a viable destination for mid-tier free agents.

It's important to recognize that this activity at the big-league level is not done in isolation. The Brewers understand their minor-league system lacks high-impact talent. Rather than replenish it through trades—as teams like the Cubs and Astros have done in recent years—Milwaukee has begun acquiring high-risk talent with massive upside. They drafted nothing but high school prospects in the first two rounds of the 2013 and 2014 drafts, and have given a series of franchise-record international bonuses in the same time period.

It's a thin tightrope being a small-market franchise, trying to compete every year without engaging in a full-scale rebuild. The Brewers have stayed upright. They'll try to roll out the barrel once again in 2015, and if they're in contention during the summer months, don't be surprised if they mortgage the future one more time. And don't be surprised if that future survives just fine. ∎

—J.P. Breen is an author at Baseball Prospectus.

Player comments by J.P. Breen and Baseball Prospectus Authors

Hitters

Orlando Arcia   SS

Born: 8/4/94   Age: 20   Bats: R   Throws: R   Height: 6' 0"   Weight: 165

YEAR	TEAM	LVL	AGE	PA	R	2B	3B	HR	RBI	BB	K	SB	CS	AVG/OBP/SLG	TAv	BABIP	BRR	FRAA	WARP
2013	WIS	A	18	486	67	14	5	4	39	35	40	20	9	.251/.314/.333	.241	.268	1.8	SS(120): 7.3	2.4
2014	BRV	A+	19	546	65	29	5	4	50	42	65	31	11	.289/.346/.392	.263	.326	4.2	SS(90): 9.9, 2B(36): 1.4	3.5
2015	MIL	MLB	20	250	26	10	1	2	17	12	45	7	3	.229/.270/.312	.223	.270	0.3	SS 4, 2B 0	0.6

Breakout: 0%   Improve: 0%   Collapse: 0%   Attrition: 0%   MLB: 0%   Comparables: *Ruben Tejada, Tyler Pastornicky, Wilfredo Tovar*

One of the more overlooked shortstop prospects in the game, Arcia has the confident swagger of a top-100 prospect and projects as a future every-day shortstop. Indeed, considering he's a glove-first prospect and was only 19 years old in the pitcher-friendly Florida State League last year, that .738 OPS should turn some heads. The brother of the Twins' Oswaldo has good bat-to-ball skills (see that strikeout rate) and an improving approach (see that walk rate). Some scouts believe he could flirt with double-digit homers down the road, but he's more of a gap-to-gap hitter who can rack up numerous doubles while adding value as a smart baserunner who gets good reads. A former relief pitcher for the Brewers once called him a "no s—t big leaguer" after seeing him in spring training as a 17-year-old in 2012. Yeah, no s—t.

Ryan Braun   RF

Born: 11/17/83   Age: 31   Bats: R   Throws: R   Height: 6' 2"   Weight: 200

YEAR	TEAM	LVL	AGE	PA	R	2B	3B	HR	RBI	BB	K	SB	CS	AVG/OBP/SLG	TAv	BABIP	BRR	FRAA	WARP
2012	MIL	MLB	28	677	108	36	3	41	112	63	128	30	7	.319/.391/.595	.327	.346	0.5	LF(151): 0.1	6.1
2013	MIL	MLB	29	253	30	14	2	9	38	27	56	4	5	.298/.372/.498	.300	.360	1.8	LF(59): 2.3	2.2
2014	MIL	MLB	30	580	68	30	6	19	81	41	113	11	5	.266/.324/.453	.280	.304	-3.1	RF(134): 3.8, CF(1): -0.0	2.4
2015	MIL	MLB	31	480	65	25	2	19	67	39	86	14	5	.288/.352/.488	.311	.319	-0.4	RF 1, LF 1	3.6

Breakout: 0%   Improve: 42%   Collapse: 2%   Attrition: 1%   MLB: 98%   Comparables: *Hank Aaron, Andre Ethier, Frank Robinson*

Braun's 114 OPS+ indicates an above-league-average hitter, but the overall numbers obfuscate his truly dreadful second half. He sunk to a .226/.295/.374 slash line, which was the gurgling gas bubble in the Brewers' second-half swamp water. He was battling a troublesome thumb injury, and without a guaranteed surgical remedy, Braun attempted to play through the discomfort—he described the pain of making contact with the baseball as similar to touching a scorching stove. He compensated by focusing on right field. Opposing pitchers responded by pounding him on the hands, where he physically couldn't handle it. The injury forced him to start his bat earlier, which explains his 10.3 percent swinging-strike rate, his highest mark since 2008. Braun finally had non-invasive surgery in October to alleviate the pain. The effectiveness of the operation will determine his value in 2015, and if he returns healthy, or at least mostly healthy, he should deliver a strong bounce-back.

Clint Coulter   C

Born: 7/30/93   Age: 21   Bats: R   Throws: R   Height: 6' 3"   Weight: 222

YEAR	TEAM	LVL	AGE	PA	R	2B	3B	HR	RBI	BB	K	SB	CS	AVG/OBP/SLG	TAv	BABIP	BRR	FRAA	WARP
2013	WIS	A	19	135	18	5	1	3	13	11	31	1	0	.207/.299/.345	.252	.250	0.8	C(28): -0.1	0.6
2014	WIS	A	20	529	84	28	3	22	89	73	103	6	6	.287/.410/.520	.335	.326	0.8	C(61): 0.7	5.6
2015	MIL	MLB	21	250	25	8	1	7	29	21	67	0	0	.216/.299/.362	.251	.269	-0.4	C 0	0.5

Breakout: 0%   Improve: 0%   Collapse: 0%   Attrition: 0%   MLB: 0%   Comparables: *Lars Anderson, Anthony Rizzo, Chris Marrero*

Coulter needed to prove two things during the 2014 season: (1) That he could handle the catcher position defensively, and (2) that the rake would bounce back. The organization wasn't satisfied with the proof of (1), so in early October, it announced a position switch for the Washington native. Coulter transitioned to right field and participated in the Arizona Fall League, where he was surprisingly believable: The body has improved since the Brewers drafted him. Fortunately, his bat still projects well in right field because (2) left no room for doubt. The 21-year-old showed his true colors at the plate, launching 22 homers and posting a .410 on-base percentage. Right-handed pitchers still give him fits at times and he can struggle to recognize quality secondary pitches, but overall Coulter displayed a valuable power/patience combination that has been sorely lacking in the Brewers' farm system for several seasons. His bat could even take another step forward now that he is free of the defensive rigors and developmental bandwidth of catching.

Khris Davis   LF

Born: 12/21/87   Age: 27   Bats: R   Throws: R   Height: 5' 11"   Weight: 190

YEAR	TEAM	LVL	AGE	PA	R	2B	3B	HR	RBI	BB	K	SB	CS	AVG/OBP/SLG	TAv	BABIP	BRR	FRAA	WARP
2012	HUN	AA	24	154	23	9	0	8	23	20	33	2	2	.383/.484/.641	.377	.471	-1.1	LF(28): 4.6	2.6
2012	NAS	AAA	24	140	23	12	0	4	24	20	27	1	0	.310/.414/.522	.327	.360	0.0	LF(27): -3.1, RF(2): -0.1	1.1
2013	NAS	AAA	25	281	35	12	1	13	37	31	59	6	4	.255/.349/.473	.295	.283	-1.3	LF(55): 4.0, RF(10): -0.1	1.9
2013	MIL	MLB	25	153	27	10	0	11	27	11	34	3	0	.279/.353/.596	.322	.293	1.2	LF(34): -1.7	1.2
2014	MIL	MLB	26	549	70	37	2	22	69	32	122	4	1	.244/.299/.457	.283	.275	-0.6	LF(134): 6.6	2.8
2015	MIL	MLB	27	470	59	25	1	20	66	36	107	5	2	.256/.324/.463	.293	.293	-0.1	LF 5, RF -0	3.1

Breakout: 5%   Improve: 48%   Collapse: 4%   Attrition: 13%   MLB: 90%   *Comparables: Chris Heisey, Matt Joyce, Mark Trumbo*

The Brewers moved their franchise player to right field to make room for Davis in the outfield, which made it all the more stressful to see him spin his wheels out of the gate, hitting .222/.250/.399 in his first 40 games. However, after a mechanical adjustment that aided his timing and helped him let pitches travel further into the zone, Davis outhit Braun (and a bunch of other good major-league corner outfielders) the rest of the way, hitting .253/.319/.483 with 17 homers from May 20th onward. Perhaps more encouraging than the overall line was his handling of right-handed pitching, which had been a concern throughout his minor-league career and into his rookie year. A .749 OPS against righties isn't going to propel him to an All-Star game anytime soon, but it's no liability and makes him an everyday guy. Defense remains an issue. His range is slightly above average in left field; however, he throws like Johnny Damon warming up. Opposing teams regularly ran on him, and by the second half Gerardo Parra had to be his late-innings defensive replacement. At this point, Davis essentially *is* the Brewers: He has his flaws, but does well for his salary and has enough pop to be dangerous.

Jake Gatewood   SS

Born: 9/25/95   Age: 19   Bats: R   Throws: R   Height: 6' 5"   Weight: 190

YEAR	TEAM	LVL	AGE	PA	R	2B	3B	HR	RBI	BB	K	SB	CS	AVG/OBP/SLG	TAv	BABIP	BRR	FRAA	WARP
2015	MIL	MLB	19	250	23	8	0	3	15	10	76	4	4	.190/.224/.261	.185	.262	-0.6	SS -2	-1.2

Breakout: 0%   Improve: 0%   Collapse: 0%   Attrition: 0%   MLB: 0%   *Comparables: Carlos Rivero, Neftali Soto, Adrian Cardenas*

Gatewood has been putting on impressive batting practice showcases for some time. His gargantuan raw power has drawn comparisons to A-Rod and Tulo, but ultimately, the 6-foot-5 "shortstop" has significant mechanical issues that could hinder his ability to get his own shortened-name moniker. His swing gets crazy long and his hit tool is much worse than par, as seen in his strikeout rates and batting averages. Furthermore, the 19-year-old doesn't project to remain at shortstop; he might even end up in the corner of an outfield. All scouts recognize the ridiculous power potential, but many see little chance things come together. It's going to be a long, arduous developmental path that will require patience, luck and a lot of hard work. On the small chance everything coalesces, though ... stud.

Scooter Gennett   2B

Born: 5/1/90   Age: 25   Bats: L   Throws: R   Height: 5' 10"   Weight: 170

YEAR	TEAM	LVL	AGE	PA	R	2B	3B	HR	RBI	BB	K	SB	CS	AVG/OBP/SLG	TAv	BABIP	BRR	FRAA	WARP
2012	HUN	AA	22	573	66	30	2	5	44	28	71	11	5	.293/.330/.385	.248	.328	-2.6	2B(127): 4.2	0.8
2013	NAS	AAA	23	350	44	10	5	3	22	21	59	10	5	.280/.327/.371	.264	.333	-1.4	2B(77): 8.5	2.0
2013	MIL	MLB	23	230	29	11	2	6	21	10	42	2	1	.324/.356/.479	.308	.380	2.2	2B(59): -2.8	1.8
2014	MIL	MLB	24	474	55	31	3	9	54	22	67	6	3	.289/.320/.434	.271	.321	-1.1	2B(119): -11.8, RF(1): -0.0	0.5
2015	MIL	MLB	25	438	42	21	2	7	45	17	72	6	3	.274/.303/.389	.257	.309	0.4	2B -3	1.0

Breakout: 2%   Improve: 39%   Collapse: 14%   Attrition: 32%   MLB: 88%   *Comparables: DJ LeMahieu, Josh Rutledge, Josh Harrison*

Many scouts dwelled on Scooter's miniature stature and his miniature range at second base, suggesting that Skipper would struggle to be anything more than a utility infielder. However, those scouts glossed over the fact that Scrappy can straight-up barrel the baseball. The 24-year-old's .271 TAv ranked ninth among second baseman (min. 400 PA) and he came within a wind gust of proving double-digit home run power. In essence, Skeeter could offer the same kind of offensive production that Howie Kendrick has provided throughout his career. Stinky won't ever approach Kendrick's defensive peak, but he proved to be fringe-average with the glove. One could easily project Skookey to hit .280-.300 with 10 homers and 10 stolen bases, which is valuable in the offensive wasteland that is second base. The question will be whether Stripper can handle southpaws well enough to receive everyday at-bats and avoid a platoon situation.

Carlos Gomez   CF

Born: 12/4/85   Age: 29   Bats: R   Throws: R   Height: 6' 3"   Weight: 220

YEAR	TEAM	LVL	AGE	PA	R	2B	3B	HR	RBI	BB	K	SB	CS	AVG/OBP/SLG	TAv	BABIP	BRR	FRAA	WARP
2012	MIL	MLB	26	452	72	19	4	19	51	20	98	37	6	.260/.305/.463	.265	.296	4.0	CF(128): 0.8	2.2
2013	MIL	MLB	27	590	80	27	10	24	73	37	146	40	7	.284/.338/.506	.293	.344	2.1	CF(145): 14.1	6.0
2014	MIL	MLB	28	644	95	34	4	23	73	47	141	34	12	.284/.356/.477	.302	.339	1.7	CF(145): 3.6	5.3
2015	MIL	MLB	29	594	87	25	4	19	62	35	138	35	9	.257/.313/.426	.273	.304	1.4	CF 4	3.0

Breakout: 4%   Improve: 42%   Collapse: 2%   Attrition: 5%   MLB: 97%   *Comparables: B.J. Upton, Andre Dawson, Carlos Beltran*

Gomez told the Brewers' coaching staff in 2012 that he no longer wanted to be the groundball speedster Baseball Men had been telling him he should be. He wanted to be himself, to swing for the fences. Since that conversation, the 28-year-old has posted the three lowest groundball rates of his career: 40.3, 40.4 and 37.5 percent, respectively. Prior to 2012, Gomez never produced an OPS higher than .700 in a single season. His past three seasons: .768, .843 and .833, in an era in which those numbers end arguments. Suddenly, the fact that he might be the best defensive center fielder in the game is almost an afterthought; dude's a bona fide superstar, all around. If his walk rate and overall plate discipline continue to improve as they have the past couple years, he'll be on all 30 MVP ballots.

Monte Harrison   OF

Born: 8/10/95   Age: 19   Bats: R   Throws: R   Height: 6' 3"   Weight: 200

YEAR	TEAM	LVL	AGE	PA	R	2B	3B	HR	RBI	BB	K	SB	CS	AVG/OBP/SLG	TAv	BABIP	BRR	FRAA	WARP
2015	MIL	MLB	19	250	27	8	0	2	14	13	74	13	2	.191/.239/.255	.191	.263	1.8	RF -3, CF 1	-1.4

Breakout: 0%   Improve: 0%   Collapse: 0%   Attrition: 0%   MLB: 0%   *Comparables: Caleb Gindl, Oswaldo Arcia, Marcell Ozuna*

Considered by some scouts to be the best pure athlete in the 2014 draft, Harrison bent to the Brewers' persuasion and passed up a football scholarship from the University of Nebraska to sign for $1.8 million. He uses a wide stance in the box, with a subtle loading mechanism in which he pivots on his toe before replanting his heel. Though many question his hit tool, his rookie-league walk rate and OBP were encouraging and suggest he could eventually provide a patience/speed combination. He has plus raw power, but it has yet to show up in games. Ultimately, he's the type of premium athlete scouts dream on, and if everything (or even most things) come together he's a potential All-Star center fielder. It's a tantalizing profile to grab in the second round.

Elian Herrera   RF

Born: 2/1/85   Age: 30   Bats: B   Throws: R   Height: 5' 10"   Weight: 195

YEAR	TEAM	LVL	AGE	PA	R	2B	3B	HR	RBI	BB	K	SB	CS	AVG/OBP/SLG	TAv	BABIP	BRR	FRAA	WARP
2012	ABQ	AAA	27	297	50	20	10	3	40	17	47	11	7	.341/.381/.520	.292	.400	0.3	SS(25): -1.6, 2B(22): -2.4	1.6
2012	LAN	MLB	27	214	26	10	1	1	17	23	50	4	2	.251/.340/.332	.256	.338	1.6	LF(22): 1.2, 3B(20): -0.9	0.7
2013	ABQ	AAA	28	476	69	13	1	7	43	48	76	16	3	.282/.367/.370	.254	.330	2.7	2B(76): 2.4, 3B(20): 0.0	1.6
2013	LAN	MLB	28	8	0	0	0	0	0	0	2	0	0	.250/.250/.250	.132	.333	-0.1	LF(2): -0.2	-0.1
2014	NAS	AAA	29	124	21	9	2	0	9	8	19	5	1	.304/.350/.417	.276	.365	0.5	CF(15): -1.0, 2B(12): -0.6	0.4
2014	MIL	MLB	29	140	14	7	1	0	5	3	36	4	1	.274/.288/.341	.235	.370	-0.5	RF(15): -0.6, SS(14): 1.4	0.2
2015	MIL	MLB	30	250	27	10	2	2	18	16	53	6	2	.250/.305/.333	.245	.310	0.5	2B 0, 3B -1	0.3

Breakout: 0%   Improve: 11%   Collapse: 10%   Attrition: 18%   MLB: 40%   Comparables: Bubba Crosby, Jason Repko, Chris Denorfia

Herrera's season could be encapsulated in a single defensive play in right field: On September 29th, the Brewers clung to a one-run lead in the seventh inning against the Cardinals. Herrera fielded the baseball near the warning track and proceeded to spike his throw directly into the ground in front of him. Herrera stood frozen with slumped shoulders, helplessly watching as the ball trickled down the first-base line toward the infield. Two runs came around to score and the Brewers lost the game.

Luis Jimenez   3B

Born: 1/18/88   Age: 27   Bats: R   Throws: R   Height: 6' 1"   Weight: 205

YEAR	TEAM	LVL	AGE	PA	R	2B	3B	HR	RBI	BB	K	SB	CS	AVG/OBP/SLG	TAv	BABIP	BRR	FRAA	WARP
2012	SLC	AAA	24	517	78	38	2	16	85	19	70	17	7	.309/.334/.495	.273	.331	-0.3	3B(118): 17.0	4.8
2013	SLC	AAA	25	218	28	9	2	4	42	12	26	11	3	.284/.326/.411	.260	.301	1.6	3B(36): 3.4, SS(6): 0.0	1.5
2013	ANA	MLB	25	110	15	6	0	0	5	2	28	0	0	.260/.291/.317	.240	.351	-1.3	3B(29): 3.6, 1B(2): -0.0	0.6
2014	SLC	AAA	26	501	67	34	3	21	76	24	75	12	4	.286/.321/.505	.272	.300	-2.0	3B(81): 4.7, 1B(11): 0.1	2.9
2014	ANA	MLB	26	41	3	2	0	0	2	0	13	0	0	.162/.205/.216	.162	.250	0.3	3B(16): 0.1	-0.1
2015	MIL	MLB	27	250	25	12	0	6	27	9	48	5	2	.242/.273/.376	.243	.274	0.0	3B 4, 1B 0	0.6

Breakout: 1%   Improve: 10%   Collapse: 4%   Attrition: 11%   MLB: 19%   Comparables: Angel Chavez, Jeff Baisley, Hector Gimenez

For the second straight season, "Lucho" had his opportunity to show what he could do in the bigs, and for the second time he stumbled. The glove continued to play above average at the hot corner, but his bat deteriorated further in the face of major-league pitching. His two primary strengths in the minors—a better-than-average contact rate and a penchant for pulling fly balls for doubles—fell victim to big-league breaking balls just beyond the outer half, ballooning his K-rate to double his minor-league mark and swelling his pop-up rate north of 22 percent. Upon returning to Salt Lake, he did his usual yeoman's work, but it was clear that his future wasn't in Anaheim. The Brewers claimed him.

Gilbert Lara   SS

Born: 10/30/97   Age: 17   Bats: R   Throws: R   Height: 6' 3"   Weight: 180

Milwaukee has traditionally tiptoed its way through the international market, shying away from big-money prospects due to a paucity of relationships with prominent buscones and the low probability of an on-the-field payoff. That narrative shifted in a big way in July. The Brewers signed Lara to a $3.1 million signing bonus, which not only blew past the Brewers' international spending record but also marked the top bonus of last year's July 2nd class. He's a 6-foot-3 slugger with massive raw power and all the normal developmental question marks associated with 16-year-old international prospects. Lara represents a new era for the organization's engagement with the foreign market, and regardless of Lara's endpoint in his baseball career, that is significant in itself.

Adam Lind   DH

Born: 7/17/83   Age: 31   Bats: L   Throws: L   Height: 6' 2"   Weight: 195

YEAR	TEAM	LVL	AGE	PA	R	2B	3B	HR	RBI	BB	K	SB	CS	AVG/OBP/SLG	TAv	BABIP	BRR	FRAA	WARP
2012	LVG	AAA	28	143	24	10	0	8	29	15	26	1	0	.392/.448/.664	.356	.436	-3.7	1B(25): -1.4	1.1
2012	TOR	MLB	28	353	28	14	2	11	45	29	61	0	0	.255/.314/.414	.256	.282	-0.1	1B(61): -4.0	-0.3
2013	TOR	MLB	29	521	67	26	1	23	67	51	103	1	0	.288/.357/.497	.301	.324	-3.2	1B(76): -1.3	2.3
2014	TOR	MLB	30	318	38	24	2	6	40	28	48	0	0	.321/.381/.479	.301	.369	2.9	1B(47): -0.8	1.9
2015	MIL	MLB	31	342	37	15	1	11	43	26	69	0	0	.262/.317/.424	.276	.300	-0.1	1B -2	0.8

Breakout: 1%   Improve: 33%   Collapse: 10%   Attrition: 9%   MLB: 95%   Comparables: Ben Broussard, Rafael Palmeiro, Seth Smith

Lind spent three years below replacement level, trying to recapture his breakout 2009, before the Blue Jays scrapped playing him full-time in 2013 and directed 81 percent of his plate appearances to left-on-right matchups, with tremendous success. Last year, that grew to 88 percent. Lind also added a staggering goatee, which surely contributed to the best on-base percentage and batting average of his career. He hit to the opposite field with much higher frequency, splashing more extra-base hits to left field than his pull side. He's still unusable at first base, which makes his acquisition by the Brewers a little mystifying, even accounting for his reasonable contract status: $7.5 million owed in 2015 and an $8 million club option (with just a $500,000 buyout) in 2016.

Jonathan Lucroy   C

Born: 6/13/86   Age: 29   Bats: R   Throws: R   Height: 6' 0"   Weight: 195

YEAR	TEAM	LVL	AGE	PA	R	2B	3B	HR	RBI	BB	K	SB	CS	AVG/OBP/SLG	TAv	BABIP	BRR	FRAA	WARP
2012	MIL	MLB	26	346	46	17	4	12	58	22	44	4	1	.320/.368/.513	.299	.338	-2.3	C(88): -2.4	2.3
2013	MIL	MLB	27	580	59	25	6	18	82	46	69	9	1	.280/.340/.455	.274	.290	-7.6	C(126): -1.4, 1B(14): -0.3	2.2
2014	MIL	MLB	28	655	73	53	2	13	69	66	71	4	4	.301/.373/.465	.306	.324	2.1	C(136): -1.4, 1B(19): -0.0	6.0
2015	MIL	MLB	29	600	63	30	2	13	67	45	85	6	2	.274/.331/.408	.278	.300	-2.7	C -2, 1B -0	2.8

Breakout: 3%   Improve: 42%   Collapse: 3%   Attrition: 5%   MLB: 99%   *Comparables: Ted Simmons, Kurt Suzuki, Yogi Berra*

How much has Lucroy progressed as a catcher? Back in 2010, he failed to make the BP Top 101 prospect list. In 2014, he was the best catcher in baseball. He might have been, for six months, the best *player* in baseball? His 6.0 WARP was tops at his position and eighth best overall, but of course that doesn't factor in framing, where steady-heady added more than two full wins, if you believe the methodology. His walk rate has risen in each of his major-league seasons, jumping to 10.1 percent last year, and his strikeout rate has plummeted to a career-low 10.8 percent. When the Brewers signed him to a long, pre-arb extension before the 2012 season, it landed somewhere between "huh" and "oh." He had produced 2.1 WARP in two seasons to that point. Three years in, he has produced about 10, and he's still under contract for $12.8 million over the next three years. The ascent has been stunning. He now represents the gold standard for the catching position.

Martin Maldonado   C

Born: 8/16/86   Age: 28   Bats: R   Throws: R   Height: 6' 0"   Weight: 230

YEAR	TEAM	LVL	AGE	PA	R	2B	3B	HR	RBI	BB	K	SB	CS	AVG/OBP/SLG	TAv	BABIP	BRR	FRAA	WARP
2012	NAS	AAA	25	138	10	6	0	4	13	9	37	0	2	.198/.270/.347	.220	.241	0.2	C(34): 0.1	0.2
2012	MIL	MLB	25	256	22	9	0	8	30	17	56	1	1	.266/.321/.408	.251	.320	1.8	C(69): 0.9, 1B(4): -0.0	1.1
2013	MIL	MLB	26	202	13	7	1	4	22	13	53	0	0	.169/.236/.284	.197	.214	0.3	C(47): 1.3, 1B(10): -0.2	-0.5
2014	MIL	MLB	27	126	14	5	0	4	16	11	32	0	0	.234/.320/.387	.258	.293	0.3	C(42): 0.7, 1B(2): 0.0	0.5
2015	*MIL*	*MLB*	*28*	*250*	*25*	*9*	*0*	*6*	*25*	*17*	*61*	*1*	*0*	*.225/.290/.350*	*.241*	*.273*	*0.7*	*C 1, 1B -0*	*0.6*

Breakout: 5%   Improve: 33%   Collapse: 14%   Attrition: 36%   MLB: 77%   *Comparables: Michael McKenry, Gerald Laird, Ronny Paulino*

If you programmed your 3D printer to generate you a near-perfect backup catcher, Maldonado could serve as its prototype. He draws a credible number of walks, produced a solid .153 isolated power, saved more runs framing on a per-pitch basis than even Jonathan Lucroy and gunned down runners at an above-average rate (as he has in each of his big-league seasons). Perhaps the greatest throw of his career came against the Red Sox in April. From his knees, he unleashed a dart to second base in time to get Jonathan Herrera, who'd had a phenomenal jump on the pitch. Maldonado's throw had no tail, no sink—it didn't even rise above the pitcher's head. The more we talk, the less Maldonado sounds like the perfect backup catcher, and the more he sounds like a pretty good starter.

Sthervin Matos   3B

Born: 2/13/94   Age: 21   Bats: R   Throws: R   Height: 6' 1"   Weight: 185

YEAR	TEAM	LVL	AGE	PA	R	2B	3B	HR	RBI	BB	K	SB	CS	AVG/OBP/SLG	TAv	BABIP	BRR	FRAA	WARP
2014	WIS	A	20	43	2	0	0	1	7	1	12	1	0	.103/.122/.179	.124	.111	0.1	3B(7): -0.1	-0.5
2015	*MIL*	*MLB*	*21*	*250*	*20*	*8*	*0*	*5*	*22*	*8*	*75*	*3*	*1*	*.192/.220/.288*	*.192*	*.252*	*0.1*	*3B -1, 1B 1*	*-1.2*

Breakout: 0%   Improve: 0%   Collapse: 0%   Attrition: 0%   MLB: 0%   *Comparables: Luis Jimenez, Charlie Culberson, Matt Tuiasosopo*

The 20-year-old third baseman has three important things going in his favor: (1) a great name, (2) a great story and (3) a great stat line. The name, Sthervin, appears to be a typo that somehow eluded the editorial staff—though a typo for *what*, exactly, isn't clear. After a July promotion to the short-season Pioneer League, the anxious and overwhelmed Matos got off his airplane a stop too early in Great Falls, Montana. A customer service agent for Alaska Airlines drove Matos nearly two hours to Helena (stopping at a grocery store to buy him "a red Powerade;" you can read all about this on Alaska Airlines' company blog, a sentence that merits two or three embedded exclamation points) and arrived 15 minutes before opening pitch. In the fourth inning on that same night, Matos clubbed a home run. From panic to elation, all in about three hours. The Dominican native ultimately hit .317/.338/.521 with six homers before being promoted to Class-A Wisconsin for the final couple weeks of the season.

Lyle Overbay   1B

Born: 1/28/77   Age: 38   Bats: L   Throws: L   Height: 6' 2"   Weight: 235

YEAR	TEAM	LVL	AGE	PA	R	2B	3B	HR	RBI	BB	K	SB	CS	AVG/OBP/SLG	TAv	BABIP	BRR	FRAA	WARP
2012	GWN	AAA	35	28	3	3	0	0	3	6	6	0	0	.273/.429/.409	.288	.375	-0.2	1B(6): -0.2	0.1
2012	ARI	MLB	35	110	11	9	0	2	10	12	26	0	0	.292/.367/.448	.278	.377	-3.5	1B(21): 0.2	0.0
2012	ATL	MLB	35	21	1	1	0	0	1	1	8	0	0	.100/.143/.150	.106	.167	0.2	1B(2): -0.0	-0.3
2013	NYA	MLB	36	485	43	24	1	14	59	36	111	2	0	.240/.295/.393	.248	.287	-0.7	1B(130): -0.2, RF(4): -0.1	-0.3
2014	MIL	MLB	37	296	24	14	0	4	35	36	60	2	0	.233/.328/.333	.250	.287	0.2	1B(83): -0.6	0.2
2015	*MIL*	*MLB*	*38*	*315*	*30*	*15*	*1*	*6*	*32*	*29*	*72*	*1*	*0*	*.226/.299/.346*	*.247*	*.279*	*-0.3*	*1B -1, RF -0*	*-0.2*

Breakout: 0%   Improve: 20%   Collapse: 20%   Attrition: 24%   MLB: 78%   *Comparables: Don Baylor, Darrell Evans, Bob Watson*

For two years, Milwaukee searched desperately for a first baseman who could fill the void left by Prince Fielder; failing to come close, they realized that, as with Fielder's britches, it might take two full-size men to fill the space. Overbay was signed to handle the strong side of a platoon in 2014, to be a veteran in the clubhouse and to scoop throws in the dirt. He excelled at the latter two, but the bat didn't carry, and the Brewers began using their regular catcher at first to avoid starting Overbay. He redeemed himself as a pinch-hitter, hitting .324/.425/.471 off the bench with some huge hits: a September 12th walk-off, a go-ahead, bases-clearing double on August 15th. The sustainability of that skill is dubious, at best, but if you're narrating his 2014 story, those hits deserve their due.

Gerardo Parra   RF

Born: 5/6/87   Age: 28   Bats: L   Throws: L   Height: 5' 11"   Weight: 200

YEAR	TEAM	LVL	AGE	PA	R	2B	3B	HR	RBI	BB	K	SB	CS	AVG/OBP/SLG	TAv	BABIP	BRR	FRAA	WARP
2012	ARI	MLB	25	430	58	21	2	7	36	33	77	15	9	.273/.335/.392	.260	.323	2.9	CF(48): -2.7, LF(47): 0.4	1.5
2013	ARI	MLB	26	663	79	43	4	10	48	48	100	10	10	.268/.323/.403	.257	.305	0.8	RF(123): 9.7, CF(33): 1.6	3.7
2014	ARI	MLB	27	440	51	18	3	6	30	24	72	5	5	.259/.305/.362	.247	.300	1.1	RF(102): -2.8, CF(3): 0.1	0.4
2014	MIL	MLB	27	134	13	4	1	3	10	8	28	4	2	.268/.318/.390	.250	.326	0.1	LF(27): 0.7, CF(9): 0.1	0.5
2015	*MIL*	*MLB*	*28*	*557*	*65*	*26*	*3*	*8*	*47*	*38*	*95*	*11*	*7*	*.263/.317/.375*	*.259*	*.302*	*1.6*	*RF 3, CF -0*	*1.7*

Breakout: 1%   Improve: 60%   Collapse: 1%   Attrition: 9%   MLB: 90%   *Comparables: Magglio Ordonez, Lyman Bostock, Terry Puhl*

Parra is a lovely fourth outfielder who can handle regular at-bats without threatening any of the game's most hallowed records. Some Arizona observers suggested his defense took a step back due to a heavier lower half, which is a polite way to suggest a player has gained undesirable weight—by which we mean dat ass—but he covered ground like a fat dude chasing a cake after he arrived in Milwaukee, which is a rude way to say he looked a lot better. Parra spent time at all three outfield positions for the Brewers, but was mostly a soft-platoon partner and defensive replacement for Khris Davis in left field. The roughness at the plate will need to be sanded down over the offseason if he wants to be anything more than a fourth outfielder in 2015. He will especially need to rein in an aggressive approach and draw a few more walks if he wants to keep his career going now that he's in his mid-30s and can no longer—wait, Gerardo Parra is only 28? Lies, damned lies and statistics.

Aramis Ramirez   3B

Born: 6/25/78   Age: 37   Bats: R   Throws: R   Height: 6' 1"   Weight: 205

YEAR	TEAM	LVL	AGE	PA	R	2B	3B	HR	RBI	BB	K	SB	CS	AVG/OBP/SLG	TAv	BABIP	BRR	FRAA	WARP
2012	MIL	MLB	34	630	92	50	3	27	105	44	82	9	2	.300/.360/.540	.303	.310	-2.5	3B(143): -4.0	4.2
2013	MIL	MLB	35	351	43	18	0	12	49	36	55	0	1	.283/.370/.461	.288	.308	-2.8	3B(80): -11.2	0.4
2014	MIL	MLB	36	531	47	23	1	15	66	21	75	3	0	.285/.330/.427	.265	.310	-3.0	3B(126): -11.2	0.6
2015	MIL	MLB	37	464	52	23	0	15	59	28	70	3	1	.264/.319/.430	.279	.282	-2.2	3B -10	0.7

Breakout: 0%   Improve: 19%   Collapse: 9%   Attrition: 13%   MLB: 77%   Comparables: Scott Rolen, Melvin Mora, Mark DeRosa

Thirty-six years old, been dealing with multiple leg injuries over the past couple seasons, produced a .142 ISO that was his lowest since an 18-game stint with the Pirates in 1999. That's not to suggest Ramirez can't still swing the bat (we're not above noticing a .285 batting average), but the overall effectiveness has waned. Knee troubles in 2013 and a strained hamstring in 2014 have caused him to rely more on his upper half, forcing him to begin his swing earlier and giving him less time to identify quality pitches. The walk rate (4 percent) is horrendous and the swinging strike rate (10.8 percent) is his worst since 2003, way back when he was still in Pittsburgh, when it was just him and Tike Redman and Pokey Reese and Adam Hyzdu and Rob Mackowiak and Jeff Reboulet and Kevin Young and—whoops, just fell into the Pirates-nostalgia spiral. Back to Ramirez: Hopefully, he arrives at spring training fully healthy, because you get the feeling that otherwise we're going to be writing the post-retirement career retrospective in this space next winter.

Victor Roache   OF

Born: 9/17/91   Age: 23   Bats: R   Throws: R   Height: 6' 1"   Weight: 225

YEAR	TEAM	LVL	AGE	PA	R	2B	3B	HR	RBI	BB	K	SB	CS	AVG/OBP/SLG	TAv	BABIP	BRR	FRAA	WARP
2013	WIS	A	21	519	62	14	4	22	74	46	137	6	2	.248/.322/.440	.274	.302	-1.0	LF(86): 1.7	1.7
2014	BRV	A+	22	481	46	17	2	18	54	37	138	11	4	.226/.298/.400	.247	.287	-0.7	LF(106): -4.6, RF(1): 0.0	-0.4
2015	MIL	MLB	23	250	24	7	1	9	29	14	85	2	1	.198/.249/.347	.223	.264	-0.2	LF -1	-0.5

Breakout: 0%   Improve: 0%   Collapse: 0%   Attrition: 0%   MLB: 0%   Comparables: Jeremy Moore, Zoilo Almonte, Corey Dickerson

Milwaukee drafted Roache in the first round in 2012, knowing he possessed gargantuan raw power and hoping he would hit enough to consistently tap into that power. It has not happened. He launched 18 homers in a very difficult offensive environment, but a .226 batting average at this level really means something for a hitter's outlook. He can't hit quality secondary offerings, and his range in the outfield limits him primarily to a left-field profile, which puts even more pressure on the utility of his bat. There exists a chance that Roache develops the hit tool and soars up the prospect rankings. Certainly, the Brewers still hope, but keeping hope for a former first-round pick is the Pascal's Wager of the baseball world.

Jean Segura   SS

Born: 3/17/90   Age: 25   Bats: R   Throws: R   Height: 5' 10"   Weight: 205

YEAR	TEAM	LVL	AGE	PA	R	2B	3B	HR	RBI	BB	K	SB	CS	AVG/OBP/SLG	TAv	BABIP	BRR	FRAA	WARP
2012	ARK	AA	22	414	50	10	5	7	40	23	57	33	13	.294/.346/.404	.291	.329	2.6	SS(80): 6.6, 2B(2): -0.0	3.8
2012	HUN	AA	22	37	7	3	0	0	4	4	4	4	0	.433/.500/.533	.345	.481	-0.8	SS(8): 0.6	0.4
2012	ANA	MLB	22	3	0	0	0	0	0	0	2	0	0	.000/.000/.000	.247	.000	-0.1	SS(1): 0.1	0.0
2012	MIL	MLB	22	163	19	4	3	0	14	13	21	7	1	.264/.321/.331	.236	.305	1.0	SS(43): -2.7	0.1
2013	MIL	MLB	23	623	74	20	10	12	49	25	84	44	13	.294/.329/.423	.265	.326	2.6	SS(144): 23.5	5.6
2014	MIL	MLB	24	557	61	14	6	5	31	28	70	20	9	.246/.289/.326	.235	.275	4.8	SS(144): 23.6	3.8
2015	MIL	MLB	25	536	67	18	6	7	43	25	75	27	9	.269/.308/.372	.259	.297	2.1	SS 16, 2B 0	4.2

Breakout: 1%   Improve: 72%   Collapse: 4%   Attrition: 12%   MLB: 100%   Comparables: Alcides Escobar, Everth Cabrera, Jose Reyes

Though he backed up his defensive breakout from 2013, Segura's campaign was otherwise a depressing montage of offensive uncomeliness. His .289 on-base percentage was the 12th worst among qualified big leaguers, while his power potential was undone by a 59 percent groundball rate, the eighth highest in the league. He features an extremely rotational swing that limits his ability to drive the ball, as he fails to stay back and produce any leverage, resulting in weak groundouts to his pull side. Prior to the end of the season, the Brewers and Segura discussed the natural limitations in his hitting mechanics, with the club encouraging him to make adjustments over the offseason. Those adjustments are non-negotiable, as he's now a year and a half removed from the electric .325/.363/.487 line he produced in the first half of 2013, and a year and a half into a second act as one of the league's worst hitters.

Tyrone Taylor   CF

Born: 1/22/94   Age: 21   Bats: R   Throws: R   Height: 6' 0"   Weight: 185

YEAR	TEAM	LVL	AGE	PA	R	2B	3B	HR	RBI	BB	K	SB	CS	AVG/OBP/SLG	TAv	BABIP	BRR	FRAA	WARP
2013	WIS	A	19	549	69	33	2	8	57	35	63	19	8	.274/.338/.400	.266	.299	2.4	CF(108): 12.2, LF(4): 0.0	3.5
2014	BRV	A+	20	559	69	36	3	6	68	39	58	22	6	.278/.331/.396	.267	.301	1.4	CF(128): 12.8, RF(1): -0.1	3.9
2015	MIL	MLB	21	250	22	12	0	3	22	10	47	5	2	.230/.268/.326	.226	.268	0.1	CF 5, LF 0	0.3

Breakout: 0%   Improve: 0%   Collapse: 0%   Attrition: 0%   MLB: 0%   Comparables: Ben Revere, Desmond Jennings, Melky Cabrera

One of the three best prospects in a weak Milwaukee system, Taylor has tallied an impressive 69 doubles over the past two seasons—nice—to go with a batting average around .275. The more optimistic scouts expect that gap power to morph into 10 or 15 homers to go with 20 stolen bases at the major-league level. The offensive profile screams "solid," not "spectacular," which—with strong defense—could reasonably develop into a quality everyday center fielder. But how much upside is there, really? He's athletic, but physically maxed out, and unless he really starts driving the ball the power will never reach "plus." Maybe that's just finding something to complain about; the 21-year-old center fielder should be a big-league regular, which is routinely undervalued when projecting minor-league players.

Rickie Weeks   2B

Born: 9/13/82   Age: 32   Bats: R   Throws: R   Height: 5' 10"   Weight: 220

YEAR	TEAM	LVL	AGE	PA	R	2B	3B	HR	RBI	BB	K	SB	CS	AVG/OBP/SLG	TAv	BABIP	BRR	FRAA	WARP
2012	MIL	MLB	29	677	85	29	4	21	63	74	169	16	3	.230/.328/.400	.262	.285	-0.9	2B(152): -14.2	0.3
2013	MIL	MLB	30	399	40	20	1	10	24	40	105	7	3	.209/.306/.357	.235	.268	0.6	2B(95): -5.0	-0.7
2014	MIL	MLB	31	286	36	19	1	8	29	25	73	3	4	.274/.357/.452	.301	.355	0.5	2B(62): -6.2	1.3
2015	MIL	MLB	32	291	33	13	1	8	33	28	72	5	2	.237/.325/.390	.274	.294	-0.2	2B -4	0.9

Breakout: 3%   Improve: 37%   Collapse: 4%   Attrition: 5%   MLB: 97%   Comparables: Dan Uggla, Ryne Sandberg, Al Rosen

Much like Vince Vaughn these days, Weeks possesses a very limited skill set that mustn't be overstretched, lest we suddenly realize how extremely unsettling he is to the eye. Weeks is dreadful defensively and struggles against right-handed pitching; to hit a competent .294/.351/.395 against them required a *.420 BABIP*. His limited value stems from his ability to crush lefties, and his non-BABIP-soaked .865 OPS against southpaws produces All Star pop—just once or twice a week, that's all. He compiled a 10.3 percent walk rate against lefties and had a .248 ISO with 18 extra-base hits in only 155 plate appearances. Again, lefty masher with no real defensive home doesn't sound appealing, but even as the guy behind the guy behind the guy, he's useful enough to carve out a big-league role for the next few seasons, especially because he's considered a positive influence in the clubhouse and a mentor to young players.

Kyle Wren   OF

Born: 4/23/91   Age: 24   Bats: L   Throws: L   Height: 5' 10"   Weight: 175

YEAR	TEAM	LVL	AGE	PA	R	2B	3B	HR	RBI	BB	K	SB	CS	AVG/OBP/SLG	TAv	BABIP	BRR	FRAA	WARP
2013	ROM	A	22	215	36	11	4	2	20	16	21	32	6	.328/.382/.456	.312	.360	3.0	CF(47): 0.7	2.2
2014	LYN	A+	23	336	46	10	4	0	27	30	39	33	9	.296/.359/.357	.267	.333	1.6	CF(76): 4.7	1.9
2014	MIS	AA	23	227	28	11	4	0	16	16	40	13	5	.283/.338/.376	.269	.352	2.2	CF(50): -1.5	0.9
2015	MIL	MLB	24	250	30	9	2	2	16	14	49	15	4	.244/.290/.323	.231	.293	1.4	CF 1, LF 0	0.2

Breakout: 0%   Improve: 0%   Collapse: 0%   Attrition: 0%   MLB: 0%   Comparables: Matthew Szczur, Abraham Almonte, Brandon Guyer

See, sometimes nepotism pays. Wren has garnered more attention for being Frank's son than he would have with the same skill set and a different last name, yet he deserves acknowledgment as one of the system's top outfield prospects. In addition to quality instincts, Wren weds plus speed with a line-drive swing. His lack of walks and power (check the HR column) means he'll need to fend off a steady diet of strikes from advanced pitchers. Should he prove able, he could be the Braves' fou—
　　Never mind, Wren was traded two months after his dad got canned.

Pitchers

Michael Blazek   RHP

Born: 3/16/89   Age: 26   Bats: R   Throws: R   Height: 6'0"   Weight: 200

YEAR	TEAM	LVL	AGE	W	L	SV	G	GS	IP	H	HR	BB	K	BB/9	K/9	GB%	BABIP	WHIP	ERA	FIP	FRA	WARP
2012	SFD	AA	23	5	8	0	40	7	80	61	11	34	83	3.8	9.3	44%	.254	1.19	4.16	4.38	6.39	-0.4
2013	SFD	AA	24	0	0	7	17	0	19²	11	0	10	25	4.6	11.4	56%	.244	1.07	0.92	2.04	2.59	0.5
2013	MEM	AAA	24	1	2	2	19	0	26	17	1	16	27	5.5	9.3	36%	.246	1.27	2.77	3.84	4.64	0.2
2013	MIL	MLB	24	0	1	0	7	0	7	6	1	3	4	3.9	5.1	40%	.208	1.29	3.86	5.02	7.20	-0.2
2013	SLN	MLB	24	0	0	0	11	0	10¹	10	2	10	10	8.7	8.7	48%	.276	1.94	6.97	6.79	6.37	-0.2
2014	NAS	AAA	25	4	4	1	37	17	102¹	106	9	40	87	3.5	7.7	49%	.317	1.43	4.13	4.40	5.01	1.1
2015	MIL	MLB	26	4	4	0	34	11	83²	79	10	38	67	4.1	7.2	46%	.298	1.39	4.48	4.81	4.87	-0.2

Breakout: 15%   Improve: 23%   Collapse: 9%   Attrition: 24%   MLB: 37%   Comparables: Francisco Cruceta, John Ennis, Adam Johnson

Blazek came to Milwaukee in the 2013 John Axford trade. He throws in the mid-90s with a couple tough breaking balls, but the 25-year-old struggles to find the strike zone and can occasionally walk too many batters, as seen in his 9 percent walk rate at Triple-A Nashville. Now that you mention it, that profile sounds eerily similar to the current version of Axford. Perhaps we should hereby refer to the trade as the Axford-for-Axford-Lite trade. Let it be written.

Jonathan Broxton   RHP

Born: 6/16/84   Age: 31   Bats: R   Throws: R   Height: 6'4"   Weight: 295

YEAR	TEAM	LVL	AGE	W	L	SV	G	GS	IP	H	HR	BB	K	BB/9	K/9	GB%	BABIP	WHIP	ERA	FIP	FRA	WARP
2012	CIN	MLB	28	3	3	4	25	0	22¹	20	1	3	20	1.2	8.1	49%	.306	1.03	2.82	2.46	2.57	0.5
2012	KCA	MLB	28	1	2	23	35	0	35²	36	1	14	25	3.5	6.3	58%	.321	1.40	2.27	3.35	4.70	0.1
2013	CIN	MLB	29	2	2	0	34	0	30²	27	4	12	25	3.5	7.3	47%	.261	1.27	4.11	4.65	5.45	-0.1
2014	CIN	MLB	30	4	2	7	51	0	48¹	32	3	17	37	3.2	6.9	46%	.221	1.01	1.86	3.50	3.68	0.3
2014	MIL	MLB	30	0	1	0	11	0	10¹	9	1	2	12	1.7	10.5	54%	.296	1.06	4.35	2.62	4.68	0.0
2015	MIL	MLB	31	3	1	4	51	0	48	42	4	16	44	3.1	8.3	47%	.308	1.22	3.49	3.70	3.79	0.4

Breakout: 25%   Improve: 44%   Collapse: 28%   Attrition: 17%   MLB: 85%   Comparables: Pedro Feliciano, John Grabow, Nick Masset

Broxton terminated the cutter experiment and returned to relevance at the back of the Reds and Brewers bullpens. One wonders how sustainable a bounce-back is when aided by a .234 BABIP—a career low by 30 points—and no uptick in velocity or swinging-strike rate. The question: How much credit does a reliever get for a league-best 10 percent line drive rate in a 60-inning sample? Russell Carleton found that line-drive rates stabilize for pitchers at around 650 balls in play; Broxton allowed 162 batted balls, so call us in three or four years.

Mike Fiers   RHP

Born: 6/15/85   Age: 30   Bats: R   Throws: R   Height: 6'2"   Weight: 190

YEAR	TEAM	LVL	AGE	W	L	SV	G	GS	IP	H	HR	BB	K	BB/9	K/9	GB%	BABIP	WHIP	ERA	FIP	FRA	WARP
2012	NAS	AAA	27	1	3	0	10	10	55	49	6	18	49	2.9	8.0	42%	.281	1.22	4.42	4.45	4.85	0.8
2012	MIL	MLB	27	9	10	0	23	22	127²	125	12	36	135	2.5	9.5	34%	.319	1.26	3.74	3.14	3.32	3.4
2013	NAS	AAA	28	1	2	0	5	5	28²	24	3	12	30	3.8	9.4	47%	.284	1.26	2.20	4.09	4.24	0.5
2013	MIL	MLB	28	1	4	0	11	3	22¹	28	8	6	15	2.4	6.0	37%	.270	1.52	7.25	7.14	6.74	-0.2
2014	NAS	AAA	29	8	5	0	17	17	102¹	80	8	17	129	1.5	11.3	46%	.289	0.95	2.55	2.90	2.95	2.7
2014	MIL	MLB	29	6	5	0	14	10	71²	46	7	17	76	2.1	9.5	36%	.224	0.88	2.13	2.96	3.47	1.0
2015	*MIL*	*MLB*	*30*	*8*	*7*	*0*	*22*	*22*	*127¹*	*106*	*14*	*33*	*122*	*2.4*	*8.6*	*40%*	*.289*	*1.10*	*3.22*	*3.73*	*3.50*	*1.8*

Breakout: 18%   Improve: 26%   Collapse: 14%   Attrition: 19%   MLB: 48%   *Comparables: Guillermo Moscoso, Buddy Carlyle, Garrett Mock*

Nobody much cared, but there was Fiers, laying waste to the Pacific Coast League with an 11.4 K/9. Finally the Brewers called him up in August to stabilize their faltering rotation. As Milwaukee crumbled, Fiers held strong, striking out batters, limiting his previous home run exposure and adding a mile per hour across his repertoire. That increased velocity translated into a higher whiff rate, especially up in the zone, adding an extra dimension to his four-pitch, strike-throwing routine; batters were thrown further off balance, and his cutter to righties and changeup to lefties played up for the extra layer of unpredictability. So: Will the improved velocity carry over, and will the BABIP regress? There's no real reason to doubt the velocity, but the BABIP is something else. At .224, his was the lowest of any starting pitcher who threw at least 70 innings, and he doesn't have a history of low BABIPs. While the double-digit infield pop-up rate is encouraging, it isn't anywhere close to being high enough to suggest sustainability. Regression is coming, but some core gains indicate he could still find success as a back-end starter going forward. This time, they'll care.

Yovani Gallardo   RHP

Born: 2/27/86   Age: 29   Bats: R   Throws: R   Height: 6'2"   Weight: 210

YEAR	TEAM	LVL	AGE	W	L	SV	G	GS	IP	H	HR	BB	K	BB/9	K/9	GB%	BABIP	WHIP	ERA	FIP	FRA	WARP
2012	MIL	MLB	26	16	9	0	33	33	204	185	26	81	204	3.6	9.0	49%	.290	1.30	3.66	3.98	4.44	2.7
2013	MIL	MLB	27	12	10	0	31	31	180²	180	18	66	144	3.3	7.2	51%	.299	1.36	4.18	3.87	4.49	1.6
2014	MIL	MLB	28	8	11	0	32	32	192¹	195	21	54	146	2.5	6.8	54%	.294	1.29	3.51	3.91	4.74	0.1
2015	*MIL*	*MLB*	*29*	*10*	*9*	*0*	*27*	*27*	*163¹*	*148*	*16*	*49*	*146*	*2.7*	*8.1*	*48%*	*.306*	*1.20*	*3.57*	*3.76*	*3.88*	*1.5*

Breakout: 14%   Improve: 36%   Collapse: 15%   Attrition: 4%   MLB: 94%   *Comparables: Matt Garza, Edwin Jackson, John Lackey*

Gallardo saw his strikeout rate drop and his swinging-strike rate match a career low, but he still enjoyed his best ERA since an injury-shortened 2008 season. This represents—well, some luck, to be honest, but also an evolution for Gallardo, who has embraced the groundball and is learning to find success with diminished stuff. In his April 6th start against Boston, he threw 6 2/3 shutout innings without a single swing and miss. That's—well, a backhanded compliment, to be honest, but also an incredible transformation for a guy who struck out a batter per inning each season from 2009 to 2012. Many folks began to throw in the towel after Gallardo's disappointing 2013 season, but it wasn't a down year so much as a transition. "Ground-ball specialist Yovani Gallardo" sounds strange. Beats being washed up at 29, though.

Matt Garza   RHP

Born: 11/26/83   Age: 31   Bats: R   Throws: R   Height: 6'4"   Weight: 215

YEAR	TEAM	LVL	AGE	W	L	SV	G	GS	IP	H	HR	BB	K	BB/9	K/9	GB%	BABIP	WHIP	ERA	FIP	FRA	WARP
2012	CHN	MLB	28	5	7	0	18	18	103²	90	15	32	96	2.8	8.3	50%	.271	1.18	3.91	4.21	5.42	-0.3
2013	CHN	MLB	29	6	1	0	11	11	71	61	8	20	62	2.5	7.9	43%	.266	1.14	3.17	3.75	4.15	0.8
2013	TEX	MLB	29	4	5	0	13	13	84¹	89	12	22	74	2.3	7.9	41%	.308	1.32	4.38	3.99	4.22	0.7
2014	MIL	MLB	30	8	8	0	27	27	163¹	143	12	50	126	2.8	6.9	46%	.268	1.18	3.64	3.51	4.27	0.5
2015	*MIL*	*MLB*	*31*	*9*	*8*	*0*	*23*	*23*	*142¹*	*126*	*15*	*39*	*120*	*2.5*	*7.6*	*43%*	*.294*	*1.16*	*3.51*	*3.92*	*3.82*	*1.4*

Breakout: 14%   Improve: 50%   Collapse: 14%   Attrition: 14%   MLB: 93%   *Comparables: John Lackey, Gavin Floyd, Jason Hammel*

When Garza's home run rate dips below 1.0 HR/9, he posts an ERA under 3.80. When it's above 1.0 HR/9, he posts an ERA above 3.80. That has held true for every season since he started 30 games for the first time in 2008 with the Rays. This year, his home run rate was only 0.7 HR/9 and his ERA was subsequently 3.64. Easy enough, right? More happened beneath the surface, though, which indicates some decline in effectiveness. His fastball velocity has dropped a mile per hour over the past two years. His swinging-strike rate fell to 8.9 percent, which is below the league average for starting pitchers. Similarly, his strikeout rate plummeted to a mere 19 percent, also worse than league average. It appears his success is beginning to be tied more intimately to his overall BABIP and home run rates, which can fluctuate significantly from year to year. He found success when both were below his career average. If either ticks up, this could get ugly now that he lacks strong peripherals for ballast.

Tom Gorzelanny   LHP

Born: 7/12/82   Age: 32   Bats: R   Throws: L   Height: 6'3"   Weight: 210

YEAR	TEAM	LVL	AGE	W	L	SV	G	GS	IP	H	HR	BB	K	BB/9	K/9	GB%	BABIP	WHIP	ERA	FIP	FRA	WARP
2012	WAS	MLB	29	4	2	1	45	1	72	65	7	30	62	3.8	7.8	43%	.283	1.32	2.88	4.01	4.18	0.6
2013	MIL	MLB	30	3	6	0	43	10	85¹	77	11	31	83	3.3	8.8	45%	.288	1.27	3.90	3.91	4.48	0.6
2014	MIL	MLB	31	0	0	0	23	0	21	22	1	8	23	3.4	9.9	47%	.344	1.43	0.86	2.96	3.50	0.3
2015	*MIL*	*MLB*	*32*	*2*	*1*	*0*	*20*	*4*	*39*	*35*	*4*	*14*	*34*	*3.2*	*7.9*	*42%*	*.301*	*1.26*	*3.87*	*4.09*	*4.20*	*0.2*

Breakout: 19%   Improve: 41%   Collapse: 17%   Attrition: 7%   MLB: 72%   *Comparables: Todd Wellemeyer, Hisashi Iwakuma, Jaret Wright*

Many folks pointed to the sparkling 0.86 ERA and wondered why Gorzelanny pitched so rarely. Part of the answer stems from his injured shoulder, which kept him on the disabled list until June 15th, but significant underlying issues were percolating. His velocity dropped nearly two miles per hour from the 2013 season. Such a decline hints that his recovery might not have been as complete as it could have been, and portends that Gorzelanny won't be the same pitcher from this point forward. Maybe he'll have to learn to cope with sub par stuff. After all, the numbers look good, but the skill set suggests severe limitations. Couple the velocity drop with a .324/.439/.353 slash line against lefties, who should be his target demographic, and question marks will hover over the southpaw heading into 2015.

Johnny Hellweg   RHP
Born: 10/29/88   Age: 26   Bats: R   Throws: R   Height: 6'9"   Weight: 210

YEAR	TEAM	LVL	AGE	W	L	SV	G	GS	IP	H	HR	BB	K	BB/9	K/9	GB%	BABIP	WHIP	ERA	FIP	FRA	WARP
2012	ARK	AA	23	5	10	0	21	21	119²	105	8	60	88	4.5	6.6	56%	.286	1.38	3.38	4.51	5.59	-0.8
2012	HUN	AA	23	2	1	0	7	2	20	16	0	15	17	6.8	7.7	69%	.291	1.55	2.70	3.84	5.27	0.2
2013	NAS	AAA	24	12	5	0	23	23	125²	103	6	81	89	5.8	6.4	59%	.270	1.46	3.15	5.04	5.41	0.5
2013	MIL	MLB	24	1	4	0	8	7	30²	40	3	26	9	7.6	2.6	58%	.319	2.15	6.75	7.03	7.45	-0.9
2014	NAS	AAA	25	1	2	0	4	4	20	21	1	15	12	6.8	5.4	62%	.323	1.80	4.95	5.70	7.10	-0.2
2015	MIL	MLB	26	2	3	0	8	8	39¹	37	4	25	28	5.7	6.5	54%	.300	1.57	5.09	5.53	5.53	-0.3

Breakout: 14%   Improve: 24%   Collapse: 4%   Attrition: 18%   MLB: 32%   *Comparables: Clint Nageotte, Lucas Harrell, Mark Rogers*

A lost season, from spring training (six runs in three innings) to Triple-A (15 walks in 20 innings) to Tommy John surgery (lots of forms to fill out). With 81 inches of body and a triple-digits fastball, he remains a tantalizing late-inning relief prospect who should return at some point in 2015, but the dream that he'd make it as a starter is probably gone for good. The upside now will depend on his ability to throw quality strikes, as he can be overpowering when pounding the lower portion of the zone.

Jim Henderson   RHP
Born: 10/21/82   Age: 32   Bats: L   Throws: R   Height: 6'5"   Weight: 220

YEAR	TEAM	LVL	AGE	W	L	SV	G	GS	IP	H	HR	BB	K	BB/9	K/9	GB%	BABIP	WHIP	ERA	FIP	FRA	WARP
2012	NAS	AAA	29	4	3	15	35	0	48	36	2	22	56	4.1	10.5	35%	.301	1.21	1.69	3.37	3.14	1.5
2012	MIL	MLB	29	1	3	3	36	0	30²	26	1	13	45	3.8	13.2	44%	.352	1.27	3.52	1.99	2.84	0.8
2013	MIL	MLB	30	5	5	28	61	0	60	44	8	24	75	3.6	11.2	29%	.261	1.13	2.70	3.55	3.14	1.0
2014	MIL	MLB	31	2	1	0	14	0	11¹	14	3	4	17	3.2	13.5	38%	.423	1.59	7.15	4.60	4.97	0.0
2015	MIL	MLB	32	2	1	9	34	0	37²	30	4	16	43	3.8	10.3	38%	.300	1.21	3.39	3.78	3.69	0.4

Breakout: 14%   Improve: 24%   Collapse: 10%   Attrition: 21%   MLB: 41%   *Comparables: Joe Nelson, Wil Ledezma, Clay Rapada*

Henderson burst onto the big-league scene in 2012 with a high-90s fastball and a monster strikeout rate, eventually taking the closer's role. As the 2014 season approached, though, Brewers coaches became concerned when he struggled to touch 94 mph in spring training. The organization attempted to ease him into the season, removing him from the ninth inning and pitching him in low-leverage situations. Finally, after a five-run implosion against the Reds on May 1st, Henderson went inactive with a sore shoulder. The vague diagnosis crystallized later in the year, though: After a setback in his minor-league rehab, he had shoulder surgery on his labrum and rotator cuff in August. Given the prescribed four-month recovery—it was only a cleanup procedure—he should be ready for spring training and another shot at a meaningful bullpen role.

Jon Huizinga   RHP
Born: 10/16/79   Age: 35   Bats: R   Throws: R   Height: 6'4"   Weight: 200

YEAR	TEAM	LVL	AGE	W	L	SV	G	GS	IP	H	HR	BB	K	BB/9	K/9	GB%	BABIP	WHIP	ERA	FIP	FRA	WARP
2015	MIL	MLB	35	1	0	1	27	0	35²	37	4	15	26	3.9	6.6	45%	.318	1.46	4.86	4.81	5.28	-0.3

Breakout: 7%   Improve: 10%   Collapse: 5%   Attrition: 9%   MLB: 20%   *Comparables: Tim Hamulack, Jason Childers, Kevin Beirne*

Huizinga appeared in five games for High-A Brevard County at 34 years old. That'll sound mundane, but his story is one of perseverance and, finally, the realization of a dream. After 11 innings with Kalamazoo in the independent leagues way back in 2003, the right-hander inked a minor-league deal with the Brewers and made 23 appearances for Class-A Beloit. He was released the following season and returned to Kalamazoo, only to suffer a serious elbow injury that doctors said would end his career. (Notably, independent teams rarely provide health insurance.) Huizinga refused to believe that. He embarked on an ambitious rehab regime, which involved physical therapy and an intense nutrition plan. He returned to baseball in 2006 for the independent Calgary Vipers. After he spent seven more seasons in indy ball—he outlasted the Vipers, who folded in 2011—the Brewers came calling once again in mid-August. When he appeared on August 18th, his baseball career had come full circle. The 1.35 ERA in five appearances was nice, but the real beauty was that he was there at all.

Jeremy Jeffress   RHP
Born: 9/21/87   Age: 27   Bats: R   Throws: R   Height: 6'1"   Weight: 205

YEAR	TEAM	LVL	AGE	W	L	SV	G	GS	IP	H	HR	BB	K	BB/9	K/9	GB%	BABIP	WHIP	ERA	FIP	FRA	WARP
2012	OMA	AAA	24	5	4	2	37	0	58	52	4	25	61	3.9	9.5	50%	.318	1.33	4.97	3.75	4.47	0.8
2012	KCA	MLB	24	0	0	0	13	0	13¹	19	0	13	13	8.8	8.8	49%	.404	2.40	6.75	4.02	4.88	0.0
2013	BUF	AAA	25	1	0	7	25	0	27¹	22	0	13	28	4.3	9.2	56%	.324	1.28	1.65	2.58	2.95	0.7
2013	TOR	MLB	25	1	0	0	10	0	10¹	8	1	5	12	4.4	10.5	69%	.280	1.26	0.87	3.46	3.87	0.2
2014	NAS	AAA	26	4	1	5	30	0	41²	33	0	18	45	3.9	9.7	64%	.317	1.22	1.51	2.84	2.93	1.0
2014	MIL	MLB	26	1	1	0	29	0	28²	27	1	7	25	2.2	7.8	65%	.321	1.19	1.88	2.54	2.68	0.5
2014	TOR	MLB	26	0	0	0	3	0	3¹	8	0	3	4	8.1	10.8	33%	.667	3.30	10.80	5.26	4.70	0.0
2015	MIL	MLB	27	3	1	0	43	2	58²	51	4	27	56	4.1	8.5	54%	.313	1.32	3.68	3.78	4.00	0.4

Breakout: 35%   Improve: 47%   Collapse: 16%   Attrition: 25%   MLB: 71%   *Comparables: Evan Meek, Javy Guerra, Dan Runzler*

Jeffress is back where he started. After being drafted by the Brewers in the first round in 2006, he struggled with his command in the minors, got traded to Kansas City in the Greinke deal and then bounced around between the majors and minors in Toronto before returning to Milwaukee on a minor-league deal. Things culminated in a successful return to the majors, as he managed a 1.88 ERA in 29 appearances out of the bullpen. He even secured some high-leverage innings when the Brewers' bullpen imploded down the stretch. It's always been the same story for Jeffress: If he can throw strikes consistently with his curveball, he can be dominant. He did that with Milwaukee. What can make the right-hander devastating on the mound is his hard, heavy fastball. He can touch triple digits, and he can get absurd amounts of groundballs. Jeffress can be frustrating to watch when he lacks command, but when he's got it, he does something amazing for a middle reliever: He keeps the ball in the park.

Taylor Jungmann RHP

Born: 12/18/89 Age: 25 Bats: R Throws: R Height: 6'6" Weight: 210

YEAR	TEAM	LVL	AGE	W	L	SV	G	GS	IP	H	HR	BB	K	BB/9	K/9	GB%	BABIP	WHIP	ERA	FIP	FRA	WARP
2012	BRV	A+	22	11	6	0	26	26	153	159	7	46	99	2.7	5.8	56%	.308	1.34	3.53	3.81	5.00	0.3
2013	HUN	AA	23	10	10	0	26	26	139¹	117	11	73	82	4.7	5.3	58%	.253	1.36	4.33	4.55	6.48	-1.8
2014	HUN	AA	24	4	4	0	9	9	52	52	4	15	46	2.6	8.0	60%	.316	1.29	2.77	3.46	4.47	0.2
2014	NAS	AAA	24	8	6	0	19	18	101²	88	7	46	101	4.1	8.9	57%	.301	1.32	3.98	4.32	4.93	0.9
2015	*MIL*	*MLB*	*25*	*7*	*9*	*0*	*23*	*23*	*127²*	*128*	*14*	*53*	*84*	*3.7*	*5.9*	*54%*	*.305*	*1.42*	*4.67*	*4.94*	*5.08*	*-0.6*

Breakout: 19% Improve: 24% Collapse: 5% Attrition: 25% MLB: 30%   *Comparables: Rob Scahill, Charlie Leesman, Kris Johnson*

The 2011 first-rounder Jungmann is struggling to adjust to his declined stuff, as he's now working in the high-80s and low-90s with a fringy breaking ball and an inconsistent changeup. One scout suggested his best days were in college at the University of Texas, and his best hope to make the big-leagues is as a back-end starter. Even then, his command must improve to make that a reality.

Brandon Kintzler RHP

Born: 8/1/84 Age: 30 Bats: R Throws: R Height: 5'10" Weight: 190

YEAR	TEAM	LVL	AGE	W	L	SV	G	GS	IP	H	HR	BB	K	BB/9	K/9	GB%	BABIP	WHIP	ERA	FIP	FRA	WARP
2012	HUN	AA	27	0	2	9	31	0	35²	35	1	12	20	3.0	5.0	63%	.306	1.32	3.28	3.56	5.26	0.0
2012	NAS	AAA	27	0	1	0	8	0	11²	8	0	2	11	1.5	8.5	70%	.267	0.86	1.54	2.29	3.09	0.2
2012	MIL	MLB	27	3	0	0	14	0	16²	18	1	7	14	3.8	7.6	51%	.340	1.50	3.78	3.50	3.82	0.2
2013	MIL	MLB	28	3	3	0	71	0	77	66	2	16	58	1.9	6.8	60%	.281	1.06	2.69	2.51	3.48	1.1
2014	MIL	MLB	29	3	3	0	64	0	58¹	62	8	16	31	2.5	4.8	59%	.293	1.34	3.24	4.65	6.17	-1.0
2015	*MIL*	*MLB*	*30*	*3*	*1*	*1*	*50*	*0*	*54²*	*50*	*5*	*14*	*42*	*2.3*	*7.0*	*56%*	*.301*	*1.16*	*3.34*	*3.80*	*3.63*	*0.6*

Breakout: 17% Improve: 44% Collapse: 18% Attrition: 18% MLB: 74%   *Comparables: Ryan Mattheus, Matt Lindstrom, Brandon Medders*

As the Brewers' bullpen imploded down the stretch, Kintzler complained he wasn't getting high-leverage looks. Okay, we'll bite. He finished the year with a 3.24 ERA, which ranked third among Brewers relievers with 50 innings. The problem, though, is that Kintzler's peripherals suggested serious underlying suck. The velocity held steady and nothing changed with his pitch mix; however, his strikeout rate tumbled and tumbled and tumbled some more, until only six pitchers in baseball were looking up at him. The right-hander continued to rack up the groundballs, but without any of the home run-suppressing benefits of such an approach: His 17 percent HR/FB ranked fifth in baseball. That just ain't workable in high-leverage spots, bruh.

Kyle Lohse RHP

Born: 10/4/78 Age: 36 Bats: R Throws: R Height: 6'2" Weight: 210

YEAR	TEAM	LVL	AGE	W	L	SV	G	GS	IP	H	HR	BB	K	BB/9	K/9	GB%	BABIP	WHIP	ERA	FIP	FRA	WARP
2012	SLN	MLB	33	16	3	0	33	33	211	192	19	38	143	1.6	6.1	43%	.262	1.09	2.86	3.55	3.98	2.1
2013	MIL	MLB	34	11	10	0	32	32	198²	196	26	36	125	1.6	5.7	44%	.276	1.17	3.35	4.05	4.30	1.5
2014	MIL	MLB	35	13	9	0	31	31	198¹	183	22	45	141	2.0	6.4	42%	.268	1.15	3.54	3.92	4.43	1.0
2015	*MIL*	*MLB*	*36*	*10*	*9*	*0*	*26*	*26*	*165²*	*163*	*19*	*35*	*109*	*1.9*	*5.9*	*42%*	*.295*	*1.19*	*3.90*	*4.25*	*4.24*	*0.7*

Breakout: 16% Improve: 38% Collapse: 19% Attrition: 20% MLB: 81%   *Comparables: Carl Pavano, Bronson Arroyo, Paul Byrd*

Lohse used to be a thrower, but then he became a pitcher, and then later he became a *pitcher*, and now he's a Pitcher with a capital P. His fastball struggles to crack 90, but he commands the strike zone, repeats his mechanics, sequences well and takes the mound every fifth day. Last year marked his fourth consecutive season with an adjusted ERA better than league average; since 2011, his 116 ERA+ slots right between those of Jon Lester and Max Scherzer. His changeup and slider each took steps forward in 2014, especially his changeup, which had a whiff rate of 18 percent (up from 14 percent). As long as the last gasps of velocity hold and the injury bug stays away, Lohse will continue to deliver mid-rotation consistency, while we try to come up with new ways of hyperbolizing the word "pitcher."

Jorge Lopez RHP

Born: 2/10/93 Age: 22 Bats: R Throws: R Height: 6'4" Weight: 165

YEAR	TEAM	LVL	AGE	W	L	SV	G	GS	IP	H	HR	BB	K	BB/9	K/9	GB%	BABIP	WHIP	ERA	FIP	FRA	WARP
2013	WIS	A	20	7	8	2	25	22	117	120	13	48	92	3.7	7.1	48%	.305	1.44	5.23	4.67	6.14	0.0
2014	BRV	A+	21	10	10	0	25	25	137²	144	12	46	119	3.0	7.8	50%	.328	1.38	4.58	3.89	5.37	-0.1
2015	*MIL*	*MLB*	*22*	*5*	*8*	*0*	*24*	*21*	*115²*	*125*	*15*	*52*	*77*	*4.0*	*6.0*	*46%*	*.318*	*1.53*	*5.40*	*5.26*	*5.87*	*-1.4*

Breakout: 0% Improve: 0% Collapse: 0% Attrition: 0% MLB: 0%   *Comparables: Jose A. Ramirez, Daryl Thompson, Wilking Rodriguez*

Lopez flashes brilliance at times. Between May 4th and July 2nd, the right-hander posted a 2.12 ERA over 68 innings and held opposing hitters to a .216 average. He nudges the mid-90s with his fastball and backs it up with a 12-to-6 curveball, but the changeup is nonexistent. That suggests a future bullpen role, as his fastball-curveball combination doesn't project to be good enough to become Ben Sheets 2.0. Lopez also struggled with personal issues in 2014. His young son has battled illness, forcing Lopez to fly back and forth between the States and Puerto Rico. The Brevard County Manatees and his teammates held a charity golf outing to help raise money to ease the travel and medical bills. Such stress perhaps puts his late-season skid in perspective. The 21-year-old father had more important things on his mind than baseball.

Kodi Medeiros LHP

Born: 5/25/96 Age: 19 Bats: L Throws: L Height: 6'2" Weight: 180

YEAR	TEAM	LVL	AGE	W	L	SV	G	GS	IP	H	HR	BB	K	BB/9	K/9	GB%	BABIP	WHIP	ERA	FIP	FRA	WARP
2015	*MIL*	*MLB*	*19*	*1*	*2*	*0*	*14*	*4*	*34*	*37*	*4*	*20*	*20*	*5.3*	*5.3*	*45%*	*.317*	*1.69*	*5.88*	*5.73*	*6.39*	*-0.5*

Breakout: 0% Improve: 0% Collapse: 0% Attrition: 0% MLB: 0%   *Comparables: Joe Wieland, Patrick McCoy, Jake Odorizzi*

Milwaukee grabbed Medeiros with the 12th overall selection in the 2014 draft, inking him to a slightly below-slot $2.7 million bonus. He has three pitches—fastball, slider and changeup—that all flash plus potential. However, considering his unorthodox sidearm delivery and slight build, some doubt Medeiros will be anything but a reliever in the future. The skeptics see an arm slot that will be too appetizing for right-handers, and a delivery that will buckle under a 200-inning workload. With that said, the delivery funk and dancing stuff suggest a safe floor as a major-league reliever. His brief professional debut was wild—he threw more wild pitches in 18 innings than Kyle Lohse has thrown over the past four *seasons*—and will likely remain in short-season ball for another go in 2015.

Jimmy Nelson   RHP

Born: 6/5/89   Age: 26   Bats: R   Throws: R   Height: 6'6"   Weight: 245

YEAR	TEAM	LVL	AGE	W	L	SV	G	GS	IP	H	HR	BB	K	BB/9	K/9	GB%	BABIP	WHIP	ERA	FIP	FRA	WARP
2012	BRV	A+	23	4	4	0	13	13	81¹	63	3	25	77	2.8	8.5	61%	.273	1.08	2.21	3.09	3.97	1.1
2012	HUN	AA	23	2	4	0	10	10	46	34	2	37	42	7.2	8.2	57%	.256	1.54	3.91	4.49	5.08	0.3
2013	HUN	AA	24	5	4	0	12	12	69	63	5	15	72	2.0	9.4	52%	.320	1.13	2.74	2.81	3.96	0.7
2013	NAS	AAA	24	5	6	0	15	15	83¹	74	2	50	91	5.4	9.8	63%	.327	1.49	3.67	3.64	3.94	1.3
2013	MIL	MLB	24	0	0	0	4	1	10	2	0	5	8	4.5	7.2	42%	.083	0.70	0.90	2.92	3.47	0.1
2014	NAS	AAA	25	10	2	0	17	16	111	70	3	32	114	2.6	9.2	62%	.241	0.92	1.46	2.97	3.56	2.1
2014	MIL	MLB	25	2	9	0	14	12	69¹	82	6	19	57	2.5	7.4	50%	.344	1.46	4.93	3.75	4.23	0.2
2015	MIL	MLB	26	9	9	0	25	25	145¹	134	12	57	120	3.5	7.5	54%	.307	1.32	4.04	4.11	4.39	0.5

Breakout: 23%   Improve: 44%   Collapse: 18%   Attrition: 31%   MLB: 72%   Comparables: Justin Wilson, J.D. Durbin, Kyle Weiland

Nelson steamrolled through the Pacific Coast League in the first half. He struck out a batter per inning, walked very few, kept the ball earthbound and, eventually, got the call to Milwaukee. His peripherals held relatively strong, but he failed to throw his slider consistently for strikes and found too much of the plate with his fastball. Opposing hitters blasted him with a .289 average, and he finished the year with a 1.46 WHIP. On the bright side, ever since his freshman year at the University of Alabama, Nelson has needed a year to adjust to each level of competition, after which he has bloomed anew. Upon transitioning to A-Ball, he posted a 4.38 ERA. The next year: 2.21 ERA. Upon transitioning to Double-A, he posted a 3.91 ERA. The next year: 2.74. Triple-A: 3.67 ERA, then 1.46. Nelson can touch 97 with the fastball and has a slider with legitimate plus potential. He generates groundballs and praise for his makeup. There's a lot to like, and if his historical trends prove reliable, he'll find success in Milwaukee this year.

Wily Peralta   RHP

Born: 5/8/89   Age: 26   Bats: R   Throws: R   Height: 6'1"   Weight: 245

YEAR	TEAM	LVL	AGE	W	L	SV	G	GS	IP	H	HR	BB	K	BB/9	K/9	GB%	BABIP	WHIP	ERA	FIP	FRA	WARP
2012	NAS	AAA	23	7	11	0	28	28	146²	154	9	78	143	4.8	8.8	54%	.351	1.58	4.66	4.29	4.60	2.2
2012	MIL	MLB	23	2	1	0	6	5	29	24	0	11	23	3.4	7.1	57%	.304	1.21	2.48	2.69	2.98	0.7
2013	MIL	MLB	24	11	15	0	32	32	183¹	187	19	73	129	3.6	6.3	52%	.293	1.42	4.37	4.27	5.14	-0.3
2014	MIL	MLB	25	17	11	0	32	32	198²	198	23	61	154	2.8	7.0	56%	.295	1.30	3.53	4.08	4.93	0.1
2015	MIL	MLB	26	10	10	0	29	29	164²	157	16	62	132	3.4	7.2	52%	.311	1.33	4.18	4.27	4.55	0.2

Breakout: 45%   Improve: 71%   Collapse: 13%   Attrition: 23%   MLB: 94%   Comparables: Wade Davis, Ivan Nova, Dana Eveland

It's tempting to see his age and velocity and see his improvement as a trendline pointing up; more likely, 2014 was him reaching his full potential. His xFIP indicators improved and, as you'd expect in such a situation, his ERA improved. But Peralta still hasn't addressed the issue that will keep him from being anything more than a no. 3: He has no answer for left-handed hitters, who hit .300/.349/.471 against him. His ongoing project is incorporating an effective changeup into his repertoire, but returns on the current iteration weren't great: Batters weren't fooled into chasing it out of the zone, and when he came into the zone they produced a 44 percent line-drive rate.

Francisco Rodriguez   RHP

Born: 1/7/82   Age: 33   Bats: R   Throws: R   Height: 6'0"   Weight: 195

YEAR	TEAM	LVL	AGE	W	L	SV	G	GS	IP	H	HR	BB	K	BB/9	K/9	GB%	BABIP	WHIP	ERA	FIP	FRA	WARP
2012	MIL	MLB	30	2	7	3	78	0	72	65	8	31	72	3.9	9.0	42%	.294	1.33	4.38	3.87	4.56	0.4
2013	MIL	MLB	31	1	1	10	25	0	24²	17	2	9	26	3.3	9.5	34%	.250	1.05	1.09	3.06	3.04	0.5
2013	BAL	MLB	31	2	1	0	23	0	22	25	5	5	28	2.0	11.5	48%	.351	1.36	4.50	4.30	4.09	0.2
2014	MIL	MLB	32	5	5	44	69	0	68	49	14	18	73	2.4	9.7	46%	.216	0.99	3.04	4.47	4.51	0.1
2015	MIL	MLB	33	3	1	22	60	0	57¹	46	6	18	62	2.8	9.8	44%	.299	1.12	3.04	3.56	3.30	0.9

Breakout: 18%   Improve: 42%   Collapse: 28%   Attrition: 8%   MLB: 88%   Comparables: Matt Thornton, Kyle Farnsworth, J.J. Putz

K-Rod was the talk of the town for much of the first half. He did not allow a single run through his first 19 outings, including 15 completed saves. His command was pristine and it translated into a gaudy strikeout rate. However, after he surrendered his first run on May 11th, Frankie was janky. He posted a 4.22 ERA in his final 49 innings, allowing 14 homers. The right-hander blew only five saves, which helped him keep his job throughout the remainder of the year, but as we all know, a closer who keeps his job isn't always a closer who's good at his job. His HR/FB rate was worst in the league (by a ton), which might strike you as a fluke if he hadn't had an even worse rate in Baltimore down the stretch in 2013. More than anything, those numbers suggest that when his fastball command isn't precisely on the corners and he cannot get to his plus changeup, big-league hitters can light him up. He'll be 33 in 2015 and can still be supremely effective when he spots his fastball, but the margin for error is just too small to feel comfortable trusting him with a lead in a pennant race.

Will Smith   LHP

Born: 7/10/89   Age: 25   Bats: R   Throws: L   Height: 6'5"   Weight: 250

YEAR	TEAM	LVL	AGE	W	L	SV	G	GS	IP	H	HR	BB	K	BB/9	K/9	GB%	BABIP	WHIP	ERA	FIP	FRA	WARP
2012	OMA	AAA	22	4	4	0	15	15	89²	104	8	22	74	2.2	7.4	44%	.340	1.41	3.61	3.98	4.48	1.4
2012	KCA	MLB	22	6	9	0	16	16	89²	111	12	33	59	3.3	5.9	43%	.340	1.61	5.32	4.61	4.95	0.5
2013	OMA	AAA	23	6	4	0	28	10	89	81	7	24	100	2.4	10.1	47%	.325	1.18	3.03	3.26	3.53	1.9
2013	KCA	MLB	23	2	1	0	19	1	33¹	24	6	7	43	1.9	11.6	44%	.243	0.93	3.24	3.56	4.61	0.1
2014	MIL	MLB	24	1	3	1	78	0	65²	62	6	31	86	4.2	11.8	46%	.350	1.42	3.70	3.22	3.26	0.8
2015	MIL	MLB	25	4	3	0	24	9	69¹	68	8	21	59	2.7	7.7	45%	.319	1.28	4.12	4.14	4.48	0.1

Breakout: 34%   Improve: 56%   Collapse: 16%   Attrition: 22%   MLB: 86%   Comparables: Aaron Crow, Carlos Carrasco, Edgar Gonzalez

Featuring what Brewers' fans dubbed the "Slider of Death"—a pitch so nasty it generated baseball's third-highest strikeout rate against left-handed hitters—Smith allowed just one earned run in his first 29 appearances. So what explains the mediocre 3.61 ERA and ghastly 1.41 WHIP you see above? Some have suggested his 78 relief appearances—which ranked second in baseball—eventually wore him down; however, that's far from clear. His velocity did not tail off over the course of the season. Instead, righties simply beat up on his fastball, slashing .339/.417/.617 against the 94 mph four-seamer. Having a world-class slider is wonderful, especially for a lefty specialist, which might be all Smith is.

Tyler Thornburg   RHP

Born: 9/29/88   Age: 26   Bats: R   Throws: R   Height: 5'11"   Weight: 190

YEAR	TEAM	LVL	AGE	W	L	SV	G	GS	IP	H	HR	BB	K	BB/9	K/9	GB%	BABIP	WHIP	ERA	FIP	FRA	WARP
2012	HUN	AA	23	8	1	0	13	13	75	57	6	24	71	2.9	8.5	41%	.250	1.08	3.00	3.33	4.51	1.3
2012	NAS	AAA	23	2	3	0	8	8	37²	38	1	13	42	3.1	10.0	53%	.356	1.35	3.58	2.98	3.53	0.9
2012	MIL	MLB	23	0	0	0	8	3	22	24	8	7	20	2.9	8.2	45%	.271	1.41	4.50	7.14	6.43	0.0
2013	NAS	AAA	24	0	9	0	15	15	74²	90	11	29	87	3.5	10.5	36%	.380	1.59	5.79	4.48	3.92	1.5
2013	MIL	MLB	24	3	1	0	18	7	66²	53	1	26	48	3.5	6.5	38%	.271	1.18	2.03	3.08	3.29	1.3
2014	MIL	MLB	25	3	1	0	27	0	29²	24	1	21	28	6.4	8.5	37%	.284	1.52	4.25	3.78	3.83	0.3
2015	*MIL*	*MLB*	*26*	*3*	*2*	*0*	*12*	*7*	*45*	*40*	*5*	*18*	*42*	*3.6*	*8.3*	*40%*	*.305*	*1.29*	*3.95*	*4.26*	*4.29*	*0.2*

Breakout: 30%   Improve: 52%   Collapse: 18%   Attrition: 22%   MLB: 82%   Comparables: Matt Riley, Angel Guzman, Esmil Rogers

For most organizations, Thornburg would have had a shot at the starting rotation, but the Brewers had enough depth that he was immediately slotted into the bullpen. He thrived in that role in April, working into high-leverage roles with 10 strikeouts per nine and a 0.61 ERA. But things fall apart, intentions shatter: The walks soared, the velocity dropped and by June he was gone with an elbow injury. The right-hander has a legitimate three-pitch mix and can throw all three for strikes; however, the elbow injury only validates concerns over the durability of his slight frame. If one really dreams, he can see a little bit of Tyler Clippard in Thornburg.

Wei-Chung Wang   LHP

Born: 4/25/92   Age: 23   Bats: L   Throws: L   Height: 6'1"   Weight: 180

YEAR	TEAM	LVL	AGE	W	L	SV	G	GS	IP	H	HR	BB	K	BB/9	K/9	GB%	BABIP	WHIP	ERA	FIP	FRA	WARP
2014	WIS	A	22	0	2	0	3	3	13²	13	0	4	10	2.6	6.6	50%	.310	1.24	3.29	2.90	3.80	0.2
2014	MIL	MLB	22	0	0	0	14	0	17¹	30	6	8	13	4.2	6.8	40%	.375	2.19	10.90	7.66	7.46	-0.5
2015	*MIL*	*MLB*	*23*	*2*	*2*	*0*	*14*	*7*	*39¹*	*42*	*5*	*14*	*27*	*3.2*	*6.1*	*44%*	*.313*	*1.42*	*4.91*	*4.88*	*5.33*	*-0.2*

Breakout: 19%   Improve: 44%   Collapse: 5%   Attrition: 22%   MLB: 57%   Comparables: Ervin Santana, Chad Gaudin, Kyle Davies

The Brewers turned some heads in the Rule 5 Draft by selecting Wang, who was 21 years old and had never pitched above Rookie ball. Team scouts saw a mature southpaw who they believed had a chance to someday develop into a major-league starter, but it was unclear whether he would actually make the 25-man roster out of spring training. Wang pitched his way onto the team with 14 walkless innings in Maryville, showing a legitimate three-pitch mix with a low-90s fastball, a curveball and a deceptive straight change. The trick was always going to be hiding him on a roster that had legitimate postseason aspirations. The Brewers successfully did so, pitching him in only 13 games in the first four months of the season before he was placed on the DL with a shoulder injury. Subsequently, Wang pitched in an extended minor-league rehab assignment, where he compiled a solid 2.33 ERA in seven games, striking out 22 and walking four.

Devin Williams   RHP

Born: 9/21/94   Age: 20   Bats: R   Throws: R   Height: 6'3"   Weight: 165

YEAR	TEAM	LVL	AGE	W	L	SV	G	GS	IP	H	HR	BB	K	BB/9	K/9	GB%	BABIP	WHIP	ERA	FIP	FRA	WARP
2015	*MIL*	*MLB*	*20*	*2*	*3*	*0*	*14*	*7*	*51*	*56*	*6*	*31*	*32*	*5.4*	*5.6*	*48%*	*.318*	*1.69*	*5.87*	*5.71*	*6.38*	*-0.8*

Breakout: 0%   Improve: 0%   Collapse: 0%   Attrition: 0%   MLB: 0%   Comparables: Rafael Dolis, Jarred Cosart, Daniel Corcino

It's easy to be swayed by minor-league numbers, but if you're looking at a Rookie ball line, keep in mind that the pitchers are backed up by defensive units that are ... well, let's just call them aspirational. Williams' Helena ERA reflects a lousy .359 BABIP, but he struck out a man per inning, walked only 7 percent of the batters he faced and mostly survived in a light-air league. He features a fastball that runs into the mid-90s and a curveball that flashes solid-average, if not better. He's tall and athletic and should add stones of muscle as he moves up the ladder. He *might* be the best pitching prospect in the system, but he certainly has the most upside. This could be a future no. 2, and 2015 could be the year he joins the national prospect conversation.

Taylor Williams   RHP

Born: 7/21/91   Age: 23   Bats: B   Throws: R   Height: 5'11"   Weight: 165

YEAR	TEAM	LVL	AGE	W	L	SV	G	GS	IP	H	HR	BB	K	BB/9	K/9	GB%	BABIP	WHIP	ERA	FIP	FRA	WARP
2014	WIS	A	22	8	1	4	22	12	107	78	4	23	112	1.9	9.4	52%	.264	0.94	2.36	2.69	3.75	1.8
2014	BRV	A+	22	1	2	0	5	5	25¹	29	4	5	25	1.8	8.9	46%	.342	1.34	4.26	4.18	4.90	0.2
2015	*MIL*	*MLB*	*23*	*4*	*5*	*0*	*22*	*13*	*98*	*98*	*11*	*37*	*75*	*3.3*	*6.8*	*46%*	*.310*	*1.37*	*4.53*	*4.59*	*4.92*	*-0.3*

Breakout: 0%   Improve: 0%   Collapse: 0%   Attrition: 0%   MLB: 0%   Comparables: Stephen Fife, Hector Noesi, Jeff Manship

At the moment, a Google Images search for "Taylor Williams" turns up almost exclusively high school girls; Taylor Williams the ballplayer doesn't show up until the 18th result. Give it another few months and search again. The right-hander turned some heads in the Midwest League, compiling a 2.36 ERA with more than a strikeout per inning—enough that some scouts now suggest he's the best arm in the system. His 5-foot-11 frame will assuredly raise questions (and forced Tim Lincecum comparisons) throughout his minor-league career; however, he sat 93-94 mph during fall instructionals and touched 97. Earlier in the season, some reports had him bumping up to 98 mph, with a good slider on the side. He throws strikes and can command his fastball within the zone. Pop-up prospects sneak up on scouts every year. Williams is the Brewers' surprise.

Rob Wooten   RHP

Born: 7/21/85   Age: 29   Bats: R   Throws: R   Height: 6'1"   Weight: 195

YEAR	TEAM	LVL	AGE	W	L	SV	G	GS	IP	H	HR	BB	K	BB/9	K/9	GB%	BABIP	WHIP	ERA	FIP	FRA	WARP
2012	HUN	AA	26	3	0	8	17	0	20²	18	1	7	21	3.0	9.1	46%	.293	1.21	1.74	2.90	2.88	0.5
2012	NAS	AAA	26	0	2	7	40	0	52²	49	4	16	49	2.7	8.4	46%	.300	1.23	3.93	3.82	4.52	0.6
2013	NAS	AAA	27	0	1	20	40	0	52	40	4	12	45	2.1	7.8	45%	.248	1.00	2.94	3.65	3.90	0.7
2013	MIL	MLB	27	3	1	0	27	0	27²	27	1	8	18	2.6	5.9	44%	.299	1.27	3.90	3.17	3.49	0.3
2014	NAS	AAA	28	0	2	14	21	0	21²	24	1	5	21	2.1	8.7	50%	.333	1.34	5.82	3.19	4.08	0.3
2014	MIL	MLB	28	1	4	0	40	0	34¹	42	1	8	29	2.1	7.6	52%	.380	1.46	4.72	2.58	3.84	0.3
2015	MIL	MLB	29	3	1	1	48	0	56²	52	5	15	47	2.4	7.5	45%	.306	1.19	3.57	3.71	3.89	0.4

Breakout: 18%   Improve: 26%   Collapse: 17%   Attrition: 23%   MLB: 46%   Comparables: Ron Flores, Josh Roenicke, Chris Hatcher

The 29-year-old reliever is a cutter specialist and a former North Carolina Tar Heel, in that order. The overwhelming reliance on the cutter led to issues against left-handed hitters. He induced a 12 percent whiff rate against righties, but merely a 7 percent against lefties. Thus, manager Ron Roenicke was quick to yank him when a lefty stepped up to the dish. Roenicke, of course, played college ball at UCLA, and one can only assume that each time he strolled to the mound to make the switch, he would callously remind Wooten that UCLA had triumphed over UNC to reach the College World Series finals the previous summer, just to sprinkle a little salt in the wounds.

Lineouts

Hitters

NAME	POS	TEAM	LVL	AGE	PA	R	2B	3B	HR	RBI	BB	K	SB	CS	AVG/OBP/SLG	TAv	BABIP	BRR	FRAA	WARP
Jeff Bianchi	SS	NAS	AAA	27	105	11	5	0	3	12	6	19	2	0	.276/.314/.418	.254	.312	-0.2	SS(9): -0.5, 2B(8): 0.1	0.0
	SS	MIL	MLB	27	74	4	1	0	0	6	3	17	0	0	.171/.203/.186	.147	.222	-0.4	SS(10): -0.0, 3B(9): 0.0	-0.5
Juan Centeno	C	BIN	AA	24	83	8	5	0	0	8	6	11	0	1	.286/.337/.351	.231	.333	-0.3	C(21): -0.4	0.2
	C	LVG	AAA	24	202	19	5	0	1	17	15	26	2	0	.291/.343/.335	.264	.329	-3.5	C(52): -0.5	0.9
	C	NYN	MLB	24	33	1	0	0	0	2	3	5	0	0	.200/.273/.200	.174	.240	-0.1	C(9): 0.1	-0.1
Matt Clark	1B	BIN	AA	27	255	32	14	0	10	46	25	45	0	0	.297/.380/.498	.322	.327	-3.4	1B(40): 0.1, LF(2): 0.2	1.7
	1B	NAS	AAA	27	213	35	9	0	16	37	15	52	0	0	.313/.371/.605	.326	.354	-0.3	1B(50): -3.0, LF(3): 0.1	1.5
	1B	MIL	MLB	27	31	4	0	0	3	7	2	8	0	0	.185/.226/.519	.272	.111	0.2	1B(9): -0.1	0.1
Nick Delmonico	3B	BRV	A+	21	150	11	8	0	4	15	7	34	2	2	.262/.300/.404	.256	.317	-2.1	3B(34): 4.8	0.8
Hector Gomez	SS	NAS	AAA	26	442	59	25	6	15	49	21	80	5	3	.282/.325/.483	.278	.315	-1.4	SS(111): 6.1, 3B(3): 0.1	3.3
	SS	MIL	MLB	26	21	2	1	0	0	1	1	9	0	0	.150/.190/.200	.145	.273	-0.9	SS(7): 0.5, 3B(6): -0.1	-0.2
Hunter Morris	1B	HUN	AA	25	27	3	0	0	0	2	1	4	0	0	.269/.296/.269	.191	.318	0.0	1B(6): 0.2	-0.2
	1B	NAS	AAA	25	356	46	21	1	11	42	20	74	0	0	.279/.323/.448	.273	.327	-1.7	1B(78): -0.4	0.7
Nathan Orf	2B	BRV	A+	24	538	66	30	4	2	43	55	74	7	6	.288/.388/.386	.289	.336	-3.3	2B(55): -3.4, RF(31): -1.1	2.6
Michael Reed	RF	BRV	A+	21	457	50	20	5	5	47	78	79	33	13	.255/.396/.378	.292	.310	-0.4	RF(99): -4.4, CF(2): -0.2	2.0
Yadiel Rivera	SS	BRV	A+	22	254	35	8	2	3	17	16	50	5	3	.255/.312/.346	.236	.311	0.0	SS(38): 5.7, 2B(28): -0.2	1.1
	SS	HUN	AA	22	196	31	9	6	2	13	10	36	5	0	.262/.304/.410	.250	.317	2.3	SS(57): 2.3	1.0
Jason Rogers	3B	HUN	AA	26	324	42	18	2	7	43	31	56	5	1	.282/.355/.432	.286	.326	2.0	3B(66): 1.9	2.4
	3B	NAS	AAA	26	232	36	11	4	11	39	22	38	0	0	.316/.379/.568	.330	.338	-1.3	3B(56): 4.3	3.1
	1B	MIL	MLB	26	10	0	1	0	0	0	1	1	0	0	.111/.200/.222	.170	.125	0.0	1B(4): -0.0	-0.1
Logan Schafer	CF	NAS	AAA	27	185	27	13	4	3	18	21	33	4	1	.273/.355/.460	.284	.325	1.2	CF(39): 2.8, LF(5): -0.0	1.7
	LF	MIL	MLB	27	136	13	9	1	0	8	15	27	2	1	.181/.278/.276	.224	.233	-0.2	LF(17): -0.0, RF(17): -0.4	-0.3
Shawn Zarraga	C	HUN	AA	25	267	34	16	0	1	30	42	23	1	4	.330/.440/.419	.337	.357	-2.1	C(51): -0.2, 1B(3): -0.1	3.1
	C	NAS	AAA	25	57	1	2	0	0	7	5	7	0	0	.213/.304/.255	.209	.238	-1.0	C(16): 0.4	-0.2

Over the past two seasons, only six players (min. 250 PA) have compiled a lower isolated power than **Jeff Bianchi**'s .046, but he's blessed to have played defense precisely well enough to be the definition of replacement level; that seems useful in an abstract sense. ❖ **Juan Centeno** gets on base at a decent clip, and his throwing and footwork are exceptional. For more information on why the Mets cut him, see Anthony Recker's comment. ❖ The 27-year-old journeyman **Matt Clark** hit at least 20, but not 30 home runs for the sixth year in a row, a streak that has spanned four minor-league levels and a couple flights over the Pacific Ocean. The big difference about this year: Three of those dongers came in the majors. Raise a toast for this cool dude. ❖ **Nick Delmonico**'s on-base percentage couldn't clear the .300 mark and he got suspended 50 games for amphetamines. The 2014 season needed to come with a reset button. Maybe a few of them. ❖ Sometimes, a player's story is one of forgottenness and perseverance. **Hector Gomez** overcame a persistent spate of injuries from 2008 through 2012, his release by Colorado in 2012 and a .198/.238/.255 Double-A slash line in 2013 to start three games at shortstop for the Brewers during a September postseason race. Just six more seasons until the big free-agency payday. ❖ The 17-year-old Dominican shortstop **Franly Mallen** failed to produce in the Dominican Summer League, but he and his J2 classmate **Nicolas Pierre** represent a change in philosophy for the Brewers' organization. Their $800,000 signing bonuses set a franchise record, since broken. ❖ Brewers first basemen have hit a combined .211/.277/.368 over the past two seasons, yet **Hunter Morris** has not been promoted to the big leagues. That should speak volumes about the organization's opinion of the 25-year-old slugger. ❖ Former second-round draft pick **Tucker Neuhaus** was considered a raw, long-term project when the Brewers drafted him. His fielding percentage is even worse than his slash line. ❖ **Nathan Orf** is a 24-year-old, 5-foot-9 prospect who came within one hustle double of hitting .288/.388/.388, which, our metrics show, is a lot of eights. Instead, he's known for playing all nine positions in one August 31st game, retiring the only batter he faced and then exiting the game early. ❖ **Michael Reed** is a classic tweener. He doesn't project well in center, but lacks the offensive profile for a corner outfielder. Patience and speed are his assets, though, and he could parlay those into a fourth-outfielder gig. ❖ The stat line sucked, but **Yadiel Rivera** featured good range, smooth actions and a strong arm at shortstop, and he hit .301/.333/.456 against lefties. It's not a starting package, but you'd certainly quit your boring job for a big-league bench role. ❖ The overall slash line highlights **Jason Rogers**' aptitude at the plate, but he's a first baseman without the ideal power profile. His .252 ISO in Nashville doesn't really count. Pete Kozma hit 11 homers in the PCL in 2012. ❖ **Logan Schafer** couldn't best Mendoza in 2014, but he plays plus defense at all three outfield positions and remains the spitting image of Aussie golfer Adam Scott, so he's still in fine shape when it comes to life. ❖ An invitation to the exclusive Arizona Fall League might qualify as the career high point for 44th-rounder **Shawn Zarraga**, who slugged in Double-A but has a bad body and doesn't project to catch in the majors.

Pitchers

NAME	TEAM	LVL	AGE	W	L	SV	G	GS	IP	H	HR	BB	K	BB/9	K/9	GB%	BABIP	WHIP	ERA	FIP	FRA	WARP
Jed Bradley	BRV	A+	24	5	2	0	10	10	60¹	54	4	10	53	1.5	7.9	68%	.296	1.06	2.98	3.04	4.51	0.4
	HUN	AA	24	5	8	0	17	17	87	106	8	36	71	3.7	7.3	62%	.359	1.63	4.55	4.16	4.61	0.5
Drew Gagnon	HUN	AA	24	11	6	0	28	28	154²	135	18	62	118	3.6	6.9	43%	.264	1.27	3.96	4.57	4.90	0.7
David Goforth	HUN	AA	25	5	4	27	54	0	64²	60	2	29	46	4.0	6.4	52%	.286	1.38	3.76	3.60	4.55	0.2
Brooks Hall	HUN	AA	24	2	1	0	5	5	26	24	1	7	16	2.4	5.5	46%	.287	1.19	2.77	3.84	4.36	0.3
Ariel Pena	NAS	AAA	25	9	8	0	25	24	128¹	96	12	75	140	5.3	9.8	35%	.266	1.33	4.56	4.60	4.76	1.1
Tyler Wagner	BRV	A+	23	13	6	0	25	25	150	118	10	48	118	2.9	7.1	54%	.259	1.11	1.86	3.66	4.54	0.9

Former first-rounder **Jed Bradley** required three goes at High-A Brevard County before finally making the jump to Double-A, with shoulda-stayed-at-High-A results. With low-90s heat and an inconsistent breaking ball, a move to the bullpen is probably his only path to the majors. ❖ **Drew Gagnon** has the three-pitch mix to project as a back-of-the-rotation starter in the majors, but the command to project as a front-of-the-rotation starter in Double-A. ❖ Considered a potential late-inning reliever down the road, **David Goforth**'s meager strikeout rate, and 1.38 WHIP in Double-A obfuscate his true power stuff, which includes a triple-digits fastball and a hard cutter. ❖ Big, tall **Brooks Hall** is still projectable, but bone spurs in his elbow kept him in stasis. ❖ The forgotten piece of the Zack Greinke trade, **Ariel Pena** is unforgettable when he throws strikes. Minor-league hitters can't hit his fastball-slider combination, but he gives them very little incentive to try. ❖ Possessing a classic back-end starter profile, **Tyler Wagner** dominated the Florida State League as a 23-year-old. He'll pick on kids his own age in 2015.

Manager

Ron Roenicke

YEAR	TEAM	W	L	Py-thag +/-	Avg PC	100+ P	120+ P	QS	BQS	REL	REL w Zero R	IBB	PH	PH Avg	PH HR	SB2	CS2	SB3	CS3	SAC Att	SAC%	POS SAC	Squeeze	Swing	In Play
2012	MIL	83	79	-3	97.1	84	0	85	3	512	370	20	315	.223	4	134	32	24	5	129	58.9%	45	8	356	90
2013	MIL	74	88	-1	91.6	45	0	82	3	501	399	29	265	.210	4	120	40	21	4	106	72.6%	35	10	352	101
2014	MIL	82	80	2	97.8	76	1	103	5	478	395	20	246	.222	4	83	41	19	2	110	63.6%	27	3	265	72

Milwaukee fans like to call him Runnin' Ron, and for good reason: The Brewers stole more than 300 bases during the 2012-13 seasons, the most for the franchise over a two-year span since the early '90s. Yet last season, with Milwaukee running less often than usual, Buntin' Ron would have been the more accurate moniker (although some invariably chose to modify his first name by adding two letters).

During Roenicke's four years in charge, the Brewers have led the majors in bunt attempts twice; they finished second and third in the other two years. In sum, the Brewers have attempted 12 more bunts than the next-closest team (the Reds). Change the measure to sacrifices by position players, and the Brewers still led the NL, though they finished second in the majors, behind the Angels.

Consider that fitting, because Roenicke worked for the Angels before he joined Milwaukee. He was plucked from the Mike Scioscia tree, same as Bud Black and Joe Maddon, meaning Gene Mauch's small-ball ways are ingrained in his baseball soul. (To wit, Roenicke loves the squeeze play.) That inheritance is an annoyance when it leads to Carlos Gomez laying one down, but is tolerable—and even logical, at times—when lesser hitters, like Jean Segura, Scooter Gennett, Martin Maldonado and Elian Herrera are the ones doing the deed, as they often were throughout last season. Hence why Doug Melvin, a self-professed critic of the bunt, lives with Roenicke as his manager. Whether you agree with Roenicke's bunt-heavy approach or not, there's one thing all can agree on: Don't call him Walkin' Ron—no NL manager issued fewer intentional walks last year.

MINNESOTA TWINS

by Steve Neuman

The riders sagged on their mounts, spent. They'd ridden for days. Paul, the older of the two, couldn't remember a time when they weren't riding. The sky hung low, a tar-black curtain heavy with old dreams of a world forsaken.

Minnie, the other rider, spoke, his voice a ragged squawk.

"I'm hungry, Paul. Horses are hungry, too."

"Goddammit, you think I don't know that."

"I know, Paul. It's just been so long. We can't go much longer."

Paul could hear his ride's labored breaths, its exhausted gait like a staggering drunk. He knew they would soon be on foot, slaughtering the beasts for whatever meager, rancid protein they could glean.

"We get over that rise there," Paul mumbled, gesturing at a barely perceptible group of hills to the east. "Could be what that old woman was talking about: fresh water, fish, game, shelter."

"She was out of her mind," shrugged Minnie. "That hag couldn't of known night from day. She wa—"

"Shut up," Paul barked, knowing Minnie was right. She had gone on about how this was going to be the year "the twins" turned it around, jabbering about "Kirby" and "Herbie" before sinking into delirium. Hadn't been any kids born in The North for as long as Paul could remember, much less two at a time.

They rode in silence.

✦✦✦

Over the rise, such as it was, there was something: a ruined cityscape, dull grey and shattered, stretched to a river choked with filth and detritus. The sludgy trickle wasn't so much water as it was a cruel reminder of a laughing, terrible god. Their thirst would not be quenched today.

"What is this place?" asked Minnie. "Musta been something."

"You know the same stories I know," said Paul. "The old-timers always talked about the two cities in the north, divided only by a great river. Reckon this is what's left."

"Damn," said Minnie. He remembered Father talking about a verdant land, all emerald and azure in the summer, stark and bitter white in the long winter.

The burned-out husk of a giant structure loomed nearby, rebar and ash mixed with garish signs, their bright colors muted in the gloaming:

"HOOTERS"

"FOREVER 21"

"MALL OF AMERICA"

"America had its own mall? Shit." Minnie dismounted, tied up the horse and walked toward the building's remains.

"Where are you going?" asked Paul.

"Ain't got anywhere better to go. Maybe there's some provisions here, like where we found that brown sugar water."

"Cola. It's called cola. And I don't see a Kwik Trip sign nowhere."

"Come on, man. This place is huge. Musta been a church or a stadium. Or both. Let's have a look."

Paul sighed. Weariness beat against him, a ceaseless punching. "I guess."

✦✦✦

They walked past storefronts, more than either of them had seen in one place before. A giant yellow shibboleth, bucktoothed and grinning like a demon lit from within by some incandescent want, welcomed them to "SPONGEBOB SQUAREPANTS ROCK BOTTOM PLUNGE."

"What's that mean?"

"Damned if I know," said Paul. "Lotta different gods out there. Devils, too."

"Do you think it's real?"

"C'mon. It's getting dark. We gotta get moving. If that yellow ... thing is real and living here, I don't want no part of it."

✦✦✦

They camped just north of the place with the banana-colored wraith. A sign said "Richfield" but it was a lie twice told. Restless sleep with throats parched and stomachs hollowed by an almost physical hunger awaited them.

"I gotta piss," said Paul.

"Careful," said Minnie. "Awful dark tonight."

"It's dark every night."

Paul started out to gain some measure of privacy. In a debased, canine world, stepping away to urinate or move his bowels kept him in touch with a world long since abandoned.

Minnie was right, though. The black wrapped around him, a suffocating embrace that shot cold, paralyzing fear through his loins. He decided he didn't have to go and turned around. That's when he noticed the stairs.

"Minnie."

"What? You okay?"

"Get over here. Bring the candle."

The stairs were all that remained of a house. They led into the

TWINS PROSPECTUS
2014 W-L: 70-92, 5TH IN AL CENTRAL

Pythag	.461	23rd	DER	.685	30th
RS/G	4.41	7th	B-Age	27.5	7th
RA/G	4.80	29th	P-Age	29.1	22nd
TAv	.258	16th	Salary	$85M	23rd
BRR	4.61	6th	M$/MW	$3.3M	19th
TAv-P	.271	28th	DL Days	490	3rd
FIP	4.00	26th	$ on DL	19%	23rd

Three-Year Park Factors

Runs	Runs/RH	Runs/LH	HR/RH	HR/LH
108	111	108	88	79

Top Hitter WARP	4.3	Brian Dozier
Top Pitcher WARP	4.7	Phil Hughes
Top Prospect		Byron Buxton

ground. There was a wooden door at the bottom.

"You figure it's a shelter?"

"Hell if I know. All I know is it's gotta be a damn sight warmer down there than it is up here. Let's go."

They descended.

◆ ◆ ◆

The door was locked but gave way with a mild shove. The smell of dead things, of the earth coming to reclaim a debt, hung in the still, putrescent air.

"Someone died here," said Minnie.

"You can say that about a lotta places," said Paul.

They moved into the room. The walls were decorated with faded, triangular flags that said "MINNESOTA TWINS." A poster of a small, stout man with a powerful trunk pumping his fist in triumph hung over a desk. Seated at the desk was a body.

The corpse had a garish, yellowed sweatshirt reading "1987 WORLD SERIES CHAMPIONS" on the front. Its left hand clutched a moldering piece of threadbare fabric, faded red on white, inscribed "Homer Hanky."

"That machine on the desk. What is it?"

"I think I know what this is. The elders spoke of a time when you'd put paper into these machines, you'd press some buttons and the paper would come out with words on it. Writetyper, I think."

"There's a piece of paper in it, it say anything? You know the big words, not me."

Paul smiled. He grabbed the paper and read.

Dear Star Tribune,

Your bias newspaper is never more bias than when you cover for the Minnesota Twins and Joe Mauer. He is a singles hitter making $23 million dollars a year, then he gets a hangnail and can't play for a week. My old man was a farmer and once got all his fingers cut off by a piece of machinery. He scooped 'em up, put 'em on ice, drove into town and had the doctors sew 'em back on. Next day he was back out in the fields, working the land. Said he could always tell when a storm was coming in with that hand afterwards.

The funny thing is, the doctors messed up and switched up his thumb and ring finger. Still, Dad didn't complain, even though he could never bowl right for the rest of his life.

Can you imagine if that was Joe Mauer? I bet he'd be like, oh, my fingers are all tore off, better sit this one out, Gardy. Maybe give me a month or two. Ha! I tell you what, Mauer could of learned a few things about toughness from my old man. And another thing, Obama is a asdl;kjasdfasidfj aejivvvvvvvvvvvvvvvvvvvvvvvvvvvvv

"And that's it. Like he died right when he was writing it."

"Damn," Minnie said. "$23 million for a year's work. He must of been a landowner or something."

Paul put the paper on the desk. Looking down, he noticed a cylinder on the floor beneath it. Dozens of them. He'd seen them before. At the Kwik Trip.

"Minnie. I count 37 'Coke Zeroes' at our feet. Tonight we will drink, and drink deep."

◆ ◆ ◆

They drank their fill of the colas, then brought some out to the bedraggled horses, who were apprehensive at first before guzzling them.

Back in the shelter (which Paul insisted on calling a "base mint"), they looked for a place to move the body. They found an adjoining room, a small bathroom, carried the corpse as gently as possible in the candlelit gloom and deposited him on the floor.

"Paul, look."

Minnie gestured to a folded-up wad of paper atop the toilet tank. Paul grabbed it. A newspaper.

"What's it say?"

Paul scanned the front page.

"'2015 MINNESOTA TWINS SEASON PREVIEW' in big letters."

"That's who the $23 million man worked for!"

Paul held the paper closer to the candle. There was a section of print highlighted in some sort of colored ink. He read aloud.

It's hard to imagine the Twins not being at least somewhat improved under new manager Paul Molitor, even though it won't necessarily be Molitor's doing. They've gone from zero starting pitchers to one in Phil Hughes. Should he regress in 2015, Ricky Nolasco being just competent instead of terrible will make up that difference, and the addition of Ervin Santana helps as well. The rest of the rotation is waiting to see if/when Alex Meyer, J.O. Berrios, Kohl Stewart and Trevor May arrive, and hoping everyone else can get them to Casey Fien and Glen Perkins in the interim.

"Waiting" is the watchword elsewhere, too. Byron Buxton and Miguel Sano's injury-riddled 2014 campaigns have pushed their arrival out to mid- or late-2015 at the earliest. Still, there's enough offense, or at least potential, from the likes of Brian Dozier, Oswaldo Arcia, Josmil Pinto, Trevor Plouffe and a healthy Joe Mauer that Molitor is not inheriting a train wreck.

Contending for the playoffs is still, at best, a season or three out. A .500 record is probably the most that can be hoped for, and should be greeted with fireworks.

"Were these guys warriors?" asked Minnie. "Was Mauer their leader?"

"Beats the hell out of me," said Paul. "Our late friend circled 'healthy Joe Mauer' and wrote 'LOL' next to it."

"What does that mean?"

◆ ◆ ◆

Morning came. Minnie's discovery of a tin of "Pringles Chips" behind the writetyper provided not nearly enough breakfast, but was welcome. They rode east and came to the river of sludge again. Minnie stopped.

"Paul."

"What?"

"I don't think I can cross."

"Sure you can. There's a path right there."

"No, it ain't that. What if there are other base mints like last night? A man could make a life out of that."

"Minnie, we've rode forever, and how many of those have we come across?"

"But we ain't been lookin', Paul. We've just been ridin' for god knows what."

Paul knew he had a point. He also knew he couldn't stay. There had to be something else out there. Anything else. Had to be.

"Okay. I'm going to keep going. There were always stories about a place in the north where they lived off mead and dairy and steaks. Old-timers called it 'Wisco.' Figure I should try and see if they were right before it gets too cold."

"Makes sense. I'll be here. You'll know where to look."

Paul dismounted. So did Minnie.

They shook hands. ■

—Steve "RandBall's Stu" Neuman is a Digital Producer for the Infinite Guest podcast network, a division of American Public Media.

Player comments by Ken Funck and Baseball Prospectus Authors

Hitters

Oswaldo Arcia   RF

Born: 5/9/91   Age: 24   Bats: L   Throws: R   Height: 6' 0"   Weight: 220

YEAR	TEAM	LVL	AGE	PA	R	2B	3B	HR	RBI	BB	K	SB	CS	AVG/OBP/SLG	TAv	BABIP	BRR	FRAA	WARP
2012	FTM	A+	21	235	22	16	3	7	31	23	45	1	3	.309/.376/.517	.300	.361	0.5	RF(51): -0.1	1.7
2012	NBR	AA	21	299	54	20	5	10	67	28	62	3	2	.328/.398/.557	.341	.392	1.3	RF(55): 1.3, CF(4): -0.1	3.6
2013	ROC	AAA	22	155	25	6	0	10	30	22	37	2	1	.313/.426/.594	.338	.366	-0.7	RF(17): -0.8, LF(2): 0.2	1.4
2013	MIN	MLB	22	378	34	17	2	14	43	23	117	1	2	.251/.304/.430	.267	.336	-1.6	LF(56): 1.9, RF(29): -1.1	0.9
2014	ROC	AAA	23	85	16	7	0	5	18	5	17	1	0	.312/.365/.597	.289	.339	0.6	RF(16): 0.3	0.5
2014	MIN	MLB	23	410	46	16	3	20	57	31	127	1	2	.231/.300/.452	.270	.292	-0.6	RF(100): -4.6	0.6
2015	MIN	MLB	24	410	48	19	3	17	57	30	115	2	2	.259/.321/.458	.282	.326	-0.6	RF -2, LF 1	1.4

Breakout: 5%   Improve: 46%   Collapse: 12%   Attrition: 16%   MLB: 88%   Comparables: *Mark Reynolds, Travis Snider, Chris Davis*

With his smoldering intensity, bizarre haircut experiments, immense raw power and Keystone Kops outfield defense, Arcia has already become the one Twin you absolutely have to watch. The young Venezuelan tries to launch every fastball he sees to the Puckett statue in Target Plaza, and while his grip-it-and-rip-it approach leads to a mountain of strikeouts and a low OBP, there's enough thunder in his bat to make the entire package work: His .291 isolated power against righties last season trailed only Edwin Encarnacion and Mike Trout. Arcia will only be 23 on Opening Day, so it's not crazy to think he could learn to make a little more contact, draw a few more walks, improve his ghastly performance against same-side pitching and grow into one of the league's more feared lefty sluggers.

Byron Buxton   CF

Born: 12/18/93   Age: 21   Bats: R   Throws: R   Height: 6' 2"   Weight: 190

YEAR	TEAM	LVL	AGE	PA	R	2B	3B	HR	RBI	BB	K	SB	CS	AVG/OBP/SLG	TAv	BABIP	BRR	FRAA	WARP
2013	CDR	A	19	321	68	15	10	8	55	44	56	32	11	.341/.431/.559	.349	.402	4.6	CF(66): 3.5	5.0
2013	FTM	A+	19	253	41	4	8	4	22	32	49	23	8	.326/.415/.472	.320	.404	5.0	CF(55): 5.1	3.6
2014	FTM	A+	20	134	19	4	2	4	16	10	33	6	2	.240/.313/.405	.254	.298	1.5	CF(28): 4.6, RF(2): -0.2	1.0
2015	MIN	MLB	21	250	33	8	3	5	21	22	66	13	5	.248/.316/.376	.255	.323	1.1	CF 5, RF -0	1.2

Breakout: 14%   Improve: 24%   Collapse: 2%   Attrition: 8%   MLB: 37%   Comparables: *Christian Yelich, Anthony Gose, Jake Marisnick*

It was a lost season for Buxton, as the league's consensus top prospect began the year recovering from wrist problems, struggled through a concussion suffered during an outfield collision and left the Arizona Fall League early with an injured finger that required offseason surgery. Buxton didn't post eye-popping numbers during his rare time between the lines, leading some to think his stock has dropped; that belief is more a comment on today's Twitter-fed baseball fandom than on Buxton himself. He remains a blur on the basepaths and in center field, with a strong, accurate arm, a lightning-quick bat and an advanced approach that gives him every opportunity to succeed. There are no guarantees, and his timeline may have been delayed, but Buxton still seems as likely to turn his exceptional tools into big-league stardom as any prospect in baseball.

Brian Dozier   2B

Born: 5/15/87   Age: 28   Bats: R   Throws: R   Height: 5' 11"   Weight: 190

YEAR	TEAM	LVL	AGE	PA	R	2B	3B	HR	RBI	BB	K	SB	CS	AVG/OBP/SLG	TAv	BABIP	BRR	FRAA	WARP
2012	ROC	AAA	25	200	15	11	1	2	17	14	34	3	2	.232/.286/.337	.228	.270	0.2	SS(42): -1.5, 2B(4): -0.8	-0.1
2012	MIN	MLB	25	340	33	11	1	6	33	16	58	9	2	.234/.271/.332	.224	.267	-2.0	SS(83): 4.2	0.4
2013	MIN	MLB	26	623	72	33	4	18	66	51	120	14	7	.244/.312/.414	.263	.278	3.9	2B(146): 6.4	3.8
2014	MIN	MLB	27	707	112	33	1	23	71	89	129	21	7	.242/.345/.416	.278	.269	4.3	2B(156): 3.2	4.3
2015	MIN	MLB	28	647	83	30	3	16	63	58	121	17	6	.245/.318/.392	.263	.279	1.7	2B 2, SS -0	2.8

Breakout: 0%   Improve: 57%   Collapse: 0%   Attrition: 3%   MLB: 95%   Comparables: *Kelly Johnson, Marcus Giles, Aaron Hill*

After playing his way into Minnesota's future plans with a solid 2013 season, Dozier spent last summer settling in as one of baseball's better second basemen. Smooth and rangy in the field, Dozier works deep counts, takes his walks and swings from the heels when he gets a pitch he likes. Strikeouts and low batting averages will always be an issue, but his dramatic improvement against same-side pitching—doubling his walk rate and adding 60 points of on-base percentage—sanded away the last significant flaw in his game. Dozier isn't a superstar, but a second baseman who can go 20/20 and is years away from free agency is a certified building block.

Eduardo Escobar   SS

Born: 1/5/89   Age: 26   Bats: B   Throws: R   Height: 5' 10"   Weight: 175

YEAR	TEAM	LVL	AGE	PA	R	2B	3B	HR	RBI	BB	K	SB	CS	AVG/OBP/SLG	TAv	BABIP	BRR	FRAA	WARP
2012	ROC	AAA	23	151	19	3	3	1	9	8	26	3	1	.217/.259/.304	.206	.259	0.7	3B(17): -3.5, SS(10): -1.0	-0.8
2012	CHA	MLB	23	97	14	4	1	0	3	9	23	2	0	.207/.281/.276	.207	.281	0.6	3B(22): 0.4, 2B(6): -0.4	-0.2
2012	MIN	MLB	23	49	4	0	0	0	6	2	8	1	0	.227/.271/.227	.190	.270	0.1	2B(8): 0.6, SS(6): 0.4	-0.1
2013	ROC	AAA	24	188	22	16	2	4	27	17	37	6	2	.307/.380/.500	.290	.373	0.1	SS(29): -0.2, 2B(6): 0.8	1.7
2013	MIN	MLB	24	179	23	5	2	3	10	11	34	0	1	.236/.282/.345	.241	.279	-2.0	SS(38): -0.8, 3B(23): -2.1	-0.3
2014	MIN	MLB	25	465	52	35	2	6	37	24	93	1	1	.275/.315/.406	.251	.336	0.7	SS(98): -7.1, 3B(25): -1.3	0.3
2015	MIN	MLB	26	402	36	20	3	4	35	22	80	4	2	.257/.298/.359	.238	.308	-0.3	SS -1, 3B -3	0.1

Breakout: 10%   Improve: 49%   Collapse: 14%   Attrition: 30%   MLB: 89%   Comparables: *Ramiro Pena, Reid Brignac, Dee Gordon*

Escobar earned the first extended playing time of his career last summer (The Eddie 400!), and the young infielder proved once and for all that he can outhit Pedro Florimon. For whatever that's worth. A switch-hitter with doubles power, Escobar can provide solid defense all over the infield but remains the free-swingingest of free-swingers, continually offering at pitches outside the zone and getting himself out at a rate that should preclude him from regular work. He's a nice utility option, but if Escobar is your starting shortstop, you're either rebuilding, settling or both.

Nick Gordon   SS

Born: 10/24/95   Age: 19   Bats: L   Throws: R   Height: 6' 0"   Weight: 160

YEAR	TEAM	LVL	AGE	PA	R	2B	3B	HR	RBI	BB	K	SB	CS	AVG/OBP/SLG	TAv	BABIP	BRR	FRAA	WARP
2015	MIN	MLB	19	250	21	9	1	1	15	7	69	3	2	.207/.232/.267	.184	.279	-0.2	SS 8	-0.1

Breakout: 0%   Improve: 0%   Collapse: 0%   Attrition: 0%   MLB: 0%   Comparables: Daniel Santana, Hector Gomez, Hernan Perez

If you dig through Gordon's numbers in his Rookie League debut, you'll find that people are staring at you, shaking their heads at the idea you can learn much digging through Rookie League numbers. It's all about the projection for last year's fifth overall pick, as Dee's little brother is still an uncarved block of tools, albeit a somewhat more polished block than most prep products. A true shortstop with soft hands, smooth actions and a plus arm, Gordon's toolbox includes plus speed and a compact lefty swing that should eventually generate significant power. We're years away from knowing if he can touch up the best pitchers in the world, but for now there's plenty to dream on.

Chris Herrmann   RF

Born: 11/24/87   Age: 27   Bats: L   Throws: R   Height: 6' 0"   Weight: 200

YEAR	TEAM	LVL	AGE	PA	R	2B	3B	HR	RBI	BB	K	SB	CS	AVG/OBP/SLG	TAv	BABIP	BRR	FRAA	WARP
2012	NBR	AA	24	558	91	25	1	10	61	58	89	2	1	.276/.350/.392	.271	.315	2.1	C(83): 0.4, LF(27): -1.0	2.9
2012	MIN	MLB	24	19	0	0	0	0	1	1	5	0	0	.056/.105/.056	.073	.077	0.0	C(3): -0.0, LF(2): -0.1	-0.4
2013	ROC	AAA	25	275	31	9	3	2	22	24	61	3	2	.227/.297/.312	.225	.292	1.2	C(40): 1.9, LF(18): -1.1	0.1
2013	MIN	MLB	25	178	16	7	0	4	18	18	49	0	1	.204/.286/.325	.218	.269	1.3	C(27): 0.2, RF(21): -2.0	-0.2
2014	ROC	AAA	26	228	31	18	4	5	26	21	45	4	1	.304/.373/.505	.287	.368	1.0	C(26): -0.5, RF(23): 0.2	1.7
2014	MIN	MLB	26	79	8	3	0	0	4	4	17	1	0	.213/.253/.253	.194	.276	0.7	RF(13): 0.2, LF(12): -0.5	-0.4
2015	MIN	MLB	27	250	26	11	1	4	21	20	57	2	1	.237/.299/.347	.238	.295	1.0	C 0, RF -1	0.2

Breakout: 1%   Improve: 12%   Collapse: 7%   Attrition: 17%   MLB: 31%   Comparables: Kory Casto, Brandon Jones, Shane Costa

You don't see many catcher/outfielders, so Herrmann's versatility has earned him a few trips to Target Field. There's one problem with building your career on versatility alone: You can't take your favorite versatility out of the versatility rack and use it to line a shot into the right-field gap, which is what Herrmann needs to do more often if he wants to stick around. The Twins don't seem convinced he has the defensive chops to be a backup catcher—mind you, this is a franchise that employed Ryan Doumit in that role—and his bat lacks the juice for an outfield corner, leaving Herrmann as a likely fixture in Rochester. Might we suggest the knuckleball?

Aaron Hicks   CF

Born: 10/2/89   Age: 25   Bats: B   Throws: R   Height: 6' 2"   Weight: 190

YEAR	TEAM	LVL	AGE	PA	R	2B	3B	HR	RBI	BB	K	SB	CS	AVG/OBP/SLG	TAv	BABIP	BRR	FRAA	WARP
2012	NBR	AA	22	563	100	21	11	13	61	79	116	32	11	.286/.384/.460	.299	.348	8.7	CF(114): 3.3, LF(3): 0.2	5.2
2013	ROC	AAA	23	82	7	4	2	0	5	10	21	1	0	.222/.317/.333	.242	.314	0.2	CF(19): 0.3	0.1
2013	MIN	MLB	23	313	37	11	3	8	27	24	84	9	3	.192/.259/.338	.237	.241	1.1	CF(81): 2.3	0.6
2014	NBR	AA	24	178	30	11	1	4	21	28	27	2	3	.297/.404/.466	.311	.336	1.9	CF(27): 2.1, RF(9): -0.2	1.8
2014	ROC	AAA	24	84	9	5	0	1	8	9	13	1	1	.278/.349/.389	.248	.317	-0.6	CF(16): -1.8, RF(4): 0.1	-0.1
2014	MIN	MLB	24	225	22	8	0	1	18	36	56	4	3	.215/.341/.274	.243	.300	-0.8	CF(57): 4.6, LF(6): 0.1	0.6
2015	MIN	MLB	25	278	34	11	2	5	24	32	67	7	3	.235/.323/.361	.254	.299	-0.1	CF 3, RF 0	0.9

Breakout: 6%   Improve: 51%   Collapse: 10%   Attrition: 30%   MLB: 85%   Comparables: Ryan Kalish, Michael Saunders, Dexter Fowler

Few players offered at a lower percentage of pitches last year than Hicks, which led to a greatly improved walk rate and on-base percentage compared to his nightmarish 2013 debut. Unfortunately, his miniscule batting average and slugging percentage and high whiff rate shows his approach isn't exactly "waiting for his pitch" so much as "waiting for something to happen." This is something Twins fans are very familiar with when it comes to Hicks. The former top pick has long flashed the speed, cannon arm, patient approach and power potential that pointed to future stardom, but his complete inability to make contact or drive the ball against advanced pitchers continues to haunt him. Hicks remains a sterling defensive center fielder and will likely get another chance to earn his keep, but with the shadow of Byron Buxton looming, time's a-wastin'.

Torii Hunter   RF

Born: 7/18/75   Age: 39   Bats: R   Throws: R   Height: 6' 2"   Weight: 225

YEAR	TEAM	LVL	AGE	PA	R	2B	3B	HR	RBI	BB	K	SB	CS	AVG/OBP/SLG	TAv	BABIP	BRR	FRAA	WARP
2012	ANA	MLB	36	584	81	24	1	16	92	38	133	9	1	.313/.365/.451	.286	.389	5.5	RF(134): -1.8	3.4
2013	DET	MLB	37	652	90	37	5	17	84	26	113	3	2	.304/.334/.465	.292	.344	0.8	RF(143): -13.0	1.8
2014	DET	MLB	38	586	71	33	2	17	83	23	89	4	3	.286/.319/.446	.266	.311	0.4	RF(128): -10.8	0.5
2015	MIN	MLB	39	564	68	27	2	14	59	35	107	5	2	.279/.329/.420	.274	.325	1.4	RF -6	1.3

Breakout: 0%   Improve: 11%   Collapse: 5%   Attrition: 13%   MLB: 71%   Comparables: Ken Griffey, Dave Winfield, Raul Ibanez

He'll tell you age is only a number. Unfortunately, so is FRAA, and in Hunter's case, both numbers pass the eye test. The good news is that it's 2015, and baseball invented the designated hitter with situations like Hunter's in mind. The bad news is that it's Minnesota and Kennys Vargas is here. Hunter still strikes the ball well and has enough bat speed to launch a curve 400 feet. His presence in both the lineup and clubhouse is the type that could be the missing piece for a young contender, which, even aside from the position issue, makes him a weird fit for a Twins team that won't contend for anything other than respectability.

Max Kepler   CF

Born: 2/10/93   Age: 22   Bats: L   Throws: L   Height: 6' 4"   Weight: 205

YEAR	TEAM	LVL	AGE	PA	R	2B	3B	HR	RBI	BB	K	SB	CS	AVG/OBP/SLG	TAv	BABIP	BRR	FRAA	WARP
2013	CDR	A	20	263	35	11	3	9	40	24	43	2	0	.237/.312/.424	.268	.254	-1.4	1B(24): -1.4, LF(15): 2.2	0.8
2014	FTM	A+	21	407	53	20	6	5	59	34	62	6	2	.264/.333/.393	.274	.304	-1.1	CF(61): -5.2, RF(18): -0.9	0.8
2015	MIN	MLB	22	250	22	10	2	5	25	15	55	1	0	.228/.280/.349	.232	.276	-0.1	CF -2, 1B -0	-0.4

Breakout: 0%   Improve: 0%   Collapse: 0%   Attrition: 0%   MLB: 0%   Comparables: Nick Markakis, Desmond Jennings, Ryan Kalish

If you were to build a word cloud describing Kepler today, it would look pretty much like it did when he signed with the Twins as a 16-year-old: "young," "German," "ballet" and "power potential" would figure prominently. Notably absent is the word "productive," as Kepler has yet to put up noteworthy numbers in the low minors despite growing into a slugger's frame. Tall and athletic, Kepler makes contact and has a good approach, but he rarely puts a charge into the ball and his fringy arm will likely limit him to left field or first base. Given his unique background, the Twins continue to show patience with him and hope he can morph into a middle-of-the-order force, but he'll need to start launching a few bombs this year if he wants to keep his prospect sheen.

Joe Mauer   1B

Born: 4/19/83   Age: 32   Bats: L   Throws: R   Height: 6' 5"   Weight: 230

YEAR	TEAM	LVL	AGE	PA	R	2B	3B	HR	RBI	BB	K	SB	CS	AVG/OBP/SLG	TAv	BABIP	BRR	FRAA	WARP
2012	MIN	MLB	29	641	81	31	4	10	85	90	88	8	4	.319/.416/.446	.297	.364	-2.1	C(74): -1.7, 1B(30): -2.2	3.1
2013	MIN	MLB	30	508	62	35	0	11	47	61	89	0	1	.324/.404/.476	.315	.383	-0.5	C(75): -0.2, 1B(8): 0.0	4.6
2014	MIN	MLB	31	518	60	27	2	4	55	60	96	3	0	.277/.361/.371	.261	.342	4.2	1B(100): 1.7	1.3
2015	MIN	MLB	32	487	52	27	2	6	50	56	75	3	1	.298/.380/.409	.289	.347	0.5	1B 1, C -0	2.5

Breakout: 1%   Improve: 32%   Collapse: 1%   Attrition: 7%   MLB: 96%   Comparables: Kent Hrbek, Mike Sweeney, Justin Morneau

Mauer's move to first base last season didn't have the desired effects on his health or his production, as The Franchise missed a month with a strained oblique and suffered through a season-long power outage. But was this just a blip, or the new normal? Optimists will wave away his first-half struggles as the after-effects of his 2013 concussion, and point to his .289/.397/.408 second-half line as a harbinger of things to come. Pessimists will note Mauer's rising strikeout and chase rates, trends that actually began in 2013 but were masked by his career-high .383 BABIP that year. Engineers will point out that a half-filled glass is twice as large as it needs to be, but that doesn't really help us. When choosing between an argument based on narrative and an argument based on statistical fact it's usually best to go with the numbers, and they're starting to whisper "decline phase." Mauer has long shown a preternatural ability to find his pitch and barrel it up, but he's now making less contact and posting more strikeouts. Once his batting average starts clocking in at .285 on a regular basis, he'll be a good player, not a great one.

Eduardo Nunez   SS

Born: 6/15/87   Age: 28   Bats: R   Throws: R   Height: 6' 0"   Weight: 185

YEAR	TEAM	LVL	AGE	PA	R	2B	3B	HR	RBI	BB	K	SB	CS	AVG/OBP/SLG	TAv	BABIP	BRR	FRAA	WARP
2012	SWB	AAA	25	172	18	4	0	2	16	7	28	16	3	.227/.256/.288	.189	.259	2.1	SS(35): 1.8	-0.1
2012	NYA	MLB	25	100	14	4	1	1	11	6	12	11	2	.292/.330/.393	.275	.313	0.8	SS(16): -0.3, 3B(9): 0.1	0.5
2013	NYA	MLB	26	336	38	17	4	3	28	20	51	10	3	.260/.307/.372	.255	.298	-0.2	SS(75): -10.6, 3B(14): -0.7	-0.1
2014	ROC	AAA	27	41	7	1	0	1	6	1	8	1	0	.282/.293/.385	.226	.323	-0.2	SS(4): -0.3, 3B(4): -0.5	-0.1
2014	MIN	MLB	27	213	26	7	4	4	24	5	31	9	3	.250/.271/.382	.224	.278	0.9	SS(20): -1.4, 3B(20): -1.3	0.1
2015	MIN	MLB	28	250	27	11	2	2	20	14	34	13	3	.266/.308/.361	.245	.298	0.4	SS -3, 3B -1	0.0

Breakout: 6%   Improve: 29%   Collapse: 6%   Attrition: 15%   MLB: 80%   Comparables: Luis Rivas, Brendan Ryan, Hector Luna

Two things changed for Nunez the instant he moved from New York to Minnesota last spring: Instead of backing up millionaires, he's now playing second fiddle to thousandaires, and instead of being crucified by a pitiless Big Apple press corps, he's being ignored by Midwestern scribes taught to say nothing at all if there was nothing nice to say. What hasn't changed is the fact that Nunez has neither the bat of an everyday player nor the dependable glove of a utility guy. Last year he was outstanding in at least one way: His 2.3 percent walk rate was the lowest in the American League. So there's that.

Chris Parmelee   RF

Born: 2/24/88   Age: 27   Bats: L   Throws: L   Height: 6' 1"   Weight: 220

YEAR	TEAM	LVL	AGE	PA	R	2B	3B	HR	RBI	BB	K	SB	CS	AVG/OBP/SLG	TAv	BABIP	BRR	FRAA	WARP
2012	ROC	AAA	24	282	45	17	1	17	49	51	52	1	1	.338/.457/.645	.381	.373	-2.7	1B(62): 7.3	4.6
2012	MIN	MLB	24	210	18	10	2	5	19	13	52	0	0	.229/.290/.380	.233	.287	-0.7	1B(38): 0.1, RF(18): -0.6	-0.4
2013	ROC	AAA	25	198	23	13	1	3	22	22	32	1	0	.231/.318/.370	.253	.264	-1.5	1B(28): 1.5, RF(18): -0.1	0.0
2013	MIN	MLB	25	333	21	13	0	8	24	33	81	1	1	.228/.309/.354	.244	.284	-5.4	RF(68): -6.9, 1B(23): -1.3	-1.1
2014	ROC	AAA	26	135	13	7	0	7	23	14	24	0	0	.305/.378/.542	.312	.326	-0.3	1B(22): -1.7, RF(9): 1.0	0.7
2014	MIN	MLB	26	270	27	11	0	7	28	17	64	0	3	.256/.307/.384	.247	.317	-2.0	1B(33): 1.3, RF(33): 0.6	0.3
2015	MIN	MLB	27	310	33	14	1	9	37	30	65	1	1	.260/.333/.416	.273	.306	-2.0	RF -1, 1B 2	0.7

Breakout: 5%   Improve: 41%   Collapse: 8%   Attrition: 13%   MLB: 78%   Comparables: Ryan Garko, Gaby Sanchez, Dan Johnson

Parmelee once again spent the summer alternately raking in Triple-A and floundering in the American League, failing to grab hold of an outfield job that's just begging to be claimed. If Parmelee could masquerade as a center fielder he could be the next Ryan Sweeney, but as a defensively challenged corner outfielder, his lack of home run thump dooms him. His pretty lefty swing and first-round pedigree will keep earning him chances, and it's possible an Age-27 Miracle could unfold, but Parmelee was preemptively swamped by the next wave of Twins prospects and designated for assignment in December.

Josmil Pinto   DH

Born: 3/31/89   Age: 26   Bats: R   Throws: R   Height: 5' 11"   Weight: 210

YEAR	TEAM	LVL	AGE	PA	R	2B	3B	HR	RBI	BB	K	SB	CS	AVG/OBP/SLG	TAv	BABIP	BRR	FRAA	WARP
2012	FTM	A+	23	393	45	22	2	12	51	39	63	0	0	.295/.361/.473	.284	.326	-2.5	C(56): 0.1	2.4
2012	NBR	AA	23	52	8	4	1	2	9	4	10	0	0	.298/.365/.553	.319	.343	0.2	C(2): -0.0	0.4
2013	NBR	AA	24	453	59	23	1	14	68	64	71	0	2	.308/.411/.482	.320	.349	-1.5	C(60): 0.0	3.9
2013	ROC	AAA	24	75	6	9	0	1	6	2	12	0	0	.314/.333/.486	.248	.356	-1.3	C(14): -0.3	0.1
2013	MIN	MLB	24	83	10	5	0	4	12	6	22	0	0	.342/.398/.566	.337	.440	-0.4	C(20): -0.2	1.1
2014	ROC	AAA	25	242	24	17	1	6	35	31	37	0	1	.279/.376/.457	.275	.313	-1.5	C(34): 0.6	1.0
2014	MIN	MLB	25	197	25	8	0	7	18	24	50	0	1	.219/.315/.391	.251	.261	-0.5	C(25): 0.1	0.1
2015	MIN	MLB	26	261	28	13	1	8	32	25	55	0	0	.264/.337/.424	.277	.311	-0.2	C -0	1.2

Breakout: 2%   Improve: 25%   Collapse: 18%   Attrition: 25%   MLB: 72%   Comparables: Ryan Lavarnway, Welington Castillo, Jeff Clement

A bat-first backstop with questionable defensive value, it was no big surprise to see Pinto struggle behind the plate in his first extended playing time. Basestealers were 20-for-20 on Pinto's watch last season, his blocking skills were poor and he was one of the worst pitch-framers in baseball, all of which contributed to his midseason demotion to Triple-A and Kurt Suzuki's extension. At the plate, Pinto continues to show patience, good contact skills and some pop, giving him an above-average bat for a catcher. Make him a full-time DH, however, and his bat is no longer special, so the Twins had best hope he can improve enough behind the dish to take on the backup catcher role, or resign themselves to a steady dose of Eric Fryer.

Trevor Plouffe 3B

Born: 6/15/86   Age: 29   Bats: R   Throws: R   Height: 6' 2"   Weight: 205

YEAR	TEAM	LVL	AGE	PA	R	2B	3B	HR	RBI	BB	K	SB	CS	AVG/OBP/SLG	TAv	BABIP	BRR	FRAA	WARP
2012	MIN	MLB	26	465	56	19	1	24	55	37	92	1	3	.235/.301/.455	.261	.244	-2.6	3B(95): -2.7, RF(15): -0.7	0.4
2013	MIN	MLB	27	522	44	22	1	14	52	34	112	2	1	.254/.309/.392	.261	.301	-0.4	3B(120): -13.7, 1B(2): -0.0	0.1
2014	MIN	MLB	28	582	69	40	2	14	80	53	109	2	1	.258/.328/.423	.271	.299	-0.6	3B(127): -0.6	2.4
2015	MIN	MLB	29	537	57	26	2	17	66	40	113	2	1	.247/.310/.415	.265	.285	-0.9	3B -6, RF -0	0.7

Breakout: 1%   Improve: 32%   Collapse: 9%   Attrition: 17%   MLB: 96%   *Comparables: David Freese, Casey McGehee, Chris Johnson*

Plouffe quietly put together a very nice season last year, establishing himself as a bona fide major-league third baseman. He finally looked comfortable in the field, showing better instincts, softer hands and a more accurate arm. At the plate, Plouffe managed to lay off more pitches out of the zone, cut down on his strikeouts, draw more walks and use the whole field, helping him rank among the league leaders in doubles. A fractured forearm suffered while applying a tag ended his season early, but he should be back from offseason surgery in time for spring training. Like Brian Dozier, Plouffe has surprisingly played his way into Minnesota's future plans, and his emergence gives the Twins a viable fallback option should Miguel Sano's glove not hold up at the hot corner.

Jorge Polanco SS

Born: 7/5/93   Age: 21   Bats: B   Throws: R   Height: 5' 11"   Weight: 165

YEAR	TEAM	LVL	AGE	PA	R	2B	3B	HR	RBI	BB	K	SB	CS	AVG/OBP/SLG	TAv	BABIP	BRR	FRAA	WARP
2013	CDR	A	19	523	76	32	10	5	78	42	59	4	4	.308/.362/.452	.297	.336	-0.4	2B(57): -0.2, SS(49): -4.5	2.9
2014	FTM	A+	20	432	61	17	6	6	45	46	60	10	8	.291/.364/.415	.282	.327	1.0	SS(86): -0.5, 2B(6): -1.0	2.8
2014	NBR	AA	20	157	13	6	0	1	16	9	28	7	3	.281/.323/.342	.246	.342	0.8	SS(33): 1.6, 2B(4): -0.1	0.6
2014	MIN	MLB	20	8	2	1	1	0	3	2	2	0	0	.333/.500/.833	.455	.500	0.1	SS(4): 0.0	0.2
2015	MIN	MLB	21	250	26	11	2	2	19	15	50	3	2	.251/.297/.347	.236	.304	-0.1	SS -1, 2B -0	0.2

Breakout: 0%   Improve: 0%   Collapse: 0%   Attrition: 0%   MLB: 0%   *Comparables: Tyler Pastornicky, Carlos Sanchez, Jose Pirela*

Polanco is a clean second draft, displaying smooth actions and good instincts in the field and a clean line-drive stroke from both sides of the plate. He's also a fast mover, holding his own as a 20-year-old in High-A, spending time in Double-A and earning a brief call-up last summer. He's more steady than spectacular in all phases of the game, with above-average speed, developing gap power and solid bat-to-ball skills. Most scouts feel he is a little stretched at shortstop, but with Brian Dozier currently manning the keystone the Twins will give Polanco every opportunity to show he can stay on the left side of the infield. At a minimum he'll have a career as an above-average utility infielder, with the possibility for more.

Eddie Rosario 2B

Born: 9/28/91   Age: 23   Bats: L   Throws: R   Height: 6' 1"   Weight: 180

YEAR	TEAM	LVL	AGE	PA	R	2B	3B	HR	RBI	BB	K	SB	CS	AVG/OBP/SLG	TAv	BABIP	BRR	FRAA	WARP
2012	BLT	A	20	429	60	32	4	12	70	31	69	11	11	.296/.345/.490	.294	.329	0.2	2B(67): -0.3, CF(19): -0.2	3.1
2013	FTM	A+	21	231	40	13	5	6	35	17	29	3	6	.329/.377/.527	.317	.350	-2.5	2B(50): 8.9	2.9
2013	NBR	AA	21	313	40	19	3	4	38	21	67	7	4	.284/.330/.412	.269	.355	-1.0	2B(65): -5.8	0.6
2014	FTM	A+	22	34	5	0	0	0	4	4	5	1	1	.300/.382/.300	.266	.360	-1.1	CF(7): -0.2, 2B(2): 0.1	0.0
2014	NBR	AA	22	336	40	20	3	8	36	17	68	8	4	.237/.277/.396	.237	.277	-1.9	CF(43): 3.8, LF(18): 1.1	0.5
2015	MIN	MLB	23	250	24	12	2	5	25	11	57	4	2	.245/.279/.372	.235	.300	-0.2	2B -0, CF 1	0.2

Breakout: 0%   Improve: 0%   Collapse: 0%   Attrition: 0%   MLB: 0%   *Comparables: Bryan Petersen, Josh Reddick, Xavier Paul*

No one has ever questioned Rosario's ability to hit a baseball. If only we could say the same about his glove, his plate approach, his commitment, his maturity and his power potential. Rosario began the season serving a 50-game suspension for his second drug policy violation, and when he finally took the field he struggled in his first taste of the high minors. He went back to lashing line drives all over the Arizona Fall League, but whereas his bat was an asset at the keystone and would remain one if he could stick in center field, his lack of power and hacktastic approach would make it a liability should he move to a corner, as some scouts expect. If Rosario can answer his critics by improving his defense, becoming more selective at the plate and showing more maturity (or even just picking two of those), he can still carve out a big-league career.

Miguel Sano 3B

Born: 5/11/93   Age: 22   Bats: R   Throws: R   Height: 6' 4"   Weight: 235

YEAR	TEAM	LVL	AGE	PA	R	2B	3B	HR	RBI	BB	K	SB	CS	AVG/OBP/SLG	TAv	BABIP	BRR	FRAA	WARP
2012	BLT	A	19	553	75	28	4	28	100	80	144	8	3	.258/.373/.521	.303	.307	1.9	3B(125): -3.0, 1B(1): -0.1	4.3
2013	FTM	A+	20	243	51	15	2	16	48	29	61	9	2	.330/.424/.655	.366	.397	2.8	3B(56): -1.4	3.6
2013	NBR	AA	20	276	35	15	3	19	55	36	81	2	1	.236/.344/.571	.312	.265	-0.9	3B(64): 2.8	2.4
2015	MIN	MLB	22	250	32	10	1	13	38	26	79	2	1	.231/.316/.464	.278	.289	-0.1	3B 0, 1B -0	1.1

Breakout: 3%   Improve: 31%   Collapse: 2%   Attrition: 10%   MLB: 55%   *Comparables: Chris Carter, Chris Davis, Evan Longoria*

It's always a shame when a prospect misses a full season of development, but in Sano's case, losing all of last summer to Tommy John surgery was especially sad. When last we saw the *Pelotero* star in game action, he was launching moonshots as a 20-year-old in Double-A, but advanced pitchers were exposing some contact issues and his defense at third base was still an open question. The lost year didn't given him the chance to provide answers, and as Sano continues to grow the belief that he'll need to move to right field or first base grows with him, though his bat, featuring 80-grade raw power, will play anywhere. His second crack at Double-A will tell us a lot about his future position, the utility of his hit tool and how well his makeup helps him overcome adversity. Sano's ceiling is as high as any prospect around, and by next fall we should have a much better idea of his chances of reaching it.

Daniel Santana   UT

Born: 11/7/90   Age: 24   Bats: B   Throws: R   Height: 5' 11"   Weight: 175

YEAR	TEAM	LVL	AGE	PA	R	2B	3B	HR	RBI	BB	K	SB	CS	AVG/OBP/SLG	TAv	BABIP	BRR	FRAA	WARP
2012	FTM	A+	21	547	70	21	9	8	60	29	77	17	11	.286/.329/.410	.267	.322	-0.4	SS(85): -8.6, 2B(32): -2.0	1.0
2013	NBR	AA	22	588	66	22	10	2	45	24	94	30	13	.297/.333/.386	.268	.353	1.5	SS(125): 0.7, 2B(3): -0.1	3.0
2014	ROC	AAA	23	105	15	7	2	0	7	6	28	4	1	.268/.311/.381	.240	.377	-0.7	SS(20): -2.9	-0.1
2014	MIN	MLB	23	430	70	27	7	7	40	19	98	20	4	.319/.353/.472	.289	.405	2.0	CF(69): 0.4, SS(34): -5.0	2.3
2015	MIN	MLB	24	406	47	18	5	4	32	14	86	15	5	.275/.303/.384	.248	.336	0.5	SS -4, CF -0	0.6

Breakout: 9%   Improve: 34%   Collapse: 8%   Attrition: 21%   MLB: 61%   Comparables: Felix Pie, Peter Bourjos, Juan Lagares

Let's start with the obvious: Charlie Kelly is more likely to correctly pronounce "Hawaiian luau" than Santana is to duplicate last year's ridiculous .405 BABIP. He clearly can hit, but he strikes out way too much and offers at too many pitches out of the zone to remain a .300 hitter. That being said, Santana's speed, gap power, defensive versatility and switch-hitting acumen should keep him in Minnesota's plans. He's an adequate if unspectacular shortstop, but last year's inevitable Aaron Hicks fail had the Twins asking Santana to learn center field on the fly; the young Dominican responded well and looked adequate if unspectacular. He'll never walk enough to hit at the top of the order or slug enough to be a run producer, but if the Twins plug him in at shortstop and slot him in the eight hole they'll be happy with the results.

Jordan Schafer   LF

Born: 9/4/86   Age: 28   Bats: L   Throws: L   Height: 6' 1"   Weight: 205

YEAR	TEAM	LVL	AGE	PA	R	2B	3B	HR	RBI	BB	K	SB	CS	AVG/OBP/SLG	TAv	BABIP	BRR	FRAA	WARP
2012	HOU	MLB	25	360	40	10	2	4	23	36	106	27	9	.211/.297/.294	.227	.304	4.2	CF(87): -3.7	-0.2
2013	GWN	AAA	26	33	0	2	0	0	2	1	4	0	0	.063/.091/.125	.056	.071	0.0	CF(5): 0.1	-0.5
2013	ATL	MLB	26	265	32	8	3	3	21	29	73	22	6	.247/.331/.346	.251	.348	1.4	CF(30): 0.3, RF(29): 1.5	0.6
2014	ATL	MLB	27	93	9	4	0	0	12	10	20	15	2	.163/.256/.213	.193	.217	1.9	LF(15): -0.1, CF(11): 0.7	-0.2
2014	MIN	MLB	27	147	17	5	1	1	13	12	28	15	5	.285/.345/.362	.264	.356	-0.5	LF(34): -0.6, CF(9): 0.0	0.2
2015	MIN	MLB	28	250	33	9	2	2	15	22	58	21	6	.239/.310/.322	.235	.302	1.3	CF 0, LF -1	0.2

Breakout: 1%   Improve: 37%   Collapse: 4%   Attrition: 13%   MLB: 94%   Comparables: Luis Matos, Gene Richards, Mike Aldrete

When Schafer stood in left field making his first start for the Twins after being waived by the Braves, no one had to tell him his role. One glance at newbie center fielder Danny Santana and putative "outfielder" Oswaldo Arcia impatiently awaiting his hacks in right told him he was there to run down fly balls, draw some walks and steal a few bases. Schafer did that and more, and while his batting average and OBP are likely to drop and he's no sane person's idea of a starting corner outfielder, his speed and solid defensive chops make him an upgrade from the Mastroianni/Presley/Fuld class of backup center fielder.

Kurt Suzuki   C

Born: 10/4/83   Age: 31   Bats: R   Throws: R   Height: 5' 11"   Weight: 230

YEAR	TEAM	LVL	AGE	PA	R	2B	3B	HR	RBI	BB	K	SB	CS	AVG/OBP/SLG	TAv	BABIP	BRR	FRAA	WARP
2012	OAK	MLB	28	278	19	15	0	1	18	9	53	1	0	.218/.250/.286	.198	.267	-1.6	C(75): -1.1	-0.3
2012	WAS	MLB	28	164	17	5	0	5	25	11	20	1	0	.267/.321/.404	.267	.274	-0.4	C(42): 0.5	0.8
2013	OAK	MLB	29	35	6	2	0	2	7	2	3	0	0	.303/.343/.545	.343	.286	-1.1	C(15): 0.4	0.5
2013	WAS	MLB	29	281	19	11	1	3	25	20	32	2	0	.222/.283/.310	.227	.240	1.0	C(78): -0.1	0.0
2014	MIN	MLB	30	503	37	34	0	3	61	34	46	0	1	.288/.345/.383	.264	.310	-4.7	C(119): 0.8	1.9
2015	MIN	MLB	31	435	42	22	1	7	42	28	53	1	1	.256/.311/.372	.251	.275	-2.0	C -1	1.0

Breakout: 1%   Improve: 32%   Collapse: 8%   Attrition: 10%   MLB: 94%   Comparables: Paul Lo Duca, Brian Schneider, A.J. Pierzynski

In baseball, timing is everything. After two years of playing roster hot-potato between Oakland and Washington, Suzuki brought his declining bat to Minnesota before last season on a make-good one-year deal to share the catcher job with Josmil Pinto. Seven months later, the Twins made Suzuki their highest-paid position player not named Mauer when they signed him to a multi-year extension. What happened? Well, the Twins soured on Pinto after watching him hand out free stolen-base coupons to every opposing batter, while Suzuki earned a trip to the All-Star Game on the strength of his defensive reputation and a BABIP-fueled .309/.365/.396 line. Of course, Suzuki's second-half .253/.313/.362 line and .280 BABIP are almost perfect matches for his career numbers, and are a better indicator of what the Twins will get going forward. If he's going to earn his salary it will likely have to be through intangibles like his reputation as a good game-caller and clubhouse leader.

Kennys Vargas   DH

Born: 8/1/90   Age: 24   Bats: B   Throws: R   Height: 6' 5"   Weight: 275

YEAR	TEAM	LVL	AGE	PA	R	2B	3B	HR	RBI	BB	K	SB	CS	AVG/OBP/SLG	TAv	BABIP	BRR	FRAA	WARP
2012	BLT	A	21	186	22	10	1	11	36	28	41	0	0	.318/.419/.610	.352	.362	-1.2	1B(33): 0.1, 3B(1): 0.2	2.0
2013	FTM	A+	22	520	68	33	1	19	93	50	105	0	0	.267/.344/.468	.284	.304	-0.9	1B(81): -3.9	1.5
2014	NBR	AA	23	405	50	17	0	17	63	43	68	0	2	.281/.360/.472	.297	.303	-1.0	1B(81): 5.9	2.6
2014	MIN	MLB	23	234	26	10	1	9	38	12	63	0	0	.274/.316/.456	.274	.340	0.1	1B(13): -0.7	0.6
2015	MIN	MLB	24	296	32	13	1	11	39	23	73	0	0	.252/.313/.425	.269	.303	0.1	1B 0, 3B 0	0.7

Breakout: 3%   Improve: 25%   Collapse: 17%   Attrition: 31%   MLB: 59%   Comparables: Nick Evans, Joey Votto, Brett Wallace

A few things about Vargas are obvious at first glance: He's huge, he's got a lot of swing and miss, his raw power from both sides of the plate is massive, he's probably best suited to DH and he's huge. A man this big can't be reduced to the singular. Vargas was a free-swinger last year, particularly at pitches outside the zone, yet still made plenty of hard contact in his big-league debut. If he can start controlling the strike zone the way he did in the minors—a big if—his walk rate should increase out of sheer pitcher terror, and he could become an above-average power bat. The Twins would be best served by sticking him in the lineup every day to find out.

Pitchers

A.J. Achter RHP

Born: 8/27/88   Age: 26   Bats: R   Throws: R   Height: 6'5"   Weight: 205

YEAR	TEAM	LVL	AGE	W	L	SV	G	GS	IP	H	HR	BB	K	BB/9	K/9	GB%	BABIP	WHIP	ERA	FIP	FRA	WARP
2012	BLT	A	23	3	1	0	18	1	40	33	5	12	49	2.7	11.0	30%	.298	1.12	2.47	3.50	3.50	0.8
2012	FTM	A+	23	2	1	6	19	0	34¹	21	0	3	37	0.8	9.7	30%	.236	0.70	0.79	1.50	2.52	1.0
2013	NBR	AA	24	2	0	3	25	0	36²	28	3	19	36	4.7	8.8	36%	.258	1.28	2.21	4.06	4.84	0.1
2013	ROC	AAA	24	1	0	0	16	0	23²	17	4	14	20	5.3	7.6	30%	.210	1.31	3.04	5.49	5.83	0.0
2014	ROC	AAA	25	4	4	6	40	0	72	44	4	24	69	3.0	8.6	34%	.220	0.94	2.38	3.25	4.20	0.8
2014	MIN	MLB	25	1	0	0	7	0	11	14	2	3	5	2.5	4.1	32%	.308	1.55	3.27	5.43	6.12	-0.1
2015	*MIN*	*MLB*	*26*	*2*	*2*	*1*	*30*	*4*	*66*	*66*	*8*	*28*	*56*	*3.8*	*7.6*	*35%*	*.297*	*1.42*	*4.51*	*4.83*	*4.90*	*0.3*

Breakout: 12%   Improve: 17%   Collapse: 0%   Attrition: 12%   MLB: 22%   Comparables: *Miguel Socolovich, Preston Guilmet, Robert Manuel*

The son of a Vikings draftee, Achter is a former 46th-round pick who came out of nowhere last year to post solid numbers in the Rochester 'pen and earn a September call-up. An extreme fly-ball pitcher, Achter uses a decent slider, changeup and cutter to mask his low-velocity four-seamer, but anything he leaves out over the plate in The Show is liable to wind up in the bleachers. There's little about Achter to differentiate him from any other candidate for low-leverage relief work, so there's no guarantee he'll ever see Target Field again. Then again, A.J.'s father was cut before the end of his first Vikings training camp, so when it comes to family bragging rights he's already playing with house money.

Jason Adam RHP

Born: 8/4/91   Age: 23   Bats: R   Throws: R   Height: 6'4"   Weight: 225

YEAR	TEAM	LVL	AGE	W	L	SV	G	GS	IP	H	HR	BB	K	BB/9	K/9	GB%	BABIP	WHIP	ERA	FIP	FRA	WARP
2012	WIL	A+	20	7	12	0	27	27	158	148	18	36	123	2.1	7.0	46%	.284	1.16	3.53	4.24	4.82	0.1
2013	NWA	AA	21	8	11	0	26	26	144	153	12	54	126	3.4	7.9	42%	.328	1.44	5.19	3.83	4.72	1.1
2014	NWA	AA	22	4	8	0	19	18	98¹	107	9	30	89	2.7	8.1	42%	.332	1.39	5.03	3.57	4.37	1.1
2014	OMA	AAA	22	1	1	0	8	0	15¹	17	0	4	11	2.3	6.5	44%	.354	1.37	2.35	3.63	3.46	0.3
2015	*MIN*	*MLB*	*23*	*5*	*8*	*0*	*19*	*19*	*103*	*125*	*13*	*39*	*64*	*3.4*	*5.6*	*42%*	*.319*	*1.59*	*5.69*	*5.36*	*6.18*	*-0.8*

Breakout: 0%   Improve: 0%   Collapse: 0%   Attrition: 0%   MLB: 0%   Comparables: *Kyle Lobstein, Anthony Swarzak, Stolmy Pimentel*

Minnesota's return for Josh Willingham, Adam is a low-risk, full-bodied innings horse with mundane stuff. He avoids ball four but doesn't generate much swing-and-miss, and average command of his low-90s fastball, curveball and changeup leads to frequent hard contact. There was a time when Adam's low walk rate would have set hearts aflutter in the Twins' front office, but with more high-octane talents like Jose Berrios, Alex Meyer and Kohl Stewart in the pipeline, the big Kansan is more likely to find work in long relief than the back of the rotation.

Jose Berrios RHP

Born: 5/27/94   Age: 21   Bats: R   Throws: R   Height: 6'0"   Weight: 187

YEAR	TEAM	LVL	AGE	W	L	SV	G	GS	IP	H	HR	BB	K	BB/9	K/9	GB%	BABIP	WHIP	ERA	FIP	FRA	WARP
2013	CDR	A	19	7	7	0	19	19	103²	105	6	40	100	3.5	8.7	45%	.330	1.40	3.99	3.58	4.69	1.5
2014	FTM	A+	20	9	3	0	16	16	96¹	78	4	23	109	2.1	10.2	38%	.297	1.05	1.96	2.51	3.33	2.1
2014	NBR	AA	20	3	4	0	8	8	40²	33	2	12	28	2.7	6.2	45%	.261	1.11	3.54	3.65	4.41	0.6
2015	*MIN*	*MLB*	*21*	*6*	*8*	*0*	*20*	*20*	*106¹*	*115*	*11*	*45*	*84*	*3.8*	*7.1*	*40%*	*.316*	*1.51*	*4.85*	*4.77*	*5.28*	*0.1*

Breakout: 0%   Improve: 0%   Collapse: 0%   Attrition: 0%   MLB: 0%   Comparables: *Jarrod Parker, Carlos Martinez, Drew Hutchison*

Berrios began last season as a teenager and continued his blazing ascent, racking up more than a strikeout per inning in High-A before holding his own through nine starts in the high minors. His stuff—a fastball that sits comfortably in the mid-90s, two breaking balls and a baffling changeup—is top shelf, but mound presence and makeup is what helps him stand out. Berrios pitches with a chip on his shoulder and continually challenges hitters; he doesn't believe he can be beaten, and rarely is. Listed at six feet flat, he doesn't generate many groundballs but maintains plus velocity over multiple innings. Berrios should open the year as a 20-year-old in Double-A, and if he continues to dominate could be in line for a September call-up.

Nick Burdi RHP

Born: 1/19/93   Age: 22   Bats: R   Throws: R   Height: 6'5"   Weight: 215

YEAR	TEAM	LVL	AGE	W	L	SV	G	GS	IP	H	HR	BB	K	BB/9	K/9	GB%	BABIP	WHIP	ERA	FIP	FRA	WARP
2014	CDR	A	21	0	0	5	13	0	13	8	0	8	26	5.5	18.0	55%	.400	1.23	4.15	1.33	2.50	0.4
2015	*MIN*	*MLB*	*22*	*2*	*1*	*1*	*34*	*0*	*34¹*	*32*	*3*	*17*	*38*	*4.4*	*10.1*	*46%*	*.321*	*1.42*	*4.12*	*4.13*	*4.48*	*0.3*

Breakout: 0%   Improve: 0%   Collapse: 0%   Attrition: 0%   MLB: 0%   Comparables: *Stephen Pryor, Tommy Kahnle, Drew Storen*

The Twins snagged the Louisville closer in the second round of last year's draft and the big right-hander was dominant during his brief pro debut, striking out more than half the righties who dared step in against him. Burdi's fastball can reach triple digits, and when he can command it alongside his sharp-breaking slider, hitters don't have a snowball's chance. His high-effort delivery limits him to the bullpen, but if he can make mincemeat of Double-A batters next year, he should be working in high-leverage situations at Target Field by 2016.

Jared Burton RHP

Born: 6/2/81   Age: 34   Bats: R   Throws: R   Height: 6'5"   Weight: 225

YEAR	TEAM	LVL	AGE	W	L	SV	G	GS	IP	H	HR	BB	K	BB/9	K/9	GB%	BABIP	WHIP	ERA	FIP	FRA	WARP
2012	MIN	MLB	31	3	2	5	64	0	62	41	5	16	55	2.3	8.0	48%	.220	0.92	2.18	3.34	3.88	0.9
2013	MIN	MLB	32	2	9	2	71	0	66	61	6	22	61	3.0	8.3	45%	.294	1.26	3.82	3.64	3.89	0.7
2014	MIN	MLB	33	3	5	3	68	0	64	58	6	25	46	3.5	6.5	41%	.271	1.30	4.36	4.25	4.73	0.3
2015	*MIN*	*MLB*	*34*	*3*	*1*	*1*	*58*	*0*	*55*	*53*	*5*	*20*	*46*	*3.2*	*7.5*	*44%*	*.291*	*1.32*	*4.02*	*4.32*	*4.37*	*0.5*

Breakout: 20%   Improve: 37%   Collapse: 27%   Attrition: 9%   MLB: 75%   Comparables: *Scott Eyre, Steve Karsay, Tyler Walker*

Middle relievers are nothing if not slaves to small sample sizes. Case in point: Burton, who once again threw 60 innings with essentially the same quality stuff he's always displayed, but who saw his walk and strikeout rates drift in the wrong direction. If a starter experiences similar struggles over a nine-start stretch, he still has 20 or so games to right the ship before his full-season numbers are judged. Not Burton, who saw his option declined at the end of the year. Armed with an excellent changeup that proofs him against lefty batters, don't be surprised if Burton is once again a seventh-inning asset this year.

Logan Darnell LHP
Born: 2/2/89   Age: 26   Bats: L   Throws: L   Height: 6'2"   Weight: 210

YEAR	TEAM	LVL	AGE	W	L	SV	G	GS	IP	H	HR	BB	K	BB/9	K/9	GB%	BABIP	WHIP	ERA	FIP	FRA	WARP
2012	NBR	AA	23	11	12	0	28	28	156	193	22	47	98	2.7	5.7	49%	.331	1.54	5.08	4.76	5.90	-0.8
2013	NBR	AA	24	6	6	0	15	15	96²	96	4	23	77	2.1	7.2	54%	.321	1.23	2.61	3.23	3.80	1.5
2013	ROC	AAA	24	4	4	0	12	11	57	63	5	22	43	3.5	6.8	49%	.339	1.49	4.26	4.20	5.18	0.2
2014	ROC	AAA	25	7	6	0	23	19	115	108	16	49	90	3.8	7.0	49%	.270	1.37	3.60	4.91	5.58	-0.1
2014	MIN	MLB	25	0	2	0	7	4	24	31	5	8	22	3.0	8.2	48%	.342	1.62	7.12	5.16	5.41	0.0
2015	*MIN*	*MLB*	*26*	*6*	*9*	*0*	*21*	*21*	*118*	*142*	*17*	*43*	*70*	*3.3*	*5.3*	*48%*	*.315*	*1.57*	*5.57*	*5.54*	*6.06*	*-0.8*

Breakout: 16%   Improve: 25%   Collapse: 10%   Attrition: 28%   MLB: 38%   *Comparables: Anthony Ortega, Chris Seddon, David Pauley*

Darnell made four starts over several trips to Minnesota last summer and didn't do much to convince the Twins' brass that he should make many more. His four-pitch arsenal and middling velocity don't stand out, and with high octane arms like Alex Meyer and Jose Berrios ready to make a splash, there won't be room for him in the future rotation unless things go badly wrong. On the plus side, Darnell continues to make same-side batters mutter to themselves in Triple-A, so he could eventually slot into the bullpen and become the new Brian Duensing.

Brian Duensing   LHP
Born: 2/22/83   Age: 32   Bats: L   Throws: L   Height: 6'0"   Weight: 205

YEAR	TEAM	LVL	AGE	W	L	SV	G	GS	IP	H	HR	BB	K	BB/9	K/9	GB%	BABIP	WHIP	ERA	FIP	FRA	WARP
2012	MIN	MLB	29	4	12	0	55	11	109	126	10	27	69	2.2	5.7	48%	.319	1.40	5.12	3.77	4.49	1.2
2013	MIN	MLB	30	6	2	1	73	0	61	68	4	22	56	3.2	8.3	43%	.348	1.48	3.98	3.27	3.13	1.1
2014	MIN	MLB	31	3	3	0	62	0	54¹	52	6	20	33	3.3	5.5	46%	.272	1.33	3.31	4.54	4.84	0.1
2015	*MIN*	*MLB*	*32*	*2*	*2*	*0*	*27*	*5*	*46²*	*53*	*5*	*14*	*32*	*2.7*	*6.2*	*47%*	*.315*	*1.43*	*4.61*	*4.56*	*5.01*	*0.2*

Breakout: 18%   Improve: 46%   Collapse: 19%   Attrition: 9%   MLB: 77%   *Comparables: Hisashi Iwakuma, Rodrigo Lopez, Kevin Millwood*

Speaking of which, Duensing should be lauded for earning the organization's Community Service Award last year for his charitable endeavors off the field, but needs to temper the extreme generosity he also shows to right-handed batters. Last season was the latest chapter in Duensing's slow, inexorable devolution from starter to swingman to middle-man to LOOGY, as the longtime Twin dominated lefty batters, holding them to a .242/.282/.305 line. Righties, however, sprinted to the plate to get in their hacks, pounding him to the tune of .264/.352/.491 and walking nearly as often as they struck out. Duensing obviously needs to be spotted carefully to provide value in a big-league bullpen, and with his walk and strikeout rates moving dangerously close to one another, he may soon struggle to stay in The Show in any role.

Casey Fien   RHP
Born: 10/21/83   Age: 31   Bats: R   Throws: R   Height: 6'2"   Weight: 205

YEAR	TEAM	LVL	AGE	W	L	SV	G	GS	IP	H	HR	BB	K	BB/9	K/9	GB%	BABIP	WHIP	ERA	FIP	FRA	WARP
2012	ROC	AAA	28	2	5	9	33	0	46	39	5	14	42	2.7	8.2	32%	.268	1.15	4.30	3.66	4.64	0.1
2012	MIN	MLB	28	2	1	0	35	0	35	25	3	9	32	2.3	8.2	26%	.229	0.97	2.06	3.19	3.76	0.4
2013	MIN	MLB	29	5	2	0	73	0	62	51	9	12	73	1.7	10.6	40%	.280	1.02	3.92	3.19	3.65	0.8
2014	MIN	MLB	30	5	6	1	73	0	63¹	64	7	10	51	1.4	7.2	35%	.297	1.17	3.98	3.46	3.19	1.4
2015	*MIN*	*MLB*	*31*	*3*	*1*	*1*	*54*	*0*	*53¹*	*53*	*7*	*13*	*46*	*2.2*	*7.8*	*37%*	*.296*	*1.24*	*3.89*	*4.33*	*4.23*	*0.6*

Breakout: 14%   Improve: 21%   Collapse: 18%   Attrition: 13%   MLB: 47%   *Comparables: Scott Strickland, Mike Adams, Vladimir Nunez*

Unlike talk-show hosts, relievers advance in their career by being tabbed to work ever later in the evening. By that measure Fien is nearing the pinnacle of his profession, as the cutter specialist has become the local news lead-in for late-night funny man Glen Perkins. Fien doesn't have overpowering stuff, and his strikeout rate is often nothing to write home about, but he is effective against both righties and lefties, would rather swallow glass than issue a walk and keeps the ball in the yard more than you'd expect for someone with his sky-high fly-ball rate. The Twins have focused on flame-throwing college relievers in recent drafts, so his days as a set-up man are likely numbered, but Fien remains one of the rare consistently productive middle relievers in the game.

Kyle Gibson   RHP
Born: 10/23/87   Age: 27   Bats: R   Throws: R   Height: 6'6"   Weight: 220

YEAR	TEAM	LVL	AGE	W	L	SV	G	GS	IP	H	HR	BB	K	BB/9	K/9	GB%	BABIP	WHIP	ERA	FIP	FRA	WARP
2013	ROC	AAA	25	7	5	0	17	17	101²	85	5	33	87	2.9	7.7	57%	.279	1.16	2.92	3.11	4.08	1.4
2013	MIN	MLB	25	2	4	0	10	10	51	69	7	20	29	3.5	5.1	51%	.350	1.75	6.53	5.19	5.48	-0.2
2014	MIN	MLB	26	13	12	0	31	31	179¹	178	12	57	107	2.9	5.4	57%	.287	1.31	4.47	3.82	4.83	0.9
2015	*MIN*	*MLB*	*27*	*8*	*10*	*0*	*28*	*28*	*146¹*	*159*	*13*	*47*	*100*	*2.9*	*6.2*	*54%*	*.309*	*1.41*	*4.41*	*4.40*	*4.80*	*1.0*

Breakout: 32%   Improve: 61%   Collapse: 12%   Attrition: 24%   MLB: 88%   *Comparables: David Huff, Armando Galarraga, Jeff Niemann*

A former top pick whose arrival was delayed by Tommy John surgery, Gibson worked his first full season in the Twins' rotation with mixed results. Tall and solid, Gibson doesn't have plus velocity, so he pitches to contact, working his sinker around the edges of the zone to induce weak ground-ball contact and deploying an improved changeup that helps keep lefties off-balance. But when he catches too much of the plate he can get tattooed, leading to occasional disasterpiece outings. He's competitive and fields his position well, and if Gibson can find a way to work in a few more offspeed pitches and up his strikeout rate, he could settle in as a reasonable innings sponge.

Stephen Gonsalves   LHP

Born: 7/8/94   Age: 20   Bats: L   Throws: L   Height: 6'5"   Weight: 190

YEAR	TEAM	LVL	AGE	W	L	SV	G	GS	IP	H	HR	BB	K	BB/9	K/9	GB%	BABIP	WHIP	ERA	FIP	FRA	WARP
2014	CDR	A	19	2	3	0	8	8	36²	31	1	11	44	2.7	10.8	36%	.326	1.15	3.19	2.50	3.32	0.9
2015	MIN	MLB	20	2	4	0	10	10	44	49	5	24	34	4.8	6.9	42%	.319	1.66	5.44	5.32	5.91	-0.2

Breakout: 0%   Improve: 0%   Collapse: 0%   Attrition: 0%   MLB: 0%   Comparables: Trevor Cahill, Chris Tillman, Jenrry Mejia

He doesn't get as much press as the more high-profile arms in the Minnesota system, but don't sleep on Gonsalves. The Twins nabbed the California prep product when he slipped to the fourth round of the 2013 draft and have been rewarded with steady progress and the promise of better things to come. Long and lean, Gonsalves is growing into his frame and posted a 4:1 strikeout-to-walk ratio last year as a teenager in the Midwest League. His breaking ball is still on back order, but his fastball can reach the low-90s and his changeup flashes plus, which helped him hold righty batters to a .220/.284/.292 line. The Twins will stretch him out in the low minors this year, and if Gonsalves continues to progress he'll take a big leap up the prospect charts.

J.R. Graham   RHP

Born: 1/14/90   Age: 25   Bats: R   Throws: R   Height: 6'0"   Weight: 195

YEAR	TEAM	LVL	AGE	W	L	SV	G	GS	IP	H	HR	BB	K	BB/9	K/9	GB%	BABIP	WHIP	ERA	FIP	FRA	WARP
2012	LYN	A+	22	9	1	0	17	17	102²	88	6	17	68	1.5	6.0	59%	.269	1.02	2.63	3.38	4.81	0.4
2012	MIS	AA	22	3	1	0	9	9	45¹	35	2	17	42	3.4	8.3	56%	.266	1.15	3.18	3.12	4.09	0.7
2013	MIS	AA	23	1	3	0	8	8	35²	39	0	10	28	2.5	7.1	68%	.348	1.37	4.04	2.18	3.14	0.7
2014	MIS	AA	24	1	5	0	27	19	71¹	79	2	26	50	3.3	6.3	53%	.328	1.47	5.55	3.50	4.47	1.1
2015	MIN	MLB	25	3	4	0	11	11	53	63	6	20	32	3.4	5.4	54%	.318	1.56	5.20	5.12	5.66	-0.1

Breakout: 17%   Improve: 23%   Collapse: 7%   Attrition: 28%   MLB: 33%   Comparables: Graham Godfrey, Cesar Valdez, Rob Scahill

Behold the margins for an undersized starting pitching prospect's starting pitching prospects. Two seasons ago, when Graham first reached Double-A, he appeared about a year away from the majors. He has since missed most of 2013 due to a shoulder injury, returned to Double-A for a third stint and taken additional time off due to arm problems. The Braves used Graham in the bullpen during the season's final month, and given how things have transpired, that's probably where his future is, provided his joints can handle even that workload. The Twins Rule 5'd him, which could look savvy in a couple of months, but it's hell on us for purposes of this book; he may be a Brave again by the time you read this.

Phil Hughes   RHP

Born: 6/24/86   Age: 29   Bats: R   Throws: R   Height: 6'5"   Weight: 240

YEAR	TEAM	LVL	AGE	W	L	SV	G	GS	IP	H	HR	BB	K	BB/9	K/9	GB%	BABIP	WHIP	ERA	FIP	FRA	WARP
2012	NYA	MLB	26	16	13	0	32	32	191¹	196	35	46	165	2.2	7.8	33%	.286	1.26	4.23	4.52	4.45	2.0
2013	NYA	MLB	27	4	14	0	30	29	145²	170	24	42	121	2.6	7.5	32%	.324	1.46	5.19	4.52	4.78	0.8
2014	MIN	MLB	28	16	10	0	32	32	209²	221	16	16	186	0.7	8.0	38%	.324	1.13	3.52	2.68	3.16	4.7
2015	MIN	MLB	29	9	10	0	29	29	165	177	19	38	137	2.0	7.5	35%	.313	1.30	4.16	4.17	4.52	1.5

Breakout: 19%   Improve: 43%   Collapse: 22%   Attrition: 5%   MLB: 96%   Comparables: Javier Vazquez, Dan Haren, Jered Weaver

Escape From New York 2: The Porch Lengthening was a blockbuster hit last summer, as the move from cozy Yankee Stadium to more spacious Target Field did Hughes a world of good. One of baseball's most extreme fly-ball pitchers, the change of venue of course helped him avoid cheap home runs, but, perhaps more importantly, it allowed him to pitch without fear. Hughes pounded the zone like never before, added a sinker to his arsenal and ditched his slider to concentrate on his curveball. Results: A few more groundballs, a continued solid strikeout rate and a walk rate under 2 percent, which clocked in as the second-lowest for a qualifying pitcher in this century. None of this looks the least bit flukish, and by signing an ace at the bargain price of $8 million per year through 2016, the Twins look to have pulled off a rare free agent coup.

Trevor May   RHP

Born: 9/23/89   Age: 25   Bats: R   Throws: R   Height: 6'5"   Weight: 215

YEAR	TEAM	LVL	AGE	W	L	SV	G	GS	IP	H	HR	BB	K	BB/9	K/9	GB%	BABIP	WHIP	ERA	FIP	FRA	WARP
2012	REA	AA	22	10	13	0	28	28	149²	139	22	78	151	4.7	9.1	43%	.294	1.45	4.87	4.88	5.47	0.3
2013	NBR	AA	23	9	9	0	27	27	151²	149	14	67	159	4.0	9.4	40%	.328	1.42	4.51	3.91	4.09	2.3
2014	ROC	AAA	24	8	6	0	18	18	98¹	75	4	39	94	3.6	8.6	38%	.270	1.16	2.84	3.16	4.29	1.5
2014	MIN	MLB	24	2	3	0	10	9	45²	59	7	22	44	4.3	8.7	39%	.377	1.77	7.88	4.80	6.17	-0.2
2015	MIN	MLB	25	6	9	0	22	22	119	122	14	62	116	4.7	8.8	38%	.317	1.55	4.94	4.86	5.37	0.0

Breakout: 25%   Improve: 38%   Collapse: 16%   Attrition: 38%   MLB: 60%   Comparables: Andy Oliver, Neil Ramirez, Chris Withrow

May fulfilled the dream that many have dreamed but precious few have lived when he made his big-league debut last August. That he walked seven Athletics in two innings doesn't diminish the accomplishment, but when viewed alongside his other seven starts down the stretch, it gives us some indication of May's future. The big right-hander has an ideal starter's frame, and while his stuff, especially his plus changeup, can sometimes look dominant, he has never commanded it very well. He can be a nibbler, leading to high pitch counts and short outings, and his extreme fly-ball tendencies will make him prone to bouts of gopheritis. The sum of those parts is a pitcher who can take 30 inconsistent turns at the back of a rotation, a job May will apply for this spring.

Alex Meyer   RHP

Born: 1/3/90   Age: 25   Bats: R   Throws: R   Height: 6'9"   Weight: 220

YEAR	TEAM	LVL	AGE	W	L	SV	G	GS	IP	H	HR	BB	K	BB/9	K/9	GB%	BABIP	WHIP	ERA	FIP	FRA	WARP
2012	HAG	A	22	7	4	0	18	18	90	68	4	34	107	3.4	10.7	54%	.292	1.13	3.10	3.01	3.54	2.4
2012	POT	A+	22	3	2	0	7	7	39	29	2	11	32	2.5	7.4	53%	.252	1.03	2.31	3.41	4.08	0.6
2013	NBR	AA	23	4	3	0	13	13	70	60	3	29	84	3.7	10.8	61%	.317	1.27	3.21	2.85	3.79	1.4
2014	ROC	AAA	24	7	7	0	27	27	130¹	116	10	64	153	4.4	10.6	49%	.321	1.38	3.52	3.66	3.74	2.8
2015	MIN	MLB	25	6	7	0	21	21	103	100	10	47	103	4.1	9.0	50%	.314	1.43	4.22	4.34	4.59	1.0

Breakout: 24%   Improve: 36%   Collapse: 17%   Attrition: 39%   MLB: 59%   Comparables: Nate Karns, Dellin Betances, Scott Barnes

Last year the towering Meyer spent a full season lobbing thunderbolts and racking up whiffs in Triple-A, yet the same nagging questions continue to nip at his heels. His stuff can be filthy, featuring a lively fastball that can reach triple digits, a high-80s breaker and an improving changeup. Yet Meyer still struggles with his mechanics and can lose control of his offerings, leading to a walk rate that climbed above 11 percent last year. The lazy comparison is to Randy Johnson, who didn't master his delivery and cut down on free passes until he turned 29. But for every one of those there are three dozen John Axfords, who never consistently find the plate but provide occasional dominance in the bullpen. Meyer will be 25 on Opening Day, so it's time to put him in the big-league rotation and see what the sorting hat says.

Tommy Milone   LHP
Born: 2/16/87   Age: 28   Bats: L   Throws: L   Height: 6'0"   Weight: 205

YEAR	TEAM	LVL	AGE	W	L	SV	G	GS	IP	H	HR	BB	K	BB/9	K/9	GB%	BABIP	WHIP	ERA	FIP	FRA	WARP
2012	OAK	MLB	25	13	10	0	31	31	190	207	24	36	137	1.7	6.5	40%	.310	1.28	3.74	3.88	4.18	2.0
2013	SAC	AAA	26	0	0	0	2	2	10¹	16	0	1	15	0.9	13.1	52%	.516	1.65	1.74	0.96	2.10	0.5
2013	OAK	MLB	26	12	9	0	28	26	156¹	160	25	39	126	2.2	7.3	36%	.284	1.27	4.14	4.33	4.28	0.9
2014	SAC	AAA	27	1	1	0	4	4	21	28	5	9	17	3.9	7.3	46%	.343	1.76	6.43	6.46	6.10	0.0
2014	OAK	MLB	27	6	3	0	16	16	96¹	91	12	26	61	2.4	5.7	39%	.262	1.21	3.55	4.45	4.38	0.5
2014	MIN	MLB	27	0	1	0	6	5	21²	37	4	11	14	4.6	5.8	46%	.393	2.22	7.06	5.93	5.96	-0.2
2015	MIN	MLB	28	7	9	0	22	22	131	149	16	29	101	2.0	6.9	39%	.318	1.36	4.57	4.36	4.97	0.5

Breakout: 18%   Improve: 45%   Collapse: 17%   Attrition: 28%   MLB: 80%   Comparables: Jo-Jo Reyes, Jason Vargas, Boof Bonser

Milone is Alex Meyer's reverse-doppelganger—a short, lefty junkballer who doesn't strike anyone out but has proven he can survive at the back of a rotation by keeping hitters guessing and avoiding ball four. Last year he posted 16 reasonably effective starts in Oakland, but the aspirational A's, despite their reputation for not selling jeans, didn't find Milone sexy enough. They demoted him and then shipped him to Minnesota, the franchise most in need of exactly the type of short-term veteran mediocrity Milone can provide. He didn't pitch well for the Twins, lost a month to a sore neck and enters the year wearing a big question mark, but as a low-priced option with a track record of success, he's a cut above the Kevin Correias of the world.

Ricky Nolasco   RHP
Born: 12/13/82   Age: 32   Bats: R   Throws: R   Height: 6'2"   Weight: 225

YEAR	TEAM	LVL	AGE	W	L	SV	G	GS	IP	H	HR	BB	K	BB/9	K/9	GB%	BABIP	WHIP	ERA	FIP	FRA	WARP
2012	MIA	MLB	29	12	13	0	31	31	191	214	18	47	125	2.2	5.9	49%	.310	1.37	4.48	3.92	4.26	1.2
2013	MIA	MLB	30	5	8	0	18	18	112¹	112	11	25	90	2.0	7.2	43%	.299	1.22	3.85	3.47	4.12	0.4
2013	LAN	MLB	30	8	3	0	16	15	87	83	6	21	75	2.2	7.8	46%	.298	1.20	3.52	3.12	3.72	1.8
2014	MIN	MLB	31	6	12	0	27	27	159	203	22	38	115	2.2	6.5	44%	.351	1.52	5.38	4.32	4.88	0.4
2015	MIN	MLB	32	8	10	0	24	24	147	174	18	32	105	2.0	6.4	45%	.325	1.40	4.88	4.49	5.30	0.0

Breakout: 13%   Improve: 33%   Collapse: 39%   Attrition: 7%   MLB: 81%   Comparables: Joe Blanton, Aaron Harang, James Shields

The Twins signed Nolasco to the richest free-agent contract in club history last year so he could provide them with quality veteran innings, but what they received was one adjective and a large quantity of noun less than they had hoped for. Nolasco struggled mightily early in the season and early in games, finally hitting the disabled list in July after admitting a sore elbow had affected his velocity and ability to get loose since spring. After resting a month, Nolasco returned with his normal low-90s velocity and provided his normal fourth-starter results. His final numbers look woeful, but a healthier Nolasco should be able to improve on them significantly this year. Whether such consistent mediocrity is worth what the Twins are paying is a separate question, but as they say in the Minnesota front office: "Hey, how 'bout that Phil Hughes signing, huh?"

Lester Oliveros   RHP
Born: 5/28/88   Age: 27   Bats: R   Throws: R   Height: 6'0"   Weight: 235

YEAR	TEAM	LVL	AGE	W	L	SV	G	GS	IP	H	HR	BB	K	BB/9	K/9	GB%	BABIP	WHIP	ERA	FIP	FRA	WARP
2012	NBR	AA	24	1	1	2	13	0	19	10	0	7	16	3.3	7.6	45%	.213	0.89	1.42	2.62	3.91	0.2
2012	ROC	AAA	24	1	2	6	19	0	29¹	24	2	8	35	2.5	10.7	39%	.306	1.09	3.07	2.48	3.10	0.7
2012	MIN	MLB	24	0	0	0	1	0	1²	1	0	1	1	5.4	5.4	20%	.200	1.20	5.40	3.65	3.99	0.0
2014	NBR	AA	26	3	1	12	26	0	30¹	17	0	14	36	4.2	10.7	46%	.236	1.02	0.89	2.66	3.39	0.6
2014	ROC	AAA	26	1	2	6	24	0	35¹	27	0	13	52	3.3	13.2	49%	.333	1.13	2.29	1.60	1.58	1.6
2014	MIN	MLB	26	0	1	0	7	0	6¹	6	2	3	5	4.3	7.1	32%	.235	1.42	7.11	7.11	7.67	-0.1
2015	MIN	MLB	27	2	1	0	37	0	49¹	46	4	23	52	4.1	9.4	45%	.311	1.40	3.93	4.01	4.28	0.5

Breakout: 16%   Improve: 28%   Collapse: 24%   Attrition: 32%   MLB: 63%   Comparables: Cory Gearrin, Jeff Stevens, Kam Mickolio

After losing most of 2013 to Tommy John surgery, Oliveros cut a wide swath through the upper minors last year and may have pitched his way into a big-league job. Short but powerfully built, Oliveras can rush it up in the mid-90s, and his slider generated a lot of awkward swings and a strikeout per inning last year. For all his fastball sizzle, Oliveros needs to hack a few chunks out of his oversized walk rate and improve his fastball command. If he can do so, he'll be the first in a new wave of hard-throwing relief prospects to earn a role in the comparatively soft-tossing Minnesota bullpen.

Mike Pelfrey   RHP
Born: 1/14/84   Age: 31   Bats: R   Throws: R   Height: 6'7"   Weight: 250

YEAR	TEAM	LVL	AGE	W	L	SV	G	GS	IP	H	HR	BB	K	BB/9	K/9	GB%	BABIP	WHIP	ERA	FIP	FRA	WARP
2012	NYN	MLB	28	0	0	0	3	3	19²	24	0	4	13	1.8	5.9	54%	.353	1.42	2.29	2.42	2.42	0.7
2013	MIN	MLB	29	5	13	0	29	29	152²	184	13	53	101	3.1	6.0	45%	.337	1.55	5.19	4.02	4.13	1.8
2014	ROC	AAA	30	1	0	0	2	2	10	9	0	3	3	2.7	2.7	41%	.250	1.20	0.90	3.96	4.69	0.1
2014	MIN	MLB	30	0	3	0	5	5	23²	29	5	18	10	6.8	3.8	45%	.286	1.99	7.99	7.60	8.05	-0.6
2015	MIN	MLB	31	2	4	0	9	9	49¹	59	5	18	27	3.2	4.9	47%	.318	1.56	5.20	5.04	5.65	-0.1

Breakout: 8%   Improve: 43%   Collapse: 21%   Attrition: 20%   MLB: 85%   Comparables: Jason Marquis, Jon Garland, Jeff Suppan

Yet another medium-risk, low-reward free-agent signing, Pelfrey proved he had both recovered from Tommy John surgery and was merely a stone's throw away from once again almost-but-not-quite being a somewhat-below-average big-league starter in 2013. The Twins duly re-upped him for two years, just in time for the longtime innings muncher to lose his appetite. After five disastrous starts, Pelfrey came up lame with a groin injury and then had surgery on his elbow, missing the remainder of the season. (The nerve! No, really, that's the part of his arm that required fixing.) He's slated to be healthy by spring training, but with the Twins ready to graduate a number of promising young fireballers into the rotation, Pelfrey will most likely earn his millions in low-leverage long relief.

Glen Perkins   LHP

Born: 3/2/83   Age: 32   Bats: L   Throws: L   Height: 6'0"   Weight: 205

YEAR	TEAM	LVL	AGE	W	L	SV	G	GS	IP	H	HR	BB	K	BB/9	K/9	GB%	BABIP	WHIP	ERA	FIP	FRA	WARP
2012	MIN	MLB	29	3	1	16	70	0	70¹	57	8	16	78	2.0	10.0	44%	.278	1.04	2.56	3.12	3.55	1.2
2013	MIN	MLB	30	2	0	36	61	0	62²	43	5	15	77	2.2	11.1	37%	.271	0.93	2.30	2.52	3.21	1.2
2014	MIN	MLB	31	4	3	34	63	0	61²	62	7	11	66	1.6	9.6	36%	.316	1.18	3.65	3.13	3.83	1.0
2015	MIN	MLB	32	3	1	30	53	0	52¹	53	5	14	50	2.4	8.7	44%	.320	1.29	3.94	3.78	4.29	0.5

Breakout: 23%   Improve: 40%   Collapse: 16%   Attrition: 12%   MLB: 64%   *Comparables: Buddy Carlyle, Justin Miller, Doug Slaten*

So Glen, let's talk. Knowing that you understand and keep track of your FIP—and, just as importantly, know what you can and can't do with that information—obviously makes you a favorite around these parts. We also love that you're a great Twitter follow, you've been known to close out games with your fly down, you earned an All-Star save at your home stadium in your home town last summer, you signed a club-friendly extension to pitch in front of your family and friends for two additional years and you quietly remain one of the game's better closers. But dude, when your arm hurts, you gotta tell somebody. Trying to pitch through a sore elbow, like you did in September before finally copping to the pain and getting some needed rest, just isn't cool. We understand how much stoicism is valued in the Upper Midwest—some of us are from there—but you can't risk greater injury and the possibility of not being a force on the mound the next time those September saves are actually meaningful for the Twins. BP out.

Ryan Pressly   RHP

Born: 12/15/88   Age: 26   Bats: R   Throws: R   Height: 6'3"   Weight: 205

YEAR	TEAM	LVL	AGE	W	L	SV	G	GS	IP	H	HR	BB	K	BB/9	K/9	GB%	BABIP	WHIP	ERA	FIP	FRA	WARP
2012	SLM	A+	23	5	3	0	20	12	76	86	9	26	61	3.1	7.2	50%	.329	1.47	6.28	4.50	5.88	-0.4
2012	PME	AA	23	2	2	0	14	0	27²	23	2	10	21	3.3	6.8	45%	.262	1.19	2.93	3.71	4.41	0.3
2013	MIN	MLB	24	3	3	0	49	0	76²	71	5	27	49	3.2	5.8	45%	.282	1.28	3.87	3.70	4.63	0.2
2014	ROC	AAA	25	1	4	6	35	0	60¹	55	1	21	63	3.1	9.4	44%	.318	1.26	2.98	2.58	3.19	1.4
2014	MIN	MLB	25	2	0	0	25	0	28¹	30	3	8	14	2.5	4.4	50%	.281	1.34	2.86	4.50	4.45	0.2
2015	MIN	MLB	26	3	3	0	30	7	70	80	8	30	42	3.9	5.4	47%	.307	1.57	5.18	5.32	5.63	-0.2

Breakout: 39%   Improve: 60%   Collapse: 13%   Attrition: 26%   MLB: 76%   *Comparables: Jim Johnson, John Koronka, Juan Gutierrez*

Pressly has found success in the Minnesota 'pen with an approach that could be described as Hippocratic. His stuff can resemble a power reliever, with a fastball that can reach the mid-90s, a power slider and a curve, but he doesn't rack up many strikeouts. Instead, Pressly does no harm with walks and keeps the ball in the yard, leading to solid run prevention despite sketchy peripherals. It's not a formula that you often see in high-leverage situations, but there's no reason Pressly can't continue to succeed in the middle innings.

Ervin Santana   RHP

Born: 12/12/82   Age: 32   Bats: R   Throws: R   Height: 6'2"   Weight: 185

YEAR	TEAM	LVL	AGE	W	L	SV	G	GS	IP	H	HR	BB	K	BB/9	K/9	GB%	BABIP	WHIP	ERA	FIP	FRA	WARP
2012	ANA	MLB	29	9	13	0	30	30	178	165	39	61	133	3.1	6.7	45%	.241	1.27	5.16	5.58	6.18	-1.6
2013	KCA	MLB	30	9	10	0	32	32	211	190	26	51	161	2.2	6.9	47%	.267	1.14	3.24	3.96	4.62	0.9
2014	ATL	MLB	31	14	10	0	31	31	196	193	16	63	179	2.9	8.2	45%	.319	1.31	3.95	3.36	4.05	1.3
2015	MIN	MLB	32	9	10	0	25	25	159²	165	21	52	123	2.9	6.9	43%	.294	1.36	4.48	4.85	4.87	0.7

Breakout: 15%   Improve: 40%   Collapse: 23%   Attrition: 6%   MLB: 76%   *Comparables: Gil Meche, Ted Lilly, Freddy Garcia*

Stranded on Qualifying Offer Island until mid-March, Santana was rescued by the Braves after they went searching for rotation help. While his ERA suggests he took a big step back from his breakout 2013 with Kansas City, his FIP rolls its eyes and sighs. The truth is, Santana was the same durable, steady no. 3 starter. He still leans on his fastball-slider combination, he still goes through stretches where his command evades him and he still has crazy hair. Unburdened of a qualifying offer, Santana showed just how much difference being a truly free agent makes by signing a four-year, $54 million contract with the Twins.

Kohl Stewart   RHP

Born: 10/7/94   Age: 20   Bats: R   Throws: R   Height: 6'3"   Weight: 195

YEAR	TEAM	LVL	AGE	W	L	SV	G	GS	IP	H	HR	BB	K	BB/9	K/9	GB%	BABIP	WHIP	ERA	FIP	FRA	WARP
2014	CDR	A	19	3	5	0	19	19	87²	75	4	24	62	2.5	6.4	57%	.270	1.14	2.59	3.73	5.26	0.2
2015	MIN	MLB	20	3	5	0	13	13	57	71	7	27	26	4.2	4.1	49%	.311	1.71	5.98	5.91	6.50	-0.5

Breakout: 0%   Improve: 0%   Collapse: 0%   Attrition: 0%   MLB: 0%   *Comparables: Jonathan Pettibone, Kyle Ryan, T.J. House*

Stewart didn't exactly dominate and posted mundane peripherals in his full-season debut, but scouts continue to file glowing reports. Competitive and athletic, Stewart turned down an offer to play quarterback for the Aggies, so his mound demeanor is pretty much a walking, talking "Don't Mess With Texas" sign. Blessed with a clean, repeatable delivery, he mixes in a curveball and changeup with his mid-90s fastball. While Stewart hasn't missed many bats as a pro, he focused on commanding his fastball last season and many expect his strikeout rate to rise as he starts to use his full, improving arsenal in game situations. More troubling are the episodes of shoulder soreness that have plagued him; the Twins don't expect this to be chronic, but any time a young starter comes up with a bum wing it's reason for concern. If Stewart can stay healthy and starts getting the results his stuff should support, he could grow into a very good second starter.

Anthony Swarzak   RHP

Born: 9/10/85   Age: 29   Bats: R   Throws: R   Height: 6'4"   Weight: 210

YEAR	TEAM	LVL	AGE	W	L	SV	G	GS	IP	H	HR	BB	K	BB/9	K/9	GB%	BABIP	WHIP	ERA	FIP	FRA	WARP
2012	MIN	MLB	26	3	6	0	44	5	96²	106	15	31	62	2.9	5.8	44%	.298	1.42	5.03	4.74	5.57	-0.1
2013	MIN	MLB	27	3	2	0	48	0	96	89	7	22	69	2.1	6.5	46%	.285	1.16	2.91	3.30	4.27	0.7
2014	MIN	MLB	28	3	2	0	50	4	86	100	5	28	47	2.9	4.9	45%	.319	1.49	4.60	3.80	4.65	0.6
2015	MIN	MLB	29	3	2	0	32	5	74²	86	8	22	46	2.7	5.5	41%	.312	1.44	4.68	4.70	5.09	0.2

Breakout: 29%   Improve: 43%   Collapse: 17%   Attrition: 16%   MLB: 76%   Comparables: Kameron Loe, Brad Thompson, Zach Miner

After a brief, exciting rendezvous with success in the bullpen, Swarzak's miniscule strikeout rate barged in on him and he was back to his old workaday self last year. The big right-hander is always a bad choice to help break in a catcher's mitt, which also makes him a bad choice to pitch high-leverage innings. Swarzak avoids walks, but it's virtually impossible to be an effective major-league pitcher when you strike out only 12.4 percent of the batters you face. Take comfort, Minnesota fans: you'll soon be able to revel in the sight of other Twins moundsmen blowing fastballs past overmatched hitters.

Caleb Thielbar   LHP

Born: 1/31/87   Age: 28   Bats: R   Throws: L   Height: 6'0"   Weight: 195

YEAR	TEAM	LVL	AGE	W	L	SV	G	GS	IP	H	HR	BB	K	BB/9	K/9	GB%	BABIP	WHIP	ERA	FIP	FRA	WARP
2012	FTM	A+	25	1	1	1	7	0	12¹	4	0	2	16	1.5	11.7	36%	.160	0.49	0.00	1.77	2.33	0.4
2012	NBR	AA	25	2	0	4	16	0	25	18	1	3	26	1.1	9.4	52%	.262	0.84	1.80	2.00	2.75	0.7
2012	ROC	AAA	25	3	1	1	25	1	40¹	42	5	16	32	3.6	7.1	44%	.298	1.44	3.57	4.45	5.96	-0.1
2013	ROC	AAA	26	1	1	1	17	0	26¹	27	1	8	34	2.7	11.6	44%	.371	1.33	3.76	2.14	2.58	0.9
2013	MIN	MLB	26	3	2	0	49	0	46	24	4	14	39	2.7	7.6	27%	.175	0.83	1.76	3.42	3.95	0.3
2014	MIN	MLB	27	2	1	0	54	0	47²	51	3	16	35	3.0	6.6	36%	.318	1.41	3.40	3.58	3.53	0.8
2015	MIN	MLB	28	2	1	0	37	0	44¹	45	4	15	35	3.0	7.1	40%	.303	1.37	4.30	4.24	4.67	0.3

Breakout: 25%   Improve: 41%   Collapse: 10%   Attrition: 22%   MLB: 61%   Comparables: Cory Wade, Clay Zavada, Royce Ring

No one expected Thielbar to duplicate his magical, BABIP-fueled 2013 performance, but in his second year in Minnesota he established himself as a dependable bullpen arm. Often deployed to face lefties but capable of retiring hitters of every flavor, Thielbar's success relies on sequencing, a deceptive delivery and a well-commanded fastball that sits in the upper-80s. His three off-speed pitches are nothing special but give hitters something else to think about during at-bats; afterwards, their thoughts are often occupied with figuring out how they were made to look so silly by a pitcher with such mundane stuff. The whole of Thielbar is greater than the sum of his parts, and that whole might just be good enough to build a long career in middle relief.

Lewis Thorpe   LHP

Born: 11/18/80   Age: 34   Bats: L   Throws: L   Height: 6'1"   Weight: 210

YEAR	TEAM	LVL	AGE	W	L	SV	G	GS	IP	H	HR	BB	K	BB/9	K/9	GB%	BABIP	WHIP	ERA	FIP	FRA	WARP
2014	CDR	A	18	3	2	0	16	16	71²	62	7	36	80	4.5	10.0	44%	.297	1.37	3.52	4.24	4.43	0.9
2015	MIN	MLB	19	3	5	0	12	12	53²	59	7	30	43	5.0	7.2	42%	.315	1.66	5.52	5.51	6.00	-0.2

Breakout: 0%   Improve: 0%   Collapse: 0%   Attrition: 0%   MLB: 0%   Comparables: Jordan Lyles, Taijuan Walker, Martin Perez

Lewis Wynn Thorpe III (not quite his real name, but we wanted to give a shout out to Dan Aykroyd fans) struck out more than a batter per inning as a teenager in the Midwest League, which bodes extremely well for the young Aussie's future. Armed with above-average lefty velocity and a plus change-up that can defang even the most dangerous righty slugger, Thorpe issued more walks than you'd like to see but has plenty of time to work on his control. Of more concern is the sore elbow that popped up late in the year, though the organization doesn't expect this to be a serious issue going forward. He's years away from The Show and needs to grow into his frame and build up his endurance, but so far he's right on target. Looking good, Lewis!

Michael Tonkin   RHP

Born: 11/19/89   Age: 25   Bats: R   Throws: R   Height: 6'7"   Weight: 220

YEAR	TEAM	LVL	AGE	W	L	SV	G	GS	IP	H	HR	BB	K	BB/9	K/9	GB%	BABIP	WHIP	ERA	FIP	FRA	WARP
2012	BLT	A	22	3	0	6	22	0	39	29	1	9	53	2.1	12.2	55%	.311	0.97	1.38	1.74	2.69	1.1
2012	FTM	A+	22	1	1	6	22	0	30¹	24	2	11	44	3.3	13.1	37%	.324	1.15	2.97	2.64	3.03	0.8
2013	NBR	AA	23	1	2	7	22	0	24¹	21	0	8	30	3.0	11.1	60%	.313	1.19	2.22	2.21	2.00	1.0
2013	ROC	AAA	23	1	2	14	30	0	32²	33	3	8	36	2.2	9.9	49%	.330	1.26	4.41	3.02	3.79	0.6
2013	MIN	MLB	23	0	0	0	9	0	11¹	9	0	3	10	2.4	7.9	44%	.265	1.06	0.79	2.10	2.10	0.3
2014	ROC	AAA	24	3	4	10	39	0	45	41	2	12	46	2.4	9.2	48%	.305	1.18	2.80	2.82	3.28	1.0
2014	MIN	MLB	24	0	0	0	25	0	19	23	2	6	16	2.8	7.6	50%	.350	1.53	4.74	4.11	5.09	0.1
2015	MIN	MLB	25	2	1	0	43	0	54¹	60	5	20	44	3.3	7.2	48%	.320	1.47	4.77	4.42	5.19	0.0

Breakout: 20%   Improve: 23%   Collapse: 14%   Attrition: 24%   MLB: 39%   Comparables: Osiris Matos, Jake Dunning, Jonathan Albaladejo

A towering right-hander with a big fastball that can reach the mid-90s, Tonkin spent last year bouncing between Target Field and Triple-A but looks like a good bet to stick this time around. The Gulf is one of the few bullpen options this spring who has both a hint of big-league seasoning and swing-and-miss stuff, and if he can maintain his admirably low walk rate while generating whiffs at a level more reminiscent of his minor-league numbers, he can be an asset in the seventh inning. Teacher says every time a 30th-round draft pick carves out a big league career an angel gets his wings, so here's hoping.

Lineouts

Hitters

NAME	POS	TEAM	LVL	AGE	PA	R	2B	3B	HR	RBI	BB	K	SB	CS	AVG/OBP/SLG	TAv	BABIP	BRR	FRAA	WARP
Niko Goodrum	3B	FTM	A+	22	504	63	19	5	3	49	58	99	35	4	.249/.337/.336	.253	.312	4.7	3B(92): -0.7, SS(26): 2.4	1.9
Travis Harrison	LF	FTM	A+	21	537	80	33	1	3	59	64	86	7	5	.269/.361/.365	.281	.318	-0.1	LF(98): -0.6, 3B(15): -2.4	1.8
Jason Kubel	LF	MIN	MLB	32	176	12	6	1	1	13	19	59	1	0	.224/.313/.295	.220	.354	0.5	LF(36): -1.1, RF(4): -0.1	-0.6
Max Murphy	CF	CDR	A	21	137	15	7	0	4	15	8	40	1	4	.242/.314/.395	.241	.325	-1.9	CF(27): 1.0, LF(2): 0.2	0.0
Shane Robinson	CF	MEM	AAA	29	216	33	12	0	2	16	22	25	4	2	.304/.380/.398	.276	.339	1.6	CF(34): 1.1, RF(10): 0.1	1.5
	RF	SLN	MLB	29	66	3	1	1	0	4	6	10	0	1	.150/.227/.200	.157	.180	0.1	RF(15): 0.3, LF(5): 0.1	-0.5
Stuart Turner	C	FTM	A+	22	364	49	16	2	7	40	31	61	7	0	.249/.322/.375	.261	.286	-1.0	C(92): -1.9	1.5
Adam Walker	RF	FTM	A+	22	555	78	19	1	25	94	44	156	9	5	.246/.307/.436	.268	.303	0.5	RF(110): 5.7	1.7

Lanky switch-hitter **Niko Goodrum** carries more tools than a Silverado commercial, with speed, smooth actions, a cannon arm and the athleticism to play all over the diamond, but until his offensive production starts to match his projection, he's a future utilityman. ❖ **Travis Harrison** spent last summer emulating Daytona manager Doug Mientkiewicz, making contact but eschewing the long ball; moving to left field significantly raises the offensive bar, so his improved approach will need to become a foundation for future power, not a replacement for it. ❖ Remember how **Jason Kubel** used to tee off on right-handed pitching and earn MVP votes? His lumber doesn't, and Kubel won't make his way back to The Show until he finds an antidote for the Forget-Me-Now coursing through his bat rack. ❖ A ninth-round pick in last summer's draft, compact center fielder **Max Murphy** positively reeks of folk-hero potential, with an alliterative name, Minnesota roots and a Kirby Puckett Award from Bradley University on his mantle. Legit power, too. ❖ Quad-A outfielder **Shane Robinson** can now add "aging" and "former Cardinal" to the group of adjectives that describe him, which is nice, since "diminutive" and "grindy" were looking for some new friends. ❖ In his first full pro season, Ole Miss standout **Stuart Turner** displayed the plus receiving skills and strong arm that will earn him membership in the International Brotherhood of Backup Catchers, and flashed just enough offensive potential to dream of more. ❖ **Adam Walker** put his massive raw power on display while winning the Florida State League home run derby, but advanced pitchers have more in their arsenal than batting practice fastballs.

Pitchers

NAME	TEAM	LVL	AGE	W	L	SV	G	GS	IP	H	HR	BB	K	BB/9	K/9	GB%	BABIP	WHIP	ERA	FIP	FRA	WARP
Tyler Duffey	FTM	A+	23	3	0	0	4	4	22¹	22	0	5	13	2.0	5.2	36%	.286	1.21	2.82	2.90	4.01	0.2
	NBR	AA	23	8	3	0	18	18	111¹	104	14	19	84	1.5	6.8	47%	.274	1.10	3.80	4.13	4.81	0.9
	ROC	AAA	23	2	0	0	3	3	16	16	3	6	16	3.4	9.0	28%	.302	1.38	3.94	5.11	5.71	0.0
Ryan Eades	CDR	A	22	10	11	0	26	25	133	147	11	50	98	3.4	6.6	43%	.323	1.48	5.14	4.44	5.12	0.3
Justin Gallant	CDR	A	25	2	1	5	21	0	28	12	0	9	46	2.9	14.8	47%	.235	0.75	0.64	1.27	1.86	1.0
Matt Guerrier	MIN	MLB	35	0	1	0	27	0	28	30	1	10	12	3.2	3.9	41%	.290	1.43	3.86	3.95	4.86	0.1
Kris Johnson	ROC	AAA	29	10	7	0	23	23	132	115	8	55	102	3.8	7.0	52%	.275	1.29	3.48	3.90	5.02	0.8
	MIN	MLB	29	0	1	0	3	3	13¹	17	2	9	12	6.1	8.1	51%	.366	1.95	4.72	5.33	5.20	0.1
Felix Jorge	CDR	A	20	2	5	0	12	8	39	57	9	20	23	4.6	5.3	43%	.358	1.97	9.00	7.00	7.76	-0.7
Mason Melotakis	FTM	A+	23	3	1	1	25	2	47	50	3	24	45	4.6	8.6	54%	.338	1.57	3.45	4.03	5.38	0.0
	NBR	AA	23	1	0	2	13	0	16	17	0	3	17	1.7	9.6	54%	.370	1.25	2.25	1.98	2.17	0.6
Brandon Peterson	CDR	A	22	1	0	3	9	0	12²	9	0	2	19	1.4	13.5	48%	.333	0.87	0.71	0.96	1.08	0.6
	FTM	A+	22	1	1	1	31	1	45	28	0	17	65	3.4	13.0	34%	.289	1.00	1.80	1.64	2.33	1.5
Stephen Pryor	TAC	AAA	24	2	1	1	24	0	31	26	4	18	27	5.2	7.8	31%	.256	1.42	4.65	5.38	5.28	0.1
	ROC	AAA	24	1	0	2	14	0	20¹	6	2	16	22	7.1	9.7	37%	.098	1.08	0.89	4.83	4.83	0.1
	SEA	MLB	24	0	0	0	1	0	1²	1	0	2	1	10.8	5.4	60%	.200	1.80	5.56	6.70	-0.1
Jacob Reed	CDR	A	21	3	0	5	16	0	25	10	0	3	31	1.1	11.2	55%	.182	0.52	0.36	1.48	3.07	0.5
Taylor Rogers	NBR	AA	23	11	6	0	24	24	145	150	4	37	113	2.3	7.0	50%	.327	1.29	3.29	3.04	3.75	2.7
Aaron Thompson	ROC	AAA	27	3	3	3	46	0	52	49	5	26	51	4.5	8.8	43%	.306	1.44	3.98	4.20	4.50	0.5
	MIN	MLB	27	0	0	0	7	0	7¹	8	0	2	6	2.5	7.4	30%	.348	1.36	2.45	2.34	2.70	0.2
Jason Wheeler	FTM	A+	23	6	5	0	13	13	79	77	2	19	57	2.2	6.5	46%	.301	1.22	2.51	3.04	4.03	0.9
	NBR	AA	23	5	4	0	12	12	74¹	69	9	16	55	1.9	6.7	36%	.271	1.14	2.78	4.26	4.26	1.0

Towering tyro **Michael Cederoth** lights up radar guns and can unleash a sharp slider, but his longstanding struggles with fastball command pushed him to the bullpen at San Diego State; he's found early success in a pro rotation against overmatched Rookie-league batsmen, but his likeliest future involves getting high-leverage outs one inning at a time. ❖ Sure, **Tyler Duffey** doesn't miss a lot of bats, but he has a plan and shows solid control of his low-90s fastball and slurvy breaking ball; it's not a sexy profile, but this is the primordial soup from which middle relievers and swingmen evolve. ❖ Last year we urged Twins fans not to panic after second-round pick **Ryan Eades** suffered through 10 nightmarish starts in Rookie ball; now that he's spent a full season struggling to repeat his delivery or command his mid-90s fastball, you have our permission. ❖ Reliever/Danielle Steel character **Dallas Gallant** has overcome a novel's worth of misfortune, including two elbow surgeries and a PED suspension, to strike out more than a batter-and-a-half per inning in the low minors, but as a 26-year-old just now hitting Double-A, time's running out for a happy ending. ❖ Aging reliever **Matt Guerrier** no longer misses bats and looked so awful in his last Twins appearance that a concerned Ron Gardenhire took the trainer with him for his final mound visit. He was released the next day, but the longtime bullpen stalwart deserves a chance to hook on somewhere else and be carried out on his shield. ❖ Journeyman lefty **Kris Johnson** made three starts for the Twins last summer, but his greatest contribution to the organization was the six-figure payment they received when he was purchased by the Hiroshima Carp. ❖ Young Dominican **Felix Jorge** lacked his normal mid-90s velocity during his first taste of Low-A, but he righted the ship somewhat back in Rookie ball; he's still only 21, but he'll need to find success in a full-season league to stay on the prospect radar. ❖ A move to the 'pen suited lefty **Mason Melotakis**, as his mid-90s fastball and power curve played up in shorter stints; elbow soreness cut his season short, but if he's healthy and can do a better job of avoiding ball four he could start generating groundball outs at Target Field as soon as this summer. ❖ Burnsville's own **Brandon Peterson** used a mid-90s fastball and developing slider to blaze his way through Cedar Rapids and Fort Myers; if he can continue to rack up the whiffs and keep his walks in check in Double-A, he could become a bullpen asset. ❖ **Stephen Pryor** once looked like a future bullpen fixture when his mid-90s heater and wipeout slider were racking up strikeouts, but shoulder surgery took his velocity and reduced his control to LaLooshian levels. ❖ Fifth-round pick **Jake Reed** earned the organization's full attention with his ridiculous 13:1 strikeout-to-walk ratio, mid-90s fastball and mid-90s run of 1,000-yard receiving seasons for the Vikings. ❖ **Taylor Rogers** passed his Double-A exam over the summer, as the lefty starter upped his strikeout rate, avoided walks and induced plenty of two-hoppers; plus command of his low-90s fastball and nondescript off-speed junk might just carry him to a swingman role. ❖ Southpaw

Aaron Thompson earned a September call-up, but fringy stuff and subpar command do not a bullpen arm make, lefty or not. ❖ Very large human **Jason Wheeler** parlayed a solid year in the upper minors into a spot on the 40-man roster. He's a lefty with upper-80s velocity and good control, and dig that hot, sexy Old School Twins strikeout rate. Dig it hard.

Manager

Paul Molitor

Not since Gene Mauch in 1976 have the Twins hired a skipper with previous experience managing in the majors. What's more, all but one of their past five managers played for the organization at some level or another. Put another way, the Twins like new blood with an old face.

It was no surprise, then, that the Twins hired another of their own over Torey Lovullo, someone with no ties to the organization. But Molitor, a Minnesota native and University of Minnesota attendee, isn't just a nostalgia play; he is, by all accounts, an intelligent, well-respected figure who is familiar with the organization and its processes. He coached under Tom Kelly back in the day, served in the minors for almost a decade and joined the big-league staff in a supervisory role last season, where he observed and instructed the Twins' baserunning, bunting, infield play and defensive positioning.

He is, at 58, getting a late start on his managerial career, and it won't be easy sledding early on. Still, there's reason to think he's capable of holding the job down for a while—and not just because of his connections to the Twin Cities.

NEW YORK METS

by Ted Berg

David Wright plays through all sorts of pain.

In 2009, Wright wanted to stay on the active roster after he suffered a concussion on a 93 mph Matt Cain fastball to the helmet. Mets brass, showing atypical prudence, sent Wright to the disabled list, but he returned after just the then-minimum 15-day absence, only to be mocked by teammates, fans and media for the massive helmet he wore to protect himself from further head trauma (though, to be fair, it was a pretty silly helmet).

In 2011, Wright broke a bone in his back during an on-field collision with Carlos Lee. He played hurt for a month before he consented to an examination and, ultimately, the disabled list.

And in 2014, Wright struggled with an injured left shoulder that affected his swing for most of the season before the Mets finally shut him down in September. Wright was off to a slow start before the first reports of the injury, and he finished with his worst-ever offensive numbers.

That's not to mention all the nicks and bruises and broken digits that never manage to keep Wright away from the field for more than a game or two.

And then, none of that considers the mental and emotional anguish of playing for the Mets. Perhaps no one in the world has more unfairly suffered for the team's recent woes than its 32-year-old franchise third baseman, who grew up a Mets fan just barely too young to remember their last World Series win, 28 years ago.

Wright helped the club to the postseason in only his second full big-league season in 2006, but watched as the team collapsed late and missed the playoffs in 2007 and 2008, then fell apart entirely in 2009 because of a rash of injuries exposing the lack of organizational depth that quietly plagued the team throughout then-GM Omar Minaya's administration.

During the team's collapses, Wright earned an unfortunate, misdirected and ever frustrating reputation for a lack of clutchness, a knock perpetuated by confirmation bias whenever Wright failed to carry a shallow team populated by too many aging and aching players. Sports-talk radio gaga targeted him even in September 2008, when the Mets' genuinely atrocious bullpen blew a series of late leads and yielded a 5.63 ERA over the season's final two weeks. (Wright hit .340/.416/.577 that September.)

Wright was there, of course, when the Mets opened Citi Field,

a new ballpark with comically deep dimensions that seemed perversely designed to rob him of home runs. When his power output dipped in part due to the gimmicky decision to put the wall in right-center field 415 feet from home plate, Wright caught heat for letting the dimensions get to his head. A FOX Sports column advised the Mets to trade Wright for prospects after that season, arguing that Wright might welcome a trade because of the "new ballpark he obviously hates."

He even took a cheap shot from Mets owner Fred Wilpon, who called Wright "not a superstar" in a 2011 *New Yorker* feature that otherwise focused on Wilpon's relationship with Bernie Madoff, whose multi-billion-dollar Ponzi scheme hamstrung the team's finances and helped slow the rebuilding process from which the Mets only now seem to be emerging.

The tradition of condemning great ballplayers for the inadequacies of the roster around them dates back to at least 1888, when Ernest Thayer and a melancholy crowd hung a Mudville Nine loss on no less a talent than Mighty Casey, even though he was marooned behind Flynn—a noted "lulu"—and Jimmy Blake, the well documented "cake" in the club's lineup.

Wright is the best homegrown position player in Mets history, but he has been forced to bear the brunt of the blame from many fans and media for failing to carry the awful players around him, his isolated failures amplified to make him a symbol of sorts for a dark era in Flushing, his stubborn positivity and typical excellence annoying some as the organization wasted away his prime seasons.

In 2011, a *Daily News* columnist told Wright he'd be best served being traded, and wrote that Wright "doesn't seem to get it" when the third baseman responded to the unsolicited career advice with only a quizzical look. An ESPN New York article in April 2012 declared the Mets' decision to commit to Wright over departed shortstop Jose Reyes a mistake less than a month after Reyes played his first game for the Miami Marlins.

When Wright sits out even a day for an injury, he is deemed soft. When he plays through the injury, he is declared stubborn. Some fans have so often clamored for his departure via trade—for no one in particular, of course—that writers at the Mets site Amazin' Avenue began ironically demanding a "traid" whenever Wright made a great play or smacked a big hit. Even former

METS PROSPECTUS
2014 W-L: 79-83, 2ND IN NL EAST

Pythag	.508	14th	DER	.705	16th
RS/G	3.88	21st	B-Age	28.3	13th
RA/G	3.81	10th	P-Age	29.2	23rd
TAv	.259	15th	Salary	$84.7M	24th
BRR	-1.79	20th	M$/MW	$2.3M	11th
TAv-P	.266	21st	DL Days	742	14th
FIP	3.72	16th	$ on DL	14%	13th

Three-Year Park Factors

Runs	Runs/RH	Runs/LH	HR/RH	HR/LH
95	93	92	92	90

Top Hitter WARP	3.6	Juan Lagares
Top Pitcher WARP	2.8	Jacob DeGrom
Top Prospect		Noah Syndergaard

teammate Paul Lo Duca got in on the action last season, calling into local radio in June to say the Mets should move Wright—"go back to their roots"—despite the massive contract extension he signed before the 2013 campaign.

Wright obviously loves playing baseball, almost as much as he obviously hates MRI machines. His patience with being a Met and his abilities to withstand both the physical toil and the onslaught of nonsense that have come with his particular circumstances all seem like admirable skills, the type we all must develop, and the type that should endear the third baseman to Mets fans everywhere. It seems like if Wright had a mustache and half as much power, he'd be the grittiest bastard to ever clean infield dirt out of his ears.

But Wright is perhaps the first American in history treated unfairly for being a handsome white guy, labeled a pretty boy just because he's pretty, his chiseled jawline obscuring his remarkably resilient chin.

The lone holdover from the club's last playoff appearance, he has been and remains the face of a franchise that has too often been a punchline—LOLMets—in recent seasons. But two years into the deal that will keep him a Met through the end of the decade, he now has the opportunity to help his club back to October, perhaps—as crazy as it may sound—as soon as this year.

✦ ✦ ✦

GM Sandy Alderson took over for Minaya after the 2010 season to build a sustainable winner on a big-market team that suddenly had neither the ability nor the willingness to pursue marquee stars in free agency. Alderson made a series of shrewd trades to secure top prospects for veterans nearing the ends of their contracts, and though the process was delayed by young ace Matt Harvey's Tommy John surgery, it now appears it's all just about ready to come to fruition.

Here's the formula: Young pitching! Young pitching! Young pitching!

There's young pitching in the rotation. In Harvey, who should be at full strength in plenty of time for opening day, reigning NL Rookie of the Year Jacob deGrom and fireballer Zack Wheeler, the Mets have a trio of cost-controlled young studs with the potential to match any in baseball.

There's young pitching in the bullpen. Righty Jenrry Mejia, now five years removed from the baffling experiment that had him working mop-up duty as a 20-year-old in 2010, moved back to the bullpen in May and pitched effectively—despite a few too many baserunners—as the team's closer for most of the season. Jeurys Familia, 25, emerged as a sturdy set-up man in his rookie season. And less-heralded arms Vic Black and Josh Edgin appear apt to fill key roles in the club's 2015 relief corps.

There's young pitching on the farm. Top prospect Noah Syndergaard, acquired with catcher Travis d'Arnaud in the R.A. Dickey trade after the 2012 season, showed good rate stats in 133 innings at Triple-A Las Vegas, a punishing environment for pitchers. Rafael Montero got his first big-league look after posting great minor-league numbers in 2012 and 2013. Lefty Steven Matz flourished in his first turn at Double-A and could be ready for the majors by midseason.

Of course, the obvious counter to all that: Young pitching. Young pitching. Young pitching. Relying on young pitching, as Mets fans know well, is sometimes like relying on a helmet against a Matt Cain fastball.

But assuming the pitching holds up—with veterans Jon Niese and Bartolo Colon providing ballast, and layers upon layers of depth—the Mets will still need to score runs to contend in 2015. And Wright is the biggest variable.

Not just because he's the Mets' best recruitment tool, though that's a little bit of it. He convinced childhood friend Michael Cuddyer to sign a two-year, $21 million deal after rejecting the Rockies' one-year, $15.3 million qualifying offer. Wright phoned Cuddyer multiple times a day to persuade him—because, again, David Wright apparently still enjoys playing for the Mets enough to tell his buddies to join him in Flushing.

The addition of Cuddyer makes the Mets' 2015 lineup look deep with viable big leaguers—a low enough bar, but one they haven't cleared often lately—but there is no one on the club, and no one likely on the way, who can hit the way Wright has in his best seasons. Even at 32 years old and coming off his rough year, Wright is still the one Met who can compete for an MVP award—a six-win player as recently as 2013, even though he missed 45 games that year with a hamstring injury (which, of course, he first tried to play through).

All of the Mets' easiest routes to contention require a rebound season from him. If there's any justice whatsoever in this world, Wright will remain healthy enough to seize this opportunity and power his club back to the postseason, rekindling his status as a franchise hero and cementing his legacy as the best position player ever to wear the uniform he has cheered since childhood.

Part of what makes baseball so engaging, I think, is the way it provides orderly, accessible, ultimately unimportant variants of the real-life trials and triumphs we all endeavor. And every single one of us, to continue existing, will be forced to shoulder pains of seemingly every variety. To live is to suffer, as Nietszche and DMX say. We are all kind of David Wright—maybe not quite so handsome, but nonetheless bravely plowing forward in the face of discomfort and disquiet far beyond our control.

And we keep going, I'm pretty certain, for the beautiful, fleeting moments of greatness and glory and happiness that punctuate all the misery. It would be redeeming to see Wright repaid in some karmic baseball sense for all the baseball nonsense he has so willingly weathered. It would remind us that sometimes it does happen, that these efforts to endure are sometimes rewarded. ■

—Ted Berg lives in New York City and writes about baseball and Taco Bell for USA TODAY Sports.

Player comments by Will Woods and Baseball Prospectus Authors

Hitters

Eric Campbell   UT
Born: 4/9/87   Age: 28   Bats: R   Throws: R   Height: 6' 3"   Weight: 205

YEAR	TEAM	LVL	AGE	PA	R	2B	3B	HR	RBI	BB	K	SB	CS	AVG/OBP/SLG	TAv	BABIP	BRR	FRAA	WARP
2012	BIN	AA	25	465	53	25	2	9	50	58	76	10	5	.297/.391/.439	.295	.344	-1.0	1B(56): 1.3, LF(45): 0.3	3.1
2013	LVG	AAA	26	425	61	25	3	8	66	66	60	12	4	.314/.435/.475	.308	.357	2.6	RF(29): 0.2, 3B(28): -1.9	3.3
2014	LVG	AAA	27	163	39	15	0	3	24	20	20	3	1	.355/.442/.525	.307	.398	2.2	1B(17): 2.1, 2B(13): 0.3	1.7
2014	NYN	MLB	27	211	16	9	0	3	16	17	55	3	0	.263/.322/.358	.265	.348	-0.7	LF(20): 0.0, 3B(19): -0.2	0.4
2015	NYN	MLB	28	250	26	12	0	4	24	27	52	4	1	.251/.338/.361	.272	.308	-0.5	1B 1, 3B 0	1.0

Breakout: 5%   Improve: 13%   Collapse: 8%   Attrition: 20%   MLB: 39%   Comparables: Jesus Guzman, Steve Pearce, Jose Morales

Campbell was a pleasant surprise at the big-league level in 2014, tearing it up until the All-Star break before going ice cold in the final two months. He showed an ability to hit the fastball, and a discerning eye that suggests an honest, no-guessing approach. Now, the problem: Like Josh Satin before him, Campbell does not provide the power to play first, or the defensive value to play anywhere else. Patience is nice, but he'd have to hit .320 to justify himself as a starter worth keeping around. The result: Campbell played everywhere but pitcher and catcher in 2014; he'll say he just wants to get on the field, but when it comes to staying on the field, versatility smacks more of desperation than confidence.

Michael Conforto   OF
Born: 3/1/93   Age: 22   Bats: L   Throws: R   Height: 6' 1"   Weight: 211

YEAR	TEAM	LVL	AGE	PA	R	2B	3B	HR	RBI	BB	K	SB	CS	AVG/OBP/SLG	TAv	BABIP	BRR	FRAA	WARP
2014	BRO	A-	21	186	30	10	0	3	19	16	29	3	0	.331/.403/.448	.314	.383	1.9	LF(41): -1.7	1.8
2015	NYN	MLB	22	250	18	9	1	3	21	13	68	0	0	.200/.250/.279	.209	.265	-0.4	LF -2	-1.0

Breakout: 0%   Improve: 0%   Collapse: 0%   Attrition: 0%   MLB: 0%   Comparables: Corey Dickerson, Michael Taylor, Adron Chambers

Scouts like to use a lot of abstract terminology that, in some cases, might only be visible to the scouts themselves—like wine experts, only tobacco-ier. Here, then, a plain-English scouting report on Michael Conforto: He is able to swing extremely hard while also being rather choosy about the pitches on which he unleashes his fury. His swing is a rare combination of short and uppercut, and he uses his entire body to muster torque, to the point that it's jarring when it doesn't result in a line drive. Conforto outclassed the New York-Penn League and should finish 2015 in the high minors. More importantly, he barely moves his arms when he runs. He would've made a fine Koopa Troopa.

Michael Cuddyer   RF
Born: 3/27/79   Age: 36   Bats: R   Throws: R   Height: 6' 2"   Weight: 220

YEAR	TEAM	LVL	AGE	PA	R	2B	3B	HR	RBI	BB	K	SB	CS	AVG/OBP/SLG	TAv	BABIP	BRR	FRAA	WARP
2012	COL	MLB	33	394	53	30	2	16	58	32	78	8	3	.260/.317/.489	.275	.287	1.3	RF(74): -2.1, 1B(26): -0.8	1.5
2013	COL	MLB	34	540	74	31	3	20	84	46	100	10	3	.331/.389/.530	.304	.382	1.0	RF(118): -12.5, 1B(15): 0.6	1.9
2014	COL	MLB	35	205	32	15	1	10	31	14	30	3	0	.332/.376/.579	.316	.351	0.6	RF(35): -1.9, 1B(14): -0.1	1.4
2015	NYN	MLB	36	265	29	14	1	7	31	21	51	4	1	.260/.320/.411	.285	.301	0.6	RF -4, 1B -0	0.7

Breakout: 0%   Improve: 22%   Collapse: 3%   Attrition: 8%   MLB: 86%   Comparables: Torii Hunter, Magglio Ordonez, Larry Walker

After leading the National League in batting average in 2013, Cuddyer led hitters in a different, far worse category last year: DL stints. Cuddyer missed 105 games with hamstring and shoulder injuries but raked when healthy, hitting for the best True Average of his career in 49 games. Nutshell: On his first day back from the 60-day DL, he became the 12th player over 35 to hit for the cycle; he returned to the disabled list seven days later. At his age, the slash lines are more magical than the card tricks he's known to bring to clubhouses, but his slow-footed defense makes most of that value disappear.

Travis d'Arnaud   C
Born: 2/10/89   Age: 26   Bats: R   Throws: R   Height: 6' 2"   Weight: 210

YEAR	TEAM	LVL	AGE	PA	R	2B	3B	HR	RBI	BB	K	SB	CS	AVG/OBP/SLG	TAv	BABIP	BRR	FRAA	WARP
2012	LVG	AAA	23	303	45	21	2	16	52	19	59	1	1	.333/.380/.595	.303	.374	0.1	C(55): 0.4, 1B(2): -0.1	2.9
2013	BIN	AA	24	30	2	2	1	1	3	3	9	0	0	.222/.300/.481	.266	.294	-0.8	C(7): 0.3	0.2
2013	LVG	AAA	24	78	19	8	0	2	12	21	12	0	0	.304/.487/.554	.355	.349	-1.2	C(18): 0.6	1.1
2013	NYN	MLB	24	112	4	3	0	1	5	12	21	0	0	.202/.286/.263	.205	.244	-0.5	C(30): -0.3	-0.2
2014	LVG	AAA	25	59	13	8	0	6	16	3	5	0	0	.436/.475/.909	.408	.409	-0.5	C(10): -0.0	1.1
2014	NYN	MLB	25	421	48	22	3	13	41	32	64	1	0	.242/.302/.416	.269	.259	-0.3	C(105): -0.3	1.9
2015	NYN	MLB	26	360	39	18	1	12	46	29	67	1	0	.251/.315/.424	.283	.280	-0.3	C -0, 1B -0	2.2

Breakout: 5%   Improve: 51%   Collapse: 4%   Attrition: 5%   MLB: 96%   Comparables: Geovany Soto, Mitch Moreland, Miguel Montero

From the Anthony Recker School of Biceps Curls comes the swing of Travis d'Arnaud, which is so arm-dependent it almost explains away his poor throwing. Still, after a rough start earned him a ticket to Triple-A, d'Arnaud recovered and made himself a mild positive at the plate in 2014, mostly thanks to a torrid September. The finale was encouraging, but the d'Arnaud show lacks a certain je ne sais quoi: For every outside fastball driven into the right-field corner, there's a toothless wave at a pitch that appeared hittable. The defense is equally flighty and uninspiring, and now there's another injury to add to the list—he had surgery to remove a bone spur in September. Overall, d'Arnaud was an average player in his first full season, but 2015 will be the year we separate what he is from what he was supposed to be.

Matt den Dekker   OF

Born: 8/10/87   Age: 27   Bats: L   Throws: L   Height: 6' 1"   Weight: 210

YEAR	TEAM	LVL	AGE	PA	R	2B	3B	HR	RBI	BB	K	SB	CS	AVG/OBP/SLG	TAv	BABIP	BRR	FRAA	WARP
2012	BIN	AA	24	268	47	21	4	8	29	20	64	10	7	.340/.397/.563	.329	.429	1.9	CF(56): -1.5, RF(1): -0.1	2.7
2012	BUF	AAA	24	317	37	10	4	9	47	14	90	11	2	.220/.256/.373	.217	.279	4.0	CF(76): -1.3	-0.1
2013	SLU	A+	25	62	8	2	0	0	4	3	6	1	0	.276/.306/.310	.238	.302	-0.2	CF(14): -1.2	-0.2
2013	LVG	AAA	25	202	34	8	4	6	38	20	46	8	1	.296/.366/.486	.282	.364	2.6	CF(49): -0.0, LF(2): 0.1	1.6
2013	NYN	MLB	25	63	7	1	0	1	6	4	23	4	1	.207/.270/.276	.211	.324	1.8	CF(16): -1.0, RF(1): 0.1	-0.1
2014	LVG	AAA	26	385	70	31	7	8	46	40	65	9	5	.334/.407/.540	.321	.392	4.9	CF(86): -9.0, LF(4): -0.3	3.3
2014	NYN	MLB	26	174	23	11	0	0	7	21	34	7	4	.250/.345/.322	.263	.322	1.9	LF(28): -1.7, CF(18): -1.7	0.6
2015	NYN	MLB	27	250	29	11	2	5	21	17	65	7	3	.240/.297/.366	.254	.310	1.8	CF -3, LF -1	0.3

Breakout: 4%   Improve: 20%   Collapse: 8%   Attrition: 20%   MLB: 52%   Comparables: Chris Aguila, Will Venable, Brandon Barnes

A defense-first player trapped behind a Gold Glove-caliber center fielder, and the owner of a loopy swing with giant holes—he has one(!) career hit on balls up in the zone, and he whiffed on fully half(!) of the breaking balls he saw in 2014—the cherubic den Dekker is just missing an organization to love him. His gaudy numbers at Triple-A Las Vegas, while partly a product of the park, do not lie; he's a nice combination of speed and gap power. Put him against major-league pitching, however, and he has the most obvious holes you'll ever see. More than most, den Dekker needs a situation that allows him extended time to acclimatize and fix his swing. N.b.: the BP Annual Style Guide allows for one use of the phrase "gaudy numbers" per team.

Lucas Duda   1B

Born: 2/3/86   Age: 29   Bats: L   Throws: R   Height: 6' 4"   Weight: 255

YEAR	TEAM	LVL	AGE	PA	R	2B	3B	HR	RBI	BB	K	SB	CS	AVG/OBP/SLG	TAv	BABIP	BRR	FRAA	WARP
2012	BUF	AAA	26	107	12	4	0	3	8	10	21	0	0	.260/.327/.396	.262	.301	-1.1	LF(18): -0.7, RF(4): 0.1	0.2
2012	NYN	MLB	26	459	43	15	0	15	57	51	120	1	0	.239/.329/.389	.261	.301	-4.7	RF(81): -7.8, LF(24): -0.7	-0.9
2013	SLU	A+	27	30	4	2	0	1	5	2	7	0	0	.250/.300/.429	.235	.300	-0.7	LF(5): 0.2	-0.1
2013	LVG	AAA	27	78	13	3	0	0	8	14	15	1	0	.306/.423/.355	.272	.388	-0.9	1B(12): 0.2, LF(3): 0.1	0.2
2013	NYN	MLB	27	384	42	16	0	15	33	55	102	0	3	.223/.352/.415	.286	.276	0.6	LF(58): -3.8, 1B(34): -0.4	1.1
2014	NYN	MLB	28	596	74	27	0	30	92	69	135	3	2	.253/.349/.481	.312	.283	-2.4	1B(146): -7.2, LF(1): 0.0	2.8
2015	NYN	MLB	29	532	63	24	1	20	69	59	123	2	1	.242/.335/.424	.289	.285	-1.8	1B -1, LF -2	1.6

Breakout: 6%   Improve: 50%   Collapse: 6%   Attrition: 8%   MLB: 88%   Comparables: Travis Hafner, Allen Craig, Dan Johnson

Duda started the season in a first-base platoon with Ike Davis—yes, they're both left handed; no, don't ask—and beat out the former first-round pick as the New York media revealed they'd kinda sorta stumped for Ike because Ike's a better interview. (Duda, on hitting his 30th home run in his final at-bat of the season: "Thirty—that's a nice number.") Once Davis left for Pittsburgh, Duda caught fire, posting MVP-caliber numbers through June and July. The big revelation for Duda is that he is no longer the only lefty slugger vulnerable to the low pitch, paving a bright future for that well-worn cliché in the years to come. N.b.: The Official BP Stylebook has it, "The DudA bides."

Wilmer Flores   SS

Born: 8/6/91   Age: 23   Bats: R   Throws: R   Height: 6' 3"   Weight: 205

YEAR	TEAM	LVL	AGE	PA	R	2B	3B	HR	RBI	BB	K	SB	CS	AVG/OBP/SLG	TAv	BABIP	BRR	FRAA	WARP
2012	SLU	A+	20	272	31	12	0	10	42	18	30	3	2	.289/.336/.463	.272	.286	-2.9	3B(61): -2.9, 2B(3): 0.2	0.6
2012	BIN	AA	20	275	37	18	2	8	33	20	30	0	0	.311/.361/.494	.289	.326	-1.4	3B(26): -2.0, 2B(24): 0.9	1.3
2013	LVG	AAA	21	463	69	36	4	15	86	25	63	1	3	.321/.357/.531	.300	.342	-1.2	2B(79): -4.8, 1B(11): 0.7	2.7
2013	NYN	MLB	21	101	8	5	0	1	13	5	23	0	0	.211/.248/.295	.200	.264	-0.3	3B(26): 1.8, 2B(2): -0.1	-0.2
2014	LVG	AAA	22	241	43	11	2	13	57	16	39	0	2	.323/.367/.568	.309	.339	-0.3	SS(32): 4.7, 2B(12): -0.2	2.8
2014	NYN	MLB	22	274	28	13	1	6	29	12	31	1	0	.251/.286/.378	.250	.265	-0.2	SS(51): 1.9, 2B(19): -1.2	0.8
2015	NYN	MLB	23	314	30	16	1	9	37	13	53	1	1	.255/.288/.403	.264	.280	-0.4	SS 1, 2B -1	1.1

Breakout: 5%   Improve: 48%   Collapse: 4%   Attrition: 18%   MLB: 75%   Comparables: Howie Kendrick, Mike Moustakas, Nolan Arenado

The acting chair of the Mets' "Shortstops Who Probably Shouldn't Be Shortstops" committee (Chairman Emeritus: Omar Quintanilla), Flores deserves a little slack despite his poor offensive numbers. After making the big club out of camp, he was twice demoted and then called back up, all the while relearning a position he hadn't played since 2011. The red flag with Flores is that he cheats on breaking pitches, and he's getting burned for it. That he swung at more fastballs out of the zone than breaking balls out of the zone is more horrifying even than watching him play shortstop. Speaking of which, with no suitable position to which they can assign Flores, the Mets should trade him as a public service. No man should be forced to live a lie, even if that lie increases his trade value.

Curtis Granderson   RF

Born: 3/16/81   Age: 34   Bats: L   Throws: R   Height: 6' 1"   Weight: 200

YEAR	TEAM	LVL	AGE	PA	R	2B	3B	HR	RBI	BB	K	SB	CS	AVG/OBP/SLG	TAv	BABIP	BRR	FRAA	WARP
2012	NYA	MLB	31	684	102	18	4	43	106	75	195	10	3	.232/.319/.492	.287	.260	2.3	CF(157): -11.7	3.1
2013	SWB	AAA	32	21	2	0	0	1	3	1	4	0	0	.400/.429/.550	.339	.467	0.4	RF(2): -0.1, LF(2): 0.0	0.2
2013	NYA	MLB	32	245	31	13	2	7	15	27	69	8	2	.229/.317/.407	.264	.302	0.6	CF(25): 1.1, RF(14): 0.7	0.9
2014	NYN	MLB	33	654	73	27	2	20	66	79	141	8	2	.227/.326/.388	.275	.265	-0.9	RF(142): 1.4, CF(15): -0.7	1.9
2015	NYN	MLB	34	538	74	18	4	21	63	58	139	10	3	.227/.315/.417	.278	.270	0.4	RF 1, CF -2	2.1

Breakout: 0%   Improve: 34%   Collapse: 8%   Attrition: 11%   MLB: 93%   Comparables: Jayson Werth, Jermaine Dye, Andruw Jones

In 2009, Granderson published a children's book entitled *All You Can Be: Dream It, Draw It, Become It!* Which is a nice thought, albeit better suited to a self-help seminar or a corporate retreat Powerpoint than a children's book; in much the same way, Granderson was a nice idea but an odd fit for the Mets, given the unlikelihood of both player and team being competitive at the same time. Granderson is regrettably but unmistakably on the decline. He is almost purely a mistake hitter now, unable to turn on the inside fastball or drive to left center with convincing power. His swings against curves and sliders are not something you talk about in polite company. He is hanging on to starter status—and he was a fringe-average starter last year, essentially—but it's difficult to see that extending past 2015.

Dilson Herrera 2B

Born: 3/3/94   Age: 21   Bats: R   Throws: R   Height: 5' 10"   Weight: 150

YEAR	TEAM	LVL	AGE	PA	R	2B	3B	HR	RBI	BB	K	SB	CS	AVG/OBP/SLG	TAv	BABIP	BRR	FRAA	WARP
2012	SCO	A-	18	29	7	1	1	1	2	1	6	1	0	.321/.345/.536	.328	.381	1.3	2B(5): 1.0	0.5
2013	SAV	A	19	24	6	0	0	0	4	3	6	3	0	.316/.417/.316	.350	.429	0.2	2B(6): -0.4	0.3
2013	WVA	A	19	479	69	27	3	11	56	37	110	11	6	.265/.330/.421	.294	.328	-0.1	2B(103): 5.5	3.6
2014	SLU	A+	20	309	48	16	2	3	23	18	44	14	3	.307/.355/.410	.272	.353	0.2	2B(43): -1.8, SS(19): 1.5	1.2
2014	BIN	AA	20	278	50	17	3	10	48	29	52	9	4	.340/.406/.560	.333	.389	0.9	2B(55): -0.6, SS(8): -0.2	2.9
2014	NYN	MLB	20	66	6	0	1	3	11	7	17	0	0	.220/.303/.407	.255	.256	-0.9	2B(17): 0.1	0.0
2015	NYN	MLB	21	250	29	10	1	6	23	15	64	4	1	.239/.289/.368	.253	.297	0.1	2B 0, SS 0	0.7

Breakout: 6%   Improve: 17%   Collapse: 4%   Attrition: 12%   MLB: 31%   Comparables: Brett Lawrie, Jonathan Schoop, Lonnie Chisenhall

Herrera was the youngest player in both the majors and the Eastern League as a 20-year-old in 2014. More impressive still, he didn't look out of place as a September call-up. Herrera was able to handle major-league fastballs with a below-average whiff rate, and generally didn't appear to be guessing or sacrificing part of the strike zone. Defensively, he's sexy and he knows it; he has range and a strong arm, and seems to take pleasure in being taken out at second base, though errors of omission abound. In the short term, the Mets have Daniel Murphy under control for another season, so Herrera can work the kinks out at Triple-A. But, by hook or by crook, he'll be back in the bigs in 2015—and he'll be ready.

Juan Lagares CF

Born: 3/17/89   Age: 26   Bats: R   Throws: R   Height: 6' 1"   Weight: 215

YEAR	TEAM	LVL	AGE	PA	R	2B	3B	HR	RBI	BB	K	SB	CS	AVG/OBP/SLG	TAv	BABIP	BRR	FRAA	WARP
2012	BIN	AA	23	548	69	29	6	4	48	37	93	21	10	.283/.334/.389	.263	.337	2.8	CF(70): 13.3, RF(47): 7.0	4.6
2013	LVG	AAA	24	82	13	3	2	3	9	4	14	2	3	.346/.378/.551	.320	.393	0.4	CF(17): 1.0	1.0
2013	NYN	MLB	24	421	35	21	5	4	34	20	96	6	3	.242/.281/.352	.232	.310	0.3	CF(108): 7.6, RF(14): 0.5	1.0
2014	NYN	MLB	25	452	46	24	3	4	47	20	87	13	4	.281/.321/.382	.276	.341	1.0	CF(112): 8.0	3.6
2015	NYN	MLB	26	433	46	20	3	4	33	20	92	10	4	.253/.292/.350	.251	.311	0.2	CF 9, RF 1	1.9

Breakout: 8%   Improve: 60%   Collapse: 11%   Attrition: 18%   MLB: 94%   Comparables: Leonys Martin, Julio Borbon, Peter Bourjos

After a bizarre early-season stint as a fourth outfielder—the hashtag #FreeLagares was starting to gain traction—the Mets' defensive marvel showed the steady improvement at the plate that should make him an everyday center fielder in the years to come. Lagares came up in 2013 unable to catch up to fastballs and utterly flummoxed by off-speed pitches; he's still flummoxed by off-speed, but he was able to sit on enough fastballs (especially inside) to make his numbers respectable. That's not the kind of approach that could lead to a breakout season down the road, but his defense is so good, and so out-of-nowhere, perhaps we can count 2014 as a breakout season in itself.

John Mayberry 1B

Born: 12/21/83   Age: 31   Bats: R   Throws: R   Height: 6' 6"   Weight: 230

YEAR	TEAM	LVL	AGE	PA	R	2B	3B	HR	RBI	BB	K	SB	CS	AVG/OBP/SLG	TAv	BABIP	BRR	FRAA	WARP
2012	PHI	MLB	28	479	53	24	0	14	46	34	111	1	0	.245/.301/.395	.257	.296	-2.4	LF(70): 4.1, CF(58): 0.5	1.3
2013	PHI	MLB	29	384	47	23	1	11	39	27	90	5	3	.227/.286/.391	.252	.273	-0.6	RF(79): -2.9, CF(46): 1.2	0.2
2014	LEH	AAA	30	38	4	2	0	1	4	3	11	0	0	.182/.289/.333	.235	.238	-0.7	1B(3): 0.2, LF(3): -0.2	-0.3
2014	PHI	MLB	30	138	11	7	0	6	21	15	30	0	0	.213/.304/.418	.274	.233	-1.9	1B(17): -0.1, LF(13): -0.2	0.4
2014	TOR	MLB	30	30	4	3	0	1	2	5	5	0	0	.208/.333/.458	.274	.211	0.6	1B(6): -0.1, LF(3): -0.0	0.0
2015	NYN	MLB	31	250	27	12	0	7	27	18	57	2	1	.232/.293/.382	.265	.275	-0.8	CF 0, RF -1	0.6

Breakout: 0%   Improve: 36%   Collapse: 7%   Attrition: 18%   MLB: 85%   Comparables: Scott Hairston, Terrmel Sledge, Fred Lewis

Mayberry Jr., owner of a 68-point career TAv split in favor of lefties, still found himself facing righties more often in Philadelphia. What's up with that? Toronto acquired him in September and deployed him as a pinch-hitter (mostly) against southpaws. His one shining moment, a bottom-of-the-ninth, two-out, game-tying, pinch-hit home run, made the trade worth it ... until the Jays lost in the 10th.

Daniel Murphy 2B

Born: 4/1/85   Age: 30   Bats: L   Throws: R   Height: 6' 1"   Weight: 215

YEAR	TEAM	LVL	AGE	PA	R	2B	3B	HR	RBI	BB	K	SB	CS	AVG/OBP/SLG	TAv	BABIP	BRR	FRAA	WARP
2012	NYN	MLB	27	612	62	40	3	6	65	36	82	10	2	.291/.332/.403	.268	.329	4.0	2B(138): -2.6, 1B(12): -0.3	2.3
2013	NYN	MLB	28	697	92	38	4	13	78	32	95	23	3	.286/.319/.415	.265	.315	7.6	2B(150): -7.9, 1B(7): 0.4	2.2
2014	NYN	MLB	29	642	79	37	2	9	57	39	86	13	5	.289/.332/.403	.277	.322	-1.3	2B(126): -5.8, 3B(16): -0.6	2.2
2015	NYN	MLB	30	614	70	36	2	8	53	33	84	14	4	.279/.318/.389	.273	.311	2.3	2B -5, 3B -0	2.5

Breakout: 1%   Improve: 47%   Collapse: 2%   Attrition: 8%   MLB: 98%   Comparables: Brandon Phillips, Aaron Hill, Orlando Hudson

The sobering reality of Murphy's "All-Star" campaign is that the gross numbers are only slightly less empty than his glove after a grounder to his left. Murphy is the prototypical "professional hitter," which is to say he's an honest hitter: He doesn't cheat, preferring to remain ready for any pitch type and location. That's a nice approach on its face, and it makes for some impressive line drives the other way, but it negates the power that could make Murphy a star. As is, he might be a star nonetheless were he not such an exquisitely poor defender. When Ruben Tejada and Lucas Duda need you to step it up on defense, you've got a big problem.

Kirk Nieuwenhuis OF

Born: 8/7/87   Age: 27   Bats: L   Throws: R   Height: 6' 3"   Weight: 225

YEAR	TEAM	LVL	AGE	PA	R	2B	3B	HR	RBI	BB	K	SB	CS	AVG/OBP/SLG	TAv	BABIP	BRR	FRAA	WARP
2012	NYN	MLB	24	314	40	12	1	7	28	25	98	4	4	.252/.315/.376	.256	.358	-0.1	CF(50): 3.7, LF(23): -0.6	1.2
2013	LVG	AAA	25	330	60	15	2	14	37	40	78	6	2	.248/.345/.465	.264	.293	4.2	CF(42): 0.1, RF(29): 2.9	1.9
2013	NYN	MLB	25	108	10	3	1	3	14	12	32	2	0	.189/.278/.337	.233	.246	-0.8	CF(25): -1.3, LF(9): -0.5	-0.1
2014	LVG	AAA	26	229	34	13	3	11	32	15	56	3	3	.265/.319/.512	.272	.310	-0.3	LF(31): 1.5, CF(25): -1.3	1.4
2014	NYN	MLB	26	130	16	14	1	3	16	16	39	4	0	.259/.346/.482	.307	.361	0.6	LF(17): -0.5, CF(14): -0.5	0.9
2015	NYN	MLB	27	250	30	11	1	7	25	22	74	4	2	.220/.292/.373	.254	.287	-0.1	CF 1, LF -0	0.6

Breakout: 5%   Improve: 35%   Collapse: 12%   Attrition: 20%   MLB: 78%   Comparables: Laynce Nix, Clete Thomas, Ryan Ludwick

Nieuwenhuis' approach is basically to attack any fastball in the zone, take all breaking pitches and occasionally look stupid on changeups he thought were fastballs. That's not the road to stardom, but it's a plan, and it'll keep him in the mix for a 25-man roster spot. He plays all three outfield positions passably, and he has enough power and patience that you'll put up with a daily strikeout. He's also been healthy for a full year following long-term knee and foot injuries. There's just a whiff of breakout potential here.

Brandon Nimmo   CF

Born: 3/27/93   Age: 22   Bats: L   Throws: R   Height: 6' 3"   Weight: 205

YEAR	TEAM	LVL	AGE	PA	R	2B	3B	HR	RBI	BB	K	SB	CS	AVG/OBP/SLG	TAv	BABIP	BRR	FRAA	WARP
2012	BRO	A-	19	321	41	20	2	6	40	46	78	1	5	.248/.372/.406	.308	.328	0.6	CF(69): 5.1	3.3
2013	SAV	A	20	480	62	16	6	2	40	71	131	10	7	.273/.397/.359	.301	.402	2.0	CF(106): -1.2	4.0
2014	SLU	A+	21	279	59	9	5	4	25	50	51	9	3	.322/.448/.458	.319	.401	1.4	CF(56): -1.6	2.6
2014	BIN	AA	21	279	38	12	4	6	26	36	54	5	1	.238/.339/.396	.260	.283	0.1	CF(44): 0.9, LF(21): -1.3	0.5
2015	NYN	MLB	22	250	27	8	2	3	19	29	72	2	1	.212/.311/.308	.245	.297	0.0	CF -0, LF -0	0.2

Breakout: 0%   Improve: 0%   Collapse: 0%   Attrition: 0%   MLB: 0%   Comparables: Aaron Hicks, Ryan Kalish, Brett Jackson

Nimmo is something of a baseball savant: He grew up in Cheyenne, Wyoming, playing American Legion ball because his state doesn't offer high school baseball. His swing aesthetic—and to some extent, everything else—reflects that lack of experience. Like a gory movie, to see him play is to realize the disturbingly mechanical nature of the human body. This is not a player you'd expect, say, to hit well to the opposite field, or post a 15 percent walk rate in his introduction to Double-A, at the age of 21. And then you see the end product and, insert local Wyoming expression of surprise here, he's really doing it.

Kevin Plawecki   C

Born: 2/26/91   Age: 24   Bats: R   Throws: R   Height: 6' 2"   Weight: 225

YEAR	TEAM	LVL	AGE	PA	R	2B	3B	HR	RBI	BB	K	SB	CS	AVG/OBP/SLG	TAv	BABIP	BRR	FRAA	WARP
2012	BRO	A-	21	252	26	8	0	7	27	25	24	0	0	.250/.345/.384	.282	.250	-0.1	C(36): -0.4, 1B(1): -0.0	1.5
2013	SAV	A	22	282	35	24	1	6	43	23	32	1	0	.314/.390/.494	.355	.336	-3.7	C(46): 0.6	3.7
2013	SLU	A+	22	239	25	14	0	2	37	19	21	0	0	.294/.391/.392	.295	.319	-1.9	C(42): -1.0, 1B(17): 1.5	1.5
2014	BIN	AA	23	249	33	18	0	6	43	16	27	0	0	.326/.378/.487	.307	.344	0.8	C(54): -0.1	2.4
2014	LVG	AAA	23	170	25	6	0	5	21	14	21	0	0	.283/.345/.421	.264	.299	-0.3	C(40): 0.6, 1B(1): -0.0	0.7
2015	NYN	MLB	24	250	23	12	0	5	26	14	43	0	0	.246/.304/.360	.260	.280	-0.5	C 0, 1B 0	0.8

Breakout: 5%   Improve: 11%   Collapse: 18%   Attrition: 22%   MLB: 39%   Comparables: John Jaso, Curtis Casali, Jonathan Lucroy

Amazin' that Travis d'Arnaud received Rookie of the Year votes, and yet Plawecki might still be the Mets' catcher of the future. The 2012 first-round pick from Purdue proved himself too advanced for Double-A and held his own at Triple-A Las Vegas for the final two months of 2014. Plawecki's exceptionally mature approach held up through the high minors, but most notable was that he logged only one game at first base. His mediocre arm masks solid receiving skills; Plawecki can absolutely stay at the position. The bigger decision concerns his facial hair, because "2 o'clock shadow" is not ever going to be a thing.

Anthony Recker   C

Born: 8/29/83   Age: 31   Bats: R   Throws: R   Height: 6' 2"   Weight: 240

YEAR	TEAM	LVL	AGE	PA	R	2B	3B	HR	RBI	BB	K	SB	CS	AVG/OBP/SLG	TAv	BABIP	BRR	FRAA	WARP
2012	SAC	AAA	28	229	29	7	0	9	29	28	56	3	1	.265/.358/.435	.280	.326	-1.7	C(44): -0.5, LF(3): 0.1	1.4
2012	OAK	MLB	28	37	3	1	0	0	0	4	13	0	0	.129/.250/.161	.180	.222	0.4	C(12): -0.2	0.0
2012	CHN	MLB	28	21	1	1	0	1	4	2	2	0	0	.167/.286/.389	.244	.133	-0.1	C(5): 0.1, 1B(1): -0.0	0.1
2013	NYN	MLB	29	151	17	7	0	6	19	13	49	0	1	.215/.280/.400	.263	.280	-1.2	C(38): -0.3, P(1): -0.0	0.4
2014	NYN	MLB	30	189	18	9	0	7	27	10	64	1	1	.201/.246/.374	.240	.267	1.2	C(52): 0.9	0.9
2015	NYN	MLB	31	250	27	10	0	8	27	23	72	2	1	.216/.291/.368	.253	.275	0.1	C 1, LF 0	0.9

Breakout: 3%   Improve: 18%   Collapse: 13%   Attrition: 28%   MLB: 56%   Comparables: Joe Borchard, Jeff Liefer, Chris Shelton

In a less enlightened time, we might have noted that five of Recker's seven home runs in 2014 gave the Mets the lead. In a less enlightened time, we might have said that of course Recker is a great clubhouse presence—he tweets about his favorite restaurants on the road! In a less enlightened time, we might have observed Recker's great baseball face, which would be code for, "He's built like a tank and he's really, really, almost insanely good-looking." In reality, Recker did little to earn himself a major-league job in 2015, but he'll be around, which makes one wonder how enlightened we really are. The man is a gorgeous, ruggedly handsome personification of the progress BP and our ilk have yet to make. He is gorgeous, though.

Amed Rosario   SS

Born: 11/20/95   Age: 19   Bats: R   Throws: R   Height: 6' 2"   Weight: 170

YEAR	TEAM	LVL	AGE	PA	R	2B	3B	HR	RBI	BB	K	SB	CS	AVG/OBP/SLG	TAv	BABIP	BRR	FRAA	WARP
2014	SAV	A	18	31	2	0	1	1	4	1	11	0	0	.133/.161/.300	.157	.167	-0.1	SS(2): -0.1, 3B(1): -0.1	-0.3
2014	BRO	A-	18	290	39	11	5	1	23	17	47	7	3	.289/.337/.380	.274	.345	0.7	SS(64): 3.2	2.0
2015	NYN	MLB	19	250	19	9	1	2	16	8	73	1	1	.192/.220/.262	.190	.262	-0.2	SS -0, 3B -0	-0.8

Breakout: 0%   Improve: 0%   Collapse: 0%   Attrition: 0%   MLB: 0%   Comparables: Hernan Perez, Daniel Santana, Arismendy Alcantara

Warm up the salivary glands. Rosario was short-season Brooklyn's only 18-year-old and acquitted himself well, earning himself a call-up to Savannah for the Sally League Playoffs. The numbers don't jump off the page—they rarely do for hitters in the New York-Penn League—but Rosario made incremental improvements in strikeouts and walks, and the five-tool ceiling remains very high. The caveats: Scouts indicate his swing needs a major overhaul before he hits the high minors, and he might have to move off shortstop as his frame fills out. The variables leave his big-league ETA in question, but Rosario is the son of a judge and graduated high school at 16, so—actually, those things probably won't help. He seems like a good guy, though.

Dominic Smith   1B

Born: 6/15/95   Age: 20   Bats: L   Throws: L   Height: 6' 0"   Weight: 185

YEAR	TEAM	LVL	AGE	PA	R	2B	3B	HR	RBI	BB	K	SB	CS	AVG/OBP/SLG	TAv	BABIP	BRR	FRAA	WARP
2014	SAV	A	19	518	52	26	1	1	44	51	77	5	4	.271/.344/.338	.262	.321	-4.8	1B(110): -1.8	-0.1
2015	NYN	MLB	20	250	17	10	0	1	19	15	60	0	0	.210/.260/.273	.213	.274	-0.5	1B -1	-1.1

Breakout: 0%   Improve: 0%   Collapse: 0%   Attrition: 0%   MLB: 0%   *Comparables: Eric Hosmer, Joc Pederson, Pablo Sandoval*

Smith played his first full pro season with Single-A Savannah and raised alarm bells by hitting just one home run in 518 plate appearances, with even some rumblings that, given his plus athleticism, he might move off first base. These concerns, for the time being, are absolutely ridiculous: Smith, who at 19 was still very young for that level, put on batting practice shows that proved the raw power just needs to carry over into games. His approach remains remarkably mature—he sees a lot of pitches and regularly drives the ball to left center—which seems to fit someone with the middle name "Rene." So let's allow puberty to end before we start worrying; if Smith ends up more John Olerud than Dave Kingman, Mets fans will gladly take it.

Ruben Tejada   SS
Born: 10/27/89   Age: 25   Bats: R   Throws: R   Height: 5' 11"   Weight: 200

YEAR	TEAM	LVL	AGE	PA	R	2B	3B	HR	RBI	BB	K	SB	CS	AVG/OBP/SLG	TAv	BABIP	BRR	FRAA	WARP
2012	BUF	AAA	22	21	3	1	0	0	2	1	3	0	0	.200/.238/.250	.152	.235	0.8	SS(6): -0.2	-0.1
2012	NYN	MLB	22	501	53	26	0	1	25	27	73	4	4	.289/.333/.351	.262	.339	2.4	SS(112): -5.4	2.0
2013	LVG	AAA	23	269	38	14	1	2	24	14	30	1	1	.288/.337/.379	.252	.316	2.7	SS(58): -2.1, 2B(1): -0.0	1.1
2013	NYN	MLB	23	227	20	12	0	0	10	15	24	2	1	.202/.259/.260	.203	.228	1.8	SS(55): 3.1	0.1
2014	NYN	MLB	24	419	30	11	0	5	34	50	73	1	2	.237/.342/.310	.261	.283	-2.5	SS(114): 10.3	2.9
2015	ANA	MLB	35	603	76	30	1	25	86	53	74	5	1	.273/.339/.472	.306	.272	-1.0	1B 5, 3B 0	4.0

Breakout: 1%   Improve: 65%   Collapse: 3%   Attrition: 4%   MLB: 100%   *Comparables: Aaron Hill, Asdrubal Cabrera, Yuniesky Betancourt*

You would think a player with Tejada's plate discipline wouldn't also be the sort of person who, on July 2nd, had his back turned on Jacob deGrom's first pitch of the game, allowing a groundball to get past him. But that's the Ruben Tejada experience; he plays a slow, steady game on both sides of the ball, and then he'll take a page out of the Yasiel Puig Playbook. Defensively, don't be fooled by the FRAA. Tejada is now just a passable short-stop—but he had to work his way up to mediocrity, and maybe that means he's growing up.

David Wright   3B
Born: 12/20/82   Age: 32   Bats: R   Throws: R   Height: 6' 0"   Weight: 205

YEAR	TEAM	LVL	AGE	PA	R	2B	3B	HR	RBI	BB	K	SB	CS	AVG/OBP/SLG	TAv	BABIP	BRR	FRAA	WARP
2012	NYN	MLB	29	670	91	41	2	21	93	81	112	15	10	.306/.391/.492	.315	.347	1.6	3B(155): -0.0, SS(1): -0.0	6.5
2013	NYN	MLB	30	492	63	23	6	18	58	55	79	17	3	.307/.390/.514	.326	.340	3.9	3B(111): 5.4	5.8
2014	NYN	MLB	31	586	54	30	1	8	63	42	113	8	5	.269/.324/.374	.259	.325	-2.2	3B(133): -3.9	1.2
2015	NYN	MLB	32	532	63	27	2	15	63	53	109	11	5	.268/.343/.426	.293	.316	0.9	3B -2, SS -0	2.9

Breakout: 1%   Improve: 32%   Collapse: 10%   Attrition: 11%   MLB: 99%   *Comparables: Morgan Ensberg, George Brett, Al Rosen*

The count is 3-1, with a man on first. The whole stadium knows a fastball is coming. The pitcher winds and delivers, and 2014 David Wright ... fouls it off back out of play. That's a miss, but it isn't a miss—at least, not in terms of whiff rate. In looking for evidence of Wright's decline, you might be surprised to find that his whiff rate held firm around the league average, in keeping with his numbers from years past. But swings and misses don't tell the whole story; whether it was the balky left shoulder that eventually ended his season, or the beginning of a permanent decline, Wright was consistently beat on fastballs in obvious fastball situations. Can he turn it around? Depends how enthused you are that he didn't miss them entirely. The good news is that Wright didn't let his struggles affect his mature approach—the amateur psychologist sees a man who knows this too shall pass.

Eric Young   LF
Born: 5/25/85   Age: 30   Bats: B   Throws: R   Height: 5' 10"   Weight: 195

YEAR	TEAM	LVL	AGE	PA	R	2B	3B	HR	RBI	BB	K	SB	CS	AVG/OBP/SLG	TAv	BABIP	BRR	FRAA	WARP
2012	COL	MLB	27	196	36	7	2	4	15	13	31	14	2	.316/.377/.448	.274	.367	5.0	CF(15): 1.9, RF(11): -0.7	1.4
2013	COL	MLB	28	180	22	9	3	1	6	11	33	8	4	.242/.290/.352	.225	.298	-2.7	RF(20): -2.5, CF(10): 0.6	-0.9
2013	NYN	MLB	28	418	48	18	4	1	26	35	67	38	7	.251/.318/.329	.239	.303	7.4	LF(88): 5.9, CF(8): -0.7	1.4
2014	NYN	MLB	29	316	48	10	5	1	17	24	60	30	6	.229/.299/.311	.251	.285	6.3	LF(73): 1.9, 2B(2): -0.0	1.5
2015	NYN	MLB	30	355	44	13	3	1	20	30	68	29	6	.235/.306/.306	.243	.287	3.8	LF 1, RF -1	0.6

Breakout: 0%   Improve: 45%   Collapse: 6%   Attrition: 12%   MLB: 94%   *Comparables: Scott Podsednik, Willie Harris, Lew Ford*

Eric Young is so fast, he snuck his way onto 99 lineup cards and Terry Collins was none the wiser. Young is a one-tool player who has been lucky to land in two great situations: the Rockies, for altitude-related reasons, and the Mets, for "We don't have anyone else"-related reasons. He remains among the best baserunners in the game, but Young's inability to improve even one other area—defense is a glaring disappointment, given his speed—should keep him off most lineup cards going forward. Still, Young stole 30 bases in 124 stolen base opportunities; that's not a ratio that leads to the unemployment line.

Pitchers

Vic Black   RHP
Born: 5/23/88   Age: 27   Bats: R   Throws: R   Height: 6'4"   Weight: 210

YEAR	TEAM	LVL	AGE	W	L	SV	G	GS	IP	H	HR	BB	K	BB/9	K/9	GB%	BABIP	WHIP	ERA	FIP	FRA	WARP
2012	ALT	AA	24	2	3	13	51	0	60	40	2	29	85	4.3	12.8	55%	.295	1.15	1.65	2.45	3.14	1.3
2013	IND	AAA	25	5	3	17	38	0	46²	28	2	21	63	4.1	12.1	44%	.252	1.05	2.51	2.48	2.85	1.1
2013	PIT	MLB	25	0	0	0	3	0	4	6	0	2	3	4.5	6.8	47%	.400	2.00	4.50	3.77	2.77	0.1
2013	NYN	MLB	25	3	0	1	15	0	13	11	1	4	12	2.8	8.3	24%	.270	1.15	3.46	3.33	4.03	0.1
2014	LVG	AAA	26	0	1	7	17	0	19²	12	0	17	18	8.2	8.7	54%	.261	1.55	1.45	4.66	5.33	0.2
2014	NYN	MLB	26	2	3	0	41	0	34²	26	2	19	32	4.9	8.3	48%	.255	1.30	2.60	3.74	3.04	0.4
2015	NYN	MLB	27	2	1	0	45	0	50¹	39	3	24	55	4.2	9.8	46%	.298	1.24	3.29	3.44	3.57	0.5

Breakout: 28%   Improve: 39%   Collapse: 19%   Attrition: 26%   MLB: 71%   *Comparables: Jake Diekman, Santiago Casilla, Dan Runzler*

"You throw 97; put it over the plate!" they begged. (We can't prove that happened; we're just assuming.) But Black wouldn't listen, walking more than a batter every two innings, with even more disturbing numbers in Triple-A. There are very few major-league pitchers for whom it's permissible for the catcher to line up straight down the middle, but Black might be one; he's fast enough to get by with a few more strikes regardless of where (or how flat) they are. Then there's his curveball, an absolute knee-buckler, but rendered useless by his inaccurate fastball, because hitters need only wait until Black falls behind in the count and then sit on the heater. The good news is that Black is a simple fix—and if he gains control of his fastball, he'll get the curveball as a bonus.

Matthew Bowman   RHP

Born: 5/31/91   Age: 24   Bats: R   Throws: R   Height: 6'0"   Weight: 165

YEAR	TEAM	LVL	AGE	W	L	SV	G	GS	IP	H	HR	BB	K	BB/9	K/9	GB%	BABIP	WHIP	ERA	FIP	FRA	WARP
2012	BRO	A-	21	2	2	3	12	1	29¹	26	1	2	30	0.6	9.2	49%	.312	0.95	2.45	2.04	3.70	0.4
2013	SAV	A	22	4	0	0	5	5	30²	28	0	4	26	1.2	7.6	66%	.301	1.04	2.64	2.27	3.08	0.5
2013	SLU	A+	22	6	4	0	16	16	96¹	83	8	31	90	2.9	8.4	63%	.283	1.18	3.18	3.54	4.62	0.4
2014	BIN	AA	23	7	6	0	17	17	98¹	102	7	27	92	2.5	8.4	63%	.331	1.31	3.11	3.35	4.41	1.3
2014	LVG	AAA	23	3	2	0	7	6	36¹	38	1	9	32	2.2	7.9	59%	.333	1.29	3.47	3.04	3.68	1.1
2015	NYN	MLB	24	6	7	0	20	20	119	112	11	37	97	2.8	7.4	56%	.309	1.25	3.79	3.94	4.12	0.4

Breakout: 13%   Improve: 25%   Collapse: 8%   Attrition: 25%   MLB: 40%   Comparables: Simon Castro, Rudy Owens, Brandon Workman

The Tim Lincecum delivery comparison is a major stretch—Bowman freely admits that Lincecum is "way more athletic than I am"—but the Princeton-educated economics major might find his way to the big leagues in 2015. No single pitch stands out, but like Dillon Gee and Rafael Montero before him, Bowman has navigated the minors with his exceptional command. He'll almost certainly get crowded out of a rotation spot, but his dead-even lefty-righty splits would be nonetheless valuable in relief. He's also a former all-Ivy League shortstop, which should put him, what, at least third or fourth on the Mets depth chart.

Bartolo Colon   RHP

Born: 5/24/73   Age: 42   Bats: R   Throws: R   Height: 5'11"   Weight: 285

YEAR	TEAM	LVL	AGE	W	L	SV	G	GS	IP	H	HR	BB	K	BB/9	K/9	GB%	BABIP	WHIP	ERA	FIP	FRA	WARP
2012	OAK	MLB	39	10	9	0	24	24	152¹	161	17	23	91	1.4	5.4	47%	.286	1.21	3.43	3.78	3.90	1.7
2013	OAK	MLB	40	18	6	0	30	30	190¹	193	14	29	117	1.4	5.5	43%	.294	1.17	2.65	3.26	3.63	2.7
2014	NYN	MLB	41	15	13	0	31	31	202¹	218	22	30	151	1.3	6.7	41%	.307	1.23	4.09	3.54	4.19	0.8
2015	NYN	MLB	42	10	10	0	28	28	175	173	17	29	123	1.5	6.3	43%	.309	1.16	3.54	3.73	3.85	1.1

Breakout: 7%   Improve: 18%   Collapse: 16%   Attrition: 8%   MLB: 63%   Comparables: Greg Maddux, John Smoltz, Andy Pettitte

Colon pitched this season like a man incensed to find that his agent had placed him with a team that only intended to trade him in the coming months. Every time he put together a little run—every time his ERA crept down toward 3.50—Colon would get bombed and throw potential trade partners off the scent. Even after the trade deadline passed, he tanked his first and last starts of August, just in case he cleared waivers, just to be safe. (And he did clear waivers.) Yet for all the starts in between, let us admire what an artist this man is: It will be a long time before we see a starting pitcher with the command to throw 84 percent fastballs, as Colon has done since 2007. And it will be a very long time before we see another pitcher decide, screw it, I'm playing my at-bats for comedy.

Jacob DeGrom   RHP

Born: 6/19/88   Age: 27   Bats: L   Throws: R   Height: 6'4"   Weight: 180

YEAR	TEAM	LVL	AGE	W	L	SV	G	GS	IP	H	HR	BB	K	BB/9	K/9	GB%	BABIP	WHIP	ERA	FIP	FRA	WARP
2012	SAV	A	24	6	3	0	15	15	89²	77	3	14	78	1.4	7.8	52%	.277	1.01	2.51	2.78	3.18	2.2
2012	SLU	A+	24	3	0	0	4	4	21²	14	1	6	18	2.5	7.5	39%	.213	0.92	2.08	3.30	4.25	0.4
2013	SLU	A+	25	1	0	0	2	2	12	12	1	2	13	1.5	9.8	47%	.333	1.17	3.00	2.91	3.80	0.1
2013	BIN	AA	25	2	5	0	10	10	60	69	4	20	44	3.0	6.6	45%	.342	1.48	4.80	3.82	4.06	0.9
2013	LVG	AAA	25	4	2	0	14	14	75²	87	6	24	63	2.9	7.5	47%	.342	1.47	4.52	3.93	4.50	1.8
2014	LVG	AAA	26	4	0	0	7	7	38¹	39	2	10	29	2.3	6.8	60%	.311	1.28	2.58	3.73	4.27	0.9
2014	NYN	MLB	26	9	6	0	22	22	140¹	117	7	43	144	2.8	9.2	47%	.297	1.14	2.69	2.64	3.27	2.8
2015	NYN	MLB	27	8	9	0	25	25	147²	134	11	42	126	2.5	7.7	47%	.308	1.19	3.47	3.51	3.77	1.2

Breakout: 36%   Improve: 57%   Collapse: 17%   Attrition: 28%   MLB: 87%   Comparables: David Phelps, Joe Saunders, Josh Collmenter

DeGrom was a revelation in every way; reminiscent of a leaner John Maine, he posted strikeout numbers beyond both his career minor-league numbers and the quality of his individual pitches. In particular his mid-90s fastball, a relatively flat pitch, yielded an ungodly 12.3 percent whiff rate. To what might we attribute this? Consider the season-long presence of Bartolo Colon, living proof of the importance of command and control over physical skills. DeGrom's changeup is an afterthought, his curve and slider essentially 87- and 80-mph versions of the same pitch; for a big man, he simply repeats his motion at an elite level. Maybe he learned from Colon or maybe he didn't, but his success was in a similar vein. Also notable: He was smart enough to learn to hit from someone who is not Bartolo Colon.

Josh Edgin   LHP

Born: 12/17/86   Age: 28   Bats: R   Throws: L   Height: 6'1"   Weight: 245

YEAR	TEAM	LVL	AGE	W	L	SV	G	GS	IP	H	HR	BB	K	BB/9	K/9	GB%	BABIP	WHIP	ERA	FIP	FRA	WARP
2012	BUF	AAA	25	3	2	1	35	0	37	34	0	18	40	4.4	9.7	43%	.324	1.41	3.89	2.54	3.20	0.8
2012	NYN	MLB	25	1	2	0	34	0	25²	19	5	10	30	3.5	10.5	42%	.233	1.13	4.56	4.73	5.58	-0.2
2013	LVG	AAA	26	2	0	0	11	0	10²	14	1	2	12	1.7	10.1	39%	.406	1.50	5.91	3.38	4.43	0.2
2013	NYN	MLB	26	1	1	1	34	0	28²	26	2	12	20	3.8	6.3	44%	.279	1.33	3.77	4.00	5.24	-0.2
2014	LVG	AAA	27	3	0	2	17	0	12²	16	1	11	12	7.8	8.5	53%	.405	2.13	4.97	5.67	6.02	0.0
2014	NYN	MLB	27	1	0	0	47	0	27¹	19	2	6	28	2.0	9.2	51%	.250	0.91	1.32	2.66	3.50	0.0
2015	NYN	MLB	28	2	1	1	40	0	37²	32	3	14	37	3.4	8.8	49%	.302	1.22	3.53	3.66	3.84	0.2

Breakout: 21%   Improve: 39%   Collapse: 10%   Attrition: 19%   MLB: 60%   Comparables: Clay Zavada, Brad Brach, Jonathan Albaladejo

Sure, he's got the fire hydrant physique and the cringe-inducing elbow torque, but don't be too quick to label Edgin a LOOGY. Lefties are helpless against him, but righties weren't much better; Edgin added a cutter last season to keep them honest, and it worked out so well he breaks it out for same-sided hitters as well. The lesson, there: Hitters, left- or right-handed, aren't used to seeing 94 with sink from the left side. The result was 27 innings' worth of breakout campaign. The other key number, of course, is the six walks. This isn't all rocket science, you know.

Jeurys Familia   RHP

Born: 10/10/89   Age: 25   Bats: R   Throws: R   Height: 6'3"   Weight: 240

YEAR	TEAM	LVL	AGE	W	L	SV	G	GS	IP	H	HR	BB	K	BB/9	K/9	GB%	BABIP	WHIP	ERA	FIP	FRA	WARP
2012	BUF	AAA	22	9	9	0	28	28	137	145	8	73	128	4.8	8.4	55%	.333	1.59	4.73	3.73	4.64	1.3
2012	NYN	MLB	22	0	0	0	8	1	12¹	10	0	9	10	6.6	7.3	48%	.303	1.54	5.84	3.70	4.17	0.1
2013	NYN	MLB	23	0	0	1	9	0	10²	12	2	9	8	7.6	6.8	54%	.303	1.97	4.22	6.49	5.35	-0.2
2014	NYN	MLB	24	2	5	5	76	0	77¹	59	3	32	73	3.7	8.5	59%	.264	1.18	2.21	3.04	3.66	0.5
2015	NYN	MLB	25	3	3	1	24	9	58²	52	5	27	55	4.2	8.4	49%	.308	1.34	4.01	4.11	4.36	0.1

Breakout: 36%   Improve: 65%   Collapse: 18%   Attrition: 26%   MLB: 89%   Comparables: Tyson Ross, Rubby De La Rosa, Chris Archer

Familia's two-seamer is unhittable—97 with decent arm-side movement, and the control is good enough to make it all work. His four-seam data shows some of that same movement, suggesting many of his supposed four-seamers are just failed sinkers. The end product is about three sinkers for every slider. Now, consider this: On 0-0 counts, Familia threw up to 266 (85 percent) fastballs in 2014. Of those, 128 were strikes, and of those, just seven were hit for line drives or fly balls. Not only can big leaguers not hit what they already know is coming, but Familia's fastball hasn't even reached its ceiling; it's easy to imagine a grade jump in control still. In a perfect world, Famila and Jenrry Mejia become a media sensation, a sort of Dominican Bash Brothers. But you know what happens when the Mets try to market themselves.

Dillon Gee   RHP

Born: 4/28/86   Age: 29   Bats: R   Throws: R   Height: 6'1"   Weight: 205

YEAR	TEAM	LVL	AGE	W	L	SV	G	GS	IP	H	HR	BB	K	BB/9	K/9	GB%	BABIP	WHIP	ERA	FIP	FRA	WARP
2012	NYN	MLB	26	6	7	0	17	17	109²	108	12	29	97	2.4	8.0	52%	.302	1.25	4.10	3.75	4.07	1.4
2013	NYN	MLB	27	12	11	0	32	32	199	208	24	47	142	2.1	6.4	45%	.296	1.28	3.62	3.98	4.12	2.1
2014	NYN	MLB	28	7	8	0	22	22	137¹	128	18	43	94	2.8	6.2	45%	.268	1.25	4.00	4.49	4.82	-0.2
2015	NYN	MLB	29	7	8	0	22	22	132²	123	15	39	107	2.6	7.2	46%	.299	1.22	3.90	4.25	4.24	0.2

Breakout: 32%   Improve: 47%   Collapse: 16%   Attrition: 11%   MLB: 77%   Comparables: Charlie Morton, Manny Parra, Boof Bonser

For the third year in a row, Gee overcame an injury to his throwing arm to have the exact same year he has every other year. For the fourth year in a row, he mixed five pitches in roughly the same proportion, without any one of them being what one might call "good." He isn't smoke and mirrors; he just works within finer margins than the rest of the league. Some have labeled Gee a trade candidate to accommodate the Mets' crowded rotation. But GMs (and prospective fantasy owners) beware: Gee's fly-ball tendencies likely make him more valuable to the Mets than to another team. On the other hand, the Mets' moving the Citi Field fences in yet again could be a sign that Gee should pack his bags. Would that be better or worse than breaking up via text message?

Gonzalez Germen   RHP

Born: 9/23/87   Age: 27   Bats: R   Throws: R   Height: 6'1"   Weight: 200

YEAR	TEAM	LVL	AGE	W	L	SV	G	GS	IP	H	HR	BB	K	BB/9	K/9	GB%	BABIP	WHIP	ERA	FIP	FRA	WARP
2012	SLU	A+	24	3	0	0	5	4	26²	25	3	8	21	2.7	7.1	56%	.289	1.24	3.04	4.18	4.02	0.2
2012	BIN	AA	24	8	12	0	20	19	119²	127	11	33	97	2.5	7.3	50%	.314	1.34	4.59	3.70	4.85	0.6
2013	LVG	AAA	25	3	3	4	35	0	44	47	7	11	51	2.2	10.4	50%	.336	1.32	5.52	4.07	4.27	0.9
2013	NYN	MLB	25	1	2	1	29	0	34¹	32	1	16	33	4.2	8.7	37%	.313	1.40	3.93	2.87	3.32	0.4
2014	LVG	AAA	26	3	1	6	18	0	22²	20	2	10	21	4.0	8.3	58%	.281	1.32	2.38	4.45	4.19	0.6
2014	NYN	MLB	26	0	0	0	25	0	30¹	30	7	14	31	4.2	9.2	38%	.287	1.45	4.75	5.54	5.36	-0.3
2015	NYN	MLB	27	3	3	0	23	6	56¹	54	7	20	47	3.1	7.5	47%	.310	1.32	4.31	4.48	4.69	-0.2

Breakout: 31%   Improve: 38%   Collapse: 10%   Attrition: 26%   MLB: 52%   Comparables: Felix Diaz, D.J. Houlton, Tony Watson

Germen threw a first-pitch strike to 54 percent of the batters he faced in 2014. It went downhill from there: a walk every two innings and seven home runs in just 30 innings of work. In terms of raw stuff, Germen illustrates the difference between control and command. His lack of control gets him behind batters; then, when he has to give them something to hit, he's often unable to command enough sink on his low-to-mid-90s fastball to get the groundballs he needs. The off-speed stuff shows flashes but was no more consistent than in 2013. Essentially, there's a Grand Canyon-sized variance between Good Germen and Bad Germen, and his pitch-to-pitch fluctuation means he can't be trusted with more than mop-up duty. He did use Justin Timberlake's "Mirrors" as a walk-in song, which at least shows he's a man of taste.

Matt Harvey   RHP

Born: 3/27/89   Age: 26   Bats: R   Throws: R   Height: 6'4"   Weight: 225

YEAR	TEAM	LVL	AGE	W	L	SV	G	GS	IP	H	HR	BB	K	BB/9	K/9	GB%	BABIP	WHIP	ERA	FIP	FRA	WARP
2012	BUF	AAA	23	7	5	0	20	20	110	97	9	48	112	3.9	9.2	46%	.295	1.32	3.68	3.66	4.65	0.9
2012	NYN	MLB	23	3	5	0	10	10	59¹	42	5	26	70	3.9	10.6	41%	.262	1.15	2.73	3.34	3.88	1.3
2013	NYN	MLB	24	9	5	0	26	26	178¹	135	7	31	191	1.6	9.6	49%	.280	0.93	2.27	1.98	2.66	4.0
2015	NYN	MLB	26	2	2	0	7	7	39	31	3	11	40	2.6	9.2	47%	.301	1.09	2.85	3.17	3.10	0.7

Breakout: 40%   Improve: 67%   Collapse: 14%   Attrition: 15%   MLB: 94%   Comparables: Alex Cobb, Ian Kennedy, Daniel Hudson

Few pitchers get more from their legs than Harvey—older Mets fans may recall Tom Seaver—but as it turned out, his smooth drop and drive wasn't enough to avoid the UCL injury that led to Tommy John surgery. Harvey's velocity rose dramatically upon his promotion to the majors; he distributes the extra torque beautifully, but it has still added stress on the body, which means increased risk. With nothing but rehab on the docket for 2014, Harvey stayed relevant with a cavalcade of model girlfriends who don't get nearly as much power from their lower bodies as he does. You can't blame the man for playing the field; when fate (and Dr. James Andrews) has your career in its hands, you may as well plow your way down 7th Avenue while you have the chance.

Daisuke Matsuzaka   RHP

Born: 9/13/80   Age: 34   Bats: R   Throws: R   Height: 6'0"   Weight: 205

YEAR	TEAM	LVL	AGE	W	L	SV	G	GS	IP	H	HR	BB	K	BB/9	K/9	GB%	BABIP	WHIP	ERA	FIP	FRA	WARP
2012	PAW	AAA	31	1	3	0	11	11	51	42	6	17	41	3.0	7.2	38%	.247	1.16	3.18	4.37	5.25	0.1
2012	BOS	MLB	31	1	7	0	11	11	45²	58	11	20	41	3.9	8.1	41%	.336	1.71	8.28	5.89	6.76	-0.5
2013	COH	AAA	32	5	8	0	19	19	103¹	93	11	39	95	3.4	8.3	36%	.290	1.28	3.92	3.97	4.96	0.4
2013	NYN	MLB	32	3	3	0	7	7	38²	32	4	16	33	3.7	7.7	33%	.259	1.24	4.42	4.29	4.78	0.0
2014	LVG	AAA	33	0	0	0	2	2	12	7	0	6	12	4.5	9.0	30%	.233	1.08	2.25	3.20	3.13	0.3
2014	NYN	MLB	33	3	3	1	34	9	83¹	62	6	50	78	5.4	8.4	43%	.256	1.34	3.89	4.18	4.14	0.4
2015	NYN	MLB	34	5	7	0	20	20	98¹	84	10	41	86	3.8	7.8	36%	.287	1.27	3.86	4.33	4.20	0.4

Breakout: 14%   Improve: 30%   Collapse: 17%   Attrition: 14%   MLB: 58%   Comparables: Ryan Vogelsong, Claudio Vargas, Eric Stults

There were times last season when Matsuzaka appeared to be the glue holding the Mets' pitching staff together. He was so versatile—along with nine starts, he made eight relief appearances of at least two innings or more—and kept the rest of the staff so fresh, it makes one wonder whether a franchise might get value out of grooming *good* pitchers for such a role. The numbers themselves were not all that special (okay, 50 walks in 83 innings with an ERA under 4.00 is special), but Matsuzaka gave the Mets that unseen added value. At press, he was getting a lucrative offer from Japan that promised the money and rotation spot he's unlikely to earn stateside.

Steven Matz   LHP

Born: 5/29/91   Age: 24   Bats: R   Throws: L   Height: 6'2"   Weight: 200

YEAR	TEAM	LVL	AGE	W	L	SV	G	GS	IP	H	HR	BB	K	BB/9	K/9	GB%	BABIP	WHIP	ERA	FIP	FRA	WARP
2013	SAV	A	22	5	6	0	21	21	106¹	86	4	38	121	3.2	10.2	55%	.315	1.17	2.62	2.91	3.42	1.8
2014	SLU	A+	23	4	4	0	12	12	69¹	66	0	21	62	2.7	8.0	59%	.328	1.25	2.21	2.73	3.98	1.0
2014	BIN	AA	23	6	5	0	12	12	71¹	66	3	14	69	1.8	8.7	48%	.317	1.12	2.27	2.64	3.07	1.9
2015	NYN	MLB	24	6	8	0	22	22	116¹	107	10	43	101	3.3	7.8	49%	.313	1.29	3.87	3.95	4.21	0.3

Breakout: 17%   Improve: 32%   Collapse: 14%   Attrition: 26%   MLB: 48%   Comparables: Chad Bettis, Andre Rienzo, Charles Brewer

Better late than never. Drafted 72nd overall in 2009, Matz didn't make his pro debut until 2012 following a long recovery from Tommy John surgery, but he's made up for lost time. He made the fateful leap from High-A to Double-A and actually performed better in the latter, with nearly a strikeout an inning and nary a walk to be seen. Matz ditched the slider to focus exclusively on the curveball this year, and made a delivery adjustment that has him working straight over the top. But the real difference, apparently, is that Matz is now "throwing [pitches] with conviction." Would that we all could be drafted 72nd overall without any conviction.

Casey Meisner   RHP

Born: 5/22/95   Age: 20   Bats: R   Throws: R   Height: 6'7"   Weight: 190

YEAR	TEAM	LVL	AGE	W	L	SV	G	GS	IP	H	HR	BB	K	BB/9	K/9	GB%	BABIP	WHIP	ERA	FIP	FRA	WARP
2014	BRO	A-	19	5	3	0	13	13	62¹	67	4	18	67	2.6	9.7	43%	.342	1.36	3.75	3.18	3.82	1.0
2015	NYN	MLB	20	2	4	0	12	9	50²	54	6	26	33	4.6	5.8	41%	.314	1.56	5.32	5.31	5.78	-0.7

Breakout: 0%   Improve: 0%   Collapse: 0%   Attrition: 0%   MLB: 0%   Comparables: Alex Sanabia, Roman Mendez, Kyle Lobstein

You cannot find a report on Meisner that does not include the word "projectable." That's what happens when you're 6-feet-7 and 190 pounds at 19 years old. We can all do the math that he'll grow into something someday, but let's have a look at what Meisner is: He's straight over the top, with the long stride of a man who assumes that, at some point, he'll grow into his frame. The young Texan had an excellent showing at short-season Brooklyn, where he allowed two earned runs or fewer in each of his last six starts. He also commented that he went "down" to Manhattan, and he "wasn't expecting how [the subway] worked." He's gonna love the 7 train one of these days.

Jenrry Mejia   RHP

Born: 10/11/89   Age: 25   Bats: R   Throws: R   Height: 6'0"   Weight: 205

YEAR	TEAM	LVL	AGE	W	L	SV	G	GS	IP	H	HR	BB	K	BB/9	K/9	GB%	BABIP	WHIP	ERA	FIP	FRA	WARP
2012	SLU	A+	22	1	0	0	2	2	11	7	1	2	8	1.6	6.5	55%	.200	0.82	2.45	3.67	5.11	0.1
2012	BUF	AAA	22	3	4	0	26	10	73²	75	4	24	39	2.9	4.8	56%	.290	1.34	3.54	3.82	5.41	-0.1
2012	NYN	MLB	22	1	2	0	5	3	16	20	2	9	8	5.1	4.5	68%	.327	1.81	5.62	5.45	5.48	0.0
2013	BIN	AA	23	0	0	0	2	2	11	6	1	4	9	3.3	7.4	41%	.192	0.91	0.82	3.96	4.44	0.1
2013	NYN	MLB	23	1	5	0	5	5	27¹	28	2	4	27	1.3	8.9	58%	.329	1.17	2.30	2.44	2.97	0.4
2014	NYN	MLB	24	6	6	28	63	7	93²	98	9	41	98	3.9	9.4	52%	.336	1.48	3.65	3.70	3.79	0.7
2015	NYN	MLB	25	4	4	8	32	11	79¹	73	7	28	66	3.2	7.5	54%	.308	1.27	3.74	3.99	4.06	0.4

Breakout: 31%   Improve: 54%   Collapse: 17%   Attrition: 17%   MLB: 94%   Comparables: Justin Masterson, Noah Lowry, Luke Hochevar

You probably heard most about Mejia for his "excessive" postgame celebrations—a laughable controversy in which the media seemed to care far more than the players themselves—but his real story of 2014 was one of self-discovery and heartwarming deliverance. After injury upon injury, role reversals and re-reversals, Mejia flourished as a closer when Bobby Parnell went down and Jose Valverde was Jose Valverde. Although his curve and slider are functionally very similar, a four-pitch offering (with no four-seam fastball) is odd for a closer and difficult to square up in a single at-bat. Mejia has taken his lumps and succeeded in spite of it; you can't blame the guy for doing a little dance.

Marcos Molina   RHP

Born: 3/8/95   Age: 20   Bats: R   Throws: R   Height: 6'3"   Weight: 188

YEAR	TEAM	LVL	AGE	W	L	SV	G	GS	IP	H	HR	BB	K	BB/9	K/9	GB%	BABIP	WHIP	ERA	FIP	FRA	WARP
2014	BRO	A-	19	7	3	0	12	12	76¹	46	2	18	91	2.1	10.7	52%	.246	0.84	1.77	2.34	3.41	1.2
2015	NYN	MLB	20	2	4	0	12	10	57¹	59	6	29	38	4.5	6.0	45%	.310	1.52	5.12	5.10	5.56	-0.7

Breakout: 0%   Improve: 0%   Collapse: 0%   Attrition: 0%   MLB: 0%   Comparables: Kyle Lobstein, Roman Mendez, J.C. Ramirez

Molina justified BP's faith in him—Jason Parks rated him 10th among Mets prospects to begin the season—with a dominant showing as a 19-year-old at Brooklyn. Molina delivers a low-to-mid-90s fastball with a violent whip that may be as injury-inducing as it is deceptive, along with a strong changeup and a promising slider. While he's getting some extra velocity from unhealthy torque, strong coaching could help him shed the mechanical flaws while making it up in other areas; at 6-feet-3 he should put on some muscle, and even now he doesn't use 100 percent of his body to drive forward. Molina could also use a Crash Davis-type catcher as a mentor—it might not help his pitching, but, son, you can't get to The Show with that Jheri curl mullet.

Rafael Montero   RHP

Born: 10/17/90   Age: 24   Bats: R   Throws: R   Height: 6'0"   Weight: 185

YEAR	TEAM	LVL	AGE	W	L	SV	G	GS	IP	H	HR	BB	K	BB/9	K/9	GB%	BABIP	WHIP	ERA	FIP	FRA	WARP
2012	SAV	A	21	6	3	0	12	12	71¹	61	4	8	54	1.0	6.8	37%	.260	0.97	2.52	3.17	3.40	1.4
2012	SLU	A+	21	5	2	0	8	8	50²	35	2	11	56	2.0	9.9	41%	.270	0.91	2.13	2.47	3.06	1.5
2013	BIN	AA	22	7	3	0	11	11	66²	51	2	10	72	1.4	9.7	40%	.277	0.92	2.43	2.00	2.57	2.1
2013	LVG	AAA	22	5	4	0	16	16	88²	85	4	25	78	2.5	7.9	40%	.316	1.24	3.05	3.24	3.59	2.5
2014	LVG	AAA	23	6	4	0	16	16	80	69	4	34	80	3.8	9.0	44%	.297	1.29	3.60	3.66	4.45	1.6
2014	NYN	MLB	23	1	3	0	10	8	44¹	44	8	23	42	4.7	8.5	36%	.298	1.51	4.06	5.11	5.01	-0.1
2015	NYN	MLB	24	7	7	0	22	22	119²	102	10	36	105	2.7	7.9	39%	.293	1.15	3.23	3.62	3.52	1.4

Breakout: 21%   Improve: 53%   Collapse: 19%   Attrition: 25%   MLB: 78%   Comparables: Erik Johnson, Alex Cobb, Jake Odorizzi

Montero made his major-league debut in 2014 with the look of a man who thought the jig might be up. For a prospect who has defied scouting evaluations at every level, Montero seemed afraid to challenge major-league hitters, leading to a walk rate that few starters' arsenal could overcome, much less his own. What should have been a polished sinker-slider-change ensemble greater than the sum of its parts became 62 percent four-seam fastballs, which led to high pitch counts and long nights for the bullpen catcher. His final three starts, however, were outstanding. Montero will never dominate on stuff alone, so he needs time at the highest level to figure out how to adapt his style. The question is whether the Mets' crowded rotation can afford him that opportunity.

Jon Niese   LHP

Born: 10/27/86   Age: 28   Bats: L   Throws: L   Height: 6'3"   Weight: 220

YEAR	TEAM	LVL	AGE	W	L	SV	G	GS	IP	H	HR	BB	K	BB/9	K/9	GB%	BABIP	WHIP	ERA	FIP	FRA	WARP
2012	NYN	MLB	25	13	9	0	30	30	190¹	174	22	49	155	2.3	7.3	49%	.272	1.17	3.40	3.85	4.16	2.6
2013	NYN	MLB	26	8	8	0	24	24	143	158	10	48	105	3.0	6.6	53%	.326	1.44	3.71	3.55	3.91	2.0
2014	NYN	MLB	27	9	11	0	30	30	187²	193	17	45	138	2.2	6.6	50%	.304	1.27	3.40	3.64	4.22	0.9
2015	NYN	MLB	28	8	10	0	26	26	155	151	15	40	128	2.3	7.4	49%	.317	1.23	3.85	3.80	4.18	0.4

Breakout: 20%   Improve: 65%   Collapse: 12%   Attrition: 9%   MLB: 90%   Comparables: Edwin Jackson, Brad Penny, Jeremy Bonderman

Everything Niese throws has some sink to it, which sounds great until he comes set and sees Ruben Tejada, Wilmer Flores, Daniel Murphy and Lucas Duda just trying to stay upright out there. All the more remarkable, then, that Niese carved out such a fine year, and while throwing the sinker about 50 percent more often than in 2013. Niese's velocity dipped significantly in 2014, more than it had the year before when he partially tore his rotator cuff. The four-seam fastball isn't generating outs the way it did, and he had to find another way to do business—this is a guy who could decline faster than most. Niese is smart and efficient enough to have continued success, of course, but we might have to reprint this comment for the 2017 Annual.

Bobby Parnell   RHP

Born: 9/8/84   Age: 30   Bats: R   Throws: R   Height: 6'3"   Weight: 205

YEAR	TEAM	LVL	AGE	W	L	SV	G	GS	IP	H	HR	BB	K	BB/9	K/9	GB%	BABIP	WHIP	ERA	FIP	FRA	WARP
2012	NYN	MLB	27	5	4	7	74	0	68²	65	4	20	61	2.6	8.0	63%	.302	1.24	2.49	3.03	3.18	1.5
2013	NYN	MLB	28	5	5	22	49	0	50	38	1	12	44	2.2	7.9	53%	.264	1.00	2.16	2.30	3.27	0.7
2014	NYN	MLB	29	0	0	0	1	0	1	2	0	1	1	9.0	9.0	25%	.500	3.00	9.00	4.10	2.90	0.0
2015	NYN	MLB	30	2	1	15	40	0	39²	33	2	11	37	2.6	8.7	55%	.307	1.14	2.97	2.97	3.23	0.5

Breakout: 33%   Improve: 56%   Collapse: 15%   Attrition: 21%   MLB: 81%   Comparables: Rafael Perez, Todd Coffey, Chad Qualls

Parnell went under the knife for Tommy John surgery after just one appearance. It might not have been just a lost season, though; unlike Matt Harvey, perhaps the best candidate ever to make a full comeback from the procedure, Parnell will return with uncertainty about both his role and whether he has the tools to play it. He never quite got the swings and misses that an upper-90s fastball usually gets, instead making himself a groundball machine. If 96 becomes 92, how many of those groundballs will be elevated? It's typically unwise to judge a pitcher by his velocity—Jon Niese, Bartolo Colon, Rafael Montero and Dillon Gee are side-eyeing us right now—but Parnell's fastball velo and bullpen role might be directly correlative.

Noah Syndergaard   RHP

Born: 8/29/92   Age: 22   Bats: L   Throws: R   Height: 6'6"   Weight: 240

YEAR	TEAM	LVL	AGE	W	L	SV	G	GS	IP	H	HR	BB	K	BB/9	K/9	GB%	BABIP	WHIP	ERA	FIP	FRA	WARP
2012	LNS	A	19	8	5	1	27	19	103²	81	3	31	122	2.7	10.6	58%	.299	1.08	2.60	2.36	3.50	2.3
2013	SLU	A+	20	3	3	0	12	12	63²	61	3	16	64	2.3	9.0	53%	.333	1.21	3.11	2.64	3.90	0.9
2013	BIN	AA	20	6	1	0	11	11	54	46	8	12	69	2.0	11.5	43%	.304	1.07	3.00	3.36	3.97	1.3
2014	LVG	AAA	21	9	7	0	26	26	133	154	11	43	145	2.9	9.8	47%	.378	1.48	4.60	3.70	4.22	3.2
2015	NYN	MLB	22	7	8	0	25	25	120¹	108	11	36	118	2.7	8.9	48%	.317	1.20	3.50	3.54	3.81	1.1

Breakout: 14%   Improve: 28%   Collapse: 2%   Attrition: 10%   MLB: 37%   Comparables: Gerrit Cole, Robbie Erlin, Danny Duffy

One of the great surprises of the 2014 Mets was that Syndergaard did not make his major-league debut. Of the three pitchers to make at least 15 starts for the Triple-A Las Vegas 51s, Syndergaard was the worst. Here's the part where we talk you off the ledge: As a 21-year-old in an almost comical hitter's haven, Syndergaard's peripheral numbers barely budged (note the 118 FRA+, an improvement over Double-A in 2013). His knee-buckling 12-to-6 curve was less effective at altitude, leaving him with upper-90s heat and an average change; he didn't fully adjust to being a three-pitch pitcher who couldn't dominate with his fastball, but that's what the minor leagues are for. He was also the victim of a .378 BABIP—while we hate to use that crutch, um, that seems like a lot.

Carlos Torres   RHP

Born: 10/22/82   Age: 32   Bats: R   Throws: R   Height: 6'1"   Weight: 180

YEAR	TEAM	LVL	AGE	W	L	SV	G	GS	IP	H	HR	BB	K	BB/9	K/9	GB%	BABIP	WHIP	ERA	FIP	FRA	WARP
2012	CSP	AAA	29	5	4	0	14	13	61	62	6	25	59	3.7	8.7	48%	.329	1.43	3.98	4.29	4.95	1.3
2012	COL	MLB	29	5	3	0	31	0	53	49	2	26	42	4.4	7.1	46%	.299	1.42	5.26	3.74	4.56	0.7
2013	LVG	AAA	30	6	3	0	12	12	71²	71	7	19	67	2.4	8.4	52%	.308	1.26	3.89	3.85	4.41	1.1
2013	NYN	MLB	30	4	6	0	33	9	86¹	79	15	17	75	1.8	7.8	45%	.266	1.11	3.44	4.27	4.89	-0.1
2014	NYN	MLB	31	8	6	2	73	1	97	89	11	38	96	3.5	8.9	49%	.302	1.31	3.06	3.83	3.68	0.6
2015	NYN	MLB	32	4	4	1	40	9	94²	83	9	33	85	3.2	8.0	46%	.299	1.23	3.62	3.91	3.94	0.5

Breakout: 14%   Improve: 29%   Collapse: 7%   Attrition: 9%   MLB: 42%   Comparables: *Dustin McGowan, Clay Hensley, Jason Grilli*

Finally armed with the information that pitchers who throw 80 percent fastballs and aren't Bartolo Colon should probably be relievers, the Mets enjoyed an even more productive Torres in 2014. More productive, that is, in fewer innings per appearance: It's easier to get people out when you only face them once a game, especially when you pretty much have one pitch. Torres deserves credit—his curveball appeared sharper and more reliable, and he threw a little harder on average—but his numbers have everything to do with being (almost) exclusively a reliever. He'll probably make another spot start somewhere down the line; don't go rushing to pick him up for your fantasy team just because he has nice peripherals.

Jose Valverde   RHP

Born: 3/24/78   Age: 37   Bats: R   Throws: R   Height: 6'4"   Weight: 265

YEAR	TEAM	LVL	AGE	W	L	SV	G	GS	IP	H	HR	BB	K	BB/9	K/9	GB%	BABIP	WHIP	ERA	FIP	FRA	WARP
2012	DET	MLB	34	3	4	35	71	0	69	59	3	27	48	3.5	6.3	36%	.264	1.25	3.78	3.57	3.97	0.9
2013	TOL	AAA	35	0	0	7	11	0	11	14	1	6	10	4.9	8.2	36%	.406	1.82	4.09	4.48	4.97	0.0
2013	DET	MLB	35	0	1	9	20	0	19¹	18	6	6	19	2.8	8.8	40%	.235	1.24	5.59	6.39	6.90	-0.3
2014	NYN	MLB	36	1	1	2	21	0	20²	24	4	10	23	4.4	10.0	34%	.345	1.65	5.66	4.84	5.30	-0.2
2015	NYN	MLB	37	2	1	8	39	0	37²	30	3	16	36	3.7	8.7	43%	.286	1.21	3.39	3.89	3.69	0.2

Breakout: 16%   Improve: 34%   Collapse: 17%   Attrition: 8%   MLB: 61%   Comparables: *Jason Isringhausen, Brendan Donnelly, Joe Borowski*

The less said, the better.

Zack Wheeler   RHP

Born: 5/30/90   Age: 25   Bats: L   Throws: R   Height: 6'4"   Weight: 195

YEAR	TEAM	LVL	AGE	W	L	SV	G	GS	IP	H	HR	BB	K	BB/9	K/9	GB%	BABIP	WHIP	ERA	FIP	FRA	WARP
2012	BIN	AA	22	10	6	0	19	19	116	92	2	43	117	3.3	9.1	48%	.300	1.16	3.26	2.80	3.78	2.1
2012	BUF	AAA	22	2	2	0	6	6	33	23	2	16	31	4.4	8.5	48%	.250	1.18	3.27	3.61	4.47	0.2
2013	LVG	AAA	23	4	2	0	13	13	68²	61	9	27	73	3.5	9.6	42%	.289	1.28	3.93	4.41	4.68	1.4
2013	NYN	MLB	23	7	5	0	17	17	100	90	10	46	84	4.1	7.6	45%	.279	1.36	3.42	4.14	3.91	0.8
2014	NYN	MLB	24	11	11	0	32	32	185¹	167	14	79	187	3.8	9.1	55%	.304	1.33	3.54	3.52	4.10	1.3
2015	NYN	MLB	25	9	10	0	28	28	155²	130	13	66	149	3.8	8.6	49%	.300	1.26	3.67	3.93	3.99	0.8

Breakout: 40%   Improve: 65%   Collapse: 18%   Attrition: 22%   MLB: 94%   Comparables: *Edinson Volquez, J.P. Howell, Dana Eveland*

The numbers look similar to 2013, but Wheeler has become—hmmm, how to say this without relying on a cliche? Okay, Wheeler has become more of a non-thrower and less of a non-pitcher than he was a year ago. With an increased emphasis on the sinker, changeup and slider (and less curveball and four-seam fastball), Wheeler is on his way to a well-rounded arsenal that will serve him well once the velocity starts to fade. In the near term, however, the ceiling has lowered slightly: His control and command improved but have a ways to go, and it doesn't seem that any of his secondary pitches will make him an All-Star by itself—you know, in that A.J. Burnett, nine-walk no-no kind of way. But if one or the other improves, he could still be an ace. Perhaps the scariest thing about Wheeler is that, in a way, he couldn't possibly pitch any worse.

Gabriel Ynoa   RHP

Born: 5/26/93   Age: 22   Bats: R   Throws: R   Height: 6'2"   Weight: 158

YEAR	TEAM	LVL	AGE	W	L	SV	G	GS	IP	H	HR	BB	K	BB/9	K/9	GB%	BABIP	WHIP	ERA	FIP	FRA	WARP
2012	BRO	A-	19	5	2	0	13	13	76²	61	1	10	64	1.2	7.5	43%	.268	0.93	2.23	2.34	3.27	1.2
2013	SAV	A	20	15	4	0	22	22	135²	123	9	16	106	1.1	7.0	41%	.278	1.02	2.72	3.16	3.73	1.6
2014	SLU	A+	21	8	2	0	14	14	82	95	7	13	64	1.4	7.0	44%	.330	1.32	3.95	3.45	4.54	0.7
2014	BIN	AA	21	3	2	0	11	11	66¹	74	9	12	42	1.6	5.7	40%	.304	1.30	4.21	4.53	5.04	0.3
2015	NYN	MLB	22	6	9	0	22	22	129²	138	16	35	75	2.4	5.2	40%	.304	1.33	4.59	4.72	4.99	-0.9

Breakout: 0%   Improve: 0%   Collapse: 0%   Attrition: 0%   MLB: 0%   Comparables: *James Parr, Jeanmar Gomez, Vance Worley*

That Ynoa has garnered so little attention speaks volumes for the Mets' organizational pitching depth. Like many of their prospects, he's mostly fastball and changeup, but where the Mets have stockpiled mid-to-upper-90s fastballs, Ynoa is out of the Rafael Montero mold: low 90s with impeccable command. It's also a relative low-effort delivery, suggesting he'll remain a starter until the big leagues tell him he can't hack it. Finally, perhaps Ynoa could use a cheeseburger once in a while; 6-feet-2 and 158 pounds suggests there's power that's yet to come to the surface. A little meat on the thighs could get him further down the mound.

Lineouts

Hitters

NAME	POS	TEAM	LVL	AGE	PA	R	2B	3B	HR	RBI	BB	K	SB	CS	AVG/OBP/SLG	TAv	BABIP	BRR	FRAA	WARP
Bobby Abreu	RF	LVG	AAA	40	91	11	8	0	1	18	16	14	0	0	.360/.473/.507	.304	.433	0.4	RF(9): 0.6	0.6
	RF	NYN	MLB	40	155	12	9	0	1	14	20	21	1	0	.248/.342/.338	.269	.283	-0.4	RF(26): -1.9, LF(5): -0.2	0.1
Jayce Boyd	1B	BIN	AA	23	477	60	22	2	8	59	52	67	2	1	.293/.382/.414	.290	.331	-2.1	1B(73): 4.0	2.3
Gavin Cecchini	SS	SAV	A	20	259	42	17	4	3	25	25	41	7	1	.259/.333/.408	.278	.299	3.5	SS(53): 2.6	2.3
	SS	SLU	A+	20	271	36	10	1	5	31	32	40	3	3	.236/.325/.352	.247	.259	0.3	SS(59): -2.7	0.2
L.J. Mazzilli	2B	SAV	A	23	284	39	9	2	7	45	29	48	11	1	.292/.363/.428	.304	.332	1.9	2B(49): 4.5, SS(14): -1.8	2.8
	2B	SLU	A+	23	274	40	20	2	4	34	16	33	3	3	.312/.363/.456	.304	.344	-1.0	2B(53): -3.1	1.5
Cesar Puello	LF	LVG	AAA	23	371	59	20	2	7	37	30	72	13	1	.252/.355/.393	.267	.305	4.6	LF(42): -0.5, RF(39): -4.6	1.2
Matthew Reynolds	SS	BIN	AA	23	242	33	5	3	1	21	29	41	6	3	.355/.430/.422	.330	.433	1.7	SS(46): 2.4, 2B(13): 0.2	3.0
	SS	LVG	AAA	23	301	54	16	4	5	40	21	60	14	4	.333/.385/.479	.297	.404	4.6	SS(58): -1.7, 2B(8): 0.9	3.1
Anthony Seratelli	2B	LVG	AAA	31	294	45	10	4	5	40	41	64	8	7	.279/.385/.414	.274	.354	-0.5	2B(43): 0.9, LF(34): 1.5	1.3
Taylor Teagarden	C	LVG	AAA	30	211	32	7	0	14	39	30	59	0	0	.303/.403/.579	.326	.374	0.6	C(44): 0.3, 1B(7): -0.4	2.5
	C	NYN	MLB	30	30	1	0	0	0	1	5	2	7	0	0	.143/.200/.250	.161	.150	0.2	C(9): 0.1	-0.1
Wilfredo Tovar	SS	SLU	A+	22	23	2	2	1	0	4	4	1	2	0	.353/.522/.588	.353	.375	-0.5	SS(3): 0.3	0.3
	SS	BIN	AA	22	285	31	8	1	2	29	21	22	8	6	.282/.345/.345	.253	.299	1.9	SS(47): 1.1, 2B(30): 4.5	1.6
	SS	NYN	MLB	22	3	0	0	0	0	0	0	0	0	0	.000/.000/.000	-.010	.000	0.0	SS(1): 0.0	-0.1
Jhoan Urena	3B	BRO	A-	19	315	30	20	1	5	47	27	58	7	9	.300/.356/.431	.303	.356	-2.1	3B(75): -3.5	2.3

Bobby Abreu so endeared himself to Mets fans that they forgot he garnered MVP votes for two of their least favorite teams, and gave him a prolonged standing ovation after his farewell game. ❖ **Jayce Boyd** hits and hits (and walks) and hits. But he doesn't hit for enough power to play first base, and when he moves to hitting haven Las Vegas, he'll be unfairly criticized when the homers don't go up. It's just not that kind of swing. ❖ **Gavin Cecchini** failed upward for the third consecutive year; when every scouting report defaults to raving about a first-rounder's "intangibles," there's a problem. Double-A will be the crossroads, with "potential starter" on one side, and "Nick Green" on the other. ❖ In a morass of Mets infield prospects pretending to be shortstops, **Luis Guillorme** not only belongs at the position but excels at it. The bat needs to come around, of course, but at age 20 he has time. ❖ **Vicente Lupo** wasn't even an everyday player to start the Appalachian League season, but he's back on the prospect radar after being named Kingsport's Player of the Year. And yes, to be fair, all outfielders in the Mets system should be considered "prospects." ❖ Son of former Mets All-Star Lee, **L.J. Mazzilli** is a well-built, powerful second baseman with the rare, Marcus Giles-esque ability to open his front shoulder and still hit to the opposite field. ❖ **Cesar Puello** had a breakout 2013, then broke out in acne because of the PEDs he took to break out in the first place. He broke into Triple-A for the first time in 2014 and returned to pre-PED numbers. ❖ A third-round pick in 2014, **Milton Ramos** is an exceptional defensive shortstop, but his swing will need an overhaul. The good news is he may not feel the need to wrap the bat as he gains strength. ❖ **Matt Reynolds** needed to stick at shortstop to have a shot at The Show … until he posted an .859 OPS between Double-A and Triple-A in 2014. Given how much he strikes out, though, sticking at shortstop would help considerably. ❖ **Anthony Seratelli** is patient at the plate, adds some power and has played at least 94 minor-league games at every position but pitcher, catcher and center field. He's now 32; a big-league call-up would be no less than he deserves. ❖ When **Taylor Teagarden** retires, he'll meet someone outside of baseball who has no idea who he is, and he'll tell that person he played major-league baseball, and that man or woman will be totally blown away by how awesome that is, and … well, that's just going to be an especially refreshing conversation for him. ❖ **Wilfredo Tovar** has been passed on the depth chart by Matt Reynolds, and at some point the Mets are going to notice he's on the 40-man roster. ❖ The big question with **Jhoan Urena** is whether he can stay at third base. If he can, the bat could carry him to the majors, and one lucky plyometrics trainer would have something for the resume.

Pitchers

NAME	TEAM	LVL	AGE	W	L	SV	G	GS	IP	H	HR	BB	K	BB/9	K/9	GB%	BABIP	WHIP	ERA	FIP	FRA	WARP
Dario Alvarez	SAV	A	25	7	1	1	20	6	61¹	43	2	14	95	2.1	13.9	55%	.315	0.93	1.32	1.70	2.01	2.4
	NYN	MLB	25	0	0	0	4	0	1¹	4	1	0	1	0.0	6.8	43%	.500	3.00	13.50	11.35	11.45	-0.2
Buddy Carlyle	LVG	AAA	36	4	2	3	30	0	33¹	27	6	12	36	3.2	9.7	32%	.250	1.17	2.16	5.14	5.26	0.3
	NYN	MLB	36	1	1	0	27	0	31	23	2	5	28	1.5	8.1	38%	.250	0.90	1.45	2.62	3.15	0.4
Dana Eveland	LVG	AAA	30	4	1	0	12	8	46	55	5	12	58	2.3	11.3	47%	.391	1.46	3.91	3.57	3.49	1.9
	NYN	MLB	30	1	1	1	30	0	27¹	24	2	6	27	2.0	8.9	55%	.289	1.10	2.63	3.18	3.07	0.2
Michael Fulmer	SLU	A+	21	6	10	0	19	19	95¹	112	7	31	86	2.9	8.1	50%	.347	1.50	3.97	3.77	4.48	1.0
Sean Gilmartin	NBR	AA	24	7	3	0	12	12	72	76	2	16	74	2.0	9.2	43%	.357	1.28	3.12	2.45	3.14	2.0
	ROC	AAA	24	2	4	0	14	14	73²	69	7	28	59	3.4	7.2	39%	.291	1.32	4.28	4.17	5.77	0.1
Erik Goeddel	LVG	AAA	25	3	2	0	49	0	63²	77	6	30	64	4.2	9.0	45%	.364	1.68	5.37	4.37	4.72	1.1
	NYN	MLB	25	0	0	0	6	0	6²	3	0	4	6	5.4	8.1	31%	.188	1.05	2.70	3.10	4.70	0.0
Jack Leathersich	BIN	AA	23	3	3	1	37	0	46	38	1	21	79	4.1	15.5	42%	.394	1.28	2.93	1.83	2.05	1.8
Cory Mazzoni	BIN	AA	24	2	0	0	2	2	12	10	0	4	10	3.0	7.5	39%	.278	1.17	4.50	2.69	3.33	0.3
	LVG	AAA	24	5	1	0	9	9	52	54	6	12	49	2.1	8.5	41%	.320	1.27	4.67	4.18	4.69	0.6
Scott Rice	NYN	MLB	32	1	2	0	32	0	13²	15	1	12	13	7.9	8.6	68%	.359	1.98	5.93	5.01	4.56	-0.1

As 2014 wore on, the Mets came around to the idea that **Dario Alvarez** is going to be a reliever. He might make a good one, too, because he has an excellent slider … and not much else. ❖ A **Buddy Carlyle** sighting! With a versatile arsenal of fastball and fastball—and he spent the last two seasons in the minors, where he added a third fastball—the best stage name in baseball will likely find itself in a bullpen, somewhere. ❖ **Dana Eveland** is not a lefty specialist, but if his sinker/slider offering keeps up this groundball rate, he won't have to be. ❖ With the body of a starter and the arsenal of a reliever—the changeup just will not cooperate—**Michael Fulmer** had a deceptively good season at High-A St. Lucie (15 earned runs over two of his first three starts). He had season-ending surgery to remove a bone spur in his pitching elbow. ❖ Former Braves first-rounder **Sean Gilmartin** continues to strain our thesaurus by using mundane stuff and a workaday approach to post forgettable numbers against mediocre Triple-A hitters and so-so blah meh, but on the bright side, last year's .201/.219/.235 line against lefties paints him as a possible LOOGY-in-waiting. ❖ **Erik Goeddel** converted to relief full-time in 2014, and it went, um, not very well. He did make his debut in September, however, showing a mid-90s fastball and an unremarkable-for-the-big-leagues curve and change. ❖ For the second straight year, **Jack Leathersich** looked strong at Double-A Binghamton and got lit up at Triple-A Las Vegas. He could crack The Show at any time; for now, look at those strikeout numbers! ❖ **Cory Mazzoni**'s season was abbreviated by a strained lat that kept him out for two months. He hasn't made a relief appearance since his first year of pro ball, but for reasons both in and out of his control, the time may be nigh. ❖ **Scott Rice** got lit up and sent down, and then missed the last three months with elbow surgery to remove bone spurs. He'll be making the rounds this spring as a LOOGY for hire.

Manager

Terry Collins

YEAR	TEAM	W	L	Py-thag +/-	Avg PC	100+ P	120+ P	QS	BQS	REL	REL w Zero R	IBB	PH	PH Avg	PH HR	SB2	CS2	SB3	CS3	SAC Att	SAC%	POS SAC	Squeeze	Swing	In Play
2012	NYN	74	88	0	95.5	69	2	101	1	505	380	29	322	.240	10	66	35	13	3	82	78.0%	19	4	321	108
2013	NYN	74	88	1	95.7	69	2	94	3	534	417	38	262	.207	4	99	31	15	4	82	64.6%	26	0	310	87
2014	NYN	79	83	-3	97.4	72	3	98	3	489	411	38	240	.181	3	90	27	10	7	86	68.6%	18	3	274	64

Collins is entering his fifth season as Mets skipper. He's held that position longer than 19 current managers have held theirs. He'll move into fourth in franchise history in games managed during the opening series, and third before the All-Star break. There's no reason to consider him more of a house-sitter than a homeowner. So why does he continue to feel like a bridge?

The oddest of Collins' 2014 decisions were how he paced New York's young arms. He allowed Zack Wheeler to cross the century mark on 23 occasions, almost twice as many times as anyone else on the Mets staff. Those 23 instances included three games where Wheeler failed to get out of the fifth inning, and another nine in which he recorded at most 18 outs. The bizarre handling extended to Jacob deGrom, who threw 122 pitches in his third big-league start, then went more than a month until topping 110 again. From there deGrom threw at least 110 pitches in two of his next four starts, before doing it just once more over his final eight.

Inconsistent workloads don't mean a pitcher is destined to blow out his arm. It just shows that Collins had an unusual, often ambiguous approach to divvying inning shares. That's a somewhat surprising development, given he reportedly obeyed a guideline that forbade pitches from throwing more than 330 pitches over a three-start span—although there were enough exceptions to suggest that was more of a rule of thumb than a law from Leviticus. Perhaps that disorganized vibe is why Collins feels like a temporary fixture; it's as if he's an on-the-job trainee rather than one of the longer-tenured managers in the game.

NEW YORK YANKEES

by Ben Lindbergh

It's been months since Derek Jeter received his last retirement gift, hit his last weak grounder and embarked upon a second career of commissioning banal blog posts for The Players' Tribune. We know, we know, the span of one winter isn't enough time for the farewell fatigue to wear off. Still, let's start with Jeter, not only because the Captain's long goodbye became the story of the Yankees' otherwise-unremarkable 2014 season, but because it tells us something about the team's predicament heading into 2015.

What was Jeter's farewell season worth? By Wins Above Replacement Player, BP's all-in-one accounting of on-field value, very little: No player produced less than Jeter's -2.1 WARP in 2014. Jeter performed like a defensive specialist at the plate and a 40-year-old in the field, with the customary offensive gap between starter and backup preserved only because the Yankees' actual defensive specialist, Brendan Ryan, hit like an NL pitcher.

However, Jeter's value to his team went well beyond the Baseball Prospectus sortables (and I'm not talking about intangibles). Aside from the Captain's Kodak moments, the Yankees weren't a compelling product. Last spring, PECOTA projected the Yankees for only 83 wins, the franchise's first sub-91 forecast in the system's 12-year history. PECOTA's pessimism was on point. An 84-win team with the run differential of a 77-win team, the Yankees fell out of first place for good on May 22th, and their playoff odds permanently sank below 50 percent on June 22nd. At no point in the season did their probability of winning the AL East reach 40 percent.

Based on our understanding of the way their money machine works, the Yankees' second consecutive finish out of the postseason picture should have inflicted a severe financial penalty that went well beyond the loss of playoff ticket sales. In *Diamond Dollars*, his 2007 book about the economics of Baseball, SABR President Vince Gennaro noted that the Yankees' years of success have made them especially susceptible to a reverse-bandwagon effect:

> Because much of the Yankee brand is built on two pillars—winning and tradition—even the mighty Yankee brand has its fragile points. Our analysis shows that few teams' fans are as punishing as Yankee fans if the team fails to play competitive baseball. … Partly through their own marketing efforts and hype, the Yankees have inadvertently increased their financial penalty for not winning.

Gennaro's analysis was borne out in 2013, when the Yankees fell short of the playoffs for the first time since 2008. Despite the buoying effect of Mariano Rivera's slightly less ostentatious retirement tour, the Yankees' ratings declined by roughly a third, and their average attendance fell by more than 3,000 fans per home game, the sixth-largest drop of any team. Theoretically, a second season of quasi-contention should have led to an additional deficit.

"I would have expected them to be down at least 200,000 fans," Gennaro said via email. "A conservative, unchallengeable expected decline would be at least 100,000 fans for 2014, under 'normal' circumstances."

Instead, the scuffling club became an even hotter ticket. The Yankees' home crowds increased by an average of more than 2,000 fans per game, despite a slight leaguewide drop in attendance. Their ratings in the New York market rose by 15 percent relative to 2013, which presumably meant more revenue from advertisers and a higher valuation for the team's substantial stake in the RSN. More New Yorkers watched Jeter's final appearance in pinstripes than any other game broadcast in YES Network history, even though the team had been eliminated from wild card contention the day before.

"I cannot see any reason other than Jeter to explain how they turned -100,000 into +120,000," Gennaro said, using his conservative, "unchallengeable" expected decline. "Even if we say he was worth 220,000 fans x $50/ticket, we're talking $11 million, but that is an unfairly conservative estimate of his impact. There would be a case to make for it to be 1.5x or 2x that amount."

Nor did the dollars stop at ticket sales and TV ratings. The revenue from Jeter's league-leading jersey sales was shared among all teams, in accordance with the Collective Bargaining Agreement, but the Yankees got to keep the extra concessions cash that flowed from higher ticket sales and, presumably, lower no-show rates and higher in-game fan retention rates. The team also received an undisclosed but undoubtedly exorbitant fortune from its partnership with Steiner Sports, the company that stopped just

YANKEES PROSPECTUS
2014 W-L: 84-78, 2ND IN AL EAST

Pythag	.478	20th	DER	.702	18th
RS/G	3.91	18th	B-Age	32.9	30th
RA/G	4.1	18th	P-Age	29.3	25th
TAv	.255	22nd	Salary	$197.2M	2nd
BRR	-5.87	25th	M$/MW	$5.2M	5th
TAv-P	.262	19th	DL Days	1,035	25th
FIP	3.70	14th	$ on DL	25%	27th

Three-Year Park Factors

Runs	Runs/RH	Runs/LH	HR/RH	HR/LH
101	98	103	90	98

Top Hitter WARP	3.6	Jacoby Ellsbury
Top Pitcher WARP	2.6	Dellin Betances
Top Prospect		Aaron Judge

short of going through Jeter's garbage (probably) in its efforts to hawk every item with a tenuous tie to the shortstop. On top of that, there's the difficult-to-calculate benefit of brand awareness generated by a steady supply of Jeter headlines, not to mention the cloying Nike and Gatorade commercials that prominently featured the pinstripes and were widely circulated online.

Superstars' impact on attendance and revenue is often overstated, an amorphous force trotted out to justify dubious contracts. Jeter, however, might have singlehandedly propped up the Yankees' profits while having the worst full season of his career. Unless his performance on the field cost the Yankees a playoff spot—a conclusion that would require us to take the most negative view of his defense, as well as to conjure an imaginary above-average shortstop who could have served in his stead— Jeter's contribution to the club's bottom line far exceeded his $12 million earnings.

"It's inconceivable that the Yankees made less than $25 million on Jeter's marquee value in 2014," Gennaro concluded. "If someone were to claim it was considerably higher, I'm not sure how to argue against it."

Even as the ship went down with its Captain, then, the Yankees' earnings stayed afloat. Unfortunately, the Yankees have run out of retiring icons who can drum up enthusiasm for a lackluster team. This season, they can count on one Jeter-inspired sellout for the inevitable number-retirement ceremony, but other than that, their box-office fortunes will rise or fall based on the quality of their play. And the stakes are high, since a third straight lackluster season might expose all the weakness that was artificially obscured by the fortuitous timing of Jeter's final fist-pumps.

What was the source of that weakness? Injuries explain some of it: The Yankees lost to injuries the third-most projected WARP (10.4) and the fifth-most games (1071) of any team in 2014, after ranking first in both categories in 2013. For them, though, that's the norm. Over the past 10 years, the period for which the BP database contains a complete account of DL stints *and* day-to-day injuries, the Yankees have ranked fourth in games missed and first in WARP lost. That's probably not just lousy luck. The Yankees are old, and old guys get hurt. Don't blame the age-induced injuries; blame the age.

Don't blame it for everything, though, because at no point in their long run of success were the Steinbrenner Yankees young. Even in 1998, with a robust roster and the Core Five firing on all cylinders, the Yankees fielded the second-oldest lineup in the league. They haven't had an average lineup age under 30 since 1993, the first year of their 22-season winning streak (the second-longest in MLB history). Nor was their 2014 team unusually ancient. Last year's Yankees' combined batter-pitcher age of 31.1 (weighted by plate appearances and batters faced) made them only the 27th-oldest team of the wild card era, younger than the 10 Yankees clubs from 1999–2006 and 2012–13.

If we filter out pitchers, last year's Yankees do look a little more wrinkled. Only four teams since 1994 have surpassed the 2014 Yankees' batter age of 32.9, led by the Barry Bonds-dependent 2006–2007 Giants and the 1998 Orioles. Even here, though, there's a recent pinstriped precedent: The 2012 Yankees, who won 95 games and featured the best offense in baseball, averaged an even 33 years, ranking fourth on the oldest-lineup list. The 2014 Yankees, although slightly younger, had the 13th-worst lineup in the league.

In other words, it's not the Yankees who've changed: They're still constructing their rosters essentially the same way that they did when they were consistently among baseball's best teams. The percentages of playing time (plate appearances plus batters faced) and WARP attributable to "homegrown" players (defined as players who debuted in the big leagues with the Yankees, a cohort that also includes some international free agents) on the 2014 team were similar to those the Yankees have sported throughout their 1993–2014 string of above-.500 finishes. (See Table 1.)

For two decades, the Yankees were old, imported and great. For two years, they've been old, imported and

Table 1: Homegrown Players

	1993–2014 Yankees	2014 Yankees
% Playing Time	39.8	38.0
% WARP	44.9	42.8

mediocre. The approach hasn't shifted, but the results have suffered, which suggests that we're looking for a lurking variable. Age and lack of homegrown talent could be behind the Yankees' decline, but they must have had an accomplice.

There's evidence to suggest that circumstances *are* conspiring against the Yankees, and not only because the luxury tax and the CBA's restrictions on amateur bonuses have made it more difficult for them to spend other teams into submission. The Yankees can still outspend almost anyone, but there are fewer wins for sale.

While the 2014 team wasn't unusually reliant on imported talent by Bronx standards, the Yankees have long been in the bottom third of teams in homegrown playing time and WARP. (See Table 2.)

That dependence on outside talent worked well when the Yankees could count on fresh meat reaching the free-agent market. After the Yankees missed the playoffs in 2008, for instance, they bought CC Sabathia, A.J. Burnett and Mark Teixeira (and stole Nick Swisher from the White Sox), and they bounced right back to win 103 games and a World Series.

Table 2: Homegrown Players

	MLB AVG	Yankees AVG	Yankees Rank
% PA	44.0	42.7	16
% TBF	44.2	36.9	27
% PA+BF	44.1	39.8	24
% BWARP	50.8	48.6	18
% PWARP	47.4	39.0	23
% WARP	49.6	44.9	21

That kind of quick fix is becoming more difficult to accomplish. The past offseason's free agent crop was the weakest in at least a decade, by projected WARP, particularly for position players. For the Yankees, that's an ominous sign. In recent years, DVR-resistant live sports have become increasingly attractive to advertisers. As a result, national and local broadcast contracts have enriched every team, pushing a higher percentage of revenue toward ownership and allowing even comparatively cash-poor teams to lock up their young talent. Roster turnover rates, which reached an all-time high in the late 1990s and early aughts, have since receded slightly. The Yankees are a net importer with no natural resources, and the rest of Major League Baseball has begun a blockade.

The dwindling supply of free agents is compounded by another problem (from the Yankees' perspective): The PED era is over, and players are once again aging at normal historical rates. (See Figure 1, next page.)

The Yankees' dynasty years coincided almost perfectly with the period when, for the first time ever, over-30 players outproduced under-30 players, and almost one in five superstars (>5 WARP) switched teams from one season to the next. There has never been a better time than that one to construct one's roster around free agents. Whatever combination of PED testing, run environment and cyclical change has restored the standard aging curve has also stripped the Yankees of an enormous advantage. Forty-year-olds still might make the All-Star team for sentimental reasons, as Jeter did last season, but it's less likely that they'll qualify for performance-related reasons, as an allegedly chemically enhanced Roger Clemens did in 2003. That's not to suggest that the Yankees employed an abnormal number of PED users, though they certainly had their share. However, the Yankees did field an abnormal number of players at the stage of their careers when they probably stood to benefit the most from amphetamines, growth hormones and other since-banned and screened substances.

It would be silly to suggest that the Yankees' way of winning will never work again, just as it would have been foolish to predict that the team's postseason streak would never end. Had Carlos Beltran and Brian McCann not undershot their combined PECOTA projections by 3.5 WARP, the Yankees might

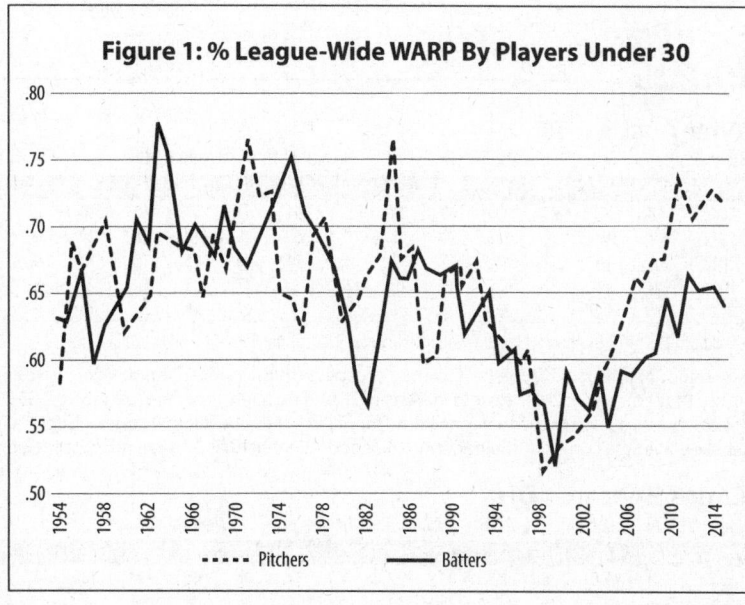

Figure 1: % League-Wide WARP By Players Under 30

- - - - Pitchers ——— Batters

have made it to October last year. Alternatively, the Yankees could have succeeded had they used the same strategy—sign expensive free agents—but applied it to different players (such as Robinson Cano, who outproduced the Yankees' motley second basemen by more than five WARP). Despite the deck being less stacked in their favor, they weren't far from holding a winning hand. Currently, though, they're constructed to excel under the anomalous conditions that prevailed more than a decade ago.

One reason that the Yankees came as close as they did—along with Dellin Betances' historic relief, Joe Girardi's bullpen management, Brett Gardner's power surge and Masahiro Tanaka's superlative 20 starts—was their willingness to use their financial resources to complete a series of astute acquisitions down the stretch, at little cost in player talent. Five players they picked up produced almost four times as much for the Yankees as they had for their previous teams, in fewer than half the games. (See Table 3.)

Table 3

Player	Pre-NYY G	Post-NYY G	Pre-NYY WARP	Post-NYY WARP
Chase Headley	77	58	0.3	2.1
Martin Prado	106	37	0	1.5
Brandon McCarthy	18	14	0.6	1.1
Chris Young	88	23	0.6	0.8
Chris Capuano	28	12	0.1	0.6
TOTAL	**317**	**144**	**1.6**	**6.1**

Not every late arrival blossomed in the Bronx. Stephen Drew, who'd been bad with Boston, was even worse with the Yankees, while speculative pickups such as Jeff Francis, Josh Outman and Scott Sizemore merely made cameos to establish their eligibility for future Old-Timers' Days. Still, during disappointing seasons by Beltran and McCann, that midseason tinkering offered some evidence that the Yankees aren't inept at evaluating veteran talent.

The Yankees have also flexed their financial muscle below the major-league level, obliterating their bonus allotment for international amateurs in 2014 and awarding above-market deals to minor-league free agents like Yangervis Solarte, who

gave them two good months and then helped them land Headley. In addition, they overhauled their player-development structure over the winter, as longtime senior VP of Baseball Operations Mark Newman retired and both director of player development Pat Roessler and Newman's no. 2, assistant director of minor league operations Billy Hart, were dismissed. The Yankees filled the vacancies from within, replacing Newman with former coach and coordinator Gary Denbo and promoting assistant director of amateur scouting Eric Schmitt to director of minor league ops. Although the Yankees' system contains some supplementary talent at the upper levels, it still ranks in baseball's bottom third, and the team has seen only 17.4 WARP from its 30 post-Jeter draft picks in the first and supplemental rounds. Only the Padres, at 17.2, have gotten less from first-rounders and supplemental picks over the same span. The Yankees tend to draft late and trade prospects (and they failed to sign draftees Mark Prior and Gerrit Cole), which excuses some of that meager output, but player development has been a problem that the personnel changes could correct.

The fruits of that labor are a long way away, though, and the attendance drop is at the door. As the offseason began, the Yankees were reportedly focusing on middle-tier free agents rather than prepping for another spending spree like the previous winter's. When asked whether he'd be bidding on the most expensive arms, given the injury questions surrounding Tanaka, Sabathia, and Michael Pineda, GM Brian Cashman demurred but did concede, "We're looking at smart ways to improve our club," seeming to distinguish the "smart" ways from the most expensive ones. In time, that intelligence might remold the roster into one that's optimized for a homegrown-heavy game. For now, though, the Yankees are a team out of time, hoping that a high payroll can keep them competitive enough to avoid their first three-season playoff drought since the early-90s dark days. ∎

—Ben Lindbergh is a staff writer at Grantland.com, where he writes about baseball and dabbles in pop-culture coverage. A former editor-in-chief of Baseball Prospectus, he continues to co-host BP's daily podcast, Effectively Wild.

Player comments by Patrick Dubuque and Baseball Prospectus Authors

Hitters

Tyler Austin   RF
Born: 9/6/91   Age: 23   Bats: R   Throws: R   Height: 6' 1"   Weight: 220

YEAR	TEAM	LVL	AGE	PA	R	2B	3B	HR	RBI	BB	K	SB	CS	AVG/OBP/SLG	TAv	BABIP	BRR	FRAA	WARP
2012	CSC	A	20	309	69	22	5	14	54	37	68	17	2	.320/.405/.598	.337	.380	2.9	RF(61): -4.0, 1B(3): -0.1	3.0
2012	TAM	A+	20	148	20	13	1	2	23	12	28	6	0	.321/.385/.478	.290	.394	0.0	RF(31): 0.8, 1B(5): 0.3	0.8
2013	TRN	AA	21	366	43	17	1	6	40	41	79	4	0	.257/.344/.373	.260	.321	-0.4	RF(69): -4.6	0.6
2014	TRN	AA	22	437	56	20	5	9	47	36	80	3	2	.275/.336/.419	.275	.323	-1.9	RF(59): -2.2, 1B(19): -1.3	1.0
2015	*NYA*	*MLB*	*23*	*250*	*24*	*10*	*1*	*6*	*27*	*18*	*64*	*1*	*0*	*.238/.295/.373*	*.253*	*.300*	*-0.2*	*RF -2, 1B -0*	*-0.1*

Breakout: 1%   Improve: 13%   Collapse: 2%   Attrition: 3%   MLB: 22%   Comparables: *J.D. Martinez, Rene Tosoni, Caleb Gindl*

The minor member of the Yankees' former prospect triumvirate, Austin has the most potential of the bunch at this point, if only by default. The wrist injury that erased his 2013 ate into 2014 as well, and through June he was hitting .254/.324/.371. He performed much better in the second half, leaving the optimists room to blame the injury for his troubles. We'll know soon enough, but keep in mind that given Austin's defensive shortcomings as a below-average corner outfielder, even the good Tyler Austin is a fringe prospect at best.

Carlos Beltran   DH
Born: 4/24/77   Age: 38   Bats: B   Throws: R   Height: 6' 1"   Weight: 210

YEAR	TEAM	LVL	AGE	PA	R	2B	3B	HR	RBI	BB	K	SB	CS	AVG/OBP/SLG	TAv	BABIP	BRR	FRAA	WARP
2012	SLN	MLB	35	619	83	26	1	32	97	65	124	13	6	.269/.346/.495	.296	.291	0.1	RF(132): -6.5, CF(9): -0.1	2.8
2013	SLN	MLB	36	600	79	30	3	24	84	38	90	2	1	.296/.339/.491	.289	.314	2.0	RF(137): 1.3	3.1
2014	NYA	MLB	37	449	46	23	0	15	49	37	80	3	1	.233/.301/.402	.258	.252	-2.8	RF(32): -1.1, 1B(1): -0.0	0.0
2015	*NYA*	*MLB*	*38*	*452*	*53*	*20*	*2*	*16*	*59*	*39*	*85*	*4*	*2*	*.256/.322/.436*	*.282*	*.282*	*-0.2*	*RF -3, CF -0*	*1.4*

Breakout: 0%   Improve: 10%   Collapse: 16%   Attrition: 22%   MLB: 78%   Comparables: *Paul Konerko, Stan Musial, Hideki Matsui*

The first eighteenth of Beltran's three-year, $45 million contract went great. Five hits in 43 at-bats later, the former All-Star was diagnosed with a bone spur in his elbow. The team determined that he could avoid surgery and rest the elbow for a couple of weeks. They were wrong; he had the surgery, but only after sinking 309 underwhelming plate appearances into the delusion. The problem shouldn't impact his preparation for 2015.

Beltran's legacy as a whole will always be greatness mingled with intermissions, but his desire to play through pain, once medically identified, can only be considered a positive for him. It was the optimism of Yankees management, and the lack of escape plans, that allowed 2014 Beltran to happen. Now that his defense is an unquestionable liability, Beltran needs to hit to earn his keep: Alex Rodriguez and Mark Teixeira could sure use those defensive innings in quiet contemplation.

Gregory Bird   1B
Born: 11/9/92   Age: 22   Bats: L   Throws: R   Height: 6' 3"   Weight: 215

YEAR	TEAM	LVL	AGE	PA	R	2B	3B	HR	RBI	BB	K	SB	CS	AVG/OBP/SLG	TAv	BABIP	BRR	FRAA	WARP
2012	STA	A-	19	47	4	4	0	2	8	6	10	0	0	.400/.489/.650	.396	.500	-0.8	1B(10): 0.5	0.7
2013	CSC	A	20	573	84	36	3	20	84	107	132	1	1	.288/.428/.511	.347	.364	-0.5	1B(90): -7.9	5.4
2014	TAM	A+	21	325	36	22	1	7	32	45	70	1	0	.277/.375/.442	.297	.342	-1.2	1B(61): -1.1	1.7
2014	TRN	AA	21	116	16	8	0	7	11	18	27	0	0	.253/.379/.558	.330	.274	-1.0	1B(24): -1.5	0.8
2015	*NYA*	*MLB*	*22*	*250*	*28*	*10*	*0*	*8*	*30*	*31*	*71*	*0*	*0*	*.227/.327/.391*	*.270*	*.294*	*-0.5*	*1B -3, C -0*	*0.2*

Breakout: 2%   Improve: 22%   Collapse: 0%   Attrition: 10%   MLB: 44%   Comparables: *Jonathan Singleton, Anthony Rizzo, Jaff Decker*

The man can hit. Nearly forgotten as a prospect after a back injury wiped out his 2012 season, Bird flew to Trenton by the end of the season and put up a passable .305 ISO in 116 plate appearances. Along with the impressive in-game power, Bird has a good view of the strike zone and acceptable contact skills. Let's put it this way: he hit for more extra bases than singles in each of the three levels he played at in 2014. That's good. Of course, we all have flaws, and Bird's is his back, which he has injured twice now, the latest flare-up biting a chunk out of his 2014 season. The injury limits him to first base, so he's basically going to have to keep hitting this well to pan out. Also, anyone who's lost a Saturday from sleeping wrong can testify that back injuries can be both spontaneous and debilitating. Still, he's just a couple of levels and a couple of coin flips away from being a contributor at the major-league level.

Stephen Drew   SS
Born: 3/16/83   Age: 32   Bats: L   Throws: R   Height: 6' 0"   Weight: 190

YEAR	TEAM	LVL	AGE	PA	R	2B	3B	HR	RBI	BB	K	SB	CS	AVG/OBP/SLG	TAv	BABIP	BRR	FRAA	WARP
2012	RNO	AAA	29	40	6	1	1	2	5	4	6	0	0	.250/.325/.500	.284	.250	-0.8	SS(9): -0.8	0.1
2012	ARI	MLB	29	155	17	8	1	2	12	19	35	0	1	.193/.290/.311	.225	.242	0.3	SS(36): -3.7	-0.4
2012	OAK	MLB	29	172	21	5	0	5	16	18	41	1	1	.250/.326/.382	.270	.306	-0.5	SS(39): -0.5	0.8
2013	PME	AA	30	23	1	2	0	1	4	2	4	0	0	.200/.261/.450	.297	.188	-0.3	SS(5): -0.4	0.1
2013	BOS	MLB	30	501	57	29	8	13	67	54	124	6	0	.253/.333/.443	.282	.320	-0.4	SS(124): -4.6	2.9
2014	BOS	MLB	31	145	11	6	1	4	11	14	39	1	1	.176/.255/.328	.212	.216	-0.4	SS(39): 2.4	0.0
2014	NYA	MLB	31	155	7	8	0	3	15	13	36	0	0	.150/.219/.271	.194	.175	-1.7	2B(34): -1.8, SS(12): -1.0	-0.9
2015	*NYA*	*MLB*	*32*	*328*	*34*	*15*	*3*	*7*	*33*	*31*	*75*	*3*	*1*	*.230/.303/.370*	*.256*	*.281*	*-0.7*	*SS -3, 2B -1*	*0.7*

Breakout: 2%   Improve: 38%   Collapse: 5%   Attrition: 9%   MLB: 93%   Comparables: *Jhonny Peralta, Mike Fontenot, Cal Ripken Jr.*

The only thing more depressing than the career treadmill is what happens when we try to step off for a moment. Drew was rewarded for his fine work in Boston in 2013 with a one-year, $14.1 million qualifying offer. He and his agent Scott Boras declined, hoping for a multiyear deal, but the cost of a draft choice deterred any suitors and he spent half a season willing the cell phone to ring. Drew then cost himself even more money by re-signing on May 20th and joining the club two weeks later, forgetting that sage aphorism: "Those who forget the experience of Bruce Bochte are doomed to repeat it." The result was a miserable season at the plate, as his timing never resurfaced and he hit everything into the sky. With a fresh start, Drew can recover; Bochte had a nice comeback year, too. But it's looking increasingly clear that 2010 and 2013 were the exceptions, not the rule.

Jacoby Ellsbury CF

Born: 9/11/83 Age: 31 Bats: L Throws: L Height: 6' 1" Weight: 195

YEAR	TEAM	LVL	AGE	PA	R	2B	3B	HR	RBI	BB	K	SB	CS	AVG/OBP/SLG	TAv	BABIP	BRR	FRAA	WARP
2012	BOS	MLB	28	323	43	18	0	4	26	19	43	14	3	.271/.313/.370	.243	.304	3.3	CF(73): -2.2	0.3
2013	BOS	MLB	29	636	92	31	8	9	53	47	92	52	4	.298/.355/.426	.277	.341	5.3	CF(134): 6.9	4.4
2014	NYA	MLB	30	635	71	27	5	16	70	49	93	39	5	.271/.328/.419	.275	.296	-1.2	CF(141): 12.0	3.6
2015	NYA	MLB	31	595	84	27	3	14	57	41	90	37	6	.276/.329/.416	.279	.305	1.4	CF 7	3.7

Breakout: 0%   Improve: 53%   Collapse: 1%   Attrition: 3%   MLB: 95%   Comparables: Angel Pagan, Vernon Wells, Shane Victorino

Ellsbury, in his first year in pinstripes, proved to be utterly sufficient. He played almost every day until the Yankees were eliminated, and posted remarkably consistent numbers across the board. He did get dinged with some BABIP luck despite a career-high line-drive rate, which brought down his offensive percentages, but he's essentially the same hitter. The defensive metrics are mixed, but FRAA is optimistic, and it's easy to forgive fewer chances with Gardner and Ichiro holding their own in the corners. All in all, this is a boring player comment, because Ellsbury is a boring player to project. He looks like he's ready to enjoy the pleasant, predictable decline of the early-30s athlete: a handful fewer steals, a handful of doubles creeping over the wall, the occasional hamstring pull. He'll earn his keep for a while yet.

Brett Gardner LF

Born: 8/24/83 Age: 31 Bats: L Throws: L Height: 5' 10" Weight: 185

YEAR	TEAM	LVL	AGE	PA	R	2B	3B	HR	RBI	BB	K	SB	CS	AVG/OBP/SLG	TAv	BABIP	BRR	FRAA	WARP
2012	NYA	MLB	28	37	7	2	0	0	3	5	7	2	2	.323/.417/.387	.294	.417	0.5	LF(15): -0.2	0.2
2013	NYA	MLB	29	609	81	33	10	8	52	52	127	24	8	.273/.344/.416	.279	.342	3.4	CF(138): -6.4	2.7
2014	NYA	MLB	30	636	87	25	8	17	58	56	134	21	5	.256/.327/.422	.276	.305	4.5	LF(126): 0.2, CF(25): -0.0	3.2
2015	NYA	MLB	31	592	75	23	7	7	47	58	120	26	8	.256/.336/.370	.266	.309	3.1	LF 4, CF -2	2.3

Breakout: 0%   Improve: 46%   Collapse: 4%   Attrition: 10%   MLB: 92%   Comparables: Minnie Minoso, Gene Woodling, Roy White

Gardner's remarkable metamorphosis continues, only he's going from butterfly to caterpillar instead of the other way around. While his speed is on the decline and the underground defensive metric supercomputers agree that he's no longer an elite defender, Gardner has compensated by swinging at more hittable pitches. His home runs doubled in 2014, and while his average home run distance remained constant, only three of the 17 could be considered "cheap"—not to mention that he's always been a historically better hitter on the road. But just because he's earning them doesn't mean it'll continue; the fastball well may dry up. Gardner is getting pitched to like an early-career Omar Vizquel, which he clearly no longer is. Will he continue to get non-star treatment? If not, will the belt-high fastball power he's developed disappear? If so, will his walk rate revert to better days? In that scenario, will he attempt to steal more often? And if so will his elite defense return? Answers: Probably, Maybe, Not all the way, No. Gardner's great, but he might need to find a new new way forward.

Didi Gregorius SS

Born: 2/18/90 Age: 25 Bats: L Throws: R Height: 6' 2" Weight: 205

YEAR	TEAM	LVL	AGE	PA	R	2B	3B	HR	RBI	BB	K	SB	CS	AVG/OBP/SLG	TAv	BABIP	BRR	FRAA	WARP
2012	PEN	AA	22	359	45	11	8	1	31	29	49	3	4	.278/.344/.373	.266	.323	-2.7	SS(80): -14.9	-0.1
2012	LOU	AAA	22	202	25	10	3	6	23	12	31	0	2	.243/.288/.427	.242	.262	1.5	SS(42): -1.6, 2B(3): 0.1	0.6
2012	CIN	MLB	22	21	1	0	0	0	2	0	5	0	0	.300/.300/.300	.228	.400	0.3	SS(6): -0.4	0.0
2013	RNO	AAA	23	33	7	2	0	2	2	2	1	1	0	.387/.424/.645	.332	.357	-0.6	SS(1): 0.2	0.3
2013	ARI	MLB	23	404	47	16	3	7	28	37	65	0	2	.252/.332/.373	.262	.290	-4.5	SS(100): -6.9	0.3
2014	RNO	AAA	24	260	42	14	4	3	25	24	26	3	0	.310/.389/.447	.278	.338	1.0	2B(38): -2.9, SS(19): 2.9	1.4
2014	ARI	MLB	24	299	35	9	5	6	27	22	52	3	0	.226/.290/.363	.244	.257	4.5	SS(67): 2.5, 2B(11): 1.0	1.4
2015	NYA	MLB	25	344	37	13	3	6	31	22	60	2	1	.245/.302/.366	.255	.278	0.2	SS -3, 2B -0	0.9

Breakout: 1%   Improve: 54%   Collapse: 10%   Attrition: 27%   MLB: 96%   Comparables: Yunel Escobar, Russ Adams, Alcides Escobar

So good on defense that he could teach a **class** on it, Gregorius failed to crack league average on offense once again. While his glovework is unquestioned, his inability to contribute on offense is why he opened the season **No. 2** on Arizona's shortstop depth chart. You have to **respect** how **gift**ed he is around the bag, and his ability to do the jump throw like he's shooting **baskets**. Those traits will keep him in the game for a long time, but unless or until he can be within shouting distance of "tolerable" on offense, he should be a backup. Not a "**my way** or the highway" type player, Gregorius should continue to progress under the tutelage of New York's coaching staff. He will work well as a defense-minded bench player who is a bit handi**capped in** the batter's box.

Chase Headley 3B

Born: 5/9/84 Age: 31 Bats: B Throws: R Height: 6' 2" Weight: 220

YEAR	TEAM	LVL	AGE	PA	R	2B	3B	HR	RBI	BB	K	SB	CS	AVG/OBP/SLG	TAv	BABIP	BRR	FRAA	WARP
2012	SDN	MLB	28	699	95	31	2	31	115	86	157	17	6	.286/.376/.498	.320	.337	-2.0	3B(159): -6.3, 1B(1): -0.0	5.9
2013	SDN	MLB	29	600	59	35	2	13	50	67	142	8	4	.250/.347/.400	.278	.319	-4.1	3B(140): -8.1	1.6
2014	SDN	MLB	30	307	27	12	1	7	32	22	73	4	1	.229/.296/.355	.245	.285	0.8	3B(76): -2.6	0.3
2014	NYA	MLB	30	224	28	8	0	6	17	29	49	3	2	.262/.371/.398	.283	.324	0.9	3B(51): 5.6, 1B(7): 0.3	2.1
2015	NYA	MLB	31	516	59	24	1	13	59	50	118	9	3	.259/.338/.402	.280	.318	-1.1	3B -4, 1B 0	1.7

Breakout: 1%   Improve: 35%   Collapse: 15%   Attrition: 16%   MLB: 98%   Comparables: Eric Chavez, Scott Rolen, Ron Santo

The Yankees threw Headley a vine and he pulled himself out of Petco's quicksand, to everyone's delight. The perpetually disappointing third baseman spent the late summer holding together the New York lineup, engineering three walkoffs and calculating the exact size and location of his future Scrooge McDuck vault. It's not as though the power came back—the power will never come back, and even if it did, 31 home runs in 2012 exchanges to about 20 in the modern scoring environment. Instead, the major adjustment appears to be selection: In a small sample, he swung at fewer pitches out of the zone and hit more of the ones he did swing at. Perhaps he finally accepted what kind of hitter he really is, because that hitter is good enough to go with a plus glove at third. Headley's never (again) going to be a star, but he'll provide nearly the value of one. If only he hadn't set expectations so high.

Eric Jagielo   3B

Born: 5/17/92   Age: 23   Bats: L   Throws: R   Height: 6' 2"   Weight: 195

YEAR	TEAM	LVL	AGE	PA	R	2B	3B	HR	RBI	BB	K	SB	CS	AVG/OBP/SLG	TAv	BABIP	BRR	FRAA	WARP
2013	STA	A-	21	218	19	14	1	6	27	26	54	0	0	.266/.376/.451	.315	.344	-1.9	3B(42): -1.3	1.6
2014	TAM	A+	22	359	43	14	0	16	54	38	93	0	0	.259/.354/.460	.283	.315	-1.1	3B(62): -9.2	0.8
2015	NYA	MLB	23	250	26	8	0	9	30	18	79	0	0	.209/.280/.365	.244	.274	-0.5	3B -6	-0.6

Breakout: 1%   Improve: 11%   Collapse: 1%   Attrition: 10%   MLB: 31%   Comparables: Josh Bell, Mike Olt, Adam Duvall

Like Gary Sanchez, Jagielo's luster as a prospect is almost entirely dependent on his ability to feign mediocrity at his given defensive assignment. So far, it doesn't look good. Fielding percentage isn't a very good measure of defensive ability, but when there's an 8 after the decimal point, a layman starts to worry. His arm is strong, but he's oversized for the position, his range is unspectacular and for Jagielo more than most it's important he not botch the ones he gets to. If he achieves defensive competency, there's plenty to like. A late first-rounder out of Notre Dame, Jagielo was hailed as a quality pick, both in terms of organizational need and developmental safety. And indeed, Jagielo's left-handed power has fans drawing arcs into the right field bleachers in their minds' eyes. His plate discipline is also strong and his contact rate is workable. He missed most of the Fall League after he took a nasty grounder to the face, but he'll be fine in time for spring.

Derek Jeter   SS

Born: 6/26/74   Age: 41   Bats: R   Throws: R   Height: 6' 3"   Weight: 195

YEAR	TEAM	LVL	AGE	PA	R	2B	3B	HR	RBI	BB	K	SB	CS	AVG/OBP/SLG	TAv	BABIP	BRR	FRAA	WARP
2012	NYA	MLB	38	740	99	32	0	15	58	45	90	9	4	.316/.362/.429	.274	.347	-1.2	SS(135): -7.8	3.0
2013	SWB	AAA	39	23	4	1	0	0	1	5	3	0	0	.222/.391/.278	.285	.267	-0.1	SS(6): 0.0	0.1
2013	NYA	MLB	39	73	8	1	0	1	7	8	10	0	0	.190/.288/.254	.201	.208	0.9	SS(13): -1.9	-0.3
2014	NYA	MLB	40	634	47	19	1	4	50	35	87	10	2	.256/.304/.313	.234	.294	-1.9	SS(130): -24.6	-2.1
2015	NYA	MLB	41	487	50	17	1	3	34	30	76	7	2	.259/.310/.321	.245	.301	-0.7	SS -12	-0.3

Breakout: 0%   Improve: 16%   Collapse: 8%   Attrition: 18%   MLB: 62%   Comparables: Omar Vizquel, Kenny Lofton, Paul Molitor

It pains to admit this, but the truth is unavoidable: Jeter is more of an org guy than a prospect at this point. A slap-first hitter, scouts are divided on his hit tool, but he displays 25-grade power at best and most feel that he'll never stick at shortstop. And while Jeter has received plenty of headlines over the years, and his intangibles are undeniable, one can't avoid the fact that he's been developing in the organization for an eternity. At this rate he might not even see time at the major-league level, in 2015 or perhaps ever.

Aaron Judge   OF

Born: 4/26/92   Age: 23   Bats: R   Throws: R   Height: 6' 7"   Weight: 230

YEAR	TEAM	LVL	AGE	PA	R	2B	3B	HR	RBI	BB	K	SB	CS	AVG/OBP/SLG	TAv	BABIP	BRR	FRAA	WARP
2014	CSC	A	22	278	36	15	2	9	45	39	59	1	0	.333/.428/.530	.343	.408	-2.8	RF(55): 4.1	3.1
2014	TAM	A+	22	285	44	9	2	8	33	50	72	0	0	.283/.411/.442	.302	.377	1.7	RF(61): 6.7	2.9
2015	NYA	MLB	23	250	26	8	1	7	28	28	75	0	0	.223/.314/.358	.256	.303	-0.3	RF 5	0.8

Breakout: 2%   Improve: 11%   Collapse: 7%   Attrition: 9%   MLB: 26%   Comparables: Nolan Reimold, Kyle Parker, Wladimir Balentien

The 32nd overall pick in 2013, Judge's debut was delayed by a quad pull until last season. He made up for lost time. Standing 6-feet-7, Judge casts an impressive shadow; he's the sort of hitter you describe not in terms of strength but in terms of torque. If he played in the early nineties, someone would have created a poster of him chopping down a tree with another tree. He's strong, is the point of this paragraph.

Judge is a big guy, but he's athlete-big and not Fielder-big, and it looks like he has the arm and the range for corner outfield. He'll likely start 2015 in Double-A Trenton, and contact issues stemming from those long arms are the biggest factor holding him back from the Bronx.

Brian McCann   C

Born: 2/20/84   Age: 31   Bats: L   Throws: R   Height: 6' 3"   Weight: 230

YEAR	TEAM	LVL	AGE	PA	R	2B	3B	HR	RBI	BB	K	SB	CS	AVG/OBP/SLG	TAv	BABIP	BRR	FRAA	WARP
2012	ATL	MLB	28	487	44	14	0	20	67	44	76	3	0	.230/.300/.399	.245	.234	-0.6	C(114): 2.9	1.5
2013	ATL	MLB	29	402	43	13	0	20	57	39	66	0	1	.256/.336/.461	.288	.261	-1.7	C(92): -0.0	2.7
2014	NYA	MLB	30	538	57	15	1	23	75	32	77	0	0	.232/.286/.406	.256	.231	-3.6	C(108): 3.4, 1B(16): -0.5	1.8
2015	NYA	MLB	31	481	57	16	0	20	66	44	82	1	0	.245/.319/.426	.280	.256	-1.7	C 2, 1B -0	2.7

Breakout: 1%   Improve: 35%   Collapse: 4%   Attrition: 8%   MLB: 97%   Comparables: Victor Martinez, Ted Simmons, Gary Carter

It wasn't the type of season anyone wanted to see, but it could have been worse. McCann stayed in the lineup nearly every day, and his defense behind the dish remains strong enough to delay the inevitable relocation for at least a few more years. But his walk rate has halved since his peak, and between shifting defenses and his footspeed approaching absolute zero, he has seen his groundball BABIPs drop to league-worst territory. When he did elevate, he saw a 25-foot drop in average home run distance, from 395 feet to 370. Fortunately, the short right porch in Turner Field taught the pull-hitting catcher to wrap his homers around the foul pole, but there's a disturbing split between his home (.254 ISO) and road (.085) numbers. Expect a similar trend going forward.

J.R. Murphy   C

Born: 5/13/91   Age: 24   Bats: R   Throws: R   Height: 5' 11"   Weight: 195

YEAR	TEAM	LVL	AGE	PA	R	2B	3B	HR	RBI	BB	K	SB	CS	AVG/OBP/SLG	TAv	BABIP	BRR	FRAA	WARP
2012	TAM	A+	21	294	39	14	1	5	28	26	41	4	3	.257/.322/.374	.238	.286	1.8	C(59): 0.6, 3B(1): -0.0	0.6
2012	TRN	AA	21	170	23	12	1	4	16	16	32	0	0	.231/.306/.408	.270	.259	1.1	C(38): 0.8	1.2
2013	TRN	AA	22	211	34	10	0	6	25	24	32	1	0	.268/.352/.421	.307	.293	1.4	C(49): 0.1	2.6
2013	SWB	AAA	22	257	26	19	0	6	21	23	41	0	1	.270/.342/.430	.264	.304	0.6	C(56): -0.8	1.5
2013	NYA	MLB	22	27	3	1	0	0	1	1	9	0	0	.154/.185/.192	.146	.235	0.0	C(15): 0.1	-0.1
2014	SWB	AAA	23	196	17	9	0	6	28	13	42	0	0	.246/.292/.397	.240	.284	1.0	C(46): -0.8	0.5
2014	NYA	MLB	23	85	7	4	0	1	9	4	22	0	0	.284/.318/.370	.265	.379	-1.1	C(30): -0.4	0.2
2015	NYA	MLB	24	250	23	11	0	6	28	16	55	0	0	.235/.286/.370	.249	.276	-0.5	C -0, 3B 0	0.6

Breakout: 8%   Improve: 14%   Collapse: 13%   Attrition: 24%   MLB: 41%   *Comparables: Bryan Anderson, Austin Romine, Tim Federowicz*

Now that Francisco Cervelli is out of the picture, Murphy finally has a job: backing up one of the most consistent and expensive backstops in the game. After rising above most of the Yankees' catching prospect morass, Murphy got some playing time in the bigs and acquitted himself nicely, smacking an unsustainable number of line drives and catching well enough to avoid major criticism. With single-digit power, Murphy isn't a bat-first or a glove-first catcher; he's just kind of okay at everything. Given what's out there on the market at the catching position, being okay at everything makes for a quality backup catcher in this league.

Eury Perez   CF

Born: 5/30/90   Age: 25   Bats: R   Throws: R   Height: 6' 0"   Weight: 190

YEAR	TEAM	LVL	AGE	PA	R	2B	3B	HR	RBI	BB	K	SB	CS	AVG/OBP/SLG	TAv	BABIP	BRR	FRAA	WARP
2012	HAR	AA	22	373	34	11	2	0	30	7	53	26	10	.299/.325/.342	.248	.351	1.8	CF(82): 8.0, RF(2): -0.0	2.1
2012	SYR	AAA	22	173	21	7	1	0	10	8	26	20	5	.333/.373/.390	.262	.398	2.1	CF(25): 2.0, LF(3): -0.0	1.1
2012	WAS	MLB	22	5	3	0	0	0	0	0	0	3	0	.200/.200/.200	.163	.200	-0.6	CF(4): -0.1, LF(3): -0.0	-0.1
2013	SYR	AAA	23	433	55	18	5	7	28	13	64	23	8	.300/.336/.422	.263	.343	2.2	CF(68): -5.6, LF(15): 0.6	1.2
2013	WAS	MLB	23	8	1	0	0	0	0	3	1	0	.125/.125/.125	.082	.200	0.1	CF(4): 0.1, LF(3): 0.1	-0.1
2014	POT	A+	24	33	6	1	0	1	4	3	4	6	1	.321/.387/.464	.310	.348	0.4	CF(9): 0.6	0.4
2014	SYR	AAA	24	238	30	13	2	1	11	13	35	20	3	.311/.372/.406	.273	.367	3.3	RF(29): -1.7, CF(18): -1.0	1.0
2014	NYA	MLB	24	10	2	0	0	0	0	0	3	1	0	.200/.200/.200	.144	.286	0.2	CF(2): 0.1, RF(2): 0.0	-0.1
2015	NYA	MLB	25	250	31	10	1	3	19	6	47	15	4	.270/.300/.360	.247	.315	1.6	CF 1, RF -1	0.5

Breakout: 6%   Improve: 26%   Collapse: 9%   Attrition: 30%   MLB: 45%   *Comparables: Clay Timpner, Gary Brown, Jim Adduci*

With baseball being a game of copycat, Perez is a prime candidate to be the next Jarrod Dyson—an elite-fleet center fielder who can't hit enough to be more than a bench bat. After spending the past two-and-a-half seasons in Triple-A, the 24-year-old is not someone who needs more development in the hopes of being an everyday starter; he needs a team that will carry him as spare outfielder now. The Yankees, who claimed him from Washington in September, just might be that team. Given the at-bats they gave to Ichiro, Chris Young and Alfonso Soriano during the 2014 season, Perez stands a good chance to get his major-league moment, however fleeting it might be.

Martin Prado   3B

Born: 10/27/83   Age: 31   Bats: R   Throws: R   Height: 6' 1"   Weight: 190

YEAR	TEAM	LVL	AGE	PA	R	2B	3B	HR	RBI	BB	K	SB	CS	AVG/OBP/SLG	TAv	BABIP	BRR	FRAA	WARP
2012	ATL	MLB	28	690	81	42	6	10	70	58	69	17	4	.301/.359/.438	.286	.322	1.4	LF(119): -8.7, 3B(25): -1.1	3.3
2013	ARI	MLB	29	664	70	36	2	14	82	47	53	3	5	.282/.333/.417	.264	.288	-5.6	3B(113): -0.6, 2B(32): -3.5	1.2
2014	ARI	MLB	30	436	44	17	4	5	42	23	57	2	1	.270/.317/.370	.245	.301	0.7	3B(99): -3.5, 2B(4): -0.1	0.0
2014	NYA	MLB	30	137	18	9	0	7	16	3	23	1	0	.316/.336/.541	.323	.340	0.3	2B(17): 2.3, 3B(11): 1.3	1.5
2015	NYA	MLB	31	556	64	27	2	11	54	34	67	5	3	.272/.319/.398	.273	.290	-1.1	3B 1, LF -2	1.8

Breakout: 0%   Improve: 34%   Collapse: 2%   Attrition: 5%   MLB: 96%   *Comparables: Bill Madlock, Alberto Callaspo, Chone Figgins*

In a quarter of a season in pinstripes, Prado doubled his career power output and topped career records in pretty much every other rate stat on the way. He also walked 2.2 percent of the time, but why trouble yourself with walking when you're hitting everything anyway? Obviously, regression is coming: That .226 ISO shall not stand. The bright note is that only one of his seven home runs after the trade could be considered "cheap." There will be no cheapies in Miami.

Robert Refsnyder   2B

Born: 3/26/91   Age: 24   Bats: R   Throws: R   Height: 6' 1"   Weight: 205

YEAR	TEAM	LVL	AGE	PA	R	2B	3B	HR	RBI	BB	K	SB	CS	AVG/OBP/SLG	TAv	BABIP	BRR	FRAA	WARP
2012	CSC	A	21	182	22	8	0	4	22	16	25	11	1	.241/.319/.364	.247	.261	0.3	RF(42): 0.3	0.1
2013	CSC	A	22	62	9	4	1	0	6	6	12	7	0	.370/.452/.481	.394	.476	0.1	2B(13): -1.7	0.9
2013	TAM	A+	22	511	66	28	2	6	51	78	70	16	6	.283/.408/.404	.303	.326	-1.6	2B(95): -9.4	2.7
2014	TRN	AA	23	244	35	19	5	6	30	14	38	5	5	.342/.385/.542	.329	.391	-2.2	2B(58): 3.8	2.8
2014	SWB	AAA	23	333	47	19	1	8	33	41	67	4	4	.300/.389/.456	.291	.364	-0.8	2B(64): -5.4, RF(9): -0.6	1.4
2015	NYA	MLB	24	250	27	12	1	5	26	22	55	4	2	.252/.326/.382	.270	.309	-0.3	2B -2, RF -0	0.7

Breakout: 4%   Improve: 19%   Collapse: 9%   Attrition: 19%   MLB: 46%   *Comparables: Ian Kinsler, Corban Joseph, Jason Kipnis*

It's finally happened: The Yankees have a hitting prospect ready to graduate. While Kelly Johnson and Brian Roberts spent 2014 disintegrating like old-timey vampires at dawn, Refsnyder, a 2012 fifth-round pick, was grinding out levels in the upper minors. He wields trace amounts of power and speed, the amount you're used to seeing out of your run-of-the-mill second baseman, but it's his quick swing and the judiciousness with which he employs it that excites the young people. Refsnyder has excellent contact skills, and is rarely fooled by bad pitches, leading to impressive on-base averages at every stop of his career. It's not an offensive approach that looks good on an outfielder, unless you adore modern Nick Markakis types, which is why the Yankees converted Refsnyder to second in 2013, which was why he wasn't promoted to the majors last year: He's still learning the position. After two seasons, he finally looks at least somewhat comfortable with the not-making-mistakes aspect of the job, and will compete for the starting second base spot in spring training.

Brian Roberts   2B
Born: 10/9/77   Age: 37   Bats: B   Throws: R   Height: 5' 9"   Weight: 175

YEAR	TEAM	LVL	AGE	PA	R	2B	3B	HR	RBI	BB	K	SB	CS	AVG/OBP/SLG	TAv	BABIP	BRR	FRAA	WARP
2012	BOW	AA	34	21	4	3	0	1	3	4	3	0	0	.250/.381/.625	.342	.231	-0.1	2B(7): -0.1	0.3
2012	NOR	AAA	34	23	2	2	0	0	1	2	4	0	0	.238/.304/.333	.219	.294	0.2	2B(5): -0.2	0.0
2012	BAL	MLB	34	74	2	0	0	0	5	5	12	1	1	.182/.233/.182	.181	.214	-0.3	2B(17): -1.0	-0.6
2013	BAL	MLB	35	296	33	12	1	8	39	26	44	3	1	.249/.312/.392	.269	.267	-1.7	2B(60): 3.9	1.1
2014	NYA	MLB	36	348	40	16	4	5	21	28	53	7	4	.237/.300/.360	.247	.269	2.9	2B(91): 1.3	0.9
2015	NYA	MLB	37	318	31	13	1	4	27	25	54	5	3	.235/.295/.334	.241	.269	0.3	2B -1	0.3

Breakout: 0%   Improve: 23%   Collapse: 22%   Attrition: 19%   MLB: 74%   Comparables: Mark Ellis, Orlando Cabrera, Jerry Hairston

At the tip of every cell are telomeres, which protect the ends of the chromosome from damage. When cells multiply, a little bit of those telomeres is lost, until they recede to the point where there is none left, the cell can no longer divide, and it dies. Millions of Brian Roberts' cells are dying as you read this, their mitochondria grinding silently to a halt, their nuclei disintegrating, their membranes taking on water until they burst. This only underscores the fact that the collection of cells that you knew as Brian Roberts, the one who hit 51 doubles and stole 40 bases in 2008, is but a biological memory.

Alex Rodriguez   3B
Born: 7/27/75   Age: 39   Bats: R   Throws: R   Height: 6' 3"   Weight: 225

YEAR	TEAM	LVL	AGE	PA	R	2B	3B	HR	RBI	BB	K	SB	CS	AVG/OBP/SLG	TAv	BABIP	BRR	FRAA	WARP
2012	NYA	MLB	36	529	74	17	1	18	57	51	116	13	1	.272/.353/.430	.281	.323	-1.6	3B(81): -4.8	1.7
2013	TAM	A+	37	20	2	1	0	0	3	1	5	0	0	.176/.300/.235	.193	.250	-0.6	3B(3): 0.0	-0.2
2013	NYA	MLB	37	181	21	7	0	7	19	23	43	4	2	.244/.348/.423	.273	.292	-1.0	3B(27): -0.3	0.7
2015	NYA	MLB	39	250	30	10	1	8	31	23	55	4	1	.247/.324/.408	.276	.288	-0.8	3B 1	0.9

Breakout: 0%   Improve: 14%   Collapse: 7%   Attrition: 17%   MLB: 72%   Comparables: Mike Schmidt, Raul Ibanez, Jeff Kent

Rodriguez poses the question that has divided many a high school debate class: Can good exist without evil? Platonic forms only qualify for their rank because some fail the ideal; if every slider were perfect, we would cease to marvel at any slider, or care about them at all. Human beings are terrible at appreciating things for what they are; they need signposts, references. This is why every novel, every wrestling federation, every theology and every sport needs its heels. A sport in which everyone gets along and tries their hardest and one team proves their fractionally greater talent is not a sport steeped in drama. Heroes need their villains, and fans will create them if necessary. Rodriguez's particular crimes against baseball are myriad but hardly unique; he is the latest of a legion of cheaters, some lionized, others tarred. Fortunately for everyone, 2015 should prove A-Rod's denouement, both as a character and as a baseball player. Teams will need to find a new dragon to slay, and will assuredly do so.

Austin Romine   C
Born: 11/22/88   Age: 26   Bats: R   Throws: R   Height: 6' 0"   Weight: 215

YEAR	TEAM	LVL	AGE	PA	R	2B	3B	HR	RBI	BB	K	SB	CS	AVG/OBP/SLG	TAv	BABIP	BRR	FRAA	WARP
2012	SWB	AAA	23	71	6	2	0	3	9	8	10	0	0	.213/.296/.393	.260	.200	-0.4	C(13): -0.1	0.3
2013	SWB	AAA	24	46	5	0	0	1	4	4	12	0	0	.333/.391/.405	.282	.448	-0.2	C(14): -0.2	0.3
2013	NYA	MLB	24	148	15	9	0	1	10	8	37	1	0	.207/.255/.296	.189	.276	1.4	C(59): 0.2	-0.2
2014	SWB	AAA	25	313	33	17	0	6	33	24	54	1	0	.242/.300/.365	.224	.279	-0.7	C(62): 0.1, 1B(13): -0.8	-0.4
2014	NYA	MLB	25	13	2	1	0	0	1	0	4	0	0	.231/.231/.308	.190	.333	-0.1	C(3): -0.0, 1B(1): -0.0	-0.1
2015	NYA	MLB	26	250	23	10	0	5	24	15	54	0	0	.231/.280/.338	.235	.277	-0.4	C -0, 1B -0	0.1

Breakout: 1%   Improve: 12%   Collapse: 17%   Attrition: 26%   MLB: 43%   Comparables: Josh Phegley, Humberto Quintero, Guillermo Quiroz

It's looking like Romine will have a better major-league career than his father Kevin, if only because he might not receive the playing time necessary to accumulate negative value. Pressed into service in 2013, the signing of McCann and the elevation of other, less-known prospects left Romine in Triple-A, where his pitch framing went unrecorded by high-speed cameras but his weak-grounder hitting was recorded by low-fi ones. With no bat and no arm, Romine is probably doomed to haunt various Triple-A rosters, quietly hoping that major leaguers get hurt and then instantly feeling bad about it.

Brendan Ryan   SS
Born: 3/26/82   Age: 33   Bats: R   Throws: R   Height: 6' 2"   Weight: 195

YEAR	TEAM	LVL	AGE	PA	R	2B	3B	HR	RBI	BB	K	SB	CS	AVG/OBP/SLG	TAv	BABIP	BRR	FRAA	WARP
2012	SEA	MLB	30	470	42	19	3	3	31	44	98	11	5	.194/.277/.278	.228	.244	-1.0	SS(138): 12.0	1.9
2013	SEA	MLB	31	287	23	10	0	3	21	21	60	4	2	.192/.254/.265	.201	.237	-2.1	SS(84): 4.9	0.1
2013	NYA	MLB	31	62	7	2	0	1	1	2	13	0	0	.220/.258/.305	.209	.267	0.7	SS(17): 2.9	0.2
2014	NYA	MLB	32	124	5	4	0	0	8	4	30	0	2	.167/.211/.202	.164	.221	-0.5	SS(25): -1.2, 2B(19): 2.2	-0.8
2015	NYA	MLB	33	250	22	9	1	2	19	17	49	4	2	.216/.278/.296	.221	.257	-0.6	SS 5, 2B 1	0.5

Breakout: 1%   Improve: 29%   Collapse: 7%   Attrition: 14%   MLB: 97%   Comparables: Adam Everett, Dick Groat, Ron Hansen

When we talk about good-field, no-hit shortstops, our imaginations immediately form around Ryan spearing a grounder deep in the hole, his body already turning into the throw. But we aren't really talking about no-hit shortstops, because the term does no justice: Ryan continues to explore new territories of offensive ineptitude with each passing season. Those who grew weary of the Jeter-topped lineup cards can blame his backup, who set lows in every offensive category, as well as some that haven't been invented yet. Ryan's never been even passable with the stick, but at least in Seattle he had the good sense to leave the bat on the shoulder; in New York, with limited opportunity, there's a suggestion that he pressed at the plate.

There must be some point where no amount of defensive value is enough, even in a utility role, and Ryan will veer toward it in the second year of a $5 million contract with the Yankees. If he can hit like Alexi Amarista, someone will keep signing checks.

Gary Sanchez   C

Born: 12/2/92   Age: 22   Bats: R   Throws: R   Height: 6' 3"   Weight: 235

YEAR	TEAM	LVL	AGE	PA	R	2B	3B	HR	RBI	BB	K	SB	CS	AVG/OBP/SLG	TAv	BABIP	BRR	FRAA	WARP
2012	CSC	A	19	289	44	19	0	13	56	22	65	11	4	.297/.353/.517	.298	.348	-1.5	C(53): -1.0	2.1
2012	TAM	A+	19	185	21	10	1	5	29	10	41	4	0	.279/.330/.436	.267	.341	-0.5	C(38): -0.8	0.7
2013	TAM	A+	20	399	38	21	0	13	61	28	71	3	1	.254/.313/.420	.259	.280	-0.3	C(76): -1.8, 1B(1): -0.0	1.8
2013	TRN	AA	20	110	12	6	0	2	10	13	16	0	0	.250/.364/.380	.285	.280	-0.5	C(20): 0.2	0.8
2014	TRN	AA	21	477	48	19	0	13	65	43	91	1	1	.270/.338/.406	.283	.314	-2.6	C(93): 1.7	2.9
2015	NYA	MLB	22	250	25	10	0	8	29	14	64	0		.231/.280/.374	.249	.281	-0.5	C 0	0.6

Breakout: 4%   Improve: 19%   Collapse: 3%   Attrition: 27%   MLB: 37%   Comparables: Hank Conger, Wilin Rosario, Tony Sanchez

Sometimes you look at a disappointing prospect and you have to remind yourself of how young he is. Sometimes a prospect won't let you forget it. Sanchez waded through an inconsistent second year in the Eastern League, continued to struggle on defense, and got suspended for a week in June due to undisclosed crimes. He's still young for his level, you say, knowing that with each sentence he grows a little older. As the vision of Brian Mc-Cann, First Basemen fades into the sepia-toned optimism of yesteryear, the Yankees can afford to give Sanchez all the time he needs. The question is whether all the time in the world will be enough; Sanchez has never been renowned for his lithe figure or his work ethic. For now, a weary cadre of sportswriters drags out their Jesus Montero comparisons: always trite, still technically accurate.

Alfonso Soriano   RF

Born: 1/7/76   Age: 39   Bats: R   Throws: R   Height: 6' 1"   Weight: 195

YEAR	TEAM	LVL	AGE	PA	R	2B	3B	HR	RBI	BB	K	SB	CS	AVG/OBP/SLG	TAv	BABIP	BRR	FRAA	WARP
2012	CHN	MLB	36	615	68	33	2	32	108	44	153	6	2	.262/.322/.499	.281	.303	-3.0	LF(145): 7.7	3.2
2013	CHN	MLB	37	383	47	24	1	17	51	15	89	10	5	.254/.287/.467	.268	.290	0.6	LF(86): 3.5	1.2
2013	NYA	MLB	37	243	37	8	0	17	50	21	67	8	4	.256/.325/.525	.300	.287	-1.4	LF(48): 2.0	2.0
2014	NYA	MLB	38	238	22	15	0	6	23	6	71	1	0	.221/.244/.367	.226	.288	1.3	RF(26): -2.9, LF(11): -0.4	-0.6
2015	NYA	MLB	39	301	35	15	0	13	40	15	79	5	2	.232/.276/.423	.261	.274	-0.5	LF 0, RF -1	0.5

Breakout: 0%   Improve: 15%   Collapse: 4%   Attrition: 18%   MLB: 67%   Comparables: Sammy Sosa, Joe Adcock, Ellis Burks

At least now we can finally agree on Soriano. As majestic and improbable as his 2013 half-season with the Yankees was, 2014 proved the exact opposite. His already terrible plate discipline shriveled along with his power, leading to his July 15th release. With no offers on the table, and unwilling to formally retire with all the negative economic repercussions therein, he withdrew from society to craft and melt down little gold statuettes of himself and hurl insults at the sea.

Ichiro Suzuki   RF

Born: 10/22/73   Age: 41   Bats: L   Throws: R   Height: 5' 11"   Weight: 170

YEAR	TEAM	LVL	AGE	PA	R	2B	3B	HR	RBI	BB	K	SB	CS	AVG/OBP/SLG	TAv	BABIP	BRR	FRAA	WARP
2012	SEA	MLB	38	423	49	15	5	4	28	17	40	15	2	.261/.288/.353	.234	.279	1.8	RF(93): 6.8	1.0
2012	NYA	MLB	38	240	28	13	1	5	27	5	21	14	5	.322/.340/.454	.279	.337	-1.3	RF(39): -2.1, LF(35): 0.1	0.5
2013	NYA	MLB	39	555	57	15	3	7	35	26	63	20	4	.262/.297/.342	.240	.285	4.1	RF(128): -5.3, CF(13): -0.2	0.0
2014	NYA	MLB	40	385	42	13	2	1	22	21	68	15	3	.284/.324/.340	.250	.346	2.6	RF(119): -1.4, LF(9): -0.1	0.4
2015	NYA	MLB	41	396	39	14	2	2	29	17	52	16	3	.265/.297/.330	.239	.298	1.4	RF -3, LF 0	-0.3

Breakout: 0%   Improve: 17%   Collapse: 9%   Attrition: 20%   MLB: 62%   Comparables: Enos Slaughter, Bob Boyd, Lou Piniella

It's hard watching any player grow old, but it's especially difficult with Ichiro. The contact skills that made him such a marvel in his relative youth have dissipated. His swing rate at pitches out of the zone has climbed, which has caused the percentage of pitches he sees in the zone to fall, which has caused his contact rates to fall, which has caused him to fall behind in more counts, which has caused him to swing at more bad pitches, which causes us to all feel our mortality, cold and tight, clenched in our throat. For all that, he didn't have a bad year. He adjusted by hitting everything straight into the ground and trusting his legs, finishing fourth in baseball in infield-hit percentage. It was enough to get the job done, and his work in the field was equally adequate. He's truly a fourth outfielder now, anonymous in all facets except in name, which is fine. We all grow old. We all fall a little short of arbitrary milestones.

Mark Teixeira   1B

Born: 4/11/80   Age: 35   Bats: B   Throws: R   Height: 6' 3"   Weight: 215

YEAR	TEAM	LVL	AGE	PA	R	2B	3B	HR	RBI	BB	K	SB	CS	AVG/OBP/SLG	TAv	BABIP	BRR	FRAA	WARP
2012	NYA	MLB	32	524	66	27	1	24	84	54	83	2	1	.251/.332/.475	.297	.250	-3.5	1B(119): 7.6	2.9
2013	NYA	MLB	33	63	5	1	0	3	12	8	19	0	0	.151/.270/.340	.231	.156	0.1	1B(14): 0.1	-0.1
2014	NYA	MLB	34	508	56	14	0	22	62	58	109	1	1	.216/.313/.398	.263	.233	0.3	1B(117): -0.9	0.3
2015	NYA	MLB	35	389	47	15	1	16	53	42	76	1	1	.233/.324/.424	.282	.249	-0.8	1B 3	1.5

Breakout: 2%   Improve: 27%   Collapse: 7%   Attrition: 14%   MLB: 95%   Comparables: Paul Konerko, Hideki Matsui, Travis Hafner

"I absolutely plan on playing 150 games this year," a healthy Teixeira told reporters on February 16th. On September 14th, he changed his mind and admitted that he probably wasn't a 150-games-a-year player, having been sidelined by a gashed left hand, a sore knee, dizziness, a strained oblique and hamstring and that same old wrist that destroyed his 2013 season. A week later, he promised that a renewed strength-training regimen would restore his power, a best shape of his life story written in the future perfect tense.

This is the true horror of old age: not that it happens, but that you don't notice it. You don't think about the fact that when you jog to the mailbox in your thirties, it's become that slow jog that isn't really any faster than walking. You notice the soreness, but you don't notice the subtle ways you limit yourself, fool yourself into preventing yourself from getting sore. Mark Teixeira is a professional athlete, and so must pursue the usual Freudian id-smothering self-psychiatry that allows a reviled public figure to fail continuously without getting down. Mark Teixeira is getting old and weak, and must justify his existence to his irrational and detached Patreon backers that are the fans.

If the Yankees are wise, they'll sign someone who can play first base and then actually do so for 60 games next season. The team can probably look forward to 60-80 games of Good Teixeira; they might as well spread them out over the season.

Luis Torrens   C

Born: 5/2/96   Age: 19   Bats: R   Throws: R   Height: 6' 0"   Weight: 175

YEAR	TEAM	LVL	AGE	PA	R	2B	3B	HR	RBI	BB	K	SB	CS	AVG/OBP/SLG	TAv	BABIP	BRR	FRAA	WARP
2014	CSC	A	18	34	4	0	0	1	3	6	7	0	0	.154/.353/.269	.222	.167	0.3	C(9): 0.2	0.0
2014	STA	A-	18	202	27	13	3	2	18	14	41	1	2	.270/.327/.405	.260	.336	0.2	C(39): 0.3	1.1
2015	NYA	MLB	19	250	22	8	1	3	18	15	74	0	0	.193/.248/.275	.201	.263	-0.4	C 1	-0.6

Breakout: 0%   Improve: 0%   Collapse: 0%   Attrition: 0%   MLB: 0%   *Comparables: Miguel Gonzalez, Brandon Snyder, Tomas Telis*

In 2012, the Yankees signed Torrens out of Venezuela as a shortstop and converted him to catcher to take advantage of his arm. He took to the tools gladly, and as an 18-year-old in Single-A, his defense was already drawing glowing reviews. If he proves decent at catcher, it leaves a lot of leeway for his hitting, which is currently described as "not getting knocked out of his hands" despite facing pitchers who are old enough to drink and to have already read *The Lottery* in their freshman Intro to Lit classes. That's enough to make a prospect list, because catching is both difficult and undesirable.

Mason Williams   CF

Born: 8/21/91   Age: 23   Bats: L   Throws: R   Height: 6' 1"   Weight: 180

YEAR	TEAM	LVL	AGE	PA	R	2B	3B	HR	RBI	BB	K	SB	CS	AVG/OBP/SLG	TAv	BABIP	BRR	FRAA	WARP
2012	CSC	A	20	311	55	19	4	8	28	21	33	19	9	.304/.359/.489	.300	.319	0.3	CF(66): 0.7	2.6
2012	TAM	A+	20	86	13	3	0	3	7	3	14	1	4	.277/.302/.422	.251	.303	0.3	CF(22): 0.5	0.3
2013	TAM	A+	21	461	56	21	3	3	24	39	61	15	9	.261/.327/.350	.245	.299	3.3	CF(98): 6.6	1.7
2013	TRN	AA	21	76	7	3	1	1	4	1	18	0	0	.153/.164/.264	.146	.189	-0.5	CF(15): 0.3	-0.7
2014	TRN	AA	22	563	67	18	4	5	40	47	68	21	8	.223/.290/.304	.216	.248	2.9	CF(106): 3.6, RF(11): -0.2	0.0
2015	NYA	MLB	23	250	27	9	1	4	19	13	49	6	3	.214/.258/.314	.214	.246	0.2	CF 2, RF -0	-0.3

Breakout: 0%   Improve: 0%   Collapse: 0%   Attrition: 0%   MLB: 0%   *Comparables: Jacoby Ellsbury, Shane Robinson, Daniel Robertson*

Williams is still the Yankees' center fielder of the future, but now it's a future containing a twisted, smoking hellscape. Makeup has always been a concern for the former top-100 prospect, who seems trapped in a cycle of disappointment. At the same time, his raw power and speed have never seemed further from his production. The organization protected him from the Rule 5 draft, since his defensive skills would make him an easy fifth outfielder to stash on a major-league roster for a year, which indicates that someone, somewhere, holds hope.

Chris Young   OF

Born: 9/5/83   Age: 31   Bats: R   Throws: R   Height: 6' 2"   Weight: 200

YEAR	TEAM	LVL	AGE	PA	R	2B	3B	HR	RBI	BB	K	SB	CS	AVG/OBP/SLG	TAv	BABIP	BRR	FRAA	WARP
2012	ARI	MLB	28	363	36	24	0	14	41	36	79	8	3	.231/.311/.434	.261	.263	-0.3	CF(87): 0.7	1.4
2013	OAK	MLB	29	375	46	18	3	12	40	36	93	10	3	.200/.280/.379	.247	.237	1.0	CF(54): 2.8, RF(26): 2.9	1.1
2014	NYN	MLB	30	287	31	12	0	8	28	25	54	7	3	.205/.283/.346	.253	.226	1.1	LF(55): 0.2, CF(27): -0.0	0.6
2014	NYA	MLB	30	79	9	8	0	3	10	7	16	1	0	.282/.354/.521	.308	.327	0.6	LF(18): 0.7, RF(1): 0.0	0.8
2015	NYA	MLB	31	350	42	16	1	12	42	35	79	9	3	.228/.309/.399	.269	.265	0.4	CF 0, LF 2	1.5

Breakout: 0%   Improve: 0%   Collapse: 0%   Attrition: 0%   MLB: 0%   *Comparables: Jacoby Ellsbury, Shane Robinson, Daniel Robertson*

If you were among the many who had given Young up for dead, few could blame you. Baseball is a constant parade of funerals, one after another, to the point where you wonder how anything else gets done. It's kind of terrifying when a guy proceeds to leap out of the coffin. We get caught up with looking forward, worrying about the future. There's nothing wrong with that; it's a survival mechanism. But stop and take a moment to enjoy the continued employment of one Chris Young, vicariously if necessary. He'll be rewarded gently for his past performance, and given a chance to regress in front of hundreds of thousands of highly expectant people. Then they'll put him back down into the ground for good, and life will be a little drearier and less troubling.

Juan De Leon   OF
Born: 9/13/97   Age: 17   Bats: R   Throws: R   Height: 6'1"   Weight: 175

Dermis Garcia   SS
Born: 1/7/98   Age: 17   Bats: R   Throws: R   Height: 6'2"   Weight: 185

Nelson Gomez   3B
Born: 10/8/97   Age: 17   Bats: R   Throws: R   Height: 6'2"   Weight: 210

It's hard to spend money these days if you're a baseball franchise. The luxury tax is oppressive, and the small-market teams have started figuring out how to lock up their arbitration-eligible talent anyway. The draft used to be a decent fallback option, but now they've capped the spending on that, too. You can still spend on scouting and coaches and facilities, but infrastructure doesn't provide that same thrill.

The Yankees found their solution in the international market. Reaching out to the lawless wilds of Latin American baseball, the Yankees went ahead and signed the top-ranked international prospect according to MLB.com. They also signed the prospects who ranked second, fifth, seventh, ninth, 13th, 14th, 16th and 25th. If the world of scouting is a raffle, the Yankees are happy to buy all the tickets. Given that these kids are literally kids, it'll be years before the strategy pays off at the major-league level. But there are names worth remembering, including Garcia and Gomez, two imposing individuals with plus power and the potential to man the left side of the infield. Another, DeLeon, is an outfielder with raw skill and the chance to wield all five tools. Whether or not they succeed, they'll make the Yankees' farm system more interesting than it's been in years.

Pitchers

Manny Banuelos   LHP

Born: 3/13/91   Age: 24   Bats: L   Throws: L   Height: 5'10"   Weight: 205

YEAR	TEAM	LVL	AGE	W	L	SV	G	GS	IP	H	HR	BB	K	BB/9	K/9	GB%	BABIP	WHIP	ERA	FIP	FRA	WARP
2012	SWB	AAA	21	0	2	0	6	6	24	29	2	10	22	3.8	8.2	43%	.360	1.62	4.50	3.78	5.09	0.2
2014	TAM	A+	23	0	0	0	5	5	12²	10	0	2	14	1.4	9.9	36%	.303	0.95	2.84	1.89	3.49	0.3
2014	TRN	AA	23	1	3	0	17	16	49	40	8	19	44	3.5	8.1	42%	.242	1.20	4.59	5.03	5.75	0.0
2014	SWB	AAA	23	1	0	0	4	4	15	14	2	10	13	6.0	7.8	39%	.273	1.60	3.60	5.56	5.90	-0.1
2015	NYA	MLB	24	3	4	0	13	13	51²	52	6	26	44	4.5	7.7	46%	.303	1.51	4.86	5.09	5.28	0.0

Breakout: 17%   Improve: 32%   Collapse: 11%   Attrition: 30%   MLB: 45%   *Comparables: Mike Kickham, Chris Dwyer, Chris Withrow*

Take the hero-at-his-lowest-moment-struggling-to-pull-it-back-together montage from any '80s movie, take out the music, and stretch it out to three years. Now you understand how Manny Banuelos has been feeling lately. Once the top prospect in the Yankees organization, Banuelos waded through his post-TJS season, and it was predictably ugly; control wasn't exactly his specialty even with the old ligament. The Yankees have one year left to find out what they have in their former future ace before the options run out. If he rediscovers enough command to return to his pre-surgery level, he can contribute. In the short term, his value lies in the bullpen, both based on team need and his own workload progression. It might be a *Rocky* ending and not a *Rocky II* ending in his future, but at least the plot should move forward again.

Heath Bell   RHP
Born: 9/29/77   Age: 37   Bats: R   Throws: R   Height: 6'3"   Weight: 250

YEAR	TEAM	LVL	AGE	W	L	SV	G	GS	IP	H	HR	BB	K	BB/9	K/9	GB%	BABIP	WHIP	ERA	FIP	FRA	WARP
2012	MIA	MLB	34	4	5	19	73	0	63²	70	5	29	59	4.1	8.3	48%	.342	1.55	5.09	3.76	4.35	0.2
2013	ARI	MLB	35	5	2	15	69	0	65²	74	12	16	72	2.2	9.9	44%	.337	1.37	4.11	4.07	3.63	0.7
2014	NOR	AAA	36	2	0	1	10	0	10²	15	0	6	11	5.1	9.3	53%	.441	1.97	4.22	3.26	3.04	0.3
2014	TBA	MLB	36	1	1	0	13	0	17¹	24	1	8	12	4.2	6.2	67%	.365	1.85	7.27	4.60	4.37	0.0
2015	NYA	MLB	37	2	1	5	40	0	38¹	38	4	13	38	3.1	9.0	46%	.313	1.33	4.01	4.10	4.36	0.2

Breakout: 20%   Improve: 46%   Collapse: 18%   Attrition: 10%   MLB: 78%   *Comparables: Brendan Donnelly, Eddie Guardado, Bob Wickman*

No closer is an island, entire of itself; every closer is a piece of the continent, a part of the main. If a clod be washed away by the sea, fantasy baseball is the less, as well as if a promontory were, as well as if a manor of thy friend's or of thine own were: Any closer's demise diminishes me, because I am involved in an 18-team redraft league, and therefore never send to know for whom the bell tolls; it tolls for Heath.

Dellin Betances   RHP
Born: 3/23/88   Age: 27   Bats: R   Throws: R   Height: 6'8"   Weight: 260

YEAR	TEAM	LVL	AGE	W	L	SV	G	GS	IP	H	HR	BB	K	BB/9	K/9	GB%	BABIP	WHIP	ERA	FIP	FRA	WARP
2012	TRN	AA	24	3	4	0	11	10	56²	73	4	30	53	4.8	8.4	41%	.392	1.82	6.51	4.15	5.32	0.2
2012	SWB	AAA	24	3	5	0	16	16	74²	71	9	69	71	8.3	8.6	43%	.298	1.88	6.39	5.84	6.98	-1.0
2013	SWB	AAA	25	6	4	5	38	6	84	52	2	42	108	4.5	11.6	45%	.269	1.12	2.68	2.69	3.84	1.7
2013	NYA	MLB	25	0	0	0	6	0	5	9	1	2	10	3.6	18.0	36%	.615	2.20	10.80	2.88	5.36	0.0
2014	NYA	MLB	26	5	0	1	70	0	90	46	4	24	135	2.4	13.5	49%	.241	0.78	1.40	1.67	1.91	2.6
2015	NYA	MLB	27	4	3	0	26	9	68²	58	7	35	78	4.6	10.3	44%	.291	1.35	3.89	4.32	4.23	0.6

Breakout: 28%   Improve: 43%   Collapse: 9%   Attrition: 26%   MLB: 62%   *Comparables: Brayan Villarreal, Michael Kirkman, Nick Hagadone*

Raise your hand if you saw that coming. Betances spent eight seasons in the minor leagues, where his mechanics recalled the monster of a survival horror game. Dan Syzmborski, creator of the projection tool ZiPS, ran the numbers and estimated a 6.24 ERA season, which he later called the worst in ZiPS' 11-year existence. Instead he had one of the best middle relief seasons since Mark Eichhorn (look it up), breaking Mariano Rivera's record for strikeouts by a reliever in a season. Starters almost always improve when they become relievers, but for Betances the move was particularly helpful: It allowed him to slough off his lesser off-speed pitches and concentrate on the good old 99 mph fastball/slider combo. Also, pitching more often helped regulate his delivery, and the short stints prevented fatigue from ruining it. Sure, it took Betances until the age of 26 to find himself, but people have gone much longer.

Jose Campos   RHP
Born: 7/27/92   Age: 22   Bats: R   Throws: R   Height: 6'4"   Weight: 195

YEAR	TEAM	LVL	AGE	W	L	SV	G	GS	IP	H	HR	BB	K	BB/9	K/9	GB%	BABIP	WHIP	ERA	FIP	FRA	WARP
2012	CSC	A	19	3	0	0	5	5	24²	20	2	8	26	2.9	9.5	44%	.269	1.14	4.01	3.62	4.25	0.4
2013	CSC	A	20	4	2	2	26	19	87	82	5	16	77	1.7	8.0	50%	.301	1.13	3.41	3.11	4.06	1.0
2015	NYA	MLB	22	2	3	0	7	7	33¹	38	5	13	21	3.5	5.6	46%	.304	1.54	5.26	5.68	5.72	-0.2

Breakout: 0%   Improve: 0%   Collapse: 0%   Attrition: 0%   MLB: 0%   *Comparables: Rudy Owens, Alex Cobb, Wilking Rodriguez*

Campos was finally felled by the Curse of Monteropineda, which robbed him of two years of his life, two ticks off his fastball and the innocent amiability of youth. Even before the fall, he wasn't the same guy who was such a steal from the Mariners' organization, as he battled to dodge the inexorable scalpel. Non-tendered by the Yanks and re-signed to a minor-league deal, we're left to discover which prize Campos can be for the gambler: The 95 mph power arm with rough secondary pitches, the 92 mph version with above-average accuracy and a promising curve or what's in the box. Inside the box is probably a middle reliever.

Chris Capuano   LHP
Born: 8/19/78   Age: 36   Bats: L   Throws: L   Height: 6'3"   Weight: 215

YEAR	TEAM	LVL	AGE	W	L	SV	G	GS	IP	H	HR	BB	K	BB/9	K/9	GB%	BABIP	WHIP	ERA	FIP	FRA	WARP
2012	LAN	MLB	33	12	12	0	33	33	198¹	188	25	54	162	2.5	7.4	43%	.284	1.22	3.72	3.99	4.29	1.4
2013	LAN	MLB	34	4	7	0	24	20	105²	125	11	24	81	2.0	6.9	48%	.334	1.41	4.26	3.52	4.37	0.6
2014	CSP	AAA	35	1	0	0	3	3	14²	12	2	3	14	1.8	8.6	51%	.256	1.02	3.07	4.18	4.02	0.3
2014	BOS	MLB	35	1	1	0	28	0	31²	34	3	15	29	4.3	8.2	41%	.326	1.55	4.55	4.08	4.46	0.1
2014	NYA	MLB	35	2	3	0	12	12	65²	67	7	19	55	2.6	7.5	44%	.297	1.31	4.25	3.88	4.33	0.6
2015	NYA	MLB	36	6	6	0	18	18	100	106	14	28	82	2.5	7.4	43%	.304	1.34	4.45	4.69	4.84	0.2

Breakout: 16%   Improve: 37%   Collapse: 14%   Attrition: 10%   MLB: 73%   *Comparables: Bartolo Colon, Roy Oswalt, Kenshin Kawakami*

Tired of paying extra for some name-brand product just to cover the company's advertising budget? Sick of being drawn in by empty promises of wealth, fame and attractive members of the gender of your choice? Then try Generic Left-Handed Swingman! Generic Left-Handed Swingman is ready to use straight off the shelf, 80 percent of the time, and works just as well as the namebrand competitor. Check the active ingredients—they're identical! Generic Left-Handed Swingman can be used on the go, whatever you need. Over-rely on young starting pitching? Toss Generic Left-Handed Swingman a dozen starts! Everybody healthy this month? Stick Generic Left-Handed Swingman in long relief; he'll probably enjoy the rest. And even if you're not satisfied, Generic Left-Handed Swingman will probably be worth more than you paid for him. (Offer not valid in Colorado.)

Preston Claiborne   RHP

Born: 1/21/88   Age: 27   Bats: R   Throws: R   Height: 6'2"   Weight: 225

YEAR	TEAM	LVL	AGE	W	L	SV	G	GS	IP	H	HR	BB	K	BB/9	K/9	GB%	BABIP	WHIP	ERA	FIP	FRA	WARP
2012	TRN	AA	24	2	2	5	30	0	48²	33	1	24	49	4.4	9.1	49%	.258	1.17	2.22	3.00	4.38	0.5
2012	SWB	AAA	24	4	0	1	20	0	33¹	31	2	12	29	3.2	7.8	47%	.305	1.29	4.05	3.28	4.86	0.1
2013	SWB	AAA	25	0	0	3	8	0	10¹	14	0	1	10	0.9	8.7	67%	.375	1.45	3.48	1.56	2.10	0.3
2013	NYA	MLB	25	0	2	0	44	0	50¹	51	7	14	42	2.5	7.5	46%	.295	1.29	4.11	4.17	4.62	0.1
2014	SWB	AAA	26	0	1	2	15	0	20¹	20	0	11	20	4.9	8.9	37%	.323	1.52	3.54	3.01	3.80	0.4
2014	NYA	MLB	26	3	0	0	18	0	21	24	1	10	16	4.3	6.9	41%	.333	1.62	3.00	3.68	4.22	0.1
2015	NYA	MLB	27	1	1	0	29	0	44	44	5	17	37	3.6	7.6	44%	.298	1.39	4.26	4.67	4.63	0.1

Breakout: 24%   Improve: 35%   Collapse: 13%   Attrition: 23%   MLB: 55%   Comparables: Marcus McBeth, Ryan Braun, Lucas Luetge

Preston Claiborne hadn't hit since college. But it was the 13th inning, the bench was empty and it was interleague play. "Just put it on the grass," he told himself. And he did. "It was crazy," he later told reporters. Luis Valbuena threw him out, but the runner advanced and went on to score the winning run. Even Jeter was impressed. Claiborne won't soon forget that day.

Ian Clarkin   LHP

Born: 2/14/95   Age: 20   Bats: L   Throws: L   Height: 6'2"   Weight: 190

YEAR	TEAM	LVL	AGE	W	L	SV	G	GS	IP	H	HR	BB	K	BB/9	K/9	GB%	BABIP	WHIP	ERA	FIP	FRA	WARP
2014	CSC	A	19	3	3	0	16	15	70	64	6	22	71	2.8	9.1	44%	.319	1.23	3.21	3.75	4.64	0.9
2015	NYA	MLB	20	3	4	0	12	12	48²	53	6	22	37	4.1	6.9	43%	.306	1.53	5.10	5.23	5.55	-0.2

Breakout: 0%   Improve: 0%   Collapse: 0%   Attrition: 0%   MLB: 0%   Comparables: Jarrod Parker, Julio Teheran, Jordan Lyles

In a way, this whole discussion about Clarkin is a lie. Lefty, low-90s fastball, good 12-6 curve, changeup needs polish, promising start. Good kid, plenty of heart, willing to work hard, keeps his head down, knows his job. A top prospect. It's the story of thousands of young pitchers over a hundred years, some now famous, most now forgotten. He's a 20-year-old pitching prospect, so we both know that he doesn't really exist in any meaningful sense. He'll either fall apart or he won't, and none of this means anything until then.

There is no such thing as a pitching prospect, but that's not enough, is it? It's not enough to wait and see. That's why you have to have prospect lists and power rankings and power ranking rankings. That's why you skipped past Chris Young and Martin Prado and Manny Banuelos to get to this comment first. That's why you look at Ian Clarkin for his value to the Yankees, those promised wins above replacement, that 2018 playoff run. You borrow his victories at interest.

Today, Ian Clarkin is a very good young pitcher. It might never be true again. But if his shoulder fails, he owes you nothing, owes himself nothing. He's a 20-year-old pitcher. Care at your own peril.

Shawn Kelley   RHP

Born: 4/26/84   Age: 31   Bats: R   Throws: R   Height: 6'2"   Weight: 220

YEAR	TEAM	LVL	AGE	W	L	SV	G	GS	IP	H	HR	BB	K	BB/9	K/9	GB%	BABIP	WHIP	ERA	FIP	FRA	WARP
2012	TAC	AAA	28	2	0	6	14	0	20	9	0	4	25	1.8	11.2	43%	.214	0.65	0.90	1.77	1.47	0.8
2012	SEA	MLB	28	2	4	0	47	0	44¹	43	5	15	45	3.0	9.1	31%	.304	1.31	3.25	3.50	3.26	0.6
2013	NYA	MLB	29	4	2	0	57	0	53¹	47	8	23	71	3.9	12.0	34%	.312	1.31	4.39	3.66	3.82	0.5
2014	NYA	MLB	30	3	6	4	59	0	51²	45	5	20	67	3.5	11.7	36%	.315	1.26	4.53	3.04	3.65	0.6
2015	NYA	MLB	31	3	1	1	47	0	47	41	5	17	54	3.2	10.4	37%	.297	1.23	3.40	3.76	3.69	0.6

Breakout: 24%   Improve: 35%   Collapse: 26%   Attrition: 17%   MLB: 86%   Comparables: Michael Wuertz, Jorge Julio, Jason Motte

On the surface it looked like Kelley's worst season in the majors; beneath it, it might have been his best yet. Kelley gave up a run in only 14 of his 59 games, but he gave up multiple runs in six of the 14. It's these kinds of meltdowns that stick to a player and turn a fan base against him; it's also the cause of surprisingly decent peripherals, because it tends to be a single extra hit or walk that does all the damage. In reality, Kelley's what he has always been: a decent enough seventh-inning guy who people ask too much of, when they even remember he exists. He threw 57 percent sliders last season, one of four pitchers to use it more than his fastball in 2014. Surprisingly, the increase was due to a newfound desire to throw it against lefties. Even more surprisingly, it actually worked: He showed a slight reverse platoon split, and maintained his seemingly outlier strikeout rate of 2013. At his current progression, Kelley will throw 100 percent sliders by his age-38 season.

Hiroki Kuroda   RHP

Born: 2/10/75   Age: 40   Bats: R   Throws: R   Height: 6'1"   Weight: 205

YEAR	TEAM	LVL	AGE	W	L	SV	G	GS	IP	H	HR	BB	K	BB/9	K/9	GB%	BABIP	WHIP	ERA	FIP	FRA	WARP
2012	NYA	MLB	37	16	11	0	33	33	219²	205	25	51	167	2.1	6.8	53%	.281	1.17	3.32	3.81	4.49	2.1
2013	NYA	MLB	38	11	13	0	32	32	201¹	191	20	43	150	1.9	6.7	47%	.282	1.16	3.31	3.59	4.00	2.9
2014	NYA	MLB	39	11	9	0	32	32	199	191	20	35	146	1.6	6.6	49%	.279	1.14	3.71	3.63	4.27	1.1
2015	NYA	MLB	40	11	9	0	26	26	169²	168	18	38	125	2.0	6.6	48%	.287	1.22	3.74	4.24	4.06	1.7

Breakout: 14%   Improve: 27%   Collapse: 13%   Attrition: 7%   MLB: 73%   Comparables: Greg Maddux, Mike Mussina, Woody Williams

Declining softly as a cloud,
Producing neither vales nor hills
When pitching 'fore his own home crowd
Or 'midst the fans of far off villes;
In August, April, or in June
In dark of night, or light of noon.

Continuous as the stars that shine
And twinkle on the Lower Bay,
The two-run, six-frame pitching line
Untouched by physical decay.
On such low heights are fortunes made
And ageless pitchers underpaid.

Jacob Lindgren   LHP

Born: 3/12/93   Age: 22   Bats: L   Throws: L   Height: 5'11"   Weight: 180

YEAR	TEAM	LVL	AGE	W	L	SV	G	GS	IP	H	HR	BB	K	BB/9	K/9	GB%	BABIP	WHIP	ERA	FIP	FRA	WARP
2014	TRN	AA	21	1	1	0	8	0	11²	6	0	9	18	6.9	13.9	73%	.273	1.29	3.86	2.58	4.27	0.1
2015	NYA	MLB	22	1	1	1	27	0	35²	28	3	16	46	4.0	11.6	53%	.302	1.24	3.20	3.55	3.48	0.5

Breakout: 0%   Improve: 0%   Collapse: 0%   Attrition: 0%   MLB: 0%   *Comparables: Andrew Carignan, Chris Perez, Craig Kimbrel*

The Strikeout Factory has a base on balls byproduct it doesn't like to advertise, but otherwise it reported a solid Q3. Though drafting college relievers with a team's first pick is never going to be popular, the Yankees felt like they had to make an exception with Lindgren, who struck out more than 16 batters per nine after moving to the 'pen his senior year. He proved equally overpowering in the minors, and the team considered having him ready for the postseason as the Royals did with Brandon Finnegan, but alas. A lefty with a low-90s fastball and a biting slider, Lindgren is basically ready to spam two true outcomes in the majors right now, but the acquisition of Justin Wilson might allow the team to give him a couple of months to learn how to aim.

Andrew Miller   LHP

Born: 5/21/85   Age: 30   Bats: L   Throws: L   Height: 6'7"   Weight: 210

YEAR	TEAM	LVL	AGE	W	L	SV	G	GS	IP	H	HR	BB	K	BB/9	K/9	GB%	BABIP	WHIP	ERA	FIP	FRA	WARP
2012	PAW	AAA	27	0	0	1	10	0	11	4	1	14	23	11.5	18.8	53%	.214	1.64	5.73	4.25	4.72	0.1
2012	BOS	MLB	27	3	2	0	53	0	40¹	28	3	20	51	4.5	11.4	43%	.269	1.19	3.35	3.12	3.45	0.6
2013	BOS	MLB	28	1	2	0	37	0	30²	25	3	17	48	5.0	14.1	57%	.338	1.37	2.64	3.08	4.02	0.2
2014	BOS	MLB	29	3	5	0	50	0	42¹	25	2	13	69	2.8	14.7	55%	.280	0.90	2.34	1.72	2.11	1.2
2014	BAL	MLB	29	2	0	1	23	0	20	8	1	4	34	1.8	15.3	36%	.219	0.60	1.35	1.16	2.10	0.5
2015	NYA	MLB	30	3	2	0	32	4	43²	39	4	24	47	4.8	9.8	47%	.301	1.43	4.25	4.38	4.62	0.2

Breakout: 16%   Improve: 42%   Collapse: 20%   Attrition: 20%   MLB: 70%   *Comparables: Tyler Yates, Wil Ledezma, Dustin Nippert*

It wasn't long ago that Miller was the lump of iron pyrite of the Miguel Cabrera trade. After finding his niche in Boston as a two-pitch lefty with scrubbed mechanics, he set off a bidding war at the trade deadline; by October it was clear he is one of the 10 best relievers in baseball. Not just against lefties, either: He held righties to a .446 OPS, and it's easy to see why. At the angle from which he throws, he dots the low corners with fastballs that don't seem to ever actually touch the strike zone until they're already in the catcher's glove. He alternates between that and a back-foot slider that enters and exits the frame like a stray paper airplane thrown from somewhere in the upper deck. He has one career save, and will spend the next four years battling Dellin Betances for the title of Best Non-Closer In Baseball. Loser is the one with the saves.

Ivan Nova   RHP

Born: 1/12/87   Age: 28   Bats: R   Throws: R   Height: 6'4"   Weight: 225

YEAR	TEAM	LVL	AGE	W	L	SV	G	GS	IP	H	HR	BB	K	BB/9	K/9	GB%	BABIP	WHIP	ERA	FIP	FRA	WARP
2012	NYA	MLB	25	12	8	0	28	28	170¹	194	28	56	153	3.0	8.1	46%	.331	1.47	5.02	4.55	4.82	0.7
2013	SWB	AAA	26	2	0	0	3	3	17²	15	1	4	17	2.0	8.7	56%	.298	1.08	2.04	2.70	3.26	0.3
2013	NYA	MLB	26	9	6	0	23	20	139¹	135	9	44	116	2.8	7.5	54%	.313	1.28	3.10	3.50	4.22	1.5
2014	NYA	MLB	27	2	2	0	4	4	20²	32	6	6	12	2.6	5.2	50%	.371	1.84	8.27	6.93	7.69	-0.5
2015	NYA	MLB	28	2	2	0	7	7	39²	41	4	12	31	2.8	7.1	50%	.306	1.35	4.21	4.37	4.57	0.2

Breakout: 20%   Improve: 53%   Collapse: 12%   Attrition: 12%   MLB: 82%   *Comparables: Gavin Floyd, Jesse Litsch, Jason Hammel*

Instead of building off of a promising second half of 2013, Nova suffered a partially torn UCL in April and spent the year learning how to cook three different rice-and-bean combinations for his wife. As accomplishments go, this is touching both in its simplicity and its lack of ambition. He'll probably return to his primary occupation in May or June, where he and the Yankees hope he can be effective combining his hittable repertoire with the usual wildness of the TJS sufferer.

David Phelps   RHP

Born: 10/9/86   Age: 28   Bats: R   Throws: R   Height: 6'2"   Weight: 200

YEAR	TEAM	LVL	AGE	W	L	SV	G	GS	IP	H	HR	BB	K	BB/9	K/9	GB%	BABIP	WHIP	ERA	FIP	FRA	WARP
2012	NYA	MLB	25	4	4	0	33	11	99²	81	14	38	96	3.4	8.7	44%	.258	1.19	3.34	4.27	4.73	0.8
2013	NYA	MLB	26	6	5	0	22	12	86²	88	8	35	79	3.6	8.2	44%	.323	1.42	4.98	3.84	4.74	0.4
2014	NYA	MLB	27	5	5	1	32	17	113	115	13	46	92	3.7	7.3	44%	.301	1.42	4.38	4.43	4.81	0.4
2015	NYA	MLB	28	5	5	0	25	14	96	94	11	32	83	3.0	7.8	44%	.297	1.32	3.99	4.49	4.33	0.7

Breakout: 21%   Improve: 50%   Collapse: 21%   Attrition: 30%   MLB: 82%   *Comparables: Josh Collmenter, Garrett Olson, Randy Wells*

In a chaotic and frightening world, Phelps is our bedrock. He's a reliable but underwhelming swingman with a reliable but underwhelming arsenal. He gets hurt each summer with such precise timing that you wonder if he has a timeshare. We should be grateful for him. In a world where the three true outcomes dominate and everyone is gradually becoming Adam Dunn, Phelps alone resists. If Crash Davis was correct when he called groundballs democratic, then flyballs are populist; they allow fans to whip their necks and imagine for a second that every one is a home run. The world is sliding into methodical, stainless excellence, and the mediocrity of one David Phelps gives it color.

Michael Pineda   RHP

Born: 1/18/89   Age: 26   Bats: R   Throws: R   Height: 6'7"   Weight: 265

YEAR	TEAM	LVL	AGE	W	L	SV	G	GS	IP	H	HR	BB	K	BB/9	K/9	GB%	BABIP	WHIP	ERA	FIP	FRA	WARP
2013	SWB	AAA	24	1	1	0	6	6	23¹	18	2	6	26	2.3	10.0	52%	.267	1.03	3.86	3.12	5.15	0.2
2014	NYA	MLB	25	5	5	0	13	13	76¹	56	5	7	59	0.8	7.0	42%	.233	0.83	1.89	2.74	3.36	1.5
2015	NYA	MLB	26	4	3	0	11	11	62¹	53	6	16	61	2.3	8.8	41%	.278	1.11	3.04	3.69	3.31	1.3

Breakout: 36%   Improve: 66%   Collapse: 13%   Attrition: 13%   MLB: 92%   *Comparables: Clay Buchholz, Daniel Hudson, Jeremy Hellickson*

The prodigal son returned, unrepentant of the sliders that stole his youth, and a city welcomed him with open arms. Pineda threw them even more than he did before, more than almost any starter in baseball. And it was glorious.

That won't be what anyone remembers about his 2014, of course. Not with that patch of pine tar, so thick that you can still see it, as though it were burned into your retinas. The glassy expression that met his sentencing, the moral handwringing of the Baylesses and the people who wished they were as famous as Bayless. But that's over now. Now, all that remains is a mid-rotation starter, one whose fastball is older and wiser, one who somehow managed to improve his changeup during all that flat-grounded catch. A starter who pounds the zone and gets ahead in the count, thanks to a slider that's easier to aim (so far) than it is to hit. It's a recipe that can work well, and it's neat that it's worked at all.

CC Sabathia   LHP

Born: 7/21/80   Age: 34   Bats: L   Throws: L   Height: 6'7"   Weight: 285

YEAR	TEAM	LVL	AGE	W	L	SV	G	GS	IP	H	HR	BB	K	BB/9	K/9	GB%	BABIP	WHIP	ERA	FIP	FRA	WARP
2012	NYA	MLB	31	15	6	0	28	28	200	184	22	44	197	2.0	8.9	50%	.288	1.14	3.38	3.29	3.71	3.6
2013	NYA	MLB	32	14	13	0	32	32	211	224	28	65	175	2.8	7.5	47%	.308	1.37	4.78	4.12	4.95	0.3
2014	NYA	MLB	33	3	4	0	8	8	46	58	10	10	48	2.0	9.4	50%	.350	1.48	5.28	4.81	5.29	-0.2
2015	NYA	MLB	34	5	4	0	11	11	74¹	72	7	19	68	2.3	8.3	48%	.302	1.22	3.64	3.81	3.96	0.8

Breakout: 21%   Improve: 45%   Collapse: 15%   Attrition: 13%   MLB: 86%   *Comparables: Josh Beckett, Wandy Rodriguez, Johan Santana*

When Sabathia was felled by a season-ending knee injury in June, it froze him in a statistical pause face. His eight starts yielded a career-worst earned run average thanks to a .350 BABIP and a home run/fly ball rate (23 percent) that would make Brandon McCarthy shudder. Behind the results were actually some strong peripherals, with the second-best walk rate and highest strikeout rate of his career, all with a fastball that averaged under 90 miles per hour.

The knee is the first major injury of Sabathia's impressive career, but it's also a major concern. Though it didn't require full microfracture surgery, and he should be ready to start 2015 on schedule—the injury is the same one that befell Russell Westbrook of an unnamable basketball team—but if Sabathia suffers any kind of setback, it could threaten his career.

Of equal interest is how this affects Sabathia's progress as a pitcher. The awful numbers masked a drastic change in his approach on the mound. Realizing that his fastball was useless, Sabathia effectively eliminated it, relying heavily on a sinker/slider/changeup combination. He'll never be an ace again, but if the home run rate regresses and he benefits from new leadership at shortstop behind him, Sabathia can still be a productive member of the rotation.

Luis Severino   RHP

Born: 2/20/94   Age: 21   Bats: R   Throws: R   Height: 6'0"   Weight: 195

YEAR	TEAM	LVL	AGE	W	L	SV	G	GS	IP	H	HR	BB	K	BB/9	K/9	GB%	BABIP	WHIP	ERA	FIP	FRA	WARP
2013	CSC	A	19	1	1	0	4	4	17²	21	1	4	21	2.0	10.7	46%	.392	1.42	4.08	2.52	2.58	0.5
2014	CSC	A	20	3	2	0	14	14	67²	62	2	15	70	2.0	9.3	53%	.321	1.14	2.79	2.70	3.90	1.4
2014	TAM	A+	20	1	1	0	4	4	20²	11	0	6	28	2.6	12.2	59%	.239	0.82	1.31	1.55	1.80	0.9
2014	TRN	AA	20	2	2	0	6	6	25	20	1	6	29	2.2	10.4	48%	.297	1.04	2.52	2.27	3.05	0.8
2015	NYA	MLB	21	5	5	0	17	17	80¹	81	9	31	69	3.5	7.8	49%	.303	1.40	4.41	4.63	4.79	0.3

Breakout: 0%   Improve: 0%   Collapse: 0%   Attrition: 0%   MLB: 0%   *Comparables: Drew Hutchison, Danny Duffy, Jarrod Parker*

Severino is the perfect rags-to-riches story, if you ignore the fact that he's still about four years away from actual riches. A low-profile international signing out of the Dominican Republic, it took him a year to become the top pitching prospect in the Yankees' system, and one more to become their top prospect overall. In 2014 he bounded from Single-A Charleston through Tampa to Double-A Trenton, showing little hesitation on the way. He has a fastball that touches 98, a good change and a hard slider, all with the potential to be plus pitches. It's actually his own development that presents his biggest obstacle: Entering his age-21 season, his body hasn't had time to catch up to his arm. At 6 feet and 195 pounds, he'll need to build on his frame to handle the rigors of starting, and the team will need to be careful with his workload in the meantime.

Masahiro Tanaka   RHP

Born: 11/1/88   Age: 25   Bats: R   Throws: R   Height: 6'2"   Weight: 205

YEAR	TEAM	LVL	AGE	W	L	SV	G	GS	IP	H	HR	BB	K	BB/9	K/9	GB%	BABIP	WHIP	ERA	FIP	FRA	WARP
2012	RAK	NPB	23	10	4	0	22	22	173	160	4	19	169	1.0	8.8	—	.327	1.03	1.87	—	—	—
2013	RAK	NPB	24	24	0	1	28	24	212	168	6	32	183	1.4	7.8	—	.280	0.94	1.27	—	—	—
2014	NYA	MLB	25	13	5	0	20	20	136¹	123	15	21	141	1.4	9.3	48%	.299	1.06	2.77	3.07	3.46	2.2
2015	NYA	MLB	26	6	4	0	13	13	95²	85	10	16	98	1.6	9.3	46%	.298	1.07	2.95	3.45	3.21	1.9

Breakout: 21%   Improve: 53%   Collapse: 20%   Attrition: 10%   MLB: 98%   *Comparables: Jeremy Bonderman, Cole Hamels, Felix Hernandez*

Tanaka simultaneously proved why the Yankees gave him a seven-year, $155 million contract and why it's insane to have given him said contract. The common sentiment held that Tanaka was slightly inferior to Yu Darvish, having excellent control but lacking his predecessor's plus fastball. Those were both true. The fastball was pretty terrible, and it's a good thing that Tanaka didn't have to work from behind in that many counts. However, his split-finger and slider were both among the best in baseball. It's generally not encouraged to reach two strikes as a batter anyway, but with Tanaka pitching, the rest of the at-bat becomes a formality. He spent three months destroying the league before succumbing to a partially torn UCL in early July. The doctors recommended rest instead of surgery, and it potentially saved one of those expensive, expensive seasons. He was able to return in time to make a few starts in September, and looks ready heading into 2015.

Adam Warren   RHP

Born: 8/25/87   Age: 27   Bats: R   Throws: R   Height: 6'1"   Weight: 200

YEAR	TEAM	LVL	AGE	W	L	SV	G	GS	IP	H	HR	BB	K	BB/9	K/9	GB%	BABIP	WHIP	ERA	FIP	FRA	WARP
2012	SWB	AAA	24	7	8	0	26	26	152²	167	11	46	107	2.7	6.3	49%	.319	1.40	3.71	3.68	4.95	0.6
2012	NYA	MLB	24	0	0	0	1	1	2¹	8	2	2	1	7.7	3.9	29%	.500	4.29	23.14	15.90	9.38	-0.1
2013	NYA	MLB	25	3	2	1	34	2	77	80	10	30	64	3.5	7.5	47%	.311	1.43	3.39	4.35	4.60	0.4
2014	NYA	MLB	26	3	6	3	69	0	78²	63	4	24	76	2.7	8.7	48%	.272	1.11	2.97	2.92	3.25	1.3
2015	NYA	MLB	27	3	3	0	22	8	65	67	7	21	49	2.9	6.8	46%	.296	1.35	4.22	4.58	4.59	0.3

Breakout: 32%   Improve: 54%   Collapse: 17%   Attrition: 32%   MLB: 82%   *Comparables: Joe Saunders, J.D. Martin, David Phelps*

In 2014, Warren had perhaps the most boring 90th-percentile season in PECOTA history, serving as the last option in one of the best bullpens in baseball. A former fourth-round pick and a starter in the minors, Warren for years had been that plan that was never quite crazy enough to work, and it says something that the organization gave 13 other starters a name on the marquee last season. Maybe the team didn't want to ruin a good thing. Maybe he was their 14th choice.

If Warren was a victim of his own success, the happy news is that said success probably won't last long; though he has a history of outperforming his peripherals, regression is almost tangible in 2015. To be fair, his move to the bullpen has come with some adjustments, including the usual up-tick in fastball speed and increased slider usage, which may explain his relative success. Long considered a poor team's fifth starter, maybe Warren violates the Peter Principle by being where he belongs: just good enough to be there.

Chase Whitley   RHP

Born: 6/14/89   Age: 26   Bats: R   Throws: R   Height: 6'3"   Weight: 215

YEAR	TEAM	LVL	AGE	W	L	SV	G	GS	IP	H	HR	BB	K	BB/9	K/9	GB%	BABIP	WHIP	ERA	FIP	FRA	WARP
2012	SWB	AAA	23	9	5	1	41	2	80¹	61	7	25	66	2.8	7.4	48%	.248	1.07	3.25	3.66	4.34	0.5
2013	SWB	AAA	24	3	2	3	29	5	67²	61	3	21	62	2.8	8.2	44%	.310	1.21	3.06	3.06	4.11	0.7
2014	SWB	AAA	25	3	2	0	10	6	31¹	22	1	8	37	2.3	10.6	56%	.286	0.96	2.01	1.76	2.81	0.9
2014	NYA	MLB	25	4	3	0	24	12	77²	94	10	18	60	2.1	7.1	46%	.353	1.48	5.23	4.16	4.79	0.3
2015	NYA	MLB	26	3	2	0	36	6	84¹	84	10	26	72	2.8	7.7	47%	.300	1.31	4.00	4.47	4.34	0.6

Breakout: 33%   Improve: 45%   Collapse: 15%   Attrition: 17%   MLB: 71%   Comparables: Kazuhito Tadano, Jose Ascanio, Josh Spence

Whitley really put the emergency in emergency starter in 2014. Thrown to the wolves in May, he held his own for a month, only to continue to pitch after that. Despite some batted-ball misfortune, the end result shouldn't surprise anyone; he's a comedy act without a punchline.

Justin Wilson   LHP

Born: 8/18/87   Age: 27   Bats: L   Throws: L   Height: 6'2"   Weight: 205

YEAR	TEAM	LVL	AGE	W	L	SV	G	GS	IP	H	HR	BB	K	BB/9	K/9	GB%	BABIP	WHIP	ERA	FIP	FRA	WARP
2012	IND	AAA	24	9	6	0	29	25	135²	91	12	66	138	4.4	9.2	37%	.232	1.16	3.78	3.89	5.06	0.3
2012	PIT	MLB	24	0	0	0	8	0	4²	10	0	3	7	5.8	13.5	25%	.625	2.79	1.93	2.06	2.83	0.1
2013	PIT	MLB	25	6	1	0	58	0	73²	50	4	28	59	3.4	7.2	55%	.229	1.06	2.08	3.39	3.84	0.5
2014	PIT	MLB	26	3	4	0	70	0	60	49	4	30	61	4.5	9.1	52%	.285	1.32	4.20	3.59	4.02	0.1
2015	NYA	MLB	27	3	2	0	26	6	52	46	5	25	46	4.3	7.9	47%	.276	1.37	4.00	4.62	4.35	0.4

Breakout: 33%   Improve: 54%   Collapse: 13%   Attrition: 27%   MLB: 76%   Comparables: Michael Kirkman, Josh Outman, Ryan Cook

Part of why relievers are volatile is their small samples on a seasonal basis, which allows one or two bad appearances to taint 45 good ones. Overall, it appears Wilson had a bad season. Dig deeper and that's not necessarily the case. In two appearances, Wilson managed to allow seven runs while only retiring two batters. Scratch those games from his seasonal line and his run average against decreases from 4.50 to 3.54, still not quite where he was in 2013, but not the nearly 120 percent change it looks like otherwise. Because the blow-ups were isolated, and because Wilson's other numbers remained strong, there's no reason to believe he won't resume being a quality late-inning reliever this season.

Lineouts

Hitters

NAME	POS	TEAM	LVL	AGE	PA	R	2B	3B	HR	RBI	BB	K	SB	CS	AVG/OBP/SLG	TAv	BABIP	BRR	FRAA	WARP
Miguel Andujar	3B	CSC	A	19	527	75	25	4	10	70	35	83	5	1	.267/.318/.397	.271	.302	-2.9	3B(120): 0.7	2.1
Jake Cave	CF	TAM	A+	21	416	50	18	4	3	24	28	80	10	3	.304/.354/.395	.269	.377	0.4	CF(89): -0.1	1.8
	CF	TRN	AA	21	197	24	10	5	4	18	18	44	2	3	.273/.344/.455	.280	.344	1.9	CF(20): -0.4, LF(8): -1.0	0.8
Ramon Flores	RF	SWB	AAA	22	271	30	17	4	7	23	33	45	3	2	.247/.339/.443	.261	.276	-0.4	RF(34): -1.4, LF(14): 2.4	0.9
Slade Heathcott	RF	TRN	AA	23	37	4	2	0	0	1	3	13	0	1	.182/.250/.242	.207	.300	-0.7	RF(5): -0.0, CF(3): -0.5	-0.3
Gosuke Katoh	2B	CSC	A	19	465	58	19	6	3	37	71	142	20	10	.222/.345/.326	.258	.339	-4.1	2B(108): 1.3	0.7
Jose Pirela	2B	SWB	AAA	24	581	87	21	11	10	60	37	74	15	7	.305/.351/.441	.280	.336	3.8	2B(60): -1.2, LF(31): -1.1	3.3
	2B	NYA	MLB	24	25	6	1	2	0	3	1	4	0	0	.333/.360/.542	.304	.400	0.5	2B(4): 0.1	0.3
Scott Sizemore	3B	SWB	AAA	29	319	31	17	5	7	41	26	87	0	0	.266/.329/.433	.255	.355	-1.9	3B(60): -4.6, 1B(6): 0.1	0.3
	3B	NYA	MLB	29	16	3	2	0	0	4	0	8	0	0	.313/.313/.438	.271	.625	0.1	3B(5): 0.0, 1B(2): 0.1	0.1
Zelous Wheeler	3B	SWB	AAA	27	338	49	25	0	9	40	28	61	1	0	.296/.367/.467	.279	.346	-1.4	3B(33): -0.0, SS(26): -0.4	1.7
	3B	NYA	MLB	27	62	6	0	0	2	5	2	12	0	0	.193/.230/.298	.199	.205	-0.2	3B(18): -0.3, RF(6): -0.4	-0.2

The numbers don't look that impressive, but only because you're not using the right arbitrary endpoints: **Miguel Andujar** hit .314/.345/.444 from July forward. The scouts swear that there's both power and defense hiding deep within him, waiting to be unlocked by a grizzled coach or a voyage of self-discovery. ❖ **Jake Cave** broke his kneecap in his first professional game and missed two years, so he's doomed to wander the lands as Old For His Level. Despite the setback, he had a nice season with the bat in 2014 and might be described as a slower Brett Gardner, which sounds better than "potential fourth outfielder." ❖ Pro tip: If you're interested in making the majors and you're not the athletic type, you should consider either hitting singles or home runs. You'll probably see **Ramon Flores** on the bench this summer, waiting for the perfect opportunity to show his stuff, one that doesn't technically exist. ❖ If all the 19-year-old talent in this chapter has you excited, here's a palate cleanser. Fifty years from now, the only evidence of **Slade Heathcott**'s professional career will be the slow, tight wince as he lifts himself out of his easy chair. ❖ After a pleasant introduction in Rookie ball, **Gosuke Katoh** fell apart in Charleston, striking out 30 percent of the time and halving his ISO. Beyond Robert Refsnyder there isn't much organizational depth in the middle infield, at least until the Latin American kids make their way stateside, so a quick revival would really be in his team's best interests. ❖ Scouts wait a long time to see a true 80 skill, and he's a Yankees prospect, so expect to hear plenty about **Jorge Mateo**. The guy can run, and it looks like the arm and glove will stick at short. ❖ **Jose Pirela** is a Bloomquist in bloom, a true pre-renaissance man. In the minors he's played seven positions; the only one he hits like, sadly, is a shortstop. If he can develop his heart and grit, he'll be a sports radio darling for years. ❖ The next time you tell your kid that he has to eat his broccoli before he can go play Pokemon, and he tells you life isn't fair, walk him over to the computer, show him **Scott Sizemore**'s career numbers, and choke back a sob you didn't even know was there. ❖ The Yankees signed 18-year-old **Carlos Vidal** out of Colombia and sent him to the DSL, where he hit .361/.482/.498. He's a long way away, literally and figuratively, but the name is short and easy enough to remember. ❖ **Zelous Wheeler** just wants to get his first major-league double, and then he'll return to his home planet.

Pitchers

NAME	TEAM	LVL	AGE	W	L	SV	G	GS	IP	H	HR	BB	K	BB/9	K/9	GB%	BABIP	WHIP	ERA	FIP	FRA	WARP
Rich Hill	PAW	AAA	34	3	3	2	25	0	39	29	0	17	45	3.9	10.4	50%	.299	1.18	3.23	2.51	3.01	0.8
	ANA	MLB	34	0	0	0	2	0	0	1	0	3	0			0%	1.000				61.18	-0.1
	NYA	MLB	34	0	0	0	14	0	5¹	6	0	3	9	5.1	15.2	42%	.500	1.69	1.69	2.03	-0.15	0.2
David Huff	NYA	MLB	29	3	1	0	30	0	39	34	3	17	28	3.9	6.5	47%	.263	1.31	1.85	4.03	3.88	0.4
	SFN	MLB	29	1	0	0	16	0	20	27	2	6	11	2.7	4.9	53%	.347	1.65	6.30	4.35	4.21	0.0
Bryan Mitchell	TRN	AA	23	2	5	0	14	13	61¹	64	6	29	60	4.3	8.8	55%	.328	1.52	4.84	4.09	4.63	0.7
	SWB	AAA	23	4	2	0	9	8	41²	45	5	16	34	3.5	7.3	52%	.325	1.46	3.67	4.44	5.43	0.4
	NYA	MLB	23	0	1	0	3	1	11	10	0	3	7	2.5	5.7	56%	.312	1.18	2.45	3.25	3.71	0.1
Jose A. Ramirez	SWB	AAA	24	3	0	1	9	0	12¹	13	0	10	16	7.3	11.7	48%	.394	1.86	1.46	3.44	2.77	0.3
	NYA	MLB	24	0	2	0	8	0	10	11	2	7	10	6.3	9.0	23%	.321	1.80	5.40	6.46	6.00	-0.2
Esmil Rogers	BUF	AAA	28	2	2	0	12	7	48²	42	2	18	41	3.3	7.6	47%	.294	1.23	3.14	3.44	4.51	0.5
	TOR	MLB	28	0	0	0	16	0	20²	28	5	7	21	3.0	9.1	46%	.371	1.69	6.97	5.43	5.83	-0.2
	NYA	MLB	28	2	0	0	18	1	25	22	3	10	23	3.6	8.3	36%	.275	1.28	4.68	4.20	3.99	0.2
Nick Rumbelow	TAM	A+	22	5	1	1	19	0	26¹	20	0	8	29	2.7	9.9	36%	.299	1.06	2.39	2.21	2.75	0.7
	SWB	AAA	22	0	1	1	10	0	15²	17	2	5	19	2.9	10.9	41%	.357	1.40	4.02	3.55	3.84	0.2
Tyler Webb	TAM	A+	23	0	0	4	13	0	13	7	0	1	17	0.7	11.8	55%	.241	0.62	2.77	1.24	1.83	0.5
	TRN	AA	23	1	6	7	23	0	35²	35	2	14	51	3.5	12.9	38%	.371	1.37	4.04	2.65	3.09	1.0
	SWB	AAA	23	2	0	1	17	0	20	17	3	7	26	3.2	11.7	40%	.286	1.20	4.05	3.76	4.49	0.2

A third-round pick out of prep school, **Austin DeCarr** has a starter's build and, at the moment, a reliever's repertoire. He has a low-90s fastball and a nice hard curve, each of which shows more promise than his mother DeCarr. ❖ Imagine playing Pin The Tail On The Donkey, but with an assault rifle. That's **Luis Garcia**, who hit 99.5 mph in a September game. ❖ **Rich Hill** is a very good pitcher, which is why it's a shame that it's nearly physically impossible for him to pitch. Moving him to the bullpen to save his arm failed, so now all that's left is to see him pitch a dozen innings a year and be pleasantly surprised, like spotting a quarter on the ground. ❖ Take everything written in the Alex Rodriguez comment, replace morality with aesthetics, and you have a description of **David Huff**. His arsenal is the canvas on which better pitches are painted. ❖ **Bryan Mitchell** has two plus pitches in a mid-90s fastball and a GIFable curve, but that annoying changeup will probably doom him to a relief role. According to the *New York Post*'s George King, the Yankees turned down a swap for Dustin Ackley in August, so they obviously have faith in him. ❖ **Jose A. Ramirez** is still talented, still as frail as the self-esteem of high school freshmen. The Yankees decided to contain his peril through the limits of relief pitching, but this too failed. He'll return to Scranton, always flinching at the next blow, just about to land. ❖ We were all prospects once, all had metaphorical 96 mph fastballs. Then we go to college and develop control problems, make a few DL trips. In the end, we all eventually become **Esmil Rogers**, the miniboss of baseball, easily defeated, always reappearing. ❖ The unheralded **Nick Rumbelow** moved up four rungs of the ladder in a single year, an impressive feat even for a college reliever. Wielding a fastball/curveball combination similar to David Robertson, it won't be long before he's working the seventh inning on the big stage. ❖ No one cares about 10th-round former college relievers, but because of the hand he uses to endorse his checks, **Tyler Webb** has a decent chance of getting big-league appearances this year. He's basically a copy of Lindgren, or maybe a copy of a copy, the kind that's blurry but still strikes out more than a batter an inning.

Manager

Joe Girardi

YEAR	TEAM	W	L	Py-thag +/-	Avg PC	100+ P	120+ P	QS	BQS	REL	REL w Zero R	IBB	PH	PH Avg	PH HR	SB2	CS2	SB3	CS3	SAC Att	SAC%	POS SAC	Squeeze	Swing	In Play
2012	NYA	95	67	-1	97.9	84	3	82	7	485	409	32	129	.148	4	77	24	16	3	50	62.0%	28	0	321	88
2013	NYA	85	77	7	95.7	82	1	84	11	428	356	34	99	.242	1	96	27	18	4	53	67.9%	35	0	302	94
2014	NYA	84	78	7	93.4	56	0	83	6	475	399	23	95	.244	2	97	23	13	3	45	64.4%	27	0	311	85

Managing the Yankees is no easy job. Girardi, sixth on the franchise's games-managed leaderboard, knows this nearly as well as anyone. Over the past two seasons, Girardi has steered the Yankees around farewell tours and a welcome tour; he's introduced most of a new lineup on Opening Day, then did it again four months later, following a trade-deadline infusion; he's even kept his head above water through the various twists and turns in the A-Rod saga.

While Girardi has handled the drama as artfully as a playwright, what's more pertinent is how deftly he manages bullpens. No longer able to go to Mo, Girardi took the second-youngest Yankees relief corps since Rivera became closer in '97 (as weighed by innings) and led them to respectable individual numbers despite heavy usage. David Robertson remained in a traditional closer role, yet standout youngsters Dellin Betances and Adam Warren were used for four or more outs 64 times—putting them one-two in the majors, with more such outings combined than the Braves' entire staff.

By now you've said, but wait, the Yankees ranked 20th in bullpen ERA—just how good is this Girardi guy really? True, there were poor performers that anchored the staff's numbers down, though most of the damage was done by long relievers and spare arms. Girardi isn't blameless—he did use them, after all, and perhaps that was an unwanted drawback to having his best relievers toss multiple innings—but a manager can only employ who he's given, and Girardi wasn't given much at the back of the bullpen.

Because Girardi manages the Yankees, he'll never receive proper credit for his tactical chops. But as his stint with the Marlins betokened—and his time with the Yankees has verified—he's high quality.

OAKLAND ATHLETICS

by Philip Michaels

On July 31st, the Oakland Athletics sat more or less snugly in first place in the American League West. They also owned baseball's best record. Having already acquired Jeff Samardzija and Jason Hammel in exchange for a collection of young talent that included their best prospect, Addison Russell, Billy Beane pulled the trigger on arguably the biggest move of the trade deadline, depending on how you feel about David Price's change of address to Detroit: The A's secured the services of Jon Lester, he of the 3.2 WARP already accrued for Boston and the steamer trunk jammed with postseason accolades. All it cost Oakland was the services of talismanic slugger Yoenis Cespedes. (The deal also sent Jonny Gomes to the A's as part of an effort to stump anyone taking sports pub quizzes 15 years from now.)

Adding Lester to an already stacked rotation wasn't just about punching Oakland's ticket to October; it was supposed to give them an answer to two consecutive seasons of win-or-go home games in which the A's took the latter option because of a shut-down performance by the opponent's ace. Now they would be able to match fire for fire and keep their fine first-half form lasting well into the postseason.

More significantly, the Lester deal—and the Samardzija/Hammel pick-up that preceded it—marked a decided departure from how Beane and his front-office staff handled player acquisitions. Past Athletics wheelings and dealings were generally conducted with an eye toward a future that never quite arrived, with star players sent away through trade in exchange for a parade of prospects. "You pile up enough tomorrows, and you'll find you are left with nothing but a lot of empty yesterdays," Harold Hill says in *The Music Man*. "I don't know about you, but I'd like to make today worth remembering." With his team in the unusual position of staring down at 29 other clubs, Beane decided the same thing. The A's were going to put the pieces in place to make the 2014 season one to remember.

It was memorable, though not for the reasons Oakland's front office was hoping: The A's played .400 baseball in their last 55 games, squandered their divisional lead over the Angels and only managed to clinch the American League's last playoff slot on the final day of the season. The subsequent wild-card game, started by Lester, saw Oakland boot away a 7-3 lead with six outs to go and lose the title of destiny's darlings to the Royals. In the end,

we gained another data point about the work history of Beane's shit vis-a-vis the playoffs. This is probably not how the A's drew it up.

Nothing else the A's did in 2014—no heroics on the field, no roster shuffling off it—will ever emerge from the long shadow cast by trading Cespedes for two months of Lester's pitching services and whatever it is that Gomes does. The sizzling Hot Take in the wake of the team's season-ending tailspin was that the A's blew it: Beane tinkered with the chemistry of a league-leading pennant favorite and wound up with yet another postseason flame-out. One Bay Area columnist even suggested that all the A's moves so shattered the fragile eggshell minds of Oakland's band of brothers that they simply couldn't battle on in the face of their heartless GM's attempts to improve the team's chances of advancing in the postseason. Even in less insane quarters, Cespedes became the team's Rebecca to the worshipful Mrs. Danvers of the fan base. *The A's did well when Cespy was on the team. The A's did poorly once Cespy was traded. Trading Cespy was a mistake. QED.*

While I stand second to none in my admiration both for Cespedes' ability to turn a misplayed bounce off the wall into an outfield assist and his proficiency at field stripping a pig, the notion that he's the magic feather the A's needed to fly is massaging the facts to fit the narrative. The combination of a number of small, gnawing problems undid what was shaping up to be a dream season for Oakland far more than Cespedes and his .287 TAv heading off to Boston ever did.

The A's were cruisin' for a regressin'. As Oakland entered the All-Star break, a driving force of their success was a powerful offense. Their 466 runs scored placed second in baseball (ominously, the Angels were the team ahead of them), and their plus-145 run differential was tickling the upper reaches of history. Much of that run-producing oomph came from Brandon Moss, who went into the break with 21 home runs and a .268/.349/.530 line, and Derek Norris, dramatically out-pacing his career numbers with a gaudy .294/.402/.477 performance. Both were selected for the All-Star Game. Meanwhile, Stephen Vogt, who wasn't even called up until June 1st, was hitting .351 and slugging .530, not numbers you'd expect from someone who entered 2014 with a

ATHLETICS PROSPECTUS
2014 W-L: 88-74, 2ND IN AL WEST

Pythag	.608	1st	DER	.728	1st
RS/G	4.5	4th	B-Age	29.6	27th
RA/G	3.53	3rd	P-Age	28.2	17th
TAv	.269	6th	Salary	$80M	26th
BRR	-12.32	29th	M$/MW	$1.7M	3rd
TAv-P	.247	2nd	DL Days	936	18th
FIP	3.7	14th	$ on DL	9%	1st

Three-Year Park Factors

Runs	Runs/RH	Runs/LH	HR/RH	HR/LH
96	96	98	85	78

Top Hitter WARP	6.7	Josh Donaldson
Top Pitcher WARP	2.2	Sonny Gray
Top Prospect	Daniel Robertson	

.213 lifetime average.

No sensible person could have expected that to continue. Then again, no sensible person could have seen the Grand Canyon-depth hole all three of those players were about to tumble into. Moss would hit four home runs the rest of the year, strike out 67 times in 58 post-break games and go the entire month of August without clearing the fences; Norris' slash line dropped off to .228/.299/.297 after the July 31st trade deadline; and Vogt's performance went similarly southward (.188/.244/.305), with a foot injury taking him out of the lineup for much of September and limiting him to first base when he did play. Among A's regulars, only Josh Donaldson, Josh Reddick and Eric Sogard saw their numbers hold steady or improve in the latter stages of the 2014 season.

Oakland's drop in production—from an average of 5.1 runs per game before Lester came to town to 3.5 afterward—wasn't due to any one person's change of address to Yawkey Way, but to a team-wide decline after a half-season in which multiple players dramatically outperformed expectations. Given Cespedes' own middling performance in the far more offensively fertile confines of Fenway Park (a .269/.296/.423 line for the Red Sox), it's unlikely, magical powers or no, that he would have been anything more than a bullet point in the What Went Wrong? postmortems had Beane never pressed Ben Cherington's number on speed dial.

The A's kept getting hurt. Injuries help explain some of that fall-off in performance. The season was barely done and dusted before Moss went under the knife to repair a hip injury that, it turned out, had bothered him most of the year and required cortisone shots during the stretch run. Vogt marked the A's annual postseason elimination with surgery of his own to fix his foot. Coco Crisp battled a neck injury throughout the year that frequently limited him to every-other-day duty but was forced into action when able-bodied teammates were few and far between; his hitting predictably suffered. Crisp's slash line after August 1st was .203/.277/.280; it was a more Crispian .274/.372/.416 before that date.

That's just the Athletics who were able to limp onto the field in August and September. John Jaso was turning in a solid offensive season at .264/.337/.430 before a foul ball off his catcher's mask cut his season short in August; it was his second consecutive season ended by a concussion. Craig Gentry, who had been spelling Crisp in center, also saw his year end early due to a concussion after a terrifying collision at first base. Jed Lowrie missed significant time in August, as did his backup, Nick Punto, leaving a stretched Sogard to start many days at shortstop. And just to prove that the pitching staff could contribute to the team-wide late-year injury bug, Sean Doolittle sat for two weeks with an intercostal muscle strain. All these bangs and bruises left the A's, who have thrived by mixing and matching players, to make do with what they had available; thanks to the aforementioned slumps, that wasn't much. August and September amounted to

a rerun of *M*A*S*H* minus the hilarity. (Which is maybe *China Beach*? Either way, depressing.)

It's not like the 2014 Angels were the Washington Generals. We focus on the A's late-season performance for the same reason most people tune into motor sports: Car crashes make for riveting viewing. But let's not ignore the role the Angels played in all this. At the time of the Lester trade, they were 2½ games behind the A's, close enough for Oakland to squander the lead over one grim weekend. All the Angels did was play .614 ball the rest of the way. Yes, seven of the Angels' 35 wins came by fattening up on the nosediving A's, but Oakland still would have needed a .581 winning percentage over that stretch to keep pace with Los Angeles. (For context, that's a 94-win pace over a full season.)

In other words, Oakland had little margin for coming off the boil. It's likely the front office spotted this in late July and figured that if a death-or-glory wild-card game was possible, best to go into it with a true front-line pitcher who knew what it took in the postseason, especially if all it cost was a player with one year left on his contract who was destined for the trading block in the winter. The decision process was sound, even if the result was nauseatingly suboptimal. That Lester didn't close out the playoff game in ace-like fashion, that the bullpen fumbled away the lead and that defensively superior catcher Geovany Soto was forced out by injury can all be filed in Oakland's Just One of Those Things folder, which by now is bursting at the seams.

✦✦✦

Still, even if the Lester trade wasn't the disaster conventional wisdom made it out to be, even if it put the A's in a better position to win the wild-card game than standing pat would have, A's fans will chew it over for some time because it represents the exact moment the hint of possibility gave way to the gnawing suspicion that this may have been good as it gets for the current version of the Athletics.

It's hard to approach the coming season without sensing a 2007-08 vibe to the whole affair. The A's came off a postseason run in 2006, one in which they actually got out of the first round, and returned much of the same cast of characters, but neither their heralded youngsters nor their seemingly canny free-agent signings panned out and they finished 18 games out of first place. Soon enough established stars like Dan Haren and Nick Swisher were peddled as part of the latest round of rebuilding for a better tomorrow. That tomorrow wouldn't come until 2012.

Every offseason in Oakland is tumultuous, but the bridge between 2014 and 2015 was more unsettled than usual, so it's too early to tell if the same multi-year run of mediocrity awaits. A's fans can be forgiven if they feel they've piled up a lot of empty yesterdays without either the promise of a few fulfilling tomorrows or the reality of a rewarding today. ∎

—Philip Michaels is a former editor for both TechHive.com *and* Macworld *and has contributed to* Previously TV *and* SixColors.com.

Player comments by Doug Thorburn and Baseball Prospectus Authors

Hitters

Franklin Barreto   SS

Born: 2/27/96   Age: 19   Bats: R   Throws: R   Height: 5' 9"   Weight: 174

YEAR	TEAM	LVL	AGE	PA	R	2B	3B	HR	RBI	BB	K	SB	CS	AVG/OBP/SLG	TAv	BABIP	BRR	FRAA	WARP
2014	VAN	A-	18	328	65	23	4	6	61	26	64	29	5	.311/.384/.481	.314	.378	2.9	SS(68): -5.8	3.1
2015	OAK	MLB	19	250	23	9	1	3	20	9	75	9	3	.203/.239/.292	.207	.277	0.9	SS -4	-0.7

Breakout: 0%   Improve: 0%   Collapse: 0%   Attrition: 0%   MLB: 0%   Comparables: *Chris Owings, Arismendy Alcantara, Hernan Perez*

Barreto led the Northwest League in five offensive categories and was named MVP of both short-season leagues by *Baseball America*. Oh, and he was the youngest player in either league, too. He has natural bat-to-barrel abilities, going consecutive games without a hit just three times. He was the upside portion of the Josh Donaldson return, and the A's appear to have a special player on their hands. So, just for a moment, why don't you quit worrying about his high leg kick and whether he can stick at shortstop?

Billy Burns   CF

Born: 8/30/89   Age: 25   Bats: B   Throws: R   Height: 5' 9"   Weight: 180

YEAR	TEAM	LVL	AGE	PA	R	2B	3B	HR	RBI	BB	K	SB	CS	AVG/OBP/SLG	TAv	BABIP	BRR	FRAA	WARP
2012	HAG	A	22	485	83	14	5	0	41	65	68	38	9	.322/.432/.382	.302	.387	4.3	CF(68): 0.8, LF(41): 1.3	4.6
2013	POT	A+	23	402	70	8	9	0	29	52	37	54	5	.312/.422/.391	.295	.349	0.1	LF(73): 3.5, CF(18): -2.2	2.7
2013	HAR	AA	23	138	26	4	0	0	8	20	17	20	2	.325/.434/.360	.305	.381	3.5	CF(17): 1.7, LF(13): -0.5	1.7
2014	MID	AA	24	421	57	20	3	1	23	44	65	51	5	.250/.333/.330	.247	.298	4.9	CF(81): 9.5, LF(6): -0.9	2.0
2014	SAC	AAA	24	121	17	2	0	0	5	9	19	3	1	.193/.254/.211	.173	.233	0.5	CF(28): 0.8	-0.7
2014	OAK	MLB	24	6	4	0	0	0	0	0	0	3	1	.167/.167/.167	.156	.167	-0.6	CF(1): -0.0	-0.1
2015	OAK	MLB	25	250	30	7	2	0	13	22	46	20	2	.236/.311/.284	.236	.288	3.0	CF 2, LF 0	0.6

Breakout: 3%   Improve: 19%   Collapse: 11%   Attrition: 29%   MLB: 37%   Comparables: *Matt Angle, Luis Durango, Darin Mastroianni*

This one-trick pony is worth a bet at the races, but his skills with the stick are still in the developmental stages, leaving him confined to a pinch-running/pinch-flycatching role during his cup of coffee last September. Burns has parlayed his true 80-grade speed into an 89 percent success rate on stolen bases in his minor-league career, including 166 thefts over the past three seasons. A right-handed hitter when the Nats drafted him in 2011, Burns has since converted to switch-hitting in order to make more of his speed by shortening the route to first base, and his first two seasons of double duty were a resounding hit. His copious singles and walks floated a Rickey-like OBP, before it fell off in 2014 despite Midland's favorable hitting environment. A key to his future success is his ability to work counts and earn the respect of opposing pitchers. Not a key to future success, but still important: His name is a true sentence.

Billy Butler   DH

Born: 4/18/86   Age: 29   Bats: R   Throws: R   Height: 6' 1"   Weight: 240

YEAR	TEAM	LVL	AGE	PA	R	2B	3B	HR	RBI	BB	K	SB	CS	AVG/OBP/SLG	TAv	BABIP	BRR	FRAA	WARP
2012	KCA	MLB	26	679	72	32	1	29	107	54	111	2	1	.313/.373/.510	.302	.341	-4.7	1B(20): -0.2	3.1
2013	KCA	MLB	27	668	62	27	0	15	82	79	102	0	0	.289/.374/.412	.283	.326	-6.3	1B(7): 0.2	1.6
2014	KCA	MLB	28	603	57	32	0	9	66	41	96	0	0	.271/.323/.379	.256	.310	-3.7	1B(37): 0.8	0.0
2015	OAK	MLB	29	579	62	29	1	13	66	54	93	1	0	.277/.347/.412	.290	.311	-3.7	1B -0	2.2

Breakout: 4%   Improve: 55%   Collapse: 6%   Attrition: 4%   MLB: 98%   Comparables: *Justin Morneau, Don Mattingly, Edwin Encarnacion*

Like many of his Royals teammates, Butler was at his best in the second half last season, filling in admirably for the injured Eric Hosmer at first base in August before sliding back to his usual role of hitting designatedly. His overall numbers were woeful for a bat-only player, as Butler was strangely impatient, swinging at far more pitches out of the zone than is normal for him and seeing commensurate drops in his on-base and slugging percentages. Last year he posted a .291/.349/.470 line when he took the field between innings instead of marinating in the dugout, and his career numbers show he may suffer from the DH penalty more than most. The sluggardly Butler may well set a record for double-play grounders hitting behind the A's assortment of table-setters. Whether he can regain enough of his patient and productive approach and line-drive stroke to overcome his total lack of other skills is harder to predict.

Matt Chapman   3B

Born: 4/28/93   Age: 22   Bats: R   Throws: R   Height: 6' 2"   Weight: 205

YEAR	TEAM	LVL	AGE	PA	R	2B	3B	HR	RBI	BB	K	SB	CS	AVG/OBP/SLG	TAv	BABIP	BRR	FRAA	WARP
2014	BLT	A	21	202	22	8	3	5	20	7	46	2	1	.237/.282/.389	.220	.288	0.4	3B(21): 1.1	0.2
2015	OAK	MLB	22	250	17	9	1	3	20	9	72	0	0	.194/.228/.273	.197	.262	-0.3	3B 2	-0.9

Breakout: 0%   Improve: 0%   Collapse: 0%   Attrition: 0%   MLB: 0%   Comparables: *Brad Emaus, Alex Castellanos, Ryan Rua*

Chosen with the 25th overall selection in the 2014 draft, Chapman inked a below-slot deal following a disappointing junior season for Cal State Fullerton. He has slugging upside but is still learning to convert his raw power to in-game utility, and there are questions surrounding his swing and how it will translate to pro ball. He has the pedigree to move quickly, but the speed with which Chapman climbs the ladder will likely depend on how he responds to instruction and failure. His right arm is a cannon that's illegal in four states, adding value with his defense during stretches where his bat goes cold. With a fastball that reportedly hits 98 mph, the former two-way player can follow the Sean Doolittle path to the mound if the bat fails to come around.

Coco Crisp CF

Born: 11/1/79 Age: 35 Bats: B Throws: R Height: 5' 10" Weight: 185

YEAR	TEAM	LVL	AGE	PA	R	2B	3B	HR	RBI	BB	K	SB	CS	AVG/OBP/SLG	TAv	BABIP	BRR	FRAA	WARP
2012	OAK	MLB	32	508	68	25	7	11	46	45	64	39	4	.259/.325/.418	.272	.280	3.1	CF(97): 2.0, LF(16): -0.8	2.3
2013	OAK	MLB	33	584	93	22	3	22	66	61	65	21	5	.261/.335/.444	.295	.258	4.1	CF(110): 5.3	4.3
2014	OAK	MLB	34	536	68	21	3	9	47	66	66	19	5	.246/.336/.363	.280	.266	0.4	CF(111): -12.8	0.9
2015	OAK	MLB	35	513	66	21	4	9	44	47	70	24	5	.255/.320/.381	.271	.275	1.5	CF -0, LF -0	2.0

Breakout: 2%   Improve: 29%   Collapse: 5%   Attrition: 13%   MLB: 82%   Comparables: Bernie Williams, Johnny Damon, Shannon Stewart

Last year was a pain in the neck for Crisp. He ended up on the losing end of multiple run-ins with the outfield wall, and though it didn't require any stints on the disabled list, his neck woes cost him games on seven different occasions for stiffness, soreness and inflammation. After years of high-value work in center field, Crisp was bad last season, and every defensive metric supports that assessment. This might be a blip caused by the neck problems, as might be his diminished power, but maybe his speed and athleticism have just fallen off because he's in his mid-30s and that happens. He will need the wheels to bounce back if he is going to carry the weight of his contract, which, if the playing-time requirements vest, will carry through his age-37 season.

Ike Davis 1B

Born: 3/22/87 Age: 28 Bats: L Throws: L Height: 6' 4" Weight: 220

YEAR	TEAM	LVL	AGE	PA	R	2B	3B	HR	RBI	BB	K	SB	CS	AVG/OBP/SLG	TAv	BABIP	BRR	FRAA	WARP
2012	NYN	MLB	25	584	66	26	0	32	90	61	141	0	2	.227/.308/.462	.272	.246	-2.5	1B(148): 2.6	1.6
2013	LVG	AAA	26	92	21	7	0	7	13	17	18	0	0	.293/.424/.667	.344	.300	-1.5	1B(19): 0.7	0.9
2013	NYN	MLB	26	377	37	14	0	9	33	57	101	4	0	.205/.326/.334	.249	.268	-0.6	1B(96): -2.6	-0.5
2014	NYN	MLB	27	30	4	1	0	1	5	6	4	0	0	.208/.367/.375	.292	.211	0.1	1B(7): 0.5	0.3
2014	PIT	MLB	27	397	39	18	0	10	46	57	74	0	4	.235/.342/.378	.266	.270	-1.7	1B(117): -0.9	0.3
2015	OAK	MLB	28	402	47	17	0	14	51	50	91	2	1	.236/.331/.412	.284	.275	-1.0	1B 1	1.4

Breakout: 1%   Improve: 54%   Collapse: 0%   Attrition: 4%   MLB: 97%   Comparables: Nick Johnson, John Mayberry, Jason Kubel

Davis escaped from New York in April, when the Pirates sprung him in exchange for two minor-league pitchers. He went on to have a season that advanced offensive metrics say equaled his 2012, but it still felt like a disappointment. While Davis upped his average by eschewing his dead-pull tendencies in favor of using center field more often, a career-best strikeout-to-walk rate boosted his numbers the most. (It also helps that Clint Hurdle micromanaged to the point that Davis faced righties in more than 90 percent of his plate appearances.) A first baseman who relies on walks for his offense is about as desirable as a computer with more viruses than programs. See Barton, Daric, a comp that probably seems a bit on-the-nose after the Pirates sent Davis to the A's and netted $250,000 in extra international slot money.

Adam Dunn DH

Born: 11/9/79 Age: 35 Bats: L Throws: R Height: 6' 6" Weight: 285

YEAR	TEAM	LVL	AGE	PA	R	2B	3B	HR	RBI	BB	K	SB	CS	AVG/OBP/SLG	TAv	BABIP	BRR	FRAA	WARP
2012	CHA	MLB	32	649	87	19	0	41	96	105	222	2	1	.204/.333/.468	.283	.246	-2.4	1B(52): -0.9, LF(5): 0.1	1.9
2013	CHA	MLB	33	607	60	15	0	34	86	76	189	1	1	.219/.320/.442	.281	.266	-5.7	1B(71): -2.0, LF(3): -0.1	1.2
2014	CHA	MLB	34	435	43	17	0	20	54	65	132	1	1	.220/.340/.433	.285	.279	-8.2	1B(23): -1.1, LF(4): 0.4	0.6
2014	OAK	MLB	34	76	6	1	0	2	10	6	27	0	0	.212/.316/.318	.262	.324	-0.7		0.0
2015	OAK	MLB	35	498	59	16	1	21	65	65	166	1	1	.203/.312/.392	.269	.269	-4.0	1B -2, LF 0	0.5

Breakout: 1%   Improve: 19%   Collapse: 10%   Attrition: 12%   MLB: 95%   Comparables: Carlos Pena, Ken Phelps, Russell Branyan

2001: A Playoff Odyssey. Our hero played 14 years in the big leagues without ever appearing in the postseason, and with his Chicago club sitting in last place in late August, the odds of his breaking that streak were approaching zero. Then the baseball gods intervened, transporting him to Oakland, where a contending team might finally fulfill his quest for playoff baseball. The A's squeaked in via the wild card, and after 2,001 career games Adam Dunn was finally granted access to the glory of meaningful October baseball. Alas, Bob Melvin omitted him from the starting lineup despite a right-handed Royals starter; Dunn could only watch as his team squandered a late lead and Melvin passed him over for other left-handed pinch-hitters. His playoff trip came to an abrupt end in a sea of blue. The silver lining was that Dunn was resilient on the bench because he remembered to put on his Himalayan walking shoes.

Nate Freiman 1B

Born: 12/31/86 Age: 28 Bats: R Throws: R Height: 6' 8" Weight: 250

YEAR	TEAM	LVL	AGE	PA	R	2B	3B	HR	RBI	BB	K	SB	CS	AVG/OBP/SLG	TAv	BABIP	BRR	FRAA	WARP
2012	SAN	AA	25	581	80	31	1	24	105	49	95	0	2	.298/.370/.502	.319	.324	-7.9	1B(129): -4.3	2.9
2013	OAK	MLB	26	208	10	8	1	4	24	14	31	0	0	.274/.327/.389	.262	.306	-2.2	1B(59): 0.9	0.1
2014	SAC	AAA	27	364	48	22	1	15	74	40	73	0	0	.284/.371/.506	.313	.319	-3.9	1B(50): 0.1	2.1
2014	OAK	MLB	27	93	12	5	0	5	15	5	23	0	0	.218/.269/.448	.255	.237	-1.2	1B(33): -0.2	-0.1
2015	OAK	MLB	28	250	27	12	1	8	31	18	52	0	0	.252/.313/.418	.279	.288	-1.4	1B -0	0.6

Breakout: 8%   Improve: 20%   Collapse: 13%   Attrition: 26%   MLB: 54%   Comparables: Steve Pearce, Jeff Clement, Jesus Guzman

The certified lefty-masher spent the first half of the season in Sacramento and, a couple U-turns aside, made a mark in Oakland with a handful of second-half homers (all against southpaws) while being deployed with the platoon advantage in 76 percent of his plate appearances. Pitchers have peppered the bottom of the zone against the towering Freiman in an attempt to get under his long swing; though the strategy works against him with breaking balls, it also plays right into his approach of dropping the hammer on heat.

Sam Fuld CF

Born: 11/20/81 Age: 33 Bats: L Throws: L Height: 5' 10" Weight: 175

YEAR	TEAM	LVL	AGE	PA	R	2B	3B	HR	RBI	BB	K	SB	CS	AVG/OBP/SLG	TAv	BABIP	BRR	FRAA	WARP
2012	DUR	AAA	30	21	0	1	0	0	0	3	3	0	1	.167/.286/.222	.172	.200	-1.2	RF(2): 0.4, LF(1): 0.1	-0.2
2012	TBA	MLB	30	107	14	3	2	0	5	8	14	7	2	.255/.318/.327	.237	.298	-0.6	RF(15): 0.1, LF(14): 0.3	0.0
2013	TBA	MLB	31	200	25	0	3	2	17	17	28	8	2	.199/.270/.267	.202	.223	1.7	LF(55): 0.3, CF(29): 0.7	-0.4
2014	MIN	MLB	32	195	15	10	0	1	17	26	29	12	3	.274/.370/.354	.271	.324	0.6	CF(40): 2.9, LF(10): 0.5	1.0
2014	OAK	MLB	32	207	25	6	4	3	19	17	34	9	1	.209/.275/.332	.236	.240	0.6	LF(26): 2.9, CF(22): 3.1	0.9
2015	OAK	MLB	33	340	35	11	4	1	23	34	52	17	4	.227/.306/.301	.241	.265	0.4	CF 5, LF 3	1.3

Breakout: 3% Improve: 23% Collapse: 13% Attrition: 19% MLB: 81% Comparables: Brady Clark, Lenny Green, Kevin Mench

Fuld fits the Oakland mold of underappreciated outfielder as a player who does the little things well yet lacks the one standout tool that gets noticed. The A's let him go via waivers in April only to reacquire him from the Twins in a trade for Tommy Milone at the July 31st deadline. Fuld responded with a .210/.275/.312 line over the final two months of the season, though he supplied enough value on the basepaths and in the field to excuse the lack of offense. As players who can cover any outfield position and steal bases with efficiency, Fuld and Craig Gentry are cut from the same (but opposite-handed) cloth.

Craig Gentry CF

Born: 11/29/83 Age: 31 Bats: R Throws: R Height: 6' 2" Weight: 190

YEAR	TEAM	LVL	AGE	PA	R	2B	3B	HR	RBI	BB	K	SB	CS	AVG/OBP/SLG	TAv	BABIP	BRR	FRAA	WARP
2012	TEX	MLB	28	269	31	12	3	1	26	14	41	13	7	.304/.367/.392	.275	.364	-1.2	CF(114): 5.5, RF(3): 0.0	1.9
2013	TEX	MLB	29	287	39	12	4	2	22	29	46	24	3	.280/.373/.386	.293	.337	4.6	CF(71): 5.9, LF(34): 0.0	3.2
2014	OAK	MLB	30	258	38	6	1	0	12	17	44	20	2	.254/.319/.289	.249	.314	4.4	CF(50): 0.0, RF(29): 1.7	0.9
2015	OAK	MLB	31	252	27	9	2	0	16	18	46	16	3	.252/.323/.313	.252	.309	1.9	CF 3, LF 1	1.1

Breakout: 1% Improve: 34% Collapse: 3% Attrition: 12% MLB: 84% Comparables: Tony Gwynn, Nyjer Morgan, Ryan Freel

The A's made a statement about their position in the success cycle with their prospect purge of 2014, a declaration that started with the offseason Gentry deal and grew louder as the season progressed. The A's landed Gentry by trading premium prospect Michael Choice to the Rangers, and though Gentry managed his usual shtick of good defense and efficient baserunning, he was beset by injuries. His bat also took a nap, and though his legwork should be applauded, the seven extra-base hits and .035 ISO were insufficient marks for a regular (even a platoon regular) on a contending club.

Gentry's weaknesses (hitting righties, hitting in general, also hitting) can be masked by the A's plug-and-play approach to roster construction. Bob Melvin strategically employed him to make the most of his skill set, with more than 30 percent of his games played coming as a defensive replacement in the late innings. The best hope for a bounceback in Gentry's batting is probably health from the outfielders ahead of him on the depth chart so that Melvin can work him in when the matchups favor it, rather than forcing him into an everyday role for which he isn't suited.

Jonny Gomes LF

Born: 11/22/80 Age: 34 Bats: R Throws: R Height: 6' 1" Weight: 230

YEAR	TEAM	LVL	AGE	PA	R	2B	3B	HR	RBI	BB	K	SB	CS	AVG/OBP/SLG	TAv	BABIP	BRR	FRAA	WARP
2012	OAK	MLB	31	333	46	10	0	18	47	44	104	3	1	.262/.377/.491	.318	.348	-1.7	LF(39): 0.4, RF(3): 0.3	2.4
2013	BOS	MLB	32	366	49	17	0	13	52	43	89	1	1	.247/.344/.426	.283	.298	2.5	LF(98): -5.3, RF(4): 0.0	1.7
2014	BOS	MLB	33	246	22	7	0	6	32	26	70	0	0	.234/.329/.354	.264	.312	-0.3	LF(65): -3.6, RF(11): 0.8	0.5
2014	OAK	MLB	33	75	6	1	0	0	5	9	18	0	0	.234/.320/.250	.234	.313	0.2	LF(19): 0.7	0.0
2015	OAK	MLB	34	311	33	10	1	9	35	32	83	1	0	.228/.319/.367	.267	.291	0.1	LF -3, RF 1	0.7

Breakout: 0% Improve: 30% Collapse: 10% Attrition: 18% MLB: 93% Comparables: Jason Bay, Bob Nieman, Eric Hinske

Gomes bleeds green and gold. He grew up wearing those colors for the Casa Grande Gauchos as a high school ballplayer in Petaluma, California; in 2012, he supported the Petaluma Little League team that donned those colors (while he was an Athletic); and in 2014, Gomes returned home for his second tour of duty with Oakland, where he immediately stepped into the cleanup spot in the lefty-killing half of the A's lineup. Perhaps Gomes playing for the A's can be the next even-year phenomenon. Platoons make it impossible to tell from a glance at the games-played column whether players have been healthy, but Gomes has avoided the disabled list since 2006. From the department of round numbers: He finished 2014 with a career total of 500 RBI and a perfect split of 250 apiece at home and on the road.

John Jaso C

Born: 9/19/83 Age: 31 Bats: L Throws: R Height: 6' 2" Weight: 205

YEAR	TEAM	LVL	AGE	PA	R	2B	3B	HR	RBI	BB	K	SB	CS	AVG/OBP/SLG	TAv	BABIP	BRR	FRAA	WARP
2012	SEA	MLB	28	361	41	19	2	10	50	56	51	5	0	.276/.394/.456	.339	.298	0.1	C(43): -0.4	3.8
2013	OAK	MLB	29	249	31	12	0	3	21	38	45	2	1	.271/.387/.372	.291	.331	-0.7	C(48): -0.0, 1B(1): -0.0	1.4
2014	OAK	MLB	30	344	42	18	3	9	40	28	60	2	0	.264/.337/.430	.290	.300	-2.2	C(54): -1.1	1.7
2015	OAK	MLB	31	304	36	14	2	5	27	36	46	2	1	.255/.350/.378	.284	.289	-0.8	C -1	1.5

Breakout: 2% Improve: 37% Collapse: 3% Attrition: 9% MLB: 97% Comparables: Victor Martinez, Ted Simmons, Yadier Molina

For the second consecutive year, Jaso's season ended prematurely due to a concussion incurred on a foul tip. Given the snowball nature of head injuries and his inadequacies behind the plate, his days of donning the tools of ignorance should be coming to an end. He nabbed just four of 36 runners attempting to steal, an 11 percent catch rate that ranked dead last in the majors among catchers with more than 20 attempts. Jaso's value will be tied to his bat, just as it was when he was nominally a catcher. The interesting question is whether the shape of that bat has changed permanently: The OBP-for-power exchange in 2014 worked out weirdly well, as Jaso posted a nearly identical TAv compared to 2013, but it's alarming to see a player change his offensive identity so radically. On the other hand, Jaso's career-high in plate appearances is 404; keep that in mind when you evaluate the fluctuation in his season lines from year to year.

Brett Lawrie 3B

Born: 1/18/90   Age: 25   Bats: R   Throws: R   Height: 6' 0"   Weight: 210

YEAR	TEAM	LVL	AGE	PA	R	2B	3B	HR	RBI	BB	K	SB	CS	AVG/OBP/SLG	TAv	BABIP	BRR	FRAA	WARP
2012	TOR	MLB	22	536	73	26	3	11	48	33	86	13	8	.273/.324/.405	.258	.311	2.4	3B(123): 20.6, SS(1): -0.0	4.0
2013	TOR	MLB	23	442	41	18	3	11	46	30	68	9	5	.254/.315/.397	.263	.280	0.3	3B(103): 3.6, 2B(6): -0.7	1.7
2014	TOR	MLB	24	282	27	9	0	12	38	16	49	0	0	.247/.301/.421	.262	.260	-0.2	3B(63): 1.3, 2B(32): 1.5	1.2
2015	OAK	MLB	25	304	34	12	2	8	35	20	52	5	2	.263/.318/.409	.280	.293	0.6	3B 7, 2B 0	2.3

Breakout: 2%   Improve: 65%   Collapse: 1%   Attrition: 5%   MLB: 100%   *Comparables: Edwin Encarnacion, Ryan Zimmerman, Hank Blalock*

Lawrie hit the disabled list for the fourth year in a row, playing just three innings in the second half, in the interlude between his two DL stints. The first resulted from a Johnny Cueto fastball that beaned his right index finger mid-swing. That happened just four days after he suffered a left-hand contusion courtesy of a Chase Whitley pitch. Lawrie's HBP history stretches back to 2011, when his call-up was delayed after Anthony Bass fractured his (guess what) left hand. It's a risk Lawrie takes by standing on top of the plate, but his supreme bat speed and strength seem to justify the danger. After the Blue Jays integrated Juan Francisco, Lawrie split time between third and second base; while he played well at second and crammed more offense into the lineup, the Blue Jays missed his speed, instincts and arm at third, an athletic package that makes him elite there. With a bat capable of 25 home runs in a full season, Lawrie has all the tools to rank among the league's best third basemen, but health is a skill, too. The A's are probably hoping on that upside more than they are banking on it after acquiring him as a co-headliner with Franklin Barreto in the Josh Donaldson trade.

Maxwell Muncy 1B

Born: 8/25/90   Age: 24   Bats: L   Throws: R   Height: 6' 0"   Weight: 205

YEAR	TEAM	LVL	AGE	PA	R	2B	3B	HR	RBI	BB	K	SB	CS	AVG/OBP/SLG	TAv	BABIP	BRR	FRAA	WARP
2012	BUR	A	21	274	34	20	2	4	23	41	37	3	1	.275/.383/.432	.289	.309	-3.5	1B(63): -1.7	0.9
2013	STO	A+	22	428	67	13	1	21	76	64	68	1	1	.285/.400/.507	.330	.295	0.6	1B(85): -2.4	3.6
2013	MID	AA	22	197	22	12	2	4	24	24	34	0	1	.250/.340/.413	.257	.289	-1.0	1B(43): 1.4	0.3
2014	MID	AA	23	530	59	23	3	7	63	87	92	7	2	.264/.385/.379	.278	.316	-0.7	1B(86): -1.6, 3B(22): 1.8	1.9
2015	OAK	MLB	24	250	24	10	1	4	24	30	52	1	0	.225/.319/.336	.256	.273	-0.3	1B -1, 3B 0	0.1

Breakout: 3%   Improve: 11%   Collapse: 7%   Attrition: 22%   MLB: 29%   *Comparables: Chris McGuiness, Kila Ka'aihue, Mike Carp*

The numbers suggest that Muncy left a sock behind in Stockton, which is a problem for a player whose power is supposed to be his carrying tool, but he was raking before a broken middle finger sidelined him for a few weeks and dulled his hitting tools upon return. His patience remained intact, as he led the Texas League in walks by a healthy margin and finished third in on-base percentage. The A's gave him 22 games at third base, but Muncy's body suggests that he will succumb to the funnel of the defensive spectrum and settle at the cold corner long term, putting the pressure on his bat to rebound in 2015.

Renato Nunez 3B

Born: 4/4/94   Age: 21   Bats: R   Throws: R   Height: 6' 1"   Weight: 185

YEAR	TEAM	LVL	AGE	PA	R	2B	3B	HR	RBI	BB	K	SB	CS	AVG/OBP/SLG	TAv	BABIP	BRR	FRAA	WARP
2013	BLT	A	19	546	69	27	0	19	85	28	136	2	2	.258/.301/.423	.248	.315	-1.6	3B(114): 3.9	1.2
2014	STO	A+	20	563	75	28	3	29	96	34	113	2	0	.279/.336/.517	.288	.303	-1.9	3B(88): 1.8	3.0
2015	OAK	MLB	21	250	22	9	1	7	28	8	71	0	0	.212/.244/.349	.227	.265	-0.4	3B 1	-0.2

Breakout: 0%   Improve: 0%   Collapse: 0%   Attrition: 0%   MLB: 0%   *Comparables: Josh Bell, Mike Moustakas, Josh Vitters*

Nunez's raw power finally translated from batting practice to game time, and though the hitter-friendly environs of the Cal League may have aided his breakout, the performance can also be attributed to an improved approach at the plate that put him in more favorable counts to showcase his pop. His glove at third base is still a work in progress (which is not to say it hasn't made progress: A nearly halved error rate is a good sign), and Nunez spent 35 games at DH in order to keep his bat in the lineup, but the 21-year-old has time on his side. He has also exhibited a heavy platoon split over the past two seasons, and lack of development against same-side arms could limit him to part-time duty at the highest level, and not the good kind of part-time. Lefty mashers aren't that hard to find.

Matt Olson 1B

Born: 3/29/94   Age: 21   Bats: L   Throws: R   Height: 6' 4"   Weight: 236

YEAR	TEAM	LVL	AGE	PA	R	2B	3B	HR	RBI	BB	K	SB	CS	AVG/OBP/SLG	TAv	BABIP	BRR	FRAA	WARP
2013	BLT	A	19	558	69	32	0	23	93	72	148	4	3	.225/.326/.435	.266	.272	0.1	1B(127): 6.5	1.9
2014	STO	A+	20	634	111	31	1	37	97	117	137	2	0	.262/.404/.543	.326	.287	0.3	1B(107): 0.3, RF(8): -0.4	5.4
2015	OAK	MLB	21	250	27	9	0	9	31	29	74	0	0	.200/.295/.371	.257	.251	-0.5	1B 1, RF -0	0.2

Breakout: 2%   Improve: 10%   Collapse: 3%   Attrition: 5%   MLB: 18%   *Comparables: Jonathan Singleton, Kyle Blanks, Anthony Rizzo*

While Kris Bryant and Joey Gallo were grabbing headlines for their prodigious home run counts, Olson was trailing close behind, finishing with the third-highest total in the minors for 2014. His 117 walks led the minor leagues, as Olson posted the type of high-ceiling output that the A's were targeting with their high school-heavy draft of 2012. His defense was a big question mark entering last season, but he made strides with his glove and athleticism to help silence some of the critics, and the former high-school pitcher can unveil a strong arm when the situation arises. He might be the best first-base prospect in the minors, which is a bit like being the coolest employee at Shenanigans.

Andy Parrino SS

Born: 10/31/85   Age: 29   Bats: B   Throws: R   Height: 6' 0"   Weight: 190

YEAR	TEAM	LVL	AGE	PA	R	2B	3B	HR	RBI	BB	K	SB	CS	AVG/OBP/SLG	TAv	BABIP	BRR	FRAA	WARP
2012	TUC	AAA	26	265	43	23	3	1	32	25	49	6	2	.328/.400/.464	.288	.409	0.9	SS(39): 2.0, 2B(11): 0.0	2.1
2012	SDN	MLB	26	138	9	5	0	1	6	17	35	1	0	.207/.316/.276	.227	.284	-0.3	SS(26): 0.0, 2B(16): -0.5	0.2
2013	SAC	AAA	27	420	43	16	3	4	36	43	102	3	1	.210/.300/.302	.227	.278	-1.2	SS(85): 2.7, 3B(18): -0.8	0.1
2013	OAK	MLB	27	36	2	2	0	0	1	2	12	0	0	.118/.167/.176	.112	.182	0.0	SS(7): 0.3, 2B(5): -0.4	-0.5
2014	ROU	AAA	28	59	4	3	0	0	5	3	12	0	0	.189/.271/.245	.191	.244	-0.3	SS(13): -1.4	-0.1
2014	SAC	AAA	28	423	57	19	2	7	52	44	97	7	0	.286/.363/.404	.287	.369	-1.2	SS(85): 1.5, 2B(5): 0.1	2.6
2014	OAK	MLB	28	51	4	3	0	1	3	3	14	0	0	.152/.216/.283	.218	.188	0.2	SS(14): -0.6, 2B(4): 0.0	-0.1
2015	OAK	MLB	29	250	23	10	1	3	20	22	64	2	0	.219/.294/.307	.236	.290	0.0	SS -1, 2B 0	0.3

Breakout: 1%   Improve: 4%   Collapse: 4%   Attrition: 12%   MLB: 17%   *Comparables:* *Steve Tolleson, Tommy Manzella, Kory Casto*

A switch-hitter who can fill in anywhere in the infield is a handy tool off the bench, but Parrino has been trapped in Triple-A for the last four seasons, as his bat has not been loud enough to get much attention during his few gasps of air at the highest level. Oakland puts a premium on versatility, and though they let Parrino go in spring training before 2014, they were ready to pounce when he was waived by Texas two months later. The lowering of league-wide offensive expectations theoretically opens a window for him to sneak onto a big-league roster for an extended visit, but there's "lowered expectations" and there's "career .216 TAv," so a long Triple-A summer seems more likely.

Shane Peterson   1B

Born: 2/11/88   Age: 27   Bats: L   Throws: L   Height: 6' 0"   Weight: 210

YEAR	TEAM	LVL	AGE	PA	R	2B	3B	HR	RBI	BB	K	SB	CS	AVG/OBP/SLG	TAv	BABIP	BRR	FRAA	WARP
2012	MID	AA	24	205	27	11	3	2	23	44	47	9	3	.274/.441/.420	.315	.380	2.5	LF(35): -0.0, RF(8): -0.4	1.7
2012	SAC	AAA	24	157	36	7	1	7	23	23	31	4	3	.389/.484/.618	.380	.473	1.4	LF(25): -2.2, RF(12): -1.4	2.0
2013	SAC	AAA	25	553	70	25	1	12	79	77	127	17	2	.251/.358/.387	.284	.315	-1.5	CF(63): -1.3, LF(33): -3.0	2.1
2013	OAK	MLB	25	8	1	0	0	0	1	1	3	0	0	.143/.250/.143	.167	.250	0.0	1B(2): 0.0	0.0
2014	SAC	AAA	26	625	101	40	5	11	90	66	139	11	2	.308/.381/.460	.314	.391	7.6	CF(83): -13.1, LF(42): -1.2	4.5
2015	OAK	MLB	27	250	26	11	1	4	25	28	64	4	1	.246/.334/.365	.272	.320	0.2	CF -3, LF -1	0.5

Breakout: 6%   Improve: 15%   Collapse: 9%   Attrition: 21%   MLB: 41%   *Comparables:* *Cole Gillespie, Chad Huffman, Ryan Raburn*

Peterson had a great season in his fourth go as a Sacramento River Cat, finishing at or near the top of the circuit in virtually every non-ratio category aside from homers and steals. His main competition for PCL notoriety was Joc Pederson (no relation), though Peterson is a few years older and has a considerably lower ceiling than the Dodgers' outfielder. Still, the fact that he wasn't playing in a bandbox gives the impression that Peterson could hold his own in the bigs if he got a clean shot at a gig.

Chad Pinder   2B

Born: 3/29/92   Age: 23   Bats: R   Throws: R   Height: 6' 2"   Weight: 195

YEAR	TEAM	LVL	AGE	PA	R	2B	3B	HR	RBI	BB	K	SB	CS	AVG/OBP/SLG	TAv	BABIP	BRR	FRAA	WARP
2013	VER	A-	21	161	14	4	0	3	8	12	41	1	0	.200/.286/.293	.262	.253	-0.9	SS(33): -3.2, 3B(2): -0.0	0.1
2014	STO	A+	22	436	61	32	5	13	55	22	99	12	9	.288/.336/.489	.286	.352	-1.1	2B(76): -4.9, SS(14): 1.7	2.2
2015	OAK	MLB	23	250	21	10	1	3	21	9	71	4	2	.213/.250/.308	.221	.285	-0.2	2B -2, SS 0	-0.4

Breakout: 0%   Improve: 0%   Collapse: 0%   Attrition: 0%   MLB: 0%   *Comparables:* *Charlie Culberson, Jordany Valdespin, Luke Hughes*

Drafted as a shortstop, Pinder slid over to second base in 2014, and after an adjustment period his defense thrived in his new infield territory. His strong arm is marginalized at the keystone and he might have the chops for the hot corner, but the presence of Renato Nunez effectively blocked the third base job in Stockton and Pinder's gap power is more appreciated from an up-the-middle spot. He still needs work on some of the secondary aspects of his game, including baserunning and pitch recognition, but the early returns have been encouraging. Expect Pinder to start the season in Midland, where he will reunite with most of his mates from the Ports' infield.

Nick Punto   2B

Born: 11/8/77   Age: 37   Bats: B   Throws: R   Height: 5' 9"   Weight: 195

YEAR	TEAM	LVL	AGE	PA	R	2B	3B	HR	RBI	BB	K	SB	CS	AVG/OBP/SLG	TAv	BABIP	BRR	FRAA	WARP
2012	BOS	MLB	34	148	14	6	0	1	10	19	33	5	0	.200/.301/.272	.206	.258	-0.2	3B(26): 2.0, 2B(15): -0.8	-0.2
2012	LAN	MLB	34	43	6	1	0	0	0	6	9	1	0	.286/.390/.314	.274	.385	0.6	2B(11): 0.8, 3B(5): -0.0	0.4
2013	LAN	MLB	35	335	34	15	0	2	21	33	67	3	3	.255/.328/.327	.236	.322	-0.5	SS(49): -1.2, 3B(35): 0.8	0.0
2014	OAK	MLB	36	224	21	7	2	2	14	25	56	3	1	.207/.296/.293	.236	.279	-0.3	2B(52): 2.2, SS(17): 0.2	0.3
2015	OAK	MLB	37	250	22	9	1	1	17	27	53	3	1	.224/.307/.287	.237	.282	-0.2	2B 1, SS -0	0.4

Breakout: 1%   Improve: 27%   Collapse: 14%   Attrition: 18%   MLB: 80%   *Comparables:* *Mark Ellis, Davey Lopes, Roberto Alomar*

Though his game is declining, the aging Punto will probably have a job as a 25th man for years to come. Assuming health, of course, and that's not as easy an assumption as it looked last offseason: Punto missed over a month late in the year with a hamstring strain; it was his first trip to the disabled list since 2011. Still, the infielder with the winning smile is ideally suited to a spare-part role. In the meantime, he can market his new cologne, "Grinder" (from the Clubhouse Collection), a scent for nice guys whose hard work and grit earns time on the field even when playing out of their league.

Josh Reddick   RF

Born: 2/19/87   Age: 28   Bats: L   Throws: R   Height: 6' 2"   Weight: 180

YEAR	TEAM	LVL	AGE	PA	R	2B	3B	HR	RBI	BB	K	SB	CS	AVG/OBP/SLG	TAv	BABIP	BRR	FRAA	WARP
2012	OAK	MLB	25	673	85	29	5	32	85	55	151	11	1	.242/.305/.463	.275	.269	1.9	RF(136): 2.4, CF(14): 0.4	3.0
2013	OAK	MLB	26	441	54	19	2	12	56	46	86	9	2	.226/.307/.379	.263	.255	2.8	RF(113): 4.2	1.9
2014	STO	A+	27	22	6	2	0	3	8	1	6	0	0	.429/.455/.952	.455	.500	0.0	RF(4): -0.5	0.4
2014	OAK	MLB	27	396	53	16	7	12	54	28	63	1	1	.264/.316/.446	.292	.289	0.4	RF(107): 2.0, CF(1): -0.0	2.4
2015	OAK	MLB	28	388	43	17	3	13	48	30	76	5	1	.245/.304/.418	.276	.274	0.8	RF 3, CF -0	1.7

Breakout: 0%   Improve: 47%   Collapse: 3%   Attrition: 15%   MLB: 96%   *Comparables:* *Jeremy Hermida, Michael Cuddyer, Xavier Nady*

Reddick's bat got back on track after a 2013 season in which his power went missing, though it was not simply a case of posting a healthy return from wrist injuries. He changed to a more aggressive approach, and after a four-year run of increasing pitches per plate appearance, Reddick went the other direction with 3.6 PPA, his lowest rate since 2010. Right-knee injuries sent him to the disabled list twice over the summer and took away his ability to contribute on the bases, while the outfield kills that previously separated him from the pack were diminished to a nondescript total. A return to the 32-homer pace of 2012 is unlikely, but Reddick still has a 20-homer campaign in the tank if he can stay healthy for a full season.

Daniel Robertson   SS

Born: 3/22/94   Age: 21   Bats: R   Throws: R   Height: 6' 0"   Weight: 190

YEAR	TEAM	LVL	AGE	PA	R	2B	3B	HR	RBI	BB	K	SB	CS	AVG/OBP/SLG	TAv	BABIP	BRR	FRAA	WARP
2012	VER	A-	18	104	9	2	0	1	8	7	31	1	1	.181/.238/.234	.185	.258	0.4	SS(18): 1.5, 3B(9): -0.5	-0.3
2013	BLT	A	19	451	59	21	1	9	46	41	79	1	7	.277/.353/.401	.272	.324	-0.6	SS(99): -8.9	1.6
2014	STO	A+	20	642	110	37	3	15	60	72	94	4	4	.310/.402/.471	.311	.349	4.3	SS(123): -2.2, 2B(8): -0.8	6.7
2015	OAK	MLB	21	250	24	10	1	3	19	18	56	0	0	.227/.291/.313	.241	.284	-0.5	SS -2, 3B -0	0.2

Breakout: 0%   Improve: 0%   Collapse: 0%   Attrition: 0%   MLB: 0%   *Comparables: Eugenio Suarez, Jose Pirela, Tyler Pastornicky*

Robertson owns a well-rounded tool kit. He has improved his defense to the point that he should be able to stick up the middle, where his blossoming power and walk-driven on-base skills will be dripping with value. The Cal League leaderboards were saturated with members of the Ports' infield last season and Robertson was no exception, pacing the circuit in hits, plate appearances and doubles. He also finished fourth in on-base percentage and sixth in walks. Robertson's breadth of skills and his long-term viability up the middle may have buffered the loss of uber-prospect Addison Russell, allowing the big-league club to go all in last season.

Marcus Semien   3B

Born: 9/17/90   Age: 24   Bats: R   Throws: R   Height: 6' 1"   Weight: 195

YEAR	TEAM	LVL	AGE	PA	R	2B	3B	HR	RBI	BB	K	SB	CS	AVG/OBP/SLG	TAv	BABIP	BRR	FRAA	WARP
2012	WNS	A+	21	487	80	31	5	14	59	55	97	11	5	.273/.362/.471	.300	.323	-1.5	SS(80): -7.5, 2B(24): 0.1	3.5
2013	BIR	AA	22	484	90	21	5	15	49	84	66	20	5	.290/.420/.483	.329	.317	2.9	SS(47): 3.3, 2B(41): -2.7	5.9
2013	CHR	AAA	22	142	20	11	1	4	17	14	24	4	0	.264/.338/.464	.275	.293	-0.9	SS(25): -3.9, 3B(6): 0.8	0.5
2013	CHA	MLB	22	71	7	4	0	2	7	1	22	2	2	.261/.268/.406	.266	.348	-0.6	3B(17): 0.1, 2B(3): 0.3	0.3
2014	CHR	AAA	23	366	57	20	3	15	52	53	59	7	2	.267/.380/.502	.285	.282	2.8	SS(42): 0.4, 3B(17): 1.7	3.2
2014	CHA	MLB	23	255	30	10	2	6	28	21	70	3	0	.234/.300/.372	.246	.310	-1.3	3B(33): 0.8, 2B(26): 0.6	0.5
2015	OAK	MLB	24	332	42	14	2	8	33	34	74	6	2	.240/.323/.389	.276	.288	-0.8	SS -0, 3B 1	1.7

Breakout: 2%   Improve: 27%   Collapse: 21%   Attrition: 29%   MLB: 77%   *Comparables: Andy LaRoche, James Darnell, Ian Stewart*

Albert Pujols. Doug Fister. Bartolo Colon. Charlie Furbush. Millions of immature fantasy enthusiasts owe the most sophomoric team names of our time to these players. Semien has the potential to headline the next wave of said talent, but first he needs to prove he can stick in the majors. For the second straight season, Semien hit well in Triple-A but was less potent in Chicago, and while he's still just 24 there have long been concerns about his power not playing at the highest level. The challenge increases in Oakland; same goes for the questions about his defense, and particularly his arm, now that he's in line to play shortstop for the A's. He can probably have a long career as a utility infielder, or even a second-division starter at the keystone, but everything about his new situation portends overextension.

Eric Sogard   2B

Born: 5/22/86   Age: 29   Bats: L   Throws: R   Height: 5' 10"   Weight: 190

YEAR	TEAM	LVL	AGE	PA	R	2B	3B	HR	RBI	BB	K	SB	CS	AVG/OBP/SLG	TAv	BABIP	BRR	FRAA	WARP
2012	SAC	AAA	26	180	29	5	2	5	22	23	17	11	3	.331/.417/.484	.321	.348	0.6	2B(30): 6.1, SS(5): 0.1	2.5
2012	OAK	MLB	26	108	8	3	1	2	7	5	17	2	0	.167/.206/.275	.185	.181	0.2	SS(15): 1.1, 3B(14): 0.2	-0.2
2013	OAK	MLB	27	410	45	24	3	2	35	27	51	10	5	.266/.322/.364	.266	.301	-1.5	2B(113): 0.4, SS(15): 0.6	1.3
2014	OAK	MLB	28	329	38	10	0	1	22	31	37	11	4	.223/.298/.268	.223	.251	0.3	2B(102): 5.7, SS(14): 0.0	0.7
2015	OAK	MLB	29	325	33	13	2	2	25	28	44	10	4	.248/.316/.327	.254	.280	-0.4	2B 3, SS 0	1.2

Breakout: 6%   Improve: 23%   Collapse: 14%   Attrition: 17%   MLB: 66%   *Comparables: Russ Adams, Will Rhymes, Kevin Frandsen*

Sogard had audiences clamoring for Nerd Power to start last season and came within a hair's breadth of being hilariously elected by Twitter users as the Face of MLB (he lost to David Wright in the finals), but his weak performance only served to reinforce the stereotype that gets geeks picked last in gym class. Sogard's bat has never been his carrying tool, but the minor-league walk rates that buoyed his on-base percentage have not translated to the highest level and an inability to hit southpaws has further marginalized his utility. He doesn't swing and miss, but he doesn't have anything close to the power to make anything useful out of all that contact. No, Nerd Power doesn't count.

Geovany Soto   C

Born: 1/20/83   Age: 32   Bats: R   Throws: R   Height: 6' 1"   Weight: 235

YEAR	TEAM	LVL	AGE	PA	R	2B	3B	HR	RBI	BB	K	SB	CS	AVG/OBP/SLG	TAv	BABIP	BRR	FRAA	WARP
2012	CHN	MLB	29	197	26	6	1	6	14	19	35	0	0	.199/.284/.347	.229	.215	1.2	C(52): -0.7	0.2
2012	TEX	MLB	29	164	19	6	0	5	25	11	41	1	0	.196/.253/.338	.228	.231	0.3	C(44): -0.1	0.1
2013	TEX	MLB	30	184	20	9	0	9	22	20	60	1	2	.245/.328/.466	.289	.330	-3.3	C(53): 0.9, 3B(1): -0.0	1.2
2014	FRI	AA	31	22	4	2	0	0	1	3	6	0	0	.368/.455/.474	.332	.538	-0.8	C(4): 0.1	0.1
2014	ROU	AAA	31	33	2	2	0	1	2	1	10	0	0	.188/.212/.344	.175	.238	0.0	C(7): -0.1	-0.2
2014	OAK	MLB	31	49	3	4	0	0	8	6	8	0	0	.262/.354/.357	.249	.324	-0.2	C(14): 0.2	0.2
2014	TEX	MLB	31	38	5	2	0	1	3	0	11	0	0	.237/.237/.368	.211	.308	-0.6	C(10): 0.0	-0.1
2015	OAK	MLB	32	250	27	11	0	7	27	25	64	1	1	.222/.304/.371	.264	.274	-0.6	C 0, 3B -0	1.1

Breakout: 3%   Improve: 32%   Collapse: 11%   Attrition: 10%   MLB: 92%   *Comparables: John Buck, Chris Snyder, Mike Stanley*

Soto endured two surgeries in spring training, the second of which sidelined him for more than half the season, and then he was back on the disabled list within five days of his late-July return. Acquired by the A's at the end of August, he was the throwing head of their catcher hydra down the stretch, a critical role on a club whose backstops were suffering from varying degrees of injury and/or noodle arm. His significance was under a microscope in the Wild Card game against Kansas City, as the Royals went wild on the basepaths after a second-inning thumb injury took Soto out of the game. There may still be some slug left in his bat, enough to give him value as a part-timer, even as it's clear he's long past his 2008-2011 heyday.

Stephen Vogt   1B

Born: 11/1/84   Age: 30   Bats: L   Throws: R   Height: 6' 0"   Weight: 215

YEAR	TEAM	LVL	AGE	PA	R	2B	3B	HR	RBI	BB	K	SB	CS	AVG/OBP/SLG	TAv	BABIP	BRR	FRAA	WARP
2012	DUR	AAA	27	396	48	18	4	9	43	42	61	1	0	.272/.350/.424	.259	.306	-2.4	C(37): -0.5, LF(23): -1.5	0.7
2012	TBA	MLB	27	27	0	0	0	0	0	2	2	0	0	.000/.074/.000	.042	.000	0.0	C(7): -0.0, LF(2): 0.0	-0.5
2013	SAC	AAA	28	338	55	21	3	13	58	38	45	0	1	.324/.398/.547	.325	.344	-0.2	C(65): 0.2	4.3
2013	OAK	MLB	28	148	18	6	1	4	16	9	28	0	1	.252/.295/.400	.255	.286	-0.4	C(44): -0.5	0.5
2014	SAC	AAA	29	97	18	8	2	3	19	8	8	1	1	.364/.412/.602	.371	.372	1.3	C(19): -0.5, LF(1): -0.1	1.7
2014	OAK	MLB	29	287	26	10	2	9	35	16	39	1	0	.279/.321/.431	.284	.297	0.4	1B(47): -2.3, RF(17): -0.5	1.2
2015	*OAK*	*MLB*	*30*	*297*	*30*	*12*	*2*	*7*	*34*	*22*	*50*	*1*	*0*	*.256/.311/.401*	*.271*	*.284*	*0.1*	*C -0, 1B -1*	*0.9*

Breakout: 1%   Improve: 17%   Collapse: 10%   Attrition: 14%   MLB: 46%   *Comparables: Steve Pearce, Andy Phillips, Micah Hoffpauir*

All Vogt does is contribute. He has the glove to cover catcher in a backup role, the versatility to play first base or the outfield and a bat that's good enough to put that versatility to use. Vogt is worthy of everyday use, whether starting the game or coming in as a pinch-hitter, while adhering to the strategic deployment that has seen him face right-handers in 87 percent of his career plate appearances. Vogt keeps the clubhouse loose with his straight-faced bit as an NBA referee, calling technical fouls for everything from wearing the wrong shirt to dissing Nick Punto, and the fans have embraced him as a rallying totem for the club. I believe in Stephen Vogt!

Joe Wendle   2B

Born: 4/26/90   Age: 25   Bats: L   Throws: R   Height: 5' 11"   Weight: 190

YEAR	TEAM	LVL	AGE	PA	R	2B	3B	HR	RBI	BB	K	SB	CS	AVG/OBP/SLG	TAv	BABIP	BRR	FRAA	WARP
2012	MHV	A-	22	267	32	15	4	4	37	15	25	4	1	.327/.375/.469	.321	.349	-0.5	2B(32): -0.2, 3B(21): 3.0	2.8
2013	CAR	A+	23	474	73	32	5	16	64	44	79	10	4	.295/.372/.513	.298	.327	3.3	2B(101): 6.7	4.1
2014	AKR	AA	24	370	46	20	5	8	50	26	56	4	2	.253/.311/.414	.262	.279	1.3	2B(80): 10.2	2.7
2015	*OAK*	*MLB*	*25*	*250*	*23*	*11*	*2*	*5*	*26*	*14*	*53*	*2*	*1*	*.231/.281/.358*	*.247*	*.275*	*-0.1*	*2B 4, 3B 0*	*1.0*

Breakout: 1%   Improve: 17%   Collapse: 10%   Attrition: 14%   MLB: 46%   *Comparables: Steve Pearce, Andy Phillips, Micah Hoffpauir*

The jump to Double-A is considered the second biggest in professional baseball (behind the one from Triple-A to MLB, which probably can go unsaid, but hey, you never know). The consistency of good stuff that hitters see there necessitates an adjustment period for all but an elite (or lucky) few prospects. For Wendle, that period lasted a month and marred what was an otherwise fine Wendle-like season. He struggled mightily in April, hitting under .200 for the month, before righting himself in May and taking off in June. Full recovery of his season line was halted by a hamate injury in August, but Wendle showed that he can hit the baseball even if nothing else about him really stands out. Hitting gets you to the majors. It also gets you to the A's in a surprising exchange for Brandon Moss.

Pitchers

Fernando Abad   LHP

Born: 12/17/85   Age: 29   Bats: L   Throws: L   Height: 6'1"   Weight: 220

YEAR	TEAM	LVL	AGE	W	L	SV	G	GS	IP	H	HR	BB	K	BB/9	K/9	GB%	BABIP	WHIP	ERA	FIP	FRA	WARP
2012	OKL	AAA	26	2	0	2	13	3	27²	33	3	7	28	2.3	9.1	34%	.366	1.45	3.90	3.92	4.37	0.4
2012	HOU	MLB	26	0	6	0	37	6	46	57	6	19	38	3.7	7.4	43%	.359	1.65	5.09	4.61	3.58	0.7
2013	SYR	AAA	27	1	0	0	17	0	17	17	0	2	12	1.1	6.4	53%	.309	1.12	1.06	2.15	2.86	0.4
2013	WAS	MLB	27	0	3	0	39	0	37²	42	3	10	32	2.4	7.6	41%	.325	1.38	3.35	3.23	3.19	0.6
2014	OAK	MLB	28	2	4	0	69	0	57¹	34	4	15	51	2.4	8.0	42%	.211	0.85	1.57	3.28	3.35	0.4
2015	*OAK*	*MLB*	*29*	*3*	*1*	*0*	*44*	*2*	*44¹*	*44*	*5*	*13*	*37*	*2.6*	*7.4*	*40%*	*.299*	*1.29*	*3.89*	*4.37*	*4.23*	*0.2*

Breakout: 26%   Improve: 49%   Collapse: 15%   Attrition: 12%   MLB: 78%   *Comparables: Wesley Wright, Dan Wheeler, Vinnie Chulk*

Oakland's defense was good last season, but it wasn't *that* good. Abad cut his ERA in half on the shoulders of a chopped hit rate driven by an outlier BABIP that jumped over the bell curve to the happy side of the mean. The key was the lefty's fastball, which went from pinball to ghost pitch despite losing a half-tick of velocity from 2013's peak. (Of course, it's often fine to lose that half-tick when you're throwing close to 95.) Sometimes regression acts as a mysterious gravitational force; sometimes you can identify the exact areas where a player is unlikely to repeat. In Abad's case, he got away with some hittable pitches: Opposing batters went just 1-for-17 on pitches in the middle of the zone. The A's weren't necessarily believers in the performance: 46 of his 69 appearances were in situations with below-average leverage, and there was no upward trend at the end of the season despite months of stellar numbers.

Raul Alcantara   RHP

Born: 12/4/92   Age: 22   Bats: R   Throws: R   Height: 6'3"   Weight: 225

YEAR	TEAM	LVL	AGE	W	L	SV	G	GS	IP	H	HR	BB	K	BB/9	K/9	GB%	BABIP	WHIP	ERA	FIP	FRA	WARP
2012	BUR	A	19	6	11	0	27	17	102²	119	12	38	57	3.3	5.0	53%	.327	1.53	5.08	5.07	6.57	-0.4
2013	BLT	A	20	7	1	0	13	13	77¹	84	3	7	58	0.8	6.8	47%	.324	1.18	2.44	2.77	3.79	1.7
2013	STO	A+	20	5	5	0	14	14	79	73	8	17	66	1.9	7.5	41%	.280	1.14	3.76	4.21	4.57	1.1
2014	MID	AA	21	2	0	0	3	3	19²	17	0	5	10	2.3	4.6	54%	.288	1.12	2.29	3.17	4.76	0.1
2015	*OAK*	*MLB*	*22*	*2*	*3*	*0*	*6*	*6*	*34²*	*41*	*4*	*13*	*15*	*3.4*	*3.9*	*46%*	*.302*	*1.56*	*5.29*	*5.56*	*5.75*	*-0.4*

Breakout: 0%   Improve: 0%   Collapse: 0%   Attrition: 0%   MLB: 0%   *Comparables: Zeke Spruill, Matt Harrison, Kyle Ryan*

The UCL virus that took down Oakland pitchers last season spread to the minor leagues, where Tommy John surgery sidetracked Alcantara after just 19 innings in Double-A. Mechanics are often the scapegoat when injury occurs, but such finger-pointing would be misguided in this case, as Alcantara has an efficient delivery that strikes a balance between power and stability. The right-hander was on a positive trajectory prior to the surgery, refining his command as well as the consistency of his secondary pitches. Those two elements will still be focal points of his development when he returns to the mound, though the return of his low-to-mid-90s velocity will garner much of the attention.

Chris Bassitt RHP

Born: 2/22/89 Age: 26 Bats: R Throws: R Height: 6'5" Weight: 210

YEAR	TEAM	LVL	AGE	W	L	SV	G	GS	IP	H	HR	BB	K	BB/9	K/9	GB%	BABIP	WHIP	ERA	FIP	FRA	WARP
2012	WNS	A+	23	5	4	4	38	10	91	74	6	54	75	5.3	7.4	51%	.258	1.41	3.66	4.51	5.29	-0.3
2013	WNS	A+	24	7	2	0	18	18	101¹	90	9	42	101	3.7	9.0	50%	.283	1.30	3.46	3.90	4.78	1.3
2013	BIR	AA	24	4	2	0	8	8	47²	35	2	17	37	3.2	7.0	48%	.254	1.09	2.27	3.23	4.36	0.2
2014	BIR	AA	25	3	1	0	6	6	34²	26	2	14	36	3.6	9.3	48%	.264	1.15	1.56	3.24	3.88	0.5
2014	CHA	MLB	25	1	1	0	6	5	29²	34	0	13	21	3.9	6.4	42%	.340	1.58	3.94	3.36	3.43	0.6
2015	OAK	MLB	26	3	4	0	22	10	73¹	72	7	35	55	4.3	6.8	47%	.289	1.46	4.48	4.94	4.87	-0.1

Breakout: 19% Improve: 29% Collapse: 14% Attrition: 28% MLB: 53% *Comparables: Clint Nageotte, Kevin Hart, Kyle Weiland*

Bassitt missed the first half of 2014 with what he would describe only as a "non-baseball related injury" to his hand, which really makes you wonder what injury is too embarrassing to share in a sport that has dealt with self-ironing mishaps, sneeze-induced strains, sandwich-related traumas and so on. The layoff slowed some of the momentum he built up in a strong 2013, but he earned a promotion quickly and made a handful of September starts. Bassitt, acquired by the A's in the Jeff Samardzija deal, relies heavily on a good sinker, along with two fringe breaking pitches. He has some funky arm action and a deep stab as he draws his arm down below his trunk before swinging it through with a low three-quarters action. The resulting command isn't great, casting doubt on his ability to start in the big-leagues. The fastball can be a plus offering, but without much else to back it up he's likely a middle reliever, assuming no more accidents with ... a Hello Kitty plush toy? His secret collection of dried scabs? Some farts and boogers? We'll probably never know.

Jesse Chavez RHP

Born: 8/21/83 Age: 31 Bats: R Throws: R Height: 6'2" Weight: 160

YEAR	TEAM	LVL	AGE	W	L	SV	G	GS	IP	H	HR	BB	K	BB/9	K/9	GB%	BABIP	WHIP	ERA	FIP	FRA	WARP
2012	LVG	AAA	28	8	5	1	19	17	95	90	10	20	86	1.9	8.1	48%	.294	1.16	3.98	3.89	4.48	2.0
2012	SAC	AAA	28	0	0	1	2	1	10	8	0	2	9	1.8	8.1	45%	.276	1.00	1.80	2.47	2.53	0.3
2012	OAK	MLB	28	0	0	0	4	0	3¹	9	1	1	3	2.7	8.1	44%	.533	3.00	18.90	6.95	7.98	-0.1
2012	TOR	MLB	28	1	1	0	9	2	21¹	25	6	10	27	4.2	11.4	36%	.333	1.64	8.44	5.86	7.07	-0.4
2013	SAC	AAA	29	2	2	0	5	5	30	35	1	5	26	1.5	7.8	41%	.351	1.33	2.70	2.87	3.10	0.8
2013	OAK	MLB	29	2	4	1	35	0	57¹	50	3	20	55	3.1	8.6	47%	.281	1.22	3.92	3.04	2.71	1.2
2014	OAK	MLB	30	8	8	0	32	21	146	142	17	49	136	3.0	8.4	43%	.302	1.31	3.45	3.92	4.29	0.4
2015	OAK	MLB	31	5	5	1	42	13	117	114	13	36	103	2.8	7.9	44%	.296	1.28	3.87	4.27	4.21	0.7

Breakout: 18% Improve: 32% Collapse: 12% Attrition: 15% MLB: 51% *Comparables: Boof Bonser, Glen Perkins, Chris Resop*

Chavez's conversion from reliever to starter was just another example of the A's parlaying their organizational depth. He was a logical choice to fill one of the injury-induced holes in the rotation, with a legit four-pitch mix that allowed for a smooth transition without any drastic change to his approach. The rub was that he could not hold the spot for the full season without an unsafe jump in innings pitched, a factor that played a role in the A's midseason trade flurry that put starting pitching at a premium. The league also knocked him around in the dog days: In his last six starts, he posted an ERA of 5.51. Chavez shifted back to the bullpen in early August and the A's effectively shut him down in September, but the final tally was still 23 more innings than he had ever thrown in a season of pro baseball.

Ryan Cook RHP

Born: 6/30/87 Age: 28 Bats: R Throws: R Height: 6'2" Weight: 215

YEAR	TEAM	LVL	AGE	W	L	SV	G	GS	IP	H	HR	BB	K	BB/9	K/9	GB%	BABIP	WHIP	ERA	FIP	FRA	WARP
2012	OAK	MLB	25	6	2	14	71	0	73¹	42	4	27	80	3.3	9.8	48%	.220	0.94	2.09	2.84	2.97	1.1
2013	OAK	MLB	26	6	4	2	71	0	67¹	62	2	25	67	3.3	9.0	46%	.306	1.29	2.54	2.76	3.14	1.1
2014	OAK	MLB	27	1	3	1	54	0	50	32	3	22	50	4.0	9.0	47%	.232	1.08	3.42	3.38	4.51	0.1
2015	OAK	MLB	28	2	1	1	46	0	46²	39	3	19	44	3.7	8.5	51%	.282	1.24	3.20	3.90	3.48	0.7

Breakout: 29% Improve: 47% Collapse: 19% Attrition: 20% MLB: 77% *Comparables: Jonny Venters, Rafael Perez, Evan Meek*

Cook got a delayed start to 2014 due to shoulder inflammation and he missed most of May with a forearm strain, a combination of arm woes that might have played a role in his drop in velocity and lack of command. The slider was his most effective pitch once again, including a whiff-per-swing rate of 41 percent, but for the first time in Cook's big-league career the pitch was taken out of the park, not once but twice. He seems to have the pure stuff to close, but there are too many cooks in the Oakland kitchen to see a clear path for future saves.

Oh, what, don't make that face. You *knew* this is where the *Too Many Cooks* joke would go.

Sean Doolittle LHP

Born: 9/26/86 Age: 28 Bats: L Throws: L Height: 6'3" Weight: 210

YEAR	TEAM	LVL	AGE	W	L	SV	G	GS	IP	H	HR	BB	K	BB/9	K/9	GB%	BABIP	WHIP	ERA	FIP	FRA	WARP
2012	STO	A+	25	0	0	0	6	0	10¹	5	0	2	21	1.7	18.3	50%	.357	0.68	0.87	0.91	-0.04	0.7
2012	MID	AA	25	0	0	1	8	0	11	2	0	4	19	3.3	15.5	47%	.118	0.55	0.82	1.19	3.19	0.2
2012	OAK	MLB	25	2	1	1	44	0	47¹	40	3	11	60	2.1	11.4	37%	.316	1.08	3.04	2.03	1.96	1.4
2013	OAK	MLB	26	5	5	2	70	0	69	53	4	13	60	1.7	7.8	35%	.262	0.96	3.13	2.74	2.52	1.5
2014	OAK	MLB	27	2	4	22	61	0	62²	38	5	8	89	1.1	12.8	24%	.246	0.73	2.73	1.74	2.45	1.7
2015	OAK	MLB	28	3	1	7	50	0	53	40	3	11	65	1.8	11.0	36%	.287	0.96	1.99	2.48	2.17	1.6

Breakout: 30% Improve: 49% Collapse: 23% Attrition: 14% MLB: 93% *Comparables: Joakim Soria, Huston Street, Bobby Jenks*

Doolittle ascended to the closer role in the wake of Jim Johnson's early-2014 meltdown, emerging from a strong bullpen committee with a performance worthy of his All-Star selection, including an eye-popping 63 strikeouts to just two walks in the first half. This dominance is achieved on the strength of a single offering, an exploding fastball he threw 87 percent of the time and which accounted for 79 of his 87 strike threes. Especially now, after three years of this, batters know it's coming, but they still come up empty on 32 percent of their hacks, the eighth-highest rate among baseball's four-seamers (min. 200 pitches). He also throws a biting slider that leaves his hand on a fastball trajectory and typically winds up well low and well glove-side, but Doolittle isn't happy unless he's going Mach 2 with his beard on fire.

Daniel Gossett   RHP

Born: 11/13/92   Age: 22   Bats: R   Throws: R   Height: 6'2"   Weight: 185

YEAR	TEAM	LVL	AGE	W	L	SV	G	GS	IP	H	HR	BB	K	BB/9	K/9	GB%	BABIP	WHIP	ERA	FIP	FRA	WARP
2014	VER	A-	21	1	0	0	12	1	24	16	1	1	25	0.4	9.4	55%	.246	0.71	2.25	2.02	3.42	0.3
2015	OAK	MLB	22	1	0	1	16	0	32²	37	4	17	20	4.6	5.4	46%	.306	1.65	5.45	5.66	5.93	-0.4

Breakout: 0%   Improve: 0%   Collapse: 0%   Attrition: 0%   MLB: 0%   Comparables: *Danny Farquhar, Ben Rowen, Stephen Fife*

The 2014 second-round pick out of Clemson had a pleasant introduction to pro baseball, breezing through the New York-Penn League for a dozen well-crafted outings of two innings apiece. He has strong command of a low-90s fastball as well as a reliable changeup, which combination should allow him to move quickly up the ladder. Gossett's slider is a certified out pitch that will drive his strikeout totals. His delivery has some funk and mechanical inefficiency, including a long arm path that features a low pick up and a tall slot, so his future might rest in the bullpen if he struggles to endure a starter's workload.

Kendall Graveman   RHP

Born: 12/21/90   Age: 24   Bats: R   Throws: R   Height: 6'2"   Weight: 195

YEAR	TEAM	LVL	AGE	W	L	SV	G	GS	IP	H	HR	BB	K	BB/9	K/9	GB%	BABIP	WHIP	ERA	FIP	FRA	WARP
2013	LNS	A	22	1	3	0	10	10	39²	41	3	13	25	2.9	5.7	64%	.295	1.36	4.31	4.12	5.65	0.2
2014	LNS	A	23	2	0	0	4	4	26¹	11	0	6	25	2.1	8.5	68%	.175	0.65	0.34	2.27	3.47	0.5
2014	DUN	A+	23	8	4	0	16	16	96²	89	1	18	64	1.7	6.0	59%	.287	1.11	2.23	2.88	4.36	0.9
2014	BUF	AAA	23	3	2	0	6	6	38¹	34	1	5	22	1.2	5.2	66%	.282	1.02	1.88	2.94	4.09	0.4
2014	TOR	MLB	23	0	0	0	5	0	4²	4	0	0	4	0.0	7.7	64%	.286	0.86	3.86	1.45	2.59	0.1
2015	OAK	MLB	24	6	8	0	21	21	118¹	124	10	36	65	2.7	4.9	55%	.292	1.35	4.04	4.59	4.39	0.5

Breakout: 17%   Improve: 28%   Collapse: 11%   Attrition: 28%   MLB: 46%   Comparables: *Dallas Keuchel, Jake Buchanan, Adam Warren*

Graveman had a Mariano Rivera moment last June in High-A: His four-seamer started cutting on its own right in the middle of a game. He added that new wrinkle to his decent sinker-slider arsenal and by season's end he had a courtesy September 1st call-up to Toronto. An eighth-rounder in 2013 (his signing "bonus" was $5,000), Graveman was the top starter on Mississippi State's College World Series runner-up roster, and he brings maturity and steadiness to the mound. He should start the year in Nashville, where a good showing will position him for fourth or fifth starter action in the majors. If he pitches well with a last name like that, he won't need a nickname, but if he pitches poorly, he'll dig his own ... well, you know.

Brett Graves   RHP

Born: 1/30/93   Age: 22   Bats: R   Throws: R   Height: 6'1"   Weight: 170

YEAR	TEAM	LVL	AGE	W	L	SV	G	GS	IP	H	HR	BB	K	BB/9	K/9	GB%	BABIP	WHIP	ERA	FIP	FRA	WARP
2014	VER	A-	21	3	2	0	8	2	21	24	1	6	18	2.6	7.7	58%	.338	1.43	6.86	3.35	4.35	0.0
2015	OAK	MLB	22	1	1	0	11	2	31²	38	4	18	15	5.0	4.4	47%	.308	1.75	5.98	6.26	6.50	-0.5

Breakout: 0%   Improve: 0%   Collapse: 0%   Attrition: 0%   MLB: 0%   Comparables: *Evan Crawford, Joe Kelly, Bobby Cassevah*

The third-rounder was the second of four consecutive picks with which the A's selected right-handed college pitchers in the 2014 draft. Graves is a Mizzou product who has had to overcome questions about his size since high school, but there is little debate about his stuff, with a low-to-mid-90s fastball that spikes 97 and a slider that flashes plus. His lack of consistency with the secondaries is a roadblock he needs to surpass. He might eventually satisfy the conventional bias against slight pitchers with a move to the bullpen. That said, the A's were perfectly content to draft and develop Sonny Gray as a starter, so any transition will likely be driven by the development pattern of Graves' arsenal rather than his size.

Sonny Gray   RHP

Born: 11/7/89   Age: 25   Bats: R   Throws: R   Height: 5'11"   Weight: 195

YEAR	TEAM	LVL	AGE	W	L	SV	G	GS	IP	H	HR	BB	K	BB/9	K/9	GB%	BABIP	WHIP	ERA	FIP	FRA	WARP
2012	MID	AA	22	6	9	0	26	26	148	148	8	57	97	3.5	5.9	57%	.302	1.39	4.14	3.91	5.11	0.3
2013	SAC	AAA	23	10	7	0	20	20	118¹	117	5	39	118	3.0	9.0	52%	.337	1.32	3.42	3.11	3.62	2.7
2013	OAK	MLB	23	5	3	0	12	10	64	51	4	20	67	2.8	9.4	52%	.276	1.11	2.67	2.73	3.30	1.2
2014	OAK	MLB	24	14	10	0	33	33	219	187	15	74	183	3.0	7.5	58%	.277	1.19	3.08	3.49	4.00	2.2
2015	OAK	MLB	25	10	10	0	30	30	179²	166	13	60	150	3.0	7.5	53%	.292	1.26	3.34	3.88	3.64	2.4

Breakout: 30%   Improve: 54%   Collapse: 19%   Attrition: 19%   MLB: 93%   Comparables: *Daniel Hudson, Matt Harvey, Homer Bailey*

Gray may not have sustained his impressive 2013 ratios, but he provided a decent copy in triple the innings. He continued to limit damage on batted balls, with low rates of hits and homers in line with 2013. Part of the recipe for this success was the evolution of Gray's slider, which he threw thrice as often as in his rookie season. It was his most effective offering, with the highest rate of whiffs per swing and the stingiest batted-ball results of the pitches in his repertoire. The right-hander has risen to the occasion in big games during his young career, and he was a rock at the front of the rotation at a time when limbs were falling off the pitching tree in Oakland. He threw a pair of complete-game shutouts that essentially book-ended his season, the first in April and the other in game 162, propelling the A's into the postseason.

A.J. Griffin   RHP

Born: 1/28/88   Age: 27   Bats: R   Throws: R   Height: 6'5"   Weight: 230

YEAR	TEAM	LVL	AGE	W	L	SV	G	GS	IP	H	HR	BB	K	BB/9	K/9	GB%	BABIP	WHIP	ERA	FIP	FRA	WARP
2012	MID	AA	24	3	1	0	7	7	43¹	31	4	7	44	1.5	9.1	44%	.250	0.88	2.49	3.00	4.06	0.5
2012	SAC	AAA	24	4	2	0	10	10	58²	48	3	11	47	1.7	7.2	41%	.260	1.01	3.07	3.50	3.80	1.3
2012	OAK	MLB	24	7	1	0	15	15	82¹	74	10	19	64	2.1	7.0	38%	.264	1.13	3.06	3.80	4.11	0.9
2013	OAK	MLB	25	14	10	0	32	32	200	171	36	54	171	2.4	7.7	33%	.242	1.12	3.83	4.58	5.06	-0.5
2015	OAK	MLB	27	2	2	0	6	6	36¹	33	5	9	30	2.3	7.4	38%	.270	1.16	3.46	4.53	3.76	0.4

Breakout: 29%   Improve: 60%   Collapse: 12%   Attrition: 13%   MLB: 85%   Comparables: *Scott Baker, Lance Lynn, Juan Nicasio*

Griffin's 2014 played out like a bad horror movie where you beg the victim DON'T OPEN THE DOOR only to watch through your fingers as predictable mayhem ensues. He tried to get through his arm woes with rest and rehabilitation, but in the end fell prey to the almighty blade; Tommy John surgery wiped out his 2014 season in late April. His desire to avoid surgery is understandable, but the baseball gods, hungering for fresh victims like an even-more-demented Wes Craven, decreed that the A's were to lose 400 innings from their projected rotation by (meat)hook or by (violent) crook, so lose them they did. Thus fell the first dominoes in the sequence that led to the team's mad dash for starting pitching during trade season. You've seen the movie. You know how it ended.

Scott Kazmir   LHP

Born: 1/24/84   Age: 31   Bats: L   Throws: L   Height: 6'0"   Weight: 185

YEAR	TEAM	LVL	AGE	W	L	SV	G	GS	IP	H	HR	BB	K	BB/9	K/9	GB%	BABIP	WHIP	ERA	FIP	FRA	WARP
2013	CLE	MLB	29	10	9	0	29	29	158	162	19	47	162	2.7	9.2	42%	.324	1.32	4.04	3.54	3.83	2.5
2014	OAK	MLB	30	15	9	0	32	32	190¹	171	16	50	164	2.4	7.8	44%	.285	1.16	3.55	3.38	4.03	1.8
2015	OAK	MLB	31	8	10	0	28	28	152²	151	16	54	128	3.2	7.6	42%	.298	1.34	4.13	4.45	4.49	0.6

Breakout: 13%   Improve: 51%   Collapse: 16%   Attrition: 25%   MLB: 86%   Comparables: *Wandy Rodriguez, Jorge De La Rosa, Brett Myers*

Kazmir continues to evolve as a pitcher, transforming from the wild thing of his youth to the modern-day iteration that favors balance, repetition and command. His penchant for the free pass was once the southpaw's greatest weakness, but he has flipped the script as part of a systematic reinvention of his approach to pitching. He picked up the slack for an Oakland rotation that was ravaged by injury in spring training, staying on the mound for the second-highest innings count of his career. He particularly shouldered the load with a dynamite first half, including a 2.38 ERA and four strikeouts per walk. However, his ERA skyrocketed to 5.42 during the second half, with secondary stats to match, as part of the Oakland house of cards that came crumbling down over the final two months of the season.

Brendan McCurry   RHP

Born: 1/7/92   Age: 23   Bats: R   Throws: R   Height: 5'10"   Weight: 165

YEAR	TEAM	LVL	AGE	W	L	SV	G	GS	IP	H	HR	BB	K	BB/9	K/9	GB%	BABIP	WHIP	ERA	FIP	FRA	WARP
2014	BLT	A	22	2	0	2	15	0	26¹	12	1	3	34	1.0	11.6	65%	.192	0.57	0.34	1.97	2.67	0.2
2015	OAK	MLB	23	1	0	1	21	0	33²	36	3	15	24	4.0	6.4	47%	.303	1.50	4.73	4.74	5.14	-0.2

Breakout: 0%   Improve: 0%   Collapse: 0%   Attrition: 0%   MLB: 0%   Comparables: *Kevin Chapman, Dylan Axelrod, Chris Bassitt*

As Oklahoma State's closer, McCurry set school records for saves in a season and in a career and posted a miniscule 0.39 ERA his senior year. The A's were willing to overlook his modest stature and spend a 22nd-round pick on the right-hander, and he responded with even better run-prevention and complete ownership of the strike zone in his pro debut. McCurry is known for his ever-changing arm slots and the unpredictable pitch trajectories that accompany them, and though his low-90s fastball is modest by today's standards, his powerful delivery, plethora of pitch types and deceptive release point—which ranges from straight sidearm to high three-quarters—will quickly take the attention off his size.

Sean Nolin   LHP

Born: 12/26/89   Age: 25   Bats: L   Throws: L   Height: 6'4"   Weight: 230

YEAR	TEAM	LVL	AGE	W	L	SV	G	GS	IP	H	HR	BB	K	BB/9	K/9	GB%	BABIP	WHIP	ERA	FIP	FRA	WARP
2012	DUN	A+	22	9	0	0	17	15	86¹	72	7	21	90	2.2	9.4	45%	.293	1.08	2.19	3.23	4.01	1.5
2012	NHP	AA	22	1	0	0	3	3	15	9	0	6	18	3.6	10.8	43%	.257	1.00	1.20	2.20	3.45	0.3
2013	NHP	AA	23	8	3	0	17	17	92²	89	6	25	103	2.4	10.0	36%	.333	1.23	3.01	2.82	2.84	3.0
2013	BUF	AAA	23	1	1	0	3	3	17²	13	1	10	13	5.1	6.6	39%	.267	1.30	1.53	4.34	4.97	0.0
2013	TOR	MLB	23	0	1	0	1	1	1¹	7	1	1	0	6.8	0.0	30%	.667	6.00	40.50	15.08	12.58	-0.1
2014	BUF	AAA	24	4	6	0	17	17	87¹	74	6	35	74	3.6	7.6	42%	.270	1.25	3.50	3.86	4.30	1.0
2014	TOR	MLB	24	0	0	0	1	1	1	1	1	0	0	0.0	0.0	25%	.000	1.00	9.00	16.16	16.46	-0.1
2015	OAK	MLB	25	5	6	0	17	17	85	83	9	32	72	3.4	7.6	41%	.297	1.36	4.05	4.49	4.40	0.5

Breakout: 20%   Improve: 36%   Collapse: 11%   Attrition: 36%   MLB: 53%   Comparables: *Matt Maloney, Brad Peacock, Alex Wilson*

Nolin might have drawn a bit more notice were it not for Daniel Norris, Aaron Sanchez and Marcus Stroman. Lucky for him, he's in Oakland now and doesn't have to deal with those comparisons anymore. He lacks the raw stuff of his former organization-mates, but he can dial his fastball up to 95 when he needs to. Nolin missed time with a groin pull last season, so the Jays sent him to the Arizona Fall League to get a few more reps. He'll use 2015, ideally at Triple-A, to prove his durability and work on his control, which needs improvement if his modest strikeout rate is going to play.

Eric O'Flaherty   LHP

Born: 2/5/85   Age: 30   Bats: L   Throws: L   Height: 6'2"   Weight: 220

YEAR	TEAM	LVL	AGE	W	L	SV	G	GS	IP	H	HR	BB	K	BB/9	K/9	GB%	BABIP	WHIP	ERA	FIP	FRA	WARP
2012	ATL	MLB	27	3	0	0	64	0	57¹	47	3	19	46	3.0	7.2	66%	.275	1.15	1.73	3.31	4.07	0.4
2013	ATL	MLB	28	3	0	0	19	0	18	12	2	5	11	2.5	5.5	59%	.192	0.94	2.50	4.08	4.63	0.0
2014	OAK	MLB	29	1	0	1	21	0	20	15	3	4	15	1.8	6.8	56%	.214	0.95	2.25	4.51	3.42	0.2
2015	OAK	MLB	30	2	1	1	39	0	36¹	31	2	11	31	2.7	7.6	56%	.277	1.17	2.96	3.52	3.22	0.6

Breakout: 36%   Improve: 54%   Collapse: 18%   Attrition: 15%   MLB: 82%   Comparables: *Sean Burnett, Jim Johnson, Brandon League*

After missing the first three months of 2014 recovering from Tommy John surgery, O'Flaherty picked up right where he left off by eating up same-side bats, though inflammation in his left elbow ominously ended his season in late September. Command is typically the last thing to return following TJS, and though O'Flaherty posted strong walk numbers, he also struggled to hit catcher targets on a consistent basis. With merely average velocity, the southpaw relies on deception and movement to induce weak contact; nothing he throws is straight, yet all of his pitches fall within a narrow velocity range. He also uses a closed stride directed toward the left-handed batter's box, an angle that helps him to mask the ball from the batter's view.

Dan Otero   RHP

Born: 2/19/85   Age: 30   Bats: R   Throws: R   Height: 6'3"   Weight: 215

YEAR	TEAM	LVL	AGE	W	L	SV	G	GS	IP	H	HR	BB	K	BB/9	K/9	GB%	BABIP	WHIP	ERA	FIP	FRA	WARP
2012	FRE	AAA	27	5	5	0	48	0	62	70	4	8	45	1.2	6.5	56%	.333	1.26	2.90	3.58	4.27	1.1
2012	SFN	MLB	27	0	0	0	12	0	12¹	19	0	2	8	1.5	5.8	67%	.422	1.70	5.84	2.81	3.04	0.2
2013	SAC	AAA	28	1	0	15	23	0	27¹	14	0	1	22	0.3	7.2	63%	.187	0.55	0.99	2.18	2.93	0.6
2013	OAK	MLB	28	2	0	0	33	0	39	42	0	6	27	1.4	6.2	56%	.333	1.23	1.38	2.15	2.73	0.9
2014	OAK	MLB	29	8	2	1	72	0	86²	80	4	15	45	1.6	4.7	58%	.269	1.10	2.28	3.31	3.92	0.4
2015	OAK	MLB	30	3	1	1	57	0	69²	69	4	12	48	1.6	6.2	53%	.294	1.17	3.25	3.48	3.53	0.9

Breakout: 16%   Improve: 40%   Collapse: 15%   Attrition: 17%   MLB: 62%   *Comparables:*   *Brad Ziegler, Geoff Geary, Doug Slaten*

"Book 'em" Dan Otero is a worm-burning machine thanks to a heavy sinker that batters struggle to lift. He didn't surrender a home run for the first 63 innings of his career, and, at 29, finally managed to spend a full year with the luxuries of big-league life (per diem above McDonald's grade; bed bug-free hotels; games in real cities like Milwaukee rather than third-rate podunks like Las Vegas). He only throws two speeds with his three-pitch repertoire, and he relies on the sinker to fuel an extreme pitch-to-contact approach (18 percent Three True Outcome rate last year). The risky strategy has paid off to the tune of a 2.01 ERA across 125 innings over the past two seasons, a nod to Otero's excellent command fueled by a repeatable release point from his low-three-quarter arm slot.

Dillon Overton   LHP
Born: 8/17/91   Age: 23   Bats: L   Throws: L   Height: 6'2"   Weight: 172

YEAR	TEAM	LVL	AGE	W	L	SV	G	GS	IP	H	HR	BB	K	BB/9	K/9	GB%	BABIP	WHIP	ERA	FIP	FRA	WARP
2014	VER	A-	22	0	1	0	5	5	15	11	0	1	22	0.6	13.2	47%	.324	0.80	2.40	0.91	1.29	0.7
2015	OAK	MLB	23	2	3	0	9	9	32²	35	3	18	25	4.9	6.8	43%	.309	1.62	5.18	5.10	5.64	-0.2

Breakout: 0%   Improve: 0%   Collapse: 0%   Attrition: 0%   MLB: 0%   *Comparables:*   *Jesse Hahn, Alex Wilson, Jimmy Barthmaier*

The 2013 second-rounder underwent Tommy John surgery soon after he was drafted, delaying his pro debut, but Overton was back on the mound just 12 months after going under the knife. The college product was more advanced than his competition in the Arizona and New York-Penn Leagues, but the performance was impressive considering the physical obstacles. The organization was understandably cautious, using Overton for three-inning stints to minimize his in-game fatigue. He was rebuilding velocity during his dozen starts, sitting in the upper 80s with the fastball, and is on track to be back at his typical low 90s by spring. Mechanically, Overton utilizes a good combination of power and stability, including a fluid pace to the plate with strong momentum that he repeated very well considering he hadn't seen the mound in a year.

Jarrod Parker   RHP
Born: 11/24/88   Age: 26   Bats: R   Throws: R   Height: 6'1"   Weight: 195

YEAR	TEAM	LVL	AGE	W	L	SV	G	GS	IP	H	HR	BB	K	BB/9	K/9	GB%	BABIP	WHIP	ERA	FIP	FRA	WARP
2012	SAC	AAA	23	1	0	0	4	4	20²	22	2	6	21	2.6	9.1	55%	.345	1.35	2.18	3.76	4.00	0.5
2012	OAK	MLB	23	13	8	0	29	29	181¹	166	11	63	140	3.1	6.9	45%	.290	1.26	3.47	3.38	3.70	2.3
2013	OAK	MLB	24	12	8	0	32	32	197	178	25	63	134	2.9	6.1	42%	.260	1.22	3.97	4.43	4.81	0.0
2015	OAK	MLB	26	2	2	0	6	6	35¹	33	3	12	27	3.0	6.9	46%	.285	1.28	3.65	4.24	3.96	0.3

Breakout: 34%   Improve: 66%   Collapse: 15%   Attrition: 15%   MLB: 94%   *Comparables:*   *Jon Lester, Jhoulys Chacin, Matt Garza*

Parker was penciled in as the Opening Day starter last year, but he fell prey to The Plague and hit the shelf before the regular season started. It was his second Tommy John surgery in less than five years, a factor that complicates his recovery timeline and clouds his long-term prognosis. Expect the A's to be careful with Parker in his first year back on the mound; a conservative approach will give him time to recover strength and flexibility while limiting his workload for the season. Miscast at the head of a rotation in any event, Parker has the profile of a quality no. 3 starter if he makes a full comeback.

Drew Pomeranz   LHP
Born: 11/22/88   Age: 26   Bats: R   Throws: L   Height: 6'5"   Weight: 240

YEAR	TEAM	LVL	AGE	W	L	SV	G	GS	IP	H	HR	BB	K	BB/9	K/9	GB%	BABIP	WHIP	ERA	FIP	FRA	WARP
2012	CSP	AAA	23	4	4	0	9	9	46²	52	2	20	46	3.9	8.9	56%	.347	1.54	2.51	3.54	4.23	1.3
2012	COL	MLB	23	2	9	0	22	22	96²	97	14	46	83	4.3	7.7	45%	.289	1.48	4.93	4.85	5.25	1.4
2013	CSP	AAA	24	8	1	0	15	15	85²	83	6	33	96	3.5	10.1	47%	.338	1.35	4.20	3.50	4.04	2.5
2013	COL	MLB	24	0	4	0	8	4	21²	25	4	19	19	7.9	7.9	55%	.339	2.03	6.23	6.44	6.58	-0.2
2014	SAC	AAA	25	3	1	0	8	8	46¹	45	6	17	54	3.3	10.5	42%	.325	1.34	3.69	4.15	4.36	0.7
2014	OAK	MLB	25	5	4	0	20	10	69	51	7	26	64	3.4	8.3	48%	.244	1.12	2.35	3.80	4.28	0.4
2015	OAK	MLB	26	5	6	0	19	19	96	87	9	40	91	3.7	8.5	46%	.291	1.32	3.68	4.23	4.00	1.0

Breakout: 42%   Improve: 70%   Collapse: 14%   Attrition: 15%   MLB: 94%   *Comparables:*   *Jake Arrieta, Manny Parra, Marc Rzepczynski*

The lefty with the funky arm action helped fill innings as the A's worked with their papier mache starting rotation, at least until he put his own self on the disabled list by punching a chair with his pitching hand when he went on tilt following a pinball-machine outing on June 16th. He was demoted to Triple-A upon his return, watching from afar as the A's traded for starters and he slid down the depth chart. Pomeranz had the platoon disadvantage 78 percent of the time, but the southpaw put those right-handers to sleep with a .196/.274/.289 line in 2014. Regression awaits.

Bobby Wahl   RHP
Born: 3/21/92   Age: 23   Bats: R   Throws: R   Height: 6'2"   Weight: 210

YEAR	TEAM	LVL	AGE	W	L	SV	G	GS	IP	H	HR	BB	K	BB/9	K/9	GB%	BABIP	WHIP	ERA	FIP	FRA	WARP
2013	VER	A-	21	0	0	2	9	4	20²	20	3	6	27	2.6	11.8	32%	.321	1.26	3.92	3.24	4.17	0.2
2014	BLT	A	22	0	4	4	20	7	42²	46	5	19	43	4.0	9.1	39%	.323	1.52	5.06	4.54	5.52	0.5
2014	STO	A+	22	0	0	0	9	0	10²	8	2	6	19	5.1	16.0	35%	.286	1.31	4.22	4.30	2.73	0.4
2015	OAK	MLB	23	2	2	1	20	5	41¹	44	5	21	32	4.6	7.1	39%	.305	1.57	5.10	5.31	5.54	-0.3

Breakout: 0%   Improve: 0%   Collapse: 0%   Attrition: 0%   MLB: 0%   *Comparables:*   *Henry Villar, Jason Miller, Seth Rosin*

Wahl dealt with an oblique injury that cost him a month during the spring, and after a quartet of ineffective starts upon his return the right-hander was sent to the bullpen. It turns out that a little relief was just what the doctor ordered. His ERA shrunk from 7.01 as a starting pitcher to 2.93 as a reliever and his strikeout rate ballooned from 16 percent to an eye-opening 35. The transition to relief takes the pressure off Wahl to develop a third pitch, allowing his fastball-curveball combination to shine as he parlays a powerful delivery into high-leverage gold. With his future role now defined, Wahl could move quickly and be on the fast track to the bigs.

Lineouts

Hitters

NAME	POS	TEAM	LVL	AGE	PA	R	2B	3B	HR	RBI	BB	K	SB	CS	AVG/OBP/SLG	TAv	BABIP	BRR	FRAA	WARP
Jeremy Barfield	RF	MID	AA	25	173	16	6	2	3	16	29	41	0	1	.261/.387/.394	.264	.343	-0.5	RF(25): -1.1, P(2): -0.0	0.4
B.J. Boyd	CF	BLT	A	20	521	57	15	5	6	38	48	94	15	9	.226/.300/.319	.246	.270	2.2	CF(64): -2.6, LF(57): 3.9	0.7
Andrew Brown	RF	LVG	AAA	29	446	65	26	1	21	69	52	87	2	0	.283/.372/.519	.299	.313	1.1	RF(83): -1.8, LF(6): -0.3	2.7
	LF	NYN	MLB	29	49	6	1	0	2	7	3	15	0	0	.182/.245/.341	.233	.214	0.2	LF(8): -0.1, RF(4): 0.0	-0.1
Jaycob Brugman	LF	BLT	A	22	287	33	19	4	8	37	35	65	5	2	.278/.371/.484	.304	.347	-1.0	LF(31): 3.3, RF(15): 1.7	2.3
	LF	STO	A+	22	214	34	6	2	13	35	16	50	3	3	.282/.332/.533	.294	.311	0.9	LF(25): -1.3, RF(18): 0.6	1.2
Mark Canha	LF	NWO	AAA	25	537	83	28	3	20	82	57	112	3	1	.303/.384/.505	.318	.356	0.1	LF(61): 2.1, 1B(40): -2.3	4.2
Bobby Crocker	LF	STO	A+	24	499	59	22	6	11	52	37	149	31	6	.271/.336/.421	.260	.378	3.4	LF(52): 5.0, CF(43): 2.9	2.6
Miles Head	3B	MID	AA	23	227	21	7	1	7	28	11	52	1	0	.219/.264/.362	.219	.253	-0.8	3B(20): 0.5, 1B(13): -0.7	-0.6
Ryon Healy	3B	STO	A+	22	600	73	28	2	16	83	28	79	0	0	.285/.318/.428	.259	.304	-1.4	3B(46): 1.6, 1B(29): -0.4	1.0
Bruce Maxwell	C	STO	A+	23	334	33	11	1	6	35	41	58	0	1	.273/.365/.381	.274	.322	0.4	C(73): -0.7	2.4
	C	MID	AA	23	94	8	3	0	0	2	9	32	0	1	.141/.223/.176	.146	.226	-0.5	C(24): 0.2	-0.6
Hiroyuki Nakajima	2B	MID	AA	31	289	30	8	0	6	31	26	56	3	3	.266/.337/.367	.250	.315	-2.1	2B(33): -3.0, 3B(8): -1.0	-0.4
	3B	SAC	AAA	31	45	3	2	0	0	4	4	10	1	0	.128/.222/.179	.173	.167	-0.7	3B(9): -0.9, 2B(1): -0.0	-0.4
Josh Phegley	C	CHR	AAA	26	467	69	30	4	23	75	31	72	0	1	.274/.331/.530	.271	.278	0.6	C(105): -0.0	3.3
	C	CHA	MLB	26	38	4	2	0	3	7	0	11	0	0	.216/.211/.514	.267	.208	-0.8	C(11): -0.0	0.1
Herschel Powell	CF	BLT	A	21	312	43	7	4	3	17	53	49	16	13	.335/.452/.429	.326	.404	-2.0	CF(66): 2.1	3.0
	CF	STO	A+	21	69	11	3	1	0	11	8	4	0	2	.377/.449/.459	.322	.404	0.3	CF(11): 0.3, RF(3): -0.0	0.6
Aaron Shipman	LF	STO	A+	22	215	30	6	6	1	16	36	39	13	2	.292/.414/.410	.290	.370	2.2	LF(42): -1.3, RF(4): 0.2	1.1

The **Jeremy Barfield** mound experiment lasted for three months and 36 innings, yielding inconclusive results before he went back to swinging a bat full-time. At 26, his career isn't dead yet, but it is time to hit or get off the pot. ❖ The 2014 campaign was a lost cause for young outfielder **B.J. Boyd**, who began the season "on the rise" but finished 50 miles from nowhere. ❖ **Andrew Brown** was predictably gangbusters at Triple-A Las Vegas, but when he got the call-up, the microwave wasn't working. He's a decent bench bat and he kills lefties. ❖ **Jaycob Brugman** hit well enough in Beloit to receive the door prize: a promotion to the Cal League that spun its black magic to convert his doubles into home runs. ❖ Too old to be a prospect, and without loud tools, the only thing that **Mark Canha** brings to the table is consistent above-average performance as a hitter at every minor-league stop. That was enough to get him to Oakland in the Rule 5 draft. ❖ **Bobby Crocker** spent 2014 treading water in Stockton, California, quite a feat in a landlocked city in the midst of a harsh drought. He repeated High-A with virtually the same results as 2013, including the same problematic strikeout-to-walk ratio. ❖ **Miles Head**'s big-league quest has stalled at Double-A, with injuries and poor performance confining him to Midland since 2012, while the power that previously buoyed his prospect status was left behind in the Cal League. Time is still on his side, but Head no longer enjoys the caveat of being young for his levels. ❖ The 100th overall pick in the 2013 draft, **Ryon Healy** held his own in his first full season of pro ball. The power is under construction, but his defense was the main focus as he worked to add the hot corner to his fielding resume. ❖ **Bruce Maxwell** keeps throwing out baserunners in his quest to be the thief-stopping caddy to an offense-oriented catcher, but even backups have to hit a *little* bit. ❖ **Hiroyuki Nakajima** climbed the wrong way down the minor-league ladder, as he was banished to Double-A after a dozen games of futility in the PCL but put up the same anemic numbers in the Texas League that he had posted in Triple-A a year earlier, dooming his MLB future. ❖ **Josh Phegley** abused Triple-A for the second straight season in 2014, but defensive limitations and Adrian Nieto's Rule 5 status prevented him from seeing much time in the majors. He's roughly 20 percent of Derek Norris. ❖ **Herschel "Boog" Powell** tore through the Midwest League, earned a promotion to High-A and continued the offensive explosion for a couple of weeks, right up until he got a 50-game suspension for amphetamines. This Boog is about half the size of the original, by the way, and no relation. ❖ Injuries have continued to plague **Aaron Shipman**'s career, and he was in the midst of his best season (including his first pro home run) when it was cut short in 2014. He has played in just 297 games over the past four seasons, and he's not such a tremendous talent that he can afford all that lost development time.

Pitchers

NAME	TEAM	LVL	AGE	W	L	SV	G	GS	IP	H	HR	BB	K	BB/9	K/9	GB%	BABIP	WHIP	ERA	FIP	FRA	WARP
Dylan Covey	BLT	A	22	4	9	0	18	17	101	99	3	26	70	2.3	6.2	59%	.308	1.24	4.81	3.41	5.00	0.1
	STO	A+	22	3	5	0	8	8	39	49	2	15	22	3.5	5.1	58%	.348	1.64	7.15	4.82	6.09	0.1
Jorge De Leon	CCH	AA	26	1	2	2	15	0	20²	18	5	7	18	3.0	7.8	36%	.224	1.21	3.92	5.68	6.43	-0.2
	OKL	AAA	26	3	3	3	31	0	48	46	0	16	43	3.0	8.1	47%	.333	1.29	2.62	2.97	3.54	1.1
	HOU	MLB	26	0	0	0	8	0	7¹	9	2	3	4	3.7	4.9	31%	.292	1.64	4.91	6.84	7.86	-0.3
Tucker Healy	STO	A+	24	2	1	3	13	0	17¹	9	1	4	29	2.1	15.1	26%	.267	0.75	1.04	2.01	1.55	0.8
	MID	AA	24	0	1	4	12	0	19¹	17	1	6	29	2.8	13.5	24%	.356	1.19	2.33	1.72	2.37	0.8
	SAC	AAA	24	1	1	0	20	0	24¹	31	4	14	28	5.2	10.4	31%	.373	1.85	8.14	5.38	5.25	0.2
Arnold Leon	SAC	AAA	25	10	7	0	27	27	145	170	12	51	128	3.2	7.9	43%	.357	1.52	4.97	4.19	4.58	1.2
Deck McGuire	NHP	AA	25	3	4	0	10	10	60¹	58	3	17	47	2.5	7.0	42%	.294	1.24	2.98	3.44	3.68	1.2
	BUF	AAA	25	3	5	0	10	10	55	57	12	23	38	3.8	6.2	41%	.269	1.45	5.56	6.12	6.74	-0.6
	SAC	AAA	25	2	4	0	7	6	34²	49	5	16	16	4.2	4.2	39%	.346	1.88	8.05	6.04	6.65	-0.4
Rudy Owens	OKL	AAA	26	8	5	1	25	21	135	136	10	33	104	2.2	6.9	42%	.304	1.25	4.33	4.03	4.52	1.9
	HOU	MLB	26	0	1	0	1	1	5²	9	1	2	1	3.2	1.6	36%	.333	1.94	7.94	6.69	6.19	-0.2
F. Rodriguez	SAC	AAA	30	3	0	0	38	0	45²	40	2	16	53	3.2	10.4	39%	.328	1.23	1.97	3.20	2.94	1.2
	OAK	MLB	30	1	0	0	7	0	9	4	0	2	4	2.0	4.0	33%	.148	0.67	1.00	2.94	3.41	0.1
Evan Scribner	SAC	AAA	28	4	1	16	40	0	47	39	4	9	72	1.7	13.8	38%	.337	1.02	3.06	2.38	2.27	1.5
	OAK	MLB	28	1	0	0	13	0	11²	11	4	0	11	0.0	8.5	37%	.226	0.94	4.63	5.99	6.69	-0.3
Seth Streich	STO	A+	23	9	6	0	22	22	114	110	7	22	116	1.7	9.2	49%	.329	1.16	3.16	3.24	3.50	3.5
Taylor Thompson	CHR	AAA	27	3	0	7	39	0	59	48	3	29	68	4.4	10.4	53%	.294	1.31	2.14	3.19	3.25	1.5
	CHA	MLB	27	0	0	0	5	0	5¹	9	1	4	4	6.8	6.8	42%	.444	2.44	10.12	6.91	7.02	-0.1
Pat Venditte	TRN	AA	29	0	1	1	15	0	22	11	2	5	30	2.0	12.3	26%	.200	0.73	0.82	2.49	2.23	0.7
	SWB	AAA	29	2	5	1	26	2	56¹	54	4	17	53	2.7	8.5	32%	.305	1.26	3.36	3.36	3.53	1.4

Dylan Covey is learning the hard way that throwing strikes will only take you so far in the pros if you lack the stuff to back it up, and his stats, including an ugly 7.15 ERA at Stockton last year, are a reflection of his diminishing repertoire. ❖ Hard-throwing **Jorge De Leon** should earn a trophy for going a whole season in the PCL without allowing a home run. He then should lose the trophy for allowing two homers in his September call-up. What a cruel hypothetical award system. ❖ **Tucker Healy** jumped two levels in 2014 but hit a wall at Triple-A; he has registered double-digit strikeouts per nine at every stop of his minor-league career. ❖ **Arnold Leon** has learned the hard way about the perils of pitching to contact, and in particular the pitfalls of such a strategy in the Pacific Coast League. ❖ **Deck McGuire** has fallen on hard times, as the former first-rounder was dealt to the A's for cash considerations midseason; his performance in Sacramento continued its impression of a snowball in hell. ❖ After watching **Rudy Owens** throw 40 of his signature changeups and record exactly one swinging strike against major-league hitters, the Astros sent him back to the PCL, then outrighted him; he signed with the A's. Or, more realistically, the Sounds. ❖ **Fernando Rodriguez** is defying the age-related gravity of velocity, throwing 95 mph heat that has been rising along with his strikeout rate since he moved permanently to the bullpen, but it wasn't enough to keep him from being designated for assignment by the A's in December. ❖ **Evan Scribner** has excellent command of a fastball-curve combination, a trait that is necessary when a right-hander averages 90 mph on his heat. His days as the perfect 26th man are over, however, as he's out of options. ❖ **Seth Streich** was in the middle of a breakout season, having halved his walk rate and passed his previous high in innings, when a shoulder injury took him down in late July and knocked him out for the rest of the season. The Padres grabbed him as a throw-in when they acquired Derek Norris. ❖ **Taylor Thompson** labored for six years as an organizational soldier with the White Sox before finally breaking through to the majors in July. As far as 2009 44th-round relievers making their debuts go, Ken Giles had the better rookie season. The A's claimed Thompson in November. ❖ **Pat Venditte** is Emmet Brickowski in baseball's Bricksburg. His numbers in Scranton were good, not great, but the A's snapped him up quickly and gave him an invitation to spring training. Cross your fingers.

Manager

Bob Melvin

YEAR	TEAM	W	L	Py-thag +/-	Avg PC	100+ P	120+ P	QS	BQS	REL	REL w Zero R	IBB	PH	PH Avg	PH HR	SB2	CS2	SB3	CS3	SAC Att	SAC%	POS SAC	Squeeze	Swing	In Play
2012	OAK	93	67	1	92.7	52	0	88	4	456	381	34	93	.231	3	87	24	33	5	42	64.3%	26	0	297	74
2013	OAK	96	66	-1	94.8	56	0	92	2	447	370	23	130	.135	5	58	24	17	3	37	56.8%	21	2	253	87
2014	OAK	88	74	-12	96.2	61	1	102	5	441	380	28	161	.201	3	67	16	16	4	41	46.3%	15	2	253	83

Melvin is a likable manager. He's open-minded about data, employs shifts and platoons, doesn't bunt, adjusts to his personnel and lets his players grow facial hair to their hearts' content. And yet, when a team skids like the A's did during the second half, you have to ask: Was the manager fueling it? It wasn't Mauch in '64—Melvin didn't run Jon Lester and Jeff Samardzija into the ground over the final week—but the A's behaved differently as the season wound down.

Most notably, the A's attempted 23 of their 41 bunts during the final two months. Likewise, Oakland became less efficient on the basepaths, going 6-for-15 on stolen-base attempts. A deeper dig suggests those performance blips had more to do with the personnel than panic. Sam Fuld, who wasn't on the roster until August, laid down five bunts; Eric Sogard, who had been there all along, added three of his own. Sogard also contributed two caught stealings, while the others were done by three players who should run (Billy Burns, Craig Gentry and Coco Crisp) and one who shouldn't (Derek Norris).

There were no bizarre changes in bullpen usage. Melvin didn't confuse Dan Otero and Luke Gregerson with Evan Scribner and Fernando Rodriguez. He didn't demote Sean Doolittle to a low-leverage role after blowing a September save. The players just didn't perform like they had throughout the year. Perhaps Melvin pressed in some other way that escapes vision, or maybe he couldn't calm a clubhouse disturbed by the Yoenis Cespedes trade. Whatever the case, it'd be difficult to finger Melvin as the reason for the collapse.

PHILADELPHIA PHILLIES

by Michael Baumann

At some point during 2013, Phillies fans realized their team out-and-out sucked and there was no hope for the immediate future. That's a feeling that could accurately describe about 100 of the franchise's first 115 years in existence, but nowadays, fans have an expectation of competitiveness that feels new historically, though it actually predates the War on Terror. Mid-2013 was the moment most Phillies fans realized that expectation wouldn't be met.

And so the chants rained down, from talk radio and empirically savvy blogs alike: Fire Ruben Amaro! Now! The Phillies had gone from a 102-win juggernaut to a laughingstock in 18 months; surely something had gone wrong in those 18 months that could be fixed just as quickly if those responsible were replaced.

If only it were that simple.

The Phillies' decline says fascinating—if not exactly groundbreaking—things about causality and human capacity for patience. In baseball more than in other sports, we feel the effects of baseball operations decisions on an extreme delay. That can be a good thing, as the Phillies won the World Series in 2008 thanks largely to a core that took an extremely long time to come together: Jimmy Rollins, Carlos Ruiz, Pat Burrell, Ryan Madson, Brett Myers, Chase Utley, Ryan Howard and Cole Hamels all joined the Phillies as amateurs between 1996 and 2002. Rollins' MVP season came 11 years after the Phillies drafted him.

Right now, the team is living the converse, thanks to decisions that were made starting in 2002. That year, they signed Jim Thome as a free agent and forfeited their first-round pick the next season. They'd lose first-round picks again in 2005 (for signing Jon Lieber), 2006 (Tom Gordon), 2009 (Raul Ibanez), 2011 (Cliff Lee) and 2012 (Jonathan Papelbon). From November 2007 to July 2010, they made five major trades for pitchers (Brad Lidge, Joe Blanton, Lee, Roy Halladay and Roy Oswalt) to set up the backbone of a staff that won 384 games, four division titles, two pennants and a World Series from 2008 to 2011. The cost was 16 young players, including Kyle Drabek (one of only five first-round picks the Phillies actually made between 2001 and 2012) and two other sandwich-round picks. In July 2011, the Phillies traded four more prospects for Hunter Pence. The cost of signing or trading for 11 major players who

helped the Phillies win from 2003 to 2011 ended up being 26 players who might have helped them win from 2011 to the present. The Phillies offloaded some established players in that time, and they also traded for veterans who didn't help them win a division title. But let's focus on signings that cost draft picks and trades that brought in major contributors from 2007 to 2011, as shown in Table 1 on the next page.

It's possible that the Phillies' turn-of-the-century draft success would have ended when it did even if they hadn't been so cavalier about giving away first-round picks. But even looking back on what those players have become (and very few of them have turned into stars), you start to appreciate the bulk value of 26 young, cost-controlled players. In 2014, the Phillies, with a very college-heavy crop of draftees, signed 28 players, so in quantity alone, the Phillies traded away an entire draft class. Twenty-six players is a full doubleheader roster, or a little more than half as many players as they used in all of 2014.

There's a personnel cost in addition to lost prospects: In 2008, when Pat Gillick retired, the Phillies promoted Amaro instead of Mike Arbuckle, their other assistant general manager. Arbuckle was a legendary scouting figure and one of the chief architects of the draft strategy that built the World Series team. Arbuckle then jumped ship for Kansas City, where he was one of the chief architects of the draft strategy that helped the Royals win the pennant in 2014. In practical terms, the result of losing Arbuckle and the Gang of 26 is that the last homegrown player who gave the Phillies multiple years of starter-level production is Carlos Ruiz, who signed in 1998, debuted in 2006 and will be 36 years old on Opening Day 2015.

Arbuckle was a key figure in the organization's construction, but once the team was assembled, the Phillies wanted Amaro to see the process through. He maximized the Phillies' chances of winning in the short term in a way Arbuckle might not have, but he did so at a long-term cost. I don't know that it's an unreasonable price to pay: The Phillies won the only title among the city's five major professional sports teams, and could easily have won at least one more if not for a series of rodent infestations (Cody Ross in 2010, the Busch Stadium Rally Squirrel in 2011). But it was a choice, and it has consequences.

PHILLIES PROSPECTUS
2014 W-L: 73-89, 5TH IN NL EAST

Pythag	.453	24th	DER	.705	16th
RS/G	3.82	23rd	B-Age	31.1	29th
RA/G	4.24	21st	P-Age	30.4	29th
TAv	.255	22nd	Salary	$174.8M	3rd
BRR	-4.36	24th	M$/MW	$6.6M	30th
TAv-P	.268	24th	DL Days	668	9th
FIP	3.79	19th	$ on DL	18%	20th

Three-Year Park Factors

Runs	Runs/RH	Runs/LH	HR/RH	HR/LH
97	97	92	99	89

Top Hitter WARP	4.5	Chase Utley
Top Pitcher WARP	2.7	Cole Hamels
Top Prospect		J.P. Crawford

Table 1. Win-Now Phillies Moves, 2002-2011

In	Out
Jim Thome	No. 18 overall pick in 2003 (Brad Snyder; could have been Chad Cordero, Carlos Quentin or Adam Jones)
Jon Lieber	No. 17 overall pick in 2005 (C.J. Henry, who was later traded for Bobby Abreu; could have been Jacoby Ellsbury, Matt Garza or Colby Rasmus)
Tom Gordon	No. 21 overall pick in 2006 (Ian Kennedy; could have been Daniel Bard or Joba Chamberlain)
Brad Lidge (and Eric Bruntlett)	Michael Bourn, Mike Costanzo, Geoff Geary
Joe Blanton	Adrian Cardenas, Matthew Spencer, Josh Outman
Raul Ibanez	No. 27 overall pick in 2009 (Nick Franklin; could have been Rex Brothers, James Paxton, Tyler Skaggs or Garrett Richards)
Cliff Lee (trade)	Carlos Carrasco, Jason Donald, Lou Marson, Jason Knapp
Roy Halladay	Kyle Drabek, Michael Taylor, Travis d'Arnaud
Roy Oswalt	J.A. Happ, Anthony Gose, Jonathan Villar
Cliff Lee (free agency)	No. 33 overall pick in 2011 (Kevin Matthews; could have been Henry Owens or Jackie Bradley)
Hunter Pence	Jarrod Cosart, Jonathan Singleton, Josh Zeid, Domingo Santana
Jonathan Papelbon	No. 31 overall pick in 2012 (Brian Johnson; could have been Jose Berrios, Kevin Plawecki, Stephen Piscotty or Joey Gallo)

✦✦✦

It's been equally fascinating to watch Phillies fans react to the new paradigm. This was clearly coming all along, perhaps sooner than we'd hoped, but it was more or less inevitable. It made me consider the difference between denial—"I don't think this will happen"—and disbelief—"I can't believe this is happening"—as well as the many layers of nuance that cover any discussion of rebuilding in baseball.

It's one thing to say that you want a team to rebuild, but another to grapple with what that means. Not every rebuilding project needs to be like the insurance fraud fire the Astros (or, across the parking lot, the NBA's 76ers) have undertaken. Whether the Phillies should have traded Lee, or whether they should still trade Hamels (he remained a Phillie despite hot pursuit by the Padres as this book was put to bed), are questions without clear-cut answers.

It is, however, clear that the rebuild is underway. Papelbon was the last win-now free agent Amaro signed, and after years of not having first-round picks and misusing what picks remained, things are turning around. The Phillies once drafted Anthony Hewitt and Larry Greene without bothering to learn if either one actually possessed usable baseball skills, but 2013 first-rounder J.P. Crawford has the makings of a potential All-Star, 2014 first-rounder Aaron Nola should be in the rotation by midseason and last year's rookie reliever Ken Giles looks like a future closer. It's still not a great farm system and the major-league team is still old and below average at almost every position, but things are turning around.

Slowly.

That's the key to understanding the direction of the franchise, because even the best-run baseball operations departments can take the better part of a decade to build a winner from within. A baseball team is like a supertanker: It moves slowly and only with great effort. It can take a long time to go from drifting aimlessly to moving in a positive direction, and once heading in the wrong direction, it takes even longer to turn around. And even among baseball teams, the Phillies seem to have more inertia and a wider turning circle than most.

✦✦✦

There's something very Old Testament about the Phillies, a thematic familiarity that goes beyond the normal cracks about their analytics department and hits on the cyclical nature of prosperity. God blesses the Phillies, then the Phillies do something dumb and God smites them. Then God smites the next three or four generations, just to make sure they get the message. Forever and ever, amen.

The Hunter Pence trade is straight out of 1 Kings, in which the Israelites say to God, "We want a king. Everyone else has a king, and we want one."

And God's all like, "No, y'all are doing okay being ruled by judges. Kings are bad news."

"But we want a king now!"

So God gives them Saul, who starts out okay, but goes slightly crazy, alienates David (Israel's top prospect, who is Jonathan Singleton in this metaphor) and kills himself. As always, the crap you're going through in the present was caused by a mistake you made years ago, and there's nothing you can do about it.

And if you're impatient with the Phillies' rebuild, remember that Moses died before he reached the Promised Land.

✦✦✦

The thing is, I'm less convinced that Ruben Amaro is bad for the Phillies now than at any point in his tenure. That's how long the causal lag is in baseball, particularly for draft picks and prospects, and that's how important patience has to be. Not because there's some grand plan that will rescue the Phillies from gerontocracy and futility—because I'm still not convinced that there is—but because what's the alternative?

Once it became clear in 2012 that the Phillies' run was over, Amaro has more or less abstained from the kind of signings that made him a laughingstock: The Phillies have ignored top-tier free agents who would be too old to contribute by the time Nola, Crawford and the rest are established. Instead, he's gone for mid-tier stopgaps like A.J. Burnett, Michael Young and Marlon Byrd, who have spanned the gulf from "Well, someone's got to play third base" to "Actually, he's been pretty good." When younger alternatives have appeared, he's been unafraid to cut bait on veterans, sometimes with surprising results: There are three legitimate prospects in the Phillies' system right now who were acquired for the combined price of John McDonald and the former Fausto Carmona. (Amaro's December comments about the Phillies being better off without Ryan Howard than with him, while shocking for their frankness and worth some point-and-laugh because Amaro's the one who signed him to that absurd extension in the first place, are fully of a piece with the way he's run the team the last three years.)

I know this is a pretty low standard for competence, but nothing Amaro has done since midseason 2012 has actively hindered the Phillies' ability to regenerate naturally, as the ecosystem does after a forest fire.

✦✦✦

The irony is that while Amaro has never done a better job than he is now, it might not be enough to save him, as winning percentages and attendance fall together. There is nothing, realistically, that the Phillies can do to compete in 2015, or likely even 2016, and you'd be shocked how comforting that is to say out loud.

That's been my standard refrain over the past two years, because it's amazingly liberating to just decide to care less about your favorite team when it's bad. Viewed through the lenses of patience and apathy, Howard and Chase Utley aren't decomposing on the field in front of us, putting off winning by another year through their refusal to accept a trade. Instead, they're living legends taking one final lap around the stadium for the benefit of the fans. So what if they suck (and Utley weren't half bad in 2014), because it's not like there's anyone better stuck in the pipeline, languishing in Triple-A because the old guy wouldn't give up his spot.

Why worry about Ben Revere's lack of power, or Domonic Brown's defense, or Jonathan Papelbon's incurable and terminal case of Punchable Face Syndrome? The Phillies aren't going to win anyway and there's no immediate and obvious replacement knocking down the door.

It's a churlish, facile and nihilistic way to be a baseball fan, and I don't care. Some people have the patience to wallow in the price we've paid for our good fortune without turning away. But for others, the only sane thing to do is to unplug emotionally for a while; even if Ruben Amaro does get fired, and even if it is the right decision, we won't feel the effects for years. ∎

—Michael Baumann is a contributor to Grantland's Triangle blog and covers college baseball in the northeast and midwest for D1Baseball.com. His book, Philadelphia Phenoms: The Most Amazing Athletes to Play in the City of Brotherly Love, *has been described as "inaccessible" and a "garbage fire."*

Player comments by Paul Sporer and Baseball Prospectus Authors

Hitters

Aaron Altherr   OF

Born: 1/14/91   Age: 24   Bats: R   Throws: R   Height: 6' 5"   Weight: 220

YEAR	TEAM	LVL	AGE	PA	R	2B	3B	HR	RBI	BB	K	SB	CS	AVG/OBP/SLG	TAv	BABIP	BRR	FRAA	WARP
2012	LWD	A	21	471	65	27	6	8	50	38	102	25	8	.252/.319/.402	.259	.310	3.5	CF(54): 10.7, LF(30): 5.0	3.3
2013	CLR	A+	22	527	57	36	6	12	69	45	140	23	5	.275/.337/.455	.285	.360	0.5	CF(64): 1.0, LF(52): 0.5	3.5
2014	CLR	A+	23	33	6	1	2	0	2	5	8	1	0	.250/.364/.429	.278	.350	0.3	CF(6): 0.8, RF(1): -0.1	0.4
2014	REA	AA	23	492	54	27	2	14	57	26	110	12	6	.236/.287/.399	.242	.279	-2.9	CF(100): -0.2, LF(12): 0.6	0.3
2014	PHI	MLB	23	5	0	0	0	0	0	0	2	0	0	.000/.000/.000	.006	.000	0.0	LF(1): 0.1	-0.1
2015	PHI	MLB	24	250	23	11	1	5	23	11	75	5	2	.209/.250/.327	.219	.280	0.3	CF 1, LF 1	-0.1

Breakout: 0%   Improve: 0%   Collapse: 0%   Attrition: 0%   MLB: 0%   Comparables: Jordan Danks, Brandon Barnes, Kevin Mattison

Sure, we all know that a $1 scratch-off lottery ticket is a terrible investment. But that's only because it probably won't win. If you had two, though, then it's only half as bad an investment, see? The best investment is lots of $1 scratch-off lottery tickets. Lots and lots and lots and lots and lots and lots and lots and lots and lots. The Phillies have a gaggle of raw, toolsy outfielders scattered throughout the system, many of whom you'll get to read about in the next 40 minutes, one of whom is Altherr. He's got great size and plus speed and if you scratch at him your brain drops a little dopamine into your blood system, but thus far the numbers haven't lined up. He got two brief tastes of the majors, but he's nowhere near ready.

Cody Asche   3B

Born: 6/30/90   Age: 25   Bats: L   Throws: R   Height: 6' 1"   Weight: 200

YEAR	TEAM	LVL	AGE	PA	R	2B	3B	HR	RBI	BB	K	SB	CS	AVG/OBP/SLG	TAv	BABIP	BRR	FRAA	WARP
2012	CLR	A+	22	270	31	13	3	2	25	12	37	10	2	.349/.378/.447	.276	.399	-0.6	3B(61): -3.1	0.6
2012	REA	AA	22	289	42	20	3	10	47	22	56	1	1	.300/.360/.513	.303	.348	-1.0	3B(67): -1.3	2.1
2013	LEH	AAA	23	446	52	24	4	15	68	35	95	11	3	.295/.352/.485	.285	.349	0.5	3B(103): 4.9	2.8
2013	PHI	MLB	23	179	18	8	1	5	22	15	43	1	0	.235/.302/.389	.250	.287	0.9	3B(44): -0.7	0.6
2014	PHI	MLB	24	434	43	25	0	10	46	33	102	0	1	.252/.309/.390	.261	.315	-0.3	3B(112): -3.3	1.4
2015	PHI	MLB	25	413	42	20	2	11	48	26	96	3	1	.258/.306/.405	.268	.314	0.4	3B -1	1.2

Breakout: 7%   Improve: 37%   Collapse: 17%   Attrition: 29%   MLB: 88%   Comparables: Andy Marte, Lonnie Chisenhall, Kyle Seager

Well, Asche won't ever be able to say he didn't get a chance. With a one-year head start on Maikel Franco, he had the third base job to himself, and with a better showing would have pushed the Phillies to consider other plans for Franco. Instead, he mustered only an average offensive line, paired it with sloppy defense, and most likely doomed himself to a career as a traveling depthman. In fairness, his major-league numbers are essentially in line with what his minor-league track record suggested, so asking for more was asking too much. His best bet at locking in playing time is reestablishing the dominance over righties that he showed in the minors, but there isn't a first-division player lurking beneath the surface here.

Aaron Brown   OF

Born: 6/20/92   Age: 23   Bats: L   Throws: L   Height: 6' 2"   Weight: 220

YEAR	TEAM	LVL	AGE	PA	R	2B	3B	HR	RBI	BB	K	SB	CS	AVG/OBP/SLG	TAv	BABIP	BRR	FRAA	WARP
2014	LWD	A	22	59	3	6	0	1	5	1	19	0	1	.309/.339/.473	.290	.444	-0.6	RF(10): 1.0, CF(3): -0.5	0.3
2014	WPT	A-	22	193	23	7	1	3	16	6	41	8	4	.256/.301/.356	.262	.314	-1.1	CF(39): 1.7	0.8
2015	PHI	MLB	23	250	18	9	1	3	20	7	80	2	2	.194/.225/.271	.192	.274	-0.4	CF -1, RF 1	-1.3

Breakout: 0%   Improve: 0%   Collapse: 0%   Attrition: 0%   MLB: 0%   Comparables: Justin Maxwell, Kevin Pillar, Matt Den Dekker

A strong junior season at Pepperdine improved Brown's draft position by 27 rounds; not only that, but he got to spend another warm winter in Malibu. A two-way collegian, Brown has started his pro career as a hitter, though most teams reportedly preferred him as a pitching prospect. The ceiling isn't terribly high, and his unimpressive plate control in college has carried over to the pro game. A live arm in the outfield and a chance at some bench pop down the line is probably the best case, but the fallback—a conversion back to the mound—provides some insurance.

Domonic Brown LF

Born: 9/3/87   Age: 27   Bats: L   Throws: L   Height: 6' 5"   Weight: 230

YEAR	TEAM	LVL	AGE	PA	R	2B	3B	HR	RBI	BB	K	SB	CS	AVG/OBP/SLG	TAv	BABIP	BRR	FRAA	WARP
2012	LEH	AAA	24	239	33	13	2	5	28	17	42	4	6	.286/.335/.432	.268	.331	-2.2	LF(43): 0.2, CF(11): -0.7	0.6
2012	PHI	MLB	24	212	21	11	2	5	26	21	34	0	0	.235/.316/.396	.251	.260	-3.5	RF(38): -0.8, LF(29): 1.1	0.0
2013	PHI	MLB	25	540	65	21	4	27	83	39	97	8	3	.272/.324/.494	.292	.287	2.7	LF(132): -13.6, RF(2): 0.1	2.0
2014	PHI	MLB	26	512	47	22	1	10	63	34	91	7	1	.235/.285/.349	.246	.269	0.3	LF(127): -6.0	-0.2
2015	PHI	MLB	27	487	54	21	2	15	58	39	94	7	2	.253/.314/.410	.276	.287	-0.4	LF -6, RF -0	1.1

Breakout: 6%   Improve: 47%   Collapse: 6%   Attrition: 13%   MLB: 96%   Comparables: Brennan Boesch, Juan Rivera, David DeJesus

Brown's brilliant two-month "I told you so" stretch of 2013 accounts for 37 percent of his career home run total. He's now 27, and for the second time has gone from "promise" to "bust," this time without sporadic playing time as an excuse. So now he moves on to Act 3, the "change-of-scenery" section of the story, where another organization that always liked him as a high schooler sees whether its coaches can shorten his swing, or persuade him to lift the ball more, or get him to be a bit choosier on pitches in the strike zone. Now that his value has *completely* bottomed out, look for Ruben Amaro Jr. to deal him for pennies on the dollar, before he gets too old for the Phillies to part with.

Marlon Byrd RF

Born: 8/30/77   Age: 37   Bats: R   Throws: R   Height: 6' 0"   Weight: 245

YEAR	TEAM	LVL	AGE	PA	R	2B	3B	HR	RBI	BB	K	SB	CS	AVG/OBP/SLG	TAv	BABIP	BRR	FRAA	WARP
2012	CHN	MLB	34	47	1	0	0	0	2	3	10	0	1	.070/.149/.070	.136	.091	-0.4	CF(13): 0.9	-0.4
2012	BOS	MLB	34	106	9	2	0	1	7	2	21	0	2	.270/.286/.320	.232	.325	-0.5	CF(33): 0.7, RF(2): -0.0	0.1
2013	NYN	MLB	35	464	61	26	5	21	71	25	124	2	4	.285/.330/.518	.311	.350	0.1	RF(111): -5.6, CF(2): -0.3	2.7
2013	PIT	MLB	35	115	14	9	0	3	17	6	20	0	0	.318/.357/.486	.291	.365	-0.6	RF(27): -1.7, LF(2): -0.1	0.4
2014	PHI	MLB	36	637	71	28	2	25	85	35	185	3	2	.264/.312/.445	.286	.341	-3.7	RF(149): 12.0	4.0
2015	PHI	MLB	37	587	57	27	2	14	66	27	137	3	3	.255/.299/.389	.266	.313	-1.5	RF 0, CF 0	1.3

Breakout: 0%   Improve: 22%   Collapse: 8%   Attrition: 10%   MLB: 83%   Comparables: Dave Winfield, Andre Dawson, Roberto Clemente

Byrd continued to be, against all odds, interesting. His mid-30s, post-PED resurgence is like a straight batting practice fastball in Amaro's wheelhouse, and the first year of his two-year deal with the Phillies went so well that the GM is probably praying that the third year (at the standard $8M AAV that PED suspendees get these days) vests. This is a guy who, two years ago, needed a strong winter ball showing just to get a spring invite. Byrd is selling out for power these days, with a sharp rise in his fly-ball rate and a near-doubling of the strikeout rate he had back when he was an All-Star with the Cubs. At this point he's basically late-career Reggie Sanders, but with a multi-year contract.

Dylan Cozens OF

Born: 5/31/94   Age: 21   Bats: L   Throws: L   Height: 6' 6"   Weight: 235

YEAR	TEAM	LVL	AGE	PA	R	2B	3B	HR	RBI	BB	K	SB	CS	AVG/OBP/SLG	TAv	BABIP	BRR	FRAA	WARP
2013	WPT	A-	19	277	50	19	2	9	35	28	64	11	6	.265/.343/.469	.305	.322	1.9	RF(60): 0.8	2.1
2014	LWD	A	20	556	69	25	6	16	62	40	147	23	7	.248/.303/.415	.250	.314	-1.5	RF(110): -2.7, LF(8): 0.4	-0.2
2015	PHI	MLB	21	250	24	9	1	6	24	13	82	5	2	.196/.238/.318	.211	.268	0.3	RF -1, LF 0	-0.9

Breakout: 0%   Improve: 0%   Collapse: 0%   Attrition: 0%   MLB: 0%   Comparables: Jamie Romak, Carlos Gonzalez, Steven Moya

The size alone is enough to intrigue, but it might also be his undoing; those long arms, leveraged well by Cozens' nice lofty swing, will produce plenty of home runs and plenty of holes. He struck out once a game in his first full-season assignment, oscillating like so: A .603 OPS, 28 percent strikeout rate and two homers in June; and .892 OPS, 20 percent strikeout rate and five bombs in July. Neat-o thing: When he was in high school, he hit a home run that a local engineer estimated traveled as far as 520 feet.

J.P. Crawford SS

Born: 1/11/95   Age: 20   Bats: L   Throws: R   Height: 6' 2"   Weight: 180

YEAR	TEAM	LVL	AGE	PA	R	2B	3B	HR	RBI	BB	K	SB	CS	AVG/OBP/SLG	TAv	BABIP	BRR	FRAA	WARP
2013	LWD	A	18	60	10	1	0	0	2	7	10	2	1	.208/.300/.226	.220	.256	-0.3	SS(14): 0.1	0.1
2014	LWD	A	19	267	37	16	0	3	19	37	37	14	7	.295/.398/.405	.291	.342	1.2	SS(59): 2.3	2.3
2014	CLR	A+	19	271	32	7	0	8	29	28	37	10	7	.275/.352/.407	.284	.292	-3.0	SS(62): 0.5	1.6
2015	PHI	MLB	20	250	28	9	0	4	19	21	55	6	4	.226/.295/.319	.241	.278	-0.4	SS 1	0.6

Breakout: 0%   Improve: 0%   Collapse: 0%   Attrition: 0%   MLB: 0%   Comparables: Jurickson Profar, Brad Harman, Ruben Tejada

The Phillies' front office gets picked on a lot, which means it doesn't always get the credit it deserves for individual moves. Crawford, the 16th overall pick in 2013, has a shot to go down as the best value-for-the-spot pick in that year's first round. Assuming they don't trade him for some 30-something former star—now, really, was that dig necessary?—the Phillies have their long-term replacement for Jimmy Rollins lined up and cost-controlled. Crawford unquestionably has the leather for short, but some questions remain about how his bat holds up at higher levels; his proponents forecast added bulk, while detractors see a contact-oriented swing and little strength. It's all a bit rough still, so don't get too excited by Rollins being traded. Crawford will need more time than that.

Kelly Dugan OF

Born: 9/18/90   Age: 24   Bats: L   Throws: R   Height: 6' 3"   Weight: 215

YEAR	TEAM	LVL	AGE	PA	R	2B	3B	HR	RBI	BB	K	SB	CS	AVG/OBP/SLG	TAv	BABIP	BRR	FRAA	WARP
2012	LWD	A	21	498	83	33	2	12	60	48	122	5	1	.300/.387/.470	.308	.391	-0.1	RF(79): 3.5, 1B(25): -3.5	3.0
2013	CLR	A+	22	248	37	12	3	10	36	24	60	1	3	.318/.401/.539	.334	.401	-0.8	RF(50): 5.6	3.1
2013	REA	AA	22	226	25	12	1	10	23	5	54	0	1	.264/.299/.472	.273	.309	-0.8	RF(28): 0.7, LF(24): 3.7	1.2
2014	REA	AA	23	290	43	18	1	5	34	28	56	1	0	.296/.383/.435	.286	.363	-0.1	RF(53): -0.2, LF(11): 0.5	1.1
2015	PHI	MLB	24	250	23	11	1	6	27	13	72	0	0	.238/.292/.369	.251	.315	-0.4	RF 1, LF 1	0.4

Breakout: 1%   Improve: 9%   Collapse: 3%   Attrition: 11%   MLB: 20%   Comparables: Casper Wells, Steven Souza, John Bowker

When Dugan plays, he rakes. When Dugan plays, he breaks. He has averaged just 70 games per season since he was drafted six years ago, and has thus never leaped a league ahead of his age cohort. That takes some of the shine off of his .819 OPS in 1,737 PA, but his hit and power tools both have league-average potential. He should appear with the big-league club at some point this season, but with only 132 games in the high minors he'll benefit from a few more reps. The problem with reps, of course, is how many injuries one can suffer per rep.

Maikel Franco   3B

Born: 8/26/92   Age: 22   Bats: R   Throws: R   Height: 6' 1"   Weight: 180

YEAR	TEAM	LVL	AGE	PA	R	2B	3B	HR	RBI	BB	K	SB	CS	AVG/OBP/SLG	TAv	BABIP	BRR	FRAA	WARP
2012	LWD	A	19	554	70	32	3	14	84	38	80	3	1	.280/.336/.439	.274	.306	-0.2	3B(122): -13.5	1.1
2013	CLR	A+	20	289	42	23	1	16	52	20	39	0	0	.299/.349/.576	.315	.297	-0.5	3B(64): -6.1	2.2
2013	REA	AA	20	292	47	13	2	15	51	10	31	1	2	.339/.363/.563	.336	.338	0.9	3B(59): 3.4, 1B(8): -0.3	3.7
2014	LEH	AAA	21	556	64	33	4	16	78	30	81	3	1	.257/.299/.428	.249	.276	2.4	3B(107): -3.8, 1B(23): 0.6	0.9
2014	PHI	MLB	21	58	5	2	0	0	5	1	13	0	0	.179/.190/.214	.147	.227	0.5	3B(12): 0.7, 1B(5): 0.2	-0.3
2015	PHI	MLB	22	250	24	12	1	8	31	8	47	0	0	.248/.273/.403	.257	.275	-0.4	3B -2, 1B 0	0.3

Breakout: 4%   Improve: 27%   Collapse: 6%   Attrition: 26%   MLB: 50%   Comparables: Josh Vitters, Brandon Laird, Lonnie Chisenhall

Dig up a time capsule from a year ago, and you'll find such mysteries of the past as an archaic third-generation Amazon Kindle (oooooh) and a ticket for the old-timey movie *Jack Ryan: Shadow Recruit* (ahhhhhh) and an article written by somebody suggesting Maikel Franco might actually break camp with the Phillies' third base job (huh?). Instead, the 21-year-old spent the bulk of his year in Triple-A as the youngest full-time hitter in the league, which certainly makes his production there more impressive but also reinforces how unrealistic it was to expect him in Philadelphia last April. (For that matter, he's no lock to start this year in Philadelphia, either.) Franco is still one of the brightest prospects in an admittedly thin system; the bat is lightning quick and thunder loud, though his guess-and-rip approach can look ugly, too. He isn't going to be an instant savior for the Phillies, but he will give fans something more exciting to watch than this old copy of *Jack Ryan: Shadow Recruit* .

Freddy Galvis   3B

Born: 11/14/89   Age: 25   Bats: B   Throws: R   Height: 5' 10"   Weight: 185

YEAR	TEAM	LVL	AGE	PA	R	2B	3B	HR	RBI	BB	K	SB	CS	AVG/OBP/SLG	TAv	BABIP	BRR	FRAA	WARP
2012	PHI	MLB	22	200	14	15	1	3	24	7	29	0	0	.226/.254/.363	.210	.253	0.7	2B(55): 3.3, SS(5): 0.7	-0.2
2013	LEH	AAA	23	266	26	14	2	3	25	11	51	3	1	.245/.274/.357	.221	.290	0.4	SS(56): -5.7, 2B(3): -0.3	-0.3
2013	PHI	MLB	23	222	13	5	4	6	19	13	45	1	0	.234/.283/.385	.238	.273	1.0	2B(23): 0.1, 3B(16): 0.6	0.4
2014	CLR	A+	24	20	4	0	2	1	3	0	2	0	0	.200/.200/.550	.248	.176	0.2	SS(2): 0.1, 2B(2): 0.1	0.1
2014	LEH	AAA	24	149	22	14	1	3	15	11	25	1	1	.267/.322/.452	.263	.308	1.1	SS(30): -2.0, 2B(3): 0.6	0.7
2014	PHI	MLB	24	128	14	3	1	4	12	8	30	1	0	.176/.227/.319	.215	.198	-0.4	SS(25): 1.9, 3B(11): -0.0	-0.1
2015	PHI	MLB	25	250	26	11	2	5	23	11	49	1	0	.230/.267/.362	.235	.262	0.3	SS 1, 2B 1	0.6

Breakout: 3%   Improve: 53%   Collapse: 12%   Attrition: 25%   MLB: 91%   Comparables: Ronny Cedeno, Jose Castillo, Stephen Drew

We try to avoid rinse-n-repeat comments in this book; after 162 games there's always something new to say, good or bad, about every player. Except for one Freddy Galvis. Same as always: He can field. He can't hit. But he can field. That makes him the 26th guy on a roster, wearing out a path between Lehigh Valley and Philadelphia. At 25, another player could reasonably add to his offense, but not Freddy Galvis, no sir, not Freddy Galvis. One comment for the 2016 Annual done.

Deivi Grullon   C

Born: 2/17/96   Age: 19   Bats: R   Throws: R   Height: 6' 1"   Weight: 180

YEAR	TEAM	LVL	AGE	PA	R	2B	3B	HR	RBI	BB	K	SB	CS	AVG/OBP/SLG	TAv	BABIP	BRR	FRAA	WARP
2014	LWD	A	18	81	9	5	0	1	7	3	13	0	0	.237/.275/.342	.221	.274	0.1	C(24): 0.1	0.0
2014	WPT	A-	18	199	14	9	1	0	18	9	39	3	0	.225/.268/.283	.213	.284	-2.1	C(53): 0.2	-0.4
2015	PHI	MLB	19	250	17	9	1	2	18	7	67	0	0	.198/.226/.263	.190	.263	-0.4	C 0	-0.9

Breakout: 0%   Improve: 0%   Collapse: 0%   Attrition: 0%   MLB: 0%   Comparables: Tomas Telis, Wilson Ramos, Francisco Pena

The Phillies depth, as it is, concentrates mostly behind the dish: Here begins a run of four Phillies farm catchers in a five-comment span. Grullon has an elite arm and plus receiving skills, which will push him faster than his bat would otherwise dictate; actually, with his slash line to date anybody but a catcher with an elite arm and plus receiving skills would be worried about his job, not hanging out in the middle of his team's Top 10 Prospects rankings. The 2012 J2 product ($575,000) will aim for an Austin Hedges-like love affair with the prospect community, but those of you who draft your keeper leagues off those lists should be careful.

Ryan Howard   1B

Born: 11/19/79   Age: 35   Bats: L   Throws: L   Height: 6' 4"   Weight: 250

YEAR	TEAM	LVL	AGE	PA	R	2B	3B	HR	RBI	BB	K	SB	CS	AVG/OBP/SLG	TAv	BABIP	BRR	FRAA	WARP
2012	PHI	MLB	32	292	28	11	0	14	56	25	99	0	0	.219/.295/.423	.246	.287	-4.1	1B(67): -3.8	-0.9
2013	PHI	MLB	33	317	34	20	2	11	43	23	95	0	0	.266/.319/.465	.278	.349	-1.6	1B(76): -1.9	0.6
2014	PHI	MLB	34	648	65	18	1	23	95	67	190	0	0	.223/.310/.380	.261	.288	-1.5	1B(141): -6.2	-0.3
2015	PHI	MLB	35	543	62	20	1	21	71	50	158	0	0	.235/.312/.413	.274	.300	-2.5	1B -4	0.6

Breakout: 0%   Improve: 21%   Collapse: 9%   Attrition: 14%   MLB: 94%   Comparables: Carlos Pena, Luke Scott, Ken Phelps

Fantasy players might try to convince you that Howard wasn't *that* bad in 2014, but once you look beyond his homers and RBIs, it all falls apart. Wait: His 29 percent strikeout rate was also a three-year best, but *now* it all falls apart.

He posted a sub-.400 SLG for the first time, with a career-worst .156 ISO. The "why?" behind this decline is the tricky part. There is nothing to suggest that he deserved such a miserable fate. His batted-ball profile held steady, he stayed healthy and he even hit lefties quite well for the first time in five years. It's hard to paint a rosy outlook going forward, but with respect to his 2014, Howard suffered through some bad luck—though his first injury-free season since 2011 was a bit of good.

Note that he is still, delightfully, a very good hitter with runners on base, with a .260/.359/.449 line in the roughly half of his plate appearances when the defense can't shift, or shift as much. His OPS is more than 100 points better in nearly 3,000 such plate appearances in his career, so even if the RBI totals are misleading, the stories you've heard are only partial lies.

Tommy Joseph C

Born: 7/16/91   Age: 23   Bats: R   Throws: R   Height: 6' 1"   Weight: 225

YEAR	TEAM	LVL	AGE	PA	R	2B	3B	HR	RBI	BB	K	SB	CS	AVG/OBP/SLG	TAv	BABIP	BRR	FRAA	WARP
2012	REA	AA	20	114	12	8	0	3	10	9	32	0	1	.250/.327/.420	.255	.333	-0.4	C(24): -0.6, 1B(2): -0.1	0.3
2012	RIC	AA	20	335	32	16	0	8	38	25	64	0	3	.260/.313/.391	.260	.300	-2.2	C(50): -0.2, 1B(14): -0.6	1.0
2013	CLR	A+	21	42	0	2	0	0	1	0	13	0	0	.095/.095/.143	.095	.138	-0.5	C(8): -0.1	-0.6
2013	LEH	AAA	21	72	6	1	0	3	14	4	15	0	1	.209/.264/.358	.209	.224	-1.2	C(21): -0.6	-0.3
2014	REA	AA	22	87	8	4	1	5	19	5	13	0	0	.282/.345/.551	.303	.279	-0.3	C(21): 0.1	0.6
2015	PHI	MLB	23	250	22	10	0	6	27	12	63	0	0	.223/.268/.355	.237	.274	-0.6	C -1, 1B -0	0.2

Breakout: 8%   Improve: 15%   Collapse: 3%   Attrition: 17%   MLB: 23%   Comparables: Jonathan Lucroy, Josh Donaldson, Miguel Montero

Another lost season has cost Joseph dearly, though when we're talking about recurring concussions there are more serious issues at hand. Once ahead of schedule as a 21-year-old with some Triple-A time under his belt, Joseph has now been limited to just 63 games over the past two years. A head injury ended his 2013 season—his third concussion, at least, he said—and a "possible concussion" knocked him foggy in April 2014. He missed a week, then returned for one before a wrist injury essentially ended his season. In that week between injuries he was catching, but a position switch seems prudent. While he has the power to carry first base, there is a substantial roadblock there—Ryan Howard's five-year, $125 million contract extension *hasn't even started yet*. (Joke.) For now, getting healthy is Joseph's biggest concern.

Andrew Knapp C

Born: 11/9/91   Age: 23   Bats: B   Throws: R   Height: 6' 1"   Weight: 190

YEAR	TEAM	LVL	AGE	PA	R	2B	3B	HR	RBI	BB	K	SB	CS	AVG/OBP/SLG	TAv	BABIP	BRR	FRAA	WARP
2013	WPT	A-	21	247	30	20	0	4	23	22	57	7	5	.253/.340/.401	.278	.325	-3.4	C(21): -0.3	0.6
2014	LWD	A	22	314	39	19	4	5	25	27	71	3	3	.290/.354/.438	.287	.368	1.0	C(42): -1.1	1.5
2014	CLR	A+	22	90	7	1	0	1	7	5	26	1	0	.157/.222/.205	.163	.214	-1.1		-1.0
2015	PHI	MLB	23	250	18	9	1	3	21	13	77	0	0	.197/.246/.283	.205	.276	-0.4	C -1	-0.9

Breakout: 0%   Improve: 0%   Collapse: 0%   Attrition: 0%   MLB: 0%   Comparables: Andrew Brown, Tyler Moore, Darin Ruf

Knapp started the season in High-A—a two-level jump because of organizational needs—and nailed the role of overmatched recent draftee getting buried in his first full-season assignment. Thankfully, June brought a demotion (strange words, we know), and he added 150 points to his BABIP against slightly lesser competition. He'll need to hit much, much better when he returns to Clearwater this year, as he's a bat-first backstop who needs to show power from both sides to keep his shine. He might also want to shave the stiff mustache he was rocking, unless he aspires to be a bullpen coach from the early 1990s.

Gabriel Lino C

Born: 5/17/93   Age: 22   Bats: R   Throws: R   Height: 6' 3"   Weight: 200

YEAR	TEAM	LVL	AGE	PA	R	2B	3B	HR	RBI	BB	K	SB	CS	AVG/OBP/SLG	TAv	BABIP	BRR	FRAA	WARP
2012	DEL	A	19	227	28	13	0	4	18	16	64	1	1	.218/.282/.340	.221	.293	0.8	C(51): -0.2	-0.3
2012	LWD	A	19	148	16	10	0	3	14	14	33	0	2	.227/.311/.371	.239	.281	0.7	C(37): -0.9	0.4
2013	LWD	A	20	37	4	3	1	0	9	1	13	0	1	.242/.297/.394	.266	.381	0.0	C(10): -0.0	0.3
2013	WPT	A-	20	167	14	6	0	4	23	10	47	2	1	.256/.305/.372	.254	.343	-1.1	C(39): 1.1, 1B(5): -0.1	1.0
2014	LWD	A	21	60	7	5	0	1	6	9	23	0	0	.180/.300/.340	.237	.296	0.1	C(16): -0.3	0.1
2014	CLR	A+	21	261	26	7	0	4	28	18	68	0	3	.223/.281/.303	.213	.292	-0.3	C(70): 0.4, 1B(1): 0.1	0.0
2015	PHI	MLB	22	250	18	9	0	4	20	12	85	0	0	.185/.228/.273	.194	.266	-0.6	C -0, 1B 0	-0.8

Breakout: 0%   Improve: 0%   Collapse: 0%   Attrition: 0%   MLB: 0%   Comparables: Anthony Recker, Steven Lerud, Ali Solis

Is Jose Molina the new Jamie Moyer? The guy to whom we comp disappointing A-Ballers, on the off chance that *this* unathletic, uninspiring guy is just as Mensa-qualified as the one unathletic, uninspiring guy who actually made it? Lino has the defense to be a major leaguer, but the bat falls somewhere around backup upside. The minors are littered with defense-only backstops who post sub-.600 OPSes in A-Ball. Jose Molina, with career earnings approaching $18 million, was one of them, and only one of them.

Cameron Perkins OF

Born: 9/27/90   Age: 24   Bats: R   Throws: R   Height: 6' 5"   Weight: 195

YEAR	TEAM	LVL	AGE	PA	R	2B	3B	HR	RBI	BB	K	SB	CS	AVG/OBP/SLG	TAv	BABIP	BRR	FRAA	WARP
2012	WPT	A-	21	293	31	23	1	1	38	14	41	5	5	.304/.352/.407	.285	.352	0.3	1B(23): 1.8, 3B(11): 0.5	1.6
2013	CLR	A+	22	424	54	30	5	6	53	25	57	4	5	.295/.346/.444	.270	.330	-1.9	RF(69): -2.1, LF(20): -1.1	1.9
2014	REA	AA	23	222	25	19	1	3	34	20	30	5	3	.342/.408/.495	.311	.393	0.0	LF(22): 0.5, RF(20): -1.9	1.8
2014	LEH	AAA	23	272	17	9	3	2	17	13	49	3	3	.216/.259/.298	.197	.260	-0.6	LF(54): 6.1, RF(19): -0.2	-0.3
2015	PHI	MLB	24	250	20	12	1	2	22	10	53	2	2	.237/.274/.330	.231	.290	-0.4	RF -1, LF 2	-0.2

Breakout: 0%   Improve: 0%   Collapse: 0%   Attrition: 0%   MLB: 0%   Comparables: Kevin Pillar, Colin Curtis, Andre Ethier

After hitting well at every stop since he was drafted in the sixth round in 2012, Perkins finally hit a bump when he reached Triple-A. He carried a strikeout-to-walk ratio of just over two through Double-A, but it shot up to almost four at Lehigh Valley. With doubles power and a high-contact approach, Perkins doesn't profile well in the four corners, but he'll get a chance to launch a career as a bench outfielder sometime this year.

Roman Quinn OF

Born: 5/14/93   Age: 22   Bats: B   Throws: R   Height: 5' 10"   Weight: 170

YEAR	TEAM	LVL	AGE	PA	R	2B	3B	HR	RBI	BB	K	SB	CS	AVG/OBP/SLG	TAv	BABIP	BRR	FRAA	WARP
2012	WPT	A-	19	309	56	9	11	1	23	28	61	30	6	.281/.370/.408	.300	.357	7.1	SS(66): -9.3	2.1
2013	LWD	A	20	298	37	7	3	5	21	27	64	32	8	.238/.323/.346	.263	.297	0.1	SS(65): -14.3	-0.6
2014	CLR	A+	21	382	51	10	3	7	36	36	80	32	12	.257/.343/.370	.259	.316	3.0	CF(69): 0.7, SS(17): -2.5	1.4
2015	PHI	MLB	22	250	31	7	2	3	16	16	69	15	5	.207/.271/.298	.220	.273	1.3	SS -6, CF 0	-0.7

Breakout: 0%   Improve: 0%   Collapse: 0%   Attrition: 0%   MLB: 0%   Comparables: Dexter Fowler, Ezequiel Carrera, Reymond Fuentes

The easy comparison is to Ben Revere, but that's lazy; beyond superspeed and body type, there's not much there. Quinn, like you, has more power than Revere, but doesn't make as much contact, and is therefore more likely to put up empty .260s than empty .305s. He makes the exciting play but is, in the dull stretches that make up life, nothing special. His reads aren't great on the bases. At his age, there is time for development, but it would take some unforeseen evolution to turn him into the sort of valuable player who future speedsters are lazily compared to.

Ben Revere   CF

Born: 5/3/88   Age: 27   Bats: L   Throws: R   Height: 5' 9"   Weight: 165

YEAR	TEAM	LVL	AGE	PA	R	2B	3B	HR	RBI	BB	K	SB	CS	AVG/OBP/SLG	TAv	BABIP	BRR	FRAA	WARP
2012	ROC	AAA	24	101	9	1	0	0	6	4	6	6	2	.330/.360/.340	.256	.348	1.6	CF(12): 0.6, LF(6): 0.4	0.5
2012	MIN	MLB	24	553	70	13	6	0	32	29	54	40	9	.294/.333/.342	.242	.325	9.6	RF(84): 2.7, CF(39): -1.0	1.5
2013	PHI	MLB	25	336	37	9	3	0	17	16	36	22	8	.305/.338/.352	.250	.344	1.5	CF(87): 6.5	1.5
2014	PHI	MLB	26	626	71	13	7	2	28	13	49	49	8	.306/.325/.361	.261	.330	6.5	CF(141): -2.7	2.1
2015	PHI	MLB	27	530	63	13	5	1	32	23	56	36	8	.280/.315/.333	.252	.309	4.6	CF 1, RF 0	1.6

Breakout: 12%   Improve: 47%   Collapse: 3%   Attrition: 13%   MLB: 96%   Comparables: Jacoby Ellsbury, Willy Taveras, Coco Crisp

The easy comparison is to Roman Quinn, but that's just lazy. It isn't wrong to say that Revere had a massive power surge in 2014, in the same way that Sochi had a massive surge in Olympics hostings, and that Princess Leonore, Duchess of Gotland, had a massive surge in instances of being born. Revere is a contact machine who relies on his incredible speed for every bit of his value, whether as a hitter or while patrolling center field. There are no tricks, no hidden value; if Revere can run, he is a sure bet to produce a couple wins. He had offseason ankle surgery in October, but it's not expected to be any sort of issue going forward.

Darin Ruf   PH

Born: 7/28/86   Age: 28   Bats: R   Throws: R   Height: 6' 3"   Weight: 240

YEAR	TEAM	LVL	AGE	PA	R	2B	3B	HR	RBI	BB	K	SB	CS	AVG/OBP/SLG	TAv	BABIP	BRR	FRAA	WARP
2012	REA	AA	25	584	93	32	1	38	104	65	102	2	0	.317/.408/.620	.345	.325	-2.2	1B(107): -3.4, LF(29): -1.5	5.8
2012	PHI	MLB	25	37	4	2	1	3	10	2	12	0	0	.333/.351/.727	.368	.400	-0.2	LF(6): -0.4, 1B(3): 0.1	0.4
2013	LEH	AAA	26	350	44	22	0	7	46	36	88	1	2	.266/.343/.407	.264	.343	-0.5	LF(60): -2.1, 1B(19): -0.3	0.7
2013	PHI	MLB	26	293	36	11	0	14	30	33	91	0	0	.247/.348/.458	.279	.324	0.7	1B(36): 0.9, RF(29): -1.7	0.8
2014	LEH	AAA	27	91	6	6	0	1	10	6	16	1	0	.265/.308/.373	.254	.309	-1.1	LF(14): -0.5, 1B(8): 0.1	0.0
2014	PHI	MLB	27	117	13	8	0	3	8	8	32	0	0	.235/.310/.402	.271	.304	0.5	1B(20): 0.5, LF(15): -0.3	0.4
2015	PHI	MLB	28	250	29	11	0	10	34	21	67	0	0	.248/.322/.435	.285	.303	0.3	1B 0, LF -1	0.9

Breakout: 6%   Improve: 30%   Collapse: 15%   Attrition: 20%   MLB: 68%   Comparables: Mike Carp, Brandon Moss, John Bowker

Were you one of those people who got really excited about Ruf's 38 homers in 2012? Do you now realize your error? Have you learned anything? Do you promise not to do it again? Have you read the Andy Wilkins comment in the White Sox chapter yet? Ruf strained his oblique and broke his wrist in his age-27 season, moving him one year further from his Double-A "breakout." When healthy he mashed lefties and darned near went hitless against righties, though all samples good or bad come with size-related caveats. He might still carve out a role as the short side of a platoon with Ryan Howard or Domonic Brown (or their equivalents on another team), but such chances are limited at his end of the defensive spectrum.

Carlos Ruiz   C

Born: 1/22/79   Age: 36   Bats: R   Throws: R   Height: 5' 10"   Weight: 205

YEAR	TEAM	LVL	AGE	PA	R	2B	3B	HR	RBI	BB	K	SB	CS	AVG/OBP/SLG	TAv	BABIP	BRR	FRAA	WARP
2012	PHI	MLB	33	421	56	32	0	16	68	29	50	4	0	.325/.394/.540	.324	.339	-1.9	C(106): 2.6	5.1
2013	PHI	MLB	34	341	30	16	0	5	37	18	39	1	0	.268/.320/.368	.246	.291	4.0	C(86): 0.7	1.6
2014	PHI	MLB	35	445	43	25	1	6	31	46	60	4	2	.252/.347/.370	.282	.281	-4.1	C(109): 4.1	2.9
2015	PHI	MLB	36	403	41	21	0	6	41	34	53	3	1	.267/.344/.378	.278	.295	-0.7	C 2	2.5

Breakout: 0%   Improve: 25%   Collapse: 6%   Attrition: 10%   MLB: 84%   Comparables: Ramon Hernandez, Mike Lieberthal, Todd Helton

In the past five years:
Carlos Ruiz has a 116 OPS+ in 569 games, with 9 fielding runs above average and 17.2 WARP
Yadier Molina has a 116 OPS+ in 659 games, with 2 fielding runs above average and 18.2 WARP
But Molina has added 39 runs with his pitch-framing, according to BP's metrics. Ruiz has *given away* 42 runs. And that right there is the difference between a superstar and a very good, slightly underrated, ultimately replaceable player.

Cord Sandberg   OF

Born: 1/2/95   Age: 20   Bats: L   Throws: L   Height: 6' 3"   Weight: 215

YEAR	TEAM	LVL	AGE	PA	R	2B	3B	HR	RBI	BB	K	SB	CS	AVG/OBP/SLG	TAv	BABIP	BRR	FRAA	WARP
2014	WPT	A-	19	284	33	5	3	6	24	11	56	8	3	.235/.267/.345	.234	.276	0.6	RF(51): 7.4, LF(9): -0.7	0.4
2015	PHI	MLB	20	250	22	7	1	3	17	10	74	2	1	.189/.225/.269	.192	.255	-0.2	RF 3, LF 1	-0.7

Breakout: 0%   Improve: 0%   Collapse: 0%   Attrition: 0%   MLB: 0%   Comparables: Lorenzo Cain, Aaron Cunningham, Rymer Liriano

Here's a weird one: In Sandberg, the Phillies have a remarkably athletic, and remarkably raw, outfield prospect. These are as rare in the Phillies ecosystem as pigeons in New York, though Sandberg is a bit more colorful than the rest: A former football player who threw 35 touchdowns and one interception in his senior year, he could've played quarterback in the SEC at Mississippi State. Sandberg has the arm for any outfield position. The bat is a project, but there's no pressure on him yet. If he's traded at age 22 for David DeJesus, watch out.

Grady Sizemore   LF

Born: 8/2/82   Age: 32   Bats: L   Throws: L   Height: 6' 2"   Weight: 200

YEAR	TEAM	LVL	AGE	PA	R	2B	3B	HR	RBI	BB	K	SB	CS	AVG/OBP/SLG	TAv	BABIP	BRR	FRAA	WARP
2014	BOS	MLB	31	205	14	10	2	2	15	19	41	5	0	.216/.288/.324	.230	.266	-0.9	LF(24): 0.8, CF(18): 0.7	-0.2
2014	LEH	AAA	31	51	5	1	0	1	2	5	7	0	0	.283/.353/.370	.267	.316	0.8	CF(5): -0.7, LF(3): -0.1	0.1
2014	PHI	MLB	31	176	21	9	2	3	12	14	35	1	1	.253/.313/.389	.270	.306	2.2	LF(28): 0.6, RF(12): -1.6	0.5
2015	PHI	MLB	32	290	27	13	2	5	28	21	71	3	1	.224/.286/.343	.243	.285	0.4	LF 1, RF -3	-0.1

Breakout: 4%   Improve: 33%   Collapse: 12%   Attrition: 17%   MLB: 89%   Comparables: Emil Brown, Dusty Baker, Ricky Ledee

The Phillies' recent history of favoring veterans makes the re-signing of Sizemore @analyticsplant fodder, but the move is sound enough. It's a one-year deal at just $2 million, and his presence isn't blocking any up-and-comers. Sizemore is coming off a terrible season that, nonetheless, has to be considered a success simply due to the fact that he suited up 112 times, a six-year high. He hits from the left side with a pretty good eye and he can play center field; put a little loft back in his swing and he's the sort of fourth outfielder who you'll happily pay $1 million to. As for the second million—well, okay, maybe that's fair game.

Carlos Tocci   OF
Born: 8/23/95   Age: 19   Bats: R   Throws: R   Height: 6' 2"   Weight: 160

YEAR	TEAM	LVL	AGE	PA	R	2B	3B	HR	RBI	BB	K	SB	CS	AVG/OBP/SLG	TAv	BABIP	BRR	FRAA	WARP
2013	LWD	A	17	459	40	17	0	0	26	22	77	6	7	.209/.261/.249	.206	.253	-0.3	CF(116): 16.4	0.5
2014	LWD	A	18	538	59	18	8	2	30	25	96	10	11	.242/.297/.324	.241	.297	1.1	CF(124): -1.9	0.5
2015	PHI	MLB	19	250	19	8	1	1	14	6	60	2	2	.197/.225/.250	.186	.253	-0.5	CF 3, LF 0	-0.9

Breakout: 0%   Improve: 0%   Collapse: 0%   Attrition: 0%   MLB: 0%   Comparables: *Reymond Fuentes, Michael Brantley, Austin Jackson*

The time to panic isn't nearly here, but Tocci has been standing still for the past two years, a problem for a player who has such a wide gap between his present skills and the promise of his tools. (On the other hand, standing still beats trying to steal second, as you can see from his success rates up there.) His plus-plus speed, solid contact abilities, baseball instincts and clean swing make for a wonderful prospect profile, but he just doesn't have the strength to handle pro pitching yet. On the positive side, he is still quite young for his level; even repeating, he was the Sally League's third-youngest hitter in 2014, and one of just five teenagers to log more than 500 plate appearances there.

Jiandido Tromp   OF
Born: 9/27/93   Age: 21   Bats: R   Throws: R   Height: 5' 11"   Weight: 175

YEAR	TEAM	LVL	AGE	PA	R	2B	3B	HR	RBI	BB	K	SB	CS	AVG/OBP/SLG	TAv	BABIP	BRR	FRAA	WARP
2012	WPT	A-	18	54	8	3	0	0	5	2	15	3	0	.208/.245/.271	.216	.286	1.1	CF(8): 0.5, RF(4): -0.4	0.0
2013	LWD	A	19	44	2	1	2	0	3	2	16	0	1	.150/.227/.275	.192	.250	-0.1	RF(8): 0.3, CF(4): -0.4	-0.2
2013	WPT	A-	19	117	9	9	1	1	8	8	25	6	2	.299/.353/.430	.299	.383	0.8	CF(17): 1.5, LF(10): 0.3	1.1
2014	LWD	A	20	95	11	4	1	1	9	6	30	3	0	.224/.287/.329	.239	.327	1.7	LF(15): 0.4, RF(5): 0.1	0.5
2014	WPT	A-	20	288	39	14	2	14	33	19	72	16	5	.266/.325/.498	.303	.316	1.5	CF(32): 3.0, LF(25): -0.2	2.4
2015	PHI	MLB	21	250	25	8	1	5	19	10	87	4	2	.188/.228/.290	.199	.270	0.2	CF 2, LF -0	-0.7

Breakout: 0%   Improve: 0%   Collapse: 0%   Attrition: 0%   MLB: 0%   Comparables: *Jeremy Moore, Alex Presley, Tyler Colvin*

Tromp is more than a good name. After hitting Low-A pitchers hard in 2013, he earned a brief, ugly finish at Class-A Lakewood. After a brief, ugly start at Class-A Lakewood in 2014, he went back to hitting Low-A pitchers hard. That palindrome isn't enough to say he can't hang at higher levels, but now that he's 21 it becomes non-optional: He *has* to hit higher or fall behind on the prospect track. He has displayed enough of all five tools to suggest it could come together in a moderately big way, though he doesn't have the size of his more athletic outfield competition in the system. But, like we said, he's more than a good name. He's a great name.

Chase Utley   2B
Born: 12/17/78   Age: 36   Bats: L   Throws: R   Height: 6' 1"   Weight: 200

YEAR	TEAM	LVL	AGE	PA	R	2B	3B	HR	RBI	BB	K	SB	CS	AVG/OBP/SLG	TAv	BABIP	BRR	FRAA	WARP
2012	CLR	A+	33	38	3	0	0	1	5	3	5	1	0	.156/.263/.250	.227	.148	0.1	2B(4): 0.3	0.0
2012	PHI	MLB	33	362	48	15	2	11	45	43	43	11	1	.256/.365/.429	.286	.261	2.9	2B(81): 4.1	2.7
2013	PHI	MLB	34	531	73	25	6	18	69	45	79	8	3	.284/.348/.475	.292	.305	1.6	2B(125): 2.6	3.4
2014	PHI	MLB	35	664	74	36	6	11	78	53	85	10	1	.270/.339/.407	.288	.295	2.8	2B(147): 6.9, 1B(1): -0.0	4.5
2015	PHI	MLB	36	598	65	25	4	13	65	53	84	11	2	.253/.333/.390	.276	.275	2.2	2B 7, 1B -0	4.0

Breakout: 0%   Improve: 27%   Collapse: 4%   Attrition: 7%   MLB: 83%   Comparables: *Carlos Guillen, Ray Durham, Lou Whitaker*

He's still pretty good, he's still pretty old, he's still pretty underrated and he's still a pretty significant injury risk, no matter what his clean 2014 health log tries to tell you. The fact that he and Ryan Howard combined for 308 games in 2014 is nothing short of a miracle, because a year or two ago you might not have bet on either mid-30s veteran to gather 308 plate appearances in a given year. He and Howard combined to produce 4.2 WARP.

Jesmuel Valentin   2B
Born: 5/12/94   Age: 21   Bats: B   Throws: R   Height: 5' 9"   Weight: 180

YEAR	TEAM	LVL	AGE	PA	R	2B	3B	HR	RBI	BB	K	SB	CS	AVG/OBP/SLG	TAv	BABIP	BRR	FRAA	WARP
2013	GRL	A	19	122	12	6	1	0	5	16	28	4	3	.212/.325/.293	.248	.292	-0.2	SS(17): -2.6, 2B(16): -0.3	-0.1
2014	GRL	A	20	462	73	22	9	7	47	38	72	24	7	.280/.349/.430	.297	.323	7.4	2B(105): 4.4, 3B(1): -0.0	4.4
2014	CLR	A+	20	49	8	2	0	0	0	3	6	1	1	.205/.255/.250	.163	.237	0.0	2B(12): -0.1	-0.6
2015	PHI	MLB	21	250	25	9	1	2	16	16	59	6	3	.206/.264/.284	.213	.259	0.2	2B 0, SS -1	-0.4

Breakout: 0%   Improve: 0%   Collapse: 0%   Attrition: 0%   MLB: 0%   Comparables: *Nate Spears, Steve Lombardozzi, Josh Harrison*

Being one of the P's T B N'd L in the Roberto Hernandez deal tells you what you need to know about Jose's kid. He isn't a blue chip prospect, more like his uncle Javier than like his dad at the plate, and less like John (unrelated) than his dad with the glove. He was unimpressive in his organizational debut, but they had jumped him a level and he was nearly three years younger than league average. He's one to watch.

Pitchers

Mike Adams   RHP
Born: 7/29/78   Age: 36   Bats: R   Throws: R   Height: 6'5"   Weight: 210

YEAR	TEAM	LVL	AGE	W	L	SV	G	GS	IP	H	HR	BB	K	BB/9	K/9	GB%	BABIP	WHIP	ERA	FIP	FRA	WARP
2012	TEX	MLB	33	5	3	1	61	0	52¹	56	4	17	45	2.9	7.7	48%	.327	1.39	3.27	3.47	3.40	1.0
2013	PHI	MLB	34	1	4	0	28	0	25	23	5	11	23	4.0	8.3	54%	.269	1.36	3.96	5.22	5.45	-0.2
2014	PHI	MLB	35	2	1	0	22	0	18²	16	1	8	21	3.9	10.1	58%	.306	1.29	2.89	2.83	1.88	0.5
2015	PHI	MLB	36	2	1	1	43	0	39	32	3	11	39	2.5	9.1	45%	.298	1.09	2.84	3.22	3.08	0.7

Breakout: 21%   Improve: 36%   Collapse: 37%   Attrition: 9%   MLB: 78%   *Comparables:* *Brendan Donnelly, Brian Fuentes, J.J. Putz*

Heartbreaking: "I said I didn't want to steal money, and that's exactly what happened," Adams said in August, after his second year battling injuries. While Adams' integrity is unquestioned, he shouldn't feel too bad: 44 total innings and a better-than-average ERA aren't what the Phillies had hoped for when they signed him to a two-year, $12 million deal, but just about every team in baseball had a reliever in rehab or released earning mid-seven figures last year. No, really: Angels, Sean Burnett. A's, Jim Johnson. Astros, Jesse Crain. Blue Jays, Sergio Santos. Braves, Jonny Venters. We could probably do the whole alphabet.

It was particularly hard to see a shoulder injury weaken Adams, the best set-up man of his generation. (Reliever generations only span three years. They're baseball's fruit fly.) When he could take the mound for the Phillies he put up quality work, which has always been the story with Adams: He has seven separate DL stints in his 10 major-league seasons, three of them on the 60-man, limiting him to fewer than 60 innings in all but three seasons. But his career ERA+ is better than those of Kenley Jansen, Huston Street and Joe Nathan. His latest shoulder maladies definitely took something from us all, but he's not the thief.

Victor Arano   RHP

Born: 2/7/95   Age: 20   Bats: R   Throws: R   Height: 6'2"   Weight: 200

YEAR	TEAM	LVL	AGE	W	L	SV	G	GS	IP	H	HR	BB	K	BB/9	K/9	GB%	BABIP	WHIP	ERA	FIP	FRA	WARP
2014	GRL	A	19	4	7	3	22	15	86	88	11	20	83	2.1	8.7	45%	.309	1.26	4.08	3.92	4.75	0.9
2015	*PHI*	*MLB*	*20*	*3*	*5*	*0*	*17*	*11*	*68²*	*74*	*9*	*29*	*45*	*3.8*	*5.9*	*44%*	*.315*	*1.49*	*5.20*	*5.20*	*5.65*	*-0.8*

Breakout: 0%   Improve: 0%   Collapse: 0%   Attrition: 0%   MLB: 0%   *Comparables:* *Joe Wieland, Stolmy Pimentel, Will Smith*

Generally, beware any items sold as "the jewel of the Roberto Hernandez deal," but Arano really does have a quality cut and a little sparkle. He cracked the Dodgers' top 10 prospects a year ago with an impressive fastball-curveball combo and good arm action, and his developing changeup gave him a good three-pitch mix in his first full-season assignment. He's a long way out, but the Phillies can already feel good about this trade.

Phillippe Aumont   RHP

Born: 1/7/89   Age: 26   Bats: L   Throws: R   Height: 6'7"   Weight: 260

YEAR	TEAM	LVL	AGE	W	L	SV	G	GS	IP	H	HR	BB	K	BB/9	K/9	GB%	BABIP	WHIP	ERA	FIP	FRA	WARP
2012	LEH	AAA	23	3	1	15	41	0	44¹	34	3	34	59	6.9	12.0	57%	.304	1.53	4.26	4.01	4.97	0.0
2012	PHI	MLB	23	0	1	2	18	0	14²	10	1	9	14	5.5	8.6	76%	.244	1.30	3.68	3.27	3.02	0.2
2013	LEH	AAA	24	0	2	2	32	0	35²	29	0	38	42	9.6	10.6	47%	.326	1.88	4.04	4.55	5.36	-0.1
2013	PHI	MLB	24	1	3	0	22	0	19¹	24	0	13	19	6.1	8.8	50%	.400	1.91	4.19	3.54	3.48	0.3
2014	LEH	AAA	25	3	3	3	35	0	55	48	2	39	65	6.4	10.6	54%	.333	1.58	3.93	3.59	4.55	0.5
2014	PHI	MLB	25	0	1	0	5	0	5²	14	3	5	6	7.9	9.5	46%	.524	3.35	19.06	10.51	11.81	-0.6
2015	*PHI*	*MLB*	*26*	*2*	*1*	*0*	*47*	*0*	*55¹*	*49*	*4*	*33*	*58*	*5.5*	*9.5*	*49%*	*.327*	*1.49*	*4.46*	*4.14*	*4.85*	*-0.3*

Breakout: 28%   Improve: 37%   Collapse: 8%   Attrition: 17%   MLB: 45%   *Comparables:* *Emiliano Fruto, Javy Guerra, Tyler Johnson*

High-90s heat earns plenty of chances, but if you don't know where it's going the answer is probably "back to Triple-A." Aumont walked 3.1 batters per nine in his pro debut back in 2008, but he hasn't been below 4.1 in a season since; the *lowest* number you see in that table up there is 5.5. Throwing 98 isn't as rare as it used to be, unless you're Aumont, who mostly tops out at 96 these days. Last year we called him "an obvious 'change of scenery' candidate," and if it doesn't happen soon he'll end up with Lehigh Valley's career wild pitches record. He has already led the team in that category three years in a row, as a reliever.

Jesse Biddle   RHP

Born: 10/22/91   Age: 23   Bats: L   Throws: L   Height: 6'5"   Weight: 220

YEAR	TEAM	LVL	AGE	W	L	SV	G	GS	IP	H	HR	BB	K	BB/9	K/9	GB%	BABIP	WHIP	ERA	FIP	FRA	WARP
2012	CLR	A+	20	10	6	0	26	26	142²	129	10	54	151	3.4	9.5	41%	.308	1.28	3.22	3.43	4.31	2.3
2013	REA	AA	21	5	14	0	27	27	138¹	104	10	82	154	5.3	10.0	44%	.278	1.34	3.64	3.88	4.28	2.7
2014	CLR	A+	22	2	0	0	2	2	10	3	0	6	9	5.4	8.1	59%	.136	0.90	0.90	3.39	4.34	0.1
2014	REA	AA	22	3	10	0	16	16	82¹	78	11	44	80	4.8	8.7	44%	.291	1.48	5.03	4.93	6.09	-0.1
2015	*PHI*	*MLB*	*23*	*5*	*7*	*0*	*17*	*17*	*89²*	*82*	*9*	*47*	*79*	*4.7*	*7.9*	*41%*	*.306*	*1.44*	*4.42*	*4.59*	*4.80*	*-0.2*

Breakout: 0%   Improve: 0%   Collapse: 0%   Attrition: 0%   MLB: 0%   *Comparables:* *Casey Crosby, Chris Archer, Dan Cortes*

Bad weather, of all things, derailed Biddle's season. He got stuck in a hailstorm on his way to the park one May day, and pellets knocked out his back window, bloodied his hands and hit him in the head, giving him concussion symptoms. He dealt with headaches, and said later, "I'm miserable out there. I'm very unhappy and I don't know why." He skipped one start but allowed a 9.86 ERA in his next five before the Phillies shut him down. It is, of course, impossible to know how much it affected him, but the before and after numbers are stark:

Before: 3.18 ERA, 25 percent strikeout rate, 2.5 K:BB ratio in 56 2/3 innings

After: 6.69 ERA, 18 percent strikeout rate, 1.2 K:BB ratio in 37 2/3 innings

There is still time for the former first-rounder to get his stuff back, but for now, all the other concerns—the iffy fastball command and release point, the changeup that misses up too often—are secondary.

David Buchanan   RHP

Born: 5/11/89   Age: 26   Bats: R   Throws: R   Height: 6'3"   Weight: 200

YEAR	TEAM	LVL	AGE	W	L	SV	G	GS	IP	H	HR	BB	K	BB/9	K/9	GB%	BABIP	WHIP	ERA	FIP	FRA	WARP
2012	REA	AA	23	3	5	0	12	12	72¹	73	7	23	40	2.9	5.0	47%	.288	1.33	3.86	4.56	5.82	0.0
2013	REA	AA	24	6	11	0	22	22	130²	142	15	41	86	2.8	5.9	48%	.304	1.40	4.82	4.58	4.93	0.9
2013	LEH	AAA	24	4	2	0	6	6	39	36	2	12	22	2.8	5.1	44%	.274	1.23	3.00	3.90	4.63	0.2
2014	LEH	AAA	25	6	2	0	12	12	57	67	3	21	46	3.3	7.3	44%	.356	1.54	3.95	3.69	4.18	0.7
2014	PHI	MLB	25	6	8	0	20	20	117²	120	12	32	71	2.4	5.4	54%	.284	1.29	3.75	4.24	4.76	-0.2
2015	*PHI*	*MLB*	*26*	*7*	*11*	*0*	*26*	*26*	*149²*	*157*	*16*	*46*	*88*	*2.8*	*5.3*	*46%*	*.307*	*1.36*	*4.55*	*4.65*	*4.95*	*-0.8*

Breakout: 31%   Improve: 48%   Collapse: 11%   Attrition: 30%   MLB: 65%   *Comparables:* *Luke French, Zach Jackson, Dustin Moseley*

Buchanan, who had always been well below the prospect radar, was one of maybe three or four bright spots on the Phillies' 2014 DVD. None of his secondary stuff makes for pretty GIFs, and the 89-91 mph fastball from the right side leaves him thin margins. But his gallimaufry does have two points in its favor: All five pitches he throws get average or better groundball rates; and the 10 mph difference between his fastball and changeup makes the latter a swing-and-miss pitch. Getting to the secondary pitches is the trouble, as he allowed the 10th-highest OPS on fastballs in baseball. It's a fourth or fifth starter's profile, but he should eat plenty of innings for a rebuilding club.

Justin De Fratus   RHP

Born: 10/21/87   Age: 27   Bats: B   Throws: R   Height: 6'4"   Weight: 225

YEAR	TEAM	LVL	AGE	W	L	SV	G	GS	IP	H	HR	BB	K	BB/9	K/9	GB%	BABIP	WHIP	ERA	FIP	FRA	WARP
2012	LEH	AAA	24	0	1	3	17	0	21²	15	2	3	22	1.2	9.1	54%	.241	0.83	2.49	2.74	3.95	0.2
2012	PHI	MLB	24	0	0	0	13	0	10²	7	0	5	8	4.2	6.8	52%	.226	1.12	3.38	3.04	3.61	0.1
2013	LEH	AAA	25	3	0	0	13	0	19	18	0	6	17	2.8	8.1	62%	.321	1.26	1.89	2.68	3.72	0.3
2013	PHI	MLB	25	3	3	0	58	0	46²	45	3	25	42	4.8	8.1	46%	.316	1.50	3.86	3.98	4.24	0.2
2014	LEH	AAA	26	0	0	3	15	0	16	20	1	4	13	2.2	7.3	45%	.396	1.50	4.50	3.48	4.69	0.1
2014	PHI	MLB	26	3	1	0	54	0	52²	45	4	12	49	2.1	8.4	41%	.272	1.08	2.39	3.08	3.05	0.5
2015	*PHI*	*MLB*	*27*	*3*	*1*	*1*	*57*	*0*	*61²*	*52*	*5*	*19*	*60*	*2.8*	*8.8*	*49%*	*.306*	*1.16*	*3.26*	*3.48*	*3.54*	*0.7*

Breakout: 31%   Improve: 40%   Collapse: 28%   Attrition: 23%   MLB: 81%   Comparables: *Mark Melancon, Jerry Blevins, Steve Cishek*

De Fratus has had the stuff to be a late-inning, high-leverage reliever since arriving in the majors four years ago, but the lack of command made him too tough to trust. In 2014, he decided to sacrifice a little bit of velocity in exchange for a ton more control. The walks went down but, even more joyously, the strikeouts went *up*, and a lesson was learned. He's a viable candidate to close when Papelbon vacates the position.

Jake Diekman   LHP

Born: 1/21/87   Age: 28   Bats: L   Throws: L   Height: 6'4"   Weight: 200

YEAR	TEAM	LVL	AGE	W	L	SV	G	GS	IP	H	HR	BB	K	BB/9	K/9	GB%	BABIP	WHIP	ERA	FIP	FRA	WARP
2012	LEH	AAA	25	1	1	7	25	0	26²	19	0	13	37	4.4	12.5	56%	.306	1.20	1.69	2.07	2.70	0.7
2012	PHI	MLB	25	1	1	0	32	0	27¹	25	1	20	35	6.6	11.5	55%	.333	1.65	3.95	3.58	3.55	0.4
2013	LEH	AAA	26	1	0	11	30	0	30	31	1	24	37	7.2	11.1	62%	.380	1.83	5.70	3.67	4.88	0.1
2013	PHI	MLB	26	1	4	0	45	0	38¹	34	1	16	41	3.8	9.6	53%	.311	1.30	2.58	2.47	2.85	0.7
2014	PHI	MLB	27	5	5	0	73	0	71	66	4	35	100	4.4	12.7	44%	.363	1.42	3.80	2.62	2.69	1.1
2015	*PHI*	*MLB*	*28*	*3*	*1*	*1*	*66*	*0*	*66¹*	*52*	*4*	*34*	*78*	*4.6*	*10.6*	*52%*	*.319*	*1.29*	*3.51*	*3.45*	*3.81*	*0.5*

Breakout: 26%   Improve: 39%   Collapse: 20%   Attrition: 16%   MLB: 71%   Comparables: *Santiago Casilla, Al Alburquerque, Pedro Strop*

Diekman has made modest improvements against right-handers, but his platoon splits are still some of the largest among baseball's non-LOOGY class. He walked righties at triple the rate that he walked lefties, and allowed double the extra-base-hit rate. The problem is that he leans on a swing-and-miss slider that he doesn't command well; when he misses with the pitch against a lefty, it's a foul ball, but when he misses to a righty it's big trouble. It's odd to suggest situational work for a pitcher who struck out 13 batters per nine with a 98 mph fastball, but unless he tightens up his breaking pitch—and keeps righties from continuing to slug over .500 against it—or comes up with a reliable changeup, or discovers untapped ambidextrousness, he'll travel dangerously in a right-handed world.

Ken Giles   RHP

Born: 9/20/90   Age: 24   Bats: R   Throws: R   Height: 6'2"   Weight: 205

YEAR	TEAM	LVL	AGE	W	L	SV	G	GS	IP	H	HR	BB	K	BB/9	K/9	GB%	BABIP	WHIP	ERA	FIP	FRA	WARP
2012	LWD	A	21	3	3	5	29	6	67¹	54	5	44	86	5.9	11.5	44%	.299	1.46	3.61	4.22	4.23	0.9
2012	CLR	A+	21	1	0	3	10	0	14²	10	1	6	25	3.7	15.3	32%	.300	1.09	3.07	2.10	1.80	0.7
2013	CLR	A+	22	2	2	6	24	0	25²	23	4	19	34	6.7	11.9	32%	.306	1.64	6.31	4.96	5.87	-0.3
2014	REA	AA	23	0	0	7	13	0	15	8	0	5	29	3.0	17.4	44%	.348	0.87	1.20	0.49	1.18	0.7
2014	LEH	AAA	23	2	0	5	11	0	13²	10	0	8	9	5.3	5.9	31%	.256	1.32	2.63	4.02	4.63	0.0
2014	PHI	MLB	23	3	1	1	44	0	45²	25	1	11	64	2.2	12.6	46%	.267	0.79	1.18	1.31	1.69	1.2
2015	*PHI*	*MLB*	*24*	*2*	*1*	*0*	*39*	*1*	*55*	*41*	*4*	*24*	*68*	*3.9*	*11.1*	*41%*	*.310*	*1.18*	*3.03*	*3.18*	*3.29*	*0.8*

Breakout: 19%   Improve: 35%   Collapse: 8%   Attrition: 22%   MLB: 56%   Comparables: *David Robertson, Stephen Pryor, Rex Brothers*

"Seventh-round pick Kenny Giles is a raw but very live-armed right-hander with some of the best velocity in the system," Kevin Goldstein wrote in early 2012, but sleepers are often sleepers because they're sleeping: Giles couldn't contain the big velocity and his slider only flashed plus on occasion. Two years later, it clicked, and the guy who allowed seven runs per nine in High-A a year earlier allowed seven baserunners per nine in the majors. Just seven of his 413 heaters came in below 95 mph, giving him a pretty nice secondary pitch. Yup, secondary: The slider was better, yielding a .113 slugging percentage and producing a whiff rate two standard deviations higher than that of the average right-handed reliever. He was born with a closer's intensity and flair, and with a newfound ability to repeat his mechanics he's going to have a closer's salary once he hits arbitration.

Miguel Gonzalez   RHP

Born: 9/23/86   Age: 28   Bats: R   Throws: R   Height: 6'3"   Weight: 200

YEAR	TEAM	LVL	AGE	W	L	SV	G	GS	IP	H	HR	BB	K	BB/9	K/9	GB%	BABIP	WHIP	ERA	FIP	FRA	WARP
2012	ART	CNS	25	0	1	0	2	2	3¹	6	1	1	1	2.7	2.7		.372	2.10	10.80			
2013	TIJ	CNS	26	0	0	0	2	2	6	5	0	0	11	0.0	16.5		.455	0.83	0.00			
2014	CLR	A+	27	0	2	0	8	3	15¹	20	0	9	11	5.3	6.5	38%	.377	1.89	4.70	3.72	6.76	0.1
2014	REA	AA	27	0	2	5	11	0	14¹	10	2	7	24	4.4	15.1	36%	.308	1.19	3.14	3.28	2.85	0.4
2014	LEH	AAA	27	0	0	2	12	0	16²	10	0	10	19	5.4	10.3	33%	.256	1.20	1.62	3.06	3.84	0.2
2014	PHI	MLB	27	0	1	0	6	0	5¹	9	1	3	5	5.1	8.4	24%	.400	2.25	6.75	5.35	4.28	0.0
2015	PHI	MLB	28	2	1	0	28	2	39²	35	4	17	39	3.8	8.9	40%	.315	1.31	3.89	4.05	4.23	0.2
2015	*PHI*	*MLB*	*28*	*2*	*3*	*0*	*9*	*7*	*39²*	*35*	*4*	*17*	*39*	*3.8*	*8.9*	*40%*	*.315*	*1.31*	*3.89*	*4.05*	*4.23*	*0.2*

Breakout: 15%   Improve: 22%   Collapse: 11%   Attrition: 22%   MLB: 40%   Comparables: *Mitch Stetter, Anthony Varvaro, Carlos Guevara*

The Phillies ended up getting Gonzalez for much less than expected—his deal was negotiated down from six years and $49 million (then a record for a Cuban import) to 3/$12M after a physical—but even that outlay wasn't made with the notion of making him a reliever. But after four months on the mend from a shoulder injury, he returned with lousy control, and his stuff "started to break down" after 30 or 40 pitches, Amaro told the *Philadelphia Daily News*. While the Phillies will try to stretch him back out as a starter, the leash will be short. He has a readymade three-pitch mix headlined by a fastball that can touch the mid-90s, along with a solid curveball and emerging changeup. But it's not a frontline package, and he's not a young man.

Severino Gonzalez   RHP

Born: 9/28/92   Age: 22   Bats: R   Throws: R   Height: 6'1"   Weight: 153

YEAR	TEAM	LVL	AGE	W	L	SV	G	GS	IP	H	HR	BB	K	BB/9	K/9	GB%	BABIP	WHIP	ERA	FIP	FRA	WARP
2013	LWD	A	20	3	0	0	4	4	21¹	10	1	3	31	1.3	13.1	46%	.214	0.61	1.69	1.75	2.91	0.5
2013	CLR	A+	20	3	5	0	20	9	75²	66	4	19	82	2.3	9.8	32%	.318	1.12	2.02	2.59	2.97	1.9
2014	REA	AA	21	9	13	0	27	27	158²	169	23	34	115	1.9	6.5	38%	.296	1.28	4.59	4.60	4.63	1.2
2015	PHI	MLB	22	6	7	0	28	18	132¹	130	16	35	103	2.4	7.0	40%	.308	1.25	4.09	4.30	4.45	0.0

Breakout: 0%   Improve: 0%   Collapse: 0%   Attrition: 0%   MLB: 0%   Comparables: *Hector Rondon, Joe Wieland, Jeremy Hellickson*

Gonzalez's first year stateside turned some heads, but he came back to earth just as quickly as 23 of his pitches left it. He is more command-and-control than pure stuff, but his fastball was playing up in the mid-90s out of the bullpen in 2013. That might be his eventual landing spot, as a pitcher who can spot a fastball at that enhanced velocity will almost always find a late-inning, high-leverage role. But there's still room to hope for more, considering he survived Double-A despite being four years younger than the average Eastern League pitcher. Let this be the 150th time you'll read this about a young pitcher mentioned in this book: He'll need to keep developing his changeup to make it as a starter.

Cole Hamels   LHP

Born: 12/27/83   Age: 31   Bats: L   Throws: L   Height: 6'3"   Weight: 195

YEAR	TEAM	LVL	AGE	W	L	SV	G	GS	IP	H	HR	BB	K	BB/9	K/9	GB%	BABIP	WHIP	ERA	FIP	FRA	WARP
2012	PHI	MLB	28	17	6	0	31	31	215¹	190	24	52	216	2.2	9.0	44%	.290	1.12	3.05	3.35	3.66	4.0
2013	PHI	MLB	29	8	14	0	33	33	220	205	21	50	202	2.0	8.3	45%	.295	1.16	3.60	3.23	3.69	3.8
2014	CLR	A+	30	0	1	0	3	3	17	12	3	1	12	0.5	6.4	67%	.214	0.76	2.12	4.63	5.27	0.0
2014	PHI	MLB	30	9	9	0	30	30	204²	176	14	59	198	2.6	8.7	50%	.295	1.15	2.46	3.04	3.59	2.7
2015	PHI	MLB	31	11	10	0	28	28	186¹	160	18	42	176	2.0	8.5	47%	.300	1.09	3.13	3.44	3.40	2.4

Breakout: 19%   Improve: 52%   Collapse: 15%   Attrition: 12%   MLB: 94%   Comparables: *Josh Beckett, James Shields, John Lackey*

Lousy run support and some early-season biceps tendinitis were all that kept Hamels from his highest-ever Cy Young finish. His season didn't start until April 23rd, and it didn't *really* start until he'd put three poor starts on his record; from start no. 4 onward, he produced a 2.06 ERA in 188 innings. He allowed more than three earned runs just once during the 27-start run, and fell short of seven innings just five times. The Phillies managed to go just 15-15 when he was on the mound.

While there's virtually no knock on Hamels as a pitcher, the career-best ERA was one of those blips more than a step forward. His peripherals have been among the game's most consistent over the past half-decade, and everything from his strike rate to his whiff rate to his batted-ball profile fits perfectly on top of his career line. That puts him in a tier slightly below the Kershaws of the world—well, the Kershaw of the world—but it also makes him one of the best multi-year pitching investments a team has made this century, and a very quiet Hall of Fame candidate. His average fastball is harder than it has ever been, and he threw 200 innings for the fifth year in a row, so there's no sign he's breaking down. Meanwhile, Hamels has begun making the adjustments that separate the pitchers who survive into their 30s from those who don't—more sinkers, more pitches down in the zone.

Matt Imhof   LHP

Born: 10/26/93   Age: 21   Bats: L   Throws: L   Height: 6'5"   Weight: 220

YEAR	TEAM	LVL	AGE	W	L	SV	G	GS	IP	H	HR	BB	K	BB/9	K/9	GB%	BABIP	WHIP	ERA	FIP	FRA	WARP
2014	WPT	A-	20	1	0	0	3	3	12	6	0	4	11	3.0	8.2	0%	.207	0.83	0.75	3.11	3.38	—
2014	LWD	A	20	0	2	0	7	7	27¹	32	3	6	27	2.0	8.9	39%	.382	1.39	4.28	3.81	3.39	0.5
2015	PHI	MLB	21	2	3	0	8	8	35²	37	4	15	25	3.8	6.3	43%	.318	1.47	4.92	4.87	5.35	-0.3

Breakout: 0%   Improve: 0%   Collapse: 0%   Attrition: 0%   MLB: 0%   Comparables: *Robbie Ray, Carter Capps, Edwin Escobar*

Imhof went undrafted out of high school before blossoming into a second-round pick out of Cal Poly. He's got a low-90s fastball that has good cut and comes out of a deceptive motion. He took turns at three levels in his first pro summer, and should earn a 2015 assignment to High-A, where the stuff will be put to its first real test. A big reverse split is a curiosity to keep an eye on.

Kyle Kendrick   RHP

Born: 8/26/84   Age: 30   Bats: R   Throws: R   Height: 6'3"   Weight: 210

YEAR	TEAM	LVL	AGE	W	L	SV	G	GS	IP	H	HR	BB	K	BB/9	K/9	GB%	BABIP	WHIP	ERA	FIP	FRA	WARP
2012	PHI	MLB	27	11	12	0	37	25	159¹	154	20	49	116	2.8	6.6	48%	.278	1.27	3.90	4.37	4.81	1.2
2013	PHI	MLB	28	10	13	0	30	30	182	207	18	47	110	2.3	5.4	52%	.306	1.40	4.70	3.99	4.35	2.3
2014	PHI	MLB	29	10	13	0	32	32	199	214	25	57	121	2.6	5.5	47%	.290	1.36	4.61	4.54	5.00	-0.6
2015	PHI	MLB	30	9	11	0	28	28	168¹	171	20	43	108	2.3	5.8	46%	.302	1.27	4.30	4.52	4.67	-0.4

Breakout: 16%   Improve: 41%   Collapse: 29%   Attrition: 14%   MLB: 85%   Comparables: *Sidney Ponson, Clayton Richard, Jeff Weaver*

Like many a fifth starter, Kendrick's ERA swings from league average on the high end to much worse on the low end, without ever really seeing his FIP budge. His latest attempt at missing the occasional bat is a curveball that he threw about once in 10 pitches; it had one of the league's worst whiff rates, and batters slugged .450 against it. He's not getting better but he is getting more work, having set career highs in innings in each of the past two seasons, and like many a fifth starter that's about 90 percent of his value. Unlike many a fifth starter, he has earned $20 million.

Cliff Lee   LHP

Born: 8/30/78   Age: 36   Bats: L   Throws: L   Height: 6'3"   Weight: 205

YEAR	TEAM	LVL	AGE	W	L	SV	G	GS	IP	H	HR	BB	K	BB/9	K/9	GB%	BABIP	WHIP	ERA	FIP	FRA	WARP
2012	PHI	MLB	33	6	9	0	30	30	211	207	26	28	207	1.2	8.8	46%	.309	1.11	3.16	3.17	3.52	3.8
2013	PHI	MLB	34	14	8	0	31	31	222²	193	22	32	222	1.3	9.0	47%	.287	1.01	2.87	2.80	3.51	4.3
2014	CLR	A+	35	0	1	0	3	3	10²	13	1	2	8	1.7	6.8	58%	.324	1.41	5.06	3.95	4.82	0.1
2014	PHI	MLB	35	4	5	0	13	13	81¹	100	7	12	72	1.3	8.0	51%	.358	1.38	3.65	2.93	3.50	1.4
2015	PHI	MLB	36	6	5	0	15	15	105²	95	10	14	100	1.2	8.5	45%	.314	1.04	2.94	3.08	3.19	1.6

Breakout: 12%   Improve: 34%   Collapse: 23%   Attrition: 16%   MLB: 84%   Comparables: *Roy Halladay, Javier Vazquez, Ted Lilly*

The biggest danger in giving a 32-year-old pitcher a five-year deal is that the risk for injury grows exponentially with each passing year. Lee was one of the sturdiest pitchers in the game from 2008 through 2013, with just a couple of brief DL stints and 30-plus starts in all but one year (28 in 2010). The math caught up: A pair of elbow injuries limited him to just 81 innings in 2014, and cast doubt over his future, which includes a $25 million salary this year. His 3.65 ERA last year was a seven-year high, though his FIP didn't change—it just got pummeled by a .358 BABIP, 60 points beyond his career figure and unaccompanied by any increase in line drive or home run frequency. He still walked almost nobody; his strikeout rate was healthy, albeit his lowest in a half-decade. But pitchers like Lee, who produce elite K:BB ratios by always being around the plate, can get hit hard when the stuff fades, and it won't be a surprise if the FIP is a lagging indicator. Hope not. Baseball is better when he's healthy.

Aaron Nola RHP

Born: 6/4/93   Age: 22   Bats: R   Throws: R   Height: 6'1"   Weight: 195

YEAR	TEAM	LVL	AGE	W	L	SV	G	GS	IP	H	HR	BB	K	BB/9	K/9	GB%	BABIP	WHIP	ERA	FIP	FRA	WARP
2014	CLR	A+	21	2	3	0	7	6	31¹	24	4	5	30	1.4	8.6	34%	.247	0.93	3.16	3.61	5.02	0.2
2014	REA	AA	21	2	0	0	5	5	24	25	4	5	15	1.9	5.6	49%	.284	1.25	2.62	4.90	4.90	0.3
2015	PHI	MLB	22	2	3	0	8	8	37²	37	4	12	28	2.8	6.7	42%	.309	1.31	4.28	4.28	4.65	0.0

Breakout: 0%   Improve: 0%   Collapse: 0%   Attrition: 0%   MLB: 0%   Comparables: *Joe Wieland, Patrick Corbin, Will Smith*

What Nola lacks in size—especially compared to the typical pitcher taken in the first third of round one—he makes up for with polish. He already moves his fastball around, adds and subtracts velocity, varies his arm angle without losing mechanical consistency and has Double-A success on his resume. What you get for such polish is, of course, a cap on the upside, and Nola has neither an overwhelming breaking pitch nor the projection to add much sizzle to his low-90s fastball. He should be pretty good, and only pretty good. Pitchers like Nola probably read complaints like these and just shake their danged heads. In conclusion: He ain't Kyle Kendrick.

Jonathan Papelbon RHP

Born: 11/23/80   Age: 34   Bats: R   Throws: R   Height: 6'4"   Weight: 215

YEAR	TEAM	LVL	AGE	W	L	SV	G	GS	IP	H	HR	BB	K	BB/9	K/9	GB%	BABIP	WHIP	ERA	FIP	FRA	WARP
2012	PHI	MLB	31	5	6	38	70	0	70	56	8	18	92	2.3	11.8	44%	.296	1.06	2.44	2.94	3.23	1.3
2013	PHI	MLB	32	5	1	29	61	0	61²	59	6	11	57	1.6	8.3	42%	.296	1.14	2.92	3.02	3.61	0.8
2014	PHI	MLB	33	2	3	39	66	0	66¹	45	2	15	63	2.0	8.5	44%	.247	0.90	2.04	2.50	2.74	1.2
2015	PHI	MLB	34	3	2	32	58	0	59	46	4	13	67	2.0	10.2	41%	.301	1.00	2.38	2.64	2.59	1.4

Breakout: 14%   Improve: 33%   Collapse: 47%   Attrition: 6%   MLB: 91%   Comparables: *Heath Bell, Matt Thornton, J.J. Putz*

With the exception of a one-week stretch in June 2013, Papelbon hasn't been anything close to bad with the Phillies, posting three straight sub-3.00 ERA seasons with the skills to back it up. So why does the $37 million they've already spent feel like such a waste? Partly it's that they're the classic example of a team that's about seven other moves away from needing a great closer. Partly it's that he no longer looks as sturdy as his final numbers, with a fastball four mph slower than in his final year in Boston and a just-average strikeout rate. Partly it's the sense that the BABIP and HR/FB rates he had last year can't possibly repeat, which leads further to the sense that he's a liability going forward. Partly it's that no fan south of the Bronx has ever thought his closer was anything but a drunk on a wobbly ladder, and partly it's that the dude just flat out isn't likable. Lay his numbers out before the contract was signed and the Phillies would have been happy with them. Lay them out now and a decent portion of the fan base sees a guy who could be replaced by Ken Giles at 1/25th the cost. Bottom line: There are plenty of teams Papelbon could have helped to reach the postseason these past three years. The Phillies weren't one of them.

Jonathan Pettibone RHP

Born: 7/19/90   Age: 24   Bats: L   Throws: R   Height: 6'6"   Weight: 225

YEAR	TEAM	LVL	AGE	W	L	SV	G	GS	IP	H	HR	BB	K	BB/9	K/9	GB%	BABIP	WHIP	ERA	FIP	FRA	WARP
2012	REA	AA	21	9	7	0	19	19	117¹	115	9	27	81	2.1	6.2	53%	.290	1.21	3.30	3.64	4.10	1.9
2012	LEH	AAA	21	4	1	0	7	7	42¹	31	0	22	32	4.7	6.8	53%	.254	1.25	2.55	3.20	4.32	0.4
2013	LEH	AAA	22	0	2	0	4	4	17¹	26	1	5	10	2.6	5.2	42%	.397	1.79	6.75	4.01	5.29	0.0
2013	PHI	MLB	22	5	4	0	18	18	100¹	109	9	38	66	3.4	5.9	52%	.313	1.47	4.04	4.16	4.38	0.8
2014	LEH	AAA	23	2	0	0	5	5	26¹	22	0	6	13	2.1	4.4	36%	.253	1.06	3.42	3.05	3.94	0.5
2014	PHI	MLB	23	0	1	0	2	2	9	17	2	3	6	3.0	6.0	53%	.417	2.22	9.00	5.66	6.70	-0.1
2015	PHI	MLB	24	2	3	0	8	8	44	45	4	15	27	3.0	5.5	47%	.306	1.35	4.31	4.48	4.69	-0.1

Breakout: 26%   Improve: 52%   Collapse: 17%   Attrition: 34%   MLB: 80%   Comparables: *Alex Sanabia, Trevor Bell, Zach Jackson*

Pettibone enjoyed an impressive debut as a groundball, pitch-to-contact guy in 2013 and appeared on his way toward a career as a generic innings-eater, but generic innings-eaters can't have bad shoulders, and Pettibone did. His outlook for 2015 is unclear, as labrum surgery's no simple fix and as generic innings-eaters don't get priority seating. For now, he's Kyle Kendrick's darkest timeline.

Lineouts

Hitters

NAME	POS	TEAM	LVL	AGE	PA	R	2B	3B	HR	RBI	BB	K	SB	CS	AVG/OBP/SLG	TAv	BABIP	BRR	FRAA	WARP
Andres Blanco	SS	LEH	AAA	30	155	16	6	0	0	11	13	25	3	5	.241/.314/.285	.214	.292	1.2	SS(39): 1.1, 2B(5): -0.2	0.1
	3B	PHI	MLB	30	53	4	5	0	1	3	2	6	0	0	.277/.306/.447	.268	.300	-0.6	3B(10): 0.6, SS(6): -0.0	0.3
Chase d'Arnaud	CF	IND	AAA	27	416	59	16	9	2	23	29	82	30	13	.250/.313/.356	.241	.312	3.9	CF(38): 2.3, LF(32): -0.3	0.8
Jeff Francoeur	RF	ELP	AAA	30	487	55	22	3	15	69	21	95	11	2	.289/.320/.450	.273	.331	0.7	RF(103): -16.7, P(8): -0.1	-0.7
	RF	SDN	MLB	30	28	2	0	0	0	1	3	7	0	0	.083/.179/.083	.141	.111	0.2	RF(7): 0.1	-0.2
Tyson Gillies	CF	LEH	AAA	25	177	13	6	0	2	10	6	44	3	2	.214/.270/.289	.211	.278	-0.4	CF(40): 7.0, LF(4): 0.6	0.3
Zach Green	1B	LWD	A	20	358	41	22	2	6	43	24	65	7	1	.268/.316/.402	.268	.313	-2.7	1B(53): 3.7, 3B(22): 0.4	0.8
Tony Gwynn	CF	LEH	AAA	31	81	7	2	0	1	7	11	12	2	4	.290/.383/.362	.268	.333	-0.7	CF(19): -1.1, LF(1): 0.1	0.2
	CF	PHI	MLB	31	127	14	2	1	0	3	15	23	3	0	.152/.264/.190	.208	.195	0.5	CF(25): 0.7, LF(16): 0.1	-0.3
Cesar Hernandez	3B	REA	AA	24	117	13	4	1	3	14	13	13	1	3	.340/.410/.485	.311	.364	0.3	3B(18): -0.4, SS(8): -0.2	1.1
	2B	LEH	AAA	24	171	23	6	3	0	10	15	34	4	4	.256/.322/.333	.231	.328	-0.4	2B(21): -3.8, SS(16): -0.4	-0.3
	3B	PHI	MLB	24	125	13	2	0	1	4	9	33	1	1	.237/.290/.281	.234	.321	-0.2	3B(14): -0.8, 2B(11): -1.2	-0.2
John Hester	C	SLC	AAA	30	273	31	16	1	6	29	26	70	3	0	.261/.338/.411	.246	.341	0.2	C(66): -1.5	0.6
Wil Nieves	C	PHI	MLB	36	128	9	8	0	1	7	1	34	1	0	.254/.270/.344	.234	.341	-1.3	C(34): 1.2, 1B(1): -0.0	0.2

After a three-year hiatus from this book, **Andres Blanco** returns just long enough for us to point out how unbelievably bad the Phillies bench was. Keep reading! ❖ **Chase d'Arnaud** can't hit but he's so fast he runs on water. And oxygen. And blood. And … ❖ **Jeff Francoeur** got duped into believing a teammate at El Paso was deaf, made the first eight relief appearances of his professional career and still couldn't hit big-league pitching. ❖ **Tyson Gillies** has been saddled with the nickname of "Hamster" because of a rash of hamstring injuries, winning him the award for the absolute worst nickname ever. Once a key part of the Cliff Lee trade, he was dropped from the 40-man this year. ❖ **Zach Green** didn't hit as much as he needs to following a move from short to third, but he dealt with back injuries that might have sapped his power, so we'll give him a pass for now. ❖ **Tony Gwynn** was 40-for-131 in his career as a pinch-hitter entering the season, but went 2-for-30 in Philadelphia. It was his sixth sub-zero WARP in eight tries. ❖ Just entering his mid-20s, **Cesar Hernandez** still holds a shred of hope to become a full-timer, though it would take quite a boost to his offense to get there. Given the state of the franchise, there's no reason to spend much effort trying to find the next Reid Brignac or Andres Blanco to take away his plate appearances. ❖ Traveling is complicated enough without having to go through the waiver wire, so when backup catcher **John Hester** used up the last of his options, the Angels cast him aside for guys who could travel more lightly from Anaheim to Salt Lake and back. ❖ They may don the tools of ignorance, but catchers are so wily they'll scam an 11-year big-league career out of a .214 TAv. **Wil Nieves** has done his best work in his mid-30s, which may well earn him a Year 12.

Pitchers

NAME	TEAM	LVL	AGE	W	L	SV	G	GS	IP	H	HR	BB	K	BB/9	K/9	GB%	BABIP	WHIP	ERA	FIP	FRA	WARP
Paul Clemens	OKL	AAA	26	6	3	1	19	5	46¹	37	4	23	41	4.5	8.0	36%	.258	1.29	4.08	4.74	4.69	0.4
	HOU	MLB	26	0	1	0	13	0	24²	28	5	13	16	4.7	5.8	44%	.280	1.66	5.84	6.20	6.70	-0.4
Brody Colvin	CLR	A+	23	0	2	0	4	4	12²	14	0	10	2	7.1	1.4	51%	.298	1.89	7.11	5.44	6.80	-0.1
Mario Hollands	PHI	MLB	25	2	2	0	50	0	47	45	3	21	35	4.0	6.7	55%	.292	1.40	4.40	3.85	4.31	0.0
Cesar Jimenez	LEH	AAA	29	3	2	3	38	2	49²	34	0	15	46	2.7	8.3	44%	.256	0.99	1.45	2.41	2.82	1.4
	PHI	MLB	29	0	0	0	16	0	16	14	1	7	8	3.9	4.5	42%	.265	1.31	1.69	4.23	5.30	-0.2
Adam Loewen	CLR	A+	30	1	0	0	2	2	10¹	7	0	7	9	6.1	7.8	52%	.259	1.35	2.61	3.68	5.49	0.0
	REA	AA	30	4	5	0	17	17	103¹	84	7	53	75	4.6	6.5	52%	.255	1.33	3.31	4.50	4.98	0.6
Ethan Martin	LEH	AAA	25	2	1	0	29	0	47²	46	2	21	45	4.0	8.5	54%	.321	1.41	4.15	3.40	4.38	0.4
	PHI	MLB	25	0	0	0	2	0	4	1	1	3	4	6.8	9.0	20%	.000	1.00	4.50	6.60	7.89	-0.1
Yoel Mecias	LWD	A	20	3	3	0	7	7	33²	29	2	9	23	2.4	6.1	43%	.270	1.13	3.21	3.97	4.92	0.3
Hoby Milner	REA	AA	23	10	6	0	25	25	143¹	146	25	56	86	3.5	5.4	38%	.270	1.41	4.21	5.62	5.76	0.2
Hector Neris	REA	AA	25	2	0	0	11	0	19¹	12	3	10	12	4.7	5.6	44%	.176	1.14	1.86	5.68	5.87	-0.1
	LEH	AAA	25	4	3	2	37	1	58	50	5	19	58	2.9	9.0	43%	.287	1.19	4.19	3.77	4.78	0.3
	PHI	MLB	25	1	0	0	1	0	1	0	0	0	1	0.0	9.0	50%	.000	0.00	0.00	1.10	1.43	0.0
Miguel Nunez	CLR	A+	21	6	7	0	25	20	122¹	125	8	44	95	3.2	7.0	37%	.310	1.38	4.49	3.87	4.26	1.8
Nefi Ogando	REA	AA	25	5	1	7	48	0	56	64	6	28	57	4.5	9.2	51%	.352	1.64	6.27	4.53	5.77	0.1
Andy Oliver	IND	AAA	26	3	4	13	48	0	64	35	3	47	85	6.6	12.0	39%	.230	1.28	2.53	3.70	4.20	0.6
B.J. Rosenberg	LEH	AAA	28	2	1	1	18	0	19	24	2	12	17	5.7	8.1	44%	.367	1.89	6.63	4.99	5.80	-0.1
	PHI	MLB	28	1	0	0	13	0	12	20	5	7	9	5.2	6.8	30%	.395	2.25	6.75	8.77	7.92	-0.4
Jerome Williams	ROU	AAA	32	0	1	0	2	2	10¹	16	3	1	3	0.9	2.6	43%	.317	1.65	6.10	7.76	8.66	-0.3
	PHI	MLB	32	4	2	0	9	9	57¹	48	5	17	38	2.7	6.0	48%	.257	1.13	2.83	3.96	4.32	0.1
	HOU	MLB	32	1	4	0	26	0	47²	59	7	16	38	3.0	7.2	48%	.335	1.57	6.04	4.67	5.74	-0.4
	TEX	MLB	32	1	1	0	2	2	10	18	0	3	6	2.7	5.4	41%	.462	2.10	9.90	2.86	3.74	0.2

Astros fans wanted to know: Is **Paul Clemens** going to be a starter? Or is he a reliever? Since the Astros outrighted him at the end of the season, the answer is "a Phillie." ❖ **Brody Colvin** was once a top-100 prospect across the industry, but the 24-year-old was released after a disastrous start to the 2014 season—actually, four disastrous starts. It usually takes more than two years for a prospect to fall *completely* off the radar, but this may well be it for Colvin. ❖ The lean lefty **Elniery Garcia** struck out 23 and walked only four in 26 Gulf Coast League innings, and has added velocity to a fastball that now sits in the low 90s with impressive tail. He could be a Dude by this time next year. ❖ **Mario Hollands** hits the mid-90s from the left side, but it's the lefty-smothering slider that'll get him paid, because he's likely all LOOGY all the way home from here. ❖ **Cesar Jimenez** has pitched in five seasons since his first call-up in 2006, but 2014 marked the first time he appeared in The Show for back-to-back seasons. He's a reliever with two strong secondaries and no velocity or command, which at least gets points for originality. ❖ Pitcher turned hitter turned pitcher **Adam Loewen** is probably a better hitter than any major-league pitcher and a better pitcher than any major-league hitter, but he made $1,500 a month because athletics are largely arbitrary. ❖ You remember **Ethan Martin** from his days as a big-time prospect in the Dodgers system, and he seems intent on keeping it that way. ❖ **Yoel Mecias** returned in June from Tommy John surgery, with his stuff mostly intact. He'll need to add to his frame and learn all the nuances to pitching now that he's a year behind developmentally. ❖ **Hoby Milner**'s 2014 ERA was 20 pounds of suck crammed into a 10 pound sack. ❖ A clean 15th inning against Houston in early August made **Hector Neris** a major leaguer, and put him ahead of Gerrit Cole, Tyson

Ross and Tim Hudson on at least one 2014 leaderboard: Win Probability Added. He should get many more innings in a bullpen this year, but most likely in much lower leverage. ❖ The huge right-hander **Miguel Nunez** has shown flashes, but with low-90s heat from the right side, he needs the secondary pitches to emerge even more than most do. Likely outcome is the bullpen, where he can ditch his sorry changeup altogether. ❖ Acquired for John McDonald in late August 2013, **Nefi Ogando** made some noise in his new organization with high-90s velocity. His ERA was crushed by bad BABIP luck, but his FIP was crushed by lousy control. ❖ Southpaw **Andy Oliver** attacks the strike zone with a ferociousness most reserve for intramural ultimate frisbee. His stuff is such that he'll probably reach the majors as a reliever anyway. ❖ **B.J. Rosenberg** allowed as many big-league home runs in 2014 as Garrett Richards. Even siphoning out the bad luck doesn't leave an interesting story. ❖ As long as **Jerome Williams** never stays in any one place for more than 60 or 70 innings, he's guaranteed to put up at least one small-sample ERA low enough to get him a spring training invite.

Manager

Ryne Sandberg

YEAR	TEAM	W	L	Py-thag +/-	Avg PC	100+ P	120+ P	QS	BQS	REL	REL w Zero R	IBB	PH	PH Avg	PH HR	SB2	CS2	SB3	CS3	SAC Att	SAC%	POS SAC	Squeeze	Swing	In Play
2013	PHI	20	22	4	89.7	15	1	22	0	135	104	10	64	.203	0	6	5	3	0	19	63.2%	3	1	57	21
2014	PHI	73	89	0	98.3	73	7	85	6	461	386	43	256	.182	5	96	22	13	4	87	67.8%	29	1	327	99

In a league where many new managers have no prior experience on the bench, Sandberg represents the rare recent hire who paid his due on the farm. The Hall of Fame second baseman toiled in the minors for six seasons before joining the Phillies' big-league staff in '13 as the third-base coach. He later replaced Charlie Manuel on an interim basis over the final 42 games, impressing the Phillies' brass enough to earn a three-year contract. Alas, Sandberg's first full year at the helm became noteworthy for the wrong reasons—and not just because he admitted to snacking on cat food as a child.

If Sandberg was expected to have an easier time dealing with players than the average rookie manager, then 2014 offered enough evidence to dismiss the theory as wishful thinking. The embarrassment started in spring training, when Sandberg benched Jimmy Rollins for three games over a misinterpreted quote. In short, Sandberg took offense to Rollins' dismissive response to a question about his exhibition-season struggles. Sandberg assumed Rollins didn't care enough about the team's overall woes, and sent him a message to get on board or get out. Those two later patched their relationship, but before the season ended Sandberg would meet in private with no fewer than three players who had vented to the press; there was even an incident with Cole Hamels, in which he left the mound before Sandberg arrived to remove him.

Sandberg's problems ramified beyond questionable interpersonal skills. Despite an uncompetitive record, Sandberg was borderline abusive toward his rotation. Philadelphia's starters scored a majors-leading eight starts with more than 120 pitches—three more than anyone else. The Phillies were also the only team to have a pitcher exceed 130 pitches in a game; they did it twice. Sandberg allowing Hamels, Cliff Lee and A.J. Burnett long leashes is reasonable, but Kyle Kendrick? In a game in which he'd thrown 33 first-inning pitches and trailed 3-0 after two? Questionable, at best; nonsensical, at worst.

It's clear that marinating in the minors didn't leave Sandberg as a finished product. Problem is, another quarrel-filled year could leave him without enough time to get this managing thing right.

PITTSBURGH PIRATES

by Sarah Sprague

We have all sorts of words for general low-grade depression and dissatisfaction. Ennui. Lassitude. Malaise. We don't have an equivalent to describe low-grade happiness. "Satisfaction" and "contentment" are too positive and reflect a general state of accomplishment, and you would be hard-pressed to find a Pirates fan who would say the 2014 campaign left them feeling *fulfilled*. This is not to sound ungrateful or displeased, as two successive winning seasons after twenty years of losing is not a terrible problem to have. Making the playoffs two years in a row (granted, just the Wild Card game in 2014, but we'll take it) means you're a contender, and who can be unhappy with a team playing exciting, winning baseball in September? Yet in the larger context of the 2014 Pirates season, winning felt like losing.

"Hey! If you guys are so great, how come you lost the big one?"

—Michael Keaton in Gung Ho

More than in other small cities, Pittsburghers like to know who "their guy" is on the field. It doesn't matter if they're actually from Western Pennsylvania (although it helps); "their guy" speaks to them in a secret language that conveys, "Hey, we're in this together. Maybe we're loud, a little rough around the edges, and others may look down at us, but no matter what I've got your back." In 2013, Pirates fans had that in a man not unlike themselves: A.J. Burnett was tattooed, older, supposedly with his best years behind him. They loved the Yankees' castoff and made him one of their own; his fire pulled everyone out of their cautious fan shells, from worrying about disaster to riding every high.

Even though he broke fans' hearts with his performance against the Cardinals in the 2013 NLDS, losing Burnett (who aside from being an object of affection was the team's best pitcher) to free agency before 2014 tempered even the most fervent expectations. You can logically explain away not throwing what limited bank the Pirates have at a pricey 37-year-old hurler, but considering Neal Huntington's biggest move to shore up the 2014 pitching staff was to bring in reclamation project Edinson Volquez, it was understandable that the letdown of the 2013 postseason would carry forward into the next year. (Are we even allowed to say "letdown" yet? A starving man given a piece of bread doesn't reflect back and say he wishes it had been an everything bagel that saved him from perishing. Then again, the 2013 Pirates didn't luck into the playoffs and by all rights were just a few breaks from continuing on.)

"Somebody tell Britta what an analogy is."
"I know what it is. It's like a thought with another thought's hat on."

—Gillian Jacobs in Community

If losing in the 2013 postseason felt disappointing, then March and April of 2014 could not have felt any worse to Pirate fans, as the team started 10-16 and dropped two series each to the Brewers and Reds. Wandy Rodriguez, Jason Grilli and Russell Martin were placed on the disabled list. Travis Snider and Martin served suspensions stemming from a bench-clearing brawl during a 3-2 loss to the Brewers late in the month that had more to do with general frustration than a Carlos Gomez bat flip. The only things that prevented April from being any worse for Pittsburgh were opening the year against the Cubs and road losses to the Orioles being postponed until May. Oh, and 2013 MVP Andrew McCutchen doing his usual (.286/.408/.500 for the month).

Early May brought a few wins, but by the end of the month Rodriguez had imploded. Pitching against the Orioles in a 9-8 win that bloodied both teams, he threw 61 pitches in 1 2/3 innings, allowing six runs on seven hits before he was mercifully pulled from the mound. When asked about Rodriguez's future after the game, manager Clint Hurdle sounded surprisingly like a *Saturday Night Live* character, responding, "I'm not even going to go there right now." What "not going there right now" eventually meant was releasing a player from the already-thin pitching staff and swallowing the $7.5 million salary that went with him. Even as the team racked up some wins, even as McCutchen, Neil Walker, Josh Harrison and Starling Marte strapped the club onto their backs and provided the offense needed to bail out the pitching staff to go 15-14 on the month, the stink of near-success hung over the clubhouse, and the collective mood among Pirates fans is best represented by a famous bowl of petunias: "Oh no, not again."

PIRATES PROSPECTUS
2014 W-L: 88-74, 2ND IN NL CENTRAL

Pythag	.535	8th	DER	.710	11th
RS/G	4.21	10th	B-Age	27.2	4th
RA/G	3.9	15th	P-Age	27.8	8th
TAv	.274	3rd	Salary	$71.9M	28th
BRR	5.2	5th	M$/MW	$1.5M	2nd
TAv-P	.260	13th	DL Days	421	1st
FIP	3.77	18th	$ on DL	12%	8th

Three-Year Park Factors

Runs	Runs/RH	Runs/LH	HR/RH	HR/LH
99	98	100	83	95

Top Hitter WARP	7.1	Andrew McCutchen
Top Pitcher WARP	1.8	Gerrit Cole
Top Prospect		Tyler Glasnow

"Oh, yeah. Oooh, ahhh, that's how it always starts. Then later there's running and screaming."

—*Jeff Goldblum in* The Lost World: Jurassic Park

June continued the slow, fitful upward trajectory for the Pirates as they scraped together enough wins to reach .500 by the end of the month. But for every good there was a bad, and the bad haunted the pitching staff in particular. Vance Worley would throw seven scoreless innings against the Marlins only to have Tony Watson and Jared Hughes blow it. The gamble on Volquez would appear to be paying off only to see 2013 All-Star Grilli shipped to the Angels for Ernesto Frieri in a change-of-scenery swap. (Frieri pitched 10 awful innings for Pittsburgh and earned his release in September.) Dreams of the Wild Card seemed far-fetched and unreasonable even as the team slid into the All-Star break 49-46. (This is where I take a moment and again thank the Cubs for their very existence; they were the only team in the division the Pirates had a winning record against in the 2014. Congratulations on your new manager, please don't get any better.)

It was also around the All-Star break that every armchair GM with a connection to the 412 area code started to wonder what the Pirates would have to do keep catcher Russell Martin on the payroll once the season ended. Fans suddenly became experts in pitch framing and started rooting around their sofas for spare change to add to the collection plate. Nearly every mention of Martin was coupled with the reminder that he was going to be a free agent at the end of the season. Of course, there never was any realistic hope of retaining Martin when top-tier catchers are hard to come by, but it's worth noting because worries about keeping talent on limited payroll start to be corrosive for fans. Yes, the team is getting better; yes, they're winning more games; yes, they're .500; but how long is it going to last if this key player leaves? No longer can fans pour their energy into the current season; they're anxious about a future that does not look to include one of the best players on the club.

Mix in a quiet trade deadline after whispers about landing a fancy Jon Lester or John Lackey and it's easy to let seeds of doubt take root. Will we ever be good enough?

"You're a killer of art, you're a killer of beauty, and you're even a killer of laughter. I can't bear your work."

—*Dutch abstract expressionist Willem de Kooning to Andy Warhol*

And yet, the Pirates were 57-51, just 2 1/2 games back of first place as the calendar flipped to August. In a season that had seemed lost, you couldn't realistically ask for more. Which is why things immediately went to hell. McCutchen was placed on the disabled list for the first time in his career after breaking his rib hitting a sacrifice fly in a game against the Diamondbacks. How does one break a rib swinging a bat after so many years of swinging bats? Easy. Dislodge a piece of costochondral cartilage from the rib the day after being plunked in the back with a 95 mph fastball by Randall Delgado in "retaliation" for a Frieri pitch that went off-track and fractured Paul Goldschmidt's left hand two days prior.

The team went 5-9 in McCutchen's absence, including a seven-game losing streak capped by an eight-run loss the day McCutchen returned. The streak knocked them from a game and a half back of the division-leading Brewers to *seven* games back. Charlie Morton also hit the disabled list for the rest of the season after struggling with a sports hernia for most of the year.

"Love isn't a state of perfect caring. It is an active noun like struggle. To love someone is to strive to accept that person exactly the way he or she is, right here and now."

—*Fred Rogers,* The World According to Mister Rogers: Important Things to Remember

But just when it felt like the season was lost, the Pirates won three consecutive series and ended August at 71-65, once again just two games back of the division lead. The team then got hot in September, creating a low-grade fever of positivity. Champagne had been popped for a winning season in 2013, the ghosts of 20 years suddenly exorcised. By 2014, reaching .500 for good in late June and hanging around the outskirts of the division race, jostling for a Wild Card, felt unsatisfying.

Yet the Pirates were on the verge of winning the division in the last month of the regular season, narrowing the lead to just one game heading into the final weekend, with an already-clinched Wild Card a reasonable fall-back position. Fans asked each other, "Can you believe we're here now? Looking back at June can you believe this team is going to the playoffs? Again?" It seemed ludicrous and inevitable that Hurdle would roll the dice on his best starters against the Reds, hoping to catch one last break to avoid a win-or-go-home contest against the Giants on October 1st. The gamble failed and the Pirates could only turn to (who else?) their "major" offseason acquisition, Volquez, in the Wild Card game.

"My heart was simultaneously broken and filled with lust, I was exhausted, and I loved every minute of it. It was strange and elating to find myself for once the weaker."

—*Michael Chabon,* The Mysteries of Pittsburgh

There is an absurdity to a one-game playoff in baseball, of all sports, but this is a well-worn track, the randomness of small-sample outcomes, and it is not worth treading again. In retrospect, knowing that it was only going to be one game and nothing was going to prevent Madison Bumgarner from plowing through opposing batters from his complete game on October 1st right through the last out of the World Series, I would have worried a lot less about which Volquez was going to show up on the mound. It didn't matter.

And as much as the 2014 Pirates had overcome, getting to the Wild Card game but no further just didn't feel like winning.

✦ ✦ ✦

Of course in the time it took me to write this essay, Martin departed for Toronto and the Pirates brought in catcher Francisco Cervelli—another notable framer—from the Yankees. This is important because that fan-favorite pitcher the Bucs let go to make more money elsewhere in 2014? He left significant money on the table to return to the Pirates and pitch for a club he enjoyed playing for and a fan base he liked. He'll replace Volquez, who decamped to Kansas City, in the rotation, but nobody has to replace Francisco Liriano, who signed a three-year deal in December to stick with the team that brought him back from the dead.

The old saw that "no one wins the offseason" is true; teams only can only add and subtract elements they believe will give them the best odds of winning the next year. So far, though, next year feels pretty good. ∎

—*Sarah Sprague is an LA-based writer; she is an editor for the Yardbarker network and has contributed to sites such as Kissing Suzy Kolber, SB Nation, Ain't It Cool News, The Awl and Deadspin.*

Player comments by R.J. Anderson and Baseball Prospectus Authors

Hitters

Pedro Alvarez   3B

Born: 2/6/87   Age: 28   Bats: L   Throws: R   Height: 6' 3"   Weight: 235

YEAR	TEAM	LVL	AGE	PA	R	2B	3B	HR	RBI	BB	K	SB	CS	AVG/OBP/SLG	TAv	BABIP	BRR	FRAA	WARP
2012	PIT	MLB	25	586	64	25	1	30	85	57	180	1	0	.244/.317/.467	.283	.308	0.5	3B(145): -5.1	2.5
2013	PIT	MLB	26	614	70	22	2	36	100	48	186	2	0	.233/.296/.473	.274	.276	0.0	3B(150): 11.9	4.5
2014	PIT	MLB	27	445	46	13	1	18	56	45	113	8	3	.231/.312/.405	.263	.277	-1.1	3B(99): 8.2, 1B(5): -0.5	2.2
2015	PIT	MLB	28	452	54	17	1	19	60	43	132	4	1	.234/.311/.420	.274	.295	-0.2	3B 5, 1B -0	2.2

Breakout: 2%   Improve: 49%   Collapse: 3%   Attrition: 4%   MLB: 93%   Comparables: *Ian Stewart, Wilson Betemit, Al Rosen*

Alvarez led the NL in home runs, won the Silver Slugger Award and made his first All-Star team in 2013. He achieved none of the above during a pitiable 2014. Not only did his power numbers decline, he went through a defensive crisis that resulted in time spent at first base. It wasn't a case of "El Toro" in a China shop, either: He entered the year with more fielding than throwing errors, but in 2014 flubbed with the glove just once, compared to a whopping 24 times with his arm. Travis Sawchik, of the *Pittsburgh Tribune-Review*, wrote an article about the shoddy marksmanship in which Steve Blass expressed sympathy toward Alvarez, a nice gesture by the always gracious Blass, but an ominous development for the receiving player. Alvarez's awful season then ended prematurely following a stress reaction in his foot. His future—not just positionally, but with the Pirates—is very much in doubt.

Josh Bell   RF

Born: 8/14/92   Age: 22   Bats: B   Throws: R   Height: 6' 2"   Weight: 235

YEAR	TEAM	LVL	AGE	PA	R	2B	3B	HR	RBI	BB	K	SB	CS	AVG/OBP/SLG	TAv	BABIP	BRR	FRAA	WARP
2012	WVA	A	19	66	6	5	0	1	11	2	21	1	0	.274/.288/.403	.229	.381	-0.1	RF(14): -1.3	-0.2
2013	WVA	A	20	519	75	37	2	13	76	52	90	1	2	.279/.353/.453	.318	.319	-1.1	RF(83): 2.9	4.1
2014	BRD	A+	21	363	45	20	4	9	53	25	43	5	4	.335/.384/.502	.309	.364	-1.8	RF(62): -6.4	1.7
2014	ALT	AA	21	102	13	2	0	0	7	8	12	4	1	.287/.343/.309	.251	.329	0.3	RF(19): 0.4	0.3
2015	PIT	MLB	22	250	23	11	1	4	25	14	51	2	1	.251/.296/.360	.250	.300	-0.3	RF -1	0.0

Breakout: 2%   Improve: 24%   Collapse: 2%   Attrition: 23%   MLB: 38%   Comparables: *Domonic Brown, Brandon Moss, Shane Peterson*

Widely considered a steal from the 2011 draft, Bell had a mixed year. He earned a promotion to Altoona after hectoring Florida State League pitching, but left his pop behind in his McKechnie Field locker. Making matters worse for Bell—who had dealt with his share of ailments before—was a knee injury that ended his regular season a few weeks early. He did play in the Arizona Fall League, where he took a test drive at first base, an experiment that hints at how he might fit onto the big-league roster some day. Of course, before Bell reaches the majors he'll need to hit for power against advanced pitching. The Pirates play their spring games at McKechnie, so he'll have a chance to recover that missing thunder from his old stomping grounds.

Keon Broxton   OF

Born: 5/7/90   Age: 25   Bats: R   Throws: R   Height: 6' 3"   Weight: 195

YEAR	TEAM	LVL	AGE	PA	R	2B	3B	HR	RBI	BB	K	SB	CS	AVG/OBP/SLG	TAv	BABIP	BRR	FRAA	WARP
2012	VIS	A+	22	536	84	24	1	19	62	40	136	21	8	.267/.326/.437	.274	.332	2.5	CF(103): -1.8, LF(18): -0.2	2.5
2013	MOB	AA	23	372	40	13	3	8	41	30	116	5	1	.231/.296/.359	.239	.325	1.8	CF(48): 1.8, RF(35): -3.4	0.1
2014	ALT	AA	24	471	67	22	9	15	52	59	122	25	6	.275/.369/.484	.303	.357	4.4	CF(80): 4.0, LF(43): 6.3	5.1
2015	PIT	MLB	25	250	26	9	1	6	25	18	77	7	2	.221/.282/.348	.238	.302	0.7	CF 0, LF 1	0.2

Breakout: 12%   Improve: 20%   Collapse: 5%   Attrition: 36%   MLB: 45%   Comparables: *Melky Mesa, Matt Den Dekker, Brian Barton*

Broxton, perhaps annealed by a spring trade to the Pirates, showed the power-speed combination that convinced the Diamondbacks to draft him in the third round years ago. Although Altoona's lineup featured a couple of hosses in Stetson Allie and Willy Garcia, it was Broxton who led the team in isolated power. He did so while showing more than enough range to patrol center field and stealing at an acceptable rate. The contact concerns remain valid, particularly on breaking balls, and will limit his ceiling, but he should have a big-league future as an extra outfielder. Not a bad return on cash considerations.

Francisco Cervelli   C

Born: 3/6/86   Age: 29   Bats: R   Throws: R   Height: 6' 1"   Weight: 205

YEAR	TEAM	LVL	AGE	PA	R	2B	3B	HR	RBI	BB	K	SB	CS	AVG/OBP/SLG	TAv	BABIP	BRR	FRAA	WARP
2012	SWB	AAA	26	417	43	15	2	2	39	39	82	6	0	.246/.341/.316	.236	.308	-2.7	C(96): 0.6	0.7
2012	NYA	MLB	26	2	1	0	0	0	0	1	0	0	0	.000/.500/.000	.278	.000	0.1	C(3): -0.0	0.0
2013	NYA	MLB	27	61	12	3	0	3	8	8	9	0	0	.269/.377/.500	.321	.275	-0.3	C(16): 0.5, 2B(1): -0.0	0.8
2014	TRN	AA	28	20	2	0	0	0	0	4	4	0	0	.133/.350/.133	.199	.182	0.1	C(2): -0.0, 1B(2): -0.1	-0.1
2014	NYA	MLB	28	162	18	11	1	2	13	11	41	1	0	.301/.370/.432	.283	.408	-2.0	C(42): -0.3, 1B(5): -0.1	0.9
2015	PIT	MLB	29	250	23	10	1	2	21	22	49	2	0	.248/.330/.327	.255	.305	-0.9	C 0, 1B -0	0.7

Breakout: 4%   Improve: 28%   Collapse: 9%   Attrition: 25%   MLB: 82%   Comparables: *John Baker, Brayan Pena, Jose Lobaton*

Cervelli didn't manage to break anything in 2014, which made the season an improvement; instead, a hamstring pull, migraines and Brian McCann limited him to 49 games. That he's only topped that number once in seven years summarizes how it's gone for Cervelli, who wears an oversized helmet to protect against concussions and a weary expression to guard against the world's myriad disappointments. Cervelli has made the most of little windows of mercy, however, and in 2014 he coasted on a .408 BABIP to a ridiculous (for him) slash. He's also worked hard to transform his statistical defense from a negative to a shrug, and he's a solid pitch framer as well. Small sample aside, the Pirates traded a decent lefty reliever for him, and the Yankees succeeded in offloading one of the 13 catchers on their 40-man roster. Everyone comes away a winner, except perhaps Cervelli once the bees get him.

Jaff Decker   OF

Born: 2/23/90   Age: 25   Bats: L   Throws: L   Height: 5' 9"   Weight: 190

YEAR	TEAM	LVL	AGE	PA	R	2B	3B	HR	RBI	BB	K	SB	CS	AVG/OBP/SLG	TAv	BABIP	BRR	FRAA	WARP
2012	SAN	AA	22	190	30	3	2	3	9	40	37	6	2	.184/.365/.293	.275	.224	-1.4	RF(36): 0.3, CF(7): -0.5	0.6
2013	TUC	AAA	23	415	63	23	1	10	40	55	94	4	6	.286/.381/.443	.284	.361	2.5	CF(66): -2.8, RF(39): -2.9	2.2
2013	SDN	MLB	23	31	3	0	0	1	2	3	4	0	1	.154/.233/.269	.196	.136	-0.5	LF(8): 0.3	-0.3
2014	IND	AAA	24	409	41	27	1	6	39	51	73	7	6	.257/.355/.391	.255	.308	3.5	LF(79): 0.4, CF(20): -1.4	1.4
2014	PIT	MLB	24	5	0	0	0	0	0	0	3	0	0	.000/.000/.000	-.002	.000	0.0	LF(2): -0.0	-0.1
2015	PIT	MLB	25	250	29	10	0	4	21	29	57	3	3	.228/.324/.338	.257	.283	-0.7	LF 0, CF -1	0.2

Breakout: 9%   Improve: 15%   Collapse: 15%   Attrition: 28%   MLB: 40%   *Comparables: Shane Peterson, Cole Gillespie, Chad Huffman*

Added as part of a three-player trade with the Padres before 2014, Decker's numbers in the International League were predictably depressed compared to those he posted a year prior in the PCL. His super-patient approach resulted in a healthy on-base percentage, but he didn't show enough power or glove to profile as more than a bench bat in the majors. Clint Hurdle used Decker as just that during his big-league appearances, but management left him on the proverbial pine after rosters expanded, an indication that he might have fallen off the depth chart in a system dappled with similar players. Nonetheless, Decker is in for a long career as teams take turns seeing if he's Matt Stairs-meets-Snake Plissken, or if he just looks like it. (It's the latter.)

Elias Diaz   C

Born: 11/17/90   Age: 24   Bats: R   Throws: R   Height: 6' 1"   Weight: 175

YEAR	TEAM	LVL	AGE	PA	R	2B	3B	HR	RBI	BB	K	SB	CS	AVG/OBP/SLG	TAv	BABIP	BRR	FRAA	WARP
2012	WVA	A	21	347	32	14	1	3	26	22	51	2	2	.208/.262/.288	.197	.234	-1.2	C(92): 2.1	-0.7
2013	BRD	A+	22	220	30	12	2	2	15	31	33	4	4	.279/.382/.399	.290	.327	-1.5	C(55): -1.4	1.3
2014	ALT	AA	23	367	41	20	0	6	54	30	51	3	2	.328/.378/.445	.296	.365	0.8	C(88): 1.2, 1B(1): 0.1	4.0
2014	IND	AAA	23	37	4	1	0	0	0	3	6	0	1	.152/.243/.182	.172	.185	0.2	C(9): -0.2	-0.2
2015	PIT	MLB	24	250	21	10	1	2	20	17	49	1	1	.232/.288/.310	.230	.281	-0.5	C -0, 1B 0	0.2

Breakout: 3%   Improve: 4%   Collapse: 2%   Attrition: 9%   MLB: 10%   *Comparables: Jordan Pacheco, Steve Clevenger, Bryan Holaday*

A catcher needn't possess more than a good arm and some defensive acumen to earn consideration for a backup job. Diaz fits both qualifications, setting a nice major-league floor, though his recent offensive improvements could have him competing for a starting job as well. He's never going to hit for much power, but he has shown an appreciable ability to make contact and reach base. Bundle those offensive skills with his work behind the plate and it's no wonder Diaz forced Tony Sanchez to first base late in the year.

Willy Garcia   OF

Born: 9/4/92   Age: 22   Bats: R   Throws: R   Height: 6' 3"   Weight: 180

YEAR	TEAM	LVL	AGE	PA	R	2B	3B	HR	RBI	BB	K	SB	CS	AVG/OBP/SLG	TAv	BABIP	BRR	FRAA	WARP
2012	WVA	A	19	497	57	17	2	18	77	32	131	10	8	.240/.286/.403	.237	.292	-1.9	LF(58): 3.6, RF(56): -3.7	-0.5
2013	BRD	A+	20	480	51	21	6	16	60	23	154	13	6	.256/.294/.437	.257	.351	-1.2	RF(114): 2.8, CF(2): -0.1	1.3
2014	ALT	AA	21	474	59	27	5	18	63	24	145	8	4	.271/.311/.478	.280	.361	1.2	RF(103): -3.7, LF(19): 0.6	2.0
2015	PIT	MLB	22	250	24	9	1	7	27	9	87	3	1	.214/.246/.355	.223	.298	0.0	RF -1, LF 1	-0.6

Breakout: 0%   Improve: 0%   Collapse: 0%   Attrition: 0%   MLB: 0%   *Comparables: Steven Moya, Marcell Ozuna, Jeremy Moore*

There's a lot to like about Garcia. His arm strength and raw power are good enough to man right field, he's continued to improve with each promotion over the past few seasons and hey, he's still a baby. But then there's his free-swinging approach, which threatens to sabotage his upside. How bad are things? Garcia's strikeout-to-walk ratio was the second-worst among Double-A hitters who fanned in at least 25 percent of their plate appearances. (Detroit's Steven Moya took first.) The rule of thumb is that it's fine to strike out a lot or walk a little, but not to do both. Should Garcia tighten his approach, he has the chance to be a fun player.

Alen Hanson   SS

Born: 10/22/92   Age: 22   Bats: B   Throws: R   Height: 5' 11"   Weight: 170

YEAR	TEAM	LVL	AGE	PA	R	2B	3B	HR	RBI	BB	K	SB	CS	AVG/OBP/SLG	TAv	BABIP	BRR	FRAA	WARP
2012	WVA	A	19	558	99	33	13	16	62	55	105	35	19	.309/.381/.528	.315	.364	6.3	SS(103): -14.0	4.2
2013	BRD	A+	20	409	51	23	8	7	48	33	70	24	14	.281/.339/.444	.283	.325	2.0	SS(92): 2.4	3.4
2013	ALT	AA	20	150	13	4	5	1	10	8	26	6	2	.255/.299/.380	.273	.306	-0.9	SS(34): -1.6	0.6
2014	ALT	AA	21	527	64	21	12	11	58	31	88	25	11	.280/.326/.442	.283	.321	-0.9	SS(100): -0.6, 2B(17): 1.3	3.5
2015	PIT	MLB	22	250	30	10	3	4	20	14	56	9	4	.245/.289/.368	.246	.297	0.7	SS -2, 2B 0	0.5

Breakout: 5%   Improve: 32%   Collapse: 4%   Attrition: 18%   MLB: 47%   *Comparables: Tim Beckham, Junior Lake, Arismendy Alcantara*

The problem with prospects is the older they get, the less they resemble their perfect-world selves. Hanson is a good example. He's never going to be an all-star shortstop: The footwork, instincts and arm strength aren't there. Knowing that, the Pirates did the smart thing and played him at second base during the season's final month. Sliding down the defensive spectrum isn't the only way Hanson has let dreamers down. His approach remains undisciplined, his power is likely to play as fringe-average and he was benched twice for not hustling. Hanson remains the odds-on favorite to succeed Neil Walker at second base; that's just not the exciting probability it was a few years ago.

Josh Harrison   3B

Born: 7/8/87   Age: 27   Bats: R   Throws: R   Height: 5' 8"   Weight: 200

YEAR	TEAM	LVL	AGE	PA	R	2B	3B	HR	RBI	BB	K	SB	CS	AVG/OBP/SLG	TAv	BABIP	BRR	FRAA	WARP
2012	PIT	MLB	24	276	34	9	5	3	16	10	37	7	3	.233/.279/.345	.238	.259	0.3	2B(28): -0.3, SS(25): -2.0	0.1
2013	IND	AAA	25	296	50	29	5	4	34	20	39	19	7	.317/.373/.507	.297	.360	1.0	2B(33): 4.6, SS(29): 3.3	3.0
2013	PIT	MLB	25	95	10	1	2	3	14	2	10	2	0	.250/.290/.409	.238	.253	0.7	RF(14): -0.8, 2B(11): 0.6	0.1
2014	PIT	MLB	26	550	77	38	7	13	52	22	81	18	6	.315/.347/.490	.308	.353	0.4	3B(72): 4.0, LF(26): -1.7	5.1
2015	PIT	MLB	27	461	57	26	4	7	42	20	64	16	6	.282/.321/.415	.274	.309	0.3	3B 2, 2B 2	2.3

Breakout: 4%   Improve: 47%   Collapse: 7%   Attrition: 19%   MLB: 96%   *Comparables: Danny Valencia, Garrett Atkins, Jorge Cantu*

This is where we apologize to Harrison, Clint Hurdle and Neal Huntington for doubting them all these years. Let's go to the highlights:

From *BP 2012*: "It's a shame Harrison has no interest in taking free passes, since he could be a useful player if his walk rate ever exceeded his height."

From *BP 2013*: "Figuring out why the Pirates like Harrison enough to keep him around is tough."

From *BP 2014*: "Realistically, it's hard to see the pipsqueak-sized Harrison hitting for much pop heading forward, and that leaves his ability to produce offensively in doubt."

We were wrong, we were wrong, we were wrong. Harrison went on to have an all-star season. He hit more home runs and stole more bases than he had in his previous seasons combined, he played better defense than Pedro Alvarez at third base and he provided energy that, while its impact was likely overstated, did make him an enjoyable viewing experience. We went from unconvinced that he should be on a big-league roster to agreeing with those who thought he deserved down-ballot MVP votes.

But us being us, we can't help but wonder if Harrison will ever approximate his production again. Usually legitimate breakouts bring with them improvements in underlying areas. Harrison's? Not so much. He did walk more, but not by much, and his career-best ISO wasn't far removed from his effort in 2013. Even his plate discipline stats are mixed: He swung about as often, made a little less contact and chased out of the zone more than he had in 2013. Viewed from a historical perspective, there's a fair chance Harrison is just the newest version of Mark Loretta or Willie Harris, neither of whom built upon their momentum.

None of this is meant to take away from Harrison or his incredible 2014. We'd just like to see a little more before we buy into the idea that he's an above-average player. And if we're underselling him, we'll be more than happy to admit it. Again.

Andrew Lambo   OF
Born: 8/11/88   Age: 26   Bats: L   Throws: L   Height: 6' 3"   Weight: 225

YEAR	TEAM	LVL	AGE	PA	R	2B	3B	HR	RBI	BB	K	SB	CS	AVG/OBP/SLG	TAv	BABIP	BRR	FRAA	WARP
2012	ALT	AA	23	108	13	3	1	4	16	14	19	0	1	.250/.346/.435	.284	.271	-0.9	RF(26): 4.1	1.0
2013	ALT	AA	24	247	35	9	4	14	46	20	60	6	1	.291/.351/.559	.319	.336	-0.3	LF(38): 3.5, 1B(18): -0.3	2.3
2013	IND	AAA	24	254	32	15	1	18	53	24	67	1	0	.272/.344/.589	.306	.303	0.7	RF(32): 0.5, LF(22): 0.2	1.9
2013	PIT	MLB	24	33	4	2	0	1	2	3	11	0	1	.233/.303/.400	.253	.333	0.4	RF(6): -0.8, LF(2): 0.1	0.0
2014	IND	AAA	25	262	44	19	2	11	42	22	47	3	2	.328/.389/.563	.308	.372	-0.8	1B(17): 0.6, LF(16): -0.2	1.7
2014	PIT	MLB	25	39	3	4	0	0	1	0	8	0	0	.256/.256/.359	.208	.323	-0.1	RF(6): 0.3, 1B(1): 0.0	-0.1
2015	PIT	MLB	26	250	30	11	1	10	35	18	62	2	1	.257/.315/.455	.284	.303	-0.2	RF 0, LF 0	1.1

Breakout: 3%   Improve: 23%   Collapse: 10%   Attrition: 20%   MLB: 55%   Comparables: *Russ Canzler, Joe Mather, Tommy Medica*

Neal Huntington collects former top prospects like your grandmother hoards gimcracks. Lambo, who somehow out-endured James McDonald as the last player still swashbuckling from the Octavio Dotel trade, is one such example. Prior to dealing for Ike Davis, the Pirates had an obvious need for a left-handed first baseman. Rather than go with Lambo, the top internal choice, they rolled with perpetual disappointment Travis Ishikawa. Ouch. Lambo did receive a promotion in late August and spent September as a pinch-hitter, meaning Clint Hurdle knows his name, or at least his number. But is that a good sign? Perhaps familiarity is working against Lambo, leaving him buried behind Huntington's ever-growing stash of busts.

Starling Marte   LF
Born: 10/9/88   Age: 26   Bats: R   Throws: R   Height: 6' 1"   Weight: 185

YEAR	TEAM	LVL	AGE	PA	R	2B	3B	HR	RBI	BB	K	SB	CS	AVG/OBP/SLG	TAv	BABIP	BRR	FRAA	WARP
2012	IND	AAA	23	431	64	21	13	12	62	28	91	21	12	.286/.347/.500	.283	.344	-2.2	CF(76): 2.0, LF(16): 2.3	2.8
2012	PIT	MLB	23	182	18	3	6	5	17	8	50	12	5	.257/.300/.437	.270	.333	-1.1	LF(43): -2.0, CF(4): -0.0	0.2
2013	PIT	MLB	24	566	83	26	10	12	35	25	138	41	15	.280/.343/.441	.286	.363	3.1	LF(124): -2.1, CF(13): -0.0	2.9
2014	PIT	MLB	25	545	73	29	6	13	56	33	131	30	11	.291/.356/.453	.315	.373	1.5	LF(114): -5.5, CF(28): -2.7	3.7
2015	PIT	MLB	26	518	73	23	7	12	49	28	125	30	12	.271/.330/.424	.285	.341	0.4	LF -2, CF -1	2.2

Breakout: 5%   Improve: 53%   Collapse: 11%   Attrition: 16%   MLB: 99%   Comparables: *Carlos Gonzalez, Hunter Pence, Matt Kemp*

The Pirates so believed in Marte following his rookie season that they extended him for six years and $31 million. Perhaps spirited by the show of confidence, Marte had an even better season than his rookie campaign: He upped his average, on-base percentage and slugging percentage, all while continuing to play left field as though he were a displaced center fielder. There remains room for improvement, particularly when it comes to his stolen-base efficiency, and his affinity for getting drilled by pitches is a pro—it helps buoy his OBP, after all—that could turn into a big con if/when he suffers a serious injury. Still, through one year, Marte looks worth the money and the risk.

Andrew McCutchen   CF
Born: 10/10/86   Age: 28   Bats: R   Throws: R   Height: 5' 10"   Weight: 190

YEAR	TEAM	LVL	AGE	PA	R	2B	3B	HR	RBI	BB	K	SB	CS	AVG/OBP/SLG	TAv	BABIP	BRR	FRAA	WARP
2012	PIT	MLB	25	673	107	29	6	31	96	70	132	20	12	.327/.400/.553	.338	.375	-0.5	CF(156): -9.9	6.4
2013	PIT	MLB	26	674	97	38	5	21	84	78	101	27	10	.317/.404/.508	.330	.353	1.0	CF(155): -8.9	6.1
2014	PIT	MLB	27	648	89	38	6	25	83	84	115	18	3	.314/.410/.542	.354	.355	1.1	CF(146): -8.0	7.1
2015	PIT	MLB	28	614	83	31	4	19	80	72	105	20	7	.294/.384/.477	.321	.331	0.4	CF -7	4.9

Breakout: 0%   Improve: 51%   Collapse: 1%   Attrition: 2%   MLB: 100%   Comparables: *Willie Mays, Frank Robinson, Hank Aaron*

Practically the perfect franchise player.

Reese McGuire   C
Born: 3/2/95   Age: 20   Bats: L   Throws: R   Height: 6' 0"   Weight: 181

YEAR	TEAM	LVL	AGE	PA	R	2B	3B	HR	RBI	BB	K	SB	CS	AVG/OBP/SLG	TAv	BABIP	BRR	FRAA	WARP
2014	WVA	A	19	428	46	11	4	3	45	24	44	7	2	.262/.307/.334	.232	.284	0.2	C(84): 0.4	1.2
2015	PIT	MLB	20	250	15	9	1	0	18	8	46	0	0	.218/.248/.265	.199	.264	-0.3	C 0	-0.7

Breakout: 0%   Improve: 0%   Collapse: 0%   Attrition: 0%   MLB: 0%   Comparables: *Miguel Gonzalez, Salvador Perez, Christian Vazquez*

His arm is strong, his feet nimble and his leadership qualities could result in a book deal down the road (working title: *Squat Down*). Oh, and he ought to hit a little, too. McGuire is so promising as a field general that we just know he wouldn't want other catchers in the system to get down after reading this comment, so here's a rundown of his negatives that ought to make everyone feel better: He doesn't project for more than a dozen homers a season thanks to a contact-oriented swing; he's at least another year away; and he's a young catcher, and those are as prone to attrition as baby turtles. But golly, isn't he just wonderful?

Austin Meadows   OF

Born: 5/3/95   Age: 20   Bats: L   Throws: L   Height: 6' 3"   Weight: 200

YEAR	TEAM	LVL	AGE	PA	R	2B	3B	HR	RBI	BB	K	SB	CS	AVG/OBP/SLG	TAv	BABIP	BRR	FRAA	WARP
2013	JAM	A-	18	22	8	0	0	2	2	5	4	0	0	.529/.636/.882	.506	.636	0.5	CF(5): 0.5	0.8
2014	WVA	A	19	167	18	13	1	3	15	14	30	2	3	.322/.388/.486	.293	.383	-0.3	CF(38): -0.0	1.2
2015	PIT	MLB	20	250	21	10	1	3	23	17	67	1	1	.219/.278/.313	.226	.289	-0.5	CF -1	-0.3

Breakout: 0%   Improve: 0%   Collapse: 0%   Attrition: 0%   MLB: 0%   Comparables: *Fernando Martinez, Aaron Hicks, Oswaldo Arcia*

Sidelined by a hamstring injury for most of the first half, Meadows joined West Virginia in mid-July and looked no worse for the missed time. He finished the season among the league leaders in average and on-base percentage, but slipped when it came to slugging. Scouts think Meadows could develop above-average power as he matures, but his flat swing plane is more conductive to the gaps than the bleachers. Fortunately, his contributions on the basepaths and in the outfield should atone for his lack of home runs. Playing center is often a concomitant of outfielder development, yet Meadows is athletic enough to stick there. His arm is well below average, though, so expect him to slide to left if he is moved to a corner. Wherever he winds up, Meadows projects as a future starter.

Jordy Mercer   SS

Born: 8/27/86   Age: 28   Bats: R   Throws: R   Height: 6' 3"   Weight: 205

YEAR	TEAM	LVL	AGE	PA	R	2B	3B	HR	RBI	BB	K	SB	CS	AVG/OBP/SLG	TAv	BABIP	BRR	FRAA	WARP
2012	IND	AAA	25	236	28	14	1	4	27	20	45	3	5	.287/.357/.421	.281	.346	1.8	SS(33): 2.5, 2B(11): 1.5	1.9
2012	PIT	MLB	25	68	7	5	1	1	5	4	14	0	1	.210/.265/.371	.232	.250	0.1	SS(28): 0.4, 2B(7): 0.7	0.1
2013	IND	AAA	26	109	11	6	1	1	19	12	17	3	1	.333/.404/.448	.293	.392	-0.3	SS(23): 3.4, 2B(2): 0.2	1.2
2013	PIT	MLB	26	365	33	22	2	8	27	22	62	3	2	.285/.336/.435	.274	.330	-4.0	SS(78): -0.9, 2B(26): 2.9	1.6
2014	PIT	MLB	27	555	56	27	2	12	55	35	89	4	1	.255/.305/.387	.259	.285	3.9	SS(144): 8.0, RF(1): -0.0	3.8
2015	PIT	MLB	28	497	51	26	2	9	50	33	87	4	2	.263/.319/.389	.267	.302	-0.1	SS 5, 2B 1	3.1

Breakout: 4%   Improve: 46%   Collapse: 3%   Attrition: 9%   MLB: 97%   Comparables: *Bobby Crosby, Jed Lowrie, Zack Cozart*

The best shortstop to make his big-league debut with the Pirates since Jack Wilson—hey, don't laugh, Josh Rodriguez might hear you. Mercer does nothing extremely well or poorly. He hits for some average, takes some walks and provides some power. He's more nimble in the field than his large frame suggests, and he took well to a shift-heavy system that asks him to obsessively shade this or that way. No, Mercer isn't a threat to play in a midsummer classic, but he's a solid, no-frills starter who can hang around the bottom of a lineup until someone better comes along.

Gregory Polanco   RF

Born: 9/14/91   Age: 23   Bats: L   Throws: L   Height: 6' 4"   Weight: 220

YEAR	TEAM	LVL	AGE	PA	R	2B	3B	HR	RBI	BB	K	SB	CS	AVG/OBP/SLG	TAv	BABIP	BRR	FRAA	WARP
2012	WVA	A	20	485	84	26	6	16	85	44	64	40	15	.325/.388/.522	.321	.352	5.7	CF(98): -2.6	4.9
2013	BRD	A+	21	241	29	17	0	6	30	16	37	24	4	.312/.364/.472	.311	.350	1.3	CF(56): -0.0	2.3
2013	ALT	AA	21	286	36	13	2	6	41	36	36	13	7	.263/.354/.407	.286	.282	1.7	CF(58): 6.3, RF(6): -0.3	2.6
2014	IND	AAA	22	305	51	17	5	7	51	28	49	16	6	.328/.390/.504	.304	.377	0.7	RF(69): 7.7	3.1
2014	PIT	MLB	22	312	50	9	0	7	33	30	59	14	5	.235/.307/.343	.247	.272	2.3	RF(83): 5.8	1.4
2015	PIT	MLB	23	339	40	14	2	7	34	27	63	15	5	.257/.318/.382	.266	.298	1.1	RF 5, CF 1	1.6

Breakout: 1%   Improve: 42%   Collapse: 5%   Attrition: 14%   MLB: 71%   Comparables: *Fernando Martinez, Dayan Viciedo, Andrew McCutchen*

"How Far We've Come" is a catchy song by Matchbox Twenty and the soundtrack to this comment. Sing along with the end if that's what you wanna do. *It was cool cool, it was just all cool.* Polanco, left to marinate in the minors until after the Super Two deadline, began his Pirates career with a franchise record 11-game hitting streak. Locals responded in measured tones by talking about how, at long last, Roberto Clemente had a real successor. (What, Jeromy Burnitz meant nothing to you people?) *Now it's over for me, and it's over for you.* Polanco then encountered some timing issues, leading him to a 1-for-30 stretch that ended with a demotion to the minors. When he returned in September, his role was minimized in favor of the streaking Travis Snider. *Let's see how far we've come* (seven times). Rookie struggles aside, Polanco should make the necessary adjustments and develop into a well rounded right fielder. Remember, even Mike Trout stumbled at first.

Sean Rodriguez   2B

Born: 4/26/85   Age: 30   Bats: R   Throws: R   Height: 6' 0"   Weight: 200

YEAR	TEAM	LVL	AGE	PA	R	2B	3B	HR	RBI	BB	K	SB	CS	AVG/OBP/SLG	TAv	BABIP	BRR	FRAA	WARP
2012	TBA	MLB	27	342	36	14	1	6	32	27	75	5	0	.213/.281/.326	.225	.260	0.9	3B(49): 4.0, SS(47): 4.2	0.8
2013	TBA	MLB	28	222	21	10	1	5	23	17	59	1	3	.246/.320/.385	.272	.323	-0.3	LF(47): 0.4, 1B(23): 0.4	0.9
2014	TBA	MLB	29	259	30	13	3	12	41	10	66	2	1	.211/.258/.443	.259	.235	-1.4	2B(23): 0.3, 1B(18): 0.4	0.1
2015	PIT	MLB	30	250	26	11	1	5	24	17	58	3	2	.233/.304/.361	.253	.284	-0.4	LF 0, 1B 1	0.6

Breakout: 2%   Improve: 47%   Collapse: 2%   Attrition: 4%   MLB: 93%   Comparables: *Ryne Sandberg, Dick McAuliffe, Orlando Hudson*

The ability to play multiple positions remains Rodriguez's key attribute. He appeared at six different spots in 2014, handling each one at least adequately. He has tremendous instincts regardless of where he lines up, and his arm plays anywhere. Though he lacked a regular position or consistent playing time, he belted double-digit home runs for the first time in his career. Unfortunately, the occasional dinger is about the only offensive skill he showed and his appetite for chasing out of the zone was awakened after a year of suppression. Still arbitration eligible, his defensive acumen and versatility make him a bargain even with the offensive warts.

Gaby Sanchez   1B

Born: 9/2/83   Age: 31   Bats: R   Throws: R   Height: 6' 1"   Weight: 235

YEAR	TEAM	LVL	AGE	PA	R	2B	3B	HR	RBI	BB	K	SB	CS	AVG/OBP/SLG	TAv	BABIP	BRR	FRAA	WARP
2012	NWO	AAA	28	144	20	7	0	5	18	22	23	2	2	.302/.431/.491	.329	.337	0.7	1B(31): -0.4	1.4
2012	MIA	MLB	28	196	12	10	0	3	17	12	36	1	0	.202/.250/.306	.201	.234	-0.1	1B(54): 5.8	-0.6
2012	PIT	MLB	28	130	18	6	0	4	13	13	20	0	0	.241/.323/.397	.245	.261	0.5	1B(41): 0.7	0.3
2013	PIT	MLB	29	320	29	18	0	7	36	44	51	1	0	.254/.361/.402	.290	.282	1.8	1B(113): -1.2, 3B(1): -0.0	1.1
2014	PIT	MLB	30	290	31	18	1	7	33	23	58	2	0	.229/.293/.385	.257	.265	-0.9	1B(96): 3.7, RF(1): -0.0	0.6
2015	PIT	MLB	31	278	29	14	0	6	31	27	44	1	0	.249/.329/.387	.273	.276	0.2	1B 1, RF -0	0.9

Breakout: 0%   Improve: 39%   Collapse: 4%   Attrition: 5%   MLB: 91%   Comparables: Lyle Overbay, Mike Sweeney, Aubrey Huff

There aren't many reserve right-handed first basemen for a reason: They add limited value and their optimal usage equates to almost no usage at all. Consider Sanchez's 2014. Though he'd spent the previous season-and-a-half with the platoon-happy Pirates, it wasn't until last year that he faced left-handed pitchers in more than 50 percent of his plate appearances. Sounds good, right? Except that religious devotion to matchups left Sanchez with a greater number of pinch-hit appearances than games started, and with a career-worst rate of complete games; even when he did start, he was often lifted for Ike Davis late. Sanchez's production versus southpaws remained respectable: His walks dipped, but the average and power were there. The poor overall numbers are part of the job, which is why Sanchez should ask for hazard pay.

Tony Sanchez   C
Born: 5/20/88   Age: 27   Bats: R   Throws: R   Height: 5' 11"   Weight: 225

YEAR	TEAM	LVL	AGE	PA	R	2B	3B	HR	RBI	BB	K	SB	CS	AVG/OBP/SLG	TAv	BABIP	BRR	FRAA	WARP
2012	ALT	AA	24	162	22	14	1	0	17	18	33	1	1	.277/.370/.390	.286	.361	-2.7	C(37): 0.4	0.8
2012	IND	AAA	24	236	21	12	0	8	26	23	46	0	0	.233/.316/.408	.248	.260	-1.7	C(59): -0.7	0.4
2013	IND	AAA	25	296	35	26	0	10	42	28	60	0	0	.288/.368/.504	.285	.339	-0.8	C(72): -0.6	1.7
2013	PIT	MLB	25	66	9	4	0	2	5	3	14	0	0	.233/.288/.400	.271	.267	0.2	C(16): -0.2	0.3
2014	IND	AAA	26	313	30	17	0	11	45	38	76	0	0	.235/.337/.422	.258	.284	-1.1	C(70): 0.5, 1B(2): -0.0	0.9
2014	PIT	MLB	26	80	3	1	0	2	13	3	28	0	0	.267/.300/.360	.248	.391	-0.3	C(20): -0.3	0.1
2015	PIT	MLB	27	250	25	12	0	6	28	20	62	0	0	.235/.307/.377	.259	.292	-0.5	C -0, 1B -0	0.9

Breakout: 5%   Improve: 17%   Collapse: 7%   Attrition: 23%   MLB: 42%   Comparables: Max Ramirez, George Kottaras, Chris Gimenez

Let's play good news, bad news. Good news: Sanchez isn't the biggest bust from the 2009 draft (he was selected between Donavan Tate and Matt Hobgood). Bad news: He's not Zack Wheeler, Mike Leake or even Victor Black, the other player the Pirates drafted in that round. Good news: Sanchez receives so well his nickname ought to be Antenna. Bad news: He threw out just 13 percent of prospective basestealers, meaning his nickname could also be Broken Antenna. Good news: Sanchez spent more time in the majors in 2014. Bad news: He was bumped to first base late in the year by a pop-up prospect. Good news: Sanchez might eke out a career as a backup catcher. Bad news: That's about the best-case scenario.

Travis Snider   OF
Born: 2/2/88   Age: 27   Bats: L   Throws: L   Height: 6' 0"   Weight: 235

YEAR	TEAM	LVL	AGE	PA	R	2B	3B	HR	RBI	BB	K	SB	CS	AVG/OBP/SLG	TAv	BABIP	BRR	FRAA	WARP
2012	DUN	A+	24	23	3	1	0	0	1	1	5	2	0	.227/.261/.273	.185	.294	0.4	LF(3): 0.0, CF(1): -0.0	-0.1
2012	LVG	AAA	24	246	49	16	0	13	56	34	42	2	4	.335/.423/.598	.321	.363	0.2	LF(34): -0.7, RF(10): -0.5	2.0
2012	PIT	MLB	24	145	17	5	1	1	9	14	34	2	0	.250/.324/.328	.250	.326	0.5	RF(33): 0.6, LF(5): 0.1	0.3
2012	TOR	MLB	24	40	6	2	0	3	8	3	14	0	0	.250/.300/.556	.302	.300	0.0	LF(10): 0.6	0.3
2013	IND	AAA	25	38	4	1	0	0	5	5	8	1	1	.344/.421/.375	.318	.440	0.2	RF(5): -0.6	0.3
2013	PIT	MLB	25	285	28	12	2	5	25	24	75	2	3	.215/.281/.333	.230	.282	-3.3	RF(79): 3.7, LF(5): -0.0	-0.4
2014	PIT	MLB	26	359	37	15	1	13	38	34	67	1	1	.264/.338/.438	.284	.298	1.9	RF(64): -3.8, LF(36): 0.7	1.5
2015	PIT	MLB	27	328	39	16	1	8	32	27	75	3	2	.250/.314/.387	.265	.305	-0.4	RF -2, LF 0	0.6

Breakout: 5%   Improve: 49%   Collapse: 7%   Attrition: 14%   MLB: 93%   Comparables: Corey Hart, Josh Reddick, Travis Buck

As if we didn't have enough to apologize for given our years of Josh Harrison-related skepticism, we were downright arctic about Snider last year. We'd love to claim that our dismissive comment was meant for motivational purposes, but come on, who thought he would do this? Even the Pirates couldn't have foreseen Snider cutting into his strikeouts and homering more times against righties in a single season than he had in the previous three combined. So where does he go from here? Snider is now 27 years old—or roughly a year and a half younger than Andrew McCutchen—and would be a lock in almost any team's lineup. The problem is the Pirates have Gregory Polanco ready to take over in right field, which leaves Snider as the odd man out. Expect a trade soon, if it didn't happen while this book was at the printer, and expect the Pirates to get more than Brad Lincoln in return.

Chris Stewart   C
Born: 2/19/82   Age: 33   Bats: R   Throws: R   Height: 6' 4"   Weight: 210

YEAR	TEAM	LVL	AGE	PA	R	2B	3B	HR	RBI	BB	K	SB	CS	AVG/OBP/SLG	TAv	BABIP	BRR	FRAA	WARP
2012	NYA	MLB	30	157	15	8	0	1	13	10	21	2	0	.241/.292/.319	.238	.273	0.4	C(54): -0.5	0.4
2013	NYA	MLB	31	340	28	6	0	4	25	30	49	4	0	.211/.293/.272	.219	.237	-2.7	C(108): 0.6, 1B(2): -0.0	-0.1
2014	PIT	MLB	32	154	9	5	0	0	10	12	27	0	1	.294/.362/.331	.263	.364	0.1	C(46): 0.5	0.8
2015	PIT	MLB	33	250	22	9	0	1	18	20	36	2	1	.232/.304/.289	.233	.266	-0.7	C 1, 1B -0	0.3

Breakout: 4%   Improve: 33%   Collapse: 10%   Attrition: 18%   MLB: 87%   Comparables: Paul Lo Duca, Tim McCarver, Gerald Laird

Starter on the Pirates turned backup on the Yankees. It's an old, tiresome dance that we've seen performed too many times before. What the whole thing does, really, is underscore how bad baseball's competitive balance is, and how much we need … wait. Stewart went from starter on the Yankees to backup on the Pirates? My oh my, do we live in strange times, times when dogs have blogs and sabermetrically inclined writers embrace offensively challenged catchers, which, it should be noted, is what Stewart remains. Despite BABIP-fueled raw numbers suggesting otherwise, his underlying indicators declined: He walked less, struck out more and produced little power. That's okay, though. Teams don't employ Stewart for his bat, but rather his mitt, arm and ability to boggle minds.

Jose Tabata   OF
Born: 8/12/88   Age: 26   Bats: R   Throws: R   Height: 5' 11"   Weight: 210

YEAR	TEAM	LVL	AGE	PA	R	2B	3B	HR	RBI	BB	K	SB	CS	AVG/OBP/SLG	TAv	BABIP	BRR	FRAA	WARP
2012	IND	AAA	23	173	21	9	0	0	15	10	20	5	2	.297/.353/.354	.248	.338	0.5	CF(25): -0.1, RF(15): 1.4	0.7
2012	PIT	MLB	23	374	43	20	3	3	16	29	58	8	12	.243/.315/.348	.246	.287	-0.2	RF(77): -0.5, LF(32): 2.3	0.2
2013	IND	AAA	24	32	1	1	0	0	0	3	7	1	0	.179/.281/.214	.180	.238	0.2	RF(8): -0.0	-0.2
2013	PIT	MLB	24	341	35	17	5	6	33	23	45	3	1	.282/.342/.429	.279	.315	0.9	RF(50): -4.4, LF(40): 1.4	1.1
2014	IND	AAA	25	163	18	10	0	0	12	10	14	1	2	.281/.337/.349	.244	.304	-0.1	RF(31): -0.0, LF(2): -0.0	0.1
2014	PIT	MLB	25	186	14	5	2	0	17	7	26	1	1	.282/.314/.333	.228	.327	0.4	RF(37): -1.9, LF(18): 0.7	-0.5
2015	PIT	MLB	26	250	28	12	1	2	19	19	36	4	3	.270/.333/.358	.264	.310	0.3	RF -3, LF 1	0.5

Breakout: 4%   Improve: 53%   Collapse: 14%   Attrition: 20%   MLB: 96%   Comparables: Matt Murton, Jacoby Ellsbury, Ryan Sweeney

Proof that life comes at you fast and not all team-friendly extensions pay dividends. Tabata, who signed a six-year deal back in 2011, was removed from the 40-man roster in June after a string of poor play; he passed through waivers untouched. He returned to the big leagues two months later, but didn't move the needle during his sporadic appearances. Owed a little less than $9 million over the next two seasons, Tabata is about to become the richest regular in the International League. He'll be the most popular, too, provided he shares the wealth and picks up all the bar tabs.

Cole Tucker   SS

Born: 7/3/96   Age: 18   Bats: B   Throws: R   Height: 6' 3"   Weight: 185

YEAR	TEAM	LVL	AGE	PA	R	2B	3B	HR	RBI	BB	K	SB	CS	AVG/OBP/SLG	TAv	BABIP	BRR	FRAA	WARP
2015	PIT	MLB	18	250	23	8	1	2	15	12	72	5	2	.196/.240/.257	.192	.268	0.0	SS -1	-0.8

Breakout: 0%   Improve: 0%   Collapse: 0%   Attrition: 0%   MLB: 0%   Comparables: *Adrian Cardenas, Argenis Diaz, Carlos Rivero*

Considered an overdraft at no. 24—a perception reinforced by his underslot agreement—Tucker is no Daniel Moskos. While he lacks a carrying tool, everything but his power grades as average or better, and given his spindly frame and extreme youth, he could add muscle as he matures. Factor in his ability to stick at shortstop and the result is a solid, if unspectacular, prospect. Besides, any carping about Tucker's underslot agreement misses an important point: The Pirates exceeded their allotted bonus pool overall. Pittsburgh's portfolio approach to the draft saw them hand out four overslot deals, including one to 11th-rounder Gage Hinsz that paid him third-round money. By the way, Peter Gammons reported Oakland would have selected Tucker with the very next pick, so the youngster has fans within the industry outside of the Steel City.

Neil Walker   2B

Born: 9/10/85   Age: 29   Bats: B   Throws: R   Height: 6' 3"   Weight: 210

YEAR	TEAM	LVL	AGE	PA	R	2B	3B	HR	RBI	BB	K	SB	CS	AVG/OBP/SLG	TAv	BABIP	BRR	FRAA	WARP
2012	PIT	MLB	26	530	62	27	0	14	69	47	104	7	5	.280/.342/.426	.283	.326	-1.1	2B(125): -0.9	2.3
2013	PIT	MLB	27	551	62	24	4	16	53	50	85	1	2	.251/.339/.418	.278	.274	0.8	2B(132): 3.6	2.9
2014	PIT	MLB	28	571	74	25	3	23	76	45	88	2	2	.271/.342/.467	.297	.288	0.4	2B(135): -3.4	3.5
2015	PIT	MLB	29	536	58	26	2	13	62	46	93	3	3	.267/.337/.412	.282	.303	0.0	2B -5	2.5

Breakout: 3%   Improve: 38%   Collapse: 2%   Attrition: 8%   MLB: 100%   Comparables: *Kelly Johnson, Ian Kinsler, Robinson Cano*

Walker, alongside Jordy Mercer, formed the tallest double-play combination this side of Colorado. When not providing baserunners with shade, Walker threw plenty of it at opposing pitchers: He had a career-best season that saw him hit 20-plus homers for the first time, majors or minors. The upped pop wasn't accompanied by a change in strikeouts or walks, and he even improved his production against lefties, which have always been a splinter in his heel. If there is a negative, from a Pittsburgh perspective, it's that Walker is increasing his price as he nears his 2016 date with free agency. Given how the Pirates haven't agreed to an extension with the hometown boy as of press time, it's looking more and more like he'll spend his 30s in another city.

Pitchers

John Axford   RHP

Born: 4/1/83   Age: 32   Bats: R   Throws: R   Height: 6'5"   Weight: 220

YEAR	TEAM	LVL	AGE	W	L	SV	G	GS	IP	H	HR	BB	K	BB/9	K/9	GB%	BABIP	WHIP	ERA	FIP	FRA	WARP
2012	MIL	MLB	29	5	8	35	75	0	69¹	61	10	39	93	5.1	12.1	48%	.307	1.44	4.67	4.10	3.91	0.7
2013	MIL	MLB	30	6	7	0	62	0	54²	62	10	23	54	3.8	8.9	46%	.331	1.55	4.45	4.74	5.49	-0.3
2013	SLN	MLB	30	1	0	0	13	0	10¹	11	0	3	11	2.6	9.6	55%	.379	1.35	1.74	2.05	2.14	0.3
2014	CLE	MLB	31	2	3	10	49	0	43²	34	6	30	51	6.2	10.5	55%	.259	1.47	3.92	4.74	5.65	-0.4
2014	PIT	MLB	31	0	1	0	13	0	11	9	0	6	12	4.9	9.8	54%	.321	1.36	4.09	2.83	3.21	0.1
2015	PIT	MLB	32	3	1	3	59	0	54¹	43	4	22	62	3.7	10.3	48%	.314	1.21	3.19	3.29	3.46	0.7

Breakout: 16%   Improve: 38%   Collapse: 24%   Attrition: 10%   MLB: 87%   Comparables: *Michael Gonzalez, Brian Fuentes, Jose Valverde*

A recurring theme throughout this section sees the Pirates, led by pitching coach Ray Searage and special assistant Jim Benedict, aiding forlorn pitchers. This strategy is forced by necessity rather than organizational choice: The Pirates can't afford pitchers with good stuff *and* results, so they gather worthy reclamation projects—those with talent who are anchored by (fixable) mechanical deficiencies—and help them fulfill their promise. Axford, an in-season waiver-claim from the Indians, seemed like a tight fit. His arsenal, late-inning worthy, has been plagued by command and pitch-tipping woes throughout his career. Yet the Pirates were unable to get him back in shape before the season ended. A failure? Perhaps. But therein lies the beauty of Pittsburgh's approach: The cost is low enough that a miss here and there won't sink the ship. As for Axford, look for him to frustrate again before getting shipped midyear to another NL Central club—the Reds, let's say—and continuing his divisional tour.

Antonio Bastardo   LHP

Born: 9/21/85   Age: 29   Bats: R   Throws: L   Height: 5'11"   Weight: 200

YEAR	TEAM	LVL	AGE	W	L	SV	G	GS	IP	H	HR	BB	K	BB/9	K/9	GB%	BABIP	WHIP	ERA	FIP	FRA	WARP
2012	PHI	MLB	26	2	5	1	65	0	52	40	7	26	81	4.5	14.0	30%	.306	1.27	4.33	3.39	3.65	0.8
2013	PHI	MLB	27	3	2	2	48	0	42²	33	2	21	47	4.4	9.9	36%	.287	1.27	2.32	2.97	2.64	1.0
2014	PHI	MLB	28	5	7	0	67	0	64	43	4	34	81	4.8	11.4	32%	.260	1.20	3.94	3.07	4.25	0.1
2015	PIT	MLB	29	3	2	1	63	0	55²	39	4	24	69	3.9	11.2	35%	.300	1.14	2.77	3.15	3.01	1.0

Breakout: 22%   Improve: 46%   Collapse: 28%   Attrition: 11%   MLB: 93%   Comparables: *David Robertson, Frank Francisco, Tyler Clippard*

Ahh, the volatility of relievers. Bastardo saw a 1.62 rise in ERA last year, while his FIP moved by only 0.10, the result being a 2014 line that more closely resembles his career output than any before it. Bastardo has avoided LOOGYdom for reasons good—he handles righties almost as well as lefties—and bad—the last person you want for your LOOGY is somebody who walks a whopping 12 percent of the lefties he faces. This is his walk year, but for Bastardo they all are.

A.J. Burnett   RHP

Born: 1/3/77   Age: 38   Bats: R   Throws: R   Height: 6'4"   Weight: 225

YEAR	TEAM	LVL	AGE	W	L	SV	G	GS	IP	H	HR	BB	K	BB/9	K/9	GB%	BABIP	WHIP	ERA	FIP	FRA	WARP
2012	PIT	MLB	35	16	10	0	31	31	202¹	189	18	62	180	2.8	8.0	58%	.294	1.24	3.51	3.57	3.70	2.8
2013	PIT	MLB	36	10	11	0	30	30	191	165	11	67	209	3.2	9.8	59%	.305	1.21	3.30	2.77	3.54	2.1
2014	PHI	MLB	37	8	18	0	34	34	213²	205	20	96	190	4.0	8.0	53%	.302	1.41	4.59	4.11	4.94	-1.0
2015	PIT	MLB	38	9	11	0	29	29	177²	169	16	69	158	3.5	8.0	52%	.322	1.34	4.24	4.10	4.61	-0.1

Breakout: 11%   Improve: 30%   Collapse: 19%   Attrition: 10%   MLB: 74%   Comparables: *Andy Pettitte, Hideo Nomo, Jose Contreras*

They all say they want to play for a contender, but how many voluntarily take a 32 percent pay cut to do it? Burnett did, after a season slogging along with the rest of the Phillies, turning down the $12.5 million player option he had and returning to Pittsburgh under a one-year, $8.5 million deal. Burnett has long been a player whose performance seems to mirror his environment, so we might not be so swayed by the one-and-a-half runs he added to his ERA and FIP as PECOTA is. He still has a 93 mph fastball, a swing-and-miss curve, a changeup that gets copious grounders and, even in his late 30s, 200-inning durability. A contender can use him as much as he can use a contender.

Gerrit Cole   RHP

Born: 9/8/90   Age: 24   Bats: R   Throws: R   Height: 6'4"   Weight: 240

YEAR	TEAM	LVL	AGE	W	L	SV	G	GS	IP	H	HR	BB	K	BB/9	K/9	GB%	BABIP	WHIP	ERA	FIP	FRA	WARP
2012	BRD	A+	21	5	1	0	13	13	67	53	5	21	69	2.8	9.3	51%	.276	1.10	2.55	3.38	4.30	1.1
2012	ALT	AA	21	3	6	0	12	12	59	54	2	23	60	3.5	9.2	50%	.315	1.31	2.90	2.88	3.93	1.1
2013	IND	AAA	22	5	3	0	12	12	68	44	4	28	47	3.7	6.2	50%	.216	1.06	2.91	4.00	4.48	0.4
2013	PIT	MLB	22	10	7	0	19	19	117¹	109	7	28	100	2.1	7.7	51%	.308	1.17	3.22	2.88	3.53	1.6
2014	IND	AAA	23	3	1	0	4	4	22¹	21	1	5	16	2.0	6.4	51%	.294	1.16	2.01	3.31	4.96	0.2
2014	PIT	MLB	23	11	5	0	22	22	138	127	11	40	138	2.6	9.0	52%	.311	1.21	3.65	3.20	3.77	1.8
2015	PIT	MLB	24	8	8	0	24	24	139¹	124	10	41	123	2.6	8.0	49%	.311	1.18	3.33	3.51	3.62	1.7

Breakout: 30%   Improve: 67%   Collapse: 10%   Attrition: 16%   MLB: 94%   Comparables: *David Price, Jered Weaver, Brett Cecil*

Everyone will remember how Cole's season ended. Hurdle, citing "human analytics," started his nominal ace in the final game of the year in an effort to force a tiebreaker for the division title rather than saving him for the Wild Card game. The Pirates, though not because of Cole, lost both contests and started their offseason early. Whatever your belief about Hurdle's choice or reasoning—and let's be clear: The difference in probabilities between the options was not large—there's no reason for everyone to pretend Cole is in the same class as Matt Harvey or Jose Fernandez just yet, and not because he lacks an elbow scar. Cole's power fastball-slider combination can overwhelm hitters, but it's puzzling how a guy with that kind of stuff, a stellar defense and a friendly ballpark hasn't yet posted a brilliant ERA. Maybe 2015. There's a first time for everything, except for the things that never happen.

Brandon Cumpton   RHP

Born: 11/16/88   Age: 26   Bats: R   Throws: R   Height: 6'2"   Weight: 220

YEAR	TEAM	LVL	AGE	W	L	SV	G	GS	IP	H	HR	BB	K	BB/9	K/9	GB%	BABIP	WHIP	ERA	FIP	FRA	WARP
2012	ALT	AA	23	12	11	0	27	27	152¹	149	9	46	88	2.7	5.2	60%	.290	1.28	3.84	4.02	5.25	0.6
2013	IND	AAA	24	6	7	0	21	19	122	115	6	44	90	3.2	6.6	62%	.298	1.30	3.32	3.65	5.03	-0.2
2013	PIT	MLB	24	2	1	0	6	5	30²	26	1	5	22	1.5	6.5	55%	.263	1.01	2.05	2.60	3.17	0.5
2014	IND	AAA	25	5	4	0	12	11	71¹	69	7	20	37	2.5	4.7	53%	.278	1.25	3.03	4.61	6.79	-0.7
2014	PIT	MLB	25	3	4	0	16	10	70	82	2	18	46	2.3	5.9	46%	.338	1.43	4.89	3.19	3.53	1.0
2015	PIT	MLB	26	6	8	0	22	22	124	128	10	37	72	2.7	5.2	53%	.310	1.33	4.32	4.35	4.70	-0.1

Breakout: 32%   Improve: 51%   Collapse: 13%   Attrition: 29%   MLB: 68%   Comparables: *Zach Jackson, Tim Stauffer, Dustin Moseley*

The ideal back-end starter—if such a thing exists—throws strikes, coerces grounders and, above all else, costs nothing. Cumpton fits the criteria. He hasn't walked more than 3.2 batters per nine at any professional stop in which he's thrown more than 20 innings, he constantly posts groundball rates exceeding 50 percent and he won't make more than the league minimum for a few years. The only thing Cumpton hasn't done—besides repeat his unsustainable 2013 performance, thanks mostly to a disastrous start against the Dodgers—is claim a rotation spot as his own. That accomplishment is coming, probably this year.

Speaking of the Dodgers, you'd be forgiven a fervent wish for a trade there, where Cumpton's entrance music would be Tupac's "California Love": "In the citaaaaay, the city of Cumpton."

Tyler Glasnow   RHP

Born: 8/23/93   Age: 21   Bats: L   Throws: R   Height: 6'7"   Weight: 195

YEAR	TEAM	LVL	AGE	W	L	SV	G	GS	IP	H	HR	BB	K	BB/9	K/9	GB%	BABIP	WHIP	ERA	FIP	FRA	WARP
2013	WVA	A	19	9	3	0	24	24	111¹	54	9	61	164	4.9	13.3	50%	.215	1.03	2.18	3.47	3.99	1.6
2014	BRD	A+	20	12	5	0	23	23	124¹	74	3	57	157	4.1	11.4	40%	.260	1.05	1.74	2.63	3.03	3.1
2015	PIT	MLB	21	6	7	0	22	22	102¹	79	8	57	114	5.0	10.0	42%	.303	1.33	3.68	3.94	4.00	0.9

Breakout: 0%   Improve: 0%   Collapse: 0%   Attrition: 0%   MLB: 0%   Comparables: *Trevor May, Joel Zumaya, Matt Moore*

The putative top arm in the system following Jameson Taillon's elbow injury, Glasnow didn't seem bothered by the increased attention. Rather, he continued to dominate the competition with his power fastball and hammer curve as if nothing had changed. While the overall results represent the good kind of stability, his continued control woes were the bad side of it. The causes of his wildness—lack of balance in his delivery, varying stride length and a tendency to fly open—remain correctable, though obviously he hasn't solved them yet. If Glasnow can become more consistent with his location, he has the chance to exceed his middle-of-the-rotation projections.

Jeanmar Gomez   RHP

Born: 5/3/91   Age: 24   Bats: R   Throws: R   Height: 6'4"   Weight: 220

YEAR	TEAM	LVL	AGE	W	L	SV	G	GS	IP	H	HR	BB	K	BB/9	K/9	GB%	BABIP	WHIP	ERA	FIP	FRA	WARP
2012	COH	AAA	24	6	5	0	11	11	69¹	75	6	17	54	2.2	7.0	55%	.319	1.33	4.41	3.50	5.40	0.3
2012	CLE	MLB	24	5	8	0	20	17	90²	95	15	34	47	3.4	4.7	50%	.271	1.42	5.96	5.42	6.20	-0.7
2013	PIT	MLB	25	3	0	0	34	8	80²	65	6	28	53	3.1	5.9	57%	.243	1.15	3.35	3.83	4.45	0.0
2014	PIT	MLB	26	2	2	1	44	0	62	70	6	23	38	3.3	5.5	48%	.318	1.50	3.19	4.34	4.84	-0.3
2015	PIT	MLB	27	3	3	0	17	8	59¹	59	5	19	39	2.9	5.9	49%	.306	1.32	4.17	4.19	4.54	0.0

Breakout: 25%   Improve: 51%   Collapse: 12%   Attrition: 14%   MLB: 73%   Comparables: Sergio Mitre, Wade Miley, Clayton Richard

Nowhere on a baseball team is meritocracy more in effect than the bullpen. Successful long relievers become middle relievers; good middle relievers turn into setup men; and, with a little luck and some good timing, accomplished setup men get looks in the ninth inning. Gomez is in the early stages of the process—he moved from designated swingman to more of a long relief role in 2014—but the results thus far suggest he won't earn many more promotions. That's okay; Gomez can still add value with his rubber arm—he pitched multiple innings in more than half his appearances—but the Pirates would be wise to proceed with caution, lest the Peter Principle come into play.

Luis Heredia   RHP

Born: 8/10/94   Age: 20   Bats: R   Throws: R   Height: 6'6"   Weight: 205

YEAR	TEAM	LVL	AGE	W	L	SV	G	GS	IP	H	HR	BB	K	BB/9	K/9	GB%	BABIP	WHIP	ERA	FIP	FRA	WARP
2012	SCO	A-	17	4	2	0	14	14	66¹	53	2	20	40	2.7	5.4	55%	.252	1.10	2.71	3.47	4.90	0.1
2013	WVA	A	18	7	3	0	14	13	65	52	5	37	55	5.1	7.6	39%	.272	1.37	3.05	4.77	4.70	0.1
2014	WVA	A	19	2	4	0	18	18	89	87	9	33	43	3.3	4.3	52%	.268	1.35	4.15	5.32	6.37	-0.3
2015	PIT	MLB	20	3	7	0	16	16	71¹	80	8	39	29	5.0	3.6	44%	.306	1.68	5.82	5.94	6.33	-1.2

Breakout: 0%   Improve: 0%   Collapse: 0%   Attrition: 0%   MLB: 0%   Comparables: Danny Salazar, Collin Balester, Jonathan Pettibone

Heredia is too young for us to feel this cold. The former bonus baby, who signed for $2.6 million as a 16-year-old, repeated West Virginia without noticeable improvement. To his credit, he reported to camp in better shape than he had in 2013. Unfortunately, the good vibes ended there, as he missed two months with a shoulder injury; neither his stats nor scouting reports showed excitement at his return. Blame it on unfulfilled promise: His fastball hasn't gained speed, his secondaries haven't developed into bat-missing weapons, etc. Those developmental failures, though perhaps not entirely his fault, have left Heredia closer to being a no. 5 starter than the no. 1 or 2 the Pirates hoped for when they signed him.

John Holdzkom   RHP

Born: 10/19/87   Age: 27   Bats: R   Throws: R   Height: 6'7"   Weight: 225

YEAR	TEAM	LVL	AGE	W	L	SV	G	GS	IP	H	HR	BB	K	BB/9	K/9	GB%	BABIP	WHIP	ERA	FIP	FRA	WARP
2014	IND	AAA	26	2	0	2	18	0	21²	14	1	10	27	4.2	11.2	47%	.260	1.11	2.49	2.99	3.57	0.4
2014	PIT	MLB	26	1	0	1	9	0	9	4	1	2	14	2.0	14.0	44%	.200	0.67	2.00	2.10	3.40	0.1
2015	PIT	MLB	27	2	1	3	32	0	38¹	28	2	17	45	3.9	10.6	47%	.309	1.18	3.09	3.10	3.36	0.5

Breakout: 19%   Improve: 28%   Collapse: 21%   Attrition: 27%   MLB: 62%   Comparables: Pedro Strop, Michael Schwimer, Billy Sadler

A classic scouting find and instructional triumph. The Pirates discovered Holdzkom pitching for the Amarillo Sox of the independent American Association, signed him and helped excavate the upside offered by his power fastball. Holdzkom appeared in 22 games in the minors before the Pirates called him up in September. Sometime during his stay on the farm, he adjusted the grip on his fastball and improved his control over the pitch. Holdzkom then captivated everyone who set eyes on him during his initial big-league run, filling the zone with mid-90 fastballs that boast natural cutting action. If the improvements are genuine, then Holdzkom—nicknamed "Sasquatch" by his teammates—could leave opposing hitters examining the video footage frame-by-frame for years.

Jared Hughes   RHP

Born: 7/4/85   Age: 29   Bats: R   Throws: R   Height: 6'7"   Weight: 245

YEAR	TEAM	LVL	AGE	W	L	SV	G	GS	IP	H	HR	BB	K	BB/9	K/9	GB%	BABIP	WHIP	ERA	FIP	FRA	WARP
2012	PIT	MLB	26	2	2	2	66	0	75²	65	7	22	50	2.6	5.9	60%	.250	1.15	2.85	4.09	5.15	-0.4
2013	IND	AAA	27	1	0	2	18	1	21	17	0	7	18	3.0	7.7	67%	.293	1.14	0.43	2.63	3.96	0.4
2013	PIT	MLB	27	2	3	0	29	0	32	37	2	16	23	4.5	6.5	58%	.333	1.66	4.78	4.08	4.41	0.0
2014	PIT	MLB	28	7	5	0	63	0	64¹	51	4	19	36	2.7	5.0	66%	.246	1.09	1.96	3.96	4.35	0.1
2015	PIT	MLB	29	3	3	2	44	2	58	55	5	19	40	3.0	6.2	57%	.303	1.29	4.08	4.28	4.44	0.0

Breakout: 17%   Improve: 35%   Collapse: 15%   Attrition: 20%   MLB: 57%   Comparables: Ruddy Lugo, Roman Colon, Sean Henn

"Most gulls don't bother to learn more than the simplest facts of flight—how to get from shore to food and back again," wrote Richard Bach. Hughes could have been one of those simple gulls. His sinker-slider combination had guided him to enough success against right-handed hitters to hover around the majors for years to come. Yet last season Hughes progressed in an effort to become a capable two-way threat. The key? Improved command of his slider, which allowed him to back-foot the pitch against left-handed hitters. Presuming Hughes continues to work at his craft, he should fly into an expanded role this year.

Nick Kingham   RHP

Born: 11/8/91   Age: 23   Bats: R   Throws: R   Height: 6'5"   Weight: 220

YEAR	TEAM	LVL	AGE	W	L	SV	G	GS	IP	H	HR	BB	K	BB/9	K/9	GB%	BABIP	WHIP	ERA	FIP	FRA	WARP
2012	WVA	A	20	6	8	0	27	27	127	115	15	36	117	2.6	8.3	50%	.286	1.19	4.39	4.34	4.96	1.7
2013	BRD	A+	21	6	3	0	13	13	70	55	6	14	75	1.8	9.6	46%	.274	0.99	3.09	3.20	4.27	0.7
2013	ALT	AA	21	3	3	0	14	12	73¹	70	1	30	69	3.7	8.5	45%	.328	1.36	2.70	2.97	3.18	1.5
2014	ALT	AA	22	1	7	0	12	12	71	71	3	25	54	3.2	6.8	46%	.305	1.35	3.04	3.34	4.32	0.6
2014	IND	AAA	22	5	4	0	14	14	88	70	6	27	65	2.8	6.6	45%	.244	1.10	3.58	3.72	5.03	0.2
2015	PIT	MLB	23	7	9	0	26	26	134²	129	12	47	99	3.1	6.6	44%	.303	1.31	4.16	4.24	4.53	0.2

Breakout: 0%   Improve: 0%   Collapse: 0%   Attrition: 0%   MLB: 0%   Comparables: Andrew Heaney, Kyle Gibson, Erik Johnson

Kingham doesn't receive as much attention as other arms in the system, but he's arguably the closest to the majors. He combines an assortment of average or better pitches with the kind of size and strength that makes scouts splutter. Like most 23-year-olds, Kingham could stand to improve his fastball command and consistency with his secondary offerings. Still, there's enough shine and polish here to expect him to develop into a middle-of-the-rotation starter. He ought to debut this summer, hopefully in front of a crowd dressed like Scout Finch on Halloween.

Francisco Liriano   LHP

Born: 10/26/83   Age: 31   Bats: L   Throws: L   Height: 6'2"   Weight: 215

YEAR	TEAM	LVL	AGE	W	L	SV	G	GS	IP	H	HR	BB	K	BB/9	K/9	GB%	BABIP	WHIP	ERA	FIP	FRA	WARP
2012	CHA	MLB	28	3	2	0	12	11	56²	54	7	32	58	5.1	9.2	42%	.307	1.52	5.40	4.46	5.15	0.4
2012	MIN	MLB	28	3	10	0	22	17	100	89	12	55	109	4.9	9.8	47%	.296	1.44	5.31	4.20	5.26	0.7
2013	IND	AAA	29	2	0	0	3	3	16	15	1	1	23	0.6	12.9	54%	.350	1.00	3.38	1.52	2.96	0.3
2013	PIT	MLB	29	16	8	0	26	26	161	134	9	63	163	3.5	9.1	52%	.290	1.22	3.02	2.90	3.61	2.2
2014	PIT	MLB	30	7	10	0	29	29	162¹	130	13	81	175	4.5	9.7	57%	.280	1.30	3.38	3.56	4.66	0.3
2015	PIT	MLB	31	8	9	0	26	26	143¹	121	10	60	147	3.8	9.2	51%	.314	1.26	3.45	3.55	3.75	1.5

Breakout: 15%   Improve: 47%   Collapse: 19%   Attrition: 18%   MLB: 87%   Comparables: A.J. Burnett, Jorge De La Rosa, Erik Bedard

More of a Pirates pitcher than we realized, Liriano pushed his career total to 196 starts without tallying a 200-inning season, earning him 13th place among pitchers who debuted later than 1950. Among the names between him and leader Bruce Kison (just 50 starts away!): Erik Bedard, Kip Wells and Kevin Correia. The pitchers ranked immediately behind Liriano? Oliver Perez and Josh Fogg. Liriano was, naturally, better than just about all those guys while wearing Wiz Khalifa's favorite colors, and more than earned his money. But sheesh, what *is* it about that franchise and inefficient pitching? His five-and-fly tendency will be in the Pirates' rotation for three more years.

Jeff Locke   LHP

Born: 11/20/87   Age: 27   Bats: L   Throws: L   Height: 6'0"   Weight: 185

YEAR	TEAM	LVL	AGE	W	L	SV	G	GS	IP	H	HR	BB	K	BB/9	K/9	GB%	BABIP	WHIP	ERA	FIP	FRA	WARP
2012	IND	AAA	24	10	5	0	24	24	141²	126	9	43	131	2.7	8.3	46%	.296	1.19	2.48	3.19	3.97	1.8
2012	PIT	MLB	24	1	3	0	8	6	34¹	36	6	11	34	2.9	8.9	50%	.312	1.37	5.50	4.48	5.33	-0.2
2013	PIT	MLB	25	10	7	0	30	30	166¹	146	11	84	125	4.5	6.8	55%	.278	1.38	3.52	4.00	4.24	0.9
2014	IND	AAA	26	3	1	0	9	9	50	51	5	22	37	4.0	6.7	55%	.299	1.46	4.14	4.62	5.49	0.1
2014	PIT	MLB	26	7	6	0	21	21	131¹	127	16	40	89	2.7	6.1	53%	.278	1.27	3.91	4.34	5.07	-0.6
2015	PIT	MLB	27	8	10	0	27	27	154²	146	15	59	121	3.4	7.0	48%	.305	1.32	4.16	4.33	4.52	0.2

Breakout: 39%   Improve: 66%   Collapse: 8%   Attrition: 16%   MLB: 85%   Comparables: Dillon Gee, Jason Vargas, Tyson Ross

No matter where Locke goes, no matter what he does, he'll always be able to call himself a former All-Star. In the short term, he ought to remain around Pittsburgh, contributing as part of the Pirates' rotation. Despite being optioned three times last season, including once as a procedural move, Locke found time to notch 13 quality starts in 21 tries. He's not imposing or thrilling and he won't put any butts in the seats, but he's a competent finesse lefty and back-end guy. And yes, a former All-Star.

Mark Melancon   RHP

Born: 3/28/85   Age: 30   Bats: R   Throws: R   Height: 6'2"   Weight: 215

YEAR	TEAM	LVL	AGE	W	L	SV	G	GS	IP	H	HR	BB	K	BB/9	K/9	GB%	BABIP	WHIP	ERA	FIP	FRA	WARP
2012	PAW	AAA	27	0	0	11	21	0	21²	15	0	3	27	1.2	11.2	63%	.278	0.83	0.83	1.36	2.52	0.6
2012	BOS	MLB	27	0	2	1	41	0	45	45	8	12	41	2.4	8.2	51%	.285	1.27	6.20	4.54	6.40	-0.3
2013	PIT	MLB	28	3	2	16	72	0	71	60	1	8	70	1.0	8.9	62%	.296	0.96	1.39	1.61	2.61	1.5
2014	PIT	MLB	29	3	5	33	72	0	71	51	2	11	71	1.4	9.0	60%	.258	0.87	1.90	2.06	3.13	1.1
2015	PIT	MLB	30	3	1	16	61	0	62	52	4	16	60	2.3	8.6	55%	.306	1.09	2.80	3.11	3.04	1.1

Breakout: 26%   Improve: 51%   Collapse: 14%   Attrition: 17%   MLB: 83%   Comparables: Darren O'Day, Manny Delcarmen, Jason Frasor

Quick, name the three pitchers with better ERA+ than Melancon over the past two seasons. The answers: Greg Holland, Craig Kimbrel and Koji Uehara, a.k.a. three of the best closers in baseball. Melancon had been more of a set-up man since leaving Houston, but returned to the ninth inning on a permanent basis following Jason Grilli's collapse. The problem is that saves inflate arbitration costs, and the Pirates can't pay a top-flight closer his market worth. That means Melancon, some two seasons away from free agency, might be headed down the Joel Hanrahan path. You know, the same Hanrahan who emerged as a lights-out closer with the Pirates, was traded a year before he qualified for free agency and in return brought Melancon to Pittsburgh. Expecting another Melancon in return might seem ambitious, but it's not like anyone thought the original deal was a robbery in progress, either. But any trade is probably a season away, so for now, Pirates fans should enjoy one of the league's best relievers.

Charlie Morton   RHP

Born: 11/12/83   Age: 31   Bats: R   Throws: R   Height: 6'5"   Weight: 235

YEAR	TEAM	LVL	AGE	W	L	SV	G	GS	IP	H	HR	BB	K	BB/9	K/9	GB%	BABIP	WHIP	ERA	FIP	FRA	WARP
2012	PIT	MLB	28	2	6	0	9	9	50¹	62	5	11	25	2.0	4.5	58%	.317	1.45	4.65	4.21	5.04	-0.5
2013	ALT	AA	29	1	1	0	4	4	18²	10	2	6	11	2.9	5.3	59%	.154	0.86	2.41	4.50	4.79	0.2
2013	IND	AAA	29	0	1	0	4	4	19	16	1	10	12	4.7	5.7	61%	.250	1.37	3.79	4.36	5.91	0.0
2013	PIT	MLB	29	7	4	0	20	20	116	113	6	36	85	2.8	6.6	65%	.306	1.28	3.26	3.57	4.56	-0.2
2014	PIT	MLB	30	6	12	0	26	26	157¹	143	9	57	126	3.3	7.2	58%	.295	1.27	3.72	3.69	4.71	-0.2
2015	PIT	MLB	31	7	9	0	23	23	132	134	10	47	92	3.2	6.3	56%	.321	1.37	4.48	4.29	4.87	-0.4

Breakout: 13%   Improve: 41%   Collapse: 15%   Attrition: 21%   MLB: 67%   Comparables: Randy Wells, Doug Davis, Armando Galarraga

Signed to a three-year, $21 million extension prior to 2014, Morton had another disappointing season from a workload perspective. He still hasn't reached 200 innings in a season, and his career-best (171) was set three whole years ago. Sadly, none of this will change in 2015 because he underwent a hip operation, the second of his career, which will sideline him for most, if not all, of the first half. Morton has all the makings of a workhorse middle-of-the-rotation starter and none of the durability. It's not his fault, of course; you just can't help but feel frustrated right alongside him.

Stolmy Pimentel   RHP

Born: 2/1/90   Age: 25   Bats: R   Throws: R   Height: 6'3"   Weight: 230

YEAR	TEAM	LVL	AGE	W	L	SV	G	GS	IP	H	HR	BB	K	BB/9	K/9	GB%	BABIP	WHIP	ERA	FIP	FRA	WARP
2012	PME	AA	22	6	7	0	22	22	115²	115	9	42	86	3.3	6.7	52%	.298	1.36	4.59	3.87	5.20	0.7
2013	ALT	AA	23	4	3	0	13	13	77¹	74	8	35	61	4.1	7.1	45%	.286	1.41	3.61	4.64	5.18	0.2
2013	IND	AAA	23	2	6	0	14	14	92	76	6	21	62	2.1	6.1	50%	.250	1.05	3.13	3.45	4.89	0.3
2013	PIT	MLB	23	0	0	0	5	0	9¹	6	0	2	9	1.9	8.7	44%	.222	0.86	1.93	1.73	1.99	0.3
2014	PIT	MLB	24	2	1	0	20	0	32²	34	5	16	38	4.4	10.5	28%	.333	1.53	5.23	4.42	4.46	0.0
2015	PIT	MLB	25	3	4	0	14	10	58¹	59	6	23	39	3.5	6.1	44%	.305	1.40	4.66	4.71	5.06	-0.3

Breakout: 22%   Improve: 36%   Collapse: 13%   Attrition: 42%   MLB: 58%   Comparables: *Lance Broadway, Mike Kickham, Clayton Mortensen*

We once likened Pimentel to an Italian sports car on the grounds that he looks amazing but never works right. He did nothing to invalidate the comparison during his first full season in the majors. His mid-90s fastball and splitter proved to be legitimate bat-missing weapons, yet his control and durability problems limited his value. Pimentel missed more than a month due to shoulder inflammation, and later suffered a well timed sprained ankle that sidelined him *juuuuust* long enough that he could return after rosters expanded. Because Pimentel wouldn't sneak through waivers, the Pirates (or whomever employs him) will have to continue to brave the stolmy weather that comes with his considerable upside.

Casey Sadler   RHP

Born: 7/13/90   Age: 24   Bats: R   Throws: R   Height: 6'4"   Weight: 215

YEAR	TEAM	LVL	AGE	W	L	SV	G	GS	IP	H	HR	BB	K	BB/9	K/9	GB%	BABIP	WHIP	ERA	FIP	FRA	WARP
2012	BRD	A+	21	4	6	2	32	17	130¹	125	7	35	93	2.4	6.4	51%	.296	1.23	3.73	3.72	5.56	0.8
2013	ALT	AA	22	11	7	0	23	23	130¹	116	11	42	67	2.9	4.6	57%	.259	1.21	3.31	4.57	5.44	0.0
2014	IND	AAA	23	11	4	0	21	21	124²	124	11	24	77	1.7	5.6	53%	.290	1.19	3.03	3.94	5.23	0.4
2014	PIT	MLB	23	0	1	0	6	0	10¹	12	0	5	7	4.4	6.1	50%	.333	1.65	7.84	3.49	4.10	0.0
2015	PIT	MLB	24	5	6	0	29	15	114²	117	11	35	62	2.7	4.9	50%	.300	1.32	4.40	4.64	4.78	-0.3

Breakout: 12%   Improve: 20%   Collapse: 6%   Attrition: 20%   MLB: 26%   Comparables: *Bobby Livingston, Stephen Fife, Justin Germano*

Hailing from Western Oklahoma State College—the same place that produced Andrelton Simmons—Sadler has outdone most 25th-round picks by reaching the majors. He could make many more appearances, but it won't be in the starting role he filled for Indianapolis. In the bullpen, his average sinker-slider combination gives him a chance against righties. Picture Jared Hughes, only shorter. Now picture Jared Hughes' ERA, only larger. That's Sadler.

Edinson Volquez   RHP

Born: 7/3/83   Age: 31   Bats: R   Throws: R   Height: 6'0"   Weight: 220

YEAR	TEAM	LVL	AGE	W	L	SV	G	GS	IP	H	HR	BB	K	BB/9	K/9	GB%	BABIP	WHIP	ERA	FIP	FRA	WARP
2012	SDN	MLB	28	11	11	0	32	32	182²	160	14	105	174	5.2	8.6	52%	.292	1.45	4.14	4.10	4.74	0.1
2013	SDN	MLB	29	9	10	0	27	27	142¹	168	14	69	116	4.4	7.3	49%	.337	1.67	6.01	4.19	4.39	1.1
2013	LAN	MLB	29	0	2	0	6	5	28	25	5	8	26	2.6	8.4	48%	.253	1.18	4.18	4.34	4.93	0.0
2014	PIT	MLB	30	13	7	0	32	31	192²	166	17	71	140	3.3	6.5	53%	.263	1.23	3.04	4.12	4.57	0.4
2015	PIT	MLB	31	8	10	0	27	27	156¹	144	14	68	133	3.9	7.7	50%	.308	1.36	4.23	4.27	4.59	0.0

Breakout: 15%   Improve: 44%   Collapse: 18%   Attrition: 25%   MLB: 74%   Comparables: *John Maine, J.A. Happ, Wade Miller*

We were pessimistic when the Pirates signed Volquez to a one-year deal before 2014; likely the new Jonathan Sanchez, we said. Could you blame us? This was a guy who, over the previous five seasons, had compiled an ERA near 5.00. But because it was the Pirates, they were able to milk a quality campaign from Volquez. Not only did he lead the team in innings, he posted a better ERA than Gerrit Cole. Jerry Crasnick, in an excellent ESPN.com profile, covered the whys and hows. In short, the team noticed Volquez had been rushing his delivery, causing his arm to drag and leading to elevated pitches. They helped him get that in order, and while he wasn't perfect (see, e.g., five runs in five innings in the Wild Card game), he resembled a big-league starter again for the first time in a long time. The Royals made a two-year, $20 million bet that Volquez can hold onto those fixes without Ray Searage around.

Tony Watson   LHP

Born: 5/30/85   Age: 30   Bats: L   Throws: L   Height: 6'4"   Weight: 225

YEAR	TEAM	LVL	AGE	W	L	SV	G	GS	IP	H	HR	BB	K	BB/9	K/9	GB%	BABIP	WHIP	ERA	FIP	FRA	WARP
2012	PIT	MLB	27	5	2	0	68	0	53¹	37	5	23	53	3.9	8.9	42%	.241	1.12	3.38	3.72	3.81	0.3
2013	PIT	MLB	28	3	1	2	67	0	71²	51	5	12	54	1.5	6.8	46%	.227	0.88	2.39	3.17	3.73	0.6
2014	PIT	MLB	29	10	2	2	78	0	77¹	64	5	15	81	1.7	9.4	51%	.298	1.02	1.63	2.66	2.87	1.6
2015	PIT	MLB	30	4	2	2	68	0	67²	54	6	19	63	2.6	8.4	42%	.285	1.09	2.99	3.63	3.25	1.0

Breakout: 19%   Improve: 49%   Collapse: 16%   Attrition: 17%   MLB: 78%   Comparables: *Craig Breslow, Kevin Gregg, Matt Lindstrom*

Watson keeps on getting better. Last season marked the third time in a row he made 60 or more appearances, and the third consecutive year he improved upon his ERA and strikeout-to-walk ratio. Remember that Mark Melancon trade possibility we floated earlier? Should it happen, Watson might be the benefactor. Yes, there's always been a weird hesitancy to use a southpaw as a closer, but look at the facts: He throws strikes, gets groundballs, has a three-pitch mix and has held righties to a .633 OPS over the past few years. Maybe the Pirates keep him in a set-up role to suppress his cost; odds are, he'd already be the closer on most teams.

Vance Worley   RHP

Born: 9/25/87   Age: 27   Bats: R   Throws: R   Height: 6'2"   Weight: 230

YEAR	TEAM	LVL	AGE	W	L	SV	G	GS	IP	H	HR	BB	K	BB/9	K/9	GB%	BABIP	WHIP	ERA	FIP	FRA	WARP
2012	PHI	MLB	24	6	9	0	23	23	133	154	12	47	107	3.2	7.2	47%	.341	1.51	4.20	3.90	4.18	1.6
2013	ROC	AAA	25	6	3	0	9	9	58	65	3	17	34	2.6	5.3	42%	.316	1.41	3.88	3.64	4.84	0.2
2013	MIN	MLB	25	1	5	0	10	10	48²	82	9	15	25	2.8	4.6	48%	.401	1.99	7.21	5.56	5.78	0.1
2014	IND	AAA	26	3	2	0	7	7	46	47	3	4	43	0.8	8.4	57%	.331	1.11	4.30	2.73	3.92	1.0
2014	PIT	MLB	26	8	4	0	18	17	110²	112	9	22	79	1.8	6.4	53%	.299	1.21	2.85	3.41	4.14	0.4
2015	PIT	MLB	27	7	8	0	21	21	125	128	10	34	92	2.5	6.6	46%	.324	1.30	4.11	3.83	4.47	0.2

Breakout: 23%   Improve: 53%   Collapse: 16%   Attrition: 15%   MLB: 80%   *Comparables: Travis Wood, Ivan Nova, Wade Davis*

Worley started for the Twins on Opening Day 2013. Not even a year later, he was dealt to the Pirates in a minor trade right before the season began. He didn't pitch in the majors until mid-June, then reeled off four consecutive quality starts to begin his Buccos career. There were some rough patches—he allowed more than a third of his seasonal run total during three starts in August—but overall he looked like a capable back-of-the-rotation starter again. The catalyst for the turnaround? You guessed it: Jim Benedict, who noticed Worley had changed his mechanics following an elbow injury. These guys are good, man. These guys are so good.

Lineouts

Hitters

NAME	POS	TEAM	LVL	AGE	PA	R	2B	3B	HR	RBI	BB	K	SB	CS	AVG/OBP/SLG	TAv	BABIP	BRR	FRAA	WARP
Stetson Allie	1B	ALT	AA	23	486	60	16	0	21	62	71	127	9	6	.246/.362/.440	.286	.303	-2.1	1B(109): 1.7, LF(1): -0.0	2.0
Barrett Barnes	CF	BRD	A+	22	24	3	2	0	0	1	3	5	1	0	.238/.333/.333	.240	.313	-0.7	CF(6): -0.3	-0.1
Jake Elmore	2B	SAC	AAA	27	211	30	15	0	0	18	27	26	9	4	.282/.374/.365	.271	.325	0.8	2B(29): -1.2, SS(11): -0.5	0.9
	2B	LOU	AAA	27	104	14	2	0	0	6	15	15	3	0	.279/.379/.302	.255	.329	1.0	2B(14): -0.1, SS(8): -0.4	0.3
	SS	CIN	MLB	27	12	0	0	0	0	0	1	4	0	0	.182/.250/.182	.178	.286	0.0	SS(3): 0.0, 2B(2): 0.0	0.0
Pedro Florimon	SS	ROC	AAA	27	314	38	17	4	4	29	30	82	12	2	.257/.328/.389	.246	.345	1.6	SS(65): 2.7, 3B(11): -0.6	1.0
	SS	MIN	MLB	27	86	7	1	1	0	1	8	22	6	0	.092/.179/.132	.136	.130	0.8	SS(31): 3.1	-0.4
JaCoby Jones	SS	WVA	A	22	501	72	21	3	23	70	33	132	17	9	.288/.347/.503	.291	.352	5.7	SS(99): 1.9	4.6
Wyatt Mathisen	3B	WVA	A	20	419	48	17	2	3	42	33	54	6	2	.280/.344/.360	.269	.318	-2.2	3B(84): -2.6	1.6
Chris McGuiness	1B	IND	AAA	26	489	60	31	2	9	54	63	72	0	1	.264/.358/.412	.264	.297	-1.2	1B(111): 5.6	1.4
Gift Ngoepe	2B	ALT	AA	24	499	58	17	9	9	52	51	135	13	8	.238/.319/.380	.252	.322	0.2	2B(86): 3.8, SS(44): -3.0	0.9
Harold Ramirez	CF	WVA	A	19	226	30	14	1	1	24	11	35	12	3	.309/.364/.402	.283	.365	2.5	CF(24): -0.0, RF(23): -2.3	1.3
Mel Rojas	CF	ALT	AA	24	220	26	11	1	5	36	23	34	6	4	.303/.379/.446	.315	.346	-1.0	CF(53): -8.2	0.9
	RF	IND	AAA	24	280	35	8	4	5	30	32	62	5	5	.277/.363/.405	.272	.350	-0.6	RF(27): 0.1, LF(24): 3.2	1.6
Sebastian Valle	C	REA	AA	23	120	4	4	0	1	10	5	19	0	0	.257/.286/.319	.211	.298	0.0	C(29): -0.0, 1B(1): -0.0	0.0
	C	LEH	AAA	23	135	17	7	0	4	22	4	33	0	0	.220/.241/.370	.206	.261	-1.2	C(36): 0.5	-0.2

Stetson Allie continues to ride the organizational escalator. He's a powerful dude with a powerful arm who has powerful limitations imposed upon him by poor bat-to-ball and ball-to-glove skills. ❖ Don't be surprised if **Barrett Barnes** files for divorce soon; sources say the relationship with his hamstrings has become strained over the past couple years due to ... um ... repeated strains. ❖ **Jake Elmore** is a beautifully replacement-level infielder: He can handle multiple defensive positions, control the strike zone and hit for no power whatsoever. ❖ Former Twin **Pedro Florimon** blinked first, losing his good-field, no-switch-hit staring contest to the younger Eduardo Escobar last summer; claimed off waivers by Washington, he'd be capable of providing the Nats with a major-league glove if he hadn't since been claimed off waivers by Pittsburgh. ❖ **Connor Joe** was taken 39th overall out of the University of San Diego on the strength of his bat; he played some catcher late in his college career, and the Pirates would like to get him reps behind the plate, but he has yet to make his pro debut due to injuries. ❖ Former second-round pick **JaCoby Jones** seems better suited for center field than shortstop, but contact woes could render his position (and your best Reggie Cleveland All-Star jokes) irrelevant. ❖ Remember the scene in *Wyatt Earp* where the titular character says, "You'd be doing me a favor to call me Wyatt or Earp, but not both"? The Pirates did **Wyatt Mathisen** a favor by calling him a third baseman or a catcher, but not both: He made himself comfortable at his new defensive home and showed offensive life in his third stint at West Virginia. ❖ **Chris McGuiness** sounds like a McDonald's meal and he's equally as readily available and unsatisfying. ❖ It's hard not to root for **Gift Ngoepe**, a slick fielder from South Africa whose bat showed signs of life last year in Altoona. ❖ Speedy young outfielder **Harold Ramirez** extended his hitting streak to 23 games on July 1st, then missed the rest of the season due to a shin injury. ❖ In addition to making everyone feel old, **Mel Rojas Jr.** excels at getting on base. He strikes out too often for someone with modest pop, but should have a future as an extra outfielder. ❖ Jeepers creepers, where'd you get those sleepers? Jeepers creepers, where'd you get those guys? The Pirates seem to find gems in the Dominican Republic on an annual basis. **Raul Siri**, a short second baseman, could be the next if he continues to hit like he has in complex ball. ❖ At 24, **Sebastian Valle** is hardly done—he has a good body and has demonstrated some raw power—but his prospect status has shown a strong negative correlation to the size of his high-minors sample.

Pitchers

NAME	TEAM	LVL	AGE	W	L	SV	G	GS	IP	H	HR	BB	K	BB/9	K/9	GB%	BABIP	WHIP	ERA	FIP	FRA	WARP
Buddy Borden	WVA	A	22	7	9	1	27	26	128	103	13	48	122	3.4	8.6	44%	.265	1.18	3.16	4.27	4.82	1.7
Preston Guilmet	NOR	AAA	26	4	2	10	40	0	48¹	42	6	10	54	1.9	10.1	41%	.283	1.08	3.91	3.36	4.42	0.5
	BAL	MLB	26	0	1	0	10	0	10¹	8	2	2	12	1.7	10.5	41%	.222	0.97	5.23	3.93	5.08	0.0
Bobby LaFromboise	ELP	AAA	28	1	2	3	58	0	53	68	4	21	45	3.6	7.6	50%	.366	1.68	4.75	4.17	5.00	0.6
	PIT	MLB	28	0	0	0	6	0	3²	3	1	0	4	0.0	9.8	20%	.222	0.82	2.45	4.47	9.84	-0.2
Joely Rodriguez	ALT	AA	22	6	11	1	30	21	134	151	10	43	73	2.9	4.9	57%	.315	1.45	4.84	4.22	5.68	-0.3
Wandy Rodriguez	PIT	MLB	35	0	2	0	6	6	26²	37	10	8	20	2.7	6.7	44%	.310	1.69	6.75	7.38	7.59	-0.6
Adrian Sampson	ALT	AA	22	10	5	0	24	24	148	125	10	30	99	1.8	6.0	51%	.256	1.05	2.55	3.62	4.39	2.0
	IND	AAA	22	1	1	0	4	4	19	29	1	7	10	3.3	4.7	33%	.389	1.89	6.16	4.25	6.32	-0.5
Rob Scahill	CSP	AAA	27	2	3	2	41	0	58¹	59	6	18	53	2.8	8.2	57%	.308	1.32	4.32	4.40	5.34	0.5
	COL	MLB	27	1	0	0	12	0	15	17	3	9	11	5.4	6.6	43%	.292	1.73	4.80	6.24	6.80	-0.3
Josh Stinson	NOR	AAA	26	5	5	1	22	13	85¹	78	14	38	80	4.0	8.4	43%	.272	1.36	5.48	5.16	5.83	0.0
	BAL	MLB	26	0	0	0	8	0	13	16	2	6	6	4.2	4.2	51%	.311	1.69	6.23	6.08	7.45	-0.3
Blake Wood	OMA	AAA	28	0	0	0	14	0	18¹	18	2	16	21	7.9	10.3	60%	.348	1.85	6.38	5.44	7.98	-0.3
	CLE	MLB	28	0	1	0	7	0	6¹	4	0	7	7	9.9	9.9	47%	.267	1.74	7.11	4.74	6.38	-0.1

Buddy Borden is a big righty whose fastball-slider combination will play in the bullpen, provided he doesn't go insane from his teammates' repeated "South Park" jokes first. ❖ After a first-week trade, Baltimore recalled **Preston Guilmet** six times before slamming down the DFA whammy. Home runs inflated his ERA, but monster whiff/walk numbers make him a viable 12th pitcher or Triple-A reserve—because he knows how to pack a darn suitcase. ❖ **Clay Holmes** is a strong righty with a good fastball-curveball combination. He'll try to pick up where he left off in 2013, having missed last season due to Tommy John surgery. ❖ Overslot signees **Mitch Keller** and **Trey Supak** are projectable righties with promising fastballs and curveballs. The Pirates sure have a type. ❖ Side-armer **Bobby LaFromboise**, an August waiver claim from the Padres, aspires to be the second or third southpaw in a bullpen one day. He's already the guy you have to triple-check to confirm he's from California, not Louisiana. ❖ Developing a worthwhile secondary pitch has eluded smallish lefty **Joely Rodriguez** for years. Another bad season like the one he just had and a big-league future will evade him, too. ❖ **Wandy Rodriguez** was released at the end of May after six starts. Odds are, his days as a productive starter are behind him, but he's left-handed so who can be sure? ❖ Though **Adrian Sampson**'s changeup lags behind his above-average fastball and curve, he ought to join Evan Meek and Dave Pagan as Bellevue Community College attendees to pitch for the Pirates. Go Bulldogs! ❖ Hittable righty **Rob Scahill**, who calls himself a "pelota chucker" on Twitter, might salvage his career if he robs (Trevor) Cahill of his changeup. ❖ If **Josh Stinson** were a sandwich, he'd be left half-eaten. ❖ Top prospect **Jameson Taillon** underwent Tommy John surgery in April, prolonging his trek to the majors. He made the best of a rotten situation by adopting Francis Underwood, a bearded dragon he named after the *House of Cards* character. ❖ His lefty gas still sits in the upper 90s, but all you need to know about his atrocious control is that **Blake Wood** is an anagram for "Walked. Boo!"

Manager

Clint Hurdle

YEAR	TEAM	W	L	Py-thag +/-	Avg PC	100+ P	120+ P	QS	BQS	REL	REL w Zero R	IBB	PH	PH Avg	PH HR	SB2	CS2	SB3	CS3	SAC Att	SAC%	POS SAC	Squeeze	Swing	In Play
2012	PIT	79	83	1	90.4	42	0	83	2	483	398	30	266	.173	2	66	45	7	3	93	66.7%	30	2	271	94
2013	PIT	94	68	5	89.7	41	0	83	2	465	395	26	285	.207	7	83	36	10	6	93	66.7%	35	1	347	100
2014	PIT	88	74	1	93.9	46	0	90	3	452	361	43	317	.218	7	99	41	5	4	101	53.5%	18	1	365	135

Hurdle used the term "human analytics" when explaining why he started Gerrit Cole in Game 162. It turns out that's a reasonable explanation for his success in Pittsburgh.

Few considered Hurdle a desirable commodity when the Pirates hired him from the retread pile. He'd spent eight years guiding the Rockies earlier in the decade, posting a winning record just once. Yet Hurdle has made the most of his second chance, enjoying success unseen in Pittsburgh since Jim Leyland's days around town. Part of his progress is due to a growth mindset, which has seen him not only embrace the Pirates' numbers-heavy approach, but welcome what amounts to a traveling quantitative secretary, in Mike Fitzgerald, whom Ben Lindbergh profiled for Grantland.

Hurdle has accepted, among other advanced concepts, defensive shifts and strict platoons. But those tastes don't mean there isn't an old-school flavor to his approach. Hit-and-runs—frowned upon by some due to their risky nature and the position they put the hitter in—were a go-to play for the Pirates last season, who led the majors by more than 15 attempts. Additionally, Hurdle deserves credit for getting his players to buy in to the new-school stratagems—including pitching inside. Hurdle still has some faults, and his quick-to-purple complexion lends itself to jokes, but he's become the ideal manager for these Pirates.

SAN DIEGO PADRES

by Miles Wray

For years now, the Padres have done what their aesthetically disastrous camouflage alternate uniforms so blatantly fail to do: hide in plain sight. The Padres have always been there, but you might have forgotten because they blend into the background so well.

Here's a fun fact about the Padres' tendency to fade into the scenery: Did you know that Bud Black is currently tied for the second-longest managerial tenure in all of baseball? In first, and by a mile, is Black's old boss, Mike Scioscia, who has been installed in Anaheim's dugout since 2000. Scioscia won a World Series ring and has led the Angels to seven seasons of at least 90 wins. In 2007, Black started managing the Padres at the same time that the man he replaced in San Diego, Bruce Bochy, took over in San Francisco. Since then, Bochy has won the World Series more times (three) than Black has finished above .500 (two).

Even more fun about Black's tenure: In four of his eight seasons with San Diego, including the last three seasons in a row, the Padres have finished within the impossibly tiny window of 75 to 77 wins. This is the perfect camo record: nowhere near an attention-grabbing playoff race, but also nowhere near the true bottom of the standings, where people might start to notice for all the wrong reasons.

Where Black's tenure gets really crazy is the total lack of continuity in every direction around him. After Adrian Gonzalez's trade to Boston, the team has had four WARP leaders in four years. With new General Manager A.J. Preller installed last August, Black is now working under his fourth different front office. Fifth if you count the significant trade-deadline moves made last year by the three-headed interim GM team of Omar Minaya, A.J. Hinch and Fred Uhlman Jr., which sent Chris Denorfia, Chase Headley and Huston Street out of town. For that matter, how many managers have had to deal with a hydra GM?

Most notably of all, Black has had to manage under three different ownership groups, which causes trickle-down chaos and leads to the Padres' primary problem: an inability to stay dedicated to a long-term plan. The impersonal carousel of comings and goings at the top of the organization is mirrored by impersonal comings and goings of the men on the field, barely acquainted with the Padres fan base before they are packaged and shipped elsewhere for a new semi-anonymous dramatis personae.

As Geoff Young put it in last year's Annual—scant months before the removal of Josh Byrnes—each successive Padres GM has spent his time "undoing the work of his predecessor." And oh my is there a mighty stack of half-complete blueprints for team success in the wastebaskets at Petco. Just about all of the Padres' GMs have made a terrifying draft blunder—2004's no. 1 overall pick Matt Bush never made it to Triple-A and is presently in prison—but what might hurt even more is the long list of viable-to-valuable major leaguers who were traded away from the organization or, even worse, lost in the Rule 5 draft, before they became contributors. For example: Jason Bay, David Freese, Eric Sogard, Joakim Soria, 2014 Cy Young winner Corey Kluber. Work undone indeed.

Let's play a game where I give you a quote from the Padres chapter in a previous *Baseball Prospectus* Annual and you guess which year the quote was published. Here's a hint: It's impossible because all four of these passages adequately diagnose the team Preller inherited last season. Good luck:

Quote 1: "The farm system is hopeless and the free agent class that follows this season is expected to be extremely thin, so even if [he] deigns to up the budget, there will be few freely available players on whom to spend the dollars."

Quote 2: "It seems likely that the majority of players who will help bring [the GM's] vision of building a championship organization to fruition are not even in the organization and in fact may still be walking the campuses of high schools and colleges around the country. Of course, [the GM] knows that, and he's young enough to invest the time to bring them in."

Quote 3: "No strategy is flawless, but extending young players for less money than equivalent talent on the open market is one way the Padres can narrow the gap between themselves and their richer competitors. They are wise to exploit it."

Quote 4: "If the ship starts to sink, they need to trade veterans for help down the road without hemming and hawing."

(Answers at the end.)

In the tradition of Padres general managers, Preller has, like

PADRES PROSPECTUS
2014 W-L: 77-85, 3RD IN NL WEST

Pythag	.467	21st	DER	.711	9th
RS/G	3.3	30th	B-Age	27.8	11th
RA/G	3.56	4th	P-Age	28.7	20th
TAv	.246	30th	Salary	$90.4M	20th
BRR	-8.06	27th	M$/MW	$2.7M	14th
TAv-P	.256	9th	DL Days	1,553	29th
FIP	3.43	2nd	$ on DL	40%	30th

Three-Year Park Factors

Runs	Runs/RH	Runs/LH	HR/RH	HR/LH
93	92	90	86	91

Top Hitter WARP	3.8	Seth Smith
Top Pitcher WARP	2.6	Ian Kennedy
Top Prospect		Austin Hedges

Godzilla romping through a metropolis, gotten to work leveling the structures built by his predecessors. In the scant weeks between the end of the World Series and the opening of presents on Christmas morn', Preller traded away five first-round picks. One of those, Trea Turner, was selected by Byrnes 13th overall just last June, and is now in the Washington Nationals' system after less than half a year with San Diego. (Sort of. Because he can't be traded until a year after he signed, Turner is technically still a Padre, and technically the Nationals got a player to be named later. As we went to press, Turner's agent was threatening a grievance over the whole situation and the chattering classes were discussing whether the one-year trade bar has outlived its utility.)

Not that Preller is breaking up a Royals-circa-2010-caliber farm system here. The Padres have one first-round pick in this century who has produced more than three career WARP (Khalil Greene). Lest I be accused of picking on the Padres' record with first-rounders while ignoring their back-end gems, each year's best pick from 2000 to 2010 looks roughly like this: Chad Cordero, Jason Bartlett, Greene, Tim Stauffer, Kyle Blanks, Headley, Mat Latos, Kluber, Jason Kipnis, Nate Freiman, Jedd Gyorko.

The difference between Preller and his predecessors is that Preller became baseball's breakout star of the hot stove season, engineering moves so splashy that SeaWorld has contemplated a lawsuit for trademark infringement. In exchange for all those first-rounders selected by evaluators of dubious reliability, Preller has acquired a pre-prime All-Star catcher (Derek Norris), a 24-year-old former Rookie of the Year (Wil Myers) and two of the game's most recognizable sluggers (Matt Kemp and Justin Upton). For the first time since their 1998 World Series appearance, the Padres aren't an extra in the background: They're commanding a speaking part at the forefront of the game.

Reasons abound to critique Preller's moves. From Kemp and Norris' lackluster defense to Myers' uninspiring 2014, these players might provide more splash value than win value. But Preller knows as well as anybody the total emptiness of the former: He was a Rangers assistant GM last winter, when Texas spent big on Shin-Soo Choo and acquired Prince Fielder's enormous contract only to see their season crumble to smithereens.

I contend that Preller should be applauded for these moves, not because each transaction will necessarily maximize the Padres' long-term success (though Norris can't be a free agent until after 2018, and Myers and Kemp 2019), but because Preller has so thoroughly and imaginatively avoided a dark, empty-bleachers era of rebuilding.

The Padres, at this writing, are not in the top tier of World Series contenders. (There are moves to come, given that there are seven major-league outfielders on the roster, but Seth Smith isn't likely to bring back enough to move the needle.) I think Preller knows that, perhaps better than anybody. But they are equally not Jeff Luhnow's Astros or Dayton Moore's Royals or Theo Epstein's Cubs: Padres fans will not have to sit through a mini-generation of knowing their major-league squad is doomed to fifth place, relying on reports of exceptional youngsters on the farm for emotional sustenance.

As we saw last fall with Moore's Royals, a top-to-bottom organizational rebuild can pay tremendous dividends. Even in the ecstatic apex of the Royals' playoff run, however, Kansas City fans had to be performing some complex calculus to figure out how many playoff wins would make all those years of cellar-dwelling truly worth it. Padres fans who are conscious of the new beginnings that come with a new general manager will, at the least, not have to do this arithmetic, as Preller's very first step has been boldly forward instead of strategically backward. That Preller has conducted all these trades while increasing the team's payroll by less than $10 million to date is an encouraging first sign.

In order for the Padres to viably succeed long-term, Preller will have to nail the draft, graduating eventual contributors from the minors and filling the Padres with young talent under cheap team control. The exact same thing has to be said about the 29 other GMs leading the 29 other teams. He hasn't even reached his first June yet, so we're a long way from knowing whether Preller will be the first Padres GM in a generation to see his draft picks make an impact in the big leagues. For a change, though, it will be exciting to see him try to get there. ∎

Trivia answers:
Quote 1: 2009
Quote 2: 2010
Quote 3: 2014
Quote 4: 2005 (!)

—Miles Wray lives in Seattle and is a regular contributor to FanGraphs, Hardwood Paroxysm, The Classical and Ploughshares Literary Magazine.

Player comments by Geoff Young and Baseball Prospectus Authors

Hitters

Abraham Almonte   CF

Born: 6/27/89   Age: 26   Bats: B   Throws: R   Height: 5'9"   Weight: 205

YEAR	TEAM	LVL	AGE	PA	R	2B	3B	HR	RBI	BB	K	SB	CS	AVG/OBP/SLG	TAv	BABIP	BRR	FRAA	WARP
2012	TRN	AA	23	359	47	17	4	4	25	37	59	30	5	.276/.350/.392	.259	.327	5.0	CF(30): -2.7, RF(27): 5.6	2.5
2013	WTN	AA	24	120	18	6	1	4	18	18	28	6	1	.255/.367/.451	.281	.314	-2.4	CF(11): -0.4, RF(8): 0.1	0.3
2013	TAC	AAA	24	396	63	17	5	11	50	49	66	20	7	.314/.403/.491	.325	.363	1.6	CF(83): -0.6, LF(5): 0.3	4.5
2013	SEA	MLB	24	82	10	4	0	2	9	6	21	1	0	.264/.313/.403	.262	.333	1.5	CF(15): -2.0, RF(7): 0.3	0.2
2014	TAC	AAA	25	312	42	10	3	6	31	28	66	7	4	.267/.333/.390	.259	.330	-0.2	CF(69): -1.3	1.1
2014	SDN	MLB	25	107	9	5	0	2	7	6	20	1	2	.265/.305/.378	.258	.312	-1.7	LF(16): -0.1, CF(15): 2.5	0.7
2014	SEA	MLB	25	113	10	5	1	1	8	6	40	3	1	.198/.248/.292	.217	.308	1.1	CF(26): -0.9	0.0
2015	SDN	MLB	26	287	34	11	2	5	24	24	68	9	3	.240/.303/.352	.254	.299	0.6	CF -1, LF 0	0.6

Breakout: 7%   Improve: 43%   Collapse: 15%   Attrition: 25%   MLB: 72%   Comparables: *Bryan Petersen, Lorenzo Cain, Chris Denorfia*

Almonte, a Warren Newson-shaped center fielder, began 2014 as Seattle's leadoff man, banging out two hits in Anaheim on Opening Day. After failing to make contact for a month, he spent the next three down the road at Tacoma, where his numbers improved to mediocre. Almonte continued down I-5 to San Diego in a deadline deal and wasn't terrible. A plus runner with gap power, he expands the strike zone too often. In the field, his speed is useful but doesn't always let him overcome curious routes and concentration lapses. Like Chris Denorfia, for whom he was traded, Almonte profiles as a role player.

Yonder Alonso   1B
Born: 4/8/87   Age: 28   Bats: L   Throws: R   Height: 6' 1"   Weight: 230

YEAR	TEAM	LVL	AGE	PA	R	2B	3B	HR	RBI	BB	K	SB	CS	AVG/OBP/SLG	TAv	BABIP	BRR	FRAA	WARP
2012	SDN	MLB	25	619	47	39	0	9	62	62	101	3	0	.273/.348/.393	.275	.318	-5.3	1B(149): 5.9	2.0
2013	SDN	MLB	26	375	34	11	0	6	45	32	47	6	0	.281/.341/.368	.262	.306	-3.0	1B(92): 2.8, LF(1): -0.0	0.6
2014	SDN	MLB	27	288	27	19	1	7	27	17	36	6	1	.240/.285/.397	.254	.251	1.3	1B(77): 2.4, 3B(3): 0.0	0.5
2015	SDN	MLB	28	293	30	15	1	6	31	25	49	4	1	.261/.323/.386	.273	.297	-1.4	1B 2, 3B -0	0.8

Breakout: 2%   Improve: 33%   Collapse: 11%   Attrition: 15%   MLB: 88%   Comparables: Ryan Garko, Gaby Sanchez, Matt LaPorta

In a make-or-break campaign, Alonso broke. Again. For the second straight season, right wrist and arm issues kept him from playing 100 games. His line during that stretch is a Torrealbaesque .263/.317/.381. Despite occasional bouts of competence (.421/.477/.737 in 15 games before his season-ending right forearm injury in August: a torn tendon, if you must know), Alonso is a large, lumbering first baseman who doesn't get on base, hit for power or stay healthy. He's Denny Walling without the mustache. We keep downgrading his comps. It's like an old *Get Smart* routine: "He's Lyle Overbay. Would you believe Bruce Bochte? How about Denny Walling? How about a loaf of bread?" You know, if the bread was hurt all the time.

Alexi Amarista   UT
Born: 4/6/89   Age: 26   Bats: L   Throws: R   Height: 5' 6"   Weight: 150

YEAR	TEAM	LVL	AGE	PA	R	2B	3B	HR	RBI	BB	K	SB	CS	AVG/OBP/SLG	TAv	BABIP	BRR	FRAA	WARP
2012	SLC	AAA	23	83	11	6	2	0	12	3	6	1	0	.273/.289/.403	.231	.284	0.7	2B(8): -0.3, 3B(6): 0.8	0.1
2012	TUC	AAA	23	51	6	1	0	1	6	1	6	3	0	.286/.300/.367	.277	.310	0.2	2B(5): -0.4, SS(3): 0.2	0.2
2012	SDN	MLB	23	300	35	15	5	5	32	17	42	8	4	.240/.282/.385	.244	.265	2.6	2B(52): -3.3, LF(27): 0.7	0.3
2013	SDN	MLB	24	396	35	14	4	5	32	22	57	4	2	.236/.282/.337	.226	.267	2.2	CF(87): 1.6, 2B(23): 0.7	0.4
2014	SDN	MLB	25	466	39	13	2	5	40	29	69	12	1	.239/.286/.314	.245	.271	0.7	SS(73): 2.5, 3B(22): 0.8	1.5
2015	SDN	MLB	26	424	39	17	3	4	34	22	67	8	2	.234/.274/.328	.235	.263	1.5	SS 2, CF -1	0.7

Breakout: 7%   Improve: 48%   Collapse: 10%   Attrition: 20%   MLB: 97%   Comparables: Cesar Izturis, Yuniesky Betancourt, Erick Aybar

Asking Amarista to set the table is like asking a Kardashian to explain quantum mechanics (or set the table). While it provides cheap laughs, the exercise ultimately wastes everyone's time. And yet, nearly 30 percent of Amarista's career plate appearances have come while batting first or second. His .279 on-base percentage makes him a poor choice for such a role. It also makes him a poor choice for any other role, raising the obvious question of why he is even here. As with the Kardashians, the answer is complicated and unsatisfying. Amarista's ability to play anywhere helps—he admirably plugged the Padres' shortstop sinkhole last year—but reaching first base less often than an actual padre limits his value.

Clint Barmes   SS
Born: 3/6/79   Age: 36   Bats: R   Throws: R   Height: 6' 1"   Weight: 200

YEAR	TEAM	LVL	AGE	PA	R	2B	3B	HR	RBI	BB	K	SB	CS	AVG/OBP/SLG	TAv	BABIP	BRR	FRAA	WARP
2012	PIT	MLB	33	493	34	16	1	8	45	20	106	0	2	.229/.272/.321	.222	.280	2.1	SS(142): 8.9, 1B(1): -0.0	0.8
2013	PIT	MLB	34	330	22	15	0	5	23	14	70	0	0	.211/.249/.309	.211	.257	0.7	SS(106): 3.2	-0.1
2014	IND	AAA	35	21	3	0	0	1	2	1	1	0	0	.158/.190/.316	.182	.111	0.1	SS(5): -0.9	-0.2
2014	PIT	MLB	35	116	15	5	0	0	7	9	18	1	1	.245/.328/.294	.242	.294	0.8	SS(27): -1.8, 2B(14): 0.4	0.1
2015	SDN	MLB	36	250	21	10	0	3	21	15	52	1	1	.216/.270/.306	.226	.259	0.8	SS 2, 2B 0	0.5

Breakout: 1%   Improve: 26%   Collapse: 13%   Attrition: 23%   MLB: 81%   Comparables: Alan Trammell, Juan Castro, Cal Ripken Jr.

Re-signed by the Pirates to a one-year deal in 2014 to serve as Plan B in the event that Jordy Mercer proved unfit, Barmes appeared in fewer than 100 games for the first time since 2007. His sparse playing time can be credited to Mercer, who proved quite fit, and a strained groin that disabled him for two months. Barmes will celebrate his 36th birthday right around the time you read this, so he's getting close to the day when he'll donate his cleats to a Goodwill and move on to the next phase of his life. We'll wish him a happy, venison-free retirement when he does, and, in the meantime, a happy hitting-free role for the Padres. He should leave deer alone one way or the other.

Everth Cabrera   SS
Born: 11/17/86   Age: 28   Bats: B   Throws: R   Height: 5' 10"   Weight: 190

YEAR	TEAM	LVL	AGE	PA	R	2B	3B	HR	RBI	BB	K	SB	CS	AVG/OBP/SLG	TAv	BABIP	BRR	FRAA	WARP
2012	TUC	AAA	25	159	27	9	1	0	15	12	28	15	0	.333/.389/.410	.301	.414	2.7	SS(17): -2.6, 3B(10): -0.5	1.4
2012	SDN	MLB	25	449	49	19	3	2	24	43	110	44	4	.246/.324/.324	.248	.336	5.8	SS(111): 7.0, 2B(6): -0.1	2.9
2013	SDN	MLB	26	435	54	15	5	4	31	41	69	37	12	.283/.355/.381	.280	.337	2.2	SS(95): 0.7	3.1
2014	ELP	AAA	27	24	4	1	0	0	1	4	3	1	0	.350/.458/.400	.026	.412	0.0	SS(6): -0.6	-0.2
2014	SDN	MLB	27	391	36	13	1	3	20	20	86	18	8	.232/.272/.300	.228	.294	-2.4	SS(90): 1.4	0.8
2015	SDN	MLB	28	380	47	14	2	2	23	30	83	26	7	.242/.305/.317	.246	.302	0.7	SS 2, 2B -0	1.3

Breakout: 4%   Improve: 45%   Collapse: 2%   Attrition: 7%   MLB: 91%   Comparables: Brendan Ryan, Felipe Lopez, Hector Luna

Cabrera is running out of chances when he should just be running. In 2012, it was domestic violence. In 2013, it was Biogenesis. Last year he completed the trifecta with a DUI. Even before the off-field issues, he brandished an OBP that would make Alcides Escobar blush. When Cabrera's ability to discern balls from strikes disappeared, it took his basestealing prowess along for the ride. One problem, which afflicted the entire Padres offense, was his futility after a first-pitch strike. His OPS after a 1-0 count was a respectable .808; after 0-1, it was .378, which has him looking up at Greg Maddux. Granted, Maddux is in the Hall of Fame, but you see the problem. A larger problem, which may prove unsolvable, is Cabrera's loss of discipline at the plate, on the bases and apparently in life.

Franchy Cordero   SS
Born: 9/2/94   Age: 20   Bats: L   Throws: R   Height: 6' 3"   Weight: 175

YEAR	TEAM	LVL	AGE	PA	R	2B	3B	HR	RBI	BB	K	SB	CS	AVG/OBP/SLG	TAv	BABIP	BRR	FRAA	WARP
2014	EUG	A-	19	259	40	8	4	9	35	14	75	13	5	.279/.329/.458	.291	.372	1.4	SS(36): -4.8, 3B(1): 0.0	1.0
2014	FTW	A	19	94	5	2	1	0	9	4	36	3	3	.188/.237/.235	.206	.314	-0.9	SS(20): -5.0	-0.7
2015	SDN	MLB	20	250	23	7	1	3	16	9	94	5	3	.182/.215/.262	.189	.279	0.2	SS -10, 3B 0	-2.0

Breakout: 0%   Improve: 0%   Collapse: 0%   Attrition: 0%   MLB: 0%   Comparables: Jonathan Villar, Reid Brignac, Junior Lake

Cordero turned heads in spring training with a quick bat and was assigned to full-season ball, where his game never materialized. He rediscovered himself in the Northwest League. As one of the circuit's youngest players, he finished 10th in slugging percentage, though a broken bone in his right hand ended his season prematurely. The power potential is real. Unfortunately, so are the holes in his swing and glove: Cordero struck out in 31 percent of his plate appearances and committed 51 errors in 56 games at shortstop. That's actually difficult to do. Still, the kid has talent, and given time and a position, he just might figure out how to use it.

Michael Gettys   CF

Born: 10/22/95   Age: 19   Bats: R   Throws: R   Height: 6' 1"   Weight: 203

YEAR	TEAM	LVL	AGE	PA	R	2B	3B	HR	RBI	BB	K	SB	CS	AVG/OBP/SLG	TAv	BABIP	BRR	FRAA	WARP
2015	SDN	MLB	19	250	18	8	1	2	19	9	81	4	1	.187/.217/.258	.188	.265	0.4	CF 3, RF 0	-0.8

Breakout: 0%   Improve: 0%   Collapse: 0%   Attrition: 0%   MLB: 0%   Comparables: Oscar Taveras, Joe Benson, Gorkys Hernandez

The Padres popped Gettys in the second round out of a Georgia high school, then signed him away from a verbal commitment to the University of Georgia. A two-way player who some felt could have been drafted as a pitcher, Gettys shows electric tools as a position player. His range and arm in center field are excellent. He has quick hands at the plate and drives the ball with authority when he makes contact, which isn't often enough, especially against anything other than a fastball. Speed and defense will get Gettys to the big leagues, with his eventual role determined by how well he makes adjustments as a hitter along the way.

Jake Goebbert   1B

Born: 9/24/87   Age: 27   Bats: L   Throws: L   Height: 6' 0"   Weight: 205

YEAR	TEAM	LVL	AGE	PA	R	2B	3B	HR	RBI	BB	K	SB	CS	AVG/OBP/SLG	TAv	BABIP	BRR	FRAA	WARP
2012	CCH	AA	24	433	71	23	6	9	53	55	57	5	3	.304/.399/.473	.305	.338	5.5	RF(48): 3.9, LF(43): 2.3	4.3
2012	OKL	AAA	24	35	2	1	0	0	1	5	7	0	0	.133/.257/.167	.155	.174	-0.5	LF(5): -0.3, RF(4): -0.4	-0.4
2013	MID	AA	25	459	57	20	5	18	75	47	83	6	3	.268/.352/.480	.289	.291	-1.8	LF(35): 4.7, RF(25): 1.0	2.6
2013	SAC	AAA	25	85	13	3	0	4	6	15	16	0	0	.229/.365/.443	.290	.240	-1.5	LF(11): 1.1, RF(4): -0.3	0.3
2014	ELP	AAA	26	207	37	13	2	8	35	33	33	0	0	.322/.435/.561	.459	.359	0.1	LF(31): 0.7, RF(11): -0.1	0.9
2014	SAC	AAA	26	132	21	7	1	6	25	19	20	1	0	.257/.371/.500	.309	.259	0.0	LF(25): 0.2	1.1
2014	SDN	MLB	26	115	12	1	3	1	10	12	32	2	1	.218/.313/.317	.237	.309	1.3	1B(25): 1.1, LF(8): 0.2	1.1
2015	SDN	MLB	27	250	26	9	2	6	28	27	53	1	1	.231/.320/.378	.269	.273	-0.1	LF 2, 1B 1	1.1

Breakout: 4%   Improve: 18%   Collapse: 15%   Attrition: 22%   MLB: 41%   Comparables: Paul McAnulty, Mike Baxter, Danny Putnam

Acquired in mid-May for perpetually injured Kyle Blanks, Goebbert is a spare outfielder who makes decent contact (although not in his first look at the majors) and has middling power. He started 19 games at first base for the Padres last year, which says more about the team than the player. He did hit a homer at Coors Field against Jair Jurrjens, who hasn't been good since 2011. That tied Goebbert with J.A. Happ for sixth in career home runs by players who attended Northwestern University. He's probably tops among those who grew up on a pumpkin farm and majored in psychology; you could call him a pioneer of sorts.

Yasmani Grandal   C

Born: 11/8/88   Age: 26   Bats: B   Throws: R   Height: 6' 2"   Weight: 225

YEAR	TEAM	LVL	AGE	PA	R	2B	3B	HR	RBI	BB	K	SB	CS	AVG/OBP/SLG	TAv	BABIP	BRR	FRAA	WARP
2012	TUC	AAA	23	235	40	18	0	6	35	37	35	0	0	.335/.443/.521	.318	.381	0.5	C(45): -1.3	2.3
2012	SDN	MLB	23	226	28	7	1	8	36	31	39	0	0	.297/.394/.469	.318	.333	-3.2	C(55): 0.3	2.1
2013	TUC	AAA	24	38	3	3	0	0	2	2	8	0	0	.306/.342/.389	.262	.393	-1.5	C(5): 0.2	-0.1
2013	SDN	MLB	24	108	13	8	0	1	9	18	18	0	0	.216/.352/.341	.260	.257	0.9	C(26): 0.8, 1B(1): -0.0	0.6
2014	SDN	MLB	25	443	47	19	1	15	49	58	115	3	0	.225/.327/.401	.287	.277	-3.1	C(76): -0.2, 1B(37): -1.5	1.9
2015	SDN	MLB	26	354	40	16	1	10	41	45	79	1	0	.244/.343/.397	.286	.295	-1.9	C 0, 1B -1	1.8

Breakout: 7%   Improve: 50%   Collapse: 1%   Attrition: 5%   MLB: 99%   Comparables: Alex Avila, Chris Iannetta, Miguel Montero

While Grandal's desire to return quickly from right-knee surgery was admirable, it may have hurt his performance. He struggled to make contact, tied for the MLB lead in passed balls despite starting only 67 games behind the dish and caught just 13 percent of basestealers. By late August, he was playing more first base than catcher. Although the switch-hitter was abused by southpaws last year, that hadn't been true in the past. With his ACL tear receding further in the rearview mirror, Grandal can still develop—as his .250/.360/.440 line over the final three months suggests—into the middle-of-the-order threat the Padres envisioned when they acquired him. His career numbers are freakishly similar to those of another former Padres catcher/first baseman, Gene Tenace, at the same age. As with Tenace, the bat is more exciting if Grandal sticks at catcher; his pitch-framing numbers are strong, at least. The Dodgers acquiring him in the Matt Kemp trade implies that he *will* stick: He's not pushing Adrian Gonzalez off first base.

Jedd Gyorko   2B

Born: 9/23/88   Age: 26   Bats: R   Throws: R   Height: 5' 10"   Weight: 210

YEAR	TEAM	LVL	AGE	PA	R	2B	3B	HR	RBI	BB	K	SB	CS	AVG/OBP/SLG	TAv	BABIP	BRR	FRAA	WARP
2012	SAN	AA	23	149	18	4	0	6	17	17	27	1	1	.262/.356/.431	.275	.289	1.2	2B(17): 0.3, 3B(17): 0.3	0.8
2012	TUC	AAA	23	408	62	24	0	24	83	34	68	4	3	.328/.380/.588	.322	.344	-1.0	3B(56): -0.4, 2B(30): 4.1	4.4
2013	SDN	MLB	24	525	62	26	0	23	63	33	123	1	1	.249/.301/.444	.264	.287	0.2	2B(117): -5.6, 3B(13): 0.6	1.3
2014	ELP	AAA	25	28	7	2	0	1	5	4	4	0	0	.292/.393/.500	.310	.316	0.2	2B(6): 0.4	0.0
2014	SDN	MLB	25	443	37	17	1	10	51	36	100	3	2	.210/.280/.333	.245	.253	0.2	2B(109): -3.8	0.0
2015	SDN	MLB	26	437	48	18	0	16	56	32	101	2	1	.241/.299/.409	.274	.280	0.2	2B -2, 3B 0	1.9

Breakout: 2%   Improve: 59%   Collapse: 7%   Attrition: 9%   MLB: 98%   Comparables: Neil Walker, Danny Espinosa, Kevin Kouzmanoff

How bad was the Padres' offense last year? Gyorko led the team in RBIs with two fewer than Hack Wilson had in August 1930 or Joe DiMaggio had in August 1939 (but one more than Pete Ward and Tommy Davis had to lead the '68 White Sox, yay!). His .333 slugging percentage was the lowest by any team's RBI leader since 1973, when Aurelio Rodriguez and his .330 mark paced the Tigers. Philosophical ruminations on the merits of the RBI aside, damn.

Gyorko's season literally got off on the wrong foot, as plantar fasciitis helped sink his numbers and then put him on the disabled list for almost all of June and July. After posting a barely believable .482 OPS before the DL stint, he went .745 the rest of the way, identical to his rookie campaign (though different shape: more OBP in 2014, less SLG). With Gyorko under contract for five more years, the Padres hope his post-injury performance provides a better gauge of what the future holds.

The drop in power from Mike Cameron levels as a rookie to Mark Ellis levels as a sophomore is a concern. On the plus side, he is the franchise's all-time leader in home runs among second basemen, and we're not even kidding. (The prior record-holder was Mark Loretta. Still not kidding.) With two good feet to stand on, Gyorko—owner of a .529 SLG in 1,500 minor-league plate appearances—should find an equilibrium somewhere between his first two seasons, likely at the higher end. That would be nice because his bat is where any value lies.

Austin Hedges   C

Born: 8/18/92   Age: 22   Bats: R   Throws: R   Height: 6' 1"   Weight: 190

YEAR	TEAM	LVL	AGE	PA	R	2B	3B	HR	RBI	BB	K	SB	CS	AVG/OBP/SLG	TAv	BABIP	BRR	FRAA	WARP
2012	FTW	A	19	373	44	28	0	10	56	23	62	14	9	.279/.334/.451	.285	.312	-1.0	C(94): 0.3	3.1
2013	LEL	A+	20	266	34	22	1	4	30	22	45	5	4	.270/.343/.425	.279	.314	0.7	C(61): 0.9	2.2
2013	SAN	AA	20	75	4	3	0	0	8	6	9	3	1	.224/.297/.269	.225	.259	0.4	C(18): 0.0	0.1
2014	SAN	AA	21	457	31	19	2	6	44	23	89	1	3	.225/.268/.321	.207	.269	-1.7	C(106): -2.6	-0.7
2015	SDN	MLB	22	250	19	11	1	3	22	11	59	2	1	.211/.249/.305	.219	.263	-0.5	C -0	-0.2

Breakout: 0%   Improve: 0%   Collapse: 0%   Attrition: 0%   MLB: 0%   Comparables: Josmil Pinto, Miguel Montero, Rob Brantly

Let's get this out of the way: Hedges didn't hit last year. At all. From May 29th to season's end, his line was a surreal .198/.235/.256. There's no way to put a positive spin on that. The good news is that he was one of the youngest players in the Texas League and remains a brilliant defensive catcher. His quick release, accurate throws and strong game-calling chops will get him to the big leagues and keep him there for a long time. Fantasy owners may end up disappointed in his production, but real-life owners will appreciate the value of Hedges' defensive prowess. And while there's no indication that he *will* hit, there's still the possibility that he *might*. Vaguely relevant and/or misleading statement of fact: Lance Parrish and Jason Varitek didn't provide much offense at Double-A.

Taylor Lindsey   2B

Born: 12/2/91   Age: 23   Bats: L   Throws: R   Height: 6' 0"   Weight: 195

YEAR	TEAM	LVL	AGE	PA	R	2B	3B	HR	RBI	BB	K	SB	CS	AVG/OBP/SLG	TAv	BABIP	BRR	FRAA	WARP
2012	INL	A+	20	589	79	26	6	9	58	29	66	8	6	.289/.328/.408	.273	.313	-4.3		2.7
2013	ARK	AA	21	567	68	22	6	17	56	48	91	4	4	.274/.339/.441	.288	.303	0.0	2B(134): -6.2	2.3
2014	ELP	AAA	22	159	18	6	1	2	17	9	15	0	2	.219/.270/.315	.203	.229	-0.8	2B(33): -3.6, 3B(6): 0.1	-0.8
2014	SLC	AAA	22	334	50	13	4	8	30	31	44	7	2	.247/.323/.400	.257	.267	0.8	2B(71): -10.6	-0.4
2015	SDN	MLB	23	250	25	9	2	4	20	14	45	2	1	.224/.269/.329	.235	.257	-0.2	2B -2, 3B 0	-0.1

Breakout: 8%   Improve: 20%   Collapse: 0%   Attrition: 9%   MLB: 22%   Comparables: Daniel Descalso, Brad Emaus, Kyle Seager

Acquired in the Huston Street trade, Lindsey is an offense-first second baseman who forgot the offense in 2014. Missing three weeks in June with concussion-like symptoms didn't help. Lindsey controls the strike zone reasonably well and flashes occasional power, but his game revolves around batting average, always a dangerous proposition. He'll need to hit .300 to crack a big-league starting lineup, and he has to be a starter to stick in the majors, as his modest defensive skill set makes a utility role unlikely. Lindsey is knocking on the proverbial door, but when it opens, it may not stay that way for long. Worse, it may lead down a long corridor, between the pit of man's fears and the summit of his knowledge, to an area we call Quadruple-A.

Rymer Liriano   RF

Born: 6/20/91   Age: 24   Bats: R   Throws: R   Height: 6' 0"   Weight: 230

YEAR	TEAM	LVL	AGE	PA	R	2B	3B	HR	RBI	BB	K	SB	CS	AVG/OBP/SLG	TAv	BABIP	BRR	FRAA	WARP
2012	LEL	A+	21	314	41	22	2	5	41	21	69	22	7	.298/.360/.443	.289	.374	-2.1	RF(66): -2.8, CF(3): 0.0	1.0
2012	SAN	AA	21	206	24	10	2	3	20	20	50	10	1	.251/.335/.377	.253	.331	1.9	RF(49): 0.7, CF(9): -0.6	0.5
2014	SAN	AA	23	415	55	20	2	14	53	35	102	17	7	.264/.335/.442	.270	.326	5.3	LF(55): 2.6, CF(37): -0.1	2.9
2014	ELP	AAA	23	71	14	11	1	0	13	8	14	3	1	.452/.521/.661	.368	.583	-1.3	RF(11): -1.1, CF(5): 0.1	0.1
2014	SDN	MLB	23	121	13	2	0	1	6	9	39	4	1	.220/.289/.266	.211	.329	1.1	RF(34): -0.7	-0.3
2015	SDN	MLB	24	250	26	11	1	4	23	17	72	8	2	.228/.288/.341	.246	.310	0.5	RF -1, LF 1	0.2

Breakout: 1%   Improve: 14%   Collapse: 9%   Attrition: 13%   MLB: 32%   Comparables: Kelly Johnson, Justin Huber, Matt Murton

Raw. Aggressive. Toolsy. After missing 2013 following Tommy John surgery, Liriano returned to Double-A and launched a career-high 14 homers. He's a strong kid, but the power has been slow to show thanks to a suspect hit tool. He has whiffed in 24 percent of his career minor-league plate appearances, ratcheting that up to 32 percent in his seven-week trial with the Padres last year. Liriano's only big-league homer was a memorable 427-foot blast at Petco Park on an inside fastball, which hints at the talent. Putting it to use every day is a different story. If he continues to make adjustments, as he has in the past after initially struggling at each new level, he'll get there. Eventually.

Cameron Maybin   CF

Born: 4/4/87   Age: 28   Bats: R   Throws: R   Height: 6' 3"   Weight: 205

YEAR	TEAM	LVL	AGE	PA	R	2B	3B	HR	RBI	BB	K	SB	CS	AVG/OBP/SLG	TAv	BABIP	BRR	FRAA	WARP
2012	SDN	MLB	25	561	67	20	5	8	45	44	110	26	7	.243/.306/.349	.249	.293	2.7	CF(145): 4.5	1.6
2013	TUC	AAA	26	56	7	1	0	4	5	10	9	1	1	.261/.393/.543	.338	.242	-0.1	CF(13): 0.5	0.7
2013	SDN	MLB	26	57	7	1	0	1	5	4	9	4	1	.157/.232/.235	.158	.171	0.8	CF(14): -0.2	-0.4
2014	ELP	AAA	27	61	8	2	1	1	6	6	10	1	0	.264/.328/.396	.239	.295	-0.7	CF(15): -0.8	-0.1
2014	SDN	MLB	27	272	24	13	4	1	15	19	56	4	3	.235/.290/.331	.234	.297	1.1	CF(86): -4.4	-0.1
2015	SDN	MLB	28	250	28	9	2	4	22	19	55	9	3	.239/.300/.351	.257	.293	0.9	CF 1	0.9

Breakout: 0%   Improve: 45%   Collapse: 3%   Attrition: 2%   MLB: 97%   Comparables: Angel Pagan, Aaron Rowand, Franklin Gutierrez

When you are drafted 10th overall, draw comparisons to Eric Davis, homer off Roger Clemens in your first big-league at-bat at age 20 and get traded for Miguel Cabrera, folks assume you are destined for greatness. Maybin displayed a wide range of skills in his first season with the Padres but hasn't come close to that performance in his last three years. Injuries have derailed his development and last July's suspension for amphetamines didn't help. If you catch Maybin at the right moment, you'll swear he's the best player on the field. He's a brilliant center fielder who runs the bases with grace and can hit baseballs very far, although the numbers don't show it. There's still time for a happy ending, but Maybin keeps veering toward the Ruben Rivera Memorial Highway of Disappointment.

Tommy Medica 1B

Born: 4/9/88   Age: 27   Bats: R   Throws: R   Height: 6' 3"   Weight: 205

YEAR	TEAM	LVL	AGE	PA	R	2B	3B	HR	RBI	BB	K	SB	CS	AVG/OBP/SLG	TAv	BABIP	BRR	FRAA	WARP
2012	LEL	A+	24	406	65	37	5	19	87	41	86	1	1	.330/.406/.623	.362	.387	0.8	1B(39): -2.3, C(1): -0.0	4.6
2013	SAN	AA	25	320	48	20	3	18	57	28	67	4	2	.296/.372/.582	.334	.327	-1.4	1B(51): 2.4, LF(1): -0.0	3.1
2013	SDN	MLB	25	79	9	2	0	3	10	10	23	0	0	.290/.380/.449	.312	.395	0.2	1B(19): 0.5	0.4
2014	ELP	AAA	26	101	8	6	2	3	18	9	24	0	0	.213/.307/.427	.390	.258	1.1	1B(15): -0.6, LF(10): 0.1	0.3
2014	SDN	MLB	26	259	31	11	2	9	27	14	75	6	1	.233/.286/.408	.282	.299	1.1	1B(46): -0.7, LF(22): -0.1	1.0
2015	SDN	MLB	27	263	30	12	1	10	34	19	72	3	1	.242/.306/.428	.282	.301	0.4	1B -0, LF -0	1.1

Breakout: 5%   Improve: 26%   Collapse: 10%   Attrition: 21%   MLB: 60%   Comparables: Mike Carp, Ryan Shealy, Jake Fox

Streakiness, thy name is Medica. After hitting .161/.212/.290 through April, he was exiled to El Paso for a month. On returning, he hit .309/.351/.559 through the end of June. Medica had his moments, but 2-for-25 and 3-for-53 stretches torpedoed his overall numbers. He doesn't have a defensive home and doesn't hit enough to justify running his glove out there every day, which makes his terrible career numbers off the bench—in an admittedly small sample—problematic. There is a place for a right-handed hitter who can swat one over the wall every so often, but whether that place is the big leagues or Triple-A depends on how well he does everything else. Medica is right on the edge.

Will Middlebrooks 3B

Born: 9/9/88   Age: 26   Bats: R   Throws: R   Height: 6' 3"   Weight: 220

YEAR	TEAM	LVL	AGE	PA	R	2B	3B	HR	RBI	BB	K	SB	CS	AVG/OBP/SLG	TAv	BABIP	BRR	FRAA	WARP
2012	PAW	AAA	23	100	18	3	1	9	27	7	18	3	1	.333/.380/.677	.371	.333	-1.6	3B(24): -2.1	1.2
2012	BOS	MLB	23	286	34	14	0	15	54	13	70	4	1	.288/.325/.509	.279	.335	-0.2	3B(72): 4.0	1.8
2013	PAW	AAA	24	196	25	5	0	10	35	16	38	1	0	.268/.327/.464	.272	.288	-0.2	3B(40): 3.6	1.2
2013	BOS	MLB	24	374	41	18	0	17	49	20	98	3	1	.227/.271/.425	.240	.263	1.5	3B(92): -0.8, 2B(2): 0.0	0.8
2014	PAW	AAA	25	112	13	1	1	4	8	6	30	0	0	.231/.277/.375	.219	.282	0.8	3B(17): 0.1	-0.1
2014	BOS	MLB	25	234	14	10	0	2	19	15	70	1	1	.191/.256/.265	.188	.273	-0.2	3B(62): -0.9, 1B(1): -0.0	-1.2
2015	SDN	MLB	26	288	32	13	0	11	37	17	74	2	1	.243/.292/.413	.261	.293	0.3	3B 1, 1B -0	0.9

Breakout: 2%   Improve: 52%   Collapse: 6%   Attrition: 14%   MLB: 96%   Comparables: Wilson Betemit, Ian Stewart, Kevin Kouzmanoff

Middlebrooks looks born to play the part, with his boyish All-American looks and his easy, high school quarterback Texas swagger. He is Adonis on a baseball diamond, but every pitch with a modicum of movement serves as a new wild boar, laying waste to his beauty. The unfortunate reality is that Middlebrooks has looked at turns unwilling or unable to make adjustments since his strong rookie campaign, and neither tendency bodes well for his future. His power is useless when he can't make contact, and he can't stay on the field long enough to make his plus defensive profile matter. He's the weak link in the Padres' offseason right-handed power splurge.

Wil Myers RF

Born: 12/10/90   Age: 24   Bats: R   Throws: R   Height: 6' 3"   Weight: 205

YEAR	TEAM	LVL	AGE	PA	R	2B	3B	HR	RBI	BB	K	SB	CS	AVG/OBP/SLG	TAv	BABIP	BRR	FRAA	WARP
2012	NWA	AA	21	152	32	11	1	13	30	16	42	4	1	.343/.414/.731	.394	.413	-0.3	CF(20): 3.6, RF(13): 0.1	3.0
2012	OMA	AAA	21	439	66	15	5	24	79	45	98	2	2	.304/.378/.554	.313	.349	-1.6	CF(67): -7.8, 3B(13): -0.9	2.8
2013	DUR	AAA	22	289	44	13	2	14	57	29	71	7	1	.286/.356/.520	.290	.335	0.3	RF(56): 8.1	2.2
2013	TBA	MLB	22	373	50	23	0	13	53	33	91	5	2	.293/.354/.478	.303	.362	0.3	RF(72): -2.3, CF(8): 0.9	2.0
2014	DUR	AAA	23	31	3	1	0	2	6	7	7	3	0	.250/.419/.542	.309	.267	0.2	LF(2): -0.1, RF(2): 0.1	0.3
2014	TBA	MLB	23	361	37	14	0	6	35	34	90	6	1	.222/.294/.320	.231	.286	-2.6	RF(78): 0.7, 1B(2): 0.0	-0.5
2015	SDN	MLB	24	381	46	16	1	14	50	34	97	6	1	.258/.325/.437	.287	.315	-0.8	RF 2, CF -0	1.8

Breakout: 3%   Improve: 41%   Collapse: 12%   Attrition: 13%   MLB: 91%   Comparables: Travis Snider, Chris Young, Justin Upton

The regressioners set out with pitchforks in hand calling for Myers' head after his rookie campaign. They celebrated victory after his sophomore season went up in flames. His downfall was more lack than luck: Little improvement against soft pitching along with a fractured wrist doomed the youngster more than any hocus pocus. Anything with tilt put Myers on axis; it's a surprise he didn't injure himself lunging for a slider in the dirt. Still, all the raw tools remain intact, from bat speed to strong wrists to ignorance of the word "failure." Outside of a mediocre (but still not bad) season in Double-A in 2011, Myers has seen only success as a professional. This bump in the road might be good for him in the long run; that's what the Padres appear to be betting on after acquiring him in a massive trade in mid-December.

Derek Norris C

Born: 2/14/89   Age: 26   Bats: R   Throws: R   Height: 6' 0"   Weight: 210

YEAR	TEAM	LVL	AGE	PA	R	2B	3B	HR	RBI	BB	K	SB	CS	AVG/OBP/SLG	TAv	BABIP	BRR	FRAA	WARP
2012	SAC	AAA	23	246	39	14	2	9	38	21	41	5	1	.271/.329/.477	.278	.287	-0.6	C(58): -0.4	1.6
2012	OAK	MLB	23	232	19	8	1	7	34	21	66	5	1	.201/.276/.349	.231	.255	-0.3	C(58): 0.0	0.1
2013	OAK	MLB	24	308	41	16	0	9	30	37	71	5	0	.246/.345/.409	.289	.301	0.3	C(91): 0.3, 1B(1): 0.0	2.4
2014	OAK	MLB	25	442	46	19	1	10	55	54	86	2	2	.270/.361/.403	.286	.324	-4.8	C(114): -0.2	2.3
2015	SDN	MLB	26	390	43	16	1	10	44	40	87	4	1	.245/.325/.391	.279	.296	-1.6	C 0, 1B 0	2.1

Breakout: 1%   Improve: 18%   Collapse: 10%   Attrition: 25%   MLB: 64%   Comparables: Cal Ripken Jr., Tony Taylor, Jamey Carroll

Norris' throwing issues were exposed in the A's Wild Card game, with the Royals running rampant on the basepaths en route to a playoff record-tying seven stolen bases, six of which came with Norris behind the dish after Geovany Soto was knocked out of the game with an injury. Things were not quite as extreme in the regular season, but opposing runners had a gaudy 83 percent success rate on 72 steal attempts, and Norris' frequent shot-put throws back to the pitcher further encouraged runners to test his arm. With solid power and a patient approach, his offensive clout makes for a worthwhile trade-off, but Norris is best used as part of an offense/defense platoon that allows him to rest against running teams or in late-and-close innings. Now paired with Tim Federowicz in San Diego, Norris will probably be just a regular old starting catcher.

Did you know: Norris has not shaved since 1973.

Dustin Peterson　3B

Born: 9/10/94　Age: 20　Bats: R　Throws: R　Height: 6' 2"　Weight: 180

YEAR	TEAM	LVL	AGE	PA	R	2B	3B	HR	RBI	BB	K	SB	CS	AVG/OBP/SLG	TAv	BABIP	BRR	FRAA	WARP
2014	FTW	A	19	564	64	31	3	10	79	25	137	1	3	.233/.274/.361	.224	.294	1.3	3B(101): -9.5	-2.1
2015	SDN	MLB	20	250	19	9	0	3	17	6	79	0	0	.184/.207/.259	.184	.257	-0.5	3B -5	-2.0

Breakout: 0%　Improve: 0%　Collapse: 0%　Attrition: 0%　MLB: 0%　　Comparables:　Will Middlebrooks, Juan Francisco, Mat Gamel

On July 1st, Peterson knocked three hits against the Dayton Dragons, bringing his season line to .270/.324/.432. Not great, but respectable for one of the younger players in a pitching-friendly league. From that point forward, the 2013 second-round pick hit .176/.190/.249 over his final 49 games, with three walks against 55 strikeouts. This is a serious problem. So are the 38 errors he committed at third base, which could push him across the diamond or to the outfield, where his offensive performance becomes even more important. Youth remains on Peterson's side for now, but he must make dramatic improvements on both sides of the ball if he wants to turn his potential into something useful.

Jace Peterson　INF

Born: 5/9/90　Age: 25　Bats: L　Throws: R　Height: 6' 0"　Weight: 210

YEAR	TEAM	LVL	AGE	PA	R	2B	3B	HR	RBI	BB	K	SB	CS	AVG/OBP/SLG	TAv	BABIP	BRR	FRAA	WARP
2012	FTW	A	22	521	78	23	9	2	48	62	63	51	13	.286/.378/.392	.285	.328	5.8	SS(107): -4.5	3.4
2013	LEL	A+	23	496	78	17	13	7	66	54	58	42	10	.303/.382/.454	.314	.332	4.7	SS(106): -4.4	4.8
2014	SAN	AA	24	83	10	3	0	1	7	9	9	4	3	.311/.386/.392	.285	.344	1.3	SS(17): -0.0, 2B(1): -0.0	0.6
2014	ELP	AAA	24	299	44	21	6	2	39	42	50	12	6	.306/.406/.464	.352	.374	0.1	SS(28): -0.6, 2B(25): 1.3	0.9
2014	SDN	MLB	24	58	3	0	0	0	2	18	2	0	.113/.161/.113	.106	.171	0.3	2B(14): 1.2, 3B(10): 0.3	-0.6
2015	SDN	MLB	25	250	28	9	2	1	15	23	49	11	4	.228/.302/.304	.239	.279	0.9	SS -1, 2B 0	0.5

Breakout: 0%　Improve: 6%　Collapse: 10%　Attrition: 19%　MLB: 33%　　Comparables:　Justin Sellers, Alejandro Machado, Brian Dozier

Exclusively a shortstop in his first two pro seasons, Peterson shifted to a utility role in 2014. His versatility landed him in San Diego after just 18 Double-A games, which turned out to be too fast: Playing third base, he went 4-for-23 before being shipped to El Paso, where he hit .330/.441/.560 for the next month. Peterson then returned to the Padres in June as a second baseman and hit 1-for-27. "Hmm," the Padres said. "Hmmmm." Peterson continued to bounce between the two locales and ended his season with a 12-game hitting streak at Triple-A that included nine multi-hit games and no cup of coffee. In theory, his on-base skills and speed could make him a productive table-setter. In practice, at the big-league level, a few forks and knives are missing. Learning to play different positions was a wise move.

Carlos Quentin　LF

Born: 8/28/82　Age: 32　Bats: R　Throws: R　Height: 6' 1"　Weight: 235

YEAR	TEAM	LVL	AGE	PA	R	2B	3B	HR	RBI	BB	K	SB	CS	AVG/OBP/SLG	TAv	BABIP	BRR	FRAA	WARP
2012	SDN	MLB	29	340	44	21	0	16	46	36	41	0	1	.261/.374/.504	.317	.252	-1.3	LF(69): -3.3, RF(3): -0.4	2.1
2013	SDN	MLB	30	320	42	21	0	13	44	31	55	0	0	.275/.363/.493	.315	.297	-0.8	LF(69): -3.0	1.8
2014	SDN	MLB	31	155	9	6	0	4	18	17	33	0	0	.177/.284/.315	.230	.196	-2.3	LF(32): -1.0	-0.7
2015	SDN	MLB	32	250	29	12	0	10	33	22	45	0	0	.239/.329/.433	.295	.256	-0.9	LF -3, RF -0	1.0

Breakout: 0%　Improve: 28%　Collapse: 3%　Attrition: 6%　MLB: 97%　　Comparables:　Chipper Jones, Brian Giles, Carl Yastrzemski

The mistake wasn't trading for Quentin—he cost the Padres almost nothing. The mistake came when they signed their brittle "left fielder" to a three-year extension that included a full no-trade clause. Already blessed with the inability to survive a season unscathed, last year he added "unproductive when healthy" to his repertoire, although "healthy" might be the wrong word to describe someone who missed the season's first seven weeks and last nine with variations on the same injury. A rebound is possible, but it's tough to bet on a guy with bad knees, no glove and a missing stick.

Hunter Renfroe　OF

Born: 1/28/92　Age: 23　Bats: R　Throws: R　Height: 6' 1"　Weight: 200

YEAR	TEAM	LVL	AGE	PA	R	2B	3B	HR	RBI	BB	K	SB	CS	AVG/OBP/SLG	TAv	BABIP	BRR	FRAA	WARP
2013	EUG	A-	21	111	20	9	0	4	18	5	26	2	0	.308/.333/.510	.335	.368	1.1	RF(25): 1.2	1.4
2013	FTW	A	21	72	6	5	0	2	7	4	23	0	0	.212/.268/.379	.230	.293	-1.0	RF(16): -1.2	-0.4
2014	LEL	A+	22	316	46	21	3	16	52	28	81	9	3	.295/.370/.565	.334	.359	-0.3	RF(62): -5.8, CF(4): 1.0	3.0
2014	SAN	AA	22	251	17	12	0	6	23	25	53	2	1	.232/.307/.353	.239	.280	-0.5	LF(30): -2.7, CF(22): -1.8	-0.2
2015	SDN	MLB	23	250	24	10	1	7	27	16	74	2	1	.213/.269/.349	.240	.278	-0.2	RF -1, LF -1	-0.3

Breakout: 2%　Improve: 5%　Collapse: 1%　Attrition: 1%　MLB: 8%　　Comparables:　Roger Kieschnick, Kyle Parker, Rene Tosoni

The easy narrative is that Renfroe thrived in the hitter-friendly California League before struggling in a tougher environment. A subtler interpretation considers that this was his first full season and that pitchers in Double-A have more moxie than their High-A counterparts. Renfroe remains a work in progress, albeit one who crushes baseballs. His aggressive approach will be exploited at higher levels, although the improved walk rate after promotion is a promising sign. Defense is less of a concern, as his athleticism and arm make him an asset in right field. If Renfroe develops a better plan at the plate, especially against off-speed stuff late in counts, he could land in the heart of a big-league lineup as early as 2016.

Franmil Reyes　RF

Born: 7/7/95　Age: 19　Bats: R　Throws: R　Height: 6' 5"　Weight: 240

YEAR	TEAM	LVL	AGE	PA	R	2B	3B	HR	RBI	BB	K	SB	CS	AVG/OBP/SLG	TAv	BABIP	BRR	FRAA	WARP
2013	EUG	A-	17	45	4	1	0	1	4	1	10	0	0	.205/.222/.295	.193	.242	0.6	RF(11): 0.1	-0.1
2014	FTW	A	18	552	67	24	2	11	59	38	118	1	5	.248/.301/.368	.242	.301	0.3	RF(106): -8.7, LF(1): -0.0	-1.3
2015	SDN	MLB	19	250	17	9	1	3	21	11	75	0	0	.196/.231/.280	.202	.267	-0.5	RF -3, LF -0	-1.4

Breakout: 0%　Improve: 0%　Collapse: 0%　Attrition: 0%　MLB: 0%　　Comparables:　Marcell Ozuna, Oswaldo Arcia, Chris Parmelee

How you view Reyes says a lot about how you view the world. The optimist sees one of the Midwest League's youngest players hold his own against more experienced competition and imagines a bright future. The pessimist sees a kid who is already 6-feet-5 and 240 pounds at age 18 and wonders how much projection he has left. Reyes made decent contact in his full-season debut, but a league-average ISO won't get you much more than a "Participant" ribbon. And while it's true that we're all participants in this world, it's equally true that the overwhelming majority of us aren't big-league hitters.

Jose Rondon   SS

Born: 3/3/94   Age: 21   Bats: R   Throws: R   Height: 6' 1"   Weight: 160

YEAR	TEAM	LVL	AGE	PA	R	2B	3B	HR	RBI	BB	K	SB	CS	AVG/OBP/SLG	TAv	BABIP	BRR	FRAA	WARP
2014	LEL	A+	20	154	18	9	0	1	12	13	23	3	1	.301/.371/.390	.284	.357	0.1	SS(36): -1.2	0.9
2014	INL	A+	20	324	40	17	5	0	24	17	50	8	6	.327/.362/.418	.287	.391	3.7		3.4
2015	SDN	MLB	21	250	21	10	1	0	15	11	55	2	2	.224/.259/.280	.213	.283	-0.3	SS 2, 3B 0	0.0

Breakout: 0%   Improve: 0%   Collapse: 0%   Attrition: 0%   MLB: 0%   Comparables: *DJ LeMahieu, Cristhian Adames, Joe Panik*

Rondon has knocked exactly one home run in each of the last three seasons. The Venezuelan shortstop, who came to San Diego in the Huston Street deal, will never be mistaken for Giancarlo Stanton. Still, Rondon's quick bat and good hand-eye coordination have conspired to keep his batting average near .300. Both of his California League managers last year lauded his defensive skills, although some observers believe a move to second base may be needed. Whichever side of the bag he ends up on, if the hit tool continues to develop at higher levels, he could start in the big leagues. More likely, he's a future utility player in the mold of Alexi Amarista, another guy the Padres once acquired from the Angels for a reliever.

Seth Smith   LF

Born: 9/30/82   Age: 32   Bats: L   Throws: L   Height: 6' 3"   Weight: 210

YEAR	TEAM	LVL	AGE	PA	R	2B	3B	HR	RBI	BB	K	SB	CS	AVG/OBP/SLG	TAv	BABIP	BRR	FRAA	WARP
2012	OAK	MLB	29	441	55	23	2	14	52	50	98	2	2	.240/.333/.420	.281	.285	1.6	LF(57): 2.0, RF(13): -0.6	2.0
2013	OAK	MLB	30	410	49	27	0	8	40	39	94	0	0	.253/.329/.391	.265	.320	1.1	LF(50): 2.3, RF(9): -0.6	1.2
2014	SDN	MLB	31	521	55	31	5	12	48	69	87	1	1	.266/.367/.440	.312	.305	-1.6	LF(102): 1.6, RF(43): -1.1	3.8
2015	SDN	MLB	32	467	48	24	3	11	52	46	97	2	1	.243/.322/.394	.277	.289	0.4	LF 3, RF -1	2.1

Breakout: 0%   Improve: 30%   Collapse: 4%   Attrition: 9%   MLB: 97%   Comparables: *David Justice, Andy Pafko, Hideki Matsui*

Excluding strike-shortened seasons, the 2014 Padres were the first team since the 1910 White Sox to have zero players collect at least 120 hits. Smith came closest, with 118, and provided more value than expected. Acquired from Oakland in December 2013 to be the team's fourth outfielder, he took on a larger role thanks to the obligatory Cameron Maybin and Carlos Quentin injuries. Smith responded by establishing career highs in TAv and WARP. He handled southpaws better than usual (in a small sample) and hit two-thirds of his home runs at Petco Park. An indifferent defender whose sole value lies in his bat, Smith hit .214/.326/.310 over the final two months, knocking his last homer on August 6th. Five weeks earlier, the Padres had extended him through 2016, not anticipating that his second-half ISO would match Alberto Callaspo's career mark.

Yangervis Solarte   UT

Born: 7/7/87   Age: 27   Bats: B   Throws: R   Height: 5' 11"   Weight: 195

YEAR	TEAM	LVL	AGE	PA	R	2B	3B	HR	RBI	BB	K	SB	CS	AVG/OBP/SLG	TAv	BABIP	BRR	FRAA	WARP
2012	ROU	AAA	24	568	69	28	0	11	54	41	44	3	1	.288/.340/.405	.261	.294	-0.1	2B(91): -7.2, LF(21): -2.6	0.6
2013	ROU	AAA	25	577	66	31	0	12	75	39	69	3	0	.276/.323/.403	.259	.294	1.4	2B(88): -4.2, 3B(20): -0.5	1.3
2014	SWB	AAA	26	21	3	3	1	0	5	1	2	0	0	.600/.619/.850	.481	.667	0.0	3B(4): -0.2, SS(1): 0.1	0.6
2014	NYA	MLB	26	289	26	14	0	6	31	30	34	0	0	.254/.337/.381	.268	.270	-1.1	3B(66): 0.9, 2B(17): -0.7	0.8
2014	SDN	MLB	26	246	30	5	1	4	17	23	24	0	1	.267/.336/.355	.269	.281	-0.1	3B(45): -5.4, 2B(10): -0.7	0.5
2015	SDN	MLB	27	468	42	21	1	7	47	33	62	1	0	.251/.304/.356	.258	.273	-0.4	3B -3, 2B -2	0.5

Breakout: 6%   Improve: 26%   Collapse: 12%   Attrition: 26%   MLB: 68%   Comparables: *Jordan Pacheco, Luis Rodriguez, Justin Turner*

Signed by the Yankees as a minor-league free agent, Solarte was hitting .299/.368/.458 on June 8th, after his second straight two-hit game against the Royals. A 4-for-51 skid ensued, resulting in a demotion to Triple-A and subsequent trade to San Diego for the more famous Chase Headley. With the Padres, Solarte did everything Headley did, but without all the strikeouts. That said, he profiles as a utility player going forward, as the most exciting aspect of his game for a small-market team is that he costs a lot less than his predecessor.

Cory Spangenberg   UT

Born: 3/16/91   Age: 24   Bats: L   Throws: R   Height: 6' 0"   Weight: 195

YEAR	TEAM	LVL	AGE	PA	R	2B	3B	HR	RBI	BB	K	SB	CS	AVG/OBP/SLG	TAv	BABIP	BRR	FRAA	WARP
2012	LEL	A+	21	426	53	12	8	1	40	26	72	27	9	.271/.324/.352	.255	.327	4.5	2B(96): 2.2	1.8
2013	LEL	A+	22	253	33	13	6	4	31	23	51	17	3	.296/.364/.460	.299	.368	1.5	2B(52): -7.2	1.3
2013	SAN	AA	22	319	35	10	3	2	20	17	61	19	11	.289/.331/.366	.270	.358	0.9	2B(75): 2.2, LF(1): -0.0	1.7
2014	EUG	A-	23	25	3	0	1	0	2	0	6	2	0	.200/.200/.280	.156	.263	0.5	2B(4): 0.5, CF(1): -0.1	-0.2
2014	SAN	AA	23	304	38	17	8	2	22	15	63	14	9	.331/.365/.470	.291	.421	-1.8	2B(48): -1.6, CF(14): 0.6	2.0
2014	SDN	MLB	23	65	7	2	1	2	9	2	14	4	2	.290/.313/.452	.280	.348	0.2	3B(9): 0.1, LF(4): -0.3	0.2
2015	SDN	MLB	24	250	28	9	3	2	16	10	60	10	5	.243/.277/.327	.233	.309	0.7	2B -1, 3B 0	0.1

Breakout: 4%   Improve: 15%   Collapse: 8%   Attrition: 26%   MLB: 39%   Comparables: *Charlie Culberson, Hernan Iribarren, Cesar Hernandez*

Don't let the two homers in his first 12 big-league plate appearances fool you. Spangenberg admitted after the first—a pinch-hit, walk-off job—that when he hits the ball out, it's a mistake. The two bombs in 300 plate appearances last year at Double-A and career .109 ISO in the minors are better barometers of his power potential. The small-ball approach would work better if he walked more and got caught stealing less often. Primarily a second baseman, Spangenberg also saw action at third base and in the outfield last year. His upside lies along the Ackley/Amarista continuum, which isn't exciting except for the fact that it might keep him gainfully employed for the next decade.

Trea Turner   SS

Born: 6/30/93   Age: 22   Bats: R   Throws: R   Height: 6' 1"   Weight: 175

YEAR	TEAM	LVL	AGE	PA	R	2B	3B	HR	RBI	BB	K	SB	CS	AVG/OBP/SLG	TAv	BABIP	BRR	FRAA	WARP
2014	EUG	A-	21	105	14	2	0	1	2	11	19	9	1	.228/.324/.283	.271	.278	0.7	SS(14): 2.7	0.7
2014	FTW	A	21	216	31	14	2	4	22	24	48	14	3	.369/.447/.529	.337	.478	2.8	SS(36): -0.2	3.0
2015	SDN	MLB	22	250	26	9	1	3	17	17	73	7	2	.215/.275/.295	.227	.298	0.4	SS 1	0.2

Breakout: 0%   Improve: 0%   Collapse: 0%   Attrition: 0%   MLB: 0%   Comparables: *Jonathan Villar, Tim Beckham, Eugenio Suarez*

Turner started the year at North Carolina State and ended it in the Arizona Fall League. Concerns about a long swing were assuaged—at least temporarily—by his wanton destruction of Midwest League pitching. Though lacking in power, he controls the strike zone and possesses 80 speed. A former third baseman, Turner has plenty of arm but is still learning the nuances of shortstop. His athleticism should keep him there, with lineup placement determined by how well the hit tool plays at higher levels. If he repeats last year's success, he'll be a dangerous leadoff man. If better pitchers thwart him, as many suspect, he'll slot toward the bottom third. Washington picked him up, along with Joe Ross, on the back end of the Wil Myers deal for the low low price of Steven Souza and Travis Ott.

Will Venable   OF

Born: 10/29/82   Age: 32   Bats: L   Throws: L   Height: 6'3"   Weight: 205

YEAR	TEAM	LVL	AGE	PA	R	2B	3B	HR	RBI	BB	K	SB	CS	AVG/OBP/SLG	TAv	BABIP	BRR	FRAA	WARP
2012	SDN	MLB	29	470	62	26	8	9	45	41	94	24	6	.264/.335/.429	.278	.320	3.8	RF(114): 4.9, CF(21): -1.3	2.5
2013	SDN	MLB	30	515	64	22	8	22	53	29	118	22	6	.268/.312/.484	.281	.313	2.1	RF(97): 1.3, CF(80): -0.6	2.2
2014	SDN	MLB	31	448	47	13	2	8	33	33	107	11	6	.224/.288/.325	.236	.283	-1.0	CF(76): 0.6, RF(75): 2.4	0.1
2015	SDN	MLB	32	434	56	16	5	11	41	31	106	17	5	.240/.298/.385	.261	.295	1.0	RF 2, CF -0	1.4

Breakout: 1%   Improve: 38%   Collapse: 1%   Attrition: 9%   MLB: 95%   Comparables: Aaron Rowand, Torii Hunter, Jim Edmonds

When locals speak of Venable, which isn't often, they sometimes call him Mr. August thanks to his career .300/.361/.529 line during that month. Last season, he was more of a July guy: On the 11th, he got his batting average to stay above .200; on the 30th, he got his slugging percentage to stay above .300. Last year's edition of this book advised against betting the farm on Venable's "breakout" 2013 campaign, noting that it was really a two-month hot streak. Some years, the streak never comes. Venable's futility against breaking balls, which had lain dormant since 2011, chose an inopportune time to re-erupt. When a hitter exposes a weakness as glaring as Venable's against pitches with spin, it removes the incentive for pitchers to throw him anything else. If the weakness persists, it removes the incentive for managers to stick him in the lineup.

Pitchers

Joaquin Benoit   RHP

Born: 7/26/77   Age: 37   Bats: R   Throws: R   Height: 6'3"   Weight: 220

YEAR	TEAM	LVL	AGE	W	L	SV	G	GS	IP	H	HR	BB	K	BB/9	K/9	GB%	BABIP	WHIP	ERA	FIP	FRA	WARP
2012	DET	MLB	34	5	3	2	73	0	71	59	14	22	84	2.8	10.6	38%	.269	1.14	3.68	4.22	4.20	0.8
2013	DET	MLB	35	4	1	24	66	0	67	47	5	22	73	3.0	9.8	44%	.256	1.03	2.01	2.90	3.09	1.3
2014	SDN	MLB	36	4	2	11	53	0	54¹	28	3	14	64	2.3	10.6	38%	.203	0.77	1.49	2.29	3.01	0.8
2015	SDN	MLB	37	3	1	9	51	0	50¹	35	4	14	60	2.5	10.7	40%	.281	0.97	2.15	2.82	2.34	1.3

Breakout: 16%   Improve: 31%   Collapse: 26%   Attrition: 19%   MLB: 86%   Comparables: J.J. Putz, Joe Nathan, Rafael Betancourt

Signed by the Padres in December 2013 to replace Luke Gregerson as Huston Street's chief setup man, Benoit assumed the closer role after Street was traded in July. Featuring a 95 mph fastball backed by an untouchable splitter that accounted for two-thirds of his strikeouts, Benoit thrived in both roles. In high-leverage situations, batters hit .110/.180/.183 against him, which is goofier than the Leidenfrost effect. Although a "cranky" shoulder cost him much of August and September, he finished strong, retiring the last 16 men he faced. With at least $9.5 million coming Benoit's way over the next two years, the Padres hope the 37-year-old can better shoulder the load in 2015.

Blaine Boyer   RHP

Born: 7/11/81   Age: 33   Bats: R   Throws: R   Height: 6'3"   Weight: 225

YEAR	TEAM	LVL	AGE	W	L	SV	G	GS	IP	H	HR	BB	K	BB/9	K/9	GB%	BABIP	WHIP	ERA	FIP	FRA	WARP
2013	OMA	AAA	31	0	1	1	13	0	15	15	3	3	18	1.8	10.8	54%	.300	1.20	3.00	4.37	6.00	0.0
2014	ELP	AAA	32	1	2	7	25	0	29	26	2	6	28	1.9	8.7	55%	.316	1.10	3.10	3.39	3.76	0.6
2014	SDN	MLB	32	0	1	0	32	0	40¹	34	2	8	29	1.8	6.5	45%	.264	1.04	3.57	2.90	3.60	0.3
2015	SDN	MLB	33	2	2	0	36	2	49¹	48	5	16	35	2.9	6.5	51%	.305	1.30	4.14	4.29	4.50	-0.1

Breakout: 20%   Improve: 26%   Collapse: 12%   Attrition: 20%   MLB: 43%   Comparables: Randy Flores, Doug Slaten, David Cortes

Last seen coughing up four runs in the 11th inning of an April 2011 contest, Boyer returned from Forgottenpitcherstan to become a productive member of the Padres' bullpen. He featured a mid-90s fastball and a breaking ball that, according to Boyer, hadn't been right since 2006 labrum and rotator cuff surgery. Working primarily in low-leverage situations, he fared well against right-handers, retiring the first 26 he faced after being re-called from Triple-A in late May. (You'd think a guy who got Troy Tulowitzki out twice could get Drew Butera out once.) Boyer fizzled late, allowing 10 of his 16 runs in his last seven outings, punctuated by a 2 1/2-week mid-September absence due to shoulder fatigue. Tough way to end the season, but after sitting out 2012 and splitting 2013 between Omaha and Japan, who's complaining?

Andrew Cashner   RHP

Born: 9/11/86   Age: 28   Bats: R   Throws: R   Height: 6'6"   Weight: 220

YEAR	TEAM	LVL	AGE	W	L	SV	G	GS	IP	H	HR	BB	K	BB/9	K/9	GB%	BABIP	WHIP	ERA	FIP	FRA	WARP
2012	SAN	AA	25	2	0	0	3	3	14¹	10	0	3	22	1.9	13.8	52%	.345	0.91	1.88	1.26	1.58	0.7
2012	SDN	MLB	25	3	4	0	33	5	46¹	42	5	19	52	3.7	10.1	56%	.311	1.32	4.27	3.59	4.07	0.5
2013	SDN	MLB	26	10	9	0	31	26	175	151	12	47	128	2.4	6.6	53%	.269	1.13	3.09	3.32	4.18	2.4
2014	SDN	MLB	27	5	7	0	19	19	123¹	110	7	29	93	2.1	6.8	50%	.275	1.13	2.55	3.06	3.85	1.2
2015	SDN	MLB	28	6	7	0	31	19	118²	100	9	32	104	2.5	7.9	51%	.294	1.12	3.02	3.42	3.28	1.7

Breakout: 27%   Improve: 51%   Collapse: 19%   Attrition: 11%   MLB: 84%   Comparables: Homer Bailey, Sean Marshall, Jeff Francis

Cashner built on his breakout 2013 campaign, looking every bit the ace through mid-May. Then, as he will do, he got hurt. He missed three weeks with "soreness and irritation" in his right elbow, made three starts in June, then missed two months with right-shoulder inflammation. Sprinkled among his 19 starts were an April 11th one-hitter and a September 15th two-hitter. The dominance is there, as is the stuff (BP's Doug Thorburn gushed over Cashner's 96 mph sinker "with ridiculous arm-side run" after the one-hitter), but he has yet to flash the health skill with consistency. Also worth noting: At Petco Park over the last two years, batters have hit .205/.246/.279 against Cashner. On the road, they've hit .263/.321/.417. If he finds durability, despite the caveats, this is a frontline starter.

Odrisamer Despaigne   RHP
Born: 4/4/87   Age: 28   Bats: R   Throws: R   Height: 6'0"   Weight: 195

YEAR	TEAM	LVL	AGE	W	L	SV	G	GS	IP	H	HR	BB	K	BB/9	K/9	GB%	BABIP	WHIP	ERA	FIP	FRA	WARP
2014	ELP	AAA	27	1	3	0	5	5	23²	36	3	13	29	4.9	11.0	0%	.440	2.07	7.61	4.67	5.08	
2014	SDN	MLB	27	4	7	0	16	16	96¹	85	6	32	65	3.0	6.1	55%	.267	1.21	3.36	3.72	4.58	-0.3
2015	SDN	MLB	28	3	5	0	15	13	66²	60	5	21	52	2.8	7.1	49%	.298	1.21	3.53	3.82	3.83	0.5

Breakout: 22%   Improve: 57%   Collapse: 22%   Attrition: 11%   MLB: 97%   Comparables: Mark Mulder, Johnny Cueto, John Danks

Junk. Lots of junk. With different movement, and from different arm angles. The Padres signed Despaigne out of Cuba for $1 million in May. He made seven uninspired minor-league starts (some suggested he may have been bored pitching at that level) before being recalled toward the end of June; he remained in the big-league rotation the rest of the way. His fastball just pushes into the 90s and he'll fling an assortment of breaking balls anywhere from the mid-80s to the mid-60s. Despaigne patterns his game after that of former Yankees hurler and countryman Orlando Hernandez, but lacks his idol's ability to put baseballs past hitters, which limits him to the back end of a rotation or perhaps long relief.

Zach Eflin   RHP
Born: 4/8/94   Age: 21   Bats: R   Throws: R   Height: 6'4"   Weight: 200

YEAR	TEAM	LVL	AGE	W	L	SV	G	GS	IP	H	HR	BB	K	BB/9	K/9	GB%	BABIP	WHIP	ERA	FIP	FRA	WARP
2013	FTW	A	19	7	6	0	22	22	118²	110	7	31	86	2.4	6.5	42%	.275	1.19	2.73	3.54	4.14	2.1
2014	LEL	A+	20	10	7	0	24	24	128	138	9	31	93	2.2	6.5	53%	.323	1.32	3.80	4.02	4.87	1.3
2015	SDN	MLB	21	5	9	0	21	21	110¹	116	11	40	63	3.2	5.1	44%	.306	1.41	4.65	4.70	5.05	-0.8

Breakout: 0%   Improve: 0%   Collapse: 0%   Attrition: 0%   MLB: 0%   Comparables: Kyle Ryan, Erasmo Ramirez, Jonathan Pettibone

Eflin, one of the California League's youngest hurlers, hid his youth well. He lasted at least five innings in 21 of his 24 starts, his ERA was better than league average and the nine homers he allowed came in bunches (three in an April contest at High Desert, the minors' most taterrific ballpark; five more in a four-game stretch in June). Featuring a low-90s fastball, plus changeup and developing slider, the long and lean Eflin works around the strike zone but doesn't miss as many bats as he could. Acquired by the Dodgers in the Matt Kemp trade and then the Phillies in the Jimmy Rollins deal, he'll continue to climb the ladder one rung at a time en route to his eventual role as a mid-rotation starter.

Robbie Erlin   LHP
Born: 10/8/90   Age: 24   Bats: R   Throws: L   Height: 6'0"   Weight: 190

YEAR	TEAM	LVL	AGE	W	L	SV	G	GS	IP	H	HR	BB	K	BB/9	K/9	GB%	BABIP	WHIP	ERA	FIP	FRA	WARP
2012	SAN	AA	21	3	1	0	11	11	52¹	53	6	14	72	2.4	12.4	40%	.353	1.28	2.92	2.99	2.93	1.4
2013	TUC	AAA	22	8	3	0	20	20	99¹	125	11	34	84	3.1	7.6	37%	.352	1.60	5.07	4.38	4.51	1.6
2013	SDN	MLB	22	3	3	0	11	9	54²	53	6	15	40	2.5	6.6	39%	.283	1.24	4.12	3.81	4.47	0.2
2014	SAN	AA	23	0	0	0	3	3	10¹	12	1	4	10	3.5	8.7	42%	.367	1.55	3.48	3.60	3.54	0.2
2014	ELP	AAA	23	0	1	0	2	2	10²	21	2	2	8	1.7	6.8	50%	.475	2.16	9.28	5.20	6.71	-0.1
2014	SDN	MLB	23	4	5	0	13	11	61¹	71	6	15	46	2.2	6.8	43%	.332	1.40	4.99	3.66	4.00	0.3
2015	SDN	MLB	24	4	7	0	17	17	87²	86	10	22	76	2.3	7.8	38%	.315	1.23	3.91	3.90	4.25	0.2

Breakout: 26%   Improve: 53%   Collapse: 8%   Attrition: 21%   MLB: 77%   Comparables: Yusmeiro Petit, Will Smith, Liam Hendriks

"Always had a thing for leggy redheads and strike-throwing southpaws," Snake says, brown eyes peering out from beneath the worn leather hat that's sat on his head as long as he's sat in that seat—late Carter administration. "Take Erlin. Kid doesn't throw hard, but he knows what he's doing out there. Gets hammered sometimes but never rattled. Just needs to stay healthy is all. Just needs 30 starts." Snake's eyes lose focus as he drifts toward the Crystal Gayle eight-track playing in his mind. Erlin. He said Erlin, right? Or did he say Ellen? It's too late to ask. Snake is long gone, his eyes turned blue.

Max Fried   LHP
Born: 1/18/94   Age: 21   Bats: L   Throws: L   Height: 6'4"   Weight: 185

YEAR	TEAM	LVL	AGE	W	L	SV	G	GS	IP	H	HR	BB	K	BB/9	K/9	GB%	BABIP	WHIP	ERA	FIP	FRA	WARP
2013	FTW	A	19	6	7	0	23	23	118²	107	7	56	100	4.2	7.6	59%	.304	1.37	3.49	4.04	5.46	0.6
2015	SDN	MLB	21	1	3	0	9	9	35¹	36	4	18	24	4.7	6.2	52%	.312	1.53	5.05	5.13	5.48	-0.4

Breakout: 0%   Improve: 0%   Collapse: 0%   Attrition: 0%   MLB: 0%   Comparables: Edgar Olmos, Jose A. Ramirez, Tyler Chatwood

In January 2014, after his first full professional season, Fried told MLB.com, "Now I can better expect and anticipate things that happen during a Minor League season." A month later, the former first-round pick was shut down due to forearm soreness that reportedly had bothered him over the winter. Although an MRI showed no damage to the elbow ligament, Fried didn't get into an actual game until July. Then he faced 50 batters in five abbreviated starts before being shut down again. He had Tommy John surgery in mid-August, likely killing most or all of his 2015 season. This cruelly falls outside the range of what Fried could have expected or anticipated only a few months earlier.

Jesse Hahn   RHP
Born: 7/30/89   Age: 25   Bats: R   Throws: R   Height: 6'5"   Weight: 190

YEAR	TEAM	LVL	AGE	W	L	SV	G	GS	IP	H	HR	BB	K	BB/9	K/9	GB%	BABIP	WHIP	ERA	FIP	FRA	WARP
2012	HUD	A-	22	2	2	0	14	14	52	38	0	15	55	2.6	9.5	66%	.273	1.02	2.77	2.20	3.81	0.9
2013	PCH	A+	23	2	1	0	19	19	67	55	1	18	63	2.4	8.5	63%	.284	1.09	2.15	2.49	3.53	1.4
2014	SAN	AA	24	2	1	0	13	10	42¹	34	1	15	38	3.2	8.1	66%	.282	1.16	1.91	2.77	3.67	0.9
2014	SDN	MLB	24	7	4	0	14	12	73¹	57	4	32	70	3.9	8.6	52%	.270	1.21	3.07	3.38	3.74	0.9
2015	SDN	MLB	25	5	7	0	22	22	92	79	7	35	84	3.4	8.2	55%	.303	1.24	3.49	3.73	3.80	0.9

Breakout: 33%   Improve: 66%   Collapse: 15%   Attrition: 19%   MLB: 91%   Comparables: Wade Davis, Alex Cobb, Zach Britton

The question with Hahn has always been health. A sixth round pick in 2010, the lanky right-hander missed 2011 following Tommy John surgery and pitched a total of 121 innings over the next two seasons. After a January 2014 trade from the Rays, he got called up to San Diego in June, well ahead of schedule. Through nine starts, Hahn had a 2.01 ERA, holding opponents to a .182/.270/.246 line. Then fatigue set in—115 innings might not seem like a lot, but it's nearly twice his previous season high—and he stumbled to the finish line. Hahn's low-90s sinker generates grounders, while his big-breaking curve generates strikeouts. Earlier talk of an eventual move to the bullpen has subsided. Assuming no further obstacles, and subject to normal development of season-long stamina, he'll stick in the middle of Oakland's rotation, where he landed as the main piece coming back for Derek Norris.

Casey Kelly   RHP

Born: 10/4/89   Age: 25   Bats: R   Throws: R   Height: 6'3"   Weight: 210

YEAR	TEAM	LVL	AGE	W	L	SV	G	GS	IP	H	HR	BB	K	BB/9	K/9	GB%	BABIP	WHIP	ERA	FIP	FRA	WARP
2012	SAN	AA	22	0	1	0	3	3	16²	11	1	3	18	1.6	9.7	45%	.244	0.84	3.78	2.62	4.02	0.2
2012	TUC	AAA	22	0	0	0	2	2	12	12	0	0	14	0.0	10.5	55%	.364	1.00	2.25	1.58	2.26	0.5
2012	SDN	MLB	22	2	3	0	6	6	29	39	5	10	26	3.1	8.1	57%	.366	1.69	6.21	4.83	5.25	0.1
2014	SAN	AA	24	1	0	0	2	2	12	11	0	1	8	0.8	6.0	49%	.297	1.00	0.75	2.54	3.55	-0.2
2015	SDN	MLB	25	2	3	0	7	7	36¹	38	3	12	27	2.8	6.8	49%	.325	1.36	4.47	3.99	4.86	-0.2

Breakout: 27%   Improve: 43%   Collapse: 11%   Attrition: 35%   MLB: 65%   Comparables: Jeff Locke, Scott Diamond, Clayton Mortensen

The good news is that Kelly pitched in games last year, something he hadn't done since September 2012. The bad news is that he was shut down after four rehab starts in May. He started long tossing again a few months later, and the Padres say he's structurally fine. Kelly has worked a total of 87 innings over the last three seasons, which is a difficult way to develop. At a time when he should be refining his craft at the highest level, he's trying to get his elbow to function properly. We keep saying mid-rotation starter, but each passing setback makes it harder to justify that stance.

Ian Kennedy   RHP

Born: 12/19/84   Age: 30   Bats: R   Throws: R   Height: 6'0"   Weight: 190

YEAR	TEAM	LVL	AGE	W	L	SV	G	GS	IP	H	HR	BB	K	BB/9	K/9	GB%	BABIP	WHIP	ERA	FIP	FRA	WARP
2012	ARI	MLB	27	15	12	0	33	33	208¹	216	28	55	187	2.4	8.1	40%	.306	1.30	4.02	4.08	4.45	2.3
2013	ARI	MLB	28	3	8	0	21	21	124	128	18	48	108	3.5	7.8	38%	.301	1.42	5.23	4.57	4.84	0.2
2013	SDN	MLB	28	4	2	0	10	10	57¹	52	9	25	55	3.9	8.6	44%	.279	1.34	4.24	4.56	4.93	0.2
2014	SDN	MLB	29	13	13	0	33	33	201	189	16	70	207	3.1	9.3	42%	.315	1.29	3.63	3.18	3.42	2.6
2015	SDN	MLB	30	8	11	0	27	27	169¹	147	18	50	159	2.7	8.4	40%	.298	1.16	3.53	3.84	3.84	1.0

Breakout: 15%   Improve: 42%   Collapse: 27%   Attrition: 12%   MLB: 89%   Comparables: Ervin Santana, Javier Vazquez, Edwin Jackson

Sometimes the narrative is right. Kennedy's mechanics got out of whack in Arizona. The Padres spotted this and thought they could fix it. Then-GM Josh Byrnes picked him up for Rosencrantz and Guildenstern and pitching coach Darren Balsley made a few tweaks that resulted in greater torque, fastball velocity and downward plane, a nice combination. Kennedy also relied less on his curve and more on his changeup. The improvement against left-handed batters was dramatic: from 19 homers and a .235 ISO in 2013, to eight and .146 last year. He established career bests in strikeouts and FIP, and his splits (including, crucially for every Padres pitcher, home/road) were nonexistent. Oscar Wilde said that consistency is the hallmark of the unimaginative, but even he never expected Kennedy to be this effective.

Kevin Quackenbush   RHP

Born: 11/28/88   Age: 26   Bats: R   Throws: R   Height: 6'4"   Weight: 220

YEAR	TEAM	LVL	AGE	W	L	SV	G	GS	IP	H	HR	BB	K	BB/9	K/9	GB%	BABIP	WHIP	ERA	FIP	FRA	WARP
2012	LEL	A+	23	3	2	27	52	0	57²	42	1	22	70	3.4	10.9	50%	.301	1.11	0.94	2.76	2.97	1.5
2013	SAN	AA	24	2	0	13	29	0	31	16	1	10	46	2.9	13.4	53%	.246	0.84	0.29	1.77	2.14	0.9
2013	TUC	AAA	24	8	2	4	28	0	34	33	0	19	38	5.0	10.1	49%	.359	1.53	2.91	3.19	3.33	0.9
2014	ELP	AAA	25	0	0	6	13	0	14¹	9	0	4	12	2.5	7.5	67%	.222	0.91	1.26	2.86	3.04	0.4
2014	SDN	MLB	25	3	3	6	56	0	54¹	42	2	18	56	3.0	9.3	41%	.278	1.10	2.48	2.62	3.04	0.6
2015	SDN	MLB	26	3	1	2	55	0	60¹	46	3	22	68	3.3	10.1	47%	.303	1.12	2.60	2.86	2.83	1.1

Breakout: 30%   Improve: 46%   Collapse: 23%   Attrition: 26%   MLB: 79%   Comparables: Greg Holland, Joe Thatcher, Luke Gregerson

Taken in the eighth round of the 2011 draft, Quackenbush abused every minor-league level he met. After a one-game call-up in late April, he stuck with the big club for good a few weeks later, proving himself in low-leverage situations before assuming a larger role toward the All-Star break. By September he was notching saves when Joaquin Benoit was unavailable. Quackenbush's fastball runs in the low 90s, and he doesn't have one knockout secondary pitch, but a deceptive delivery makes him tough to hit. He held opponents to a .178/.252/.206 line at Petco Park, had a 1.96 ERA from May 27th to season's end and in August confessed to FOX Sports San Diego's Scott Miller that his favorite Mighty Ducks movie is the second one.

Tyson Ross   RHP

Born: 4/22/87   Age: 28   Bats: R   Throws: R   Height: 6'5"   Weight: 225

YEAR	TEAM	LVL	AGE	W	L	SV	G	GS	IP	H	HR	BB	K	BB/9	K/9	GB%	BABIP	WHIP	ERA	FIP	FRA	WARP
2012	SAC	AAA	25	6	2	0	15	13	78¹	69	4	29	64	3.3	7.4	61%	.283	1.25	2.99	3.92	4.45	1.0
2012	OAK	MLB	25	2	11	0	18	13	73¹	96	7	37	46	4.5	5.6	52%	.360	1.81	6.50	4.75	5.18	0.1
2013	TUC	AAA	26	1	1	0	4	2	11²	12	0	6	9	4.6	6.9	60%	.343	1.54	4.63	3.57	4.08	0.3
2013	SDN	MLB	26	3	8	0	35	16	125	100	8	44	119	3.2	8.6	57%	.282	1.15	3.17	3.17	4.18	0.8
2014	SDN	MLB	27	13	14	0	31	31	195²	165	13	72	195	3.3	9.0	59%	.291	1.21	2.81	3.22	4.05	2.1
2015	SDN	MLB	28	8	10	0	28	28	155¹	137	11	56	144	3.2	8.4	54%	.314	1.24	3.48	3.58	3.78	1.2

Breakout: 23%   Improve: 54%   Collapse: 16%   Attrition: 13%   MLB: 85%   Comparables: Tom Gorzelanny, Dustin McGowan, Manny Parra

Ross followed his breakout 2013 season with an All-Star encore. Tall and lean like younger brother Joe, he relied on his slider more often last year, and although it remains his strikeout pitch, it was less devastating than in 2013, especially against right-handers. He and Darren Balsley tweaked his release point on the sinker, which led to the death of many worms and made the four-seamer more effective. With this shift in repertoire, his platoon splits disappeared. His home/road splits didn't, but such is the nature of Petco Park. After two rough September outings, he was shut down early due to "a slight strain of the flexor in his forearm." Although team doctors were not concerned, Ross did exceed his previous high in innings pitched by 44. Still, that's a helluva return on investment for a guy who cost the Padres nothing.

Tim Stauffer   RHP

Born: 6/2/82   Age: 33   Bats: R   Throws: R   Height: 6'1"   Weight: 210

YEAR	TEAM	LVL	AGE	W	L	SV	G	GS	IP	H	HR	BB	K	BB/9	K/9	GB%	BABIP	WHIP	ERA	FIP	FRA	WARP
2012	LEL	A+	30	0	1	0	4	4	13¹	15	0	2	11	1.4	7.4	50%	.357	1.27	3.38	2.61	2.86	0.4
2012	SDN	MLB	30	0	0	0	1	1	5	7	1	3	5	5.4	9.0	56%	.400	2.00	5.40	5.54	5.42	0.0
2013	TUC	AAA	31	2	2	0	8	8	42²	50	1	15	38	3.2	8.0	51%	.377	1.52	3.16	3.22	4.24	1.1
2013	SDN	MLB	31	3	1	0	43	0	69²	59	7	20	64	2.6	8.3	53%	.275	1.13	3.75	3.52	4.23	0.3
2014	SDN	MLB	32	6	2	0	44	3	64¹	67	4	23	67	3.2	9.4	44%	.356	1.40	3.50	2.99	3.18	0.9
2015	SDN	MLB	33	3	3	0	22	8	65	61	6	17	53	2.4	7.3	51%	.314	1.22	3.64	3.77	3.96	0.3

Breakout: 10%   Improve: 33%   Collapse: 12%   Attrition: 18%   MLB: 63%   Comparables: Claudio Vargas, Jeff Francis, Bruce Chen

There goes Stauffer again, doing whatever is asked of him, usually well. Remove a disastrous May 28th start at Arizona and his ERA drops to 2.53. He hasn't had the career you'd expect from a fourth pick overall, and it's easy to dream on what might have been if not for a cavalcade of injuries, but his 3.37 ERA over the last six seasons ain't bad. Despite making just four starts since 2012, Stauffer retains rotation dreams. That might be too much to ask of a 33-year-old who has cracked triple digits in innings once in nine big-league seasons, but if we've learned anything over the years, it's that you don't want to underestimate baseball's version of the Energizer Bunny.

Eric Stults   LHP

Born: 12/9/79   Age: 35   Bats: L   Throws: L   Height: 6'2"   Weight: 220

YEAR	TEAM	LVL	AGE	W	L	SV	G	GS	IP	H	HR	BB	K	BB/9	K/9	GB%	BABIP	WHIP	ERA	FIP	FRA	WARP
2012	CHR	AAA	32	1	1	0	5	5	28²	25	0	10	26	3.1	8.2	42%	.316	1.22	2.20	2.39	2.75	0.8
2012	CHA	MLB	32	0	0	0	2	1	6²	6	0	4	4	5.4	5.4	57%	.286	1.50	2.70	4.10	4.13	0.1
2012	SDN	MLB	32	8	3	0	18	14	92¹	86	7	23	51	2.2	5.0	41%	.262	1.18	2.92	3.80	4.06	1.2
2013	SDN	MLB	33	11	13	0	33	33	203²	219	18	40	131	1.8	5.8	42%	.302	1.27	3.93	3.50	3.88	2.6
2014	SDN	MLB	34	8	17	0	32	32	176	197	26	45	111	2.3	5.7	46%	.296	1.38	4.30	4.60	4.96	-0.7
2015	SDN	MLB	35	7	10	1	37	24	157	157	17	35	107	2.0	6.1	42%	.303	1.23	3.96	4.11	4.31	0.0

Breakout: 12%   Improve: 42%   Collapse: 10%   Attrition: 10%   MLB: 69%   Comparables: Rodrigo Lopez, Jason Johnson, Paul Byrd

After going 3-13 with a 5.22 ERA over the first four months, Stults went 5-4 with a 2.74 ERA over the final two. It's tempting to say he turned the pro-verbial corner, but his track record suggests otherwise. One problem is that, as Beyond the Box Score's Justin Schultz so eloquently put it, "Stults' curveball is terrible." Hitters and their .400-plus ISO against that pitch last year might disagree, but as hitters, they are not to be trusted in such matters. Can Stults continue to survive at the highest level? Without getting into lengthy discussions about the nature of survival, either improving or ditching the curve might help. So might long walks on the beach with Jamie Moyer.

Dale Thayer   RHP

Born: 12/17/80   Age: 34   Bats: R   Throws: R   Height: 6'0"   Weight: 210

YEAR	TEAM	LVL	AGE	W	L	SV	G	GS	IP	H	HR	BB	K	BB/9	K/9	GB%	BABIP	WHIP	ERA	FIP	FRA	WARP
2012	SDN	MLB	31	2	2	7	64	0	57²	53	4	12	47	1.9	7.3	43%	.287	1.13	3.43	3.08	3.85	0.5
2013	SDN	MLB	32	3	5	1	69	0	65	59	8	22	64	3.0	8.9	42%	.293	1.25	3.32	3.76	3.74	0.3
2014	SDN	MLB	33	4	5	0	70	0	65¹	53	9	16	62	2.2	8.5	42%	.250	1.06	2.34	3.82	3.72	0.2
2015	SDN	MLB	34	3	1	1	58	0	58¹	51	6	15	52	2.3	8.0	45%	.295	1.13	3.17	3.75	3.44	0.6

Breakout: 17%   Improve: 27%   Collapse: 21%   Attrition: 7%   MLB: 54%   Comparables: John Bale, Geoff Geary, Brian Sanches

In a 1976 American Journal of Sociology article, Dwight E. Robinson noted a relationship between beard frequency in men and skirt width in women. One wonders what Robinson might have discovered about the fuzz on Thayer's face and on his fastball if given enough grant money. Brooks Baseball, which shows that Thayer brings the heat at 93 mph and throws it three-quarters of the time, is woefully deficient in facial hair data. Ancient Greeks viewed beards as a sign of virility, with Thetis touching Zeus' hirsute chin while praying for her son, Achilles. Similarly, by the power of Zeus, the effective but obscure Thayer has made 203 appearances since 2012. Alexander the Great eventually forbade his soldiers from wearing beards. There's no telling what would happen to Thayer's fastball if he were to meet a similar fate.

Alex Torres   LHP

Born: 12/8/87   Age: 27   Bats: L   Throws: L   Height: 5'10"   Weight: 175

YEAR	TEAM	LVL	AGE	W	L	SV	G	GS	IP	H	HR	BB	K	BB/9	K/9	GB%	BABIP	WHIP	ERA	FIP	FRA	WARP
2012	DUR	AAA	24	3	7	0	26	14	69	70	6	63	91	8.2	11.9	47%	.368	1.93	7.30	4.52	5.99	0.5
2013	DUR	AAA	25	2	2	0	9	9	46	34	2	21	61	4.1	11.9	50%	.288	1.20	3.52	2.62	3.90	1.0
2013	TBA	MLB	25	4	2	0	39	0	58	32	1	20	62	3.1	9.6	46%	.221	0.90	1.71	2.35	2.42	1.2
2014	SDN	MLB	26	2	1	0	70	0	54	46	2	33	51	5.5	8.5	50%	.291	1.46	3.33	3.70	4.37	-0.1
2015	SDN	MLB	27	3	3	0	26	8	56²	47	4	29	60	4.5	9.5	48%	.313	1.32	3.63	3.76	3.95	0.3

Breakout: 32%   Improve: 51%   Collapse: 13%   Attrition: 30%   MLB: 72%   Comparables: Michael Kirkman, David Purcey, Brayan Villarreal

The wild streaks that plagued Torres in the minors returned in his first season with the Padres. He was often used as a LOOGY despite being less effective against left-handed batters, who accounted for three-quarters of his walks despite an even split in batters faced from each side of the plate. If you're called on to get one man out and can't throw strikes, that's a problem. So is unraveling after the All-Star break, which he also did. On June 21st, Torres became the first big leaguer to wear the new isoBLOX cap designed to protect a pitcher from line drives. Although many people mocked him for it, he had a different view: "I don't care about how it's going to look. I want to be safe." You could say he used his head.

Nick Vincent RHP

Born: 7/12/86 Age: 28 Bats: R Throws: R Height: 5'11" Weight: 180

YEAR	TEAM	LVL	AGE	W	L	SV	G	GS	IP	H	HR	BB	K	BB/9	K/9	GB%	BABIP	WHIP	ERA	FIP	FRA	WARP
2012	TUC	AAA	25	1	1	2	23	0	21²	27	2	11	19	4.6	7.9	43%	.368	1.75	5.82	4.91	4.97	0.3
2012	SDN	MLB	25	2	0	0	27	0	26¹	19	2	7	28	2.4	9.6	39%	.254	0.99	1.71	2.91	3.89	0.2
2013	TUC	AAA	26	4	3	0	24	0	25¹	26	4	12	24	4.3	8.5	35%	.297	1.50	3.55	5.27	4.67	0.4
2013	SDN	MLB	26	6	3	1	45	0	46¹	33	1	11	49	2.1	9.5	46%	.274	0.95	2.14	2.03	2.44	1.0
2014	SDN	MLB	27	1	2	0	63	0	55	44	5	11	62	1.8	10.1	38%	.289	1.00	3.60	2.74	2.77	0.7
2015	SDN	MLB	28	3	1	0	51	0	52	41	4	14	53	2.5	9.1	41%	.292	1.07	2.80	3.18	3.04	0.8

Breakout: 27%   Improve: 41%   Collapse: 14%   Attrition: 19%   MLB: 67%   Comparables: Rich Thompson, Brad Brach, Clay Zavada

Among the 354 pitchers who have faced at least 200 right-handed batters over the last two seasons, only Craig Kimbrel owns a lower OPS against than Vincent, who has held them to a .162/.199/.227 line, with a nearly 10-to-1 strikeout-to-walk ratio. Lefties have been less kind (.288/.358/.445). Vincent's 2014 numbers ballooned in a four-game stretch in June that accounted for 41 percent of the runs he allowed all year. After watching video during that stretch, he noted that "the arm slot looked a little lower" and that he and Darren Balsley "tried to get it back up, but we couldn't." Vincent speculated that a sore elbow the previous month may have led to the change and subsequent right shoulder fatigue, which put him on the shelf. After a month of rest, he resumed being a dominant late-inning option, posting a 1.61 ERA over his final 33 appearances.

Matt Wisler RHP

Born: 3/22/84 Age: 31 Bats: R Throws: R Height: 6'2" Weight: 205

YEAR	TEAM	LVL	AGE	W	L	SV	G	GS	IP	H	HR	BB	K	BB/9	K/9	GB%	BABIP	WHIP	ERA	FIP	FRA	WARP
2012	FTW	A	19	5	4	0	24	23	114	95	1	28	113	2.2	8.9	45%	.299	1.08	2.53	2.35	3.51	2.9
2013	LEL	A+	20	2	1	0	6	6	31	22	1	6	28	1.7	8.1	43%	.253	0.90	2.03	3.06	3.46	0.7
2013	SAN	AA	20	8	5	0	20	20	105	85	7	27	103	2.3	8.8	39%	.281	1.07	3.00	2.79	3.42	1.8
2014	SAN	AA	21	1	0	0	6	6	30	26	2	6	35	1.8	10.5	47%	.312	1.07	2.10	2.25	3.33	0.6
2014	ELP	AAA	21	9	5	0	22	22	116²	131	19	36	101	2.8	7.8	44%	.317	1.43	5.01	5.14	5.11	0.8
2015	SDN	MLB	22	5	7	0	26	19	130²	118	13	39	112	2.7	7.7	42%	.302	1.21	3.66	3.90	3.98	0.6

Breakout: 12%   Improve: 27%   Collapse: 5%   Attrition: 17%   MLB: 37%   Comparables: Cesar Carrillo, Eric Hurley, Michael Pineda

"Mid-rotation starter." The description applies to many Padres farmhands, including Wisler, who is closer to the big leagues than most. His numbers suffered at El Paso, where the legendary LaVel Freeman once hit .395. After four awful starts to begin his Triple-A career, Wisler fashioned a sub-4 ERA over his final 18, a slick trick in a league where the ERA last year was 4.64. Lefties still confound him, although the gap between them and right-handers is narrowing. He has no single outstanding pitch, but thanks to the Fort Wayne TinCaps, for whom he pitched in 2012, he has a bobblehead in his likeness. Wisler will compete for a rotation spot in 2015. If he doesn't start the season in the big leagues, he'll end it there.

Lineouts

Hitters

NAME	POS	TEAM	LVL	AGE	PA	R	2B	3B	HR	RBI	BB	K	SB	CS	AVG/OBP/SLG	TAv	BABIP	BRR	FRAA	WARP
Yeison Asencio	RF	SAN	AA	24	486	51	21	3	10	44	24	57	8	4	.284/.323/.409	.262	.306	0.0	RF(97): -0.1, LF(16): -1.7	1.2
	LF	ELP	AAA	24	86	16	4	0	5	15	4	9	0	1	.333/.372/.568	.287	.328	1.1	LF(18): -0.2, RF(4): 0.1	0.7
Cody Decker	1B	ELP	AAA	27	510	68	25	4	27	79	51	150	0	3	.261/.337/.514	.279	.324	-3.9	1B(92): 4.3, 3B(15): 1.9	0.8
Alex Dickerson	RF	SAN	AA	24	147	20	11	2	3	24	9	28	0	1	.321/.367/.496	.295	.387	-0.5	RF(28): 0.5	0.9
Gabriel Quintana	3B	LEL	A+	21	566	77	35	0	18	84	21	150	4	1	.263/.302/.431	.268	.331	-1.1	3B(98): -5.4, 3B(12): -5.4	1.1
Mallex Smith	CF	FTW	A	21	303	56	13	6	0	15	38	55	48	16	.295/.393/.394	.286	.373	3.9	CF(63): 5.8	2.5
	CF	LEL	A+	21	261	43	16	1	5	16	31	48	40	10	.327/.414/.475	.336	.400	2.5	CF(33): -0.6, CF(4): -0.6	2.7

Yeison Asencio has hit at every level, and while he is strong and has a quick bat, that hasn't yet translated into usable power for the right fielder whose name is an anagram for the world's worst rapper, Easy Ice Onions. ❖ As a former 22nd round pick who is always old for his level, struggles to make contact and offers little defensive value, **Cody Decker** often gets overlooked in favor of sexier prospects despite owning a career .262 ISO in 2,500 minor-league plate appearances and 80-grade viral video chops. ❖ Local product **Alex Dickerson** came to the Padres from Pittsburgh in November 2013. Surgery on his left heel kept him out until mid-July, but he showed a strong stick, albeit one lacking the home run punch required of a range-challenged corner outfielder. ❖ It's not often you hear someone referred to as a poor man's Dustin Peterson, but **Gabriel Quintana** might fit the bill; although he has some pop, he isn't a stellar third baseman, and his 83-to-6 strikeout-to-walk ratio from June onward shouldn't be mentioned in polite company. ❖ "Something was revealed about a person's nature by the way he tried to run," Paul Theroux once said. For **Mallex Smith**, "something" was the desire and ability to steal bases; he got caught a little too often last year, but 88 steals and a .403 OBP reveal a potential future table-setter.

Pitchers

NAME	TEAM	LVL	AGE	W	L	SV	G	GS	IP	H	HR	BB	K	BB/9	K/9	GB%	BABIP	WHIP	ERA	FIP	FRA	WARP
R.J. Alvarez	ARK	AA	23	0	0	1	21	0	27	13	0	10	38	3.3	12.7	49%	.265	0.85	0.33	1.75	2.64	0.6
	SAN	AA	23	0	1	6	17	0	16¹	16	0	3	23	1.7	12.7	38%	.381	1.16	2.76	1.04	2.02	0.6
	SDN	MLB	23	0	0	0	10	0	8	3	0	5	9	5.6	10.1	28%	.167	1.00	1.12	3.10	3.46	0.0
Leonel Campos	SAN	AA	26	2	7	1	31	14	72¹	69	6	38	95	4.7	11.8	44%	.352	1.48	5.60	3.27	4.83	1.3
	ELP	AAA	26	0	0	0	11	0	10	20	2	13	13	11.7	11.7	33%	.529	3.30	11.70	7.60	8.12	-0.2
	SDN	MLB	26	0	0	0	6	0	7	9	0	4	9	5.1	11.6	35%	.450	1.86	5.14	2.25	2.66	0.2
Frank Garces	SAN	AA	24	2	5	8	51	0	65¹	46	3	24	74	3.3	10.2	44%	.262	1.07	1.93	2.69	2.97	1.6
	SDN	MLB	24	0	0	0	15	0	9	8	1	1	10	1.0	10.0	16%	.292	1.00	2.00	2.99	3.75	0.0
Tayron Guerrero	FTW	A	23	6	1	1	25	0	36	22	2	12	42	3.0	10.5	51%	.233	0.94	1.00	2.87	3.77	0.7
	LEL	A+	23	0	0	3	14	0	13²	10	1	8	14	5.3	9.2	44%	.257	1.32	2.63	4.62	5.58	0.0
Jason Lane	ELP	AAA	37	9	9	0	24	24	149²	183	16	26	77	1.6	4.6	43%	.323	1.40	4.51	4.64	5.59	1.1
	SDN	MLB	37	0	1	0	3	1	10¹	7	1	0	6	0.0	5.2	46%	.188	0.68	0.87	3.20	3.32	0.2
Zechariah Lemond	EUG	A-	21	2	3	0	11	8	38	39	1	5	34	1.2	8.1	66%	.330	1.16	3.79	3.08	3.92	0.7
Juan Oramas	SAN	AA	24	3	0	0	4	4	25²	24	0	6	23	2.1	8.1	36%	.324	1.17	1.05	2.15	2.62	0.7
	ELP	AAA	24	7	7	0	23	21	110²	135	14	45	93	3.7	7.6	40%	.354	1.63	5.61	5.07	5.79	1.0
Adys Portillo	SAN	AA	22	1	4	0	46	0	55²	44	2	43	68	7.0	11.0	41%	.311	1.56	3.23	3.46	3.76	0.8
Keyvius Sampson	ELP	AAA	23	2	5	0	38	14	91²	91	19	68	94	6.7	9.2	40%	.297	1.73	6.68	6.67	7.91	-0.8
Joe Wieland	ELP	AAA	24	2	1	0	4	4	23²	22	1	4	20	1.5	7.6	43%	.296	1.10	3.42	3.07	4.60	0.5
	SDN	MLB	24	1	0	0	4	2	11¹	16	3	5	8	4.0	6.4	37%	.342	1.85	7.15	6.46	6.92	-0.2

R.J. Alvarez was traded twice in five months without ever leaving California (from the Angels for Huston Street; from the Padres for Derek Norris). He delivers mid-90s heat and a mid-80s slider that makes right-handers—who had a .117 slugging percentage (!) against him in 2014—less comfortable than the Persians at Plataea. ❖ **Leonel Campos** arrived at spring training without his velocity, got rocked at Triple-A and continued to struggle after a May demotion and June move to the rotation, but the Padres were encouraged enough by the former soccer player's in-season development to give him a September summons. ❖ Formerly a starter who couldn't get righties out, **Frank Garces** moved to the bullpen, where his low-90s fastball and breaking ball neutralized left-handed batters (.150/.254/.221) at San Antonio and in a September cameo in San Diego. ❖ **Tayron Guerrero** is, as they say, a tall drink of water. The 6-foot-7 right-hander from Colombia features a mid-90s fastball (occasionally reaching triple digits) and high-80s sharp slider that could eventually make him a late-inning drink of water. ❖ After signing a one-year, $8 million deal with the Padres in November 2013, oft-injured **Josh Johnson** almost survived spring training. Almost. He required a second Tommy John surgery in April, not to mention a great big hug. ❖ **Jason Lane** completed an improbable comeback by reaching the big leagues as a pitcher seven years after he left as an outfielder; he didn't embarrass himself on the mound, and even got in some work at first base and in left field in the minors, hitting .362/.444/.580 in 81 Triple-A plate appearances. ❖ **Zech Lemond** broke the single-season saves record at Rice in 2013, previously held by David Aardsma and Tony Cingrani; although Lemond made five starts for the Owls last year, the third-round pick's mid-90s moving fastball and sharp slider are better suited to the bullpen, where he could soar, à la Quackenbush. ❖ We ended last year's **Cory Luebke** comment by noting that his contract "becomes less [of a bargain] if he can't actually throw a baseball." He underwent a second Tommy John surgery in February 2014, so no bargain unless his latest procedure makes the Padres eligible for a group discount on elbows. ❖ **Juan Oramas** is a squat southpaw whose best pitch is his changeup, which helps explain last year's severe reverse platoon split; he could work his way to the back end of a rotation, but first he must stop allowing four-plus runs every third start. ❖ The Padres finally moved long-limbed right-hander **Adys Portillo** to the bullpen, where he continued to throw as hard and erratic as an angry frat guy slinging darts after too many Fireballs. ❖ **Keyvius Sampson** got off to a decent start in his second PCL stint before four disastrous outings in May and June pushed him to the bullpen, where the results weren't much better. Even as a reliever, he'll need to face lefties, who went '94 Barry Bonds on him last year. ❖ **Joe Wieland** got shelled in his return to the big leagues, and nobody cared; the fact that he pitched in actual games for the first time since May 2012 was victory enough, as Tommy John surgery has limited him to 85 innings over the last three years. If he can stay healthy, he could pitch in the rotation when Brett Anderson gets hurt.

Manager

Bud Black

YEAR	TEAM	W	L	Py-thag +/-	Avg PC	100+ P	120+ P	QS	BQS	REL	REL w Zero R	IBB	PH	PH Avg	PH HR	SB2	CS2	SB3	CS3	SAC Att	SAC%	POS SAC	Squeeze	Swing	In Play
2012	SDN	76	86	2	92.2	49	1	75	5	529	449	48	278	.248	6	129	42	25	2	107	58.9%	30	1	396	88
2013	SDN	76	86	5	93.9	59	2	87	2	488	402	31	266	.206	8	105	31	13	3	92	56.5%	23	1	284	75
2014	SDN	77	85	2	94.6	52	1	91	2	481	417	32	311	.218	11	75	31	16	3	90	62.2%	32	2	248	70

The most unusual situation in the league. Managers seldom survive one GM change, let alone two; Black is on GM no. 4. He was hired by Kevin Towers and has been retained by Jed Hoyer, Josh Byrnes and now A.J. Preller. The only other active manager with that kind of staying power is Black's mentor, Mike Scioscia, who has outlasted two GMs. Difference is Scioscia won a ring; Black hasn't even reached the postseason. In fact, he's overseen just two winning seasons in eight tries.

Shy of owning the team, Connie Mack-style, or playing for it, Jimmy Dykes-like, how do you explain Black retaining his job with that record? The same way you explain the gap between his reputation as one of the best and his career winning percentage, which places him south of Ned Yost: Managers have a limited impact on their team's success. Black has worked miracles throughout his tenure with San Diego rosters that were average on the rare occasions when they were healthy. Factor in the constant change above him—at the management and ownership levels—and he's been the franchise's lone stabilizing force for most of the past decade.

A closer look reveals why many industry folk adore Black. Whether it's his California cool personality, allowing him to relate to the modern player, or his willingness to eschew tradition in favor of logic—i.e. bat the spot-starter eighth so he can be pinch-hit for earlier, as was the case with Donn Roach in May—it's easy to wonder just how good he would be with a better roster at his disposal. Turns out we might get an answer soon. Black's contract expires after the '15 season, and Preller reportedly identified possible replacement candidates during his interview process. If and when Black is done with the Padres, expect him to land another gig with no trouble.

SAN FRANCISCO GIANTS

by Grant Brisbee

Look, I don't know either.

You opened this chapter and hoped a professional writer would break down the 2014 Giants in a way that was satisfactory, illuminating and easy to understand. A distillation of their strengths that would explain why their perceived weaknesses were overblown. A rousing tale of adversity, persistence and talent.

I'm telling you, though. I have no idea.

Because if you told me before the season that the Giants had a shot, an honest shot, to make the World Series, it wouldn't have been an implausible twist in an unlikely movie. The Giants had talent, alright. It was clear before the Cactus League started that the Giants had a shot. They just needed a few things to happen.

- Matt Cain needed to build on his strong second half from 2013 and make everyone forget about the miserable first half.
- Tim Lincecum needed to take the next step back from the abyss and settle into a no. 3 role, actively helping the team more than he hurt it.
- Angel Pagan needed to stay healthy, considering the Giants stopped winning when he was out in the previous season, and started again when he returned.
- Marco Scutaro needed to return from his serious back problems, considering the Giants had absolutely no reasonable backup plans.
- Brandon Belt needed to build on his promising finish from 2013 and turn into a middle-of-the-order weapon.

That verb up there wasn't chosen lightly. Those things needed to happen if the Giants were going to do well in the postseason. If they were going to make the postseason, even. There was no path to the World Series that could have happened without those things—and scores of others—going the Giants' way. Instead, they made the World Series because Travis Ishikawa hit a pennant-winning home run.

So, seriously, I have no idea.

Except, hold on, there were several Giants on the World Series-winning team who weren't out of place on a championship roster. It wasn't Travis Ishikawa all the way down, like so many turtles. Buster Posey was supposed to be good, and he was. He

followed the weird I'll-get-stronger-as-the-season-progresses pattern that catchers shouldn't follow, but whatever. Hunter Pence was supposed to be good, and he turned in one of the best seasons of his career. Pablo Sandoval overcame a ghastly start (below the Mendoza Line halfway through May) to enjoy a perfectly proper Panda season. Brandon Crawford caught the ball like he was supposed to, threw it like he was supposed to and even hit a little bit more than expected, to boot. The Giants survived because they had an overqualified fourth outfielder in Gregor Blanco, an overqualified long reliever in Yusmeiro Petit and an overqualified setup man in Santiago Castilla all ready to step in when the varsity bus went wayward.

So maybe I have some idea. There was talent on the team. It's not like the 2013 Astros won a title after an inspirational speech that was followed by a montage. The Giants spent a lot of time and money accumulating talented players, including an unprecedented run of successful first-round picks.

Still, it was mostly Bumgarner this time. He appeared in 41 percent of the Giants' postseason games, which is absurd. That's just how the off-days and universe aligned. That, along with his freakish ability/willingness to come back on two days' rest and dominate, helped the Giants advance the even-year narrative. The Bochy-is-a-genius narrative. The knows-how-to-win narrative. It's a lot easier when an ace settles into his mechanics on the last day of September and never loses them, then gets to pitch a third of the innings during a ridiculous postseason run.

Now that he's been knighted and the statues have been erected, it feels weird to point out that Bumgarner was adrift at different points during the season, that his command/control/stuff didn't have the same je ne sais cut that it normally did. The same goes for every member of the 2014 Giants. There were ups, downs, laughs, better than Catseses, slumps, extended slumps and worse slumps. The season was split into three parts.

Phase I

In which Morse gets his oats. The Giants were unstoppable in the first part of the season. They were the Pythagorean Theorem smoking four-leaf clovers with a sprite. They had ninth-inning comebacks, 10th-inning twists and 11th-inning turns. Mike

---

GIANTS PROSPECTUS

2014 W-L: 88-74, 2ND IN NL WEST

Pythag	.536	7th	DER	.718	5th
RS/G	4.1	12th	B-Age	28.4	14th
RA/G	3.79	9th	P-Age	31.5	30th
TAv	.263	9th	Salary	$146.9M	7th
BRR	-1.52	19th	M$/MW	$3.4M	20th
TAv-P	.253	6th	DL Days	686	10th
FIP	3.55	8th	$ on DL	20%	24th

Three-Year Park Factors

Runs	Runs/RH	Runs/LH	HR/RH	HR/LH
97	92	99	86	88

Top Hitter WARP	5.9	Buster Posey
Top Pitcher WARP	3.5	Madison Bumgarner
Top Prospect		Adalberto Mejia

Morse was a veritable fount of dingers, a fan-favorite revelation. Hudson was a legitimate Cy Young candidate. Belt was a threat to hit 30 home runs. Why not 40? The Giants swept the Mets in early June to run their record to 43-21. They were probably the best team in baseball, everybody. Probably the best team in baseball.

Suddenly, a pirate ship appeared on the horizon! While millions of people were starving, the king lived in luxury. Meanwhile, on a small farm in Kansas, a boy was growing up.

(This is when the bad times came.)

Phase II

The Giants were 10 games up after the Mets series. Ten games. They could have gone 20-20 over their next 40 games, the Dodgers could have played like a 100-win team over the same stretch, and the Giants still would have had a substantial lead on the other side. Instead, they frittered that lead away in 21 games. Poof. They would jostle back and forth with the Dodgers for a bit, reclaiming and relosing the lead at different points, but they lost the division for good when the Dodgers swept them at AT&T Park right before the trade deadline. It was the third time the Dodgers had swept the Giants at AT&T Park in the last five years, having previously done so in 2010 and 2012.

It's hard to elaborate on what was happening during this stretch. The line drives were caught when the Giants were batting. The bloops fell in when the Giants were pitching. The Giants couldn't buy a two-out hit with runners in scoring position; every hitter and his pitcher could get a two-out hit with someone in scoring position against the Giants. Hitters went to the plate with six donuts still on the bat, wondering why they couldn't swing as hard. Pitchers were throwing rosin bags instead of baseballs, hoping for the best. Runners were getting picked off and yelling at the umpires that they had claimed no pickoffs no tags no backsies. Nothing was working, whereas in Phase I, everything was.

Phase III

I don't know if there was a Phase III. After getting swept by the Royals in Kansas City and dropping a series opener to the White Sox, the Giants were 5½ games back in the NL West. That wasn't their biggest deficit of the season. That would come on the last day of the season. But after that loss to the White Sox, the Giants won on a controversial implementation of the Buster Posey Rule, stealing a game they might not have deserved, but sorely needed. After that win, they were 19-17. Good enough for government work. Let's get the participatory ribbon of the Wild Card Game out of the way. Here's your ribbon. Thanks for showing up, Giants. Take the damned ribbon. Now go home.

Phase IV

In which Bruce Bochy was smarter than everyone else, and Madison Bumgarner is one of the greatest postseason pitchers of all time. It's a dandy story when you put it like that. The right general and the right soldier went over the hill and took the encampment on the other side. It's that simple.

I keep going back to the winning run of the World Series, though.

Sandoval started the inning with an infield hit. He had 10 on the season, his best mark since 2010. Pence dunked one in front of the center fielder. There was a gutsy sacrifice fly mixed in. Morse broke his bat—on a good swing, mind you—to drive in the winning run of the 2014 World Series.

It was the black-and-white picture next to the dictionary entry of baseball. Sometimes you eat the BABIP, and sometimes the BABIP eats you. That same inning could have happened for the Royals in any of the nine innings, especially the ninth. It could have happened to Bumgarner before he ascended and refused to take us with him. It happened to the Giants, though, and we watched it happen. The Giants were lucky.

Except the Giants had Bumgarner and Posey in the first place. Except they traded for Pence, and except they extended him before some other dumb team could whisper "guaranteed sixth year" into his ear. Except they drafted Joe Panik and had him in a glass case for just the right emergency. Except they found mid-round steals in Crawford and Belt, and dominated the minor-league free agent market over the previous offseasons, signing key contributors every winter.

And yet the Giants don't make it to the World Series without Travis Ishikawa, an ex-prospect from the dark years, who came through while he was playing a position he had no business playing. They don't make it there without Matt Williams being the only person on the planet who thought Jordan Zimmermann was out of gas in the NLDS, without Clint Hurdle thinking, "Nah. Edinson Volquez will be just fine, no need to bring Gerrit Cole into this."

Except the Giants navigated the seas of the postseason deftly, with Bochy as their skipper. The right moves were made. The wrong moves were papered over just perfectly. They had Bumgarner, who truly put in a performance that baseball nerds will talk about next century. There was talent, and there was execution. It was a cool mix of player development and cagey acquisitions.

Both are right. What is a World Series champion without a mix of talent and luck? Show me the World Series winner that was 90 percent brute force, and I'll show you a mid-50s Yankees team that used another major-league team as a de facto farm system, in an era when players had no choice where they would play. That's the last time a collection of players could be *that much better* than the other team's. Since those days, it's been a combination of talent and luck. It was for a lot of the postseasons before 2014, sure, but it's like that for all of them now. The ball bounced the right way for the Giants. The Giants made sure they had the right players in place to field it. Or, in the case of Sandoval, the right player in place to swing at the ball when it bounced the right way. It's a delicate balance.

It's elegant and oafish at the same time. The 2014 Giants won the World Series, and I'm not sure how they did it. They did it because of talent, unless they did it because of luck. It's Schrödinger's championship, everyone. Just don't open the box, and we'll all have a much deeper understanding of all this. ∎

—Grant Brisbee is the senior baseball writer for SB Nation, and he writes about the Giants at McCovey Chronicles.

Player comments by Daniel Rathman and Baseball Prospectus Authors

Hitters

Joaquin Arias　3B

Born: 9/21/84　Age: 30　Bats: R　Throws: R　Height: 6' 1"　Weight: 165

YEAR	TEAM	LVL	AGE	PA	R	2B	3B	HR	RBI	BB	K	SB	CS	AVG/OBP/SLG	TAv	BABIP	BRR	FRAA	WARP
2012	FRE	AAA	27	74	14	5	0	2	17	3	11	0	1	.400/.432/.557	.340	.456	0.1	SS(16): -0.2	0.8
2012	SFN	MLB	27	344	30	13	5	5	34	13	44	5	1	.270/.304/.389	.249	.295	2.0	3B(74): 1.7, SS(50): -1.6	1.1
2013	SFN	MLB	28	236	17	9	2	1	19	4	33	1	0	.271/.284/.342	.230	.311	-0.2	3B(55): 1.3, SS(24): -0.6	-0.1
2014	SFN	MLB	29	204	18	9	0	0	15	8	23	1	0	.254/.281/.301	.217	.285	1.2	3B(44): 0.6, 1B(16): -0.7	-0.1
2015	SFN	MLB	30	250	21	10	2	2	21	8	38	2	0	.261/.289/.347	.243	.299	0.6	3B 1, SS -1	0.3

Breakout: 3%　Improve: 41%　Collapse: 1%　Attrition: 5%　MLB: 95%　　Comparables: Carney Lansford, Buddy Bell, Don Money

Arias has special powers to make professional baseball decision-makers do inexplicable things. Perhaps it's his high-effort swing, which, by slightly misunderstanding the Law of Conservation of Energy in physics, one might assume *has to* result in heavy contact. Or maybe it's his strenuous exertion when he runs, making it nearly impossible to believe he's moving no faster than an airport autowalk. Whatever *it* is, *it* led the Giants to hand a multi-year guarantee to a replacement-level, part-time player. Lest you think Arias' sorcery affects only his employer, other teams were so spooked by *it* that they twice gifted him an intentional pass to first base during a 100-PA stretch in which he never earned his way to second. In case there is any lingering doubt, a manager now regarded as a lock for Hall of Fame induction was so amazed by *it*, that he gave Arias four first-half starts at first base. Now, thanks to the Giants' aversion to arbitration—they haven't gone to a hearing since 2004—they'll have the pleasure of paying Arias $1.45 million this year to keep finding out what *it* is.

Christian Arroyo　MI

Born: 5/30/95　Age: 20　Bats: R　Throws: R　Height: 6' 1"　Weight: 180

YEAR	TEAM	LVL	AGE	PA	R	2B	3B	HR	RBI	BB	K	SB	CS	AVG/OBP/SLG	TAv	BABIP	BRR	FRAA	WARP
2014	AUG	A	19	125	10	3	1	1	14	4	22	1	2	.203/.226/.271	.189	.237	-0.8	2B(26): 5.7, SS(5): -0.2	0.0
2014	SLO	A-	19	267	39	14	2	5	48	18	31	6	1	.333/.378/.469	.310	.360	0.1	SS(58): 6.1	3.0
2015	SFN	MLB	20	250	17	9	1	2	21	7	61	1	0	.214/.237/.292	.205	.272	-0.3	SS 5, 2B 2	0.3

Breakout: 0%　Improve: 0%　Collapse: 0%　Attrition: 0%　MLB: 0%　　Comparables: Trevor Plouffe, Lonnie Chisenhall, Charlie Culberson

The most surprising selection in the first round of the 2013 draft, Arroyo boasts one exceptional trait: his pure hitting ability, which was on display when the Giants reneged on an overly aggressive assignment to Low-A Augusta and let him keep raking at Salem-Keizer following rehab for a sprained thumb. Less clear is whether Arroyo has the athleticism to stay at shortstop, a concern because his above-average arm would be wasted at second base, and because his gap power might not stand out on the right side of the infield. The Giants handed the Floridian $1.87 million to prove cynical evaluators wrong, and while the results have leaned in the club's favor so far, Arroyo will need to fare better in a second try at Augusta to keep his stock from falling.

Brandon Belt　1B

Born: 4/20/88　Age: 27　Bats: L　Throws: L　Height: 6' 5"　Weight: 220

YEAR	TEAM	LVL	AGE	PA	R	2B	3B	HR	RBI	BB	K	SB	CS	AVG/OBP/SLG	TAv	BABIP	BRR	FRAA	WARP
2012	SFN	MLB	24	472	47	27	6	7	56	54	106	12	2	.275/.360/.421	.302	.351	-0.7	1B(139): -2.6, LF(4): -0.1	2.6
2013	SFN	MLB	25	571	76	39	4	17	67	52	125	5	2	.289/.360/.481	.310	.351	2.5	1B(143): 6.1	4.4
2014	FRE	AAA	26	20	2	3	0	2	5	1	5	0	1	.526/.550/1.000	.563	.667	-0.1	1B(4): 0.0	0.7
2014	SFN	MLB	26	235	30	8	0	12	27	18	64	3	1	.243/.306/.449	.278	.288	-0.4	1B(59): 6.7, RF(1): -0.0	1.6
2015	SFN	MLB	27	292	34	14	2	9	36	29	70	4	2	.265/.343/.437	.293	.329	0.0	1B 2, LF -0	1.6

Breakout: 5%　Improve: 54%　Collapse: 7%　Attrition: 6%　MLB: 98%　　Comparables: Ike Davis, Adrian Gonzalez, Mark Teixeira

With five home runs in his first eight games of the 2014 campaign, Belt seemed poised to build on his breakout the previous year. But those long balls quickly gave way to lots and lots of strikeouts, then a broken thumb, then more strikeouts, then a concussion, then more strikeouts, then a recurrence of concussion symptoms, then fewer strikeouts in September and October, but also less of the early-season thunder. His contact rate on pitches in the zone plunged from 88 percent to 79 percent, so pitchers pounded him with strikes. Always most dangerous when he can use his nine-iron swing down and in, Belt will need to restore his ability to fight off pitches on the outer half to rediscover his 2013 form at the plate. The good news is, amid the injuries, he was still among the best defenders at his position.

Gregor Blanco　CF

Born: 12/24/83　Age: 31　Bats: L　Throws: L　Height: 5' 11"　Weight: 175

YEAR	TEAM	LVL	AGE	PA	R	2B	3B	HR	RBI	BB	K	SB	CS	AVG/OBP/SLG	TAv	BABIP	BRR	FRAA	WARP
2012	SFN	MLB	28	453	56	14	5	5	34	51	104	26	6	.244/.333/.344	.265	.318	5.1	RF(54): -2.4, LF(53): -2.8	1.5
2013	SFN	MLB	29	511	50	17	6	3	41	52	95	14	9	.265/.341/.350	.259	.328	0.2	CF(76): -3.2, LF(72): -1.6	0.9
2014	SFN	MLB	30	444	51	18	6	5	38	41	77	16	5	.260/.333/.374	.272	.311	4.0	CF(72): -2.2, LF(64): 2.6	2.2
2015	SFN	MLB	31	430	50	15	4	3	30	42	88	16	6	.251/.328/.339	.257	.311	2.0	CF -3, LF -0	0.8

Breakout: 0%　Improve: 42%　Collapse: 6%　Attrition: 12%　MLB: 92%　　Comparables: Ryan Freel, Coco Crisp, Rajai Davis

When Angel Pagan went down in 2013, the Giants' ship sank with him in part because Blanco was dead weight. A year later, Blanco was one of the most valuable fourth outfielders in the league when Pagan and Michael Morse succumbed to injuries. The difference: Three more extra-base hits, some timely baserunning, a half-dozen fewer GIDPs and a handful of extra runs on defense (according to FRAA, at least). Those are the margins in this game, sometimes.

The speedy left-handed hitter showed better plate discipline on pitches outside the zone and more aggression on pitches in the zone, leading not to more walks but harder contact. That, plus a better line-drive rate, plus assuredly a bit of luck, led to a 63-point BABIP improvement from the first half to the second. From the All-Star break onward, Blanco's .814 OPS ranked 11th among National League outfielders, outshining more-acclaimed center fielders like Carlos Gomez and Yasiel Puig. Iffy instincts have hindered the utility of Blanco's tools at times, but when he slows down the game and takes the uppercut out of his swing, he is a competent reserve who has proven himself capable of holding down the fort for a contender.

Gary Brown   CF

Born: 9/28/88   Age: 26   Bats: R   Throws: R   Height: 6' 1"   Weight: 190

YEAR	TEAM	LVL	AGE	PA	R	2B	3B	HR	RBI	BB	K	SB	CS	AVG/OBP/SLG	TAv	BABIP	BRR	FRAA	WARP
2012	RIC	AA	23	610	73	32	2	7	42	40	87	33	18	.279/.347/.385	.278	.318	3.7	CF(127): -2.0, LF(6): -0.1	3.7
2013	FRE	AAA	24	608	79	29	6	13	50	33	135	17	11	.231/.286/.375	.228	.282	0.4	CF(133): -0.6, LF(3): -0.2	0.2
2014	FRE	AAA	25	596	89	24	6	10	53	36	119	36	20	.271/.329/.394	.265	.328	1.7	CF(128): -3.7, RF(7): -0.0	2.6
2014	SFN	MLB	25	7	1	0	0	0	1	0	0	0	0	.429/.429/.429	.325	.429	0.1	CF(6): 0.1	0.1
2015	SFN	MLB	26	250	29	10	2	3	17	11	57	10	5	.227/.275/.323	.230	.282	0.2	CF -1, RF -0	-0.2

Breakout: 0%   Improve: 11%   Collapse: 17%   Attrition: 21%   MLB: 31%   Comparables: Craig Gentry, Kevin Mattison, Adam Stern

Elite speed might be the surest way for a position player to reach the majors, and Brown finally wet his feet in September, four years after the Giants plucked him 24th overall out of Cal State Fullerton. Trouble is, elite speed is just about all Brown has going for him these days. He is 26, has not hit well at any minor-league stop since High-A, and is not particularly adroit on the dirt. Once a top-100 prospect, Brown is likely to settle for a career as a glove-first extra outfielder whose skill set could take on heightened importance in the postseason if he becomes a more efficient base thief. Notably, the Giants played four rounds in the postseason this year and Brown appeared once. In the 18th inning.

Brandon Crawford   SS

Born: 1/21/87   Age: 28   Bats: L   Throws: R   Height: 6' 2"   Weight: 215

YEAR	TEAM	LVL	AGE	PA	R	2B	3B	HR	RBI	BB	K	SB	CS	AVG/OBP/SLG	TAv	BABIP	BRR	FRAA	WARP
2012	SFN	MLB	25	476	44	26	3	4	45	33	95	1	4	.248/.304/.349	.245	.307	0.8	SS(139): 12.7	2.9
2013	SFN	MLB	26	550	52	24	3	9	43	42	96	1	2	.248/.311/.363	.247	.290	2.1	SS(147): -1.1	1.6
2014	SFN	MLB	27	564	54	20	10	10	69	59	129	5	3	.246/.324/.389	.269	.307	-0.2	SS(149): 9.3	3.9
2015	SFN	MLB	28	527	50	22	5	7	48	43	106	3	3	.239/.303/.352	.250	.288	0.9	SS 8	2.6

Breakout: 2%   Improve: 59%   Collapse: 0%   Attrition: 7%   MLB: 96%   Comparables: Felipe Lopez, Toby Harrah, J.J. Hardy

That Crawford became the first shortstop ever to hit a postseason grand slam is surprising more because he was the first than because *he* was the first: He did, after all, crank 10 homers in the regular season. The shocking facet of *him* doing it is that it came on a curveball, because Crawford is chiefly a fastball hitter whose career slugging percentage on breaking stuff is just .287. The UCLA product is no Andrelton Simmons, but he's slick enough with the leather to compensate for shortcomings with the lumber—and, as the round-tripper in the wild-card playoff game suggested, he's making incremental improvements in the box. The total package made Crawford the fifth-most-valuable shortstop in the majors last year, a level that, when he came up a few years ago, seemed out of reach.

Matthew Duffy   MI

Born: 1/15/91   Age: 24   Bats: R   Throws: R   Height: 6' 2"   Weight: 170

YEAR	TEAM	LVL	AGE	PA	R	2B	3B	HR	RBI	BB	K	SB	CS	AVG/OBP/SLG	TAv	BABIP	BRR	FRAA	WARP
2012	SLO	A-	21	216	31	4	0	1	16	26	22	10	1	.247/.361/.286	.248	.275	1.3	SS(45): 2.2	0.8
2013	AUG	A	22	339	48	14	3	4	43	45	41	22	6	.307/.405/.418	.321	.346	5.8	SS(74): 11.3	5.6
2013	SJO	A+	22	115	17	6	1	5	14	7	16	3	1	.292/.342/.509	.302	.306	0.0	SS(25): 0.9	1.1
2014	RIC	AA	23	417	53	24	4	3	62	42	66	20	4	.332/.398/.444	.308	.391	1.9	SS(89): 5.4, 3B(3): -0.1	4.7
2014	SFN	MLB	23	64	5	2	0	0	8	1	14	0	1	.267/.302/.300	.242	.348	-0.5	2B(9): 0.3, SS(7): -0.9	0.2
2015	SFN	MLB	24	250	28	10	2	2	18	18	50	7	2	.258/.315/.343	.255	.316	0.5	SS 3, 2B 0	1.3

Breakout: 4%   Improve: 19%   Collapse: 12%   Attrition: 27%   MLB: 50%   Comparables: Chase d'Arnaud, Yamaico Navarro, Greg Garcia

If bat knobs were indicative of a player's talent, Duffy might be a perennial MVP candidate. In reality, the infielder's Duffman decals belie a modest offensive profile tempered by 30-grade raw power. Duffy is also just an average runner, but he boasts precocious instincts on the basepaths, which were on display when he scored from second without hesitating on a game-tying, ninth-inning wild pitch in the NLCS. Duffy made the most of his skill set to soar past the competition for the batting title in the pitcher-friendly Eastern League, topping career minor leaguer Niuman Romero by 12 points and toolsy Nationals prospect Michael Taylor by 19. The former Long Beach State Dirtbag might never become more than a steady utility infielder, but for an 18th-round pick just two years removed from a .625 OPS in college ball, his 2014 accomplishments deserve a hearty "Oh, yeah!"

Adam Duvall   1B

Born: 9/4/88   Age: 26   Bats: R   Throws: R   Height: 6' 1"   Weight: 205

YEAR	TEAM	LVL	AGE	PA	R	2B	3B	HR	RBI	BB	K	SB	CS	AVG/OBP/SLG	TAv	BABIP	BRR	FRAA	WARP
2012	SJO	A+	23	598	101	24	4	30	100	47	116	8	2	.258/.327/.487	.301	.274	2.4	3B(117): 3.0, 1B(1): -0.0	5.1
2013	RIC	AA	24	430	61	23	4	17	58	35	72	2	1	.252/.320/.465	.288	.268	0.2	3B(90): 6.1, 1B(7): -0.2	3.3
2014	FRE	AAA	25	394	67	21	3	27	90	30	82	2	0	.298/.360/.599	.321	.320	1.7	3B(52): 1.8, 1B(41): 0.5	4.2
2014	SFN	MLB	25	77	8	2	0	3	5	3	20	0	0	.192/.234/.342	.222	.220	0.4	1B(21): -1.4, 3B(1): -0.0	-0.3
2015	SFN	MLB	26	250	27	10	2	10	34	14	58	0	0	.233/.281/.423	.265	.263	-0.2	3B 1, 1B -1	0.7

Breakout: 1%   Improve: 18%   Collapse: 4%   Attrition: 19%   MLB: 38%   Comparables: Jake Fox, Clint Robinson, Matthew Brown

Duvall has plus right-handed power, which can be difficult to find, and he plays a decent first base. He can also stand at the hot corner for two innings of a 17-0 blowout without embarrassing himself, assuming that the ball is not hit his way. Asking any more than that of Duvall at third base is begging for trouble—as his .915 fielding percentage in Fresno can attest—and the narrow defensive profile docks his utility. That could make it difficult for the Kentuckian to stick on a 25-man roster, so Duvall would do well to hone his reactions and throws if he hopes to avoid the Capital Corridor commute.

Aramis Garcia   C

Born: 1/12/93   Age: 22   Bats: R   Throws: R   Height: 6' 2"   Weight: 195

YEAR	TEAM	LVL	AGE	PA	R	2B	3B	HR	RBI	BB	K	SB	CS	AVG/OBP/SLG	TAv	BABIP	BRR	FRAA	WARP
2014	SLO	A-	21	76	5	3	0	2	12	5	19	0	0	.229/.289/.357	.217	.286	-0.1	C(18): 0.2	-0.1
2015	SFN	MLB	22	250	17	8	1	2	19	12	75	1	0	.189/.231/.260	.191	.263	-0.2	C 0	-0.8

Breakout: 0%   Improve: 0%   Collapse: 0%   Attrition: 0%   MLB: 0%   Comparables: J.P. Arencibia, Eddy Rodriguez, Drew Butera

Considered a modest reach in a 2014 draft class low on college catchers, the second-round pick has the plus makeup and defensive tools to stay in the squat. At the plate, Garcia's compact swing gives him the potential for a solid-average hit tool, and he could slug 12-15 homers a year with some offseason time in the weight room. The reigning Conference USA Player of the Year will try to follow in the footsteps of Buster Posey and Andrew Susac in a farm system that has quietly built a nice track record of refining mature backstops. If he succeeds, he could give Florida International University its best-known athletic alumnus since four-time All-Star Mike Lowell.

Tyler Horan   OF

Born: 12/2/90   Age: 24   Bats: L   Throws: R   Height: 6' 2"   Weight: 230

YEAR	TEAM	LVL	AGE	PA	R	2B	3B	HR	RBI	BB	K	SB	CS	AVG/OBP/SLG	TAv	BABIP	BRR	FRAA	WARP
2013	SLO	A-	22	199	25	11	3	4	25	20	34	4	0	.295/.372/.460	.297	.345	0.4	RF(24): -0.0, LF(14): -1.0	1.3
2014	AUG	A	23	417	59	22	5	15	54	39	97	9	4	.273/.350/.481	.313	.331	0.0	RF(95): -1.3, CF(8): -0.0	3.2
2014	SJO	A+	23	117	17	5	1	10	27	9	31	6	4	.321/.376/.670	.344	.364	-0.8	LF(16): -1.7, RF(7): -0.8	1.1
2015	SFN	MLB	24	250	26	9	2	8	29	15	74	3	2	.221/.271/.375	.244	.286	0.0	RF -1, LF -1	-0.2

Breakout: 0%   Improve: 5%   Collapse: 2%   Attrition: 7%   MLB: 13%   Comparables: Casper Wells, John Mayberry, Bryce Brentz

An eighth-round pick out of Virginia Tech in 2013, Horan had opened eyes the previous summer when he tied a Cape Cod League record with 16 home runs. The Massachusetts native was too advanced for Low-A ball, but he quieted some doubters by producing what would have been the California League's second-best OPS had he logged enough plate appearances to qualify. In a system that's low on playable power, Horan stands out, but he will need to carry over his production to the less-accommodating Eastern League yards to garner serious attention on prospect lists.

Travis Ishikawa   1B

Born: 9/24/83   Age: 31   Bats: L   Throws: L   Height: 6' 3"   Weight: 220

YEAR	TEAM	LVL	AGE	PA	R	2B	3B	HR	RBI	BB	K	SB	CS	AVG/OBP/SLG	TAv	BABIP	BRR	FRAA	WARP
2012	NAS	AAA	28	21	1	3	0	0	5	3	2	0	0	.222/.333/.389	.279	.250	0.0	1B(4): -0.1	0.1
2012	MIL	MLB	28	174	19	12	1	4	30	13	42	0	0	.257/.329/.428	.249	.327	-0.5	1B(43): -1.1, RF(3): -0.0	-0.1
2013	CHR	AAA	29	140	17	5	2	2	23	15	31	0	0	.250/.353/.375	.264	.322	1.0	RF(21): -2.4, 1B(7): -0.2	0.0
2013	NOR	AAA	29	208	29	16	0	7	31	29	43	1	0	.316/.413/.525	.316	.383	-0.5	1B(43): -2.2	1.0
2013	BAL	MLB	29	18	0	0	0	0	1	1	8	0	0	.118/.167/.118	.116	.222	0.0	1B(4): -0.1	-0.2
2013	NYA	MLB	29	2	0	0	0	0	0	0	2	0	0	.000/.000/.000	.026	--	0.0	1B(1): -0.1	-0.1
2014	FRE	AAA	30	272	34	9	0	11	45	24	62	0	0	.271/.349/.446	.277	.320	-1.3	1B(56): 2.7, RF(10): 0.0	1.0
2014	PIT	MLB	30	38	2	1	1	1	3	3	11	0	0	.206/.263/.382	.234	.261	1.2	1B(11): 0.5	0.2
2014	SFN	MLB	30	81	7	3	0	2	15	6	23	0	0	.274/.337/.397	.273	.367	0.6	1B(31): -0.7, LF(8): 0.4	0.3
2015	SFN	MLB	31	250	24	11	1	5	26	21	62	0	0	.238/.309/.363	.255	.302	0.6	1B -0, RF -0	0.2

Breakout: 3%   Improve: 18%   Collapse: 9%   Attrition: 17%   MLB: 53%   Comparables: Steve Pearce, Eric Munson, Jeff Liefer

From now on, whenever coaches encourage veterans to continue their careers until no one gives them a uniform, to endure the long bus rides, meager pay and minor-league anonymity, they'll tell Ishikawa's story. After the Pirates cut him loose in April, the long-ago Giants prospect, now on the wrong side of 30, thought about hanging 'em up.

Then, the Giants came calling, and he reluctantly accepted a Triple-A offer. Three months later, with the team in a tailspin, Ishikawa got a shot to provide juice off the bench. A month and a handful of timely hits after that, Bochy had little choice but to gamble on Ishikawa, almost exclusively a first baseman to that point, handling left. He met that threshold *just* well enough to be on the field in late innings of Game Five of the NLCS, and, well, you know the rest.

"With a little luck, that could be you," 60-something baseball lifers will say, as down-on-their-luck 30-somethings shake their heads, and someday, one of them will be proven right. When that happens, both euphoric player and beaming coach will have Travis Ishikawa to thank.

Ryder Jones   INF

Born: 6/7/94   Age: 21   Bats: L   Throws: R   Height: 6' 2"   Weight: 200

YEAR	TEAM	LVL	AGE	PA	R	2B	3B	HR	RBI	BB	K	SB	CS	AVG/OBP/SLG	TAv	BABIP	BRR	FRAA	WARP
2014	AUG	A	20	399	43	21	1	7	49	18	93	6	1	.220/.272/.339	.221	.274	0.6	3B(50): -0.5, SS(34): -7.5	-1.0
2014	SLO	A-	20	117	17	5	1	3	18	7	21	1	0	.243/.293/.393	.242	.274	0.6	3B(27): -0.6	0.1
2015	SFN	MLB	21	250	21	9	1	3	18	6	75	1	0	.192/.220/.278	.191	.262	-0.2	3B -0, SS -3	-1.5

Breakout: 0%   Improve: 0%   Collapse: 0%   Attrition: 0%   MLB: 0%   Comparables: Luis Jimenez, Charlie Culberson, Russell Mitchell

Scouts who really like Jones, and there are plenty, look past his prolonged funk in Augusta and the pedestrian results following his late-July demotion to Salem-Keizer. They see easy-plus raw power and a plus-plus arm—an excellent tandem from which to build a first-division future at the hot corner. But Jones also has his doubters, and there are plenty, who scoffed at the Giants for using a top-65 selection on a player whose other tools lagged well behind. They question the former Stanford commit's bat speed and wonder if the armbar in his swing, which leaves him exposed over the inner half and mutes his raw power, is correctable. Jones' supporters will tell you that it is—that he will eventually wield above-average hit and power tools to become the first prep bat the Giants have drafted and groomed into a 10-career-win player since Royce Clayton in 1989. He will need to perform better in round two at the Low-A level to keep them on the bandwagon.

Angel Pagan   CF

Born: 7/2/81   Age: 33   Bats: B   Throws: R   Height: 6' 2"   Weight: 200

YEAR	TEAM	LVL	AGE	PA	R	2B	3B	HR	RBI	BB	K	SB	CS	AVG/OBP/SLG	TAv	BABIP	BRR	FRAA	WARP
2012	SFN	MLB	30	659	95	38	15	8	56	48	97	29	7	.288/.338/.440	.289	.329	1.4	CF(151): 5.5	4.7
2013	FRE	AAA	31	22	1	0	0	0	3	2	2	0	0	.278/.364/.278	.237	.294	0.2	CF(5): -0.2	0.0
2013	SFN	MLB	31	305	44	16	3	5	30	23	36	9	4	.282/.334/.414	.277	.307	2.6	CF(71): -4.5	1.2
2014	SFN	MLB	32	413	56	21	2	3	27	25	53	16	6	.300/.342/.389	.277	.339	0.3	CF(91): 1.8	2.1
2015	SFN	MLB	33	373	44	18	4	4	30	25	55	14	5	.271/.319/.381	.267	.308	0.6	CF 1	1.5

Breakout: 2%   Improve: 33%   Collapse: 3%   Attrition: 7%   MLB: 96%   Comparables: Coco Crisp, Johnny Damon, Reed Johnson

Pagan is no stranger to the operating table—his elbow, shoulder, hamstring and now lower back have all required a surgeon's care. When he's on the field, he's an underrated all-around player who chips in positively at the plate, in the field and on the basepaths. The sum of those contributions is a first-division player, one who would be vastly underpaid at $19 million over the next two years. But while Pagan's previous nicks, strains and tears have healed seamlessly, a bulging disk and spinal stenosis are no walk in the park. If the Giants head to spring training counting on Pagan to be an everyday player, they'd be wise to shore up their outfield depth, i.e., don't head to spring training counting on Pagan to be an everyday player.

Joe Panik 2B

Born: 10/30/90   Age: 24   Bats: L   Throws: R   Height: 6' 1"   Weight: 190

YEAR	TEAM	LVL	AGE	PA	R	2B	3B	HR	RBI	BB	K	SB	CS	AVG/OBP/SLG	TAv	BABIP	BRR	FRAA	WARP
2012	SJO	A+	21	605	93	27	4	7	76	58	54	10	4	.297/.368/.402	.300	.317	4.2	SS(122): 9.5	6.0
2013	RIC	AA	22	599	64	27	4	4	57	58	68	10	5	.257/.333/.347	.260	.285	-0.8	2B(117): -5.8, SS(20): 0.2	1.0
2014	FRE	AAA	23	326	50	14	4	5	45	27	33	3	2	.321/.382/.447	.286	.346	-0.6	2B(61): -5.0, SS(10): -0.5	1.3
2014	SFN	MLB	23	287	31	10	2	1	18	16	33	0	0	.305/.343/.368	.263	.343	1.1	2B(70): -2.8	0.5
2015	SFN	MLB	24	333	32	14	2	1	24	22	46	2	1	.257/.307/.333	.248	.293	0.6	2B -4, SS 1	0.5

Breakout: 6%   Improve: 20%   Collapse: 10%   Attrition: 21%   MLB: 51%   *Comparables:* *Steve Lombardozzi, Tyler Pastornicky, Daniel Descalso*

In a 2011 draft class teeming with toolsy bats and electric arms, the Giants made a second baseman whose baseball acumen far exceeds his physical gifts the 29th overall pick. Draft analysts panned Panik as the boring choice, but boring and bad aren't always synonymous. The St. John's University product understands his strengths—a compact swing and excellent infield technique—well enough to shield his weaknesses—nonexistent game power and middling athleticism in the field—and that maturity stabilized the keystone for a reeling Giants club last year. In an era where the mean performance at second was a .686 OPS, Panik's short stroke yielded a .385 average on balls hit to the opposite field, driving the overall profile to above-average heights. With the bar at the plate set so low, simply sustaining his 2014 output could make Panik a two-win regular, an awesomely boring outcome.

Hunter Pence RF

Born: 4/13/83   Age: 32   Bats: R   Throws: R   Height: 6' 4"   Weight: 220

YEAR	TEAM	LVL	AGE	PA	R	2B	3B	HR	RBI	BB	K	SB	CS	AVG/OBP/SLG	TAv	BABIP	BRR	FRAA	WARP
2012	PHI	MLB	29	440	59	15	2	17	59	37	85	4	2	.271/.336/.447	.277	.305	0.0	RF(101): -8.4	0.7
2012	SFN	MLB	29	248	28	11	2	7	45	19	60	1	0	.219/.287/.384	.258	.261	-0.2	RF(58): -1.2	0.1
2013	SFN	MLB	30	687	91	35	5	27	99	52	115	22	3	.283/.339/.483	.294	.308	-0.4	RF(162): 14.8	5.1
2014	SFN	MLB	31	708	106	29	10	20	74	52	130	13	6	.277/.332/.445	.289	.318	2.0	RF(161): 1.0, CF(1): -0.0	3.9
2015	SFN	MLB	32	661	75	29	5	19	80	46	127	13	4	.270/.322/.428	.285	.309	0.1	RF 1, CF -0	3.0

Breakout: 0%   Improve: 39%   Collapse: 0%   Attrition: 4%   MLB: 96%   *Comparables:* *Scott Hairston, Jose Guillen, Cody Ross*

Watching Pence's fundamentals—in the words of a fictional amateur scout created by SB Nation's Grant Brisbee, he's like "a rotary phone thrown into a running clothes dryer"—might explain why, in July 2012, the Phillies traded him to the Giants for a package devoid of blue-chip assets. But Pence has overcome Scheuermann's Disease to be a true five-tool talent, a contributor in all three phases in which position players partake and a top-20 outfielder overall. The Texan's 2013 is likely to stand as a career year, but he should remain an above-average player throughout his early 30s, with surplus value on the front end justifying San Francisco's $90 million total outlay through 2018. The aforementioned swap with the Phillies will be remembered as one of the most lopsided deals of the decade.

Juan Perez OF

Born: 11/13/86   Age: 28   Bats: R   Throws: R   Height: 5' 11"   Weight: 185

YEAR	TEAM	LVL	AGE	PA	R	2B	3B	HR	RBI	BB	K	SB	CS	AVG/OBP/SLG	TAv	BABIP	BRR	FRAA	WARP
2012	RIC	AA	25	513	65	26	4	11	53	22	85	18	15	.302/.341/.441	.291	.349	3.4	RF(94): 3.2, CF(16): 0.4	4.1
2013	FRE	AAA	26	409	52	27	5	10	50	15	75	18	6	.291/.323/.466	.282	.337	2.6	RF(50): 9.0, 3B(34): -0.4	3.1
2013	SFN	MLB	26	97	8	5	0	1	8	6	21	2	0	.258/.302/.348	.232	.324	-0.3	CF(20): 2.0, LF(11): 0.4	0.6
2014	FRE	AAA	27	196	33	13	0	7	25	14	32	7	4	.316/.372/.508	.317	.350	-0.4	RF(33): -1.9, LF(8): 0.9	1.4
2014	SFN	MLB	27	109	13	7	0	1	3	5	25	0	1	.170/.224/.270	.186	.216	0.3	LF(40): 0.1, CF(17): 0.2	-0.5
2015	SFN	MLB	28	250	25	12	2	4	25	9	55	7	3	.252/.285/.374	.253	.306	-0.4	RF 1, CF 2	0.7

Breakout: 3%   Improve: 13%   Collapse: 17%   Attrition: 28%   MLB: 36%   *Comparables:* *Scott Cousins, Matt Cepicky, Trent Oeltjen*

You wouldn't know it from looking at him now, but less than seven years ago, Perez clubbed 37 home runs for Western Oklahoma State College, shattering the previous Division II junior college record of 23. A late bloomer who played high school ball a stone's throw from Yankee Stadium, these days Perez earns his living with speed and defense. He still evokes his JuCo thump once in a blue moon—like, say, in Game Five of the World Series, when he came closer than anyone all year to hitting a home run against Royals reliever Wade Davis—but Perez's calling card is serving as a late-inning substitute for lumbering brutes like Michael Morse. That's what he did in 2014, and it's what he'll continue to do if he makes a big-league roster this spring.

Buster Posey C

Born: 3/27/87   Age: 28   Bats: R   Throws: R   Height: 6' 1"   Weight: 215

YEAR	TEAM	LVL	AGE	PA	R	2B	3B	HR	RBI	BB	K	SB	CS	AVG/OBP/SLG	TAv	BABIP	BRR	FRAA	WARP
2012	SFN	MLB	25	610	78	39	1	24	103	69	96	1	1	.336/.408/.549	.346	.368	-3.6	C(114): -0.6, 1B(29): -2.1	7.5
2013	SFN	MLB	26	595	61	34	1	15	72	60	70	2	1	.294/.371/.450	.296	.312	-4.5	C(121): 0.3, 1B(21): -0.6	4.1
2014	SFN	MLB	27	605	72	28	2	22	89	47	69	0	1	.311/.364/.490	.316	.319	-3.5	C(111): 1.6, 1B(35): 1.4	5.9
2015	SFN	MLB	28	566	67	29	2	18	75	51	79	1	1	.301/.366/.471	.314	.323	-3.0	C 0, 1B -0	4.7

Breakout: 0%   Improve: 44%   Collapse: 1%   Attrition: 4%   MLB: 99%   *Comparables:* *Brian McCann, Carlos Santana, Joe Mauer*

The downside of having a swing that belongs in the Louvre is that when any element is the tiniest bit askew, it's apparent even to untrained observers. Fretful questions are inevitable. Is he hurt? Tired? Declining? Is it time for a position change? Is his $164 million contract about to become an albatross?

The upside of having such a picturesque swing is the ability to halt the inquisition, to clobber any fastball, to add 94 points to one's OPS in a 15-game span more than three-quarters of the way through the season. From August 21st to September 6th, Posey clubbed six doubles, a triple and seven homers while striking out only four times. Weeks after discussing his demise, talk radio was musing about his MVP clout.

Posey cooled off by season's end and morphed into a pure singles hitter come October, though his blocking, framing and throwing prowess remained intact. As he broke David Eckstein's record for postseason plate appearances without an extra-base knock, the armchair coaches and postgame skeptics sprung back to life. After all, when there's a chip in the Mona Lisa, everyone notices. But a minor fix—or four months of rest—should make him priceless again.

Hector Sanchez   C

Born: 11/17/89   Age: 25   Bats: B   Throws: R   Height: 6' 0"   Weight: 235

YEAR	TEAM	LVL	AGE	PA	R	2B	3B	HR	RBI	BB	K	SB	CS	AVG/OBP/SLG	TAv	BABIP	BRR	FRAA	WARP
2012	SFN	MLB	22	227	22	15	0	3	34	5	52	0	0	.280/.295/.390	.246	.349	-1.8	C(56): -1.1	0.2
2013	FRE	AAA	23	99	10	4	0	3	11	12	15	0	0	.271/.364/.424	.275	.294	-0.3	C(18): -0.3	0.6
2013	SFN	MLB	23	140	8	4	0	3	19	7	29	0	0	.248/.300/.349	.241	.296	-0.9	C(33): 0.0	0.1
2014	FRE	AAA	24	20	1	0	0	1	3	1	3	0	0	.158/.200/.316	.187	.133	-0.1	C(5): -0.0	-0.1
2014	SFN	MLB	24	177	8	8	0	3	28	8	55	0	1	.196/.237/.301	.209	.266	-0.2	C(45): 0.0, 1B(1): 0.1	-0.3
2015	SFN	MLB	25	250	21	11	1	4	25	12	58	0	0	.236/.275/.345	.236	.291	-0.8	C -0, 1B 0	0.2

Breakout: 4%   Improve: 28%   Collapse: 11%   Attrition: 23%   MLB: 72%   *Comparables:*   *John Buck, Austin Romine, Chris Snyder*

Oh, 2014 wasn't kind to Sanchez: With Andrew Susac breathing down his neck for the backup catcher duties, the switch-hitter performed poorly at the plate and took a beating behind it. A foul ball off the mask in late July sent Sanchez to the shelf with a concussion, and another during his late-August rehab assignment ended his season. Sanchez has improved his framing, grading positively in that department last year for the first time, but he is a subpar blocker and a league-average thrower, so the overall defensive skill set doesn't atone for his undisciplined approach at the plate. This isn't quite a case of Lou Gehrig unseating Wally Pipp, but with Andrew Susac in the majors, Sanchez's clearest route to big-league playing time this year might be a ticket out of town.

Marco Scutaro   2B

Born: 10/30/75   Age: 39   Bats: R   Throws: R   Height: 5' 10"   Weight: 185

YEAR	TEAM	LVL	AGE	PA	R	2B	3B	HR	RBI	BB	K	SB	CS	AVG/OBP/SLG	TAv	BABIP	BRR	FRAA	WARP
2012	COL	MLB	36	415	47	16	3	4	30	27	35	7	3	.271/.324/.361	.236	.287	1.2	2B(72): 5.5, SS(27): 3.1	1.2
2012	SFN	MLB	36	268	40	16	1	3	44	13	14	2	1	.362/.385/.473	.310	.366	0.5	2B(46): -4.0, 3B(15): 1.7	1.9
2013	SFN	MLB	37	547	57	23	3	2	31	45	34	2	1	.297/.357/.369	.271	.314	1.2	2B(121): -0.9	2.0
2014	SFN	MLB	38	13	1	0	0	0	0	1	3	0	0	.091/.167/.091	.103	.125	0.0	2B(3): -0.3	-0.2
2015	SFN	MLB	39	250	25	11	1	1	18	16	26	2	1	.267/.315/.336	.252	.290	0.5	2B -0, SS 0	0.7

Breakout: 0%   Improve: 22%   Collapse: 17%   Attrition: 23%   MLB: 76%   *Comparables:*   *Jamey Carroll, Craig Counsell, Eric Young*

The Giants won the 2010 World Series with Freddy Sanchez as their second baseman. Two years later, Sanchez cashed a $6 million check while sitting out the season following shoulder and back surgery, from which he still has not sufficiently recovered. To fill that hole, the Giants acquired Scutaro, with whom they won the 2012 Fall Classic, and to whom they paid $6 million two years later for a grand total of one hit. Owed another $6 million this year, Scutaro is still on the mend. And if history is any guide, his replacement, Panik, might want to start looking for a chiropractor.

Andrew Susac   C

Born: 3/22/90   Age: 25   Bats: R   Throws: R   Height: 6' 1"   Weight: 215

YEAR	TEAM	LVL	AGE	PA	R	2B	3B	HR	RBI	BB	K	SB	CS	AVG/OBP/SLG	TAv	BABIP	BRR	FRAA	WARP
2012	SJO	A+	22	426	58	16	3	9	52	55	100	1	1	.244/.351/.380	.279	.311	-0.7	C(97): 0.3	3.1
2013	RIC	AA	23	310	32	17	0	12	46	42	68	1	0	.256/.362/.458	.310	.299	-0.6	C(71): -0.5, 1B(9): -0.7	3.0
2014	FRE	AAA	24	253	34	9	0	10	32	34	50	0	1	.268/.379/.451	.292	.305	0.4	C(56): 1.2	2.3
2014	SFN	MLB	24	95	13	8	0	3	19	7	28	0	0	.273/.326/.466	.291	.368	0.5	C(29): -0.1	0.8
2015	SFN	MLB	25	250	25	10	1	6	28	25	66	0	0	.227/.311/.367	.261	.289	-0.3	C 0, 1B -0	0.9

Breakout: 7%   Improve: 23%   Collapse: 8%   Attrition: 27%   MLB: 52%   *Comparables:*   *Geovany Soto, Chris Gimenez, Josmil Pinto*

Susac's first extended major-league stint began in late July, when Sanchez succumbed to a concussion, and the replacement quickly emerged as one of the team's best hitters, trailing only Posey and Morse in True Average in unduly limited action. The former Oregon State Beaver only garnered six pinch-hit chances during the regular season and saw the field only four times altogether in October: Such is life backing up an elite starter, particularly playing for a manager whose emergency-catcher phobia weighs heavily on his choice of pinch-hitting assignments. With a strong arm and solid-average thunder in the stick, Susac has the tools to be a regular behind the dish and is already a first-rate backup. Assuming the Sacramento-area native is not used as a trade chit, finding ways to increase his playing time should be a priority for Bochy in 2015.

Dan Uggla   2B

Born: 3/11/80   Age: 35   Bats: R   Throws: R   Height: 5' 11"   Weight: 210

YEAR	TEAM	LVL	AGE	PA	R	2B	3B	HR	RBI	BB	K	SB	CS	AVG/OBP/SLG	TAv	BABIP	BRR	FRAA	WARP
2012	ATL	MLB	32	630	86	29	0	19	78	94	168	4	3	.220/.348/.384	.272	.283	0.5	2B(152): 14.6	4.0
2013	ATL	MLB	33	537	60	10	3	22	55	77	171	2	0	.179/.309/.362	.252	.225	-3.8	2B(133): -12.9	-0.9
2014	ATL	MLB	34	145	13	3	0	2	10	10	40	0	0	.162/.241/.231	.195	.213	0.7	2B(35): 2.0	-0.4
2014	SFN	MLB	34	12	1	0	0	0	0	1	6	0	0	.000/.083/.000	.051	.000	0.0	2B(4): 0.4	-0.2
2015	SFN	MLB	35	250	28	8	1	9	31	28	67	1	1	.218/.313/.383	.268	.268	-0.4	2B -1	0.9

Breakout: 2%   Improve: 27%   Collapse: 11%   Attrition: 16%   MLB: 93%   *Comparables:*   *Bobby Grich, Jeff Kent, Jason Bay*

After so revolting the Braves that they chose to eat the $18 million or so remaining on his contract, Uggla latched on with the Giants, who prayed for the sort of lightning-in-a-bottle renaissance that Pat Burrell enjoyed in San Francisco in 2010. Instead, Uggla appeared in four games, all losses, and logged more errors than times on base. The Giants forgave and forgot his "contributions" in key July defeats to the Dodgers and Pirates when they won the World Series. In doing so, they earned Uggla a ring by which to remember them.

Pitchers

Jeremy Affeldt   LHP
Born: 6/6/79   Age: 36   Bats: L   Throws: L   Height: 6'4"   Weight: 225

YEAR	TEAM	LVL	AGE	W	L	SV	G	GS	IP	H	HR	BB	K	BB/9	K/9	GB%	BABIP	WHIP	ERA	FIP	FRA	WARP
2012	SFN	MLB	33	1	2	3	67	0	63¹	57	1	23	57	3.3	8.1	62%	.306	1.26	2.70	2.77	3.96	0.5
2013	SFN	MLB	34	1	5	0	39	0	33²	27	2	17	21	4.5	5.6	57%	.245	1.31	3.74	4.42	5.47	-0.3
2014	SFN	MLB	35	4	2	0	62	0	55¹	47	1	14	41	2.3	6.7	68%	.279	1.10	2.28	2.83	3.69	0.3
2015	SFN	MLB	36	3	1	2	53	0	48²	43	3	16	42	3.0	7.7	57%	.307	1.22	3.42	3.56	3.72	0.4

Breakout: 18%   Improve: 41%   Collapse: 28%   Attrition: 9%   MLB: 71%   Comparables: *Scott Downs, Fernando Rodney, Ricardo Rincon*

If Comeback Player of the Year accolades were distributed based on sheer quantity of injuries and surgeries endured, Affeldt would have been a shoo-in to take home the hardware in 2014. Between the end of the 2012 season and his first official outing last year, he underwent LASIK eye treatment, strained his oblique, pulled his groin, had surgery to repair a sports hernia and sprained the MCL in his right knee. With all of that in the rearview mirror, Affeldt compiled the best walk rate and the highest groundball rate of his major-league career—and then turned in 11 straight scoreless postseason appearances, running his active streak to 22, one shy of Mariano Rivera's all-time record. Two years into a three-year, $18 million deal, whoever employs the lefty in 2015 will hope that Good Affeldt takes the rubber match.

Martin Agosta   RHP
Born: 4/7/91   Age: 24   Bats: R   Throws: R   Height: 6'1"   Weight: 180

YEAR	TEAM	LVL	AGE	W	L	SV	G	GS	IP	H	HR	BB	K	BB/9	K/9	GB%	BABIP	WHIP	ERA	FIP	FRA	WARP
2013	AUG	A	22	9	3	0	18	18	91²	57	4	43	109	4.2	10.7	37%	.254	1.09	2.06	3.31	4.17	0.6
2014	SJO	A+	23	3	3	0	11	11	39	51	5	34	25	7.8	5.8	43%	.346	2.18	9.23	6.82	8.04	-0.5
2015	SFN	MLB	24	3	5	0	13	13	56	56	5	32	44	5.2	7.1	42%	.319	1.57	5.10	4.79	5.54	-0.5

Breakout: 0%   Improve: 0%   Collapse: 0%   Attrition: 0%   MLB: 0%   Comparables: *Frank Garces, Duane Below, Jose A. Ramirez*

Organizations often invent injuries to get players a mental break. In Agosta's case, it was done to send him from San Jose to the complex league so that he could iron out his command, which became intolerable a month into the season. The Giants found the right-hander in their backyard at St. Mary's College, selecting him in the second round exactly one year after they did the same with his high school catcher, Andrew Susac. The ex-Gael needs a bounceback season if the battery's ever going to get back together.

Tyler Beede   RHP
Born: 5/23/93   Age: 22   Bats: R   Throws: R   Height: 6'4"   Weight: 200

YEAR	TEAM	LVL	AGE	W	L	SV	G	GS	IP	H	HR	BB	K	BB/9	K/9	GB%	BABIP	WHIP	ERA	FIP	FRA	WARP
2015	SFN	MLB	22	1	3	0	9	9	34	38	3	19	21	4.9	5.6	48%	.326	1.65	5.59	5.17	6.07	-0.5

Breakout: 0%   Improve: 0%   Collapse: 0%   Attrition: 0%   MLB: 0%   Comparables: *Nick Maronde, Buddy Boshers, Adam Warren*

A maddening collegian at Vanderbilt, Beede can flash three plus pitches and dominate in one start but fail to hit the broad side of a barn the next. He is an excellent, high-payoff project for an organization that prides itself on grooming pitchers, with a ceiling that might have warranted a top-10 pick. On the other hand, Beede struggles to repeat his delivery, and he went from Golden Spikes Award finalist as a sophomore to a 4.05 ERA as a junior, when he was expected to front the eventual College World Series champion Vanderbilt's staff. If the Giants can help Beede rediscover his fleeting power curveball and up his fastball command from fringy to solid average, the Massachusetts native could blossom into a no. 2 starter. If it all goes south, he might lean back on an amateur hobby as a YouTube rapper. (He goes by the rap name Young Beedah.)

Ty Blach   LHP
Born: 10/20/90   Age: 24   Bats: R   Throws: L   Height: 6'1"   Weight: 210

YEAR	TEAM	LVL	AGE	W	L	SV	G	GS	IP	H	HR	BB	K	BB/9	K/9	GB%	BABIP	WHIP	ERA	FIP	FRA	WARP
2013	SJO	A+	22	12	4	0	22	20	130¹	124	8	18	117	1.2	8.1	48%	.304	1.09	2.90	3.23	3.70	2.5
2014	RIC	AA	23	8	8	0	25	25	141	142	8	39	91	2.5	5.8	47%	.295	1.28	3.13	3.70	3.95	2.4
2015	SFN	MLB	24	6	8	0	21	21	121¹	126	10	32	75	2.4	5.6	46%	.312	1.30	4.11	4.04	4.47	0.1

Breakout: 23%   Improve: 31%   Collapse: 7%   Attrition: 29%   MLB: 44%   Comparables: *Dallas Keuchel, Elih Villanueva, Seth Maness*

Any time a pitcher posts a sub-3.00 ERA and fans more than six batters for every walk in the bandboxes of the California League, pacing the circuit in both categories, fans sit up and take notice. When the same pitcher sees his walk rate double and his strikeout rate plunge following a promotion to more pitcher-friendly environs in Double-A, the excitement wanes. Those are the last two chapters in Blach's development story. Readers who thought it might conclude with the Creighton product emerging as the second coming of Tom Glavine have already been disappointed. Those who see his average pitch menu (highlighted by a plus changeup) for the fifth-starter promise it holds might yet be smiling when they turn the last page.

Raymond Black   RHP
Born: 6/26/90   Age: 25   Bats: R   Throws: R   Height: 6'5"   Weight: 225

YEAR	TEAM	LVL	AGE	W	L	SV	G	GS	IP	H	HR	BB	K	BB/9	K/9	GB%	BABIP	WHIP	ERA	FIP	FRA	WARP
2014	AUG	A	24	1	3	1	33	0	31¹	16	1	14	64	4.0	18.4	39%	.333	0.96	3.73	1.45	2.01	1.2
2015	SFN	MLB	25	2	1	2	40	0	38	28	3	17	51	4.0	12.1	42%	.326	1.18	2.98	3.13	3.24	0.6

Breakout: 9%   Improve: 17%   Collapse: 7%   Attrition: 20%   MLB: 27%   Comparables: *Anthony Slama, John Gaub, Clay Zavada*

Shoulder surgery to repair a torn labrum forced Black—a seventh-round pick in 2011 who underwent Tommy John surgery in high school—to wait nearly three years to make his professional debut. The delay spared radar guns around the minors the need to light up a third digit. Finally healthy, Black blew hitters away at a breakneck pace to earn a midseason promotion to San Jose. If his arm stays attached, the plus-plus fastballs and big-tilt sliders it hurls should propel him to the majors by September. Black's stuff is undeniably good enough for late-inning work, and a modest control improvement could make him a closer. Assuming, of course, that he can stay off the operating table.

Clayton Blackburn   RHP

Born: 1/6/93   Age: 22   Bats: L   Throws: R   Height: 6'2"   Weight: 260

YEAR	TEAM	LVL	AGE	W	L	SV	G	GS	IP	H	HR	BB	K	BB/9	K/9	GB%	BABIP	WHIP	ERA	FIP	FRA	WARP
2012	AUG	A	19	8	4	0	22	22	131¹	116	3	18	143	1.2	9.8	60%	.315	1.02	2.54	2.29	3.06	2.9
2013	SJO	A+	20	7	5	0	23	23	133	111	12	35	138	2.4	9.3	49%	.280	1.10	3.65	3.86	4.25	2.0
2014	RIC	AA	21	5	6	0	18	18	93	94	1	20	85	1.9	8.2	57%	.341	1.23	3.29	2.54	3.33	2.2
2015	SFN	MLB	22	5	6	0	17	17	91	89	7	26	73	2.6	7.2	52%	.319	1.26	3.90	3.71	4.24	0.4

Breakout: 14%   Improve: 27%   Collapse: 3%   Attrition: 20%   MLB: 38%   *Comparables:*   *Patrick Corbin, Nick Tropeano, David Holmberg*

There are many ways to describe a 6-foot-2, 260-pound frame, some kinder than others. Scouts are typically generous when it comes to Blackburn, using terms like "workhorse build" and "country strong," instead of calling him "fat" or comparing him to late-career Bartolo Colon. A 16th-round pick in 2011 who caved on his threat to attend the University of Oklahoma, Blackburn has moved more swiftly through the minors than most of his prep-school contemporaries thanks to a plus command profile that amplifies his solid-average stuff. Born in Texas and raised in Oklahoma, Blackburn spins a true 12-6 curveball and can spot his low-90s fastball in all four corners of the strike zone. He profiles as an innings chewer whose durability and precocious polish will make him a valuable mid-rotation asset. Having pitched well in Richmond in 2014, Blackburn should debut sometime this year.

Brett Bochy   RHP

Born: 8/27/87   Age: 27   Bats: R   Throws: R   Height: 6'2"   Weight: 200

YEAR	TEAM	LVL	AGE	W	L	SV	G	GS	IP	H	HR	BB	K	BB/9	K/9	GB%	BABIP	WHIP	ERA	FIP	FRA	WARP
2012	RIC	AA	24	7	3	14	41	0	53¹	29	3	18	69	3.0	11.6	33%	.232	0.88	2.53	2.53	4.02	0.5
2013	FRE	AAA	25	1	1	2	45	0	56¹	51	2	16	57	2.6	9.1	31%	.304	1.19	3.99	3.02	3.16	1.4
2014	FRE	AAA	26	4	4	0	35	2	54	53	8	27	47	4.5	7.8	28%	.297	1.48	3.83	5.38	4.41	0.5
2014	SFN	MLB	26	0	0	0	3	0	3¹	1	1	2	3	5.4	8.1	38%	.000	0.90	5.40	7.90	13.49	-0.2
2015	SFN	MLB	27	2	1	1	41	0	52¹	44	4	18	53	3.1	9.2	34%	.304	1.18	3.26	3.42	3.54	0.6

Breakout: 4%   Improve: 11%   Collapse: 15%   Attrition: 19%   MLB: 31%   *Comparables:*   *C.C. Lee, Rob Delaney, Rob Wooten*

What's in a name? Thirty seconds of fame on a Sunday Night Baseball telecast in September, apparently, because the ESPN crew was so excited to see Bochy warming up that they didn't realize the pitcher they were focusing on was actually Erik Cordier. Now that he has trudged up the organizational ladder, the manager's son will face a perennial uphill battle to stick as the last man in a big-league bullpen: He's a high-80s right-hander who saw all three of his FIP stats decay from 2013 (when he actually merited a promotion). Bochy is the seventh major leaguer to have the privilege of calling his skipper "dad." In the midst of a 17-0 September blowout, his father became the first manager to hand the ball to his kid on a big-league mound.

Madison Bumgarner   LHP

Born: 8/1/89   Age: 25   Bats: R   Throws: L   Height: 6'5"   Weight: 235

YEAR	TEAM	LVL	AGE	W	L	SV	G	GS	IP	H	HR	BB	K	BB/9	K/9	GB%	BABIP	WHIP	ERA	FIP	FRA	WARP
2012	SFN	MLB	22	16	11	0	32	32	208¹	183	23	49	191	2.1	8.3	49%	.276	1.11	3.37	3.54	4.11	2.4
2013	SFN	MLB	23	13	9	0	31	31	201¹	146	15	62	199	2.8	8.9	49%	.252	1.03	2.77	3.03	3.58	3.0
2014	SFN	MLB	24	18	10	0	33	33	217¹	194	21	43	219	1.8	9.1	46%	.296	1.09	2.98	3.02	3.76	3.5
2015	SFN	MLB	25	10	10	0	28	28	180²	157	15	38	172	1.9	8.6	47%	.307	1.08	3.03	3.20	3.29	2.7

Breakout: 10%   Improve: 17%   Collapse: 7%   Attrition: 20%   MLB: 25%   *Comparables:*   *Geno Espineli, Chuckie Fick, Mike McClendon*

There are places where one might be expected to yawn—a history lecture, perhaps, or a redeye flight. The visitors dugout during the seventh game of the World Series, when you are the pitcher, throwing on two days of rest, tasked with preserving a one-run lead? That's not one of them. But nothing better epitomizes Bumgarner's demeanor than that moment FOX cameras caught in the top of the seventh inning. He's large and in charge on the mound, pumping fastball and cutter strikes, then snapping off 69 mph slow curves while keeping a straight face, whether the stage is Scottsdale in March or Kansas City in October. Bumgarner set career bests in walk and strikeout rates last year, and he's one of baseball's most valuable assets, a true no. 1 starter who can be retained through 2019 for $52 million. Expect the Giants to manage his workload early in 2015, on the heels of a 270-inning burden that Bumgarner brought on himself by treating the playoffs like an afternoon nap.

Matt Cain   RHP

Born: 10/1/84   Age: 30   Bats: R   Throws: R   Height: 6'3"   Weight: 230

YEAR	TEAM	LVL	AGE	W	L	SV	G	GS	IP	H	HR	BB	K	BB/9	K/9	GB%	BABIP	WHIP	ERA	FIP	FRA	WARP
2012	SFN	MLB	27	16	5	0	32	32	219¹	177	21	51	193	2.1	7.9	41%	.259	1.04	2.79	3.44	3.66	3.2
2013	SFN	MLB	28	8	10	0	30	30	184¹	158	23	55	158	2.7	7.7	39%	.260	1.16	4.00	3.90	4.47	1.2
2014	SFN	MLB	29	2	7	0	15	15	90¹	81	13	32	70	3.2	7.0	46%	.265	1.25	4.18	4.55	5.51	-0.6
2015	SFN	MLB	30	5	5	0	14	14	92	77	8	23	77	2.3	7.5	40%	.281	1.09	3.14	3.62	3.41	1.2

Breakout: 9%   Improve: 37%   Collapse: 30%   Attrition: 13%   MLB: 88%   *Comparables:*   *Jered Weaver, Freddy Garcia, Gavin Floyd*

If you are squeamish and reading this over a meal, skip this comment and move on to the next one. Cain made at least 30 starts in each of his first eight full big-league seasons, but he did so while, in his words, "manipulating" bone chips around his throwing elbow to alleviate discomfort. As if that were not nauseating enough, Cain also revealed that he has not had full range of motion in his right arm since high school. These are the things one must do to get nicknamed "The Horse." With the pain from those loose bodies worsening and taking Cain's performance along with it, he finally acceded to surgery, spent the second half of the season in the stable, and then underwent another arthroscopic procedure in October to remove bone chips from his ankle. A prime candidate for Comeback Player of the Year honors, Cain will aim to rediscover his FIP-defying ways when he returns to the mound in spring training—and with $70 million left on his contract, the Giants had better hope he does.

Santiago Casilla RHP

Born: 7/25/80   Age: 34   Bats: R   Throws: R   Height: 6'0"   Weight: 210

YEAR	TEAM	LVL	AGE	W	L	SV	G	GS	IP	H	HR	BB	K	BB/9	K/9	GB%	BABIP	WHIP	ERA	FIP	FRA	WARP
2012	SFN	MLB	31	7	6	25	73	0	63¹	55	8	22	55	3.1	7.8	55%	.254	1.22	2.84	4.18	4.84	-0.3
2013	SFN	MLB	32	7	2	2	57	0	50	39	2	25	38	4.5	6.8	55%	.262	1.28	2.16	3.64	3.77	0.3
2014	SFN	MLB	33	3	3	19	54	0	58¹	35	3	15	45	2.3	6.9	57%	.211	0.86	1.70	3.15	3.94	0.4
2015	SFN	MLB	34	3	1	6	53	0	50²	40	3	18	45	3.3	8.1	51%	.287	1.16	3.09	3.48	3.36	0.7

Breakout: 14%   Improve: 29%   Collapse: 38%   Attrition: 10%   MLB: 84%   Comparables: Dennys Reyes, Jason Isringhausen, Brandon Lyon

With easy 95 mph cheddar and a hook from hell, Casilla has all the components to be a closer, though he does get more groundballs than strikeouts. Thrust into that ninth inning role for the second time in three years, he quickly developed the requisite death stare and rewarded Bochy by going 17-for-18 in save chances after taking over for Sergio Romo. Casilla amassed the lowest walk rate of his career and, at 21 percent, his highest strikeout rate since 2011, two feathers in the cap of one of the senior circuit's most underrated relievers. More importantly, perhaps, he produced another gods-defyingly low BABIP, moving his to 11th-lowest in baseball since he joined the Giants in 2010. He did nothing to cede ninth-inning duties during his four months on the job and figures to get the ball in the defending champs' first save opportunity of 2015.

Erik Cordier RHP

Born: 2/25/86   Age: 29   Bats: R   Throws: R   Height: 6'4"   Weight: 250

YEAR	TEAM	LVL	AGE	W	L	SV	G	GS	IP	H	HR	BB	K	BB/9	K/9	GB%	BABIP	WHIP	ERA	FIP	FRA	WARP
2012	GWN	AAA	26	1	1	0	8	4	24²	27	1	21	15	7.7	5.5	51%	.347	1.95	4.38	5.14	6.65	-0.1
2013	IND	AAA	27	4	2	4	44	0	53	51	3	28	65	4.8	11.0	48%	.351	1.49	4.58	3.19	4.18	0.5
2014	FRE	AAA	28	4	3	3	47	0	52²	40	4	31	68	5.3	11.6	40%	.295	1.35	3.59	4.04	4.04	1.0
2014	SFN	MLB	28	0	0	0	7	0	6	5	0	2	9	3.0	13.5	43%	.357	1.17	1.50	2.60	2.93	0.1
2015	SFN	MLB	29	2	2	0	29	5	51	48	4	27	44	4.8	7.7	45%	.320	1.48	4.55	4.42	4.95	-0.2

Breakout: 5%   Improve: 6%   Collapse: 3%   Attrition: 8%   MLB: 13%   Comparables: Bill Murphy, Jimmy Barthmaier, Brian Slocum

Cordier can throw a baseball 100 mph (which makes confusing him for Brett Bochy even funnier). Most humans who can do that find their way to the major leagues, but the majority do not take the road less traveled, a road that takes them through four organizations over nine professional seasons before one finally offers a September audition. Cordier was once a polished cold-weather prep-schooler with merely decent velocity and advanced secondary stuff. But while he regained and even bolstered his gas after undergoing Tommy John surgery in 2007, his slider and changeup regressed. Despite the caliber of bullets in his right arm, Cordier is a long shot to secure a stable bullpen role unless his command or breaking ball takes a step forward. He'll only turn 29 in February, though, and with a brief taste of The Show to motivate him, there is no reason to give up yet.

Kyle Crick RHP

Born: 11/30/92   Age: 22   Bats: L   Throws: R   Height: 6'2"   Weight: 220

YEAR	TEAM	LVL	AGE	W	L	SV	G	GS	IP	H	HR	BB	K	BB/9	K/9	GB%	BABIP	WHIP	ERA	FIP	FRA	WARP
2012	AUG	A	19	7	6	0	23	22	111¹	75	1	67	128	5.4	10.3	48%	.279	1.28	2.51	3.53	3.33	2.5
2013	SJO	A+	20	3	1	0	14	14	68²	48	1	39	95	5.1	12.5	44%	.324	1.27	1.57	2.94	2.96	2.2
2014	RIC	AA	21	6	7	0	23	22	90¹	78	7	61	111	6.1	11.1	47%	.326	1.54	3.79	3.96	3.53	2.0
2015	SFN	MLB	22	4	6	0	16	16	75¹	64	5	45	81	5.4	9.6	45%	.322	1.44	4.07	3.96	4.42	0.2

Breakout: 0%   Improve: 0%   Collapse: 0%   Attrition: 0%   MLB: 0%   Comparables: Trevor May, Zack Wheeler, Mauricio Robles

If a workhorse build, elite arm speed and plus-plus gas were all the boxes a pitching prospect needed to check to graduate as a frontline starter, Crick might be the most coveted blue-chipper in the minors. But command matters, and Crick's is below average. Secondary pitches matter, and Crick doesn't spin a consistent put-away breaker. Mechanics matter, and Crick is prone to opening up early. All of these issues might be correctable, but the Fort Worth native is three-plus years into his professional career, and his walk rate tells the story of his (poor) progress. Crick will be a big leaguer, and with a bulldog mentality and high-octane stuff, he could rack up saves and strikeouts. Barring a big step forward in control, however, he won't stick as a starter.

Kendry Flores RHP

Born: 11/24/91   Age: 23   Bats: R   Throws: R   Height: 6'2"   Weight: 175

YEAR	TEAM	LVL	AGE	W	L	SV	G	GS	IP	H	HR	BB	K	BB/9	K/9	GB%	BABIP	WHIP	ERA	FIP	FRA	WARP
2012	SLO	A-	20	1	3	0	10	8	42¹	44	4	11	34	2.3	7.2	35%	.296	1.30	4.46	3.73	5.40	0.3
2013	AUG	A	21	10	6	0	22	22	141²	113	11	17	137	1.1	8.7	39%	.267	0.92	2.73	3.00	3.74	1.7
2014	SJO	A+	22	4	6	0	20	20	105²	101	14	32	112	2.7	9.5	41%	.307	1.26	4.09	4.39	4.62	1.7
2015	SFN	MLB	23	5	7	0	18	18	97²	101	11	32	71	2.9	6.5	38%	.313	1.36	4.64	4.45	5.04	-0.5

Breakout: 0%   Improve: 0%   Collapse: 0%   Attrition: 0%   MLB: 0%   Comparables: Josh Banks, Barry Enright, Hector Rondon

What scouts think of Flores sometimes depends on the day they see him, because his velocity has a tendency to hop up to 94 one start and drop down to 89 the next. The jig was a bit calmer in 2014, and any concerns about his velo-volatility are further mitigated by Flores' great command and control, which help to play up his stuff even on days when nothing he throws is plus. More worrisome now is the shoulder soreness that cost Flores the last month of 2014. If that checks out fine, his deep assortment of pitches and ability to formulate a plan on the hill should make him a rotation option by the middle of 2016.

Joan Gregorio RHP

Born: 1/12/92   Age: 23   Bats: R   Throws: R   Height: 6'7"   Weight: 180

YEAR	TEAM	LVL	AGE	W	L	SV	G	GS	IP	H	HR	BB	K	BB/9	K/9	GB%	BABIP	WHIP	ERA	FIP	FRA	WARP
2012	SLO	A-	20	7	7	0	16	16	76¹	85	9	23	69	2.7	8.1	43%	.321	1.41	5.54	4.07	4.67	1.4
2013	AUG	A	21	6	3	0	14	13	69²	65	3	17	84	2.2	10.9	35%	.341	1.18	4.00	2.45	2.94	1.8
2014	AUG	A	22	2	7	1	13	12	68	50	2	27	65	3.6	8.6	41%	.259	1.13	3.57	3.47	4.46	0.9
2014	SJO	A+	22	2	2	0	6	5	22²	27	2	13	27	5.2	10.7	27%	.391	1.76	6.75	4.23	3.85	0.4
2015	SFN	MLB	23	3	6	0	16	16	76	78	7	34	58	4.1	6.9	38%	.323	1.48	4.85	4.50	5.27	-0.5

Breakout: 0%   Improve: 0%   Collapse: 0%   Attrition: 0%   MLB: 0%   Comparables: A.J. Achter, Corey Kluber, James Houser

Being tall has its advantages, like the ability to reach the cookies on the top shelf of the kitchen cupboard or to play basketball competitively beyond one's bar mitzvah. It's also an advantage on the mound, and Gregorio has the potential to generate serious downhill plane, but, like many of his towering colleagues, he struggles to repeat his mechanics. As a result, his command is below average at present and might not come around enough for him to pitch out of a big-league rotation, where he'd have third-starter upside if all broke right. More likely, Gregorio will eventually settle into a relief role, where his lankiness would be less of a detriment and his low-90s fastball could more frequently scrape 95. Now 23, Gregorio needs to fare better in a second try at High-A to resurface on the organization's top 10 list.

Juan Gutierrez   RHP

Born: 7/14/83   Age: 31   Bats: R   Throws: R   Height: 6'3"   Weight: 245

YEAR	TEAM	LVL	AGE	W	L	SV	G	GS	IP	H	HR	BB	K	BB/9	K/9	GB%	BABIP	WHIP	ERA	FIP	FRA	WARP
2012	OMA	AAA	28	0	1	0	10	0	11	13	2	3	7	2.5	5.7	23%	.297	1.45	8.18	5.57	6.00	0.0
2013	ANA	MLB	29	1	4	0	28	0	26	26	3	12	28	4.2	9.7	42%	.315	1.46	5.19	3.81	4.28	0.1
2013	KCA	MLB	29	0	1	0	25	0	29¹	30	2	8	17	2.5	5.2	42%	.304	1.30	3.38	3.72	4.07	0.3
2014	SFN	MLB	30	1	2	0	61	0	63²	60	7	16	44	2.3	6.2	39%	.266	1.19	3.96	4.00	4.66	-0.4
2015	SFN	MLB	31	3	1	0	54	0	55¹	53	6	17	46	2.8	7.4	40%	.305	1.26	4.00	4.12	4.35	0.0

Breakout: 24%   Improve: 45%   Collapse: 23%   Attrition: 17%   MLB: 81%   *Comparables: Luis Vizcaino, Travis Harper, Esteban Yan*

Gutierrez is a multitasking graduate student's dream: His pace is slow enough for one to get a page of reading done between pitches. When he gets into trouble, as he frequently did during the second half, an entire chapter could be put to bed by the time he was removed from the game. From April through early August, the hard-throwing journeyman looked like the Giants' latest bullpen scavenging revelation, but he spent the final two months turning everyone into the 2013 version of Miguel Cabrera. Designated for assignment in November, Gutierrez will have to fight for a middle-relief job in spring training.

Tim Hudson   RHP

Born: 7/14/75   Age: 39   Bats: R   Throws: R   Height: 6'1"   Weight: 175

YEAR	TEAM	LVL	AGE	W	L	SV	G	GS	IP	H	HR	BB	K	BB/9	K/9	GB%	BABIP	WHIP	ERA	FIP	FRA	WARP
2012	GWN	AAA	36	2	0	0	2	2	10²	8	0	5	8	4.2	6.8	62%	.235	1.22	0.84	3.06	4.41	0.1
2012	ATL	MLB	36	16	7	0	28	28	179	168	12	48	102	2.4	5.1	56%	.270	1.21	3.62	3.82	5.09	0.1
2013	ATL	MLB	37	8	7	0	21	21	131¹	120	10	36	95	2.5	6.5	57%	.281	1.19	3.97	3.43	4.07	1.6
2014	SFN	MLB	38	9	13	0	31	31	189¹	199	15	34	120	1.6	5.7	54%	.300	1.23	3.57	3.51	4.55	-0.5
2015	SFN	MLB	39	8	9	0	24	24	152	142	11	38	99	2.2	5.9	56%	.296	1.18	3.49	3.86	3.80	1.3

Breakout: 7%   Improve: 31%   Collapse: 10%   Attrition: 4%   MLB: 70%   *Comparables: Derek Lowe, Hiroki Kuroda, Andy Pettitte*

If you ever doubt that there's a silver lining to every cloud, Hudson's year might change your mind. The old man sustained a gruesome ankle injury in July 2013 that threatened his career, but it also depressed his value enough to tempt the Giants, who were searching for affordable mid-rotation arms. The weakened ankle prevented Hudson from pushing off the rubber as forcefully as he once did, but that kept his mechanics in check such that he walked only two batters in 45 2/3 April innings. A bum hip dogged Hudson throughout September, but he contributed to victories in the Division and Championship Series. Then, as the oldest pitcher to start Game Seven of the World Series, Hudson departed without finishing the second inning—which helped get his new best friend, Madison Bumgarner, into the game, and you know the rest. Hudson will turn 40 during the coming year, but throwing strikes and coaxing grounders are skills that age well, and the old man should remain a useful starter in what he says will be his last year.

Christian Jones   LHP

Born: 1/27/91   Age: 24   Bats: L   Throws: L   Height: 6'3"   Weight: 210

YEAR	TEAM	LVL	AGE	W	L	SV	G	GS	IP	H	HR	BB	K	BB/9	K/9	GB%	BABIP	WHIP	ERA	FIP	FRA	WARP
2013	SLO	A-	22	2	0	0	11	0	13²	14	1	2	14	1.3	9.2	69%	.317	1.17	3.29	2.88	3.70	0.3
2014	AUG	A	23	5	9	0	22	22	110²	96	6	26	100	2.1	8.1	59%	.288	1.10	3.33	3.43	5.03	0.7
2015	SFN	MLB	24	4	6	0	23	14	79²	83	8	31	54	3.5	6.1	52%	.318	1.43	4.75	4.64	5.16	-0.5

Breakout: 0%   Improve: 0%   Collapse: 0%   Attrition: 0%   MLB: 0%   *Comparables: Yohan Flande, Jason Berken, Tobi Stoner*

Born and raised in the East Bay suburb of Danville, Jones' path to the Giants organization took him through Eugene, Oregon, where he enjoyed a fine sophomore year as a starter for the Ducks before succumbing to Tommy John surgery and returning as a reliever. The Giants remembered pre-operation Jones when they snagged him in the 18th round and could not have been more pleased with the southpaw's first full professional season. At 23, Jones was old for Low-A, but he has the stuff and the frame to start, and would be further up the chain if not for the elbow trouble that is now more than two years in the rearview. Once regarded as a potential top-three-round talent, Jones has fourth starter upside and could eventually be regarded as one of the steals of the 2013 draft.

Tim Lincecum   RHP

Born: 6/15/84   Age: 31   Bats: L   Throws: R   Height: 5'11"   Weight: 170

YEAR	TEAM	LVL	AGE	W	L	SV	G	GS	IP	H	HR	BB	K	BB/9	K/9	GB%	BABIP	WHIP	ERA	FIP	FRA	WARP
2012	SFN	MLB	28	10	15	0	33	33	186	183	23	90	190	4.4	9.2	47%	.309	1.47	5.18	4.22	4.77	0.0
2013	SFN	MLB	29	10	14	0	32	32	197²	184	21	76	193	3.5	8.8	47%	.300	1.32	4.37	3.71	3.96	1.2
2014	SFN	MLB	30	12	9	1	33	26	155²	154	19	63	134	3.6	7.7	49%	.299	1.39	4.74	4.28	5.09	-1.2
2015	SFN	MLB	31	7	9	0	23	23	140	126	14	51	140	3.3	9.0	47%	.317	1.27	3.83	3.80	4.17	0.6

Breakout: 18%   Improve: 50%   Collapse: 15%   Attrition: 22%   MLB: 90%   *Comparables: Ted Lilly, Ervin Santana, Jorge De La Rosa*

The Giants gave Lincecum $35 million to stay in San Francisco, rewarding him for past glories and hoping against hope for even a small rebound. Unfortunately, while hope springs eternal, velocity does not, and Lincecum's continued to decline. As troubling as the fastball's recession toward the Reagan era is the downtrend in the power of Lincecum's breaking stuff: Both the curve and slider have seen a five-mph drop since 2011, and the whiff rate on the latter tumbled from over 18 percent in 2013 to less than 15 percent last year. The Giants have 18 million reasons to try to fix Lincecum, but all the money and effort in the world can't make a cooked goose waddle again.

Javier Lopez   LHP

Born: 7/11/77   Age: 37   Bats: L   Throws: L   Height: 6'4"   Weight: 220

YEAR	TEAM	LVL	AGE	W	L	SV	G	GS	IP	H	HR	BB	K	BB/9	K/9	GB%	BABIP	WHIP	ERA	FIP	FRA	WARP
2012	SFN	MLB	34	3	0	7	70	0	70	36	37	1	14	28	3.5	7.0	60%	.318	1.42	2.50	3.11	2.94	0.4
2013	SFN	MLB	35	4	2	1	69	0	39¹	30	1	12	37	2.7	8.5	65%	.261	1.07	1.83	2.38	2.02	0.7
2014	SFN	MLB	36	1	1	0	65	0	37²	31	2	19	22	4.5	5.3	68%	.238	1.33	3.11	4.30	4.74	-0.3
2015	SFN	MLB	37	3	1	1	62	0	37²	33	2	14	30	3.3	7.3	58%	.301	1.23	3.35	3.61	3.65	0.4

Breakout: 24%   Improve: 43%   Collapse: 19%   Attrition: 9%   MLB: 73%   Comparables: Salomon Torres, Scott Downs, Fernando Rodney

On May 12, 2014, at AT&T Park, Freddie Freeman hit the shot heard 'round the LOOGY world: a mammoth splash hit, and the first long ball Lopez had ever allowed to a lefty while wearing the Giants' home colors. Considering that Lopez came to the Giants at the 2010 trading deadline, the blast was nearly four years in the making, and it presaged the sidewinding southpaw's worst year in San Francisco to date. Lopez still clamped down on like-handed batters, but his command wavered, forcing him into fastball counts and limiting the extent to which he could lean on his bread-and-butter slider. With two years and $10 million left on his contract, the Giants will hope that Lopez can resume keeping lefties at bay instead of watching as the ball flies into it.

Jean Machi   RHP

Born: 2/1/82   Age: 33   Bats: R   Throws: R   Height: 6'0"   Weight: 255

YEAR	TEAM	LVL	AGE	W	L	SV	G	GS	IP	H	HR	BB	K	BB/9	K/9	GB%	BABIP	WHIP	ERA	FIP	FRA	WARP
2012	FRE	AAA	30	2	1	15	53	0	56²	67	7	17	44	2.7	7.0	52%	.323	1.48	3.97	4.78	6.30	0.3
2012	SFN	MLB	30	0	0	0	8	0	6²	7	2	1	4	1.4	5.4	39%	.238	1.20	6.75	6.29	6.54	-0.1
2013	FRE	AAA	31	3	1	2	16	0	18¹	13	0	3	19	1.5	9.3	47%	.289	0.87	0.98	2.15	2.94	0.4
2013	SFN	MLB	31	3	1	0	51	0	53	46	2	12	51	2.0	8.7	54%	.301	1.09	2.38	2.27	3.10	1.0
2014	SFN	MLB	32	7	1	2	71	0	66¹	45	5	18	51	2.4	6.9	55%	.230	0.95	2.58	3.40	4.07	0.6
2015	SFN	MLB	33	3	1	1	55	0	56¹	49	5	16	49	2.6	7.9	49%	.302	1.15	3.28	3.70	3.57	0.6

Breakout: 24%   Improve: 29%   Collapse: 13%   Attrition: 19%   MLB: 45%   Comparables: Dale Thayer, Pat Neshek, Chris Bootcheck

As goes Machi's splitter, so goes Machi, whose fastball touches 95 but tends to find barrels, and whose—no, what you're about to read is not a misprint—4.1 speed from home-to-first rarely sees the light of day. From April through June 21st, he feasted on opponents with his forkball, en route to a league-leading 0.29 ERA and zero home runs allowed. Five days later, Brandon Phillips blasted off at Machi's expense, setting off a second-half spiral that carried through a disappointing October. The right-hander lost his feel for the off-speed weapon, repeatedly sailing it thigh-high, where it was about as effective as a cafeteria spork against a well-done steak. A longtime minor leaguer who took a decade to reach The Show, Machi can only hope that a winter of rest brings the bite back to his forkball, because hangers in March could mean more bus rides and motel stays until it returns.

Adalberto Mejia   LHP

Born: 6/20/93   Age: 22   Bats: R   Throws: L   Height: 6'3"   Weight: 195

YEAR	TEAM	LVL	AGE	W	L	SV	G	GS	IP	H	HR	BB	K	BB/9	K/9	GB%	BABIP	WHIP	ERA	FIP	FRA	WARP
2012	AUG	A	19	10	7	0	30	14	106²	122	4	21	79	1.8	6.7	44%	.332	1.34	3.97	3.29	4.16	1.2
2013	SJO	A+	20	7	4	0	16	16	87	75	11	23	89	2.4	9.2	38%	.277	1.13	3.31	4.20	4.50	1.2
2014	RIC	AA	21	7	9	0	22	21	108	119	9	31	82	2.6	6.8	36%	.326	1.39	4.67	3.78	4.38	1.3
2015	SFN	MLB	22	4	7	0	17	17	90²	98	10	29	59	2.9	5.9	39%	.320	1.40	4.72	4.52	5.13	-0.6

Breakout: 0%   Improve: 0%   Collapse: 0%   Attrition: 0%   MLB: 0%   Comparables: Jeanmar Gomez, Vance Worley, Will Smith

Keury Mella   RHP

Born: 8/2/93   Age: 21   Bats: R   Throws: R   Height: 6'2"   Weight: 200

YEAR	TEAM	LVL	AGE	W	L	SV	G	GS	IP	H	HR	BB	K	BB/9	K/9	GB%	BABIP	WHIP	ERA	FIP	FRA	WARP
2014	AUG	A	20	3	3	0	12	12	66¹	69	1	13	63	1.8	8.5	62%	.337	1.24	3.93	2.79	3.49	1.4
2014	SLO	A-	20	1	1	0	6	6	19²	16	0	6	20	2.7	9.2	47%	.302	1.12	1.83	3.00	3.82	0.6
2015	SFN	MLB	21	3	6	0	14	14	66¹	71	6	29	47	3.9	6.4	51%	.326	1.50	4.93	4.58	5.36	-0.5

Breakout: 0%   Improve: 0%   Collapse: 0%   Attrition: 0%   MLB: 0%   Comparables: Edwin Escobar, Jordan Walden, Kyle Lobstein

It's been 20 years since a Dominican pitcher last logged 100 innings in a Giants uniform. It's been even longer since the Giants—currently regarded as one of the most adept organizations in the league at developing pitching talent—have signed and groomed a hurler from the baseball hotbed into a rotation fixture. The Dominican Dandy, who left for Boston after the 1973 season, has lived long enough to see his statue erected outside of the team's ballpark but is still waiting for a fellow countryman to follow in his footsteps.

San Francisco's homegrown pitching drought actually extends to Venezuela, too, as Yusmeiro Petit—originally signed by the Mets in 2001—last year became the first pitcher from the Land of Grace to reach the 100-inning plateau in orange and black since Ramon Monzant in 1958, the Giants' first year on the west coast. The current composition of the club's farm system suggests that Monzant's trail might remain unhiked for years. Juan Marichal, on the other hand, could soon see his blazed again.

Born 43 days apart in Bonao, a city of some 125,000 in the center of the Dominican Republic, Mejia and Mella are two of the organization's most highly regarded international pitching prospects. Two levels ahead on the minor-league chain, Mejia is likely to reach the majors sooner, and either he or Kendry Flores should have first crack at snapping the streak. Mella, who battled a minor rotator-cuff ailment in 2014, might boast more upside but also faces a path fraught with injury and stuff-progression risk.

The left-handed Mejia is a three-pitch southpaw who ranks as the top arm in the system, but he'll sit out the first 50 games of the year after testing positive for a banned stimulant in November. His fastball sits in the low 90s and can light up 95, though the life and location on the heater erode when he amps up. His changeup plays well off the fastball and his curve is slowly becoming more consistent. All three offerings should be above average, and all three have plus potential. Still just 21, Mejia could round into a no. 3 starter, and he's a safer bet to reach his ceiling than either Tyler Beede or Kyle Crick.

Mella's arsenal is more explosive: His fastball has plus-plus potential with the velocity and bowling-ball sink to be a weapon, and his curveball already flashes plus shape when he snaps it off properly. The changeup is the laggard here, mooching off the heater but failing to impress on its own. Besides the shoulder trouble, the main concern with Mella is his delivery, which contains significant crossfire and arm recoil in his follow through. He might have more upside than Mejia if he sticks in the rotation, but the medicals and mechanics point to a bullpen future, where he could thrive in the late innings but would leave Marichal's footsteps unfollowed.

Steven Okert   LHP

Born: 7/9/91   Age: 23   Bats: L   Throws: L   Height: 6'3"   Weight: 210

YEAR	TEAM	LVL	AGE	W	L	SV	G	GS	IP	H	HR	BB	K	BB/9	K/9	GB%	BABIP	WHIP	ERA	FIP	FRA	WARP
2012	SLO	A-	20	2	0	0	15	0	26²	26	0	11	22	3.7	7.4	67%	.306	1.39	2.36	3.36	3.80	0.6
2013	AUG	A	21	2	2	2	44	0	60²	55	3	24	59	3.6	8.8	48%	.302	1.30	2.97	3.42	3.95	0.4
2014	SJO	A+	22	1	2	19	33	0	35¹	33	2	11	54	2.8	13.8	45%	.373	1.25	1.53	2.52	1.13	2.0
2014	RIC	AA	22	1	0	5	24	0	33	24	3	11	38	3.0	10.4	43%	.266	1.06	2.73	3.23	3.83	0.5
2015	SFN	MLB	23	2	1	2	44	0	58²	55	5	24	54	3.7	8.3	46%	.321	1.35	4.15	3.93	4.51	-0.1

Breakout: 0%   Improve: 0%   Collapse: 0%   Attrition: 0%   MLB: 0%   Comparables: Daniel Stange, Gus Schlosser, C.C. Lee

The Giants plucked Okert out of the University of Oklahoma, where he flashed the makings of two plus pitches but never got the instruction he needed to settle on a stable delivery. The 2011 fourth-rounder has come a long way with two and a half years of professional coaching and is now on the fast track to the major-league bullpen. Okert's easy-plus fastball has him ticketed for the late innings, and his solid-average slider is already lethal against arm-side batters. With a bit more polish on the breaking ball, he could tackle the southpaw side of a setup tandem by the end of the year.

Jake Peavy   RHP

Born: 5/31/81   Age: 34   Bats: R   Throws: R   Height: 6'1"   Weight: 195

YEAR	TEAM	LVL	AGE	W	L	SV	G	GS	IP	H	HR	BB	K	BB/9	K/9	GB%	BABIP	WHIP	ERA	FIP	FRA	WARP
2012	CHA	MLB	31	11	12	0	32	32	219	191	27	49	194	2.0	8.0	37%	.272	1.10	3.37	3.69	4.41	2.7
2013	BOS	MLB	32	4	1	0	10	10	64²	56	6	19	45	2.6	6.3	30%	.256	1.16	4.04	3.82	3.99	0.8
2013	CHA	MLB	32	8	4	0	13	13	80	74	14	17	76	1.9	8.6	36%	.278	1.14	4.28	4.13	4.72	0.3
2014	BOS	MLB	33	1	9	0	20	20	124	131	20	46	100	3.3	7.3	42%	.301	1.43	4.72	4.83	5.18	-0.2
2014	SFN	MLB	33	6	4	0	12	12	78²	65	3	17	58	1.9	6.6	40%	.270	1.04	2.17	3.00	3.68	0.5
2015	SFN	MLB	34	10	10	0	28	28	175	158	16	39	152	2.0	7.8	38%	.303	1.13	3.35	3.54	3.65	1.8

Breakout: 20%   Improve: 42%   Collapse: 18%   Attrition: 8%   MLB: 81%   Comparables: Colby Lewis, Ben Sheets, Ted Lilly

Traded to the eventual World Series winner in back-to-back years, Peavy now has a mobile cable-car bar to go with his duck boat. The Alabaman debuted at the legal drinking age and is younger than you think, but he also has mileage and a unique shoulder surgery on his arm. Still almost as good as he once was a time or two through the order, Peavy can navigate five or six solid innings, but opponents read him like a bad tell in their third trips to the box. If you're in the market for a 170-inning back-end starter, Peavy's your man; those seeking a workhorse are advised to look elsewhere.

Yusmeiro Petit   RHP

Born: 11/22/84   Age: 30   Bats: R   Throws: R   Height: 6'1"   Weight: 250

YEAR	TEAM	LVL	AGE	W	L	SV	G	GS	IP	H	HR	BB	K	BB/9	K/9	GB%	BABIP	WHIP	ERA	FIP	FRA	WARP
2012	FRE	AAA	27	7	7	0	28	28	166²	178	14	36	153	1.9	8.3	32%	.330	1.28	3.46	3.59	3.70	4.6
2012	SFN	MLB	27	0	0	0	1	1	4²	7	0	4	1	7.7	1.9	41%	.412	2.36	3.86	5.28	4.42	0.0
2013	FRE	AAA	28	5	6	0	15	15	87²	92	16	13	91	1.3	9.3	38%	.315	1.20	4.52	4.31	4.72	1.1
2013	SFN	MLB	28	4	1	0	8	7	48	46	4	11	47	2.1	8.8	33%	.313	1.19	3.56	2.83	3.04	1.0
2014	SFN	MLB	29	5	5	0	39	12	117	97	12	22	133	1.7	10.2	36%	.290	1.02	3.69	2.75	3.58	1.1
2015	SFN	MLB	30	5	5	0	22	15	101¹	92	10	20	98	1.8	8.7	34%	.312	1.11	3.30	3.26	3.58	1.2

Breakout: 16%   Improve: 22%   Collapse: 13%   Attrition: 17%   MLB: 43%   Comparables: Buddy Carlyle, Guillermo Moscoso, Garrett Mock

Half a decade ago, Petit's dreams of a major-league career were on life support. He was two years removed from his last big-league trial, and his middling stuff was as poor a fit for the desert as it was for the bandboxes of the Pacific Coast League, where he toiled aimlessly in 2010 before crossing the border. For many players, like Greg Aquino, Benji Gil and Josh Towers—with whom Petit shared the 2011 Guerreros de Oaxaca clubhouse—a trip to the Mexican League represents the twilight of their days in uniform. For Petit, it turned out to be the sunrise.

The Venezuelan caught the Giants' eye in Oaxaca, and the organization tendered a minor-league offer that put Petit in the hands of its instructors. Suddenly, in 2012, the PCL was no longer so scary. A year later, Petit came within an out of throwing a perfect game. The next year, he broke a record by retiring 46 consecutive hitters. Two months after that, he became the first pitcher ever to log three scoreless relief appearances of three or more innings in the same postseason.

Joining the Giants was Petit's saving grace, as major-league pitching coach Dave Righetti was the late-bloomer's Miracle-Gro. When Petit came to Scottsdale three springs ago, Righetti tweaked his fizzling curveball, advising him to throw it harder and with a slurvier shape. That breaking ball rapidly blossomed into one of the league's best. In 2014, Petit's curve lapped the circuit in both opponents' swing rate and their whiffs-per-swing ratio, a deadly combination made even more lethal by the deception in his delivery and his pinpoint fastball command.

Thanks to Righetti's tutelage, Petit now stands alongside Gregor Blanco and Ryan Vogelsong in Sabean's string of recent junkyard finds. If Madison Bumgarner was the most valuable player in the Giants' run to their third title in five years, Petit was the unsung hero. And the evolution of his curveball into a dominant secondary pitch provides reason to believe that he won't break down as suddenly as he broke out.

Sergio Romo   RHP

Born: 3/4/83   Age: 32   Bats: R   Throws: R   Height: 5'10"   Weight: 185

YEAR	TEAM	LVL	AGE	W	L	SV	G	GS	IP	H	HR	BB	K	BB/9	K/9	GB%	BABIP	WHIP	ERA	FIP	FRA	WARP
2012	SFN	MLB	29	4	2	14	69	0	55¹	37	5	10	63	1.6	10.2	50%	.239	0.85	1.79	2.74	2.85	0.8
2013	SFN	MLB	30	5	8	38	65	0	60¹	53	5	12	58	1.8	8.7	42%	.276	1.08	2.54	2.82	3.31	0.8
2014	SFN	MLB	31	6	4	23	64	0	58	43	9	12	59	1.9	9.2	38%	.233	0.95	3.72	3.91	4.50	-0.1
2015	SFN	MLB	32	4	2	29	64	0	54	41	5	9	62	1.6	10.2	41%	.291	0.93	2.30	2.79	2.50	1.3

Breakout: 22%   Improve: 40%   Collapse: 30%   Attrition: 5%   MLB: 92%   Comparables: Jonathan Papelbon, Rafael Soriano, Dan Wheeler

An atypical closer with a subpar fastball for the job, Romo set out last spring to learn a changeup to combat lefties and complement his Frisbee slider. It was an admirable idea, but the best-laid plans of mice and men often go thigh-high. As Romo tried to gain feel for the cambio, his slider stopped sliding and Bochy lost faith after a June 28th loss to the Reds in which Romo blew his fifth save and surrendered his fifth homer on a slider. A move back to setup duties relaxed the need for the changeup, and suddenly, the slider was making foes look foolish again, as the offering's 29-to-1 K:BB ratio from July through September will attest. (He throws the slider more on three-ball counts than the fastball, incidentally.) After a first-half blip, Romo should return to being one of the game's elite set-up men as long as the slider is back for good.

Chris Stratton   RHP

Born: 8/22/90   Age: 24   Bats: R   Throws: R   Height: 6'3"   Weight: 186

YEAR	TEAM	LVL	AGE	W	L	SV	G	GS	IP	H	HR	BB	K	BB/9	K/9	GB%	BABIP	WHIP	ERA	FIP	FRA	WARP
2012	SLO	A-	21	0	1	0	8	5	16¹	14	1	10	16	5.5	8.8	50%	.302	1.47	2.76	4.37	5.41	0.2
2013	AUG	A	22	9	3	0	22	22	132	128	5	47	123	3.2	8.4	49%	.327	1.33	3.27	3.25	4.05	1.0
2014	SJO	A+	23	7	8	0	19	18	99¹	103	13	36	102	3.3	9.2	49%	.328	1.40	5.07	4.54	4.92	1.2
2014	RIC	AA	23	1	1	0	5	5	23	29	2	12	18	4.7	7.0	53%	.360	1.78	3.52	4.49	4.57	0.1
2015	SFN	MLB	24	5	9	0	21	21	109	116	11	47	79	3.9	6.5	46%	.326	1.49	4.97	4.61	5.40	-1.0

Breakout: 0%   Improve: 0%   Collapse: 0%   Attrition: 0%   MLB: 0%   *Comparables:*   *Jose A. Ramirez, Alex Wilson, Rob Rasmussen*

Some saw Stratton as a draft-day steal when the Giants nabbed him 20th overall in 2012, pointing to a high-upside college arm that would fit on a no. 2 starter. However, the former Mississippi State Bulldog's fastball has not progressed as hoped, chiefly because his arm speed has dwindled and the arm tends to play catch-up in the delivery. On the bright side, Stratton's slider still has plus projection and he stands a good chance of staying in the rotation with a modest grade jump in his changeup. This is more of a finesse profile than some envisioned when Stratton sliced through the SEC as a junior, but there are worse outcomes for a top-20 selection than untold hundreds of innings as a back-end starter.

Hunter Strickland   RHP

Born: 9/24/88   Age: 26   Bats: R   Throws: R   Height: 6'4"   Weight: 220

YEAR	TEAM	LVL	AGE	W	L	SV	G	GS	IP	H	HR	BB	K	BB/9	K/9	GB%	BABIP	WHIP	ERA	FIP	FRA	WARP
2012	BRD	A+	23	2	2	0	10	9	45¹	47	5	8	25	1.6	5.0	44%	.292	1.21	2.98	4.65	5.45	0.2
2012	ALT	AA	23	2	2	2	23	0	42¹	50	5	15	33	3.2	7.0	51%	.352	1.54	4.46	4.45	4.91	0.1
2013	SJO	A+	24	1	0	9	20	0	21	10	1	5	23	2.1	9.9	51%	.196	0.71	0.86	3.06	3.44	0.4
2014	RIC	AA	25	1	1	11	38	0	35²	25	3	4	48	1.0	12.1	41%	.275	0.81	2.02	2.09	2.86	0.9
2014	SFN	MLB	25	1	0	1	9	0	7	5	0	0	9	0.0	11.6	56%	.312	0.71	0.00	0.53	1.49	0.2
2015	SFN	MLB	26	2	1	1	25	2	37¹	37	4	11	29	2.5	7.0	45%	.320	1.28	4.19	4.24	4.56	0.0

Breakout: 13%   Improve: 16%   Collapse: 3%   Attrition: 9%   MLB: 21%   *Comparables:*   *Jeremy Horst, Sandy Rosario, Bryan Price*

As you're reading this, the bomb Bryce Harper hit off Strickland in Game One of the NLDS is landing somewhere in eastern Maryland. The righty learned the hard way in October that major-league hitters can turn around a high-90s fastball if it comes in straight—and whether you prefer to call it life, movement, run, tail or wiggle, the Georgia native's heater doesn't have it. After briefly looking like the Giants' closer of the future, the former Red Sox and Pirate reminded the world why he was once cut in favor of Jonathan Sanchez—the 2013 version. With tight break on his slider and good fade on his changeup, Strickland could work his way back into a high-leverage bullpen role, but he'll need to impress some sink or cut upon his fastball to realize that potential in 2015.

Ryan Vogelsong   RHP

Born: 7/22/77   Age: 37   Bats: R   Throws: R   Height: 6'4"   Weight: 215

YEAR	TEAM	LVL	AGE	W	L	SV	G	GS	IP	H	HR	BB	K	BB/9	K/9	GB%	BABIP	WHIP	ERA	FIP	FRA	WARP
2012	FRE	AAA	34	1	0	0	2	2	10	9	0	4	12	3.6	10.8	48%	.360	1.30	1.80	2.47	2.48	0.4
2012	SFN	MLB	34	14	9	0	31	31	189²	171	17	62	158	2.9	7.5	44%	.284	1.23	3.37	3.74	3.84	1.8
2013	RIC	AA	35	2	0	0	2	2	11	10	1	2	8	1.6	6.5	38%	.290	1.09	0.82	3.60	3.52	0.2
2013	SFN	MLB	35	4	6	0	19	19	103²	124	15	38	67	3.3	5.8	42%	.320	1.56	5.73	4.88	5.26	-0.4
2014	SFN	MLB	36	8	13	0	32	32	184²	178	18	58	151	2.8	7.4	41%	.294	1.28	4.00	3.82	4.36	0.8
2015	SFN	MLB	37	7	10	0	25	25	143¹	142	14	50	115	3.1	7.3	43%	.318	1.34	4.37	4.20	4.75	-0.4

Breakout: 5%   Improve: 30%   Collapse: 16%   Attrition: 19%   MLB: 64%   *Comparables:*   *Chan Ho Park, Kenshin Kawakami, Jason Schmidt*

On October 7th at AT&T Park, in Game Four of the NLDS, Vogelsong kicked and dealt, and the ball came out of his hand traveling faster than 95 mph. The last time the right-hander had thrown a major-league pitch that hard was more than two years earlier, on September 21st, 2012. In between, Vogelsong turned into a pumpkin whose days as a big leaguer seemed numbered. His heater wavered between 88 and 91 in 2013, and hitters slugged over .470 against four of Vogelsong's five offerings, sparing only his cutter. Curiously, though, Vogelsong's velocity bounced back last year and brought his performance up with it. Then, adrenaline kicked in, and the mid-90s were no longer a distant afterthought. Those are reserved for the October stage, it appears, but even consistent 92s make Vogelsong a useful back-end starter.

Luis Ysla   LHP

Born: 4/27/92   Age: 23   Bats: L   Throws: L   Height: 6'1"   Weight: 185

YEAR	TEAM	LVL	AGE	W	L	SV	G	GS	IP	H	HR	BB	K	BB/9	K/9	GB%	BABIP	WHIP	ERA	FIP	FRA	WARP
2014	AUG	A	22	6	7	0	24	23	121¹	104	8	45	115	3.3	8.5	47%	.287	1.23	2.45	3.93	4.28	1.5
2015	SFN	MLB	23	4	8	0	19	19	93	96	9	43	66	4.2	6.4	45%	.317	1.49	4.97	4.77	5.40	-0.8

Breakout: 0%   Improve: 0%   Collapse: 0%   Attrition: 0%   MLB: 0%   *Comparables:*   *Bryan Mitchell, Jose A. Ramirez, Wilking Rodriguez*

Any time a pitcher goes straight from the Arizona League to full-season ball and proceeds to lead his circuit in ERA, he is bound to open eyes. That was the case for Ysla, an older international addition signed out of Venezuela in 2012 for the cost of a used Ford Focus. At 22, Ysla handled the age-appropriate assignment well, but his two-pitch arsenal and herky-jerky mechanics temper scouts' expectations. Both his fastball and slider could play up to plus in a bullpen role, giving Ysla a LOOGY floor and a setup ceiling with a late-2016 ETA. A more patient approach would entail smoothing out the delivery and honing what is currently a nascent changeup to mold him into a starter, though scouts diverge on whether Ysla's back-end upside would justify that time investment. The role in which he is used this year will reveal his club's intentions.

Lineouts

Hitters

NAME	POS	TEAM	LVL	AGE	PA	R	2B	3B	HR	RBI	BB	K	SB	CS	AVG/OBP/SLG	TAv	BABIP	BRR	FRAA	WARP
Ehire Adrianza	2B	FRE	AAA	24	22	6	0	0	1	1	2	4	0	0	.316/.381/.474	.338	.357	0.3	2B(3): 0.5, SS(2): 0.3	0.5
	2B	SFN	MLB	24	106	10	6	0	0	5	5	22	1	1	.237/.279/.299	.230	.303	0.1	2B(25): 0.7, SS(7): 0.2	0.1
Daniel Carbonell	CF	SJO	A+	23	100	17	3	3	3	12	6	19	7	2	.344/.390/.538	.325	.408	0.3	CF(19): 1.9	1.2
Tyler Colvin	RF	FRE	AAA	28	176	21	9	2	2	18	11	43	1	0	.227/.278/.344	.205	.294	1.4	RF(26): 1.0, LF(12): 0.8	-0.4
	LF	SFN	MLB	28	149	16	10	3	2	18	8	45	1	0	.223/.268/.381	.239	.312	1.7	LF(43): -2.1, CF(3): -0.1	0.1
Dylan Davis	RF	SLO	A-	20	93	11	0	0	4	7	7	23	1	0	.200/.269/.341	.210	.224	0.4	RF(10): -1.0, LF(5): -0.9	-0.5
Chris Dominguez	RF	FRE	AAA	27	528	66	23	3	21	85	22	143	21	10	.274/.307/.460	.266	.340	0.0	RF(39): -0.5, SS(33): 1.7	2.2
	LF	SFN	MLB	27	18	1	0	0	1	2	1	4	0	0	.059/.111/.235	.150	.000	0.0	LF(5): 0.5, 3B(1): -0.0	-0.2
Johneshwy Fargas	CF	SLO	A-	19	208	33	6	0	3	13	24	27	15	6	.240/.373/.329	.276	.268	0.7	CF(25): -3.6, LF(20): 0.8	0.6
Brandon Hicks	2B	FRE	AAA	28	152	18	11	0	6	17	14	49	0	0	.218/.311/.436	.248	.295	-0.1	2B(28): -1.1, 3B(10): -0.2	0.0
	2B	SFN	MLB	28	242	27	6	1	8	22	32	77	0	1	.162/.280/.319	.231	.208	1.9	2B(61): -0.3, LF(1): -0.0	0.3
Brett Jackson	RF	IOW	AAA	25	252	23	8	4	5	20	24	94	4	6	.210/.298/.348	.228	.336	-1.6	RF(48): 3.0, LF(14): -0.2	-0.4
	RF	ARI	MLB	25	5	0	0	0	0	0	0	1	1	0	0	.000/.200/.000	.118	.000	-0.2	RF(4): 0.1, CF(1): 0.0	-0.1
Nick Noonan	2B	SJO	A+	25	20	1	1	0	1	2	1	4	0	0	.158/.300/.368	.170	.143	-0.1	2B(4): 0.1	-0.1
	SS	FRE	AAA	25	406	38	16	0	3	24	20	98	6	5	.237/.282/.303	.204	.312	2.1	SS(77): 1.6, 3B(14): 0.6	-0.7
Jarrett Parker	RF	RIC	AA	25	419	52	20	6	12	58	45	103	11	4	.275/.370/.463	.293	.353	-0.5	RF(70): -3.3, CF(30): -2.0	1.9
	RF	FRE	AAA	25	89	13	5	0	3	10	9	23	1	2	.278/.360/.456	.302	.358	1.1	RF(22): 0.4	0.8
Carlos Triunfel	SS	ABQ	AAA	24	321	28	12	4	4	40	12	55	2	1	.223/.256/.330	.194	.258	0.2	SS(59): 1.8, 2B(24): -0.6	-0.8
	SS	LAN	MLB	24	16	3	0	0	1	1	1	5	0	0	.133/.188/.333	.201	.111	0.2	SS(10): -0.5	-0.1
Angel Villalona	1B	RIC	AA	23	400	35	18	4	10	54	23	94	1	1	.227/.290/.381	.239	.278	0.8	1B(85): -1.5	-0.6
Mac Williamson	DH	SJO	A+	23	100	16	7	0	3	11	13	14	6	1	.318/.420/.506	.336	.353	0.9		1.0

Ehire Adrianza is a quick-twitch athlete with smooth infield actions, but he is prone to mental errors and will not hit enough to be more than a glove-first utility man. ❖ A low-profile Cuban defector signed in June for $1.4 million, **Daniel Carbonell** brings plus-plus speed and decent raw power, but his awkwardly mechanical swing might not work against upper-level pitching. ❖ Injuries are a part of the game, and thus so is **Tyler Colvin**, who can park one on occasion while filling in at left, right or first. ❖ **Dylan Davis** was a two-way player at Oregon State, and by coupling the plus arm he used on the mound with his plus raw pop at the plate, he might emerge as a power-hitting right fielder down the road. ❖ The Giants tried to nurture **Chris Dominguez**'s versatility, even giving him 33 games at shortstop for Fresno, but the 6-foot-4, 235-pounder is miscast beyond the corners and will struggle to shed the Quad-A tag. ❖ Puerto Rico Baseball Academy product **Johneshwy Fargas** exhibited fine plate discipline and could emerge as a fourth outfielder with the ability to handle all three positions. Bonus: His given name already resembles a ballplayer's illegible signature. ❖ **Brandon Hicks** slugged seven homers in his first 114 Giants plate appearances, earning comparisons to yesteryear Dan Uggla; he proceeded to hit like present-day Dan Uggla and eventually lost his job. (Eight days later, the Giants signed Dan Uggla.) ❖ In August, Kevin Towers collected **Brett Jackson**, a former crown jewel in the Cubs' collection, in hopes that a fresh start would lead to better results. In his debut with his new organization Jackson went 0-5 with four strikeouts. Arizona quickly moved on from both people named in this lineout. ❖ Outrighted on August 3rd, **Nick Noonan** will remain in extra-infielder conversations thanks mainly to his left-handedness. ❖ Left-handed thump might keep **Jarrett Parker** around as an extra outfielder, but the holes in his swing will prevent him from emerging as a regular. ❖ This is **Carlos Triunfel**'s eighth book comment. The first five noted how young he was for his level. This one will note that he's terrible. ❖ Keeping **Angel Villalona** on your 40-man roster is like storing a long-ago ex-girlfriend's number in your cell phone; you'll probably never call, but you just can't let go. ❖ Johnathan Mackensey Williamson, or **Mac Williamson** in baseball parlance, has oodles of raw power, but Tommy John surgery in April stunted his development, and he might lack the pitch recognition to become more than a dangerous bench bat.

Pitchers

NAME	TEAM	LVL	AGE	W	L	SV	G	GS	IP	H	HR	BB	K	BB/9	K/9	GB%	BABIP	WHIP	ERA	FIP	FRA	WARP
Mike Kickham	FRE	AAA	25	8	8	0	27	27	148.1	171	8	64	131	3.9	7.9	56%	.355	1.58	4.43	4.03	4.19	2.8
	SFN	MLB	25	0	0	0	2	0	8	8	1	1	1	4.5	4.5	57%	.538	4.50	22.50	10.10	8.25	-0.1
George Kontos	FRE	AAA	29	3	3	4	30	0	47.2	41	4	11	58	2.1	11.0	41%	.303	1.09	2.08	3.05	3.11	1.4
	SFN	MLB	29	4	0	0	24	0	32.1	24	1	11	27	3.1	7.5	39%	.267	1.08	2.78	2.86	2.96	0.4
Derek Law	RIC	AA	23	2	0	13	27	0	28	19	1	14	29	4.5	9.3	51%	.265	1.18	2.57	3.35	3.49	0.5

The Giants were pleased to see Canadian righty **Dylan Brooks**' progress in the Arizona League in 2014, but the 2013 30th-rounder is still very much a raw pitcher whose most intriguing asset—a 6-foot-7 frame—could be a detriment when it comes to repeating his delivery. ❖ Last year's fifth-rounder **Sam Coonrod** touches 98 with a plus slider to boot, but he needs to find more consistency to develop into a late-inning bullpen option. ❖ The Braves thought they had a Peter Moylan clone in **Cory Gearrin**, but a faulty elbow begat Tommy John surgery, leaving the side-arming righty barren. ❖ A well proportioned lefty who was once viewed as a back-end starter, **Mike Kickham** now looks like a reliever whose solid-average fastball and slider could work—but most likely won't—in a specialist or middle-inning role. ❖ **George Kontos** has good control for a middle-inning guy, but his hard stuff is below average and he hangs too many sliders to hold his manager's trust. ❖ Best known for his 45-to-1 K:BB rate in San Jose in 2013, **Derek Law** was one of the organization's top relief prospects before he tore his UCL and underwent Tommy John surgery in June; assuming his recovery goes smoothly, he should be in the majors by 2016. ❖ Keep an eye on **Michael Santos**, a loose-armed right-hander who oozes projection and might be ready to give full-season ball a try after impressing scouts in the Arizona League. ❖ A two-sport high school star who also played quarterback—they all did—**Logan Webb** was a spring pop-up prospect in Rocklin, Calif.—some 100 miles northeast of AT&T Park—whose velocity shot up to 96. That earned him $600,000 as a fourth-round pick, the Giants' largest overslot outlay of the 2014 draft.

Manager

Bruce Bochy

YEAR	TEAM	W	L	Py-thag +/-	Avg PC	100+ P	120+ P	QS	BQS	REL	REL w Zero R	IBB	PH	PH Avg	PH HR	SB2	CS2	SB3	CS3	SAC Att	SAC%	POS SAC	Squeeze	Swing	In Play
2012	SFN	94	68	5	100	91	3	93	6	526	440	42	214	.217	3	111	35	6	2	100	69.0%	27	0	382	123
2013	SFN	76	86	3	96.1	79	2	80	2	524	429	64	258	.213	4	64	24	3	1	86	76.7%	25	2	329	119
2014	SFN	88	74	1	94.9	62	1	86	6	475	412	35	233	.222	4	52	24	4	2	66	68.2%	20	5	268	97

Sam Miller calls Bochy the Chase Utley of managers: brilliant, yet underrated (especially in end-of-year voting) in favor of his flashier peers. Everyone else calls him a three-time champion. Forget about winning three World Series in five seasons, winning three period is an impressive feat. How impressive? Bochy became the 10th skipper to do it, joining nine Hall of Fame managers, including recent inductees Joe Torre and Tony La Russa—will Bochy earn enshrinement next to them some day?

Some might hesitate, and score the Hall of Fame talk as just the emotion of the moment, given Bochy has the second-worst winning percentage among the 10. The truth is, folks were making the case for him even before the latest World Series win. Chris Jaffe ranked Bochy as the 30th-best manager of all-time in his book, *Evaluating Baseball Managers*, and that was without considering Bochy's Giants tenure. Jonah Keri has since made the case on Grantland, citing Bochy's deft bullpen usage, his ability to coax more from veteran hitters while trusting youngsters and his consistent outperforming of his expected records.

Another World Series win would place Bochy in the select company of Joe McCarthy, Casey Stengel, Connie Mack, Walter Alston and Torre. Whether that's enough to earn him a spot in Cooperstown can be debated later; for now, he's one of the best and most successful managers in baseball.

SEATTLE MARINERS

by Patrick Dubuque

In the mid-'70s, a large man regularly wandered through the Capitol Hill district of downtown Seattle. He wore a sandwich board decrying the creation of a brand-new, publicly funded structure dubbed "The Kingdome." The man was Jeff Heath: former All-Star, former Pilots broadcaster-turned-realtor. He loved baseball, he would tell people over and over, shaking their hands and handing them an ink-stained petition. He loved Seattle. But he'd seen the terms of the financing in the Kingdome deal and it wasn't right, he said.

The deal went through. Heath felt a throb in his left arm, and died. They built the Kingdome, a very minor wonder of the modern world. The Seattle Mariners were established to inhabit that concrete cylinder, and they lost baseball games there, over and over. Twenty-five years later, 15 years ago, the city grew tired of gray and Astroturf green and razed it. Next year, taxpayers will finally pay off the last of the municipal bonds.

Debt is a difficult concept for people; it's hard to contrast the immediate reward for an action against its eventual returns. People don't add the finance charges from the credit card to the sticker price when they make purchases. Instead they have the evolutionary survival feature of brains set to YOLO. Baseball teams are no different: They have executives with jobs to worry about, budgets to fulfill. Knowing exactly when to go into debt, and how much, is no easy question.

✦ ✦ ✦

At the close of the 2013 season, the Seattle Mariners found themselves teetering on the edge of the void. Only the AL-Westward migration of the hapless Astros prevented the Mariners' fourth consecutive cellar finish. In the modern era of the general manager as the general and hero of a team, Geoff Baker of the *Seattle Times* exposed Jack Zduriencik as insufferable and Machiavellian, forcing out managers and assistants over personal and philosophical conflicts. The team's attendance, once the strongest in the league, withered, and its payrolls stagnated until the Padres and Indians were outspending Seattle. The long-awaited wave of young talent had crashed against the sand and receded.

The team's primary asset in that post-2013 darkness was its lack of debt; what would save them was less a windfall of talent than a line of credit. The heavy yokes of the Bavasi-era contracts, as well as the once-hailed Chone Figgins deal, were lifted from the team's shoulders, and attempts in previous offseasons to lure Prince Fielder and Josh Hamilton northwesterly had been happy failures. With a deserving Felix as the team's only long-term contract, and pre-arbitration players around the diamond, the Mariners forcibly hurled money at free agent Robinson Cano and, surprisingly, succeeded. Trembling from sticker shock, the team failed to make any other moves, and ownership nixed a completed one-year, $7.5 million deal with Nelson Cruz over post-steroid trauma concerns. The hesitance proved all the difference, as the well-meaning duo of Endy Chavez and Stefen Romero claimed 448 plate appearances. The Mariners improved by 16 wins but were eliminated from the wild card race on the final afternoon of the regular season.

Zduriencik this winter appeared at first to have learned his fiscal lesson. He locked up his best all-around offensive player, Kyle Seager, to a deal fair for both sides, and then apologized to Nelson Cruz by providing him with $57 million over four years. It's the Richie Sexson contract of yesteryear, minus the innocence: a move that helps the team win in 2015, and perhaps the year after, with the promise of contemptuous familiarity by 2018. But this is the way the world of baseball works now: The nature of the modern long-term contract mandates these final years of regret, of quadragenarians collecting the paychecks of a prime scarcely remembered. This is the modern baseball economy, a fair reflection of the real world. Debt is a necessity.

And so, still flush with the ill-gotten gains of cable television, ripe with the adolescent exuberance, the Mariners turned to Melky Cabrera, yet underbid by a couple of million dollars. The contradictory approach to Cruz and Cabrera surprised analysts and frustrated some fans. The Mariners have the opportunity and the means to go for broke, and yet they hesitate.

✦ ✦ ✦

It's the age-old fourth-beer debate: Would you accept X straight losing seasons to enjoy one championship? Tears in their eyes, the fans almost always say yes; they live for the moment. In a universe without genies or guarantees, they want action,

MARINERS PROSPECTUS
2014 W-L: 87-75, 3RD IN AL WEST

Pythag	.559	6th	DER	.725	2nd
RS/G	3.91	18th	B-Age	27.5	7th
RA/G	3.42	1st	P-Age	28.6	19th
TAv	.262	10th	Salary	$90.9M	19th
BRR	6.83	3rd	M$/MW	$2M	8th
TAv-P	.251	3rd	DL Days	626	8th
FIP	3.64	13th	$ on DL	9%	1st

Three-Year Park Factors

Runs	Runs/RH	Runs/LH	HR/RH	HR/LH
91	89	94	84	85

Top Hitter WARP	7.3	Kyle Seager
Top Pitcher WARP	4.1	Felix Hernandez
Top Prospect		D.J. Peterson

evidence of a plan even it's one they don't understand. Any action, as evidenced by laboratory rats and adolescents, is superior to boredom.

This is the problem with past success: It's in the past, a place where people generally don't like to live. They want to think about now, or at the very most, how now is going to feel in a couple of minutes. Fans of championship teams don't tend to spend their days watching reruns of the World Series; they start thinking about the next one. It's easy to sell your soul for a championship until the bill comes due, just as it is to put a television on the credit card.

The correlation between the desires of the fan and his or her corporate baseball entity of choice has always been a tenuous one. Flags fly forever. Ticket sales operate under somewhat different rules. The financial benefits of postseason success are plentiful, certainly, but it's not a true/false dichotomy: An 80-win season is hardly equal to a 60-win season. And while the average fan may not fully sympathize with the plight of the shareholder, and say they want championships, it's the possibility of championships that brings vigor to life. As the Astros and their 0.1 cable ratings have proved, there's good reason for all concerned to avoid being miserable.

+ + +

It took a while for the philosophers for consider the pursuit of happiness; they spent their first millennia pursuing justice and the good, then the next one worried about sin and the bad. But when they finally got around to what everyone actually cared about, pleasure, it kept them in business for quite a while. Most of the time it was pretty clear that people weren't happy because they were starving or freezing, but eventually less of them were, and the rich started realizing that they weren't particularly pleased with life either, even with all their gilded candlesticks. The Utilitarians tried to quantify happiness, breaking it up into units called utiles, the Wins Above Replacement Player of philosophy. People generally liked the utile thing, but they didn't really want to do math every time they picked a breakfast cereal, so it never really stuck. People went on being unhappy.

It turned out that they were going about it the wrong way. By the time Bertrand Russell wrote *The Conquest of Happiness* in 1930, he didn't start tackling the means to be happy until three-fifths of the way through. Instead he detailed all the sources of unhappiness, and how they have to be eliminated before people can really get anywhere. Unhappiness isn't just the opposite of happiness, nor does it work that way in J.S. Mill's algebraic equations. Human brains don't work like that. When there's something making someone unhappy, no matter how many loved ones or vaults of swimmable money they have, they tend to focus on it.

+ + +

Debt receives a lot of criticism for ruining people, and it deserves it as much as an abstract concept can. But there's an aspect to the modern deluge of debt that is often underrated: the flexibility it provides. Used responsibly, credit provides a personal safety net, smoothing out the rough edges of life. In the past, a farmer or merchant who stumbled across bad fortune could be destroyed; the loss of a man's job could throw a family into ruin. Debt delays misery by allowing people the chance to right their own ships.

Translating this to baseball, one could make the argument, based on the principle of avoiding unhappiness, that it's the low times when teams should sink their money in the free agent pool, and use those periods of success to lie low and pay off past debts. It was the humble 2011 Mariners, and not the 2014 or 2015 editions, that needed to open up the pocketbook, to avoid the downward spiral of talent and enthusiasm that repeated losing creates. Instead, stories will abound this summer of a very good team winning in front of half-sold stadiums, mocking a fan base still cradling a decade-long hangover.

No team would ever undertake such an iconoclastic roster philosophy, of course; the fans would riot. Witness the reaction to CEO Howard Lincoln's 2013 emphasis of Safeco Field itself as the franchise's selling point, and the $15 million in renovations it made that offseason. The sparkling new videoboard had no effect on payroll, and Lincoln wasn't wrong that his team wasn't much of a draw in itself, but the timing of his comments, at the end of yet another aimless season, irritated.

Such are the perils of every December and January, where inaction is equated with failure. But consider the Royals and Giants. Their glorious playoff runs proved that regular-season dominance is overrated: Set two good teams against each other for seven games, and all is chance. Windows aren't completely extinct yet—though the Chicago White Sox this year are certainly out to prove it—but they're no longer nearly so rigid. The model for success in the Wild Card Era is the St. Louis Cardinals: Build a strong foundation, roll out very good but non-elite teams, and show up for the dance. The Mariners appear to head into at least this season on similar footing.

This is why the Mariners, as of this publication, have Nelson Cruz and Robinson Cano on their roster, but also Taijuan Walker and James Paxton; the team is trying to avoid being neither timid nor foolhardy. Whether the plan succeeds, of course, depends on the performance of the players; another season of falling just short would rankle, but no more than a scenario involving a 2015 first-round exit and Walker pitching for the 2016 NL All-Star team. The organization can hope that by 2017, when its stars grow grizzled, they'll have underpaid replacements in the wings. In the meantime, their biggest debt remains owed to their expectant, weary fans. ∎

—Patrick Dubuque has written for The Classical, The Hardball Times, NotGraphs, Pitchers & Poets and Lookout Landing.

Player comments by Patrick Dubuque and Baseball Prospectus Authors

Hitters

Dustin Ackley LF

Born: 2/26/88   Age: 27   Bats: L   Throws: R   Height: 6' 1"   Weight: 195

YEAR	TEAM	LVL	AGE	PA	R	2B	3B	HR	RBI	BB	K	SB	CS	AVG/OBP/SLG	TAv	BABIP	BRR	FRAA	WARP
2012	SEA	MLB	24	668	84	22	2	12	50	59	124	13	3	.226/.294/.328	.243	.265	3.2	2B(142): -1.9, 1B(11): -0.2	0.4
2013	TAC	AAA	25	126	21	8	0	2	14	19	14	0	0	.365/.472/.500	.339	.409	0.5	2B(12): -1.0, CF(9): -0.7	1.4
2013	SEA	MLB	25	427	40	18	2	4	31	37	72	2	3	.253/.319/.341	.251	.301	1.8	2B(53): 3.5, CF(50): -1.8	1.2
2014	SEA	MLB	26	542	64	27	4	14	65	32	90	8	4	.245/.293/.398	.261	.273	0.3	LF(133): 3.9	1.6
2015	SEA	MLB	27	501	57	21	3	9	44	43	90	7	3	.248/.314/.365	.268	.288	1.3	LF 2, 2B -2	1.8

Breakout: 11%   Improve: 44%   Collapse: 6%   Attrition: 13%   MLB: 98%   Comparables: David DeJesus, Conor Jackson, Floyd Robinson

By the end of June, Ackley looked like a dead duck. He was performing all the Ackley cliches: watching strike three just outside the zone, rolling over weak grounders to second and staring into the middle distance with cold, empty eyes. Suddenly, something changed. Ackley has repeated in the past that he struggles with confidence, but his second-half success was almost a violent change in approach. He stopped walking (4.5 percent in the second half) and started hitting fly balls, which actually went pretty far. His second-half ISO of .207 was 21st in the league and highest on the Mariners. Ackley has been a second-half player in his short career, and prone to violent streaks, but if he's true to this new mini-slugger identity, his newfound power and clumsy-yet-effective defense in left combine to make a valuable player, if not a star. The eyes remain dead.

Willie Bloomquist SS

Born: 11/27/77   Age: 37   Bats: R   Throws: R   Height: 5' 11"   Weight: 190

YEAR	TEAM	LVL	AGE	PA	R	2B	3B	HR	RBI	BB	K	SB	CS	AVG/OBP/SLG	TAv	BABIP	BRR	FRAA	WARP
2012	ARI	MLB	34	338	47	21	5	0	23	12	55	7	10	.302/.325/.398	.262	.362	0.3	SS(64): -8.8, 3B(11): 0.3	0.6
2013	RNO	AAA	35	23	5	0	1	0	9	2	2	0	0	.429/.478/.524	.310	.474	0.7	2B(5): -0.1, SS(1): 0.1	0.3
2013	ARI	MLB	35	150	16	5	1	0	14	8	11	0	2	.317/.360/.367	.262	.341	2.2	2B(15): -0.9, SS(9): -0.3	0.5
2014	SEA	MLB	36	139	15	6	0	1	14	4	32	1	1	.278/.297/.346	.248	.356	-0.4	SS(16): -1.7, 2B(10): -0.5	-0.1
2015	SEA	MLB	37	250	24	9	1	1	16	10	42	4	4	.256/.288/.316	.241	.304	0.7	SS -4, 2B -1	-0.1

Breakout: 1%   Improve: 30%   Collapse: 12%   Attrition: 19%   MLB: 81%   Comparables: John McDonald, Alan Trammell, Damion Easley

There are fans who felt chagrin at giving literally nonzero dollars to a statistically replacement level baseball player for multiple years. But those people simply don't see all the things that Bloomquist does for the franchise. Like going around the stadium after home games checking all the doors to make sure they're locked. Or calling all the rookies the day before to make sure they've prepared discussion questions for *Siddhartha* for the team book club. These things don't happen by themselves; they require quiet veteran leadership. The 2003 Tigers took a laissez-faire attitude toward literary discussion, and you can see what happened there. That's why you need Willie Bloomquist.

Is it worth mentioning his extreme "clutch" statistics of late? Since 2012, he has hit .388/.419/.483 with men on. Maybe, like *Siddhartha*, he has found enlightenment?

Robinson Cano 2B

Born: 10/22/82   Age: 32   Bats: L   Throws: R   Height: 6' 0"   Weight: 210

YEAR	TEAM	LVL	AGE	PA	R	2B	3B	HR	RBI	BB	K	SB	CS	AVG/OBP/SLG	TAv	BABIP	BRR	FRAA	WARP
2012	NYA	MLB	29	697	105	48	1	33	94	61	96	3	2	.313/.379/.550	.319	.326	-1.6	2B(154): 6.3	6.9
2013	NYA	MLB	30	681	81	41	0	27	107	65	85	7	1	.314/.383/.516	.324	.327	-0.9	2B(153): -1.8, SS(1): -0.0	6.3
2014	SEA	MLB	31	665	77	37	2	14	82	61	68	10	3	.314/.382/.454	.315	.335	2.8	2B(150): 2.3	6.2
2015	SEA	MLB	32	628	74	34	2	19	80	47	87	6	2	.293/.350/.460	.312	.315	0.0	2B 2, SS -0	5.6

Breakout: 0%   Improve: 29%   Collapse: 2%   Attrition: 6%   MLB: 99%   Comparables: Chase Utley, Aramis Ramirez, Vladimir Guerrero

One year down, nine to go. The Mariners' big offseason acquisition was worth the money for the first tenth of his contract, hitting well and taking the team to the cusp of the playoffs. Moving to Safeco did affect his power, but not quite in the manner expected: It was a sudden jump in his groundball rate (52.6 percent, highest of his career) that essentially killed his power. Things did improve after May, when his ISO reverted to a more palatable .164 and the Jay-Z jokes died down. Other than the power, his offensive production was essentially identical to 2013. What you probably care about is exactly how painful, in terms of dols, Cano's retirement tour will be in 2023. But you shouldn't, not only because you may be dead by then, but because 2015 comes first, and Cano will remain a great ballplayer in 2015, even if he hits 18 home runs.

Endy Chavez RF

Born: 2/7/78   Age: 37   Bats: L   Throws: L   Height: 5' 11"   Weight: 170

YEAR	TEAM	LVL	AGE	PA	R	2B	3B	HR	RBI	BB	K	SB	CS	AVG/OBP/SLG	TAv	BABIP	BRR	FRAA	WARP
2012	NOR	AAA	34	53	2	3	0	0	4	2	6	0	0	.149/.192/.213	.163	.163	-0.8	RF(10): 0.3, LF(4): -0.1	-0.5
2012	BAL	MLB	34	169	15	6	0	2	12	6	24	3	2	.203/.236/.278	.195	.227	-1.2	LF(35): -1.0, RF(21): 0.9	-0.9
2013	TAC	AAA	35	31	8	1	0	0	1	3	3	0	2	.429/.484/.464	.389	.480	-0.1	CF(5): -0.2, LF(1): -0.0	0.5
2013	SEA	MLB	35	279	22	10	0	2	14	9	31	1	3	.267/.290/.327	.232	.295	0.8	RF(50): 2.5, CF(24): 0.5	0.2
2014	TAC	AAA	36	134	16	2	0	0	6	13	17	0	4	.272/.346/.289	.234	.313	-1.1	CF(10): 0.1, RF(8): -0.0	-0.1
2014	SEA	MLB	36	258	22	12	2	2	23	15	30	5	2	.276/.317/.371	.277	.307	-1.5	RF(46): -2.5, LF(11): 0.2	0.3
2015	SEA	MLB	37	270	25	10	1	1	17	11	38	4	3	.245/.276/.305	.233	.274	-0.7	RF 0, CF -1	-0.4

Breakout: 2%   Improve: 34%   Collapse: 9%   Attrition: 20%   MLB: 74%   Comparables: Scott Podsednik, Jim Eisenreich, Felipe Alou

Chavez is the sort of guy your casual-fan uncle loves to watch play. "Seems like he gets a hit every game," he says, and your uncle is right, but it's next to impossible to explain to him how 1-for-4 with a single translates into a slash line. There's no way Chavez earns this much playing time next year, but there was no way last year, and no way the year before that. He's a "break glass in emergency" case that's empty inside, except for shards of the glass you just broke.

Ji-Man Choi   1B

Born: 5/19/91   Age: 24   Bats: B   Throws: R   Height: 6' 1"   Weight: 225

YEAR	TEAM	LVL	AGE	PA	R	2B	3B	HR	RBI	BB	K	SB	CS	AVG/OBP/SLG	TAv	BABIP	BRR	FRAA	WARP
2012	CLN	A	21	294	43	14	1	8	43	39	55	0	2	.298/.420/.463	.320	.358	-3.2	1B(35): -2.8	1.5
2013	HDS	A+	22	211	34	24	3	7	40	27	33	0	1	.337/.427/.619	.336	.380	-0.2	1B(41): 2.3, 3B(4): -0.1	2.2
2013	WTN	AA	22	236	21	10	3	9	39	32	28	2	2	.268/.377/.485	.307	.270	-0.7	1B(43): -2.3	1.1
2013	TAC	AAA	22	52	9	2	0	2	6	4	7	0	0	.244/.333/.422	.264	.250	0.1	1B(10): 0.5	0.1
2014	TAC	AAA	23	281	41	7	2	5	30	36	42	2	2	.283/.381/.392	.274	.323	0.2	1B(40): -0.1, LF(25): -1.1	0.7
2015	SEA	MLB	24	250	25	10	1	5	27	24	50	1	1	.238/.320/.364	.270	.280	-0.4	1B -1, LF -0	0.4

Breakout: 3%   Improve: 16%   Collapse: 10%   Attrition: 20%   MLB: 38%   Comparables: Chris Carter, Conor Jackson, Mike Carp

Choi spent 50 games repenting for Bad Things after being caught using a steroid that makes Arnold Schwarzenegger feel nostalgic. It put a dent in what was, to that point, a pretty interesting prospect arc. It's actually fairly difficult to find a successful first baseman with as little home run power as Choi seems to present: Even Sean Casey hit a dozen dingers a year. Choi's best bet, other than the boring way of developing power as he ages, is a Magadanian path of walking and continuing to hit copious doubles, as he did up until his post-steroid Tacoma stint. Or move to the outfield, which he tried in the fall league. Either way, like his national comrade and former Mariners prospect Shin-Soo Choo, Choi does enough well to be worth watching.

Austin Cousino   CF

Born: 4/17/93   Age: 22   Bats: L   Throws: L   Height: 5' 10"   Weight: 178

YEAR	TEAM	LVL	AGE	PA	R	2B	3B	HR	RBI	BB	K	SB	CS	AVG/OBP/SLG	TAv	BABIP	BRR	FRAA	WARP
2014	EVE	A-	21	309	40	17	1	6	28	28	54	23	4	.266/.341/.402	.273	.310	3.2	CF(62): -6.7	1.0
2015	SEA	MLB	22	250	25	8	1	3	15	10	68	8	2	.196/.232/.269	.201	.256	0.8	CF -5	-1.3

Breakout: 0%   Improve: 0%   Collapse: 0%   Attrition: 0%   MLB: 0%   Comparables: Clete Thomas, Colin Curtis, Adam Eaton

After selecting a pair of sluggers with their top two choices in the 2014 draft, the Mariners averaged it out in the third by reaching for Cousino, a short-ish outfielder from Kentucky. He's got a center fielder's range and instincts as well as a center fielder's arm, and he's fleet enough on the bases to look like a center fielder there, too. Whether he's a good one will depend on the bat, which was inconsistent even in college. It's been said that Cousino flashed just enough power to fall in love with it, pulling him away from his real athletic strengths. The organization will have to fix his swing and perhaps teach him the value of the humble groundball.

Nelson Cruz   DH

Born: 7/1/80   Age: 34   Bats: R   Throws: R   Height: 6' 2"   Weight: 230

YEAR	TEAM	LVL	AGE	PA	R	2B	3B	HR	RBI	BB	K	SB	CS	AVG/OBP/SLG	TAv	BABIP	BRR	FRAA	WARP
2012	TEX	MLB	31	642	86	45	0	24	90	48	140	8	4	.260/.319/.460	.278	.301	-0.7	RF(151): 5.6, LF(6): -0.2	3.1
2013	TEX	MLB	32	456	49	18	0	27	76	35	109	5	1	.266/.327/.506	.294	.295	-0.9	RF(102): -2.5	1.9
2014	BAL	MLB	33	678	87	32	2	40	108	55	140	4	5	.271/.333/.525	.312	.288	-4.0	LF(60): 0.8, RF(11): 0.1	4.2
2015	SEA	MLB	34	593	71	28	1	26	82	40	140	6	3	.252/.304/.448	.291	.289	-1.7	RF 3, LF 1	3.2

Breakout: 0%   Improve: 28%   Collapse: 11%   Attrition: 15%   MLB: 94%   Comparables: Derrek Lee, Ryan Howard, Marcus Thames

There's no more terrifying slugger than a contract-year slugger. After sitting out 50 games to Biogenesis chicanery in 2013, Cruz declined a qualifying offer from Texas and sought a small European country's GDP on the free-agent market. Whether it was the severity of his demands or the draft pick chained to him we'll never know, but come February he reluctantly accepted Baltimore's one-year, $8 million deal, then flipped the market the bird by leading the AL in homers. Don't call it a breakout year, though: His batting splits were only slightly better than his career average, and 40 homers can be attributed to playing almost every game, something he couldn't do back when his hamstring barked through previous summers. There's not a single injury mark, not a strain or soreness or a flu bug or anything on his injury log for 2014. Even if injury is no longer a concern, age still is; there's no more terrifying DH acquisition than a multi-year, mid-30s DH acquisition. The Mariners presumably are aware of that but signed him to a four-year deal for $57 million anyway, a year after ownership rejected a much shorter, much cheaper deal because of the Biogenesis problem.

Gabriel Guerrero   RF

Born: 12/11/93   Age: 21   Bats: R   Throws: R   Height: 6' 3"   Weight: 190

YEAR	TEAM	LVL	AGE	PA	R	2B	3B	HR	RBI	BB	K	SB	CS	AVG/OBP/SLG	TAv	BABIP	BRR	FRAA	WARP
2013	CLN	A	19	499	60	23	3	4	50	21	113	12	3	.271/.303/.358	.251	.344	1.8	RF(121): 10.0	1.3
2014	HDS	A+	20	580	97	28	2	18	96	34	131	18	6	.307/.347/.467	.275	.373	3.8	RF(109): 1.2, CF(12): -1.4	1.9
2015	SEA	MLB	21	250	19	8	1	4	22	5	73	3	1	.222/.238/.307	.217	.297	-0.1	RF 1, CF -0	-0.6

Breakout: 0%   Improve: 0%   Collapse: 0%   Attrition: 0%   MLB: 0%   Comparables: Yorman Rodriguez, Avisail Garcia, Rymer Liriano

The Guerrero of Our Generation, and nephew of Vladimir, showed enough at Single-A Clinton as a 19-year-old to move to High Desert in 2014. As so many hitters do, he found it to his liking. His power resurfaced in the arid climes and, more importantly, his strikeout rate remained identical a rung up the ladder. Guerrero wields a Goliath-slaying arm and can apply speed in addition to the power. The question is, and always will be, whether he can get by with his open-minded attitude toward the strike zone. So far, he's emulating old Vlad, putting those hard-to-reach pitches into play and making good on them. If the bat speed can hold up against advanced pitching, look forward to happy chaos.

Corey Hart   DH

Born: 3/24/82   Age: 33   Bats: R   Throws: R   Height: 6' 6"   Weight: 230

YEAR	TEAM	LVL	AGE	PA	R	2B	3B	HR	RBI	BB	K	SB	CS	AVG/OBP/SLG	TAv	BABIP	BRR	FRAA	WARP
2012	MIL	MLB	30	622	91	35	4	30	83	44	151	5	0	.270/.334/.507	.278	.318	-0.9	1B(103): 0.9, RF(53): -3.4	1.6
2014	TAC	AAA	32	77	8	4	2	4	9	7	13	0	0	.286/.351/.571	.350	.302	-1.5	LF(1): 0.0	0.6
2014	SEA	MLB	32	255	17	9	0	6	21	16	59	2	0	.203/.271/.319	.245	.244	-0.6	RF(7): 0.1, 1B(2): -0.2	-0.3
2015	SEA	MLB	33	250	28	11	1	9	32	16	60	2	1	.247/.303/.422	.283	.291	-0.5	1B -0, RF -0	0.8

Breakout: 1%   Improve: 31%   Collapse: 3%   Attrition: 6%   MLB: 92%   Comparables: Garrett Jones, Adam LaRoche, Derrek Lee

According to Bertrand Russell, a proper noun is a set of properties that distinguish that noun from others; in other words, when we name something, we are intrinsically describing it as well. We attach inherent value to the word "apple" so that when I call something an apple, it may not be the exact apple you have presupposed, but it will certainly match your expectations in basic ways. The purpose of this statement is to underscore the fact that Corey Hart needs a new name. He is no longer Corey Hart, because the words "Corey" and "Hart," when put together, insinuate a person of reasonable strength and character who also wields two functioning knees. This, sadly, is and probably forevermore will be untrue.

Alex Jackson   RF
Born: 12/25/95   Age: 19   Bats: R   Throws: R   Height: 6' 2"   Weight: 215

YEAR	TEAM	LVL	AGE	PA	R	2B	3B	HR	RBI	BB	K	SB	CS	AVG/OBP/SLG	TAv	BABIP	BRR	FRAA	WARP
2015	SEA	MLB	19	250	16	7	0	2	18	11	80	1	0	.180/.220/.240	.188	.258	-0.4	RF -0	-1.5

Breakout: 0%   Improve: 0%   Collapse: 0%   Attrition: 0%   MLB: 0%   Comparables: Cedric Hunter, Caleb Gindl, Matt Davidson

The 2014 sixth overall pick and the first high school position player drafted, Jackson is everything the Mariners love in a player, meaning that he bats right-handed and hits the ball hard. He spent his time in high school as a catcher before being drafted as an outfielder, proving that he also has an arm worthy of right field. Things were going well for Jackson generally until he lost a ball in the lights while making a diving play on a liner, resulting in a broken face. He healed himself up by the end of the season, and the scouts and the stats agree that he's fulfilling his promise to this point. The Mariners plan to promote him aggressively, as they're wont to do, and it may not be long before we see him wearing teal. With James Paxton and Taijuan Walker having exceeded the rookie limits, Jackson immediately vies for a place atop the Seattle prospect rankings.

Austin Jackson   CF
Born: 2/1/87   Age: 28   Bats: R   Throws: R   Height: 6' 1"   Weight: 185

YEAR	TEAM	LVL	AGE	PA	R	2B	3B	HR	RBI	BB	K	SB	CS	AVG/OBP/SLG	TAv	BABIP	BRR	FRAA	WARP
2012	DET	MLB	25	617	103	29	10	16	66	67	134	12	9	.300/.377/.479	.302	.371	2.9	CF(137): 8.0	5.7
2013	DET	MLB	26	614	99	30	7	12	49	52	129	8	4	.272/.337/.417	.277	.333	4.4	CF(129): -6.0	2.8
2014	DET	MLB	27	420	52	25	5	4	33	35	85	9	4	.273/.332/.398	.265	.334	2.4	CF(100): -3.7	1.3
2014	SEA	MLB	27	236	19	5	1	0	14	12	59	11	2	.229/.267/.260	.195	.309	0.4	CF(54): 1.3	-0.8
2015	SEA	MLB	28	610	69	25	6	7	49	48	153	14	6	.254/.315/.360	.267	.331	2.9	CF 0	2.5

Breakout: 2%   Improve: 41%   Collapse: 1%   Attrition: 3%   MLB: 99%   Comparables: Cesar Cedeno, Merv Rettenmund, Ellis Burks

At the time, the trade that brought Jackson to Seattle looked like it couldn't be any more reasonable: He was a cost-effective upgrade, signed through 2015, playing capable defense in center field, where the team needed it most, all at the price of an expendable prospect at a surplus position. The result was unreasonable. Jackson began his Mariners career cold and continued even colder, working counts only to flail weakly at breaking pitches below the zone. Generally a weaker second-half hitter anyway (career .256 TAv versus .271 in the first half), Jackson's groundball rate and strikeout rate rose after July and his walk rate plummeted as desperation grew. It's telling that his finest moment of the season came in game 161, keeping the team alive with an extra-innings walkoff by barely beating out a double-play ball. These things happen sometimes; one need only look at Rickey Henderson's tenure with the Blue Jays and Angels. Jackson will have another year to prove that his late summer was a poorly timed fluke, and the Mariners have few options other than to let him make his case.

James Jones   CF
Born: 9/24/88   Age: 26   Bats: L   Throws: L   Height: 6' 4"   Weight: 200

YEAR	TEAM	LVL	AGE	PA	R	2B	3B	HR	RBI	BB	K	SB	CS	AVG/OBP/SLG	TAv	BABIP	BRR	FRAA	WARP
2012	HDS	A+	23	559	109	28	12	14	76	54	124	26	17	.306/.378/.497	.292	.382	-0.1	CF(77): -8.5, RF(42): -0.1	2.5
2013	WTN	AA	24	405	44	14	10	6	45	40	72	28	9	.275/.347/.419	.273	.330	-2.6	RF(53): 0.2, CF(18): 0.5	1.0
2014	TAC	AAA	25	173	24	6	3	2	15	13	31	7	3	.282/.341/.397	.266	.341	1.8	CF(32): -1.5, RF(6): 0.0	0.9
2014	SEA	MLB	25	328	46	9	5	0	9	12	67	27	1	.250/.278/.311	.234	.318	3.4	CF(85): -7.7, RF(9): -0.3	-0.6
2015	SEA	MLB	26	319	36	11	4	2	21	18	74	17	3	.238/.281/.322	.241	.304	0.7	CF -6, RF -1	-0.5

Breakout: 8%   Improve: 39%   Collapse: 12%   Attrition: 27%   MLB: 64%   Comparables: Gorkys Hernandez, Angel Pagan, Tony Gwynn

Here's an easy formula for projecting Mariner rookies: Take their minor-league walk rate and divide by two. Jones arrived to replace Abe Almonte with the promise of being a young, cheap Juan Pierre, and finished the season with the production of a young, current Juan Pierre. Jones is undeniably fast, but in every other facet of the game, he's cringe-inducingly unpolished. He has the range for center but his arm is weak and his routes are circuitous. He abandoned any hope of the power he hinted at in the minors by swinging down on everything (54 percent groundball rate). Unfortunately, he simply doesn't make enough contact to rely on the ball in play to get to first. Entering his age-26 season, it's probably too late to expect any of these skills to develop, and even with some regression, he's a fourth outfielder and pinch-running specialist at best. At worst, he and Juan Pierre have the same production by 2016.

Patrick Kivlehan   OF
Born: 12/22/89   Age: 25   Bats: R   Throws: R   Height: 6' 2"   Weight: 210

YEAR	TEAM	LVL	AGE	PA	R	2B	3B	HR	RBI	BB	K	SB	CS	AVG/OBP/SLG	TAv	BABIP	BRR	FRAA	WARP
2012	EVE	A-	22	316	46	17	3	12	52	19	93	14	1	.301/.373/.511	.308	.412	-0.2	3B(69): -6.9	2.2
2013	CLN	A	23	247	26	12	1	3	31	17	42	5	3	.283/.344/.386	.271	.333	-2.1	3B(49): -2.5	0.8
2013	HDS	A+	23	302	48	13	2	13	59	26	65	10	3	.320/.384/.530	.314	.373	-3.0	3B(66): 3.9	2.9
2014	HDS	A+	24	157	24	9	2	9	35	12	32	2	0	.282/.331/.563	.289	.298	0.0	3B(14): -0.6, 1B(13): -0.1	0.8
2014	WTN	AA	24	431	60	23	7	11	68	44	78	9	4	.300/.374/.485	.309	.348	0.2	3B(58): -8.8, 1B(26): -0.1	2.7
2015	SEA	MLB	25	250	24	9	1	6	26	13	67	3	1	.234/.280/.358	.252	.298	0.0	3B -3, 1B -0	0.0

Breakout: 14%   Improve: 25%   Collapse: 9%   Attrition: 32%   MLB: 41%   Comparables: Danny Valencia, Luke Hughes, Russ Canzler

Economics and sports are both about specialization: Consuming your life in the pursuit of a single skill, and then leveraging that facet to the best of your ability. This is fine, but Kivlehan chose the wrong one. After devoting the majority of his college career to the special teams unit of the Rutgers football team, he gave baseball a shot and showed enough to warrant a fourth-round draft choice by the Mariners. Since then, he's been Bo Jackson and Hector rolled into one. The organization is throwing him into every league they can find to catch up on his development, and so far there have been no speed bumps. He'll probably begin 2015 in Tacoma, adjusting to corner outfield while continuing to polish his offensive skills. If it all works, the Mariners will soon have a little more of that right-handed power they so badly covet.

Ketel Marte   SS

Born: 10/12/93   Age: 21   Bats: B   Throws: R   Height: 6' 1"   Weight: 180

YEAR	TEAM	LVL	AGE	PA	R	2B	3B	HR	RBI	BB	K	SB	CS	AVG/OBP/SLG	TAv	BABIP	BRR	FRAA	WARP
2012	EVE	A-	18	269	36	4	2	0	22	12	35	14	4	.247/.281/.279	.214	.287	0.5	SS(41): -0.4, 2B(25): 0.5	-0.3
2013	CLN	A	19	406	61	15	5	0	29	15	39	16	8	.304/.330/.370	.263	.336	-1.3	SS(70): 3.1, 2B(24): -1.4	1.7
2013	HDS	A+	19	92	18	0	2	1	8	4	11	4	3	.256/.289/.337	.244	.284	1.6	SS(15): -0.0, 2B(2): 0.2	0.3
2014	WTN	AA	20	472	63	27	6	2	46	19	65	23	10	.302/.334/.404	.269	.346	0.2	SS(102): -2.3, 2B(7): 1.4	2.2
2014	TAC	AAA	20	90	16	5	0	2	9	8	13	6	0	.313/.367/.450	.293	.343	1.2	SS(19): 0.8	1.2
2015	SEA	MLB	21	250	24	9	1	1	15	4	49	8	3	.243/.256/.305	.223	.292	0.6	SS 1, 2B 1	0.3

Breakout: 0%   Improve: 0%   Collapse: 0%   Attrition: 0%   MLB: 0%   Comparables: Joaquin Arias, Alcides Escobar, Carlos Triunfel

When the days get dark, the Mariners are prepared to reach into their bottomless Bag of League-Average Shortstops and pull out Marte, who reached Tacoma by the end of his age-20 season. Defensively, he's already basically there: He has the range and hands of a quality defender, though his arm is a little weak for short. He's the embodiment of that adjective seemingly reserved for the young talented shortstop: slick. The other half of Marte's game is more of a patchwork affair. He has excellent speed that has translated more to reaching first and tripling than stealing second—though that skill is coming along, too. The question, as with so many Mariners youths, lies in his plate discipline: In its current form, he's entirely dependent on BABIP for his offensive production, much like his predecessor Chris Taylor. Even if his bat never improves, Marte has the glove to contribute in the majors right now. And remember: He was born nearly a year into the Bill Clinton presidency.

Brad Miller   SS

Born: 10/18/89   Age: 25   Bats: L   Throws: R   Height: 6' 2"   Weight: 200

YEAR	TEAM	LVL	AGE	PA	R	2B	3B	HR	RBI	BB	K	SB	CS	AVG/OBP/SLG	TAv	BABIP	BRR	FRAA	WARP
2012	HDS	A+	22	473	89	33	5	11	56	52	79	19	6	.339/.412/.524	.301	.394	1.9	SS(97): 6.1	5.1
2012	WTN	AA	22	170	21	7	2	4	12	22	26	4	1	.320/.406/.476	.305	.364	-0.3	SS(37): -2.2	1.3
2013	WTN	AA	23	175	27	7	1	6	25	20	30	4	3	.294/.379/.471	.313	.333	-0.4	SS(29): 0.9, 2B(6): -0.4	1.3
2013	TAC	AAA	23	122	26	5	1	6	28	15	18	2	1	.356/.426/.596	.369	.373	1.8	SS(22): 1.8, 2B(3): 0.0	2.5
2013	SEA	MLB	23	335	41	11	6	8	36	24	52	5	3	.265/.318/.418	.279	.294	2.3	SS(68): -3.8, 2B(13): -0.7	1.6
2014	SEA	MLB	24	411	47	15	4	10	36	34	95	4	2	.221/.288/.365	.261	.268	0.9	SS(107): 0.2, 2B(13): 0.2	1.9
2015	SEA	MLB	25	405	48	15	3	9	39	31	83	5	3	.251/.309/.383	.272	.295	1.2	SS -1, 2B -0	2.1

Breakout: 2%   Improve: 53%   Collapse: 9%   Attrition: 17%   MLB: 96%   Comparables: Kyle Seager, Ian Kinsler, Yunel Escobar

Miller has logged three half-seasons of baseball now, two of them great and the other a Lovecraftian nightmare dimension. After handing Miller's starting gig to Chris Taylor, the Mariners lost Willie Bloomquist for the year and decided to just make a better one. Miller henceforth broke out of his slump and had a productive second half, filling in around the infield and hitting as expected, albeit with a few more strikeouts and a touch more power than before.

The team now faces a happy dilemma: two capable starting shortstops. Barring a trade or another Nick Franklin debacle, the Mariners have spoken about making Miller a "super sub" in the mold of Ben Zobrist. He's capable, if inconsistent, at short, and plenty fine at second or third. And although he hasn't technically played outfield since childhood, coaches dubbed him a "natural" in drills. There's also the problem that Kyle Seager and Robinson Cano, playing two of Miller's natural positions, play more than most regulars. But unless Miller's bat goes through another snowy April, the team will find a place for him somewhere most days of the week. There's too much offensive potential to let him rot.

Jesus Montero   DH

Born: 11/28/89   Age: 25   Bats: R   Throws: R   Height: 6' 3"   Weight: 235

YEAR	TEAM	LVL	AGE	PA	R	2B	3B	HR	RBI	BB	K	SB	CS	AVG/OBP/SLG	TAv	BABIP	BRR	FRAA	WARP
2012	SEA	MLB	22	553	46	20	0	15	62	29	99	0	2	.260/.298/.386	.254	.292	-6.6	C(56): -0.6	0.0
2013	TAC	AAA	23	82	12	6	2	1	9	8	24	0	0	.247/.317/.425	.256	.347	-0.3	1B(16): -1.3, C(1): -0.0	0.0
2013	SEA	MLB	23	110	6	1	1	3	9	8	21	0	1	.208/.264/.327	.227	.231	-0.4	C(26): -0.1	-0.1
2014	TAC	AAA	24	409	55	24	1	16	74	37	79	1	0	.286/.350/.489	.293	.320	-3.6	1B(44): -3.6	1.2
2014	SEA	MLB	24	17	1	0	0	1	2	0	3	0	0	.235/.235/.412	.234	.231	0.0	1B(1): 0.0	0.0
2015	SEA	MLB	25	250	25	10	1	7	30	15	53	0	0	.252/.298/.396	.272	.294	-1.5	C -0, 1B -1	0.5

Breakout: 5%   Improve: 46%   Collapse: 4%   Attrition: 17%   MLB: 83%   Comparables: Jason Kubel, John Bowker, Brett Wallace

Given how much America glorifies athletes and athletics, it's surprisingly easy to understand why anyone would not want to be a baseball player. It requires focus, not the good kind of focus that keeps kids from drawing dinosaurs on their Social Studies tests, but the kind that requires utterly subsuming every other facet of a person's life. It demands pain and disappointment and an almost unfair amount of risk.

It's beginning to look like Jesus Montero does not want to be a baseball player. After getting suspended as part of the Biogenesis investigation, Montero returned to Venezuela for the offseason, where, in his own words, "all [he] did was eat." He arrived at camp 40 pounds overweight and was banished to Tacoma before an infamous ice cream sandwich ended his season. Montero did cash half a million dollars in checks to play baseball, so technically it's permissible for fans to castigate him for violating a contract in which they're not personally involved. It's a tired argument, and not a very good one; there are plenty of players who were born with die rolls that allowed them to be both lazy and successful, and people still root for them. Maybe Montero does want to be a baseball player, but he wants to define that concept differently than we do, in a way that doesn't include all the in-between sadness. The Mariners, for their part, have completely misread his psychological profile, behaving like the distant father who pushes his son away. At this point, the situation is untenable. Montero needs to be traded for a 19-year-old with control problems and placed in a new environment with no expectations and no grudges. Or he needs to be at home with a big dinner, a couple of beers and some peace.

Gareth Morgan   RF

Born: 4/12/96   Age: 19   Bats: R   Throws: R   Height: 6' 4"   Weight: 220

YEAR	TEAM	LVL	AGE	PA	R	2B	3B	HR	RBI	BB	K	SB	CS	AVG/OBP/SLG	TAv	BABIP	BRR	FRAA	WARP
2015	SEA	MLB	19	250	16	7	0	2	18	8	85	1	1	.175/.207/.239	.181	.255	-0.2	LF 2, CF -0	-1.2

Breakout: 0%   Improve: 0%   Collapse: 0%   Attrition: 0%   MLB: 0%   Comparables: Gregory Polanco, Ender Inciarte, Zoilo Almonte

For all the talk of Alex Jackson, the success of the 2014 draft will ultimately hinge on Morgan, the team's second-round choice. The M's picked the Canadian 74th and then threw boatloads of money at him, tripling his slot and forcing them to draft cheap college seniors with their next seven picks. Morgan is a lumberjack in the batter's box, both through his strength and his woodcutting swing. He was exposed in his brief stint in Rookie ball, where he struck out 41 percent of the time. It's early, but baseball's past is littered with the bones of batting practice wonders.

Logan Morrison   1B

Born: 8/25/87   Age: 27   Bats: L   Throws: L   Height: 6' 3"   Weight: 245

YEAR	TEAM	LVL	AGE	PA	R	2B	3B	HR	RBI	BB	K	SB	CS	AVG/OBP/SLG	TAv	BABIP	BRR	FRAA	WARP
2012	MIA	MLB	24	334	30	15	1	11	36	31	58	1	0	.230/.308/.399	.253	.248	-0.7	LF(59): -4.1, 1B(21): 2.6	0.1
2013	JUP	A+	25	27	0	0	0	0	3	4	0	0	1	.174/.296/.174	.218	.174	-1.4	1B(3): 0.4	-0.2
2013	JAX	AA	25	35	5	0	0	2	7	2	4	0	0	.182/.229/.364	.212	.148	0.1	1B(7): 0.0	-0.2
2013	MIA	MLB	25	333	32	13	4	6	36	38	56	0	0	.242/.333/.375	.262	.281	-0.1	1B(79): -1.6	0.4
2014	TAC	AAA	26	77	13	2	0	3	8	11	8	2	0	.308/.416/.477	.320	.315	0.3	1B(6): 0.1	0.7
2014	SEA	MLB	26	365	41	20	0	11	38	24	59	5	2	.262/.315/.420	.281	.287	-2.5	1B(79): -5.9, RF(8): 0.5	0.6
2015	SEA	MLB	27	355	39	16	2	10	42	35	63	3	1	.244/.323/.402	.284	.273	-0.9	1B -1, LF -0	1.0

Breakout: 4%   Improve: 48%   Collapse: 6%   Attrition: 9%   MLB: 98%   Comparables: James Loney, Justin Smoak, Nick Johnson

Morrison didn't have a fantastic year: Compare his line to local pariah Justin Smoak's 2013 effort. (If you're lazy and don't want to flip four chapters ahead: They're basically the same.) But he did get hot exactly when the rest of the team curled into the fetal position, racking up several clutch hits to propel the team just short of the finish line. By agreeing to the Mariners Hitter Written Agreement's "swing at everything" clause, Morrison has turned himself into a strange type of player, one whose offensive value is almost entirely predicated on hitting line drives. This makes him the new James Loney, as long as he's seeing the ball well; it makes him the old Eric Hosmer when he isn't. None of the comparisons in this comment are exciting for any of the people involved.

D.J. Peterson   1B

Born: 12/31/91   Age: 23   Bats: R   Throws: R   Height: 6' 1"   Weight: 190

YEAR	TEAM	LVL	AGE	PA	R	2B	3B	HR	RBI	BB	K	SB	CS	AVG/OBP/SLG	TAv	BABIP	BRR	FRAA	WARP
2013	EVE	A-	21	123	20	6	0	6	27	13	18	0	1	.312/.382/.532	.331	.326	-0.6	3B(24): -2.9, 1B(1): -0.0	0.9
2013	CLN	A	21	107	16	5	1	7	20	7	24	1	0	.293/.346/.576	.321	.324	-0.1	3B(21): -0.6	0.9
2014	HDS	A+	22	299	51	23	1	18	73	23	65	6	0	.326/.381/.615	.321	.372	1.4	3B(45): -0.4, 1B(10): 0.7	2.9
2014	WTN	AA	22	248	32	8	0	13	38	22	51	1	1	.261/.335/.473	.291	.283	-0.8	3B(45): -3.0, 1B(9): 0.5	1.4
2015	SEA	MLB	23	250	27	9	0	10	33	13	69	0	0	.231/.273/.406	.264	.278	-0.4	3B -3, 1B 0	0.3

Breakout: 1%   Improve: 21%   Collapse: 2%   Attrition: 13%   MLB: 49%   Comparables: Alex Liddi, Alex Gordon, Allen Craig

Can he play third? Given the axiom that all the world hates a first base prospect, Peterson's trade value hinges on whether he can scrape by at the hot corner. No one disputes that his bat is major league-caliber, despite a second-half slump; he was the safest hitting prospect in the 2013 draft. Most promising is Peterson's strikeout rate, unusually low for a power hitter, which reduces the chance of him busting entirely. The organization thus far has chosen to hedge its bets, giving him about 80 percent of his starts at third and the rest at first. Now that Kyle Seager will be wearing Northwest "Green" for the rest of Peterson's twenties, he'll probably become a first baseman for life when the Mariners find themselves in their time of need.

Stefen Romero   RF

Born: 10/17/88   Age: 26   Bats: R   Throws: R   Height: 6' 2"   Weight: 220

YEAR	TEAM	LVL	AGE	PA	R	2B	3B	HR	RBI	BB	K	SB	CS	AVG/OBP/SLG	TAv	BABIP	BRR	FRAA	WARP
2012	HDS	A+	23	276	47	19	3	11	51	13	35	6	2	.357/.391/.581	.309	.379	-1.2	2B(53): -1.8	1.8
2012	WTN	AA	23	240	38	15	4	12	50	14	37	6	3	.347/.392/.620	.339	.366	0.1	2B(54): -0.1	2.6
2013	HDS	A+	24	21	1	1	0	0	2	2	1	0	0	.278/.381/.333	.229	.294	-0.1	3B(4): -0.0	0.0
2013	TAC	AAA	24	411	51	23	4	11	74	28	87	8	4	.277/.331/.448	.273	.331	0.6	LF(73): 2.3, RF(2): 0.2	1.4
2014	TAC	AAA	25	163	26	7	2	12	36	8	28	1	3	.358/.387/.669	.352	.368	-2.5	RF(30): -1.6, LF(3): 0.1	1.7
2014	SEA	MLB	25	190	19	6	2	3	11	4	48	0	4	.192/.234/.299	.195	.244	0.3	RF(42): 0.2, LF(11): -0.1	-0.9
2015	SEA	MLB	26	250	26	10	2	7	29	8	56	3	3	.249/.282/.399	.264	.293	-0.5	RF -0, LF 0	0.5

Breakout: 7%   Improve: 26%   Collapse: 12%   Attrition: 20%   MLB: 55%   Comparables: Chris Heisey, Steve Pearce, Cody Ross

The good news: Romero absolutely destroyed Triple-A in his second stint there, mashing for a 1.056 OPS. The bad news: He didn't spend the whole season at Triple-A. Romero began and ended the season in the majors, where he was one of the worst players in baseball, struggling in the field and looking absolutely lost at the plate. Romero's minor-league numbers reflect a guy who can hit and PECOTA is similarly optimistic. Additionally, the Mariners aren't exactly teeming with outfielders, which is why Romero kept getting chances to fail in 2014. It wouldn't be hard to imagine the team calling Xavier Avery or Jabari Blash's name when the team needs an outfielder in May.

Justin Ruggiano   RF

Born: 4/12/82   Age: 33   Bats: R   Throws: R   Height: 6' 1"   Weight: 210

YEAR	TEAM	LVL	AGE	PA	R	2B	3B	HR	RBI	BB	K	SB	CS	AVG/OBP/SLG	TAv	BABIP	BRR	FRAA	WARP
2012	OKL	AAA	30	138	21	13	1	5	29	18	24	5	3	.325/.409/.581	.327	.367	0.3	CF(21): -2.1, RF(7): 0.1	1.3
2012	MIA	MLB	30	320	38	23	1	13	36	29	84	14	8	.313/.374/.535	.322	.401	-0.1	CF(52): 2.3, LF(31): -1.1	2.9
2013	MIA	MLB	31	472	49	18	1	18	50	41	114	15	8	.222/.298/.396	.253	.260	1.0	CF(84): -2.7, LF(23): -0.4	0.7
2014	IOW	AAA	32	25	3	1	0	0	0	3	6	0	0	.143/.280/.190	.193	.200	0.3	RF(5): 0.1	-0.2
2014	CHN	MLB	32	250	29	13	1	6	28	18	70	2	4	.281/.337/.429	.291	.375	0.5	RF(34): -1.9, CF(18): 0.3	1.3
2015	SEA	MLB	33	283	34	14	1	9	33	23	75	7	5	.249/.314/.413	.273	.312	0.2	CF -0, RF -1	1.1

Breakout: 1%   Improve: 26%   Collapse: 5%   Attrition: 9%   MLB: 91%   Comparables: Ryan Raburn, Jermaine Dye, Casey Blake

Ruggiano's 2014 was cut short by left-ankle surgery, but while on the field, he bounced back nicely from a disappointing 2013. He hasn't been used with a platoon partner much in his career, but his numbers against lefties indicate that he could thrive in a role that lets him focus on mashing them. Ruggiano entered the season slugging over .500 against southpaws for his career and continued that trend in 2014, posting a .305/.333/.512 line. He's not unplayable against righties, but as he ages into his mid-30s it may behoove his handlers to pick his matchups ever more carefully. That he can handle all three outfield spots (for now, anyway) makes it easier to develop a sort of full-time-against-lefties super-outfield-sub role.

Kyle Seager   3B

Born: 11/3/87   Age: 27   Bats: L   Throws: R   Height: 6' 0"   Weight: 210

YEAR	TEAM	LVL	AGE	PA	R	2B	3B	HR	RBI	BB	K	SB	CS	AVG/OBP/SLG	TAv	BABIP	BRR	FRAA	WARP
2012	SEA	MLB	24	651	62	35	1	20	86	46	110	13	5	.259/.316/.423	.274	.286	0.5	3B(138): -2.8, 2B(18): 1.6	3.0
2013	SEA	MLB	25	695	79	32	2	22	69	68	122	9	3	.260/.338/.426	.290	.290	0.9	3B(160): 2.0	4.9
2014	SEA	MLB	26	654	71	27	4	25	96	52	118	7	5	.268/.334/.454	.304	.296	-0.8	3B(157): 20.5	7.3
2015	SEA	MLB	27	623	69	30	2	17	73	47	111	9	4	.261/.321/.413	.287	.293	0.0	3B 7, 2B 0	3.9

Breakout: 5%   Improve: 43%   Collapse: 6%   Attrition: 9%   MLB: 100%   Comparables: *Edwin Encarnacion, George Brett, Pablo Sandoval*

Everyone's favorite utilityman and high-floor/low-ceiling prospect keeps raising the ceiling year after year. In 2012 he didn't crack the team's Opening Day lineup; two years later, he was a clear All-Star. His TAv over the last four years reads like a crescendo: .263, .274, .290, .304. Last year's massive improvement, though, came on the defensive side, where he netted his first Gold Glove. Seager credits practice and coaching for his improvement, as well as finally having a stable position. Spiteful people will point out that it was a drop in errors that accounted for the majority of his improvement, but even with regression Seager remains one of the best third basemen in baseball, and one of the unlikeliest. The Mariners, recognizing the former, signed him to an extension through 2021, buying three arbitration years and four free-agent years, plus a club option for 2022. Seager gets to say he has a nine-figure contract and the Mariners get to win baseball games.

Jesus Sucre   C

Born: 4/30/88   Age: 27   Bats: R   Throws: R   Height: 6' 0"   Weight: 225

YEAR	TEAM	LVL	AGE	PA	R	2B	3B	HR	RBI	BB	K	SB	CS	AVG/OBP/SLG	TAv	BABIP	BRR	FRAA	WARP
2012	WTN	AA	24	349	27	11	0	1	30	20	39	1	1	.271/.319/.315	.230	.305	0.1	C(88): 3.1	1.1
2013	TAC	AAA	25	95	10	3	0	0	8	7	10	1	1	.299/.351/.333	.277	.338	1.5	C(23): -0.3	0.8
2013	SEA	MLB	25	29	1	0	0	0	3	2	1	0	0	.192/.241/.192	.162	.192	0.3	C(8): 0.3	-0.1
2014	TAC	AAA	26	181	13	7	1	2	16	4	29	0	1	.274/.293/.360	.230	.317	-0.2	C(47): -0.2	0.6
2014	SEA	MLB	26	64	4	2	0	0	5	0	17	0	0	.213/.213/.246	.176	.295	-0.3	C(21): -0.1	-0.3
2015	SEA	MLB	27	250	18	8	0	1	18	7	44	0	0	.233/.256/.285	.218	.275	-0.4	C 1	0.0

Breakout: 5%   Improve: 10%   Collapse: 9%   Attrition: 15%   MLB: 23%   Comparables: *Wilkin Castillo, Humberto Quintero, Drew Butera*

There are worse gigs out there than backup catcher. You basically play on Sundays, when everyone is out mowing the lawn, and as a defensive replacement after a pinch-hitter, when the game's probably already decided. You get plenty of time to actually heal from all that catching. And expectations are even lower than for backup quarterbacks. Take Sucre. He's about as worthless a hitter as you're likely to stumble across: His swinging-strike rate of 14 percent means that basically every pitcher he faces has Clayton Kershaw's stuff; he has forgotten how to take a base on balls; and his swings have five frames of animation. Yet thanks to the defensive legacy of the law firm of Olivo, Shoppach, Buck & Montero, Sucre's sure glove and fully articulating right arm make grown Seattlites weep. As long as Mike Zunino remains hale and hearty and can shoulder the majority of life's burdens, Sweet Jesus will make a passable sidekick.

Chris Taylor   SS

Born: 8/29/90   Age: 24   Bats: R   Throws: R   Height: 6' 1"   Weight: 190

YEAR	TEAM	LVL	AGE	PA	R	2B	3B	HR	RBI	BB	K	SB	CS	AVG/OBP/SLG	TAv	BABIP	BRR	FRAA	WARP
2012	EVE	A-	21	165	26	12	1	2	18	21	18	13	5	.328/.430/.474	.318	.361	-3.2	SS(30): 0.8, 2B(6): 0.9	1.5
2012	CLN	A	21	53	5	0	0	0	4	2	4	4	1	.304/.373/.304	.258	.333	-0.1	SS(8): -1.0	0.0
2013	HDS	A+	22	319	62	16	7	7	44	44	62	20	2	.335/.426/.524	.320	.407	5.2	SS(61): 3.6, 2B(2): 0.2	4.1
2013	WTN	AA	22	300	46	12	4	1	16	40	55	18	3	.293/.391/.383	.296	.368	5.3	SS(39): 1.6, 2B(25): -0.4	3.3
2014	TAC	AAA	23	346	63	22	7	5	37	35	74	14	6	.328/.397/.497	.314	.412	2.1	SS(53): 2.5, 2B(21): 1.7	4.2
2014	SEA	MLB	23	151	16	8	0	0	9	11	39	5	2	.287/.347/.346	.289	.398	2.4	SS(47): 3.8	1.8
2015	SEA	MLB	24	250	28	10	2	1	17	21	59	9	2	.257/.323/.337	.265	.336	0.7	SS 3, 2B 0	1.6

Breakout: 2%   Improve: 26%   Collapse: 17%   Attrition: 22%   MLB: 65%   Comparables: *Ian Desmond, Yamaico Navarro, Chase d'Arnaud*

It took Taylor less than two years to go from being a fifth-round draft pick to big-league starting shortstop. The defense is no surprise: Taylor was projected to wield a strong glove along with above-average range. He showed a pleasant aptitude toward the stolen base, developing the instincts to steal more than his pure speed might lead one to guess. But it's the pop in his bat that has upgraded his prospect luster, not the pop that puts the ball over the wall but the pop that puts the ball over infielder's gloves. Taylor's approach and quick hands keep him from being overmatched at the plate. He heads into 2015 competing with Brad Miller for the starting shortstop role, one for which both candidates, though different in their strengths, are fully capable. Either way, Taylor's next step will be to improve his contact rate to match his batting eye, giving him more opportunities to put that beautiful BABIP of his to use.

Austin Wilson   OF

Born: 2/7/92   Age: 23   Bats: R   Throws: R   Height: 6' 4"   Weight: 249

YEAR	TEAM	LVL	AGE	PA	R	2B	3B	HR	RBI	BB	K	SB	CS	AVG/OBP/SLG	TAv	BABIP	BRR	FRAA	WARP
2013	EVE	A-	21	226	22	11	3	6	27	17	42	2	4	.241/.319/.414	.297	.277	-0.3	RF(45): -1.9, CF(3): 0.1	1.2
2014	CLN	A	22	299	38	17	3	12	54	26	65	1	1	.291/.376/.517	.321	.346	1.0	RF(51): 1.2, LF(9): 0.1	2.7
2015	SEA	MLB	23	250	22	9	1	7	27	11	70	0	0	.212/.260/.344	.238	.270	-0.4	RF 0, LF 0	-0.2

Breakout: 0%   Improve: 0%   Collapse: 0%   Attrition: 0%   MLB: 0%   Comparables: *Roger Kieschnick, Andrew Lambo, J.D. Martinez*

Whenever people say "this guy looks like a baseball player," there's generally an unspoken "even though he isn't hitting yet." And while Wilson remains rough for a college draft choice, his age-22 season saw his stats and skills begin to converge. His athleticism makes him a natural fit for right field, and the power is there, flickering like a warning light. He still strikes out a lot (though not at Joey Gallo levels), he doesn't even try to run and he can be inconsistent, so the team will take him slowly, even if he is already 23. But the peripherals are slowly congealing. It shouldn't be long before people stop needing to explain his choice of vocation.

Mike Zunino   C

Born: 3/25/91   Age: 24   Bats: R   Throws: R   Height: 6' 2"   Weight: 220

YEAR	TEAM	LVL	AGE	PA	R	2B	3B	HR	RBI	BB	K	SB	CS	AVG/OBP/SLG	TAv	BABIP	BRR	FRAA	WARP
2012	EVE	A-	21	133	29	10	0	10	35	18	26	1	0	.373/.474/.736	.385	.413	-0.6	C(19): 0.3	2.4
2012	WTN	AA	21	57	6	4	0	3	8	5	7	0	0	.333/.386/.588	.319	.333	0.1	C(12): 0.1	0.6
2013	TAC	AAA	22	229	38	12	3	11	43	17	66	0	0	.227/.297/.478	.285	.269	2.1	C(50): 0.2	1.9
2013	SEA	MLB	22	193	22	5	0	5	14	16	49	1	0	.214/.290/.329	.247	.267	-0.8	C(50): 0.0	0.4
2014	SEA	MLB	23	476	51	20	2	22	60	17	158	0	3	.199/.254/.404	.241	.248	1.5	C(130): -0.2	1.5
2015	SEA	MLB	24	418	46	15	2	17	51	22	126	1	1	.215/.272/.393	.260	.269	0.6	C 0	1.7

Breakout: 5%   Improve: 52%   Collapse: 11%   Attrition: 20%   MLB: 98%   *Comparables:* *Jarrod Saltalamacchia, Wilin Rosario, Alex Gordon*

No one created more strikes in 2014 than Zunino, who contributed with the glove, where he was one of the best pitch framers in the game, and with the bat, where he swung at everything as if Kenobi told him to put down the blast shield on his helmet. It's not every day you see a hitter accumulate more home runs and HBPs than unintentional walks. So maybe "Olivo, but with defense" isn't exactly what fans were looking for out of their heralded first-round pick, and the strikeout-to-walk ratio approaching double figures isn't exactly an indication of superstardom. But he turns 24 right before the season starts, and his defense and power will make him valuable while he catches up on the whole plate discipline thing, or even if he never does.

Pitchers

Joe Beimel   LHP

Born: 4/19/77   Age: 38   Bats: L   Throws: L   Height: 6'3"   Weight: 205

YEAR	TEAM	LVL	AGE	W	L	SV	G	GS	IP	H	HR	BB	K	BB/9	K/9	GB%	BABIP	WHIP	ERA	FIP	FRA	WARP
2013	GWN	AAA	36	1	2	0	30	0	33	34	6	16	24	4.4	6.5	38%	.272	1.52	4.36	5.75	6.29	-0.4
2014	SEA	MLB	37	3	1	0	56	0	45	39	4	14	25	2.8	5.0	51%	.250	1.18	2.20	4.20	4.26	0.0
2015	SEA	MLB	38	2	1	1	42	0	35²	37	4	12	22	3.0	5.6	45%	.285	1.37	4.26	4.91	4.63	-0.1

Breakout: 17%   Improve: 29%   Collapse: 19%   Attrition: 11%   MLB: 65%   *Comparables:* *Brian Boehringer, Matt Herges, Brian Shouse*

Everyone complains about small sample size, but it's what allowed Beimel to feel like a king for a couple of months. The non-roster invitee had missed 2012 completely, been lit up at Triple-A in 2013, but in 2014 held lefties to a .188/.217/.288 line. His FIP suggests he doesn't belong, but, shoot, his being Joe Beimel suggested he doesn't belong. We all deserve a little undeserved praise once in a while.

Edwin Diaz   RHP

Born: 3/22/94   Age: 21   Bats: R   Throws: R   Height: 6'2"   Weight: 178

YEAR	TEAM	LVL	AGE	W	L	SV	G	GS	IP	H	HR	BB	K	BB/9	K/9	GB%	BABIP	WHIP	ERA	FIP	FRA	WARP
2014	CLN	A	20	6	8	0	24	24	116¹	96	5	42	111	3.2	8.6	44%	.289	1.19	3.33	3.48	4.21	1.3
2015	SEA	MLB	21	4	6	0	17	17	85	89	9	42	59	4.4	6.3	43%	.298	1.54	4.88	5.26	5.30	-0.7

Breakout: 0%   Improve: 0%   Collapse: 0%   Attrition: 0%   MLB: 0%   *Comparables:* *Jordan Walden, Jeremy Hellickson, Jose A. Ramirez*

You know those little capsules you got as a kid? The kind they don't sell anymore and no one under the age of thirty has any idea about? You take the capsule, fill up your sink, throw it in and watch it slowly expand and take shape as some random object, maybe a dinosaur or a gorilla. It always went way too slow and most of the time you didn't even like the end result. Just like pitching prospects! So maybe that's not fair to Diaz. He's doing everything he's supposed to do: putting on weight, polishing his secondary pitches, learning what it is to be a man in a troubled world. His fastball is mid-90s with room to improve, his slider is strong and he has plenty of time to figure out a third pitch, starting in Double-A Jackson. Of course, he'll probably have some sort of tear once he's fully grown and you won't want him.

Roenis Elias   LHP

Born: 8/1/88   Age: 26   Bats: L   Throws: L   Height: 6'1"   Weight: 190

YEAR	TEAM	LVL	AGE	W	L	SV	G	GS	IP	H	HR	BB	K	BB/9	K/9	GB%	BABIP	WHIP	ERA	FIP	FRA	WARP
2012	HDS	A+	23	11	6	0	26	26	148¹	136	19	41	128	2.5	7.8	45%	.281	1.19	3.76	4.74	5.27	2.6
2013	WTN	AA	24	6	11	0	22	22	130	112	9	50	121	3.5	8.4	44%	.286	1.25	3.18	3.20	3.82	1.7
2014	SEA	MLB	25	10	12	0	29	29	163²	151	16	64	143	3.5	7.9	48%	.294	1.31	3.85	4.06	4.23	0.7
2015	SEA	MLB	26	8	8	0	24	24	137	130	14	50	113	3.3	7.4	44%	.288	1.31	3.98	4.47	4.32	0.4

Breakout: 30%   Improve: 59%   Collapse: 19%   Attrition: 22%   MLB: 91%   *Comparables:* *Dillon Gee, Carlos Carrasco, Boof Bonser*

With three-fifths of its starting rotation injured and another pitcher claiming secret surprise free agency, Elias was thrown to the wolves at the beginning of the season. He fought said wolves to a draw. Despite being a consensus non-prospect, Elias continued putting up league-average numbers even while being leaned on more and more heavily as the year went by. He throws a passable 92 mph with his left arm and has a decent enough changeup, but it's his curve that will win or lose his legacy. When he spotted it, he looked as good as any of the more famous Mariners prospects of recent times. PECOTA has all his minor-league numbers in front of it and isn't particularly impressed, and there's a reason the experts didn't pull his name out of the hat at the bottom of their lists. Though it's probably in everyone's best interest for the Mariners to thank Elias kindly for the conscription and return him to Tacoma to learn, the team does have something valuable on its hands.

Danny Farquhar   RHP

Born: 2/17/87   Age: 28   Bats: R   Throws: R   Height: 5'9"   Weight: 185

YEAR	TEAM	LVL	AGE	W	L	SV	G	GS	IP	H	HR	BB	K	BB/9	K/9	GB%	BABIP	WHIP	ERA	FIP	FRA	WARP
2012	NHP	AA	25	0	1	1	20	0	30¹	28	2	10	33	3.0	9.8	42%	.306	1.25	2.97	3.17	3.81	0.5
2012	TRN	AA	25	1	0	4	6	0	11	2	0	0	14	0.0	11.5	48%	.095	0.18	0.00	0.66	2.13	0.3
2012	TAC	AAA	25	1	0	4	12	0	16²	9	0	5	16	2.7	8.6	48%	.214	0.84	0.54	2.83	2.60	0.5
2013	TAC	AAA	26	0	1	6	15	0	20	17	1	4	30	1.8	13.5	50%	.340	1.05	2.25	1.82	2.35	0.7
2013	SEA	MLB	26	0	3	16	46	0	55²	44	2	22	79	3.6	12.8	43%	.336	1.19	4.20	1.89	2.42	1.4
2014	SEA	MLB	27	3	1	1	66	0	71	58	5	22	81	2.8	10.3	45%	.298	1.13	2.66	2.89	3.25	1.0
2015	SEA	MLB	28	3	1	4	51	0	61²	51	4	21	67	3.1	9.7	46%	.291	1.17	2.93	3.35	3.19	0.9

Breakout: 25%   Improve: 38%   Collapse: 16%   Attrition: 15%   MLB: 66%   *Comparables:*   *Pedro Strop, Clay Zavada, Rich Thompson*

Closers are made and not born, but they can also be unmade. In a surprising move last offseason, the Mariners demoted their newly minted closer to obtain capital-V veteran Fernando Rodney. The move worked out well: Rodney earned his keep and the Mariners were able to obtain equal value from the green, short, vivacious Farquhar without having to pay him for those expensive saves. As Farquhar reaches arbitration, the Mariners may have found themselves saving nearly as much on his contracts as they spent on Rodney, a neat little trick. In an attempt to appear more mild-mannered, Farquhar held back a little on his fastball; the results were pleasing overall. The strikeouts dropped to mortal levels, but he cut nearly a full walk off his BB/9 and added 4.5 percent to his first-pitch strikes. Given that control was the weakness that saw him get shuttled through five organizations in the minors, it's looking like the Mariners won at least one trade with the Yankees.

Charlie Furbush   LHP

Born: 4/11/86   Age: 29   Bats: L   Throws: L   Height: 6'5"   Weight: 215

YEAR	TEAM	LVL	AGE	W	L	SV	G	GS	IP	H	HR	BB	K	BB/9	K/9	GB%	BABIP	WHIP	ERA	FIP	FRA	WARP
2012	TAC	AAA	26	1	0	0	7	0	10	7	1	3	13	2.7	11.7	33%	.261	1.00	3.60	3.27	4.18	0.1
2012	SEA	MLB	26	5	2	0	48	0	46¹	28	3	16	53	3.1	10.3	45%	.231	0.95	2.72	2.77	3.41	0.6
2013	SEA	MLB	27	2	6	0	71	0	65	48	5	29	80	4.0	11.1	42%	.264	1.18	3.74	3.09	3.40	0.7
2014	SEA	MLB	28	1	5	1	67	0	42¹	40	4	9	51	1.9	10.8	39%	.327	1.16	3.61	2.83	2.70	0.7
2015	SEA	MLB	29	2	2	1	31	3	40²	37	5	13	42	2.8	9.3	41%	.292	1.22	3.54	4.19	3.85	0.3

Breakout: 21%   Improve: 46%   Collapse: 13%   Attrition: 17%   MLB: 74%   *Comparables:*   *Juan Gutierrez, Jon Rauch, Rich Hill*

Furbush is as oppressed as a near-millionaire athlete gets. Break out your "Underrated Baseball Player Bingo" cards. Obtained in an unpopular and regrettable trade: check. Left-handed pitcher who gets left-handed batters out really well: check. Unimpressive stint as a starter before settling into a relief role: check. Entendre-filled last name that everyone has already made too many jokes about: check. The world has grown cynical toward the poor southpaw. As games stretch into the four-hour mark and relieving sessions grow increasingly short-lived, a weary fan base projects its hatred of commercials on the lefty who mows down his apportioned like-winged opponents. It's reached the point where every left-handed middle reliever is treated with equal bile. Yet despite Furbush's ridiculous numbers against his countrymen (13.5 K/BB ratio in 2014), he's no slouch against right-handers, either. In a shallow bullpen, he'd make a popular setup man, but in Seattle he's just a guy who threw 42 innings because they didn't need more.

J.A. Happ   LHP

Born: 10/19/82   Age: 32   Bats: L   Throws: L   Height: 6'5"   Weight: 205

YEAR	TEAM	LVL	AGE	W	L	SV	G	GS	IP	H	HR	BB	K	BB/9	K/9	GB%	BABIP	WHIP	ERA	FIP	FRA	WARP
2012	HOU	MLB	29	7	9	0	18	18	104¹	112	17	39	98	3.4	8.5	48%	.315	1.45	4.83	4.53	4.78	0.5
2012	TOR	MLB	29	3	2	0	10	6	40¹	35	2	17	46	3.8	10.3	38%	.317	1.29	4.69	2.75	2.61	1.4
2013	BUF	AAA	30	0	2	0	3	3	13¹	17	2	8	13	5.4	8.8	44%	.385	1.88	6.75	5.00	5.62	0.0
2013	TOR	MLB	30	5	7	0	18	18	98²	91	10	45	77	4.4	7.5	38%	.288	1.47	4.56	4.34	4.45	0.9
2014	TOR	MLB	31	11	11	0	30	26	158	160	22	51	133	2.9	7.6	42%	.297	1.34	4.22	4.29	4.76	0.8
2015	SEA	MLB	32	8	9	0	24	24	134	132	15	53	112	3.6	7.5	40%	.294	1.38	4.26	4.59	4.63	-0.1

Breakout: 19%   Improve: 35%   Collapse: 18%   Attrition: 10%   MLB: 65%   *Comparables:*   *Randy Wolf, Claudio Vargas, Brandon Backe*

Clap along! Because Happ performed precisely to fifth-starter expectations, which shouldn't be too surprising because he's done it for five years now. Clap along! Because Happ gained two mph on his fastball last year, snapping up a few extra strikeouts and the best walk rate of his career. Don't clap along! His middling secondary stuff didn't follow suit, leaving him with plain, fifth-starter stuff. Clap along again! Because Happ broke Ian Snell's record for the most (pitching) starts to begin a career without committing an error. Happ beat Snell's streak of 127 and ended his own at 138 when he logged a throwing error on September 22nd. If that piece of Happ trivia doesn't impress your friends, nothing can make them happy.

Felix Hernandez   RHP

Born: 4/8/86   Age: 29   Bats: R   Throws: R   Height: 6'3"   Weight: 225

YEAR	TEAM	LVL	AGE	W	L	SV	G	GS	IP	H	HR	BB	K	BB/9	K/9	GB%	BABIP	WHIP	ERA	FIP	FRA	WARP
2012	SEA	MLB	26	13	9	0	33	33	232	209	14	56	223	2.2	8.7	50%	.308	1.14	3.06	2.79	3.29	3.7
2013	SEA	MLB	27	12	10	0	31	31	204¹	185	15	46	216	2.0	9.5	53%	.313	1.13	3.04	2.63	3.41	3.2
2014	SEA	MLB	28	15	6	0	34	34	236	170	16	46	248	1.8	9.5	57%	.258	0.92	2.14	2.59	3.11	4.1
2015	SEA	MLB	29	13	8	0	28	28	193²	164	14	42	194	2.0	9.0	52%	.291	1.07	2.58	3.18	2.80	4.1

Breakout: 12%   Improve: 34%   Collapse: 18%   Attrition: 4%   MLB: 94%   *Comparables:*   *CC Sabathia, Jon Lester, Matt Garza*

The King had yet another superlative season, riding the deflated offensive environment to new bests in many categories. At one point he set a record of 16 consecutive starts with seven-plus innings and two or fewer runs, which is probably called a Mathewson or a Fidrych or something. Everything about his 2014 season was an incremental improvement; in fact, you can really just read last year's edition and underline all the compliments. The only concern at this point is his workload: Hernandez topped 230 innings for the fifth time in six years. Lloyd McClendon actually showed commendable restraint, lifting him with shutouts and complete games within reach. No pitcher is immortal, as CC Sabathia recently proved, but Felix has as a good a shot as any due to reliance on movement rather than speed and avoiding all those pesky postseason innings.

Hisashi Iwakuma   RHP

Born: 4/12/81   Age: 34   Bats: R   Throws: R   Height: 6'3"   Weight: 210

YEAR	TEAM	LVL	AGE	W	L	SV	G	GS	IP	H	HR	BB	K	BB/9	K/9	GB%	BABIP	WHIP	ERA	FIP	FRA	WARP
2012	SEA	MLB	31	9	5	2	30	16	125¹	117	17	43	101	3.1	7.3	54%	.282	1.28	3.16	4.30	4.87	-0.3
2013	SEA	MLB	32	14	6	0	33	33	219²	179	25	42	185	1.7	7.6	50%	.252	1.01	2.66	3.47	4.03	2.2
2014	SEA	MLB	33	15	9	0	28	28	179	167	20	21	154	1.1	7.7	52%	.287	1.05	3.52	3.28	3.91	1.6
2015	SEA	MLB	34	10	8	0	24	24	161	148	18	31	133	1.7	7.5	50%	.280	1.11	3.13	3.97	3.40	2.1

Breakout: 22%   Improve: 44%   Collapse: 14%   Attrition: 10%   MLB: 80%   *Comparables:*   *Johan Santana, Josh Beckett, Kevin Millwood*

Iwakuma hurt himself in one of the most Mariner of ways outside of getting eaten by a whale: He snagged his finger in some netting and tore a tendon. The injury robbed him of March, April and perhaps September, as he faded badly at the end of the season without a proper spring training. But in between, he was as good as his Cy Young finalist 2013 season, maybe better. He gave up more runs, mostly thanks to the usual suspects: a jump in BABIP, HR/FB rate and a drop in strand rate. But he also cut his walks down to a minuscule rate that was good for fourth in baseball and particularly good for a guy who needs to get ahead in the count to expand hitter's strike zones.

Dominic Leone   RHP
Born: 10/26/91   Age: 23   Bats: R   Throws: R   Height: 5'11"   Weight: 210

YEAR	TEAM	LVL	AGE	W	L	SV	G	GS	IP	H	HR	BB	K	BB/9	K/9	GB%	BABIP	WHIP	ERA	FIP	FRA	WARP
2012	EVE	A-	20	3	0	5	19	0	33	20	0	19	39	5.2	10.6	51%	.260	1.18	1.36	2.78	3.19	0.9
2013	HDS	A+	21	0	1	12	29	0	39²	31	2	9	37	2.0	8.4	57%	.274	1.01	2.50	3.32	3.72	1.1
2013	WTN	AA	21	1	2	4	16	0	18	12	2	5	17	2.5	8.5	49%	.213	0.94	2.50	3.30	4.10	0.1
2014	SEA	MLB	22	8	2	0	57	0	66¹	52	4	25	70	3.4	9.5	57%	.282	1.16	2.17	3.10	3.61	0.5
2015	SEA	MLB	23	2	1	1	42	0	55²	48	4	20	54	3.2	8.8	49%	.288	1.22	3.12	3.71	3.40	0.7

Breakout: 18%   Improve: 25%   Collapse: 12%   Attrition: 16%   MLB: 45%   Comparables: *Drew Storen, Chance Ruffin, Kelvin Herrera*

Leone was a weekend starter in college, and a reliever in the minors, so it makes perfect sense that the undersized former 16th-rounder would leap from Double-A to the majors and dominate after adding seven mph on his fastball and mastering a cutter by watching YouTube videos of Mariano Rivera. He had the best ERA in the Mariners' bullpen, and a higher ERA+ than 19 of 30 full-time closers. Writing this down, kids?

Brandon Maurer   RHP
Born: 7/3/90   Age: 24   Bats: R   Throws: R   Height: 6'5"   Weight: 220

YEAR	TEAM	LVL	AGE	W	L	SV	G	GS	IP	H	HR	BB	K	BB/9	K/9	GB%	BABIP	WHIP	ERA	FIP	FRA	WARP
2012	WTN	AA	21	9	2	0	24	24	137²	133	4	48	117	3.1	7.6	48%	.322	1.31	3.20	3.00	3.94	2.2
2013	TAC	AAA	22	3	4	0	10	10	46²	48	2	26	47	5.0	9.1	39%	.341	1.59	5.21	4.11	3.83	0.9
2013	SEA	MLB	22	5	8	0	22	14	90	114	16	27	70	2.7	7.0	45%	.346	1.57	6.30	4.93	5.19	-0.3
2014	TAC	AAA	23	1	0	3	12	1	19¹	18	2	8	24	3.7	11.2	40%	.333	1.34	2.79	3.80	3.72	0.4
2014	SEA	MLB	23	1	4	0	38	7	69²	74	6	19	55	2.5	7.1	41%	.308	1.33	4.65	3.52	4.23	0.2
2015	SEA	MLB	24	5	5	0	24	13	86	89	9	27	69	2.8	7.2	43%	.308	1.34	4.14	4.41	4.50	0.1

Breakout: 29%   Improve: 60%   Collapse: 15%   Attrition: 23%   MLB: 87%   Comparables: *Jon Niese, Homer Bailey, Alex White*

The former 23rd-round pick had a heartwarming 2013, in the tire-fire sense, and it looked as though 2014 would be no different. It was clear that Maurer had been rushed badly, and the intention was to keep him in Tacoma to learn how pitching is performed, but the plague hit Seattle and Maurer relived his greatest hits for seven starts in April and May. By the time Hisashi Iwakuma was ready to take his spot back, Maurer's ERA was 7.52 and he was gibbering uncontrollably. It took three weeks for the team to solve that problem: They converted him to reliever and told him to forget that "learning to pitch" stuff, ditch the sinker and the curve and throw his slider as hard and as often as possible. Somehow, it worked: Maurer posted a 1.90 FIP the rest of the way and settled in as a strong seventh-inning reliever. As is so often the case, the confidence that the bullpen can bring a young pitcher can intoxicate a club, and it looks like Maurer's days of starting are behind him.

Yoervis Medina   RHP
Born: 7/27/88   Age: 26   Bats: R   Throws: R   Height: 6'3"   Weight: 245

YEAR	TEAM	LVL	AGE	W	L	SV	G	GS	IP	H	HR	BB	K	BB/9	K/9	GB%	BABIP	WHIP	ERA	FIP	FRA	WARP
2012	WTN	AA	23	5	5	5	46	1	69¹	63	5	35	77	4.5	10.0	55%	.320	1.41	3.25	3.59	4.80	1.1
2013	SEA	MLB	24	4	6	1	63	0	68	49	5	40	71	5.3	9.4	55%	.257	1.31	2.91	3.88	4.34	0.1
2014	SEA	MLB	25	5	3	0	66	0	57	48	3	28	60	4.4	9.5	56%	.298	1.33	2.68	3.48	3.93	0.3
2015	SEA	MLB	26	3	2	0	32	4	51²	48	5	23	45	4.0	7.8	48%	.291	1.38	4.11	4.61	4.46	0.0

Breakout: 36%   Improve: 57%   Collapse: 20%   Attrition: 19%   MLB: 84%   Comparables: *Jose Capellan, Blake Wood, Jorge De La Rosa*

For years Medina sat on the 40-man roster while other, bigger names came and went. He's turned out to be somewhat worth the wait, given that most people didn't realize they had been waiting. Medina's got a live arm and a power sinker that nets a nice groundball rate, and he would seem ideal for mid-inning jams. Unfortunately, many of the double plays that Medina induced were of his own making. Despite powerful stuff, he's never posted elite K:BB ratios because he can't steer the ball close enough to the zone to tempt them into swinging. What he is now is good enough to be a sixth- or seventh-inning guy, but even average control would make him a great reliever.

James Paxton   LHP
Born: 11/6/88   Age: 26   Bats: L   Throws: L   Height: 6'4"   Weight: 220

YEAR	TEAM	LVL	AGE	W	L	SV	G	GS	IP	H	HR	BB	K	BB/9	K/9	GB%	BABIP	WHIP	ERA	FIP	FRA	WARP
2012	WTN	AA	23	9	4	0	21	21	106¹	96	5	54	110	4.6	9.3	49%	.322	1.41	3.05	3.24	3.89	2.3
2013	TAC	AAA	24	8	11	0	28	26	145²	158	10	58	131	3.6	8.1	51%	.338	1.48	4.45	3.92	4.07	2.3
2013	SEA	MLB	24	3	0	0	4	4	24	15	2	7	21	2.6	7.9	59%	.203	0.92	1.50	3.28	4.40	0.2
2014	TAC	AAA	25	0	1	0	3	3	10¹	13	2	6	14	5.2	12.2	53%	.393	1.84	4.35	5.25	5.03	0.1
2014	SEA	MLB	25	6	4	0	13	13	74	60	3	29	59	3.5	7.2	57%	.270	1.20	3.04	3.31	3.55	0.9
2015	SEA	MLB	26	5	5	0	16	16	87²	81	7	34	80	3.5	8.2	50%	.298	1.31	3.57	3.98	3.88	0.8

Breakout: 33%   Improve: 53%   Collapse: 20%   Attrition: 24%   MLB: 84%   Comparables: *John Maine, Josh Collmenter, Juan Gutierrez*

Paxton earned a spot in the rotation in the spring and then almost instantly moved to the disabled list for four months with a strained lat muscle and the naturally corresponding shoulder inflammation. Once he returned in August, he was great. The mavens have always been split on Paxton, who for health reasons found himself a year or two behind his ideal development path. Some see a lefty throwing a mid-90s fastball and a well-above-50 percent groundball rate and get cartoon dollar signs over their eyes. Others note his underwhelming peripherals and that amateur curveball, the elusive third pitch, the one he needs in order to get strikeouts.

Muddying things further are the health issues, arising from mechanics that might charitably be described as "flamboyant." The question may not be whether Paxton can dominate, but whether he can afford to: The higher release point he needs for an effective curve could be leading to injury. In the meantime, he's graduated from possible reliever to definite starter, though whether as a no. 2 or a back-end type remains to be seen.

Erasmo Ramirez   RHP

Born: 5/2/90   Age: 25   Bats: R   Throws: R   Height: 5'11"   Weight: 200

YEAR	TEAM	LVL	AGE	W	L	SV	G	GS	IP	H	HR	BB	K	BB/9	K/9	GB%	BABIP	WHIP	ERA	FIP	FRA	WARP
2012	TAC	AAA	22	6	3	0	15	15	77¹	81	5	18	58	2.1	6.8	48%	.299	1.28	3.72	3.86	4.53	1.1
2012	SEA	MLB	22	1	3	0	16	8	59	47	6	12	48	1.8	7.3	41%	.243	1.00	3.36	3.50	3.58	0.9
2013	TAC	AAA	23	3	3	0	7	7	43²	43	4	14	42	2.9	8.7	44%	.315	1.31	3.09	3.87	3.75	0.9
2013	SEA	MLB	23	5	3	0	14	13	72¹	79	12	26	57	3.2	7.1	44%	.300	1.45	4.98	4.86	5.18	-0.4
2014	TAC	AAA	24	6	5	0	15	14	86¹	92	8	13	67	1.4	7.0	41%	.313	1.22	3.65	3.94	4.06	1.4
2014	SEA	MLB	24	1	6	0	17	14	75¹	82	13	34	60	4.1	7.2	40%	.307	1.54	5.26	5.40	5.66	-0.9
2015	SEA	MLB	25	8	9	0	25	25	141¹	145	16	34	101	2.2	6.5	46%	.292	1.26	3.93	4.48	4.27	0.5

Breakout: 30%   Improve: 52%   Collapse: 15%   Attrition: 25%   MLB: 84%   Comparables: Jeanmar Gomez, Justin Grimm, Alex Cobb

Not too long ago, Ramirez was the team's fourth starter of the future: an undersized pitcher who got by on a plus changeup and a willingness to throw it in the zone. Now he's older and wiser and not as good at baseball. His walk rate rose to over 10 percent in the majors and his home run problem grew even worse as hitters feasted on his off-speed pitches. Is Ramirez avoiding the plate because he's so hittable in the zone? Is he hittable in the zone because he's lost control and constantly behind in the count? His declining fastball cries the former, while his numbers in Tacoma make it look like the latter. Either way, he has one last chance to pull himself out of this spiral, at least in the M's organization. If he were left-handed, he'd have infinitely more opportunities.

Fernando Rodney   RHP

Born: 3/18/77   Age: 38   Bats: R   Throws: R   Height: 5'11"   Weight: 220

YEAR	TEAM	LVL	AGE	W	L	SV	G	GS	IP	H	HR	BB	K	BB/9	K/9	GB%	BABIP	WHIP	ERA	FIP	FRA	WARP
2012	TBA	MLB	35	2	2	48	76	0	74²	43	2	15	76	1.8	9.2	59%	.220	0.78	0.60	2.08	2.42	1.8
2013	TBA	MLB	36	5	4	37	68	0	66²	53	3	36	82	4.9	11.1	50%	.298	1.34	3.38	2.87	2.83	1.3
2014	SEA	MLB	37	1	6	48	69	0	66¹	61	3	28	76	3.8	10.3	51%	.330	1.34	2.85	2.86	2.94	0.9
2015	SEA	MLB	38	3	1	40	61	0	58	50	3	25	59	3.9	9.2	51%	.294	1.29	3.24	3.61	3.53	0.6

Breakout: 19%   Improve: 37%   Collapse: 21%   Attrition: 8%   MLB: 81%   Comparables: Francisco Cordero, Trever Miller, Randy Choate

The Mariners paid Rodney to repeat 2013, in terms of value, and that's just about what he did. The Fernando Rodney Experience always seemed to involve a couple of baserunners but it also nearly always ended in another of those imaginary arrows into the sky. Mariners fans were never quite content with the process. Entering his age-37 season, Rodney's fastball lost a little fire and he grew more hittable as a result. He faded in the second half, his season punctuated by a grisly one-inning, four-walk loss that effectively ended the Mariners' season. But closers are like that. They're human. They throw hard and make mistakes and ruin people's evenings. That doesn't mean they should all be treated like Jose Mesa.

Taijuan Walker   RHP

Born: 8/13/92   Age: 22   Bats: R   Throws: R   Height: 6'4"   Weight: 230

YEAR	TEAM	LVL	AGE	W	L	SV	G	GS	IP	H	HR	BB	K	BB/9	K/9	GB%	BABIP	WHIP	ERA	FIP	FRA	WARP
2012	WTN	AA	19	7	10	0	25	25	126²	124	12	50	118	3.6	8.4	43%	.313	1.37	4.69	3.98	4.96	0.8
2013	WTN	AA	20	4	7	0	14	14	84	58	6	30	96	3.2	10.3	47%	.259	1.05	2.46	2.84	3.66	1.2
2013	TAC	AAA	20	5	3	0	11	11	57¹	54	5	27	64	4.2	10.0	49%	.331	1.41	3.61	3.99	3.87	1.2
2013	SEA	MLB	20	1	0	0	3	3	15	11	0	4	12	2.4	7.2	39%	.250	1.00	3.60	2.28	2.72	0.4
2014	TAC	AAA	21	6	4	0	14	14	73	68	13	25	74	3.1	9.1	37%	.281	1.27	4.81	5.30	5.68	0.2
2014	SEA	MLB	21	2	3	0	8	5	38	31	2	18	34	4.3	8.1	49%	.282	1.29	2.61	3.71	3.84	0.5
2015	SEA	MLB	22	7	7	0	21	21	110	99	11	40	104	3.3	8.5	44%	.288	1.26	3.68	4.22	4.00	0.8

Breakout: 21%   Improve: 33%   Collapse: 7%   Attrition: 19%   MLB: 52%   Comparables: Chris Tillman, Carlos Martinez, Tyler Skaggs

Walker took his glove and went home after two healthy starts in the Arizona Fall League, but it's not hard to see why he'd want to call it a year. After nothing but smooth sailing throughout his short minor-league career, he caught Shoulder Disease early in spring and spent half a season recovering. Even afterward it took longer than expected to shake off the rust, leaving the year almost lost save for the obstacles of life's petty pace. A healthy Walker remains one of the most promising rookie pitchers on the planet, so much that even though he's still a work in progress—his secondary pitches are hit and miss, especially the curve and the changeup—he has the plus slider along with the fastball velocity and command to get by in the majors right now. Barring any heavy-handed plot twists, Walker is ready to fulfill expectations.

Tom Wilhelmsen   RHP

Born: 12/16/83   Age: 31   Bats: R   Throws: R   Height: 6'6"   Weight: 220

YEAR	TEAM	LVL	AGE	W	L	SV	G	GS	IP	H	HR	BB	K	BB/9	K/9	GB%	BABIP	WHIP	ERA	FIP	FRA	WARP
2012	SEA	MLB	28	4	3	29	73	0	79¹	59	5	29	87	3.3	9.9	48%	.266	1.11	2.50	2.84	2.93	1.3
2013	TAC	AAA	29	0	1	0	8	2	12	19	3	5	15	3.8	11.2	42%	.485	2.00	10.50	6.07	7.49	0.0
2013	SEA	MLB	29	0	3	24	59	0	59	45	2	33	45	5.0	6.9	44%	.253	1.32	4.12	3.72	4.26	0.2
2014	SEA	MLB	30	3	2	1	57	2	79¹	47	6	36	72	4.1	8.2	53%	.204	1.05	2.27	3.76	3.57	0.6
2015	SEA	MLB	31	3	2	6	47	3	64¹	56	6	27	55	3.7	7.7	44%	.275	1.28	3.54	4.47	3.84	0.5

Breakout: 19%   Improve: 23%   Collapse: 17%   Attrition: 16%   MLB: 52%   Comparables: Matt Thornton, Matt Wise, Brian Bruney

The Bartender enjoyed a pleasant return to form last season after wasting 2013 away searching for his lost curveball. He found it, but it was the introduction of a cutter that made him so deadly: Batters failed to secure a single hit against it after April, and hit just .168 as whole for the season. Whether it's a long-term upgrade remains to be seen: Wilhelmsen actually throws a surprisingly high percentage of pitches in the zone (a smidge below 50 percent) for someone who walks so many batters. His out pitches, first the curve and now the cutter, rely on getting ahead in the count before making batters flail at those two-strike pitches at the laces. His struggles in 2013 were due to batters just not buying, even when he had two strikes. Perhaps he's a better salesman now. Stuff like this always makes one think of pitch-tipping, mostly because everyone loves an easy fix.

Chris Young   RHP

Born: 5/25/79   Age: 36   Bats: R   Throws: R   Height: 6'10"   Weight: 255

YEAR	TEAM	LVL	AGE	W	L	SV	G	GS	IP	H	HR	BB	K	BB/9	K/9	GB%	BABIP	WHIP	ERA	FIP	FRA	WARP
2012	SLU	A+	33	1	0	0	3	3	17	17	1	2	7	1.1	3.7	26%	.286	1.12	3.18	3.86	4.01	0.3
2012	NYN	MLB	33	4	9	0	20	20	115	119	16	36	80	2.8	6.3	25%	.287	1.35	4.15	4.54	4.08	1.6
2013	SYR	AAA	34	1	2	0	7	7	32	50	9	14	16	3.9	4.5	30%	.342	2.00	7.88	7.17	7.61	-0.6
2014	SEA	MLB	35	12	9	0	30	29	165	143	26	60	108	3.3	5.9	25%	.238	1.23	3.65	5.04	4.39	0.4
2015	SEA	MLB	36	7	8	0	22	22	119	118	17	43	78	3.3	5.9	29%	.271	1.36	4.37	5.33	4.75	-0.3

Breakout: 21%   Improve: 41%   Collapse: 14%   Attrition: 12%   MLB: 69%   Comparables: Russ Ortiz, Shawn Estes, Robert Person

If you were among the many who had given Young up for dead, few could blame you. Baseball is a constant parade of funerals, one after another, to the point where you wonder how anything else gets done. It's kind of terrifying when a guy proceeds to leap out of the coffin. We get caught up with looking forward, worrying about the future. There's nothing wrong with that; it's a survival mechanism. But stop and take a moment to enjoy the continued employment of one Chris Young, vicariously if necessary. He'll be rewarded gently for his past performance, and given a chance to regress in front of hundreds of thousands of highly expectant people. Then they'll put him back down into the ground for good, and life will be a little drearier and less troubling.

Lineouts

Hitters

NAME	POS	TEAM	LVL	AGE	PA	R	2B	3B	HR	RBI	BB	K	SB	CS	AVG/OBP/SLG	TAv	BABIP	BRR	FRAA	WARP
Jabari Blash	RF	WTN	AA	24	163	27	7	1	6	22	28	35	4	1	.236/.387/.449	.319	.270	-0.6	RF(21): 1.7, LF(2): -0.1	1.4
	RF	TAC	AAA	24	189	23	8	0	12	37	17	57	2	2	.210/.312/.481	.282	.232	1.6	RF(41): 0.0	0.8
Chris Denorfia	RF	SDN	MLB	33	268	25	10	3	1	16	18	51	8	1	.242/.293/.319	.222	.301	1.6	RF(55): 6.2, LF(26): 0.0	0.3
	RF	SEA	MLB	33	90	11	2	1	2	5	7	19	1	2	.195/.256/.317	.222	.226	-0.3	RF(21): -0.2, LF(7): 0.0	-0.1
Jabari Henry	LF	HDS	A+	23	511	79	26	5	30	95	69	109	6	9	.291/.398/.584	.319	.324	-3.9	LF(59): 0.1, RF(8): 0.7	4.1
John Hicks	C	WTN	AA	24	211	29	10	2	3	27	20	42	6	3	.296/.362/.418	.287	.366	0.0	C(43): 0.5	1.5
	C	TAC	AAA	24	112	13	2	1	2	20	7	24	1	0	.277/.330/.376	.255	.338	1.2	C(28): 0.7	0.7
Jordy Lara	1B	HDS	A+	23	447	77	26	5	22	80	38	82	1	3	.353/.413/.609	.333	.398	2.4	1B(70): 0.6, 1B(5): 0.6	4.5
	RF	WTN	AA	23	138	14	14	0	4	24	8	19	0	0	.286/.326/.492	.286	.302	-0.8	RF(15): 1.0, 1B(7): 0.0	0.5
Tyler Marlette	C	HDS	A+	21	339	51	23	0	15	49	24	61	9	2	.301/.351/.519	.286	.332	0.6	C(70): 0.3, C(7): 0.3	2.9
	C	WTN	AA	21	36	3	2	0	2	2	4	10	0	0	.250/.333/.500	.294	.300	-0.4	C(9): -0.1	0.2
Julio Morban	RF	WTN	AA	22	128	14	5	1	1	11	9	35	0	0	.252/.307/.339	.240	.346	-0.9	RF(26): -0.7	0.0
	LF	TAC	AAA	22	109	10	4	1	0	7	10	32	0	0	.242/.312/.303	.222	.358	0.0	LF(8): 0.2, RF(8): -0.1	-0.4
Tyler O'Neill	LF	CLN	A	19	245	31	9	0	13	38	20	79	5	0	.247/.322/.466	.294	.320	0.3	LF(36): -0.1, RF(13): -1.6	1.2
Carlos Rivero	3B	PME	AA	26	130	14	6	0	2	17	8	24	0	0	.214/.285/.316	.205	.250	0.2	3B(13): -0.1, LF(11): 0.7	-0.3
	3B	PAW	AAA	26	302	32	14	2	5	36	23	66	0	2	.286/.341/.407	.274	.354	-0.5	3B(37): 1.6, SS(17): 0.6	2.0
	3B	BOS	MLB	26	8	1	2	0	1	3	1	0	0	0	.571/.625/1.286	.623	.500	0.0	3B(3): -0.0	0.3

Voted the franchise's Most Onomatopoeic Name for the third year running, **Jabari Blash** undid years of progress chipping away at his walk and strikeout problems in a mere 45 games at Tacoma. Entering his age-25 season, he needs to get back on track to tapping his power quickly. ❖ With Michael Saunders out and Endy Chavez waving his hand frantically at the end of the bench, the Mariners looked at **Chris Denorfia**'s .612 OPS as a Padre and figured it couldn't be true. They were right: Thanks to BABIP luck and some overswinging, Denorfia's offense fell apart completely. ❖ **Franklin Gutierrez** swears that he'll be ready to participate in spring training this year, but what will follow will almost certainly be an exhausting demonstration of mortality. Gutierrez is the stepped-on ant with one good leg who can only labor in circles, over and over. ❖ **Jabari** the Technically Younger (**Henry**) spent his age-23 season in High Desert beating up opposing pitchers not yet old enough to buy alcohol and stealing their lunch money. The fact that the organization left him there all year tells you how vital he is to their future plans. ❖ A highly ranked international prospect by the shadowy international prospect-ranking cabal, **Brayan Hernandez** is a center fielder who might become a right fielder, a balanced hitter who might become a power hitter and a baseball player who might become an airplane pilot. The kid's only sixteen, after all. ❖ The Mariners risked losing more talented players in the Rule 5 draft to protect **John Hicks** because he's the second-most-easily stashed commodity: a backup catcher; he has a strong defensive reputation and a decent shot of someday outhitting Jesus Sucre. ❖ **Jordy Lara** spent a college career in Rookie ball before taking a deep breath of the thin air at High Desert, where he suddenly decided to try hitting. ❖ **Tyler Marlette** converted from third base to catcher late in high school, and his defensive skills are a work in progress, albeit a pleasant one; he's currently the best catching prospect in the organization. ❖ **Julio Morban** is finally healthy entering his age-23 season after a broken leg that sapped his development time and power, and he still has time to improve. He also has time to decline, as do we all. ❖ The kind of player who gets called "slugger" instead of "hitter," **Tyler O'Neill** shook off a self-inflicted broken hand and hit some dingers as a teenager in Single-A Clinton. ❖ **Carlos Rivero** had been bouncing between organizations and Double- and Triple-A for the better part of four seasons before finally reaching the majors last year. He's no more than Quad-A depth, but he got his first MLB hit and his first MLB homer in 2014 and that's pretty damn cool.

Pitchers

NAME	TEAM	LVL	AGE	W	L	SV	G	GS	IP	H	HR	BB	K	BB/9	K/9	GB%	BABIP	WHIP	ERA	FIP	FRA	WARP
Anthony Fernandez	TAC	AAA	24	1	1	0	5	5	25²	24	3	14	27	4.9	9.5	39%	.313	1.48	3.86	4.75	5.54	0.0
Luiz Gohara	EVE	A-	17	0	6	0	11	11	37¹	46	6	24	37	5.8	8.9	60%	.348	1.88	8.20	6.25	6.74	-0.1
Mayckol Guaipe	WTN	AA	23	1	3	12	40	0	56	45	4	9	56	1.4	9.0	42%	.266	0.96	2.89	2.76	3.54	1.0
Lucas Luetge	TAC	AAA	27	3	2	3	42	0	62¹	58	6	27	70	3.9	10.1	48%	.323	1.36	3.32	4.24	4.13	0.8
	SEA	MLB	27	0	0	0	12	0	9	6	3	5	7	5.0	7.0	42%	.130	1.22	5.00	7.60	8.39	-0.4
Tyler Pike	HDS	A+	20	2	4	0	14	14	61¹	56	10	46	57	6.8	8.4	41%	.277	1.66	5.72	6.59	7.01	0.4
	WTN	AA	20	3	4	0	13	13	49	57	5	34	33	6.2	6.1	46%	.333	1.86	7.35	5.74	6.82	-0.6
Victor Sanchez	WTN	AA	19	7	6	0	23	23	124²	128	17	34	97	2.5	7.0	39%	.294	1.30	4.19	4.39	5.21	0.0
Carson Smith	TAC	AAA	24	1	3	10	39	0	43	44	1	13	45	2.7	9.4	70%	.352	1.33	2.93	2.89	3.49	0.9
	SEA	MLB	24	1	0	0	9	0	8¹	7	2	3	10	3.2	10.8	81%	.125	0.60	0.00	1.84	1.86	0.2
Ryan Yarbrough	EVE	A-	22	0	1	0	12	10	38²	25	1	4	53	0.9	12.3	60%	.263	0.75	1.40	1.87	2.22	0.7

Anthony Fernandez spent the year rehabbing from May Tommy John surgery; some thought before the injury that he might be ready to contribute in the majors last year. ❖ When **Luiz Gohara** isn't collecting Dragon Balls and saving the earth, he's putting up a 6.66 ERA across Rookie and short-season ball; still, he's only 18 and his stuff remains electric. ❖ The organization gave up on hard-throwing righty **Mayckol Guaipe** as a starter early in 2013 and in the two years since, he's responded by giving up on being terrible. ❖ **Danny Hultzen** spent 2014 recovering from rotator cuff surgery. He did start three games in the fall instructional league, and Jack Zduriencik declared that he should be 100 percent for 2015, though it's not clear if he intended the statement as predictive or imperative. ❖ Joe Beimel's first-half antics doomed **Lucas Luetge** to a year in the fair city of Tacoma, where he pitched to faceless lefties and dreamed of someday returning to the majors, wearing a beard twice as thick as Beimel's. Three times. ❖ The Angels acquired **Brian Moran** in intriguing fashion, having Toronto claim him in the Rule 5 draft and then swapping an international bonus slot for the lefty. They got almost three full spring training innings out of him before his elbow came apart, resulting in Tommy John surgery and his eventual return to the Mariners. ❖ **Tyler Pike** used to get Tom Glavine comparisons, which is the prospect equivalent of having a nice personality, but he'll need to fix his mechanics to get compared to anyone you've heard of again. ❖ **Victor Sanchez** regressed a little in his third season of pro ball, mainly due to quadruple the home runs and a more human walk rate, but he's still a 19-year-old who held his own in Double-A. ❖ As if the Mariners needed another good reliever, **Carson Smith** showed up in September and knocked them all down. They'll lock him back in the cloning facility until the time comes. ❖ Chosen in the fourth round in 2014 as much for his price as his pedigree, **Ryan Yarbrough** was immediately hailed by the intelligentsia as a LOOGY at best.

Manager

Lloyd McClendon

YEAR	TEAM	W	L	Py-thag +/-	Avg PC	100+ P	120+ P	QS	BQS	REL	REL w Zero R	IBB	PH	PH Avg	PH HR	SB2	CS2	SB3	CS3	SAC Att	SAC%	POS SAC	Squeeze	Swing	In Play
2014	SEA	87	75	-5	91.8	41	0	83	5	498	418	36	80	.186	1	85	36	11	3	57	61.4%	30	0	334	98

Who says there are no mulligans in baseball? The Mariners passed on McClendon when they hired Eric Wedge before the 2011 season. Three losing seasons and a Wedge resignation later, the Mariners tabbed McClendon as the third permanent manager under Jack Zduriencik. The results in year one were mixed.

McClendon, who suffered with the Pirates for parts of five seasons, enjoyed the best season of his managerial career. Not only was it the first time he posted a winning record, but it was the first time he finished better than fourth place. Early on, McClendon earned Robinson Cano's trust by defending his new keystone cornerstone against the Yankees' criticism. Later on, McClendon earned Seattle fans' trust through creative application of his bullpen. Last season, just 27 major-league relievers made at least 20 multi-inning appearances; the Mariners housed three of them, in Dominic Leone, Danny Farquhar and Tom Wilhelmsen.

Negatively, McClendon allowed his team to run (ninth most stolen-base attempts) more often than their success rate deserved (22nd best). He was also too unyielding with his lineup. Allowing Austin Jackson and Kendrys Morales to break out their slumps is one thing, but by keeping them at leadoff and cleanup, McClendon limited his lineup's ability to cash in on Cano's on-base percentage or place runners aboard for Kyle Seager—who, it must be noted, spent his fantastic season batting fifth. Assuming McClendon's skillfulness with the bullpen can translate to the lineup, the Mariners should continue to be happy with their do-over."

St. Louis Cardinals

by Howard Megdal

Back in June, the Cardinals then-scouting director Dan Kantrovitz and I sat in the draft room at Busch Stadium, just before day two of the MLB amateur draft began. Kantrovitz explained his mindset as he scanned the draft board, which was set up with magnets around the room representing various positions and experience. Kantrovitz said he has a Plan A, B, C and D for every single pick, every single round. "They laughed at me for having Plan C and D," Kantrovitz said, referring to the room of scouts and executives who gather inside Busch Stadium to see which 40 amateurs will be given the opportunity to join the Cardinals. "And then last year, one round, we needed D. So they don't laugh anymore."

This approach to drafting is an essential window into how the Cardinals, under the stewardship of General Manager John Mozeliak and owner Bill DeWitt, have approached the larger question of how to properly run a baseball team. That approach is why the Cardinals were, once again, playing deeper into October than 13 other National League teams in 2014.

It was amusing to see the Cardinals receive so much resentment from other fan bases last year, the essential idea being that the Cardinals have struck some deal with a higher power (the devil is cited more frequently than God), allowing for everything to go right in St. Louis. Playoff appearances, Clydesdale horsies marching around the warning track and happy Midwesterners follow. Satan is supposedly to blame, perhaps due to color scheme.

But realistically, 2014 was a Plan D kind of year for the Cardinals—though the total number of permutations made it more like Plan R—with little consistency at any position for the duration of the season. If anything, that's even scarier for the rest of baseball, given that the Cardinals managed to win 90 games and advance to the NLCS even as so much went contrary to plan—or, at any rate, Plan A.

Consider what the Cardinals needed to overcome in 2014.

- Their most important player, Yadier Molina, missed seven weeks with a thumb injury, had a .626 OPS upon returning and was shelved by oblique injury in the NLCS.
- Opening Day second baseman Kolten Wong was demoted after producing a .544 OPS in April.
- Their big free agent acquisition, shortstop Jhonny Peralta, didn't clear the Mendoza line until May.
- Their third baseman, Matt Carpenter, had one home run, total, in the season's first two months.
- Their best power threat, Matt Holliday, hit six home runs and slugged below .400 in the first half.
- Opening Day center fielder Peter Bourjos was benched; he finished with an OPS+ of 79.
- Opening Day right fielder Allen Craig dropped from a 129 OPS+ in 2013 to 78. He was traded in July.
- That opened right field for Oscar Taveras. Then Taveras didn't hit, either.
- Ace Adam Wainwright pitched all season with an elbow injury that eventually required surgery.
- Their 2013 postseason hero, Michael Wacha, missed months with a rare shoulder injury that had no template for rehab and recovery.
- Closer Trevor Rosenthal's walk rate more than doubled.
- Setup man/top prospect Carlos Martinez struggled with command for much of the season.
- Shutdown lefty Kevin Siegrist pitched through forearm pain. His 6.82 ERA was a 15-fold increase from 2013.

Even the deadline deals for pitching didn't work how the Cardinals hoped. John Lackey's ERA+ after coming over was a pedestrian 86. Justin Masterson, acquired for talented outfield prospect James Ramsey, saw his ERA climb over 7 after the deal.

And yet, as everything crumbled, one notable streak continued: Since 2011, the Cardinals have either won the World Series or lost to the team that did in every postseason.

So how did it happen? How does Plan D get you 90 wins, to within a few wins of the World Series?

Well, let's start with what they didn't do. They didn't jettison Wong. He returned from his demotion in mid-May and ended up a Rookie of the Year contender (despite playing through a shoulder injury all season). He's a deeply compelling talent, just 23, and the Cardinals knew better than to cast him aside for long.

They didn't budge with Carpenter at third, and some power came—he was named an All-Star and, on the season, was a four-win player. When the postseason rolled around, he and Wong each slugged over .700.

They didn't panic with Peralta or Holliday, each of whom

CARDINALS PROSPECTUS
2014 W-L: 90-72, 1st in NL Central

Pythag	.512	12th	DER	.714	7th
RS/G	3.82	23rd	B-Age	28.7	18th
RA/G	3.72	7th	P-Age	27	2nd
TAv	.255	22nd	Salary	$109.7M	14th
BRR	-7.87	26th	M$/MW	$2.3M	10th
TAv-P	.252	4th	DL Days	614	7th
FIP	3.62	11th	$ on DL	16%	18th

Three-Year Park Factors

Runs	Runs/RH	Runs/LH	HR/RH	HR/LH
101	97	99	92	92

Top Hitter WARP	4.5	Jhonny Peralta
Top Pitcher WARP	4.2	Adam Wainwright
Top Prospect		Stephen Piscotty

found career norms after a slow start. But they also didn't hesitate with Bourjos, plugging in Jon Jay, who had played himself into irrelevance in 2013 but who then hit exactly as he has every other season. His batting averages, 2010-2012 and 2014: .300, .297, .305, .303. His OPS+, same years: 113, 112, 113, 111.

They didn't get complacent in right field, first cashing in the last value of Craig and then quickly acting to bolster Taveras. In September, they plugged unheralded Randal Grichuk in as a platoon partner, and in September he (.866 OPS in the final month) and Taveras (.727 OPS) produced a cumulative .316/.362/.418 line that was well better than the league's average right fielder. (It's worth noting that the Cardinals added Grichuk—and Bourjos—in the deal for David Freese and Fernando Salas last winter. To complete the trade, they gave Freese's number to Jon Hamm when he was honored with a bobblehead last August.)

But perhaps the best example of the Plan A, B, C, D check-off came in the Masterson-Ramsey trade. Mozeliak believed his team needed more pitching, and he turned out to be correct, when Wainwright broke down in October and Wacha couldn't get healthy in time to do more than deliver the home run ball that ended the NLCS. But consider for a moment how many teams could afford to trade their first-round pick in 2012, one with a .916 OPS in Double-A at the time of the deal. But the Cardinals, incredibly, didn't have room for Ramsey in St. Louis. They didn't even have room for Ramsey in *Triple-A Memphis*. Between trade-acquisition Grichuk, international signee Taveras and compensation draft pick Stephen Piscotty, the Memphis Redbirds were already struggling to find playing time for Tommy Pham, a late-blooming outfielder with center field range who hit .324/.395/.491 down there. Trading Ramsey wasn't just a smart transaction; it was an act of grace.

Most notable about this depth is what it says about the team's farm system, and about Kantrovitz's stewardship of it. Under Jeff Luhnow and Sig Mejdal, the Cardinals completely rebuilt their drafting philosophy and created a comprehensive system for evaluating amateur players. Generally speaking, you won't see the results of a given approach for roughly five years. So it should come as no surprise that Luhnow's 2009 draft essentially won the 2014 NLDS against the Dodgers. Shelby Miller (first round, 2009) dueled Clayton Kershaw to a draw in Game Four. Matt Adams (23rd round, 2009) hit the three-run homer against the Cy Young winner to account for St. Louis' scoring. Rosenthal (21st round, 2009) finished the Dodgers in the ninth. And the guy with three homers and a 1.537 OPS in the series? Matt Carpenter (13th round, 2009).

Kantrovitz has overseen just three drafts, yet the Cardinals have already enjoyed success from those hauls. Wacha was the top pick in 2012. Marco Gonzales, a first-round pick in 2013, had five scoreless appearances in six tries during the postseason. (The other top pick, 2013 first-rounder Rob Kaminsky, dominated in Class-A Peoria and should move quickly through the system, too.)

The Cardinals march on. The pipeline is as fertile than ever. Revenues are up, and DeWitt should be able to authorize increased payroll in the coming years. Mozeliak, who always seems to know precisely what everybody is thinking, is signed through 2018. According to Derrick Goold of the *St. Louis Post-Dispatch*, the team's television deal runs through 2017, so another significant revenue stream should be added to the team's array of alternatives shortly.

But no matter how good the team, the need for Plan Bs—and Cs, and Ds—pop up. It's—well, it's hard to even think about this for its baseball implications, but the Cardinals already had one horrifying and shocking challenge to deal with, when Oscar Taveras and his girlfriend, 18-year-old Edilia Arvelo, died in an offseason automobile accident. They traded from their pitching surplus, swapping Miller and Tyrell Jenkins for Jason Heyward.

But there will be more. They will have to find a way to get Molina more rest. He turned 32 in July, and after three seasons averaging 138 games and a 130 OPS+ (plus remarkable defense and pitch-calling), he dropped to 110 games and a 101 OPS+. The Cardinals are going to have to field a replacement for Molina more of the time during the season, or expedite the day they'll need to replace him entirely.

The well-traveled Mark Reynolds and internal option Xavier Scruggs will battle to become the right-hander to supplement Adams at first. And they'll need a middle infielder who can provide more than Mark Ellis did (or Daniel Descalso, Pete Kozma or Tyler Greene did) if a first-stringer goes down.

But more important than middle infielders and backup catchers was the challenge the Cardinals faced this offseason, when the A's poached Kantrovitz to serve as Billy Beane's Assistant GM. (Be prepared to hear Kantrovitz's name brought up for every GM opening from now until he receives one.) Kantrovitz was the perfect replacement for Luhnow, having been a big part of Luhnow's statistical revolution. But now that three-man crew—Luhnow, Mejdal and Kantrovitz—are no longer in St. Louis, the Cardinals were faced with finding the perfect Plan D, the replacement who could take over without anybody noticing the drop off.

Notably, the Cardinals named Chris Correa as Kantrovitz's replacement. It's fascinating because of what it shows Mozeliak most values in his scouting director at this point. Luhnow was, at heart, a corporate turnaround master. Kantrovitz balanced a playing background with advanced knowledge of analytics. But Correa, who came through that analytics department founded by Luhnow, has spent his career with the Cardinals focused on the data. Mozeliak knows this, and didn't hesitate to promote Correa.

The depth on hand means another Plan D kind of season won't sink the Cardinals—it'll just mean a lower playoff seed. The Cardinals, the most successful team in National League history, just completed four straight seasons in the postseason. That's never happened before. Not with Rogers Hornsby, not with Dizzy Dean, not with Stan Musial, not with Lou Brock and Bob Gibson, not with Vince Coleman and Willie McGee.

Even accounting for bad luck, it doesn't look like that streak is ending anytime soon. Because while fans of 29 other teams don't want to hear this, the St. Louis Cardinals are actually due for a few breaks to come their way. ∎

—Howard Megdal is a writer-at-large for Capital New York, contributes to Sports Illustrated, USA Today *and other outlets, and his book about the remaking of the Cardinals' farm system will be published in October 2015 by St. Martin's Press.*

Player comments by Ken Funck and Baseball Prospectus Authors

Hitters

Matt Adams   1B

Born: 8/31/88   Age: 26   Bats: L   Throws: R   Height: 6' 3"   Weight: 260

YEAR	TEAM	LVL	AGE	PA	R	2B	3B	HR	RBI	BB	K	SB	CS	AVG/OBP/SLG	TAv	BABIP	BRR	FRAA	WARP
2012	MEM	AAA	23	276	41	22	0	18	50	15	57	3	1	.329/.362/.624	.339	.360	0.5	1B(59): 2.7	3.0
2012	SLN	MLB	23	91	8	6	0	2	13	5	24	0	0	.244/.286/.384	.228	.317	-1.6	1B(24): 0.6	-0.3
2013	SLN	MLB	24	319	46	14	0	17	51	23	80	0	1	.284/.335/.503	.289	.337	-1.6	1B(74): -0.2	1.1
2014	SLN	MLB	25	563	55	34	5	15	68	26	114	3	2	.288/.321/.457	.282	.338	-2.6	1B(133): -2.6	1.3
2015	SLN	MLB	26	484	55	27	2	18	65	27	108	2	1	.272/.315/.457	.281	.319	-2.0	1B 1	1.5

Breakout: 4%   Improve: 52%   Collapse: 4%   Attrition: 9%   MLB: 97%   Comparables: Adrian Gonzalez, Justin Morneau, Adam Lind

It's been three years since Albert Pujols left for warmer climes and the St. Louis first base position is just fine, thank you. "Big City" Adams settled in last summer, and while the slow-footed slugger from Slippery Rock will never flash the all-around game of his Hall of Fame predecessor, his power bat provides enough production to make him an asset at the cold corner. The big lefty has improved defensively and can pound right-handed pitching, posting a higher TAv against them last year than Pujols did. Postseason glory against Clayton Kershaw and Madison Bumgarner aside, Adams still needs to improve on his execrable .190/.231/.298 line against lefties or risk becoming a platoon player. There's always the concern that big-bodied sluggers don't age well, but for the next few years Adams should provide middle-of-the-order thump for pennies on the dollar.

Peter Bourjos   CF

Born: 3/31/87   Age: 28   Bats: R   Throws: R   Height: 6' 1"   Weight: 185

YEAR	TEAM	LVL	AGE	PA	R	2B	3B	HR	RBI	BB	K	SB	CS	AVG/OBP/SLG	TAv	BABIP	BRR	FRAA	WARP
2012	SLC	AAA	25	32	4	1	3	0	3	3	6	0	0	.310/.375/.552	.289	.391	1.5	CF(4): -0.2	0.3
2012	ANA	MLB	25	195	27	7	0	3	19	15	44	3	1	.220/.291/.315	.231	.274	1.5	CF(90): 7.2	1.2
2013	SLC	AAA	26	55	13	4	0	2	7	4	19	0	0	.208/.291/.417	.248	.286	0.9	CF(7): 0.5	0.2
2013	ANA	MLB	26	196	26	3	3	3	12	10	43	6	0	.274/.333/.377	.259	.346	1.9	CF(53): -0.4	0.6
2014	SLN	MLB	27	294	32	9	5	4	24	20	78	9	3	.231/.294/.348	.243	.311	3.5	CF(104): 3.3	1.2
2015	SLN	MLB	28	265	29	10	4	5	26	16	60	7	2	.247/.307/.384	.257	.301	1.7	CF 1	1.0

Breakout: 0%   Improve: 43%   Collapse: 8%   Attrition: 8%   MLB: 92%   Comparables: Franklin Gutierrez, Aaron Rowand, Drew Stubbs

Watching Bourjos chase down gappers in center field remains one of baseball's great joys, as the former Angel routinely posts such ridiculously high run-prevention scores that he single-handedly casts doubt on the accuracy of modern defensive metrics. Yet despite benefiting from the guarantee that he will never have to hit into a defense that features Peter Bourjos patrolling the outfield, his bat hasn't quite blossomed: He rarely makes enough contact or draws enough walks to maintain a solid on-base percentage. And if it's not his anemic bat keeping him out of the lineup, it's a litany of health woes, with end-of-season hip surgery now stacked on top of earlier wrist and hamstring problems. Bourjos is so valuable with the leather that even a slight improvement at the plate will make him an above-average player, but he's running out of time to prove he should be penciled in every day.

Matt Carpenter   3B

Born: 11/26/85   Age: 29   Bats: L   Throws: R   Height: 6' 3"   Weight: 215

YEAR	TEAM	LVL	AGE	PA	R	2B	3B	HR	RBI	BB	K	SB	CS	AVG/OBP/SLG	TAv	BABIP	BRR	FRAA	WARP
2012	SLN	MLB	26	340	44	22	5	6	46	34	63	1	1	.294/.365/.463	.293	.346	-0.7	1B(44): -1.2, 3B(33): -0.9	1.2
2013	SLN	MLB	27	717	126	55	7	11	78	72	98	3	3	.318/.392/.481	.312	.359	8.4	2B(132): 1.8, 3B(42): 0.4	7.3
2014	SLN	MLB	28	709	99	33	2	8	59	95	111	5	3	.272/.375/.375	.289	.318	-1.6	3B(156): 0.2, RF(2): 0.0	3.8
2015	SLN	MLB	29	668	80	38	4	10	62	80	105	4	3	.276/.367/.406	.288	.315	2.0	3B 4, 2B 0	4.3

Breakout: 2%   Improve: 42%   Collapse: 5%   Attrition: 7%   MLB: 97%   Comparables: Garrett Atkins, Ben Zobrist, Chipper Jones

After earning MVP votes for his 2013 campaign, Carpenter came back to earth last summer, hitting for a lower average and losing some of his extra-base pop. Yet even at this more sustainable level of production, his approach and skill set is such that every single team in baseball history would be improved if they had him on their roster. Carpenter is the game's most patient hitter, working deep counts and making hard contact when he gets his pitch, taking his walks when he doesn't. His on-base percentage in the leadoff spot fuels the Cardinals' offense, and his lack of a platoon split allows him to play every day. He's sure-handed and steady at multiple positions, and even if he weren't a starter Carpenter would be the one bench bat every pitcher would hate to face with the game on the line. Expect a few more doubles and a higher batting average this year, and a few more classic postseason at-bats over the next decade.

Tony Cruz   C

Born: 8/18/86   Age: 28   Bats: R   Throws: R   Height: 5' 11"   Weight: 215

YEAR	TEAM	LVL	AGE	PA	R	2B	3B	HR	RBI	BB	K	SB	CS	AVG/OBP/SLG	TAv	BABIP	BRR	FRAA	WARP
2012	SLN	MLB	25	131	11	9	1	1	11	3	19	0	0	.254/.267/.365	.223	.287	-0.8	C(47): 0.4, 1B(2): 0.0	0.1
2013	SLN	MLB	26	129	13	6	1	1	13	4	25	0	1	.203/.240/.293	.178	.247	0.7	C(44): -0.5, 3B(3): -0.0	-0.5
2014	SLN	MLB	27	150	11	5	0	1	17	13	28	0	3	.200/.270/.259	.191	.245	-0.2	C(47): -0.6, 1B(2): 0.0	-0.7
2015	SLN	MLB	28	250	21	12	1	3	21	15	47	1	2	.230/.281/.325	.228	.274	0.1	C -0, 3B 0	0.1

Breakout: 3%   Improve: 36%   Collapse: 7%   Attrition: 17%   MLB: 95%   Comparables: Drew Butera, Jesus Flores, Joe Azcue

Over four seasons in St. Louis, Cruz has posted a .225/.271/.310 batting line, which slots him somewhere between Yovani Gallardo and Zack Greinke on career batting leaderboards. While the Cardinals have long considered defense to be the most important attribute of a catcher, there is a limit, and Cruz proved to be so punchless during Yadier Molina's most recent trip to the infirmary that the organization deigned to allow the unclean hands of A.J. Pierzynski to handle their pitching staff. Cruz is familiar to St. Louis hurlers, so that should give him a leg up on a roster spot, but with Molina likely to miss more time with each passing year, the Cardinals might want to invest in a better insurance policy.

Aledmys Diaz   SS

Born: 8/1/90   Age: 24   Bats: R   Throws: R   Height: 6' 1"   Weight: 195

YEAR	TEAM	LVL	AGE	PA	R	2B	3B	HR	RBI	BB	K	SB	CS	AVG/OBP/SLG	TAv	BABIP	BRR	FRAA	WARP
2014	PMB	A+	23	54	5	2	0	2	6	7	10	1	0	.227/.352/.409	.289	.242	1.2		0.3
2014	SFD	AA	23	125	15	8	1	3	18	2	24	6	2	.291/.311/.453	.274	.341	-0.7	SS(17): -3.1	0.2
2015	SLN	MLB	24	250	26	11	1	5	25	12	57	7	2	.237/.284/.359	.239	.287	0.5	SS 0	-0.2

Breakout: 0%   Improve: 0%   Collapse: 0%   Attrition: 0%   MLB: 0%   Comparables: *Scott Thorman, Rhyne Hughes, Russ Canzler*

A riddle wrapped in a mystery inside a Cuban shortstop, Diaz lied about his age when he defected in 2012, causing the league to rule him ineligible for a year before he signed a four-year, $8 million contract with St. Louis last spring. His stateside debut shed little light, as chronic shoulder woes kept him off the field for much of the year, and the long layoff from baseball made him rusty when he did play. The book on Diaz when he signed was that of a contact hitter with little power who might be stretched defensively at shortstop, and while the club is happy with what they've seen of his bat so far, he's even more of a wild card than your typical maybe-24-or-so-year-old infield prospect.

Mark Ellis   2B

Born: 6/6/77   Age: 38   Bats: R   Throws: R   Height: 5' 10"   Weight: 190

YEAR	TEAM	LVL	AGE	PA	R	2B	3B	HR	RBI	BB	K	SB	CS	AVG/OBP/SLG	TAv	BABIP	BRR	FRAA	WARP
2012	LAN	MLB	35	464	62	21	1	7	31	40	70	5	0	.258/.333/.364	.263	.296	-1.2	2B(110): 1.2	1.4
2013	LAN	MLB	36	480	46	13	2	6	48	26	74	4	1	.270/.323/.351	.260	.310	3.1	2B(119): 3.3, 3B(1): -0.0	2.1
2014	SLN	MLB	37	202	15	6	0	0	12	14	38	4	1	.180/.253/.213	.195	.225	0.7	2B(50): -0.2, 1B(3): 0.1	-0.8
2015	SLN	MLB	38	250	26	10	1	2	18	16	39	3	1	.244/.305/.323	.241	.280	0.4	2B 1, 1B 0	0.5

Breakout: 1%   Improve: 25%   Collapse: 12%   Attrition: 16%   MLB: 65%   Comparables: *Chris Gomez, Jamey Carroll, Mark Grudzielanek*

Overheard at a Cardinals game last summer: "He may be a vacuum at second base, but in the batter's box, he just sucks." Whenever a veteran player posts a ridiculously low batting average on balls in play there's a temptation to chalk it up to bad luck, but Ellis earned his .225 mark through copious routine groundballs and contact soft enough to post the lowest isolated slugging mark this side of Jose Molina. When Ellis hits even a little his nifty leatherwork makes him a useful player, but players his age with walk, strikeout and contact rates moving in the wrong direction aren't ideal bounce-back candidates, leaving his best hope going forward the sudden implementation of a Designated Fielder rule.

Randal Grichuk   RF

Born: 8/13/91   Age: 23   Bats: R   Throws: R   Height: 6' 1"   Weight: 195

YEAR	TEAM	LVL	AGE	PA	R	2B	3B	HR	RBI	BB	K	SB	CS	AVG/OBP/SLG	TAv	BABIP	BRR	FRAA	WARP
2012	INL	A+	20	575	79	30	9	18	71	23	92	16	6	.298/.335/.488	.300	.329	3.2		4.6
2013	ARK	AA	21	542	85	27	8	22	64	28	92	9	5	.256/.306/.474	.285	.272	3.0	RF(95): 13.0, CF(23): -0.8	4.3
2014	MEM	AAA	22	472	73	23	2	25	71	28	108	8	5	.259/.311/.493	.278	.289	-0.9	LF(53): -4.1, CF(36): -3.3	1.3
2014	SLN	MLB	22	116	11	6	1	3	8	5	31	0	2	.245/.278/.400	.245	.316	-1.5	RF(28): -0.6, CF(5): 0.8	0.1
2015	SLN	MLB	23	250	26	11	2	8	31	10	55	3	2	.240/.276/.410	.255	.276	-0.2	RF 1, CF -0	0.4

Breakout: 0%   Improve: 14%   Collapse: 1%   Attrition: 10%   MLB: 28%   Comparables: *Zoilo Almonte, Michael Taylor, Marc Krauss*

It's been a magical 18 months for Grichuk, who went from "That Guy The Angels Drafted [Just] Ahead Of Mike Trout" to "That Guy Who Came Over With Peter Bourjos" to "Hey, Who's That Dude Starting In Right Field in The NLCS?" Along the way he's continued to show off both the impressive home run thump that got him to The Show and the lack of contact that will keep him from reaching his full potential. Grichuk's over-aggressive approach and aversion to ball four have led to a low on-base percentage in the upper minors, a weakness big-league pitchers are paid handsomely to exploit. An excellent defensive outfielder who is stretched in center but an asset in right, Grichuk doesn't profile as a long-term starter but should carve out a long career as a fourth outfielder ideal for the short side of a platoon.

Jason Heyward   RF

Born: 8/9/89   Age: 25   Bats: L   Throws: L   Height: 6' 5"   Weight: 245

YEAR	TEAM	LVL	AGE	PA	R	2B	3B	HR	RBI	BB	K	SB	CS	AVG/OBP/SLG	TAv	BABIP	BRR	FRAA	WARP
2012	ATL	MLB	22	651	93	30	6	27	82	58	152	21	8	.269/.335/.479	.296	.319	7.2	RF(154): 15.5, CF(2): -0.1	6.3
2013	GWN	AAA	23	26	1	1	0	0	6	4	7	1	0	.300/.423/.350	.308	.429	0.0	RF(3): 0.3	0.2
2013	ATL	MLB	23	440	67	22	1	14	38	48	73	2	4	.254/.349/.427	.280	.281	1.2	RF(86): 7.6, CF(20): -0.6	2.7
2014	ATL	MLB	24	649	74	26	3	11	58	67	98	20	4	.271/.351/.384	.288	.308	1.0	RF(149): 26.4	6.0
2015	SLN	MLB	25	571	79	26	3	16	61	64	103	14	5	.261/.351/.424	.292	.296	2.6	RF 12, CF -0	4.4

Breakout: 3%   Improve: 58%   Collapse: 1%   Attrition: 3%   MLB: 100%   Comparables: *Nick Markakis, Justin Upton, Jack Clark*

The Gulf of Tonkin for defensive-metric skeptics, who see in Heyward's WAR(P)s nothing but inconsistencies in the official accounts. At least one of the total-value metrics measured Heyward to be a top-three player in the NL, a controversial rank given that he was a slightly above-average hitter playing right field. The biggest problem—okay, the *second*-biggest problem, behind imperfect defensive metrics—is Heyward's body. As stupid as it sounds, his look doesn't match his skill set. It's hard to accept that anyone is worth the defensive runs that Heyward purportedly was, but *especially* someone built like a slugger. If he swapped bodies with B.J. Upton, the world might be more accepting of the numbers. But he can't, so it isn't. Don't take any of this as a knock on Heyward; he's a good player who adds value with his bat, with his legs and, certainly, with his glove. The argument is about *how much* value he adds, which is what teams will have to decide for themselves when he hits the open market in November. That a brainy team like the Cardinals were willing to give up Shelby Miller for just one guaranteed year of Heyward suggests that the dollar figures might go quite high.

Matt Holliday   LF

Born: 1/15/80   Age: 35   Bats: R   Throws: R   Height: 6' 4"   Weight: 250

YEAR	TEAM	LVL	AGE	PA	R	2B	3B	HR	RBI	BB	K	SB	CS	AVG/OBP/SLG	TAv	BABIP	BRR	FRAA	WARP
2012	SLN	MLB	32	688	95	36	2	27	102	75	132	4	4	.295/.379/.497	.309	.337	0.7	LF(152): -9.6	4.1
2013	SLN	MLB	33	602	103	31	1	22	94	69	86	6	1	.300/.389/.490	.300	.322	3.0	LF(136): -4.6	3.4
2014	SLN	MLB	34	667	83	37	0	20	90	74	100	4	1	.272/.370/.441	.293	.298	3.2	LF(150): -6.2	2.9
2015	SLN	MLB	35	614	76	33	1	20	81	66	103	4	2	.278/.367/.457	.305	.309	1.9	LF -6	3.6

Breakout: 2%   Improve: 27%   Collapse: 5%   Attrition: 8%   MLB: 93%   Comparables: *Sid Gordon, Barry Bonds, Carlos Beltran*

When Holliday signed his seven-year, $120 million contract before the 2010 season, there was some fear that he was a product of Coors Field getting paid as the best of a weak crop of free agents. Five years and 20-ish WARP later, Big Daddy's contract is not only a bargain compared to the Carl Crawfords and Mark Teixeiras of the world, it seems almost quaint. Last year Holliday soldiered through his usual litany of minor complaints and remained one of the most quietly productive hitters in baseball, earning down-ballot MVP votes for the fourth time in five years. His power, batting average and defensive range showed a little wobble, but he still draws walks, avoids strikeouts and makes consistent hard contact. Since the Cardinals are the Cardinals, Holliday's contract will likely run out before his game misses a shift on the long decline.

Jon Jay   CF
Born: 3/15/85   Age: 30   Bats: L   Throws: L   Height: 5' 11"   Weight: 195

YEAR	TEAM	LVL	AGE	PA	R	2B	3B	HR	RBI	BB	K	SB	CS	AVG/OBP/SLG	TAv	BABIP	BRR	FRAA	WARP
2012	SLN	MLB	27	502	70	22	4	4	40	34	71	19	7	.305/.373/.400	.283	.355	-0.5	CF(116): 12.1	3.9
2013	SLN	MLB	28	628	75	27	2	7	67	52	103	10	5	.276/.351/.370	.263	.325	3.6	CF(152): -3.0	1.9
2014	SLN	MLB	29	468	52	16	3	3	46	28	78	6	3	.303/.372/.378	.279	.363	-1.6	CF(98): -3.5, RF(33): -0.6	1.5
2015	SLN	MLB	30	472	55	22	2	5	39	34	77	8	4	.280/.348/.380	.273	.322	0.1	CF 2, RF -0	2.1

Breakout: 1%   Improve: 45%   Collapse: 2%   Attrition: 9%   MLB: 99%   Comparables: Angel Pagan, Jacoby Ellsbury, Shane Victorino

A late bloomer who was never considered a top prospect or a true center fielder, at what point do we stop calling Jay an overachiever and just admit he's an achiever? With more than four full seasons now in the ledger, The Federalist has posted a .295/.359/.396 career batting line with average-at-worst defense in center, yet rarely gets recognition as the key contributor he has been. Jay lashes line drives from gap to gap, hits for a high average, is always among the league's hit-by-pitch leaders and last year torched the lefty pitching that has sometimes plagued him. He might just be the most Cardinals of players, lacking recognition but continuing to produce year after year. That is, until he struggles, breaks down or grows too expensive, at which point The Player Development Appliance will serve up his replacement.

Carson Kelly   C
Born: 7/14/94   Age: 20   Bats: R   Throws: R   Height: 6' 2"   Weight: 200

YEAR	TEAM	LVL	AGE	PA	R	2B	3B	HR	RBI	BB	K	SB	CS	AVG/OBP/SLG	TAv	BABIP	BRR	FRAA	WARP
2013	PEO	A	18	168	18	6	0	2	13	13	25	0	0	.219/.288/.301	.242	.248	0.2	3B(31): -4.9	-0.3
2013	SCO	A-	18	299	35	16	1	4	32	20	31	1	0	.277/.340/.387	.260	.301	-0.9	3B(64): -7.2	-0.1
2014	PEO	A	19	415	41	17	4	6	49	37	54	1	0	.248/.326/.366	.264	.274	-2.2	C(79): -0.5	1.5
2015	SLN	MLB	20	250	19	10	1	3	22	13	50	0	0	.208/.258/.297	.211	.247	-0.4	C -0, 3B -4	-1.0

Breakout: 0%   Improve: 0%   Collapse: 0%   Attrition: 0%   MLB: 0%   Comparables: Travis d'Arnaud, J.R. Murphy, Christian Vazquez

His bat has yet to set the world on fire, but a successful move behind the plate makes it more likely Kelly will have a big-league career. He still has a lot to learn about game-calling, pitch framing and the other nuances of baseball's most demanding defensive position, but his strong arm and solid frame give him a chance, and reviews so far have been positive. At the plate Kelly is far more projection than production, but if he can tap into his impressive raw power during games his bat will be at least adequate for a backup. A cool-climate high school draftee, the development clock on Kelly was going to be a long one even before he was handed a facemask, so the Cardinals will have plenty of patience with him. You'd be advised to follow their lead.

Yadier Molina   C
Born: 7/13/82   Age: 32   Bats: R   Throws: R   Height: 5' 11"   Weight: 220

YEAR	TEAM	LVL	AGE	PA	R	2B	3B	HR	RBI	BB	K	SB	CS	AVG/OBP/SLG	TAv	BABIP	BRR	FRAA	WARP
2012	SLN	MLB	29	563	65	28	0	22	76	45	55	12	3	.315/.373/.501	.315	.316	-4.3	C(136): 2.3, 1B(3): 0.1	6.6
2013	SLN	MLB	30	541	68	44	0	12	80	30	55	3	2	.319/.359/.477	.297	.338	-5.6	C(131): -0.7, 1B(5): -0.2	4.2
2014	SLN	MLB	31	445	40	21	0	7	38	28	55	1	1	.282/.333/.386	.258	.307	-2.5	C(107): -1.2, 1B(1): 0.0	1.9
2015	SLN	MLB	32	438	46	24	0	9	49	30	48	4	2	.286/.339/.417	.281	.300	-3.1	C 0, 1B -0	2.3

Breakout: 1%   Improve: 26%   Collapse: 4%   Attrition: 10%   MLB: 97%   Comparables: Victor Martinez, Kenji Johjima, Ramon Hernandez

"It's almost like he can look right into a hitter's soul," Shelby Miller said about Molina's game-calling ability last spring. It's exactly that sort of intangible quality that has made Molina the beating heart of the Cardinals, and with the retirement of Derek Jeter, perhaps all of baseball. Molina has never led the Cardinals in quantifiable value measures like WARP, although the inclusion of his fantastic career marks in our new pitch framing and blocking metrics might have changed that. Instead, it's been his other contributions—leadership, game-calling and the pitcher confidence it spawns, the suppression of the running game—that continue to make him one of the most valuable players in baseball. Last year his offense began its inevitable decline from his recent MVP-level peak to a more modest level of production, and as he moves later into his thirties St. Louis fans can expect more episodes like last October's postseason oblique strain, but Molina will remain the best all-around catcher in baseball for as long as he can will himself into the lineup.

Jhonny Peralta   SS
Born: 5/28/82   Age: 33   Bats: R   Throws: R   Height: 6' 2"   Weight: 215

YEAR	TEAM	LVL	AGE	PA	R	2B	3B	HR	RBI	BB	K	SB	CS	AVG/OBP/SLG	TAv	BABIP	BRR	FRAA	WARP
2012	DET	MLB	30	585	58	32	3	13	63	49	105	1	2	.239/.305/.384	.240	.275	-0.8	SS(149): -6.0	0.6
2013	DET	MLB	31	448	50	30	0	11	55	35	98	3	3	.303/.358/.457	.293	.374	-2.8	SS(106): 8.6, LF(3): -0.0	4.0
2014	SLN	MLB	32	628	61	38	0	21	75	58	112	3	2	.263/.336/.443	.286	.292	-3.1	SS(152): 3.6	4.5
2015	SLN	MLB	33	554	56	29	1	13	62	46	105	3	2	.255/.320/.395	.268	.295	-1.8	SS 2, LF -0	2.8

Breakout: 1%   Improve: 27%   Collapse: 4%   Attrition: 6%   MLB: 93%   Comparables: Miguel Tejada, Alan Trammell, Mike Lamb

Peralta has had one of the more interesting careers around, as the former Indian was exiled to third base due to defensive woes, found success at shortstop in Detroit, was suspended 50 games due to his link to Biogenesis, signed a surprisingly large four-year deal with St. Louis and led the Cardinals in WARP last year while earning a few down-ballot MVP votes. Through it all he's exhibited prodigious thump for a shortstop, especially against lefties, but the most surprising development is his transformation into a plus defensive player. Shortstops' gloves are supposed to turn to vinegar, not wine, but Peralta has become more reliable in the field each year, making up for lackluster range with soft hands and good instincts. As long as he can stick on the left side of the infield, Peralta's bat will earn his pay.

Thomas Pham   OF

Born: 3/8/88   Age: 27   Bats: R   Throws: R   Height: 6' 1"   Weight: 175

YEAR	TEAM	LVL	AGE	PA	R	2B	3B	HR	RBI	BB	K	SB	CS	AVG/OBP/SLG	TAv	BABIP	BRR	FRAA	WARP
2012	SFD	AA	24	43	3	2	0	1	3	4	19	0	0	.154/.233/.282	.183	.263	0.1	CF(2): 0.1	-0.3
2013	SFD	AA	25	188	27	6	6	6	28	20	42	6	3	.301/.388/.521	.303	.371	0.0	CF(36): 2.8, RF(1): -0.0	1.8
2013	MEM	AAA	25	113	6	6	1	1	13	7	25	2	1	.264/.310/.368	.261	.338	0.3	CF(28): 2.8, LF(2): 0.0	0.5
2014	MEM	AAA	26	390	63	16	6	10	44	38	81	20	2	.324/.395/.491	.316	.397	-1.3	CF(59): -0.9, LF(29): 2.3	3.5
2014	SLN	MLB	26	2	0	0	0	0	0	0	2	0	0	.000/.000/.000	-.006	--	0.0	LF(2): 0.0, RF(1): -0.0	0.0
2015	*SLN*	*MLB*	*27*	*250*	*30*	*10*	*3*	*4*	*22*	*20*	*62*	*7*	*2*	*.251/.317/.376*	*.261*	*.325*	*1.0*	*CF 2, LF 0*	*1.0*

Breakout: 5%   Improve: 14%   Collapse: 4%   Attrition: 15%   MLB: 30%   *Comparables: Denis Phipps, Matt Carson, Kenny Kelly*

An oft-overlooked late bloomer in the Craig/Freese/Carpenter mold, Pham was finally healthy last summer after almost a decade of injury and mis-fortune. He took out his frustrations on Triple-A pitchers, earning his first September call-up. Pham's offense is predicated on waiting for his pitch and attacking, stroking line drives from gap to gap. He's also an excellent defender at each outfield position. With Randal Grichuk ahead of him and Stephen Piscotty coming up behind, Pham has a narrow window to prove himself in St. Louis, but however things play out he looks like a legitimate fourth outfielder or second-division starter.

A.J. Pierzynski   C

Born: 12/30/76   Age: 38   Bats: L   Throws: R   Height: 6' 3"   Weight: 235

YEAR	TEAM	LVL	AGE	PA	R	2B	3B	HR	RBI	BB	K	SB	CS	AVG/OBP/SLG	TAv	BABIP	BRR	FRAA	WARP
2012	CHA	MLB	35	520	68	18	4	27	77	28	78	0	0	.278/.326/.501	.279	.280	-3.1	C(126): -2.3	2.7
2013	TEX	MLB	36	529	48	24	1	17	70	11	76	1	0	.272/.297/.425	.262	.288	-2.8	C(119): -1.2	1.8
2014	BOS	MLB	37	274	19	10	1	4	31	9	40	0	0	.254/.286/.348	.232	.282	-2.0	C(64): -0.8	0.1
2014	SLN	MLB	37	88	6	2	0	1	6	5	14	0	1	.244/.295/.305	.224	.284	-1.0	C(23): -0.2	-0.2
2015	*SLN*	*MLB*	*38*	*374*	*33*	*17*	*1*	*7*	*39*	*13*	*48*	*0*	*0*	*.256/.290/.371*	*.245*	*.274*	*-1.9*	*C -1*	*0.5*

Breakout: 0%   Improve: 17%   Collapse: 22%   Attrition: 24%   MLB: 74%   *Comparables: Yogi Berra, Walker Cooper, Jose Molina*

Love him or hate him, there's no denying that few players seem to enjoy themselves on the field more than Pierzynski. Unfortunately, not every team-mate enjoys the A.J. show as much as A.J. himself, and with his bad defensive reputation and his bat no longer providing the consistent mediocrity on which he built his career, teams are becoming more and more reticent to keep him around. Pierzynski has been a better player for longer than any of us might have imagined, but he's past getting regular playing time and doesn't seem likely to hang on in a mentor role. He'll likely end his career with a WARP total between Tony Pena and Rick Dempsey, and the same career TAv as Benito Santiago and Jim Sundberg, all of which feels about right.

Stephen Piscotty   RF

Born: 1/14/91   Age: 24   Bats: R   Throws: R   Height: 6' 3"   Weight: 210

YEAR	TEAM	LVL	AGE	PA	R	2B	3B	HR	RBI	BB	K	SB	CS	AVG/OBP/SLG	TAv	BABIP	BRR	FRAA	WARP
2012	QUD	A	21	237	29	18	1	4	27	18	25	3	0	.295/.376/.448	.293	.320	0.3	3B(36): -0.3	1.4
2013	PMB	A+	22	264	30	14	2	9	35	18	27	4	5	.292/.348/.477	.296	.300	1.1	RF(59): -1.7	1.4
2013	SFD	AA	22	207	17	9	0	6	24	19	19	7	3	.299/.364/.446	.292	.304	-4.3	RF(48): 0.6	0.6
2014	MEM	AAA	23	556	70	32	0	9	69	43	61	11	5	.288/.355/.406	.276	.313	-1.0	RF(113): 7.0, LF(8): 0.3	2.5
2015	*SLN*	*MLB*	*24*	*250*	*24*	*13*	*0*	*4*	*25*	*16*	*36*	*4*	*2*	*.256/.312/.367*	*.258*	*.285*	*-0.3*	*RF 1, 3B -0*	*0.5*

Breakout: 5%   Improve: 19%   Collapse: 12%   Attrition: 30%   MLB: 45%   *Comparables: Alex Romero, Caleb Gindl, Adrian Cardenas*

The top prospect in the Cardinals' system, Piscotty impresses with his advanced approach and excellent bat-to-ball skills, but his in-game power has yet to show up with any regularity. The Stanford product is a work in progress in right field, with a strong arm but fringy range that will likely keep him from being better than average with the glove. No one questions his ability to hit, as Piscotty works himself into good counts before making loud contact and he should post solid on-base percentages at the highest level. Power is often the last tool to develop, and if Piscotty can learn to loft more of those line shots out of the yard he could grow into a prototypical corner outfielder.

Mark Reynolds   1B

Born: 8/3/83   Age: 31   Bats: R   Throws: R   Height: 6' 2"   Weight: 220

YEAR	TEAM	LVL	AGE	PA	R	2B	3B	HR	RBI	BB	K	SB	CS	AVG/OBP/SLG	TAv	BABIP	BRR	FRAA	WARP
2012	BAL	MLB	28	538	65	26	0	23	69	73	159	1	3	.221/.335/.429	.266	.282	-1.2	1B(108): -14.0, 3B(15): -1.4	-0.7
2013	CLE	MLB	29	384	40	8	0	15	48	43	123	3	0	.215/.307/.373	.255	.285	0.0	1B(41): 0.5, 3B(40): -3.1	0.2
2013	NYA	MLB	29	120	15	6	0	6	19	8	31	0	1	.236/.300/.455	.271	.274	-0.2	1B(24): -1.1, 3B(14): 0.3	0.2
2014	MIL	MLB	30	433	47	9	0	22	45	47	122	5	1	.196/.287/.394	.258	.218	1.0	1B(91): 2.2, 3B(42): 1.8	1.2
2015	*SLN*	*MLB*	*31*	*421*	*54*	*14*	*1*	*19*	*54*	*51*	*129*	*3*	*1*	*.209/.314/.405*	*.268*	*.262*	*-0.1*	*1B -3, 3B -2*	*0.5*

Breakout: 5%   Improve: 39%   Collapse: 8%   Attrition: 12%   MLB: 95%   *Comparables: Craig Wilson, Brad Wilkerson, Ken Phelps*

Only three big-league hitters have clubbed at least 20 homers in each of the past six seasons, and this wouldn't be much of a comment if one of them wasn't Reynolds. (The others: David Ortiz and Nelson Cruz.) Once again, though, the batting average proved unplayable, and so, down the stretch, he was unplayed. So that was the downer part of his season. The good part was that he proved more than capable defensively, even rating above-average at first by most metrics. That combination of plus power and plus defense—okay, okay, blend-into-the-background defense—should allow him to carve out consistent playing time, though you'd expect it to come with teams desperate for a body, not a player-producing machine like St. Louis. He's got an intriguing profile from afar, but, as he showed in Milwaukee, it's a profile that can get old quickly.

Xavier Scruggs   1B

Born: 9/23/87   Age: 27   Bats: R   Throws: R   Height: 6' 1"   Weight: 220

YEAR	TEAM	LVL	AGE	PA	R	2B	3B	HR	RBI	BB	K	SB	CS	AVG/OBP/SLG	TAv	BABIP	BRR	FRAA	WARP
2012	SFD	AA	24	522	64	26	1	22	91	58	150	8	4	.235/.331/.442	.275	.297	1.0	1B(123): 5.0	1.9
2013	SFD	AA	25	546	67	18	1	29	81	82	177	11	7	.248/.376/.487	.302	.335	-1.1	1B(129): 1.3, LF(1): -0.0	3.3
2014	MEM	AAA	26	538	82	29	3	21	87	53	114	3	5	.286/.370/.494	.301	.336	0.3	1B(133): 0.3, RF(1): -0.0	3.3
2014	SLN	MLB	26	18	0	1	0	0	2	2	7	0	0	.200/.333/.267	.221	.375	-0.7	1B(5): -0.0	-0.1
2015	*SLN*	*MLB*	*27*	*250*	*29*	*10*	*1*	*9*	*31*	*26*	*74*	*2*	*1*	*.228/.320/.402*	*.269*	*.297*	*-0.5*	*1B 1, RF -0*	*0.5*

Breakout: 0%   Improve: 3%   Collapse: 6%   Attrition: 14%   MLB: 30%   *Comparables: Josh Whitesell, Joe Koshansky, Juan Miranda*

It's not particularly rare for 26-year-old first basemen to post gaudy numbers in the Pacific Coast League, but it is rare for them to have a name as awesome as Xavier Scruggs. Never a top prospect, the former late-round pick from UNLV has legitimate power and made a meal of minor-league hurlers the last two seasons, earning a brief call-up last September. Scruggs cut down on his formerly disastrous strikeout rate last year and laid a .345/.404/.669 beat-down on lefty hurlers, providing hope he could stick as a bench bat or platoon partner. That would be so Cardinals.

Charlie Tilson   CF

Born: 12/2/92   Age: 22   Bats: L   Throws: L   Height: 5'11"   Weight: 175

YEAR	TEAM	LVL	AGE	PA	R	2B	3B	HR	RBI	BB	K	SB	CS	AVG/OBP/SLG	TAv	BABIP	BRR	FRAA	WARP
2013	PEO	A	20	411	49	8	6	4	30	25	58	15	6	.303/.349/.388	.269	.349	2.5	CF(71): -4.1, LF(17): -0.1	1.7
2013	PMB	A+	20	39	1	1	1	0	0	5	6	0.	0	.294/.385/.382	.290	.357	-0.9	CF(9): -0.4	0.2
2014	PMB	A+	21	402	54	8	8	5	36	24	76	10	7	.308/.357/.414	.280	.377	3.7	CF(83): -9.9	1.2
2014	SFD	AA	21	145	19	4	1	2	17	6	28	2	3	.237/.269/.324	.217	.284	2.8	CF(26): -1.0, LF(6): 0.3	0.0
2015	*SLN*	*MLB*	*22*	*250*	*25*	*7*	*2*	*3*	*19*	*11*	*57*	*3*	*2*	*.240/.277/.326*	*.225*	*.300*	*0.0*	*CF -4, LF 0*	*-0.7*

Breakout: 2%   Improve: 7%   Collapse: 7%   Attrition: 12%   MLB: 18%   *Comparables: Peter Bourjos, Gorkys Hernandez, Eury Perez*

The start of his pro career was delayed by a shoulder injury and he ended last season rehabbing a broken foot, but in between Tilson has flashed the tools that made him a second-round pick. Speed is his calling card, as the Illinois prep product can outrun his mistakes, but his game still has plenty of rough edges, especially his routes in center field and his limited base-stealing acumen. At the plate Tilson projects to have little more than gap power and his aggressive approach can cause him trouble: It may preclude him from hitting at the top of a big-league lineup. Still, there's a chance Tilson could grow into the next Jon Jay, minus the copious beanball welts.

Kolten Wong   2B

Born: 10/10/90   Age: 24   Bats: L   Throws: R   Height: 5'9"   Weight: 185

YEAR	TEAM	LVL	AGE	PA	R	2B	3B	HR	RBI	BB	K	SB	CS	AVG/OBP/SLG	TAv	BABIP	BRR	FRAA	WARP
2012	SFD	AA	21	579	79	23	6	9	52	44	74	21	11	.287/.348/.405	.281	.318	4.1	2B(123): 2.6	3.4
2013	MEM	AAA	22	463	68	21	8	10	45	41	60	20	1	.303/.369/.466	.307	.332	0.7	2B(102): 12.9	4.9
2013	SLN	MLB	22	62	6	1	0	0	0	3	12	3	0	.153/.194/.169	.143	.191	0.6	2B(18): 1.3	-0.4
2014	MEM	AAA	23	80	16	4	0	3	13	5	9	6	0	.360/.400/.533	.348	.381	1.0	2B(18): 1.6	1.3
2014	SLN	MLB	23	433	52	14	3	12	42	21	71	20	4	.249/.292/.388	.242	.275	6.7	2B(107): -3.8	0.6
2015	*SLN*	*MLB*	*24*	*400*	*50*	*16*	*3*	*7*	*35*	*24*	*63*	*16*	*3*	*.259/.309/.382*	*.259*	*.289*	*3.6*	*2B 3*	*2.0*

Breakout: 3%   Improve: 32%   Collapse: 8%   Attrition: 17%   MLB: 80%   *Comparables: Luis Valbuena, Steve Lombardozzi, Josh Barfield*

Not every player can be Mike Trout—in fact, the laws of time and space dictate that only Mike Trout can be—so it was no big surprise that Wong didn't become an instant superstar and instead struggled through an up-and-down rookie season. Double-digit home runs and 20 stolen bases speak well of Wong's well-rounded offensive game, but the former top pick was uncharacteristically impatient at the plate, struck out more than usual and posted a low batting average when he did make contact. His defense at the keystone was as sharp as advertised, however, and there's every reason to expect Wong's postseason heroics will carry him into a 2015 campaign that paints him as one of the league's better second sackers.

Pitchers

Matt Belisle   RHP

Born: 6/6/80   Age: 35   Bats: R   Throws: R   Height: 6'4"   Weight: 225

YEAR	TEAM	LVL	AGE	W	L	SV	G	GS	IP	H	HR	BB	K	BB/9	K/9	GB%	BABIP	WHIP	ERA	FIP	FRA	WARP
2012	COL	MLB	32	3	8	3	80	0	80	91	5	18	69	2.0	7.8	52%	.340	1.36	3.71	3.01	3.83	1.3
2013	COL	MLB	33	5	7	0	72	0	73	76	6	15	62	1.8	7.6	50%	.321	1.25	4.32	3.01	3.83	1.2
2014	COL	MLB	34	4	7	0	66	1	64²	74	5	19	43	2.6	6.0	48%	.322	1.44	4.87	3.71	4.57	0.7
2015	*SLN*	*MLB*	*35*	*3*	*1*	*1*	*64*	*0*	*62²*	*57*	*4*	*13*	*54*	*1.9*	*7.8*	*49%*	*.314*	*1.12*	*3.14*	*3.11*	*3.41*	*0.9*

Breakout: 19%   Improve: 36%   Collapse: 25%   Attrition: 14%   MLB: 84%   *Comparables: LaTroy Hawkins, Hideki Okajima, Rafael Betancourt*

Belisle, who was the only Rockies reliever remaining from their 92-win playoff team in 2009, lost more than 15 points on his ERA+ for the fourth straight year. His hard put-away slider is no longer dominant against righties; after inducing whiffs on 38 percent of swings with it in 2013, he drew whiffs on just 20 percent last year. Instead, those swings became balls hit in the air, the death sentence that keeps on killing in Colorado. Second in the majors in relief innings since 2010, he should find employment for a few more years, but his salary with the Cardinals ($3.5 million) shows the truth: He's less Mr. Reliable than Mr. Belisleable these days.

Randy Choate   LHP

Born: 9/5/75   Age: 39   Bats: L   Throws: L   Height: 6'1"   Weight: 210

YEAR	TEAM	LVL	AGE	W	L	SV	G	GS	IP	H	HR	BB	K	BB/9	K/9	GB%	BABIP	WHIP	ERA	FIP	FRA	WARP
2012	LAN	MLB	36	0	0	0	36	0	13¹	13	1	9	11	6.1	7.4	69%	.293	1.65	4.05	4.94	5.06	-0.2
2012	MIA	MLB	36	0	0	1	44	0	25¹	16	0	9	27	3.2	9.6	62%	.246	0.99	2.49	2.43	2.75	0.4
2013	SLN	MLB	37	2	1	0	64	0	35¹	26	0	11	28	2.8	7.1	68%	.260	1.05	2.29	2.54	3.72	0.2
2014	SLN	MLB	38	2	2	0	61	0	36	27	2	13	32	3.2	8.0	63%	.260	1.11	4.50	3.55	3.57	0.2
2015	*SLN*	*MLB*	*39*	*4*	*2*	*1*	*73*	*0*	*37²*	*31*	*3*	*14*	*35*	*3.4*	*8.2*	*57%*	*.296*	*1.19*	*3.32*	*3.86*	*3.61*	*0.5*

Breakout: 16%   Improve: 40%   Collapse: 15%   Attrition: 11%   MLB: 69%   *Comparables: Trever Miller, Arthur Rhodes, Mike Stanton*

Choate is more than just a LOOGY. He's the LOOGY to end all LOOGYs, a LOOGY Supreme complete with sour cream, tangy red sauce and a ridiculous .160 TAv against lefties last year. When he faces righties, however, disaster on a level usually reserved for Russian dashboard camera footage frequently ensues. Choate is an old dog who isn't about to learn any new tricks, so in this, the last year of his contract, the Cardinals had best continue to spot him wisely or suffer the painful consequences.

Tim Cooney   LHP

Born: 12/19/90   Age: 24   Bats: L   Throws: L   Height: 6'3"   Weight: 195

YEAR	TEAM	LVL	AGE	W	L	SV	G	GS	IP	H	HR	BB	K	BB/9	K/9	GB%	BABIP	WHIP	ERA	FIP	FRA	WARP
2012	BAT	A-	21	3	3	0	13	11	55²	56	4	8	43	1.3	7.0	57%	.319	1.15	3.40	3.26	4.90	0.2
2013	PMB	A+	22	3	3	0	6	6	36	38	1	4	23	1.0	5.8	43%	.316	1.17	2.75	2.74	4.16	0.2
2013	SFD	AA	22	7	10	0	20	20	118¹	132	8	18	125	1.4	9.5	49%	.366	1.27	3.80	2.43	3.29	3.1
2014	MEM	AAA	23	14	6	0	26	25	158	158	21	47	119	2.7	6.8	48%	.291	1.30	3.47	4.93	4.67	2.0
2015	SLN	MLB	24	9	8	0	24	24	136¹	140	14	35	98	2.3	6.5	47%	.317	1.29	4.16	4.14	4.52	0.3

Breakout: 19%   Improve: 30%   Collapse: 8%   Attrition: 26%   MLB: 44%   Comparables: *Kyle Gibson, Tommy Milone, Rudy Owens*

A low-ceiling, high-floor prospect, Cooney doesn't have the eye-popping velocity or filthy stuff that sets tongues a-waggin'. Instead, the young lefty uses excellent control and solid command of his low-90s fastball and standout changeup to rack up innings and keep his team in games. His strike-out rate plummeted and his walk rate climbed last year in Triple-A, and while he was still comparatively stingy with ball four, pitchers like Cooney often don't miss enough bats to stick in a big-league rotation over the long haul. More likely he'll carve out a long career as a swingman, doing solid work filling in for a few starts and working multiple innings in middle relief.

Jack Flaherty   RHP

Born: 10/15/95   Age: 19   Bats: R   Throws: R   Height: 6'4"   Weight: 205

YEAR	TEAM	LVL	AGE	W	L	SV	G	GS	IP	H	HR	BB	K	BB/9	K/9	GB%	BABIP	WHIP	ERA	FIP	FRA	WARP
2015	SLN	MLB	19	2	3	0	8	8	33²	37	4	20	19	5.3	5.0	46%	.318	1.70	5.93	5.81	6.45	-0.6

Breakout: 0%   Improve: 0%   Collapse: 0%   Attrition: 0%   MLB: 0%   Comparables: *Jenrry Mejia, Edwin Escobar, Jonathan Pettibone*

Unlike the stereotypical prep pitching prospect with million-dollar velocity and hit-the-bull control, Flaherty stands out by showing surprising command of his four-pitch arsenal. His fastball rarely reaches into the low 90s, although the organization expects more instruction will lead to additional heat, and he already shows advanced feel for his slider, curveball and changeup. With height, athleticism and an easy, repeatable delivery, Flaherty enters his first full pro season with a sturdy foundation on which to build toward his mid-rotation ceiling.

Sam Freeman   LHP

Born: 6/24/87   Age: 28   Bats: R   Throws: L   Height: 5'11"   Weight: 165

YEAR	TEAM	LVL	AGE	W	L	SV	G	GS	IP	H	HR	BB	K	BB/9	K/9	GB%	BABIP	WHIP	ERA	FIP	FRA	WARP
2012	SFD	AA	25	1	3	1	15	0	17¹	12	1	4	12	2.1	6.2	48%	.216	0.92	1.56	3.51	4.25	0.1
2012	MEM	AAA	25	2	2	0	27	0	30¹	25	3	12	27	3.6	8.0	42%	.272	1.22	2.08	4.36	4.54	0.3
2012	SLN	MLB	25	0	2	0	24	0	20	17	2	10	18	4.5	8.1	46%	.273	1.35	5.40	4.29	4.40	0.1
2013	MEM	AAA	26	7	2	2	49	0	69²	57	4	27	66	3.5	8.5	48%	.273	1.21	2.97	3.71	3.73	1.3
2013	SLN	MLB	26	1	0	0	13	0	12¹	8	0	5	8	3.6	5.8	40%	.216	1.05	2.19	2.94	3.19	0.2
2014	MEM	AAA	27	0	1	0	16	0	20¹	25	1	7	26	3.1	11.5	48%	.393	1.57	3.54	2.96	2.98	0.7
2014	SLN	MLB	27	2	0	0	44	0	38	34	1	19	35	4.5	8.3	61%	.294	1.39	2.61	3.76	3.67	0.5
2015	SLN	MLB	28	3	1	0	53	0	59¹	52	5	24	50	3.7	7.6	46%	.299	1.29	3.79	4.12	4.12	0.3

Breakout: 15%   Improve: 32%   Collapse: 11%   Attrition: 21%   MLB: 54%   Comparables: *Craig Breslow, Cory Gearrin, Ehren Wassermann*

When prospect evaluators discuss the depth of a system and the value it can provide, they're talking about players like Freeman. Never a top prospect, the lefty reliever has kicked around the Cardinals' farm for seven years, overpowering the kids with mid-90s heat and a baffling splitter. Then last summer, when Kevin Siegrist—himself a product of the Cardinals' enviable depth—went down with shoulder woes, Freeman was plugged right into the second lefty role and held his own. His split piece allows him to neutralize righty batters, and while he will always issue too many walks to expand his role he should continue to find success in the middle innings.

Jaime Garcia   LHP

Born: 7/8/86   Age: 28   Bats: L   Throws: L   Height: 6'2"   Weight: 215

YEAR	TEAM	LVL	AGE	W	L	SV	G	GS	IP	H	HR	BB	K	BB/9	K/9	GB%	BABIP	WHIP	ERA	FIP	FRA	WARP
2012	SFD	AA	25	1	0	0	2	2	10¹	8	2	0	11	0.0	9.6	50%	.231	0.77	5.23	3.67	5.13	0.0
2012	SLN	MLB	25	7	7	0	20	20	121²	136	7	30	98	2.2	7.2	56%	.339	1.36	3.92	3.01	3.94	2.3
2013	SLN	MLB	26	5	2	0	9	9	55¹	57	6	15	43	2.4	7.0	64%	.300	1.30	3.58	3.69	4.82	-0.1
2014	SLN	MLB	27	3	1	0	7	7	43²	39	6	7	39	1.4	8.0	54%	.270	1.05	4.12	3.79	4.64	0.4
2015	SLN	MLB	28	3	2	0	7	7	43¹	41	4	12	35	2.4	7.3	54%	.316	1.22	3.69	3.81	4.01	0.4

Breakout: 23%   Improve: 64%   Collapse: 12%   Attrition: 9%   MLB: 91%   Comparables: *CC Sabathia, Matt Harrison, Matt Garza*

The only group Garcia frustrates more than opposing batters is the organization that relies on him to work a full season in the rotation. Last year he checked yet another box on his pitcher injury card, adding thoracic outlet surgery to his previous rotator cuff, labrum and elbow ligament woes. On the rare occasions he's been healthy, Garcia has continued to be productive and aesthetically pleasing, changing speeds and keeping hitters off balance with a never-ending assortment of cutters, sliders, changeups, curves and sinkers. Former teammate Chris Carpenter never really made it back from similar surgery (though others have) and the organization threw a fit last July over the perceived lack of communication between Garcia and the Cardinals about his treatment, the latest of several player-team dust-ups. Garcia is expected to compete for a rotation spot this spring, but whether he can stay there is an open question.

Marco Gonzales   LHP

Born: 2/16/92   Age: 23   Bats: L   Throws: L   Height: 6'1"   Weight: 195

YEAR	TEAM	LVL	AGE	W	L	SV	G	GS	IP	H	HR	BB	K	BB/9	K/9	GB%	BABIP	WHIP	ERA	FIP	FRA	WARP
2013	PMB	A+	21	0	0	0	4	4	16²	10	1	5	13	2.7	7.0	33%	.214	0.90	1.62	3.36	4.48	0.1
2014	PMB	A+	22	2	2	0	6	6	37²	34	1	8	32	1.9	7.6	53%	.303	1.12	1.43	2.67	3.34	0.6
2014	SFD	AA	22	3	2	0	7	7	38²	33	2	10	46	2.3	10.7	45%	.304	1.11	2.33	2.19	3.28	1.0
2014	MEM	AAA	22	4	1	0	8	8	45²	43	7	9	39	1.8	7.7	43%	.279	1.14	3.35	4.77	5.01	0.5
2014	SLN	MLB	22	4	2	0	10	5	34²	32	4	21	31	5.5	8.0	39%	.283	1.53	4.15	4.72	4.57	0.4
2015	SLN	MLB	23	7	7	0	22	22	114	105	11	40	95	3.2	7.5	43%	.304	1.27	3.95	4.12	4.29	0.7

Breakout: 23%   Improve: 58%   Collapse: 7%   Attrition: 26%   MLB: 85%   Comparables: *Chris Tillman, Randall Delgado, Alex White*

Gonzales was tabbed as a fast mover when he was drafted in the first round out of Gonzaga, and true to form he made his big-league debut last June, 382 days after signing. His quick ascent was due primarily to his beast of a changeup, a true Bugs Bunny pitch that he can throw in any count and generate whiffs. None of his other offerings have as much sizzle, but he commands his upper-80s fastball and 12-6 breakers reasonably well; he seems likely to cut down on the walks that troubled him at times last summer. Mature beyond his years, Gonzales doesn't have the jaw-dropping arsenal of a Carlos Martinez but makes the most of what he has and is a good bet to reach his mid-rotation ceiling.

Nick Greenwood   LHP

Born: 9/28/87   Age: 27   Bats: R   Throws: L   Height: 6'1"   Weight: 180

YEAR	TEAM	LVL	AGE	W	L	SV	G	GS	IP	H	HR	BB	K	BB/9	K/9	GB%	BABIP	WHIP	ERA	FIP	FRA	WARP
2012	MEM	AAA	24	4	3	0	49	4	77²	87	6	23	47	2.7	5.4	60%	.318	1.42	4.40	4.54	5.14	0.6
2013	SFD	AA	25	3	4	0	11	7	40²	50	3	11	22	2.4	4.9	58%	.326	1.50	3.98	3.89	5.58	0.3
2013	MEM	AAA	25	2	8	0	22	7	54¹	65	9	19	24	3.1	4.0	57%	.296	1.55	5.63	5.94	6.77	-0.1
2014	MEM	AAA	26	4	4	0	27	5	50²	42	4	10	37	1.8	6.6	64%	.257	1.03	3.02	3.98	4.86	0.7
2014	SLN	MLB	26	2	1	0	19	1	36	36	5	5	17	1.2	4.2	62%	.265	1.14	4.75	4.46	5.95	-0.2
2015	SLN	MLB	27	3	2	1	41	5	73¹	79	8	21	36	2.6	4.5	56%	.306	1.37	4.74	4.84	5.15	-0.4

Breakout: 10%   Improve: 17%   Collapse: 7%   Attrition: 20%   MLB: 25%   *Comparables: Geno Espineli, Chuckie Fick, Mike McClendon*

Yet another testament to the Cardinals' pitching depth, injuries helped elevate Greenwood from swingman duty in Triple-A to bullpen action with the big club, and the Rhode Island product spent the summer earning big-league meal money. A dedicated worm-killer, Greenwood works his upper-80s fastball low in the zone and generates plenty of groundballs with his slider, but too much exposure to righty batters will leave permanent scars. Even when better options are available, it's comforting to know a steady hand like Greenwood can be stowed behind glass in case there's another bullpen emergency.

Rob Kaminsky   LHP

Born: 9/2/94   Age: 20   Bats: R   Throws: L   Height: 5'11"   Weight: 191

YEAR	TEAM	LVL	AGE	W	L	SV	G	GS	IP	H	HR	BB	K	BB/9	K/9	GB%	BABIP	WHIP	ERA	FIP	FRA	WARP
2014	PEO	A	19	8	2	0	18	18	100²	71	2	31	79	2.8	7.1	53%	.239	1.01	1.88	3.28	4.07	0.9
2015	SLN	MLB	20	4	5	0	14	14	71	75	7	34	38	4.3	4.9	48%	.305	1.52	5.07	5.22	5.51	-0.5

Breakout: 0%   Improve: 0%   Collapse: 0%   Attrition: 0%   MLB: 0%   *Comparables: Jeurys Familia, T.J. House, Ian Krol*

Kaminsky handled his full-season debut with remarkable aplomb, using his low-90s fastball, plus curve and developing change to post a miniscule ERA as a teenager in the Midwest League. Whether the vertically challenged lefty can pull the same tricks as he moves up in class is a matter of debate among scouts. Some look askance at his height, iffy command and low strikeout rate and see a future middle reliever, while others expect his curveball to eventually generate enough swing-and-miss to reach his mid-rotation potential. The jury is out, but advanced hitters will render their verdict soon enough.

John Lackey   RHP

Born: 10/23/78   Age: 36   Bats: R   Throws: R   Height: 6'6"   Weight: 235

YEAR	TEAM	LVL	AGE	W	L	SV	G	GS	IP	H	HR	BB	K	BB/9	K/9	GB%	BABIP	WHIP	ERA	FIP	FRA	WARP
2013	BOS	MLB	34	10	13	0	29	29	189¹	179	26	40	161	1.9	7.7	48%	.281	1.16	3.52	3.89	4.33	1.9
2014	BOS	MLB	35	11	7	0	21	21	137¹	137	15	32	116	2.1	7.6	49%	.298	1.23	3.60	3.59	3.99	1.6
2014	SLN	MLB	35	3	3	0	10	10	60²	69	9	15	48	2.2	7.1	43%	.319	1.38	4.30	4.24	4.65	0.1
2015	SLN	MLB	36	11	9	0	28	28	174¹	172	18	47	134	2.4	6.9	45%	.313	1.26	4.11	4.11	4.47	0.4

Breakout: 16%   Improve: 43%   Collapse: 14%   Attrition: 20%   MLB: 78%   *Comparables: Kevin Millwood, Cory Lidle, Ted Lilly*

When the Red Sox signed Lackey to his windfall five-year deal prior to the 2010 season, they wrote in some protection in the form of a team option at the league minimum should he miss significant time with an elbow injury. Fast forward to the easiest decision John Mozeliak has ever made, as the Cardinals exercised Lackey's option this year and will benefit from his veteran steadiness and league-average production for a cool $500k. The big right-hander has never been dominant but remains a premier strike-thrower who slots comfortably into the middle of a rotation. His bulldog demeanor and postseason heroics play well in the heartland. Midway through his Boston career, who could have imagined Google would someday auto-complete "John Lackey is" with the phrase "the poster boy for redemption?"

Lance Lynn   RHP

Born: 5/12/87   Age: 28   Bats: R   Throws: R   Height: 6'5"   Weight: 240

YEAR	TEAM	LVL	AGE	W	L	SV	G	GS	IP	H	HR	BB	K	BB/9	K/9	GB%	BABIP	WHIP	ERA	FIP	FRA	WARP
2012	SLN	MLB	25	18	7	0	35	29	176	168	16	64	180	3.3	9.2	46%	.321	1.32	3.78	3.53	3.71	2.8
2013	SLN	MLB	26	15	10	0	33	33	201²	189	14	76	198	3.4	8.8	45%	.314	1.31	3.97	3.25	3.48	3.6
2014	SLN	MLB	27	15	10	0	33	33	203²	185	13	72	181	3.2	8.0	46%	.290	1.26	2.74	3.32	3.63	2.9
2015	SLN	MLB	28	11	9	0	29	29	173²	154	14	61	164	3.1	8.5	45%	.314	1.24	3.65	3.69	3.96	1.5

Breakout: 26%   Improve: 54%   Collapse: 15%   Attrition: 15%   MLB: 85%   *Comparables: Felipe Paulino, Bud Norris, Tom Gorzelanny*

Conventional wisdom states that starters need to rely on their changeup to find success against opposite-side batters, but don't tell that to Lynn. Last year, the Ole Miss alum started rationing his dodgy off-speed stuff and instead pounded lefty hitters with two- and four-seamers, improving his platoon splits and emerging as a bona fide third starter. Lynn threw a fastball almost 80 percent of the time, by far the most in baseball among starters unless you're willing to accept that whatever it is Bartolo Colon throws can be classified as a "heater." The best offering in any pitcher's arsenal is a fastball thrown to the right spot, and by winning 48 games over the last three seasons Lynn is seemingly bent on proving that fastball command isn't everything, it's the only thing.

Tyler Lyons   LHP

Born: 2/21/88   Age: 27   Bats: B   Throws: L   Height: 6'4"   Weight: 200

YEAR	TEAM	LVL	AGE	W	L	SV	G	GS	IP	H	HR	BB	K	BB/9	K/9	GB%	BABIP	WHIP	ERA	FIP	FRA	WARP
2012	SFD	AA	24	5	4	0	12	12	64¹	70	6	19	54	2.7	7.6	57%	.330	1.38	3.92	3.75	4.63	0.6
2012	MEM	AAA	24	4	9	0	15	15	88¹	87	9	18	89	1.8	9.1	40%	.315	1.19	4.28	3.65	3.45	2.6
2013	MEM	AAA	25	7	2	0	17	16	100¹	85	6	19	86	1.7	7.7	52%	.280	1.04	3.32	3.38	4.22	1.4
2013	SLN	MLB	25	2	4	0	12	8	53	49	5	16	43	2.7	7.3	50%	.282	1.23	4.75	3.70	4.37	0.3
2014	MEM	AAA	26	8	2	0	14	14	81¹	94	9	18	75	2.0	8.3	44%	.348	1.38	4.43	3.96	4.29	1.8
2014	SLN	MLB	26	0	4	0	11	4	36²	33	4	11	36	2.7	8.8	43%	.284	1.20	4.42	3.62	3.92	0.3
2015	SLN	MLB	27	7	5	0	24	17	108	104	11	28	87	2.3	7.2	46%	.312	1.23	3.98	3.96	4.32	0.5

Breakout: 35%   Improve: 43%   Collapse: 17%   Attrition: 30%   MLB: 67%   Comparables: John Ely, Brad Lincoln, Zach Stewart

Lyons has nothing left to prove in the minors, and if he were, say, a Twin, he'd be earning a long look-see in the big-league rotation instead of serving as a Triple-A insurance policy. A solidly built lefty who abets his average fastball with a nice slider, Lyons has never found the magical elixir to proof him against the right-handed bats who posted a .303/.335/.485 against him last year, limiting his upside to that of a fourth starter, a role he's not likely to fill in St. Louis.

Seth Maness   RHP

Born: 10/14/88   Age: 26   Bats: R   Throws: R   Height: 6'0"   Weight: 190

YEAR	TEAM	LVL	AGE	W	L	SV	G	GS	IP	H	HR	BB	K	BB/9	K/9	GB%	BABIP	WHIP	ERA	FIP	FRA	WARP
2012	PMB	A+	23	3	1	0	7	7	46	45	5	1	29	0.2	5.7	58%	.282	1.00	2.15	3.61	5.32	0.0
2012	SFD	AA	23	11	3	0	20	20	123²	122	13	9	83	0.7	6.0	54%	.278	1.06	3.27	3.67	4.92	0.8
2013	MEM	AAA	24	2	2	0	4	4	25	34	2	3	18	1.1	6.5	40%	.376	1.48	4.32	3.65	4.39	0.2
2013	SLN	MLB	24	5	2	1	66	0	62	65	4	13	35	1.9	5.1	70%	.311	1.26	2.32	3.41	4.10	0.3
2014	SLN	MLB	25	6	4	3	73	0	80¹	77	7	11	55	1.2	6.2	57%	.289	1.10	2.91	3.35	4.31	0.6
2015	SLN	MLB	26	4	3	0	33	7	68²	70	7	12	42	1.6	5.5	55%	.306	1.19	3.86	4.10	4.19	0.4

Breakout: 44%   Improve: 67%   Collapse: 11%   Attrition: 13%   MLB: 88%   Comparables: Scott Baker, Taylor Buchholz, Dave Bush

In this era of increased pitcher specialization, big-league bullpens come stocked with closers, set-up men, middle men, swingmen, LOOGYs, ROOGYs and players like Maness whose role is to induce double-play grounders: the TOOGY. Primarily a sinkerballer, Maness equates walks with treason, generates plenty of groundballs and can dominate same-side hitters, but when he makes a mistake to lefties it often leaves the yard. You'll know Maness is being used properly if he's brought in to end a key late-inning threat and removed before he ignites a new one.

Carlos Martinez   RHP

Born: 9/21/91   Age: 23   Bats: R   Throws: R   Height: 6'0"   Weight: 185

YEAR	TEAM	LVL	AGE	W	L	SV	G	GS	IP	H	HR	BB	K	BB/9	K/9	GB%	BABIP	WHIP	ERA	FIP	FRA	WARP
2012	PMB	A+	20	2	2	0	7	7	33	29	0	10	34	2.7	9.3	50%	.319	1.18	3.00	2.79	3.62	0.6
2012	SFD	AA	20	4	3	0	15	14	71¹	62	6	22	58	2.8	7.3	63%	.276	1.18	2.90	3.92	4.63	0.6
2013	SFD	AA	21	1	0	0	3	3	11²	11	1	1	9	0.8	6.9	57%	.278	1.03	2.31	3.14	3.52	0.3
2013	MEM	AAA	21	5	3	0	13	13	68	54	3	27	63	3.6	8.3	56%	.268	1.19	2.51	3.75	4.03	1.0
2013	SLN	MLB	21	2	1	1	21	1	28¹	31	1	9	24	2.9	7.6	55%	.345	1.41	5.08	3.06	4.11	0.2
2014	MEM	AAA	22	1	0	0	2	2	10¹	6	0	1	7	0.9	6.1	48%	.207	0.68	0.00	2.63	2.89	0.2
2014	SLN	MLB	22	2	4	1	57	7	89¹	90	4	36	84	3.6	8.5	55%	.333	1.41	4.03	3.15	3.27	2.0
2015	SLN	MLB	23	5	4	0	30	14	87²	80	6	33	75	3.4	7.7	52%	.312	1.29	3.86	3.84	4.20	0.6

Breakout: 23%   Improve: 64%   Collapse: 16%   Attrition: 22%   MLB: 92%   Comparables: Rubby De La Rosa, Brett Cecil, Brian Matusz

The question entering last season was whether Martinez should help the Cardinals win a championship by dominating the eighth inning or start his career in the rotation. As it turned out none of those things happened, as the lightning-armed Dominican was used in multiple bullpen roles, made seven starts, spent some time in Triple-A and never found the space to let his natural raw talent dominate. And dominate he can, as Martinez misses bats and generates groundballs with a moving high-90s fastball and a plus slider. His stuff is filthy and at times unhittable, good enough to front a rotation, but continuing concerns about his durability, high-effort delivery and a dodgy changeup that gives lefty batters a chance have kept St. Louis from committing to him as a starter. Martinez could one day start an All-Star Game, but he'll first need to be trusted to start every fifth day in April.

Jason Motte   RHP

Born: 6/22/82   Age: 33   Bats: R   Throws: R   Height: 6'0"   Weight: 205

YEAR	TEAM	LVL	AGE	W	L	SV	G	GS	IP	H	HR	BB	K	BB/9	K/9	GB%	BABIP	WHIP	ERA	FIP	FRA	WARP
2012	SLN	MLB	30	4	5	42	67	0	72	49	9	17	86	2.1	10.8	41%	.242	0.92	2.75	3.16	3.74	0.7
2014	SLN	MLB	32	1	0	0	29	0	25	29	7	9	17	3.2	6.1	37%	.286	1.52	4.68	6.46	6.59	-0.5
2015	SLN	MLB	33	2	1	1	41	0	39	31	4	11	39	2.5	9.1	42%	.290	1.08	2.96	3.65	3.22	0.7

Breakout: 19%   Improve: 44%   Collapse: 29%   Attrition: 10%   MLB: 89%   Comparables: Pedro Feliciano, J.J. Putz, Heath Bell

Motte returned last May after missing more than a year to elbow surgery, and it soon become clear that both the Cardinals' bullpen and Motte himself had changed significantly while he was away. All his old running mates (Boggsy and 'Nando and Scrabble) were gone, replaced by young flamethrowers who could light up radar guns at a rate Motte could only dream of now that the surgeons had hacked a few ticks off his formerly elite velocity. The former closer struggled pitching in low-leverage situations, relied more on his cutter and never got back on track. Another year removed from surgery should help him, though he's edging into dicey territory age-wise, and Motte's Proven Closer imprimatur should help get him more chances to reinvent himself in a set-up role.

Alex Reyes   RHP

Born: 8/29/94   Age: 20   Bats: R   Throws: R   Height: 6'3"   Weight: 185

YEAR	TEAM	LVL	AGE	W	L	SV	G	GS	IP	H	HR	BB	K	BB/9	K/9	GB%	BABIP	WHIP	ERA	FIP	FRA	WARP
2014	PEO	A	19	7	7	0	21	21	109¹	82	6	61	137	5.0	11.3	40%	.295	1.31	3.62	3.45	3.84	1.7
2015	SLN	MLB	20	5	6	0	17	17	86	81	8	51	75	5.4	7.9	40%	.315	1.54	4.87	4.77	5.29	-0.5

Breakout: 0%   Improve: 0%   Collapse: 0%   Attrition: 0%   MLB: 0%   Comparables: Trevor May, Tyler Matzek, Trevor Cahill

Reyes arrived in Peoria for his full-season debut carrying a lot of bad weight and struggled to control his elite stuff, but when he was on, Midwest League hitters couldn't handle his truth. Blessed with easy mid-90s gas and an impressive power curve, Reyes has the goods to be an ace if he can learn to command his offerings and develop his changeup into more than a show-me offering. His route to the big leagues is almost as unique as his talent, as Reyes moved from New Jersey to live with his grandparents in the Dominican Republic as a high school senior, thus avoiding the draft and sitting out a year before signing with the Cardinals in 2012. If he can improve his conditioning and build on the consistency he showed down the stretch last season, Reyes could make a dramatic jump up prospect lists this summer.

Trevor Rosenthal   RHP

Born: 5/29/90   Age: 25   Bats: R   Throws: R   Height: 6'2"   Weight: 220

YEAR	TEAM	LVL	AGE	W	L	SV	G	GS	IP	H	HR	BB	K	BB/9	K/9	GB%	BABIP	WHIP	ERA	FIP	FRA	WARP
2012	SFD	AA	22	8	6	0	17	17	94	67	6	37	83	3.5	7.9	47%	.243	1.11	2.78	3.59	4.67	0.8
2012	MEM	AAA	22	0	0	0	3	3	15	11	1	5	21	3.0	12.6	61%	.312	1.07	4.20	3.13	3.25	0.4
2012	SLN	MLB	22	0	2	0	19	0	22²	14	2	7	25	2.8	9.9	55%	.222	0.93	2.78	3.14	2.96	0.4
2013	SLN	MLB	23	2	4	3	74	0	75¹	63	4	20	108	2.4	12.9	46%	.341	1.10	2.63	1.88	1.80	2.3
2014	SLN	MLB	24	2	6	45	72	0	70¹	57	2	42	87	5.4	11.1	39%	.318	1.41	3.20	2.96	3.80	0.6
2015	SLN	MLB	25	4	3	7	35	7	67¹	54	5	26	73	3.5	9.8	47%	.309	1.19	3.26	3.44	3.54	1.0

Breakout: 15%   Improve: 27%   Collapse: 10%   Attrition: 25%   MLB: 38%   Comparables: *Anthony Ranaudo, Andrew Chafin, Kyle Weiland*

Credit St. Louis for crafting a plan and sticking to it, as the progression of Rosenthal from minor-league starter to late-season bullpen reinforcement to set-up man to closer has worked perfectly for both the player and the club. Rosenthal's wall-denting fastball looks and sounds lethal, but the Missouri native was less dominant than his 45 saves might lead you to believe. He racked up plenty of whiffs, of course, but his .249 TAv allowed was two ticks higher than Seth Maness, due mostly to a sharp escalation in his walk rate. Control problems will likely always be just a few outings away for Rosenthal, which is why he's destined for a long career as a second-tier closer rather than a mid-rotation starter.

Kevin Siegrist   RHP

Born: 7/20/89   Age: 25   Bats: L   Throws: L   Height: 6'5"   Weight: 215

YEAR	TEAM	LVL	AGE	W	L	SV	G	GS	IP	H	HR	BB	K	BB/9	K/9	GB%	BABIP	WHIP	ERA	FIP	FRA	WARP
2012	PMB	A+	22	6	0	0	10	10	55¹	33	3	22	41	3.6	6.7	41%	.200	0.99	2.28	4.13	5.08	0.1
2012	SFD	AA	22	1	2	0	8	5	32¹	26	4	9	27	2.5	7.5	54%	.244	1.08	3.62	4.52	5.94	-0.1
2013	SFD	AA	23	1	1	1	13	0	20	8	2	7	35	3.2	15.8	42%	.207	0.75	2.25	2.06	2.77	0.6
2013	SLN	MLB	23	3	1	0	45	0	39²	17	1	18	50	4.1	11.3	41%	.195	0.88	0.45	2.26	2.24	0.9
2014	SLN	MLB	24	1	4	0	37	0	30¹	32	5	16	37	4.7	11.0	33%	.338	1.58	6.82	4.59	5.41	-0.3
2015	SLN	MLB	25	2	2	0	21	5	42¹	35	4	19	38	4.1	8.2	44%	.289	1.29	3.81	4.28	4.14	0.3

Breakout: 36%   Improve: 62%   Collapse: 19%   Attrition: 23%   MLB: 85%   Comparables: *James McDonald, Josh Outman, Hector Santiago*

Siegrist was well on his way to building on his breakout 2013 campaign when a left forearm strain followed by nerve pain in his shoulder cost him two months of the season; the aches continued to bedevil him after he returned. When he's right the long-levered lefty is as subtle as a thunderstorm, blowing his mid-90s gas past hitters and racking up enough strikeouts to overcome his chronically sketchy walk rate. The organization expects him to be ready for spring training, and if he's healthy he can provide a big lift in the middle innings.

Samuel Tuivailala   RHP

Born: 10/19/92   Age: 22   Bats: R   Throws: R   Height: 6'3"   Weight: 195

YEAR	TEAM	LVL	AGE	W	L	SV	G	GS	IP	H	HR	BB	K	BB/9	K/9	GB%	BABIP	WHIP	ERA	FIP	FRA	WARP
2013	PEO	A	20	0	3	1	28	0	35¹	31	0	20	50	5.1	12.7	58%	.365	1.44	5.35	2.55	3.23	0.8
2014	PMB	A+	21	0	1	3	29	0	37²	29	1	18	64	4.3	15.3	47%	.364	1.25	3.58	1.93	2.16	1.3
2014	SFD	AA	21	2	1	1	17	0	21	18	0	9	30	3.9	12.9	56%	.375	1.29	2.57	1.69	1.44	0.9
2014	SLN	MLB	21	0	0	0	2	0	1	5	2	2	1	18.0	9.0	0%	.600	7.00	36.00	33.10	22.34	-0.3
2015	SLN	MLB	22	2	1	1	42	0	52	43	4	26	62	4.6	10.6	45%	.327	1.33	3.80	3.60	4.13	0.3

Breakout: 0%   Improve: 0%   Collapse: 0%   Attrition: 0%   MLB: 0%   Comparables: *Jhan Marinez, Andrew Carignan, Tommy Kahnle*

Drafted in the first round back in 2010, Tuivailala hopes to follow in the footsteps of Trevor Rosenthal and Jason Motte as a converted position player working high-leverage innings in the Cardinals' bullpen. He punched out nearly 37 percent of the batters he faced last year over four levels, including two innings in St. Louis, and his stuff looks to be tailor-made for late-game work. Tuivailala can amp his fastball up near triple digits, and his power curve can make overmatched batters look silly, although he still needs to work on his command. The organization will likely let him make his bones in Memphis, but Tuivailala may start his apprenticeship in the big-league 'pen later this summer.

Michael Wacha   RHP

Born: 7/1/91   Age: 23   Bats: R   Throws: R   Height: 6'6"   Weight: 210

YEAR	TEAM	LVL	AGE	W	L	SV	G	GS	IP	H	HR	BB	K	BB/9	K/9	GB%	BABIP	WHIP	ERA	FIP	FRA	WARP
2013	MEM	AAA	21	5	3	0	15	15	85	65	9	19	73	2.0	7.7	38%	.241	0.99	2.65	3.90	3.69	1.5
2013	SLN	MLB	21	4	1	0	15	9	64²	52	5	19	65	2.6	9.0	46%	.275	1.10	2.78	2.90	3.55	0.9
2014	SLN	MLB	22	5	6	0	19	19	107	95	6	33	94	2.8	7.9	44%	.288	1.20	3.20	3.14	3.61	1.5
2015	SLN	MLB	23	7	4	0	22	17	100²	83	8	28	94	2.5	8.4	43%	.294	1.11	3.03	3.39	3.30	1.8

Breakout: 33%   Improve: 70%   Collapse: 15%   Attrition: 11%   MLB: 97%   Comparables: *Madison Bumgarner, Mat Latos, Phil Hughes*

Equipped with a well-commanded low-90s fastball and a devastating changeup, Wacha began last summer as the safest bet to eventually assume the mantle of staff ace whenever Adam Wainwright tires of it, but that was before his shoulder started to bother him. Dominant early in the season, Wacha struggled in June before being diagnosed with a scapular stress fracture. Two months of rest got him back on the mound in time for the stretch run and playoffs, seemingly as good as new, but with this particular injury there are no guarantees. Brandon McCarthy has suffered recurrent stress reactions over the years and there's no way of knowing whether Wacha will suffer many, few or none going forward. Of course, the same can be said about any other complaint, but this just adds to the always-present injury risk inherent in throwing a baseball 95 miles per hour.

Adam Wainwright   RHP

Born: 8/30/81   Age: 33   Bats: R   Throws: R   Height: 6'7"   Weight: 235

YEAR	TEAM	LVL	AGE	W	L	SV	G	GS	IP	H	HR	BB	K	BB/9	K/9	GB%	BABIP	WHIP	ERA	FIP	FRA	WARP
2012	SLN	MLB	30	14	13	0	32	32	198²	196	15	52	184	2.4	8.3	52%	.315	1.25	3.94	3.14	3.96	2.8
2013	SLN	MLB	31	19	9	0	34	34	241²	223	15	35	219	1.3	8.2	50%	.305	1.07	2.94	2.52	3.30	5.1
2014	SLN	MLB	32	20	9	0	32	32	227	184	10	50	179	2.0	7.1	49%	.267	1.03	2.38	2.85	3.37	4.2
2015	SLN	MLB	33	13	8	0	29	29	193	165	13	42	168	1.9	7.8	50%	.301	1.07	2.87	3.19	3.12	3.7

Breakout: 4%   Improve: 42%   Collapse: 25%   Attrition: 24%   MLB: 90%   Comparables: Chris Carpenter, Roy Oswalt, Johan Santana

We're starting to wonder whether it was actually Tommy John's ligament that was sewn into Wainwright's reconstructed elbow several years ago, as the Cardinals ace looks to be following the same post-surgical path John himself blazed in the seventies: John followed up his solid post-surgical comeback season with four straight campaigns that earned strong Cy Young consideration, winning 80 games. Wainwright has followed up *his* solid post-surgical comeback season with 39 wins in two years, placing no lower than third in Cy Young balloting. If you believe in destiny, you won't let Wainwright's postseason cartilage trim spook you and you'll bet heavily on two more 20-win seasons; after all, Vegas loves it when you believe in destiny. If you don't, expect Wainwright to be dominant as long as he remains healthy, and hedge your bets accordingly.

Jordan Walden   RHP

Born: 11/16/87   Age: 27   Bats: R   Throws: R   Height: 6'5"   Weight: 250

YEAR	TEAM	LVL	AGE	W	L	SV	G	GS	IP	H	HR	BB	K	BB/9	K/9	GB%	BABIP	WHIP	ERA	FIP	FRA	WARP
2012	ANA	MLB	24	3	2	1	45	0	39	35	3	18	48	4.2	11.1	40%	.311	1.36	3.46	2.97	3.60	0.6
2013	ATL	MLB	25	4	3	1	50	0	47	39	4	14	54	2.7	10.3	33%	.292	1.13	3.45	2.79	2.51	1.1
2014	ATL	MLB	26	0	2	3	58	0	50	33	2	27	62	4.9	11.2	45%	.272	1.20	2.88	2.76	3.29	0.4
2015	SLN	MLB	27	3	1	1	50	0	46²	37	3	19	51	3.7	10.0	44%	.311	1.21	3.17	3.23	3.45	0.6

Breakout: 30%   Improve: 51%   Collapse: 23%   Attrition: 12%   MLB: 89%   Comparables: Boone Logan, Joe Smith, Sean Doolittle

"As with our colleges, so with a hundred 'modern improvements'; there is an illusion about them; there is not always a positive advance." Thoreau was talking about the facade of progress, so he might as well have been addressing Walden's control. In 2013, Walden posted a career-low walk rate; in 2014, he regressed to his feral roots, throwing fewer strikes than he had during his Angels days. False gains or not, he limited contact like a restraining order, allowing him to persevere as a valuable reliever, albeit one who seems to miss a few weeks each season with some ailment or another.

Luke Weaver   RHP

Born: 8/21/93   Age: 21   Bats: R   Throws: R   Height: 6'2"   Weight: 170

YEAR	TEAM	LVL	AGE	W	L	SV	G	GS	IP	H	HR	BB	K	BB/9	K/9	GB%	BABIP	WHIP	ERA	FIP	FRA	WARP
2015	SLN	MLB	21	2	3	0	9	9	34²	37	4	17	22	4.4	5.8	45%	.318	1.56	5.28	5.28	5.74	-0.3

Breakout: 0%   Improve: 0%   Collapse: 0%   Attrition: 0%   MLB: 0%   Comparables: Edwin Escobar, Kyle Lobstein, Jose A. Ramirez

The Cardinals have an unquenchable thirst for polished college starters and the developmental certainty they often represent, but in Weaver's case the cost of his high floor is a relatively low ceiling for a first-round pick. The Florida State alumnus knows how to pitch and flashes plus command of his low-90s fastball and an advanced changeup, but lacks elite velocity and a true wipeout offering. Of course, that's what people said about Michael Wacha a few years ago, and these are the Cardinals, so you never know.

Lineouts

Hitters

NAME	POS	TEAM	LVL	AGE	PA	R	2B	3B	HR	RBI	BB	K	SB	CS	AVG/OBP/SLG	TAv	BABIP	BRR	FRAA	WARP
Vaughn Bryan	LF	PEO	A	21	350	47	17	9	1	15	27	73	11	7	.262/.326/.382	.249	.337	0.2	LF(28): 0.6, CF(24): 1.9	0.2
Danny Diekroeger	3B	SCO	A-	22	287	41	13	4	5	35	16	34	2	2	.286/.331/.424	.294	.307	1.4	3B(22): -3.2, 2B(2): 0.0	0.6
Ed Easley	C	MEM	AAA	28	312	43	17	1	10	43	22	46	0	4	.296/.359/.473	.286	.321	-2.7	C(79): -0.5, LF(1): -0.0	2.3
Greg Garcia	2B	MEM	AAA	24	441	60	12	3	8	40	41	95	7	5	.272/.358/.382	.272	.342	-1.6	2B(90): 3.8, SS(13): -0.9	2.2
	2B	SLN	MLB	24	18	2	1	0	0	1	1	6	0	0	.143/.333/.214	.231	.250	-0.2	2B(4): -0.1, SS(1): 0.0	-0.1
Juan Herrera	SS	PEO	A	21	416	50	22	3	2	56	24	57	27	13	.274/.320/.364	.279	.314	-0.3	SS(92): -4.6	2.1
	SS	PMB	A+	21	32	3	0	0	0	0	1	5	1	0	.194/.219/.194	.167	.231	0.3	SS(9): 1.0	0.0
Tyler Kelly	2B	TAC	AAA	25	549	81	19	2	15	80	85	96	11	3	.263/.381/.412	.298	.303	2.1	2B(64): -11.8, 3B(36): -0.2	2.9
Pete Kozma	SS	MEM	AAA	26	437	59	23	0	8	54	41	61	10	7	.248/.330/.372	.263	.275	1.6	SS(96): 7.5, 3B(11): 0.7	2.8
	SS	SLN	MLB	26	26	4	3	0	0	0	3	4	0	0	.304/.385/.435	.298	.368	0.8	SS(8): 0.3, 2B(6): -0.2	0.3
Mike O'Neill	LF	SFD	AA	26	408	57	17	4	1	26	41	37	5	7	.269/.343/.347	.259	.295	0.1	LF(83): 3.0, CF(2): -0.1	1.2
	LF	MEM	AAA	26	65	3	1	1	0	8	7	4	0	1	.333/.400/.386	.284	.352	-1.4	LF(16): 0.6	0.2
Cody Stanley	C	SFD	AA	25	434	47	16	2	12	43	35	68	13	2	.283/.340/.429	.277	.309	-2.1	C(76): 2.7	2.6
Oscar Taveras	LF	MEM	AAA	22	262	36	18	1	8	49	19	31	1	1	.318/.370/.502	.305	.337	-0.2	LF(22): -0.9, RF(17): 0.2	1.6
	RF	SLN	MLB	22	248	18	8	0	3	22	12	37	0	1	.239/.278/.312	.218	.272	-1.0	RF(62): -4.0, CF(3): 0.3	-1.2
Breyvic Valera	2B	PMB	A+	22	323	35	8	4	0	37	25	13	13	10	.333/.385/.388	.291	.346	-3.2	2B(52): 1.0, 3B(10): 0.7	2.0
	2B	SFD	AA	22	247	31	8	2	0	20	15	22	4	5	.286/.329/.339	.238	.316	0.0	2B(58): -2.5	0.3
Gerwuins Velazco	1B	PEO	A	22	24	2	2	0	1	2	1	6	0	0	.409/.435/.636	.367	.533	-0.3	1B(3): 0.1	0.3
	C	PMB	A+	22	113	13	6	1	1	16	15	15	0	0	.281/.384/.396	.304	.325	-0.4	C(33): -0.3, P(1): -0.0	1.0
Rowan Wick	RF	PEO	A	21	157	21	8	2	6	22	13	60	4	0	.220/.299/.433	.265	.333	-0.1	RF(28): -3.2, LF(7): -0.2	0.3
	RF	SCO	A-	21	141	30	8	1	14	38	20	34	1	1	.378/.475/.815	.426	.437	-1.8	RF(33): 6.7	3.5
Jacob Wilson	3B	PMB	A+	23	138	18	12	0	0	20	12	24	0	0	.298/.358/.397	.275	.360	0.1	3B(15): 0.1, 2B(12): 1.6	0.9
	2B	SFD	AA	23	145	15	13	0	5	21	11	23	3	1	.305/.366/.519	.309	.337	-0.5	2B(31): -3.1, 3B(5): 0.2	0.8
Patrick Wisdom	3B	SFD	AA	22	498	49	19	4	14	53	39	149	5	1	.215/.277/.367	.236	.282	0.7	3B(125): 5.7	0.8

Switch-hitting burner **Vaughn Bryan** spent his first full pro season proving that his drool-inducing tools will play in Peoria, though there are plenty of rough edges to sand away; his in-game power is all projection, but with plus speed, range enough for center and some contact skill, he's one to keep an eye on. ❖ Stanford Cardinal **Danny Diekroeger** transitioned from color to bird with aplomb as the lanky 10th-round gamer played both second and third and displayed an advanced lefty bat during a 21-game hitting streak; he's not a future starter, but defensive versatility will improve his odds of earning a bench role. ❖ Veteran minor-league backstop **Ed Easley** parlayed a solid year in Triple-A into a spot on the 40-man roster; he might find himself summoned to the Victory Motel this spring for a roster shootout with Tony Cruz and Cody Stanley, but you should keep that off the record, on the QT and very hush-hush. ❖ Descalso-in-waiting **Greg Garcia** is stretched at shortstop and hopeless against lefty pitching, but his combination of infield steadiness, solid approach and occasional pop makes him an excellent utility option as soon as this summer. ❖ **Juan Herrera** came to St. Louis as part of the Marc Rzepczynski trade, and while his full-season debut wasn't quite a triple word score, the young Dominican flashed speed, gap-power potential and enough range and arm to stick at shortstop. ❖ **Ty Kelly** can take a walk like a boss, and he spent 2014 splitting between the infield and the outfield, mastering the utility trade. ❖ Former big-league starter **Pete Kozma** remains an outstanding defensive infielder, a true shortstop with soft hands and excellent instincts, yet his career .238/.311/.348 minor-league line tells you all you need to know about his offensive potential; he may compete for a utility spot this year, but if his glove regresses even a nanometer it won't cover for his anemic bat. ❖ Fun-sized **Mike O'Neill** isn't exactly a one-trick pony, since he can draw walks *and* hit singles, but that's about five tricks shy of a big-league outfielder. ❖ As delighted as **Cody Stanley** looked posing with his shin guards and Texas League All-Star Game MVP belt last summer (seriously, Google that), being added to the 40-man roster had to feel even better; he's not a future starter, but with a dollop of patience and power, he might well outhit Tony Cruz in a backup role. ❖ The deaths of **Oscar Taveras** and Edilia Arvelo on a roadside in the Dominican Republic were tragic both for the loss of such young and valuable lives and for the ease with which they could have been avoided. ❖ One False Outcome enthusiast **Breyvic Valera** rarely walks, whiffs or launches a home run, using tremendous contact skills and plus speed to consistently hit for a high average. As a switch-hitter with a steady glove at the keystone, there are likely a lot of double-switches in his big-league future. ❖ It's possible we're writing him up because any catcher who shows an advanced approach and posts a .304 TAv in the Florida State League deserves the attention, never mind sketchy catch-and-throw skills, but really it's because his name is **Gerwuins Velazco**. His saddle's waiting. ❖ After posting video-game numbers in short-season ball, **Rowan Wick** struggled to make contact in the Midwest League [insert lame candle-lighting joke here]. The power is real, so if he can bring a plan to the plate at higher levels, he has the arm to be a solid right fielder. ❖ **Jacob Wilson** continued to show an advanced approach and some thunder in his stick during his first taste of the high minors; he's not a future star, but an infielder with his bat should someday find work on a big-league bench. ❖ **Patrick Wisdom** continued his spot-on Patrick Wisdom impersonation with occasional flashes of brilliance in the field, sufficient power for third and way too many strikeouts to convince us his bat has turned the corner; he needs another crack at the Double-A weeder class.

Pitchers

NAME	TEAM	LVL	AGE	W	L	SV	G	GS	IP	H	HR	BB	K	BB/9	K/9	GB%	BABIP	WHIP	ERA	FIP	FRA	WARP
Keith Butler	MEM	AAA	25	1	0	0	9	0	10²	8	0	2	13	1.7	11.0	30%	.348	0.94	0.84	1.82	1.80	0.4
	SLN	MLB	25	0	0	0	2	0	2	6	0	1	2	4.5	9.0	60%	.600	3.50	27.00	4.10	7.00	-0.1
John Gast	MEM	AAA	25	3	2	0	12	11	59¹	55	8	22	36	3.3	5.5	36%	.254	1.30	4.85	5.45	5.57	-0.1
Corey Littrell	PMB	A+	22	0	2	0	5	5	31²	45	4	10	19	2.8	5.4	49%	.383	1.74	4.55	4.78	5.94	-0.3
	SLM	A+	22	5	5	0	19	18	100	101	8	38	91	3.4	8.2	43%	.325	1.39	3.60	4.09	4.69	1.1
Dixon Llorens	PMB	A+	21	0	1	9	33	0	43²	22	1	27	74	5.6	15.3	53%	.288	1.12	2.06	2.57	3.76	0.7
Andrew Morales	PMB	A+	21	1	0	0	2	0	7¹	2	0	0	6	0.0	7.4	0%	.111	0.27	1.23	—	0.00	0.0
Nick Petree	PEO	A	23	2	0	0	4	4	21	15	2	10	24	4.3	10.3	36%	.255	1.19	1.29	3.87	4.13	0.2
	PMB	A+	23	6	5	0	17	17	103¹	98	5	22	80	1.9	7.0	42%	.300	1.16	2.44	3.17	3.59	1.5
Zachary Petrick	SFD	AA	24	2	0	0	3	3	18²	9	0	5	15	2.4	7.2	46%	.161	0.75	0.48	2.32	3.18	0.4
	MEM	AAA	24	7	6	1	24	20	115	119	16	36	82	2.8	6.4	46%	.292	1.35	4.62	5.13	5.61	0.2
Miguel Socolovich	LVG	AAA	27	2	2	3	51	0	59¹	68	5	19	68	2.9	10.3	42%	.375	1.47	3.64	3.46	3.13	2.3
Boone Whiting	MEM	AAA	24	4	7	0	21	20	96²	96	9	44	99	4.1	9.2	35%	.319	1.45	4.19	4.26	4.47	1.5

Fringy middle man **Keith Butler** broke camp with the big club last spring but pitched his way back to Triple-A before undergoing season-ending Tommy John surgery; he may or may not be back on the mound before the leaves turn. ❖ Who is **John Gast**? A low-velocity lefty who returned from shoulder surgery and made 11 starts between additional DL stints; he showed flashes in July and August, but has to stay healthy to fulfill his swing man potential. ❖ Lefty **Corey Littrell** came to the Cardinals in the John Lackey trade and has a chance to be more than a throw-in; he shows solid command of a fastball that can reach the low 90s, and if he can continue to miss bats with his curve and change, he could eventually slot into the end of a rotation. ❖ Reliever **Dixon Llorens** continues to be a strikeout machine, slinging mid-90s heat and a sharp slider from a sidearm delivery that held righties to a .172/.297/.273 line; if he keeps this up in the high minors he could grow into the 2018 version of Pat Neshek, bringing joy to both the Cardinals and the 2018 version of Michael Morse. ❖ The Cardinals nabbed UC-Irvine starter **Andrew Morales**, his low-90s fastball and his impressive slider in the second round of last year's draft; since the only prejudice that remains socially acceptable to express in public pertains to short right-handed pitchers, he may wind up in the bullpen. ❖ Lightning-armed **Frederis Parra** oozed potential during his stateside debut, with a projectable frame, easy heat and secondary stuff that can flash plus; he's a long way from St. Louis, but if everything breaks right he could become a mid-rotation stalwart. ❖ Low-velocity right-hander **Nick Petree** has mundane stuff but can hit his target with the best of them; more advanced hitters may have their way with him this year in Double-A, but at least he has the organization watching to make sure. ❖ **Zach Petrick** may have bumped his head on the ceiling, as the undrafted free agent stopped missing bats and posted journeyman numbers in his Triple-A debut; he'll need to fool more of the people more of the time if he wants to become a swing man with the big club. ❖ **Miguel Socolovich** used his sinker-slider combo to keep the ball in the yard at Triple-A Las Vegas, where a 3.64 ERA is no small feat. If the Cardinals' bullpen struggles, he'll be the call-up your friends who don't buy the Annual have never heard of. ❖ **Boone Whiting** possesses the sort of well-commanded low-velocity arsenal that can fool the kids in Triple-A but would likely get tattooed by the best hitters in the world. With a name straight out of Faulkner, he appears destined for a long career in Memphis with occasional low-leverage duty upriver. ❖ Second-round teenager **Ronnie Williams** impressed in his pro debut, commanding his mid-90s fastball and displaying surprisingly good feel for his changeup and curve; short righties will always hear whispers about a move to the 'pen, but the Cardinals will let him start until he proves he can't.

Manager

Mike Matheny

YEAR	TEAM	W	L	Py-thag +/-	Avg PC	100+ P	120+ P	QS	BQS	REL	REL w Zero R	IBB	PH	PH Avg	PH HR	SB2	CS2	SB3	CS3	SAC Att	SAC%	POS SAC	Squeeze	Swing	In Play
2012	SLN	88	74	-6	94.2	49	1	99	4	506	400	28	279	.190	1	72	27	18	5	104	66.3%	34	0	287	100
2013	SLN	97	65	-6	96.0	67	5	88	3	483	411	26	234	.202	3	33	20	11	2	94	59.6%	17	0	242	87
2014	SLN	90	72	7	94.2	61	2	91	2	485	393	35	251	.225	2	48	25	9	7	97	66.0%	24	2	306	112

Matheny has reached the NLCS in each of his first three seasons at the reins, and owns the best winning percentage among skippers with 400-plus games managed since Earl Weaver retired. Yet nobody seems to care or give him credit for those accomplishments. Instead Matheny has succeeded Dusty Baker as the winningest, most-oft-second-guessed manager in baseball.

In a sense, Matheny has become the whipping boy for the organization; the goat whenever the otherwise perfect Cardinals do something disagreeable or unpopular. Take the spring decision to move Carlos Martinez to the bullpen. It was Matheny who received the blame—as if a front office that many consider the best in sports would permit him to make such big personnel decisions entirely on his own.

Of course Matheny has his warts, like any other manager, but for the Cardinals to continue to employ him suggests one or two of three things: 1) they're ignorant of his abilities and mistakes; 2) they believe his qualitative value outweighs those missteps; or 3) they think his on-the-field skills can mature with more experience. Odds are, the answer lies somewhere between the second and third choices. When faced with the toughest challenge of his young career, Oscar Taveras' passing, Matheny crafted a touching statement that hit the right notes, focusing on the young man rather than the ballplayer. The cynic might point to it as a PR creation, but if that's how Matheny treats and addresses his players, then St. Louis' decision to stand by him, flaws and all, becomes a lot more understandable.

TAMPA BAY RAYS

by Adam Sobsey

---

*"Oh, I never want it to end," she says.
"It's the lasting that makes the game."*

—Lucas Mann, Class A: Baseball in the
Middle of Everywhere

At a Durham Bulls game last April, I was chatting with a scout I'm friendly with. He's a straight-talking but cheerful former first baseman, built big and ruddy. He's also something of a savant, as seasoned scouts often are. To wit: In July, I sat next to him at the Triple-A All-Star Game. He exchanged greetings with an acquaintance during Dodgers prospect Joc Pederson's at-bat, and when he turned his attention back to the game he asked me what the count was.

"3-1," I told him.

"Home run," he said, with the chipper offhand certainty of a longtime martini drinker naming his gin for a bartender at 5:30 p.m. Pederson hit a home run on the next pitch.

On April 12th, the scout and I were discussing the breaking news that Matt Moore needed Tommy John surgery. Tampa Bay had already lost Alex Cobb and Jeremy Hellickson to injury.

"The Rays are finished," he said, sympathetically but decisively. "I hope I'm wrong, but they're finished."

And so they were, although he happened to have the wrong cause; all the more evidence of his savant quality: knowledge beyond mere facts. The Rays' pitching turned out to be fine, even though they added a fourth lost starter in July, fellow by the name of Price. Pitching is never Tampa Bay's problem. Since 2008, the Rays have allowed the fewest runs in the American League. The disappointment of 2014 was quite simple, and quite the opposite: The Rays scored the fewest runs in the American League.

The day after the scout made his pronouncement, the Rays began a four-game losing streak that augured a two-month plunge. On June 10th, Tampa Bay had the worst record in baseball. Finished. During the skid, they lost four different outfielders to hand and wrist injuries, including reigning Rookie of the Year Wil Myers. Finished.

Not so fast. The Rays had baseball's best record for the next two months. They became just the fourth team in history to fall 18 games below .500 and then return. Hope surged, but the Rays leveled off, and on July 31st David Price was traded. Finished—

again. What the scout had identified was not so much the Rays' demise as their habit. All through 2014, they kept enacting different ways of being finished.

The big finishes, of course, came after the season, appropriately, with the departures of Andrew Friedman and Joe Maddon for greener bank accounts, the latter not long after speaking publicly about his expectation of working out an extension with the Rays. The two-week tumult of surprise and intrigue that surrounded their exits was a fittingly unpredictable finish to a season of jolts, extremes and contradictions. The Rays became the sixth team in the last quarter-century to have a 10-game winning streak and 10-game losing streak in the same season. They threw the most shutouts by any American League team since the introduction of the designated hitter. They were also shut out more times than any other team. The pitching staff broke the big-league record for strikeouts in a season—again. The infielders turned the fewest double plays in baseball and had the lowest GIDP rate. The hitters left the most runners on base, despite an only middling OBP: They were bad at starting rallies and bad at consummating them. Evan Longoria had his worst season and his highest swing rate on pitches outside the zone, perhaps partly owing to Wil Myers' absence as lineup protection. Grant Balfour, signed to a costly (for the Rays) two-year deal, also had his worst season. Stuart Sternberg gave Andrew Friedman the biggest payroll allowance in franchise history; at the trade deadline, Friedman dealt his highest-paid player, throwing in the towel and cutting some of Sternberg's losses before the Rays had even flagged.

That is all to say that you could not swing a dead bat in 2014 without hitting a singular Rays statistic, or a freak streak (or hand injury), or a surprising rumor or suspension or trade or Joe Maddon quote. Although the Rays weren't a good baseball team, they may have been baseball's most *interesting* team. The Sternberg/Friedman/Maddon engine has not consistently manufactured runs, but its seasonal production has unfailingly given its audiences plenty of drama (and comedy). The Rays are always a great *story*, even in a losing year, and they pose a deceptively profound sports question: Does a team have to win games in order to win attention and loyalty—that is, hearts?

RAYS PROSPECTUS
2014 W-L: 77-85, 4TH IN AL EAST

Pythag	.491	16th	DER	.714	7th
RS/G	3.78	27th	B-Age	29.3	23rd
RA/G	3.86	13th	P-Age	28.0	14th
TAv	.260	14th	Salary	$76.7M	27th
BRR	-2.59	23rd	M$/MW	$2.2M	9th
TAv-P	.253	6th	DL Days	822	16th
FIP	3.59	9th	$ on DL	12%	8th

Three-Year Park Factors

Runs	Runs/RH	Runs/LH	HR/RH	HR/LH
98	96	96	81	74

Top Hitter WARP	4.6	Ben Zobrist
Top Pitcher WARP	2.4	Jake Odorizzi
Top Prospect		Willy Adames

Here is another extreme Rays stat. It isn't about batting, pitching, fielding or payroll—or perhaps it's about all of them, in a way. The Rays played the slowest games in baseball in 2014, averaging 3:19. That set a new record. In September, they played the longest nine-inning, 1-0 game in recorded history. About a week later, Maddon was asked for his opinion about Major League Baseball's newly formed Pace of Game committee. His response was quick and unequivocal: "To put a clock out there is really an abhorrent thought."

Baseball has no clock. Baseball has no clock. Baseball has no clock. Have you heard this truism so often that it sounds nonsensical, like a word repeated over and over? If you wanted to see it in (in)action, though, you had only to watch Joe Maddon's baseball team. From 2008 to 2014, the Rays finished in the top five (or bottom five, if you prefer) in time of game every year but one, and it wasn't because they shared a division with the Red Sox and Yankees; the Blue Jays and Orioles weren't among the leaders. It was because that was how Maddon wanted it.

Six of the 20 slowest-working pitchers to throw 60 innings last year were Rays. Joel Peralta, a de facto second pitching coach for the Rays' young staff, was the slowest in baseball (32 seconds between pitches!). Three of the 11 slowest qualifying starters were Rays. David Price was the slowest starter in the majors. Erik Bedard and Jeremy Hellickson would have placed in the top 10 had they thrown enough innings to qualify. Former Ray Matt Garza, always pokey, was 10th. Eight of the 24 slowest qualifying starters in the majors since 2010 are or have been Rays.

Baseball has no clock—not yet, anyway—but another newly approved gadget allowed Maddon to make games even longer: He issued more instant replay challenges than any other manager except, ah, the Cubs' Rick Renteria. (If you can't beat 'em, unseat 'em?) Maddon had the fifth-worst success rate. He was, it seems, just dallying, dilating, delaying: buying time.

Why would he do this? My beat is the International League, with its constant up-and-down of players to and from the majors. I ask them all the time about the difference between Triple-A and The Show. The game moves faster up there, they say. The game speeds up on you. This, too, is a truism. Maddon slows it down for them. He makes baseball easier for his youth-heavy teams to play. Of all his innovations—defensive shifts, constant lineup shuffling and platoon subbing, penguins and pythons in the clubhouse, themed-dress road trips—this has been the greatest, and the hardest to detect; the greatest because hardest to detect. And it was especially potent last year, when Maddon's hoarding of seconds and minutes seemed like increasingly desperate measures to keep time from running out on his erratic, unpredictable team. That is, to keep the Rays from being finished.

In a way, they weren't; in another, baseball does have a clock, or clocks. If you have the 2014 Annual handy, re-read R.J. Anderson's account of the 2013 Rays. It begins:

> There are three clocks overseeing all business in Andrew Friedman's office, ticking in different directions and in different dimensions. One counts up, keeping track of David Price's service time [...] Another counts down from Price's free agent eligibility [...] And the final clock—complete with a blurry display, wonky wiring and uncertain rhythm—predicts when league-wide trends and rule changes will conspire to steal every conceivable advantage that the Rays hold over big-market teams.

It was the third clock that finished the Rays: It stole, if not their "every conceivable advantage over big-market teams," then certainly the two biggest. The clock turned out not to have to do with league trends and rules at all, but with the very man in whose office it hung: In October, its blurry face resolved to an image of Andrew Friedman himself. His time was up, and up to him: He opted out. Perhaps the Rays' peculiarly disappointing season, especially in Wall Street terms—high investment, low yield—had something to do with it. Or it could have indicated Friedman's desire for a radically new kind of challenge after building from limited resources for nearly a decade in Tampa Bay. He went from one of baseball's lowest payrolls and attendances to its very highest. Or maybe it was just for a bigger paycheck. Finished, in any case.

Then came the great reveal. Behind Friedman's clock lurked a fourth one, unseen; readers of classic juvenile fiction may imagine the Trop as *The House with a Clock in its Walls*. Maddon's agent informed his client that Friedman's departure triggered an out clause in Maddon's own contract, but it only stayed open for two weeks. How perfect: a clock on Maddon's field of employment, which he could not control, moving abhorrently fast. Unable to manipulate time, he put himself in a new place.

Friedman and Maddon couldn't last in Tampa Bay forever, although it sometimes seemed they would. The Rays' knack for thinking a measure ahead—an extra 2%, let's say—resulted, paradoxically, in an almost achingly sweet (and sometimes bitter) lengthiness. The franchise lived on what you might call Rays Time. Adepts have long known it by another name: The Process. Under it, games, seasons and years moved slowly, and often in a cyclical motion that seemed to give Rays Time not just extra horizontal width but also vertical depth. Think of Dan Johnson hitting a giant home run in 2008 and then reappearing three years later to hit another one; or of Grant Balfour's disastrous return in 2014, inverting his excellent first go-round with Tampa Bay. Think of the Rays' three-game, three-city, four-day odyssey at the end of 2013, at once epic and whirlwind, that landed them in the Division Series. Think of the front office's constant habit of signing character risks and the farm system's seemingly endless player suspensions, with first-rounder Josh Sale's transgressions alone creating two seasons' worth of drama (to say nothing of Matt Bush and Josh Lueke). Reflect on all the ascendant players who hit the trade-rumor wire and then stayed there for months or even years until a high-impact, high-profile deal would finally splash into the tank, sending waves of change through the organization. Everything about the Rays' modus operandi has worked to manufacture persistent, complex drama—*patient* drama—in prolonged time. It's the lasting that makes the game. And in this lasting, a few near-magical punctuations have formed the bright coordinates on which the team's rich story has been plotted.

Without Friedman and Maddon, the game is likely to speed up on Tampa Bay. (It seemed symbolic that Friedman sent for slowpoke Peralta shortly after arriving in Los Angeles.) Before it does, adherents of baseball's most interesting franchise might find it comforting to take a moment to register the loss of the two men responsible for bringing it out of its early darkness. Implied in the very name Baseball Prospectus is the directive to look forward. This is, perhaps, one moment to look back.

If you do, you'll see that some of what lies behind stretches ahead, too. Despite trading David Price, Friedman left the Rays a healthy, competitive roster with surprisingly firm continuity: Tampa Bay was one of just three teams to end 2014 with no free agents. The front office is also stable. Friedman's job went to *consiglieri* Matt Silverman, and trusted advisers Chaim Bloom and Erik Neander were promoted. The farm system lacks the gleam it had at its peak, but it's still fertile and constantly restocked via trades. The Rays retained their hitting and pitching coaches, who are steeped in (and contributors to) Maddon's methods, and filled a pair of field staff vacancies from within, appointing Charlie Montoyo, their longtime Triple-A manager, and franchise fixture Rocco Baldelli as base coaches. They appeared to start a brand new managerial clock by replacing Maddon with the young, inexperienced Kevin Cash, but in fact Cash has a legacy here. He grew up in Tampa, went to Florida State and was with the franchise in 2005-06. (Seekers after mystical mojo will note that he homered in his very first at-bat as a (Devil) Ray.)

Yet isn't all that steady-as-she-goes sailing a little, well, boring for the most interesting franchise in baseball? Sure enough, just before Christmas two alarming new clocks were hung over the hot stove—and on the very same day, no less. On December 18, 2014—count it as Day One of Rays Mark III—Silverman announced his presence with authority by sending Wil Myers to San Diego as part of a three-team, multi-player deal, the consequences of which may take years to assess. More

immediately, it was a controversial sell-low of young, cheap talent, not only swerving sharply away from Friedman's staunch approach but also undoing the splashiest trade of his tenure. In 2012, Friedman cast Myers as the Shaggy to Longoria's Scooby Doo in a heavier-hitting, pitching-lightened Rays New World. Removing Myers from the frame more than merely meddled with Boy Wonder's mystery machine. Silverman's Brave New Whirl seemed to signal a significant change, perhaps even a reversion, of organizational philosophy.

That very same afternoon, the St. Petersburg city council voted against a payout deal Sternberg had made with Mayor Rick Kriseman to allow the Rays to explore new ballpark sites in the Tampa Bay area. Sternberg had already warned that if the agreement was rejected, he'd sell the team within a decade and the new owner would surely pack up the franchise and leave Florida. This threat, and the council's veto, may have simply been bargaining tactics in a longer-ticking and ultimately happier negotiation that keeps the Rays' timeline active in Tampa Bay. But if not, if they do move—to Montreal, Montclair, Mexico or Mars—only then can we really call the Rays finished. ■

—Adam Sobsey, a Baseball Prospectus writer since 2011, started covering the Durham Bulls in 2008 and has written for The Paris Review, The Classical *and* Town & Country, *among others.*

Player comments by Tommy Rancel, Adam Sobsey and Baseball Prospectus Authors

Hitters

Ryan Brett 2B
Born: 10/9/91 Age: 23 Bats: R Throws: R Height: 5' 9" Weight: 180

YEAR	TEAM	LVL	AGE	PA	R	2B	3B	HR	RBI	BB	K	SB	CS	AVG/OBP/SLG	TAv	BABIP	BRR	FRAA	WARP
2012	BGR	A	20	456	77	20	3	6	35	37	73	48	8	.285/.348/.393	.272	.332	4.5	2B(88): -11.3	0.9
2013	PCH	A+	21	225	38	11	4	4	22	15	27	22	7	.340/.396/.490	.307	.377	1.0	2B(47): -2.0	1.5
2013	MNT	AA	21	114	19	6	1	3	16	8	14	4	0	.238/.289/.400	.257	.247	1.8	2B(25): 1.1	0.5
2014	MNT	AA	22	459	64	25	6	8	38	24	74	27	7	.303/.346/.448	.287	.350	4.4	2B(100): 4.0	3.3
2015	TBA	MLB	23	250	30	10	1	3	19	11	53	12	3	.247/.285/.344	.241	.301	1.4	2B -1	0.4

Breakout: 6% Improve: 16% Collapse: 2% Attrition: 10% MLB: 24%   Comparables: Stefen Romero, Josh Barfield, Jose Pirela

Brett will not top any prospect lists, but he is on track to become a big-league starter at the keystone. His size keeps him from sending many balls over the wall, but he can pepper the field with extra-base hits backed by plus speed, keeping his batting average from being empty. He's a steady defender at second base, but needs further training in the nuances of the position, especially considering the variety of shifts employed at the top level. Brett is, in short, a good reminder that unexciting players without star upside can still be worth tracking through the minors.

Curtis Casali C
Born: 11/9/88 Age: 26 Bats: R Throws: R Height: 6' 2" Weight: 225

YEAR	TEAM	LVL	AGE	PA	R	2B	3B	HR	RBI	BB	K	SB	CS	AVG/OBP/SLG	TAv	BABIP	BRR	FRAA	WARP
2012	WMI	A	23	206	25	12	0	8	25	27	18	2	1	.288/.402/.500	.334	.283	-1.2	C(46): -0.5	2.6
2012	LAK	A+	23	179	18	13	0	1	18	11	28	0	0	.250/.322/.350	.233	.298	-2.9	C(41): 0.7	0.4
2013	PCH	A+	24	184	15	6	1	5	22	18	31	1	0	.267/.342/.406	.255	.302	-1.7	C(37): -0.3	0.4
2013	MNT	AA	24	145	25	11	0	5	31	21	18	0	0	.383/.483/.600	.385	.418	-0.7	C(25): 1.0	2.6
2014	MNT	AA	25	96	7	5	0	1	13	23	16	0	0	.314/.500/.429	.361	.396	-1.0	C(15): 0.2	1.2
2014	DUR	AAA	25	183	11	10	0	3	15	22	50	0	0	.237/.335/.359	.236	.324	-1.5	C(41): -0.3	0.1
2014	TBA	MLB	25	84	10	3	0	0	3	8	23	0	0	.167/.268/.208	.198	.245	1.0	C(29): -0.5	-0.1
2015	TBA	MLB	26	250	24	10	0	4	25	25	58	0	0	.231/.321/.340	.257	.289	-0.5	C 0	0.8

Breakout: 1% Improve: 16% Collapse: 15% Attrition: 25% MLB: 40%   Comparables: Tony Sanchez, Eric Fryer, Dan Butler

There was little risk in putting Casali, a defense-first catcher in his mid-20s, on the fast track. The former Tigers farmhand moved quickly through the Rays' system, starting 2013 in High-A and progressing to the majors midway through 2014. The physical attributes of his defense lag behind the mental: His movement behind the plate needs improvement but his ability to handle a staff and call a game are already solid. If you wanted to be nice about his offense, you'd call it nondescript, but that oversells it. It's actually quite descript in its ugliness. Casali's plate appearances were better against left-handers, leaving the door slightly ajar for a platoon role down the road.

David DeJesus   DH

Born: 12/20/79   Age: 35   Bats: L   Throws: L   Height: 5' 11"   Weight: 190

YEAR	TEAM	LVL	AGE	PA	R	2B	3B	HR	RBI	BB	K	SB	CS	AVG/OBP/SLG	TAv	BABIP	BRR	FRAA	WARP
2012	CHN	MLB	32	582	76	28	8	9	50	61	89	7	8	.263/.350/.403	.278	.301	2.8	RF(100): -2.8, CF(50): -0.8	2.0
2013	CHN	MLB	33	318	39	19	3	6	27	29	55	3	0	.250/.330/.401	.268	.291	3.0	CF(73): 5.8, LF(3): 0.2	2.1
2013	TBA	MLB	33	117	13	10	0	2	11	10	23	2	3	.260/.328/.413	.279	.313	-0.8	LF(27): -0.6, CF(7): -0.2	0.4
2013	WAS	MLB	33	4	0	0	0	0	0	0	1	0	0	.000/.000/.000	.079	.000	0.0	RF(2): -0.1, CF(1): -0.0	-0.1
2014	PCH	A+	34	28	1	0	0	0	2	4	4	1	1	.227/.357/.227	.248	.263	0.4	LF(3): -0.1	0.0
2014	TBA	MLB	34	273	24	15	2	6	19	30	43	0	3	.248/.344/.403	.275	.280	0.9	LF(13): 0.3, CF(3): -0.2	0.9
2015	TBA	MLB	35	296	33	14	2	4	24	27	51	3	3	.248/.328/.358	.267	.290	1.0	CF 0, RF 0	1.0

Breakout: 3%   Improve: 32%   Collapse: 3%   Attrition: 19%   MLB: 88%   Comparables: Kevin Millar, Doug Mientkiewicz, Mike Sweeney

DeJesus has entered the envious portion of life where he is free of most worries. He is an accomplished major leaguer with an annual salary that includes two commas. He has established strengths and weakness, and the Rays have tailored his usage accordingly. He faces right-handers almost exclusively and is still an above-average hitter against them, littering the gaps with liners. He is spry enough to turn some doubles into triples or flip some singles into doubles with the occasional bag swipe. With younger legs available to roam the outfield, he spends most of his nights as a fan dispensing high-fives and encouragement except for the four times his name is announced as the team's designated hitter. He's also married to a former model. Things are good.

Yunel Escobar   SS

Born: 11/2/82   Age: 32   Bats: R   Throws: R   Height: 6' 2"   Weight: 215

YEAR	TEAM	LVL	AGE	PA	R	2B	3B	HR	RBI	BB	K	SB	CS	AVG/OBP/SLG	TAv	BABIP	BRR	FRAA	WARP
2012	TOR	MLB	29	608	58	22	1	9	51	35	70	5	1	.253/.300/.344	.230	.273	1.4	SS(143): 5.9	1.5
2013	TBA	MLB	30	578	61	27	1	9	56	57	73	4	4	.256/.332/.366	.264	.281	1.0	SS(153): -2.2	2.8
2014	TBA	MLB	31	529	33	18	0	7	39	43	60	1	1	.258/.324/.340	.255	.282	1.5	SS(136): -14.4, LF(1): -0.0	0.5
2015	TBA	MLB	32	508	47	19	1	4	41	44	64	3	2	.252/.321/.324	.255	.279	0.9	SS -2	1.7

Breakout: 2%   Improve: 40%   Collapse: 5%   Attrition: 10%   MLB: 97%   Comparables: Ryan Theriot, David Eckstein, Orlando Cabrera

The Rays invested in Escobar early in the season, reworking his previous arrangement (one remaining club option) into two guaranteed years with a new club option on top. After a productive two-way season in 2013, the shortstop failed to get things going at the plate and appeared a step slow in the field, though his arm strength remains top notch. Perhaps nagging injuries (quadriceps and shoulder) prevented him from getting in a rhythm, but the lack of positive contributions on either side of the ball is cause for concern about a player on the wrong end of 30. In addition to the physical aspect of his game, he appeared to fall into a mental slump toward the end of the season. There is no true heir apparent on the horizon, so a changing of the guard does not appear imminent.

Logan Forsythe   2B

Born: 1/14/87   Age: 28   Bats: R   Throws: R   Height: 6' 1"   Weight: 195

YEAR	TEAM	LVL	AGE	PA	R	2B	3B	HR	RBI	BB	K	SB	CS	AVG/OBP/SLG	TAv	BABIP	BRR	FRAA	WARP
2012	TUC	AAA	25	74	12	2	3	1	9	13	18	3	0	.259/.419/.448	.309	.359	-0.5	3B(7): 0.8, SS(5): 0.5	0.8
2012	SDN	MLB	25	350	45	13	3	6	26	28	57	8	2	.273/.343/.390	.272	.316	0.0	2B(81): -3.0, SS(5): 0.1	1.0
2013	TUC	AAA	26	33	6	2	2	2	5	8	7	0	0	.360/.515/.840	.378	.438	0.6	SS(4): -0.3, 2B(3): -0.1	0.6
2013	SDN	MLB	26	243	22	6	1	6	19	19	54	6	1	.214/.281/.332	.234	.255	1.5	2B(34): 0.9, 3B(11): 0.2	0.2
2014	TBA	MLB	27	336	32	12	1	6	26	25	71	2	0	.223/.287/.329	.238	.268	0.0	2B(74): 3.1, 3B(6): 0.2	0.3
2015	TBA	MLB	28	301	35	11	2	6	27	27	64	5	1	.239/.317/.358	.263	.289	0.3	2B -1, SS 0	1.0

Breakout: 2%   Improve: 54%   Collapse: 3%   Attrition: 6%   MLB: 96%   Comparables: Neil Walker, Marcus Giles, Kelly Johnson

Forsythe was the best known of the four players acquired by the Rays in a January 2014 seven-player swap with the Padres. A second baseman by trade, he made appearances at five different positions in his first year with Tampa Bay, including first base for the first time as a professional. The right-handed batter holds his own against southpaws but is below average against same-siders, as the Rays know all too well after injuries forced him into too much action. At his best, he puts together good at-bats with an understanding of balls and strikes and good contact skills. He makes nearly every routine play in the field with the occasional highlight grab. Being cheap, flexible and dependable is an underrated skill set.

Nick Franklin   SS

Born: 3/2/91   Age: 24   Bats: B   Throws: R   Height: 6' 1"   Weight: 195

YEAR	TEAM	LVL	AGE	PA	R	2B	3B	HR	RBI	BB	K	SB	CS	AVG/OBP/SLG	TAv	BABIP	BRR	FRAA	WARP
2012	WTN	AA	21	239	25	17	4	4	26	24	38	9	2	.322/.394/.502	.302	.378	-0.3	SS(39): -4.3, 2B(14): 2.0	1.7
2012	TAC	AAA	21	296	39	15	5	7	29	24	68	3	2	.243/.310/.416	.247	.301	-0.1	2B(34): -2.9, SS(30): 0.4	0.3
2013	TAC	AAA	22	177	28	9	0	4	20	30	20	7	0	.324/.440/.472	.339	.350	0.9	2B(23): 1.0, SS(15): 0.2	2.2
2013	SEA	MLB	22	412	38	20	1	12	45	42	113	6	1	.225/.303/.382	.260	.290	-1.3	2B(96): 14.8, SS(3): 0.1	2.5
2014	DUR	AAA	23	113	8	2	0	2	9	10	34	2	0	.210/.288/.290	.218	.297	0.2	2B(16): -0.4, SS(7): 0.7	-0.1
2014	TAC	AAA	23	333	45	16	1	9	47	47	60	5	5	.294/.392/.455	.307	.340	1.2	2B(34): -3.6, SS(34): 1.2	2.8
2014	SEA	MLB	23	52	3	0	1	0	2	3	21	1	0	.128/.192/.170	.147	.222	0.1	SS(7): 0.4, 2B(5): 0.6	-0.3
2014	TBA	MLB	23	38	4	2	0	1	4	3	11	1	0	.206/.263/.353	.228	.261	0.1	2B(7): -0.6, SS(3): 0.1	-0.1
2015	TBA	MLB	24	250	30	11	1	5	22	24	60	5	1	.235/.312/.361	.258	.294	-0.5	2B 2, SS -1	0.9

Breakout: 2%   Improve: 34%   Collapse: 8%   Attrition: 17%   MLB: 78%   Comparables: Luis Valbuena, Sean Rodriguez, Dustin Ackley

Detractors may carp that Franklin is currently closer to Elliot Johnson than Ben Zobrist: a switch-hitter with nearly all his pop from the left side; worrisome strikeout tendencies against big-league pitching; questions about his shortstop skills. They may also grumble that they expected more in return for David Price, notwithstanding Drew Smyly and an intriguing 18-year-old prospect. Look deeper: A second baseman with lefty power is an asset, especially one with Franklin's competitive edge and confidence. He has natural leadership qualities and the intensity to rise to the challenges he faces. He struggled on arrival in Durham in early August, but rallied with a strong Triple-A postseason. The Rays gave Franklin ample September reps in the bigs and a major-league job is probably his to lose in 2015.

Brandon Guyer   LF

Born: 1/28/86   Age: 29   Bats: R   Throws: R   Height: 6' 2"   Weight: 195

YEAR	TEAM	LVL	AGE	PA	R	2B	3B	HR	RBI	BB	K	SB	CS	AVG/OBP/SLG	TAv	BABIP	BRR	FRAA	WARP
2012	DUR	AAA	26	97	9	3	1	3	13	7	15	2	0	.294/.365/.459	.295	.324	1.0	RF(12): 1.3, CF(6): -0.1	0.7
2012	TBA	MLB	26	7	2	0	0	1	1	0	1	0	0	.143/.143/.571	.329	.000	0.0	LF(3): -0.0	0.1
2013	DUR	AAA	27	405	73	23	6	7	41	29	62	22	3	.301/.374/.458	.285	.346	0.7	RF(41): 1.3, LF(29): -0.6	2.7
2014	DUR	AAA	28	26	8	2	2	0	1	6	4	0	0	.400/.538/.700	.399	.500	0.2	RF(1): 0.1, LF(1): -0.0	0.5
2014	TBA	MLB	28	294	37	15	1	3	26	16	52	6	1	.266/.334/.367	.273	.322	3.5	LF(62): 1.3, CF(11): 0.1	1.6
2015	TBA	MLB	29	270	29	13	2	5	28	17	50	7	1	.263/.328/.392	.277	.307	1.8	LF 3, CF 1	1.7

Breakout: 0%   Improve: 15%   Collapse: 17%   Attrition: 22%   MLB: 57%   Comparables: Matt Diaz, Chris Denorfia, Jesus Guzman

Out of options and room for development, Guyer made the club in spring training and served as a valuable member of the roster. Filling in for Wil Myers and David DeJesus, Guyer's play went largely unnoticed in the way you're not supposed to notice umpires and long snappers. A former two-sport star in high school, he is a smart runner with good speed who can play all three outfield positions in a pinch, though left field is his best position. Fans appreciate his work ethic and his respect for the 90 feet between home and first, to borrow a phase from Joe Maddon. All this may leave some yearning for more Guyer, but not everyone in the band can be the lead singer; somebody's got to man the rhythm section.

Desmond Jennings   CF

Born: 10/30/86   Age: 28   Bats: R   Throws: R   Height: 6' 2"   Weight: 200

YEAR	TEAM	LVL	AGE	PA	R	2B	3B	HR	RBI	BB	K	SB	CS	AVG/OBP/SLG	TAv	BABIP	BRR	FRAA	WARP
2012	TBA	MLB	25	563	85	19	7	13	47	46	120	31	2	.246/.314/.388	.261	.298	5.6	LF(111): 0.2, CF(21): -0.1	2.4
2013	TBA	MLB	26	602	82	31	6	14	54	64	115	20	8	.252/.334/.414	.287	.295	5.7	CF(136): 1.7	4.3
2014	TBA	MLB	27	542	64	30	2	10	36	47	108	15	6	.244/.319/.378	.271	.296	1.1	CF(118): 4.3	2.1
2015	TBA	MLB	28	522	67	23	4	9	45	50	103	20	6	.247/.327/.375	.271	.293	2.7	CF 3, LF 0	2.6

Breakout: 1%   Improve: 51%   Collapse: 3%   Attrition: 11%   MLB: 95%   Comparables: Nate McLouth, Shane Victorino, David DeJesus

Those who have failed to reset their expectations of Jennings becoming a superstar leadoff hitter continue to be disappointed. Meanwhile, those who are comfortable with an above-average hitter, steady defender and speedy runner should be content, although that crowd may too be unsatisfied after a nagging knee injury ended Jennings' season without much improvement in any area. The sum of the parts is a good center fielder under team control for three more seasons. Remember the Damon Hollins-Joey Gathright year?

Kevin Kiermaier   RF

Born: 4/22/90   Age: 25   Bats: L   Throws: R   Height: 6' 1"   Weight: 195

YEAR	TEAM	LVL	AGE	PA	R	2B	3B	HR	RBI	BB	K	SB	CS	AVG/OBP/SLG	TAv	BABIP	BRR	FRAA	WARP
2012	PCH	A+	22	212	16	7	6	0	12	26	38	10	4	.260/.361/.367	.260	.331	-2.8	CF(53): 5.1, RF(4): 0.0	0.9
2013	MNT	AA	23	417	65	14	9	5	28	31	61	14	11	.307/.370/.434	.302	.354	2.5	CF(89): 10.5	5.1
2013	DUR	AAA	23	154	24	7	6	1	13	14	26	7	1	.263/.338/.423	.258	.315	3.6	CF(38): 7.6	1.7
2014	DUR	AAA	24	143	28	7	2	3	13	12	23	11	1	.305/.362/.461	.284	.350	1.5	CF(33): 5.8	1.5
2014	TBA	MLB	24	364	35	16	8	10	35	23	71	5	4	.263/.315/.450	.283	.306	-1.4	RF(68): 5.1, CF(42): 3.2	2.8
2015	TBA	MLB	25	359	42	14	5	5	31	24	71	10	4	.259/.315/.384	.264	.306	-0.6	CF 7, RF 3	2.1

Breakout: 6%   Improve: 47%   Collapse: 9%   Attrition: 34%   MLB: 87%   Comparables: Ryan Kalish, Peter Bourjos, Juan Lagares

During a season in which the team grossly underperformed, Kiermaier, a former 31st-round pick, did the opposite. The rookie produced an above-average slash line even if most of the production was clustered early in his big-league stint. He showed much more power than expected and his speed is game-changing (though it's worth noting that he was caught stealing way too many times). His fast-paced style of play makes for an aggressive approach at the plate that was exposed with more playing time. Kiermaier is referred to as an "outlaw" on defense: His plus speed covers up mistakes, allowing him to make difficult catches with little regard for his own well-being even though his route-running rivals a cowboy on an unbridled stallion over rough terrain. His arm is the same: It's strong, but his throws lack accuracy or common sense. Even as a slightly overhyped fourth outfielder, he provides tremendous value to the team considering his salary.

Patrick Leonard   3B

Born: 10/20/92   Age: 22   Bats: R   Throws: R   Height: 6' 4"   Weight: 225

YEAR	TEAM	LVL	AGE	PA	R	2B	3B	HR	RBI	BB	K	SB	CS	AVG/OBP/SLG	TAv	BABIP	BRR	FRAA	WARP
2013	BGR	A	20	493	52	26	0	9	57	42	118	4	1	.225/.303/.345	.233	.286	-1.1	1B(99): -6.2, 3B(12): 0.2	-1.8
2014	PCH	A+	21	515	79	26	5	13	58	49	107	14	0	.284/.359/.448	.288	.342	-2.2	1B(104): 1.0, 3B(6): -0.3	1.6
2015	TBA	MLB	22	250	22	9	1	5	24	16	74	1	0	.204/.263/.314	.223	.272	-0.1	1B -1, 3B 1	-0.7

Breakout: 0%   Improve: 0%   Collapse: 0%   Attrition: 0%   MLB: 0%   Comparables: Tyler Flowers, Jerry Sands, C.J. Cron

No longer just the fourth piece of the James Shields trade, Leonard established himself as a prospect to watch with a strong season in the Florida State League. Every bit of his 6-feet-4 listed height, he has no standout tool offensively but hit for both power and average with a good feel of the strike zone in 2014. Despite his size, he is light on his feet and has surprising in-game speed. He spent most of the year playing a solid first base and made cameo appearances at the hot corner, where his arm is strong enough to cross the diamond. He hasn't played the outfield yet, but he could wind up a four-corners type.

James Loney   1B

Born: 5/7/84   Age: 31   Bats: L   Throws: L   Height: 6' 3"   Weight: 235

YEAR	TEAM	LVL	AGE	PA	R	2B	3B	HR	RBI	BB	K	SB	CS	AVG/OBP/SLG	TAv	BABIP	BRR	FRAA	WARP
2012	BOS	MLB	28	106	5	2	0	2	8	5	12	0	0	.230/.264/.310	.212	.241	-0.3	1B(28): 2.6	-0.2
2012	LAN	MLB	28	359	32	18	0	4	33	23	39	0	3	.254/.302/.344	.224	.277	-2.2	1B(105): 1.4	-1.0
2013	TBA	MLB	29	598	54	33	0	13	75	44	77	3	1	.299/.348/.430	.282	.326	-2.7	1B(154): -3.0	1.5
2014	TBA	MLB	30	651	59	27	0	9	69	41	80	4	0	.290/.336/.380	.269	.319	-5.5	1B(152): -5.5	0.1
2015	TBA	MLB	31	601	56	29	1	8	60	42	78	3	1	.270/.322/.371	.265	.299	-3.0	1B -1	0.4

Breakout: 0%   Improve: 32%   Collapse: 5%   Attrition: 6%   MLB: 92%   Comparables: Sean Casey, Don Mattingly, Casey Kotchman

The Rays broke the mold with Loney, signing him to a three-year, $21 million deal, the largest free agent contract ever by pre-Dodgers Andrew Friedman. Whereas Tampa Bay has passed on rewarding one-hit wonders like Casey Kotchman and Jeff Keppinger in the past, the club invested in Loney because his "breakout" with the Rays was more of a return to normalcy than an anomaly. Once again he provided above-average contact skills along with a batting average and on-base percentage within points of career levels. His weakness continues to be power output. He also regressed against lefties, but continued to play every day because of his glovework. Defensive metrics fail to capture the grace and poetic nature of his fielding. Using soft hands, a strong arm and willingness to extend his limbs beyond the playing boundaries, he routinely composes outs like a troubadour of infield defense.

Evan Longoria 3B

Born: 10/7/85 Age: 29 Bats: R Throws: R Height: 6' 2" Weight: 210

YEAR	TEAM	LVL	AGE	PA	R	2B	3B	HR	RBI	BB	K	SB	CS	AVG/OBP/SLG	TAv	BABIP	BRR	FRAA	WARP
2012	DUR	AAA	26	39	0	0	0	0	3	7	9	0	0	.200/.359/.200	.239	.273	-0.1		-0.1
2012	TBA	MLB	26	312	39	14	0	17	55	33	61	2	3	.289/.369/.527	.322	.313	-1.2	3B(50): -1.5	2.5
2013	TBA	MLB	27	693	91	39	3	32	88	70	162	1	0	.269/.343/.498	.309	.312	-0.8	3B(147): 7.9	6.2
2014	TBA	MLB	28	700	83	26	1	22	91	57	133	5	0	.253/.320/.404	.281	.285	1.7	3B(155): 4.2	4.3
2015	TBA	MLB	29	656	80	31	2	25	89	68	131	3	1	.262/.343/.451	.301	.295	0.0	3B 6	4.9

Breakout: 6%   Improve: 53%   Collapse: 1%   Attrition: 14%   MLB: 98%   Comparables: Ryan Zimmerman, David Wright, Hanley Ramirez

The curse of the superstar: A well-above-average 2014 for anybody else was a disappointment for Longoria. The franchise player set a career low in several offensive categories, including on-base and slugging percentage. Longoria tinkered with some mechanical adjustments—perhaps in an attempt to regain control over the inner third of the plate—but didn't make any changes radical enough to be noticeable by a casual observer. Nor was health an issue: He played in all 162 games and there were no reports of nagging injuries that might have sapped effectiveness while leaving him on the field. It's an uneasy feeling not having a reason for a drop-off like this, especially with nearly a decade left on Longoria's contract, but with youth and talent on his side it is very likely that 2014, viewed in hindsight, is just going to be an outlier, not a harbinger.

Mikie Mahtook RF

Born: 11/30/89 Age: 25 Bats: R Throws: R Height: 6' 1" Weight: 200

YEAR	TEAM	LVL	AGE	PA	R	2B	3B	HR	RBI	BB	K	SB	CS	AVG/OBP/SLG	TAv	BABIP	BRR	FRAA	WARP
2012	PCH	A+	22	386	44	15	7	5	37	29	71	19	6	.290/.358/.419	.276	.347	2.2	RF(57): 9.1, CF(37): 0.8	2.8
2012	MNT	AA	22	169	17	10	1	4	25	11	31	4	3	.248/.308/.405	.242	.283	-0.3	RF(33): -1.4, CF(1): 0.1	-0.1
2013	MNT	AA	23	568	71	30	8	7	68	43	102	25	8	.254/.322/.386	.261	.303	-0.1	RF(85): 0.9, CF(43): 0.4	1.7
2014	DUR	AAA	24	550	56	33	6	12	68	46	137	18	5	.292/.362/.458	.275	.380	3.2	CF(74): 2.7, RF(41): 0.4	3.4
2015	TBA	MLB	25	250	25	11	2	4	23	14	61	7	2	.239/.292/.351	.247	.305	0.6	RF 1, CF 1	0.5

Breakout: 8%   Improve: 24%   Collapse: 4%   Attrition: 27%   MLB: 44%   Comparables: Xavier Paul, Scott Cousins, Jason Pridie

Or, "What We Talk About When We Talk About All-Around Players." We tend to be disappointed when they don't turn out to be stars, but there's a place for guys like Mahtook and Desmond Jennings and Brandon Guyer, who have similar profiles. The question is where Mahtook falls on the spectrum. He plays more like Guyer: aggressive style; high strikeout rate, which owes more to pitch recognition than to undisciplined hacking; imperfect outfield routes. Yet Mahtook had his best minor-league season in his first year of Triple-A (and just his third overall as a pro), an encouraging sign that he's quick to adapt and perhaps has the deeper baseball instinct that unifies the tools into a complete package. A late-season power surge kept Mahtook's corner-outfield projection alive, relieving concerns about his viability in center. His promise gives the Rays some flexibility with their sudden surplus of outfielders.

Jose Molina C

Born: 6/3/75 Age: 40 Bats: R Throws: R Height: 6' 0" Weight: 250

YEAR	TEAM	LVL	AGE	PA	R	2B	3B	HR	RBI	BB	K	SB	CS	AVG/OBP/SLG	TAv	BABIP	BRR	FRAA	WARP
2012	TBA	MLB	37	274	27	9	0	8	32	20	60	3	1	.223/.286/.355	.245	.262	-3.0	C(102): -1.9	0.4
2013	TBA	MLB	38	313	26	14	0	2	18	22	63	2	1	.233/.290/.304	.222	.290	-0.4	C(96): -1.6	-0.2
2014	TBA	MLB	39	247	4	2	0	0	10	14	55	3	0	.178/.230/.187	.160	.233	-1.9	C(80): -0.1	-1.8
2015	TBA	MLB	40	250	21	8	0	2	18	16	57	2	1	.214/.270/.282	.217	.270	-1.2	C -1	-0.4

Breakout: 3%   Improve: 19%   Collapse: 9%   Attrition: 28%   MLB: 63%   Comparables: Walker Cooper, Elston Howard, Carlton Fisk

In 1947, private investigator Eddie Valiant was declared a hero for his work in the murder cases of Marvin Acme and R.K. Maroon. With help from his girlfriend Dolores, Baby Herman and Maroon Cartoon Studio star Jessica Rabbit, Valiant discovered that Judge Doom killed Acme and Maroon in an attempt to take over Toontown. Unfortunately, Valiant's investigation came before the time of detectives Mike Fast and Max Marchi. The case was re-opened in 2011 when it was determined that Jose Molina was indeed the one who framed Roger Rabbit.

Justin O'Conner C

Born: 3/31/92 Age: 23 Bats: R Throws: R Height: 6' 0" Weight: 190

YEAR	TEAM	LVL	AGE	PA	R	2B	3B	HR	RBI	BB	K	SB	CS	AVG/OBP/SLG	TAv	BABIP	BRR	FRAA	WARP
2012	HUD	A-	20	257	39	18	1	5	29	18	73	2	0	.223/.276/.370	.249	.298	0.1		0.0
2013	BGR	A	21	439	49	17	0	14	56	31	111	5	0	.233/.290/.381	.244	.283	1.4	C(62): 0.8	1.2
2014	PCH	A+	22	340	40	31	2	10	44	15	78	0	0	.282/.321/.486	.269	.343	-1.5	C(68): -0.2	1.9
2014	MNT	AA	22	84	9	4	0	2	3	1	20	0	0	.263/.298/.388	.249	.328	0.6	C(14): 0.2	0.4
2015	TBA	MLB	23	250	20	10	0	6	26	9	79	0	0	.205/.239/.327	.215	.275	-0.4	C 0	-0.4

Breakout: 0%   Improve: 0%   Collapse: 0%   Attrition: 0%   MLB: 0%   Comparables: Josh Phegley, Welington Castillo, Yan Gomes

It took longer than expected but O'Conner, a 2010 first-round pick, is finally on the right rung of the organizational ladder. Surgery on both hips along with other maladies have hampered his progress, but he thrived both at the plate and behind it in 2014. He still struggles receiving the ball but earns high praise from those around him for his ability to call a game. His arm is a bona fide weapon, using a quick release to cut down would-be basestealers or even those that may have strayed a foot too far off the bag. He stands a chance to make the big leagues on defense alone. On offense, he showed an improved approach and slightly more than gap-to-gap power, especially considering he played most of his games in the thick humidity of Southern Florida. He's also a grinder who doesn't mind a tattered uniform; it'll be summer's hottest look, sure to sweep Montgomery's impressionable youth off its collective feet.

Rene Rivera   C

Born: 7/31/83   Age: 31   Bats: R   Throws: R   Height: 5' 10"   Weight: 215

YEAR	TEAM	LVL	AGE	PA	R	2B	3B	HR	RBI	BB	K	SB	CS	AVG/OBP/SLG	TAv	BABIP	BRR	FRAA	WARP
2012	ROC	AAA	28	326	31	14	1	10	34	30	62	0	1	.226/.307/.385	.248	.255	-2.1	C(81): 2.2, 1B(7): -0.2	1.1
2013	TUC	AAA	29	276	36	18	0	5	38	17	42	0	2	.343/.382/.474	.289	.388	-1.9	C(68): 0.3, 1B(3): 0.1	2.5
2013	SDN	MLB	29	71	4	3	1	0	7	2	16	0	0	.254/.268/.328	.224	.321	-1.4	C(21): -0.1	0.2
2014	SDN	MLB	30	329	27	18	1	11	44	27	76	0	0	.252/.319/.432	.277	.301	-1.3	C(89): 1.9, 1B(3): 0.1	2.4
2015	TBA	MLB	31	291	27	13	1	6	29	19	67	0		.230/.285/.353	.247	.278	-1.1	C 1, 1B 0	0.8

Breakout: 1%   Improve: 11%   Collapse: 18%   Attrition: 30%   MLB: 57%   *Comparables: Robby Hammock, Koyie Hill, Bobby Wilson*

Rivera has played pro ball for teams in 12 different states and semipro ball in his native Puerto Rico; sadly, his trade to the Rays in the Wil Myers deal won't add one to his resume because he already spent a stint in Jacksonville. Before 2014, he owned a .531 OPS in a half-season's worth of MLB plate appearances spread across a decade. He started the year as the Padres' third catcher and finished as the starter, posting respectable numbers at the plate and shining behind it. Among NL backstops, only Pittsburgh's Russell Martin (who caught 200 more innings) nailed more would-be basestealers. Rivera's pitch-framing prowess is well documented, as is his rapport with pitchers: Count ex-batterymates Andrew Cashner and Tyson Ross among his biggest fans. It's been a long strange trip, but the 49th player taken in the 2001 draft appears to have found himself.

Adrian Rondon   SS

Born: 7/7/98   Age: 16   Bats: R   Throws: R   Height: 6' 2"   Weight: 180

What did you get for your 16th birthday? Standout Dominican prospect Rondon signed for a $3 million bonus from Tampa Bay on his big day. The Rays were so taken with him that they traded a minor leaguer in exchange for another team's draft pool money and used it to exceed their spending share; they'll have to pay a luxury tax on top of what they gave Rondon. Are they *that* sure of Rondon's well-scouted potential—smooth rather than flashy glovework, good plate discipline (*for a 15-year-old!*), all-fields hitting—or are they still throwing good money after Tim Beckham?

Steven Souza   OF

Born: 4/24/89   Age: 26   Bats: R   Throws: R   Height: 6' 4"   Weight: 225

YEAR	TEAM	LVL	AGE	PA	R	2B	3B	HR	RBI	BB	K	SB	CS	AVG/OBP/SLG	TAv	BABIP	BRR	FRAA	WARP
2012	HAG	A	23	293	48	20	2	17	72	22	49	7	7	.290/.346/.576	.320	.294	2.9	RF(44): 2.4	2.9
2012	POT	A+	23	107	16	2	1	6	13	13	25	7	1	.319/.421/.560	.337	.383	0.2	CF(16): -0.3, RF(9): -0.6	1.0
2013	HAR	AA	24	323	54	23	1	15	44	41	76	20	6	.300/.396/.557	.348	.360	0.5	RF(72): -2.0, CF(5): -0.1	3.8
2014	SYR	AAA	25	407	62	25	2	18	75	52	75	26	4	.350/.432/.590	.351	.398	0.0	RF(63): 6.5, CF(27): 3.3	6.1
2014	WAS	MLB	25	26	2	0	0	2	2	3	7	0	0	.130/.231/.391	.225	.071	0.0	RF(8): 0.1, LF(4): -0.0	0.0
2015	TBA	MLB	26	250	35	11	0	10	33	23	62	11	3	.270/.340/.460	.299	.325	0.7	RF 1, CF 1	1.8

Breakout: 5%   Improve: 26%   Collapse: 15%   Attrition: 29%   MLB: 68%   *Comparables: Russ Canzler, Justin Ruggiano, Ryan Shealy*

There's no getting around mentioning The Catch; unfortunately, science has yet to come up with a way to embed GIFs into print. As amazing as it is to close a season with a no-hitter-saving dive, Souza had a year to remember from start to finish. It's been a strange journey, from toolsy draft pick to bad seed (he was suspended for PEDs in 2010, then quit his team after an altercation with his manager in 2011) to rededicated born-again Christian to legitimate prospect. With a full outfield in Washington and two prospects with better defensive skills (Michael Taylor and Brian Goodwin) in the upper minors, Souza is probably happy to be in Tampa, where he landed in the second half of the Wil Myers trade; he should have a clean look at a corner outfield job this year, though Mikie Mahtook looms.

Andrew Velazquez   SS

Born: 7/14/94   Age: 20   Bats: B   Throws: R   Height: 5' 8"   Weight: 175

YEAR	TEAM	LVL	AGE	PA	R	2B	3B	HR	RBI	BB	K	SB	CS	AVG/OBP/SLG	TAv	BABIP	BRR	FRAA	WARP
2013	SBN	A	18	257	23	10	4	0	16	21	59	7	2	.260/.319/.336	.251	.345	-0.6	SS(48): -6.8, 2B(14): -0.9	-0.3
2014	SBN	A	19	623	94	18	15	9	56	62	136	50	15	.290/.367/.428	.297	.369	4.2	SS(129): -1.6	4.9
2015	TBA	MLB	20	250	27	7	2	2	16	17	74	9	3	.212/.268/.289	.217	.297	0.9	SS -3, 2B -0	-0.3

Breakout: 0%   Improve: 0%   Collapse: 0%   Attrition: 0%   MLB: 0%   *Comparables: Brad Harman, Tim Beckham, Eugenio Suarez*

Repeating a league generally isn't good, especially in the lower minors, but a second round of A-Ball for a player as young as Velazquez isn't a knock on his comer status and he showed plenty for the Rays to target him in the Jeremy Hellickson trade. He lacks enough power to be considered a big-time prospect, but it plays up thanks to his keen eye, which puts him ahead in the count early and often. His 50 stolen bases overstate his speed, which grades out as just plus; he just took advantage of inept Midwest League batteries. Velazquez is a heady player with good baseball instincts, so while his realistic role is utility infielder, his only slightly unrealistic role is second-division regular. His last name is worth 39 points in Scrabble, but everybody will know you pocketed that second Z, cheater.

Ben Zobrist   2B

Born: 5/26/81   Age: 34   Bats: B   Throws: R   Height: 6' 3"   Weight: 210

YEAR	TEAM	LVL	AGE	PA	R	2B	3B	HR	RBI	BB	K	SB	CS	AVG/OBP/SLG	TAv	BABIP	BRR	FRAA	WARP
2012	TBA	MLB	31	668	88	39	7	20	74	97	103	14	9	.270/.377/.471	.311	.296	-5.2	RF(71): 1.7, 2B(58): -7.4	4.7
2013	TBA	MLB	32	698	77	36	3	12	71	72	91	11	3	.275/.354/.402	.283	.303	-0.9	2B(125): 0.4, RF(39): 0.4	3.4
2014	TBA	MLB	33	654	83	34	3	10	52	75	84	10	5	.272/.354/.395	.286	.301	2.4	2B(79): 4.7, LF(38): 3.0	4.6
2015	TBA	MLB	34	624	76	31	3	10	55	74	101	11	5	.256/.346/.381	.281	.293	-1.0	2B -3, RF 1	3.2

Breakout: 0%   Improve: 28%   Collapse: 12%   Attrition: 12%   MLB: 99%   *Comparables: Orlando Hudson, Brian Roberts, Chase Utley*

Zobrist continues to be one of the best all-around players in the game despite celebrating his 33rd birthday in the middle of the season. He manned five positions, starting at least 15 games at four of them, and he plays all of them well, even transitioning seamlessly from one to the other. In fact, he played multiple positions in nearly a quarter of his games. It is becoming increasingly unlikely that Zobrist approaches 20 home runs in a season again, but he continues to pump out extra-base hits like a southern rap album. He was named the team MVP by the local chapter of the BBWAA, but at this point is deserving of a lifetime achievement award for the near-decade he has produced as a member of the organization.

Pitchers

Matthew Andriese   RHP

Born: 8/28/89   Age: 25   Bats: R   Throws: R   Height: 6'3"   Weight: 210

YEAR	TEAM	LVL	AGE	W	L	SV	G	GS	IP	H	HR	BB	K	BB/9	K/9	GB%	BABIP	WHIP	ERA	FIP	FRA	WARP
2012	LEL	A+	22	10	8	0	27	26	146	140	9	38	131	2.3	8.1	58%	.312	1.22	3.58	3.68	4.20	2.6
2013	SAN	AA	23	8	2	0	15	15	76	71	3	17	63	2.0	7.5	61%	.298	1.16	2.37	2.70	3.55	1.5
2013	TUC	AAA	23	3	5	0	12	10	58²	64	2	12	42	1.8	6.4	57%	.332	1.30	4.45	3.30	5.00	0.7
2014	DUR	AAA	24	11	8	0	28	25	162¹	153	18	48	129	2.7	7.2	53%	.291	1.24	3.77	4.24	5.52	-0.1
2015	TBA	MLB	25	7	9	0	24	24	130¹	134	13	40	90	2.8	6.2	54%	.294	1.33	4.08	4.54	4.43	0.7

Breakout: 21%   Improve: 27%   Collapse: 6%   Attrition: 24%   MLB: 42%   Comparables: David Phelps, Chris Rusin, Adam Warren

The UC Riverside product, who came to the Rays with Logan Forsythe et al., has trouble gaining notice with his soft stuff, but he has a varied repertoire and a cool head. His five-pitch mix includes a sinker and cutter; as he matures he'll get savvier about how to use all of it and miss more bats. The question is whether he'll get a fair shot to crack Tampa Bay's crowded rotation, or anyone's for that matter.

Chris Archer   RHP

Born: 9/26/88   Age: 26   Bats: R   Throws: R   Height: 6'3"   Weight: 190

YEAR	TEAM	LVL	AGE	W	L	SV	G	GS	IP	H	HR	BB	K	BB/9	K/9	GB%	BABIP	WHIP	ERA	FIP	FRA	WARP
2012	DUR	AAA	23	7	9	0	25	25	128	99	6	62	139	4.4	9.8	49%	.293	1.26	3.66	3.21	4.16	1.9
2012	TBA	MLB	23	1	3	0	6	4	29¹	23	3	13	36	4.0	11.0	44%	.290	1.23	4.60	3.35	4.70	0.1
2013	DUR	AAA	24	5	3	0	10	10	50	50	6	23	52	4.1	9.4	57%	.312	1.46	3.96	4.18	5.03	0.5
2013	TBA	MLB	24	9	7	0	23	23	128²	107	15	38	101	2.7	7.1	47%	.253	1.13	3.22	4.09	4.42	0.7
2014	TBA	MLB	25	10	9	0	32	32	194²	177	12	72	173	3.3	8.0	48%	.296	1.28	3.33	3.42	4.08	2.0
2015	TBA	MLB	26	9	11	0	29	29	162²	147	14	70	146	3.9	8.1	47%	.290	1.33	3.73	4.32	4.05	1.6

Breakout: 41%   Improve: 67%   Collapse: 18%   Attrition: 16%   MLB: 95%   Comparables: Jake Arrieta, Travis Wood, Wade Davis

The Dalai Lama of the diamond, Archer is cool as a cucumber off the field, engaging in philosophical debates and juggling book club memberships. Between the chalk, however, he is a fiery competitor, chucking hardballs in the upper 90s with a sharp slider. Casual observers may still clamor for a third pitch, but Archer's fastball-slider duo actually works as a quartet: He throws a straight four-seam fastball for command and a two-seamer with serious arm-side boogie, and in addition to a two-plane slider that sweeps to his glove-side, he has added a shorter version that gives him a legitimate option to throw away from left-handed batters. The result was a significant improvement against lefties in 2014. It is clear why the thrifty Rays decided to make a long-term investment in his right arm.

Grant Balfour   LHP

Born: 12/30/77   Age: 37   Bats: R   Throws: R   Height: 6'2"   Weight: 200

YEAR	TEAM	LVL	AGE	W	L	SV	G	GS	IP	H	HR	BB	K	BB/9	K/9	GB%	BABIP	WHIP	ERA	FIP	FRA	WARP
2012	OAK	MLB	34	3	2	24	75	0	74²	41	4	28	72	3.4	8.7	36%	.201	0.92	2.53	2.98	3.88	0.7
2013	OAK	MLB	35	1	3	38	65	0	62²	48	7	27	72	3.9	10.3	40%	.263	1.20	2.59	3.52	4.07	0.4
2014	TBA	MLB	36	2	6	12	65	0	61¹	49	3	41	57	5.9	8.2	45%	.274	1.44	4.91	3.98	4.91	-0.1
2015	TBA	MLB	37	3	1	17	57	0	55²	45	4	24	56	3.9	9.1	39%	.277	1.24	3.18	3.80	3.46	0.8

Breakout: 17%   Improve: 35%   Collapse: 23%   Attrition: 12%   MLB: 77%   Comparables: Arthur Rhodes, J.J. Putz, Trever Miller

Balfour returned to the Rays after three seasons in the other Bay Area, but it was an ill-fated homecoming, as he resembled the wild middle reliever Tampa Bay first acquired back in 2007 and not the relief ace who left in 2010. In an ironic twist, the fiery Australian was often passive in his pitch selection, settling for sliders over fastballs, perhaps because he has lost a tick or two on the heater. A lack of control got him bounced from the closer's gig, as he walked nearly as many as he struck out, and when he did throw a strike, it was in a hittable location. He's 37, doesn't have premium velocity, and can't throw a strike; it's hard not to see this as the end of the road.

Jeff Beliveau   RHP

Born: 1/17/87   Age: 28   Bats: L   Throws: L   Height: 6'1"   Weight: 195

YEAR	TEAM	LVL	AGE	W	L	SV	G	GS	IP	H	HR	BB	K	BB/9	K/9	GB%	BABIP	WHIP	ERA	FIP	FRA	WARP
2012	IOW	AAA	25	4	5	0	37	0	44	44	4	18	52	3.7	10.6	35%	.345	1.41	3.89	3.71	3.70	1.0
2012	CHN	MLB	25	1	0	0	22	0	17²	21	5	12	17	6.1	8.7	41%	.314	1.87	4.58	7.10	7.17	-0.4
2013	DUR	AAA	26	2	3	1	38	0	44²	41	1	22	76	4.4	15.3	37%	.404	1.41	2.62	1.64	1.98	1.9
2013	TBA	MLB	26	0	0	0	1	0	0²	1	0	1	0	13.5	0.0	33%	.333	3.00	0.00	7.58	6.65	0.0
2014	DUR	AAA	27	0	0	11	30	0	36	19	0	14	51	3.5	12.8	51%	.253	0.92	1.50	1.69	2.13	1.2
2014	TBA	MLB	27	0	0	1	30	0	24	19	1	7	28	2.6	10.5	41%	.290	1.08	2.62	2.49	2.32	0.5
2015	TBA	MLB	28	2	1	1	42	0	48¹	40	4	20	58	3.8	10.7	40%	.298	1.25	3.25	3.56	3.53	0.7

Breakout: 12%   Improve: 16%   Collapse: 18%   Attrition: 31%   MLB: 49%   Comparables: Mike Zagurski, Brandon Gomes, Kam Mickolio

A typical flight between Raleigh-Durham and Tampa costs about $330 without advance notice. Based on that figure, Beliveau has booked over $4,000 in flights since joining the Rays in 2013. His most recent recall, on July 22nd, could end up being his last. A slender left-hander with marginal velocity, he does not stand out, especially in a 'pen with live arms. As you'd expect, though, he has pitchability, good control and enough stuff to get outs at the highest level. His fastball, which barely touches 90, is typically thrown up and away regardless of the batter. He also features a pair of breaking balls: a curve in the mid-70s and a harder slider. He uses all three against lefties and righties alike. The slider is shorter and gets more swings and misses, while the curve has more length and often ends plate appearances. As a second lefty who can get outs on both sides, Beliveau may finally stop living out of his suitcase.

Brad Boxberger   LHP

Born: 5/27/88   Age: 27   Bats: R   Throws: R   Height: 6'2"   Weight: 220

YEAR	TEAM	LVL	AGE	W	L	SV	G	GS	IP	H	HR	BB	K	BB/9	K/9	GB%	BABIP	WHIP	ERA	FIP	FRA	WARP
2012	TUC	AAA	24	2	2	5	37	0	43¹	37	0	19	62	3.9	12.9	50%	.370	1.29	2.70	2.26	2.09	1.8
2012	SDN	MLB	24	0	0	0	24	0	27²	22	3	18	33	5.9	10.7	40%	.297	1.45	2.60	4.33	4.53	-0.1
2013	TUC	AAA	25	2	4	5	42	0	57¹	50	3	19	89	3.0	14.0	35%	.376	1.20	3.61	2.14	2.74	2.0
2013	SDN	MLB	25	0	1	1	18	0	22	19	3	13	24	5.3	9.8	49%	.296	1.45	2.86	4.38	4.77	-0.1
2014	TBA	MLB	26	5	2	2	63	0	64²	34	9	20	104	2.8	14.5	44%	.227	0.84	2.37	2.87	3.21	0.7
2015	TBA	MLB	27	3	1	1	52	0	60²	46	5	27	82	4.0	12.2	44%	.298	1.20	3.06	3.36	3.33	1.0

Breakout: 29%   Improve: 42%   Collapse: 16%   Attrition: 23%   MLB: 71%   Comparables: Edwar Ramirez, Pat Neshek, Alex Hinshaw

Acquired from the Padres in a multi-player trade, Boxberger is unlike most of the other Tampa Bay bullpen breakouts: He is healthy and did not have a track record of major-league success. He arrived with a mid-90s fastball and a devastating changeup, along with a lack of command and plan for how to use those offerings. Jim Hickey and crew got him turned around, and Boxberger set the club's single-season record for strikeouts by a reliever. The former starter finally dropped the windup and made a full-time commitment to the stretch. His newfound ability to place fastballs, particularly to his glove side, enhanced the effectiveness of his changeup; we usually save "Mjölnir" for curveballs, but Boxberger's change is good enough to deserve the name. His long-term role is in the back end of the bullpen even if saves never become his thing.

Alex Cobb   RHP

Born: 10/7/87   Age: 27   Bats: R   Throws: R   Height: 6'3"   Weight: 200

YEAR	TEAM	LVL	AGE	W	L	SV	G	GS	IP	H	HR	BB	K	BB/9	K/9	GB%	BABIP	WHIP	ERA	FIP	FRA	WARP
2012	DUR	AAA	24	1	4	0	8	8	41¹	44	1	18	44	3.9	9.6	57%	.355	1.50	4.14	2.79	3.38	1.0
2012	TBA	MLB	24	11	9	0	23	23	136¹	130	11	40	106	2.6	7.0	60%	.295	1.25	4.03	3.62	4.34	0.9
2013	TBA	MLB	25	11	3	0	22	22	143¹	120	13	45	134	2.8	8.4	57%	.279	1.15	2.76	3.39	4.03	1.2
2014	TBA	MLB	26	10	9	0	27	27	166¹	142	11	47	149	2.5	8.1	56%	.282	1.14	2.87	3.26	4.34	1.2
2015	TBA	MLB	27	8	8	0	24	24	139²	130	10	44	126	2.8	8.1	54%	.299	1.24	3.39	3.75	3.69	1.9

Breakout: 22%   Improve: 50%   Collapse: 22%   Attrition: 12%   MLB: 90%   Comparables: Ian Kennedy, Clay Buchholz, Homer Bailey

Though he lacks the prestige of some of his rotation mates, Cobb will enter this season as the unofficial leader of the Rays' staff. A calm but serious competitor, he uses a deceptive delivery (which includes an outstretched left leg and a long pause at the apex) and a three-pitch mix to baffle batters on both sides of the plate. His 90 mph fastball is pedestrian, but it is also the key ingredient in Cobb's salad: Locating the pitch on the edges of the zone amplifies the effectiveness of his low-80s curveball that he commands to both sides and a mid-80s splitter that is one of the best pitches in baseball. The "thing," as it is called, comes out of the chute like a fastball, but is depressed by about 5 mph and dives like Greg Louganis. As impressive as the pitch's movement is, the precision with which Cobb deploys the pitch is remarkable: He locates it in exactly the spots to induce swings while minimizing damage on contact. The major piece missing for Cobb is health: For a third straight season, the right-hander landed on the disabled list with an injury unrelated to his arm, this time to his oblique.

Alex Colome   RHP

Born: 12/31/88   Age: 26   Bats: R   Throws: R   Height: 6'2"   Weight: 210

YEAR	TEAM	LVL	AGE	W	L	SV	G	GS	IP	H	HR	BB	K	BB/9	K/9	GB%	BABIP	WHIP	ERA	FIP	FRA	WARP
2012	MNT	AA	23	8	3	0	14	14	75	69	2	34	75	4.1	9.0	47%	.332	1.37	3.48	2.85	4.04	1.1
2012	DUR	AAA	23	0	1	0	3	3	16²	12	1	9	15	4.9	8.1	44%	.262	1.26	3.24	3.94	4.60	0.2
2013	DUR	AAA	24	4	6	0	14	14	70¹	63	5	29	72	3.7	9.2	42%	.301	1.31	3.07	3.49	4.01	1.2
2013	TBA	MLB	24	1	1	0	3	3	16	14	2	9	12	5.1	6.8	45%	.255	1.44	2.25	5.08	5.64	-0.1
2014	PCH	A+	25	0	1	0	3	3	11	7	0	5	10	4.1	8.2	45%	.241	1.09	1.64	2.94	2.87	0.3
2014	DUR	AAA	25	7	6	0	15	15	86	84	2	30	73	3.1	7.6	42%	.319	1.33	3.77	3.25	4.18	1.3
2014	TBA	MLB	25	2	0	0	5	3	23²	19	1	10	13	3.8	4.9	40%	.247	1.23	2.66	3.88	4.81	0.1
2015	TBA	MLB	26	5	7	0	18	18	95²	92	9	44	73	4.1	6.9	43%	.288	1.42	4.26	4.82	4.63	0.3

Breakout: 19%   Improve: 32%   Collapse: 15%   Attrition: 38%   MLB: 57%   Comparables: Kyle Weiland, Eric Surkamp, Jeff Niemann

Colome served a 50-game PED suspension to begin 2014 and had inconsistent results on returning. There are flashes of a dominant starter with a four-pitch mix, but even if he can't maintain his command—a problem throughout the minors—he'll certainly see significant action out of the bull-pen, where the Rays were already considering relocating him late last season. (He has the mechanics of a reliever, too.) Colome is out of options, so he's almost sure to be on the 25-man roster in some capacity.

Jose Dominguez   RHP

Born: 8/7/90   Age: 24   Bats: R   Throws: R   Height: 6'0"   Weight: 200

YEAR	TEAM	LVL	AGE	W	L	SV	G	GS	IP	H	HR	BB	K	BB/9	K/9	GB%	BABIP	WHIP	ERA	FIP	FRA	WARP
2012	GRL	A	21	4	3	4	33	5	72	77	4	47	78	5.9	9.8	46%	.349	1.72	5.25	4.07	5.19	0.5
2013	CHT	AA	22	1	0	5	14	0	17¹	8	0	8	28	4.2	14.5	52%	.258	0.92	2.60	1.24	1.84	0.6
2013	LAN	MLB	22	0	0	0	9	0	8¹	11	0	3	4	3.2	4.3	39%	.355	1.68	2.16	3.50	4.20	0.1
2014	ABQ	AAA	23	1	2	10	31	0	33¹	31	1	18	39	4.9	10.5	51%	.337	1.47	3.24	3.73	3.22	1.1
2014	LAN	MLB	23	0	0	0	5	0	6¹	7	2	3	8	4.3	11.4	33%	.312	1.58	11.37	6.58	7.70	-0.3
2015	TBA	MLB	24	1	1	0	20	3	34	32	3	18	33	4.8	8.6	45%	.305	1.49	4.41	4.54	4.79	0.0

Breakout: 12%   Improve: 22%   Collapse: 6%   Attrition: 17%   MLB: 38%   Comparables: Fernando Cabrera, Waldis Joaquin, Phillippe Aumont

Dominguez received a surprising 2013 promotion to the Dodgers and was expected to do big things in 2014. He made the team's opening trip to Australia, went to the minors shortly after and returned shortly after that due to Brian Wilson's injury, but his season never really got on track. The pitcher who had the best fastball in Los Angeles' system has yet to learn command of the pitch and didn't earn a September call-up. He was rehabbing an injury, but even healthy, a promotion wasn't likely because he didn't display enough developmental progress. He still has a late-inning ceiling, high enough that the Rays acquired him in the Joel Peralta trade, but it's looking less and less likely that the flame-throwing reliever reaches it.

Ernesto Frieri   LHP

Born: 7/19/85   Age: 29   Bats: R   Throws: R   Height: 6'2"   Weight: 205

YEAR	TEAM	LVL	AGE	W	L	SV	G	GS	IP	H	HR	BB	K	BB/9	K/9	GB%	BABIP	WHIP	ERA	FIP	FRA	WARP
2012	ANA	MLB	26	4	2	23	56	0	54¹	26	7	26	80	4.3	13.3	27%	.188	0.96	2.32	3.49	3.48	0.9
2012	SDN	MLB	26	1	0	0	11	0	11²	9	2	4	18	3.1	13.9	27%	.292	1.11	2.31	3.82	4.04	0.0
2013	ANA	MLB	27	2	4	37	67	0	68²	55	11	30	98	3.9	12.8	26%	.293	1.24	3.80	3.75	3.12	1.1
2014	ANA	MLB	28	0	3	11	34	0	31	33	8	9	38	2.6	11.0	36%	.325	1.35	6.39	5.03	5.69	-0.3
2014	PIT	MLB	28	1	1	0	14	0	10²	14	3	5	10	4.2	8.4	26%	.344	1.78	10.12	6.57	7.14	-0.3
2015	TBA	MLB	29	2	1	16	47	0	46²	36	5	21	61	4.1	11.7	29%	.285	1.22	3.32	3.86	3.61	0.6

Breakout: 25%   Improve: 50%   Collapse: 23%   Attrition: 11%   MLB: 88%   Comparables: *Tony Sipp, David Riske, Frank Francisco*

Frieri moved very quickly from closer to "sort of like closer but without the c." He misplaced his fastball command, causing the Angels to relocate him away from the ninth inning and then away from Anaheim, dealing him to Pittsburgh for another fallen closer, Jason Grilli. The Pirates tried to turn him around, couldn't, and relocated him off the 40-man and then out of the organization entirely, releasing him before the season ended. Frieri would have been non-tendered anyway, so the Pirates essentially did him a favor by allowing him to shop for a new home earlier. The Rays picked him up on a cheap major-league deal before Thanksgiving, hoping Jim Hickey can fix what ails him, but it's worth asking what the odds of that are given that Ray Searage has already taken his best shot.

Kevin Jepsen   LHP

Born: 7/26/84   Age: 30   Bats: R   Throws: R   Height: 6'3"   Weight: 235

YEAR	TEAM	LVL	AGE	W	L	SV	G	GS	IP	H	HR	BB	K	BB/9	K/9	GB%	BABIP	WHIP	ERA	FIP	FRA	WARP
2012	SLC	AAA	27	2	2	2	23	0	25	18	1	9	35	3.2	12.6	39%	.321	1.08	3.24	2.47	3.34	0.7
2012	ANA	MLB	27	3	2	2	49	0	46²	39	3	12	38	2.4	7.7	37%	.293	1.14	3.02	3.16	3.74	0.6
2013	ANA	MLB	28	1	3	0	45	0	36	41	3	14	36	3.5	9.0	42%	.345	1.53	4.50	3.41	4.17	0.3
2014	ANA	MLB	29	0	2	2	74	0	65	45	4	23	75	3.2	10.4	50%	.263	1.05	2.63	2.81	3.61	0.6
2015	TBA	MLB	30	3	1	1	55	0	50	45	4	20	50	3.6	8.9	46%	.300	1.29	3.41	3.90	3.71	0.6

Breakout: 27%   Improve: 51%   Collapse: 14%   Attrition: 13%   MLB: 80%   Comparables: *Santiago Casilla, Manny Delcarmen, Jason Frasor*

So what ever happens to those teenagers who flash dominant in A-Ball with mid-90s heat and power breaking balls? The high-risk, mid-round guys who make a couple of team prospect rankings with scouting reports that always end with "needs to polish command and changeup"? The ones who then disappear for years into the void of fallen prospects? If they're lucky, they wind up being Kevin Jepsen. He had a career year in 2014 while basically cutting the use of his signature hard stuff by 20 percent. That changeup he never developed in his teenage years? It's become his go-to pitch. He's under club control through 2016 and was the Rays' return on Matt Joyce.

Nate Karns   RHP

Born: 11/25/87   Age: 27   Bats: R   Throws: R   Height: 6'3"   Weight: 230

YEAR	TEAM	LVL	AGE	W	L	SV	G	GS	IP	H	HR	BB	K	BB/9	K/9	GB%	BABIP	WHIP	ERA	FIP	FRA	WARP
2012	HAG	A	24	3	0	2	11	5	44¹	23	1	21	61	4.3	12.4	50%	.237	0.99	2.03	2.74	3.80	1.1
2012	POT	A+	24	8	4	0	13	13	71²	47	1	26	87	3.3	10.9	53%	.287	1.02	2.26	2.39	3.01	1.9
2013	HAR	AA	25	10	6	0	23	23	132²	109	14	48	155	3.3	10.5	47%	.289	1.18	3.26	3.60	3.87	1.7
2013	WAS	MLB	25	0	1	0	3	3	12	17	5	6	11	4.5	8.2	37%	.316	1.92	7.50	8.35	7.62	-0.4
2014	DUR	AAA	26	9	9	0	27	27	145¹	142	16	62	153	3.8	9.5	47%	.323	1.40	5.08	4.03	5.00	1.0
2014	TBA	MLB	26	1	1	0	2	2	12	7	3	4	13	3.0	9.8	47%	.148	0.92	4.50	5.74	6.34	-0.1
2015	TBA	MLB	27	7	9	0	25	25	132¹	122	15	57	129	3.9	8.8	46%	.294	1.35	4.07	4.52	4.42	0.7

Breakout: 28%   Improve: 32%   Collapse: 11%   Attrition: 25%   MLB: 50%   Comparables: *Corey Kluber, Joel Carreno, P.J. Walters*

Karns has three big league-quality pitches: a lively fastball that sits comfortably at 93 mph, a hard changeup and a power curve. He's big and durable. He dominated in his Rays debut in September. So why do you sense a caution flag coming? In Karns' second big-league start, he was tagged for three homers in five innings, victimized by his typically untrustworthy command. Although he tinkered with his delivery in Triple-A to throw less cross-body, the issue isn't really mechanical. As one scout put it in Durham, Karns "comes with baggage," which is to say: head case as suitcase. Or: You don't have to throw left-handed to be a lefty; it's a state of mind.

Merrill Kelly   RHP

Born: 10/14/88   Age: 26   Bats: R   Throws: R   Height: 6'2"   Weight: 190

YEAR	TEAM	LVL	AGE	W	L	SV	G	GS	IP	H	HR	BB	K	BB/9	K/9	GB%	BABIP	WHIP	ERA	FIP	FRA	WARP
2012	MNT	AA	23	8	3	0	32	9	88¹	84	4	28	61	2.9	6.2	42%	.294	1.27	3.57	3.44	4.36	0.8
2013	MNT	AA	24	5	6	0	13	12	73²	54	3	31	41	3.8	5.0	43%	.231	1.15	4.15	3.71	4.71	0.1
2013	DUR	AAA	24	8	4	0	15	14	84²	74	4	34	70	3.6	7.4	42%	.281	1.28	3.19	3.48	4.93	0.6
2014	DUR	AAA	25	9	4	0	28	15	114	107	10	37	108	2.9	8.5	49%	.298	1.26	2.76	3.73	4.86	1.2
2015	TBA	MLB	26	5	6	0	24	15	102²	103	9	40	63	3.5	5.5	45%	.283	1.40	4.25	4.82	4.62	0.3

Breakout: 10%   Improve: 20%   Collapse: 3%   Attrition: 15%   MLB: 25%   Comparables: *Brooks Brown, D.J. Mitchell, Graham Godfrey*

Guess who had the best overall numbers among the Rays' six Triple-A starters in 2014? And who uncomplainingly toggled between the rotation and the bullpen all season? And who set a career-high strikeout rate and career-low walk rate? And added a couple miles an hour to his modest fastball by season's end? Kelly will get no love for his stuff, so he can only attract attention with results, and perhaps not even with those. He's the kind of low-profile (literally: That listed height is a whopper), highly effective non-prospect who always gets passed over for the guy with the big arm, until one day someone finally notices he's been quietly succeeding in Triple-A for years. Then they also notice he's now 28 or 29, a different set of assumptions is slapped on him and he passes from one kind of anonymity into another, his status changing in letter but not in spirit. Kelly escaped that path this winter and opted for a different kind of anonymity, heading to Korea to play for SK Wyverns.

Jake McGee   RHP

Born: 8/6/86   Age: 28   Bats: L   Throws: L   Height: 6'3"   Weight: 235

YEAR	TEAM	LVL	AGE	W	L	SV	G	GS	IP	H	HR	BB	K	BB/9	K/9	GB%	BABIP	WHIP	ERA	FIP	FRA	WARP
2012	TBA	MLB	25	5	2	0	69	0	55¹	33	3	11	73	1.8	11.9	44%	.244	0.80	1.95	1.76	1.51	1.6
2013	TBA	MLB	26	5	3	1	71	0	62²	52	8	22	75	3.2	10.8	43%	.286	1.18	4.02	3.44	3.80	0.6
2014	TBA	MLB	27	5	2	19	73	0	71¹	48	2	16	90	2.0	11.4	38%	.280	0.90	1.89	1.76	1.86	2.1
2015	TBA	MLB	28	3	2	5	63	0	57²	47	4	18	67	2.7	10.5	42%	.293	1.11	2.67	3.11	2.90	1.3

Breakout: 36%   Improve: 50%   Collapse: 22%   Attrition: 17%   MLB: 87%   Comparables: Rafael Soriano, Tyler Clippard, Greg Holland

For years, McGee has been the Rays' best reliever even though the save opportunities went elsewhere. In a move that was likely financially driven, the club used cost-certain veterans in the ninth inning while McGee, an arbitration-eligible player, did the heavy lifting outside the saves. After Grant Balfour's failure in the role, though, the team—in the midst of a free fall—finally turned to McGee to finish victories. Despite the increased responsibility, the lefty turned in another stellar performance, his fastball filling the strike zone like the farmer's breakfast at Bob Evans. He added a curve in the spring, but, like the pancakes, it's a bonus pitch more than an integral part of the plate. There's no particular reason beyond the normal level of capriciousness associated with relief pitching to think McGee won't keep doing this for at least a few more years.

Mike Montgomery   LHP

Born: 7/1/89   Age: 25   Bats: L   Throws: L   Height: 6'4"   Weight: 200

YEAR	TEAM	LVL	AGE	W	L	SV	G	GS	IP	H	HR	BB	K	BB/9	K/9	GB%	BABIP	WHIP	ERA	FIP	FRA	WARP
2012	NWA	AA	22	2	6	0	10	10	58	69	12	21	44	3.3	6.8	49%	.318	1.55	6.67	5.69	7.27	-1.0
2012	OMA	AAA	22	3	6	0	17	17	91²	110	12	43	67	4.2	6.6	49%	.323	1.67	5.69	5.41	6.10	0.1
2013	DUR	AAA	23	7	8	0	20	19	108²	111	9	48	77	4.0	6.4	50%	.305	1.46	4.72	4.36	5.75	0.1
2014	DUR	AAA	24	10	5	0	25	25	126	117	9	48	98	3.4	7.0	51%	.285	1.31	4.29	3.99	5.10	0.7
2015	TBA	MLB	25	5	8	0	20	20	105	108	11	43	74	3.7	6.3	49%	.293	1.43	4.54	4.91	4.94	-0.1

Breakout: 20%   Improve: 22%   Collapse: 5%   Attrition: 23%   MLB: 33%   Comparables: Alex Wilson, Chaz Roe, Roenis Elias

Montgomery's overall numbers in 2014 suggest an incremental improvement over 2013, but they're actually the aggregate of two starkly different halves. Nothing changed much last year—mechanics, arsenal, velocity—except a few months of results. In April, he nearly threw a no-hitter and cruised onto the International League All-Star Game with a 3.21 ERA. Then he collapsed, producing a 7.63 ERA and failing to reach the fifth inning in five of his final eight starts. He didn't see the seventh inning after June 9th, and not because his arm tired out: He's inefficient with his pitches and is prone to early trouble that drives him from games. Montgomery doesn't dominate lefties enough to convert him into a situational reliever, but he's still left-handed enough to reach the majors at some point, in some capacity.

Matt Moore   LHP

Born: 6/18/89   Age: 26   Bats: L   Throws: L   Height: 6'3"   Weight: 200

YEAR	TEAM	LVL	AGE	W	L	SV	G	GS	IP	H	HR	BB	K	BB/9	K/9	GB%	BABIP	WHIP	ERA	FIP	FRA	WARP
2012	TBA	MLB	23	11	11	0	31	31	177¹	158	18	81	175	4.1	8.9	39%	.294	1.35	3.81	3.88	3.75	2.7
2013	TBA	MLB	24	17	4	0	27	27	150¹	119	14	76	143	4.5	8.6	41%	.259	1.30	3.29	3.98	4.33	1.2
2014	TBA	MLB	25	0	2	0	2	2	10	10	1	5	6	4.5	5.4	42%	.281	1.50	2.70	4.76	4.48	0.0
2015	TBA	MLB	26	2	2	0	6	6	35¹	30	3	15	38	3.9	9.6	41%	.290	1.28	3.38	3.84	3.68	0.5

Breakout: 39%   Improve: 71%   Collapse: 13%   Attrition: 13%   MLB: 95%   Comparables: Edinson Volquez, Francisco Liriano, Gio Gonzalez

Remember the part in The Lion King where young Simba disappears for a while but comes back a little older, a little more mature and a whole lot stronger, so he can become the leader everyone hoped he would be? That's basically what the Rays are hoping for with Moore, who missed most of the season after undergoing Tommy John surgery. Especially important is the part where he defeats the evil scar on his left arm.

Jake Odorizzi   RHP

Born: 3/27/90   Age: 25   Bats: R   Throws: R   Height: 6'2"   Weight: 185

YEAR	TEAM	LVL	AGE	W	L	SV	G	GS	IP	H	HR	BB	K	BB/9	K/9	GB%	BABIP	WHIP	ERA	FIP	FRA	WARP
2012	NWA	AA	22	4	2	0	7	7	38	27	2	10	47	2.4	11.1	36%	.269	0.97	3.32	2.28	3.38	1.0
2012	OMA	AAA	22	11	3	0	19	18	107¹	105	12	40	88	3.4	7.4	30%	.292	1.35	2.93	4.65	4.46	2.0
2012	KCA	MLB	22	0	1	0	2	2	7¹	8	1	4	4	4.9	4.9	38%	.280	1.64	4.91	5.36	5.90	0.0
2013	DUR	AAA	23	9	6	0	22	22	124¹	101	12	40	124	2.9	9.0	37%	.282	1.13	3.33	3.45	4.54	1.6
2013	TBA	MLB	23	0	1	1	7	4	29²	28	3	8	22	2.4	6.7	34%	.287	1.21	3.94	3.92	3.61	0.4
2014	TBA	MLB	24	11	13	0	31	31	168	156	20	59	174	3.2	9.3	32%	.295	1.28	4.12	3.78	3.73	2.4
2015	TBA	MLB	25	8	9	0	26	26	142²	132	16	50	130	3.2	8.2	35%	.287	1.28	3.72	4.35	4.05	1.4

Breakout: 33%   Improve: 62%   Collapse: 19%   Attrition: 22%   MLB: 91%   Comparables: Anthony Reyes, Dan Straily, Marc Rzepczynski

Odorizzi came into the season with a new off-speed pitch, a splitter learned from Alex Cobb. Blending his new weapon with the arsenal he already had, the right-hander flourished like a cocker spaniel riding with the windows down on Biscayne Boulevard on a warm summer afternoon. The splitter worked twofold for Odorizzi: It was a valuable offering on its own, serving as an out pitch that he previously lacked, and it greatly enhanced the low-90s fastball that he routinely elevated above the hands of the opposition. Improved command of the fastball also led to more efficient at-bats and, in turn, deeper outings. Odorizzi also throws a nifty curve with velocity and is tenacious and athletic on the mound. Nobody will mistake him for an ace, but he'll fit just fine in the rotation for the five years of team control he has left.

Enny Romero   LHP

Born: 1/24/91   Age: 24   Bats: L   Throws: L   Height: 6'3"   Weight: 210

YEAR	TEAM	LVL	AGE	W	L	SV	G	GS	IP	H	HR	BB	K	BB/9	K/9	GB%	BABIP	WHIP	ERA	FIP	FRA	WARP
2012	PCH	A+	21	5	7	0	25	23	126	89	5	76	107	5.4	7.6	47%	.244	1.31	3.93	4.19	5.80	0.0
2013	MNT	AA	22	11	7	0	27	27	140¹	110	9	73	110	4.7	7.1	44%	.252	1.30	2.76	3.78	4.49	0.8
2013	TBA	MLB	22	0	0	0	1	1	4²	1	0	4	0	7.7	0.0	64%	.071	1.07	0.00	5.65	5.26	0.0
2014	DUR	AAA	23	5	11	0	25	25	126	128	13	52	117	3.7	8.4	42%	.312	1.43	4.50	4.13	4.93	1.1
2015	TBA	MLB	24	5	9	0	22	22	109²	107	11	61	83	5.0	6.8	46%	.287	1.53	4.68	5.18	5.08	-0.2

Breakout: 15%   Improve: 27%   Collapse: 10%   Attrition: 25%   MLB: 38%   Comparables: Anthony Ranaudo, Andrew Chafin, Kyle Weiland

Romero started 2014 as the Rays' no. 1 prospect and ended it as the sixth-best starter on his Triple-A team. Two problems: 1) mechanics! 2) starting! Romero is the kind of pitcher who throws a fastball, peeps the **99** readout on the stadium gun and pumps his fist. That's a reliever. He's still young and will get more time to prove himself as a starter, but Romero is destined for the bullpen.

Mark Sappington   LHP

Born: 11/17/90   Age: 24   Bats: R   Throws: R   Height: 6'5"   Weight: 210

YEAR	TEAM	LVL	AGE	W	L	SV	G	GS	IP	H	HR	BB	K	BB/9	K/9	GB%	BABIP	WHIP	ERA	FIP	FRA	WARP
2013	INL	A+	22	11	4	0	22	22	130²	103	10	62	110	4.3	7.6	47%	.262	1.26	3.38	4.62	4.97	0.9
2013	ARK	AA	22	1	1	0	5	5	25²	23	1	20	26	7.0	9.1	52%	.306	1.68	3.86	4.11	4.30	0.2
2014	INL	A+	23	3	7	5	33	8	70¹	80	11	43	80	5.5	10.2	37%	.359	1.75	5.76	5.42	5.97	0.3
2014	ARK	AA	23	1	4	0	9	9	43¹	44	2	36	34	7.5	7.1	33%	.328	1.85	6.44	4.64	5.27	0.0
2015	TBA	MLB	24	4	8	0	28	19	102²	108	11	68	74	5.9	6.5	43%	.300	1.71	5.47	5.69	5.94	-1.1

Breakout: 0%   Improve: 0%   Collapse: 0%   Attrition: 0%   MLB: 0%   Comparables: *Jimmy Nelson, Joel Hanrahan, Shane Greene*

Sappington threw just enough strikes and decent changeups in 2013 to look like a viable starting prospect, but poor mechanics caught up with him last year. By July, he was exiled to the Inland Empire bullpen—the role scouts had envisioned from the beginning—where he cut his walk rate from nearly one an inning to just one per three. Other high-octane arms had already lapped him in the system, so the Angels capitalized on his second half by swapping him for the now-value of Cesar Ramos. Sappington hails from Peculiar, Missouri, a community with at least two founding myths, so in addition to his mid-90s heat he brings a plus-plus trivia tidbit and enough unsolved mystery to beguile the most fanatic Tampa fans.

Drew Smyly   RHP

Born: 6/13/89   Age: 26   Bats: L   Throws: L   Height: 6'3"   Weight: 190

YEAR	TEAM	LVL	AGE	W	L	SV	G	GS	IP	H	HR	BB	K	BB/9	K/9	GB%	BABIP	WHIP	ERA	FIP	FRA	WARP
2012	TOL	AAA	23	0	2	0	7	7	17²	22	3	8	25	4.1	12.7	35%	.413	1.70	6.11	4.06	4.67	0.3
2012	DET	MLB	23	4	3	0	23	18	99¹	93	12	33	94	3.0	8.5	42%	.295	1.27	3.99	3.78	4.23	1.6
2013	DET	MLB	24	6	0	2	63	0	76	62	4	17	81	2.0	9.6	43%	.291	1.04	2.37	2.34	2.95	1.6
2014	DET	MLB	25	6	9	0	21	18	105¹	111	14	31	89	2.6	7.6	40%	.313	1.35	3.93	4.11	3.83	1.8
2014	TBA	MLB	25	3	1	0	7	7	47²	25	4	11	44	2.1	8.3	36%	.184	0.76	1.70	3.10	3.25	0.8
2015	TBA	MLB	26	6	6	1	36	18	117¹	103	10	36	115	2.7	8.9	42%	.291	1.18	3.23	3.66	3.51	1.9

Breakout: 30%   Improve: 58%   Collapse: 14%   Attrition: 11%   MLB: 93%   Comparables: *Mike Minor, Max Scherzer, Tommy Hanson*

The Tigers thought so highly of Smyly that they traded Doug Fister in part to clear a spot in the rotation for him. The Rays showed how much they valued the lanky lefty, acquiring him as a key piece of the David Price trade. Tampa Bay inherited a 25-year-old southpaw with a low-90s fastball, a knee-buckling curveball in the high 70s, a cutter-slider hybrid in the mid-80s and a change more for show than use. In lieu of sweeping changes to their new addition, the club took the available pieces and rearranged them a bit. This included encouraging Smyly to let the fastball fly high and to put the cutter in the back door to right-handers. The latter helped narrow a sizable platoon split while the former led to quicker outs and an uptick in whiffs. Concerns over workload resulted in an early September shutdown, but the seven-start introduction was enough to get those in and around the organization excited to see what Smyly can do full-time in 2015.

Kirby Yates   RHP

Born: 3/25/87   Age: 28   Bats: L   Throws: R   Height: 5'10"   Weight: 195

YEAR	TEAM	LVL	AGE	W	L	SV	G	GS	IP	H	HR	BB	K	BB/9	K/9	GB%	BABIP	WHIP	ERA	FIP	FRA	WARP
2012	MNT	AA	25	4	2	16	50	0	68	48	4	39	94	5.2	12.4	43%	.299	1.28	2.65	2.91	3.03	1.7
2013	DUR	AAA	26	3	2	20	51	0	61²	38	2	23	93	3.4	13.6	41%	.286	0.99	1.90	1.97	2.43	1.9
2014	DUR	AAA	27	1	0	16	21	0	25	10	0	9	35	3.2	12.6	45%	.196	0.76	0.36	1.76	1.97	0.9
2014	TBA	MLB	27	0	2	1	37	0	36	33	4	15	42	3.8	10.5	34%	.315	1.33	3.75	3.77	4.34	0.2
2015	TBA	MLB	28	2	1	1	40	0	51	42	4	24	59	4.3	10.5	40%	.294	1.30	3.44	3.82	3.74	0.6

Breakout: 14%   Improve: 18%   Collapse: 12%   Attrition: 20%   MLB: 37%   Comparables: *Christian Garcia, Jeff Stevens, Billy Sadler*

Yates completed his journey from an undrafted free agent to major-league pitcher when he took the mound in a Rays uniform on June 7, 2014. Standing under six feet tall, he creates some deception with his release that comes inches away from his right ear. He works primarily off of a low-to-mid-90s fastball and a mid-80s slider. His third pitch, a changeup, shows promise but lags, and Yates added a curve later in the season as compensation. The lack of weapons against left-handed batters put more emphasis on his fastball, which in turn resulted in an unfortunate split and an area to focus on if the right-hander wants to become a complete reliever. Yates is calm on the bump, without fear of the moment, which bodes well for his ability to handle higher leverage work if he can incorporate the changeup regularly.

Lineouts

Hitters

NAME	POS	TEAM	LVL	AGE	PA	R	2B	3B	HR	RBI	BB	K	SB	CS	AVG/OBP/SLG	TAv	BABIP	BRR	FRAA	WARP
Willy Adames	SS	BGR	A	18	114	15	5	2	2	11	15	30	3	0	.278/.377/.433	.291	.379	2.1	SS(25): -1.2	0.8
	SS	WMI	A	18	400	40	14	12	6	50	39	96	3	6	.269/.346/.428	.307	.353	0.7	SS(97): -0.4	3.8
Jake Bauers	1B	FTW	A	18	467	59	18	3	8	64	51	80	5	6	.296/.376/.414	.283	.347	0.9	1B(103): 7.4	2.7
Tim Beckham	2B	DUR	AAA	24	65	8	2	0	0	4	2	14	0	0	.258/.281/.290	.191	.333	-0.2	2B(7): -1.1, SS(5): 0.3	-0.5
Wilson Betemit	1B	DUR	AAA	32	453	53	17	0	18	50	49	144	1	0	.217/.298/.396	.237	.281	-1.9	1B(47): -3.9, 3B(7): 0.9	-1.2
Allan Dykstra	1B	LVG	AAA	27	439	62	23	3	16	74	84	97	0	0	.280/.426/.504	.309	.340	-3.1	1B(61): -1.8	2.5
Johnny Field	CF	BGR	A	22	362	62	23	5	7	41	33	74	18	4	.290/.367/.461	.316	.356	1.3	CF(67): 2.9, RF(6): 0.3	3.6
	CF	PCH	A+	22	169	33	13	3	5	17	13	28	5	4	.320/.396/.547	.337	.368	0.0	CF(40): 1.4	2.0
Cole Figueroa	3B	DUR	AAA	27	312	33	13	3	3	33	39	29	4	1	.282/.371/.389	.275	.302	-1.2	3B(43): 3.2, SS(21): 2.6	2.2
	2B	TBA	MLB	27	49	6	2	1	0	6	4	4	0	0	.233/.286/.326	.248	.244	0.9	2B(16): -0.5	0.1
Casey Gillaspie	1B	HUD	A-	21	308	27	16	1	7	42	42	65	2	3	.262/.364/.411	.267	.321	-2.5	1B(63): 3.0	0.3
Tyler Goeddel	3B	PCH	A+	21	479	41	25	8	6	61	46	98	20	9	.269/.349/.408	.277	.335	-3.0	3B(106): 7.8	2.9
Hak-Ju Lee	SS	DUR	AAA	23	357	36	9	1	4	23	37	86	12	5	.203/.287/.276	.203	.267	1.9	SS(92): -7.9	-1.2
Luke Maile	C	MNT	AA	23	393	43	19	4	5	37	35	76	1	1	.268/.341/.387	.264	.327	-1.4	C(80): -0.6	1.5
Josh Sale	LF	PCH	A+	22	361	34	14	4	4	46	35	109	0	4	.238/.313/.344	.241	.344	-2.5	LF(56): -4.4, RF(23): 0.8	-0.8
Richie Shaffer	3B	MNT	AA	23	491	58	28	4	19	64	56	119	4	0	.222/.318/.440	.271	.261	-0.5	3B(109): -4.5	1.8
Andrew Toles	CF	PCH	A+	22	218	28	10	1	1	13	12	31	18	10	.261/.302/.337	.234	.300	1.7	CF(46): -3.5	-0.1
Justin Williams	RF	SBN	A	18	112	16	6	3	2	23	7	23	0	1	.284/.348/.461	.293	.351	-0.9	RF(20): -0.3, LF(7): -0.0	0.6
Kean Wong	2B	BGR	A	19	454	56	15	3	2	24	27	73	13	9	.306/.347/.370	.273	.364	0.4	2B(97): 0.8	1.8

Willy Adames was the young-prospect return from the Tigers for David Price, and he already has some folks convinced he's a real-deal shortstop; he's also a teenager, though, so don't hold your breath. Seriously, you'll pass out. ❖ **Jake Bauers** set the Midwest League on fire in his first 50 games, hitting .379/.453/.563 as the circuit's youngest regular. Then pitchers extinguished him to the tune of .233/.316/.302 in his final 62 and wished for better metaphors. ❖ **Tim Beckham** returned from his torn ACL in late July, just in time to get himself up to speed for his fifth season in Triple-A. Buster Posey led the Giants to their third World Series title in five years. ❖ You know how Kelly Johnson only hits left-handed, and you can play him at first base if you really have to, and last season he achieved the American League East Career Slam (playing for each team)? Change that last one to International League South and you have **Wilson Betemit**. ❖ **Nick Ciuffo**'s defense behind the plate remains ahead of his hitting, which is undermined by an uppercut swing that produces power but also copious whiffs. ❖ **Allan Dykstra** continues to mash in the high minors, but is for some reason considered organizational filler by whoever's in charge of self-fulfilling prophecies. ❖ If your name is **Johnny Field** you get to be in this book, although it helps if you Johnny Hit your way up to High-A midway through your second season out of the University of Arizona and win the Rays' Minor-League Player of the Year award. ❖ **Cole Figueroa** earned his first call-up for the Rays, spent a couple of months occupying the Honorary Joe Dillon Chair of Bench Studies and got released a few weeks after Joe Maddon signed with the Cubs. Now he's a Yankee. ❖ The Rays' top pick in 2014, **Casey Gillaspie** made a smooth transition from metal to wooden bats over the summer. Conor's switch-hitting brother projects to be average across the board without a standout tool, but with enough to play every day at the cold corner. ❖ **Tyler Goeddel** sometimes struggles with throws on the run and balls have a tendency to eat him up at third; at the plate he showed some pitch-recognition improvement and inside-the-park power. ❖ **Hak-Ju Lee** "recovered" from his gruesome knee injury in medicalspeak only; he lost several steps off his plus speed, reverted to tentative habits in the batter's box and looked increasingly tired after the All-Star break. He's quite likely a lost cause, and another blot on the record of Tim Beckham, who made the bad throw that put Lee's knee in harm's way two seasons ago. ❖ **Luke Maile** (rhymes with Bailey), the most advanced catcher in the Rays' system, may not have a big enough frame to stick behind the plate, but he has both physical and mental agility and a promising bat that might play at Evan Longoria's position. ❖ **Josh Sale** is a bozo. ❖ **Richie Shaffer** shows power potential with a quick bat and strong hands, but there's no real star potential, which is disappointing for a first-round pick. ❖ **Andrew Toles**, the organization's Minor League Player of the Year in 2013, was benched in late May for not hustling. Four days later he left the Charlotte Stone Crabs for personal reasons and did not return, though he reappeared in the Gulf Coast League at the end of the season. ❖ Considered Monday Night-level raw out of the draft, **Justin Williams**, who came to the Rays for Jeremy Hellickson, actually reached Low-A during his age-18 season and acquitted himself quite well. He's got huge power, and he'll need it, as he's already limited to the outfield corners. ❖ **Kean Wong** skipped a level, making him the fourth-youngest regular in the Midwest League; he nonetheless had its second-highest batting average, and was named Bowling Green's MVP by the Rays. Look out, Kolten.

Pitchers

NAME	TEAM	LVL	AGE	W	L	SV	G	GS	IP	H	HR	BB	K	BB/9	K/9	GB%	BABIP	WHIP	ERA	FIP	FRA	WARP
Erik Bedard	TBA	MLB	35	4	6	0	17	15	75²	84	10	29	64	3.4	7.6	36%	.312	1.49	4.76	4.42	4.15	1.0
Jacob Faria	BGR	A	20	7	9	0	23	23	119²	113	9	32	107	2.4	8.0	44%	.300	1.21	3.46	3.55	4.35	1.2
Dylan Floro	MNT	AA	23	11	13	0	28	28	178²	209	4	24	112	1.2	5.6	62%	.341	1.30	3.48	2.68	3.65	2.9
Grayson Garvin	MNT	AA	24	1	8	0	20	20	74	76	5	15	60	1.8	7.3	46%	.327	1.23	3.77	3.34	3.76	1.6
Steven Geltz	DUR	AAA	26	3	3	1	29	0	41²	27	3	17	60	3.7	13.0	32%	.276	1.06	2.38	2.71	3.25	1.0
	TBA	MLB	26	0	1	0	11	0	8¹	6	3	5	14	5.4	15.1	25%	.231	1.32	3.24	7.00	9.64	-0.4
Brandon Gomes	DUR	AAA	29	0	2	0	27	0	37¹	36	4	12	42	2.9	10.1	36%	.320	1.29	3.62	3.63	3.90	0.7
	TBA	MLB	29	2	2	0	29	0	34	28	5	11	24	2.9	6.4	33%	.235	1.15	3.71	4.63	5.74	-0.3
Josh Lueke	DUR	AAA	29	0	1	12	32	0	37¹	32	3	9	40	2.2	9.6	38%	.287	1.10	3.38	3.06	4.58	0.3
	TBA	MLB	29	1	2	0	25	0	30¹	38	7	5	19	1.5	5.6	43%	.301	1.42	5.64	5.50	5.75	-0.4
German Marquez	BGR	A	19	5	7	0	22	18	98	83	5	29	95	2.7	8.7	53%	.294	1.14	3.21	3.22	4.24	1.0
Juan Oviedo	TBA	MLB	32	3	3	1	32	0	31²	27	3	16	26	4.5	7.4	36%	.261	1.36	3.69	4.55	4.28	0.0
C.J. Riefenhauser	DUR	AAA	24	3	3	1	39	0	57²	41	3	25	53	3.9	8.3	37%	.242	1.14	1.40	3.60	4.16	0.7
	TBA	MLB	24	0	0	0	7	0	5¹	6	3	3	2	5.1	3.4	32%	.316	1.69	8.44	4.10	4.20	0.0
Blake Snell	BGR	A	21	3	2	0	8	8	40¹	26	1	19	42	4.2	9.4	69%	.253	1.12	1.79	3.14	4.40	0.3
	PCH	A+	21	5	6	0	16	16	75¹	69	1	37	77	4.4	9.2	54%	.325	1.41	3.94	3.19	4.00	1.1
Ryne Stanek	BGR	A	22	3	4	0	9	9	44²	47	2	13	46	2.6	9.3	52%	.363	1.34	3.63	2.95	3.94	0.7
	PCH	A+	22	1	1	0	3	3	13	13	0	5	4	3.5	2.8	33%	.283	1.38	5.54	3.93	5.54	0.0

Erik Bedard has thrown nearly 500 above-replacement innings after labrum surgery, a testament to medicine and to him; he can probably keep filling the "hold down a starting spot until a better option becomes available" role as long as he feels like it. ❖ **Jake Faria** used average stuff to get outs in a league in which he was the ninth-youngest qualified starter. And he won the Rays' nice-guy award. ❖ **Dylan Floro** continues to ride a low-90s sinker through the Rays' system, gathering groundballs in bunches as he advances. A finesse righty, he has the control aspect down but his aggressiveness in the zone will hurt him at higher levels if he doesn't work the edges. ❖ Until his body says otherwise, the Rays will continue to call **Grayson Garvin** a starter because of his good control and average offerings from the left side. Five years ago, we'd have said Garvin was a future member of the Padres' since-disassembled Yacht Club Bullpen. ❖ **Steve Geltz** wasn't on the 40-man and looked like Triple-A filler—especially after sitting out 50 games on a party-drug suspension—but got a surprise late-season call to the majors, where more than half the hitters he faced produced one of the three true outcomes. ❖ **Brandon Gomes** has spent the last four years as a split resident of Durham and St. Petersburg, but that's about to come to an end: he has neither options nor a pitch to get lefties out. ❖ Former top-100 prospect **Taylor Guerreri** returned very briefly to the mound in the GCL last year after Tommy John surgery; he also served a suspension for a drug of abuse during his rehab period. ❖ **Brent Honeywell**, the Rays' 2014 competitive balance pick, throws a screwball (!) that he learned from his father's cousin, Mike Marshall—he also features a good fastball, conventional change and curveball—and wowed wonks while dominating the Appy League and winning his team MVP award. ❖ **Josh Lueke** aims to play in Japan in 2015, which may be far enough for him to escape the shadow of his 2008 rape charge. ❖ Hey, wake up, you're lining out! **German Marquez** is a sleeper! He was Bowling Green's best starter last year *and* the fifth-youngest in the Midwest League. ❖ **Juan Carlos Oviedo** made his major-league debut in 2014, then, like Leo Nunez before him, vanished and was not heard from again. ❖ **C.J. Riefenhauser** missed time with a strained oblique, pushing him down the depth chart on his return, but his late-season call-up indicates that the Rays still have him and his nasty breaking ball in their plans. ❖ Expected to compete for a Padres rotation spot in 2014, **Burch Smith** instead got shelled in two April starts at Triple-A and then missed the rest of the season with a flexor muscle strain in his right forearm before heading to the Arizona Fall League to make up for lost innings. Now he's a Ray after serving as 9 percent of the Wil Myers trade. ❖ **Blake Snell** bounced most of the way back from a walk-plagued 2013, earned a midseason promotion, and was named the Rays' Minor League Pitcher of the Year. ❖ Between injuries, **Ryne Stanek** was promoted to High-A; he has a plus fastball, hammer breaking ball and nifty lip sweater, the latter of which will help him transition to the bullpen if he can't stay healthy as a starter. ❖ The Rays gave 2014 second-rounder **Cameron Varga** an over-slot signing bonus because he might be a first-round talent with solid velocity and a power curve, but he comes with injury questions.

Manager

Kevin Cash

The most unexpected managerial search of the winter was prompted by Joe Maddon opting out of his contract and jetting to Chicago. The Rays then conducted a lengthy, deliberate and surprisingly transparent (relative to the organization's lips-sewn-shut nature) search that included among the candidates multiple ESPN on-air personalities, a mixture of veteran and first-time managerial types and a player who hadn't announced his retirement.

Cash, by virtue of going through the interview process (and almost landing the job) with the Rangers, wasn't the greenest of the bunch. He was, however, deemed the best by the Rays, who made him the fifth manager in franchise history, much to the delight of the local media. Not only does Cash come with a headline-friendly last name, but he's a local product, having been born and raised in Tampa. He went undrafted out of Florida State University, yet still carved out a lengthy big-league career, which included a stint with the Devil Rays.

Cash's post-playing career included time spent with the Blue Jays and Indians. He comes as a well-regarded communicator and talent evaluator, but those are common traits for most new managers. We'll just have to wait to see if Cash is indeed money for the Rays.

TEXAS RANGERS

by Russell A. Carleton

There is a tide in the affairs of men,
Which, taken at the flood, leads on to fortune,
Omitted, all the voyage of their life
Is bound in shallows and in miseries.
On such a full sea are we now afloat;
And we must take the current when it serves,
Or lose our ventures.

—Shakespeare, Julius Caesar, Act IV, Scene 3

I briefly considered writing a three-word essay on the 2014 Rangers' season. "Everyone got hurt." No team suffered the slings and arrows of outrageous fortune more. A quick recap:

The Rangers traded Ian Kinsler to the Tigers for Prince Fielder, which was supposed to simultaneously clear the way for future Hall of Famer Jurickson Profar and get Mitch Moreland to politely take the hint and exit stage left. Profar, Fielder and (insult to injuries) Moreland all got hurt. Kinsler was an All-Star for the Tigers.

They splashed cash (and seven years) on Shin-Soo Choo. He spent some time on the disabled list but did hit a decent .242/.340/.374. The problem was that the Rangers were expecting (and paying for) something more on the order of his 2012 line (.283/.373/.441), if not 2013 (.285/.423/.462). The fact that Choo's defense was well below average meant that he barely functioned above replacement level. To quote someone else from Texas, "Oops."

Martin Perez threw back-to-back three-hit shutouts early in April, then had Tommy John surgery about a month later. He joined Tanner Scheppers, Alexi Ogando, Matt Harrison and Derek Holland in the "We had a season-ending injury" Facebook group.

Colby Lewis led the team in starts. Colby. Lewis.

✦✦✦

If you can look into the seeds of time, and say which grain will grow and which will not, speak then unto me.

—Macbeth, Act I, Scene 3

RANGERS PROSPECTUS
2014 W-L: 67-95, 5TH IN AL WEST

Pythag	.411	30th	DER	.690	26th
RS/G	3.93	17th	B-Age	28.4	14th
RA/G	4.77	28th	P-Age	27.8	8th
TAv	.256	21st	Salary	$132.7M	10th
BRR	4.3	7th	M$/MW	$6.5M	29th
TAv-P	.281	30th	DL Days	2,218	30th
FIP	4.25	29th	$ on DL	38%	29th

Three-Year Park Factors

Runs	Runs/RH	Runs/LH	HR/RH	HR/LH
101	101	101	81	85

Top Hitter WARP	4.9	Adrian Beltre
Top Pitcher WARP	3.8	Yu Darvish
Top Prospect		Joey Gallo

It's a rite of spring to make predictions about the upcoming season. "The Rangers will win 91 games" rolls off the tongue easily, followed by a reflexive "assuming no major injuries." Funny that so much can rest on a few tiny ligaments. What happened to the Rangers last year was a reminder of just how much can change thanks to random events. It's the sort of tragic tale that might inspire a play.

But we're left with a frustrating question afterward. Other than the nice side effect that the Rangers will own the fourth pick in the 2015 draft, we might as well simply pretend 2014 didn't happen at The Globe. It was all a tale told by an idiot, full of sound and fury signifying nothing. (*Macbeth*, Act V, Scene 5.) What do we make of a team that basically lost an entire year? Most of the wounded are coming back, but what can we expect from them in 2015? Are the days of the Rangers winning 90 games a thing of the past? That is the question.

In 2013, I did some #GoryMath on what best predicts pitcher injuries. I came to the not-at-all-surprising conclusion that the best predictor for starting pitchers is having previously been injured. The effect size was huge. Pitchers who had an injury in the year prior were eight to 10 times more likely to have an injury to that same body part in the next year. It's not a guarantee that the Rangers will be running an ER triage unit in their clubhouse, but any sober assessment of the their chances in 2015 can't end with the usual glib "assuming no injuries." It needs to end with a terrified and somber "if they get lucky and avoid the injury bug." The good news is that the Rangers do have a lot of talent coming back, and that core was good enough to win 91 games in 2013, so the ceiling is there.

It's more likely than not that the person reading this essay is a Rangers fan who opened the book and quickly turned to the Rangers chapter to root root root for the home team. Hopefully, you didn't stop reading at the end of that last paragraph. Yes, it's entirely possible that last year's rash of injuries was a run of bad luck and that even with the increased injury risk, everyone is coming back at roughly the same talent level as before. So yeah, the ceiling for 91 wins is there. But injuries can also be a sign of a sneakily aging team. Fielder is 31. Choo is 32. Even Holland, Moreland and Yu Darvish are now past 27. If there's something that can be said for the Rangers, it's that they have to be considered one of the highest-variance teams for 2015. They have the talent to win 90 games, but they have the risk factors to lose 90 again.

✦✦✦

There should be a sonnet about Adrian Beltre. In fact ...

O brave third baseman known in Texas
But less well known than certain pandas
O'er the past four years thou were the nexus
Of Ranger wins, so hear these stanzas
Thy glove still with flecks of golden heaven
Thy bat as constant as the waves on the shore(p)
And since you came in 2011
Few have matched your total WAR(P).
This skill set a joy in many layers
But oh, Fair Adrian hast not received due
Whene'er they mention the "Top 10 players"
They ne'er seem to mention you.
Yet once your career has squelched its flame
Dude, you belong in the Hall of Fame!

✦✦✦

Reputation is an idle and most false imposition;
oft got without merit, and lost without deserving.

—*Othello, Act II, Scene 3*

Hidden among the injuries were some worrying signs for the healthy. Elvis Andrus played 157 games, but for the second straight year saw a dip in his walk rate and on-base percentage, and his defensive numbers took a rather steep plunge. Most people probably stopped watching Rangers games on MLB.tv around June and most likely still assume Andrus is slick shortstop who can put up a .340 OBP. His season was emblematic of other hitters on the team. It's not that he has reached the level of awful player. It's that he (and Choo and Fielder) have reached the most maddening level there is: "Not bad." If Choo had fallen below the Mendoza line, or Andrus had gone full-on Dan Uggla, it would be easy enough to start picking out a replacement from the waiver wire. But the reality is that Andrus is a top-25 shortstop; he might be no. 23, so you'd like more production out of that spot, but who is available to actually give it to you? Unfortunately, he'll make $15 million doing "not bad" in each of the next eight years.

Neftali Feliz, acquired alongside Andrus in the Mark Teixeira trade way back in 2007, is another example. His strikeout-an-inning, Rookie of the Year campaign was in 2010. Five years ago. Since then, his strikeout rates per nine innings have read 7.8, 7.8, 7.7 and 6.0. More importantly, his innings pitched over that time have been 62 in 2011, 43 (in eight games, seven of them starts) in 2012, then five and 32. I'm not arguing that he is now a desiccated shell of his former self, but that we need to be tempered in our expectations. He's a good reliever (assuming no major ... oh right) just not an elite one.

✦✦✦

The fault, dear Brutus, is not in our stars, but in ourselves,
that we are underlings.

—*Julius Caesar, Act I, Scene 2*

And then there was Darvish. At this point, it's well known that he's a legitimate ace. There's a GIF out there of Darvish throwing five separate pitches superimposed on one another, and all five break in a different direction. It doesn't quite work here on the printed page, but you have Google, right? Let's get overly excited about something. Where do Darvish's stikeout totals fit historically?

He came to MLB at age 25 and in his three major-league seasons has struck out 680 batters. He's been pitching professionally since he was 18. In six and a half years in the Japanese Pacific League, he struck out 1,250 batters in 1,268 innings. While the Japanese season is shorter, Darvish regularly pitched 200 innings, so we know an MLB workload wasn't going to be much of an issue for him. The general consensus is that the quality of the Japanese professional leagues is not on par with MLB, but Darvish would surely have racked up a few strikeouts in the bigs even if he'd come over prior to 2012. Given that he stepped in at age 25 and fanned 221 in his first season, it's not likely that his age-23 and -24 seasons would have been much different. But let's discount his Japanese strikeout total by a third to compensate for the difference in quality. That would leave him with nearly 1,500 strikeouts entering his age-28 season. Of all pitchers since 1950, that would sandwich him in ninth place between Fernando Valenzuela and Sandy Koufax at that age. Others on that list? Sam McDowell, Bert Blyleven, Don Drysdale, Felix Hernandez, Dwight Gooden, Nolan Ryan and Pedro Martinez. Some Hall of Fame names (and a couple of cautionary tales!).

Even if we believe Darvish would have "only" 1,400 strikeouts to his name at this point, it drops him below Clayton Kershaw, Roger Clemens and Tom Seaver, while keeping him ahead of Catfish Hunter, Don Sutton and Vida Blue. There's no guarantee that Darvish will continue at his current rate with the strikeouts, but it's a real shame that more people aren't having this conversation about him.

But there's a lesson in all of this, Rangers fans. Darvish worked out great. International exchanges like this are always difficult because they cost a lot of money and the returns are not guaranteed. Remember Daisuke Matsuzaka? If you find yourself feeling down and out about all the bad luck your team has been handed in the past year, you've had your moments of good fortune as well. As Cassius points out to Brutus, if you accept that you are an underling because of the stars, then you give up your claim to say that your success is your own.

Good night, good night! Parting is such sweet sorrow, that
I shall say good night till it be morrow.

—*Romeo and Juliet, Act II, Scene 2* ∎

—*Russell A. Carleton is an author at Baseball Prospectus*
and previously consulted for two MLB teams.

Player comments by Bret Sayre and Baseball Prospectus Authors

Hitters

Jorge Alfaro   C

Born: 6/11/93   Age: 22   Bats: R   Throws: R   Height: 6' 2"   Weight: 185

YEAR	TEAM	LVL	AGE	PA	R	2B	3B	HR	RBI	BB	K	SB	CS	AVG/OBP/SLG	TAv	BABIP	BRR	FRAA	WARP
2012	HIC	A	19	300	40	21	5	5	34	16	84	7	3	.261/.320/.430	.264	.355	1.2	C(29): -0.2, 1B(17): -0.0	0.8
2013	HIC	A	20	420	63	22	1	16	53	28	111	16	3	.258/.338/.452	.280	.324	-0.4	C(82): 1.4, 1B(17): -1.2	2.8
2014	MYR	A+	21	437	63	22	5	13	73	23	100	6	5	.261/.318/.440	.263	.315	-1.7	C(75): 1.6, 1B(17): 0.2	1.7
2014	FRI	AA	21	99	12	4	0	4	14	6	23	0	0	.261/.343/.443	.264	.311	0.1	C(15): 0.1, 1B(1): 0.1	0.4
2015	TEX	MLB	22	250	22	10	1	6	26	8	77	2	1	.214/.257/.341	.227	.287	-0.1	C 1, 1B -0	0.0

Breakout: 0%   Improve: 0%   Collapse: 0%   Attrition: 0%   MLB: 0%   Comparables: *Max Stassi, Luke Montz, Wilin Rosario*

If most catching prospects are Ferris wheels, Alfaro is a funhouse, but his distortions are less amusing than they are downright dangerous. Armed with two weapons-grade tools (raw power and arm strength), Alfaro offers upside rarely seen at the position, but his flaws are equally real. For all of the concerns around his plate discipline, one would expect a large variance in Alfaro's minor-league performances, but his OPS at each level since 2011 has never been lower than .751 (High-A) or higher than .826 (short-season ball), and he's reduced his strikeout rate with each promotion. For a prospect who has already attained a certain legendary status, an extended taste of the upper minors in 2015 will give us key clues about whether he'll blossom into a star or merely be a fun player to watch.

Elvis Andrus   SS

Born: 8/26/88   Age: 26   Bats: R   Throws: R   Height: 6' 0"   Weight: 200

YEAR	TEAM	LVL	AGE	PA	R	2B	3B	HR	RBI	BB	K	SB	CS	AVG/OBP/SLG	TAv	BABIP	BRR	FRAA	WARP
2012	TEX	MLB	23	711	85	31	9	3	62	57	96	21	10	.286/.349/.378	.258	.332	5.7	SS(153): 3.0	3.6
2013	TEX	MLB	24	698	91	17	4	4	67	52	97	42	8	.271/.328/.331	.251	.312	6.8	SS(146): -5.2	2.4
2014	TEX	MLB	25	685	72	35	1	2	41	46	96	27	15	.263/.314/.333	.241	.305	5.8	SS(153): -7.8	1.5
2015	TEX	MLB	26	645	75	25	4	2	42	49	88	29	11	.270/.331/.336	.257	.306	4.4	SS -2	2.7

Breakout: 4%   Improve: 51%   Collapse: 2%   Attrition: 5%   MLB: 99%   Comparables: *John Valentin, Barry Larkin, Yunel Escobar*

In the two seasons since signing his $120 million contract extension, Andrus has seen his TAv decline twice and the only two negative FRAA seasons of his career. Good thing the extension hasn't actually kicked in yet. Andrus' problems started before the season even began, as his dedication to the Rangers' offseason program was questioned and he showed up overweight in the spring. With a new manager in town, it remains to be seen whether his very old-school two-hole skills keep him chained to that spot in a league moving more toward the new school. Andrus also embodied the presumed spirit of former Texas shortstop Alex Rodriguez by registering a cool .483 OPS in close-and-late situations against an .808 OPS when the margin was five runs or more.

J.P. Arencibia   C

Born: 1/5/86   Age: 29   Bats: R   Throws: R   Height: 6' 0"   Weight: 205

YEAR	TEAM	LVL	AGE	PA	R	2B	3B	HR	RBI	BB	K	SB	CS	AVG/OBP/SLG	TAv	BABIP	BRR	FRAA	WARP
2012	TOR	MLB	26	372	45	16	0	18	56	18	108	1	0	.233/.275/.435	.250	.281	0.1	C(94): 1.0	1.5
2013	TOR	MLB	27	497	45	18	0	21	55	18	148	0	2	.194/.227/.365	.217	.231	-1.9	C(131): 0.4	-0.5
2014	ROU	AAA	28	203	31	8	0	14	41	10	53	1	0	.279/.320/.542	.291	.315	0.5	C(23): 0.6, 1B(20): 0.5	1.5
2014	TEX	MLB	28	222	20	9	0	10	35	10	62	0	0	.177/.239/.369	.228	.195	-1.8	C(22): -0.5, 1B(22): -0.9	-0.7
2015	TEX	MLB	29	294	31	12	1	13	39	15	80	1	0	.219/.265/.406	.252	.258	-0.6	C 0, 1B -0	0.6

Breakout: 5%   Improve: 40%   Collapse: 9%   Attrition: 14%   MLB: 93%   Comparables: *Jarrod Saltalamacchia, Wily Mo Pena, Eliezer Alfonzo*

The story of the 2014 Rangers can be told through side-by-side pictures of Arencibia and Prince Fielder with their respective first baseman's mitts. While demoting a catcher and bringing him back solely as a 1B/DH is a strange conceit, getting Arencibia at-bats against southpaws is not: His .840 OPS with the platoon advantage was third best on the team. Unfortunately, he received most of his at-bats against righties. When you combine a moderately lefty-mashing offensive profile with poor defense behind the plate, it's no surprise he was more valuable as a pitcher in 2014 than as either a hitter or defender.

Adrian Beltre   3B

Born: 4/7/79   Age: 36   Bats: R   Throws: R   Height: 5' 11"   Weight: 220

YEAR	TEAM	LVL	AGE	PA	R	2B	3B	HR	RBI	BB	K	SB	CS	AVG/OBP/SLG	TAv	BABIP	BRR	FRAA	WARP
2012	TEX	MLB	33	654	95	33	2	36	102	36	82	1	0	.321/.359/.561	.322	.319	0.0	3B(129): -6.2	5.7
2013	TEX	MLB	34	690	88	32	0	30	92	50	78	1	0	.315/.371/.509	.312	.322	-1.7	3B(146): -5.2	5.7
2014	TEX	MLB	35	614	79	33	1	19	77	57	74	1	1	.324/.388/.492	.320	.345	-1.5	3B(136): -5.2	4.9
2015	TEX	MLB	36	592	70	30	1	22	83	35	77	1	0	.299/.343/.481	.307	.311	-0.9	3B -0	4.1

Breakout: 1%   Improve: 29%   Collapse: 2%   Attrition: 7%   MLB: 90%   Comparables: *Aramis Ramirez, Chipper Jones, Vladimir Guerrero*

In 2014, Beltre continued to glare at the aging curve like it had just rubbed his head. Few players have been more reliably great this decade, but pegging Beltre as merely reliable—even in combination with other descriptors—undersells him. He finished 2014 with the highest TAv among third baseman, and it wasn't particularly close. In the field he shows slightly diminished range from his peak, but his actions are still smooth and the arm a weapon.

He's currently in the "underappreciated" tier in career WARP, surrounded by players like Larry Walker, Dick Allen, Buddy Bell and Edgar Martinez. One hopes post-retirement discussion about Beltre, whenever that occurs, does not include an unfortunate narrative about his move from tough hitters' environments in Los Angeles and Seattle into happier homes in Boston and Texas, because his park-adjusted stats show that his hitting isn't a mirage: Those .310-plus TAvs you see above are legit. It's the odd shape of his performance that we should be studying: From his debut at 19 through his age-30 season, Beltre accumulated a solid 34 WARP, but a quarter of that came in his massive 2004 season. In just five seasons since, he's added 28 WARP. (Other WAR calculations rate him and his defense even higher.) He's having, in other words, a Hall of Famer's decline without the typical precursor: a Hall of Famer's peak.

Engel Beltre RF

Born: 11/1/89 Age: 25 Bats: L Throws: L Height: 6' 2" Weight: 180

YEAR	TEAM	LVL	AGE	PA	R	2B	3B	HR	RBI	BB	K	SB	CS	AVG/OBP/SLG	TAv	BABIP	BRR	FRAA	WARP
2012	FRI	AA	22	614	80	17	17	13	55	26	118	36	10	.261/.307/.420	.262	.307	2.3	CF(119): 12.8, RF(2): 0.2	3.9
2012	ESP	INT	22	21	4	0	1	0	3	4	1	3	0	.375/.524/.500	.377	.400	0.0		0.0
2013	ROU	AAA	23	439	58	19	1	7	34	28	84	15	12	.292/.340/.398	.277	.351	-3.9	CF(94): 1.7	2.2
2013	TEX	MLB	23	42	7	1	0	0	2	0	5	1	2	.250/.268/.275	.227	.286	0.5	RF(6): 0.0, CF(5): 0.4	0.1
2014	ROU	AAA	24	50	2	1	0	0	2	1	7	0	0	.106/.143/.128	.086	.125	0.3	RF(10): -0.4, CF(2): -0.0	-0.9
2015	TEX	MLB	25	250	28	9	3	3	19	8	52	8	4	.244/.274/.346	.234	.291	0.4	CF 3, RF 0	0.4

Breakout: 4%   Improve: 10%   Collapse: 2%   Attrition: 14%   MLB: 20%   Comparables: Francisco Peguero, Joey Butler, James Jones

The entire organization had a season to forget, but Beltre's face-plant sits toward the top of the horrifying list. The two-time Top 101 prospect was struggling to make the 25-man roster out of spring training before a fractured right tibia sidelined him for three months. There are certainly less painful stays of execution. With the carrot of real playing time dangling in front of him due to the Rangers' never-ending supply of injuries, Beltre spat out a .315 OPS over two rehab assignments. Then, like a bookie who finally lost his patience, the 2014 season came back for Beltre's other leg. Having undergone the knife during his September stress fracture surgery, he'll face the axe if he doesn't earn a roster spot this spring, as he's out of minor league options.

Kyle Blanks 1B

Born: 9/11/86 Age: 28 Bats: R Throws: R Height: 6' 6" Weight: 265

YEAR	TEAM	LVL	AGE	PA	R	2B	3B	HR	RBI	BB	K	SB	CS	AVG/OBP/SLG	TAv	BABIP	BRR	FRAA	WARP
2012	SDN	MLB	25	6	0	0	0	0	0	1	2	0	0	.200/.333/.200	.230	.333	-0.2	LF(1): -0.0, 1B(1): -0.0	0.0
2013	TUC	AAA	26	46	8	3	0	1	4	6	10	0	0	.237/.370/.395	.271	.296	-0.5	1B(7): 0.0, LF(5): 0.2	0.2
2013	SDN	MLB	26	308	31	14	0	8	35	21	85	1	1	.243/.305/.379	.256	.317	1.5	RF(37): 2.2, LF(35): -1.2	0.7
2014	ELP	AAA	27	99	15	5	0	9	20	10	24	0	0	.265/.364/.651	.292	.250	-0.2	1B(20): 1.0, LF(3): 0.0	0.1
2014	SAC	AAA	27	28	4	0	0	1	3	6	3	0	0	.429/.536/.571	.397	.444	0.3	1B(5): -0.2, LF(1): -0.0	0.6
2014	SDN	MLB	27	10	1	0	0	0	0	0	3	0	0	.200/.200/.200	.159	.286	0.0	1B(3): 0.1, LF(1): -0.0	-0.1
2014	OAK	MLB	27	56	9	1	0	2	7	8	13	0	0	.333/.446/.489	.351	.419	-2.2	1B(17): -0.1, RF(1): -0.0	0.4
2015	TEX	MLB	28	250	27	11	1	8	31	20	68	1	0	.241/.313/.406	.273	.305	-0.2	1B 0, RF 1	0.9

Breakout: 2%   Improve: 37%   Collapse: 9%   Attrition: 22%   MLB: 77%   Comparables: Hee-Seop Choi, Josh Phelps, Casper Wells

Acquired by the A's from the Padres midseason, Blanks was a great fit due to his penchant for knocking left-handers around the yard. He was quite productive for his first month before a calf injury took him out of action for the rest of the season. An inability to stay healthy has marginalized a once-promising career, with a laundry list of injuries that include Tommy John surgery to his throwing elbow, labrum surgery to the non-throwing shoulder, a busted Achilles, torn plantar fascia and now the calf strain that slammed the brakes on his 2014. He's on a minor-league contract in Texas but could stick as a useful platoon player to give Mitch Moreland, Prince Fielder and Shin-Soo Choo breaks.

Lewis Brinson CF

Born: 5/8/94 Age: 21 Bats: R Throws: R Height: 6' 3" Weight: 170

YEAR	TEAM	LVL	AGE	PA	R	2B	3B	HR	RBI	BB	K	SB	CS	AVG/OBP/SLG	TAv	BABIP	BRR	FRAA	WARP
2013	HIC	A	19	503	64	18	2	21	52	48	191	24	7	.237/.322/.427	.268	.362	-0.1	CF(119): 4.0	2.5
2014	HIC	A	20	186	36	8	1	10	28	18	46	7	4	.335/.405/.579	.329	.413	3.0	CF(43): 3.7	3.0
2014	MYR	A+	20	199	17	8	1	3	22	15	50	5	5	.246/.307/.350	.248	.323	-0.9	CF(33): 2.8, LF(3): -0.1	0.5
2015	TEX	MLB	21	250	29	8	1	7	23	14	92	5	3	.205/.256/.336	.224	.299	-0.1	CF 2, LF -0	0.0

Breakout: 0%   Improve: 0%   Collapse: 0%   Attrition: 0%   MLB: 0%   Comparables: Michael Choice, Greg Halman, Brett Jackson

Somewhere in the shadow of Joey Gallo there lives another position player who overcame historic strikeout tendencies in 2013 to take a step toward a major-league future. Repeating the Sally League, Brinson cut his strikeout rate by 35 percent and raised his OPS by nearly 250 points before being promoted to High-A. Despite the improvement at the plate, Brinson's best attribute is likely to be his center field defense, which projects to be at least plus due to his high-end athleticism. The first-round pick from 2012 continues to be a high-risk proposition and will likely continue his slow climb by starting 2015 back at High-A.

Mike Carp 1B

Born: 6/30/86 Age: 29 Bats: L Throws: R Height: 6' 2" Weight: 210

YEAR	TEAM	LVL	AGE	PA	R	2B	3B	HR	RBI	BB	K	SB	CS	AVG/OBP/SLG	TAv	BABIP	BRR	FRAA	WARP
2012	TAC	AAA	26	154	13	8	0	2	17	12	31	1	3	.223/.286/.324	.210	.269	-0.8	1B(10): -0.2, LF(3): 0.0	-0.8
2012	SEA	MLB	26	189	17	6	0	5	20	21	46	1	0	.213/.312/.341	.242	.263	-1.2	LF(24): 1.0, 1B(23): -0.1	-0.1
2013	BOS	MLB	27	243	34	18	2	9	43	22	67	1	0	.296/.362/.523	.322	.385	-0.5	LF(41): -1.7, 1B(29): -1.0	1.6
2014	PAW	AAA	28	22	2	1	0	1	3	1	7	0	0	.238/.273/.429	.199	.308	-0.5	1B(3): -0.2, LF(2): -0.3	-0.2
2014	BOS	MLB	28	103	9	5	1	0	9	11	17	0	1	.198/.320/.279	.231	.243	-0.5	1B(20): 0.4, LF(12): -0.6	-0.3
2014	TEX	MLB	28	46	2	0	0	0	4	5	14	0	0	.125/.217/.125	.151	.185	0.6	1B(12): -0.7, LF(1): -0.0	-0.5
2015	TEX	MLB	29	250	28	11	1	9	32	20	59	1	1	.247/.313/.418	.276	.293	-0.6	1B -1, LF 0	0.7

Breakout: 5%   Improve: 22%   Collapse: 10%   Attrition: 21%   MLB: 69%   Comparables: Chris Shelton, Matt LaPorta, Travis Ishikawa

After the Red Sox acquired Yoenis Cespedes and Allen Craig, Carp became unnecessary, so they cut him on August 1st. The Rangers swooped in because they had already tried J.P. Arencibia and Carlos Pena at first base. In other words: Why not? Incredibly, Carp ended up being the worst of that trio, with a .342 OPS and zero extra-base hits. Keep an eye out, though: He's been above replacement level, with at least a .279 TAv, in every odd-numbered year of his career.

Robinson Chirinos   C

Born: 6/5/84   Age: 31   Bats: R   Throws: R   Height: 6' 1"   Weight: 205

YEAR	TEAM	LVL	AGE	PA	R	2B	3B	HR	RBI	BB	K	SB	CS	AVG/OBP/SLG	TAv	BABIP	BRR	FRAA	WARP
2013	ROU	AAA	29	311	35	10	2	8	40	38	55	2	0	.257/.356/.400	.287	.294	1.7	C(51): -0.3, 3B(10): -0.6	2.2
2013	TEX	MLB	29	30	3	3	0	0	0	2	6	0	0	.179/.233/.286	.183	.227	-0.4	1B(4): 0.0, 3B(3): 0.0	-0.2
2014	TEX	MLB	30	338	36	15	0	13	40	17	71	0	1	.239/.290/.415	.267	.265	-0.3	C(91): 1.1	2.2
2015	TEX	MLB	31	293	29	12	1	7	30	21	63	1	0	.234/.299/.359	.252	.279	-0.1	C 0, 3B -0	0.9

Breakout: 1%   Improve: 13%   Collapse: 19%   Attrition: 29%   MLB: 59%   Comparables: Robby Hammock, Chris Gimenez, Koyie Hill

The 30-year-old late bloomer (and late catcher) was a forgettable piece of the Matt Garza-to-the-Cubs trade before becoming the first player ever to be traded from Tampa Bay to Texas. Chirinos, who has one of those names built for a pun-laced fantasy team, began the season third on the depth chart behind the plate, but found plenty of playing time due to Geovany Soto's lack of health and J.P. Arencibia's lack of baseball skills. In fact, Chirinos wound up putting together a season not unlike what was expected from the man whose job he took (good power, low OBP), with the huge exception of his above-average defense. Jon Daniels came out early in the offseason in support of Chirinos as the full-time catcher in 2015, but his leash is not likely to be long and he'll be brushed aside soon enough if Jorge Alfaro is who scouts think he is.

Michael Choice   LF

Born: 11/10/89   Age: 25   Bats: R   Throws: R   Height: 6' 0"   Weight: 215

YEAR	TEAM	LVL	AGE	PA	R	2B	3B	HR	RBI	BB	K	SB	CS	AVG/OBP/SLG	TAv	BABIP	BRR	FRAA	WARP
2012	MID	AA	22	402	59	15	2	10	58	33	88	5	1	.287/.356/.423	.282	.352	1.7	CF(85): -7.9	1.2
2013	SAC	AAA	23	600	90	29	1	14	89	69	115	1	2	.302/.390/.445	.303	.358	-4.9	LF(55): -4.5, CF(52): -2.5	3.0
2013	OAK	MLB	23	19	2	1	0	0	0	1	6	0	0	.278/.316/.333	.294	.417	0.0	RF(4): 0.1, LF(2): -0.0	0.1
2014	ROU	AAA	24	182	25	8	0	7	31	23	47	2	1	.267/.379/.460	.284	.333	2.4	LF(22): -0.2, RF(12): -0.2	1.0
2014	TEX	MLB	24	280	20	6	1	9	36	21	69	1	0	.182/.250/.320	.216	.208	-1.5	LF(41): 0.6, RF(17): 0.0	-1.1
2015	TEX	MLB	25	310	31	11	1	8	34	24	75	1	0	.241/.310/.372	.260	.297	-0.9	LF -1, CF -1	0.3

Breakout: 15%   Improve: 35%   Collapse: 12%   Attrition: 32%   MLB: 69%   Comparables: Brandon Jones, Shin-Soo Choo, Caleb Gindl

The never-ending string of injuries in Texas should have been welcome news for Choice, but it ended up exposing his weaknesses and leaving fans longing for the smooth stylings of Craig Gentry. Though you can squint and strain and make feeble noises about how his .138 isolated power wasn't bad, all things considered, Choice's issues might run deep: When a prospect posts double-digit walk percentages in the minor leagues, it's generally accepted as a good thing, but as we've learned with Aaron Hicks and others, sometimes it's more a result of passivity and minor-league pitchers' inability to consistently throw strikes than it is about true selectivity. Choice will have to prove his low swing rate (42 percent in 2014) was a feature, not a bug, as he fights for playing time again in 2015.

Shin-Soo Choo   LF

Born: 7/13/82   Age: 32   Bats: L   Throws: L   Height: 5' 11"   Weight: 205

YEAR	TEAM	LVL	AGE	PA	R	2B	3B	HR	RBI	BB	K	SB	CS	AVG/OBP/SLG	TAv	BABIP	BRR	FRAA	WARP
2012	CLE	MLB	29	686	88	43	2	16	67	73	150	21	7	.283/.373/.441	.293	.353	-0.2	RF(154): 0.2	3.7
2013	CIN	MLB	30	712	107	34	2	21	54	112	133	20	11	.285/.423/.462	.318	.338	1.1	CF(150): -4.5, LF(3): -0.1	6.3
2014	TEX	MLB	31	529	58	19	1	13	40	58	131	3	4	.242/.340/.374	.267	.308	0.3	LF(64): -6.8, RF(12): 0.5	0.5
2015	TEX	MLB	32	533	72	23	2	12	52	63	115	11	6	.264/.366/.403	.291	.326	0.0	CF -2, RF -0	2.3

Breakout: 0%   Improve: 28%   Collapse: 3%   Attrition: 4%   MLB: 98%   Comparables: Carl Yastrzemski, Brian Giles, Chipper Jones

When the Rangers spent $130 million on Choo as a free agent last winter, it was surely with full knowledge of the risk that he'd only play 129 games in 2014. No one was ever going to confuse him for Cal Ripken. (Choo has 70-grade hair.) But Jon Daniels was certainly hoping for more than an average offensive player who gave back most of his value on defense. Choo's biggest shortcoming in 2014 had previously been his biggest strength: hitting with the platoon advantage. The .732 OPS he posted against right-handers was not only a near-300 point drop from 2013, it was the worst of his career. Choo will set out to prove that his contract is not one of the worst in baseball in 2015, but with his speed and defense hurtling toward oblivion, that will have to manifest itself in a batters-box bounce back.

Travis Demeritte   2B

Born: 9/30/94   Age: 20   Bats: R   Throws: R   Height: 6' 0"   Weight: 178

YEAR	TEAM	LVL	AGE	PA	R	2B	3B	HR	RBI	BB	K	SB	CS	AVG/OBP/SLG	TAv	BABIP	BRR	FRAA	WARP
2014	HIC	A	19	466	77	16	2	25	66	50	171	7	2	.211/.310/.450	.262	.286	1.6	2B(92): 4.2, 3B(12): -0.3	1.9
2015	TEX	MLB	20	250	24	6	1	9	29	19	101	0	0	.180/.252/.335	.221	.266	-0.3	2B 1, 3B -0	0.0

Breakout: 0%   Improve: 0%   Collapse: 0%   Attrition: 0%   MLB: 0%   Comparables: Mike Carp, Domingo Santana, Travis Denker

Yawn, just another first-round pick who racked up homers and strikeouts in Hickory. In fact, Demeritte finished his full-season debut with essentially the same walk-strikeout profile as Joey Gallo's 2013 performance at the level, though he also came up 13 bombs short. The Georgia prep product's power is not the result of size or strength, but the torque that generates his plus bat speed and the backspin he pairs with it. Defensively, he's a work in progress, as the Rangers have been giving him reps at both second and third. He's unlikely to develop into a Gold Glover anywhere, but has enough arm to stick at the hot corner and the footwork to play at the keystone.

Delino DeShields   2B

Born: 8/16/92   Age: 22   Bats: R   Throws: R   Height: 5' 9"   Weight: 210

YEAR	TEAM	LVL	AGE	PA	R	2B	3B	HR	RBI	BB	K	SB	CS	AVG/OBP/SLG	TAv	BABIP	BRR	FRAA	WARP
2012	LEX	A	19	523	96	22	5	10	52	70	108	83	14	.298/.401/.439	.296	.373	7.3	2B(108): -8.3	3.4
2012	LNC	A+	19	114	17	2	3	2	9	13	23	18	5	.237/.336/.381	.244	.288	2.0	2B(24): -2.8	0.0
2013	LNC	A+	20	534	100	25	14	5	54	57	91	51	18	.317/.405/.468	.296	.387	7.1	2B(107): -9.5	3.4
2014	CCH	AA	21	507	75	14	2	11	57	61	112	54	14	.236/.346/.360	.268	.293	8.7	CF(78): -2.0, LF(29): -0.9	2.3
2015	TEX	MLB	22	250	34	8	2	3	16	22	62	21	5	.230/.307/.319	.238	.293	2.3	2B -3, CF -1	0.0

Breakout: 0%   Improve: 0%   Collapse: 0%   Attrition: 0%   MLB: 0%   Comparables: Andrew McCutchen, Desmond Jennings, Ryan Kalish

DeShields Senior—Dad, if you will—hit .250/.376/.379 while posting a 21 percent strikeout rate and averaging 0.4 stolen bases per game over his minor-league career. DeShields Junior—Son—has hit .267/.362/.396 with a 20 percent strikeout rate while swiping 0.5 bags per game in the Astros system. Son had his issues in Double-A—his contact rate slipped and too many fly balls led to weak BABIP—but this is the same tremendous athlete who swiped 101 bags back in 2012, when he challenged Billy Hamilton for the crown. The Rangers took him in the Rule 5 draft and he could stick as a utility type with starter upside; he has the tools and burgeoning skills to be a major leaguer. If he winds up back with the Astros, he might have to settle for being one of baseball's most gifted fourth outfielders.

Prince Fielder   1B

Born: 5/9/84   Age: 31   Bats: L   Throws: R   Height: 5' 11"   Weight: 275

YEAR	TEAM	LVL	AGE	PA	R	2B	3B	HR	RBI	BB	K	SB	CS	AVG/OBP/SLG	TAv	BABIP	BRR	FRAA	WARP
2012	DET	MLB	28	690	83	33	1	30	108	85	84	1	0	.313/.412/.528	.321	.321	-8.0	1B(159): 0.8	4.4
2013	DET	MLB	29	712	82	36	0	25	106	75	117	1	1	.279/.362/.457	.297	.307	-5.5	1B(151): -6.4	2.4
2014	TEX	MLB	30	178	19	8	0	3	16	25	24	0	0	.247/.360/.360	.256	.274	-1.2	1B(39): -1.8	-0.3
2015	TEX	MLB	31	274	35	12	0	10	37	35	44	0	0	.274/.378/.457	.311	.297	-2.1	1B -1	1.3

Breakout: 1%   Improve: 39%   Collapse: 4%   Attrition: 7%   MLB: 99%   *Comparables: Nick Johnson, Frank Thomas, Edwin Encarnacion*

First they came for the left-handed pitchers, and I did not speak out because I was not a left-handed pitcher. Then they came for Fielder, the man who had missed only one game over the past five seasons. The slugger was limited to just 42 games in 2014 due to a herniated disc in his neck that required cervical fusion surgery in May. While his sidelining was surprising, what he did on the field before the injury was slightly less so: His on-base and slugging percentages both continued their four-year decline, the latter settling nearly 100 points below his previous career low despite the moderate bump you'd expect moving from Comerica to Globe Life Park. For an offense-only player in his 30s with $144 million remaining on his contract, this is as unsettling as watching Nolan Ryan slaughter, grind and pack his own meat products. Fielder should be fully recovered by spring training and looking to replicate the path of Peyton Manning, who returned from a similar procedure to his previous glory.

Joey Gallo   3B

Born: 11/19/93   Age: 21   Bats: L   Throws: R   Height: 6' 5"   Weight: 205

YEAR	TEAM	LVL	AGE	PA	R	2B	3B	HR	RBI	BB	K	SB	CS	AVG/OBP/SLG	TAv	BABIP	BRR	FRAA	WARP
2012	SPO	A-	18	67	9	2	0	4	9	11	26	0	0	.214/.343/.464	.292	.308	-0.9	3B(16): 1.6	0.5
2013	HIC	A	19	446	82	19	5	38	78	48	165	14	1	.245/.334/.610	.316	.305	3.1	3B(100): -3.6	3.7
2014	MYR	A+	20	246	53	9	3	21	50	51	64	5	3	.323/.463/.735	.390	.370	1.0	3B(54): 3.5	4.9
2014	FRI	AA	20	291	44	10	0	21	56	36	115	2	0	.232/.334/.524	.297	.322	-1.3	3B(53): 1.0, 1B(7): -0.0	1.8
2015	TEX	MLB	21	250	35	7	1	17	43	26	98	1	0	.218/.303/.488	.288	.289	-0.1	3B 0, 1B -0	1.3

Breakout: 5%   Improve: 24%   Collapse: 8%   Attrition: 7%   MLB: 40%   *Comparables: Giancarlo Stanton, Javier Baez, Domingo Santana*

Gallo in the minors has thus far been akin to Maximus at the Colosseum. The thunder in the Las Vegas native's bat is as real as it gets, with some scouts not only pegging him for the best raw power in the minors today, but the best they've ever seen. Defensively, he has plus-plus arm strength and, despite playing seven games at first base toward the end of the season, there is no current need to move him off third from a talent standpoint. From a depth chart perspective, however, with Adrian Beltre under contract for one more season Gallo will need to find another spot (right field and first base are the most likely options) if he's going to force the Rangers' hand in 2015. Most importantly, given just how hard hitting baseballs in the majors is, Gallo's work ethic and aptitude for the game receive constant praise.

Leonys Martin   CF

Born: 3/6/88   Age: 27   Bats: L   Throws: R   Height: 6' 2"   Weight: 190

YEAR	TEAM	LVL	AGE	PA	R	2B	3B	HR	RBI	BB	K	SB	CS	AVG/OBP/SLG	TAv	BABIP	BRR	FRAA	WARP
2012	ROU	AAA	24	260	48	18	2	12	42	24	39	10	9	.359/.422/.610	.351	.392	2.1	CF(46): 2.9, LF(8): -0.6	3.9
2012	TEX	MLB	24	52	6	5	2	0	6	4	12	3	0	.174/.235/.370	.191	.229	-0.2	CF(14): 0.4, LF(4): 0.3	-0.2
2013	TEX	MLB	25	508	66	21	6	8	49	28	104	36	9	.260/.313/.385	.256	.319	4.1	CF(127): 4.2, RF(21): -0.4	2.5
2014	TEX	MLB	26	583	68	13	7	7	40	39	114	31	12	.274/.325/.364	.259	.336	4.3	CF(152): 8.8	4.2
2015	TEX	MLB	27	533	64	21	5	8	47	33	101	29	10	.265/.317/.381	.261	.312	2.0	CF 5, RF -0	2.3

Breakout: 9%   Improve: 38%   Collapse: 5%   Attrition: 15%   MLB: 93%   *Comparables: Franklin Gutierrez, Peter Bourjos, Cameron Maybin*

With two major-league seasons under his belt, Martin hasn't quite hit as well as hoped considering his minor-league track record, but he has been a great $15.5 million investment for the Rangers. Without the flashy tools of higher-profile Cuban signings, Martin has built his value and reputation on strong center field defense and baserunning skills. In fact, he's played at a near-All-Star level against right-handed pitching, which serves to indict his career .575 OPS against southpaws more than anything else. The 26-year-old, who was named after Lionel Richie, has certainly been more Stuck On You than Endless Love to this point, but he's a good bet to continue Running With the Ni—[This author has now been located and moved to a safe house]

Nomar Mazara   RF

Born: 4/26/95   Age: 20   Bats: L   Throws: L   Height: 6' 4"   Weight: 195

YEAR	TEAM	LVL	AGE	PA	R	2B	3B	HR	RBI	BB	K	SB	CS	AVG/OBP/SLG	TAv	BABIP	BRR	FRAA	WARP
2013	HIC	A	18	506	48	23	2	13	62	44	131	1	2	.236/.310/.382	.254	.301	-2.5	RF(114): -4.7	0.4
2014	HIC	A	19	461	68	21	2	19	73	57	99	4	3	.264/.358/.470	.291	.304	-3.5	RF(91): -11.2	0.9
2014	FRI	AA	19	97	10	7	1	3	16	9	22	0	0	.306/.381/.518	.305	.377	-3.1	RF(23): -0.7	0.1
2015	TEX	MLB	20	250	22	9	1	6	26	18	74	0	0	.210/.270/.336	.231	.277	-0.4	RF -4	-0.8

Breakout: 0%   Improve: 0%   Collapse: 0%   Attrition: 0%   MLB: 0%   *Comparables: Caleb Gindl, Chris Parmelee, Travis Snider*

It was somewhat surprising to see Mazara start the 2014 season back at Hickory, repeating the level, but that was less surprising than the Rangers giving him a two-level jump in August. Maybe Mazara really hates Myrtle Beach? The last time the organization skipped a teenage prospect over the Carolina League, it was Jurickson Profar, which gives some insight into what the organization thinks of the young outfielder. Everything Mazara does on the field is done with ease, and the power that earned him his record $5 million bonus is no exception.

Mitch Moreland   DH

Born: 9/6/85   Age: 29   Bats: L   Throws: L   Height: 6' 2"   Weight: 230

YEAR	TEAM	LVL	AGE	PA	R	2B	3B	HR	RBI	BB	K	SB	CS	AVG/OBP/SLG	TAv	BABIP	BRR	FRAA	WARP
2012	TEX	MLB	26	357	41	18	0	15	50	23	71	1	1	.275/.321/.468	.271	.306	-1.9	1B(95): 7.1, RF(3): 0.1	1.6
2013	TEX	MLB	27	518	60	24	1	23	60	45	117	0	0	.232/.299/.437	.269	.255	-2.1	1B(146): 3.4, RF(1): -0.0	1.2
2014	TEX	MLB	28	184	18	9	1	2	23	12	43	0	0	.246/.297/.347	.237	.315	-0.9	1B(22): -0.7, LF(2): 0.0	-0.4
2015	TEX	MLB	29	250	27	11	1	7	29	20	52	0	0	.248/.311/.404	.268	.285	-0.9	1B 0, LF 0	0.4

Breakout: 6%   Improve: 43%   Collapse: 10%   Attrition: 11%   MLB: 94%   *Comparables:*   *Ben Broussard, Ty Wigginton, Ryan Garko*

Coming off a career-high 23 homers, Moreland's power fell off a cliff in 2014, as only Jake Peavy and R.A. Dickey watched him circle the bases before an ankle injury in June ended his season. While he's expected to be at full strength by spring training, the power outage is a concern because he doesn't do enough else to add value if he's not popping a dinger every 25 plate appearances. In fact, with Prince Fielder at first base, Moreland is unlikely to see much of the field at all as he looks to reprise his role of designated hitter against right-handed pitching. With Joey Gallo steaming up hard behind him, Moreland will have to put a strong hold on that spot if he wants to stay on the roster at all.

Rougned Odor   2B

Born: 2/3/94   Age: 21   Bats: L   Throws: R   Height: 5' 11"   Weight: 170

YEAR	TEAM	LVL	AGE	PA	R	2B	3B	HR	RBI	BB	K	SB	CS	AVG/OBP/SLG	TAv	BABIP	BRR	FRAA	WARP
2012	HIC	A	18	471	60	23	4	10	47	25	65	19	10	.259/.313/.400	.263	.284	0.8	2B(85): 0.9, SS(15): -0.7	1.6
2013	MYR	A+	19	425	65	33	4	5	59	26	67	27	8	.305/.369/.454	.293	.355	1.4	2B(84): 4.3	3.6
2013	FRI	AA	19	144	20	8	2	6	19	9	24	5	2	.306/.354/.530	.314	.337	-0.4	2B(30): 2.5	1.6
2014	FRI	AA	20	138	21	2	1	6	17	7	22	6	3	.279/.314/.450	.266	.294	0.0	2B(31): 2.7	0.8
2014	TEX	MLB	20	417	39	14	7	9	48	17	71	4	7	.259/.297/.402	.254	.294	1.6	2B(110): -0.4	1.3
2015	TEX	MLB	21	397	40	17	4	8	41	13	76	8	5	.253/.285/.381	.252	.291	1.1	2B 3, SS -0	1.4

Breakout: 6%   Improve: 24%   Collapse: 3%   Attrition: 12%   MLB: 33%   *Comparables:*   *Ryan Zimmerman, Brett Lawrie, Kolten Wong*

The 2014 season was supposed to be one of continued minor-league development for the 20-year-old Venezuelan infielder, but the Rangers got aggressive when Jurickson Profar went down in May. Odor stuck the whole season and showed glimpses of what made him the top prospect in the Rangers' system heading into the year. Many of the descriptors used on Odor—scrappy, plucky—are, for better or worse, affiliated with players who are lacking in talent, but don't let that fool you: He is a talented and supremely confident player, capable of hitting for a high average with surprising pop and above-average defense at the keystone. He's the kind of player Mariners, A's, Astros and Angels fans will grow to despise, yet respect.

Jurickson Profar   2B

Born: 2/20/93   Age: 22   Bats: B   Throws: R   Height: 6' 0"   Weight: 165

YEAR	TEAM	LVL	AGE	PA	R	2B	3B	HR	RBI	BB	K	SB	CS	AVG/OBP/SLG	TAv	BABIP	BRR	FRAA	WARP
2012	FRI	AA	19	562	76	26	7	14	62	66	79	16	4	.281/.368/.452	.299	.306	-0.8	SS(97): -8.9, 2B(25): -1.8	3.3
2012	TEX	MLB	19	17	2	2	0	1	2	0	4	0	0	.176/.176/.471	.202	.167	-0.4	2B(5): -0.2, SS(3): -0.1	-0.2
2013	ROU	AAA	20	166	27	7	2	4	19	21	24	6	1	.278/.370/.438	.289	.310	1.5	SS(30): 0.6, 2B(7): -0.6	1.3
2013	TEX	MLB	20	324	30	11	0	6	26	26	63	2	4	.234/.308/.336	.248	.280	-0.8	2B(32): -2.2, SS(18): 0.1	0.2
2015	TEX	MLB	22	250	29	11	2	5	23	21	44	4	2	.250/.317/.375	.263	.285	-0.1	SS -1, 2B -2	0.6

Breakout: 6%   Improve: 41%   Collapse: 8%   Attrition: 19%   MLB: 65%   *Comparables:*   *Melky Cabrera, Ruben Tejada, Troy Tulowitzki*

For all of the injuries and disappointing performance Profar has been associated with thus far, he'll still arrive at camp this spring at just 21, though that makes him the older of the two players aiming for the starting job at second base. Middle infield remains a position of strength for the Rangers, but the former no. 1 prospect in baseball has been the prize of that group for years. The culprit during 2014 was a teres major tear in his shoulder, which was aggravated more often than William Foster (the fictional character, not the pioneering cinematographer who died of syphilis, probably) and kept him sidelined for all of 2014. After receiving a PRP injection in late September, causing him to miss the Arizona Fall League, Profar expects to be 100 percent by spring training, but it's hard to rely on this being behind him until he's on the field for an extended period of time.

Alex Rios   RF

Born: 2/18/81   Age: 34   Bats: R   Throws: R   Height: 6' 5"   Weight: 210

YEAR	TEAM	LVL	AGE	PA	R	2B	3B	HR	RBI	BB	K	SB	CS	AVG/OBP/SLG	TAv	BABIP	BRR	FRAA	WARP
2012	CHA	MLB	31	640	93	37	8	25	91	26	92	23	6	.304/.334/.516	.292	.323	5.8	RF(156): 14.3	5.2
2013	CHA	MLB	32	465	57	22	2	12	55	32	78	26	6	.277/.328/.421	.267	.314	3.0	RF(108): 3.2	2.1
2013	TEX	MLB	32	197	26	11	2	6	26	9	30	16	1	.280/.315/.457	.276	.305	2.1	RF(47): 2.2, CF(1): -0.0	1.2
2014	TEX	MLB	33	521	54	30	8	4	54	23	93	17	9	.280/.311/.398	.254	.335	-2.5	RF(114): 5.4	0.4
2015	TEX	MLB	34	517	57	25	4	10	52	23	84	21	6	.264/.299/.391	.259	.299	1.4	RF 7	1.7

Breakout: 0%   Improve: 24%   Collapse: 13%   Attrition: 19%   MLB: 91%   *Comparables:*   *Randy Winn, Emil Brown, Moises Alou*

It seemed like a foregone conclusion at the outset of 2014 that the Rangers would pick up Rios' $13.5 million option for 2015, but after a season that saw his power disappear, the team reversed course and moved on. An Alex Rios stat line is like a foreign-language movie with no subtitles: It looks like something you should appreciate, but you can't make any sense of it. At the very least, there should be some level of confidence that he won't be able to maintain an Elvis Andrus-like 3 percent homer-per-fly rate, although that would still double up Nori Aoki, the man he'll be replacing in the Royals outfield.

Adam Rosales 1B

Born: 5/20/83 Age: 32 Bats: R Throws: R Height: 6' 1" Weight: 195

YEAR	TEAM	LVL	AGE	PA	R	2B	3B	HR	RBI	BB	K	SB	CS	AVG/OBP/SLG	TAv	BABIP	BRR	FRAA	WARP
2012	SAC	AAA	29	310	46	21	1	8	47	26	57	4	2	.280/.340/.451	.286	.319	0.9	SS(57): -2.1, 2B(13): 3.0	2.7
2012	OAK	MLB	29	111	12	5	0	2	8	11	24	0	0	.222/.297/.333	.234	.270	-0.9	2B(21): -2.0, SS(11): 0.0	-0.2
2013	SAC	AAA	30	42	4	2	0	0	6	3	7	1	1	.211/.262/.263	.218	.250	-0.3	SS(7): -0.3, 2B(1): 0.1	0.0
2013	OAK	MLB	30	154	11	5	0	4	8	10	31	0	0	.191/.267/.316	.223	.218	0.0	SS(36): 5.0, 2B(13): 0.6	0.5
2013	TEX	MLB	30	12	4	0	0	1	4	0	3	0	0	.182/.167/.455	.311	.125	0.5	1B(4): 0.1, SS(3): 0.0	0.1
2014	ROU	AAA	31	307	42	16	3	7	43	28	61	3	0	.276/.349/.434	.277	.329	0.5	3B(50): 1.5, 1B(15): 0.2	1.6
2014	TEX	MLB	31	181	20	7	0	4	19	13	42	4	2	.262/.328/.378	.272	.331	0.4	1B(32): 2.6, 3B(7): -0.1	0.9
2015	TEX	MLB	32	250	24	10	1	5	23	16	57	2	1	.234/.289/.346	.247	.285	0.1	SS 0, 1B 1	0.5

Breakout: 3% Improve: 24% Collapse: 8% Attrition: 25% MLB: 64% *Comparables: Mark Teahen, Brendan Harris, Keith Ginter*

After bouncing between Oakland and Texas more often than American Airlines Flight 2433 in 2013, Rosales finally got settled in Round Rock last year before making Arlington his summer home. Sure, it may have been horribly depressing injuries to the first string that got him extended playing time, but the utilityman made the most of it early on, securing Rangers' Player of the Month honors in August by hitting a cool .352/.417/.537 during the month. As is often the case when a career backup has a little success in the spotlight, Rosales then got bad fast. His September .536 OPS was especially sad because he spent most of the month as the starting first baseman. If he's anything more than the last man on the bench in 2015, something will have gone terribly wrong. Again.

Ryan Rua 3B

Born: 3/11/90 Age: 25 Bats: R Throws: R Height: 6' 2" Weight: 205

YEAR	TEAM	LVL	AGE	PA	R	2B	3B	HR	RBI	BB	K	SB	CS	AVG/OBP/SLG	TAv	BABIP	BRR	FRAA	WARP
2012	SPO	A-	22	320	40	16	1	7	43	29	64	4	1	.293/.368/.432	.302	.354	0.6	3B(38): -4.5, 1B(14): 0.6	1.9
2013	HIC	A	23	430	70	24	1	29	82	49	91	13	2	.251/.356/.559	.332	.253	0.3	2B(87): 3.3, 3B(8): -0.8	4.9
2013	FRI	AA	23	95	19	2	1	3	9	7	24	1	0	.233/.305/.384	.244	.288	0.8	3B(23): -2.2	-0.1
2014	FRI	AA	24	288	34	13	1	10	38	30	55	5	3	.300/.375/.475	.300	.349	-0.7	3B(50): -3.2, 1B(6): -0.1	1.4
2014	ROU	AAA	24	241	31	13	2	8	36	21	42	1	2	.313/.382/.505	.308	.355	-1.2	3B(27): -0.3, LF(24): -1.9	1.5
2014	TEX	MLB	24	109	11	7	0	2	14	2	18	1	0	.295/.321/.419	.269	.341	0.9	LF(17): -1.2, 1B(9): 0.5	0.2
2015	TEX	MLB	25	250	27	11	1	8	30	17	58	2	1	.250/.307/.406	.270	.298	-0.3	3B -2, 2B 0	0.5

Breakout: 10% Improve: 31% Collapse: 15% Attrition: 39% MLB: 69% *Comparables: Kevin Kouzmanoff, Zach Lutz, Adam Duvall*

A nominal prospect before landing smack in the middle of the power display put on by the Hickory Crawdads in 2013, Rua continued his climb toward age-appropriate levels before ending up in Texas for an extended cup of coffee last summer. When a prospect plays four positions in the upper minors it's for one of two reasons: He's either being prepped for a bench role where versatility is key or the team is trying to find a workable way to get his bat in the big-league lineup. No one watching Rua on defense will believe it's the former, but his power *is* a carrying tool. With nowhere to play on a healthy Rangers squad, he'll likely start 2015 back in Round Rock, but he should be one of the first bats called upon if injury strikes.

Luis Sardinas 2B

Born: 5/16/93 Age: 22 Bats: B Throws: R Height: 6' 1" Weight: 150

YEAR	TEAM	LVL	AGE	PA	R	2B	3B	HR	RBI	BB	K	SB	CS	AVG/OBP/SLG	TAv	BABIP	BRR	FRAA	WARP
2012	HIC	A	19	412	65	14	2	2	30	29	52	32	9	.291/.346/.356	.259	.331	3.7	SS(76): 2.4, 2B(14): -0.5	2.1
2013	MYR	A+	20	432	69	15	3	1	31	32	54	27	8	.298/.358/.360	.261	.339	3.9	SS(92): -3.6, 2B(1): -0.1	2.0
2013	FRI	AA	20	141	12	4	0	1	15	4	21	5	2	.259/.286/.311	.225	.301	-1.7	SS(29): 0.9	0.0
2014	FRI	AA	21	90	12	5	1	0	9	3	12	1	1	.253/.278/.333	.239	.293	1.7	SS(20): -1.2, 2B(1): 0.0	0.2
2014	ROU	AAA	21	273	39	15	2	1	28	12	39	9	4	.290/.310/.374	.236	.336	-0.9	SS(60): 1.3	0.4
2014	TEX	MLB	21	125	12	6	0	0	8	5	21	5	1	.261/.303/.313	.228	.319	0.7	2B(19): -2.3, SS(13): 0.7	0.0
2015	TEX	MLB	22	250	24	10	1	0	15	7	44	8	3	.246/.271/.300	.220	.295	0.4	SS 0, 2B -1	-0.1

Breakout: 5% Improve: 17% Collapse: 5% Attrition: 18% MLB: 28% *Comparables: Joaquin Arias, Freddy Galvis, Jose Iglesias*

Just another in a never-ending parade of Latin shortstops that continues to climb out of the clown car known as the Rangers' development system, Sardinas was pressed into major-league action for parts of the 2014 season. Unfortunately, it didn't agree with him in the short term, but the plus defensive shortstop should return to Triple-A to start 2015. He'll look to either force his way into the Rangers' plans or force his exit from the organization as a strong trade chip. If he lives up to his potential, he could be a large fraction of Elvis Andrus at a very small fraction of the cost.

Nick Williams LF

Born: 9/8/93 Age: 21 Bats: L Throws: L Height: 6' 3" Weight: 195

YEAR	TEAM	LVL	AGE	PA	R	2B	3B	HR	RBI	BB	K	SB	CS	AVG/OBP/SLG	TAv	BABIP	BRR	FRAA	WARP
2013	HIC	A	19	404	70	19	12	17	60	15	110	8	5	.293/.337/.543	.303	.371	-0.4	LF(73): -3.7, CF(8): -1.8	2.3
2014	MYR	A+	20	408	61	28	4	13	68	19	117	5	7	.292/.343/.491	.281	.391	-1.4	LF(44): -0.4, CF(25): -2.2	1.6
2014	FRI	AA	20	64	4	2	1	0	4	2	21	1	1	.226/.250/.290	.201	.341	0.1	LF(11): -0.4, CF(4): -0.1	-0.3
2015	TEX	MLB	21	250	22	10	2	6	27	5	83	2	2	.226/.252/.360	.228	.313	-0.2	LF -1, CF -1	-0.7

Breakout: 0% Improve: 0% Collapse: 0% Attrition: 0% MLB: 0% *Comparables: Chris Davis, Marcell Ozuna, Greg Halman*

Usually when an outfield prospect enters pro ball raw, it's because he's more of an athlete than a hitter, someone who can run down balls in center and make strong throws but can't hit to save his life. Williams is something of an exception. An inconsistent outfielder at best, he will not be an option in center and will have to rely on his bat to carry the weight of his potential. Fortunately, he's a naturally gifted hitter with the Adam Jones starter kit at the plate. Unfortunately, the instructions are in Aramaic, the pages are out of order and his go-go-go approach isn't conducive to remedying those problems. After a successful Arizona Fall League campaign, Williams will return to Frisco in 2015 and match wits and bat speed against a group of opposing pitchers with vastly better secondary stuff than he's seen so far.

Pitchers

Scott Baker RHP
Born: 9/19/81 Age: 33 Bats: R Throws: R Height: 6'4" Weight: 215

YEAR	TEAM	LVL	AGE	W	L	SV	G	GS	IP	H	HR	BB	K	BB/9	K/9	GB%	BABIP	WHIP	ERA	FIP	FRA	WARP
2013	KNC	A	31	1	2	0	6	6	23¹	29	4	8	14	3.1	5.4	36%	.325	1.59	6.17	5.40	6.74	-0.1
2013	CHN	MLB	31	0	0	0	3	3	15	9	3	4	6	2.4	3.6	30%	.136	0.87	3.60	5.62	7.05	-0.2
2014	ROU	AAA	32	4	1	0	6	6	38	35	5	11	30	2.6	7.1	38%	.280	1.21	3.32	4.86	5.03	0.3
2014	TEX	MLB	32	3	4	0	25	8	80²	82	15	14	55	1.6	6.1	26%	.272	1.19	5.47	4.81	5.15	-0.1
2015	TEX	MLB	33	4	5	0	20	14	88¹	90	12	21	71	2.2	7.2	35%	.296	1.26	4.12	4.54	4.48	0.5

Breakout: 13% Improve: 38% Collapse: 15% Attrition: 14% MLB: 76% Comparables: Bruce Chen, Jeff Weaver, Brett Tomko

In this installment of "Really, He's Still a Major-League Pitcher?" Baker made just three starts between 2012 and 2013 (mostly due to Tommy John surgery), but surfaced for the Rangers last season because, well, let's face it, who didn't? Baker stayed true to his Minnesota form by limiting walks and groundballs (he was one of only two pitchers with a fly-ball rate over 50 percent in at least 70 innings), but losing nearly two mph off his fastball really hurt his bottom line.

Daniel Bard RHP
Born: 6/25/85 Age: 30 Bats: R Throws: R Height: 6'4" Weight: 215

YEAR	TEAM	LVL	AGE	W	L	SV	G	GS	IP	H	HR	BB	K	BB/9	K/9	GB%	BABIP	WHIP	ERA	FIP	FRA	WARP
2012	PAW	AAA	27	3	2	0	31	1	32	31	2	29	32	8.2	9.0	56%	.322	1.88	7.03	5.63	6.78	-0.7
2012	BOS	MLB	27	5	6	0	17	10	59¹	60	9	43	38	6.5	5.8	45%	.285	1.74	6.22	6.32	6.93	-0.6
2013	PME	AA	28	0	1	0	13	0	12²	13	1	17	6	12.1	4.3	51%	.300	2.37	6.39	7.43	8.70	-0.4
2013	BOS	MLB	28	0	0	0	2	0	1	1	0	2	1	18.0	9.0	33%	.333	3.00	9.00	7.08	10.69	-0.1
2015	TEX	MLB	30	2	1	1	26	2	34	30	3	19	31	4.9	8.1	48%	.281	1.43	4.12	4.85	4.48	0.2

Breakout: 21% Improve: 44% Collapse: 19% Attrition: 14% MLB: 72% Comparables: Brian Bruney, J.C. Romero, Manny Delcarmen

In four games in the Sally League, Bard recorded two outs, walked nine batters and hit seven with pitches. (He allowed no hits, though he did get one of those two outs on a batted ball, which is probably a story in itself.) Much is made of the wonder of batters standing in against 90 mph pitches, but most professional pitchers know to a reasonable degree where the ball is going; Bard's lack of control is as dangerous as it is mystifying and sad.

Lisalverto Bonilla RHP
Born: 6/18/90 Age: 25 Bats: B Throws: R Height: 6'0" Weight: 175

YEAR	TEAM	LVL	AGE	W	L	SV	G	GS	IP	H	HR	BB	K	BB/9	K/9	GB%	BABIP	WHIP	ERA	FIP	FRA	WARP
2012	CLR	A+	22	1	1	1	10	0	13¹	9	0	4	18	2.7	12.1	48%	.290	0.98	1.35	1.59	2.22	0.5
2012	REA	AA	22	2	1	3	21	0	33	22	1	17	46	4.6	12.5	42%	.309	1.18	1.64	2.44	2.38	1.1
2013	FRI	AA	23	2	0	6	21	0	30¹	16	0	9	50	2.7	14.8	55%	.286	0.82	0.30	0.85	1.44	1.3
2013	ROU	AAA	23	5	5	0	26	2	43	52	8	24	56	5.0	11.7	54%	.376	1.77	7.95	5.13	4.77	0.4
2014	ROU	AAA	24	4	2	1	39	6	74²	73	9	25	92	3.0	11.1	41%	.337	1.31	4.10	3.85	4.00	1.6
2014	TEX	MLB	24	3	0	0	5	3	20²	13	2	12	17	5.2	7.4	42%	.216	1.21	3.05	4.66	4.35	0.1
2015	TEX	MLB	25	3	3	1	36	6	77¹	74	8	32	77	3.7	9.0	47%	.306	1.37	4.09	4.27	4.44	0.4

Breakout: 25% Improve: 34% Collapse: 8% Attrition: 23% MLB: 46% Comparables: Ernesto Frieri, Jordan Norberto, Harvey Garcia

Yet another relief prospect who the Rangers wedged into the rotation in a pinch, Bonilla started more major-league games in 2014 than minor-league games in 2012-2013. Because baseball remains baseball, he won each of his three September starts, allowing just four earned runs total. His profile does not support a rotation projection in the long run, though, as below-average control and the lack of a quality breaking pitch are limiting factors. The Rangers sent Bonilla to the AFL to continue working as a starter, so he might get a chance to compete for the no. 5 spot this spring.

Neal Cotts LHP
Born: 3/25/80 Age: 35 Bats: L Throws: L Height: 6'1" Weight: 200

YEAR	TEAM	LVL	AGE	W	L	SV	G	GS	IP	H	HR	BB	K	BB/9	K/9	GB%	BABIP	WHIP	ERA	FIP	FRA	WARP
2012	ROU	AAA	32	2	1	3	25	0	31²	32	2	15	41	4.3	11.7	40%	.361	1.48	4.55	3.41	1.78	1.6
2013	ROU	AAA	33	3	1	2	15	0	23	13	1	5	42	2.0	16.4	54%	.353	0.78	0.78	1.13	1.37	1.0
2013	TEX	MLB	33	8	3	1	58	0	57	36	2	18	65	2.8	10.3	46%	.246	0.95	1.11	2.20	2.50	1.4
2014	TEX	MLB	34	2	9	2	73	0	66²	66	6	23	63	3.1	8.5	36%	.314	1.34	4.32	3.61	3.51	0.8
2015	TEX	MLB	35	3	1	2	58	0	60²	52	4	20	67	2.9	9.9	42%	.302	1.19	3.03	3.24	3.29	1.1

Breakout: 22% Improve: 37% Collapse: 24% Attrition: 18% MLB: 73% Comparables: Joe Borowski, Tyler Walker, Joe Nelson

When Cotts buys a car, it's either a Maserati or a used Kia. When he plays golf, he's all eagles and double bogies. He has a sprawling estate on Nantucket but spends most of his time in a tumbledown shack in Fresno. You get the gist. In his nine major-league seasons, the left-handed veteran has twice posted an ERA under 2.00 and the other seven times finished at 4.29 or higher. Unsurprisingly for a reliever who developed under the tutelage of Don Cooper, Cotts heavily features a cutter, which is part of the reason he maintains a career reverse OPS split of 50 points. He doesn't throw his slider much anymore, but he hasn't allowed an extra-base hit to a left-handed batter on the pitch since Prince Fielder doubled off him the week after Lehman Brothers went under.

Yu Darvish RHP
Born: 8/16/86 Age: 28 Bats: R Throws: R Height: 6'5" Weight: 215

YEAR	TEAM	LVL	AGE	W	L	SV	G	GS	IP	H	HR	BB	K	BB/9	K/9	GB%	BABIP	WHIP	ERA	FIP	FRA	WARP
2012	TEX	MLB	25	16	9	0	29	29	191¹	156	14	89	221	4.2	10.4	48%	.295	1.28	3.90	3.24	3.77	3.1
2013	TEX	MLB	26	13	9	0	32	32	209²	145	26	80	277	3.4	11.9	42%	.264	1.07	2.83	3.30	3.78	3.2
2014	TEX	MLB	27	10	7	0	22	22	144¹	133	13	49	182	3.1	11.3	37%	.334	1.26	3.06	2.87	2.91	3.8
2015	TEX	MLB	28	8	6	0	19	19	135²	108	11	49	167	3.3	11.1	42%	.297	1.16	2.94	3.29	3.20	2.7

Breakout: 19% Improve: 47% Collapse: 31% Attrition: 13% MLB: 98% Comparables: Rich Harden, Tim Lincecum, Jake Peavy

Another year for Darvish means enough wind power generated to keep Globe Life Park lit up all summer long. It also means another silly controversy. The flavor of the month for those looking to tear down the 28-year-old ace was his supposed unwillingness to rush back from an elbow injury to lead a last-place squad through September. While his elbow let him down from mid-August on, the defense behind him had been managing that feat all season long: The Rangers were a bottom-five team in defensive efficiency, which obviously made a strong contribution to Darvish's .334 BABIP. On the other hand, Darvish continued to improve his control, as his walk rate hit a career-low 8 percent. In a vacuum, that's an okay figure, not an ace figure, except that Darvish's strikeout rate looks more like a back-end reliever's than a 200-inning starter's: Over 2012-2014 (i.e. Darvish's time in MLB), he leads all starters with a 30 percent strikeout rate, and that's without setting any innings or games-started minimum on the query.

Darvish's array of offerings is as dizzying for a PITCHf/x analyst as it is for a hitter (Brooks Baseball counts no fewer than *eight*). He had kicked his slider usage up above 30 percent in 2013, dropped back to 2012 levels (about half that) early in 2014, then jumped back up to the high 20s in his seven starts before his injury. Now, pitches cannot simply be taken out of their arsenal and sequential contexts, but Darvish's slider was such a beast in 2013 that its re-disappearance early last year was akin to Gallagher shrugging, "You know what, too many watermelons." Slider or no, Darvish's health will play a huge role in determining whether the Rangers can return to contention a year after finishing with the worst record in the American League.

Ross Detwiler   LHP

Born: 3/6/86   Age: 29   Bats: R   Throws: L   Height: 6'5"   Weight: 210

YEAR	TEAM	LVL	AGE	W	L	SV	G	GS	IP	H	HR	BB	K	BB/9	K/9	GB%	BABIP	WHIP	ERA	FIP	FRA	WARP
2012	WAS	MLB	26	10	8	0	33	27	164^1	149	15	52	105	2.8	5.8	52%	.263	1.22	3.40	4.09	4.82	0.5
2013	WAS	MLB	27	2	7	0	13	13	71^1	92	5	14	39	1.8	4.9	48%	.344	1.49	4.04	3.64	3.79	0.8
2014	WAS	MLB	28	2	3	1	47	0	63	68	5	21	39	3.0	5.6	47%	.309	1.41	4.00	4.13	4.75	0.1
2015	TEX	MLB	29	3	3	0	15	8	54^2	60	5	17	32	2.8	5.4	49%	.301	1.40	4.56	4.70	4.95	0.0

Breakout: 38%   Improve: 51%   Collapse: 17%   Attrition: 16%   MLB: 80%   Comparables: Sergio Mitre, Roberto Hernandez, Jason Vargas

Life's just a little bit harder for the southpaw drafted three picks before Madison Bumgarner, and after losing Washington's fifth starter job in the spring to Tanner Roark, Detwiler went without making a start for the first time in his career. In the bullpen, he continued his fastball-heavy ways, as he combined to throw his four- and two-seamers more than 85 percent of the time for the second season in a row. The left-hander was a high-quality LOOGY when required, giving up only one extra-base hit to that population all season. Unfortunately, Detwiler also played the role against right-handers, getting hit around to the tune of an .848 OPS, and he was left off the Nats' postseason roster. In the end, it was a blah season for a blah reliever, and the Rangers added him in December in a blah trade.

Neftali Feliz   RHP

Born: 5/2/88   Age: 27   Bats: R   Throws: R   Height: 6'3"   Weight: 225

YEAR	TEAM	LVL	AGE	W	L	SV	G	GS	IP	H	HR	BB	K	BB/9	K/9	GB%	BABIP	WHIP	ERA	FIP	FRA	WARP
2012	TEX	MLB	24	3	1	0	8	7	42^2	28	5	23	37	4.9	7.8	38%	.213	1.20	3.16	4.59	5.78	0.1
2013	TEX	MLB	25	0	0	0	6	0	4^2	5	0	2	4	3.9	7.7	29%	.357	1.50	0.00	3.29	4.30	0.0
2014	ROU	AAA	26	1	1	7	24	0	28^2	19	6	8	31	2.5	9.7	30%	.203	0.94	3.14	5.20	5.75	0.1
2014	TEX	MLB	26	2	1	13	30	0	31^2	20	5	11	21	3.1	6.0	29%	.176	0.98	1.99	4.93	5.17	-0.2
2015	TEX	MLB	27	2	1	6	32	3	42^1	33	4	16	41	3.3	8.7	37%	.266	1.16	2.92	4.12	3.17	0.9

Breakout: 26%   Improve: 47%   Collapse: 25%   Attrition: 10%   MLB: 91%   Comparables: Kyle McClellan, Joe Smith, Byung-Hyun Kim

Having made just 14 appearances in the prior two seasons, Feliz came into 2014 with something to prove; during the first three months of the season, he either completely failed to prove it or had a different idea of what he was trying to prove than the rest of us. After losing a battle for a roster spot in the spring, he didn't even get his first Triple-A save until June. When he arrived in Texas at the outset of July, he was a wisp of a shell of his diminished self. In three of his first six outings, he did not even reach 93 mph with his fastball, a stark change from the pitcher who averaged 91 with his *changeup* in July 2011. But a funny thing happened on the way to irrelevance: Feliz got better. He stopped allowing home runs. He started throwing harder (96 mph fastball in September). The old Neftali had returned. The Rangers, who have no obvious internal alternative to close games, will be hoping he's back for good.

Kyuji Fujikawa   RHP

Born: 7/21/80   Age: 33   Bats: L   Throws: R   Height: 6'0"   Weight: 190

YEAR	TEAM	LVL	AGE	W	L	SV	G	GS	IP	H	HR	BB	K	BB/9	K/9	GB%	BABIP	WHIP	ERA	FIP	FRA	WARP
2012	HNS	NPB	30	2	2	24	48	0	47^2	34	1	15	58	2.8	10.9	–	.300	1.03	1.32	–	–	–
2013	CHN	MLB	32	1	1	2	12	0	12	11	1	2	14	1.5	10.5	50%	.323	1.08	5.25	2.77	3.69	0.1
2014	CHN	MLB	33	0	0	0	15	0	13	18	2	6	17	4.2	11.8	46%	.432	1.85	4.85	4.33	3.71	0.1
2015	TEX	MLB	34	2	1	1	33	0	35^2	34	3	11	35	2.7	8.8	45%	.307	1.25	3.69	3.75	4.01	0.3

Breakout: 21%   Improve: 31%   Collapse: 24%   Attrition: 6%   MLB: 65%   Comparables: Brendan Donnelly, Justin Miller, Trever Miller

With 25 big-league innings to his name and a Tommy John surgery sandwiched in between, it isn't clear whether Fujikawa can survive as a major-league reliever. He has shown the ability to strike out hitters at a solid clip, but he'll need to regain his pre-surgery command and the zip on his fastball to take the late-inning role he was once expected to fill.

Chi Chi Gonzalez   RHP

Born: 1/15/92   Age: 23   Bats: R   Throws: R   Height: 6'2"   Weight: 195

YEAR	TEAM	LVL	AGE	W	L	SV	G	GS	IP	H	HR	BB	K	BB/9	K/9	GB%	BABIP	WHIP	ERA	FIP	FRA	WARP
2013	SPO	A-	21	0	4	0	9	9	23^2	30	1	7	20	2.7	7.6	69%	.382	1.56	4.56	3.19	3.77	0.6
2013	MYR	A+	21	0	0	0	5	5	19	15	1	9	15	4.3	7.1	59%	.264	1.26	2.84	3.88	5.59	0.1
2014	MYR	A+	22	5	2	0	11	11	65^1	56	3	16	49	2.2	6.8	55%	.262	1.10	2.62	3.62	4.13	0.8
2014	FRI	AA	22	7	4	0	15	14	73^1	67	3	25	64	3.1	7.9	55%	.300	1.25	2.70	3.09	4.22	1.0
2015	TEX	MLB	23	5	8	0	22	22	100^1	108	9	37	65	3.3	5.8	52%	.302	1.44	4.62	4.71	5.02	0.2

Breakout: 0%   Improve: 0%   Collapse: 0%   Attrition: 0%   MLB: 0%   Comparables: Robbie Ross, Jarred Cosart, Bobby Livingston

It's fitting that the prospect who continued to chug along like the Little Engine That Could would be nicknamed "Chi Chi." Rodriguez didn't lose his stride at all while moving from High-A to Double-A midseason, allowing more than two earned runs only three times in 15 starts at his new level. There's no top-of-the-rotation projection here, and in this era of high strikeout totals and extreme velocity, it's not surprising that Gonzalez has flown under the radar. However, he features a three-way fastball (he can both cut and sink it) as well as a slider and change that could each be plus pitches. Add a repeatable delivery and a body built to log innings and you've got the whole set for a valuable no. 3 starter.

Matt Harrison   LHP

Born: 9/16/85   Age: 29   Bats: L   Throws: L   Height: 6'4"   Weight: 240

YEAR	TEAM	LVL	AGE	W	L	SV	G	GS	IP	H	HR	BB	K	BB/9	K/9	GB%	BABIP	WHIP	ERA	FIP	FRA	WARP
2012	TEX	MLB	26	18	11	0	32	32	213¹	210	22	59	133	2.5	5.6	50%	.284	1.26	3.29	3.98	4.63	1.5
2013	TEX	MLB	27	0	2	0	2	2	10²	14	2	7	12	5.9	10.1	47%	.400	1.97	8.44	5.23	5.71	0.0
2014	FRI	AA	28	1	0	0	3	3	16	12	0	4	10	2.2	5.6	49%	.245	1.00	1.69	2.62	3.62	0.2
2014	TEX	MLB	28	1	1	0	4	4	17¹	20	1	12	10	6.2	5.2	51%	.317	1.85	4.15	5.01	5.05	0.0
2015	TEX	MLB	29	2	2	0	6	6	35²	36	3	11	24	2.8	6.0	48%	.294	1.32	3.92	4.32	4.26	0.3

Breakout: 21%   Improve: 41%   Collapse: 21%   Attrition: 11%   MLB: 90%   Comparables: *John Danks, Mark Mulder, Anibal Sanchez*

It's hard enough for a pitcher to come back from either thoracic outlet syndrome surgery or spinal fusion surgery; Harrison is trying to navigate with both in his rear view. The left-hander has been anything but sharp in the meager 28 innings he's thrown for the Rangers over the last two seasons, dealing with both diminished velocity (he averaged only 91 mph in 2014, a far cry from his 93-94 mark in 2012) and dissolving control. The future is as unknown for Harrison as it's been for any pitcher in the last decade, and the Rangers still owe him at least $41 million through 2017, spanning the second half of his "team-friendly" contract.

Derek Holland   LHP

Born: 10/9/86   Age: 28   Bats: B   Throws: L   Height: 6'2"   Weight: 210

YEAR	TEAM	LVL	AGE	W	L	SV	G	GS	IP	H	HR	BB	K	BB/9	K/9	GB%	BABIP	WHIP	ERA	FIP	FRA	WARP
2012	TEX	MLB	25	12	7	0	29	27	175¹	162	32	52	145	2.7	7.4	44%	.261	1.22	4.67	4.71	5.50	0.1
2013	TEX	MLB	26	10	9	0	33	33	213	210	20	64	189	2.7	8.0	43%	.307	1.29	3.42	3.46	3.99	2.4
2014	ROU	AAA	27	2	1	0	4	4	15¹	20	5	8	19	4.7	11.2	52%	.349	1.83	5.87	7.03	7.38	-0.2
2014	TEX	MLB	27	2	0	0	6	5	37	34	0	5	25	1.2	6.1	42%	.296	1.05	1.46	2.21	2.35	1.1
2015	TEX	MLB	28	4	4	0	12	12	73²	71	8	21	63	2.6	7.7	44%	.294	1.25	3.77	4.19	4.10	0.7

Breakout: 24%   Improve: 55%   Collapse: 17%   Attrition: 10%   MLB: 87%   Comparables: *Matt Garza, James Shields, John Lackey*

The southpaw with the 20-grade mustache kicked off the Rangers of Sadness parade in January 2014 when he injured his left knee in an accident involving his dog and a staircase, requiring microfracture surgery. (In retrospect, it seems obvious that no non-Cub should name his pet "Wrigley.") An All-Star break target return date became August and August became September 2nd before Holland finally made his 2014 debut. What happened from that point on may not necessarily be predictive, but it was incredible: In one month, he became the Rangers' third-most-valuable pitcher for the entire season (1. Yu Darvish; 2. Joakim Soria) by slicing his previous career-best walk rate in half and declining to surrender even a single homer. Holland actually had the *lowest* strike percentage of his career, hitting the zone just two out of every five times, but he got hitters to chase at a rate significantly higher than in previous seasons by peppering the target just off the low, glove-side corner. Sample-size issues abound, but if Holland continues to trade strikeouts for weak contact in 2015, he could be setting himself up for a career year.

Luke Jackson   RHP

Born: 8/24/91   Age: 23   Bats: R   Throws: R   Height: 6'2"   Weight: 205

YEAR	TEAM	LVL	AGE	W	L	SV	G	GS	IP	H	HR	BB	K	BB/9	K/9	GB%	BABIP	WHIP	ERA	FIP	FRA	WARP
2012	HIC	A	20	5	5	0	13	13	64	63	4	33	72	4.6	10.1	48%	.347	1.50	4.92	3.92	4.50	1.3
2012	MYR	A+	20	5	2	0	13	13	65²	67	2	32	74	4.4	10.1	42%	.376	1.51	4.39	3.17	4.04	0.8
2013	MYR	A+	21	9	4	0	19	19	101	79	6	47	104	4.2	9.3	48%	.284	1.25	2.41	3.55	4.22	1.6
2013	FRI	AA	21	2	0	0	6	4	27	13	0	12	30	4.0	10.0	48%	.213	0.93	0.67	2.17	2.58	0.7
2014	FRI	AA	22	8	2	1	15	14	83¹	58	5	24	83	2.6	9.0	44%	.242	0.98	3.02	2.92	3.24	1.7
2014	ROU	AAA	22	1	3	0	11	10	40	56	9	28	43	6.3	9.7	45%	.395	2.10	10.35	6.72	8.20	-0.7
2015	TEX	MLB	23	5	8	0	21	21	102	105	11	53	88	4.6	7.7	43%	.307	1.54	4.92	4.98	5.35	-0.3

Breakout: 0%   Improve: 0%   Collapse: 0%   Attrition: 0%   MLB: 0%   Comparables: *Chris Withrow, Scott Barnes, Jered Weaver*

After ten weeks of continuing his impressive run against Double-A batters to start the season, Jackson looked so lost at Triple-A that he needed a GPS to find the dugout between innings. In 11 starts at Round Rock, not only did he have a double-digit ERA, he saw the sixth inning only once. There's plenty to like about the right-hander from a velocity standpoint, but he continues to battle command issues with his fastball and has still not developed a real put-away breaking pitch. Jackson will likely return to Triple-A, where he'll continue trying to prove he can cut it as a starting pitcher.

Corey Knebel   RHP

Born: 11/26/91   Age: 23   Bats: R   Throws: R   Height: 6'3"   Weight: 195

YEAR	TEAM	LVL	AGE	W	L	SV	G	GS	IP	H	HR	BB	K	BB/9	K/9	GB%	BABIP	WHIP	ERA	FIP	FRA	WARP
2013	WMI	A	21	2	1	15	31	0	31	14	0	10	41	2.9	11.9	56%	.212	0.77	0.87	1.66	2.69	0.8
2014	ERI	AA	22	3	0	1	11	0	15	8	1	8	23	4.8	13.8	53%	.241	1.07	1.20	2.75	2.65	0.5
2014	ROU	AAA	22	1	0	0	9	0	12	9	2	5	20	3.8	15.0	42%	.318	1.17	3.75	4.03	3.70	0.3
2014	TOL	AAA	22	1	1	2	14	0	18¹	6	0	9	20	4.4	9.8	55%	.158	0.82	1.96	2.98	3.86	0.3
2014	DET	MLB	22	0	0	0	8	0	8²	11	0	3	11	3.1	11.4	56%	.440	1.62	6.23	1.66	3.07	0.2
2015	TEX	MLB	23	2	1	0	36	0	41²	33	3	17	50	3.7	10.7	48%	.297	1.21	3.09	3.41	3.35	0.7

Breakout: 18%   Improve: 20%   Collapse: 12%   Attrition: 20%   MLB: 35%   Comparables: *Eduardo Sanchez, Stephen Pryor, Bruce Rondon*

Half of the package the Rangers received from Detroit for Joakim Soria, the hard-throwing Texan (stop me if you've heard that before) has the potential to fire two plus-plus pitches, his fastball and curve, in a high-leverage bullpen role. Health willing, he could do that as soon as this season. Of course that's anything but a given considering Knebel was shut down in mid-August with the harbinger of doom that is a UCL sprain, though surgery is not currently planned and his rehabilitation progress has been encouraging. The raw skills are there for Knebel to choose his own entrance music. And no matter what, his place in baseball history is secure: He was selected with the first MLB draft pick to be included in a trade.

Colby Lewis   RHP

Born: 8/2/79   Age: 35   Bats: R   Throws: R   Height: 6'4"   Weight: 240

YEAR	TEAM	LVL	AGE	W	L	SV	G	GS	IP	H	HR	BB	K	BB/9	K/9	GB%	BABIP	WHIP	ERA	FIP	FRA	WARP
2012	TEX	MLB	32	6	6	0	16	16	105	99	16	14	93	1.2	8.0	34%	.279	1.08	3.43	3.83	3.82	2.0
2013	FRI	AA	33	0	1	0	5	5	18	23	4	4	15	2.0	7.5	37%	.328	1.50	7.00	4.95	5.29	0.0
2014	TEX	MLB	34	10	14	0	29	29	170¹	211	25	48	133	2.5	7.0	35%	.339	1.52	5.18	4.49	4.79	0.2
2015	TEX	MLB	35	7	8	0	22	22	133¹	136	17	35	115	2.4	7.7	36%	.299	1.28	4.19	4.42	4.56	0.6

Breakout: 10%   Improve: 35%   Collapse: 14%   Attrition: 12%   MLB: 81%   Comparables: *Ted Lilly, Bartolo Colon, Aaron Harang*

After the right-hander had two surgeries in 2013 and failed to pitch in the majors, the Rangers were just hoping for him to eat innings should they need them. And boy did they need them. Lewis gorged himself on plateful after plateful, faithfully taking his turn in the rotation and his lumps on the mound in a lost season. If you look at Lewis' two halves, you can talk yourself into him as a major-league starter: His 3.86 ERA in the second half is absolutely playable. The problem is that no study has found split-halves analysis to result in better projections than taking all the data into account, and all the data (plus Lewis being 35) add up to "ehhhhhh."

Nick Martinez   LHP

Born: 8/5/90   Age: 24   Bats: L   Throws: R   Height: 6'1"   Weight: 175

YEAR	TEAM	LVL	AGE	W	L	SV	G	GS	IP	H	HR	BB	K	BB/9	K/9	GB%	BABIP	WHIP	ERA	FIP	FRA	WARP
2013	MYR	A+	22	10	7	0	22	21	119¹	106	5	38	105	2.9	7.9	54%	.294	1.21	2.87	3.27	4.49	1.6
2013	FRI	AA	22	2	0	0	5	4	32	11	1	7	23	2.0	6.5	49%	.123	0.56	1.12	2.68	3.73	0.4
2014	TEX	MLB	23	5	12	0	29	24	140¹	150	18	55	77	3.5	4.9	35%	.289	1.46	4.55	4.97	5.03	0.1
2015	TEX	MLB	24	6	8	0	28	22	128	135	13	48	79	3.4	5.6	43%	.295	1.43	4.62	4.92	5.02	0.0

Breakout: 25%   Improve: 53%   Collapse: 21%   Attrition: 31%   MLB: 85%   Comparables: *Matt Harrison, Casey Coleman, Ryan Feierabend*

The first Fordham product to play in the majors since the eminently useful and forgettable Pete Harnisch, Martinez was equally useful and forgettable in his first major-league season. In a perfect world, he could have spent all of 2014 in the upper minors, preparing to compete for a back-end rotation spot in 2015, but after just six starts at Double-A, this is what ended up being in Martinez's instruction manual for the season: Fill in for Darvish, go to Triple-A, fill in for Scheppers, go to the bullpen, fill in for Perez, throw as many innings as you can, please. The 24-year-old won't miss many bats or keep the ball on the ground, but in the second half his home run and walk rates dropped, leading to a 4.05 ERA that's tolerably mediocre. In the end, 2014 was still preparation for the 2015 rotation spot, but presented as a crash course rather than gentle introduction.

Miles Mikolas   RHP

Born: 8/23/88   Age: 26   Bats: R   Throws: R   Height: 6'5"   Weight: 220

YEAR	TEAM	LVL	AGE	W	L	SV	G	GS	IP	H	HR	BB	K	BB/9	K/9	GB%	BABIP	WHIP	ERA	FIP	FRA	WARP
2012	SAN	AA	23	1	1	4	12	0	12¹	16	0	3	11	2.2	8.0	46%	.410	1.54	2.92	2.23	3.14	0.3
2012	TUC	AAA	23	2	1	0	17	0	19²	20	1	8	17	3.7	7.8	52%	.311	1.42	3.20	3.82	3.81	0.5
2012	SDN	MLB	23	2	1	0	25	0	32¹	32	4	15	23	4.2	6.4	55%	.280	1.45	3.62	4.90	6.28	-0.5
2013	TUC	AAA	24	4	2	26	54	0	61	62	6	17	40	2.5	5.9	51%	.287	1.30	3.25	4.37	4.88	0.5
2013	SDN	MLB	24	0	0	0	2	0	1²	0	0	1	1	5.4	5.4	0%	.000	0.60	0.00	5.42	5.40	0.0
2014	ROU	AAA	25	5	1	2	16	6	44²	53	3	3	38	0.6	7.7	49%	.342	1.25	3.22	3.07	3.80	1.1
2014	TEX	MLB	25	2	5	0	10	10	57¹	64	8	18	38	2.8	6.0	40%	.299	1.43	6.44	4.80	4.71	0.1
2015	TEX	MLB	26	4	3	1	54	4	82²	87	8	23	56	2.5	6.1	48%	.299	1.33	4.14	4.42	4.50	0.4

Breakout: 33%   Improve: 46%   Collapse: 14%   Attrition: 21%   MLB: 71%   Comparables: *Cory Wade, Alberto Arias, Aaron Loup*

On the bright side, Mikolas made 10 starts and posted his lowest major-league FIP in 2014. On the other side, everything else. He was one of just five pitchers to make double-digit starts with at least a 6.00 ERA, alongside Andre Rienzo, Edwin Jackson, Robbie Ross and Jacob Turner. Of course, coming off his best start on August 25th (eight shutout innings against Seattle), Mikolas was shut down with shoulder fatigue. He'll probably never pitch well enough to make people forget he ate a live lizard during an Arizona Fall League game in 2011. To be fair, even Clayton Kershaw couldn't pitch that well. He's headed off to the Yomiuri Giants along with Aaron Poreda.

Alexi Ogando   RHP

Born: 10/5/83   Age: 31   Bats: R   Throws: R   Height: 6'4"   Weight: 200

YEAR	TEAM	LVL	AGE	W	L	SV	G	GS	IP	H	HR	BB	K	BB/9	K/9	GB%	BABIP	WHIP	ERA	FIP	FRA	WARP
2012	TEX	MLB	28	2	0	3	58	1	66	49	9	17	66	2.3	9.0	39%	.237	1.00	3.27	3.68	4.22	0.7
2013	ROU	AAA	29	0	1	0	3	3	13	12	4	4	4	2.8	2.8	38%	.186	1.23	6.23	7.88	9.47	-0.4
2013	TEX	MLB	29	7	4	0	23	18	104¹	87	11	41	72	3.5	6.2	43%	.254	1.23	3.11	4.39	4.60	0.6
2014	TEX	MLB	30	2	3	1	27	0	25	33	1	15	22	5.4	7.9	37%	.386	1.92	6.84	3.84	4.53	0.1
2015	TEX	MLB	31	2	2	0	15	6	40	36	3	12	33	2.8	7.3	40%	.278	1.20	3.27	3.91	3.56	0.7

Breakout: 16%   Improve: 45%   Collapse: 20%   Attrition: 17%   MLB: 84%   Comparables: *Brian Duensing, Ryan Dempster, Scott Feldman*

A 2014 return to the bullpen for Ogando didn't bring back the velocity he lost in 2013, when his fastball dropped around 3 mph. And despite the big spike in walk rate, he probably didn't deserve the .386 BABIP or 63 percent strand rate that contributed to his inflated ERA. The big right-hander was heavily used at the outset of the season, appearing in 17 of the Rangers' first 30 games. A month later, he was sidelined with right-elbow inflammation and disappeared into the abyss known as the Rangers' 60-day disabled list. (Seriously, have they checked there for Jimmy Hoffa?) Ogando was non-tendered and hadn't signed anywhere before we sent this book to press.

Luis Ortiz   RHP

Born: 9/22/95   Age: 19   Bats: R   Throws: R   Height: 6'3"   Weight: 230

The Rangers' first-round pick in 2014, Ortiz is a high-upside arm who fell in the draft due to concerns about forearm tightness that cropped up last spring and weight issues that dogged him during his high school career. The right-hander features a low-to-mid-90s fastball and a sharp slider that both currently project as plus pitches. If his delivery looks slightly familiar, it's because he modeled it after Felix Hernandez, which will surely in no way create unrealistic expectations. The Rangers will likely be aggressive with Ortiz and start him out in Low-A, where he impressed in short bursts during a brief August stay.

Martin Perez   LHP

Born: 4/4/91   Age: 24   Bats: L   Throws: L   Height: 6'0"   Weight: 190

YEAR	TEAM	LVL	AGE	W	L	SV	G	GS	IP	H	HR	BB	K	BB/9	K/9	GB%	BABIP	WHIP	ERA	FIP	FRA	WARP
2012	ROU	AAA	21	7	6	0	22	21	127	122	10	56	69	4.0	4.9	52%	.277	1.40	4.25	5.02	5.44	0.4
2012	TEX	MLB	21	1	4	0	12	6	38	47	3	15	25	3.6	5.9	50%	.333	1.63	5.45	4.10	4.23	0.4
2013	ROU	AAA	22	5	1	0	6	6	36	29	1	8	28	2.0	7.0	59%	.280	1.03	1.75	3.21	3.26	0.8
2013	TEX	MLB	22	10	6	0	20	20	124¹	129	15	37	84	2.7	6.1	49%	.292	1.34	3.62	4.26	4.54	1.0
2014	TEX	MLB	23	4	3	0	8	8	51¹	50	3	19	35	3.3	6.1	53%	.315	1.34	4.38	3.72	4.43	0.4
2015	*TEX*	*MLB*	*24*	*3*	*4*	*0*	*10*	*10*	*58²*	*62*	*5*	*21*	*41*	*3.3*	*6.2*	*50%*	*.304*	*1.43*	*4.47*	*4.46*	*4.86*	*0.1*

Breakout: 22%   Improve: 55%   Collapse: 19%   Attrition: 28%   MLB: 86%   Comparables: *Vin Mazzaro, Alex White, Sean West*

A former top prospect whose stock seemed to be in perpetual decline since he turned heads as an 18-year-old at Low-A in 2009, Perez was all set to build off his strong 2013 campaign before the Rangers' curse struck. Despite making only eight starts on the season, Perez was the only pitcher in 2014 to throw three consecutive games of at least eight scoreless innings. Of course, the domination that implies doesn't quite bear out in reality as the left-hander showed diminished velocity right out of the gate, and it only got worse as his season went on. As it turns out, concerns were warranted: After undergoing Tommy John surgery on May 19th, Perez is not expected back until at least two months into the 2015 season. He remains a good bet to outperform the very team-friendly contract that could keep him in Texas through 2020, but see Matt Harrison for an example of how these contracts can go south.

Aaron Poreda   LHP

Born: 10/1/86   Age: 28   Bats: L   Throws: L   Height: 6'6"   Weight: 240

YEAR	TEAM	LVL	AGE	W	L	SV	G	GS	IP	H	HR	BB	K	BB/9	K/9	GB%	BABIP	WHIP	ERA	FIP	FRA	WARP
2012	ALT	AA	25	2	0	0	3	3	16	12	0	11	11	6.2	6.2	54%	.261	1.44	2.25	4.08	5.49	-0.1
2014	ROU	AAA	27	0	1	3	16	0	16¹	21	0	7	28	3.9	15.4	56%	.488	1.71	6.06	1.92	1.63	0.9
2014	TEX	MLB	27	2	1	0	26	0	21¹	30	2	7	21	3.0	8.9	47%	.424	1.73	5.91	3.53	3.61	0.3
2015	*TEX*	*MLB*	*28*	*1*	*1*	*0*	*23*	*1*	*32²*	*30*	*2*	*23*	*31*	*6.3*	*8.6*	*50%*	*.305*	*1.63*	*4.78*	*4.78*	*5.19*	*-0.1*

Breakout: 19%   Improve: 21%   Collapse: 8%   Attrition: 16%   MLB: 32%   Comparables: *Kevin Barry, Anthony Varvaro, Leyson Septimo*

Five years removed from his last taste of the majors, and two years removed from *any* action after Tommy John surgery, the most notable prospect in the 2009 Jake Peavy trade finally resurfaced throwing smoke. In fact, he had the third-highest fastball velocity among southpaws in 2014, clocking in at 96.5 mph, behind only Aroldis Chapman and Jake McGee. Poreda's FIP may point toward utility ahead in the Rangers' bullpen, but a bout of tendinitis got him shut down in late July. "Expected to be fully healthy for spring training, Poreda gives Texas another potentially exciting high-leverage option" is what we would have said except that the team sold his contract to the Yomiuri Giants.

Robbie Ross   LHP

Born: 6/24/89   Age: 26   Bats: L   Throws: L   Height: 5'11"   Weight: 215

YEAR	TEAM	LVL	AGE	W	L	SV	G	GS	IP	H	HR	BB	K	BB/9	K/9	GB%	BABIP	WHIP	ERA	FIP	FRA	WARP
2012	TEX	MLB	23	6	0	0	58	0	65	55	3	23	47	3.2	6.5	63%	.274	1.20	2.22	3.35	4.11	0.8
2013	TEX	MLB	24	4	2	0	65	0	62¹	63	4	19	58	2.7	8.4	45%	.326	1.32	3.03	3.20	3.57	0.9
2014	ROU	AAA	25	5	4	0	12	9	60¹	66	7	16	43	2.4	6.4	58%	.319	1.36	4.33	4.73	5.69	0.2
2014	TEX	MLB	25	3	6	0	27	12	78¹	103	9	30	51	3.4	5.9	54%	.352	1.70	6.20	4.77	5.34	-0.2
2015	*TEX*	*MLB*	*26*	*6*	*5*	*0*	*49*	*12*	*110¹*	*117*	*9*	*35*	*75*	*2.9*	*6.1*	*54%*	*.307*	*1.38*	*4.27*	*4.38*	*4.64*	*0.4*

Breakout: 45%   Improve: 73%   Collapse: 13%   Attrition: 18%   MLB: 94%   Comparables: *Joe Kelly, Jeanmar Gomez, Garrett Richards*

Of all the players summoned to fill the Rangers' rotation in 2014, Ross had both the best major-league track record (albeit in the bullpen) and the best prospect pedigree. So, naturally, he was bad as a starter and even worse (7.85 ERA in 18 innings) in relief. Power and strikeouts have never been part of his game, so Ross has to channel the man he shares a name with and paint the strike zone. A more complete arsenal would have helped, but he struggled to integrate all his pitches, including his happy little two-seamer and his fluffy curve. On the bright side, he will likely return to a relief role in 2015, and he's still never given up a hit on his change (though he'll have to use it more than 90 times for that fun fact to be impressive). Here's to fewer mistakes from Ross and more happy accidents.

Tanner Scheppers   RHP

Born: 1/17/87   Age: 28   Bats: R   Throws: R   Height: 6'4"   Weight: 200

YEAR	TEAM	LVL	AGE	W	L	SV	G	GS	IP	H	HR	BB	K	BB/9	K/9	GB%	BABIP	WHIP	ERA	FIP	FRA	WARP
2012	ROU	AAA	25	1	2	11	27	0	31	30	2	4	31	1.2	9.0	39%	.322	1.10	3.48	3.18	3.71	0.6
2012	TEX	MLB	25	1	1	1	39	0	32¹	47	6	9	30	2.5	8.4	44%	.390	1.73	4.45	4.62	4.47	0.3
2013	TEX	MLB	26	6	2	1	76	0	76²	58	6	24	59	2.8	6.9	51%	.252	1.07	1.88	3.77	3.86	0.8
2014	TEX	MLB	27	0	1	0	8	4	23	31	6	10	17	3.9	6.7	54%	.333	1.78	9.00	6.77	8.25	-0.7
2015	*TEX*	*MLB*	*28*	*2*	*1*	*0*	*30*	*1*	*35*	*35*	*3*	*11*	*30*	*2.9*	*7.8*	*45%*	*.306*	*1.32*	*4.02*	*4.15*	*4.37*	*0.2*

Breakout: 29%   Improve: 47%   Collapse: 13%   Attrition: 21%   MLB: 73%   Comparables: *Shawn Kelley, Brandon Medders, Yhency Brazoban*

With the Scheppers-as-starting-pitcher experiment lasting about as long as *The Paul Reiser Show*, the big right-hander is bullpen-bound once again in 2015. That is, assuming his elbow inflammation subsides: Scheppers missed 140 games last season with two bouts of it. Only one season removed from being a key cog of the Rangers' relief corps, Scheppers used to fire a high-90s four-seamer but has mostly shelved it for a sinker that has nearly the same velocity but shatters the hopes and dreams of infield worms everywhere. Paired with a slider that he uses as a put-away pitch to batters of all persuasions, it's not hard to see why the Rangers wanted to give him a shot in the rotation. Unfortunately, the body wants what the body wants. If healthy, he could challenge Neftali Feliz for first chair.

Nick Tepesch   RHP

Born: 10/12/88   Age: 26   Bats: R   Throws: R   Height: 6'4"   Weight: 225

YEAR	TEAM	LVL	AGE	W	L	SV	G	GS	IP	H	HR	BB	K	BB/9	K/9	GB%	BABIP	WHIP	ERA	FIP	FRA	WARP
2012	MYR	A+	23	5	3	0	12	12	71²	68	3	18	59	2.3	7.4	61%	.307	1.20	2.89	3.33	4.29	0.5
2012	FRI	AA	23	6	3	0	16	14	90¹	97	10	26	68	2.6	6.8	52%	.316	1.36	4.28	4.18	5.07	0.1
2013	TEX	MLB	24	4	6	0	19	17	93	100	12	27	76	2.6	7.4	48%	.309	1.37	4.84	4.22	4.68	0.3
2014	ROU	AAA	25	6	1	0	7	7	45²	36	1	9	41	1.8	8.1	55%	.280	0.99	1.58	2.91	3.24	1.2
2014	TEX	MLB	25	5	11	0	23	22	126	128	15	44	56	3.1	4.0	43%	.272	1.37	4.36	5.03	5.55	-0.6
2015	TEX	MLB	26	7	9	0	23	23	132¹	143	14	40	82	2.7	5.6	47%	.300	1.38	4.54	4.81	4.93	0.1

Breakout: 39%   Improve: 64%   Collapse: 12%   Attrition: 21%   MLB: 89%   Comparables: Jeanmar Gomez, Zach McAllister, Glen Perkins

In this new age of low-contact baseball, Tepesch was truly a throwback in 2014. Unlike in clothes or cars, that's not a good thing. His 10 percent strikeout rate was the worst in baseball among pitchers who threw at least 100 innings. With his sinker-slider tendencies and pitch-to-contact style, it's a surprise he's not a member of the Twins' organization along with his Missouri teammate Kyle Gibson. Tepesch is likely to be in the running for the no. 5 starter spot in Texas, but if the Rangers want to be competitive, he's a much better fit as a "break glass in case of emergency" guy they can keep around in either Triple-A or the bullpen.

Jake Thompson   RHP

Born: 1/31/94   Age: 21   Bats: R   Throws: R   Height: 6'4"   Weight: 235

YEAR	TEAM	LVL	AGE	W	L	SV	G	GS	IP	H	HR	BB	K	BB/9	K/9	GB%	BABIP	WHIP	ERA	FIP	FRA	WARP
2013	WMI	A	19	3	3	0	17	16	83¹	79	4	32	91	3.5	9.8	45%	.325	1.33	3.13	3.33	3.91	1.6
2014	LAK	A+	20	6	4	0	16	16	83	75	3	25	79	2.7	8.6	44%	.316	1.20	3.14	3.11	3.61	1.5
2014	ERI	AA	20	1	0	0	2	2	11	10	0	4	7	3.3	5.7	40%	.286	1.27	2.45	3.45	4.00	0.2
2014	FRI	AA	20	3	1	0	7	6	35²	28	3	18	44	4.5	11.1	46%	.305	1.29	3.28	3.34	5.35	0.3
2015	TEX	MLB	21	5	7	0	20	20	98²	101	10	44	83	4.1	7.6	43%	.309	1.47	4.56	4.78	4.96	0.1

Breakout: 0%   Improve: 0%   Collapse: 0%   Attrition: 0%   MLB: 0%   Comparables: Jarrod Parker, Carlos Martinez, Chris Tillman

The big-bodied Texan arrived back home via a July trade that sent Joakim Soria from the Rangers to Detroit. With a body built for black ink in the innings column, Thompson took a step forward over the course of the season, both in terms of results and stuff. While he features two fastballs, two breaking balls and a developing changeup, Thompson won't be confused for Yu Darvish, but he could find himself in the Rangers' rotation in the second half of 2015, sooner if the pitching hex on the franchise still hasn't been lifted.

Shawn Tolleson   RHP

Born: 1/19/88   Age: 27   Bats: R   Throws: R   Height: 6'2"   Weight: 210

YEAR	TEAM	LVL	AGE	W	L	SV	G	GS	IP	H	HR	BB	K	BB/9	K/9	GB%	BABIP	WHIP	ERA	FIP	FRA	WARP
2012	CHT	AA	24	0	0	5	11	0	13	8	2	4	19	2.8	13.2	58%	.250	0.92	1.38	3.14	3.39	0.3
2012	LAN	MLB	24	3	1	0	40	0	37²	30	4	20	39	4.8	9.3	42%	.271	1.33	4.30	4.12	4.35	-0.1
2013	LAN	MLB	25	0	0	0	1	0	0	0	0	2	0	—	—	0%	—	—	—	—	4572.53	-0.2
2014	TEX	MLB	26	3	1	0	64	0	71²	56	10	28	69	3.5	8.7	40%	.245	1.17	2.76	4.26	4.36	0.3
2015	TEX	MLB	27	2	1	0	46	0	51¹	43	5	19	55	3.4	9.7	46%	.290	1.22	3.41	3.89	3.71	0.7

Breakout: 35%   Improve: 47%   Collapse: 20%   Attrition: 27%   MLB: 78%   Comparables: Louis Coleman, Shawn Kelley, Clay Zavada

A former Dodgers farmhand who put up gaudy numbers throughout the minors, Tolleson finally put that practice to good use on the way to being the most valuable reliever, and third-most valuable pitcher, on the 2014 Rangers. Maybe the former Baylor and Texas high school star just needed to be back on his native soil, though his 87 percent strand rate certainly didn't hurt. The right-hander has a fastball-heavy approach that leaves him without much of a platoon split, though it also leaves him vulnerable to the long ball. With the dearth of established (read: good) options in the Texas bullpen, Tolleson could continue his march toward a late-inning role in 2015.

Lineouts

Hitters

NAME	POS	TEAM	LVL	AGE	PA	R	2B	3B	HR	RBI	BB	K	SB	CS	AVG/OBP/SLG	TAv	BABIP	BRR	FRAA	WARP
Jim Adduci	1B	FRI	AA	29	23	3	1	1	1	6	0	5	1	0	.318/.304/.591	.313	.353	0.1	1B(4): 0.0, CF(1): -0.1	0.2
	1B	ROU	AAA	29	29	3	1	0	0	3	2	8	2	1	.296/.345/.333	.245	.421	0.2	1B(6): 0.0, CF(1): -0.0	0.0
	LF	TEX	MLB	29	114	13	3	0	1	8	10	27	3	1	.168/.239/.228	.193	.213	0.7	LF(20): 2.1, RF(8): 0.1	-0.1
Jairo Beras	LF	HIC	A	19	427	38	18	0	7	33	33	133	5	6	.242/.305/.342	.240	.348	-1.8	LF(49): -0.6, RF(33): 2.1	0.4
Michael De Leon	SS	HIC	A	17	373	42	10	2	1	26	28	40	3	3	.244/.302/.295	.262	.272	-0.9	SS(26): 0.6, 2B(4): 0.3	0.4
	SS	MYR	A+	17	28	5	3	0	1	6	3	4	0	0	.292/.370/.542	.339	.316	0.2	SS(7): 0.4	0.5
Chris Gimenez	C	ROU	AAA	31	156	18	4	2	6	22	19	30	0	1	.284/.365/.478	.291	.317	0.0	C(18): -0.4, 1B(14): -0.4	1.1
	C	TEX	MLB	31	118	13	10	0	0	11	11	26	0	1	.262/.331/.355	.247	.346	0.0	C(26): -0.0, 1B(5): -0.2	0.2
	1B	CLE	MLB	31	10	0	0	0	0	0	1	3	0	0	.000/.100/.000	.067	.000	0.0	1B(5): -0.2, C(2): 0.0	-0.2
Ronald Guzman	1B	HIC	A	19	492	46	32	0	6	63	37	107	6	3	.218/.283/.330	.226	.270	-1.5	1B(115): -9.7, LF(2): 0.4	-2.5
Kevin Kouzmanoff	3B	TEX	MLB	32	51	8	6	0	2	10	2	7	0	0	.362/.412/.617	.347	.395	0.1	3B(13): -0.3	0.5
Josh Morgan	2B	SPO	A-	18	102	11	1	0	0	9	10	10	1	0	.303/.392/.315	.281	.342	-0.6	2B(13): -0.2, SS(10): -0.8	0.4
Carlos Pena	1B	ROU	AAA	36	80	12	3	0	4	8	5	15	0	0	.297/.350/.500	.280	.327	-0.1	1B(14): 0.6	0.4
	1B	TEX	MLB	36	63	4	3	0	1	2	4	11	1	0	.136/.190/.237	.176	.149	-1.6	1B(16): 0.6	-0.5
Guilder Rodriguez	SS	FRI	AA	30	349	36	7	1	0	20	37	45	10	7	.269/.347/.298	.242	.314	0.8	SS(45): 2.7, 3B(19): 0.1	1.0
	2B	ROU	AAA	30	35	4	1	0	0	1	4	5	0	0	.167/.265/.200	.164	.200	-0.5	2B(4): -0.7, SS(2): -0.2	-0.3
	3B	TEX	MLB	30	14	2	0	0	0	1	1	5	0	0	.167/.231/.167	.167	.286	0.0	3B(3): -0.1, 2B(2): -0.0	-0.1
Jake Smolinski	LF	FRI	AA	25	307	43	15	3	10	35	32	54	6	2	.267/.349/.459	.296	.295	-0.7	LF(49): 0.7, 1B(4): 0.2	2.0
	LF	ROU	AAA	25	34	7	6	0	0	6	4	5	0	0	.267/.353/.467	.287	.320	1.0	LF(7): 0.3, CF(1): -0.1	0.2
	LF	TEX	MLB	25	92	12	5	0	3	12	3	24	0	0	.349/.391/.512	.336	.458	-0.6	LF(12): -1.1, RF(9): 0.7	0.6
Tomas Telis	C	FRI	AA	23	295	31	16	2	2	33	17	29	7	1	.303/.339/.401	.267	.325	-2.7	C(46): 0.8, 1B(1): 0.1	1.1
	C	ROU	AAA	23	147	18	7	2	3	17	6	12	1	1	.345/.377/.489	.294	.363	0.2	C(19): -0.2, 1B(9): 0.6	1.0
	C	TEX	MLB	23	71	7	2	0	0	8	1	10	0	0	.250/.271/.279	.234	.293	-0.1	C(17): -0.3	0.0
Josh Wilson	SS	ROU	AAA	33	332	37	11	1	5	33	16	87	1	2	.246/.295/.338	.220	.323	-2.5	SS(45): -6.0, 3B(33): -0.9	-1.2
	2B	TEX	MLB	33	72	7	4	0	0	8	2	14	1	0	.239/.271/.299	.206	.302	0.5	2B(19): 2.0, 3B(4): 0.4	0.2

After nearly 10 years toiling in the minors, **Jim Adduci**, a 42nd-rounder from British Columbia, finally got his first cup of coffee in 2013, but with a .467 OPS last season, he's already made the transition from "great story" to "depth guy" to "will play 2015 in Korea." ❖ **Jairo Beras** has not performed well enough on the field to distance himself from the scandal and subsequent suspension that resulted from lying about his age before signing, but he'll play the season at 20, so there's still time to make up for the lost year of development. ❖ **Michael de Leon** is a shortstop with a line-drive stroke who spent most of the season as the youngest player in the South Atlantic League before becoming the first 17-year-old position player to appear at Double-A since Wil Cordero in 1989. ❖ **Ti'Quan Forbes**, the Rangers' second-round pick last year, was one of the youngest players in the draft; with patience, lots and lots and lots of patience, the hope is that he's a five-tool up-the-middle player. ❖ After his cross-country tour took him through Seattle, Tampa and Arlington, **Chris Gimenez** went back to where it all started (Cleveland) in hopes that his defensive versatility would be put to good use. He's in Texas again as of this writing, but don't be surprised if that's already outdated. ❖ A repeat trip to Hickory for **Ronald Guzman** did not bring the step forward that many were hoping for out of the 2011 international bonus baby, but his hit tool still projects as plus, so the seven-figure promise isn't gone yet. ❖ Well-traveled third baseman **Kevin Kouzmanoff** recorded a .347 TAv in 13 games in 2014 before missing the rest of the season with a herniated disk in his back. ❖ **Josh Morgan**, 2014's third-round pick, may not stick at shortstop and isn't likely to hit for more than fringy power, but his advanced hit tool and approach could make him a top-of-the-lineup presence. ❖ A two-time MVP vote recipient, **Carlos Pena** lasted all of two months in an organization that was absolutely decimated by injuries at first and DH and needed power in a bad way. He's joined MLB Network as a studio analyst and presumably does not plan to play baseball at the same time. ❖ After 12 years in the minors, **Guilder Rodriguez** finally got 12 at-bats in the majors in September; known for his mentoring ability, don't be surprised if he sticks with the organization when his playing days come to a close. ❖ **Jake Smolinski**'s 2014 major-league BABIP was higher than any single-season *slugging percentage* he posted in the minors from 2007 to 2013. ❖ **Tomas Telis** is a 24-year-old Venezuelan backstop who makes contact at a strong rate but is unlikely to stick in the majors due to his inability to control runners or frame pitches. ❖ When **Josh Wilson** got the Opening Day start for the Rangers at second base, they became the eighth team he's played for in his 10-year career. Amazingly, none of those eight organizations was a part of Major League Baseball in 1960.

Pitchers

NAME	TEAM	LVL	AGE	W	L	SV	G	GS	IP	H	HR	BB	K	BB/9	K/9	GB%	BABIP	WHIP	ERA	FIP	FRA	WARP
Nathan Adcock	ROU	AAA	26	1	0	2	18	0	21¹	14	1	11	22	4.6	9.3	60%	.250	1.17	2.95	4.07	4.12	0.3
	TEX	MLB	26	0	0	0	7	0	10	11	2	5	9	4.5	8.1	41%	.333	1.60	4.50	6.06	5.29	-0.1
Alec Asher	FRI	AA	22	11	11	0	28	28	154	139	18	32	122	1.9	7.1	36%	.265	1.11	3.80	3.74	4.79	1.1
Anthony Bass	OKL	AAA	26	0	2	1	14	0	16¹	15	3	6	14	3.3	7.7	44%	.267	1.29	3.31	5.47	5.66	0.0
	HOU	MLB	26	1	1	2	21	0	27	32	6	7	7	2.3	2.3	52%	.268	1.44	6.33	6.53	7.98	-0.8
Alexander Claudio	MYR	A+	22	4	0	4	17	2	49¹	38	2	9	56	1.6	10.2	64%	.298	0.95	1.09	2.44	3.04	1.3
	FRI	AA	22	2	2	0	8	6	37¹	31	1	2	22	0.5	5.3	52%	.246	0.88	2.17	2.53	3.99	0.5
	TEX	MLB	22	0	0	0	15	0	12¹	14	0	4	14	2.9	10.2	58%	.389	1.46	2.92	1.86	1.76	0.4
Jon Edwards	FRI	AA	26	1	2	0	22	0	33¹	27	4	23	36	6.2	9.7	34%	.277	1.50	5.13	4.59	6.02	-0.2
	ROU	AAA	26	1	1	0	12	0	15²	15	0	9	26	5.2	14.9	34%	.429	1.53	2.87	2.30	1.58	0.8
	TEX	MLB	26	0	0	0	9	0	8¹	13	0	5	9	5.4	9.7	46%	.464	2.16	4.32	3.16	2.30	0.2
Andrew Faulkner	MYR	A+	21	10	1	1	21	18	104¹	86	1	31	100	2.7	8.6	46%	.298	1.12	2.07	2.70	3.12	2.9
	FRI	AA	21	2	4	0	7	6	30²	28	3	14	33	4.1	9.7	48%	.298	1.37	4.99	3.61	5.09	0.4
Alfredo Figaro	NAS	AAA	29	5	2	2	42	2	70¹	80	5	22	55	2.8	7.0	50%	.341	1.45	3.71	4.04	4.51	0.8
	MIL	MLB	29	0	1	0	6	0	8²	11	2	1	8	1.0	8.3	52%	.333	1.38	7.27	4.60	5.09	-0.1
Keone Kela	MYR	A+	21	0	1	5	8	0	10¹	7	0	4	13	3.5	11.3	37%	.333	1.26	2.61	2.16	3.10	0.2
	FRI	AA	21	2	1	5	36	0	38²	22	1	27	55	6.3	12.8	50%	.259	1.27	1.86	2.86	3.72	0.8
Michael Kirkman	ROU	AAA	27	5	5	1	36	4	54¹	50	6	29	62	4.8	10.3	68%	.312	1.45	4.47	4.56	6.93	0.5
	TEX	MLB	27	0	1	0	12	0	5²	5	0	1	3	1.6	4.8	62%	.312	1.06	1.59	3.69	3.29	0.0

NAME	TEAM	LVL	AGE	W	L	SV	G	GS	IP	H	HR	BB	K	BB/9	K/9	GB%	BABIP	WHIP	ERA	FIP	FRA	WARP
Phil Klein	FRI	AA	25	3	0	10	24	0	33.1	15	0	14	42	3.8	11.3	61%	.208	0.87	0.81	1.95	2.92	0.9
	ROU	AAA	25	0	0	0	9	0	18.1	7	0	6	28	2.9	13.7	39%	.226	0.71	0.00	1.95	1.50	0.8
	TEX	MLB	25	1	2	0	17	0	19	15	3	10	23	4.7	10.9	43%	.195	1.11	2.84	4.69	3.72	0.2
Will Lamb	MYR	A+	23	1	1	2	14	0	18.2	17	0	9	25	4.3	12.1	34%	.362	1.39	2.41	2.29	2.65	0.6
	FRI	AA	23	4	2	3	26	0	33	18	1	26	34	7.1	9.3	46%	.224	1.33	1.09	3.91	3.69	0.5
David Martinez	OKL	AAA	26	5	6	0	22	13	83	94	5	30	62	3.3	6.7	45%	.337	1.49	5.64	4.18	4.89	1.0
	HOU	MLB	26	0	0	0	3	0	7	5	1	2	6	2.6	7.7	40%	.211	1.00	5.14	4.16	3.98	0.0
Shane McCain	SPO	A-	22	2	0	3	15	0	28.2	17	0	1	39	0.3	12.2	20%	.200	0.63	0.31	1.30	2.09	0.3
Roman Mendez	ROU	AAA	23	0	1	3	25	0	31.1	39	4	12	30	3.4	8.6	41%	.365	1.63	4.02	4.78	5.60	0.1
	TEX	MLB	23	0	1	0	30	0	33	20	2	17	22	4.6	6.0	44%	.194	1.12	2.18	4.34	4.78	0.0
Spencer Patton	ROU	AAA	26	1	1	4	15	0	16	16	1	3	25	1.7	14.1	44%	.395	1.19	3.38	1.95	2.92	0.5
	OMA	AAA	26	4	3	14	34	0	46.1	26	9	22	60	4.3	11.7	43%	.179	1.04	4.08	5.19	5.61	0.2
	TEX	MLB	26	1	0	0	9	0	9.1	6	0	2	8	1.9	7.7	52%	.240	0.86	0.96	2.09	2.60	0.2
Ben Rowen	ROU	AAA	25	3	0	5	34	0	47	47	2	9	31	1.7	5.9	62%	.290	1.19	3.45	3.89	4.86	0.5
	TEX	MLB	25	0	0	0	8	0	8.2	10	0	4	7	4.2	7.3	61%	.357	1.62	4.15	2.93	2.69	0.2
Matthew West	FRI	AA	25	2	0	3	8	0	13.1	7	1	2	10	1.4	6.8	31%	.176	0.68	0.68	3.27	2.96	0.3
	ROU	AAA	25	3	3	1	33	1	43.1	52	4	16	54	3.3	11.2	44%	.400	1.57	4.15	3.86	3.92	1.1
	TEX	MLB	25	0	0	0	3	0	4	6	0	1	3	2.2	6.8	50%	.429	1.75	6.75	2.41	2.94	0.1

Nate Adcock came back from thoracic outlet syndrome surgery throwing his sinker at 94 mph, a couple of ticks higher than in his previous major-league stints, albeit in just 10 big-league innings. ❖ **Alec Asher** is a 2012 fourth-rounder who lost some of his prospect luster last year as both his performance and raw stuff took a step back at Double-A, but you can never have too many up-and-down starter types. ❖ Although hard-throwing righty **Anthony Bass** missed two months to injury, a total of seven strikeouts, seven walks and six home runs in a season is as good a reason as any to drop the Bass. ❖ **Alex Claudio** is a soft-tossing southpaw with a GIF-tastic changeup who made a brief cameo in the majors in 2014 and will fight for the LOOGY role this year. ❖ A great story of perseverance, **Jon Edwards** was a 14th-rounder who flamed out in the Cardinals' system as an outfielder before playing for the Alpine Cowboys of the Pecos League in 2011 and remaking himself as a pitcher. ❖ **Andrew Faulkner**, a South Carolina native, shined near his old hamlet at Myrtle Beach, leaning on a heavy fastball and a splitter that can miss bats, but his sanctuary will probably be the bullpen due to an inconsistent breaking ball; if he leaves Double-A hitters unvanquished, he's more likely to be receiving soldiers' pay in 2017 than living in a mansion. ❖ **Alfredo Figaro** owns a 98 mph fastball and a 1.9 HR/9 rate. ❖ Any reliever who can touch triple digits with his fastball is automatically worth paying attention to; if he can bring his control even within hailing distance of average, **Keone Kela** can pitch high-leverage innings in the majors. ❖ Not even the Rangers playing a Wrath of God card on their pitching staff could get **Michael Kirkman** more than a September call-up in 2014; the southpaw succeeded in a small sample and was perfect against right-handed batters. ❖ **Phil Klein** is a 6-foot-7 righty who has cruised since being drafted in the 30th round in 2011; he joined the Texas bullpen in August and promptly slew every same-side hitter he saw with a slider-heavy approach. ❖ **Will Lamb**, whose middle initial is not "I," is a 6-foot-6 southpaw now working full time out of the bullpen; if he can get a handle on his control issues in the high minors, he could find a home in middle relief. ❖ Kicking strike-throwing organizational depth to the curb is a luxury the Astros can now afford, so they DFA'd **David Martinez** in September to make room for bigger, badder arms; he signed a minor-league deal a couple hours up I-45. ❖ **Shane McCain** is an undrafted free agent lefty who struck out 39 against just one walk in his professional debut and has a future throwing down rockin' bro country hits when he's done with baseball. ❖ A hard-throwing right-hander who got his first taste of the majors in 2014, **Roman Mendez** had four strikeouts for every walk against righties but more than two walks for every strikeout against lefties. ❖ **Spencer Patton** was acquired from the Royals for Jason Frasor last July and has put up strong minor-league numbers based on deception, but he acquitted himself well in a September call-up and could compete for a bullpen role this year. ❖ **Ben Rowen**, a 26-year-old submarining reliever who debuted in 2014 with an 80 mph fastball, has issued more intentional walks in his career than Derek Holland. ❖ **Matt West** is a hard-throwing right-hander who was converted from third base to the mound in 2011 and surfaced in the majors for three appearances last season. ❖

Manager

Jeff Banister

Following Ron Washington's mysterious late-season resignation, the Rangers elevated bench coach Tim Bogar to interim manager. Bogar oversaw a 14-8 finish, yet the organization elected to conduct a full search once the season concluded. In the end, they opted for an external candidate.

Banister is perhaps the least likely manager in the game, not because he lacks merit or potential, but because of his background story. He has defeated bone cancer and osteomyelitis, endured seven surgeries on his leg and ankle and recovered from a home-plate collision that left him temporarily paralyzed. That last incident led a doctor to tell Banister his playing days were over, according to a 2013 Tyler Kepner feature in the *New York Times*. Yet Banister played on, eventually reaching the majors for one at-bat, in which he singled.

Banister has since filled various roles with the Pirates, including serving as Clint Hurdle's bench coach for the past four years. Perseverance is an obvious strength of his, as is his open-minded approach toward new ideas. Rangers fans tired of Washington's antiquated ways should take a liking to the new skipper in town, and those who weren't should find sufficient reason to root for Banister anyway."

TORONTO BLUE JAYS

by Andrew Stoeten

On a Friday night in early July 1993, 39-year-old Garry Hoy, a partner with leading Toronto law firm Holden Day Wilson, was at a reception in his firm's offices on the 24th story of the Toronto-Dominion Centre. Three blocks away, at SkyDome, the Blue Jays were playing the Rangers, on their way to a rare loss in what would be their second straight World Series championship season, and to date their final playoff appearance.

Among those gathered with Hoy were several prospective articling students, most of whom had yet to see the company's tony digs, which also meant they hadn't seen Hoy's favorite office trick. With boasts about unbreakable glass, the 160-pound Hoy delighted in hurling himself full force into the windows, always harmlessly bouncing back.

On this night Hoy again charged the glass. Stepping. Leaping. For a fraction of a moment he must have seemed subsumed by the crystal as it bent and shuddered. Then, as always, it strained, pushed back against him and set him gently back down on the safe concrete of the 24th floor.

With the confidence of a man who was an engineer before entering the world of corporate and securities law and a veteran of several heart-in-throat moments like the one he'd just perpetrated on the students, Hoy stepped back and readied himself to perform the trick again.

The glass again held its shape, but while it didn't shatter, it did it slip from its frame, tumbling out into the Toronto night. And along with it, Hoy, to his death.

Todd Stottlemyre took the loss.

Holden Day Wilson went under three years later.

✦ ✦ ✦

In reports from the time, Hoy is described as one of the best and the brightest minds employed by the firm. A young senior partner who had steadily climbed the ladder through the '80s and early '90s, his peak was short-lived, literally, undone by a burst of overconfidence, miscalculation and misunderstanding of forces beyond his control.

After winning the World Series a little over three months later, the Blue Jays would also reach their zenith as a franchise. Soon after, and for many of the same reasons, they would begin a descent of their own, one they continue to struggle to pull themselves out of.

The Blue Jays of that era could do no wrong, it seemed, but cracks in the foundation had already begun to deepen as the club won its second World Series. In retrospect, those cracks may date to the groundbreaking ceremony for the SkyDome in 1986. The stadium, opened in 1989, was a state-of-the-art multipurpose cash cow funded to a significant extent by government, but as much as that gift propelled the club through their World Series years—the sheer novelty of the building, and civic pride in it as a symbol of Toronto's coming of age as a modern, glamorous city that had moved beyond its "Hogtown" roots, helped it become a hotspot for local scenesters as the club smashed attendance records—it wouldn't be long before the facility became a relic and a drag on the franchise.

Camden Yards in Baltimore opened in 1992, bringing with it the proliferation of small, beautiful, "retro" single-sport ballparks. SkyDome, with its cookie-cutter shape, concrete and AstroTurf, quickly began to appear dated. The 1994 strike hit as the defending champs languished on the field for the first time in a decade, and by the time baseball returned, the glory years were over.

In 1995, General Manager Pat Gillick jumped ship and landed in Baltimore. The club's well-liked owner, the Labatt Brewing Company, was sold to foreign multinational Interbew, ushering in an era of passive and indifferent conglomerate ownership that still persists.

Arrogance and miscalculation played their role, too. Part of the funding for the SkyDome was through multimillion-dollar contributions from several of Canada's largest companies, who were granted luxury boxes in return, with the option to renew the lease in 10 years' time. During the halcyon days of 1989, when money rolled in and the greatness of the on-field product seemed inevitable, perhaps nothing about this set off alarm bells. A decade later, with the club down on its luck, the city still adjusting in the wake of an early-'90s recession, the stadium facing myriad financial problems and the nearby Air Canada Centre newly built to host the NHL's Maple Leafs and NBA's Raptors, many of the expected renewals didn't happen.

✦ ✦ ✦

As the late '90s turned to the early 2000s, GM Gord Ash tried to spend the club out of trouble—remember Roger Clemens?—

BLUE JAYS PROSPECTUS
2014 W-L: 83-79, 3RD IN AL EAST

Pythag	.524	10th	DER	.706	14th
RS/G	4.46	5th	B-Age	29.3	23rd
RA/G	4.23	20th	P-Age	30	27th
TAv	.267	8th	Salary	$137.2M	8th
BRR	1.81	14th	MS/MW	$3.6M	22nd
TAv-P	.263	20th	DL Days	715	11th
FIP	4.00	26th	$ on DL	15%	15th

Three-Year Park Factors

Runs	Runs/RH	Runs/LH	HR/RH	HR/LH
105	102	107	94	91

Top Hitter WARP	6.0	Jose Bautista
Top Pitcher WARP	2.7	Mark Buehrle
Top Prospect		Aaron Sanchez

before J.P. Ricciardi was hired away from Oakland to import their small-market strategies to combat a sagging Canadian dollar, which bottomed out at 61.79 cents US in January 2002.

The glass had shucked its restraints and was tumbling toward earth: The club was full-on into a 21-year playoff dry spell during which it would finish higher than third in the AL East only once.

By the mid-2000s, when Ricciardi's methods stopped gaining traction as the rest of the sport caught on, the club was given a major bump in payroll, dubiously presented as a last civic-minded whim of the elderly billionaire behind the corporation that owns the club, the late Ted Rogers. In the winters following 2006 and 2007 the Jays were spenders again, inking major long-term free-agent deals with A.J. Burnett, B.J. Ryan and Frank Thomas, and working out a massive extension for Vernon Wells.

That sure went swimmingly, eh?

✦✦✦

After two more ineffectual years—which featured, among other indignities, the release of both Ryan and Thomas, Burnett opting out after the third year of a five-year deal to join the Yankees, Wells beginning his long journey into the abyss and the planting of the seeds of the Roy Halladay trade—Ricciardi was out, fired by the club's new-old president, Paul Beeston.

Much like then-manager Cito Gaston, Beeston (who was initially brought in on an interim basis to help the club find a new president after the firing of Paul Godfrey, but eventually took the gig himself) had all the credentials you could ever want, including the perceived shine of the club's marvelous Labatt days. Yet the hiring gave off the odor of cynical, fan-appeasing nostalgia designed to foster goodwill and consumer confidence in a brand that had, by end of the Riccardi years, become increasingly poisoned. The fact that Ricciardi's successor, Alex Anthopoulos, is Canadian—something that always plays in this market—fed further into the idea.

Still, slow-building with homegrown talent had, thirty years earlier, transformed the club from a run-of-the-mill expansion team into one of the model franchises of the sport. Could it happen again? That was the promise of Beeston and his hand-picked general manager, Anthopoulos. Or at the very least the hope. And in the fall of 2009 they had the mandate from fans to do it and do it right, to begrudgingly trade Halladay, to reenter the Latin American amateur market that Ricciardi had abandoned to cut costs and to build from within like the sickeningly smart Rays.

The front-office team was enthusiastic, confident and publicly praised ownership at every turn, insisting that financial resources would be available when needed. In reality, glimpses of those resources have been fleeting, and when financial muscles have been flexed, as they were after the club's extraordinarily calculated, payroll-inflating offseason deals two winters ago, their strength has ultimately proved to be a mirage. Try as he might, "AA"'s tenure has more resembled the constant shape-shifting and excuse-making of the Ricciardi years than anything Gillick ever touched, and he now faces the very real possibility of hurtling out the window, clutching at that illusion.

✦✦✦

What are the Toronto Blue Jays heading into 2015, then? They are a team at a crossroads.

They are some strange marriage between two clubs: the one that went all in for 2013 and tried to build around the superstar who fell into their laps, Jose Bautista, only to find they didn't yet have a strong enough foundation, and the preceding iteration that loaded up on scouts and hoarded prospects, emphasizing loud tools and high ceilings with a view to some far-away future when they might spend again to complement the core pieces. A conflicted mix: on the one hand, the team whose biggest free-agent deal over a four-year span was the $4.5 million paid to Francisco Cordero; on the other, the team that lavished $82 million on a 31-year-old Russell Martin. Somewhere between the traditionalist club of scouts and Cito—one that inexplicably curbed its use of defensive shifts in 2013, after the departure of third base coach Brian Butterfield, who had been doing it without computer assistance!—and the forward-thinking organization now banking on pitch framing.

✦✦✦

After a year almost completely on the sidelines transactions-wise, the Blue Jays have gone back to the 2013 well and again traded young assets for someone else's star. In this case, Josh Donaldson.

"Trade" is a frightening word in Toronto given some of the names that have been dealt away by the organization in deals for better-established players in the last two years—Yan Gomes, Noah Syndergaard, Travis d'Arnaud, Henderson Alvarez, Adeiny Hechavarria—yet you can understand the need to keep pushing and acquire Donaldson for Brett Lawrie, 19-year-old Franklin Barreto and two young arms.

The 2015 Jays were supposed to be in a honeymoon period after two years of success stemming from Anthopoulos' acquisition of Jose Reyes, Mark Buehrle, Josh Johnson and R.A. Dickey for 2013. Instead Johnson is gone, Buehrle is too expensive, Dickey is a disappointment and Reyes is too expensive *and* a disappointment.

Realistically, it's hard to complain about the 5.3 WARP from Buehrle and the 6.1 WARP produced by Reyes in 2013-14, but if you're playing "stars and scrubs" as hard as the Jays were, you need your stars to truly shine. (Dickey's 101 ERA+ over the last two years is fair game for complaints.) As we head into the diminishing returns phase of Reyes' deal, and the twilight years for Dickey, Buehrle and eventually Bautista, star performances from the existing roster become increasingly unlikely, leading to the need for replenishment from outside.

✦✦✦

All of this was just as obvious heading into 2014 as it is now. Speaking to reporters at the end of the 2013 season, Anthopoulos identified the starting rotation as the "number one area" where the club needed to improve. "That has to get better," he said. "We're going to look to improve. No doubt about it, we have to."

But then came nothing. Unlike the starbursts of the 2012-13 offseason, the club found itself banking on Brandon Morrow's health. Strong performances from Marcus Stroman, Drew Hutchison and Aaron Sanchez in the Arizona Fall League allowed Anthopoulos to walk back his comments about needing pitching, but the cynical grumbled that this went above the general manager, that ownership was uneasy about the lack of returns from raising the club's 2013 payroll to $119 million from $84 million, and was tightening the purse strings again.

At the same time, Rogers Communications, the Canadian telecom giant that owns both the club and the network holding their TV rights—a relationship fans view with suspicion at the best of times, given the Jays' frequent crying poor despite the skyrocketing value of the content they're obligated to provide the parent company's network—bet massively on hockey, announcing a 12-year, $5.2 billion broadcast and multimedia rights deal with the NHL at the end of November. And while all that was going on, the organization was preparing for a change of leadership, with Guy Laurence, the former head of Vodafone UK and a man with a reputation for drastic cost-cutting, taking over as CEO.

Whether it was ownership's dissatisfaction with 2013 revenue, a lack of funds following the hockey deal, paralysis from having to wait for the new honcho to survey his territory or some other reason, it eventually became clear as the 2013-14 offseason wore on with nary a major move that the Blue Jays were again in a payroll bind.

Nothing illustrated this better than the Ervin Santana situation. Still available after months of rumored interest from the Jays as he languished in Qualifying Offer limbo, Santana was very close to completing a deal in Toronto when the Braves' Kris Medlen blew out his elbow in a spring training game. Santana spurned the Jays and went to Atlanta. Toronto did not have the ability to suddenly react with a better offer: The Jays had only been in a position to sign Santana in the first place because several of their highest-paid players were willing to defer salary.

✦ ✦ ✦

So into 2014 the Jays went, doubling down on the same strange cast that had done so little in 2013, supplemented neither by youngsters, who had been traded away, nor outsiders, who Anthopolous could not afford. The result was a strange journey to exactly the place anybody would have predicted: an 83-79 record, the Platonic ideal of a Blue Jays season.

It's baseball, so some aspects were fresh: Juan Francisco helped carry the club in a torrid first half, for instance. Most of the rest you should have seen coming, though. Bautista was spectacular. Buehrle was steady. Dickey was consistently inconsistent, and averaged out to … average. Brett Lawrie couldn't stay healthy. Adam Lind handled right-handers like few others can, but spent time on the disabled list. Edwin

Encarnacion and Melky Cabrera were very good. Colby Rasmus followed a terrific 2013 by being a total mess.

✦ ✦ ✦

Then again, the two least surprising events would lead to Anthopolous' saving grace. The club began 2014 with the oft-injured duo of Morrow and Dustin McGowan in the starting rotation, the latter by default after a spring battle for the fifth spot turned up nothing but dreck. That was never going to last. McGowan—who entered the year having thrown just 76 competitive innings since 2008—couldn't hold up to the rigors of the starting rotation and Morrow lasted just six starts before succumbing to a torn tendon sheath at the base of his index finger.

Their absences set the stage for Stroman to join the rotation; he embarked on a stellar rookie campaign, amassing 1.9 WARP while striking out 108 in 120 innings (as a starter), walking just 27 and—most importantly, considering the concerns about his stature and ability to keep the ball down in the zone—kept the ball in the ballpark. Couple Stroman's breakout with a strong return from Tommy John surgery for youngster Drew Hutchison and a superb bullpen cameo beginning in August for Aaron Sanchez and the Jays had found themselves three pitchers who they think can provide enough, alongside the dependable-if-unspectacular Buehrle and Dickey (and perhaps heralded youngster Daniel Norris), to justify a continued push for the playoffs centered around the current core and its main catalyst, the brilliant Bautista, who remains under contract for just two more years. His previous five, easily among the greatest in franchise history, are already wasted.

The Jays will continue to gamble with the same basic roster construction, and surely will continue to say they have faith in the strength of ownership's commitment and their ability to build a winner with the pieces they have. Perhaps, realistically, that's all they can do. But perhaps it's just another miscalculation to contemplate while impact with the cold, hard, inescapable concrete rushes closer. ∎

—Andrew Stoeten covers the Blue Jays for his own site, AndrewStoeten.com (formerly Drunk Jays Fans), and is a contributor to the National Post.

Player comments by Adam Sobsey, Andrew Koo and Baseball Prospectus Authors

Hitters

Daric Barton 1B

Born: 8/16/85   Age: 29   Bats: L   Throws: R   Height: 6' 0"   Weight: 205

YEAR	TEAM	LVL	AGE	PA	R	2B	3B	HR	RBI	BB	K	SB	CS	AVG/OBP/SLG	TAv	BABIP	BRR	FRAA	WARP
2012	SAC	AAA	26	336	49	14	3	8	35	66	53	7	1	.255/.411/.425	.302	.286	0.9	1B(57): -1.4, 3B(1): -0.0	1.6
2012	OAK	MLB	26	136	8	7	0	1	6	22	32	1	0	.204/.338/.292	.247	.275	0.2	1B(43): -1.0	-0.1
2013	SAC	AAA	27	488	77	29	1	7	69	87	57	1	2	.297/.423/.430	.310	.327	-0.2	1B(80): 12.0, 3B(29): -1.3	4.4
2013	OAK	MLB	27	120	15	2	0	3	16	13	18	0	0	.269/.350/.375	.296	.294	0.9	1B(36): 3.3	1.2
2014	SAC	AAA	28	375	46	18	1	9	56	51	40	0	1	.261/.371/.411	.284	.271	-1.9	1B(42): 6.2	1.9
2014	OAK	MLB	28	64	7	1	0	0	5	5	14	0	0	.158/.234/.175	.174	.205	-0.6	1B(30): 0.2	-0.5
2015	*TOR*	*MLB*	*29*	*250*	*26*	*12*	*1*	*4*	*25*	*37*	*43*	*1*	*0*	*.242/.359/.363*	*.271*	*.282*	*0.1*	*1B 3, 3B -0*	*0.9*

Breakout: 4%   Improve: 36%   Collapse: 9%   Attrition: 17%   MLB: 82%   Comparables: *John Jaso, Dan Johnson, Gaby Sanchez*

Coincidence that the A's switched their Triple-A affiliation from Sacramento to Nashville and Barton signed a minor-league contract with Toronto in the same offseason? *We think not!* Raley Field had become a home for Barton, a Sacto regular since 2006, and he will surely miss the familiarity of the yellow Tower Bridge and The Ziggurat looming beyond the outfield, providing the perfect backdrop for Saturday night fireworks. He'll spend the summer in Buffalo instead, though as before, he'll be just 100 miles from the big leagues should disaster strike.

Jose Bautista RF

Born: 10/19/80   Age: 34   Bats: R   Throws: R   Height: 6' 0"   Weight: 205

YEAR	TEAM	LVL	AGE	PA	R	2B	3B	HR	RBI	BB	K	SB	CS	AVG/OBP/SLG	TAv	BABIP	BRR	FRAA	WARP
2012	TOR	MLB	31	399	64	14	0	27	65	59	63	5	2	.241/.358/.527	.307	.215	3.8	RF(90): 1.1, 1B(4): 0.1	3.5
2013	TOR	MLB	32	528	82	24	0	28	73	69	84	7	2	.259/.358/.498	.307	.259	-1.5	RF(109): -8.5, 3B(3): -0.3	3.1
2014	TOR	MLB	33	673	101	27	0	35	103	104	96	6	2	.286/.403/.524	.329	.287	-2.8	RF(131): 1.0, 1B(12): -0.5	6.0
2015	*TOR*	*MLB*	*34*	*603*	*91*	*24*	*1*	*34*	*99*	*91*	*105*	*6*	*2*	*.264/.381/.521*	*.330*	*.267*	*-0.3*	*RF -4, 1B -0*	*4.9*

Breakout: 2%   Improve: 26%   Collapse: 6%   Attrition: 7%   MLB: 96%   Comparables: *Stan Musial, Frank Robinson, Barry Bonds*

With his best and healthiest season since his MVP-level 2011, Bautista padded his five-year home run lead, shipping another 35 bullets to left field bleachers around the league. He's like FedEx: He delivers anywhere, and fast. His trademark torque-unleashing swing hasn't slowed with age, and his superb batting eye had pitchers expending severe effort to avoid mistakes. Bautista saw the sixth-most pitches in the AL, content with walking and letting Edwin Encarnacion clean up behind him. He topped right fielders in outfield assists too, his arm making up for lesser range. Going into his age-34 season, any prolonged slump might be a signal of permanent decline, but Bautista's patience and approach should withstand a steep drop-off. So how long can he keep this up? Is he the right-handed David Ortiz?

Ezequiel Carrera CF

Born: 6/11/87   Age: 28   Bats: L   Throws: L   Height: 5' 10"   Weight: 185

YEAR	TEAM	LVL	AGE	PA	R	2B	3B	HR	RBI	BB	K	SB	CS	AVG/OBP/SLG	TAv	BABIP	BRR	FRAA	WARP
2012	COH	AAA	25	438	65	19	6	6	42	29	60	26	7	.294/.345/.419	.252	.332	0.2	CF(93): 5.0, RF(1): -0.1	1.3
2012	CLE	MLB	25	158	20	6	3	2	11	8	35	8	1	.272/.312/.395	.249	.342	1.6	LF(36): 2.4, CF(15): 1.6	0.5
2013	COH	AAA	26	464	57	16	5	5	31	38	87	43	12	.248/.312/.346	.245	.301	2.7	CF(41): 2.3, LF(38): 4.4	1.5
2013	CLE	MLB	26	5	1	0	0	0	0	1	0	1	0	.500/.500/.500	.291	.667	0.6	RF(1): -0.1	0.1
2013	PHI	MLB	26	16	2	0	0	0	0	1	4	0	0	.077/.250/.077	.146	.111	0.0	RF(5): 0.0, LF(1): 0.0	-0.1
2014	TOL	AAA	27	434	68	15	5	6	41	48	65	43	13	.307/.387/.422	.284	.355	1.5	CF(69): 2.5, RF(25): 0.2	2.6
2014	DET	MLB	27	73	12	4	1	0	2	3	14	7	1	.261/.301/.348	.242	.327	0.9	CF(38): -0.2, LF(1): 0.1	0.2
2015	*TOR*	*MLB*	*28*	*250*	*32*	*9*	*3*	*2*	*18*	*18*	*48*	*18*	*4*	*.254/.313/.351*	*.246*	*.303*	*1.2*	*CF 2, LF 1*	*0.7*

Breakout: 5%   Improve: 33%   Collapse: 11%   Attrition: 26%   MLB: 59%   Comparables: *Shane Robinson, Jason Ellison, Craig Gentry*

In 2013, the city of Toledo ran a "You Will Do Better In Toledo" campaign to stimulate economic growth. It really should be the theme for Carrera, who was named an International League All-Star, leading the circuit in stolen bases and posting his first .300 batting line since 2009, in Double-A. After Austin Jackson was freighted out of town by the Tigers in July, Carrera found himself on the big-league roster platooning in center field for two months, but his subpar instincts and routes cost the team a few defensive runs, and other than occasionally bunting a single or stealing a base, he has little offensive value. He was signed to a minor-league deal by Toronto, but he would do better in Toledo.

Chris Colabello 1B

Born: 10/24/83   Age: 31   Bats: R   Throws: R   Height: 6' 4"   Weight: 220

YEAR	TEAM	LVL	AGE	PA	R	2B	3B	HR	RBI	BB	K	SB	CS	AVG/OBP/SLG	TAv	BABIP	BRR	FRAA	WARP
2012	NBR	AA	28	562	78	37	1	19	98	47	94	0	0	.284/.358/.478	.291	.314	-1.0	1B(124): 5.7	2.9
2013	ROC	AAA	29	391	58	25	0	24	76	43	89	2	1	.352/.427/.639	.350	.413	-2.0	1B(67): -1.9, RF(14): -0.5	3.9
2013	MIN	MLB	29	181	14	3	0	7	17	20	58	0	1	.194/.287/.344	.240	.253	-0.9	1B(26): 1.0, RF(11): -0.5	-0.3
2014	ROC	AAA	30	238	28	13	0	10	38	21	55	0	0	.268/.336/.469	.267	.313	-0.6	1B(54): 3.0, RF(2): -0.1	0.9
2014	MIN	MLB	30	220	17	13	0	6	39	14	66	0	2	.229/.282/.380	.244	.308	0.2	1B(23): -1.2, RF(19): -1.8	-0.4
2015	*TOR*	*MLB*	*31*	*281*	*31*	*14*	*0*	*11*	*37*	*22*	*76*	*1*	*1*	*.244/.311/.427*	*.272*	*.303*	*0.1*	*1B 1, RF -1*	*0.6*

Breakout: 4%   Improve: 12%   Collapse: 6%   Attrition: 18%   MLB: 34%   Comparables: *Ryan Shealy, Micah Hoffpauir, Kevin Witt*

After more than a decade in the minors and independent ball, Colabello made the Twins' Opening Day roster, earned the season's first AL Player of the Week award, set a team record for RBIs in a month and posted a .346/.386/.577 line through April 23rd. Then fate, transubstantiated as a Grant Balfour fastball, intervened. Colabello was jammed on the pitch, suffered nerve damage in his thumb, stayed in the lineup and went into a tailspin that culminated in a May demotion to Triple-A. An offseason of rest may help heal his hand, and if he's right Colabello could work as a bench bat or short-term fill-in at first base or in an outfield corner, but if (as seems likely) last April was his peak, it's as much as any Worcester Tornado could have asked for.

Andy Dirks   LF

Born: 1/24/86   Age: 29   Bats: L   Throws: L   Height: 6' 0"   Weight: 195

YEAR	TEAM	LVL	AGE	PA	R	2B	3B	HR	RBI	BB	K	SB	CS	AVG/OBP/SLG	TAv	BABIP	BRR	FRAA	WARP
2012	TOL	AAA	26	41	4	1	0	2	5	4	8	2	0	.216/.293/.405	.235	.222	0.2	RF(6): -0.8, CF(2): -0.1	0.1
2012	DET	MLB	26	344	56	18	5	8	35	23	53	1	1	.322/.370/.487	.297	.365	2.0	LF(59): -1.0, RF(24): -2.2	1.5
2013	DET	MLB	27	484	60	16	2	9	37	42	84	7	1	.256/.323/.363	.255	.298	-2.5	LF(116): 7.4, RF(15): 0.1	1.0
2015	TOR	MLB	29	250	31	12	1	6	25	19	46	3	1	.264/.324/.407	.268	.304	-0.1	LF 3, RF -0	1.0

Breakout: 4%   Improve: 37%   Collapse: 7%   Attrition: 13%   MLB: 100%   Comparables: *David Murphy, Chris Coghlan, Ben Francisco*

Dirks was projected to lose only two months of 2014 to back surgery, but a malevolent series of hamstring setbacks kept interrupting his rehab assignments; it made Lucy holding the ball for Charlie Brown look like Mother Teresa bathing the blind. Mostly suited for left, Dirks still has the knack to play a fourth outfielder and the neck to be a centurion, but none of it matters if he can't successfully complete a rehab assignment. Big necks *are* respected in certain cultures, though.

Josh Donaldson   3B

Born: 12/8/85   Age: 29   Bats: R   Throws: R   Height: 6' 0"   Weight: 220

YEAR	TEAM	LVL	AGE	PA	R	2B	3B	HR	RBI	BB	K	SB	CS	AVG/OBP/SLG	TAv	BABIP	BRR	FRAA	WARP
2012	SAC	AAA	26	234	38	12	2	13	45	23	34	5	2	.335/.402/.598	.342	.350	-0.2	3B(26): -1.8, C(22): -0.0	2.8
2012	OAK	MLB	26	294	34	16	0	9	33	14	61	4	1	.241/.289/.398	.257	.278	0.5	3B(71): 5.5, C(3): -0.0	1.7
2013	OAK	MLB	27	668	89	37	3	24	93	76	110	5	2	.301/.384/.499	.326	.333	-2.9	3B(155): 1.2, 1B(1): -0.0	6.2
2014	OAK	MLB	28	695	93	31	2	29	98	76	130	8	2	.255/.342/.456	.302	.278	-2.5	3B(150): 19.4	6.7
2015	TOR	MLB	29	648	81	32	2	26	90	64	131	6	1	.264/.342/.464	.296	.297	-1.7	3B 9, C 0	4.8

Breakout: 3%   Improve: 48%   Collapse: 3%   Attrition: 6%   MLB: 96%   Comparables: *Chase Headley, David Freese, Ryan Zimmerman*

Donaldson seemed like the perfect Athletic. He came to the A's as part of the return for Rich Harden in 2008, was unable to cut it behind the plate after six years catching in the minors, transitioned to third base and voila! All-Star, MVP votes, screaming fans. He exhibits outstanding plate coverage with a swing designed for line drives and the strength to drive the ball out of any part of the park, all of which is enhanced by a patient approach (see? Perfect Athletic) that results in frequent free passes. His defense (ibid.) garners universal love from the metrics and fueled the fifth-highest WARP in the majors last season. Donaldson literally limped to the finish line in an attempt to resurrect a crumbling A's offense, playing through a knee injury that he suffered on the final weekend of the regular season.

Of course, to truly be the perfect Athletic required Donaldson to be sacrificed via trade to feed the machine of market efficiency. With his Super Two status this offseason and his late bloom suggesting that his peak could end any moment, Billy Beane and crew decided the time was right (after previously laughing off the notion that Donaldson would be traded) and the Blue Jays, who aren't as handicapped by the penny ante ways of Oakland's ownership group, were happy to snap him up for a collection of talent headlined by Brett Lawrie and Franklin Barreto.

Edwin Encarnacion   1B

Born: 1/7/83   Age: 32   Bats: R   Throws: R   Height: 6' 1"   Weight: 230

YEAR	TEAM	LVL	AGE	PA	R	2B	3B	HR	RBI	BB	K	SB	CS	AVG/OBP/SLG	TAv	BABIP	BRR	FRAA	WARP
2012	TOR	MLB	29	644	93	24	0	42	110	84	94	13	3	.280/.384/.557	.324	.266	-3.9	1B(68): -6.3, LF(3): -0.0	3.8
2013	TOR	MLB	30	621	90	29	1	36	104	82	62	7	1	.272/.370/.534	.319	.247	1.8	1B(79): -5.5, 3B(10): 1.1	4.4
2014	TOR	MLB	31	542	75	27	2	34	98	62	82	2	0	.268/.354/.547	.307	.260	-0.1	1B(80): -3.2, LF(2): -0.1	2.6
2015	TOR	MLB	32	527	72	25	1	26	80	56	80	5	1	.263/.347/.490	.306	.265	-0.7	1B -6, 3B -0	2.3

Breakout: 0%   Improve: 25%   Collapse: 2%   Attrition: 5%   MLB: 98%   Comparables: *Adrian Gonzalez, Mark Teixeira, Justin Morneau*

In the past three years, Encarnacion's 112 homers trails only Miguel Cabrera, by just one. More remarkable is that Hit Tracker Online has labeled 43 of them "no-doubters"—they "cleared the fence by at least 20 vertical feet and landed at least 50 feet past the fence"—12 more than Jose Bautista, who places second in that category. That Encarnacion has lapped the league in no-doubters is remarkable for someone who doesn't receive the superstar treatment, the "did you see that Vine" spotlight, yet his home runs indeed leave parks in a hurry, often pulled high to left field. Encarnacion doesn't possess Bryce Harper-level power, but he is one of the few true fly-ball, aim-for-the-fences batters in the league who also makes contact at an above-average rate, traits he shares with hitters like Bautista, David Ortiz and Mike Trout. If Encarnacion doesn't lose his bat speed as he ages—and pitchers continue testing the inner half with him—expect to see the parrot take another 30 trips around the bases.

Juan Francisco   3B

Born: 6/24/87   Age: 28   Bats: L   Throws: R   Height: 6' 2"   Weight: 245

YEAR	TEAM	LVL	AGE	PA	R	2B	3B	HR	RBI	BB	K	SB	CS	AVG/OBP/SLG	TAv	BABIP	BRR	FRAA	WARP
2012	ATL	MLB	25	205	17	11	0	9	32	11	70	1	1	.234/.278/.432	.241	.316	-1.9	3B(49): -1.5	-0.1
2013	ATL	MLB	26	115	10	2	0	5	16	7	43	0	1	.241/.287/.398	.244	.350	-1.0	3B(30): 2.4	0.3
2013	MIL	MLB	26	270	26	10	1	13	32	25	95	0	1	.221/.300/.433	.256	.299	0.8	1B(67): -2.3, 3B(4): -0.2	0.1
2014	BUF	AAA	27	50	9	2	1	2	11	6	9	0	0	.341/.420/.568	.324	.394	-0.1	3B(7): -0.3	0.5
2014	TOR	MLB	27	320	40	16	2	16	43	27	116	0	2	.220/.291/.456	.267	.297	-0.7	3B(74): -3.5, 1B(20): -0.6	1.0
2015	TOR	MLB	28	321	36	16	1	14	44	21	102	1	1	.239/.292/.439	.265	.312	-0.5	3B -2, 1B -1	0.3

Breakout: 2%   Improve: 42%   Collapse: 6%   Attrition: 12%   MLB: 82%   Comparables: *Josh Fields, Josh Phelps, Chris Johnson*

On May 10th, Francisco smashed a pitch from Cliff Lee for his first major-league home run off a left-handed pitcher. Thirty-five had come before against righties, making Francisco an obvious platoon half. The Blue Jays signed him soon after his release from the Brewers in spring training and Francisco delivered as advertised, his True Average .285 against righties, .168 against southpaws—how did he manage to sneak 49 plate appearances there? As pitchers left and right began to figure out he couldn't hit any breaking ball, Francisco's ride slowed down, coming to a stop in September, when he ceded all but five at-bats to Danny Valencia. With the league's second-highest strikeout rate and little defensive value, Francisco should make his career hitting mistakes in Triple-A.

Ryan Goins   2B

Born: 2/13/88   Age: 27   Bats: L   Throws: R   Height: 5' 10"   Weight: 185

YEAR	TEAM	LVL	AGE	PA	R	2B	3B	HR	RBI	BB	K	SB	CS	AVG/OBP/SLG	TAv	BABIP	BRR	FRAA	WARP
2012	NHP	AA	24	618	66	33	4	7	61	47	78	15	9	.289/.342/.403	.268	.323	-0.7	SS(114): 0.2, 2B(23): 1.8	3.6
2013	BUF	AAA	25	418	42	22	1	6	46	29	85	3	5	.257/.311/.369	.242	.316	0.6	SS(101): 6.5, 2B(9): -1.0	1.3
2013	TOR	MLB	25	121	11	5	0	2	8	2	28	0	0	.252/.264/.345	.231	.315	-1.4	2B(32): 1.0, SS(2): 0.0	-0.1
2014	BUF	AAA	26	402	36	21	2	0	30	28	64	4	4	.284/.337/.353	.249	.342	0.2	SS(51): 2.2, 2B(49): 1.5	1.3
2014	TOR	MLB	26	193	14	6	3	1	15	5	42	0	1	.188/.209/.271	.190	.237	-0.7	2B(57): 1.3, SS(15): 0.1	-0.7
2015	TOR	MLB	27	277	27	13	1	3	22	14	57	2	2	.244/.283/.340	.230	.291	-1.1	2B 1, SS 1	0.3

Breakout: 4%   Improve: 11%   Collapse: 4%   Attrition: 20%   MLB: 34%   Comparables: *Pete Orr, Anderson Hernandez, Chris Valaika*

Goins is the kind of player who can appear to make a whole season out of a single web gem—or rather, hand gem: Go check out his insane barehand stab and leaping throw on a bad-hop bouncer on September 8th. You only have to hit a little bit if you can field like that, but unfortunately Goins cannot hit a little bit; in fact, he got worse in his second big-league trial, and was demoted to Triple-A after a month as the Jays' second baseman. If he doesn't show improvement this season, the Jays may have to relegate him to late-inning replacement duties.

A.J. Jimenez   C

Born: 5/1/90   Age: 25   Bats: R   Throws: R   Height: 6' 0"   Weight: 225

YEAR	TEAM	LVL	AGE	PA	R	2B	3B	HR	RBI	BB	K	SB	CS	AVG/OBP/SLG	TAv	BABIP	BRR	FRAA	WARP
2012	NHP	AA	22	113	14	4	1	2	10	5	14	2	3	.257/.295/.371	.240	.278	-1.2	C(27): 0.2	0.3
2013	DUN	A+	23	29	5	3	0	1	9	1	3	0	0	.429/.448/.643	.391	.458	-2.4	C(7): -0.1	0.3
2013	NHP	AA	23	223	28	15	0	3	29	16	37	1	2	.276/.327/.394	.271	.319	-0.7	C(40): 1.9	1.3
2013	BUF	AAA	23	31	0	1	0	0	0	1	2	0	1	.233/.258/.267	.189	.250	-0.5	C(7): -0.0	-0.1
2014	NHP	AA	24	102	11	8	0	1	13	6	19	1	0	.223/.275/.340	.214	.267	1.7	C(24): 0.8	0.2
2014	BUF	AAA	24	237	21	13	1	2	24	13	33	1	1	.260/.295/.356	.233	.291	0.3	C(48): 0.2	0.3
2015	TOR	MLB	25	250	20	13	1	3	24	11	49	1	1	.238/.274/.341	.229	.283	-0.5	C 1	0.2

Breakout: 7%   Improve: 9%   Collapse: 14%   Attrition: 21%   MLB: 28%   Comparables: *Josh Phegley, Caleb Joseph, Wyatt Toregas*

Jimenez has big-league skills behind the plate. The questions are about his bat and, perhaps more importantly in this age of the punchless catcher, his health. Jimenez bulked up before 2014 to absorb the toll of the job, but still missed most of August with an undisclosed injury. If he's healthy, he should get a chance in the majors this season. The Jays have Dioner Navarro under contract in 2015 to buy Jimenez a year of development.

Dan Johnson   1B

Born: 8/10/79   Age: 35   Bats: L   Throws: R   Height: 6' 2"   Weight: 210

YEAR	TEAM	LVL	AGE	PA	R	2B	3B	HR	RBI	BB	K	SB	CS	AVG/OBP/SLG	TAv	BABIP	BRR	FRAA	WARP
2012	CHR	AAA	32	589	77	21	1	28	85	94	94	1	0	.267/.388/.492	.304	.272	0.3	1B(89): -1.8, 3B(15): 1.3	3.6
2012	CHA	MLB	32	31	8	1	0	3	6	9	3	0	0	.364/.548/.818	.441	.313	0.5	1B(3): 0.0	0.7
2013	SWB	AAA	33	560	57	26	0	21	69	93	82	1	0	.253/.379/.447	.294	.264	-5.1	1B(113): 3.7, 3B(5): -0.1	2.5
2013	BAL	MLB	33	5	0	0	0	0	0	0	1	0	0	.000/.000/.000	.027	.000	0.0	1B(1): -0.0	-0.1
2014	BUF	AAA	34	460	62	19	0	18	56	86	81	0	0	.232/.381/.434	.285	.245	-2.2	1B(81): -6.8, 3B(1): 0.0	1.0
2014	TOR	MLB	34	48	8	2	0	1	7	7	10	0	0	.211/.333/.342	.264	.241	-1.6	1B(8): 0.1	-0.1
2015	TOR	MLB	35	250	31	10	0	10	34	36	49	0	0	.231/.347/.423	.284	.250	-0.5	1B -0, 3B 0	0.8

Breakout: 4%   Improve: 21%   Collapse: 15%   Attrition: 23%   MLB: 72%   Comparables: *Roberto Petagine, Andy Tracy, Bobby Scales*

The Annual harvests The Great Pumpkin yet again, but not because of any late-season heroics (which he did not provide) or because he logged more big-league service time than in any season since 2007 (which he did). No, he's in here because last fall he revealed his secret, three-year project to extend his big-league career: He's been learning a knuckleball. (Pause while you rub your eyes.) It's too bad Johnson earned a big chunk of last year's major-league salary while he was on the disabled list with a hamstring strain, reducing the amount of tutelage he could get from R.A. Dickey. Here's hoping Johnson leads Triple-A in walks drawn *and* walks allowed in 2015.

Munenori Kawasaki   2B

Born: 6/3/81   Age: 34   Bats: L   Throws: R   Height: 5' 11"   Weight: 175

YEAR	TEAM	LVL	AGE	PA	R	2B	3B	HR	RBI	BB	K	SB	CS	AVG/OBP/SLG	TAv	BABIP	BRR	FRAA	WARP
2012	SEA	MLB	31	115	13	1	0	0	7	8	18	2	2	.192/.257/.202	.185	.233	-0.7	SS(38): -1.9, 2B(10): 0.4	-0.7
2013	BUF	AAA	32	81	9	0	0	0	3	14	12	3	0	.250/.400/.250	.234	.313	-0.9	SS(12): -0.1, 2B(11): -0.1	-0.1
2013	TOR	MLB	32	289	27	6	5	1	24	32	41	7	1	.229/.326/.308	.245	.269	0.9	SS(60): -3.1, 2B(18): 1.5	0.5
2014	BUF	AAA	33	129	12	11	1	0	9	8	17	1	1	.276/.320/.388	.255	.320	-0.3	SS(28): 0.2, 2B(13): 1.2	0.4
2014	TOR	MLB	33	274	31	7	1	0	17	22	49	1	0	.258/.327/.296	.238	.323	1.3	2B(64): 1.8, 3B(19): 1.9	0.8
2015	TOR	MLB	34	289	26	10	2	1	20	25	51	4	1	.237/.312/.301	.231	.281	0.5	2B 2, SS -2	0.4

Breakout: 2%   Improve: 29%   Collapse: 13%   Attrition: 17%   MLB: 83%   Comparables: *Jamey Carroll, Aaron Miles, Alfredo Amezaga*

According to PITCHf/x, Kawasaki saw fastballs on over 68 percent of pitches last year, "bettered" only by Austin Romine among hitters with 250 plate appearances. Hitting for no power, nor even fly balls, limited any serious damage from Kawasaki; he produced an absurd line drive rate that lifted his batting average, but that was it. The rest of his production was mediocre, including a walk rate that regressed to league average after a 2013 spike. That left his contributions to his ability to work a count, play middle infield and provide between-inning entertainment.

Russell Martin   C

Born: 2/15/83   Age: 32   Bats: R   Throws: R   Height: 5' 10"   Weight: 215

YEAR	TEAM	LVL	AGE	PA	R	2B	3B	HR	RBI	BB	K	SB	CS	AVG/OBP/SLG	TAv	BABIP	BRR	FRAA	WARP
2012	NYA	MLB	29	485	50	18	0	21	53	53	95	6	1	.211/.311/.403	.255	.222	1.2	C(128): -0.6	2.0
2013	PIT	MLB	30	506	51	21	0	15	55	58	108	9	5	.226/.327/.377	.260	.266	0.4	C(120): 1.5, 3B(3): -0.1	2.8
2014	PIT	MLB	31	460	45	20	0	11	67	59	78	4	4	.290/.402/.430	.312	.336	-1.1	C(107): 3.7	5.2
2015	TOR	MLB	32	441	51	18	0	13	51	50	87	6	3	.238/.336/.386	.273	.273	0.0	C 1, 3B -0	2.4

| | Breakout: 1% | Improve: 28% | Collapse: 8% | Attrition: 13% | MLB: 97% | | *Comparables:* | *Ted Simmons, Gary Carter, Victor Martinez* |

Had Zora Neale Hurston worried about baseball, she might have written, "Free agents at a distance have every team's wish on board." Martin's tenure with the Pirates made him the rare free-agent signing who exceeded expectations. He missed about a month with thigh issues in 2014 and had the best offensive season of his career anyway. His trademark defense remained strong, headed by excellent receiving. When the Pirates signed Martin, some wondered why they would do that. With the Pirates letting him walk in free agency, those same people are wondering why they would do *that*. It's a testament to Martin that he became a piece of the Pittsburgh tapestry so quickly. Now, two years older than the last time around, he'll try to repeat the feat in Toronto after the Blue Jays signed him to a backloaded five-year deal.

Dioner Navarro   C

Born: 2/9/84   Age: 31   Bats: B   Throws: R   Height: 5' 9"   Weight: 205

YEAR	TEAM	LVL	AGE	PA	R	2B	3B	HR	RBI	BB	K	SB	CS	AVG/OBP/SLG	TAv	BABIP	BRR	FRAA	WARP
2012	LOU	AAA	28	240	24	12	0	5	32	23	24	0	0	.319/.382/.449	.281	.332	-3.8	C(49): -0.5	1.3
2012	CIN	MLB	28	73	6	3	1	2	12	2	12	0	0	.290/.306/.449	.260	.321	0.9	C(21): -0.2	0.5
2013	CHN	MLB	29	266	31	7	0	13	34	23	36	0	1	.300/.365/.492	.301	.307	-5.3	C(55): 0.2	1.6
2014	TOR	MLB	30	520	40	22	0	12	69	32	76	3	0	.274/.317/.395	.257	.301	-1.3	C(112): -1.7	1.4
2015	TOR	MLB	31	438	45	18	1	11	49	34	70	2	0	.259/.320/.391	.262	.285	-2.1	C -0	1.4

| | Breakout: 5% | Improve: 28% | Collapse: 10% | Attrition: 14% | MLB: 85% | | *Comparables:* | *Josh Bard, Brayan Pena, Carlos Ruiz* |

On his fifth team in five years, Navarro arrived in Toronto with a simple task: Improve on the precedent set by his heirs. Blue Jays catchers (J.P. Arencibia and Josh Thole) accrued -1.3 WARP at the position in 2013, setting the bar politely low for Navarro to clear. And despite wide career platoon splits, he cleared it and more, hitting near league average while starting regularly for the first time since 2009. At times, his wild whiffs looked like physical precursors to stumbling over, but look, no one said it'd be pretty. The Jays were just looking for an upgrade over their previous situation and Navarro was an easy improvement for $3 million. With his play, he's now the most popular Dion in Toronto sports, too. Again, low bar to clear.

Max Pentecost   C

Born: 3/10/93   Age: 22   Bats: R   Throws: R   Height: 6' 2"   Weight: 191

YEAR	TEAM	LVL	AGE	PA	R	2B	3B	HR	RBI	BB	K	SB	CS	AVG/OBP/SLG	TAv	BABIP	BRR	FRAA	WARP
2014	VAN	A-	21	87	15	2	3	0	9	2	18	2	1	.313/.322/.410	.266	.388	0.3	C(6): -0.1	0.1
2015	TOR	MLB	22	250	17	9	1	2	19	10	74	1	1	.197/.233/.271	.189	.272	-0.2	C -0	-1.3

| | Breakout: 0% | Improve: 0% | Collapse: 0% | Attrition: 0% | MLB: 0% | | *Comparables:* | *Ben Paulsen, Tyler Moore, Donald Lutz* |

Pentecost was the Jays' top pick in the 2014 draft, taken 11th overall out of Kennesaw State in Georgia (also the alma mater of fellow Blue Jay Chad Jenkins). A smallish, bat-first catcher, Pentecost nonetheless has shown good pop times behind the plate, and he's already gotten his Tommy John surgery out of the way. He projects as a solid rather than spectacular big-league regular. Pentecost's first half-season saw him spend most of his time at DH and visit the Jays' doctors in Florida with nicks and dents; he reportedly wound up having labrum surgery in October. If he doesn't ultimately have the body to withstand the load at catcher, the Jays will hope that his professional, line-drive swing will add homers and make him a corner infield candidate. And if *that* doesn't work, he can always retire to a quiet life as a vigilante with a grim mien, a dark trench coat and a Saint Edmund the Martyr medal tucked into his shirt.

Kevin Pillar   LF

Born: 1/4/89   Age: 26   Bats: R   Throws: R   Height: 6' 0"   Weight: 205

YEAR	TEAM	LVL	AGE	PA	R	2B	3B	HR	RBI	BB	K	SB	CS	AVG/OBP/SLG	TAv	BABIP	BRR	FRAA	WARP
2012	LNS	A	23	375	49	20	4	5	57	35	53	35	6	.322/.390/.451	.290	.371	0.1	LF(49): 3.9, RF(15): 2.7	2.9
2012	DUN	A+	23	178	16	8	2	1	34	5	17	16	3	.323/.339/.415	.284	.342	1.6	RF(18): -0.7, CF(16): -0.5	1.1
2013	NHP	AA	24	327	44	20	2	5	30	19	31	15	8	.313/.361/.441	.284	.336	1.3	CF(53): 2.2, LF(20): -1.3	2.4
2013	BUF	AAA	24	218	30	19	4	4	27	12	39	8	5	.299/.341/.493	.294	.350	1.9	LF(21): 2.5, CF(20): -0.7	1.9
2013	TOR	MLB	24	110	11	4	0	3	13	4	29	0	1	.206/.250/.333	.219	.257	-1.7	LF(33): 1.2, RF(1): -0.0	-0.2
2014	BUF	AAA	25	434	57	39	6	10	59	21	48	27	6	.323/.359/.509	.299	.345	3.2	LF(47): 0.3, CF(31): -4.0	3.5
2014	TOR	MLB	25	122	19	9	0	2	7	4	28	1	2	.267/.295/.397	.258	.333	-0.1	LF(30): 0.5, CF(16): -0.2	0.3
2015	TOR	MLB	26	250	27	15	1	5	26	10	46	9	3	.269/.303/.403	.261	.313	-0.5	LF 2, CF -1	0.7

| | Breakout: 4% | Improve: 26% | Collapse: 9% | Attrition: 23% | MLB: 57% | | *Comparables:* | *Alex Presley, Xavier Paul, David Lough* |

Pillar had a minor-league tantrum when he was pulled for a pinch-hitter in a game in late June, throwing his bat in the dugout—not the best idea when you have a .520 OPS and no walks in 40 plate appearances. He was promptly demoted to Triple-A, where he raked thanks to an adjustment not only to his attitude but also to his swing: Pillar moved his hands in and down, giving him more compact mechanics and minimizing the loop in his cut. Recalled in late August, he raised his batting average nearly 50 points and his status out of Gibbons' doghouse by the end of the year. He ought to be a valuable fourth-outfielder type this season.

Dalton Pompey   CF

Born: 12/11/92   Age: 22   Bats: B   Throws: R   Height: 6' 2"   Weight: 195

YEAR	TEAM	LVL	AGE	PA	R	2B	3B	HR	RBI	BB	K	SB	CS	AVG/OBP/SLG	TAv	BABIP	BRR	FRAA	WARP
2012	LNS	A	19	24	1	0	1	0	3	1	5	1	1	.227/.261/.318	.260	.294	-0.8	CF(5): 0.0	0.0
2012	VAN	A-	19	44	11	3	1	0	4	9	7	3	0	.294/.442/.441	.371	.370	1.8	CF(10): 1.2	0.9
2013	LNS	A	20	511	68	22	9	6	40	63	106	38	10	.261/.358/.394	.266	.329	2.7	CF(102): -5.3, LF(6): 0.0	1.3
2014	DUN	A+	21	317	49	12	6	6	34	35	56	29	2	.319/.397/.471	.306	.380	6.5	CF(70): 1.8	3.7
2014	NHP	AA	21	127	20	5	3	2	12	14	18	8	5	.295/.378/.473	.305	.330	2.3	CF(30): -2.1	1.1
2014	BUF	AAA	21	56	15	5	0	0	5	3	10	6	0	.358/.393/.453	.302	.442	0.7	CF(11): 0.1	0.5
2014	TOR	MLB	21	43	5	1	2	1	4	4	12	1	0	.231/.302/.436	.253	.308	0.8	LF(9): -0.5, CF(5): -0.1	0.1
2015	TOR	MLB	22	250	31	10	3	4	19	21	64	12	3	.235/.303/.348	.244	.307	1.6	CF -2, LF -0	0.2

| | Breakout: 4% | Improve: 28% | Collapse: 2% | Attrition: 14% | MLB: 43% | | *Comparables:* | *Ryan Kalish, Austin Jackson, Nick Markakis* |

After Pompey got his first big-league hit in September, Derek Jeter gave him the Emerson-to-Whitman "I greet you at the beginning of a great career" anointment. Four nights later, he hit his first career homer off no less a luminary than Felix Hernandez. Not bad for a kid who began the season in High-A. With Anthony Gose and Kevin Pillar failing to convince the Jays of their centerfieldworthiness (that's a 21-letter "word," kids), Pompey has a chance to seize the job. The switch-hitter has no worrisome platoon split (though he's a better hitter from the left side), and his fielding and speed grade out plus. The former 16th-rounder's sudden emergence recalls that of another low-round 2010 center field draftee, the Rays' Kevin Kiermaier. Pompey also happens to be as nice a kid as you can imagine, and—be still your hearts, Jays fans—from Ontario.

Colby Rasmus   CF

Born: 8/11/86   Age: 28   Bats: L   Throws: L   Height: 6' 2"   Weight: 195

YEAR	TEAM	LVL	AGE	PA	R	2B	3B	HR	RBI	BB	K	SB	CS	AVG/OBP/SLG	TAv	BABIP	BRR	FRAA	WARP
2012	TOR	MLB	25	625	75	21	5	23	75	47	149	4	3	.223/.289/.400	.240	.259	0.6	CF(145): -9.1	0.1
2013	TOR	MLB	26	458	57	26	1	22	66	37	135	0	1	.276/.338/.501	.297	.356	1.0	CF(114): 7.6	4.1
2014	BUF	AAA	27	24	0	0	0	0	2	1	9	0	0	.130/.167/.130	.126	.214	0.0	CF(4): 0.4	-0.3
2014	TOR	MLB	27	376	45	21	1	18	40	29	124	4	0	.225/.287/.448	.268	.294	-0.5	CF(87): 4.2	1.7
2015	TOR	MLB	28	373	44	17	2	14	47	32	102	2	1	.239/.309/.429	.270	.298	0.3	CF -3	1.1

Breakout: 1%   Improve: 58%   Collapse: 0%   Attrition: 3%   MLB: 99%   Comparables: Chris Young, Bobby Murcer, Fred Lynn

Adjusting for 2013's inflated BABIP, Rasmus has posted the same numbers for three years now: low on-base percentage, high strikeout rate, big power for a center fielder. His fielding utility used to offset his awful performance against southpaws, but his range disappeared in 2014, and John Gibbons benched him in September in favor of Kevin Pillar. Besides his weakness to left-handers, he's easily fooled by breaking balls, restricting his hitting value to squaring up a fastball. That's still valuable, especially for Rasmus, who hits so many fly balls. Striking out a third of the time mounts intense frustration though, and the Blue Jays, with three-and-a-half years of it, set him free to the open market.

Jose Reyes   SS

Born: 6/11/83   Age: 32   Bats: B   Throws: R   Height: 6' 0"   Weight: 195

YEAR	TEAM	LVL	AGE	PA	R	2B	3B	HR	RBI	BB	K	SB	CS	AVG/OBP/SLG	TAv	BABIP	BRR	FRAA	WARP
2012	MIA	MLB	29	716	86	37	12	11	57	63	56	40	11	.287/.347/.433	.293	.298	4.3	SS(160): -15.0	4.1
2013	TOR	MLB	30	419	58	20	0	10	37	34	47	15	6	.296/.353/.427	.283	.315	2.2	SS(92): 1.4	3.3
2014	TOR	MLB	31	655	94	33	4	9	51	38	73	30	2	.287/.328/.398	.271	.312	6.4	SS(142): -11.1	2.8
2015	TOR	MLB	32	573	74	29	6	9	53	39	62	26	5	.287/.335/.421	.279	.306	3.4	SS -8	3.1

Breakout: 1%   Improve: 42%   Collapse: 4%   Attrition: 10%   MLB: 98%   Comparables: Jimmy Rollins, Rafael Furcal, Jason Bartlett

Reyes' season could not have begun more disastrously: First game, first inning, first plate appearance, he strained his hamstring. Again. The Blue Jays' leadoff man, lost for nearly a third of 2013, visited the disabled list for the ninth time in his career. He left the shortstop reins to Jonathan Diaz and Ryan Goins, who, if given 10 seasons, likely wouldn't combine to match Reyes' production in one. Fortunately for Toronto, Reyes missed just 16 games recovering from the strain and played nearly every other once healthy. His speed took time to return but once it did, he stole 17 consecutive bases without getting caught, a three-month stretch that contributed to the best success rate of his career. With the sluggers behind him, pitchers fed Reyes more fastballs than ever and he appropriately swung more, still showing a knack for quality contact. At age 32, that skill will be essential as his power, speed and defense slip away. There's not much else otherwise, despite his status as baseball's highest-paid shortstop.

Michael Saunders   RF

Born: 11/19/86   Age: 28   Bats: L   Throws: R   Height: 6' 4"   Weight: 225

YEAR	TEAM	LVL	AGE	PA	R	2B	3B	HR	RBI	BB	K	SB	CS	AVG/OBP/SLG	TAv	BABIP	BRR	FRAA	WARP
2012	SEA	MLB	25	553	71	31	3	19	57	43	132	21	4	.247/.306/.432	.281	.297	1.7	CF(113): -3.3, LF(22): 0.6	2.5
2013	SEA	MLB	26	468	59	23	3	12	46	54	118	13	5	.236/.323/.397	.281	.298	2.1	CF(78): -2.1, RF(34): 0.8	2.2
2014	TAC	AAA	27	71	11	3	1	1	9	16	15	0	0	.327/.479/.473	.367	.436	1.0	RF(10): -0.3	1.0
2014	SEA	MLB	27	263	38	11	3	8	34	26	59	4	5	.273/.341/.450	.316	.327	0.1	RF(68): 0.3, CF(12): 0.1	1.9
2015	TOR	MLB	28	300	36	14	2	8	32	32	76	8	3	.237/.320/.395	.266	.296	0.5	CF -0, RF 0	1.0

Breakout: 2%   Improve: 53%   Collapse: 4%   Attrition: 15%   MLB: 98%   Comparables: Jeremy Hermida, Michael Cuddyer, Corey Hart

One of the unfortunate outcomes of our dumb human brains is that our drive to connect cause and effect also drives us to attach a moral weight to that cause. Paradoxically, with our modern medical and chemical knowledge, the responsibility of health and welfare has shifted increasingly toward the control of the individual. When one becomes sick, the tendency is to ask what they did wrong to fall prey to their illness, whether they failed to wash their hands or licked the subway car. So it is with obliques, which is why the Mariners publicly castigated the Condor for a regime that led to his various maladies over the past several years. This might have been arbitration maneuvering, a campaign on public opinion with the subtlety of late-October political television advertisements, but the timing and the public venting of these laments are undeniable; the Mariners simply wished he were someone he is not. It's worth asking whether Seattle could have gotten more than J.A. Happ in return for him without the carping.

Ryan Schimpf   2B

Born: 4/11/88   Age: 27   Bats: L   Throws: R   Height: 5' 9"   Weight: 190

YEAR	TEAM	LVL	AGE	PA	R	2B	3B	HR	RBI	BB	K	SB	CS	AVG/OBP/SLG	TAv	BABIP	BRR	FRAA	WARP
2012	DUN	A+	24	419	59	29	3	14	61	48	89	4	2	.266/.353/.479	.286	.311	-1.6	2B(69): -1.1, 3B(16): 0.5	2.2
2012	NHP	AA	24	137	21	8	0	8	15	23	32	3	1	.279/.412/.568	.329	.324	0.7	3B(16): -0.2, LF(12): -0.4	1.5
2013	NHP	AA	25	529	67	21	3	23	65	79	138	3	3	.210/.338/.428	.271	.248	-1.7	3B(49): -3.8, 2B(38): 1.4	1.5
2014	NHP	AA	26	219	35	17	1	15	37	28	56	1	0	.270/.370/.616	.337	.299	0.4	LF(14): -0.8, 2B(13): 0.9	2.4
2014	BUF	AAA	26	246	29	7	1	9	21	24	59	0	1	.189/.290/.358	.232	.212	1.0	2B(38): 2.1, RF(12): 0.3	0.6
2015	TOR	MLB	27	250	29	10	1	10	33	27	73	1	0	.209/.303/.406	.261	.256	-0.4	2B 0, 3B -0	0.6

Breakout: 0%   Improve: 4%   Collapse: 9%   Attrition: 17%   MLB: 22%   Comparables: Mike Hollimon, Brooks Conrad, Kevin Melillo

It's fun to misread this little sport ute's name as "Schimpf," but he was a big fish on LSU's national championship team in 2009, and even then his coach was calling him a lunchpail player. Schimpf has some patience at the plate and pop in his bat, although the uppercut swing will be exploited in the big leagues, driving up an already high strikeout rate. But given the Jays' second base options (a team-worst .634 OPS from keystone-sackers like Goins, Kawasaki and Tolleson) and their lack of a dependable utility player, Schimpf—who can play outfield, too—could work his way into a useful role.

Justin Smoak   1B

Born: 12/5/86   Age: 28   Bats: B   Throws: L   Height: 6' 4"   Weight: 230

YEAR	TEAM	LVL	AGE	PA	R	2B	3B	HR	RBI	BB	K	SB	CS	AVG/OBP/SLG	TAv	BABIP	BRR	FRAA	WARP
2012	TAC	AAA	25	82	10	6	1	0	4	16	16	1	0	.242/.390/.364	.266	.320	0.4	1B(19): -0.2	0.1
2012	SEA	MLB	25	535	49	14	0	19	51	49	111	1	0	.217/.290/.364	.239	.242	-2.5	1B(131): -9.4	-2.0
2013	TAC	AAA	26	22	2	2	0	0	1	0	5	0	0	.238/.273/.333	.266	.313	0.3	1B(3): -0.2	0.0
2013	SEA	MLB	26	521	53	19	0	20	50	64	119	0	0	.238/.334/.412	.281	.278	-5.1	1B(125): -8.1	0.2
2014	TAC	AAA	27	249	29	13	0	7	40	33	41	0	2	.337/.422/.502	.349	.376	-0.9	1B(42): -0.8	2.5
2014	SEA	MLB	27	276	28	13	0	7	30	24	66	0	1	.202/.275/.339	.235	.243	-0.4	1B(79): -2.9	-0.8
2015	TOR	MLB	28	347	38	15	0	11	42	40	77	0	0	.237/.328/.400	.271	.279	-1.7	1B -4	0.1

Breakout: 0%   Improve: 40%   Collapse: 1%   Attrition: 14%   MLB: 92%   Comparables: Mitch Moreland, Dan Johnson, Kevin Youkilis

A modern point of debate in etiquette is the act of ghosting, in which a guest, rather than making a formal departure from a party and its host, simply slips out unseen. The idea is that while you would think it's rude to not say goodbye, the act of saying it not only interrupts the flow of the party, it draws attention to itself and makes a connotative statement, like it or not, about the proceedings. Someone who ghosts may irk people at the end of the night, when the crime is discovered, but at least the important part, the night itself, remains intact.

In 2014, Justin Smoak left his coat on the Mariners' bed and went out for a cigarette. He will be missed, in a way.

Rowdy Tellez   1B

Born: 3/16/95   Age: 20   Bats: L   Throws: L   Height: 6' 4"   Weight: 220

YEAR	TEAM	LVL	AGE	PA	R	2B	3B	HR	RBI	BB	K	SB	CS	AVG/OBP/SLG	TAv	BABIP	BRR	FRAA	WARP
2014	LNS	A	19	49	6	0	0	2	7	7	10	0	0	.357/.449/.500	.369	.433	0.3	1B(8): -0.3	0.7
2015	TOR	MLB	20	250	21	9	1	5	24	15	67	0	0	.211/.263/.320	.218	.271	-0.3	1B -4	-1.4

Breakout: 0%   Improve: 0%   Collapse: 0%   Attrition: 0%   MLB: 0%   Comparables: Eric Hosmer, Logan Morrison, Anthony Rizzo

Sounds like what happens after bankers' hours in the party vault; is actually a much quieter but just as moneyed phenomenon. Before the 2013 draft, Tellez was mum about both his contract demands and his commitment to USC, so he fell all the way to the 30th round, where the Jays gave him a whopping $850,000 signing bonus. He has light-tower power and isn't done growing. After a slow start in Rookie ball, Tellez started mashing in late July and hopped to Low-A, where he continued making big deposits during the season's final week and a half. He'll take a walk, too. We know what you're thinking: Yes, it's his real name; and no, he's actually the *third* Rowdy in professional baseball history.

Josh Thole   C

Born: 10/28/86   Age: 28   Bats: L   Throws: R   Height: 6' 1"   Weight: 205

YEAR	TEAM	LVL	AGE	PA	R	2B	3B	HR	RBI	BB	K	SB	CS	AVG/OBP/SLG	TAv	BABIP	BRR	FRAA	WARP
2012	NYN	MLB	25	354	24	15	0	1	21	27	50	0	0	.234/.294/.290	.207	.273	1.3	C(100): 0.6	-0.1
2013	BUF	AAA	26	167	18	5	1	7	31	14	25	0	1	.322/.383/.510	.293	.345	-2.2	C(37): 0.1, 1B(1): 0.1	1.1
2013	TOR	MLB	26	135	11	3	1	1	8	12	25	0	0	.175/.256/.242	.190	.213	0.4	C(39): -0.6, 1B(2): -0.1	-0.6
2014	TOR	MLB	27	150	11	4	0	0	7	14	25	0	3	.248/.320/.278	.223	.306	-1.2	C(53): 0.1	0.0
2015	TOR	MLB	28	250	24	11	1	3	22	22	38	1	1	.251/.322/.351	.250	.284	0.2	C 0, 1B -0	0.8

Breakout: 2%   Improve: 47%   Collapse: 2%   Attrition: 15%   MLB: 92%   Comparables: Dioner Navarro, Yadier Molina, Tim McCarver

Throughout the first half of 2014, the Blue Jays had a running joke they broke out when Thole was in the lineup: Next to his name, every time, was the team's highest batting average. On and on this went, as he was batting .400 as late as May 7th. (In 37 plate appearances, granted.) "He's a different guy," John Gibbons said. "He really adjusted his swing." Or true talent was taking an extended holiday. Thole went back to hitting like himself soon enough, making weak contact, going hitless through June and letting a larger sample size apply its statistical effects. When he wasn't catching R.A. Dickey and benefitting from his ability to hold runners, Thole didn't throw out a single basestealer in 16 attempts: Of four caught runners on his watch, three didn't involve him, and the fourth was slowpoke Derek Jeter, caught standing up after Dickey's quick delivery. But R.A. needs a personal catcher, so all is forgiven, Josh.

Devon Travis   2B

Born: 2/21/91   Age: 24   Bats: R   Throws: R   Height: 5' 9"   Weight: 195

YEAR	TEAM	LVL	AGE	PA	R	2B	3B	HR	RBI	BB	K	SB	CS	AVG/OBP/SLG	TAv	BABIP	BRR	FRAA	WARP
2012	ONE	A-	21	107	17	2	2	3	11	8	10	3	1	.280/.352/.441	.320	.284	0.1	2B(23): 0.8	0.9
2013	WMI	A	22	339	55	17	2	6	42	35	32	14	3	.352/.430/.486	.341	.375	3.3	2B(68): 8.4	5.2
2013	LAK	A+	22	237	38	11	2	10	34	18	32	8	1	.350/.401/.561	.340	.371	2.4	2B(53): -5.9	2.5
2014	ERI	AA	23	441	68	20	7	10	52	37	60	16	5	.298/.358/.460	.277	.327	2.7	2B(95): 0.8, CF(3): 0.1	2.5
2015	TOR	MLB	24	250	27	11	2	6	28	16	48	5	1	.262/.315/.404	.265	.302	0.4	2B 0, CF 0	1.0

Breakout: 5%   Improve: 29%   Collapse: 8%   Attrition: 21%   MLB: 49%   Comparables: Ian Kinsler, Jason Kipnis, David Adams

Blocked at second by Ian Kinsler and just about due for a call-up, Travis was moved to center field by the Tigers ridiculously late in the season, then suffered a core muscle injury that required surgery and wiped out his previously scheduled Arizona Fall League experience. The short-lived outfield experiment is likely over; after moving to Canada in the Anthony Gose trade, he's got a clear path to playing time in the Toronto infield. His right-handed power could peak in the dozen-homer range at Rogers Centre. He has other skills too, but nothing wholly impressive, not unlike a Hickory Farms gift basket.

Danny Valencia   3B

Born: 9/19/84   Age: 30   Bats: R   Throws: R   Height: 6' 2"   Weight: 220

YEAR	TEAM	LVL	AGE	PA	R	2B	3B	HR	RBI	BB	K	SB	CS	AVG/OBP/SLG	TAv	BABIP	BRR	FRAA	WARP
2012	PAW	AAA	27	53	3	3	0	1	8	3	12	0	2	.306/.358/.429	.275	.389	-0.9	3B(12): 0.8	0.2
2012	ROC	AAA	27	284	30	17	1	7	37	15	40	1	2	.250/.289/.399	.246	.270	0.9	3B(56): 0.1	0.3
2012	BOS	MLB	27	29	1	0	0	1	4	0	6	0	0	.143/.138/.250	.163	.136	0.0	3B(10): -0.3	-0.3
2012	MIN	MLB	27	132	13	6	1	2	17	3	32	0	1	.198/.212/.310	.180	.242	0.1	3B(34): 0.5	-0.8
2013	NOR	AAA	28	282	40	20	1	14	51	17	48	1	1	.286/.326/.531	.306	.300	1.6	3B(48): -2.5, 1B(6): -0.4	2.1
2013	BAL	MLB	28	170	20	14	1	8	23	8	33	0	2	.304/.335/.553	.307	.339	-0.4	3B(6): -0.4	1.0
2014	KCA	MLB	29	119	8	5	0	2	11	7	27	0	0	.282/.328/.382	.277	.354	-2.8	3B(26): 0.6, 2B(6): -0.2	0.2
2014	TOR	MLB	29	165	12	11	1	2	19	7	35	0	1	.240/.273/.364	.223	.292	-1.3	3B(40): 1.3, 1B(20): 0.2	-0.2
2015	TOR	MLB	30	279	27	15	1	7	32	16	55	1	2	.254/.297/.400	.259	.294	-1.3	3B -1, 1B -0	0.4

Breakout: 3%   Improve: 32%   Collapse: 5%   Attrition: 9%   MLB: 82%   Comparables: *Jayson Nix, Brendan Harris, Jeff Baker*

At the time, Valencia was worth Liam Hendriks and Erik Kratz, the pieces sent to Kansas City to ship him to Toronto. He brought a career .310 TAv against lefties and settled into a comfortable platoon with Juan Francisco at third base. Valencia against lefties, Francisco against righties, reap the benefits, including the option to pinch-hit. Yay! That lasted until the end of August, when the Blue Jays entered an exclusive relationship with Valencia at third because, John Gibbons said, "I like the way he looks." Do you mean his handsome countenance or the direction his eyes focus, Gibby? Valencia's resulting True Average in September was .188, about the worst possible outcome because even a full-time Francisco wouldn't have seen many lefties. At least the experiment, conducted mostly out of playoff contention, yielded the answer to whether Valencia could replace Brett Lawrie at the hot corner. Nope.

Pitchers

Matt Boyd   LHP

Born: 2/2/91   Age: 24   Bats: L   Throws: L   Height: 6'3"   Weight: 215

YEAR	TEAM	LVL	AGE	W	L	SV	G	GS	IP	H	HR	BB	K	BB/9	K/9	GB%	BABIP	WHIP	ERA	FIP	FRA	WARP
2013	LNS	A	22	0	1	0	5	3	14	7	0	1	12	0.6	7.7	37%	.184	0.57	0.64	1.84	2.62	0.5
2013	DUN	A+	22	0	2	0	3	2	10	7	2	3	11	2.7	9.9	39%	.238	1.00	5.40	4.54	9.39	-0.1
2014	DUN	A+	23	5	3	0	16	16	90²	65	4	20	103	2.0	10.2	42%	.270	0.94	1.39	2.49	3.12	2.5
2014	NHP	AA	23	1	4	0	10	10	42²	55	5	13	44	2.7	9.3	31%	.379	1.59	6.96	3.94	4.65	0.6
2015	TOR	MLB	24	6	5	0	19	19	94	93	11	33	87	3.1	8.4	39%	.307	1.34	4.14	4.45	4.50	0.9

Breakout: 20%   Improve: 39%   Collapse: 11%   Attrition: 31%   MLB: 56%   Comparables: *Sean Nolin, David Huff, Scott Barnes*

Instead of signing with the Reds after a 13th-round selection in 2012, Boyd used his senior year at Oregon State to transform from a reliever into a starter and improve his draft stock: The Jays took him in the sixth round in 2013. A big lefty with a high leg kick, Boyd throws a low-90s fastball and a good curve. Like every mound prospect, he's working on a changeup in the same way that everyone in Los Angeles is working on a screenplay: Sure, let us know when you have something to pitch. Boyd's advanced control and feel dominated High-A, but two stints in Double-A went poorly and kicked him back down to Dunedin. Nonetheless, his college pedigree should speed him up the system, faster still if his left-handedness encourages the Jays to move him back to the bullpen.

Mark Buehrle   LHP

Born: 3/23/79   Age: 36   Bats: L   Throws: L   Height: 6'2"   Weight: 240

YEAR	TEAM	LVL	AGE	W	L	SV	G	GS	IP	H	HR	BB	K	BB/9	K/9	GB%	BABIP	WHIP	ERA	FIP	FRA	WARP
2012	MIA	MLB	33	13	13	0	31	31	202¹	197	26	40	125	1.8	5.6	43%	.270	1.17	3.74	4.22	4.88	0.3
2013	TOR	MLB	34	12	10	0	33	33	203²	223	24	51	139	2.3	6.1	48%	.305	1.35	4.15	4.13	4.34	2.6
2014	TOR	MLB	35	13	10	0	32	32	202	228	15	46	119	2.0	5.3	45%	.316	1.36	3.39	3.69	4.00	2.7
2015	TOR	MLB	36	11	9	0	27	27	173	195	19	40	106	2.1	5.5	45%	.307	1.36	4.42	4.55	4.80	0.6

Breakout: 15%   Improve: 39%   Collapse: 16%   Attrition: 14%   MLB: 80%   Comparables: *Bronson Arroyo, Carl Pavano, Derek Lowe*

There's not much more to say about Buehrle's consistency, is there? Last year was his 14th consecutive season with 30 starts, 200 innings, 800 batters faced, 15-plus quality starts, sub-5 ERA, sub-7 percent walk rate, zero missed starts, blah, blah, blah. He pitched the league's first nine-inning game under two hours since June 2012. He led the league in pitcher pace, *again*. He made the All-Star team, *again*. And his fastball dropped a half-mile an hour, *again*.

Yet at age 35, Buehrle still set two new career records: his lowest home run rate to date and the fewest steal attempts off him in a season. Just four runners took off all year, and calling them *attempts* overstates the matter because the three caught runners were picked off by Buehrle himself. The one successful thief, Javier Baez, took third on a delayed steal as Buehrle delivered an 83 mph cutter. Buehrle wasn't the only pitcher to allow zero straight steal attempts, but the feat is more impressive considering he doesn't even throw high-80s heat like Doug Fister, much less upper-90s rage like Yordano Ventura. He does his thing with the league's slowest four-seamer, a mid-80s traveler that scouts disqualified way back when he was a 38th-round pick.

In this era, baseball likely won't see 14 straight 200-inning seasons again soon: James Shields and Justin Verlander would need to hit the mark for six more seasons, until they're 38; Felix Hernandez, more feasibly, for seven years until he's 35. They just don't build them like Buehrle anymore, making his career an achievement in consistency and durability. He's a perfect pitcher in every aspect but velocity. He costs $20 million this year, but wouldn't you pay that for a near-guarantee of 200 solid innings?

Turns out there was a lot to say.

Brett Cecil   LHP

Born: 7/2/86   Age: 28   Bats: R   Throws: L   Height: 6'3"   Weight: 220

YEAR	TEAM	LVL	AGE	W	L	SV	G	GS	IP	H	HR	BB	K	BB/9	K/9	GB%	BABIP	WHIP	ERA	FIP	FRA	WARP
2012	NHP	AA	25	3	2	0	9	9	42²	44	2	14	34	3.0	7.2	45%	.318	1.36	3.38	3.34	3.65	0.9
2012	LVG	AAA	25	1	2	0	6	6	43⁹²	36	1	7	33	1.6	7.5	50%	.312	1.08	2.50	2.93	3.25	1.2
2012	TOR	MLB	25	2	4	0	21	9	61¹	70	11	23	51	3.4	7.5	40%	.324	1.52	5.72	4.99	5.05	0.2
2013	TOR	MLB	26	5	1	1	60	0	60²	44	4	23	70	3.4	10.4	53%	.267	1.10	2.82	2.91	3.18	1.1
2014	TOR	MLB	27	2	3	5	66	0	53¹	46	2	27	76	4.6	12.8	55%	.344	1.37	2.70	2.37	2.29	1.3
2015	TOR	MLB	28	3	2	0	21	6	49¹	48	6	16	43	2.9	7.9	44%	.296	1.30	4.04	4.50	4.39	0.4

Breakout: 21%   Improve: 45%   Collapse: 14%   Attrition: 13%   MLB: 81%   Comparables: *Luke Hochevar, Tom Gorzelanny, Jason Hammel*

Cecil's curves are temptation at its finest. *Curveballs*, we mean. Thrown with a knuckle grip, Cecil whips it to both lefties and righties. It's near certain to fall to the dirt before it reaches the plate, yet hitters couldn't resist swinging: He induced cuts over half the time he threw the pitch thanks to 12-to-6 movement and mid-80s velocity. Armed with that formidable weapon, Cecil competently handled set-up duties for the Blue Jays, running into occasional trouble with command or hitters smartly holstering their bats. He finished the season with 21 straight scoreless appearances.

R.A. Dickey   RHP

Born: 10/29/74   Age: 40   Bats: R   Throws: R   Height: 6'3"   Weight: 215

YEAR	TEAM	LVL	AGE	W	L	SV	G	GS	IP	H	HR	BB	K	BB/9	K/9	GB%	BABIP	WHIP	ERA	FIP	FRA	WARP
2012	NYN	MLB	37	20	6	0	34	33	233²	192	24	54	230	2.1	8.9	48%	.275	1.05	2.73	3.31	3.71	3.7
2013	TOR	MLB	38	14	13	0	34	34	224²	207	35	71	177	2.8	7.1	42%	.265	1.24	4.21	4.61	4.81	1.8
2014	TOR	MLB	39	14	13	0	34	34	215²	191	26	74	173	3.1	7.2	45%	.263	1.23	3.71	4.35	4.86	0.5
2015	TOR	MLB	40	12	9	0	29	29	188¹	179	22	55	145	2.6	7.0	47%	.281	1.25	3.92	4.58	4.26	1.8

Breakout: 16%   Improve: 30%   Collapse: 13%   Attrition: 7%   MLB: 73%   Comparables: *Mike Mussina, Woody Williams, Tim Wakefield*

Now the first pitcher since Greg Maddux to pitch 200 innings four times above age 36, Dickey added more Black Ink to his resume, tying for the AL leads in starts (again) and hit batters. His vaunted knuckler showed signs of Mets-time velocity early on but never quite reached those heights, instead declining in the second half. Fewer fly balls left the park and a slight overall velocity tick induced more whiffs; otherwise, Dickey repeated his initial season with the Blue Jays: passable, sturdy, yet hardly elite. Like Mark Buehrle, Dickey was among the best in holding runners (just five steal attempts, one picked off), giving the Jays the odd pairing of durable steal-preventing starters who throw at the slowest speeds in the league. Only James Shields has thrown more pitches in the past two regular seasons, but while Dickey might be slowing down, he isn't stopping.

Kyle Drabek   RHP

Born: 12/8/87   Age: 27   Bats: R   Throws: R   Height: 6'2"   Weight: 205

YEAR	TEAM	LVL	AGE	W	L	SV	G	GS	IP	H	HR	BB	K	BB/9	K/9	GB%	BABIP	WHIP	ERA	FIP	FRA	WARP
2012	TOR	MLB	24	4	7	0	13	13	71¹	67	10	47	47	5.9	5.9	55%	.274	1.60	4.67	5.57	6.47	-0.4
2013	DUN	A+	25	0	1	0	8	6	20²	14	2	3	20	1.3	8.7	61%	.231	0.82	2.61	3.14	3.98	0.3
2013	BUF	AAA	25	1	2	0	4	3	14¹	14	1	2	12	1.3	7.5	52%	.302	1.12	3.77	2.86	4.44	0.2
2013	TOR	MLB	25	0	0	0	3	0	2¹	4	1	2	3	7.7	11.6	50%	.429	2.57	7.71	9.93	8.79	-0.1
2014	BUF	AAA	26	7	7	0	32	13	99	116	12	30	68	2.7	6.2	45%	.326	1.47	4.18	4.50	5.24	0.4
2014	TOR	MLB	26	0	0	0	2	0	3	2	0	2	5	6.0	15.0	17%	.333	1.33	0.00	1.83	0.20	0.2
2015	TOR	MLB	27	4	5	0	20	14	76²	81	10	36	54	4.2	6.4	48%	.298	1.53	5.15	5.39	5.59	-0.2

Breakout: 32%   Improve: 49%   Collapse: 14%   Attrition: 27%   MLB: 77%   Comparables: *Mitchell Boggs, Brandon Claussen, Mitch Talbot*

In June, the Jays made a reliever out of Drabek. That's not the outcome you want for the key piece in the 2009 Roy Halladay trade, but no amount of tinkering with Drabek's mechanics helped him throw strikes as a major-league starter. The question is how to use Drabek's low strikeout and average groundball rates in short appearances. He might make a good long man or spot starter if the Jays want to split the difference between the rotation and the bullpen.

Marco Estrada   RHP

Born: 7/5/83   Age: 31   Bats: R   Throws: R   Height: 6'0"   Weight: 200

YEAR	TEAM	LVL	AGE	W	L	SV	G	GS	IP	H	HR	BB	K	BB/9	K/9	GB%	BABIP	WHIP	ERA	FIP	FRA	WARP
2012	MIL	MLB	28	5	7	0	29	23	138¹	129	18	29	143	1.9	9.3	37%	.298	1.14	3.64	3.39	4.02	2.3
2013	MIL	MLB	29	7	4	0	21	21	128	109	19	29	118	2.0	8.3	39%	.262	1.08	3.87	3.83	4.51	1.0
2014	MIL	MLB	30	7	6	0	39	18	150²	137	29	44	127	2.6	7.6	34%	.257	1.20	4.36	4.85	5.89	-0.9
2015	TOR	MLB	31	7	5	0	31	17	118²	113	17	33	107	2.5	8.1	37%	.285	1.23	3.92	4.54	4.27	1.2

Breakout: 18%   Improve: 50%   Collapse: 16%   Attrition: 22%   MLB: 88%   Comparables: *Brett Myers, Jeff Karstens, Randy Wolf*

Estrada lost his role in the starting rotation after allowing a home run every four innings—every four innings!—through July 7th. The right-hander struggled to command anything, fell behind in the count, turned to a below-average fastball when he was backed into that corner and from there too often missed up in the hittrackeronline.com part of the zone. His overall 4.36 ERA, though, masks his effective stint in the bullpen. After the transition to a relief role, Estrada compiled a sparkling 2.89 ERA, which actually makes sense: Batters have hit just .215/.263/.383 against Estrada the first time through the order in his career. The Mexico native has an effective three-pitch mix and generated a healthy swinging-strike rate—which leads one to believe he could succeed as a starter—but a permanent move to the bullpen might ultimately lead to more consistent effectiveness. One step at a time: The Blue Jays hope a permanent move to Toronto, where he'll fight for a spot in the rotation this spring, will do the trick.

Drew Hutchison   RHP

Born: 8/22/90   Age: 24   Bats: L   Throws: R   Height: 6'3"   Weight: 195

YEAR	TEAM	LVL	AGE	W	L	SV	G	GS	IP	H	HR	BB	K	BB/9	K/9	GB%	BABIP	WHIP	ERA	FIP	FRA	WARP
2012	NHP	AA	21	2	1	0	3	3	16²	16	1	3	12	1.6	6.5	45%	.312	1.14	2.16	3.08	3.91	0.3
2012	TOR	MLB	21	5	3	0	11	11	58²	59	8	20	49	3.1	7.5	46%	.291	1.35	4.60	4.43	5.37	0.0
2013	BUF	AAA	22	0	3	0	5	5	19	28	2	6	20	2.8	9.5	27%	.433	1.79	6.63	4.05	5.80	0.0
2014	TOR	MLB	23	11	13	0	32	32	184²	173	23	60	184	2.9	9.0	37%	.293	1.26	4.48	3.87	4.50	1.6
2015	*TOR*	*MLB*	*24*	*9*	*7*	*0*	*25*	*25*	*136*	*130*	*15*	*44*	*131*	*2.9*	*8.6*	*42%*	*.301*	*1.28*	*3.96*	*4.18*	*4.31*	*1.5*

Breakout: 31%   Improve: 65%   Collapse: 12%   Attrition: 16%   MLB: 94%   Comparables: *David Price, Tommy Hanson, Jered Weaver*

Hutchison showed no ill effects in his major-league return from Tommy John surgery, making every start and ranking eighth among AL starters in strikeout rate. There's little "elite" anything with Hutchison, but the arsenal, velocity, delivery and command each earn solid marks. Managers consciously stacked lefties in their lineups against Hutchison, exploiting his most notable weakness; 17 of his 23 home runs allowed were hit from the left side of the plate. That could improve if he can get more velocity separation on his changeup, but even if he remains a splitsy starter, he'll fulfill his mid-rotation projection. Not bad for a 15th-round pick.

Casey Janssen   RHP

Born: 9/17/81   Age: 33   Bats: R   Throws: R   Height: 6'4"   Weight: 205

YEAR	TEAM	LVL	AGE	W	L	SV	G	GS	IP	H	HR	BB	K	BB/9	K/9	GB%	BABIP	WHIP	ERA	FIP	FRA	WARP
2012	TOR	MLB	30	1	1	22	62	0	63²	44	7	11	67	1.6	9.5	44%	.240	0.86	2.54	3.03	3.51	1.2
2013	TOR	MLB	31	4	1	34	56	0	52²	39	3	13	50	2.2	8.5	49%	.254	0.99	2.56	2.77	3.40	0.8
2014	TOR	MLB	32	3	3	25	50	0	45²	47	6	7	28	1.4	5.5	38%	.273	1.18	3.94	4.17	4.45	0.3
2015	*TOR*	*MLB*	*33*	*2*	*1*	*23*	*44*	*0*	*43²*	*40*	*4*	*10*	*40*	*2.2*	*8.3*	*45%*	*.293*	*1.16*	*3.24*	*3.71*	*3.52*	*0.8*

Breakout: 19%   Improve: 42%   Collapse: 33%   Attrition: 11%   MLB: 91%   Comparables: *Keith Foulke, Hideki Okajima, LaTroy Hawkins*

Janssen's 10-year career in the Blue Jays organization ended with a poor second-half performance, though that shouldn't erase the ninth-inning relief he's brought them. For Toronto, it's been relief in both senses of the word, much needed after B.J. Ryan's sour, volatile time. Janssen has led the Jays in saves over the past three years, stability the team hasn't seen since Billy Koch's reign from 2000-2002. His velocity has fallen for three straight years now—the only closers with lower velocity were Koji Uehara and Sergio Romo, both non-reliant on fastballs—but he has remained dependable and consistent with his signature command and cutter. His finesse should carry him into his mid-30s as a high-leverage reliever even if he doesn't remain in a ninth-inning role.

Chad Jenkins   RHP

Born: 12/22/87   Age: 27   Bats: R   Throws: R   Height: 6'4"   Weight: 235

YEAR	TEAM	LVL	AGE	W	L	SV	G	GS	IP	H	HR	BB	K	BB/9	K/9	GB%	BABIP	WHIP	ERA	FIP	FRA	WARP
2012	NHP	AA	24	5	9	0	20	20	114¹	145	17	31	57	2.4	4.5	49%	.322	1.54	4.96	5.08	6.13	-0.9
2012	TOR	MLB	24	1	3	0	13	3	32	32	5	11	16	3.1	4.5	44%	.262	1.34	4.50	5.20	5.40	0.0
2013	NHP	AA	25	0	0	0	4	3	15	11	0	2	9	1.2	5.4	65%	.224	0.87	1.20	2.52	3.23	0.4
2013	BUF	AAA	25	0	3	0	5	5	21²	33	6	4	8	1.7	3.3	55%	.329	1.71	7.48	6.62	8.40	-0.7
2013	TOR	MLB	25	1	0	0	10	3	33¹	31	3	6	15	1.6	4.1	47%	.262	1.11	2.70	3.98	4.37	0.3
2014	BUF	AAA	26	1	3	2	21	4	44	45	5	9	27	1.8	5.5	48%	.282	1.23	4.70	4.29	6.14	0.1
2014	TOR	MLB	26	1	1	0	21	0	31²	34	2	6	18	1.7	5.1	58%	.294	1.26	2.56	3.51	4.31	0.3
2015	*TOR*	*MLB*	*27*	*3*	*3*	*0*	*17*	*9*	*62¹*	*73*	*9*	*18*	*31*	*2.6*	*4.4*	*49%*	*.300*	*1.47*	*5.24*	*5.46*	*5.69*	*-0.3*

Breakout: 20%   Improve: 35%   Collapse: 10%   Attrition: 26%   MLB: 48%   Comparables: *Tim Stauffer, Greg Reynolds, Chris Rusin*

Jenkins was the Jays' option scapegoat on the pitching side last year, like Anthony Gose among the position players, sent to Triple-A five different times. For his part, Jenkins didn't pitch badly. The big-bodied accounting major efficiently knocked down batters with his sinker, generating groundballs with high frequency. No pitcher with 30 innings recorded fewer pitches per plate appearance than Jenkins' 3.24. He memorably went six herculean innings in the 19-inning affair with Detroit on August 10th and was rewarded with not getting demoted, though he couldn't escape that fate five days later. He never spent more than six weeks with Toronto or Buffalo all year, and didn't even make it to expanded rosters in September due to a hand fracture, sadly finishing his season with surgery.

Aaron Loup   LHP

Born: 12/19/87   Age: 27   Bats: L   Throws: L   Height: 5'11"   Weight: 205

YEAR	TEAM	LVL	AGE	W	L	SV	G	GS	IP	H	HR	BB	K	BB/9	K/9	GB%	BABIP	WHIP	ERA	FIP	FRA	WARP
2012	NHP	AA	24	0	3	3	37	0	45¹	46	4	14	43	2.8	8.5	51%	.318	1.32	2.78	3.71	3.88	0.7
2012	TOR	MLB	24	0	2	0	33	0	30²	26	0	2	21	0.6	6.2	57%	.277	0.91	2.64	1.87	2.69	0.8
2013	TOR	MLB	25	4	6	2	64	0	69¹	66	5	13	53	1.7	6.9	61%	.299	1.14	2.47	3.35	4.38	0.4
2014	TOR	MLB	26	4	4	4	71	0	68²	50	4	30	56	3.9	7.3	56%	.246	1.17	3.15	3.86	3.86	0.6
2015	*TOR*	*MLB*	*27*	*3*	*1*	*2*	*51*	*0*	*56²*	*56*	*5*	*19*	*46*	*3.0*	*7.2*	*49%*	*.299*	*1.33*	*4.13*	*4.30*	*4.49*	*0.4*

Breakout: 30%   Improve: 41%   Collapse: 24%   Attrition: 21%   MLB: 74%   Comparables: *Fu-Te Ni, Gary Majewski, Ramon Troncoso*

Loup led the Blue Jays in appearances once again, pitching occasionally in LOOGY duty, but often in L4OGY duty, retiring the next inning after working out of his starter's mess. Despite his side-armed delivery and left-leaning splits, Loup coerces outs of all kinds. Loup abides by another common abbreviation: KISS. He Keeps It Simple pitching down and away with his sinker and two off-speed pitches: a changeup against righties with arm-side movement and a curveball against lefties that dives glove-side. He used each pitch almost exclusively against its intended batting hand, minimizing hits and inducing weak contact. In his last appearance of the year, Loup saved Todd Redmond from a two-on, two-out jam, and finished atop the leaderboard in games entered with inherited runners.

Dustin McGowan   RHP

Born: 3/24/82   Age: 33   Bats: R   Throws: R   Height: 6'3"   Weight: 240

YEAR	TEAM	LVL	AGE	W	L	SV	G	GS	IP	H	HR	BB	K	BB/9	K/9	GB%	BABIP	WHIP	ERA	FIP	FRA	WARP
2013	TOR	MLB	31	0	0	0	25	0	25²	19	2	12	26	4.2	9.1	47%	.236	1.21	2.45	3.70	3.89	0.3
2014	TOR	MLB	32	5	3	1	53	8	82	80	13	33	61	3.6	6.7	39%	.275	1.38	4.17	5.05	4.90	0.3
2015	TOR	MLB	33	4	3	1	37	8	62²	62	8	27	53	4.0	7.7	42%	.293	1.43	4.68	5.00	5.09	0.1

Breakout: 14%   Improve: 29%   Collapse: 10%   Attrition: 18%   MLB: 51%   Comparables: *Gary Glover, Chad Durbin, Nelson Cruz*

McGowan has resided in the Blue Jays organization for 14 years. On the team's roster tree, you can trace his first-round selection in 2000 back to Roger Clemens (traded away for Graeme Lloyd, who yielded a compensation pick when he departed for the Expos via free agency in 1999—that pick became McGowan). Since his big-league promotion in 2005, injuries have held him back: He has actually pitched more career innings in the minor leagues. Last year was his first completely healthy season since 2007 and McGowan pitched serviceably as a medium-leverage reliever. For someone who has undergone four surgeries, the Jays couldn't have asked for more. (Well, they actually did try to ask for more, experimenting with a starting role, but that was scrapped.) McGowan will always be haunted by what could have been, but at 33 and still throwing in the mid-90s, let's call this a happy result.

Juan Meza   RHP

Last summer, the Jays signed Meza out of Carlos Guillen's Venezuelan baseball academy for $1.6 million, just what a 16-year-old needs to go with a fastball that already tops 90 mph, a decent slider and—unusually for such a young hurler—a changeup. The bonus was no great surprise given that Meza was generally regarded as a top-10 international prospect and that the Jays had lavished similar money on his fellow Venezuelan Franklin Barreto at the same age in 2013. Meza has a smooth delivery and room to build out his lanky frame. He's also 16 and a pitcher, so anything can happen between the bonus and the majors, if he gets there.

Brandon Morrow   RHP

Born: 7/26/84   Age: 30   Bats: R   Throws: R   Height: 6'3"   Weight: 210

YEAR	TEAM	LVL	AGE	W	L	SV	G	GS	IP	H	HR	BB	K	BB/9	K/9	GB%	BABIP	WHIP	ERA	FIP	FRA	WARP
2012	NHP	AA	27	1	0	0	3	3	14¹	10	2	3	12	1.9	7.5	38%	.216	0.91	2.51	3.97	4.69	0.2
2012	TOR	MLB	27	10	7	0	21	21	124²	98	12	41	108	3.0	7.8	42%	.252	1.11	2.96	3.60	4.14	2.2
2013	TOR	MLB	28	2	3	0	10	10	54¹	63	12	18	42	3.0	7.0	39%	.302	1.49	5.63	5.45	5.48	0.1
2014	TOR	MLB	29	1	3	0	13	6	33¹	37	2	18	30	4.9	8.1	52%	.357	1.65	5.67	3.76	4.46	0.2
2015	TOR	MLB	30	2	2	0	7	7	35²	33	4	14	37	3.4	9.4	40%	.304	1.31	3.97	4.29	4.32	0.4

Breakout: 18%   Improve: 39%   Collapse: 24%   Attrition: 16%   MLB: 83%   Comparables: *Jorge De La Rosa, Daisuke Matsuzaka, Gil Meche*

For the third straight year, Morrow found himself on the 60-day disabled list. This time, a torn tendon sheath in his right index finger cost him four months of play. He was pitching erratically even before reporting to duty where baseball knows him best (the DL), failing to break six innings even once. In a late-April start against the Red Sox, he unforgettably walked eight of 14 batters ... while allowing no hits. He recovered by September to pitch late-inning relief, pumping high-90s velocity, but the Blue Jays decided enough was enough with the righty's injury-prone body and declined their $10 million option.

Daniel Norris   LHP

Born: 4/25/93   Age: 22   Bats: L   Throws: L   Height: 6'2"   Weight: 180

YEAR	TEAM	LVL	AGE	W	L	SV	G	GS	IP	H	HR	BB	K	BB/9	K/9	GB%	BABIP	WHIP	ERA	FIP	FRA	WARP
2013	LNS	A	20	1	7	0	23	22	85²	84	6	44	99	4.6	10.4	51%	.342	1.49	4.20	3.62	4.08	2.0
2014	DUN	A+	21	6	0	0	13	13	66¹	50	0	18	76	2.4	10.3	48%	.298	1.03	1.22	1.91	2.77	2.1
2014	NHP	AA	21	3	1	0	8	8	35²	32	5	17	49	4.3	12.4	39%	.329	1.37	4.54	4.03	4.60	0.4
2014	BUF	AAA	21	3	1	0	5	4	22²	14	2	8	38	3.2	15.1	51%	.324	0.97	3.18	2.21	3.26	0.6
2014	TOR	MLB	21	0	0	0	5	1	6²	5	1	5	4	6.8	5.4	38%	.200	1.50	5.40	6.16	6.20	-0.1
2015	TOR	MLB	22	7	7	0	24	24	99¹	96	11	49	104	4.5	9.4	44%	.311	1.46	4.49	4.52	4.88	0.6

Breakout: 17%   Improve: 23%   Collapse: 3%   Attrition: 11%   MLB: 30%   Comparables: *Tommy Hanson, Shelby Miller, Christian Friedrich*

Norris enjoyed the pitcher's version of Dalton Pompey's season: He started 2014 in High-A and ended it with an All-Star encounter in The Show, making David Ortiz his first major-league strikeout victim on September 5th. Norris has a Matt Moore-like power arsenal: fastball that sits at 92-94 but regularly reaches 95-96, plus curve and changeup, and a slider Moore lacks. The Surfer Boy (from Tennessee?) who lives most of the year in his camper van has a good chance to be the Page to Marcus Stroman's Plant (or Cheech to his Chong, if you must) in Toronto's rotation; if the Jays can get Aaron Sanchez tuned up, there's John Paul Jones, too. Norris has room on his frame to add some muscle. He had minor elbow surgery in the offseason (if you discover "loose bodies" in your elbow, stop taking Viagra immediately), but he's expected to be ready for spring training.

Todd Redmond   RHP

Born: 5/17/85   Age: 30   Bats: R   Throws: R   Height: 6'3"   Weight: 200

YEAR	TEAM	LVL	AGE	W	L	SV	G	GS	IP	H	HR	BB	K	BB/9	K/9	GB%	BABIP	WHIP	ERA	FIP	FRA	WARP
2012	GWN	AAA	27	6	6	0	18	18	105²	107	11	28	96	2.4	8.2	34%	.312	1.28	3.58	3.55	4.42	1.1
2012	LOU	AAA	27	2	5	0	8	7	43	43	7	11	40	2.3	8.4	36%	.303	1.26	3.77	4.25	6.04	0.0
2012	CIN	MLB	27	0	1	0	1	1	3¹	7	1	5	2	13.5	5.4	33%	.429	3.60	10.80	10.34	7.21	-0.1
2013	BUF	AAA	28	3	1	0	6	5	26²	29	2	5	29	1.7	9.8	39%	.370	1.27	5.06	2.57	3.96	0.4
2013	TOR	MLB	28	4	3	0	17	14	77	70	13	23	76	2.7	8.9	31%	.277	1.21	4.32	4.43	4.60	0.6
2014	TOR	MLB	29	1	4	1	42	0	75	73	5	27	60	3.2	7.2	34%	.309	1.33	3.24	3.59	4.02	0.8
2015	TOR	MLB	30	4	3	0	16	10	67¹	69	9	21	56	2.8	7.6	36%	.299	1.34	4.49	4.72	4.88	0.2

Breakout: 14%   Improve: 19%   Collapse: 7%   Attrition: 14%   MLB: 31%   Comparables: *Fernando Nieve, Guillermo Moscoso, Jason Hirsh*

Redmond trotted in from the bullpen 42 times in 2014; the Blue Jays were trailing in all but 10 of those games. This particular deployment claimed for Redmond the league's lowest average leverage index among relievers with at least 40 innings. He was the team's designated long man, often stretched for three innings to mop up out-of-hand games. In fact, when Redmond pitched with higher leverage, he made sure it *got* out of hand. In the five tie games he entered, he wound up with the loss in three of them. In two other games he entered with a small lead, he allowed all of his inherited runners to score, then tacked on additional runs for good (bad) measure. That makes Redmond's season evaluable in two ways: His respectable WARP, mostly accrued with effective garbage innings, or his grotesque -1.6 win probability added, derived from his tendency to fall apart in key situations. Either way, he's found his role as a sixth starter.

Sean Reid-Foley RHP

Born: 8/30/95 Age: 19 Bats: R Throws: R Height: 6'3" Weight: 220

YEAR	TEAM	LVL	AGE	W	L	SV	G	GS	IP	H	HR	BB	K	BB/9	K/9	GB%	BABIP	WHIP	ERA	FIP	FRA	WARP
2015	TOR	MLB	19	1	2	0	9	5	31¹	37	4	20	19	5.8	5.5	48%	.312	1.83	6.40	6.22	6.96	-0.4

Breakout: 0%   Improve: 0%   Collapse: 0%   Attrition: 0%   MLB: 0%   Comparables: *Brad Hand, Stolmy Pimentel, Aaron Sanchez*

Reid-Foley was considered a first-round talent in last year's draft, but he fell to the second due to signability concerns: He had a commitment to Florida State. The Jays nonetheless managed to land him without going over the slot value. Reid-Foley's fastball sits in the low 90s. He's got a big frame to handle a starter's workload and already sports a four-pitch arsenal. If he lives up to his pre-draft rankings, he could be a steal.

Aaron Sanchez RHP

Born: 7/1/92 Age: 22 Bats: R Throws: R Height: 6'4" Weight: 200

YEAR	TEAM	LVL	AGE	W	L	SV	G	GS	IP	H	HR	BB	K	BB/9	K/9	GB%	BABIP	WHIP	ERA	FIP	FRA	WARP
2012	LNS	A	19	8	5	0	25	18	90¹	64	3	51	97	5.1	9.7	62%	.279	1.27	2.49	3.56	4.68	1.2
2013	DUN	A+	20	4	5	0	22	20	86¹	63	4	40	75	4.2	7.8	61%	.250	1.19	3.34	3.67	5.19	0.3
2014	NHP	AA	21	3	4	0	14	14	66	52	2	40	57	5.5	7.8	69%	.279	1.39	3.82	4.16	5.56	0.3
2014	BUF	AAA	21	0	3	0	8	6	34¹	36	4	17	27	4.5	7.1	62%	.317	1.54	4.19	4.87	6.15	-0.3
2014	TOR	MLB	21	2	2	3	24	0	33	14	1	9	27	2.5	7.4	67%	.157	0.70	1.09	2.83	3.56	0.5
2015	TOR	MLB	22	6	5	0	29	18	100²	95	10	57	84	5.1	7.5	56%	.289	1.50	4.52	5.10	4.91	0.5

Breakout: 21%   Improve: 26%   Collapse: 6%   Attrition: 19%   MLB: 45%   Comparables: *Nathan Eovaldi, Franklin Morales, Sean Gallagher*

Sanchez's major-league debut confirmed that he'll destroy hitters in relief, at the least. Not only did his fastball sit in the upper 90s but the explosion of arm-side movement had hitters waving fruitlessly: If they were lucky enough to make contact, the ball sputtered weakly on the ground for an easy out. Its dominance may have been detrimental to Sanchez's overall development, as he threw it nearly 90 percent of the time, hardly calling on his undeveloped changeup, the pitch he'll need to graduate to a starting role. Other red flags also surfaced, however. His failure to repeat his delivery often resulted in the fastball flying all over the place, especially up. This isn't an issue when it's so hard to hit, but it's likely to produce regular free passes when he's starting. That was the troubling case in the high minors, where Sanchez walked 14 percent of batters as a starter before his call-up. He'll make his no. 2/no. 3 starter potential if pitching coaches can help him find consistent mechanics—while retaining his velocity—*and* bump his changeup to an average grade. Those are two big ifs and they're the same ifs that have followed Sanchez his entire career.

Marcus Stroman RHP

Born: 5/1/91 Age: 24 Bats: R Throws: R Height: 5'9" Weight: 185

YEAR	TEAM	LVL	AGE	W	L	SV	G	GS	IP	H	HR	BB	K	BB/9	K/9	GB%	BABIP	WHIP	ERA	FIP	FRA	WARP
2012	VAN	A-	21	1	0	0	7	0	11¹	8	0	3	15	2.4	11.9	48%	.296	0.97	3.18	1.47	3.12	0.3
2013	NHP	AA	22	9	5	0	20	20	111²	99	13	27	129	2.2	10.4	46%	.301	1.13	3.30	3.33	4.11	2.1
2014	BUF	AAA	23	2	4	0	7	7	35²	32	1	9	45	2.3	11.4	54%	.348	1.15	3.03	2.12	3.02	1.0
2014	TOR	MLB	23	11	6	1	26	20	130²	125	7	28	111	1.9	7.6	55%	.306	1.17	3.65	2.87	3.88	1.9
2015	TOR	MLB	24	9	6	0	24	24	133²	126	12	33	129	2.2	8.7	48%	.305	1.19	3.35	3.61	3.64	2.5

Breakout: 27%   Improve: 64%   Collapse: 13%   Attrition: 16%   MLB: 93%   Comparables: *Tommy Hanson, Drew Smyly, Patrick Corbin*

For two years, Stroman answered every doubt about his height with simply dominant stuff. Last year, he took it to the majors and showed he was serious, in case you weren't. Like many potential front-line starters, Stroman initially pitched in relief, a disappointing two-week spell that sentenced him to two starts in Triple-A. He returned and in his first big-league start flashed his vicious hard slider against Eric Hosmer, a two-plane diver that incited a "wow" from the lefty. Then the rookie took over as the Blue Jays' most consistent starter, showing command of three plus pitches and a quick, strong delivery that discouraged any running game. He closed his season with a four-inning save, becoming the first pitcher since 2004 to record a shutout and save in his debut season. Sorry to inform you that you've missed your window for arguing that Stroman is better than Aaron Sanchez: Everyone already knows; you don't get points for it anymore.

Lineouts ———————————————————————

Hitters

NAME	POS	TEAM	LVL	AGE	PA	R	2B	3B	HR	RBI	BB	K	SB	CS	AVG/OBP/SLG	TAv	BABIP	BRR	FRAA	WARP
Jonathon Berti	2B	NHP	AA	24	594	69	21	7	7	50	35	82	40	15	.270/.323/.373	.264	.305	7.6	2B(84): 7.7, LF(30): -1.6	2.8
D.J. Davis	CF	LNS	A	19	542	56	13	7	8	52	36	167	19	20	.213/.268/.316	.228	.299	-6.8	CF(114): 2.0, LF(2): -0.4	-1.1
Roemon Fields	CF	VAN	A-	23	328	64	13	4	1	26	27	61	48	9	.269/.338/.350	.269	.333	3.6	CF(55): 5.4	2.1
Caleb Gindl	RF	NAS	AAA	25	408	40	20	1	8	32	42	88	2	2	.227/.310/.354	.245	.277	-4.5	RF(43): -1.4, LF(38): -0.4	-0.5
	RF	MIL	MLB	25	23	0	0	0	0	0	4	5	0	0	.158/.304/.158	.201	.214	-0.3	RF(6): -0.1	-0.2
Brad Glenn	RF	NHP	AA	27	206	31	10	1	9	23	20	53	0	0	.231/.311/.445	.273	.270	0.9	RF(32): -1.4, 1B(4): 0.4	0.6
	RF	BUF	AAA	27	244	26	13	1	6	37	19	54	2	1	.303/.360/.452	.283	.377	-1.8	RF(33): -0.2, LF(18): 1.0	1.1
	RF	TOR	MLB	27	16	0	0	0	0	0	1	5	0	0	.067/.125/.067	.091	.100	-0.1	RF(4): 0.0	-0.3
Maicer Izturis	2B	TOR	MLB	33	38	3	1	0	0	1	2	4	1	0	.286/.324/.314	.239	.323	0.1	2B(10): -0.2	-0.1
Ryan Kalish	CF	IOW	AAA	26	319	34	14	3	8	37	28	74	12	4	.251/.322/.404	.260	.312	-1.0	CF(31): -3.9, LF(26): 0.8	0.0
	LF	CHN	MLB	26	130	13	4	4	0	5	8	28	3	2	.248/.295/.347	.248	.323	0.4	LF(18): -0.2, CF(11): -0.2	0.0
George Kottaras	C	COH	AAA	31	47	4	0	0	1	5	4	18	0	1	.119/.196/.190	.146	.174	0.3	C(14): -0.3	-0.4
	C	BUF	AAA	31	49	6	1	0	3	8	7	14	0	0	.262/.367/.500	.290	.320	-0.6	C(11): -0.3	0.3
	C	TOR	MLB	31	5	0	0	0	0	0	1	3	0	0	.000/.200/.000	.115	.000	0.0	C(3): -0.0	-0.1
	C	CLE	MLB	31	27	4	0	0	3	4	4	11	0	0	.286/.385/.714	.378	.375	0.1	C(9): -0.1	0.4
	C	SLN	MLB	31	6	0	0	0	0	1	1	2	0	0	.200/.333/.200	.323	.333	-0.5	C(3): -0.0	0.0
Mitch Nay	3B	LNS	A	20	518	57	34	3	9	59	39	79	6	2	.285/.342/.389	.287	.335	-1.4	3B(104): 10.0	3.7
	3B	DUN	A+	20	40	2	1	0	0	1	3	9	0	0	.189/.250/.216	.176	.250	-0.2	3B(11): -1.0	-0.3
Dwight Smith	LF	DUN	A+	21	533	83	28	8	12	60	58	69	15	4	.284/.363/.453	.285	.311	1.5	LF(78): -0.9, CF(39): -3.1	2.7
Steve Tolleson	SS	BUF	AAA	30	84	12	2	1	1	9	12	13	6	1	.236/.345/.333	.239	.276	-0.3	SS(9): -1.0, 2B(7): 0.3	0.0
	2B	TOR	MLB	30	189	21	7	2	3	16	12	49	3	1	.253/.308/.371	.251	.336	-2.8	2B(55): 0.5, 3B(43): -0.7	0.1
Brett Wallace	1B	BUF	AAA	27	151	12	5	0	7	23	15	33	0	0	.323/.404/.519	.311	.387	-1.4	1B(29): 0.8	1.0
	1B	NOR	AAA	27	374	50	12	0	10	35	29	98	0	1	.265/.329/.389	.254	.343	-0.9	1B(72): 1.5, 3B(7): -0.7	0.3

Jonathon Berti is an Ecksteinian who got basestealing tutelage from Tim Raines and then an assignment to the Arizona Fall League, i.e. the Jays have taken notice of their former 18th-rounder out of Bowling Green—no surprise, given the state of second base in Toronto. ❖ Former first-rounder **D.J. Davis'** astonishingly lopsided combination of strikeouts, walks, power outage and stolen-base "success" rate no doubt made the Jays even happier that Dalton Pompey rocketed up the farm system last year. ❖ **Roemon Fields** roamed outfields for the Swedes of NAIA Bethany College (enrollment less than 1,000) in Lindsborg, Kansas, and was running from dogs as a mailman back home in Seattle when a Blue Jays scout discovered him playing summer ball. Then Fields broke the Northwest League's single-season stolen-base record by the season's midpoint. ❖ Scouts once thought **Caleb Gindl** would righty-mash his way to a permanent role in the big leagues, but he didn't even get a token September promotion after a lousy Triple-A campaign and now he's in *Canada*. ❖ **Brad Glenn**, who started the season as a 27-year-old in his third year at Double-A, got called up in late June for a week, an early indication that the Jays' wheels were already falling off. ❖ In the middle of a three-year deal, **Maicer Izturis'** slow bat didn't hurt the team for long. A left knee sprain tripping on stairs ended his season early, less than eight months after spraining his left ankle the previous season. Safe recovery, dude. ❖ **Ryan Kalish** returned in 2014 after not playing in a game in 2013 because of back problems, but he's little more than outfield depth at this point. ❖ **George Kottaras** signed with the Cubs before last year's winter meetings; by the end of the season, three other teams had rostered him. He'll be designated for assignment when you finish reading this comment. ❖ **Mitch "Double-a-Day" Nay**, a 2012 supplemental first-rounder, shows plenteous gap power, and if it turns into anticipated home run pop, third base will be waiting for him in Toronto. ❖ **Dwight Smith Jr.**'s dad was the runner-up for 1989 National League Rookie of the Year, and although the son started to hit homers in 2014, making him look like a viable left fielder, the Jays had him take reps at second base in the AFL. ❖ **Steve Tolleson** played the role of Maicer Izturis perfectly as an injury fill-in, playing multiple positions and hitting for negative value. ❖ **Brett Wallace**, at various times the heir apparent to Albert Pujols in St. Louis and Lance Berkman in Houston, didn't sign with the Jays when they drafted him out of high school and didn't stick when they traded for him in 2010 (he was flipped for Anthony Gose), but returned midway through 2014 as the heir apparent to, um, Dan Johnson.

Pitchers

NAME	TEAM	LVL	AGE	W	L	SV	G	GS	IP	H	HR	BB	K	BB/9	K/9	GB%	BABIP	WHIP	ERA	FIP	FRA	WARP
Cory Burns	MNT	AA	26	1	1	4	16	0	18	9	2	3	21	1.5	10.5	65%	.184	0.67	2.00	2.80	4.11	0.2
	ROU	AAA	26	2	2	0	20	1	32²	55	6	10	29	2.8	8.0	52%	.430	1.99	7.44	5.41	5.62	0.1
	DUR	AAA	26	2	2	1	7	0	13	17	0	3	8	2.1	5.5	53%	.362	1.54	2.77	2.82	2.69	0.4
Miguel Castro	LNS	A	19	1	1	0	4	4	21²	10	2	7	20	2.9	8.3	55%	.151	0.78	3.74	3.95	5.53	0.0
	VAN	A-	19	6	2	0	10	10	50¹	36	2	20	53	3.6	9.5	49%	.272	1.11	2.15	3.48	3.84	1.1
Taylor Cole	DUN	A+	24	8	9	0	24	23	132	114	4	39	171	2.7	11.7	45%	.344	1.16	3.07	2.22	3.01	4.0
	NHP	AA	24	0	2	0	2	2	12¹	12	1	7	10	5.1	7.3	53%	.297	1.54	7.30	4.73	5.51	0.0
Steve Delabar	BUF	AAA	30	2	2	1	24	0	28	21	3	18	38	5.8	12.2	33%	.295	1.39	2.89	4.29	3.46	0.5
	TOR	MLB	30	3	0	0	30	0	25²	19	3	19	21	6.7	7.4	37%	.235	1.48	4.91	5.61	6.97	-0.5
Liam Hendriks	OMA	AAA	25	4	1	0	5	5	35	33	1	6	35	1.5	9.0	49%	.337	1.11	2.83	2.59	3.62	0.8
	BUF	AAA	25	8	1	0	18	16	108¹	92	6	7	91	0.6	7.6	54%	.279	0.91	2.33	2.67	3.74	1.7
	TOR	MLB	25	1	0	0	3	3	13¹	12	3	4	8	2.7	5.4	35%	.225	1.20	6.07	6.23	7.43	-0.2
	KCA	MLB	25	0	2	0	6	3	19¹	26	3	3	15	1.4	7.0	46%	.388	1.50	4.66	2.23	3.74	0.3
Colt Hynes	ABQ	AAA	29	1	3	2	42	0	53	56	6	10	46	1.7	7.8	51%	.316	1.25	4.08	4.06	5.03	0.3
Jairo Labourt	LNS	A	20	0	0	0	6	3	14	15	1	20	11	12.9	7.1	42%	.359	2.50	6.43	7.77	9.20	-0.4
	VAN	A-	20	5	3	0	15	15	71¹	47	3	37	82	4.7	10.3	54%	.278	1.18	1.77	3.41	3.84	1.5
Wilton Lopez	CSP	AAA	30	1	2	0	23	1	43¹	58	4	6	35	1.2	7.3	56%	.375	1.48	4.57	3.77	4.69	0.5
	COL	MLB	30	0	0	0	4	0	6¹	18	3	0	4	0.0	5.7	50%	.517	2.84	11.37	8.00	6.68	0.0
Roberto Osuna	DUN	A+	19	0	2	0	7	7	22	28	3	9	30	3.7	12.3	37%	.446	1.68	6.55	4.07	5.55	0.2
Rob Rasmussen	BUF	AAA	25	1	1	1	35	0	43	32	0	17	44	3.6	9.2	44%	.278	1.14	2.72	2.57	3.19	0.9
	TOR	MLB	25	0	0	0	10	0	11¹	8	1	7	13	5.6	10.3	43%	.259	1.32	3.18	4.40	6.52	-0.1
Ricky Romero	BUF	AAA	29	0	3	0	9	9	37²	37	4	42	28	10.0	6.7	59%	.297	2.10	5.50	6.76	7.20	-0.5
Sergio Santos	BUF	AAA	30	1	0	2	11	0	10²	3	0	6	16	5.1	13.5	55%	.150	0.84	0.00	2.33	2.16	0.3
	TOR	MLB	30	0	3	5	26	0	21	28	5	18	29	7.7	12.4	41%	.426	2.19	8.57	6.06	4.91	0.0
Bo Schultz	RNO	AAA	28	10	8	0	28	23	135¹	174	17	46	82	3.1	5.5	56%	.334	1.63	6.18	5.23	6.79	0.4
	ARI	MLB	28	0	1	0	4	0	8	13	1	1	5	1.1	5.6	50%	.414	1.75	7.88	3.85	6.57	-0.1
John Stilson	BUF	AAA	23	2	0	1	25	0	34	37	2	18	32	4.8	8.5	45%	.337	1.62	3.18	3.92	4.81	0.1
Alberto Tirado	LNS	A	19	1	2	1	13	7	40	45	3	39	40	8.8	9.0	55%	.359	2.10	6.30	5.61	6.15	-0.1
	VAN	A-	19	1	0	0	17	3	35²	25	1	28	36	7.1	9.1	58%	.255	1.49	3.53	4.77	5.89	0.1
Frank Viola	LNS	A	30	2	2	0	5	5	23¹	24	1	15	13	5.8	5.0	45%	.319	1.67	3.86	5.63	6.46	-0.2
	DUN	A+	30	1	2	0	4	4	15²	26	1	15	4	8.6	2.3	36%	.397	2.62	12.06	7.73	9.55	-0.5

It's fun to watch roly-poly **Cory Burns** throw his screwball-ish changeup and needle younger guys in the Triple-A clubhouse about their green interviewing skills! ❖ **Miguel Castro** has a big arm that can deal near 100 mph, and if his development as a lower-velocity starter stalls out, he'll go back to doing that as often as he can out of the bullpen. ❖ **Taylor Cole**, a 2011 29th-rounder without a power arm or plus pitch, finished up his 2010 Mormon mission in, of all places, Toronto; so, even though he's been dominating guys he's too old to be facing, it does kind of seem like destiny, doesn't it? ❖ From High-A flameout to indy ball starter to high school substitute teacher to major-league All-Star, **Steve Delabar** took another big turn in 2014 as he gained a massive beard. In exchange, he lost his control and finished the year in Triple-A. ❖ **Liam Hendriks** is a walking advertisement for the gulf between Triple-A hitters (career 3.19 ERA, 5.1 K/BB) and big-league hitters (5.92 ERA, 2.3 K/BB). ❖ **Jeff Hoffman** had Tommy John surgery a month before the 2014 draft, in which the Jays made him the no. 9 overall pick and signed him for $3 million out of East Carolina. See ya in 2016. ❖ **Colt Hynes**, an August waiver claim by the Jays, has a neat first name and went to the same Texas high school as two other ballplayers with neat first names: Hippo and Boob. The fourth ballplayer who went to that high school is Zach Britton, and he doesn't think that's very funny. ❖ **Jairo Labourt** had a disastrous start to the year in the Midwest League, went back to extended spring training for re-education, and came correct in Vancouver. He needs to work on his control, but his upside has some pundits thinking he might be the best lefty in the system after Daniel Norris. ❖ On a warm April night, **Wilton Lopez**, fulfilling his $2.2 million contract, jogged in to pitch the eighth inning for the Rockies. He faced 10 batters, allowed eight hits, including three homers, and was never seen in Coors Field again. They say his ghost still haunts the place, though. ❖ **Roberto Osuna** returned from Tommy John surgery looking svelte and ready for the Arizona Fall League after a month at High-A, but we'll let him tweet for himself: "You do not forget to smile today and show everyone that you're stronger than yesterday." Excelsior! ❖ **Rob Rasmussen** reached the major leagues in 2014! Bet you didn't. He's also been traded for Carlos Lee and Michael Young. Bet you haven't been. ❖ **Ricky Romero** had knee surgery in June and missed the rest of the season, which unfortunately was kind of a relief. ❖ **Sergio Santos** could maybe go back to playing shortstop? ❖ **Bo Schultz** made his major-league debut in Arizona as a reliever with a mid-90s fastball. He was claimed off waivers in October. ❖ Promising but oft-injured **John Stilson** had labrum surgery in August and may not be ready in time for spring training. ❖ **Alberto Tirado** went from being our no. 3 Blue Jays prospect to heading our "Season's Most Disappointing Prospects" list last September; that's what eight walks per nine innings and

demotions to (a) short-season ball in June and (b) the Vancouver bullpen will do. Dare you to look up Spanish-to-English definitions of "tirado." ❖
Frank Viola III—son of *that* Frank Viola—doesn't want to go into the "'stuff' he went through, the forces that dragged him down and out of baseball and into selling timeshares," as one sportswriter put it, but he'll happily tell you that he returned to baseball for the first time since 2007 by learning to throw a knuckler with help from R.A. Dickey.

Manager

John Gibbons

YEAR	TEAM	W	L	Py-thag +/-	Avg PC	100+ P	120+ P	QS	BQS	REL	REL w Zero R	IBB	PH	PH Avg	PH HR	SB2	CS2	SB3	CS3	SAC Att	SAC%	POS SAC	Squeeze	Swing	In Play
2013	TOR	74	88	-2	92.3	56	1	67	6	487	391	33	102	.220	3	87	38	25	3	44	65.9%	26	0	353	99
2014	TOR	83	79	-2	96.7	69	4	86	7	449	367	23	176	.220	9	64	16	14	5	61	57.4%	34	1	309	102

You have to feel bad for Gibbons. Last year he led Toronto to its first winning season since 2010, yet remained on the hot seat due to the gulf between expectations and results. He made mistakes last season, that much is undeniable—most notably, he succeeded on just 33 percent of his replay challenges, the worst mark in the majors—but placing all or most of the blame on him for the Jays' disappointing season is absurd. In addition to one of the worst bullpens in the league—thanks to unexpectedly poor performances by the likes of Steve Delabar and Sergio Santos—Gibbons had to deal with a gimpy roster that was without Jose Bautista, Melky Cabrera, Edwin Encarnacion and Adam Lind for stretches. No manager in the majors can keep a team afloat with so many key pieces missing time due to injuries.

Besides, focusing on the negatives ignores the good Gibbons did. Those positives range from keeping Lind and Juan Francisco away from left-handed pitchers (each faced more than 85 percent righties) to eschewing tradition and batting Bautista second after Cabrera. Also worth a mention: Gibbons had one of the best post-ejection quips of the season, when he told the *Toronto Star*'s Brendan Kennedy in July, "[I got] a little tired of seeing bunts not getting down, [and thought I'd go] have a beer." Realistically, another season without a playoff appearance could leave Gibbons without a job. If that happens, it probably won't be of his own doing.

WASHINGTON NATIONALS

by Chris Cwik

For the second time in three years, the Nationals finished with the most wins in the National League. While the season ultimately ended in disappointment, the franchise had certainly come a long way in its decade in Washington: From a laughingstock that took eight years to produce its first winning record, the Nationals are now one of the premier organizations in the game. While there are a number of moves that could be highlighted as the turning point for the franchise, perhaps no deal exemplifies the Nationals' rise to prominence better than the "absolutely batshit crazy" Jayson Werth contract.

That's right, Werth's seven-year, $126 million deal is the reason for the Nationals' recent success. At the time of the signing, the move was met with immediate ridicule. A rival GM gave the now famous "batshit" quote to Fox Sports just after the signing. Mets General Manager Sandy Alderson actually went on the record, saying the deal made "some of [the Mets] contracts look pretty good." ESPN's Buster Olney tweeted that rival general managers and executives were "going nuts about the terms." Nobody outside of the organization thought this was a good deal.

Washington's General Manager Mike Rizzo didn't necessarily disagree, telling the *Washington Post* "we have to do a little bit more than the championship-caliber, win-today teams. I think that it's kind of a two-fold process. Sometimes you have to give the years to get the player." Rizzo had a point. Since moving to the Capital, the club's most recognizable moments were probably the Jose Rijo bonus-skimming scandal, Jim Bowden's Segway and the infamous "Natinals" jerseys. The product on the field was correspondingly forgettable: After winning 81 games in their inaugural season, they went 331-478 over the next five years, better than only the Pirates. That was the state and perception of the franchise on the day they signed Werth. Rizzo knew he'd have to overpay, or else change the narrative, to sign premium players.

The move looked awful on paper. Teams can often justify overpaying for a player in free agency when that player pushes them into contention. That was not the case here. The Nationals won just 80 games in 2011, their first year with Werth. Signing one marquee player was not going to suddenly push them to 90 wins.

But while the on-field ramifications of the deal were puzzling, the impact it had on the perception of the Nationals organization was immediate. The signing signaled a change in direction. There would be no more dumpster diving for headaches like Elijah Dukes and Lastings Milledge. The Nationals believed in their young core and were willing to spend the money to compete. With Werth buying into the team's long-term goals, there was at least hope that other free agents would follow him.

On top of that, Werth was tasked with changing the culture in the clubhouse. Rizzo regularly cited the fact that Werth came from the Phillies, who had been the toast of the NL East for the previous three seasons. Werth had played for a winner, and knew what it was like to be in a winning clubhouse. That was something no player had experienced in Washington. Werth was responsible for turning around the culture of losing.

We can roll our eyes a bit at this, but to his credit, Werth took on the challenge, and with tangible success. In a 2013 profile by the *Washington Post*, Werth was credited with numerous changes within the organization. He was responsible for the team overhauling the weight room, putting a nutritionist in the clubhouse kitchen and suggesting alternative medical therapies be made available for players. "I came here for a reason," Werth said. "I was told this place was going to be right. So when you see things that aren't right, you speak up."

The approach ruffled some feathers early, but, eventually, his teammates came around. "At the beginning, people are like, 'God, this guy,'" third baseman Ryan Zimmerman said. "At the end, they're like, 'Man, he was kind of right.'"

Culture, leadership and the nutritional value of a good diet might not be the type of things you expect to read about in a Baseball Prospectus annual. There's a reason for that. Until the next brilliant baseball mind creates Food Out Of Replacement Kitchen (FOORK), we are pretty limited in our ability to measure the impact of such soft factors. There's certainly something to be said for Werth's changes within the organization, but we can't definitively say they led to wins on the field.

We can, however, evaluate Werth's play. In order to do so, we need to figure out how much a win is worth on the free agent market. There are differing opinions on the subject, which will

NATIONALS PROSPECTUS
2014 W-L: 96-66, 1ST IN NL EAST

Pythag	.594	2nd	DER	.706	14th
RS/G	4.23	9th	B-Age	28.7	18th
RA/G	3.43	2nd	P-Age	27.9	10th
TAv	.268	7th	Salary	$136.5M	9th
BRR	5.97	4th	M$/MW	$2.6M	12th
TAv-P	.244	1st	DL Days	992	20th
FIP	3.15	1st	$ on DL	15%	15th

Three-Year Park Factors

Runs	Runs/RH	Runs/LH	HR/RH	HR/LH
99	94	94	85	81

Top Hitter WARP	5.7	Denard Span
Top Pitcher WARP	3.9	Jordan Zimmermann
Top Prospect		Lucas Giolito

impact the outcome of the analysis. The general thought is that a win has cost between $5 million and about $9 million. The high end comes from Indians President Mark Shapiro, who told FOX Sports Ohio that the cost of a win in 2012 was $9 million. Shapiro also put the value of a win at $8 million in 2010, the year the Nationals signed Werth. Lewie Pollis of Beyond The Box Score also did an in-depth study in October 2013 and determined the cost of a win in 2010 to be closer to $6 million.

With those three valuations as our guide, the Werth contract doesn't look as bad with hindsight. If you buy Shapiro's $8 million figure, Werth has basically lived up to the deal already, according to WARP. In this scenario, Werth would have to produce just over a win in his next three seasons to merit his seven years of salaries. Even at a much lower estimate—say, $5 million per win—Werth has already provided $73.5 million to the Nationals. He would need to produce 6.6 WARP over the next three seasons to reach $126 million; PECOTA thinks he'll cut into that even more, projecting him for about 3 WARP this year.

And that's at the lowest estimated value of a win. As Shapiro noted, the cost of a win is constantly changing, and if the cost was $5 million in 2010 it's certainly higher now. It's foolish to think teams don't factor inflation into contracts, and with that understanding the deal only gets better. The Nationals might have overpaid for Werth when all is said and done, but this deal was far from the colossal failure people thought it would be in 2010.

Even now, on the back end of the contract, Werth is nothing like an albatross. At 35 years old, he's coming off a 5-WARP year, his second consecutive season as a down-ballot MVP candidate. While $21.5 million per year is a significant chunk of money to spend on an aging outfielder, it's not likely the Nationals would opt to shed the contract if they had the chance.

In fact, you could argue that the Werth deal has progressed at the perfect pace for the Nationals. Given the team's roster makeup at the time of the signing—high-upside prospects all around—Rizzo knew he wouldn't have to hand out another nine-figure contract for some time. And Werth's deal expires following the 2017 season, ideal timing to provide the Nationals flexibility to lock up some of their young core.

They won't be able to keep everyone from that core, of course, but they are rich in opportunity. Jordan Zimmermann, Stephen Strasburg and Ian Desmond will become free agents in the two years immediately before Werth's contract expires; Bryce Harper, Anthony Rendon and Tanner Roark in the two years immediately after. As Werth ages gracefully into his twilight years, his contract promises one final gift to his club: $21 million in shed payroll that they can count on three years from now.

In that sense, the Werth deal was the perfect bridge for the franchise. He came in at a time when the young core needed guidance, a veteran advocate and an example of how to go about their business. He came at a cost that, in retrospect, he earned with his play on the field, and that, given the youth and affordability of the team's young core, the Nationals could well afford. What seemed prohibitively expensive at the time didn't keep the Nationals from acquiring and/or extending Adam LaRoche, Gio Gonzalez, Doug Fister, Rafael Soriano and Ryan Zimmerman. And by the time the stars of their promising young core are too expensive to coexist on a payroll with an aging $21 million corner outfielder, Werth will be all but gone.

There's still work to be done. Werth has to show he can provide value over the next three seasons, and his team has to win a postseason series or three. But a few years ago, both ideas would have seemed impossible. Today, Werth is one of the great stars of Washington's decade-long history, and the Nationals are one of the game's premier franchises. And it's all due to an "absolutely batshit crazy" contract. ■

—Chris Cwik is a writer at CBSSports.com and occasional freelancer. He can be found on Twitter @Chris_Cwik.

Player comments by Bret Sayre and Baseball Prospectus Authors

Hitters

Asdrubal Cabrera   SS

Born: 11/13/85   Age: 29   Bats: B   Throws: R   Height: 6' 0"   Weight: 205

YEAR	TEAM	LVL	AGE	PA	R	2B	3B	HR	RBI	BB	K	SB	CS	AVG/OBP/SLG	TAv	BABIP	BRR	FRAA	WARP
2012	CLE	MLB	26	616	70	35	1	16	68	52	99	9	4	.270/.338/.423	.265	.303	3.3	SS(136): 2.7	2.9
2013	CLE	MLB	27	562	66	35	2	14	64	35	114	9	3	.242/.299/.402	.262	.283	-2.8	SS(129): -3.9	1.5
2014	CLE	MLB	28	416	54	22	2	9	40	27	79	7	2	.246/.305/.386	.254	.286	-0.7	SS(92): 1.1	1.1
2014	WAS	MLB	28	200	20	9	2	5	21	22	29	3	0	.229/.312/.389	.275	.245	0.7	2B(48): -2.2, SS(1): 0.0	0.6
2015	WAS	MLB	29	568	68	28	2	12	54	40	102	10	3	.260/.320/.390	.268	.298	0.1	SS -4, 2B -1	2.2

Breakout: 3%   Improve: 36%   Collapse: 3%   Attrition: 7%   MLB: 100%   Comparables: Stephen Drew, John Valentin, J.J. Hardy

The long-range outlook of Jason Kipnis and Francisco Lindor in Cleveland made Cabrera expendable well before he was traded to the Nationals at the trading deadline, though he played a large part in that himself. Rising swing rates and rising whiff rates generally do not make great bedfellows, and Cabrera is no exception, as career-highs in both led to yet another year of declining TAv. The middle infielder entered free agency as a below-average shortstop, a bit of an unknown at the keystone and an eternity away from his surprising 25-homer season in 2011. If either the bat or glove doesn't start to reverse course, he'll play his way into permanent stopgap status.

Ian Desmond   SS

Born: 9/20/85   Age: 29   Bats: R   Throws: R   Height: 6' 3"   Weight: 215

YEAR	TEAM	LVL	AGE	PA	R	2B	3B	HR	RBI	BB	K	SB	CS	AVG/OBP/SLG	TAv	BABIP	BRR	FRAA	WARP
2012	WAS	MLB	26	547	72	33	2	25	73	30	113	21	6	.292/.335/.511	.286	.332	0.8	SS(128): -15.0	1.8
2013	WAS	MLB	27	655	77	38	3	20	80	43	145	21	6	.280/.331/.453	.273	.336	0.2	SS(158): 5.0	3.8
2014	WAS	MLB	28	648	73	26	3	24	91	46	183	24	5	.255/.313/.430	.273	.326	1.8	SS(154): 4.0	4.5
2015	WAS	MLB	29	610	70	29	2	15	68	37	143	22	6	.262/.309/.404	.268	.319	0.4	SS -4	2.7

Breakout: 1%   Improve: 34%   Collapse: 2%   Attrition: 9%   MLB: 97%   Comparables: Robin Yount, Khalil Greene, Derek Jeter

The list of shortstops who have accumulated three 20/20 seasons is short and impressive: Alex Rodriguez, Hanley Ramirez and Ian Desmond. At the plate, his on-base ability was slightly hampered by a strikeout rate that jumped more than six percentage points over his previous career high. The driving force behind this increase was a drag in contact outside the zone; he's always been below average, but dropped below B.J. Upton levels last year. Away from the batter's box, Desmond remains an above-average defender and baserunner, and those enviable traits pushed him to the best season of his career. The last Expos draft pick on the Nationals' 40-man roster head into his walk year a man of confidence after reportedly rejecting a seven-year, $107 million deal prior to the 2014 season. That confidence suits him well.

Danny Espinosa   2B

Born: 4/25/87   Age: 28   Bats: B   Throws: R   Height: 6' 0"   Weight: 205

YEAR	TEAM	LVL	AGE	PA	R	2B	3B	HR	RBI	BB	K	SB	CS	AVG/OBP/SLG	TAv	BABIP	BRR	FRAA	WARP
2012	WAS	MLB	25	658	82	37	2	17	56	46	189	20	6	.247/.315/.402	.255	.333	-0.3	2B(126): 2.7, SS(36): 3.1	2.1
2013	SYR	AAA	26	313	32	12	1	2	22	19	101	6	1	.216/.280/.286	.210	.324	1.3	2B(41): -3.0, SS(35): -0.6	-0.8
2013	WAS	MLB	26	167	11	9	0	3	12	4	47	1	0	.158/.193/.272	.178	.202	-0.3	2B(43): 0.7, SS(1): -0.1	-1.0
2014	WAS	MLB	27	364	31	14	3	8	27	18	122	8	1	.219/.283/.351	.234	.319	-1.3	2B(89): 0.0, SS(12): 0.1	-0.1
2015	WAS	MLB	28	340	37	14	1	8	34	22	99	8	2	.224/.290/.358	.245	.297	-0.5	2B 1, SS 0	0.8

Breakout: 2%   Improve: 52%   Collapse: 10%   Attrition: 16%   MLB: 91%   Comparables: Dan Uggla, Jayson Nix, Jeff Baker

After a relatively hot start—fueled, in part, by seven bunt hits in eight April attempts—Espinosa settled into a diminished role and career-high 34 percent strikeout rate. (He didn't bunt for a hit in the entire second half.) The book on the former third-round pick is largely the same: free swinger, free misser, good defender and hard to watch against right-handed pitching. In fact, his career .271/.343/.460 line against southpaws was raised across the board in 2014, which only serves to highlight his paltry .532 OPS from the left-hand side of the plate. On the bright side, he didn't make it back to the Erie Canal Museum this year. Espinosa will have another shot at a starting job in 2015.

Kevin Frandsen   PH

Born: 5/24/82   Age: 33   Bats: R   Throws: R   Height: 6' 0"   Weight: 190

YEAR	TEAM	LVL	AGE	PA	R	2B	3B	HR	RBI	BB	K	SB	CS	AVG/OBP/SLG	TAv	BABIP	BRR	FRAA	WARP
2012	LEH	AAA	30	418	38	34	0	1	33	14	31	2	4	.302/.337/.396	.251	.323	0.5	2B(81): 0.1, 1B(10): -0.8	0.7
2012	PHI	MLB	30	210	24	10	3	2	14	9	18	0	1	.338/.383/.451	.293	.366	-1.7	3B(52): -3.0	0.8
2013	PHI	MLB	31	278	27	10	1	5	26	12	29	1	0	.234/.296/.341	.233	.245	-1.6	1B(40): -0.1, 2B(20): -0.6	-0.5
2014	WAS	MLB	32	236	17	8	0	1	17	6	26	0	0	.259/.299/.309	.222	.289	0.7	LF(21): 0.0, 3B(16): -0.3	-0.4
2015	WAS	MLB	33	250	23	12	1	1	17	9	28	1	0	.262/.305/.329	.244	.290	-0.7	3B -1, 2B -0	-0.1

Breakout: 2%   Improve: 21%   Collapse: 8%   Attrition: 12%   MLB: 64%   Comparables: Timo Perez, Kevin Mench, Jason Tyner

The aging utility man played another full year in the majors, despite not doing anything particularly well, and was rewarded with his sixth negative WARP season in eight tries. Frandsen played more outfield in 2014 than he ever had (due to injuries to Bryce Harper and Nate McLouth), but it didn't suit him any better than the infield did. On the bright side, he did get to participate in the playoffs, popping out on two pitches against Yusmeiro Petit in the 15th inning of Game 2 of the NLDS.

Brian Goodwin   CF

Born: 11/2/90   Age: 24   Bats: L   Throws: R   Height: 6' 0"   Weight: 200

YEAR	TEAM	LVL	AGE	PA	R	2B	3B	HR	RBI	BB	K	SB	CS	AVG/OBP/SLG	TAv	BABIP	BRR	FRAA	WARP
2012	HAG	A	21	266	47	18	1	9	38	43	39	15	4	.324/.438/.542	.342	.357	0.4	CF(55): 2.6	3.4
2012	HAR	AA	21	186	17	8	1	5	14	18	50	3	3	.223/.306/.373	.245	.288	0.0	CF(42): -5.3	-0.1
2013	HAR	AA	22	533	82	19	11	10	40	66	121	19	11	.252/.355/.407	.286	.321	2.0	CF(116): -0.7	3.4
2014	SYR	AAA	23	329	31	10	4	4	32	50	95	6	4	.219/.342/.328	.255	.320	0.1	CF(65): 1.1, RF(14): -0.8	1.0
2015	WAS	MLB	24	250	29	9	2	4	20	26	69	5	3	.223/.309/.332	.248	.302	0.0	CF -1, RF -0	0.2

Breakout: 5%   Improve: 15%   Collapse: 8%   Attrition: 15%   MLB: 30%   Comparables: Thomas Pham, Jaff Decker, Xavier Paul

One of the great inevitabilities in baseball is that many prospects with athleticism and tools end up unable to translate those key ingredients into baseball skills. The pull is undeniable—the ones who hit are the all-stars, the household names. Goodwin is now extremely unlikely to fulfill that promise, and has tumbled from the Nationals' center fielder of the future to possibly second in line for an outfield opening, behind Michael Taylor. His ability to play up the middle will likely keep him on a roster for several years, even if he struggles to make the sort of contact he was once projected to.

Scott Hairston   PH

Born: 5/25/80   Age: 35   Bats: R   Throws: R   Height: 6' 0"   Weight: 200

YEAR	TEAM	LVL	AGE	PA	R	2B	3B	HR	RBI	BB	K	SB	CS	AVG/OBP/SLG	TAv	BABIP	BRR	FRAA	WARP
2012	NYN	MLB	32	398	52	25	3	20	57	19	83	8	2	.263/.299/.504	.289	.287	0.3	LF(59): -4.9, RF(48): 2.1	1.9
2013	CHN	MLB	33	112	13	2	0	8	19	7	25	2	0	.172/.232/.434	.245	.129	-0.1	RF(29): -2.9, LF(1): 0.0	-0.3
2013	WAS	MLB	33	62	5	3	0	2	7	2	19	0	0	.224/.246/.379	.223	.289	-0.6	LF(15): -0.1, RF(2): -0.2	-0.3
2014	WAS	MLB	34	87	6	4	0	1	8	4	26	0	0	.208/.253/.299	.221	.278	-1.7	LF(15): 1.1, RF(1): -0.0	-0.3
2015	WAS	MLB	35	250	27	11	1	9	30	15	58	4	1	.233/.285/.397	.260	.271	-0.6	LF -1, RF -1	0.3

Breakout: 1%   Improve: 24%   Collapse: 15%   Attrition: 22%   MLB: 92%   Comparables: Ryan Ludwick, Bob Nieman, Matt Diaz

Maybe the most surprising thing about the Nationals' season was that Hairston, a recently renowned lefty masher, spent 136 games on the active roster and hit exactly zero home runs against southpaws. That's a far cry from the 21 he hit between 2012 and 2013. After missing most of April with an abdominal strain, Hairston fell on hard times as the season progressed—his .123/.188/.158 line from June through September is colloquially known as The Sad Trombone. In the end, Hairston has turned out to be yet another cautionary tale about giving a part-time player a multi-year contract.

Bryce Harper   LF

Born: 10/16/92   Age: 22   Bats: L   Throws: R   Height: 6' 3"   Weight: 225

YEAR	TEAM	LVL	AGE	PA	R	2B	3B	HR	RBI	BB	K	SB	CS	AVG/OBP/SLG	TAv	BABIP	BRR	FRAA	WARP
2012	SYR	AAA	19	84	8	4	1	1	3	9	14	1	1	.243/.325/.365	.257	.288	-0.3	CF(13): -1.1, RF(6): -0.2	0.1
2012	WAS	MLB	19	597	98	26	9	22	59	56	120	18	6	.270/.340/.477	.288	.310	5.6	CF(92): 2.2, RF(65): 2.8	5.1
2013	WAS	MLB	20	497	71	24	3	20	58	61	94	11	4	.274/.368/.486	.303	.306	-0.6	LF(97): -1.2, RF(16): 1.1	3.4
2014	WAS	MLB	21	395	41	10	2	13	32	38	104	2	2	.273/.344/.423	.290	.352	-1.9	LF(90): -1.3, RF(10): -0.4	1.9
2015	WAS	MLB	22	396	50	16	3	14	52	40	86	7	3	.269/.346/.450	.297	.315	0.4	LF -1, CF -0	2.4

Breakout: 4%   Improve: 59%   Collapse: 1%   Attrition: 1%   MLB: 93%   Comparables: Frank Robinson, Jason Heyward, Albert Pujols

If Helen of Troy was the face that launched a thousand ships, Harper's is the swing that launched a thousand expletives. The beautiful violence in that swing is the perfect complement to his aggressive style of play, which makes him both exhilarating to watch and a constant threat to hit the disabled list. Assessing his 2014 season is an exercise in perspective. On one hand, he was a 21-year old with a .290 TAv and 1.9 WARP in only 100 games; most high-end prospects his age are in Double-A. Conversely, it was a down season for the third-year slugger, who had a career-high strikeout rate and a career-low slugging percentage. And there lies the problem. Harper's youth relative to performance has gotten plenty of print and airspace, but it's nearly impossible to overstate. When Harper was on a rehab assignment in Potomac last June after tearing a ligament in his thumb, he was still nearly two years younger than the average player in the High-A Carolina League. The Twitter fun facts are nearly endless. In fact, the next time Harper faces a pitcher younger than him in a professional game will be the first.

Jose Lobaton   C

Born: 10/21/84   Age: 30   Bats: B   Throws: R   Height: 6' 0"   Weight: 215

YEAR	TEAM	LVL	AGE	PA	R	2B	3B	HR	RBI	BB	K	SB	CS	AVG/OBP/SLG	TAv	BABIP	BRR	FRAA	WARP
2012	TBA	MLB	27	197	16	10	0	2	20	24	46	0	1	.222/.323/.317	.238	.289	-1.5	C(66): 0.6	0.2
2013	TBA	MLB	28	311	38	15	2	7	32	30	65	0	1	.249/.320/.394	.280	.300	-3.2	C(96): -0.0	1.5
2014	WAS	MLB	29	230	18	9	0	2	12	15	61	0	0	.234/.287/.304	.224	.318	-1.0	C(64): 0.9	0.3
2015	WAS	MLB	30	250	24	11	1	3	22	24	59	0	0	.238/.315/.338	.252	.305	-1.2	C 0	0.7

Breakout: 2%   Improve: 36%   Collapse: 13%   Attrition: 16%   MLB: 84%   Comparables: John Baker, Landon Powell, Eric Munson

The Nationals dealt for the Venezuelan backstop just prior to spring training, adding a layer of depth in case of Wilson Ramos injury. And like only Carnac the Magnificent could have predicted, Ramos would end up on the disabled list twice, allowing Lobaton to start 58 games. Unfortunately, his strikeout rate ballooned, while his walk rate and isolated power shrank, leading to a 115-point drop in OPS and 56-point drop in TAv. Perhaps some of the struggles at the plate can be attributed to learning a new pitching staff, but even with depressed offensive output, Lobaton still brings above-average defense and framing to the table. He even took a big step forward in controlling baserunners, which had been the weakest part of his glove game.

Nate McLouth   PH

Born: 10/28/81   Age: 33   Bats: L   Throws: R   Height: 5' 10"   Weight: 190

YEAR	TEAM	LVL	AGE	PA	R	2B	3B	HR	RBI	BB	K	SB	CS	AVG/OBP/SLG	TAv	BABIP	BRR	FRAA	WARP
2012	BAL	MLB	30	236	35	12	1	7	18	22	43	12	1	.268/.342/.435	.273	.306	4.0	LF(55): 0.2, CF(6): -0.0	1.2
2012	NOR	AAA	30	209	29	5	2	10	33	18	26	5	0	.244/.325/.461	.278	.231	2.6	CF(28): -0.7, RF(12): -1.6	1.0
2012	PIT	MLB	30	62	4	2	0	0	2	5	18	0	0	.140/.210/.175	.151	.205	0.5	LF(9): -0.5, CF(4): 0.2	-0.6
2013	BAL	MLB	31	593	76	31	4	12	36	53	86	30	7	.258/.329/.399	.269	.288	4.0	LF(136): 1.9, CF(3): 0.0	2.5
2014	WAS	MLB	32	162	10	6	0	1	7	16	35	4	1	.173/.280/.237	.218	.221	0.7	LF(28): -0.6, RF(16): -0.4	-0.3
2015	WAS	MLB	33	250	31	10	1	4	19	24	45	10	2	.231/.313/.337	.248	.269	1.5	LF -0, CF -0	0.3

Breakout: 2%   Improve: 31%   Collapse: 10%   Attrition: 12%   MLB: 87%   Comparables: Roy White, Luis Gonzalez, Floyd Robinson

Yet another cautionary tale about two-year contracts for reserve players, McLouth was both terrible and hurt during a 2014 campaign he'd like to forget. Unfortunately, the Nationals won't be able to forget the $5.75 million he is still owed: No matter how much outfield depth they promote to the upper minors, McLouth just keeps hanging around. He underwent surgery to repair the labrum in his throwing shoulder, which will just serve to diminish an already weak arm. He'd be a fine fit as a fourth outfielder on a team with fewer internal options than the Nationals have, with decent on-base skills and a penchant for stealing bases carefully, but he's average at best in left field and worse everywhere else. McLouth has likely permanently fallen into "more valuable for immeasurable things than what he does on the field" territory.

Tyler Moore   1B

Born: 1/30/87   Age: 28   Bats: R   Throws: R   Height: 6' 2"   Weight: 220

YEAR	TEAM	LVL	AGE	PA	R	2B	3B	HR	RBI	BB	K	SB	CS	AVG/OBP/SLG	TAv	BABIP	BRR	FRAA	WARP
2012	SYR	AAA	25	115	15	6	1	9	26	12	26	1	0	.307/.374/.653	.338	.324	-1.9	1B(24): 1.9, LF(3): -0.3	1.2
2012	WAS	MLB	25	171	20	9	0	10	29	14	46	3	0	.263/.327/.513	.273	.310	-2.2	LF(40): -3.7, 1B(14): -0.4	-0.1
2013	SYR	AAA	26	200	26	14	1	10	46	23	39	1	0	.318/.395/.584	.336	.354	-1.3	LF(21): -0.2, 1B(19): 0.2	1.9
2013	WAS	MLB	26	178	16	9	0	4	21	8	58	0	0	.222/.260/.347	.238	.311	-0.2	LF(29): -3.1, 1B(14): -0.2	-0.9
2014	SYR	AAA	27	354	45	21	0	10	44	47	77	0	2	.265/.367/.434	.281	.323	-3.7	1B(64): -3.3, LF(15): 0.4	0.5
2014	WAS	MLB	27	100	8	2	0	4	14	7	29	0	0	.231/.300/.385	.257	.293	0.0	1B(24): 0.5, LF(4): 0.2	0.2
2015	WAS	MLB	28	250	28	11	0	9	32	22	68	1	0	.248/.317/.421	.278	.311	-0.9	1B 1, LF -2	0.5

Breakout: 6%   Improve: 27%   Collapse: 10%   Attrition: 23%   MLB: 65%   Comparables: Ryan Shealy, Josh Phelps, Jake Fox

He spent most of his minor-league career as the "but he's old for his level" guy, but that preface doesn't change the fact that Moore has hit at every stop. Which made the .801 OPS he registered in Syracuse during 2014—his lowest mark since graduating to full-season ball—all the more surprising. At the plate, he's a right-handed power hitter with holes in his swing and a poor rate of contact on pitches out of the zone. In the field, he's a first baseman, even when he's playing the outfield. With the next wave of outfielders ready to contribute for the Nats, the best chance for Moore to be relevant in Washington during 2015 is to be the first-baseman-in-waiting at Triple-A. Assuming he's understudying the recently brittle Ryan Zimmerman, a lot of patience might not be required.

Wilson Ramos   C

Born: 8/10/87   Age: 27   Bats: R   Throws: R   Height: 6' 0"   Weight: 235

YEAR	TEAM	LVL	AGE	PA	R	2B	3B	HR	RBI	BB	K	SB	CS	AVG/OBP/SLG	TAv	BABIP	BRR	FRAA	WARP
2012	WAS	MLB	24	96	11	2	0	3	10	12	19	0	0	.265/.354/.398	.284	.306	0.6	C(24): 0.3	0.6
2013	WAS	MLB	25	303	29	9	0	16	59	15	42	0	1	.272/.307/.470	.268	.270	-1.1	C(77): -0.3	1.8
2014	WAS	MLB	26	361	32	12	0	11	47	17	57	0	0	.267/.299/.399	.251	.290	1.9	C(87): 0.1	1.9
2015	WAS	MLB	27	334	36	14	0	10	39	20	57	0	0	.264/.310/.408	.271	.290	0.5	C -0	1.7

Breakout: 5%   Improve: 52%   Collapse: 4%   Attrition: 10%   MLB: 99%   Comparables: *Miguel Montero, Jason Castro, Ronny Paulino*

After the oft-injured catcher made it just three plate appearances into the 2014 season before requiring surgery—this time for a hamate injury—expectations for both his playing time and power were depressed. But even after a subsequent DL stint for a hamstring strain, Ramos hit double-digit homers and played the second most games of his career (though, admittedly, the second most games of *his* career). The 27-year-old catcher still loves to swing, as he took a hack more than 58 percent of the time he saw a pitch in 2014, which would have ranked second in baseball behind Pablo Sandoval had he qualified. With two seasons left before his chance at a real payday, Ramos will have to get that pesky on-base percentage back over .300 and show that his one-year dip as a framer was a fluke.

Anthony Rendon   3B

Born: 6/6/90   Age: 25   Bats: R   Throws: R   Height: 6' 1"   Weight: 200

YEAR	TEAM	LVL	AGE	PA	R	2B	3B	HR	RBI	BB	K	SB	CS	AVG/OBP/SLG	TAv	BABIP	BRR	FRAA	WARP
2012	AUB	A-	22	32	7	2	0	1	3	4	6	0	0	.259/.375/.444	.290	.300	0.4	3B(5): 0.3	0.2
2012	POT	A+	22	32	5	2	3	0	0	5	4	0	0	.333/.438/.630	.417	.391	-0.1	3B(6): 0.3	0.6
2012	HAR	AA	22	82	14	3	1	3	3	11	16	0	0	.162/.305/.368	.248	.163	1.6	3B(18): 1.5	0.5
2013	HAR	AA	23	152	17	11	2	6	24	30	25	1	0	.319/.461/.603	.376	.352	-0.5	3B(24): 3.5, 2B(5): -0.5	2.8
2013	WAS	MLB	23	394	40	23	1	7	35	31	69	1	1	.265/.329/.396	.261	.307	1.3	2B(82): 0.9, 3B(15): 0.5	1.3
2014	WAS	MLB	24	683	111	39	6	21	83	58	104	17	3	.287/.351/.473	.302	.314	4.9	3B(134): 0.9, 2B(28): -2.0	5.5
2015	WAS	MLB	25	604	78	32	3	15	63	55	103	10	2	.270/.341/.427	.287	.304	2.6	3B 4, 2B -1	3.9

Breakout: 1%   Improve: 58%   Collapse: 0%   Attrition: 5%   MLB: 100%   Comparables: *Edwin Encarnacion, Pablo Sandoval, Logan Morrison*

With a face that Merces would fall for and the swordsmanship of Porthos, Rendon is a superstar straight out of Dumas. When Ryan Zimmerman hit the shelf for a good portion of the year, Rendon stepped back into his natural position and let his bat (if he's not calling it Balizarde, he should be) do the talking. The exact words were "Little pimple ... meet me behind the Luxembourg at 1 o'clock and bring a long wooden box."

The 2011 first-round pick showed the type of approach and bat control that drove draft prognosticators to project him as the top talent in the class, allowing his power to play consistently in games, as he finished top five in extra-base hits. Given the concerns that have dogged him since his sophomore year at Rice, his most important stat was 153, as in how many games he played. A healthy Rendon is a year-in, year-out MVP candidate (FRAA is an outlier in rating his defense) and makes a formidable core with Bryce Harper and Stephen Strasburg in Washington. If they were both as dashing as Rendon, they'd truly be the Three Musketeers.

Nate Schierholtz   RF

Born: 4/19/90   Age: 24   Bats: L   Throws: R   Height: 5' 10"   Weight: 195

YEAR	TEAM	LVL	AGE	PA	R	2B	3B	HR	RBI	BB	K	SB	CS	AVG/OBP/SLG	TAv	BABIP	BRR	FRAA	WARP
2012	PHI	MLB	28	73	5	4	0	1	5	5	10	0	0	.273/.319/.379	.257	.304	-0.1	RF(28): -0.6, CF(7): -0.2	0.1
2012	SFN	MLB	28	196	15	4	5	5	16	18	36	3	2	.251/.321/.417	.280	.287	-1.4	RF(52): -1.5	0.4
2013	CHN	MLB	29	503	56	32	3	21	68	29	94	6	3	.251/.301/.470	.274	.270	2.1	RF(126): 3.2	2.1
2014	CHN	MLB	30	341	29	10	3	6	33	18	76	4	4	.192/.240/.300	.210	.228	-2.2	RF(81): 1.0	-1.3
2014	WAS	MLB	30	42	3	1	1	1	4	2	8	0	1	.225/.262/.375	.256	.258	0.1	RF(6): -0.4, LF(4): -0.0	0.0
2015	WAS	MLB	31	387	39	17	2	9	41	23	74	5	4	.245/.294/.380	.255	.281	-0.6	RF -0, CF -0	0.4

Breakout: 1%   Improve: 41%   Collapse: 7%   Attrition: 6%   MLB: 88%   Comparables: *Ron Northey, Kevin Bass, Juan Encarnacion*

For the second time in two years, Washington relieved the Cubs of a platoon player whose contract had soured. In 2013 it was Hairston, but the Nationals' investment was smaller this time, as Schierholtz was so bad in the first half they didn't even have to give up a prospect for him. For a corner outfielder who is totally prohibited from facing left-handed pitching, even above-average defense can't come close to compensating for the .566 OPS he produced against righties. He'll be 31 this year, and it'll be a surprise if he ever again sees 379 plate appearances (his average over the last four years), but he could still be a useful extra guy.

Matt Skole   3B

Born: 7/30/89   Age: 25   Bats: L   Throws: R   Height: 6' 3"   Weight: 225

YEAR	TEAM	LVL	AGE	PA	R	2B	3B	HR	RBI	BB	K	SB	CS	AVG/OBP/SLG	TAv	BABIP	BRR	FRAA	WARP
2012	HAG	A	22	448	73	18	0	27	92	94	116	10	0	.286/.438/.574	.336	.345	-3.0	3B(95): -7.7	4.5
2012	POT	A+	22	76	11	10	1	0	12	5	17	1	0	.314/.355/.486	.299	.407	0.6	3B(12): 0.0	0.6
2014	HAR	AA	24	544	58	29	1	14	68	78	127	3	1	.241/.352/.399	.271	.301	-0.6	1B(97): -1.6, 3B(29): -5.6	0.7
2015	WAS	MLB	25	250	26	10	0	7	28	32	73	0	0	.220/.320/.358	.258	.295	-0.5	1B -1, 3B -3	-0.2

Breakout: 6%   Improve: 10%   Collapse: 5%   Attrition: 15%   MLB: 22%   Comparables: *Jeff Larish, Tommy Medica, Chris McGuiness*

There's only so much hope for a 25-year old first baseman in Double-A, but there is enough potential in Skole's bat to keep him on the prospect radar. After missing nearly the entire 2013 season with a torn UCL in his non-throwing arm, he was both rusty and not quite 100 percent at the beginning of 2014. But after registering a .512 OPS through the first month and a half of 2014 (62 points lower than his *slugging percentage* during a breakout 2012 season), things started to turn around for the aspiring power threat. From May 15th on, Skole hit .262/.382/.448 with 13 homers in 100 games. Now just about a full-time first baseman, on account of having the range of Aramis Ramirez in cement shoes, Skole can still carve out a career as a second-division first baseman on the strong side of a platoon. Don't everybody all line up at once.

Denard Span   CF

Born: 2/27/84   Age: 31   Bats: L   Throws: L   Height: 6' 0"   Weight: 210

YEAR	TEAM	LVL	AGE	PA	R	2B	3B	HR	RBI	BB	K	SB	CS	AVG/OBP/SLG	TAv	BABIP	BRR	FRAA	WARP
2012	MIN	MLB	28	568	71	38	4	4	41	47	62	17	6	.283/.342/.395	.261	.315	-1.0	CF(125): 8.3	2.5
2013	WAS	MLB	29	662	75	28	11	4	47	42	77	20	6	.279/.327/.380	.251	.313	0.3	CF(153): 8.8	2.7
2014	WAS	MLB	30	668	94	39	8	5	37	50	65	31	7	.302/.355/.416	.289	.330	6.8	CF(147): 8.0	5.7
2015	WAS	MLB	31	627	71	29	6	2	44	47	78	23	6	.273/.328/.356	.262	.306	1.6	CF 8	2.9

Breakout: 0%   Improve: 39%   Collapse: 4%   Attrition: 9%   MLB: 94%   Comparables: Coco Crisp, Shane Victorino, Len Dykstra

Generally, when a player is considered underrated, it means he lacks fan support or media coverage, but Span's underratedness ranges as far as he does in the outfield—all the way to his own teammates. At the end of June, Bryce Harper backhandedly called for Span to be benched for Danny Espinosa, which seemed foolish at the time and was made even more foolish by Span's .339/.398/.445 line after the comments were made. A career-best contact rate pushed his batting average back to his early Minnesota levels, and although he doesn't get on base via the walk as much anymore, the hits and his plus defense made him (by WARP) the third-most-valuable center fielder in baseball, ahead of Carlos Gomez and Adam Jones. The Nationals picked up his no-brainer $9 million option, which makes this his walk year.

Michael Taylor   OF

Born: 3/26/91   Age: 24   Bats: R   Throws: R   Height: 6' 3"   Weight: 210

YEAR	TEAM	LVL	AGE	PA	R	2B	3B	HR	RBI	BB	K	SB	CS	AVG/OBP/SLG	TAv	BABIP	BRR	FRAA	WARP
2012	POT	A+	21	431	51	33	2	3	37	40	113	19	9	.242/.318/.362	.246	.335	0.7	CF(108): 13.0, RF(1): -0.1	2.7
2013	POT	A+	22	581	79	41	6	10	87	55	131	51	7	.263/.340/.426	.265	.331	7.5	CF(117): 14.3, RF(4): 0.1	5.0
2014	HAR	AA	23	441	74	17	2	22	61	50	130	34	8	.313/.396/.539	.327	.421	3.5	CF(87): 13.1, RF(1): 0.1	6.9
2014	SYR	AAA	23	52	7	3	1	1	3	7	14	3	1	.227/.333/.409	.261	.310	0.8	CF(12): 1.4	0.5
2014	WAS	MLB	23	43	5	3	0	1	5	3	17	0	2	.205/.279/.359	.235	.333	-0.8	CF(10): 0.0, RF(5): 0.8	0.5
2015	WAS	MLB	24	250	32	11	1	5	21	19	79	13	3	.229/.292/.351	.245	.321	1.1	CF 4, RF 0	0.9

Breakout: 2%   Improve: 12%   Collapse: 5%   Attrition: 9%   MLB: 24%   Comparables: Justin Maxwell, Melky Mesa, Matt Den Dekker

Toolsy outfielders with contact issues are not supposed to skip through the upper minors the way that Taylor did in 2014. They're also not supposed to put up stat lines that would merit first-round roto attention if duplicated in the majors. Offensive glitz aside, the aspect of his game most likely to keep him in a major-league lineup is his center field defense, which is strong enough that he could take over for Denard Span without advanced metrics even noticing. How the hit tool plays at the highest level will determine whether Taylor becomes a potential All-Star or someone the fans hate for the strikeouts, both being eminently achievable outcomes. The glut of outfielders in Washington will force Taylor to get more time in the upper minors, working on his approach and contact issues—not a bad thing for his development.

Jayson Werth   RF

Born: 5/20/79   Age: 36   Bats: R   Throws: R   Height: 6' 5"   Weight: 240

YEAR	TEAM	LVL	AGE	PA	R	2B	3B	HR	RBI	BB	K	SB	CS	AVG/OBP/SLG	TAv	BABIP	BRR	FRAA	WARP
2012	SYR	AAA	33	27	4	2	0	0	4	6	5	0	0	.238/.407/.333	.247	.313	-0.2	RF(5): -0.2, CF(2): -0.1	0.0
2012	WAS	MLB	33	344	42	21	3	5	31	42	57	8	2	.300/.387/.440	.299	.356	-1.0	RF(76): 5.8, CF(11): -1.0	2.3
2013	POT	A+	34	20	6	1	0	2	8	2	0	0	0	.556/.600/.944	.464	.500	-0.8	RF(6): 0.5	0.5
2013	WAS	MLB	34	532	84	24	0	25	82	60	101	10	1	.318/.398/.532	.325	.358	3.2	RF(126): -0.9	4.7
2014	WAS	MLB	35	629	85	37	1	16	82	83	113	9	1	.292/.394/.455	.320	.343	2.5	RF(139): -5.3	5.0
2015	WAS	MLB	36	574	69	28	1	15	68	67	126	10	2	.269/.359/.420	.294	.327	1.4	RF -0, CF 0	3.2

Breakout: 1%   Improve: 25%   Collapse: 3%   Attrition: 11%   MLB: 87%   Comparables: Carlos Beltran, Lance Berkman, Frank Robinson

We've finally moved beyond the point where Werth's contact needs to be mentioned constantly; we can only hope the beard follows suit. The rejuvenated outfielder whiffed less in 2014 than in any previous year of his career, riding his strong plate discipline and patient approach like a photoshopped motorcycle. Werth is one of only three players to post an on-base percentage over .380 in each of the past three seasons. The other two: Joey Votto and Andrew McCutchen. Unfortunately, he failed to cap off the year with a strong postseason, as his 1-for-17 performance against the Giants failed to remind us all of his past playoff glory. (See? You'd forgotten.) Suddenly, he is owed only a very reasonable $63 million over the final three years of his contract. Guess it does need to be mentioned occasionally.

Ryan Zimmerman   LF

Born: 9/28/84   Age: 30   Bats: R   Throws: R   Height: 6' 3"   Weight: 220

YEAR	TEAM	LVL	AGE	PA	R	2B	3B	HR	RBI	BB	K	SB	CS	AVG/OBP/SLG	TAv	BABIP	BRR	FRAA	WARP
2012	WAS	MLB	27	641	93	36	1	25	95	57	116	5	2	.282/.346/.478	.286	.313	-0.2	3B(145): 5.6	4.7
2013	WAS	MLB	28	633	84	26	2	26	79	60	133	6	0	.275/.344/.465	.284	.316	0.9	3B(141): 1.2	3.9
2014	WAS	MLB	29	240	26	19	1	5	38	22	37	0	0	.280/.342/.449	.295	.313	-3.1	LF(30): -1.3, 3B(23): 0.8	1.2
2015	WAS	MLB	30	306	36	15	0	9	39	29	58	2	1	.276/.344/.438	.294	.316	-0.5	3B -0, LF -1	1.6

Breakout: 1%   Improve: 57%   Collapse: 2%   Attrition: 6%   MLB: 100%   Comparables: Milton Bradley, Carl Yastrzemski, Josh Hamilton

In some reference books, 2014 will go down as the year the face of the franchise became just "the other Zimm." This Zimm's performance was strong enough when he was on the field—his OPS+ has been shockingly consistent, settling between 117 and 121 in each of the past four seasons—but once again, staying on the field was the problem. He missed 101 games, split equally between a fractured thumb and a strained thigh muscle. When he wasn't hurt, he still wasn't healthy, as a bum shoulder forced him to play more left field than third base; it's clear he'll be peddling his own line of first baseman's gloves very soon. With four years left on the extension he signed prior to the 2012 season, Zimmerman's bat should at least provide some value for the cost. Wait, let's all say it together. Ready? If he can stay on the field.

Pitchers

Aaron Barrett   RHP

Born: 1/2/88   Age: 27   Bats: R   Throws: R   Height: 6'3"   Weight: 225

YEAR	TEAM	LVL	AGE	W	L	SV	G	GS	IP	H	HR	BB	K	BB/9	K/9	GB%	BABIP	WHIP	ERA	FIP	FRA	WARP
2012	POT	A+	24	0	0	1	11	0	17	9	0	3	21	1.6	11.1	45%	.237	0.71	1.06	1.80	1.65	0.7
2012	HAG	A	24	3	2	16	31	0	34²	25	2	11	52	2.9	13.5	51%	.311	1.04	2.60	2.28	2.96	1.1
2013	HAR	AA	25	1	1	26	51	0	50¹	40	2	15	69	2.7	12.3	54%	.325	1.09	2.15	1.99	2.55	1.5
2014	SYR	AAA	26	1	0	2	10	0	10¹	5	0	1	8	0.9	7.0	57%	.179	0.58	0.00	2.10	2.39	0.3
2014	WAS	MLB	26	3	0	0	50	0	40²	33	1	20	49	4.4	10.8	47%	.311	1.30	2.66	2.56	3.10	0.5
2015	WAS	MLB	27	2	1	1	43	0	45	37	3	17	51	3.5	10.1	46%	.322	1.22	3.21	3.08	3.49	0.6

Breakout: 24%   Improve: 35%   Collapse: 19%   Attrition: 28%   MLB: 67%   Comparables: *Josh Roenicke, Jim Hoey, Michael Schwimer*

The 26-year-old reliever did not garner the Rookie of the Year support that fellow 2010 ninth-rounder Jacob deGrom did, but he worked his way into a key bullpen role at the end of the season. Barrett features a fastball he can run up to 96-plus and a wipeout slider that he went to more than a third of the time in 2014. Unsurprisingly, given his repertoire, Barrett held right-handed batters to a .532 OPS in his rookie season, making it even more befuddling that Matt Williams let him pitch to Pablo Sandoval in the seventh inning of NLDS Game Four. That one matchup—which included a series-icing wild pitch, then a misfired intentional ball—will likely be what his career is remembered for, but he's got enough time and enough stuff to paper over it. He'll be a seventh-inning bridge to Drew Storen and Tyler Clippard this year.

Jerry Blevins   LHP

Born: 9/6/83   Age: 31   Bats: L   Throws: L   Height: 6'6"   Weight: 185

YEAR	TEAM	LVL	AGE	W	L	SV	G	GS	IP	H	HR	BB	K	BB/9	K/9	GB%	BABIP	WHIP	ERA	FIP	FRA	WARP
2012	OAK	MLB	28	5	1	1	63	0	65¹	45	7	25	54	3.4	7.4	39%	.224	1.07	2.48	4.16	4.27	0.2
2013	OAK	MLB	29	5	0	0	67	0	60	47	7	17	52	2.5	7.8	33%	.242	1.07	3.15	3.91	4.43	-0.2
2014	WAS	MLB	30	2	3	0	64	0	57¹	48	3	23	66	3.6	10.4	41%	.306	1.24	4.87	2.74	3.37	0.7
2015	WAS	MLB	31	3	1	0	53	0	52	44	5	17	52	2.9	9.0	39%	.306	1.18	3.31	3.66	3.59	0.6

Breakout: 30%   Improve: 43%   Collapse: 26%   Attrition: 18%   MLB: 87%   Comparables: *Darren O'Day, Santiago Casilla, Juan Rincon*

The left-hander's first foray into the National League resulted in the highest ERA of his career and the lowest FIP. Most of the discrepancy can be attributed to a 61 percent strand rate, a far cry from his 74 percent career rate. The curveball was as fun to watch as ever, with Blevins getting nothing but a cool breeze more than half the time he threw it to left-handed batters. He was much more of a LOOGY in 2014 than in years past, which may be a role he settles into in his 30s. Somewhere down the list of fun things to watch for on the 2015 Nationals—how *far* down the list depends on your level of fun fact appreciation—is the continued race between Blevins and fellow 'pen-mate Craig Stammen to be the all-time WAR leader among University of Dayton alumni.

Tyler Clippard   RHP

Born: 2/14/85   Age: 30   Bats: R   Throws: R   Height: 6'3"   Weight: 200

YEAR	TEAM	LVL	AGE	W	L	SV	G	GS	IP	H	HR	BB	K	BB/9	K/9	GB%	BABIP	WHIP	ERA	FIP	FRA	WARP
2012	WAS	MLB	27	2	6	32	74	0	72²	55	7	29	84	3.6	10.4	32%	.259	1.16	3.72	3.36	3.49	1.1
2013	WAS	MLB	28	6	3	0	72	0	71	37	9	24	73	3.0	9.3	29%	.170	0.86	2.41	3.80	4.51	0.2
2014	WAS	MLB	29	7	4	1	75	0	70¹	47	5	23	82	2.9	10.5	38%	.251	1.00	2.18	2.72	3.30	0.9
2015	WAS	MLB	30	3	2	1	61	0	63	44	5	21	76	3.0	10.9	32%	.281	1.02	2.37	3.00	2.58	1.5

Breakout: 35%   Improve: 43%   Collapse: 28%   Attrition: 9%   MLB: 90%   Comparables: *Jonathan Papelbon, Francisco Rodriguez, Rafael Soriano*

The rubber-armed right-hander's 393 innings over the past five seasons are tops in the major leagues among pitchers who have not made a single start, and whether you think he's going to blow out in 2015 largely depends on what side of the Gambler's Fallacy you fall. Philosophy aside, there was a new element to Clippard's repertoire: the splitter. He introduced it briefly the previous September, but threw it nearly 10 percent of the time last season. This helped the spectacled one spike his groundball rate eight percentage points higher than his career level, as the split induced a grounder at a 50 percent clip. He will turn 30 before Opening Day, but there's no reason to suspect Clippard will be anything other than the sturdy bridge he's been for years.

A.J. Cole   RHP

Born: 1/5/92   Age: 23   Bats: R   Throws: R   Height: 6'5"   Weight: 200

YEAR	TEAM	LVL	AGE	W	L	SV	G	GS	IP	H	HR	BB	K	BB/9	K/9	GB%	BABIP	WHIP	ERA	FIP	FRA	WARP
2012	STO	A+	20	0	7	0	8	8	38	60	7	10	31	2.4	7.3	37%	.405	1.84	7.82	5.60	5.48	0.2
2012	BUR	A	20	6	3	0	19	19	95²	78	7	19	102	1.8	9.6	47%	.291	1.01	2.07	2.89	3.87	2.0
2013	HAR	AA	21	4	2	0	7	7	45¹	31	3	10	49	2.0	9.7	39%	.248	0.90	2.18	2.68	2.84	1.1
2013	POT	A+	21	6	3	0	18	18	97¹	96	12	23	102	2.1	9.4	38%	.317	1.22	4.25	3.69	4.44	1.8
2014	SYR	AAA	22	7	0	0	11	11	63	69	9	17	50	2.4	7.1	40%	.316	1.37	3.43	4.48	5.36	-0.2
2014	HAR	AA	22	6	3	0	14	14	71	79	1	15	61	1.9	7.7	40%	.342	1.32	2.92	2.58	3.14	2.2
2015	WAS	MLB	23	7	8	0	23	23	119²	124	12	35	100	2.6	7.5	39%	.329	1.32	4.29	3.94	4.66	0.0

Breakout: 0%   Improve: 0%   Collapse: 0%   Attrition: 0%   MLB: 0%   Comparables: *Burch Smith, Hector Rondon, Jeremy Sowers*

Cole was drafted as an arm strength bet in the fourth round of the 2010 draft, and in some ways, that's still how he can be characterized. Of course, he's on the verge of the majors because that arm strength has surrounded itself with good fastball command and a potential plus change. Despite a sterling 5.7 percent career walk rate, he'll need his breaking ball to take a step forward to keep right-handed hitters from sitting on the heat. Cole will get more time to develop in 2015, as the Nationals are as full in the rotation as any team in the majors, but should injury strike after the Super Two deadline he is likely to be the one to get the call.

Erick Fedde   RHP

Born: 2/25/93   Age: 22   Bats: R   Throws: R   Height: 6' 4"   Weight: 180

The Nationals now have an established tradition of overlooking near-term injury concerns to draft the most talented players on their draft board, so when Fedde had Tommy John surgery the day before the 2014 draft, the fit seemed natural. In hoping to replicate the success of 2012 first-rounder Lucas Giolito, Fedde will look to make his professional debut during the first half of the 2015 season. Prior to undergoing surgery, Fedde's slider was one of the best breaking balls in the draft class; in combination with a fastball that can touch the mid-90s and a change that can get to above average in time, it gives him a solid mid-rotation ceiling. If all goes well, Fedde could join Las Vegas High teammate Bryce Harper in Washington at some point during the 2017 season.

Doug Fister   RHP

Born: 2/4/84   Age: 31   Bats: L   Throws: R   Height: 6'8"   Weight: 210

YEAR	TEAM	LVL	AGE	W	L	SV	G	GS	IP	H	HR	BB	K	BB/9	K/9	GB%	BABIP	WHIP	ERA	FIP	FRA	WARP
2012	DET	MLB	28	10	10	0	26	26	161²	156	15	37	137	2.1	7.6	53%	.296	1.19	3.45	3.37	4.17	2.4
2013	DET	MLB	29	14	9	0	33	32	208²	229	14	44	159	1.9	6.9	56%	.332	1.31	3.67	3.29	3.63	3.8
2014	WAS	MLB	30	16	6	0	25	25	164	153	18	24	98	1.3	5.4	51%	.262	1.08	2.41	3.90	4.70	0.2
2015	WAS	MLB	31	9	8	0	24	24	153¹	148	10	28	113	1.6	6.6	50%	.314	1.15	3.36	3.36	3.65	1.7

Breakout: 11%   Improve: 46%   Collapse: 17%   Attrition: 12%   MLB: 88%   Comparables: *Roy Halladay, Mark Buehrle, Roy Oswalt*

If you judge Fister's season solely by the statistics that Murray Chass clings to when he sleeps at night, then the trade that brought him to Washington was even more lopsided than it seemed at the time. But if you peel away the first few layers of that onion, it reveals some signs of Dave Dombrowski Devil Magic. First, the vertically unchallenged right-hander missed the opening six weeks of the season with a shoulder strain. When he did return, he did so with a 1.2 mph drop in fastball velocity and four-year lows in strikeout percentage and swinging strike rate. Add to that a career-high home run rate (among qualifying seasons) and a five percentage point drop in groundball rate, and these factors led to Fister throwing barely better than a replacement-level pitcher in his first National League season. If some of these underlying numbers don't start moving in the opposite direction, there's going to be a limit to his suitors when he reaches free agency after the 2015 season.

Lucas Giolito   RHP

Born: 7/14/94   Age: 20   Bats: R   Throws: R   Height: 6'6"   Weight: 255

YEAR	TEAM	LVL	AGE	W	L	SV	G	GS	IP	H	HR	BB	K	BB/9	K/9	GB%	BABIP	WHIP	ERA	FIP	FRA	WARP
2013	AUB	A-	18	1	0	0	3	3	14	9	1	4	14	2.6	9.0	67%	.250	0.93	0.64	3.31	3.56	0.3
2014	HAG	A	19	10	2	0	20	20	98	70	7	28	110	2.6	10.1	51%	.262	1.00	2.20	3.16	4.13	1.8
2015	WAS	MLB	20	4	5	0	16	16	72	69	7	31	62	3.9	7.8	47%	.319	1.39	4.31	4.31	4.68	0.1

Breakout: 0%   Improve: 0%   Collapse: 0%   Attrition: 0%   MLB: 0%   Comparables: *Julio Teheran, Robbie Ray, Jenrry Mejia*

"How do you know you're looking at a Giolito scouting report?" the young scout in the thrift-store-vintage polo shirt and the Sperry Top-Siders asked the grizzled old scout. The scout tried to ignore him, as he had for the past three innings, but eventually looked up with defeated eyes and grumbled, "How?" "Because it has more 80s than the Slaughter/Winger concert I saw last year at the casino." The old scout nodded, not knowing what any of that meant.

The fact that the 2014 season firmly established Giolito as one of the top pitching prospects in baseball, even though the proverbial training wheels haven't come off, speaks to the extreme height of his ceiling—the same ceiling that might have made him the first prep right-handed pitcher to go first overall in the draft in 2012, if not for a pre-draft elbow injury. Giolito climbs the hill with a fastball that has a devastating combination of velocity and plane; a curveball many scouts believe to be the top breaking ball in the minors; and a developing change that could give him another out pitch at the major-league level. Now that he's made it through a full, healthy season, the Nationals could move him as quickly as his talent will allow, which could lead to a 2016 debut. As the young scout might say, Lucas Giolito is the balls.

Gio Gonzalez   RHP

Born: 9/19/85   Age: 29   Bats: R   Throws: L   Height: 6'0"   Weight: 205

YEAR	TEAM	LVL	AGE	W	L	SV	G	GS	IP	H	HR	BB	K	BB/9	K/9	GB%	BABIP	WHIP	ERA	FIP	FRA	WARP
2012	WAS	MLB	26	21	8	0	32	32	199¹	149	9	76	207	3.4	9.3	50%	.267	1.13	2.89	2.87	3.36	3.9
2013	WAS	MLB	27	11	8	0	32	32	195²	169	17	76	192	3.5	8.8	44%	.286	1.25	3.36	3.38	3.50	2.9
2014	WAS	MLB	28	10	10	0	27	27	158²	134	10	56	162	3.2	9.2	48%	.294	1.20	3.57	3.00	3.96	1.4
2015	WAS	MLB	29	9	8	0	24	24	146¹	122	10	55	144	3.4	8.9	47%	.306	1.21	3.26	3.43	3.55	1.9

Breakout: 11%   Improve: 40%   Collapse: 20%   Attrition: 6%   MLB: 92%   Comparables: *Ubaldo Jimenez, Carlos Zambrano, Jon Lester*

The fact that a pitcher as good as Gonzalez was arguably the least interesting member—and the worst, by some standards—of the Nationals' rotation in 2014 is a big reason they finished with home-field advantage in the National League playoffs. When he returned from a month-long absence due to shoulder inflammation in June, he was as good as expected, but was a slightly different model. His velocity never quite returned during the second half of the season: His average fastball registered at 94.2 mph prior to the injury, and 92.8 after. Fortunately, he also returned with sharper control. His 8.6 percent walk rate on the season was a career low, but over the final three months, it sat at 7.4 percent. If the velocity and walk rate drops continue to go hand-in-hand, Gonzalez might actually age better than originally anticipated, which is well timed good news, since he turns 30 this season.

Jake Johansen   RHP

Born: 1/23/91   Age: 24   Bats: R   Throws: R   Height: 6'6"   Weight: 235

YEAR	TEAM	LVL	AGE	W	L	SV	G	GS	IP	H	HR	BB	K	BB/9	K/9	GB%	BABIP	WHIP	ERA	FIP	FRA	WARP
2013	AUB	A-	22	1	1	0	10	10	42¹	22	1	18	44	3.8	9.4	71%	.200	0.94	1.06	2.67	3.84	0.7
2014	HAG	A	23	5	6	0	29	18	100²	120	3	55	89	4.9	8.0	62%	.376	1.74	5.19	4.05	5.69	0.5
2015	WAS	MLB	24	4	6	0	22	16	82²	93	8	46	54	5.0	5.8	54%	.336	1.68	5.57	5.17	6.05	-1.2

Breakout: 0%   Improve: 0%   Collapse: 0%   Attrition: 0%   MLB: 0%   Comparables: *Tom Koehler, Humberto Sanchez, Josh Butler*

After being drafted in the second round in 2013, the big right-hander dominated in short-season ball, taking many by surprise given his underwhelming college career. But his full-season debut with Hagerstown proved just as disappointing, given the strength of his fastball, as those three years at Dallas Baptist had been. Johansen is essentially an old furnace, firing off heat without much regard for situation or utility. The inconsistency of his secondary pitches plays it down further. A rotation future is not out of the picture yet, but letting him air it out one inning at a time is a tempting proposition, given the huge development curve ahead of him.

Taylor Jordan   RHP

Born: 1/17/89   Age: 26   Bats: R   Throws: R   Height: 6'5"   Weight: 200

YEAR	TEAM	LVL	AGE	W	L	SV	G	GS	IP	H	HR	BB	K	BB/9	K/9	GB%	BABIP	WHIP	ERA	FIP	FRA	WARP
2012	HAG	A	23	3	4	0	9	9	40	52	2	9	28	2.0	6.3	59%	.376	1.52	4.05	3.95	4.65	0.8
2012	AUB	A-	23	0	3	0	6	6	14¹	19	0	2	17	1.3	10.7	68%	.404	1.47	8.16	2.22	4.00	0.3
2013	HAR	AA	24	7	0	0	9	8	54	37	0	9	43	1.5	7.2	56%	.243	0.85	0.83	2.51	3.14	1.4
2013	POT	A+	24	2	1	0	6	6	36¹	31	1	6	29	1.5	7.2	56%	.280	1.02	1.24	2.61	3.23	1.1
2013	WAS	MLB	24	1	3	0	9	9	51²	59	3	11	29	1.9	5.1	58%	.322	1.35	3.66	3.47	4.37	0.3
2014	SYR	AAA	25	0	2	0	6	6	31	31	3	8	28	2.3	8.1	55%	.311	1.26	4.06	3.78	4.87	0.1
2014	WAS	MLB	25	0	3	0	5	5	25²	34	3	8	17	2.8	6.0	55%	.330	1.64	5.61	4.47	4.62	0.1
2015	WAS	MLB	26	3	4	0	12	12	62²	68	5	17	39	2.5	5.5	53%	.323	1.35	4.49	4.09	4.89	-0.1

Breakout: 34%   Improve: 52%   Collapse: 11%   Attrition: 26%   MLB: 69%   Comparables: *Craig Stammen, Joe Saunders, Burke Badenhop*

In retrospect, the preseason battle between Jordan and Tanner Roark for the fifth starter job looks more like Little Mac vs. Glass Joe than the even-handed competition it was at the time. The tall right-hander made the rotation due to Doug Fister's injury, but could not recapture the success of his nine-start run in 2013. In fact, the most notable event of his season was giving up Albert Pujols' 500th home run. Things only got worse from there for Jordan, as he was demoted to Triple-A and then shut down in early June with lingering elbow soreness, which is even more of a concern than usual, as Jordan already has a 2011 Tommy John surgery on his resume. When he's right, he throws strikes, keeps the ball on the ground and misses enough bats to survive in the back of a rotation.

Reynaldo Lopez   RHP

Born: 1/4/94   Age: 21   Bats: R   Throws: R   Height: 6'0"   Weight: 185

YEAR	TEAM	LVL	AGE	W	L	SV	G	GS	IP	H	HR	BB	K	BB/9	K/9	GB%	BABIP	WHIP	ERA	FIP	FRA	WARP
2014	HAG	A	20	4	1	0	9	9	47¹	27	1	11	39	2.1	7.4	65%	.211	0.80	1.33	2.91	3.68	1.0
2014	AUB	A-	20	3	2	0	7	7	36	15	0	15	31	3.8	7.8	62%	.167	0.83	0.75	3.14	4.09	0.3
2015	WAS	MLB	21	3	4	0	12	10	53	56	5	24	35	4.1	6.0	51%	.320	1.52	4.90	4.76	5.33	-0.4

Breakout: 0%   Improve: 0%   Collapse: 0%   Attrition: 0%   MLB: 0%   Comparables: *Jhoulys Chacin, Jose A. Ramirez, Jordan Walden*

In this day and age of prospect coverage across all four quadrants of the internet, it's increasingly rare for a true pop-up prospect to appear on the scene. Yet, here we are with Lopez. Signed out of the Dominican Republic for a meager $17,000 in the summer of 2012, he was both unimpressive and often injured prior to the 2014 season. When he showed up in the New York-Penn League last summer, he had two extra ticks of velocity on his pitches and a pretty clear idea of where they were going. With a curveball that flashes plus and a change that could be usable in time, Lopez has gone from unknown to a name in discussion for the back end of prospect lists. His slight frame will make it an uphill climb to a major-league rotation, but there's no doubting the trajectory of his stuff.

Ryan Mattheus   RHP

Born: 11/10/83   Age: 31   Bats: R   Throws: R   Height: 6'3"   Weight: 220

YEAR	TEAM	LVL	AGE	W	L	SV	G	GS	IP	H	HR	BB	K	BB/9	K/9	GB%	BABIP	WHIP	ERA	FIP	FRA	WARP
2012	WAS	MLB	28	5	3	0	66	0	66¹	57	8	19	41	2.6	5.6	49%	.253	1.15	2.85	4.46	5.13	-0.2
2013	WAS	MLB	29	0	2	0	37	0	35¹	52	1	15	22	3.8	5.6	57%	.398	1.90	6.37	3.42	4.17	0.2
2014	SYR	AAA	30	1	3	2	34	0	40¹	47	5	12	32	2.7	7.1	57%	.321	1.46	5.80	4.28	6.16	-0.5
2014	WAS	MLB	30	0	0	0	7	0	8²	7	0	4	4	4.2	4.2	50%	.269	1.27	1.04	3.91	4.87	0.0
2015	WAS	MLB	31	2	1	1	46	0	47²	47	4	16	34	3.1	6.4	51%	.312	1.33	4.09	4.14	4.45	0.0

Breakout: 16%   Improve: 19%   Collapse: 14%   Attrition: 14%   MLB: 40%   Comparables: *Mike Koplove, Brad Ziegler, Willie Eyre*

Here's a fun quirk of the fielding-independent-stats era: Mattheus has produced ERAs in his career of 2.81, 2.85, 6.37 and 1.04; yet the only season with a positive WARP was the one that probably kept him up at nights. The reliever spent the season getting unlucky in Triple-A and lucky in the majors, riding his heavy sinker usage to a strong groundball rate in Washington. At this point none of us can keep track of whether he's charmed or cursed, but he's not very good, that much is certain.

Ross Ohlendorf   RHP

Born: 8/8/82   Age: 32   Bats: R   Throws: R   Height: 6'4"   Weight: 240

YEAR	TEAM	LVL	AGE	W	L	SV	G	GS	IP	H	HR	BB	K	BB/9	K/9	GB%	BABIP	WHIP	ERA	FIP	FRA	WARP
2012	PAW	AAA	29	4	3	0	10	10	52²	57	5	15	37	2.6	6.3	39%	.310	1.37	4.61	4.30	5.11	0.1
2012	TUC	AAA	29	1	1	0	3	0	17	19	2	3	17	1.6	9.0	40%	.354	1.29	4.24	3.90	5.08	0.3
2012	SDN	MLB	29	4	4	0	13	9	48²	62	7	24	39	4.4	7.2	32%	.340	1.77	7.77	4.94	4.56	0.1
2013	SYR	AAA	30	4	6	0	14	13	74²	65	5	30	71	3.6	8.6	42%	.284	1.27	4.22	3.50	4.17	0.7
2013	WAS	MLB	30	4	1	0	16	7	60¹	56	8	14	45	2.1	6.7	41%	.268	1.16	3.28	4.00	4.18	0.5
2015	WAS	MLB	32	2	2	0	8	6	36	38	4	12	28	3.0	7.0	39%	.323	1.38	4.65	4.42	5.05	-0.1

Breakout: 15%   Improve: 24%   Collapse: 7%   Attrition: 13%   MLB: 36%   Comparables: *Tim Redding, Runelvys Hernandez, Armando Galarraga*

The right-hander who was once traded for Randy Johnson had a tough season in 2014, as he was limited to 15 minor-league innings wedged between recurring lumbar strains in his back. Now, as a general rule, another person's back pain is never interesting. So we'll focus on those things about Ohlendorf that are. One: He has recorded one of the 77 instances of a pitcher striking out the side on nine pitches, accomplishing this feat in September 2009 against a veritable Murderer's Row of Khalil Greene, Julio Lugo and Jason LaRue. Two: His Princeton thesis, a sabermetric look at draft return on investment. Three: His mid-career internship with the U.S. Department of Agriculture. If he were a better pitcher, he'd be your favorite pitcher.

Matt Purke   LHP

Born: 7/17/90   Age: 24   Bats: L   Throws: L   Height: 6'4"   Weight: 215

YEAR	TEAM	LVL	AGE	W	L	SV	G	GS	IP	H	HR	BB	K	BB/9	K/9	GB%	BABIP	WHIP	ERA	FIP	FRA	WARP
2012	HAG	A	21	0	2	0	3	3	15¹	15	1	12	14	7.0	8.2	49%	.318	1.76	5.87	5.14	5.81	0.2
2013	POT	A+	22	5	3	0	12	12	61	67	3	18	41	2.7	6.0	50%	.325	1.39	4.43	3.73	5.19	0.6
2013	HAG	A	22	1	1	0	6	6	29	25	3	7	41	2.2	12.7	46%	.333	1.10	2.48	2.83	3.61	0.7
2014	HAR	AA	23	1	6	0	8	8	31¹	42	5	18	22	5.2	6.3	53%	.356	1.91	8.04	5.84	7.13	-0.4
2015	WAS	MLB	24	2	3	0	8	8	37¹	42	4	17	25	4.0	6.0	47%	.331	1.56	5.27	4.88	5.73	-0.4

Breakout: 0%   Improve: 0%   Collapse: 0%   Attrition: 0%   MLB: 0%   Comparables: *Alex Wilson, Armando Galarraga, Bryan Morris*

When you're a 24-year-old prospect with a career 5.00 ERA and you've seen barely more minor-league levels (3) than arm surgeons (2), things aren't quite going according to plan. His most recent surgery was Tommy John in May, which will likely sideline him for the start of the 2015 season. When he's been on the field, Purke has been a shell of the pitcher scouts imagined in 2009, when he was considered a steal at the 14th overall pick, or the pitcher Purke surely imagined, when he turned down the Rangers' $4 million offer that year. The best-case scenarios for the former Horned Frog are that he pitches his way into the back of a rotation someday or he airs it out in short bursts as a reliever. Neither plan guarantees success.

Tanner Roark   RHP

Born: 10/5/86   Age: 28   Bats: R   Throws: R   Height: 6'2"   Weight: 230

YEAR	TEAM	LVL	AGE	W	L	SV	G	GS	IP	H	HR	BB	K	BB/9	K/9	GB%	BABIP	WHIP	ERA	FIP	FRA	WARP
2012	SYR	AAA	25	6	17	0	28	26	147²	161	14	47	130	2.9	7.9	45%	.332	1.41	4.39	3.81	5.03	0.7
2013	SYR	AAA	26	9	3	2	33	11	105²	85	6	20	84	1.7	7.2	47%	.255	0.99	3.15	3.01	4.28	1.7
2013	WAS	MLB	26	7	1	0	14	5	53²	38	1	11	40	1.8	6.7	50%	.243	0.91	1.51	2.39	3.04	1.1
2014	WAS	MLB	27	15	10	0	31	31	198²	178	16	39	138	1.8	6.3	42%	.270	1.09	2.85	3.44	4.15	1.3
2015	WAS	MLB	28	8	8	1	31	23	154	154	14	40	113	2.3	6.6	44%	.314	1.26	3.94	3.92	4.28	0.6

Breakout: 29%   Improve: 45%   Collapse: 11%   Attrition: 33%   MLB: 64%   Comparables: *Brad Lincoln, Dylan Axelrod, Cory Luebke*

There were 752 players selected ahead of Roark in the 2008 draft, and he has surpassed nearly all of them. There were 752 players who tried to hit their way on against him in 2014, and he bettered most of them, too. The pitcher who was once traded as part of a package for Cristian Guzman (yes, really) will need to continue limiting walks, as his fastball barely scrapes 92 and his overall whiff rate was a percentage point below league average. It was easy to yell "REGRESSION" at his 2013 numbers, especially in ERA and home run rate, but each fell only down to above-average, leaving him with a rotation spot firmly in hand for 2015. The major win metrics were very split on Roark's overall value last season, ranging from a WARP of 1.3 to a bWAR of 5.1; the biggest statement on his value might come from the Nationals, who dropped him to the bullpen for the postseason. But for the pitcher who was dumped from the University of Illinois baseball team and knocked around in the Frontier League, mild adversity or calls for further regression will go no further than strike one.

Joe Ross   RHP

Born: 5/21/93   Age: 22   Bats: R   Throws: R   Height: 6'4"   Weight: 205

YEAR	TEAM	LVL	AGE	W	L	SV	G	GS	IP	H	HR	BB	K	BB/9	K/9	GB%	BABIP	WHIP	ERA	FIP	FRA	WARP
2012	EUG	A-	19	0	2	0	8	8	26²	16	1	9	28	3.0	9.4	62%	.238	0.94	2.03	2.84	4.34	0.4
2012	FTW	A	19	0	2	0	6	6	27¹	33	2	11	27	3.6	8.9	48%	.365	1.61	6.26	3.53	4.65	0.3
2013	FTW	A	20	5	8	0	23	23	122¹	124	7	40	79	2.9	5.8	52%	.298	1.34	3.75	3.89	5.19	0.8
2014	LEL	A+	21	8	6	0	19	19	101²	101	6	28	87	2.5	7.7	55%	.308	1.27	3.98	3.83	4.40	1.7
2014	SAN	AA	21	2	0	0	4	3	20	23	2	1	19	0.4	8.6	47%	.339	1.20	3.60	2.67	3.13	0.3
2015	WAS	MLB	22	5	9	0	22	22	108¹	112	11	41	69	3.4	5.7	49%	.310	1.41	4.59	4.67	4.99	-0.7

Breakout: 0%   Improve: 0%   Collapse: 0%   Attrition: 0%   MLB: 0%   Comparables: *Brett Marshall, Collin Balester, Jeanmar Gomez*

Ross' ERA looks better when you consider that five of his starts came at High Desert and Lancaster, two of the planet's most hitter-friendly ballparks. His ERA in those games, including a 10-run implosion on July 12th, was a Luciferian 6.66. Tall and lean like older brother Tyson, he pumps mid-90s fastballs on a downward plane. Last year he worked on keeping them in on the hands to prevent hitters from extending. Secondary pitches have been slower to develop, but Ross' changeup showed signs of improvement, leading to better success against lefties. Another promising sign is the uptick in strikeouts and decline in walks at higher levels. If he keeps refining the off-speed and breaking stuff, Ross will be a no. 3 or 4 starter. He should start the year in Harrisburg after the Nats grabbed him from the Rays in the Wil Myers kerfuffle.

Rafael Soriano   RHP

Born: 12/19/79   Age: 35   Bats: R   Throws: R   Height: 6'4"   Weight: 230

YEAR	TEAM	LVL	AGE	W	L	SV	G	GS	IP	H	HR	BB	K	BB/9	K/9	GB%	BABIP	WHIP	ERA	FIP	FRA	WARP
2012	NYA	MLB	32	2	1	42	69	0	67²	55	6	24	69	3.2	9.2	38%	.274	1.17	2.26	3.27	3.17	1.3
2013	WAS	MLB	33	3	3	43	68	0	66²	65	7	17	51	2.3	6.9	35%	.287	1.23	3.11	3.62	4.44	0.3
2014	WAS	MLB	34	4	1	32	64	0	62	51	4	19	59	2.8	8.6	32%	.280	1.13	3.19	3.05	3.55	0.7
2015	WAS	MLB	35	3	1	36	59	0	57¹	48	4	16	54	2.6	8.5	36%	.302	1.13	3.08	3.21	3.35	0.8

Breakout: 19%   Improve: 35%   Collapse: 28%   Attrition: 17%   MLB: 85%   Comparables: *Rafael Betancourt, Hideki Okajima, Eddie Guardado*

Things could not have been going any more smoothly, as he reached the All-Star break with a 0.97 ERA and 22 saves in 24 tries. He stumbled so badly in the second half that he was removed from the closer's role on September 5th, immediately after an outing in which he allowed homers to noted power threats Carlos Ruiz and Ben Revere. There were the standard rumblings of mechanical adjustments being made and his head being cleared, but Soriano's biggest issue was that he'd lost command of his slider: By the time he got the playoffs, he had nearly scrapped it entirely, throwing it just twice in 2¹ᐟ³ innings. Based on his track record and overall 2014 numbers, Soriano is likely to get saves somewhere in 2015, as are 75 or so other pitchers.

Craig Stammen   RHP

Born: 3/9/84   Age: 31   Bats: R   Throws: R   Height: 6'4"   Weight: 225

YEAR	TEAM	LVL	AGE	W	L	SV	G	GS	IP	H	HR	BB	K	BB/9	K/9	GB%	BABIP	WHIP	ERA	FIP	FRA	WARP
2012	WAS	MLB	28	6	1	1	59	0	88¹	70	7	36	87	3.7	8.9	47%	.265	1.20	2.34	3.49	3.72	1.2
2013	WAS	MLB	29	7	6	0	55	0	81²	78	4	27	79	3.0	8.7	62%	.326	1.29	2.76	2.79	3.27	1.0
2014	WAS	MLB	30	4	5	0	49	0	72²	78	5	14	56	1.7	6.9	50%	.323	1.27	3.84	3.16	3.76	0.6
2015	WAS	MLB	31	3	2	0	32	4	64	63	5	19	53	2.6	7.4	51%	.324	1.28	3.97	3.61	4.32	0.2

Breakout: 19%   Improve: 38%   Collapse: 12%   Attrition: 13%   MLB: 57%   Comparables: *Glen Perkins, Matt Belisle, Justin Miller*

While teammate Tyler Clippard gets most of the recognition for throwing a ton of innings perennially, Stammen has actually thrown nearly 30 more frames from the Nationals' bullpen over the past three years, and the most in baseball over that span by nearly 20. Perhaps the two consecutive seasons of 80-plus innings were wearing on the 30-year-old, as his strikeout rate dipped by five percentage points in 2014. Stammen has settled into a pretty defined role in the Nationals' bullpen, usually throwing when the Nationals are behind, but still within striking distance. There's been no upward trajectory in his average-leverage index, and there's unlikely to be, considering how valuable he is in this role.

Drew Storen   RHP

Born: 8/11/87   Age: 27   Bats: B   Throws: R   Height: 6'1"   Weight: 195

YEAR	TEAM	LVL	AGE	W	L	SV	G	GS	IP	H	HR	BB	K	BB/9	K/9	GB%	BABIP	WHIP	ERA	FIP	FRA	WARP
2012	WAS	MLB	24	3	1	4	37	0	30¹	22	0	8	24	2.4	7.1	52%	.265	0.99	2.37	2.44	2.59	0.7
2013	WAS	MLB	25	4	2	3	68	0	61²	65	7	19	58	2.8	8.5	44%	.319	1.36	4.52	3.59	3.99	0.6
2014	WAS	MLB	26	2	1	11	65	0	56¹	44	2	11	46	1.8	7.3	54%	.259	0.98	1.12	2.68	3.36	0.7
2015	WAS	MLB	27	3	1	4	57	0	53	44	4	13	52	2.3	8.9	46%	.305	1.08	2.81	3.16	3.06	1.0

Breakout: 17%   Improve: 37%   Collapse: 28%   Attrition: 6%   MLB: 93%   Comparables: *Chris Perez, Manny Corpas, Huston Street*

After stumbling in the shadows of Rafael Soriano and Tyler Clippard in 2013, Storen claimed his second act as Nationals' closer in just his fifth professional season. He did this by following some pieces of the reliever doctrine, and by ignoring others. It doesn't take a degree in mechanical engineering from Stanford, which Storen is just a few credits shy of completing, to know that managers become more trusting of relievers who keep walks and home runs to a minimum; Storen saw vast improvements in both, including a career-best 4.9 percent walk rate. However, he broke the mold and expanded his repertoire to a full four-pitch arsenal, worthy of a starting pitcher. The right-hander threw more changeups in 2014 (147) than in the previous four years combined (132). It was a legit weapon against left-handed batters, inducing whiffs 38 percent of the time, ground-balls 57 percent of the time on contact and extra-base hits zero percent of the time. Storen will return to what is once again his rightful job in 2015, at the head of one of the deepest bullpens in baseball.

Stephen Strasburg   RHP

Born: 4/19/90   Age: 24   Bats: L   Throws: R   Height: 5' 10"   Weight: 195

YEAR	TEAM	LVL	AGE	W	L	SV	G	GS	IP	H	HR	BB	K	BB/9	K/9	GB%	BABIP	WHIP	ERA	FIP	FRA	WARP
2012	WAS	MLB	23	15	6	0	28	28	159¹	136	15	48	197	2.7	11.1	44%	.311	1.15	3.16	2.87	3.17	4.5
2013	WAS	MLB	24	8	9	0	30	30	183	136	16	56	191	2.8	9.4	52%	.263	1.05	3.00	3.18	4.12	3.0
2014	WAS	MLB	25	14	11	0	34	34	215	198	23	43	242	1.8	10.1	48%	.315	1.12	3.14	2.91	3.83	2.8
2015	WAS	MLB	26	12	9	0	31	31	178²	141	14	42	207	2.1	10.4	48%	.312	1.03	2.65	2.77	2.88	4.0

Breakout: 21%   Improve: 53%   Collapse: 15%   Attrition: 8%   MLB: 93%   Comparables: *Yovani Gallardo, Mark Prior, Jake Peavy*

The 2014 season was a very important one in the development of the most hyped young arm of the past 20 years, as Strasburg accumulated black ink in both games started and strikeouts and garnered Cy Young votes for the first time, albeit the third-most votes in his own rotation. The inability to throw "ace innings" was the knock on Strasburg heading into the season, which proves that it's pretty hard to knock the 26-year-old for anything. The Nationals still didn't let him top 120 pitches in a game, and he still has only one complete game in his career (a shutout in 2013), but he finished fifth in the NL in innings, in part because of a career-best 3.8 pitches per plate appearances. The biggest change in his repertoire during 2014 was just that—he bumped his cambio usage to a career-high 20 percent. If you're wondering whether that's good news, last season was the second time in three years that Strasburg led all of baseball in changeup whiff rate, so, yeah. He's not quite at the top of the sport yet, so the 2015 season will be a very important one in the development of the most hyped young arm of the ...

Matt Thornton   LHP

Born: 9/15/76   Age: 38   Bats: L   Throws: L   Height: 6'6"   Weight: 235

YEAR	TEAM	LVL	AGE	W	L	SV	G	GS	IP	H	HR	BB	K	BB/9	K/9	GB%	BABIP	WHIP	ERA	FIP	FRA	WARP
2012	CHA	MLB	35	4	10	3	74	0	65	63	4	17	53	2.4	7.3	55%	.317	1.23	3.46	3.14	4.41	0.5
2013	BOS	MLB	36	0	1	0	20	0	15¹	22	0	5	9	2.9	5.3	61%	.386	1.76	3.52	2.88	3.76	0.2
2013	CHA	MLB	36	0	3	0	40	0	28	25	4	10	21	3.2	6.8	45%	.266	1.25	3.86	4.72	4.51	-0.1
2014	NYA	MLB	37	0	3	0	46	0	24²	23	0	6	20	2.2	7.3	57%	.299	1.18	2.55	2.75	3.48	0.3
2014	WAS	MLB	37	1	0	0	18	0	11¹	10	0	2	8	1.6	6.4	56%	.294	1.06	0.00	2.48	4.02	0.0
2015	WAS	MLB	38	3	1	1	48	0	38	34	2	11	37	2.5	8.7	48%	.326	1.18	3.07	2.97	3.34	0.6

Breakout: 22%   Improve: 38%   Collapse: 24%   Attrition: 8%   MLB: 82%   Comparables: *Francisco Cordero, Mariano Rivera, Trever Miller*

The big left-hander made his presence known in Washington with 18 scoreless appearances after being plucked off waivers in early August. Of course, it was curious that he ended up on waivers in the first place, as both ERA and FIP suggest a pitcher worth more than the $3.5 million he's still owed in 2015. While Thornton was used very situationally in 2014, both his yearly and career stats show no glaring weakness against righties. Despite the positives, it will be a long offseason for Thornton, who was given the loss in the game that eliminated the Nationals from the postseason.

Blake Treinen   RHP

Born: 6/30/88   Age: 27   Bats: R   Throws: R   Height: 6'5"   Weight: 215

YEAR	TEAM	LVL	AGE	W	L	SV	G	GS	IP	H	HR	BB	K	BB/9	K/9	GB%	BABIP	WHIP	ERA	FIP	FRA	WARP
2012	STO	A+	24	7	7	0	24	15	103	116	11	23	92	2.0	8.0	58%	.330	1.35	4.37	4.20	4.93	1.3
2013	HAR	AA	25	6	7	0	21	20	118²	125	9	33	86	2.5	6.5	58%	.310	1.33	3.64	3.79	4.33	1.5
2014	SYR	AAA	26	8	2	0	16	16	80²	78	4	20	64	2.2	7.1	58%	.301	1.21	3.35	3.31	4.59	0.7
2014	WAS	MLB	26	2	3	0	15	7	50²	57	1	13	30	2.3	5.3	60%	.333	1.38	2.49	3.06	3.99	0.4
2015	WAS	MLB	27	6	6	0	28	17	110²	120	9	30	72	2.5	5.8	55%	.328	1.36	4.37	4.01	4.75	-0.2

Breakout: 26%   Improve: 38%   Collapse: 13%   Attrition: 35%   MLB: 62%   Comparables: *Doug Mathis, Stephen Fife, Brian Duensing*

It's almost as if the Nationals were incapable of producing a starting pitcher who struggled at the major-league level in 2014. No Gio Gonzalez for a few weeks? Want to rest a few guys down the stretch? Sure, here's a seventh-round draft pick with a 3.70 career minor-league ERA and pretty much just one pitch. He starts seven games and allows 12 earned runs. To be fair, when that one pitch is a sinker that can touch 99 mph and generates groundballs at a 65 percent clip, simple is sexy. There's no place for him in Washington as a starting pitcher in 2015, but that's more of a reflection on the Nationals than on Treinen.

Jordan Zimmermann   RHP

Born: 5/23/86   Age: 29   Bats: R   Throws: R   Height: 6'2"   Weight: 220

YEAR	TEAM	LVL	AGE	W	L	SV	G	GS	IP	H	HR	BB	K	BB/9	K/9	GB%	BABIP	WHIP	ERA	FIP	FRA	WARP
2012	WAS	MLB	26	12	8	0	32	32	195²	186	18	43	153	2.0	7.0	44%	.288	1.17	2.94	3.55	3.83	3.8
2013	WAS	MLB	27	19	9	0	32	32	213¹	192	19	40	161	1.7	6.8	49%	.271	1.09	3.25	3.33	3.98	2.5
2014	WAS	MLB	28	14	5	0	32	32	199²	185	13	29	182	1.3	8.2	42%	.302	1.07	2.66	2.65	3.25	3.9
2015	WAS	MLB	29	10	9	0	27	27	169¹	155	14	31	142	1.6	7.5	44%	.307	1.10	3.21	3.36	3.49	2.3

Breakout: 19%   Improve: 41%   Collapse: 21%   Attrition: 5%   MLB: 95%   Comparables: *Josh Johnson, John Danks, Roy Oswalt*

There's this magical point that pitchers sometimes reach when their command is so good that they can almost shelve their secondary offerings, dominating opponents with fastballs dotted on the edges and saving the wiggly stuff for maximum giffability. That's where Zimmermann is: He threw his four-seamer a stunning 77 percent of the time to lefties, riding that simple approach to the best walk rate in the league. But it wasn't by necessity that he handed out more cheese in the nation's capital than Andrew Jackson; he managed to go the entire season without allowing a home run on a breaking ball, in some 800 pitches. He's entering his walk year, and the only thing that could keep him from getting paid would be if he saw that Andrew Jackson/cheese simile and just sort of lost the will to keep living.

Lineouts

Hitters

NAME	POS	TEAM	LVL	AGE	PA	R	2B	3B	HR	RBI	BB	K	SB	CS	AVG/OBP/SLG	TAv	BABIP	BRR	FRAA	WARP
Osvaldo Abreu	SS	AUB	A-	20	231	31	7	3	1	15	9	41	10	6	.229/.279/.305	.247	.278	1.7	SS(57): -4.9	0.4
Rafael Bautista	CF	HAG	A	21	543	97	20	5	5	54	33	72	69	15	.290/.341/.382	.266	.328	8.5	CF(117): 5.5, RF(16): 1.6	3.7
Emmanuel Burriss	SS	SYR	AAA	29	510	80	18	7	6	46	48	41	22	10	.300/.377/.412	.285	.319	2.5	SS(103): 5.4, 2B(11): -0.7	4.4
Wilmer Difo	SS	HAG	A	22	610	91	31	7	14	90	37	65	49	9	.315/.360/.470	.293	.333	6.5	SS(70): 4.2, 2B(66): 4.3	5.6
Greg Dobbs	1B	SYR	AAA	35	102	12	4	0	2	11	5	23	0	0	.247/.284/.351	.222	.306	0.9	1B(16): -0.3	-0.2
	PH	MIA	MLB	35	13	0	0	0	0	0	0	4	0	0	.077/.077/.077	.060	.111	0.0		-0.2
	1B	WAS	MLB	35	30	0	1	0	0	2	1	4	0	0	.214/.233/.250	.187	.240	-0.9	1B(3): 0.1	-0.3
Jeff Kobernus	LF	HAR	AA	26	26	2	1	0	0	3	2	4	2	0	.292/.346/.333	.236	.350	0.3	LF(6): 1.2	0.2
	CF	SYR	AAA	26	235	28	13	1	2	23	23	44	15	3	.257/.338/.359	.240	.315	-0.1	CF(24): -1.1, LF(20): 1.6	0.0
	2B	WAS	MLB	26	8	2	0	0	0	0	1	1	0	0	.000/.250/.000	.149	.000	0.4	2B(3): 0.3	0.0
Brandon Laird	3B	SYR	AAA	26	506	67	32	1	18	85	34	96	1	0	.300/.350/.490	.292	.343	-1.5	3B(116): 22.6, 1B(4): 0.2	5.8
Sandy Leon	C	SYR	AAA	25	193	26	9	0	5	25	23	36	1	0	.229/.321/.371	.238	.264	-0.7	C(42): -0.3	0.4
	C	WAS	MLB	25	70	7	1	0	1	3	6	20	0	0	.156/.229/.219	.184	.209	0.0	C(20): -0.1	-0.2
Will Rhymes	2B	SYR	AAA	31	437	55	22	5	5	42	33	54	5	2	.255/.313/.375	.249	.280	2.6	2B(70): 2.8, 3B(12): 1.7	1.2
Pedro Severino	C	POT	A+	20	326	41	15	1	9	36	21	57	2	0	.247/.306/.399	.252	.276	-0.8	C(93): 2.0	1.6
Drew Vettleson	RF	AUB	A-	22	26	3	1	1	0	2	3	5	1	0	.318/.423/.455	.309	.412	-1.0	RF(7): 0.2	0.1
	RF	HAR	AA	22	267	24	14	3	8	28	11	75	3	3	.246/.275/.423	.255	.312	-0.8	RF(63): -1.0, CF(9): -0.6	0.1
Drew Ward	3B	HAG	A	19	478	45	26	3	10	73	42	121	2	2	.269/.341/.413	.260	.353	-5.0	3B(92): -4.3	0.8

The 20-year-old shortstop **Osvaldo Abreu** has a good shot to stick at the position but did not take the step forward at the plate his organization was hoping for. ❖ **Rafael Bautista** is yet more proof that you don't need to be a burner to put up gaudy stolen-base numbers in Low-A; it'll be his plus defense in center, not the basestealing, that pledges a major-league future. ❖ **Emmanuel Burriss** hit six home runs for Syracuse in Triple-A; his previous *career* total, majors and minors, 2,900 plate appearances in all, was six. ❖ Sally League Player of the Year **Wilmer Difo** came out of nowhere to claim legit prospect status in 2014, but he'll have to prove it wasn't just a 22-year-old-in-Low-A illusion. He could hop straight to Double-A so the Nats can see if it's just sand. ❖ An OPS+ of 6 might mean the end for **Greg Dobbs**. Yes, you read that right. Six. He made 10 times as much money as Ira Glass. ❖ The 26-year-old utility man **Jeff Kobernus** got the all-access tour of the Nationals' minor-league system, spending time at all four full-season affiliates before receiving a September call-up. Now he's on their email list. ❖ After 134 minor-league home runs and 138 major-league plate appearances, the most interesting thing about **Brandon Laird** is still that his name was called in the 27th round of the MLB draft, twice. ❖ The most rewarding thing about **Sandy Leon**'s 2014 season was that he wasn't the only Nationals position player with an OPS+ lower than his jersey number. He wore number 41. ❖ In addition to having an unnecessarily difficult name, 2014 third-rounder **Jakson Reetz** brings the potential at and behind the plate to develop into a true two-way catcher. ❖ **Will Rhymes** might have played in 130 major-league games between 2010 and 2012, but he's now spent the past two seasons lingering in Syracuse with a .700 OPS. ❖ The strength of **Pedro Severino**'s defense will likely carry him to the majors one day, but unless he learns to make more consistent contact the second day is in doubt. ❖ Former day-one pick **Drew Vettleson** tasted the upper minors and found it bitter. That strikeout-to-walk ratio could be overlooked if he was hitting 30 home runs, but he wasn't hitting 30 home runs. He was hitting eight. Eight is not enough. ❖ The raw power from big-bodied Oklahoman **Drew Ward** is appealing, but he has a long way to go with the hit tool and his defense at third base won't ever be a point in his favor. Gosh dang is his name ever close to being a palindrome.

Pitchers

NAME	TEAM	LVL	AGE	W	L	SV	G	GS	IP	H	HR	BB	K	BB/9	K/9	GB%	BABIP	WHIP	ERA	FIP	FRA	WARP
Xavier Cedeno	SYR	AAA	27	5	1	4	35	0	39¹	22	3	12	57	2.7	13.0	61%	.247	0.86	2.29	2.37	3.29	0.8
	WAS	MLB	27	0	0	0	9	0	7	10	1	0	5	0.0	6.4	40%	.375	1.43	3.86	3.53	3.26	0.0
Eric Fornataro	MEM	AAA	26	4	5	15	44	0	56	46	3	20	35	3.2	5.6	55%	.254	1.18	2.57	4.27	4.53	0.5
	SLN	MLB	26	0	0	0	8	0	9²	11	0	1	3	0.9	2.8	51%	.297	1.24	4.66	3.10	4.11	0.0
Matthew Grace	HAR	AA	25	3	1	3	22	0	35¹	32	0	12	32	3.1	8.2	74%	.291	1.25	1.02	2.56	3.44	1.0
	SYR	AAA	25	2	0	0	28	0	41²	28	1	13	30	2.8	6.5	65%	.237	0.98	1.30	3.31	4.59	0.2
Taylor Hill	SYR	AAA	25	11	7	1	25	24	144	136	15	25	86	1.6	5.4	49%	.268	1.12	2.81	4.23	5.47	0.2
	WAS	MLB	25	0	1	0	3	1	9	16	0	3	5	3.0	5.0	54%	.457	2.11	9.00	3.66	3.81	0.1
Felipe Rivero	HAR	AA	22	2	7	0	10	10	43²	45	4	18	38	3.7	7.8	52%	.304	1.44	4.12	4.18	4.09	0.6
Jefry Rodriguez	HAG	A	20	0	2	0	4	4	17	27	0	5	11	2.6	5.8	49%	.443	1.88	6.88	3.88	5.18	0.1
	AUB	A-	20	1	0	0	3	3	16¹	16	0	4	9	2.2	5.0	61%	.314	1.22	2.76	3.07	4.70	0.0
Austin Voth	HAG	A	22	4	3	0	13	13	69²	51	1	22	74	2.8	9.6	54%	.281	1.05	2.45	2.68	3.23	2.0
	POT	A+	22	2	1	0	6	6	37²	16	2	7	40	1.7	9.6	43%	.163	0.61	1.43	2.64	3.52	0.8
	HAR	AA	22	1	3	0	5	5	19¹	22	4	9	19	4.2	8.8	43%	.333	1.60	6.52	5.63	5.92	-0.1
Jake Walsh	HAG	A	23	1	2	10	23	0	31	17	1	10	27	2.9	7.8	45%	.190	0.87	1.45	3.33	4.17	0.4
	POT	A+	23	3	0	2	14	0	21	12	1	4	27	1.7	11.6	52%	.224	0.76	1.71	2.28	2.85	0.6

Failed starting pitching prospect **Xavier Cedeno** has been largely unsuccessful as a LOOGY (.689 career OPS versus left-handed batters). He could try ROOGY work next, except those guys collectively hit like Jose Bautista against him. ❖ After missing all of the 2014 season due to Tommy John surgery, **Erik Davis** will look to break back into a Nationals' bullpen that's gotten a lot more crowded in his absence. ❖ Triple-A closer **Eric Fornataro** made his big-league debut last summer, showing off a heavy mid-90s sinker that generates plenty of groundball outs, but until he starts missing more bats Washington fans won't grow familiar with his entrance music. ❖ **Mathew Grace** took a big step toward finding a spot in the Nationals' bullpen by holding left-handed hitters to a .144/.198/.173 line between Double-A and Triple-A. Well, *in* Double-A and *in* Triple-A. Between Double-A and Triple-A he mostly just read the in-flight magazines. ❖ There's hitting rock bottom, and then there's having an ERA twice as high as Tracy Mc-Grady for the Sugar Land Skeeters. **Clay Hensley** is likely to be the next great Atlantic League comeback story. ❖ The quintessential Triple-A starter you hope to never use, **Taylor Hill** is a sinkerballer who doesn't miss bats; he got nine innings of work in Washington and allowed nine runs to match. ❖ One-third of the return for Nate Karns last offseason, **Felipe Rivero** missed three months of the season with an elbow injury, but returned to close the year strong at Double-A. "Nationals rotation depth" is famous last words for fringy starters, so we'll say he could be an option for the Washington bullpen this year. ❖ **Jefry Rodriguez** was limited to 33 innings in 2014 due to tendonitis, but when he's right, he still flashes a mid-90s fastball and a plus curve. ❖ Since being drafted in the second round of the 2010 draft, **Sammy Solis** had thrown a whopping 179 innings between Tommy John surgery and other various arm injuries; he's Brett Anderson after a few rounds in the Pit of Despair. ❖ The 2013 fifth-rounder **Austin Voth** had continued success with a fastball-heavy approach, blazing through both levels of A-Ball before finally getting knocked around for the first time as a pro in five Double-A starts. ❖ The 34th-rounder **Jake Walsh** has put up some gaudy stats in his two years of pro ball (1.49 ERA across three levels), but with a fastball in the 80s and no LOOGY-worthy breaking ball, his major-league future is questionable, at best.

Manager

Matt Williams

YEAR	TEAM	W	L	Py-thag +/-	Avg PC	100+ P	120+ P	QS	BQS	REL	REL w Zero R	IBB	PH	PH Avg	PH HR	SB2	CS2	SB3	CS3	SAC Att	SAC%	POS SAC	Squeeze	Swing	In Play
2014	WAS	96	66	-2	94.6	59	0	106	2	458	386	26	240	.145	5	89	16	12	6	105	57.1%	12	1	261	76

The weird truth is that fans are more willing to accept (and expect) growth from players than from managers and executives; probably because the progress is easier to observe and compare. Williams seemed like the exception. He had transitioned from the guy who benched Bryce Harper over hustle-related concerns—either irritating the franchise player or setting an egalitarian tone for the roster, depending on your views—to a promising rookie manager. "Seemed like" because his bullpen usage during the postseason sabotaged any chance he had of ending the year on a high note. The same folks who were praising his progress were left begging for his dismissal. He was so close, too.

If there is something everyone can agree on about Williams, it's that he doesn't fit the image of the typical hothead-turned-manager. Last year Chris Jaffe expressed surprise that Kirk Gibson, a similar case and Williams' mentor, had eschewed small-ball tactics. Williams was the same way in '14. Washington's position players sacrificed the fewest times in the majors—three fewer than Bob Melvin's Athletics. Williams also avoided running his relievers into the ground, as the Nationals tallied the game's fewest amount of appearances on zero days' rest. What's it mean? Perhaps nothing, or perhaps that he's more thoughtful than his appearance and nickname suggest.

I Was Promised Flying Cars and Managers Who Used Their Closers Correctly

by Russell A. Carleton

I suppose that if humanity really wanted flying cars, they could happen. In some parts of the world, where traffic is heavy and roads are poor, the super-wealthy fly around in helicopters to get from Point A to Point B. Imagine if 30 or 40 years ago, the powers that be had decided to bring helicopters to the same scale as cars now. In the same way that cars went from playthings of the rich to fairly common issue, perhaps a helicopter would be cheap enough that owning one was within the reach of a good chunk of the population. In this alternate world, people would wake up in the morning and fly to work or school or the baseball stadium.

It takes me about 20 minutes to drive in my car from my house to my "real" job every morning, and 20 minutes home at night, depending on how the highway is doing. I suppose that if I had a helicopter, I could skip the meandering roads and just zip in a straight line to work in something like 10 or 15 minutes. I don't know anything about helicopters. I assume that there's some takeoff and landing time that goes along with them, and I'm just assuming that if humanity had dedicated itself to this effort, then mass producing helicopters could be done. And it would be a quicker commute for me and for everyone. Without being restricted to two dimensions, people would realize their dreams of being able to get to places much faster.

We brought it to scale on the inter-city level with airplanes, and only a few decades after the Wright brothers made their maiden flight. It's much quicker to fly from one city to the next than to drive. Why not on the local level with helicopters or small airplanes or anti-gravity pods? You can probably guess the answer. The entire infrastructure of transportation within a city is based on cars. We have garages attached to our houses that are shaped for cars. We have parking lots in front of stores and buildings, not helipads. We have fuel stations designed for cars to drive in and fuel up. We have 3,980,817 miles of road built already, in the United States alone. Switching over to helicopters might be technically feasible, and would save some time, but is it worth rebuilding an entire infrastructure just to save 10 minutes on my commute?

✦✦✦

For those of you who read the Baseball Prospectus annual for the articles, you've probably had this moment while watching a game: A manager does something so splendiferously stupid that you end up shaking your head. All of the research that's been done, and he still hits that guy with the .268 on-base percentage in the two-hole.

One of the things that I've always found rather interesting about how the game has changed in response to the sabermetric movement is that it's been rather uneven. It's true that teams are still using the sacrifice bunt a little too much, and that they are far too rigid when it comes to bullpen roles. Even the "enlightened" managers are loathe to use the closer in the ninth inning of a tie game on the road. You'll still see a few awful "professional hitters" in the second spot of a lineup, and managers rarely juggle their lineups much at all. When will they ever learn?

Then again, before you lose all hope, consider that teams aren't completely oblivious. In 2014, the infield shift had its moment, mostly because teams took a good long look at the data and realized that they could convert more balls into outs if they used it. Jose Molina finally got a full-time job in his late 30s because someone recognized his otherworldly pitch-framing abilities. On-base percentage has more or less defeated batting average. Teams seem much more likely now to play a good defender who can't hit much, but they understand that the defense can be that valuable.

If you wanted to make a case that the sabermetric movement has been a failure, there are several points in your favor. If you want to make the case that it's a great success, you can do that too. Some stratagems have been quickly adopted and some have been completely ignored. There's something of a truism that everything that exists does so for a reason. It may not be a good reason, but there's always some sort of reason, and I think exploring that reason might teach us something about the game and how sabermetrics might come to influence baseball in the next decade.

✦✦✦

Let's assume that teams are, at the end of the day, rational to the ends of the knowledge that they have. They may have imperfect knowledge (don't we all?) but they honestly believe, after a cost-benefit analysis, that they are making decisions that will lead to wins. Let's look at one example of a particularly maddening strategy that teams still use, despite the fact that research has shown it is not optimal: the "inefficient" use of relievers.

In theory, a manager should use his closer during the most important point in a game. Now, to do that properly would require the manager to have a crystal ball to be able to see all possible situations that might arise, but there's a general understanding that a tie game in the eighth inning is hanging more in the balance than a three-run lead at the beginning of the ninth. Why don't teams insert the closer earlier in the game?

It turns out that when you do the #GoryMath on these sorts of alternate bullpen arrangements, you actually don't get much of an effect. I once looked into a strategy in which a team would commit to using its closer in the eighth inning if it was winning by one run, and to have him pitch two innings; correspondingly, the team would let his set-up man handle any three-run saves in the ninth. In the event of a two-run lead, the set-up man and closer handled the eighth and ninth in the manner to which we have become accustomed. After some modeling, I estimated that a team might squeeze out some small fraction of a win by doing this. It would be an improvement, just not a huge one. It's tempting to say "Well, even if the effects are small, every little bit helps. Why not do it?" The fact that it's rare for even the most "progressive" teams to deviate from a fairly standard bullpen model tells us teams believe there is a greater cost to be paid.

What could that cost possibly be? It's certainly not financial. This sort of strategy utilizes pitchers already on the roster. In the past, analysts would have said that the "cost" is just teams and managers being overly attached to tradition and being unwilling to try something new. Still, if there's a demonstrable way to win more games, you'd figure that one of the 30 managers out there might be willing to give it a chance. The answer usually comes back that a strategy for bullpen usage based on leverage would require pitchers to pitch in different situations from game to game, likely in different innings. Pitchers prefer to have a defined role. The most common response to that one is "Get over it, you millionaire."

But is it a preference or a necessity? Consider the life of a relief pitcher. He travels a lot across time zones. He lives out of a suitcase. I'm guessing there are days when he wakes up and has no idea what city he's in. Sleep is at a premium. He goes to the ballpark and, unlike a starting pitcher, he doesn't know if his number will be called that day. There's very little about his day that's predictable. It's hot. He's been doing this now for months. And yeah, that million-dollar salary for playing a kids game is nice, but he is a human being. After a while, the constant travel and uncertainty take their toll. People don't do well when they don't know what's coming next. Can you blame the manager for adopting a strategy that might not be completely optimal if you did everything according to the computer model, but at least gives his relievers some sense of control over their day?

Research has shown that plate discipline for hitters tends to get a little bit worse as the season goes on, probably because of fatigue. It's not something immediately visible to the eye, but it's there and it steals value a little at a time. Over the course of 162 games though, that can add up. I've done research showing that certain managers tend to be good, and reliably so, at stopping this erosion of plate discipline, with the best managers being worth something on the order of one win just based on this one skill. It's reasonable that relievers feel the same grind, suffer the same sort of erosion in their performance, and maybe, just maybe it's more important for a manager to do everything he can to solve that problem than to make tiny little marginal gains here and there by trying weird new strategies.

✦ ✦ ✦

I think there's a common theme that distinguishes the sabermetric strategies that have been fully adopted from those that haven't. Front offices now seem much more willing to think in terms of overall value rather than just the same 100-year-old stats. Front offices have clearly noticed the development of catcher defense metrics. Front offices… notice a theme here?

Front offices have clearly evolved in how they decide which players to put on the roster. Managers, on the other hand, have been slower to play around with players' job descriptions on a day-to-day basis. I think up to this point, the assumption has been that the managers out there did this because they were hard-headed and silly. But that doesn't explain how the infield shift has largely caught on.

I'd suggest that managers are actually behaving quite rationally. The infield shift requires little more than directing players to "stand over there for this play." But playing around with reliever roles (and other "strategies" that might be technically correct) ignores the larger ecosystem in which baseball players live. Not knowing whether you'll be in for the fifth or the eighth inning means an hour or so of your day is spent sitting on the edge of your chair. That's a small stress, but small stressors add up.

Yes, we could have flying cars and they would make things a bit quicker, but we'd need an entirely different infrastructure to support them. Given what we have now, the flying cars would be useless, or at least they would be more of a hassle than just dealing with regular roads. In the same way, we could have a leverage-based bullpen, but the fact that it hasn't happened tells you a lot about how strong the pull is for keeping things a little more predictable. Maybe the effect isn't as big as managers and relievers think it is, but the benefits of using a leverage-based bullpen are actually not that great either, and we have indirect evidence that how a manager handles things can make a big impact on the grind that players feel as the season wears on. Maybe managers really are choosing wisely.

✦ ✦ ✦

I think there's a message buried in there somewhere. Those of us who come up with crazy ideas for teams to implement need to first think about the ecosystem in which the players actually live. What works great on paper might not work out in the wild. The human element can have a huge impact on how a player performs. That effect might be much bigger than we imagine. What if "The Grind" is actually the most powerful force in baseball? What if giving relievers a little bit of comfort by giving them a firm idea of when they will pitch is the best way to fight that?

The truth is that we haven't really gone there yet. I don't suggest giving managers a free pass on the topic, but clearly their actions point to… something, and if we are to be good scientists, we need to figure out what that something is. And given that information, it might make complete sense that managers aren't running their bullpens—or doing a few other things—the way that we thought they would in "the future." ■

—Russell A. Carleton is an author at Baseball Prospectus and previously consulted for two MLB teams

Delivery Angle Determines Pitch Movement

Evidence from Biomechanics and Pitch Tracking

By Daniel I. Brooks, Glenn S. Fleisig and Harry Pavlidis

Modern pitching analysis has largely taken three independent approaches. First, and most common to the everyday baseball fan, has been the sabermetric analysis of actual and predicted outcomes, which has resulted in statistics such as FIP (fielding independent pitching) and WARP (wins above replacement player). The second approach has been pitch tracking, largely via the PITCHf/x system developed by Sportvision and Major League Baseball, in which researchers have analyzed the actual trajectory that the ball takes from pitcher to batter. The third approach has been biomechanical analysis, studying the body motions and joint forces of the pitcher. Integrating analysis from these three approaches will not only have major consequences for player evaluation in the front offices of major-league baseball clubs but also for doctors, coaches and development personnel. Here, we present new data that link two of these approaches: biomechanics and pitch tracking.

Physics and Pitch Classification

This article is not intended to be a primer on baseball physics. For that, we direct the reader to Robert K. Adair's wonderful *Physics of Baseball* or Alan Nathan's website of the same name. As any baseball fan who has watched a biting curveball or tailing fastball knows, pitched baseballs have "movement;" that is, they deviate from the trajectories normally observed for a round object affected only by gravity. This movement is caused by air resistance related to the *spin* of the ball. The amount of spin generally predicts the magnitude of this movement, while the axis of this spin generally predicts the angle or direction of this movement. For example, four-seam fastballs are thrown with backspin, creating Magnus force to counteract the effect of gravity. Thus, typical fastballs "rise" (that is, they do not actually rise, but they fall less than expected).

Of critical importance is the direction or angle of the spin axis: A fastball thrown with pure backspin will generate only upward force, but a fastball thrown with a tilted spin axis will also generate sideways force. Thus, a cutter thrown by a right-handed pitcher has some amount of leftward spin, a slider or slurve has a larger leftward spin component and a curveball has an almost entirely topspin component. A sinker thrown by a right-handed pitcher tilts rightward, which effectively trades some amount of the force normally given to making the ball "rise" and translates that force into horizontal, directional force, making the ball appear to sink and giving these pitches their characteristic "tailing" action.

These physics models (like most models of the world!) actually create somewhat of a mismatch between theory and what happens in practice. For instance, while four-seam fastballs are generally thrown with nearly pure backspin *with respect to the hand*, the hand itself is actually tilted. Thus, although these

pitch concepts detail the spin of the ball relative to the hand, they don't explain the measured ball trajectory.

Given these principles, Matt Lentzner published and presented a set of essential analyses which asserted that the angle of the arm as the ball was released provided an important piece of information when classifying pitch types. Using data derived from PITCHf/x as well as photographs of pitchers at the moment of release, Lentzner provided preliminary evidence that the movement of fastballs (and indeed, other pitches) could be predicted by arm angle. Below, we present findings using more sophisticated measurements to evaluate this theory. Specifically, we combined PITCHf/x and full-body biomechanics data captured for 25 major-league pitchers.

How do we measure biomechanics and pitch movement?

The American Sports Medicine Institute (ASMI), under the guidance of Dr. Glenn Fleisig and Dr. James Andrews, hosts one of the best-equipped biomechanics laboratories and the largest dataset of baseball pitching biomechanics data. At this facility, biomechanics can be directly measured using a system in which reflective markers are attached to various positions on a player's body and high-speed cameras track the location of those markers while the pitcher throws (Figure 1, next page, left panel). The data from these marker locations are then used to compute the orientation of each part of the body during the throwing motion and the forces and torques created about the throwing shoulder and elbow. Details of this analysis are available in the extensive body of publications from Fleisig, Andrews and colleagues.

For the purposes of this project, the goal was to create an accurate representation of how the hand and arm are tilted at the point of release. Although release point is often thought of as a two-dimensional coordinate (often represented and reported from x0 and z0 in the PITCHf/x data), release point (and arm tilt) is really a three-dimensional angle that depends on a variety of interconnected parts. According to Lentzner's theory, the critical variable is the tilt of the arm and hand at release. To construct that tilt, we need to know four pieces of biomechanical data. Figure 1 depicts angles superimposed onto photographs that represent each piece of biomechanical data analyzed here. We need to know three critical angles: The angle of the upper arm relative to the body (shoulder abduction), the angle of the forearm relative to the elbow (elbow flexion) and how much the pitcher tilts to his left or right. We also need to know how much the pitcher tilts forward. Trunk-tilt angles, while not intuitive or obvious to the casual baseball fan, are important because bending to the side globally alters the shoulder and elbow angles relative to the body, and bending forward at release changes the degree to which shoulder-tilt angle is translated into the important measurement plane. Here, we will call the combination of each of these features *Delivery Angle*. We use the term delivery angle,

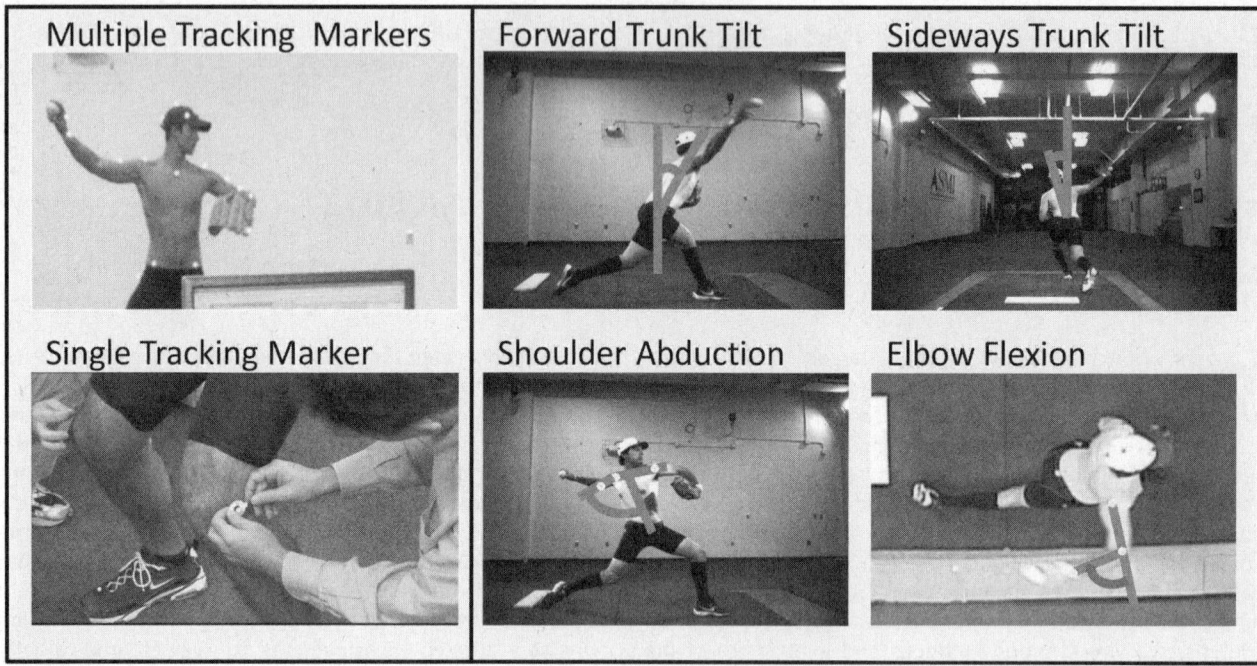

Figure 1

rather than arm angle, to emphasize that although the effort is to predict something about arm path, other variables, such as body tilt, must be incorporated into the measurement to create an accurate predictor.

For pitch-tracking data, we use the reclassified and recalibrated dataset that is maintained by Pitch Info. This dataset also powers BrooksBaseball.net and many of the pitching analyses at Baseball Prospectus. If you are unfamiliar with this dataset, it is fundamentally built on PITCHf/x. Since 2008, every major-league park has been home to a set of cameras and associated hardware installed by Sportvision and MLBAM that operate as part of the PITCHf/x product. These cameras sample the location of the ball as it is delivered by the pitcher to home plate; sophisticated algorithms then fit a nine-parameter trajectory to each pitch that can be used to accurately recreate the flight of the ball. These flight paths are used for broadcast and media purposes across baseball (e.g., to create the graphics seen on MLB Gameday and ESPN's K-Zone product).

PITCHf/x data are also available for research purposes. At Pitch Info, we download the PITCHf/x raw data, reclassify the pitches and recalibrate the tracking information from each pitch to remove movement inconsistencies introduced by the various systems across years and parks. After recalibrating these nine-parameter fits, we recalculate several critical variables, such as the amount of movement due to the spin of each pitch. Our critical variable here will be movement angle; that is, the angular direction of the Magnus force exerted on each pitch that is caused by the spin of the baseball.

From the extensive dataset collected at ASMI (more than 2,000 pitchers), we've identified a subset of 25 professional pitchers for the analysis here. These 25 pitchers have all been tested in ASMI's biomechanics lab, have been tracked with PITCHf/x during major-league games and throw both four-seam and two-seam (or sinking) fastballs (at least 100 fastballs recorded in a major-league game, and with at least 10 percent frequency of each type of fastball). We also documented the

percentage of four-seam and two-seam fastballs each pitcher throws. The reasoning was that pitchers who get more "natural" or additional movement are more likely to favor sinkers, which are pitches that further exaggerate movement. Perhaps these pitchers fit the general trend, but some additional component of variance can be explained by attending to their pitch-usage patterns.

Fastballs and Sinkers

For the 25 players who met the inclusion criteria, we fit a simple model in which we predicted actual movement angle based on two predictors: delivery angle and four-seam percentage. This model revealed that the combination of these two factors overwhelmingly predicted fastball movement. Figure 2 (next page) depicts the very high correlation (R = .85) between the actual movement angle and the model-predicted movement angle. Delivery angle was a highly significant predictor ($p <$ .001), although four-seam percentage was also significant ($p <$ .01). Without including the four-seam percentage variable, there was still a very strong correlation (R = .75) between delivery angle and pitch movement alone.

We also fit data from their two-seam or sinking fastballs (Figure 3, next page). This set of data also produced a strong correlation (R = .86). Again, there was a strong correlation between delivery angle and pitch movement alone (R = .79) that was marginally improved by including the percentage of four-seam fastballs thrown by that pitcher.

These data strongly demonstrate that for four-seam and two-seam fastballs the direction of pitch movement is almost entirely predicted from biomechanics, and that this prediction can be slightly improved by including the usage patterns of each pitcher's fastball. Given the physical explanation for pitch movement and the hypothesized interaction between biomechanics (and release angle) and spin angle, these data are not particularly surprising. However, it is important to note that if so much of the variance in pitch movement can be explained by biomechanics, differences in fastball grip do not seem to play more than a marginal role in determining overall pitch movement for these pitch types.

Putting it all together

These analyses relate and connect two traditionally disconnected datasets: biomechanics and pitch-tracking data. Here, we show a strong relationship between delivery angle as measured by biomechanical analysis and pitch movement measured by pitch-tracking systems.

This provides further support for the use of biomechanical analyses in player evaluation and development. Because ball-

movement angle can be predicted following a biomechanical analysis and accurate representation of delivery angle, teams could use biomechanical information for reasons beyond the obvious medical value of understanding the forces acting on key joints and ligaments. For example, given the relationship described here, tweaks or changes to a delivery to reduce stress on the arm should have highly predicable changes in ball movement.

Delivery angle is critical to understanding ball movement, so having the best representation possible of a player's delivery angle seems fundamental to a good understanding of that pitcher. Because a pitcher's delivery is a highly visible, repeated event, it should be possible to describe that delivery with enough detail to provide a coarse representation of the angles discussed in this article. Perhaps when evaluators from organizations like Baseball Prospectus describe pitching talent, we should capture a representation of that delivery in a way that goes beyond generalities like "3/4" or "overhand" and be more descriptive about the actual angles of the arm and tilt of the body involved. Not only will this serve the reader by creating a better picture of each player, but it will also serve the analyst because it will provide critical information on how each pitch is predicted to move.

A secondary possibility raised by this research is translating from pitch movement to biomechanics. Pitch-tracking systems are quickly becoming ubiquitous features in baseball stadiums, both in the major and minor leagues and even at many amateur showcases and colleges. Thus, whereas top-end biomechanical analyses currently require a suite of specialized hardware and trained personnel in a controlled environment, utilizing pitch tracking to predict biomechanics might cast a much wider net with which to produce biomechanical analyses of players. Current pitch-tracking data is almost certainly too limited to produce an accurate representation of biomechanics. For example, knowing that a pitcher's sinker breaks a particular way gives you clues as to his overall delivery angle, but doesn't identify whether his body or arm is relatively tilted. Poorer-resolution systems for measuring biomechanics exist; these work by software analysis of pictures and video. Perhaps combining data from these lower-quality biomechanics systems with pitch-tracking information would yield more stable analysis.

Although the results here prove that the direction of pitch movement is predictable from biomechanical variables, there are several concerns. First, N is somewhat low. The reason is that we're restricted to using sets of publicly available PITCHf/x data and, although the ASMI dataset is large it includes many players who have not pitched in major-league games or who have not thrown sufficiently large numbers of pitches. Furthermore, the correlation reported here might dramatically *underestimate* the correlation between pitching biomechanics and

Figure 2: Fastball Movement Can Be Predicted from Biomechanics

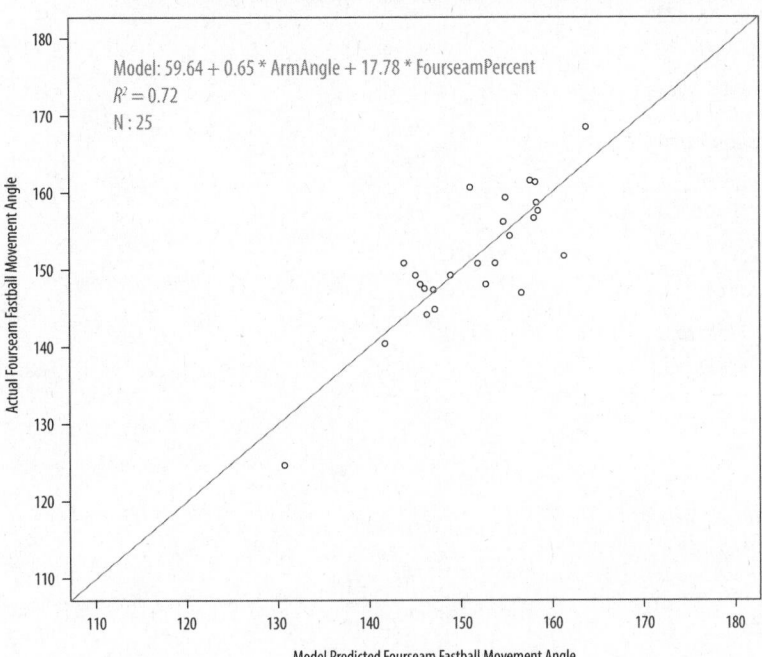

Model: 59.64 + 0.65 * ArmAngle + 17.78 * FourseamPercent
$R^2 = 0.72$
N : 25

Figure 3: Sinker Movement Can Be Predicted from Biomechanics

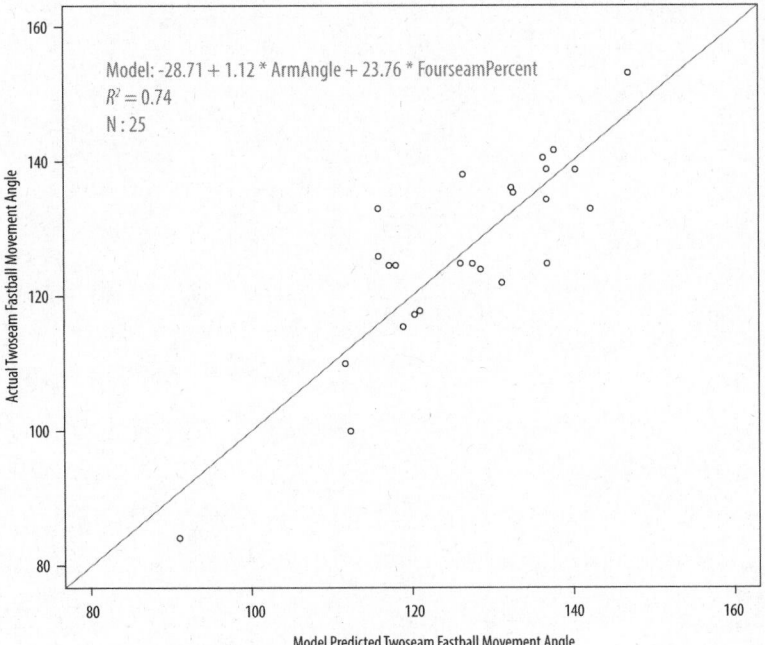

Model: -28.71 + 1.12 * ArmAngle + 23.76 * FourseamPercent
$R^2 = 0.74$
N : 25

ball movement because the biomechanical tracking sessions and pitches recorded during actual games sometimes took place *years* apart. Mechanics might change over time, and these later mechanics might predict ball movement better than the ones measured in our dataset. One obvious solution to both of these limitations is to repeat this study while recording biomechanical data and pitch movement simultaneously. Such a scenario is difficult to arrange: Biomechanics labs are difficult to move, and pitch-tracking systems are costly to set up and maintain. But such future testing is not impossible. Advances in biomechanics now allow for tracking in outdoor settings such as spring training facilities. Also pitch-tracking systems might soon be added to biomechanics labs like ASMI. Synchronizing ball-movement data with biomechanics data may allow more exact extrapolations. ■

–Dan Brooks is an experimental psychologist at Tufts University, chief scientist at Pitch Info and maintains the baseball analysis website BrooksBaseball.net.

–Glenn Fleisig, Ph.D., is the research director of the American Sports Medicine Institute. He is also chairman of the Medical & Safety Committee for USA Baseball, a member of Major League Baseball's Elbow Task Force, a safety consultant for Little League Baseball & Softball and a board member of Motus Global.

–Harry Pavlidis, a Chicagoan, is the founder of Pitch Info and Director of Technology for Baseball Prospectus.

A Little Advice

by Robert Whiting

It had long been a fundamental tenet of the Japanese game that baseball players should practice longer and harder than their counterparts in the U.S. Introduced to Japan in the late 19th century by visiting American professors, Japanese besuboru—or yakyuu (field ball), as it is also known—was heavily influenced by the martial arts, with their emphasis on endless training and development of spirit. An integral part of preseason practice was drills that forced a player to his limit, like the 1,000-fungo drill, which took two to three hours, and nagekomi, where a pitcher threw until he couldn't throw anymore. These exercises built stamina and confidence, but there was also Zen element: It was necessary to wear a player out to strengthen his fighting spirit, to teach him that he can do more than he thinks he is capable. In this way were great players born.

Two of Japan's top pitchers in history, Kazuhisa Inao and Hiroshi Gondo, endured enormous workloads. Inao, who pitched for the Nishitetsu Lions in the 1950s and 1960s, averaged nearly 350 innings per year over his first eight seasons. He won 30 games three times and 42 in 1961. In the 1958 Japan Series, he pitched in six of seven games, and this after appearing in 18 of 25 contests down the stretch. He inspired a saying: "Kamisama, Hoteksama and Inao sama." ("God, Buddha and Inao.") Gondo, for his part, won 35 games in his rookie 1960 season for the Chunichi Dragons, pitching a record 429 innings, and followed that with 30 wins the following year. His heroics gave rise to a poetic mantra of his own: Gondo, Gondo, Ame, Gondo, Ame, Ame, Gondo, Ame, Gondo, Ame. (Ame—pronounced ah-may—means rain.) But Inao was finished as a full-time starter in 1964 at the age of 26 and Gondo was out of baseball in 1965 at age 25, both with damaged arms.

Neither complained.

"Many times my arm and fingers ached with pain," Gondo recalled. "But I could not refuse my manager's request. The manager wanted me to pitch and I could not say no."

"Heart is the most important thing," said Inao, rejecting the suggestion that he was overworked.

In the early 1980s, Choji Murata, an overworked ace for the Lotte Orions, busted a ligament and traveled to Los Angeles to become the first Japanese player to undergo Tommy John surgery, performed by famed surgeon Frank Jobe. In a subsequent series of interviews with the Japanese media, Jobe lectured Japanese pitchers and pitching coaches about overthrowing in games and practice. "The human arm is not a piece of rubber," he said, referring to Murata's habit (and the habit of many other Japanese hurlers) of throwing 100 pitches every day on the sidelines. "It was not designed to throw a baseball and must have three to four days rest after pitching a nine-inning game of 100 pitches or more."

As Japan began to produce MLB stars—starting with Hideo Nomo in 1995—and became more familiar with the U.S. way of doing things, pressure arose to re-examine the traditional system of throwing hundreds of pitches a day and pushing players to the point of physical collapse. As a result, things began to change.

Now it is not unusual for Japanese starting pitchers to throw once a week and often go light on practice during the season (although nagekomi—marathon pitching to build stamina, confidence and fighting spirit, and to refine control—is still popular in spring camp, and pitch counts during the season are not nearly as restrictive as they are in MLB). Says Itaru Kobayashi, general manager of the 2014 Japan Champion Softbank Hawks, "Our starters now only throw 40-50 pitches in practice between starts. Sadaharu Oh, our honorary chairman, thinks our pitchers should throw a lot more in training than they do. But most of the younger generation believe more in science than spirit."

A number of high schools have also instituted pitch counts both in games and in practice. Says Kobayashi, "We drafted a pitcher in 2012—he was our second-round pick—who had never thrown over 100 pitches in his life, either in a game or in practice. The coaches had to push him to do it."

Now, ironically, it is Japanese who are giving advice to Americans.

✦ ✦ ✦

In the past five years, major-league teams have lost more than $1 billion due to highly paid pitchers being on the disabled list. Roughly a third of major-league pitchers have undergone Tommy John surgery. In 2014, according to accounting kept by the Hardball Times' Jon Roegele, American professional leagues saw a record number of such operations. This was far in excess of what the NPB experienced.

When Masahiro Tanaka went on the DL in July with a partially torn UCL, the American media focused on Pitcher Abuse Points from the 160-pitch games Tanaka pitched in Japan and his overuse of the split-finger fastball. The split-finger is notoriously hard on the elbow and Tanaka threw it twice as often in the States as he did in Japan. However, Yu Darvish stepped forward to argue that, in this case, it was the American system that was the cause of the problem. In an interview with reporters at the All-Star game in Minneapolis—an interview that occupied the entire front page of Japan's popular Nikkan Sports and was prominently featured in other Japanese sports dailies—Darvish said that the root of Tanaka's arm troubles was not throwing the splitter or throwing too much in Japan but having to switch from throwing once a week to pitching once every five days. He wasn't getting proper rest, according to Darvish. "Four days rest is too short," he said. "You need at least five to heal the inflammation. With six days rest you can also pitch longer into the game: 120-140 pitches is not unreasonable." He added that he thought the changeup and the forkball were harder on the arm than the split-finger. Darvish himself missed the last two months of the 2014 season with arm trouble.

Shortly after that, a Japanese orthopedic surgeon named Daisuke Nakai opined to the Wall Street Journal that Americans have bad mechanics. "Americans count on upper-body strength to propel the ball," he said in a video interview, "whereas Japanese who sometimes aren't as strong use their entire bodies, including their legs, reducing strain on the arms."

Koji Uehara, whose money pitch is the split-finger, echoed that view in an interview with the Tokyo Broadcasting System. "All breaking pitches put a strain on the elbow. It's a question of form, of using the entire body," he said.

For many Japanese, this is an interesting turn of events. As Osamu Nagatani, a reporter for the evening tabloid *Yukan Fuji*, put it, "If Darvish had made his remarks several years ago, he would have been roundly condemned by both Japan and U.S. media for being so outspoken. For many years now, the American system of using starting pitchers—roughly 100-pitch limits followed by four days of rest—was thought to be the last word. But now, with this outbreak of damaged ligaments, maybe the American approach isn't so great after all. Maybe Japan knows better."

There are, in fact, a growing number of Americans with knowledge of or experience in Japan who are willing to argue the value of the Japanese approach. In a Sports On Earth article headlined "The Joys of the Six-Man Rotation," former major-league pitcher Brian Bannister—who played briefly in Japan—praised the "extended recovery cycle" for pitchers in Japanese ball, with its characteristic six days of rest, its accompanying massages and its practice of long, leisurely soaks in alternating hot and cold water. Bannister also lauded the pregame warm-up system in NPB, saying "the standard practice session and pregame dynamic warm-up in Japan is extremely thorough in both duration and number of unique motions [...] This makes sure the body is warm and stretched out prior to throwing." He further praised the weight-training approach of the Japanese, which avoids "beach muscle" bodies by focusing on balanced muscle-development.

✦✦✦

It should also be noted that despite these changes in the Japanese approach, the old way has not exactly disappeared. There is still tension between the traditional ways of doing things and more modern approaches, particularly in high school baseball.

U.S. media gave extensive exposure to high schooler Tomohiro Anraku, who threw 772 pitches in nine days at the spring version of the national high school tournament, held at Koshien Stadium in Kobe a year ago, labeling it "child abuse" in some quarters. That is still routine for the annual spring and summer tournaments, where it is common for ace pitchers to throw four complete games in four days as the tournament reaches its climax.

Glenn S. Fleisig, research director at the American Sports Medicine Institute in Alabama, has said, among others things, that 100-200 pitches a day is far too many for adolescent and adult pitchers. Like smoking, he has said, the damage doesn't happen immediately or uniformly, but the danger is incontrovertible. (The rules for the California Interscholastic Federation limit game pitches to 130 per week, with recommendations that a pitcher who throws 76 pitches be required to rest for a minimum of four days.)

The problem in Japan, however, is that the media and the public glorify Koshien-style demonstrations of fighting spirit as heroic, so few high school teams have limits on pitching. The summer tournament is Japan's version of the NCAA basketball tournament: Teams emerging victorious from the 49 prefectural elimination playoffs meet in a single-elimination tournament lasting two weeks to determine the national champion. Supporters of this system complain that cutting back on training and instituting strict American-style pitch counts would strip what is special and unique about the Japanese game, which centers on discipline, self-sacrifice, perseverance and team spirit. Daisuke Matsuzaka's performance in the 1998 Koshien summer tournament is considered one of the greatest feats in the history of Japanese sports: He threw 250 pitches in 17 innings, following a 148-pitch performance the previous day. Two days later he pitched a complete-game no-hitter to lead his team to victory. Equally revered was the performance of Yuki Saito in the 2006 summer tourney: He threw 948 pitches in 69 innings to bring his school a championship, defeating arch-rival (and future Yankee) Tanaka in the final game. Without such displays of endurance and suffering, you will hear, the Koshien tourney would simply not be the same.

In fact, Matsuzaka was recently quoted as saying that he personally enjoyed throwing as many as 200 pitches a day in high school and that it didn't hurt him at all, although he does now say that he thinks it is important for coaches and mangers to take control and educate the players on how much the body can withstand. Matsuzaka's high school pitching coach still makes his pitchers throw more than 100 pitches a day in practice—every day of the year. "If a student's motion is flawless," he said, "then it's not a strain on the body." At Komazawa High School in Tokyo, a major schoolboy power, pitchers are expected to throw 200 pitches every other day.

✦✦✦

This way of thinking still exists In the pro ranks. Dave Okubo, the newly appointed manager of the Rakuten Golden Eagles, is a devotee of the 1,000-fungo drill and other aspects of the traditional Japanese system, and says that the American obsession with pitch counts is a bad thing. In the Golden Eagles' month-long autumn camp, which began November 1st with dawn-to-dusk workouts and evening practice indoors, Okubo instituted something called the 15-minute drill. Batters have to stand in against two BP pitchers who alternate, delivering a ball every two seconds for the 15-minute period. The batters are exhausted by the end (as are, presumably, the coaches who have to do the throwing). Okubo promised a regime of no days off for the coming year.

Bobby Valentine, who initially opposed the Japanese system during his early years as a manager with the Chiba Lotte Marines, eventually came to allow high pitch counts and *nagekomi* in camp, if a pitcher's core mechanics and conditioning were in top form. In the spring of 2014, a number of NPB pitchers threw *nagekomi* sessions in camp that would make American coaches wince. Among them were Daisuke Miura of Yokohama, who threw 311 pitches on February 16th in camp, and Takuma Achira of Chunichi, who threw 341 on February 25th. (That same spring, infielder Takahiro Kakizawa passed out while undergoing a 1,000-fungo drill and required a cardiac massage from a trainer. Yomiuri Giants infielder Harutomo Tsuji swung the bat 2,044 times during one eight-hour session.)

Said Shigetoshi Hasegawa, the former Angel and Mariner, "Honestly, Japanese guys have better mechanics than Americans. You know why? Because they throw (so) many balls. If you don't have good mechanics, you're done."

How this will all play out remains to be seen. In youth baseball, for example, many Japanese coaches, players and doctors have come to support limits on pitching. The Japanese Society for Clinical Sports and Medicine, for example, has, since 1995, recommended limits of no more than 50 pitches a day, or 200 pitches a week, for Japanese 11- and 12-year-olds (although it is not clear how many Little League coaches actually follow them). This compares unfavorably to rules in the U.S., which limit 11- and 12-year-olds to 75 pitches per game and 100 per week.

Officials of Japan's High School Baseball Federation, which oversees the Koshien championship, says they are now considering whether to introduce such measures as pitch counts, and perhaps take steps to limit long extra-inning games, but a nationwide survey conducted in mid-2014 revealed most fans and participants prefer high school baseball just the way it is..

Tradition dies hard. For the foreseeable future, the old and the new will continue to run on parallel courses. ■

–Robert Whiting is the author of
You Gotta Have Wa *and* The Meaning of Ichiro

Top 101 Prospects

by Nick J. Faleris, Chris Mellen, Mark Anderson, Tucker Blair, Craig Goldstein, Jordan Gorosh, Jeff Moore, Ethan Purser and Bret Sayre

1. Byron Buxton, OF, Minnesota Twins

Dear Byron, Please stay on the field. Love, everyone who watches baseball. Buxton's health failed him last year—from a nagging wrist issue to a nasty collision in the outfield. When 2012's second overall pick did play, he flashed the same elite pre-injury skill set that made him our top prospect before the season, though his offense was clearly restricted by the wrist, and the need for continued refinement handling breaking stuff does stick out. The upside is a top-of-the-scale runner, a plus-plus glove in center, a plus hitter with power that can peak as above-average: a player who can take over the game in every situation. If Buxton can make up for lost time in 2015, he might see the majors before the year ends.

2. Addison Russell, SS, Chicago Cubs

Russell is the current flag-bearer for a cadre of standout shortstops clustered atop the minor-league ranks, providing an elite blend of offensive upside, defensive stability at a high-value position, athleticism and strength. Through his first 233 professional contests Russell has shown an ability to impact the game in all facets, hitting for average and power while providing steady defense at short and impressing on the bases. He's close to major-league ready and possesses the skill set, makeup and natural ability to step in as a contributor immediately upon arrival.

3. Carlos Correa, SS, Houston Astros

Though a broken right fibula ended his season prematurely, Correa showcased electrifying tools and impressive game-awareness. The first overall selection in the 2012 draft has a well-rounded offensive package with an advanced approach, remarkable feel to hit and projectable raw power. Even at 6-feet-4 he should have the ability to stick at shortstop for the foreseeable future. With elite makeup, he figures to be one of the main building blocks in Houston going forward.

4. Francisco Lindor, SS, Cleveland Indians

Close your eyes for a second and imagine the ideal shortstop prospect. Without knowing it, you just conjured Lindor. Yes, we're positive. The 2011 first-rounder is a switch-hitting contact-oriented batter who possesses an approach well beyond his years, and sneaky pop to boot. He's otherwordly in the field, a player whose elite skills are obvious even in pregame infield practice. Really, head out to Columbus this year and get to the game early: His youthful exuberance and pillow-quality hands are worth the price of admission.

5. Kris Bryant, 3B, Chicago Cubs

Through his minor-league career, which covers a shade more than one full season's worth of plate appearances, Bryant has posted steroids-era numbers at the plate, with a slash line of .327/.428/.666 and a home run almost every three games. The former first-rounder is ready to bring his act to The Show, where he should eventually settle in as a fixture in the middle of the Cubs lineup, joining Russell as foundational talents for the up-and-comer Cubbies. Both are set to debut in 2015 as the North Siders look to effect the transition from loveable losers to feared frontrunners.

6. Lucas Giolito, RHP, Washington Nationals

There are major-league teams that don't currently have a better pitcher than Giolito, a 20-year-old who spent his summer pitching in front of three-digit hometown crowds at Hagerstown. The Nationals have paced his development slowly, a reasonable precaution for a pitcher with a Tommy John surgery on his resume, but it created an unreasonable mismatch for Low-A hitters: Giolito flashed an elite fastball/curveball combination on his way to 10 strikeouts per nine innings and a 2.20 ERA. The changeup is still a work in progress, but he replicates arm speed and has shown steady improvement with it. He is the full package, the best pitching prospect in baseball and a future ace whose only red flag is his job title.

7. Corey Seager, SS, Los Angeles Dodgers

While Seager's unrestricted offensive march through the California League seemed all but predetermined, it was his assault on Double-A arms upon promotion that pushed him firmly into the upper echelon of the prospect-scape. In spite of a placid setup featuring minimal load, the former first-rounder excels at driving the ball and should supplement his solid over-the-fence pop with plenty of doubles. At present his advanced feel for the game offsets his limited range at short, and his soft hands and strong, accurate arm are left-side assets, be it at the six- or five-spot.

8. Dylan Bundy, RHP, Baltimore Orioles

After missing all of 2013 following Tommy John surgery, Bundy took the mound again in June with the same exceptional shape on his up-and-down curveball, but without the full suite that had made him electric pre-injury. He lacked feel for the rest of his arsenal and his velocity was a bit slower to return (though he did notch 96 in his later starts). He still has the makeup and mentality to reestablish his front-line potential, so now he has to prove he still has the stuff.

9. Noah Syndergaard, RHP, New York Mets

Spending too much time in Vegas can drag anyone down, but Syndergaard's 2014 stats belie his true talent. The big right-hander still flashes the same huge stuff, including a potential double-plus curve and a fastball that sits in the mid-90s while touching higher. The fact that his changeup is constantly improving and can miss major-league bats makes it hard not to envision a top-of-the-rotation workhorse. Even with a full rotation ahead of him in Queens, expect him to force the issue before the All-Star break.

10. Julio Urias, LHP, Los Angeles Dodgers

There's no truth to the rumor that Urias, born in 1996, was inspired to pitch by Robert Rodriguez's 1995 masterpiece *Desperado*. There's every reason to believe it though, as he packs multiple weapons into an unassuming frame and toys with hitters as deftly as El Mariachi plucks his guitar. Urias' impressive arsenal is further bolstered by his ability to cut, run and sink his fastball and vary the length and bite on his breaking ball. The cambio gives him a chance for three above-average pitches, and his feel for the craft at such a young age instills confidence he'll approach his overall future projection of a no. 2 starter.

11. Archie Bradley, RHP, Arizona Diamondbacks

Bradley endured a bevy of challenges in 2014, including an extended DL stint and mechanical issues ranging from a variable arm slot to inconsistent posture, timing and landing, all combining to throw off his release and complicate his execution. Evaluators remain bullish, however, and the Arizona Fall League found the Oklahoman showing renewed confidence and a notably impactful cutter, broadening a repertoire that already included some of the filthiest raw stuff in the game. Recent hiccups notwithstanding, this is an elite arm capable of bridging the gap between his lackluster 2014 performance and a front-end future in the blink of an eye.

12. Miguel Sano, 3B, Minnesota Twins

Tommy John surgery took his 2014 season, but the good news is that Sano is not a pitcher and this injury is unlikely to negatively affect his long-term potential. If baseball held its own version of a "longest drive" contest, Sano would contend for the crown, with top-of-the-scale raw power that already shows up in games. The only thing that might prevent production is a lack of hit-tool refinement. It remains to be seen whether he can stick at third: The action and hands are major-league quality, but he has Tommy John surgery and size working against him. Even in right field or at the cold corner, he'd be an impact prospect.

13. Jonathan Gray, RHP, Colorado Rockies

Gray continued to showcase power stuff in 2014, headlined by an elite fastball/slider combo and an emerging changeup that could give the former Oklahoma Sooner a third plus offering with which to attack major-league bats. The Rockies limited Gray in his pitch selection and counts, encouraging a pitch-to-contact approach that drew soft contact from Texas League bats and mild angst from evaluators longing to see the burly right-hander unleashed and unrestricted. Gray should provide major-league value in short order, with anything shy of no. 3 production, even in the challenging Coors environs, coming as a surprise.

14. Alex Meyer, RHP, Minnesota Twins

It's easy to imagine Meyer, a 6-foot-9 flamethrower with a plus-plus slider, becoming an impact closer chasing 400 saves. He's abnormally large, with tree-trunk legs, and his stuff would play up in short bursts. But the fastball command started to take a step forward in 2014, and despite the lack of consistent changeup, Meyer's two main pitches add up to four pluses, so a ceiling as a no. 2 starter is not out of the question. Meyer is entering his age-25 season, but large pitchers take a longer time to develop.

15. Joey Gallo, 3B, Texas Rangers

It's been some time since minor-league pitchers have seen natural raw power like this. More impressive is that Gallo has had no trouble putting that power into play in games; despite the swing-and-miss, he has hit 104 bombs in just 296 career minor-league games. (For context, Giancarlo Stanton hit 91 in 333 games, though Gallo *has* been a year or so behind Stanton's promotion schedule.) Power is the headliner, but Gallo's baseball IQ and work ethic have been praised since he was drafted in 2012, and he could stick at third or work in right field due to his huge arm. Just watch where you park when he's playing.

16. Robert Stephenson, RHP, Cincinnati Reds

Stephenson survived the year at Double-A Pensacola, but in the process showed there is work to be done before he can tackle his next set of developmental challenges. Almost all of the righty's issues can be traced back to a propensity to go through on-field obstacles, rather than negotiating them via precise execution and craft. The fastball-curve combo has the potential to miss bats at every level, but in order to fully tap into that potential, Stephenson is going to have to rein things in and place a higher premium on spotting and execution.

17. Blake Swihart, C, Boston Red Sox

Stumbles out of the gate by previous top Red Sox prospects should in no way factor into one's opinion of Swihart. The latest player bestowed with the honor has everything you want in a prospect, with plus defensive ability up the middle, a major league-caliber bat and elite makeup, the latter of which is extremely important given his position and home ballpark. While not necessarily a middle-of-the-order slugger, Swihart will hit enough to be a first-division regular, and the defensive profile grades out even better than his bat. He should be an everyday catcher for the better part of a decade, and could be the best player on a contending team.

18. Joc Pederson, OF, Los Angeles Dodgers

With a patient approach that borders on passive, Pederson pairs his stellar walk rate with a strikeout-heavy profile. It's a strategy that worked last year as he rode a 30/30 season in Triple-A all the way to his major-league debut, quelling concerns about his ability to hit same-side pitching in the process. While there's no carrying tool in his profile, he grades out as average or a tick above across the board and should be a starting-caliber player, whether he sticks in center or shifts to a corner down the line.

19. Jorge Soler, OF, Chicago Cubs

Soler put together a solid but checkered showing in his first taste of major-league ball to close out 2014, and should be ready to step in full time for the Cubs on Opening Day. If he's to reach his upside as a true middle-of-the-order masher, he'll need to prove capable of adjusting to major-league arms who work with a book and a gameplan. But even if the hit tool never fully materializes, Soler could thrive as a dangerous five- or six-hole bat capable of punishing mistakes en route to 25-plus home runs per season.

20. Hunter Harvey, RHP, Baltimore Orioles

Harvey was shut down with shoulder soreness late in the season, which is the last thing one wants to read in the first sentence of a prospect write-up. But his season was otherwise impeccable, as he feasted on Low-A hitters in 17 starts at Delmarva. He can make his electric fastball cut or run, and his hammer curveball won't find a fair fight until he reaches the upper levels. Hunter showed mild improvements in arm-speed repetition and overall feel for his changeup. That pitch will struggle to keep up as the rest of his arsenal pushes him up the Orioles' system toward a possible 2016 debut.

21. Tyler Glasnow, RHP, Pittsburgh Pirates

Glasnow's a huge guy with a huge fastball, and he racked up huge strikeout totals with High-A Bradenton. The heater is hard to square up due to his long limbs and extreme plane, and his hammer curve has deep break and plus potential. Taming such a big delivery will be a challenge, and for now he struggles with his release point and consistency. Glasnow needs to improve his command and the consistency of his secondaries, but the first signs of pitching-not-throwing are already flashing, and the upside is impressive.

22. Braden Shipley, RHP, Arizona Diamondbacks

Shipley accomplished a great deal in 2014: He increased proficiency with his breaking ball, managed a solid jump in workload and showed more comfort mixing and matching his offerings in variable game situations. His mechanics work for him and his repertoire. His athleticism is an asset, both in implementing tweaks suggested by player development staff and in self-correcting when his motion slides slightly out of whack within outings. With a chance for three plus or better offerings and the strength and arm to shoulder a major-league starter's workload, Shipley represents one of the more exciting profiles in the minors.

23. Austin Hedges, C, San Diego Padres

When you are the best defensive catcher in the minor leagues, the expectations for big-league arrival are accelerated. Hedges is on track to debut in San Diego this year based on his glove-work alone. It truly is his glove-work alone, though: He hit .225/.268/.321 line in his first full exposure to Double-A, where his approach unraveled and pitchers challenged him with impunity. He has shown good strike-zone judgment, a balanced swing and plenty of strength in the past, so some offensive development isn't out of the question, but Hedges' impact will almost certainly be limited to what he does behind the plate.

24. David Dahl, OF, Colorado Rockies

After missing much of 2013 due to injury and some disciplinary issues (neither of which poses any concern moving forward), Dahl slid into the full-season routine this summer with nary a missed step, showcasing true five-tool talent and an impressive combination of athleticism and baseball acumen. There is work to be done smoothing out the reads and routes in the outfield,

as well as the overall approach at the plate, but many of these concerns should abate with continued reps, leaving the talented center fielder poised to emerge as an elite talent.

25. Aaron Sanchez, RHP, Toronto Blue Jays

After starting the year in Double-A, Sanchez climbed to the major leagues and spent the latter part of the season in Toronto's bullpen. He generates easy fastball velocity that can reach elite levels out of the bullpen with generous arm-side life. His low-80s curveball flashes late, hard bite and projects as at least a plus offering. Sanchez has made strides with the changeup, and though he rarely used it out of the bullpen the pitch flashes above-average potential. Though his ultimate role has yet to be determined, the talented righty has the requisite stuff to impact a staff in either capacity.

26. Jameson Taillon, RHP, Pittsburgh Pirates

Though Taillon missed the entire season after Tommy John surgery and still hasn't thrown off a mound as the book goes to press, signs point toward a healthy return heading into the 2015 season. He offers a four-pitch arsenal and potentially dominant stuff, and was inching close to a major-league debut before Dr. Altchek cut him open. Development is rarely linear, but Taillon will be looking to prove good health this spring before reminding everybody why he was (and is) one of the premier pitching talents in the minors.

27. Raul Mondesi, SS, Kansas City Royals

Last year's Top 101 stated that "it might take some time for [Mondesi's] numbers to catch up with the scouting," and so it remains. He started the year like a house on fire before turning into ash in May and June. He recovered toward season's end, curtailing his free-swinging ways in favor of a more patient approach. His plus-plus bat speed allows him to generate thump despite a frame that's more lithe than powerful. That pop is more evident from the left side, but hard contact is a constant from either side of the plate. He's a good defender who projects to average or better tools across the board, a valuable skill set in an up-the-middle package.

28. Kohl Stewart, RHP, Minnesota Twins

Shoulder impingement, we abhor thee. Any time a pitcher's name is mentioned alongside the word "shoulder," sirens should start going off. The good news is that Stewart required no surgery and he should resume a full workload at High-A. An excellent athlete and former Division I quarterback recruit, he features repeatable mechanics and plus fastball life. Backing up a low-to-mid-90s heater with a potential plus slider, average curve and feel for a changeup, the ceiling is way up there.

29. Chi Chi Gonzalez, RHP, Texas Rangers

The consistently underrated Gonzalez has done nothing but impress since being drafted late in the first round in 2013. It all starts with a fastball that he can cut and sink, and that he learned to command better over the course of the season. There's no wow pitch in the package, but he can miss bats from either side of the plate with his hard slider and developing change, both of which could be plus in time. Gonzalez might not face adversity until he reaches The Show, which could happen in the second half.

30. A.J Cole, RHP, Washington Nationals

It's been almost five years since Cole was drafted, and four since he first appeared on a BP Top 101, but he continues to make steady progress. He pounds the strike zone with an effortless mid-90s fastball, spotting the pitch on either side of the plate while mixing in two average-or-better secondaries. The command could still use refinement and the slider still needs to find a shape if he's to reach his mid-rotation upside. He handled Triple-A in 2014 and has logged at least 25 starts in each of the past three seasons, so he'll eat major-league innings soon.

31. Jorge Alfaro, C, Texas Rangers

The tools have been legendary since he was an 18-year-old in the Northwest League, and slowly and steadily Alfaro has harnessed those tools. Gifted with a plus-plus arm that makes scouts recalibrate their stopwatches, Alfaro also has the athleticism to project to above-average defense behind the plate. Perhaps more impressive is what he does at the plate, where he boasts 70 raw power and potential to regularly knock 25-plus homers. Catchers this dynamic are as rare in today's game as they were in previous eras, and it might be some time before we see this collection of tools and upside in a backstop again.

32. Stephen Piscotty, OF, St. Louis Cardinals

Regular hard contact is a fixture in Piscotty's game, and his ability to rack up extra bases, be it by home run or double, will determine whether he reaches his first-division upside. The former Stanford Cardinal has the raw strength to drive the ball, but merely average bat speed will place increased importance on continued refinement of his approach. He must learn which situations allow for added length and leverage in the swing. His feel for the craft and a professional approach should aid Piscotty in making the requisite adjustments as he finishes baking in the majors.

33. Steven Matz, LHP, New York Mets

The southpaw from Long Island finally showed he could stay on the mound for a full season and saw his prospect status go through the roof. Drafted in the second round in 2009, he threw more innings in 2014 than he had in his entire career up to that point. He remains a health risk (with Tommy John already on his resume) and he needs to work on sharpening his command and working down in the zone, but three potential plus pitches from the left-hand side and Double-A success breed excitement.

34. Daniel Norris, LHP, Toronto Blue Jays

Norris flew through three minor-league levels before making five appearances in the majors in September. The 21-year-old showcased a quality four-pitch mix at every stop, including a plus fastball/slider combination, a changeup that shows at least above-average potential and an average curveball that can change sightlines. The 2011 second-rounder showcased much better strike-throwing ability in 2014 and projects to have an average command/control profile, though the 6-foot-2, 180-pound lefty throws across his body and falls off significantly toward third base. He projects as a solid no. 3 starter and is nearly major-league ready.

35. Mark Appel, RHP, Houston Astros

A year after being selected first overall by the Astros, Appel remains an enigma. With a durable 6-foot-5, 225-pound frame and a relatively clean delivery, the Stanford product looks the part of a front-end innings eater, and at his best he flashes a double-plus fastball and a plus slider and changeup that can make hitters on either side of the plate look foolish. The command is often loose and the stuff has a tendency to play down, with the results not always backing the arsenal and some evaluators questioning the ultimate upside. The quality of the repertoire gives him a high floor and he should be in line for a Houston debut in the near future.

36. J.P. Crawford, SS, Philadelphia Phillies

Crawford marries an exciting ceiling with a high floor. There are very few questions about his ability to remain at shortstop, and thus near certainty that he'll be a big leaguer. He doesn't offer the power projection of some of the top shortstop prospects in the game, but he also doesn't have massive strikeout numbers burning a hole through his hit tool. Crawford still needs some polish, but his flaws are far from glaring and he's handled the Phillies' aggressive promotions with aplomb thus far. He should continue to be pushed this season.

37. Andrew Heaney, LHP, Los Angeles Angels

The former Marlin (and Dodger for a half-hour) should snag a rotation spot with the Angels this season. Heaney had moved quickly through Miami system, failing to find a challenge at any minor-league level before finally scuffling in the majors. He profiles as a mid-rotation starter whose fastball/slider combination could carry him into a no. 2 role. There's not much left for Heaney in the minors, and there's little reason to believe that his struggles will carry over. He's as major-league ready as pitching prospects come and should benefit from the Angels' pitcher-friendly ballpark.

38. Albert Almora, OF, Chicago Cubs

Almora is a complicated assortment of high-level baseball skills, natural ability and unrefined approach that has thus far resulted in uneven offensive production through his first two full seasons of pro ball. There is solid foundational value built into the profile, however, with the 20-year-old providing plus defense up the middle and serving as an asset on the bases. While there's work to be done on his approach, the bat-to-ball is top shelf, allowing Almora to post elite contact rates that should buoy the hit tool moving forward.

39. Tim Anderson, SS, Chicago White Sox

Potential drips off this former first-rounder and puddles at his feet. Be patient with him, as he has fewer baseball reps than most do at his stage of development, but the tools are loud: Plus-plus run, potential plus hit tool wrapped up with some pop and dynamic athleticism offer mountainous upside. It'll fit at an up-the-middle position, more likely second base or center field than shortstop. This is one of the most naturally gifted players in the minor leagues, and Double-A will present an interesting challenge for his skill set.

40. Nomar Mazara, OF, Texas Rangers

Before A.J. Preller was San Diego's GM, he was the international scouting savant who gave Mazara $4.95 million in 2011; at the time, it was the largest amateur signing bonus ever. Mazara struggled in his full-season debut in 2013, but after making mechanical adjustments, he took off in 2014, reaching Double-A as a teenager. A prototypical right-fielder, his presence looms large on both sides of the ball, with a plus arm and power potential to match. A plus work ethic and above-average hit tool could make him truly special.

41. Carlos Rodon, LHP, Chicago White Sox

Just a few months into his pro career—during which he struck out 14 batters per nine while reaching Triple-A—and Rodon is already suffering from prospect fatigue. Despite one of the game's best sliders, an electric fastball and precocious feel for his changeup, Rodon reached Peak Prospect back in college and has since left scouts wanting to see more refinement. In the prospect world, staying the same can be viewed as taking a step backward, but Rodon could have a chance to impress anew with a big-league debut this year.

42. Dalton Pompey, OF, Toronto Blue Jays

Pompey is an impressive athlete who shows plus speed and instinctive routes in center field, utilizing an above-average arm to keep runners honest. He wields a line-drive stroke with above-average bat speed, particularly from the left side, controlling the zone well and projecting for low-teens home run output with plenty of gap power. The former 16th-round pick jumped from High-A to the majors in 2014, making enough progress at the plate that he should be an above-average regular in short order.

43. Aaron Blair, RHP, Arizona Diamondbacks

Blair's deception, size and ability to create a sharp plane in spite of a low three-quarters slot proved too much for low-minors bats this summer, especially once the Marshall University product was able to tap into his two-plane breaker with regularity. He releases each of his offerings with uniformity, and the well-shielded release complicates hitters' ability to pick up the secondaries. The improved consistency of the curve has given Blair a vertical weapon to pair with his already solid fastball/changeup combo. If the command tightens enough to avoid regular mistakes up in the zone, he could flirt with no. 2 status.

44. Jesse Winker, OF, Cincinnati Reds

Winker is a polarizing prospect with a bat-first profile. He has a feel for the barrel but less-than-impactful bat speed and some issues identifying soft stuff. The whiff rates have thus far exceeded what one would expect from a player with an advanced approach and a comfortable and loving relationship with the strike zone, but supporters note Winker's strong work ethic at the professional level and count as a given that he will put in the requisite time and effort to continue making adjustments as he progresses toward Cincy.

45. Raimel Tapia, OF, Colorado Rockies

Tapia utilizes an unconventional set-up, variable swing and innate ability to find the ball with the barrel regardless of quadrant or pitch type, producing one of the most interesting hit tools in the minors. The native Dominican possesses natural bat speed and hand-eye coordination, with steady balance throughout his swing serving as the foundation for regular impactful barrel delivery. Tapia lacks the same level of feel on the defensive side, though his foot speed and arm could make for average or better production in center or right with continued work.

46. Henry Owens, LHP, Boston Red Sox

Much has been made of Owens' ascent through the Red Sox system, and while expectations seem to be trending toward frontline starter, it is far more likely Owens settles in as a mid-rotation arm. Owens' changeup is a standout pitch that earns easy plus grades, and it helps his average fastball play to a slightly more impressive level. Owens is continuing to develop both his curveball and command, two items that will need to step forward if he is to cement himself as a no. 3 starter; if he does, it could happen as early as the second half of this year.

47. Jake Thompson, RHP, Texas Rangers

A second-rounder in 2012, Thompson returned home to Texas in the Joakim Soria trade and continued posting big strikeout totals, microscopic home run rates and an ERA in the low 3s. He's big-bodied and holds his velocity extremely well throughout his starts, but it's the slider that will launch a thousand GIFs. With eight starts already at Double-A, Thompson could force his way to Arlington before 2015 is over.

48. Jose Berrios, RHP, Minnesota Twins

The word is "electric." Berrios took huge strides in 2014 and has put himself in position for a late-2015 arrival. As is said about many slight hurlers who have success at the lower levels, the 6-foot Dominican must show the requisite durability for a 200-inning role and continue to hold his velocity late in games. The stuff isn't in question: Berrios' three-pitch mix, including a filthy hard slider that sets him apart, is comparable to any in the minors today.

49. Aaron Judge, OF, New York Yankees

The first thing you notice about Judge is his massive size, but watching him reveals a portfolio of skills that go deeper. He doesn't have many of the same flaws that plague other behemoths, moving extremely well for his size and pretty well even for humans of normal dimensions. He keeps his swing as short as his long arms will allow. In right field, he's presently an average defender, aided by a strong, accurate arm that can be a true asset. He will hit for above-average power without even trying; he knows this and chooses not to sell out for power, lifting the entire offensive approach. The result is an advanced hitter who could jump from High-A to the majors within the year.

50. Hunter Renfroe, OF, San Diego Padres

The club's top pick in the 2013 draft, Renfroe is part of an increasingly rare group of prospects in the minor leagues with legitimate 70-grade raw power and the potential to post 25-plus home runs annually at his peak. Renfroe clearly needs refinement at the plate, and the degree to which his power plays in game situations will ultimately depend on how his approach develops and how he handles quality spin. If everything comes together, Renfroe could become a prototypical right-field bat with solid defense and a powerful arm.

51. Luis Severino, RHP, New York Yankees

Severino's fastball has the potential to be an elite pitch, and when paired with a potential plus changeup, he generates the swinging strikes that make scouts drool. Many of those evaluators are split, however, on whether or not he will be able to remain a starter given his build and lack of a third pitch. It's far too early for the Yankees to have to make that decision; for now, he's simply the most exciting arm in the system, categories be damned. He'll continue to start and should spend most of the season in Double-A. Regardless of his role, Severino has a big-league arm with impact potential.

52. Marco Gonzales, LHP, St. Louis Cardinals

Gonzales took his share of knocks during a 2014 cup of coffee, but generally impressed both as a starter and out of the 'pen. Despite lacking an impact breaking ball, the former Gonzaga Bulldog has been able to keep left- and right-handed hitters alike at bay thanks to advanced feel and a prime change piece. He'll have the opportunity to compete for a spot in the St. Louis rotation to start 2015, but with the Cardinals' robust collection of starters returning the lefty could be forced to the bullpen or back down to Memphis to begin the season.

53. Matt Wisler, RHP, San Diego Padres

Wisler didn't dominate in 2014, but maintains no. 3 upside and at a minimum should help in the back of a big-league rotation. He has enough fastball to avoid being labeled a finesse right-hander, and is at his best when he's filling up the bottom of the zone with the lively heater and secondaries. The slider earns some plus scores from scouts, giving him a pitch that can miss bats and induce weak contact, and the changeup might prove his most useful offering, flashing late fade and deception. Wisler is a good bet to settle in as a solid no. 4 starter and with some incremental improvements could reach his mid-rotation ceiling.

54. Lucas Sims, RHP, Atlanta Braves

Don't be scared off by a less-than-impressive stat line from 2014, as Sims still showed all the potential of a major-league starter. He shows the promise of three plus pitches, though command jumps are needed across the set. The most important developmental need, as it is with most young pitchers, is fastball command. Still, he's handled a workload that few pitchers his age can take on and he did so while maintaining a live arm all season. A few steps forward here and there and Sims will take off.

55. Alex Reyes, RHP, St. Louis Cardinals

Reyes disappointed early in the year, arriving in the Midwest League with a bulky lower half and a jarring inability to repeat his mechanics and execute with any regularity. The young power arm self-corrected as the season progressed, crescendoing in his final 11 starts as he blended top-shelf swing-and-miss stuff with drastically improved control. Had that caliber of performance carried his entire 2014 season there would be a strong case for his ranking some 20 spots higher on this list. This is a potential front-end arm who will be on the way to elite status with improved conditioning and a sharper focus on game prep and execution.

56. Miguel Almonte, RHP, Kansas City Royals

You rarely hear "fluid" mentioned this often outside of medical recovery scenarios, but Almonte's smooth, effortless delivery elicits the same assessment time and again. The ease with which he throws belies a mid-90s fastball that he carries deep into games. His changeup is a major league-quality offering that features more fade than Patrick Ewing circa 1994. The curve lags at present but has shown considerable development already and projects to be an average third offering. Despite not lighting up A-Ball, Almonte is ready for the rigors of the upper minors.

57. Michael Taylor, OF, Washington Nationals

After two years marinating quietly in High-A, Taylor sizzled in Double-A Harrisburg, flashing impact tools across the board. Propelled throughout his career by his toolsy athleticism, he finally lessened the noise in his swing, turning his plus bat speed and raw power into production. His defense alone provides a second-division floor in the majors, but the bat now gives hope for much more. A bit more contact, and a bit more *hard* contact, will make him a first-division center fielder.

58. Josh Bell, OF, Pittsburgh Pirates

Bell had his second (mostly) healthy season, putting the knee injury that cost him almost all of 2012 further in the rear view. He had been making up quickly for the lost time until reaching Double-A Altoona, where his power disappeared over 102 plate appearances. The physically mature outfielder has plenty of raw tools, including plus power and an arm that's plenty strong enough for right field. His swing has noise from both sides of the plate, which will need to be quieted before he consistently taps into his tools. The Pirates sent him to the AFL with instructions to play first base, which increases his flexibility moving forward but limits the value of his arm.

59. Reese McGuire, C, Pittsburgh Pirates

McGuire is such a talented defensive catcher that some writer is probably already working on a "future major-league manager" profile about him. His polished receiving skills are paired with athletic movements behind the plate and a strong arm, which gunned down 39 percent of attempted basestealers. There were, and will be, hiccups at the plate, but the underlying skills are enough to expect a competent hitter in the long term: barrel feel, good bat speed. The defense creates a very high floor, but he'll look to prove his value isn't entirely tied to what he does *behind* the plate.

60. Aaron Nola, RHP, Philadelphia Phillies

Perhaps the most major league-ready arm in the 2014 draft, Nola was in Double-A within two months of draft day. The results were reassuring, as Nola handled advanced batters with the same alacrity he had in the SEC. His advanced skills make up for a moderate ceiling as a mid-rotation starter. His biggest strength is his ability to throw strikes at an elite level, but his future will depend on the development of at least one of his off-speed offerings as a legitimate weapon to keep hitters honest.

61. Manuel Margot, OF, Boston Red Sox

The Dominican center fielder's fast-twitch athleticism was on full display during his time split between Low-A Greenville and High-A Salem. He pairs loose hands and strong barrel skills with above-average bat speed and surprising pop. His strong defensive instincts suggests enough talent to provide impact with his glove at an up-the-middle position. The raw tools are not quite refined, but the skill set is one that carries tremendous value at full potential.

62. D.J. Peterson, 3B, Seattle Mariners

Eventually Peterson will be forced to the other side of the diamond by his limited quickness and poor range, so he will need to really slug if he's to maintain his prospect status. The 12th pick in the 2013 draft has the potential to develop into a plus hitter with plus power, and the gains should happen rapidly thanks to his solid approach and college experience. He already passed the Double-A test, showing a knack for hard contact to all fields and substantial in-game power.

63. Michael Lorenzen, RHP, Cincinnati Reds

It was a hugely successful summer for the one-time two-way standout, as Lorenzen showed he could hold his own as a starter while sprinkling in flashes of dominance. The big question is whether the strong-armed righty will be able to build up the arm and the body to the point that he consistently delivers his power arsenal later into starts, and more importantly later into the season. If more conservative pacing causes the stuff to tick down, it's still a solid no. 4 starter profile, with a fallback in high-leverage relief.

64. Eddie Butler, RHP, Colorado Rockies

After breaking out with a dominant 2013, Butler struggled through much of 2014 due to shoulder issues and discomfort with mechanical tweaks. At his best, the lanky righty wields a mid-to-upper-90s heater with multiple looks and lots of weight, and a plus or better change piece that aids in keeping balls off barrels and on the ground. If questions about Butler's ability to hold up to a major-league starter's workload prove valid, the Radford product could thrive in a late-innings role pounding the bottom of the strike zone with his heavy fastball/changeup pairing.

65. Eduardo Rodriguez, LHP, Boston Red Sox

The Venezuelan lefty dominated the Eastern League after Boston acquired him in the Andrew Miller trade. Rodriguez sits comfortably in the low 90s but topped out at 96 a few times down the stretch. While the delivery is smooth and repeatable, the inconsistencies with the command, velocity and secondary arsenal are all areas for improvement if Rodriguez is to hit his mid-rotation ceiling. At his best, he flashes three above-average pitches and could be capable of working through a major-league lineup as early as this season.

66. Daniel Robertson, SS, Oakland Athletics

There was a brief moment, in between the Addison Russell and Josh Donaldson trades, when Robertson was the "shortstop of the future" for the Athletics. It was a tenuous title at best given his lack of lateral quickness, though his heady play and soft hands should work well at either the keystone or the hot corner if he can't stick at the six-spot. At the plate Robertson has solid contact skills that play up thanks to an advanced approach, and fringe power that could be major-league average at his peak.

67. Nick Kingham, RHP, Pittsburgh Pirates

Kingham projects to be a workhorse who can eat innings in the middle or back of a rotation. The 6-foot-5 righty has good mechanics for somebody of his size, leading to above-average control and, when he's on, the ability to effortlessly command his fastball on both sides of the plate. That, combined with his poise on the mound, makes for a pitchability profile, though he'll need to improve his changeup to make it all work. There's no out pitch in his repertoire, and his strikeout rates were worse than his leagues' averages last year, but he should see time in the majors this season.

68. Alex Jackson, OF, Seattle Mariners

The Mariners moved the 2014 first-rounder to the outfield permanently, rather than even attempt to develop him as a backstop, but Jackson's offensive potential is so vast that he still maintains his status as a very good prospect. Indeed, the simpler development path of an outfield prospect could help ensure that his offensive game flourishes. While evaluators are divided as to quality of the approach and ultimate contact ability, Jackson is roundly lauded for his 60- to 70-grade raw power, which can already flash in games. Through reps and instruction he could eventually develop into a dominant force in the middle of a major-league lineup.

69. Brandon Nimmo, OF, New York Mets

The Wyoming native's prospect package leaves plenty of room for doubt, but the weight of his overall tools still makes him an extremely strong prospect. He might not be a center fielder in the long term, but he could be an easy plus defender in a corner. Even without the strongest hit tool, but can get on base via a strong approach, and he flashes above-average power potential. More of the focus should be on what he can do, and Nimmo can do almost everything.

70. Nick Gordon, SS, Minnesota Twins

The top prep hitter in the 2014 draft, Gordon's great makeup and high baseball IQ—Did you know he has family who played in the majors? Totally new fact!—have given scouts reason to believe he's got an excellent chance to be a first-division big leaguer, or a tick more. While the tools are more solid-average across the board than impact, he's a "sum of his parts" prospect who could play a premium position for a decade and contribute in all facets of the game.

71. Nick Williams, OF, Texas Rangers

Williams' ceiling is immense due to an aesthetically pleasing left-handed swing built for power and grace. Yet the approach is about two steps away from qualifying even as rudimentary. (At least his OBP gets a boost from plentiful HBPs.) In order to reach his ultimate ceiling, Williams needs to get himself into better hitting counts and find a way to be a non-liability in the field. Even if he never develops that baseball acumen or focus, he'll hit some big-league pitches a long way.

72. Reynaldo Lopez, RHP, Washington Nationals

The Dominican flamethrower entered the season with five stateside innings and virtually no prospect profile, but he dominated two levels of the low minors. Beyond leading all Sally League starters in ERA (he was second in the New York-Penn League), he had scouts raving about his elite fastball, a mid-90s pitch with heavy sink and late life. The command isn't always there, but he has the physical foundation to suggest it will come. It's a very long trek from Hagerstown to the majors, but Lopez displayed enough to forecast an impact arm who could front a rotation if everything breaks right.

73. Jeff Hoffman, RHP, Toronto Blue Jays

Hoffman emerged as a legitimate 1:1 candidate early last spring before Tommy John surgery in May caused him to fall to the ninth overall pick. Prior to the injury, Hoffman flashed a double-plus fastball, sitting comfortably in the mid-90s with arm-side life and sink. His secondary arsenal features a changeup and a hard curveball that flash at least plus potential, sometimes higher. The 6-foot-4, 185-pound East Carolina product is a lithe athlete, utilizing a drop-and-drive delivery with plenty of momentum throughout. He has a track record of throwing strikes and could have a plus command profile at the end of the day, giving him the ceiling of frontline starter if his arm recovers to full strength.

74. Franklin Barreto, SS, Oakland Athletics

While the diminutive Barreto stands just 5-feet-9, he packs a punch at a physically maxed-out 175 pounds. Despite the solid frame, he isn't thick, and maintains plus speed on the basepaths and in the field. At the plate he features a swing smoother than your cool uncle and bat-to-ball skills significantly more natural than your uncle's second wife. He could see double-digit home runs in his prime thanks to a fluid, powerful weight transfer. Barreto has yet to reach full-season ball, but he has drawn plus hit-tool grades from scouts, and is known to be a hard worker.

75. Vincent Velasquez, RHP, Houston Astros

A groin injury sidelined him for two months, but Velasquez showcased bat-missing stuff across 64 innings in the California League. The broad, athletic Californian possesses a fastball that comfortably works in the mid-90s to go along with a swing-and-miss changeup, a true plus offering. His curveball is inconsistent but flashes average, giving him three pitches he can throw for strikes with a solid command/control profile. He will likely begin the 2015 season in Double-A, giving him a legitimate shot at an extended look by 2016, with health being the most important caveat.

76. Kyle Freeland, LHP, Colorado Rockies

Freeland easily overmatched collegiate competition and low-minors bats alike in 2014 and could ascend quickly through the minor-league ranks. The southpaw is distinctive for the chameleonic manner in which he wields his three-pitch arsenal: He can give different looks or vary the cut and sink of the pitches, effectively turning the three pitches into seven, covering a velocity band that stretches cleanly from the low 80s to the mid-90s. Provided Freeland can maintain that quality of stuff over a long pro season, the former Purple Ace should provide an impressive left-handed complement to power righties Jonathan Gray and Eddie Butler, perhaps as early as 2016.

77. Kyle Schwarber, C/OF, Chicago Cubs

The former Hoosier had little trouble raking through three levels of A-Ball, slashing .344/.428/.560 over his first 311 pro plate appearances (60 percent of which came in the pitcher-friendly Florida State League). The true test will come in 2015 when Schwarber gets his first taste of advanced pro arms on both sides of the ball. If the 2014 first-rounder can prove capable of handling even a 60-game workload behind the dish while otherwise providing passable defense in left field he could become an immensely valuable asset for Chicago, be it in the lineup or as a trade chip.

78. Amed Rosario, SS, New York Mets

He is still years away from reaching it, but Rosario's future has more upside than any position prospect in the Mets' system, and it starts with his glove. A strong bet to stay at shortstop, he could develop into a plus defender in time due to his high baseball IQ and fluid actions, though he's getting by on pure athleticism right now. At the plate, he shows a strong aptitude for contact and the foundation for average power projection, but he is overly aggressive and will chase. It will be a slow burn, but one with a possible All-Star payoff.

79. Grant Holmes, RHP, Los Angeles Dodgers

A last name isn't the only thing connecting Grant with John, given the former's X-rated breaking ball. Holmes' power curve generated rave reviews on top of copious whiffs and ranked as one of the best among prep products in the 2014 draft class. He's not a one-trick pony, as his long arm action begets a fastball that sits in the mid-90s and can touch 98, along with a developing changeup that flashes above-average potential. His growth will have to come from improved command and sequencing, as there isn't much projection in his 6-foot-1, 215-pound frame.

80. Kevin Plawecki, C, New York Mets

There's nothing overly exciting about Plawecki's game—he's the vanilla of catching prospects—but this downplays the delectability of said flavor. Four average tools (he's not going to be a threat on the basepaths) from a catcher is extremely valuable, and there's a chance he could bring that hit tool up over time. He's a grinder in all aspects of the game, and a tough out, which likely endear him to fans and members of the media alike.

81. Billy McKinney, OF, Chicago Cubs

McKinney drew mixed reviews from scouts throughout the summer and during instructs, but supporters believe strongly in the hit tool and on-base skill set. As he ascends to the Southern League in 2015, more advanced sequencing and consistent execution could expose some coverage blips on the 21-year-old's inner half. But with a preternatural feel for both the barrel and the strike zone, there's good reason to bet on the sweet-swinging lefty making the necessary adjustments. Incremental developments on the power front could solidify McKinney as one of the minors' top corner bats, with some already putting him on par with Jesse Winker.

82. Dilson Herrera, 2B, New York Mets

The undersized second baseman flew through the Mets' system in 2014 before arriving in August as the youngest player in the majors, and even held his own with a .255 TAv in 18 games for the Metropolitans. Last season's success might lead to unrealistic short-term expectations for Herrera, who will too willingly chase breaking balls and who still needs to slow down the game on defense. Another year of development wouldn't hurt, which matches nicely with Daniel Murphy's impending free agency this winter.

83. Pierce Johnson, RHP, Chicago Cubs

After struggling with his mechanics early in 2014, Johnson found his stride in the second half, putting together 65 highly impressive innings over his final 12 starts. The key to unlocking a future spot in the Cubs rotation will be continued growth in his command profile and more consistency working the lower "U" of the strike zone with the heater. The Missouri State product should get significant exposure to Triple-A bats over the course of next summer, with a focus on staying healthy, logging innings and finding consistency in execution.

84. Francisco Mejia, C, Cleveland Indians

Mejia is a switch-hitting catcher with feel for the barrel and solid-average defensive chops, a profile that produces less risk than you'd typically associate with a 19-year-old in short-season ball. The Dominican signee could rank significantly higher on the 2016 list if his ultra-aggressive approach proves not to be a liability against Midwest League pitching, and if he continues to refine his receiving behind the plate. The raw skills jump off the field, but patience is key, as catchers typically take longer to develop. There will be some bumps ahead, but Mejia offers All-Star upside at a premium defensive position.

85. Sean Manaea, LHP, Kansas City Royals

Manaea faced an adjustment period in High-A before taking command of the reins over the final three months of the season, as he simplified his delivery and was able to better limit the inconsistencies in his control and execution. Manipulation and deception feature into every facet of Manaea's game, as his ideal pitcher's frame (6-feet-5, 235 pounds) and slight crossfire delivery allow him to hide the ball until the last possible frame. His fastball features sink or run, depending on grip and velocity band, and his slider and change can both flash above-average with bat-missing ability. He could be a fast mover if he can hold his mechanics together.

86. Adalberto Mejia, RHP, San Francisco Giants

Arguably the most polished of the high-profile arms in the Giants system, Mejia has the fine skills to make his impressive arsenal play against advanced competition. Armed with a low-90s fastball from the left side, Mejia can induce plenty of weak contact just by mixing his two-seam and four-seam fastballs. Mejia's slider and changeup earn unanimous praise from scouts, with opinions divided as to which will settle as the most effective secondary. The promising lefty will miss developmental time in 2015 due to a 50-game suspension for a drug violation. Once back in the fold, Mejia should continue his progression toward San Francisco and could settle in as a no. 3 starter in short order.

87. Brandon Finnegan, LHP, Kansas City Royals

Finnegan was introduced to the world as a reliever, and that's a role many think he's destined for long term. Still, the only player to ever appear in the College and Major League World Series in the same season has the pure arsenal to hang as starter, provided he can maintain the quality of stuff through his second and third spins through the lineup. Despite a stocky 5-foot-11, 185-pound frame, Finnegan creates downhill plane from a high-three-quarters arm slot, and while his delivery features effort he repeats it well. His unproven durability is the only obstacle standing between him and a major-league rotation, but at present that obstacle looms large.

88. Kyle Crick, RHP, San Francisco Giants

Crick represents the latest in a long line of high-end pitching prospects to pass through the Giants system, and while he offers extreme upside he also carries more risk than the typical high-minors arm. Crick's profile is headlined by a near-elite fastball that explodes on hitters and can be difficult to square. Both his breaking ball and changeup flash at an above-average level, but neither consistently shows in that range. Many scouts believe Crick is destined for the bullpen because of his lack of control,

though some believe he can survive in a rotation thanks to his electric stuff alone.

89. Clint Frazier, OF, Cleveland Indians

Frazier puts on a batting practice display like few others in the lower levels. He has preposterous wrists and power-lifter hand strength, which he uses to lift balls deep into or over the bleachers in left-center field. The hit tool and approach each need to take steps forward; otherwise, he'll suffer after breaking balls down and away as so many disappointing prospects before him have. Whether he sticks in center is not an existential issue, as the power and secondary skills could carry a corner.

90. Rafael Devers, 3B, Boston Red Sox

One of the prize signings of the 2013 J2 class, Devers commanded a bonus of $1.5 million that already looks like a bargain. The third baseman has quickly made a name for himself at the plate, drawing raves from evaluators for his effortless bat speed and a hit/power package that few in the minors match. With a physically maxed-out body, his defense needs to improve at the hot corner, particularly in his lateral quickness. But if the bat keeps coming it won't matter which position Devers plays; even a player with no defensive utility can provide elite value, as all Bostonians know.

91. Lewis Thorpe, LHP, Minnesota Twins

Thorpe rounded out the Top 101 last offseason, with his projectable build, loose delivery and versatile arsenal providing fertile ground for the development of an impact lefty starter. Through 72 Low-A innings across 16 starts this year, the teenaged Aussie saw an uptick in velocity to the 91-to-94 mph range, as well as further growth across his full complement of secondaries. Having gained firm developmental traction over the past 12 months, the southpaw can now set his sights on a true breakout this summer, likely to be split between Low- and High-A.

92. Jose Peraza, 2B, Atlanta Braves

To get away with having virtually no power, a prospect typically needs to have near-elite speed, as Peraza does. He embraces his small-ball role and makes contact at an incredibly high rate, giving his legs a chance to help get him on base. That speed, coupled with plus defense at second base, gives him a chance to be a valuable everyday player even if he never produces double-digit home run totals. Peraza handled Double-A last season without missing a beat, and should head straight to Triple-A to begin the 2015 season; from there, he could top the Braves' depth chart by this time next year.

93. Orlando Arcia, SS, Milwaukee Brewers

Arcia has established a profile with a firm foundational value thanks to a major league-quality glove at a high-worth position and advanced feel for the game on the bases. The approach at the plate is improving, and as he continues to add strength it will help his frequent contact become more productive. Ultimately, though, reining in his approach will most help Arcia push his offensive game from interesting to impactful. In the field, the Venezuela product continues to refine and should provide a steady presence at shortstop when his time comes.

94. Willy Adames, SS, Tampa Bay Rays

Acquired in the David Price trade, Adames performed well for two teams in his Midwest League debut. He has an easy, balanced swing that allows for at least average projections on both his hit and power tools. At 6-feet-1 and 180 pounds, he is an average runner at present but projects to get bigger down the line, though most believe he'll retain the ability to stick at shortstop. If he is forced to slide off the position eventually, he has the requisite arm strength to profile at third base. It's a solid all-around skill set at a premium position.

95. Hunter Dozier, 3B, Kansas City Royals

Grab your best Russian friend and take him to see Dozier, just so you can hear the phrase "strong like bull" as it's meant to be heard. His strength and tremendous hands enable him to barrel the ball with authority, though the swing plays more to doubles at present. While Dozier struggled upon his promotion to Double-A, the former first-rounder displays an understanding of how opposing pitchers work him and he should be able to make adjustments with further exposure. In the field he shows good mobility for his size and a strong arm, and shouldn't have any trouble sticking at the hot corner.

96. Maikel Franco, 3B, Philadelphia Phillies

Franco made his major-league debut last year and figures to get regular playing time at both infield corners in Philly this year. His natural bat-to-ball skills are near elite, but his aggressive approach gets him in trouble and leads to extremely streaky production, especially when he gets long with his swing. When he's on, he can carry an offense. How he responds to a healthy dose of major-league off-speed stuff will determine where on that streaky spectrum he spends the majority of his career. He has plenty of arm to handle third base and his range should be enough for a few years, though eventually he'll shift across the diamond.

97. Andrew Susac, C, San Francisco Giants

Often overlooked on the prospect scene, Susac nevertheless proved a welcome addition to the 2014 champions, affording the club the freedom to rest all-world backstop Buster Posey without ceding offensive production from the catcher position. While the former OSU Beaver is a capable receiver with enough catch-and-throw to keep baserunners honest, he makes his bones with above-average pop and a methodical approach at the plate, allowing for above-average on-base and power production out of a defensive spot traditionally light in both departments. There's first-division upside here, with a solid floor as an offensive-minded backup and bench bat.

98. Derek Hill, OF, Detroit Tigers

Premium defensive skills, plus-plus speed and natural hand-eye coordination make for a wonderful starting point. Hill's hit tool is a work in progress, but he often makes sharp contact and is already driving balls to the gaps. Over-the-fence power might never come, but even without that he could produce extreme value with his run-saving in center field and top-of-the-lineup skill set. The Tigers will be aggressive with the high-IQ prospect.

99. Nick Burdi, RHP, Minnesota Twins

With an upper-90s fastball that can pop triple digits on the Stalker, mid- to upper-80s wipeout slider and promising changeup, this 2014 draftee is already in possession of enough firepower to step into late-inning work and thrive in the majors. He'll need to refine aspects of his game, including improving his fastball command and picking better spots to elevate the heater, and evaluators would like to see him maintain his stuff better on back-to-back nights. Nevertheless, it shouldn't be long before Louisville's all-time saves leader starts making his case to rack up finishes in Minnesota.

100. Ryan McMahon, 3B, Colorado Rockies

McMahon's calling card is his raw power, which he comes by honestly thanks to good bat speed, solid strength and wrists capable of producing whip in the barrel. The approach is still loose and he remains particularly susceptible to same-side spin, but when McMahon is locked in and comfortable he comes by hard contact with ease and demonstrates an organic ability to use the whole field. While a thickening body carries with it the risk of limiting his actions at third, his overall athleticism and arm strength should allow him to stick at the five-spot.

101. Chance Sisco, C, Baltimore Orioles

The young catcher led the South Atlantic League in average and OBP in his full-season debut, and the 2013 second-rounder now has a .345 batting average in 600 pro at-bats. His swing is relaxed and easy, with minimal movement in the hands and a quick stroke through the zone. The early consensus is that the power will likely come once he adds strength and durability to his frame, though the developmental demands placed on young catchers could challenge his offensive growth. His receiving and blocking skills do not match his athleticism, and he allowed a whopping 95 stolen bases in 74 games last year.

Team Codes

CODE	TEAM	LEAGUE	AFFIL.	NAME
ABE	Aberdeen	NYP	Orioles	IronBirds
ABQ	Albuquerque	PCL	Dodgers	Isotopes
AKR	Akron	EAS	Indians	RubberDucks
ALT	Altoona	EAS	Pirates	Curve
ANA	Los Angeles	AL	-	Angels
ANG	AZL Angels	AZL	Angels	-
ARI	Arizona	NL	-	D-backs
ARK	Arkansas	TEX	Angels	Travelers
ART	Artemisa	CNS	-	
ASH	Asheville	SAL	Rockies	Tourists
AST	GCL Astros	GCL	Astros	GCL Astros
ATH	AZL Athletics	AZL	Athletics	-
ATL	Atlanta	NL	-	Braves
AUB	Auburn	NYP	Nationals	Doubledays
AUG	Augusta	SAL	Giants	GreenJackets
BAK	Bakersfield	CAL	Reds	Blaze
BAL	Baltimore	AL	-	Orioles
BAT	Batavia	NYP	Marlins	Muckdogs
BGR	Bowling Green	MID	Rays	Hot Rods
BIL	Billings	PIO	Reds	Mustangs
BIN	Binghamton	EAS	Mets	Mets
BIR	Birmingham	SOU	White Sox	Barons
BLJ	GCL Blue Jays	GCL	Blue Jays	GCL Blue Jays
BLT	Beloit	MID	Athletics	Snappers
BLU	Bluefield	APP	Blue Jays	Blue Jays
BNC	Burlington	APP	Royals	Royals
BOI	Boise	NOR	Cubs	Hawks
BOS	Boston	AL	-	Red Sox
BOW	Bowie	EAS	Orioles	Baysox
BRA	GCL Braves	GCL	Braves	GCL Braves
BRD	Bradenton	FSL	Pirates	Marauders
BRI	Bristol	APP	Pirates	Pirates
BRO	Brooklyn	NYP	Mets	Cyclones
BRR	AZL Brewers	AZL	Brewers	-
BRV	Brevard County	FSL	Brewers	Manatees
BUF	Buffalo	INT	Blue Jays	Bisons
BUR	Burlington	MID	Angels	Bees
CAR	Carolina	CAR	Indians	Mudcats
CCH	Corpus Christi	TEX	Astros	Hooks
CDR	Cedar Rapids	MID	Twins	Kernels
CFG	Cienfuegos	CNS	-	
CHA	Chicago	AL	-	White Sox
CHB	Chiba Lotte	NPB	-	Marines
CHN	Chicago	NL	-	Cubs
CHR	Charlotte	INT	White Sox	Knights
CHT	Chattanooga	SOU	Dodgers	Lookouts
CHU	Chunichi	NPB	-	Dragons
CIN	AZL Reds	AZL	Reds	-
CIN	Cincinnati	NL	-	Reds
CLE	AZL Indians	AZL	Indians	-

CODE	TEAM	LEAGUE	AFFIL.	NAME
CLE	Cleveland	AL	-	Indians
CLN	Clinton	MID	Mariners	LumberKings
CLR	Clearwater	FSL	Phillies	Threshers
COH	Columbus	INT	Indians	Clippers
COL	Colorado	NL	-	Rockies
CRD	GCL Cardinals	GCL	Cardinals	GCL Cardinals
CSC	Charleston	SAL	Yankees	RiverDogs
CSP	Colorado Springs	PCL	Rockies	Sky Sox
CUB	AZL Cubs	AZL	Cubs	-
DAN		DSL	Angels	
DAR		DSL	Astros	
DAS		DSL	Astros	
DAT		DSL	Athletics	
DAY	Daytona	FSL	Cubs	Cubs
DBA		DSL	Orioles	
DBL		DSL	Blue Jays	
DBR		DSL	Braves	
DBW		DSL	Brewers	
DCA		DSL	Cardinals	
DCU		DSL	Cubs	
DDI		DSL	D-backs	
DDO		DSL	Dodgers	
DDR		DSL	Rays	
DEL	Delmarva	SAL	Orioles	Shorebirds
DET	Detroit	AL	-	Tigers
DGI		DSL	Giants	
DIA	AZL D-backs	AZL	D-backs	-
DIN		DSL	Indians	
DME		DSL	Mets	
DML		DSL	Marlins	
DMR		DSL	Mariners	
DNV	Danville	APP	Braves	Braves
DOD	AZL Dodgers	AZL	Dodgers	-
DOR		DSL	Orioles	
DPA		DSL	Padres	
DPH		DSL	Phillies	
DPI		DSL	Pirates	
DPT		DSL	Pirates	
DRD		DSL	Reds	
DRG		DSL	Rangers	
DRJ		DSL	Reds	
DRO		DSL	Rockies	
DRS		DSL	Red Sox	
DRY		DSL	Royals	
DTI		DSL	Tigers	
DTW		DSL	Twins	
DUN	Dunedin	FSL	Blue Jays	Blue Jays
DUR	Durham	INT	Rays	Bulls
DWA		DSL	Nationals	

CODE	TEAM	LEAGUE	AFFIL.	NAME
DWS		DSL	White Sox	
DYA		DSL	Yankees	
DYN		DSL	Yankees	
DYT	Dayton	MID	Reds	Dragons
ELP	El Paso	PCL	Padres	Chihuahuas
ELZ	Elizabethton	APP	Twins	Twins
ERI	Erie	EAS	Tigers	SeaWolves
EUG	Eugene	NOR	Padres	Emeralds
EVE	Everett	NOR	Mariners	AquaSox
FKU	Fukuoka	NPB	-	Hawks
FRD	Frederick	CAR	Orioles	Keys
FRE	Fresno	PCL	Giants	Grizzlies
FRI	Frisco	TEX	Rangers	RoughRiders
FTM	Fort Myers	FSL	Twins	Miracle
FTW	Fort Wayne	MID	Padres	TinCaps
GIA	AZL Giants	AZL	Giants	-
GJR	Grand Junction	PIO	Rockies	Rockies
GRB	Greensboro	SAL	Marlins	Grasshoppers
GRF	Great Falls	PIO	White Sox	Voyagers
GRL	Great Lakes	MID	Dodgers	Loons
GRN	Greenville	SAL	Red Sox	Drive
GRV	Greeneville	APP	Astros	Astros
GWN	Gwinnett	INT	Braves	Braves
HAB	La Habana	CNS	-	
HAG	Hagerstown	SAL	Nationals	Suns
HAR	Harrisburg	EAS	Nationals	Senators
HDS	High Desert	CAL	Mariners	Mavericks
HEL	Helena	PIO	Brewers	Brewers
HIC	Hickory	SAL	Rangers	Crawdads
HNS	Hanshin	NPB	-	Tigers
HOU	Houston	AL	-	Astros
HRO	Hiroshima Toyo	NPB	-	Carp
HUD	Hudson Valley	NYP	Rays	Renegades
HUN	Huntsville	SOU	Brewers	Stars
IDA	Idaho Falls	PIO	Royals	Chukars
IND	Indianapolis	INT	Pirates	Indians
INL	Inland Empire	CAL	Angels	66ers
IOW	Iowa	PCL	Cubs	Cubs
JAM	Jamestown	NYP	Pirates	Jammers
JAX	Jacksonville	SOU	Marlins	Suns
JCY	Johnson City	APP	Cardinals	Cardinals
JUP	Jupiter	FSL	Marlins	Hammerheads
KAN	Kannapolis	SAL	White Sox	Intimidators
KCA	Kansas City	AL	-	Royals
KNC	Kane County	MID	Cubs	Cougars
KNG	Kingsport	APP	Mets	Mets
LAK	Lakeland	FSL	Tigers	Flying Tigers
LAN	Los Angeles	NL	-	Dodgers
LEH	Lehigh Valley	INT	Phillies	IronPigs
LEL	Lake Elsinore	CAL	Padres	Storm

CODE	TEAM	LEAGUE	AFFIL.	NAME
LEX	Lexington	SAL	Royals	Legends
LKC	Lake County	MID	Indians	Captains
LNC	Lancaster	CAL	Astros	JetHawks
LNS	Lansing	MID	Blue Jays	Lugnuts
LOU	Louisville	INT	Reds	Bats
LOW	Lowell	NYP	Red Sox	Spinners
LTU	Las Tunas	CNS	-	
LVG	Las Vegas	PCL	Mets	51s
LWD	Lakewood	SAL	Phillies	BlueClaws
LYN	Lynchburg	CAR	Braves	Hillcats
MEM	Memphis	PCL	Cardinals	Redbirds
MET		DSL	Mets	
MHV	Mahoning Valley	NYP	Indians	Scrappers
MIA	Miami	NL	-	Marlins
MID	Midland	TEX	Athletics	RockHounds
MIL	Milwaukee	NL	-	Brewers
MIN	Minnesota	AL	-	Twins
MIS	Mississippi	SOU	Braves	Braves
MNT	Montgomery	SOU	Rays	Biscuits
MOB	Mobile	SOU	D-backs	BayBears
MOD	Modesto	CAL	Rockies	Nuts
MRL	GCL Marlins	GCL	Marlins	GCL Marlins
MRN	AZL Mariners	AZL	Mariners	-
MSO	Missoula	PIO	D-backs	Osprey
MTS	GCL Mets	GCL	Mets	GCL Mets
MYR	Myrtle Beach	CAR	Rangers	Pelicans
NAS	Nashville	PCL	Brewers	Sounds
NAT	GCL Nationals	GCL	Nationals	GCL Nationals
NBR	New Britain	EAS	Twins	Rock Cats
NHP	New Hampshire	EAS	Blue Jays	Fisher Cats
NIP	Nippon Ham	NPB	-	Fighters
NOR	Norfolk	INT	Orioles	Tides
NWA	NW Arkansas	TEX	Royals	Naturals
NWO	New Orleans	PCL	Marlins	Zephyrs
NYA	New York	AL	-	Yankees
NYN	New York	NL	-	Mets
OAK	Oakland	AL	-	Athletics
OGD	Ogden	PIO	Dodgers	Raptors
OKL	Oklahoma City	PCL	Astros	RedHawks
OMA	Omaha	PCL	Royals	Storm Chasers
ONE	Connecticut	NYP	Tigers	Tigers
ORI	GCL Orioles	GCL	Orioles	GCL Orioles
ORM	Orem	PIO	Angels	Owlz
ORX	Orix	NPB	-	Buffaloes
PAW	Pawtucket	INT	Red Sox	Red Sox
PCH	Charlotte	FSL	Rays	Stone Crabs
PDR	AZL Padres	AZL	Padres	-
PEN	Pensacola	SOU	Reds	Blue Wahoos
PEO	Peoria	MID	Cardinals	Chiefs
PHI	Philadelphia	NL	-	Phillies
PHL	GCL Phillies	GCL	Phillies	GCL Phillies
PIR	GCL Pirates	GCL	Pirates	GCL Pirates
PIT	Pittsburgh	NL	-	Pirates
PMB	Palm Beach	FSL	Cardinals	Cardinals

CODE	TEAM	LEAGUE	AFFIL.	NAME
PME	Portland	EAS	Red Sox	Sea Dogs
POT	Potomac	CAR	Nationals	Nationals
PRI	Princeton	APP	Rays	Rays
PUL	Pulaski	APP	Mariners	Mariners
QUD	Quad Cities	MID	Astros	River Bandits
RAK	Rakuten	NPB	-	Golden Eagles
RAY	GCL Rays	GCL	Rays	GCL Rays
RCU	Rancho Cucamonga	CAL	Dodgers	Quakes
REA	Reading	EAS	Phillies	Fightin Phils
RIC	Richmond	EAS	Giants	Flying Squirrels
RNG	AZL Rangers	AZL	Rangers	-
RNO	Reno	PCL	D-backs	Aces
ROC	Rochester	INT	Twins	Red Wings
ROM	Rome	SAL	Braves	Braves
ROU	Round Rock	PCL	Rangers	Express
RSX	GCL Red Sox	GCL	Red Sox	GCL Red Sox
SAC	Sacramento	PCL	Athletics	River Cats
SAN	San Antonio	TEX	Padres	Missions
SAV	Savannah	SAL	Mets	Sand Gnats
SBN	South Bend	MID	D-backs	Silver Hawks
SCO	State College	NYP	Cardinals	Spikes
SDN	San Diego	NL	-	Padres
SEA	Seattle	AL	-	Mariners
SEI	Seibu	NPB	-	Lions
SFD	Springfield	TEX	Cardinals	Cardinals
SFN	San Francisco	NL	-	Giants
SJO	San Jose	CAL	Giants	Giants
SLC	Salt Lake	PCL	Angels	Bees
SLM	Salem	CAR	Red Sox	Red Sox
SLN	St. Louis	NL	-	Cardinals
SLO	Salem-Keizer	NOR	Giants	Volcanoes
SLU	St. Lucie	FSL	Mets	Mets
SPO	Spokane	NOR	Rangers	Indians
STA	Staten Island	NYP	Yankees	Yankees
STO	Stockton	CAL	Athletics	Ports
SWB	Scranton/WB	INT	Yankees	RailRiders
SYR	Syracuse	INT	Nationals	Chiefs
TAC	Tacoma	PCL	Mariners	Rainiers
TAM	Tampa	FSL	Yankees	Yankees
TBA	Tampa Bay	AL	-	Rays
TCV	Tri-City	NYP	Astros	ValleyCats
TEN	Tennessee	SOU	Cubs	Smokies
TEX	Texas	AL	-	Rangers
TGR	GCL Tigers	GCL	Tigers	GCL Tigers
TOL	Toledo	INT	Tigers	Mud Hens
TOR	Toronto	AL	-	Blue Jays
TRI	Tri-City	NOR	Rockies	Dust Devils
TRN	Trenton	EAS	Yankees	Thunder
TUL	Tulsa	TEX	Rockies	Drillers
TWI	GCL Twins	GCL	Twins	GCL Twins
VAN	Vancouver	NOR	Blue Jays	Canadians
VCU	VSL CHN	VSL	Cubs	VSL Cubs
VER	Vermont	NYP	Athletics	Lake Monsters

CODE	TEAM	LEAGUE	AFFIL.	NAME
VIS	Visalia	CAL	D-backs	Rawhide
VPH	VSL PHI	VSL	Phillies	VSL Phillies
VSE	VSL SEA	VSL	Mariners	VSL Mariners
VTB	VSL TB	VSL	Rays	VSL Rays
VTI	VSL DET	VSL	Tigers	VSL Tigers
WAS	Washington	NL	-	Nationals
WIL	Wilmington	CAR	Royals	Blue Rocks
WIS	Wisconsin	MID	Brewers	Timber Rattlers
WMI	West Michigan	MID	Tigers	Whitecaps
WNS	Winston-Salem	CAR	White Sox	Dash
WPT	Williamsport	NYP	Phillies	Crosscutters
WSX	AZL White Sox	AZL	White Sox	-
WTN	Jackson	SOU	Mariners	Generals
WVA	West Virginia	SAL	Pirates	Power
YAK	Hillsboro	NOR	D-backs	Hops
YAN	GCL Yankees1	GCL	Yankees	GCL Yankees
YAT	GCL Yankees2	GCL	Yankees	GCL Yankees2
YKL	Yakult	NPB	-	Swallows
YKO	Yokohama DeNA	NPB	-	BayStars
YOM	Yomiuri	NPB	-	Giants

PECOTA Leaderboards

Hitters

Home Runs

Rank	NAME	Team	HR
1	Jose Bautista	TOR	34
2	Giancarlo Stanton	MIA	33
3	Miguel Cabrera	DET	31
4	Chris Carter	HOU	27
5	Edwin Encarnacion	TOR	26
5	Nelson Cruz	SEA	26
5	Chris Davis	BAL	26
5	Josh Donaldson	TOR	26
5	Mike Trout	ANA	26
10	Albert Pujols	ANA	25
10	Brandon Moss	CLE	25
10	Evan Longoria	TBA	25
10	Anthony Rizzo	CHN	25
14	David Ortiz	BOS	24
14	Adam Jones	BAL	24
16	Yoenis Cespedes	DET	23
16	Jose Abreu	CHA	23
18	Adrian Beltre	TEX	22
18	Matt Kemp	LAN	22
18	Jay Bruce	CIN	22
18	Justin Upton	ATL	22
18	Todd Frazier	CIN	22
18	Paul Goldschmidt	ARI	22

Runs

Rank	NAME	Team	R
1	Mike Trout	ANA	106
2	Miguel Cabrera	DET	92
3	Jose Bautista	TOR	91
4	Carlos Gomez	MIL	87
5	Ian Kinsler	DET	84
5	Jacoby Ellsbury	NYA	84
5	Jose Altuve	HOU	84
5	Giancarlo Stanton	MIA	84
5	Yasiel Puig	LAN	84
10	Andrew McCutchen	PIT	83
10	Brian Dozier	MIN	83
12	Josh Donaldson	TOR	81
13	Evan Longoria	TBA	80
13	Matt Carpenter	SLN	80
15	Jason Heyward	SLN	79
16	Anthony Rendon	WAS	78
17	Albert Pujols	ANA	76
17	Matt Holliday	SLN	76
17	Adam Jones	BAL	76
17	Ben Zobrist	TBA	76
17	Carlos Santana	CLE	76
17	Justin Upton	ATL	76
17	Freddie Freeman	ATL	76
17	Anthony Rizzo	CHN	76
17	Billy Hamilton	CIN	76

Batting Average

Rank	NAME	Team	AVG
1	Miguel Cabrera	DET	.318
2	Troy Tulowitzki	COL	.306
3	Victor Martinez	DET	.302
4	Buster Posey	SFN	.301
5	Jose Altuve	HOU	.300
6	Adrian Beltre	TEX	.299
7	Joe Mauer	MIN	.298
7	Mike Trout	ANA	.298
9	Jose Abreu	CHA	.295
10	Andrew McCutchen	PIT	.294
11	Robinson Cano	SEA	.293
11	Corey Dickerson	COL	.293
13	Melky Cabrera	CHA	.291
14	Yasiel Puig	LAN	.289
15	Joey Votto	CIN	.288
15	Ryan Braun	MIL	.288
17	Jose Reyes	TOR	.287
18	Yadier Molina	SLN	.286
18	Michael Brantley	CLE	.286
20	Adrian Gonzalez	LAN	.284

Runs Batted In

Rank	NAME	Team	RBI
1	Miguel Cabrera	DET	103
2	Jose Bautista	TOR	99
3	Giancarlo Stanton	MIA	96
4	Josh Donaldson	TOR	90
5	Evan Longoria	TBA	89
6	Albert Pujols	ANA	86
6	Mike Trout	ANA	86
8	Adam Jones	BAL	85
9	Freddie Freeman	ATL	84
9	Anthony Rizzo	CHN	84
11	Adrian Beltre	TEX	83
11	David Ortiz	BOS	83
13	Adrian Gonzalez	LAN	82
13	Nelson Cruz	SEA	82
15	Matt Holliday	SLN	81
15	Yoenis Cespedes	DET	81
17	Edwin Encarnacion	TOR	80
17	Robinson Cano	SEA	80
17	Hunter Pence	SFN	80
17	Andrew McCutchen	PIT	80

Stolen Bases

Rank	NAME	Team	SB
1	Billy Hamilton	CIN	58
2	Dee Gordon	MIA	52
3	Rajai Davis	DET	40
4	Jose Altuve	HOU	39
5	Jacoby Ellsbury	NYA	37
6	Ben Revere	PHI	36
7	Carlos Gomez	MIL	35
8	Starling Marte	PIT	30
9	Elvis Andrus	TEX	29
9	Eric Young	NYN	29
9	Jarrod Dyson	KCA	29
9	Leonys Martin	TEX	29
13	Mike Trout	ANA	28
14	Emilio Bonifacio	ATL	27
14	Jean Segura	MIL	27
16	Jose Reyes	TOR	26
16	Brett Gardner	NYA	26
16	Alcides Escobar	KCA	26
16	Everth Cabrera	SDN	26
20	Coco Crisp	OAK	24
20	Jonathan Villar	HOU	24

On-Base Percentage

Rank	NAME	Team	OBP
1	Joey Votto	CIN	.408
2	Miguel Cabrera	DET	.399
3	Andrew McCutchen	PIT	.384
4	Mike Trout	ANA	.383
5	Jose Bautista	TOR	.381
6	Joe Mauer	MIN	.380
7	Troy Tulowitzki	COL	.378
8	Paul Goldschmidt	ARI	.372
9	Matt Holliday	SLN	.367
9	Matt Carpenter	SLN	.367
11	Shin-Soo Choo	TEX	.366
11	Carlos Santana	CLE	.366
11	Buster Posey	SFN	.366
14	David Ortiz	BOS	.362
14	Yasiel Puig	LAN	.362
16	Jose Abreu	CHA	.360
17	Jayson Werth	WAS	.359
17	Giancarlo Stanton	MIA	.359
19	Victor Martinez	DET	.358
20	Freddie Freeman	ATL	.354

Slugging Percentage

Rank	NAME	Team	SLG
1	Miguel Cabrera	DET	.557
2	Troy Tulowitzki	COL	.534
3	Giancarlo Stanton	MIA	.531
4	Jose Abreu	CHA	.528
5	Jose Bautista	TOR	.521
6	Mike Trout	ANA	.518
7	Paul Goldschmidt	ARI	.512
8	Corey Dickerson	COL	.507
9	Edwin Encarnacion	TOR	.490
10	Ryan Braun	MIL	.488
11	David Ortiz	BOS	.485
12	Matt Kemp	LAN	.482
13	Adrian Beltre	TEX	.481
13	Joey Votto	CIN	.481
15	Andrew McCutchen	PIT	.477
16	Yasiel Puig	LAN	.476
17	Chris Davis	BAL	.473
18	Albert Pujols	ANA	.472
19	Mark Trumbo	ARI	.471
19	Buster Posey	SFN	.471

Isolated Slugging Percentage

Rank	NAME	Team	ISO
1	Giancarlo Stanton	MIA	.262
2	Jose Bautista	TOR	.257
3	Miguel Cabrera	DET	.239
4	Jose Abreu	CHA	.233
5	Paul Goldschmidt	ARI	.229
6	Troy Tulowitzki	COL	.228
7	Edwin Encarnacion	TOR	.227
8	Chris Davis	BAL	.222
9	Mike Trout	ANA	.220
9	Chris Carter	HOU	.220
11	Mark Trumbo	ARI	.218
11	Evan Gattis	ATL	.218
13	Brandon Moss	CLE	.215
14	Corey Dickerson	COL	.214
14	David Ortiz	BOS	.214
16	George Springer	HOU	.213
17	Matt Kemp	LAN	.208
17	Anthony Rizzo	CHN	.208
19	Khris Davis	MIL	.207
20	Mike Napoli	BOS	.204

True Average

Rank	NAME	Team	TAv
1	Miguel Cabrera	DET	.340
2	Mike Trout	ANA	.337
3	Joey Votto	CIN	.331
4	Jose Bautista	TOR	.330
5	Giancarlo Stanton	MIA	.326
5	Jose Abreu	CHA	.326
7	Andrew McCutchen	PIT	.321
8	Paul Goldschmidt	ARI	.320
9	Yasiel Puig	LAN	.316
10	Buster Posey	SFN	.314
11	Troy Tulowitzki	COL	.313
12	Robinson Cano	SEA	.312
13	Ryan Braun	MIL	.311
14	David Ortiz	BOS	.309
15	Adrian Beltre	TEX	.307
16	Albert Pujols	ANA	.306
16	Edwin Encarnacion	TOR	.306
18	Matt Holliday	SLN	.305
18	Anthony Rizzo	CHN	.305
20	Freddie Freeman	ATL	.304

Wins Above Replacement Player—AL

Rank	NAME	Team	WARP
1	Mike Trout	ANA	7.4
2	Robinson Cano	SEA	5.6
3	Miguel Cabrera	DET	5.5
4	Jose Bautista	TOR	4.9
4	Evan Longoria	TBA	4.9
6	Josh Donaldson	TOR	4.8
7	Adrian Beltre	TEX	4.1
7	Ian Kinsler	DET	4.1
9	Albert Pujols	ANA	4.0
9	Alex Gordon	KCA	4.0

WARP—Catcher

Rank	NAME	Team	WARP
1	Buster Posey	SFN	4.7
2	Jonathan Lucroy	MIL	2.8
3	Brian McCann	NYA	2.7
4	Yan Gomes	CLE	2.6
5	Carlos Ruiz	PHI	2.5
5	Salvador Perez	KCA	2.5
7	Miguel Montero	CHN	2.4
7	Russell Martin	TOR	2.4
9	Yadier Molina	SLN	2.3
10	Travis d'Arnaud	NYN	2.2
10	Devin Mesoraco	CIN	2.2
10	Evan Gattis	ATL	2.2

WARP—First Base

Rank	NAME	Team	WARP
1	Albert Pujols	ANA	4.0
2	Anthony Rizzo	CHN	3.9
2	Paul Goldschmidt	ARI	3.9
4	Carlos Santana	CLE	3.7
5	Jose Abreu	CHA	3.5
6	Adrian Gonzalez	LAN	3.4
7	David Ortiz	BOS	3.2
7	Joey Votto	CIN	3.2
7	Freddie Freeman	ATL	3.2
10	Victor Martinez	DET	2.6

WARP—Second Base

Rank	NAME	Team	WARP
1	Robinson Cano	SEA	5.6
2	Ian Kinsler	DET	4.1
3	Chase Utley	PHI	4.0
4	Dustin Pedroia	BOS	3.3
5	Ben Zobrist	TBA	3.2
5	Jose Altuve	HOU	3.2
7	Howie Kendrick	LAN	2.8
7	Brian Dozier	MIN	2.8
9	Jason Kipnis	CLE	2.7
10	Neil Walker	PIT	2.5
10	Daniel Murphy	NYN	2.5

WARP—Third Base

Rank	NAME	Team	WARP
1	Miguel Cabrera	DET	5.5
2	Evan Longoria	TBA	4.9
3	Josh Donaldson	TOR	4.8
4	Matt Carpenter	SLN	4.3
5	Adrian Beltre	TEX	4.1
6	Kyle Seager	SEA	3.9
6	Anthony Rendon	WAS	3.9
8	David Wright	NYN	2.9
9	Pablo Sandoval	BOS	2.7
9	Manny Machado	BAL	2.7

Wins Above Replacement Player—NL

Rank	NAME	Team	WARP
1	Giancarlo Stanton	MIA	5.8
2	Andrew McCutchen	PIT	4.9
3	Buster Posey	SFN	4.7
3	Andrelton Simmons	ATL	4.7
5	Jason Heyward	SLN	4.4
6	Matt Carpenter	SLN	4.3
7	Jean Segura	MIL	4.2
8	Chase Utley	PHI	4.0
8	Yasiel Puig	LAN	4.0
10	Justin Upton	ATL	3.9
10	Anthony Rizzo	CHN	3.9
10	Paul Goldschmidt	ARI	3.9
10	Anthony Rendon	WAS	3.9

WARP—Shortstop

Rank	NAME	Team	WARP
1	Andrelton Simmons	ATL	4.7
2	Jean Segura	MIL	4.2
3	Troy Tulowitzki	COL	3.8
4	Jose Reyes	TOR	3.1
4	Jordy Mercer	PIT	3.1
6	Starlin Castro	CHN	2.9
7	Jhonny Peralta	SLN	2.8
8	Ian Desmond	WAS	2.7
8	Elvis Andrus	TEX	2.7
8	Alexei Ramirez	CHA	2.7

WARP—Left Field

Rank	NAME	Team	WARP
1	Alex Gordon	KCA	4.0
2	Justin Upton	ATL	3.9
3	Matt Holliday	SLN	3.6
4	Khris Davis	MIL	3.1
5	Yoenis Cespedes	DET	2.8
5	Christian Yelich	MIA	2.8
7	Josh Hamilton	ANA	2.6
8	Michael Brantley	CLE	2.4
8	Bryce Harper	WAS	2.4
10	Brett Gardner	NYA	2.3

WARP—Center Field

Rank	NAME	Team	WARP
1	Mike Trout	ANA	7.4
2	Andrew McCutchen	PIT	4.9
3	Jacoby Ellsbury	NYA	3.7
4	Adam Jones	BAL	3.4
5	Carlos Gomez	MIL	3.0
6	Denard Span	WAS	2.9
7	Matt Kemp	LAN	2.8
8	Desmond Jennings	TBA	2.6
9	Austin Jackson	SEA	2.5
9	Billy Hamilton	CIN	2.5

WARP—Right Field

Rank	NAME	Team	WARP
1	Giancarlo Stanton	MIA	5.8
2	Jose Bautista	TOR	4.9
3	Jason Heyward	SLN	4.4
4	Yasiel Puig	LAN	4.0
5	Ryan Braun	MIL	3.6
6	Jayson Werth	WAS	3.2
6	Nelson Cruz	SEA	3.2
8	Hunter Pence	SFN	3.0
9	Jay Bruce	CIN	2.8
10	Kole Calhoun	ANA	2.5

WARP—AL Rookies

Rank	NAME	Team	WARP
1	Rusney Castillo	BOS	1.8
2	Antoan Richardson	TEX	1.2
3	Luke Montz	OAK	0.9
3	Zelous Wheeler	NYA	0.9
3	Christian Colon	KCA	0.9
6	Jose Pirela	NYA	0.8
6	Curtis Casali	TBA	0.8
8	Dan Butler	BOS	0.7
9	Melky Mesa	TOR	0.6
9	Jesus Aguilar	CLE	0.6
9	Lane Adams	KCA	0.6
9	Alex Hassan	BAL	0.6
9	J.R. Murphy	NYA	0.6
9	Billy Burns	OAK	0.6

WARP—NL Rookies

Rank	NAME	Team	WARP
1	Steven Souza	WAS	1.8
2	Joc Pederson	LAN	1.4
3	Matthew Duffy	SFN	1.3
4	Dean Anna	SLN	1.1
5	Thomas Pham	SLN	1.0
5	Nick Ahmed	ARI	1.0
7	Alex Castellanos	NYN	0.9
7	Corban Joseph	ATL	0.9
7	Michael Taylor	WAS	0.9
7	Greg Garcia	SLN	0.9
7	Andrew Susac	SFN	0.9
7	Jorge Soler	CHN	0.9

WARP—Declines

Rank	NAME	Team	2014 WARP	2015 WARP	WARP Diff.
1	Michael Brantley	CLE	6.0	2.4	-3.6
2	Kyle Seager	SEA	7.3	3.9	-3.4
3	J.D. Martinez	DET	4.0	0.7	-3.3
4	Steve Pearce	BAL	4.8	1.6	-3.2
4	Jonathan Lucroy	MIL	6.0	2.8	-3.2
6	Justin Turner	LAN	4.0	1.1	-2.9
7	Denard Span	WAS	5.7	2.9	-2.8
7	Josh Harrison	PIT	5.1	2.3	-2.8
7	Russell Martin	TOR	5.2	2.4	-2.8
10	Marlon Byrd	PHI	4.0	1.3	-2.7

WARP—Improvements

Rank	NAME	Team	2014 WARP	2015 WARP	WARP Diff.
1	Omar Infante	KCA	-1.2	2.1	3.3
2	Allen Craig	BOS	-2.0	1.0	3.0
3	Nick Swisher	CLE	-1.0	1.7	2.7
4	A. Simmons	ATL	2.1	4.7	2.6
5	Jay Bruce	CIN	0.4	2.8	2.4
6	Carlos Gonzalez	COL	-0.7	1.6	2.3
6	Wil Myers	TBA	-0.5	1.8	2.3
8	Billy Butler	OAK	-0.0	2.2	2.2
9	Javier Baez	CHN	-1.0	1.1	2.1
9	Will Middlebrooks	BOS	-1.2	0.9	2.1

Pitchers

Wins

Rank	NAME	Team	W
1	Jered Weaver	ANA	13
1	David Price	DET	13
1	Felix Hernandez	SEA	13
1	Adam Wainwright	SLN	13
5	Justin Verlander	DET	12
5	Max Scherzer	DET	12
5	James Shields	KCA	12
5	R.A. Dickey	TOR	12
5	Jon Lester	CHN	12
5	Clayton Kershaw	LAN	12
5	Stephen Strasburg	WAS	12
12	C.J. Wilson	ANA	11
12	Rick Porcello	BOS	11
12	Danny Salazar	CLE	11
12	Corey Kluber	CLE	11
12	Hiroki Kuroda	NYA	11
12	Mark Buehrle	TOR	11
12	Julio Teheran	ATL	11
12	Zack Greinke	LAN	11
12	Cole Hamels	PHI	11
12	John Lackey	SLN	11
12	Lance Lynn	SLN	11

Strikeouts

Rank	NAME	Team	K
1	Stephen Strasburg	WAS	207
2	Max Scherzer	DET	201
3	Felix Hernandez	SEA	194
4	David Price	DET	193
5	Jon Lester	CHN	191
5	Clayton Kershaw	LAN	191
7	Chris Sale	CHA	182
8	Danny Salazar	CLE	181
8	Corey Kluber	CLE	181
10	Justin Verlander	DET	177
11	Cole Hamels	PHI	176
12	Madison Bumgarner	SFN	172
13	Jeff Samardzija	CHA	171
14	James Shields	KCA	168
14	Adam Wainwright	SLN	168
16	Yu Darvish	TEX	167
17	Lance Lynn	SLN	164
18	Zack Greinke	LAN	162
19	Ian Kennedy	SDN	159
20	Julio Teheran	ATL	158
20	A.J. Burnett	PIT	158

ERA

Rank	NAME	Team	ERA
1	Clayton Kershaw	LAN	2.17
2	Felix Hernandez	SEA	2.58
3	Chris Sale	CHA	2.65
3	Stephen Strasburg	WAS	2.65
5	Adam Wainwright	SLN	2.87
6	Yu Darvish	TEX	2.94
7	Johnny Cueto	CIN	2.96
8	Jered Weaver	ANA	3.00
9	Madison Bumgarner	SFN	3.03
10	Alex Wood	ATL	3.12
11	Hisashi Iwakuma	SEA	3.13
11	Cole Hamels	PHI	3.13
13	Zack Greinke	LAN	3.14
13	Hyun-jin Ryu	LAN	3.14
15	Jordan Zimmermann	WAS	3.21
16	Jon Lester	CHN	3.22
16	Mike Fiers	MIL	3.22
18	David Price	DET	3.23
19	Justin Verlander	DET	3.24
20	Gio Gonzalez	WAS	3.26

WHIP

Rank	NAME	Team	WHIP
1	Clayton Kershaw	LAN	0.94
2	Stephen Strasburg	WAS	1.03
3	Chris Sale	CHA	1.07
3	Felix Hernandez	SEA	1.07
3	Johnny Cueto	CIN	1.07
3	Adam Wainwright	SLN	1.07
7	Madison Bumgarner	SFN	1.08
8	Zack Greinke	LAN	1.09
8	Cole Hamels	PHI	1.09
10	Mike Fiers	MIL	1.10
10	Jordan Zimmermann	WAS	1.10
12	Hisashi Iwakuma	SEA	1.11
13	Jered Weaver	ANA	1.12
13	Hyun-jin Ryu	LAN	1.12
15	Jake Peavy	SFN	1.13
16	Kyle Hendricks	CHN	1.14
16	Brandon McCarthy	LAN	1.14
16	Alex Wood	ATL	1.14
19	Jon Lester	CHN	1.15
19	Doug Fister	WAS	1.15

Strikeouts per 9 Innings

Rank	NAME	Team	K/9
1	Yu Darvish	TEX	11.1
2	Chris Sale	CHA	10.5
3	Stephen Strasburg	WAS	10.4
4	Danny Salazar	CLE	9.8
4	Max Scherzer	DET	9.8
6	Clayton Kershaw	LAN	9.7
7	Henry Owens	BOS	9.5
8	Francisco Liriano	PIT	9.2
9	Shelby Miller	ATL	9.1
10	Felix Hernandez	SEA	9.0
10	Jeff Samardzija	CHA	9.0
10	Tim Lincecum	SFN	9.0
10	Corey Kluber	CLE	9.0
10	Alex Wood	ATL	9.0
10	Cody Martin	ATL	9.0
16	Trevor Bauer	CLE	8.9
16	Gio Gonzalez	WAS	8.9
18	Nate Karns	TBA	8.8
19	Jon Lester	CHN	8.7
19	Marcus Stroman	TOR	8.7
19	Drew Hutchison	TOR	8.7

Saves

Rank	NAME	Team	SV
1	Craig Kimbrel	ATL	46
2	Fernando Rodney	SEA	40
3	Rafael Soriano	WAS	36
4	Joe Nathan	DET	35
4	Greg Holland	KCA	35
6	Jonathan Papelbon	PHI	32
7	Huston Street	ANA	31
7	Addison Reed	ARI	31
7	Kenley Jansen	LAN	31
10	Glen Perkins	MIN	30
11	Mariano Rivera	NYA	29
11	Sergio Romo	SFN	29
13	Steve Cishek	MIA	28
14	Casey Janssen	TOR	23
15	Francisco Rodriguez	MIL	22
16	Jim Johnson	ATL	20
17	Rafael Betancourt	COL	18
18	Grant Balfour	TBA	17
19	Jason Grilli	ANA	16
19	Ernesto Frieri	TBA	16
19	Mark Melancon	PIT	16

Wins Above Replacement Player

Rank	NAME	Team	WARP
1	Clayton Kershaw	LAN	5.0
2	Felix Hernandez	SEA	4.1
2	Chris Sale	CHA	4.1
4	Stephen Strasburg	WAS	4.0
5	David Price	DET	3.9
6	Adam Wainwright	SLN	3.7
7	Justin Verlander	DET	3.6
8	Max Scherzer	DET	3.3
9	Jered Weaver	ANA	3.1
10	Johnny Cueto	CIN	2.9
11	Madison Bumgarner	SFN	2.7
11	Yu Darvish	TEX	2.7
13	Jon Lester	CHN	2.5
13	Marcus Stroman	TOR	2.5
15	Sonny Gray	OAK	2.4
15	Cole Hamels	PHI	2.4
17	Zack Greinke	LAN	2.3
17	Jordan Zimmermann	WAS	2.3
19	Craig Kimbrel	ATL	2.2
19	Danny Salazar	CLE	2.2
19	Jose Quintana	CHA	2.2

WARP—AL Rookies

Rank	NAME	Team	WARP
1	Nick Tropeano	ANA	1.1
1	Andrew Heaney	ANA	1.1
3	Steven Geltz	TBA	0.8
4	Nate Karns	TBA	0.7
4	Corey Knebel	TEX	0.7
4	Carson Smith	SEA	0.7
4	Spencer Patton	TEX	0.7
4	Alexander Claudio	TEX	0.7
9	Matt Barnes	BOS	0.6
9	Daniel Norris	TOR	0.6
9	Heath Hembree	BOS	0.6
9	Phil Klein	TEX	0.6

WARP—NL Rookies

Rank	NAME	Team	WARP
1	Rafael Montero	NYN	1.4
2	Yimi Garcia	LAN	0.8
3	Preston Guilmet	PIT	0.7
3	Marco Gonzales	SLN	0.7
5	R.J. Alvarez	SDN	0.6
5	Brett Bochy	SFN	0.6
7	John Holdzkom	PIT	0.5
7	Juan Jaime	ATL	0.5
9	Ian Thomas	ATL	0.4
9	Dario Alvarez	NYN	0.4
9	Leonel Campos	SDN	0.4
9	Miguel Socolovich	SLN	0.4

WARP—Declines

Rank	NAME	Team	2014 WARP	2015 WARP	WARP Diff.
1	Corey Kluber	CLE	6.0	1.4	-4.7
2	Phil Hughes	MIN	4.7	1.5	-3.1
3	Jake Arrieta	CHN	4.0	1.2	-2.7
4	Zack Greinke	LAN	4.7	2.3	-2.4
4	Jose Quintana	CHA	4.5	2.2	-2.4
6	Tyler Matzek	COL	1.8	-0.5	-2.3
6	Aaron Harang	ATL	1.4	-0.9	-2.3
8	Mark Buehrle	TOR	2.7	0.6	-2.0
8	Dellin Betances	NYA	2.6	0.6	-2.0
8	Wade Davis	KCA	2.4	0.4	-2.0

WARP—Improvements

Rank	NAME	Team	2014 WARP	2015 WARP	WARP Diff.
1	Jered Weaver	ANA	0.5	3.1	2.6
2	Marco Estrada	TOR	-0.9	1.2	2.1
3	Matt Cain	SFN	-0.6	1.2	1.8
3	Tim Hudson	SFN	-0.5	1.3	1.8
3	Tim Lincecum	SFN	-1.2	0.6	1.8
6	C.J. Wilson	ANA	-0.1	1.6	1.6
6	Brandon Kintzler	MIL	-1.0	0.6	1.6
8	Rafael Montero	NYN	-0.1	1.4	1.5
8	Dan Straily	CHN	-0.6	0.9	1.5
8	Jake Peavy	SFN	0.3	1.8	1.5
8	Doug Fister	WAS	0.2	1.7	1.5
8	Andrew Heaney	ANA	-0.4	1.1	1.4

Contributors

R.J. Anderson lives in Florida and joined Prospectus in 2011. In the past, Anderson's work has appeared on ESPN and Wired. com, as well as in *Newsweek*. His nightmares include running out of baseball-related quips to use here.

J.P. Breen is a graduate student at the University of Chicago, studying U.S. history, religion and nativism. He lives in Hyde Park with his beautiful wife, Sarah, who somehow tolerates his baseball addiction.

Ben Carsley is a senior fantasy writer at Baseball Prospectus, host of the TINO podcast and a bad influence at The Dynasty Guru. Born, raised and living in Boston, his past work has appeared on NESN.com, Over The Monster, Fire Brand of the AL, Bleacher Report and other sites. When he's not writing about baseball, Ben is generally cooking, sampling IPAs, arguing about sandwiches and catering to his niche Twitter following of William Faulkner-loving Red Sox fans with a high tolerance for sarcasm.

Patrick Dubuque is a wastrel and a general layabout. In the past he's written for The Classical, The Hardball Times, NotGraphs, Pitchers & Poets and Lookout Landing. He will be survived by his wife Kjersten, his daughter Sylvie and the admirable futility of human existence.

Ken Funck contributes his "Changing Speeds" column to the Baseball Prospectus website so infrequently that he clearly wants to be considered the Terrence Malick of sabermetrics. He has also written for the Baseball Prospectus annual every year since 2009. Ken spends his days managing business intelligence systems and lives outside Madison, Wisconsin with his ever-supportive wife Stephanie, their children Max and Abby, one cat, two dogs and a room full of exercise equipment in various states of disrepair.

Ryan Ghan lives in Portland, Oregon with his wife, Sarah, and twin girls, Cleo and Annabel. He coaxes teenagers into solving for "x" by day and coaxes toddlers into eating their veggies by night. He spends his remaining time watching, thinking and writing about minor-league baseball.

Craig Goldstein is an author at Baseball Prospectus, The Dynasty Guru and SB Nation's MLB Newsdesk. He formerly wrote for MLB Draft Insider and SB Nation's Fake Teams. He lives outside Washington, DC, and spends just the right amount of time thinking about sandwiches.

Bryan Grosnick is the Managing Editor and lead writer at SB Nation's sabermetrics blog, Beyond the Box Score. He lives in Michigan with his lovely wife, Sarah, and his non-baseball hobbies include eating, running and eating while running.

Andrew Koo is responsible for the 1/20th of jokes in this book that aren't funny. He joined BP's technical team in 2012, working to provide data for the site's content; occasionally, he steps out from the back-end shadows to write. His love for sports tussles with the demands of his studies as a math student, neither subject ever willing to return his love. (Andrew has cheered for the Blue Jays since 2001.) He attends the University of Waterloo and resides in wondrous Toronto, Ontario. When he's not in school, he makes his living talking to computers in SQL and R, which he does claim to be funny at, somehow.

Sam Miller (@SamMillerBP) is the editor-in-chief of Baseball Prospectus, the co-host of the daily BP podcast Effectively Wild and a contributor to *ESPN the Magazine*. He lives in California with his wife, his daughter and his concerns about hyphenation standards.

Dustin Nosler (@DustinNosler) is a writer at Dodgers Digest, co-host of the Dugout Blues podcast, prospect maven, FanGraphs contracts intern and Hardball Times contributor/editor.

Daniel Rathman is a Master of Urban Planning candidate at New York University and a research assistant at the Rudin Center for Transportation Policy and Management. He lives in San Francisco when he's not away studying.

Tommy Rancel has written for Bloomberg Sports, FanGraphs, Gammons Daily and ESPN.com. He lives in the Tampa Bay area with his wife (Jamie) and their three children (Alexis, Vincent and Jarek).

Mauricio Rubio Jr. is a Chicago-based data analyst and a multimedia freelancer who enjoys obscure and nuanced jokes only three people would get. He also has a soft spot for dead authors, live music and documentary binges.

Bret Sayre is the Fantasy Manager and Prospect Coordinator at Baseball Prospectus. He's known to be a bit verbose, so he's really trying to keep this brief. By day, he is quite adept at telling investment professionals what not to do. By night, he is a full-time family man, part-time cook, part-time nurse, full-time baseball writer and part-time musician. As an eight-year-old, he was knocked over by a grown man as he tried to catch a dead ball thrown by Kevin Mitchell at Shea Stadium. Now, he lives in New Jersey with his wife, Carolyn, his daughter, Alyson, and his son, Joshua, who learned to switch-hit before he could walk. And no, that's not a reflection of his plate discipline.

Sahadev Sharma is an editor and writer for Baseball Prospectus. When not at Wrigley Field or The Cell, he carves out time to spend with his family, which includes his wife, Andrea Caruso, an amazing NICU nurse, his son, Sawyer, a future fireman/doctor/truck driver/baseball writer/vacuum repairman (all according to him), his sweet but very opinionated daughter, Penny, and two Italian Greyhounds, Harper and Maya. He is also a beer snob, but readily admits there is a time for a PBR or High Life, usually when all other options are exhausted or you're almost out of money.

Adam Sobsey has been writing for Baseball Prospectus since 2011 and covering the Durham Bulls since 2009. He is the principal author of *Bull City Summer* (Daylight Books, 2014), a documentary project about the Bulls' 2013 season. He has written about baseball for *The Paris Review* and The Classical, among others, and he is at work on a book about Triple-A. His biography of the rock musician Chrissie Hynde is forthcoming from University of Texas Press in 2016.

Paul Sporer's work can be found at various outlets on the internet, primarily Rotowire.com, as well as on TV as a guest of MLB Network's MLB Now. His own website, PaulSporer.com, has been around since 2006 and still houses his work, including the well-known *Starting Pitcher Guide*, the ninth edition of which will be released in 2015. He and his beloved beagle Curtis (named after former Detroit Tiger Granderson) spend their summers enjoying the blistering Texas heat while glued to the MLB At-Bat app on the computer, iPhone and iPad, watching or listening to as many games as possible, including every Tigers one.

Matt Sussman (@suss2hyphens) is an IT professional from Toledo, Ohio. During the season he co-authors replacement-level jokes for the Prospectus Hit List.

Doug Thorburn is a pitching junkie. He writes the "Raising Aces" column at Baseball Prospectus, a series that studies the science of pitching though the trifocal lenses of mechanics, stuff and stats. Thorburn has trained in the dual arts of coaching and scouting, directed the motion analysis program at the National Pitching Association and co-authored a book about pitching, *Arm Action, Arm Path, and the Perfect Pitch*. Thorburn resides in Morgan Hill, California, with his 80-grade wife, Caitlin, and a pair of mischievous huskies that are trained to kill … gophers beware.

Jason Wojciechowski (@jlwoj) is a labor lawyer in Los Angeles. He founded the A's blog Beaneball in 2003 and tells a lot of lies on Twitter.

Will Woods is a copywriter living in New York City. He sings in a choir and plays lots of soccer, but he still makes time for baseball because you can't really chew tobacco doing any of those things.

Geoff Young founded Ducksnorts, publishing online content and three books about the Padres under that title from 1997 to 2011. He currently writes for PadresPublic.com, and has previously written for Baseball Prospectus, The Hardball Times, ESPN. com and others. This is his fourth appearance in the BP annual. He also edited *Baseball Prospectus Futures Guide 2014* and contributed to *Best of Baseball Prospectus: 1996-2011*. Geoff lives in San Diego with his patient wife, Sandra.

Acknowledgments

Ben Carsley: My Red Sox-crazed family, the ever-patient Allyson Clancy, Bret Sayre, Craig Goldstein, Mauricio Rubio, Jordon Gorosh, Sam Miller, Jason Wojciechowski, Joe Hamrahi, Jason Parks, Evan Brunell, Xander Bogaerts, Mary Donovan, Daniel Ohman, the generous Marc Normandin

Patrick Dubuque: Chris Crawford, Scott Weber, Nathan Bishop, Logan Davis, Michael Barr, Marc W, Eric Nusbaum, Tanya Bondurant, Jeff Sullivan, Eno Sarris, Jason Cohen, Andrew Mearns, Caitlin Rogers, William Wordsworth

Ken Funck: Sam Miller, Jason Wojciechowski, Ben Lindbergh, Steven Goldman, John Perrotto, Christina Kahrl, Rany Jazayerli, Harry Pavlidis, Joe Hamrahi, Doug Ross, Zach Eveland, Richard Chao, Kevin Moore, Mike Atherton

Craig Goldstein: Laurie Gross, Harvey Goldstein, Alexis Goldstein, Katherine Pappas, Jason Wojciechowski, Sam Miller, Taylor Swift, Bret Sayre, Ian Miller, Riley Breckenridge, Jason Parks, The BP Prospect Team, Marc Normandin, RJ Anderson, Chris Crawford, Meghan Trainor, Mauricio Rubio, Ben Carsley, Jacob Raim, Zach Mortimer, Jason Cole, Josh Herzenberg, Mike Ferrin, Stu Wallace, Tommy Rancel, Matt Sussman, Joe Hamrahi

Bryan Grosnick: Sarah Grosnick, Phil and Debbie Grosnick, Stuart Wallace, Andrew Ball, Ben Horrow, Neil Weinberg, Sam Miller and Jason Wojciechowski, Michael Jong, Andrew Snyder, Sam Evans, Tucker Blair, Mark Anderson, Patrick Ebert, Mark Simon, the entire Beyond the Box Score staff

Andrew Koo: BP's Prospect Team, Dan Brooks, Harry Pavlidis, Dan Rozenson, Rob McQuown, Sam Miller, Jason Wojciechowski, Dave Pease, Ben Lindbergh, Adam Sobsey, Bryan Kilpatrick

Sam Miller: R.J. Anderson, Dan Brooks, Jit Fong Chin, Sean Forman, Ken Funck, Joe Hamrahi, Ben Lindbergh, Rob McQuown, Rod Miller, Bret Sayre, the BP Prospect staff

Tommy Rancel: Sam Miller, Jason Wojciechowski, R.J. Anderson, Jonah Keri, Keith Law, Barry Eugene Carter, Craig Goldstein, Chris Crawford, Jason Collette, Erik Hahmann, Dave L.D. Burd, Carl Reed, Chaim Bloom, Erik Neander, Rebecca Basse, Carlos Alvarez, Jamie, Alexis, Vincent, Jarek

Daniel Rathman: Nick J. Faleris, Joe Hamrahi, Chris Mellen, Sam Miller, Jason Parks, Chris Rodriguez, Hank Schulman

Mauricio Rubio: To my mother and father for encouraging and pushing me, mi abuelo y abuela for guiding me, Pablo and Jess for encouraging me, Jason, Joe, Bret and Craig for taking a chance on me, my friends for being a stable support network, and to my brother for inspiring me, thank you.

Bret Sayre: Carolyn, Alyson, and Joshua, for always making me smile. Lynn and Peter Sayre. Joe Hamrahi. Jason Parks. Marc Normandin. Ray Guilfoyle. The BP Fantasy and Prospect teams. The Gentlemen of TINO. Ryan Westmoreland. Brock Landers. John Roderick. Howard Johnson. Jack Johnson (the boxer). All of my friends and family not mentioned above. Sam, Jason and editors everywhere for making me look better than I am.

Sahadev Sharma: My wife for putting up with me when I forgot a deadline and had to abandon the family to go write a thousand words on the Cubs. My kids for reminding me why I must stay driven when my focus started to drift. My mother (for so many things, but in particular this) and mother-in-law, each for watching my children when I needed to get writing done while my wife was at work. The front office executives and scouts who have taught me things about the game of baseball that I could have never learned on my own. Joe Hamrahi, Sam Miller, Mike Ferrin, the BP Prospect team and so many more friends and colleagues who helped me glean some bit of knowledge that aided in my writing of this chapter.

Adam Sobsey: Heather Mallory, R.J. Anderson, Jason Collette, Tommy Rancel, Neil Solondz, Chaim Bloom, Charlie Caskey, David Laurila, Shi Davidi, Noah Pransky, Marc Topkin

Paul Sporer: Curtis the Beagle, Sean Forman, Doug Thorburn, Dana Cummings, Melissa Parks, Cody Sporer, Dorothy Sporer, Paul Sporer Sr., Chandler Parks, Kendrick Lamar (whose music underscored all of my writing sessions for the annual)

Matt Sussman: My super-cool wife Brittany, my newborn son Maxwell for taking a copious amount of naps during my writing spells and Play Index and Brooks Baseball for being magic databases of baseball wisdom.

Doug Thorburn: Joe Hamrahi, Tom House, Ryan Sienko, Eric Andrews, Paul Sporer, Mike Ferrin, Dan Brooks, Harry Pavlidis, anyone who is dedicated to life on the mound

Jason Wojciechowski: R.J. Anderson, Patrick Dubuque, Ken Funck, Craig Goldstein, Joe Hamrahi, Andrew Koo, Ben Lindbergh, Rob McQuown, Marc Normandin, Eric Nusbaum, Dave Pease, Austen Rachlis, everybody on Weird Baseball Twitter

Geoff Young: Corey Brock, Keith Carter, Bill Center, Jerry Coleman, John Conniff, Jeff Creps, Scott Dunsmore, Nick Faleris, Sean Forman, Tony Gwynn, Matthew Kory, Tom Krasovic, Patrick Kurish, Anne Lamott, Dennis Lin, Rob McQuown, Mike Metzger, Jeff Moore, John Nolan, Dustin Palmateer, Jason Parks, Harry Pavlidis, David Pinto, Mark Salfi, Eno Sarris, Bret Sayre, Doug Thorburn, Sandra Tokashiki, Alan Yates and anyone else inadvertently missed

Index of Names